The New Routledge & Van Dale Dutch Dictionary

This comprehensive and contemporary two-way dictionary is ideal for Dutch language learners and users at all levels. Key features of the dictionary include:

- Over 32,000 Dutch entries
- The use of colloquial and idiomatic language
- Useful contextual information within glosses
- Phonetic transcription for all Dutch headwords, aiding pronunciation
- Gender marked for all Dutch nouns
- Appendix of Dutch irregular verbs

This second edition has been systematically revised and updated throughout to provide:

- 9,000 new headwords and definitions, supported by 18,000 translations and helpful pronunciation aid
- Expanded and updated information for a number of the previously existing headwords, including the addition of 3,000 new examples
- An improved layout and format for clearer and easier referencing
- Articles for Dutch nouns presented at a glance, in the margin before the headwords
- Conjugational information added to the Dutch verbs after the headwords

The New Routledge & Van Dale Dutch Dictionary

Dutch–English/English–Dutch

Second Edition

Routledge
Taylor & Francis Group

LONDON AND NEW YORK

Utrecht - Antwerpen

Second English edition published 2014
by Routledge
2 Park Square, Milton Park, Abingdon, Oxon OX14 4RN

and by Routledge
711 Third Avenue, New York, NY 10017

Routledge is an imprint of the Taylor & Francis Group, an informa business

First published by Van Dale Lexicografie bv 2001 as *Ster Woordenboek Engels–Nederlands/
Nederlands–Engels*, Third edition, by R. Hempelman and N.E. Osselton
First English edition published by Routledge 2003

Editorial consultant for English edition: Sarah Butler

British Library Cataloguing in Publication Data
A catalogue record for this book is available from the British Library

Library of Congress Cataloging in Publication Data
The new Routledge & Van Dale Dutch dictionary. -- Second English edition.
       pages cm
1. English language--Dictionaries--Dutch. 2. Dutch language--Dictionaries--English.
I. Title: New Routledge and Van Dale Dutch dictionary.
  PF640.N66 2014
  439.313'21--dc23
                                     2014012138

ISBN: 978-1-138-78580-9 (hbk)
ISBN: 978-1-138-78579-3 (pbk)

Typeset in Frutiger
by Pre Press Media Groep, Zeist, The Netherlands

Contents

Foreword for the First Edition

This dictionary includes the past tense and past participle forms of Dutch irregular verbs.

In this dictionary all words appear in British spelling. To avoid confusion, American spellings have not been included. However, in many cases American spelling can easily be predicted on the basis of British spellings. For example, many words ending in *–our (humour)* and *–tre (centre)* are spelt *–or (humor)* and *–ter (center)* in American English. Also, unlike British spelling, American spelling does not always use double consonants, thus American English has "trave*l*er" and "jewe*l*er" rather than British "trave*ll*er" and "jewe*ll*er".

However, where British and American English differ lexically, there are entries for both: so for *apotheek* both chemist's, and [Am] drugstore are given.

The pronunciation of entries is represented by means of easy-to-understand symbols.

Detailed information about the layout of this dictionary is to be found in the Guide to the dictionary.

To make it easy to look up words, each entry appears at the beginning of a new line; in addition, all entries are printed in full.

Foreword for the Second Edition

For the second edition the dictionary has been systematically revised and updated throughout to offer two main improvements.

Firstly, there has been a substantial expansion of the headwords in the dictionary. In keeping with changes in the Dutch and English languages, the dictionary features 9,000 new headwords (an increase by 18% since the previous edition), supported by pronunciation aids. These new headwords are also accompanied by 9,000 new definitions, 18,000 translations and 3,000 new examples. A number of existing entries have also been revised and updated to reflect new developments in Dutch.

Secondly, the dictionary offers a substantially improved new layout design for clearer and easier referencing. Articles for Dutch nouns are presented at a glance, in the margin before the headwords, and conjugational information follows the Dutch verbs, after the headwords.

List of Abbreviations

abbrev	*abbreviation*	int	*interjection*
adj	*adjective*	iron	*ironical*
adv	*adverb*	lit	*literal*
Am	*American, in the USA*	maths	*mathematics*
approx	*approximate*	m.b.t.	*met betrekking tot*
art	*article*	med	*medical*
Austr	*Australian, in Australia*	mil	*military*
aux vb	*auxiliary verb*	mus	*music*
Belg	*Belgian, in Belgium*	n	*noun*
bldg	*building*	num	*numeral*
bot	*botany*	oft	*often*
chem	*chemistry*	pers	*person*
com	*commerce*	pers pron	*personal pronoun*
comp	*computer*	pl	*plural*
conj	*conjunction*	pol	*politics*
dem pron	*demonstrative pronoun*	poss pron	*possessive pronoun*
depr	*depreciatory*	prep	*preposition*
econ	*economics*	pron	*pronoun*
educ	*education*	ref pron	*reflexive pronoun*
eg	*for example*	ref vb	*reflexive verb*
elec	*electricity*	rel	*religion*
esp	*especially*	shipp	*shipping*
euph	*euphemism*	s.o.	*someone*
fig	*figurative*	socc	*soccer*
fin	*finance*	sth.	*something*
form	*formal*	techn	*technics*
geog	*geography*	telecom	*telecommunication*
graph	*graphics*	traf	*traffic*
iem.	*iemand*	vb	*verb*
ind pron	*indefinite pronoun*	vulg	*vulgar*
inform	*informal*		

Pronunciation Symbols

ɑ	as in French chat
a	as in after
ɛ	as in bed
e	as in late
ə	as in about
ɪ	as in bid
i	as in French ici
ɔ	as in lot
o	as in German Boot
ʏ	as in sun
y	as in French fumé
u	as in foot
b	as in back
c	as in cheek
d	as in door
f	as in far
ɣ	as in loch (but voiced)
χ	as in loch
g	as in goal
h	as in help
j	as in yet
k	as in car
l	as in like
m	as in mouse
n	as in nose
ŋ	as in wrong
ɲ	as in French campagne
p	as in paper
r	as in room
s	as in son
ʃ	as in fish
ʒ	as in pleasure
t	as in town
θ	as in thriller
v	as in verb
w	as in wax
z	as in zip
ø	as in German schön
ɛi	approx as in table, vein
œy	as in Latin neutrum
ɑu	as in mouth
oe:	as in nurse
ã	as in French chanson
ɛ̃	as in French vin
ɔ̃	as in French chanson
:	lengthening symbol, lenghtens the preceding vowel
ɑ:	as in barbecue
ɛ:	as in wear
i:	as in jeans
ɔ:	as in corner
u:	as in jury
ʏ:	as in service
y:	as in French pur

Guide to the Dictionary

The abbreviations and the pronunciation symbols used in this dictionary are explained in the *List of abbreviations* and the *Pronunciation symbols* on the preceding pages.

All entries appear in bold type

aunt tante

The vowel or vowels of stressed syllables of the English entries are underlined

ab̲olish afschaffen, een eind maken aan
acr̲oss-the-b̲oard algemeen (geldend)

The pronunciation of the Dutch entries appears between slashes. The vowel or vowels of stressed syllables are underlined

België /bɛlɣijə/ Belgium

Dutch entries which are nouns, are preceded by the article **de** or **het** at the beginning of the line. If applicable, the plural form is given between brackets

de **satésaus** /satesɑus/ (pl: -sauzen) satay sauc
het **satéstokje** /satestɔkjə/ (pl: -s) skewer

Dutch entries which are verbs, are followed by their conjugated forms (imperfect and past participle with the applicable auxiliary)

creëren /krejerə(n)/ (creëerde, heeft gecreëerd) create
doorschuiven /dorsχœyvə(n)/ (schoof door, heeft/is doorgeschoven) pass on

Entries with identical spelling but different stress, pronunciation patterns or grammar are identified by a superscript numeral **1**, **2** etc.

de **¹achteruit** /ɑχtərœyt/ reverse (gear): *een auto in zijn ~ zetten* put a car into reverse (gear)
²achteruit /ɑχtərœyt/ (adv) back(wards)
het **¹aas** /as/ bait: *levend ~* live bait; *van ~ voorzien* bait (the hook, trap)
het/de **²aas** /as/ [cards] ace: *de ~ van harten, ruiten* the ace of hearts, diamonds

In the translations of English nouns the Dutch neuter nouns are marked with a superior h to mark the use of the Dutch article *het*
In case the articles *het* and *de* are both allowed, the nouns are marked with +h

accelerator gaspedaalʰ
ace 1 [cards] aas⁺ʰ, één; [fig] troef **2** [sport, esp tennis] ace **3** [inform] uitblinker: *an ~ at arithmetic* een hele piet in het rekenen

In entries which are abbreviations, the explanation is given first, printed in italics

a.u.b. /aybe/ (abbrev) *alstublieft* please

Commas are used to separate translations which are very close in meaning

de **aardbol** /ardbɔl/ (pl: -len) earth, world, globe

Semicolons are used to separate translations which are less close in meaning. In many cases information about this small difference in meaning appears between brackets

shutdown sluiting; stopzetting [of business]
spotless brandschoon, vlekkeloos; [fig also] onberispelijk

If an entry has significantly different translations, these are numbered **1**, **2** etc.

¹auxiliary (n) **1** helper, hulpkracht, assisten **2** hulpmiddelʰ **3** hulpwerkwoordʰ

In some cases a translation requires clarification: eg restrictions as to the usage of a word, a field label, a brief explanation. This additional information appears between brackets

acoustics 1 geluidsleer **2** akoestiek [in concert hall etc]
defuse onschadelijk maken [also fig]; demonteren [explosives]: *~ a crisis* een crisis bezweren

In a number of cases the translation is followed by examples and expressions. These are in italics; the entry is represented by the symbol ~. To help you find your way through the examples, the most important word is printed in bold

For some entries no translations are given; they appear in one or more expressions

Expressions which do not clearly fit any of the given translations of an entry are dealt with at the end, after the || symbol

In case an expression has several meanings, these meanings are seperated by the letters **a)** and **b)**

Alternative forms appear between brackets and are introduced by *or*

Some entries are only used in fixed combinations with another word. In these cases the latter word is introduced by the sign +

Translations which are mainly used in American English are preceded by the abbreviation [Am]. This notation is also used in compounds and examples.

de **voorlichting** /vo̲rlɪχtɪŋ/ (pl: -en) information: *de afdeling* ~ public relations department; *seksuele* ~ sex education; *goede* ~ *geven* give good advice

apegapen /a̲pəɣapə(n)/: *op* ~ *liggen* be at one's last gasp

de **balk** /bɑlk/ (pl: -en) beam || *het geld over de ~ gooien* spend money like water

de **groet** […]: *de ~en!* **a)** [greeting] see you!; **b)** [forget it] not on your life!, no way!
de **aanplant** /a̲mplɑnt/ plantings, plants: *nieuwe* (or: *jonge*) ~ new (*or:* young) plantings

all-time van alle tijden: *an* ~ *high* (or: *low*) een absoluut hoogtepunt (*or:* dieptepunt)

accessible (+ to) toegankelijk (voor), bereikbaar (voor); [fig] begrijpelijk (voor)

het **appartement** /ɑpɑrtəmɛnt/ (pl: -en) flat; [Am] apartment
de **etage** /eta̲ʒə/ (pl: -s) floor, storey: *op de eerste* ~ on the first floor; [Am] on the second floor

Dutch Irregular Verbs

Conjugated forms shown between brackets are regular.
Numbered forms represent the first, second and third person singular in the present tense.

infinitive	imperfect sing	imperfect pl	past participle
bakken	(bakte)		gebakken
bannen	(bande)		gebannen
barsten	(barstte)		gebarsten
bederven	bedierf	bedierven	bedorven
bedriegen	bedroog	bedrogen	bedrogen
beginnen	begon	begonnen	begonnen
begrijpen	begreep	begrepen	begrepen
belijden	beleed	beleden	beleden
bergen	borg		geborgen
bevelen	beval	bevalen	bevolen
bewegen	bewoog	bewogen	bewogen
bezwijken	bezweek	bezweken	bezweken
bidden	bad	baden	gebeden
bieden	bood	boden	geboden
bijten	beet	beten	gebeten
binden	bond		gebonden
blazen	blies	bliezen	geblazen
blijken	bleek	bleken	gebleken
blijven	bleef	bleven	gebleven
blinken	blonk		geblonken
braden	(braadde)		gebraden
breken	brak	braken	gebroken
brengen	bracht		gebracht
brouwen	(brouwde)		gebrouwen
buigen	boog	bogen	gebogen
delven	(delfde)/dolf	(delfden)/dolven	gedolven
denken	dacht		gedacht
dingen	dong		gedongen
doen	deed	deden	gedaan
1. doe 2. doet 3. doet			
dragen	droeg		gedragen
drijven	dreef	dreven	gedreven
dringen	drong		gedrongen
drinken	dronk		gedronken
druipen	droop	dropen	gedropen
duiken	dook	doken	gedoken
dunken	(dunkte)/docht		(gedunkt)/gedocht
dwingen	dwong		gedwongen
eten	at	aten	gegeten
fluiten	floot	floten	gefloten
gaan	ging		gegaan
1. ga 2. gaat 3. gaat			
gelden	gold		gegolden
genezen	genas	genazen	genezen
genieten	genoot	genoten	genoten
geven	gaf	gaven	gegeven
gieten	goot	goten	gegoten
glijden	gleed	gleden	gegleden
glimmen	glom	glommen	geglommen
graven	groef	groeven	gegraven
grijpen	greep	grepen	gegrepen
hangen	hing		gehangen
hebben	had	hadden	gehad
1. heb 2. hebt 3. heeft			
heffen	hief	hieven	geheven

infinitive	imperfect sing	imperfect pl	past participle
helpen	hielp		geholpen
heten	(heette)		geheten
hijsen	hees	hesen	gehesen
houden	hield		gehouden
houwen	hieuw		gehouwen
jagen	(jaagde)/joeg		(gejaagd)
kiezen	koos	kozen	gekozen
kijken	keek	keken	gekeken
klimmen	klom	klommen	geklommen
klinken	klonk		geklonken
kluiven	kloof	kloven	gekloven
knijpen	kneep	knepen	geknepen
komen	kwam	kwamen	gekomen
kopen	kocht		gekocht
krijgen	kreeg	kregen	gekregen
krimpen	kromp		gekrompen
kruipen	kroop	kropen	gekropen
kunnen	kon	konden	(gekund)
1. kan 2. kan/kunt 3. kan			
kwijten	kweet	kweten	gekweten
lachen	(lachte)		gelachen
laden	(laadde)		geladen
laten	liet		gelaten
lezen	las	lazen	gelezen
liegen	loog	logen	gelogen
liggen	lag	lagen	gelegen
lijden	leed	leden	geleden
lijken	leek	leken	geleken
lopen	liep		gelopen
malen	(maalde)		gemalen
melken	molk/(melkte)		gemolken
meten	mat/(meette)	maten/(meetten)	gemeten
mijden	meed	meden	gemeden
moeten	moest		gemoeten
mogen	mocht		gemogen
1. mag 2. mag 3. mag			
napluizen	ploos na	plozen na	nageplozen
nemen	nam	namen	genomen
ontginnen	ontgon	ontgonnen	ontgonnen
ontluiken	ontlook	ontloken	ontloken
ontspruiten	ontsproot	ontsproten	ontsproten
plegen			
- be in habit of	placht		-
- commit	(pleegde)		(gepleegd)
pluizen	(pluisde)		geplozen/(gepluisd)
prijzen			
- praise	prees	prezen	geprezen
- price	(prijsde)		(geprijsd)
raden	(raadde)		geraden
rieken	(riekte)/rook		geroken
rijden	reed	reden	gereden
rijgen	reeg	regen	geregen
rijten	reet	reten	gereten
rijzen	rees	rezen	gerezen
roepen	riep		geroepen
ruiken	rook	roken	geroken
scheiden	(scheidde)		gescheiden
schelden	schold		gescholden
schenden	schond		geschonden
schenken	schonk		geschonken

infinitive	imperfect sing	imperfect pl	past participle
scheppen			
- create	schiep		geschapen
- shovel	(schepte)		(geschept)
scheren			
- shave	schoor	schoren	geschoren
- skim	(scheerde)		(gescheerd)
schieten	schoot	schoten	geschoten
schijnen	scheen	schenen	geschenen
schijten	scheet	scheten	gescheten
schrijden	schreed	schreden	geschreden
schrijven	schreef	schreven	geschreven
schrikken			
- be scared	schrok	schrokken	geschrokken
- be quenched	(schrikte)		(geschrikt)
schuilen			
- hide	school	scholen	gescholen
- shelter	(schuilde)		(geschuild)
schuiven	schoof	schoven	geschoven
slaan	sloeg		geslagen
1. sla 2. slaat 3. slaat			
slapen	sliep		geslapen
slijpen	sleep	slepen	geslepen
slijten	sleet	sleten	gesleten
slinken	slonk		geslonken
sluipen	sloop	slopen	geslopen
sluiten	sloot	sloten	gesloten
smelten	smolt		gesmolten
smijten	smeet	smeten	gesmeten
snijden	sneed	sneden	gesneden
snuiten	snoot	snoten	gesnoten
snuiven	snoof	snoven	gesnoven
spannen	(spande)		gespannen
spijten	speet	speten	gespeten
spinnen	(spinde)/spon	(spinden)/sponnen	gesponnen
splijten	spleet	spleten	gespleten
spreken	sprak	spraken	gesproken
springen	sprong		gesprongen
spugen	(spuugde)		(gespuugd)/gespogen
spruiten	sproot	sproten	gesproten
spuiten	spoot	spoten	gespoten
staan	stond		gestaan
1. sta 2. staat 3. staat			
steken	stak	staken	gestoken
stelen	stal	stalen	gestolen
sterven	stierf	stierven	gestorven
stijgen	steeg	stegen	gestegen
stinken	stonk		gestonken
strijden	streed	streden	gestreden
strijken	streek	streken	gestreken
stuiven	stoof	stoven	gestoven
treden	trad	traden	getreden
treffen	trof	troffen	getroffen
trekken	trok	trokken	getrokken
vallen	viel		gevallen
vangen	ving		gevangen
varen	voer		gevaren
vechten	vocht		gevochten
verdwijnen	verdween	verdwenen	verdwenen
vergeten	vergat	vergaten	vergeten
verliezen	verloor	verloren	verloren

infinitive	imperfect sing	imperfect pl	past participle
verschuilen	verschool	verscholen	verscholen
verslinden	verslond		verslonden
verzinnen	verzon	verzonnen	verzonnen
vinden	vond		gevonden
vlechten	vlocht		gevlochten
vliegen	vloog	vlogen	gevlogen
vouwen	(vouwde)		gevouwen
vragen	vroeg		gevraagd
vreten	vrat	vraten	gevreten
vriezen	vroor	vroren	gevroren
waaien	(waaide)/woei		gewaaid
wassen			
- grow	wies		gewassen
- wash	(waste)		gewassen
wegen	woog	wogen	gewogen
werpen	wierp		geworpen
werven	wierf	wierven	geworven
weten	wist		geweten
weven	weefde		geweven
wezen	was	waren	(geweest)
wijken	week	weken	geweken
wijten	weet	weten	geweten
wijzen	wees	wezen	gewezen
willen	(wilde)/wou	(wilden)/wouden	(gewild)
1. wil 2. wilt 3. wil			
winden	wond		gewonden
winnen	won	wonnen	gewonnen
worden	werd		geworden
wreken	(wreekte)		gewroken
wrijven	wreef	wreven	gewreven
wringen	wrong		gewrongen
zeggen	zei/(zegde)	zeiden/(zegden)	(gezegd)
zenden	zond		gezonden
zien	zag	zagen	gezien
1. zie 2. ziet 3. ziet			
zijgen	zeeg	zegen	gezegen
zijn	was	waren	geweest
1. ben 2. bent 3. is			
zingen	zong		gezongen
zinken	zonk		gezonken
zinnen	zon/(zinde)	zonnen/(zinden)	gezonnen
zitten	zat	zaten	gezeten
zoeken	zocht		gezocht
zouten	(zoutte)		gezouten
zuigen	zoog	zogen	gezogen
zuipen	zoop	zopen	gezopen
zullen	zou	zouden	-
1. zal 2. zult 3. zal			
zwelgen	zwolg		gezwolgen
zwellen	zwol	zwollen	gezwollen
zwemmen	zwom	zwommen	gezwommen
zweren			
- swear	zwoer		gezworen
- fester	zwoor/(zweerde)	zworen/(zweerden)	gezworen
zwerven	zwierf	zwierven	gezworven
zwijgen	zweeg	zwegen	gezwegen

Dutch–English

a

de **a** /a/ (pl: a's) a, A: *van a tot z kennen* know from A to Z (*or:* from beginning to end); *wie a zegt, moet ook b zeggen* in for a penny, in for a pound

à /a/ (prep) **1** [roughly] (from …) to, [roughly] or: *2 à 3 maal* 2 or 3 times; *er waren zo'n 10 à 15 personen* there were some 10 to 15 people **2** at (the rate of): *5 meter à 6 euro, is 30 euro* 5 metres at 6 euros is 30 euros

het **A4'tje** /aviːrcə/ **1** A4 page **2** side

de **AA** /aa/ (pl) *Anonieme Alcoholisten* Alcoholics Anonymous

de **aai** /aj/ (pl: -en) stroke; caress; pet

aaien /ajə(n)/ (aaide, heeft geaaid) stroke; caress

de **aak** /ak/ (pl: aken) barge

de **aal** /al/ (pl: alen) eel

de **aalbes** /albɛs/ (pl: -sen) currant

de **aalmoes** /almus/ (pl: aalmoezen) alms

de **aalmoezenier** /almuzənir/ chaplain

de **aalscholver** /alsxɔlvər/ (pl: -s) cormorant

het **aambeeld** /ambelt/ (pl: -en) anvil

de **aambeien** /ambɛiə(n)/ (pl) piles

¹**aan** /an/ (adj) on: *een vrouw met een groene jurk* ~ a woman in (*or:* wearing) a green dress; *de kachel is* ~ the stove is on ‖ *het is weer dik* ~ *tussen hen* it's on again between them; *daar is niets* ~ **a)** there's nothing to it; **b)** it's dead easy; **c)** it's a waste of time

²**aan** /an/ (adv) (+ wat) about, around, away: *ik rotzooi maar wat* ~ I'm just messing about ‖ *stel je niet zo* ~*!* stop carrying on like that!; *daar heeft zij niets* ~ that's no use to her; *daar zijn we nog niet* ~ *toe* we haven't got that far yet; [fig] *zij weet niet waar zij* ~ *toe is* she doesn't know where she stands; *rustig* ~*!* calm down!, take it easy!; *van nu af* ~ from now on; *van voren af* ~ from the beginning; *van jongs af* ~ from childhood; *jij kunt ervan op* ~ *dat …* you can count on it that …

³**aan** /an/ (prep) **1** on, at, by: *vruchten* ~ *de bomen* fruit on the trees; ~ *een verslag werken* work on a report; ~ *zee* (or: *de kust*) *wonen* live by the sea (*or:* on the coast) **2** by, with: *dag* ~ *dag* day by day; *doen* ~ do, go in for; *twee* ~ *twee* two by two **3** to: *hij geeft les* ~ *de universiteit* he lectures at the university; ~ *wal gaan* go ashore; *hoe kom je* ~ *dat spul?* how did you get hold of that stuff? **4** of, from: *sterven* ~ *een ziekte* die of a disease **5** of: *een tekort* ~ *kennis* a lack of knowledge **6** up to: *het is* ~ *mij ervoor te zorgen dat …* it is up to me to see that …; *dat ligt* ~ *haar* that's

her fault ‖ *hij heeft het* ~ *zijn hart* he has got heart trouble; *hij is* ~ *het joggen* he's out jogging; *hij is* ~ *het strijken* he's (busy) ironing; *ze zijn* ~ *vakantie toe* they could do with (*or:* are badly in need of) a holiday

aanbakken /ambakə(n)/ (bakte aan, is aangebakken) burn, get burnt

aanbellen /ambɛlə(n)/ (belde aan, heeft aangebeld) ring (at the door): *bij iem.* ~ ring s.o.'s doorbell

aanbesteden /ambəstedə(n)/ (besteedde aan, heeft aanbesteed) put out to tender: *werk* ~ put work out to tender, call for (*or:* invite) tenders for work

de **aanbesteding** /ambəstedɪŋ/ (pl: -en) tender; contract: *inschrijven* op een ~ (submit a) tender for a contract

de **aanbetaling** /ambətalɪŋ/ (pl: -en) down payment; deposit: *een* ~ *doen van 200 euro* make a down payment of 200 euros

aanbevelen /ambəvelə(n)/ (beval aan, heeft aanbevolen) recommend: *dat kan ik je warm* ~ I can recommend it warmly to you; *voor suggesties houden wij ons aanbevolen* we welcome any suggestions

aanbevelenswaardig /ambəvelə(n)swardəχ/ (adj) recommendable, advisable

de **aanbeveling** /ambəvelɪŋ/ (pl: -en) recommendation: *het verdient* ~ *om …* it is advisable to …

aanbidden /ambɪdə(n)/ (aanbad, heeft aanbeden) **1** worship; venerate **2** [fig] worship; adore: *Jan aanbad zijn vrouw* Jan worshipped (*or:* adored) his wife

de **aanbidder** /ambɪdər/ (pl: -s) **1** worshipper **2** admirer: *een stille* ~ a secret admirer

aanbieden /ambidə(n)/ (bood aan, heeft aangeboden) **1** offer, give: *iem. een geschenk* ~ present a gift to s.o.; *hulp* (*or:* *diensten*) ~ offer help (*or:* services); *zijn ontslag* ~ tender one's resignation; *zijn verontschuldigingen* ~ offer one's apologies **2** offer: *iets te koop* (or: *huur*) ~ put sth. up for sale (*or:* rent)

de **aanbieding** /ambidɪŋ/ (pl: -en) special offer, bargain: *goedkope* (or: *speciale*) ~ special offer, bargain; *koffie is in de* ~ *deze week* coffee is on special offer this week, coffee's reduced this week

aanbinden /ambɪndə(n)/ (bond aan, heeft aangebonden) **1** fasten on **2** engage

aanblijven /amblɛivə(n)/ (bleef aan, is aangebleven) stay on: *zij blijft aan als minister* she is staying on as minister

de **aanblik** /amblɪk/ **1** sight, glance: *bij de eerste* ~ at first sight (*or:* glance) **2** sight; [pers] appearance: *een troosteloze* ~ *opleveren* be a sorry sight, make a sorry spectacle

het **aanbod** /ambɔt/ **1** offer: *iem. een* ~ *doen* make s.o. an offer; *zij nam het* ~ *aan* she accepted (*or:* took up) the offer; *zij sloeg het* ~

af she rejected the offer; *een ~ dat je niet kunt weigeren* an offer you can't refuse **2** supply: *vraag en ~* supply and demand

aanboren /ˈambɔrə(n)/ (boorde aan, heeft aangeboord) tap, broach: *een nieuw vat ~* tap (*or:* broach) a new barrel; [fig] *nieuwe belastingbronnen ~* tap new sources of taxation

de **aanbouw** /ˈambɑu/ **1** building; construction: *dit huis is in ~* this house is under construction **2** extension, annexe: *een ~ aan een huis* an extension (*or:* annexe) to a house

aanbouwen /ˈambɑuwə(n)/ (bouwde aan, heeft aangebouwd) build on, add: *een aangebouwde keuken* a built-on kitchen

aanbranden /ˈambrɑndə(n)/ (brandde aan, is aangebrand) burn (on): *laat de aardappelen niet ~* mind the potatoes don't boil dry (*or:* get burnt)

¹**aanbreken** /ˈambrekə(n)/ (brak aan, is aangebroken) come, break; dawn; fall: *het moment was aangebroken om afscheid te nemen* the moment had come to say goodbye

²**aanbreken** /ˈambrekə(n)/ (brak aan, heeft aangebroken) break into; break (into); open (up): *er staat nog een aangebroken fles* there's a bottle that's already been opened

aanbrengen /ˈambrɛŋə(n)/ (bracht aan, heeft aangebracht) **1** put in, put on, install; introduce; apply: *verbeteringen ~* make improvements; *make-up ~* put on make-up **2** inform on; report: *een zaak ~* report a matter

de **aandacht** /ˈandɑxt/ attention, notice: *(persoonlijke) ~ besteden aan* give (*or:* pay) (personal) attention to; *aan de ~ ontsnappen* escape notice; *al zijn ~ richten op ...* focus all one's attention on ...; *iemands ~ trekken* attract s.o.'s attention, catch s.o.'s eye; *de ~ vestigen op* draw attention to; *onder de ~ komen* (*or:* *brengen*) *van* come (*or:* bring) to the attention of

aandachtig /ˈandɑxtəx/ (adj, adv) attentive, intent: *~ luisteren* listen attentively (*or:* intently); *iets ~ bestuderen* examine sth. carefully (*or:* closely)

het **aandachtspunt** /ˈandɑx(t)spʏnt/ (pl: -en) point of (special (*or:* particular)) interest: *een ~ van iets maken* draw special (*or:* particular) attention to sth.

het **aandeel** /ˈandel/ (pl: aandelen) **1** share, portion: *~ hebben in een zaak* (*or:* *de winst*) have a share in a business (*or:* the profits) **2** contribution, part: *een actief ~ hebben in iets take* an active part in sth. **3** share (certificate); [Am] stock (certificate); *~ op naam* nominative share, registered share

de **aandeelhouder** /ˈandelhɑudər/ (pl: -s) shareholder

het **aandenken** /ˈandɛŋkə(n)/ keepsake, memento: *iets bewaren als ~* keep sth. as a keepsake

zich **aandienen** /ˈandinə(n)/ (diende zich aan, heeft zich aangediend) present o.s. (as): *er diende zich een mogelijkheid aan om ... an* opportunity to ... presented itself

aandikken /ˈandɪkə(n)/ (dikte aan, heeft aangedikt) embroider, pile (it) on

aandoen /ˈandun/ (deed aan, heeft aangedaan) **1** put on **2** do to, cause: *iem. een proces ~* take s.o. to court; *iem. verdriet, onrecht ~* cause s.o. grief, do s.o. an injustice; *dat kun je haar niet ~!* you can't do that to her! **3** turn on, switch on

de **aandoening** /ˈandunɪŋ/ (pl: -en) disorder, complaint

aandoenlijk /ˈandunlək/ (adj, adv) moving, touching

aandraaien /ˈandrajə(n)/ (draaide aan, heeft aangedraaid) tighten, screw tighter

aandragen /ˈandraɣə(n)/ (droeg aan, heeft aangedragen) carry, bring (up/along/to)

de **aandrang** /ˈandrɑŋ/ insistence, instigation: *~ uitoefenen op* exert pressure on; *~ hebben* need to go

aandrijven /ˈandrɛivə(n)/ (dreef aan, heeft aangedreven) drive: *door een elektromotor aangedreven* driven by an electric motor

de **aandrijving** /ˈandrɛivɪŋ/ (pl: -en) drive, power: *elektrische ~* electric drive (*or:* power)

aandringen /ˈandrɪŋə(n)/ (drong aan, heeft aangedrongen) **1** urge: *niet verder ~* not press the point, not insist; *bij iem. op hulp ~* urge s.o. to help **2** insist: *er sterk op ~ dat* strongly insist that; *~ op iets* insist on sth.

aanduiden /ˈandœydə(n)/ (duidde aan, heeft aangeduid) indicate: *niet nader aangeduid* unspecified; *iem. ~ als X* refer to s.o. as X

aandurven /ˈandʏrvə(n)/ (durfde aan, heeft aangedurfd) dare to (do), feel up to: *een taak ~* feel up to a task; *het ~ om* dare (*or:* presume) to

aanduwen /ˈandywə(n)/ (duwde aan, heeft aangeduwd) **1** push (on) **2** push home, press firm

aaneen /aˈnen/ (adv): *jaren ~* (for) years on end (*or:* at a time, stretch); *dicht ~* close together; *kilometers ~* kilometres at a stretch

aaneengesloten /aˈnenɣəslotə(n)/ (adj) unbroken, connected, continuous; [fig] united

de **aaneenschakeling** /aˈnensxakəlɪŋ/ (pl: -en) chain, succession, sequence: *een ~ van ongelukken* a series (*or:* sequence) of accidents

aanflitsen /ˈanflɪtsə(n)/ (flitste aan, heeft aangeflitst) flash on

de **aanfluiting** /ˈanflœytɪŋ/ (pl: -en) mockery

¹**aangaan** /ˈaŋɑn/ (ging aan, is aangegaan) **1** go (towards), head (for/towards): *achter iem. (iets) ~* **a)** chase s.o. (sth.) (up); **b)** [fig] go

after s.o., go for sth. **2** go on; switch on; light turned himself in **4** indicate, mark: *de thermometer geeft 30* **graden** *aan* the thermometer is registering 30 degrees; *de* **maat** *~ beat time* **5** [socc] feed; [volleyball] set

²**aangaan** /ˈaŋɣan/ (ging aan, is aangegaan) **1** enter into; contract: *een lening* ~ contract a loan; *de* **strijd** *~* enter into combat (with), fight (with) **2** concern: *dat gaat hem niets aan* that's none of his business; *wat mij aangaat* as far as I'm concerned

aangaande /ˈaŋɣandə/ (prep) as regards, regarding, with regard (or: respect) to, concerning

de **aangever** /ˈaŋɣevər/ (pl: -s) **1** informant; person submitting a declaration **2** [socc] feeder

aangewezen /ˈaŋɣəwezə(n)/ (adj): *de ~* **persoon** the obvious (or: right) person (for the job); *op iets ~ zijn* rely on sth.; *op zichzelf ~ zijn* be left to one's own devices; *zij zijn* **op** *elkaar ~* they depend (or: rely) on each other

het **aangezicht** /ˈaŋɣəzɪxt/ (pl: -en) countenance, face

aangapen /ˈaŋɣapə(n)/ (gaapte aan, heeft aangegaapt) gape (at), gawp at, gawk at: *sta me niet zo dom aan te gapen!* stop gaping at me like an idiot!

aangeboren /ˈaŋɣəborə(n)/ (adj) innate, inborn; [med] congenital

aangezien /ˈaŋɣəzin/ (conj) since, as, seeing (that)

de **aangifte** /ˈaŋɣɪftə/ (pl: -n) declaration; report; registration: *~* **inkomstenbelasting** income tax return; *~* **doen** *van een misdrijf* report a crime; *~* **doen** make a declaration; *~* **doen** *van geboorte* register a birth; *bij diefstal* **wordt** *altijd* **gedaan** shoplifters will be prosecuted

aangedaan /ˈaŋɣədan/ (adj) **1** moved, touched **2** affected

aangeharkt /ˈaŋɣəharkt/ (adj) [fig] manicured, immaculate: *het landschap* **ligt er** *~* **bij** the landscape looks well manicured

de **aangeklaagde** /ˈaŋɣəklaɣdə/ (pl: -n) accused, defendant

het **aangifteformulier** /ˈaŋɣɪftəformylir/ (pl: -en) tax form; declaration; registration form

aangelegd /ˈaŋɣəlɛxt/ (adj) -minded: *artistiek ~ zijn* have an artistic bent

aangrenzend /ˈaŋɣrɛnzənt/ (adj) adjoining; adjacent; neighbouring

de **aangelegenheid** /ˈaŋɣəleɣənhɛit/ (pl: -heden) affair, business, matter

aangrijpen /ˈaŋɣrɛipə(n)/ (greep aan, heeft aangegrepen) **1** grip; move; make a deep impression on: *dit* **boek** *heeft me zeer aangegrepen* this book has made a deep impression on me **2** seize (at/upon), grip: *een* **gelegenheid** *met beide handen ~* seize (at/upon) an opportunity with both hands

aangenaam /ˈaŋɣənam/ (adj, adv) pleasant; pleasing; congenial: *ze was ~* **verrast** she was pleasantly surprised; *~ (met u kennis te maken)* pleased to meet you

aangenomen /ˈaŋɣənomə(n)/ (adj): *~* **werk** contract work

aangrijpend /ˈaŋɣrɛipənt/ (adj, adv) moving, touching, poignant

aangepast /ˈaŋɣəpast/ (adj) (specially) adapted; adjusted: *een ~e* **versie** an adapted version; *een ~e* **ingang** a specially adapted entrance; *goed ~ zijn* be well-adapted (or: well-adjusted); *slecht ~ zijn* be poorly adapted (or: adjusted)

aangroeien /ˈaŋɣrujə(n)/ (groeide aan, is aangegroeid) **1** grow, increase **2** grow again: **doen** *~* regenerate

aanhaken /ˈanhakə(n)/ (haakte aan, heeft/is aangehaakt): *hij kon* **bij** *de kopgroep ~* he was able to join the leading group; *ik wilde graag even* **bij** *het zojuist gezegde ~* I would like to come in here, could I just follow up on that?

aangeschoten /ˈaŋɣəsxotə(n)/ (adj) **1** under the influence, tipsy **2** unintentional: *~* **hands** unintentional hands

aanhalen /ˈanhalə(n)/ (haalde aan, heeft aangehaald) **1** caress, fondle **2** quote: *als* **voorbeeld** (or: **bewijs**) *~* quote as an example (or: as evidence) **3** pull in; haul in: *we moeten allemaal de* **buikriem** *~* we'll all have to tighten our belts

aangeslagen /ˈaŋɣəslaɣə(n)/ (adj) affected; shaken: *hij was ~* **door** *het nieuws* he was shaken (or: deeply affected) by the news

aangetekend /ˈaŋɣətekənt/ (adj) registered: *je moet die stukken ~* **versturen** you must send those items by registered mail

aanhalig /ˈanhaləɣ/ (adj, adv) affectionate: *hij kon zeer ~* **doen** he could be very affectionate

aangetrouwd /ˈaŋɣətraut/ (adj) related by marriage: *~e* **familie** in-laws

de **aanhaling** /ˈanhalɪŋ/ (pl: -en) quotation; [inform] quote

aangeven /ˈaŋɣevə(n)/ (gaf aan, heeft aangegeven) **1** hand, pass **2** indicate, declare: *de trein vertrok op de aangegeven* **tijd** the train left on time; *tenzij* **anders** *aangegeven* except where otherwise specified, unless stated otherwise **3** report, notify; declare: *een* **diefstal** *~* report a theft (to the police); *een* **geboorte** (or: **huwelijk**) *~* register a birth (or: marriage); *hebt u nog iets aan te geven?* do you have anything (else) to declare?; *de dader heeft* **zichzelf** *aangegeven* the culprit

het **aanhalingsteken** /ˈanhalɪŋstekə(n)/ (pl: -s) quotation mark; [inform] quote; inverted comma: *tussen ~s* in quotation marks, in inverted commas

de **aanhang** /ˈanhaŋ/ following; supporters: *over een grote ~ beschikken* have a large following; *veel ~ vinden onder* find considerable support among, have a large following among

aanhangen /ɑnhɑŋə(n)/ (hing aan, heeft aangehangen) adhere to, be attached to, support: *een geloof ~* adhere to a faith; *een partij ~* support a party

de **aanhanger** /ɑnhɑŋər/ (pl: -s) **1** follower; supporter: *een vurig* (or: *trouw*) *~ van* an ardent (or: a faithful) supporter of **2** trailer

aanhangig /ɑnhɑŋəχ/ (adj) pending, before the courts: *een kwestie ~ maken bij de autoriteiten* take a matter up with the authorities

het **aanhangsel** /ɑnhɑŋsəl/ (pl: -s) appendix: *een ~ bij een polis* an appendix to a policy; *het wormvormig ~* the vermiform appendix

de **aanhangwagen** /ɑnhɑŋwaɣə(n)/ (pl: -s) trailer

aanhankelijk /ɑnhɑŋkələk/ (adj, adv) affectionate, devoted

aanhebben /ɑnhɛbə(n)/ (had aan, heeft aangehad) have on, be wearing

aanhechten /ɑnhɛχtə(n)/ (hechtte aan, heeft aangehecht) attach; fasten on; affix

de **aanhechting** /ɑnhɛχtɪŋ/ (pl: -en) attachment

de **aanhef** /ɑnhɛf/ opening words; [letter] salutation

aanheffen /ɑnhɛfə(n)/ (hief aan, heeft aangeheven) start, begin; break into; raise

aanhoren /ɑnhorə(n)/ (hoorde aan, heeft aangehoord) listen to, hear: *iemands relaas geduldig ~* listen patiently to s.o.'s story

¹**aanhouden** /ɑnhɑudə(n)/ (hield aan, heeft aangehouden) **1** keep on, go on, persist (in): *blijven ~* persevere, insist; *je moet niet zo ~* you shouldn't keep going on about it (like that) **2** go on, continue; hold, last, keep up **3** (+ op) keep [left or right]; make (for), head (for): *links* (or: *rechts*) *~* keep to the left (or: right); bear left (or: right)

²**aanhouden** /ɑnhɑudə(n)/ (hield aan, heeft aangehouden) **1** stop; arrest; hold: *een verdachte ~* take a suspect into custody **2** hold on to, keep; continue; stick to **3** keep on **4** keep on, keep up; leave on; keep going || *als je het recept aanhoudt, kan er niets misgaan* if you stick to the recipe, nothing can go wrong

aanhoudend /ɑnhɑudənt/ (adj, adv) **1** continuous, persistent, constant, all the time: *een ~e droogte* a prolonged period of drought **2** continual, repeated, time and again, always

de **aanhouder** /ɑnhɑudər/ (pl: -s) sticker, go-getter: *de ~ wint* it's dogged that (or: as) does it; if at first you don't succeed, try, try, try again

de **aanhouding** /ɑnhɑudɪŋ/ (pl: -en) arrest
aanjagen /ɑɲjaɣə(n)/ (jaagde aan/joeg aan,

heeft aangejaagd) fill with: *iem. schrik ~* frighten (or: terrify) s.o.

aankaarten /ɑnkartə(n)/ (kaartte aan, heeft aangekaart) raise: *een zaak ~ bij* raise a matter with

aankijken /ɑnkɛikə(n)/ (keek aan, heeft aangekeken) look at: *elkaar veelbetekenend ~* give each other a meaningful look; *het ~ niet waard* not worth looking at

de **aanklacht** /ɑnklɑχt/ (pl: -en) charge; indictment; complaint: *een ~ indienen tegen iem. (bij)* lodge a complaint against s.o. (with); *de ~ werd ingetrokken* the charge was dropped

aanklagen /ɑnklaɣə(n)/ (klaagde aan, heeft aangeklaagd) bring charges against, lodge a complaint against: *iem. ~ wegens diefstal* (or: *moord*) charge s.o. with theft (or: murder)

de **aanklager** /ɑnklaɣər/ (pl: -s) accuser; complainant; plaintiff; prosecutor: *openbare ~* public prosecutor, Crown Prosecutor

aanklampen /ɑnklɑmpə(n)/ (klampte aan, heeft aangeklampt) stop; [fig] approach, apply to || *~ bij de kopgroep* join the leaders

aankleden /ɑnkledə(n)/ (kleedde aan, heeft aangekleed) dress, get dressed; clothe; fit out: *je moet die jongen warm ~* you must wrap the boy up well; *zich ~* get dressed

de **aankleding** /ɑnkledɪŋ/ (pl: -en) furnishing; decor; furnishings; decor; set(ting)

aanklikken /ɑnklɪkə(n)/ (klikte aan, heeft aangeklikt) click (on)

aankloppen /ɑnklɔpə(n)/ (klopte aan, heeft aangeklopt) knock (at the door); [fig] come with a request; appeal (to): *tevergeefs bij iem. ~ om hulp* appeal to s.o. for help in vain

aanknopen /ɑnknopə(n)/ (knoopte aan, heeft aangeknoopt) **1** tie on **2** enter into: *betrekkingen ~ met* establish relations with; *onderhandelingen ~ met* enter into negotiations with; *een gesprek ~ met* begin (or: strike up) a conversation with

het **aanknopingspunt** /ɑnknopɪŋspʏnt/ (pl: -en) clue, lead; starting point

aankoeken /ɑnkukə(n)/ (koekte aan, is aangekoekt) cake, stick: *het eten was aangekoekt* the food had caked (or: stuck) on to the pan

¹**aankomen** /ɑnkomə(n)/ (kwam aan, is aangekomen) **1** arrive, reach; come in, pull in; [sport] finish: *de trein kan elk ogenblik ~* the train is due at any moment; *daar komt iem. aan* s.o. is coming; *als derde ~* come in third **2** hit hard: *de klap is hard aangekomen* a) it was a heavy blow; b) [fig] it was a great blow to him **3** come (with): *en daar kom je nu pas mee aan?* and now you tell me!; *je hoeft met dat plan bij hem niet aan te komen* it's no use going to him with that plan **4** come (along), approach: *ik zag het ~* I could see it coming **5** touch, hit, come up (against): *niet* (or: *ner-*

gens) ~*!* don't touch!, hands off! **6** put on weight

²**aankomen** /a̱ŋkomə(n)/ (kwam aan, is aangekomen) come (down) (to): *als het op betalen aankomt* when it comes to paying; *waar het op aankomt* what really matters ‖ *als het erop aan komt* when it comes to the crunch

aankomend /a̱ŋkomənt/ (adj) prospective, future; budding; apprentice; trainee: *een ~ actrice* a starlet, an up-and-coming actress; *een ~ schrijver* a budding author

de **aankomst** /a̱ŋkomst/ arrival, coming (in); [sport] finish(ing); [aeroplane] landing: *in volgorde van ~* in (the) order of finishing; *bij ~* on arrival

de **aankomsttijd** /a̱ŋkomstɛit/ (pl: -en) time of arrival

aankondigen /a̱ŋkondəɣə(n)/ (kondigde aan, heeft aangekondigd) announce: *de volgende plaat ~* announce (or: introduce) the next record; *~ iets te zullen doen* announce that one will do sth.

de **aankondiging** /a̱ŋkondəɣɪŋ/ (pl: -en) announcement, notice; signal; foreboding; proclamation: *tot nadere ~* until further notice

de **aankoop** /a̱ŋkop/ (pl: aankopen) **1** buying: *bij ~ van drie flacons krijgt u een poster cadeau* (you get a) free poster with every three bottles **2** purchase(s): *grote aankopen doen* make large purchases

aankopen /a̱ŋkopə(n)/ (kocht aan, heeft aangekocht) buy, purchase, acquire

aankrijgen /a̱ŋkrɛiɣə(n)/ (kreeg aan, heeft aangekregen) get going: *ik krijg de kachel niet aan* I can't get the stove to burn (or: light)

aankruisen /a̱ŋkrœysə(n)/ (kruiste aan, heeft aangekruist) tick: *~ wat van toepassing is* tick where appropriate

aankunnen /a̱ŋkʏnə(n)/ (kon aan, heeft aangekund) **1** be a match for, (be able to) hold one's own against: *het alleen ~* hold one's own **2** be equal (or: up) to, be able to manage (or: cope with): *zij kon het werk niet aan* she couldn't cope (with the work) ‖ *kan ik ervan op aan, dat je komt?* can I rely on your coming?

aanlanden /a̱nlandə(n)/ (landde aan, is aangeland) land (up), arrive at: *waar zijn we nu aangeland?* where have we got to now?

aanlandig /a̱nlandəx/ (adj) onshore: *de wind is ~* there is an onshore wind, the wind is blowing home

de **aanleg** /a̱nlɛx/ **1** construction, building; laying; digging; layout: *in ~* under construction; *~ van elektriciteit* installation of electricity **2** talent; aptitude: *~ tonen voor talen* show an aptitude for languages; *~ voor muziek* a talent for music; *daar moet je ~ voor hebben* it's a gift **3** tendency, predisposition, inclina-

tion: *~ voor griep hebben* be susceptible to flu ‖ [Belg] *rechtbank van eerste ~* [roughly] county court

¹**aanleggen** /a̱nlɛɣə(n)/ (legde aan, heeft aangelegd) [shipp] moor, tie up; touch (at); berth

²**aanleggen** /a̱nlɛɣə(n)/ (legde aan, heeft aangelegd) **1** construct, build; lay; dig; lay out; install; build up: *een spoorweg* (or: *weg*) *~* construct a railway (or: road); *een nieuwe wijk ~* build a new estate; [Am] build a new development; *voorraden ~* build up stocks, stock up on provisions **2** aim

de **aanlegplaats** /a̱nlɛxplats/ (pl: -en) landing stage, landing place, mooring place; berth

de **aanleiding** /a̱nlɛidɪŋ/ (pl: -en) occasion, reason, cause: *er bestaat geen ~ om* (or: *tot*) there is no reason to (or: for); *iem. (geen) ~ geven* give s.o. (no) cause; *~ zijn (geven) tot* give rise to; *naar ~ van* as a result of

aanlengen /a̱nlɛŋə(n)/ (lengde aan, heeft aangelengd) dilute

aanleren /a̱nlerə(n)/ (leerde aan, heeft aangeleerd) **1** learn, acquire: *slechte manieren ~* acquire bad manners **2** teach: *een hond kunstjes ~* teach a dog tricks

aanleunen /a̱nlønə(n)/ (leunde aan, heeft aangeleund) lean (against/towards): *~ tegen* bear (close) resemblance to ‖ [Belg] *~ bij* seek support (or: protection) from; *zich iets laten ~* take (or: put up with, swallow) sth.

de **aanleunwoning** /a̱nlønwonɪŋ/ granny house, sheltered accommodation

aanlijnen /a̱nlɛinə(n)/ (lijnde aan, heeft aangelijnd) leash: *aangelijnd houden* keep on the leash (or: lead)

aanlokkelijk /a̱nlɔkələk/ (adj) tempting, alluring, attractive

de **aanloop** /a̱nlop/ (pl: aanlopen) **1** run-up: *een ~ nemen* take a run-up; *een sprong met* (or: *zonder*) *~* a running (or: standing) jump; *in de ~ naar de verkiezingen* in the build-up to the elections **2** visitors, callers; customers: *zij hebben altijd veel ~* they always have lots of visitors

de **aanloopkosten** /a̱nlopkɔstə(n)/ (pl) initial costs (or: expenses)

aanlopen /a̱nlopə(n)/ (liep aan, is aangelopen) **1** walk (towards), come (towards); drop in, drop by: *tegen iets ~* **a)** walk into sth.; **b)** [fig] chance (or: stumble) on sth. **2** rub; drag **3** turn … (in the face): *rood ~* turn red in the face

de **aanmaak** /a̱mak/ manufacture, production

aanmaken /a̱makə(n)/ (maakte aan, heeft aangemaakt) **1** mix; prepare: *sla ~* dress a salad **2** light: *een vuur* (or: *de kachel*) *~* light a fire (or: the stove)

aanmanen /a̱manə(n)/ (maande aan, heeft aangemaand) **1** urge: *tot voorzichtigheid ~* urge caution **2** order: *iem. tot betaling ~* demand payment from s.o.

de **aanmaning** /ˈaːmanɪŋ/ (pl: -en) **1** reminder: *een vriendelijke ~* a gentle reminder **2** request for payment, notice to pay: *~ tot betaling* a) reminder; b) final notice

zich **aanmatigen** /ˈaːmatəɣə(n)/ (matigde zich aan, heeft zich aangematigd): *zich een oordeel ~* take it upon o.s. to pass judgement

aanmatigend /ˈaːmatəɣənt/ (adj, adv) presumptuous, arrogant, high-handed: *op ~e toon spreken* speak arrogantly (or: in a high-handed manner)

aanmelden /ˈaːmɛldə(n)/ (meldde aan, heeft aangemeld) **1** announce, report **2** present, enter forward (s.o.'s name), put forward (s.o.'s name)

de **aanmelding** /ˈaːmɛldɪŋ/ (pl: -en) entry; application; enlistment; enrolment: *de ~ is gesloten* applications will no longer be accepted

aanmeren /ˈaːmerə(n)/ (meerde aan, heeft aangemeerd) moor, tie up

aanmerkelijk /aːmˈɛrkələk/ (adj, adv) considerable; appreciable; marked, noticeable: *een ~ verschil met vroeger* a considerable change from the past; *het gaat ~ beter* things have improved noticeably

aanmerken /ˈaːmɛrkə(n)/ (merkte aan, heeft aangemerkt) comment, criticize: *op zijn gedrag valt niets aan te merken* his conduct is beyond reproach

de **aanmerking** /ˈaːmɛrkɪŋ/ (pl: -en) comment, criticism, remark: *~en maken (hebben) op* find fault with, criticize || *in ~ nemen* consider; *in ~ komen voor* qualify for

aanmeten /ˈaːmetə(n)/: *zich een nieuw kapsel laten ~* change one's hairdo; [fig] *zich een beleefde houding ~* assume a polite attitude, strike a polite pose

aanmodderen /ˈaːmɔdərə(n)/ (modderde aan, heeft aangemodderd) muddle on: *maar wat ~* mess around

aanmoedigen /ˈaːmudəɣə(n)/ (moedigde aan, heeft aangemoedigd) encourage; cheer on: *iem. tot iets ~* encourage s.o. to do sth.

de **aanmoediging** /ˈaːmudəɣɪŋ/ (pl: -en) encouragement; cheers: *onder ~ van het publiek* while the spectators cheered him (or: her, them) on; *hij had weinig ~ nodig* he needed little encouragement

aanmonsteren /ˈaːmɔnstərə(n)/ (monsterde aan, heeft aangemonsterd) sign on

aannaaien /ˈaːnajə(n)/ (naaide aan, heeft aangenaaid) sew on || *ik laat mij niets ~* I wasn't born yesterday

aannemelijk /aːnˈemələk/ (adj) **1** plausible: *een ~e verklaring geven voor iets* give a plausible explanation for sth. **2** acceptable, reasonable: *tegen elk ~ bod* any reasonable offer accepted; *iets ~ maken* make a reasonable case for sth.

aannemen /ˈaːnemə(n)/ (nam aan, heeft aangenomen) **1** take, accept; pick up; answer: *kan ik een boodschap ~?* can I take a message? **2** accept, take (on); pass; carry: *een aanbod met beide handen ~* jump at an offer; *een opdracht* (or: *voorstel*) *~* accept a commission (or: proposal); *met algemene stemmen ~* carry unanimously; *de uitdaging ~* accept (or: take on) the challenge **3** accept, believe: *iets voor waar ~* accept (or: believe) sth.; *stilzwijgend ~* tacitly accept; *u kunt het van mij ~* you can take it from me **4** assume, suppose: *algemeen werd aangenomen dat ...* it was generally assumed that ...; *als vaststaand (vanzelfsprekend) ~* take for granted **5** accept, take, contract for **6** engage, take on: *iem. op proef ~* appoint s.o. for a trial period || *vaste vorm ~* take (definite) shape, crystallize

de **aannemer** /ˈaːnemər/ (pl: -s) (building) contractor, builder

de **aanpak** /ˈaːmpɑk/ approach: *de ~ van dit probleem* the way to deal with (or: tackle) this problem; *een zakelijke ~* a pragmatic approach

aanpakken /ˈaːmpɑkə(n)/ (pakte aan, heeft aangepakt) **1** take, take, catch, get hold of **2** go (or: set) about (it); deal with; handle; tackle; seize; take: *een probleem ~* tackle a problem; *hoe zullen we dat ~?* how shall we set about it?; *een zaak goed* (or: *verkeerd*) *~* go the right (or: wrong) way about a matter; *hij weet van ~* he's a tremendous worker **3** deal with; attack; [law] proceed against: *iem. flink ~* take a firm line with s.o., be tough on s.o.

aanpappen /ˈaːmpɑpə(n)/ (papte aan, heeft aangepapt) chum (or: pal) up (with)

¹**aanpassen** /ˈaːmpɑsə(n)/ (paste aan, heeft aangepast) **1** try on, fit on: *een nieuwe jas ~* try on a new coat **2** adapt (to), adjust (to), fit (to): *de lonen zullen opnieuw aangepast worden* wages will be readjusted

zich ²**aanpassen** /ˈaːmpɑsə(n)/ (paste zich aan, heeft zich aangepast) adapt o.s. (to)

de **aanpassing** /ˈaːmpɑsɪŋ/ (pl: -en) adaptation (to), adjustment (to)

het **aanpassingsvermogen** /ˈaːmpɑsɪŋsfərmoɣə(n)/ adaptability (to); accommodation: *gebrek aan ~* lack of flexibility

het **aanplakbiljet** /ˈaːmplɑɡbɪljɛt/ (pl: -ten) poster, bill

het **aanplakbord** /ˈaːmplɑɡbɔrt/ (pl: -en) notice board; boarding; [Am] billboard

aanplakken /ˈaːmplɑkə(n)/ (plakte aan, heeft aangeplakt) affix, paste (up); post (up): *verboden aan te plakken* no billposting

de **aanplant** /ˈaːmplɑnt/ plantings, plants: *nieuwe* (or: *jonge*) *~* new (or: young) plantings

aanplanten /ˈaːmplɑntə(n)/ (plantte aan, heeft aangeplant) plant (out), cultivate, grow; afforest

aanpoten /ˈampotə(n)/ (pootte aan, heeft aangepoot) hurry (up), slog away

aanpraten /ˈampratə(n)/ (praatte aan, heeft aangepraat) palm off on, talk into: *iem.* **iets** ~ talk s.o. into (doing) sth., palm sth. off on s.o.

aanprijzen /ˈamprɛizə(n)/ (prees aan, heeft aangeprezen) recommend, praise

het **aanraakscherm** /ˈanraksχɛrm/ (pl: -en) [comp] touchscreen

aanraden /ˈanradə(n)/ (raadde aan, heeft aangeraden) advise; recommend; suggest: *iem.* **dringend** ~ *iets te doen* advise s.o. urgently to do sth.; *dat* **is** *niet aan te raden* that is not advisable, to be recommended

aanraken /ˈanrakə(n)/ (raakte aan, heeft aangeraakt) touch: *verboden aan te raken* (please) do not touch; *met geen vinger* ~ not lay a finger on

de **aanraking** /ˈanrakɪŋ/ (pl: -en) touch ‖ *hij is nog nooit met de politie* **in** ~ *geweest* he has never been in trouble with the police (*or:* the law)

aanranden /ˈanrandə(n)/ (randde aan, heeft aangerand) assault

de **aanrander** /ˈanrandər/ (pl: -s) assailant

de **aanranding** /ˈanrandɪŋ/ (pl: -en) (criminal, indecent) assault

het/de **aanrecht** /ˈanrɛχt/ (pl: -en) kitchen (sink) unit

het **aanrechtblad** /ˈanrɛχtblɑt/ (pl: -en) worktop, working top

aanreiken /ˈanrɛikə(n)/ (reikte aan, heeft aangereikt) pass, hand; reach: *informatie* ~ supply information; *iem.* **oplossingen** ~ steer (*or:* direct) s.o. towards a solution strategy

aanrekenen /ˈanrekənə(n)/ (rekende aan, heeft aangerekend) blame (for)

aanrichten /ˈanrɪχtə(n)/ (richtte aan, heeft aangericht) cause, bring about: *een* **bloedbad** ~ *(onder)* bring about a massacre (among); *grote* **verwoestingen** ~ *(bij)* create (*or:* wreak) havoc (on)

aanrijden /ˈanrɛidə(n)/ (reed aan, heeft aangereden) collide (with), crash (into), run into: *hij heeft een* **hond** *aangereden* he hit a dog; *tegen een muur* ~ run (*or:* crash) into a wall

de **aanrijding** /ˈanrɛidɪŋ/ (pl: -en) collision, crash: *een* ~ **hebben** be involved in a collision (*or:* crash)

aanroepen /ˈanrupə(n)/ (riep aan, heeft aangeroepen) call on/upon; invoke

aanroeren /ˈanrurə(n)/ (roerde aan, heeft aangeroerd) **1** touch: *het* **eten** *was nauwelijks aangeroerd* the food had hardly been touched **2** touch upon

aanrommelen /ˈanrɔmələ(n)/ (rommelde aan, heeft aangerommeld) mess around

aanrukken /ˈanrykə(n)/: *nog een* **fles** *laten* ~ have another bottle (up); *versterkingen laten* ~ move up (*or:* call in) reinforcements

de **aanschaf** /ˈansχɑf/ purchase, buy, acquisition

aanschaffen /ˈansχɑfə(n)/ (schafte aan, heeft aangeschaft) purchase, acquire

aanscherpen /ˈansχɛrpə(n)/ (scherpte aan, heeft aangescherpt) **1** sharpen **2** [fig] accentuate, highlight

aanschieten /ˈansχitə(n)/ (schoot aan, heeft aangeschoten) **1** hit: *een aangeschoten* **hert** a wounded deer **2** buttonhole, accost: *een voorbijganger* ~ buttonhole a passer-by

aanschouwelijk /ansˈχɑuwələk/ (adj) clear: *iets* ~ **maken** illustrate sth.; demonstrate sth.

aanschouwen /ansˈχɑuwə(n)/ (aanschouwde, heeft aanschouwd) behold, see: *het* **levenslicht** ~ (first) see the light; *met eigen ogen* ~ behold (*or:* see) with one's own eyes

aanschuiven /ˈansχœyvə(n)/ (schoof aan, heeft aangeschoven) draw up, pull up: ~ *bij een overleg* join (in on) the meeting

¹**aanslaan** /ˈanslan/ (sloeg aan, is aangeslagen) **1** start **2** catch on, be successful: *dat plan is* **bij** *hen goed aangeslagen* that plan has caught on (well) with them

²**aanslaan** /ˈanslan/ (sloeg aan, heeft aangeslagen) **1** touch, strike, hit: *een* **toets** ~ strike a key; *een* **snaar** ~ touch a string **2** estimate; assess; tax: *iem.* **hoog** ~ think highly of s.o.

de **aanslag** /ˈanslɑχ/ (pl: -en) **1** [mus] touch: *een lichte* (*or:* **zware**) ~ a light (*or:* heavy) touch **2** ready: *met het geweer* **in** *de* ~ with one's rifle at the ready **3** attempt, attack, assault: *een* ~ **op** *iemands leven plegen* make an attempt on s.o.'s life **4** deposit; moisture: *een* **vieze** ~ *op het plafond* a filthy (smoke) deposit on the ceiling **5** assessment: *een* ~ **van** *€1000,- ontvangen* get assessed €1000.00 ‖ [fig] *een* ~ *doen* **op** *iemands portemonnee* make inroads upon s.o.'s budget, hurt s.o.'s pocketbook

het **aanslagbiljet** /ˈanslɑχbɪljɛt/ (pl: -ten) assessment (notice); (income) tax return (*or:* form)

aanslibben /ˈanslɪbə(n)/ (slibde aan, is aangeslibd) form a deposit: *aangeslibd* **land** alluvium, alluvial land

aansluipen /ˈanslœypə(n)/: *komen* ~ come sneaking along/up

¹**aansluiten** /ˈanslœytə(n)/ (sloot aan, heeft aangesloten) connect, join, link: *een nieuwe* **abonnee** ~ connect a new subscriber ‖ *wilt u daar* ~? will you queue up there, please?

zich ²**aansluiten** /ˈanslœytə(n)/ (sloot zich aan, heeft zich aangesloten) join (in), become a member of: *zich* **bij** *de vorige spreker* ~ agree with the preceding speaker; *zich* **bij** *een partij* ~ join a party; *daar sluit ik me graag* **bij** *aan* I would like to second that

de **aansluiting** /ˈanslœytɪŋ/ (pl: -en) **1** joining, association (with): ~ **vinden** *bij iem. (iets)* join in with s.o. (sth.); [fig] ~ *zoeken bij* seek contact with **2** [traf] connection: *de ~ missen* miss the connection **3** connection: *~ op het gasnet* connection to the gas mains

aansmeren /ɑnsmerə(n)/ (smeerde aan, heeft aangesmeerd) palm off (on): *iem. een veel te dure auto ~* cajole s.o. into buying far too expensive a car

aansnijden /ɑnsnɛidə(n)/ (sneed aan, heeft aangesneden) **1** cut (into) **2** [fig] broach, bring up

aanspannen /ɑnspɑnə(n)/ (spande aan, heeft aangespannen) institute: *een proces (tegen iem.) ~* institute (legal) proceedings (against s.o.)

aanspelen /ɑnspelə(n)/ (speelde aan, heeft aangespeeld) pass, feed, play to

aanspoelen /ɑnspulə(n)/ (spoelde aan, is aangespoeld) wash ashore, be washed ashore: *er is een fles met een briefje erin aangespoeld* a bottle containing a letter has been washed ashore

aansporen /ɑnsporə(n)/ (spoorde aan, heeft aangespoord) urge (on); spur (on): *iem. ~ tot grotere inspanning* incite s.o. to greater efforts

de **aansporing** /ɑnsporɪŋ/ (pl: -en) incentive: *die beloning was een echte ~ voor hem* that reward was a real incentive to him

de **aanspraak** /ɑnsprak/ (pl: aanspraken) **1** claim: *geen ~ kunnen doen gelden (op iets)* not be able to lay any claim (to sth.); *~ maken op iets* lay claim to sth. **2** contacts: *weinig ~ hebben* have few contacts

aansprakelijk /ɑnsprakələk/ (adj) responsible (for); [law] liable (for): *zich voor iets ~ stellen* take responsibility for sth.; *iem. ~ stellen voor iets* hold s.o. responsible for sth.

de **aansprakelijkheid** /ɑnsprakələkhɛit/ (pl: -heden) liability (for), responsibility: *wettelijke ~*, [Belg] *burgerlijke aansprakelijkheid* (legal) liability, liability in law; *~ tegenover derden* third-party liability

de **aansprakelijkheidsverzekering** /ɑnsprakələkhɛitsfərzekərɪŋ/ (pl: -en) liability insurance, third party insurance

aanspreekbaar /ɑnsprekbar/ (adj) approachable; get-at-able

aanspreken /ɑnsprekə(n)/ (sprak aan, heeft aangesproken) **1** draw on, break into: *zijn kapitaal ~* break into one's capital **2** speak to, talk to, address: *iem. (op straat) ~* approach s.o. (in the street); *ik voel mij niet aangesproken* it doesn't concern me; *iem. met mevrouw (or: meneer) ~* address s.o. as madam (or: sir); *iem. over zijn gedrag ~* talk to s.o. about his conduct **3** appeal to: *het boek sprak me niet erg aan* the book had little appeal for me

aanstaan /ɑnstan/ (stond aan, heeft aangestaan) **1** please: *zijn gezicht staat mij niet*

aan I do not like the look of him **2** be running; be (turned) on

de **¹aanstaande** /ɑnstandə/ (pl: -n) fiancé; fiancée

²aanstaande /ɑnstandə/ (adj) **1** next; this: *~ vrijdag* this Friday **2** (forth)coming; approaching: *een ~ moeder* an expectant mother, a mother-to-be

de **aanstalten** /ɑnstɑltə(n)/ (pl): *~ maken om te vertrekken* get ready to leave; *geen ~ maken (om)* show no sign (or: intention) (of)

aanstampen /ɑnstɑmpə(n)/ (stampte aan, heeft aangestampt) tamp (down)

aanstaren /ɑnstarə(n)/ (staarde aan, heeft aangestaard) stare at, gaze at: *iem. met open mond ~* stare open-mouthed at s.o., gape at s.o.; *iem. vol bewondering ~* gaze at s.o. admiringly

aanstekelijk /ɑnstekələk/ (adj, adv) infectious, contagious, catching

aansteken /ɑnstekə(n)/ (stak aan, heeft aangestoken) **1** light; kindle; turn on, switch on: *die brand is aangestoken* that fire was started deliberately; *een kaars ~* light a candle **2** infect, contaminate: [fig] *ze steken elkaar aan* they are a bad (or: good) influence on one another

de **aansteker** /ɑnstekər/ (pl: -s) (cigarette) lighter

¹aanstellen /ɑnstɛlə(n)/ (stelde aan, heeft aangesteld) appoint: *iem. vast ~* appoint s.o. permanently

zich **²aanstellen** /ɑnstɛlə(n)/ (stelde zich aan, heeft zich aangesteld) show off, put on airs, act: *zich belachelijk ~* make a fool of o.s.; *stel je niet aan!* be your age!, stop behaving like a child!

de **aansteller** /ɑnstɛlər/ (pl: -s) poseur; [someone behaving childishly] baby

aanstellerig /ɑnstɛlərəx/ (adj) affected, theatrical

de **aanstellerij** /ɑnstɛlərɛi/ (pl: -en) affectation, pose, showing off ‖ *is het nu uit met die ~?* are you quite finished?

de **aanstelling** /ɑnstɛlɪŋ/ (pl: -en) appointment: *een vaste (or: tijdelijke) ~ hebben* have a permanent (or: temporary) appointment

aansterken /ɑnstɛrkə(n)/ (sterkte aan, is aangesterkt) get stronger, recuperate, regain one's strength

aanstichten /ɑnstɪxtə(n)/ (stichtte aan, heeft aangesticht) instigate

de **aanstichter** /ɑnstɪxtər/ (pl: -s) instigator, originator: *de ~ van alle kwaad* the source of all evil

aanstippen /ɑnstɪpə(n)/ (stipte aan, heeft aangestipt) **1** mention briefly, touch on **2** [med] dab

aanstoken /ɑnstokə(n)/ (stak aan, heeft aangestoken) stir up, incite

aanstonds /ɑnstɔn(t)s/ (adv): *zo ~* presently, in a little while

de **aanstoot** /ˈanstot/ offence: ~ **geven** give offence; ~ **nemen** *aan* take offence at

aanstootgevend /ˈanstotxevənt/ (adj, adv) offensive, objectionable; [stronger] scandalous; [stronger] shocking: ~*e passages in een boek* offensive passages in a book

¹**aanstoten** /ˈanstotə(n)/ (stootte aan, is aangestoten) knock (against), bump (into): *hij stootte **tegen** de tafel aan* he bumped into the table

²**aanstoten** /ˈanstotə(n)/ (stootte aan, heeft aangestoten) nudge: *zijn **buurman** ~* nudge one's neighbour

aanstrepen /ˈanstrepə(n)/ (streepte aan, heeft aangestreept) mark, check (off), tick (off): *een **plaats** in een boek* ~ mark a place in a book

aansturen /ˈanstyrə(n)/ (stuurde aan, heeft aangestuurd) (+ op) aim for, aim at, steer towards; drive at: *ik zou niet weten waar hij **op** aanstuurt* I don't know what he is driving at

het **aantal** /ˈantɑl/ (pl: -len) number: *een ~ **jaren** lang* for a number of years; *een ~ **gasten** kwam te laat* a number of guests were late; *een **flink** ~ boeken* quite a few books; *het **totale** ~ werkende kinderen* the total number of working children

aantasten /ˈantɑstə(n)/ (tastte aan, heeft aangetast) **1** affect; harm, attack: *dit zuur tast metalen aan* this acid corrodes metals; *die roddels tasten onze goede **naam** aan* those rumours damage (*or:* harm) our reputation **2** attack: *door een **ziekte** aangetast worden* be stricken with a disease

aantekenen /ˈantekənə(n)/ (tekende aan, heeft aangetekend) **1** take (*or:* make) a note of, note down, write down, record; register: *brieven **laten** ~* have letters registered **2** comment, note, remark: *daarbij tekende hij aan, dat … he further observed that … ‖ **hoger beroep** ~* enter (*or:* lodge) an appeal

de **aantekening** /ˈantekənɪŋ/ (pl: -en) note: ~*en **maken*** take notes

de **aantijging** /ˈantɛiɣɪŋ/ (pl: -en) allegation, imputation, accusation: [Belg] *lasterlijke ~* false allegation

de **aantocht** /ˈantɔxt/: *in ~ zijn* be on the way

aantonen /ˈantonə(n)/ (toonde aan, heeft aangetoond) demonstrate, prove, show: *er werd **ruimschoots** aangetoond dat …* ample evidence was given to show that …

aantoonbaar /ˈantombar/ (adj) demonstrable: *dat is ~ onjuist* that is patently incorrect

aantreden /ˈantredə(n)/ (trad aan, is aangetreden): *de manschappen **laten** ~* fall the men in; *sinds het ~ van het **kabinet*** since the government took office

aantreffen /ˈantrɛfə(n)/ (trof aan, heeft aangetroffen) **1** meet, encounter, find: *iem. in bed ~* find s.o. in bed; *iem. niet **thuis** ~* find

s.o. out **2** find, come across

aantrekkelijk /ˈantrɛkələk/ (adj) attractive; inviting: *ik vind ze **erg** ~* I find them very attractive

¹**aantrekken** /ˈantrɛkə(n)/ (trok aan, heeft aangetrokken) **1** attract, draw: *de **aarde** wordt door de zon aangetrokken* the earth gravitates towards the sun **2** tighten: *een **knoop** ~* tighten a knot **3** draw, attract: *zich aangetrokken **voelen** door* (*or: tot*) *iem. (iets)* feel attracted to s.o. (sth.); *dat trekt **mij** wel aan* that appeals to me **4** attract; draw: *nieuwe **medewerkers** ~* take on (*or:* recruit) new staff **5** put on: *andere **kleren** ~* change one's clothes; *ik heb niets om aan te trekken* I have nothing to wear

zich ²**aantrekken** /ˈantrɛkə(n)/ (trok zich aan, heeft zich aangetrokken) be concerned about, take seriously: *zich iemands **lot** ~* be concerned about s.o.('s fate); *trek **het** je niet aan* don't let that worry you; *zich alles **persoonlijk** ~* take everything personally

de **aantrekking** /ˈantrɛkɪŋ/ **1** attraction; gravitation **2** [fig] attraction, appeal

de **aantrekkingskracht** /ˈantrɛkɪŋskrɑxt/ **1** attraction, appeal: *een grote ~ **bezitten** voor iem.* hold (a) great attraction for s.o.; ~ **uitoefenen** *op iem.* attract s.o. **2** (force of) attraction; gravitational force

aanvaardbaar /ˌanˈvardbar/ (adj) acceptable: ~ **voor** acceptable to

aanvaarden /anˈvardə(n)/ (aanvaardde, heeft aanvaard) **1** accept, agree to; take: *ik aanvaard uw **aanbod*** I accept your offer; *de **consequenties** ~* take (*or:* accept) the consequences; *een **voorstel** ~* accept a proposal **2** accept, assume: *de **verantwoordelijkheid** ~* assume the responsibility

de **aanval** /ˈanvɑl/ (pl: -len) **1** attack, assault, offensive: *een ~ **ondernemen*** (*or: **afslaan***) launch (*or:* beat off) an attack; *tot de ~ **overgaan*** take the offensive; *in de ~ **gaan*** go on the offensive; *de ~ is de beste verdediging* attack is the best form of defence **2** [med] attack, fit: *een ~ van **koorts*** an attack of fever; *een ~ van **woede*** an attack of anger

aanvallen /ˈanvɑlə(n)/ (viel aan, heeft aangevallen) attack, assail, assault: *de vijand **in de rug** ~* attack (*or:* take) the enemy from the rear

aanvallend /ˈanvɑlənt/ (adj, adv) offensive, aggressive

de **aanvaller** /ˈanvɑlər/ (pl: -s) **1** assailant, attacker **2** [sport] attacker; [socc] forward; striker

de **aanvang** /ˈanvɑŋ/ beginning; commencement: *bij ~* at the start, at the onset; *een ~ **nemen*** commence, begin

aanvangen /ˈanvɑŋə(n)/ (ving aan, heeft aangevangen) begin, start, commence

aanvankelijk /anˈvɑŋkələk/ (adv) initially,

at first, in (or: at) the beginning
aanvaren /ˈanvarə(n)/ (voer aan, heeft aangevaren) run into, collide with: *een ander schip ~* collide with another ship
de **aanvaring** /ˈanvarɪŋ/ (pl: -en) collision, crash: *in ~ komen met* collide with
aanvechtbaar /anvɛxtbar/ (adj) contestable, disputable: *een ~ standpunt* a debatable point of view
aanvechten /ˈanvɛxtə(n)/ (vocht aan, heeft aangevochten) dispute: *een beslissing ~* challenge a decision
de **aanvechting** /anvɛxtɪŋ/ (pl: -en) [fig] temptation, impulse: *een ~ van (de) slaap* an attack of sleepiness
aanvegen /ˈanveɣə(n)/ (veegde aan, heeft aangeveegd) sweep, sweep out
aanverwant /anvərwɑnt/ (adj) related, allied: *de geneeskunde en ~e vakken* medicine and related professions
aanvinken /ˈanvɪŋkə(n)/ (vinkte aan, heeft aangevinkt) check (or: tick) off
¹**aanvliegen** /ˈanvliɣə(n)/ (vloog aan, heeft/is aangevlogen) fly (towards): *tegen iets ~* fly (towards) against sth.; crash into sth.
²**aanvliegen** /ˈanvliɣə(n)/ (vloog aan, heeft aangevlogen) fly at, attack: *de hond vloog de postbode aan* the dog flew at the postman
de **aanvliegroute** /ˈanvliɣrutə/ (pl: -s) approach route
aanvoegend /anvuɣənt/ (adj): *de ~e wijs* the subjunctive mood
aanvoelen /ˈanvulə(n)/ (voelde aan, heeft aangevoeld) feel, sense: *iem. ~* understand s.o.; [stronger] empathize with s.o.; *een stemming ~* sense an atmosphere; *elkaar goed ~* speak the same language || *het voelt koud aan* it feels cold
de **aanvoer** /ˈanvur/ supply, delivery: *de ~ van levensmiddelen* food supplies
de **aanvoerder** /ˈanvurdər/ (pl: -s) leader, captain
de **aanvoerdersband** /ˈanvurdərzbɑnt/ captain's arm band
aanvoeren /ˈanvurə(n)/ (voerde aan, heeft aangevoerd) **1** lead, command, captain: *een leger ~* command an army **2** supply; import: *hulpgoederen werden per vliegtuig aangevoerd* relief supplies were flown in **3** bring forward, advance; produce; argue: *iets als verontschuldiging ~* put forward sth. in one's defence, by way of an excuse
de **aanvoering** /ˈanvurɪŋ/ command, leadership, captaincy: *onder ~ van* under the command (or: leadership) of
de **aanvraag** /ˈanvraχ/ (pl: aanvragen) **1** application, request; inquiry: *een ~ indienen* submit an application; *op ~ te vertonen* to be shown on demand; *~ voor een uitkering* application for social welfare payment **2** request, demand, order: *wij konden niet aan alle*

aanvragen voldoen we couldn't meet the demand; *op ~ verkrijgbaar* available on request
aanvragen /ˈanvraɣə(n)/ (vroeg aan, heeft aangevraagd) **1** apply for, request: *ontslag ~* apply for permission to make redundant; *een vergunning ~* apply for a licence **2** request, order: *vraag een gratis folder aan* send for free brochure; *informatie ~ over treinen in Engeland* inquire about trains in England
de **aanvrager** /ˈanvraɣər/ (pl: -s) applicant
aanvreten /ˈanvretə(n)/ (vrat aan, heeft aangevreten) eat away (at), eat into: *door roest aangevreten* corroded by rust; *door gifgas aangevreten longen* lungs attacked by toxic gas
aanvullen /ˈanvʏlə(n)/ (vulde aan, heeft aangevuld) complete, finish, fill (up): *de voorraad ~* replenish stocks; *zij vullen elkaar goed aan* they complement each other well
aanvullend /ˈanvʏlənt/ (adj) supplementary, additional: *een ~e cursus* a follow-up course; *een ~ pensioen* a supplementary pension
de **aanvulling** /ˈanvʏlɪŋ/ (pl: -en) supplement, addition
aanvuren /ˈanvyrə(n)/ (vuurde aan, heeft aangevuurd) fire; rouse; incite: *de troepen ~* rouse the troops
aanwaaien /ˈanwajə(n)/ (waaide/woei aan, is aangewaaid) come naturally to: *alles waait hem zomaar aan* everything just falls into his lap
aanwakkeren /ˈanwɑkərə(n)/ (wakkerde aan, heeft aangewakkerd) **1** stir up: *het vuur ~* fan the fire **2** stimulate, stir up: *de kooplust ~* stimulate buying
de **aanwas** /ˈanwɑs/ (pl: -sen) growth, accretion
aanwenden /ˈanwɛndə(n)/ (wendde aan, heeft aangewend) apply, use: *zijn gezag ~* use one's authority; *zijn invloed ~* exert one's influence
zich **aanwennen** /ˈanwɛnə(n)/ (wende zich aan, heeft zich aangewend) get into the habit of: *zich slechte gewoonten ~* fall into (or: acquire) bad habits
aanwerven /ˈanwɛrvə(n)/ (wierf aan, heeft aangeworven) [Belg] recruit
aanwezig /anwezəχ/ (adj) present: *Trudie is vandaag niet ~* Trudie is not in (or: here) today; *~ zijn bij* be present at; *niet ~* absent
de **aanwezige** /anwezəɣə/ (pl: -n) person present: *alle ~n keurden het plan goed* all (those) present approved the plan; *onder de ~n bevonden zich …* those present included, among those present were …
de **aanwezigheid** /anwezəχhɛit/ presence; attendance: *uw ~ is niet noodzakelijk* your presence is not necessary (or: required); *in ~ van* in the presence of
aanwijsbaar /anwɛizbar/ (adj) demonstrable, provable, apparent

de **aanwijsstok** /ɑnwɛɪstɔk/ (pl: -ken) pointer
aanwijzen /ɑnwɛɪzə(n)/ (wees aan, heeft aangewezen) **1** point to, point out, indicate, show: *de dader* ~ point out (*or:* to) the culprit; *een fout* ~ point out a mistake; *gasten hun plaats* ~ show guests to their seats **2** designate, assign, allocate: *een acteur* ~ *voor een rol* cast an actor for a part; *een erfgenaam* ~ designate an heir **3** indicate, point to, show: *de klok wijst de tijd aan* the clock shows the time
aanwijzend /ɑnwɛɪzənt/ (adj): ~ *voornaamwoord* demonstrative pronoun
de **aanwijzing** /ɑnwɛɪzɪŋ/ (pl: -en) **1** indication, sign, clue: *er bestaat geen enkele* ~ *dat …* there is no indication whatever that … **2** instruction, direction: *hij gaf nauwkeurige ~en* he gave precise instructions; *de ~en opvolgen* follow the directions; *~en voor het gebruik* directions for use
de **aanwinst** /ɑnwɪnst/ (pl: -en) **1** acquisition, addition: *een mooie* ~ *voor het museum* a beautiful acquisition for the museum **2** gain, improvement, asset: *de computer is een* ~ *voor ieder bedrijf* the computer is an asset in every business
¹**aanwrijven** /ɑnvrɛɪvə(n)/ (wreef aan, heeft aangewreven) rub against; graze against (*or:* past)
²**aanwrijven** /ɑnvrɛɪvə(n)/ (wreef aan, heeft aangewreven) impute, blame: *iem. iets* ~ impute sth. to s.o.
aanzeggen /ɑnzɛɣə(n)/ (zegde aan/zei aan, heeft aangezegd) give notice, notify, announce: [fig] *iem. de wacht* ~ issue a (serious) warning to s.o., give s.o. a talking to
de **aanzet** /ɑnzɛt/ (pl: -ten) start, initiative: *de (eerste)* ~ *geven tot iets* initiate sth., give the initial impetus to sth.
aanzetten /ɑnzɛtə(n)/ (zette aan, heeft aangezet) **1** put on, sew on, stitch on **2** start up, turn on: *de radio* ~ turn on the radio **3** spur on, urge, incite, instigate: *iem. tot diefstal* ~ incite s.o. to steal ‖ *ergens laat komen* ~ turn up late somewhere; *met iets komen* ~ turn up with sth., come up with sth.
het **aanzicht** /ɑnzɪxt/ (pl: -en) aspect, look, view: *nu krijgt de zaak een ander* ~ that puts a different light on the matter
het ¹**aanzien** /ɑnzin/ **1** looking (at), watching: *dat is het* ~ *waard* that is worth watching (*or:* looking at); *ten* ~ *van* with regard (*or:* respect) to **2** look, aspect, appearance: *iets een ander* ~ *geven* put a different complexion on sth. **3** standing, regard: *een man van* ~ a man of distinction; *hij is sterk in* ~ *gestegen* his prestige has risen sharply
²**aanzien** /ɑnzin/ (zag aan, heeft aangezien) **1** look at, watch, see: *die film is niet om aan te zien* it's an awful film; *ik kon het niet langer* ~ I couldn't bear to watch it any longer; *ik wil*

het nog even ~ I want to wait a bit, I want to await further developments **2** consider, regard: *waar zie je mij voor aan?* what do you take me for?; *iem. voor een ander* ~ (mis)take s.o. for s.o. else ‖ *ik zie haar er best voor aan* I think she's quite capable of it
aanzienlijk /ɑnzinlək/ (adj, adv) considerable, substantial: *~e schade* serious damage; *een ~e verbetering* a substantial improvement
het **aanzoek** /ɑnzuk/ (pl: -en) proposal: *de knappe prins deed het meisje een* ~ the handsome prince proposed to the girl
aanzuigen /ɑnzœyɣə(n)/ (zoog aan, heeft aangezogen) suck in ‖ *een ~de werking hebben* draw in more and more people
aanzuiveren /ɑnzœyvərə(n)/ (zuiverde aan, heeft aangezuiverd) pay off (*or:* up), settle: *een tekort* ~ make up (*or:* good) a deficit
aanzwellen /ɑnzwɛlə(n)/ (zwol aan, is aangezwollen) swell (up, out), rise
de **aap** /ap/ (pl: apen) monkey; ape ‖ *~jes kijken* gawk at people
de **aar** /ar/ (pl: aren) ear
de **aard** /art/ **1** nature, disposition, character: *zijn ware* ~ *tonen* show one's true character **2** nature, sort, kind: *iets van dien* ~ sth. of the sort, that sort, that nature; *schilderijen van allerlei* ~ various kinds (*or:* all kinds) of paintings
de **aardappel** /ardɑpəl/ (pl: -s, -en) potato: *gekookte* (or: *gebakken*) *~s* boiled (*or:* fried) potatoes
het **aardappelmeel** /ardɑpəlmel/ potato flour
het **aardappelmesje** /ardɑpəlmɛʃə/ (pl: -s) potato peeler
de **aardappelpuree** /ardɑpəlpyre/ mashed potato(es)
de **aardas** /artɑs/ (pl: -sen) axis of the earth
de **aardbei** /ardbɛi/ (pl: -en) strawberry
de **aardbeving** /ardbevɪŋ/ (pl: -en) earthquake
de **aardbodem** /ardbodəm/ surface (*or:* face) of the earth: *honderden huizen werden van de* ~ *weggevaagd* hundreds of houses were wiped off the face of the earth; [fig] *van de* ~ *verdwijnen* disappear off the face of the earth
de **aardbol** /ardbɔl/ (pl: -len) earth, world, globe
de **aarde** /ardə/ **1** earth, world: *in een baan om de* ~ in orbit round the earth; *op* ~ on earth, under the sun **2** ground; earth [electricity] **3** earth, soil: *dat zal bij haar niet in goede* ~ *vallen* she is not going to like that; *het plan viel in goede* ~ the plan was well received; *ter* ~ *bestellen* commit to the earth, inhume, inter
het ¹**aardedonker** /ardədɔŋkər/ pitch-darkness: *in het* ~ in pitch-darkness
²**aardedonker** /ardədɔŋkər/ (adj) pitch-dark
¹**aarden** /ardə(n)/ (adj) earthen, clay

²**aarden** /ˈɑrdə(n)/ (aardde, heeft geaard)
thrive: *zij **kan** hier niet ~* she can't settle in
here, she can't find her niche; *ik aard hier **best***
I fit in here, I feel at home here; *dit diertje
aardt hier **goed*** this animal thrives here

³**aarden** /ˈɑrdə(n)/ (aardde, heeft geaard)
[electricity] earth

het ¹**aardewerk** /ˈɑrdəwɛrk/ earthenware, pottery

²**aardewerk** /ˈɑrdəwɛrk/ (adj): *een ~ **schotel***
an earthenware dish

het **aardgas** /ˈɑrtxɑs/ natural gas

¹**aardig** /ˈɑrdəx/ (adj) **1** nice, friendly: [iron]
*wat **doe** je ~!* charming!, how charming you
are!; *dat **is** ~ van je!* how nice of you! **2** nice,
pretty: *het is een ~e **meid*** she's a nice girl; *een
~ **tuintje*** a nice (*or:* pretty) garden **3** fair,
nice: *een ~ **inkomen*** a nice income

²**aardig** /ˈɑrdəx/ (adv) nicely, pretty, fairly: *dat
komt ~ in de richting* that's more like it; *~ **wat**
mensen* quite a few people; *hij is ~ op weg om
… te worden* he is well on his way to becoming …

de **aardigheid** /ˈɑrdəxhɛit/ (pl: -heden) small
present: *ik **heb** een ~je **meegebracht*** I have
brought a little sth.

de **aardkorst** /ˈɑrtkɔrst/ earth's crust

de **aardlekschakelaar** /ˈɑrtlɛksxakəlar/ (pl: -s)
earth leakage circuit breaker

de **aardolie** /ˈɑrtoli/ petroleum

de **aardrijkskunde** /ˈɑrdrɛikskɵndə/ geography

aardrijkskundig /ˈɑrdrɛikskɵndəx/ (adj)
geographic(al)

aards /arts/ (adj) earthly, worldly: *~e **machten*** earthly powers; *een ~ **paradijs*** paradise
on earth; *~e **genoegens*** worldly pleasures

de **aardschok** /ˈɑrtsxɔk/ (pl: -ken) earthquake;
[fig] upheaval, shock

de **aardverschuiving** /ˈɑrtfərsxœyvɪŋ/ (pl:
-en) landslide; [fig also] upheaval

de **aardworm** /ˈɑrtwɔrm/ (pl: -en) (earth)worm

de **aars** /ars/ (pl: aarzen) arse

het **aartsbisdom** /ˈartsbɪzdɔm/ (pl: -men) arch-
bishopric

de **aartsbisschop** /ˈartsbɪsxɔp/ (pl: -pen) archbishop

de **aartsengel** /ˈartsɛŋəl/ (pl: -en) archangel

de **aartshertog** /ˈartshɛrtɔx/ (pl: -en) archduke

de **aartsvader** /ˈartsfadər/ (pl: -s, -en) patriarch

de **aartsvijand** /ˈartsfɛiɑnt/ (pl: -en) arch-en-
emy

aarzelen /ˈarzələ(n)/ (aarzelde, heeft geaar-
zeld) hesitate: *~ iets te **doen*** hesitate about
doing sth.; *ik aarzel **nog*** I am still in doubt

de **aarzeling** /ˈarzəlɪŋ/ (pl: -en) hesitancy; hesitation; shilly-shallying; doubt: *na enige ~* after some hesitation

het ¹**aas** /as/ bait: *levend ~* live bait; *van ~ **voorzien*** bait (the hook, trap)

het/de ²**aas** /as/ [cards] ace: *de ~ van **harten, ruiten***

the ace of hearts, diamonds

de **aasgier** /ˈasxir/ (pl: -en) vulture

het **abattoir** /abɑtwar/ (pl: -s) abattoir, slaughterhouse

het **abc** /abeseˈ/ (pl: -'s) ABC

het **abces** /ɑpsɛs/ (pl: -sen) abscess

de **abdij** /ɑbdɛi/ (pl: -en) abbey

abject /ɑpjɛkt/ (adj) despicable, abject

het **ABN** /abeɛn/ *Algemeen Beschaafd Nederlands* (received) standard Dutch

abnormaal /ɑpnɔrmal/ (adj, adv) abnormal; deviant; aberrant; deformed: *een ~
groot **hoofd*** an abnormally large head

de **abonnee** /abɔneˈ/ (pl: -s) subscriber (to)

het **abonneenummer** /abɔnenʏmər/ (pl: -s)
subscriber('s) number

de **abonneetelevisie** /abɔnetelevizi/ pay television (*or:* cable), subscription television

het **abonnement** /abɔnəmɛnt/ (pl: -en) **1** subscription (to); taking (*or:* buying) a season
ticket: *een ~ **nemen** op …* subscribe to …; *een
~ **opzeggen*** (or: **vernieuwen**) cancel (*or:* renew) a subscription **2** season ticket

zich **abonneren** /abɔnerə(n)/ (abonneerde zich,
heeft zich geabonneerd) subscribe (to), take
out a subscription (to)

de **Aboriginal** /ɛbərɪdʒənəl/ (pl: -s) Aboriginal

aborteren /abɔrterə(n)/ (aborteerde, heeft
geaborteerd) abort (a pregnancy), perform
an abortion (on): *zij **liet** zich ~* she had an
abortion

de **abortus** /abɔrtʏs/ (pl: -sen) abortion

het **abracadabra** /abrakadabra/ abracadabra:
[fig] *dat **is** ~ voor hem* that is all mumbo-jumbo (*or:* Chinese, double Dutch) to him

Abraham /abrahɑm/ Abraham ‖ *hij **heeft** ~
gezien* he won't see fifty again; *hij weet waar
~ de mosterd haalt* he has been around

de **abri** /abri/ (pl: -'s) bus shelter

de **abrikoos** /abrikos/ apricot

abrupt /aprʏpt/ (adj, adv) abrupt, sudden: *~
halt houden* stop abruptly (*or:* suddenly)

abseilen /ˈɑbzɑjlən/ (seilde ab, heeft abge-
seild) abseil

absent /ɑpsɛnt/ (adj) absent

de **absentie** /ɑpsɛnsi/ (pl: -s) absence

de **absolutie** /ɑpsolʏ(t)si/ absolution: *~ **geven***
absolve

absoluut /ɑpsolyt/ (adj, adv) absolute, perfect: *~ **gehoor*** perfect pitch; *dat is ~ **onmogelijk*** that's absolutely impossible; *~ **niet***
definitely (*or:* absolutely) not; *ik heb ~ **geen**
tijd* I simply have no time; *weet je het zeker? ~!*
are you sure? absolutely!; *op het absolute
hoogtepunt van haar carrière* at the absolute
peak (*or:* very height) of her career

absorberen /ɑpsɔrberə(n)/ (absorbeerde,
heeft geabsorbeerd) absorb: *~d **middel*** absorbent, absorbing agent

de **absorptie** /ɑpsɔrpsi/ (pl: -s) absorption

abstract /ɑpstrɑkt/ (adj, adv) abstract: *~e*

denkbeelden abstract (*or:* theoretical) ideas; ~ *schilderen* paint abstractly

de **abstractie** /ɑpstrɑksi/ (pl: -s) abstraction: *onder* ~ *van* abstracting (from)

abstraheren /ɑpstrahɛrə(n)/ (abstraheerde, heeft geabstraheerd) abstract (from)

absurd /ɑpsʏrt/ (adj, adv) absurd, ridiculous, ludicrous: ~ *toneel* theatre of the absurd

de **absurditeit** /ɑpsʏrditɛɪt/ (pl: -en) absurdity; incongruity

de **abt** /ɑpt/ (pl: -en) abbot

het **¹abuis** /ɑbœys/ mistake: *per (bij)* ~ by mistake

²abuis /ɑbœys/ (adj) mistaken: *u bent* ~ you are mistaken

abusievelijk /ɑbysivələk/ (adv) mistakenly, erroneously

de **acacia** /ɑkasia/ locust (tree), (false) acacia

de **academicus** /ɑkademikʏs/ (pl: academici) university (*or:* college) graduate; academic

de **academie** /ɑkademi/ (pl: -s) university, college: *pedagogische* ~ college of education; *sociale* ~ college of social studies

academisch /ɑkademis/ (adj, adv) academic, university: *een* ~*e graad* a university degree; ~ *ziekenhuis* university (*or:* teaching) hospital; ~ *kwartiertje* [roughly] break between lectures; *een* ~*e vraag* an academic question

de **acceleratie** /ɑksɛlərɑ(t)si/ acceleration

accelereren /ɑksələrɛrə(n)/ (accelereerde, heeft/is geaccelereerd) accelerate

het **accent** /ɑksɛnt/ (pl: -en) accent; stress: *een sterk* (or: *licht*) *noordelijk* ~ a strong (*or:* slight) northern accent; *het* ~ *hebben op de eerste lettergreep* have the accent on the first syllable; *het* ~ *leggen op* stress

accentueren /ɑksɛntywɛrə(n)/ (accentueerde, heeft geaccentueerd) stress, emphasize, accentuate

acceptabel /ɑksɛptabəl/ (adj, adv) acceptable

accepteren /ɑksɛptɛrə(n)/ (accepteerde, heeft geaccepteerd) accept, take: *een wissel* ~ accept a bill (of exchange); *zijn gedrag kan ik niet* ~ I can't accept (*or:* condone) his behaviour

de **acceptgiro** /ɑksɛptxiro/ (pl: -'s) giro form (*or:* slip), payment slip

het **accessoire** /ɑsəswarə/ (pl: -s) accessory

de **accijns** /ɑksɛɪns/ (pl: accijnzen) excise (duty, tax): *accijnzen heffen (op)* charge excise (on)

de **acclamatie** /ɑklamɑ(t)si/ (pl: -s): *bij* ~ *aannemen* carry (*or:* pass) by acclamation; *bij* ~ *verkiezen* elect by acclamation

acclimatiseren /ɑklimatizɛrə(n)/ (acclimatiseerde, is geacclimatiseerd) acclimatize, become acclimatized

de **accolade** /ɑkoladə/ (pl: -s) brace, bracket

de **accommodatie** /ɑkomodɑ(t)si/ (pl: -s) accommodation; facilities: *er is* ~ *voor tien pas-*

sagiers there are facilities for ten passengers

het/de **accordeon** /ɑkɔrdejɔn/ (pl: -s) accordion

de **account** /əkaunt/ (pl: -s) **1** account: *een* ~ *aanmaken* make a new account **2** client meeting, client contact: *een* ~ *beheren* manage an account

de **accountant** /əkauntənt/ (pl: -s) accountant; auditor

de **accountmanager** /əkauntmɛnədʒər/ (pl: -s) account manager

accrediteren /ɑkreditɛrə(n)/ (accrediteerde, heeft geaccrediteerd) acknowledge, recognize

de **accu** /ɑky/ (pl: -'s) battery: *de* ~ *is leeg* the battery is dead; *de* ~ *opladen* charge (up) the battery; [fig] recharge one's batteries

accuraat /ɑkyrat/ (adj, adv) accurate, precise, meticulous: ~ *werken* work accurately

de **accuratesse** /ɑkyratɛsə/ accuracy, precision, meticulousness

de **ace** /es/ (pl: -s) ace

het/de **aceton** /ɑsetɔn/ acetone

ach /ɑχ/ (int) oh, ah: ~ *wat, ik doe het gewoon!* oh who cares, I'll just do it!; ~*, je kunt niet alles hebben!* oh well, you can't have everything!

de **achilleshiel** /ɑχɪləshil/ (pl: -en) weakness, flaw, failing; [person also] Achilles heel; [plan also] (soft) underbelly

de **achillespees** /ɑχɪləspes/ (pl: -pezen) Achilles tendon

de **¹acht** /ɑχt/ (pl: -en) attention, consideration: ~ *slaan op* a) pay attention to; b) take notice of; *de regels* ~ *nemen* comply with (*or:* observe) the rules; *voorzichtigheid in* ~ *nemen* take due care

²acht /ɑχt/ (num) eight: *nog* ~ *dagen* another eight days, eight more days; *iets in* ~*en breken* break sth. into eight pieces; *zij kwamen met hun* ~*en* eight of them came; *zij zijn met hun* ~*en* there are eight of them

de **achtbaan** /ɑχtban/ (pl: -banen) roller coaster: [fig] *een emotionele* ~ an emotional roller coaster

achteloos /ɑχtəlos/ (adj, adv) careless; negligent, casual; inconsiderate

achten /ɑχtə(n)/ (achtte, heeft geacht) **1** esteem, respect **2** consider, think

¹achter /ɑχtər/ (adv) **1** behind, at the rear (*or:* back): ~ *in de tuin* at the bottom of the garden **2** slow, behind(hand): *jouw horloge loopt* ~ your watch is slow ‖ *ik ben* ~ *met mijn werk* I am behind(hand) with my work; [sport] ~ *staan* be behind (*or:* trailing); [sport] *vier punten* ~ *staan* be four points down

²achter /ɑχtər/ (prep) **1** behind, at the back (*or:* rear) of: ~ *het huis* behind (*or:* at the back of) the house; ~ *haar ouders' rug om* behind her parents' back; *zet een kruisje* ~ *je naam* put a tick against your name; ~ *zijn*

computer at his computer; ~ *de **tralies*** behind bars; *pas op, ~ **je!*** mind your back **2** after: ~ ***elkaar*** one after the other, in succession, in a row ‖ ~ *iets **komen*** find out about sth.; get to the bottom of sth.; ~ *iem. **staan*** stand behind s.o.; ~ *iets **staan*** approve of sth., back sth.; *er **zit (steekt)** meer ~* there is more to it

achteraan /ɑχtərãn/ (adv) at the back, at (*or:* in) the rear: *wij **wandelden*** ~ we were walking at the back; *~ **in** de zaal* at the back of the hall

achteraangaan /ɑχtəraηɣan/ go after: *ik zou **er** maar eens ~* you'd better look into that, I'd do sth. about it if I were you

achteraankomen /ɑχtəraηkomə(n)/ (kwam achteraan, is achteraangekomen) come last: *wij **komen** wel achteraan* we'll follow on after

achteraanlopen /ɑχtəraãnlopə(n)/ (liep achteraan, heeft achteraangelopen) walk on behind

achteraf /ɑχtərɑf/ (adv) **1** at the back, in (*or:* at) the rear; [remote] out of the way: ~ ***wonen*** live out in the sticks, live in the middle of nowhere **2** afterwards, later (on), now, as it is: *~ **bekeken** zou ik zeggen dat …* looking back I would say that …; *~ is het makkelijk praten* it is easy to be wise after the event; *~ ben ik blij dat …* now I'm glad that …

de **achterbak** /ɑχtərbɑk/ (pl: -ken) boot

achterbaks /ɑχtərbɑks/ (adj, adv) underhand, sneaky

de **achterban** /ɑχtərbɑn/ (pl: -nen) supporters, backing; grassroots (support)

de **achterband** /ɑχtərbɑnt/ (pl: -en) back (*or:* rear) tyre

de **achterbank** /ɑχtərbɑŋk/ (pl: -en) back seat

achterblijven /ɑχtərblɛivə(n)/ (bleef achter, is achtergebleven) **1** stay behind, remain (behind) **2** be (*or:* get) left (behind) **3** be left: *zij bleef achter **met** drie kinderen* she was left with three children ‖ *toen iedereen trakteerde, **wou** hij niet ~* when everyone else paid their round, he felt he had to follow suit

de **achterblijvende** /ɑχtərblɛivəndə/ (pl: -n) surviving relative

de **achterblijver** /ɑχtərblɛivər/ (pl: -s) **1** stay-behind; stay-at-home **2** slow (*or:* late) developer, backward child

de **achterbuurt** /ɑχtərbyrt/ (pl: -en) slum

de **achterdeur** /ɑχtərdør/ (pl: -en) back door; rear door [car]

de **achterdocht** /ɑχtərdɔχt/ suspicion (of, about): *hij begon ~ te **krijgen*** he began to get suspicious

achterdochtig /ɑχtərdɔχtəχ/ (adj, adv) suspicious

achtereen /ɑχtərẽn/ (adv) in succession: *hij won het kampioenschap **driemaal** ~* he won the championship three times in succession

(*or:* in a row); ***weken*** ~ (for) weeks on end, week after week

achtereenvolgend /ɑχtərenvɔlɣənt/ (adj) successive, consecutive

achtereenvolgens /ɑχtərenvɔlɣəns/ (adv) successively

het **achtereind** /ɑχtərɛint/ (pl: -en) rear end; hindquarters

achteren /ɑχtərə(n)/ (adv) (the) back: *verder naar* ~ further back(wards); *van* ~ from behind; *van* ~ *naar voren* back to front; backwards

achtergebleven /ɑχtərχəblevə(n)/ (adj) backward, underdeveloped: ~ ***gebieden*** backward (*or:* underdeveloped) areas

de **achtergrond** /ɑχtərɣrɔnt/ (pl: -en) background: *de ~en van een **conflict*** the background to (*or:* of) a dispute ‖ *zich **op** de ~ houden* keep in the background

de **achtergrondinformatie** /ɑχtərɣrɔntɪnforma(t)si/ background (information)

de **achtergrondmuziek** /ɑχtərɣrɔntmyzik/ background music; muzak

achterhaald /ɑχtərhalt/ (adj) out of date, irrelevant

achterhalen /ɑχtərhalə(n)/ (achterhaalde, heeft achterhaald) **1** overtake; catch up with: *de politie heeft de **dief** kunnen* ~ the police were able to run down the thief **2** retrieve: *die **gegevens** zijn niet meer te* ~ those data can no longer be accessed (*or:* retrieved) ‖ *die **gegevens** zijn allang achterhaald* that information is totally out of date

de **achterhoede** /ɑχtərhudə/ (pl: -s) [sport] defence

het **achterhoedegevecht** /ɑχtərhudəɣəvɛχt/ (pl: -en) rearguard action

het **achterhoofd** /ɑχtərhoft/ (pl: -en) back of the head: *iets **in** zijn ~ houden* keep sth. at the back of one's mind; *hij is niet **op** zijn ~ gevallen* he was not born yesterday, there are no flies on him

achterhouden /ɑχtərhaudə(n)/ (hield achter, heeft achtergehouden) **1** keep back, withhold **2** hold back

achterin /ɑχtərɪn/ (adv) in the back (*or:* rear); at the back (*or:* rear)

de **achterkamertjespolitiek** /ɑχtərkamərcəspolitik/ backroom (*or:* closed-door) politics

de **achterkant** /ɑχtərkɑnt/ (pl: -en) back, rear (side), reverse (side): *op de ~ van het **papier*** on the back of the paper

de **achterklap** /ɑχtərklɑp/ backbiting, gossip, slander

de **achterkleindochter** /ɑχtərklɛindɔχtər/ (pl: -s) great-granddaughter

het **achterkleinkind** /ɑχtərklɛiŋkɪnt/ (pl: -eren) great-grandchild

de **achterkleinzoon** /ɑχtərklɛinzon/ (pl: -zonen, -s) great-grandson de **achterklep** /ɑχtərklɛp/ (pl: -pen) lid of the boot [car]; hatchback, liftback

het **achterland** /ɑχtərlɑnt/ (pl: -en) hinterland

achterlaten /ɑχtərlatə(n)/ (liet achter, heeft achtergelaten) leave (behind): *een **be- richt** (or: **boodschap**) ~ leave (behind) a note (or: message)*

het **achterlicht** /ɑχtərlɪχt/ (pl: -en) back (or: rear) light; rear lamp

achterliggen /ɑχtərlɪχə(n)/ (lag achter, heeft achtergelegen) lie behind; lag (behind): *drie **ronden** ~ be three laps behind, be trailing by three laps*

het **achterlijf** /ɑχtərlɛif/ (pl: -lijven) **1** rump; abdomen **2** back

¹**achterlijk** /ɑχtərlək/ (adj) backward, (mentally) retarded: *hij is **niet** ~ he's no fool*

²**achterlijk** /ɑχtərlək/ (adv) like a moron, like an idiot: *doe niet zo ~ don't be such a moron*

achterlopen /ɑχtərlopə(n)/ (liep achter, heeft achtergelopen) **1** be slow, lose time; be behind, lag behind **2** be behind the times

achterna /ɑχtərna/ (adv) **1** after, behind **2** afterwards, after the event

de **achternaam** /ɑχtərnam/ (pl: -namen) surname, last name, family name

achternagaan /ɑχtərnaɣan/ (ging achterna, is achternagegaan) go after, follow (behind)

achternalopen /ɑχtərnalopə(n)/ (liep achterna, heeft/is achternagelopen) follow

achternazitten /ɑχtərnazɪtə(n)/ (zat achterna, heeft achternagezeten) chase: *de **politie** zit ons achterna the police are after us (or: on our heels, on our tail)*

de **achterneef** /ɑχtərnef/ (pl: -neven) second cousin; great-nephew

de **achternicht** /ɑχtərnɪχt/ (pl: -en) second cousin; great-niece

achterom /ɑχtərɔm/ (adv) round the back: *een **blik** ~ a backward glance*

achterop /ɑχtərɔp/ (adv) **1** at (or: on) the back: *spring maar ~! jump on behind me!* **2** behind

achteropraken /ɑχtərɔprakə(n)/ (raakte achterop, is achteropgeraakt) get (or: fall) behind; drop behind

achterover /ɑχtərɔvər/ (adv) back(wards): *hij **viel** ~ op de stenen he fell back(wards) onto the stones*

achteroverdrukken /ɑχtərɔvərdrʏkə(n)/ (drukte achterover, heeft achterovergedrukt) pinch

de **achterpoot** /ɑχtərpot/ (pl: -poten) hind leg

de **achterruit** /ɑχtərœyt/ (pl: -en) rear window, back window

de **achterruitverwarming** /ɑχtərœytfərwɑrmɪŋ/ (rear window) demister

de **achterspeler** /ɑχtərspelər/ (pl: -s) back

achterst /ɑχtərst/ (adj) back, rear, hind(most): *de ~e **rijen** the back rows*

achterstaan /ɑχtərstan/ (stond achter, heeft achtergestaan) be behind (or: down): *bij de rust stonden we **met** 3-1 achter at half-time we were down 3 to 1*

achterstallig /ɑχtərstɑləχ/ (adj) back, overdue, in arrears: *~e **huur** rent arrears, back rent; ~ **onderhoud** overdue maintenance*

de **achterstand** /ɑχtərstɑnt/ arrears: [sport] *een **grote** ~ hebben be well down (or: behind); de ~ **inlopen** make up arrears, catch up; een ~ **oplopen** fall behind; de ploeg probeerde de ~ **weg te werken** the team tried to draw level*

de **achterstandswijk** /ɑχtərstan(t)swɛik/ (pl: -en) disadvantaged urban area

het ¹**achterste** /ɑχtərstə/ (pl: -n) **1** back (part): *niet het ~ van zijn **tong** laten zien keep one's cards close to one's chest, not commit o.s.* **2** backside, rear (end): *op zijn ~ vallen fall on one's bottom*

het/de ²**achterste** /ɑχtərstə/ (pl: -n) back one, hindmost one, rear(most) one

achterstellen /ɑχtərstɛlə(n)/ (stelde achter, heeft achtergesteld) slight, neglect: *hij **voelde** zich achtergesteld he felt discriminated against*

de **achtersteven** /ɑχtərstevə(n)/ (pl: -s) stern

achterstevoren /ɑχtərstəvɔrə(n)/ (adv) back to front

de **achtertuin** /ɑχtərtœyn/ **1** back garden; [Am] backyard **2** backyard

de ¹**achteruit** /ɑχtərœyt/ reverse (gear): *een auto **in** zijn ~ zetten put a car into reverse (gear)*

²**achteruit** /ɑχtərœyt/ (adv) back(wards)

achteruitgaan /ɑχtərœytχan/ (ging achteruit, is achteruitgegaan) **1** go back(wards); go astern [ship]; reverse [car]; back [car]: *ga eens **wat** achteruit! stand back a little!* **2** [fig] decline, get worse, grow worse; fail: *zijn **prestaties** gaan achteruit his performance is on the decline; haar gezondheid gaat **snel** achteruit her health is failing rapidly; ik ben er per maand honderd euro **op** achteruitgegaan I am a hundred euros worse off per month*

de ¹**achteruitgang** /ɑχtərœytχɑn/ back exit, rear exit, back door

de ²**achteruitgang** /ɑχtərœytχɑn/ decline: *de huidige **economische** ~ the present economic decline*

de **achteruitkijkspiegel** /ɑχtərœytkɛikspiɣəl/ (pl: -s) rear-view mirror

achteruitlopen /ɑχtərœytlopə(n)/ (liep achteruit, heeft/is achteruitgelopen) **1** walk backwards: *de **barometer** loopt achteruit the barometer is falling* **2** [fig] decline

achteruitrijden /ɑχtərœytrɛidə(n)/ (reed achteruit, heeft/is achteruitgereden) reverse (into), back (into)

achteruitwijken /ɑχtərœytwɛikə(n)/ (week achteruit, is achteruitgeweken) back away, step back, fall back

achtervolgen /ɑχtərvɔlɣə(n)/ (achtervolg-de, heeft achtervolgd) **1** follow: *die gedachte achtervolgt mij* that thought haunts (*or:* obsesses) me **2** pursue; persecute

de **achtervolger** /ɑχtərvɔlɣər/ (pl: -s) pursuer

de **achtervolging** /ɑχtərvɔlɣɪŋ/ (pl: -en) pursuit; chase; persecution: *de ~ inzetten* pursue, set off in pursuit (of)

de **achtervolgingswaanzin** /ɑχtərvɔlɣɪŋswanzɪn/ persecution complex (*or:* mania), paranoia

¹**achterwaarts** /ɑχtərwarts/ (adj) backward, rearward: *een ~e beweging* a backward movement

²**achterwaarts** /ɑχtərwarts/ (adv) back-(wards): *een stap ~* a step back(wards)

de **achterwand** /ɑχtərwɑnt/ (pl: -en) back wall, rear wall

achterwege /ɑχtərweɣə/ (adv): *een antwoord bleef ~* an answer was not forthcoming; *~ laten* omit; leave undone

het **achterwerk** /ɑχtərwɛrk/ (pl: -en) backside, rear (end)

het **achterwiel** /ɑχtərwil/ (pl: -en) back wheel, rear wheel

de **achterzak** /ɑχtərzɑk/ (pl: -ken) back pocket

de **achterzijde** /ɑχtərzɛidə/ (pl: -n) back, rear

de **achting** /ɑχtɪŋ/ regard, esteem: *~ voor iem. hebben* have respect for s.o.; *in (iemands) ~ dalen* come down in s.o.'s estimation; *in (iemands) ~ stijgen* go up in s.o.'s estimation

achtste /ɑχtstə/ (adj) eighth: *een ~ liter* one eighth of a litre

achttien /ɑχtin/ (num) eighteen

achttiende /ɑχtində/ (num) eighteenth

achttiende-eeuws /ɑχtindəews/ (adj) eighteenth-century

achturig /ɑχtyrəχ/ (adj) eight-hour: *de ~e werkdag* the eight-hour (working) day

de **acne** /ɑkne/ acne

de **acquisitie** /akwizi(t)si/ (pl: -s) acquisition

de **acrobaat** /akrobat/ (pl: acrobaten) acrobat

de **acrobatiek** /akrobatik/ acrobatics

acrobatisch /akrobatis/ (adj, adv) acrobatic

het **acryl** /akril/ acrylic (fibre)

acteren /aktɛrə(n)/ (acteerde, heeft geacteerd) act, perform

de **acteur** /aktœr/ (pl: -s) actor, performer

de **actie** /ɑksi/ (pl: -s) **1** action, activity: *er zit geen ~ in dat toneelstuk* there's no action in that play; *in ~ komen* go into action **2** (protest) campaign: *~ voeren* [just once] hold a demonstration; *~ voeren tegen* campaign against

het **actiecomité** /ɑksikɔmite/ (pl: -s) action committee

actief /ɑktif/ (adj, adv) active [finance]; busy; energetic: *in actieve dienst* **a)** on active duty; **b)** [mil] on active service; *een actieve handelsbalans* a favourable balance of

trade; *iets ~ en passief steunen* support sth. (both) directly and indirectly ‖ *actieve handel* export (trade)

de **actiegroep** /ɑksiɣrup/ (pl: -en) action group; [roughly] pressure group

het **actiepunt** /ɑksipʏnt/ point of action

de **actieradius** /ɑksiradijʏs/ radius of action, range

de **actievoerder** /ɑksivurdər/ (pl: -s) campaigner, activist

actievoeren /ɑksivurə(n)/ (voerde actie, heeft actiegevoerd): *~ tegen* agitate (*or:* campaign) against, carry on a campaign against

de **activa** /ɑktiva/ (pl) assets: *~ en passiva* assets and liabilities; *vaste ~* fixed assets; *vlottende ~* current assets

activeren /ɑktivɛrə(n)/ (activeerde, heeft geactiveerd) activate

de **activist** /ɑktivɪst/ (pl: -en) activist, crusader

de **activiteit** /ɑktivitɛit/ (pl: -en) activity: *~en ontplooien* undertake activities; *buitenschoolse ~en* extramural activities, extracurricular activities

de **actrice** /ɑktrisə/ (pl: -s) actress

actualiseren /ɑktywalizɛrə(n)/ (actualiseerde, heeft geactualiseerd) update

de **actualiteit** /ɑktywalitɛit/ (pl: -en) topical matter (*or:* subject); current event; news; current affairs

het **actualiteitenprogramma** /ɑktywalitɛitə(n)proɣrama/ (pl: -'s) current affairs programme

actueel /ɑktywel/ (adj) current, topical: *een ~ onderwerp* a topical subject; current affairs

de **acupunctuur** /akypʏŋktyr/ (pl: acupuncturen) acupuncture

¹**acuut** /akyt/ (adj) acute, critical: *~ gevaar* acute danger

²**acuut** /akyt/ (adv) immediately, right away, at once

A.D. (abbrev) *anno Domini* AD

de **adamsappel** /adɑmsɑpəl/ (pl: -s) Adam's apple

het **adamskostuum** /adɑmskɔstym/: *in ~* in one's birthday suit

de **adapter** /adɑptər/ (pl: -s) adapter

de **adder** /ɑdər/ (pl: -s) viper, adder: [fig] *er schuilt een ~(tje) onder het gras* there's a snake in the grass, there's a catch in it somewhere

additioneel /adi(t)ʃonel/ (adj) additional, accessory

de **adel** /adəl/ nobility, peerage: *hij is van ~* he is a peer, he belongs to the nobility

de **adelaar** /adəlar/ (pl: -s) eagle

adellijk /adələk/ (adj) noble: *van ~e afkomst* of noble birth; *~ bloed* noble blood

de **adelstand** /adəlstɑnt/ nobility: *iem. in (or: tot) de ~ verheffen* ennoble s.o., raise s.o. to the peerage de **adem** /<u>a</u>dəm/ breath: *de laatste ~ uitblazen* breathe one's last; *slechte ~* bad breath, halitosis; *zijn ~ inhouden* [also fig] hold one's breath; *naar ~ happen* gasp for breath; *buiten ~ zijn* be out of breath; *in één ~* in the same breath; *weer op ~ komen* catch one's breath

adembenemend /adəmbən<u>e</u>mənt/ (adj, adv) breathtaking: *een ~ schouwspel* a breathtaking scene

ademen /<u>a</u>dəmə(n)/ (ademde, heeft geademd) breathe, inhale: *vrij ~* [also fig] breathe freely; *de lucht die we hier ~ is verpest* the air we are breathing here is poisoned

ademhalen /<u>a</u>dəmhalə(n)/ (haalde adem, heeft ademgehaald) breathe: *weer adem kunnen halen* be able to breathe again; *haal eens diep adem* take a deep breath

de **ademhaling** /<u>a</u>dəmhalıŋ/ (pl: -en) breathing, respiration: *kunstmatige ~* artificial respiration; *een onrustige ~* irregular breathing

ademloos /<u>a</u>dəmlos/ (adj, adv) breathless: *een ademloze stilte* a breathless hush

de **ademnood** /<u>a</u>dəmnot/: *in ~ verkeren* be gasping for breath, find it difficult to breathe

de **adempauze** /<u>a</u>dəmpauzə/ (pl: -s) breathing space, breather

de **ademtest** /<u>a</u>dəmtɛst/ (pl: -s) breath test: *iem. de ~ afnemen* breathalyse s.o.

de **adept** /adɛpt/ (pl: -en) follower, adherent, disciple

adequaat /adəkw<u>a</u>t/ (adj, adv) appropriate, effective; adequate: *~ reageren* react appropriately (*or:* effectively)

de **ader** /<u>a</u>dər/ (pl: -s, -en) vein, blood vessel; artery: *een gesprongen ~* a burst blood vessel

de **aderlating** /<u>a</u>dərlatıŋ/ (pl: -en) bleeding; [fig] drain (on resources): *dat was een behoorlijke ~* it made a big hole in the budget

de **aderverkalking** /<u>a</u>dərvərkalkıŋ/ arteriosclerosis, hardening of the arteries

ADHD /adehad<u>e</u>/ *attention deficit hyperactivity disorder* ADHD

de **adhesie** /ath<u>e</u>zi/ adherence

a.d.h.v. (abbrev) *aan de hand van* using, by means of

het **¹adjectief** /atjɛkt<u>i</u>f/ (pl: adjectieven) adjective

²adjectief /atjɛkt<u>i</u>f/ (adj) adjectival, adjective

de **adjudant** /atjyd<u>a</u>nt/ (pl: -en) **1** adjutant, aide(-de-camp) **2** [roughly] warrant officer

de **adjunct-directeur** /atjʏŋgdirɛktǫr/ (pl: -en) deputy director (*or:* manager); [educ] deputy headmaster

de **administrateur** /atministrat<u>ø</u>r/ (pl: -en, -s) administrator: *de ~ van een universiteit* the administrative director of a university

de **administratie** /atministr<u>a</u>(t)si/ (pl: -s) **1** administration; management; accounts: *de ~ voeren* do the administrative work; keep the accounts **2** administrative department; [bldg] administrative building (*or:* offices): *hij zit op de ~* he's in the administrative (*or:* clerical) department

administratief /atministrat<u>i</u>f/ (adj, adv) administrative; clerical: *~ personeel* administrative (*or:* clerical) staff; [Belg] *~ centrum* administrative centre

de **administratiekosten** /atministr<u>a</u>(t)sikostə(n)/ (pl) administrative costs, service charge(s)

administreren /atministr<u>e</u>rə(n)/ (administreerde, heeft geadministreerd) administer; manage, run; keep accounts: *een ~d lichaam* an administrative body

de **admiraal** /atmir<u>a</u>l/ (pl: -s) admiral

de **adolescent** /adolɛsɛnt/ (pl: -en) adolescent; youngster

de **adonis** /ad<u>o</u>nıs/ (pl: -sen) Adonis; Greek god

adopteren /adopt<u>e</u>rə(n)/ (adopteerde, heeft geadopteerd) adopt

de **adoptie** /ad<u>o</u>psi/ (pl: -s) adoption

het **adoptiekind** /ad<u>o</u>psikınt/ (pl: -eren) adopted child

de **adoptieouder** /ad<u>o</u>psiaudər/ (pl: -s) adoptive parent

de **adrenaline** /adrenal<u>i</u>nə/ adrenaline

het **adres** /adr<u>ɛ</u>s/ (pl: -sen) address, (place of) residence: [fig] *je bent aan het juiste ~* you've come to the right place; *hij verhuisde zonder een ~ achter te laten* he moved without leaving a forwarding address; *per ~* care of; [abbr] c/o

de **adresbalk** /adr<u>ɛ</u>zbɑlk/ (pl: -en) address bar, location bar

adresseren /adrɛs<u>e</u>rə(n)/ (adresseerde, heeft geadresseerd) address: *een brief vergeten te ~* forget to address a letter

de **adreswijziging** /adr<u>ɛ</u>swɛizəɣıŋ/ (pl: -en) change of address

Adriatisch /adrij<u>a</u>tis/ (adj) Adriatic: *~e Zee* Adriatic Sea

ADSL /adeɛs<u>ɛ</u>l/ *asymmetric digital subscriber line* ADSL

de **advent** /atf<u>ɛ</u>nt/ Advent

de **adverteerder** /atfərt<u>e</u>rdər/ (pl: -s) advertiser

de **advertentie** /atfərt<u>ɛ</u>nsi/ (pl: -s) advertisement, ad(vert): *een ~ plaatsen* put an advertisement in the paper('s)

adverteren /atfərt<u>e</u>rə(n)/ (adverteerde, heeft geadverteerd) advertise; announce: *er wordt veel geadverteerd voor nieuwe computerspelletjes* new computer games are being heavily advertised

het **advies** /atf<u>i</u>s/ (pl: adviezen) advice: *~ geven* give advice; *iemands ~ opvolgen* follow s.o.'s advice; *iem. om ~ vragen* ask s.o.'s advice; *een ~* a piece of advice; a recommendation; *het ~ van deskundigen inwinnen* obtain expert advice, get the opinion of experts

het **adviesbureau** /ɑtfiːzbyro/ (pl: -s) consultancy

de **adviesprijs** /ɑtfiːsprɛɪs/ (pl: -prijzen) recommended selling (or: retail) price
adviseren /ɑtfizeːrə(n)/ (adviseerde, heeft
geadviseerd) **1** recommend, advise (s.o.): *hij
adviseerde mij de auto te laten repareren* he ad-
vised me to have the car mended **2** advise,
counsel: *ik kan je in deze lastige kwestie niet ~* I
can't offer you advice in this complicated
matter

de **adviseur** /ɑtfizøːr/ (pl: -s) adviser, advisor,
counsellor; consultant: *rechtskundig ~* legal
advisor, lawyer; solicitor

de **advocaat** /ɑtfokaːt/ (pl: advocaten) lawyer;
barrister; solicitor: *een ~ nemen* engage a
lawyer ‖ [fig] *~ van de duivel* the devil's advocate

het **advocatenkantoor** /ɑtfokaːtə(n)kɑntor/
(pl: -kantoren) lawyer's office

de **advocatuur** /ɑtfokatyːr/ Bar; legal profession: *de sociale ~* [roughly] legal aid lawyers

de **aerobics** /ɛːrɔbɪks/ aerobics
aerodynamisch /ɛːrodinaːmis/ (adj) aerodynamic

¹**af** /ɑf/ (adj) **1** finished, done, completed;
polished; well-finished: *het werk is af* the
work is done (or: finished) **2** [game] out: *hij is
af* he's out ‖ *teruggaan naar af* go back to
square one

²**af** /ɑf/ (adv) **1** off, away: *mensen liepen af en
aan* people came and went; *af en toe* (every)
now and then; *klaar? af!* ready, steady, go!;
get set! go! **2** (+ van) from: *van die dag af*
from that day (on, onwards); *van kind af (aan)
woon ik in deze straat* since I was a child I have
been living in this street; *van de grond af*
from ground level **3** away, off: [fig] *dat kan
er bij ons niet af* we can't afford that; *de verf is
er af* the paint has come off; *ver af* a long
way off; *hij woont een eindje van de weg af* he
lives a little way away from the road; *van
iem. af zijn* be rid of s.o.; *u bent nog niet van
me af* you haven't seen (or: heard) the last of
me; I haven't finished with you yet **4** down:
de trap af down the stairs **5** to; towards; up
to: *ze komen op ons af* they are coming towards us ‖ *goed* (or: *beter, slecht*) *af zijn* have
come off well (or: better, badly); *ik weet er
niets van af* I don't know anything about it;
van voren af aan beginnen start from scratch;
start all over again

de **afasie** /afaziː/ aphasia
afbakenen /ɑvbakənə(n)/ (bakende af,
heeft afgebakend) mark out; stake out; define; demarcate; mark off
afbakken /ɑvbɑkə(n)/ (bakte af, heeft af-
gebakken) finish off in the oven: *broodjes
om zelf af te bakken* par(t)-baked rolls
afbeelden /ɑvbeldə(n)/ (beeldde af, heeft
afgebeeld) depict, portray, picture

de **afbeelding** /ɑvbeldɪŋ/ (pl: -en) picture, i-
mage; illustration; figure
afbekken /ɑvbɛkə(n)/ (bekte af, heeft af-
gebekt): [inform] *iem. ~ snap* (or: snarl) at
s.o., jump down s.o.'s throat
afbellen /ɑvbɛlə(n)/ (belde af, heeft afge-
beld) **1** cancel (by telephone) **2** ring round:
hij belde de halve stad af om een taxi he rang
round half the city for a taxi
afbestellen /ɑvbəstɛlə(n)/ (bestelde af,
heeft afbesteld) cancel
afbetalen /ɑvbətaːlə(n)/ (betaalde af, heeft
afbetaald) pay off; pay for [goods]: *het huis is
helemaal afbetaald* the house is completely
paid for

de **afbetaling** /ɑvbətalɪŋ/ (pl: -en) hire purchase, payment by instalment (or: in instalments): *op ~* on hire purchase
afbeulen /ɑvbølə(n)/ (beulde af, heeft af-
gebeuld) drive into the ground, work to
death: *zich ~ slave*; work one's guts out;
knacker o.s.
afbieden /ɑvbidə(n)/ (bood af, heeft afge-
boden) [Belg] bring (or: knock, beat) down
afbijten /ɑvbɛitə(n)/ (beet af, heeft afgebe-
ten) **1** bite off **2** strip, remove ‖ *van zich ~*
stick up for o.s.
afbinden /ɑvbɪndə(n)/ (bond af, heeft af-
gebonden) **1** tie off **2** untie, undo: *de
schaatsen ~* untie (or: undo) one's skates
afbladderen /ɑvbladərə(n)/ (bladderde af,
is afgebladderd) flake (off), peel (off): *de
verf bladdert af* the paint is flaking (or: peeling) off
afblazen /ɑvblaːzə(n)/ (blies af, heeft afgeblazen) blow off (or: away): *stof van de tafel ~*
blow the dust off the table ‖ *de scheidsrechter had (de wedstrijd) al afgeblazen* the referee
had already blown the final whistle
afblijven /ɑvblɛivə(n)/ (bleef af, is afgeble-
ven) keep off, leave alone, let alone, keep
(or: stay) away (from): *blijf van de koekjes af*
leave the biscuits alone
afboeken /ɑvbukə(n)/ (boekte af, heeft af-
geboekt) **1** transfer **2** write off
afborstelen /ɑvbɔrstələ(n)/ (borstelde af,
heeft afgeborsteld) brush (down): *zijn kleren
~* give one's clothes a brush
afbouwen /ɑvbɑuwə(n)/ (bouwde af, heeft
afgebouwd) **1** cut back (on), down (on),
phase out: *we zijn de therapie aan het ~* we're
phasing out the therapy **2** complete, finish

de **afbraak** /ɑvbrak/ demolition
afbranden /ɑvbrɑndə(n)/ (brandde af,
heeft/is afgebrand) burn down
afbreekbaar /ɑvbreɡbar/ (adj) decomposa-
ble, degradable; biodegradable: *biologisch
afbreekbare wasmiddelen* biodegradable de-
tergents

¹**afbreken** /ɑvbrekə(n)/ (brak af, is afgebroken) break off (or: away); snap (off): *de punt*

brak (van de stok) af the end broke off (the stick)

²**afbreken** /ɑvbrekə(n)/ (brak af, heeft afgebroken) **1** break off, interrupt; cut short: *onderhandelingen ~* break off negotiations; *de wedstrijd werd afgebroken* the game was stopped **2** pull down, demolish; break down, tear down; break up; dismantle: *de boel ~* smash the place up **3** decompose, degrade ‖ *afvalstoffen worden in het lichaam afgebroken* waste-products are broken down in the body

afbrengen /ɑvbrɛŋə(n)/ (bracht af, heeft afgebracht) put off: *ze zijn er niet van af te brengen* they can't be put off (*or:* deterred) ‖ *het er goed ~* do well; *het er slecht ~* come off badly, be badly off; *het er levend ~* escape with one's life; *het er heelhuids ~* come out of it unscathed

de **afbreuk** /ɑvbrøk/: *~ doen aan* harm, injure, damage

afbrokkelen /ɑvbrɔkələ(n)/ (brokkelde af, is afgebrokkeld) crumble (off, away), fragment: *het plafond brokkelt af* the ceiling is crumbling

afbuigen /ɑvbœyɣə(n)/ (boog af, is afgebogen) turn off, bear off, branch off: *hier buigt de weg naar rechts af* here the road bears (to the) right

het **afdak** /ɑvdɑk/ (pl: -en) lean-to

afdalen /ɑvdalə(n)/ (daalde af, is afgedaald) go down, come down, descend: *een berg ~* go (*or:* come) down a mountain

de **afdaling** /ɑvdalɪŋ/ (pl: -en) **1** descent **2** [skiing] downhill

afdanken /ɑvdɑŋkə(n)/ (dankte af, heeft afgedankt) **1** discard; cast off; (send for) scrap **2** dismiss; disband: *personeel ~* pay off staff

het **afdankertje** /ɑvdɑŋkərcə/ (pl: -s) cast-off, hand-me-down

afdekken /ɑvdɛkə(n)/ (dekte af, heeft afgedekt) cover (over, up)

de **afdeling** /ɑvdelɪŋ/ (pl: -en) department, division; section; ward: *de ~ Utrecht van onze vereniging* the Utrecht branch of our society; *Kees werkt op de ~ financiën* Kees works in the finance department

de **afdelingschef** /ɑvdelɪŋʃɛf/ (pl: -s) department(al) manager, head of department; floor manager

afdingen /ɑvdɪŋə(n)/ (dong af, heeft afgedongen) bargain (*or:* haggle) (with s.o.)

afdoen /ɑvdun/ (deed af, heeft afgedaan) **1** take off, remove: *zijn hoed ~* take off one's hat **2** take off: *iets van de prijs ~* knock a bit off the price, come down a bit (in price) ‖ [fig] *dat doet niets af aan het feit dat ...* that doesn't alter the fact that …

afdoend /ɑvdunt/ (adj, adv) sufficient, adequate; effective: *een ~ middel* an effective method

afdraaien /ɑvdrajə(n)/ (draaide af, heeft afgedraaid) twist off: *de dop van een vulpen ~* unscrew the cap of a fountain pen ‖ *hier moet u rechts ~* you turn right (*or:* turn off to the right) here

afdragen /ɑvdraɣə(n)/ (droeg af, heeft afgedragen) **1** make over, transfer, hand over, turn over **2** wear out: *afgedragen schoenen* worn-out shoes

afdrijven /ɑvdrɛivə(n)/ (dreef af, is afgedreven) drift off; [shipp] go adrift ‖ *de bui drijft af* the shower is blowing over

afdrogen /ɑvdroɣə(n)/ (droogde af, heeft afgedroogd) dry (up); wipe dry: *zijn handen ~* dry one's hands (on a towel); *zich ~* dry o.s. (off)

de **afdronk** /ɑvdrɔŋk/ aftertaste

afdruipen /ɑvdrœyp ə(n)/ (droop af, is afgedropen) slink off (*or:* away), clear off

de **afdruk** /ɑvdrʏk/ (pl: -ken) print; imprint; mould; cast: *de wielen lieten een ~ achter* the wheels left an impression

afdrukken /ɑvdrʏkə(n)/ (drukte af, heeft afgedrukt) print (off); copy; run off

afdwalen /ɑvdwalə(n)/ (dwaalde af, is afgedwaald) stray (off) (from), go astray; [fig also] wander (off): *zijn gedachten dwaalden af naar haar* his thoughts wandered off to her; *van zijn onderwerp ~* stray from one's subject

afdwingen /ɑvdwɪŋə(n)/ (dwong af, heeft afgedwongen) exact (from); extort (from)

de **affaire** /ɑfɛ:rə/ (pl: -s) affair

het/de **affiche** /ɑfiʃə/ (pl: -s) poster; (play)bill

afgaan /ɑfxan/ (ging af, is afgegaan) **1** go down, descend: *de trap ~* go down the stairs **2** (+ op) [fig] rely on, depend on: *~de op wat hij zegt* judging by what he says; *op zijn gevoel ~* play it by ear **3** come off; be deducted: *daar gaat 10 % van af* 10 % is taken off that **4** go off: *een geweer doen ~* fire a rifle **5** lose face, flop, fail ‖ *van school ~* leave school

de **afgang** /ɑfxɑŋ/ (pl: -en) (embarrassing) failure, flop

afgedraaid /ɑfxədrajt/ (adj) worn-out, completely exhausted

afgeladen /ɑfxəladə(n)/ (adj) (jam-)packed, crammed

afgelasten /ɑfxəlɑstə(n)/ (gelastte af, heeft afgelast) cancel; call off; [sport] postpone

afgeleefd /ɑfxəleft/ (adj) used up, worn-out, spent

afgelegen /ɑfxəleɣə(n)/ (adj, adv) remote, far(-away), far-off: *een ~ dorp* a remote (*or:* an out-of-the-way) village

afgeleid /ɑfxəlɛit/ (adj) diverted, distracted: *hij is gauw ~* he is easily distracted

afgelopen /ɑfxəlopə(n)/ (adj) last, past: *de ~ maanden hadden wij geen woning* for the last few months we haven't had anywhere to live; *de ~ tijd* recently; *de ~ weken* the past weeks, the last few weeks ‖ *~!* stop it!, that's enough!

afgemeten /ɑfxəmetə(n)/ (adj, adv) measured (off, out): *met ~ **passen*** with measured steps

afgepeigerd /ɑfxəpɛiɣərt/ (adj) knackered, exhausted

afgericht /ɑfxərɪxt/ (adj) (well-)trained

afgerond /ɑfxərɔnt/ (adj) **1** (well-)rounded: *het vormt een ~ **geheel*** it forms a complete whole **2** round

afgesproken /ɑfxəsprokə(n)/ (adj) agreed, settled || *dat is dan ~* it's a deal!

afgestompt /ɑfxəstɔmt/ (adj) dull(ed), deadened

de **afgestudeerde** /ɑfxəstyderdə/ (pl: -n) graduate

de **afgevaardigde** /ɑfxəvardəɣdə/ (pl: -n) delegate, representative; member (of parliament): *de **geachte** ~* the honourable member

¹**afgeven** /ɑfxevə(n)/ (gaf af, heeft afgegeven) **1** run **2** (+ op) run down: *op iem. (iets) ~* run s.o. (sth.) down

²**afgeven** /ɑfxevə(n)/ (gaf af, heeft afgegeven) **1** hand in; deliver; leave; hand over; give up: *hij weigerde zijn **geld** af te geven* he refused to part with his money; *een **pakje** bij iem. ~* leave a parcel with s.o. **2** give off: *de kachel geeft veel **warmte** af* the stove gives off a lot of heat

afgewerkt /ɑfxəwɛrkt/ (adj) used (up), spent: *~e **olie*** used oil

afgewogen /ɑfxəwoɣə(n)/ (adj) balanced

afgezaagd /ɑfxəzaxt/ (adj) [fig] stale; hackneyed

de **afgezant** /ɑfxəzɑnt/ (pl: -en) envoy, ambassador

afgezien /ɑfxəzin/: *~ van* besides, apart from; *~ van de kosten* (or: *moeite*) apart from the cost (or: trouble)

afgezonderd /ɑfxəzɔndərt/ (adj, adv) isolated, cut off; segregated; remote

de **Afghaan** /ɑfxan/ (pl: Afghanen) Afghan

Afghaans /ɑfxans/ (adj) Afghan

Afghanistan /ɑfxanistɑn/ Afghanistan

afgieten /ɑfxitə(n)/ (goot af, heeft afgegoten) pour off; strain; drain: *aardappels ~* drain potatoes; *groente ~* strain vegetables

het **afgietsel** /ɑfxitsəl/ (pl: -s) cast, mould

de **afgifte** /ɑfxɪftə/ delivery; issue [tickets etc]

de **afgod** /ɑfxɔt/ (pl: -en) idol

afgooien /ɑfxojə(n)/ (gooide af, heeft afgegooid) throw down; fling down: *pas op dat je het **er** niet afgooit* take care that you don't knock it off

afgraven /ɑfxravə(n)/ (groef af, heeft afgegraven) dig up, dig off; level

afgrendelen /ɑfxrɛndələ(n)/ (grendelde af, heeft afgegrendeld) [fig] seal off, close off; [literally] bolt up

afgrijselijk /ɑfxrɛisələk/ (adj, adv) **1** horrible, horrid, atrocious: *een ~e **moord*** a grue-

some murder **2** hideous, ghastly

het **afgrijzen** /ɑfxrɛizə(n)/ horror, dread: *met ~ vervullen* horrify

de **afgrond** /ɑfxrɔnt/ (pl: -en) abyss, chasm

de **afgunst** /ɑfxynst/ envy, jealousy

afgunstig /ɑfxynstəx/ (adj) envious

de **afhaalmaaltijd** /ɑfhalmaltɛit/ takeaway; [Am] take-out

het **afhaalrestaurant** /ɑfhalrɛstorɑnt/ (pl: -s) takeaway (restaurant); [Am] take-out (restaurant)

afhaken /ɑfhakə(n)/ (haakte af, heeft/is afgehaakt) pull out, drop out

afhakken /ɑfhɑkə(n)/ (hakte af, heeft afgehakt) chop off, cut off

afhalen /ɑfhalə(n)/ (haalde af, heeft afgehaald) **1** collect, call for **2** collect, meet: *ik **kom** je over een uur ~* I'll pick you up in an hour; *iem. **van** de trein ~* meet s.o. at the station || *bedden ~* strip the beds

afhandelen /ɑfhɑndələ(n)/ (handelde af, heeft afgehandeld) settle, conclude, deal with, dispose of: *de spreker handelde eerst de **bezwaren** af* the speaker first dealt with the objections

de **afhandeling** /ɑfhɑndəlɪŋ/ settlement, transaction

afhandig /ɑfhɑndəx/ (adj): *iem. iets ~ **maken*** trick s.o. out of sth.

afhangen /ɑfhɑŋə(n)/ (hing af, heeft afgehangen) depend (on): *hij danste alsof zijn leven **ervan** afhing* he danced for dear life (or: as though his life depended on it); *het hangt **van** het weer af* it depends on the weather

afhankelijk /ɑfhɑŋkələk/ (adj) dependent (on), depending (on): *ik **ben** van niemand ~* I am quite independent; *de beslissing **is** ~ van het weer* the decision is dependent on (or: depends on) the weather

de **afhankelijkheid** /ɑfhɑŋkələkhɛit/ dependence

afhelpen /ɑfhɛlpə(n)/ (hielp af, heeft afgeholpen) rid (of); cure (of): *iem. **van** zijn geld ~* relieve s.o. of his money

afhouden /ɑfhaudə(n)/ (hield af, heeft afgehouden) **1** keep off, keep out: *zij kon haar **ogen** niet van de taart ~* she couldn't keep her eyes off the cake; *iem. **van** zijn werk ~* keep s.o. from his work **2** keep back: *een **deel** van het loon ~* withhold a part of the wages

afhuren /ɑfhyrə(n)/ (huurde af, heeft afgehuurd) hire, rent

afijn /ɑfɛin/ (int) so, well

afkalven /ɑfkɑlvə(n)/ (kalfde af, is afgekalfd) cave in; [fig] be eroded

afkammen /ɑfkɑmə(n)/ (kamde af, heeft afgekamd) run down, tear (to pieces); [book also] slash (to shreds); slate

afkappen /ɑfkɑpə(n)/ (kapte af, heeft afgekapt) **1** chop off **2** cut (s.o.) short: *een **gesprek** ~* break off (or: cut short) a conversa-

tion

de **afkeer** /ɑfker/ aversion (to), dislike (of): *een ~ hebben* (or: *tonen*) have (or: display) an aversion (to)

afkeren /ɑfkerə(n)/ (keerde af, heeft afgekeerd) turn away (or: aside), avert: *het hoofd ~* turn one's head away; *zich ~ van iem. (iets)* turn away from s.o. (sth.)

afkerig /ɑfkerəx/ (adj) averse (to): *~ zijn van iets* be abhorrent of sth., abhor sth.; *niet ~ zijn van iets* not be ill-disposed toward sth.

afketsen /ɑfkɛtsə(n)/ (ketste af, is afgeketst) **1** bounce off, glance off **2** [fig] fall through, fail: *het plan is afgeketst op geldgebrek* the plan fell through because of a lack of money; *iets laten ~* reject sth.; defeat sth.; frustrate sth.

afkeuren /ɑfkørə(n)/ (keurde af, heeft afgekeurd) **1** reject, turn down, declare unfit: *hij is voor 70 % afgekeurd* he has a 70 % disability **2** disapprove of, condemn ‖ *een doelpunt ~* disallow a goal

de **afkeuring** /ɑfkørɪŋ/ (pl: -en) disapproval, condemnation: *zijn ~ uitspreken over* express one's disapproval of

afkicken /ɑfkɪkə(n)/ (kickte af, heeft/is afgekickt) kick the habit; dry out: *hij is afgekickt* he has kicked the habit

de **afkickverschijnselen** /ɑfkɪkfərsxɛɪnsələ(n)/ (pl) withdrawal symptoms

afkijken /ɑfkɛikə(n)/ (keek af, heeft afgekeken) **1** copy, crib **2** see out, see to the end: *we hebben die film niet afgekeken* we didn't see the film out ‖ *bij* (or: *van*) *zijn buurman ~* copy (or: crib) from one's neighbour

afkleden /ɑfkledə(n)/ (kleedde af, heeft afgekleed) be slimming

afkloppen /ɑfklɔpə(n)/ (klopte af, heeft afgeklopt) knock on wood, touch wood: *even ~!* touch wood!

afkluiven /ɑfklœyvə(n)/ (kloof af, heeft afgekloven) gnaw off/on: *een botje ~* pick a bone

afknappen /ɑfknɑpə(n)/ (knapte af, is afgeknapt) break down, have a breakdown: *~ op iem. (iets)* get fed up with s.o. (sth.)

afknippen /ɑfknɪpə(n)/ (knipte af, heeft afgeknipt) cut (off); trim

afkoelen /ɑfkulə(n)/ (koelde af, is afgekoeld) cool (off, down); chill; refrigerate: *iets laten ~* leave sth. to cool

de **afkoeling** /ɑfkulɪŋ/ cooling (off (or: down))

afkoersen /ɑfkursə(n)/ (koerste af, heeft/is afgekoerst) (+ op) head straight for

afkomen /ɑfkomə(n)/ (kwam af, is afgekomen) **1** (+ op) come up to (or: towards): *(dreigend) op iem. ~* approach s.o. (menacingly); *zij zag de auto recht op zich ~* she saw the car heading straight for her (or: coming straight at her); [fig] *de dingen op zich laten ~* wait and see, let things take their course **2** get rid of;

be done (or: finished) with; get off (or: away); get out of: *er gemakkelijk ~* get off easily (or: lightly)

de **afkomst** /ɑfkɔmst/ descent, origin; birth; [word] derivation: *Jean is van Franse ~* Jean is French by birth

afkomstig /ɑfkɔmstəx/ (adj) **1** from, coming (from), originating (from): *~ uit Spanje* of Spanish origin **2** originating (from), derived (from): *dat woord is ~ uit het Turks* that word is derived (or: borrowed) from Turkish

afkondigen /ɑfkɔndəɣə(n)/ (kondigde af, heeft afgekondigd) proclaim, give notice of

de **afkondiging** /ɑfkɔndəɣɪŋ/ (pl: -en) proclamation; declaration

de **afkoopsom** /ɑfkopsɔm/ (pl: -men) redemption money, compensation

afkopen /ɑfkopə(n)/ (kocht af, heeft afgekocht) buy (from), purchase (from), buy off; redeem; ransom: *een hypotheek ~* redeem a mortgage; *een polis ~* surrender a policy

afkoppelen /ɑfkɔpələ(n)/ (koppelde af, heeft afgekoppeld) uncouple; disconnect

afkorten /ɑfkɔrtə(n)/ (kortte af, heeft afgekort) shorten; abbreviate

de **afkorting** /ɑfkɔrtɪŋ/ (pl: -en) abbreviation, shortening

afkrabben /ɑfkrɑbə(n)/ (krabde af, heeft afgekrabd) scratch off, scrape off (or: from)

afkraken /ɑfkrakə(n)/ (kraakte af, heeft afgekraakt) run down: *de criticus kraakte haar boek volledig af* the reviewer ran her book into the ground

afkrijgen /ɑfkrɛiɣə(n)/ (kreeg af, heeft afgekregen) **1** get off, get out: *hij kreeg de vlek er niet af* he couldn't get the stain out **2** get done (or: finished): *het werk op tijd ~* get the work done (or: finished) in time

afkunnen /ɑfkʏnə(n)/ be able to get through, be able to cope with: *ik kan het zonder jou wel af* I can get along (very well) without you

de **aflaat** /ɑflat/ (pl: aflaten) indulgence

aflandig /ɑflɑndəx/ (adj) offshore

afleggen /ɑflɛɣə(n)/ (legde af, heeft afgelegd) **1** take off; lay down **2** make; take: *een bezoek ~* pay a visit; *een examen ~* take an exam(ination); sit (for) an examination; *een getuigenis ~* give evidence; testify **3** cover: *500 mijl per dag ~* cover 500 miles a day ‖ *het (moeten) ~ tegen iem./iets op het gebied van* lose out to s.o./sth. on

afleiden /ɑflɛidə(n)/ (leidde af, heeft afgeleid) **1** lead (or: guide) away (from); divert (from) [road etc]; conduct [lightning]: *de stroom ~* divert the stream; *de bliksem ~* conduct lightning **2** divert, distract: *ik leidde hem af van zijn werk* I kept him from doing his work **3** trace back (to); derive (from): *'spraak' is afgeleid van 'spreken'* 'spraak' is derived from 'spreken'

de **afleiding** /ɑflɛidɪŋ/ (pl: -en) distraction, diversion: *ik heb echt ~ nodig* I really need sth. to take my mind off it (*or:* things); *voor ~ zorgen* take s.o.'s mind off things

de **afleidingsmanoeuvre** /ɑflɛidɪŋsmanœːvrə/ (pl: -s) diversion; [fig] red herring

afleren /ɑflerə(n)/ (leerde af, heeft afgeleerd) **1** unlearn, get out of (a habit): *ik heb het stotteren afgeleerd* I have overcome my stammer **2** cure of, break of: *ik zal je dat liegen wel ~* I'll teach you to tell lies ‖ *nog eentje om het af te leren* one for the road

afleveren /ɑfleverə(n)/ (leverde af, heeft afgeleverd) **1** deliver: *de bestelling is op tijd afgeleverd* the order was delivered on time **2** [Belg] award, grant

de **aflevering** /ɑfleverɪŋ/ (pl: -en) **1** delivery: *bij ~ betalen* cash on delivery **2** episode

aflezen /ɑflezə(n)/ (las af, heeft afgelezen) **1** read out (the whole of) **2** read (off) ‖ [fig] *de woede van iemands gezicht ~* tell the anger from, see the anger on s.o.'s face

aflikken /ɑflɪkə(n)/ (likte af, heeft afgelikt) lick: *zijn vingers* (*or: een lepel*) *~* lick one's fingers (*or:* a spoon)

de **afloop** /ɑflop/ (pl: aflopen) **1** end, close: *na ~ van de voorstelling* after the performance **2** result, outcome: *ongeluk met dodelijke ~* fatal accident

aflopen /ɑflopə(n)/ (liep af, is afgelopen) **1** (come to an) end, finish; expire: *de cursus is afgelopen* the course is finished; *dit jaar loopt het huurcontract af* the lease expires this year; *het verhaal liep goed af* the story had a happy ending **2** run (*or:* go, walk) down

aflopend /ɑflopənt/ (adj): *het is een ~e zaak* we're fighting a losing battle

aflossen /ɑflɔsə(n)/ (loste af, heeft afgelost) **1** relieve: *laten we elkaar ~* let's take turns **2** pay off: *een bedrag op een lening ~* pay off an part of a loan

de **aflossing** /ɑflɔsɪŋ/ (pl: -en) **1** changing, change: *de ~ van de wacht* the changing of the guard **2** (re)payment **3** (re)payment (period), instalment: *een maandelijkse* (*or: jaarlijkse*) *~* a monthly (*or:* an annual) payment

afluisteren /ɑflœystərə(n)/ (luisterde af, heeft afgeluisterd) eavesdrop (on), listen in to (*or:* in on), monitor; (wire-)tap: *iem. ~* eavesdrop on s.o.; monitor s.o.; *een telefoongesprek ~* listen in to a phone call

afmaken /ɑfmakə(n)/ (maakte af, heeft afgemaakt) **1** finish, complete: *een werkje ~* finish (*or:* complete) a bit of work **2** kill: *ze hebben de hond moeten laten ~* they had to have the dog put down ‖ *hij maakte er zich met een grap van af* he brushed it aside with a joke; *zich er wat al te gemakkelijk van ~* shrug sth. off too lightly

afmatten /ɑfmɑtə(n)/ (matte af, heeft afgemat) exhaust, wear out, tire out

afmelden /ɑfmɛldə(n)/ (meldde af, heeft afgemeld) cancel: *zich ~* check (*or:* sign) (o.s.) out

afmeten /ɑfmetə(n)/ (mat af/meette af, heeft afgemeten) measure, judge: *de kwaliteit van een opleiding ~ aan het aantal geslaagden* judge the quality of a course from (*or:* by) the number of passes

de **afmeting** /ɑfmetɪŋ/ (pl: -en) dimension, proportion, size: *de ~en van de kamer* the dimensions (*or:* size) of the room

de **afname** /ɑfnamə/ **1** purchase: *bij ~ van 25 exemplaren* for quantities of 25, if 25 copies are ordered (*or:* bought) **2** sale **3** decline, decrease: *de ~ van de werkloosheid* the reduction in unemployment

afneembaar /ɑfnembar/ (adj) detachable, removable

¹**afnemen** /ɑfnemə(n)/ (nam af, is afgenomen) decrease, decline: *onze belangstelling nam af* our interest faded; *in gewicht ~* lose weight

²**afnemen** /ɑfnemə(n)/ (nam af, heeft afgenomen) **1** take off (*or:* away), remove (from): *zijn hoed ~* take off one's hat; raise one's hat; *het kleed van de tafel ~* take (*or:* remove) cloth from the table **2** remove: *iem. bloed ~* take blood (*or:* a blood sample) **3** clean: *de tafel met een natte doek ~* wipe the table with a damp cloth **4** deprive: *iem. zijn rijbewijs ~* take away s.o.'s driving licence **5** hold, administer: *iem. de biecht ~* hear s.o.'s confession; *iem. een eed ~* administer an oath to s.o.; swear s.o. in; *iem. een examen ~* examine s.o. **6** buy, purchase

de **afnemer** /ɑfnemər/ (pl: -s) buyer, customer: *Duitsland is onze grootste ~ van snijbloemen* Germany is our largest customer for cut flowers

afpakken /ɑfpɑkə(n)/ (pakte af, heeft afgepakt) take (away), snatch (away): *iem. een mes ~* take away a knife from s.o.

afpassen /ɑfpɑsə(n)/ (paste af, heeft afgepast) measure (out): *een afgepaste portie* a measured (*or:* an adjusted) portion

afpersen /ɑfpɛrsə(n)/ (perste af, heeft afgeperst) extort (*or:* wring), force: *iem. geld ~* extort money from s.o.

de **afperser** /ɑfpɛrsər/ (pl: -s) blackmailer

de **afpersing** /ɑfpɛrsɪŋ/ (pl: -en) extortion; blackmail

afpikken /ɑfpɪkə(n)/ (pikte af, heeft afgepikt) [inform] pinch (from)

afpingelen /ɑfpɪŋələ(n)/ (pingelde af, heeft afgepingeld) haggle: *proberen af te pingelen* try to beat down the price

afplakken /ɑfplɑkə(n)/ (plakte af, heeft afgeplakt) tape up, cover with tape

afplukken /ɑfplʏkə(n)/ (plukte af, heeft afgeplukt) pick, pluck: *de veren van een kip ~* pluck a chicken

afpoeieren /ɑfpujərə(n)/ (poeierde af, heeft afgepoeierd) brush off, put off

afprijzen /ɑfprɛizə(n)/ (prijsde af, heeft afgeprijsd) reduce, mark down: *alles is afgeprijsd* everything is reduced (in price)

afraden /ɑfradə(n)/ (raadde af, heeft afgeraden) advise against: *(iem.) iets ~* dissuade (*or:* discourage) s.o. from (doing) sth.

afraffelen /ɑfrɑfələ(n)/ (raffelde af, heeft afgeraffeld) rush (through): *zijn huiswerk ~* rush (through) one's homework

de **aframmeling** /ɑfrɑməlɪŋ/ (pl: -en) beating, hiding

afranselen /ɑfrɑnsələ(n)/ (ranselde af, heeft afgeranseld) beat (up); flog; cane

de **afrastering** /ɑfrɑstərɪŋ/ (pl: -en) fencing, fence; railings

afreageren /ɑfrejaɣerə(n)/ (reageerde af, heeft afgereageerd) work off (*or:* vent) one's emotions, let off steam: *iets op iem. ~* take sth. out on s.o.

afrekenen /ɑfrekənə(n)/ (rekende af, heeft afgerekend) settle (up), settle (*or:* pay) one's bill, settle one's account(s): *ober, mag ik ~!* waiter, the bill please! ‖ *met iem. ~* deal with (*or:* polish off) one's enemies; *iem. ~ op zijn resultaten* judge s.o. on his results

de **afrekening** /ɑfrekənɪŋ/ (pl: -en) **1** payment **2** receipt; statement

afremmen /ɑfrɛmə(n)/ (remde af, heeft afgeremd) **1** slow down, brake, put the brake(s) on: *hij kon niet meer ~* it was too late for him to brake; *voor een bocht ~* slow down to take a curve **2** [fig] curb, check: *iem. in zijn enthousiasme ~* curb s.o.'s enthusiasm

africhten /ɑfrɪxtə(n)/ (richtte af, heeft afgericht) train: *valken ~ voor de jacht* train falcons for hunting

¹**afrijden** /ɑfrɛidə(n)/ (reed af, heeft afgereden) drive down; ride down [on horseback]: *een heuvel ~* ride (*or:* drive) down a hill

²**afrijden** /ɑfrɛidə(n)/ (reed af, heeft afgereden) drive to the end of; ride to the end of: *de hele stad ~* ride (*or:* drive) all over town

Afrika /ɑfrika/ Africa

de **Afrikaan** /afrikan/ (pl: Afrikanen) African

Afrikaans /afrikans/ (adj, adv) **1** African **2** South African

het **afrikaantje** /afrikancə/ (pl: -s) [bot] African marigold

de **Afrikaner** /afrikanər/ Afrikaner, Boer

de **afrit** /ɑfrɪt/ (pl: -ten) exit: *op- en ~ten* slip roads; *bij de volgende ~* at the next exit

de **afritsbroek** /ɑfrɪt(s)bruk/ zip-off trousers

de **afroep** /ɑfrup/: *op ~ beschikbaar* available on demand; on call

afroepen /ɑfrupə(n)/ (riep af, heeft afgeroepen) call out; call off

afrollen /ɑfrɔlə(n)/ (rolde af, heeft afgerold) **1** unwind; unroll **2** roll down

afromen /ɑfromə(n)/ (roomde af, heeft af-

geroomd) **1** skim **2** [fig] cream off

afronden /ɑfrɔndə(n)/ (rondde af, heeft afgerond) **1** wind up, round off: *wilt u (uw betoog) ~?* would you like to wind up (what you have to say)?; *een afgerond geheel vormen* form a complete whole **2** round off: *naar boven* (or: *beneden*) *~* round up (*or:* down); *een bedrag op hele euro ~* round off an amount to the nearest euro

de **afronding** /ɑfrɔndɪŋ/ (pl: -en) winding up, rounding off, completion, conclusion: *als ~ van je studie moet je een werkstuk maken* to complete your study, you have to do a project

afruimen /ɑfrœymə(n)/ (ruimde af, heeft afgeruimd) clear (away), clear the table

afschaffen /ɑfsxɑfə(n)/ (schafte af, heeft afgeschaft) abolish, do away with: *de doodstraf ~* abolish capital punishment

de **afschaffing** /ɑfsxɑfɪŋ/ abolition: *de ~ van de slavernij* the abolition of slavery

het **afscheid** /ɑfsxɛit/ parting, leaving, farewell, departure: *van iem. ~ nemen* take leave of s.o.; *officieel ~ nemen (van)* take formal leave (of); *bij zijn ~ kreeg hij een gouden horloge* when he left he received a gold watch

afscheiden /ɑfsxɛidə(n)/ (scheidde af, heeft afgescheiden) **1** divide (off), partition off: *een ruimte met een gordijn ~* curtain off an area **2** discharge; secrete: *sommige bomen scheiden hars af* some trees secrete (*or:* produce) resin

de **afscheiding** /ɑfsxɛidɪŋ/ (pl: -en) **1** separation; secession; schism; demarcation **2** partition; dividing line: *een ~ aanbrengen* put up a partition **3** discharge, secretion

afschepen /ɑfsxepə(n)/ (scheepte af, heeft afgescheept) (+ met) palm (sth.) off on (s.o.), fob (s.o.) off with (sth.): *zij laat zich niet zo gemakkelijk ~* she is not so easily put off; *zich niet laten ~ (met een smoesje)* not be fobbed off (with an excuse)

afscheren /ɑfsxerə(n)/ (schoor af, heeft afgeschoren) shave (off); shear (off)

afschermen /ɑfsxɛrmə(n)/ (schermde af, heeft afgeschermd) screen; protect (from)

afscheuren /ɑfsxørə(n)/ (scheurde af, heeft afgescheurd) tear off

afschieten /ɑfsxitə(n)/ (schoot af, heeft afgeschoten) **1** fire (off); discharge: *een geweer ~* fire a gun **2** shoot: *wild ~* shoot game

afschilderen /ɑfsxɪldərə(n)/ (schilderde af, heeft afgeschilderd) **1** paint **2** portray, depict: *iem. ~ als* portray s.o. as, make s.o. out to be

afschilferen /ɑfsxɪlfərə(n)/ (schilferde af, heeft/is afgeschilferd) flake off; peel off

afschminken /ɑfʃmɪŋkə(n)/ (schminkte af, heeft afgeschminkt) remove make-up

afschrapen /ɑfsxrapə(n)/ (schraapte af, heeft afgeschraapt) scrape off het **afschrift** /ɑfsχrɪft/ (pl: -en) copy: *een ~ van een (lopende) rekening* a current account statement

afschrijven /ɑfsχrɛivə(n)/ (schreef af, heeft afgeschreven) **1** debit: *geld van een rekening ~* withdraw money from an account **2** write off: *die auto kun je wel ~* you might as well write that car off; *we hadden haar al afgeschreven* we had already written her off **3** write down; write off (as depreciation)

de **afschrijving** /ɑfsχrɛivɪŋ/ (pl: -en) **1** debit **2** [fixed assets] depreciation; write-off; [intangible assets] amortization: *voor ~ op de machines* for depreciation of the machines

afschrikken /ɑfsχrɪkə(n)/ (schrikte af, heeft afgeschrikt) deter, put off; frighten off, scare off: *zo'n benadering schrikt de mensen af* an approach like that scares (*or:* puts) people off; *hij liet zich door niets ~* he was not to be put off (*or:* deterred)

het **afschrikkingsmiddel** deterrent

afschrikwekkend /ɑfsχrɪkwɛkənt/ (adj, adv) frightening, off-putting: *een ~ voorbeeld* a warning, a deterrent

afschudden /ɑfsχʏdə(n)/ (schudde af, heeft afgeschud) shake off; cast off: *een tegenstander van zich ~* shake off an opponent

afschuimen /ɑfsχœymə(n)/ (schuimde af, heeft afgeschuimd) scour, comb: *de stad ~* scour (*or:* comb) the city

afschuiven /ɑfsχœyvə(n)/ (schoof af, heeft afgeschoven) pass (on to s.o.): *de verantwoordelijkheid op een ander ~* pass the buck; *zijn verantwoordelijkheid van zich ~* shirk one's responsibility

afschuren /ɑfsχyrə(n)/ (schuurde af, heeft afgeschuurd) rub down; sand down

de **afschuw** /ɑfsχyw/ horror, disgust: *een ~ hebben van iets* loathe (*or:* detest) sth.; *van ~ vervuld* horrified, appalled

afschuwelijk /ɑfsχywələk/ (adj, adv) **1** horrible **2** shocking, awful, appalling: *ik heb een ~e dag gehad* I've had an awful day; *die rok staat je ~* that dress looks awful on you

¹**afslaan** /ɑfslan/ (sloeg af, is afgeslagen) **1** turn (off); branch off **2** cut out, stall ‖ *van zich ~* hit out

²**afslaan** /ɑfslan/ (sloeg af, heeft afgeslagen) turn down; refuse; decline: *nou, een kopje koffie sla ik niet af* I won't say no to a cup of coffee

afslachten /ɑfslɑχtə(n)/ (slachtte af, heeft afgeslacht) slaughter, massacre

de **afslag** /ɑfslɑχ/ (pl: -en) **1** turn(ing); exit: *de volgende ~ rechts nemen* take the next turning on the right **2** Dutch auction: *~ van vis* fish auction; *bij ~ veilen* sell by Dutch auction

afslanken /ɑfslɑŋkə(n)/ (slankte af, is afgeslankt) slim (down), trim down: *het bedrijf moet aanzienlijk ~* the company has to slim

down considerably

¹**afslijten** /ɑfslɛitə(n)/ (sleet af, is afgesleten) wear out, wear off

²**afslijten** /ɑfslɛitə(n)/ (sleet af, heeft afgesleten) wear (off, down)

afsloven /ɑfslovə(n)/ (sloofde zich af, heeft zich afgesloofd) wear out: *zich voor iem. ~* wear o.s. out (of: kill o.s.) for s.o.

de **afsluitdijk** /ɑfslœydɛik/ (pl: -en) dam, causeway: *de Afsluitdijk* the IJsselmeer Dam

afsluiten /ɑfslœytə(n)/ (sloot af, heeft afgesloten) **1** close (off, up): *een weg ~ voor verkeer* close a road to traffic **2** lock (up); close: *heb je de voordeur goed afgesloten?* have you locked the front door? **3** cut off, shut off, turn off, disconnect; exit: *de stroom ~* cut off the electricity **4** conclude; enter into; negotiate: *een levensverzekering ~* take out a life insurance policy **5** close, conclude: *een (dienst)jaar ~* close a year ‖ *zich ~* cut o.s. off

de **afsluiting** /ɑfslœytɪŋ/ (pl: -en) **1** closing off, closing up **2** locking (up, away) **3** shut-off, cut-off, disconnection **4** conclusion **5** closing; close; balancing **6** seclusion, isolation

afsnauwen /ɑfsnɑuwə(n)/ (snauwde af, heeft afgesnauwd) snap (*or:* snarl) at: *iem. ~* snap s.o.'s head off

afsnijden /ɑfsnɛidə(n)/ (sneed af, heeft afgesneden) cut off ‖ *de bocht ~* cut the corner; *een stuk ~* take a short cut

afsnoepen /ɑfsnupə(n)/ (snoepte af, heeft afgesnoept) steal

¹**afspelen** /ɑfspelə(n)/ (speelde af, heeft afgespeeld) play

zich ²**afspelen** /ɑfspelə(n)/ (speelde zich af, heeft zich afgespeeld) happen, take place, occur

afspiegelen /ɑfspiɣələ(n)/ (spiegelde af, heeft afgespiegeld) depict, portray: *men spiegelt hem af als een misdadiger* he is represented as a criminal

de **afspiegeling** /ɑfspiɣəlɪŋ/ (pl: -en) reflection, mirror image

¹**afsplitsen** /ɑfsplɪtsə(n)/ (splitste af, heeft afgesplitst) split off, separate

zich ²**afsplitsen** /ɑfsplɪtsə(n)/ (splitste zich af, heeft zich afgesplitst) split off

afspoelen /ɑfspulə(n)/ (spoelde af, heeft afgespoeld) rinse (down, off), wash (down, off): *het stof van zijn handen ~* rinse the dust off one's hands

de **afspraak** /ɑfsprak/ (pl: afspraken) appointment; engagement; agreement: *een ~ maken (or: hebben) bij de tandarts* make (*or:* have) an appointment with the dentist; *een ~ nakomen, zich aan een ~ houden* a) keep an appointment; b) stick to an agreement

het **afspraakje** /ɑfsprakjə/ (pl: -s) date

¹**afspreken** /ɑfsprekə(n)/ (sprak af, heeft afgesproken) make an appointment

²**afspreken** /ɑfsprekə(n)/ (sprak af, heeft af-

gesproken) agree (on), arrange: *een **plan** ~* agree on a plan; *dat **is** dus afgesproken* that's a deal, that's settled then; *~ iets te **zullen doen*** agree to do sth.; *zoals afgesproken* as agreed

afspringen /ɑfsprɪŋə(n)/ (sprong af, is afgesprongen) **1** jump down/off **2** fall through; break down

afstaan /ɑfstan/ (stond af, heeft afgestaan) give up; hand over: *zijn **plaats** ~* [eg to a younger colleague] step down

de **afstammeling** /ɑfstaməlɪŋ/ (pl: -en) descendant

afstammen /ɑfstamə(n)/ (stamde af, is afgestamd) descend (from)

de **afstamming** /ɑfstamɪŋ/ descent: *van **Italiaanse** ~* of Italian extraction

de **afstand** /ɑfstɑnt/ (pl: -en) **1** distance (to, from): *een ~ **afleggen*** cover a distance; *~ **houden*** (or: *bewaren*) keep one's distance; [fig also] keep aloof; *~ **nemen** van een onderwerp* distance o.s. from a subject; *op een ~* **a)** at a distance; **b)** [fig] distant, aloof; *iem. op een ~ houden* [fig also] keep s.o. at arm's length **2** renunciation: *~ **doen** van iets* renounce, disclaim; give up; *~ **doen** van zijn bezit* part with one's possessions

afstandelijk /ɑfstɑndələk/ (adj, adv) distant, aloof

de **afstandsbediening** /ɑfstɑntsbədinɪŋ/ remote control (unit)

het **afstandsonderwijs** /ɑfstɑntsɔndərwɛis/ distance learning

het **afstapje** /ɑfstapjə/ (pl: -s) step: *denk om het ~* mind the step

afstappen /ɑfstapə(n)/ (stapte af, is afgestapt) step down, come down, come off, dismount; get off (one's bike)

¹**afsteken** /ɑfstekə(n)/ (stak af, heeft afgestoken) stand out: *de kerktoren stak (donker) af tegen de hemel* the church tower stood out against the sky

²**afsteken** /ɑfstekə(n)/ (stak af, heeft afgestoken) **1** let off: *vuurwerk ~* let off fireworks **2** deliver: *een **speech** ~* hold forth, make a speech

het **afstel** /ɑfstɛl/ cancellation

afstellen /ɑfstɛlə(n)/ (stelde af, heeft afgesteld) adjust (to), set; tune (up)

afstemmen /ɑfstɛmə(n)/ (stemde af, heeft afgestemd) **1** tune af tune (to); tune in (to): *een radio **op** een zender ~* tune a radio in to a station **3** tune (to): *alle werkzaamheden zijn **op** elkaar afgestemd* all activities are geared to one another

afstempelen /ɑfstɛmpələ(n)/ (stempelde af, heeft afgestempeld) stamp, cancel, postmark: *een **paspoort** (or: **kaartje**) ~* stamp a passport (or: ticket)

afsterven /ɑfstɛrvə(n)/ (stierf af, is afgestorven) die (off); die back

afstevenen /ɑfstevənə(n)/ (stevende af, is afgestevend) (+ op) make for, head for (or: towards)

afstoffen /ɑfstɔfə(n)/ (stofte af, heeft afgestoft) dust (off)

¹**afstompen** /ɑfstɔmpə(n)/ (stompte af, is afgestompt) become blunt(ed) (or: numb)

²**afstompen** /ɑfstɔmpə(n)/ (stompte af, heeft afgestompt) blunt, dull, numb

afstotelijk /ɑfstotələk/ (adj) repulsive, repellent; off-putting

afstoten /ɑfstotə(n)/ (stootte af, heeft afgestoten) **1** dispose of; reject; hive off: *arbeidsplaatsen ~* cut jobs **2** repel: *zo'n onvriendelijke **behandeling** stoot af* such unfriendly treatment is off-putting

afstraffen /ɑfstrafə(n)/ (strafte af, heeft afgestraft) punish

afstrijken /ɑfstrɛikə(n)/ (streek af, heeft afgestreken) **1** strike, light **2** wipe off, level (off): *een afgestreken **eetlepel*** a level tablespoonful

afstropen /ɑfstropə(n)/ (stroopte af, heeft afgestroopt) **1** strip (off): *een haas de **huid** ~* skin a hare **2** pillage, ransack: *enkele benden strooten het **platteland** af* a few bands pillaged the countryside

de **afstudeerscriptie** /ɑfstyderskrɪpsi/ (pl: -s) (Master's) thesis

afstuderen /ɑfstyderə(n)/ (studeerde af, heeft/is afgestudeerd) graduate (from), complete (or: finish) one's studies (at)

afstuiten /ɑfstœytə(n)/ (stuitte af, is afgestuit) rebound; be frustrated: *de bal stuit af tegen de paal* the ball rebounds off the post; *het voorstel stuitte af **op** haar koppigheid* the proposal fell through owing to her obstinacy

afsturen /ɑfstyrə(n)/ (stuurde af, heeft afgestuurd op) (+ op) send (towards): *de hond **op** iem. ~* set the dog on s.o.

aftakelen /ɑftakelə(n)/ (takelde af, is afgetakeld) go (or: run) to seed, go downhill: *hij **begint** al flink af te takelen* he really is starting to go downhill; [mentally] he is really starting to lose his faculties

de **aftakeling** /ɑftakəlɪŋ/ (pl: -en) deterioration, decline

de **aftakking** /ɑftɑkɪŋ/ (pl: -en) branch, fork

aftands /ɑftɑnts/ (adj) broken down, worn out: *een ~e **piano*** a worn-out (or: dilapidated) piano

aftappen /ɑftɑpə(n)/ (tapte af, heeft afgetapt) **1** draw off, drain: *als het hard vriest, moet je de **waterleiding** ~* when it freezes hard you have to drain the pipes **2** tap: *stroom ~* tap electricity; *de **benzine** ~* siphon (off) the petrol; *een **telefoonlijn** ~* tap a telephone line

aftasten /ɑftɑstə(n)/ (tastte af, heeft afgetast) **1** feel, sense: *een **oppervlak** ~* explore a surface with one's hands **2** [fig] feel out,

sound out
¹aftekenen /ɑftekənə(n)/ (tekende af, heeft afgetekend) **1** outline, mark off: *de platte-grond van een plein* ~ map out a (town) square **2** register, record: *ik heb mijn gewerkte uren laten* ~ I've had my working hours registered

zich **²aftekenen** /ɑftekənə(n)/ (tekende zich af, heeft zich afgetekend) stand out, become visible: *zich* ~ *tegen* stand out against

aftellen /ɑftɛlə(n)/ (telde af, heeft afgeteld) count (out, off): *de dagen* ~ count the days

de **afterparty** /ɑːftərpɑːrti/ after party

de **aftershave** /ɑftərʃef/ (pl: -s) aftershave

de **aftersun** /ɑːftərsʏn/ after sun

aftikken /ɑftɪkə(n)/ (tikte af, heeft afgetikt) tag (out)

de **aftiteling** /ɑftitəlɪŋ/ (pl: -en) credit titles, credits

de **aftocht** /ɑftɔxt/ (pl: -en) retreat: *de* ~ *slaan* (or: *blazen*) beat a retreat

de **aftrap** /ɑftrɑp/ (pl: -pen) kick-off: *de* ~ *doen* kick off

aftrappen /ɑftrɑpə(n)/ (trapte af, heeft afgetrapt) kick off

aftreden /ɑftredə(n)/ (trad af, is afgetreden) resign (one's post)

de **aftrek** /ɑftrɛk/ **1** deduction: ~ *van voorarrest* reduction in sentence for time already served; *na* ~ *van onkosten* less expenses **2** deduction; allowance || *gretig* ~ *vinden* sell like hot cakes; *geen* ~ *vinden* not sell

aftrekbaar /ɑftrɛgbar/ (adj) deductible; tax-deductible

aftrekken /ɑftrɛkə(n)/ (trok af, heeft afgetrokken) **1** subtract: *als je acht van veertien aftrekt houd je zes over* if you take eight from fourteen you have six left **2** deduct **3** masturbate, jerk off

de **aftrekpost** /ɑftrɛkpɔst/ (pl: -en) deduction, tax-deductible item (or: expense)

het **aftreksel** /ɑftrɛksəl/ (pl: -s) extract, infusion: [fig] *een slap* ~ *van het origineel* a poor substitute for (or: rendering of) the original

de **aftreksom** /ɑftrɛksɔm/ (pl: -men) subtraction (sum)

aftroeven /ɑftruvə(n)/ (troefde af, heeft afgetroefd) score (points) off

aftroggelen /ɑftrɔɣələ(n)/ (troggelde af, heeft afgetroggeld) wheedle out of: *iem. iets weten af te troggelen* succeed in wheedling sth. out of s.o.

aftuigen /ɑftœyɣə(n)/ (tuigde af, heeft afgetuigd) beat up, mug

afvaardigen /ɑfardəɣə(n)/ (vaardigde af, heeft afgevaardigd) send (or: appoint) as delegate: *hij was naar de leerlingenraad afgevaardigd* he had been appointed as delegate to the students' council

de **afvaardiging** /ɑfardəɣɪŋ/ (pl: -en) delegation

de **afvaart** /ɑfart/ (pl: -en) sailing, departure

het **afval** /ɑfɑl/ waste (matter); refuse; rubbish: *radioactief* ~ radioactive waste

de **afvalbak** /ɑfɑlbɑk/ litter bin (or: basket); dustbin; rubbish bin

afvallen /ɑfɑlə(n)/ (viel af, is afgevallen) **1** fall off (or: down): *de bladeren vallen af* the leaves are falling **2** drop out: *dat alternatief viel af* that option was dropped (or: was no longer available) **3** lose weight: *ik ben drie kilo afgevallen* I've lost three kilos || *iem.* ~ let s.o. down, desert (or: abandon) s.o.

afvallig /ɑfɑləx/ (adj) unfaithful, disloyal; lapsed

het **afvalproduct** /ɑfɑlprodʏkt/ (pl: -en) by-product, waste product

de **afvalrace** /ɑfɑlres/ (pl: -s) elimination race

de **afvalstof** /ɑfɑlstɔf/ (pl: -fen) waste product; waste (matter): *schadelijke ~fen* harmful (or: noxious) waste

de **afvalverwerking** /ɑfɑlvərwɛrkɪŋ/ (pl: -en) processing of waste, waste disposal (or: treatment)

het **afvalwater** /ɑfɑlwatər/ waste water

de **afvalwedstrijd** /ɑfɑlwɛtstrɛɪt/ (pl: -en) heat, knock-out (or: elimination) competition

afvegen /ɑfeɣə(n)/ (veegde af, heeft afgeveegd) wipe (off), brush away, wipe away: *de tafel* ~ wipe (off) the table

afvinken /ɑfɪŋkə(n)/ (vinkte af, heeft afgevinkt) check (or: tick) off

afvloeien /ɑflujə(n)/ (vloeide af, is afgevloeid) be made redundant, be laid off; be given early retirement

de **afvloeiing** /ɑflujɪŋ/ (pl: -en) release, gradual dismissal (or: discharge)

de **afvloeiingsregeling** /ɑflujɪŋsreɣəlɪŋ/ (pl: -en) redundancy pay (or: scheme)

de **afvoer** /ɑfur/ **1** transport, conveyance: *de* ~ *van goederen* transport (or: removal) of goods **2** drain(pipe), outlet; exhaust (pipe): *de* ~ *is verstopt* the drain is blocked

de **afvoerbuis** /ɑfurbœys/ (pl: -buizen) discharge (or: outlet) pipe; soil (or: waste) pipe; exhaust (pipe)

afvoeren /ɑfurə(n)/ (voerde af, heeft afgevoerd) **1** transport; drain away, drain off; lead away **2** carry off (or: down), lead down

zich **afvragen** /ɑfraɣə(n)/ (vroeg zich af, heeft zich afgevraagd) wonder, ask o.s.; (be in) doubt (as to): *ik vraag mij af, wie* … I wonder who …; *ik vraag mij af of dat juist is* I wonder if (or: whether) that is correct

afvuren /ɑfyrə(n)/ (vuurde af, heeft afgevuurd) fire, let off, discharge; launch

afwachten /ɑfwɑxtə(n)/ (wachtte af, heeft afgewacht) wait (for), await; anticipate: *zijn beurt* ~ wait (for) one's turn; *we moeten maar* ~ we'll have to wait and see

de **afwachting** /ɑfwɑxtɪŋ/ expectation; anticipation: *in* ~ *van uw antwoord* we look forward to receiving your reply

de **afwas** /ɑfwɑs/ **1** dishes, washing-up **2** doing (*or:* washing) the dishes, washing-up: *hij is* ***aan*** *de* ~ he is washing up (*or:* doing) the dishes

afwasbaar /ɑfwɑzbar/ (adj) washable

de **afwasborstel** /ɑfwɑzbɔrstəl/ (pl: -s) washing-up brush

de **afwasmachine** /ɑfwɑsmɑʃinə/ (pl: -s) dishwasher, washing-up machine

het **afwasmiddel** /ɑfwɑsmɪdəl/ (pl: -en) washing-up liquid; [Am] dishwashing liquid

¹**afwassen** /ɑfwɑsə(n)/ (waste af, heeft afgewassen) do (*or:* wash) the dishes

²**afwassen** /ɑfwɑsə(n)/ (waste af, heeft afgewassen) **1** wash (up) **2** wash off (*or:* away): *bloed* ***van*** *zijn handen* ~ wash blood from his hands

de **afwatering** /ɑfwatərɪŋ/ (pl: -en) **1** drainage **2** drainage, drains

de **afweer** /ɑfwer/ defence

het **afweergeschut** /ɑfweɣəsχʏt/ anti-aircraft guns

het **afweersysteem** /ɑfwersistem/ (pl: -systemen) defence system; immune system

afwegen /ɑfweɣə(n)/ (woog af, heeft afgewogen) **1** weigh **2** weigh (up), consider: *de* ***voor-*** *en* ***nadelen*** *(tegen elkaar)* ~ weigh the pros and cons (against each other)

de **afweging** /ɑfweɣɪŋ/ (pl: -en) assessment; determination: *een* ~ ***maken*** consider the pros and cons, make a comparative assessment

afwenden /ɑfwɛndə(n)/ (wendde af, heeft afgewend) **1** turn away (*or:* aside); avert: *het* ***hoofd*** (or: *de* ***ogen***) ~ turn one's head (*or:* eyes) away, look away; *de ogen niet* ~ ***van*** *iem. (iets)* not take one's eyes off s.o. (sth.) **2** avert, ward off, stave off; parry

afwennen /ɑfwɛnə(n)/ (wende af, heeft afgewend) cure of, break of: *iem. het* ***nagelbijten*** *proberen af te wennen* try to get s.o. out of the habit of biting his nails

afwentelen /ɑfwɛntələ(n)/ (wentelde af, heeft afgewenteld) shift (on to), transfer (to)

afweren /ɑfwerə(n)/ (weerde af, heeft afgeweerd) keep off (*or:* away), hold off; [fig] fend off, ward off: *nieuwsgierigen* ~ keep bystanders at a distance; *een* ***aanval*** (or: ***aanvaller***) ~ repel an attack (*or:* attacker)

afwerken /ɑfwɛrkə(n)/ (werkte af, heeft afgewerkt) **1** finish (off): *een* ***opstel*** (or: ***roman***) ~ add the finishing touches to an essay (*or:* a novel) **2** finish (off), complete: *een* ***programma*** ~ complete a programme

de **afwerking** /ɑfwɛrkɪŋ/ (pl: -en) finish(ing), finishing touch

afwerpen /ɑfwɛrpə(n)/ (wierp af, heeft afgeworpen) throw off

afweten /ɑfwetə(n)/: *het laten* ~ fail, refuse

to work; not show up

afwezig /ɑfwezəχ/ (adj) **1** absent; away; gone: *Jansen* ***is*** *op het ogenblik* ~ Jansen is away at the moment **2** absent-minded, preoccupied

de **afwezigheid** /ɑfwezəχhɛit/ **1** absence: ***tijdens*** *Pauls* ~ during Paul's absence; *in (bij)* ~ *van* in the absence of **2** absent-mindedness: *in een* ***ogenblik*** *van* ~ in a forgetful moment, in a momentary fit of absent-mindedness

afwijken /ɑfwɛikə(n)/ (week af, is afgeweken) **1** deviate (from); depart (from); diverge (from): *doen* ~ divert, turn (away); [fig] *van het rechte pad* ~ deviate from the straight and narrow **2** differ, deviate, vary; disagree (with)

afwijkend /ɑfwɛikənt/ (adj) different: ~ ***gedrag*** abnormal behaviour; *~e* ***mening*** different opinion

de **afwijking** /ɑfwɛikɪŋ/ (pl: -en) **1** defect, abnormality, aberration: *een* ***geestelijke*** ~ a mental abnormality; *een* ***lichamelijke*** ~ a physical defect **2** difference, deviation: *dit horloge* ***vertoont*** *een* ~ *van één seconde* this watch is accurate to within one second

afwijzen /ɑfwɛizə(n)/ (wees af, heeft afgewezen) **1** not admit, turn away: *een* ***bezoeker*** ~ turn away a visitor; *iem.* ***als*** *lid (van een vereniging)* ~ refuse s.o. membership (of an association) **2** refuse, decline, reject; repudiate

de **afwijzing** /ɑfwɛizɪŋ/ (pl: -en) refusal, rejection; repudiation

afwikkelen /ɑfwɪkələ(n)/ (wikkelde af, heeft afgewikkeld) complete, settle: *een* ***contract*** (or: ***kwestie***) ~ settle a contract (*or:* question)

afwimpelen /ɑfwɪmpələ(n)/ (wimpelde af, heeft afgewimpeld) not follow up, pass over; find an excuse (not to accept), get out of

afwinden /ɑfwɪndə(n)/ (wond af, heeft afgewonden) unwind

afwisselen /ɑfwɪsələ(n)/ (wisselde af, heeft afgewisseld) **1** alternate with, take turns; relieve: *elkaar* ~ take turns **2** vary: *zijn werk* ~ ***met*** *ontspanning* alternate one's work with relaxation

¹**afwisselend** /ɑfwɪsələnt/ (adj) **1** alternate **2** varied

²**afwisselend** /ɑfwɪsələnt/ (adv) alternately, in turn

de **afwisseling** /ɑfwɪsəlɪŋ/ (pl: -en) variety, variation, change: *een* ***welkome*** ~ *vormen* make a welcome change; *voor de* ~ for a change

afzakken /ɑfsɑkə(n)/ (zakte af, is afgezakt) **1** come down: *zich* ***laten*** ~ fall behind; go with (or: be taken by) the current **2** fall back

het **afzakkertje** /ɑfsɑkərcə/ (pl: -s) [inform] one for the road; nightcap

afzeggen /ɑfsɛɣə(n)/ (zei af/zegde af, heeft

afgezegd) cancel, call off: *de staking werd af-gezegd* the strike was called off

afzeiken /ɑfsɛɪkə(n)/ (zeikte af, heeft afge-zeikt/gezeken) [inform] put down; [vulg] shit all over: *zich niet laten* ~ not let o.s. be put down, not let people shit all over one

de **afzender** /ɑfsɛndər/ (pl: -s) sender; shipper [goods]: ~ ... [on letter] from ...

de **afzet** /ɑfsɛt/ **1** sale, market **2** sales

het **afzetgebied** /ɑfsɛtχəbit/ (pl: -en) outlet, opening, market

afzetten /ɑfsɛtə(n)/ (zette af, heeft afge-zet) **1** switch off, turn off; disconnect **2** cut off, amputate **3** cheat, swindle; overcharge: *een klant voor tien euro* ~ cheat a customer out of ten euros **4** enclose, fence off, fence in; block off, close off: *een bouwterrein* ~ fence off a building site **5** push off: [fig] *zich* ~ *tegen (iets, iem.)* react against (sth., s.o.); *zich* ~ *voor een sprong* take off **6** dismiss, remove: *een koning* ~ depose a king **7** drop, set down, put down: *een vriend thuis* ~ drop a friend at his home ‖ *dat moet je van je af (kunnen) zetten* (you should be able to) get that out of your mind

de **afzetter** /ɑfsɛtər/ (pl: -s) cheat, swindler

de **afzetterij** /ɑfsɛtərɛɪ/ swindle, cheat; rip-off

de **afzetting** /ɑfsɛtɪŋ/ (pl: -en) enclosure, fence; cordon

afzichtelijk /ɑfsɪχtələk/ (adj, adv) ghastly, hideous

afzien /ɑfsin/ (zag af, heeft afgezien) **1** (+ van) abandon, give up; renounce: *naderhand zagen ze toch van samenwerking af* afterwards they decided not to cooperate **2** have a hard time (of it), sweat it out: *dat wordt* ~ we'd better roll up our sleeves

afzienbaar /ɑfsimbar/ (adj): *binnen afzien-bare tijd* in the near future, within the fore-seeable (*or:* not too distant) future

afzijdig /ɑfsɛidəɣ/ (adj) aloof: *zich* ~ *houden van,* ~ *blijven van* keep aloof from

zich **afzonderen** /ɑfsɔndərə(n)/ (zonderde zich af, heeft zich afgezonderd) separate (*or:* se-clude) o.s. (from), retire (from), withdraw (from): *zich van de wereld* ~ withdraw from the world

de **afzondering** /ɑfsɔndərɪŋ/ (pl: -en) separa-tion, isolation, seclusion: *in strikte (strenge)* ~ in strict isolation

afzonderlijk /ɑfsɔndərlək/ (adj) separate, individual, single: *de keuze wordt aan ieder* ~ *kind overgelaten* the choice is left to each in-dividual child

de **afzuigkap** /ɑfsœyχkɑp/ (pl: -pen) (cooker) hood

¹**afzwakken** /ɑfswɑkə(n)/ (zwakte af, is af-gezwakt) subside, decrease

²**afzwakken** /ɑfswɑkə(n)/ (zwakte af, heeft afgezwakt) weaken, tone (*or:* play) down: *de scherpe toon* ~ soften the sharp tone (of),

tone down the sharpness (of)

afzwemmen /ɑfswɛmə(n)/ (zwom af, heeft afgezwommen) take a swimming test

afzweren /ɑfswerə(n)/ (zwoer af, heeft af-gezworen) renounce, forswear: *de drank* ~ a) give up drink(ing); b) swear off drink(ing); *zijn geloof* (or: *beginselen*) ~ renounce one's faith (*or:* principles)

de **agenda** /aɣɛnda/ (pl: -'s) **1** [notebook] diary **2** agenda: *op de* ~ *staan* be on the agenda; *geheime* (or: *verborgen*) ~ hidden agenda

de **agent** /aɣɛnt/ (pl: -en) **1** policeman, consta-ble: *een stille* ~, *een* ~ *in burger* a plain-clothes policeman **2** agent ‖ *een geheim* ~ a secret agent

het **agentschap** /aɣɛntsχɑp/ (pl: -pen) branch (office)

ageren /aɣerə(n)/ (ageerde, heeft ge-ageerd) agitate (*or:* manoeuvre) (against), (carry on a) campaign (against)

de **agglomeratie** /aɣlomərɑ(t)si/ (pl: -s) con-urbation

de **aggregatietoestand** /aɣreɣa(t)situstɑnt/ (pl: -en) physical state

de **agrariër** /aɣrarijər/ (pl: -s) farmer

agrarisch /aɣraris/ (adj) agrarian, agricul-tural, farming: *~e school* school of agricul-ture

de **agressie** /aɣrɛsi/ (pl: -s) aggression: *een daad van* ~ an act of aggression; ~ *opwekken* provoke aggression

agressief /aɣrɛsif/ (adj, adv) aggressive: *een agressieve politiek voeren* pursue an aggres-sive policy

de **agressor** /aɣrɛsɔr/ (pl: -s) aggressor, attack-er

ah /a/ (int) ah, oh

aha /aha/ (int) aha

de **ahorn** /ahɔrn/ (pl: -en, -s) maple

a.h.w. (abbrev) *als het ware* as it were

ai /aj/ (int) ouch; ow; ah; oh ‖ *ai!, dat was maar net mis* oops! that was a close shave

de **aids** /ets/ Aids

de **aidspatiënt** /etspaʃɛnt/ (pl: -en) AIDS pa-tient

de **aidsremmer** /etsrɛmər/ (pl: -s) AIDS inhibi-tor

de **aio** /ajo/ (pl: -'s) *assistent in opleiding* PhD student, research trainee

het **air** /ɛːr/ (pl: -s) air, look: *met het* ~ *van* with an air of

de **airbag** /ɛːrbɛːk/ (pl: -s) air bag

de **airconditioning** /ɛːrkɔndɪʃənɪŋ/ air-condi-tioning

de **ajuin** /ajœyn/ (pl: -en) [Belg] onion

akelig /akələɣ/ (adj) **1** unpleasant, nasty, dismal; dreary; bleak; ghastly: *een* ~ *gezicht* (or: *beeld*) a nasty sight (*or:* picture); *een* ~ *verhaal* a ghastly story; ~ *weer* nasty weath-er **2** ill, sick: *ik word er* ~ *van* it turns my stomach het **akkefietje** /ɑkəfiˌcə/ (pl: -s) **1** chore **2** (little) job **3** trifle || *een ~ **hebben** met iem.* have a slight disagreement/misunderstanding with s.o., have a spat with s.o.

de **akker** /ɑkər/ (pl: -s) field

de **akkerbouw** /ɑkərbɑu/ (arable) farming, agriculture

de **akkerbouwer** /ɑkərbɑuwər/ (pl: -s) (crop) farmer, cultivator

het **akkerland** /ɑkərlɑnt/ arable land, plough land

het **akkoord** /ɑkort/ (pl: -en) **1** agreement, arrangement, settlement; bargain: *een ~ **aangaan*** (or: *sluiten*) come to an arrangement; *tot een ~ **komen*** reach an agreement **2** [mus] chord || *~ **gaan** (met)* agree (to), be agreeable (to); *niet ~ **gaan** (met)* disagree (with)

de **akoestiek** /akustik/ acoustics

akoestisch /akustis/ (adj) acoustic, sonic

de **akte** /ɑktə/ (pl: -n, -s) **1** deed; contract: *~ van geboorte* (or: *overlijden, huwelijk*) birth (or: death, marriage) certificate; *een ~ **opmaken*** draw up a deed; *~ **opmaken** van* make a record of **2** certificate; diploma; licence **3** [theatre, film] act || *waarvan ~* duly noted, acknowledged

de **aktetas** /ɑktətɑs/ (pl: -sen) briefcase

¹**al** /ɑl/ (ind pron) **1** all, whole: *al de **moeite*** all our (or: their) trouble; *het was **één** en al geweld op tv gisteren* there was nothing but violence on TV yesterday **2** all (of)

²**al** /ɑl/ (adv) **1** yet; already: *al een hele **tijd*** for a long time now; *al enige **tijd**, al vanaf juli* for some time past (or: now), (ever) since July; *dat **dacht** ik al* I thought so; *is zij er nu al?* is she here already?; *is Jan er al?* is John here yet?; *ik heb het **altijd** al geweten* I've known it all along; *daar heb je het al* there you are **2** all: *dat **alleen** al* that alone; *al **te** snel* (or: *spoedig*) far too fast (or: soon); *ze weten het maar al **te** goed* they know only too well; *hij had het **toch** al moeilijk* he had enough problems as it was || *het is al **laat*** (or: *duur*) genoeg it is late (or: expensive) enough as it is; *dat lijkt er al meer op, dat is al beter* that's more like it

³**al** /ɑl/ (num) all (of); every; each: *al zijn **gedachten*** his every thought; *al de **kinderen*** all (of) the children

⁴**al** /ɑl/ (conj) though, although, even though, even if: *al ben ik arm, ik ben gelukkig* I may be poor, but I'm happy; *al zeg ik het zelf* even though I say so myself; *al was het alleen maar omdat* if only because; *ook al is het erg* bad as it is (or: may be); *ik deed het niet, al kreeg ik een miljoen* I wouldn't do it for a million pounds

het **alarm** /ɑlɑrm/ alarm: *groot ~* full (or: red) alert; *loos (vals) ~* false alarm; *een stil ~* a silent alarm; *~ **slaan*** (or: *geven*) give (or: sound) the alarm

de **alarmbelprocedure** /ɑlɑrmbɛlprosedyrə/ [Belg] constitutionally mandated procedure in Belgium to prevent discrimination against minorities

de **alarmcentrale** /ɑlɑrmsɛntralə/ (pl: -s) emergency centre, (general) emergency number

alarmeren /ɑlɑrmerə(n)/ (alarmeerde, heeft gealarmeerd) **1** alert, call out: *de **brandweer** ~* call (out) the fire brigade **2** alarm: *~de **berichten*** disturbing reports

het **alarmnummer** /ɑlɑrmnʏmər/ (pl: -s) emergency number

het **alarmpistool** /ɑlɑrmpistol/ (pl: -pistolen) alarm gun

de ¹**Albanees** /ɑlbanes/ (pl: Albanezen) [person] Albanian

het ²**Albanees** /ɑlbanes/ [language] Albanian

³**Albanees** /ɑlbanes/ (adj) Albanian

Albanië /ɑlbanijə/ Albania

het **albast** /ɑlbɑst/ (pl: -en) alabaster

de **albatros** /ɑlbatrɔs/ (pl: -sen) albatross

de **albino** /ɑlbino/ (pl: -'s) albino

het **album** /ɑlbʏm/ (pl: -s) album

de **alchemie** /ɑlxemi/ alchemy

de **alcohol** /ɑlkohɔl/ alcohol: *pure ~* pure alcohol; *verslaafd aan ~* addicted to alcohol

alcoholhoudend /ɑlkohɔlhɑudənt/ (adj) alcoholic: *~e **dranken*** alcoholic beverages, spirits

alcoholisch /ɑlkohɔlis/ (adj) alcoholic: *~e **dranken*** alcoholic drinks; *een **niet** ~ drankje* a non-alcoholic drink

het **alcoholisme** /ɑlkohɔlɪsmə/ alcoholism

de **alcoholist** /ɑlkohɔlɪst/ (pl: -en) alcoholic

alcoholvrij /ɑlkohɔlvrɛi/ (adj) non-alcoholic, soft: *~e **dranken*** non-alcoholic beverages, soft drinks

aldaar /ɑldar/ (adv) there, at (or: of) that place

aldoor /ɑldor/ (adv) all along, all the time: *zij **dacht** ~ dat …* she kept thinking that …

aldus /ɑldʏs/ (adv) thus, so: *~ **geschiedde*** and so (or: thus) it happened; *~ de **minister*** according to (or: said) the minister

alert /ɑlɛrt/ (adj) alert: *~ zijn **op** spelfouten* be on the alert (or: lookout) for spelling mistakes

de **alfa** /ɑlfa/ (pl: -'s) [educ] [roughly] languages, humanities, arts || *zij is een **echte** ~* all her talents are on the arts side

het **alfabet** /ɑlfabɛt/ (pl: -ten) alphabet: *alle **letters** van het ~* all the letters in the alphabet; *de boeken staan **op** ~* the books are arranged in alphabetical order

alfabetisch /ɑlfabetis/ (adj, adv) alphabetical: *in ~e **volgorde*** in alphabetical order

alfabetiseren /ɑlfabɛtizerə(n)/ (alfabetiseerde, heeft gealfabetiseerd) alphabetize

alfanumeriek /ɑlfanymerik/ (adj) alphanumeric(al)

de **alg** /ɑlx/ (pl: -en) alga

de **algebra** /ɑlɣəbra/ algebra
algebraïsch /ɑlɣəbrɑis/ (adj, adv) algebraic(al)
algeheel /ɑlɣəhel/ (adj) complete, total: *met algehele steun* with (everyone's) full support; *met mijn algehele instemming* with my wholehearted consent; *tot algehele tevredenheid* to everyone's satisfaction
algemeen /ɑlɣəmen/ (adj, adv) **1** public, general, universal, common: *een algemene regel* a general rule; *voor ~ gebruik* for general use; *algemene ontwikkeling* general knowledge; *in algemene zin* in a general sense; *algemene middelen* public funds; *het is ~ bekend* it is common knowledge; *~ beschouwd worden als* be generally known as **2** general(ized), broad: *in algemene bewoordingen* in general terms ‖ *in het ~ hebt u gelijk* on the whole, you're right; *zij zijn in het ~ betrouwbaar* for the most part they are reliable; *in (over) het ~* in general

de **algemeenheid** /ɑlɣəmenhɛit/ (pl: -heden) generality; indefiniteness ‖ [Belg] *met ~ van stemmen* unanimously
Algerije /ɑlɣərɛiə/ Algeria

de **Algerijn** /ɑlɣərɛin/ (pl: -en) Algerian
Algerijns /ɑlɣərɛins/ (adj) Algerian
alhoewel /ɑlhuwɛl/ (conj) although
alias /alijɑs/ (adv) alias, also (or: otherwise) known as

het/de **alibi** /alibi/ (pl: -'s) alibi; excuse: *iem. een ~ bezorgen (geven)* cover up for s.o.

de **alien** /elijən/ alien

de **alimentatie** /alimɛntɑ(t)si/ maintenance (allowance, money); alimony

de **alinea** /alineja/ (pl: -'s) paragraph: *een nieuwe ~ beginnen* start a new paragraph
alla /ɑla/ (int) that's one thing
Allah /ɑla/ Allah
allang /ɑlɑŋ/ (adv) for a long time, a long time ago: *ik ben ~ blij dat je er bent* I'm pleased that you're here at all

¹**alle** /ɑlə/ (ind pron) all, every, each: *uit ~ macht iets proberen* try one's utmost; *hij had ~ reden om* he had every reason to; *boven ~ twijfel* beyond all doubt; *voor ~ zekerheid* to make quite (or: doubly) sure

²**alle** /ɑlə/ (num) all, every, each; everyone; everybody: *van ~ kanten* from all sides, from every side; *in ~ opzichten* in all respects; *zij gingen met hun ~n naar het zwembad* they went all together to the swimming pool; *geen van ~n wist het* not one of them knew
allebei /ɑləbɛi/ (num) both; either: *~ de kinderen waren bang* both (of the) children were afraid; *het was ~ juist geweest* either would have been correct
alledaags /ɑlədaxs/ (adj) daily, everyday: *de ~e beslommeringen* day-to-day worries; *de kleine, ~e dingen van het leven* the little everyday things of life; *dat is niet iets ~* that's not

an everyday occurrence

¹**alleen** /alen/ (adj, adv) **1** alone, by o.s., on one's own: *hij is graag ~* he likes to be alone (or: by himself); *het ~ klaarspelen* manage it alone (or: on one's own); *helemaal ~* all (or: completely) alone; *een kamer voor hem ~* a room (all) to himself **2** only, alone: *~ in het weekeinde geopend* only open at weekends

²**alleen** /alen/ (adv) only, merely, just: *de gedachte ~ al* the mere (or: very) thought; *ik wilde u ~ maar spreken* I just wanted to talk to you; *~ maar aan zichzelf denken* only think of o.s.; *niet ~ … maar ook* not only … but also

de **alleenheerschappij** /alenhersxɑpɛi/ absolute power; [fig] monopoly: *de ~ voeren (over)* reign supreme (over)

de **alleenheerser** /alenhersər/ (pl: -s) absolute sovereign, autocrat

het **alleenrecht** /alenrɛxt/ (pl: -en) exclusive right(s)
alleenstaand /alenstant/ (adj) single: *een ~e ouder* a single parent

de **alleenverdiener** /alenvərdinər/ (pl: -s) sole wage-earner

het **allegaartje** /aleɣarcə/ (pl: -s) mishmash, hotchpotch, jumble

de **allegorie** /aleɣori/ (pl: -ën) allegory
allegorisch /aleɣoris/ (adj, adv) allegorical

¹**allemaal** /ɑləmal/ (adv) all, only: *hij zag ~ sterretjes* all he saw was little stars

²**allemaal** /ɑləmal/ (num) all; everybody; everyone; everything: *beste van ~* best of all; *~ onzin* all nonsense; *ik houd van jullie ~* I love you all; *zoals wij ~* like all of us; *~ samen (tegelijk)* all together; *tot ziens ~* goodbye everybody
allemachtig /ɑləmɔxtəx/ (adv) amazingly: *een ~ groot huis* an amazingly big house
alleman /ɑləmɑn/ (ind pron) everybody: *Jan en ~* one and all, all and sundry; *met Jan en ~ naar bed gaan* sleep around
allengs /ɑlɛŋs/ (adv) gradually, little by little
allerbest /ɑlərbɛst/ (adj, adv) very best: *zijn ~e vrienden* his very best friends; *ik wens je het ~e* I wish you all the best
allereerst /ɑlərerst/ (adj, adv) first of all, very first: *vanaf het ~e begin* from the very beginning

het **allergeen** /alɛrɣen/ (pl: allergenen) allergen

de **allergie** /alɛrɣi/ (pl: -ën) allergy
allergisch /alɛrɣis/ (adj) allergic (to)
allerhande /ɑlərhɑndə/ (adj) all sorts (of), all kinds (of)
Allerheiligen /ɑlərhɛiləɣə(n)/ All Saints' (Day)
allerhoogst /ɑlərhoxst/ (adj) highest of all; very highest; supreme; paramount; maximum; top: *van het ~e belang* of supreme (or: paramount) importance; *het is de ~e tijd* it's

high time

allerijl /ɑlərɛɪl/: *in* ~ with all speed, in great haste

allerlaatst /ɑlərlatst/ (adj, adv) last of all, very last, very latest: *de ~e bus* the (very) last bus; *de ~e mode* the very latest style; *op het* ~ at the very last moment; *tot op het* ~ right up to the (very) end

allerlei /ɑlərlɛi/ (adj) all sorts (*or:* kinds) of: ~ *speelgoed* all sorts of toys

allerliefst /ɑlərlifst/ (adj, adv) **1** (very) dearest (*or:* sweetest): *een ~ kind* a very dear (*or:* sweet) child **2** more than anything: *hij wil het ~ acteur worden* he wants to be an actor to be an actor more than anything

allerminst /ɑlərmɪnst/ (adj) **1** least (of all): *ik heb er niet het ~e op aan te merken* I don't have the slightest objection **2** (very) least, (very) slightest: *op zijn* ~ at the very least

Allerzielen /ɑlərzilə(n)/ All Souls' (Day)

alles /ɑləs/ (ind pron) everything, all, anything: *hij heeft (van)* ~ *geprobeerd* he has tried everything; *is dat* ~? will that be all?; *dat is* ~ that's it (*or:* everything); *ik weet er* ~ *van* I know all about it; *(het is)* ~ *of niets* (it's) all or nothing; ~ *op* ~ *zetten* go all out; *van* ~ *(en nog wat)* all sorts of things; ~ *bij elkaar viel het mee* all in all (*or:* all things considered) it was better than expected; ~ *op zijn tijd* all in due course, all in good time; *dat slaat* ~ that takes the cake

allesbehalve /ɑləzbəhɑlvə/ (adv) anything but: *het was ~ een succes* it was anything but a success; ~ *vriendelijk* anything but friendly

de **alleseter** /ɑləsetər/ (pl: -s) omnivore

allesomvattend /ɑləsɔmvɑtənt/ (adj) all-embracing, comprehensive, universal

allesoverheersend /ɑləsovərhersənt/ (adj) overpowering: *een ~e smaak van knoflook* an overpowering taste of garlic

de **allesreiniger** /ɑləsrɛinəyər/ (pl: -s) all-purpose cleaner

alleszins /ɑləsɪns/ (adv) in every way, completely, in all respects, fully: *dat is ~ redelijk* that is perfectly reasonable

de **alliantie** /ɑlijɑnsi/ (pl: -s) alliance

allicht /ɑlɪxt/ (adv) most probably (*or:* likely), of course: *ja* ~ yes, of course

de **alligator** /ɑliɣatɔr/ (pl: -s) alligator

all-in /ɔ:lɪn/ (adj, adv) all-in(clusive): *dat is € 1000* ~ that is € 1000 everything included

de **all-inreis** (pl: -reizen) all-inclusive trip

de ¹**allochtoon** /ɑlɔxton/ (pl: allochtonen) immigrant, foreigner

²**allochtoon** /ɑlɔxton/ (adj) foreign

allrisk /ɔ:lrɪsk/ (adj, adv) comprehensive: ~ *verzekerd zijn* have a comprehensive policy

de **allriskverzekering** /ɔ:lrɪskfərzekərɪŋ/ comprehensive insurance policy

allround /ɔ:lrɑunt/ (adj) all-round

de **allure** /ɑlyrə/ (pl: -s) air, style: ~ *hebben* have

style; *iem. van* ~ a striking personality; *een gebouw met* ~ an imposing building

de **allusie** /ɑlyzi/ (pl: -s) allusion: [Belg] ~*(s) maken op* hint at, allude to

almaar /ɑlmar/ (adv) constantly, continuously, all the time: *kinderen die* ~ *om snoep vragen* children who are always asking for sweets

de **almacht** /ɑlmɑxt/ omnipotence

almachtig /ɑlmɑxtəx/ (adj) almighty, all-powerful: *de Almachtige* the Almighty

de **almanak** /ɑlmɑnɑk/ (pl: -ken) almanac

de **alo** /alo/ *academie voor lichamelijke opvoeding* college of physical education

alom /ɑlɔm/ (adv) everywhere, on all sides: ~ *gevreesd* (*or:* *bekend*) generally feared (*or:* known)

de **alp** /ɑlp/ (pl: -en) alp

de **alpineskiën** /ɑlpinəskijə(n)/ alpine (*or:* downhill) skiing

het **alpinisme** /ɑlpinɪsmə/ alpinism, mountaineering

de **alpinist** /ɑlpinɪst/ (pl: -en) alpinist, mountaineer

de **alpino** /ɑlpino/ (pl: -'s) (Basque) beret

als /ɑls/ (conj) **1** like, as: *zich* ~ *een dame gedragen* behave like a lady; *hetzelfde* ~ *ik* the same as me, just like me; *hij is even groot* ~ *jij* he is as tall as you; *de brief luidt* ~ *volgt* the letter reads as follows; *zowel in de stad* ~ *op het land* both in the city and in the country **2** as, as if: ~ *bij toverslag veranderde alles* as if by magic everything changed; ~ *ware het je eigen kind* as if it were your own child **3** for, as: *poppen* ~ *geschenk* dolls for presents; *ik heb die man nog* ~ *jongen gekend* I knew that man when he was still a boy; ~ *vrienden uit elkaar gaan* part as friends **4** when: *telkens* ~ *wij elkaar tegenkomen keert hij zich af* whenever we meet, he turns away **5** if, as long as: ~ *zij er niet geweest was …* if she had not been there …; *maar wat* ~ *het regent,* ~ *het nu eens regent?* but what if it rains?; ~ *het mogelijk is* if possible; ~ *ze al komen* if they come at all

alsmaar /ɑlsmar/ (adv) constantly, all the time: ~ *praten* talk constantly

alsmede /ɑlsmedə/ (conj) as well as, and also

alsnog /ɑlsnɔx/ (adv) still, yet: *je kunt ~ van studie veranderen* you can still change your course

alsof /ɑlsɔf/ (conj) as if: *je doet maar* ~ you're just pretending; *hij keek* ~ *hij mij niet begreep* he looked as if he didn't understand me

alsook /ɑlsok/ (conj) as well as

¹**alstublieft** /ɑlstyblift/ (adv) please: *een ogenblikje* ~ just a minute, please; *wees* ~ *rustig* please be quiet

²**alstublieft** /ɑlstyblift/ (int) please; here you are: ~*, dat is dan €6,50* (thank you,) that will be €6.50

de **¹alt** /ɑlt/ [mus] [singer] alto

de **²alt** /ɑlt/ [mus] [voice] alto

het **altaar** /ɑltar/ (pl: altaren) altar

het **alternatief** /ɑltɛrnatif/ (pl: alternatieven) alternative: *er is* **geen** *enkel* ~ there is no alternative; *als* ~ as an alternative; *alternatieve* **geneeswijze** alternative treatment

althans /ɑltɑns/ (adv) at least

altijd /ɑltɛit/ (adv) always, forever: *ik* **heb** *het* ~ *wel* **gedacht** I've thought so all along; I've always thought so; *je* **kunt** *niet* ~ **winnen** you can't win them all; ~ **weer** again and again; *wat je ook doet, je* **verliest** ~ no matter what you do, you always lose; *bijna* ~ nearly always; *wonen ze* **nog** ~ *in Almere?* are they still living in Almere?; **voor** *eens en* ~ once and for all; *hetzelfde* **als** ~ the same as always, the usual; *ze ging* ~ *op woensdag winkelen* she always went shopping on Wednesdays

altijddurend /ɑltɛɪdyrənt/ (adj) everlasting

de **altsaxofoon** /ɑltsaksofon/ (pl: -s, altsaxofonen) alto saxophone

de **altviolist** /ɑltfijolɪst/ violist

de **altviool** /ɑltfijol/ viola

de **aluin** /alœyn/ (pl: -en) alum

het **¹aluminium** /alyminijʏm/ aluminium

²aluminium /alyminijʏm/ (adj) aluminium

het/de **aluminiumfolie** /alyminijʏmfoli/ aluminium (*or:* tin, kitchen) foil

alvast /ɑlvɑst/ (adv) meanwhile, in the meantime: *jullie* **hadden** ~ **kunnen** *beginnen zonder mij* you could have started without me

de **alvleesklier** /ɑlvlesklir/ (pl: -en) pancreas

alvorens /ɑlvorə(n)s/ (adv) before: ~ *te* **vertrekken,** *graag het licht uitdoen* before you leave, please switch the light off

alweer /ɑlwer/ (adv) again, once more: *het wordt* ~ **herfst** autumn has come round again

alwetend /ɑlwetənt/ (adj) omniscient, all-knowing

de **alzheimer** /ɑltshɛimər/ Alzheimer's (disease)

de **ama** /ama/ single under-aged asylum seeker

het **amalgaam** /amɑlɣam/ (pl: amalgamen) amalgam

de **amandel** /amɑndəl/ (pl: -en) **1** almond **2** tonsil: *zijn ~en* **laten knippen** have one's tonsils (taken) out

de **amanuensis** /amanywɛnsɪs/ (pl: -sen, amanuenses) laboratory assistant

de **amateur** /amatør/ (pl: -s) amateur

amateuristisch /amatørɪstis/ (adj, adv) amateur(ish): ~*e* **sportbeoefening** amateur sports; *dat* **is** *zeer* ~ **gedaan** that was done very amateurishly

de **amazone** /amazo:nə/ (pl: -s) horsewoman

de **Amazone** /amazo:nə/ Amazon

het **ambacht** /ɑmbɑχt/ (pl: -en) trade, (handi)craft: *het* ~ **uitoefenen** *van ...* practise the trade of ... || *het is met hem* **twaalf** *~en, dertien ongelukken* he is a jack-of-all-trades (and master of none)

ambachtelijk /ɑmbɑχtələk/ (adj) according to traditional methods: *op ~e* **wijze** *bereid* prepared according to traditional methods

de **ambachtsman** /ɑmbɑχ(t)sman/ (pl: ambachtslieden) artisan, craftsman

de **ambassade** /ɑmbɑsadə/ (pl: -s) embassy

de **ambassadeur** /ɑmbɑsadør/ (pl: -s) ambassador

de **amber** /ɑmbər/ amber

de **ambiance** /ɑmbijɑ̃sə/ ambiance

ambiëren /ɑmbijerə(n)/ (ambieerde, heeft geambieerd) aspire to: *een* **baan** ~ aspire to a job

de **ambitie** /ɑmbi(t)si/ (pl: -s) ambition: *een man* **van** *grote* ~ a man with great ambitions

ambitieus /ɑmbi(t)jøs/ (adj) ambitious: *ambitieuze* **plannen** ambitious plans

ambivalent /ɑmbivalɛnt/ (adj) ambivalent

het **ambt** /ɑmt/ (pl: -en) office: *een* ~ **uitoefenen** carry out one's duties; *iem.* **uit** *een* ~ *ontzetten* discharge s.o. from office

ambtelijk /ɑmtələk/ (adj, adv) official: *~e* **stukken** official documents

ambteloos /ɑmtəlos/ (adj) private: *een* ~ **burger** a private citizen

de **ambtenaar** /ɑmtənar/ (pl: ambtenaren) official, civil servant, public servant: ~ *van de burgerlijke* **stand** registrar; [Am] county clerk; **burgerlijk** ~ civil (*or:* public) servant

het **ambtenarenapparaat** /ɑmtənarə(n)aparat/ civil service

de **ambtenarij** /ɑmtənarɛi/ bureaucracy, red tape

de **ambtgenoot** /ɑmtχənot/ (pl: -genoten) colleague

de **ambtsaanvaarding** /ɑm(t)sanvardɪŋ/ accession to office, acceptance (*or:* assumption) of duties

de **ambtsdrager** /ɑm(t)sdraɣər/ (pl: -s) office holder

het **ambtsgeheim** /ɑm(t)sχəhɛɪm/ (pl: -en) professional secrecy (*or:* confidentiality); official secrecy

ambtshalve /ɑm(t)shɑlvə/ (adv) by virtue of one's office; in one's official capacity, officially

de **ambtstermijn** /ɑmtstɛrmɛin/ (pl: -en) term of office: *zijn* ~ **loopt af** his term of office is drawing to a close, his term of office is nearing its end

ambtswege /ɑm(t)sweɣə/: **van** ~ officially, ex officio, by virtue of one's office

de **ambtswoning** /ɑm(t)swonɪŋ/ (pl: -en) official residence

de **ambulance** /ɑmbylɑ̃sə/ (pl: -s) ambulance

ambulant /ɑmbylɑnt/ (adj) ambulatory, ambulant: *~e* **zorg** ambulatory care

het **amen** /amə(n)/ amen || [fig] *ja* **en** ~ *op iets zeggen* bow to sth.; [Belg] ~ *en* **uit** that's enough!, stop it!

het **amendement** /amɛndəmɛ̱nt/ (pl: -en) amendment

amenderen /amɛnde̱rə(n)/ (amendeerde, heeft geamendeerd) amend

Amerika /ame̱rika/ America

de **Amerikaan** /amerika̱n/ (pl: Amerikanen) American: *tot ~ naturaliseren* naturalize as an American

Amerikaans /amerika̱ns/ (adj) American: *de ~e burgeroorlog* the American Civil War; *het ~e congres* Congress; *~e whiskey* bourbon, rye, corn whiskey

de **Amerikaanse** /amerika̱nsə/ American (woman)

het/de **amfetamine** /amfetami̱nə/ (pl: -n) amphetamine

de **amfibie** /amfibi̱/ (pl: -ën) amphibian

het **amfibievoertuig** /amfibivurtœyx/ (pl: -en) amphibious vehicle, amphibian

het **amfitheater** /amfiteja̱tər/ (pl: -s) amphitheatre

amicaal /amika̱l/ (adj, adv) amicable, friendly: *~ omgaan met iem.* be on friendly terms with s.o.

het **aminozuur** /ami̱nozyr/ (pl: -zuren) amino acid

de **ammonia** /amo̱nija/ ammonia (water)

de **ammoniak** /amonija̱k/ ammonia

de **amnestie** /amnɛsti̱/ (pl: -ën) amnesty: *~ verlenen (aan)* grant an amnesty (to)

de **amoebe** /amø̱bə/ (pl: -n) amoeba

amok /amo̱k/: *~ maken* run amok

amoreel /amore̱l/ (adj, adv) amoral

amorf /amo̱rf/ (adj) amorphous

ampel /a̱mpəl/ (adj, adv) ample: *na ~e overweging* after careful (*or:* full) consideration

amper /a̱mpər/ (adv) scarcely, barely, hardly: *hij kon ~ schrijven* he could barely write

de **ampère** /ampɛ̱:rə/ (pl: -s) ampere

de **ampul** /ampy̱l/ (pl: -len) ampoule

de **amputatie** /ampyta̱(t)si/ (pl: -s) amputation

amputeren /ampyte̱rə(n)/ (amputeerde, heeft geamputeerd) amputate

de **amulet** /amylɛ̱t/ (pl: -ten) amulet

amusant /amyza̱nt/ (adj, adv) amusing: *een ~ verhaal* an amusing story; *iets ~ vinden* find sth. amusing (*or:* entertaining)

het **amusement** /amyzəmɛ̱nt/ (pl: -en) amusement, entertainment

de **amusementshal** /amyzəmɛ̱n(t)shal/ (pl: -len) amusement arcade

zich **amuseren** /amyze̱rə(n)/ (amuseerde zich, heeft zich geamuseerd) amuse o.s., entertain o.s., enjoy o.s.: *zich kostelijk (uitstekend) ~* thoroughly enjoy o.s.

anaal /ana̱l/ (adj, adv) anal

anabool /anabo̱l/ (adj) anabolic: *anabole steroïden* anabolic steroids

het **anachronisme** /anaxroni̱smə/ (pl: -n) anachronism

het **anagram** /anaɣra̱m/ (pl: -men) anagram:

een ~ vormen van make an anagram of

de **analfabeet** /analfabe̱t/ (pl: analfabeten) illiterate

het **analfabetisme** /analfabeti̱smə/ illiteracy

de **analist** /anali̱st/ (pl: -en) (chemical) analyst, lab(oratory) technician

de **analogie** /analoɣi̱/ (pl: -ën) analogy: *naar ~ van* by analogy with

analoog /analo̱x/ (adj, adv) analogue

de **analyse** /anali̱zə/ (pl: -s) analysis: *een kritische ~ van een roman* a critical analysis of a novel

analyseren /analize̱rə(n)/ (analyseerde, heeft geanalyseerd) analyse: *grondig ~* a) analyse thoroughly; b) [fig] dissect

analytisch /anali̱tis/ (adj, adv) analytical: *~ denken* think analytically

de **ananas** /a̱nanas/ (pl: -sen) pineapple

de **anarchie** /anarxi̱/ anarchy

het **anarchisme** /anarxi̱smə/ anarchism

de **anarchist** /anarxi̱st/ (pl: -en) anarchist

anarchistisch /anarxi̱stis/ (adj) **1** anarchist(ic) **2** anarchic

de **anatomie** /anatomi̱/ anatomy

anatomisch /anato̱mis/ (adj) anatomical

de **ancien** /ãsjɛ̱̃/ (pl: -s) [Belg] veteran, ex-serviceman

de **anciënniteit** /ãʃɛnitɛ̱ɪt/ seniority, length of service

Andalusië /andaly̱sijə/ Andalusia

¹**ander** /a̱ndər/ (adj) **1** other, another: *aan de ~e kant* on the other hand; *een ~e keer misschien!* maybe some other time!; (de) een of ~e voorbijganger* some passer-by; *met ~e woorden* in other words; *om de één of ~e reden* for some reason, for one reason or another **2** different: *ik voel me nu een ~ mens* I feel a different man (*or:* woman) now; *dat is een heel ~e zaak* that's quite a different matter, that's a different matter altogether

²**ander** /a̱ndər/ (ind pron) **1** other, others: *de een of ~* somebody, s.o.; *sommigen wel, ~en niet* some do (*or:* are); some don't (*or:* aren't); *de ene of de ~e* (choose) one thing or the other **2** another matter (*or:* thing); other matters (*or:* things): *als geen ~* more than anybody else; *je hebt het een en ~ nodig om te …* you need a few things in order to …; *onder ~e* among other things, including; *of het één, of het ~!* you can't have it both ways

³**ander** /a̱ndər/ (num) next, other: *om de ~e dag* every other day, on alternative days

anderhalf /a̱ndərha̱lf/ (num) one and a half: *~ maal zoveel* half as much (*or:* many) again; *~ maal zo hoog* one and a half times as high; *~ uur* an hour and a half

¹**anders** /a̱ndərs/ (adj) different (from): *niemand ~* nobody else; *wilt u nog iets ~?* do you want anything else?; *over iets ~ beginnen (te praten)* change the subject; *er zit niets ~ op dan …* there is nothing for it but to …; *het is*

(nu eenmaal) **niet** ~ that's how it is (and there's nothing can be done about it)
²**anders** /ɒndərs/ (adv) **1** normally, differently: *het* ~ **aanpakken** handle it differently; ~ *gezegd,* … in other words …; *in jouw geval* **liggen** *de zaken* ~ in your case things are different; *(zo is het) en* **niet** ~ that's the way it is *(or:* how things are); *net* **als** ~ just as usual; *niet meer zo vaak* **als** ~ less often than usual **2** otherwise, else: *wat* **kon** *ik* ~ *(doen) (dan* …)? what else could I do (but …); ~ *niets?* will that be all? || *ergens* ~ somewhere else
andersdenkend /andərzdɛŋkənt/ (adj) dissentient, dissident
andersom /andərsɔm/ (adv) the other way round
de **anderstalige** /andərstaləɣə/ non-native speaker
anderszins /ɒndərsɪns/ (adv) otherwise: *en/of* ~ and/or otherwise
anderzijds /ɒndərzɛits/ (adv) on the other hand
de **andijvie** /andɛivi/ endive
Andorra /andɔra/ Andorra
de ¹**Andorrees** /andɔres/ (pl: Andorrezen) Andorran
²**Andorrees** /andɔres/ (adj) Andorran
het **andreaskruis** /andrejaskrœys/ (pl: -en) cross of St Andrew
de **anekdote** /anɛɣdotə/ (pl: -s) anecdote
de **anemoon** /anəmon/ (pl: anemonen) anemone
de **anesthesie** /anɛstezi/ anaesthesia: *lokale (or: totale)* ~ local *(or:* general) anaesthesia
de **anesthesist** /anɛstezɪst/ (pl: -en) anaesthetist
de **angel** /aŋəl/ (pl: -s) sting
Angelsaksisch /aŋəlsɑksis/ (adj) **1** English(-speaking) **2** Anglo-Saxon
de **angina** /aŋɣina/ tonsillitis
de **anglicaan** /aŋxlikan/ (pl: anglicanen) Anglican
anglicaans /aŋɣlikans/ (adj) Anglican: *de ~e* **kerk** the Church of England
de **anglist** /aŋɣlɪst/ (pl: -en) specialist *(or:* student) of English (language and literature)
Angola /aŋɣola/ Angola
de **Angolees** /aŋɣoles/ Angolan
de **angst** /aŋst/ (pl: -en) fear (of); dread, terror (of); anxiety: ~ **aanjagen** frighten; [stronger] terrify; ~ **hebben** *voor* be afraid *(or:* scared) of; *uit* ~ *voor straf* for fear of punishment; *verlamd van* ~ numb with fear
angstaanjagend /aŋstanjaɣənt/ (adj, adv) terrifying, frightening
de **angsthaas** /aŋsthas/ (pl: -hazen) scaredy-cat
angstig /aŋstəx/ (adj) **1** anxious; [after vb] afraid: *een ~e* **schreeuw** an anxious cry; *dat* **maakte** *mij* ~ that frightened me, that made me afraid **2** fearful, anxious, terrifying: *~e*

gedachten anxious thoughts; *het waren ~e* **tijden** those were anxious times
angstvallig /aŋstfɑləx/ (adj, adv) **1** scrupulous, meticulous: *zij* **vermeed** ~ *alle vreemde woorden* she scrupulously *(or:* carefully) avoided all foreign words **2** anxious, nervous
angstwekkend /aŋstwɛkənt/ (adj, adv) frightening, terrifying
het **angstzweet** /aŋstswet/ cold sweat
de **anijs** /anɛis/ aniseed
de **animatie** /anima(t)si/ (pl: -s) animation: [Belg] *kinder~* children's activities (during an event)
het/de **animo** /animo/ zest (for), enthusiasm (for): *er is weinig* ~ *voor* … there is little enthusiasm for …
de **anjer** /ɑɲər/ (pl: -s) carnation
het **anker** /aŋkər/ (pl: -s) anchor: *het* ~ **lichten** raise (the) anchor; [also fig] get under way; *voor* ~ *liggen* be anchored, lie at anchor
de **ankerketting** /aŋkərkɛtɪŋ/ (pl: -en) chain
de **ankerplaats** /aŋkərplats/ (pl: -en) anchorage, berth
annex /anɛks/ (conj) cum; and; slash
de **annexatie** /anɛksa(t)si/ (pl: -s) annexation; incorporation [esp municipalities]
annexeren /anɛksɣerə(n)/ (annexeerde, heeft geannexeerd) annex; incorporate [esp municipalities]
anno /ɑno/ (prep) in the year: ~ *1981* in the year 1981
de **annonce** /anɔ̃sə/ (pl: -s) advertisement, announcement
annonceren /anɔnsɣerə(n)/ (annonceerde, heeft geannonceerd) **1** announce **2** bid; call
annuleren /anylɣerə(n)/ (annuleerde, heeft geannuleerd) cancel: *een* **bestelling** ~ cancel an order
de **annulering** /anylɣerɪŋ/ (pl: -en) cancellation: ~ *van een* **reservering** cancellation of a reservation
de **annuleringsverzekering** /anylɣerɪŋsfərzekərɪŋ/ (pl: -en) cancellation insurance
de **anode** /anodə/ (pl: -n, -s) anode
anoniem /anonim/ (adj) anonymous, nameless, incognito
de **anonimiteit** /anonimitɛit/ anonymity
de **anorak** /ɑnorak/ (pl: -s) anorak
de **anorexia** /anorɛksija/ anorexia
de **ansichtkaart** /ɒnzɪxtkart/ (pl: -en) (picture) postcard
de **ansjovis** /aɲovɪs/ (pl: -sen) anchovy
Antarctica /ɑntɑrktika/ Antarctica
het **antecedent** /antəsədɛnt/ (pl: -en) antecedent: *iemands ~en* **natrekken** look into s.o.'s past record
de **antenne** /ɑntɛnə/ (pl: -s) aerial; antenna
het **antibioticum** /antibijotikʏm/ (pl: antibiotica) antibiotic: *ik* **neem** *antibiotica* I'm taking antibiotics
anticiperen /antisipɣerə(n)/ (anticipeerde,

heeft geanticipeerd) anticipate

de **anticlimax** /ɑntiklimɑks/ (pl: -en) anticlimax

de **anticonceptie** /ɑntikɔnsɛpsi/ contraception, birth control

het **anticonceptiemiddel** /ɑntikɔnsɛpsimɪdəl/ (pl: -en) contraceptive

de **anticonceptiepil** /ɑntikɔnsɛpsipɪl/ (pl: -len) contraceptive pill

het ¹**antiek** /ɑntik/ antiques

²**antiek** /ɑntik/ (adj) antique, ancient: ~e meubels antique furniture

de **antiglobalist** /ɑntiɣlobalɪst/ antiglobalist

de **antiheld** /ɑntihɛlt/ (pl: -en) antihero

het **antilichaam** /ɑntilɪxɑm/ (pl: -lichamen) antibody

de **Antillen** /ɑntɪlə(n)/ (pl) (the) Antilles: de **Nederlandse** ~ the Netherlands Antilles

de **Antilliaan** /ɑntɪl(i)jan/ (pl: Antillianen) Antillean

Antilliaans /ɑntɪlijans/ (adj) Antillean

de **antilope** /ɑntilopə/ (pl: -n) antelope

de **antipathie** /ɑntipati/ (pl: -ën) antipathy (towards)

de **antiquair** /ɑntikɛ:r/ (pl: -s) antique dealer

het **antiquariaat** /ɑntikwarijat/ (pl: antiquariaten) antiquarian (or: second-hand) bookshop

de **antireclame** /ɑntirəklamə/ [roughly] bad (or: negative) publicity

de **antisemiet** /ɑntisemit/ (pl: -en) anti-Semite

antisemitisch /ɑntisemitis/ (adj) anti-Semitic

het **antisemitisme** /ɑntisemitɪsmə/ anti-Semitism

antiseptisch /ɑntisɛptis/ (adj) antiseptic

de **antistof** /ɑntistɔf/ (pl: -fen) antibody

de **antithese** /ɑntitezə/ (pl: -n, -s) antithesis

het/de **antivries** /ɑntivris/ antifreeze

het/de **antraciet** /ɑntrasit/ anthracite (coal)

de **antropologie** /ɑntropoloɣi/ anthropology: **culturele** ~ cultural anthropology, ethnology

de **antropoloog** /ɑntropolox/ (pl: -logen) anthropologist

de **antroposofie** /ɑntroposofi/ anthroposophy

Antwerpen /ɑntwɛrpə(n)/ Antwerp

het **antwoord** /ɑntwort/ (pl: -en) answer, reply: een **afwijzend** (ontkennend) ~ a negative answer; een **bevestigend** ~ an affirmative answer; een **positief** ~ a favourable answer; ~ **geven** op reply to, answer; een ~ **geven** give an answer; het ~ schuldig (moeten) **blijven** give no reply, remain silent; in ~ **op** uw brief (schrijven) in reply to your letter; dat is **geen** ~ op mijn vraag that doesn't answer my question

het **antwoordapparaat** /ɑntwortɑparat/ (pl: -apparaten) answering machine, answerphone

antwoorden /ɑntwordə(n)/ (antwoordde, heeft geantwoord) answer, reply, respond:

bevestigend (positief) ~ answer in the affirmative; ik antwoord niet **op** zulke vragen I don't answer such questions

het **antwoordnummer** /ɑntwortnʏmər/ (pl: -s) [roughly] Freepost

de **anus** /anʏs/ anus

de **ANWB** /aɛnwebe/ Algemene Nederlandse Wielrijdersbond [roughly] Dutch AA, Royal Dutch Touring Club; [Am] Dutch AAA

de **aorta** /aɔrta/ (pl: -'s) aorta

de **AOW** /aowe/ **1** Algemene Ouderdomswet general retirement pensions act **2** (old-age retirement) pension

de **AOW'er** /aowejər/ (pl: -s) OAP (old-age pensioner), senior citizen

apart /apɑrt/ (adj, adv) **1** separate, apart: elk geval ~ **behandelen** deal with each case individually; iem. ~ **nemen (spreken)** take s.o. aside; onderdelen ~ **verkopen** sell parts separately **2** special, exclusive: zij vormen een **klasse** ~ they are in a class of their own **3** different, unusual: hij ziet er **wat** ~ uit he looks a bit unusual

de **apartheid** /apɑrthɛit/ apartheid

apathisch /apatis/ (adj, adv) apathetic, impassive, indifferent

apegapen /apəɣapə(n)/: **op** ~ liggen be at one's last gasp

de **apenkop** /apə(n)kɔp/ (pl: -pen) monkey, brat

de **Apennijnen** /apənɛinə(n)/ (pl) Apennines

de **apennoot** /apənot/ peanut, monkey nut

het **apenstaartje** /apə(n)starcə/ (pl: -s) at sign

het **aperitief** /aperitif/ (pl: aperitieven) aperitif

de **apk-keuring** /apekakørɪŋ/ (pl: -en) motor vehicle test, MOT test

de **Apocalyps** /apokalɪps/ Apocalypse

de **apostel** /apɔstəl/ (pl: -en) apostle

de **apostrof** /apostrɔf/ (pl: -s) apostrophe

de **apotheek** /apotek/ (pl: apotheken) (dispensing) chemist's; [Am] drugstore

de **apotheker** /apotekər/ (pl: -s) pharmacist, dispenser

de **apothekersassistent** /apotekərsɑsistɛnt/ (pl: -en) pharmacist's assistant

de **app** /ɛp/ (pl: -s) app

het **apparaat** /apɑrat/ (pl: apparaten) machine, appliance, device: **huishoudelijke** apparaten household appliances ‖ het **ambtelijk** ~ the administrative system, the Civil Service

de **apparatuur** /apɑratʏr/ apparatus, equipment, machinery; hardware

het **appartement** /apɑrtəmɛnt/ (pl: -en) flat; [Am] apartment: een **driekamerappartement** a 2-bedroom flat

het **appartementsgebouw** /apɑrtəmɛntsxəbɑu/ (pl: -en) [Belg] block of flats

de ¹**appel** /ɑpəl/ (pl: -s) apple: een ~tje voor de **dorst** a nest egg

het ²**appel** /apɛl/ (pl: -s) **1** call: ~ **houden** call the roll **2** appeal: in ~ **gaan** appeal ‖ een ~ **voor** *hands* an appeal for hands

de **appelboom** /ɑpəlbom/ (pl: -bomen) apple tree

de **appelflap** /ɑpəlflɑp/ (pl: -pen) apple turnover

de **appelflauwte** /ɑpəlflɑutə/ (pl: -s): *een ~ krijgen* go off in a swoon, swoon, sham a faint

het **appelgebak** /ɑpəlɣəbɑk/ [roughly] apple tart

appelleren /ɑpɛleːrə(n)/ (appelleerde, heeft geappelleerd) appeal: *~ aan* appeal to; *~ voor hands* appeal for hands

de **appelmoes** /ɑpəlmus/ apple-sauce

het **appelsap** /ɑpəlsɑp/ apple juice

de **appelsien** /ɑpəlsin/ (pl: -en) [Belg] orange

de **appelstroop** /ɑpəlstrop/ apple spread

de **appeltaart** /ɑpəltart/ (pl: -en) apple pie

het/de **appendix** /ɑpɛndɪks/ (pl: appendices) appendix

appetijtelijk /ɑpətɛrtələk/ (adj, adv) appetizing

applaudisseren /ɑplɑudiseːrə(n)/ (applaudisseerde, heeft geapplaudisseerd) applaud, clap: *~ voor iem.* applaud s.o.

het **applaus** /ɑplɑus/ applause, clapping: *de motie werd met ~ begroet* the motion was received with applause; *een ~je voor Marleen!* let's give a big hand to Marleen!

appreciëren /ɑpreʃeːrə(n)/ (apprecieerde, heeft geapprecieerd) appreciate

het/de **après-ski** /ɑprɛskiː/ après-ski

après-skiën /ɑprɛskijə(n)/ (après-skiede, heeft geaprès-skied) indulge in amusements after skiing

de **april** /ɑprɪl/ (pl: -s) April: *één ~* April Fools' Day

de **aprilgrap** /ɑprɪlɣrɑp/ (pl: -pen) April Fool's joke

het/de **¹à propos** /ɑpropoː/: *van zijn ~ raken (zijn)* lose the thread of one's argument

²à propos /ɑpropoː/ (int) apropos, by the way, incidentally

het **aquaduct** /ɑkwadʏkt/ (pl: -en) aqueduct

aquajoggen /ɑkwadʒɔɣə(n)/ (aquajogde, heeft/is geaquajogd) aquajog

de **aquaplaning** /ɑkwaplenɪŋ/ aquaplaning; skidding

de **aquarel** /ɑkwarɛl/ (pl: -len) water colour, aquarelle

het **aquarium** /ɑkwarijʏm/ (pl: -s, aquaria) aquarium

de **¹ar** /ɑr/ (pl: arren) sleigh

²ar /ɑr/ (adj): *in arren moede iets doen* do sth. out of desperation

Arabië /ɑrabijə/ Arabia

de **Arabier** /ɑrabir/ (pl: -en) **1** Saudi (Arabian) **2** Arab

het **¹Arabisch** /ɑrabis/ Arabic: *in het ~* in Arabic

²Arabisch /ɑrabis/ (adj) Arabic; Arabian; Arab: *de ~e literatuur* Arabic literature

de **arbeid** /ɑrbɛit/ labour, work: *de Dag van de Arbeid* Labour Day; *de Partij van de Arbeid* the Labour Party; *(on)geschoolde ~* (un)skilled labour (*or:* work); *~ verrichten* labour, work

de **arbeider** /ɑrbɛidər/ (pl: -s) worker, workman: *landarbeiders* agricultural labourers; *geschoolde ~s* skilled workers; *ongeschoolde ~s* unskilled workers

de **arbeidersklasse** /ɑrbɛidərsklɑsə/ working class(es)

de **arbeiderspartij** /ɑrbɛidərspɑrtɛi/ (pl: -en) Labour Party, Socialist Party

de **arbeidsbemiddeling** /ɑrbɛitsbəmɪdəlɪŋ/ employment-finding

het **arbeidsbureau** /ɑrbɛitsbyro/ (pl: -s) employment office, jobcentre: *zich inschrijven bij het ~* sign on at the employment office

het **arbeidsconflict** /ɑrbɛitskɔnflɪkt/ (pl: -en) labour dispute (*or:* conflict)

het **arbeidscontract** /ɑrbɛitskɔntrɑkt/ (pl: -en) employment contract

de **arbeidsinspectie** /ɑrbɛitsɪnspɛksi/ (pl: -s) labour inspectorate: *een ambtenaar van de ~* a labour inspector

arbeidsintensief /ɑrbɛitsɪntɛnzif/ (adj) labour-intensive

de **arbeidsmarkt** /ɑrbɛitsmɑrkt/ (pl: -en) labour market, job market: *de situatie op de ~* the employment situation

arbeidsongeschikt /ɑrbɛitsɔŋɣəsxɪkt/ (adj) disabled, unable to work: *gedeeltelijk ~ verklaard worden* be declared partially disabled

de **arbeidsongeschiktheid** /ɑrbɛitsɔŋɣəsxɪkthɛit/ disability, inability to work: *volledige, gedeeltelijke ~* full, partial disability

de **arbeidsovereenkomst** /ɑrbɛitsovərənkɔmst/ (pl: -en) employment contract: *een collectieve ~* a collective agreement; *een individuele ~* an individual employment contract

de **arbeidsplaats** /ɑrbɛitsplats/ (pl: -en) job: *nieuwe ~en scheppen* create new jobs; *er gaan 20 ~en verloren* 20 jobs will be lost

de **arbeidstijdverkorting** /ɑrbɛitstɛitfərkortɪŋ/ reduction of working hours, shorter working week

de **arbeidsvoorwaarden** /ɑrbɛitsforwardə(n)/ (pl) terms (*or:* conditions) of employment: *secundaire ~* fringe benefits

arbeidzaam /ɑrbɛitsam/ (adj) industrious, hard-working, laborious: *na een ~ leven* after a useful life (*or:* a life of hard work)

de **arbiter** /ɑrbitər/ (pl: -s) [sport] referee; umpire

de **arbitrage** /ɑrbitraʒə/ **1** [sport] refereeing **2** [law] arbitration **3** [com] arbitrage

arbitrair /ɑrbitrɛːr/ (adj, adv) arbitrary: *~ te werk gaan* act arbitrarily

de **Arbowet** /ɑrbowɛt/ (Dutch) occupational health and safety act, Factories Act; [Am] [roughly] Labor Law

arceren /ɑrsɛ̯rə(n)/ (arceerde, heeft gearceerd) shade: *het gearceerde* **gedeelte** the shaded area

archaïsch /ɑrχai̯s/ (adj) archaic; antiquated

het **archeologie** /ɑrχejoloɣi̯/ archaeology

archeologisch /ɑrχejoloχis/ (adj, adv) archaeological; *~e* **opgravingen** archaeological excavation(s)

de **archeoloog** /ɑrχejoloχ/ (pl: -logen) archaeologist

het **archief** /ɑrχif/ (pl: archieven) archives; record office; registry (office); files: *iets* **in** *het ~* **opbergen** file sth. (away)

de **archiefkast** /ɑrχifkɑst/ (pl: -en) filing cabinet

de **archipel** /ɑrχipɛl/ (pl: -s) archipelago

de **architect** /ɑrʃitɛkt/ (pl: -en) architect

architectonisch /ɑrʃitɛktonis/ (adj, adv) architectonic

de **architectuur** /ɑrʃitɛktyr/ architecture, building (style): *voorbeelden van* **moderne** *~* examples of modern architecture

de **archivaris** /ɑrχivɑrɪs/ (pl: -sen) archivist, keeper of the archives (*or:* records); registrar

Arctisch /ɑrktis/ (adj) Arctic

de **Ardennen** /ɑrdɛnə(n)/ (pl) (the) Ardennes

de **are** /ɑrə/ (pl: -n) are: *één ~ is honderd vierkante meter* one are is a hundred square metres

de **arena** /ɑrena/ (pl: -'s) arena

de **arend** /ɑrənt/ (pl: -en) eagle

argeloos /ɑrɣəlos/ (adj, adv) unsuspecting, innocent

de **Argentijn** /ɑrɣəntɛi̯n/ (pl: -en) Argentine, Argentinian

Argentijns /ɑrɣəntɛi̯ns/ (adj) Argentine, Argentinian

Argentinië /ɑrɣəntini̯jə/ Argentina

arglistig /ɑrχlistəχ/ (adj, adv) crafty, cunning

het **argument** /ɑrɣymɛnt/ (pl: -en) argument: *een* **steekhoudend** *~* a watertight argument; *~en* **aanvoeren** *voor iets* make out a case for sth.; *~en* **voor** *en* **tegen** pros and cons; *dat is* **geen** *~* that's no reason

de **argumentatie** /ɑrɣymɛnta(t)si/ (pl: -s) **1** argumentation, reasoning, line of reasoning **2** argument

argumenteren /ɑrɣymɛntɛrə(n)/ (argumenteerde, heeft geargumenteerd) argue: *~* **voor** (*or:* **tegen**) argue (*or:* make out a case) for (*or:* against)

de **argusogen** /ɑrɣʏsoɣə(n)/ (pl): *iets* **met** *~ bekijken* look at sth. with Argus' eyes

de **argwaan** /ɑrχwan/ suspicion: *~* **koesteren** *tegen iem. (omtrent iets)* be suspicious of s.o. (sth.); *~* **krijgen** grow suspicious; *~* **wekken** arouse (*or:* excite) suspicion

argwanend /ɑrχwanənt/ (adj, adv) suspicious: *een ~e* **blik** a suspicious look

de **aria** /ɑrija/ (pl: -'s) aria

de **aristocraat** /ɑrɪstokrat/ (pl: aristocraten) aristocrat

de **aristocratie** /ɑrɪstokra(t)si/ (pl: -ën) aristocracy

aristocratisch /ɑrɪstokratis/ (adj, adv) aristocratic

de **ark** /ɑrk/ (pl: -en) **1** houseboat **2** Ark: *de ~ van* **Noach** Noah's Ark

de ¹**arm** /ɑrm/ (pl: -en) **1** arm: *een* **gebroken** *~* a broken (*or:* fractured) arm; *met* **open** *~en ontvangen* receive (*or:* welcome) with open arms; *hij* **sloeg** *zijn ~en om haar heen* he threw his arms around her; *zij liepen ~* **in** *~* they walked arm in arm; *een advocaat* **in** *de ~ nemen* consult a solicitor **2** arm, sleeve

²**arm** /ɑrm/ (adj) **1** poor: *de ~e* **landen** the poor countries; *de ~en en de rijken* the rich and the poor **2** poor (in), lacking **3** poor, wretched: *het ~e* **schaap** the poor thing (*or:* soul)

de **armatuur** /ɑrmatyr/ (pl: armaturen) fitting, bracket

de **armband** /ɑrmbɑnt/ (pl: -en) bracelet

het ¹**Armeens** /ɑrmens/ Armenian

²**Armeens** /ɑrmens/ (adj) Armenian

Armenië /ɑrmeni̯jə/ Armenia

de **Armeniër** /ɑrmeni̯jər/ (pl: -s) Armenian

armetierig /ɑrmətirəχ/ (adj, adv) miserable, paltry

armlastig /ɑrmlɑstəχ/ (adj) poverty-stricken, needy

de **armleuning** /ɑrmlønɪŋ/ (pl: -en) arm(rest)

de **armoede** /ɑrmudə/ poverty; [stronger] destitution: *geestelijke ~* intellectual (*or:* spiritual) poverty; *~* **lijden** be poverty-stricken, be in need; *schrijnende* (or: **bittere**) *~* abject (*or:* grinding) poverty

armoedig /ɑrmudəχ/ (adj, adv) poor; shabby: *~* **gekleed** shabbily dressed; *dat* **staat** *zo ~* that looks so shabby

de **armoedzaaier** /ɑrmutsajər/ (pl: -s) down-and-out(er); [Am] bum

het **armsgat** /ɑrmsχɑt/ (pl: -en) armhole

de **armslag** /ɑrmslɑχ/ (pl: -en) elbow room

armzalig /ɑrmzaləχ/ (adj, adv) poor, paltry, miserable: *een ~* **pensioentje** a meagre pension

het **aroma** /ɑroma/ aroma, flavour

aromatisch /ɑromatis/ (adj) aromatic

het **arrangement** /ɑrãʒəmɛnt/ (pl: -en) arrangement; format; order: *een ~* **voor** *piano* an arrangement for piano

arrangeren /ɑrãʒerə(n)/ (arrangeerde, heeft gearrangeerd) **1** arrange; set out **2** arrange, organize, get up **3** arrange, score: *voor orkest ~* orchestrate, score

de **arrenslee** /ɑrə(n)sle/ (pl: -ën) horse sleigh

het **arrest** /ɑrɛst/ (pl: -en) arrest, detention; custody: *u staat* **onder** *~* you are under arrest

de **arrestant** /ɑrɛstɑnt/ (pl: -en) arrested man (*or:* woman); detainee; prisoner de **arrestatie** /ɑrɛsta(t)si/ (pl: -s) arrest: *een ~ verrichten* make an arrest

het **arrestatiebevel** /ɑrɛsta(t)sibəvɛl/ (pl: -en) arrest warrant

arresteren /ɑrɛsterə(n)/ (arresteerde, heeft gearresteerd) arrest; detain: *iem. laten ~* have s.o. arrested; place s.o. in charge

arriveren /ɑrivɛrə(n)/ (arriveerde, is gearriveerd) arrive

arrogant /ɑroɣɑnt/ (adj, adv) arrogant; superior: *een ~e houding hebben* have a haughty manner

de **arrogantie** /ɑroɣɑn(t)si/ arrogance, presumptuousness, superiority: *de ~ van de macht* the arrogance of rank (or: power)

het **arrondissement** /ɑrɔndisəmɛnt/ (pl: -en) district

de **arrondissementsrechtbank** /ɑrɔndisəmɛntsrɛxtbɑŋk/ (pl: -en) district court

het **arsenaal** /ɑrsenal/ (pl: arsenalen) arsenal

het **arsenicum** /ɑrsenikʏm/ arsenic

articuleren /ɑrtikylerə(n)/ (articuleerde, heeft gearticuleerd) articulate, enunciate: *goed* (or: *duidelijk*) ~ articulate well (or: distinctly); *slecht ~* articulate badly (or: poorly)

de **artiest** /ɑrtist/ (pl: -en) artist, entertainer; performer

het **artikel** /ɑrtikəl/ (pl: -en) **1** article, paper; story: *een redactioneel ~* an editorial; *de krant wijdde er een speciaal ~ aan* the newspaper ran a feature on it **2** article, item: *huishoudelijke ~en* household goods (or: items) **3** [law] article, section, clause: *~ 80 van de Grondwet* section 80 of the constitution

de **artillerie** /ɑrtɪləri/ (pl: -ën) artillery: *lichte* (or: *zware*) ~ light (or: heavy) artillery

¹**artisanaal** /ɑrtizanal/ (adj) [Belg] craft-

²**artisanaal** /ɑrtizanal/ (adv) [Belg] by craftsmen, by traditional methods

de **artisjok** /ɑrtiʃɔk/ (pl: -ken) artichoke

artistiek /ɑrtɪstik/ (adj, adv) artistic: *de ~ leider* the artistic director

de **artrose** /ɑrtrozə/ arthrosis, articular degeneration

de **arts** /ɑrts/ (pl: -en) doctor, physician: *zijn ~ raadplegen* consult one's doctor

de **artsenbezoeker** /ɑrtsə(n)bəzukər/ (pl: -s) medical representative; [Am esp] drug salesman (or: saleswoman)

Aruba /aruba/ Aruba

de **Arubaan** /aruban/ (pl: Arubanen) Aruban

Arubaans /arubans/ (adj) Aruban

de **as** /ɑs/ (pl: assen) **1** ashes; ash: *gloeiende as* (glowing) embers; *een stad in de as leggen* reduce a city to ashes **2** axle; shaft **3** [geometry] axis: *om zijn as draaien* revolve on its axis **4** [mus] A-flat

a.s. (abbrev) *aanstaande* next: *~ maandag* next Monday

de **asbak** /ɑzbɑk/ (pl: -ken) ashtray

het **asbest** /ɑzbɛst/ asbestos

asblond /ɑzblɔnt/ (adj) ash blond

de **asceet** /ɑset/ (pl: asceten) ascetic

ascetisch /ɑsetis/ (adj, adv) ascetic

aselect /ɑselɛkt/ (adj, adv) random, indiscriminate: *een ~e steekproef* a random sample (or: sampling)

het **asfalt** /ɑsfɑlt/ (pl: -en) asphalt

asfalteren /ɑsfɑlterə(n)/ (asfalteerde, heeft geasfalteerd) asphalt; [Am] blacktop

het **asiel** /azil/ (pl: -en) **1** asylum, sanctuary: *politiek ~ vragen* (or: *krijgen*) seek (or: obtain) political asylum **2** animal home (or: shelter); pound

de **asielzoeker** /azilzukər/ (pl: -s) asylum seeker

het **asielzoekerscentrum** /azilzukərsɛntrʏm/ (pl: -centra) asylum seekers' (or: refugee) centre

asjemenou /ɑʃəmənɑu/ (int) oh dear!, my goodness!

de ¹**aso** /aso/ (pl: -'s) [inform] antisocial (person)

²**aso** /aso/ (adj) [inform] antisocial

het **a.s.o.** /aɛso/ [Belg] general secondary education

asociaal /asoʃal/ (adj) antisocial, unsociable; asocial: *~ gedrag* antisocial behaviour

het **aspect** /ɑspɛkt/ (pl: -en) aspect: *we moeten alle ~en van de zaak bestuderen* we must consider every aspect of the matter

de **asperge** /ɑspɛrʒə/ (pl: -s) asparagus

de **asperger** Asperger's syndrome

de **aspirant** /ɑspirɑnt/ (pl: -en) **1** trainee, student **2** junior: *hij speelt nog bij de ~en* he is still (playing) in the junior league

aspirant- prospective: *~student* prospective student

de **aspirant-koper** /ɑspirɑntkopər/ (pl: -s) prospective buyer

de **aspiratie** /ɑspira(t)si/ (pl: -s): *hij heeft ~s om voorzitter te worden* it is his ambition to be chairman, he aspires to be chairman

de **aspirine** /ɑspirinə/ aspirin

de **assemblage** /ɑsɛmblaʒə/ (pl: -s) assembly, assembling

assembleren /ɑsɛmblerə(n)/ (assembleerde, heeft geassembleerd) assemble

het **assenstelsel** /ɑsə(n)stɛlsəl/ (pl: -s) co-ordinate system

Assepoester /ɑsəpustər/ Cinderella

assertief /ɑsɛrtif/ (adj) assertive: *~ gedrag* assertive behaviour

de **assertiviteit** /ɑsɛrtivitɛit/ assertiveness

het **assessment** /əsɛsmənt/ (pl: -s) assessment

de **assessor** /ɑsɛsɔr/ (pl: -s) assessor

de **assisen** /ɑsizə(n)/: [Belg] *hof van ~* [roughly] Crown Court

de **assist** /əsɪst/ assist

de **assistent** /ɑsɪstɛnt/ (pl: -en) assistant, aid, helper: [Belg] *sociaal ~* social worker

de **assistentie** /ɑsɪstɛnsi/ assistance, aid, help: *~ verlenen* give assistance; *de politie verzocht*

om ~ the police asked for assistance
assisteren /ɑsɪstɛrə(n)/ (assisteerde, heeft geassisteerd) assist, help, aid

de **associatie** /ɑsoʃa(t)si/ (pl: -s) association

associëren /ɑsoʃerə(n)/ (associeerde, heeft geassocieerd) (+ met) associate (with) ‖ *zich ~ met* associate with

het **assortiment** /ɑsɔrtimɛnt/ (pl: -en) assortment, selection: *een ruim* (or: *beperkt*) *~ hebben* have a broad (or: limited) assortment

de **assurantie** /ɑsyrɑnsi/ (pl: assurantiën) insurance

de **aster** /ɑstər/ (pl: -s) aster

de **asterisk** /ɑstərɪsk/ (pl: -en) asterisk

het/de **astma** /ɑsma/ asthma: *~ hebben* suffer from (or: have) asthma

astmatisch /ɑsmatis/ (adj) asthmatic

de **astrologie** /ɑstroloɣi/ astrology

de **astroloog** /ɑstroloχ/ (pl: -logen) astrologer

de **astronaut** /ɑstronɑut/ (pl: -en) astronaut

de **astronomie** /ɑstronomi/ astronomy

astronomisch /ɑstronomis/ (adj) **1** astronomical: *~e kijker* astronomical telescope **2** astronomic(al): *~e bedragen* astronomic amounts

de **astronoom** /ɑstronom/ (pl: -nomen) astronomer

Aswoensdag /ɑswunzdɑχ/ Ash Wednesday

asymmetrisch /ɑsimetris/ (adj, adv) asymmetric(al)

het **at** /ɛt/ at; at-sign

de **atalanta** /ɑtalɑnta/ (pl: -'s) [zoology] red admiral

de **ATB** /atebe/ (pl: -'s) ATB *(all-terrain bike)*

atechnisch /ɑtɛχnis/ (adj) untechnical

het **atelier** /ɑtəlje/ (pl: -s) studio; workshop: *werken op een ~* work in a studio

Atheens /ɑtens/ (adj) Athenian

het **atheïsme** /ɑtejɪsma/ atheism

de **atheïst** /ɑtejɪst/ (pl: -en) atheist

Athene /ɑtenə/ Athens

het **atheneum** /ɑtənejʏm/ (pl: -s) [Dutch] [roughly] grammar school; [Am] high school: *op het ~ zitten* [roughly] be at grammar school

Atlantisch /ɑtlɑntis/ (adj) Atlantic: *de ~e Oceaan* the Atlantic (Ocean)

de **atlas** /ɑtlɑs/ (pl: -sen) atlas

de **atleet** /ɑtlet/ (pl: -leten) athlete

de **atletiek** /ɑtletik/ athletics

atletisch /ɑtletis/ (adj) athletic

de **atmosfeer** /ɑtmɔsfer/ (pl: atmosferen) atmosphere; environment: *de hogere* (or: *lagere*) *~* the upper (or: lower) atmosphere

atmosferisch /ɑtmɔsferis/ (adj) atmospheric: *~e druk* atmospheric pressure; *~e storing* static interference, atmospheric disturbance

het **atol** /ɑtɔl/ (pl: -len) atoll

het **atoom** /ɑtom/ (pl: atomen) atom

de **atoombom** /ɑtɔmbɔm/ (pl: -men) atom bomb, A-bomb

de **atoomenergie** /ɑtomenɛrʒi/ nuclear (or: atomic) energy (or: power)

het **atoomtijdperk** /ɑtomtɛɪtpɛrk/ nuclear (or: atomic) age

het **atoomwapen** /ɑtomwapə(n)/ (pl: -s) nuclear (or: atomic) weapon

het **atrium** /ɑtrijʏm/ (pl: -s, atria) atrium

de **attaché** /ɑtaʃe/ (pl: -s) [Belg] ministerial adviser

het/de **attachment** /ətɛtʃmənt/ (pl: -s) attachment

de **attaque** /ɑtɑk/ (pl: -s) **1** attack **2** stroke: *een ~ krijgen* suffer (or: have) a stroke

het **at-teken** /ɛtekə(n)/ at-sign

attenderen /ɑtɛndɛrə(n)/ (attendeerde, heeft geattendeerd) point out, draw attention to: *ik attendeer u erop dat ...* I draw your attention to (the fact that) ...

attent /ɑtɛnt/ (adj, adv) **1** attentive: *iem. ~ maken op iets* draw s.o.'s attention to sth. **2** considerate, thoughtful: *hij was altijd heel ~ voor hen* he was always very considerate towards them

de **attentie** /ɑtɛnsi/ (pl: -s) attention, mark of attention; present: *ik heb een kleine ~ meegebracht* I've brought a small present; *ter ~ van* for the attention of

het **attest** /ɑtɛst/ (pl: -en) certificate

de **attractie** /ɑtrɑksi/ (pl: -s) attraction: *zij is de grootste ~ vanavond* she is the main attraction this evening

attractief /ɑtrɑktif/ (adj, adv) attractive, catching

het **attractiepark** /ɑtrɑksipɑrk/ (pl: -en) amusement park

het **attribuut** /ɑtribyt/ (pl: attributen) attribute, characteristic

de **atv** /ɑteve/ *arbeidstijdverkorting* reduction of working hours

au /ɑu/ (int) ow, ouch

a.u.b. /aybe/ (abbrev) *alstublieft* please

de **aubade** /obɑdə/ (pl: -s) aubade: *een ~ brengen* perform an aubade, sing an aubade (to s.o.)

de **aubergine** /oberʒinə/ (pl: -s) aubergine, eggplant

de **audiëntie** /ɑud(i)jɛnsi/ (pl: -s) audience: *~ geven (verlenen)* grant an audience (to s.o.); *op ~ gaan bij* have an audience with

het **audioboek** /ɑudijobuk/ (pl: -en) audio book

audiovisueel /ɑudijovizywel/ (adj) audiovisual

de **audit** /ɔːdɪt/ audit

de **auditie** /ɑudi(t)si/ (pl: -s) audition, try-out; screen test: *een ~ doen* (do an) audition

auditief /ɑuditif/ (adj, adv) auditive

de ¹**auditor** (pl: -s)

de ²**auditor** /ɑuditɔr/ (pl: -en) (student) listener

het **auditorium** /ɑuditorijʏm/ (pl: auditoria, -s)

auditorium

de **augurk** /ɑuɣʏrk/ (pl: -en) gherkin

de **augustus** /ɑuɣʏstʏs/ August

de **aula** /ɑula/ (pl: -'s) great hall, auditorium

de **au pair** /opɛːr/ (pl: -s) au pair

de **aura** /ɑura/ (pl: -'s) aura, charisma: *de ~ van een groot kunstenaar* the aura (*or:* charisma) of a great artist; *iemands ~ lezen* read s.o.'s aura

het/de **aureool** /ɑurejol/ (pl: aureolen) **1** aureole, aureola, halo **2** [fig] aura: *een ~ van roem* an aura of fame

de **auspiciën** /ɑuspisijə(n)/ (pl) auspices, aegis: *onder ~ van* under the auspices (*or:* aegis) of, sponsored by

de **ausputzer** /ɑusputsər/ (pl: -s) sweeper

Australië /ɑustralijə/ Australia

de **Australiër** /ɑustralijər/ (pl: -s) Australian

Australisch /ɑustralis/ (adj) Australian

de **auteur** /ɑutør/ (pl: -s) author, writer

het **auteursrecht** /ɑutørsrɛxt/ (pl: -en) copyright: *overtreding van het ~* infringement of copyright

de **authenticiteit** /ɑutɛntisitɛɪt/ authenticity

authentiek /ɑutɛntik/ (adj) authentic; legitimate; genuine: *een ~e tekst* an authentic text; *een ~ kunstwerk* an original (*or:* authentic) work of art

de **autist** /ɑutɪst/ (pl: -en) autistic person

autistisch /ɑutɪstis/ (adj) autistic

de **auto** /ɑuto/ (pl: -'s) car: *in een ~ rijden* drive, go by car; *het is een uur rijden met de ~* it's an hour's drive by car; *een zuinige ~* an economy car

de **autoband** /ɑutobant/ (pl: -en) (car) tyre

de **autobiografie** /ɑutobijoɣrafi/ (pl: -ën) autobiography

de **autobom** /ɑutobɔm/ (pl: -men) car bomb

de **autobotsing** /ɑutobɔtsɪŋ/ (pl: -en) car crash

de **autobus** /ɑutobʏs/ (pl: -sen) bus

de **¹autochtoon** /ɑutɔxton/ (pl: autochtonen) autochthon, indigene, native

²autochtoon /ɑutɔxton/ (adj) autochthonous, indigenous, native

de **autocontrole** /ɑutokɔntroːlə/ (pl: -s) [Belg] MOT (test) [UK]; (state) motor vehicle inspection [USA]

de **autocoureur** /ɑutokurør/ (pl: -s) racing(-car) driver

de **autocratie** /ɑutokra(t)si/ (pl: -ën) autocracy, dictatorship, autarchy

de **autocue** /ɑutokju/ (pl: -s) autocue; [Am] teleprompter

de **autodidact** /ɑutodidɑkt/ (pl: -en) autodidact, self-taught person

de **autodiefstal** /ɑutodifstɑl/ (pl: -len) car theft

het **autogas** /ɑutoɣɑs/ (pl: -sen) LPG [liquefied petroleum gas]

de **autogordel** /ɑutoɣɔrdəl/ (pl: -s) seat belt, safety belt: *het dragen van ~s is verplicht* the

wearing of seat belts is compulsory

de **autohandelaar** /ɑutohɑndəlɑr/ (pl: -s, -handelaren) car dealer

de **autokaart** /ɑutokart/ (pl: -en) road map; road atlas

het **autokerkhof** /ɑutokɛrkhɔf/ (pl: -hoven) junkyard, (used) car dump

de **autokeuring** /ɑutokørɪŋ/ (pl: -en) MOT (test); (state) motor vehicle inspection: *verplichte, periodieke ~* (compulsory, periodical) MOT (test), yearly (motor vehicle) inspection

de **autokraak** /ɑutokrak/ (pl: -kraken) car break-in

autoluw /ɑutolyw/ (adj) low-traffic: *de binnenstad ~ maken* limit (*or:* reduce) traffic in the city centre, make the city centre a low-traffic area (*or:* zone)

de **automaat** /ɑutomat/ (pl: automaten) **1** automaton, robot **2** slot machine, vending machine; ticket machine: *munten in een ~ gooien* feed coins into a slot machine

de **automatenhal** /ɑutomatə(n)hɑl/ (pl: -len) [roughly] amusement arcade

de **automatiek** /ɑutomatik/ (pl: -en) automat

automatisch /ɑutomatis/ (adj, adv) automatic: *machtiging voor ~e afschrijving* standing order; *een ~e piloot* an automatic pilot, an autopilot; *iets ~ doen* do sth. automatically; *~ sluitende deuren* self-closing doors

automatiseren /ɑutomatizerə(n)/ (automatiseerde, heeft geautomatiseerd) automate, automatize; computerize: *een administratie ~* computerize an accounting department

de **automatisering** /ɑutomatizerɪŋ/ automation, computerization

het **automatisme** /ɑutomatɪsmə/ (pl: -n) automatism

de **automobiel** /ɑutomobil/ (pl: -en) (motor) car

de **automobilist** /ɑutomobilɪst/ (pl: -en) motorist, driver

de **automonteur** /ɑutomɔntør/ (pl: -s) car mechanic

de **autonomie** /ɑutonomi/ autonomy, self-government

autonoom /ɑutonom/ (adj, adv) autonomous

het **auto-ongeluk** /ɑutoɔŋɣəlʏk/ (pl: -ken) car crash, (road) accident: *bij het ~ zijn drie mensen gewond geraakt* three people were injured in the car crash

de **autopapieren** /ɑutopapirə(n)/ (pl) car (registration) papers

de **autopech** /ɑutopɛx/ breakdown, car trouble

de **autoped** /ɑutopɛt/ (pl: -s) scooter

de **autopsie** /ɑutopsi/ (pl: -s, -ën) autopsy: *(een) ~ verrichten op* perform an autopsy on

de **autorace** /ɑutores/ (pl: -s) car race

de **autoradio** /au̯toradijo/ (pl: -'s) car radio

autorijden /au̯tɔrɛɪdə(n)/ (reed auto, heeft autogereden) drive (a car)

de **autorijschool** /au̯tɔrɛisχol/ (pl: -scholen) driving school

de **autorisatie** /au̯toriza(t)si/ (pl: -s) authorization, sanction, authority: *de ~ van de **regering** verkrijgen om* be authorized by the government to

autoritair /au̯toritɛːr/ (adj, adv) authoritarian

de **autoriteit** /au̯toritɛit/ (pl: -en) authority: *de **plaatselijke** ~en* the local government; *een ~ op het gebied van slakken* an authority on snails

de **autoruit** /au̯torœyt/ (pl: -en) car window; windscreen

de **autosnelweg** /au̯tosnɛlwɛχ/ (pl: -en) motorway

de **autostop** /au̯tostɔp/: [Belg] *~ doen* hitchhike

de **autostrade** /au̯tostradə/ [Belg] motorway

het **autoverkeer** /au̯tovərker/ car traffic

de **autowasstraat** /au̯towɑstrat/ automatic car wash

de **autoweg** /au̯towɛχ/ (pl: -en) motorway

het **autowrak** /au̯tovrɑk/ (pl: -ken) wreck

de **avance** /avā̯sə/ (pl: -s) advance, approach: *~s doen* make advances (*or*: approaches) (to)

de **avenue** /avəny/ (pl: -s) avenue

¹**averechts** /avərɛχts/ (adj) **1** misplaced, wrong: *een ~e **uitwerking** hebben* have a contrary effect, be counter-productive **2** unsound, contrary, wrong

²**averechts** /avərɛχts/ (adv) **1** back-to-front, inside out, upside down **2** (all) wrong: *het valt ~ uit* it goes all wrong

de **averij** /avərɛi/ (pl: -en) damage; average: *zware ~ oplopen* sustain heavy damage

de **aversie** /avɛrsi/ aversion: *een ~ krijgen **tegen*** take an aversion to

de **avocado** /avokado/ (pl: -'s) avocado

de **avond** /avɔnt/ (pl: -en) evening, night: *in de loop van de ~* during the evening; *de **hele** ~* all evening, the whole evening; *het is zijn **vrije** ~* it is his night off; *een ~je tv kijken* (*or*: *lezen*) spend the evening watching TV (*or*: reading); *een ~je uit* a night out, an evening out; *tegen de ~* towards the evening; *de ~ **voor** de grote wedstrijd* the eve of the big match; *'s ~s* at night, in the evening

het **avondblad** /avɔndblɑt/ (pl: -en) evening paper

de **avondcursus** /avɔntkʏrzʏs/ (pl: -sen) evening classes

de **avonddienst** /avɔndinst/ (pl: -en) evening shift; evening duty: *~ **hebben*** be on the evening shift (*or*: duty)

het **avondeten** /avɔntetə(n)/ dinner, supper, evening meal: *het ~ **klaarmaken*** prepare dinner (*or*: supper)

de **avondjurk** /avɔntjʏrk/ (pl: -en) evening gown (*or*: frock)

de **avondkleding** /avɔntkledɪŋ/ evening dress (*or*: wear)

de **avondklok** /avɔntklɔk/ (pl: -ken) curfew

het **Avondland** /avɔntlɑnt/ Occident

het **avondmaal** /avɔntmal/ dinner, supper: *het **Laatste** Avondmaal* the Last Supper; *het ~ **vieren*** celebrate (Holy) Communion

de **avondmens** /avɔntmɛns/ (pl: -en) night person; night owl

het **avondrood** /avɔntrot/ sunset (glow), evening glow, sunset sky

de **avondschool** /avɔntsχol/ (pl: -scholen) night school; evening classes: *op een ~ zitten* go to night school

de **avondspits** /avɔntspɪts/ (pl: -en) evening rush-hour

de **avonturier** /avɔntyrir/ (pl: -s) adventurer, adventuress

het **avontuur** /avɔntyr/ (pl: avonturen) **1** adventure: *een **vreemd** ~ beleven* have a strange adventure; *op ~ (uit)gaan* set off on adventures; go solo **2** venture: *niet **van** avonturen **houden*** not like risky ventures **3** luck, chance: *het **rad** van ~* the wheel of fortune

avontuurlijk /avɔntyrlək/ (adj, adv) **1** adventurous **2** full of adventure, exciting

het **avontuurtje** /avɔntyrcə/ (pl: -s) affair: *een ~ hebben met …* have an affair with …

het **axioma** /ɑks(i)joma/ (pl: -'s) axiom

de **ayatollah** /ajatɔla/ (pl: -s) ayatollah

het **AZ** /azɛt/ (pl: AZ's) [Belg] *Algemeen/Academisch Ziekenhuis* University Hospital, General Hospital

de **azalea** /azaleja/ (pl: -'s) azalea

azen /azə(n)/ (aasde, heeft geaasd) have one's eye on

de **Azerbeidzjaan** /ɑzɛrbɛidʒan/ Azerbaijani

Azerbeidzjaans /ɑzɛrbɛidʒans/ (adj) Azerbaijani

Azerbeidzjan /ɑzɛrbɛidʒɑn/ Azerbaijan

de **Azeri** /azɛri/ (pl: -'s) Azeri

de **Aziaat** /azijat/ (pl: Aziaten) Asian

Aziatisch /azijatis/ (adj) Asian

Azië /azijə/ Asia

de **azijn** /azɛin/ (pl: -en) vinegar

het **azijnzuur** /azɛinzyr/ acetic acid

de **Azoren** /azorə(n)/ (pl) Azores

de **Azteken** /ɑstekə(n)/ (pl) Aztecs

het **azuur** /azyr/ azure

b

de **b** /be/ (pl: b's) b; B ‖ *wie a zegt, moet ook b zeggen* in for a penny, in for a pound

de **baai** /baj/ (pl: -en) bay; [small] cove; inlet

de **baal** /bal/ (pl: balen) bag, sack; bale: *een ~ katoen* a bale of cotton

de **baaldag** /baldɑχ/ (pl: -en) off-day

de **baan** /ban/ (pl: banen) **1** job: *een vaste ~ hebben* have a permanent job **2** path; lane: *iets op de lange ~ schuiven* shelve sth. **3** [sport] track; court; rink; speed-skating track; course: *starten in ~ drie* start in lane three **4** orbit: *een ~ om de aarde maken* orbit the earth

baanbrekend /bambrekənt/ (adj) pioneering, groundbreaking, pathbreaking: *~ werk verrichten* do pioneering work, break new ground

het **baanvak** /banvak/ (pl: -ken) section (of track)

de **baar** /bar/ **1** litter, stretcher **2** ingot, bar: *een ~ goud* a gold bar (*or:* ingot)

de **baard** /bart/ (pl: -en) beard: *hij krijgt de ~ in de keel* his voice is breaking; *zijn ~ laten staan* grow a beard

de **baarmoeder** /barmudər/ (pl: -s) womb

de **baars** /bars/ (pl: baarzen) perch, bass

de **baas** /bas/ (pl: bazen) **1** boss: *de situatie de ~ zijn* be in control of the situation; *je hebt altijd ~ boven ~* there's always s.o. bigger, better, …, there's always a bigger fish **2** boss, owner: *eigen ~ zijn* be one's own boss (*or:* master)

de **baat** /bat/ (pl: baten) **1** benefit, advantage **2** profit(s), benefit

de **babbel** /bɑbəl/ (pl: -s) chat: *hij heeft een vlotte ~* he's a smooth talker

babbelen /bɑbələ(n)/ (babbelde, heeft gebabbeld) chatter, chat

de **babe** /beb/ babe

de **baby** /bebi/ (pl: -'s) baby: *een te vroeg geboren ~* a premature baby

het **babybedje** (baby's) cot

de **babyboom** /bebibu:m/ baby boom

de **babyboomer** /bebibu:mər/ baby boomer

de **babyface** /bebifes/ baby face

de **babyfoon** /bebifon/ (pl: -s) baby alarm

de **babysit** /bebisɪt/ (pl: -s) babysitter

babysitten /bebisɪtə(n)/ (babysitte, heeft gebabysit) babysit

de **babyverzorgingsruimte** (pl: -n, -s) baby care room

de **bachelor** /bɛtʃələr/ (pl: -s) **1** BA, BSc, LL B: *~ zijn* hold a Bachelor's degree **2** Bachelor's degree course; [Am] Bachelor's degree program

de **bacheloropleiding** (pl: -en) bachelor study

de **bacil** /bɑsɪl/ (pl: -len) bacillus, bacterium, germ; bug

de **back** /bɛk/ (pl: -s) back

de **backhand** /bɛkhɛnt/ backhand(er), backhand stroke

de **backpacker** /bɛkpɛkər/ (pl: -s) backpacker

de **backslash** /bɛkslɛʃ/ (pl: -es) backslash

de **back-up** /bɛkʏp/ (pl: -s) backup: *een ~ maken van* make a backup of

het **bacon** /bekən/ bacon

de **bacterie** /bɑkteri/ (pl: bacteriën) bacterium, microbe

bacteriologisch /bɑkterijoloɣis/ (adj) bacteriological, bacterial, microbial

het **bad** /bɑt/ (pl: -en) **1** bath **2** pool

¹**baden** /badə(n)/ (baadde, heeft gebaad) **1** bath; [Am] bathe; (go for a) swim; bathe; take a dip **2** roll (in), wallow (in), swim (in)

²**baden** /badə(n)/ (baadde, heeft gebaad) bath

de **badgast** /bɑtχɑst/ (pl: -en) seaside visitor, bather

het/de **badge** /bɛdʒ/ (pl: -s) (name) badge, (name) tag; insignia

de **badhanddoek** /bɑthɑnduk/ (pl: -en) bath towel

de **badjas** /bɑtjɑs/ (pl: -sen) (bath)robe, bath(ing) wrap

de **badkamer** /bɑtkamər/ (pl: -s) bathroom

de **badkleding** /bɑtkledɪŋ/ swimwear, bathing wear (*or:* gear)

de **badkuip** /bɑtkœyp/ (pl: -en) bathtub, bath

het **badlaken** /bɑtlakə(n)/ (pl: -s) bath towel (*or:* sheet)

de **badmeester** /bɑtmestər/ (pl: -s) bath superintendent (*or:* attendant), lifeguard

het **badminton** /bɛtmɪntɔn/ badminton

badmintonnen /bɛtmɪntɔnə(n)/ (badmintonde, heeft gebadmintond) play badminton

de **badmuts** /bɑtmʏts/ (pl: -en) bathing (*or:* swimming) cap

het **badpak** /bɑtpɑk/ (pl: -ken) swimsuit, bathing suit

de **badplaats** /bɑtplats/ (pl: -en) seaside resort

de **badstof** /bɑtstɔf/ (pl: -fen) towelling, terry (cloth) (*or:* towelling)

het **badwater** /bɑtwatər/ bath water

de **bagage** /baɣaʒə/ (pl: -s) **1** luggage **2** intellectual baggage, stock-in-trade

de **bagagedrager** /baɣaʒədraɣər/ (pl: -s) (rear) carrier

de **bagagekluis** /baɣaʒəklœys/ (pl: -kluizen) (luggage) locker

de **bagageruimte** /baɣaʒərœymtə/ (pl: -n, -s) boot; [Am] trunk

het/de **bagatel** /baɣatɛl/ (pl: -len) bagatelle, trifle

bagatelliseren /baɣatɛlizerə(n)/ (bagatel-

de **bagger** /bɑɣər/ (pl: -s) **1** mud; dredgings **2** rubbish, junk

baggeren /bɑɣərə(n)/ (baggerde, heeft gebaggerd) dredge

bah /bɑ/ (int) ugh!, yuck!

de **Bahama's** /bahamas/ (pl) the Bahamas

de **bahco** /bako/ (pl: -'s) adjustable spanner

Bahrein /bɑxrɛɪn/ Bahrain, Bahrein

de **Bahreiner** /bɑxrɛɪnər/ (pl: -s) Bahraini

Bahreins /bɑxrɛɪns/ (adj) Bahraini

de **bajes** /bajəs/ [inform] can, cooler, jug, stir

de **bajesklant** /bajəsklɑnt/ (pl: -en) [inform] jailbird, lag, con

de **bajonet** /bajonɛt/ (pl: -ten) bayonet

de **bak** /bɑk/ (pl: -ken) **1** (storage) bin; cistern; tank; tray; trough; dish; bowl; tray **2** joke **3** can, jug, clink: *de ~ in* **draaien** go down, be put inside, be put locked up **4** cup (of coffee) || *(vol) aan de ~* **moeten** (have to) pull out all the stops

het **bakbeest** /bɑgbest/ (pl: -en) whopper, monster

het **bakblik** /bɑgblɪk/ (pl: -ken) baking tin, cake tin

het **bakboord** /bɑgbort/ port

het **bakeliet®** /bakəlit/ bakelite

het **baken** /bakə(n)/ (pl: -s) [shipp] beacon

de **bakermat** /bakərmɑt/ (pl: -ten) cradle, origin

de **bakfiets** /bɑkfits/ (pl: -en) **1** carrier tricycle **2** delivery bicycle, carrier cycle

de **bakkebaard** /bɑkəbart/ (pl: -en) (side) whiskers; sideboards; muttonchop; muttonchop whisker

bakkeleien /bɑkəlɛɪə(n)/ (bakkeleide, heeft gebakkeleid) [inform] squabble, wrangle

bakken /bɑkə(n)/ (bakte, heeft gebakken) **1** bake: *vers gebakken* **brood** freshly-baked bread **2** fry; deep-fry: *friet* ~ deep-fry chips

de **bakker** /bɑkər/ (pl: -s) **1** baker **2** bakery, baker's shop: *een* **warme** ~ a fresh bakery || *(dat is)* **voor** *de* ~ that's settled (*or:* fixed)

de **bakkerij** /bɑkərɛɪ/ (pl: -en) bakery, baker's shop

het **bakkie** /bɑki/ (pl: -s) [inform] rig

het **bakmeel** /bɑkmel/ self-raising flour

de **bakpan** /bɑkpɑn/ (pl: -nen) frying pan

de **bakplaat** /bɑkplat/ (pl: bakplaten) baking sheet (*or:* tray)

het **bakpoeder** /bɑkpudər/ baking powder

de **baksteen** /bɑksten/ (pl: bakstenen) brick: *zinken* **als** *een* ~ sink (*or:* swim) like a stone; [fig] *iem. laten vallen* **als** *een* ~ drop s.o. like a hot potato, let s.o. down hard

de **bakvorm** /bɑkfɔrm/ (pl: -en) baking tin, cake tin

het **bakzeil** /bɑksɛɪl/: ~ **halen** back down, climb down (from)

de **¹bal** /bɑl/ (pl: -len) **1** [sport] ball: *iem. de ~* **toespelen** pass (the ball to s.o.); [fig] *een ~letje over iets* **opgooien** put out feelers about sth.; *een ~(letje)* **gehakt** a meatball; *een ~letje* **slaan** hit a ball; [fig] *toen is het ~letje gaan* **rollen** then the ball got rolling; *het kan me* **geen** ~ *schelen* I don't give a damn, I couldn't care less; *wie* **kaatst** *moet de* ~ *verwachten* those who play at bowls must look out for rubbers; [roughly] do as you would be done by **2** snob

het **²bal** /bɑl/ (pl: -s) ball: *gekostumeerd* ~ fancy-dress ball

balanceren /bɑlɑnserə(n)/ (balanceerde, heeft gebalanceerd) balance: ~ **op** *de rand van de dood* hover between life and death

de **balans** /bɑlɑns/ (pl: -en) **1** balance, equilibrium: *uit* *zijn* ~ *zijn* be out of balance **2** (pair of) scales; balance **3** balance sheet, audit (report): *de* ~ **opmaken** a) draw up the balance sheet; b) [fig] take stock (of sth.)

baldadig /bɑldadəx/ (adj, adv) rowdy, boisterous

het/de **baldakijn** /bɑldakɛɪn/ (pl: -en) canopy, baldachin

de **balein** /bɑlɛɪn/ (pl: -en) whalebone, rib

balen /balə(n)/ (baalde, heeft gebaald) be fed up (with), be sick (and tired) (of)

de **balg** /bɑlx/ (pl: -en) bellows

de **balie** /bali/ (pl: -s) **1** counter; desk: *aan de* ~ *verstrekt men u graag alle informatie* you can obtain all the information you need at the desk **2** bar

de **baliemedewerker** /balimedəwɛrkər/ (pl: -s) desk clerk, receptionist

de **balk** /bɑlk/ (pl: -en) beam || *het geld* **over** *de* ~ *gooien* spend money like water

de **Balkan** /bɑlkɑn/ (the) Balkans

balken /bɑlkə(n)/ (balkte, heeft gebalkt) bray

het **balkon** /bɑlkɔn/ (pl: -s) **1** balcony **2** [theatre] balcony, (dress) circle, gallery **3** platform

de **ballade** /bɑladə/ (pl: -n, -s) ballad

de **ballast** /bɑlɑst/ **1** ballast **2** lumber, dead weight; [of people] dead wood

¹ballen /bɑlə(n)/ (balde, heeft gebald) play (with a) ball

²ballen /bɑlə(n)/ (balde, heeft gebald) clench: *de* **vuist(en)** ~ clench one's fist(s)

de **ballenbak** /bɑlə(n)bɑk/ (pl: -ken) ball pit

de **ballenjongen** /bɑlə(n)jɔŋə(n)/ (pl: -s) ball boy

ballerig /adj/ arrogant, loudmouthed, snooty

de **ballerina** /bɑlərina/ ballerina

het **ballet** /bɑlɛt/ (pl: -ten) ballet: *op* ~ *zitten* take ballet lessons

de **balletdanser** /bɑlɛdɑnsər/ (pl: -s) (ballet) dancer

de **balletdanseres** /bɑlɛdɑnsərɛs/ (pl: -sen) ballet dancer het **balletje-balletje** /bɑləcəbɑləcə/ shell game

de **balling** /bɑlɪŋ/ (pl: -en) exile

de **ballingschap** /bɑlɪŋsxɑp/ exile, banishment: *in ~ gaan* go into exile

de **ballon** /bɑlɔn/ (pl: -nen) balloon: *een ~ opblazen* blow up a balloon

de **ballpoint** /bɑlpɔjnt/ (pl: -s) ballpoint

balorig /bɑlorəx/ (adj) contrary, refractory, recalcitrant

de **balpen** /bɑlpɛn/ (pl: -nen) ballpoint (pen)

de **balsamicoazijn** /bɑlsɑmikoazɛɪn/ balsamic vinegar

de **balsem** /bɑlsəm/ (pl: -s) balm, balsam, ointment, salve

balsemen /bɑlsəmə(n)/ (balsemde, heeft gebalsemd) embalm, mummify

Baltisch /bɑltis/ (adj) Baltic: *~e Zee* Baltic (Sea), the Baltic

de **balts** /bɑlts/ display, courtship

de **balustrade** /bɑlystrɑdə/ (pl: -s) balustrade, railing; banister(s)

de **balzaal** /bɑlzal/ (pl: balzalen) ballroom

de **balzak** /bɑlzɑk/ (pl: -ken) scrotum, bag

de **bamastructuur** two-cycle university system

het/de **¹bamboe** /bɑmbu/ bamboo

²bamboe /bɑmbu/ (adj) bamboo

de **bami** /bɑmi/ chow mein: *~ goreng* chow mein, fried noodles

de **ban** /bɑn/ (pl: -nen) **1** excommunication, ban: *in de ~ doen* (put under the) ban, outlaw **2** spell, fascination: *in de ~ van iets raken* fall under the spell of sth.

banaal /bɑnal/ (adj, adv) banal, trite

de **banaan** /bɑnan/ (pl: bananen) banana

de **banaliteit** /bɑnalitɛɪt/ (pl: -en) platitude, cliché

de **bananenschil** /bɑnanə(n)sxɪl/ (pl: -len) banana peel (or: skin): *uitglijden over een ~* slip on a banana skin

bancair /bɑŋkɛːr/ (adj) bank(ing), in (or: of, through) the bank(s): *~ geldverkeer* monetary exchange via the banks

de **¹band** /bɑnt/ (pl: -en) **1** band, ribbon, tape; [karate, judo] belt: *een ~ afspelen* play a tape back; *iets op de ~ opnemen* tape sth.; *zwarte ~* black belt **2** tyre: *een lekke ~* a flat tyre, a puncture **3** conveyor (belt): *de lopende ~* the conveyor belt **4** tie, bond, link, alliance, association: *~en van vriendschap* ties of friendship **5** (wave)band, wave **6** cushion, bank || *aan de lopende ~ doelpunten scoren* pile on scores; *uit de ~ springen* get out of hand; *iets aan ~en leggen* check, curb, restrain sth.

de **²band** /bɛnt/ (pl: -en) band, orchestra; group; combo

het **³band** /bɑnt/ (pl: -en) tape; ribbon; string; band

de **bandage** /bɑndaʒə/ (pl: -s) bandage

bandeloos /bɑndəlos/ (adj) lawless; undisciplined; wild

de **bandenlichter** /bɑndə(n)lɪxtər/ (pl: -s) tyre lever

de **bandenpech** /bɑndə(n)pɛx/ tyre trouble; flat (tyre); puncture

de **bandiet** /bɑndit/ (pl: -en) **1** bandit; brigand **2** hooligan

het **bandje** /bɑncə/ (pl: -s) **1** band, strip, ribbon, string **2** tape **3** tape recording **4** strap

de **bandleider** /bɛntlɛidər/ (pl: -s) bandleader

de **bandopname** /bɑntɔpnamə/ (pl: -n, -s) tape recording

de **bandrecorder** /bɑntrikɔːrdər/ (pl: -s) tape recorder

banen /banə(n)/ (baande, heeft gebaand): *zich een weg ~* work (or: edge) one's way through; *gebaande wegen* beaten track(s)

bang /bɑŋ/ (adj) **1** afraid (of), frightened (of), scared (of); terrified (of): *~ maken* scare, frighten; *~ in het donker* afraid of the dark **2** frightening, anxious, scary **3** timid, fearful **4** afraid, anxious: *ik ben ~ dat het niet lukt* I'm afraid it won't work; *wees daar maar niet ~ voor* don't worry about it

bangelijk /bɑŋələk/ (adj) timid, fearful, chicken-hearted: *~ zijn* be a nervous type, be easily frightened

de **bangerd** /bɑŋərt/ (pl: -s) coward, chicken

Bangladesh /bɑŋladɛʃ/ Bangladesh

de **banier** /bɑnir/ (pl: -en) banner

de **banjo** /bɑnjo/ (pl: -'s) banjo

de **bank** /bɑŋk/ (pl: -en) **1** bench; couch; settee, sofa; seat **2** bank: *geld op de ~ hebben* have money in the bank **3** desk **4** pew **5** bank, shoal || *door de ~ (genomen)* on average

het **bankafschrift** /bɑŋkafsxrɪft/ bank statement

het **bankbiljet** /bɑŋkbɪljɛt/ (pl: -ten) (bank)-note; paper currency

de **bankemployé** /bɑŋkɑmplwaje/ (pl: -s) bank employee

het **banket** /bɑŋkɛt/ (pl: -ten) **1** banquet, feast **2** [roughly] (almond) pastry

de **banketbakker** /bɑŋkɛdbɑkər/ (pl: -s) confectioner, pastry-cook

de **banketbakkerij** /bɑŋkɛdbɑkərɛi/ (pl: -en) confectionery, patisserie, confectioner's (shop)

de **banketletter** /bɑŋkɛtlɛtər/ (pl: -s) (almond) pastry letter

het **bankgeheim** /bɑŋkxəhɛɪm/ bank(ing) secrecy

de **bankhanger** /bɑŋkhaŋər/ (pl: -s) couch potato

de **bankier** /bɑŋkir/ (pl: -s) banker

het **bankje** /bɑŋkjə/ (pl: -s) bench; stool, footrest

de **bankkaart** /bɑŋkart/ (pl: -en) [Belg] bank-(er's) card

de **bankkluis** /bɑŋklœys/ (pl: -kluizen) bank vault (or: strongroom); [for client] safe-deposit box de **bankoverval** /bɑŋkovərvɑl/ (pl: -len) bank hold-up, bank robbery

de **bankpas** /bɑŋkpɑs/ (pl: -sen) bank(er's) card

de **bankrekening** /bɑŋkrekənɪŋ/ (pl: -en) bank account: *een ~ openen bij een bank* open an account with a bank

het **¹bankroet** /bɑŋkrut/ (pl: -en) bankruptcy

²bankroet /bɑŋkrut/ (adj) bankrupt, broke; bust: *~ gaan* go bankrupt; (go) bust

de **bankroof** /bɑŋkrof/ bank robbery

de **bankschroef** /bɑŋksχruf/ (pl: -schroeven) vice

het **bankstel** /bɑŋkstɛl/ (pl: -len) lounge suite

de **bankwerker** /bɑŋkwɛrkər/ (pl: -s) (bench) fitter, benchman

de **banneling** /bɑnəlɪŋ/ (pl: -en) exile

bannen /bɑnə(n)/ (bande, heeft gebannen) exile (from), expel (from); [esp fig] banish: *ban de bom* ban the bomb; *iets uit zijn geheugen ~* efface sth. from one's memory

de **banner** /bɛnər/ (pl: -s) banner

het **bantamgewicht** /bɑntɑmɣəwɪχt/ bantam-(weight)

de **bapao** /bɑpɑu/ Chinese steamed bread

de **¹bar** /bɑr/ (pl: -s) bar: *aan de ~ zitten* sit at the bar; *wie staat er achter de ~?* who's behind the bar?; *hakkenbar* heel bar

²bar /bɑr/ (adj) **1** barren **2** severe: *~ weer* severe weather **3** rough, gross: *jij maakt het wat al te ~* you are carrying things too far ‖ *~ en boos* really dreadful

³bar /bɑr/ (adv) extremely, awfully

de **barak** /bɑrɑk/ (pl: -ken) shed, hut; barracks

de **barbaar** /bɑrbar/ (pl: barbaren) barbarian

barbaars /bɑrbars/ (adj, adv) barbarian, barbarous; barbaric; savage

de **Barbadaan** /bɑrbadan/ (pl: Barbadanen) Barbadian

Barbados /bɑrbedɔs/ Barbados

de **barbecue** /bɑːrbəkju/ (pl: -s) barbecue (party)

barbecueën /bɑːrbəkjuwə(n)/ (barbecuede, heeft gebarbecued) barbecue

de **barbediende** /bɑrbədɪndə/ (pl: -n, -s) barman, barwoman

de **barcode** /bɑrkodə/ (pl: -s) bar code

de **bareel** /bɑrel/ (pl: barelen) [Belg] barrier

het **barema** /bɑrema/ (pl: -'s) [Belg] wage scale, salary scale

baren /bɑrə(n)/ (baarde, heeft gebaard) bear, give birth to

de **barensnood** /bɑrə(n)snot/ labour: *in ~ verkeren* be in labour; be in travail, labour

de **baret** /bɑrɛt/ (pl: -ten) beret, (academic) cap

het **¹Bargoens** /bɑrɣuns/ **1** (thieves') slang, argot **2** jargon

²Bargoens /bɑrɣuns/ (adj) slangy

de **bariton** /bɑritɔn/ (pl: -s) baritone (singer)

de **barjuffrouw** /bɑrjʏfrɑu/ (pl: -en) barmaid

de **barkeeper** /bɑrkipər/ (pl: -s) barman

de **barkruk** /bɑrkrʏk/ (pl: -ken) bar stool

barmhartig /bɑrmhɑrtəχ/ (adj, adv) merciful, charitable: *de ~e Samaritaan* the Good Samaritan

de **barmhartigheid** /bɑrmhɑrtəχɦɛit/ mercy, clemency; charity

het/de **¹barok** /bɑrɔk/ baroque

²barok /bɑrɔk/ (adj) baroque

de **barometer** /bɑrometər/ (pl: -s) barometer: *de ~ staat op mooi weer* (or: *storm*) **a)** the barometer is set fair (*or:* is pointing to storm); **b)** [fig] things are looking good (*or:* bad)

de **baron** /bɑrɔn/ (pl: -nen) baron: *meneer de ~* his (*or:* your) Lordship

de **barones** /bɑrɔnɛs/ (pl: -sen) baroness

de **barrage** /bɑraʒə/ (pl: -s) [sport] decider, play-off

de **barricade** /bɑrikadə/ (pl: -n) **1** barricade: *voor iets op de ~ gaan staan* [fig] fight on the barricades for sth.; *~n opwerpen* raise (*or:* throw up) barricades **2** [fig] barrier

barricaderen /bɑrikadərə(n)/ (barricadeerde, heeft gebarricadeerd) barricade; bar

de **barrière** /bɑrijɛːrə/ (pl: -s) barrier: *een onoverkomelijke ~* an insurmountable barrier

bars /bɑrs/ (adj, adv) stern, grim; forbidding; harsh

de **barst** /bɑrst/ (pl: -en) crack; chap: *er komen ~en in* it is cracking ‖ *ik geloof er geen ~ van* I'm not buying that, I don't believe a single word of it

barsten /bɑrstə(n)/ (barstte, is gebarsten) **1** crack, split; burst; chap; get chapped **2** burst, explode ‖ *het barst hier van de cafés* the place is full of pubs; *iem. laten ~* leave s.o. in the lurch

de **bas** /bɑs/ (pl: -sen) **1** bass (singer, player); basso **2** double bass, (contra)bass: *~ spelen* play the bass **3** bass (guitar)

basaal /bɑzal/ (adj) basal, fundamental, basic

het **basalt** /bɑzɑlt/ basalt

de **¹base** /bɑzə/ (pl: -n) base

de **²base** /bes/ free-base cocaine

het **baseball** /bezbɔːl/ baseball

baseballen /bezbɔlə(n)/ (baseballde, heeft gebaseballd) play baseball

¹baseren /bɑzerə(n)/ (baseerde, heeft gebaseerd) base (on), found (on)

zich **²baseren** /bɑzerə(n)/ (baseerde zich, heeft zich gebaseerd) base o.s. on, go on: *we hadden niets om ons op te ~* we had nothing to go on

de **basgitaar** /bɑsχitar/ (pl: basgitaren) bass (guitar)

het **basilicum** /bɑzilikʏm/ basil

de **basiliek** /bɑzilik/ (pl: -en) basilica

de **basis** /bɑzɪs/ (pl: bases) **1** basis, foundation: *de ~ leggen voor iets* lay the foundation of sth. **2** base, basis

de **basisbeurs** /bɑzɪzbørs/ (pl: -beurzen) basic grant

basisch /bazis/ (adj, adv) alkaline, basic: ~
reageren give (*or:* show) an alkaline reaction; ~*e zouten* basic salts

de **basiscursus** /bazɪskʏrzʏs/ (pl: -sen) basic
course, elementary course

het **basisinkomen** /bazɪsɪŋkomə(n)/ (pl: -s)
1 guaranteed minimum income **2** basic income

het **basisonderwijs** /bazɪsɔndərwɛis/ primary
education

de **basisopstelling** /bazɪsɔpstɛlɪŋ/ (pl: -en)
(the team's) starting line-up

de **basisoptie** /bazɪsɔpsi/ (pl: -s) [Belg] orientation subjects

de **basisschool** /bazɪsχol/ (pl: -scholen) primary school

de **basisverzekering** /bazɪsfərzekərɪŋ/ (pl:
-en) basic (health) insurance (*or:* policy)

de **basisvorming** /bazɪsfɔrmɪŋ/ basic (secondary school) curriculum

de **Bask** /bɑsk/ (pl: -en) Basque
Baskenland /bɑskə(n)lɑnt/ the Basque
Country

het **basketbal** /bɑːskədbɑl/ basketball
basketballen /bɑːskədbɑlə(n)/ (basketbalde, heeft gebasketbald) play basketball

het **Baskisch** /bɑskis/ Basque

het **bassin** /bɑsɛ̃/ (pl: -s) **1** (swimming) pool
2 basin

de **bassist** /bɑsɪst/ (pl: -en) bass player

de **bassleutel** /bɑsløtəl/ (pl: -s) bass clef, F clef

de **bast** /bɑst/ (pl: -en) **1** bark; husk **2** [inform]
skin, hide
basta /bɑsta/ (int) stop!, enough!: *en daarmee* ~*!* and there's an end to it!

de **bastaard** /bɑstart/ (pl: -s) **1** bastard
2 mongrel, cross-breed **3** hybrid, cross(-breed)

de **basterdsuiker** /bɑstərtsœykər/ soft brown
sugar

het **bastion** /bɑstijɔn/ (pl: -s) bastion

het **bat** /bɛt/ (pl: -s) bat

het **bataljon** /bɑtaljɔn/ (pl: -s) battalion

de **Batavier** /bɑtavir/ (pl: -en) Batavian

de **bate** /bɑtə/: *ten ~ van* for the benefit of
baten /bɑtə(n)/ (baatte, heeft gebaat) avail:
wij zouden erbij gebaat zijn it would be very
helpful to us; *baat het niet, dan schaadt het
niet* no harm in trying
batig /bɑtəχ/ (adj): ~ *saldo* surplus, credit
balance
batikken /bɑtɪkə(n)/ (batikte, heeft gebatikt) batik: *gebatikte stoffen* batiks

het **batje** /bɛcə/ bat

de **batterij** /bɑtərɛi/ (pl: -en) battery: *lege* ~
dead battery

de **batterijlader** battery charger

het **bauxiet** /bouksit/ bauxite

de **baviaan** /bɑvijan/ (pl: bavianen) baboon

de **baxter** /bɛkstər/ (pl: -s) [Belg; med] drip

de **bazaar** /bazɑr/ (pl: -s) bazaar; (fancy)fair

bazelen /bazələ(n)/ (bazelde, heeft gebazeld) drivel (on), waffle
bazig /bazəχ/ (adj, adv) overbearing, domineering, bossy

de **bazin** /bazɪn/ (pl: -nen) **1** mistress **2** lady of
the house

het **beachvolleybal** /biːtʃfɔlibɑl/ beach volleyball
beademen /bəademə(n)/ (beademde,
heeft beademd) **1** breathe air into **2** apply
artificial respiration to

de **beademing** /bəadəmɪŋ/ (pl: -en) **1** breathing of air into **2** artificial respiration: *aan de* ~
liggen be on a ventilator

de **beambte** /bəɑmtə/ (pl: -n, -s) functionary,
(junior) official
beamen /bəamə(n)/ (beaamde, heeft beaamd) endorse; agree (with): *een bewering* ~
endorse a claim

de **beamer** /biːmər/ data projector
beangstigen /bəɑŋstəχə(n)/ (beangstigde,
heeft beangstigd) alarm; frighten

¹**beantwoorden** /bəɑntwordə(n)/ (beantwoordde, heeft beantwoord) answer, meet,
comply with: *aan* al de vereisten ~ meet all the
requirements; *niet* ~ *aan* de verwachtingen fall
short of expectations

²**beantwoorden** /bəɑntwordə(n)/ (beantwoordde, heeft beantwoord) answer; reply
to
beargumenteren /bəɑrɣʏmɛnterə(n)/ (beargumenteerde, heeft beargumenteerd)
substantiate: *zijn standpunt kunnen* ~ be able
to substantiate one's point of view

de **beat** /biːt/ (pl: -s) beat

de **beatbox** /biːdbɔks/ (pl: -en) beatbox

de **beauty** /bjuːti/ (pl: -'s) beauty: *een ~ van een
doelpunt* a lovely (*or:* beautiful) goal, a beauty

de **beautycase** /bjuːtikes/ (pl: -s) vanity case
bebloed /bəblut/ (adj) bloody, blood-stained: *zijn gezicht* was geheel ~ his face was
completely covered in blood
beboeten /bəbutə(n)/ (beboette, heeft beboet) fine: *beboet worden* be fined, incur a
fine; *iem.* ~ *met* 100 euro fine s.o. 100 euros
bebossen /bəbɔsə(n)/ (beboste, heeft bebost) (af)forest: *bebost terrein* woodland
bebouwd /bəbɑut/ (adj) built-on: *de* ~*e
kom* the built-up area
bebouwen /bəbɑuwə(n)/ (bebouwde,
heeft bebouwd) **1** build on **2** cultivate, farm:
de grond ~ cultivate the land

de **bebouwing** /bəbɑuwɪŋ/ (pl: -en) buildings:
[Belg] *halfopen* ~ semidetached house
becijferen /bəsɛifərə(n)/ (becijferde, heeft
becijferd) calculate; compute; estimate: *de
schade valt niet te* ~ it is impossible to calculate the damage
becommentariëren /bəkɔmɛntarijerə(n)/
(becommentarieerde, heeft becommentari-

eerd) comment (on)

beconcurreren /bəkɔŋkyrɛ̲rə(n)/ (beconcurreerde, heeft beconcurreerd) compete with: *de banken ~ elkaar scherp* there is fierce competition among the banks

het **bed** /bɛt/ (pl: -den) bed: *het ~ (moeten) houden* be confined to bed; *haar ~je is gespreid* she has got it made; *het ~ opmaken* make the bed; *naar ~ gaan* go to bed; *naar ~ gaan met iem.* go to bed with s.o.; *hij gaat ermee naar ~ en staat er weer mee op* he can't stop thinking about it; *dat is ver van mijn ~* that does not concern me; *een ~ rozen* a bed of roses

bedaard /bəda̲rt/ (adj, adv) **1** composed, collected **2** calm, quiet: *~ optreden* act calmly

bedacht /bəda̲xt/ (adj) prepared (for): *op zoveel verzet waren ze niet ~ geweest* they had not bargained for so much resistance

bedachtzaam /bəda̲xtsam/ (adj, adv) cautious, circumspect; deliberate: *heel ~ te werk gaan* set about sth. with great caution

de **bedankbrief** /bəda̲ŋkbrif/ (pl: -brieven) letter of thanks

¹**bedanken** /bəda̲ŋkə(n)/ (bedankte, heeft bedankt) decline, refuse

²**bedanken** /bəda̲ŋkə(n)/ (bedankte, heeft bedankt) thank: *iem. voor iets ~* thank s.o. for sth.

het **bedankje** /bəda̲ŋkjə/ (pl: -s) thank-you; letter of thanks; word of thanks: *er kon nauwelijks een ~ af!* (and) small thanks I got (for it)!

bedankt /bəda̲ŋkt/ (int) thanks: *reuze ~* thanks a lot

bedaren /bəda̲rə(n)/ (bedaarde, heeft bedaard) quiet down, calm down: *iem. tot ~ brengen* calm (or: quieten) s.o. down

het **beddengoed** /bɛ̲də(n)ɣut/ (bed)clothes, bedding

de **beddensprei** /bɛ̲də(n)sprɛi/ (pl: -en) bedspread

de **bedding** /bɛ̲dɪŋ/ (pl: -en) bed, channel

bedeesd /bəde̲st/ (adj) shy, diffident, timid

bedekken /bəde̲kə(n)/ (bedekte, heeft bedekt) cover; cover up; cover over: *geheel ~ met iets* cover in sth.

de **bedekking** /bəde̲kɪŋ/ (pl: -en) cover(ing)

bedekt /bəde̲kt/ (adj) **1** covered; overcast **2** covert: *in ~e termen* in guarded terms

de **bedelaar** /be̲dəlar/ (pl: -s) beggar

de **bedelarij** /bedəlarɛi̲/ begging

de **bedelarmband** /be̲dəlɑrmbɑnt/ (pl: -en) charm bracelet

de **bedelbrief** /be̲dəlbrif/ (pl: -brieven) begging-letter

bedelen /be̲dələ(n)/ (bedelde, heeft gebedeld) beg (for)

de **bedelstaf** /be̲dəlstɑf/: *aan de ~ raken* be reduced to beggary, be left a pauper

het **bedeltje** /be̲dəlcə/ (pl: -s) charm

bedelven /bədɛ̲lvə(n)/ (bedolf, heeft bedolven) bury; [fig also] swamp: *zij werden door het puin bedolven* they were buried under the rubble

bedenkelijk /bəde̲ŋkələk/ (adj, adv) **1** worrying; dubious; questionable; serious: *een ~ geval* a worrying (or: serious) case **2** doubtful, dubious: *een ~ gezicht* a doubtful (or: serious) face

¹**bedenken** /bəde̲ŋkə(n)/ (bedacht, heeft bedacht) **1** think (about), consider: *als je bedenkt, dat …* considering (or: bearing in mind) (that) … **2** think of, think up, invent, devise

zich ²**bedenken** /bəde̲ŋkə(n)/ (bedacht zich, heeft zich bedacht) **1** think (about), consider: *zij zal zich wel tweemaal ~ voordat …* she'll think twice before …; *zonder zich te ~* without a moment's thought **2** change one's mind, have second thoughts

de **bedenking** /bəde̲ŋkɪŋ/ (pl: -en) objection: *~en hebben tegen iets* have objections to sth.

het **bedenksel** /bəde̲ŋksəl/ (pl: -s) fabrication

de **bedenktijd** /bəde̲ŋktɛit/ time for reflection: *hij kreeg drie dagen ~* he was given three days to think (the matter over) (or: to consider (the matter))

het **bederf** /bəde̲rf/ decay, rot

bederfelijk /bəde̲rfələk/ (adj) perishable: *~e goederen* perishables

¹**bederven** /bəde̲rvə(n)/ (bedierf, is bedorven) decay, rot

²**bederven** /bəde̲rvə(n)/ (bedierf, heeft bedorven) spoil: *die jurk is totaal bedorven* that dress is completely ruined; *iemands plezier ~* spoil s.o.'s fun

de **bedevaart** /be̲dəvart/ (pl: -en) pilgrimage: *een ~ doen* make (or: go) on a pilgrimage

de **bedevaartganger** /be̲dəvartɣɑŋər/ (pl: -s) pilgrim

het **bedevaartsoord** /be̲dəvartsort/ (pl: -en) place of pilgrimage

de **bediende** /bədi̲ndə/ (pl: -n, -s) **1** employee; clerk; assistant; attendant: *jongste ~* a) office junior; b) dogsbody **2** servant: *eerste ~* butler **3** [Belg] official

¹**bedienen** /bədi̲nə(n)/ (bediende, heeft bediend) **1** serve: *iem. op zijn wenken ~* wait on s.o. hand and foot; *aan tafel ~* wait at (the) table **2** operate

zich ²**bedienen** /bədi̲nə(n)/ (bediende zich, heeft zich bediend) use, make use of

de **bediening** /bədi̲nɪŋ/ (pl: -en) **1** service: *al onze prijzen zijn inclusief ~* all prices include service (charges) **2** operation: *de ~ van een apparaat* the operation of a machine

het **bedieningspaneel** /bədi̲nɪŋspanel/ (pl: -panelen) control panel; dash(board); [comp] console

het **beding** /bədɪ̲ŋ/ (pl: -en) condition, stipulation: *onder geen ~* under no circumstances

bedingen /bədɪŋə(n)/ (bedong, heeft bedongen) stipulate (for, that); insist on; require; agree (on)

bedisselen /bədɪsələ(n)/ (bedisselde, heeft bedisseld) fix (up), arrange

het **bedlampje** /bɛtlɑmpjə/ (pl: -s) bedside lamp, bedhead light

bedlegerig /bɛtleɣərəx/ (adj) ill in bed; bedridden

de **bedoeïen** /beduwin/ (pl: -en) Bedouin

bedoelen /bədulə(n)/ (bedoelde, heeft bedoeld) mean, intend: *wat bedoel je?* what do you mean?; *het was goed bedoeld* it was meant well (*or:* well meant); ~ **met** mean by

de **bedoeling** /bədulɪŋ/ (pl: -en) **1** intention, aim, purpose, object: *dat was niet de ~* that was not intended (*or:* the intention); *met de ~ om te …* with a view to (…ing); *hij zei dat zonder kwade ~en* he meant no harm by saying that **2** meaning; drift

de **bedoening** /bədunɪŋ/ (pl: -en) to-do, job, fuss: *het was een hele ~* it was quite a business

bedolven /bədɔlvə(n)/ (adj) **1** covered (with) **2** snowed under (with), swamped (with): *~ onder het werk* snowed under with work, up to one's ears in work

bedompt /bədɔmt/ (adj) stuffy; close; airless; stale: *een ~e atmosfeer* a stuffy atmosphere

bedonderen /bədɔndərə(n)/ (bedonderde, heeft bedonderd) [inform] cheat (on), trick, do (in the eye): *de kluit ~* take everybody for a ride

bedorven /bədɔrvə(n)/ (adj) bad, off; [fig] spoilt: *de melk is ~* the milk has gone off

bedotten /bədɔtə(n)/ (bedotte, heeft bedot) fool, take in

bedplassen /bɛtplɑsə(n)/ bed-wetting

de **bedrading** /bədradɪŋ/ (pl: -en) wiring, circuit

het **bedrag** /bədrɑx/ (pl: -en) **1** amount **2** sum: *een rond ~* a round sum; *een ~ ineens* a lump sum

bedragen /bədraɣə(n)/ (bedroeg, heeft bedragen) amount to; number; come to be

bedreigen /bədrɛiɣə(n)/ (bedreigde, heeft bedreigd) threaten: *bedreigde (dier- of planten)soorten* endangered species

de **bedreiging** /bədrɛiɣɪŋ/ (pl: -en) threat: *onder ~ van een vuurwapen* at gunpoint

bedreven /bədrevə(n)/ (adj) adept (at, in); skilled (in); skilful (in); (well-)versed (in): *niet ~ zijn in iets* lack experience in sth.

bedriegen /bədriɣə(n)/ (bedroog, heeft bedrogen) deceive, cheat; swindle: *als mijn ogen me niet ~* if my eyes do not deceive me; *hij bedriegt zijn vrouw* he cheats on his wife

de **bedrieger** /bədriɣər/ (pl: -s) cheat, fraud, impostor; swindler

bedrieglijk /bədrixlək/ (adj, adv) deceptive, false; deceitful; fraudulent: *dit licht is ~* this light is deceptive

het **bedrijf** /bədrɛif/ (pl: bedrijven) **1** business, company, enterprise, firm; [large] concern; farm: *gemengd ~* mixed farm; *openbare bedrijven* public services **2** act **3** operation; (working) order: *buiten ~ zijn* be out of order

de **bedrijfsadministratie** /bədrɛifsɑtministra(t)si/ business administration; business accountancy, industrial accountancy

de **bedrijfsarts** /bədrɛifsɑrts/ (pl: -en) company doctor, company medical officer

de **bedrijfscultuur** /bədrɛifskʏltyr/ (pl: -culturen) corporate culture

de **bedrijfseconomie** /bədrɛifsekonomi/ business economics, industrial economics

het **bedrijfskapitaal** /bədrɛifskapital/ (pl: -kapitalen) working capital

bedrijfsklaar /bədrɛifsklar/ (adj) in working order, in running order: *~ maken* put into working (*or:* running) order

de **bedrijfskunde** /bədrɛifskʏndə/ business administration, management

de **bedrijfsleider** /bədrɛifslɛidər/ (pl: -s) manager

de **bedrijfsleiding** /bədrɛifslɛidɪŋ/ (pl: -en) management, board (of directors)

het **bedrijfsleven** /bədrɛifslevə(n)/ business, trade and industry: *het particuliere ~* private enterprise

het **bedrijfsongeval** /bədrɛifsɔŋɣəval/ (pl: -len) industrial accident; [fig] unfortunate accident

het **bedrijfsresultaat** /bədrɛifsrezʏltat/ trading results, company results

de **bedrijfsrevisor** /bədrɛifsrevizɔr/ (pl: -s, -en) [Belg] auditor

de **bedrijfsruimte** /bədrɛifsrœymtə/ (pl: -n, -s) working (*or:* business) accommodation, work(ing) space

de **bedrijfssluiting** /bədrɛifslœytɪŋ/ (pl: -en) shutdown, close-down

de **bedrijfstak** /bədrɛifstɑk/ (pl: -ken) sector, industry, trade (*or:* business) (sector)

de **bedrijfsvereniging** /bədrɛifsfərenəɣɪŋ/ (pl: -en) industrial insurance board

de **bedrijfsvoering** /bədrɛifsfurɪŋ/ management

bedrijfszeker /bədrɛifsekər/ (adj) reliable

bedrijven /bədrɛivə(n)/ (bedreef, heeft bedreven) commit, perpetrate

bedrijvend /bədrɛivənt/ (adj): *de ~e vorm van een werkwoord* the active voice of a verb

het **bedrijvenpark** /bədrɛivə(n)park/ (pl: -en) business park; industrial estate; [Am] industrial park

bedrijvig /bədrɛivəx/ (adj) active, busy; industrious; bustling: *een ~ type* an industrious type

de **bedrijvigheid** /bədrɛivəxhɛit/ activity, busyness, industriousness: *economische ~* economic activity; *koortsachtige* ~ feverish activity

zich **bedrinken** /bədrɪ̃ŋkə(n)/ (bedronk zich, heeft zich bedronken) get drunk

bedroefd /bədru̱ft/ (adj) sad (about), dejected; upset (about), distressed (about)

de **bedroefdheid** /bədru̱ftɦɛit/ sadness, sorrow, dejection, distress

bedroeven /bədru̱və(n)/ (bedroefde, heeft bedroefd) [form] sadden, grieve

¹**bedroevend** /bədru̱vənt/ (adj) **1** sad(dening), depressing **2** pathetic: *~e resultaten* pitiful results

²**bedroevend** /bədru̱vənt/ (adv) pathetically, miserably: *zijn werk is ~ slecht* his work is lamentable

het **bedrog** /bədrɔ̱x/ **1** deceit, deception; fraud; swindle: *~ plegen* cheat, swindle, deceive, commit fraud **2** deception, delusion: *optisch ~* optical illusion

bedruipen /bədrœy̯pə(n)/ (bedroop, heeft bedropen): *zichzelf (kunnen) ~* be able to pay one's way (*or:* support) o.s.

bedrukken /bədry̱kə(n)/ (bedrukte, heeft bedrukt) print, inscribe

bedrukt /bədry̱kt/ (adj) dejected, depressed

de **bedtijd** /bɛ̱tɛit/ bedtime

beducht /bədy̱xt/ (adj) anxious (for): *~ zijn voor zijn reputatie* be concerned (*or:* anxious) for one's reputation

beduiden /bədœy̯də(n)/ (beduidde, heeft beduid) signal, motion, indicate: *de agent beduidde mij te stoppen* the policeman signalled (to) me to stop

beduidend /bədœy̯dənt/ (adj, adv) significant, considerable: *~ minder* considerably less

beduimeld /bədœy̯məlt/ (adj) well-thumbed: *een ~ boek* a well-thumbed book

beduusd /bədy̱st/ (adj) taken aback, flabbergasted

beduvelen /bədy̱vələ(n)/ (beduvelde, heeft beduveld) [inform] cheat (on), trick, do (in the eye); [fin also] swindle

het **bedwang** /bədwɑ̱ŋ/ control, restraint: *iem. in ~ houden* keep s.o. in check

bedwelmen /bədwɛ̱lmə(n)/ (bedwelmde, heeft bedwelmd) stun, stupefy; intoxicate

bedwingen /bədwɪ̱ŋə(n)/ (bedwong, heeft bedwongen) suppress, subdue; restrain: *zijn tranen ~* hold back one's tears; *zich niet langer kunnen ~* lose control (of (*or:* over) o.s.)

beëdigd /bəe̱dəxt/ (adj) sworn; chartered: *~ getuige* sworn witness

beëdigen /bəe̱dəɣə(n)/ (beëdigde, heeft beëdigd) swear (in), administer an oath to: *een getuige ~* swear (in) a witness

de **beëdiging** /bəe̱dəxɪŋ/ (pl: -en) **1** swearing, confirmation on oath **2** swearing (in), administration of the oath

beëindigen /bəɛ̱indəɣə(n)/ (beëindigde,

heeft beëindigd) **1** end, finish; complete: *een vriendschap ~* break off a friendship **2** end; close; discontinue; terminate

de **beek** /bek/ (pl: beken) brook, stream

het **beeld** /belt/ (pl: -en) **1** statue, sculpture **2** picture, image; view; illustration: *in ~ zijn* be on (the screen); *in ~ brengen* show (a picture, pictures of); *zich een ~ van iets vormen* form a picture (*or:* an image) of sth., visualize sth. **3** picture, description

de **beeldbuis** /be̱ltbœys/ (pl: -buizen) **1** cathode ray tube **2** screen; box: *elke avond voor de ~ zitten* sit in front of the box every evening

beeldend /be̱ldənt/ (adj, adv) plastic, expressive: *~e kunst* visual arts

de **beeldenstorm** /be̱ldə(n)stɔrm/ (pl: -en) **1** [fig] image breaking **2** iconoclasm

beeldhouwen /be̱lthɑuwə(n)/ (beeldhouwde, heeft gebeeldhouwd) sculpture, sculpt; carve

de **beeldhouwer** /be̱lthɑuwər/ (pl: -s) sculptor, sculptress; woodcarver

de **beeldhouwkunst** /be̱lthɑukʏnst/ sculpture

het **beeldhouwwerk** /be̱lthɑuwɛrk/ (pl: -en) sculpture; carving

beeldig /be̱ldəx/ (adj, adv) gorgeous, adorable: *die jas staat je ~* that coat looks gorgeous on you

het **beeldmerk** /be̱ltmɛrk/ (pl: -en) logo(type)

het/de **beeldpunt** /be̱ltpʏnt/ (pl: -en) pixel

het **beeldscherm** /be̱ltsxɛrm/ (pl: -en) (TV, television) screen; [comp] display

beeldschoon /beltsxo̱n/ (adj) gorgeous, ravishingly (*or:* stunningly) beautiful

de **beeldspraak** /be̱ltsprak/ (pl: -spraken) metaphor, imagery, metaphorical language, figurative language

de **beeldvorming** /be̱ltfɔrmɪŋ/ formation of an image: *bijdragen tot een bepaalde ~* help to create (*or:* establish) a certain image

de **beeltenis** /be̱ltənɪs/ (pl: -sen) likeness; effigy, image

het **been** /ben/ (pl: benen) **1** leg; [in expressions often] foot: *op eigen benen staan* stand on one's own (two) feet; *hij is met het verkeerde ~ uit bed gestapt* he got out of bed on the wrong side; *de benen nemen* run for it; *met beide benen op de grond staan* [fig] have one's feet firmly on the ground; *op de ~ blijven* remain on one's feet, keep going; [fig] *op zijn achterste benen gaan staan* rise up in arms **2** leg **3** bone **4** bones **5** [maths] side, leg: *de benen van een driehoek* the sides of an triangle

de **beenbeschermer** /be̱mbəsxɛrmər/ (pl: -s) leg-guard, pad

de **beenbreuk** /be̱mbrøk/ (pl: -en) fracture of the leg: *gecompliceerde ~* compound fracture (of the leg) de **beenham** /bεnhɑm/ ham off the bone

de **beenhouwer** /bεnhɑuwər/ (pl: -s) [Belg] butcher

de **beenhouwerij** /benhɑuwərεi̯/ (pl: -en) [Belg] butcher's shop

het **beenmerg** /bεmεrχ/ bone marrow

de **beenruimte** /bεnrœymtə/ legroom

de **beer** /ber/ (pl: beren) **1** bear; (bear) cub **2** boar

de **beerput** /berpʏt/ (pl: -ten) cesspool; cesspit: [fig] *de ~ opentrekken* blow (*or:* take) the lid off

het **beest** /best/ (pl: -en) **1** beast; animal: [fig] *het ~je bij zijn naam noemen* call a spade a spade **2** animal; beast; cattle **3** creepy-crawly ‖ [fig] *de ~ uithangen* behave like an animal; paint the town red

¹**beestachtig** /bestɑχtəχ/ (adj) bestial; brutal; savage

²**beestachtig** /bestɑχtəχ/ (adv) terribly, dreadfully

de **beet** /bet/ (pl: beten) bite

beetgaar /betχɑr/ (adj) al dente

¹**beethebben** /bεthεbə(n)/ (had beet, heeft beetgehad) [fishing] have a bite

²**beethebben** /bεthεbə(n)/ (had beet, heeft beetgehad) **1** have (got) (a) hold of **2** take in, cheat, fool; make a fool of

het ¹**beetje** /becə/ (pl: -s) (little) bit, little: *een ~ Frans kennen* know a little French, have a smattering of French; *een ~ melk graag* a little milk (*or:* a drop of milk), please; *bij stukjes en bij ~s* bit by bit, little by little; *alle ~s helpen* every little helps; *een ~ technicus verhelpt dat zo* anyone who calls himself a technician could fix that in a jiffy; *een ~ kantoor heeft een koffieautomaat* any self-respecting office has got a coffee machine

²**beetje** /becə/ (adv) (a) (little) bit, (a) little, rather: *dat is een ~ weinig* that's not very much; *een ~ vervelend zijn* a) be a bit of a nuisance, be rather annoying; b) be rather boring, be a bit of a bore; *een ~ opschieten* get a move on

beetnemen /betnemə(n)/ (nam beet, heeft beetgenomen) take in, make a fool of, fool: *je bent beetgenomen!* you've been had!

beetpakken /betpɑkə(n)/ (pakte beet, heeft beetgepakt) lay hold of, get one's (*or:* lay) hands on

befaamd /bəfɑmt/ (adj) famous, renowned

begaafd /bəɣɑft/ (adj) **1** gifted, talented **2** gifted (with), endowed (with)

de **begaafdheid** /bəɣɑfthεit/ **1** talent, ability; intelligence; genius **2** talent (for), gift (for)

¹**begaan** /bəɣɑn/: *iem. laten ~* let s.o. do as he/she likes (*or:* pleases)

²**begaan** /bəɣɑn/ (beging, heeft begaan) commit; [mistakes also] make

begaanbaar /bəɣɑmbɑr/ (adj) passable, practicable

begeerlijk /bəɣerlək/ (adj, adv) desirable; eligible

de **begeerte** /bəɣertə/ (pl: -n) desire (for), wish (for), craving (for)

begeleiden /bəɣəlεidə(n)/ (begeleidde, heeft begeleid) **1** accompany, escort **2** guide, counsel, support; supervise; coach **3** accompany [mus also]; go with

begeleidend /bəɣəlεidənt/ (adj) accompanying, attendant: *~e muziek* incidental music

de **begeleider** /bəɣəlεidər/ (pl: -s) **1** companion; escort **2** guide, counsellor; supervisor; coach **3** [mus] accompanist

de **begeleiding** /bəɣəlεidɪŋ/ (pl: -en) **1** accompaniment, accompanying; escort(ing) **2** guidance, counselling, support; supervision; coaching: *de ~ na de operatie was erg goed* the follow-up care after the operation was very good; *onder ~ van* under the guidance of **3** [mus] accompaniment

begeren /bəɣerə(n)/ (begeerde, heeft begeerd) desire, crave, long for: *alles wat zijn hartje maar kon ~* all one could possibly wish for

begerenswaardig /bəɣerənswɑrdəχ/ (adj) desirable; eligible; enviable

begerig /bəɣerəχ/ (adj, adv) desirous (of), longing (for), eager (for); hungry (for): *~e blikken* hungry looks

¹**begeven** /bəɣevə(n)/ (begaf, heeft begeven) **1** break down, fail; collapse; give way: *de auto kan het elk ogenblik ~* the car is liable to break down any minute **2** forsake, leave, fail: *zijn stem begaf het* his voice broke

zich ²**begeven** /bəɣevə(n)/ (begaf zich, heeft zich begeven) proceed; embark (on, upon); adjourn (to): *zich op weg ~ (naar)* set out (for)

begieten /bəɣitə(n)/ (begoot, heeft begoten) water, wet

begiftigd /bəɣɪftəχt/ (adj): *~ met grote muzikaliteit* endowed (*or:* gifted) with great musical talent

het **begin** /bəɣɪn/ beginning, start; opening: *~ mei* early in May, (at) the beginning of May; *een veelbelovend ~* a promising start; *dit is nog maar het ~* this is only the beginning; *een ~ maken met iets* begin (*or:* start) sth.; *(weer) helemaal bij het ~ beginnen* (have to) start from scratch; *in het ~* at the beginning; at first, initially; *een boek van ~ tot eind lezen* read a book from cover to cover; *een goed ~ is het halve werk* well begun is half done; the first blow is half the battle

de **beginletter** /bəɣɪnlεtər/ (pl: -s) initial letter, first letter; initial

de **beginneling** /bəɣɪnəlɪŋ/ (pl: -en) beginner, novice

¹**beginnen** /bəɣɪnə(n)/ (begon, is begonnen) **1** begin, start (to do sth., doing sth.); commence; set about (doing): [inform] *begin maar!* go ahead!; fire away!; *laten we ~* let's

get started; *het begint er op te lijken* that's more like it; *weer van voren af aan moeten ~* go back to square one; *hij begon met te zeggen …* he began by saying …; *het begint donker te worden* it is getting dark; *je weet niet waar je aan begint* you don't know what you are letting yourself in for **2** (+ over) bring up, raise: *over politiek ~* bring up politics; *over iets anders ~* change the subject ‖ *daar kunnen we niet aan ~* that's out of the question; *om te ~ …* for a start …; *voor zichzelf ~* start one's own business

²**beginnen** /bəɣɪnə(n)/ (begon, is begonnen) begin, start; open: *een gesprek ~* begin (*or:* start) a conversation; *een zaak ~* start a business

de **beginner** /bəɣɪnər/ (pl: -s) beginner: *cursus voor ~s* beginners' course

het **beginpunt** /bəɣɪmpʏnt/ (pl: -en) starting point, point of departure

het **beginsalaris** /bəɣɪnsalarɪs/ starting (*or:* initial) salary

het **beginsel** /bəɣɪnsəl/ (pl: -en) principle, rudiment: *in ~* in principle

de **beginselverklaring** /bəɣɪnsəlvərklarɪŋ/ (pl: -en) statement (*or:* declaration) of principles; manifesto

de **beglazing** /bəɣlazɪŋ/ (pl: -en) glazing

begluren /bəɣlyrə(n)/ (begluurde, heeft begluurd) peep at, spy on

de **begonia** /bəɣonija/ (pl: -'s) begonia

de **begraafplaats** /bəɣrafplats/ (pl: -en) cemetery, graveyard, burial ground

de **begrafenis** /bəɣrafənɪs/ (pl: -sen) **1** funeral **2** burial

de **begrafenisondernemer** /bəɣrafənɪsɔndərnemər/ (pl: -s) undertaker, funeral director

de **begrafenisonderneming** /bəɣrafənɪsɔndərnemɪŋ/ (pl: -en) undertaker's (business), funeral parlour; [Am] funeral home

de **begrafenisstoet** /bəɣrafənɪstut/ (pl: -en) funeral procession

begraven /bəɣravə(n)/ (begroef, heeft begraven) bury: *dood en ~ zijn* be dead and gone

begrensd /bəɣrɛnst/ (adj) limited, finite, restricted

begrenzen /bəɣrɛnzə(n)/ (begrensde, heeft begrensd) **1** border: *door de zee begrensd* bordered by the sea **2** [fig] define **3** limit, restrict

¹**begrijpelijk** /bəɣrɛipələk/ (adj) **1** understandable, comprehensible, intelligible **2** natural, obvious: *dat is nogal ~* that is hardly surprising; *het is heel ~ dat hij bang is* it's only natural that he should be frightened

²**begrijpelijk** /bəɣrɛipələk/ (adv) clearly

begrijpen /bəɣrɛipə(n)/ (begreep, heeft begrepen) **1** understand, comprehend, grasp: *hij begreep de hint* he took the hint, he

got the message; *dat kan ik ~* I (can) understand that; *o, ik begrijp het* oh, I see; *laten we dat goed ~* let's get that clear; *begrijp je me nog?* are you still with me?; *dat laat je voortaan, begrepen!* I'll have no more of that, is that clear? (*or:* do you hear?); *als je begrijpt wat ik bedoel* if you see what I mean **2** understand, gather: *begrijp me goed* don't get me wrong; *iem. (iets) verkeerd ~* misunderstand s.o. (sth.)

het **begrip** /bəɣrɪp/ (pl: -pen) **1** understanding, comprehension, conception: *vlug van ~* quick-witted **2** concept, idea, notion **3** understanding, sympathy: *~ voor iets kunnen opbrengen* appreciate; *ze was vol ~* she was very understanding

begroeid /bəɣruit/ (adj) grown over (with), overgrown (with); wooded

begroeten /bəɣrutə(n)/ (begroette, heeft begroet) greet; hail; salute: *elkaar ~* exchange greetings; *het voorstel werd met applaus begroet* the proposal was greeted with applause

de **begroeting** /bəɣrutɪŋ/ (pl: -en) greeting, salutation

begroten /bəɣrotə(n)/ (begrootte, heeft begroot) estimate (at), cost (at): *de kosten van het gehele project worden begroot op 12 miljoen* the whole project is costed at 12 million

de **begroting** /bəɣrotɪŋ/ (pl: -en) estimate, budget: *een ~ maken* make an estimate

het **begrotingstekort** /bəɣrotɪŋstəkɔrt/ (pl: -en) budget deficit

de **begunstigde** /bəɣʏnstəɣdə/ (pl: -n) beneficiary; payee

begunstigen /bəɣʏnstəɣə(n)/ (begunstigde, heeft begunstigd) favour

de **beha** /beha/ (pl: -'s) bra

behaaglijk /bəhaxlək/ (adj, adv) **1** pleasant, comfortable: *een ~ gevoel* a comfortable feeling **2** comfortable, relaxed **3** cosy, snug

behaagziek /bəhaxsik/ (adj, adv) coquettish

behaard /bəhart/ (adj) hairy: *de huid is daar ~* the skin is covered with hair there; *zwaar ~* very hairy

het ¹**behagen** /bəhaɣə(n)/ pleasure, delight: *~ scheppen in* take (a) pleasure (*or:* delight) in

²**behagen** /bəhaɣə(n)/ (behaagde, heeft behaagd) please: *het heeft Hare Majesteit behaagd om …* Her Majesty has been graciously pleased to …

behalen /bəhalə(n)/ (behaalde, heeft behaald) gain, obtain, achieve, score, win: *een hoog cijfer ~* get (*or:* obtain) a high mark; *de overwinning ~* be victorious, carry the day

behalve /bəhɑlvə/ (prep) **1** except (for), but (for), with the exception of, excepting: *~ mij heeft hij geen enkele vriend* except for me he hasn't got a single friend **2** besides, in addition to

behandelen /bəhɑndələ(n)/ (behandelde, heeft behandeld) **1** handle, deal with, treat; attend to: *dergelijke* **aangelegenheden** *behandelt de rector zelf* the director attends to such matters himself; *eerlijk behandeld worden* be treated fairly; *de dieren werden* **goed** *behandeld* the animals were well looked after; *iem.* **oneerlijk** ~ *do s.o.* (a) wrong; *iem.* **voorzichtig** ~ *go easy with s.o.* **2** treat (of), discuss, deal with: *een* **onderwerp** ~ *discuss a subject* **3** treat; nurse

de **behandeling** /bəhɑndəlɪŋ/ (pl: -en) **1** treatment, use, handling; operation; handling; management: *een wetsontwerp* **in** ~ *nemen* discuss a bill; *in* ~ *nemen* deal with **2** treatment, discussion **3** [med] treatment, attention: *zich* **onder** ~ *stellen* go to a doctor

de **behandelkamer** /bəhɑndəlkamər/ (pl: -s) surgery

het **behang** /bəhɑŋ/ wallpaper

¹behangen /bəhɑŋə(n)/ (behing, heeft behangen) (wall)paper (a room), hang (wallpaper)

²behangen /bəhɑŋə(n)/ (behing, heeft behangen) (+ met) hang (with), drape (with)

de **behanger** /bəhɑŋər/ (pl: -s) paperhanger

behappen /bəhɑpə(n)/: *dat* **kan** *ik niet in m'n eentje* ~ I can't handle that all at once on my own

behartigen /bəhɑrtəɣə(n)/ (behartigde, heeft behartigd) look after, promote

de **behartiging** /bəhɑrtəɣɪŋ/ promotion (of), protection (of)

het **beheer** /bəher/ **1** management; control; supervision: *de penningmeester heeft het* ~ **over** *de kas* the treasurer is in charge of the funds **2** administration, management, rule: *dat eiland staat onder* **Engels** ~ that island is under British administration

de **beheerder** /bəherdər/ (pl: -s) **1** administrator, trustee **2** manager

beheersen /bəhersə(n)/ (beheerste, heeft beheerst) control, govern, rule; dominate: *die gedachte beheerst zijn* **leven** that thought dominates his life ‖ *een vreemde* **taal** ~ have a thorough command of a foreign language

de **beheersing** /bəhersɪŋ/ control; command: *de* ~ **over** *zichzelf verliezen* lose one's self-control

beheerst /bəherst/ (adj, adv) controlled, composed

beheksen /bəhɛksə(n)/ (behekste, heeft behekst) **1** bewitch, bedevil **2** [fig] bewitch, cast (or: put) a spell (or: charm) on

zich **behelpen** /bəhɛlpə(n)/ (behielp zich, heeft zich beholpen) manage, make do: *hij* **weet** *zich te* ~ he manages, he can make do; *het is* **erg** ~ *zonder stroom* it's really roughing it without electricity

behelzen /bəhɛlzə(n)/ (behelsde, heeft behelsd) contain, include, comprehend: *we weten niet wat het* **plan** *behelst* we don't know what the plan amounts to; *het voorstel behelst het* **volgende** the proposal (*or:* suggestion) is this

behendig /bəhɛndəɣ/ (adj, adv) dexterous; adroit; skilful; clever; smart: *een* ~*e* **jongen** an agile boy; ~ **klom** *ze achterop* she climbed nimbly up on the back

de **behendigheid** /bəhɛndəɣhɛit/ dexterity, agility, skill

behept /bəhɛpt/ (adj) cursed (with), -ridden: *met* **vooroordelen** ~ prejudice-ridden

beheren /bəherə(n)/ (beheerde, heeft beheerd) **1** manage; administer: *de* **financiën** ~ control the finances **2** manage, run

behoeden /bəhudə(n)/ (behoedde, heeft behoed) **1** guard (from), keep (from), preserve (from): *iem.* **voor** *gevaar* ~ keep s.o. from danger **2** guard, watch over

behoedzaam /bəhutsam/ (adj, adv) cautious, wary

de **behoefte** /bəhuftə/ (pl: -n) need (of, for); demand (for): *in* **eigen** ~ (*kunnen*) *voorzien* be self-sufficient; ~ *hebben* **aan** *rust* have a need for quiet ‖ *zijn* ~ **doen** relieve o.s.

behoeftig /bəhuftəɣ/ (adj) needy, destitute; distressed: *de armen en* **de** ~*en* the poor and the needy (*or:* destitute); *in* ~*e* **omstandigheden** *verkeren* find o.s. in needy (*or:* reduced) circumstances

het **behoeve** /bəhuvə/: **ten** ~ **van** for the benefit of

behoeven /bəhuvə(n)/ (behoefde, heeft behoefd) need, be in need of; require: *hulp* ~ be in need of aid (*or:* support); *dit behoeft enige* **toelichting** this requires some explanation

¹behoorlijk /bəhorlək/ (adj) **1** decent, appropriate, proper, fitting: *producten van* ~*e* **kwaliteit** good quality products **2** adequate, sufficient **3** decent, respectable, presentable **4** considerable, substantial: *dat is een* ~ **eind** *lopen* that's quite a distance to walk

²behoorlijk /bəhorlək/ (adv) **1** decently, properly: *gedraag je* ~ behave yourself **2** adequately, enough **3** pretty, quite: ~ **wat** *a* fair amount (of) **4** decently, well (enough): *je kunt hier heel* ~ **eten** you can get a very decent meal here

behoren /bəhorə(n)/ (behoorde, heeft behoord) **1** belong (to); be owned by; be part of: *dat behoort nu* **tot** *het verleden* that's past history **2** require, need, be necessary, be needed: *naar* ~ as it should be **3** should, ought (to): *jongeren* ~ **op** *te staan voor ouderen* young people should stand up for older people **4** belong (to), go together (*or:* with): *een tafel met de* **daarbij** ~*de stoelen* a table and the chairs to go with it; *hij behoort* **tot** *de*

het **behoud** /bəhɑut/ **1** preservation, maintenance; conservation **2** preservation, conservation, care

behouden /bəhɑudə(n)/ (behield, heeft behouden) **1** preserve, keep; conserve; retain: *zijn zetel* ~ retain one's seat **2** maintain, keep: *zijn vorm* ~ keep fit ‖ *ik wens u een* ~ *vaart* I wish you a safe journey

behoudend /bəhɑudənt/ (adj, adv) conservative: *hij behoort tot de ~e vleugel van de partij* he belongs to the conservative section of the party; ~ *spelen* play a defensive game

behoudens /bəhɑudə(n)s/ (prep) **1** subject to: ~ *goedkeuring door de gemeenteraad* subject to the council's approval **2** except (for): ~ *enkele wijzigingen werd het plan goedgekeurd* except for (*or:* with) a few alterations, the plan was approved

de **behuizing** /bəhœyzɪŋ/ (pl: -en) housing, accommodation; house; dwelling: *passende zoeken* look for suitable accommodation

het **behulp** /bəhʏlp/: *met ~ van iets* with the help (*or:* aid) of sth.

behulpzaam /bəhʏlpsam/ (adj) helpful: *zij is altijd* ~ she's always ready to help

de **beiaard** /bɛiart/ (pl: -s) carillon

beide /bɛidə/ (num) both, either (one); two: *het is in ons ~r belang* it's in the interest of both of us; *een opvallend verschil tussen hun ~ dochters* a striking difference between their two daughters; *in ~ gevallen* in either case, in both cases; *ze zijn ~n getrouwd* they are both married, both (of them) are married; *wij ~n* both of us, the two of us; *ze weten het geen van ~n* neither of them knows

het ¹**beige** /bɛːʒə/ beige
²**beige** /bɛːʒə/ (adj) beige

de **beignet** /bɛːnɛ/ (pl: -s) fritter

zich **beijveren** /bɛivərə(n)/ (beijverde zich, heeft zich beijverd) apply o.s. (to)

beïnvloeden /bəɪnvludə(n)/ (beïnvloedde, heeft beïnvloed) influence, affect: *zich door iets laten* ~ be influenced by sth.

de **beïnvloeding** /bəɪnvludɪŋ/: ~ *van de jury* influencing the jury

Beiroet /bɛirut/ Beirut

de **beitel** /bɛitəl/ (pl: -s) chisel

beitelen /bɛitələ(n)/ (beitelde, heeft gebeiteld) **1** chisel **2** carve

het/de **beits** /bɛits/ (pl: -en) stain

beitsen /bɛitsə(n)/ (beitste, heeft gebeitst) stain

bejaard /bəjart/ (adj) elderly, aged, old

de **bejaarde** /bəjardə/ (pl: -n) elderly (*or:* old) person, senior citizen

het **bejaardentehuis** /bəjardə(n)təhœys/ (pl: -tehuizen) old people's home, home for the elderly

de **bejaardenverzorger** /bəjardə(n)vərzɔrɣər/ (pl: -s) geriatric helper

de **bejaardenzorg** /bəjardə(n)zɔrɣ/ care of the elderly (*or:* old)

bejegenen /bəjeɣənə(n)/ (bejegende, heeft bejegend) treat: *iem. onheus* ~ snub (*or:* rebuff) s.o.

de **bek** /bɛk/ (pl: -ken) **1** bill; beak **2** snout, muzzle **3** mouth, trap, gob: *een grote ~ hebben* be loud-mouthed; *hou je grote ~* shut up!; *op zijn ~ gaan* come a cropper, fall flat on one's face **4** mug: *(gekke) ~ken trekken* make (silly) faces

bekaaid /bəkajt/ (adj): *er ~ afkomen* come off badly, get the worst of it, get a raw deal

bekaf /bɛkɑf/ (adj) all-in, knackered, dead tired

bekakt /bəkɑkt/ (adj, adv) affected, snooty

de **bekeerling** /bəkerlɪŋ/ (pl: -en) convert

bekend /bəkɛnt/ (adj) **1** known: *dit was mij ~* I knew (of) this; *het is algemeen ~* it's common knowledge; *voor zover mij ~* as far as I know; *voor zover ~* as far as is known **2** well-known, noted (for), known (for); notorious (for): ~ *van radio en tv* of radio and TV fame **3** familiar: *u komt me ~ voor* haven't we met (somewhere) (before)?

de **bekende** /bəkɛndə/ (pl: -n) acquaintance

de **bekendheid** /bəkɛnthɛit/ **1** familiarity (with), acquaintance (with), experience (of) **2** reputation, name, fame

bekendmaken /bəkɛntmakə(n)/ (maakte bekend, heeft bekendgemaakt) **1** announce **2** publish, make public (*or:* known): *de verkiezingsuitslag ~* declare the results of the election **3** familiarize (with), acquaint

de **bekendmaking** /bəkɛntmakɪŋ/ (pl: -en) **1** announcement **2** publication; notice; declaration

bekendstaan /bəkɛntstan/ (stond bekend, heeft bekendgestaan) be known (as), be known (*or:* reputed) (to be): *goed, slecht* ~ have a good, bad reputation; ~ *om* be noted (*or:* known) for

bekennen /bəkɛnə(n)/ (bekende, heeft bekend) **1** [law] confess; plead guilty (to) **2** confess, admit, acknowledge: *schuld* ~ admit one's guilt; *je kunt beter eerlijk* ~ you'd better come clean **3** see, detect: *hij was nergens te ~* there was no sign (*or:* trace) of him (anywhere)

de **bekentenis** /bəkɛntənɪs/ (pl: -sen) confession, admission, acknowledgement; plea of guilty: *een volledige ~ afleggen* make a full confession

de **beker** /bekər/ (pl: -s) beaker, cup; mug: *de ~ winnen* win the cup

bekeren /bəkerə(n)/ (bekeerde, heeft bekeerd) convert; reform

de **bekerfinale** /bekərfinalə/ (pl: -s) cup final

de **bekering** /bəkerɪŋ/ (pl: -en) conversion

de **bekerwedstrijd** /bekərwɛtstrɛit/ (pl: -en) cup-tie

bekeuren /bəkø̲rə(n)/ (bekeurde, heeft bekeurd) fine (on the spot): *bekeurd worden* ***voor*** *te hard rijden* be fined for speeding

de **bekeuring** /bəkø̲rɪŋ/ (pl: -en) (on-the-spot) fine, ticket

bekijken /bəkɛ̲ikə(n)/ (bekeek, heeft bekeken) **1** look at, examine: *iets* ***vluchtig*** *~* glance at sth.; *van dichtbij ~* take a close(r) look at **2** look at, consider **3** see, look at, consider, view: ***hoe*** *je het ook bekijkt* whichever way you look at it || *je bekijkt* ***het*** *maar!* please yourself!; ***goed*** *bekeken!* well done!; good thinking!

het **bekijks** /bəkɛ̲ɪks/: ***veel*** *~ hebben* attract a great deal of (*or:* a lot of) attention

het **bekken** /bɛ̲kə(n)/ (pl: -s) **1** basin **2** [biology] pelvis **3** [mus] cymbal

de **beklaagde** /bəkla̲ɣdə/ (pl: -n) accused, defendant; prisoner (at the bar)

de **beklaagdenbank** /bəkla̲ɣdə(n)bɑŋk/ (pl: -en) dock

bekladden /bəklɑ̲də(n)/ (bekladde, heeft beklad) blot; daub; plaster

het **beklag** /bəklɑ̲χ/ complaint

[1]**beklagen** /bəkla̲ɣə(n)/ (beklaagde, heeft beklaagd) pity

zich [2]**beklagen** /bəkla̲ɣə(n)/ (beklaagde zich, heeft zich beklaagd) complain (to s.o.), make a complaint (to s.o.)

beklagenswaardig /bəklaɣə(n)swa̲rdəχ/ (adj) pitiable, pitiful, piteous, lamentable, deplorable: *hij* ***is*** *~* he is (much) to be pitied

bekleden /bəkle̲də(n)/ (bekleedde, heeft bekleed) **1** cover; coat; line: *een kamer ~* carpet a room **2** hold, occupy: *een hoge* ***positie*** *~* hold a high position

de **bekleding** /bəkle̲dɪŋ/ (pl: -en) covering, coating, lining

beklemd /bəklɛ̲mt/ (adj) jammed, wedged, stuck, trapped

beklemmen /bəklɛ̲mə(n)/ (beklemde, heeft beklemd) **1** jam **2** oppress

beklemtonen /bəklɛ̲mtonə(n)/ (beklemtoonde, heeft beklemtoond) stress, accent(uate); emphasize

beklimmen /bəklɪ̲mə(n)/ (beklom, heeft beklommen) climb, ascend, scale

beklinken /bəklɪ̲ŋkə(n)/ (beklonk, heeft/is beklonken) settle, clinch: *de* ***zaak*** *is beklonken* the matter's settled; the deal's sewn up

bekneld /bəknɛ̲lt/ (adj) trapped: *door een botsing ~* ***raken*** *in een auto* be trapped in a car after a collision

beknibbelen /bəknɪ̲bələ(n)/ (beknibbelde, heeft beknibbeld) **1** cut back (on); skimp (on), stint (on) **2** [Belg] meddle with, interfere with

beknopt /bəknɔ̲pt/ (adj, adv) brief(ly-worded), concise, succinct || *een ~e* ***uitgave*** an abridged edition

beknotten /bəknɔ̲tə(n)/ (beknotte, heeft beknot) curtail, cut short, restrict: *iemands* ***vrijheid*** *~* curtail (*or:* restrict) s.o.'s freedom

bekocht /bəkɔ̲χt/ (adj) cheated; taken in, taken for a ride: *zich ~* ***voelen*** feel cheated (*or:* taken in)

bekoelen /bəku̲lə(n)/ (bekoelde, is bekoeld) **1** cool (off, down) **2** [fig] cool (off), dampen

bekogelen /bəko̲ɣələ(n)/ (bekogelde, heeft bekogeld) pelt, bombard

bekokstoven /bəkɔ̲kstovə(n)/ (bekokstoofde, heeft bekokstoofd) cook up: *wat ben je nu weer* ***aan*** *'t ~?* what are you cooking up now?

bekomen /bəko̲mə(n)/ (bekwam, is bekomen) **1** agree with; suit; disagree with: *dat zal je* ***slecht*** *~* you'll be sorry (for that) **2** recover, get over; come round, come to: ***van*** *de (eerste) schrik ~* get over the (initial) shock

zich **bekommeren** /bəkɔ̲mərə(n)/ (bekommerde zich, heeft zich bekommerd) worry (about), bother (about), concern (*or:* trouble) o.s. (with, about)

de **bekomst** /bəkɔ̲mst/: *zijn ~ van iets* ***hebben*** have had one's fill of sth.; be fed up with (*or:* sick and tired of) sth.

bekonkelen /bəkɔ̲ŋkələ(n)/ (bekonkelde, heeft bekonkeld) cook up; wheel and deal

bekoorlijk /bəko̲rlək/ (adj, adv) charming, lovely

bekopen /bəko̲pə(n)/ (bekocht, heeft bekocht) pay for

bekoren /bəko̲rə(n)/ (bekoorde, heeft bekoord) charm, seduce: *dat* ***kan*** *mij niet ~* it doesn't appeal to me; I don't think much of it

de **bekoring** /bəko̲rɪŋ/ (pl: -en) charm(s), appeal

bekorten /bəkɔ̲rtə(n)/ (bekortte, heeft bekort) cut short, shorten, curtail: *zijn reis* ***met*** *een week ~* cut one's journey short by a week, cut a week off one's journey

bekostigen /bəkɔ̲stəɣə(n)/ (bekostigde, heeft bekostigd) bear the cost of, pay for, fund: *ik* ***kan*** *dat niet ~* I can't afford that

bekrachtigen /bəkrɑ̲χtəɣə(n)/ (bekrachtigde, heeft bekrachtigd) ratify, confirm; pass; assent to: *bekrachtigd* ***worden*** be passed

de **bekrachtiging** /bəkrɑ̲χtəχɪŋ/ (pl: -en) **1** ratification, confirmation **2** upholding || ***stuurbekrachtiging*** power steering

bekritiseren /bəkritize̲rə(n)/ (bekritiseerde, heeft bekritiseerd) criticize, find fault with

bekrompen /bəkrɔ̲mpə(n)/ (adj, adv) narrow(-minded), petty, blinkered; [stronger] bigoted

bekronen /bəkro̲nə(n)/ (bekroonde, heeft bekroond) award a prize to: *een bekroond* ***ontwerp*** a prizewinning design, an award-winning design de **bekroning** /bəkro̱nɪŋ/ (pl: -en) award

bekruipen /bəkrœ̱ypə(n)/ (bekroop, heeft bekropen) come over, steal over: *het spijt me, maar nu bekruipt me toch het gevoel dat …* I'm sorry, but I've got a sneaking feeling that …

bekvechten /bɛ̱kfɛχtə(n)/ (bekvechtte, heeft gebekvecht) argue, bicker

bekwaam /bəkwa̱m/ (adj) competent, capable, able

de **bekwaamheid** /bəkwa̱mhɛit/ (pl: -heden) competence, (cap)ability, capacity, skill

zich **bekwamen** /bəkwa̱mə(n)/ (bekwaamde zich, heeft zich bekwaamd) qualify, train (o.s.), study, teach: *zich in iets ~* train for sth.

de **bel** /bɛl/ (pl: -len) **1** bell; chime; gong (bell): *de ~ gaat* there's s.o. at the door; *op de ~ drukken* press the bell **2** bubble: *~len blazen* blow bubbles

belabberd /bəla̱bərt/ (adj, adv) [inform] rotten, lousy, rough: *ik voel me nogal ~* I feel pretty rough (*or:* lousy)

belachelijk /bəla̱χələk/ (adj, adv) ridiculous, absurd, laughable, ludicrous: *op een ~ vroeg uur* at some ungodly hour; *doe niet zo ~* stop making such a fool of yourself

¹**beladen** /bəla̱də(n)/ (adj) emotionally charged

²**beladen** /bəla̱də(n)/ (belaadde, heeft beladen) load; burden

belagen /bəla̱ɣə(n)/ (belaagde, heeft belaagd) **1** beset; [stronger] besiege **2** menace, endanger

belanden /bəla̱ndə(n)/ (belandde, is beland) land (up), end up, finish, find o.s.: *~ bij* end up at, finish at; *waardoor hij in de gevangenis belandde* which landed him in prison

het **belang** /bəla̱ŋ/ (pl: -en) **1** interest, concern; good: *het algemeen ~* the public interest; *~ bij iets hebben* have an interest in sth.; *in het ~ van uw gezondheid* for the sake of your health; *het is van het grootste ~ …* it is imperative to … **2** interest (in): *~ stellen in* be interested in, take an interest in **3** importance, significance: *veel ~ hechten aan iets* set great store by sth.

belangeloos /bəla̱ŋəlos/ (adj, adv) unselfish, selfless: *belangeloze hulp* disinterested help

de **belangengroep** /bəla̱ŋə(n)ɣrup/ (pl: -en) interest group, lobby, pressure group

de **belangenvereniging** /bəla̱ŋə(n)vərenəɣɪŋ/ (pl: -en) interest group, pressure group, lobby

de **belangenverstrengeling** /bəla̱ŋə(n)vərstrɛŋəlɪŋ/ conflict of interest

belanghebbend /bəla̱ŋhɛ̱bənt/ (adj) interested, concerned

de **belanghebbende** /bəla̱ŋhɛ̱bəndə/ (pl: -n) interested party, party concerned

belangrijk /bəla̱ŋrɛik/ (adj) **1** important: *de ~ste gebeurtenissen* the main (*or:* major) events; *zijn gezin ~er vinden dan zijn carrière* put one's family before one's career; *en wat nog ~er is …* and, more important(ly), …; *lekker ~* hip, who cares **2** considerable, substantial, major: *in ~e mate* considerably, substantially

¹**belangstellend** /bəla̱ŋstɛ̱lənt/ (adj) interested: *ze waren heel ~* they were very attentive

²**belangstellend** /bəla̱ŋstɛ̱lənt/ (adv) interestedly, with interest

de **belangstellende** /bəla̱ŋstɛ̱ləndə/ person interested, interested party

de **belangstelling** /bəla̱ŋstɛ̱lɪŋ/ interest (in): *in het middelpunt van de ~ staan* be the focus of attention; *een man met een brede ~* a man of wide interests; *zijn ~ voor iets verliezen* lose interest in sth.; *daar heb ik geen ~ voor* I'm not interested (in that)

belangwekkend /bəla̱ŋwɛ̱kənt/ (adj) interesting; of interest; conspicuous, prominent: *een ~e figuur* a conspicuous (*or:* prominent) person

belast /bəla̱st/ (adj) responsible (for), in charge (of)

belastbaar /bəla̱stbar/ (adj) taxable: *~ inkomen* taxable income

belasten /bəla̱stə(n)/ (belastte, heeft belast) **1** load: *iets te zwaar ~* overload sth. **2** (place a) load (on) **3** make responsible (for), put in charge (of): *iem. te zwaar ~* overtax s.o. **4** tax

belastend /bəla̱stənt/ (adj) aggravating; [law] incriminating; damning; damaging

belasteren /bəla̱stərə(n)/ (belasterde, heeft belasterd) slander; [written] libel

de **belasting** /bəla̱stɪŋ/ (pl: -en) **1** load, stress: *~ van het milieu met chemische producten* burdening of the environment with chemicals **2** burden, pressure: *de studie is een te grote ~ voor haar* studying is too much for her **3** tax, taxation; rate(s): *~ heffen* levy taxes; *~ ontduiken* evade tax

de **belastingaangifte** /bəla̱stɪŋaŋɣɪftə/ (pl: -n) tax return

de **belastingaanslag** /bəla̱stɪŋanslɑχ/ (pl: -en) tax assessment

de **belastingaftrek** /bəla̱stɪŋaftrɛk/ tax deduction

de **belastingbetaler** /bəla̱stɪŋbətalər/ (pl: -s) taxpayer

de **belastingdienst** /bəla̱stɪŋdinst/ (pl: -en) tax department, Inland Revenue; [Am] IRS; Internal Revenue Service

de **belastingfraude** /bəla̱stɪŋfrɑudə/ tax fraud

de **belastingheffing** /bəla̱stɪŋhɛfɪŋ/ (pl: -en) taxation, levying of taxes

de **belastinginspecteur** /bəla̱stɪŋɪnspɛktør/ (pl: -s) tax inspector, inspector of taxes

de **belastingontduiking** /bəla̱stɪŋɔndœykɪŋ/

(pl: -en) tax evasion, tax dodging

het **belastingparadijs** /bəlɑstɪŋparadɛis/ (pl: -paradijzen) tax haven

de **belastingplichtige** /bəlɑstɪŋplɪxtəɣə/ (pl: -n) taxpayer

het **belastingstelsel** /bəlɑstɪŋstɛlsəl/ (pl: -s) tax system, system of taxation

het **belastingtarief** /bəlɑstɪŋtarif/ (pl: -tarieven) revenue tariff, tax rate

belastingvrij /bəlɑstɪŋvrɛi/ (adj) tax-free, duty-free; duty-paid; untaxed

belazeren /bəlazərə(n)/ (belazerde, heeft belazerd) [inform] cheat, make a fool of

beledigen /bəledəɣə(n)/ (beledigde, heeft beledigd) offend; [stronger] insult: *zich beledigd voelen door* be (or: feel) offended by

beledigend /bəledəɣənt/ (adj, adv) offensive (to), insulting (to), abusive

de **belediging** /bəledəɣɪŋ/ (pl: -en) insult, affront: *een grove (zware)* ~ a gross insult

beleefd /bəleft/ (adj, adv) polite, courteous; well-mannered; civil: *dat is niet* ~ that's bad manners, that's not polite

de **beleefdheid** /bəleftheit/ (pl: -heden) politeness, courtesy

het **beleg** /bəlɛx/ **1** siege: *de staat van* ~ *afkondigen* declare martial law **2** (sandwich) filling

belegen /bəleɣə(n)/ (adj) mature(d); ripe; [fig] stale: *jong (licht)* ~ *kaas* semi-mature(d) cheese

belegeren /bəleɣərə(n)/ (belegerde, heeft belegerd) besiege, lay siege to

de **belegering** /bəleɣərɪŋ/ (pl: -en) siege

¹**beleggen** /bəlɛɣə(n)/ (belegde, heeft belegd) invest: *in effecten* ~ invest in stocks and shares

²**beleggen** /bəlɛɣə(n)/ (belegde, heeft belegd) **1** convene, call: *een vergadering* ~ call a meeting **2** cover, fill; put meat (or: cheese) on [slice of bread]: *belegde broodjes* (ham, cheese etc.) rolls

de **belegger** /bəlɛɣər/ (pl: -s) investor

de **belegging** /bəlɛɣɪŋ/ (pl: -en) investment

het **beleggingsfonds** /bəlɛɣɪŋsfon(t)s/ (pl: -en) **1** investment trust (or: fund) **2** [roughly] gilt-edged (or: government) securities

het **beleid** /bəlɛit/ **1** policy: *het* ~ *van deze regering* the policies of this government; *verkeerd (slecht)* ~ mismanagement **2** tact, discretion: *met* ~ *te werk gaan* handle things tactfully

belemmeren /bəlɛmərə(n)/ (belemmerde, heeft belemmerd) hinder, hamper; [stronger] impede; interfere with; [stronger] obstruct; block: *iem. het uitzicht* ~ obstruct (or: block) s.o.'s view; *de rechtsgang* ~ obstruct the course of justice

de **belemmering** /bəlɛmərɪŋ/ (pl: -en) hindrance, impediment, interference, obstruction: *een* ~ *vormen voor* stand in the way of

belendend /bəlɛndənt/ (adj) adjoining, adjacent, neighbouring

belenen /bəlenə(n)/ (beleende, heeft beleend) pawn; borrow money on, raise a loan on

het **beletsel** /bəlɛtsəl/ (pl: -s) obstacle, impediment

beletten /bəlɛtə(n)/ (belette, heeft belet) prevent (from), obstruct

beleven /bəleβə(n)/ (beleefde, heeft beleefd) go through, experience: *de spannendste avonturen* ~ have the most exciting adventures; *plezier* ~ *aan* enjoy

de **belevenis** /bəleβənɪs/ (pl: -sen) experience, adventure

belezen /bəlezə(n)/ (adj) well-read, widely-read: *een (zeer)* ~ *man* a man of wide reading

de **Belg** /bɛlx/ (pl: -en) Belgian

België /bɛlɣijə/ Belgium

Belgisch /bɛlɣis/ (adj) Belgian

Belgrado /bɛlɣrado/ Belgrade

belichamen /bəlɪxamə(n)/ (belichaamde, heeft belichaamd) embody

de **belichaming** /bəlɪxamɪŋ/ (pl: -en) embodiment

belichten /bəlɪxtə(n)/ (belichtte, heeft belicht) **1** illuminate, light (up) **2** discuss, shed (or: throw) light on: *een probleem van verschillende kanten* ~ discuss different aspects of a problem **3** expose

de **belichting** /bəlɪxtɪŋ/ lighting

¹**believen** /bəliβə(n)/ (beliefde, heeft beliefd) please

²**believen** /bəliβə(n)/ (beliefde, heeft beliefd) want, desire: *wat belieft u?* (I beg your) pardon?

belijden /bəlɛidə(n)/ (beleed, heeft beleden) profess, avow

de **belijdenis** /bəlɛidənɪs/ (pl: -sen) confession (of faith); confirmation

de **Belizaan** /belizan/ (pl: Belizanen) Belizian

Belizaans /belizans/ (adj) Belizian

Belize /beli:zə/ Belize

de **belkaart** /bɛlkart/ phone card

¹**bellen** /bɛlə(n)/ (belde, heeft gebeld) ring (the bell): *de fietser belde* the cyclist rang his bell

²**bellen** /bɛlə(n)/ (belde, heeft gebeld) ring (up), call: *kan ik even* ~? may I use the (tele)phone?

bellenblazen /bɛlə(n)blazə(n)/ blow bubbles

het **belletje** /bɛləcə/ (pl: -s) buzz, call, ring

de **belminuut** /bɛlminyt/ (pl: -minuten) (time) unit

de **belofte** /bəlɔftə/ (pl: -n) promise; pledge: *iem. een* ~ *doen* make s.o. a promise; *zijn* ~ *(ver)breken* break one's promise; *zijn* ~ *houden* keep (or: live up) to one's promise (to s.o.), be as good as one's word; ~ *maakt schuld* promise is debt

belonen /bəlonə(n)/ (beloonde, heeft beloond) pay, reward, repay

de **beloning** /bəlonɪŋ/ (pl: -en) reward; pay-(ment): *als* ~ *(van, voor)* in reward (for)

het **beloop** /bəlop/ (pl: belopen) course, way: *iets op zijn* ~ *laten* let sth. take (*or:* run) its course; let things slide

belopen /bəlopə(n)/ (beliep, heeft belopen) **1** walk: *die afstand is in één dag niet te* ~ it's not a distance you can walk in one day **2** amount (*or:* come) to, total; run (in)to

beloven /bəlovə(n)/ (beloofde, heeft beloofd) promise; vow; pledge: *dat belooft niet veel goeds* that does not augur well; *het belooft een mooie dag te worden* it looks as if it'll be a lovely day; *dat belooft wat!* that's promising!; that spells trouble!

het **belspel** (pl: -len) phone-in programme, phone-in contest

het **beltegoed** /bɛltəɣut/ (pl: -en) credit (on prepaid phonecard)

de **beltoon** /bɛlton/ (pl: beltonen) ringtone

beluisteren /bəlœystərə(n)/ (beluisterde, heeft beluisterd) **1** listen to; listen in to: *het programma is iedere zondag te* ~ the pro-gramme is broadcast every Sunday **2** hear, overhear

belust /bəlʏst/ (adj) (+ op) bent (on); out (for)

de **belwaarde** /bɛlwardə/ (pl: -n) [Belg] credit (on prepaid phonecard)

bemachtigen /bəmɑxtəɣə(n)/ (bemachtig-de, heeft bemachtigd) **1** get hold of, get (*or:* lay) one's hands on: *een zitplaats* ~ secure a seat **2** seize, capture, take (possession of); acquire

bemalen /bəmalə(n)/ (bemaalde, heeft be-maald/bemalen) drain

bemannen /bəmɑnə(n)/ (bemande, heeft bemand) man, staff; crew: *een bemand ruim-tevaartuig* a manned spacecraft

de **bemanning** /bəmɑnɪŋ/ (pl: -en) crew; ship's company; complement; garrison

het **bemanningslid** /bəmɑnɪŋslɪt/ (pl: -leden) crewman, member of the crew, hand

bemerken /bəmɛrkə(n)/ (bemerkte, heeft bemerkt) notice, note

bemesten /bəmɛstə(n)/ (bemestte, heeft bemest) manure; fertilize

bemeubelen /bəmøbələ(n)/ (bemeubelde, heeft bemeubeld) [Belg] furnish

de **bemiddelaar** /bəmɪdəlar/ (pl: -s) interme-diary; mediator; go-between

bemiddelbaar /bəmɪdəlbar/ (adj) employ-able

bemiddeld /bəmɪdəlt/ (adj) affluent, well-to-do

bemiddelen /bəmɪdələ(n)/ (bemiddelde, heeft bemiddeld) mediate: *~d optreden (in)* act as a mediator (*or:* an arbitrator) (in)

de **bemiddeling** /bəmɪdəlɪŋ/ mediation

bemind /bəmɪnt/ (adj) dear (to), loved (by),

much-loved: *door zijn charme maakte hij zich bij iedereen* ~ his charm endeared him to eve-ryone

de **beminde** /bəmɪndə/ (pl: -n) beloved, sweetheart

beminnelijk /bəmɪnələk/ (adj) amiable

beminnen /bəmɪnə(n)/ (beminde, heeft bemind) love, hold dear

bemoedigen /bəmudəɣə(n)/ (bemoedig-de, heeft bemoedigd) encourage, hearten

de **bemoeial** /bəmujal/ (pl: -len) busybody

zich **bemoeien** /bəmujə(n)/ (bemoeide zich, heeft zich bemoeid) (+ met) meddle (in), in-terfere (in): *bemoei je niet overal mee!* mind your own business!; *daar bemoei ik me niet mee* I don't want to get mixed up in that

de **bemoeienis** /bəmujənɪs/ (pl: -sen) **1** con-cern: *geen* ~ *hebben met* not be concerned with, have nothing to do with **2** interference

bemoeilijken /bəmujləkə(n)/ (bemoeilijk-te, heeft bemoeilijkt) hamper, hinder; im-pede; aggravate; complicate

bemoeiziek /bəmujzik/ (adj) interfering, meddling: ~ *zijn* be a meddler (*or:* busy-body); be a nos(e)y parker

de **bemoeizucht** /bəmujzʏxt/ meddlesome-ness, interference

benadelen /bənadelə(n)/ (benadeelde, heeft benadeeld) harm, put at a disadvan-tage, handicap; [law] prejudice: *iem. in zijn rechten* ~ infringe s.o.'s rights

benaderen /bənadərə(n)/ (benaderde, heeft benaderd) **1** approach; [fig also] ap-proximate to; come close to: *moeilijk te* ~ unapproachable **2** approach, get in touch with: *iem.* ~ *over een kwestie* approach s.o. on a matter **3** calculate (roughly), estimate (roughly)

de **benadering** /bənadərɪŋ/ (pl: -en) **1** ap-proach; [fig also] approximation (to) **2** (rough) calculation, (rough) estimate, ap-proximation || *bij* ~ approximately, roughly

benadrukken /bənadrʏkə(n)/ (benadruk-te, heeft benadrukt) emphasize, stress, un-derline

de **benaming** /bənamɪŋ/ (pl: -en) name, desig-nation

benard /bənɑrt/ (adj) awkward, perilous, distressing

benauwd /bənɑut/ (adj) **1** short of breath **2** close, muggy; stuffy: *een* ~ *gevoel op de borst* a tight feeling in one's chest; ~ *warm* close, muggy, oppressive **3** anxious, afraid: *het* ~ *krijgen* feel anxious **4** upsetting **5** nar-row, cramped

de **benauwdheid** /bənɑuthɛit/ **1** tightness of the chest **2** closeness, stuffiness **3** fear, anxi-ety

benauwen /bənɑuwə(n)/ (benauwde, heeft benauwd) weigh down on

de **bende** /bɛndə/ (pl: -s) **1** mess, shambles

2 mass; swarm; crowd **3** gang, pack

¹beneden /bəne̱də(n)/ (adv) down, below; downstairs; at the bottom: *(via de trap) naar ~ gaan* go down(stairs); *de vijfde regel van ~* the fifth line up, the fifth line from the bottom

²beneden /bəne̱də(n)/ (prep) under, below, beneath: *kinderen ~ de zes jaar* children under six (years of age)

de **benedenverdieping** /bəne̱də(n)vərdipɪŋ/ (pl: -en) ground floor; lower floor

benedenwinds /bənedə(n)wɪnts/ (adj) leeward

de **benefietwedstrijd** /benəfi̱twɛtstrɛɪt/ (pl: -en) benefit (match)

de **Benelux** /benəlyks/ Benelux, the Benelux countries

benemen /bənemə(n)/ (benam, heeft benomen) take away (from)

benen /be̱nə(n)/ (adj) bone

benepen /bənepə(n)/ (adj) **1** small-minded, petty **2** anxious, timid

benevelen /bəne̱vələ(n)/ (benevelde, heeft beneveld) cloud, (be)fog: *licht(elijk) beneveld* tipsy, woozy

Bengaals /bɛŋa̱ls/ (adj) Bengal; Bengali

de **Bengalees** /bɛŋyale̱s/ (pl: Bengalezen) Bangladeshi, Bengali

de **bengel** /bɛ̱ŋəl/ (pl: -s) (little) rascal, scamp, (little) terror

bengelen /bɛ̱ŋələ(n)/ (bengelde, heeft gebengeld) dangle, swing (to and fro)

benieuwd /bəni̱wt/ (adj) curious: *ik ben ~ wat hij zal zeggen* I wonder what he'll say; *ze was erg ~ (te horen) wat hij ervan vond* she was dying to hear what he thought of it

benieuwen /bəni̱wə(n)/ arouse curiosity: *het zal mij ~ of hij komt* I wonder if he'll come

benijden /bəni̱də(n)/ (benijdde, heeft benijd) envy, be envious (of), be jealous (of): *al onze vrienden ~ ons om ons huis* our house is the envy of all our friends

benijdenswaardig /bənɛɪdənswa̱rdəx/ (adj, adv) enviable

Benin /beni̱n/ Benin

de **Beniner** /beni̱nər/ (pl: -s) Beninese

benodigd /bəno̱dəxt/ (adj) required, necessary, wanted

de **benodigdheden** /bəno̱dəxthedə(n)/ requirements, necessities

benoemen /bənu̱mə(n)/ (benoemde, heeft benoemd) appoint, assign (to), nominate: *iem. tot burgemeester ~* appoint s.o. mayor

de **benoeming** /bənu̱mɪŋ/ (pl: -en) appointment, nomination

het **benul** /bənʏl/ notion, inkling, idea: *hij heeft er geen (flauw) ~ van* he hasn't got the foggiest idea

benutten /bənʏtə(n)/ (benutte, heeft benut) utilize, make use of: *zijn kansen ~* make the most of one's opportunities; *een strafschop ~* score from a penalty

B en W /beɛnwe̱/ (pl) *Burgemeester en Wethouders* Mayor and Aldermen

de **benzine** /bɛnzi̱nə/ petrol; [Am] gas(oline): *gewone (normale) ~* two star petrol; *loodvrije ~* unleaded petrol

de **benzinemotor** /bɛnzi̱nəmotər/ (pl: -en) petrol engine

de **benzinepomp** /bɛnzi̱nəpomp/ (pl: -en) **1** petrol station, filling station **2** fuel pump

het **benzinestation** /bɛnzi̱nəsta(t)ʃon/ (pl: -s) petrol station, filling station

de **benzinetank** /bɛnzi̱nətɛŋk/ (pl: -s) petrol tank; [Am] gas(oline) tank

de **beoefenaar** /bəu̱fənar/ (pl: -s) student; practitioner

beoefenen /bəu̱fənə(n)/ (beoefende, heeft beoefend) practise, pursue, follow, study; go in for: *sport ~* go in for sports

beogen /bəo̱ɣə(n)/ (beoogde, heeft beoogd) have in mind, aim at, intend: *het beoogde resultaat* the intended (*or:* desired) result, the result aimed at

de **beoordelaar** /bəo̱rdelar/ (pl: -s) judge, assessor; reviewer

beoordelen /bəo̱rdelə(n)/ (beoordeelde, heeft beoordeeld) judge, assess: *een boek ~* criticize a book; *dat kan ik zelf wel ~!* I can judge for myself (, thank you very much)!; *dat is moeilijk te ~* that's hard to say; *iem. verkeerd ~* misjudge s.o.

de **beoordeling** /bəo̱rdelɪŋ/ judg(e)ment, assessment, evaluation; [educ] mark; review

¹bepaald /bəpalt/ (adj) **1** particular, specific: *heb je een ~ iem. in gedachten?* are you thinking of anyone in particular? **2** specific, fixed, set, specified; given: *vooraf ~* predetermined **3** certain, particular: *om ~e redenen* for certain reasons

²bepaald /bəpalt/ (adv) definitely: *niet ~ slim* not particularly clever

de **bepakking** /bəpɑkɪŋ/ (pl: -en) pack; (marching) kit

bepalen /bəpa̱lə(n)/ (bepaalde, heeft bepaald) **1** prescribe, lay down, determine, stipulate: *zijn keus ~* make one's choice; *vooraf ~* predetermine; *de prijs werd bepaald op €100,-* the price was set at 100 euros **2** determine, ascertain: *u mag de dag zélf ~* (you can) name the day; *het tempo ~* set the pace

de **bepaling** /bəpa̱lɪŋ/ (pl: -en) **1** definition **2** provision, stipulation, regulation: *een wettelijke ~* a legal provision (*or:* stipulation) **3** condition **4** determination

¹beperken /bəpɛ̱rkə(n)/ (beperkte, heeft beperkt) **1** limit, restrict **2** (+ tot) restrict (to), limit (to), confine (to), keep (to): *de uitgaven ~* keep expenditure down; *tot het minimum ~* keep (down) to a minimum

zich **²beperken** /bəpɛ̱rkə(n)/ (beperkte zich, heeft zich beperkt) restrict (o.s. to), confine

(o.s. to)

de **beperking** /bəpɛrkɪŋ/ (pl: -en) **1** limitation, restriction: *zijn ~en* **kennen** know one's limitations; *~en* **opleggen** *aan* impose limits (*or:* limitations) on **2** reduction, cutback

beperkt /bəpɛrkt/ (adj, adv) limited, restricted, confined; reduced: *~* **blijven** *tot* be restricted to; *een ~e* **keuze** a limited choice; *verstandelijk ~* mentally challenged (*or:* disabled)

beplanten /bəplɔntə(n)/ (beplantte, heeft beplant) plant (with); sow (with)

de **beplanting** /bəplɔntɪŋ/ (pl: -en) planting, plants, crop(s)

bepleiten /bəplɛitə(n)/ (bepleitte, heeft bepleit) argue, plead, advocate: *iemands* **zaak** *~ (bij iem.)* plead s.o.'s case (with s.o.)

beppen /bɛpə(n)/ (bepte, heeft gebept) yack, chat

bepraten /bəpratə(n)/ (bepraatte, heeft bepraat) talk over/about, discuss: *wij zullen die* **zaak** *nader ~* we will talk the matter over

beproefd /bəpruft/ (adj): *een ~e* **methode** a tried and tested (*or:* well-tried, approved) method

beproeven /bəpruvə(n)/ (beproefde, heeft beproefd) (put to the) test, try: *zijn* **geluk** *~* try one's luck

de **beproeving** /bəpruvɪŋ/ (pl: -en) **1** testing **2** ordeal, trial

het **beraad** /bərat/ consideration, deliberation; consultation: *na* **rijp** *~* after careful consideration

beraadslagen /bəratslaɣə(n)/ (beraadslaagde, heeft beraadslaagd) deliberate (upon), consider: *met iem.* **over** *iets ~* consult with s.o. about sth.

de **beraadslaging** /bəratslaɣɪŋ/ (pl: -en) deliberation, consideration, consultation

zich **beraden** /bəradə(n)/ (beraadde zich, heeft zich beraden) consider, think over: *zich ~* **over (op)** deliberate about

beramen /bəramə(n)/ (beraamde, heeft beraamd) **1** devise, plan: *een* **aanslag** *~* plot an attack **2** estimate, calculate

de **beraming** /bəramɪŋ/ (pl: -en) **1** planning, design **2** estimate, calculation, budget

de **Berber** /bɛrbər/ (pl: -s) Berber

het **berde** /bɛrdə/: *iets* **te** *~ brengen* bring up a matter, raise a point

berechten /bərɛχtə(n)/ (berechtte, heeft berecht) try

de **berechting** /bərɛχtɪŋ/ (pl: -en) trial; judgement; adjudication

bereden /bəredə(n)/ (adj) mounted

beredeneren /bərədənerə(n)/ (beredeneerde, heeft beredeneerd) argue, reason (out)

bereid /bərɛit/ (adj) **1** prepared **2** ready, willing, disposed: *tot* **alles** *~ zijn* be prepared to do anything

bereiden /bərɛidə(n)/ (bereidde, heeft bereid) prepare, get ready; cook; make, fix: *een* **maaltijd** *~* prepare a meal; *iem. een hartelijke (warme)* **ontvangst** *~* give s.o. a warm welcome

de **bereidheid** /bərɛithɛit/ readiness, preparedness, willingness

de **bereiding** /bərɛidɪŋ/ (pl: -en) preparation, making, manufacture, production

de **bereidingswijze** /bərɛidɪŋswɛizə/ (pl: -n) method of preparation, process of manufacture, procedure

bereidwillig /bərɛitwɪləɣ/ (adj, adv) obliging, willing; helpful: *~ iets* **doen** do sth. willingly

het **bereik** /bərɛik/ reach; range: *buiten (het) ~ van kinderen bewaren* keep away from children; *ik heb* **geen** *~* I haven't got a signal, I'm not getting a signal

bereikbaar /bərɛigbar/ (adj) accessible, attainable, within reach: *bent u* **telefonisch** *~?* can you be reached by phone?

bereiken /bərɛikə(n)/ (bereikte, heeft bereikt) **1** reach, arrive in, arrive at, get to **2** reach, achieve, attain, gain: *zijn* **doel** *~* attain one's goal **3** reach, contact; get through (to)

berekend /bərekənt/ (adj) meant for, designed for; equal to, suited to: *hij is niet ~* **voor** *zijn taak* he is not up to his job

berekenen /bərekənə(n)/ (berekende, heeft berekend) **1** calculate, compute, determine, figure out; add up **2** charge: *iem. te* **veel** (or: **weinig**) *~* overcharge (*or:* undercharge) s.o.

berekenend /bərekənənt/ (adj) calculating, scheming

de **berekening** /bərekənɪŋ/ (pl: -en) **1** calculation, computation: *naar (volgens) een ruwe ~* at a rough estimate **2** calculation, evaluation, assessment: *een huwelijk* **uit** *~* a marriage of convenience

de **berg** /bɛrχ/ (pl: -en) mountain; hill: *~en* **verzetten** move mountains; *ik zie er* **als** *een ~ tegenop* I'm not looking forward to it one little bit; [fig] iem. **gouden** *~en beloven* promise s.o. the moon

bergachtig /bɛrχaχtəχ/ (adj) mountainous, hilly

bergafwaarts /bɛrχɑfwarts/ (adv) downhill

bergbeklimmen /bɛrɣbəklɪmə(n)/ mountaineering, (rock)climbing

de **bergbeklimmer** /bɛrɣbəklɪmər/ (pl: -s) mountaineer, (mountain-)climber

¹**bergen** /bɛrɣə(n)/ (borg, heeft geborgen) **1** store, put away; stow (away): *mappen* **in** *een la ~* put files away in a drawer **2** [shipp] salvage **3** rescue, save; shelter; recover

zich ²**bergen** /bɛrɣə(n)/ (borg zich, heeft zich geborgen) get out of harm's (*or:* the) way, take cover

de **berggeit** /bɛrχɛit/ (pl: -en) chamois, mountain goat

de **berghelling** /bɛrχhɛlɪŋ/ (pl: -en) mountain slope, mountainside

het **berghok** /bɛrχhɔk/ (pl: -ken) shed; storeroom; boxroom

de **berghut** /bɛrχhʏt/ (pl: -ten) mountain hut, climbers' hut, mountain refuge

de **berging** /bɛrχɪŋ/ (pl: -en) **1** [shipp] salvage, recovery **2** storeroom, boxroom; shed

de **bergkam** /bɛrχkɑm/ (pl: -men) (mountain) ridge

de **bergketen** /bɛrχketə(n)/ (pl: -s) mountain range (or: chain)

het **bergmeubel** /bɛrχmøbəl/ (pl: -s) storage cabinet

bergop /bɛrχɔp/ (adv) uphill

de **bergpas** /bɛrχpɑs/ (pl: -sen) (mountain) pass, col

de **bergplaats** /bɛrχplɑts/ (pl: -en) storage (space); storeroom; shed

de **bergschoen** /bɛrχsχun/ (pl: -en) mountaineering (or: climbing) boot

de **bergsport** /bɛrχsport/ mountaineering, (mountain) climbing; alpinism

de **bergtop** /bɛrχtɔp/ (pl: -pen) summit, mountain top, peak; pinnacle

de **bergwand** /bɛrχwɑnt/ (pl: -en) mountain side, face of a mountain, mountain wall

het **bericht** /bərɪχt/ (pl: -en) message, notice, communication; report; news: *volgens de laatste* ~en according to the latest reports; *tot nader* ~ until further notice; *u krijgt schriftelijk* ~ you will receive written notice (or: notification); ~ *krijgen over* receive information about; ~ *achterlaten dat* leave a message that

berichten /bərɪχtə(n)/ (berichtte, heeft bericht) report, send word, inform, advise

de **berichtgeving** /bərɪχtχevɪŋ/ reporting, (news) coverage, report(s)

berijden /bərɛidə(n)/ (bereed, heeft bereden) **1** ride **2** ride (on), drive (on)

de **berijder** /bərɛidər/ rider

berispen /bərɪspə(n)/ (berispte, heeft berispt) reprimand, admonish

de **berisping** /bərɪspɪŋ/ (pl: -en) reprimand, reproof

de **berk** /bɛrk/ (pl: -en) birch

Berlijn /bɛrlɛin/ Berlin

de **berm** /bɛrm/ (pl: -en) verge, roadside, shoulder

de **bermbom** /bɛrmbɔm/ (pl: -men) IED (*improvised explosive device)*; roadside bomb

de **bermuda** /bɛrmydɑ/ (pl: -'s) Bermuda shorts, Bermudas

beroemd /bərumt/ (adj) famous, renowned, celebrated, famed: ~ *om* famous for

de **beroemdheid** /bərumthɛit/ (pl: -heden) **1** fame, renown **2** celebrity

zich **beroemen** /bərumə(n)/ (beroemde zich, heeft zich beroemd) boast (about), take pride (in), pride o.s. (on)

het **beroep** /bərup/ (pl: -en) **1** occupation, profession, vocation; trade; business: *in de uitoefening van zijn* ~ in the exercise of one's profession; *wat ben jij van* ~? what do you do for a living? **2** appeal: *raad van* ~ **a)** Court of Appeal; **b)** [Am] Court of Appeals; *in (hoger) gaan* appeal (to a higher court), take one's case to a higher court || *een* ~ *doen op iem. (iets)* (make an) appeal to s.o. (sth.)

zich **beroepen** /bərupə(n)/ (beriep zich, heeft zich beroepen) (+ op) call (upon), appeal (to), refer (to)

beroeps /bərups/ (adj) professional: ~ *worden* turn professional

de **beroepsbevolking** /bərupsbəvɔlkɪŋ/ employed population, working population, labour force

de **beroepsdeformatie** /bərupsdeforma(t)si/ (pl: -s) occupational (or: job-related) disability

het **beroepsgeheim** /bərupsχəhɛim/ (pl: -en) duty of professional confidentiality: *het* ~ *schenden* breach one's duty of professional confidentiality

beroepshalve /bərupshɑlvə/ (adv) professionally, in one's professional capacity

de **beroepskeuze** /bərupskøzə/ choice of (a) career (or: of profession): *begeleiding bij de* ~ careers counselling

de **beroepskeuzeadviseur** /bərupskøzəɑtfizør/ (pl: -s) counsellor, careers master

de **beroepsmilitair** /bərupsmilitɛːr/ (pl: -en) regular (soldier)

het **beroepsonderwijs** /bərupsɔndərwɛis/ vocational training, professional training

de **beroepsopleiding** /bərupsɔplɛidɪŋ/ (pl: -en) professional (or: vocational, occupational) training

de **beroepsschool** /bərupsχol/ (pl: -scholen) [Belg] technical school

de **beroepsvoetballer** /bərupsfudbɑlər/ (pl: -s) professional football player

de **beroepsziekte** /bərupsiktə/ (pl: -n, -s) occupational disease (or: illness)

beroerd /bərurt/ (adj, adv) **1** miserable, wretched, rotten: *ik word er* ~ *van* it makes me sick; *hij ziet er* ~ *uit* he looks terrible **2** lazy: *hij is nooit te* ~ *om mij te helpen* he is always willing to help me

beroeren /bərurə(n)/ (beroerde, heeft beroerd) **1** touch **2** trouble, agitate

de **beroering** /bərurɪŋ/ (pl: -en) trouble, agitation, unrest, commotion

de **beroerte** /bərurtə/ (pl: -s) stroke

berokkenen /bərɔkənə(n)/ (berokkende, heeft berokkend) cause: *iem. schade* ~ cause s.o. harm

berooid /bərojt/ (adj) destitute

het **berouw** /bərou/ remorse: ~ *hebben over* regret; ~ *tonen* show remorse (*or*: contrition)

berouwen /bərouwə(n)/ (berouwde, heeft berouwd) regret, rue, feel sorry for

beroven /bərovə(n)/ (beroofde, heeft beroofd) **1** rob: *iem. ~ van iets* rob s.o. of sth. **2** deprive of, strip: *iem. van zijn vrijheid ~* deprive s.o. of his freedom; *zich van het leven ~* take one's own life

de **beroving** /bərovɪŋ/ (pl: -en) robbery

berucht /bəryχt/ (adj) notorious (for), infamous

berusten /bərystə(n)/ (berustte, heeft berust) **1** (+ op) rest on, be based on, be founded on: *dit moet op een misverstand ~* this must be due to a misunderstanding **2** resign o.s. to **3** rest with, be deposited with: *de wetgevende macht berust bij het parlement* legislative power rests with parliament

de **berusting** /bərystɪŋ/ resignation, acceptance, acquiescence

de **bes** /bɛs/ **1** berry; currant **2** [mus] B-flat

beschaafd /bəsχaft/ (adj) cultured, civilized, refined, well-bred

beschaamd /bəsχamt/ (adj, adv) ashamed, shamefaced

beschadigd /bəsχadəχt/ (adj) damaged

beschadigen /bəsχadəɣə(n)/ (beschadigde, heeft beschadigd) damage: *door brand beschadigde goederen* fire-damaged goods

de **beschadiging** /bəsχadəɣɪŋ/ (pl: -en) damage

beschamen /bəsχamə(n)/ (beschaamde, heeft beschaamd) **1** (put to) shame **2** disappoint, betray: *iemands vertrouwen (niet) ~* (not) betray s.o.'s confidence

beschamend /bəsχamənt/ (adj) shameful, humiliating, ignominious: *een ~e vertoning* a humiliating spectacle

de **beschaving** /bəsχavɪŋ/ (pl: -en) **1** civilization **2** culture, refinement, polish

bescheiden /bəsχɛidə(n)/ (adj, adv) **1** modest, unassuming: *zich ~ terugtrekken* withdraw discreetly; *naar mijn ~ mening* in my humble opinion **2** modest, unpretentious: *een ~ optrekje* a modest little place

de **bescheidenheid** /bəsχɛidə(n)hɛit/ modesty, unpretentiousness: *valse ~* false modesty

de **beschermeling** /bəsχɛrmə lɪŋ/ (pl: -en) ward, protégé

beschermen /bəsχɛrmə(n)/ (beschermde, heeft beschermd) protect, shield, preserve, (safe)guard, shelter: *een beschermd leventje* a sheltered life; ~ *tegen de zon* screen from the sun

de **beschermengel** /bəsχɛrmɛnəl/ (pl: -en) guardian angel

de **beschermer** /bəsχɛrmər/ (pl: -s) defender, protector, protector

de **beschermheer** /bəsχɛrmher/ (pl: -heren)

patron

de **beschermheilige** /bəsχɛrmhɛiləɣə/ (pl: -n) patron saint, patron, patroness

de **bescherming** /bəsχɛrmɪŋ/ (pl: -en) protection, (safe)guarding, shelter, cover: ~ *bieden aan* offer protection to; *iem. in ~ nemen* take s.o. under one's protection; [fig] take s.o. under one's wing

de **beschermlaag** /bəsχɛrmlaχ/ protective layer (*or*: coating)

beschieten /bəsχitə(n)/ (beschoot, heeft beschoten) fire on, fire at, shell, bombard, pelt

beschikbaar /bəsχɪgbar/ (adj) available, at one's disposal, free

de **beschikbaarheid** /bəsχɪgbarhɛit/ availability

beschikken /bəsχɪkə(n)/ (beschikte, heeft beschikt) (+ over) dispose of, have (control of), have at one's disposal: *over genoeg tijd ~* have enough time at one's disposal; *over iemands lot ~* determine s.o.'s fate

de **beschikking** /bəsχɪkɪŋ/ (pl: -en) disposition, disposal: *ik sta tot uw ~* I am at your disposal; *ter ~ stellen* provide, supply, make available

beschilderen /bəsχɪldərə(n)/ (beschilderde, heeft beschilderd) paint

de **beschildering** /bəsχɪldərɪŋ/ (pl: -en) painting

beschimmeld /bəsχɪmə lt/ (adj) mouldy: *~e papieren* musty papers

beschimmelen /bəsχɪmələ(n)/ (beschimmelde, is beschimmeld) become mouldy

beschimpen /bəsχɪmpə(n)/ (beschimpte, heeft beschimpt) taunt, jeer at, call names

beschonken /bəsχɔŋkə(n)/ (adj) drunk; intoxicated: *in ~ toestand* under the influence (of alcohol)

beschouwen /bəsχɑuwə(n)/ (beschouwde, heeft beschouwd) **1** consider, contemplate **2** consider, regard as, look upon as: *iets als zijn plicht ~* consider sth. (as, to be) one's duty

de **beschouwing** /bəsχɑuwɪŋ/ (pl: -en) consideration, view: *iets buiten ~ laten* leave sth. out of account, ignore sth.

beschrijven /bəsχrɛivə(n)/ (beschreef, heeft beschreven) **1** write (on) **2** describe, portray: *dat is met geen pen te ~* it defies description **3** describe, trace: *een baan om de aarde ~* trace a path around the earth

de **beschrijving** /bəsχrɛivɪŋ/ (pl: -en) description; depiction; sketch: *dat gaat alle ~ te boven* that defies description

beschroomd /bəsχromt/ (adj) timid, diffident, bashful

de **beschuit** /bəsχœyt/ (pl: -en) Dutch rusk, biscuit rusk, zwieback

de **beschuldigde** /bəsχyldəɣdə/ (pl: -n) accused, defendant

beschuldigen /bəsχyldəɣə(n)/ (beschuldig-

de, heeft beschuldigd) accuse (of), charge (s.o. with sth.), blame (s.o. for sth.): *ik beschuldig **niemand**, maar ...* I won't point a finger, but ...
beschuldigend /bəsχɣldəχənt/ (adj) accusatory, denunciatory

de **beschuldiging** /bəsχɣldəɣɪŋ/ (pl: -en) accusation, imputation; charge; indictment: *iem. in **staat** van ~ stellen (wegens)* indict s.o. (for); *onder (op) ~ van diefstal (gearresteerd)* (arrested) on a charge of theft
beschut /bəsχɣt/ (adj) sheltered, protected ‖ [Belg] ~*te **werkplaats*** sheltered workshop
beschutten /bəsχɣtə(n)/ (beschutte, heeft beschut) (+ tegen) shelter (from), protect (from, against); shield (from)

de **beschutting** /bəsχɣtɪŋ/ (pl: -en) shelter, protection: *(geen) ~ **bieden*** offer (no) protection; *~ **tegen** de regen* protection from the rain

het **besef** /bəsɛf/ understanding, idea; sense: *tot het ~ **komen** dat* come to realize that
beseffen /bəsɛfə(n)/ (besefte, heeft beseft) realize, be aware (of); grasp; be conscious (of): *voor ik **het** besefte, had ik ja gezegd* before I knew it, I had said yes

¹**beslaan** /bəslan/ (besloeg, is beslagen) mist up (*or:* over), steam up (*or:* over): *toen ik binnenkwam, besloeg mijn **bril*** when I entered, my glasses steamed up

²**beslaan** /bəslan/ (besloeg, heeft beslagen) **1** take up, cover; run to: *deze kast beslaat de halve **kamer*** this cupboard takes up half the room **2** shoe

het **beslag** /bəslɑχ/ (pl: -en) **1** batter **2** fitting(s); ironwork; metalwork; shoe **3** possession: *iemands tijd **in** ~ nemen* take up s.o.'s time; *deze tafel neemt te veel ruimte **in** ~* this table takes up too much space **4** attachment: *smokkelwaar **in** ~ nemen* confiscate contraband ‖ *~ **leggen** op iets* take possession of sth., lay (one's) hands on sth.

de **beslaglegging** /bəslɑχlɛɣɪŋ/ (pl: -en) attachment, seizure, distress (on)
beslechten /bəslɛχtə(n)/ (beslechtte, heeft beslecht) settle: *het **pleit** is beslecht* the dispute has been settled
beslissen /bəslɪsə(n)/ (besliste, heeft beslist) decide, resolve: *dit doelpunt zou de **wedstrijd** ~* this goal was to decide the match
beslissend /bəslɪsənt/ (adj) decisive, conclusive; final; crucial: *in een ~ **stadium** zijn* have come to a head, be at a critical stage

de **beslissing** /bəslɪsɪŋ/ (pl: -en) decision; ruling

de **beslissingswedstrijd** /bəslɪsɪŋswɛtstrɛɪt/ (pl: -en) decider, play-off: *een ~ **spelen*** play off

¹**beslist** /bəslɪst/ (adj) **1** definite **2** decided

²**beslist** /bəslɪst/ (adv) certainly, definitely

de **beslommering** /bəslɔmərɪŋ/ (pl: -en) wor-

ry: *de **dagelijkse** ~en* the day-to-day worries
besloten /bəslotə(n)/ (adj) closed, private: *een ~ **vergadering*** a meeting behind closed doors; *in ~ **kring*** in a closed (*or:* private) circle, private(ly)
besluipen /bəslœypə(n)/ (besloop, heeft beslopen) steal up on, creep up on; stalk: *de **vrees** besloop hen* (the) fear crept over them

het **besluit** /bəslœyt/ (pl: -en) **1** decision, resolution, resolve: *een ~ **nemen*** take a decision; *mijn ~ **staat vast*** I'm quite determined **2** conclusion **3** order, decree
besluiteloos /bəslœytəlos/ (adj) indecisive, irresolute
besluiten /bəslœytə(n)/ (besloot, heeft besloten) **1** conclude, close, end **2** decide, resolve
besluitvaardig /bəslœytfardəχ/ (adj) decisive, resolute
besmeren /bəsmerə(n)/ (besmeerde, heeft besmeerd) butter; daub [with paint]
besmet /bəsmɛt/ (adj) **1** infected, contaminated **2** tainted, contaminated, polluted
besmettelijk /bəsmɛtələk/ (adj) **1** infectious, contagious, catching: *een ~e **ziekte*** an infectious disease **2** (be) easily soiled
besmetten /bəsmɛtə(n)/ (besmette, heeft besmet) **1** infect (with), contaminate (with): *met griep besmet **worden** (door iem.)* catch the flu (from s.o.) **2** taint, soil

de **besmetting** /bəsmɛtɪŋ/ (pl: -en) infection; contagion; disease: *radioactieve ~* radioactive contamination
besmeuren /bəsmørə(n)/ (besmeurde, heeft besmeurd) stain, soil: *met **bloed** besmeurde handen* blood-stained hands
besneden /bəsnedə(n)/ (adj) circumcised
besnijden /bəsnɛidə(n)/ (besneed, heeft besneden) circumcise

de **besnijdenis** /bəsnɛidənɪs/ circumcision

¹**besnoeien** /bəsnuje(n)/ (besnoeide, heeft besnoeid) cut down (on): *op de **uitgaven** ~* cut down (on) expenses

²**besnoeien** /bəsnuje(n)/ (besnoeide, heeft besnoeid) prune; lop; trim
bespannen /bəspɑnə(n)/ (bespande, heeft bespannen) **1** stretch; string **2** harness (a horse to a cart): *een rijtuig **met** paarden ~* put horses to a carriage
besparen /bəsparə(n)/ (bespaarde, heeft bespaard) **1** save **2** spare, save: *de **rest** zal ik je maar ~* I'll spare you the rest; *die **moeite** had u zich wel kunnen ~* you could have spared yourself the trouble

de **besparing** /bəsparɪŋ/ (pl: -en) **1** saving, economy **2** saving(s), economies: *een ~ **op** a* saving on
bespelen /bəspelə(n)/ (bespeelde, heeft bespeeld) **1** [sport] play on, play in [field] **2** [mus] play (on) **3** manipulate; play on: *een **gehoor** ~* play to an audience

bespeuren /bəspø̞rə(n)/ (bespeurde, heeft bespeurd) sense, notice, perceive, find

bespieden /bəspi̯də(n)/ (bespiedde, heeft bespied) spy (on), watch

bespioneren /bəspijon̩erə(n)/ (bespioneerde, heeft bespioneerd) spy on

bespoedigen /bəspu̯dəɣə(n)/ (bespoedigde, heeft bespoedigd) accelerate, speed up

bespottelijk /bəspɔtələk/ (adj, adv) ridiculous, absurd: *een ~ figuur* slaan (make o.s.) look ridiculous

bespotten /bəspɔtə(n)/ (bespotte, heeft bespot) ridicule, mock, deride, scoff at

bespreekbaar /bəspreɡbar/ (adj) debatable, discussible

bespreken /bəsprekə(n)/ (besprak, heeft besproken) **1** discuss, talk about; consider: *een probleem ~* go into a problem **2** discuss, comment on, examine; review **3** book, reserve: *kaartjes (plaatsen) ~* make reservations

de **bespreking** /bəsprekɪŋ/ (pl: -en) **1** discussion, talk **2** meeting, conference, talks **3** review **4** booking, reservation

besprenkelen /bəsprɛŋkələ(n)/ (besprenkelde, heeft besprenkeld) sprinkle

bespringen /bəsprɪŋə(n)/ (besprong, heeft besprongen) pounce on, jump

besproeien /bəspru̯jə(n)/ (besproeide, heeft besproeid) **1** sprinkle **2** irrigate; spray; water

bespuiten /bəspœytə(n)/ (bespoot, heeft bespoten) spray

het **bessensap** /bɛsə(n)sɑp/ (red)currant juice; blackcurrant juice

¹best /bɛst/ (adj) **1** best, better, optimum: *met de ~e bedoelingen* with the best of intentions; *~e maatjes zijn met* be very thick with; *Peter ziet er niet al te ~ uit* Peter is looking the worse for wear; *hij kan koken als de ~e* he can cook with the best of them; *op een na de ~e* the second best; *het ~e ermee!* good luck!; best wishes! **2** well, all right: *(het is) mij ~* I don't mind **3** dear, good: *Beste Jan* Dear Jan ‖ *de eerste, de ~e* anyone, anything, any; *hij overnacht niet in het eerste het ~e hotel* he doesn't stay at just any (old) hotel

²best /bɛst/ (adv) **1** best: *jij kent hem het ~e* you know him best **2** fine **3** sure: *je weet het ~* you know perfectly well; *het zal ~ lukken* it'll work out (all right) **4** really **5** possibly, well: *dat zou ~ kunnen* that's quite possible; *ze zou ~ willen …* she wouldn't mind … ‖ *zijn ~ doen* do one's best; *hij is op zijn ~* he is at his best; *ze is op haar ~ (gekleed)* she looks her best

het **¹bestaan** /bəstan/ **1** existence: *die firma viert vandaag haar vijftigjarig ~* that firm is celebrating its fiftieth anniversary today **2** living, livelihood

²bestaan /bəstan/ (bestond, heeft bestaan)

1 exist, be (in existence): *laat daar geen misverstand over ~* let there be no mistake about it; *onze liefde zal altijd blijven ~* our love will live on forever; *ophouden te ~* cease to exist **2** (+ uit) consist (of); be made up (of): *dit werk bestaat uit drie delen* this work consists of three parts **3** be possible: *hoe bestaat het!* can you believe it!

bestaand /bəstant/ (adj) existing, existent, current

het **bestaansminimum** /bəstansminimʏm/ (pl: -minima) subsistence level

het **bestaansrecht** /bəstansrɛxt/ right to exist: *geen ~ hebben* have no right to exist; *zijn ~ ontlenen aan* be justified by

het **¹bestand** /bəstɑnt/ (pl: -en) **1** truce, armistice **2** file

²bestand /bəstɑnt/ (adj): *~ zijn tegen* withstand, resist; be immune to; *tegen hitte ~* heat-resistant

het **bestanddeel** /bəstɑndel/ (pl: -delen) constituent, element; component (part); ingredient

besteden /bəstedə(n)/ (besteedde, heeft besteed) **1** spend, devote (to), give (to), employ for: *geen aandacht ~ aan* pay no attention to; *zorg ~ aan (werk)* take care over (work); *zoiets is niet aan haar besteed* such things are lost (or: wasted) on her **2** spend (on): *ik besteed elke dag een uur aan mijn huiswerk* every day I spend one hour on my homework

de **besteding** /bəstedɪŋ/ (pl: -en) spending: *~en doen* spend money, invest

besteedbaar /bəstedbar/ (adj) disposable

het **bestek** /bəstɛk/ (pl: -ken) **1** cutlery: *(een) zilveren ~* a set of silver cutlery **2** specifications ‖ *iets in kort ~ uiteenzetten* explain sth. in brief

het **bestel** /bəstɛl/ (established) order

de **bestelauto** /bəstɛlɑuto/ (pl: -'s) delivery van; [Am] (panel) truck

bestelen /bəstelə(n)/ (bestal, heeft bestolen) rob

bestellen /bəstɛlə(n)/ (bestelde, heeft besteld) **1** order, place an order (for); send for: *een taxi ~* call a taxi; *iets ~ bij* order sth. from **2** deliver **3** book, reserve

de **besteller** /bəstɛlər/ (pl: -s) **1** delivery man; postman **2** customer

de **bestelling** /bəstɛlɪŋ/ (pl: -en) **1** delivery **2** order: *een ~ doen bij, voor* place an order with, for **3** order, goods ordered: *~en afleveren* deliver goods ordered

de **bestemmeling** /bəstɛmməlɪŋ/ (pl: -en) [Belg] addressee

bestemmen /bəstɛmə(n)/ (bestemde, heeft bestemd) mean, intend; design: *dit boek is voor John bestemd* this book was meant for John

de **bestemming** /bəstɛmɪŋ/ (pl: -en) **1** intention, purpose; allocation **2** destination:

plaats van ~ destination; *hij is met **onbekende** ~ vertrokken* he has gone without leaving a forwarding address **3** destiny

het **bestemmingsplan** /bəstɛmɪŋsplɑn/ (pl: -nen) zoning plan (*or:* scheme)

bestempelen /bəstɛmpələ(n)/ (bestempelde, heeft bestempeld): *iets ~ **als*** designate sth. as, label (*or:* call) sth.

bestendig /bəstɛndəx/ (adj, adv) **1** durable; lasting, enduring **2** stable, steady: ~ **weer** settled weather **3** -proof, -resistant: *hittebestendig* heat-resistant

bestendigen /bəstɛndəɣə(n)/ (bestendigde, heeft bestendigd) continue: *als de **economische** groei wordt bestendigd* if economic growth continues

besterven /bəstɛrvə(n)/ (bestierf, is bestorven) [roughly] hang, [roughly] age || *het ~ van schrik* die of fright

bestijgen /bəstɛiɣə(n)/ (besteeg, heeft bestegen) **1** mount; ascend **2** climb, ascend

de **bestijging** /bəstɛixɪŋ/ (pl: -en) **1** mounting; ascent; accession (to) **2** climbing, ascent

bestoken /bəstokə(n)/ (bestookte, heeft bestookt) harass, press, shell; bomb(ard): *iem. **met** vragen* ~ bombard s.o. with questions

bestormen /bəstɔrmə(n)/ (bestormde, heeft bestormd) storm

de **bestorming** /bəstɔrmɪŋ/ (pl: -en) storming, assault

bestraffen /bəstrɑfə(n)/ (bestrafte, heeft bestraft) punish

de **bestraffing** /bəstrɑfɪŋ/ (pl: -en) punishing, chastisement

bestralen /bəstralə(n)/ (bestraalde, heeft bestraald) give radiation treatment (*or:* radiotherapy)

de **bestraling** /bəstralɪŋ/ (pl: -en) irradiation; radiotherapy; radiation treatment

bestraten /bəstratə(n)/ (bestraatte, heeft bestraat) pave; surface; cobble

de **bestrating** /bəstratɪŋ/ (pl: -en) pavement, paving, surface, cobbles

bestrijden /bəstrɛidə(n)/ (bestreed, heeft bestreden) **1** dispute, challenge, contest; oppose; resist **2** combat, fight, counteract; control: *het **alcoholisme** ~* combat alcoholism

het **bestrijdingsmiddel** /bəstrɛidɪŋsmɪdəl/ (pl: -en) pesticide; herbicide; weed killer

bestrijken /bəstrɛikə(n)/ (bestreek, heeft bestreken) **1** cover: *deze krant bestrijkt de hele **regio*** this newspaper covers the entire area **2** spread; coat

bestrooien /bəstrojə(n)/ (bestrooide, heeft bestrooid) sprinkle (with); cover (with), spread (with); powder (with), dust (with): *gladde wegen **met** zand ~* sand icy roads

de **bestseller** /bɛ(st)sɛlər/ (pl: -s) best seller

bestuderen /bəstyderə(n)/ (bestudeerde, heeft bestudeerd) **1** study, pore over

2 study, investigate, explore

bestuiven /bəstœyvə(n)/ (bestoof, heeft bestoven) pollinate; dust; powder

besturen /bəstyrə(n)/ (bestuurde, heeft bestuurd) **1** drive, steer, navigate: *een **schip** ~* steer a ship **2** control, operate **3** govern, administrate, manage, run

de **besturing** /bəstyrɪŋ/ (pl: -en) control(s), steering, drive

het **besturingssysteem** /bəstyrɪŋsistem/ (pl: -systemen) operating system

het **bestuur** /bəstyr/ (pl: besturen) **1** government; rule; administration; management: *de **raad** van ~ van deze school* the Board of Directors of this school **2** administration, government; management **3** government; council; corporation: *iem. **in** het ~ kiezen* elect s.o. to the board

bestuurbaar /bəstyrbar/ (adj) controllable, manageable; navigable: *gemakkelijk ~ zijn* be easy to steer (*or:* control); *niet meer ~ zijn* be out of control

de **bestuurder** /bəstyrdər/ (pl: -s) **1** driver; pilot; operator **2** administrator, manager: *de ~s van een **instelling*** the governors (*or:* managers) of an institution **3** director, manager

bestuurlijk /bəstyrlək/ (adj) administrative, governmental, managerial

het **bestuurslid** /bəstyrslɪt/ (pl: -leden) member of the board; committee member

de **bestwil** /bɛstwɪl/: *ik zeg het **voor** je (eigen) ~* I'm saying this for your own good

de **bèta** /bɛːta/ science (side, subjects)

de **betaalautomaat** /bətalɑutomat/ (pl: -automaten) point-of-sale terminal, point-of-pay(ment) terminal; ticket machine

betaalbaar /bətalbar/ (adj) affordable, reasonably priced

de **betaalcheque** /bətalʃɛk/ (pl: -s) (bank-)guaranteed cheque

betaald /bətalt/ (adj) paid (for), hired, professional: ~ **voetbal** professional soccer || *iem. iets ~ **zetten*** get even with s.o., get back at (*or:* on) s.o.

de **betaalkaart** /bətalkart/ (pl: -en) (guaranteed) giro cheque

het **betaalmiddel** /bətalmɪdəl/ (pl: -en) tender, currency, circulating medium

de **betaalpas** /bətalpɑs/ (pl: -sen) cheque card

de **betaal-tv** /bətalteve/ pay TV

de **bètablokker** /bɛːtablokər/ (pl: -s) betablocker

betalen /bətalə(n)/ (betaalde, heeft betaald) pay; pay for: *de **kosten** ~* bear the cost; *(nog) te ~* balance due; *contant ~* pay (in) cash; *die huizen zijn **niet** te ~* the price of these houses is prohibitive; *met cheques ~* pay by cheque; *dit werk betaalt **slecht*** this work pays badly

de **betaler** /bətalər/ (pl: -s) payer

de **betaling** /bətalɪŋ/ (pl: -en) payment; re-

ward; remuneration; settlement: ~ *in termijnen* payment in instalments

de **betalingsbalans** /bətaⱼlɪnzbalɑns/ (pl: -en)
balance of payments

het **betalingsbewijs** /bətaⱼlɪnzbəwɛis/ (pl: -be-
wijzen) receipt

de **betalingstermijn** /bətaⱼlɪnstɛrmɛin/ (pl:
-en) instalment

betamelijk /bətaⱼmələk/ (adj, adv) decent,
fit(ting), seemly, proper

betasten /bətɑstə(n)/ (betastte, heeft be-
tast) feel, finger

betegelen /bəteⱼɣələ(n)/ (betegelde, heeft
betegeld) tile

betekenen /bəteⱼkənə(n)/ (betekende,
heeft betekend) **1** mean, stand for, signify:
*wat **heeft** dit te ~?* what's the meaning of
this?; *wat betekent NN?* what does N.N. stand
for? **2** mean, count, matter: *mijn auto betekent **alles** voor mij* my car means everything to
me; *niet **veel (weinig)** ~* be of little importance; *die baan betekent **veel** voor haar* that
job means a lot to her **3** mean, entail: *dat betekent nog niet **dat** …* that does not mean
that …

de **betekenis** /bəteⱼkənɪs/ (pl: -sen) **1** meaning,
sense **2** significance, importance: *van **door-
slaggevende** ~* of decisive importance

beter /beⱼtər/ (adj, adv) **1** better: *het **is** ~ dat
je nu vertrekt* you'd better leave now; *ze **is** ~ in
wiskunde dan haar broer* she's better at maths
than her brother; *dat **is** al ~* that's more like
it; *~ **maken** improve; ~ **worden** improve; *wel
wat ~s te doen hebben* have better things to
do; *~ laat dan nooit* better late than never; *hij
is weer helemaal ~* he has completely recov-
ered; *~ **maken**, weer ~ **maken** cure; ~ **worden,** weer ~ **worden** recover, get well again;
*het ~ **doen** (dan een ander)* do better than s.o.
else; *je **had** ~ **kunnen** helpen* you would have
done better to help; *de leerling **kon** ~* the student could do better; *John **tennist** ~ dan ik*
John is a better tennis-player than me; [iron]
*het ~ **weten*** know best; *ze **weten** niet ~ of …*
for all they know …; *des te ~ (voor ons)* so
much the better (for us); *hoe eerder **hoe** ~* the
sooner the better; *de volgende keer ~* better
luck next time **2** better (class of), superior: *uit
~e **kringen*** upper-class

de **beterschap** /beⱼtərsxɑp/ recovery (of
health): *~!* get well soon!

beteugelen /bətøⱼɣələ(n)/ (beteugelde,
heeft beteugeld) curb, check, suppress, control

beteuterd /bətøⱼtərt/ (adj) taken aback, dismayed: *~ **kijken*** look dismayed

de **betichte** /bətɪxtə/ (pl: -n) [Belg; law] accused, defendant

betichten /bətɪxtə(n)/ (betichtte, heeft beticht) accuse (of): *hij werd **ervan** beticht dat hij
…* he was alleged to have …

betijen /bətɛijə(n)/: *laat hem maar ~* let him
be, leave him alone

betimmeren /bətɪmərə(n)/ (betimmerde,
heeft betimmerd) board, panel

betitelen /bətitələ(n)/ (betitelde, heeft be-
titeld) call, label: *iets **als** onzin ~* call (or: label)
sth. nonsense

de **betoelaging** /bətulaɣɪŋ/ [Belg] subsidy

betogen /bətoⱼɣə(n)/ (betoogde, heeft be-
toogd) demonstrate, march

de **betoger** /bətoⱼɣər/ (pl: -s) demonstrator,
marcher

de **betoging** /bətoⱼɣɪŋ/ (pl: -en) demonstration,
march

het **beton** /bətɔn/ concrete: *gewapend ~* reinforced concrete; *~ **storten*** pour concrete

betonen /bətoⱼnə(n)/ (betoonde, heeft be-
toond) show, display; extend

de **betonmolen** /bətɔnmolə(n)/ (pl: -s) concrete
mixer

betonnen /bətɔnə(n)/ (adj) concrete

het **betonrot** /bətɔnrɔt/ concrete cancer

het **betoog** /bətox/ (pl: betogen) argument;
plea

betoveren /bətoⱼvərə(n)/ (betoverde, heeft
betoverd) **1** put (or: cast) a spell on, bewitch:
*betoverd **door** haar ogen* bewitched by her
eyes **2** enchant

de **betovering** /bətoⱼvərɪŋ/ (pl: -en) **1** spell,
bewitchment **2** enchantment, charm

betraand /bətrant/ (adj) tearfilled; bleary

betrachten /bətrɑxtə(n)/ (betrachtte, heeft
betracht) practise, exercise; observe; show

de **betrachting** /bətrɑxtɪŋ/ (pl: -en) [Belg] aim,
intention

betrappen /bətrɑpə(n)/ (betrapte, heeft
betrapt) catch, surprise: *op heterdaad betrapt*
caught redhanded

betreden /bətreⱼdə(n)/ (betrad, heeft betreden) **1** enter: *het is verboden dit **terrein** te ~*
no entry, keep out (or: off) **2** tread: *nieuwe
paden ~* break new (or: fresh) ground

betreffen /bətrɛfə(n)/ (betrof, heeft be-
troffen) **1** concern, regard: *waar het **politiek**
betreft* when it comes to politics; *wat mij betreft is het in orde* as far as I'm concerned it's
all right; *wat betreft je broer* with regard to
your brother **2** concern, relate to

betreffende /bətrɛfəndə/ (prep) concerning, regarding

¹**betrekkelijk** /bətrɛkələk/ (adj) relative: *dat
is ~* that depends (on how you look at it); *alles **is** ~* everything is relative

²**betrekkelijk** /bətrɛkələk/ (adv) relatively,
comparatively

de **betrekkelijkheid** /bətrɛkələkhɛit/ relativity

¹**betrekken** /bətrɛkə(n)/ (betrok, is betrokken) **1** become overcast (or: cloudy), cloud
over **2** cloud over; darken

²**betrekken** /bətrɛkə(n)/ (betrok, heeft be-

trokken) involve, concern: *zij deden alles zonder de anderen* **erin** *te ~ they did everything without consulting the others; betrokken zijn* **bij** *be involved (or: implicated, mixed up) in ‖ iets* **op** *zichzelf ~ take sth. personally*

de **betrekking** /bətrɛkɪŋ/ (pl: -en) **1** post, job, position; office: *iem.* **aan** *een ~* **helpen** *engage s.o., help s.o. find a job* **2** relation(ship): *nauwe ~en met iem.* **onderhouden** *maintain close ties (or: connections) with s.o.* **3** relation, connection: *met ~* **tot** *with regard to, with respect to; ~* **hebben** *op relate (or: refer) to, concern*

betreuren /bətrørə(n)/ (betreurde, heeft betreurd) **1** regret, be sorry for: *een* **vergissing** *~ regret a mistake* **2** mourn (for, over), be sorry for

betreurenswaardig /bətrørənswɑrdəχ/ (adj) regrettable, sad

betrokken /bətrɔkə(n)/ (adj) **1** concerned; involved: *de ~* **docent** *the teacher concerned* **2** overcast, cloudy

de **betrokkenheid** /bətrɔkənhɛit/ involvement, commitment, concern

betrouwbaar /bətrɑubar/ (adj) reliable, trustworthy, dependable: *uit betrouwbare* **bron** *on good authority*

de **betrouwbaarheid** /bətrɑubarhɛit/ reliability, dependability; trustworthiness

betuigen /bətœyɣə(n)/ (betuigde, heeft betuigd) express: *iem. zijn* **deelneming** *(or:* **medeleven**) *~ express one's condolences (or: sympathy) to s.o.*

betwijfelen /bətwɛifələ(n)/ (betwijfelde, heeft betwijfeld) doubt, (call in) question: *het valt te ~* **of** *… it is doubtful whether …*

betwisten /bətwɪstə(n)/ (betwistte, heeft betwist) dispute, contest, challenge

beu /bø/ (adj): *iets ~* **zijn** *be sick of sth.*

de **beugel** /bøɣəl/ (pl: -s) brace: *een ~* **dragen** *wear braces, wear a brace ‖ dat kan niet* **door** *de ~ that cannot pass (muster), that won't do*

het **beugelslot** /bøɣəlslɔt/ U-lock

de **beuk** /bøk/ (pl: -en) beech

¹**beuken** /bøkə(n)/ (adj) beech

²**beuken** /bøkə(n)/ (beukte, heeft gebeukt) batter, pound; lash: *op (or: tegen) iets ~ hammer on sth., batter (away) at sth.*

het **beukennootje** /bøkənocə/ (pl: -s) beechnut

de **beul** /bøl/ (pl: -en) **1** executioner; hangman **2** [fig] tyrant, brute

beunen /bønə(n)/ (beunde, heeft gebeund) moonlight

de **beunhaas** /bønhas/ (pl: -hazen) moonlighter

beunhazen /bønhazə(n)/ (beunhaasde, heeft gebeunhaasd) **1** bungle, botch **2** moonlight

de ¹**beurs** /børs/ (pl: beurzen) **1** scholarship, grant: *een ~* **hebben, van** *een ~* **studeren** *have a grant; een ~* **krijgen** *get a grant* **2** exchange, market; [bldg] Stock Exchange **3** fair, show, exhibition: *antiekbeurs antique(s) fair* **4** purse

²**beurs** /børs/ (adj) overripe, mushy

de **beursindex** /børsɪndɛks/ (pl: -en) stock market price index

de **beurskoers** /børskurs/ share price, (exchange) rate

de **beursnotering** /børsnoterɪŋ/ (pl: -en) quotation, share price; foreign exchange rate

de **beursstudent** /børstydɛnt/ (pl: -en) student on a grant, scholar

de **beurswaarde** /børswardə/ quoted value, stock exchange value

de **beurt** /børt/ (pl: -en) turn: *een* **goede** *~ maken make a good impression; een* **grote** *~ [car] a big service; de kamer een grondige ~* **geven** *give the room a good cleaning; hij is* **aan** *de ~ it's his turn, he's next; om de ~ iets* **doen** *take turns doing sth.; om de ~ in turn; te ~ vallen fall to s.o.'s lot (or: share)*

beurtelings /børtəlɪŋs/ (adv) alternately, by turns, in turn: *het ~ warm en koud* **krijgen** *go hot and cold (all over)*

de **beurtrol** /børtrɔl/ (pl: -len) [Belg] see *toerbeurt*

bevaarbaar /bəvarbar/ (adj) navigable

bevallen /bəvɑlə(n)/ (beviel, is bevallen) **1** give birth (to): *zij is* **van** *een dochter ~ she gave birth to a daughter* **2** please, suit; give satisfaction: *hoe* **bevalt** *het je op school? how do you like school?*

bevallig /bəvɑləχ/ (adj, adv) graceful, charming

de **bevalling** /bəvɑlɪŋ/ (pl: -en) delivery, childbirth

het **bevallingsverlof** /bəvɑlɪŋsfərlɔf/ (pl: -verloven) [Belg] maternity leave

bevangen /bəvɑŋə(n)/ (beving, heeft bevangen) seize, overcome: *hij werd* **door** *angst ~ he was panic-stricken*

bevaren /bəvarə(n)/ (bevoer, heeft bevaren) navigate; sail

bevattelijk /bəvɑtələk/ (adj, adv) intelligible, comprehensible; see *vatbaar*

bevatten /bəvɑtə(n)/ (bevatte, heeft bevat) **1** contain, hold **2** comprehend, understand: *niet te ~ incomprehensible*

het **bevattingsvermogen** /bəvɑtɪŋsfərmoɣə(n)/ comprehension: *zijn ~ te boven gaan be beyond one's comprehension*

bevechten /bəvɛχtə(n)/ (bevocht, heeft bevochten) **1** gain: *een* **zwaar** *bevochten positie a hard-won (or: dearly won) position* **2** fight (against)

beveiligen /bəvɛiləɣə(n)/ (beveiligde, heeft beveiligd) protect, secure; [fig also] safeguard

de **beveiliging** /bəvɛiləɣɪŋ/ (pl: -en) **1** protection, security; [fig also] safeguard(s) **2** safety (*or:* protective, security) device

de **beveiligingsdienst** /bəvɛɪləɣɪŋzdinst/ (pl: -en) (private) security service

het **bevel** /bəvɛl/ (pl: -en) order, command; warrant: ~ *geven* tot give the order to; *het* ~ *voeren over een leger* be in command of an army

bevelen /bəvelə(n)/ (beval, heeft bevolen) order, command

de **bevelhebber** /bəvɛlhɛbər/ (pl: -s) commander, commanding officer

beven /bevə(n)/ (beefde, heeft gebeefd) **1** shake, tremble, shiver: ~ *van kou* shiver with cold **2** tremble, quake

de **bever** /bevər/ (pl: -s) beaver

bevestigen /bəvɛstəɣə(n)/ (bevestigde, heeft bevestigd) **1** fix, fasten, attach **2** confirm, affirm: *de uitzondering bevestigt de* **regel** the exception proves the rule

bevestigend /bəvɛstəɣənt/ (adj, adv) affirmative

de **bevestiging** /bəvɛstəɣɪŋ/ (pl: -en) **1** fixing, fastening, attachment **2** confirmation **3** affirmation, confirmation

het **bevind** /bəvɪnt/: *naar* ~ *van zaken handelen* act according to circumstances, use one's judgment

¹**bevinden** /bəvɪndə(n)/ (bevond, heeft bevonden) find: *gezien en* **goed** *bevonden* seen and approved; *schuldig* ~ *(aan een misdaad)* find guilty (of a crime)

zich ²**bevinden** /bəvɪndə(n)/ (bevond zich, heeft zich bevonden) be, find o.s.: *zich* **in** *gevaar* ~ be in danger

de **bevinding** /bəvɪndɪŋ/ (pl: -en) finding, result; experience; conclusion

de **beving** /bevɪŋ/ (pl: -en) trembling; shiver

bevlekken /bəvlɛkə(n)/ (bevlekte, heeft bevlekt) soil, stain, spot: *met bloed bevlekt* bloodstained

de **bevlieging** /bəvliɣɪŋ/ (pl: -en) whim, impulse

bevloeien /bəvlujə(n)/ (bevloeide, heeft bevloeid) irrigate, water

bevlogen /bəvloɣə(n)/ (adj) animated, inspired, enthusiastic

bevochtigen /bəvɔxtəɣə(n)/ (bevochtigde, heeft bevochtigd) moisten, wet; humidify

de **bevochtiger** /bəvɔxtəɣər/ (pl: -s) humidifier

bevoegd /bəvuxt/ (adj) competent, qualified, authorized: *de ~e* **overheden (autoriteiten)** the proper authorities; *~e* **personen** authorized persons; ~ **zijn** be qualified

de **bevoegdheid** /bəvuxtheɪt/ (pl: -heden) competence, qualification, authority; jurisdiction: *de bevoegdheden van de* **burgemeester** the powers of the mayor; *de* ~ **hebben** *om* have the power to; *zonder* ~ unauthorized

bevoelen /bəvulə(n)/ (bevoelde, heeft bevoeld) feel, finger

bevolken /bəvɔlkə(n)/ (bevolkte, heeft bevolkt) populate, people

de **bevolking** /bəvɔlkɪŋ/ (pl: -en) population, inhabitants: *de* **inheemse** ~ the native population

de **bevolkingsdichtheid** /bəvɔlkɪŋzdɪxthɛit/ population density

de **bevolkingsgroep** /bəvɔlkɪŋsxrup/ (pl: -en) community, section of the population

het **bevolkingsonderzoek** /bəvɔlkɪŋsɔndərzuk/ (pl: -en) screening

het **bevolkingsregister** /bəvɔlkɪŋsrəɣɪstər/ (pl: -s) register (of births, deaths and marriages)

bevolkt /bəvɔlkt/ (adj) populated: *een dicht-* (or: *dunbevolkte*) *streek* a densely (*or:* sparsely) populated region

bevoogden /bəvoɣdə(n)/ (bevoogdde, heeft bevoogd) patronize (s.o.)

bevoordelen /bəvordelə(n)/ (bevoordeelde, heeft bevoordeeld) benefit, favour: *familieleden* ~ *boven anderen* favour relatives above others

bevooroordeeld /bəvorordelt/ (adj) prejudiced, bias(s)ed: ~ *zijn* **tegen** (or: **voor**) be prejudiced against (*or:* in favour of)

bevoorraden /bəvoradə(n)/ (bevoorraadde, heeft bevoorraad) provision, supply, stock up

bevoorrechten /bəvorɛxtə(n)/ (bevoorrechtte, heeft bevoorrecht) privilege, favour: *een bevoorrechte* **positie** *innemen* occupy a privileged position

bevorderen /bəvordərə(n)/ (bevorderde, heeft bevorderd) **1** promote, further, advance; boost; aid; encourage; stimulate; lead to; be conducive to: *dat bevordert de* **bloedsomloop** that stimulates one's blood circulation; *de* **verkoop** *van iets* ~ boost the sale of sth., push sth. **2** promote: *bevorderd worden* go up (to the next class); *een leerling* **naar** *een hogere klas* ~ move a pupil up to a higher class; *hij werd* **tot** *kapitein bevorderd* he was promoted to (the rank of) captain

de **bevordering** /bəvordərɪŋ/ (pl: -en) **1** promotion, advancement; encouragement: **ter** ~ *van* for the promotion (*or:* advancement) of **2** promotion: *voor* ~ *in aanmerking komen* be eligible for promotion

bevorderlijk /bəvordərlək/ (adj) beneficial (to), conducive (to), good (for): ~ *zijn* **voor** a) promote, further, advance; b) boost, aid; c) lead to, be conducive to

bevredigen /bəvredəɣə(n)/ (bevredigde, heeft bevredigd) satisfy; gratify: *zijn* **nieuwsgierigheid** ~ gratify one's curiosity; *moeilijk te* ~ hard to please ‖ *zichzelf* ~ masturbate

bevredigend /bəvredəɣənt/ (adj) satisfactory, satisfying; gratifying: *een ~e* **oplossing** a satisfactory solution

de **bevrediging** /bəvredəɣɪŋ/ (pl: -en) satisfaction, fulfilment; gratification: ~ *in iets* **vinden** find satisfaction in sth.

bevreemden /bəvrɛ̱mdə(n)/ (bevreemdde, heeft bevreemd) surprise: *dat bevreemdt **mij*** I'm surprised at it

bevreesd /bəvre̱st/ (adj) afraid, fearful

bevriend /bəvri̱nt/ (adj) friendly (with): *een ~e* **mogendheid** a friendly nation (*or:* power); *goed ~ zijn (met iem.)* be close friends (with s.o.)

bevriezen /bəvri̱zə(n)/ (bevroor, heeft/is bevroren) **1** freeze (up, over), become (*or:* be frozen) (up, over): *het **water** is bevroren* the water is frozen; *alle **leidingen** zijn bevroren* all the pipes are (*or:* have) frozen (up) **2** frost (up, over), become frosted **3** freeze; block

de **bevriezing** /bəvri̱zɪŋ/ **1** freezing (over), frost, frostbite **2** freeze

bevrijden /bəvrɛ̱idə(n)/ (bevrijdde, heeft bevrijd) free (from), liberate; release; set free; rescue; emancipate: *een **land** ~* free (*or:* liberate) a country; *iem. **uit** zijn benarde positie ~* rescue s.o. from a desperate position

de **bevrijding** /bəvrɛ̱idɪŋ/ **1** liberation; release; rescue; emancipation: *~ **uit** slavernij* emancipation from slavery **2** [fig] relief: *een **gevoel** van ~* a feeling of relief

Bevrijdingsdag /bəvrɛ̱idɪŋzdɑx/ Liberation Day

bevruchten /bəvrʏxtə(n)/ (bevruchtte, heeft bevrucht) fertilize; impregnate; inseminate

de **bevruchting** /bəvrʏxtɪŋ/ (pl: -en) fertilization, impregnation, insemination: *kunstmatige ~* artificial insemination; *~ **buiten** de baarmoeder* in vitro fertilization

bevuilen /bəvœ̱ylə(n)/ (bevuilde, heeft bevuild) soil, dirty, foul: *het eigen **nest** ~* foul one's own nest

de **bewaarder** /bəwa̱rdər/ (pl: -s) **1** keeper, guardian; jailer; warder: *ordebewaarder* keeper of the peace **2** keeper

het **bewaarmiddel** /bəwa̱rmɪdəl/ (pl: -en) [Belg; culinary] preservative

bewaken /bəwa̱kə(n)/ (bewaakte, heeft bewaakt) guard, watch (over); monitor; [fig] watch; [fig] mind: *het **budget** ~* watch the budget; *een **gevangene** ~* guard a prisoner; *een **terrein** ~* guard (over) an area; *zwaar* (*or: licht*) *bewaakte gevangenis* maximum (*or:* minimum) security prison

de **bewaker** /bəwa̱kər/ (pl: -s) **1** guard **2** security guard

de **bewaking** /bəwa̱kɪŋ/ guard(ing), watch(ing), surveillance, control: *onder strenge ~ staan* be kept under strict surveillance

de **bewakingscamera** /bəwa̱kɪŋskamərɑ/ security camera

bewandelen /bəwɑndələ(n)/ (bewandelde, heeft bewandeld) **1** walk (on, over) **2** [fig] take (*or:* follow, steer) a … course: *de*

middenweg ~ steer a middle course; *de officiële **weg** ~* take the official line

bewapenen /bəwa̱pənə(n)/ (bewapende, heeft bewapend) arm: *zich ~* arm; *zwaar bewapend* heavily armed

de **bewapening** /bəwa̱pənɪŋ/ armament, arms

bewaren /bəwa̱rə(n)/ (bewaarde, heeft bewaard) **1** keep, save **2** keep, store; stock (up): *appels ~* store apples; *een **onderwerp** tot de volgende keer ~* leave a topic for the next time; *~ **voor** later* save up for a rainy day **3** keep, maintain: *zijn **kalmte** ~* keep calm; *zijn **evenwicht** ~* keep (*or:* maintain) one's balance **4** preserve (from), save (from), guard (from, against) || *een **geheim** ~* keep (*or:* guard) a secret

de **bewaring** /bəwa̱rɪŋ/ **1** keeping, care; storage; custody: *in ~ **geven** (aan, bij)* deposit (at, with); entrust (to), leave (with) **2** custody, detention: *huis van ~* house of detention

beweegbaar /bəwe̱xbar/ (adj) movable: *beweegbare **delen*** moving parts

beweeglijk /bəwe̱xlək/ (adj) agile, lively, active: *een zeer ~ **kind*** a very active child

de **beweegreden** /bəwe̱xredə(n)/ (pl: -en) motive; grounds: *de ~en van zijn **gedrag*** the motives underlying his behaviour

bewegen /bəwe̱xə(n)/ (bewoog, heeft bewogen) move, stir: *op en **neer*** (*or: **heen** en weer*) *~* move up and down (*or:* to and fro); *zich ~* move, stir; *ik **kan** me nauwelijks ~* I can hardly move; *geen **blad** bewoog* not a leaf stirred; *~de **delen*** moving parts; *niet ~!* don't move!

de **beweging** /bəwe̱xɪŋ/ (pl: -en) movement, move, motion; gesture: *een **verkeerde** ~ maken* make a wrong move; *er is geen ~ in te **krijgen*** it won't budge (*or:* move); *in ~ **brengen**, in ~ **zetten*** set in motion; start; *in ~ **blijven*** keep moving; *in ~ **zijn*** be moving, be in motion || *de **vredesbeweging*** the peace movement

bewegingloos /bəwe̱xɪŋlos/ (adj) motionless, immobile

de **bewegingsvrijheid** /bəwe̱xɪŋsfrɛihɛit/ freedom of movement

bewegwijzeren /bəwɛ̱xwɛizərə(n)/ (bewegwijzerde, heeft bewegwijzerd) signpost

beweren /bəwe̱rə(n)/ (beweerde, heeft beweerd) claim; contend; allege: *durven te ~ dat* dare to claim that; *dat zou ik niet **willen** ~* I wouldn't (go as far as to) say that; *zij beweerde onschuldig te **zijn*** she claimed to be innocent; *dat is precies **wat** wij ~* that's the very point we're making; *hij beweert **dat** hij niets gehoord heeft* he maintains that he did not hear anything

de **bewering** /bəwe̱rɪŋ/ (pl: -en) assertion, statement; allegation; claim; contention: *bij zijn ~ **blijven*** stick to one's claim; *kun je deze ~*

hard maken? can you substantiate this claim?

bewerkelijk /bəwɛrkələk/ (adj) laborious

bewerken /bəwɛrkə(n)/ (bewerkte, heeft bewerkt) treat; work; process; edit; rewrite; revise; adapt: *een studieboek voor het Nederlandse taalgebied* ~ adapt a textbook for the Dutch user; *de grond* ~ till the land (*or:* soil); *geheel opnieuw bewerkt door* completely revised by; ~ *tot een film* adapt for the screen

de **bewerker** /bəwɛrkər/ (pl: -s) redactor; editor; orchestrator

de **bewerking** /bəwɛrkɪŋ/ (pl: -en) **1** treatment; cultivation; process(ing); manufacturing; editing: *de derde druk van dit schoolboek is in* ~ the third edition of this textbook is in preparation **2** adaptation; version; arrangement; revision: *de Nederlandse* ~ *van dit boek* the Dutch version of this book; ~ *voor toneel* (*or: de film*) adaptation for stage (*or:* the screen) **3** manipulation, influencing **4** processing

bewerkstelligen /bəwɛrkstɛləɣə(n)/ (bewerkstelligde, heeft bewerkstelligd) bring about, effect, realize: *een ontmoeting* (*or: verzoening*) ~ bring about a meeting (*or:* reconciliation)

het **bewijs** /bəwɛis/ (pl: bewijzen) **1** proof, evidence: [Belg] ~ *van goed gedrag en zeden* [roughly] certificate of good character; *het* ~ *leveren (dat, van)* produce evidence (that, of); *als* ~ *aanvoeren* quote (in evidence) **2** proof, evidence, sign: *als* ~ *van erkentelijkheid* as a token of gratitude; *het levende* ~ *zijn van* be the living proof of **3** proof, certificate: *betalingsbewijs* proof of payment, receipt; ~ *van goed gedrag* certificate of good conduct

de **bewijslast** /bəwɛislɑst/ (pl: -en) burden of proof

het **bewijsmateriaal** /bəwɛismaterijal/ evidence, proof

bewijzen /bəwɛizə(n)/ (bewees, heeft bewezen) **1** prove, establish, demonstrate: *dit bewijst dat* this proves that **2** render, show, prove: *de laatste eer* ~ *aan iem.* render the last honours to s.o., pay s.o. one's last respects || *zichzelf moeten* ~ have to prove o.s.

het **bewind** /bəwɪnt/ **1** government, regime, rule: *aan het* ~ *komen* come to power; *het* ~ *voeren over* govern, rule (over); manage, administer **2** administration, government

de **bewindsman** /bəwɪn(t)smɑn/ (pl: -lieden, -personen) member of government (*or:* cabinet); minister, secretary

de **bewindsvrouw** /bəwɪn(t)sfrɑu/ *see bewindsman*

de **bewindvoerder** /bəwɪntfurdər/ (pl: -s) administrator, director

bewogen /bəwoɣə(n)/ (adj) **1** moved: *tot tranen toe* ~ moved to tears **2** stirring, eventful

de **bewolking** /bəwɔlkɪŋ/ (pl: -en) cloud(s):

laaghangende ~ low cloud(s)

bewolkt /bəwɔlkt/ (adj) cloudy, overcast

de **bewonderaar** /bəwɔndərar/ (pl: -s) admirer; [inform] fan

bewonderen /bəwɔndərə(n)/ (bewonderde, heeft bewonderd) admire, look up to

bewonderenswaardig /bəwɔndərənswardəx/ (adj, adv) admirable, wonderful

de **bewondering** /bəwɔndərɪŋ/ admiration, wonder

bewonen /bəwonə(n)/ (bewoonde, heeft bewoond) inhabit, occupy; live in

de **bewoner** /bəwonər/ (pl: -s) inhabitant; occupant; resident

de **bewoning** /bəwonɪŋ/ occupation, residence

bewoonbaar /bəwombar/ (adj) (in)habitable; liveable

de **bewoordingen** /bəwordɪŋə(n)/ (pl) terms: *in krachtige* ~ strongly worded; warmly expressed

¹**bewust** /bəwʏst/ (adj) **1** concerned, involved: *op die ~e dag* on the day in question **2** aware, conscious: *ik ben me niet ~ van enige tekortkomingen* I am not aware of any shortcomings

²**bewust** /bəwʏst/ (adv) consciously, knowingly

bewusteloos /bəwʏstələos/ (adj) unconscious, senseless: ~ *raken* pass out

de **bewusteloosheid** /bəwʏstələoshɛit/ unconsciousness

de **bewustwording** /bəwʏstwordɪŋ/ awakening (to), realization

het **bewustzijn** /bəwʏstsɛin/ consciousness; awareness: *zijn* ~ *verliezen* lose consciousness; *buiten* ~ *zijn* be unconscious; *weer tot* ~ *komen* regain (*or:* recover) consciousness

bezaaien /bəzajə(n)/ (bezaaide, heeft bezaaid) strew, stud: *bezaaid met* strewn with; studded with; littered with; dotted with

bezadigd /bəzadəxt/ (adj) sober, level-headed, dispassionate

bezegelen /bəzeɣələ(n)/ (bezegelde, heeft bezegeld) seal

de **bezem** /bezəm/ (pl: -s) broom

de **bezemsteel** /bezəmstel/ (pl: -stelen) broomstick, broomhandle

¹**bezeren** /bəzerə(n)/ (bezeerde, heeft bezeerd) hurt, bruise

zich ²**bezeren** /bəzerə(n)/ (bezeerde zich, heeft zich bezeerd) hurt o.s., get hurt; [stronger] injure o.s.

bezet /bəzɛt/ (adj) **1** occupied; taken: ~ *gebied* occupied territory; *geheel* ~ full (up) **2** taken up, occupied **3** engaged, occupied, busy || *de lijn is* ~ the line is engaged, busy

bezeten /bəzetə(n)/ (adj) **1** possessed (by): *als een ~e tekeergaan* go berserk **2** obsessed (by)

de **bezetene** /bəzetənə/ (pl: -n) possessed per-

bezetten

son: *als* een ~ frenetically, madly

bezetten /bəzɛtə(n)/ (bezette, heeft bezet) occupy, take, fill: *een belangrijke* **plaats** ~ *in* occupy an important place in; feature in

de **bezetter** /bəzɛtər/ (pl: -s) occupier(s), occupying force(s)

de **bezetting** /bəzɛtɪŋ/ (pl: -en) **1** occupation; sit-in; filling; filling up **2** [theatre] cast

bezichtigen /bəzɪxtəɣə(n)/ (bezichtigde, heeft bezichtigd) (pay a) visit (to); see; tour; inspect: *een* **huis** ~ view a house

de **bezichtiging** /bəzɪxtəɣɪŋ/ (pl: -en) visit, view, inspection, tour

bezield /bəzilt/ (adj) **1** alive, living **2** animated, inspired

bezielen /bəzilə(n)/ (bezielde, heeft bezield) inspire, animate: *wat bezielt je!* what has got into you!

de **bezieling** /bəzilɪŋ/ inspiration, animation

bezien /bəzin/ (bezag, heeft bezien) see, consider, look on

de **bezienswaardigheid** /bəzinswardəxhɛit/ (pl: -heden) place of interest, sight

bezig /bezəx/ (adj) busy (with sth., doing sth.), working (on), preoccupied (with), engaged (in): *de wedstrijd* **is** *al* ~ the match has already started; *als je* **er** *toch* **mee** ~ *bent* while you are at it (*or*: about it); *vreselijk lang* **met** *iets* ~ *zijn* be an awful long time over sth. ‖ *waar* **ben** *je eigenlijk mee* ~*!* what do you think you're up to?; *hij* **is** *weer* ~ he's at it again

bezigen /bezəɣə(n)/ (bezigde, heeft gebezigd) [form] employ, use: *verstandige* **taal** ~ talk sense

de **bezigheid** /bezəxhɛit/ (pl: -heden) activity, occupation, work

de **bezigheidstherapie** /bezəxhɛitsterapi/ occupational therapy

¹**bezighouden** /bezəxhɑudə(n)/ (hield bezig, heeft beziggehouden) occupy, keep busy

zich ²**bezighouden** /bezəxhɑudə(n)/ (hield zich bezig, heeft zich beziggehouden) occupy (*or*: busy) o.s. (with), engage (o.s.) (in)

bezinken /bəzɪŋkə(n)/ (bezonk, is bezonken) **1** settle (down), sink (to the bottom) **2** clarify, settle (out)

het **bezinksel** /bəzɪŋksəl/ (pl: -s) sediment, deposit, residue

zich **bezinnen** /bəzɪnə(n)/ (bezon zich, heeft zich bezonnen) **1** contemplate, reflect (on): *bezint eer ge begint* look before you leap **2** change one's mind

de **bezinning** /bəzɪnɪŋ/ reflection, contemplation

het **bezit** /bəzɪt/ possession, property: *in* ~ *houden* keep in one's possession

bezittelijk /bəzɪtələk/ (adj) possessive: ~ *voornaamwoord* possessive pronoun

bezitten /bəzɪtə(n)/ (bezat, heeft bezeten) possess, own, have

de **bezitter** /bəzɪtər/ (pl: -s) owner; holder; possessor

de **bezitting** /bəzɪtɪŋ/ (pl: -en) property, possession, belongings; estate: *persoonlijke* ~*en* personal belongings; **waardevolle** ~*en* valuables

bezocht /bəzɔxt/ (adj) visited, attended, frequented: *een druk* ~*e* **receptie** a busy reception

bezoedelen /bəzudələ(n)/ (bezoedelde, heeft bezoedeld) defile, besmirch, sully

het **bezoek** /bəzuk/ (pl: -en) **1** visit; call: *op* ~ *gaan bij iem.* pay s.o. a visit **2** visitor(s), guest(s), caller(s)

bezoeken /bəzukə(n)/ (bezocht, heeft bezocht) visit, pay a visit to: *een* **school** ~ attend a school; *een* **website** ~ visit a website

de **bezoeker** /bəzukər/ (pl: -s) visitor, guest: *een site met een miljoen* ~*s per week* a site with a million visitors a week

het **bezoekerscentrum** /bəzukərsɛntrʏm/ (pl: -centra) visitors centre

de **bezoekregeling** /bəzukreɣəlɪŋ/ (pl: -en) visiting arrangements

het **bezoekuur** /bəzukyr/ (pl: -uren) visiting hour(s) (*or*: time)

de **bezoldiging** /bəzɔldəɣɪŋ/ (pl: -en) pay, salary

zich **bezondigen** /bəzɔndəɣə(n)/ (bezondigde zich, heeft zich bezondigd) be guilty of

bezopen /bəzopə(n)/ (adj) [inform] **1** sloshed, plastered **2** absurd

bezorgd /bəzɔrxt/ (adj, adv) **1** concerned (for, about): *de* ~*e* **moeder** the caring mother **2** worried (about): *wees* maar niet ~ don't worry

de **bezorgdheid** /bəzɔrxthɛit/ (pl: -heden) concern (for, about), worry

bezorgen /bəzɔrɣə(n)/ (bezorgde, heeft bezorgd) **1** get, provide: *iem. een* **baan** ~ get s.o. a job; *dat bezorgt ons heel wat extra* **werk** that lands us with a lot of extra work **2** give, cause: *iem. een hoop* **last** ~ put s.o. to great inconvenience **3** deliver: *de* **post** ~ deliver the post

de **bezorger** /bəzɔrɣər/ (pl: -s) delivery man (*or*: woman)

de **bezorging** /bəzɔrɣɪŋ/ (pl: -en) delivery

bezuinigen /bəzœynəɣə(n)/ (bezuinigde, heeft bezuinigd) economize, save

de **bezuiniging** /bəzœynəɣɪŋ/ (pl: -en) **1** economy, cut(back) **2** saving(s)

de **bezuinigingsmaatregel** /bəzœynəɣɪŋsmatreɣəl/ (pl: -en) economy measure; expenditure (*or*: spending) cut

bezuren /bəzyrə(n)/: *dat zal je* you'll regret (*or*: pay for, suffer for) that

het **bezwaar** /bəzwar/ (pl: bezwaren) **1** drawback **2** objection; scruple: ~ *maken tegen iets* object to sth.; *zonder enig* ~ without any objection

bezwaard /bəzwart/ (adj) troubled

bezwaarlijk /bəzwarlək/ (adj) troublesome

het **bezwaarschrift** /bəzwarsχrɪft/ (pl: -en) protest, petition

bezweet /bəzwet/ (adj) sweaty, sweating

bezweren /bəzwerə(n)/ (bezwoer, heeft bezworen) **1** implore **2** avert

bezwijken /bəzwɛikə(n)/ (bezweek, is bezweken) **1** give (way, out): *onder* een last ~ [also fig] collapse under a load **2** succumb, yield: *voor* de verleiding ~ yield to (or: give in) to the temptation **3** go under: *aan* een ziekte ~ succumb to a disease

de **Bhutaan** /butan/ (pl: Bhutanen) Bhutanese

Bhutaans /butans/ (adj) Bhutan(ese)

Bhutan /butan/ Bhutan

bibberen /bɪbərə(n)/ (bibberde, heeft gebibberd) shiver (with)

de **bibliografie** /biblijoɣrafi/ (pl: -ën) bibliography

de **bibliothecaris** /biblijotekarəs/ (pl: -sen) librarian

de **bibliotheek** /biblijotek/ (pl: bibliotheken) library

de **biceps** /bisɛps/ (pl: -en) biceps

de ¹**bicultureel** /bikʏltyrel/ (pl: biculturelen) bicultural

²**bicultureel** /bikʏltyrel/ (adj) bicultural

bidden /bɪdə(n)/ (bad, heeft gebeden) **1** pray, say one's prayers: *tot* God ~ *om* pray to God for **2** implore

de **biecht** /biχt/ (pl: -en) confession: *iem. de ~ afnemen* hear s.o.'s confession

biechten /biχtə(n)/ (biechtte, heeft gebiecht) confess, go to confession

de **biechtstoel** /biχtstul/ (pl: -en) confessional (box)

bieden /bidə(n)/ (bood, heeft geboden) **1** offer; present **2** [cards] bid: *het is jouw beurt om te* ~ it's your (turn to) bid now **3** (make an) offer, (make a) bid: *ik bied er twintig euro voor* I'll give you twenty euros for it

de **bieder** /bidər/ (pl: -s) bidder

de **biefstuk** /bifstʏk/ (pl: -ken) steak: *~ van de haas* fillet steak

de **biels** /bils/ (pl: bielzen) (railway) sleeper; [Am] railroad tie

het **bier** /bir/ (pl: -en) beer: [Belg] *klein* ~ small beer; *~ van het vat* draught beer

het **bierblikje** /birblɪkjə/ (pl: -s) beer can

de **bierbrouwerij** /birbrɑuwərɛi/ (pl: -en) brewery

de **bierbuik** /birbœyk/ (pl: -en) **1** beer belly, beer gut **2** beer guzzler

het **bierglas** /birɣlɑs/ (pl: -glazen) beer glass

de **bierkeet** /birket/ (pl: -keten) beer barn, beer joint

het **bierviltje** /birvɪltjə/ (pl: -s) beer mat, coaster

de **bies** /bis/ (pl: biezen) **1** piping, border, edg-

ing **2** rush ‖ *zijn biezen* **pakken** make o.s. scarce

het **bieslook** /bislok/ chives

de **biet** /bit/ (pl: -en) beet

bietsen /bitsə(n)/ (bietste, heeft gebietst) [inform] scrounge, cadge

biezen /bizə(n)/ (adj) rush: *een ~ zitting* a rush(-bottomed) seat; *see bies*

de **big** /bɪχ/ (pl: -gen) piglet; piggy

biggelen /bɪɣələ(n)/ (biggelde, heeft/is gebiggeld) trickle

de ¹**bij** /bɛi/ (pl: -en) (honey) bee

²**bij** /bɛi/ (adj) **1** up-to-date: *de leerling is* weer (or: *nog niet*) ~ *met wiskunde* the pupil has now caught up on (or: is still behind in) mathematics **2** up-to-date: *(goed)* ~ *zijn* be (thoroughly) on top of things

³**bij** /bɛi/ (prep) **1** near (to), close (by, to): ~ *iem. gaan zitten* sit next to s.o. **2** at, to: ~ *een kruispunt komen* come to an intersection **3** to, with: *alles blijft* ~ *het oude* everything stays the same; *we zullen het er maar* ~ *laten* let's leave it at that **4** while, during: ~ *zijn dood* at his death **5** at: *zij was* ~ *haar tante* she was at her aunt's; *er niet* ~ *zijn met zijn gedachten* have only half one's mind on it **6** for, with: ~ *een baas werken* work for a boss; ~ *de marine* in the navy; *~ ons* at our house; back home; in our country (or: family) **7** with, along: *zij had haar dochter* ~ *zich* she had her daughter with her; *ik heb geen geld* ~ *me* I have no money on me **8** with, to: *inlichtingen* ~ *de balie inwinnen* request information at the desk; ~ *zichzelf (denken, zeggen)* (think, say) to o.s. **9** by: *iem.* ~ *naam kennen* know s.o. by name **10** by, at: ~ *het lezen van de krant* (when) reading the newspaper; ~ *het ontbijt* at breakfast **11** in case of, if **12** for, in the eyes of: *zij kan* ~ *de buren geen goed doen* she can do no good as far as the neighbours are concerned ‖ *de kamer is 6* ~ *5* the room is 6 by 5; *je bent er* ~ the game is up; gotcha!

het **bijbaantje** /bɛibantʃə/ (pl: -s) job on the side, second (or: secondary) job: *een ~ heb-ben* moonlight

de **bijbedoeling** /bɛibədulɪŋ/ ulterior motive (or: design)

bijbehorend /bɛibəhorənt/ (adj) accompanying, matching

de **Bijbel** /bɛibəl/ (pl: -s) Bible

Bijbels /bɛibəls/ (adj) biblical

het **Bijbelvers** /bɛibəlvɛrs/ (pl: -verzen) Bible verse

bijbenen /bɛibenə(n)/ keep up (with)

bijbetalen /bɛibətalə(n)/ (betaalde bij, heeft bijbetaald) pay extra, pay an additional (or: extra) charge

bijblijven /bɛiblɛivə(n)/ (bleef bij, is bijgebleven) **1** keep pace, keep up **2** stick in one's memory: *dat zal mij altijd* ~ I shall never forget it

bijboeken /bɛɪbukə(n)/ (boekte bij, heeft bijgeboekt) post; enter, write up: *een bedrag* ~ transfer an amount, credit an amount to s.o.'s account; *een* **weekje** ~ book an extra week, add a week (to one's stay)

bijbrengen /bɛɪbrɛŋə(n)/ (bracht bij, heeft bijgebracht) impart (to), convey (to), instil (into): *iem. bepaalde* **kennis** ~ convey (certain) knowledge to s.o.

bijdehand /bɛɪdəhɑnt/ (adj) bright, sharp

de **bijdrage** /bɛɪdraɣə/ (pl: -n) contribution, offering

bijdragen /bɛɪdraɣə(n)/ (droeg bij, heeft bijgedragen) contribute, add: *zijn* **steentje** ~ do one's bit

bijeen /bɛɪen/ (adv) together

bijeenbrengen /bɛɪembrɛŋə(n)/ (bracht bijeen, heeft bijeengebracht) bring together, get together, raise

bijeenkomen /bɛɪeŋkomə(n)/ (kwam bijeen, is bijeengekomen) meet, assemble

de **bijeenkomst** /bɛɪeŋkomst/ (pl: -en) meeting, gathering

bijeenroepen /bɛɪenrupə(n)/ (riep bijeen, heeft bijeengeroepen) call together, convene

het ¹**bijeenzijn** /bɛɪenzɛɪn/ gathering

²**bijeenzijn** /bɛɪenzɛɪn/ (was bijeen, is bijeengeweest) be together (*or:* gathered): *de* **commissie** *is bijeengeweest* the commission has met

de **bijenhouder** /bɛɪə(n)hɑudər/ (pl: -s) beekeeper

de **bijenkoningin** /bɛɪə(n)konɪŋɪn/ (pl: -nen) queen bee

de **bijenkorf** /bɛɪə(n)kɔrf/ (pl: -korven) (bee)hive

de **bijenteelt** /bɛɪə(n)telt/ apiculture

het **bijenvolk** /bɛɪə(n)vɔlk/ (pl: -en) (swarm of, hive of) bees

het/de **bijenwas** /bɛɪə(n)wɑs/ beeswax

¹**bijgaand** /bɛɪɣant/ (adj) enclosed: *de* ~*e* **stukken** the enclosures

²**bijgaand** /bɛɪɣant/ (adv) enclosed: ~ *treft u aan ...* please find enclosed ...

het **bijgebouw** /bɛɪɣəbɑu/ (pl: -en) annex, outbuilding

de **bijgedachte** /bɛɪɣədɑxtə/ (pl: -n) **1** association **2** ulterior motive (*or:* design)

het **bijgeloof** /bɛɪɣəlof/ superstition

bijgelovig /bɛɪɣəlovəx/ (adj, adv) superstitious

de **bijgelovigheid** /bɛɪɣəlovəxhɛit/ (pl: -heden) superstition, superstitiousness

bijgenaamd /bɛɪɣənamt/ (adj) called; nicknamed

bijhouden /bɛɪhɑudə(n)/ (hield bij, heeft bijgehouden) **1** hold out (*or:* up) (to): *houd je* **bord** *bij* hold out your plate **2** keep up (with), keep pace (with): *het* **onderwijs** *niet kunnen* ~ be unable to keep up at school **3** keep up to

date: *de* **stand** ~ keep count (*or:* the score)

het **bijhuis** /bɛɪhœys/ (pl: bijhuizen) [Belg] branch

het **bijkantoor** /bɛɪkɑntor/ (pl: bijkantoren) branch (office)

de **bijkeuken** /bɛɪkøkə(n)/ (pl: -s) scullery

bijklussen /bɛɪklʏsə(n)/ (kluste bij, heeft bijgeklust) have a sideline

bijkomen /bɛɪkomə(n)/ (kwam bij, is bijgekomen) **1** come to (*or:* round) **2** (re)gain (one's) breath, recover (o.s.): *niet meer* ~ *(van het lachen)* be overcome (with laughter)

bijkomend /bɛɪkomənt/ (adj) additional, incidental; subordinate

bijkomstig /bɛɪkɔmstəx/ (adj) accidental, incidental; inessential; secondary; subordinate

de **bijkomstigheid** /bɛɪkɔmstəxhɛit/ (pl: -heden) incidental circumstance

de **bijl** /bɛɪl/ (pl: -en) axe ‖ *het* ~*tje erbij* **neerleggen** knock off, call it a day; call it quits

de **bijlage** /bɛɪlaɣə/ (pl: -n) **1** enclosure, appendix; supplement **2** [comp] attachment

bijlange /bɛɪlɑŋə/ (adv): ~ *na* **niet** not anything like (as nice, good, ...), not nearly (so nice, good, ...); not by a long shot (*or:* chalk)!

bijleggen /bɛɪlɛɣə(n)/ (legde bij, heeft bijgelegd) **1** contribute, pay; make up **2** settle: *het* ~ make up

de **bijles** /bɛɪlɛs/ (pl: -sen) coaching; [Am also] tutoring

bijlichten /bɛɪlɪxtə(n)/ (lichtte bij, heeft bijgelicht) light: *iem.* ~ give (a) light to s.o.

bijna /bɛɪna/ (adv) almost, nearly; close on; near: ~ **nooit** (or: **geen**) almost never (*or:* none), hardly ever (*or:* any)

de **bijnaam** /bɛɪnam/ (pl: bijnamen) nickname

de **bijna-doodervaring** /bɛɪnadotɛrvarɪŋ/ (pl: -en) near-death experience

het **bijou** /biʒu/ (pl: -s) jewel

bijpassen /bɛɪpɑsə(n)/ (paste bij, heeft bijgepast) pay; make up (the difference): *je zult* **moeten** ~ you will have to pay (*or:* make up) the difference

bijpassend /bɛɪpɑsənt/ (adj) matching; to match

bijpraten /bɛɪpratə(n)/ (praatte bij, heeft bijgepraat) catch up: *iem.* ~ bring s.o. up to date

het **bijproduct** /bɛɪprodʏkt/ (pl: -en) by-product, spin-off

de **bijrijder** /bɛɪrɛɪdər/ (pl: -s) substitute-driver, driver's mate

de **bijrol** /bɛɪrɔl/ (pl: -len) supporting role (*or:* part) [also fig]

bijschaven /bɛɪsxavə(n)/ (schaafde bij, heeft bijgeschaafd) **1** plane (down) **2** [fig] polish: *een* **opstel** ~ polish up an essay

bijscholen /bɛɪsxolə(n)/ (schoolde bij, heeft bijgeschoold) give further training

de **bijscholing** /bɛɪsxolɪŋ/ (extra) training

het **bijschrift** /bɛisχrɪft/ (pl: -en) **1** caption, legend **2** note

bijschrijven /bɛisχrɛivə(n)/ (schreef bij, heeft bijgeschreven) enter, include

de **bijschrijving** /bɛisχrɛivɪŋ/ (pl: -en) **1** entering (in the books) **2** amount entered, item entered

de **bijsluiter** /bɛislœytər/ (pl: -s) information leaflet, instruction leaflet

de **bijsmaak** /bɛismak/ (pl: bijsmaken) taste: *deze soep heeft een ~je* this soup has a funny taste to it, this soup doesn't taste right

bijspijkeren /bɛispɛikərə(n)/ (spijkerde bij, heeft bijgespijkerd) brush up: *een zwakke leerling* ~ bring a weak pupil up to standard

bijspringen /bɛisprɪŋə(n)/ (sprong bij, heeft/is bijgesprongen) support, help out

¹**bijstaan** /bɛistan/ (stond bij, heeft bijgestaan) dimly recollect: *er staat me iets bij van een vergadering waar hij heen zou gaan* I seem to remember that he was to go to a meeting

²**bijstaan** /bɛistan/ (stond bij, heeft bijgestaan) assist, aid

de **bijstand** /bɛistɑnt/ **1** assistance, aid; social security: *hij leeft van de* ~ he's on social security; ~ *verlenen* render assistance **2** Social Security

de **bijstandsmoeder** /bɛistɑntsmudər/ (pl: -s) mother on social security

de **bijstandsuitkering** /bɛistɑntsœytkerɪŋ/ (pl: -en) social security (payment)

de **bijstandswet** /bɛistɑntswɛt/ social security act

bijstellen /bɛistɛlə(n)/ (stelde bij, heeft bijgesteld) (re-)adjust

de **bijstelling** /bɛistɛlɪŋ/ (pl: -en) (re-)adjustment

bijster /bɛistər/ (adv) unduly, (none) too: *de tuin is niet ~ groot* the garden is none too large ‖ *het spoor ~ zijn* have lost one's way

bijsturen /bɛistyrə(n)/ (stuurde bij, heeft bijgestuurd) **1** steer (away from, clear of, towards) **2** [fig] steer away from (*or:* clear of); adjust

de **bijt** /bɛit/ (pl: -en) hole (in the ice)

bijtanken /bɛitɛŋkə(n)/ (tankte bij, heeft bijgetankt) **1** refuel **2** [fig] replenish one's reserves, recharge one's battery

bijten /bɛitə(n)/ (beet, heeft gebeten) **1** bite: *van zich af* ~ give as good as one gets, stick up for o.s. **2** sting, smart

bijtend /bɛitənt/ (adj, adv) biting; corrosive

bijtijds /bɛitɛits/ (adv) **1** early **2** early, (well) in advance

bijtreden /bɛitredə(n)/ (trad bij, is bijgetreden) [Belg] agree (with)

bijtrekken /bɛitrɛkə(n)/ (trok bij, is bijgetrokken) **1** straighten (out), improve **2** come (a)round

bijv. (abbrev) *bijvoorbeeld* e.g.

het **bijvak** /bɛivak/ (pl: -ken) subsidiary (subject)

de **bijval** /bɛivɑl/ approval; support

bijvallen /bɛivɑlə(n)/ (viel bij, is bijgevallen) agree (with), support, back up: *iem.* ~ *go* along with s.o., agree with s.o.

bijverdienen /bɛivərdinə(n)/ (verdiende bij, heeft bijverdiend) have an additional income: *een paar pond* ~ earn a few pounds extra (*or:* on the side)

de **bijverdienste** /bɛivərdinstə/ (pl: -n) extra earnings, extra income, additional income

het **bijverschijnsel** /bɛivərsχɛinsəl/ (pl: -en) side effect

bijvoegen /bɛivuɣə(n)/ (voegde bij, heeft bijgevoegd) add; enclose; attach

bijvoeglijk /bɛivuχlək/ (adj): ~ *naamwoord* adjective

het **bijvoegsel** /bɛivuχsəl/ (pl: -s) supplement, addition

bijvoorbeeld /bɛivorbelt/ (adv) for example, for instance, e.g.

bijvullen /bɛivγlə(n)/ (vulde bij, heeft bijgevuld) top up (with); fill up (with)

bijwerken /bɛiwɛrkə(n)/ (werkte bij, heeft bijgewerkt) improve, catch up (on); bring up to date; update

de **bijwerking** /bɛiwɛrkɪŋ/ (pl: -en) side effect

bijwonen /bɛiwonə(n)/ (woonde bij, heeft bijgewoond) attend, be present at

het **bijwoord** /bɛiwort/ (pl: -en) adverb

de **bijzaak** /bɛizak/ (pl: bijzaken) side issue, (minor) detail

bijzetten /bɛizɛtə(n)/ (zette bij, heeft bijgezet) **1** add **2** inter, bury

bijziend /bɛizint/ (adj) short-sighted

de **bijziendheid** /bɛizinthɛit/ short-sightedness

het **bijzijn** /bɛizɛin/: *in (het)* ~ *van* in the presence of

de **bijzin** /bɛizɪn/ (pl: -nen) (subordinate) clause: *betrekkelijke* ~ relative clause

¹**bijzonder** /bizɔndər/ (adj) **1** particular: *in het* ~ in particular, especially **2** special, unique **3** strange, peculiar **4** private

²**bijzonder** /bizɔndər/ (adv) **1** very (much) **2** particularly, in particular, especially

de **bijzonderheid** /bizɔndərhɛit/ (pl: -heden) detail, particular

de **bikini** /bikini/ (pl: -'s) bikini

bikkelhard /bɪkəlhɑrt/ (adj) **1** rock-hard **2** very hard

bikken /bɪkə(n)/ (bikte, heeft gebikt) chip (away)

de **bil** /bɪl/ (pl: -len) buttock: *dikke* (or: *blote*) ~*len* a fat (or: bare) bottom

de/het **bila** /bila/ (pl: -'s) tête-à-tête, face-to-face (*or:* one-to-one) meeting

bilateraal /bilateral/ (adj) bilateral

biljard /bɪljɑrt/ (num) thousand billion(s); [Am] quadrillion

het **biljart** /bɪljɑrt/ (pl: -s) billiards, billiard table

de **biljartbal** /bɪljɑrdbɑl/ (pl: -len) billiard ball:

*zo kaal **als** een ~* as bald as a coot

biljarten /bɪljɑrtə(n)/ (biljartte, heeft gebiljart) play billiards

de **biljarter** /bɪljɑrtər/ billiards player

de **biljartkeu** /bɪljɑrtkø/ (pl: -s, -en) billiard cue

het **biljet** /bɪljɛt/ (pl: -ten) **1** ticket; bill; poster **2** note; [Am] bill

het **biljoen** /bɪljun/ (pl: -en) trillion

het/de **billboard** /bɪlbɔːrd/ (pl: -s) billboard

de **billenkoek** /bɪlə(n)kuk/: *~ **krijgen*** get a smacking, get a spanking

billijk /bɪlək/ (adj, adv) fair, reasonable; moderate

billijken /bɪləkə(n)/ (billijkte, heeft gebillijkt) approve of: *dat **kan** ik ~* I approve of that; *dat **valt** te ~* that is quite reasonable

de **billijkheid** /bɪləkhɛit/ fairness, reasonableness

binair /binɛːr/ (adj) binary

¹**binden** /bɪndə(n)/ (bond, heeft gebonden) **1** tie (up), knot, bind, fasten; strap **2** tie (up) **3** bind: *door **voorschriften** gebonden zijn* be bound by regulations **4** bind **5** [culinary] thicken

zich ²**binden** /bɪndə(n)/ (bond zich, heeft zich gebonden) commit o.s. (to), bind (*or:* pledge) o.s. (to)

bindend /bɪndənt/ (adj) binding

de **binding** /bɪndɪŋ/ (pl: -en) bond, tie

het **bindmiddel** /bɪntmɪdəl/ (pl: -en) binding agent, binder

het **bindweefsel** /bɪntwefsəl/ connective (*or:* interstitial) tissue

het **bingo** /bɪŋɡo/ bingo

de **bink** /bɪŋk/ (pl: -en) hunk: *de ~ **uithangen*** show off, play the tough guy

¹**binnen** /bɪnə(n)/ (adv) inside, in; indoors: *hij **is** ~* he has got it made; *daar ~* inside, in there; *naar ~ gaan* go in, go inside, enter; *het wil me niet **te** ~ schieten* I can't bring it to mind; *van ~* (on the) inside; *'~!'* come in!

²**binnen** /bɪnə(n)/ (prep) inside, within: *het ligt ~ mijn **bereik*** [also fig] it is within my reach

de **binnenbaan** /bɪnə(n)ban/ (pl: -banen) **1** inside lane **2** indoor track; indoor court

het **binnenbad** /bɪnə(n)bɑt/ (pl: -en) indoor (swimming) pool

de **binnenband** /bɪnə(n)bɑnt/ (pl: -en) (inner) tube

de **binnenbocht** /bɪnə(n)bɔχt/ (pl: -en) inside bend

binnenboord /bɪnə(n)bɔrt/ (adv) inboard ‖ *zijn benen ~ **houden*** keep one's legs in(side)

binnenbrengen /bɪnə(n)brɛŋə(n)/ (bracht binnen, heeft binnengebracht) bring in, take in, carry in

binnendoor /bɪnə(n)dor/ (adv): *~ **gaan*** take the direct route

binnendringen /bɪnə(n)drɪŋə(n)/ (drong binnen, is binnengedrongen) penetrate

(into), enter; break in(to); force one's way in(to)

binnendruppelen /bɪnə(n)drvpələ(n)/ (druppelde binnen, is binnengedruppeld) [also fig] trickle in(to)

binnengaan /bɪnə(n)ɣan/ (ging binnen, is binnengegaan) enter, go in(to), walk in(to)

binnenhalen /bɪnə(n)halə(n)/ (haalde binnen, heeft binnengehaald) fetch in, bring in; land

de **binnenhaven** /bɪnə(n)havə(n)/ (pl: -s) inland harbour (*or:* port); inner harbour

het **Binnenhof** /bɪnə(n)hɔf/ the Dutch Parliament

binnenhouden /bɪnə(n)haudə(n)/ (hield binnen, heeft binnengehouden) keep in(doors)

de **binnenhuisarchitect** /bɪnə(n)hœysɑrʃitɛkt/ (pl: -en) interior designer (and decorator)

binnenin /bɪnə(n)ɪn/ (adv) inside

de **binnenkant** /bɪnə(n)kɑnt/ (pl: -en) inside, interior

binnenkomen /bɪnə(n)komə(n)/ (kwam binnen, is binnengekomen) come in(to), walk in(to), enter; arrive: *zij mocht **niet** ~* she was not allowed (to come) in

de **binnenkomst** /bɪnə(n)kɔmst/ entry, entrance; arrival

binnenkort /bɪnə(n)kɔrt/ (adv) soon, shortly, before (very) long

binnenkrijgen /bɪnə(n)krɛiɣə(n)/ (kreeg binnen, heeft binnengekregen) **1** get down, swallow **2** get, obtain

het **binnenland** /bɪnə(n)lɑnt/ (pl: -en) **1** interior, inland **2** home

binnenlands /bɪnə(n)lɑnts/ (adj) home, internal, domestic

binnenlaten /bɪnə(n)latə(n)/ (liet binnen, heeft binnengelaten) let in(to), admit (to); show in(to), usher in(to)

binnenlopen /bɪnə(n)lopə(n)/ (liep binnen, is binnengelopen) go in(to), walk in(to)

de **binnenmarkt** /bɪnəmɑrkt/ internal market

de **binnenmuur** /bɪnə(n)myr/ (pl: -muren) interior wall, inside wall

de **binnenplaats** /bɪnə(n)plats/ (pl: -en) (inner) court(yard); yard

het **binnenpretje** /bɪnə(n)prɛcə/ (pl: -s) secret amusement

de **binnenschipper** /bɪnə(n)sχɪpər/ (pl: -s) skipper of a barge

binnenshuis /bɪnənshœys/ (adv) indoors, inside, within doors

binnensmonds /bɪnənsmɔnts/ (adv) inarticulately, indistinctly

de **binnensport** /bɪnə(n)spɔrt/ (pl: -en) indoor sport

de **binnenstad** /bɪnə(n)stɑt/ (pl: -steden) town centre; city centre; inner city

het **binnenste** /bɪnə(n)stə/ inside, in(ner)most

part, inner part

binnenstebuiten /bɪnənstəbœytə(n)/ (adv) inside out, wrong side out

binnenstormen /bɪnə(n)stɔrmə(n)/ (stormde binnen, is binnengestormd): *zij kwam de **kamer** ~ she came storming (or: dashing, rushing) into the room*

binnenstromen /bɪnə(n)stromə(n)/ (stroomde binnen, is binnengestroomd) [also fig] pour in(to), flow in(to); rush in(to), surge in(to)

binnentrekken /bɪnə(n)trɛkə(n)/ (trok binnen, is binnengetrokken) march in(to), enter

de **binnenvaart** /bɪnə(n)vart/ inland shipping

binnenvallen /bɪnə(n)valə(n)/ (viel binnen, is binnengevallen) burst in(to), barge in(to); invade: *bij iem. **komen** ~ descend on s.o.*

de **binnenvetter** /bɪnə(n)vɛtər/ (pl: -s) introvert

het **binnenwater** /bɪnə(n)watər/ (pl: -en) **1** inland waterway, canal, river **2** polder water

de **binnenweg** /bɪnə(n)wɛx/ (pl: -en) byroad; short cut

de **binnenzak** /bɪnə(n)zak/ (pl: -ken) inside pocket

de **binnenzee** /bɪnə(n)ze/ (pl: -ën) inland sea

het **bint** /bɪnt/ (pl: -en) beam; joist

de **biobak** /bijobak/ (pl: -ken) compost bin

de **bioboer** biological farmer, organic farmer

de **biobrandstof** /bijobrɑntstɔf/ (pl: -fen) biofuel

de **biochemicus** /bijoxemikʏs/ (pl: biochemici) biochemist

de **biochemie** /bijoxemi/ biochemistry

biodynamisch /bijodinamis/ (adj) biodynamic

de **bio-energie** /bijoenɛrʒi/ bioenergy

de **biograaf** /bijoɣraf/ (pl: biografen) biographer

de **biografie** /bijoɣrafi/ (pl: -ën) biography

biografisch /bijoɣrafis/ (adj) biographic(al)

de **bio-industrie** /bijoɪndʏstri/ (pl: -ën) factory farming; agribusiness

de **biologie** /bijoloɣi/ biology

biologisch /bijoloɣis/ (adj, adv) biological, organic

de **bioloog** /bijolox/ (pl: biologen) biologist

het **bioritme** /bijorɪtmə/ (pl: -s) biorhythm

de **bioscoop** /bijoskop/ (pl: bioscopen) cinema

de **bips** /bɪps/ (pl: -en) bottom, backside, buttocks

Birma /bɪrma/ Burma

de **Birmaan** /bɪrman/ (pl: Birmanen) Burmese

Birmaans /bɪrmans/ (adj) Burmese

bis /bis/ (adv) (once) again, encore

het **biscuitje** /bɪskwicə/ biscuit; [Am] cookie

het **bisdom** /bɪzdɔm/ (pl: -men) diocese, bishopric

biseksueel /bisɛksywel/ (adj) bisexual

de **bisschop** /bɪsxɔp/ (pl: -pen) bishop

bisschoppelijk /bɪsxɔpələk/ (adj) episcopal

bissen /bɪsə(n)/ (biste, heeft gebist) [Belg; educ] repeat (the year)

de **bisser** /bɪsər/ (pl: -s) [Belg; educ] pupil who repeats a class

de **bistro** /bistro/ (pl: -'s) bistro

de **¹bit** /bɪt/ bit

het **²bit** /bɪt/ bit

de **bitch** /bɪtʃ/ bitch

bits /bɪts/ (adj, adv) snappish, short(-tempered)

het/de **¹bitter** /bɪtər/ (gin and) bitters

²bitter /bɪtər/ (adj) **1** bitter **2** bitter, sour

de **bitterbal** /bɪtərbɑl/ (pl: -len) type of croquette served as an appetizer

de **bitterheid** /bɪtərhɛit/ (pl: -heden) bitterness

het **bitterkoekje** /bɪtərkukjə/ (pl: -s) (bitter) macaroon

het **bivak** /bivɑk/ (pl: -ken) bivouac: *zijn ~ **opslaan** [fig] pitch one's tent*

bivakkeren /bivɑkerə(n)/ (bivakkeerde, heeft gebivakkeerd) **1** bivouac **2** lodge, stay

bizar /bizɑr/ (adj, adv) bizarre

de **bizon** /bizɔn/ (pl: -s) bison

het **blaadje** /blacə/ (pl: -s) **1** leaf(let); sheet (of paper), piece (of paper); paper; tray **2** [bot] leaflet; petal ‖ *bij iem. in een **goed** ~ staan be in s.o.'s good books*

de **blaam** /blam/ blame

de **blaar** /blar/ (pl: blaren) blister

de **blaas** /blas/ (pl: blazen) bladder, cyst

de **blaasbalg** /blazbɑlx/ (pl: -en) (pair of) bellows

het **blaasinstrument** /blasɪnstrymɛnt/ (pl: -en) wind instrument

de **blaaskaak** /blaskak/ (pl: -kaken) bighead, stuffed shirt, windbag

de **blaasontsteking** /blasɔntstekɪŋ/ (pl: -en) bladder infection, cystitis

het **blaasorkest** /blasɔrkɛst/ (pl: -en) wind orchestra; brass band

het **blaaspijpje** /blaspɛipjə/ (pl: -s) breathalyser

de **blaastest** /blastɛst/ (pl: -en) breathalyser (or: breath) test

de **blabla** /blablɑ/ **1** blah(-blah) **2** fuss

het **blad** /blɑt/ (pl: -en, -eren) **1** [bot] leaf; petal **2** tray **3** sheet, leaf; page **4** (news)paper; magazine **5** sheet; top; blade

de **bladblazer** /blɑdblazər/ leaf blower

bladderen /blɑdərə(n)/ (bladderde, heeft/is gebladderd) blister; bubble; flake; peel

het **bladerdeeg** /bladərdex/ puff pastry (or: paste)

bladeren /bladərə(n)/ (bladerde, heeft gebladerd) thumb, leaf

het **bladgoud** /blɑtxaut/ gold leaf

het **bladgroen** /blɑtxrun/ chlorophyll

de **bladgroente** /blɑtxruntə/ (pl: -n, -s) green vegetables

de **bladluis** /blɑtlœys/ (pl: -luizen) greenfly,

blackfly, aphis

de **bladmuziek** /bl*a*tmyzik/ sheet music

bladstil /bl*a*tstɪl/ (adj) dead calm: *het was ~* not a leaf stirred, it was dead calm

de **bladvulling** /bl*a*tfʏlɪŋ/ (pl: -en) in-fill, fill-up (article)

de **bladwijzer** /bl*a*twɛizər/ (pl: -s) bookmark(er)

de **bladzijde** /bl*a*tsɛidə/ (pl: -n) page: *ik sloeg het boek open op ~ 58* I opened the book at page 58

blaffen /bl*a*fə(n)/ (blafte, heeft geblaft) bark

blaken /bl*a*kə(n)/ (blaakte, heeft geblaakt) burn (with), glow (with)

blakeren /bl*a*kərə(n)/ (blakerde, heeft geblakerd) scorch, burn: *door de zon geblakerd* sun-baked

de **blamage** /blama*ʒ*ə/ (pl: -s) disgrace

blancheren /blã*ʃ*erə(n)/ (blancheerde, heeft geblancheerd) blanch

blanco /bl*a*ŋko/ (adj, adv) blank

blank /blaŋk/ (adj) **1** white: *~ hout* natural wood **2** flooded: *de kelder staat ~* the cellar is flooded

de **blanke** /bl*a*ŋkə/ (pl: -n) white (man, woman): *de ~n* the whites

blasé /bla*z*e/ (adj) blasé

de **blasfemie** /blɑsfemi/ (pl: -ën) blasphemy

blaten /bl*a*tə(n)/ (blaatte, heeft geblaat) bleat

blauw /blɑu/ (adj) **1** blue: *in het ~ gekleed* dressed in blue **2** black, dark: *een ~e plek* a bruise; *iem. bont en ~ slaan* beat s.o. black and blue

de **blauwalg** /bl*a*uɑlx/ (pl: -en) blue algae

de **blauwbaard** /bl*a*ubart/ (pl: -en) bluebeard

de **blauwdruk** /bl*a*udrʏk/ (pl: -ken) blueprint

de **blauwhelm** /bl*a*uhɛlm/ (pl: -en) blue helmet

het **blauwtje** /bl*a*ucə/ (pl: -s): *een ~ lopen* be turned down, be rejected

de **blauwtong** /bl*a*utɔŋ/ bluetongue (disease)

¹**blazen** /bl*a*zə(n)/ (blies, heeft geblazen) **1** blow: *op de trompet, de fluit, het fluitje, de hoorn ~* sound the trumpet, play the flute, blow the whistle, play the horn **2** breathe into a breathalyser ǁ *katten ~ als ze kwaad zijn* cats hiss when they are angry

²**blazen** /bl*a*zə(n)/ (blies, heeft geblazen) blow ǁ *het is oppassen geblazen* we (*or:* you) need to watch out

de **blazer** /bl*a*zər/ (pl: -s) player of a wind instrument

het **blazoen** /blazu*n*/ (pl: -en) blazon

bleek /blek/ (adj) **1** pale; wan: *~ zien* look pale (*or:* wan) **2** pale, white

de **bleekheid** /bl*e*khɛit/ paleness; pallor

het **bleekmiddel** /bl*e*kmɪdəl/ (pl: -en) bleach, bleaching agent

de **bleekselderij** /bl*e*ksɛldərɛi/ celery

het **bleekwater** /bl*e*kwatər/ bleach, bleaching agent

bleken /bl*e*kə(n)/ (bleekte, heeft gebleekt) bleach

blèren /blɛ:rə(n)/ (blèrde, heeft geblèrd) **1** squall, howl **2** bleat

de **bles** /blɛs/ (pl: -sen) blaze, star

blesseren /blɛs*e*rə(n)/ (blesseerde, heeft geblesseerd) injure, hurt; wound

de **blessure** /blɛsy*r*ə/ (pl: -s) injury

de **blessuretijd** /blɛsy*r*ətɛit/ injury time

bleu /blø/ (adj) timid

blieven /bl*i*və(n)/ (bliefde, heeft gebliefd) **1** like **2** please

blij /blɛi/ (adj) **1** glad, happy, pleased, cheerful, merry: *daar ben ik ~ om* I'm pleased about it; *~ zijn voor iem.* be glad for s.o.'s sake **2** happy, joyful, joyous

de **blijdschap** /bl*ɛ*itsxɑp/ joy, gladness, cheer(fulness), happiness

blijf /blɛif/: [Belg] *geen ~ met iets weten* be at a loss, not know what to do about sth.

het **blijf-van-mijn-lijfhuis** /blɛifɑmənlɛifhœys/ women's refuge centre, shelter (for battered women)

de **blijheid** /bl*ɛ*ihɛit/ gladness, joy, happiness

het **blijk** /blɛik/ (pl: -en) mark, token: *~ geven van belangstelling* show one's interest

¹**blijkbaar** /bl*ɛ*igbar/ (adj) evident, obvious, clear

²**blijkbaar** /bl*ɛ*igbar/ (adv) apparently, evidently

blijken /bl*ɛ*ikə(n)/ (bleek, is gebleken) prove, turn out: *doen ~ van* show, express; *hij liet er niets van ~* he gave no sign of it; *dat moet nog ~* that remains to be seen

blijkens /bl*ɛ*ikə(n)s/ (prep) according to, as appears from, as is evident from

blijmoedig /blɛimu*d*əx/ (adj, adv) cheerful, merry, gay

het **blijspel** /bl*ɛ*ispɛl/ (pl: -en) comedy

blijven /bl*ɛ*ivə(n)/ (bleef, is gebleven) **1** remain: *het blijft altijd gevaarlijk* it will always be dangerous; *rustig ~* keep quiet; *deze appel blijft lang goed* this apple keeps well; *jong ~* stay young **2** remain (doing), stay (on) (doing), continue (doing), keep (doing): *~ logeren* stay the night (in the house); *blijft u even aan de lijn?* hold the line, please; *blijf bij de reling vandaan* keep clear of the railings; *je moet op het voetpad ~* you have to keep to the footpath **3** be, keep: *~ staan* a) stand still, stop; b) remain standing; *waar zijn we gebleven?* where were we?; *waar is mijn portemonnee gebleven?* where has my purse got to? **4** perish, be left (*or:* remain) behind: *ergens in ~ (van het lachen)* a) choke; b) [fig] die (laughing)

blijvend /bl*ɛ*ivənt/ (adj) lasting; enduring, permanent; durable

de ¹**blik** /blɪk/ **1** look; glance: *een ~ op iem. wer-*

pen take a look at s.o., look s.o. over **2** look (in one's eyes), expression **3** view, outlook ‖ *een geoefende* (or: *scherpe*) ~ a trained (*or:* sharp) eye

het **²blik** /blɪk/ **1** tin(plate): *in* ~ tinned **2** tin; [Am] can **3** dustpan

de **blikgroente** /blɪkχruntə/ (pl: -n, -s) tinned vegetables

¹blikken /blɪkə(n)/ (adj) tin: ~ *doosjes* tin boxes (*or:* canisters)

²blikken /blɪkə(n)/ (blikte, heeft geblikt): *zonder* ~ *of blozen* without batting an eyelid

de **blikopener** /blɪkopənər/ (pl: -s) tin-opener

de **blikschade** /blɪksχadə/ bodywork damage

de **bliksem** /blɪksəm/ (pl: -s) lightning: *als door de* ~ *getroffen* thunderstruck; *de* ~ *slaat in* lightning strikes ‖ *er als de gesmeerde* ~ *vandoor gaan* take off like greased lightning

de **bliksemafleider** /blɪksəmɑflɛidər/ (pl: -s) lightning conductor

het **bliksembezoek** /blɪksəmbəzuk/ (pl: -en) flying visit, lightning visit

de **bliksemcarrière** /blɪksəmkɑrijɛːrə/ (pl: -s) lightning career: *een* ~ *maken* rise rapidly

bliksemen /blɪksəmə(n)/ (bliksemde, heeft gebliksemd) flash, blaze

de **bliksemflits** /blɪksəmflɪts/ (pl: -en) (flash of) lightning

de **bliksemic inslag** /blɪksəmɪnslɑχ/ (pl: -en) stroke (*or:* bolt) of lightning, thunderbolt

bliksemsnel /blɪksəmsnɛl/ (adj, adv) lightning, at (*or:* with) lightning speed, quick as lightning, like greased lightning

de **bliksemstart** /blɪksəmstɑrt/ lightning start

de **bliksemstraal** /blɪksəmstral/ (pl: -stralen) thunderbolt

de **blikvanger** /blɪkfɑŋər/ (pl: -s) eye-catcher

het **blikveld** /blɪkfɛlt/ field of vision; [fig] horizon, perspective

de **¹blind** /blɪnt/ (pl: -en) (window) shutter, blind

²blind /blɪnt/ (adj) blind: *zich* ~ *staren (op)* concentrate too much on sth.; ~ *typen* touch-type; *zij is aan één oog* ~ she is blind in one eye

de **blind date** /blɑjndɛt/ blind date

de **blinddoek** /blɪnduk/ (pl: -en) blindfold

blinddoeken /blɪndukə(n)/ (blinddoekte, heeft geblinddoekt) blindfold

de **blinde** /blɪndə/ (pl: -n) blind person, blind man, blind woman: *de* ~*n* the blind

de **blindedarm** /blɪndədɑrm/ (pl: -en) appendix

de **blindedarmontsteking** /blɪndədɑrmontstekɪŋ/ (pl: -en) appendicitis

blindelings /blɪndəlɪŋs/ (adv) blindly: ~ *volgen* follow blindly

de **blindengeleidehond** /blɪndə(n)γəlɛidəhɔnt/ (pl: -en) guide dog (for the blind)

blinderen /blɪndərə(n)/ (blindeerde, heeft geblindeerd) armour

de **blindganger** /blɪntχɑŋər/ (pl: -s) dud, unexploded bomb (*or:* shell)

de **blindheid** /blɪnthɛit/ blindness

zich **blindstaren** /blɪntstarə(n)/ (staarde zich blind, heeft zich blindgestaard): *zich* ~ *op* be fixed on, be obsessed by, concentrate too much on; *je moet je niet* ~ *op details* don't let yourself be put off (*or:* obsessed) by details

het/de **blingbling** bling-bling

blinken /blɪŋkə(n)/ (blonk, heeft geblonken) shine, glisten, glitter: *alles blinkt er* everything is spotless (*or:* spick and span)

blits /blɪts/ (adj) trendy, hip

de **blocnote** /blɔknot/ (pl: -s) (writing) pad

het **bloed** /blut/ blood: *mijn eigen vlees en* ~ my own flesh and blood; ~ *vergieten* shed (*or:* spill) blood; *geen* ~ *kunnen zien* not be able to stand the sight of blood ‖ *in koelen* ~*e* in cold blood; *kwaad* ~ *zetten* breed (*or:* create) bad blood; *iem. het* ~ *onder de nagels vandaan halen* get under s.o.'s skin, exasperate s.o.

de **bloedarmoede** /blutɑrmudə/ anaemia

de **bloedbaan** /blutban/ (pl: -banen) bloodstream

het **bloedbad** /blutbɑt/ (pl: -en) bloodbath, massacre: *een* ~ *aanrichten onder de inwoners* massacre the inhabitants

de **bloedbank** /blutbɑŋk/ (pl: -en) blood bank

de **bloedcel** /blutsɛl/ (pl: -len) blood cell (*or:* corpuscle)

de **bloeddonor** /bludonɔr/ (pl: -en, -s) blood donor

bloeddoorlopen /bludorlopə(n)/ (adj) bloodshot: *met* ~ *ogen* with bloodshot eyes

bloeddorstig /bludɔrstəχ/ (adj, adv) bloodthirsty

de **bloeddruk** /bludrʏk/ blood pressure: *de* ~ *meten* take s.o.'s blood pressure

bloedeigen /blutɛiχə(n)/ (adj) (very) own: *mijn* ~ *kind* my own child

bloedeloos /bludolos/ (adj) lifeless

bloeden /bludə(n)/ (bloedde, heeft gebloed) bleed

bloederig /bludərəχ/ (adj) bloody, gory

de **bloedgroep** /blutχrup/ (pl: -en) blood group (*or:* type)

bloedheet /bluthet/ (adj) sweltering (hot), boiling (hot)

bloedhekel /bluthekəl/: *een* ~ *hebben aan iets* absolutely hate sth.

de **bloedhond** /bluthɔnt/ (pl: -en) bloodhound

bloedig /bludəχ/ (adj) bloody, gory

de **bloeding** /bludɪŋ/ (pl: -en) bleeding; haemorrhage

het **bloedlichaampje** /blutlɪχampjə/ (pl: -s) blood corpuscle (*or:* cell)

bloedlink /blutlɪŋk/ (adj, adv) [inform] **1** bloody dangerous **2** hopping mad, furious: *hij werd* ~ *toen hij ervan hoorde* he went into a rage when he heard about it

de **bloedneus** /blutnøs/ (pl: -neuzen) bloody

nose

het **bloedonderzoek** /blu̲tɔndərzuk/ (pl: -en) blood test(s)

het **bloedplaatje** /blu̲tplacə/ (pl: -s) (blood) platelet, thrombocyte

het **bloedplasma** /blu̲tplɑsma/ (blood) plasma

de **bloedproef** /blu̲tpruf/ (pl: -proeven) blood test

de **bloedprop** /blu̲tprɔp/ (pl: -pen) blood clot, thrombus

bloedrood /blu̲trot/ (adj, adv) blood-red

bloedserieus /blutserijø̲s/ (adj) dead (or: utterly) serious

de **bloedsomloop** /blu̲tsɔmlop/ (blood) circulation

bloedstollend /blutstɔ̲lənt/ (adj) blood-curdling

de **bloedsuiker** /blu̲tsœykər/ (pl: -s) blood sugar

de **bloedsuikerspiegel** /blu̲tsœykərspiɣəl/ blood sugar level

de **bloedtransfusie** /blu̲trɑnsfyzi/ (pl: -s) (blood) transfusion

de **bloeduitstorting** /blu̲tœytstɔrtɪŋ/ (pl: -en) extravasation (of blood)

het **bloedvat** /blu̲tfɑt/ (pl: -en) blood vessel

de **bloedverdunner** /blu̲tfərdynər/ (pl: -s) blood diluent

bloedvergieten /blu̲tfərɣitə(n)/ bloodshed: *een revolutie zonder ~* a bloodless revolution

de **bloedvergiftiging** /blu̲tfərɣɪftəɣɪŋ/ (pl: -en) blood poisoning

het **bloedverlies** /blu̲tfərlis/ loss of blood

de **bloedverwant** /blu̲tfərwɑnt/ (pl: -en) (blood) relation, relative, kinsman, kinswoman: *naaste ~en* close relatives, next of kin

de **bloedworst** /blu̲twɔrst/ (pl: -en) black pudding

de **bloedwraak** /blu̲tvrak/ blood feud, vendetta

de **bloedzuiger** /blu̲tsœyɣər/ (pl: -s) leech, bloodsucker

de **bloei** /bluj/ bloom, flower(ing); blossoming: *iem. in de ~ van zijn leven* s.o. in the prime of (his) life; *tot ~ komen* thrive, blossom

bloeien /blu̲jə(n)/ (bloeide, heeft gebloeid) **1** bloom, flower; blossom **2** [fig] prosper, flourish

de **bloeiperiode** /blu̲jperijodə/ (pl: -n, -s) **1** [bot] flowering time (or: season) **2** [fig] prime

de **bloem** /blum/ (pl: -en) **1** flower, bloom, blossom **2** flour

de **bloembak** /blu̲mbɑk/ (pl: -ken) planter, flower box; window box

het **bloembed** /blu̲mbɛt/ (pl: -den) flowerbed

de **bloembol** /blu̲mbɔl/ (pl: -len) bulb

het/de **bloemencorso** /blu̲mə(n)kɔrso/ (pl: -'s) flower parade

de **bloemenhandelaar** /blu̲mə(n)hɑndəlar/ (pl: -s, -handelaren) florist

het **bloemenstalletje** /blu̲mə(n)stɑləcə/ (pl: -s) flower stand, flower stall

de **bloemenvaas** /blu̲mə(n)vas/ (pl: -vazen) (flower) vase

de **bloemenwinkel** /blu̲mə(n)wɪŋkəl/ (pl: -s) florist's (shop), flower shop

het **bloemetje** /blu̲məcə/ (pl: -s) **1** (little) flower **2** flowers, nosegay ‖ *de ~s buiten zetten* paint the town red

de **bloemist** /blumɪ̲st/ (pl: -en) florist

de **bloemkool** /blu̲mkol/ (pl: -kolen) cauliflower

de **bloemkroon** /blu̲mkron/ (pl: -kronen) corolla

de **bloemkwekerij** /blumkwekərɛ̲i/ (pl: -en) **1** nursery, florist's (business) **2** floriculture, flower-growing industry

de **bloemlezing** /blu̲mlezɪŋ/ (pl: -en) anthology

de **bloempot** /blu̲mpɔt/ (pl: -ten) flowerpot

bloemrijk /blu̲mrɛik/ (adj) flowery [also fig]

het **bloemschikken** /blu̲msxɪkə(n)/ (art of) flower arrangement

het **bloemstuk** /blu̲mstʏk/ (pl: -ken) flower arrangement

de **bloemsuiker** /blu̲msœykər/ [Belg] icing sugar

de **bloes** /blus/ (pl: bloezen) blouse; shirt

de **bloesem** /blu̲səm/ (pl: -s) blossom, bloom, flower

het/de **blog** /blɔx/ blog

de **blogger** /blɔ̲ɣər/ blogger

het **blok** /blɔk/ (pl: -ken) **1** block, chunk; log: *slapen als een ~* sleep like a log; *een ~je omlopen* walk around the block; *een doos met ~ken* a box of building blocks **2** block; check **3** [pol] bloc(k) ‖ *iem. voor het ~ zetten* put a person on the spot

de **blokfluit** /blɔ̲kflœyt/ (pl: -en) recorder

de **blokhut** /blɔ̲khʏt/ (pl: -ten) log cabin

het **blokje** /blɔ̲kjə/ (pl: -s) cube, square

de **blokkade** /blɔkka̲də/ (pl: -s) blockade

blokken /blɔ̲kə(n)/ (blokte, heeft geblokt) cram, swot: *~ voor een tentamen* cram for an examination

de **blokkendoos** /blɔ̲kə(n)dos/ (pl: -dozen) box of building blocks

blokkeren /blɔkke̲rə(n)/ (blokkeerde, heeft geblokkeerd) **1** blockade, block **2** freeze: *een creditcard ~* put a stop on a card, stop (or: cancel) a card **3** block, jam, lock **4** [sport] block, obstruct

de **blokletter** /blɔ̲klɛtər/ (pl: -s) block letter, printing

blokletteren /blɔ̲klɛtərə(n)/ (blokletterde, heeft geblokletterd) [Belg] headline, splash (news on the front page)

het **blokuur** /blɔ̲kyr/ (pl: blokuren) [roughly] double period (or: lesson)

blond /blɔnt/ (adj) **1** blond, fair **2** golden

blonderen /blɔndərə(n)/ (blondeerde, heeft geblondeerd) bleach, peroxid(e)

de **blondine** /blɔndinə/ (pl: -s) blonde

het **¹bloot** /blot/ nudity

²bloot /blot/ (adj) bare, naked, nude: *op blote voeten* lopen go barefoot(ed); *uit het blote hoofd spreken* speak off the cuff, speak extempore; *met het blote oog iets waarnemen* observe sth. with the naked eye; *onder de blote hemel* in the open (air); *een jurk met blote rug* a barebacked dress

zich **blootgeven** /blotχevə(n)/ (gaf zich bloot, heeft zich blootgegeven) **1** expose o.s. **2** give o.s. away: *zich niet* ~ not commit o.s., be non-committal

het **blootje** /bloːcə/: *in zijn* ~ in the nude

blootleggen /blotlɛχə(n)/ (legde bloot, heeft blootgelegd) lay open (*or:* bare), expose; [fig also] reveal

blootshoofds /blotshoːfts/ (adv) bareheaded

blootstaan /blotstan/ (stond bloot, heeft blootgestaan) be exposed (to); be subject (to), be open (to)

blootstellen /blotstɛlə(n)/ (stelde bloot, heeft blootgesteld) expose (to): *zich aan gevaar* ~ expose o.s. to danger

blootsvoets /blotsfuts/ (adv) barefoot(ed): ~ *lopen* go (*or:* walk) barefoot(ed)

de **blos** /blɔs/ (pl: -sen) **1** bloom: *een gezonde* ~ a rosy complexion **2** flush; blush

de **blouse** /bluzə/ (pl: -s) blouse

blowen /blowə(n)/ (blowde, heeft geblowd) smoke dope

blozen /blozə(n)/ (bloosde, heeft gebloosd) **1** bloom (with) **2** flush (with); blush (with)

de **blubber** /blʏbər/ mud

de **blues** /bluːs/ blues

de **bluf** /blʏf/ **1** bluff(ing) **2** boast(ing), brag-(ging), big talk

bluffen /blʏfə(n)/ (blufte, heeft gebluft) bluff; boast; brag, talk big

de **bluffer** /blʏfər/ (pl: -s) bluffer, boaster, braggart

het **blufpoker** /blʏfpokər/: *hij speelde een partijtje* ~ he tried to brazen it out (*or:* bluff his way out)

de **blunder** /blʏndər/ (pl: -s) blunder

blunderen /blʏndərə(n)/ (blunderde, heeft geblunderd) blunder, make a blunder

het **blusapparaat** /blʏsɑparat/ (pl: -apparaten) fire extinguisher

blussen /blʏsə(n)/ (bluste, heeft geblust) extinguish; put out

het **blusvliegtuig** /blʏsflixtœyx/ (pl: -en) fire-fighting plane

blut /blʏt/ (adj) broke, skint: *volkomen* ~ stony-broke, flat broke

blz. (abbrev) *bladzijde* p.; pp.

de **BN'er** /beɛnər/ *bekende Nederlander* celebrity, famous Dutch person

bnp (abbrev) *bruto nationaal product* GNP

het **bo** /beo/ [Belg] *bijzonder onderwijs* special needs education

de **boa** /bowa/ (pl: -'s) boa

het **board** /bɔːrd/ (pl: -s) hardboard, (fibre)board

de **¹bob** /bɔp/ bobsleigh, bobsled

de **²bob**® /bɔp/ designated driver

de **bobbel** /bɔbəl/ (pl: -s) bump, lump

de **bobo** /bobo/ bigwig, big shot

de **bobslee** /bɔpsle/ (pl: -ën) bob(sleigh)

bobsleeën /bɔpslejən/ bobsleigh

de **bochel** /bɔχəl/ (pl: -s) hump; hunchback

de **bocht** /bɔχt/ bend, curve: *zich in allerlei ~en wringen* try to wriggle one's way out of sth.; *uit de* ~ *vliegen* run off the road ǁ *dat is te kort door de* ~ that's jumping to conclusions

bochtig /bɔχtəχ/ (adj) winding

het **bod** /bɔt/ offer, bid: *een* ~ *doen* (*or:* uitbrengen) make a bid (*or:* an offer); *niet aan* ~ *komen* [fig] not get a chance

de **bode** /bodə/ (pl: -n, -s) messenger, postman

de **bodem** /bodəm/ (pl: -s) **1** bottom; base: *een dubbele* ~ a hidden meaning **2** ground, soil **3** territory, soil: *producten van eigen* ~ home-grown products ǁ *op de* ~ *van de zee* at the bottom of the sea; [fig] *iets tot de* ~ *uitzoeken* examine sth. down to the last detail

de **bodemgesteldheid** /bodəmχəstɛlthɛit/ condition (*or:* composition) of the soil

bodemloos /bodəmlos/ (adj) bottomless

de **bodemprijs** /bodəmprɛis/ (pl: -prijzen) minimum price

de **bodemverontreiniging** /bodəmvərɔntrɛinəɣɪn/ (pl: -en) soil pollution

de **bodybuilder** /bɔdibɪldər/ (pl: -s) bodybuilder, muscleman

het/de **bodybuilding** /bɔdibɪldɪn/ body building

de **bodyguard** /bɔdiɡaːrd/ (pl: -s) bodyguard

de **bodylotion** /bɔdilo(t)ʃɔn/ (pl: -s) body lotion

de **bodypainting** /bɔdipentɪn/ body painting

de **bodywarmer** /bɔdiwɔrmər/ (pl: -s) body warmer

boe /bu/ (int) boo; moo: ~ *roepen* boo, jeer ǁ *zonder* ~ *of bah te zeggen* without saying (*or:* uttering) a word, without opening one's mouth

Boedapest /budapɛst/ Budapest

Boeddha /buda/ Buddha

het **boeddhisme** /budɪsmə/ Buddhism

de **boeddhist** /budɪst/ (pl: -en) Buddhist

boeddhistisch /budɪstis/ (adj) Buddhist

de **boedel** /budəl/ (pl: -s) property, household effects

de **boef** /buf/ (pl: boeven) scoundrel, rascal

de **boeg** /buχ/ (pl: -en) bow(s), prow: *het over een andere* ~ *gooien* change (one's) tack; change the subject

het **boegbeeld** /buχbelt/ (pl: -en) figurehead

het **boegeroep** /buɣərup/ booing, hooting: *de*

premier moest **onder** ~ het podium verlaten the prime minister was booed off the stage

de **boei** /buj/ (pl: -en) **1** buoy: een kop (or: een kleur) **als** een ~ (a face) as red as a beetroot **2** chain, handcuff: iem. **in** de ~en slaan clap (or: put) s.o. in irons, (hand)cuff s.o.

boeien /buje(n)/ (boeide, heeft geboeid) **1** chain, (hand)cuff **2** fascinate, captivate: het stuk **kon** ons niet (blijven) ~ the play failed to hold our attention

boeiend /bujent/ (adj, adv) fascinating, gripping, captivating

het **boek** /buk/ (pl: -en) book: altijd met zijn neus **in** de ~en zitten always have one's nose in a book, always be at one's books; een ~ **over** a book on

Boekarest /bukarɛst/ Bucharest

de **boekbespreking** /bugbəsprekɪŋ/ (pl: -en) book review

het **boekbinden** /bugbɪndə(n)/ (book)binding

de **boekbinder** /bugbɪndər/ (pl: -s) (book)-binder

de **boekbinderij** /bugbɪndərɛi̯/ (pl: -en) bindery, (book)binder's

het **boekdeel** /bugdel/ (pl: -delen) volume

de **boekdrukkerij** /bugdrʏkərɛi̯/ (pl: -en) **1** printing house (or: office), print shop **2** printer's

de **boekdrukkunst** /bugdrʏkʏnst/ (art of) printing, typography

boeken /buke(n)/ (boekte, heeft geboekt) book, post, enter (up)

de **boekenbeurs** /buke(n)børs/ (pl: -beurzen) book fair

de **boekenbon** /buke(n)bɔn/ (pl: -nen) book token

het **boekenfonds** /buke(n)fɔn(t)s/ (pl: -en) (educational) book fund

de **boekenkast** /buke(n)kɑst/ (pl: -en) book-case

de **boekenlegger** /buke(n)lɛɣər/ (pl: -s) book-mark(er)

de **boekenlijst** /buke(n)lɛist/ (pl: -en) (required) reading list, booklist

de **boekenplank** /buke(n)plɑŋk/ (pl: -en) bookshelf

het **boekenrek** /buke(n)rɛk/ (pl: -ken) book-shelves

de **boekensteun** /buke(n)støn/ (pl: -en) book-end

de **boekentaal** /buke(n)tal/ **1** literary language **2** bookish language

de **Boekenweek**® /buke(n)wek/ (pl: -weken) book week

de **boekenwurm** /buke(n)wʏrm/ (pl: -en) bookworm

het **boeket** /bukɛt/ (pl: -ten) bouquet: een ~je a posy, a nosegay

de **boekhandel** /bukhɑndəl/ (pl: -s) bookshop

de **boekhandelaar** /bukhɑndəlar/ (pl: -s, -handelaren) bookseller

het **¹boekhouden** /bukhɑudə(n)/ bookkeeping, accounting

²boekhouden /bukhɑudə(n)/ keep the books, do the accounting, do (or: keep) the accounts

de **boekhouder** /bukhɑudər/ (pl: -s) accountant, bookkeeper

de **boekhouding** /bukhɑudɪŋ/ (pl: -en) **1** accounting, bookkeeping **2** accounting department (or: section), accounts department

boekhoudkundig /bukhɑutkʏndəx/ (adj, adv) accounting, bookkeeping

de **boeking** /bukɪŋ/ (pl: -en) **1** booking, reservation **2** [socc] booking, caution **3** entry

het **boekjaar** /bukjar/ (pl: -jaren) fiscal year, financial year

het **boekje** /bukjə/ (pl: -s) (small, little) book, booklet ‖ **buiten** zijn ~ gaan exceed one's authority; **volgens** het ~ according to the book

boekstaven /bukstavə(n)/ (boekstaafde, heeft geboekstaafd) **1** (put on) record **2** substantiate

de **boekwaarde** /bukwardə/ book value, balance sheet value

de **boekweit** /bukwɛit/ buckwheat

het **boekwerk** /bukwɛrk/ (pl: -en) book, work

de **boekwinkel** /bukwɪŋkəl/ (pl: -s) bookshop

de **boel** /bul/ **1** things, matters; mess: hij kan zijn ~tje wel **pakken** he can (or: might) as well pack it in (now); de ~ aan **kant** maken straighten (or: tidy) things up **2** affair, business, matter, situation: er een **dolle** ~ van maken make quite a party of it; een **mooie** ~ a fine mess; het is er een **saaie** (or: **dooie**) ~ it's a dead-and-alive place **3** a lot, heaps, lots, loads

de **boeman** /bumɑn/ (pl: -nen) bogeyman

de **boemel** /buməl/ (pl: -s): **aan** de ~ gaan go (out) on the razzle

de **boemeltrein** /buməltrɛin/ (pl: -en) slow train, stopping train

de **boemerang** /buməraŋ/ (pl: -s) boomerang

de **boender** /bundər/ (pl: -s) scrubbing brush; [Am] scrub-brush

boenen /bunə(n)/ (boende, heeft geboend) **1** polish **2** scrub

het/de **boenwas** /bunwɑs/ beeswax, wax polish

de **boer** /bur/ (pl: -en) **1** farmer, peasant; [Am] rancher **2** boor, (country) bumpkin **3** burp, belch **4** jack

de **boerderij** /burdərɛi̯/ (pl: -en) farm

boeren /burə(n)/ (boerde, heeft geboerd) **1** farm, run a farm **2** burp, belch ‖ hij heeft **goed** (or: **slecht**) geboerd dit jaar he has done well (or: badly) this year

het **boerenbedrog** /burə(n)bədrɔx/ [inform] fraud, humbug, bunk: dat is je **reinste** ~ that is clearly humbug (or: total bunk)

de **boerenknecht** /burə(n)knɛxt/ (pl: -en) (farm)hand

de **boerenkool** /burə(n)kol/ (pl: -kolen) kale

het **boerenverstand** /buːrə(n)vərstɑnt/ [in-
form] horse sense
de **boerin** /buːrɪn/ (pl: -nen) **1** farmer's wife
2 woman farmer
de **boerka** /buːrka/ burqa, burk(h)a
boers /buːrs/ (adj, adv) rustic, rural, peasant:
een ~ accent a rural accent
de **boete** /buːtə/ (pl: -s) **1** fine: *een ~ krijgen van*
€100 be fined 100 euros; *iem. een ~ opleggen*
fine s.o. **2** [rel] penance: ~ *doen* do penance
(for sins) **3** penalty
het **boetekleed** /buːtəkleːt/: *het ~ aantrekken*
put on the hair shirt
boeten /buːtə(n)/ (boette, heeft geboet) pay
((the penalty, price) for); [rel] atone (for);
[rel] do penance (for): *zwaar voor iets ~* pay a
heavy penalty for sth.
de **boetiek** /butik/ (pl: -s) boutique
de **boetseerklei** /butseːrklɛi/ modelling clay
boetseren /butseːrə(n)/ (boetseerde, heeft
geboetseerd) model
boetvaardig /butfaːrdəχ/ (adj, adv) penitent
de **boeventronie** /buːvə(n)troni/ (pl: -s) [in-
form] villain's face
de **boezem** /buːzəm/ (pl: -s) **1** bosom, breast:
een zware (flinke) ~ hebben be full-bosomed
2 bosom, heart
de **boezemvriend** /buːzəmvrint/ (pl: -en) bosom friend
de **bof** /bɔf/ (pl: -fen) **1** (good) luck: *wat een ~,*
dat ik hem nog thuis tref I'm lucky (*or:* what
luck) to find him still at home **2** mumps: *de ~*
hebben have mumps
boffen /bɔfə(n)/ (bofte, heeft geboft) be
lucky
de **bofkont** /bɔfkɔnt/ (pl: -en) lucky dog
bogen /boːɣə(n)/ (boogde, heeft geboogd):
kunnen ~ op boast, pride o.s. ((up)on)
Bohemen /boh(e)mə(n)/ Bohemia
de **boiler** /bɔjlər/ (pl: -s) water heater, boiler
de **bok** /bɔk/ (pl: -ken) **1** (male) goat; billy goat;
buck; stag **2** buck
de **bokaal** /bokaːl/ (pl: bokalen) **1** goblet
2 beaker
bokken /bɔkə(n)/ (bokte, heeft gebokt) sulk
de **bokkensprong** /bɔkə(n)sprɔŋ/ (pl: -en) caper ‖ *(rare)* ~*en maken* behave unpredictably
(*or:* in a ridiculous way)
de **bokking** /bɔkɪŋ/ (pl: -en) smoked herring
de **boksbal** /bɔksbɑl/ (pl: -len) punchball
de **boksbeugel** /bɔksbøːɣəl/ (pl: -s) knuckle-
duster
boksen /bɔksə(n)/ (bokste, heeft gebokst)
box
de **bokser** /bɔksər/ (pl: -s) boxer
de **bokshandschoen** /bɔkshɑntsχun/ (pl: -en)
boxing glove
bokspringen /bɔksprɪŋə(n)/ **1** (play) leapfrog **2** (squat) vaulting; vaulting exercise
de **bokswedstrijd** /bɔkswɛtstrɛit/ (pl: -en)

boxing match, (prize)fight
de ¹**bol** /bɔl/ (pl: -len) **1** ball; bulb **2** [maths]
sphere ‖ *uit zijn ~ gaan* go crazy, go out of
one's mind
²**bol** /bɔl/ (adj, adv) round: *een ~le lens* a convex lens
de **boleet** /boleːt/ (pl: boleten) boletus
de **bolero** /boleːro/ bolero
de **bolhoed** /bɔlhut/ (pl: -en) bowler (hat)
de **bolide** /bolidə/ racing car
Bolivia /bolivija/ Bolivia
de **Boliviaan** /bolivijaːn/ (pl: Bolivianen) Bolivian
Boliviaans /bolivijaːns/ (adj) Bolivian
de **bolleboos** /bɔləbos/ (pl: bollebozen) high-
flyer
de **bollenkweker** /bɔlə(n)kweːkər/ (pl: -s) bulb
grower
de **bollenteelt** /bɔlə(n)telt/ bulb-growing (industry)
het **bollenveld** /bɔlə(n)vɛlt/ (pl: -en) bulb field
het **bolletje** /bɔləcə/ (pl: -s) **1** (little) ball; globule **2** (soft) roll
de **bolletjesslikker** /bɔləcəslɪkər/ (pl: -s) body
packer, mule
de **bolsjewiek** /bɔlʃəwik/ (pl: -en) Bolshevik
het **bolsjewisme** /bɔlʃəwɪsmə/ Bolshevism
de **bolster** /bɔlstər/ (pl: -s) shell: *ruwe ~, blanke*
pit a rough diamond
bolvormig /bɔlvɔrməχ/ (adj) spherical
de **bolwassing** /bɔlwasɪŋ/ (pl: -en) [Belg]
dressing down
het **bolwerk** /bɔlwɛrk/ (pl: -en) bulwark; [fig
also] stronghold; bastion
bolwerken /bɔlwɛrkə(n)/ manage, pull off;
stick it out; hold one's own: *het (kunnen) ~*
manage (it), pull it off; stick it out
de **bom** /bɔm/ (pl: -men) bomb: *het bericht sloeg*
in als een ~ the news came like a bombshell
de **bomaanslag** /bɔmanslaχ/ (pl: -en) bomb
attack; bombing; bomb outrage
het **bomalarm** /bɔmalɑrm/ bomb alert; air-raid
warning; bomb scare
het **bombardement** /bɔmbardəmɛnt/ (pl: -en)
bombardment
bombarderen /bɔmbardeːrə(n)/ (bombar-
deerde, heeft gebombardeerd) **1** bomb
2 bombard; shell **3** [fig] bombard, shower
de **bombrief** /bɔmbrif/ (pl: bombrieven) letter
bomb, mail bomb
de **bommelding** /bɔmɛldɪŋ/ (pl: -en) bomb
alert
bommen /bɔmə(n)/ (bomde, heeft ge-
bomd): [inform] *(het) kan mij niet ~!* I couldn't
care less (about it)!
de **bommenwerper** /bɔmə(n)wɛrpər/ (pl: -s)
bomber
het **bommetje** /bɔməcə/ (pl: -s) cannonball
de **bommoeder** /bɔmudər/ (pl: -s) [roughly]
bachelor mother
bomvol /bɔmvɔl/ (adj) chock-full, cram-full,

packed

de **bon** /bɔn/ (pl: -nen) **1** bill, receipt; cash-register slip **2** voucher, coupon; token; credit slip **3** ticket

bonafide /bonafidə/ (adj, adv) bona fide, in good faith

de **bonbon** /bɔmbɔn/ (pl: -s) chocolate, bonbon

de **bond** /bɔnt/ (pl: -en) **1** (con)federation, confederacy, alliance, union **2** union

de **bondgenoot** /bɔntxənot/ (pl: -genoten) ally; confederate

het **bondgenootschap** /bɔntxənotsxap/ (pl: -pen) alliance; confederacy, (con)federation

bondig /bɔndəx/ (adj, adv) concise, terse; pithy

het **bondsbestuur** /bɔn(t)sbəstyr/ society (or: association) executive; union executive

de **bondscoach** /bɔntskotʃ/ (pl: -es) national coach

de **Bondsdag** /bɔn(t)sdɑx/ Bundestag, (the Lower House of) the German Parliament

het **bondselftal** /bɔn(t)sɛlftal/ (pl: -len) national team

de **bondskanselier** /bɔntskɑnsəlir/ (pl: -s) Federal Chancellor

de **Bondsrepubliek** /bɔntsrepyblik/: ~ *Duitsland* Federal Republic (of Germany)

de **bonenstaak** /bonə(n)stak/ (pl: -staken) beanpole

het **boni** /boni/ profit, gains

de **bonje** /bɔnə/ rumpus, row

de **bonk** /bɔnk/ (pl: -en) lump: *één ~ zenuwen* a bundle of nerves

bonken /bɔŋkə(n)/ (bonkte, heeft/is gebonkt) **1** crash (against, into), bump (against, into) **2** bang, pound

bonkig /bɔŋkəx/ (adj): *een ~e stijl* a rough style

de **bonnefooi** /bonəfoj/: *op de ~ ergens heen gaan* go somewhere on the off chance

de **bons** /bɔns/ (pl: bonzen) **1** thud, thump **2** (big) boss || *iem. de ~ geven* give s.o. the push

de **bonsai** /bɔnsaj/ (pl: -s) bonsai

het **¹bont** /bɔnt/ (pl: -en) fur: *met ~ gevoerd* fur-lined

²bont /bɔnt/ (adj, adv) **1** multicoloured; variegated: *~e kleuren* bright colours; *iem. ~ en blauw slaan* beat s.o. black and blue **2** colourful: *een ~ gezelschap* a) a colourful group of people; b) [depr] a motley crew || *het te ~ maken* go too far

het **bontgoed** /bɔntxut/ (cotton) prints

de **bonthandel** /bɔnthɑndəl/ fur trade

de **bonthandelaar** /bɔnthɑndəlar/ (pl: -s, -handelaren) furrier

de **bontjas** /bɔntjɑs/ (pl: -sen) fur coat

de **bontmuts** /bɔntmʏts/ (pl: -en) fur cap, fur hat

de **bonus** /bonʏs/ (pl: -sen) bonus, premium

bonzen /bɔnzə(n)/ (bonsde, heeft gebonsd) **1** bang, hammer **2** bump (against, into), crash (against, into): *tegen iem. aan ~* bump into s.o., crash against (or: into) s.o. **3** pound

de **boodschap** /botsxɑp/ (pl: -pen) **1** purchase: *die kun je wel om een ~ sturen* [fig] you can leave things to him (or: her) **2** message: *een ~ voor iem. achterlaten* leave a message for s.o.; *een ~ krijgen* get a message **3** errand; mission

het **boodschappenlijstje** /botsxɑpə(n)lɛiʃə/ (pl: -s) shopping list

de **boodschappentas** /botsxɑpə(n)tɑs/ (pl: -sen) shopping bag

de **boodschapper** /botsxɑpər/ (pl: -s) messenger, courier

de **boog** /box/ (pl: bogen) **1** bow: *met pijl en ~* with bow and arrow **2** arch; span **3** arc; curve: *met een (grote) ~ om iets heenlopen* go out of one's way to avoid sth.

de **boogbal** /boxbal/ (pl: -len) lob

de **boogscheut** /boxsxøt/ (pl: -en) [Belg] stone's throw: *op een ~ van* a stone's throw from

boogschieten /boxsxitə(n)/ archery

de **boogschutter** /boxsxʏtər/ (pl: -s) archer

de **Boogschutter** /boxsxʏtər/ (pl: -s) Sagittarius

de **bookmaker** /bukmekər/ bookmaker

de **bookmark** /bukmɑːrk/ bookmark

de **boom** /bom/ (pl: bomen) **1** tree: *ze zien door de bomen het bos niet meer* they can't see the wood for the trees **2** bar, barrier, gate

de **boomgaard** /bomɣart/ (pl: -en) orchard

de **boomgrens** /bomɣrɛns/ tree line

de **boomkwekerij** /bomkwekərɛi/ (pl: -en) tree nursery

de **boomschors** /bomsxɔrs/ (pl: -en) (tree) bark

de **boomstam** /bomstɑm/ (pl: -men) (tree) trunk

de **boomstronk** /bomstrɔŋk/ (pl: -en) tree stump

de **boon** /bon/ (pl: bonen) bean: *witte bonen* haricot beans; *honger maakt rauwe bonen zoet* hunger is the best sauce

het **boontje** /bonə/ (pl: -s): *~ komt om zijn loontje* serves him right; *een heilig ~* a goody-goody (or: prig)

de **boor** /bor/ (pl: boren) **1** brace **2** bit **3** drill

het/de **boord** /bort/ (pl: -en) **1** band, trim **2** collar **3** board: *van ~ gaan* disembark || [Belg] *iets goed (or: slecht) aan ~ leggen* set about it in the right (or: wrong) way

de **boordcomputer** /bortkɔmpjutər/ (pl: -s) (on)board computer

boordevol /bordəvol/ (adj) full (or: filled) to overflowing: *~ nieuwe ideeën* bursting with new ideas; *~ mensen* packed (or: crammed) with people

de **boordwerktuigkundige** /bortwɛrktœyɣkʏndəɣə/ (pl: -n) flight engineer

het **booreiland** /boɾɛilɑnt/ (pl: -en) drilling rig (or: platform), oilrig

de **boormachine** /boɾmɑʃinə/ (pl: -s) (electric) drill

het **boorplatform** /boɾplɑtfɔrm/ (pl: -s) drilling rig (or: platform); oil rig

de **boortoren** /boɾtoɾə(n)/ (pl: -s) derrick, drilling rig

boos /bos/ (adj, adv) **1** angry, cross, hostile: ~ *kijken (naar iem.)* scowl (at s.o.); ~ *worden op iem.* get angry at s.o. **2** evil, bad, malicious, wicked; vicious: *het was geen boze opzet* no harm was intended; *de (grote) boze wolf* the big bad wolf **3** evil, foul, vile: *de boze geesten* evil spirits

boosaardig /bosaɾdəχ/ (adj, adv) **1** malignant **2** malicious, vicious

de **boosdoener** /bozdunər/ (pl: -s) wrongdoer: *de ~ was een doorgebrande zekering* the culprit was a blown fuse, a blown fuse was to blame

de **boosheid** /bosɦɛit/ (pl: -heden) anger; fury

de **boot** /bot/ (pl: boten) boat, vessel; [large] steamer; [large] ship; ferry: *de ~ missen* [also fig] miss the boat; *de ~ afhouden* [fig] refuse to commit o.s., keep one's distance

het **boothuis** /boɦœys/ (pl: -huizen) boathouse

de **bootreis** /botrɛis/ (pl: -reizen) voyage, cruise

de **bootsman** /botsmɑn/ (pl: bootslui, bootslieden) boatswain

de **boottocht** /botɔχt/ (pl: -en) boat trip (or: excursion)

de **bootvluchteling** /botflʏχtəlɪŋ/ (pl: -en) boat person (or: refugee); boat people

het **bord** /bɔrt/ (pl: -en) **1** plate: *alle probleemgevallen komen op zijn ~je terecht* he ends up with all the difficult cases on his plate; *van een ~ eten* eat off a plate **2** sign, notice: *de hele route is met ~en aangegeven* it is signposted all the way **3** board; (black)board; notice board ∥ *een ~ voor zijn kop hebben* be thick-skinned

de **bordeaux** /bordo/ (pl: -s) bordeaux; claret

het **bordeel** /bordel/ (pl: bordelen) brothel, whorehouse

de **bordenwasser** /bordə(n)wɑsər/ (pl: -s) dishwasher

de **border** /bɔːrdər/ (pl: -s) border

de **borderliner** /bɔːrdərlɑjnər/ borderliner

het **bordes** /bordɛs/ (pl: -sen) [roughly] steps

het **bordkrijt** /bɔrtkrɛit/ chalk

het **borduren** /bordyɾə(n)/ (borduurde, heeft geborduurd) embroider

het **borduurwerk** /bordyrwɛrk/ (pl: -en) embroidery

boren /boɾə(n)/ (boorde, heeft geboord) bore, drill

de **borg** /bɔrχ/ (pl: -en) **1** surety; bail: *zich ~*

stellen *voor een gevangene* stand bail for a prisoner **2** security; deposit

de **borgsom** /bɔrχsɔm/ (pl: -men) deposit, security (money)

de **borgtocht** /bɔrχtɔχt/ (pl: -en) bail, recognizance

de **boring** /boɾɪŋ/ (pl: -en) boring, drilling

de **borrel** /bɔrəl/ (pl: -s) drink ∥ *iem. voor een ~ uitnodigen* ask s.o. round (or: invite s.o.) for a drink

borrelen /bɔrələ(n)/ (borrelde, heeft geborreld) **1** bubble; gurgle **2** have a drink

het **borrelhapje** /bɔrəlhɑpjə/ (pl: -s) snack, appetizer

het **borrelnootje** /bɔrəlnocə/ (pl: -s) nut (to go with cocktails)

de **borst** /bɔrst/ **1** chest: *uit volle ~ zingen* sing lustily; *zich op de ~ slaan* (or: *kloppen*) congratulate o.s.; *dat stuit mij tegen de ~* that goes against the grain with me, that sticks in my gizzard; *maak je ~ maar nat!* prepare yourself for the worst! **2** breast: *een kind de ~ geven* breastfeed a child

het **borstbeeld** /bɔrstbelt/ (pl: -en) bust

het **borstbeen** /bɔrstben/ (pl: -benen) breastbone; sternum

de **borstcrawl** /bɔrstkrɔːl/ (front) crawl

de **borstel** /bɔrstəl/ (pl: -s) **1** brush **2** [Belg] broom ∥ [Belg] *ergens met de grove ~ door gaan* tackle sth. in a rough-and-ready way

borstelen /bɔrstələ(n)/ (borstelde, heeft geborsteld) brush

borstelig /bɔrstələχ/ (adj) bristly, bushy

de **borstkanker** /bɔrstkɑŋkər/ breast cancer

de **borstkas** /bɔrstkɑs/ (pl: -sen) chest

de **borstslag** /bɔr(st)slɑχ/ (pl: -en) breaststroke; (front) crawl

de **borstvin** /bɔrs(t)fɪn/ (pl: -nen) pectoral fin

de **borstvoeding** /bɔrstfudɪŋ/ (pl: -en) breastfeeding

de **borstwering** /bɔrstwerɪŋ/ (pl: -en) parapet

de **borstwijdte** /bɔrstwɛitə/ (pl: -s) (width of the) chest; bust (measurement)

de **borstzak** /bɔrstsɑk/ (pl: -ken) breast pocket

de **¹bos** /bɔs/ bundle; bunch: *een flinke ~ haar* a fine head of hair

het **²bos** /bɔs/ wood(s), forest

het **bosbeheer** /bɔzbəɦeʔr/ forestry

de **bosbes** /bɔzbɛs/ (pl: -sen) bilberry; [Am] blueberry

de **bosbouw** /bɔzbɑu/ forestry

de **bosbrand** /bɔzbrɑnt/ (pl: -en) forest fire

het **bosje** /bɔʃə/ (pl: -s) **1** bundle, tuft; wisp **2** grove, coppice **3** bush, shrub

de **Bosjesman** /bɔʃəsmɑn/ (pl: -nen) Bushman

de **bosklas** /bɔsklɑs/ (pl: -sen) [Belg] nature class (in the woods)

de **bosneger** /bɔsneɣər/ (pl: -s) maroon

Bosnië en Herzegovina /bɔsnijəenhɛrtʃeɣovina/ Bosnia and Herzegovina

de **Bosniër** /bɔsnijər/ (pl: -s) Bosnian

Bosnisch /bɔsnis/ (adj) Bosnian

het **bospad** /bɔspat/ (pl: -en) woodland path, forest path (or: trail)

de **Bosporus** /bɔspoɾʏs/ Bosp(h)orus

bosrijk /bɔsrɛik/ (adj) woody

de **bosvrucht** /bɔsfrʏxt/ forest fruit, fruit of the forest

de **boswachter** /bɔswaxtər/ (pl: -s) forester; [Am] (forest) ranger; gamekeeper

de ¹**bot** /bɔt/ flounder || [fig] ~ **vangen** draw a blank, come away empty-handed

het ²**bot** /bɔt/ bone: *tot op het ~ verkleumd zijn* chilled to the bone

³**bot** /bɔt/ (adj) **1** blunt, dull **2** blunt, curt: *een ~te opmerking* a blunt (or: curt) remark

de **botanicus** /botanikʏs/ (pl: botanici) botanist

botanisch /botanis/ (adj) botanic(al)

de **botbreuk** /bɔdbrøk/ (pl: -en) break, broken bone

de **boter** /botər/ (pl: -s) butter: *~ bij de vis* cash on the nail || *hij heeft ~ op zijn hoofd* listen who's talking; *met zijn neus in de ~ vallen* find one's bread buttered on both sides, be in luck

de **boterbloem** /botərblum/ (pl: -en) buttercup

het **boterbriefje** /botərbrifjə/ (pl: -s) marriage lines, marriage certificate

boteren /botərə(n)/ (boterde, heeft geboterd): *het wil tussen hen niet ~* they can't get on

de **boterham** /botərham/ (pl: -men) **1** slice (or: piece) of bread: [fig] *iets op zijn ~ krijgen* get sth. on one's plate; *een ~ met ham* a ham sandwich **2** living, livelihood: *zijn ~ verdienen met ...* earn one's living by ...

de **boterhamworst** /botərhamwɔrst/ [roughly] luncheon meat

het **boter-kaas-en-eieren** /botərkasɛnɛijərə(n)/ noughts and crosses; [Am] tic-tac-toe

de **boterkoek** /botərkuk/ (pl: -en) **1** butter biscuit **2** [Belg] brioche

de **botervloot** /botərvlot/ (pl: -vloten) butter dish

boterzacht /botərzɑxt/ (adj) (as) soft as butter

de **botheid** /bɔthɛit/ **1** bluntness, dullness **2** bluntness, gruffness

de **botkanker** /bɔtkɑŋkər/ bone cancer

de **botontkalking** /bɔtɔntkɑlkɪŋ/ osteoporosis

het **botsautootje** /bɔtsɑutocə/ (pl: -s) dodgem (car), bumper car

botsen /bɔtsə(n)/ (botste, heeft/is gebotst) **1** collide (with), bump into (or: against); crash into (or: against): *twee wagens botsten tegen elkaar* two cars collided **2** [fig] clash (with)

de **botsing** /bɔtsɪŋ/ (pl: -en) collision; crash: *met*

elkaar in ~ komen collide with one another, run into one another

de **Botswaan** /bɔtswan/ (pl: Botswanen) Botswanan

Botswaans /bɔtswans/ (adj) Botswanan

Botswana /bɔtswana/ Botswana

bottelen /bɔtələ(n)/ (bottelde, heeft gebotteld) bottle

botten /bɔtə(n)/ (botte, is gebot) bud (out), put out buds

de **botter** /bɔtər/ (pl: -s) smack, fishing boat

de **bottleneck** /bɔtəlnɛk/ (pl: -s) bottleneck

het **botulisme** /botylɪsmə/ botulism

botvieren /bɔtfirə(n)/ (vierde bot, heeft botgevierd): *zijn frustraties ~* give (full) vent to one's frustrations; *let o.s. go; dat moet je niet op haar ~* you mustn't take it out on her

botweg /bɔtwɛx/ (adv) bluntly, flatly

boud /bɑut/ (adj, adv) bold, impudent: *een ~e/boute bewering* an impudent (or: a bold) assertion

de **bougie** /buʒi/ (pl: -s) sparking plug

de **bouillon** /bujɔn/ (pl: -s) broth

het **bouillonblokje** /bujɔmblɔkjə/ (pl: -s) beef cube

de **boulevard** /buləvar/ (pl: -s) **1** boulevard, avenue **2** promenade

de **boulevardblad** /buləvarblɑt/ (pl: -en) [roughly] tabloid

de **boulimia nervosa** /bulimijanɛrvoza/ bulimia nervosa; [Am] bulimarexia

het **bouquet** /bukɛ/ bouquet

de **bourgogne** /burgɔɲə/ (pl: -s) burgundy

de **Bourgondiër** /burɣɔndijər/ (pl: -s) Burgundian

bourgondisch /burxɔndis/ (adj, adv) exuberant

de **bout** /bɑut/ (pl: -en) **1** (screw) bolt, pin **2** leg, quarter; drumstick

de **bouvier** /buvje/ (pl: -s) Bouvier des Flandres

de **bouw** /bɑu/ **1** building, construction **2** building industry (or: trade) **3** structure, construction; build

het **bouwbedrijf** /bɑubədrɛif/ (pl: -bedrijven) construction firm, builders

¹**bouwen** /bɑuwə(n)/ (bouwde, heeft gebouwd) (+ op) rely on

²**bouwen** /bɑuwə(n)/ (bouwde, heeft gebouwd) build, construct; erect; put up

de **bouwer** /bɑuwər/ (pl: -s) builder; (building) contractor; shipbuilder

de **bouwgrond** /bɑuɣrɔnt/ (pl: -en) building land

het **bouwjaar** /bɑujar/ (pl: -jaren) year of construction (or: manufacture): *te koop: auto van het ~ 1981* for sale: 1981 car

de **bouwkunde** /bɑukʏndə/ architecture

bouwkundig /bɑukʏndəx/ (adj, adv) architectural, constructional, structural: *~ ingenieur* structural engineer

de **bouwkundige** /bɑukʏndəɣə/ (pl: -n) architect, structural engineer

de **bouwkunst** /b<u>au</u>kʏnst/ building, construction, architecture

het **bouwland** /b<u>au</u>lɑnt/ farmland: *stuk* ~ field

het **bouwmateriaal** /b<u>au</u>materijal/ (pl: -materialen) building material

het **bouwpakket** /b<u>au</u>pɑkɛt/ (pl: -ten) (do-it-yourself) kit

de **bouwpromotor** /b<u>au</u>promotər/ (pl: -en, -s) [Belg] (property) developer

de **bouwput** /b<u>au</u>pʏt/ (pl: -ten) (building) excavation

bouwrijp /b<u>au</u>rɛɪp/ (adj) ready for building: *een terrein* ~ *maken* prepare a site (for building)

de **bouwsteen** /b<u>au</u>sten/ (pl: -stenen) **1** brick **2** building block

de **bouwstijl** /b<u>au</u>stɛɪl/ (pl: -en) architecture

de **bouwstof** /b<u>au</u>stɔf/ (pl: -fen) building material; [fig] material(s)

de **bouwtekening** /b<u>au</u>tekənɪŋ/ (pl: -en) floor plan, drawing(s)

het **bouwterrein** /b<u>au</u>tɛrɛin/ (pl: -en) **1** building land **2** building site, construction site

de **¹bouwvak** /b<u>au</u>vak/ construction industry holiday

het **²bouwvak** /b<u>au</u>vak/ building (*or:* construction) industry

de **bouwvakker** /b<u>au</u>vɑkər/ (pl: -s) construction worker

de **bouwval** /b<u>au</u>vɑl/ (pl: -len) ruin

bouwvallig /bɑuvɑləx/ (adj) crumbling, dilapidated, rickety

de **bouwvergunning** /b<u>au</u>vərɣʏnɪŋ/ (pl: -en) building (*or:* construction) permit

het **bouwwerk** /b<u>au</u>wɛrk/ (pl: -en) building, structure, construction

¹boven /b<u>o</u>və(n)/ (adv) **1** above, up; upstairs: *(naar)* ~ *brengen* take (*or:* carry) up; bring back; *woon je* ~ *of beneden?* do you live upstairs or down(stairs)?; *naar* ~ *afronden* round up **2** on top: *dat gaat mijn verstand (begrip) te* ~ that is beyond me; that's over my head; *de vierde regel van* ~ the fourth line from the top **3** above **4** (+ aan) on top, at the top: ~ *aan de lijst staan* be at the top (*or:* head) of the list || *te* ~ *komen* get over, overcome, recover from

²boven /b<u>o</u>və(n)/ (prep) **1** above; over: *hij woont* ~ *een bakker* he lives over a baker's shop; ~ *water komen* **a)** surface, come up for air; **b)** [fig] turn up; *de flat* ~ *ons* the flat overhead **2** above, beyond: *dat gaat* ~ *mijn verstand* that is beyond me **3** above, over: *hij stelt zijn carrière* ~ *zijn gezin* he puts his career before his family; *er gaat niets* ~ *Belgische friet* there's nothing like Belgian chips; *veiligheid* ~ *alles* safety first **4** over, above, beyond: *kinderen* ~ *de drie jaar* children over three; ~ *alle twijfel* beyond (all) doubt

bovenaan /bovə(n)<u>a</u>n/ (adv) at the top: ~ *staan* be (at the) top

de **bovenal** /bovə(n)<u>a</u>l/ (adv) above all

de **bovenarm** /b<u>o</u>və(n)ɑrm/ (pl: -en) upper arm

het **bovenbeen** /b<u>o</u>və(n)ben/ (pl: -benen) upper leg, thigh

de **bovenbouw** /b<u>o</u>və(n)bɑu/ **1** [educ] last 2 or 3 classes (of secondary school) **2** superstructure

de **bovenbuur** /b<u>o</u>və(n)byr/ (pl: -buren) upstairs neighbour

bovendien /bovəndin/ (adv) moreover, in addition, furthermore, besides: ~, *hij is niet meerderjarig* besides, he's a minor

bovendrijven /b<u>o</u>və(n)drɛɪvə(n)/ float: *komen* ~ float (*or:* rise) to the surface, surface

bovengenoemd /bovə(n)ɣən<u>u</u>mt/ (adj) above(-mentioned), mentioned above, stated above; [law] (afore)said

de **bovengrens** /b<u>o</u>və(n)ɣrɛns/ (pl: -grenzen) upper limit

bovengronds /bovə(n)ɣr<u>o</u>nts/ (adj, adv) aboveground, surface, overhead

bovenin /bovə(n)ɪn/ (adv) at the top, on top

de **bovenkaak** /b<u>o</u>və(n)kak/ (pl: -kaken) upper jaw

de **bovenkant** /b<u>o</u>və(n)kɑnt/ (pl: -en) top

de **bovenkleding** /b<u>o</u>və(n)kledɪŋ/ outer clothes, outerwear

bovenkomen /b<u>o</u>və(n)komə(n)/ (kwam boven, is bovengekomen) **1** come up, come to the surface, break (the) surface, surface **2** come up(stairs)

de **bovenlaag** /b<u>o</u>və(n)lax/ (pl: -lagen) upper layer, surface layer; top coat

de **bovenleiding** /b<u>o</u>və(n)lɛidɪŋ/ (pl: -en) overhead (contact) wire

het **bovenlijf** /b<u>o</u>və(n)lɛif/ (pl: -lijven) upper part of the body: *met ontbloot* ~ stripped to the waist

de **bovenlip** /b<u>o</u>və(n)lɪp/ (pl: -pen) upper lip

bovenmatig /bovəm<u>a</u>təx/ (adj, adv) extreme, excessive

bovenmenselijk /bovə(n)m<u>ɛ</u>nsələk/ (adj, adv) superhuman

bovennatuurlijk /bovənat<u>y</u>rlək/ (adj, adv) supernatural

bovenop /bovə(n)<u>ɔ</u>p/ (adv) **1** on top: [fig] *ergens* ~ *springen* pounce on sth.; *het er te dik* ~ *leggen* lay it on too thick **2** on one's feet: *de zieke kwam* er snel weer ~ the patient made a quick recovery

bovenst /b<u>o</u>vənst/ (adj) top, topmost, upper(most): *van de* ~*e plank* first class; *de* ~*e verdieping* [also fig] the top storey

bovenstaand /b<u>o</u>və(n)stant/ (adj) above, above-mentioned

de **boventoon** /b<u>o</u>və(n)ton/ (pl: -tonen) dominant tone: [fig] *de* ~ *voeren* [pers] play first fiddle, monopolize the conversation; [feeling] predominate

bovenuit

bovenuit /bovə(n)œyt/ (adv) above: *zijn stem **klonk** overal ~* his voice could be heard above everything

de **bovenverdieping** /bovə(n)vərdipɪŋ/ (pl: -en) upper storey, upper floor; top floor (*or:* storey)

bovenvermeld /bovə(n)vərmɛlt/ (adj) above(-mentioned)

bovenwinds /bovə(n)wɪnts/ (adj, adv) windward

de **bovenwoning** /bovə(n)wonɪŋ/ (pl: -en) upstairs flat

de **bovenzijde** /bovə(n)zɛidə/ (pl: -n) *see bovenkant*

de **bowl** /bowl/ (pl: -s) punch

bowlen /bowlə(n)/ (bowlde, heeft gebowld) bowl

de **bowlingbaan** /bolɪŋban/ (pl: -banen) bowling alley

de **box** /bɔks/ (pl: -en) **1** (loud)speaker **2** (loose) box, stall **3** storeroom **4** (play)pen

de **boxer** /bɔksər/ (pl: -s) boxer

de **boxershort** /bɔksərʃɔːrt/ (pl: -s) boxer shorts

de **boycot** /bɔjkɔt/ (pl: -s) boycott

boycotten /bɔjkɔtə(n)/ (boycotte, heeft geboycot) boycott; freeze out

de **¹boze** /bozə/ wicked person: *het is **uit** den ~* it is fundamentally wrong, it is absolutely forbidden

het **²boze** /bozə/ evil

de **braadpan** /bratpɑn/ (pl: -nen) casserole

de **braadworst** /bratwɔrst/ (pl: -en) **1** (frying) sausage **2** German sausage

braaf /braf/ (adj, adv) **1** good, honest; [oft iron] respectable; decent **2** well-behaved, obedient: [fig] *het ~ste **jongetje** van de klas* best in the class; best performing country

de **braafheid** /brafhɛit/ goodness, decency, honesty; [sometimes iron] respectability; obedience

braak /brak/ (adj) **1** waste; fallow: *~ **laten** liggen* leave (*or:* lay) fallow **2** [fig] fallow, undeveloped, unexplored

braakliggend /braklɪɣənt/ (adj) fallow

het **braakmiddel** /brakmɪdəl/ (pl: -en) emetic, vomitive

het **braaksel** /braksəl/ vomit

de **braam** /bram/ (pl: bramen) blackberry, bramble

brabbelen /brɑbələ(n)/ (brabbelde, heeft gebrabbeld) babble, jabber, gibber

braden /bradə(n)/ (braadde, heeft gebraden) roast; fry; pot-roast; grill

de **braderie** /bradəri/ (pl: -ën) fair

het **braille** /brɑjə/ braille: *in ~* in braille, brailled

brainstormen /brɛnstɔrmə(n)/ (brainstormde, heeft gebrainstormd) do some brainstorming: *~ **over*** brainstorm on

brak /brak/ (adj) saltish, brinish

braken /brakə(n)/ (braakte, heeft gebraakt) vomit, be sick, throw up, regurgitate

brallen /brɑlə(n)/ (bralde, heeft gebrald) brag, boast

de **brancard** /brɑŋkar/ (pl: -s) stretcher

de **branche** /brãʃ/ (pl: -s) branch, department; line (of business); (branch of) trade

de **brand** /brɑnt/ (pl: -en) fire, blaze: *er is **gevaar** voor ~* there is a fire hazard; *~ **stichten*** commit arson; *in ~ **staan*** be on fire; *in ~ **vliegen*** catch fire, burst into flames; ignite; *iets **in** ~ steken* set sth. on fire, set fire to sth. || *iem. **uit** de ~ helpen* help s.o. out

het **brandalarm** /brɑntalɑrm/ fire alarm (*or:* call)

brandbaar /brɑndbar/ (adj) combustible; (in)flammable

de **brandblusinstallatie** /brɑndblʏsɪnstala(t)si/ (pl: -s) sprinkler system

de **brandblusser** /brɑndblʏsər/ (pl: -s) (fire) extinguisher

de **brandbom** /brɑndbɔm/ (pl: -men) fire bomb

de **brandbrief** /brɑndbrif/ (pl: -brieven) appeal letter, letter of appeal

¹branden /brɑndə(n)/ (brandde, heeft gebrand) burn, be on fire; blaze: *de **lamp** brandt* the lamp is on || *ze was het huis niet uit te ~* there was no way of getting her out of the house

²branden /brɑndə(n)/ (brandde, heeft gebrand) burn; scald; roast: *zich de **vingers** ~* [fig] burn one's fingers

de **brander** /brɑndər/ (pl: -s) burner

branderig /brɑndərəx/ (adj) irritant, caustic

de **brandewijn** /brɑndəwɛin/ (pl: -en) brandy

de **brandgang** /brɑntxɑŋ/ (pl: -en) fire lane, firebreak

het **brandgevaar** /brɑntxəvar/ fire hazard, fire risk

brandgevaarlijk /brɑntxəvarlək/ (adj) flammable

het **brandglas** /brɑntxlɑs/ (pl: -glazen) burning-glass

de **brandhaard** /brɑnthart/ (pl: -en) seat of a fire; [fig] hotbed

het **brandhout** /brɑnthaut/ (pl: -en) firewood

de **branding** /brɑndɪŋ/ (pl: -en) surf; breakers

de **brandkast** /brɑntkɑst/ (pl: -en) safe

de **brandkraan** /brɑntkran/ (pl: -kranen) (fire) hydrant, fireplug

de **brandladder** /brɑntladər/ (pl: -s) escape ladder

de **brandlucht** /brɑntlʏxt/ smell of burning

de **brandmelder** /brɑntmɛldər/ (pl: -s) fire alarm (system)

het **brandmerk** /brɑntmɛrk/ (pl: -en) brand

brandmerken /brɑntmɛrkə(n)/ (brandmerkte, heeft gebrandmerkt) brand

de **brandnetel** /brɑntnetəl/ (pl: -s) nettle

het **brandpunt** /brɑntpʏnt/ (pl: -en) **1** focus [also maths] **2** [fig] centre

het **brandraam** /brɑntram/ (pl: -ramen) [Belg]

stained-glass window
brandschoon /brɑntsxon/ (adj) spotless
de **brandslang** /brɑntslɑŋ/ (pl: -en) fire hose
de **brandspiritus** /brɑntspiritʏs/ methylated
spirit(s)
de **brandspuit** /brɑntspœyt/ (pl: -en) fire engine: *drijvende* ~ fireboat
de **brandstapel** /brɑntstapəl/ (pl: -s) stake
brandstichten /brɑntstɪxtə(n)/ (stichtte
brand, heeft brandgesticht) commit arson
de **brandstichter** /brɑntstɪxtər/ (pl: -s) arson-
ist
de **brandstichting** /brɑntstɪxtɪŋ/ (pl: -en) arson
de **brandstof** /brɑntstɔf/ (pl: -fen) fuel
de **brandtrap** /brɑntrɑp/ (pl: -pen) fire escape
de **brandweer** /brɑntwer/ fire brigade
de **brandweerauto** /brɑntwerauto/ (pl: -'s)
fire engine
de **brandweerkazerne** /brɑntwerkazɛrnə/
(pl: -s) fire station
de **brandweerman** /brɑntwermɑn/ (pl: -lie-
den) fireman
brandwerend /brɑntwerənt/ (adj) fire-re-
sistant
de **brandwond** /brɑntwɔnt/ (pl: -en) burn
brassen /brɑsə(n)/ (braste, heeft gebrast)
binge, guzzle
de **brasserie** /brɑsəri/ (pl: -ën) brasserie
bravo /bravo/ (int) bravo!; hear! hear!
de **bravoure** /bravur/ bravura: *met veel* ~
dashing
de **Braziliaan** /brazilijan/ (pl: Brazilianen) Brazilian
Braziliaans /brazilijans/ (adj) Brazilian
Brazilië /brazilijə/ Brazil
het **break-evenpoint** /brekiːvəmpɔjnt/ (pl: -s)
break-even point
¹**breed** /bret/ (adj) wide, broad: *de kamer is 6
m lang en 5 m* ~ the room is 6 metres (long)
by 5 metres (wide); *niet breder dan twee meter*
not more than two metres wide (*or:* in
width)
²**breed** /bret/ (adv) widely; loosely: *een* ~
omgeslagen kraag a wide (*or:* loose) collar
de **breedband** /bredbɑnt/ [comp] broadband
het **breedbandinternet** /bredbɑntɪntərnɛt/
broadband (Internet access)
de **breedbeeld-tv** /bredbelteve/ (pl: -'s) wide-
screen TV
breedgebouwd /bretxəbɑut/ (adj)
broad(ly-built), square-built
breedgedragen /bretxədraɣə(n)/ (adj)
widely supported: *een* ~ *plan* a widely supported plan
breedsprakig /bretsprakəx/ (adj, adv)
long-winded
de **breedte** /bretə/ (pl: -s) **1** width, breadth: *in
de* ~ breadthways **2** [geog] latitude
de **breedtegraad** /bretəɣrat/ (pl: -graden)
parallel, degree of latitude

breeduit /bretœyt/ (adv) **1** spread (out): ~
gaan zitten sprawl (on) **2** out loud
breedvoerig /bretfurəx/ (adj, adv) circumstantial; detailed
breekbaar /bregbar/ (adj) fragile; brittle
het **breekijzer** /brekɛizər/ (pl: -s) crowbar
het **breekpunt** /brekpʏnt/ (pl: -en) breaking
point
de **breezer** /briːzər/ breezer
breien /brɛiə(n)/ (breide, heeft gebreid)
knit
het **brein** /brɛin/ brain; [fig also] brains: *het* ~ *zijn
achter een project* be the brain(s) behind a
project, mastermind a project
de **breinaald** /brɛinalt/ (pl: -en) knitting needle
het **breiwerk** /brɛiwɛrk/ (pl: -en) knitting
¹**breken** /brekə(n)/ (brak, is gebroken) break;
fracture ‖ *met iem.* ~ break off (relations)
with s.o.; break up with s.o.; *met een gewoonte* ~ break a habit
²**breken** /brekə(n)/ (brak, heeft gebroken)
break; [light] refract ‖ *een record* ~ break a
record; *de betovering* (*or: het verzet*) ~ break
the spell (*or:* resistance)
de **brem** /brɛm/ broom
brengen /brɛŋə(n)/ (bracht, heeft gebracht)
1 bring; take: *mensen (weer) bij elkaar* ~ bring
(*or:* get) people together (again); *naar huis* ~
take home; *een kind naar bed* ~ put a child to
bed **2** bring, take, give: *zijn mening naar voren* ~ put forward, come out with one's
opinion; *iets naar voren* ~ bring sth. up; *een
zaak voor het gerecht* ~ take a matter to court
3 bring, send, put: *iem. tot een daad* ~ drive
s.o. to (sth.); *iem. aan het twijfelen* ~ raise
doubt(s) in s.o.'s mind ‖ *het ver* ~ go far
de **bres** /brɛs/ (pl: -sen) breach; hole: *voor iem. in
de* ~ *springen* step into the breach for s.o.
Bretagne /brətɑɲə/ Brittany
de **bretel** /brətɛl/ (pl: -s) braces; [Am] suspend-
ers
de **breuk** /brøk/ (pl: -en) **1** break(ing), breakage **2** crack, split, fault **3** [med] fracture,
hernia **4** rift, breach **5** [maths] fraction: *decimale (tiendelige)* ~ decimal fraction; *samengestelde* ~ complex (*or:* compound)
fraction
de **breuklijn** /brøklɛin/ (pl: -en) (line of a)
break; line of fracture [also med]; [geology]
fault line
het **brevet** /brəvɛt/ (pl: -ten) certificate; [avia-
tion] licence
bridgen /brɪdʒə(n)/ (bridgede/bridgete,
heeft gebridged/gebridget) play bridge
de **brief** /brif/ (pl: brieven) letter: *aangetekende* ~ registered letter; *in antwoord op uw* ~
van de 25e in reply to your letter of the 25th
briefen /briːfə(n)/ (briefte, heeft gebrieft)
brief
het **briefgeheim** /brifxəhɛim/ confidentiality

of the mail(s)

het **briefhoofd** /brifhoft/ (pl: -en) letterhead, letter-heading

de **briefing** /bri:fɪŋ/ (pl: -s) briefing

het **briefje** /brifjə/ (pl: -s) note: *dat geef ik je op een ~* you can take it from me

de **briefkaart** /brifkart/ (pl: -en) postcard

de **briefopener** /brifopənər/ (pl: -s) paper-knife, letter-opener

het **briefpapier** /brifpapir/ writing paper, stationery

de **briefwisseling** /brifwɪsəlɪŋ/ (pl: -en) correspondence: *een ~ voeren (met)* correspond (with)

de **bries** /bris/ breeze

briesen /brisə(n)/ (brieste, heeft gebriest) roar; snort

de **brievenbus** /brivə(n)bʏs/ (pl: -sen) **1** post-box, letter box **2** letter box; [Am] mailbox

de **brigade** /briɣadə/ (pl: -s) **1** brigade **2** squad, team

de **brigadier** /briɣadir/ (pl: -s) **1** police sergeant **2** (school) crossing guard

de **brij** /brɛi/ **1** pulp **2** porridge || *om de hete ~ heen draaien* beat about the bush

de **brik** /brɪk/ (pl: -ken): [Belg] *melk in ~* milk in cartons

de **bril** /brɪl/ (pl: -len) **1** (pair of) glasses; (pair of) goggles: *alles door een donkere* (or: *roze*) *~ zien* take a gloomy (or: rosy) view of everything **2** (toilet) seat

de **brildrager** /brɪldraɣər/ (pl: -s): *hij, zij is ~* he, she wears glasses

de ¹**briljant** /brɪljɑnt/ (pl: -en) (cut) diamond
²**briljant** /brɪljɑnt/ (adj, adv) brilliant

de **brillenkoker** /brɪlə(n)kokər/ (pl: -s) glasses case

het/de **brilmontuur** /brɪlmɔntyr/ (pl: -monturen) glasses frame

de **brilslang** /brɪlslɑŋ/ (pl: -en) (spectacled) cobra

de **Brit** /brɪt/ (pl: -ten) Briton; Brit

de **brits** /brɪts/ (pl: -en) plank bed, wooden bed
Brits /brɪts/ (adj) British

de **broccoli** /brɔkoli/ broccoli

de **broche** /brɔʃ/ (pl: -s) brooch

de **brochure** /brɔʃyrə/ (pl: -s) pamphlet

het **broddelwerk** /brɔdəlwɛrk/ botch-job, botch-up

brodeloos /brodəlos/ (adj) without means of support: *iem. ~ maken* leave s.o. without means of support

broeden /brudə(n)/ (broedde, heeft gebroed) brood || *hij zit op iets te ~* he is working on sth.

de **broeder** /brudər/ (pl: -s) **1** brother **2** [Roman Catholicism] brother, friar **3** (male) nurse

broederlijk /brudərlək/ (adj, adv) fraternal; like brothers

de **broedermoord** /brudərmort/ (pl: -en) fratricide

de **broederschap** /brudərsχɑp/ (pl: -pen) brotherhood, fraternity

de **broedmachine** /brutmaʃinə/ (pl: -s) incubator, brooder

de **broedplaats** /brutplats/ (pl: -en) breeding ground

broeien /brujə(n)/ (broeide, heeft gebroeid) **1** heat, get heated, get hot **2** be sultry || *er broeit iets* there is sth. brewing

broeierig /brujərəχ/ (adj, adv) **1** sultry, sweltering, muggy **2** sultry, sensual

de **broeikas** /brujkɑs/ (pl: -sen) hothouse, greenhouse

het **broeikaseffect** /brujkɑsɛfɛkt/ greenhouse effect

het **broeikasgas** /brujkɑsχɑs/ (pl: -sen) greenhouse gas

het **broeinest** /brujnɛst/ (pl: -en) hotbed

de **broek** /bruk/ (pl: -en) (pair of) trousers; shorts || *het in zijn ~ doen* wet one's pants; *een proces aan zijn ~ krijgen* get taken to court; *iem. achter de ~ zitten* keep s.o. up to the mark, see that s.o. gets on with his work

het **broekje** /brukjə/ (pl: -s) briefs; panties; knickers

het **broekpak** /brukpɑk/ (pl: -ken) trouser suit

de **broekriem** /brukrim/ (pl: -en) belt: [also fig] *de ~ aanhalen* tighten one's belt

de **broekrok** /brukrɔk/ (pl: -ken) culottes, pantskirt

de **broekspijp** /brukspɛip/ (pl: -en) (trouser-)leg

de **broekzak** /bruksɑk/ (pl: -ken) trouser(s) pocket: *iets kennen als zijn ~* know sth. inside out (or: like the back of one's hand)
broekzakbellen pocket-dial

de **broer** /brur/ (pl: -s) brother

het **broertje** /brurcə/ (pl: -s) little brother || *een ~ dood aan iets hebben* hate sth., detest sth.

het/de **brok** /brɔk/ (pl: -ken) piece, fragment, chunk: *~ken maken* a) smash things up; b) [fig] mess things up; *hij had een ~ in zijn keel* he had a lump in his throat

het **brokaat** /brokat/ brocade

brokkelen /brɔkələ(n)/ (brokkelde, heeft/is gebrokkeld) crumble

het **brokstuk** /brɔkstʏk/ (pl: -ken) (broken) fragment, piece; debris

de **brom** /brɔm/ buzz

de **bromfiets** /brɔmfits/ (pl: -en) moped

de **bromfietser** /brɔmfitsər/ (pl: -s) moped rider (or: driver)

brommen /brɔmə(n)/ (bromde, heeft/is gebromd) **1** hum; growl **2** mutter **3** ride a moped

de **brommer** /brɔmər/ (pl: -s) moped

de **bromscooter** /brɔmskutər/ (pl: -s) (motor) scooter

de **bromvlieg** /brɔmvliχ/ (pl: -en) bluebottle, blowfly

de **bron** /brɔn/ (pl: -nen) **1** well, spring: *hete ~* hot springs **2** source; spring, cause: *~nen van bestaan* means of existence; *een ~ van ergernis* an annoyance, a nuisance ‖ *hij heeft het uit betrouwbare ~* he has it from a reliable source; *een rijke (onuitputtelijke) ~ van informatie* a mine of information

de **bronchitis** /brɔnxitəs/ bronchitis

het **brons** /brɔns/ (pl: bronzen) bronze

de **bronstijd** /brɔnstɛit/ Bronze Age

de **bronvermelding** /brɔnvərmɛldɪŋ/ (pl: -en) acknowledgement of (one's) sources: *iets zonder ~ overnemen* copy sth. without acknowledgement (*or:* crediting the source)

het **bronwater** /brɔnwatər/ (pl: -en) spring water; [in bottle] mineral water

bronzen /brɔnzə(n)/ (adj) bronze: *een ~ medaille* a bronze (medal)

het **brood** /brot/ (pl: broden) **1** bread: *daar is geen droog ~ mee te verdienen* you won't (*or:* wouldn't) make a penny out of it; [fig] *~ op de plank hebben* be able to make ends meet **2** loaf (of bread): *een snee ~* a slice of bread; *twee broden* two loaves (of bread) **3** living

het **broodbeleg** /brodbələx/ sandwich filling

het **brooddeeg** /brodex/ (bread) dough

het **broodje** /brocə/ (pl: -s) (bread) roll, bun: *~ aap* monkey's sandwich ‖ *als warme ~s over de toonbank gaan* go (*or:* sell) like hot cakes

de **broodjeszaak** /brocəzak/ (pl: -zaken) sandwich bar

de **broodkruimel** /brotkrœymøl/ (pl: -s) breadcrumb

de **broodmaaltijd** /brotmaltɛit/ (pl: -en) cold meal (*or:* lunch)

broodmager /brotmaɣər/ (adj) skinny, bony

broodnodig /brotnodəx/ (adj) much-needed, badly needed, highly necessary

het/de **broodrooster** /brotrostər/ (pl: -s) toaster

de **broodtrommel** /brotrɔməl/ (pl: -s) **1** breadbin **2** lunch box

de **broodwinner** /brotwɪnər/ (pl: -s) breadwinner

de **broodwinning** /brotwɪnɪŋ/ (pl: -en) livelihood

broos /bros/ (adj, adv) fragile, delicate, frail

bros /brɔs/ (adj) brittle, crisp(y)

brossen /brɔsə(n)/ (broste, heeft gebrost) [Belg] play truant, skip classes

brouwen /brɑuwə(n)/ (brouwde, heeft gebrouwen) brew; mix; concoct

de **brouwer** /brɑuwər/ (pl: -s) brewer

de **brouwerij** /brɑuwərɛi/ (pl: -en) brewery

het **brouwsel** /brɑusəl/ (pl: -s) brew, concoction

de **brownie** /brɑuni/ brownie

browsen /brɑuzə(n)/ (browsede/browsete, heeft gebrowsed/gebrowset) browse

de **browser** /brɑuzər/ browser

de **brug** /brʏx/ (pl: -gen) **1** bridge **2** bridge-(work) **3** [sport] parallel bars **4** [shipp]

bridge ‖ *hij moet over de ~ komen* he has to deliver the goods (*or:* pay up)

Brugge /brʏɣə/ Bruges

het **bruggenhoofd** /brʏɣə(n)hoft/ (pl: -en) abutment; bridgehead

de **brugklas** /brʏxklɑs/ (pl: -sen) first class (*or:* form) (at secondary school)

de **brugklasser** /brʏxklɑsər/ (pl: -s) first-form-er

de **brugleuning** /brʏxlønɪŋ/ (pl: -en) bridge railing; parapet

het **brugpensioen** /brʏxpɛnʃun/ (pl: -en) [Belg] early retirement

de **brugwachter** /brʏxwɑxtər/ (pl: -s) bridge-keeper

de **brui** /brœy/: *er de ~ aan geven* chuck it (in)

de **bruid** /brœyt/ (pl: -en) bride

de **bruidegom** /brœydəɣɔm/ (pl: -s) (bride)-groom

het **bruidsboeket** /brœytsbukɛt/ (pl: -ten) bridal bouquet

de **bruidsjapon** /brœytsjapɔn/ (pl: -nen) bridal gown, wedding dress

het **bruidsmeisje** /brœytsmɛiʃə/ bridesmaid

de **bruidsnacht** /brœytsnɑxt/ (pl: -en) wedding night

het **bruidspaar** /brœytspar/ (pl: -paren) bride and (bride)groom, bridal couple

de **bruidsschat** /brœytsxɑt/ (pl: -ten) dowry

de **bruidssuite** /brœytswitə/ (pl: -s) bridal suite

de **bruidstaart** /brœytstart/ (pl: -en) wedding cake

bruikbaar /brœyɣbar/ (adj) usable; useful; serviceable; employable

de **bruikleen** /brœyklen/ loan: *iets aan iem. in ~ geven* lend sth. to s.o.

de **bruiloft** /brœylɔft/ (pl: -en) wedding

bruin /brœyn/ (adj, adv) brown ‖ *wat bak je ze weer ~* you're really going to town on it

het **bruinbrood** /brœymbrot/ (pl: -broden) brown bread

bruinen /brœynə(n)/ (bruinde, heeft/is gebruind) brown; tan; bronze: *de zon heeft zijn vel gebruind* the sun has tanned his skin

de **bruinkool** /brœynkol/ brown coal, lignite

de **bruinvis** /brœynvɪs/ (pl: -sen) porpoise

bruisen /brœysə(n)/ (bruiste, heeft gebruist) foam, effervesce: *~ van geestdrift* (*or:* *energie*) bubble with enthusiasm (*or:* energy)

bruisend /brœysənt/ (adj) exuberant

het/de **bruistablet** /brœystablɛt/ (pl: -ten) effervescent tablet

brullen /brʏlə(n)/ (brulde, heeft gebruld) roar, bawl, howl: *~ van het lachen* roar (*or:* howl) with laughter

de **brunch** /brʏnʃ/ (pl: -es) brunch

brunchen /brʏnʃə(n)/ (brunchte, heeft gebruncht) have brunch

Brunei /brunɛi/ Brunei

de **Bruneier** /brunɛijər/ (pl: -s) Bruneian

Bruneis /brunɛɪs/ (adj) Bruneian

de **brunette** /brynɛtə/ (pl: -s) brunette

Brussel /brysəl/ Brussels

Brussels /brysəls/ (adj) Brussels

brutaal /brytal/ (adj, adv) **1** insolent; cheeky; impudent: *zij was zo ~ om …* she had the cheek (*or:* nerve) to … **2** bold, forward

de **brutaliteit** /brytalitɛit/ (pl: -en) cheek, impudence

bruto /bryto/ (adv) gross: *het concert heeft ~ €1100 opgebracht* the concert raised 1100 euros gross

het **brutogewicht** /brytoɣəwɪxt/ (pl: -en) gross weight

het **brutoloon** /brytolon/ (pl: -lonen) gross income

het **brutosalaris** /brytosalarɪs/ gross salary

de **brutowinst** /brytowɪnst/ (pl: -en) gross profit

bruusk /brysk/ (adj, adv) brusque, abrupt, curt: *een ~ antwoord* an abrupt (*or:* curt) answer; *een ~ optreden* a brusque manner

bruut /bryt/ (adj, adv) brute; brutal

BSE /beːɛze/ bovine spongiform encephalopathy BSE, mad cow disease

het **bsn** /beːɛsɛn/ (pl: -'s) [Dutch] *burgerservicenummer* Citizen Service Number (CSN)

het **bso** /beːɛso/ [Belg] *beroepssecundair onderwijs* secondary vocational education

de **btw** /betewe/ *belasting op de toegevoegde waarde* VAT, value added tax: *ex ~* excluding (*or:* plus VAT)

het **bubbelbad** /bybəlbɑt/ (pl: -en) whirlpool, jacuzzi

het **budget** /bydʒɛt/ (pl: -ten) budget: *dat past niet in mijn ~* that doesn't suit my budget

de **budgetbewaking** /bydʒɛdbəwakɪŋ/ budgetary control

de **budgetmaatschappij** (pl: -en) budget airline, low-cost carrier

budgettair /bydʒɛtɛːr/ (adj) budgetary

budgetteren /bydʒɛtərə(n)/ (budgetteerde, heeft gebudgetteerd) budget

de **buffel** /byfəl/ (pl: -s) buffalo

buffelen /byfələ(n)/ (buffelde, heeft gebuffeld) [inform] **1** wolf (down) **2** beaver away

de **buffer** /byfər/ (pl: -s) buffer

de **bufferstaat** /byfərstat/ (pl: -staten) buffer state

de **buffervoorraad** /byfərvorat/ (pl: -voorraden) buffer stock

de **bufferzone** /byfərzoːnə/ (pl: -s) buffer zone

het **buffet** /byfɛt/ (pl: -ten) sideboard; buffet

de **bug** /byk/ (pl: -s) bug

de **bugel** /byɣəl/ (pl: -s) bugle

de **buggy** /bygi/ (pl: -'s) buggy

de **bühne** /byːnə/ boards, stage

de **bui** /bœy/ (pl: -en) **1** shower; (short) storm: *schuilen voor* een ~ take shelter from a storm; *de ~ zien hangen* [fig] see the storm

coming; *hier* en *daar* een ~ scattered showers **2** mood: *in een driftige ~* in a fit of temper

de **buidel** /bœydəl/ (pl: -s) **1** purse **2** pouch

het **buideldier** /bœydəldir/ (pl: -en) marsupial

¹**buigen** /bœyɣə(n)/ (boog, heeft/is gebogen) **1** bow: *voor iem. ~* bow to s.o. **2** (+ voor) bow (to), bend (before) **3** bend (over)

²**buigen** /bœyɣə(n)/ (boog, heeft gebogen) bend: *het hoofd ~* [fig] bow (to), submit (to); *de weg buigt naar links* the road curves (*or:* bends) to the left; *zich over de balustrade ~* lean over the railing

de **buiging** /bœyɣɪŋ/ (pl: -en) **1** bend, curve **2** bow; curtsy: *een ~ maken* bow, curtsy

buigzaam /bœyxsam/ (adj) **1** flexible, supple **2** [fig] flexible, adaptable, compliant

buiig /bœyəx/ (adj) showery, gusty

de **buik** /bœyk/ (pl: -en) belly, stomach; abdomen: [fig] *er de ~ van vol hebben* be fed up (with it), be sick and tired of it; [fig] *schrijf iem maar op je ~* not on your life, forget it

buikdansen /bœyɡdɑnsə(n)/ (do a) belly dance

de **buikdanseres** /bœyɡdɑnsərɛs/ (pl: -sen) belly dancer

de **buikholte** /bœykhɔltə/ (pl: -n, -s) abdomen

het **buikje** /bœykjə/ (pl: -s) paunch, pot belly

de **buikkramp** /bœykrɑmp/ (pl: -en) stomach (*or:* abdominal) cramp

de **buiklanding** /bœyklɑndɪŋ/ (pl: -en) pancake landing, belly landing

de **buikloop** /bœyklop/ diarrhoea; the runs

de **buikpijn** /bœykpɛin/ (pl: -en) stomach-ache, bellyache

de **buikriem** /bœykrim/ (pl: -en) belt

de **buikspier** /bœykspir/ (pl: -en) stomach muscle, abdominal muscle

buikspreken /bœyksprekə(n)/ ventriloquize, throw one's voice

de **buikspreker** /bœyksprekər/ (pl: -s) ventriloquist

de **buikvliesontsteking** /bœykflisɔntstekɪŋ/ (pl: -en) peritonitis

de **buil** /bœyl/ (pl: -en) bump

de **buis** /bœys/ (pl: buizen) **1** tube, pipe; valve **2** box, TV **3** [Belg; inform] fail (mark)

de **buit** /bœyt/ **1** booty, spoils, loot **2** catch: *met een flinke ~ thuiskomen* come home with a big catch

buitelen /bœytələ(n)/ (buitelde, heeft/is gebuiteld) tumble, somersault

de **buiteling** /bœytəlɪŋ/ (pl: -en) tumble: *een lelijke ~ maken* take a nasty spill (*or:* tumble)

¹**buiten** /bœytə(n)/ (adv) outside, out, outdoors: *een dagje ~* a day in the country; *daar wil ik ~ blijven* I want to stay out of that; *naar ~ gaan* **a)** go outside (*or:* outdoors); **b)** go into the country (*or:* out of town); *naar ~ brengen* take out; lead (*or:* show) out [pers]; *een gedicht van ~ leren* (or: *kennen*) learn (*or:* know) a poem by heart ‖ *zich te ~ gaan (aan)* overin-

dulge (o.s.) (in); *hou* je er ~*!* stay (*or:* keep) out of it!

²buiten /bœytə(n)/ (prep) **1** outside, beyond: ~ *het bereik van* out of reach of; *hij was* ~ *zichzelf van woede* he was beside himself with anger **2** out of: *iets* ~ *beschouwing laten* leave sth. out of consideration **3** without: *het is* ~ *mijn medeweten gebeurd* it happened without my knowledge

buitenaards /bœytə(n)a̱rts/ (adj) extraterrestrial

buitenaf /bœytənaf/ (adv) outside, external, from (*or:* on) the outside

de **buitenbaan** /bœytə(n)ban/ (pl: -banen) outside lane

buitenbaarmoederlijk /bœytə(n)barmu̱dərlək/ (adj) ectopic; ~*e zwangerschap* ectopic pregnancy

het **buitenbad** /bœytə(n)bat/ (pl: -en) open-air (*or:* outdoor) pool

de **buitenband** /bœytə(n)bant/ (pl: -en) tyre

het **buitenbeentje** /bœytə(n)bencə/ (pl: -s) odd man out, outsider

de **buitenbocht** /bœytə(n)bɔχt/ (pl: -en) outside curve (*or:* bend)

de **buitenboordmotor** /bœytə(n)bo̱rtmotər/ (pl: -en) outboard motor

de **buitendeur** /bœytə(n)dør/ (pl: -en) front door, outside door

buitenechtelijk /bœytə(n)ɛ̱χtələk/ (adj) extramarital: ~ *kind* illegitimate child

¹buitengewoon /bœytə(n)ɣəwo̱n/ (adj) special, extra; exceptional, unusual

²buitengewoon /bœytə(n)ɣəwo̱n/ (adv) extremely, exceptionally

het **buitenhuis** /bœytə(n)hœys/ (pl: -huizen) country house

buitenissig /bœytəni̱səχ/ (adj) unusual, strange, eccentric

het **buitenkansje** /bœytə(n)kanʃə/ (pl: -s) stroke of luck

de **buitenkant** /bœytə(n)kant/ (pl: -en) outside, exterior: *op de* ~ *afgaan* judge by appearances

het **buitenland** /bœytə(n)lant/ foreign country (*or:* countries): *van* (or: *uit*) *het* ~ *terugkeren* return (*or:* come back) from abroad

de **buitenlander** /bœytə(n)landər/ (pl: -s) foreigner, alien

buitenlands /bœytə(n)lants/ (adj) foreign, international: *een* ~*e reis* a trip abroad

de **buitenlucht** /bœytə(n)lʏχt/ open (air); country air

buitenom /bœytə(n)ɔ̱m/ (adv) around; round the house, town, ...

buitenparlementair /bœytə(n)parləmɛntɛ̱ːr/ (adj, adv) extraparliamentary

buitenschools /bœytə(n)sχo̱ls/ (adj, adv) extracurricular, extramural: ~*e opvang* out-of-school care; after-school care

buitenshuis /bœytənshœys/ (adv) outside, out(side) of the house, outdoors: ~ *eten* eat out

buitensluiten /bœytə(n)slœytə(n)/ (sloot buiten, heeft buitengesloten) shut out; lock out

het **buitenspel** /bœytə(n)spɛl/ offside ‖ [fig] *hij werd* ~ *gezet* he was sidelined

de **buitenspiegel** /bœytə(n)spiɣəl/ (pl: -s) outside (*or:* wing) mirror

buitensporig /bœytənspo̱rəχ/ (adj, adv) extravagant, excessive, exorbitant, inordinate

de **buitensport** /bœytə(n)spɔrt/ (pl: -en) outdoor sports

buitenst /bœytə(n)st/ (adj) out(er)most, exterior, outer

de **buitenstaander** /bœytə(n)standər/ (pl: -s) outsider

het **buitenverblijf** /bœytə(n)vərblɛɪf/ (pl: -verblijven) countryhouse, country place

de **buitenwacht** /bœytə(n)waχt/ outside world, public; outsiders

de **buitenwereld** /bœytə(n)werəlt/ public (at large), outside world

de **buitenwijk** /bœytə(n)wɛik/ (pl: -en) suburb; outskirts

de **buitenwipper** /bœytə(n)wɪpər/ (pl: -s) [Belg] bouncer

de **buitenzijde** /bœytə(n)zɛidə/ (pl: -n) outside, exterior; [esp fig] surface

buitmaken /bœytmakə(n)/ (maakte buit, heeft buitgemaakt) seize; capture [ship]

buizen /bœyzə(n)/ (buisde, heeft/is gebuisd) [Belg; inform] fail

de **buizerd** /bœyzərt/ (pl: -s) buzzard

¹bukken /bʏkə(n)/ (bukte, heeft gebukt) stoop; duck: *hij gaat gebukt onder veel zorgen* he is weighed down by many worries

zich **²bukken** /bʏkə(n)/ (bukte zich, heeft zich gebukt) stoop, bend down

de **buks** /bʏks/ (pl: -en) (short) rifle

de **bul** /bʏl/ degree certificate

bulderen /bʏldərə(n)/ (bulderde, heeft gebulderd) roar, bellow

de **buldog** /bʏldɔχ/ (pl: -gen) bulldog

de **Bulgaar** /bʏlɣa̱r/ (pl: Bulgaren) Bulgarian

Bulgaars /bʏlɣa̱rs/ (adj) Bulgarian

Bulgarije /bʏlɣarɛi̱ə/ Bulgaria

de **bulkartikelen** /bʏlkartikələ(n)/ (pl) bulk, bulk(ed) goods

bulken /bʏlkə(n)/ (bulkte, heeft gebulkt): *hij bulkt van het geld* he is rolling in money

de **bulldozer** /bʏldozər/ (pl: -s) bulldozer

de **bullebak** /bʏləbak/ (pl: -ken) bully, ogre

het **bulletin** /bʏlətɛ̃/ (pl: -s) bulletin, report

de **bult** /bʏlt/ (pl: -en) **1** lump; bump **2** hunch, hump: *met een* ~ hunchbacked, humpbacked

de **bumper** /bʏmpər/ (pl: -s) bumper

de **bumperklever** /bʏmpərklevər/ tailgater

de **bundel** /bʏndəl/ (pl: -s) **1** bundle; sheaf **2** collection, volume

bundelen /bʏndələ(n)/ (bundelde, heeft gebundeld) bundle, cluster; combine: *krachten* ~ join forces

de **bungalow** /bʏŋgalow/ (pl: -s) bungalow; (summer) cottage; chalet

het **bungalowpark** /bʏŋgalowpɑrk/ (pl: -en) holiday park

de **bungalowtent** /bʏŋgalowtɛnt/ (pl: -en) family (frame) tent

bungeejumpen /bʏndʒidʒʏmpə(n)/ bungee jump

bungelen /bʏŋələ(n)/ (bungelde, heeft gebungeld) dangle, hang

de **bunker** /bʏŋkər/ (pl: -s) bunker, bomb shelter, air-raid shelter

bunkeren /bʏŋkərə(n)/ (bunkerde, heeft gebunkerd) 1 refuel 2 stoke up, stuff o.s.

de **bunzing** /bʏnzɪŋ/ (pl: -s, -en) polecat

de **burcht** /bʏrxt/ (pl: -en) castle, fortress, citadel, stronghold

het **bureau** /byro/ (pl: -s) 1 (writing) desk, bureau 2 office, bureau, department, (police) station; agency

het **bureaublad** /byroblɑt/ (pl: -en) desktop

de **bureaucraat** /byrokrat/ (pl: bureaucraten) bureaucrat

de **bureaucratie** /byrokra(t)si/ (pl: -ën) bureaucracy, officialdom

bureaucratisch /byrokratis/ (adj, adv) bureaucratic: *~e rompslomp* red tape

de **bureaula** /byrola/ (pl: -'s, -den) (desk) drawer

de **bureaulamp** /byrolamp/ (pl: -en) desk lamp

de **bureaustoel** /byrostul/ office chair, desk chair

het **bureel** /byrel/ (pl: burelen) [Belg] office

het **burengerucht** /byrə(n)ɣərʏxt/ [roughly] disturbance

de **burgemeester** /bʏrɣəmestər/ (pl: -s) mayor; [Scotland] provost: ~ *en wethouders* mayor and aldermen; municipal executive

de **burger** /bʏrɣər/ (pl: -s) 1 citizen 2 civilian: *militairen en ~s* soldiers and civilians || *een agent in* ~ a plain-clothes policeman

de **burgerbevolking** /bʏrɣərbəvɔlkɪŋ/ civilian population

de **burgerij** /bʏrɣərɛi/ (pl: -en) citizens; (petty) bourgeoisie, middle class

burgerlijk /bʏrɣərlək/ (adj, adv) 1 middle-class, bourgeois 2 [depr] bourgeois, conventional, middle-class; philistine; smug 3 civil, civic: *~e staat* marital status; *(bureau van de) ~e stand* Registry of Births, Deaths and Marriages; Registry Office 4 civil(ian)

de **burgerluchtvaart** /bʏrɣərlʏxtfart/ civil aviation

de **burgeroorlog** /bʏrɣərorlɔx/ (pl: -en) civil war

de **burgerplicht** /bʏrɣərplɪxt/ civic duty

het **burgerrecht** /bʏrɣərɛxt/ (pl: -en) civil rights

het **burgerservicenummer** /bʏrɣərsy-

rvɪsnʏmər/ [Dutch] Citizen Service Number

de **burgervader** /bʏrɣərvadər/ (pl: -s) mayor

de ¹**burgerwacht** /bʏrɣərwɑxt/ (pl: -en) neighbourhood watch volunteer

de ²**burgerwacht** /bʏrɣərwɑxt/ (pl: -en) neighbourhood watch group

Burkina Faso /burkinafɑso/ Burkina Faso

de ¹**Burkinees** /burkines/ Burkinabe

²**Burkinees** /burkines/ (adj) Burkinabe

de **burn-out** /bʏːrnɑut/ burn-out

de ¹**Burundees** /burundes/ (pl: Burundezen) Burundian

²**Burundees** /burundes/ (adj) Burundian

Burundi /burundi/ Burundi

de **bus** /bʏs/ (pl: -sen) 1 bus; coach: *met de* ~ *gaan* go by bus; *~je* minibus; van 2 tin; [large] drum 3 box: *u krijgt de folders morgen in de* ~ you will get the brochures in the post tomorrow || *als winnaar uit de* ~ *komen* (turn out to) be the winner

de **busbaan** /bʏzban/ (pl: -banen) bus lane

de **buschauffeur** /bʏsʃofør/ (pl: -s) bus driver, coach driver

de **busdienst** /bʏzdinst/ (pl: -en) bus service, coach service

de **bushalte** /bʏshɑltə/ (pl: -n, -s) bus stop, coach stop

het **bushokje** /bʏshɔkjə/ (pl: -s) bus shelter

het **busje** /bʏʃə/ (pl: -s) minibus; van

het **buskruit** /bʏskrœyt/ gunpowder

de **buslichting** /bʏslɪxtɪŋ/ (pl: -en) collection

de **buslijn** /bʏslɛin/ (pl: -en) bus route; coach route

het **busstation** /bʏsta(t)ʃɔn/ (pl: -s) bus station; coach station

de **buste** /bʏstə/ (pl: -s, -n) bust, bosom

de **bustehouder** /bʏstəhɑudər/ (pl: -s) brassiere

de **bustocht** /bʏstɔxt/ (pl: -en) coach trip; bus trip

het **butaan** /bytan/ butane

het **butagas** /bytaɣɑs/ butane (gas)

de **butler** /bʏtlər/ (pl: -s) butler

de **button** /bʏtən/ (pl: -s) badge

de **buur** /byr/ (pl: buren) neighbour: *de buren* the (next-door) neighbours

het **buurland** /byrlɑnt/ (pl: -en) neighbouring country

de **buurman** /byrmɑn/ (pl: buurlieden) (next-door) neighbour, man next door

de **buurt** /byrt/ (pl: -en) neighbourhood, area, district: *rosse* ~ red-light district || *de hele* ~ *bij elkaar schreeuwen* shout the place down; *in* (or: *uit*) *de* ~ *wonen* live nearby (or: at a distance away); *je kunt maar beter bij hem uit de* ~ *blijven* you'd better give him a wide berth

de **buurtbewoner** /byrdbəwonər/ (pl: -s) local resident

het **buurtcentrum** /byrtsɛntrʏm/ (pl: -centra) community centre

buurten /byrtə(n)/ (buurtte, heeft gebuurt)

visit the neighbours: *jullie moeten eens* **komen**
~ you must come round (*or:* over) some time

het **buurthuis** /bу̠rthœys/ (pl: -huizen) community centre

de **buurtschap** /bу̠rtsχɑp/ (pl: -pen) hamlet

de **buurvrouw** /bу̠rvrɑu/ (pl: -en) neighbour,
woman next door

de **buxus** /bу̠ksʏs/ (pl: -sen) box (tree)

de **buzzer** /bу̠zər/ buzzer, pager

de **bv** /beve̠/ (pl: bv's) *besloten vennootschap*
Ltd; [Am] Inc

  bv. (abbrev) *bijvoorbeeld* e.g.

de **BV** *bekende Vlaming* celebrity, famous
Flemish person

de **bvba** /bevebea̠/ [Belg] *besloten vennootschap met beperkte aansprakelijkheid* private company with limited liability

de **B-weg** /be̠wɛχ/ (pl: -en) B-road, secondary
(*or:* minor) road

de **bypass** /bɑ̠jpɑːs/ (pl: -es) bypass; (traffic) bypass

de **byte** /bɑjt/ (pl: -s) byte

  Byzantijns /bizɑntɛ̠ins/ (adj) Byzantine

C

de **c** /se/ (pl: c's) c; C
ca. (abbrev) *circa* approx.; ca.
het **cabaret** /kabarɛ(t)/ (pl: -s) cabaret
de **cabaretier** /kabarɛce/ (pl: -s) cabaret performer, cabaret artist(e)
de **cabine** /kabinə/ (pl: -s) **1** cabin **2** booth
de **cabriolet** /kabrijolɛt/ (pl: -s) convertible, drophead coupé
de **cacao** /kakɑu/ cocoa, (drinking) chocolate
het **cachegeheugen** /kɛʃχəhøɣə(n)/ (pl: -s) cache memory
het **cachet** /kaʃɛ/ (pl: -ten) cachet, (touch of) prestige: ~ *geven aan iets* lend style to sth.
de **cactus** /kɑktʏs/ (pl: -sen) cactus
het **CAD** /seadə/ (pl: -'s) *Computer Assisted Design* CAD
de **cadans** /kadɑns/ (pl: -en) cadence, rhythm
de **¹caddie**® /kɛdi/ (pl: -s) caddie, (shopping) trolley; [Am] pushcart
de **²caddie** /kɛdi/ (pl: -s) **1** (golf-)trolley; [Am] caddie (cart) **2** caddie, caddy
het **cadeau** /kado/ (pl: -s) present, gift: *iem. iets* ~ *geven* give a person sth. as a present; [iron] *dat krijg je van me* ~*!* you can keep it!; *iets niet* ~ *geven* not give sth. away
de **cadeaubon** /kadobɔn/ (pl: -nen) gift voucher
de **cadet** /kadɛt/ (pl: -ten, -s) [Belg] junior member of sports club
het **cadmium** /kɑtmijʏm/ cadmium
het **café** /kafe/ (pl: -s) café, pub, bar
de **caféhouder** /kafehaudər/ (pl: -s) café proprietor (*or:* owner)
de **cafeïne** /kafejinə/ caffeine
cafeïnevrij /kafejinəvrɛi/ (adj) decaffeinated
het **café-restaurant** /kaferɛstorɑnt/ (pl: -s) restaurant; café
de **cafetaria** /kafetarija/ (pl: -'s) cafeteria, snack bar
het **cahier** /kaje/ (pl: -s) exercise book
de **caissière** /kaʃɛːrə/ (pl: -s) cashier, check-out assistant
de **caisson** /kɛsɔ̃/ (pl: -s) caisson
de **caissonziekte** /kɛsɔ̃ziktə/ caisson disease, decompression sickness
de **cake** /kek/ (pl: -s) (madeira) cake
de **calamiteit** /kalamitɛit/ (pl: -en) calamity, disaster
het **calcium** /kɑlsijʏm/ calcium
de **calculatie** /kɑlkyla(t)si/ (pl: -s) calculation, computation
de **calculator** /kɑlkylator/ (pl: -s) calculator

de **calculeren** /kɑlkylerə(n)/ (calculeerde, heeft gecalculeerd) calculate, compute: [fig] *de* ~*de* **burger** the canny consumer, the citizen-consumer
de **caleidoscoop** /kalɛidoskop/ (pl: -scopen) kaleidoscope
Californië /kalifɔrnijə/ California
het **callcenter** /kɔːlsɛntər/ (pl: -s) call centre
de **calorie** /kalori/ (pl: -ën) calorie
caloriearm /kaloriɑrm/ (adj) low-calorie, low in calories
calorierijk /kalorirɛik/ (adj) high-calorie, rich in calories
het **calvinisme** /kɑlvinɪsmə/ Calvinism
de **calvinist** /kɑlvinɪst/ (pl: -en) Calvinist
calvinistisch /kɑlvinɪstis/ (adj, adv) calvinistic(al)
Cambodja /kɑmbɔca/ Cambodia
de **Cambodjaan** /kɑmbɔcan/ (pl: Cambodjanen) Cambodian
Cambodjaans /kɑmbɔcans/ (adj) Cambodian
de **camcorder** /kɛmkɔːrdər/ (pl: -s) camcorder
de **camembert** /kɑmɑmbɛːr/ Camembert (cheese)
de **camera** /kaməra/ (pl: -'s) camera: *verborgen* ~ hidden camera; candid camera
de **camerabewaking** /kamərabəwakɪŋ/ closed circuit tv, CCTV: *dit winkelgebied kent* ~ this shop area is protected by CCTV
de **cameraman** /kaməramɑn/ (pl: -nen) cameraman
de **cameraploeg** /kaməraplux/ (pl: -en) camera crew (*or:* team)
het **cameratoezicht** /kaməratuzɪxt/ closed circuit tv, CCTV
de **camouflage** /kamuflaʒə/ (pl: -s) camouflage; [fig] cover; front
camoufleren /kamuflerə(n)/ (camoufleerde, heeft gecamoufleerd) camouflage, cover up, disguise
de **campagne** /kɑmpɑɲə/ (pl: -s) campaign, drive: ~ *voeren* (voor, tegen) campaign (for, against)
de **camper** /kɛmpər/ (pl: -s) camper
de **camping** /kɛmpɪŋ/ (pl: -s) camping site
de **campus** /kɑmpʏs/ (pl: -sen) campus
Canada /kanada/ Canada
de **Canadees** /kanadeːs/ Canadian
de **canapé** /kanape/ (pl: -s) sofa, settee, couch
de **Canarische Eilanden** /kanarisəɛilɑndə(n)/ (pl) (the) Canaries, (the) Canary Islands
cancelen /kɛnsələ(n)/ (cancelde, heeft geanceld) cancel, annul
de **cannabis** /kɑnabɪs/ cannabis, hemp, marijuana
de **canon** /kanɔn/ (pl: -s) round, canon: *in* ~ *zingen* sing in a round (*or:* in canon) ‖ *de historische* ~ *van Nederland* [roughly] the historical canon of the Netherlands
CANS /kɑns/ complaints of the arm, neck

and/or shoulder

de **cantate** /kɑntɑtə/ (pl: -s, -n) cantata

de **cantharel** /kɑntɑrɛl/ (pl: -len) chanterelle

het **canvas** /kɑnvɑs/ canvas, tarpaulin

de **canyon** /kɛnjən/ (pl: -s) canyon, gorge

de **cao** /seaʊ/ (pl: -'s) *collectieve arbeidsovereenkomst* collective wage agreement

de **cao-onderhandelingen** /seaʊɔndərhɑndəlɪŋə(n)/ (pl) collective bargaining

capabel /kɑpabəl/ (adj) capable, able; competent; qualified: *voor die functie **leek** hij uiterst ~* he seemed very well qualified for the job; *ik acht hem ~ **om** die klus uit te voeren* I reckon he can cope with that job

de **capaciteit** /kɑpasitɛit/ (pl: -en) **1** capacity, power: *een motor **met** kleine ~* a low-powered engine **2** ability, capability: *Ans is een vrouw van **grote** ~en* Ans is a woman of great ability

de **cape** /kep/ (pl: -s) cape

de **capitulatie** /kɑpitylɑ(t)si/ (pl: -s) capitulation, surrender

capituleren /kɑpitylerə(n)/ (capituleerde, heeft gecapituleerd) capitulate, surrender

de **cappuccino** /kɑputʃino/ (pl: -'s) cappuccino

de **capriool** /kɑprijol/ (pl: capriolen) prank, caper

de **capsule** /kɑpsylə/ (pl: -s) capsule

de **capuchon** /kɑpyʃɔn/ (pl: -s) hood

de **carambole** /karɑmbɔl/ (pl: -s) cannon

de **caravan** /kɛrəvɛn/ (pl: -s) caravan; [Am] trailer (home)

de **carburator** /kɑrbyratɔr/ (pl: -en) carburettor

het **cardiogram** /kɑrdijoɣrɑm/ (pl: -men) cardiogram

de **cardiologie** /kɑrdijoloɣi/ cardiology

de **cardioloog** /kɑrdijolox/ (pl: -logen) cardiologist

Caribisch /karibis/ (adj) Caribbean: *het ~ **gebied*** the Caribbean

de **cariës** /karijɛs/ caries, tooth decay, dental decay

het/de **carillon** /karɪljɔn/ (pl: -s) carillon, chimes: *het **spelen** van het ~* the ringing of the bells

het **carnaval** /kɑrnaval/ (pl: -s) carnival (time)

de **carnavalsvakantie** /kɑrnavalsfakɑn(t)si/ carnival holiday, Shrovetide holiday

de **carnivoor** /kɑrnivor/ (pl: carnivoren) carnivore

carpoolen /kɑːrpulə(n)/ (carpoolde, heeft/is gecarpoold) [Am] carpool

de **carport** /kɑːrpɔːrt/ (pl: -s) carport

de **carrière** /kariɛːrə/ (pl: -s) career

de **carrosserie** /karɔsəri/ (pl: -ën) body, bodywork

het/de **carrousel** /karusɛl/ (pl: -s) merry-go-round; [Am] carousel

de **cartografie** /kɑrtoɣrafi/ cartography, mapmaking

de **cartoon** /kɑrtuːn/ (pl: -s) cartoon

de **cartoonist** /kɑrtunɪst/ (pl: -en) cartoonist

de **cartridge** /kɑːrtrɪtʃ/ cartridge

het **casco** /kɑsko/ (pl: -'s) body, vessel; hull

de **casemanager** /kesmɛnədʒər/ (pl: -s) case manager

de **casestudy** /kestydi/ (pl: -'s) case study

de **¹cash** /kɛʃ/ cash

²cash /kɛʃ/ (adv) cash

de **cashewnoot** /kɛʃunot/ (pl: -noten) cashew (nut)

het **casino** /kazino/ (pl: -'s) casino

de **cassatie** /kɑsa(t)si/ (pl: -s) annulment: *hof van ~* court of appeal

de **casselerrib** /kɑsələrɪp/ cured side of pork

de **cassette** /kɑsɛtə/ (pl: -s) **1** box, casket; coffer; slip case; money box **2** cassette (tape)

het **cassettebandje** /kɑsɛtəbɑncə/ (pl: -s) cassette (tape)

de **cassettedeck** /kɑsɛtədɛk/ (pl: -s) cassette deck, tape deck

de **cassetterecorder** /kɑsɛtərikɔːrdər/ (pl: -s) cassette (*or*: tape) recorder

de **cassis** /kɑsɪs/ cassis, black currant drink

de **castagnetten** /kɑstɑɲɛtə(n)/ (pl) castanets

castreren /kɑstrerə(n)/ (castreerde, heeft gecastreerd) castrate, neuter; doctor

de **catacomben** /katakɔmbə(n)/ (pl) catacombs

Catalaans /katalaːns/ (adj) Catalan, Catalonian

catalogiseren /kataloɣizerə(n)/ (catalogiseerde, heeft gecatalogiseerd) catalogue, record

de **catalogus** /kataloɣys/ (pl: catalogi) catalogue

Catalonië /katalonijə/ Catalonia

de **catamaran** /katamaran/ (pl: -s) catamaran

catastrofaal /katastrofal/ (adj, adv) catastrophic, disastrous

de **catastrofe** /katastroːfə/ (pl: -s, -n) catastrophe, disaster

de **catechese** /katəxezə/ catechesis

de **catechisatie** /katəxiza(t)si/ (pl: -s) catechism, confirmation classes

de **catechismus** /katəxɪsmys/ (pl: -sen) catechism

de **categorie** /katəɣori/ (pl: -ën) category, classification; bracket: *in drie ~ën **indelen*** distinguish into three categories

categorisch /katəɣoris/ (adj, adv) categorical: *iets ~ **weigeren*** refuse sth. categorically

categoriseren /katəɣorizerə(n)/ (categoriseerde, heeft gecategoriseerd) categorize, class

cateren /ketərə(n)/ (caterde, heeft gecaterd) cater (for)

de **catering** /ketərɪŋ/ catering

de **catharsis** /katɑrsɪs/ (pl: -sen) catharsis

de **catwalk** /kɛtwɔːk/ (pl: -s) catwalk

causaal /kauzal/ (adj) causal, causative: *~ **verband*** causal connection

de **cavalerie** /kavələri/ (pl: -s) cavalry, tanks

de **cavia** /ka̲vija/ (pl: -'s) guinea pig, cavia
de **cayennepeper** /kajɛ̲nəpepər/ cayenne (pepper), red pepper
cc /sese̲/ (abbrev) **1** *kubieke centimeter* cc **2** *kopie conform* [roughly] certified copy
cc'en /sese̲jə(n)/ (cc'de, heeft ge-cc'd) cc
de **cd** /sede̲/ *compact disc* CD
de **cd-box** (pl: -en) CD box
de **cd-r** /sede̲ɛr/ (pl: -'s) *compact disc - recordable* CD-R
het **cd-rek** (pl: -ken) CD rack
de **cd-rom** /sederɔ̲m/ CD-ROM
de **cd-speler** /sede̲spelər/ (pl: -s) CD player
de **ceder** /se̲dər/ (pl: -s) cedar
de **cedille** /sedijə/ (pl: -s) cedilla
de **ceintuur** /sɛnty̲r/ (pl: ceinturen) belt, waistband
de **cel** /sɛl/ (pl: -len) cell, (call) box; booth: *hij heeft een jaar ~ gekregen* he has been given a year; *in een ~ opsluiten* lock up in a cell
de **celdeling** /sɛ̲ldelɪŋ/ (pl: -en) fission, cell division
het **celibaat** /seliba̲t/ celibacy
de **celkern** /sɛ̲lkɛrn/ (pl: -en) (cell) nucleus
de **cellist** /sɛlɪ̲st/ (pl: -en) cellist
de **cello** /sɛ̲lo/ (pl: -'s) (violon)cello
het **cellofaan** /sɛlofa̲n/ cellophane: *in ~ verpakt* wrapped in cellophane
cellulair /sɛlylɛ̲r/ (adj) cellular
de **cellulitis** /sɛlylɪ̲tɪs/ cellulite; cellulitis
het **¹celluloid** /sɛlylɔ̲jt/ celluloid
²celluloid /sɛlylɔ̲jt/ (adj) celluloid
de **cellulose** /sɛlylo̲zə/ cellulose
Celsius /sɛ̲lsijʏs/ Celsius, centigrade
de **celstraf** /sɛ̲lstrɑf/ (pl: -fen) solitary confinement: *iem. ~ geven* place s.o. in solitary confinement
de **celtherapie** /sɛ̲lterapi/ cell therapy
de **celwand** /sɛ̲lwɑnt/ cell wall
het/de **cement** /səmɛ̲nt/ cement
censureren /sɛnzyre̲rə(n)/ (censureerde, heeft gecensureerd) censor; [fig] black out
de **censuur** /sɛnzy̲r/ censorship
de **cent** /sɛnt/ (pl: -en) **1** cent: *iem. tot op de laatste ~ betalen* pay s.o. to the full **2** [inform] penny, farthing: *ik vertrouw hem voor geen ~* I don't trust him an inch **3** money, cash ‖ *zonder een ~ zitten* be penniless
de **centiliter** /sɛ̲ntilitər/ (pl: -s) centilitre
de **centime** /sɛntim/ (pl: -s) centime
de **centimeter** /sɛ̲ntimetər/ (pl: -s) **1** centimetre: *een kubieke ~* a cubic centimetre; *een vierkante ~* a square centimetre **2** tape-measure
centraal /sɛntra̲l/ (adj, adv) central: [fig] *een centrale figuur* a central (or: key) figure; *een ~ gelegen punt* a centrally situated point; *~ staan* be (the) central (point), be at the centre (stage)
de **Centraal-Afrikaan** /sɛntralafrika̲n/ (pl: Centraal-Afrikanen) Central African

Centraal-Afrikaans /sɛntralafrika̲ns/ (adj) Central African
de **Centraal-Afrikaanse Republiek** /sɛntralafrikansərepybli̲k/ Central African Republic
de **centrale** /sɛntra̲lə/ (pl: -s) **1** power station, powerhouse **2** (telephone) exchange; switchboard
de **centralisatie** /sɛntraliza̲(t)si/ (pl: -s) centralization
centraliseren /sɛntralize̲rə(n)/ (centraliseerde, heeft gecentraliseerd) centralize
centreren /sɛntre̲rə(n)/ (centreerde, heeft gecentreerd) centre
de **centrifuge** /sɛntrify̲:ʒə/ (pl: -s) centrifuge; spin-dryer
centrifugeren /sɛntrifyɣe̲rə(n)/ (centrifugeerde, heeft gecentrifugeerd) centrifuge; spin-dry
het **centrum** /sɛ̲ntrʏm/ (pl: centra) centre: *in het ~ van de belangstelling staan* be the centre of attention; [pol] *links (or: rechts) van het ~* left (or: right) of centre
de **centrumspits** /sɛ̲ntrʏmspɪts/ (pl: -en) centre forward
de **ceremonie** /serəmo̲ni/ (pl: -s, ceremoniën) ceremony
ceremonieel /serəmon(i)je̲l/ (adj, adv) ceremonial, formal: *een ceremoniële ontvangst* a formal reception
de **ceremoniemeester** /serəmo̲nimestər/ (pl: -s) Master of Ceremonies; best man
het **certificaat** /sɛrtifika̲t/ (pl: certificaten) certificate
Ceylon /sɛilɔ̲n/ Ceylon; Sri Lanka
de **cfk** /seɛfka̲/ (pl: -'s) *chloorfluorkoolwaterstof* CFC
de **chador** /tʃa̲dor/ (pl: -s) chador, chuddar
het **¹chagrijn** /ʃɑɣrɛ̲ɪn/ chagrin, annoyance
het/de **²chagrijn** /ʃɑɣrɛ̲ɪn/ (pl: -en) grouch, grumbler, sourpuss
chagrijnig /ʃɑɣrɛ̲ɪnəx/ (adj, adv) miserable, grouchy: *doe niet zo ~* stop being such a misery; *~ zijn* sulk
het/de **chalet** /ʃalɛ̲/ (pl: -s) chalet, Swiss cottage
de **champagne** /ʃɑmpɑ̲ɲə/ (pl: -s) champagne
de **champignon** /ʃɑmpijɔ̲n/ (pl: -s) mushroom
het/de **chanson** /ʃɑ̃sõ̲/ (pl: -s) song, chanson
de **chansonnier** /ʃɑ̃sɔ̃nje̲/ (pl: -s) (cabaret) singer
de **chantage** /ʃɑnta̲ʒə/ (pl: -s) blackmail
chanteren /ʃɑnte̲rə(n)/ (chanteerde, heeft gechanteerd) blackmail
de **chaoot** /xao̲t/ (pl: chaoten) **1** scatterbrain **2** anarchist
de **chaos** /xa̲ɔs/ chaos, disorder, havoc: *er heerst ~ in het land* the country is in chaos
chaotisch /xao̲tis/ (adj, adv) chaotic
de **chaperon** /ʃapərɔ̲n/ (pl: -s) chaperon(e)
de **charcuterie** /ʃɑrkytəri/ [Belg] cold cooked meats

de **charge** /ʃɑrʒə/ (pl: -s) charge [also sport]: *een ~ uitvoeren (met de wapenstok)* make a (baton) charge
chargeren /ʃɑrʒerə(n)/ (chargeerde, heeft gechargeerd) overdo, exaggerate (it)
het **charisma** /xɑrɪsma/ (pl: -'s) charisma
charitatief /xɑritɑtif/ (adj) charitable: *charitatieve instelling* charity, charitable institution
de **charlatan** /ʃɑrlɑtɑn/ (pl: -s) charlatan, quack
charmant /ʃɑrmɑnt/ (adj) charming, engaging; winning; delightful, attractive: *een ~e jongeman* a charming young man
de **charme** /ʃɑrmə/ (pl: -s) charm
charmeren /ʃɑrmerə(n)/ (charmeerde, heeft gecharmeerd) charm: *hij weet iedereen te ~* he's a real charmer
de **charmeur** /ʃɑrmør/ (pl: -s) charmer; Prince Charming, ladies' man
het **charter** /tʃɑːrtər/ (pl: -s) **1** charter flight, charter(ed) plane **2** charter
charteren /ʃɑrtərə(n)/ (charterde, heeft gecharterd) charter, enlist, commission
het **chartervliegtuig** /ʃɑːrtərvliχtœyx/ (pl: -en) charter(ed) aircraft
de **chartervlucht** /ʃɑːrtərvlvχt/ (pl: -en) charter flight
het **chassis** /ʃɑsi/ chassis
de **chat** /tʃɛt/ (pl: -s) chat
de **chatbox** /tʃɛdbɔks/ chatbox
de **chatroom** /tʃɛtruːm/ chat room
chatten /tʃɛtə(n)/ (chatte, heeft gechat) chat
de **chatter** (pl: -s) chatter
chaufferen /ʃoferə(n)/ (chauffeerde, heeft gechauffeerd) drive
de **chauffeur** /ʃofør/ (pl: -s) driver, chauffeur
het **chauvinisme** /ʃovinɪsmə/ chauvinism
de **chauvinist** /ʃovinɪst/ (pl: -en) chauvinist
chauvinistisch /ʃovinɪstis/ (adj, adv) chauvinist(ic)
checken /tʃɛkə(n)/ (checkte, heeft gecheckt) check (up, out), verify
de **check-up** /tʃɛkʏp/ (pl: -s) check-up
de **cheeta** /tʃita/ (pl: -'s) cheetah
de **chef** /ʃɛf/ (pl: -s) leader; boss; head; chief; superior (officer); manager; stationmaster: *~ van een afdeling* head (*or:* manager) of a department; *~ d'équipe* team manager; *~ de mission* head of the delegation
de **chef-kok** /ʃɛfkɔk/ (pl: -s) chef
de **chef-staf** /ʃɛfstɑf/ (pl: -s, chefs van staven) Chief of Staff
de **chemicaliën** /xemikɑlijə(n)/ (pl) chemicals, chemical products
de **chemicus** /xemikʏs/ (pl: chemici) chemist
de **chemie** /xemi/ chemistry
chemisch /xemis/ (adj, adv) chemical: *kleren ~ reinigen* dry-clean clothes; *~ toilet* chemical lavatory; *~e wapens* chemical weapons
de **chemobak** /xemobɑk/ (pl: -ken) chemical

waste bin
de **chemokuur** /xemokyr/ (pl: -kuren) course of chemotherapy
de **chemotherapie** /xemoterapi/ chemotherapy
de **cheque** /ʃɛk/ (pl: -s) cheque: *een blanco ~* a blank cheque; [fig also] carte blanche; *een ongedekte ~* a dud cheque; *een ~ innen* cash a cheque
het **chequeboek** /tʃɛɡbuk/ (pl: -en) chequebook
de **¹chic** /ʃik/ chic, stylishness, elegance
²chic /ʃik/ (adj, adv) **1** chic, stylish, smart: *er ~ uitzien* look (very) smart **2** elegant, distinguished; fashionable
chicaneren /ʃikɑnerə(n)/ (chicaneerde, heeft gechicaneerd) quibble (over)
de **Chileen** /ʃilen/ (pl: Chilenen) Chilean
Chileens /ʃilens/ (adj) Chilean
Chili /ʃili/ Chile
de **chili con carne** /ʃilikɔnkɑrnə/ chilli con carne
chill /tʃɪl/ (adj) cool
chillen /tʃɪlə(n)/ (childe, heeft gechild) chill
de **chimpansee** /ʃɪmpɑnse/ (pl: -s) chimpanzee; chimp
China /ʃina/ China
de **¹Chinees** /ʃines/ (pl: Chinezen) **1** Chinese, Chinaman **2** Chinese restaurant; Chinese takeaway
het **²Chinees** /ʃines/ [language] Chinese
³Chinees /ʃines/ (adj) Chinese: *Chinese wijk (buurt)* Chinatown
de **Chinese** /ʃinesə/ Chinese (woman)
de **chip** /tʃɪp/ (pl: -s) **1** chip, integrated circuit **2** chip, microprocessor
de **chipkaart** /tʃɪpkart/ (pl: -en) smart card, intelligent card
de **chippas** /tʃɪpɑs/ chip card
chippen /tʃɪpə(n)/ (chipte, is gechipt) pay by chip card
de **chips** /tʃɪps/ (pl) (potato) crisps; [Am] (potato) chips
de **Chiro** /xiro/ [Belg] Christian youth movement
de **chirurg** /ʃirʏrx/ (pl: -en) surgeon
de **chirurgie** /ʃirʏrɣi/ surgery
chirurgisch /ʃirʏrɣis/ (adj, adv) surgical: *een ~e ingreep* a surgical operation, surgery
de **chlamydia** /xlɑmidija/ chlamydia
het/de **chloor** /xlor/ **1** chlorine **2** bleach
de **chloroform** /xlorofɔrm/ chloroform
het **chocolaatje** /ʃokolacə/ (pl: -s) chocolate
de **chocolade** /ʃokoladə/ **1** chocolate; choc: *pure ~* plain chocolate **2** (drinking) chocolate, cocoa
de **chocoladeletter** /ʃokoladələtər/ (pl: -s) chocolate letter
de **chocolademelk** /ʃokoladəmɛlk/ (drinking) chocolate, cocoa
de **chocoladepasta** /ʃokoladəpasta/ (pl: -'s)

chocolate spread
de **choke** /ʃok/ (pl: -s) choke
de **cholera** /ҳolərɑ/ cholera
de **cholesterol** /ҳolɛstərɔl/ cholesterol
choqueren /ʃokerə(n)/ (choqueerde, heeft gechoqueerd) shock, give offence: *gechoqueerd zijn (door)* be shocked (at, by)
de **choreograaf** /ҳorejoɣraf/ (pl: -grafen) choreographer
de **choreografie** /ҳorejoɣrafi/ choreography
¹**christelijk** /krɪstələk/ (adj) Christian: *een ~e school* a protestant school
²**christelijk** /krɪstələk/ (adv) decently
de **christen** /krɪstə(n)/ (pl: -en) Christian
de **christendemocraat** /krɪstə(n)demokrat/ (pl: -democraten) Christian Democrat
het **christendom** /krɪstə(n)dom/ Christianity
Christus /krɪstʏs/ Christ ‖ *na ~* AD, after Christ; *voor ~* BC, before Christ
het **chromosoom** /ҳromozom/ (pl: chromosomen) chromosome
chronisch /ҳronis/ (adj, adv) chronic, lingering; recurrent: *een ~ zieke* a chronically sick patient
de **chronologie** /ҳronoloҳi/ chronology
chronologisch /ҳronoloɣis/ (adj, adv) chronological
de **chronometer** /ҳronometər/ (pl: -s) stopwatch, chronograph
het **chroom** /ҳrom/ chrome
de **chrysant** /ҳrizɑnt/ (pl: -en) chrysanthemum
de **ciabatta** /tʃabɑta/ (pl: -'s) ciabatta (bread)
de **cider** /sidər/ cider
het **cijfer** /sɛifər/ (pl: -s) **1** figure, numeral, digit, cipher: *Romeinse ~s* Roman numerals; *twee ~s achter de komma* two decimal places; *getallen die in de vijf ~s lopen* five-figure numbers **2** mark, grade: *het hoogste ~* the highest mark
de **cijfercode** /sɛifərkodə/ (pl: -s) numeric code
cijferen /sɛifərə(n)/ (cijferde, heeft gecijferd) do (or: make) calculations
de **cijferlijst** /sɛifərlɛist/ (pl: -en) list of marks, (school) report
de **cilinder** /silɪndər/ (pl: -s) cylinder
de **cilinderinhoud** /silɪndərɪnhaut/ cylinder capacity
de **cilinderkop** /silɪndərkɔp/ (pl: -pen) cylinder head
cilindrisch /silɪndris/ (adj) cylindrical
de **cineast** /sinejɑst/ (pl: -en) film maker (or: director)
de **cipier** /sipir/ (pl: -s) warder, jailer
de **cipres** /siprɛs/ (pl: -sen) cypress
circa /sɪrka/ (adv) approximately, about; circa
het **circuit** /sɪrkwi/ (pl: -s) **1** [sport] circuit, (race)track **2** scene: *het zwarte ~* the black economy
de **circulaire** /sɪrkylɛːrə/ (pl: -s) circular (letter)
de **circulatie** /sɪrkyla(t)si/ (pl: -s) circulation:

geld in ~ brengen put money into circulation
circuleren /sɪrkylerə(n)/ (circuleerde, heeft gecirculeerd) circulate, distribute: *geruchten laten ~* put about (or: circulate) rumours
het/de **circumflex** /sɪrkumflɛks/ (pl: -en) circumflex (accent)
het **circus** /sɪrkʏs/ (pl: -sen) circus
de **circustent** /sɪrkʏstɛnt/ (pl: -en) circus tent, big top, canvas
de **cirkel** /sɪrkəl/ (pl: -s) circle: *halve ~* semicircle; *een vicieuze ~* a vicious circle
cirkelen /sɪrkələ(n)/ (cirkelde, heeft/is gecirkeld) circle, orbit
de **cirkelomtrek** /sɪrkələmtrɛk/ (pl: -ken) perimeter
de **cirkelzaag** /sɪrkəlzaҳ/ (pl: -zagen) circular saw
het **citaat** /sitat/ (pl: citaten) quotation, quote; citation: *einde ~* unquote, close quotes
de **citer** /sitər/ (pl: -s) zither
citeren /siterə(n)/ (citeerde, heeft geciteerd) quote, cite
de **Cito-toets** /sitotuts/ (pl: -en) secondary education aptitude test; [roughly] 11 plus test
de **citroen** /sitrʏn/ (pl: -en) lemon
het **citroensap** /sitrʏnsɑp/ (fresh) lemon juice
de **citrusvrucht** /sitrʏsfrʏҳt/ (pl: -en) citrus fruit
de **city** /sɪti/ (pl: -'s) city centre
civiel /sivil/ (adj, adv) civil; civilian: *~ ingenieur* civil engineer; *een politieman in ~* plainclothes officer
de **civielrechtelijk** /sivilrɛҳtələk/ (adj, adv) civil: *iem. ~ vervolgen* bring a civil suit (or: action) against s.o.
de **civilisatie** /siviliza(t)si/ (pl: -s) civilization
civiliseren /sivilizerə(n)/ (civiliseerde, heeft geciviliseerd) civilize
de **ckv** /sekavé/ *culturele en kunstzinnige vorming* [roughly] culture and art classes
de **claim** /klem/ (pl: -s) claim: *een ~ indienen (bij)* lodge a claim (with)
claimen /klemə(n)/ (claimde, heeft geclaimd) (lay) claim (to), file (or: lodge) a claim: *een bedrag ~ bij de verzekering* claim on one's insurance
de **clamshell** /klɛmʃɛl/ (pl: -s) clamshell
de **clan** /klɛn/ (pl: -s) clan, clique, coterie
clandestien /klɑndɛstin/ (adj, adv) clandestine, illicit: *de ~e pers* underground press; *~ gestookte whisky* bootleg whiskey, moonshine
de **clark** /klɑːrk/ (pl: -s) [Belg] fork-lift truck
de **classeur** /klɑsør/ (pl: -s) [Belg] file
het **classicisme** /klɑsisɪsmə/ classicism, classicalism
de **classicus** /klɑsikʏs/ (pl: classici) classicist
de **classificatie** /klɑsifika(t)si/ (pl: -s) classification, ranking, rating
classificeren /klɑsifiserə(n)/ (classificeerde, heeft geclassificeerd) classify, class, rank

de **claustrofobie** /klɑustrofobi/ claustrophobia

de **clausule** /klɑuzylə/ (pl: -s) clause, proviso, stipulation: *een ~ opnemen in* build a clause into

de **claxon** /klɑksɔn/ (pl: -s) (motor) horn: *op de ~ drukken* sound one's horn

claxonneren /klɑksɔnerə(n)/ (claxonneerde, heeft geclaxonneerd) sound one's horn, hoot

clean /kli:n/ (adj, adv) **1** clean, clinical **2** clean, off (drugs)

clement /klemɛnt/ (adj, adv) lenient

de **clementie** /klemɛn(t)si/ leniency: *~ betrachten* be lenient, show mercy

de **clerus** /klerʏs/ clergy

het **cliché** /kliʃe/ (pl: -s) **1** cliché **2** plate, block

clichématig /kliʃematəx/ (adj, adv) cliché'd, commonplace, trite

de **cliënt** /klijɛnt/ (pl: -en) **1** client **2** customer, patron

de **clientèle** /klijɛntɛːlə/ clientele, custom(ers)

de **cliffhanger** /klɪfhɛŋər/ (pl: -s) cliffhanger

de **clignoteur** /klinotør/ (pl: -s) (direction) indicator, blinker

de **climax** /klimɑks/ (pl: -en) climax: *naar een ~ toewerken* build (up) to a climax

de **clinch** /klɪnʃ/: *in de ~ liggen met iem.* be at loggerheads with someone

de **clinicus** /klinikʏs/ (pl: clinici) clinician

de **clip** /klɪp/ (pl: -s) **1** paper clip; [large] bulldog clip **2** clip, pin **3** (video)clip

de **clitoris** /klitɔrɪs/ (pl: clitores) clitoris

close /klos/ (adj) close

het **closet** /klozɛt/ (pl: -s) lavatory, toilet

het **closetpapier** /klozɛtpɑpir/ toilet paper

de **closetrol** /klozɛtrɔl/ (pl: -len) toilet roll

de **close-up** /klosʏp/ (pl: -s) close-up

de **clou** /klu/ point, essence; punch line: *de ~ van iets niet snappen* miss the point (of sth.)

de **clown** /klɑun/ (pl: -s) clown, buffoon: *de ~ uithangen* clown around

clownesk /klɑunɛsk/ (adj, adv) clownish: *een ~ gebaar* a comic(al) gesture

de **club** /klʏp/ (pl: -s) **1** club [also golf]; society, association **2** crowd, group, gang

het **clubhuis** /klʏphœys/ (pl: -huizen) **1** club(house); pavilion **2** community centre; youth centre

de **clubkas** /klʏpkɑs/ (pl: -sen) club funds

de **cluster** /klʏstər/ (pl: -s) cluster

de **clusterbom** /klʏstərbɔm/ (pl: -men) cluster bomb

cm (abbrev) *centimeter* cm

de **co** /ko/ (pl: co's) *compagnon* partner

CO₂ CO2, CO_2 *(carbon dioxide)*

CO₂-neutraal /seotwenøtrɑl/ (adj) carbon-neutral

de **coach** /kotʃ/ (pl: -es) coach, trainer; supervisor; tutor

coachen /kotʃə(n)/ (coachte, heeft gecoacht) coach, train; tutor

de **coalitie** /kowali(t)si/ (pl: -s) coalition

de **coalitiepartner** /kowali(t)sipɑrtnər/ (pl: -s) coalition partner

de **coassistent** /koɑsistɛnt/ (pl: -en) (assistant) houseman; [Am] intern(e)

de **cobra** /kobrɑ/ (pl: -'s) cobra

de **cocaïne** /kokɑinə/ cocaine: *~ snuiven* snort (*or:* sniff) cocaine

de **cockpit** /kɔkpɪt/ (pl: -s) cockpit; flight deck

de **cocktail** /kɔktel/ (pl: -s) cocktail

de **cocktailbar** /kɔktelbɑːr/ cocktail lounge

de **cocktailparty** /kɔktelpɑːrti/ (pl: -'s) cocktail party

de **cocktailprikker** /kɔktelprɪkər/ (pl: -s) cocktail stick; [Am] cocktail pick

de **cocon** /kokɔn/ (pl: -s) cocoon; pod

de **code** /kodə/ (pl: -s) code, cipher: *een ~ ontcijferen* crack a code

coderen /koderə(n)/ (codeerde, heeft gecodeerd) (en)code, encipher

het **codicil** /kodisɪl/ (pl: -len) codicil

de **coëfficiënt** /koɛfiʃɛnt/ (pl: -en) coefficient

de **co-existentie** /koɛksɪstɛn(t)si/ coexistence: *vreedzame ~* peaceful coexistence

de **coffeeshop** /kɔfiʃɔp/ (pl: -s) coffee shop

de **cognac** /kɔɲɑk/ (pl: -s) cognac

cognitief /kɔɲnitif/ (adj, adv) cognitive

coherent /koherɛnt/ (adj, adv) coherent; consistent

de **cohesie** /kohezi/ cohesion

de **coïtus** /koitʏs/ (pl: -sen) coitus, coition, sexual intercourse

de **coke** /kok/ coke; snow

de **cokes** /koks/ coke

de **col** /kɔl/ (pl: -s) **1** roll-neck, polo neck **2** col, (mountain) pass

de **cola** /kolɑ/ (pl: -'s) coke

de **cola-tic** /kolɑtɪk/ rum (*or:* gin) and coke

het/de **colbert** /kɔlbɛːr/ (pl: -s) jacket

de **collaborateur** /kɔlɑborɑtør/ (pl: -s) collaborator, quisling

de **collaboratie** /kɔlɑborɑ(t)si/ collaboration

collaboreren /kɔlɑborerə(n)/ (collaboreerde, heeft gecollaboreerd) collaborate; work together

de **collage** /kɔlaʒə/ (pl: -s) collage, montage, paste-up

de **collectant** /kɔlɛktɑnt/ (pl: -en) collector; sidesman

de **collect call** /kɔlɛktkɔːl/ reverse charge call; [Am] collect call

de **collecte** /kɔlɛktə/ (pl: -s) collection; whip-round

collecteren /kɔlɛkterə(n)/ (collecteerde, heeft gecollecteerd) collect, make a collection; [in church] take the collection

de **collectie** /kɔlɛksi/ (pl: -s) **1** collection, show: *een fraaie ~ schilderijen* a fine collection of paintings **2** collection, accumulation

het ¹**collectief** /kɔlɛktif/ (pl: collectieven) collective

²**collectief** /kɔlɛktif/ (adj, adv) collective, corporate, joint, communal: *collectieve **arbeidsovereenkomst*** collective wage agreement; *collectieve **uitgaven*** public expenditure

het **collector's item** /kɔlɛktərsɔjtəm/ (pl: -s) collector's item, collectible

de **collega** /kɔleɣa/ (pl: -'s, collegae) colleague, associate; workmate

het **college** /kɔleʒə/ (pl: -s) **1** college; (university) class; (formal) lecture: *de ~s zijn weer **begonnen*** term has started again; *~ **geven** (over)* lecture (on), give lectures (on); *~ **lopen*** attend lectures **2** board: *~ van **bestuur** a)* Board of Governors; [Am] Board of Regents; **b)** Board of Directors; *het ~ van **burgemeester** en **wethouders*** the (City, Town) Council

het **collegegeld** /kɔleʒəɣɛlt/ tuition fee

de **collegezaal** /kɔleʒəzal/ (pl: -zalen) lecture-room; lecture-hall; lecture-theatre

collegiaal /kɔleɣi(j)al/ (adj, adv) fraternal, brotherly, comradely: *zich ~ **opstellen*** be loyal to one's colleagues

de **collie** /kɔli/ (pl: -s) collie

het/de **collier** /kɔlje/ (pl: -s) necklace

het/de **colofon** /kolofɔn/ (pl: -s) colophon

Colombia /kɔlɔmbija/ Colombia

de **Colombiaan** /kolɔmbijan/ (pl: Colombianen) Colombian

Colombiaans /kolɔmbijans/ (adj) Colombian

de **colonne** /kɔlɔnə/ (pl: -s) column

colporteren /kɔlpɔrterə(n)/ (colporteerde, heeft gecolporteerd) sell door-to-door, hawk

de **coltrui** /kɔltrœy/ (pl: -en) roll-neck (pullover, sweater); [Am] turtleneck (pullover, sweater)

de **column** /kɔlʏm/ (pl: -s) column

de **columnist** /kɔlʏmnɪst/ (pl: -en) columnist

het **coma** /koma/ (pl: -'s) coma: *in (een) ~ raken* lapse into a coma

de **comapatiënt** /komapaʃɛnt/ (pl: -en) comatose patient, patient in a coma

de **combi** /kɔmbi/ (pl: -'s) estate car, station wagon

de **combiketel** /kɔmbiketəl/ (pl: -s) combination boiler

de **combinatie** /kɔmbina(t)si/ (pl: -s) combination

de **combinatietang** /kɔmbina(t)sitɑŋ/ (pl: -en) combination pliers, electrician's pliers

de **combine** /kɔmbɔjn/ (pl: -s) combine (harvester)

¹**combineren** /kɔmbinerə(n)/ (combineerde, heeft gecombineerd) go (together), match: *deze **kleuren** ~ niet* these colours don't go (together), match: *deze **kleuren** ~ niet* these colours don't go (together) (or: don't match), these colours clash

²**combineren** /kɔmbinerə(n)/ (combineerde,

heeft gecombineerd) **1** combine (with): *twee banen ~* combine two jobs **2** associate (with), link (with)

de **comeback** /kɔmbɛk/ (pl: -s) comeback: *een ~ **maken*** make (or: stage) a comeback

het **comfort** /kɔmfoːr/ comfort; convenience: *dit huis is voorzien van het **modernste** ~* this house is fully equipped with the latest conveniences

comfortabel /kɔmfɔrtabəl/ (adj, adv) comfortable

de **coming-out** /kɔmɪŋɑut/ coming out

het **comité** /komite/ (pl: -s) committee: *uitvoerend ~* executive committee

de **commandant** /komɑndɑnt/ (pl: -en) **1** commander, commandant **2** chief (fire) officer, (fire) chief

commanderen /komɑnderə(n)/ (commandeerde, heeft gecommandeerd) **1** command, be in command (of) **2** give orders; [depr] boss about, order about

het **commando** /komɑndo/ (pl: -'s) **1** command: *het ~ **voeren** (over)* be in command (of) **2** (word of) command, order; [comp] command: *iets **op** ~ **doen*** do sth. to order; *huilen **op** ~* cry at will **3** [mil] commando

de **commandopost** /komɑndopɔst/ (pl: -en) command post

het **commentaar** /komɛntar/ (pl: commentaren) **1** comment(s), remark(s), observation(s); commentary (on): *~ op iets **geven** (or: **leveren**)* comment (or: make comments) on sth.; *geen ~* no comment **2** (unfavourable) comment, criticism: *een **hoop** ~ krijgen* receive a lot of unfavourable comment || *rechtstreeks ~* (running) commentary

de **commentaarstem** /komɛntarstɛm/ (pl: -men) voice-over

de **commentator** /komɛntator/ (pl: -en) commentator

commenten /kɔmɛntə(n)/ (commentte, heeft gecomment) comment, leave a comment

de **commercie** /komɛrsi/ commerce, trade

commercieel /komɛrʃel/ (adj, adv) commercial: *op **niet-commerciële** basis* on a non-profit(-making) basis

het **commissariaat** /kɔmɪsarijat/ (pl: commissariaten) **1** commissionership: *een ~ **bekleden** bij een bedrijf* sit on the board of a company **2** commissioner's office

de **commissaris** /kɔmɪsarɪs/ (pl: -sen) **1** commissioner, governor: *~ van de **Koningin*** (Royal) Commissioner, governor; *~ van **politie*** Chief Constable, Chief of Police, police commissioner; *raad van ~sen* board of commissioners **2** official, officer

de **commissie** /kɔmɪsi/ (pl: -s) **1** committee, board, commission: *de **Europese** Commissie* the European Commission; *een ~ **instellen*** appoint (or: set up) a committee **2** [com] commission

de **commissiebasis** /kɔmɪsibazɪs/: *werken op* ~ work on a commission basis

zich **committeren** /kɔmiterə(n)/ (committeerde zich, heeft zich gecommitteerd) commit o.s.

de **commode** /kɔmodə/ (pl: -s) chest of drawers

de **commotie** /kɔmo(t)si/ (pl: -s) commotion; fuss: ~ *veroorzaken* cause a commotion, make a fuss

communautair /kɔmynotɛːr/ (adj) **1** communal; Community: *~e* **wetgeving** Community legislation **2** [Belg] community, communal: *de ~e* **kwestie** the community question; *~e* **relaties** relations between the linguistic communities

de **commune** /kɔmynə/ (pl: -s) commune

de **communicant** /kɔmynikɑnt/ (pl: -en) **1** s.o. making his (*or:* her) first Communion **2** communicant

de **communicatie** /kɔmynika(t)si/ (pl: -s) communication

communicatief /kɔmynikatif/ (adj, adv) communicative

het **communicatiemiddel** /kɔmynika(t)si-mɪdəl/ (pl: -en) means of communication

de **communicatiestoornis** /kɔmynika(t)si-stornɪs/ (pl: -sen) breakdown in communication(s)

communiceren /kɔmyniserə(n)/ (communiceerde, heeft gecommuniceerd) communicate (with): *~de* **vaten** communicating vessels

de **communie** /kɔmyni/ (pl: -s) (Holy) Communion: *eerste* (*or:* **plechtige**) ~ first (*or:* solemn) Communion

het **communiqué** /kɔmynike/ (pl: -s) communiqué, statement: *een ~* **uitgeven** issue a communiqué, put out a statement

het **communisme** /kɔmynɪsmə/ Communism

de **communist** /kɔmynɪst/ (pl: -en) Communist

communistisch /kɔmynɪstis/ (adj, adv) communist: *de ~e* **partij** the communist party

compact /kɔmpɑkt/ (adj, adv) compact

de **compact disc** /kɔmpɑkdɪsk/ (pl: -s) compact disc

de **compagnie** /kɔmpaɲi/ (pl: -s) company; partnership: *de* **Oost-Indische** *Compagnie* the Dutch East India Company

de **compagnon** /kɔmpaɲɔn/ (pl: -s) **1** partner, (business) associate: *de ~ van* **iem.** *worden* go into partnership with s.o. **2** pal, buddy, chum

het **compartiment** /kɔmpartimɛnt/ (pl: -en) compartment

de **compassie** /kɔmpɑsi/ compassion

compatibel /kɔmpatibəl/ (adj) compatible

de **compensatie** /kɔmpɛnza(t)si/ (pl: -s) compensation: *als ~* **voor**, *ter ~ van* by way of compensation for

compenseren /kɔmpɛnserə(n)/ (compenseerde, heeft gecompenseerd) compensate for, counterbalance, make good: *dit compen-*

seert de **nadelen** this outweighs the disadvantages; *een* **tekort** ~ make good a deficiency (*or:* deficit)

competent /kɔmpətɛnt/ (adj) **1** competent, able, capable: *hij is (niet) ~* **op** *dat gebied* he is (not) competent in that field **2** competent, qualified, authorized: *dit hof is in deze kwestie* **niet** ~ this court is not competent to settle this matter

de **competentie** /kɔmpətɛnsi/ (pl: -s) competence; capacity

competentiegericht /kɔmpətɛn(t)si-ɣərɪxt/ (adj) competency-based, skill-based: ~ **leren** competency-based teaching (*or:* learning)

de **competitie** /kɔmpəti(t)si/ (pl: -s) league

de **compilatie** /kɔmpila(t)si/ (pl: -s) compilation

compleet /kɔmplet/ (adj, adv) **1** complete: *deze jaargang is* **niet** ~ this volume is incomplete **2** complete, total, utter: *complete* **onzin** utter (*or:* sheer) nonsense; *ik was ~* **vergeten** *de oven aan te zetten* I'd clean (*or:* completely) forgotten to switch the oven on

het **complement** /kɔmpləmɛnt/ (pl: -en) complement

complementair /kɔmplemɛntɛːr/ (adj) complementary

completeren /kɔmpleterə(n)/ (completeerde, heeft gecompleteerd) complete, make up

het **¹complex** /kɔmplɛks/ (pl: -en) complex, aggregate: *een heel ~ van* **regels** a whole complex of rules

²complex /kɔmplɛks/ (adj) complex, complicated, intricate: *een ~* **probleem** a complex problem; *een ~* **verschijnsel** a complex phenomenon

de **complicatie** /kɔmplika(t)si/ (pl: -s) complication: *bij dit soort operaties* **treden** *zelden ~s* **op** with this type of surgery complications hardly ever arise

compliceren /kɔmpliserə(n)/ (compliceerde, heeft gecompliceerd) complicate: *een gecompliceerde* **breuk** a compound fracture

het **compliment** /kɔmplimɛnt/ (pl: -en) **1** compliment: *iem. een ~* **maken** *over iets* pay s.o. a compliment on sth., compliment s.o. on sth. **2** regard; respect: *de ~en van* **vader** *en of u even wilt komen* father sends his regards and would you mind calling around

complimenteren /kɔmplimɛnterə(n)/ (complimenteerde, heeft gecomplimenteerd) compliment: *iem. ~* **met** *iets* compliment s.o. on sth.

complimenteus /kɔmplimɛntøs/ (adj, adv) complimentary

het **complot** /kɔmplɔt/ (pl: -ten) **1** plot: *een ~* **smeden** hatch a plot, conspire **2** conspiracy

de **component** /kɔmponɛnt/ (pl: -en) component

componeren /kɔmpone̱rə(n)/ (componeer-
de, heeft gecomponeerd) compose

de **componist** /kɔmponi̱st/ (pl: -en) composer

de **compositie** /kɔmpozi̱(t)si/ (pl: -s) composition

de **compositiefoto** /kɔmpozi̱(t)sifoto/ (pl: -'s)
composition photo

het/de **compost** /kɔmpɔ̱st/ compost

composteren /kɔmpɔste̱rə(n)/ (compos-
teerde, heeft gecomposteerd) compost

de **compote** /kɔmpɔ̱:t/ (pl: -s) stewed fruit

de **compressie** /kɔmprɛ̱si/ (pl: -s) compression

de **compressor** /kɔmprɛ̱sɔr/ (pl: -en) compressor

comprimeren /kɔmprime̱rə(n)/ (compri-
meerde, heeft gecomprimeerd) compress,
condense

het **compromis** /kɔmpromi̱/ (pl: -sen) compromise: *een ~ aangaan* (or: *sluiten*) come to (*or:*
reach) a compromise

compromitteren /kɔmpromite̱rə(n)/
(compromitteerde, heeft gecompromitteerd) compromise

compromitterend /kɔmpromite̱rənt/
(adj) compromising, incriminating: *~e verklaringen* (or: *papieren*) incriminating statements (*or:* documents)

de **computer** /kɔmpju̱tər/ (pl: -s) computer:
achter de ~ zitten sit at (*or:* in front of) the
computer; *gegevens invoeren in een ~* feed
data into a computer

het **computerbestand** /kɔmpju̱tərbəstɑnt/
(pl: -en) computer file

computeren /kɔmpju̱tərə(n)/ (computer-
de, heeft gecomputerd) be at (*or:* work on,
play on) the computer

de **computerfanaat** /kɔmpju̱tərfanat/ computer fanatic (*or:* freak)

computergestuurd /kɔmpju̱tərɣəstyrt/
(adj) computer-controlled

de **computerkraker** /kɔmpju̱tərkrakər/ (pl: -s)
hacker

het **computernetwerk** /kɔmpju̱tərnɛtwɛrk/
(pl: -en) computer network

het **computerprogramma** /kɔmpju̱tər-
proɣrɑma/ (pl: -'s) computer program

het **computerspelletje** /kɔmpju̱tərspɛləcə/
(pl: -s) computer game

het **computervirus** /kɔmpju̱tərvirʏs/ computer
virus

het **concentraat** /kɔnsɛntra̱t/ (pl: concentra-
ten) concentrate, extract

de **concentratie** /kɔnsɛntra̱(t)si/ (pl: -s) concentration: *~ van het gezag* concentration of
authority; *zijn ~ verliezen* lose one's concentration

het **concentratiekamp** /kɔnsɛntra̱(t)sikɑmp/
(pl: -en) concentration camp

de **concentratieschool** /kɔnsɛntra̱(t)sisxol/
(pl: -scholen) [Belg] school for ethnic minority children

[1] **concentreren** /kɔnsɛntre̱rə(n)/ (concentreerde, heeft geconcentreerd) concentrate,
centre; mass; strengthen: *een geconcentreer-
de oplossing* a concentrated solution

zich [2] **concentreren** /kɔnsɛntre̱rə(n)/ (concentreerde zich, heeft zich geconcentreerd)
concentrate (on): *zijn hoop concentreerde zich
op de zomervakantie* his hopes were pinned
on the summer holidays

concentrisch /kɔnsɛ̱ntris/ (adj, adv) con-
centric

het **concept** /kɔnsɛ̱pt/ (pl: -en) **1** (rough, first)
draft, outline: *een ~ maken van* draft **2** concept

de **conceptie** /kɔnsɛ̱psi/ (pl: -s) conception

het **concern** /kɔnsʏ̱:rn/ (pl: -s) group

het **concert** /kɔnsɛ̱rt/ (pl: -en) **1** concert; recital:
naar een ~ gaan go to a concert **2** concerto

concerteren /kɔnsɛrte̱rə(n)/ (concerteerde,
heeft geconcerteerd) perform (*or:* give) a
concert

het **concertgebouw** /kɔnsɛ̱rtxəbɑu/ (pl: -en)
concert hall

de **concertmeester** /kɔnsɛ̱rtmestər/ (pl: -s)
(orchestra) leader

de **concertzaal** /kɔnsɛ̱rtsal/ (pl: -zalen) concert
hall, auditorium

de **concessie** /kɔnsɛ̱si/ (pl: -s) concession; franchise; licence ‖ *~s doen aan iem.* make con-
cessions to s.o.

de **conciërge** /kɔnʃɛ̱:rʒə/ (pl: -s) caretaker, janitor, porter

het **concilie** /kɔnsi̱li/ (pl: -s, conciliën) council

het **conclaaf** /kɔŋkla̱f/ (pl: conclaven) conclave

concluderen /kɔŋklyde̱rə(n)/ (concludeer-
de, heeft geconcludeerd) conclude, deduce:
wat kunnen we daaruit ~? what can we conclude from that?

de **conclusie** /kɔŋkly̱zi/ (pl: -s) conclusion, deduction; findings: *de ~ trekken* draw the
conclusion

het/de **concours** /kɔŋku̱r/ (pl: -en) competition,
contest

concreet /kɔŋkre̱t/ (adj, adv) **1** concrete,
material, real, actual, tangible: *een ~ begrip*
a concrete term; *een ~ geval van* a specific
case of **2** definite: *concrete toezeggingen*
definite promises; *het overleg heeft niets ~s
opgeleverd* the discussion did not result in
anything concrete

concretiseren /kɔŋkretize̱rə(n)/ (concreti-
seerde, heeft geconcretiseerd) concretize;
make concrete

de **concurrent** /kɔŋkʏrɛ̱nt/ (pl: -en) competitor; rival

de **concurrentie** /kɔŋkʏrɛ̱nsi/ competition,
contest, rivalry

de **concurrentiepositie** /kɔŋkʏrɛ̱nsipozi(t)si/
(pl: -s) competitive position, competitiveness

de **concurrentievervalsing** /kɔŋkʏrɛ̱n(t)si-
vərvɑlsɪŋ/ distortion of competition, unfair

competition

concurreren /kɔŋkyrɛrə(n)/ (concurreerde, heeft geconcurreerd) compete

concurrerend /kɔŋkyrɛrənt/ (adj, adv) competitive [price]; competing; rival; conflicting

het **condens** /kɔndɛns/ condensation

de **condensatie** /kɔndɛnsa(t)si/ condensation

condenseren /kɔndɛnzɛrə(n)/ (condenseerde, heeft/is gecondenseerd) condense; boil down; evaporate

het **condenswater** /kɔndɛnswatər/ (water from) condensation

de **conditie** /kɔndi(t)si/ (pl: -s) **1** condition, proviso; terms: *een ~ stellen* make a condition; *onder (op) ~ dat* on (the) condition that **2** condition, state; form; shape: *de speler is in goede ~* the player is in good shape (*or:* is fit); *je hebt geen ~* you're (badly) out of condition

de **conditietraining** /kɔndi(t)sitrenɪŋ/ fitness training: *aan ~ doen* work out

conditioneel /kɔndi(t)ʃonel/ (adj, adv) conditional

de **condoleance** /kɔndolejɑ̃sə/ (pl: -s) condolence, sympathy: *mag ik u mijn ~s aanbieden* may I offer my condolences

condoleren /kɔndolɛrə(n)/ (condoleerde, heeft gecondoleerd) offer one's condolences (to s.o.)

het **condoom** /kɔndom/ (pl: -s) condom; rubber

de **condor** /kɔndɔr/ (pl: -s) (Andean) condor

de **conducteur** /kɔndʏktør/ (pl: -s) conductor, ticket collector

de **confectie** /kɔnfɛksi/ ready-to-wear clothes, ready-made clothes

de **confederatie** /kɔnfedəra(t)si/ (pl: -s) confederation, confederacy

de **conference** /kɔnferɑ̃sə/ **1** (solo) act, (comic) monologue **2** talk

de **conferencier** /kɔnferɑ̃ʃe/ (pl: -s) entertainer

de **conferentie** /kɔnferɛnsi/ (pl: -s) conference, meeting

de **confessie** /kɔnfɛsi/ (pl: -s) confession, admission

confessioneel /kɔnfɛʃonel/ (adj) confessional; denominational

de **confetti** /kɔnfɛti/ confetti

confidentieel /kɔnfidɛnʃel/ (adj, adv) confidential

de **configuratie** /kɔnfiɣyra(t)si/ (pl: -s) configuration

confisqueren /kɔnfɪskɛrə(n)/ (confisqueerde, heeft geconfisqueerd) confiscate

de **confituren** /kɔnfityrə(n)/ (pl) conserves

de **confituur** /kɔnfityr/ [Belg] jam

het **conflict** /kɔnflɪkt/ (pl: -en) conflict, clash: *in ~ komen met* come into conflict with

conform /kɔnfɔrm/ (adj, adv) in accordance with

zich **conformeren** /kɔnfɔrmɛrə(n)/ (confor-

meerde zich, heeft zich geconformeerd) conform (to), comply (with): *zich ~ aan de publieke opinie* bow to public opinion

de **conformist** /kɔnfɔrmɪst/ (pl: -en) conformist

de **confrontatie** /kɔnfrɔnta(t)si/ (pl: -s) confrontation

confronteren /kɔnfrɔntɛrə(n)/ (confronteerde, heeft geconfronteerd) confront (with): *met de werkelijkheid geconfronteerd worden* be faced (*or:* confronted) with reality

confuus /kɔnfys/ (adj) confused

het **conglomeraat** /kɔŋɣlomera̱t/ (pl: conglomeraten) conglomerate

Congo /kɔŋɣo/ Congo

de **¹Congolees** /kɔŋɣoles/ (pl: Congolezen) Congolese

²Congolees /kɔŋɣoles/ (adj) Congolese

de **congregatie** /kɔŋɣreɣa(t)si/ (pl: -s) congregation

het **congres** /kɔŋɣrɛs/ (pl: -sen) conference; congress

het **congresgebouw** /kɔŋɣrɛsxəbɑu/ conference hall

congruent /kɔŋɣrywɛnt/ (adj) congruent

de **conifeer** /konifer/ (pl: coniferen) conifer

conjunctureel /kɔnʏŋktyrel/ (adj, adv) cyclical: *problemen van conjuncturele aard* cyclical problems, problems caused by fluctuations in the market

de **conjunctuur** /kɔnjʏŋktyr/ (pl: conjuncturen) economic situation, market conditions, trade cycle

de **connectie** /kɔnɛksi/ (pl: -s) connection, link || *goede ~s hebben* be well connected

de **conrector** /kɔnrɛktɔr/ (pl: -s) [roughly] deputy headmaster

consciëntieus /kɔnʃɛnʃøs/ (adj, adv) conscientious, scrupulous, painstaking

de **consecratie** /kɔnsekra(t)si/ (pl: -s) consecration

de **consensus** /kɔnsɛnzʏs/ consensus

consequent /kɔnsəkwɛnt/ (adj, adv) **1** logical: *~ handelen* act logically, be consistent **2** consistent (with)

de **consequentie** /kɔnsəkwɛnsi/ (pl: -s) implication, consequence: *de ~s trekken* draw the obvious conclusion

de **conservatie** /kɔnsɛrva(t)si/ conservation, preservation

de **¹conservatief** /kɔnsɛrvatif/ (pl: conservatieven) conservative; Tory

²conservatief /kɔnsɛrvatif/ (adj, adv) conservative; [pol] Conservative: *de conservatieve partij* the Conservative (*or:* Tory) Party

de **conservator** /kɔnsɛrvatɔr/ (pl: -s, -en) curator; keeper; custodian

het **conservatorium** /kɔnsɛrvatoriʏm/ (pl: conservatoria) academy of music, conservatory

de **conserven** /kɔnsɛrvə(n)/ (pl) canned

food(s), tinned food(s), preserved food(s)

het **conservenblik** /kɔnsɛrvə(n)blɪk/ (pl: -ken) can, tin (can)

conserveren /kɔnsɛrvērə(n)/ (conserveerde, heeft geconserveerd) preserve, conserve; can; tin: *goed geconserveerd zijn* be well preserved

de **conservering** /kɔnzɛrvērɪŋ/ **1** preservation; conservation **2** preserving; canning

het **conserveringsmiddel** /kɔnsɛrvērɪŋsmɪdəl/ (pl: -en) preservative

de **consideratie** /kɔnsidərā(t)si/ (pl: -s) consideration: *geen enkele ~ hebben* be completely inconsiderate

de **consignatie** /kɔnsiɲā(t)si/ (pl: -s) consignment

consolideren /kɔnsolidērə(n)/ (consolideerde, heeft geconsolideerd) **1** consolidate, strengthen **2** consolidate, fund

de **consorten** /kɔnsōrtə(n)/ (pl) confederates, associates, buddies: *Hans en ~* Hans and his pals

het **consortium** /kɔnsōr(t)sijʏm/ (pl: -s) consortium, syndicate

constant /kɔnstɑnt/ (adj, adv) constant, steady, continuous; staunch; loyal: *een ~e grootheid* (or: *waarde*) a constant quantity (*or:* value); *hij houdt me ~ voor de gek* he is forever pulling my leg (*or:* making a fool of me)

de **constante** /kɔnstɑntə/ (pl: -n) constant

constateren /kɔnstatērə(n)/ (constateerde, heeft geconstateerd) establish; ascertain; record; detect; observe: *ik constateer slechts het feit dat* I'm merely stating the fact that, all I'm saying is that

de **constatering** /kɔnstatērɪŋ/ (pl: -en) observation; establishment

de **consternatie** /kɔnstɛrnā(t)si/ (pl: -s) consternation, alarm: *dat gaf heel wat ~* it caused quite a stir

de **constipatie** /kɔnstipā(t)si/ constipation: *last hebben van ~* be constipated

de **constitutie** /kɔnstitū(t)si/ (pl: -s) **1** constitution, physique: *een slechte ~ hebben* have a weak constitution **2** constitution

constitutioneel /kɔnstity(t)jonēl/ (adj, adv) constitutional: *constitutionele monarchie* constitutional monarchy

de **constructeur** /kɔnstrʏktōr/ (pl: -s) designer

de **constructie** /kɔnstrʏksi/ (pl: -s) construction, building, erection, structure

constructief /kɔnstrʏktīf/ (adj, adv) **1** constructive, useful: *~ te werk gaan* go about sth. in a constructive way **2** constructional, structural

de **constructiefout** /kɔnstrʏksifɑut/ (pl: -en) structural (*or:* construction) defect (*or:* fault)

construeren /kɔnstrywērə(n)/ (construeerde, heeft geconstrueerd) construct; build; erect; design

de **consul** /kɔnsʏl/ (pl: -s) consul

het **consulaat** /kɔnsylāt/ (pl: consulaten) consulate

de **consulent** /kɔnsylɛnt/ (pl: -en) consultant, adviser

het **consult** /kɔnsʏlt/ (pl: -en) consultation; visit

de **consultant** /kɔnsʏltənt/ consultant

het **consultatiebureau** /kɔnsʏltā(t)sibyro/ (pl: -s) clinic, health centre: *~ voor zuigelingen* infant welfare centre, child health centre; well-baby clinic

consulteren /kɔnsʏltērə(n)/ (consulteerde, heeft geconsulteerd) **1** consult **2** confer, discuss

de **consument** /kɔnsymɛnt/ (pl: -en) consumer

de **consumentenbond** /kɔnsymɛntə(n)bɔnt/ (pl: -en) consumers' organization

consumeren /kɔnsymērə(n)/ (consumeerde, heeft geconsumeerd) **1** consume, eat, drink **2** deplete, exhaust

de **consumptie** /kɔnsʏmpsi/ (pl: -s) **1** consumption: *(on)geschikt voor ~* (un)fit for (human) consumption **2** food, drink(s), refreshment(s)

de **consumptiebon** /kɔnsʏmsibɔn/ (pl: -nen) food voucher

consumptief /kɔnsʏmptīf/ (adj) consumptive: *~ krediet* consumer credit

de **consumptiegoederen** /kɔnsʏmpsiɣudərə(n)/ (pl) consumer goods: *duurzame ~* consumer durables

het **contact** /kɔntɑkt/ (pl: -en) **1** contact, connection, touch: *telefonisch ~ opnemen* get in touch by phone; *~ opnemen met iem. (over iets)* contact s.o., get in touch with s.o. (about sth.); *in ~ blijven met* keep in touch with **2** contact, terms: *een goed ~ met iem. hebben* have a good relationship with s.o. **3** contact (man); connection: *~en hebben in bepaalde kringen* have connections in certain circles **4** contact, switch; ignition: *het sleuteltje in het ~ steken* put the key in(to) the ignition

de **contactadvertentie** /kɔntɑktɑtfərtɛnsi/ (pl: -s) personal ad(vert), advert in the personal column

contactarm /kɔntɑktɑrm/ (adj) socially inhibited; socially isolated

de **contactdoos** /kɔntɑɡdos/ (pl: -dozen) socket; appliance inlet

de **contactlens** /kɔntɑktlɛns/ (pl: -lenzen) contact lens; contacts

de **contactlijm** /kɔntɑktlɛim/ contact adhesive

de **contactpersoon** /kɔntɑktpɛrson/ (pl: -personen) contact (person)

de **contactsleutel** /kɔntɑktsløtəl/ (pl: -s) ignition key

contactueel /kɔntɑktywēl/ (adj, adv) contactual

de **container** /kɔntēnər/ (pl: -s) **1** container **2** (rubbish) skip

het **containerpark** /kɔntēnərpɑrk/ (pl: -en)

[Belg] recycling centre, amenity centre

de **contaminatie** /kɔntamina(t)si/ (pl: -s) contamination

contant /kɔntɑnt/ (adj, adv) cash, ready: *tegen ~e betaling* on cash payment; cash down; *~ geld* ready money

de **contanten** /kɔntɑntə(n)/ (pl) cash, ready money, cash in hand

content /kɔntɛnt/ (adj) content (with), satisfied (with)

de **context** /kɔntɛkst/ (pl: -en) context, framework, background: *je moet dat in de juiste ~ zien* you must put that into its proper context

het **continent** /kɔntinɛnt/ (pl: -en) continent

continentaal /kɔntinɛntal/ (adj) continental

het **contingent** /kɔntɪŋɣɛnt/ (pl: -en) **1** contingent **2** quota, share, proportion; allocation; allotment

¹**continu** /kɔntiny/ (adj) continuous; unbroken

²**continu** /kɔntiny/ (adv) continuously: *hij loopt ~ te klagen* he is always complaining

het **continubedrijf** /kɔntinybədrɛif/ (pl: -bedrijven) continuous working plant

continueren /kɔntinywerə(n)/ (continueerde, heeft gecontinueerd) **1** continue (with), carry on (with) **2** continue, retain

de **continuïteit** /kɔntinywitɛit/ **1** continuity **2** continuation

het **conto** /kɔnto/ (pl: -'s) account: [fig] *iets op iemands ~ schrijven* hold s.o. accountable for sth.; [fig] *iets op zijn ~ schrijven* achieve

de **contour** /kɔntur/ (pl: -en) contour

contra /kɔntra/ (prep) contra, against; [law] versus: *alle argumenten pro en ~ bekijken* consider all the arguments for and against

de **contrabas** /kɔntrabɑs/ (pl: -sen) (double) bass

de **contraceptie** /kɔntrasɛpsi/ contraception

het **contract** /kɔntrɑkt/ (pl: -en) contract, agreement: *zijn ~ loopt af* his contract is running out; *een ~ opzeggen* (or: *verbreken*) terminate (or: break) a contract; *volgens ~* according to contract

de **contractbreuk** /kɔntrɑktbrøk/ breach of contract

contracteren /kɔntrɑkterə(n)/ (contracteerde, heeft gecontracteerd) **1** engage; sign (up, on) **2** contract: *~de partijen* contracting parties

de ¹**contractueel** /kɔntrɑktywel/ (pl: contractuelen) [Belg] contractual worker

²**contractueel** /kɔntrɑktywel/ (adj, adv) contractual: *iets ~ vastleggen* lay sth. down (or: stipulate sth.) in a contract

de **contradictie** /kɔntradɪksi/ (pl: -s) contradiction

de **contramine** /kɔntraminə/: *in de ~ zijn* be perverse, be contrary

contraproductief /kɔntraprodʏktif/ (adj) counterproductive

de **Contrareformatie** Counter Reformation

de **contraspionage** /kɔntraspijonaʒə/ (pl: -s) counter-espionage

het **contrast** /kɔntrɑst/ (pl: -en) contrast: *een schril ~* a harsh contrast

contrasteren /kɔntrɑsterə(n)/ (contrasteerde, heeft gecontrasteerd) contrast (with), be in contrast (with/to)

contrastief /kɔntrɑstif/ (adj, adv) contrastive

de **contreien** /kɔntrɛiə(n)/ (pl) parts, regions

de **contributie** /kɔntribyy(t)si/ (pl: -s) subscription; contribution

de **controle** /kɔntro:lə/ (pl: -s) **1** check (on), checking, control; supervision (of, over); [med] check-up; monitoring: *~ van de bagage* baggage check; *de ~ van de boekhouding* the audit of accounts, the examination of the books; *de ~ over het stuur verliezen* lose control of the steering-wheel **2** control (point), checkpoint; (ticket) gate: *zijn kaartje aan de ~ afgeven* hand in one's ticket at the gate

controleerbaar /kɔntrolerbar/ (adj) verifiable

de **controlepost** /kɔntro:ləpɔst/ (pl: -en) control (point), checkpoint

controleren /kɔntrolerə(n)/ (controleerde, heeft gecontroleerd) **1** supervise, superintend; monitor: *~d geneesheer* [roughly] medical officer **2** check (up, on), inspect, examine; verify: *de boeken ~* audit the books (or: accounts); *kaartjes ~* inspect tickets; *iets extra (dubbel) ~* double-check sth.

de **controleur** /kɔntrolør/ (pl: -s) inspector, controller, checker; ticket inspector (or: collector); auditor

de **controller** /kɔntro:lər/ controller

de **controverse** /kɔntrovɛrsə/ (pl: -n, -s) controversy

controversieel /kɔntrovɛrsjel/ (adj) controversial; contentious, much debated

het **convenant** /kɔnvənɑnt/ (pl: -en) covenant

het **convent** /kɔnvɛnt/ (pl: -en) monastery; convent

de **conventie** /kɔnvɛnsi/ (pl: -s) convention: *in strijd met de ~ zijn* go against the accepted norm

conventioneel /kɔnvɛnʃonel/ (adj, adv) conventional

de **conversatie** /kɔnvɛrsa(t)si/ (pl: -s) conversation, talk

converseren /kɔnvɛrserə(n)/ (converseerde, heeft geconverseerd) converse (with), engage in conversation (with)

de **conversie** /kɔnvɛrsi/ (pl: -s) conversion

converteren /kɔnvɛrterə(n)/ (converteerde, heeft geconverteerd) convert (into, to)

cool /ku:l/ (adj) cool

de **coolingdown** /ku:lɪŋdaun/ cooling down

de **coöperatie** /koopəra(t)si/ (pl: -s) **1** cooper-

ation, collaboration **2** cooperative (society)
coöperatief /koopərat<u>i</u>f/ (adj, adv) cooperative

de **coördinaat** /ko<u>o</u>rdin<u>a</u>t/ (pl: coördinaten) co-ordinate

de **coördinatie** /ko<u>o</u>rdin<u>a</u>(t)si/ (pl: -s) coordination

de **coördinator** /ko<u>o</u>rdin<u>a</u>tɔr/ (pl: -en) coordinator

coördineren /ko<u>o</u>rdin<u>e</u>rə(n)/ (coördineerde, heeft gecoördineerd) coordinate, arrange, organize: *werkzaamheden* ~ supervise work

COPD *chronic obstructive pulmonary disease* COPD

copieus /kopi<u>j</u><u>ø</u>s/ (adj, adv) copious, abundant: *een* ~ *diner* a lavish dinner

de **copiloot** /k<u>o</u>pilot/ (pl: copiloten) co-pilot

de **coproductie** /k<u>o</u>prodʏksi/ (pl: -s) joint production, co-production

copuleren /kopyl<u>e</u>rə(n)/ (copuleerde, heeft gecopuleerd) copulate; mate

het **copyright** /k<u>ɔ</u>pirɑjt/ (pl: -s) copyright

corduroy /k<u>ɔ</u>rdyrɔj/ (adj) cord(uroy); corded

het **cornedbeef** /k<u>ɔ</u>rnɛdbif/ corned beef, bully (beef)

de **corner** /k<u>ɔ</u>ːrnər/ (pl: -s) corner

de **corporatie** /kɔrpor<u>a</u>(t)si/ (pl: -s) corporation, corporate body

het **corps** /kɔːr/ (pl: corpora) corps

de **corpsstudent** /k<u>ɔ</u>ːrstydɛnt/ (pl: -en) member of a student association

corpulent /kɔrpyl<u>ɛ</u>nt/ (adj) corpulent

correct /kɔr<u>ɛ</u>kt/ (adj, adv) **1** correct; right; exact: ~ *antwoorden* get the answer(s) right, answer correctly **2** correct, right, proper: *~e houding* proper conduct (*or:* behaviour); *~e kleding* suitable dress

de **correctheid** /kɔr<u>ɛ</u>ktheit/ (pl: -heden) **1** correctness, precision **2** correctness, propriety

de **correctie** /kɔr<u>ɛ</u>ksi/ (pl: -s) correction; adjustment; revision; marking: *~s aanbrengen* make corrections; adjust, make adjustments

correctioneel /kɔrɛkʃon<u>e</u>l/ (adj) [Belg] criminal: *correctionele rechtbank* [roughly] Crown Court

de **corrector** /kɔr<u>ɛ</u>ktɔr/ (pl: -s, -en) proofreader, corrector, reviser

de **correlatie** /kɔrel<u>a</u>(t)si/ (pl: -s) correlation

de **correspondent** /kɔrɛspond<u>ɛ</u>nt/ (pl: -en) correspondent: *van onze* ~ *in Parijs* from our Paris correspondent

de **correspondentie** /kɔrɛspond<u>ɛ</u>nsi/ (pl: -s) correspondence: *een drukke* ~ *voeren* carry on a lively correspondence

het **correspondentieadres** /kɔrɛspond<u>ɛ</u>n(t)siadrɛs/ (pl: -sen) postal (*or:* mailing) address

corresponderen /kɔrɛspond<u>e</u>rə(n)/ (correspondeerde, heeft gecorrespondeerd) **1** correspond (with), write (to) **2** correspond (to, with), match (with), agree (with)

de **corridor** /korid<u>ɔ</u>ːr/ corridor

corrigeren /kɔriʒ<u>e</u>rə(n)/ (corrigeerde, heeft gecorrigeerd) **1** correct; adjust **2** correct; mark

de **corrosie** /kɔr<u>o</u>zi/ (pl: -s) corrosion

corrumperen /kɔrʏmp<u>e</u>rə(n)/ (corrumpeerde, heeft gecorrumpeerd) corrupt, pervert: *macht corrumpeert* power corrupts

corrupt /kɔr<u>ʏ</u>pt/ (adj, adv) corrupt, dishonest

de **corruptie** /kɔr<u>ʏ</u>psi/ (pl: -s) corruption

het/de **corsage** /kɔrs<u>a</u>ʒə/ (pl: -s) corsage

Corsica /k<u>ɔ</u>rsika/ Corsica

het **corso** /k<u>ɔ</u>rso/ (pl: -'s) pageant, parade, procession

de **corvee** /kɔrv<u>e</u>/ (pl: -s) (household) chores: ~ *hebben* do the chores

de **coryfee** /korif<u>e</u>/ (pl: -ën) star, lion, celebrity

het **coschap** /k<u>ɔ</u>sxɑp/ (pl: -pen) clerkship; (assistant) housemanship; [Am] intern(e)ship

de **cosinus** /k<u>o</u>sinʏs/ cosine

de **cosmetica** /kɔsm<u>e</u>tika/ (pl) cosmetics

cosmetisch /kɔsm<u>e</u>tis/ (adj) cosmetic

Costa Rica /kɔstar<u>i</u>ka/ Costa Rica

de **Costa Ricaan** /kɔstarik<u>a</u>n/ (pl: Costa Ricanen) Costa Rican

Costa Ricaans /kɔstarik<u>a</u>ns/ (adj) Costa Rican

de **couchette** /kuʃ<u>ɛ</u>t(ə)/ (pl: -s) couchette, berth

de **coulance** /kul<u>ɑ̃</u>sə/ considerateness

coulant /kul<u>ɑ</u>nt/ (adj, adv) accommodating, obliging, reasonable

de **coulisse** /kul<u>i</u>sə/ (pl: -n) (side) wing

de **counter** /k<u>au</u>ntər/ (pl: -s) counter-attack, countermove: *op de* ~ *spelen* rely on the counter-attack

counteren /k<u>au</u>ntərə(n)/ (counterde, heeft gecounterd) counter(-attack)

de **countrymuziek** /k<u>au</u>ntrimyzik/ country music

de **coup** /kup/ (pl: -s) coup (d'état): *een* ~ *plegen* stage a coup

de **coupe** /kup/ (pl: -s) **1** cut; style **2** coupe: ~ *royale* [roughly] sundae

de **coupé** /kup<u>e</u>/ (pl: -s) **1** compartment **2** coupé

couperen /kup<u>e</u>rə(n)/ (coupeerde, heeft gecoupeerd) cut: *een hond* ~ dock a dog's tail

de **coupe soleil** /kupsɔl<u>ɛ</u>i/ (pl: coupes soleils) highlights

het **couplet** /kupl<u>ɛ</u>t/ (pl: -ten) stanza, verse; couplet

de **coupon** /kup<u>ɔ</u>n/ (pl: -s) **1** remnant **2** coupon

de **coupure** /kupy<u>r</u>ə/ (pl: -s) **1** cut, deletion **2** [finance] denomination

courant /kur<u>ɑ</u>nt/ (adj) current

de **coureur** /kur<u>ø</u>r/ (pl: -s) (racing) cyclist; racing motorcyclist; racing car driver

de **courgette** /kurʒ<u>ɛ</u>t(ə)/ (pl: -s) courgette; [Am] zucchini de **courtage** /kurtaʒə/ (pl: -s) brokerage, (broker's) commission

de **couscous** /kuskus/ couscous

de **couture** /kutyrə/ couture, dressmaking

de **couturier** /kutyrje/ (pl: -s) couturier, (fashion) designer

het **couvert** /kuvɛːr/ (pl: -s) **1** cover, envelope **2** cover; cutlery

de **couveuse** /kuvøzə/ (pl: -s) incubator

het **couveusekind** /kuvøzəkɪnt/ (pl: -eren) premature baby

het/de **cover** /kɔvər/ (pl: -s) **1** cover **2** cover (version), remake

de **cowboy** /kɑubɔj/ (pl: -s) cowboy

de **coyote** /kojotə/ (pl: -s) coyote

c.q. /seky/ (abbrev) *casu quo* and, or

de **crack** /krɛk/ (pl: -s) **1** crack player, ace; [Am] hotshot **2** crack

de **cracker** /krɛkər/ (pl: -s) cracker

de **crash** /krɛʃ/ (pl: -es) crash

crashen /krɛʃə(n)/ (crashte, heeft/is gecrasht) **1** crash: *het* ***toestel*** *crashte bij de landing* the plane crashed on landing **2** crash, go bankrupt

de **crawl** /krɔːl/ crawl

crawlen /krɔːlə(n)/ (crawlde, heeft/is gecrawld) do the crawl

de **creatie** /kreja(t)si/ (pl: -s) creation: *de* ***nieuwste*** *~s van Dior* Dior's latest creations

creatief /krejatif/ (adj, adv) creative, original, imaginative: *~ bezig zijn* do creative work

de **creativiteit** /krejativitɛit/ creativity, creativeness: [fig] *haar oplossingen* ***getuigen van*** *~* her solutions show creative talent

de **crèche** /krɛʃ/ (pl: -s) crèche, day-care centre, day nursery

het **credit** /krɛdɪt/ credit: ***debet*** *en ~* debit and credit; *iets* ***op*** *iemands ~ schrijven* [also fig] put sth. to s.o.'s credit, credit s.o. with sth.

de **creditcard** /krɛdɪtkɑːrt/ (pl: -s) credit card

crediteren /kredɪterə(n)/ (crediteerde, heeft gecrediteerd) credit

de **crediteur** /kreditør/ (pl: -en) creditor; accounts payable

de **creditnota** /krɛdɪtnota/ (pl: -'s) credit note (*or:* slip)

het **credo** /kredo/ (pl: -'s) **1** credo, creed **2** Credo, Creed

creëren /krejerə(n)/ (creëerde, heeft gecreëerd) create

de **crematie** /krema(t)si/ (pl: -s) cremation

het **crematorium** /krematorijʏm/ (pl: crematoria) crematorium

de **crème** /krɛːm/ (pl: -s) cream: *~ op zijn gezicht* ***smeren*** rub cream on one's face **2** crème ‖ *een ~ japon* a cream(-coloured) dress

cremeren /krəmerə(n)/ (cremeerde, heeft gecremeerd) cremate

de **creool** /krejol/ (pl: creolen) Creole

het **¹creools** /krejols/ creole
²creools /krejols/ (adj) creole

het **crêpepapier** /krɛːpapir/ crêpe paper

creperen /kreperə(n)/ (crepeerde, is gecrepeerd) **1** die: *ze lieten* ***haar*** *gewoon ~* they let her die like a dog **2** suffer: *~ van de pijn* be racked with pain

het **cricket** /krɪkət/ cricket
cricketen /krɪkətə(n)/ (crickette, heeft gecricket) play cricket

de **crime** /krim/ disaster: *het is een ~* it is a disaster

de **criminaliteit** /kriminalitɛit/ (pl: -en) criminality: *de* ***kleine*** *~* petty crime

de **¹crimineel** /kriminel/ (pl: criminelen) criminal
²crimineel /kriminel/ (adj) criminal
³crimineel /kriminel/ (adv) [inform] horribly, terribly: *het is ~ koud* it's wickedly cold

de **criminologie** /kriminoloyi/ criminology

de **crisis** /krizɪs/ (pl: crises) crisis: *de ~ van de* ***jaren*** *dertig* the depression of the 1930s; *een ~* ***doormaken*** go through a crisis; *een ~* ***doorstaan*** weather a crisis

de **crisismanager** /krizɪsmɛnədʒər/ (pl: -s) crisis manager

het **criterium** /kriterijʏm/ (pl: criteria) **1** criterion: *aan* de *criteria* ***voldoen*** meet the criteria; *een ~* ***vaststellen*** lay down a criterion **2** [cycling] criterium

de **criticaster** /kritikɑstər/ (pl: -s) criticaster

de **criticus** /kritikʏs/ (pl: critici) critic, reviewer: *door de critici* ***toegejuicht worden*** receive critical acclaim

de **croissant** /krwɑsɔ/ (pl: -s) croissant

de **croque-monsieur** /krɔkməsjø/ (pl: -s) [Belg] toasted ham and cheese sandwich

de **cross** /krɔs/ (pl: -es) cross
crossen /krɔsə(n)/ (croste, heeft/is gecrost) **1** take part in a cross-country (event); do cross-country; do autocross (*or:* rallycross) [car] **2** tear about: *hij crost heel wat af op die fiets* he is always tearing about on that bike of his

de **crossfiets** /krɔsfits/ (pl: -en) cyclo-cross bike; BMX bike

de **crossmotor** /krɔsmotər/ cross-country motorcycle

de **croupier** /krupje/ (pl: -s) croupier

de **¹cru** /kry/ (pl: -'s) vintage
²cru /kry/ (adj, adv) **1** crude, rude; rough: *dat klinkt misschien ~, maar ...* that sounds a bit harsh, but ... **2** blunt; cruel
cruciaal /krys(i)jal/ crucial

het **crucifix** /krysifɪks/ (pl: -en) crucifix

de **cruise** /kruːs/ (pl: -s) cruise

de **cruisecontrol** /kruːskəntrol/ cruise control
cryptisch /krɪptis/ (adj, adv) cryptic(al), obscure

het **cryptogram** /krɪptoyrɑm/ (pl: -men) cryptogram

Cuba /kуba/ Cuba

de **Cubaan** /kyban/ (pl: Cubanen) Cuban

Cubaans /kybans/ (adj) Cuban

culinair /kylinɛːr/ (adj) culinary

culmineren /kʏlminɛrə(n)/ (culmineerde, heeft geculmineerd) culminate (in)

cultiveren /kʏltivɛrə(n)/ (cultiveerde, heeft gecultiveerd) **1** cultivate; till **2** cultivate, improve: *gecultiveerde kringen* cultured (*or:* sophisticated) circles

cultureel /kʏltyrel/ (adj, adv) cultural: *~ werk* cultural activities, social and creative activities

de **cultus** /kʏltʏs/ (pl: culten) cult

de **cultuur** /kʏltyr/ (pl: culturen) **1** culture, cultivation: *een stuk grond in ~ brengen* bring land into cultivation **2** culture, civilization: *de oosterse ~* eastern civilization

de **cultuurbarbaar** /kʏltyrbɑrbɑr/ (pl: -barbaren) Philistine

de **cultuurdrager** /kʏltyrdraɣər/ (pl: -s) vehicle of culture; purveyor of culture

de **cultuurgeschiedenis** /kʏltyrɣəsxidənɪs/ (pl: -sen) history of civilization; cultural history

cultuurhistorisch /kʏltyrhɪstoris/ (adj) connected with the history of civilization; historico-cultural, cultural-historical

cum laude /kumlɑudə/ (adv) with distinction

de **cumulatie** /kymyla(t)si/ (pl: -s) (ac)cumulation: *~ van ambten* plurality

cumulatief /kymylatif/ (adj) cumulative

¹**cumuleren** /kymylɛrə(n)/ (cumuleerde, heeft gecumuleerd) [Belg] have several jobs

²**cumuleren** /kymylɛrə(n)/ (cumuleerde, heeft gecumuleerd) (ac)cumulate: *verschillende functies ~* pluralize

de **cup** /kʏp/ (pl: -s) cup

Cupido /kypido/ Cupid, Eros

de **curatele** /kyratɛlə/ legal restraint; wardship; receivership

de **curator** /kyrator/ (pl: -s, -en) curator || *de firma staat onder het beheer van een ~* the firm is in receivership

curieus /kyrijøs/ (adj, adv) curious, strange: *ik vind het maar ~* I find it rather strange

de **curiositeit** /kyrijozitɛit/ (pl: -en) curiosity, oddity, strangeness: *... en andere ~en ...* and other curiosities (*or:* curiosa)

het **curriculum** /kyrikylʏm/ (pl: curricula) curriculum: *~ vitae* curriculum vitae; [Am] résumé

cursief /kʏrsif/ (adj, adv) italic, italicized, cursive: *~ drukken* print in italics

de **cursist** /kʏrsɪst/ (pl: -en) student

de **cursor** /kʏrsor/ (pl: -s) cursor

de **cursus** /kʏrzʏs/ (pl: -sen) course (of study, lectures): *zich opgeven voor een ~ Frans* sign up for a French course; *een schriftelijke ~* a correspondence course; *een ~ volgen (bij*

iem.) take a course (with s.o.); *een ~ voor beginners* a beginners' course; *een ~ voor gevorderden* an advanced course

het **cursusboek** /kʏrzʏzbuk/ (pl: -en) textbook; coursebook

de **curve** /kʏrvə/ (pl: -n) curve

de **custard** /kʏstɑrt/ custard (powder)

de **cut** /kʏt/ (pl: -s) cut(ting)

de **cutter** /kʏtər/ (pl: -s) **1** slicer **2** cutter, editor

de ¹**cv** /sevɛ/ (pl: cv's) **1** *commanditaire vennootschap* Limited Partnership, Special Partnership **2** *coöperatieve vereniging* co-op

de ²**cv** /sevɛ/ *centrale verwarming* central heating

het ³**cv** /sevɛ/ *curriculum vitae* cv; [Am] résumé

CVA /seveɑ/ *cerebrovasculair accident* CVA, cerebrovascular accident

de **cv-ketel** /sevɛketəl/ (pl: -s) central-heating boiler

CVS /seveɛs/ *chronischevermoeidheidssyndroom* Chronic Fatigue Syndrome, CFS

het **CWI** *Centrum voor Werk en Inkomen* [roughly] Job Centre

het **cyanide** /sijanidə/ (pl: -n) cyanide

de **cybernetica** /sibɛrnɛtika/ cybernetics

cyberpesten /sɑjbərpɛstə(n)/ cyber-bully

de **cyberspace** /sɑjbərspes/ cyberspace

de **cyclaam** /siklam/ (pl: cyclamen) cyclamen

de **cyclocross** /sɑjkɑlkrɔs/ (pl: -es) cyclo-cross

cyclisch /siklis/ (adj, adv) cyclic(al): *~e verbindingen* cyclic compounds

de **cycloon** /siklon/ (pl: cyclonen) cyclone, hurricane

de **cycloop** /siklop/ (pl: cyclopen) Cyclops

de **cyclus** /siklʏs/ (pl: cycli) cycle

de **cynicus** /sinikʏs/ (pl: cynici) cynic

cynisch /sinis/ (adj, adv) cynical

het **cynisme** /sinɪsmə/ cynicism

de **Cyprioot** /siprijot/ (pl: Cyprioten) Cypriot

Cyprus /siprʏs/ Cyprus

cyrillisch /sirɪlis/ (adj) Cyrillic

de **cyste** /kɪstə/ (pl: -n) cyst

d

de **d** /de/ (pl: d's) d; D

de **daad** /dat/ (pl: daden) act(ion), deed, activity: *een goede ~ verrichten* do a good deed; *de ~ bij het woord voegen* suit the action to the word

de **daadkracht** /d<u>a</u>tkraχt/ decisiveness, energy, vigour

daadwerkelijk /datw<u>ɛ</u>rkələk/ (adj, adv) actual, active, practical

¹daags /daχs/ (adj) daily, everyday

²daags /daχs/ (adv) a day, per day, daily: *tweemaal ~* twice a day

¹daar /dar/ (adv) **1** (over) there: *zie je dat huis ~* (do you) see that house (over there)?; *tot ~* up to there **2** (just, over, right) there: *wie is ~?* who is it? (or: there?)

²daar /dar/ (conj) as, because, since

daaraan /dar<u>a</u>n/ (adv) on (to) it (or: them): *wat heb je ~* what good is that

daarachter /darαχtər/ (adv) **1** behind (it, that, them, there): [fig] *wat zou ~ zitten?* I wonder what's behind it **2** beyond (it, that, them, there)

daarbij /darb<u>ɛi</u>/ (adv) **1** with it (or: that); with these (or: those): *~ blijft het* that's how it is, we'll keep it like that **2** besides, moreover, furthermore: *~ komt, dat …* what's more …

daarbinnen /darb<u>ɪ</u>nə(n)/ (adv) in there, inside, in it (or: that); in these (or: those): *~ is het warm* it's warm in there

daarboven /darb<u>o</u>və(n)/ (adv) up there, above it

daardoor /d<u>a</u>rdor/ (adv) **1** through it (or: that); through these (or: those) **2** therefore; so, consequently; by this (or: that) means: *zij weigerde, en ~ gaf zij te kennen … she refused, and by doing so made it clear …; ~ werd hij ziek* that is (or: was) what made him ill, because of this (or: that) he became ill

daarenboven /darə(n)b<u>o</u>və(n)/ (adv) besides, moreover, in addition, furthermore: *hij was knap en ~ rijk* he was handsome and rich besides

daarentegen /darənt<u>e</u>ɣə(n)/ (adv) on the other hand: *hij is zeer radicaal, zijn broer ~ conservatief* he is a strong radical, his brother, on the other hand, is conservative

daarheen /d<u>a</u>rhen/ (adv) (to) there: *wij willen ~* we want to go (over) there

daarin /dar<u>ɪ</u>n/ (adv) **1** in there (or: it, those) **2** in that: *hij is ~ handig* he is good at it

daarlangs /darl<u>ɑ</u>ŋs/ (adv) by (or: past,

along) that: *we kunnen beter ~ gaan* we had better go that way

daarmee /darm<u>e</u>/ (adv) with, by that (or: it, those): *~ kun je het vastzetten* you can fasten it with that (or: those); *en ~ uit!* and that's that! (or: all there is to it!)

daarna /darn<u>a</u>/ (adv) after(wards), next, then: *de dag ~* the day after (that); *snel* (or: *kort*) *~* soon (or: shortly) after (that); *eerst … en ~ …* first … and then …

daarnaar /darn<u>a</u>r/ (adv) **1** at (or: to, for) that **2** accordingly, according to that: *~ moet je handelen* you must act accordingly

daarnaast /darn<u>a</u>st/ (adv) **1** beside it, next to it **2** besides, in addition (to this): *~ is hij nog brutaal ook* what's more he is cheeky (too)

daarnet /darn<u>ɛ</u>t/ (adv) just now, only a little while ago, only a minute ago

daarom /d<u>a</u>rɔm/ (adv) **1** around it **2** therefore, so, because of this (or: that), for that reason: *hij wil het niet hebben, ~ doe ik het juist* he doesn't like it, and that's exactly why I do it; *waarom niet? ~ niet!* why not? because (I say so)!; that's why!

daaromheen /darɔmh<u>e</u>n/ (adv) around it (or: them): *een tuin met een hek ~* a garden with a fence around it

daaromtrent /d<u>a</u>rɔmtrɛnt/ (adv) **1** about that: *ik kan u ~ geen inlichtingen geven* I can't give you any information about that **2** thereabout, or so: *€ 100 of ~* a hundred euros or thereabout (or: so); *rond vier uur of ~* around four o'clock

daaronder /dar<u>ɔ</u>ndər/ (adv) under(neath) it

daarop /dar<u>ɔ</u>p/ (adv) **1** (up)on that, on top of that (or: those): *de tafel en het kleed ~* the table and the cloth on top of it **2** on that, to that: *uw antwoord* (or: *reactie*) *~* your reply (or: reaction) (to that) **3** thereupon: *de dag ~* the next (or: following) day, the day after (that); *kort ~* shortly afterwards, soon after (that)

daaropvolgend /darɔpf<u>ɔ</u>lɣənt/ (adj, adv) next, following: *hij kwam in juli en vertrok in juni ~* he arrived in July and left the following June

daarover /dar<u>o</u>vər/ (adv) **1** on top of it, on (or: over, above) that: *~ lag een zeil* there was a tarpaulin on top of (or: over, across) it **2** about that: *genoeg ~* enough said, enough of that

daartegen /dart<u>e</u>ɣə(n)/ (adv) **1** against it, next to it **2** against it (or: them): *eventuele bezwaren ~* any objections to it

daartegenaan /dart<u>e</u>ɣə(n)<u>a</u>n/ (adv) (right) up against it (or: them), (right) onto it (or: them): *onze schuur is ~ gebouwd* our shed is built up against (or: onto) it

daartegenover /dart<u>e</u>ɣə(n)<u>o</u>vər/ (adv) **1** opposite (or: facing) it/them: *de kerk met de *pastorie* ~ the church with the vicarage opposite it (*or:* facing it) **2** on the other hand, (but) then again ...: ~ *staat dat dit systeem duurder is* (but) on the other hand this system costs more

daartoe /dɑrtu/ (adv) **1** for that, to that **2** for that (purpose), to that end: ~ *gemachtigd zijn* be authorized to do it

daartussen /dɑrtʏsə(n)/ (adv) **1** between them, among them: *die twee ramen en de* **ruimte** ~ those two windows and the space between (them) **2** between them: *wat is het* **verschil** ~? what's the difference (between them)?

daaruit /dɑrœʏt/ (adv) **1** out of that (*or:* those): *het water* **spuit** ~ the water spurts out of it **2** from that: ~ *kan men* **afleiden** *dat ...* from this it can be deduced that ...

daarvan /dɑrvɑn/ (adv) **1** from it (*or:* that, there) **2** of it (*or:* that), thereof **3** of it (*or:* that): ~ *maakt men plastic* plastic is made of that, that is used for making plastic ‖ *niets* ~ nothing of the sort

daarvandaan /dɑrvɑndɑn/ (adv) **1** (away) from there, away (from it) **2** hence, therefore

daarvoor /dɑrvor/ (adv) **1** in front of it, before that (*or:* those) **2** before (that): *de* **week** ~ the week before (that), the previous week **3** for that (purpose): ~ *heb ik geen tijd* I've no time for that **4** for it (*or:* them): ~ *(in de plaats)* **heb** *ik een boek gekregen* I got a book instead **5** that's why: ~ *ben ik ook* **gekomen** that's what I've come for; *daar* **zijn** *het kinderen voor* that's children for you

de **dadel** /dadəl/ date

dadelijk /dadələk/ (adv) **1** immediately, at once, right away **2** directly, presently: *ik* **kom** *(zo)* ~ *bij u* I'll be right with you

de **dadelpalm** /dadəlpɑlm/ (pl: -en) date palm

de **dadendrang** /dadə(n)drɑŋ/ dynamism, thirst for action

de **dader** /dadər/ (pl: -s) perpetrator, offender: *de vermoedelijke* ~ the suspect

het **daderprofiel** /dadərprofil/ (pl: -en) offender profile: *een* ~ **opstellen** compile an offender profile

de **¹dag** /dɑx/ (pl: -en) **1** day, daybreak, daytime: ~ *en* **nacht** *bereikbaar* available day and night; *bij* **klaarlichte** ~ in broad daylight; *het is* **kort** ~ time is running out (fast), there is not much time (left); *het is morgen* **vroeg** ~ we must get up early (*or:* an early start) tomorrow; *iem. de* ~ *van zijn* **leven** *bezorgen* give s.o. the time of his life; *lange* ~*en maken* work long hours; *er* **gaat** *geen* ~ **voorbij** *of ik denk aan jou* not a day passes but I think of you; *het* **is** *vandaag mijn* ~ it just isn't my day (today); *wat* **is** *het voor* ~? what day (of the week) is it?; *morgen* **komt** *er weer een* ~ tomorrow is another day; ~ *in,* ~ *uit* day in day out; ~ *na* ~

day by day, day after day; *het wordt* **met** *de* ~ *slechter* it gets worse by the day; *om de drie* ~*en* every three days; *24 uur* **per** ~ 24 hours a day; *van* ~ *tot* ~ daily, from day to day; *van de ene* ~ *op de andere* from one day to the next; *over* **veertien** ~*en* in two weeks' time; in a fortnight **2** daylight: *voor de* ~ *komen* come to light, surface, appear; *met iets* **voor** *de* ~ *komen* **a)** come up with sth.; **b)** come forward, present o.s.; *voor de* ~ *ermee!* **a)** out with it!; **b)** show me!; *goed* **voor** *de* ~ *komen* make a good impression **3** day(s), time: *ouden van* ~*en* the elderly **4** hello; hi (there); bye(-bye); goodbye

²dag /dɑx/ (int) hello, hi; bye(-bye); goodbye: *dáág!* bye(-bye)!, bye then; *ja, dáág!* forget it!

de **dagbehandeling** /dɑxbəhɑndəlɪŋ/ (pl: -en) outpatients' treatment

het **dagblad** /dɑxblɑt/ (pl: -en) (daily) newspaper, (daily) paper

het **dagboek** /dɑxbuk/ (pl: -en) diary, journal: *een* ~ *(bij)houden* keep a diary

het **dagdeel** /dɑxdel/ (pl: -delen) part of the day; shift; morning; afternoon; evening; night

dagdromen /dɑxdromə(n)/ (dagdroomde, heeft gedagdroomd) daydream

¹dagelijks /daɣələks/ (adj) **1** daily: *zijn* ~*e bezigheden* his daily routine; *voor* ~ **gebruik** for everyday use **2** everyday, ordinary: ~ *bestuur* executive (committee); *in het* ~ *leven* in everyday life; *dat is* ~ **werk** *voor hem* that's routine for him

²dagelijks /daɣələks/ (adv) daily, each day, every day: *dat komt* ~ **voor** it happens every day

dagen /daɣə(n)/ (daagde, heeft gedaagd) **1** summon(s); subpoena: *iem. voor het* **gerecht** ~ summon(s) s.o. **2** dawn: *het begon mij te* ~ it began to dawn on me

dagenlang /daɣə(n)lɑŋ/ (adj) lasting (for) days

de **dageraad** /daɣərat/ dawn, daybreak, break of day

het **dagje** /dɑxjə/ (pl: -s) day: *een* ~ **ouder** *worden* be getting on (a bit); *een* ~ *uit* a day out

de **dagjesmensen** /dɑxjəsmɛnsə(n)/ (pl) (day) trippers

de **dagkaart** /dɑxkart/ (pl: -en) day-ticket

het **daglicht** /dɑxlɪxt/ daylight, light of day: *bij iem. in een* **kwaad** ~ *staan* be in s.o.'s bad books; *iem. in een* **kwaad** ~ *stellen* put s.o. in the wrong (with)

het **dagmenu** /dɑxməny/ daily menu

de **dagopvang** /dɑxɔpfɑŋ/ day nursery, day-care centre

het **dagretour** /dɑxrətur/ (pl: -s) day return, day (return) ticket

de **dagschotel** /dɑxsxotəl/ (pl: -s) plat du jour, dish of the day; today's special

de **dagtaak** /dɑxtak/ (pl: dagtaken) **1** daily

work **2** day's work: *daar **heb** ik een ~ aan* that is a full day's work (*or:* a full-time job)

de **dagtekening** /dɑ̈xtekənɪŋ/ date

de **dagtocht** /dɑ̈xtɔxt/ (pl: -en) day trip

dagvaarden /dɑ̈xfardə(n)/ (dagvaardde, heeft gedagvaard) summon: *gedagvaard **worden*** be summoned (to appear in court)

de **dagvaarding** /dɑ̈xfardɪŋ/ (pl: -en) (writ of) summons, writ; subpoena

het **dagverblijf** /dɑ̈xfərblɛif/ (pl: dagverblijven) **1** day room: *een ~ voor **kinderen*** a day-care centre, a day nursery, a crèche **2** outdoor enclosure, outside cage, outside pen

dagvers /dɑ̈xfɛrs/ (adj) fresh daily, fresh each day

de **dahlia** /dɑ̈lija/ (pl: -'s) dahlia

het **dak** /dɑk/ (pl: -en) roof: *auto met **open** ~* convertible; soft-top; *een ~ boven het hoofd **hebben*** have a roof over one's head; *iets **van** de ~en schreeuwen* shout sth. from the rooftops; [fig] *het ~ **gaat eraf*** it's going to be one big party

de **dakbedekking** /dɑ̈gbədɛkɪŋ/ (pl: -en) roofing material

de **dakdekker** /dɑ̈gdɛkər/ (pl: -s) roofer

de **dakgoot** /dɑ̈kxot/ (pl: dakgoten) gutter

het **dakje** /dɑ̈kjə/ (pl: -s) **1** rooflet **2** circumflex (accent) ‖ *het ging van een **leien** ~* it was plain (*or:* smooth) sailing all the way

de **dakkapel** /dɑ̈kapɛl/ (pl: -len) dormer (window)

dakloos /dɑ̈klos/ (adj) homeless, (left) without a roof over one's head

de **dakloze** /dɑ̈klozə/ homeless person; street people

de **daklozenkrant** /dɑ̈klozə(n)krant/ [roughly] Big Issue

de **dakpan** /dɑ̈kpɑn/ (pl: -nen) (roof(ing)) tile

het **dakraam** /dɑ̈kram/ (pl: dakramen) skylight, attic window, garret window

het **dakterras** /dɑ̈ktɛrɑs/ (pl: -sen) terrace, roof garden

het **dal** /dɑl/ (pl: -en) valley, dale ‖ *hij is door een **diep** ~ gegaan* he has had a very hard (*or:* rough) time

dalen /dɑ̈lə(n)/ (daalde, is gedaald) **1** descend, go down, come down, drop, fall: *het **vliegtuig** daalt* the (aero)plane is descending; *de temperatuur daalde **tot** beneden het vriespunt* the temperature fell below zero **2** fall, go down, come down, drop; decline; decrease: *de prijzen zijn een paar **euro** gedaald* prices are down by a couple of euros

de **daling** /dɑ̈lɪŋ/ (pl: -en) **1** descent, fall(ing), drop: *~ van de **zeespiegel*** drop in the sea level **2** slope, incline, descent, drop; [small] dip **3** decrease, drop, slump: *de ~ van het **geboortecijfer*** the fall in the birth rate

de **daluren** /dɑ̈lyrə(n)/ (pl) off-peak hours

de **dam** /dɑm/ **1** dam: *een ~ **leggen*** build a dam **2** [draughts] king, crowned man: *een ~ **halen*** *(maken)* crown a man

het **damast** /dɑmɑst/ (pl: -en) damask

het **dambord** /dɑmbɔrt/ (pl: -en) draughtboard

de **dame** /dɑmə/ (pl: -s) **1** lady: *~s en **heren*** ladies and gentlemen **2** [chess, cards] queen: *een ~ **halen*** queen a pawn

het **damesblad** /dɑməzblɑt/ (pl: -en) women's magazine

de **damesfiets** /dɑməsfits/ (pl: -en) women's (*or:* lady's) bike

de **dameskapper** /dɑməskɑpər/ (pl: -s) ladies' hairdresser

de **damesmode** /dɑməsmodə/ (pl: -s) **1** ladies' fashion **2** ladies' clothing

het **damhert** /dɑmhɛrt/ (pl: -en) fallow deer

dammen /dɑmə(n)/ (damde, heeft gedamd) play draughts; [Am] play checkers

de **dammer** /dɑmər/ (pl: -s) draughts player; [Am] checkers player

de **damp** /dɑmp/ (pl: -en) **1** steam; vapour; mist **2** smoke; [oft pl] fume: *schadelijke ~en* noxious fumes

dampen /dɑmpə(n)/ (dampte, heeft gedampt) **1** steam **2** smoke

de **dampkap** /dɑmpkap/ (pl: -pen) [Belg] cooker hood, extractor hood

de **dampkring** /dɑmpkrɪŋ/ (pl: -en) (earth's) atmosphere

de **damschijf** /dɑmsxɛif/ (pl: damschijven) draught(sman)

het **damspel** /dɑmspɛl/ (pl: -len) **1** draughts **2** set of draughts

de **damwand** /dɑmwɑnt/ (pl: -en) sheet piling

¹**dan** /dɑn/ (adv) **1** then: *morgen zijn we vrij, ~ **gaan** we uit* we have a day off tomorrow, so we're going out; *nu eens dit, ~ **weer** dat* first one thing, then another; *tot ~* till then; see you then; *hij zei dat hij ~ **en** ~ zou komen* he said he'd come at such and such a time; *en je **broer** ~?* and what about your brother then?; *wat ~ **nog**?* so what!; *ook goed, ~ **niet*** all right, we won't then; *al ~ **niet** groen* green or otherwise, whether green or not; *en ~ zeggen ze **nog** dat …* and still they say that …; *hij heeft niet gewerkt; hij is ~ **ook** gezakt* he didn't work, so not surprisingly he failed **2** then; besides: *eerst werken, ~ **spelen*** business before pleasure; *zelfs ~ gaat het niet* even so it won't work; *en ~?* and then what?

²**dan** /dɑn/ (conj) than: *hij is **groter** ~ ik* he is bigger than me ‖ *een **ander** ~ hij heeft het me verteld* I heard it from s.o. other than him

de **dance** /dɛːns/ dance

de **dancing** /dɛnsɪŋ/ (pl: -s) dance hall, discotheque

danig /dɑnəx/ (adv) soundly, thoroughly, well: *~ in de knoei zitten* be in a terrible mess

de **dank** /dɑŋk/ thanks, gratitude: *iets niet **in** ~ afnemen* take sth. in bad part; *geen ~* you're welcome; *stank voor ~ krijgen* get little thanks for one's pains; *bij voorbaat ~* thank you in advance; *tegen* **wil** *en* ~ unwilling, willy-nilly

dankbaar /dɑŋgbar/ (adj, adv) **1** grateful, thankful: *ik zou u zeer* ~ **zijn** *als …* I should be most grateful to you (*or:* obliged) if … **2** rewarding, grateful: *een dankbare* **taak** a rewarding task

de **dankbaarheid** /dɑŋgbarhɛit/ gratitude, thankfulness: *uit* ~ *voor* in appreciation of

de **dankbetuiging** /dɑŋgbətœyɣɪŋ/ (pl: -en) expression of gratitude (*or:* thanks)

¹**danken** /dɑŋkə(n)/ (dankte, heeft gedankt) decline (with thanks)

²**danken** /dɑŋkə(n)/ (dankte, heeft gedankt) **1** thank: *ja graag, dank* **je** yes, please, thank you; *niet(s)* **te** ~ not at all, you're welcome **2** owe, be indebted: *dit heb ik* **aan** *jou te* ~ I owe this to you; I have you to thank for this

het **dankwoord** /dɑŋkwort/ (pl: -en) word(s) of thanks

dankzeggen /dɑŋksɛɣə(n)/ (zegde dank/zei dank, heeft dankgezegd) thank, express (one's) thanks (*or:* gratitude) to

dankzij /dɑŋksɛi/ (prep) thanks to

de **dans** /dɑns/ (pl: -en) dance, dancing: *iem.* **ten** ~ *vragen* ask s.o. to dance (*or:* for a dance) ‖ *de* ~ **ontspringen** get off scot-free

dansen /dɑnsə(n)/ (danste, heeft/is gedanst) dance: *uit* ~ **gaan** go (out) dancing; ~ **op** *muziek* (*or:* *een plaat*) dance to music (*or:* a record)

de **danser** /dɑnsər/ (pl: -s) dancer

de **danseres** /dɑnsərɛs/ (pl: -sen) dancer

de **dansles** /dɑnslɛs/ (pl: -sen) dancing class (*or:* lesson); dancing classes

het **dansorkest** /dɑnsɔrkɛst/ (pl: -en) dance band

de **danspas** /dɑnspɑs/ (pl: -sen) (dance) step

de **dansschool** /dɑnsχol/ (pl: -scholen) dancing school

de **dansvloer** /dɑnsflur/ (pl: -en) dance floor

de **danszaal** /dɑnsal/ (pl: -zalen) dance hall; ballroom

dapper /dɑpər/ (adj, adv) **1** brave, courageous: *zich* ~ **verdedigen** put up a brave fight **2** plucky, tough: *klein maar* ~ small but tough

de **dapperheid** /dɑpərhɛit/ bravery, courage

de **dar** /dɑr/ (pl: -ren) drone

de **darm** /dɑrm/ (pl: -en) intestine, bowel: **twaalfvingerige** ~ duodenum

de **darmflora** /dɑrmflora/ intestinal flora

dartel /dɑrtəl/ (adj, adv) playful, frisky, frolicsome

dartelen /dɑrtələ(n)/ (dartelde, heeft/is gedarteld) romp, frolic, gambol

het **darts** /dɑːrts/ darts

het **dartsbord** /dɑːrtsbɔrt/ dartboard

de **das** /dɑs/ **1** badger **2** tie: *dat deed hem de* ~ *om* that did for him, that finished him **3** scarf

het **dashboard** /dɛʃbɔːrt/ (pl: -s) dashboard

het **dashboardkastje** /dɛʒbɔːrtkɑʃə/ (pl: -s) glove compartment

¹**dat** /dɑt/ (dem pron) that: *ben ik* ~? is that me?; ~ **is** *het hem nu juist* that's just it, that's the problem; *ziezo,* ~ **was** ~ right, that's that (then), so much for that; ~ **lijkt** *er meer op* that's more like it; *mijn boek en* ~ **van** *jou* my book and yours; ~ **mens** that (dreadful) woman

²**dat** /dɑt/ (pron) **1** that, which; [of pers] that; who, whom: *het* **bericht** ~ *mij gebracht werd …* the message that (*or:* which) was brought me …; *het* **jongetje** ~ *ik een appel heb gegeven* the little boy (that, who) I gave an apple to **2** which; [of pers] who; [of pers] whom: *het* **huis**, ~ *onlangs opgeknapt was, werd verkocht* the house, which had recently been done up, was sold

³**dat** /dɑt/ (conj) **1** that [usually not translated]: *in* **plaats** *(van)* ~ *je me het vertelt …* instead of telling me, you …; *de* **reden** ~ *hij niet komt is …* the reason (why) he is not coming is …; *ik* **denk** ~ *hij komt* I think (that) he'll come; **zonder** ~ *ik het wist* without me knowing; *het regende* ~ *het goot* it was pouring (down) **2** that, because: *hij is kwaad* ~ *hij niet mee mag* he is angry that (*or:* because) he can't come **3** so that: *doe het* **zo**, ~ *hij het niet merkt* do it in such a way that he won't notice **4** as far as: *is hier ook een bioscoop? niet* ~ *ik weet* is there a cinema here? not that I know **5** that: ~ *mij nu juist zoiets moest overkomen!* that such a thing should happen to me now!

de **data** /data/ (pl) **1** data **2** dates

de **databank** /databɑŋk/ (pl: -en) data bank

de **datacompressie** /datakɔmprɛsi/ data compression

de **datalimiet** /datalimit/ data limit

de **date** /det/ (pl: -s) date

daten /detə(n)/ (datete, heeft gedatet) date

¹**dateren** /daterə(n)/ (dateerde) date (from), go back (to): *het huis dateert al* **uit** *de veertiende eeuw* the house goes all the way back to the fourteenth century; *de brief dateert* **van** *6 mei* the letter is dated 6th May

²**dateren** /daterə(n)/ (dateerde, heeft gedateerd) date

datgene /dɑtχenə/ (dem pron) what, that which: ~ **wat** *je zegt, is waar* what you say is true

dato /dato/ (adv) date, dated: *drie weken* **na** ~ three weeks later

de **datum** /datym/ (pl: data) date, time: *zonder* ~ undated; *er staat geen* ~ *op* there is no date on it; *over* ~ past its date, past its sell-by date

de **dauw** /dɑu/ dew ‖ [Belg] *van de* **hemelse** ~ *leven* live the life of Riley

dauwtrappen /dɑutrɑpə(n)/ [roughly] taking a walk at dawn

daveren /davərə(n)/ (daverde, heeft gedaverd) thunder, shake, roar; resound: *de vrachtwagen daverde* **voorbij** the truck thundered (*or:* roared) past

daverend /dαvərənt/ (adj, adv) resounding, thunderous: *een ~* ***applaus*** thunderous applause; *een ~* ***succes*** a resounding success

de **davidster** /dαvɪtstɛr/ (pl: -ren) Star of David

d.d. (abbrev) *de dato* dd

de /də/ (art) the: *eens in de* ***week*** once a week; *ze kosten twintig euro de* ***kilo*** they are twenty euros a kilo; *dat is dé* ***man*** *voor dat karwei* he is (just) the man for the job

de **deadline** /dɛtlαjn/ (pl: -s) deadline

dealen /diːlə(n)/ (dealde, heeft gedeald) deal (in), push: *hij dealt* ***in*** *heroïne* he deals in (*or:* pushes) heroin

de **dealer** /diːlər/ (pl: -s) dealer; pusher

het/de **debacle** /debαkəl/ (pl: -s) disaster; failure; downfall

het **debat** /dəbαt/ (pl: -ten) debate; argument

debatteren /debαtɛrə(n)/ (debatteerde, heeft gedebatteerd) debate; argue

het **debet** /debɛt/ debit(s), debtor side, debit side: *~ en* ***credit*** debit(s) and credit(s)

de ¹**debiel** /dəbiːl/ (pl: -en) mental defective, moron; imbecile; cretin

²**debiel** /dəbiːl/ (adj, adv) mentally deficient; feeble-minded

debiteren /debitɛrə(n)/ (debiteerde, heeft gedebiteerd) debit, charge

de **debiteur** /debitøːr/ (pl: -en) debtor, debt receivable, account(s) receivable

de **debriefing** /dɪbriːfɪ̃/ (pl: -s) debriefing

de **debutant** /debytɑnt/ (pl: -en) novice; newcomer

debuteren /debytɛrə(n)/ (debuteerde, heeft gedebuteerd) make a (*or:* one's) debut

het **debuut** /dəbyt/ (pl: debuten) debut: *zijn ~* ***maken*** make one's debut (*or:* first appearance)

de **decaan** /dekαn/ (pl: decanen) **1** dean **2** student counsellor

decadent /dekadɛnt/ (adj) decadent

de **decadentie** /dekadɛn(t)si/ decadence, degeneration

de **decafé** /dekαfe/ decaf(f), decaffeinated coffee

de **decameter** /dekametər/ decametre

de **december** /desɛmbər/ December

het **decennium** /desɛnijʏm/ (pl: decennia) decade

de **decentralisatie** /desɛntralizα(t)si/ decentralization; deconcentration; localization

decentraliseren /desɛntralizɛrə(n)/ (decentraliseerde, heeft gedecentraliseerd) decentralize; deconcentrate; localize

de **deceptie** /desɛpsi/ (pl: -s) disappointment; disillusionment

de **decharge** /deʃαrʒə/: *iem. ~* ***verlenen*** release (*or:* relieve) s.o. (from/of); ***getuige*** *à ~* witness for the defence

de **decibel** /desibɛl/ (pl: -s) decibel

de **deciliter** /desilitər/ (pl: -s) decilitre

de ¹**decimaal** /desimαl/ (pl: decimalen) decimal

(place): *tot op* zes decimalen uitrekenen calculate to six decimal places

²**decimaal** /desimαl/ (adj) decimal: *decimale* ***breuk*** decimal fraction, decimal

decimeren /desimɛrə(n)/ (decimeerde, heeft gedecimeerd) decimate

de **decimeter** /desimetər/ (pl: -s) decimetre

de **declamatie** /deklamα(t)si/ (pl: -s) declamation; recitation

declameren /deklamɛrə(n)/ (declameerde, heeft gedeclameerd) declaim, recite

de **declaratie** /deklarα(t)si/ (pl: -s) expenses claim; account; claim (form): *zijn ~* ***indienen*** put in one's claim

declareren /deklarɛrə(n)/ (declareerde, heeft gedeclareerd) declare: *een* ***bedrag*** (*or:* *driehonderd* ***euro***) *~* charge an amount (*or:* three hundred euros); *heeft* u nog iets te ~? have you anything to declare?

de **decoder** /dikoːdər/ decoder

decoderen /dekodɛrə(n)/ (decodeerde, heeft gedecodeerd) decode

het **decolleté** /dekɔləte/ (pl: -s) low neckline, cleavage

het **decor** /dekoːr/ (pl: -s) **1** decor, scenery, setting(s); [film] set: *~ en* ***kostuums*** scenery and costumes **2** [fig] background

de **decoratie** /dekorα(t)si/ (pl: -s) decoration, adornment

decoratief /dekoratiːf/ (adj, adv) decorative, ornamental

decoreren /dekorɛrə(n)/ (decoreerde, heeft gedecoreerd) decorate

het **decorum** /dekoːrʏm/ decorum, propriety: *het ~* ***bewaren*** maintain decorum (*or:* the proprieties)

de **decoupeerzaag** /dekupɛrzαx/ (pl: -zagen) jigsaw

het **decreet** /dəkret/ (pl: decreten) decree

het **deeg** /dex/ (pl: degen) dough; pastry

de **deegrol** /dexrɔl/ (pl: -len) rolling pin

de **deegwaren** /dexwarə(n)/ (pl) pasta

de **deejay** /diːdʒe/ (pl: -s) deejay

het **deel** /del/ **1** part, piece: *één ~* ***bloem*** *op één ~* ***suiker*** one part (of) flour to one part (of) sugar; *voor een* ***groot*** *~* to a great extent; *voor het* ***grootste*** *~* for the most part; *~* ***uitmaken*** *van* be part of, belong to **2** share: *zijn ~ van de* ***winst*** his share of the profits **3** volume ‖ *het viel hem ten ~* it fell to him (*or:* to his lot)

deelbaar /delbar/ (adj) divisible: *tien is ~* ***door*** *twee* ten is divisible by two

de **deelgenoot** /delɣənot/ (pl: -genoten) partner (in), sharer (in): *iem. ~* ***maken*** *van een geheim* confide a secret to s.o.

de **deelname** /delnαmə/ participation: *~* ***aan*** *een wedstrijd* taking part in a contest (*or:* competition, race)

deelnemen /delnemə(n)/ (nam deel, heeft deelgenomen) participate (in), take part (in); attend; enter; compete (in); join (in): *aan een* *wedstrijd* ~ take part in a contest; ~ *aan een examen* take an exam

de **deelnemer** /dɛlnemər/ (pl: -s) participant; conferee; competitor; entrant; contestant: *een beperkt aantal* ~*s* a limited number of participants

de **deelneming** /dɛlnemɪŋ/ **1** participation, attendance, entry: *bij voldoende* ~ if there are enough entries **2** sympathy; condolence(s): *zijn* ~ *betuigen* extend one's sympathy

de **deelregering** /dɛlrəɣerɪŋ/ (pl: -en) [Belg] regional government (*or:* administration)

deels /dels/ (adv) partly, part

de **deelstaat** /dɛlstat/ (pl: -staten) (federal) state

het **deelteken** /dɛltekə(n)/ (pl: -s) division sign

de **deeltijd** /dɛltɛit/ part-time, half-time

de **deeltijdbaan** /dɛltɛidban/ (pl: -banen) part-time job

het **deeltijdwerk** /dɛltɛitwɛrk/ part-time work, half-time work

het **deeltje** /dɛlcə/ (pl: -s) particle

het **deelwoord** /dɛlwort/ (pl: -en) participle: *het onvoltooid* ~ the present participle; *het voltooid* ~ the past participle

de **Deen** /den/ (pl: Denen) Dane

het **¹Deens** /dens/ Danish

²Deens /dens/ (adj) Danish

deerniswekkend /dernɪswɛkənt/ (adj) pitiful, pitiable, pathetic: *in* ~*e toestand* in a pitiful (*or:* sorry) state

het **¹defect** /defɛkt/ (pl: -en) fault, defect; flaw: *we hebben het* ~ *aan de machine kunnen verhelpen* we've managed to sort out the trouble with the machine

²defect /defɛkt/ (adj) faulty, defective; out of order; damaged: ~ *out of order*

de **defensie** /defɛnsi/ defence: *de minister van* ~ the Minister of Defence

het **defensief** /defɛnsif/ defensive

de **defibrillator** /defibrilatɔr/ (pl: -en, -s) defibrillator

het **defilé** /defile/ (pl: -s) parade

definiëren /defin(i)jerə(n)/ (definieerde, heeft gedefinieerd) define: *iets nader* ~ define sth. more closely, be more specific about sth.

de **definitie** /defini(t)si/ (pl: -s) definition: *per* ~ by definition

definitief /definitif/ (adj, adv) definitive, final: *de definitieve versie* the definitive version

de **deflatie** /defla(t)si/ (pl: -s) deflation

deftig /dɛftəɣ/ (adj, adv) distinguished, fashionable, stately: *een* ~*e buurt* a fashionable quarter

¹degelijk /deɣələk/ (adj) **1** reliable, respectable, solid, sound: *een* ~ *persoon* a respectable person **2** sound, reliable, solid: *een* ~ *fabricaat* a reliable product

²degelijk /deɣələk/ (adv) thoroughly, sound-

ly, very much || *wel* ~ really, actually, positively; *ik meen het wel* ~ I am quite serious

de **degen** /deɣə(n)/ (pl: -s) sword; foil

degene /dəɣenə/ (dem pron) he, she; those: ~ *die …* he who, she who

de **degeneratie** /deɣenəra(t)si/ (pl: -s) degeneration

de **degradatie** /deɣrada(t)si/ (pl: -s) demotion; [esp sport] relegation

de **degradatiewedstrijd** /deɣrada(t)siwɛtstrɛit/ (pl: -en) relegation match

¹degraderen /deɣraderə(n)/ (degradeerde, is gedegradeerd) be relegated (to), be downgraded (to)

²degraderen /deɣraderə(n)/ (degradeerde, heeft gedegradeerd) degrade, downgrade (to); demote (to); [esp sport] relegate (to)

deinen /dɛinə(n)/ (deinde, heeft gedeind) **1** heave: *de zee deinde sterk* the sea surged wildly **2** bob, roll

de **deining** /dɛinɪŋ/ (pl: -en) **1** swell, roll **2** rocking motion **3** commotion: ~ *veroorzaken* cause a stir

het **dek** /dɛk/ (pl: -ken) **1** cover(ing); horse-cloth **2** [shipp] deck: *alle hens aan* ~ all hands on deck

het **dekbed** /dɛgbɛt/ (pl: -den) continental quilt, duvet

het/de **dekbedovertrek** /dɛgbɛtovərtrɛk/ (pl: -ken) eiderdown cover

de **deken** /dekə(n)/ **1** blanket: *onder de* ~*s kruipen* pull the blankets over one's head **2** dean

de **dekhengst** /dɛkhɛŋst/ (pl: -en) stud(-horse), (breeding) stallion

dekken /dɛkə(n)/ (dekte, heeft gedekt) **1** cover; coat: *de tafel* ~ set the table **2** agree (with), correspond (with, to) **3** cover (for), protect: *iem. in de rug* ~ support s.o., stand up for s.o.; *zich* ~ cover (*or:* protect) o.s. **4** cover, meet: *deze cheque is niet gedekt* this cheque is not covered; *de verzekering dekt de schade* the insurance covers the damage **5** cover; service

de **dekking** /dɛkɪŋ/ **1** [mil] cover, shelter: ~ *zoeken* seek (*or:* take) cover (from) **2** service **3** [fin] cover **4** cover: *ter* ~ *van de (on)kosten* to cover (*or:* meet, make up) the expenses **5** coverage **6** [socc] marking; cover; guard [boxing etc]

de **deklaag** /dɛklaɣ/ (pl: -lagen) **1** finishing coat **2** covering layer

de **dekmantel** /dɛkmɑntəl/ (pl: -s) cover, cloak; blind; front: *iem. (iets) als* ~ *gebruiken* use s.o. (sth.) as a front

het/de **deksel** /dɛksəl/ (pl: -s) lid; top; cover: *het* ~ *op zijn neus krijgen* get the door slammed in one's face

het **dekzeil** /dɛksɛil/ (pl: -en) tarpaulin, canvas

de **delegatie** /deleɣa(t)si/ (pl: -s) delegation

delegeren /deleɣerə(n)/ (delegeerde, heeft gedelegeerd) delegate

delen /de̱lə(n)/ (deelde, heeft gedeeld) **1** divide, split **2** share, divide: *het **verschil** ~* split the difference; *je moet **kiezen** of ~* take it or leave it; *eerlijk ~* share and share alike; *samen ~* go halves **3** divide; [educ] do division: *honderd ~ **door** tien* divide one hundred by ten || *een **mening** ~* share an opinion; *iem. in zijn vreugde **laten** ~* share one's joy with s.o.

de **deler** /de̱lər/ (pl: -s) divisor

deleten /dili̱ːtə(n)/ (deletete, heeft gedeletet) delete

de **delfstof** /de̱lfstɔf/ (pl: -fen) mineral

delicaat /delika̱t/ (adj) delicate

de **delicatesse** /delikatsə̱/ (pl: -n) delicacy

het **delict** /deli̱kt/ (pl: -en) offence; indictable offence: *plaats ~* scene of the crime

de **deling** /de̱lɪŋ/ (pl: -en) division

de **delinquent** /delɪŋkwε̱nt/ (pl: -en) delinquent, offender

het **delirium** /deli̱rijʏm/ (pl: deliria) delirium

de **delta** /dε̱lta/ (pl: -'s) **1** delta **2** delta wing

deltavliegen /dε̱ltavliɣə(n)/ hang-gliding

delven /dε̱lvə(n)/ (delfde/dolf, heeft gedolven) **1** dig **2** extract: *goud* (or: *grondstoffen*) *~* mine gold (or: raw materials)

de **demagogie** /demaɣoɣi̱/ demagogy

de **demagoog** /demaɣo̱x/ (pl: demagogen) demagogue

demarreren /demareṟə(n)/ (demarreerde, heeft/is gedemarreerd) break away, take a flyer

dement /demε̱nt/ (adj) demented

dementeren /demεntə̱rə(n)/ (dementeerde, is gedementeerd) grow demented, get demented

de **dementie** /demεnsi̱/ dementia

demilitariseren /demilitarize̱rə(n)/ (demilitariseerde, heeft gedemilitariseerd) demilitarize

demissionair /demɪʃonε̱ːr/ (adj) outgoing: *het **kabinet** is ~* the cabinet has resigned (or: tendered) its resignation

de **demo** /de̱mo/ (pl: -'s) **1** demo (tape) **2** demo

de **demobilisatie** /demobiliza̱(t)si/ demobilization

de **democraat** /demokra̱t/ (pl: democraten) democrat

de **democratie** /demokra(t)si̱/ (pl: -ën) democracy, self-government

democratisch /demokra̱tis/ (adj, adv) democratic

democratiseren /demokratize̱rə(n)/ (democratiseerde, heeft/is gedemocratiseerd) democratize

de **demografie** /demoɣrafi̱/ demography

de **demon** /de̱mɔn/ (pl: -en) demon, devil, evil spirit

demoniseren /demonize̱rə(n)/ (demoniseerde, heeft gedemoniseerd) demonize

de **demonstrant** /demɔnstrɑ̱nt/ (pl: -en) demonstrator, protester

de **demonstratie** /demɔnstra̱(t)si/ (pl: -s) **1** demonstration, display, show(ing), exhibition **2** demonstration, (protest) march: *een ~ **tegen** kernwapens* a demonstration against nuclear arms

demonstratief /demɔnstrati̱f/ (adj, adv) ostentatious, demonstrative, showy: *zij liet op demonstratieve **wijze** haar ongenoegen blijken* she pointedly showed her displeasure

¹**demonstreren** /demɔnstre̱rə(n)/ (demonstreerde, heeft gedemonstreerd) demonstrate, march, protest: *~ **tegen*** (or: ***voor***) *iets* demonstrate against (or: in support of) sth.

²**demonstreren** /demɔnstre̱rə(n)/ (demonstreerde, heeft gedemonstreerd) demonstrate, display, show, exhibit

de **demontage** /demɔnta̱ʒə/ (pl: -s) dismantling, disassembling, taking apart; removal; defusing

demonteren /demɔntе̱rə(n)/ (demonteerde, heeft gedemonteerd) **1** disassemble, dismantle, take apart; remove; knock down **2** deactivate; defuse; disarm

demoraliseren /demoralize̱rə(n)/ (demoraliseerde, heeft gedemoraliseerd) demoralize

demotiveren /demotive̱rə(n)/ (demotiveerde, heeft gedemotiveerd) remove (or: reduce) (s.o.'s) motivation, discourage, dishearten

dempen /dε̱mpə(n)/ (dempte, heeft gedempt) **1** fill (up, in), close (up), stop (up) **2** subdue; tone down; muffle; deaden; dim; shade [light]: *gedempt **licht*** subdued (or: dimmed, soft) light

de **demper** /dε̱mpər/ (pl: -s) silencer; [Am] muffler

de **den** /dεn/ (pl: -nen) pine (tree), fir

denderen /dε̱ndərə(n)/ (denderde, heeft/is gedenderd) rumble, thunder; hurtle; roar

denderend /dε̱ndərənt/ (adj, adv): *ik vind dat boek **niet** ~* I don't think that book is so marvellous, I'm not exactly wild about that book

Denemarken /de̱nəmɑrkə(n)/ Denmark

denigrerend /deniɣre̱rənt/ (adj, adv) disparaging, belittling

het **denim** /dе̱nɪm/ denim

denkbaar /dε̱ŋɡbar/ (adj) conceivable, imaginable, possible

het **denkbeeld** /dε̱ŋɡbelt/ (pl: -en) **1** concept, idea, thought, notion: *zich een ~ **vormen van*** form some idea of; *een **verkeerd** ~ hebben van* have a wrong conception (or: idea) of **2** opinion, idea, view: *hij houdt er **verouderde** ~en op na* he has some antiquated ideas

denkbeeldig /dε̱ŋɡbeldəx/ (adj) **1** notional, theoretical, hypothetical **2** imaginary, illusory, unreal; fictitious: *het gevaar is **niet** ~ dat …* there's a (very) real danger that …

¹**denken** /dε̱ŋkə(n)/ (dacht, heeft gedacht)

denken

1 think, consider, reflect, ponder: *het doet ~ aan* it reminds one of …; *dit doet sterk aan omkoperij* ~ this savours strongly of bribery; *waar zit je aan te ~?* what's on your mind?; *ik moet er niet aan ~* I can't bear to think about it; *ik denk er net zo over* I feel just the same about it; *ik zal eraan ~* I'll bear it in mind; *nu ik eraan denk* (now I) come to think of it; *aan iets ~* think (or: be thinking) of sth.; *ik probeer er niet aan te ~* I try to put it out of my mind; *iem. aan het ~ zetten* set s.o. thinking; *ik dacht bij mezelf* I thought (or: said) to myself; *denk om je hoofd* mind your head; *er verschillend (anders) over ~* take a different view (of the matter); *zij denkt er nu anders over* she feels differently about it (now); *dat had ik niet van hem gedacht* I should never have thought it of him **2** think of (or: about), intend (to), plan (to): *ik denk erover met roken te stoppen* I'm thinking of giving up smoking ‖ *geen ~ aan!* it's out of the question!

²**denken** /dɛŋkə(n)/ (dacht, heeft gedacht) **1** think, be of the opinion, consider: *ik weet niet wat ik ervan moet ~* I don't know what to think; *wat dacht je van een ijsje?* what would you say to an ice cream?; *dat dacht je maar, dat had je maar gedacht* that's what you think!; *ik dacht van wel* (or: *van niet*) I thought it was (or: wasn't); *wie denk je wel dat je bent?* (just) who do you think you are? **2** think, suppose, expect, imagine: *wie had dat kunnen ~* who would have thought it?; *u moet niet ~ (that) …* you mustn't suppose (or: think) (that) …; *dat dacht ik al* I thought so; *dacht ik het niet!* just as I thought! **3** think, understand, imagine, appreciate, consider: *de beste arts die men zich maar kan ~* the best (possible) doctor; *denk eens (aan) imagine!*, just think of it! **4** think of (or: about), intend, be going (to), plan: *wat denk je nu te doen?* what do you intend to do now?

de **denker** /dɛŋkər/ (pl: -s) thinker

de **denkfout** /dɛŋkfɑut/ (pl: -en) logical error, error of reasoning

de **denkpiste** /dɛŋkpistə/ (pl: -s, -n) [Belg] cast of mind

de **denksport** /dɛŋksport/ (pl: -en) puzzle solving, problem solving

de **denktank** /dɛŋktɛŋk/ (pl: -s) think tank

de **denkwijze** /dɛŋkwɛizə/ (pl: -n) way of thinking, mode of thought

de **dennenappel** /dɛnə(n)ɑpəl/ (pl: -s) pine cone; fir cone

de **dennenboom** /dɛnə(n)bom/ (pl: -bomen) pine (tree), fir

de **deodorant** /dejodorɑnt/ (pl: -s, -en) deodorant

depanneren /depɑnərə(n)/ (depanneerde, heeft gedepanneerd) [Belg] repair, put back on the road

het **departement** /depɑrtəmɛnt/ (pl: -en) department, ministry

depenaliseren /depenalizerə(n)/ (depenaliseerde, heeft gedepenaliseerd) [Belg] decriminalize

de **dependance** /depɛndɑ̃s/ (pl: -s) annex(e)

deplorabel /deplorɑbəl/ (adj) deplorable, lamentable

deponeren /depoŋerə(n)/ (deponeerde, heeft gedeponeerd) **1** deposit, place, put (down): *documenten bij de notaris ~* deposit documents with the notary's **2** file; lodge

deporteren /deportɛrə(n)/ (deporteerde, heeft gedeporteerd) deport; transport: *een gedeporteerde* a deportee (or: transportee)

het **deposito** /depozito/ (pl: -'s) deposit

het/de **depot** /depo/ (pl: -s) **1** deposit(ing), committing to safe keeping **2** (goods on) deposit, deposited goods (or: documents) **3** depot, store

deppen /dɛpə(n)/ (depte, heeft gedept) dab; pat (dry)

de **depressie** /deprɛsi/ (pl: -s) depression

depressief /deprɛsif/ (adj) depressed, depressive, low, dejected

depri /depri/ (adj) down, depressed: *zich ~ voelen* feel down (or: depressed)

deprimeren /deprimerə(n)/ (deprimeerde, heeft gedeprimeerd) depress, deject; oppress; dishearten

de **deputatie** /depyta(t)si/ (pl: -s) deputation, delegation: [Belg] *bestendige ~* provincial council, executive

der /dɛr/ (art) of (the)

de **derby** /dyrbi/ (pl: derbies) local derby

de ¹**derde** /dɛrdə/ (pl: -n) **1** third party: *in aanwezigheid van ~n* in the presence of a third party **2** third form: *in de ~ zitten* be in the third form

het ²**derde** /dɛrdə/ (pl: -n) third: *twee ~ van de kiezers* two thirds of the voters

³**derde** /dɛrdə/ (num) third: *de ~ mei* the third of May

derdegraads /dɛrdəɣrats/ (adj) third-rate

derderangs /dɛrdərɑŋs/ (adj) third-rate, third-class

de **derde wereld** /dɛrdəwerəlt/ Third World

het **derdewereldland** /dɛrdəwerəltlɑnt/ Third World country, developing country

dereguleren /dereɣylerə(n)/ (dereguleerde, heeft gedereguleerd) deregulate

deren /derə(n)/ (deerde, heeft gedeerd) hurt, harm, injure

dergelijk /dɛrɣələk/ (dem pron) similar, (the) like, such(like): *wijn, bier en ~e dranken* wine, beer and drinks of that sort; *iets ~s heb ik nog nooit meegemaakt* I have never experienced anything like it

derhalve /dɛrhɑlvə/ (adv) therefore, so

het **derivaat** /derivat/ (pl: derivaten) derivative

dermate /dɛrmatə/ (adv) so (much), to such an extent, such (that)

de **dermatologie** /dɛrmatoloɣi/ dermatology

de **dermatoloog** /dɛrmatolox/ (pl: -logen) dermatologist

dertien /dɛrtin/ (num) thirteen; [in dates] thirteenth: ~ *is* een ongeluksgetal thirteen is an unlucky number; zo gaan er ~ in een dozijn they are two a penny

dertiende /dɛrtində/ (num) thirteenth

dertig /dɛrtəχ/ (num) thirty; [in dates] thirtieth: zij is *rond* de ~ she is thirtyish

dertigste /dɛrtəχstə/ (num) thirtieth

derven /dɛrvə(n)/ (derfde, heeft gederfd) lose, miss

¹**des** /dɛs/ (adv) wherefore, on that (or: which) count ‖ ~ *te* beter all the better; hoe meer mensen er komen, ~ *te* beter ik me voel the more people come, the better I feel

²**des** /dɛs/ (art) of (the), (the) …'s: de heer ~ *huizes* the master of the house

desalniettemin /dɛsalnitəmɪn/ (adv) nevertheless, nonetheless

desastreus /dezastrøs/ (adj, adv) disastrous: de wedstrijd *verliep* ~ the match turned into a disaster

desbetreffend /dɛzbətrɛfənt/ (adj) relevant; appropriate; respective: de ~e *afdelingen* the departments concerned (or: in question)

deserteren /dezɛrterə(n)/ (deserteerde, is gedeserteerd) desert: *uit* het leger ~ desert (the army)

de **deserteur** /dezɛrtør/ (pl: -s) deserter

de **desertie** /dezɛr(t)si/ (pl: -s) desertion

desgevraagd /dɛsχəvraχt/ (adv) if required (or: requested): ~ *deelde* zij *mee* on being asked, she declared

desgewenst /dɛsχəwɛnst/ (adv) if required (or: desired)

het **design** [dizɑjn/ design; designer: *design-jeans* designer jeans

de **desillusie** /dɛsɪlyzi/ (pl: -s) disillusion; disillusionment

desinfecteren /dɛsɪnfɛkterə(n)/ (desinfecteerde, heeft gedesinfecteerd) disinfect

de **desintegratie** /dɛsɪnteɣra(t)si/ (pl: -s) disintegration, decomposition

de **desinteresse** /dɛsɪntərɛsə/ lack of interest

deskundig /dɛskʏndəχ/ (adj, adv) expert (in, at), professional: een zaak ~ *beoordelen* judge a matter expertly; zij is zeer ~ *op* het gebied van she's an authority on

de **deskundige** /dɛskʏndəɣə/ (pl: -n) expert (in, at), authority (on), specialist (in)

de **deskundigheid** /dɛskʏndəχhɛit/ expertise, professionalism: zijn *grote* ~ op dit gebied his great expertise in this field

desnoods /dɛsnots/ (adv) if need be, if necessary; in an emergency, at a pinch

desolaat /dezolat/ (adj) desolate

desondanks /dɛsondɑnks/ (adv) in spite of this, in spite of (all) that, all the same, for all

that: ~ *protesteerde* hij niet in spite of all that he did not protest

de **desoriëntatie** /dɛsorijɛnta(t)si/ disorientation

desperaat /dɛsperat/ (adj, adv) desperate

de **despoot** /dɛspot/ (pl: despoten) despot, autocrat, tyrant

het **dessert** /dɛsɛːr/ (pl: -en) dessert, pudding: wat wil je *als* ~? what would you like for dessert?

het **dessin** /dɛsɛ̃/ (pl: -s) design, pattern

destabiliseren /destabilizerə(n)/ (destabiliseerde, heeft/is gedestabiliseerd) destabilize

destijds /dɛstɛits/ (adv) at the (or: that) time, then, in those days

de **destructie** /dɛstrʏksi/ (pl: -s) destruction

destructief /dɛstrʏktif/ (adj, adv) destructive

detacheren /detaʃerə(n)/ (detacheerde, heeft gedetacheerd) **1** second, send on secondment **2** attach (to), second, post (to)

het **detail** /detɑj/ (pl: -s) detail, particular; specifics: *in* ~s treden go into detail

de **detailhandel** /detɑjhɑndəl/ retail trade

de **detaillist** /detɑjɪst/ (pl: -en) retailer

detecteren /detɛkterə(n)/ (detecteerde, heeft gedetecteerd) detect, discover

de **detectiepoort** /detɛksiport/ (pl: -en) security gate, metal detector

de **detective** /ditɛktɪf/ (pl: -s) **1** detective: *particulier* ~ private detective (or: investigator) **2** detective novel, whodunit

de **detector** /detɛktɔr/ (pl: -s, -en) detector

de **detentie** /detɛnsi/ (pl: -s) detention, arrest, custody

determineren /detɛrminerə(n)/ (determineerde, heeft gedetermineerd) **1** determine, establish **2** [biology] identify

detineren /detinerə(n)/ (detineerde, heeft gedetineerd) detain: *in* Scheveningen gedetineerd zijn be on remand in Scheveningen (prison)

detoneren /detonerə(n)/ (detoneerde, heeft/is gedetoneerd) **1** be out of tune [also fig]: het gebouw detoneert *met* de omgeving the building is out of tune with (or: clashes with) its surroundings **2** detonate, explode

het **deuce** /djus/ deuce

de **deugd** /døχt/ (pl: -en) **1** virtuousness, morality **2** virtue, merit

deugdelijk /døɣdələk/ (adj) sound, good, reliable

deugdzaam /døχtsam/ (adj, adv) virtuous, good, upright, honest

de **deugdzaamheid** /døχtsamhɛit/ virtuousness, uprightness, honesty

deugen /døɣə(n)/ (deugde, heeft gedeugd) **1** be no good; be good for nothing: die jongen *heeft* nooit willen ~ that boy has always been a bad lot **2** be wrong (or: unsuitable, unfit): *die man deugt niet **voor** zijn werk* that man's no good at his job

de **deugniet** /dǫχnɪt/ (pl: -en) rascal, scamp, scallywag

de **deuk** /døk/ (pl: -en) **1** dent **2** [fig] blow, shock: *zijn zelfvertrouwen heeft een **flinke** ~ gekregen* his self-confidence took a terrible knock **3** fit: *we lagen **in** een ~* we were in stitches

deuken /dǫkə(n)/ (deukte, heeft gedeukt) dent; [fig] damage

de **deun** /døn/ (pl: -en) tune

de **deur** /dør/ (pl: -en) door: *voor een **gesloten** ~ komen* find no one in; *de ~ voor iemands neus **dichtdoen (dichtgooien)*** shut (or: slam) the door in s.o.'s face; *zij **komt** de ~ niet meer **uit*** she never goes out any more; *iem. de ~ **uitzetten*** turn s.o. out of the house; ***aan** de ~ kloppen* knock at (or: on) the door; *vroeger kwam de bakker bij ons **aan** de ~* the baker used to call at the house; ***buiten** de ~ eten* eat out; ***met** de ~en gooien* slam doors; ***met** de ~ in huis vallen* come straight to the point

de **deurbel** /dørbɛl/ (pl: -len) doorbell

de **deurdranger** /dørdraŋər/ (pl: -s) doorspring

de **deurknop** /dørknɔp/ (pl: -pen) doorknob

de **deurmat** /dørmɑt/ (pl: -ten) doormat

de **deuropening** /døropənɪŋ/ (pl: -en) doorway

de **deurpost** /dørpɔst/ (pl: -en) doorpost

de **deurwaarder** /dørwardər/ (pl: -s) processserver, bailiff; usher

de **devaluatie** /devalywa(t)si/ (pl: -s) devaluation

devalueren /devalywerə(n)/ (devalueerde, heeft gedevalueerd) devalue: *de **yen** is 10 % gedevalueerd* the yen has been devalued by 10 %

het **devies** /dəvis/ (pl: deviezen) motto, device

de **deviezen** /dəvizə(n)/ (foreign) exchange

de **¹devoot** /devot/ (pl: devoten) devotee

²devoot /devot/ (adj, adv) devout

de **devotie** /devo(t)si/ (pl: -s) devotion

deze /dezə/ (dem pron) this; these; this one; these (ones): *wil je ~ (hier)?* do you want this one? (or: these ones?); *een ~r **dagen** one of these days || **bij** ~n meld ik u I herewith inform you

dezelfde /dəzɛlvdə/ (dem pron) the same: *van ~ **datum** of the same date; **wil** je weer ~?* (would you like the) same again?; *op **precies** ~ dag* on the very same day

dhr. (abbrev) *de heer* Mr

de **dia** /dija/ (pl: -'s) slide, transparency

de **diabetes** /dijabetəs/ diabetes

de **diabeticus** /dijabetɪkʏs/ (pl: diabetici) diabetic

het/de **diadeem** /dijadem/ (pl: diademen) diadem

het **diafragma** /dijafrɑɣma/ (pl: -'s) diaphragm, stop

de **diagnose** /dijaɣnozə/ (pl: -n, -s) diagnosis

diagnosticeren /dijaɣnɔstiserə(n)/ (diagnosticeerde, heeft gediagnosticeerd) diagnose

de **¹diagonaal** /dijaɣonal/ diagonal

²diagonaal /dijaɣonal/ (adj) diagonal

het **diagram** /dijaɣrɑm/ (pl: -men) diagram, graph, chart

de **diaken** /dijakə(n)/ (pl: -s, -en) deacon

het **dialect** /dijalɛkt/ (pl: -en) dialect

de **dialoog** /dijalox/ (pl: dialogen) dialogue

het **dialoogvenster** /dijaloxfɛnstər/ (pl: -s) dialog box

de **dialyse** /dijalizə/ (pl: -n) dialysis, (haemo)dialysis

het/de **diamant** /dijamɑnt/ (pl: -en) diamond: *een ~ **slijpen** polish (or: cut) a diamond

diamanten /dijamɑntə(n)/ (adj) diamond: *een ~ **broche** a diamond brooch

de **diameter** /dijametər/ (pl: -s) diameter

diametraal /dijametral/ (adj, adv) diametral: [fig] *dat staat er ~ **tegenover*** that is diametrically opposed to it

de **diaprojector** /dijaprojɛktor/ (pl: -s) slide projector

de **diarree** /dijare/ diarrhoea

de **diaspora** /dijɔspora/ Diaspora

¹dicht /dɪχt/ (adj) **1** closed, shut; drawn; off: *mondje ~* mum's the word; *de afvoer **zit** ~* the drain is blocked (up) **2** tight **3** close-lipped, tight-lipped, close(-mouthed) **4** close, thick, dense, compact: *een gebied met een ~e **bevolking*** a densely populated area; *~e **mist** thick (or: dense) fog

²dicht /dɪχt/ (adv) close (to), near: *ze zaten ~ **opeengepakt*** they sat tightly packed together; *hij woont ~ **in** de buurt* he lives near here

dichtbegroeid /dɪχtbəɣrujt/ (adj) thick, dense, thickly wooded

dichtbevolkt /dɪχtbəvɔlkt/ (adj) densely populated

dichtbij /dɪχtbɛi/ (adv) close by, near by, nearby: *van ~* from close up

dichtbinden /dɪχtbɪndə(n)/ (bond dicht, heeft dichtgebonden) tie up

de **dichtbundel** /dɪχtbʏndəl/ (pl: -s) collection of poems, book of poetry

dichtdoen /dɪχdun/ (deed dicht, heeft dichtgedaan) close, shut; draw: *geen **oog** ~* not sleep a wink

dichtdraaien /dɪχdrajə(n)/ (draaide dicht, heeft dichtgedraaid) turn off; close

dichten /dɪχtə(n)/ (dichtte, heeft gedicht) **1** write poetry, compose verses **2** stop (up), fill (up); seal: *een **gat** ~* stop a gap; mend a hole

de **dichter** /dɪχtər/ (pl: -s) poet

dichterbij /dɪχtərbɛi/ (adv) nearer, closer

dichterlijk /dɪχtərlək/ (adj, adv) poetic(al): *~e **vrijheid** poetic licence

dichtgaan /dɪҳtҳan/ (ging dicht, is dichtgegaan) close; shut; heal: *de deur gaat niet dicht* the door won't shut; *op zaterdag gaan de winkels vroeg dicht* the shops close early on Saturdays

dichtgooien /dɪҳtҳojə(n)/ (gooide dicht, heeft dichtgegooid) **1** slam (to, shut); bang **2** fill up, fill in

dichtgroeien /dɪҳtҳrujə(n)/ (groeide dicht, is dichtgegroeid) **1** close; heal (up); grow thick **2** get fat, gain weight

de **dichtheid** /dɪҳtheit/ density; thickness, compactness

dichtklappen /dɪҳtklapə(n)/ (klapte dicht, heeft/is dichtgeklapt) snap shut, snap to; slam (shut)

dichtknijpen /dɪҳtknɛipə(n)/ (kneep dicht, heeft dichtgeknepen) squeeze

dichtknopen /dɪҳtknopə(n)/ (knoopte dicht, heeft dichtgeknoopt) button (up), fasten

de **dichtkunst** /dɪҳtkʏnst/ (art of) poetry

dichtmaken /dɪҳtmakə(n)/ (maakte dicht, heeft dichtgemaakt) close, fasten

dichtplakken /dɪҳtplakə(n)/ (plakte dicht, heeft dichtgeplakt) seal (up); stick down; close; stop

¹**dichtslaan** /dɪҳtslan/ (sloeg dicht, is dichtgeslagen) slam shut, bang shut

²**dichtslaan** /dɪҳtslan/ (sloeg dicht, heeft dichtgeslagen) bang (shut), slam (shut); snap shut: *de deur voor iemands neus ~* slam the door in s.o.'s face

dichtslibben /dɪҳtslɪbə(n)/ (slibde dicht, is dichtgeslibd) silt up, become silted up

dichtspijkeren /dɪҳtspɛikərə(n)/ (spijkerde dicht, heeft dichtgespijkerd) nail up (or: down), board up

dichtstbijzijnd /dɪҳstbɛizɛint/ (adj) nearest

dichtstoppen /dɪҳtstɔpə(n)/ (stopte dicht, heeft dichtgestopt) stop (up); fill (up); plug (up)

dichttrekken /dɪҳtrɛkə(n)/ (trok dicht, heeft dichtgetrokken) close; draw: *de deur achter zich ~* pull the door to behind one

de **dichtvorm** /dɪҳtfɔrm/: *in ~* in poetic form, in verse

dichtvouwen /dɪҳtfɑuwə(n)/ (vouwde dicht, heeft dichtgevouwen) fold up

dichtvriezen /dɪҳtfrizə(n)/ (vroor dicht, is dichtgevroren) freeze (over, up); be frozen (up); be frozen over

dichtzitten /dɪҳtsɪtə(n)/ (zat dicht, heeft dichtgezeten) be closed, be blocked (or: locked): *mijn neus zit dicht* my nose is blocked up

het **dictaat** /dɪktat/ (pl: dictaten) **1** (lecture) notes **2** dictation

de **dictator** /dɪktatɔr/ (pl: -s) dictator

dictatoriaal /dɪktatorijal/ (adj, adv) dictatorial

de **dictatuur** /dɪktatyr/ (pl: dictaturen) dictatorship

het **dictee** /dɪkte/ (pl: -s) dictation

dicteren /dɪkterə(n)/ (dicteerde, heeft gedicteerd) dictate

de **didacticus** /didɔktikʏs/ (pl: didactici) didactician

de **didactiek** /didɔktik/ didactics

didactisch /didɔktis/ (adj, adv) didactic

¹**die** /di/ (dem pron) **1** that; those; that one; those (ones): *heb je ~ nieuwe film van Spielberg al gezien?* have you seen this new film by Spielberg?; *~ grote* of *~ kleine?* the big one or the small one?; *niet deze maar ~ (daar)* not this one, that one; *mevrouw ~ en ~* Mrs so and so, Mrs such and such **2** that; those; that one; those (ones): *mijn boeken en ~ van mijn zus* my books and my sister's (or: those of my sister); *~ tijd is voorbij* those times are over; *~ van mij, jou, hem, haar, ons, jullie, hen* mine, yours, his, hers, ours, yours, theirs; *ze draagt altijd van ~ korte rokjes* she always wears (those) short skirts; *ken je ~ van ~ Belg ~ …* do you know the one about the Belgian who …?; *~ is goed* that's a good one; *o, ~!* oh, him! (or: her!); *waar is je auto? ~ staat in de garage* where's your car? it's in the garage; *~ zit!* bullseye!, touché!

²**die** /di/ (pron) that; [pers also] who; whom; which: *de kleren ~ u besteld heeft* the clothes (that, which) you ordered; *de man ~ daar loopt, is mijn vader* the man (that is, who is) walking over there is my father; *de mensen ~ ik spreek, zijn heel vriendelijk* the people (who, that) I talk to are very nice; *dezelfde ~ ik heb* the same one (as) I've got; *zijn vrouw, ~ arts is, rijdt in een grote Volvo* his wife, who's a doctor, drives a big Volvo

het **dieet** /dijet/ (pl: diëten) diet: *op ~ zijn* be on a diet

de **dief** /dif/ (pl: dieven) thief, robber; burglar: *houd de ~!* stop thief!

de **diefstal** /difstal/ (pl: -len) theft; robbery; burglary

diegene /diɣenə/ (pron) he, she: *~n die* those who

dienaangaande /dinaŋɣandə/ (adv) as to that, with respect (or: reference) to that

de **dienaar** /dinar/ (pl: dienaren) servant

het **dienblad** /dimblɑt/ (pl: -en) (dinner-)tray, (serving) tray

¹**dienen** /dinə(n)/ (diende, heeft gediend) **1** serve: *dat dient nergens toe* that is (of) no use **2** serve as, serve for, be used as (or: for): *vensters ~ om licht en lucht toe te laten* windows serve the purpose of letting in light and air **3** need, should, ought to: *u dient onmiddellijk te vertrekken* you are to leave immediately

²**dienen** /dinə(n)/ (diende, heeft gediend)

1 serve, attend (to), minister: *dat dient het algemeen belang* it is in the public interest **2** serve, help ‖ *iem. van advies ~* give s.o. advice; *hij was er niet van gediend* none of that with him, he didn't want that
dienovereenkomstig /dinovərenkᴐmstəx/ (adv) accordingly
diens /dins/ (dem pron) his
de **dienst** /dinst/ (pl: -en) **1** service: *zich in ~ stellen van* place o.s. in the service of; *ik ben een maand geleden als verkoper in ~ getreden bij deze firma* a month ago I joined this company as a salesman; *in ~ nemen* take on, engage; *in ~ zijn* do one's military service **2** duty: *ik heb morgen geen ~* I am off duty tomorrow **3** service, department: *de ~ openbare werken* the public works department **4** service, office: *iem. een goede ~ bewijzen* do s.o. a good turn; *je kunt me een ~ bewijzen* you can do me a favour **5** place, position: *in vaste* (or: *tijdelijke*) *~ zijn* hold a permanent (or: temporary) appointment; *iem. in ~ hebben* employ s.o.; *in ~ zijn bij iem.* be in s.o.'s service ‖ *~ doen (als)* serve (as, for); *de ~ uitmaken* run the show, call the shots; *tot uw ~* you're welcome; *iem. van ~ zijn met* be of service to s.o. with
de **dienstauto** /dinstɑuto/ (pl: -'s) official car; company car
dienstbaar /dinstbar/ (adj) helpful: *zich ~ opstellen* be of service
de **dienstbode** /dinstbodə/ (pl: -n, -s) servant (girl), maid(servant)
dienstdoen /dinsdun/ (deed dienst, heeft dienstgedaan) serve (as/for), be used (as/for)
dienstdoend /dinzdunt/ (adj) on duty; in charge; acting
het **dienstencentrum** /dinstə(n)sɛntrʏm/ (pl: -centra) social service centre
de **dienstencheque** /dinstə(n)ʃɛk/ (pl: -s) [Belg] service voucher
de **dienstensector** /dinstə(n)sɛktᴐr/ services sector, service industries
het **dienstjaar** /dinstjar/ (pl: -jaren) year of service; seniority
de **dienstlift** /dinstlɪft/ (pl: -en) service lift
de **dienstmededeling** /dinstmedədelɪŋ/ (pl: -en) staff announcement
het **dienstmeisje** /dinstmɛiʃə/ maid(servant), housemaid
de **dienstorder** /dinstᴐrdər/ (pl: -s) (official) order, instructions
het **dienstpistool** /dinstpistol/ (pl: -pistolen) duty weapon
de **dienstplicht** /dinstplɪxt/ (compulsory) military service, conscription: *vervangende ~* alternative national service; community service
dienstplichtig /dinstplɪxtəx/ (adj) eligible for military service: *de ~e leeftijd bereiken* become of military age; *niet ~* exempt from

military service
de **dienstplichtige** /dinstplɪxtəyə/ conscript
de **dienstregeling** /dinstreyəlɪŋ/ (pl: -en) timetable: *een vlucht met vaste ~* a scheduled flight
de **diensttijd** /dinstɛit/ (period, length of) service, term of office: *buiten* (or: *onder*) *~* when off (or: on) duty
het **dienstverband** /dinstfərbɑnt/ employment: *in los* (or: *vast*) *~ werken* be employed on a temporary (or: permanent) basis
de **dienstverlening** /dinstfərlenɪŋ/ service(s)
de **dienstweigeraar** /dinstwɛiyərar/ (pl: -s) conscientious objector
dientengevolge /dintɛŋyəvᴐlyə/ (adv) consequently, as a consequence
¹**diep** /dip/ (adj) deep; [fig also] profound; total, impenetrable: *twee meter ~* two metres deep; *~er maken* deepen; *in het ~e gegooid worden* be thrown in at the deep end; *een ~e duisternis* utter darkness; *in ~ gepeins verzonken* (sunk) deep in thought; *alles was in ~e rust* everything was utterly peaceful; *een ~e slaap* a deep sleep; *~ in zijn hart* deep (down) in one's heart; *uit het ~ste van zijn hart* from the bottom of one's heart ‖ *een ~e stem* a deep voice; *~ blauw* deep blue
²**diep** /dip/ (adv) **1** deep(ly), low: *~ zinken (vallen)* sink low; *~ ongelukkig zijn* be deeply unhappy; *hij is ~ verontwaardigd* he is deeply (or: mortally) indignant; *~ ademhalen* breathe deeply; take a deep breath; *~ nadenken* think hard; *de haat zit ~* the hatred runs deep **2** deep, far
diepgaand /dipxɑnt/ (adj, adv) profound, searching, in-depth: *~e discussie* in-depth (or: deep) discussion
de **diepgang** /dipxɑŋ/ **1** draught **2** depth, profundity
de **diepte** /diptə/ (pl: -n, -s) **1** depth, depth(s), profundity **2** trough, hollow
het **diepte-interview** /diptəɪntərvjuː/ (pl: -s) in-depth interview
het **dieptepunt** /diptəpʏnt/ (pl: -en) **1** (absolute) low **2** all-time low, rock bottom: *een ~ in een relatie* a low point in a relationship
de **diepvries** /dipfris/ deep-freeze, freezer
de **diepvrieskist** /dipfriskɪst/ (pl: -en) (chest-type) freezer, deep-freeze
de **diepvriesmaaltijd** /dipfrismaltɛit/ (pl: -en) freezer meal; [Am] TV dinner
diepvriezen /dipfrizə(n)/ (vroor diep, heeft diepgevroren) (deep-)freeze
de **diepvriezer** /dipfrizər/ (pl: -s) deepfreeze, freezer
diepzeeduiken /dipsedœykə(n)/ deep-sea diving
diepzinnig /dipsɪnəx/ (adj, adv) **1** profound, discerning **2** profound, pensive: *een ~e blik* a thoughtful (or: pensive) look
de **diepzinnigheid** /dipsɪnəxhɛit/ profundity,

profoundness, depth

het **dier** /dir/ (pl: -en) animal, creature; beast
dierbaar /dirbar/ (adj) dear, much-loved, beloved
de **dierenambulance** /dirə(n)ambyläsə/ (pl: -s) animal ambulance
de **dierenarts** /dirə(n)ɑrts/ (pl: -en) veterinary surgeon, vet
het **dierenasiel** /dirə(n)azil/ (pl: -en) animal home (or: shelter)
de **dierenbescherming** /dirə(n)bəsχɛrmɪŋ/ animal protection, prevention of cruelty to animals
de **dierenbeul** /dirə(n)bøl/ (pl: -en) s.o. who is cruel to animals
de **dierendag** /dirə(n)dɑχ/ [roughly] animal day, pets' day
de **dierenmishandeling** /dirə(n)mɪshɑndəlɪŋ/ cruelty to animals, maltreatment of animals
het **dierenpension** /dirə(n)pɛnʃɔn/ (pl: -s) (boarding) kennel(s)
de **dierenriem** /dirə(n)rim/ zodiac
het **dierenrijk** /dirə(n)rɛɪk/ animal kingdom (or: world)
de **dierentemmer** /dirə(n)tɛmər/ (pl: -s) animal trainer; lion-tamer
de **dierentuin** /dirə(n)tœyn/ (pl: -en) zoo, animal park
de **dierenvriend** /dirə(n)vrint/ (pl: -en) animal (or: pet) lover
de **dierenwinkel** /dirə(n)wɪŋkəl/ (pl: -s) pet shop
de **diergeneeskunde** /dirɣəneskyndə/ veterinary medicine
dierlijk /dirlək/ (adj) animal; [depr] bestial; brute; brutish: de ~e **aard (natuur)** animal nature
de **dierproef** /dirpruf/ (pl: -proeven) animal experiment (or: test)
de **diersoort** /dirsort/ (pl: -en) animal species: bedreigde ~en endangered species (of animals)
de **diesel** /dizəl/ (pl: -s, -s) diesel (oil, fuel), derv: op ~ rijden take diesel
de **dieselmotor** /dizəlmotər/ (pl: -en) diesel engine
de **dieselolie** /dizəloli/ diesel oil (or: fuel)
de **diëtist** /dijetɪst/ (pl: -en) dietitian
de **dievegge** /divɛɣə/ (pl: -s) thief; shoplifter
de **dievenklauw** /divə(n)klɑu/ (pl: -en) security lock
het **dievenpoortje** /divə(n)porcə/ (pl: -s) security label detector, anti-shoplifting alarm
diezelfde /dizɛlvdə/ (dem pron) the same, this same, that same
de **differentiaal** /dɪfərɛnʃal/ (pl: differentialen) differential
de **differentiaalrekening** /dɪfərɛn(t)ʃalrekənɪŋ/ differential calculus
de **differentiatie** /dɪfərɛn(t)ʃa(t)si/ (pl: -s) differentiation

het **differentieel** /dɪfərɛn(t)ʃel/ differential (gear)
differentiëren /dɪfərɛnʃerə(n)/ (differentieerde, heeft gedifferentieerd) differentiate (between), distinguish (between)
de **diffusie** /dɪfyzi/ diffusion, mixture
diffuus /dɪfys/ (adj) diffuse; scattered
de **difterie** /dɪftəri/ diphtheria
de **diggelen** /dɪɣələ(n)/ (pl): aan ~ slaan smash to smithereens
de **digibeet** /diɣibet/ (pl: digibeten) computer illiterate
digitaal /diɣital/ (adj, adv) digital
digitaliseren /diɣitalizerə(n)/ (digitaliseerde, heeft gedigitaliseerd) digit(al)ize
de **dij** /dɛi/ (pl: -en) thigh; ham
het **dijbeen** /dɛiben/ (pl: dijbenen) thigh bone
de **dijk** /dɛik/ (pl: -en) bank, embankment; [in the Netherlands] dike: een ~ **(aan)leggen** throw up a bank (or: an embankment) ‖ iem. **aan** de ~ zetten sack s.o., lay s.o. off
de **dijkdoorbraak** /dɛɪgdorbrak/ (pl: -braken) bursting of a dike, giving way of a dike
¹**dik** /dɪk/ (adj) **1** thick: 10 **cm** ~ 10 cm thick; de ~ke **darm** the large intestine; ze stonden tien **rijen** ~ they stood ten (rows) deep; ~ **worden** thicken, set, congeal **2** thick, fat, bulky: een ~ke **buik** a paunch **3** fat, stout, corpulent: een ~ke **man** a fat man **4** swollen: ~ke **vingers** plump fingers **5** thick, close, great: ~ke **vrienden** zijn be great (or: close) friends ‖ ~ **doen** swank, swagger, boast
²**dik** /dɪk/ (adv) **1** thick, ample, good: ~ **tevreden** (zijn) (be) well-satisfied; ~ **onder** het stof thick with dust; het er ~ bovenop leggen lay it on thick; dat zit er ~ in that's quite on the cards **2** thick, heavy, dense ‖ door ~ en dun gaan go through thick and thin
de **dikdoenerij** /dɪgdunərɛi/ bragging, boasting
dikhuidig /dɪkhœydəχ/ (adj) pachyderm(at)ous, thick-skinned
de **dikkerd** /dɪkərt/ (pl: -s) fatty, piggy: dat is een **gezellige** ~ he/she is round (or: fat) and cuddly
de **dikkop** /dɪkɔp/ (pl: -pen) tadpole
de **dikte** /dɪktə/ (pl: -s) **1** fatness, thickness **2** thickness; gauge: een ~ **van** vier voet four feet thick **3** thickness, density
dikwijls /dɪkwəls/ (adv) often, frequently
de **dikzak** /dɪksɑk/ (pl: -ken) fatty, fatso
het **dilemma** /dilɛma/ (pl: -'s) dilemma
de **dilettant** /dilɛtɑnt/ (pl: -en) dilettante, amateur
de **dille** /dɪlə/ (pl: -n) dill
de **dimensie** /dimɛnsi/ (pl: -s) **1** dimension, measurement, meaning **2** dimension, perspective
het **dimlicht** /dɪmlɪχt/ (pl: -en) dipped headlights

¹dimmen /dɪmə(n)/ (dimde, heeft gedimd) cool it: *effe ~, da's niet leuk meer* cool it, it's not funny any more

²dimmen /dɪmə(n)/ (dimde, heeft gedimd) dip (the headlights), shade

de **dimmer** /dɪmər/ (pl: -s) dimmer(-switch)

de **dimsum** /dɪmsum/ (pl: -) dimsum

het **diner** /dine/ (pl: -s) dinner: *aan het ~* at dinner

dineren /dinerə(n)/ (dineerde, heeft gedineerd) dine, have dinner

het **ding** /dɪŋ/ (pl: -en) **1** thing, object; gadget: *en (al) dat soort ~en* and (all) that sort of thing **2** thing, matter, affair: *doe geen gekke ~en* don't do anything foolish; *de ~en bij hun naam noemen* call a spade a spade ‖ *een lekker ~* a nice (*or:* sweet) little thing

dingen /dɪŋə(n)/ (dong, heeft gedongen) compete (for), strive (after/for)

de **dinges** /dɪŋəs/ [inform] thingummy, what's-his-name, what's-her-name

de **dinosaurus** /dinosaurəs/ (pl: -sen) dinosaur

de **dinsdag** /dɪnzdɑx/ (pl: -en) Tuesday: [Belg] *vette ~* Shrove Tuesday

dinsdags /dɪnzdɑxs/ (adj) Tuesday

de **diode** /dijodə/ (pl: -n, -s) diode

het **dioxine** /dijoksinə/ dioxin

de **dip** /dɪp/ (pl: -s) dip: *in een ~ zitten* be going through a bad patch

het **diploma** /diplomə/ (pl: -'s) diploma, certificate: *een ~ behalen* qualify, graduate

de **diplomaat** /diplomat/ (pl: diplomaten) diplomat

het **diplomatenkoffertje** /diplomɑtə(n)kɔfərcə/ (pl: -s) attaché case

de **diplomatie** /diploma(t)si/ **1** diplomacy **2** diplomatic corps, diplomats: *hij gaat in de ~* he is going to enter the diplomatic service

diplomatiek /diplomatik/ (adj, adv) **1** diplomatic: *langs ~e weg* by diplomacy **2** diplomatic, tactful

diplomeren /diplomerə(n)/ (diplomeerde, heeft gediplomeerd) certificate: *niet gediplomeerd* unqualified, untrained

dippen /dɪpə(n)/ (dipte, heeft gedipt) **1** dip **2** dip, insert

de **dipsaus** /dɪpsaus/ (pl: -sauzen) dip

¹direct /dirɛkt/ (adj) **1** direct, immediate, straight: *zijn ~e chef* his immediate superior; *de ~e oorzaak* the immediate cause; *~e uitzending* live broadcast **2** prompt, immediate: *~e levering* prompt delivery

²direct /dirɛkt/ (adv) **1** direct(ly), at once: *kom ~* come at once (*or:* straightaway); *per ~* straightaway; [Am] right now **2** presently, directly: *ik ben ~ klaar* I'll be ready in a minute ‖ *niet ~ vriendelijk* not exactly kind

de **directeur** /dirɛktør/ (pl: -en, -s) manager; (managing) director; principal; headmaster; superintendent; governor

de **directie** /dirɛksi/ (pl: -s) management

het **directielid** /dirɛksilɪt/ member of the board (of directors)

de **directiesecretaresse** /dirɛksisɪkrətarɛsə/ (pl: -s) executive secretary

de **directory** /dɑjrɛktəri/ (pl: -'s) directory

de **directrice** /dirɛktrisə/ (pl: -s) *see* directeur

de **dirigeerstok** /diriɣerstɔk/ (pl: -ken) baton

de **dirigent** /diriɣɛnt/ (pl: -en) conductor; choirmaster

dirigeren /diriɣerə(n)/ (dirigeerde, heeft gedirigeerd) conduct; control

de **dis** /dɪs/ (pl: -sen) [form] table

de **discipel** /disipəl/ (pl: -en) disciple, follower

disciplinair /disiplinɛ:r/ (adj, adv) disciplinary: *een ~e maatregel* a disciplinary measure

de **discipline** /disiplinə/ discipline

disciplineren /disiplinerə(n)/ (disciplineerde, heeft gedisciplineerd) discipline, train: *hij werkt zeer gedisciplineerd aan zijn nieuwe roman* he applies himself to his new novel with strict self-discipline

de **discman** /dɪskmɛːn/ (pl: -s) discman

de **disco** /dɪsko/ (pl: -'s) disco

het **disconto** /dɪskɔnto/ (pl: -'s) discount

de **discotheek** /dɪskotek/ (pl: discotheken) **1** record library (*or:* collection) **2** record library **3** discotheque

discreet /dɪskret/ (adj, adv) **1** discreet, delicate, tactful **2** discreet, unobtrusive: *een ~ tikje op de kamerdeur* a discreet tap on the door **3** delicate, secret

de **discrepantie** /dɪskrepɒnsi/ discrepancy

de **discretie** /dɪskreti/ **1** discretion, tact **2** discretion, secrecy

de **discriminatie** /dɪskrimina(t)si/ discrimination

discrimineren /dɪskriminerə(n)/ (discrimineerde, heeft gediscrimineerd) discriminate (against); [with direct object] segregate

de **discus** /dɪskys/ (pl: -sen) discus, disc

de **discussie** /dɪskysi/ (pl: -s) discussion, debate: *(het) onderwerp van ~ (zijn)* (be) under discussion; *een hevige (verhitte) ~* a heated discussion; *ter ~ staan* be under discussion, be open to discussion; *iets ter ~ stellen* **a)** bring sth. up for discussion; **b)** call sth. into question

discussiëren /dɪskyʃerə(n)/ (discussieerde, heeft gediscussieerd) discuss, debate, argue

de **discuswerpen** /dɪskyswɛrpə(n)/ discus throwing

discutabel /dɪskytabəl/ (adj) debatable, dubious, disputable

de **disk** /dɪsk/ (pl: -s) disk

de **diskdrive** /dɪsgdrɑjf/ (pl: -s) disk drive

de **diskette** /dɪskɛtə/ (pl: -s) diskette, floppy (disk)

de **diskjockey** /dɪskdʒɔki/ (pl: -s) disc jockey

het **diskrediet** /dɪskrədit/ discredit: *in ~ geraken* fall into discredit

diskwalificeren /dɪskwalifisẹrə(n)/ (diskwalificeerde, heeft gediskwalificeerd) disqualify

de **dispensatie** /dɪspɛnsạ(t)si/ (pl: -s) dispensation, exemption: ~ *verlenen (van)* grant dispensation (*or:* exemption) (from)

de **display** /dɪsplẹj/ (pl: -s) display

het **dispuut** /dɪspyt/ (pl: disputen) debating society

dissen /dɪsə(n)/ (diste, heeft gedist) insult, diss

de **dissertatie** /dɪsɛrtạ(t)si/ (pl: -s) (doctoral) dissertation, (doctoral) thesis

de **¹dissident** /dɪsidẹnt/ (pl: -en) dissident
   ²dissident /dɪsidẹnt/ (adj) dissident

de **dissonant** /dɪsonɑnt/ (pl: -en) dissonance, discord: [fig] *er was geen ~ te **horen*** not a note of discord was heard

zich **distantiëren** /dɪstɑnʃẹrə(n)/ (distantieerde zich, heeft zich gedistantieerd) distance, dissociate

de **distel** /dɪstəl/ (pl: -s) thistle

de **distillatie** /dɪstilạ(t)si/ distillation

distilleren /dɪstilẹrə(n)/ (distilleerde, heeft gedistilleerd) **1** distil **2** deduce, infer: *iets **uit** iemands woorden ~* deduce sth. from what s.o. says

distribueren /dɪstribywẹrə(n)/ (distribueerde, heeft gedistribueerd) distribute, dispense, hand out

het **district** /dɪstrɪkt/ (pl: -en) district, county

dit /dɪt/ (dem pron) this; these: *in ~ geval* in this case; *wat **zijn** ~?* what are these?

ditmaal /dɪtmal/ (adv) this time, for once

de **diva** /dịva/ (pl: -'s) diva

Divali /divạli/ Diwali

de **divan** /divạn/ (pl: -s) divan, couch

divers /divɛrs/ (adj) **1** diverse, various **2** various, several

de **diversen** /divɛrsə(n)/ (pl) sundries, miscellaneous

de **diversiteit** /divɛrsitẹit/ diversity, variety

het **dividend** /dividẹnt/ (pl: -en) dividend

de **divisie** /divịzi/ (pl: -s) division; league; class

dizzy /dɪzi/ (adj) dizzy: *ik **word** ~ van die stortvloed aan informatie* there's such a torrent of information it makes me dizzy

de **dj** /diːdʒe/ (pl: dj's) *diskjockey* DJ

de **djellaba** /djɛlaba/ (pl: -'s) djellaba

de **djembé** /djɛmbe/ djembe

Djibouti /djibụti/ Djibouti

de **Djiboutiaan** /djibucạn/ (pl: Djiboutianen) Djiboutian

Djiboutiaans /djibucạns/ (adj) Djiboutian

dm (abbrev) *decimeter* dm

d.m.v. (abbrev) *door middel van* by means of

het **DNA** /deɛnạ/ DNA: *ondernemen zit **in** zijn ~* business is in his genes, he's a born entrepreneur

het **DNA-onderzoek** /deɛnạɔndərzuk/ DNA-test

de **do** /do/ (pl: do's) do(h)

dobbelen /dɔbələ(n)/ (dobbelde, heeft gedobbeld) dice, play (at) dice

het **dobbelspel** /dɔbəlspɛl/ (pl: -len) dicing, game of dice

de **dobbelsteen** /dɔbəlsten/ (pl: -stenen) **1** dice: *met **dobbelstenen** gooien* throw the dice **2** dice, cube

de **dobber** /dɔbər/ (pl: -s) float || *hij had er een **zware** ~ aan* he found it a tough job

dobberen /dɔbərə(n)/ (dobberde, heeft gedobberd) float, bob: *op het water ~* bob up and down on the water

de **dobermannpincher** /dobərmɑnpɪnʃər/ (pl: -s) Doberman(n)(pinscher)

de **docent** /dosɛnt/ (pl: -en) teacher, instructor: *~ **aan** de universiteit* university lecturer

de **docentenkamer** /dosɛntə(n)kamər/ (pl: -s) staffroom

doceren /dosẹrə(n)/ (doceerde, heeft gedoceerd) teach; lecture

doch /dɔχ/ (conj) yet, but: *hij had haar gewaarschuwd, ~ zij wilde niet luisteren* he had warned her, yet (*or:* but, still) she wouldn't listen

de **dochter** /dɔχtər/ (pl: -s) daughter, (little) girl

de **dochtermaatschappij** /dɔχtərmatsχɑpɛi/ (pl: -en) subsidiary (company)

de **doctor** /dɔktɔr/ (pl: -en, -s) doctor

het **¹doctoraal** /dɔktorạl/ Master's (degree (*or:* exam)); [roughly] MA
   ²doctoraal /dɔktorạl/ (adj) [roughly] Master's, (post)graduate

het **doctoraat** /dɔktorạt/ (pl: doctoraten) doctorate

de **doctorandus** /dɔktorɑndʏs/ (pl: -sen, doctorandi) (title of) university graduate

de **doctrine** /dɔktrịnə/ (pl: -s) doctrine, dogma

het **document** /dokymɛnt/ (pl: -en) document, paper

documentair /dokymɛntɛːr/ (adj) documentary

de **documentaire** /dokymɛntɛːrə/ (pl: -s) documentary

de **documentatie** /dokymɛntạ(t)si/ documentation

documenteren /dokymɛntẹrə(n)/ (documenteerde, heeft gedocumenteerd) document, support with evidence

de **dode** /dọdə/ (pl: -n) dead person, the deceased

de **dodehoekspiegel** /dodəhụkspiɣəl/ (pl: -s) blind spot mirror

dodelijk /dọdələk/ (adj, adv) **1** deadly, mortal, lethal, fatal: *een ~ **ongeluk**, een ongeval met ~e **afloop*** a fatal accident **2** deadly, deathly, killing || *~ **vermoeid*** dead beat, dead tired

doden /dọdə(n)/ (doodde, heeft gedood) kill, murder, slay

de **dodencel** /dodə(n)sɛl/ (pl: -len) death cell
(or: row)

de **dodenherdenking** /dodə(n)hɛrdɛŋkɪŋ/
(pl: -en) commemoration of the dead

het **dodental** /dodə(n)tal/ (pl: -len) number of
deaths (or: casualties), death toll

de **doedelzak** /dudəlzɑk/ (pl: -ken) bagpipes:
op een ~ **spelen** play the bagpipes

de **doe-het-zelfzaak** /duətsɛlfsɑk/ (pl: -zaken)
do-it-yourself shop, DIY shop

de **doe-het-zelver** /duətsɛlvər/ (pl: -s) do-it-
yourselfer, DIY
doei /duj/ (int) [inform] bye(-bye), cheerio,
cheers: *dikke* ~ bye, catch ya later, see ya

het/de **doek** /duk/ **1** cloth, fabric **2** screen: *het witte*
~ the silver screen **3** canvas, painting **4** curtain; backcloth: *het ~ gaat op* the curtain rises ‖ *iets uit de* ~en doen disclose sth.

het **doekje** /dukjə/ (pl: -s) (piece of) cloth; tissue

het **doel** /dul/ (pl: -en) **1** target, purpose, ob-
ject(ive), aim, goal; destination **2** goal; net:
in eigen ~ schieten score an own goal; *zijn ~
bereiken* achieve one's aim; *het ~ heiligt de
middelen (niet)* the end justifies (or: does not
justify) the means
doelbewust /dulbəwʏst/ (adj, adv) determined, resolute

het **doeleinde** /dulɛində/ (pl: -n) **1** purpose,
aim, design **2** end, aim, purpose, destination: *voor eigen* (or: *privé*) ~*n* for one's own
(or: private) ends
doelen /dulə(n)/ (doelde, heeft gedoeld)
aim (at), refer (to), mean: *waar ik op doel is dit*
what I mean (or: am referring to, am driving
at) is this

het **doelgebied** /dulɣəbit/ (pl: -en) goal area
doelgericht /dulɣərɪxt/ (adj, adv) purposeful, purposive

de **doelgroep** /dulɣrup/ (pl: -en) target group
(or: audience)

de **doellijn** /dulɛin/ (pl: -en) goal line: *de bal
van de* ~ *halen* kick the ball from the line,
(make a) save on the line
doelloos /dulos/ (adj, adv) aimless, idle;
pointless

de **doelman** /dulmɑn/ (pl: -nen) goalkeeper
doelmatig /dulmatəx/ (adj, adv) suitable,
appropriate, functional, effective

de **doelmatigheid** /dulmatəxhɛit/ suitability,
expediency, effectiveness

de **doelpaal** /dulpal/ (pl: -palen) (goal)post

het **doelpunt** /dulpʏnt/ (pl: -en) goal, score: *een
~ afkeuren* disallow a goal; *een ~ maken* kick
(or: score) a goal; *met twee ~en verschil verliezen* lose by two goals

het **doelsaldo** /dulsaldo/ (pl: -'s, -saldi) goal difference

de **doelstelling** /dulstɛlɪŋ/ (pl: -en) aim, ob-
ject(ive)

de **doeltrap** /dultrɑp/ (pl: -pen) goal kick
doeltreffend /dultrɛfənt/ (adj, adv) effec-

tive, efficient

de **doelverdediger** /dulvərdedəɣər/ (pl: -s)
(goal)keeper; [Am] (goal)tender; goalie

het **doelwit** /dulwɪt/ (pl: -ten) target, aim, object: *een dankbaar* ~ *vormen* make an easy
victim (or: target)

de **doem** /dum/ doom

de **Doema** /duma/ duma
doemdenken /dumdɛŋkə(n)/ doom-mong-
ering, defeatism
doemen /dumə(n)/ doom, destine

het **doemscenario** /dumsənarijo/ worst-case
scenario

¹**doen** /dun/ (deed, heeft gedaan) **1** do, act,
behave: *gewichtig* ~ act important; ~ *alsof*
pretend; *je doet maar* go ahead, suit yourself
2 do, be: *ik doe er twee uur over* it takes me
two hours; *aan sport* ~ do sport(s), take part
in sport(s) ‖ *dat is geen manier van* ~ that's no
way to behave

²**doen** /dun/ (deed, heeft gedaan) **1** do,
make, take: *een oproep* ~ make an appeal;
uitspraak ~ pass judgement; *doe mij maar een
witte wijn* for me a white wine, I'll have a
white wine; *wat kom jij* ~? what do you
want?; *wat doet hij (voor de kost)?* what does
he do (for a living)? **2** put: *iets in zijn zak* ~ put
sth. in one's pocket **3** make, do: *dat doet me
plezier* I'm glad about that; *iem.* ~ *verdriet* (or:
pijn) ~ hurt s.o., cause s.o. grief (or: pain) **4** (+
het) work: *de remmen* ~ *het niet* the brakes
don't work **5** make: *we weten wat ons te* ~
staat we know what (we have, are) to do ‖
anders krijg je met mij te ~ or else you'll have
me to deal with; *dat doet er niet(s) toe* that's
beside the point; *niets aan te* ~ can't be
helped

het **doetje** /ducə/ (pl: -s) softy, milksop, wet

de **doevakantie** /duvakan(t)si/ (pl: -s) action
holiday; [Am] action vacation
dof /dɔf/ (adj, adv) **1** dim, dull; mat(t); tar-
nished: ~*fe tinten* dull (or: muted) hues (or:
tints) **2** dull, muffled: *een* ~*fe knal (dreun)* a
muffled boom

de **doffer** /dɔfər/ (pl: -s) cock-pigeon

de **dofheid** /dɔfhɛit/ dullness, dimness

de **dog** /dɔx/ (pl: -gen) mastiff

het **dogma** /dɔxma/ (pl: -'s) dogma
dogmatisch /dɔxmatis/ (adj, adv) dogmati-
c(al)

het **dok** /dɔk/ (pl: -ken) dock(yard)

de **doka** /doka/ (pl: -'s) darkroom
dokken /dɔkə(n)/ (dokte, heeft gedokt) [in-
form] fork out, cough up

de **dokter** /dɔktər/ (pl: -s, doktoren) doctor; GP:
een ~ *roepen (laten komen)* send for (or: call
in) a doctor ‖ ~*tje spelen* play doctors and
nurses
dokteren /dɔktərə(n)/ (dokterde, heeft ge-
dokterd) **1** practise **2** tinker (with (or: at)):
aan iets ~ tinker with sth.

het **doktersadvies** /dɔktərsɑtfis/ (pl: -adviezen) doctor's advice, medical advice

de **doktersassistente** /dɔktərsɑsistɛntə/ (medical) receptionist

het **doktersattest** /dɔktərsɑtɛst/ (pl: -en) medical (*or:* doctor's) certificate

de **doktersbehandeling** /dɔktərzbəhandəlɪŋ/ medical treatment

het **doktersvoorschrift** /dɔktərsforsxrɪft/ medical instructions, doctor's orders

dol /dɔl/ (adj) **1** mad, crazy: *het is om ~ van te **worden*** it is enough to drive you crazy; *~ **op** iets (iem.) zijn* be crazy about sth. (s.o.) **2** mad, wild, crazy: *door **het** ~le heen zijn* be beside o.s. with excitement (*or:* joy) **3** foolish, silly, daft: *~le **pret** hebben* have great fun **4** worn, slipping, stripped: *die **schroef** is ~* the screw is stripped (*or:* slipping) **5** crazy, whirling (round in circles): *het **kompas** is ~* the compass has gone crazy **6** mad, rabid

dolblij /dɔlblɛɪ/ (adj) overjoyed (about): *~ **zijn** met iets* be over the moon about sth.

doldwaas /dɔldwa̠s/ (adj) nutty, potty, absolutely crazy: *doldwaze **verwikkelingen*** hilarious twists and turns, a crazy mix-up

dolen /do̠lə(n)/ (doolde, heeft/is gedoold) wander (about), roam

de **dolfijn** /dɔlfɛin/ (pl: -en) dolphin

het **dolfinarium** /dɔlfina̠rijʏm/ (pl: -s, dolfinaria) dolphinarium

dolgraag /dɔlyra̠x/ (adv) with the greatest of pleasure: *ga je mee? ~* are you coming? I'd love to

de **dolk** /dɔlk/ (pl: -en) dagger

de **dolksteek** /dɔlkstek/ (pl: -steken) daggerthrust, stab

de **dollar** /dɔlɑr/ (pl: -s) dollar

het **dollarteken** /dɔlɑrtekə(n)/ (pl: -s) dollar sign || *~s **in** de ogen hebben* see a lot of dollar signs in front of s.o.'s eyes; have a pound sign for a brain

de **dolleman** /dɔləmɑn/ (pl: -nen) madman, lunatic

dollen /dɔlə(n)/ (dolde, heeft gedold) lark about, horse around

de ¹**dom** /dɔm/ (pl: -men) cathedral

²**dom** /dɔm/ (adj, adv) **1** stupid, simple, dumb: *zo ~ **als** het achtereind van een varken* as thick as two (short) planks **2** silly, daft: *sta niet zo ~ te **grijnzen!*** wipe that silly grin off your face! **3** sheer, pure: *~ **geluk*** sheer luck, a fluke **4** ignorant: *zich van de ~me houden* play ignorant, play (the) innocent

de **dombo** /dɔmbo/ (pl: -'s) [inform] dumbo

het **domein** /dɔmɛin/ (pl: -en) domain, territory

de **domeinnaam** /dɔmɛinam/ domain name

de **domheid** /dɔmhɛit/ (pl: -heden) stupidity, idiocy

het **domicilie** /domisi̠li/ domicile: *~ **kiezen** ten kantore van* elect domicile at the office of

dominant /dominɑnt/ (adj) dominant, overriding

de **dominee** /do̠mine/ (pl: -s) minister

domineren /domine̠rə(n)/ (domineerde, heeft gedomineerd) dominate

Dominica /domi̠nika/ Dominica

de **Dominicaan** /dominika̠n/ (pl: Dominicanen) Dominican

Dominicaans /dominika̠ns/ (adj) Dominican || *de ~e **Republiek*** the Dominican Republic

de **Dominicaanse Republiek** /dominika̠nsərepybli̠k/ Dominican Republic

het **domino** /do̠mino/ (pl: -'s) dominoes

het **domino-effect** /do̠minoɛfɛkt/ (pl: -en) knock-on effect; domino effect

het **dominospel** /do̠minospɛl/ **1** dominoes **2** set of dominoes

de **dominosteen** /do̠minosten/ (pl: -stenen) domino

dommelen /dɔmələ(n)/ (dommelde, heeft gedommeld) doze, drowse

de **domoor** /do̠mor/ (pl: domoren) idiot, fool, blockhead, dunce

dompelen /dɔmpələ(n)/ (dompelde, heeft gedompeld) plunge, dip, immerse

de **domper** /dɔmpər/ (pl: -s): *dit onverwachte bericht zette een ~ **op** de feestvreugde* this unexpected news put a damper on the party

de **dompteur** /dɔmtør/ (pl: -s) animal trainer (*or:* tamer)

domweg /dɔmwɛx/ (adv) (quite) simply, without a moment's thought, just

de **donateur** /donatør/ (pl: -s) donor; contributor; supporter

de **donatie** /dona̠(t)si/ (pl: -s) donation, gift

de **Donau** /do̠nɑu/ Danube

de **donder** /dɔndər/ (pl: -s) **1** thunder **2** [inform] carcass; [pers] devil: *op zijn ~ **krijgen*** get a roasting **3** [inform] hell, damn(ation) || *daar kun je ~ op **zeggen*** you can bet your boots on that, you can bank on that

de **donderbui** /dɔndərbœy/ (pl: -en) thunderstorm, thunder-shower

de **donderdag** /dɔndərdɑx/ (pl: -en) Thursday: *Witte Donderdag* Maundy Thursday

donderdags /dɔndərdɑxs/ (adj) Thursday

¹**donderen** /dɔndərə(n)/ (donderde, heeft/is gedonderd) **1** thunder away, bluster **2** tumble (down): *hij is **van** de trap gedonderd* he tumbled down the stairs

²**donderen** /dɔndərə(n)/ (donderde, heeft gedonderd) thunder

donderjagen /dɔndərjaɣə(n)/ (donderjaagde, heeft gedonderjaagd) [inform] be a nuisance, be a pain (in the neck)

de **donderslag** /dɔndərslɑx/ (pl: -en) **1** thunderclap, thunderbolt, roll (*or:* crack) of thunder **2** [fig] thunderbolt, bombshell: *als een ~ **bij** heldere hemel* like a bolt from the blue

doneren /done̠rə(n)/ (doneerde, heeft gedoneerd) donate

het [1]**donker** /dɔŋkər/ dark(ness), gloom
[2]**donker** /dɔŋkər/ (adj) **1** dark, gloomy **2** dark, dismal, gloomy: *een ~e* ***toekomst*** a gloomy future **3** dark, dusky **4** low(-pitched)
[3]**donker** /dɔŋkər/ (adv) dismally, gloomily: *de toekomst ~* ***inzien*** take a gloomy view of the future
donkerblauw /dɔŋkərblau/ (adj) dark (*or:* deep) blue
de **donor** /donɔr/ (pl: -en, -s) donor
het **donorcodicil** /donɔrkodisil/ (pl: -len) donor card
het **donororgaan** /donɔrɔrɣan/ donor organ
het **dons** /dɔns/ down, fuzz
de **donut** /donʏt/ (pl: -s) doughnut
donzen /dɔnzə(n)/ (adj) down(-filled): *een ~* ***dekbed*** a down(-filled) quilt (*or:* duvet)
de [1]**dood** /dot/ death, end: ***aan*** *de ~* ***ontsnappen*** escape death; *dat* ***wordt*** *zijn ~* that will be the death of him; *iem.* ***ter*** *~ veroordelen* condemn (*or:* sentence) s.o. to death; *de een zijn ~ is de ander zijn brood* one man's death is another man's breath || *(zo bang)* ***als*** *de ~ voor iets zijn* be scared to death of sth.
[2]**dood** /dot/ (adj) **1** dead, killed: *hij* ***was*** *op slag ~* he died (*or:* was killed) instantly **2** dead, extinct: *een dooie* ***boel*** a dead place; *op een ~* ***spoor*** *zitten* be at a dead end; *een dode* ***vulkaan*** an extinct volcano || *op zijn dooie* ***gemak*** at one's leisure; *een dode* ***hoek*** a blind angle
doodbloeden /dodbludə(n)/ (bloedde dood, is doodgebloed) **1** bleed to death **2** [fig] run down, peter out
de **dooddoener** /dodunər/ (pl: -s) unanswerable remark, bromide
doodeenvoudig /dotenvaudəχ/ (adj, adv) perfectly simple, quite simple
doodeng /dotɛŋ/ (adj, adv) really scary; dead scary: *ik* ***vind*** *het allemaal ~* it really gives me the creeps
zich **doodergeren** /dotɛrɣərə(n)/ (ergerde zich dood, heeft zich doodgeërgerd) be (*or:* get) exasperated (with); be extremely annoyed
doodernstig /dotɛrnstəχ/ (adj) deadly serious, solemn
doodgaan /dotχan/ (ging dood, is doodgegaan) die: ***van*** *de honger ~* starve to death
doodgeboren /dotχəborə(n)/ (adj) stillborn
doodgemoedereerd /dotχəmudərert/ (adj, adv) quite (*or:* perfectly) calm; dead calm (*or:* cool), (as) cool as a cucumber
doodgewoon /dotχəwon/ (adj, adv) perfectly common (ordinary): ***iets*** *~s* sth. quite ordinary
doodgooien /dotχojə(n)/ (gooide dood, heeft doodgegooid) bombard, swamp
de **doodgraver** /dotχravər/ (pl: -s) gravedigger, sexton
doodkalm /dotkalm/ (adj, adv) quite (*or:* perfectly) calm
de **doodkist** /dotkɪst/ (pl: -en) coffin
de **doodklap** /dotklɑp/ (pl: -pen) **1** death blow, final blow, coup de grâce **2** almighty blow
zich **doodlachen** /dotlɑχə(n)/ (lachte zich dood, heeft zich doodgelachen) kill o.s. (laughing), split one's sides: *het is* ***om*** *je dood te lachen* it's a scream
doodleuk /dotløk/ (adv) coolly, blandly
doodlopen /dotlopə(n)/ (liep dood, is doodgelopen) **1** come to an end (*or:* a dead end), peter out: *~d* ***steegje*** blind alley; *een ~de* ***straat*** a dead end **2** lead nowhere, lead to nothing
doodmaken /dotmakə(n)/ (maakte dood, heeft doodgemaakt) kill
doodmoe /dotmu/ (adj) dead tired, dead on one's feet, worn out
doodongerust /dotɔŋɣərʏst/ (adj) worried to death, worried sick
doodop /dotɔp/ (adj) worn out, washed-out
doodrijden /dotrɛidə(n)/ (reed dood, heeft doodgereden) run over and kill
doods /dots/ (adj) **1** deathly, deathlike: *een ~e* ***stilte*** a deathly silence **2** dead, dead-and-alive
de **doodsangst** /dotsɑŋst/ (pl: -en) agony, mortal fear
doodsbang /dotsbɑŋ/ (adj, adv) (+ voor) terrified (of), scared to death: *iem. ~* ***maken*** terrify s.o.
doodsbleek /dotsblek/ (adj) deathly pale, as white as a sheet: *er ~* ***uitzien*** look as white as a sheet
zich **doodschamen** /dotsχamə(n)/ (schaamde zich dood, heeft zich doodgeschaamd) be terribly embarrassed
doodschieten /dotsχitə(n)/ (schoot dood, heeft doodgeschoten) shoot (dead), shoot and kill: ***zichzelf*** *~* shoot o.s.
het **doodseskader** /dotsɛskadər/ (pl: -s) death squad
het **doodsgevaar** /dotsχəvar/ deadly peril, mortal danger: ***in*** *~ zijn (verkeren)* be in mortal danger
het **doodshoofd** /dotshoft/ (pl: -en) skull
de **doodskist** /dotskɪst/ (pl: -en) coffin
doodslaan /dotslan/ (sloeg dood, heeft doodgeslagen) kill; beat to death; strike dead: *een* ***vlieg*** *~* swat a fly
de **doodslag** /dotslɑχ/ (pl: -en) manslaughter
de **doodsnood** /dotsnot/ death agony; [fig] death throes, fight to survive: ***in*** *~ verkeren* be in one's death agony, be fighting to survive
de **doodsoorzaak** /dotsorzak/ (pl: -oorzaken) cause of death
de **doodsstrijd** /dotstrɛɪt/ death agony
de **doodsteek** /dotstek/ coup de grâce, death blow, final blow: *dat* ***betekende*** *de ~ voor het*

vredesproces that dealt a death blow to the peace process

doodsteken /d<u>o</u>tsteke(n)/ (stak dood, heeft doodgestoken) stab to death, stab and kill

doodstil /d<u>o</u>tst<u>ɪ</u>l/ (adj) deathly quiet (*or:* still); quite still; dead silent: *het **werd** opeens ~ toen hij binnenkwam* there was a sudden hush when he came in

de **doodstraf** /d<u>o</u>tstrɑf/ (pl: -fen) death penalty: *hier **staat** de ~ op* this is punishable by death

de **doodsverachting** /d<u>o</u>tsferɑχtɪŋ/ contempt (*or:* disregard) for death

doodvallen /d<u>o</u>tfɑle(n)/ (viel dood, is doodgevallen) drop (*or:* fall) dead: *ik **mag** ~ als het niet waar is* if that isn't so I'll eat my hat; *val dood!* drop dead!, go to hell!

het **doodvonnis** /d<u>o</u>tfɔnɪs/ (pl: -sen) death sentence

doodziek /d<u>o</u>tsik/ (adj) **1** critically ill, terminally ill **2** sick and tired: *ik **word** ~ van die kat* I'm (getting) sick and tired of that cat

de ¹**doodzonde** /d<u>o</u>tsɔnde/ **1** mortal sin **2** mortal sin, deadly sin

²**doodzonde** /d<u>o</u>tsɔnde/ (adj) a terrible pity; a terrible waste

doodzwijgen /d<u>o</u>tswɛɪɣe(n)/ (zweeg dood, heeft doodgezwegen) hush up, smother, keep quiet

doof /dof/ (adj, adv) deaf: *~ **blijven** voor* turn a deaf ear to; *~ **aan** één oor* deaf in one ear

de **doofheid** /d<u>o</u>fhɛit/ deafness

de **doofpot** /d<u>o</u>fpɔt/ (pl: -ten) extinguisher, cover-up: *die hele zaak is **in** de ~ (gestopt)* that whole business has been hushed up

doofstom /dofst<u>o</u>m/ (adj) deaf-and-dumb, deaf mute

de **doofstomme** /dofst<u>o</u>me/ (pl: -n) deaf mute

de **dooi** /doj/ thaw

dooien /d<u>o</u>je(n)/ (dooide, heeft gedooid) thaw: *het **begon** te ~* the thaw set in

de **dooier** /d<u>o</u>jer/ (pl: -s) (egg) yolk

de **doolhof** /d<u>o</u>lhɔf/ (pl: -hoven) maze, labyrinth

de **doop** /dop/ (pl: dopen) **1** christening, baptism **2** [fig] inauguration, christening: *de ~ van een **schip*** the naming of a ship **3** [Belg] initiation (of new students)

het/de **doopceel** /d<u>o</u>psel/ (pl: doopcelen): *iemands ~ **lichten*** bring out s.o.'s past

de **doopnaam** /d<u>o</u>pnam/ (pl: -namen) Christian name, baptismal name, given name

het **doopsel** /d<u>o</u>psel/ (pl: -s) baptism, christening

de **doopsuiker** /d<u>o</u>psœykǝr/ [Belg] sugared almonds

het **doopvont** /d<u>o</u>pfɔnt/ (pl: -en) font

¹**door** /dor/ (adv) through: *de hele **dag** ~* all day long, throughout the day; *het kan **ermee** ~* it's passable; *de tunnel gaat **onder** de rivier ~* the tunnel passes under the river ‖ *tussen de buien ~* between showers; *ik ben ~ **en** ~ nat* I'm wet through (and through); *~ **en** ~ slecht* rotten to the core

²**door** /dor/ (prep) **1** through: *~ heel **Europa*** throughout Europe; *~ **rood (oranje)** rijden* jump the lights **2** through, into: *zout ~ het **eten** doen* mix salt into the food; *alles lag ~ **elkaar*** everything was in a mess **3** by (means of): *~ ijverig te **werken,** kun je je doel bereiken* you can reach your goal by working hard; *~ **haar** heb ik hem leren kennen* it was thanks to her that I met him **4** because of, owing to, by, with: *~ het slechte **weer*** because of (*or:* owing to) the bad weather; *~ **ziekte** verhinderd* prevented by illness from coming (*or:* attending, going); *dat **komt** ~ jou* that's (all) because of you **5** by: *zij werden ~ de **menigte** toegejuicht* they were cheered by the crowd; *~ **wie** is het geschreven?* who was it written by? ‖ *~ de **jaren** heen* over the years; *~ de **week*** through the week

doorbakken /dorb<u>ɑ</u>ke(n)/ (adj) well-done

doorberekenen /d<u>o</u>rbǝrekene(n)/ (berekende door, heeft doorberekend) pass on, on-charge

doorbetalen /d<u>o</u>rbǝtale(n)/ (betaalde door, heeft doorbetaald) keep paying, continue paying

doorbijten /d<u>o</u>rbɛite(n)/ (beet door, heeft doorgebeten) **1** bite (hard): *de **hond** beet niet door* the dog didn't bite hard **2** keep biting, continue biting (*or:* to bite); [fig] keep trying; [fig] keep at it: *even ~!* just grin and bear it!

doorbladeren /d<u>o</u>rbladere(n)/ (bladerde door, heeft doorgebladerd) leaf through, glance through; thumb through

doorboren /dorb<u>o</u>re(n)/ (doorboorde, heeft doorboord) drill (through), bore (a hole in); tunnel; pierce; stab

de **doorbraak** /d<u>o</u>rbrak/ (pl: -braken) **1** bursting, collapse **2** breakthrough; [sport] break: *~ van een politieke **partij*** the breakthrough of a political party

doorbranden /d<u>o</u>rbrɑnde(n)/ (brandde door, heeft/is doorgebrand) **1** burn through, burn properly **2** burn out: *een doorgebrande **lamp*** a blown (light) bulb

¹**doorbreken** /dorbr<u>e</u>ke(n)/ (doorbrak, heeft doorbroken) break (through), burst (through); breach: *de **sleur** ~* get out of the rut

²**doorbreken** /d<u>o</u>rbreke(n)/ (brak door, is doorgebroken) **1** break (apart, in two), break up, burst, perforate: *het **gezwel** brak door* the swelling ruptured **2** break through, come through: *de **tandjes** zullen snel ~* the teeth will come through fast **3** break through, make it

³**doorbreken** /d<u>o</u>rbreke(n)/ (brak door, heeft doorgebroken) break (in two); snap (in

two): *ze brak zijn wandelstok door (in tweeën)* she broke his walking stick in two

doorbrengen / do̯rbrɛŋə(n)/ (bracht door, heeft doorgebracht) spend: *ergens de nacht ~* spend the night (*or:* stay overnight) somewhere

doorbuigen /do̯rbœyɣə(n)/ (boog door, is doorgebogen) **1** bend, sag: *de vloer boog sterk door* the floor sagged badly **2** bend further (over), bow deeper

doordacht /dordo̯xt/ (adj) well-thought-out, well-considered

doordat /dordo̯t/ (conj) because (of the fact that), owing to, as a result of, on account of (the fact that), in that: *~ er gebrek aan geld was* through lack of money

doordenken /do̯rdɛŋkə(n)/ (dacht door, heeft doorgedacht) reflect, think, consider: *als je even doordenkt* (or: *door had gedacht*) if you think (*or:* had thought) for a moment

doordeweeks /dordəwe̯ks/ (adj) weekday, workaday

doordraaien /do̯rdrajə(n)/ (draaide door, heeft/is doorgedraaid) **1** keep turning, continue turning (*or:* to turn); [fig] go on; [fig] keep moving: *de motor laten ~* keep the engine running (*or:* on) **2** slip, not bite, have stripped, be stripped

doordrammen /do̯rdramə(n)/ (dramde door, heeft doorgedramd) nag, go on: *~ over iets* keep harping on (about) sth.

de **doordrammer** /do̯rdramər/ (pl: -s) nagger, pest

doordraven /do̯rdravə(n)/ (draafde door, heeft/is doorgedraafd) rattle on

doordrenken /do̯rdrɛŋkə(n)/ (doordrenkte, heeft doordrenkt) soak (through), saturate, drench

¹doordrijven /do̯rdrɛivə(n)/ (dreef door, heeft doorgedreven) nag: *je moet niet zo ~* stop nagging!

²doordrijven /do̯rdrɛivə(n)/ (dreef door, heeft doorgedreven) push through, force through, enforce, impose: *iets te ver ~* carry things too far

¹doordringen /dordrɪŋə(n)/ (doordrong, is doordrongen) penetrate; permeate

²doordringen /dordrɪŋə(n)/ (doordrong, heeft doordrongen) persuade, convince: *doordrongen zijn van de noodzaak ... be convinced of the necessity of ...*

³doordringen /do̯rdrɪŋə(n)/ (drong door, is doorgedrongen) penetrate, get through, occur: *~ in* penetrate; [fig] filter through; *het drong niet tot me door dat hij mij wilde spreken* it didn't occur to me that he wanted to see me; *niet tot iem. kunnen ~* not be able to get through to s.o.

doordringend /dordrɪŋənt/ (adj) piercing; penetrating; pungent: *iem. ~ aankijken* give s.o. a piercing look

doordrukken /do̯rdrʏkə(n)/ (drukte door, heeft doorgedrukt) push through, force through: *zijn eigen mening ~* impose one's own view

dooreen /do̯re̯n/ (adv) jumbled up, higgledy-piggledy

dooreten /do̯retə(n)/ (at door, heeft doorgegeten) carry on eating, keep (on) eating: *eet eens even door!* eat up now!

¹doorgaan /do̯rɣan/ (ging door, is doorgegaan) **1** go on, walk on, continue: *deze trein gaat door tot Amsterdam* this train goes on to Amsterdam **2** continue (doing, with), go (*or:* carry) on (doing, with), persist (in, with), proceed (with): *hij bleef er maar over ~* he just kept on about it; *dat gaat in één moeite door* we can do that as well while we're about it **3** continue, go on, last **4** go through, pass through, pass **5** take place, be held: *het feest gaat door* the party is on; *niet ~* be off **6** pass for, pass o.s. off as; be considered (as): *zij gaat voor erg intelligent door* she is said to be very intelligent

²doorgaan /do̯rɣan/ (ging door, is doorgegaan) go through, pass through

doorgaand /do̯rɣant/ (adj) through: *~ verkeer* through traffic

doorgaans /do̯rɣans/ (adv) generally, usually

de **doorgang** /do̯rɣaŋ/ (pl: -en) **1** occurrence: *(geen) ~ hebben* (not) take place **2** passage(-way), way through, gangway; aisle

het **doorgeefluik** /do̯rɣeflœyk/ (pl: -en) (serving-)hatch; [fig] intermediary, middleman

doorgestoken /do̯rɣəstokə(n)/ (adj): *dat is ~ kaart* it's been arranged behind our backs, it's fixed, it's a put-up job

doorgeven /do̯rɣevə(n)/ (gaf door, heeft doorgegeven) **1** pass (on, round), hand on (*or:* round): *geef de fles eens door* pass the bottle round (*or:* on) **2** pass (on): *een boodschap aan iem. ~* pass a message on to s.o. **3** pass on, hand on, hand over **4** pass on, let (s.o.) know about: *dat zal ik moeten ~ aan je baas* I will have to tell your boss about this

doorgewinterd /do̯rɣəwɪntərt/ (adj) seasoned, experienced

doorgronden /do̯rɣrɔndə(n)/ (doorgrondde, heeft doorgrond) fathom, penetrate

doorhakken /do̯rhakə(n)/ (hakte door, heeft doorgehakt) chop in half (*or:* two), split

doorhalen /do̯rhalə(n)/ (haalde door, heeft doorgehaald) cross out, delete

doorhebben /do̯rhɛbə(n)/ (had door, heeft doorgehad) see (through), be on to: *hij had het dadelijk door dat ... he saw at once that ...*

doorheen /do̯rhe̯n/ (adv) through: *zich er ~ slaan* get through (it) somehow or other

doorkijken /do̯rkɛikə(n)/ (keek door, heeft doorgekeken) look through

doorklikken /dọrklɪkə(n)/ (klikte door, heeft doorgeklikt) click (on the link)

doorklinken /dọrklɪŋkə(n)/ (klonk door, heeft doorgeklonken) be heard: *de berusting die **uit** zijn woorden doorklinkt* the resignation that can be heard in his words

doorkneed /dorknẹt/ (adj) experienced

doorknippen /dọrknɪpə(n)/ (knipte door, heeft doorgeknipt) cut through, cut in half (*or:* in two)

doorkomen /dọrkomə(n)/ (kwam door, is doorgekomen) **1** come through (*or:* past, by), pass (through, by): *de **stoet** moet hier* ~ the procession must come past here **2** get through (to the end): *de **dag** ~* make it through the day; *er is geen ~ aan* **a)** [book, work etc] there is no way I'm going to get this finished; **b)** [crowd, traffic] I don't stand a hope of getting through **3** come through, get through: *de **zon** komt door* the sun is breaking through

doorkruisen /dorkrọeysə(n)/ (doorkruiste, heeft doorkruist) **1** traverse, roam; scour: *hij heeft heel **Frankrijk** doorkruist* he has travelled all over France **2** thwart: *dat voorstel doorkruist mijn **plannen*** that proposal has thwarted my plans

doorlaten /dọrlatə(n)/ (liet door, heeft doorgelaten) let through (*or:* pass), allow through (*or:* to pass): *geen **geluid** ~* be soundproof

doorleefd /dorlẹft/ (adj) wrinkled, aged

doorleren /dọrlerə(n)/ (leerde door, heeft doorgeleerd) keep (on) studying, continue with one's studies, stay on at school

doorleven /dorlẹvə(n)/ (doorleefde, heeft doorleefd) live through, spend

¹**doorlezen** /dọrlezə(n)/ (las door, heeft doorgelezen) read on, keep (on) reading

²**doorlezen** /dọrlezə(n)/ (las door, heeft doorgelezen) read (to the end (*or:* through)): *ik heb dat **boek** slechts vluchtig doorgelezen* I have only glanced (*or:* skimmed) through that book

doorlichten /dọrlɪχtə(n)/ (lichtte door, heeft doorgelicht) investigate, examine carefully; screen [pers]

doorliggen /dọrlɪχə(n)/ (lag door, heeft/is doorgelegen) have bedsores, get bedsores: *zijn **rug** is doorgelegen* he has (got) bedsores on his back

¹**doorlopen** /dọrlopə(n)/ (doorliep, heeft/is doorlopen) **1** walk through, go through, pass through **2** go through, pass through; complete: *alle **stadia** ~* pass through (*or:* complete) every stage **3** run through, glance through

²**doorlopen** /dọrlopə(n)/ (liep door, heeft/is doorgelopen) **1** walk (*or:* go, pass) through: *hij liep **tussen** de struiken door* he walked (*or:* went) through the bushes **2** keep (on) walking (*or:* going/moving); continue walking (*or:* going/moving); continue to walk (*or:* to go/move); walk on (*or:* go/move on): *~ a.u.b.!* move along now, please! **3** run: *het **blauw** is doorgelopen* the blue has run **4** run on, carry on through, continue; be consecutive: *de eetkamer loopt door **in** de keuken* the dining room runs through into the kitchen **5** hurry up

doorlopend /dorlọpənt/ (adj, adv) continuous, continuing; continual; consecutive: *~ **krediet** revolving (*or:* continuous) credit; *hij is ~ **dronken*** he is constantly drunk

doormaken /dọrmakə(n)/ (maakte door, heeft doorgemaakt) go through, pass through, live through, experience, undergo: *een moeilijke **tijd** ~* have a hard time (of it)

doormidden /dormɪdə(n)/ (adv) in two, in half

de **doorn** /dorn/ (pl: -en) thorn: *dat is mij een ~ in het oog* that is a thorn in my flesh

doornat /dornạt/ (adj) wet through, soaked (through)

doornemen /dọrnemə(n)/ (nam door, heeft doorgenomen) **1** go through (*or:* over): *een artikel **vluchtig** ~* skim through an article **2** go over: *iets **met** elkaar ~* go over sth. together

Doornroosje /dornrọʃə/ Sleeping Beauty

doorprikken /dọrprɪkə(n)/ (prikte door, heeft doorgeprikt) burst, prick, puncture

de **doorreis** /dọrɛɪs/ stopover, stopoff: *hij is **op** ~ (naar Rome)* he is passing through (*or:* stopping over) (on his way to Rome)

doorrijden /dọrɛɪdə(n)/ (reed door, heeft/is doorgereden) **1** keep on (*or:* continue) driving/riding: *rijdt deze bus door **naar** het station?* does this bus go on to the station? **2** drive on, ride on, proceed, continue: *~ **na** een aanrijding* fail to stop after an accident **3** drive faster, ride faster, increase speed: *als we **wat** ~, zijn we er in een uur* if we step on it, we will be there in an hour

de **doorrijhoogte** /dọrɛɪhoχtə/ (pl: -n) clearance, headway

doorschemeren /dọrsχemərə(n)/ (schemerde door, heeft/is doorgeschemerd) be hinted at, be implied: *hij **liet** ~ dat hij trouwplannen had* he hinted that he was planning to marry

doorscheuren /dọrsχørə(n)/ (scheurde door, heeft/is doorgescheurd) tear up; tear in half

doorschieten /dọrsχitə(n)/ (schoot door, is doorgeschoten) shoot through (*or:* past)

doorschijnend /dorsχẹinənt/ (adj, adv) translucent; see-through; transparent

doorschuiven /dọrsχœyvə(n)/ (schoof door, heeft/is doorgeschoven) pass on

doorslaan /dọrslan/ (sloeg door, heeft/is doorgeslagen) **1** tip, dip: *de **balans** doen ~* tip

the scales **2** blow, melt; fuse; break down: *de*
stop *is doorgeslagen* the fuse has blown
3 talk

doorslaand /dorslant/ (adj) conclusive, decisive: *een ~ succes* a resounding success

de **doorslag** /dorslɑx/ (pl: -en) **1** turn (*or:* tip)
(of the scale): *dat **gaf** bij mij de ~* that decided
me; *dat **geeft** de ~* that settles it **2** carbon
(copy), duplicate

doorslaggevend /dorslɑxevənt/ (adj) decisive: *van ~ **belang*** of overriding importance

doorslikken /dorslɪkə(n)/ (slikte door,
heeft doorgeslikt) swallow

doorsmeren /dorsmerə(n)/ (smeerde door,
heeft doorgesmeerd) lubricate: *de auto **laten**
~* have the car lubricated

de **doorsnede** /dorsnedə/ (pl: -n) **1** section,
cross-section, profile: *een ~ van een **bol** maken*
make a cross-section of a sphere **2** diameter:
*die bal **heeft** een ~ van 5 cm* this ball has a diameter of 5 cm

doorsnee /dorsne/ (adj) average, mean: *de*
*~ **burger*** the man in (*or:* on) the street

¹**doorsnijden** /dorsnɛidə(n)/ (sneed door,
heeft doorgesneden) cut, sever; cut in(to)
two; bisect: *hij heeft alle **banden** met zijn familie doorgesneden* he has severed (*or:* cut) all
ties with his family

²**doorsnijden** /dorsnɛidə(n)/ (doorsneed,
heeft doorsneden) cut (through)

doorspekken /dorspɛkə(n)/ (doorspekte,
heeft doorspekt) interlard (with), intersperse
(with), punctuate (with)

¹**doorspelen** /dorspelə(n)/ (speelde door,
heeft doorgespeeld) play on, continue to
play: *het orkest speelde door alsof er niets gebeurd was* the orchestra played on as if nothing had happened

²**doorspelen** /dorspelə(n)/ (speelde door,
heeft doorgespeeld) pass on, leak: *informatie*
aan *een krant ~* pass on information to a
newspaper; *de bal ~ **naar** ...* pass (the ball) to
...

doorspoelen /dorspulə(n)/ (spoelde door,
heeft doorgespoeld) **1** wash down (*or:* out,
through): *je **eten** ~ met wijn* wash down your
food with wine **2** flush out; flush **3** wind on

doorspreken /dorsprekə(n)/ (sprak door,
heeft doorgesproken) discuss, go into (in
depth)

doorstaan /dorstan/ (doorstond, heeft
doorstaan) endure, bear, (with)stand, come
through: *een **proef** ~* come through a test

de **doorstart** /dorstɑrt/ (pl: -s) **1** aborted landing **2** [economics] new start; bankruptcy restructuring

¹**doorstarten** (startte door, heeft/is doorgestart) **1** abort a landing **2** start up again

²**doorstarten** /dorstɑrtə(n)/ (startte door,
heeft/is doorgestart) start up again

doorstoten /dorstotə(n)/ (stootte door,

heeft/is doorgestoten) **1** keep on (*or:* continue) pushing **2** advance, push on (*or:*
through); break through, burst through: *~
tot de kern van de zaak* get to the heart of the
matter

doorstrepen /dorstrepə(n)/ (streepte door,
heeft doorgestreept) cross out, delete, strike
out (*or:* through)

doorstromen /dorstromə(n)/ (stroomde
door, is doorgestroomd) **1** move up, move
on **2** flow (through)

de **doorstroming** /dorstromɪŋ/ **1** moving up,
moving on **2** flow, circulation: *een vlottere ~
van het verkeer* a freer flow of traffic

doorstuderen /dorstydərə(n)/ (studeerde
door, heeft doorgestudeerd) continue (with)
one's studies

doorsturen /dorstyrə(n)/ (stuurde door,
heeft doorgestuurd) send on; send away: *een
brief ~* forward a letter; *een **patiënt** naar een
specialist ~* refer a patient to a specialist

doortastend /dortɑstənt/ (adj, adv) vigorous, bold

de **doortocht** /dortɔxt/ (pl: -en) **1** crossing,
passage through, way through **2** passage,
thoroughfare: *de ~ **versperren*** block the way
through

doortrapt /dortrɑpt/ (adj, adv) **1** cunning,
crafty **2** base, villainous

¹**doortrekken** /dortrɛkə(n)/ (trok door,
heeft/is doorgetrokken) travel through, pass
through, journey through, roam

²**doortrekken** /dortrɛkə(n)/ (trok door,
heeft doorgetrokken) **1** extend, continue:
*een **lijn** ~* follow the same line (*or:* course);
*een **vergelijking** ~* carry a comparison (further) **2** flush

doorverbinden /dorvərbɪndə(n)/ (verbond door, heeft doorverbonden) connect;
put through (to)

doorvertellen /dorvərtɛlə(n)/ (vertelde
door, heeft doorverteld) pass on: *aan niemand ~, hoor!* don't tell anyone else!

doorverwijzen /dorvərwɛizə(n)/ (verwees
door, heeft doorverwezen) refer

de **doorvoer** /dorvur/ (pl: -en) transit

de **doorvoerhaven** /dorvurhavə(n)/ (pl: -s)
transit port

doorwaadbaar /dorwadbar/ (adj) forda-
ble, wad(e)able: *doorwaadbare **plaats*** ford

doorweekt /dorwekt/ (adj) wet through,
soaked, drenched

¹**doorwerken** /dorwɛrkə(n)/ (werkte door,
heeft doorgewerkt) **1** go (*or:* keep) on
working, continue to work, work on; work
overtime: *er werd **dag** en **nacht** doorgewerkt*
they worked night and day **2** make headway, get on (the job): *je **kunt** hier nooit ~*
you can never get on with your work here
3 affect sth., make itself felt: *zijn **houding**
werkt door op anderen* his attitude has its ef-

²**doorwerken** /d<u>o</u>rwɛrkə(n)/ (werkte door, heeft doorgewerkt) work (one's way) through, get through, go through: *een heleboel stukken door moeten werken* have to plough through a mass of documents

¹**doorzagen** /d<u>o</u>rzaɣə(n)/ (zaagde door, heeft doorgezaagd) keep (*or:* go, moan) on (about sth.)

²**doorzagen** /d<u>o</u>rzaɣə(n)/ (zaagde door, heeft doorgezaagd) saw (sth.) through, saw in two ‖ *iem. over iets blijven ~* force sth. down s.o.'s throat; question s.o. closely, grill s.o.

doorzakken /d<u>o</u>rzakə(n)/ (zakte door, is doorgezakt) **1** sag, give (way) **2** go on drinking (*or:* boozing), make a night of it

¹**doorzetten** /d<u>o</u>rzɛtə(n)/ (zette door, heeft doorgezet) **1** become stronger, become more intense: *de weeën zetten door* the contractions are increasing (in intensity) **2** persevere: *nog even ~!* don't give up now!; *van ~ weten* not give up easily

²**doorzetten** /d<u>o</u>rzɛtə(n)/ (zette door, heeft doorgezet) **1** press (*or:* go) ahead with **2** go through with: *iets tot het einde toe ~* see sth. through

de **doorzetter** /d<u>o</u>rzɛtər/ (pl: -s) go-getter, stayer

het **doorzettingsvermogen** /d<u>o</u>rzɛtɪŋsfərmoɣə(n)/ perseverance, drive

doorzeven /d<u>o</u>rzevə(n)/ (doorzeefde, heeft doorzeefd) riddle: *met kogels doorzeefd* bullet-riddled

doorzichtig /dorz<u>ɪ</u>xtəx/ (adj) **1** transparent; see-through: *gewoon glas is ~, matglas doorschijnend* plain glass is transparent, frosted glass is translucent **2** [fig] transparent, thin, obvious

de **doorzichtigheid** /dorz<u>ɪ</u>xtəxhɛit/ transparency

doorzien /dorz<u>i</u>n/ (doorzag, heeft doorzien) see through; be on to [pers]: *hij doorzag haar bedoelingen* he saw what she was up to

doorzoeken /dorz<u>u</u>kə(n)/ (doorzocht, heeft doorzocht) search through, go through; ransack: *zijn zakken ~* turn one's pockets (inside) out

de **doos** /dos/ (pl: dozen) box; case: [aviation] *de zwarte ~* the black box

de **dop** /dɔp/ (pl: -pen) **1** shell; pod; husk **2** cap; top **3** [Belg; inform] dole, unemployment benefit ‖ *een advocaat in de ~* a budding lawyer; *kijk uit je ~pen!* watch where you're going!

de ¹**dope** /dop/ dope: *helemaal onder de ~ zitten* be stoned, be doped up to the eyeballs

²**dope** (adj) [inform] (really) dope, awesome

dopen /d<u>o</u>pə(n)/ (doopte, heeft gedoopt) **1** sop, dunk (in): *zijn pen in de inkt ~* dip one's pen in the ink **2** [rel] baptize, christen: *iem. tot christen ~* baptize s.o. **3** [Belg] initiate,

rag

de **doper** /d<u>o</u>pər/ (pl: -s) baptizer: *Johannes de Doper* John the Baptist

de **doperwt** /d<u>o</u>pɛrt/ (pl: -en) green pea

de **doping** /d<u>o</u>pɪŋ/ drug(s)

de **dopingcontrole** /d<u>o</u>pɪŋkɔntrɔːlə/ (pl: -s) dope test

het **dopje** /d<u>o</u>pjə/ (pl: -s) cap, top

¹**doppen** /d<u>o</u>pə(n)/ (dopte, heeft gedopt) [Belg] be on benefit, be on the dole

²**doppen** /d<u>o</u>pə(n)/ (dopte, heeft gedopt) (un)shell; pod; hull; peel; (un)husk; hull

dor /dɔr/ (adj) **1** barren, arid **2** withered

het **dorp** /dɔrp/ (pl: -en) village; [Am] town: *het hele ~ weet het* it's all over town

de **dorpel** /d<u>o</u>rpəl/ (pl: -s) threshold, doorstep

de **dorpeling** /d<u>o</u>rpəlɪŋ/ (pl: -en) villager; village people

de **dorpsbewoner** /d<u>o</u>rpsbəwonər/ (pl: -s) villager

het **dorpshuis** /d<u>o</u>rpshœys/ (pl: -huizen) community centre

dorsen /d<u>o</u>rsə(n)/ (dorste, heeft gedorsen) thresh

de **dorst** /dɔrst/ thirst: *ik verga van de ~* I'm dying of thirst; *zijn ~ lessen* quench one's thirst

dorstig /d<u>o</u>rstəx/ (adj) thirsty, parched

doseren /dozerə(n)/ (doseerde, heeft gedoseerd) dose

de **dosering** /doz<u>e</u>rɪŋ/ (pl: -en) quantity; dose; dosage

de **dosis** /d<u>o</u>zɪs/ (pl: doses) dose, measure: *een flinke ~ gezond verstand* a good measure of common sense

het **dossier** /dɔsj<u>e</u>/ (pl: -s) file, documents, records: *een ~ bijhouden van iets (iem.)* keep a file on sth. (s.o.)

de **dot** /dɔt/ (pl: -ten) tuft ‖ *een flinke ~ slagroom* a dollop of cream; *een ~ van een kans* a golden opportunity

de **douane** /duw<u>a</u>nə/ (pl: -n, -s) customs

de **douanebeambte** /duw<u>a</u>nəbəamtə/ (pl: -n) customs officer

de **douanerechten** /duw<u>a</u>nərɛxtə(n)/ (pl) customs duties

de **double** /d<u>a</u>bəl/ (pl: -s) double

doubleren /dubl<u>e</u>rə(n)/ (doubleerde, heeft gedoubleerd) repeat (a class)

de **douche** /duʃ/ (pl: -s) shower: [fig] *een koude ~* a rude awakening

de **douchecel** /d<u>u</u>ʃɛl/ (pl: -len) shower (cubicle)

de **douchekop** /d<u>u</u>ʃkɔp/ (pl: -pen) shower head

douchen /d<u>u</u>ʃə(n)/ (douchte, heeft gedoucht) shower, take (*or:* have) a shower

douwen /d<u>ou</u>wə(n)/ (douwde, heeft gedouwd) shove, push; crowd

de **dove** /d<u>o</u>və/ (pl: -n) deaf person

de **dovemansoren** /d<u>o</u>vəmansorə(n)/ (pl): *dat is niet aan ~ gezegd* that did not fall on deaf ears; *voor ~ spreken* not find any hearing

doven /dˈoːvə(n)/ (doofde, heeft gedoofd) extinguish, put out; turn out, turn off [light]

de **dovenetel** /dˈoːvənetəl/ (pl: -s) dead nettle

down /daun/ (adj) down, down-hearted ‖ ~ **gaan** fail, go down

de **download** /dˈaunlot/ (pl: -s) download

downloaden /dˈaunlodə(n)/ (downloadde, heeft gedownload) download

het **downsyndroom** /dˈaunsɪndrom/ Down's syndrome

het **dozijn** /dozˈɛin/ dozen: *een ~ eieren* one dozen eggs

de **draad** /drat/ (pl: draden) **1** thread; fibre: *tot op de ~ versleten* worn threadbare; *de ~ weer opnemen* pick up the thread; *de ~ kwijt zijn* flounder **2** fibre; string

het **draadje** /drˈacə/ (pl: -s) **1** thread, strand, fibre: *aan een zijden ~ hangen* hang by a thread; *er zit een ~ los bij hem* he has a screw loose **2** wire, piece of wiring

draadloos /drˈatlos/ (adj) wireless: *~ internet* wireless Internet; *draadloze telefoon* cellular (tele)phone

draagbaar /drˈaɣbar/ (adj) portable, transportable

de **draagbalk** /drˈaɣbɑlk/ (pl: -en) breastsummer, girder

de **draagkracht** /drˈaxkrɑxt/ capacity, strength: *financiële ~* financial strength (*or:* capacity, means)

draaglijk /drˈaxlək/ (adj, adv) bearable, endurable

de **draagmoeder** /drˈaxmudər/ (pl: -s) surrogate mother

de **draagstoel** /drˈaxstul/ (pl: -en) sedan (chair)

de **draagtas** /drˈaxtas/ (pl: -sen) carrier bag; [Am] bag

het **draagvermogen** /drˈaxfərmoɣə(n)/ bearing (*or:* supporting) power; lift

het **draagvlak** /drˈaxflɑk/ (pl: -ken) [literally] bearing surface, basis; support: *het maatschappelijk ~ van een wetsontwerp* the public support for a bill

de **draagwijdte** /drˈaxwɛitə/ range; [fig also] scope, bearing

de **draai** /draj/ (pl: -en) **1** turn, twist, bend: *een ~ van 180° maken* make an about-turn **2** turn, twist; screw: *iem. een ~ om de oren geven* box s.o.'s ears ‖ *hij kon zijn ~ niet vinden* he couldn't settle down

draaibaar /drˈajbar/ (adj) revolving, rotating, swinging: *een draaibare (bureau)stoel* a swivel chair

de **draaibank** /drˈajbɑŋk/ (pl: -en) (turning) lathe

het **draaiboek** /drˈajbuk/ (pl: -en) script, screenplay, scenario

de **draaicirkel** /drˈajsɪrkəl/ (pl: -s) turning circle

de **draaideur** /drˈajdør/ (pl: -en) revolving door

¹**draaien** /drˈajə(n)/ (draaide, heeft/is gedraaid) **1** turn (around), revolve, rotate; or-bit; pivot: *in het rond ~* turn round, spin round; *daar draait het om* that's what it's all about **2** turn, swerve: *de wind draait* the wind is changing **3** work, run, do: *met winst (or: verlies) ~* work at a profit (*or:* loss) ‖ *die film draait nog steeds* that film is still on; *aan de knoppen ~* turn the knobs; *er omheen ~* evade the question

²**draaien** /drˈajə(n)/ (draaide, heeft gedraaid) **1** turn (around); twirl; spin: *het gas hoger (or: lager) ~* turn the gas up (*or:* down); *een deur op slot ~* lock a door **2** turn (around), swerve **3** roll; turn **4** dial **5** play: *een film ~* show a film ‖ *een nachtdienst ~* work a night shift; *de zaak ~de houden* keep things going

draaierig /drˈajərəx/ (adj) dizzy

het **draaihek** /drˈajhɛk/ turnstile, swing gate

de **draaikolk** /drˈajkɔlk/ (pl: -en) whirlpool

de **draaimolen** /drˈajmolə(n)/ (pl: -s) merry-go-round

het **draaiorgel** /drˈajɔrɣəl/ (pl: -s) barrel organ; hand organ: *de orgelman speelde zijn ~* the organgrinder was grinding his barrel organ

de **draaischijf** /drˈajsxɛif/ (pl: -schijven) **1** dial **2** potter's wheel

de **draaistoel** /drˈajstul/ (pl: -en) swivel chair, revolving chair

de **draaitafel** /drˈajtafəl/ (pl: -s) turntable

de **draak** /drak/ (pl: draken) dragon

het/de **drab** /drap/ **1** dregs, sediment **2** ooze

het/de **drachme** /drɑxmə/ (pl: -n) drachma

de **dracht** /drɑxt/ (pl: -en) **1** gestation; pregnancy **2** costume, dress

drachtig /drˈɑxtəx/ (adj) with young, bearing: *~ zijn* be with young

draconisch /drakˈonis/ (adj, adv) draconian

de **draf** /draf/ trot: *in volle ~* at full trot; *op een ~je lopen* run along, trot

¹**dragen** /drˈaɣə(n)/ (droeg, heeft gedragen) rest on, be supported: *een ~de balk* a supporting beam

²**dragen** /drˈaɣə(n)/ (droeg, heeft gedragen) **1** support, bear, carry; [fig also] sustain: *iets bij zich ~* have sth. on one **2** wear, have on: *die schoenen kun je niet bij die jurk ~* those shoes don't go with that dress **3** take, have: *de gevolgen ~* bear (*or:* take) the consequences **4** bear, endure: *de spanning was niet langer te ~* the tension had become unbearable

de **drager** /drˈaɣər/ (pl: -s) bearer; carrier

de **dragon** /drˈaɣɔn/ tarragon

de **drain** /dren/ (pl: -s) drain

draineren /drɛnˈerə(n)/ (draineerde, heeft gedraineerd) drain

dralen /drˈalə(n)/ (draalde, heeft gedraald) linger, hesitate

het **drama** /drˈama/ (pl: -'s) **1** tragedy, drama: *de Griekse ~'s* the Greek tragedies; *een ~ opvoeren* perform a tragedy **2** tragedy, catastrophe ‖ *een ~ van iets maken* make a drama

of sth.
dramatisch /dramatis/ (adj, adv) **1** dramatic: *~e effecten* theatrical effects **2** tragic; theatrical: *doe niet zo ~* don't make such a drama of it
dramatiseren /dramatizera(n)/ (dramatiseerde, heeft gedramatiseerd) **1** dramatize, make a drama of **2** dramatize; adapt for the stage
drammen /drɑmə(n)/ (dramde, heeft gedramd) nag, go on
drammerig /drɑmərəx/ (adj, adv) nagging, insistent, tiresome
de **drang** /drɑŋ/ **1** urge, instinct: *de ~ tot zelfbehoud* the survival instinct **2** pressure, force: *met zachte ~* with gentle insistence
het **dranghek** /drɑŋhɛk/ (pl: -ken) barrier
de **drank** /drɑŋk/ (pl: -en) drink; beverage: *alcoholhoudende ~en* alcoholic beverages; [Belg] *korte ~* spirits, liquor
het **drankje** /drɑŋkjə/ (pl: -s) drink: *een ~ klaarmaken* mix a drink
het **drankmisbruik** /drɑŋkmɪzbrœyk/ alcohol abuse
het **drankorgel** /drɑŋkɔrɣəl/ (pl: -s) drunk(ard), hard drinker
de **drankvergunning** /drɑŋkfərɣʏnɪŋ/ (pl: -en) liquor licence
draperen /drapera(n)/ (drapeerde, heeft gedrapeerd) drape
drassig /drɑsəx/ (adj) boggy, swampy
drastisch /drɑstis/ (adj, adv) drastic: *de prijzen* (or: *belastingen*) *~ verlagen* slash prices (or: taxes)
draven /drɑvə(n)/ (draafde, heeft/is gedraafd) **1** trot **2** hurry about
de **dreef** /dref/ (pl: dreven) **1** (+ op) in form, in one's stride: *niet op ~ zijn* be off form; *hij is aardig* (or: *geweldig*) *op ~* he's in good (or: splendid) form **2** avenue, lane
dreggen /drɛɣə(n)/ (dregde, heeft gedregd) drag
de **dreigbrief** /drɛɪɣbrif/ (pl: -brieven) threatening letter
het **dreigement** /drɛiɣəmɛnt/ (pl: -en) threat
¹**dreigen** /drɛiɣə(n)/ (dreigde, heeft gedreigd) **1** threaten, menace: *~ met straf* threaten punishment **2** threaten, be in danger: *de vergadering dreigt uit te lopen* the meeting threatens to go on longer than expected
²**dreigen** /drɛiɣə(n)/ (dreigde, heeft gedreigd) threaten
dreigend /drɛiɣənt/ (adj) **1** threatening, ominous, menacing: *iem. ~ aankijken* scowl at s.o. **2** imminent, threatening
de **dreiging** /drɛiɣɪŋ/ (pl: -en) threat, menace
de **drek** /drɛk/ dung, muck; manure
de **drempel** /drɛmpəl/ (pl: -s) **1** threshold, doorstep **2** threshold, barrier
de **drenkeling** /drɛŋkəlɪŋ/ (pl: -en) drowning

person; drowned body (*or:* person)
drenken /drɛŋkə(n)/ (drenkte, heeft gedrenkt) drench, soak, saturate
drentelen /drɛntələ(n)/ (drentelde, heeft/is gedrenteld) saunter, stroll
de **dresscode** /drɛskodə/ dress code
dresseren /drɛserə(n)/ (dresseerde, heeft gedresseerd) train
de **dresseur** /drɛsør/ (pl: -s) (animal) trainer
het/de **dressoir** /drɛswɑr/ (pl: -s) sideboard, buffet
de **dressuur** /drɛsyr/ training, drilling; dressage; schooling
de **dreumes** /drømes/ (pl: -en) toddler, tot
de **dreun** /drøn/ (pl: -en) **1** boom, rumble; drone: *er klonk een doffe ~* there was a dull boom (*or:* rumble) **2** drone, monotone **3** blow, thump: *iem. een ~ verkopen (geven)* sock s.o. one
dreunen /drønə(n)/ (dreunde, heeft gedreund) **1** hum, drone, rumble: *het hele huis dreunt ervan* the whole house is rocking with it **2** boom, crash, thunder, roar: *hij sloeg de deur ~d dicht* he slammed the door shut
dribbelen /drɪbələ(n)/ (dribbelde, heeft/is gedribbeld) dribble
drie /dri/ (num) three; [in dates] third: *een auto in z'n ~ zetten* put a car into third gear; *met ~ tegelijk* in threes; *zij waren met hun ~ën* there were three of them; *het is tegen* (or: *bij*) *~ën* it's almost three o'clock; *met 3-0 verliezen* lose by three goals to nil
driedaags /dridaxs/ (adj) three-day
driedelig /dridelex/ (adj) tripartite; threepiece
driedimensionaal /dridimɛnʃonal/ (adj) three-dimensional
driedubbel /dridʏbəl/ (adj, adv) **1** threefold, triple **2** treble, triple
de **Drie-eenheid** /driɛnhɛɪt/ the (Blessed (*or:* Holy)) Trinity
de **driehoek** /drihuk/ (pl: -en) triangle
driehoekig /drihukəx/ (adj, adv) triangular, three-cornered
de **driehoeksverhouding** /drihuksfərhɑudɪŋ/ (pl: -en) triangular (*or:* three-cornered) relationship
driehonderd /drihɔndərt/ (num) three hundred
driehoog /drihox/ (adv) three floors up; [Am] four floors up: *driehoog-achter* a garret (room)
driejarig /drijarəx/ (adj) **1** three-year-old: *op ~e leeftijd* at the age of three **2** threeyear
de **driekleur** /driklør/ tricolour
Driekoningen /drikɔnɪŋə(n)/ (feast of (the)) Epiphany, Twelfth Night
driekwart /drikwɑrt/ (adj, adv) three-quarter: *(voor) ~ leeg* three parts empty; *(voor) ~ vol* three-quarters full
de **driekwartsmaat** /drikwɑrtsmat/ three-

four (time)

drieledig /drilẹdəχ/ (adj) three-part: *een ~ doel* a threefold purpose

de **drieling** /drilɪŋ/ (pl: -en) (set of) triplets: *de geboorte van een ~* the birth of triplets

het **drieluik** /drilœyk/ (pl: -en) triptych

driemaal /drimal/ (adv) three times: *~ zo veel (groot) geworden* increased threefold; *~ is scheepsrecht* third time lucky

driemaandelijks /drimạndələks/ (adj, adv) quarterly, three-monthly: *een ~ tijdschrift* a quarterly

de **driemaster** /drimastər/ (pl: -s) three-master

de **driesprong** /drisprɔŋ/ (pl: -en) three-forked road

driest /drist/ (adj, adv) reckless, foolhardy

het **driesterrenrestaurant** /dristɛrə(n)-rɛstorɑnt/ (pl: -s) three-star restaurant

het **drietal** /drital/ (pl: -len) threesome, trio, triad

de **drietand** /dritɑnt/ (pl: -en) **1** trident: *de ~ van Neptunus* Neptune's trident **2** three-pronged, three-tined fork

de **drietrapsraket** /dritrɑpsrakɛt/ (pl: -ten) three-stage rocket

het **drievoud** /drivɑut/ (pl: -en) **1** treble, triplicate: *een formulier in ~ ondertekenen* sign a form in triplicate **2** multiple of three

drievoudig /drivɑudəχ/ (adj) treble, triple: *we moesten het ~e (bedrag) betalen* we had to pay three times as much

de **driewieler** /driwilər/ (pl: -s) tricycle; [car] three-wheel car

de **drift** /drɪft/ (pl: -en) **1** (fit of) anger, (hot) temper, rage: *in ~ ontsteken* fly into a rage **2** passion, urge **3** drift

de **driftbui** /drɪftbœy/ (pl: -en) fit (or: outburst) of anger

¹**driftig** /drɪftəχ/ (adj) **1** angry, heated: *je moet je niet zo ~ maken* you must not lose your temper **2** short-tempered

²**driftig** /drɪftəχ/ (adv) **1** angry, hot-headed: *~ spreken* speak in anger **2** vehement, heated: *hij stond ~ te gebaren* he was making vehement gestures; *zij maakte ~ aantekeningen* she was busily taking notes

de **driftkop** /drɪftkɔp/ (pl: -pen) hothead

het **drijfgas** /drɛifχɑs/ (pl: -sen) propellant

het **drijfijs** /drɛifɛis/ drift ice

de **drijfjacht** /drɛifjɑχt/ (pl: -en) drive, battue

drijfnat /drɛifnɑt/ (adj) soaking wet, sopping wet, drenched, soaked

de **drijfveer** /drɛifer/ (pl: -veren) motive, mainspring

het **drijfzand** /drɛifsɑnt/ quicksand(s)

¹**drijven** /drɛivə(n)/ (dreef, heeft/is gedreven) **1** float, drift: *het pakje bleef ~* the package remained afloat **2** float, drift, glide **3** be soaked: *~ van het zweet* be dripping with sweat

²**drijven** /drɛivə(n)/ (dreef, heeft gedreven)

1 drive, push, move: *de menigte uit elkaar ~* break up the crowd **2** drive, push, compel: *iem. tot het uiterste ~* push s.o. to the extreme **3** run, conduct, manage: *handel ~ met een land* trade with a country; *de spot met iem. ~* make fun of s.o. **4** drive; propel; operate: *door stoom gedreven schepen* steam-driven (or: steam-propelled) ships

drijvend /drɛivənt/ (adj) floating, drifting

de **drijver** /drɛivər/ (pl: -s) **1** driver; drover; beater **2** float: *~s van een watervliegtuig* floats of a seaplane

de **drilboor** /drɪlbor/ (pl: -boren) drill

drillen /drɪlə(n)/ (drilde, heeft gedrild) drill

¹**dringen** /drɪŋə(n)/ (drong, is gedrongen) **1** push, shove, penetrate: *hij drong door de menigte heen* he pushed (or: elbowed, forced) his way through the crowd; *naar voren ~* push forward **2** push, press: *het zal wel ~ worden om een goede plaats* we'll probably have to fight for a good seat **3** press, urge, compel: *de tijd dringt* time is short

²**dringen** /drɪŋə(n)/ (drong, heeft gedrongen) push, force

¹**dringend** /drɪŋənt/ (adj) **1** urgent; pressing; acute; dire **2** urgent; earnest; insistent, pressing: *op ~ verzoek van* at the urgent request of

²**dringend** /drɪŋənt/ (adv) urgently, acutely, direly: *ik moet u ~ spreken* I must speak to you immediately

drinkbaar /drɪŋbar/ (adj) drinkable; potable

de **drinkbeker** /drɪŋbekər/ (pl: -s) drinking cup, goblet

drinken /drɪŋkə(n)/ (dronk, heeft gedronken) **1** drink; sip: *wat wil je ~?, wat drink jij?* what are you having?, what'll it be?; *ik drink op ons succes* here's to our success! **2** soak (up) **3** drink: *te veel ~* drink (to excess)

de **drinker** /drɪŋkər/ (pl: -s) drinker

de **drinkplaats** /drɪŋkplats/ (pl: -en) watering place

het **drinkwater** /drɪŋkwatər/ drinking water, potable water

de **drinkyoghurt** /drɪŋkjɔχʏrt/ (pl: -s) drinking yoghurt

de **drive-inbioscoop** /drɑjvɪmbijoskop/ (pl: -bioscopen) drive-in-cinema

droef /druf/ (adj, adv) sad, sorrowful

de **droefenis** /drufənɪs/ [form] sadness, sorrow, grief: *in diepe ~* in deep distress

droefgeestig /drufχestəχ/ (adj) melancholy, mournful; doleful

de **droefheid** /drufhɛit/ sorrow, sadness, grief

de **droesem** /drusəm/ (pl: -s) dregs, lees

¹**droevig** /druvəχ/ (adj) **1** sad, sorrowful, miserable **2** sad, melancholy: *een ~e blik* a sad (or: melancholy) look **3** depressing, saddening: *een ~ lied* a sad (or: melancholy) song **4** depressing, miserable

²droevig /drᴜvəx/ (adv) **1** sadly, dolefully, sorrowfully **2** depressingly, pathetically: *het is ~ gesteld met hem* he's in a distressing situation

¹drogen /droɣə(n)/ (droogde, heeft/is gedroogd) dry: *de was **te** ~ hangen* hang out the laundry to dry

²drogen /droɣə(n)/ (droogde, heeft gedroogd) dry, air; wipe: *iets **laten** ~ leave sth. to dry

de **droger** /droɣər/ (pl: -s) drier

drogeren /droɣerə(n)/ (drogeerde, heeft gedrogeerd) dope

de **drogist** /droɣɪst/ (pl: -en) **1** chemist **2** chemist's

de **drogisterij** /droɣɪstərɛi/ (pl: -en) chemist's

de **drogreden** /droxredə(n)/ (pl: -en) fallacy, sophism

de **drol** /drɔl/ (pl: -len) turd

de **drom** /drɔm/ (pl: -men) crowd, horde, throng

de **dromedaris** /drɔmədarəs/ (pl: -sen) dromedary, (Arabian) camel

¹dromen /dromə(n)/ (droomde, heeft gedroomd) **1** dream **2** (day)dream, muse

²dromen /dromə(n)/ (droomde, heeft gedroomd) dream, imagine

de **dromer** /dromər/ (pl: -s) dreamer, stargazer, rainbow chaser

¹dromerig /dromərəx/ (adj) **1** dreamy, faraway **2** dreamy, dreamlike, illusory: *een ~e sfeer* a dreamlike feeling

²dromerig /dromərəx/ (adv) dreamily: *~ uit zijn ogen **kijken*** gaze dreamily

de **dronk** /drɔŋk/ (pl: -en) **1** toast **2** drinking

de **dronkaard** /drɔŋkart/ (pl: -s) drunk(ard)

dronken /drɔŋkə(n)/ (adj) drunken, drunk: *de wijn **maakt** hem ~* the wine is making him drunk; *iem. ~ **voeren*** ply s.o. with liquor

de **dronkenlap** /drɔŋkə(n)lɑp/ drunk

de **dronkenman** /drɔŋkəmɑn/ drunk

de **dronkenschap** /drɔŋkənsxɑp/ drunkenness, intoxication, inebriety: *in kennelijke staat van ~ (verkeren)* (be) under the influence of drink

droog /drox/ (adj) dry; arid; dried out: *hij zit **hoog** en ~* he is sitting high and dry

de **droogbloem** /droxblum/ (pl: -en) dried flower

de **droogdoek** /droxduk/ (pl: -en) tea towel

de **droogkap** /droxkɑp/ (pl: -pen) (hair)dryer (hood)

droogkoken /droxkokə(n)/ (kookte droog, is drooggekookt) boil dry

de **droogkuis** /droxkœys/ [Belg] dry-cleaning

droogleggen /droxlɛɣə(n)/ (legde droog, heeft drooggelegd) reclaim; [esp in the Netherlands]

het **droogrek** /droxrɛk/ (pl: -ken) drying rack

de **droogte** /droxtə/ (pl: -n) dryness; aridity; drought

de **droogtrommel** /droxtrɔməl/ (pl: -s) dryer, drying machine, tumble(r) dryer

droogzwemmen /droxswɛmə(n)/ (zwom droog, heeft drooggezwommen) **1** practise swimming on (dry) land **2** [fig] do a dry run

de **droom** /drom/ (pl: dromen) dream, fantasy: *het **meisje** van zijn dromen* the girl of his dreams; *een **natte** ~* a wet dream ‖ *iem. **uit** de ~ helpen* disillusion (or: disenchant) s.o.

het **droombeeld** /drombelt/ (pl: -en) picture from a dream; fantasy, illusion

de **droomprins** /dromprɪns/ (pl: -en) Prince Charming

de **droomwereld** /dromwerəlt/ dream-world, fantasy world, fool's paradise

het/de **drop** /drɔp/ liquorice: *Engelse ~* liquorice all-sorts

droppen /drɔpə(n)/ (dropte, heeft gedropt) drop off

de **dropping** /drɔpɪŋ/ (pl: -s) drop

de **drug** /drʏɣ/ (pl: -s) drug, narcotic: *handelen in ~s, ~s **verkopen*** deal in (or: sell) drugs

de **drugsdealer** /drʏksdi:lər/ (pl: -s) (drug) dealer, pusher

het **drugsgebruik** /drʏksxəbrœyk/ use of drugs, drug abuse

de **drugsgebruiker** /drʏːɡsxəbrœykər/ (pl: -s) drug user

de **drugshandel** /drʏkshɑndəl/ dealing (in drugs), drug trade

de **drugsrunner** /drʏːɡsrʏnər/ drug trafficker

de **drugsverslaafde** /drʏksfərslavdə/ (pl: -n) drug addict, junkie

de **druïde** /drywidə/ (pl: -n) druid

de **druif** /drœyf/ grape: *een tros druiven* a bunch of grapes

druilerig /drœylərəx/ (adj) drizzly

de **druiloor** /drœylor/ (pl: -oren) mope(r)

druipen /drœypə(n)/ (droop, heeft gedropen) drip, trickle

de **druiper** /drœypər/ (pl: -s) the clap, gonorrhoea

druipnat /drœypnɑt/ (adj) soaking wet, soaked through

de **druipneus** /drœypnøs/ (pl: -neuzen) runny nose: *ik **heb** een ~* my nose is running

het/de **druipsteen** /drœypsten/ stalactite; [hanging] stalagmite [standing]

de **druivenoogst** /drœyvə(n)oxst/ (pl: -en) grape harvest, vintage

het **druivensap** /drœyvə(n)sɑp/ grape-juice

de **druivensuiker** /drœyvə(n)sœykər/ grape sugar, dextrose

de **druiventros** /drœyvə(n)trɔs/ (pl: -sen) bunch of grapes

de **¹druk** /drʏk/ (pl: -ken) **1** pressure: *~ **uitoefenen** (op)* exert pressure (on) **2** strain, stress **3** edition: *een **herziene** ~* a revised edition

²druk /drʏk/ (adj) **1** busy, demanding, active, lively: *een ~ke **baan*** a demanding job; *een ~ **leven** hebben* lead a busy life **2** active, lively, boisterous: ~*ke* **kinderen** boisterous children; *zich ~* **maken** *over iets* worry about sth.

³druk /drʏk/ (adv) **1** busily: ~ *bezet* busy; ~ *bezig zijn (met iets)* be very busy (with, doing sth.) **2** busily, noisily, excitedly

drukbezet /drʏɣbəzɛt/ (adj) busy

de **drukfout** /drʏkfaut/ (pl: -en) misprint, printing error, erratum

¹drukken /drʏkə(n)/ (drukte, heeft gedrukt) press, push

²drukken /drʏkə(n)/ (drukte, heeft gedrukt) **1** push, press: *iem. de* **hand** ~ shake hands with s.o. **2** force: *iem.* **tegen** *zich aan* ~ hold s.o. close (to o.s.) **3** push down: *de prijzen* (or: *kosten*) ~ keep down prices (*or:* costs) **4** print: *10.000 exemplaren van een boek* ~ print (*or:* run off) 10,000 copies of a book **5** stamp, impress

drukkend /drʏkənt/ (adj) **1** oppressive, heavy, burdensome **2** sultry; close

de **drukker** /drʏkər/ (pl: -s) printer

de **drukkerij** /drʏkərɛi/ (pl: -en) printer, printing office (*or:* business), printer's

de **drukkingsgroep** /drʏkɪŋsxrup/ (pl: -en) [Belg] pressure group

de **drukknoop** /drʏknop/ (pl: -knopen) press stud, press fastener, popper

de **drukknop** /drʏknɔp/ (pl: -pen) push-button

de **drukletter** /drʏklɛtər/ (pl: -s) **1** (block, printed) letter **2** type, letter

de **drukpers** /drʏkpɛrs/ (pl: -en) printing press

de **drukproef** /drʏkpruf/ (pl: -proeven) proof, galley (proof), printer's proof

de **drukte** /drʏktə/ **1** busyness, pressure (of work): *door de* ~ *heb ik de bestelling vergeten* it was so busy (*or:* hectic) I forgot the order **2** bustle, commotion, stir: *de* ~ *voor Kerstmis* the Christmas rush **3** fuss, ado: *veel* ~ *over iets* **maken** make a big fuss about sth.

de **druktemaker** /drʏktəmakər/ (pl: -s) noisy (*or:* rowdy) person, show-off

de **druktoets** /drʏktuts/ (pl: -en) (push-)button

het **drukwerk** /drʏkwɛrk/ (pl: -en) printed matter (*or:* papers)

de **drum** /drʏm/ (pl: -s) drum

de **drumband** /drʏmbɛnt/ (pl: -s) drum band

drummen /drʏmə(n)/ (drumde, heeft gedrumd) **1** drum, play the drum(s) **2** [Belg] push and shove

de **drummer** /drʏmər/ (pl: -s) drummer

het **drumstel** /drʏmstɛl/ (pl: -len) drum set, (set of) drums

de **druppel** /drʏpəl/ (pl: -s) drop(let); bead: *alles tot de* **laatste** ~ *opdrinken* drain to the (very) last drop; *zij lijken op elkaar als twee ~s water* they are as like as two peas in a pod; [fig] *dat is de* ~ *die de* **emmer** *doet overlopen* that's the straw that breaks the camel's back

druppelen /drʏpələ(n)/ (druppelde, heeft gedruppeld) drip, trickle, ooze: *iets* **in** *het oog* ~ put drops in one's eye

het **dualisme** /dywalɪsmə/ dualism

¹dubbel /dʏbəl/ (adj) **1** double, duplicate, dual: *een ~e* **bodem** a double (*or:* hidden) meaning **2** double (the size), twice (as big) ‖ *een ~* **leven** *leiden* lead a double life

²dubbel /dʏbəl/ (adv) **1** double, twice: *ik* **heb** *dat boek* ~ I have two copies of that book; ~ *liggen* be doubled up **2** doubly, twice: *dat is* ~ *erg* that's twice as bad; *hij verdient het* ~ *en dwars* he deserves every bit of it

de **dubbeldekker** /dʏbəldɛkər/ (pl: -s) double-deck(er) (bus)

de **dubbelepunt** /dʏbələpʏnt/ (pl: -en) colon

de **dubbelganger** /dʏbəlɣaŋər/ (pl: -s) double, lookalike, doppelgänger

dubbelklikken /dʏbəlklɪkə(n)/ (dubbelklikte, heeft gedubbelklikt) double-click

het **dubbelleven** /dʏbəleva(n)/: *een ~* **leiden** lead a double life

dubbelop /dʏbəlɔp/ (adv) double

dubbelparkeren /dʏbəlparkerə(n)/ double-park

de **dubbelrol** /dʏbəlrɔl/ (pl: -len) double role, twin roles

het **dubbelspel** /dʏbəlspɛl/ (pl: -en) [sport] doubles

de **dubbelspion** /dʏbəlspijɔn/ (pl: -nen) double agent

het **dubbeltje** /dʏbəlcə/ (pl: -s) ten-cent piece: *zo plat* **als** *een* ~ (as) flat as a pancake; [fig] *het is een* ~ *op zijn kant* it's a toss-up, it's touch and go

dubbelvouwen /dʏbəlvauwə(n)/ (vouwde dubbel, heeft dubbelgevouwen) fold in two, bend double (*or:* in two)

dubbelzinnig /dʏbəlzɪnəx/ (adj) **1** ambiguous: *een ~* **antwoord** an ambiguous (*or:* evasive) answer **2** suggestive, with a double meaning

de **dubbelzinnigheid** /dʏbəlzɪnəxhɛit/ (pl: -heden) **1** ambiguity **2** ambiguous remark; suggestive remark

dubben /dʏbə(n)/ (dubde, heeft gedubd) brood, ponder: ~ *over iets* brood about sth.

dubieus /dybijøs/ (adj) **1** dubious, doubtful **2** dubious, questionable

duchten /dʏxtə(n)/ (duchtte, heeft geducht) fear

het **duel** /dywɛl/ (pl: -s) duel, fight, single combat

duelleren /dywɛlerə(n)/ (duelleerde, heeft geduelleerd) duel, fight

het **duet** /dywɛt/ (pl: -ten) duet, duo

duf /dʏf/ (adj, adv) **1** musty, stuffy, mouldy: *het* **rook** *daar* ~ it smelled musty **2** [fig] stuffy, stale

de **dug-out** /dʏɣaut/ (pl: -s) dugout

duidelijk /dœydələk/ (adj, adv) **1** clear, clear-cut, plain: *zich in ~e* **bewoordingen** *(taal)* *uitdrukken* speak plainly; *ik heb hem* ~ *gemaakt* **dat** ... I made it clear to him that ...;

*om ~ te **zijn**, om het maar eens ~ te **zeggen*** to put it (quite) plainly **2** clear, distinct, plain: *een ~e **voorkeur** hebben voor iets* have a distinct preference for sth.; *~ **zichtbaar*** (or: *te merken*) *zijn* be clearly visible (*or:* noticeable)

de **duidelijkheid** /dœydələkhɛit/ clearness, clarity, obviousness

duiden /dœydə(n)/ (duidde, heeft geduid) **1** point (to, at) **2** point (to), indicate: *verschijnselen die **op** tuberculose ~* symptoms that indicate tuberculosis

de **duif** /dœyf/ (pl: duiven) pigeon, dove

duigen /dœyɣə(n)/: *in ~ vallen* fall to pieces, collapse

de **duik** /dœyk/ (pl: -en) dive, diving, plunge: *een ~ **nemen*** take a dip

de **duikboot** /dœyɡbot/ (pl: -boten) submarine; sub; U-boat

de **duikbril** /dœyɡbrɪl/ (pl: -len) diving goggles

duikelen /dœykələ(n)/ (duikelde, is geduikeld) **1** (turn a) somersault, go (*or:* turn) head over heels, tumble **2** (take a) tumble, fall head over heels **3** drop, dive; plunge (downward)

de **duikeling** /dœykəlɪŋ/ (pl: -en) **1** somersault, roll **2** fall, tumble

duiken /dœykə(n)/ (dook, heeft/is gedoken) **1** dive, plunge, duck, go under; submerge: [sport] *naar een bal ~* dive for (*or:* after) a ball **2** duck (down, behind): *in een onderwerp ~* go (deeply) into a subject

de **duiker** /dœykər/ (pl: -s) diver

het **duikerpak** /dœykərpak/ (pl: -ken) wetsuit, diving suit

de **duikplank** /dœykplɑŋk/ (pl: -en) diving board

de **duiksport** /dœykspɔrt/ diving

de **duikvlucht** /dœykflʏχt/ (pl: -en) (nose) dive

de **duim** /dœym/ (pl: -en) **1** thumb: *de ~ **opsteken*** give the thumbs up; *onder de ~ houden* keep under one's thumb **2** inch ‖ [Belg] *de ~en **leggen*** surrender; throw in the sponge; *iets **uit** zijn ~ zuigen* dream sth. up

het **duimbreed** /dœymbret/ inch: *geen ~ toegeven* not budge an inch

duimen /dœymə(n)/ (duimde, heeft geduimd) **1** keep one's fingers crossed **2** suck one's thumb

duimendik /dœymə(n)dɪk/ (adv): [fig] *het ligt **er** ~ **bovenop*** it's as plain as the nose on your face, it sticks out a mile

het **duimpje** /dœympjə/ (pl: -s): *Klein Duimpje* Tom Thumb; *iets **op** zijn ~ kennen* know sth. like the back of one's hand; know sth. (off) by heart

de **duimschroef** /dœymsχruf/ (pl: -schroeven) thumbscrew: *(iem.) de duimschroeven **aandraaien*** tighten the screws (on s.o.); turn on the heat on (s.o.)

de **duimstok** /dœymstɔk/ (pl: -ken) folding ruler

de **duimzuigen** /dœymzœyɣə(n)/ thumb sucking

het/de **duin** /dœyn/ (pl: -en) (sand) dune, sand hill

Duinkerken /dœynkɛrkə(n)/ Dunkirk

de **duinpan** /dœympɑn/ (pl: -nen) dip (in the dunes)

het **¹duister** /dœystər/ dark, darkness: *in het ~ tasten* be in the dark

²duister /dœystər/ (adj, adv) **1** dark; gloomy; [fig] dim; black **2** shady, dubious

de **duisternis** /dœystərnɪs/ (pl: -sen) darkness, dark

de **duit** /dœyt/ (pl: -en): *ook een ~ in het zakje doen* put in a word

Duits /dœyts/ (adj) German ‖ *~e **herdershond*** Alsatian

de **Duitse** /dœytsə/ German woman, German girl: *zij is **een** ~* she is German

de **Duitser** /dœytsər/ (pl: -s) German

Duitsland /dœytslɑnt/ Germany

Duitstalig /dœytstaləχ/ (adj) **1** German-speaking **2** German

de **duivel** /dœyvəl/ (pl: -s) **1** [rel] devil **2** demon

duivels /dœyvəls/ (adj, adv) **1** diabolic(al), devilish, demonic: *een ~ **plan*** a diabolical plan **2** livid, (raving) mad, furious

de **duivelskunstenaar** /dœyvəlskʏnstənar/ (pl: -s) wizard

de **duivenmelker** /dœyvə(n)mɛlkər/ (pl: -s) pigeon fancier; pigeon flyer

de **duiventil** /dœyvə(n)tɪl/ (pl: -len) dovecote, pigeon house

duizelen /dœyzələ(n)/ (duizelde, heeft geduizeld) become dizzy, reel: *het duizelt **mij*** my head is spinning (*or:* swimming)

duizelig /dœyzələχ/ (adj) dizzy (with), giddy (with): *de drukte **maakte** hem ~* the crowds made his head spin

de **duizeligheid** /dœyzələχhɛit/ dizziness

de **duizeling** /dœyzəlɪŋ/ (pl: -en) dizziness, dizzy spell; vertigo: *soms last hebben van ~en* suffer from dizzy spells

duizelingwekkend /dœyzəlɪŋwɛkənt/ (adj, adv) dizzy, giddy; staggering

duizend /dœyzənt/ (num) (a, one) thousand: *~ **pond*** (or: **dollar**) a thousand pounds (*or:* dollars); *dat werk **heeft** (vele) ~en gekost* that work cost thousands; *~ **tegen** één* a thousand to one; *hij is er één **uit** ~(en)* he is one in a thousand

de **duizendpoot** /dœyzəntpot/ (pl: -poten) **1** centipede **2** jack of all trades

duizendste /dœyzəntstə/ (num) thousandth

het **duizendtal** /dœyzəntɑl/ (pl: -len) **1** thousand **2** thousands

de **dukaat** /dykat/ (pl: dukaten) ducat

dulden /dʏldə(n)/ (duldde, heeft geduld) **1** endure, bear, put up with: *geen **tegenspraak** ~* not bear being contradicted **2** tolerate, permit, allow: *de leraar duldt geen **te-***

genspraak the teacher won't put up with any contradiction

dumpen /dy̲mpə(n)/ (dumpte, heeft gedumpt) dump

de **dumpprijs** /dy̲mprɛɪs/ (pl: -prijzen) bulk-purchase price; clearance (*or:* knockdown) price

¹**dun** /dʏn/ (adj) **1** thin; slender; fine: *~ne darm* small intestine **2** sparse, light, fine, scant **3** thin, light, runny

²**dun** /dʏn/ (adv) thinly, sparsely, lightly; meanly

dunbevolkt /dy̲mbəvɔlkt/ (adj) thinly populated, sparsely populated

de **dunk** /dʏŋk/ **1** opinion **2** [basketball] dunk (shot)

dunken /dy̲ŋkə(n)/ (docht/dunkte, heeft gedocht/gedunkt): *mij dunkt, dat …* it seems to me that …, I think that …

de **dunne** /dy̲nə/: *aan de ~ zijn* have the trots (*or:* runs)

dunnetjes /dy̲nəcəs/ (adv) thin(ly) ‖ *iets nog eens ~ overdoen* go ahead and do it all over again

het **duo** /dy̲wo/ (pl: -'s) duo, pair

de **dupe** /dy̲pə/ victim, dupe: *wie zal daar de ~ van zijn?* who will be the one to suffer for it? (*or:* pay for it?)

duperen /dype̲rə(n)/ (dupeerde, heeft gedupeerd) let down, fail

de **duplex** /dy̲plɛks/ (pl: -en) [Belg] [roughly] duplex (appartment)

het **duplicaat** /dyplika̲t/ (pl: duplicaten) duplicate (copy), transcript, facsimile

duplo /dy̲plo/: *in ~* in duplicate

duren /dy̲rə(n)/ (duurde, heeft geduurd) last, take, go on: *het duurt nog een jaar* it will take another year; *het duurde uren* (or: *eeuwen, een eeuwigheid*) it lasted hours (*or:* ages, an eternity); *het duurt nog wel even (voor het zover is)* it will be a while yet (before that happens); *de tentoonstelling duurt nog tot oktober* the exhibition runs until October; *zolang als het duurt* as long as it lasts

de **durf** /dʏrf/ daring, nerve, guts

de **durfal** /dy̲rfɑl/ (pl: -len) daredevil

durven /dy̲rvə(n)/ (durfde, heeft gedurfd) dare, venture (to, upon): *hoe durf je!* how dare you!; *als het erop aan kwam durfde hij niet* he got cold feet when it came to the crunch

dus /dʏs/ (conj) so, therefore, then: *ik kan ~ op je rekenen?* I can count on you then?

dusdanig /dy̲zdanəx/ (adv) so, in such a way (*or:* manner); to such an extent

de **duster** /dy̲stər/ (pl: -s) housecoat; [Am] duster

dusver /dʏsfɛ̲r/ (adv): *tot ~* so far, up to now; *tot ~ is alles in orde* so far so good

het **dutje** /dy̲cə/ nap, snooze, forty winks

de ¹**duur** /dyr/ duration, length; life; term: *van korte ~* short-lived; *op de lange ~* in the long run; finally

²**duur** /dyr/ (adj) expensive, dear, costly: *die auto is ~ (in het gebruik)* that car is expensive to run; *hoe ~ is die fiets?* how much is that bicycle?; *dat is te ~ voor mij* I can't afford it

³**duur** /dyr/ (adv) expensively, dearly: *iets ~ betalen* pay a high price for sth.; pay dearly for sth.; [fig] *~ te staan komen* cost (s.o.) dearly

de **duurloop** /dy̲rlop/ (pl: -lopen) endurance race

¹**duurzaam** /dy̲rzam/ (adj) **1** durable; hard-wearing; (long-)lasting; enduring; permanent: *duurzame kleuren* permanent (*or:* fast) colours; *duurzame energie* renewable energy; *duurzame verbruiksgoederen* durable consumer goods **2** permanent, (long-)lasting: *voor ~ gebruik* for permanent use

²**duurzaam** /dy̲rzam/ (adv) permanently, durably: *~ gescheiden* permanently separated

de **duurzaamheid** /dy̲rzamhɛit/ durability, endurance; (useful, service) life

de **duw** /dyw/ (pl: -en) push, shove; nudge; poke; jab; dig: *hij gaf me een ~ (met de elleboog)* he nudged me; *de zaak een ~tje geven* help the matter along; *iem. een ~tje (omhoog, in de rug) geven* give s.o. a boost

de **duwboot** /dy̲wbot/ (pl: duwboten) pusher tug

¹**duwen** /dy̲wə(n)/ (duwde, heeft geduwd) press, push, jostle: *een ~de en dringende massa* a jostling crowd

²**duwen** /dy̲wə(n)/ (duwde, heeft geduwd) **1** push; shove; wheel: *een kinderwagen ~* wheel (*or:* push) a pram **2** push, thrust, shove; nudge: *iem. opzij ~* push (*or:* elbow) s.o. aside

de **duwvaart** /dy̲wvart/ push-towing, pushing

de **dvd** /devede̲/ DVD

de **dvd-brander** /devede̲brɑndər/ (pl: -s) DVD burner

de **dvd-recorder** /devede̲riko:rdər/ DVD recorder

de **dvd-speler** /devede̲spelər/ DVD player

het **dwaalspoor** /dwa̲lspor/ (pl: -sporen) wrong track, false scent: *iem. op een ~ brengen* mislead (*or:* misguide) s.o.

de ¹**dwaas** /dwas/ (pl: dwazen) fool, idiot, ass, dope, dummy, nincompoop

²**dwaas** /dwas/ (adj) foolish, silly, stupid: *een ~ idee* a crazy idea

³**dwaas** /dwas/ (adv) foolishly, stupidly, crazily

de **dwaasheid** /dwa̲shɛit/ (pl: -heden) foolishness, folly, stupidity

dwalen /dwa̲lə(n)/ (dwaalde, heeft gedwaald) **1** stray, wander **2** wander, roam: *wij dwaalden twee uur in het bos* we wandered through the forest for two hours **3** stray, travel

de **dwaling** /dwalɪŋ/ (pl: -en) error, mistake: *een rechterlijke* ~ a miscarriage of justice

de **dwang** /dwɑŋ/ compulsion, coercion; force; obligation; pressure: *onder* ~ under duress, involuntarily; *met zachte* ~ by persuasion

de **dwangarbeid** /dwɑŋɑrbɛit/ hard labour, forced labour

de **dwangarbeider** /dwɑŋɑrbɛidər/ (pl: -s) convict

het **dwangbevel** /dwɑŋbəvɛl/ (pl: -en) injunction, enforcement order: *iem. een ~ betekenen* serve a writ on s.o., slap an injunction on s.o.

het **dwangbuis** /dwɑŋbœys/ (pl: -buizen) straitjacket

de **dwangsom** /dwɑŋsɔm/ (pl: -men) penalty (*or:* damages) (imposed on a daily basis in case of non-compliance)

dwarrelen /dwɑrələ(n)/ (dwarrelde, heeft/ is gedwarreld) whirl; twirl; swirl; flutter

dwars /dwɑrs/ (adj, adv) transverse, diagonal, crosswise: ~ *tegen iets ingaan* go right against sth.; *ergens ~ doorheen gaan* go right through (*or:* across) sth.; ~ *door het veld* straight across the field; ~ *door iem. heen kijken* look straight through s.o.

de **dwarsbalk** /dwɑrzbɑlk/ (pl: -en) transverse beam, crossbeam

dwarsbomen /dwɑrzbomə(n)/ (dwarsboomde, heeft gedwarsboomd) thwart; frustrate

de **dwarsdoorsnede** /dwɑrzdorsnedə/ (pl: -n) cross-section

de **dwarsfluit** /dwɑrsflœyt/ (pl: -en) flute

de **dwarslaesie** /dwɑrslezi/ spinal cord lesion; paraplegia

dwarsliggen /dwɑrslɪɣə(n)/ (lag dwars, heeft dwarsgelegen) be obstructive, be contrary, be a troublemaker

de **dwarsligger** /dwɑrslɪɣər/ (pl: -s) **1** obstructionist, troublemaker **2** sleeper; [Am] railroad tie

de **dwarsstraat** /dwɑrstrat/ (pl: -straten) side street: [fig] *ik noem maar een* ~ just to give an example

dwarszitten /dwɑrsɪtə(n)/ (zat dwars, heeft dwarsgezeten) cross, thwart, hamper: *iem.* ~ frustrate s.o.('s plans); *wat zit je dwars?* what's worrying (*or:* bugging) you?

de **dweil** /dwɛil/ (pl: -en) (floor-)cloth, rag; mop

dweilen /dwɛilə(n)/ (dweilde, heeft gedweild) mop (down); mop (up): *dat is* ~ *met de kraan open* it's like swimming against the tide

het **dweilorkest** /dwɛilɔrkɛst/ (pl: -en) Carnival band, Oompah band

dwepen /dwepə(n)/ (dweepte, heeft gedweept) be enthusiastic: ~ *met* be enthusiastic about

de **dwerg** /dwɛrx/ (pl: -en) **1** gnome, dwarf, elf: *Sneeuwwitje en de zeven ~en* Snow White and the Seven Dwarfs **2** dwarf, midget

de **dwergstaat** /dwɛrxstat/ (pl: -staten) microstate, ministate

dwingen /dwɪŋə(n)/ (dwong, heeft gedwongen) force, compel, oblige, coerce, make (s.o. do sth.): *hij was wel gedwongen (om) te antwoorden* he was obliged to answer; *iem.* ~ *een overhaast besluit te nemen* rush s.o. into making a hasty decision; *niets dwingt je daartoe* you are not obliged to do it; *iem.* ~ *tot gehoorzaamheid* force s.o. to obey

¹**dwingend** /dwɪŋənt/ (adj) compelling, compulsory: ~*e redenen* compelling reasons

²**dwingend** /dwɪŋənt/ (adv) authoritatively: *iem. iets* ~ *voorschrijven* make sth. compulsory for s.o.

d.w.z. (abbrev) *dat wil zeggen* i.e.

de **dynamica** /dinɑmika/ dynamics

de **dynamiek** /dinɑmik/ dynamics, vitality, dynamism

het **dynamiet** /dinɑmit/ dynamite

dynamisch /dinɑmis/ (adj) dynamic, energetic, forceful

de **dynamo** /dinɑmo/ (pl: -'s) dynamo, generator

de **dynastie** /dinɑsti/ dynasty

de **dysenterie** /dɪsɛntəri/ dysentery

dyslectisch /dɪslɛktis/ (adj) dyslexic

de **dyslexie** /dɪslɛksi/ dyslexia

e

de **e** /e/ (pl: e's) e, E: *E groot* (or: *klein*) E major (or: minor)
e.a. (abbrev) *en andere(n)* et al.

de **eau de cologne** /odəkolɔnə/ (pl: eaux de cologne) cologne, eau de Cologne

de **eb** /ɛp/ **1** ebb(-tide), outgoing tide: *het is eb* the tide is out **2** low tide

het **ebbenhout** /ɛbə(n)hɑut/ ebony

het **e-book** /iːbuk/ (pl: -s) e-book

de **echo** /ɛxo/ (pl: -'s) echo, reverberation; blip: *de ~ weerkaatste zijn stem* his voice was echoed
echoën /ɛxowə(n)/ (echode, heeft geëchood) echo, reverberate, resound, ring

de **echoscopie** /ɛxoskopi/ (pl: -ën) ultrasound scan

¹**echt** /ɛxt/ (adj) **1** real, genuine; authentic; true; actual: *een ~e vriend* a true (or: real) friend **2** real, regular, true (blue, born): *het is een ~ schandaal* it's an absolute scandal **3** legitimate

²**echt** /ɛxt/ (adv) **1** really, truly, genuinely, honestly: *dat is ~ Hollands* that's typically Dutch; *dat is ~ iets voor hem* that's him all over; *ik heb het ~ niet gedaan* I honestly didn't do it **2** real, genuine(ly)

de **echtbreuk** /ɛxtbrøk/ (pl: -en) adultery
echtelijk /ɛxtələk/ (adj) conjugal, marital: *een ~e ruzie* a domestic quarrel
echter /ɛxtər/ (adv) however, nevertheless, yet, but: *dat is ~ niet gebeurd* however, that did not happen

de **echtgenoot** /ɛxtxənot/ (pl: -genoten) husband: *de aanstaande echtgenoten* the husband and wife to be

de **echtgenote** /ɛxtxənotə/ (pl: -n, -s) wife

de **echtheid** /ɛxthɛit/ authenticity, genuineness

het **echtpaar** /ɛxtpar/ (pl: -paren) married couple: *het ~ Keizers* Mr and Mrs Keizers

de **echtscheiding** /ɛxtsxɛidɪŋ/ (pl: -en) divorce

de **eclips** /eklɪps/ (pl: -en) eclipse

de **ecologie** /ekoloɣi/ ecology
ecologisch /ekoloɣis/ (adj, adv) ecological; biological

de **econometrie** /ekonometri/ econometry

de **economie** /ekonomi/ (pl: -ën) **1** economy **2** economy, frugality, thrift **3** economics, political economy
economisch /ekonomis/ (adj, adv) **1** economical, frugal, thrifty **2** economic: *de ~e aspecten van het uitgeversbedrijf* the economics of publishing

de **econoom** /ekonom/ (pl: economen) economist

het **ecosysteem** /ekosistem/ eco system

de **ecu** /eky/ (pl: -'s) ecu
Ecuador /ekwadɔr/ Ecuador

de **Ecuadoraan** /ekwadoran/ (pl: Ecuadoranen) Ecuadorian
Ecuadoraans /ekwadorans/ (adj) Ecuadorian

het **eczeem** /ɛksem/ (pl: eczemen) eczema
e.d. (abbrev) *en dergelijke* and the like

de **edammer** /edɑmər/ Edam (cheese)
edel /edəl/ (adj, adv) **1** noble, aristocratic: *van ~e geboorte* high-born **2** noble, magnanimous
edelachtbaar /edəlɑxtbar/ (adj): *Edelachtbare* Your Honour

het **edelgas** /edəlɣɑs/ (pl: -sen) inert gas

het **edelhert** /edəlhɛrt/ (pl: -en) red deer

de **edelman** /edəlmɑn/ (pl: edellieden) noble, nobleman, peer

het **edelmetaal** /edəlmetal/ (pl: -metalen) precious metal
edelmoedig /edəlmudəx/ (adj, adv) noble, generous, magnanimous

de **edelsmid** /edəlsmɪt/ (pl: -smeden) worker in precious metals

de **edelsteen** /edəlsten/ (pl: -stenen) precious stone, gem(stone)

de **editie** /edi(t)si/ (pl: -s) edition; issue; version

de **educatie** /edyka(t)si/ (pl: -s) education
educatief /edykatif/ (adj, adv) educational

de **eed** /et/ (pl: eden) oath, vow: *een ~ afleggen* take (or: swear) an oath, swear; *iets onder ede verklaren* declare sth. on oath

het **eeg** /eeɣe/ (pl: -'s) *elektro-encefalogram* EEG

de **EEG** /eeɣe/ *Europese Economische Gemeenschap* EEC

de **eekhoorn** /ekhorn/ (pl: -s) squirrel

het **eekhoorntjesbrood** /ekhorncəzbrot/ cep, boletus

het **eelt** /elt/ hard skin; callus

¹**een** /ən/ (art) **1** a; an: *op ~ (goeie) dag* one (fine) day; *neem ~ Oprah Winfrey* take s.o. like an Oprah Winfrey **2** a, some: *over ~ dag of wat* in a few days **3** a, some: *wat ~ mooie bloemen!* what beautiful flowers!; *wat ~ idee!* what an idea!

²**een** /en/ (num) one: *het ~ en ander* this and that; *van het ~ komt het ander* one thing leads to another; *op één dag* in one day; on the same day; *~ en dezelfde* one and the same; *de weg is ~ en al modder* the road is nothing but mud; *op ~ na* de laatste the last but one; *op ~ na de beste* the second best; *~ voor ~* one by one; one at a time || *~ april* April Fools' Day; *hij gaf hem er ~ op de neus* he gave him one on the nose; *geef me er nog ~* give me another (one), give me one more; *zich ~ voelen met de natuur* be at one with nature

de **eenakter** /enɑktər/ (pl: -s) one-act play

eencellig /ensɛ̱ləχ/ (adj) unicellular, single-celled

de **eend** /ent/ (pl: -en) **1** duck; duckling; drake: *zich een vreemde ~ in de bijt voelen* feel the odd man out **2** (Citroën) 2 CV, deux-chevaux

eendaags /enda̱χs/ (adj) **1** (once) daily **2** one-day

de **eendagsvlieg** /e̱ndɑχsfliχ/ (pl: -en) **1** mayfly **2** nine days' wonder

het **eendenkroos** /e̱ndə(n)kros/ duckweed

de **eendracht** /e̱ndrɑχt/ harmony, concord

eendrachtig /endrɑ̱χtəχ/ (adj, adv) united: *~ samenwerken* work together in unison, work harmoniously together

eenduidig /endœ̱ydəχ/ (adj, adv) unequivocal, unambiguous

eeneiig /ene̱iəχ/ (adj) monovular, monozygotic: *een ~e tweeling* identical twins

de **eengezinswoning** /eŋɣezɪnswonɪŋ/ (pl: -en) (small) family dwelling

de **eenheid** /e̱nhɛit/ (pl: -heden) **1** unity, oneness; uniformity: *de ~ herstellen* (or: *verbreken*) restore (or: destroy) unity **2** unit: *eenheden en tientallen* units and tens **3** unit, entity: *de mobiele ~* riot police; *een (hechte, gesloten) ~ vormen* form a (tight, closed) group

de **eenheidsprijs** /e̱nhɛitsprɛis/ (pl: -prijzen) **1** unit price, price per unit **2** uniform price

de **eenheidsworst** /e̱nhɛitsworst/ (pl: -en) sameness

de **eenhoorn** /e̱nhorn/ (pl: -s) unicorn

eenjarig /enja̱rəχ/ (adj) **1** one-year(-old), yearling **2** one-year('s): *een ~e plant* an annual

de **eenkamerflat** /e̱ŋkɑmərflɛt/ (pl: -s) single-room flat; [Am] single-room apartment

eenkennig /e̱ŋkɛnəχ/ (adj) shy

de **eenling** /e̱nlɪŋ/ (pl: -en) (solitary) individual, lone wolf, loner

eenmaal /e̱mal/ (adv) **1** once, one time: *~, andermaal, voor de derdemaal, verkocht* going, going, gone! **2** once; one day; some day: *als het ~ zover komt* if it ever comes to it **3** just, simply: *dat is nu ~ zo* that's just the way it is; *ik ben nu ~ zo* that's the way I am

eenmalig /emaḻəχ/ (adj) once-only, one-off: *een ~ optreden (concert)* a single performance

de **eenmanszaak** /e̱mɑnsak/ (pl: -zaken) one-man business

eenmotorig /emoto̱rəχ/ (adj) single-engine(d)

het **eenoudergezin** /eno̱udərɣəzɪn/ (pl: -nen) single-parent family

eenparig /empa̱rəχ/ (adj, adv) uniform: *~ versneld* uniformly accelerated

het **eenpersoonsbed** /empɛrso̱nzbɛt/ (pl: -den) single bed

de **eenpersoonskamer** /empɛrso̱nskamər/ (pl: -s) single room; single

het **eenrichtingsverkeer** /enrɪ̱χtɪŋsfərker/ one-way traffic: *straat met ~* one-way street

[1] **eens** /ens/ (adj) agreed, in agreement: *het over de prijs ~ worden* agree on a (or: about the) price; *het niet ~ zijn met iem.* disagree with s.o.

[2] **eens** /ens/ (adv) **1** once: *voor ~ en altijd* once and for all; *~ in de week* (or: *drie maanden*) once a week (or: every three months) **2** some day, one day; sometime; once: *kom ~ langs* drop in (or: by) sometime; *er was ~* once upon a time there was **3** just: *denk ~ even (goed) na* just think (carefully); *niet ~ tijd hebben om* not even have the time to; *nog ~* once more, (once) again

eensgezind /ensχəzɪ̱nt/ (adj, adv) unanimous, united; concerted: *~ voor* (or: *tegen*) *iets zijn* be unanimously for (or: against) sth.

de **eensgezindheid** /ensχəzɪ̱nthɛit/ unanimity, consensus, harmony, accord

eensklaps /e̱nsklɑps/ (adv) suddenly, all of a sudden

eensluidend /enslœ̱ydənt/ (adj) identical (in content), uniform (with): *tot een ~ oordeel komen* come to a uniform (or: unanimous) opinion (or: judgment)

eenstemmig /enste̱məχ/ (adj, adv) **1** unanimous, by common assent (or: consent) **2** in unison, for one voice

eentje /e̱ncə/ (ind pron) one: *neem er nog ~* have another (one, glass); *op* (or: *in*) *z'n ~* (by) o.s.; (on) one's own

eentonig /ento̱nəχ/ (adj, adv) monotonous, monotone; drab; dull: *een ~ leven (bestaan) leiden* lead a humdrum (or: dull) existence; *~ werk* tedious (or: monotonous) work; drudgery

de **eentonigheid** /ento̱nəχhɛit/ monotony, monotonousness, tedium

een-twee-drie /entwedri̱/ (adv) just like that: *niet ~* not just like that

het **een-tweetje** /entwe̱cə/ (pl: -s) one-two; wall pass

de **eenvoud** /e̱nvɑut/ **1** simplicity, simpleness; plainness **2** simplicity, straightforwardness, naivety, innocence: *hij zei dat in zijn ~* he said that in his naivety (or: innocence)

[1] **eenvoudig** /envɑ̱udəχ/ (adj) **1** simple, uncomplicated; plain; easy: *dat is het ~ste* that's the easiest way; *zo ~ ligt dat niet* it's not that simple **2** simple, unpretentious, ordinary **3** simple, plain, ordinary; low(ly); humble; modest, unpresuming, simple-hearted

[2] **eenvoudig** /envɑ̱udəχ/ (adv) **1** simply, plainly: *(al) te ~ voorstellen* (over)simplify **2** simply, just

eenvoudigweg /envɑ̱udəχwɛχ/ (adv) simply, just

de **eenwording** /e̱nwordɪŋ/ (pl: -en) unification, integration: *de politieke ~ van Europa* the political unification (or: integration) of Europe

eenzaam /ẹnzam/ (adj, adv) **1** solitary, isolated, lonely, lone(some): *een ~ leven leiden* live a solitary life **2** solitary, isolated, lonely, secluded

de **eenzaamheid** /ẹnzamhɛit/ solitude, solitariness, loneliness; isolation; retirement, seclusion

eenzelvig /enzẹlvəχ/ (adj, adv) self-contained, introverted

eenzijdig /enzẹidəχ/ (adj, adv) **1** one-sided, unilateral, limited: *hij is erg ~* he is very one-sided **2** one-sided, biased, partial

de **eer** /er/ **1** honour, respect: *de ~ redden* save one's face; *aan u de ~ (om te beginnen)* you have the honour (of starting); *naar ~ en geweten antwoorden* answer to the best of one's knowledge; *op mijn (woord van) ~* I give you my word (of honour); *de ~ aan zichzelf houden* take the honourable way out **2** honour(s), credit: *iem. de laatste ~ bewijzen* pay s.o. one's last respects; *het zal me een (grote, bijzondere) ~ zijn* I will be (greatly) honoured; *ter ere van* in honour of (s.o., sth.)

eerbaar /ẹrbar/ (adj, adv) honourable

het **eerbetoon** /ẹrbətoːn/ (mark of) honour: *met veel ~ ontvangen* receive with full honours

de **eerbied** /ẹrbit/ respect, esteem, regard; reverence; veneration; worship: *iem. ~ verschuldigd zijn* owe s.o. respect

eerbiedig /erbịdəχ/ (adj, adv) respectful

eerbiedigen /erbịdəγə(n)/ (eerbiedigde, heeft geëerbiedigd) respect, regard; observe: *de mening van anderen ~* respect the opinions of others

eerbiedwaardig /erbitwạrdəχ/ (adj) respectable

eerdaags /ẹrdaχs/ (adv) one of these days

¹**eerder** /ẹrdər/ (adj) earlier

²**eerder** /ẹrdər/ (adv) **1** before (now), sooner, earlier: *ik heb u al eens ~ gezien* I have seen you (somewhere) before; *hoe ~ hoe beter (liever)* the sooner the better **2** rather, sooner, more (likely): *ik zou ~ denken dat* I am more inclined to think that

het **eergevoel** /ẹrγəvul/ (sense, feeling of) honour, pride

eergisteren /erɣịstərə(n)/ (adv) the day before yesterday

het **eerherstel** /ẹrhɛrstɛl/ rehabilitation

¹**eerlijk** /ẹrlək/ (adj) **1** honest, fair, sincere: *~ is ~* fair is fair **2** honest, true, genuine: *een ~e zaak* a square deal **3** fair, square, honest: *~ spel* fair play

²**eerlijk** /ẹrlək/ (adv) **1** sincerely; honestly; frankly: *~ gezegd* to be honest **2** honestly, really and truly: *ik heb het niet gedaan, ~ (waar)!* honestly, I didn't do it! **3** fairly, squarely: *~ delen!* fair shares!

de **eerlijkheid** /ẹrləkhɛit/ honesty, fairness, sincerity

eerst /erst/ (adv) **1** first: *hij zag de brand het ~* he was the first to see the fire; *(het) ~ aan de beurt zijn* be first (*or:* next); *voor het ~* for the first time, first **2** first(ly), at first: *~ was hij verlegen, later niet meer* at first he was shy, but not later

eerste /ẹrstə/ (num) first; chief; prime; senior; earliest: *de ~ vier dagen* (for) the next four days; *informatie uit de ~ hand* first-hand information; *de ~ die aankomt krijgt de prijs* the first to get there gets the prize; *één keer moet de ~ zijn* there's a first time for everything; *van de ~ tot de laatste* down to the last one, every man jack (of them); *hij is niet de ~ de beste* he is not just anybody; *ten ~* first(ly), in the first place

eerstegraads /ẹrstəɣrats/ (adj, adv) first-degree

de **eerstehulppost** /erstəhỵlpɔst/ (pl: -en) first-aid post (*or:* station)

eerstejaars /ẹrstəjars/ (adj) first-year

het **Eerste Kamerlid** /ẹrstəkạmərlɪt/ (pl: -leden) Member of the Upper Chamber (*or:* Upper House) (of the Dutch Parliament)

eersteklas /erstəklọs/ (adj, adv) first-rate, first-class

de **eersteklasser** /erstəklọsər/ (pl: -s) first-former

de **eerstelijnszorg** /ẹrstəlɛɪnsɔrχ/ primary health care

eersterangs /erstərǫns/ (adj) first-rate, top-class

eerstkomend /erstkọmənt/ (adj) next: *~e woensdag* next Wednesday

eerstvolgend /erstfọlɣənt/ (adj) next: *de ~e trein* the next train due

¹**eervol** /ẹrvɔl/ (adj) **1** honourable, glorious, creditable: *de ~le verliezers* the worthy losers; *een ~le vermelding* an honourable mention **2** with honour, without loss of face

²**eervol** /ẹrvɔl/ (adv) honourably, worthily, gloriously, creditably

de **eerwraak** /ẹrvrak/ honour killing

eerzaam /ẹrzam/ (adj, adv) respectable, virtuous, decent, honest

de **eerzucht** /ẹrzʏχt/ ambition

eerzuchtig /erzỵχtəχ/ (adj, adv) ambitious, aspiring

eetbaar /ẹdbar/ (adj) edible, fit for (human) consumption, fit to eat; eatable; palatable

het **eetcafé** /ẹtkɑfe/ (pl: -s) pub serving meals; beanery

de **eetgelegenheid** /ẹtχəleɣə(n)hɛɪt/ (pl: -gelegenheden) place to eat, eating-house

het **eetgerei** /ẹtχərɛi/ cutlery, tableware

de **eetgewoonte** /ẹtχəwontə/ (pl: -n, -s) eating habit; diet

de **eethoek** /ẹthuk/ (pl: -en) **1** dinette **2** dining table and chairs

het **eethuis** /ẹthœys/ (pl: eethuizen) eating house, (small) restaurant de **eetkamer** /ˈetkamər/ dining room

de **eetlepel** /ˈetlepəl/ (pl: -s) soup spoon; dessertspoon; tablespoon(ful)

de **eetlust** /ˈetlʏst/ appetite

het **eetservies** /ˈetsɛrvis/ (pl: -serviezen) dinner service, dinner set, tableware

het **eetstokje** /ˈetstɔkjə/ (pl: -s) chopstick

de **eetstoornis** /ˈetstornɪs/ eating disorder

de **eetwaar** /ˈetwar/ (pl: eetwaren) foodstuff(s), eatables, food

de **eetzaal** /ˈetsal/ (pl: eetzalen) dining room (or: hall); canteen

de **eeuw** /ew/ (pl: -en) **1** century: *in de loop der ~en* through the centuries (or: ages); *in het Londen van de achttiende ~* in eighteenth-century London **2** ages, (donkey's) years: *het is ~en geleden dat ik van haar iets gehoord heb* I haven't heard from her for ages; *dat heeft een ~ geduurd* that took ages **3** age, era, epoch: *de gouden ~* the golden age

eeuwenlang /ˈewə(n)lɑŋ/ (adv) for centuries (or: ages)

eeuwenoud /ˈewə(n)ɑut/ (adj) age-old, centuries-old

¹**eeuwig** /ˈewəχ/ (adj) **1** eternal, everlasting, perennial, perpetual, never-ending: *~e sneeuw* perpetual snow **2** lifelong, undying: *~e vriendschap* undying (or: lifelong) friendship **3** endless, incessant, interminable, never-ending: *een ~e optimist* an incorrigible optimist

²**eeuwig** /ˈewəχ/ (adv) **1** forever, eternally, perpetually **2** forever, incessantly, endlessly, interminably, eternally

eeuwigdurend /ˈewəχdyrənt/ (adj) perpetual, everlasting

de **eeuwigheid** /ˈewəχhɛit/ (pl: -heden) ages, eternity: *ik heb je in geen ~ gezien* I haven't seen you for ages

de **eeuwwisseling** /ˈewɪsəlɪŋ/ (pl: -en) turn of the century

het **effect** /ɛfɛkt/ (pl: -en) **1** effect, result, outcome, consequence: *een averechts ~ hebben* have a contrary effect, be counter-productive **2** spin; side: *een bal ~ geven* put spin on a ball **3** [com] stock, share, security

het **effectbejag** /ɛfɛktbəjɑχ/ aiming at effect, straining after effect: *uit ~ for (the sake of) effect*

de **effectenbeurs** /ɛfɛktə(n)børs/ (pl: -beurzen) stock exchange

de **effectenmarkt** /ɛfɛktəmɑrkt/ stock market

effectief /ɛfɛktif/ (adj, adv) **1** real, actual, effective, active **2** effective, efficacious **3** [Belg; law] non-suspended

effen /ˈɛfə(n)/ (adj, adv) **1** even, level, smooth **2** plain, uniform, unpatterned: *~ rood* solid red

effenen /ˈɛfənə(n)/ (effende, heeft geëffend) level, smooth: *de weg ~ voor iem.* pave the way for s.o.

de **efficiency** /ɛfɪʃənsi/ efficiency

efficiënt /ɛfiʃɛnt/ (adj, adv) efficient, businesslike

de **efficiëntie** /ɛfiʃɛn(t)si/ efficiency

de **eg** /ɛχ/ (pl: eggen) harrow

de **EG** /eˈχe/ *Europese Gemeenschap* EC

egaal /eˈχal/ (adj, adv) even, level, smooth; uniform; solid

egaliseren /eˈχalizerə(n)/ (egaliseerde, heeft geëgaliseerd) level, equalize, smooth

Egeïsch /eˈχeis/ (adj) Aegean

de **egel** /ˈeχəl/ (pl: -s) hedgehog

eggen /ˈɛχə(n)/ (egde, heeft geëgd) harrow

het **ego** /ˈeχo/ ego

¹**egocentrisch** /eˈχosɛntris/ (adj) egocentric, self-centred

²**egocentrisch** /eˈχosɛntris/ (adv) in an egocentric (or: a self-centred) way

het **egoïsme** /eˈχowɪsmə/ egoism, selfishness

de **egoïst** /eˈχowɪst/ (pl: -en) egoist

egoïstisch /eˈχowɪstis/ (adj, adv) egoistic(al), selfish

Egypte /eˈχɪptə/ Egypt

de **Egyptenaar** /eˈχɪptənar/ (pl: Egyptenaren) Egyptian

Egyptisch /eˈχɪptis/ (adj) Egyptian

eh /ə/ (int) er

de **EHBO** /ehabeo/ *Eerste Hulp Bij Ongelukken* first aid; first-aid post (or: station); accident and emergency ward (or: department)

het **ei** /ɛi/ (pl: eieren) **1** egg: *een hard(gekookt) ei* a hard-boiled egg; *dat is voor haar een zacht-(gekookt) eitje* it's a piece of cake for her; *dat is het hele eieren eten* that's all there is to it; *een ei leggen* (or: *uitbroeden*) lay (or: hatch) an egg **2** ovum, egg ǁ [Belg] *ei zo na* very nearly

de **eicel** /ˈɛisɛl/ (pl: -len) egg cell, ovum, female germ cell

de **eierdooier** /ˈɛiərdojər/ (pl: -s) egg yolk

de **eierdop** /ˈɛiərdɔp/ (pl: -pen) eggshell

het **eierdopje** /ˈɛiərdɔpjə/ (pl: eierdopjes) eggcup

de **eierschaal** /ˈɛiərsχal/ (pl: -schalen) eggshell

de **eierstok** /ˈɛiərstɔk/ (pl: -ken) ovary

de **eierwekker** /ˈɛiərwɛkər/ (pl: -s) egg-timer

de **Eiffeltoren** /ˈɛifəltorə(n)/ Eiffel Tower

het **eigeel** /ˈɛiχel/ egg yolk

eigen /ˈɛiχə(n)/ (adj) **1** own; private; personal: *voor ~ gebruik* for one's (own) private use; *mensen met een ~ huis* people who own their own house; *wij hebben ieder een ~ (slaap)kamer* we have separate (bed)rooms; *~ weg* private road; *op zijn geheel ~ wijze* in his very own way; *bemoei je met je ~ zaken* mind your own business **2** typical, characteristic, individual: *bier met een geheel ~ smaak* beer with a distinctive taste **3** own, native, domestic

de **eigenaar** /ˈɛiχənar/ (pl: eigenaren) owner, possessor; holder: *de rechtmatige ~* the rightful owner; *deze auto is drie keer van ~*

veranderd this car changed hands three times
¹eigenaardig /ɛiɣənardəɣ/ (adj) **1** peculiar, personal, idiosyncratic: *een ~ geval* a peculiar case **2** peculiar, strange, odd, curious: *hij was een ~e jongen* he was a strange boy
²eigenaardig /ɛiɣənardəɣ/ (adv) peculiarly, oddly
het **eigenbelang** /ɛiɣə(n)bəlɑŋ/ self-interest
de **eigendom** /ɛiɣəndɔm/ (pl: -men) **1** ownership, title: *in ~ hebben* own (sth.) **2** property, possession; belongings: *dat boek is mijn ~* that book belongs to me
de **eigendunk** /ɛiɣə(n)dʏŋk/ (self-)conceit, self-importance, arrogance
eigengemaakt /ɛiɣə(n)ɣəmakt/ (adj) home-made
eigengereid /ɛiɣə(n)ɣərɛit/ (adj) headstrong, self-willed
eigenhandig /ɛiɣə(n)hɑndəɣ/ (adj, adv) (made, done) with one's own hand(s), (do sth.) o.s., personally
¹eigenlijk /ɛiɣə(n)lək/ (adj) real, actual, true, proper: *de ~e betekenis van een woord* the true meaning of a word
²eigenlijk /ɛiɣə(n)lək/ (adv) really, in fact, exactly, actually: *u heeft ~ gelijk* you are right, really; *wat is een pacemaker ~?* what exactly is a pacemaker?; *~ mag ik je dat niet vertellen* actually, I'm not supposed to tell you
eigenmachtig /ɛiɣəmɑxtəɣ/ (adj, adv) self-willed, self-opinionated: *~ handelen* act on one's own authority
de **eigennaam** /ɛiɣənam/ (pl: -namen) proper name
de **eigenschap** /ɛiɣənsxɑp/ (pl: -pen) quality; property; [comp] attribute: *goede ~pen* qualities (or: strong points, strengths)
eigentijds /ɛiɣə(n)tɛits/ (adj) contemporary, modern
de **eigenwaarde** /ɛiɣə(n)wardə/ self-respect, self-esteem
eigenwijs /ɛiɣə(n)wɛis/ (adj, adv) cocky, conceited, pigheaded: *doe niet zo ~* don't think you know it all
eigenzinnig /ɛiɣə(n)zɪnəɣ/ (adj, adv) self-willed; stubborn; obstinate; unamenable; wayward
de **eik** /ɛik/ (pl: -en) oak (tree)
de **eikel** /ɛikəl/ (pl: -s) **1** acorn **2** [anatomy] glans penis
het **¹eiken** /ɛikə(n)/ oak
²eiken /ɛikə(n)/ (adj) oak
de **eikenboom** /ɛikə(n)bom/ (pl: -bomen) oak (tree)
het **eiland** /ɛilɑnt/ (pl: -en) island: *op het ~ Man* on (or: in) the Isle of Man; *een kunstmatig ~* an artificial island, a man-made island
de **eilandbewoner** /ɛilɑndbəwonər/ (pl: -s) islander, island dweller
de **eilandengroep** /ɛilɑndə(n)ɣrup/ (pl: -en) archipelago, group of islands

de **eileider** /ɛilɛidər/ (pl: -s) Fallopian tube
het **eind** /ɛint/ (pl: -en) **1** way; distance; piece: *het is een heel ~* it's a long way; *het is nog een heel ~* it's still a long way; *daar kom ik een heel ~ mee* that will go a long way **2** end, extremity; ending: *~ mei* at the end of May; *het andere ~ van de stad* the other end of the town || *het bij het rechte ~ hebben* be right
de **eindbestemming** /ɛindbəstɛmɪŋ/ (pl: -en) final destination; terminal
het **eindcijfer** /ɛintsɛifər/ (pl: -s) final figure, grand total; final mark
het **einddiploma** /ɛindiploma/ (pl: -'s) diploma, certificate; certificate of qualification
het **einde** /ɛində/ (pl: -n) **1** end: *er komt geen ~ aan* there's no end to it; *ten ~ lopen* come to an end; *expire* **2** end; ending: *een verhaal met een open ~* an story with an open ending; *aan zijn ~ komen* meet one's end; *laten we er nu maar een ~ aan maken* let's finish off now; *aan het ~ van de middag* in the late afternoon; *ten ~ raad zijn* be at one's wits' end; *van het begin tot het ~* from beginning to end; *eind goed, al goed* all's well that ends well
de **eindejaarspremie** /ɛɪndəjarspremi/ (pl: -s) [Belg] end-of-year bonus
de **eindejaarsuitkering** /ɛɪndəjarsœytkerɪŋ/ (pl: -en) year-end bonus
eindelijk /ɛindələk/ (adv) finally, at last, in the end
eindeloos /ɛindəlos/ (adj) **1** endless, infinite, interminable **2** endless, perpetual, interminable, unending: *ik moest ~ lang wachten* I had to wait for ages
de **einder** /ɛindər/ horizon
het **eindexamen** /ɛintɛksamə(n)/ (pl: -s) final exam: *voor zijn ~ slagen* (or: *zakken*) pass (or: fail) one's final exams
de **eindexamenkandidaat** /ɛintɛksamə(n)kɑndidat/ (pl: -kandidaten) examinee, A-level candidate
het **eindexamenvak** /ɛintɛksamə(n)vɑk/ (pl: -ken) final examination subject, school certificate subject
eindig /ɛindəɣ/ (adj) **1** finite: *~e getallen* (or: *reeksen*) finite numbers (or: progressions) **2** limited
¹eindigen /ɛindəɣə(n)/ (eindigde, is geëindigd) **1** end, finish, come to an end, stop: *~ waar men begonnen is* end up where one started (from) **2** end, finish, come to an end, terminate; run out; expire: *dit woord eindigt op een klinker* this word ends in a vowel || *zij eindigde als eerste* she finished first
²eindigen /ɛindəɣə(n)/ (eindigde, heeft geëindigd) finish (off), end, bring to a close, terminate
het **eindje** /ɛincə/ (pl: -s) **1** piece, bit: *een ~ touw* a length of rope; a piece of string **2** short distance: *een ~ verder* a bit further **3** (loose) end: *de ~s met moeite aan elkaar kunnen kno-*

pen be hardly able to make (both) ends meet

de **eindmeet** /ɛintmet/ (pl: -meten) [Belg] finishing line

het **eindoordeel** /ɛintordel/ (pl: -oordelen) final judgement; final conclusion(s)

het **eindproduct** /ɛintprodʏkt/ (pl: -en) final product, end-product, final result, end-result

het **eindpunt** /ɛintpʏnt/ (pl: -en) end; terminus

het **eindrapport** /ɛintraport/ (pl: -en) **1** (school) leaving report **2** final report

de **eindredacteur** /ɛintredɑktør/ (pl: -en, -s) [roughly] editor-in-chief

het **eindresultaat** /ɛintrezʏltat/ (pl: -resultaten) final result, end result; conclusion; final total

de **eindsignaal** /ɛintsɪnal/ (pl: -signalen) final whistle

de **eindsprint** /ɛintsprɪnt/ (pl: -s) final sprint

het **eindstadium** /ɛintstadijʏm/ (pl: -stadia) final stage; terminal stage

de **eindstand** /ɛintstɑnt/ (pl: -en) final score

het **eindstation** /ɛintsta(t)ʃɔn/ (pl: -s) terminal (station)

de **eindstreep** /ɛintstrep/ (pl: -strepen) finish(ing line): *de ~ niet halen* [fig] not make it

de **eindstrijd** /ɛintstrɛit/ final(s), final contest

de **eindterm** /ɛintɛrm/ final attainment level

de **eindzege** /ɛintseɣə/ (pl: -s) first place

de **eis** /ɛis/ (pl: -en) **1** requirement, demand, claim: *hoge ~en stellen aan iem.* make great demands of s.o.; *aan de ~en voldoen* meet the requirements, be up to standard; *iemands ~en inwilligen* comply with s.o.'s demands **2** demand, terms: *akkoord gaan met iemands ~en* agree to s.o.'s demands **3** [law] claim, suit; sentence demanded

eisen /ɛisə(n)/ (eiste, heeft geëist) **1** demand, require, claim: *iets van iem. ~* demand sth. from s.o. **2** [law] demand, sue for: *schadevergoeding ~* claim damages

de **eiser** /ɛisər/ (pl: -s) **1** requirer, claimer **2** [law] plaintiff; prosecutor; claimant

het **eitje** /ɛicə/ (pl: -s, eiertjes) (small) egg; ovum: [fig] *een zacht(gekookt) ~* a soft-boiled egg

eivormig /ɛivɔrməx/ (adj) egg-shaped, oval

het **eiwit** /ɛiwɪt/ (pl: -ten) **1** egg white, white of an egg **2** protein, albumin

de **ejaculatie** /ejɑkylɑ(t)si/ (pl: -s) ejaculation

het/de **EK** /eka/ *Europees kampioenschap* European Championship

de **ekster** /ɛkstər/ (pl: -s) magpie

het **eksteroog** /ɛkstəroɣ/ (pl: -ogen) corn

het **elan** /elɑ̃/ élan, panache, zest

de **eland** /elɑnt/ (pl: -en) elk, moose

de **elasticiteit** /elastisitɛit/ elasticity

het **elastiek** /elastik/ (pl: -en) **1** rubber, elastic **2** rubber band, elastic band

het **elastiekje** /elastikjə/ (pl: -s) rubber band

elastisch /elastis/ (adj) elastic

elders /ɛldərs/ (adv) elsewhere

het **eldorado** /ɛldorado/ eldorado

electoraal /elɛktoral/ (adj) electoral

het **electoraat** /elɛktorat/ (pl: electoraten) electorate

elegant /eləɣɑnt/ (adj, adv) elegant; refined

de **elegantie** /eləɣɑnsi/ elegance

het/de **elektra** /elɛktra/ electricity

de **elektricien** /elɛktriʃɛ̃/ (pl: -s) electrician

de **elektriciteit** /elɛktrisitɛit/ electricity: *de ~ is nog niet aangesloten* we aren't connected to the mains yet

de **elektriciteitscentrale** /elɛktrisitɛitsɛntralə/ power station

elektrificeren /elɛktrifisərə(n)/ (elektrificeerde, heeft geëlektrificeerd) electrify

elektrisch /elɛktris/ (adj, adv) electric(al): *een ~e centrale* a power station; *een ~e deken* an electric blanket; *~ koken* cook with electricity

het **elektrocardiogram** /elɛktrokɑrdijoɣrɑm/ (pl: -men) electrocardiogram

elektrocuteren /elɛktrokytərə(n)/ (elektrocuteerde, heeft geëlektrocuteerd) electrocute

de **elektrocutie** /elɛktroky(t)si/ (pl: -s) electrocution

de **elektrode** /elɛktrodə/ (pl: -n, -s) electrode

de **elektrolyse** /elɛktroli:zə/ electrolysis

de **elektromagneet** /elɛktromaɣnet/ (pl: -magneten) electromagnet

de **elektromotor** /elɛktromotər/ (pl: -en, -s) electric motor

het **elektron** /elɛktrɔn/ (pl: -en) electron

de **elektronica** /elɛktrɔnika/ electronics

elektronisch /elɛktrɔnis/ (adj, adv) electronic: *~e post* electronic mail; e-mail

de **elektroshock** /elɛktroʃɔk/ (pl: -s) electroshock

de **elektrotechniek** /elɛktrotɛxnik/ electrotechnology

elektrotechnisch /elɛktrotɛxnis/ (adj) electrical: *~ ingenieur* electrical engineer

het **element** /eləmɛnt/ (pl: -en) element, component

elementair /eləmɛntɛːr/ (adj) elementary; fundamental, basic

de ¹**elf** /ɛlf/ (pl: -en, elven) elf, pixie, fairy

²**elf** /ɛlf/ (num) eleven; [in dates] eleventh: *het is bij elven* it's close on eleven

elfde /ɛlvdə/ (num) eleventh

elfendertigst /ɛlfəndɛrtəxst/ (num): *op zijn ~* at a snail's pace; in a roundabout way

het **elfje** /ɛlfjə/ fairy

de **Elfstedentocht** /ɛlfstedə(n)tɔxt/ (pl: -en) 11-city race; skating marathon in Friesland

het **elftal** /ɛlftal/ (pl: -len) team: *het nationale ~* the national team; *het tweede ~* the reserves

de **eliminatie** /elimina(t)si/ (pl: -s) elimination, removal

elimineren /eliminərə(n)/ (elimineerde, heeft geëlimineerd) eliminate, remove

elitair /elitɛːr/ (adj) elitist

de **elite** /elitə/ elite

het **elitekorps** /eli̯təkɔrps/ elite troop
het **elixer** /elɪ̯ksər/ (pl: -s) elixir
elk /ɛlk/ (ind pron) **1** each (one); every one: *van ~ vier (stuks)* four of each **2** everyone, everybody; *~e tweede* every other one **3** each; every; any: *ze kunnen ~e dag komen* they can come any day; *ze komen ~e dag* they come every day; *~e keer dat hij komt* every time he comes
elkaar /ɛlkɑ̯r/ (pron) each other, one another: *in ~s gezelschap* in each other's company; *uren achter ~* for hours on end; *vier keer achter ~* four times in a row; *bij ~ komen* meet, come together; *meer dan alle anderen bij ~* more than all the others put together; *wij blijven bij ~* we stick (*or:* keep) together; *door ~ raken* get mixed up (*or:* confused); *zij werden het met ~ eens* they came to an agreement; *naast ~ zitten* (*or:* *liggen*) sit (*or:* lie) side by side; *op ~ liggen* lie one on top of the other; *die auto valt bijna (van ellende) uit ~* that car is dropping to bits; *(personen of zaken) (goed) uit ~ kunnen houden* be able to tell (people, things) apart; *uit ~ gaan* **a)** break up; **b)** split up, break up; *zij zijn familie van ~* they are related; *iets niet voor ~ kunnen krijgen* not manage (to do) sth.
de **elleboog** /ɛ̯ləboːx/ (pl: ellebogen) **1** elbow **2** forearm: *ze moesten zich met de ellebogen een weg uit de winkel banen* they had to elbow their way out of the shop
de **ellende** /ɛ̯lɛndə/ **1** misery **2** trouble, bother: *dat geeft alleen maar (een hoop) ~* that will only cause (a lot of) trouble
de **ellendeling** /ɛ̯lɛndəlɪŋ/ (pl: -en) wretch, pain in the neck
¹**ellendig** /ɛ̯lɛndəχ/ (adj) **1** awful, dreadful, miserable: *ik voelde me ~* I felt rotten **2** wretched, miserable **3** awful, dreadful: *ik kan die ~e sommen niet maken* I can't do those awful sums
²**ellendig** /ɛ̯lɛndəχ/ (adv) awfully, miserably
de **ellepijp** /ɛ̯ləpɛip/ (pl: -en) ulna
de **ellips** /ɛlɪ̯ps/ (pl: -en) ellipse, oval
de **els** /ɛls/ (pl: elzen) alder
El Salvador /ɛlsɑ̯lvadɔr/ El Salvador
de **Elzas** /ɛ̯lzɑs/ Alsace
het **elzenhout** /ɛ̯lzə(n)hɑut/ alder-wood
het **email** /emɑ̯j/ enamel
de **e-mail** /iːmel/ e-mail
het **e-mailadres** /iːmeladrɛs/ e-mail address
e-mailen /iːmelə(n)/ (e-mailde, heeft ge-e-maild) e-mail
de **emancipatie** /emɑnsipa(t)si/ (pl: -s) emancipation, liberation
emanciperen /emɑnsipe̯rə(n)/ (emancipeerde, heeft geëmancipeerd) emancipate
de **emballage** /ɑmbɑla̯ʒə/ packing, packaging
het **embargo** /ɛmbɑ̯rɣoː/ (pl: -'s) (trade) embargo ‖ *een ~ opheffen* lift an embargo
het **embleem** /ɛmble̯m/ (pl: emblemen) em-

blem
de **embolie** /ɛmboli̯/ embolism
het **embryo** /ɛ̯mbrijoː/ (pl: -'s) embryo
embryonaal /ɛmbrijona̯l/ (adj) embryonic, embryonal: *in embryonale toestand* in embryo (*or:* germ), in the embryo stage
het **emeritaat** /emerita̯t/ superannuation, [roughly] retirement: *met ~ gaan* [roughly] retire
emeritus /eme̯ritʏs/ (adj) emeritus, retired: *een ~ hoogleraar* an emeritus professor, a professor emeritus
de **emigrant** /emiɣrɑ̯nt/ (pl: -en) emigrant
de **emigratie** /emiɣra̯(t)si/ (pl: -s) emigration
emigreren /emiɣre̯rə(n)/ (emigreerde, is geëmigreerd) emigrate
eminent /eminɛ̯nt/ (adj) eminent, distinguished
de **emir** /e̯mir/ (pl: -s) emir
het **emiraat** /emira̯t/ (pl: emiraten) emirate
de **emissie** /emɪ̯si/ (pl: -s) emission, issue
het **emissierecht** (pl: -en) emissions rights
de **emmer** /ɛ̯mər/ (pl: -s) bucket, pail: *met hele ~s tegelijk* by the bucketful
de **emoe** /e̯mu/ (pl: -s) emu
het **emoticon** /emo̯tikɔn/ (pl: -s) emoticon
de **emotie** /emo̯(t)si/ (pl: -s) emotion, feeling; excitement: *~s losmaken* release emotions; *de ~s liepen hoog op* emotions (*or:* feelings) were running high; *zij liet haar ~s de vrije loop* she let herself go
de **emotie-tv** /emo̯(t)siteve/ emotion tv
¹**emotioneel** /emo(t)ʃone̯l/ (adj) emotional, sensitive: *een emotionele benadering vermijden* avoid an emotional approach
²**emotioneel** /emo(t)ʃone̯l/ (adv) emotionally
het **emplacement** /ɑ̃plɑsəmɛ̯nt/ (pl: -en) yard
de **employé** /ɑmplwaje̯/ (pl: -s) employee
de **EMU** /eːmy/ *Economische en Monetaire Unie* EMU, Economic and Monetary Union
en /ɛn/ (conj) **1** and; plus: *twee en twee is vier* two and two is four; two plus two is four **2** and: *én boete én gevangenisstraf krijgen* get both a fine and a prison sentence **3** and, but, so: *en waarom doe je het niet?* so why don't you do it?; *en toch* and still; *nou en?* so what?, and …? ‖ *vind je het fijn? (nou) en of!* do you like it? I certainly do!, I'll say!
de **enclave** /ɑ̃kla̯və/ (pl: -s) enclave
de **encycliek** /ɛnsiklɪ̯k/ (pl: -en) encyclical
de **encyclopedie** /ɑ̃siklopedi̯/ (pl: -ën) encyclopaedia
de **endeldarm** /ɛ̯ndəldɑrm/ (pl: -en) rectum
endogeen /ɛndoɣe̯n/ (adj) endogenous
ene /e̯nə/ (ind pron) a, an, one: *woont hier ~ Bertels?* does a Mr (*or:* Ms) Bertels live here?
enenmale /e̯nənmalə/ (adv): *dat is ten ~ onmogelijk* that is absolutely (*or:* entirely, completely) impossible
de **energie** /enɛrʒi̯/ (pl: -ën) energy, power:

schone ~ clean energy; *overlopen van* ~ be bursting with energy

het **energiebedrijf** /ɛnɛrʒibədrɛif/ (pl: -bedrijven) electricity company, power company

de **energiebesparing** /ɛnɛrʒibəsparɪŋ/ energy saving

energiebewust /ɛnɛrʒibəwʏst/ (adj) energy-conscious

de **energiebron** /ɛnɛrʒibrɔn/ (pl: -nen) source of energy (*or:* power)

de **energiedrank** (pl: -en) energy drink

energiek /ɛnɛrʒik/ (adj, adv) energetic, dynamic

de **energievoorziening** /ɛnɛrʒivorzinɪŋ/ power supply

enerverend /ɛnɛrvɛrənt/ (adj) exciting, nerve-racking

enerzijds /enərzɛits/ (adv) on the one hand: ~ ..., *anderzijds* ... on the one hand ..., on the other (hand) ...

eng /ɛŋ/ (adj, adv) **1** scary, creepy: *een* ~ *beest* a nasty (*or:* creepy, scary) animal; a creepy-crawly **2** narrow

het **engagement** /ɑŋɡaʒəmɛnt/ (pl: -en) commitment, involvement

de **engel** /ɛŋəl/ (pl: -en) angel

Engeland /ɛŋələnt/ England

de **engelbewaarder** /ɛŋəlbəwardər/ (pl: -s) guardian angel

het **engelengeduld** /ɛŋələ(n)ɣədʏlt/ patience of a saint

Engels /ɛŋəls/ (adj) English ‖ *iets van het Nederlands in het* ~ *vertalen* translate sth. from Dutch into English

de **Engelse** /ɛŋəlsə/ Englishwoman: *zij is een* ~ she is English

de **Engelsman** /ɛŋəlsmɑn/ (pl: Engelsen) Englishman

Engelstalig /ɛŋəlstaləχ/ (adj) **1** English-language, English **2** English-speaking

de **engerd** /ɛŋərt/ (pl: -s) creep, ghoul

de **engte** /ɛŋtə/ (pl: -n, -s) narrow(s)

¹**enig** /enəχ/ (adj) only, sole: ~ *erfgenaam* sole heir; *dit was de* ~e *keer dat* ... this was the only time that ...; *hij is de* ~e *die het kan* he is the only one who can do it; *het* ~e *wat ik kon zien was* all I could see was

²**enig** /enəχ/ (adj, adv) wonderful, marvellous, lovely

³**enig** /enəχ/ (ind pron) **1** some: ~e *moeite doen* go to some trouble; *zonder* ~e *twijfel* without any doubt **2** any, a single: *zonder* ~ *incident* without a single incident **3** some, a few: *er kwamen* ~e *bezoekers* a few visitors came

enigerlei /enəɣərlɛi/ (adj) any: *in* ~ *mate* to any extent; *in* ~ *vorm* in any form, in some form or other

enigermate /enəɣərmatə/ (adv) somewhat, a bit, a little, to some extent

enigszins /enəχsɪns/ (adv) **1** somewhat,

rather: *hij was* ~ *verlegen* he was rather (*or:* somewhat) shy **2** at all, in any way: *indien (ook maar)* ~ *mogelijk* if at all possible

de ¹**enkel** /ɛŋkəl/ (pl: -s) ankle: *een verstuikte* ~ a sprained ankle

²**enkel** /ɛŋkəl/ (adj) single: *een kaartje* ~e *reis* a single (ticket)

³**enkel** /ɛŋkəl/ (adv) **1** singly **2** only, just: *hij doet het* ~ *voor zijn plezier* he only does it for fun; *ik doe het* ~ *en alleen om jou* I'm doing it simply and solely for you

⁴**enkel** /ɛŋkəl/ (num) **1** sole, solitary, single: *in één* ~e *klap* at one blow; *er is geen* ~ *gevaar* there is not the slightest danger; *geen* ~e *kans hebben* have no chance at all; *op geen* ~e *manier* (in) no way **2** a few: *in slechts* ~e *gevallen* in only a few cases **3** a few: *in* ~e *dagen* in a few days

de **enkelband** /ɛŋkəlbɑnt/ (pl: -en) **1** ankle ligament: *zijn* ~en *scheuren* tear one's ankle ligaments **2** anklet **3** electronic tag, ankle tag

de **enkeling** /ɛŋkəlɪŋ/ (pl: -en) individual: *slechts een* ~ *weet hiervan* only one or two people know about this

het **enkelspel** /ɛŋkəlspɛl/ (pl: -en) singles

het **enkeltje** /ɛŋkəlcə/ (pl: -s) single (ticket)

het **enkelvoud** /ɛŋkəlvɑut/ (pl: -en) singular

enorm /enɔrm/ (adj, adv) **1** enormous, huge: *een* ~ *succes* an enormous success **2** tremendous: ~ *groot* gigantic, immense

de **enquête** /ɑŋkɛːtə/ (pl: -s) **1** poll, survey: *een* ~ *houden* conduct (*or:* do, make) a survey of **2** inquiry, investigation

het **enquêteformulier** /ɑŋkɛːtəfɔrmylir/ (pl: -en) questionnaire

ensceneren /ɑ̃sənɛra(n)/ (ensceneerde, heeft geënsceneerd) stage, put on

het **ensemble** /ɑ̃sɑ̃blə/ (pl: -s) ensemble, company, troupe

de **ent** /ɛnt/ (pl: -en) graft

enten /ɛntə(n)/ (entte, heeft geënt) graft

de **enter** /ɛntər/ [comp] enter

enteren /ɛntərə(n)/ (enterde, heeft geënterd) board

de **entertoets** /ɛntərtuts/ (pl: -en) enter (key)

het **enthousiasme** /ɑntuʒɑsmə/ enthusiasm

enthousiast /ɑntuʒɑst/ (adj, adv) enthusiastic

de **entourage** /ɑnturaːʒə/ (pl: -s) entourage

de **entrecote** /ɑntrəkoːt/ (pl: -s) entrecôte

de **entree** /ɑ̃trɛ/ (pl: -s) **1** entrance, entrance hall **2** entry, entrance, admission: *vrij* ~ admission free; free entrance **3** admission: ~ *heffen* charge for admission

de **entreeprijs** /ɑ̃trɛprɛis/ (pl: -prijzen) admission (price)

de **envelop** /ɛnvəlɔp/ (pl: -n) envelope

enz. (abbrev) *enzovoort* etc.

enzovoorts /ɛnzovorts/ et cetera, and so on, etc.

het **enzym** /ɛnzi̱m/ (pl: -en) enzyme
het **epicentrum** /episɛ̱ntrʏm/ epicentre
de **epidemie** /epidemi̱/ (pl: -ën) epidemic
de **epilepsie** /epilɛpsi̱/ epilepsy
   epileptisch /epilɛ̱ptis/ (adj) epileptic
   epileren /epile̱rə(n)/ (epileerde, heeft geëpileerd) depilate
de **epiloog** /ɛrbo̱x/ (pl: epilogen) epilogue
   episch /e̱pis/ (adj, adv) epic(al), heroic
de **episode** /epizo̱də/ (pl: -n, -s) episode
het/de **epistel** /epi̱stəl/ (pl: -s) epistle
de **epo** /e̱po/ EPO
het **epos** /e̱pos/ (pl: epen) epic (poem), epos
de **equator** /ekwa̱tor/ equator
   Equatoriaal-Guinea /ekwatorijalɣine̱ja/ Equatorial Guinea
de **Equatoriaal-Guineeër** /ekwatorijalɣine̱jər/ (pl: -s) Equatorial Guinean
   Equatoriaal-Guinees /ekwatorijalɣine̱s/ (adj) Equatorial Guinean
de **equipe** /eki̱p/ (pl: -s) team
het **¹equivalent** /ek(w)ivalɛ̱nt/ (pl: -en) equivalent: *een ~ vinden voor* find an equivalent for
   ²equivalent /ek(w)ivalɛ̱nt/ (adj) equivalent (to)
   ¹er /ɛr/ (pron) of them [often not translated]: *ik heb er nog* (or: *nóg*) *twee* I have got two left (or: more); *ik heb er geen (meer)* I haven't got any (left); *hij kocht er acht* he bought eight (of them); *er zijn er die ...* there are those who ...
   ²er /ɛr/ (adv) **1** there: *ik zal er even langsgaan* I'll just call in (or: look in, drop in); *dat boek is er niet* that book isn't there; *wie waren er?* who was (or: were) there?; *we zijn er* here we are, we've arrived **2** there [often not translated]: *er gebeuren rare dingen* strange things (can) happen; *heeft er iem. gebeld?* did anybody call?; *wat is er?* what is it?, what's the matter?; *is er iets?* is anything wrong? (or: the matter?); *er is* (or: *zijn*) ... there is (or: are) ...; *er wordt gezegd dat ...* it is said that ...; *er was eens een koning* once upon a time there was a king ‖ *het er slecht afbrengen* make a bad job of it; *er slecht afkomen* come off badly; *ik zit er niet mee* it doesn't worry me
   eraan /ɛra̱n/ (adv) on (it), attached (to it): *kijk eens naar het kaartje dat ~ zit* have a look at the card that's on it (or: attached to it) ‖ *de hele boel ging ~* the whole lot was destroyed; *wat kan ik ~ doen?* what can I do about it?; *ik kom ~* I'm on my way
   erachter /ɛra̱xtər/ (adv) behind (it): *het hek en de tuin ~* the hedge and the garden behind (it)
   eraf /ɛra̱f/ (adv) off (it): *het knopje is ~* the button has come off; *de lol is ~* the fun has gone out of it
   erbarmelijk /ɛrba̱rmələk/ (adj, adv) abominable, pitiful, pathetic

de **erbij** /ɛrbɛi̱/ (adv) **1** there, included at (or: with) it **2** at it, to it: *ik blijf ~ dat ...* I still believe (or: maintain) that ...; *zout ~ doen* add salt; *hoe kom je ~!* the very idea!, what can you be thinking of!; *het ~ laten* leave it at that (or: there) ‖ *je bent ~* your game (or: number) is up
   erboven /ɛrbo̱və(n)/ (adv) above, over (it)
   erbovenop /ɛrbo̱və(n)o̱p/ (adv) on (the) top, on top of it (or: them) ‖ *nu is hij ~* **a)** he has got over it now; **b)** he has pulled through; **c)** [finance] he is on his feet again
   erdoor /ɛrdo̱r/ (adv) **1** through it: *die saaie zondagen, hoe zijn we ~ gekomen?* those boring Sundays, however did we get through them? **2** by (or: because) of it: *hij raakte zijn baan ~ kwijt* it cost him his job ‖ *ik ben ~* I've passed; *ik wil ~* I'd like to get past (or: through)
   erdoorheen /ɛrdorhe̱n/ (adv) through, through it
de **e-reader** /i̱ːriːdər/ (pl: -s) e-book reader, e-reader
de **ereburger** /e̱rəbʏrɣər/ (pl: -s) freeman; honorary citizen
de **erecode** /e̱rəkodə/ (pl: -n, -s) code of honour
de **erectie** /erɛ̱ksi/ (pl: -s) erection
de **eredienst** /e̱rədinst/ (pl: -en) worship, service
de **eredivisie** /e̱rədivizi/ premier league
het **eredoctoraat** /e̱rədɔktorat/ (pl: eredoctoraten) honorary doctorate
de **eregast** /e̱rəɣast/ (pl: -en) guest of honour
het **erelid** /e̱rəlɪt/ (pl: ereleden) honorary member
het **ereloon** /e̱rəlon/ (pl: erelonen) [Belg] fee
het **eremetaal** /e̱rəmetal/ medal of honour
   eren /e̱rə(n)/ (eerde, heeft geëerd) honour
de **ereplaats** /e̱rəplats/ (pl: -en) place of honour: *een ~ innemen* have an honoured place
het **erepodium** /e̱rəpodijʏm/ (pl: erepodia) rostrum, podium
de **eretitel** /e̱rətitəl/ (pl: -s) honorary title, title of honour
de **eretribune** /e̱rətribynə/ seats of honour, grandstand
het **erewoord** /e̱rəwort/ word of honour
het **erf** /ɛrf/ (pl: erven) **1** property **2** (farm)yard, estate; grounds: *huis en ~* property
het **erfdeel** /ɛ̱rvdel/ (pl: erfdelen) inheritance, portion: *het cultureel ~* the cultural heritage
   erfelijk /ɛ̱rfələk/ (adj, adv) hereditary
de **erfelijkheid** /ɛ̱rfələkhɛit/ heredity
de **erfelijkheidsleer** /ɛ̱rfələkhɛitsler/ genetics
de **erfenis** /ɛ̱rfənɪs/ (pl: -sen) **1** inheritance; [esp fig] heritage: *een ~ krijgen* be left an inheritance (or: a legacy) **2** legacy, inheritance; estate
de **erfgenaam** /ɛ̱rfɣənam/ (pl: erfgenamen) heir: *iem. tot ~ benoemen* appoint s.o. (one's)

heir

het **erfgoed** /ɛrfχut/ (pl: -eren) inheritance

de **erfpacht** /ɛrfpɑχt/ (pl: -en) [roughly] long lease

het **erfstuk** /ɛrfstʏk/ (pl: -ken) (family) heirloom

de **erfzonde** /ɛrfsɔndə/ original sin

¹**erg** /ɛrχ/ (adj) bad: *in het ~ste geval* if the worst comes to the worst; *vind je het ~ als ik er niet ben?* do you mind if I'm not there?; *wat ~!* how awful!; *het is (zo) al ~ genoeg* it's bad enough as it is

²**erg** /ɛrχ/ (adv) very: *het spijt me ~* I'm very sorry; *hij ziet er ~ slecht uit* he looks awful (*or:* dreadful, terrible)

ergens /ɛrχəns/ (adv) 1 somewhere, anywhere: *~ anders* somewhere else 2 somewhere: *ik heb dat ~ gelezen* I've read that somewhere 3 somehow: *ik kan hem ~ toch wel waarderen* (I have to admit that) he has his good points 4 sth.: *hij zocht ~ naar* he was looking for sth. (or other)

¹**ergeren** /ɛrχərə(n)/ (ergerde, heeft geërgerd) annoy, irritate

zich ²**ergeren** /ɛrχərə(n)/ (ergerde zich, heeft zich geërgerd) feel (*or:* get) annoyed (at); be shocked; take offence

ergerlijk /ɛrχərlək/ (adj, adv) annoying, aggravating

de **ergernis** /ɛrχərnɪs/ (pl: -sen) annoyance, irritation: *tot (grote) ~ van de aanwezigen* to the (great) annoyance of those present

ergonomisch /ɛrχonomis/ (adj, adv) ergonomic; [Am] biotechnological

de **ergotherapeut** /ɛrχoterapœyt/ (pl: -en) occupational therapist

de **ergotherapie** /ɛrχoterapi/ (pl: -ën) occupational therapy

erheen /ɛrhen/ (adv) there

erin /ɛrɪn/ (adv) in(to) it, (in) there: *~ lopen* [fig] walk right into it; fall for it

Eritrea /eritrɛja/ Eritrea

de **Eritreeër** /eritrejər/ (pl: -s) Eritrean

Eritrees /eritres/ (adj) Eritrean

erkend /ɛrkɛnt/ (adj) 1 recognized, acknowledged 2 recognized; authorized; certified: *een internationaal ~ diploma* an internationally recognized certificate

erkennen /ɛrkɛnə(n)/ (erkende, heeft erkend) recognize, acknowledge; admit: *zijn ongelijk ~* admit to being (in the) wrong; *iets niet ~* disown sth.; *een natuurlijk kind ~* acknowledge a natural child; *een document als echt ~* recognize a document as genuine

de **erkenning** /ɛrkɛnɪŋ/ (pl: -en) recognition, acknowledgement

erkentelijk /ɛrkɛntələk/ (adj) thankful, grateful

de **erkentelijkheid** /ɛrkɛntələkhɛit/ appreciation, recognition: *iem. zijn ~ voor iets betuigen* show one's appreciation of sth. to s.o.; *uit ~ voor* in recognition of, in gratitude for

de **erker** /ɛrkər/ (pl: -s) bay (window)

erlangs /ɛrlɑŋs/ (adv) past (it), alongside (it): *wil je deze brief even op de bus doen als je ~ komt?* could you pop this letter in the (post)box when you're passing?

de **erlenmeyer** /ɛrlə(n)mɛijər/ (pl: -s) Erlenmeyer flask

ermee /ɛrme/ (adv) with it: *hij bemoeide zich ~* he concerned himself with it; he interfered with it; *wat doen we ~?* what shall we do about (*or:* with) it?

erna /ɛrna/ (adv) afterwards, after (it), later: *de morgen ~* the morning after

ernaar /ɛrnar/ (adv) to (*or:* towards, at) it: *~ kijken* look at it

ernaast /ɛrnast/ (adv) 1 beside it, next to it: *de fabriek en de directeurswoning ~* the factory and the manager's house next to it 2 off the mark: *~ zitten* be wide of the mark, be wrong

de **ernst** /ɛrnst/ 1 seriousness, earnest(ness): *in volle (alle) ~* in all seriousness; *het is bittere ~* it is dead serious; a serious matter 2 seriousness, gravity: *de ~ van de toestand inzien* recognize the seriousness of the situation

¹**ernstig** /ɛrnstəχ/ (adj) 1 serious, grave: *de situatie wordt ~* the situation is becoming serious 2 serious, earnest, sincere: *dat is mijn ~e overtuiging* that is my sincere conviction 3 serious, severe, grave: *~e gevolgen hebben* have grave (*or:* serious) consequences

²**ernstig** /ɛrnstəχ/ (adv) 1 seriously, gravely: *iem. ~ toespreken* have a serious talk with s.o. 2 seriously, earnestly, sincerely: *het ~ menen* be serious

erom /ɛrɔm/ (adv) 1 around it, round (about) it: *een tuin met een schutting ~* a garden enclosed by a fence 2 for it: *als hij ~ vraagt* if he asks for it ǁ *denk je ~?* you won't forget, will you?; *het gaat ~ dat ...* the thing is that ...

eromheen /ɛrɔmhen/ (adv) around it, round (about) it

eronder /ɛrɔndər/ (adv) 1 under it, underneath (it), below it: *hij zat op een bank en zijn hond lag ~* he sat on a bench and his dog lay underneath (*or:* under) it 2 as a result of it, because of it, under it: *hij lijdt ~* he suffers from it ǁ *(iem.) ~ krijgen* beat, defeat (s.o.)

eronderdoor /ɛrɔndərdor/ (adv) underneath it: *~ gaan* a) go to pieces; b) go bust

erop /ɛrɔp/ (adv) 1 on it, on them: *~ of eronder* all or nothing 2 up it, up them, on(to) it: *~ slaan* hit it, bang on it; hit out 3 up it, up then: *~ klimmen* climb up it; mount it 4 to it: *het vervolg ~* the sequel to it ǁ *de dag ~* the following day; *~ staan* insist on it; *het zit ~* that's it (then)

eropaan /ɛrɔpan/ (adv) to(wards) it ǁ *als het ~ komt* when it comes to the crunch

eropaf /ɛrɔpɑf/ (adv) to (it): *~ gaan* go towards it

eropuit /ɛrɔpœyt/ (adv): *een dagje ~ **gaan*** go off (*or*: away) for the day; *hij **is** ~ mij dwars te zitten* he is out to frustrate me

de **erosie** /erozi/ (pl: -s) erosion

de **erotica** /erotika/ (pl) erotica

de **erotiek** /erotik/ eroticism

erotisch /erotis/ (adj, adv) erotic

erover /erover/ (adv) **1** over it, across it: *het kleed dat ~ **ligt*** the cloth which covers it **2** over it: *hij **gaat** ~* he is in charge of it **3** about it, of it: *hoe **denk** je ~?* what do you think about it?

eroverheen /eroverhen/ (adv) over it, across it: *het heeft lang geduurd eer ze ~ **waren*** it took them a long time to get over it

ertegen /ɛrteyə(n)/ (adv) **1** against it, at it: *hij gooide de **bal** ~* he threw the ball at it **2** against (it): *ik **ben** ~* I am against it; *~ **vechten*** fight (against) it, oppose it ‖ *~ **kunnen*** feel up to it; be able to put up with it

ertegenover /ɛrteyə(n)over/ (adv) **1** opposite (to) it: *het **huis** ~* the house opposite **2** against it; towards it: *~ **staat** dat ...* on the other hand ... ‖ *hoe **sta** je ~?* where do you stand on that?

ertoe /ɛrtu/ (adv) **1** to: *de **moed** ~ hebben* have the courage for it (*or*: to do it); *iem. ~ **brengen** om iets te doen* persuade s.o. to do sth.; *~ **komen*** get round to it; *hoe **kwam** je ~?* what made you do it? **2** to (it): *de vogels die ~ **behoren*** the birds which belong to it ‖ *wat **doet** dat ~?* what does it matter?; what has that got to do with it?

het **erts** /ɛrts/ (pl: -en) ore

ertussen /ɛrtysə(n)/ (adv) **1** (in) between (it): *het lukte me niet ~ te **komen*** I couldn't get a word in (edgeways) **2** in the middle, among other things

ertussenuit /ɛrtysə(n)œyt/ (adv) **1** out (of it) **2** out, loose: *een dagje ~ **gaan*** slip off for the day; *~ **knijpen*** slip off (*or*: away, out) (unnoticed), slope off

eruit /erœyt/ (adv) **1** out: *~!* (get) out! **2** out, gone: *~ **liggen*** be out of favour; [sport] be eliminated

eruitzien /erœytzin/ (zag eruit, heeft eruitgezien) **1** look **2** look like, look as if: *hij is niet zo dom **als** hij eruitziet* he's not as stupid as he looks **3** look a mess

de **eruptie** /erypsi/ (pl: -s) eruption

ervan /ɛrvɑn/ (adv) from it, of it: *dat is het **aantrekkelijke** ~* that's what is so attractive about it; *ik **ben** ~ **overtuigd*** I am convinced of it; *ik **schrok** ~* it gave me a fright

ervandaan /ɛrvɑndɑn/ (adv) **1** away (from there) **2** from there: *hij **woont** dertig kilometer ~* he lives twenty miles from there

ervandoor /ɛrvɑndor/ (adv) off: *met het geld ~ **gaan*** make off with the cash; *zij **ging** ~ met een zeeman* she ran off with a sailor

ervanlangs /ɛrvɑnlɑŋs/: *iem. ~ **geven*** let s.o. have it; *~ **krijgen*** (really) get (*or*: catch) it

[1]**ervaren** /ɛrvarə(n)/ (adj) experienced (in); skilled (in)

[2]**ervaren** /ɛrvarə(n)/ (ervoer/ervaarde, heeft ervaren) experience; discover

de **ervarenheid** /ɛrvarənhɛɪt/ skill, experience, practice

de **ervaring** /ɛrvarɪŋ/ (pl: -en) experience: *veel ~ **hebben*** be highly experienced; *de nodige ~ **opdoen*** (or: ***missen***) gain (*or*: lack) the necessary experience

erven /ɛrvə(n)/ (erfde, heeft geërfd) inherit: *iets (van iem.) ~* inherit sth. (from s.o.)

ervoor /ɛrvor/ (adv) **1** in front (of it) **2** before (it) **3** for it: *dat **dient** ~ om ...* that is for ..., that serves to ...; *hij **moet** ~ **boeten*** he will pay for it (*or*: this); *~ **zorgen** dat ...* see to it that ... **4** for it, in favour (of it): *ik **ben** ~* I am in favour of it **5** for it, instead (of it): *~ **doorgaan*** pass for (sth. else); *wat **krijg** ik ~?* what will I get for it? ‖ *er alleen voor **staan*** be on one's own; *zoals de zaken ~ **staan*** as things stand

de **erwt** /ɛrt/ (pl: -en) pea

de **erwtensoep** /ɛrtə(n)sup/ pea soup

de **es** /ɛs/ ash

de **escalatie** /ɛskala(t)si/ (pl: -s) escalation

[1]**escaleren** /ɛskalerə(n)/ (escaleerde, is geëscaleerd) escalate; rocket; shoot up

[2]**escaleren** /ɛskalerə(n)/ (escaleerde, heeft geëscaleerd) (cause to) escalate; force up

de **escapade** /ɛskapadə/ (pl: -s) escapade

de **escapetoets** /ɛskeptuts/ (pl: -en) escape (key)

het **escorte** /ɛskortə/ (pl: -s) escort

de **esculaap** /ɛskylap/ (pl: esculapen) staff of Aesculapius

de **esdoorn** /ɛzdorn/ (pl: -s) maple; sycamore

het **eskader** /ɛskadər/ (pl: -s) squadron

de **Eskimo** /ɛskimo/ (pl: -'s) Eskimo

de **esp** /ɛsp/ (pl: -en) aspen

het **Esperanto** /ɛsperɑnto/ Esperanto

de **espresso** /ɛsprɛso/ (pl: -'s) espresso

de **espressobar** /ɛsprɛsobɑːr/ café, coffee bar

het **essay** /ɛse/ (pl: -s) essay

de **essentie** /ɛsɛnsi/ essence

essentieel /ɛsɛnʃel/ (adj, adv) essential: *een ~ **verschil*** a fundamental difference

de **Est** /ɛst/ (pl: -en) Estonian

het **establishment** /ɛstɛblɪʃmənt/ establishment

de **estafette** /ɛstafɛtə/ (pl: -s) relay (race)

het **estafettestokje** /ɛstafɛtəstɔkjə/ (pl: -s) baton

esthetisch /ɛstetis/ (adj, adv) aesthetic

Estland /ɛstlɑnt/ Estonia

de **Estlander** /ɛstlɑndər/ (pl: -s) Estonian

Estlands /ɛstlɑn(t)s/ (adj) Estonian

de **etage** /etaʒə/ (pl: -s) floor, storey: *op de **eerste** ~* on the first floor; [Am] on the second floor

de **etalage** /etalaʒə/ (pl: -s) shop window, display window: *~s (gaan)* **kijken** (go) window-shopping

de **etalagepop** /etalaʒəpɔp/ (pl: -pen) (shopwindow) dummy, mannequin

etaleren /etalerə(n)/ (etaleerde, heeft geëtaleerd) display

de **etaleur** /etalør/ (pl: -s) window dresser

de **etappe** /etɑpə/ (pl: -s) **1** stage; lap **2** [sport] stage, leg

etc. (abbrev) *et cetera* etc.

het **¹eten** /etə(n)/ **1** food: *hij houdt van* **lekker** *~* he is fond of good food **2** meal; dinner: *warm ~* hot meal, dinner; *het ~* **is klaar** dinner is ready; *ik ben niet thuis* **met** *het ~* I won't be home for dinner

²eten /etə(n)/ (at, heeft gegeten) eat, dine: *blijf je ~?* will you stay for dinner?; *wij* **zitten** *net te ~* we've just sat down to dinner; *uit ~ gaan* go out for a meal

³eten /etə(n)/ (at, heeft gegeten) eat: *het* **is** *niet te ~* it's inedible; it tastes awful; *wat ~ we vandaag?* what's for dinner today?; *je kunt hier* **lekker** *~* the food is good here; *eet* **smakelijk** enjoy your meal

de **etensbak** /etə(n)zbɑk/ trough; food bowl

de **etensresten** /etənsrɛstə(n)/ (pl) leftovers

de **etenstijd** /etənstɛit/ dinnertime, time for dinner

de **etenswaren** /etənswarə(n)/ (pl) foodstuff(s), eatables, food

het **etentje** /etəncə/ (pl: -s) dinner, meal

de **eter** /etər/ (pl: -s) eater

de **ether** /etər/ **1** ether **2** air: *in de ~ zijn* be on the air

de **ethiek** /etik/ ethics

Ethiopië /etijopijə/ Ethiopia

de **Ethiopiër** /etijopijər/ (pl: -s) Ethiopian

Ethiopisch /etijopis/ (adj) Ethiopian

ethisch /etis/ (adj, adv) ethical, moral

het **etiket** /etikɛt/ (pl: -ten) label; ticket; tag; sticker

de **etiquette** /etikɛtə/ etiquette, good manners

het **etmaal** /ɛtmal/ (pl: etmalen) twenty-four hours

etnisch /ɛtnis/ (adj) ethnic

de **ets** /ɛts/ (pl: -en) etching

etsen /ɛtsə(n)/ (etste, heeft geëtst) etch

ettelijke /ɛtələkə/ (num) dozens of, masses of

de **etter** /ɛtər/ pus

etteren /ɛtərə(n)/ (etterde, heeft geëtterd) fester

de **etude** /etydə/ (pl: -s) étude

het **etui** /etwi/ (pl: -s) case

de **etymologie** /etimoloɣi/ (pl: -ën) etymology

etymologisch /etimoloɣis/ (adj, adv) etymological

de **EU** /ey/ *Europese Unie* EU

de **eucalyptus** /øykalɪptʏs/ (pl: -sen) eucalyptus (tree)

de **eucharistie** /øyχarɪsti/ Eucharist, celebration of the Eucharist; (the) Mass; (Holy) Communion

het **eufemisme** /øyfemɪsmə/ (pl: -n) euphemism

de **euforie** /øyfori/ euphoria

euforisch /øyforis/ (adj) euphoric

de **Eufraat** /øfrat/ Euphrates

de **eunuch** /øynʏχ/ (pl: -en) eunuch

de **euregio** /øreɣijo/ (pl: -'s) Euregio

eureka /øyreka/ (int) eureka

de **euro** /øro/ euro: *dat* **kost** *drie ~* that's three euros

de **eurocent** /ørosɛnt/ (pl: -en) (euro) cent

de **eurocheque** /øroʃɛk/ (pl: -s) Eurocheque

de **eurocommissaris** /ørokɔmɪsarɪs/ (pl: -sen) Member of the European Commission

de **eurocommissie** /ørokɔmɪsi/ (pl: -s) European Commission

het **euroland** /ørolant/ (pl: -en) euro country

de **euromunt** /øromʏnt/ (pl: -en) **1** euro **2** euro coin

Europa /øropa/ Europe

het **Europarlement** /øroparləmɛnt/ European Parliament

de **Europarlementariër** /øroparləmɛntarijər/ (pl: -s) member of the European Parliament; Euro-MP

de **Europeaan** /øropejan/ (pl: Europeanen) European

Europees /øropes/ (adj, adv) European

het **euroteken** /ørotekə(n)/ (pl: -s) euro symbol

het **Eurovisiesongfestival** /ørovizisɔŋfɛstival/ (pl: -s) Eurovision Song Contest

de **eurozone** /ørozːnə/ eurozone

de **euthanasie** /øytanazi/ euthanasia

het **euvel** /øvəl/ (pl: -s) fault, defect: *aan hetzelfde ~ mank gaan* suffer from the same flaw (*or:* fault); *een ~* **verhelpen** remedy a fault (*or:* defect)

Eva /eva/ Eve

de **evacuatie** /evakywa(t)si/ (pl: -s) evacuation

de **evacué** /evakywe/ (pl: -s) evacuee

¹evacueren /evakywerə(n)/ (evacueerde, is geëvacueerd) be evacuated

²evacueren /evakywerə(n)/ (evacueerde, heeft geëvacueerd) evacuate

de **evaluatie** /evalywa(t)si/ (pl: -s) **1** evaluation, assessment **2** evaluation

evalueren /evalywerə(n)/ (evalueerde, heeft geëvalueerd) evaluate, assess

het **evangelie** /evɑŋɣeli/ (pl: evangeliën) **1** gospel **2** Gospel: *het ~ van* **Marcus** the Gospel according to St Mark

evangelisch /evɑŋɣelis/ (adj, adv) evangelical

de **evangelist** /evɑŋɣelɪst/ (pl: -en) evangelist

¹even /evə(n)/ (adj) even ‖ *om het ~* **wie** whoever, no matter who

²**even** /e̯və(n)/ (adv) **1** (just) as: *ze zijn ~ groot* they're equally big; *in ~ grote aantallen* in equal numbers; *hij is ~ oud als ik* he is (just) as old as I am **2** just: *zij is altijd ~ opgewekt* she's always nice and cheerful **3** just, just a moment (*or:* while): *het duurt nog wel ~* it'll take a bit (*or:* while) longer; *mag ik u ~ storen?* may I disturb you just for a moment?; *eens ~ zien* let me see; *heel ~* just for a second (*or:* minute); *~ later (daarna)* shortly afterwards **4** (only) just, barely **5** just (a bit): *nog ~ doorzetten* go on for just a bit longer ‖ *als het maar éven kan* if it is at all possible

de **evenaar** /e̯vənar/ (pl: -s) equator

evenals /evəna̯ls/ (conj) (just) like; (just) as: *hun zaak ging failliet, ~ die van veel andere kleine ondernemers* their business went bankrupt, just like many other small businesses

evenaren /evəna̯rə(n)/ (evenaarde, heeft geëvenaard) equal, (be a) match (for)

het **evenbeeld** /e̯və(n)belt/ (pl: -en) image: *zij is het ~ van haar moeder* she is the spitting image of her mother; she is a carbon copy of her mother

eveneens /evə(n)e̯ns/ (adv) also, too, as well

het **evenement** /evənəme̯nt/ (pl: -en) event

evengoed /evə(n)ɣu̯t/ (adv) **1** just as: *jij bent ~ schuldig als je broer* you are just as guilty as your brother **2** just as well: *je kunt dat ~ zo doen* you can just as well do it like this **3** all the same, just the same: *ik weet van niets, maar word er ~ wel op aangekeken* I know nothing about it, but I am suspected all the same

evenmin /evə(n)mı̯n/ (adv) (just) as little as, no(t any) more than; neither; nor: *ik kom niet en mijn broer ~* I am not coming and neither is my brother

evenredig /evə(n)re̯dəχ/ (adj, adv) proportional (to); commensurate (with): *het loon is ~ aan de inspanning* the pay is in proportion to the effort; [maths] *omgekeerd ~ met* inversely proportional to

eventjes /e̯və(n)cəs/ (adv) **1** (only) just: *~ aanraken* (only) just touch **2** (for) (just) a little while: *hij is ~ hier geweest* he was here for (just) a little while **3** only, merely: *het kostte maar ~ € 1200* it only cost 1200 euros, it cost a mere 1200 euros

¹**eventueel** /evə(n)tywe̯l/ (adj) any (possible), such … as, potential: *eventuele klachten indienen bij …* (any) complaints should be lodged with …; *eventuele klanten* prospective (*or:* potential) customers

²**eventueel** /evə(n)tywe̯l/ (adv) possibly, if necessary; alternatively: *alles of ~ de helft* all of it, or alternatively half; *wij zouden ~ bereid zijn om …* we might be prepared to …

evenveel /evə(n)ve̯l/ (num) (just) as much; just as; equally: *iedereen heeft er ~ recht op*

everyone is equally entitled to it; *ieder krijgt ~ everyone* gets the same amount

evenwel /evə(n)we̯l/ (adv) however, nevertheless, nonetheless, yet

het **evenwicht** /e̯və(n)wıχt/ balance: *wankel ~* unsteady balance; *zijn ~ bewaren* (*or:* *verliezen*) keep (*or:* lose) one's balance; *het juiste ~ vinden* achieve the right balance; *de twee partijen houden elkaar in ~* the two parties balance each other out; *in ~ zijn* be well-balanced, be in equilibrium; *zijn ~ kwijt zijn* have lost one's balance

¹**evenwichtig** /evə(n)wı̯χtəχ/ (adj) (well-)balanced, steady, stable; [fig] level-headed

²**evenwichtig** /evə(n)wı̯χtəχ/ (adv) evenly, equally, uniformly

de **evenwichtsbalk** /e̯və(n)wıχtsbalk/ (pl: -en) (balance) beam

het **evenwichtsorgaan** /e̯və(n)wıχ(t)sɔrɣan/ (pl: -organen) organ of balance

evenwijdig /evə(n)we̯idəχ/ (adj, adv) parallel (to, with)

evenzeer /evə(n)ze̯r/ (adv) **1** (just) as much (as) **2** likewise, also

evenzo /evə(n)zo̯/ (adv) likewise

evenzogoed /evə(n)zoɣu̯t/ (adv) **1** just as well, equally well: *het had ~ mis kunnen gaan* it could just as well have gone wrong **2** just (*or:* all) the same, nevertheless: *hij had er totaal geen zin in, ~ ging hij* he didn't feel like it at all, but he still went (*or:* went all the same)

het **everzwijn** /e̯vərzwɛin/ (pl: -en) wild boar

evident /evidɛ̱nt/ (adj, adv) obvious, (self-)evident; [as adverb also] clearly

evolueren /evolywe̯rə(n)/ (evolueerde, heeft/is geëvolueerd) evolve

de **evolutie** /evoly(t)si/ (pl: -s) evolution

de **evolutieleer** /evoly(t)siler/ theory of evolution, evolutionism

de **ex** /ɛks/ (pl: exen) ex

¹**exact** /ɛksa̱kt/ (adj) exact, precise: *~e wetenschap* (exact) science

²**exact** /ɛksa̱kt/ (adv) accurately, precisely

ex aequo /ɛkse̱kwo/ (adv) joint: *Short en Anand eindigden ~ op de tweede plaats* Short and Anand finished joint second

het **examen** /ɛksa̱mə(n)/ (pl: -s) exam(ination): *mondeling* (*or:* *schriftelijk*) *~* oral (*or:* written) exam; *een ~ afleggen, ~ doen* take (*or:* sit) an exam; *zakken voor een ~* fail an exam

de **examenkandidaat** /ɛksa̱mə(n)kandidat/ (pl: -kandidaten) examinee, examination candidate

het **examenvak** /ɛksa̱mə(n)vak/ (pl: -ken) examination subject

de **examenvrees** /ɛksa̱mə(n)vres/ fear of exam(ination)s; (pre-)exam nerves

de **examinator** /ɛksamina̱tɔr/ (pl: -en) examiner

examineren /ɛksamine̯rə(n)/ (examineerde, heeft geëxamineerd) examine

excellent /ɛksɛlɛnt/ (adj, adv) excellent, splendid

de **excellentie** /ɛksɛlɛnsi/ (pl: -s) Excellency

excentriek /ɛksɛntrik/ (adj, adv) eccentric

exceptioneel /ɛksɛpʃonel/ (adj) exceptional

het **exces** /ɛksɛs/ (pl: -sen) excess; extravagance

excessief /ɛksɛsif/ (adj) excessive; extravagant

¹**exclusief** /ɛksklyzif/ (adj) exclusive

²**exclusief** /ɛksklyzif/ (adv) excluding, excl.: ~ *btw* excluding VAT, plus VAT

excommuniceren /ɛkskɔmynisərə(n)/ (excommuniceerde, heeft geëxcommuniceerd) excommunicate

de **excursie** /ɛkskyrsi/ (pl: -s) **1** excursion **2** (study) visit; field trip

excuseren /ɛkskyzerə(n)/ (excuseerde, heeft geëxcuseerd) excuse, pardon: *Jack vraagt of we* **hem** *willen ~, hij voelt zich niet lekker* Jack asks to be excused, he is not feeling well; *wilt u* **mij** *even ~* please excuse me for a moment; *zich ~ voor* offer one's excuses (*or:* apologies) for

het **excuus** /ɛkskys/ (pl: excuses) **1** apology: *zijn excuses* **aanbieden** apologize **2** excuse: *een slap ~* a poor excuse

executeren /ɛksekytərə(n)/ (executeerde, heeft geëxecuteerd) execute

de **executie** /ɛkseky(t)si/ (pl: -s) execution: *uitstel van ~* stay of execution

het **exemplaar** /ɛksɛmplar/ (pl: exemplaren) **1** specimen, sample **2** copy

exemplarisch /ɛksɛmplaris/ (adj, adv) exemplary, illustrative

de **exercitie** /ɛksɛrsi(t)si/ (pl: -s) exercise, drill

het **exhibitionisme** /ɛksibi(t)ʃonɪsmə/ exhibitionism

de **exhibitionist** /ɛksibiʃonɪst/ (pl: -en) exhibitionist

existentieel /ɛksistɛn(t)ʃel/ (adj) existential

exit /ɛksɪt/ exit: *~ John* exit John, farewell (to) John, that's the end of John

de **exitpoll** /ɛksɪtpɔl/ exit poll

de **exodus** /ɛksodys/ (pl: -sen) exodus

exogeen /ɛksoɣen/ (adj) exogenous

exorbitant /ɛksɔrbitɑnt/ (adj, adv) exorbitant, excessive, extravagant

het **exorcisme** /ɛksɔrsɪsmə/ exorcism

exotisch /ɛksotis/ (adj) exotic

de **expansie** /ɛkspɑnsi/ (pl: -s) expansion

het **expansievat** /ɛkspɑnsivɑt/ (pl: -en) expansion tank

de **expat** /ɛkspɛt/ expat

de **expediteur** /ɛkspeditør/ (pl: -en) shipping agent, forwarding agent; shipper; carrier

de **expeditie** /ɛkspedi(t)si/ (pl: -s) **1** shipping department, forwarding department **2** expedition: *op ~ gaan (naar)* go on an expedition (to) **3** dispatch, shipping, forwarding: *voor een* **snelle** *~ van de goederen* **zorgen** en-

sure that the goods are forwarded rapidly

het **experiment** /ɛksperimɛnt/ (pl: -en) experiment: *een wetenschappelijk ~* **uitvoeren** *(op)* perform a scientific experiment (on)

experimenteel /ɛksperimɛntel/ (adj, adv) experimental

experimenteren /ɛksperimɛntərə(n)/ (experimenteerde, heeft geëxperimenteerd) experiment

de **expert** /ɛkspɛːr/ (pl: -s) expert

de **expertise** /ɛkspɛrtiːzə/ (pl: -s, -n) (expert's) assessment

expliciet /ɛksplisit/ (adj, adv) explicit

exploderen /ɛksplodərə(n)/ (explodeerde, is geëxplodeerd) explode

de **exploitant** /ɛksplwɑtɑnt/ proprietor, owner, licensee

de **exploitatie** /ɛksplwɑta(t)si/ (pl: -s) exploitation; development

exploiteren /ɛksplwɑtərə(n)/ (exploiteerde, heeft geëxploiteerd) exploit; develop: *een stuk* **grond** *~* develop a plot of land

de **explosie** /ɛksplozi/ (pl: -s) explosion

het ¹**explosief** /ɛksplozif/ (pl: explosieven) explosive

²**explosief** /ɛksplozif/ (adj, adv) explosive: *explosieve* **stoffen** explosives

de **exponent** /ɛkspɔnɛnt/ (pl: -en) exponent

exponentieel /ɛkspɔnɛn(t)ʃel/ (adj, adv) exponential

de **export** /ɛkspɔrt/ export

exporteren /ɛkspɔrtərə(n)/ (exporteerde, heeft geëxporteerd) export

de **exporteur** /ɛkspɔrtør/ (pl: -s) exporter

exposeren /ɛkspozərə(n)/ (exposeerde, heeft geëxposeerd) exhibit, display, show

de **expositie** /ɛkspozi(t)si/ (pl: -s) exhibition, show

expres /ɛksprɛs/ (adv) on purpose, deliberately

de **expressie** /ɛksprɛsi/ (pl: -s) expression

het **expressionisme** /ɛksprɛʃonɪsmə/ expressionism

de **expresweg** /ɛksprɛswɛɣ/ (pl: -en) [Belg] [roughly] major arterial road

de **extase** /ɛkstazə/ ecstasy, rapture

¹**extatisch** /ɛkstatis/ (adj, adv) ecstatic

²**extatisch** /ɛkstatis/ (adv) ecstatically; in ecstasy

de **extensie** /ɛkstɛnsi/ (pl: -s) (file) extension

extensief /ɛkstɛnsif/ (adj) extensive

het ¹**exterieur** /ɛkster(i)jør/ (pl: -en) exterior

²**exterieur** /ɛkster(i)jør/ (adj) exterior, external, outside

extern /ɛkstɛrn/ (adj) **1** non-resident; living-out **2** external, outside

¹**extra** /ɛkstra/ (adj) extra, additional: *er zijn geen ~ kosten aan verbonden* there are no extras (involved); *iets ~'s* sth. extra

²**extra** /ɛkstra/ (adv) **1** extra: *hij kreeg 20* **euro** *~* he got 20 euros extra **2** specially: *de leerlin-*

gen hadden ~ hun best gedaan the pupils had made a special effort

het **extraatje** /ɛkstracə/ (pl: -s) bonus

het **extract** /ɛkstrɑkt/ (pl: -en) extract; excerpt, abstract

extrapoleren /ɛkstrapolerə(n)/ (extrapoleerde, heeft geëxtrapoleerd) extrapolate

de **extra's** /ɛkstras/ (pl) **1** bonuses; perquisites; perks **2** extras

extravagant /ɛkstravaɣɑnt/ (adj, adv) extravagant, outrageous

extravert /ɛkstravɛrt/ (adj) extrovert(ed), outgoing

¹**extreem** /ɛkstrem/ (adj) extreme

²**extreem** /ɛkstrem/ (adv) **1** extremely **2** ultra-, far: *extreemlinks* extreme left-wing

het ¹**extreemrechts** /ɛkstremrɛχ(t)s/ (the) extreme (*or:* far) right

²**extreemrechts** /ɛkstremrɛχ(t)s/ (adj) extreme right, ultra-right

het **extremisme** /ɛkstremɪsmə/ extremism

de **extremist** /ɛkstremɪst/ (pl: -en) extremist

de **ezel** /ezəl/ (pl: -s) **1** donkey: *zo koppig als een ~ be* as stubborn as a mule; *een ~ stoot zich in 't gemeen geen tweemaal aan dezelfde steen* once bitten, twice shy **2** easel

het **ezelsbruggetje** /ezəlzbrʏɣəcə/ memory aid, mnemonic

het **ezelsoor** /ezəlsor/ (pl: -oren) dog-ear

f

de **f** /ɛf/ (pl: f's) f, F
de **fa** /fa/ (pl: fa's) [mus] fa(h)
de **faalangst** /falɑŋst/ fear of failure
de **faam** /fam/ fame, renown
de **fabel** /fabəl/ (pl: -s) fable, fairy-tale
fabelachtig /fabəlɑxtəx/ (adj, adv) fantastic, incredible
het **fabricaat** /fabrikat/ (pl: fabricaten) manufacture, make: *Nederlands* ~ made in the Netherlands
de **fabricage** /fabrikaʒə/ manufacture, production
fabriceren /fabriserə(n)/ (fabriceerde, heeft gefabriceerd) **1** manufacture, produce **2** make, construct
de **fabriek** /fabrik/ (pl: -en) factory
de **fabrieksarbeider** /fabriksɑrbɛidər/ (pl: -s) factory worker
de **fabriekshal** /fabrikshɑl/ (pl: -len) **1** factory (building) **2** workshop
het **fabrieksterrein** /fabrikstɛrɛin/ factory site
de **fabrikant** /fabrikɑnt/ (pl: -en) manufacturer, producer; factory owner
de **façade** /fasadə/ (pl: -s) façade, front
de **facelift** /feslɪft/ (pl: -s) face-lift: *het bedrijf heeft een ~ ondergaan* the company has had a face-lift
het **facet** /fasɛt/ (pl: -ten) aspect, facet
de **faciliteit** /fasilitɛit/ (pl: -en) facility, convenience, amenity
de **faciliteitengemeente** /fasilitɛitə(n)ɣəmentə/ (pl: -n, -s) [Belg] municipality with (linguistic) facilities
de **factor** /fɑktɔr/ (pl: -en) factor
factureren /fɑktyrerə(n)/ (factureerde, heeft gefactureerd) invoice, bill
de **factuur** /fɑktyr/ (pl: facturen) invoice, bill
facultatief /fɑkyltatif/ (adj) optional, elective
de **faculteit** /fɑkyltɛit/ (pl: -en) faculty
de **fagot** /faɣɔt/ (pl: -ten) bassoon
Fahrenheit /farənhɑjt/ Fahrenheit
failliet /fajit/ (adj, adv) bankrupt: ~ *gaan* go bankrupt
het **faillissement** /fajisəmɛnt/ (pl: -en) bankruptcy
fair /fɛːr/ (adj, adv) fair: *iem. ~ behandelen* treat s.o. fairly; *dat is niet ~* that's not playing the game
de **fair trade** /fɛːrtreːt/ fair trade
de **¹fake** /fek/ (pl: -s) fake
²fake /fek/ (adj) fake: *dat hele verhaal is* ~ the whole story's a fake, the whole story's a sham

de **fakir** /fakir/ (pl: -s) fakir
de **fakkel** /fɑkəl/ (pl: -s) torch
de **fakkeldrager** /fɑkəldraɣər/ (pl: -s) torch-bearer
de **falafel** /falɑfɛl/ falafel
falen /falə(n)/ (faalde, heeft gefaald) fail; make an error (of judgment), make a mistake
de **faling** /falɪŋ/ [Belg] bankruptcy
de **fall-out** /fɔlɑut/ fall-out
de **fallus** /fɑlys/ (pl: -sen) phallus
de **falsetstem** /fɑlsɛtstɛm/ falsetto
fameus /famøs/ (adj, adv) famous, celebrated
familiaal /familijal/ (adj) familial: [Belg] *familiale verzekering* family insurance
familiair /familijɛːr/ (adj, adv) (over-)familiar: *al te ~ met iem. omgaan* treat s.o. with too much familiarity, take liberties with s.o.
de **familie** /famili/ (pl: -s) **1** family: [fig] *het is één grote* ~ they are one great big happy family; [Belg] *een politieke* ~ a political family; *bij de* ~ *Jansen* at the Jansens **2** family, relatives, (blood) relations: *wij zijn verre* ~ *(van elkaar)* we are distant relatives; *het zit in de* ~ it runs in the family
het **familiedrama** /familidrama/ (pl: -'s) family tragedy, family murder-suicide
het **familielid** /famililɪt/ (pl: -leden) member of the family; relative; relation: *zijn naaste familieleden* his next of kin
de **familienaam** /familinam/ (pl: -namen) family name, surname; [esp Am] last name
het **familiewapen** /familiwapə(n)/ (pl: -s) family (coat) of arms
familieziek /familizik/ (adj) overfond of one's relations
de **fan** /fɛn/ (pl: -s) fan
de **fanaat** /fanat/ (pl: fanaten) fanatic
de **fanaticus** /fanatikys/ (pl: fanatici) *see fanaat*
fanatiek /fanatik/ (adj, adv) fanatical, crazy: *een ~ schaker* a chess fanatic
de **fanatiekeling** /fanatikəlɪŋ/ (pl: -en) [iron] fanatic
het **fanatisme** /fanatɪsmə/ fanaticism; zealotry
de **fanclub** /fɛnklʏp/ (pl: -s) fan club
de **fancy fair** /fɛnsifɛːr/ (pl: -s) bazaar, jumble sale
de **fanfare** /fɑnfarə/ (pl: -s) brass band
de **fanmail** /fɛnmel/ fan mail
¹fantaseren /fɑntazerə(n)/ (fantaseerde, heeft gefantaseerd) fantasize (about), dream (about)
²fantaseren /fɑntazerə(n)/ (fantaseerde, heeft gefantaseerd) dream up, make up, imagine, invent
de **fantasie** /fɑntazi/ (pl: -ën) imagination
de **fantast** /fɑntɑst/ (pl: -en) dreamer, visionary, storyteller; liar

de **¹fantastisch** /fɑntɑstis/ (adj) **1** fantastic, fanciful: ~*e* **verhalen** fanciful (*or:* wild) stories **2** fantastic, marvellous

²fantastisch /fɑntɑstis/ (adv) fantastically, terrifically

de **fantasy** /fɛntəzi/ fantasy

het **fantoom** /fɑntom/ (pl: fantomen) phantom

de **fantoompijn** /fɑntompɛin/ phantom limb pain

de **farao** /farao/ (pl: -'s) pharaoh

de **farce** /fɑrs/ (pl: -n, -s) farce

de **farde** /fɑrdə/ [Belg] **1** file **2** carton (of cigarettes)

de **farizeeën** /farizejə(n)/ (pl) Pharisees

farmaceutisch /fɑrmasœytis/ (adj) pharmaceutic(al)

de **fascinatie** /fɑsina(t)si/ (pl: -s) fascination

fascineren /fɑsinerə(n)/ (fascineerde, heeft gefascineerd) fascinate, captivate

fascinerend /fɑsinerənt/ (adj) fascinating

het **fascisme** /fɑʃɪsmə/ fascism

de **fascist** /fɑʃɪst/ (pl: -en) fascist

fascistisch /fɑʃɪstis/ (adj, adv) fascist

de **fase** /fazə/ (pl: -s, -n) phase: *eerste* ~ undergraduate course of studies; *tweede* ~ postgraduate course of studies

faseren /fazerə(n)/ (faseerde, heeft gefaseerd) phase

het **fastfood** /fɑːstfuːt/ fast food

de **fat** /fɑt/ (pl: -ten) dandy, fop

fataal /fatal/ (adj, adv) fatal; terminal; lethal; mortal: *dat zou* ~ *zijn* **voor** *mijn reputatie* that would ruin my reputation

fatalistisch /fatalɪstis/ (adj, adv) fatalistic

de **fata morgana** /fatamɔrɣana/ (pl: -'s) fata morgana, mirage

het **fatsoen** /fɑtsun/ decorum, decency, propriety: *geen enkel* ~ **hebben** lack all basic sense of propriety (*or:* decency); *zijn* ~ **houden** behave (o.s.)

fatsoeneren /fɑtsunerə(n)/ (fatsoeneerde, heeft gefatsoeneerd) **1** (re-)model, shape **2** lick into shape, civilize

fatsoenlijk /fɑtsunlək/ (adj, adv) **1** decent; respectable: *op een* ~*e* **manier** *aan de kost komen* make an honest living **2** decent; respectable; fair

fatsoenshalve /fɑtsunshɑlvə/ (adv) for decency's sake, for the sake of decency

de **fatwa** /fɑtwa/ fatwa(h)

de **fauna** /fɑuna/ fauna

de **fauteuil** /fotœy/ (pl: -s) armchair, easy chair

de **¹favoriet** /favorit/ (pl: -en) favourite

²favoriet /favorit/ (adj) favourite; [pers] favoured

de **fax** /fɑks/ (pl: -en) fax

faxen /fɑksə(n)/ (faxte, heeft gefaxt) fax

de **fazant** /fazɑnt/ (pl: -en) pheasant

het **fbo** /ɛfbeo/ [Dutch] basic secondary education

de **februari** /febrywari/ February

de **fecaliën** /fekalijə(n)/ (pl) faeces

federaal /federal/ (adj) federal

federaliseren /federalizerə(n)/ (federaliseerde, heeft gefederaliseerd) federalize, (con)federate

het **federalisme** /federalɪsmə/ federalism

de **federatie** /federa(t)si/ (pl: -s) federation, confederation

de **fee** /fe/ (pl: -ën) fairy

de **feedback** /fiːdbɛk/ feedback: *iem.* ~ **geven** give s.o. feedback

feeëriek /fejərik/ (adj) enchanting, magic(al), fairylike

de **feeks** /feks/ (pl: -en) shrew, vixen

de **feeling** /fiːlɪŋ/ feel(ing), knack: ~ **hebben** **voor** *iets* have a feel(ing) for sth.

het **feest** /fest/ (pl: -en) **1** party **2** feast, treat: *dat* ~ **gaat** *niet* **door** you can put that (idea) right out of your head

de **feestartikelen** /festɑrtikələ(n)/ (pl) party goods (*or:* gadgets)

de **feestavond** /festavɔnt/ (pl: -en) gala night; social evening

de **feestdag** /fezdɑx/ (pl: -en) holiday: *op zonen* ~*en* on Sundays and public holidays; *prettige* ~*en* a) Merry Christmas; b) Happy Easter

feestelijk /festələk/ (adj, adv) festive: *een* ~*e* **jurk** a party dress

de **feestelijkheden** /festələkhedə(n)/ (pl) festivities, celebrations

feesten /festə(n)/ (feestte, heeft gefeest) celebrate, make merry

de **feestganger** /festxɑŋər/ (pl: -s) party-goer, guest

het **feestmaal** /festmal/ (pl: -malen) feast, banquet

de **feestneus** /festnøs/ (pl: -neuzen) **1** false nose **2** party-goer

het **feestvarken** /festfɑrkə(n)/ (pl: -s) birthday boy (*or:* girl), guest of honour

feestvieren /festfirə(n)/ (vierde feest, heeft feestgevierd) celebrate

feilbaar /fɛilbar/ (adj) fallible, liable to error

feilloos /fɛilos/ (adj, adv) infallible; unerring; faultless; flawless: ~ *de weg terug* **vinden** find one's way back unerringly

het **feit** /fɛit/ (pl: -en) fact; circumstance; event: *het* **is** (or: **blijft**) *een* ~ *dat* ... the fact is (*or:* remains) that ...; *de* ~*en* **spreken** *voor zichzelf* the facts speak for themselves; *in* ~*e* in fact, actually

¹feitelijk /fɛitələk/ (adj) actual: *de* ~*e* **macht** the de facto (*or:* real, actual) power

²feitelijk /fɛitələk/ (adv) actually, practically

de **feitenkennis** /fɛitə(n)kɛnɪs/ knowledge of (the) facts, factual knowledge

fel /fɛl/ (adj, adv) **1** fierce; bitter; sharp; bright; vivid; blazing [light]; glaring [light]: *een felroze jurk* a brilliant pink dress **2** fierce, sharp; keen; violent; bitter: *een* ~*le* **brand** a

blazing (*or:* raging) fire **3** fierce; fiery; vehement; spirited [pers]; scathing; biting: ~ *te-*
gen iets zijn be dead set against sth.

de **felicitatie** /felisita(t)si/ (pl: -s) congratula-
tion(s)

feliciteren /felisiterə(n)/ (feliciteerde,
heeft gefeliciteerd) congratulate on: *iem.* ~
met iets congratulate s.o. on sth.; *gefeliciteerd*
en nog vele jaren happy birthday and many
happy returns (of the day)

het **feminisme** /feminɪsmə/ feminism, Wom-
en's Liberation

de **feminist** /feminɪst/ (pl: -en) feminist
feministisch /feminɪstis/ (adj, adv) feminist

het **fenomeen** /fenomen/ (pl: fenomenen)
phenomenon

fenomenaal /fenomenal/ (adj, adv) phenomenal

feodaal /fejodal/ (adj, adv) feudal

het **feodalisme** /fejodalɪsmə/ feudalism, feudal system

ferm /fɛrm/ (adj, adv) firm; resolute

fermenteren /fɛrmɛnterə(n)/ (fermenteer-
de, heeft gefermenteerd) ferment

de **fermette** /fɛrmɛtə/ (pl: -s) [Belg] restored
farmhouse (as second home)

fervent /fɛrvɛnt/ (adj, adv) fervent, ardent

het **festijn** /fɛstɛin/ (pl: -en) feast, fête

het **festival** /fɛstival/ (pl: -s) festival

de **festiviteit** /fɛstivitɛit/ (pl: -en) festivity, celebration

de **fetisj** /fetiʃ/ (pl: -en) fetish

de **fetisjist** /fetiʃɪst/ (pl: -en) fetishist

het/de **feuilleton** /fœyətɔn/ (pl: -s) serial (story)

de **fez** /fɛs/ (pl: -zen) fez

het **fiasco** /fijasko/ (pl: -'s) fiasco, disaster

het **fiat** /fijɑt/ fiat, authorization: *zijn* ~ *geven*
authorize; give the green light

fiatteren /fijɑterə(n)/ (fiatteerde, heeft gefiatteerd) authorize; attach (*or:* give) one's
fiat to

het/de **fiche** /fiʃə/ (pl: -s) **1** counter, token, chip
2 index card, filing card

de **fictie** /fɪksi/ (pl: -s) fiction
fictief /fɪktif/ (adj, adv) fictitious, imaginary: *een* ~ *bedrag* an imaginary sum

de **fiducie** /fidysi/ faith: *ik heb er geen* ~ *in* I've
no faith in it

fier /fir/ (adj, adv) proud

de **fierheid** /firhɛit/ pride, high spirits

de **fiets** /fits/ (pl: -en) bike, bicycle, cycle: *we*
gaan op (or: *met*) *de* ~ we're going by bike;
een elektrische ~ an electric bicycle, an e-bike
‖ *op die* ~*!* like that, in that way

de **fietsband** /fitsbɑnt/ (pl: -en) bike (*or:* bicycle, cycle) tyre

de **fietsbel** /fitsbɛl/ bicycle bell

fietsen /fitsə(n)/ (fietste, heeft/is gefietst)
ride (a bike, bicycle), cycle, bike: *het is een uur*
~ it takes an hour (to get there) by bike

de **fietsenmaker** /fitsə(n)makər/ (pl: -s) bicy-

cle repairer (*or:* mender)

het **fietsenrek** /fitsə(n)rɛk/ (pl: -ken) **1** bike (*or:*
bicycle, cycle) stand **2** [roughly] gappy teeth

de **fietsenstalling** /fitsə(n)stɑlɪŋ/ bicycle
shed, bicycle stands, bicycle park

de **fietser** /fitsər/ (pl: -s) (bi)cyclist

het **fietspad** /fitspɑt/ (pl: -en) bicycle track (*or:*
path)

de **fietspomp** /fitspɔmp/ (pl: -en) bicycle pump

de **fietstas** /fitstɑs/ (pl: -sen) saddlebag

de **fietstocht** /fitstɔχt/ (pl: -en) bicycle ride (*or:*
trip, tour), cycling trip (*or:* tour): *een* ~*je gaan*
maken go for a bicycle ride

fiftyfifty /fɪftifɪfti/ (adv) fifty-fifty: ~ *doen*
split (sth.) fifty-fifty (with s.o.), go halves
(with s.o.)

de **figurant** /fiɣyrɑnt/ (pl: -en) extra, walk-on

figureren /fiɣyrerə(n)/ (figureerde, heeft
gefigureerd) **1** act, perform **2** be an extra

het/de **figuur** /fiɣyr/ (pl: figuren) figure; character;
individual: *een goed* ~ a good figure; *geen*
gek ~ *slaan* naast not come off badly compared with; *wat is hij voor een* ~*?* what sort of
person is he?

figuurlijk /fiɣyrlək/ (adj, adv) figurative,
metaphorical: ~ *gesproken* metaphorically
speaking

de **figuurzaag** /fiɣyrzaχ/ (pl: -zagen) fretsaw;
jigsaw

figuurzagen /fiɣyrzaɣə(n)/ do fretwork;
jigsaw

Fiji /fidʒi/ Fiji

de **Fiji-eilanden** /fidʒiɛilɑndə(n)/ (pl) Fiji Islands

de **Fijiër** /fidʒijər/ (pl: -s) Fijian
Fijisch /fidʒis/ (adj) Fijian

¹**fijn** /fɛin/ (adj) **1** fine: ~*e instrumenten* delicate instruments; *de* ~*e keuken* fine cooking
2 delicate **3** nice, lovely, fine, great, grand:
een ~*e tijd* a good time **4** subtle, fine: *een* ~*e*
neus a fine (*or:* subtle) nose ‖ *ik weet er het* ~*e*
niet van I don't know the finer (*or:* specific)
details

²**fijn** /fɛin/ (adv) nice: *ons huis is* ~ *groot* our
house is nice and big

³**fijn** /fɛin/ (int) that's nice, lovely: *we gaan op*
vakantie, ~*!* we're going on holiday, great!

fijnbesnaard /fɛimbəsnart/ (adj) highly-
strung, delicate(ly balanced), sensitive

fijngevoelig /fɛiŋɣəvuləχ/ (adj, adv) **1** sensitive **2** tactful

fijnmaken /fɛimakə(n)/ (maakte fijn, heeft
fijngemaakt) crush (fine); pulverize

fijnmalen /fɛimalə(n)/ (maalde fijn, heeft
fijngemalen) grind (up/down), crush

fijnmazig /fɛimazəχ/ (adj) fine(-meshed):
een ~*e structuur* a finely-woven structure

de **fijnproever** /fɛimpruvər/ (pl: -s) connoisseur; gourmet

fijnsnijden /fɛinsnɛidə(n)/ (sneed fijn,
heeft fijngesneden) cut fine(ly), slice thinly

fijnstampen /fɛinstɑmpə(n)/ (stampte fijn, heeft fijngestampt) crush, pound, pulverize; mash

fijntjes /fɛincəs/ (adv): ~ *opmerken* make a subtle remark

de **fik** /fɪk/ (pl: -ken) [inform] fire: *in de ~ steken* set fire to

fikken /fɪkə(n)/ (fikte, heeft gefikt) [inform] burn

fiks /fɪks/ (adj) sturdy, firm

fiksen /fɪksə(n)/ (fikste, heeft gefikst) [inform] fix (up), manage

de **filantroop** /filɑntrop/ (pl: filantropen) philanthropist

de **filatelist** /filatəlɪst/ (pl: -en) philatelist

de **file** /filə/ (pl: -s) queue; line; row; tailback; traffic jam: *in een ~ staan* (or: *raken*) be in (or: get into) a traffic jam

fileren /filerə(n)/ (fileerde, heeft gefileerd) 1 fillet 2 pick holes in, tear to shreds

het/de **filet** /filə/ (pl: -s) fillet

de **filevorming** /filəvɔrmɪŋ/ buildup (of traffic): *er is ~ over 3 km* traffic is backed up for 3 km

filharmonisch /filhɑrmonis/ (adj) philharmonic

het **filiaal** /filijɑl/ (pl: filialen) branch; chain store

de **filiaalhouder** /filijɑlhɑudər/ (pl: -s) branch manager

de **Filipijn** /filipɛin/ (pl: -en) Filipino

de **Filipijnen** /filipɛinə(n)/ (pl) (the) Philippines

Filipijns /filipɛins/ (adj) Philippine, Filipino

de **film** /fɪlm/ (pl: -s) film: *een stomme* ~ a silent film (or: picture); *welke ~ draait er in die bioscoop?* what's on at that cinema?; *een ~(pje) ontwikkelen* develop a film

de **filmacademie** /fɪlmakademi/ (pl: -s) film academy (or: school)

de **filmacteur** /fɪlmɑktør/ (pl: -s) film actor

de **filmcamera** /fɪlmkamərɑ/ (pl: -'s) (cine-)camera; (film)camera; motion-picture camera

filmen /fɪlmə(n)/ (filmde, heeft gefilmd) film, make (a film), shoot (a film)

de **filmer** /fɪlmər/ (pl: -s) film-maker

het **filmhuis** /fɪlmhœys/ (pl: -huizen) art cinema, cinema club

de **filmkeuring** /fɪlmkørɪŋ/ (pl: -en) film censorship; film censorship board; board of film censors

de **filmmuziek** /fɪlmyzik/ soundtrack

de **filmopname** /fɪlmɔpnamə/ (pl: -n, -s) shot, sequence, take: *een ~ maken van* make (or: shoot) a film of

de **filmproducent** /fɪlmprodysɛnt/ (pl: -en) film producer

de **filmregisseur** /fɪlmreɣisør/ (pl: -s) film director

de **filmrol** /fɪlmrɔl/ (pl: -len) 1 role (or: part) in a film 2 reel of film

de **filmster** /fɪlmstɛr/ (pl: -ren) (film) star, movie star

filosoferen /filozofɛrə(n)/ (filosofeerde, heeft gefilosofeerd) philosophize

de **filosofie** /filozofi/ (pl: -ën) philosophy: *de ~ van Plato* Plato's philosophy

filosofisch /filozofis/ (adj, adv) philosophic(al)

de **filosoof** /filozof/ (pl: filosofen) philosopher

het/de **filter** /fɪltər/ (pl: -s) filter

¹**filteren** /fɪltərə(n)/ (filterde, is gefilterd) filter through (or: into); percolate (through)

²**filteren** /fɪltərə(n)/ (filterde, heeft gefilterd) filter; percolate

de **filtersigaret** /fɪltərsiɣarɛt/ (pl: -ten) filter (tip), filter-tipped cigarette

het **filterzakje** /fɪltərzɑkjə/ (pl: -s) (coffee) filter

de **Fin** /fɪn/ (pl: -nen) Finn, Finnish woman

finaal /final/ (adj, adv) 1 final 2 complete, total: *ik ben het ~ vergeten* I clean forgot (it)

de **finale** /finalə/ (pl: -s) [mus] finale; [sport] final(s)

de **finalist** /finalɪst/ (pl: -en) finalist

financieel /finɑnʃel/ (adj, adv) financial

de **financiën** /finɑnsijə(n)/ (pl) finance, finances, funds

de **financier** /finɑnsir/ (pl: -s) financier

financieren /finɑnsirə(n)/ (financierde, heeft gefinancierd) finance, fund; back

de **financiering** /finɑnsirɪŋ/ financing

het **financieringstekort** /finɑnsirɪŋstəkɔrt/ (pl: -en) financing deficit, [roughly] budget deficit

het **fineer** /finer/ veneer

fineren /finerə(n)/ (fineerde, heeft gefineerd) veneer, finish, overlay, face

de **finesse** /finɛsə/ (pl: -s) nicety, subtlety: *de ~s van iets* the ins and outs of sth.

fingeren /fɪnɣerə(n)/ (fingeerde, heeft gefingeerd) 1 feign, sham; stage: *een gefingeerde overval* a staged robbery 2 invent, make up, dream up: *een gefingeerde naam* a fictitious name; an assumed name

de **finish** /fɪnɪʃ/ finish, finishing line

finishen /fɪnɪʃə(n)/ (finishte, heeft/is gefinisht) finish: *als tweede ~* finish second, come (in) second

Finland /fɪnlɑnt/ Finland

het ¹**Fins** /fɪns/ Finnish

²**Fins** /fɪns/ (adj) Finnish

de **firewall** /fɑjərwɔːl/ firewall

de **firma** /fɪrma/ (pl: -'s) firm, partnership, company: *de ~ Smith & Jones* the firm of Smith and Jones

het **firmament** /fɪrmamɛnt/ [form] firmament, heaven(s)

de **fis** /fis/ (pl: -sen) [mus] F sharp

fiscaal /fiskal/ (adj, adv) tax(-), fiscal: *~ aftrekbaar* tax-deductible

de **fiscus** /fɪskʏs/ the Inland Revenue, the Treasury; the taxman

fit /fɪt/ (adj) fit; fresh: *niet ~ zijn* be out of condition; be under the weather

de **fitness** /fɪtnəs/ fitness training; keep-fit exercises: *aan ~ doen* do fitness training; work out

het **fitnesscentrum** /fɪtnəsɛntrʏm/ (pl: -centra) fitness club, health club

de **fitting** /fɪtɪŋ/ (pl: -s, -en) socket; screw(cap); fitting

het **fixeer** /fɪksẹr/ fixer, fixative

fixeren /fɪksẹrə(n)/ (fixeerde, heeft gefixeerd) fix

de **fjord** /fjɔrt/ (pl: -en) fjord, fiord

de **flacon** /flakọn/ (pl: -s) bottle, flask; flagon

fladderen /flɑdərə(n)/ (fladderde, heeft/is gefladderd) **1** flap about; flutter **2** flutter; flap; stream

flagrant /flaɣrɑnt/ (adj) flagrant, blatant, glaring: *dat is een ~e leugen* that is a blatant (or: bald, barefaced) lie; *in ~e tegenspraak met* in flat contradiction to (or: with)

flakkeren /flɑkərə(n)/ (flakkerde, heeft geflakkerd) flicker

flamberen /flɑmbẹrə(n)/ (flambeerde, heeft geflambeerd) flambé

flamboyant /flɑmbwajɑnt/ (adj) flamboyant

de **flamenco** /flamɛŋko/ (pl: -'s) flamenco

de **flamingo** /flamɪŋo/ (pl: -'s) flamingo

het **flanel** /flanẹl/ (pl: -len) flannel; flannelette

flaneren /flanẹrə(n)/ (flaneerde, heeft/is geflaneerd) stroll, parade

de **flank** /flɑŋk/ (pl: -en) flank, side

flankeren /flɑŋkẹrə(n)/ (flankeerde, heeft geflankeerd) flank

flansen /flɑnsə(n)/ (flanste, heeft geflanst) (+ in elkaar) knock together, put together

de **flap** /flɑp/ (pl: -pen) **1** flap **2** turnover **3** (bank) note **4** flysheet

de **flapdrol** /flɑbdrɔl/ (pl: -len) [inform] wally

het **flapoor** /flɑpor/ protruding ear, sticking-out ear

flappen /flɑpə(n)/ (flapte, heeft geflapt) fling down, bang down, plonk down ‖ *eruit ~* blab(ber), blurt out

de **flapuit** /flɑpœyt/ (pl: -s) blab, blabber

de **flard** /flɑrt/ (pl: -en) **1** shred, tatter: *aan ~en scheuren* tear to shreds **2** fragment; scrap: *enkele ~en van het gesprek* a few fragments (or: snatches) of the conversation

de **flashback** /flɛʃbɛk/ (pl: -s) flashback

de **flat** /flɛt/ (pl: -s) **1** block of flats; block of apartments **2** flat; [Am] apartment: *op een ~ in a flat

de **flater** /flatər/ (pl: -s) blunder, howler

het **flatgebouw** /flɛtχəbʌu/ (pl: -en) see *flat*

het/de **flatscreen** /flɛtskri:n/ flat screen

flatteren /flatẹrə(n)/ (flatteerde, heeft geflatteerd) flatter: *een geflatteerd portret* a flattering portrait; *een geflatteerde voorstelling van iets geven* paint (or: present) a rosy picture of sth.

de **flatteus** /flɑtọs/ (adj) **1** becoming, flattering **2** flattering

flauw /flɑu/ (adj, adv) **1** bland, tasteless; washy; watery **2** faint, feeble, weak; dim: *ik heb geen ~ idee* I haven't the faintest idea **3** feeble: *een ~e grap* a feeble (or: corny, silly) joke **4** silly; chicken(-hearted); unsporting; faint-hearted **5** gentle, slight

de **flauwekul** /flɑuwəkʏl/ [inform] rubbish, nonsense

de **flauwte** /flɑutə/ (pl: -s) faint, fainting fit: *van een ~ bijkomen* come round (or: to)

flauwtjes /flɑucəs/ (adj, adv) faint; [light] dim; bland; dull; silly: *~ glimlachen* smile weakly

flauwvallen /flɑuvɑlə(n)/ (viel flauw, is flauwgevallen) faint, pass out: *~ van de pijn* faint with pain

de [1]**fleece** /fli:s/ (pl: -s) fleece

het/de [2]**fleece** /fli:s/ fleece

het **flensje** /flɛnʃə/ (pl: -s) crêpe, thin pancake

de **fles** /flɛs/ (pl: -sen) bottle; jar: *een melkfles* a milk bottle; *de baby krijgt de ~* the baby is bottle-fed

de **flesopener** /flɛsopənər/ (pl: -s) bottle-opener

[1]**flessen** /flɛsə(n)/ (fleste, is geflest) [Belg] fail

[2]**flessen** /flɛsə(n)/ (fleste, heeft geflest) **1** swindle, con, cheat, rip off **2** fool, pull s.o.'s leg

de **flessentrekkerij** /flɛsə(n)trɛkərɛɪ/ (pl: -en) swindle, con(fidence trick), fraud

flets /flɛts/ (adj, adv) **1** pale, wan: *er ~ uitzien* look pale (or: washed-out) **2** pale, dull: *~e kleuren* pale (or: faded, dull) colours

fleurig /flọrəχ/ (adj, adv) colourful, cheerful

flexibel /flɛksibəl/ (adj) flexible, pliable; [fig also] supple; [fig also] elastic: *~e werktijden* flexible hours; flexitime

de **flexibiliteit** /flɛksibilitɛɪt/ flexibility; [fig also] elasticity

de **flexplek** /flɛksplɛk/ (pl: -ken) hot desk

de **flexwerker** /flɛkswɛrkər/ (pl: -s) flexiworker, flex worker

de **flik** /flɪk/ (pl: -ken) [Belg; inform] cop

flikflooien /flɪkflojə(n)/ (flikflooide, heeft geflikflooid) pet, cuddle: *met iem. ~* get off (or: neck, snog) with s.o.

flikken /flɪkə(n)/ (flikte, heeft geflikt) bring off, pull off; get away with: *dat moet je me niet meer ~* don't you dare try that one on me again

de **flikker** /flɪkər/ (pl: -s) queen, poofter; [Am] faggot, fag ‖ *het kan hem geen ~ schelen* he doesn't give a damn; *hij heeft geen ~ uitgevoerd* he hasn't done a fucking, bloody thing; *iem. op zijn ~ geven* give s.o. a good hiding; give s.o. a proper dressing-down

[1]**flikkeren** /flɪkərə(n)/ (flikkerde, heeft ge-

flikkerd) **1** flicker; blink: *het ~de licht van een kaars* the flickering light of a candle **2** glitter, sparkle: *de zon flikkert op het water* the sun shimmers on the water

²**flikkeren** /flɪkərə(n)/ (flikkerde, is geflikkerd) [inform] fall, tumble: *van de trap ~* nosedive (*or:* tumble) down the stairs

¹**flink** /flɪŋk/ (adj) **1** robust, stout, sturdy **2** considerable, substantial: *een ~e dosis* a stiff dose; *een ~e wandeling* a good (long) walk **3** firm; plucky: *een ~e meid* a big girl; *zich ~ houden* put on a brave front (*or:* face)

²**flink** /flɪŋk/ (adv) considerably, thoroughly, soundly: *~ wat mensen* quite a number of people, quite a few people; *iem. er ~ van langs geven* give s.o. what for

flinterdun /flɪntərdy̯n/ (adj) wafer-thin, paper-thin

flipperen /flɪpərə(n)/ (flipperde, heeft geflipperd) play pinball

de **flipperkast** /flɪpərkɑst/ (pl: -en) pinball machine

de **flirt** /flʏːrt/ (pl: -s, -en) flirtation

de **flirten** /flʏːrtə(n)/ (flirtte, heeft geflirt) flirt

de **flits** /flɪts/ (pl: -en) **1** [photography] flash(-bulb), flash(light) **2** flash, streak **3** flash; split second **4** clip, flash: *~en van een voetbalwedstrijd* highlights of a football match

¹**flitsen** /flɪtsə(n)/ (flitste, heeft/is geflitst) flash: *er flitste een bliksemstraal in de lucht* (a bolt of) lightning flashed through the sky

²**flitsen** /flɪtsə(n)/ (flitste, heeft geflitst) flash: *geflitst worden* get flashed

flitsend /flɪtsənt/ (adj) **1** stylish, snappy, snazzy **2** brilliant

het **flitslicht** /flɪtslɪxt/ flash(light)

de **flitspaal** /flɪtspal/ speed camera, camera speed trap

de **flodder** /flɔdər/ (pl: -s): *losse ~s* dummy (*or:* blank) cartridges, blanks

flodderig /flɔdərəx/ (adj, adv) **1** baggy, floppy **2** sloppy, shoddy, messy

flonkeren /flɔŋkərə(n)/ (flonkerde, heeft geflonkerd) twinkle; sparkle; glitter: *~de ogen* sparkling eyes

de **flonkering** /flɔŋkərɪŋ/ (pl: -en) sparkle; sparkling; twinkling

de **flop** /flɔp/ (pl: -s) flop

floppen /flɔpə(n)/ (flopte, is geflopt) flop

de **floppydisk** /flɔpidɪsk/ (pl: -s) floppy disk, diskette

de **floppydrive** /flɔpidrɑjf/ (pl: -s) disk drive

de **flora** /flɔra/ flora

floreren /florerə(n)/ (floreerde, heeft gefloreerd) flourish, bloom, thrive

het/de **floret** /florɛt/ (pl: -ten) foil

de **florijn** /florɛin/ (pl: -en) florin, guilder

florissant /florisɑnt/ (adj) flourishing, blooming, thriving; well; healthy: *dat ziet er niet zo ~ uit* that doesn't look so good

flossen /flɔsə(n)/ (floste, heeft geflost) floss

one's teeth

de **fluctuatie** /flʏktywa̯(t)si/ (pl: -s) fluctuation; swing

fluctueren /flʏktywe̯rə(n)/ (fluctueerde, heeft gefluctueerd) fluctuate

fluisteren /flœystərə(n)/ (fluisterde, heeft gefluisterd) whisper

de **fluit** /flœyt/ (pl: -en) **1** flute; fife **2** whistle

het **fluitconcert** /flœytkɔnsɛrt/ (pl: -en) **1** flute concerto, concerto for flute; flute recital (*or:* concert) **2** catcalls, hissing: *op een ~ onthaald worden* be catcalled

¹**fluiten** /flœytə(n)/ (floot, heeft gefloten) **1** whistle, blow a whistle **2** play the flute **3** whistle; sing; [ship] pipe; hiss

²**fluiten** /flœytə(n)/ (floot, heeft gefloten) **1** whistle; play; sing: *een deuntje ~* whistle a tune **2** referee, act as referee in

de **fluitist** /flœytɪst/ (pl: -en) flautist, flute(-player)

het **fluitje** /flœycə/ (pl: -s) whistle ‖ *een ~ van een cent* a doddle; a piece of cake

de **fluitketel** /flœytketəl/ (pl: -s) whistling kettle

het **fluitsignaal** /flœytsɪnal/ whistle(-signal)

de **fluittoon** /flœyton/ (pl: -tonen) whistle, whistling; whine; b(l)eep

het **fluor** /flywɔr/ fluorine

het **fluweel** /flywe̯l/ (pl: fluwelen) velvet

fluwelen /flywe̯lə(n)/ (adj) velvet, velvety

flyeren /flɑjərə(n)/ (flyerde, heeft geflyerd) distribute (*or:* hand out) flyers

de **fly-over** /flɑjovər/ (pl: -s) overpass, flyover

fnuikend /fnœykənt/ (adj) fatal, destructive: *~ voor* fatal to

de **fobie** /fobi̯/ (pl: -ën) phobia: *een ~ voor katten* a phobia about cats

het/de **focus** /fokʏs/ (pl: -sen) focal point, focus

focussen /fokʏsə(n)/ (focuste, heeft gefocust) focus, focalize: *~ op een probleem* focus on a problem; *alle belangstelling was op hem gefocust* all attention was focussed on him

de **FOD** [Belg] *Federale Overheidsdienst* Federal Government Service

het **foedraal** /fudra̯l/ (pl: foedralen) case, cover, sheath

foefelen /fufələ(n)/ (foefelde, heeft gefoefeld) [Belg] cheat, fiddle

het **foefje** /fufjə/ (pl: -s) trick

foei /fuj/ (int) naughty naughty!

foeilelijk /fujlelək/ (adj) hideous, ugly as sin (*or:* hell)

de **foelie** /fuli̯/ mace

foeteren /futərə(n)/ (foeterde, heeft gefoeterd) grumble, grouse

foetsie /futsi/ (adv) [inform] gone, vanished (into thin air): *ineens was mijn portemonnee ~* suddenly my purse was gone (*or:* had vanished)

het/de **foetus** /fotʏs/ (pl: -sen) fetus

de **foetushouding** /fotʏshɑudɪŋ/ foetus posi-

tion
de **föhn** /føn/ (pl: -s) **1** [meteorology] föhn **2** blow-dryer
föhnen /fønə(n)/ (föhnde, heeft geföhnd) blow-dry
de ¹**fok** breeding
de ²**fok** /fɔk/ (pl: -ken) foresail
³**fok** (int) fuck!
fokken /fɔkə(n)/ (fokte, heeft gefokt) breed; rear; raise
de **fokker** /fɔkər/ (pl: -s) breeder; stockbreeder; cattle-raiser; fancier
de **fokkerij** /fɔkərɛi/ (pl: -en) **1** (cattle-)breeding, cattle-raising; (live)stock farming **2** breeding farm, stock farm; breeding kennel(s); stud farm
fokking (adj) [inform] [vulg] fucking: *een ~ hekel hebben aan iets* fucking hate sth.
de **fokstier** /fɔkstir/ (pl: -en) (breeding) bull
de **folder** /fɔldər/ (pl: -s) leaflet, brochure, folder
het/de **folie** /foli/ (pl: -s) (tin)foil
de **folk** /fɔk/ folk (music)
de **folklore** /fɔlklorə/ folklore
folkloristisch /fɔlklorɪstis/ (adj) folklor(-ist)ic
de **folkmuziek** /fɔkmyzik/ folk music
de **folteraar** /fɔltərar/ (pl: -s) torturer
de **folteren** /fɔltərə(n)/ (folterde, heeft gefolterd) torture; [fig also] rack; [fig also] torment
de **foltering** /fɔltərɪŋ/ (pl: -en) torture, torment
de **fondant** /fɔndɑnt/ fondant
het **fonds** /fɔnts/ (pl: -en) **1** fund, capital, resources, funds **2** fund, trust
de **fondue** /fɔndy/ (pl: -s) fondue
fonduen /fɔndywə(n)/ (fondude, heeft gefonduud) eat fondue, have fondue
de **fonetiek** /fonetik/ phonetics
fonetisch /fonetis/ (adj, adv) phonetic
fonkelen /fɔŋkələ(n)/ (fonkelde, heeft gefonkeld) **1** sparkle, glitter; twinkle **2** sparkle, effervesce
fonkelnieuw /fɔŋkəlniw/ (adj) brand-new
de **fontein** /fɔntɛin/ (pl: -en) fountain
de **fooi** /foj/ (pl: -en) **1** tip, gratuity **2** [fig] pittance; starvation wages
de **foor** /for/ (pl: foren) [Belg] fair
foppen /fɔpə(n)/ (fopte, heeft gefopt) fool, hoax, trick
de **fopspeen** /fɔpspen/ (pl: fopspenen) dummy (teat), soother; [Am] pacifier
¹**forceren** /fɔrserə(n)/ (forceerde, heeft geforceerd) **1** force; enforce: *de zaak ~ force* the issue, rush things **2** force, strain, overtax, overwork: *zijn stem ~* (over)strain one's voice
zich ²**forceren** /fɔrserə(n)/ (forceerde zich, heeft zich geforceerd) force o.s., overtax o.s., overwork o.s.
de **forel** /fɔrɛl/ (pl: -len) trout

de **forens** /forɛns/ (pl: forenzen) commuter
forensisch /forɛnzis/ (adj) forensic: *~e geneeskunde* forensic medicine
het **forfait** /fɔrfɛ/ (pl: -s): [Belg; sport] *~ geven* fail to turn up
het **formaat** /fɔrmat/ (pl: formaten) size; format; [fig] stature; [fig] class: [fig] *een prestatie van ~* a feat
formaliseren /fɔrmalizerə(n)/ (formaliseerde, heeft geformaliseerd) formalize, standardize
formalistisch /fɔrmalɪstis/ (adj, adv) formalist(ic), legalistic
de **formaliteit** /fɔrmalitɛit/ (pl: -en) formality, matter of routine: *de nodige ~en vervullen* go through the necessary formalities
format /fɔrmɑt/ format
de **formateur** /fɔrmatør/ (pl: -s) person charged with forming a new government
de **formatie** /fɔrma(t)si/ (pl: -s) **1** formation **2** band, group
formatteren /fɔrmɑterə(n)/ (formatteerde, heeft geformatteerd) format
formeel /fɔrmel/ (adj, adv) formal; official: *~ heeft u gelijk* technically speaking you are right
formeren /fɔrmerə(n)/ (formeerde, heeft geformeerd) **1** form, create **2** form, create, make **3** form, shape
het ¹**formica** /fɔrmika/ formica
²**formica** /fɔrmika/ (adj) formica
formidabel /fɔrmidabəl/ (adj, adv) formidable, tremendous
de **formule** /fɔrmylə/ (pl: -s) formula: *de ~ van water is H₂O* the formula for water is H_2O
de **formule 1** /fɔrmylen/ formula 1
de **formule 1-coureur** /fɔrmylenkurør/ formula 1 driver
formuleren /fɔrmylerə(n)/ (formuleerde, heeft geformuleerd) formulate, phrase: *iets anders ~* rephrase sth.
de **formulering** /fɔrmylerɪŋ/ (pl: -en) formulation, phrasing, wording: *de juiste ~ is als volgt* the correct wording is as follows
het **formulier** /fɔrmylir/ (pl: -en) form: *een ~ invullen* fill in a form; [Am] fill out a form
het **fornuis** /fɔrnœys/ (pl: fornuizen) **1** cooker **2** furnace
fors /fɔrs/ (adj, adv) **1** sturdy; robust; loud; vigorous; forceful; massive [bldg]; heavy: *een ~e kerel* a big fellow **2** substantial, considerable: *een ~ bedrag* a substantial sum
forsgebouwd /fɔrsxəbɑut/ (adj) sturdily (or: strongly, solidly) built
het **fort** /fɔrt/ (pl: -en) fort(ress)
het **fortuin** /fɔrtœyn/ (pl: -en) **1** (good) fortune, (good) luck: *zijn ~ zoeken* seek one's fortune **2** fortune
fortuinlijk /fɔrtœynlək/ (adj, adv) fortunate, lucky: *erg ~ zijn* be very lucky, have very good luck

het **forum** /fo̱rʏm/ (pl: -s) **1** forum, panel discussion **2** panel

forumen (forumde, heeft geforumd) participate in internet forums

het **fosfaat** /fɔsfa̱t/ (pl: fosfaten) phosphate

het/de **fosfor** /fɔ̱sfɔr/ phosphorus

fossiel /fɔsi̱l/ (adj) fossil, fossilized

de **foto** /fo̱to/ (pl: -'s) photograph, picture, photo: *een ~ nemen van iem.* take a photo (*or:* picture) of s.o.; *wil je niet op de ~?* don't you want to be in the picture?

het **fotoalbum** /fo̱toalbʏm/ (pl: -s) photo album

de **fotocamera** /fo̱tokamǝra/ (pl: -'s) camera

de **fotofinish** /fo̱tofɪnɪʃ/ photo finish

fotogeniek /fotoʒǝni̱k/ (adj) photogenic

de **fotograaf** /fotoɣra̱f/ (pl: -grafen) photographer

fotograferen /fotoɣrafe̱rǝ(n)/ (fotografeerde, heeft gefotografeerd) photograph, take a photograph (of)

de **fotografie** /fotoɣrafi̱/ (pl: -ën) photography

fotografisch /fotoɣra̱fis/ (adj) photographic(al): *een ~ geheugen* a photographic memory

de **fotokopie** /fotokopi̱/ (pl: -ën) photocopy, xerox: *een ~ maken van iets* photocopy sth.

fotokopiëren /fotokopije̱rǝ(n)/ (fotokopieerde, heeft gefotokopieerd) photocopy, xerox

het **fotomodel** /fo̱tomodɛl/ (pl: -len) model, photographer's model, cover girl

de **fotoreportage** /fo̱torǝpɔrtaʒǝ/ (pl: -s) photo-reportage

fotoshoppen /fo̱toʃɔpǝ(n)/ (fotoshopte, heeft gefotoshopt) photo shop

het **fototoestel** /fo̱totustɛl/ (pl: -len) camera

fouilleren /fujere̱(n)/ (fouilleerde, heeft gefouilleerd) search; frisk

de **fouillering** (body) search

de ¹**fout** /faut/ (pl: -en) **1** fault, flaw, defect: *zijn ~ is dat ...* the trouble with him is that ...; *niemand is zonder ~en* nobody's perfect **2** mistake, error; foul; fault: *menselijke ~* human error; *in de ~ gaan* a) make a mistake; b) slip up; *zijn ~ goedmaken* make good one's mistake

²**fout** /faut/ (adj, adv) wrong; incorrect; erroneous: *de boel ging ~* everything went wrong; *een ~ antwoord* a wrong answer ‖ *~e humor* tasteless humour

foutief /fauti̱f/ (adj, adv) wrong, incorrect

foutloos /fa̱utlos/ (adj, adv) faultless, perfect

de **foutmelding** /fa̱utmɛldɪŋ/ (pl: -en) error message

foutparkeren /fa̱utparkerǝ(n)/ park illegally

de **foyer** /fwaje̱/ (pl: -s) foyer

fraai /fraj/ (adj, adv) **1** pretty; fine **2** fine, splendid

de **fractie** /fra̱ksi/ (pl: -s) fraction: *in een ~ van een seconde* in a fraction of a second

de **fractieleider** /fra̱ksilɛidǝr/ (pl: -s) [roughly] leader of the (*or:* a) parliamentary party; [Am] [roughly] floor leader

de **fractuur** /fraktyr/ (pl: fracturen) fracture

fragiel /fraʒi̱l/ (adj) fragile

het **fragment** /fraɣmɛnt/ (pl: -en) fragment, section

fragmentarisch /fraɣmɛnta̱ris/ (adj) fragmentary

de **framboos** /frambo̱s/ raspberry

het **frame** /frem/ (pl: -s) frame

de **Française** /frɑ̃sɛ̱ːzǝ/ (pl: -s) Frenchwoman

de **franchise** /franʃi̱zǝ/ franchise

franco /frɑ̱ŋko/ (adv) prepaid; postage paid; [goods] carriage paid

de **franje** /frɑ̱ɲǝ/ (pl: -s) **1** fringe, fringing **2** [fig] frill, trimmings: *zonder (overbodige) ~* stripped of all its frills

de **frank** /frɑŋk/ (pl: -en) franc ‖ [Belg] *zijn ~ valt* the penny has dropped

frankeren /frɑŋke̱rǝ(n)/ (frankeerde, heeft gefrankeerd) stamp; frank; [Am] meter; pre-pay: *onvoldoende gefrankeerd* understamped; postage due

Frankrijk /frɑ̱ŋkrɛik/ France

het ¹**Frans** /frɑns/ French: *in het ~* in French

²**Frans** /frɑns/ (adj) French: *de ~en* the French; *twee ~en* two French people; two Frenchmen

de **Fransman** /frɑ̱nsmɑn/ (pl: Fransen) Frenchman

frappant /frapɑ̱nt/ (adj, adv) striking, remarkable

de **frase** /fra̱zǝ/ (pl: -n) phrase

de **frater** /fra̱tǝr/ (pl: -s) friar, brother

de **fratsen** /frɑ̱tsǝ(n)/ (pl) whims, fads, caprices

de **fraude** /fra̱udǝ/ (pl: -s) fraud; embezzlement

frauderen /fraude̱rǝ(n)/ (fraudeerde, heeft gefraudeerd) commit fraud

de **fraudeur** /fraudø̱r/ (pl: -s) fraud, cheat

frauduleus /fraudylø̱s/ (adj, adv) fraudulent; crooked

de **freak** /fri:k/ (pl: -s) **1** freak, nut, fanatic, buff: *een filmfreak* a film buff **2** freak, weirdo

freelance /friḻɑ̃s/ (adj, adv) freelance

de **freelancer** /friḻɑ̃sǝr/ (pl: -s) freelance(r)

de **frees** /fres/ (pl: frezen) fraise

de **freeware** /fri̱ːwɛːr/ freeware

het **fregat** /frǝɣɑ̱t/ (pl: -ten) frigate

frêle /frɛ̱ːlǝ/ (adj, adv) frail, delicate

frequent /frekwɛ̱nt/ (adj, adv) frequent

de **frequentie** /frekwɛ̱nsi/ (pl: -s) frequency: *de ~ van zijn hartslag* his pulse (rate)

het **fresco** /frɛ̱sko/ (pl: -'s) fresco

de **fresia** /fre̱zija/ (pl: -'s) freesia

de ¹**fret** /frɛt/ (pl: -ten) fret

het **²fret** /frɛt/ (pl: -ten) ferret
freudiaans /frɔjdijaːns/ (adj) Freudian: *een ~ vergissing (verspreking)* a Freudian slip
de **freule** /frøːlə/ (pl: -s) [roughly] gentlewoman, lady: *~ Jane A.* [roughly] the Honourable Jane A.
frezen /freːzə(n)/ (freesde, heeft gefreesd) mill
de **fricandeau** /frikandoː/ (pl: -s) fricandeau
de **frictie** /frɪksi/ (pl: -s) friction
friemelen /friːmələ(n)/ (friemelde, heeft gefriemeld) fiddle: *~ aan (met)* fiddle with
de **Fries** /fris/ Frisian
Friesland /frislɑnt/ Friesland
de **friet** /frit/ (pl: -en) chips; [Am] French fries: *~je oorlog* chips with mayonnaise and peanut sauce; *~je zonder* just chips (no sauce)
de **frigo** /friɣoː/ (pl: -'s) [Belg] fridge
de **frigobox** /friɣobɔks/ (pl: -en) [Belg] cool box
de **frik** /frɪk/ (pl: -ken) schoolmaster, schoolmistress
de **frikandel** /frikandɛl/ (pl: -len) minced-meat hot dog
het **¹fris** /frɪs/ soft drink; pop: *een glaasje ~* a soft drink, a glass of pop
²fris /frɪs/ (adj) **1** fresh; fit; lively: *met ~se moed* with renewed vigour **2** fresh, airy, breezy: *het ruikt hier niet ~* it's stuffy (in) here **3** clean **4** cool(ish), chilly
het **frisbee** /frɪzbi/ (pl: -s) frisbee
frisbeeën /frɪzbijə(n)/ (frisbeede, heeft gefrisbeed) frisbee
de **frisdrank** /frɪzdrɑŋk/ (pl: -en) soft drink; pop
frisjes /frɪʃəs/ (adj) chilly, nippy
de **friteuse** /fritøzə/ (pl: -s) deep fryer, chip pan
frituren /frityrə(n)/ (frituurde, heeft gefrituurd) deep-fry
de **frituur** /frityr/ chip shop
de **frituurpan** /frityrpɑn/ (pl: -nen) deep frying pan; deep fryer; chip pan
het **frituurvet** /frityrvɛt/ (pl: -ten) frying fat
frivool /frivoːl/ (adj, adv) frivolous
¹frommelen /frɔmələ(n)/ (frommelde, heeft gefrommeld) fiddle, fumble: *aan het tafelkleed ~* fiddle with the tablecloth
²frommelen /frɔmələ(n)/ (frommelde, heeft gefrommeld) **1** crumple (up), rumple, crease: *iets in elkaar ~* crumple sth. up **2** stuff away
de **frons** /frɔns/ (pl: -en) **1** wrinkle **2** frown; scowl
fronsen /frɔnsə(n)/ (fronste, heeft gefronst) frown; scowl: *de wenkbrauwen ~* frown; knit one's brow(s)
het **front** /frɔnt/ (pl: -en) front; façade; forefront: *het vijandelijke* (or: *oostelijke*) *~* the enemy (or: eastern) front
frontaal /frɔntaːl/ (adj, adv) frontal; head-on
het **fruit** /frœyt/ fruit ‖ *Turks ~* Turkish delight
de **fruitautomaat** /frœytɑutomaːt/ (pl: -auto-maten) fruit machine; [Am] slot machine; one-armed bandit
fruiten /frœytə(n)/ (fruitte, heeft gefruit) fry, sauté
het **fruithapje** /frœythɑpjə/ (pl: -s) fruit purée
fruitig /frœytəχ/ (adj) fruity ‖ *fris en ~* bright-eyed and bushy-tailed, full of beans
de **fruitsalade** /frœytsaladə/ (pl: -s) fruit salad
het **fruitsap** /frœytsɑp/ (pl: -pen) [Belg] fruit juice
de **fruitteler** /frœytelər/ fruit grower, fruit farmer
frunniken /frʏnəkə(n)/ (frunnikte, heeft gefrunnikt) fiddle
de **frustraat** /frʏstraːt/ frustrated person
de **frustratie** /frʏstra(t)si/ (pl: -s) frustration
frustreren /frʏstreːrə(n)/ (frustreerde, heeft gefrustreerd) **1** frustrate **2** thwart
de **f-sleutel** /ɛfsløtəl/ F clef
de **fte** /ɛfteː/ *fulltime-equivalent* fte, full-time equivalent
de **fuchsia** /fʏksija/ (pl: -'s) fuchsia
de **fuga** /fʏɣa/ (pl: -'s) fugue
de **fuif** /fœyf/ (pl: fuiven) party; bash: *een ~ geven (houden)* give (or: have) a party
het **fuifnummer** /fœyfnʏmər/ (pl: -s) partygoer, merrymaker: *hij is een echt ~* he's a party-going type
de **fuik** /fœyk/ (pl: -en) fyke (net); [fig] snare, trap: [fig] *in de ~ lopen* walk (or: fall) into a trap
full colour /fulkɔlər/ (adj) full colour
fulltime /fʏltɑjm/ (adj, adv) full-time
de **fulltimer** /fʏltɑjmər/ (pl: -s) full-timer
de **functie** /fʏŋksi/ (pl: -s) post, position, duties: *een hoge ~ bekleden* hold an important position; *in ~ treden* take up office ‖ [maths] *x is een ~ van* x is a function of y
de **functiebeschrijving** /fʏŋksibəsχrɛiviŋ/ (pl: -en) job description, job specification
de **functie-eis** /fʏŋksiɛis/ (pl: -en) job requirement
de **functionaris** /fʏŋkʃonɑrɪs/ (pl: -sen) official
functioneel /fʏŋkʃonel/ (adj) functional
functioneren /fʏŋkʃonerə(n)/ (functioneerde, heeft gefunctioneerd) **1** act, function, serve **2** work, function, perform: *niet* (or: *goed*) *~d* out of order, in working order
het **functioneringsgesprek** /fʏŋkʃonerɪŋsχəsprɛk/ (pl: -ken) performance interview
het **fundament** /fʏndamɛnt/ (pl: -en) foundation; [fig also] fundamental(s): *de ~en leggen (voor)* lay the foundations (for)
het **fundamentalisme** /fʏndamɛntalɪsmə/ fundamentalism
de **fundamentalist** /fʏndamɛntalɪst/ (pl: -en) fundamentalist
fundamenteel /fʏndamɛntel/ (adj, adv) fundamental, basic
funderen /fʏnderə(n)/ (fundeerde, heeft gefundeerd) **1** found, build **2** [fig also] base,

ground

de **fundering** /fʏndɐrɪŋ/ (pl: -en) foundation(s); [fig also] basis; groundwork: *de ~(en)* ***leggen*** lay the foundation(s)

funest /fynɛst/ (adj) disastrous, fatal: *de droogte is ~* ***voor*** *de tuin* (the) drought is disastrous for the garden

fungeren /fʏnɣɛrə(n)/ (fungeerde, heeft gefungeerd) **1** act as, function as **2** be the present … (*or:* acting …, officiating …)

de **furie** /fyri/ (pl: -s, furiën) fury, shrew: *tekeergaan* ***als*** *een ~* go raving mad

furieus /fyrijøs/ (adj, adv) furious, enraged

de **furore** /fyrɔrə/ furore

fuseren /fyzɛrə(n)/ (fuseerde, is gefuseerd) merge (with), incorporate

de **fusie** /fyzi/ (pl: -s) merger

fusilleren /fyzijɛrə(n)/ (fusilleerde, heeft gefusilleerd) execute by firing squad

de **fusion** /fjuːʒən/ fusion

het **fust** /fʏst/ (pl: -en) cask, barrel: *een ~* ***aanslaan*** broach a cask

de **fut** /fʏt/ go, energy, zip: *de ~ is* ***eruit*** *bij hem* there's no go in him anymore; *geen ~* ***hebben*** *om iets te doen* not have the energy (*or:* strength) to do sth.

futiel /fytil/ (adj) futile

de **futiliteit** /fytilitɛit/ (pl: -en) trifle, futility

het **futsal** /fʏtsɑl/ futsal, indoor soccer

futuristisch /fytyrɪstis/ (adj, adv) futurist(ic)

de **fuut** /fyt/ (pl: futen) great crested grebe

de **fysica** /fizika/ physics

de **fysicus** /fizikʏs/ (pl: fysici) physicist

fysiek /fizik/ (adj, adv) physical

de **fysiologie** /fizijoloɣi/ physiology

de **fysiotherapeut** /fizijoterapœyt/ (pl: -en) physiotherapist

de **fysiotherapie** /fizijoterapi/ **1** physiotherapy **2** [Belg] rehabilitation

fysisch /fizis/ (adj, adv) physical

g

de **g** /ɣe/ (pl: g's) g, G
  gaaf /ɣaf/ (adj) **1** whole, intact; sound: *een ~ gebit* a perfect set of teeth **2** great, super: *Sampras speelde een gave **partij*** Sampras played a great game
de **gaai** /ɣaj/ jay: *Vlaamse ~* jay
  ¹**gaan** /ɣan/ (ging, is gegaan) **1** go, move: *hé, waar ga jij **naartoe?*** where are you going?; where do you think you're going?; *het gaat niet zo best* (or: *slecht*) *met de patiënt* the patient isn't doing so well (or: so badly) **2** leave; be off: *hoe laat gaat de **trein?*** what time does the train go?; *ik **moet** nu –* I must go now, I must be going (or: off) now; *ik ga **ervandoor*** I'm going (or: off); *ga nu maar* off you go now **3** go, be going to: *~ **kijken*** go and (have a) look; *~ **liggen*** lie down; *~ **staan*** stand up; *ze ~ **trouwen*** they're getting married; *~ **zwemmen*** go for a swim, go swimming; *aan het werk ~* set to work **4** be, run: *de zaken ~ **goed*** business is going well; *als alles **goed** gaat* if all goes well; *dat kon toch nooit **goed** ~* that was bound to go wrong; *hoe is het gegaan?* how was it?, how did it (or: things) go? **5** (+ over) run, be in charge (of): *daar ga ik niet **over*** that's not my responsibility **6** (+ over) be (about): *waar gaat die film **over?*** what's that film about? ‖ *zich **laten** ~* let o.s. go; [fig] *dat gaat mij te **ver*** I think that is going too far; *eraan ~* have had it; [pers also] be (in) for it; *daar ~ we **weer*** (t)here we go again; *we hebben nog twee uur te **gaan*** we've got two hours to go; *aan de kant ~* move aside; *zijn gezin gaat bij hem **boven** alles* his family comes first (with him)
  ²**gaan** /ɣan/ (ging, is gegaan) **1** be, go, happen: *het is toch nog **gauw** gegaan* things went pretty fast (after all) **2** (+ om) be (about): *daar gaat het niet **om*** that's not the point; *daar gaat het juist **om*** that's the whole point; *het gaat **erom** of …* the point is whether …; *het gaat **om** het principe* it's the principle that matters; *het gaat hier **om** een nieuw type* we're talking about a new type ‖ *het ga je **goed*** all the best; *hoe gaat het **met** (met u)?* how are you?, how are things with you?; *hoe gaat het op het werk?* how is your work (going)?, how are things (going) at work?; *het gaat* it's all right; it's OK; *dat **zal** niet ~* that just won't work; I'm afraid that's not on
  gaande /ɣandə/ (adj) **1** going, running: *een gesprek ~ **houden*** keep a conversation going **2** going on, up: *~ **zijn*** be going on, be in progress
  gaandeweg /ɣandəwɛχ/ (adv) gradually
  gaans /ɣans/ walk: *nog geen tien **minuten** ~ van* within ten minutes walk from/of; *een **uur** ~* an hour's walk
de **gaap** /ɣap/ (pl: gapen) yawn
  gaar /ɣar/ (adj) **1** done; cooked: *de **aardappels** zijn ~* the potatoes are cooked (or: done); *het **vlees** is goed* (or: *precies*) *~* the meat is well done (or: done to a turn); *iets ~ koken* cook sth. **2** done, tired (out)
de **gaarheid** /ɣarhɛɪt/ readiness (to serve, eat, …)
de **gaarkeuken** /ɣarkøkə(n)/ (pl: -s) soup kitchen
  gaarne /ɣarnə/ (adv) gladly, with pleasure
het **gaas** /ɣas/ (pl: gazen) **1** gauze; net(ting): *fijn* (or: *grof*) *~* fine-meshed (or: large-meshed) gauze **2** wire mesh; (wire) netting; (wire) gauze: *het ~ van een **hor*** the wire gauze of a screen
het **gaatje** /ɣacə/ (pl: -s) (little, small) hole; puncture: *~s **in** de oren laten prikken* have one's ears pierced; *ik had **geen** ~* I had no cavities ‖ *ik zal eens kijken of ik voor u nog een ~ **kan vinden*** I'll see if I can fit (or: squeeze) you in
de **gabber** /ɣɔbər/ (pl: -s) [inform] mate, pal, chum, buddy
  Gabon /ɣabɔn/ Gabon
de ¹**Gabonees** /ɣabones/ (pl: Gabonezen) Gabonese
  ²**Gabonees** /ɣabones/ (adj) Gabonese
  gadeslaan /ɣadəslan/ (sloeg gade, heeft gadegeslagen) **1** observe, watch **2** follow, watch (closely)
de **gading** /ɣadɪŋ/: *hij kon niets **van** zijn ~ vinden* he couldn't find anything to suit him (or: to his liking, he wanted); *was er iets **van** je ~ bij?* was there anything you fancied there?
de **gaffel** /ɣɔfəl/ (pl: -s) (two-pronged) fork
de **gage** /ɣaʒə/ (pl: -s) pay; fee; salary
het **gajes** /ɣajəs/ [inform] rabble, riff-raff
de **gal** /ɣɔl/ (pl: -len) bile; gall
het **gala** /ɣala/ gala
de **gala-avond** /ɣalaavɔnt/ (pl: -en) gala night
het **galadiner** /ɣaladine/ (pl: -s) state banquet, gala dinner
  galant /ɣalɔnt/ (adj, adv) chivalrous, gallant: *~e **manieren*** elegant manners
de **galavoorstelling** /ɣalavorstɛlɪŋ/ (pl: -en) gala performance
de **galblaas** /ɣɔlblas/ (pl: galblazen) gall bladder: *een operatie **aan** de ~* a gall bladder operation
de **galei** /ɣalɛi/ (pl: -en) galley
de **galeislaaf** /ɣalɛislaf/ (pl: -slaven) galley slave
de **galerie** /ɣaləri/ (pl: -s) (art) gallery
de **galeriehouder** /ɣalərihaudər/ (pl: -s) gal-

lery owner; manager of a gallery

de **galerij** /ɣalərɛi̯/ (pl: -en) gallery; walkway; (shopping) arcade

de **galg** /ɣalɣ/ (pl: -en) gallows: *aan de ~ ophangen* hang on the gallows; *~je spelen* play hangman; *hij groeit voor ~ en rad op* he'll come to no good

de **galgenhumor** /ɣɑlɣə(n)hymɔr/ gallows humour

het **galgenmaal** /ɣɑlɣəmal/ (pl: -malen) last meal: *het ~ nuttigen* eat one's last meal

Galilea /ɣaliley̯a/ Galilee

het **galjoen** /ɣaljun/ (pl: -en) galleon

de **galm** /ɣalm/ (pl: -en) sound; peal(ing) ‖ *de luide ~ van zijn stem* his booming voice

¹**galmen** /ɣɑlmə(n)/ (galmde, heeft gegalmd) resound, boom; peal: *de klokken ~* the bells peal

²**galmen** /ɣɑlmə(n)/ (galmde, heeft gegalmd) bellow

de **galop** /ɣalɔp/ (pl: -s) gallop: *in ~* at a gallop; *in ~ overgaan* break into a gallop

galopperen /ɣalɔpɛrə(n)/ (galoppeerde, heeft/is gegaloppeerd) gallop: *een paard laten ~* gallop a horse

de **galsteen** /ɣɑlsten/ (pl: -stenen) gallstone, bilestone

Gambia /ɣɑmbija/ (The) Gambia

de **Gambiaan** /ɣɑmbijan/ (pl: Gambianen) Gambian

Gambiaans /ɣɑmbijans/ (adj) Gambian

de **game** /gem/ (pl: -s) game

de **gamepad** /gempɛt/ (pl: -s) game pad

het/de **gamma** /ɣɔma/ (pl: -'s) [mus] scale, gamut

gammel /ɣɔməl/ (adj) 1 rickety, wobbly, ramshackle: *een ~e constructie* a ramshackle construction 2 shaky, faint: *ik ben een beetje ~* I don't feel up to much

de **gang** /ɣaŋ/ (pl: -en) 1 passage(way), corridor, hall(way) 2 passage(way), tunnel: *een ondergrondse ~* an underground passage-(way) 3 walk, gait: *herkenbaar aan zijn moeizame ~* recognizable by his laboured gait 4 movement; speed: *er ~ achter zetten* speed it up; *de les was al aan de ~* the lesson had already started (or: got going); *een motor aan de ~ krijgen* get an engine going; *goed op ~ komen* [also fig] get into one's stride; *iem. op ~ helpen* help s.o. to get going, give s.o. a start 5 course, run: *de ~ van zaken is als volgt* the procedure is as follows; *de dagelijkse ~ van zaken* the daily routine; *verantwoordelijk zijn voor de goede ~ van zaken* be responsible for the smooth running of things; *het feest is in volle ~* the party is in full swing; *alles gaat weer zijn gewone ~* everything's back to normal 6 course: *het diner bestond uit vijf ~en* it was a five-course dinner ‖ *ga je ~ maar* a) (just, do) go ahead; b) (just, do) carry on; c) after you; *zijn eigen ~ gaan* go one's own way

gangbaar /ɣɑnbar/ (adj) 1 current, contemporary, common: *een gangbare uitdrukking* a common expression 2 popular: *een gangbare maat* a common size

de **Ganges** /ɣɑŋəs/ the (River) Ganges

het **gangetje** /ɣɑŋəcə/ (pl: -s) 1 pace, rate 2 alley(way); passage(way); narrow corridor (or: passage) ‖ *alles gaat z'n ~* things are going all right

de **gangmaker** /ɣɑŋmakər/ (pl: -s) (the) life and soul of the party

het **gangpad** /ɣɑŋpat/ (pl: -en) aisle

het **gangreen** /ɣɑŋɣren/ gangrene: *~ krijgen* get gangrene; [part of the body] become gangrenous

de **gangster** /gɛŋstər/ (pl: -s) gangster

de **gans** /ɣans/ (pl: ganzen) goose: *de sprookjes van Moeder de Gans* the (fairy) tales of Mother Goose

het **ganzenbord** /ɣɑnzə(n)bɔrt/ (pl: -en) (game of) goose

de **ganzenlever** /ɣɑnzə(n)levər/ (pl: -s) goose liver, foie gras

de **ganzenpas** /ɣɑnzə(n)pas/ (pl: -sen) goose step

gapen /ɣapə(n)/ (gaapte, heeft gegaapt) 1 yawn: *~ van verveling* yawn with boredom 2 gape, gawk (at) 3 yawn, gape: *een ~de afgrond* [also fig] a yawning abyss

gappen /ɣɔpə(n)/ (gapte, heeft gegapt) pinch, swipe

de **garage** /ɣaraʒə/ (pl: -s) garage: *de auto moet naar de ~* the car has to go to the garage

de **garagedeur** /ɣaraʒədør/ garage door

de **garagehouder** /ɣaraʒəhaudər/ (pl: -s) garage owner; garage manager

de **garagist** /ɣaraʒɪst/ (pl: -en) [Belg] 1 garage owner 2 motor mechanic

garanderen /ɣarandɛrə(n)/ (garandeerde, heeft gegarandeerd) guarantee, warrant: *gegarandeerd echt goud* guaranteed solid gold; *ik kan niet ~ dat je slaagt* I cannot guarantee that you will succeed; *dat garandeer ik je* I guarantee you that

de **garant** /ɣarɑnt/ (pl: -en) guarantor; guarantee underwriter; [law] surety: *~ staan voor de schulden van zijn vrouw* stand surety for one's wife's debts; *zijn aanwezigheid staat ~ voor een gezellige avond* his presence ensures an enjoyable evening

de **garantie** /ɣarɑnsi/ (pl: -s) guarantee, warranty: *dat valt niet onder de ~* that is not covered by the guarantee; *drie jaar ~ op iets krijgen* get a three-year guarantee on sth.

het **garantiebewijs** /ɣarɑnsibəwɛis/ guarantee (card), warranty, certificate of guarantee

de **garde** /ɣardə/ (pl: -n) 1 guard: *de nationale ~* the national guard 2 whisk, beater

de **garderobe** /ɣardəro:bə/ (pl: -s) 1 wardrobe: *een uitgebreide ~ bezitten* possess an extensive wardrobe 2 cloakroom; [Am] checkroom

het **gareel** /ɣarel/ (pl: garelen): *iem. (weer) in het ~ brengen* bring s.o. to heel, make s.o. toe the line; *in het ~ lopen* toe the line

het **garen** /ɣarə(n)/ (pl: -s) thread, yarn: *een klosje ~* a reel of thread

de **garnaal** /ɣarnal/ (pl: garnalen) shrimp; prawn

de **garnalencocktail** /ɣarnalə(n)kɔktel/ (pl: -s) shrimp cocktail, prawn cocktail

garneren /ɣarnerə(n)/ (garneerde, heeft gegarneerd) garnish

de **garnering** /ɣarnerɪŋ/ (pl: -en) garnishing

het **garnituur** /ɣarnityr/ (pl: garnituren) **1** garnishing, trim, trimming(s) **2** accessories; set, ensemble

het **garnizoen** /ɣarnizun/ (pl: -en) garrison

het **gas** /ɣɑs/ (pl: -sen) **1** gas: *~, water en elektra* gas, water and electricity; *vloeibaar ~* liquid gas; *het ~ aansteken* (or: *uitdraaien*) light (*or:* turn) off the gas; *op ~ koken* cook with (*or:* by) gas **2** mixture; gas: *~ geven* step on the gas; *vol ~ de bocht door* (round the bend) at full speed; *de auto rijdt op ~* the car runs on LPG

de **gasbel** /ɣɑzbɛl/ (pl: -len) **1** gas bubble (*or:* pocket) **2** gasfield, gas deposit

de **gasbrander** /ɣɑzbrɑndər/ (pl: -s) gas burner

de **gasfitter** /ɣɑsfɪtər/ (pl: -s) gas fitter; plumber

de **gasfles** /ɣɑsflɛs/ (pl: -sen) gas cylinder

het **gasfornuis** /ɣɑsfɔrnœys/ (pl: gasfornuizen) gas cooker

de **gaskachel** /ɣɑskɑxəl/ (pl: -s) gas heater

de **gaskamer** /ɣɑskamər/ (pl: -s) gas chamber, gas oven

de **gaskraan** /ɣɑskran/ (pl: gaskranen) gas tap: *de ~ opendraaien* (or: *dichtdraaien*) turn on (*or:* off) the gas (tap)

de **gasleiding** /ɣɑslɛidɪŋ/ (pl: -en) gas pipe(s); service pipe; gas main(s)

het **gaslek** /ɣɑslɛk/ (pl: -ken) gas leak(age)

de **gaslucht** /ɣɑslʏxt/ smell of gas

het **gasmasker** /ɣɑsmɑskər/ (pl: -s) gas mask

de **gasmeter** /ɣɑsmetər/ (pl: -s) gas meter

het/de **gaspedaal** /ɣɑspədal/ (pl: gaspedalen) accelerator (pedal): *het ~ indrukken* (or: *intrappen*) step on (*or:* press down) the accelerator

de **gaspit** /ɣɑspɪt/ (pl: -ten) gas ring, gas burner

het **gasstel** /ɣɑstɛl/ (pl: -len) gas ring (*or:* burner)

de **gast** /ɣɑst/ (pl: -en) **1** guest, visitor: *~en ontvangen* entertain (guests); *bij iem. te ~ zijn* be s.o.'s guest **2** customer: *vaste ~en* a) regular guests; b) regular customers **3** [inform] bloke, chap; [Am] guy, bro, dude

de **gastarbeider** /ɣɑstɑrbɛidər/ (pl: -s) immigrant worker

het **gastcollege** /ɣɑstkɔleʒə/ (pl: -s) guest lecture

de **gastdocent** /ɣɔzdosɛnt/ (pl: -en) visiting lecturer

het **gastenboek** /ɣɑstə(n)buk/ (pl: -en) visitors' book, guest book

het **gastgezin** /ɣɑstxəzɪn/ (pl: -nen) host family

de **gastheer** /ɣɑsther/ (pl: -heren) host: *als ~ optreden* act as host

het **gastland** /ɣɑstlɑnt/ (pl: -en) host country

het **gastoptreden** /ɣɑstɔptredə(n)/ guest appearance (*or:* performance)

de **gastrol** /ɣɑstrɔl/ (pl: -len) guest appearance

de **gastronomie** /ɣɑstronomi/ gastronomy

gastronomisch /ɣɑstronomis/ (adj, adv) gastronomic

de **gastspreker** /ɣɑstsprekər/ (pl: -s) guest speaker

gastvrij /ɣɑstfrɛi/ (adj, adv) hospitable, welcoming: *iem. ~ onthalen* entertain s.o. well; *iem. ~ ontvangen (opnemen)* extend a warm welcome to s.o.

de **gastvrijheid** /ɣɑstfrɛihɛit/ hospitality: *bij iem. ~ genieten* enjoy s.o.'s hospitality

de **gastvrouw** /ɣɑstfrɑu/ (pl: -en) hostess

gasvormig /ɣɑsfɔrməx/ (adj) gaseous

het **gat** /ɣɑt/ (pl: -en) **1** hole, gap: *zwart ~* black hole; *een ~ dichten* stop (*or:* fill) a hole; *een ~ maken in* make a hole in (sth.) **2** opening: [fig] *een ~ in de markt ontdekken* discover a gap (*or:* hole) in the market **3** hole, cavity: *een ~ in je kies* a hole (*or:* cavity) in your tooth **4** hole, dump **5** cut, gash: *zij viel een ~ in haar hoofd* she fell and cut her head ‖ *hij heeft een ~ in z'n hand* he spends money like water; *iets in de ~en hebben* realize sth., be aware of sth.; *iem. (iets) in de ~en houden* keep an eye on s.o. (sth.); *niets in de ~en hebben* be quite unaware of anything; *in de ~en lopen* attract (too much) attention

de **gate** /ɡet/ (pl: -s) gate

¹**gauw** /ɣɑu/ (adj, adv) quick, fast; hasty: *ga zitten en ~ een beetje* sit down and hurry up about it! (*or:* and make it snappy!); *dat heb je ~ gedaan, dat is ~* that was quick (work); *ik zou maar ~ een jurk aantrekken* (if I were you) I'd just slip into a dress

²**gauw** /ɣɑu/ (adv) **1** soon, before long: *hij had er al ~ genoeg van* he had soon had enough (of it); *hij zal nu wel ~ hier zijn* he won't be long now; *dat zou ik zo ~ niet weten* I couldn't say offhand **2** easily: *ik ben niet ~ bang, maar ...* I'm not easily scared, but ...; *dat kost al ~ €100* that can easily cost 100 euros ‖ *zo ~ ik iets weet, zal ik je bellen* as soon as I hear anything I'll ring you

de **gauwigheid** /ɣɑuwəxhɛit/ hurriedness, hurry

de **gave** /ɣavə/ (pl: -n) **1** gift, donation, endowment **2** gift, talent

de **gayscene** /ɡesi:n/ gay scene

de **Gazastrook** /ɣazastrok/ Gaza Strip

de **gazelle** /ɣazɛlə/ (pl: -n) gazelle

de **gazet** /ɣaz**ɛ**t/ (pl: -ten) [Belg] newspaper

het **gazon** /ɣaz**ɔ**n/ (pl: -s) lawn

ge /ɣə/ (pers pron) **1** thou **2** [Belg] you: *wat zegt* ge? what did you say?

geaard /ɣə**a**rt/ (adj) **1** earthed: *een ~ stop-contact* an earthed socket **2** natured, in-clined, tempered

de **geaardheid** /ɣə**a**rthɛit/ disposition, nature, inclination: *seksuele ~* sexual orientation

geabonneerd /ɣəabɔn**e**rt/ (adj): *~ zijn (op)* have a subscription (to)

geacht /ɣə**ɑ**xt/ (adj) respected, esteemed: *Geachte* **Heer** (or: **Mevrouw**) Dear Sir (*or:* Madam); *~e* **luisteraars** Ladies and Gentle-men

de **geadresseerde** /ɣəadrɛs**e**rdə/ (pl: -n) ad-dressee; consignee

geaffecteerd /ɣəafɛkt**e**rt/ (adj, adv) affect-ed, mannered: *~* **spreken** talk posh; *~* **Engels** *spreken* mince one's English

geagiteerd /ɣəaɣit**e**rt/ (adj, adv) excited, agitated: *~ zijn* be in a flutter

de **geallieerden** /ɣəali**je**rdə(n)/ (pl) Allies

geamuseerd /ɣəamyz**e**rt/ (adj, adv) amused: *~ naar iets* **kijken** watch sth. in amusement

geanimeerd /ɣəanim**e**rt/ (adj) animated, lively, warm: *een ~* **gesprek** an animated (*or:* a lively) conversation

gearmd /ɣə**ɑ**rmt/ (adj, adv) arm in arm

geavanceerd /ɣəavans**e**rt/ (adj) advanced, latest: *~e* **technieken** advanced techniques

het **gebaar** /ɣəb**a**r/ (pl: gebaren) **1** gesture, sig-n(al): *expressie in* **woord** *en ~* expression in word and gesture; *door een ~ beduidde zij hem bij haar te komen* she motioned him to come over; *met gebaren iets duidelijk maken* signal sth. (by means of gestures) **2** gesture, move: *een vriendelijk ~ aan zijn adres* a ges-ture of friendliness towards him

het **gebak** /ɣəb**ɑ**k/ pastry, confectionery, cake(s): *~ van* **bladerdeeg** puff (pastry); *vers ~* fresh pastry (*or:* confectionery); *koffie* **met** *~* coffee and cake(s)

het **gebakje** /ɣəb**ɑ**kjə/ (pl: -s) (fancy) cake, pas-try: *op ~s trakteren* treat (s.o.) to cake(s)

gebakken /ɣəb**ɑ**kə(n)/ (adj) baked; fried: *~ aardappelen* (*or:* **vis**) fried potatoes (*or:* fish)

gebaren /ɣəb**a**rə(n)/ (gebaarde, heeft ge-baard) gesture, gesticulate; signal; motion: *met armen en benen ~* gesticulate wildly

de **gebarentaal** /ɣəb**a**rə(n)tal/ sign language

de **gebarentolk** /ɣəb**a**rəntɔlk/ sign (language) interpreter

het **gebed** /ɣəb**ɛ**t/ (pl: -en) prayer, devotions; grace: *mijn ~en* **werden verhoord** my prayers were answered; *het ~* **vóór** *de maaltijd* (say-ing) grace

het **gebedel** /ɣəb**e**dəl/ begging

de **gebedsgenezer** /ɣəb**ɛ**tsɣ**ə**nezər/ (pl: -s) faith healer

het **gebedskleedje** /ɣəb**ɛ**tsklecə/ prayer mat

het **gebeente** /ɣəb**e**ntə/ (pl: -n) bones: *wee je ~!* woe betide you!, don't you dare!

gebeiteld /ɣəb**ɛ**itəlt/ (adj): *hij zit ~* he's sit-ting pretty, he's got it made

het **gebergte** /ɣəb**ɛ**rxtə/ (pl: -n, -s) **1** mountains **2** mountain range, chain of mountains

het **gebeurde** /ɣəb**ø**rdə/ incident, event: *hij wist zich niets* **van** *~ te herinneren* he couldn't remember anything of what had happened

het **¹gebeuren** /ɣəb**ø**rə(n)/ (pl: -s) event, inci-dent, happening: *een* **eenmalig** *~* a unique event

²gebeuren /ɣəb**ø**rə(n)/ (gebeurde, is ge-beurd) **1** happen, occur, take place: *er is een* **ongeluk** *gebeurd* there's been an accident; *voor ze (goed) wist wat* **er** *gebeurde* (the) next thing she knew; *er gebeurt hier nooit iets* nothing ever happens here; *alsof er* **niets** *ge-beurd was* as if nothing had happened; *wat is er* **met** *jou gebeurd?* what's happened to you?; *voor als er iets gebeurt* just in case; *er* **moet** *nog heel wat ~, voor het zover is* we have a long way to go yet; *het is* **zó** *gebeurd* it'll only take a second (*or:* minute); *er moet nog het een en ander* **aan** *~* it needs a bit more doing to it; *dat gebeurt wel meer* these things do happen **2** happen, occur: *dat* **kan** *de beste ~* it could happen to anyone; *er kan* **niets** *(mee) ~* nothing's can happen (to it)

de **gebeurtenis** /ɣəb**ø**rtənɪs/ (pl: -sen) **1** event, occurrence, incident: *dat is een* **be-langrijke** *~* that's a major event; *een* **onvoor-ziene** *~* an unforeseen occurrence (*or:* inci-dent) **2** event: *een* **eenmalige** *~* a unique oc-casion

het **gebied** /ɣəb**i**t/ (pl: -en) **1** territory, domain **2** area, district, region: *onderontwikkelde* (or: **achtergebleven**) *~en* underdeveloped (*or:* depressed) areas/regions **3** field, depart-ment: *op* **ecologisch** *~* in the field of ecology; *vragen op* **financieel** *~* financial problems; *wij verkopen alles* **op** *het ~ van …* we sell every-thing (which has) to do with … **4** territory, land

gebieden /ɣəb**i**də(n)/ (gebood, heeft gebo-den) **1** order, dictate: *iem. ~* **te zwijgen** im-pose silence on s.o., bind s.o. to secrecy **2** compel, necessitate: *de grootste* **voorzich-tigheid** *is geboden* the situation calls for the utmost caution, great caution is required

gebiedend /ɣəb**i**dənt/ (adj, adv) impera-tive, vital, compulsive ‖ *op ~e* **toon** with a voice of command, in a peremptory tone; *~e* **wijs** imperative mood, imperative

het **gebiedsdeel** /ɣəb**i**tsdel/ (pl: -delen) territo-ry: *de* **overzeese** *gebiedsdelen* the overseas territories

het **gebit** /ɣəb**ɪ**t/ (pl: -ten) **1** (set of) teeth: *een* **goed** *~ hebben* have a good set of teeth; *een* **regelmatig** (or: **onregelmatig, sterk**) *~* regu-lar (*or:* irregular, strong) teeth **2** (set of) dentures, (set of) false teeth

de **gebitsverzorging** /ɣəbɪ̆tsfərzɔrɣɪŋ/ dental care

het **gebladerte** /ɣəbladərtə/ foliage

het **geblaf** /ɣəblɑf/ barking, baying

geblesseerd /ɣəblɛsert/ (adj) injured

de **geblesseerde** /ɣəblɛserdə/ (pl: -n) injured player

geblindeerd /ɣəblɪndert/ (adj) shuttered; blacked out; armoured

gebloemd /ɣəblumt/ (adj) floral (patterned), flowered: ~ **behang** floral (patterned) wallpaper

geblokkeerd /ɣəblɔkert/ (adj) **1** blockaded; ice-bound **2** blocked **3** blocked, frozen: *een ~e* **rekening** a frozen account ‖ *de wielen* **raakten** ~ the wheels locked

geblokt /ɣəblɔkt/ (adj) chequered

gebocheld /ɣəbɔxəlt/ (adj) hunchbacked, humpbacked

het **gebod** /ɣəbɔt/ (pl: -en) order, command: *~en en* **verboden** do's and don'ts; *een ~* **uitvaardigen** issue an order (*or:* injunction); *de* **tien** *~en* the Ten Commandments

gebogen /ɣəboɣə(n)/ (adj) bent, curved: *met ~* **hoofd** with bowed head, with head bowed

gebonden /ɣəbɔndə(n)/ (adj) **1** bound, tied (up), committed: *niet* **contractueel** ~ not bound by contract; *aan huis* ~ housebound; *niet* **aan** *regels* ~ not bound by rules **2** bound: *een ~* **boek** a hardback ‖ *~* **aspergesoep** cream of asparagus (soup)

de **geboorte** /ɣəbortə/ (pl: -n, -s) birth; delivery: *bij de ~* **woog** *het kind …* the child weighed … at birth

de **geboorteakte** /ɣəbortəɑktə/ (pl: -n, -s) birth certificate, certificate of birth

de **geboortebeperking** /ɣəbortəbəpɛrkɪŋ/ (pl: -en) **1** birth control, family planning **2** contraception, family-planning methods

het **geboortecijfer** /ɣəbortəsɛifər/ (pl: -s) birth rate

de **geboortedag** /ɣəbortədɑx/ (pl: -en) **1** birthday: *de* **honderdste** (*or:* **tweehonderdste**) *~* the centenary (*or:* bicentenary) of s.o.'s birth **2** day of birth

de **geboortedatum** /ɣəbortədatʏm/ date of birth, birth date

de **geboortegolf** /ɣəbortəɣɔlf/ (pl: -golven) baby boom

het **geboortejaar** /ɣəbortəjar/ (pl: -jaren) year of birth

het **geboortekaartje** /ɣəbortəkarcə/ (pl: -s) birth announcement card

het **geboorteland** /ɣəbortəlɑnt/ (pl: -en) native country, country of origin

het **geboorteoverschot** /ɣəbortəovərsxɔt/ (pl: -ten) excess (of) births (over deaths)

de **geboorteplaats** /ɣəbortəplats/ (pl: -en) place of birth, birthplace

de **geboorteregeling** /ɣəbortəreɣəlɪŋ/ birth control

het **geboorteregister** /ɣəbortərəɣɪstər/ (pl: -s) register of births

geboren /ɣəborə(n)/ (adj) born: *een ~* **leraar** a born teacher; *mevrouw Jansen, ~* **Smit** Mrs Jansen née Smit; *~ en* **getogen** *in Amsterdam* born and bred in Amsterdam; *waar* (*or:* *wanneer*) **bent** *u ~?* where (*or:* when) were you born?; *een te* **vroeg** *~ kind* a premature baby

de **geborgenheid** /ɣəbɔrɣənhɛit/ security, safety

het **gebouw** /ɣəbɑu/ (pl: -en) building, structure, construction: *een* **groot** (*or:* **ruim**) *~* a large (*or:* spacious) building; *een* **houten** *~(tje)* a wooden structure

gebouwd /ɣəbɑut/ (adj) built, constructed: *hij is* **fors (stevig)** *~* he is well-built; *mooi ~ zijn* have a fine figure, be well-proportioned

het **gebouwencomplex** /ɣəbɑuwə(n)kɔmplɛks/ (pl: -en) block (*or:* group) of buildings

het **gebral** /ɣəbrɑl/ bragging, bluster, tubthumping

gebrand /ɣəbrɑnt/ (adj) roasted, burnt: *~e* **amandelen** burnt (*or:* roasted) almonds ‖ *erop ~* **zijn** *te* be keen on, be eager for

het **gebrek** /ɣəbrɛk/ (pl: -en) **1** lack, shortage, deficiency: *groot ~* **hebben** *aan* be greatly lacking in; [stronger] be in desperate need of; *~* **aan** *personeel hebben* be short-handed, be understaffed; *bij ~* **aan** *beter* for want of anything (*or:* sth.) better **2** want, need: *~* **hebben (lijden)** be in want (*or:* need), go short **3** ailment, infirmity: *de ~en van de* **ouderdom** the ailments of old age **4** shortcoming, weakness: *alle mensen* **hebben** *hun ~en* we all have our faults, no one is perfect **5** flaw, fault, defect: *een ~* **verhelpen** correct a fault; (*ernstige*) *~en* **vertonen** be (seriously) defective, show serious flaws ‖ *zonder ~en* flawless, faultless, perfect; *in ~e blijven* **a)** fail (to do sth.); **b)** (be in) default

¹**gebrekkig** /ɣəbrɛkəx/ (adj, adv) **1** infirm, ailing; lame: *een ~* **mens** an ailing person **2** faulty, defective; inadequate; poor: *~e* **huisvesting** poor housing; *een ~e* **kennis** *van het Engels* poor (knowledge of) English

²**gebrekkig** /ɣəbrɛkəx/ (adv) poorly, inadequately: *een taal ~* **spreken** speak a language poorly

de **gebroeders** /ɣəbrudərs/ (pl) brothers: *de ~* **Jansen**, *handelaren in wijnen* Jansen Brothers (*or:* Bros.), wine merchants

gebroken /ɣəbrokə(n)/ (adj) **1** broken; fractured: *~* **lijn** broken line; *een ~* **rib** a broken (*or:* fractured) rib **2** broken: *zich ~* **voelen** be a broken man (*or:* woman) **3** broken: *hij sprak haar in ~* **Frans** *aan* he addressed her in broken French

het **gebruik** /ɣəbrœyk/ (pl: -en) **1** use, applica-

tion; consumption; be on; take; taking: *het ~
van sterkedrank* (the) consumption of spirits;
voor algemeen ~ for general use; *voor eigen
~* for personal use; *alleen voor uitwendig
~* for external use (*or:* application) only; *(geen)
~ van iets maken* (not) make use of sth.; *van
de gelegenheid ~ maken* take (*or:* seize) the
opportunity; *iets in ~ nemen* put sth. into use
2 custom, habit: *de ~en van een land* the customs of a country

gebruikelijk /ɣəbrœykələk/ (adj) usual,
customary; common: *de ~e naam van een
plant* the common name of a plant; *op de ~e
wijze* in the usual way

¹gebruiken /ɣəbrœykə(n)/ (gebruikte, heeft
gebruikt) be on drugs, take drugs

²gebruiken /ɣəbrœykə(n)/ (gebruikte, heeft
gebruikt) use, apply; take: *de auto gebruikt
veel brandstof* the car uses (*or:* consumes) a
lot of fuel; *slaapmiddelen ~* take sleeping
pills (*or:* tablets); *zijn verstand ~* use one's
common sense; *dat kan ik net goed ~* I could
just use that; *dat kan ik goed ~* that comes in
handy; *ik zou best wat extra geld kunnen ~* I
could do with some extra money; *zich gebruikt voelen* feel used; *zijn tijd goed ~* make
good use of one's time, put one's time to
good use

de **gebruiker** /ɣəbrœykər/ (pl: -s) **1** user; consumer: *de ~s van een computer* computer users **2** drug user; drug addict

de **gebruikersnaam** /ɣəbrœykərsnam/ (pl:
-namen) user name

gebruikersvriendelijk /ɣəbrœykərs-
frindələk/ (adj, adv) user-friendly, easy to
use; convenient

gebruikmaken /ɣəbrœykmakə(n)/ (maakte gebruik, heeft gebruikgemaakt) (+ van)
use, make use of: *van de gelegenheid ~* take
(*or:* seize) the opportunity; *~ van een mogelijkheid* use a possibility

de **gebruikmaking** /ɣəbrœykmakɪŋ/ use: *met
~ van* (by) using, with the benefit of

de **gebruiksaanwijzing** /ɣəbrœyksanwɛizɪŋ/
(pl: -en) directions (for use); instructions (for
use)

gebruiksklaar /ɣəbrœyksklar/ (adj) ready
for use

gebruiksvriendelijk /ɣəbrœyksfrindələk/
(adj, adv) user-friendly

de **gebruikswaarde** /ɣəbrœykswardə/ practical value, utility value

gebruind /ɣəbrœynt/ (adj) tanned, sunburnt

het **gebrul** /ɣəbrʏl/ roar(ing), howling

gebukt /ɣəbʏkt/ (adj): *~ gaan onder zorgen*
be weighed down (*or:* be burdened) with
worries

gecharmeerd /ɣəʃarmert/ (adj): *van iem.
(iets) ~ zijn* be taken with s.o. (sth.)

geciviliseerd /ɣəsivilizert/ (adj) civilized

gecompliceerd /ɣəkɔmplisert/ (adj) complicated, involved: *een ~e breuk* a compound
fracture; *een ~ geval* a complicated case

geconcentreerd /ɣəkɔnsɛntrert/ (adj, adv)
1 concentrated **2** concentrated, intent; [as
adverb also] with concentration: *~ werken*
work with (great) concentration

geconserveerd /ɣəkɔnsɛrvert/ (adj) preserved; canned: *goed ~ zijn* be well-preserved

de **gedaagde** /ɣədaɣdə/ (pl: -n) defendant; respondent

gedaan /ɣədan/ (adj) **1** done, finished, over:
dan is het ~ met de rust then there won't be
any peace and quiet **2** done, finished, over
(with): *ik kan alles van hem ~ krijgen* he'll do
anything for me; *iets ~ krijgen* get sth. done;
van iem. iets ~ krijgen get sth. out of s.o.

de **gedaante** /ɣədantə/ (pl: -n, -s) form, figure,
shape; [fig esp] guise: *een andere ~ aannemen*
take on another form, change (its) shape; *in
menselijke ~* in human form (*or:* shape); *zijn
ware ~ tonen* show (o.s. in) one's true colours

de **gedaanteverwisseling** /ɣədantəvərwɪsə-
lɪŋ/ (pl: -en) transformation, metamorphosis:
een ~ ondergaan be(come) transformed

de **gedachte** /ɣədɑxtə/ (pl: -n) **1** thought: *iemands ~n ergens van afleiden* take s.o.'s mind
off sth.; *(diep) in ~n zijn* be deep in thought;
iets in ~n doen do sth. absent-mindedly, do
sth. with one's mind elsewhere; *iets in ~n
houden* keep one's mind on sth.; bear sth. in
mind; *er niet bij zijn met zijn ~n* have one's
mind on sth. else **2** thought, idea: *de achter-
liggende ~ is dat ...* the underlying idea (*or:*
thought) is that ...; *zijn ~n bij iets houden*
keep one's mind on sth.; *de ~ niet kunnen
verdragen dat ...* not be able to bear the
thought (*or:* bear to think) that ...; *de ~ alleen al ...* the very thought (*or:* idea) ...; *(iem.)
op de ~ brengen* give (s.o.) the idea; *van ~n
wisselen over* exchange ideas on, discuss
3 opinion, view: *iem. tot andere ~n brengen*
make s.o. change his mind **4** idea: *van ~n
veranderen* change one's mind

de **gedachtegang** /ɣədɑxtəɣɑŋ/ (pl: -en) train
of thought; (line of) reasoning

het **gedachtegoed** /ɣədɑxtəɣut/ range of
thought (*or:* ideas)

gedachtelezen /ɣədɑxtəlezə(n)/ mind-
reading, thought-reading

gedachteloos /ɣədɑxtəlos/ (adj, adv) unthinking, thoughtless

de **gedachtenis** /ɣədɑxtənɪs/ memory: *ter ~
van iem.* in memory of s.o.

de **gedachtesprong** /ɣədɑxtəsprɔŋ/ (pl: -en)
mental leap (*or:* jump): *een ~ maken* make a
mental leap (*or:* jump), jump from one idea
to another

de **gedachtewisseling** /ɣədɑxtəwɪsəlɪŋ/ (pl:
-en) exchange of ideas (*or:* opinions): *een ~
houden over* exchange ideas on, compose

notes on

gedag /ɣədɔx/ (int): ~ *zeggen* say hello (*or:* goodbye)

de **gedagvaarde** /ɣədɔxfardə/ (pl: -n) person summon(s)ed

gedateerd /ɣədate̯rt/ (adj) (out)dated, archaic

gedecideerd /ɣədeside̯rt/ (adj, adv) decisive, resolute

het **gedeelte** /ɣəde̯ltə/ (pl: -n, -s) part, section; instalment: *het bovenste* (or: *onderste*) ~ the top (*or:* bottom) part; *het grootste* ~ *van het jaar* most of the year; *voor* een ~ partly

¹**gedeeltelijk** /ɣəde̯ltələk/ (adj) partial: *een ~e vergoeding voor geleden schade* partial compensation for damage sustained

²**gedeeltelijk** /ɣəde̯ltələk/ (adv) partly, partially: *dat is slechts ~ waar* that is only partly (*or:* partially) true

gedegen /ɣəde̯ɣə(n)/ (adj) thorough: *een ~ studie* a thorough study

gedeisd /ɣəde̯ist/ (adj, adv) quiet, calm: *zich ~ houden* lie low

gedekt /ɣədɛkt/ (adj) **1** covered **2** [fin] covered: *een ~e cheque* a covered cheque

de **gedelegeerde** /ɣədeleɣe̯rdə/ (pl: -n) delegate, representative: *een ~ bij de VN* a delegate to the UN

gedemotiveerd /ɣədemotive̯rt/ (adj) demoralized, dispirited: ~ *raken* lose one's motivation

gedempt /ɣədɛmpt/ (adj) subdued, faint; muffled; hushed: *op ~e toon* in a low (*or:* subdued) voice

gedenken /ɣədɛŋkə(n)/ (gedacht, heeft gedacht) commemorate; remember: *iem. in zijn testament ~* remember s.o. in one's will

de **gedenksteen** /ɣədɛŋksten/ (pl: -stenen) memorial stone

het **gedenkteken** /ɣədɛŋktekə(n)/ (pl: -en, -s) memorial: *een ~ voor* a memorial to

gedenkwaardig /ɣədɛŋkwardəx/ (adj) memorable: *een ~e gebeurtenis* a memorable event

gedeprimeerd /ɣədeprime̯rt/ (adj) depressed

gedeputeerd /ɣədepyte̯rt/ (adj): *Gedeputeerde Staten* [roughly] the provincial executive

de **gedeputeerde** /ɣədepyte̯rdə/ (pl: -n) **1** delegate, representative **2** member of parliament **3** [roughly] member of the provincial executive

gedesillusioneerd /ɣədɛsɪlyʃone̯rt/ (adj) disillusioned

gedesoriënteerd /ɣədɛsorijənte̯rt/ (adj) disorient(at)ed

¹**gedetailleerd** /ɣədetɑje̯rt/ (adj) detailed: *een ~ verslag* a detailed report

²**gedetailleerd** /ɣədetɑje̯rt/ (adv) in detail

de **gedetineerde** /ɣədetine̯rdə/ (pl: -n) prisoner, inmate

het **gedicht** /ɣədɪxt/ (pl: -en) poem: *een ~ maken* (or: *voordragen*) write (*or:* recite) a poem

de **gedichtenbundel** /ɣədɪxtə(n)bʏndəl/ (pl: -s) volume of poetry (*or:* verse), collection of poems

gedienstig /ɣədinstəx/ (adj, adv) obliging, helpful

gedijen /ɣədɛiə(n)/ (gedijde, heeft gedijd) thrive, prosper, do well

het **geding** /ɣədɪŋ/ (pl: -en) (law)suit, (legal) action, (legal) proceedings: *in kort ~ behandelen* discuss in summary proceedings; *een ~ aanspannen (beginnen) tegen* institute proceedings against

gediplomeerd /ɣədiplome̯rt/ (adj) qualified, certified; registered

het **gedistilleerd** /ɣədɪstile̯rt/ spirits; [esp Am] liquor: *handel in ~ en wijnen* trade in wines and spirits

gedistingeerd /ɣədɪstɪŋe̯rt/ (adj, adv) distinguished: *een ~ voorkomen* a distinguished appearance

gedocumenteerd /ɣədokymɛnte̯rt/ (adj) documented: *een goed ~ rapport* a well-documented report

het **gedoe** /ɣədu̯/ business, stuff, carry on: *zenuwachtig* ~ fuss

gedogen /ɣədo̯ɣə(n)/ (gedoogde, heeft gedoogd) tolerate, put up with

het **gedonder** /ɣədɔndər/ **1** thunder(ing), rumble: *het ~ weerklonk door het gebergte* the thunder rolled through the mountains **2** trouble, hassle: *daar kun je een hoop ~ mee krijgen* that can land you in a good deal of trouble

gedoodverfd /ɣədo̯tfɛrft/ (adj): *een ~e winnaar* a hot favourite, a dead certainty; *de ~e winnaar zijn* be tipped to win

het **gedrag** /ɣədrɑx/ behaviour, conduct: *een bewijs van goed ~* evidence of good behaviour; *certificate of good character; wegens slecht ~* for bad behaviour (*or:* misconduct); *iemands ~ goedkeuren* (or: *afkeuren*) approve of (*or:* disapprove of) s.o.'s behaviour

zich **gedragen** /ɣədraɣə(n)/ (gedroeg zich, heeft zich gedragen) behave; behave o.s.: *hij beloofde zich voortaan beter te zullen ~* he promised to behave better in future; *zich goed* (or: *slecht*) ~ behave well (*or:* badly); *zich niet (slecht)* ~ misbehave (o.s.); *gedraag je!* behave (yourself)!

de **gedragslijn** /ɣədrɑxslɛin/ (pl: -en) course (of action), line of conduct: *een ~ volgen* persue a course of action

het **gedragspatroon** /ɣədrɑxspatron/ (pl: -patronen) pattern of behaviour

de **gedragsregel** /ɣədrɑxsreɣəl/ (pl: -s) rule of conduct (*or:* behaviour)

de **gedragswetenschappen** /ɣədrɑxswetənsχɑpə(n)/ (pl) behavioural sciences

het **gedrang** /ɣədrɑ̯ŋ/ jostling, pushing: *in het ~ komen* a) end up (*or:* find o.s.) in a crush; b) get into a tight corner

gedreven /ɣədre̯və(n)/ (adj) passionate; fanatic(al): *een ~ kunstenaar* s.o. who lives for his art

gedrieën /ɣədrijə(n)/ (num) (the) three (of): *zij zaten ~ op de bank* the three of them sat on the bench

het **gedrocht** /ɣədrɔ̯χt/ (pl: -en) monster, freak

gedrongen /ɣədrɔ̯ŋə(n)/ (adj): *een ~ gestalte* a stocky (*or:* thickset, squat) figure

gedrukt /ɣədrʏkt/ (adj) **1** printed **2** [com] depressed, dull: *de markt was ~* the market was depressed

geducht /ɣədyχt/ (adj, adv) formidable, fearsome: *een ~e tegenstander* a formidable opponent

het **geduld** /ɣədʏlt/ patience: *zijn ~ bewaren* remain patient; *~ hebben met iem.* be patient with s.o.; *zijn ~ verliezen* lose (one's) patience; *even ~ a.u.b.* one moment, please; *veel van iemands ~ vergen, iemands ~ op de proef stellen* try s.o.'s patience

geduldig /ɣədʏldəχ/ (adj, adv) patient: *~ afwachten* wait patiently

gedupeerd /ɣədype̯rt/ (adj) duped

de **gedupeerde** /ɣədype̯rdə/ victim, dupe

gedurende /ɣədyrəndə/ (prep) during, for, over; in the course of: *~ de hele dag* all through the day; *~ het hele jaar* throughout the year; *~ vier maanden* for (a period of) four months; *~ het onderzoek* during the enquiry; *~ de laatste (afgelopen) drie weken* over the past three weeks

gedurfd /ɣədʏrft/ (adj) daring; provocative: *een zeer ~ optreden* a highly provocative performance

gedwee /ɣədwe̯/ (adj) meek, submissive

gedwongen /ɣədwɔ̯ŋə(n)/ (adj, adv) (en)forced, compulsory, involuntary: *~ ontslag* compulsory redundancy; *een ~ verkoop* a forced sale; *~ ontslag nemen* be forced to resign

geel /ɣel/ (adj) yellow ‖ *(in de Ronde van Frankrijk) in het ~ rijden* be wearing the yellow jersey (in the Tour de France); *de scheidsrechter toonde hem het ~* the referee showed him the yellow card

de **geelzucht** /ɣe̯lzʏχt/ jaundice

geëmancipeerd /ɣəemɑnsipe̯rt/ (adj) liberated, emancipated

geëmotioneerd /ɣəemo(t)ʃone̯rt/ (adj, adv) emotional, touched, moved

¹geen /ɣen/ (num) none; not a, not any; no: *hij heeft ~ auto* he doesn't have a car, he hasn't got a car; *hij heeft ~ geld* he doesn't have any money, he has no money; *er zijn bijna ~ koekjes meer* we're nearly out of cookies; *bijna ~* almost none, hardly any; *~ van die*

jongens (or: beiden) none of those lads, neither (of them)

²geen /ɣen/ (art) **1** not a, no: *nog ~ tien minuten later* not ten minutes later; *nog ~ twee jaar geleden* less than two years ago; *~ enkele reden hebben om te* have no reason whatsoever to **2** not a(ny), no: *hij kent ~ Engels* he doesn't know (any) English; *~ één* not (a single) one

geeneens /ɣene̯ns/ (adv) [inform] not even, not so much as

geëngageerd /ɣəɑŋɡaʒe̯rt/ (adj) committed

geenszins /ɣe̯nsɪns/ (adv) by no means, not at all

de **geest** /ɣest/ (pl: -en) **1** mind, consciousness: *iets voor de ~ halen* call sth. to mind **2** soul **3** spirit, character: *jong van ~ zijn* be young at heart **4** ghost, spirit: *de Heilige Geest* the Holy Ghost (*or:* Holy Spirit); *een boze (kwade) ~* an evil spirit, a demon; *in ~en geloven* believe in ghosts **5** spirit, vein, intention

geestdodend /ɣe̯sdo̯dənt/ (adj) stultifying; monotonous; dull

de **geestdrift** /ɣe̯zdrɪft/ enthusiasm, passion; zeal

geestdriftig /ɣe̯zdrɪftəχ/ (adj) enthusiastic

geestelijk /ɣe̯stələk/ (adj, adv) **1** mental, intellectual; psychological; spiritual: *~e aftakeling* mental deterioration; *een ~ gehandicapte* a mentally handicapped person; *~e inspanning* mental effort; *~ gestoord* mentally disturbed (*or:* deranged) **2** spiritual: *~e bijstand verlenen aan iem.* a) give (spiritual) counselling to s.o.; b) [rel] minister to s.o. **3** clerical

de **geestelijke** /ɣe̯stələkə/ (pl: -n) clergyman; [Protestantism] minister; [esp Roman Catholicism] priest

de **geestelijkheid** /ɣe̯stələkhɛɪt/ **1** clergy **2** spirituality

de **geestesgesteldheid** /ɣe̯stəsχəstɛlthɛɪt/ state (*or:* frame) of mind

het **geesteskind** /ɣe̯stəskɪnt/ (pl: -eren) brainchild

de **geestestoestand** /ɣe̯stəstustɑnt/ state of mind, mental state

de **geesteswetenschappen** /ɣe̯stəswetənsχɑpə(n)/ (pl) humanities, arts

geestesziek /ɣe̯stəsik/ (adj) mentally ill

geestig /ɣe̯stəχ/ (adj, adv) witty, humorous, funny

de **geestigheid** /ɣe̯stəχhɛɪt/ (pl: -heden) witticism, quip

geestrijk /ɣe̯strɛɪk/ (adj): *~ vocht* hard liquor, strong drink

geestverruimend /ɣe̯stfərœymənt/ (adj) mind-expanding; hallucinogenic

de **geestverschijning** /ɣe̯stfərsχɛɪnɪŋ/ (pl: -en) apparition, phantom, spectre, ghost

de **geestverwant** /ɣe̯stfərwɑnt/ (pl: -en) kindred spirit; [pol] sympathizer

de **geeuw** /ɣew/ (pl: -en) yawn

geeuwen /ɣewə(n)/ (geeuwde, heeft ge-
geeuwd) yawn: ~ *van slaap* yawn with sleepiness

de **geeuwhonger** /ɣewhɔnər/ ravenous hunger

gefaseerd /ɣəfazert/ (adj) phased, in
phases

gefingeerd /ɣəfɪnɣert/ (adj) fictitious,
fake(d); feigned

geflatteerd /ɣəflɑtert/ (adj) flattering

het **geflirt** /ɣəflɪ:rt/ flirtation, flirting

het **gefluister** /ɣəflœystər/ whisper(ing)(s),
murmur

het **gefluit** /ɣəflœyt/ whistling; warbling; singing

geforceerd /ɣəfɔrsert/ (adj, adv) forced,
contrived, artificial

gefortuneerd /ɣəfɔrtynert/ (adj) moneyed,
monied, wealthy: *een ~ man* a man of means

gefrustreerd /ɣəfrʏstrert/ (adj) frustrated

gefundeerd /ɣəfʏndert/ (adj) (well-)found-
ed, (well-)grounded

de **gegadigde** /ɣəɣadəydə/ (pl: -n) applicant;
candidate; prospective buyer; interested
party: *een ~ voor iets vinden* find a (potential)
buyer for sth.

¹**gegarandeerd** /ɣəɣarɑndert/ (adj, adv)
guaranteed

²**gegarandeerd** /ɣəɣarɑndert/ (adv) [fig]
definitely: *dat gaat ~ mis* that's bound (*or:*
sure) to go wrong

gegeneerd /ɣəʒənert/ (adj) embarrassed,
uncomfortable: *zich ~ voelen* feel embarrassed (*or:* uncomfortable)

het ¹**gegeven** /ɣəɣevə(n)/ (pl: -s) **1** data, datum,
fact, information; data; entry, item: *nadere
~s* further information; *persoonlijke ~s* personal details; *~s opslaan* (*or:* *invoeren, opvragen*) store (*or:* input, retrieve) data
2 theme, subject

²**gegeven** /ɣəɣevə(n)/ (adj) given, certain: *op
een ~ moment begin je je af te vragen …* there
comes a time when you begin to wonder …

het **gegevensbestand** /ɣəɣevə(n)zbəstɑnt/
(pl: -en) database, data file

de **gegevensverwerking** /ɣəɣevənsfər-
wɛrkɪŋ/ data processing

het **gegiechel** /ɣəɣixəl/ giggle(s), giggling;
snigger(ing): *onderdrukt ~* stifled giggling

de **gegijzelde** /ɣəɣɛizəldə/ (pl: -n) hostage

het **gegil** /ɣəɣɪl/ screaming, screams

gegoed /ɣəɣut/ (adj) well-to-do, well-off,
moneyed, monied: *de ~e burgerij* the upper
middle class

het **gegoochel** /ɣəɣoxəl/ juggling

gegoten /ɣəɣotə(n)/ (adj): *die jurk zit als ~*
that dress fits you like a glove

het **gegrinnik** /χəχrɪnək/ snigger, grinning

gegrond /ɣəɣrɔnt/ (adj) (well-)founded,

valid, legitimate

gehaaid /ɣəhajt/ (adj, adv) smart, sharp

gehaast /ɣəhast/ (adj, adv) hurried, hasty,
in a hurry

gehaat /ɣəhat/ (adj) hated, hateful: *zich (bij
iem.) ~ maken* incur s.o.'s hatred

het **gehakt** /ɣəhɑkt/ minced meat, mince

de **gehaktbal** /ɣəhɑktbɑl/ (pl: -len) meatball

de **gehaktmolen** /ɣəhɑktmolə(n)/ (pl: -s)
mincer

het **gehalte** /ɣəhɑltə/ (pl: -s) content, percentage, proportion: *een hoog* (*or:* *laag*) *~ aan* a
high (*or:* low) content of

gehandicapt /ɣəhɛndikɛpt/ (adj) handicapped; disabled

de **gehandicapte** /ɣəhɛndikɛptə/ (pl: -n)
handicapped person; mentally handicapped
person: *de (lichamelijk) ~n* the (physically)
handicapped, the disabled

het **gehannes** /ɣəhɔnəs/ fumbling

gehard /ɣəhɑrt/ (adj) **1** tough, hardened,
seasoned: *~ tegen* hardened against **2** tempered

het **geharrewar** /ɣəhɑrəwɑr/ squabble(s), bick-
ering(s), squabbling

gehavend /ɣəhavənt/ (adj) battered, tattered

gehecht /ɣəhɛxt/ (adj) attached (to);
[stronger] devoted (to)

het ¹**geheel** /ɣəhel/ **1** whole, entity, unit(y)
2 whole, entirety ‖ *over het ~ genomen* on
the whole

²**geheel** /ɣəhel/ (adv) entirely, fully, completely, totally: *ik voel mij een ~ ander mens* I
feel a different person altogether; revised

de **geheelonthouder** /ɣəhelɔnthaudər/ (pl:
-s) teetotaller

geheid /ɣəhɛit/ (adj, adv): *die strafschop
gaat er ~ in* he can't miss that penalty, that
penalty's a (dead) cert; *dat wordt ~ een succes*
it's bound to be a success

het ¹**geheim** /ɣəhɛim/ (pl: -en) **1** secret: *een ~
toevertrouwen* (*or:* *bewaren*) confide (*or:*
keep) a secret; *een ~ verraden* give away a
secret, let the cat out of the bag **2** secrecy: *in
het ~* secretly

²**geheim** /ɣəhɛim/ (adj) **1** secret, hidden,
concealed, clandestine; undercover: *dat
moet ~ blijven* this must remain private (*or:* a
secret); *een ~e bijeenkomst* a secret meeting
2 secret, classified, confidential, private: *uiterst ~e documenten* top-secret documents ‖
een ~ telefoonnummer an unlisted telephone number

geheimhouden /ɣəhɛimhaudə(n)/ (hield
geheim, heeft geheimgehouden) keep (a)
secret, keep under cover, keep dark

de **geheimhouding** /ɣəhɛimhaudɪŋ/ secrecy,
confidentiality, privacy

het **geheimschrift** /ɣəhɛimsxrɪft/ (pl: -en) (secret) code, cipher

de **geheimtaal** /ɣəhɛɪmtal/ (pl: -talen) secret (or: private) language

¹**geheimzinnig** /ɣəhɛimzɪnəɣ/ (adj) mysterious, unexplained, cryptic

²**geheimzinnig** /ɣəhɛimzɪnəɣ/ (adv) mysteriously, secretly: *erg ~ doen (over iets)* be very secretive (about sth.)

de **geheimzinnigheid** /ɣəhɛimzɪnəɣhɛit/ **1** secrecy, stealth **2** mysteriousness, mystery

het **gehemelte** /ɣəheməltə/ (pl: -s) palate, roof of the mouth

het **geheugen** /ɣəhøɣə(n)/ (pl: -s) **1** memory; mind: *dat ligt nog vers in mijn ~* it's still fresh in my memory (or: mind); *iemands ~ opfrissen* refresh s.o.'s memory; *mijn ~ laat me in de steek* my memory is letting me down **2** memory, storage

de **geheugenkaart** /ɣəhøɣə(n)kart/ (pl: -en) memory card

het **geheugensteuntje** /ɣəhøɣə(n)støncə/ (pl: -s) reminder, prompt

de **geheugenstick** memory stick

het **geheugenverlies** /ɣəhøɣə(n)vərlis/ amnesia, loss of memory: *tijdelijk ~* a blackout

het **gehoor** /ɣəhor/ (sense of) hearing, ear(s): *bij geen ~* if there's no reply; *geen muzikaal ~ hebben* have no ear for music

het **gehoorapparaat** /ɣəhorɑparat/ (pl: -apparaten) hearing aid

het **gehoorbeentje** /ɣəhorbencə/ auditory ossicle

de **gehoorgang** /ɣəhorɣɑŋ/ (pl: -en) auditory duct (or: passage)

gehoorgestoord /ɣəhorɣəstort/ (adj) hearing-impaired, hard of hearing, deaf

het **gehoororgaan** /ɣəhororɣan/ (pl: -organen) ear, auditory organ, organ of hearing

de **gehoorsafstand** /ɣəhorsɑfstɑnt/ earshot, hearing

gehoorzaam /ɣəhorzam/ (adj, adv) obedient

de **gehoorzaamheid** /ɣəhorzamhɛɪt/ obedience

gehoorzamen /ɣəhorzamə(n)/ (gehoorzaamde, heeft gehoorzaamd) obey; comply (with)

gehorig /ɣəhorəɣ/ (adj) noisy, thin-walled

gehouden /ɣəhɑudə(n)/ (adj) obliged (to), liable (to): *~ zijn tot* be obliged (or: liable) to

het **gehucht** /ɣəhʏxt/ (pl: -en) hamlet, settlement

het **gehuil** /ɣəhœyl/ crying: *het ~ van de wind* the howling (or: moaning) of the wind

gehuisvest /ɣəhœysfɛst/ (adj) housed, lodged

gehuwd /ɣəhywt/ (adj) married

de **geigerteller** /ɡɑjɡərtɛlər/ (pl: -s) Geiger counter

geijkt /ɣəɛɪkt/ (adj) **1** calibrated **2** standard: *hij komt altijd met het ~e antwoord* he always comes up with the standard reply

geil /ɣɛil/ (adj, adv) [inform] randy, horny

geilen /ɣɛɪlə(n)/ (geilde, heeft gegeild) [inform] be hot for; [Am] have the hots (for)

geïmproviseerd /ɣəɪmprovizɛrt/ (adj) improvised, ad lib

de **gein** /ɣɛin/ [inform] fun, merriment: *~ trappen* make merry

geinig /ɣɛinəɣ/ (adj, adv) [inform] funny, cute

geïnteresseerd /ɣəɪntərɛsɛrt/ (adj, adv) interested

de **geïnterneerde** /ɣəɪntɛrnɛrdə/ (pl: -n) detainee, inmate

het **geintje** /ɣɛɪncə/ (pl: -s) joke, prank, (wise)-crack: *~s uithalen* play jokes

de **geiser** /ɣɛizər/ (pl: -s) geyser

de **geisha** /ɡɛiʃa/ (pl: -'s) geisha

de **geit** /ɣɛit/ (pl: -en) goat

de **geitenkaas** /ɣɛɪtə(n)kas/ goat's cheese

gejaagd /ɣəjaxt/ (adj, adv) hurried, agitated

het **gejammer** /ɣəjɑmər/ moaning, lamentation(s)

het **gejank** /ɣəjɑŋk/ whining, whine; whimper

het **gejoel** /ɣəjul/ shouting, cheering, cheers; jeering

het **gejuich** /ɣəjœyx/ cheer(ing)

de ¹**gek** /ɣɛk/ (pl: -ken) **1** lunatic; loony; nut-(case): *rijden als een ~* drive like a maniac **2** fool, idiot: *iem. voor de ~ houden* pull s.o.'s leg, make a fool of s.o.; *iem. voor ~ zetten* make a fool of s.o. **3** clown: *voor ~ lopen* look absurd (or: ridiculous)

²**gek** /ɣɛk/ (adj) **1** mad, crazy (with), insane: *je lijkt wel ~* you must be mad **2** mad; silly; stupid; foolish: *dat is geen ~ idee* that's not a bad idea; *je zou wel ~ zijn als je het niet deed* you'd be crazy (or: mad) not to (do it) **3** crazy, ridiculous; bad: *op de ~ste plaatsen* in the oddest (or: most unlikely) places; *~ genoeg* oddly (or: strangely) enough; *niet ~, hè?* not bad, eh? **4** fond (of), keen (on), mad (about), crazy (about): *hij is ~ op die meid* he's crazy about that girl

³**gek** /ɣɛk/ (adv) silly; badly: *doe niet zo ~* don't act (or: be) so silly

gekant /ɣəkɑnt/ (adj): *tegen iets ~ zijn* be set against sth., be opposed to sth.

gekarteld /ɣəkɑrtəlt/ (adj) [bot] crenated, serrated

de **gekheid** /ɣɛkhɛit/ joking, banter: *alle ~ op een stokje* (all) joking apart

het **gekibbel** /ɣəkɪbəl/ squabbling, bickering(s), squabble(s)

de **gekkekoeienziekte** /ɣɛkəkujə(n)zəiktə/ mad cow disease; [scientific] BSE

het **gekkenhuis** /ɣɛkə(n)hœys/ (pl: -huizen) [inform] madhouse, nuthouse: *wat is dat hier voor een ~?* what kind of a madhouse is this?

het **gekkenwerk** /ɣɛkə(n)wɛrk/ [inform] a mug's game, madness de **gekkigheid** /ɣɛkəχhɛit/ (pl: -heden) folly, foolishness, madness

het **geklaag** /ɣəklaχ/ complaining, moaning

gekleed /ɣəklet/ (adj) dressed: *hij is* **slecht** *(slordig)* ~ he is badly dressed

het **geklets** /ɣəklɛts/ chatter, waffle: ~ *in de ruimte* hot air

gekleurd /ɣəklørt/ (adj) coloured; [fig also] colourful: *iets door een ~e* **bril** *zien* have a coloured view of sth.

het **geklungel** /χəklʏŋəl/ [inform] fiddling (about), bungling

geknipt /ɣəknɪpt/ (adj): *ergens* **voor** ~ *zijn* be cut out for sth.

het **geknoei** /ɣəknuj/ **1** messing, splashing about **2** mess(-up): *dat* ~ **kun** *je niet* **inleveren** you can't hand that mess in **3** fraud: ~ *bij de verkiezingen* rigging (*or:* fraudulent practices) in the elections; ~ *met de boekhouding* juggling with the accounts

gekoeld /ɣəkult/ (adj) cooled, frozen

gekostumeerd /ɣəkɔstymert/ (adj): *een ~ bal* a fancy dress ball, a costume ball

het **gekrakeel** /ɣəkrakel/ squabbling(s), wrangling

gekreukeld /ɣəkrøkəlt/ (adj) wrinkled, wrinkly, (c)rumpled, creased

het **gekreun** /ɣəkrøn/ groan(s), moan(s), groaning, moaning

het **gekrijs** /ɣəkrɛis/ scream(ing); screech(ing)

het **gekrioel** /ɣəkrijul/ swarming

gekruid /ɣəkrœyt/ (adj) spiced, spicy, seasoned

gekruist /ɣəkrœyst/ (adj) crossed; crossbred

gekscherend /ɣɛksχerənt/ (adj, adv) joking, bantering

gekuist /ɣəkœyst/ (adj) expurgated, edited, cut

gekunsteld /ɣəkʏnstəlt/ (adj, adv) artificial, affected

gekwalificeerd /ɣəkwalifisert/ (adj) qualified, skilled

het **gekwebbel** /ɣəkwɛbəl/ chatter

gekweld /ɣəkwɛlt/ (adj) tormented, anguished

gekwetst /ɣəkwɛtst/ (adj) **1** hurt, wounded, injured **2** hurt, offended: *zich* ~ **voelen** take offence

het/de **gel** /dʒɛl/ (pl: -s) gel, jelly

gelaagd /ɣəlaχt/ (adj) layered: *een ~e* **maatschappij** a stratified society

gelaarsd /ɣəlarst/ (adj) booted: *de Gelaarsde Kat* Puss in Boots

het **gelaat** /ɣəlat/ (pl: gelaten) countenance, face

de **gelaatskleur** /ɣəlatsklør/ complexion

de **gelaatsscan** /ɣəlatskɛn/ facial scan

de **gelaatstrekken** /ɣəlatstrɛkə(n)/ (pl) features: *scherpe* ~ sharp (*or:* chiselled) features

de **gelaatsuitdrukking** /ɣəlatsœydrʏkɪŋ/ (pl: -en) (facial) expression

het **gelach** /ɣəlɒχ/ laughter: *in luid* ~ *uitbarsten* burst out laughing

geladen /ɣəladə(n)/ (adj) loaded, charged

het **gelag** /ɣəlɒχ/ (pl: -en): *het* ~ **betalen** foot the bill; *een hard* ~ a bad break, a raw deal

gelasten /ɣəlɒstə(n)/ (gelastte, heeft gelast) order, direct, instruct, charge: *iem.* ~ *het pand* **te ontruimen** order s.o. to vacate the premises

gelaten /ɣəlatə(n)/ (adj) resigned, uncomplaining

de **gelatine** /ʒelatinə/ gelatine; gel; jelly

het **geld** /ɣɛlt/ (pl: -en) **1** money, currency, cash: *je* ~ *of je* **leven** your money or your life!; *klein* ~ (small) change; *vals* ~ counterfeit money; *zwart* ~ undisclosed income; *bulken van* (*or:* *zwemmen in*) *het* ~ be loaded, be rolling in money (*or:* in it); *het* ~ **groeit** *mij niet op de rug* I'm not made of money; *iem.* ~ *uit de zak* **kloppen** wheedle money out of s.o.; *waar* **voor** *zijn* ~ *krijgen* get value for money **2** money, cash, funds, resources: *iem.* ~ **afpersen** extort money from s.o.; *zonder* ~ *zitten* be broke **3** money, amount, sum, price, rate: *kinderen betalen* **half** ~ children halfprice; *voor* *geen* ~ *ter wereld* not for love or money

de **geldautomaat** /ɣɛltɑutomat/ (pl: -automaten) cash dispenser, cashpoint

de **geldboete** /ɣɛltbutə/ (pl: -s) fine

geldelijk /ɣɛldələk/ (adj, adv) financial

gelden /ɣɛldə(n)/ (gold, heeft gegolden) **1** count **2** apply, obtain, go for: *hetzelfde geldt* **voor** *jou* that goes for you too

geldend /ɣɛldənt/ (adj) valid, applicable, current: *een* **algemeen** *~e regel* a universal rule

het **geldgebrek** /ɣɛltχəbrɛk/ lack of money, shortage (*or:* want) of money

geldig /ɣɛldəχ/ (adj) valid, legitimate; current

de **geldigheid** /ɣɛldəχhɛit/ validity, legitimacy, currency

de **geldingsdrang** /ɣɛldɪŋzdrɑŋ/ assertiveness

de **geldinzameling** /ɣɛltɪnzaməlɪŋ/ (pl: -en) fund-raising

de **geldmarkt** /ɣɛltmɑrkt/ (pl: -en) **1** money-market **2** stock exchange

de **geldmiddelen** /ɣɛltmɪdələ(n)/ (pl) funds, (financial) resources, (financial) means

de **geldnood** /ɣɛltnot/ financial trouble, financial problems

de **geldontwaarding** /ɣɛltɔntwardɪŋ/ inflation

de **geldschieter** /ɣɛltsχitər/ (pl: -s) moneylender; sponsor

de **geldsom** /ɣɛltsɔm/ (pl: -men) sum of money

het **geldstuk** /ɣɛltstʏk/ (pl: -ken) coin

geldverslindend /ɣɛltfərslɪndənt/ (adj, adv) costly, expensive de **geldverspilling** /ɣɛltfərspɪlɪŋ/ (pl: -en) waste of money, extravagance

de **geldwolf** /ɣɛltwɔlf/ (pl: -wolven) money-grubber

de **geldzorgen** /ɣɛltsɔrɣə(n)/ (pl) financial worries (or: problems), money troubles

geleden /ɣəle̯də(n)/ (adj) ago, back, before, previously, earlier: *het is een hele tijd ~, dat …* it has been a long time since …; *ik had het een week ~ nog gezegd* I had said so a week before; *het is donderdag drie weken ~ gebeurd* it happened three weeks ago this (or: last Thursday)

de **geleding** /ɣəle̯dɪŋ/ (pl: -en) section, part

geleed /ɣəle̯t/ (adj) jointed, articulate(d): *een ~ dier* a segmental animal

geleerd /ɣəle̯rt/ (adj) learned, scholarly; erudite; academic

de **geleerde** /ɣəle̯rdə/ (pl: -n) scholar, man of learning; scientist: *daarover zijn de ~n het nog niet eens* the experts are not yet agreed on the matter

gelegen /ɣəle̯ɣə(n)/ (adj) **1** situated, lying: *op het zuiden ~* facing south **2** convenient, opportune: *kom ik ~?* are you busy?, am I disturbing you?

de **gelegenheid** /ɣəle̯ɣənhɛit/ (pl: -heden) **1** place, site **2** opportunity, chance, facilities: *een gunstige ~ afwachten* wait for the right moment; *die streek biedt volop ~ voor fietstochten* that area offers ample facilities for cycling; *als de ~ zich voordoet* when the opportunity presents itself; *in de ~ zijn om …* be able to, have the opportunity to …; *ik maak van de ~ gebruik om …* I take this opportunity to … **3** eating place; [roughly] restaurant; eating house: *openbare gelegenheden* public places **4** occasion: *een feestelijke ~* a festive occasion; *ter ~ van* on the occasion of

de **gelegenheidskleding** /ɣəle̯ɣənhɛits-kledɪŋ/ formal dress, full dress

de **gelei** /ʒəlɛi/ (pl: -en) jelly, preserve

geleid /ɣəlɛit/ (adj) guided: *~e projectielen* guided missiles; *~e economie* planned economy

het **geleide** /ɣəlɛidə/ escort: *onder militair ~* under military escort; *ten ~* introduction

de **geleidehond** /ɣəlɛidəhɔnt/ (pl: -en) guide-dog

geleidelijk /ɣəlɛidələk/ (adj, adv) gradual, by degrees, by (or: in) (gradual) stages

geleiden /ɣəlɛidə(n)/ (geleidde, heeft geleid) **1** guide, conduct, accompany, lead **2** conduct, transmit: *koper geleidt goed* copper is a good conductor

de **geleider** /ɣəlɛidər/ (pl: -s) conductor

het **gelid** /ɣəlɪt/ (pl: gelederen) [mil] rank, file, order: *in het ~ staan* stand in line; *in de voorste gelederen* in the front ranks, in the forefront

geliefd /ɣəlift/ (adj) **1** beloved, dear, well-liked **2** favourite, cherished, pet: *zijn ~ onderwerp* his favourite subject **3** favourite, popular: *hij is niet erg ~ bij de leerlingen* he is not very popular with the pupils

de **geliefde** /ɣəlivdə/ (pl: -n) sweetheart; lover

gelieven /ɣəli̯və(n)/ (geliefde, heeft geliefd): *gelieve geen fietsen te plaatsen* please do not park bicycles here

het **¹gelijk** /ɣəlɛik/ right: *iem. ~ geven* agree with s.o.; *(groot, volkomen) ~ hebben* be (perfectly) right

²gelijk /ɣəlɛik/ (adj) **1** equal, the same: *twee mensen een ~e behandeling geven* treat two people (in) the same (way); [sport] *~ spel* a draw; *tweemaal twee is ~ aan vier* two times two is four **2** equal, equivalent: *veertig ~* deuce, forty all **3** right

³gelijk /ɣəlɛik/ (adv) **1** likewise, alike, in the same way (or: manner), similarly: *zij zijn ~ gekleed* they are dressed alike (or: the same) **2** equally: *~ (op)delen* share equally, [+ direct object] divide equally **3** level **4** simultaneously, at the same time: *de twee treinen kwamen ~ aan* the two trains came in simultaneously (or: at the same time) **5** at once, straightaway, immediately; in a minute: *ik kom ~ bij u* I'll be with you in a moment; I'll be right with you

gelijkaardig /ɣəlɛikardəx/ (adj) [Belg] similar

gelijkbenig /ɣəlɛigbe̯nəx/ (adj) isosceles

de **gelijke** /ɣəlɛikə/ (pl: -n) equal, peer

gelijkelijk /ɣəlɛikələk/ (adv) equally, evenly

gelijken /ɣəlɛikə(n)/ (geleek, heeft geleken) [form] resemble

de **gelijkenis** /ɣəlɛikənɪs/ (pl: -sen) resemblance, similarity, likeness: *~ vertonen met* bear (a) resemblance to

de **gelijkheid** /ɣəlɛikhɛit/ equality

gelijklopen /ɣəlɛiklopə(n)/ (liep gelijk, heeft gelijkgelopen) be right, keep (good) time

¹gelijkmaken /ɣəlɛikmakə(n)/ (maakte gelijk, heeft gelijkgemaakt) [sport] equalize, draw level, tie (or: level) the score

²gelijkmaken /ɣəlɛikmakə(n)/ (maakte gelijk, heeft gelijkgemaakt) **1** level, make even, smooth (out), even (out) **2** equate, make even (or: equal), even up, level up, bring into line (with)

de **gelijkmaker** /ɣəlɛikmakər/ (pl: -s) equalizer, a game-tying goal

gelijkmatig /ɣəlɛikmatəx/ (adj, adv) even, equal, constant; smooth: *een ~e druk* (a) steady pressure; *~ verdelen* distribute evenly

gelijknamig /ɣəlɛiknaməx/ (adj) of the same name

gelijkschakelen /ɣəlɛiksxakələ(n)/ (schakelde gelijk, heeft gelijkgeschakeld) regard (or: treat) as equal(s)

gelijksoortig /ɣəlɛiksɔrtəx/ (adj) similar,

geluk

het **gelijkspel** /ɣəlɛikspɛl/ (pl: gelijke spelen) draw, tie(d game)
gelijkspelen /ɣəlɛikspelə(n)/ (speelde gelijk, heeft gelijkgespeeld) draw, tie; halve: *A. speelde gelijk tegen F. A.* drew with F.
gelijkstaan /ɣəlɛikstan/ (stond gelijk, heeft gelijkgestaan) **1** be equal (to); be tantamount (to) **2** be level (with); be all square (with): *op punten* ~ be level(-pegging)
gelijkstellen /ɣəlɛikstɛlə(n)/ (stelde gelijk, heeft gelijkgesteld) equate (with); put on a par (*or:* level) (with); give equal rights (to): *voor de wet* ~ make equal before the law
de **gelijkstroom** /ɣəlɛikstrom/ direct current, DC
gelijktijdig /ɣəlɛiktɛidəχ/ (adj, adv) simultaneous, at the same time: ~ *vertrekken* leave at the same time
de **gelijktijdigheid** /χəlɛiktɛidəχhɛit/ simultaneity
gelijktrekken /ɣəlɛiktrɛkə(n)/ (trok gelijk, heeft gelijkgetrokken) level (up), equalize
gelijkvloers /ɣəlɛikflurs/ (adj, adv) on the ground floor, ground-floor; [Am also] first-floor
gelijkvormig /ɣəlɛikfɔrməχ/ (adj) identical: ~*e driehoeken* similar triangles
gelijkwaardig /ɣəlɛikwardəχ/ (adj) equal (to, in), equivalent (to), of the same value (*or:* quality) (as), equally matched, evenly matched
de **gelijkwaardigheid** /χəlɛikwardəχhɛit/ equivalence, equality, parity
gelijkzetten /ɣəlɛikzɛtə(n)/ (zette gelijk, heeft gelijkgezet) set (by): *laten we onze horloges (met elkaar)* ~ let's synchronize (our) watches
gelijkzijdig /ɣəlɛikzɛidəχ/ (adj) equilateral
gelikt /ɣəlɪkt/ (adj) licked, highly finished; slick
gelinieerd /χəlinijert/ (adj) lined; ruled
de **gelofte** /ɣəlɔftə/ (pl: -n, -s) vow, oath, pledge
het **geloof** /ɣəlof/ (pl: geloven) **1** faith, belief, trust; conviction: *een vurig* ~ *in God* ardent faith in God; ~ *in de mensheid hebben* have faith in humanity; *van zijn* ~ *vallen* lose one's faith; lose one's moral compass **2** faith, religion, creed, (religious) belief: *zijn* ~ *belijden* profess one's faith
de **geloofsbelijdenis** /ɣəlofsbəlɛidənɪs/ (pl: -sen) profession of faith: *zijn* ~ *afleggen* (solemnly) profess one's faith
de **geloofsovertuiging** /ɣəlofsovərtœyɣɪŋ/ (pl: -en) religious conviction
geloofwaardig /ɣəlofwardəχ/ (adj, adv) credible; reliable; plausible, convincing
¹**geloven** /ɣəlovə(n)/ (geloofde, heeft geloofd) **1** (+ in) believe (in), have faith (in): ~ *in God* believe in God **2** (+ aan) believe (in) ‖

ik geloof van wel I think so; *je zult eraan moeten* ~ you'll just have to, you'd better face (up to) it
²**geloven** /ɣəlovə(n)/ (geloofde, heeft geloofd) **1** believe, credit: *je kunt me* ~ *of niet* believe it or not; *niet te* ~! incredible!; *iem. op zijn woord* ~ take s.o. at his word **2** think, believe: *hij is het er, geloof ik, niet mee eens* I don't think he agrees
gelovig /ɣəlovəχ/ (adj, adv) religious; pious; faithful: *een* ~ *christen* a faithful Christian
de **gelovige** /ɣəlovəɣə/ (pl: -n) believer
het **geluid** /ɣəlœyt/ (pl: -en) **1** sound: *sneller dan het* ~ faster than sound; supersonic **2** sound; noise: *het* ~ *van krekels* the sound of crickets; *verdachte* ~*en* suspicious noises **3** tone, timbre, sound: *er zit een mooi* ~ *in die viool* that violin has a beautiful tone
geluiddempend /ɣəlœydɛmpənt/ (adj) soundproof(ing), muffling
de **geluiddemper** /ɣəlœydɛmpər/ (pl: -s) silencer; mute
geluiddicht /ɣəlœydɪχt/ (adj) soundproof
geluidloos /ɣəlœytlos/ (adj, adv) silent
de **geluidsbarrière** /ɣəlœytsbarijɛːrə/ (pl: -s) sound barrier
het **geluidseffect** /ɣəlœytsɛfɛkt/ (pl: -en) sound effect
de **geluidshinder** /ɣəlœytshɪndər/ noise nuisance
de **geluidsinstallatie** /ɣəlœytsɪnstala(t)si/ (pl: -s) sound (reproducing) equipment, stereo; public-address system
de **geluidsisolatie** /ɣəlœytsizola(t)si/ sound insulation, soundproofing
de **geluidsman** /ɣəlœytsman/ sound recordist
de **geluidsmuur** /ɣəlœytsmyr/ (pl: -muren) [Belg] **1** sound barrier **2** noise barrier
de **geluidsoverlast** /ɣəlœytsovərlast/ noise nuisance
het **geluidsscherm** /ɣəlœytsχɛrm/ (pl: -en) noise-reducing wall
de **geluidssterkte** /ɣəlœytstɛrktə/ (pl: -s) sound intensity; volume
de **geluidstechnicus** /ɣəlœytstɛχnikʏs/ (pl: -technici) sound engineer (*or:* technician)
de **geluidswal** /ɣəlœytswal/ (pl: -len) noise barrier
de **geluidsweergave** /ɣəlœytsweryavə/ (pl: -n) sound reproduction
het **geluk** /ɣəlʏk/ **1** (good) luck, (good) fortune: *dat brengt* ~ that will bring (good) luck; *iem.* ~ *toewensen* wish s.o. luck (*or:* happiness); *veel* ~! good luck!; *dat is meer* ~ *dan wijsheid* that is more (by) good luck than good judgement **2** happiness, good fortune; [stronger] joy: *hij kon zijn* ~ *niet op* he was beside himself with joy **3** lucky thing, piece (*or:* bit) of luck; lucky break: *wat een* ~ *dat je thuis was* a lucky thing you were (at) home; *hij mag van* ~ *spreken dat ...* he can count

yourself lucky that ..., he can thank your (lucky) stars that ...

¹gelukkig /ɣəlʏkəχ/ (adj) **1** lucky, fortunate: *de ~e eigenaar* the lucky owner **2** happy, lucky: *een ~e keuze* a happy choice **3** fortunate; happy; successful; prosperous: *~ kerstfeest* happy (*or:* merry) Christmas || *een ~ paar* a happy couple

²gelukkig /ɣəlʏkəχ/ (adv) **1** well, happily: *zijn woorden ~ kiezen* choose one's words well **2** luckily, fortunately: *~ was het nog niet te laat* luckily (*or:* fortunately) it wasn't too late

de **gelukkige** /ɣəlʏkəɣə/ (pl: -n) happy man (*or:* woman); lucky one; winner: *tot de ~n behoren* be one of the lucky ones

het **geluksgetal** /ɣəlʏksχətal/ (pl: -len) lucky number

het **geluksspel** /ɣəlʏkspɛl/ (pl: -en) game of chance

het **gelukstelegram** /ɣəlʏksteləɣram/ (pl: -men) telegram of congratulation

de **geluksvogel** /ɣəlʏksfoɣəl/ (pl: -s) lucky devil, lucky dog

de **gelukwens** /ɣəlʏkwɛns/ (pl: -en) congratulation; birthday wish

gelukwensen /ɣəlʏkwɛnsə(n)/ (wenste geluk, heeft gelukgewenst) (+ met) congratulate (on), offer one's congratulations (on): *iem. met zijn verjaardag ~* wish s.o. many happy returns (of the day)

gelukzalig /ɣəlʏksaləχ/ (adj) blissful, blessed, beatific: *een ~e glimlach* a beatific smile

de **gelukzoeker** /ɣəlʏksukər/ (pl: -s) fortune-hunter, adventurer

het **gelul** /ɣəlʏl/ [inform] (bull)shit

gemaakt /ɣəmakt/ (adj, adv) **1** pretended, sham: *een ~e glimlach* an artificial (*or:* a forced) smile **2** affected

de **¹gemaal** /ɣəmal/ consort

het **²gemaal** /ɣəmal/ **1** pumping-engine **2** fuss, bother

de **gemachtigde** /ɣəmɑχtəɣdə/ (pl: -n) deputy, authorized representative; endorsee; [law] proxy

het **gemak** /ɣəmɑk/ (pl: -ken) **1** ease, leisure: *zijn ~ (ervan) nemen* take things easy **2** quiet, calm: *zich niet op zijn ~ voelen* feel ill at ease, feel awkward; *iem. op zijn ~ stellen* put (*or:* set) s.o. at his ease **3** ease, facility: *met ~ winnen* win easily; win hands down, have a walkover; *voor het ~* for convenience's sake

¹gemakkelijk /ɣəmɑkələk/ (adj, adv) **1** easy; easygoing: *de ~ste weg kiezen* take the line of least resistance; *~ in de omgang* easy to get on with **2** comfortable; convenient

²gemakkelijk /ɣəmɑkələk/ (adv) **1** easily: *dat is ~er gezegd dan gedaan* that's easier said than done **2** comfortably

gemakshalve /ɣəmɑkshɑlvə/ (adv) for convenience('s sake), for the sake of convenience

de **gemakzucht** /ɣəmɑksʏχt/ laziness: *uit (pure) ~ from* (*or:* out) of (pure) laziness

gemakzuchtig /ɣəmɑksʏχtəχ/ (adj) lazy, easygoing

de **gemalin** /ɣəmalɪn/ (pl: -nen) consort

gemankeerd /ɣəmɑŋkert/ (adj) failed, broken down: *een ~ dichter* a failed (*or:* would-be) poet

gemarineerd /ɣəmarinert/ (adj) marinaded, pickled, soused

gemaskerd /ɣəmɑskərt/ (adj) masked

gematigd /ɣəmatəχt/ (adj, adv) moderate; measured

de **gember** /ɣɛmbər/ ginger

¹gemeen /ɣəmen/ (adj) **1** nasty; vicious; malicious; low; vile; shabby: *een gemene hond* a vicious dog; *een gemene streek* a dirty trick; *dat was ~ van je* that was a mean (*or:* rotten) thing to do **2** common, joint: *niets met iem. ~ hebben* have nothing in common with s.o.

²gemeen /ɣəmen/ (adv) nastily; viciously; maliciously; shabbily: *iem. ~ behandelen* **a)** treat s.o. badly (*or:* shabbily); **b)** give s.o. a raw deal

gemeend /ɣəment/ (adj) sincere

het **gemeengoed** /ɣəmenɣut/ common (*or:* public) property: *die denkbeelden zijn ~ geworden* those ideas have become generally accepted

de **gemeenplaats** /ɣəmemplats/ (pl: -en) commonplace, cliché

de **gemeenschap** /ɣəmensχɑp/ (pl: -pen) **1** community: *in ~ van goederen trouwen* have community of property **2** [Belg] federal region **3** intercourse

gemeenschappelijk /ɣəmensχɑpələk/ (adj) **1** common, communal: *een ~e bankrekening* a joint bank account; *een ~e keuken* a communal kitchen **2** joint, common; concerted; united || *onze ~e kennissen* our mutual acquaintances

het **gemeenschapsgeld** /ɣəmensχɑpsχɛlt/ (pl: -en) public funds (*or:* money)

het **gemeenschapsonderwijs** /ɣəmensχɑps-ɔndərwɛis/ [Belg] education controlled by regional authorities

de **gemeenschapsraad** /ɣəmensχɑpsrat/ (pl: -raden) [Belg] community council

de **gemeenschapszin** /ɣəmensχɑpsɪn/ community (*or:* public) spirit

de **gemeente** /ɣəmentə/ (pl: -n, -s) **1** local authority (*or:* council); metropolitan city (*or:* town, parish) council: *bij de ~ werken* work for the local council **2** district, borough, city, town, parish: *de ~ Eindhoven* the city of Eindhoven

gemeente- [also] municipal

de **gemeenteadministratie** /ɣəmentəatministra(t)si/ local government

de **gemeenteambtenaar** /ɣəmentəamtənar/ (pl: -ambtenaren) local government official het **gemeentebedrijf** /ɣəmˌɛntəbədrɛif/ (pl: -bedrijven): *de gemeentebedrijven* public works

de **gemeentebelasting** /ɣəmˌɛntəbəlɑstɪŋ/ (pl: -en) council tax

het **gemeentebestuur** /ɣəmˌɛntəbəstyr/ (pl: -besturen) district council, local authority (*or*: authorities)

het **gemeentehuis** /ɣəmˌɛntəhœys/ (pl: -huizen) local government offices; town hall, city hall

gemeentelijk /ɣəmˌɛntələk/ (adj) local authority, council, community, municipal: *het ~ vervoerbedrijf* the municipal (*or*: corporation, city) transport company

de **gemeentepolitie** /ɣəmˌɛntəpoli(t)si/ municipal police; [Am] city police

de **gemeenteraad** /ɣəmˌɛntərat/ (pl: -raden) council, town (*or*: city, parish) council: *in de ~ zitten* be on the council

het **gemeenteraadslid** /ɣəmˌɛntəratslɪt/ (pl: -raadsleden) local councillor, member of the (local) council

de **gemeenteraadsverkiezing** /ɣəmˌɛntəratsfərkizɪŋ/ (pl: -en) local election(s)

de **gemeentereiniging** /ɣəmˌɛntərɛinəɣɪŋ/ environmental (*or*: public) health department

de **gemeentesecretaris** /ɣəmˌɛntəsɪkrətarɪs/ (pl: -sen) [roughly] Town Clerk

de **gemeenteverordening** /ɣəmˌɛntəvərɔrdənɪŋ/ (pl: -en) by(e)law; [Am] city ordinance

de **gemeentewerken** /ɣəmˌɛntəwɛrkə(n)/ (pl) public works (department)

gemêleerd /ɣəmɛːlˌɛrt/ (adj) mixed, blended: *een ~ gezelschap* a mixed bunch of people

het **gemenebest** /ɣəmenəbˌɛst/ (pl: -en) commonwealth: *het Gemenebest van Onafhankelijke Staten* the Commonwealth of Independent States; *het Britse Gemenebest* the (British) Commonwealth of Nations

gemengd /ɣəmˌɛŋt/ (adj, adv) mixed; blended; miscellaneous

gemeubileerd /ɣəməbilˌɛrt/ (adj) furnished

¹**gemiddeld** /ɣəmˌɪdəlt/ (adj) 1 average: *iem. van ~e grootte* s.o. of average (*or*: medium) height 2 average, mean: *de ~e hoeveelheid regen per jaar* the average (*or*: mean) annual rainfall

²**gemiddeld** /ɣəmˌɪdəlt/ (adv) on average, an average (of)

het **gemiddelde** /ɣəmˌɪdəldə/ average, mean: *boven* (*or*: *onder*) *het ~* above (*or*: below) (the) average

het **gemis** /ɣəmˌɪs/ 1 lack, want, absence, deficiency 2 loss: *zijn dood wordt als een groot ~ gevoeld* his death is felt as a great loss

het **gemodder** /ɣəmˌɔdər/ muddling, bungling, messing

het **gemoed** /ɣəmˌut/ (pl: -eren) mind, heart: *de ~eren raakten verhit* feelings started running high; *de ~eren sussen* pour oil on troubled waters

gemoedelijk /ɣəmˌudələk/ (adj, adv) agreeable, pleasant; amiable; easygoing

de **gemoedsrust** /ɣəmˌutsrʏst/ peace (*or*: tranquillity) of mind, inner peace (*or*: calm)

de **gemoedstoestand** /ɣəmˌutstustɔnt/ state of mind, frame of mind

gemoeid /ɣəmˌujt/ (adj): *alsof haar leven er mee ~ was* as if her life depended on it (*or*: were at stake); *er is een hele dag mee ~* it will take a whole day

het **gemompel** /ɣəmˌɔmpəl/ murmur, murmuring: *er ging een verontwaardigd ~ op onder het publiek* an indignant murmur (*or*: a murmur of indignation) rose from the audience

het **gemopper** /ɣəmˌɔpər/ grumbling, grousing, complaints

gemotiveerd /ɣəmotivˌɛrt/ (adj) 1 reasoned, well-founded 2 motivated

gemotoriseerd /ɣəmotorizˌɛrt/ (adj) motorized

de **gems** /ɣɛms/ (pl: gemzen) chamois

gemunt /ɣəmˌʏnt/ (adj) coined ‖ *het op iem. ~ hebben* have it in for s.o.

het **gen** /ɣɛn/ (pl: -en) gene: [fig] *het zit in zijn ~en* it's in his genes, it's part of his genetic make-up

genaamd /ɣənˌamt/ (adj) 1 named, called 2 (also) known as, alias, going by the name of

de **genade** /ɣənˌadə/ 1 mercy, grace; quarter: *geen ~ hebben met* have no mercy on 2 mercy, pardon, forgiveness

genadeloos /ɣənˌadəlos/ (adj, adv) merciless, ruthless

de **genadeslag** /ɣənˌadəslɑx/ (pl: -en) death blow

genadig /ɣənˌadəx/ (adj, adv) merciful: *een ~e straf* a light punishment; *er ~ (van) afkomen* get off (*or*: be let off) lightly

gênant /ʒɛnˌɑnt/ (adj) embarrassing

de **gendarme** /ʒɑndɑrmˌ(ə)/ (pl: -s, -n) [Belg] member of national police force

de **gender** /dʒɛndər/ gender

gene /ɣenˌə/ (dem pron) that, the other: *deze of ~* somebody (or other)

de **gêne** /ʒɛːnˌə/ embarrassment, discomfiture: *zonder enige ~* without embarrassment, unashamedly, without (any) inhibition

de **genealogie** /ɣenejalˌoɣi/ (pl: -ën) genealogy

de **geneesheer** /ɣənˌesher/ (pl: -heren) physician, doctor

geneeskrachtig /ɣəneskrˌɑxtəx/ (adj) therapeutic, healing: *~e bronnen* medicinal springs

de **geneeskunde** /ɣənˌeskyndə/ medicine, medical science: *een student in de ~* a medical student

geneeskundig /ɣənˌeskyndəx/ (adj, adv)

medical, medicinal, therapeutic

het **geneesmiddel** /ɣəneːsmɪdəl/ (pl: -en) medicine, drug, remedy: *rust is een **uitstekend** ~* rest is an excellent cure

de **geneeswijze** /ɣəneːswɛizə/ (pl: -n) (form of) treatment, therapy

genegen /ɣəneːɣə(n)/ (adj) willing, prepared: *hij **is** niet ~ toestemming te geven* he is not prepared to give permission

de **genegenheid** /ɣəneːɣənhɛit/ affection, fondness, attachment

geneigd /ɣənɛixt/ (adj) **1** inclined, apt, prone: *~ tot luiheid* inclined to be lazy (*or:* to laziness) **2** inclined, disposed: *ik **ben** ~ je te geloven* I am inclined to believe you

de **¹generaal** /ɣenəral/ (pl: -s) general

²generaal /ɣenəral/ (adj) general: *de generale **repetitie*** (the) (full) dress-rehearsal

de **generalisatie** /ɣenəraliza(t)si/ (pl: -s) generalization, sweeping statement

generaliseren /ɣenəralizeːrə(n)/ (generaliseerde, heeft gegeneraliseerd) generalize

de **generatie** /ɣenəra(t)si/ (pl: -s) generation

de **generatiekloof** /ɣenəra(t)sikloːf/ (pl: -kloven) generation gap: *de ~ **overbruggen*** bridge the generation gap

de **generator** /ɣenəratɔr/ (pl: -en) generator, dynamo

zich **generen** /ʒenəre(n)/ (geneerde zich, heeft zich gegeneerd) be embarrassed, feel embarrassed, feel shy (*or:* awkward)

genereren /ɣenəreːrə(n)/ (genereerde, heeft gegenereerd) generate

genereus /ɣenərøs/ (adj, adv) generous

de **generiek** /ʒenərik/ [Belg] credits, credit titles

Genesis /ɣeːnəzɪs/ Genesis

de **genetica** /ɣəneːtika/ genetics

genetisch /ɣəneːtis/ (adj, adv) genetic: *~e manipulatie* genetic engineering, gene splicing

de **geneugte** /ɣənøxtə/ (pl: -n) pleasure, delight(s)

Genève /ʒɛnɛːvə/ Geneva

¹genezen /ɣəneːzə(n)/ (genas, is genezen) recover, get well again: *van een ziekte ~* recover from an illness

²genezen /ɣəneːzə(n)/ (genas, heeft genezen) cure; heal

de **genezing** /ɣəneːzɪŋ/ (pl: -en) cure; recovery; healing

geniaal /ɣenijaːl/ (adj, adv) brilliant: *een geniale **vondst (zet)*** a stroke of genius

de **genialiteit** /ɣenijalitɛit/ ingenuity, brilliance, brilliancy

de **¹genie** /ʒeni/ (pl: -ën) [mil] military engineering

het **²genie** /ʒeni/ (pl: -ën) genius: *een **groot** ~* an absolute genius

het **geniep** /ɣənip/: *in het ~* on the sly, on the quiet; sneakily

geniepig /ɣənipəx/ (adj, adv) sly; sneaky: *op een ~e **manier*** on the sly

¹genieten /ɣənitə(n)/ (genoot, heeft genoten) enjoy o.s., have a good time, have fun: *van het leven ~* enjoy life; *ik heb genoten!* I really enjoyed myself!

²genieten /ɣənitə(n)/ (genoot, heeft genoten) enjoy, have the advantage of: *een goede **opleiding** genoten hebben* have received a good training (*or:* education) ‖ *hij **is** vandaag niet te ~* he's unbearable today, he's in a bad mood today

de **genieter** /ɣənitər/ (pl: -s) **1** sensualist: *hij is een **echte** ~* he really knows how to enjoy life **2** recipient, beneficiary

de **genietroepen** /ʒənitrupə(n)/ (pl) (Military (*or:* Royal)) Engineers

de **genitaliën** /ɣenitaːlijə(n)/ (pl) genitals

de **genocide** /ɣenoːsidə/ genocide

de **genodigde** /ɣənoːdəɣdə/ (pl: -n) (invited) guest, invitee

¹genoeg /ɣənux/ (adv) enough, sufficiently: *ben ik **duidelijk** ~ geweest* have I made myself clear; *jammer ~* regrettably, unfortunately; *men kan niet **voorzichtig** ~ zijn* one can't be too careful; *vreemd ~* strangely enough, strange to say

²genoeg /ɣənux/ (num) enough, plenty, sufficient; adequate: *er is **eten** ~* there is plenty of food; *ik **heb** ~ aan een gekookt ei* a boiled egg will do for me; *ik **weet** ~* I've heard enough; *er is ~ **voor** allemaal* there is enough to go round; *er zijn al **slachtoffers** ~* there are too many victims (as it is); *er schoon ~ van hebben* have had it up to here, be heartily sick of it; *zo is het wel ~* that will do

de **genoegdoening** /ɣənuxdunɪŋ/ redress, restitution, satisfaction: *~ van iem. **eisen** voor iets* claim redress from s.o. for sth.

het **genoegen** /ɣənuɣə(n)/ (pl: -s) **1** satisfaction, gratification: *~ **nemen** met iets* put up with sth. **2** pleasure, satisfaction: *iem. een ~ **doen*** do s.o. a favour, oblige s.o.; *het was mij een **waar** ~* it was a real pleasure

genoeglijk /ɣənuxlək/ (adj, adv) enjoyable, pleasant: *zij **zaten** ~ bij elkaar* they were sitting happily together

genoegzaam /ɣənuxsam/ (adj, adv) sufficient, satisfactory: *dat is toch ~ **bekend*** that is (surely) sufficiently well known (*or:* well enough known)

genoemd /ɣənumt/ (adj) (above-)mentioned, said

het **genootschap** /ɣənoːtsxap/ (pl: -pen) society, association, fellowship

het **genot** /ɣənɔt/ (pl: genietingen) enjoyment, pleasure, delight, benefit, advantage: *onder het ~ van een glas wijn* over a glass of wine

het **genotmiddel** /ɣənɔtmɪdəl/ (pl: -en) stimulant; [pl] luxury foods

het **genre** /ʒɑ̃rə/ (pl: -s) genre

Gent /ɣɛnt/ Ghent

de **gentechnologie** /ɣɛntɛxnoloɣi/ genetic engineering

de **gentherapie** /ɣɛnterapi/ gene therapy

genuanceerd /ɣənywɑnse̲rt/ (adj, adv) subtle

het **genus** /ɣe̲nʏs/ (pl: genera) **1** genus **2** gender

de **geodriehoek** /ɣe̲jodrihuk/ (pl: -en) combination of a protractor and a setsquare

geoefend /ɣəu̲fənt/ (adj) experienced, trained: een ~ **pianist** an accomplished pianist

de **geografie** /ɣejoɣrafi̲/ geography

geografisch /ɣejoɣra̲fis/ (adj) geographic(al)

geolied /ɣəo̲lit/ (adj) oiled; lubricated

de **geologie** /ɣejoloɣi̲/ geology

geologisch /ɣejolo̲ɣis/ (adj) geological: een ~ **tijdperk** a geological age

de **geoloog** /ɣejolo̲x/ (pl: geologen) geologist

de **geometrie** /ɣejometri̲/ geometry

geometrisch /ɣejome̲tris/ (adj) geometric(al)

geoorloofd /ɣəo̲rloft/ (adj) permitted, permissible: een ~ **middel** lawful means, a lawful method

georganiseerd /ɣəorɣanize̲rt/ (adj) organized: een ~e **reis** a package tour

Georgië /ɣejo̲rɣijə/ Georgia

de **Georgiër** /ɣejo̲rɣijər/ Georgian

het ¹**Georgisch** /ɣejo̲rɣis/ Georgian

²**Georgisch** /ɣejo̲rɣis/ (adj) Georgian

georiënteerd /ɣəorijɛnte̲rt/ (adj) oriented, orientated

gepaard /ɣəpa̲rt/ (adj) coupled (with), accompanied (by), attendant (on), attached (to): de risico's die daarmee ~ **gaan** the risks involved

gepakt /ɣəpɑ̲kt/ (adj): ~ en **gezakt** ready for off, all ready to go

gepantserd /ɣəpɑ̲ntsərt/ (adj) armoured, in armour: een ~e auto an armour-plated car

geparfumeerd /ɣəpɑrfyme̲rt/ (adj) perfumed, scented

gepast /ɣəpɑ̲st/ (adj, adv) **1** (be)fitting, becoming, proper: dat is **niet** ~ that is not done **2** exact: met ~ **geld** betalen pay the exact amount

gepatenteerd /ɣəpatɛnte̲rt/ (adj) patent(ed) ‖ [fig] een ~ **leugenaar** a patent (or: an arrant) liar

het **gepeins** /ɣəpɛ̲ins/ musing(s), meditation(s), pondering

gepensioneerd /ɣəpɛnʃone̲rt/ (adj) retired, pensioned-off, superannuated

de **gepensioneerde** /ɣəpɛnʃone̲rdə/ (pl: -n) (old age) pensioner; [Am] retiree

gepeperd /ɣəpe̲pərt/ (adj) peppery, peppered; [fig also] spicy: zijn rekeningen zijn nogal ~ his bills are a bit steep

het **gepeupel** /ɣəpø̲pəl/ mob, rabble

het **gepiep** /ɣəpi̲p/ **1** squeak(ing) **2** peep(ing); chirp, cheep(ing); squeak(ing); squeal(ing); screech(ing) **3** wheeze, wheezing

gepikeerd /ɣəpike̲rt/ (adj) piqued, nettled: gauw ~ **zijn** be touchy

geplaatst /ɣəpla̲tst/ (adj) qualified, qualifying

het **geploeter** /ɣəplu̲tər/ drudgery, slaving; plodding

gepokt /ɣəpɔ̲kt/ (adj): ~ en **gemazeld** zijn be tried and tested

het **gepraat** /ɣəpra̲t/ talk, gossip, chat, (tittle-)tattle: hun huwelijk leidde tot **veel** ~ their marriage caused a lot of talk

geprefabriceerd /ɣəprefabrise̲rt/ (adj) prefabricated, prefab

geprikkeld /ɣəpri̲kəlt/ (adj) irritated, irritable: gauw ~ **zijn** be huffish (or: huffy)

geprononceerd /ɣəpronɔnse̲rt/ (adj, adv) pronounced

geraakt /ɣəra̲kt/ (adj) **1** offended, hurt **2** moved, touched

het **geraamte** /ɣəra̲mtə/ (pl: -n, -s) **1** skeleton: [fig] een **wandelend** (or: **levend**) ~ a walking (or: living) skeleton **2** [fig] frame(work)

het **geraas** /ɣəra̲s/ din, roar(ing), noise

geradbraakt /ɣəra̲dbrakt/ (adj) shattered, exhausted; [Am] bushed ‖ ~ **Frans** broken French

geraden /ɣəra̲də(n)/ (adj, adv) advisable, expedient ‖ dat is je ~ **ook!** you'd better!

geraffineerd /ɣərafine̲rt/ (adj, adv) **1** refined **2** refined, subtle: een ~ **plan** an ingenious plan **3** crafty, clever

geraken /ɣəra̲kə(n)/ (geraakte, is geraakt) [Belg] see ¹**raken**

de **gerammel** /ɣərɑ̲məl/ rattle, rattling, clank(ing) jingling, clatter(ing)

de **geranium** /ɣəra̲nijʏm/ (pl: -s) geranium

de **gerant** /ʒera̲/ (pl: -en, -s) manager

geraspt /ɣərɑ̲spt/ (adj) grated

het ¹**gerecht** /ɣərɛ̲xt/ (pl: -en) dish; course: als **volgende** ~ hebben we ... the next course is ...

het ²**gerecht** /ɣərɛ̲xt/ (pl: -en) court (of justice), court of law, law court, tribunal: **voor** het ~ gedaagd worden be summoned (to appear in court); **voor** het ~ verschijnen appear in court

¹**gerechtelijk** /ɣərɛ̲xtələk/ (adj) **1** judicial, legal, court: [Belg] ~e **politie** criminal investigation department; ~e **stappen** ondernemen take legal action (or: proceedings) **2** forensic, legal: ~e **geneeskunde** forensic medicine

²**gerechtelijk** /ɣərɛ̲xtələk/ (adv) legally, judicially: iem. ~ **vervolgen** take (or: institute) (legal) proceedings against s.o.; prosecute s.o.

gerechtigd /ɣərɛ̲xtəxt/ (adj) authorized; qualified; entitled: hij **is** ~ dat te doen he is authorized to do that

de **gerechtigheid** /ɣərɛxtəxhɛit/ justice

het **gerechtshof** /ɣərɛxtshɔf/ (pl: -hoven) court (of justice)

gerechtvaardigd /ɣərɛxtfardəxt/ (adj, adv) justified, warranted: ~e *eisen* just (*or*: legitimate) claims

gereed /ɣərет/ (adj) (all) ready; finished

de **gereedheid** /ɣəретhɛit/ readiness: *alles in ~ brengen (maken)* get everything ready (*or*: in readiness)

gereedmaken /ɣəretmakə(n)/ (maakte gereed, heeft gereedgemaakt) make ready, get ready, prepare

het **gereedschap** /ɣəretsxɑp/ (pl: -pen) tools, equipment, apparatus; utensils: *een stuk ~* a tool, a piece of equipment

de **gereedschapskist** /ɣəretsxɑpskɪst/ (pl: -en) toolbox

gereedstaan /ɣəretstan/ (stond gereed, heeft gereedgestaan) be ready, stand ready, be waiting; [pers also] stand by

gereformeerd /ɣəreformет/ (adj) (Dutch) Reformed

geregeld /ɣəreɣəlt/ (adj) **1** regular, steady: *hij komt ~ te laat* he is often (*or*: nearly always) late **2** orderly, well-ordered: *een ~ leven gaan leiden* settle down, start keeping regular hours

het **gerei** /ɣərɛi/ gear, things; tackle; kit: *keukengerei* kitchen utensils; *scheergerei* shaving things (*or*: kit); *schrijfgerei* writing materials

geremd /ɣərɛmt/ (adj, adv) inhibited

gerenommeerd /ɣərenomет/ (adj) renowned, illustrious; well-established: *een ~ hotel* a reputable hotel

gereserveerd /ɣərezɛrvет/ (adj, adv) **1** reserved, distant: *een ~e houding aannemen* keep one's distance **2** reserved, booked

gerespecteerd /ɣərɛspɛktет/ (adj) respected

geribbeld /ɣərɪbəlt/ (adj) *see* geribd

geribd /ɣərɪpt/ (adj) ribbed; corded; corrugated: *~ katoen* corduroy

gericht /ɣərɪxt/ (adj, adv) directed (at, towards), aimed (at, towards); [fig] specific: *~e vragen* carefully chosen (*or*: selected) questions

het **gerief** /ɣərif/ [Belg] accessories: *schoolgerief* school needs

gerieflijk /ɣəriflək/ (adj, adv) comfortable

gerimpeld /ɣərɪmpəlt/ (adj) wrinkled, wrinkly; shrivelled: *een ~ voorhoofd* a furrowed brow

gering /ɣərɪŋ/ (adj) **1** small, little: *een ~e kans* a slim (*or*: remote) chance; *in ~e mate* to a small extent (*or*: degree) **2** petty, slight, minor: *een ~ bedrag* a petty (*or*: trifling) sum

geringschattend /ɣərɪŋsxɑtənt/ (adj, adv) disparaging: *iem. ~ behandelen* slight s.o., be disparaging towards s.o.

het **geritsel** /ɣərɪtsəl/ rustling, rustle

het **¹Germaans** /ɣɛrmans/ Germanic

²Germaans /ɣɛrmans/ (adj) Germanic, Teutonic

de **Germanen** /ɣɛrmanə(n)/ (pl) Germans, Teutons

het **gerochel** /ɣərɔxəl/ hawk(ing)

het **geroddel** /ɣərɔdəl/ gossip(ing), tittle-tattle

het **geroep** /ɣərup/ calling, shouting, crying, call(s), shout(s), cries, cry: *hij hoorde hun ~ niet* he did not hear them calling

geroepen /ɣərupə(n)/ (adj) called: *je komt als ~* you're just the person we need

het **geroezemoes** /ɣəruzəmus/ buzz(ing), hum: *met al dat ~ kan ik jullie niet verstaan* I can't make out what you're saying with all the din

het **gerommel** /ɣərɔməl/ **1** rumbling, rumble: *~ in de buik* rumbling in one's stomach **2** rummaging (about, around) **3** messing, fiddling about

geronnen /ɣərɔnə(n)/ (adj) clotted

gerookt /ɣərokt/ (adj) smoked

geroutineerd /ɣərutinет/ (adj, adv) experienced, practised

de **gerst** /ɣɛrst/ barley

het **gerucht** /ɣəryxt/ (pl: -en) rumour: *het ~ gaat dat ...* there is a rumour that ...; *dat zijn maar ~en* it is only hearsay

geruchtmakend /ɣəryxtmakənt/ (adj) controversial, sensational

geruim /ɣərœym/ (adj) considerable

geruisloos /ɣərœyslos/ (adj, adv) noiseless, silent; [fig] quietly

geruit /ɣərœyt/ (adj) check(ed)

¹gerust /ɣərүst/ (adj) easy, at ease: *een ~ geweten* (or: *gemoed*) an easy (*or*: a clear) conscience, an easy mind; *met een ~ hart* de toekomst tegemoet zien face the future with confidence

²gerust /ɣərүst/ (adv) safely, with confidence, without any fear (*or*: problem): *ga ~ je gang* (do) go ahead!, feel free to ...; *vraag ~ om hulp* don't hesitate to ask for help

geruststellen /ɣərүstɛlə(n)/ (stelde gerust, heeft geruststeld) reassure, put (*or*: set) (s.o.'s) mind at rest

geruststellend /ɣərүstɛlənt/ (adj) reassuring

de **geruststelling** /ɣərүstɛlɪŋ/ (pl: -en) reassurance, comfort; relief

het **geruzie** /ɣərуzi/ arguing, quarrelling, bickering

het **geschater** /ɣəsxatər/ peals (*or*: roars) of laughter

gescheiden /ɣəsxɛidə(n)/ (adj) **1** separated, apart: *twee zaken strikt ~ houden* keep two things strictly separate; *~ leven (van)* live apart (from) **2** divorced: *~ gezin* broken home

het **geschenk** /ɣəsxɛŋk/ (pl: -en) present, gift

geschieden /ɣəsxidə(n)/ (geschiedde, is geschied) occur, take place, happen

de **geschiedenis** /ɣəsxidənɪs/ (pl: -sen) **1** history: *de ~ herhaalt zich* history repeats itself **2** tale, story: *dat is een andere ~* that's another story

geschiedkundig /ɣəsxitkʏndəx/ (adj, adv) historical

de **geschiedvervalsing** /ɣəsxitfərvalsɪŋ/ (pl: -en) falsification (or: rewriting) of history

geschift /ɣəsxɪft/ (adj) **1** crazy, nuts **2** curdled

geschikt /ɣəsxɪkt/ (adj, adv) suitable, fit, appropriate: *is twee uur een ~e tijd?* will two o'clock be convenient?; *~ zijn voor het doel* serve the purpose; *dat boek is niet ~ voor kinderen* that book is not suitable for children

het **geschil** /ɣəsxɪl/ (pl: -len) dispute, disagreement, quarrel: *een ~ bijleggen* settle a dispute (with s.o.)

geschoold /ɣəsxolt/ (adj) trained, skilled

het **geschreeuw** /ɣəsxrew/ shouting, yelling, shouts: *hou op met dat ~* stop yelling || *veel ~ maar weinig wol* much cry and little wool; much ado about nothing

het **geschrift** /ɣəsxrɪft/ (pl: -en) writing: *de heilige ~en* the Scriptures; *in woord en ~* orally and in written form; *valsheid in ~e plegen* commit forgery

het **geschut** /ɣəsxʏt/ artillery

de **gesel** /ɣesəl/ (pl: -s, -en) **1** whip **2** [fig] scourge

geselen /ɣesələ(n)/ (geselde, heeft gegeseld) whip, flog

gesetteld /ɣəsɛtəlt/ (adj) settled: *~ zijn* be settled

het **gesis** /ɣəsɪs/ hiss(ing); fizz(le); sizzle

gesitueerd /ɣəsitywert/ (adj) situated: *de beter ~e klassen* the better-off classes

het **gesjoemel** /ɣəʃuməl/ dirty tricks, trickery

geslaagd /ɣəslaxt/ (adj) successful

het **geslacht** /ɣəsloxt/ (pl: -en) **1** family, line, house: *uit een nobel* (or: *vorstelijk*) *~ stammen* be of noble (or: royal) descent **2** sex **3** generation

geslachtelijk /ɣəsloxtələk/ (adj) sexual: *~e voortplanting* sexual reproduction

de **geslachtsdaad** /ɣəsloxtsdat/ sex(ual) act; [med] coitus

de **geslachtsdelen** /ɣəsloxtsdelə(n)/ (pl) genitals, sex organs, genital organs; private parts

de **geslachtsdrift** /ɣəslox(t)sdrɪft/ sex(ual) drive, sexual urge, libido

de **geslachtsgemeenschap** /ɣəsloxtsxəmensxɑp/ sexual intercourse (or: relations), sex

het **geslachtsorgaan** /ɣəslox(t)sorɣan/ (pl: -organen) sex(ual) organ, genital organ; [pl also] genitals

de **geslachtsverandering** /ɣəslox(t)sfərɑndərɪŋ/ (pl: -en) sex change

het **geslachtsverkeer** /ɣəslox(t)sfərker/ sexual intercourse (or: relations)

de **geslachtsziekte** /ɣəsloxtsiktə/ (pl: -n, -s) venereal disease, VD

geslepen /ɣəslepə(n)/ (adj, adv) sly, cunning, sharp

gesloten /ɣəslotə(n)/ (adj) **1** closed, shut; drawn: *achter ~ deuren* behind closed doors, in private; in camera; *een ~ geldkist* (or: *enveloppe, goederenwagon*) a sealed chest (or: envelope, goods wagon); *een hoog ~ bloes* a high-necked blouse **2** close(-mouthed), tight-lipped: *dat kind is nogal ~* that child doesn't say much (for himself, herself); *een ~ circuit* a closed circuit

gesmeerd /ɣəsmert/ (adj, adv) **1** greased, buttered **2** smoothly: *ervoor zorgen dat het ~ gaat* make sure everything goes smoothly

gesmoord /ɣəsmort/ (adj) **1** stifled, smothered **2** [culinary] braised

het **gesnauw** /ɣəsnɑu/ snarling, snapping

het **gesnik** /ɣəsnɪk/ sobbing, sobs

het **gesnurk** /ɣəsnʏrk/ snore, snoring

het **gesoebat** /ɣəsubɑt/ imploring (for)

gesorteerd /ɣəsortert/ (adj) sorted: *op kleur ~ sorted* according to colour; *~e koekjes* assorted biscuits

de **gesp** /ɣɛsp/ (pl: -en) buckle, clasp

gespannen /ɣəspɑnə(n)/ (adj, adv) **1** tense(d), taut; bent **2** tense, strained; [pers also] nervous; on edge: *te hoog ~ verwachtingen* exaggerated expectations; *~ luisteren* listen intently; *tot het uiterste ~* at full strain

gespecialiseerd /ɣəspeʃalizert/ (adj) specialized; specializing

gespeend /ɣəspent/ (adj): *~ van* devoid of, utterly lacking (in)

gespen /ɣɛspə(n)/ (gespte, heeft gegespt) buckle; strap

gespierd /ɣəspirt/ (adj) muscular; brawny; beefy

gespikkeld /ɣəspɪkəlt/ (adj) spotted, speckled; dotted

gespitst /ɣəspɪtst/ (adj) keen || *met ~e oren* with one's ears pricked up, all ears

gespleten /ɣəspletə(n)/ (adj) split; cleft; cloven

het **gesprek** /ɣəsprɛk/ (pl: -ken) **1** talk, conversation; call: *het ~ van de dag zijn* be the talk of the town; *het ~ op iets anders brengen* change the subject; *een ~ voeren* hold a conversation; *(het nummer is) in ~* (the number's) engaged; *een ~ onder vier ogen* a private discussion **2** discussion, consultation: *inleidende ~ken* introductory talks

de **gesprekskosten** /ɣəsprɛkskostə(n)/ (pl) call charge(s)

de **gespreksstof** /ɣəsprɛkstof/ topic(s) of conversation, subject(s) for discussion

het **gespuis** /ɣəspœys/ riff-raff, rabble, scum

gestaag /ɣəstax/ (adj, adv) steady: *gestage*

arbeid steady work; *het aantal **nam** ~ **toe*** the number rose steadily; *het werk **vordert*** ~ the work is progressing steadily

de **gestalte** /ɣəstɑltə/ (pl: -n, -s) **1** figure; build: *fors van* ~ heavily-built; *een **slanke*** ~ a slim figure **2** shape, form ‖ ~ *geven (aan)* give shape (to)

gestampt /χəstɑmt/ (adj) crushed; mashed: *~e muisjes* aniseed (sugar) crumble

het/de **gestand** /ɣəstɑnt/: *zijn belofte ~ **doen*** be as good as one's word, keep one's promise

gestationeerd /ɣəsta(t)ʃonert/ (adj) stationed, based

de **geste** /ʒɛstə/ (pl: -s) gesture: *een ~ **doen*** make a gesture

het **gesteente** /ɣəstentə/ (pl: -n, -s) rock, stone

het **gestel** /ɣəstɛl/ (pl: -len) **1** constitution **2** system: *het zenuwgestel* the nervous system

gesteld /ɣəstɛlt/ (adj) **1** keen (on), fond (of): *zij zijn erop ~ (dat)* they would like it (if), they are set on (…-ing); *erg **op** comfort ~ zijn* like one's comfort **2** appointed: *binnen de ~e tijd* within the time specified

de **gesteldheid** /ɣəstɛlthɛit/ state, condition; constitution

gestemd /ɣəstɛmt/ (adj) disposed: *hij is **goed** ~* he's in a good mood; ***gunstig*** *~* favourably disposed (towards)

gesteriliseerd /ɣəsterilizert/ (adj) sterilized

het **gesticht** /ɣəstɪχt/ (pl: -en) mental home (*or:* institution)

gesticuleren /ɣɛstikylerə(n)/ (gesticuleerde, heeft gegesticuleerd) gesticulate

gestippeld /ɣəstɪpəlt/ (adj) **1** dotted: *een ~e lijn* a dotted line **2** spotted, speckled; dotted

gestoffeerd /ɣəstɔfert/ (adj) **1** upholstered **2** (fitted) with curtains and carpets

gestoord /ɣəstort/ (adj) disturbed: [fig] *ergens ~ van **worden*** be sick to one's back teeth of sth.; *prettig ~* slightly eccentric

het **gestotter** /χəstɔtər/ stammer(ing), stutter(ing)

gestreept /ɣəstrept/ (adj) striped

gestrekt /ɣəstrɛkt/ (adj) (out)stretched

gestrest /χəstrɛst/ (adj) stressed

gestroomlijnd /ɣəstromlɛint/ (adj) streamlined, aerodynamic: *een ~e organisatie* a streamlined organization

het **gesuis** /ɣəsœys/ sough(ing), murmur(ing); ringing

het **gesukkel** /ɣəsʏkəl/ **1** ailing **2** difficulties

het **getal** /ɣətɑl/ (pl: -len) number, figure: *een rond* ~ a round number (*or:* figure); *een ~ van drie cijfers* a three-digit (*or:* three-figure) number

getalenteerd /ɣətɑlɛntert/ (adj) talented

het **getalm** /ɣətɑlm/ lingering

getalsmatig /ɣətɑlsmatəχ/ (adj) numerical

getand /ɣətɑnt/ (adj) [bot] dentate, denti-

culate

getapt /ɣətɑpt/ (adj) popular (with)

het **geteisem** /ɣətɛisəm/ riff-raff, scum

getekend /ɣətekənt/ (adj) **1** marked, branded: *een fraai ~e kat* a cat with beautiful markings; *voor het leven ~ **zijn*** be marked for life **2** lined

het **getier** /ɣətir/ howl(ing), roar(ing): *gevloek en ~* cursing and swearing

het **getij** /ɣətɛi/ (pl: -en) tide

het **getik** /χətɪk/ tick(ing); tapping

getikt /ɣətɪkt/ (adj) **1** crazy, cracked, nuts: *hij is **compleet*** ~ he's completely off his rocker **2** typed

getint /ɣətɪnt/ (adj) tinted, dark

getiteld /ɣətitəlt/ (adj) entitled

het **getob** /χətɔp/ worry(ing), brooding

het **getoeter** /ɣətutər/ hoot(ing), honk(ing), beep(ing)

getralied /ɣətralit/ (adj) latticed, grated; barred

getrapt /ɣətrɑpt/ (adj) multi-stage; indirect

getraumatiseerd (adj) traumatized

het **getreiter** /ɣətrɛitər/ vexation, nagging, teasing

getroebleerd /ɣətrublert/ (adj): *~e verhoudingen* troubled (*or:* difficult) relations

getroffen /ɣətrɔfə(n)/ (adj) **1** hit, struck **2** stricken, afflicted: *de ~ ouders* the stricken parents; the bereaved parents

zich **getroosten** /ɣətrostə(n)/ (getroostte zich, heeft zich getroost) undergo, suffer: *zich de **moeite** van iets te doen* take (the) trouble (*or:* put o.s. out) to do sth.

getrouw /ɣətrɑu/ (adj) faithful, true: *een ~e vertaling* (*or:* *weergave*) a faithful translation (*or:* representation)

getrouwd /ɣətrɑut/ (adj) married; wed(ded): *hij is ~ **met** zijn werk* he is married to his work

het **getto** /ɣɛto/ (pl: -'s) ghetto

de **gettoblaster** /ɣɛtoblɑːstər/ (pl: -s) ghetto blaster

de **getuige** /ɣətœyɣə/ (pl: -n) witness

de **getuige-deskundige** /ɣətœyɣədɛskʏndəɣə/ (pl: -n) expert witness

[1]**getuigen** /ɣətœyɣə(n)/ (getuigde, heeft getuigd) **1** give evidence (*or:* testimony), testify (to) **2** speak: *alles getuigt **voor*** (*or:* ***tegen***) *haar* everything speaks in her favour (*or:* against her) **3** be evidence (*or:* a sign) (of), show, indicate: *die daad getuigt **van** moed* that act shows courage

[2]**getuigen** /ɣətœyɣə(n)/ (getuigde, heeft getuigd) testify (to), bear witness (to)

het/de **getuigenis** /ɣətœyɣənɪs/ (pl: -sen) **1** evidence **2** testimony, evidence, statement

het **getuigenverhoor** /ɣətœyɣə(n)vərhor/ (pl: -verhoren) hearing (*or:* examination) of witnesses

de **getuigenverklaring** /ɣətœyɣə(n)vərklarɪŋ/ (pl: -en) testimony, deposition

het **getuigschrift** /ɣətœyxsχrɪft/ (pl: -en) certificate; report; reference

de **geul** /ɣøl/ (pl: -en) **1** channel **2** trench, ditch, gully

de **geur** /ɣør/ (pl: -en) smell; perfume; scent; aroma: *een onaangename ~ verspreiden (afgeven)* give off an unpleasant smell ‖ *iets in ~en en kleuren vertellen* tell all the (gory) details of sth.

geuren /ɣørə(n)/ (geurde, heeft gegeurd) **1** smell **2** show off, flaunt

geurig /ɣørəχ/ (adj) fragrant, sweet-smelling

de **geus** /ɣøs/ (pl: geuzen) Beggar

het **gevaar** /ɣəvar/ (pl: gevaren) danger, risk: *hij is een ~ op de weg* he's a menace on the roads; *~ bespeuren* (or: *ruiken*) sense (or: scent) danger; *~ voor brand* fire hazard; *het is niet zonder ~* it is not without its dangers; *er bestaat (het) ~ dat* there is a risk that ‖ *iem. (iets) in ~ brengen* endanger s.o. (sth.)

gevaarlijk /ɣəvarlək/ (adj) dangerous; hazardous; risky: *zich op ~ terrein begeven* tread on thin ice

het **gevaarte** /ɣəvartə/ (pl: -n, -s) monster, colossus

het **geval** /ɣəval/ (pl: -len) **1** case, affair: *een lastig ~* an awkward case **2** circumstances, position: *in uw ~ zou ik het nooit doen* in your position I'd never do that **3** case, circumstances: *in het uiterste ~* at worst, if the worst comes to the worst; *in ~ van oorlog* (or: *brand, ziekte*) in the event of war (or: fire, illness); *in negen van de tien ~len* nine times out of ten; *in enkele ~len* in some cases; *voor het ~ dat* (just) in case **4** chance, luck: *wat wil nou het ~?* guess what

gevallen /ɣəvalə(n)/ (adj) fallen: *de ~en* the dead

gevangen /ɣəvaŋə(n)/ (adj) caught, captive; imprisoned

de **gevangenbewaarder** /ɣəvaŋə(n)bəwardər/ (pl: -s) warder, jailer

de **gevangene** /ɣəvaŋənə/ (pl: -n) prisoner, inmate; convict; captive

gevangenhouden /ɣəvaŋə(n)haudə(n)/ (hield gevangen, heeft gevangengehouden) imprison, detain, keep in confinement (or: prison)

de **gevangenis** /ɣəvaŋənɪs/ (pl: -sen) prison, jail: *hij heeft tien jaar in de ~ gezeten* he has served ten years in prison (or: jail)

de **gevangenisstraf** /ɣəvaŋənɪstraf/ (pl: -fen) imprisonment, prison sentence, jail sentence, prison term: *tot één jaar ~ veroordeeld worden* be sentenced to one year's imprisonment; *levenslange ~* life imprisonment

gevangennemen /ɣəvaŋənemə(n)/ (nam gevangen, heeft gevangengenomen) arrest; capture; take prisoner (or: captive)

de **gevangenschap** /ɣəvaŋə(n)sχap/ captivity, imprisonment

de **gevarendriehoek** /ɣəvarə(n)drihuk/ (pl: -en) warning triangle, emergency triangle; [Am] [roughly] flares

gevarieerd /ɣəvarijert/ (adj) varied

gevat /ɣəvat/ (adj, adv) quick(-witted), sharp; quick, ready: *een ~ antwoord* a ready (or: quick) retort

het **gevecht** /ɣəvɛχt/ (pl: -en) **1** [mil] fight(ing), combat: *een ~ van man tegen man* hand-to-hand combat **2** fight, struggle: *een ~ op leven en dood* a life-or-death struggle

het **gevechtsvliegtuig** /ɣəvɛχ(t)sfliχtœyχ/ (pl: -en) fighter (plane (or: aircraft))

geveinsd /ɣəvɛinst/ (adj) pretended, feigned

de **gevel** /ɣevəl/ (pl: -s) façade, (house)front; outside wall, outer wall

¹**geven** /ɣevə(n)/ (gaf, heeft gegeven) **1** be fond of: *niets (geen cent) om iem. ~* not care a thing about s.o. **2** matter: *dat geeft niks* it doesn't matter a bit (or: at all)

²**geven** /ɣevə(n)/ (gaf, heeft gegeven) give; donate; hand: *geschiedenis ~* teach history; *geef mij maar een glaasje wijn* I'll have a glass of wine; *kunt u me de secretaresse even ~?* can I please speak to the secretary?; *kun je me het zout ~?* could you give (or: pass, hand) me the salt?; [cards] *wie moet er ~?* whose deal is it?; *geef op!* (come on,) hand it over!

de **gever** /ɣevər/ (pl: -s) giver, donor: *een gulle ~* a generous giver

gevestigd /ɣəvɛstəχt/ (adj) old-established, long-standing: *de ~e orde* the established order

gevierd /ɣəvirt/ (adj) celebrated

gevlekt /ɣəvlɛkt/ (adj) spotted, specked; stained; mottled

gevleugeld /ɣəvløɣəlt/ (adj) winged

het **gevlij** /ɣəvlɛi/: *bij iem. in het ~ proberen te komen* butter s.o. up

gevlogen /ɣəvloɣə(n)/ (adj) flown, gone

gevoeglijk /ɣəvuχlək/ (adv) properly, suitably: *dat kun je ~ vergeten* you can simply rule that out

het **gevoel** /ɣəvul/ (pl: -ens) **1** touch, feel(ing): *op het ~ af* by feel (or: touch) **2** feeling, sensation: *een brandend ~ in de maag* a burning sensation in one's stomach; *ik vind het wel een lekker ~* I like the feeling; *ik heb geen ~ meer in mijn vinger* my finger's gone numb, I've got no feeling left in my finger **3** feeling, sense: *het ~ hebben dat ...* have a feeling that ..., feel that ... **4** feeling(s), emotion(s): *op zijn ~ afgaan* play it by ear; *zijn ~ens tonen* show one's feelings **5** sense (of), feeling (for): *geen ~ voor humor hebben* have no sense of humour ‖ *~ens van spijt* feelings of regret

het **gevoelen** /ɣəvulə(n)/ (pl: -s) **1** feeling, emotion: *zijn ~s tonen* show one's feelings

2 feeling, sentiment: ~s van spijt feelings of regret **3** feeling, opinion

gevoelig /ɣəvulǝx/ (adj) **1** sensitive (to); sore; tender; allergic (to) **2** sensitive (to), susceptible (to); touchy: een ~ mens a sensitive person **3** tender, sore: een ~e klap a painful (or: nasty) blow

de **gevoeligheid** /ɣəvulǝxhɛit/ (pl: -heden) sensitivity (to), susceptibility (to)

gevoelloos /ɣəvulos/ (adj) **1** numb **2** insensitive (to), unfeeling: een ~ mens an unfeeling person

de **gevoelloosheid** /ɣəvuloshɛit/ numbness; insensitivity; callousness

het **gevoelsleven** /ɣəvulslevǝ(n)/ emotional (or: inner) life

gevoelsmatig /ɣəvulsmatǝx/ (adj, adv) instinctive

de **gevoelsmens** /ɣəvulsmɛns/ (pl: -en) man (or: woman) of feeling; emotional person

de **gevoelstemperatuur** /ɣəvulstɛmpəratyr/ windchill factor

de **gevoelswaarde** /ɣəvulswardə/ **1** sentimental (or: emotional) value **2** connotation

het **gevogelte** /ɣəvoɣəltə/ poultry, fowl: wild en ~ game and fowl

het **gevolg** /ɣəvɔlx/ (pl: -en) consequence; result; effect; outcome; success: met goed ~ examen doen pass an exam; ~ geven (or: gevend) aan een opdracht carry out (or: according to) instructions; (geen) nadelige ~en hebben have (no) adverse effects; met alle ~en van dien with all its consequences; tot ~ hebben result in

de **gevolgtrekking** /ɣəvɔlxtrɛkɪŋ/ (pl: -en) conclusion, deduction

gevolmachtigd /ɣəvɔlmɔxtǝxt/ (adj) authorized, having (full) power of attorney

gevorderd /ɣəvɔrdərt/ (adj) advanced

gevormd /ɣəvɔrmt/ (adj) **1** -formed, (-)shaped: een stel fraai ~e benen a pair of shapely legs; een goed ~e neus a regular nose **2** fully formed: een ~ karakter a fully developed character

gevraagd /ɣəvraxt/ (adj) in demand: een ~ boek a book that is much (or: greatly) in demand

gevreesd /ɣəvrest/ (adj) dreaded

gevuld /ɣəvʏlt/ (adj) **1** full, plump: een ~ figuur a full figure **2** stuffed, filled: een ~ kies a filled tooth; ~e tomaten stuffed tomatoes

het **gewaad** /ɣəwat/ (pl: gewaden) garment, attire, robe, gown

gewaagd /ɣəwaxt/ (adj) **1** hazardous, risky: een ~e sprong a daring leap **2** daring, suggestive

gewaarworden /ɣəwarwɔrdə(n)/ (werd gewaar, is gewaargeworden) perceive, observe, notice

de **gewaarwording** /ɣəwarwɔrdɪŋ/ (pl: -en) perception; sensation

het **gewag** /ɣəwɔx/: ~ maken van mention, report

gewapend /ɣəwapənt/ (adj) armed; reinforced: ~ beton reinforced concrete

gewapenderhand /ɣəwapəndərhɔnt/ (adv) by force of arms: ~ tussenbeide komen intervene militarily

het **gewas** /ɣəwɔs/ (pl: -sen) plant

gewatteerd /ɣəwɔtert/ (adj) quilted: een ~e deken a quilt; a duvet

het **gewauwel** /ɣəwɔuwəl/ claptrap, drivel

het **geweer** /ɣəwer/ (pl: geweren) rifle, gun: een ~ aanleggen aim a rifle (or: gun)

het **geweervuur** /ɣəwervyr/ gunfire

het **gewei** /ɣəwɛi/ (pl: -en) antlers

het **geweld** /ɣəwɛlt/ violence, force; strength: grof ~ brute force (or: strength); huiselijk ~ domestic violence; verbaal ~ verbal violence (or: assault); de waarheid ~ aandoen stretch the truth ‖ hij wilde met alle ~ naar huis he wanted to go home at all costs

de **gewelddaad** /ɣəwɛldat/ (pl: -daden) (act of) violence, outrage

gewelddadig /ɣəwɛldadəx/ (adj, adv) violent, forcible

geweldig /ɣəwɛldəx/ (adj, adv) **1** tremendous, enormous: een ~ bedrag a huge sum; een ~e eetlust an enormous appetite; zich ~ inspannen go to great lengths **2** terrific, fantastic, wonderful: je hebt me ~ geholpen you've been a great help; hij is ~ he's a great guy; die jurk staat haar ~ that dress looks smashing on her; hij zingt ~ he sings wonderfully; ~! great!, terrific! **3** tremendous, terrible

geweldloos /ɣəwɛltlos/ (adj, adv) nonviolent: ~ verzet nonviolent (or: peaceful) resistance

het **gewelf** /ɣəwɛlf/ (pl: gewelven) **1** vault(ing), arch **2** vault

gewelfd /ɣəwɛlft/ (adj) vaulted, arched

gewend /ɣəwɛnt/ (adj) used (to), accustomed (to); in the habit (of); inured (to): ~ raken aan zijn nieuwe huis settle down in one's new house; dat zijn we niet van hem ~ that's not like him at all, that's quite unlike him!

gewenst /ɣəwɛnst/ (adj) desired, wished for

gewerveld /ɣəwɛrvəlt/ (adj) vertebrate

het **gewest** /ɣəwɛst/ (pl: -en) **1** district, region **2** province, county; [Belg] region: overzeese ~en overseas territories

gewestelijk /ɣəwɛstələk/ (adj, adv) regional, provincial

het **geweten** /ɣəwetə(n)/ conscience: een slecht ~ hebben have a bad (or: guilty) conscience; veel op zijn ~ hebben have a lot to answer for

gewetenloos /ɣəwetənlos/ (adj, adv) unscrupulous, unprincipled

het **gewetensbezwaar** /ɣəwetə(n)zbɛzwar/ (pl: -bezwaren) scruple, conscientious objec-

gezellig

tion

de **gewetensnood** /ɣəwe̲tə(n)snot/ moral dilemma

gewetensvol /ɣəwe̲tənsfɔl/ (adj, adv) conscientious, scrupulous; painstaking

de **gewetensvraag** /ɣəwe̲tə(n)sfraɣ/ (pl: -vragen): *dat* **is** *een* ~ now you're asking me one, that's quite a question

gewettigd /ɣəwɛ̲təɣt/ (adj) **1** legitimate, justified; well-founded **2** legitimated

gewezen /ɣəwe̲zə(n)/ (adj) former, ex-

het **gewicht** /ɣəwɪ̲ɣt/ (pl: -en) weight; importance: *maten en ~en* weights and measures; *zaken van het grootste* ~ matters of the utmost importance; *soortelijk* ~ specific gravity; *op zijn* ~ *letten* watch one's weight; *beneden het* ~ underweight

gewichtheffen /ɣəwɪ̲ɣthɛfə(n)/ weightlifting

¹**gewichtig** /ɣəwɪ̲ɣtəɣ/ (adj) weighty, important; grave: *~e gebeurtenissen* important events; *hij zette een ~ gezicht* he put on a grave face

²**gewichtig** /ɣəwɪ̲ɣtəɣ/ (adv) (self-)importantly, pompously: ~ *doen* be important (about sth.)

de **gewichtsklasse** /ɣəwɪ̲ɣtsklɑsə/ (pl: -n) weight

gewiekst /ɣəwi̲kst/ (adj) sharp, shrewd, fly

gewijd /ɣəwɛ̲it/ (adj) **1** consecrated, holy: ~ *water* holy water **2** ordained

gewild /ɣəwɪ̲lt/ (adj) sought-after, popular; in demand

¹**gewillig** /ɣəwɪ̲ləɣ/ (adj) **1** willing; docile; obedient: *zich* ~ *tonen* show (one's) willingness **2** willing, ready: *een ~ oor lenen aan iem.* lend a ready ear to s.o.

²**gewillig** /ɣəwɪ̲ləɣ/ (adv) willingly, readily, voluntarily: *hij ging ~ mee* he came along willingly

het **gewin** /ɣəwɪ̲n/ gain, profit

het **gewoel** /ɣəwu̲l/ **1** tossing (and turning); struggling **2** bustle

gewond /ɣəwɔ̲nt/ (adj) injured; wounded; hurt: ~ *aan het been* injured (*or:* wounded) in the leg

de **gewonde** /ɣəwɔ̲ndə/ injured person, wounded person, casualty

gewonnen /ɣəwɔ̲nə(n)/ (adj): *zich* ~ *geven* admit defeat

¹**gewoon** /ɣəwo̲n/ (adj) **1** usual, regular, customary, ordinary: *in zijn gewone doen zijn* be o.s.; *zijn gewone gang gaan* go about one's business, carry on as usual **2** common: *dat is* ~ that's natural **3** ordinary, common(place), plain: *het gewone leven* everyday life; *de gewone man* the common man; *de ~ste zaak ter wereld* (sth.) perfectly normal

²**gewoon** /ɣəwo̲n/ (adv) **1** normally: *doe maar* ~ (do) act normal(ly), behave yourself **2** normally, ordinarily, usually **3** simply, just:

zij praatte er heel ~ over she was very casual about it

gewoonlijk /ɣəwo̲nlək/ (adv) usually, normally: *zoals* ~ *kwam ze te laat* as usual, she was late

de **gewoonte** /ɣəwo̲ntə/ (pl: -n, -s) **1** custom, practice **2** habit, custom: *de macht der* ~ the force of habit; *tegen zijn* ~ contrary to his usual practice; *hij heeft de* ~ *om* he has a habit (*or:* way) of

het **gewoontedier** /ɣəwo̲ntədir/ (pl: -en) creature of habit

gewoontegetrouw /ɣəwo̲ntəɣətrɑu̲/ (adv) as usual, according to custom

gewoonweg /ɣəwo̲nwɛɣ/ (adv) simply, just

het **gewricht** /ɣəvrɪ̲ɣt/ (pl: -en) joint, articulation

de **gewrichtsontsteking** /ɣəvrɪ̲ɣ(t)sɔntstekɪŋ/ rheumatoid arthritis

het **gewriemel** /ɣəvri̲məl/ fiddling (with)

gezaagd /ɣəza̲ɣt/ (adj) [bot] serrate

het **gezag** /ɣəza̲ɣ/ **1** authority, power; [mil] command; rule; dominion: *ouderlijk* ~ parental authority; *het* ~ *voeren* over command, be in command of **2** authority, authorities: *het bevoegd* ~ the competent authorities **3** authority, weight: *op* ~ *van* on the authority of

de **gezagdrager** /ɣəza̲ɣdraɣər/ (pl: -s) person in charge (*or:* authority)

gezaghebbend /ɣəza̲ɣhɛbənt/ (adj, adv) authoritative, influential: *iets vernemen uit ~e bron* have sth. on good authority

de **gezagvoerder** /ɣəza̲ɣfurdər/ (pl: -s) captain; skipper

¹**gezamenlijk** /ɣəza̲mə(n)lək/ (adj) collective, combined, united, joint: *met ~e krachten* with united forces

²**gezamenlijk** /ɣəza̲mə(n)lək/ (adv) together

het **gezang** /ɣəzɑ̲ŋ/ (pl: -en) song, singing

het **gezanik** /ɣəza̲nək/ **1** nagging, moaning **2** trouble: *dat geeft een hoop* ~ that causes a lot of trouble

de **gezant** /ɣəzɑ̲nt/ (pl: -en) envoy, ambassador, representative, delegate

het **gezantschap** /ɣəzɑ̲ntsχɑp/ (pl: -pen) mission

gezapig /ɣəza̲pəɣ/ (adj) lethargic, indolent, complacent

het **gezegde** /ɣəze̲ɣdə/ (pl: -n, -s) **1** saying, proverb **2** [linguistics] predicate: *naamwoordelijk* ~ nominal predicate

gezegend /ɣəze̲ɣənt/ (adj, adv) blessed; fortunately; luckily

de **gezel** /ɣəzɛ̲l/ (pl: -len) companion; mate

gezellig /ɣəzɛ̲ləɣ/ (adj, adv) **1** enjoyable, pleasant; sociable; companionable: *het zijn ~e mensen* they are good company (*or:* very sociable) **2** pleasant, comfortable; cosy: *een ~ hoekje* a snug (*or:* cosy) corner

de **gezelligheid** /ɣəzɛləɣhɛit/ **1** sociability: *hij houdt van* ~ he is fond of company **2** cosiness, snugness

het **gezelschap** /ɣəzɛlsɣɑp/ (pl: -pen) **1** company, companionship: *iem.* ~ *houden* keep s.o. company **2** company, society **3** company, party: *zich bij het* ~ *voegen* join the party

het **gezelschapsspel** /ɣəzɛlsɣɑpspɛl/ (pl: -en) party game

gezet /ɣəzɛt/ (adj) **1** set, regular **2** stout, thickset

het **gezeur** /ɣəzør/ moaning, nagging; fuss(ing): *hou nu eens op met dat eeuwige* ~*!* for goodness' sake stop that perpetual moaning!

het **gezicht** /ɣəzɪɣt/ (pl: -en) **1** sight: *liefde op het eerste* ~ love at first sight; *een vreselijk* ~ a gruesome sight; *dat is geen* ~*!* you look a fright, that is hideous **2** face: *iem. in zijn* ~ *uitlachen* laugh in s.o.'s face; *iem. van* ~ *kennen* know s.o. by sight **3** face, expression, look(s): *een* ~ *zetten alsof* look as if; *ik zag aan zijn* ~ *dat* I could tell by the look on his face that **4** view, sight: *aan het* ~ *onttrekken* conceal

het **gezichtsbedrog** /ɣəzɪɣtsbədrɔɣ/ optical illusion

het **gezichtspunt** /ɣəzɪɣtspʏnt/ (pl: -en) point of view, angle ‖ *een heel nieuw* ~ an entirely fresh perspective (*or:* viewpoint, angle)

de **gezichtssluier** /ɣəzɪɣ(t)slœyjər/ (face) veil

het **gezichtsveld** /ɣəzɪɣtsfɛlt/ (pl: -en) field (*or:* range) of vision, sight

het **gezichtsverlies** /ɣəzɪɣtsfərlis/ loss of face

het **gezichtsvermogen** /ɣəzɪɣtsfərmoɣə(n)/ (eye)sight

gezien /ɣəzin/ (adj) **1** esteemed, respected, popular **2** seen (by me), endorsed ‖ *het voor* ~ *houden* pack it in

het **gezin** /ɣəzɪn/ (pl: -nen) family

gezind /ɣəzɪnt/ (adj) (pre)disposed (to), inclined (to): *iem. vijandig* ~ *zijn* be hostile toward s.o.

de **gezindheid** /ɣəzɪnthɛit/ (pl: gezindheden) inclination, disposition: *vijandige* ~ hostility (towards)

de **gezindte** /ɣəzɪntə/ (pl: -n, -s) denomination

de **gezinsbijslag** /ɣəzɪnzbɛislaɣ/ [Belg] child benefit (*or:* allowance)

het **gezinsdrama** /ɣəzɪnzdrama/ (pl: -'s) family tragedy, family murder-suicide

de **gezinshereniging** /ɣəzɪnshɛrenəɣɪŋ/ (pl: -en) reunification (*or:* reuniting) of the family

het **gezinshoofd** /ɣəzɪnshoft/ (pl: -en) head of the family

de **gezinshulp** /ɣəzɪnshʏlp/ (pl: -en) home help

het **gezinsleven** /ɣəzɪnslevə(n)/ family life

het **gezinslid** /ɣəzɪnslɪt/ (pl: -leden) member of the family, family member

de **gezinsuitbreiding** /ɣəzɪnsœydbrɛidɪŋ/

(pl: -en) addition to the family

de **gezinsverpakking** /ɣəzɪnsfərpɑkɪŋ/ (pl: -en) family(-size(d)) pack(age), king-size(d) pack(age), jumbo pack(age)

de **gezinsverzorgster** /ɣəzɪnsfərzɔrɣstər/ (pl: -s) home help

de **gezinszorg** /ɣəzɪnsɔrɣ/ (pl: -en) home help

gezocht /ɣəzɔɣt/ (adj) strained, contrived, forced; far-fetched

¹gezond /ɣəzɔnt/ (adj) **1** able-bodied, fit: ~ *en wel* safe and sound **2** robust: ~*e wangen* rosy cheeks

²gezond /ɣəzɔnt/ (adj, adv) **1** healthy, sound; well [after vb]: *zo* ~ *als een vis* as fit as a fiddle **2** sound, good: ~ *verstand* common sense

de **gezondheid** /ɣəzɔnthɛit/ health: *naar iemands* ~ *vragen* inquire after s.o.('s health); *op uw* ~*!* here's to you!, here's to your health!, cheers!; *zijn* ~ *gaat achteruit* his health is failing ‖ ~*!* (God) bless you!

de **gezondheidsdienst** /ɣəzɔnthɛitsdinst/ (pl: -en) (public) health service

de **gezondheidsredenen** /ɣəzɔnthɛitsredənə(n)/ (pl): *om* ~ for health reasons, for reasons of health

de **gezondheidstoestand** /ɣəzɔnthɛitstustɑnt/ health, state of health

de **gezondheidszorg** /ɣəzɔnthɛitsɔrɣ/ **1** health care, medical care **2** health service(s)

gezouten /ɣəzɑutə(n)/ (adj) salt(ed), salty

de **gezusters** /ɣəzʏstərs/ (pl) sisters

het **gezwam** /ɣəzwɑm/ drivel, piffle: ~ *in de ruimte* hot air

het **gezwel** /ɣəzwɛl/ (pl: -len) swelling; growth; tumour: *een goedaardig* (or: *kwaadaardig*) ~ a benign (*or:* malignant) tumour

het **gezwets** /ɣəzwɛts/ drivel, rubbish

gezwollen /ɣəzwɔlə(n)/ (adj) swollen

gezworen /ɣəzwɔrə(n)/ (adj) sworn

het **gft-afval** /ɣeɛftəafal/ [roughly] organic waste

de **gft-bak** /ɣeɛftɛbɑk/ (pl: -ken) bin for organic waste

Ghana /ɣana/ Ghana

de **¹Ghanees** /ɣanes/ (pl: Ghanezen) Ghanaian

²Ghanees /ɣanes/ (adj) Ghanaian

de **ghostwriter** /ɡostrajtər/ (pl: -s) ghostwriter

de **gids** /ɣɪts/ (pl: -en) **1** guide; mentor: *iemands* ~ *zijn* be s.o.'s guide (*or:* mentor) **2** guide(book); handbook; manual **3** (Girl) Guide; [Am] Girl Scout **4** (telephone) directory, telephone book: *de gouden* ~® the yellow pages

giechelen /ɣixələ(n)/ (giechelde, heeft gegiecheld) giggle, titter

de **giek** /ɣik/ (pl: -en) **1** [shipp] boom **2** jib

de **¹gier** /ɣir/ (pl: -en) liquid manure, slurry

de **²gier** /ɣir/ (pl: -en) vulture

gieren /ɣirə(n)/ (gierde, heeft gegierd) shriek, scream, screech

gierig /ɣirəx/ (adj) miserly, stingy

de **gierigaard** /ɣirəxart/ (pl: -s) miser, skinflint

de **gierigheid** /ɣirəxhɛit/ miserliness, stinginess

de **gierst** /ɣirst/ millet

gieten /ɣitə(n)/ (goot, heeft gegoten) **1** pour: *het regent dat het giet* it's pouring (down (*or:* with rain)) **2** cast; found; mould: *die kleren zitten (hem) als gegoten* his clothes fit (him) like a glove **3** water

de **gieter** /ɣitər/ (pl: -s) watering can

de **gieterij** /ɣitərɛi/ (pl: -en) foundry

het **gietijzer** /ɣitɛizər/ cast iron

het **gif** /ɣɪf/ (pl: -fen) poison; venom; toxin

de **gifbeker** /ɣɪvbekər/ (pl: -s) poisoned cup

de **gifbelt** /ɣɪvbɛlt/ (pl: -en) (illegal) dump for toxic waste

het **gifgas** /ɣɪfxas/ (pl: -sen) poison(ous) gas

gifgroen /ɣɪfxrun/ (adj) bilious (*or:* fluorescent) green

de **gifslang** /ɣɪfslaŋ/ (pl: -en) poisonous (*or:* venomous) snake

de **gift** /ɣɪft/ (pl: -en) gift; donation; contribution

de **giftand** /ɣɪftant/ (pl: -en) poison fang, venom tooth

giftig /ɣɪftəx/ (adj) **1** poisonous; venomous **2** venomous, vicious: *toen hij dat hoorde, werd hij ~* when he heard that he was furious

gifvrij /ɣɪfrɛi/ (adj) non-toxic, non-poisonous

de **gifwolk** /ɣɪfwolk/ (pl: -en) toxic cloud

giga (adv) mega, huge

de **gigabyte** /ɣiɣabajt/ (pl: -s) gigabyte

de **gigant** /ɣiɣɑnt/ (pl: -en) giant

gigantisch /ɣiɣɑntis/ (adj, adv) gigantic, huge

de **gigolo** /dʒiɣolo/ (pl: -'s) gigolo

gij /ɣɛi/ (pers pron) thou

de **gijzelaar** /ɣɛizəlar/ (pl: -s) hostage

gijzelen /ɣɛizələ(n)/ (gijzelde, heeft gegijzeld) take hostage; kidnap; hijack

de **gijzeling** /ɣɛizəlɪŋ/ (pl: -en) taking of hostages; kidnapping; hijack(ing): *iem. in ~ houden* hold s.o. hostage

de **gijzelnemer** /ɣɛizəlnemər/ (pl: -s) hostage taker

de **gil** /ɣɪl/ (pl: -len) scream, yell; screech; squeal; shriek: *als je me nodig hebt, geef dan even een ~* if you need me just give (me) a shout

het/de **gilde** /ɣɪldə/ (pl: -n) guild

het **gilet** /ʒilɛt/ (pl: -s) gilet

gillen /ɣɪlə(n)/ (gilde, heeft gegild) **1** scream; screech; squeal; shriek: *het is om te ~* it's a (perfect) scream; *~ als een mager speenvarken* squeal like a (stuck) pig **2** [train, siren, machine] scream; [brakes] screech

de **giller** /ɣɪlər/ (pl: -s) [inform]: *het is een ~!* what a scream (*or:* howl, gas)!

ginds /ɣɪns/ (adj, adv) over there; up there, down there

ginnegappen /ɣɪnəɣapə(n)/ (ginnegapte, heeft geginnegapt) giggle, snigger: *wat zitten jullie weer te ~?* (just) what are you sniggering about/at?, what's so funny?

de **gin-tonic** /dʒɪntɔnɪk/ gin and tonic

het **gips** /ɣɪps/ **1** plaster (of Paris): *zijn been zit in het ~* his leg is in plaster; *~ aanmaken* mix plaster **2** plaster cast

de **gipsafdruk** /ɣɪpsavdrʏk/ (pl: -ken) plaster cast

gipsen /ɣɪpsə(n)/ (adj) plaster

het **gipsverband** /ɣɪpsfərbant/ (pl: -en) (plaster) cast

giraal /ɣiral/ (adj) giro

de **giraffe** /ʒiraf/ (pl: -n, -s) giraffe

gireren /ɣirerə(n)/ (gireerde, heeft gegireerd) pay (*or:* transfer) by giro

de **giro** /ɣiro/ **1** giro **2** giro account **3** transfer by bank (*or:* giro), bank transfer, giro transfer

het **gironummer** /ɣironʏmər/ (pl: -s) Girobank (account) number

de **giropas** /ɣiropas/ (pl: -sen) (giro cheque) guarantee card

de **girorekening** /ɣirorekənɪŋ/ (pl: -en) Girobank/giro account; Check account

gissen /ɣɪsə(n)/ (giste, heeft gegist) guess (at), estimate

de **gissing** /ɣɪsɪŋ/ (pl: -en) guess; guesswork; speculation: *dit zijn allemaal (maar) ~en* this is just (*or:* mere) guesswork

de **gist** /ɣɪst/ yeast

gisten /ɣɪstə(n)/ (gistte, heeft gegist) ferment

gisteravond /ɣɪstərav̞ont/ (adv) last night, yesterday evening

gisteren /ɣɪstərə(n)/ (adv) yesterday: *de krant van ~* yesterday's paper; *~ over een week* yesterday week, a week from yesterday; *[fig] hij is niet van ~* he wasn't born yesterday, he's nobody's fool

gistermiddag /ɣɪstərmɪdɑx/ (adv) yesterday afternoon

gisternacht /ɣɪstərnɑxt/ (adv) last night

gisterochtend /ɣɪstərɔxtənt/ (adv) yesterday morning

de **gisting** /ɣɪstɪŋ/ (pl: -en) fermentation, ferment; effervescence

de **gitaar** /ɣitar/ (pl: gitaren) guitar

de **gitarist** /ɣitarɪst/ (pl: -en) guitarist, guitar player

gitzwart /ɣɪtswɑrt/ (adj) jet-black

het **glaasje** /ɣlaʃə/ (pl: -s) **1** (small) glass; slide **2** drop, drink: *(wat) te diep in het ~ gekeken hebben* have had one too many

¹**glad** /ɣlɑt/ (adj) **1** slippery; icy: *het is ~ op de wegen* the roads are slippery **2** [fig] slippery, slick: *hij heeft een ~de tong* he has a glib tongue **3** shiny; glossy; polished **4** smooth, even: *~de banden* bald tyres; *een ~de kin* a clean-shaven chin (*or:* face)

²**glad** /ɣlɑt/ (adv) smoothly
gladgeschoren /ɣlɑtχəsχorə(n)/ (adj) clean-shaven
de **gladheid** /ɣlɑthɛit/ slipperiness; iciness: ~ op de **wegen** icy patches on the roads
de **gladiator** /ɣlɑdijɑtɔr/ (pl: -en) gladiator
de **gladiool** /ɣlɑdijol/ (pl: gladiolen) gladiolus
de **gladjanus** /ɣlɑtjanʏs/ (pl: -sen) smooth operator (or: customer); smoothie
gladmaken /ɣlɑtmakə(n)/ (maakte glad, heeft gladgemaakt) smooth(en), even; polish
gladstrijken /ɣlɑtstrɛikə(n)/ (streek glad, heeft gladgestreken) smooth (out, down); iron out: *moeilijkheden* ~ iron out difficulties; *zijn* **veren** ~ preen one's feathers
de **glamour** /ɣlɛmər/ glamour
de **glans** /ɣlɑns/ (pl: -en, glanzen) **1** glow **2** gleam, lustre; gloss; sheen: *P. geeft uw meubelen een* **fraaie** ~ P. gives your furniture a beautiful shine
het **glansmiddel** /ɣlɑnsmɪdəl/ polish
glansrijk /ɣlɑnsrɛik/ (adj, adv) splendid, brilliant; glorious
de **glansrol** /ɣlɑnsrɔl/ (pl: -len) star part, star role
de **glansverf** /ɣlɑnsfɛrf/ gloss (paint)
¹**glanzen** /ɣlɑnzə(n)/ (glansde, heeft geglansd) **1** gleam, shine: *~d* **papier** glossy (or: high-gloss) paper **2** shine, glow; twinkle: *~d* **haar** glossy (or: sleek) hair
²**glanzen** /ɣlɑnzə(n)/ (glansde, heeft geglansd) polish; glaze; gloss
het **glas** /ɣlɑs/ (pl: glazen) glass; (window-)pane: *een* ~ **bier** a (glass of) beer; *dubbel* ~ double glazing; *geslepen* ~ cut glass; *laten we het* ~ *heffen op …* let's drink to …; *~ in lood* leaded glass; stained glass
de **glasbak** /ɣlɑzbɑk/ (pl: -ken) bottle bank
glasblazen /ɣlɑzblazə(n)/ glassblowing
de **glascontainer** /ɣlɑskɔntenər/ (pl: -s) bottle bank
glashard /ɣlɑshɑrt/ (adj, adv) unfeeling: *hij ontkende* ~ he flatly denied
glashelder /ɣlɑshɛldər/ (adj, adv) crystal-clear; as clear as a bell
het **glas-in-loodraam** /ɣlɑsɪnlotram/ (pl: -ramen) leaded window; stained-glass window
de **glasplaat** /ɣlɑsplat/ (pl: -platen) sheet of glass; glass plate; glass top
de **glastuinbouw** /ɣlɑstœymbɑu/ greenhouse farming
de **glasverzekering** /ɣlɑsfərzekərɪŋ/ glass insurance
de **glasvezel** /ɣlɑsfezəl/ (pl: -s) glass fibre, fibreglass
het **glaswerk** /ɣlɑswɛrk/ glass(ware)
de **glaswol** /ɣlɑswɔl/ glass wool
glazen /ɣlazə(n)/ (adj) glass
de **glazenwasser** /ɣlazə(n)wɑsər/ (pl: -s) window cleaner

glazig /ɣlazəχ/ (adj) **1** glassy **2** waxy
glazuren /ɣlazyrə(n)/ (glazuurde, heeft geglazuurd) glaze; enamel
het **glazuur** /ɣlazyr/ **1** glaze, glazing; enamel **2** icing
de **gletsjer** /ɣlɛtʃər/ (pl: -s) glacier
de **gleuf** /ɣløf/ (pl: gleuven) **1** groove; slot; slit **2** trench, ditch; fissure
glibberen /ɣlɪbərə(n)/ (glibberde, heeft geglibberd) slither, slip, slide
glibberig /ɣlɪbərəχ/ (adj) slippery, slithery; slimy; greasy: [fig] *zich op* ~ **terrein** *bevinden* have got onto a tricky subject
de **glijbaan** /ɣlɛiban/ (pl: -banen) slide, chute
glijden /ɣlɛidə(n)/ (gleed, heeft/is gegleden) **1** slide, glide **2** slip, slide: *het boek was* **uit** *haar handen gegleden* the book had slipped from her hands
glijdend /ɣlɛidənt/ (adj) sliding, flexible: *een ~e* **belastingschaal** a sliding tax scale
de **glijvlucht** /ɣlɛivlʏχt/ (pl: -en) gliding flight; glide(-down)
de **glimlach** /ɣlɪmlɑχ/ smile; grin: *een stralende* ~ a radiant smile
glimlachen /ɣlɪmlɑχə(n)/ (glimlachte, heeft geglimlacht) smile; grin: *blijven* ~ keep (on) smiling
glimmen /ɣlɪmə(n)/ (glom, heeft geglommen) **1** glow, shine **2** shine, gleam: *de tafel glimt* **als** *een spiegel* the table is shining like a mirror **3** shine, glitter: *haar ogen glommen* **van** *blijdschap* her eyes shone with pleasure
de **glimp** /ɣlɪmp/ (pl: -en) glimpse: [fig] *een ~ van iem.* **opvangen (zien)** catch a glimpse of s.o.
glinsteren /ɣlɪnstərə(n)/ (glinsterde, heeft geglinsterd) **1** glitter, sparkle; glisten **2** shine, gleam, sparkle
glippen /ɣlɪpə(n)/ (glipte, is geglipt) **1** slide: *naar buiten* ~ sneak (or: steal) out **2** slip, drop: *hij liet het glas* **uit** *de handen* ~ he let the glass slip from his hands
de **glitter** /ɣlɪtər/ (pl: -s) glitter: *een bloes* **met** ~ a sequined blouse ‖ ~ *en* **glamour** glitter and glamour, tinsel
globaal /ɣlobal/ (adj, adv) rough, broad
de **globalisering** /ɣlobalizɛrɪŋ/ globalization
de **globe** /ɣlobə/ (pl: -s) globe
de **globetrotter** /ɣlobətrɔtər/ (pl: -s) globetrotter
de **gloed** /ɣlut/ **1** glow; blaze: *in* ~ *zetten* (or: *staan*) set (or: be) aglow **2** glow; glare; blush
gloednieuw /ɣlutniw/ (adj) brand new
gloedvol /ɣlutfɔl/ (adj, adv) glowing, fervent, impassioned: *een* ~ **betoog** a glowing speech, an impassioned speech
gloeien /ɣlujə(n)/ (gloeide, heeft gegloeid) **1** glow, shine, burn **2** smoulder, glow **3** be red-hot (or: white-hot), glow
gloeiend /ɣlujənt/ (adj, adv) **1** glowing, red-hot, white-hot **2** scalding hot, boiling

hot; scorching: *het was* ~ *heet vandaag* today was a scorcher **3** glowing, fervent || *je bent er* ~ *bij* you're in for it now, (I) caught you red-handed; *een* ~*e* **hekel** *aan iem. hebben* hate s.o.'s guts

de **gloeilamp** /ɣlujlɑmp/ (pl: -en) (light) bulb

glooien /ɣlojə(n)/ (glooide, heeft geglooid) slope, slant

glooiend /ɣlojənt/ (adj) sloping, slanted; rolling

de **glooiing** /ɣlojɪŋ/ (pl: -en) slope, slant

gloren /ɣlorə(n)/ (gloorde, heeft gegloord) gleam, glimmer: *de ochtend* **begon** *te* ~ day was breaking (*or:* dawning); *er gloorde* **iets** *van hoop* there was a glimmer of hope

de **glorie** /ɣlori/ (pl: gloriën, -s) glory; [rel] gloria

glorierijk /ɣlorirɛɪk/ (adj, adv) glorious

de **glorietijd** /ɣloritɛit/ (pl: -en) heyday, golden age: *in zijn* ~ in his heyday

glorieus /ɣlorijøs/ (adj, adv) glorious

de **gloss** /ɡlɔs/ gloss

de **glossy** /ɡlɔsi/ glossy

de **glucose** /ɣlykozə/ glucose, grape-sugar

de **gluiperd** /ɣlœypərt/ (pl: -s) shifty character, sneak

gluiperig /ɣlœypərəɣ/ (adj, adv) shifty, sneaky

glunderen /ɣlʏndərə(n)/ (glunderde, heeft geglunderd) smile happily

gluren /ɣlʏrə(n)/ (gluurde, heeft gegluurd) peep, peek

het **gluten** /ɣlʏtə(n)/ gluten

de **gluurder** /ɣlʏrdər/ (pl: -s) peeping Tom

de **glycerine** /ɣlisərinə/ glycerine

gniffelen /ɣnɪfələ(n)/ (gniffelde, heeft gegniffeld) snigger, chuckle

de **gnoe** /ɣnu/ (pl: -s) gnu

de **go** /ɡo/ (pl: go's) go-ahead: *een go* **krijgen** get the go-ahead

de **goal** /ɡol/ (pl: -s) goal: *een* ~ **maken** score a goal

de **god** /ɣɔt/ (pl: -en) god; idol

God /ɣɔt/ God: *in* ~ **geloven** believe in God; *leven* **als** ~ *in Frankrijk* be in the clover, have a place in the sun

goddank /ɣɔdɑŋk/ (int) thank God (*or:* goodness)

goddelijk /ɣɔdələk/ (adj, adv) divine

goddeloos /ɣɔdəlos/ (adj) **1** irreligious, godless **2** wicked

de **godheid** /ɣɔthɛit/ (pl: -heden) deity, god-(head)

de **godin** /ɣodɪn/ (pl: -nen) goddess

godlasterend /ɣɔtlɑstərənt/ (adj) blasphemous

de **godsdienst** /ɣɔtsdinst/ (pl: -en) religion

godsdienstig /ɣɔtsdinstəɣ/ (adj, adv) religious, devout

het **godsdienstonderwijs** /ɣɔtsdinstɔndərwɛis/ religious education (*or:* instruction)

de **godsdienstvrijheid** /ɣɔtsdinstfrɛihɛit/ freedom of religion

het **godshuis** /ɣɔtshœys/ (pl: -huizen) house of God, place of worship, church

de **godslastering** /ɣɔtslɑstərɪŋ/ (pl: -en) **1** blasphemy **2** profanity

godswil /ɣɔtswɪl/: *om* ~ for heaven's sake!; *hoe is het* **om** ~ *mogelijk* how on earth is it possible?

het **¹goed** /ɣut/ (pl: -eren) **1** goods, ware(s) **2** goods, property; estate: *onroerend* ~ real estate **3** clothes: *schoon* ~ *aantrekken* put on clean clothes **4** material, fabric, cloth: *wit* (*or:* *bont*) ~ white (*or:* coloured) wash; whites, coloureds

²goed /ɣut/ (adj) **1** good; kind; nice: *ik ben wel* ~ *maar niet gek* I'm not as stupid as you think; *ik* **voel** *me heel* ~ I feel fine (*or:* great); *zou u zo* ~ **willen zijn** … would (*or:* could) you please …, would you be so kind as to …, do (*or:* would) you mind … **2** well, fine: *daar* **word** *ik niet* ~ *van* [also fig] that makes me (feel) sick || ~ *en* **kwaad** good and evil, right and wrong

³goed /ɣut/ (adj, adv) **1** good; well; right, correct: *alle* **berekeningen** *zijn* ~ all the calculations are correct; *hij* **bedoelt (meent)** *het* ~ he means well; *begrijp* me ~ don't get me wrong; *als je* ~ **kijkt** if you look closely; *dat zit wel* ~ that's all right, don't worry about it; *net* ~*!* serves you right!; *het is ook* **nooit** ~ *bij hem* nothing's ever good enough for him; *precies* ~ just (*or:* exactly) right **2** well: *hij was* ~ **nijdig** he was really annoyed; *het* **betaalt** ~ it pays well; *toen ik* ~ *en* **wel** *in bed lag* when I finally (*or:* at last) got into bed; ~ *bij zijn* be clever || *we* **hebben** *het nog nooit zo* ~ **gehad** we've never had it so good; *(heel)* ~ *Engels* **spreken** speak English (very) well, speak (very) good English; *die jas* **staat** *je* ~ that coat suits you (*or:* looks good on you); *de melk* **is** *niet* ~ *meer* the milk has gone off; *dat* **komt** ~ *uit* that's (very) convenient; *hij* **maakt** *het* ~ he is doing well (*or:* all right); [fig] *hij* **staat** *er* ~ **voor** his prospects are good; *de rest hou je nog* **te** ~ I'll owe you the rest; *dat hebben we nog* **te** ~ that's still in store for us; ~ *zo!* good!, that's right!; well done!, that's the way!; **ook** ~ very well, all right; *de opbrengst komt* **ten** ~*e van het Rode Kruis* the proceeds go to the Red Cross; *zij is* ~ *in wiskunde* she is good at mathematics; *dat is te veel van* **het** ~*e* that is too much of a good thing; *het is maar* ~ *dat* … it's a good thing that …; ~ *dat je 't zegt* that reminds me; *dat* **was** *maar* ~ *ook* it was just as well

goedaardig /ɣutardəɣ/ (adj) **1** good-natured, kind-hearted **2** [med] benign

goeddoen /ɣudun/ (deed goed, heeft goedgedaan) do good, help

het **goeddunken** /ɣudʏŋkə(n)/: *naar eigen* ~

handelen act on one's own discretion, act as one sees fit

goedemiddag /ɣudəmɪdɑχ/ (int) good afternoon

goedemorgen /ɣudəmɔrɣə(n)/ (int) good morning

goedenacht /ɣudənɑχt/ (int) good night

goedenavond /ɣudə(n)avɔnt/ (int) good evening; good night

goedendag /ɣudə(n)dɑχ/ (int) **1** good day, hello **2** goodbye, good day **3** hello!, well now!

de **goederen** /ɣudərə(n)/ (pl) **1** goods; [economics] commodities; merchandise: ~ *laden* (or: *lossen*) load (or: unload) goods **2** goods, property

de **goederenlift** /ɣudərə(n)lɪft/ (pl: -en) goods lift; [Am] service elevator

de **goederentrein** /ɣudərə(n)trɛin/ (pl: -en) goods train; [Am] freight train

de **goederenwagen** /ɣudərə(n)waɣə(n)/ (pl: -s) goods carriage; [Am] freight car

goedgeefs /ɣutχefs/ (adj) generous, liberal

goedgehumeurd /ɣutχəhymørt/ (adj) good-humoured, good-natured

goedgelovig /ɣutχəlovəχ/ (adj) credulous, gullible

goedgemutst /ɣutχəmɤtst/ (adj) good-humoured, good-natured

goedgezind /ɣutχəzɪnt/ (adj): *iem.* ~ *zijn* be well-disposed towards s.o.

goedhartig /ɣuthɑrtəχ/ (adj, adv) kind(ly), friendly

de **goedheid** /ɣuthɛit/ **1** goodness: *hij is de* ~ *zelf* he is goodness personified **2** benevolence, indulgence

¹**goedhouden** /ɣuthɑudə(n)/ (hield goed, heeft goedgehouden) keep, preserve: *melk kun je niet zo lang* ~ you can't keep milk very long

zich ²**goedhouden** /ɣuthɑudə(n)/ (hield zich goed, heeft zich goedgehouden) control o.s.; keep a straight face; keep a stiff upper lip: *hij kon zich niet* ~ he couldn't help laughing (or: crying, …)

goedig /ɣudəχ/ (adj, adv) gentle; meek

het **goedje** /ɣucə/ stuff

goedkeuren /ɣutkørə(n)/ (keurde goed, heeft goedgekeurd) **1** approve (of); pass: [med] *goedgekeurd worden* pass one's medical **2** approve; adopt

goedkeurend /ɣutkørənt/ (adj, adv) approving, favourable: ~ *knikken* (or: *glimlachen*) nod (or: smile) (one's) approval

de **goedkeuring** /ɣutkørɪŋ/ (pl: -en) approval, consent

¹**goedkoop** /ɣutkop/ (adj) **1** cheap, inexpensive: ~ *tarief* cheap rate; off-peak tariff **2** [fig] cheap

²**goedkoop** /ɣutkop/ (adv) cheaply, at a low price: *er* ~ *afkomen* get off cheap(ly)

goedlachs /ɣutlɑχs/ (adj) cheery

goedmaken /ɣutmakə(n)/ (maakte goed, heeft goedgemaakt) **1** make up (or: amends) for: *iets weer* ~ *bij* iem. make amends to s.o. for sth. **2** make up for, compensate (for) **3** cover, make good

goedmoedig /ɣutmudəχ/ (adj, adv) good-natured, good-humoured

goedpraten /ɣutpratə(n)/ (praatte goed, heeft goedgepraat) explain away, justify; gloss over

goedschiks /ɣutsχɪks/ (adv) willingly: ~ *of kwaadschiks* willing(ly) or unwilling(ly)

het ¹**goedvinden** /ɣutfɪndə(n)/ permission, consent; agreement

²**goedvinden** /ɣutfɪndə(n)/ (vond goed, heeft goedgevonden) approve (of), consent (to): *als jij het goedvindt* if you agree

de **goedzak** /ɣutsɑk/ (pl: -ken) softy: *'t is een echte* ~ he's soft as butter

de **goegemeente** /ɣuɣəmentə/ the ordinary man in the street

de **goeroe** /ɣuru/ (pl: -s) guru

de **goesting** /ɣustɪŋ/ [Belg] liking, fancy, appetite

de **gok** /ɣɔk/ gamble: *zullen we een ~je wagen?* shall we have a go (at it)?

de **gokautomaat** /ɣɔkɑutomat/ (pl: -automaten) gambling (or: gaming) machine

gokken /ɣɔkə(n)/ (gokte, heeft gegokt) gamble, (place a) bet (on): ~ *op* een paard (place a) bet on a horse

de **gokker** /ɣɔkər/ (pl: -s) gambler

het **gokpaleis** /ɣɔkpalɛis/ casino

het **gokspel** /ɣɔkspɛl/ (pl: -en) game of chance, gambling (game)

gokverslaafd /ɣɔkfərslaft/ (adj) addicted to gambling

de **gokverslaafde** /ɣɔkfərslavdə/ (pl: -n) gambling addict

de **gokverslaving** /ɣɔkfərslavɪŋ/ gambling addiction

de ¹**golden goal** /ɡoldənɡol/ golden goal; [inform] sudden death

de ¹**golf** /ɣɔlf/ (pl: golven) **1** wave: *korte* (or: *lange*) ~ short (or: long) wave **2** gulf, bay **3** stream, flood **4** [fig] wave; surge: *een ~ van geweld* a wave of violence

het ²**golf** /ɡɔlf/ (pl: golven) golf

de **golfbaan** /ɣɔlvban/ (pl: -banen) golf course (or: links)

de **golfbreker** /ɣɔlvbrekər/ (pl: -s) breakwater, mole

golfen /ɡɔlfə(n)/ (golfde/golfte, heeft gegolfd/gegolft) play golf

de **golflengte** /ɣɔlflɛŋtə/ (pl: -n, -s) wavelength: *(niet) op dezelfde* ~ *zitten* [also fig] (not) be on the same wavelength

de **golfslag** /ɣɔlfslɑχ/ surge, swell: *sterke* ~ heavy sea

de **golfstok** /ɣɔlfstɔk/ (pl: -ken) golf club

de **Golfstroom** /ɣɔlfstrom/ Gulf Stream
golven /ɣɔlvə(n)/ (golfde, heeft gegolfd)
1 undulate, wave; heave; surge: *de wind deed het water* ~ the wind ruffled the surface of the water **2** gush, flow
golvend /ɣɔlvənt/ (adj) undulating, wavy ||
een ~ *terrein* rolling terrain
het **gom** /ɣɔm/ rubber; [esp Am] eraser
de **gondel** /ɣɔndəl/ (pl: -s) gondola
de **gong** /ɣɔŋ/ (pl: -s) gong
de **goniometrie** /ɣonijometri/ goniometry
de **gonorroe** /ɣonorø/ gonorrhoea
gonzen /ɣɔnzə(n)/ (gonsde, heeft gegonsd) buzz, hum
de **goochelaar** /ɣoxəlar/ (pl: -s) conjurer, magician
goochelen /ɣoxələ(n)/ (goochelde, heeft gegoocheld) **1** conjure, do (conjuring, magic) tricks: ~ *met kaarten* do (*or:* perform) card tricks **2** juggle (with): ~ *met cijfers* juggle with figures
de **goochelkunst** /ɣoxəlkʏnst/ conjuring
de **goocheltruc** /ɣoxəltrʏk/ (pl: -s) conjuring trick, magic trick
goochem /ɣoxəm/ (adj) smart, crafty
de **goodwill** /ɡutwɪl/ goodwill
googelen® /ɡuɡələ(n)/ (googelde, heeft gegoogeld) google
de **gooi** /ɣoj/ (pl: -en) throw, toss: [fig] *een* ~ *doen naar het presidentschap* make a bid for the Presidency
gooien /ɣojə(n)/ (gooide, heeft gegooid) throw, toss; fling (at), hurl (at): *geld ertegen-aan* ~ spend a lot of money on (sth.); *iem. eruit* ~ throw s.o. out; *met de deur* ~ slam the door
het **gooi-en-smijtwerk** /ɣojɛnsmɛrtwɛrk/ knockabout, slapstick
goor /ɣor/ (adj, adv) **1** filthy, foul **2** bad, nasty: ~ *smaken* (*or:* *ruiken*) taste (*or:* smell) revolting
de **goot** /ɣot/ (pl: goten) **1** wastepipe, drain(pipe); gutter **2** gutter, drain: [fig] *in de* ~ *terechtkomen* end up in the gutter
de **gootsteen** /ɣotsten/ (pl: -stenen) (kitchen) sink: *iets door de* ~ *spoelen* pour sth. down the sink
de **gordel** /ɣɔrdəl/ (pl: -s) belt
de **gordelroos** /ɣɔrdəlros/ shingles
het/de **gordijn** /ɣɔrdɛin/ (pl: -en) curtain
de **gordijnrail** /ɣɔrdɛinrel/ (pl: -s) curtain rail (*or:* track)
gorgelen /ɣɔrɣələ(n)/ (gorgelde, heeft gegorgeld) gargle
de **gorilla** /ɣorɪla/ (pl: -'s) gorilla
de **gort** /ɣɔrt/ pearl barley, groats
gortig /ɣɔrtəx/ (adj): *dat is (me) al te* ~ it's too much (for me), it's more than I can take
gothic /ɡɔθɪk/ (adj) gothic
de **gotiek** /ɣotik/ Gothic
gotisch /ɣotis/ (adj) Gothic

het **goud** /ɣaut/ gold: *zulke kennis is* ~ *waard* such knowledge is invaluable; *voor* geen ~ not for all the tea in China; *ik zou me daar voor* geen ~ *vertonen* I wouldn't be seen dead there; *het is niet alles* ~ *wat er blinkt* all that glitters is not gold
goudbruin /ɣaudbrœyn/ (adj) golden brown, auburn
goudeerlijk /ɣauterlək/ (adj) honest through and through
gouden /ɣaudə(n)/ (adj) **1** gold; [esp fig] golden: *een* ~ *ring* a gold ring **2** golden
de **goudkoorts** /ɣautkorts/ gold fever, gold rush
de **goudmijn** /ɣautmɛin/ (pl: -en) gold mine: *een* ~ *ontdekken* [fig] strike oil
de **goudsmid** /ɣautsmɪt/ (pl: -smeden) goldsmith
het **goudstuk** /ɣautstʏk/ (pl: -ken) gold coin
de **goudvis** /ɣautfɪs/ (pl: -sen) goldfish
de **goulash** /ɡulɑʃ/ goulash
de **gourmet** /ɡurmɛ/ (pl: -s) **1** gourmet, epicure **2** fondue Bourguignonne
gourmetten /ɡurmɛtə(n)/ (gourmette, heeft gegourmet) [roughly] have a fondue Bourguignonne
de **gouvernante** /ɣuvərnɑntə/ (pl: -s) governess; nanny
het **gouvernement** /ɣuvɛrnəmɛnt/ (pl: -en) [Belg] provincial government (*or:* administration)
de **gouverneur** /ɣuvərnør/ (pl: -s) **1** governor **2** [Belg] provincial governor
de **gozer** /ɣozər/ (pl: -s) [inform] guy, fellow: *een leuke* ~ a nice guy (*or:* fellow)
het **gps** /ɣepeɛs/ *global positioning system* gps
de **graad** /ɣrat/ (pl: graden) degree; [mil] rank: *een academische* ~ a university degree; *de vader is eigenwijs, maar de zoon is nog een ~je erger* the father is conceited, but the son is even worse; *18° Celsius* 18 degrees Celsius; *een draai van 180 graden maken* make a 180-degree turn; *tien graden onder nul* ten degrees below zero
de **graadmeter** /ɣratmetər/ (pl: -s) graduator, gauge, measure
de **graaf** /ɣraf/ (pl: graven) count, earl
de **graafmachine** /ɣrafmaʃinə/ (pl: -s) excavator
het **graafschap** /ɣrafsxɑp/ (pl: -pen) county
graag /ɣrax/ (adv) **1** gladly, with pleasure: ~ *gedaan* you're welcome; *ik wil je* ~ *helpen* I'd be glad to help (you); *hoe* ~ *ik het ook zou doen* much as I would like to do it; ~ *of niet* take it or leave it; *(heel)* ~*!* (okay) thank you very much!, yes please! **2** willingly, readily: *zij praat niet* ~ *over die tijd* she dislikes talking about that time; *dat wil ik* ~ *geloven* I can quite believe that, I'm not surprised
graaien /ɣrajə(n)/ (graaide, heeft gegraaid) grabble, rummage

de **graal** /ɣral/ the (Holy) Grail

het **graan** /ɣran/ (pl: granen) grain, corn ‖ *een ~tje meepikken* get one's share, get in on the act

de **graanschuur** /ɣransxyr/ (pl: -schuren) granary

de **graat** /ɣrat/ (pl: graten) **1** (fish) bone **2** bones ‖ [Belg] *ergens geen graten in zien* see nothing wrong with

grabbel /ɣrɑbəl/: *zijn goede naam te ~ gooien* throw away one's reputation

grabbelen /ɣrɑbələ(n)/ (grabbelde, heeft gegrabbeld) rummage (about, around), grope (about, around): *de kinderen ~ naar de pepernoten* the children are scrambling for the ginger nuts

de **grabbelton** /ɣrɑbəltɔn/ (pl: -nen) lucky dip; [Am] grab bag

de **gracht** /ɣrɑxt/ (pl: -en) canal; moat: *aan een ~ wonen* live on a canal

gracieus /ɣraʃøs/ (adj, adv) graceful, elegant

de **gradatie** /ɣrada(t)si/ (pl: -s) degree, level: *in verschillende ~s van moeilijkheid* with different steps (or: levels) of difficulty

de **gradenboog** /ɣradə(n)box/ (pl: -bogen) protractor

gradueel /ɣradywel/ (adj, adv) of degree, in degree, gradual

het **graf** /ɣraf/ (pl: graven) grave, tomb: *zijn eigen ~ graven* dig one's own grave ‖ *zwijgen als het ~* be quiet (or: silent) as the grave

de **graffiti** /ɣrɛfiti/ graffiti

de **grafiek** /ɣrafik/ (pl: -en) graph, diagram

het **grafiet** /ɣrafit/ graphite

grafisch /ɣrafis/ (adj, adv) graphic

de **grafkelder** /ɣrɑfkɛldər/ (pl: -s) tomb; vault; crypt

de **grafrede** /ɣrɑfredə/ funeral oration

de **grafschennis** /ɣrɑfsxɛnɪs/ desecration of graves

het **grafschrift** /ɣrɑfsxrɪft/ (pl: -en) epitaph

de **grafsteen** /ɣrɑfsten/ (pl: -stenen) gravestone, tombstone

de **grafstem** /ɣrɑfstɛm/ (pl: -men) sepulchral voice

het/de **gram** /ɣrɑm/ (pl: -men) gram: *vijf ~ zout* five grams of salt

de **grammatica** /ɣrɑmɑtika/ grammar

grammaticaal /ɣrɑmatikal/ (adj, adv) grammatical

de **grammofoon** /ɣrɑmofon/ (pl: -s) gramophone

de **grammofoonplaat** /ɣrɑmofomplat/ (pl: -platen) (gramophone) record

de **granaat** /ɣranat/ grenade; shell

de **granaatappel** /ɣranatapəl/ (pl: -en, -s) pomegranate

de **granaatscherf** /ɣranatsxɛrf/ (pl: -scherven) piece of shrapnel, shell fragment; shrapnel

het **grand café** /ɡrãkafe/ grand café

grandioos /ɣrɑndijoːs/ (adj, adv) monumental, mighty

het **graniet** /ɣranit/ granite

granieten /ɣranitə(n)/ (adj) granite

de **grap** /ɣrɑp/ (pl: -pen) joke, gag: *een flauwe ~* a feeble (or: poor) joke; *~pen vertellen* tell (or: crack) jokes; *een ~ met iem. uithalen* play a joke on s.o.; *ze kan wel tegen een ~* she can take a joke ‖ *dat wordt een dure ~* that will be an expensive business

de **grapefruit** /ɡrepfrut/ (pl: -s) grapefruit

de **grapjas** /ɣrɑpjɑs/ (pl: -sen) see grappenmaker

het **grapje** /ɣrɑpjə/ (pl: -s) (little) joke: *het was maar een ~* I was only joking (or: kidding); *~?!* you must be joking!; *iets met een ~ afdoen* shrug sth. off with a joke; *kun je niet tegen een ~?* can't you take a joke?

de **grappenmaker** /ɣrɑpə(n)makər/ (pl: -s) joker, wag

grappig /ɣrɑpəx/ (adj, adv) **1** funny, amusing: *zij probeerden ~ te zijn* they were trying to be funny **2** funny, comical, amusing; humorous: *het was een ~ gezicht* it was a funny (or: comical) sight; *een ~e opmerking* a humorous remark; *wat is daar nou zo ~ aan?* what's so funny about that? **3** attractive; [Am] cute

het **gras** /ɣrɑs/ (pl: -sen) grass: *het ~ maaien* mow the lawn; [fig] *iem. het ~ voor de voeten wegmaaien* cut the ground from under s.o.'s feet; [fig] *ze hebben er geen ~ over laten groeien* they did not let the grass grow under their feet

grasduinen /ɣrɑzdœynə(n)/ (grasduinde, heeft gegrasduind) browse (through)

het **grasland** /ɣrɑslɑnt/ grassland, meadow; pasture

de **grasmaaier** /ɣrɑsmajər/ (pl: -s) (lawn)mower

de **grasmat** /ɣrɑsmɑt/ (pl: -ten) grass, turf; field, pitch: *de ~ lag er prachtig bij* the grass looked fantastic

de **graspriet** /ɣrɑsprit/ (pl: -en) blade of grass

het **grasveld** /ɣrɑsfɛlt/ (pl: -en) field (of grass)

de **graszode** /ɣrɑsodə/ (pl: -n) turf, sod

de **gratie** /ɣra(t)si/ **1** grace **2** favour: *bij iem. uit de ~ raken* fall out of favour with s.o. **3** mercy **4** pardon: *~ krijgen* be pardoned

de **gratificatie** /ɣratifika(t)si/ (pl: -s) gratuity, bonus

gratineren /ɣratinerə(n)/ (gratineerde, heeft gegratineerd) cover with breadcrumbs (or: cheese): *gegratineerde schotel* dish au gratin

gratis /ɣratɪs/ (adj, adv) free (of charge): *~ en voor niks* gratis, absolutely free

grauw /ɣrɑu/ (adj) grey, ashen

het **gravel** /ɡrɛvəl/ gravel

de **gravelbaan** /ɡrɛvəlban/ (pl: -banen) clay court

graven /ɣr̲a̲və(n)/ (groef, heeft gegraven)
1 dig; excavate; delve; mine: *een put* ~ sink a
well; *een tunnel* ~ dig a tunnel, tunnel **2** dig;
burrow

graveren /ɣrave̲rə(n)/ (graveerde, heeft ge-
graveerd) engrave

de **graveur** /ɣravø̲r/ (pl: -s) engraver

de **gravin** /ɣravɪ̲n/ (pl: -nen) countess

de **gravure** /ɣravy̲rə/ (pl: -s) engraving, print

grazen /ɣra̲zə(n)/ (graasde, heeft gegraasd)
graze, (be at) pasture: *het vee laten* ~ let the
cattle out to graze ǁ *te* ~ *genomen worden* be
had, be taken in; *iem. te* ~ *nemen* take s.o. for
a ride, take s.o. in

de **greep** /ɣrep/ **1** grasp, grip, grab: ~ *krijgen*
op iets get a grip on sth.; *vast in zijn* ~ *hebben*
have firmly in one's grasp **2** random selection (*or:* choice): *doe maar een* ~ take your
pick

het **greintje** /ɣrɛ̲incə/ (pl: -s) (not) a bit (of): *geen*
~ *hoop* not a ray of hope; *geen* ~ *gezond ver-*
stand not a grain of common sense

de **grendel** /ɣrɛ̲ndəl/ (pl: -s) bolt: *achter slot en*
~ *zitten* be under lock and key

grendelen /ɣrɛ̲ndələ(n)/ (grendelde, heeft
gegrendeld) bolt

grenen /ɣre̲nə(n)/ (adj) pine(wood), deal

het **grenenhout** /ɣre̲nə(n)hɑut/ pine(wood)

de **grens** /ɣrɛns/ (pl: grenzen) border; boundary; limit; bounds: *aan de Duitse* ~ at the German border; *we moeten ergens een* ~ *trekken*
we have to draw the line somewhere; *bin-*
nen *redelijke grenzen* within reason; [fig] *een*
~ *overschrijden* pass a limit; [fig] *grenzen*
verleggen push back frontiers

de **grenscontrole** /ɣrɛ̲nskɔntroːlə/ (pl: -s) border (*or:* customs) check

het **grensgebied** /ɣrɛ̲nsχəbit/ (pl: -en) **1** border
region **2** [fig] borderline, grey area; fringe
(area)

het **grensgeval** /ɣrɛ̲nsχəval/ (pl: -len) borderline case

de **grenslijn** /ɣrɛ̲nslɛin/ (pl: -en) boundary line;
[fig] dividing line

de **grensovergang** /ɣrɛ̲nsovərɣɑŋ/ (pl: -en)
border crossing(-point)

grensoverschrijdend /ɣrɛnsovər-
sχrɛ̲idənt/ (adj) cross-border, international

de **grensrechter** /ɣrɛ̲nsrɛχtər/ (pl: -s) linesman
[socc]; line judge

de **grensstreek** /ɣrɛ̲nstrek/ (pl: -streken) border region

grensverleggend /ɣrɛnsfərlɛ̲ɣənt/ (adj)
pushing back frontiers, opening new hori-
zons, revealing

grenzeloos /ɣrɛ̲nzəlos/ (adj, adv) infinite,
boundless

grenzen /ɣrɛ̲nzə(n)/ (grensde, heeft ge-
grensd) **1** border (on); be adjacent to: *hun*
tuinen ~ *aan elkaar* their gardens border on
one another **2** [fig] border (on), verge (on);

approach: *dat grenst aan het ongelofelijke* that
verges on the incredible

de **greppel** /ɣrɛ̲pəl/ (pl: -s) channel; trench;
ditch

gretig /ɣre̲təχ/ (adj, adv) eager; greedy ǁ ~
aftrek vinden sell like hot cakes

de **grief** /ɣrif/ (pl: grieven) objection, grievance,
complaint

de **Griek** /ɣrik/ (pl: -en) Greek

Griekenland /ɣri̲kə(n)lɑnt/ Greece

Grieks /ɣriks/ (adj) Greek

grienen /ɣri̲nə(n)/ (griende, heeft gegriend)
snivel, blub(ber)

de **griep** /ɣrip/ (the) flu; (a) cold: ~ *oplopen*
catch the flu

grieperig /ɣri̲pərəχ/ (adj) ill with flu: *ik ben*
wat ~ I've got a touch of flu

de **griepprik** /ɣri̲prɪk/ (pl: -ken) influenza vaccination

het **griesmeel** /ɣri̲smel/ semolina

de **griet** /ɣrit/ bird, chick, doll

grieven /ɣri̲və(n)/ (griefde, heeft gegriefd)
hurt, offend

grievend /ɣri̲vənt/ (adj, adv) hurtful, offensive, cutting: *een* ~*e opmerking* a cutting remark

de **griezel** /ɣri̲zəl/ (pl: -s) ogre, terror; [pers]
creep; [pers] weirdo

griezelen /ɣri̲zələ(n)/ (griezelde, heeft ge-
griezeld) shudder, shiver, get the creeps

de **griezelfilm** /ɣri̲zəlfɪlm/ (pl: -s) horror film

griezelig /ɣri̲zələχ/ (adj, adv) gruesome,
creepy

het **griezelverhaal** /ɣri̲zəlvərhal/ (pl: -verha-
len) horror story

grif /ɣrɪf/ (adj, adv) ready; adept; rapid;
prompt: *ik geef* ~ *toe dat ...* I readily admit to
... (-ing); ~ *van de hand gaan* sell like hot cakes

de **griffie** /ɣrɪ̲fi/ (pl: -s) registry; clerk of the
court's office

de **griffier** /ɣrɪfi̲r/ (pl: -s) [roughly] registrar,
clerk

de **grijns** /ɣrɛins/ grin, smirk; sneer

grijnzen /ɣrɛ̲inzə(n)/ (grijnsde, heeft ge-
grijnsd) **1** smirk, sneer **2** grin: *sta niet zo dom*
te ~! wipe that silly grin off your face!

¹**grijpen** /ɣrɛ̲ipə(n)/ (greep, heeft gegrepen)
grab; reach (for): *dat is te hoog gegrepen* that
is aiming too high; *naar de fles* ~ reach for
(*or:* turn to) the bottle

²**grijpen** /ɣrɛ̲ipə(n)/ (greep, heeft gegrepen)
grab (hold of), seize, grasp; snatch: *de dief*
werd gegrepen the thief was nabbed; *hij greep*
zijn kans he grabbed (*or:* seized) his chance;
[fig] *door iets gegrepen zijn* be affected (*or:*
moved) by sth.; *voor het* ~ *liggen* be there for
the taking

de **grijper** /ɣrɛ̲ipər/ (pl: -s) bucket, claw, grab

het ¹**grijs** /ɣrɛis/ grey

²**grijs** /ɣrɛis/ (adj) grey: *hij wordt* al aardig ~ he
is getting quite grey; *in een* ~ *verleden* in the

dim and distant past

de **grijsaard** /ɣrɛisart/ (pl: -s) old man

de **gril** /ɣrɪl/ (pl: -len) whim, fancy

de **grill** /ɣrɪl/ (pl: -s) grill

grillen /ɣrɪlə(n)/ (grilde, heeft gegrild) grill

grillig /ɣrɪləɣ/ (adj, adv) whimsical, fanciful, capricious: ~ *weer* changeable weather

de **grilligheid** /ɣrɪləɣhɛit/ (pl: -heden) capriciousness, whimsicality, fickleness

de **grimas** /ɣrimɑs/ (pl: -sen) grimace

de **grime** /ɣrim/ (pl: -s) make-up, greasepaint

grimeren /ɣrimerə(n)/ (grimeerde, heeft gegrimeerd) make up

de **grimeur** /ɣrimør/ (pl: -s) make-up artist

grimmig /ɣrɪməɣ/ (adj, adv) **1** furious, irate **2** fierce, forbidding: *een ~e kou* a severe cold

het **grind** /ɣrɪnt/ gravel; shingle

grinniken /ɣrɪnəkə(n)/ (grinnikte, heeft gegrinnikt) chuckle; snigger: *zit niet zo dom te ~!* stop that silly sniggering!

de **grip** /ɣrɪp/ grip; traction: ~ *hebben op* [also fig] have a grip on

grissen /ɣrɪsə(n)/ (griste, heeft gegrist) snatch, grab

de **grizzlybeer** /ɣrɪzliber/ (pl: -beren) grizzly (bear)

de **groef** /ɣruf/ (pl: groeven) groove, furrow; slot

de **groei** /ɣruj/ **1** growth, development: *een broek die op de ~ gemaakt is* trousers which allow for growth **2** growth, increase; expansion: *economische ~* economic growth

groeien /ɣrujə(n)/ (groeide, is gegroeid) grow, develop: *zijn baard laten ~* grow a beard; *hij groeit als kool* a) he is shooting up; b) he's coming on well; *het geld groeit mij niet op de rug* I am not made of money

het **groeihormoon** /ɣrujhɔrmon/ (pl: -hormonen) growth hormone

de **groeikern** /ɣrujkɛrn/ (pl: -en) centre of urban growth

de **groeipijn** /ɣrujpɛin/ (pl: -en) growing pains

de **groeistuip** /ɣrujstœyp/ (pl: -en) growing pain; [fig also] teething troubles, initial problems

groeizaam /ɣrujzam/ (adj, adv) favourable (to growth): ~ *weer* growing weather

groen /ɣrun/ (adj) green: *deze aardbeien zijn nog ~* these strawberries are still green; *het signaal sprong op ~* the signal changed to green ‖ *ze was in het ~ (gekleed)* she was (dressed) in green

Groenland /ɣrunlɑnt/ Greenland

de **Groenlander** /ɣrunlɑndər/ (pl: -s) Greenlander

Groenlands /ɣrunlɑn(t)s/ (adj) Greenland(ic)

de **groenstrook** /ɣrunstrok/ (pl: -stroken) **1** green belt, green space (*or:* area) **2** grass strip, centre strip

de **groente** /ɣruntə/ (pl: -n, -s) vegetable: *vlees en twee verschillende soorten ~* meat and two vegetables

de **groenteboer** /ɣruntəbur/ (pl: -en) greengrocer, greengrocer's (shop)

de **groentesoep** /ɣruntəsup/ vegetable soup

de **groentetuin** /ɣruntətœyn/ (pl: -en) vegetable garden, kitchen garden

de **groentewinkel** /ɣruntəwɪŋkəl/ (pl: -s) greengrocer's (shop), greengrocery

het **groentje** /ɣruncə/ (pl: -s) greenhorn; new boy, new girl; fresher; freshman

de **groep** /ɣrup/ (pl: -en) group; party: *een grote ~ van de bevolking* a large section of the population; *leeftijdsgroep* age group (*or:* bracket); *in ~jes van vijf of zes* in groups of five or six; *we gingen in een ~ rond de gids staan* we formed a group round the guide

¹groeperen /ɣruperə(n)/ (groepeerde, heeft gegroepeerd) group: *anders (opnieuw) ~* regroup

zich **²groeperen** /ɣruperə(n)/ (groepeerde zich, heeft zich gegroepeerd) **1** cluster (round), gather (round); huddle (round) **2** group (together), form a group

de **groepering** /ɣruperɪŋ/ (pl: -en) grouping, faction

de **groepsdruk** peer pressure

de **groepsleider** /ɣrupslɛidər/ (pl: -s) group leader

de **groepspraktijk** /ɣrupsprɑktɛik/ group practice

de **groepsreis** /ɣrupsrɛis/ (pl: -reizen) group travel

het **groepsverband** /ɣrupsfərbɑnt/: *in ~* in a group (*or:* team); *werken in ~* work as a team

de **groet** /ɣrut/ (pl: -en) greeting; [mil] salute: *een korte ~ tot afscheid* a parting word; *met vriendelijke ~en* yours sincerely; *doe hem de ~en van mij* give him my best wishes; say hello to him for me; *je moet de ~en van haar hebben. O, doe haar de ~en terug* she sends (you) her regards (*or:* love). Oh, the same to her; *de ~en!* a) [greeting] see you!; b) [forget it] not on your life!, no way!

groeten /ɣrutə(n)/ (groette, heeft gegroet) greet, say hello: *wees gegroet Maria* Hail Mary

de **groeve** /ɣruvə/ (pl: -n) quarry

groezelig /ɣruzələɣ/ (adj) grubby, grimy, dirty

grof /ɣrɔf/ (adj, adv) **1** coarse, hefty **2** coarse, rough, crude: *grove gelaatstrekken* coarse features; *iets ~ schetsen* a) make a (rough) sketch of sth.; b) [fig also] sketch sth. in broad outlines **3** gross; rude: *een grove fout* a glaring error; *je hoeft niet meteen ~ te worden* there's no need to be rude

grofgebouwd /ɣrɔfχəbaut/ (adj) heavily-built

de **grofheid** /ɣrɔfhɛit/ (pl: -heden) coarseness; rudeness; roughness; grossness

grofvuil /ɣrofœyl/ (adv) (collection of) bulky refuse

grofweg /ɣrɔfwɛɣ/ (adv) roughly, about, in the region of

de **grog** /ɣrɔk/ (pl: -s) grog, (hot) toddy

groggy /ɣrɔ̱gi/ (adj) groggy, dazed; punch-drunk

de **grol** /ɣrɔl/ (pl: -len) joke, gag

¹**grommen** /ɣrɔ̱mə(n)/ (gromde, heeft gegromd) growl, snarl: *de hond begon **tegen** mij te ~* the dog began to growl at me

²**grommen** /ɣrɔ̱mə(n)/ (gromde, heeft gegromd) grumble, mutter: *hij gromde iets onduidelijks* he muttered sth. indistinct

de **grond** /ɣrɔnt/ (pl: -en) **1** ground, land: *er zit een flink **stuk** ~ bij het huis* the house has considerable grounds; *een **stuk** ~* a plot of land; *braakliggende* ~ waste land; *iem. **tegen** de ~ slaan* knock s.o. flat; *zij heeft haar bedrijf **van** de ~ af opgebouwd* she built up her firm from scratch **2** ground, earth: *schrale* (or: *on-vruchtbare*) ~ barren (or: poor) soil; *iem. nog verder de ~ **in** trappen* kick s.o. when he is down **3** ground; floor: *de **begane** ~* the ground floor; [Am] the first floor; *ik had wel **door** de ~ kunnen gaan* I wanted the ground to open up and swallow me **4** bottom: *aan de ~ zitten* be on the rocks **5** ground, foundation, basis: *op* ~ *van zijn huidskleur* because of (or: on account of) his colour; *op* ~ *van artikel 461* by virtue of section 461 **6** bottom; essence: *dat komt **uit** de ~ van zijn hart* that comes from the bottom of his heart || *zichzelf **te** ~e richten* dig one's own grave, cut one's own throat

het **grondbeginsel** /ɣrɔndbəɣɪnsəl/ (pl: -en) (basic, fundamental) principle; [pl also] fundamentals; basics

het **grondbezit** /ɣrɔndbəzɪt/ **1** landownership, ownership of land **2** landed property, (landed, real) estate

de **grondbezitter** /ɣrɔndbəzɪtər/ (pl: -s) landowner

het **grondgebied** /ɣrɔntxəbit/ (pl: -en) [also fig] territory; soil

de **grondgedachte** /ɣrɔntxədɑxtə/ basic idea, underlying idea, fundamental idea

grondig /ɣrɔ̱ndəx/ (adj, adv) thorough; radical: *een ~e **hekel** aan iets hebben* loathe sth., dislike sth. intensely; *iets ~ **bespreken*** talk sth. out (or: through); *iets ~ **onderzoeken*** examine sth. thoroughly

de **grondigheid** /ɣrɔ̱ndəxhɛit/ thoroughness; soundness; validity

de **grondlaag** /ɣrɔ̱ntlaχ/ (pl: -lagen) undercoat

de **grondlegger** /ɣrɔ̱ntlɛɣər/ (pl: -s) founder, (founding) father

de **grondlegging** /ɣrɔ̱ntlɛɣɪŋ/ foundation, establishment, founding

het **grondpersoneel** /ɣrɔ̱ntpɛrsonel/ ground crew

de **grondprijs** /ɣrɔntprɛis/ (pl: -prijzen) the price of land

het **grondrecht** /ɣrɔntrɛχt/ (pl: -en) basic right; civil rights

de **grondregel** /ɣrɔntreɣəl/ (pl: -s) basic rule, fundamental rule, cardinal rule

de **grondslag** /ɣrɔntslɑχ/ (pl: -en) [fig] basis, foundation(s): *de ~ **leggen** van iets* lay the foundation for sth.; *ten ~ **liggen** aan* **a)** be at the bottom of; **b)** underlie

de **grondsoort** /ɣrɔntsort/ (pl: -en) (type, kind of) soil

de **grondstewardess** /ɣrɔntscuwɑrdɛs/ (pl: -en) ground hostess; [Am] ground stewardess

de **grondstof** /ɣrɔntstɔf/ (pl: -fen) raw material; raw produce

de **grondverf** /ɣrɔntfɛrf/ primer

de **grondvest** /ɣrɔntfɛst/ (pl: -en) foundation

grondvesten /ɣrɔntfɛstə(n)/ (grondvestte, heeft gegrondvest) **1** lay the foundations of **2** [fig] found, base: *gegrondvest **op*** based on

het **grondvlak** /ɣrɔntflɑk/ (pl: -ken) base

het **grondwater** /ɣrɔntwatər/ groundwater

het **grondwerk** /ɣrɔntwɛrk/ (pl: -en) groundwork

de **grondwet** /ɣrɔntwɛt/ (pl: -ten) constitution

grondwettelijk /ɣrontwɛtələk/ (adj) constitutional

het **grondzeil** /ɣrɔntsɛil/ (pl: -en) groundsheet

groot /ɣrot/ (adj) **1** big, large: *een tamelijk grote **kamer*** quite a big (or: large) room; *de **kans** is ~ dat …* there's a good chance that …; *op één na **de** ~ste* the second to largest **2** big, tall: *wat **ben** jij ~ **geworden!*** how you've grown!; *de ~ste van de twee* the bigger of the two **3** big; grown-up: *zij heeft al grote **kinderen*** she has (already) got grown-up children; *daar ben je **te** ~ **voor*** you're too big for that (sort of thing) **4** in size: *het stuk land is twee **hectare** ~* the piece of land is two hectares in area; *twee keer zo ~ **als** deze kamer* twice as big as this room **5** great, large: *een ~ **gezin*** a large family; *een **steeds** groter aantal* an increasing (or: a growing) number; *in **het** ~ inkopen* (or: *verkopen*) buy (or: sell) in bulk || *Karel **de** Grote* Charlemagne; *Alexander **de** Grote* Alexander the Great; *je hebt ~ **gelijk!*** you are quite (or: perfectly) right!

het **grootboek** /ɣro̱dbuk/ (pl: -en) ledger

grootbrengen /ɣro̱dbrɛŋə(n)/ (bracht groot, heeft grootgebracht) bring up, raise: *een kind **met** de fles ~* bottle-feed a child

Groot-Brittannië /ɣrodbrɪtɑn(i)jə/ Great Britain

het **grootgrondbezit** /ɣrotxrɔ̱ndbəzɪt/ large(-scale) landownership

de **grootgrondbezitter** /ɣrotxrɔ̱ndbəzɪtər/ (pl: -s) large landowner

de **groothandel** /ɣro̱thɑndəl/ (pl: -s) wholesaler's, wholesale business de **grootheid** /ɣroːthɛit/ quantity

de **grootheidswaan** /ɣroːthɛitswaːn/ megalomania

de **groothertog** /ɣroːthɛrtɔɣ/ (pl: -en) grand duke

het **groothertogdom** /ɣroːthɛrtɔɣdɔm/ (pl: -men) grand duchy

de **groothoeklens** /ɣroːthukllɛns/ (pl: -lenzen) wide-angle lens

zich **groothouden** /ɣroːthɑudə(n)/ (hield zich groot, heeft zich grootgehouden) **1** bear up (well, bravely) **2** keep up appearances, keep a stiff upper lip

de **grootmacht** /ɣroːtmɑχt/ (pl: -en) superpower

de **grootmeester** /ɣroːtmeːstər/ (pl: -s) **1** grandmaster **2** (great, past) master

de **grootmoeder** /ɣroːtmudər/ (pl: -s) grandmother

grootmoedig /ɣroːtmudəχ/ (adj, adv) magnanimous, generous: *dat was erg ~ van hem* that was very noble of him

de **grootouders** /ɣroːtɑudərs/ (pl) grandparents

groots /ɣroːts/ (adj, adv) **1** grand, magnificent, majestic **2** spectacular, large-scale; ambitious: *~e plannen hebben* have ambitious plans; *het ~ aanpakken* a) go about it on a grand scale; b) [inform] think big

grootschalig /ɣroːtsχaːləχ/ (adj, adv) large-scale, ambitious

grootscheeps /ɣroːtsχeːps/ (adj, adv) large-scale, great, massive; full-scale

de **grootspraak** /ɣroːtspraːk/ **1** boast(ing): *waar blijf je nu met al je ~!* where's all your boasting now? **2** hyperbole, overstatement

de **grootte** /ɣroːtə/ (pl: -n, -s) size: *onder de normale* ~ undersize(d); *een model op ware ~* a life-size model; *ter ~ van* the size of

de **grootvader** /ɣroːtfaːdər/ (pl: -s) grandfather

de **grootverbruiker** /ɣroːtfərbrœykər/ (pl: -s) large-scale consumer, bulk consumer

het **gros** /ɣrɔs/ (pl: -sen) **1** majority, larger part: *het ~ van de mensen* the majority of the people, the people at large **2** gross

de **grossier** /ɣrɔsiːr/ (pl: -s) wholesaler

de **grot** /ɣrɔt/ (pl: -ten) cave

grotendeels /ɣroːtəndeːls/ (adv) largely

grotesk /ɣroːtɛsk/ (adj, adv) grotesque

het **gruis** /ɣrœys/ grit

het **grut** /ɣrʏt/ toddlers, small fry, young fry

de **grutto** /ɣrʏtoː/ (pl: -'s) (black, bar-tailed) godwit

de **gruwel** /ɣrywəl/ (pl: -en) horror

de **gruweldaad** /ɣrywəldaːt/ (pl: -daden) atrocity: *gruweldaden bedrijven* commit atrocities

gruwelijk /ɣrywələk/ (adj, adv) **1** horrible, gruesome: *een ~e misdaad* a horrible crime; an atrocity **2** terrible, enormous: *een ~e hekel aan iem. hebben* hate s.o.'s guts; *zich ~*

vervelen be bored stiff (*or:* to death)

gruwen /ɣrywə(n)/ (gruwde, heeft gegruwd) be horrified (by): *ik gruw bij de gedachte aan al die ellende* I'm horrified by the thought of all this misery

de **gruzelementen** /ɣryzələmɛntə(n)/ (pl): *iets aan ~ slaan* knock sth. to pieces (*or:* matchwood), shatter sth.; *aan ~ liggen* have fallen to pieces (*or:* smithereens)

de **g-sleutel** /ɣeːsløːtəl/ (pl: -s) G clef, Treble clef

de **gsm**® /ɣeːɛsɛm/ (pl: -'s) GSM

Guatemala /ɣuwatəmaːla/ Guatemala

de **Guatemalteek** /ɣwɑtəmɑltɛk/ (pl: Guatemalteken) Guatemalan

Guatemalteeks /ɣwɑtəmɑltɛks/ (adj) Guatemalan

de **guerrilla** /ɡərɪlja/ (pl: -'s) guer(r)illa (warfare)

de **guerrillaoorlog** /ɡerɪljaorlɔɣ/ (pl: -en) guer(r)illa war(fare)

de **guerrillastrijder** /ɡərɪljastrɛidər/ (pl: -s) guer(r)illa (fighter)

de **guillotine** /ɡijotɪnə/ (pl: -s) guillotine

Guinee /ɣineː/ Guinea

Guinee-Bissau /ɣinebisɑu/ Guinea-Bissau

de **Guinee-Bissauer** /ɣinebisɑuwər/ (pl: -s) inhabitant (*or:* native) of Guinea Bissau

Guinee-Bissaus /ɣinebisɑus/ (adj) of/from Guinea Bissau

de **Guineeër** /ɣineːjər/ (pl: -s) Guinean

Guinees /ɣineːs/ (adj) Guinean

de **guirlande** /ɡirlãdə/ (pl: -s) festoon, garland

guitig /ɣœytəχ/ (adj, adv) roguish, mischievous

¹**gul** /ɣʏl/ (adj) **1** generous: *met ~le hand (geven)* (give) generously; *~ zijn met iets* be liberal with sth. **2** cordial: *een ~le lach* a hearty laugh

²**gul** /ɣʏl/ (adv) cordially

de **gulden** /ɣʏldə(n)/ (pl: -s) (Dutch) guilder, florin; [abbr] Dfl; NLG

de **gulheid** /ɣʏlhɛit/ **1** generosity **2** cordiality

de **gulp** /ɣʏlp/ (pl: -en) fly (front); zip: *je ~ staat open* your fly is open

gulpen /ɣʏlpə(n)/ (gulpte, is gegulpt) gush: *het bloed gulpte uit de wond* blood gushed from the wound

gulzig /ɣʏlzəχ/ (adj, adv) greedy: *met ~e blikken* with greedy eyes

het/de **gum** /ɣʏm/ rubber; [Am] eraser

het/de **gummi** /ɣʏmi/ rubber

de **gummiknuppel** /ɣʏmiknʏpəl/ (pl: -s) baton; [Am] club

de **gummistok** /ɣʏmistɔk/ (pl: -ken) baton

gunnen /ɣʏnə(n)/ (gunde, heeft gegund) **1** grant: *iem. een blik op iets ~* let s.o. have a look at sth.; *hij gunde zich de tijd niet om te eten* he did not allow himself time to eat **2** not begrudge: *het is je van harte gegund* you're very welcome to it

de **gunst** /ɣʏnst/ (pl: -en) favour: *iem. een ~ be-*

wijzen do s.o. a favour

gunstig /ɣʏnstəɣ/ (adj, adv) **1** favourable, kind: ~ *staan tegenover* sympathize with **2** favourable, advantageous: *een ~e gelegenheid* a good (*or:* favourable) opportunity; *in het ~ste geval* at best; *met ~e uitslag* with a favourable (*or:* satisfactory) result; *~e voortekenen* favourable (*or:* hopeful) signs; *~ voor* … favourable (*or:* good) for … **3** favourable, agreeable: *~ bekendstaan* have a good reputation

het **gunsttarief** /ɣʏnstarif/ (pl: -tarieven) [Belg] concessionary rate

gutsen /ɣʏtsə(n)/ (gutste, heeft gegutst) gush, pour

guur /ɣyr/ (adj, adv) bleak; rough; wild; cutting

de **Guyaan** /ɣijan/ (pl: Guyanen) Guyanese

Guyaans /ɣijans/ (adj) Guyanese

Guyana /ɣijana/ Guyana

de **¹gym** /ɣɪm/ gym

het **²gym** /ɣɪm/ [roughly] grammar school; [Am] high school; [in Netherlands etc] gymnasium

gymmen /ɣɪmə(n)/ (gymde, heeft gegymd) **1** do gym(nastics) **2** have gym

de **gymnasiast** /ɣɪmnaʒɔst/ (pl: -en) [roughly] grammar-school student; [Am] [roughly] high-school student; [Dutch etc.] gymnasium student

het **gymnasium** /ɣɪmnazijʏm/ (pl: -s, gymnasia) [roughly] grammar school; [Am] high school; [Dutch] gymnasium

de **gymnast** /ɣɪmnɔst/ (pl: -en) gymnast

de **gymnastiek** /ɣɪmnɔstik/ gymnastics: *op ~ zijn* be at gymnastics

de **gynaecologie** /ɣinekoloɣi/ gynaecology

de **gynaecoloog** /ɣinekoloɣ/ (pl: -logen) gynaecologist

de **gyros** /ɣirɔs/ gyros

h

de **h** /ha/ (pl: h's) h, H, aitch
 ha /ha/ (int) ah!: *ha! ben je daar?* ah! so there
 you are; *ha! dat dacht je maar!* aha! that's
 what you thought || *haha, die is goed!* ha, ha
 that's (a) good (one)!
de **haag** /haχ/ (pl: hagen) hedge(row)
de **haai** /haj/ (pl: -en) shark: *naar de ~en gaan* go
 down the drain
de **haaientanden** /hajə(n)tɑndə(n)/ **1** shark's
 teeth **2** triangular road marking (at junction)
de **haaienvinnensoep** /hajə(n)vɪnə(n)sup/
 shark-fin soup
de **haak** /hak/ (pl: haken) hook: *er zitten veel ha-
 ken en* **ogen** *aan* it's a tricky business || *dat is
 niet* **in** *de ~* that's not quite right; *de hoorn*
 van *de ~ nemen* take the receiver off the
 hook
het **haakje** /hakjə/ (pl: -s) bracket, parenthesis: *~
 openen* (or: *sluiten*) open (or: close) (the)
 brackets; *tussen (twee) ~s* **a)** in brackets;
 b) [fig] incidentally, by the way
de **haaknaald** /haknalt/ (pl: -en) crochet hook
 (or: needle)
 haaks /haks/ (adj, adv) square(d) || *hou je ~*
 (keep your) chin up
het **haakwerk** /hakwɛrk/ (pl: -en) crochet
 (work), crocheting
de **haal** /hal/ (pl: halen) **1** tug, pull: *met een
 flinke ~ trok hij het schip aan de wal* with a
 good tug he pulled the boat ashore **2** stroke
 || *aan de ~ gaan met* run off with
 haalbaar /halbar/ (adj) attainable, feasible
de **haalbaarheid** /halbarhɛit/ feasibility
de **haan** /han/ (pl: hanen) cock: *daar kraait geen
 ~ naar* no one will know a thing; *de ~* **spannen (overhalen)** cock the gun
het **haantje** /hancə/ (pl: -s) young cock; chicken
de **haantje-de-voorste** /hancədəvorstə/
 ringleader: *~ zijn* be (the) cock-of-the-walk
het **¹haar** /har/ hair: *met lang ~, met kort ~* long-
 haired, short-haired; *z'n ~* **laten knippen**
 have a haircut; *z'n ~* **verven** dye one's hair
het/de **²haar** /har/ hair: *iets* **met** *de haren erbij slepen*
 drag sth. in; **geen** *~ op m'n hoofd die eraan
 denkt* I would not dream of it; *elkaar* **in** *de haren vliegen* fly at each other; *het* **scheelde**
 maar een ~ of ik had hem geraakt I only just
 missed hitting him; *op een ~* **na** very nearly
 ³haar /har/ (pers pron) her; it: *vrienden van ~*
 friends of hers; *hij* **gaf** *het ~* he gave it to her;
 die **van** *~ is wit* hers is white
 ⁴haar /har/ (poss pron) her; its: *Els ~ schoenen*
 Elsie's shoes

de **haarborstel** /harbɔrstəl/ (pl: -s) hairbrush
het **haarbreed** /harbret/: *hij week* **geen** *~* he did
 not give an inch
de **haard** /hart/ (pl: -en) **1** stove: *eigen ~ is goud
 waard* there's no place like home **2** hearth:
 huis en ~ hearth and home; *een* **open** *~* a
 fireplace; *bij de ~* by (or: at) the fireside
de **haardos** /hardɔs/ (pl: -sen) (head of) hair:
 een **dichte** (or: **volle**) *~* a thick head of hair
de **haardracht** /hardrɑχt/ (pl: -en) hair style
de **haardroger** /hardroɣər/ (pl: -s) hairdryer
het **haardvuur** /hartfyr/ (pl: -vuren) open fire,
 fire on the hearth
 haarfijn /harfɛin/ (adv): *iets ~* **uitleggen** explain sth. in great detail, explain the ins and
 outs of sth.
de **haargroei** /harɣruj/ hair growth
de **haarkloverij** /harkloʋərɛi/ **1** hairsplitting
 2 quibbling
het/de **haarlak** /harlɑk/ (pl: -ken) hair spray
de **haarlok** /harlɔk/ (pl: -ken) lock (of hair)
 haarscherp /harsχɛrp/ (adj, adv) very sharp;
 exact
het **haarscheurtje** /harsχørcə/ (pl: -s) haircrack
de **haarspeld** /harspɛlt/ (pl: -en) **1** hairslide;
 [Am] hair clasp **2** hairpin
de **haarspeldbocht** /harspɛldbɔχt/ hairpin
 bend
de **haarspoeling** /harspulɪŋ/ hair colouring
de **haarspray** /harspre/ (pl: -s) hair spray
het **haarstukje** /harstʏkjə/ (pl: -s) hairpiece
de **haaruitval** /harœytfɑl/ hair loss
het **haarvat** /harvɑt/ (pl: -en) capillary
de **haarversteviger** /harʋərsteʋəɣər/ (pl: -s)
 hair conditioner
de **haarwortel** /harwɔrtəl/ (pl: -s) **1** hair-root:
 kleuren **tot in** *de ~s* blush to the roots of one's
 hair **2** [bot] root-hair
de **haas** /has/ (pl: hazen) **1** hare **2** fillet: *een
 biefstuk van de ~* fillet steak **3** [sport] pace-
 maker || *het ~je* **zijn** be for it; *mijn naam is ~*
 I'm saying nothing, I know nothing about it
het **haasje-over** /hajəoʋər/: *~ springen* (play)
 leapfrog
de **¹haast** /hast/ hurry, haste: *in grote ~* in a
 great hurry, in haste; *~ hebben* be in a hurry;
 waarom **zo'n** *~?* what's the rush?
 ²haast /hast/ (adv) almost, nearly; hardly:
 men zou ~ denken dat ... one would almost
 think that ...; *hij was ~ gevallen* he nearly
 fell; *hij zei ~ niets toen hij wegging* he said
 hardly anything when he left; *~ niet* hardly;
 ~ nooit scarcely ever
zich **haasten** /hastə(n)/ (haastte zich, heeft zich
 gehaast) hurry; hurry up: *we* **hoeven** *ons niet
 te ~* there's no need to hurry; *haast je maar
 niet!* don't hurry!, take your time!
 haastig /hastəχ/ (adj, adv) hasty, rash: *niet
 zo ~!* (take it) easy!
het **haastwerk** /hastwɛrk/ **1** hasty (or: rushed)
 work **2** urgent (or: pressing) work

de **haat** /hat/ hatred, hate: *blinde* ~ blind hate; ~ *zaaien* stir up (*or:* sow) hatred

haatdragend /hadrayənt/ (adj) resentful, rancorous, spiteful

de **haat-liefdeverhouding** /hatlivdəvərhaudɪŋ/ love-hate relationship

de **habbekrats** /hɑbəkrɑts/ [inform]: *voor een* ~ for a song

het **habijt** /habɛit/ (pl: -en) habit

de **habitat** /habitɑt/ (pl: -s) habitat

het/de **hachee** /haʃe/ stew, hash

hachelijk /hɑxələk/ (adj) precarious

het **hachje** /hɑxjə/ (pl: -s) skin: *zijn* ~ *redden* save one's skin; *alleen aan zijn eigen* ~ *denken* only think of one's own safety

hacken /hɛkə(n)/ (hackte, heeft gehackt) hack

de **hacker** /hɛkər/ hacker

de **hadj** /hɑdʒ/ hadj

de **hadji** /hɑdʒi/ hadji

de **hagedis** /haɣədɪs/ (pl: -sen) lizard

de **hagel** /haɣəl/ (pl: -s) hail **2** (lead, ball) shot

de **hagelbui** /haɣəlbœy/ (pl: -en) hailstorm

hagelen /haɣələ(n)/ (hagelde, heeft gehageld) hail: *het hagelt* it hails, it is hailing

de **hagelslag** /haɣəlslɑx/ chocolate strands

de **hagelsteen** /haɣəlsten/ (pl: -stenen) hailstone

hagelwit /haɣəlwɪt/ (adj) (as) white as snow: ~*te tanden* pearly-white teeth

de **haiku** /hɑjku/ (pl: -'s) haiku

de **hairextension** /hɛːrɛkstɛnʃən/ (hair) extension

Haïti /hajti/ Haiti

de **Haïtiaan** /haitijan/ (pl: Haïtianen) Haitian

Haïtiaans /haitijans/ (adj) Haitian

de **hak** /hɑk/ **1** heel: *schoenen met hoge* (or: *lage*) ~*ken* high-heeled (*or:* flat-heeled) shoes; *met de* ~*ken over de sloot slagen* pass by the skin of one's teeth **2** cut || *van de* ~ *op de tak springen* skip from one subject to another; *iem. een* ~ *zetten* play s.o. a nasty trick, do s.o. a bad turn

de **hakbijl** /hɑgbɛɪl/ (pl: -en) hatchet, chopper

het **hakblok** /hɑgblɔk/ (pl: -ken) chopping block, butcher's block

¹**haken** /hakə(n)/ (haakte, heeft gehaakt) catch: *hij bleef met zijn jas aan een spijker* ~ he caught his coat on a nail

²**haken** /hakə(n)/ (haakte, heeft gehaakt) crochet

het **hakenkruis** /hakə(n)krœys/ (pl: -kruizen) swastika

hakkelen /hɑkələ(n)/ (hakkelde, heeft gehakkeld) stammer (out), stumble (over one's words)

¹**hakken** /hɑkə(n)/ (hakte, heeft gehakt) hack (at) || *dat hakt erin* a) that costs a packet, that's a nasty blow to our budget; b) that's a big blow

²**hakken** /hɑkə(n)/ (hakte, heeft gehakt)

1 chop (up): *in stukjes* ~ cut (*or:* chop) (up) **2** cut (off, away) **3** cut (out)

het **hakmes** /hɑkmɛs/ (pl: -sen) **1** chopper, machete **2** chopping knife

de **hal** /hɑl/ (pl: -len) (entrance) hall: *in de* ~ *van het hotel* in the hotel lobby (*or:* lounge, foyer)

halal /halɑl/ (adj) halal

halen /halə(n)/ (haalde, heeft gehaald)

1 pull; drag: *ervan alles bij* ~ drag in everything (but the kitchen sink); *ik kan er mijn kosten niet uit* ~ it doesn't cover my expenses; *eruit* ~ *wat erin zit* get the most out of sth.; *overhoop* ~ turn upside down; *waar haal ik het geld vandaan?* where shall I find the money?; *zijn zakdoek uit zijn zak* ~ pull out one's handkerchief; *iem. uit zijn concentratie* ~ break s.o.'s concentration; *geld van de bank* ~ (with)draw money from the bank **2** fetch, get: *de post* ~ collect the mail; *ik zal het gaan* ~ I'll go and get it; *ik zal je morgen komen* ~ I'll come for you tomorrow; *iem. van de trein* ~ meet s.o. at the station; *twee* ~ *een betalen* two for the price of one **3** fetch, go for: *de dokter* ~ go for the doctor; *iem. (iets) laten* ~ send for s.o. (sth.) **4** get; take; pass: *goede cijfers* ~ get good marks **5** reach; catch; get; make; compare; pull through: *hij heeft de finish niet gehaald* he did not make it to the finish; *daar haalt niets (het) bij* nothing can touch (*or:* beat) it || *je haalt twee zaken door elkaar* you are mixing up two things

het ¹**half** /hɑlf/ (pl: halven) half: *twee halven maken een heel* two halves make a whole

²**half** /hɑlf/ (adj) **1** half: *voor* ~ *geld* (at) half price; *vier en een halve mijl* four and a half miles; *de halve stad spreekt ervan* half the town is talking about it **2** halfway up/down (*or:* along, through): *ik ga* ~ *april* I'm going in mid-April; *er is een bus telkens om vier minuten vóór* ~ there is a bus every four minutes to the half-hour; *het is* ~ *elf* **a)** it is half past ten; **b)** it is half ten

³**half** /hɑlf/ (adv) half, halfway: *een glas* ~ *vol schenken* pour half a glass; *met het raam* ~ *dicht* with the window halfway down (*or:* open)

halfbakken /hɑlvbɑkə(n)/ (adj, adv) half-baked: *hij deed alles maar* ~ he did everything in a half-baked way (*or:* by halves)

halfbewolkt /hɑlvbəwɔlkt/ (adj) rather cloudy, with some clouds

de **halfbloed** /hɑlvblut/ (pl: -en) half-breed, half-blood

de **halfbroer** /hɑlvbrur/ (pl: -s) half-brother

het **halfdonker** /hɑlvdɔŋkər/ semidarkness, half-dark(ness)

halfdood /hɑlvdot/ (adj) half-dead

de **halfedelsteen** /hɑlfedəlsten/ (pl: -stenen) semiprecious stone

het **halffabricaat** /hɑlfabrikat/ (pl: -fabricaten)

semimanufacture

halfgaar /halfxaːr/ (adj) **1** half-done **2** half-witted

de **halfgeleider** /hɑlfxələɛidər/ (pl: -s) semiconductor

de **halfgod** /hɑlfxɔt/ (pl: -en) demigod

halfhartig /hɑlfhɑrtəx/ (adj, adv) half-hearted

het **halfjaar** /hɑlfjaːr/ (pl: -jaren) six months, half a year

halfjaarlijks /hɑlfjaːrləks/ (adj, adv) half-yearly, biannual: *te betalen in ~e termijnen* payable in biannual instalments, payable every six months

het **halfpension** /hɑlfpɛnʃɔn/ half board

het **halfrond** /hɑlfrɔnt/ (pl: -en) hemisphere

halfslachtig /hɑlfslɑxtəx/ (adj, adv) half-hearted, half: *~e maatregelen* half(way) measures

halfstok /hɑlfstɔk/ (adv) half-mast

het **halfuur** /hɑlfyr/ half (an) hour

halfvol /hɑlfɔl/ (adj) **1** half-full: *bij hem is het glas altijd ~* for him the glass is always half-full **2** low-fat, half-fat

de **halfwaardetijd** /hɑlfwaːrdətɛɪt/ half-life

halfweg /hɑlfwɛx/ (prep) halfway: *~ Utrecht en Amersfoort heeft hij een huis gekocht* he has bought a house halfway between Utrecht and Amersfoort ‖ *ik kwam hem ~ tegen* I met him halfway

halfzacht /hɑlfsɑxt/ (adj) **1** soft-boiled **2** soft-headed, soft (in the head)

de **halfzuster** /hɑlfsystər/ (pl: -s) half-sister

halleluja /hɑlelyjaː/ (int) alleluia, halleluja(h)

hallo /hɑloː/ (int) hello, hallo, hullo

de **hallucinatie** /hɑlysinaː(t)si/ (pl: -s) hallucination

hallucineren /hɑlysinerə(n)/ (hallucineerde, heeft gehallucineerd) hallucinate, hear things, see things

de **halm** /hɑlm/ (pl: -en) stalk; blade

de **halo** /haːloː/ (pl: -'s) halo; [around moon] corona

het **halogeen** /haːloyeːn/ (pl: halogenen) halogen

de **halogeenlamp** /haːloyeːnlɑmp/ (pl: -en) halogen lamp

de **hals** /hɑls/ (pl: halzen) **1** neck: *de ~ van een gitaar* the neck of a guitar; *iem. om de ~ vallen* throw one's arms round s.o.'s neck; *een japon met laag uitgesneden ~* a low-necked dress **2** throat **3** nape ‖ *hij heeft het zichzelf op de ~ gehaald* he has brought it on himself

de **halsband** /hɑlzbɑnt/ (pl: -en) **1** collar **2** necklace

halsbrekend /hɑlzbrekənt/ (adj) daredevil

de **halsdoek** /hɑlzduk/ (pl: -en) scarf

de **halsketting** /hɑlskɛtɪŋ/ (pl: -en) **1** necklace **2** collar

de **halsmisdaad** /hɑlsmɪzdaːt/ (pl: -misdaden)

capital crime (*or:* offence)

halsoverkop /hɑlsoverkɔp/ (adv) in a hurry (*or:* rush); headlong; head over heels: *~ over kop verliefd worden* fall head over heels in love; *~ naar het ziekenhuis gebracht worden* be rushed to hospital; *~ de trap af komen* come tumbling downstairs

halsreikend /hɑlsrɛɪkənt/ (adv) eagerly: *~ naar iets uitzien* look forward eagerly to sth.

de **halsslagader** /hɑlslɑxadər/ (pl: -s, -en) carotid (artery)

halsstarrig /hɑlstɑrəx/ (adj) obstinate, stubborn

het/de **halster** /hɑlstər/ (pl: -s) halter

het **¹halt** /hɑlt/ stop: *iem. een ~ toeroepen* stop s.o.; *~ houden* halt

²halt /hɑlt/ (int) halt!, stop!, wait!

de **halte** /hɑltə/ (pl: -s) stop

de **halter** /hɑltər/ (pl: -s) dumb-bell; bar bell

de **halvarine** /hɑlvarinə/ (pl: -s) low-fat margarine

de **halvemaan** /hɑlvəmaːn/ (pl: -manen) **1** half-moon **2** crescent

halveren /hɑlverə(n)/ (halveerde, heeft gehalveerd) **1** divide into halves **2** halve

halverwege /hɑlvərweyə/ (adv) halfway, halfway through ‖ *~ blijven steken* in een boek get stuck halfway through a book

de **ham** /hɑm/ (pl: -men) ham: *een broodje ~* a ham roll

de **hamam** /hɑmɑm/ hammam

de **hamburger** /hɑmbyrɣər/ (pl: -s) hamburger, beefburger: *~ met kaas* cheeseburger

de **hamer** /haːmər/ (pl: -s) hammer

hameren /haːmərə(n)/ (hamerde, heeft gehamerd) hammer: *er bij iem. op blijven ~* keep on at s.o. about sth.

de **hamster** /hɑmstər/ (pl: -s) hamster

de **hamsteraar** /hɑmstərar/ (pl: -s) hoarder

hamsteren /hɑmstərə(n)/ (hamsterde, heeft gehamsterd) hoard (up)

de **hamstring** /hɛmstrɪŋ/ (pl: -s) hamstring

de **hamvraag** /hɑmvraːx/ (pl: -vragen) key question

de **hand** /hɑnt/ (pl: -en) hand: *blote ~en* bare hands; *in goede* (or: *verkeerde*) *~en vallen* fall into the right (*or:* wrong) hands; *iem. de helpende ~ bieden* lend s.o. a (helping) hand; *de laatste ~ aan iets leggen* put the finishing touches to sth.; *niet met lege ~en komen* not come empty-handed; *iem. (de) ~en vol werk geven* give s.o. no end of work (*or:* trouble); *de ~en vol hebben aan iem. (iets)* have one's hands full with s.o. (sth.); *dat kost ~en vol geld* that costs lots of money; *iem. de ~ drukken* (*or:* *geven, schudden*) shake hands with s.o., give s.o. one's hand; *iemands ~ lezen* read s.o.'s palm; *de ~ ophouden* [fig] hold out one's hand for a tip; beg; *zijn ~en uit de mouwen steken* [fig] roll up one's sleeves, get down to it; *hij kan zijn ~en niet thuishouden* he can't keep his hands to himself; *zijn ~ uit-steken* indicate; *~en omhoog! (of ik schiet)* hands up! (or I'll shoot); *~en thuis!* hands off!; *niks aan de ~!* there's nothing the matter; *wat geld achter de ~ houden* keep some money for a rainy day; *in de ~en klappen* clap one's hands; [fig] *iets in de ~ hebben* have sth. under control; *de macht in ~en hebben* have power, be in control; *in ~en vallen van de politie* fall into the hands of the police; *met de ~ gemaakt* hand-made; *iets omhanden hebben* have sth. to do; *iem. onder ~en nemen* take s.o. in hand (or: to task); *uit de ~ lopen* get out of hand; *iem. het werk uit (de) ~en nemen* take work off s.o.'s hands; *iets van de ~ doen* sell sth., part with sth., dispose of sth.; *dat ligt voor de ~* that speaks for itself, is self-evident; *aan de winnende ~ zijn* be winning; *iem. op zijn ~ hebben* have s.o. on one's side ‖ *wat is er daar aan de ~?* what's going on there?; *er is iets aan de ~* there's sth. the matter (or: up)

de **handbagage** /hɑndbaɣaʒə/ (pl: -s) hand-luggage

het **handbal** /hɑndbɑl/ handball

handballen /hɑndbɑlə(n)/ (handbalde, heeft gehandbald) play handball

het **handbereik** /hɑndbərɛik/ reach: *onder* (or: *binnen*) ~ within reach

de **handboei** /hɑndbuj/ (pl: -en) handcuffs

het **handboek** /hɑndbuk/ (pl: -en) **1** handbook **2** reference book

het **handbreed** /hɑndbret/ hand('s-)breadth: *geen ~ wijken* not budge, give an inch

de **handdoek** /hɑnduk/ (pl: -en) towel

de **handdruk** /hɑndrʏk/ (pl: -ken) handshake

de **handel** /hɑndəl/ **1** trade, business: *~ drijven* trade (with), do business (with); *binnenlandse ~* domestic trade; *zwarte ~* black market; *~ in verdovende middelen* drug trafficking **2** merchandise, goods **3** business; shop

de **handelaar** /hɑndəlar/ (pl: -s, handelaren) trader; merchant; dealer; [depr] trafficker

handelbaar /hɑndəlbar/ (adj) manageable, docile

handelen /hɑndələ(n)/ (handelde, heeft gehandeld) **1** trade, do business, transact business; [depr] traffic: *hij handelt in drugs* he traffics in drugs **2** act: *~d optreden* take action; *ik zal naar eer en geweten ~* I shall act in all conscience **3** (+ over) treat (of), deal (with)

de **handeling** /hɑndəlɪŋ/ (pl: -en) **1** act, deed **2** action, plot: *de plaats van ~* the scene (of the action)

handelingsbekwaam /hɑndəlɪŋzbəkwam/ (adj) having capacity (or: competence) to act

het **handelsakkoord** /hɑndəlsakort/ (pl: -en) trade agreement

het **handelsartikel** /hɑndəlsartikəl/ (pl: -en) commodity; goods; merchandise

de **handelsbalans** /hɑndəlzbalɑns/ (pl: -en) balance of trade, trade balance

de **handelsbetrekkingen** /hɑndəlzbətrɛkɪŋ/ (pl) trade relations, commercial relations

de **handelskamer** /hɑndəlskamər/ (pl: -s) **1** producers' cooperative **2** Commercial Court

de **handelskennis** /hɑndəlskɛnɪs/ knowledge of commerce (or: business); business studies

het **handelsmerk** /hɑndəlsmɛrk/ (pl: -en) trademark; brand name

de **handelsmissie** /hɑndəlsmɪsi/ (pl: -s) trade mission (or: delegation)

de **handelsonderneming** /hɑndəlsɔndər-nemɪŋ/ (pl: -en) commercial enterprise, business enterprise

de **handelsovereenkomst** /hɑndəlsovər-eŋkɔmst/ (pl: -en) trade agreement (or: pact)

de **handelspartner** /hɑndəlspɑrtnər/ (pl: -s) business partner, trading partner

het **handelsrecht** /hɑndəlsrɛχt/ commercial law

de **handelsrechtbank** /hɑndəlsrɛχtbɑŋk/ (pl: -en) [Belg] commercial court

het **handelsregister** /hɑndəlsrəɣɪstər/ (pl: -s) company (or: commercial, trade) register

de **handelsreiziger** /hɑndəlsrɛizəɣər/ (pl: -s) sales representative

het **handelstekort** /hɑndəlstəkɔrt/ (pl: -en) trade deficit

het **handelsverdrag** /hɑndəlsfərdrɑχ/ (pl: -en) commercial treaty

het **handelsverkeer** /hɑndəlsfərker/ trade, business

de **handelswaar** /hɑndəlswar/ (pl: -waren) commodity, article; merchandise; goods

de **handenarbeid** /hɑndə(n)ɑrbɛit/ hand(i)-craft, industrial art, manual training

de **hand-en-spandiensten** /hɑntɛnspɑn-dinstə(n)/ (pl): *~ verrichten* lend a helping hand; aid and abet

handenwringend /hɑndə(n)vrɪŋənt/ (adj) [fig] beside o.s. with despair

het **handgebaar** /hɑntχəbar/ (pl: -gebaren) gesture

het **handgemeen** /hɑntχəmen/ (hand-to-hand) fight

de **handgranaat** /hɑntχranat/ (pl: -granaten) (hand) grenade

de **handgreep** /hɑntχrep/ handle; grip

¹**handhaven** /hɑnthavə(n)/ (handhaafde, heeft gehandhaafd) **1** maintain; keep up; uphold; enforce: *de orde ~* maintain (or: keep, preserve) order **2** maintain, stand by: *zijn bezwaren ~* stand by one's objections

zich ²**handhaven** /hɑnthavə(n)/ (handhaafde zich, heeft zich gehandhaafd) hold one's own

de **handhaving** /hɑnthavɪŋ/ maintenance; upholding; enforcement

de **handicap** /hɛndikɛp/ (pl: -s) handicap: *spe-*

ciale voorzieningen voor mensen **met** een ~ special facilities for the disabled

handig /hɑndəx/ (adj, adv) **1** skilful; dexterous; handy: een ~ **formaat** a handy size; ~ **in (met)** iets zijn be good (or: handy) at sth. **2** clever: hij **legde** het ~ **aan** he set about it cleverly

de **handigheid** /hɑndəxhɛit/ (pl: -heden) **1** skill **2** knack

het **handje** /hɑncə/ (pl: -s) hand(shake) ‖ een ~ **helpen** give (or: lend) a (helping) hand

de **handkar** /hɑntkɑr/ (pl: -ren) handcart

de **handkus** /hɑntkʏs/ (pl: -sen) kiss on the hand: iem. een ~ **geven** kiss s.o.'s hand

de **handlanger** /hɑntlɑŋər/ (pl: -s) accomplice

de **handleiding** /hɑntlɛidɪŋ/ (pl: -en) manual, handbook; directions (or: instructions) (for use)

handlezen /hɑntlezə(n)/ palmistry, palmreading

handmatig /hɑntmatəx/ (adj) manual

de **handomdraai** /hɑntɔmdraj/: in een ~ in (less than) no time

de **handoplegging** /hɑntɔplɛɣɪŋ/ (pl: -en) laying on of hands; faith healing

de **hand-out** /hɛndaʊt/ (pl: -s) hand-out

de **handpalm** /hɑntpɑlm/ (pl: -en) palm (of the hand)

de **handreiking** /hɑntrɛikɪŋ/ (pl: -en) help(ing hand), assistance

de **handrem** /hɑntrɛm/ (pl: -men) handbrake

het **hands** /hɛnts/ hands, handling (the ball), handball: aangeschoten ~ unintentional hands

de **handschoen** /hɑntsxun/ (pl: -en) glove: een **paar** ~en a pair of gloves; iem. met **fluwelen** ~en aanpakken handle s.o. with kid gloves

het **handschoenenkastje** /hɑntsxunə(n)kɑʃə/ (pl: -s) glove compartment

het **handschrift** /hɑntsxrɪft/ (pl: -en) **1** handwriting **2** manuscript

handsfree /hɛn(t)sfri:/ (adj) handsfree

de **handstand** /hɑntstɑnt/ (pl: -en) handstand

de **handtas** /hɑntɑs/ (pl: -sen) (hand)bag

handtastelijk /hɑntɑstələk/ (adj) free, (over)familiar: ~ **worden** paw s.o.

de **handtekening** /hɑntekənɪŋ/ (pl: -en) signature; autograph

de **handtekeningenactie** /hɑntekənɪŋə(n)-ɑksi/ (pl: -s) petition

de **handvaardigheid** /hɑntfardəxhɛit/ (handi)craft(s)

het **handvat** /hɑntfɑt/ (pl: -ten) handle; hilt; butt: het ~ van een **koffer** the handle of a suitcase

het **handvest** /hɑntfɛst/ (pl: -en) charter

de **handvol** /hɑntfɔl/ handful

handwarm /hɑntwɑrm/ (adj) lukewarm

het **handwerk** /hɑntwɛrk/ (pl: -en) **1** handiwork: dit tapijt **is** ~ this carpet is handmade **2** needlework; embroidery; crochet(ing)

3 manual work; trade

de **handwerksman** /hɑntwɛrksmɑn/ (pl: handwerkslieden, handwerkslui) craftsman, artisan

handzaam /hɑntsam/ (adj) handy

de **hanenkam** /hanə(n)kɑm/ (pl: -men) **1** (cocks)comb **2** Mohawk haircut

de **hanenpoot** /hanə(n)pot/ (pl: -poten) **1** cock's foot **2** [illegible handwriting] scrawl

de **hang** /hɑŋ/: de ~ **naar** vrijheid the longing for freedom; zij heeft een sterke ~ **naar** luxe she has a strong craving for luxury

de **hangar** /hɑŋɑr/ (pl: -s) hangar

de **hangbrug** /hɑŋbrʏx/ (pl: -gen) suspension bridge

de **hangbuik** /hɑŋbœyk/ (pl: -en) pot-belly

het **hangbuikzwijn** /hɑŋbœykswɛin/ potbellied pig

¹hangen /hɑŋə(n)/ (hing, heeft gehangen) **1** hang: de zeilen ~ **slap** the sails are slack, the sails are hanging (loose); het schilderij hangt **scheef** the painting is (hanging) crooked; **aan** het plafond ~ hang (or: swing, be suspended) from the ceiling; de hond liet zijn **staart** ~ the dog hung its tail **2** sag: het koord hangt **slap** the rope is sagging (or: slack) **3** lean (over), hang (over); loll; slouch; hang around: hij hing **op** zijn stoel he lay sprawled in a chair, he lolled in his chair **4** stick (to), cling (to); be (or: get) stuck (in): [fig] **blijven** ~ linger (or: stay, hang) (on); get hung up (or: stuck); [fig] ze ~ erg **aan** elkaar they are devoted to (or: wrapped up in) each other ‖ de wolken ~ **laag** the clouds are (hanging) low; de **bloemen** zijn gaan ~ the flowers are wilting

²hangen /hɑŋə(n)/ (hing, heeft gehangen) **1** hang (up): de was **buiten** ~ hang out the washing (to dry); zijn jas **aan** de kapstok ~ hang (up) one's coat on the peg **2** hang

hangend /hɑŋənt/ (adj) hanging; drooping

het **hang-en-sluitwerk** /hɑŋɛnslœytwɛrk/ fastenings, hinges and locks

de **hanger** /hɑŋər/ (pl: -s) **1** (clothes) hanger, coat-hanger **2** pendant, pendent; pendant earring, drop earring

hangerig /hɑŋərəx/ (adj) listless

het **hangijzer** /hɑŋɛizər/ (pl: -s) pot-hook: een **heet** ~ a controversial issue, hot potato

de **hangjongere** /hɑŋjɔŋərə/ (pl: -n) loitering teen; mallrat

de **hangjongeren** (pl) [roughly] mall rats

de **hangkast** /hɑŋkɑst/ (pl: -en) wardrobe

de **hanglamp** /hɑŋlɑmp/ (pl: -en) hanging lamp

de **hangmap** /hɑŋmɑp/ (pl: -pen) suspension file

de **hangmat** /hɑŋmɑt/ (pl: -ten) hammock

de **hangplant** /hɑŋplɑnt/ (pl: -en) hanging plant

de **hangplek** /hɑŋplɛk/ hangout

het **hangslot** /hɑŋslɔt/ (pl: -en) padlock
hannesen /hɑnəsə(n)/ (hanneste, heeft ge-
hannest) [inform] mess about (or: around):
wat zit je toch te ~ you are making a mess of it
de **hansworst** /hɑnswɔrst/ (pl: -en) buffoon,
clown
hanteerbaar /hɑnterbar/ (adj) manageable
hanteren /hɑnterə(n)/ (hanteerde, heeft
gehanteerd) **1** handle, operate, employ;
wield: *de botte bijl ~* take heavy-handed,
crude measures; *moeilijk te ~* unwieldy, difficult (or: awkward) to handle, unmanageable
2 manage, manoeuvre
de **Hanzestad** /hɑnzəstɑt/ Hanseatic town
de **hap** /hɑp/ (pl: -pen) **1** bite; peck: *in één ~ was
het op* it was gone in one (or: in a single) bite
2 bite, mouthful: *een ~ nemen* take a bite
(or: mouthful)
haperen /hapərə(n)/ (haperde, heeft geha-
perd) **1** stick, get stuck: *de conversatie haperde* the conversation flagged **2** have sth.
wrong (or: the matter) with o.s.
het **hapje** /hɑpjə/ (pl: -s) **1** bite, mouthful: *wil je
ook een ~ mee-eten?* would you like to join
us (for a bite, meal)? **2** snack, bite to eat,
hors d'oeuvre, appetizer: *voor (lekkere) ~s
zorgen* serve refreshments
hapklaar /hɑpklar/ (adj) ready-to-eat
happen /hɑpə(n)/ (hapte, heeft gehapt)
1 bite (at), snap (at): *naar lucht ~* gasp for air
2 bite (into), take a bite (out of)
de **happening** /hɛpənɪŋ/ (pl: -s) happening
happig /hɑpəχ/ (adj) (+ op) keen (on), eager
(for)
het **happy end** /hɛpiɛnt/ happy ending
het **harakiri** /harakiri/ hara-kiri
haram /haram/ (adj) haram
¹**hard** /hɑrt/ (adj) **1** hard; firm; solid: *~e bewijzen* firm proof, hard evidence; *~ worden*
harden, become hard; set **2** stiff, rigid: *~e
schijf* hard disk **3** hard; loud: *~e muziek* loud
music; *~e wind* strong (or: stiff) wind **4** hard;
harsh: *een ~e politiek* a tough policy; *een ~
vonnis* a severe sentence **5** harsh; garish: *~e
trekken* harsh features
²**hard** /hɑrt/ (adv) **1** hard: *~ lachen* laugh
heartily; *een band ~ oppompen* pump a tyre
up hard; *hij ging er nogal ~ tegenaan* he went
at it rather hard; *zijn rust ~ nodig hebben* be
badly in need of a rest; *dit onderdeel is ~ aan
vervanging toe* this part is in urgent need of
replacement **2** loudly: *niet zo ~ praten!* keep
your voice down!; *de tv ~er zetten* turn up
the TV **3** fast, quickly: *~ achteruitgaan* deteriorate rapidly (or: fast); *te ~ rijden* drive (or:
ride) too fast, speed **4** hard, harshly: *iem. ~
aanpakken* be hard on s.o.
het **hardboard** /hɑrdbɔːrd/ hardboard
de **hardcore** /hɑːrtkɔːr/ hardcore
de **harddisk** /hɑrdɪsk/ (pl: -s) hard disk

de **harddiskrecorder** /hɑːrdɪskrikɔːrdər/ hard
disk recorder
¹**harden** /hɑrdə(n)/ (hardde, is gehard) hard-
en, become hard; dry; set
²**harden** /hɑrdə(n)/ (hardde, heeft gehard)
1 harden, temper **2** toughen (up): *hij is gehard door weer en wind* he has been hardened (or: seasoned) by wind and weather
3 bear, stand; take; stick: *deze hitte is niet te ~*
this heat is unbearable
hardgekookt /hɑrtχəkokt/ (adj) hard-
boiled
hardhandig /hɑrthɑndəχ/ (adj, adv) hard-
handed, rough; heavy-handed: *~ optreden*
take hard-handed (or: harsh, drastic) action,
use strong-arm tactics
de **hardheid** /hɑrthɛit/ hardness; toughness;
harshness
hardhorend /hɑrthorənt/ (adj) hard of
hearing: *~ zijn* be hard of hearing
het **hardhout** /hɑrthaut/ hardwood
hardleers /hɑrtlers/ (adj) **1** dense, slow,
thick(-skulled) **2** headstrong, stubborn
de **hardliner** /hɑːrdlɑjnər/ (pl: -s) hard liner
hardlopen /hɑrtlopə(n)/ (liep hard, heeft
hardgelopen) run, race, run a race
de **hardloper** /hɑrtlopər/ (pl: -s) runner
hardmaken /hɑrtmakə(n)/ (maakte hard,
heeft gehard) prove: *kun je dat ook ~?* have
you got any proof for that?, can you prove
that (with figures)?
hardnekkig /hɑrtnɛkəχ/ (adj, adv) stubborn, obstinate; persistent: *een ~ gerucht* a
persistent rumour
de **hardnekkigheid** /hɑrtnɛkəχhɛit/ obstinacy, stubbornness
hardop /hɑrtɔp/ (adv) aloud, out loud: *~
denken* (or: *lachen*) think/laugh aloud (or:
out loud); *iets ~ zeggen* say sth. out loud
hardrijden /hɑrtrɛidə(n)/ (reed hard, heeft
hardgereden) [sport] race; speed-skate
de **hardrijder** /hɑrtrɛidər/ (pl: -s) racer;
speedskater; racing cyclist
hardvochtig /hɑrtfɔχtəχ/ (adj, adv) hard(-
hearted); unfeeling
de **hardware** /hɑːrdwɛːr/ hardware
de **harem** /harəm/ (pl: -s) harem
harentwil /harəntwɪl/: *om ~* for her sake
harig /harəχ/ (adj) hairy; furry
de **haring** /harɪŋ/ (pl: -en) **1** herring; kipper:
een school ~en a shoal of herring; *nieuwe*
(or: *zure*) *~* new (or: pickled) herring; *als
~(en) in een ton* (packed) like sardines **2** tent
peg, tent stake
de **hark** /hɑrk/ (pl: -en) rake
harken /hɑrkə(n)/ (harkte, heeft geharkt)
rake (up, together)
de **harlekijn** /harləkɛin/ (pl: -s) **1** harlequin
2 jumping jack **3** clown
de **harmonica** /hɑrmonika/ (pl: -'s) **1** accordion **2** harmonica, mouth-organ

de **harmonicawand** /hɑrmo̱nikawɑnt/ (pl: -en) folding partition

de **harmonie** /hɑrmoni̱/ (pl: -ën, -s) **1** harmony, concord, agreement: *in* (or: *niet in*) *~ zijn met* be in (or: out of) harmony with **2** (brass)band

harmonieus /hɑrmonijø̱s/ (adj, adv) harmonious, melodious

harmonisch /hɑrmo̱nis/ (adj, adv) **1** harmonic: *een ~ geheel vormen* blend (in), go well (together) **2** harmonious

harmoniseren /hɑrmonize̱rə(n)/ (harmoniseerde, heeft geharmoniseerd) harmonize: *de belastingen in Europa ~* harmonize taxes within Europe

het **harnas** /hɑ̱rnɑs/ (pl: -sen) (suit of) armour: *in het ~ sterven* die in harness; *iem. tegen zich in het ~ jagen* put s.o.'s back up

de **harp** /hɑrp/ (pl: -en) harp

de **harpist** /hɑrpi̱st/ (pl: -en) harpist, harp player

de **harpoen** /hɑrpu̱n/ (pl: -en) harpoon

harpoeneren /hɑrpune̱rə(n)/ (harpoeneerde, heeft geharpoeneerd) harpoon

het/de **hars** /hɑrs/ (pl: -en) resin; rosin

de **harses** /hɑ̱rsəs/ (pl) [inform] nut, conk, skull: *hou je ~!* shut your trap!

het **hart** /hɑrt/ (pl: -en) **1** heart: *uit de grond van zijn ~* from the bottom of one's heart; *hij is een jager in ~ en nieren* he is a hunter in heart and soul; *met ~ en ziel* with all one's heart; *met een gerust ~* with an easy mind; *een zwak ~ hebben* have a weak heart; *iemands ~ breken* break s.o.'s heart; *het ~ op de juiste plaats hebben* have one's heart in the right place; *ik hield mijn ~ vast* my heart missed a beat; *je kunt je ~ ophalen* you can enjoy it to your heart's content; *zijn ~ uitstorten* pour out (or: unburden, open) one's heart (to s.o.); *(diep) in zijn ~ hield hij nog steeds van haar* in his heart (of hearts) he still loved her; *waar het ~ van vol is, loopt de mond van over* what the heart thinks, the tongue speaks **2** heart, nerve: *heb het ~ eens!* don't you dare!, just you try it!; *het ~ zonk hem in de schoenen* he lost heart **3** heart, centre || *iets niet over zijn ~ kunnen verkrijgen* not find it in one's heart to do sth.; *van ~e gefeliciteerd* my warmest congratulations

de **hartaanval** /hɑ̱rtanvɑl/ (pl: -len) heart attack

de **hartchirurgie** /hɑ̱rtʃirʏrɣi/ cardiac (or: heart) surgery

¹**hartelijk** /hɑ̱rtələk/ (adj) **1** hearty, warm: *~ dank voor …* many thanks for …; *~e groeten aan je vrouw* kind regards to your wife **2** warm-hearted, open-hearted, cordial: *~ tegen iem. zijn* be friendly towards s.o.

²**hartelijk** /hɑ̱rtələk/ (adv) heartily, warmly: *~ bedankt voor …* thank you very much for …; *~ gefeliciteerd* sincere congratulations

de **hartelijkheid** /hɑ̱rtələkhɛit/ (pl: -heden) **1** cordiality, warm-heartedness, open-heartedness **2** cordiality, hospitality

de **harten** /hɑ̱rtə(n)/ (pl: -) hearts: *hartenboer* jack (or: knave) of hearts

de **hartenlust** /hɑ̱rtə(n)lʏst/: *naar ~* to one's heart's content

de **hart- en vaatziekten** /hɑrtɛnva̱tsiktə(n)/ (pl) cardiovascular diseases

de **hartenwens** /hɑ̱rtə(n)wɛns/ (pl: -en) heart's desire, fondest wish

hartgrondig /hɑrtxro̱ndəx/ (adj) wholehearted, hearty

hartig /hɑ̱rtəx/ (adj, adv) **1** tasty; well-seasoned; hearty **2** salt(y)

het **hartinfarct** /hɑ̱rtɪnfɑrkt/ (pl: -en) coronary (thrombosis)

het **hartje** /hɑ̱rcə/ (pl: -s) **1** (little) heart: *hij heeft een grote mond, maar een klein ~* he's not all what he makes out to be **2** heart, centre: *~ winter* the dead of winter; *~ zomer* the height of summer

de **hartkamer** /hɑ̱rtkamər/ (pl: -s) ventricle (of the heart)

de **hartklacht** /hɑ̱rtklɑxt/ (pl: -en) heart complaint (or: condition)

de **hartklep** /hɑ̱rtklɛp/ (pl: -pen) heart valve, valve (of the heart)

de **hartklopping** /hɑ̱rtklɔpɪŋ/ (pl: -en) palpitation (of the heart)

de **hartkwaal** /hɑ̱rtkwal/ (pl: -kwalen) heart condition

de **hartpatiënt** /hɑ̱rtpaʃɛnt/ (pl: -en) cardiac patient

de **hartritmestoornis** /hɑrtrɪtməstornɪs/ (pl: -sen) cardiac arrhythmia

de **hartslag** /hɑ̱rtslɑx/ (pl: -en) heartbeat, pulse; heart rate

hartstikke /hɑ̱rtstɪkə/ (adv) awfully, terribly; completely: *~ gek* stark staring mad; crazy; *~ goed* fantastic, terrific, smashing; *~ bedankt!* thanks awfully (or: ever so much)

de **hartstilstand** /hɑ̱rtstɪlstɑnt/ (pl: -en) cardiac arrest

de **hartstocht** /hɑ̱rtstɔxt/ (pl: -en) passion; emotion [esp pl]

¹**hartstochtelijk** /hɑrtsto̱xtələk/ (adj) **1** passionate, emotional; excitable **2** passionate, ardent, fervent: *hij is een ~ skiër* he is an ardent skier

²**hartstochtelijk** /hɑrtsto̱xtələk/ (adv) passionately, ardently

de **hartstreek** /hɑ̱rtstrek/ heart (or: cardiac) region

de **hartverlamming** /hɑ̱rtfərlɑmɪŋ/ heart failure

hartverscheurend /hɑrtfərsxø̱rənt/ (adj, adv) heartbreaking, heart-rending

hartverwarmend /hɑrtfərwɑ̱rmənt/ (adj, adv) heart-warming

de **hashtag** /hɛ̱ʃtɛk/ (pl: -s) hashtag

de **hasj** /hɑʃ/ hash
de **haspel** /hɑspəl/ (pl: -s) reel; spool
hatelijk /haːtələk/ (adj, adv) nasty, spiteful; snide
de **hatelijkheid** /haːtələkhɛit/ (pl: -heden) nasty remark, snide remark, gibe, (nasty) crack
de **hatemail** /hɛtmeːl/ hatemail
haten /haːtə(n)/ (haatte, heeft gehaat) hate
hatsjie /hɑtʃi/ (int) atishoo
de **hattrick** /hɛtrɪk/ (pl: -s) hat trick: *een zuivere* ~ *scoren* score a pure hat trick
hautain /hoːtɛ̃/ (adj, adv) haughty, arrogant
de **have** /haːvə/: *levende* ~ livestock; ~ *en goed verliezen* lose everything
haveloos /haːvəloːs/ (adj) **1** shabby, scruffy; delapidated: *wat ziet hij er* ~ *uit* how scruffy he looks **2** shabby, beggarly; down-and-out
de **haven** /haːvə(n)/ (pl: -s) harbour; port; [fig] (safe) haven: [fig] *een veilige* ~ *vinden* find refuge; *een* ~ *binnenlopen (aandoen)* put into a port
de **havenarbeider** /haːvə(n)ɑrbɛidər/ (pl: -s) dockworker
het **havenhoofd** /haːvə(n)hoft/ (pl: -en) mole, jetty
de **havenmeester** /haːvəmeːstər/ (pl: -s) harbour master; [Am] port warden
de **havenstad** /haːvə(n)stɑt/ (pl: -steden) port; seaport (town)
de **haver** /haːvər/ oat; oats
de **haverklap** /haːvərklɑp/: *om de* ~ **a)** every other minute, continually; **b)** at the drop of a hat
de **havermout** /haːvərmɑut/ **1** rolled oats, oatmeal **2** (oatmeal) porridge
de **havik** /haːvɪk/ (pl: -en) **1** goshawk **2** [pol] hawk
de **haviksneus** /haːvɪksnøs/ (pl: -neuzen) hooked nose
de **havo** /haːvo/ (pl: -'s) *hoger algemeen voortgezet onderwijs* school for higher general secondary education
de **hazelaar** /haːzəlaːr/ (pl: -s) hazel
de **hazelnoot** /haːzəlnoːt/ **1** hazel **2** hazelnut
de **hazenlip** /haːzə(n)lɪp/ (pl: -pen) harelip
het **hazenpad** /haːzə(n)pɑt/ (pl: -en): *het* ~ *kiezen* take to one's heels
de **hazenpeper** /haːzə(n)pepər/ [roughly] jugged hare
het **hazenslaapje** /haːzə(n)slaːpjə/ power nap
de **hazewind** /haːzəwɪnt/ (pl: -en) greyhound
het/de **hbo** /habeːo/ *hoger beroepsonderwijs* (school for) higher vocational education
hé /he/ (int) hey!, hello; oh (really)?
hè /hɛ/ (int) oh (dear); ah: *hè, dat doet zeer!* oh (or: ouch), that hurts!; *hè, blij dat ik zit!* phew, glad I can take the weight off my feet! ‖ *lekker weertje, hè?* nice day, isn't it?
headbangen /hɛːdbɛŋə(n)/ (headbangde, heeft geheadbangd) headbanging
de **headhunter** /hɛːthʏntər/ (pl: -s) headhunter
de **headset** /hɛːtsɛt/ headset
het/de **heao** /heaːo/ (pl: -'s) *hoger economisch en administratief onderwijs* school (institute) for business administration and economics
heavy /hɛvi/ (adj) [inform] heavy
het **hebbeding** /hɛbədɪŋ/ (pl: -en) thingummy, gadget
de **hebbelijkheid** /hɛbələkhɛit/ (pl: -heden) habit: *de* ~ *hebben om* have the (nasty (or: annoying)) habit of …
¹**hebben** /hɛbə(n)/ (had, heeft gehad) **1** have (got), own: *geduld* ~ be patient; *iets moeten* ~ need sth.; *iets bij zich* ~ be carrying sth., have sth. with (or: on) one **2** have: *die pantoffels heb ik van mijn vrouw* I got those slippers from my wife; *van wie heb je dat?* who told (or: gave) you that? **3** (+ aan) be of use (to): *je weet niet wat je aan hem hebt* you never know where you are with him ‖ *verdriet* ~ be sad; *wat heb je?* what's the matter (or: wrong) with you?; *wat heb je toch?* what's come over you?; *het koud* (or: *warm*) ~ be cold (or: hot); *hij heeft iets tegen mij* he has a grudge against me; *ik heb nooit Spaans gehad* I've never learned Spanish; *ik moet er niets van* ~ I want nothing to do with it; *dat heb je ervan* that's what you get; *daar heb je het al* I told you so; *zo wil ik het* ~ that's how I want it; *iets gedaan willen* ~ want (to see) sth. done; *ik weet niet waar je het over hebt* I don't know what you're talking about; *daar heb ik het straks nog over* I'll come (back) to that later on (or: in a moment); *nu we het daar toch over* ~ now that you mention it …
²**hebben** /hɛbə(n)/ (aux vb, had) have: *had ik dat maar geweten* if (only) I had known (that); *had dat maar gezegd* if only you'd told me (that); *ik heb met Marco B. op school gezeten* I was at school with Marco B.
hebberig /hɛbərəχ/ (adj) greedy
hebbes /hɛbəs/ (int) got you; gotcha!; got it
het ¹**Hebreeuws** /hebreːws/ Hebrew
²**Hebreeuws** /hebreːws/ (adj) Hebrew
de **Hebriden** /hebridə(n)/ (pl) Hebrides
de **hebzucht** /hɛpsʏχt/ greed: *uit* ~ out of greed
hebzuchtig /hɛpsʏχtəχ/ (adj) greedy, avaricious
hecht /hɛχt/ (adj, adv) solid; [fig] strong; tight; tightly-knit; close(ly)-knit: *een ~e vriendschap* a close friendship
¹**hechten** /hɛχtə(n)/ (hechtte, heeft gehecht) **1** adhere, stick **2** be attached (to), devoted (to), adhere (to): *ik hecht niet aan deze dure auto* I'm not very attached to this expensive car
²**hechten** /hɛχtə(n)/ (hechtte, heeft gehecht) **1** stitch, suture: *een wond* ~ sew up, stitch a wound **2** attach, fasten, (af)fix: *een prijskaartje aan iets* ~ put a price tag on sth. **3** at-

tach: *waarde* (or: *belang*) *aan iets* ~ attach value (*or:* importance) to sth.

zich **³hechten** /hɛxtə(n)/ (hechtte zich, heeft zich gehecht) (+ aan) become attached to, cling to: *hij hecht zich gemakkelijk **aan** mensen* he gets attached to people easily

de **hechtenis** /hɛxtənɪs/ **1** custody, detention **2** imprisonment, prison

de **hechting** /hɛxtɪŋ/ (pl: -en) stitches, suture(s): *de ~en **verwijderen*** take out the stitches

de **hechtpleister** /hɛxtplɛɪstər/ (pl: -s) adhesive plaster

de **hectare** /hɛktarə/ (pl: -n) hectare
hectisch /hɛktis/ (adj, adv) hectic

het **hectogram** /hɛktoɣrɑm/ hectogram

de **hectoliter** /hɛktolitər/ hectolitre

de **hectometer** /hɛktometər/ hectometre

het **¹heden** /hedə(n)/ present (day)
²heden /hedə(n)/ (adv) [form] today, now-(adays), at present: *tot op* ~ up to (*or:* till/until) now; *vanaf ~, met ingang van* ~ as from today
hedendaags /hedə(n)daxs/ (adj) contemporary, present-day: *woordenboeken voor ~ taalgebruik* dictionaries of current usage

het **hedonisme** /hedonɪsmə/ (pl: -n) hedonism
¹heel /hel/ (adj) **1** intact: *het ei was nog* ~ the egg was unbroken **2** whole, entire, all: ~ *Engeland* all England; *een ~ jaar* a whole year **3** quite a, quite some: *het is een ~ eind (weg)* it's a good way (off); *een hele tijd* quite some time
²heel /hel/ (adv) **1** very (much), really: *dat is ~ gewoon* that's quite normal; *een ~ klein beetje* a tiny bit; *dat kostte ~ wat moeite* that took a great deal of effort; *je weet het ~ goed!* you know perfectly well!; ~ *vaak* very often (*or:* frequently) **2** completely, entirely, wholly: *dat is iets ~ anders* that's a different matter altogether

het **heelal** /helɑl/ universe
heelhuids /helhœyts/ (adv) unharmed, unscathed, whole: ~ *terugkomen* return safe and sound

de **heelmeester** /helmestər/ (pl: -s) surgeon: *zachte ~s maken stinkende wonden* [roughly] desperate diseases need desperate remedies

het **heemraadschap** /hemratsxɑp/ **1** polder (*or:* dike) board **2** polder (district)
heen /hen/ (adv) **1** gone, away: ~ *en weer lopen* walk/pace up and down (*or:* back and forth) **2** on the way there, out ‖ *je kunt daar niet ~* you cannot go there; *langs elkaar ~ praten* talk at cross purposes; *je kunt niet om hem ~* you can't ignore him

het **¹heengaan** /heŋɣan/ **1** passing away **2** departure
²heengaan /heŋɣan/ (ging heen, is heengegaan) **1** depart, leave **2** pass away

het **heenkomen** /heŋkomə(n)/: *een goed ~ zoeken* seek safety in flight

de **heenreis** /henrɛis/ way there, outward journey, journey out

de **heenwedstrijd** /henwɛtstrɛɪt/ (pl: -en) [Belg] first game (*or:* match)

de **heenweg** /henwɛx/ way there, way out

de **heer** /her/ (pl: heren) **1** man **2** Mr; Sir; gentlemen: *(mijne) dames en heren!* ladies and gentlemen! **3** gentleman: *een echte* ~ a real gentleman **4** Lord: *als de Heer het wil* God (*or:* the Lord) willing **5** lord, master: *mijn oude* ~ my old man **6** [cards] king
heerlijk /herlək/ (adj, adv) **1** delicious, gorgeous **2** delightful, lovely, wonderful, splendid: *het is een ~ gevoel* it feels great

de **heerschappij** /hersxɑpɛi/ dominion, mastery, rule
heersen /hersə(n)/ (heerste, heeft geheerst) **1** rule (over); reign **2** dominate **3** be, be prevalent: *er heerst griep* there's a lot of flu about
heersend /hersənt/ (adj) ruling, prevailing: *de ~e klassen* the ruling class(es); *de ~e mode* the current fashion

de **heerser** /hersər/ (pl: -s) ruler
heerszuchtig /hersʏxtəx/ (adj) imperious, domineering
hees /hes/ (adj) hoarse: *een hese keel* a sore throat

de **heesheid** /heshɛit/ hoarseness; huskiness

de **heester** /hestər/ (pl: -s) shrub
heet /het/ (adj) **1** hot: *een hete adem* a fiery breath; *in het ~st van de strijd* in the thick (*or:* heat) of the battle **2** [fig] hot; heated; fiery **3** hot, spicy: *hete kost* spicy food **4** [inform] hot, horny
heetgebakerd /hetxəbakərt/ (adj) hot-tempered, quick-tempered

de **heethoofd** /hethoft/ (pl: -en) hot-head, hot-heated person

de **hefboom** /hɛvbom/ (pl: hefbomen) lever

de **hefbrug** /hɛvbrʏx/ (pl: -gen) **1** (vertical) lift bridge **2** (hydraulic) lift
heffen /hɛfə(n)/ (hief, heeft geheven) **1** lift, raise: *het glas* ~ raise one's glass (to), drink (to) **2** levy, impose: *belasting* ~ levy taxes (on s.o.)

de **heffing** /hɛfɪŋ/ (pl: -en) levy, charge

het **heft** /hɛft/ (pl: -en) handle; haft; hilt: *het ~ in handen hebben* be in control, command
heftig /hɛftəx/ (adj, adv) violent; fierce; furious; intense; severe; heated: ~ *protesteren* protest vigorously

de **heftruck** /hɛftryk/ (pl: -s) fork-lift truck

de **heg** /hɛx/ (pl: -gen) hedge

de **heggenschaar** /hɛɣə(n)sxar/ (pl: -scharen) garden shears, hedge trimmer

de **hei** /hɛi/ (pl: -en) **1** heath(land) **2** [bot] heather

de **heibel** /hɛibəl/ row, racket

de **heide** /hɛidə/ heath

de **heidedag** policy day

de **heiden** /hɛɪdə(n)/ (pl: -en) heathen, pagan

heidens /hɛɪdəns/ (adj, adv) **1** heathen, pagan **2** atrocious, abominable; infernal; rotten

heien /hɛɪə(n)/ (heide, heeft geheid) drive (piles)

heiig /hɛɪəx/ (adj) hazy

het **heil** /hɛɪl/ good: *ik zie er geen ~ in* I do not see the point of it || *het Leger des Heils* the Salvation Army

de **Heiland** /hɛɪlɑnt/ Saviour

de **heilbot** /hɛɪlbɔt/ (pl: -ten) halibut

heilig /hɛɪləx/ (adj) holy, sacred: *iem. ~ verklaren* canonize s.o.; *~e koe* sacred cow || *hem is niets ~* nothing is sacred to him

het **heiligdom** /hɛɪləxdɔm/ (pl: -men) sanctuary

de **heilige** /hɛɪləxə/ (pl: -n) saint

het **heiligenbeeld** /hɛɪləxə(n)belt/ (pl: -en) image of a saint, holy figure

de **heiligschennis** /hɛɪləxsxɛnɪs/ sacrilege, desecration

heilloos /hɛɪlos/ (adj, adv) fatal, disastrous

heilzaam /hɛɪlzam/ (adj) **1** curative, healing; wholesome; healthful **2** salutary, beneficial: *een heilzame werking* (or: *invloed*) *hebben* have a beneficial effect (or: influence)

heimelijk /hɛɪmələk/ (adj, adv) secret; clandestine; surreptitious; sneaking

het **heimwee** /hɛɪmwe/ homesickness: *ik kreeg ~ (naar)* I became homesick (for)

Hein /hɛɪn/: *Magere ~* the Grim Reaper

heinde /hɛɪndə/ (adv): *van ~ en verre* from far and near (or: wide)

de **heipaal** /hɛɪpal/ (pl: heipalen) pile

het **hek** /hɛk/ (pl: -ken) **1** fence; barrier **2** gate; wicket(-gate)

de **hekel** /hekəl/ hackle || *een ~ aan iem. (iets) hebben* hate s.o. (sth.)

hekelen /hekələ(n)/ (hekelde, heeft gehekeld) criticize, denounce

het **hekje** /hɛkjə/ (pl: -s) **1** small gate (or: door) **2** [comp, telecom] hash; number sign

de **hekkensluiter** /hɛkə(n)slœytər/ (pl: -s) last comer: *hij* (or: *is*) *de ~ op de ranglijst* he is last on the list, he is at the bottom of the list

de **heks** /hɛks/ (pl: -en) **1** witch **2** shrew **3** hag

de **heksenjacht** /hɛksə(n)jɑxt/ (pl: -en) witchhunt

de **heksenketel** /hɛksə(n)ketəl/ (pl: -s) bedlam, pandemonium

de **heksenkring** /hɛksə(n)krɪŋ/ (pl: -en) fairy ring

de **heksentoer** /hɛksə(n)tur/ (pl: -en) tough job, complicated job

de **hekserij** /hɛksərɛɪ/ (pl: -en) sorcery, witchcraft

het **hekwerk** /hɛkwɛrk/ (pl: -en) fencing; railings

de **¹hel** /hɛl/ hell

²hel /hɛl/ (adj, adv) vivid, bright

helaas /helas/ (adv) unfortunately: *~ kunnen wij u niet helpen* I'm afraid (or: sorry) we can't help you

de **held** /hɛlt/ (pl: -en) hero || *hij is geen ~ in rekenen* he is not much at figures

de **heldendaad** /hɛldə(n)dat/ (pl: -daden) heroic deed (or: feat), act of heroism; exploit

het **heldendicht** /hɛldə(n)dɪxt/ (pl: -en) heroic poem, epic poem, epic

de **heldendood** /hɛldə(n)dot/ heroic death: *de ~ sterven* die a hero, die a hero's death

de **heldenmoed** /hɛldəmut/ heroism: *met ~* heroically, with heroism

de **heldenrol** /hɛldə(n)rɔl/ hero's part (or: role)

helder /hɛldər/ (adj, adv) **1** clear: *een ~e lach* a ringing laugh **2** clear, bright: *~ wit* (or: *groen*) brilliant white, bright green **3** clear, lucid || *zo ~ als kristal* (or: *glas*) as clear as crystal, crystal-clear

de **helderheid** /hɛldərhɛɪt/ **1** clearness, clarity **2** brightness, vividness **3** brightness **4** clarity, lucidity

helderziend /hɛldərzint/ (adj) clairvoyant

de **helderziende** /hɛldərzində/ (pl: -n) clairvoyant: *ik ben toch geen ~* I'm not a mindreader

de **helderziendheid** /hɛldərzinthɛit/ clairvoyance, second sight

heldhaftig /hɛlthɑftəx/ (adj, adv) heroic, valiant

de **heldin** /hɛldɪn/ (pl: -nen) heroine

de **heleboel** /heləbul/ (quite) a lot, a whole lot: *een ~ mensen zouden het niet met je eens zijn* an awful lot of people wouldn't agree with you

helemaal /heləmal/ (adv) **1** completely, entirely: *ik heb het ~ alleen gedaan* I did it all by myself; *~ nat zijn* be wet through; *ben je nu ~ gek geworden?* are you completely out of your mind?; *~ niets* nothing at all; *het kan mij ~ niets schelen* I couldn't care less; *~ niet* absolutely not; *niet ~ juist* not quite correct; *~ in het begin* right at the beginning (or: start) **2** right; all the way: *~ bovenaan* right at the top; *~ in het noorden* way up in the north

¹helen /helə(n)/ (heelde, is geheeld) heal: *de wond heelt langzaam* the wound is healing slowly

²helen /helə(n)/ (heelde, heeft geheeld) **1** [law] receive **2** [med] heal: *de tijd heelt alle wonden* time cures all things; time is the great healer

de **heler** /helər/ (pl: -s) receiver; [fig] fence

de **helft** /hɛlft/ (pl: -en) half: *ieder de ~ betalen* pay half each, go halves, go Dutch; *meer dan de ~* more than half; *de ~ minder* half as much (or: many); *de ~ van tien is vijf* half of ten is five; *de tweede ~ van een wedstrijd* the second half of a match

de **helikopter** /helikɔptər/ (pl: -s) helicopter; chopper

de **heling** /hɛlɪŋ/ receiving

het **helium** /helijʏm/ helium

hellen /hɛlə(n)/ (helde, heeft geheld) slope, lean (over), slant: *de muur helt naar links* the wall is leaning

het **hellenisme** /hɛlenɪsmə/ Hellenism

de **helleveeg** /hɛləvex/ (pl: -vegen) shrew, hellcat

de **helling** /hɛlɪŋ/ (pl: -en) **1** slope, incline; ramp **2** inclination

de **hell's angel** /hɛlsɛndʒəl/ Hells Angel

de **helm** /hɛlm/ (pl: -en) helmet; hard hat

het **helmgras** /hɛlmɣrɑs/ marram (grass)

help /hɛlp/ (int): *lieve* ~ oh, Lord/dear!, good heavens!, dear me!

de **helpdesk** /hɛlbdɛsk/ (pl: -s) help desk

helpen /hɛlpə(n)/ (hielp, heeft geholpen) **1** help, aid: *kun je mij aan honderd euro ~?* can you let me have a hundred euros?; *help!* help! **2** attend to: *welke specialist heeft u geholpen?* which specialist did you see? (*or:* have?); *u wordt morgen geholpen* you are having your operation tomorrow **3** help, assist: *iem. een handje ~* give (*or:* lend) s.o. a hand; *help me eraan denken, wil je?* remind me, will you? **4** help (out): *iem. aan een baan ~* get s.o. fixed up with a job **5** help, serve: *wordt u al geholpen?* are you being served? ‖ *kan ik 't ~ dat hij zich zo gedraagt?* is it my fault if he behaves like that?; *wat helpt het?* what good would it do?, what is the use?; *dat helpt tegen hoofdpijn* that's good for a headache

de **helper** /hɛlpər/ (pl: -s) helper, assistant

hels /hɛls/ (adj, adv) infernal: *een ~ karwei* a (*or:* the) devil of a job

hem /hɛm/ (pers pron) him; it: *dit boek is van ~* this book is his; *vrienden van ~* friends of his ‖ *dat is het ~ nu juist* that's just it (*or:* the point)

het **hemd** /hɛmt/ (pl: -en) **1** vest; [Am] undershirt: *iem. het ~ van zijn lijf vragen* want to know everything (from s.o.); pester s.o. (with questions); [fig] *iem. in zijn ~ zetten* make s.o. look a fool **2** shirt

de **hemdsmouw** /hɛm(t)smɑu/ (pl: -en) shirt-sleeve: *in ~en* in one's shirt-sleeves

de **hemel** /heməl/ (pl: -en) sky, heaven(s): *hij heeft er ~ en aarde om bewogen* he moved heaven and earth for it; *een heldere* (*or: blauwe, bewolkte*) ~ a clear (*or:* blue, cloudy) sky; *Onze Vader die in de ~en zijt* Our Father who (*or:* which) art in heaven; *hij was in de zevende ~* he was in seventh heaven

het **hemellichaam** /heməlɪxɑm/ (pl: -lichamen) heavenly body, celestial body

hemels /heməls/ (adj, adv) sublime, divine

hemelsblauw /heməlzblɑu/ (adj) sky-blue

hemelsbreed /heməlzbret/ (adj, adv) **1** vast, enormous **2** as the crow flies, in a straight line

hemeltergend /heməltɛrɣənt/ (adj, adv) outrageous

Hemelvaartsdag /heməlvartsdɑx/ (pl: -en) Ascension Day

de **hemofilie** /hemofili/ haemophilia

de ¹**hen** /hɛn/ (pl: -nen) hen

²**hen** /hɛn/ (pers pron) them: *hij gaf het ~* he gave it to them; *dit boek is van* ~ this book is theirs; *vrienden van* ~ friends of theirs

het/de **hendel** /hɛndəl/ (pl: -s) handle, lever

de **hengel** /hɛŋəl/ (pl: -s) fishing rod

de **hengelaar** /hɛŋəlar/ (pl: -s) angler

hengelen /hɛŋələ(n)/ (hengelde, heeft gehengeld) angle, fish

het **hengsel** /hɛŋsəl/ (pl: -s) **1** handle **2** hinge

de **hengst** /hɛŋst/ (pl: -en) stallion; stud (horse)

de **hennep** /hɛnəp/ hemp; cannabis

de **hens** /hɛns/ (pl): *alle ~ aan dek!* all hands on deck!

de **hepatitis** /hepatitɪs/ hepatitis

her /hɛr/ (adv) hither, here

de **heraldiek** /heraldik/ heraldry

het **herbarium** /hɛrbarijʏm/ (pl: -s, herbaria) herbarium

herbebossen /hɛrbəbɔsə(n)/ (herbeboste, heeft herbebost) reafforest; [esp Am] reforest

herbenoemen /hɛrbənumə(n)/ (herbenoemde, heeft herbenoemd) reappoint

de **herberg** /hɛrbɛrx/ (pl: -en) inn, tavern

herbergen /hɛrbɛrɣə(n)/ (herbergde, heeft geherbergd) accommodate, house; harbour: *de zaal kan 2000 mensen ~* the hall seats 2000 people

de **herbergier** /hɛrbɛryir/ (pl: -s) innkeeper, publican, victualler

herbewapenen /hɛrbəwapənə(n)/ (herbewapende, heeft herbewapend) rearm, remilitarize

de **herbivoor** /hɛrbivor/ (pl: herbivoren) herbivore

herboren /hɛrborə(n)/ (adj) reborn, born again

de **herbouw** /hɛrbɑu/ rebuilding, reconstruction

herbouwen /hɛrbɑuwə(n)/ (herbouwde, heeft herbouwd) rebuild, reconstruct

herdenken /hɛrdɛnkə(n)/ (herdacht, heeft herdacht) commemorate

de **herdenking** /hɛrdɛŋkɪŋ/ (pl: -en) commemoration

de **herder** /hɛrdər/ (pl: -s) **1** cowherd; shepherd **2** pastor

de **herdershond** /hɛrdərshɔnt/ (pl: -en) sheepdog; Alsatian; [Am] German shepherd (dog)

de **herdruk** /hɛrdrʏk/ (pl: -ken) (new) edition; reprint

herdrukken /hɛrdrʏkə(n)/ (herdrukte, heeft herdrukt) reprint

de **heremiet** /herəmit/ (pl: -en) hermit

het **herenakkoord** /herə(n)ɑkort/ (pl: -en) gentleman's agreement het **herendubbel** /herə(n)dỵbəl/ men's doubles

het **herenenkelspel** /herə(n)ɛŋkəlspɛl/ men's singles

de **herenfiets** /hɛrə(n)fits/ (pl: -en) men's bike (*or:* bicycle)

het **herenhuis** /hɛrə(n)hœys/ (pl: -huizen) mansion, (imposing) town house, (desirable) residence

herenigen /hɛrɛnəɣə(n)/ (herenigde, heeft herenigd) reunite; reunify

de **hereniging** /hɛrɛnəɣɪŋ/ (pl: -en) reunification, reunion

de **herenkapper** /hɛrə(n)kɑpər/ (pl: -s) men's hairdresser's

de **herenkleding** /hɛrə(n)kledɪŋ/ menswear, men's clothes (*or:* clothing)

het **herexamen** /hɛrɛksamə(n)/ (pl: -s) re-examination, resit

de **herfst** /hɛrfst/ autumn; [Am] fall: *in de ~* in (the) autumn, in the fall

de **herfstkleur** /hɛrfstklør/ (pl: -en) autumn(al) colour; [Am] fall coulour

de **herfstvakantie** /hɛrfstfakɑnsi/ (pl: -s) autumn half-term (holiday); [Am] fall break, mid-term break

het **hergebruik** /hɛrɣəbrœyk/ **1** reuse **2** recycling

hergebruiken /hɛrɣəbrœykə(n)/ (hergebruikte, heeft hergebruikt) reuse; recycle

hergroeperen /hɛrɣruperə(n)/ (hergroepeerde, heeft gehergroepeerd) regroup, reform

herhaald /hɛrhalt/ (adj) repeated: *~e pogingen doen* make repeated attempts

herhaaldelijk /hɛrhaldələk/ (adv) repeatedly: *dat komt ~ voor* that happens time and again

[1]**herhalen** /hɛrhalə(n)/ (herhaalde, heeft herhaald) repeat, redo; revise; [Am] review: *iets in het kort ~* summarize sth.

zich [2]**herhalen** /hɛrhalə(n)/ (herhaalde zich, heeft zich herhaald) repeat o.s.; recur

de **herhaling** /hɛrhalɪŋ/ (pl: -en) **1** recurrence, repetition; replay; repeat; rerun: *voor ~ vatbaar zijn* bear repetition (*or:* repeating) **2** repetition; revision; [Am] review: *in ~en vervallen* repeat o.s.

de **herhalingscursus** /hɛrhalɪŋskỵrzʏs/ refresher course

het **herhalingsrecept** /hɛrhalɪŋsrəsɛpt/ (pl: -en) repeat prescription

het **herhalingsteken** /hɛrhalɪŋstekə(n)/ (pl: -s) repeat (mark)

herindelen /hɛrɪndelə(n)/ (herindeelde, heeft geherindeeld) regroup

de **herindeling** /hɛrɪndelɪŋ/ (pl: -en) redivision, regrouping

[1]**herinneren** /hɛrɪnərə(n)/ (herinnerde, heeft herinnerd) remind, recall: *die geur herinnerde mij aan mijn jeugd* that smell reminded me of my youth; *herinner mij eraan dat ...* remind me that ... (*or:* to ...)

zich [2]**herinneren** /hɛrɪnərə(n)/ (herinnerde zich, heeft zich herinnerd) remember, recall: *kun je je die Ier nog ~?* do you remember that Irishman?; *als ik (het) me goed herinner* if I remember correctly (*or:* rightly); *zich iets vaag ~* have a vague recollection of sth.; *voor zover ik mij herinner* as far as I can remember

de **herinnering** /hɛrɪnərɪŋ/ (pl: -en) **1** recollection, remembrance: *iets in ~ brengen* recall sth.; *in ~ roepen* bring (*or:* call) to mind **2** memory: *iets in zijn ~ voor zich zien* see sth. before one **3** memory, reminiscence: *ter ~ aan* in memory of **4** souvenir, reminder || *een tweede ~ van de bibliotheek* a second reminder from the library

herintreden /hɛrɪntredə(n)/ (trad herin, is heringetreden) return to work || *een ~de vrouw* a (woman) returner

de **herkansing** /hɛrkɑnsɪŋ/ (pl: -en) repêchage; extra heat

herkauwen /hɛrkɑuwə(n)/ (herkauwde, heeft herkauwd) ruminate

de **herkauwer** /hɛrkɑuwər/ (pl: -s) ruminant

herkenbaar /hɛrkɛmbar/ (adj) recognizable: *een herkenbare situatie* a familiar situation

herkennen /hɛrkɛnə(n)/ (herkende, heeft herkend) recognize, identify, spot: *ik herkende hem aan zijn manier van lopen* I recognized him by his walk; *iem. ~ als de dader* identify s.o. as the culprit

de **herkenning** /hɛrkɛnɪŋ/ (pl: -en) recognition, identification

de **herkenningsmelodie** /hɛrkɛnɪŋsmelodi/ (pl: -ën) signature tune, theme song

het **herkenningsteken** /hɛrkɛnɪŋstekə(n)/ (pl: -s) distinguishing (*or:* identifying) mark

de **herkeuring** /hɛrkørɪŋ/ (pl: -en) re-examination, reinspection

herkiesbaar /hɛrkizbar/ (adj) eligible for re-election

herkiezen /hɛrkizə(n)/ (herkoos, heeft herkozen) re-elect

de **herkomst** /hɛrkɔmst/ (pl: -en) origin, source: *het land van ~* the country of origin

herleidbaar /hɛrlɛidbar/ (adj) reducible (to): *die breuk is niet ~* that fraction is irreducible

herleiden /hɛrlɛidə(n)/ (herleidde, heeft herleid) reduce (to), convert (into): *een breuk ~* reduce (to) a fraction

herleven /hɛrlevə(n)/ (herleefde, is herleefd) revive: *~d fascisme* resurgent fascism

herlezen /hɛrlezə(n)/ (herlas, heeft herlezen) reread

de **hermafrodiet** /hɛrmafrodit/ (pl: -en) hermaphrodite

de [1]**hermelijn** /hɛrmələin/ (pl: -en) [animal] ermine

het ²**hermelijn** /hɛrməlɛin/ [fur] ermine
hermetisch /hɛrmetis/ (adj, adv) hermetic:
~ *gesloten* hermetically sealed
hernemen /hɛrnemə(n)/ (hernam, heeft
hernomen) resume, regain
de **hernia** /hɛrnija/ (pl: -'s) slipped disc
hernieuwen /hɛrniwə(n)/ (hernieuwde,
heeft hernieuwd) renew: *met hernieuwde*
kracht with renewed strength
de **heroïne** /herowinə/ heroin
heroïsch /herowis/ (adj, adv) heroic
herontdekken /hɛrɔndɛkə(n)/ (herontdek-
te, heeft herontdekt) rediscover
heropenen /hɛropənə(n)/ (heropende,
heeft heropend) reopen
de **heropvoeding** /hɛrɔpfudɪŋ/ re-education
heroriënteren /hɛrorijɛnterə(n)/ (her-
oriënteerde, heeft geheroriënteerd) reori-
ent(ate)
heroveren /hɛrovərə(n)/ (heroverde, heeft
heroverd) recapture; recover; retake; regain:
*hij wilde zijn oude **plaats** ~* he wanted to regain his old seat (*or:* place)
de **herovering** /hɛrovərɪŋ/ recapture
heroverwegen /hɛrovərweɣə(n)/ (her-
overwoog, heeft heroverwogen) reconsider,
rethink
de **herpes** /hɛrpɛs/ herpes
de **herrie** /hɛri/ **1** noise, din, racket: *maak niet*
zo'n ~ don't make such a racket **2** bustle;
commotion; turmoil; fuss: *~ schoppen* make
trouble
de **herriemaker** /hɛrimakər/ (pl: -s) noisy person
de **herrieschopper** /hɛrisχɔpər/ (pl: -s) troublemaker
herrijzen /hɛrɛizə(n)/ (herrees, is herrezen)
rise again: *hij is als **uit** de dood herrezen* it is as
if he has come back from the dead
de **herrijzenis** /hɛrɛizənɪs/ resurrection
herroepen /hɛrupə(n)/ (herriep, heeft herroepen) revoke; repeal; retract; reverse
herscheppen /hɛrsχɛpə(n)/ (herschiep,
heeft herschapen) transform, convert
herscholen /hɛrsχolə(n)/ (herschoolde,
heeft herschoold) retrain
herschrijven /hɛrsχrɛivə(n)/ (herschreef,
heeft herschreven) rewrite
de **hersenbloeding** /hɛrsə(n)bludɪŋ/ (pl: -en)
cerebral haemorrhage
de **hersenen** /hɛrsənə(n)/ (pl) brain
de **hersenhelft** /hɛrsə(n)hɛlft/ (pl: -en) (cerebral) hemisphere, half of the brain
het **herseninfarct** /hɛrsə(n)ɪnfɑrkt/ (pl: -en) cerebral infarction
het **hersenletsel** /hɛrsə(n)lɛtsəl/ brain damage
de **hersens** /hɛrsəns/ (pl) **1** brain(s): *een goed*
stel ~ hebben have a good head on one's
shoulders; *hoe haal je het in je ~!* have you
gone off your rocker? **2** skull: *iem. de ~ in-*
slaan beat s.o.'s brains out

de **hersenschim** /hɛrsə(n)sχɪm/ (pl: -men)
chim(a)era: *~men najagen* run after (*or:*
chase) a shadow
de **hersenschudding** /hɛrsə(n)sχʏdɪŋ/ (pl:
-en) concussion
de **hersenspoeling** /hɛrsə(n)spulɪŋ/ (pl: -en)
brainwashing
de **hersenvliesontsteking** /hɛrsə(n)vlisɔnt-
stekɪŋ/ (pl: -en) meningitis
herstarten /hɛrstɑrtə(n)/ (herstartte, heeft
herstart) start again, restart; reboot
het **herstel** /hɛrstɛl/ **1** repair, mending; rectification; correction **2** recovery; convalescence;
recuperation: *het ~ van de **economie*** the recovery of the economy; *voor ~ van zijn **ge-***
zondheid to recuperate, to convalesce **3** restoration
herstelbaar /hɛrstɛlbar/ (adj) reparable
¹**herstellen** /hɛrstɛlə(n)/ (herstelde, is hersteld) recover, recuperate: *snel (or: goed) ~*
van een ziekte recover quickly (*or:* well) from
an illness
²**herstellen** /hɛrstɛlə(n)/ (herstelde, heeft
hersteld) **1** repair, mend; restore **2** restore;
re-establish: *de rust ~* restore quiet; *een ge-*
*bruik **in** ere ~* re-establish a custom **3** right;
repair; rectify; correct: *een **onrecht** ~* right a
wrong; *de heer Blaak, herstel: Braak* Mr Blaak,
correction: Braak
de **herstelwerkzaamheden** /hɛrstɛlwɛrk-
samhedə(n)/ (pl) repairs
herstructureren /hɛrstrʏktyrerə(n)/ (her-
structureerde, heeft geherstructureerd) restructure, remodel, reorganize
de **herstructurering** /hɛrstrʏktyrerɪŋ/ restructuring, reorganization
het **hert** /hɛrt/ (pl: -en) deer; red deer
de **hertenkamp** /hɛrtə(n)kɑmp/ (pl: -en) deer
park, deer forest
de **hertog** /hɛrtɔχ/ (pl: -en) duke
het **hertogdom** /hɛrtɔχdɔm/ (pl: -men) duchy,
dukedom
de **hertogin** /hɛrtoɣɪn/ (pl: -nen) duchess
hertrouwen /hɛrtrɑuwə(n)/ (hertrouwde,
is hertrouwd) remarry, marry again
hervatten /hɛrvɑtə(n)/ (hervatte, heeft
hervat) resume, continue, restart: *onderhan-*
delingen ~ resume (*or:* reopen) negotiations;
het spel ~ resume (*or:* continue) the game;
het werk ~ return to work, go back to work
de **herverdeling** /hɛrvərdelɪŋ/ (pl: -en) redistribution, reorganization, reshuffle
de **herverkaveling** /hɛrvərkavəlɪŋ/ realloca-
tion (of land)
herverzekeren /hɛrvərzekərə(n)/ (herver-
zekerde, heeft herverzekerd) reinsure
hervormd /hɛrvɔrmt/ (adj) **1** reformed
2 [rel] Reformed; Protestant [as opposed to
Catholicism]: *de ~e kerk* the Reformed
Church
hervormen /hɛrvɔrmə(n)/ (hervormde,

heeft hervormd) reform

de **hervormer** /hɛrvɔrmər/ (pl: -s) reformer

de **hervorming** /hɛrvɔrmɪŋ/ (pl: -en) **1** reformation **2** reform

herwaarderen /hɛrwardərə(n)/ (herwaardeerde, heeft geherwaardeerd) revalue; [fig] reassess

de **herwaardering** /hɛrwardərɪŋ/ revaluation, reassessment

herwinnen /hɛrwɪnə(n)/ (herwon, heeft herwonnen) recover, regain

herzien /hɛrzin/ (herzag, heeft herzien) revise: *een nieuwe, ~e* **uitgave** a new, revised edition ‖ *een* **beslissing** ~ reconsider a decision

de **herziening** /hɛrzinɪŋ/ (pl: -en) revision, review: *een ~ van de* **grondwet** an amendment to the constitution

de **hes** /hɛs/ (pl: -sen) smock, blouse

de **hesp** /hɛsp/ (pl: -en) [Belg] ham

¹het /ət/ (pron) it: *ik* **denk** (or: *hoop*) ~ I think (or: hope) so; *wie* **is** ~? **ben** *jij* ~? ja, *ik* **ben** ~ who is it? is that you? yes, it is me; *zij* **waren** ~ *die ...* it were they who ...; *als jij* ~ **zegt** if you say so; ~ *kind heeft honger; geef* ~ *een boterham* the child is hungry; give him (or: her) a sandwich; *de machine* **doet** ~ the machine works; *hoe* **gaat** ~? ~ **gaat** how are you? I'm all right (or: O.K.); *wat* **geeft** ~? *wat* **zou** ~? what does it matter? who cares?; ~ **regent** it is raining

²het /ət/ (art) the: *in* ~ **zwart** *gekleed* dressed in black; *Nederland is* ~ **land** *van de tulpen* Holland is the country for tulips; *die vind ik* ~ **leukst** that's the one I like best; *zij was er* ~ **eerst** she was there first

¹heten /hetə(n)/ (heette, heeft geheten) be called (or: named): *een jongen, David geheten* a boy by the name of David; *het* **boek** *heet ...* the book is called ...; *hoe* **heet** *dat?, hoe heet dat in het Arabisch?* what is that called?, what is that in Arabic? (or: the Arabic for that?)

²heten /hetə(n)/ (heette, heeft geheten) bid: *ik heet u* **welkom** I bid you welcome

de **heterdaad** /hetərdat/: *iem.* **op** ~ *betrappen* catch s.o. in the act, catch s.o. red-handed

de **¹hetero** /hetəro/ (pl: -'s) hetero

²hetero /hetəro/ (adj) hetero, straight

heterogeen /hetəroɣen/ (adj) heterogeneous

de **¹heteroseksueel** /hetərosɛksywel/ (pl: -seksuelen) heterosexual

²heteroseksueel /hetərosɛksywel/ (adj) heterosexual

hetgeen /ətɣen/ (pron) **1** that which, what: *ik blijf bij* ~ *ik gezegd heb* I stand by what I said **2** which: *hij kon niet komen,* ~ *hij betreurde* he could not come, which he regretted

de **hetze** /hɛtsə/ (pl: -s) witch hunt: *een ~* **voeren** *tegen* conduct a witch hunt (or: smear campaign) against

hetzelfde /ətsɛlvdə/ (dem pron) the same: *wie zou niet ~* **doen?** who wouldn't (do the same)?; *het* **is (blijft)** *mij ~* it's all the same to me; *(van)* ~ (the) same to you

hetzij /ətsɛi/ (conj) either, whether: ~ **warm** *of* **koud** either hot or cold

heuglijk /høxlək/ (adj) happy, glad, joyful

heulen /hølə(n)/ (heulde, heeft geheuld) collaborate, be in league with

de **heup** /høp/ (pl: -en) hip

het **heupgewricht** /høpɣəvrɪxt/ (pl: -en) hip joint

heupwiegen /høpwiɣə(n)/ (heupwiegde, heeft geheupwiegd) sway (or: wiggle) one's hips, waggle

heus /høs/ (adj, adv) real, true: *hij doet het ~* **wel** he is sure to do it; *maar* **niet** ~! but not really!, just kidding!

de **heuvel** /høvəl/ (pl: -s) hill; [small] hillock; mound

heuvelachtig /høvəlɑxtəx/ (adj) hilly

de **heuvelrug** /høvəlrʏx/ (pl: -gen) **1** ridge **2** range (of hills)

¹hevig /hevəx/ (adj) **1** violent, intense: *~e* **angst** acute terror; *een ~e* **brand** a raging fire; *een ~e* **koorts** a raging fever; *~e* **pijnen** severe pains **2** violent, vehement, fierce: *onder ~* **protest** under strong (or: vehement) protest; *~e* **uitvallen** violent outbursts

²hevig /hevəx/ (adv) violently, fiercely, intensely: *hij was ~* **verontwaardigd** he was highly indignant; ~ **bloeden** bleed profusely; *zij* **snikte** ~ she cried her eyes out.

de **hevigheid** /hevəxhɛit/ violence, vehemence, intensity, fierceness, acuteness

de **hiel** /hil/ (pl: -en) heel: *iem.* **op** *de ~en zitten* be (close) on s.o.'s heels

de **hielenlikker** /hilə(n)lɪkər/ (pl: -s) bootlick(er)

hier /hir/ (adv) **1** here: *dit* **meisje** ~ this girl; *ik* **ben** ~ *nieuw* I'm new here; *wie* **hebben** *we ~!* look who's here!; ~ *is het* **gebeurd** this is where it happened; ~ **is** *de krant* here's the newspaper; ~ **staat** *dat ...* it says here that ...; ~ *of* **daar** *vinden wij wel wat* we'll find sth. somewhere or other; *het zit me* **tot** ~ I've had it up to here **2** this: ~ *moet je het* **mee** *doen* you'll have to make do with this

hieraan /hiran/ (adv) to this, at/on (or: by, from) this: ~ *valt niet* **te twijfelen** there is no doubt about this

hierachter /hirɑxtər/ (adv) behind this; after this: ~ **ligt** *een grote tuin* there is a large garden at the back

de **hiërarchie** /hijərɑrxi/ (pl: -ën) hierarchy

hiërarchisch /hijərɑrxis/ (adj, adv) hierarchic(al)

hierbeneden /hirbənedə(n)/ (adv) down here

hierbij /hirbɛi/ (adv) at this, with this; herewith; hereby: ~ **bericht** *ik u, dat ...* I hereby inform you that ...; ~ **komt** nog dat hij ... in addition (to this), he ...

hierbinnen /hirbɪnə(n)/ (adv) in here, inside

hierboven /hirbɔvə(n)/ (adv) up here; above: ~ **woont** een drummer a drummer lives upstairs

hierbuiten /hirbœytə(n)/ (adv) outside

hierdoor /hirdor/ (adv) **1** through here, through this, by doing so: ~ wil hij ervoor **zorgen** dat ... by doing so he wants to ensure that ... **2** because of this: ~ **werd** ik **opgehouden** this held me up

hierheen /hirhen/ (adv) (over) here, this way: op de **weg** ~ on the way here; hij **kwam** helemaal ~ om ... he came all this way ...

hierin /hirɪn/ (adv) in here, within, in this

hierlangs /hirlɑŋs/ (adv) past here, along here, by here

hiermee /hirme/ (adv) with this, by this: in **verband** ~ in this connection

hierna /hirnɑ/ (adv) **1** after this **2** below

hiernaast /hirnɑst/ (adv) next door; alongside: de illustratie op de **bladzijde** ~ the illustration on the facing page; ~ **hebben** ze twee auto's the next-door neighbours have two cars

het **hiernamaals** /hirnɑmals/ hereafter, next world, (great) beyond

de **hiëroglief** /hijəroɣlif/ (pl: -en) hieroglyph; hieroglyphics

hierom /hirɔm/ (adv) **1** (a)round this: dat ringetje **moet** ~ that ring belongs around this **2** because of this, for this reason: ~ **blijf** ik thuis this is why I'm staying at home

hieromheen /hirɔmhen/ (adv) (a)round this: ~ **loopt** een gracht there is a canal surrounding this

hieronder /hirɔndər/ (adv) **1** under here, underneath, below: zoals ~ **aangegeven** as stated below **2** among these: ~ **zijn** veel personen van naam among them there are many people of note ǁ ~ **versta** ik ... by this I understand ...

hierop /hirɔp/ (adv) **1** (up)on this: het komt ~ **neer** it comes down to this **2** after this, then

hierover /hirɔvər/ (adv) **1** over this **2** about this, regarding this, on this

hiertegen /hirteɣə(n)/ (adv) against this

hiertegenover /hirteɣə(n)ɔvər/ (adv) opposite; across the street; over the way

hiertoe /hirtu/ (adv) **1** (up to) here: tot ~ so far, up to now **2** to this, for this: wat heeft u ~ **gebracht?** what brought you to do this?

hieruit /hirœyt/ (adv) **1** out of here: van ~ vertrekken depart from here **2** from this: ~ **volgt**, dat ... it follows (from this) that ...

hiervan /hirvɑn/ (adv) of this

hiervandaan /hirvɑndɑn/ (adv) from here, away

hiervoor /hirvor/ (adv) **1** in front (of this); before this **2** of this: ~ hoeft u niet bang te zijn you needn't be afraid of this **3** for this purpose, to this end **4** (in exchange, return) for this

de **hifi-installatie** /hɑjfɑjɪnstɑla(t)si/ (pl: -s) hifi (set)

de **high five** /hɑjfɑjf/ high five

het/de **highlight** /hɑjlɑjt/ (pl: -s) highlight: de ~s van de rondreis the highlights of the trip

hightech /hɑjtɛk/ (adj) high-tech, hi-tech

hij /hɛi/ (pers pron) he; it: iedereen is trots op het werk dat ~ zelf **doet** everyone is proud of the work they do themselves; ~ **is** het it's him; ~ **daar** him over there

hijgen /hɛiɣə(n)/ (hijgde, heeft gehijgd) pant, gasp

de **hijger** /hɛiɣər/ (pl: -s) heavy breather: ik **had** weer een ~ vandaag I had another obscene phone-call today

de **hijs** /hɛɪs/ (pl: -en) whack

hijsen /hɛisə(n)/ (hees, heeft gehesen) **1** hoist, lift: de **vlag** (in top) ~ hoist (or: run up) the flag **2** haul, heave

de **hijskraan** /hɛiskrɑn/ (pl: -kranen) crane

de **hik** /hɪk/ (pl: -ken) hiccup

hikken /hɪkə(n)/ (hikte, heeft gehikt) hiccup ǁ **tegen** iets aan ~ shrink from sth.

de **hilariteit** /hilaritɛit/ hilarity, mirth

de **Himalaya** /himalɑjɑ/ (the) Himalayas

de **hinde** /hɪndɑ/ (pl: -n) hind, doe

de **hinder** /hɪndər/ nuisance, bother; hindrance; obstacle: het verkeer **ondervindt** veel ~ van de sneeuw traffic is severely disrupted by the snow

hinderen /hɪndərə(n)/ (hinderde, heeft gehinderd) impede, hamper, obstruct: zijn lange jas hinderde hem **bij** het lopen his long coat got in his way as he walked

de **hinderlaag** /hɪndərlaɣ/ (pl: -lagen) ambush; [fig also] trap: de vijand **in** een ~ lokken lure the enemy into an ambush

[1]**hinderlijk** /hɪndərlək/ (adj) **1** annoying, irritating **2** objectionable, disturbing **3** unpleasant, disagreeable: ik vind de **warmte** niet ~ the heat does not bother me

[2]**hinderlijk** /hɪndərlək/ (adv) annoyingly, blatantly

de **hindernis** /hɪndərnɪs/ (pl: -sen) obstacle, barrier; [fig also] hindrance; [fig also] impediment

de **hindernisloop** /hɪndərnɪslop/ (pl: -lopen) steeplechase

de **hinderpaal** /hɪndərpal/ (pl: -palen) obstacle, impediment

de **Hinderwet** /hɪndərwɛt/ [roughly] Nuisance Act

de **hindoe** /hɪndu/ Hindu

het **hindoeïsme** /hɪnduwɪsmə/ Hinduism

de **Hindoestaan** /hɪndustɑn/ (pl: Hindoestanen) Hindu(stani)

hinkelen /hɪŋkələ(n)/ (hinkelde, heeft/is gehinkeld) hop; play hopscotch
hinken /hɪŋkə(n)/ (hinkte, heeft/is gehinkt) **1** limp, have a limp, walk with a limp, hobble (along) **2** hop
de **hink-stap-sprong** /hɪŋkstɑpsprɔŋ/ triple jump, hop, step and jump
hinniken /hɪnəkə(n)/ (hinnikte, heeft gehinnikt) neigh; whinny
de **hint** /hɪnt/ (pl: -s) hint, tip(-off): *(iem.) een ~ geven* drop (s.o.) a hint
de **hiphop** /hɪphɔp/ hip hop
de **hippie** /hɪpi/ (pl: -s) hippie
de **historicus** /hɪstorikʏs/ (pl: historici) historian
de **historie** /hɪstori/ (pl: historiën) **1** history **2** story, anecdote **3** affair, business
historisch /hɪstoris/ (adj) **1** historic: *wij beleven een ~ moment* we are witnessing a historic moment **2** historical; period: *een ~e roman* a historical novel **3** historical, true: *dat is ~* that's a historical fact (*or:* a true story)
de **hit** /hɪt/ (pl: -s) hit (record)
de **hitlijst** /hɪtlɛist/ (pl: -en) chart(s), hit parade
de **hitsig** /hɪtsəx/ (adj, adv) **1** hot-blooded **2** [inform] hot; randy; horny
de **hitte** /hɪtə/ heat
hittebestendig /hɪtəbəstɛndəx/ (adj) heat-resistant, heatproof
de **hittegolf** /hɪtəɣɔlf/ (pl: -golven) heatwave
het **hiv** /haive/ human immunodeficiency virus HIV
hm /həm/ (int) (a)hem
ho /ho/ (int) **1** stop: *zeg maar 'ho'* say when **2** come on!, that's not fair!
de **hoax** /hoks/ (pl: -es, -en) hoax
de **hobbel** /hɔbəl/ (pl: -s) bump
hobbelen /hɔbələ(n)/ (hobbelde, heeft/is gehobbeld) bump, jolt, lurch
hobbelig /hɔbələx/ (adj) bumpy, irregular
het **hobbelpaard** /hɔbəlpart/ (pl: -en) rocking horse
de **hobby** /hɔbi/ (pl: -'s) hobby
de **hobo** /hobo/ (pl: -'s) oboe
de **hoboïst** /hobowɪst/ (pl: -en) oboist
het **hobu** /hoby/ [Belg] *hoger onderwijs buiten de universiteit* non-university higher education
het **hockey** /hɔki/ hockey
hockeyen /hɔkijə(n)/ (hockeyde, heeft gehockeyd) play hockey
de **hockeystick** /hɔkistɪk/ (pl: -s) hockey stick
het/de **hocus pocus** /hokʏspokʏs/ hocus-pocus; mumbo-jumbo
hoe /hu/ (adv) **1** how: *je kunt wel nagaan ~ blij zij was* you can imagine how happy she was; *~ eerder ~ beter* the sooner the better; *het gaat ~ langer ~ beter* it is getting better all the time; *~ ouder ze wordt, ~ minder ze ziet* the older she gets, the less she sees; *~ fietst zij naar school?* which way does she cycle to

school?; *~ moet het nu verder?* where do we go from here?; *~ dan ook* a) anyway, anyhow; b) no matter how; c) by hook or by crook; d) no matter what; *~ vreemd het ook lijkt* strange as it may seem; *~ kom je erbij?* how can you think such a thing?; *hoezo?, ~ dat zo?* how (*or:* what) do you mean?, why do you ask?; *~ vind je mijn kamer?* what do you think of my room? **2** what: *~ noemen jullie de baby?* what are you going to call the baby? || *Dorine danste, en ~!* Dorine danced, and how!
de **hoed** /hut/ (pl: -en) hat: *een hoge ~* a top hat
de **hoedanigheid** /hudanəxhɛit/ (pl: -heden) capacity: *in de ~ van* in one's capacity as
de **hoede** /hudə/ **1** care, protection; custody; charge; (safe) keeping: *iem. onder zijn ~ nemen* take charge of s.o., take a person under one's care (*or:* protection) **2** guard: *op zijn ~ zijn (voor)* be on one's guard (against)
¹**hoeden** /hudə(n)/ (hoedde, heeft gehoed) tend, keep watch over, look after
zich ²**hoeden** /hudə(n)/ (hoedde zich, heeft zich gehoed) (+ voor) guard (against), beware (of), be on one's guard (against)
de **hoedenplank** /hudə(n)plɑŋk/ (pl: -en) shelf; [car] rear (*or:* parcel, back) shelf
het **hoedje** /hucə/ (pl: -s) (little) hat: *onder één ~ spelen met* be in league with
de **hoef** /huf/ (pl: hoeven) hoof
het **hoefijzer** /hufɛizər/ (pl: -s) (horse)shoe
de **hoefsmid** /hufsmɪt/ (pl: -smeden) farrier, blacksmith
hoegenaamd /huɣənamt/ (adv) at all, absolutely, completely
de **hoek** /huk/ (pl: -en) **1** corner: *in de ~ staan* (*or:* zetten) stand (*or:* put) in the corner; *de ~ omslaan* turn the corner; *(vlak) om de ~ (van de straat)* (just) around the corner **2** [maths] angle: [fig] *iets vanuit een andere ~ bekijken* look at sth. from a different angle; *in een rechte ~* at right angles; *een scherpe* (*or:* *een stompe*) *~* an acute (*or:* obtuse) angle; *die lijnen snijden elkaar onder een ~ van 45°* those lines meet at an angle of 45° **3** quarter, point of the compass || *dode ~* blind spot
het **hoekhuis** /hukhœys/ (pl: -huizen) corner house; end house
hoekig /hukəx/ (adj, adv) angular; craggy; rugged; jagged
het **hoekje** /hukjə/ (pl: -s) corner; nook || *het ~ omgaan* kick the bucket
het **hoekpunt** /hukpʏnt/ (pl: -en) vertex, angular point
de **hoekschop** /huksxɔp/ (pl: -pen) corner (kick)
de **hoeksteen** /huksten/ (pl: -stenen) cornerstone; [fig] keystone; linchpin; pillar
de **hoektand** /huktɑnt/ (pl: -en) canine tooth, eye-tooth; fang
hoelang /hulɑŋ/ (adv) how long

het **hoen** /hun/ (pl: -ders) hen, chicken; poultry; (domestic) fowl

de **hoepel** /h<u>u</u>pəl/ (pl: -s) hoop

hoepla /h<u>u</u>pla/ (int) whoops; oops(-a-daisy); ups-a-daisy; here we go

de **hoer** /hur/ (pl: -en) [inform] whore

hoera /hura/ (int) hooray, hurray, hurrah

de **hoes** /hus/ (pl: hoezen) cover(ing), case

de **hoest** /hust/ cough

de **hoestbui** /h<u>u</u>stbœy/ (pl: -en) fit of coughing, coughing fit

hoesten /h<u>u</u>stə(n)/ (hoestte, heeft gehoest) cough

de **hoestsiroop** /h<u>u</u>(st)sirop/ cough syrup

de **hoeve** /h<u>u</u>və/ (pl: -n) farm(stead); farmhouse; homestead

hoeveel /huv<u>e</u>l/ (num) how much, how many: ~ *appelen zijn er?* how many apples are there?; ~ *geld heb je bij je?* how much money do you have on you?; ~ *is vier plus vier?* what do four and four make?; how much is four plus four?; *met hoevelen waren jullie?* how many of you were there?; how many were you?

de **hoeveelheid** /huv<u>e</u>lhɛit/ (pl: -heden) amount, quantity; volume; dose

hoeveelste /huv<u>e</u>lstə/ (num): *de ~ juli ben je jarig?* when in July is your birthday?; *voor de ~ keer vraag ik het je nu?* how many times have I asked you?; *de ~ is het vandaag?* what day of the month is it today?; *het ~ deel van een liter is 10 cm³?* what fraction of a litre is 10cc?

¹**hoeven** /h<u>u</u>və/ (hoefde, heeft gehoefd) matter, be necessary: *het had niet gehoeven* you didn't have to do that, you shouldn't have done that; *het mag wel, maar het hoeft niet* you can but you don't have to

²**hoeven** /h<u>u</u>və(n)/ (hoefde, heeft gehoefd) need (to), have to: *dat had je niet ~ (te) doen* you shouldn't have (done that); *daar hoef je niet bang voor te zijn* you needn't worry about that

hoever /huv<u>e</u>r/ (adv) how far: *in ~re* to what extent

hoewel /huw<u>e</u>l/ (conj) 1 (al)though, even though: *~ het pas maart is, zijn de bomen al groen* even though it's only March the trees are already in leaf 2 (al)though, however

hoezeer /huz<u>e</u>r/ (adv) how much: *ik kan je niet zeggen ~ het mij spijt* I can't tell you how sorry I am

hoezo /huz<u>o</u>/ (int) what (or: how) do you mean?, in what way? (or: respect?)

het **hof** /hɔf/ 1 [law] court 2 court, royal household

de **hofdame** /h<u>ɔ</u>vdamə/ (pl: -s) lady-in-waiting; maid of honour

hoffelijk /h<u>ɔ</u>fələk/ (adj, adv) courteous, polite

de **hofhouding** /h<u>ɔ</u>fhɑudɪŋ/ (pl: -en) (royal) household, court

de **hofleverancier** /h<u>ɔ</u>flevərɑnsir/ (pl: -s) purveyor to the Royal Household, purveyor to His (Her) Majesty the King (Queen), Royal Warrant Holder

de **hofnar** /h<u>ɔ</u>fnɑr/ (pl: -ren) court jester, fool

het **hogedrukgebied** /hoɣədrykxəbit/ (pl: -en) anticyclone

de **hogedrukspuit** /hoɣədrykspœyt/ (pl: -en) high-pressure paint spray, high-pressure spraying pistol

de **hogepriester** /h<u>oɣ</u>əpristər/ (pl: -s) high priest

de **hogerhand** /hoɣərh<u>ɑ</u>nt/: *op bevel van ~* by order of the authorities

het **Hogerhuis** /h<u>oɣ</u>ərhœys/ House of Lords, Upper House

hogerop /hoɣər<u>ɔ</u>p/ (adv) higher up: *hij wil ~* he wants to get on

de **hogeschool** /hoɣəsx<u>o</u>l/ (pl: -scholen) college (of advanced, higher education), polytechnic, academy: *Economische ~* School of Economics; *Technische ~* College (or: Institute) of Technology; Polytechnic (College)

de **hogesnelheidstrein** /hoɣəsn<u>e</u>lhɛitstrɛin/ (pl: -en) high-speed train

hoi /hɔj/ (int) hi, hello; hurray; whoopee

het **hok** /hɔk/ (pl: -ken) 1 shed; storeroom 2 pen; (dog) kennel; (pig)sty; dovecote; hen house, hen-coop

het **hokje** /h<u>ɔ</u>kjə/ (pl: -s) 1 cabin; (sentry) box; cubicle; booth 2 compartment; pigeon-hole; square; box: *het ~ aankruisen (invullen)* put a tick in the box

hokken /h<u>ɔ</u>kə(n)/ (hokte, heeft gehokt) shack up (with)

het ¹**hol** /hɔl/ (pl: -en) 1 cave, cavern, grotto: *een donker ~* a dark, gloomy hole 2 hole; lair; den; burrow: *zich in het ~ van de leeuw wagen* beard (or: brave) the lion in his den 3 hole; haunt || *een op ~ geslagen paard* a runaway (horse)

²**hol** /hɔl/ (adj, adv) 1 hollow; female; sunken; gaunt: *een ~ geslepen brillenglas* a concave lens; *het ~le van de hand* (or: *voet*) the hollow of the hand, the arch of the foot 2 hollow; empty 3 hollow, cavernous || *in het ~st van de nacht* at dead of night

de **holbewoner** /h<u>ɔ</u>lbəwonər/ (pl: -s) cave-dweller

de **holding** /h<u>ɔ</u>ldɪŋ/ (pl: -s) holding

de **holebi** /h<u>o</u>lebi/ (pl: -'s) [Belg] *homo, lesbienne of biseksueel* LGB *(lesbian, gay, bisexual)*: *~'s en transgenders* LGBT *(lesbian, gay, bisexual, transgender)*

Holland /h<u>ɔ</u>lɑnt/ the Netherlands, Holland

de **Hollander** /h<u>ɔ</u>lɑndər/ (pl: -s) 1 Dutchman 2 inhabitant of North or South Holland

Hollands /h<u>ɔ</u>lɑnts/ (adj) 1 from (the province of) North or South Holland 2 Dutch, Netherlands: *~e nieuwe* Dutch (or: salted) herring

de **Hollandse** /hɔlɑntsə/ Dutchwoman
hollen /hɔlə(n)/ (holde, heeft/is gehold)
1 bolt, run away **2** run, race: *het is met hem ~ of stilstaan* it's always all or nothing with him
de **holocaust** /holokɔ:st/ (pl: -en) holocaust
het **hologram** /holoɣrɑm/ (pl: -men) hologram
de **holster** /hɔlstər/ (pl: -s) holster
de **holte** /hɔltə/ (pl: -s, -n) **1** cavity, hollow, hole; niche **2** hollow; socket; pit; crook **3** draught, depth
de **hom** /hɔm/ (pl: -men) milt: [fig] *~ of kuit willen hebben* want to know, one way or the other
de **homeopathie** /homejopati/ homoeopathy
homeopathisch /homejopatis/ (adj, adv) homoeopathic
de **homepage** /hɔmpetʃ/ (pl: -s) home page
de **hometrainer** /hɔmtrenər/ (pl: -s) home trainer
de **hommage** /ɔmaʒə/ (pl: -s) homage
de **hommel** /hɔməl/ (pl: -s) bumblebee
de **homo** /homo/ (pl: -'s) gay; fairy; queen
de ¹**homofiel** /homofil/ (pl: -en) homosexual
²**homofiel** /homofil/ (adj) homosexual
homogeen /homoɣen/ (adj) homogeneous, uniform
het **homohuwelijk** /homohywələk/ (pl: -en) same-sex marriage, gay marriage; (gay) blessing
de **homoseksualiteit** /homosɛksywalitɛit/ homosexuality; lesbianism
de ¹**homoseksueel** /homosɛksywel/ (pl: -seksuelen) homosexual
²**homoseksueel** /homosɛksywel/ (adj) homosexual
de **homp** /hɔmp/ (pl: -en) chunk, hunk, lump
de **hond** /hɔnt/ (pl: -en) **1** dog; hound: *pas op voor de* ~ beware of the dog; *de ~ uitlaten* take the dog (out) for a walk; let the dog out; *~en aan de lijn!* dogs must be kept on the lead (leash)!; *geen ~* not a soul, nobody; *men moet geen slapende ~en wakker maken* let sleeping dogs lie; *blaffende ~en bijten niet* [roughly] his bark is worse than his bite; [fig] *de ~ in de pot vinden* come too late for dinner **2** dog, cur: *ondankbare ~!* ungrateful swine!
het **hondenasiel** /hɔndə(n)azil/ (pl: -en) dogs' home
de **hondenbaan** /hɔndə(n)ban/ (pl: -banen) lousy (or: rotten, awful) job
het **hondenhok** /hɔndə(n)hɔk/ (pl: -ken) (dog) kennel
het **hondenras** /hɔndə(n)rɑs/ (pl: -sen) breed of dog
het **hondenweer** /hɔndə(n)wer/ foul weather, filthy weather
het ¹**honderd** /hɔndərt/ (pl: -en) hundred, hundred(s): *~en jaren* (or: *keren*) hundreds of years (or: times); *zij sneuvelden bij ~en* they died in their hundreds || *alles loopt in het ~*

everything is going haywire
²**honderd** /hɔndərt/ (num) hundred: *een bankbiljet van ~ euro* a hundred-euro (bank)-note; *dat heb ik nu al (minstens) ~ keer gezegd* (if I've said it once) I've said it a hundred times; *ik voel me niet helemaal ~ procent* I'm feeling a bit under the weather; *~ procent zeker zijn (van)* be absolutely positive; *er zijn er over de ~* there are more than a hundred
honderdduizend /hɔndərdœyzənt/ (num) a (or: one) hundred thousand: *(enige) ~en (mensen)* hundreds of thousands (of people)
honderdduizendste /hɔndərdœyzəntstə/ (num) (one) hundred thousandth
het **honderdje** /hɔndərcə/ (pl: -s) hundred-guilder note
honderdste /hɔndərstə/ (num) hundredth: *ik probeer het nu al voor de ~ maal* I've tried it a hundred times
het **hondje** /hɔncə/ (pl: -s) doggy, little dog; bo-wow
honds /hɔnts/ (adj, adv) despicable, shameful, scandalous
de **hondsdolheid** /hɔntsdɔlhɛit/ rabies
Honduras /hɔnduras/ Honduras
de ¹**Hondurees** /hɔndures/ (pl: Hondurezen) Honduran
²**Hondurees** /hɔndures/ (adj) Honduran
honen /honə(n)/ (hoonde, heeft gehoond) jeer
de **Hongaar** /hɔnɣar/ (pl: Hongaren) Hungarian
het ¹**Hongaars** /hɔnɣars/ Hungarian
²**Hongaars** /hɔnɣars/ (adj) Hungarian
Hongarije /hɔnɣarɛiə/ Hungary
de **honger** /hɔnər/ appetite, hunger: *ik heb toch een ~!* I'm starving; *~ hebben* be (or: feel) hungry; *van ~ sterven* die of hunger, starve to death
de **hongerdood** /hɔnərdot/ death by starvation: *de ~ sterven* starve to death, die of starvation
hongeren /hɔnərə(n)/ (hongerde, heeft gehongerd) starve, hunger: *~ naar* hanker after; hunger (or: be hungry) for
hongerig /hɔnərəx/ (adj, adv) hungry, famished; peckish
het **hongerloon** /hɔnərlon/ (pl: -lonen) pittance, subsistence wages, starvation wages
de **hongersnood** /hɔnərsnot/ (pl: -noden) famine, starvation; dearth
de **hongerstaking** /hɔnərstakɪn/ (pl: -en) hunger strike
de **honing** /honɪn/ honey
de **honingraat** /honɪnrat/ (pl: -raten) honeycomb
het **honk** /hɔnk/ (pl: -en) base
het **honkbal** /hɔnkbɑl/ baseball
de **honkbalknuppel** /hɔnkbɑlknypəl/ (pl: -s) (baseball) bat
honkballen /hɔnkbɑlə(n)/ (honkbalde,

heeft gehonkbald) play baseball

de **honneurs** /hɔnœrs/ (pl): *de ~ waarnemen* do the honours

honorair /honorɛːr/ (adj): *~ consul* honorary consul

het **honorarium** /honorarijʏm/ (pl: honoraria, -s) fee, salary; royalty; honorarium

honoreren /honorɛrə(n)/ (honoreerde, heeft gehonoreerd) **1** pay, remunerate; fee **2** honour, give due recognition; recognize

het **hoofd** /hoft/ (pl: -en) **1** head: *met gebogen ~* with head bowed; *een ~ groter* (or: *kleiner*) *zijn dan* be a head taller (*or:* shorter) than; *een hard ~ in iets hebben* have grave doubts about sth.; *het ~ laten hangen* hang one's head, be downcast; *het ~ boven water houden* [fig] keep one's head above water, keep afloat; *het werk is hem boven het ~ gegroeid* he can't cope with his work any more; *het succes is hem naar het ~ gestegen* success has gone to his head; *iets over het ~ zien* overlook sth. **2** head, mind, brain(s): *mijn ~ staat er niet naar* I'm not in the mood for it; *hij heeft veel aan zijn ~* he has a lot of things on his mind; *iets uit het ~ kennen* learn sth. by heart (*or:* rote); *uit het ~ zingen* sing from memory; *iem. het ~ op hol brengen* turn s.o.'s head; *per ~ van de bevolking* per head of (the) population **3** head; top **4** head, front, vanguard **5** head, chief, leader; principal; headmaster; headmistress **6** main, chief: *hoofdbureau* head office

de **hoofdagent** /hoftaɣɛnt/ (pl: -en) senior police officer

het **hoofdartikel** /hoftartikəl/ (pl: -en) editorial, leading article, leader

de **hoofdbrekens** (pl): *dat zal mij heel wat ~ kosten* I shall have to rack my brains over that, that's going to take a lot of thought

de **hoofdcommissaris** /hoftkɔmısarıs/ (pl: -sen) (chief) superintendent (of police), commissioner

het **hoofddeksel** /hovdɛksəl/ (pl: -s) headgear; headwear

de **hoofddoek** /hovduk/ (pl: -en) (head)scarf

het **hoofdeind** /hofteint/ head

hoofdelijk /hovdələk/ (adj, adv): *~e stemming* poll, voting by call; *~ aansprakelijk zijn* be severally liable (*or:* responsible)

het **hoofdgebouw** /hoftχəbau/ (pl: -en) main (*or:* central) building

het **hoofdgerecht** /hoftχərɛχt/ (pl: -en) main course

het/de **hoofdhaar** /hofthar/ hair (of the head)

de **hoofdhuid** /hofthœyt/ scalp

de **hoofding** /hovdıŋ/ (pl: -en) [Belg] letterhead

de **hoofdinspecteur** /hoftınspɛktør/ (pl: -s) chief inspector; chief medical officer; inspector general

het **hoofdkantoor** /hoftkantor/ (pl: -kantoren) head office, headquarters

het **hoofdkussen** /hoftkʏsə(n)/ (pl: -s) pillow

het **hoofdkwartier** /hoftkwartir/ (pl: -en) headquarters

de **hoofdletter** /hoftlɛtər/ (pl: -s) capital (letter)

de **hoofdlijn** /hoftlɛin/ (pl: -en) outline

de **hoofdluis** /hoftlœys/ (pl: -luizen) head louse

de **hoofdmaaltijd** /hoftmaltɛit/ main meal

de **hoofdmoot** /hoftmot/ (pl: -moten) principal part

de **hoofdpersoon** /hoftpɛrson/ (pl: -personen) principal person, leading figure; main character

de **hoofdpijn** /hoftpɛin/ (pl: -en) headache: *barstende ~* splitting headache

de **hoofdprijs** /hoftprɛis/ (pl: -prijzen) first prize

de **hoofdredacteur** /hoftredaktør/ (pl: -en) editor(-in-chief)

het **hoofdrekenen** /hoftrekənə(n)/ mental arithmetic

de **hoofdrol** /hoftrol/ (pl: -len) leading part: *de ~ spelen* play the leading part, be the leading man (*or:* lady)

de **hoofdrolspeler** /hoftrolspelər/ (pl: -s) leading man, star; [fig] main figure

de **hoofdschakelaar** /hoftsχakəlar/ (pl: -s) main switch

hoofdschuddend /hoftsχʏdənt/ (adv) shaking one's head

de **hoofdstad** /hoftstat/ (pl: -steden) capital (city); provincial capital

hoofdstedelijk /hoftstedələk/ (adj) metropolitan

de **hoofdsteun** /hoftstøn/ (pl: -en) headrest

de **hoofdstraat** /hoftstrat/ (pl: -straten) high street, main street

het **hoofdstuk** /hoftstʏk/ (pl: -ken) chapter

het **hoofdtelwoord** /hoftɛlwort/ (pl: -en) cardinal number

het **hoofdvak** /hoftfak/ (pl: -ken) main subject

de **hoofdverpleegkundige** /hoftfərpleyˌkʏndəɣə/ charge nurse

de **hoofdvogel** /hoftfoɣəl/ (pl: -s) [Belg] main prize ‖ *de ~ afschieten* make (*or:* commit) a serious blunder

de **hoofdweg** /hoftwɛχ/ (pl: -en) main road

de **hoofdwond** /hoftwont/ (pl: -en) head wound (*or:* injury)

de **hoofdzaak** /hoftsak/ (pl: -zaken) main point (*or:* thing); essentials: *~ is, dat we slagen* what matters is that we succeed

hoofdzakelijk /hoftsakələk/ (adv) mainly

de **hoofdzin** /hoftsın/ (pl: -nen) main sentence (*or:* clause)

de **hoofdzonde** /hoftsondə/ (pl: -n) cardinal sin

de **hoofdzuster** /hoftsʏstər/ (pl: -s) charge nurse

hoofs /hofs/ (adj, adv): *de ~e liefde* courtly love

hoog /hoɣ/ (adj, adv) high, tall: *een hoge bal* a high ball; *een hoge C* a high C, a top C; *de ~ste verdieping* the top floor; *het water staat ~* the water is high; *~ in de lucht* high up in the air; *een stapel van drie voet ~* a three-foot high pile; *hij woont drie ~* he lives on the third floor; [Am] he lives on the second floor; *een hoge ambtenaar* a senior official; *naar een hogere klas overgaan* move up (*or:* be moved up) to a higher class; *een ~ stemmetje* (*or: geluid*) a high-pitched voice (*or:* sound); *de ruzie liep ~ op* the quarrel became heated; *de verwarming staat ~* the heating is on high; *de temperatuur mag niet hoger zijn dan 60°* the temperature must not go above (*or:* exceed) 60°

hoogachten /hoɣɑxtə(n)/ (achtte hoog, heeft hooggeacht) esteem highly, respect highly: *~d* yours faithfully

hoogbegaafd /hoɣbəɣaːft/ (adj) highly gifted (*or:* talented): *scholen voor ~e kinderen* schools for highly-gifted children

de **hoogbouw** /hoɣbɑu/ high-rise building (*or:* flats)

de **hoogconjunctuur** /hoɣkɔnyŋktyr/ (period of) boom

de **hoogdag** /hoɣdɑx/ (pl: -en) [Belg] feast day

hoogdravend /hoɣdraːvənt/ (adj) high-flown, bombastic

het **hooggebergte** /hoɣəbɛrxtə/ (pl: -n, -s) high mountains

hooggeëerd /hoɣəeːrt/ (adj) highly honoured: *~ publiek!* Ladies and Gentlemen!

hooggeplaatst /hoɣəplaːtst/ (adj) high-placed, highly placed

het **hooggerechtshof** /hoɣərɛx(t)shɔf/ (pl: -hoven) Supreme Court

hooghartig /hoɣhɑrtəx/ (adj, adv) haughty

de **hoogheid** /hoɣhɛit/ (pl: -heden) highness

hooghouden /hoɣhɑudə(n)/ (hield hoog, heeft hooggehouden) honour; keep up: *de eer ~* keep one's honour

de **hoogleraar** /hoɣleːraːr/ (pl: -leraren) professor

hooglopend /hoɣloːpənt/ (adj) violent

de **hoogmis** /hoɣmɪs/ (pl: -sen) high mass

de **hoogmoed** /hoɣmut/ pride: *~ komt voor de val* pride goes before a fall

de **hoogmoedswaanzin** /hoɣmutswaːnzɪn/ megalomania

hoognodig /hoɣnoːdəx/ (adj, adv) highly necessary, much needed, urgently needed: *er moet ~ iets gebeuren* sth. needs to be done urgently

hoogoplopend /hoɣoplopənt/ (adj): *een ~e ruzie* a screaming row

de **hoogoven** /hoɣoːvə(n)/ (pl: -s) blast furnace

het **hoogseizoen** /hoɣsɛizun/ (pl: -en) high season: *buiten het ~* out of season

de **hoogspanning** /hoɣspɑnɪŋ/ high tension (*or:* voltage)

hoogspringen /hoɣsprɪŋə(n)/ high-jump, high-jumping

het ¹**hoogst** /hoɣst/ **1** top, highest **2** utmost: *je krijgt op zijn ~ wat strafwerk* at the very worst you'll be given some lines

²**hoogst** /hoɣst/ (adv) highly, extremely: *~ (on)waarschijnlijk* highly (un)likely

hoogstaand /hoɣstaːnt/ (adj) high-minded; edifying: *het was geen ~ schouwspel* it was a rather unedifying spectacle

het **hoogstandje** /hoɣstɑncə/ (pl: -s) tour de force

hoogsteigen /hoɣstɛiɣə(n)/ (adj): *de Koningin in ~ persoon* the Queen, no less; no less a person than the Queen

hoogstens /hoɣstəns/ (adv) **1** at the most, at (the very) most, up to, no(t) more than: *~ twaalf* twelve at the (very) most **2** at worst: *~ kan hij u de deur wijzen* the worst he can do is show you the door **3** at best

hoogstnodig /hoɣstnoːdəx/ (adj) absolutely necessary, strictly necessary: *alleen het ~e kopen* buy only the bare necessities

hoogstpersoonlijk /hoɣs(t)pɛrsoːnlək/ (adv) in person, personally

hoogstwaarschijnlijk /hoɣstwaːrsxɛinlək/ (adj, adv) most likely (*or:* probable), in all probability

de **hoogte** /hoɣtə/ (pl: -n, -s) **1** height: *de ~ ingaan* go up, rise; ascend; *hij deed erg uit de ~* he was being very superior; *lengte, breedte en ~* length, breadth and height **2** height; level: *de ~ van de waterspiegel* the water level; *tot op zekere ~ hebt u gelijk* up to a point you're right **3** level, latitude; elevation, altitude: *er staat een file ter ~ van Woerden* there is a traffic jam near Woerden ‖ *zich van iets op de ~ stellen* acquaint o.s. with sth.; *op de ~ blijven* keep o.s. informed; keep in touch; *ik kan geen ~ van hem krijgen* I don't understand him; I can't figure him out

de **hoogtelijn** /hoɣtəlɛin/ (pl: -en) altitude

het **hoogtepunt** /hoɣtəpʏnt/ (pl: -en) height, peak, highlight: *naar een ~ voeren, een ~ doen bereiken* bring to a climax

de **hoogtevrees** /hoɣtəvreːs/ fear of heights

de **hoogteziekte** /hoɣtəziktə/ altitude sickness

de **hoogtezon** /hoɣtəzɔn/ (pl: -nen) sun lamp

het **hoogtij** /hoɣtɛi/: *~ vieren* be (*or:* run) rampant

hooguit /hoɣœyt/ (adv) at the most, at (the very) most, no(t) more than

het **hoogverraad** /hoɣfəraːt/ high treason

de **hoogvlakte** /hoɣflɑktə/ (pl: -n, -s) plateau

de **hoogvlieger** /hoɣfliɣər/ (pl: -s) highflyer; whizz kid: *het is geen ~* he's no genius

hoogwaardig /hoɣwaːrdəx/ (adj) high-quality

de **hoogwaardigheidsbekleder** /ho͜oxwar-
dəxhɛɪtsbəkledər/ (pl: -s) dignitary

het **hoogwater** /ho͜oxwatər/ high water, high
tide: *bij (met)* ~ at high tide

de **hoogwerker** /ho͜oxwɛrkər/ (pl: -s) tower
waggon

het **hooi** /hoj/ hay: *te veel* ~ *op zijn vork nemen*
bite off more than one can chew

de **hooiberg** /hojbɛrx/ (pl: -en) haystack
hooien /hojə(n)/ (hooide, heeft gehooid)
make hay

de **hooikoorts** /hojkorts/ hay fever

de **hooimijt** /hojmɛit/ (pl: -en) haystack

de **hooivork** /hojvɔrk/ (pl: -en) pitchfork

de **hooiwagen** /hojwayə(n)/ (pl: -s) **1** haycart,
hay-wagon **2** daddy-long-legs

de **hooligan** /hulɪɡən/ (pl: -s) hooligan

het **hoongelach** /honɣəlɑx/ jeering, jeers

de **¹hoop** /hop/ (pl: hopen) **1** heap, pile: *op een*
~ *leggen* pile up, stack up; *je kunt niet alles* (or:
iedereen) *op één* ~ *gooien* you can't lump everything (*or:* everyone) together **2** great deal,
good deal, lot: *een hele* ~ a good many; *ik*
heb nog een ~ *te doen* I've still got a lot (*or:*
lots) to do **3** business

de **²hoop** /hop/ (pl: hopen) hope: *goede* ~ *heb-*
ben have high hopes; *valse* ~ *wekken* raise
false hopes; *zolang er leven is, is er* ~ while
there's life there's hope; *weer (nieuwe)* ~ *krij-*
gen regain hope; *op* ~ *van zegen* … and hoping for the best; with one's fingers crossed;
de ~ *opgeven* (or: *verliezen*) *dat* … give up
(*or:* lose) hope that …
hoopgevend /hopxevənt/ (adj) hopeful
hoopvol /hopfɔl/ (adj) hopeful; promising:
de toekomst zag er niet erg ~ *uit* the future did
not look very promising
hoorbaar /horbar/ (adj, adv) audible

het **hoorcollege** /horkɔleʒə/ (pl: -s) (formal)
lecture

de **hoorn** /horn/ (pl: -s) **1** horn: *de stier nam hem*
op zijn ~s the bull tossed him (on his horns)
2 receiver: *de* ~ *erop gooien* slam down the
receiver; *de* ~ *van de haak nemen* lift the receiver **3** horn **4** conch

de **hoornist** /hornɪst/ (pl: -en) horn player

het **hoornvlies** /hornvlis/ (pl: -vliezen) cornea

het **hoorspel** /horspɛl/ (pl: -en) radio play

de **hoorzitting** /horzɪtɪŋ/ (pl: -en) hearing

de **hop** /hop/ (pl: -pen) hop(plant), hops
hopelijk /hopələk/ (adv) I hope, let's hope,
hopefully: ~ *komt* hij morgen I hope (*or:* let's
hope) he is coming tomorrow
hopeloos /hopəlos/ (adj, adv) hopeless,
desperate: *hij is* ~ *verliefd op* he's hopelessly
(*or:* desperately) in love with

¹hopen /hopə(n)/ (hoopte, heeft gehoopt)
hope (for): ~ *op betere tijden* hope for better
times

²hopen /hopə(n)/ (hoopte, heeft gehoopt)
1 hope (for): *dat is niet te* ~ I hope (*or:* let's

hope) not; *ik hoop van wel* (or: *van niet*) I
hope so (*or:* hope not); *ik hoop dat het goed*
met u gaat I hope you are well; *tegen beter*
weten in (blijven) ~ hope against hope; *blijven*
~ keep (on) hoping **2** pile (up): *op elkaar ge-*
hoopt heaped

de **hopman** /hopmɑn/ (pl: -nen) Scoutmaster

de **hor** /hor/ (pl: -ren) screen

de **horde** /hordə/ (pl: -s) **1** horde: *de hele* ~ *komt*
hierheen the whole horde is coming here
2 [sport] hurdle

de **hordeloop** /hordəlop/ hurdle race

de **horeca** /horəka/ (hotel and) catering (industry)

¹horen /horə(n)/ (hoorde, heeft gehoord)
1 hear: *hij hoort slecht* he is hard of hearing
2 belong: *wij* ~ *hier niet* we don't belong
here; *de kopjes* ~ *hier* the cups go here **3** be
done, should be **4** belong (to) || *dat hoor je te*
weten you should (*or:* ought to) know that;
dat hoort niet it is not done; *dat hoort zo*
that's how it should be

²horen /horə(n)/ (hoorde, heeft gehoord)
1 hear: *we hoorden de baby huilen* we heard
the baby crying; *nu kun je het me vertellen, hij*
kan ons niet meer ~ you can tell me now, he is
out of earshot; *ik heb het alleen van* ~ *zeggen* I
only have it on hearsay; *ik hoor het hem nog*
zeggen I can still hear him saying it; *hij deed*
alsof hij het niet hoorde he pretended not to
hear (it); *ik kon aan zijn stem* ~ *dat hij zenuw-*
achtig was I could tell by his voice that he was
nervous **2** listen to **3** hear, be told, get to
know: *Johan kreeg te* ~ *dat het zo niet langer*
kon Johan was told that it can't go on like
that; *wij kregen heel wat te* ~ we were given a
hard time of it; *laat eens iets van je* ~ keep in
touch; *zij wil geen nee* ~ she won't take no for
an answer; *hij vertelde het aan iedereen die het*
maar ~ *wilde* he told it to anyone who would
listen; *toevallig* ~ overhear; *hij wilde er niets*
meer over ~ he didn't want to hear any more
about it; *daar heb ik nooit van gehoord* I've
never heard of it; *daarna hebben we niets meer*
van hem gehoord that was the last we heard
from him; *u hoort nog van ons* you'll be hearing from us; *nou hoor je het ook eens van een*
ander so I'm not the only one who says so; *ik*
hoor het nog wel let me know (about it) **4** listen (to): *moet je ~!* just listen!, listen to this!;
moet je ~ *wie het zegt!* look who is talking!;
hoor eens listen, I say

de **horizon** /horizɔn/ (pl: -nen) horizon: *zijn* ~
verruimen (uitbreiden) broaden one's hori-
zons
horizontaal /horizɔntal/ (adj) horizontal;
[crossword puzzle] across

het **horloge** /horloʒə/ (pl: -s) watch

het **horlogebandje** /horloʒəbɑncə/ (pl: -s)
watchband, watch strap

het **hormoon** /hormon/ (pl: hormonen) hormone

de **horoscoop** /horɔskop/ (pl: horoscopen) horoscope: *een ~ trekken (opmaken)* cast a horoscope

de **horrorfilm** /hɔrɔrfɪlm/ (pl: -s) horror film

de **hort** /hɔrt/ (pl: -en) jerk: *met ~en en stoten spreken* speak haltingly || *de ~ op zijn* be on a spree, be on the loose

de **hortensia** /hɔrtɛnsija/ (pl: -'s) hydrangea

de **horzel** /hɔrzəl/ (pl: -s) hornet

de **hospes** /hɔspɛs/ (pl: -sen) landlord; host

de **hospita** /hɔspita/ (pl: -'s) landlady

het **hospitaal** /hɔspital/ (pl: hospitalen) hospital

hospitaliseren /hɔspitalizerə(n)/ (hospitaliseerde, heeft/is gehospitaliseerd) hospitalize

de **hospitant** /hɔspitɑnt/ (pl: -en) student teacher

hospiteren /hɔspiterə(n)/ (hospiteerde, heeft gehospiteerd) **1** do one's teaching practice **2** be interviewed for a room in a student residence

hossen /hɔsə(n)/ (hoste, heeft/is gehost) dance (*or:* leap) about (arm in arm)

de **host** /host/ [comp] host

de **hostess** /hostəs/ (pl: -es) hostess

de **hostie** /hɔsti/ (pl: -s) host

de **hosting** /hostɪŋ/ [comp] hosting

de **hotdog** /hɔdɔɡ/ (pl: -s) hotdog

het **hotel** /hotɛl/ (pl: -s) hotel

de **hotelhouder** /hotɛlhɑudər/ (pl: -s) hotel-keeper

de **hotelschool** /hotɛlsxol/ (pl: -scholen) hotel and catering school: *hogere ~* hotel management school

de **hotspot** /hɔtspɔt/ hotspot

houdbaar /hɑudbar/ (adj) **1** not perishable: *ten minste ~ tot* best before **2** tenable

de **houdbaarheid** /hɑudbarhɛit/ shelf life, storage life [of foods etc]

de **houdbaarheidsdatum** /hɑudbarhɛitsdatʏm/ use-by date, best-before date

¹**houden** /hɑudə(n)/ (hield, heeft gehouden) **1** (+ van) love: *wij ~ van elkaar* we love each other **2** (+ van) like, care for: *ik hou van dansen* ~ not like dancing; *hij houdt wel van een grapje* he can stand a joke; *ik hou meer van bier dan van wijn* I prefer beer to wine **3** hold; stick: *het ijs houdt nog niet* the ice isn't yet strong enough to hold your weight

²**houden** /hɑudə(n)/ (hield, heeft gehouden) **1** keep: *je mag het ~* you can keep (*or:* have) it; *kippen* (*or:* *duiven*) ~ keep hens (*or:* pigeons); *de blik op iets gericht* ~ keep looking at sth.; *laten we het gezellig ~* let's keep it (*or:* the conversation) pleasant; *ik zal het kort ~* I'll keep it short; *iem. aan de praat* ~ keep s.o. talking; *hij kon er zijn gedachten niet bij* ~ he couldn't keep his mind on it; *iets tegen het licht* ~ hold sth. up to the light; *ik kon hun na-*

men niet uit elkaar ~ I kept getting their names mixed up; *contact met iem.* ~ keep in touch with s.o.; *orde* ~ keep order **2** hold: [sport] *die had hij gemakkelijk kunnen* ~ he could have easily stopped that one; *de balk hield het niet* the beam didn't hold; the beam gave way **3** hold; organize; give: *een lezing* ~ give (*or:* deliver) a lecture **4** (+ voor) take to be, consider to be (*or:* as): *iets voor gezien* ~ leave it at that, call it a day **5** take, stand: *het was er niet om te* ~ *van de hitte* the heat was unbearable; *ik hou het niet meer* I can't take it any more (*or:* longer) || *rechts* ~ keep (to the) right; *William houdt nooit zijn woord* (*or:* *beloften*) William never keeps his word (*or:* promises); *we* ~ *het op de 15e* let's make it the 15th, then

zich ³**houden** /hɑudə(n)/ (hield zich, heeft zich gehouden) **1** (+ aan) keep to; adhere to; abide by; comply with; observe **2** keep: *hij kon zich niet goed* ~ he couldn't help laughing (*or:* crying)

de **houder** /hɑudər/ (pl: -s) **1** holder; bearer: *een record~* a record-holder **2** [law] keeper; holder **3** keeper, manager; proprietor **4** holder, container

de **houdgreep** /hɑutxrep/ (pl: -grepen) hold

de **houding** /hɑudɪŋ/ (pl: -en) **1** position, pose: *in een andere* ~ *gaan liggen (zitten)* assume a different position **2** pose, air: *zich geen* ~ *weten te geven* feel awkward **3** attitude, manner

de **house** /hɑus/ house (music)

de **houseparty** /hɑuspaːrti/ (pl: -'s) house party

de **housewarming** /hɑuswɔːrmɪŋ/ (pl: -s) housewarming (party)

het **hout** /hɑut/ wood: ~ *sprokkelen* gather wood (*or:* sticks) || [fig] *hij is uit het goede ~ gesneden* he is made of the right stuff; [Belg] *niet meer weten van welk ~ pijlen te maken* not know which way to turn, be at a complete loss

de **houtblazers** /hɑudblazərs/ (pl) woodwinds

houten /hɑutə(n)/ (adj) wooden

houterig /hɑutərəx/ (adj, adv) wooden: *zich ~ bewegen* move woodenly

de **houthakker** /hɑuthɑkər/ (pl: -s) lumberjack

de **houthandel** /hɑuthɑndəl/ (pl: -s) **1** timber trade **2** timber yard

het **houtje** /hɑucə/ (pl: -s) bit of wood || *iets op eigen ~ doen* do sth. on one's own (initiative); *op een ~ bijten* have difficulty in keeping body and soul together

de **houtlijm** /hɑutlɛim/ wood glue

de **houtskool** /hɑutskol/ charcoal

de **houtsnede** /hɑutsnedə/ (pl: -n, -s) woodcut

het **houtsnijwerk** /hɑutsnɛiwɛrk/ (pl: -en) woodcarving

het **houtvuur** /hɑutfyr/ wood (*or:* log) fire

de **houtworm** /hɑutwɔrm/ (pl: -en) woodworm

de **houtzagerij** /hɑutsaɣərɛi/ (pl: -en) sawmill

het **houvast** /hɑuvɑst/ hold, grip: *niet veel* (or: *geen enkel*) ~ *geven* provide little (or: no) hold; *iem.* ~ *bieden* [also fig] give s.o. sth. to hold on to

de **houw** /hɑu/ gash: *iem. een* ~ *geven* gash s.o.

de **houwdegen** /hɑudeɣə(n)/ (pl: -s) **1** backsword **2** [fig] old war-horse

het **houweel** /hɑuwel/ (pl: houwelen) pickaxe

houwen /hɑuwə(n)/ (hieuw, heeft gehouwen) **1** chop, hack; carve; hew: *uit marmer gehouwen* carved out of marble **2** chop down

de **hovenier** /hovənir/ (pl: -s) horticulturist, gardener

hozen /hozə(n)/ (hoosde, heeft gehoosd) bail (out) ‖ *het hoost* it is pouring down (or: with rain)

de **hsl** /hɑɛsɛl/ (pl: -'s) hogesnelheidslijn high-speed rail link

het **hso** /hɑɛso/ [Belg] *hoger secundair onderwijs* senior general secondary education

de **hst** /hɑɛste/ *hogesnelheidstrein* high-speed train, HST

de **hts** /hɑteɛs/ (pl: -'en) *hogere technische school* Technical College

de **hufter** /hʏftər/ (pl: -s) [inform] shithead, asshole

hufterproof /hʏftərpruːf/ (adj) vandal proof

de **hugenoot** /hyɣənot/ (pl: hugenoten) Huguenot

huggen /hyɡə(n)/ (hugde, heeft gehugd) hug

de **huichelaar** /hœyxəlar/ (pl: -s) hypocrite

de **huichelarij** /hœyxəlarɛi/ (pl: -en) hypocrisy

¹**huichelen** /hœyxələ(n)/ (huichelde, heeft gehuicheld) play the hypocrite, be hypocritical

²**huichelen** /hœyxələ(n)/ (huichelde, heeft gehuicheld) feign, sham

de **huid** /hœyt/ (pl: -en) **1** skin: *hij heeft een dikke* ~ he is thick-skinned; *zijn* ~ *duur verkopen* fight to the bitter end; *iem. de* ~ *vol schelden* call s.o. everything under the sun; *iem. op zijn* ~ *zitten* keep on at s.o. **2** hide; skin

de **huidarts** /hœytɑrts/ (pl: -en) dermatologist

huidig /hœydəx/ (adj) present, current

de **huidkanker** /hœytkɑŋkər/ skin cancer

de **huiduitslag** /hœytœytslɑx/ rash

de **huidziekte** /hœytsiktə/ (pl: -n, -s) skin disease

de **huifkar** /hœyfkɑr/ (pl: -ren) covered wagon

de **huig** /hœyx/ (pl: -en) uvula

de **huilbaby** /hœylbebi/ (pl: -'s) whiny baby

de **huilbui** /hœylbœy/ (pl: -en) crying fit

de **huilebalk** /hœyləbɑlk/ (pl: -en) cry-baby

huilen /hœylə(n)/ (huilde, heeft gehuild) **1** cry; whine; snivel: *ze kon wel* ~ she could have cried; *half lachend, half ~d* between

laughing and crying; ~ *om iets* cry about sth.; ~ *van blijdschap* (or: *pijn*) cry with joy (or: pain) **2** howl

het **huis** /hœys/ (pl: huizen) **1** house, home: ~ *van bewaring* remand centre; ~ *en haard* hearth and home; *halfvrijstaand* ~ semi-detached; [Am] duplex; *open* ~ *houden* have an open day; [Am] have an open house; *het ouderlijk* ~ *verlaten, uit* ~ *gaan* leave home; *dicht bij* ~ near home; *heel wat in* ~ *hebben* [fig] have a lot going for one; *nu de kinderen het* ~ *uit zijn* now that the children have all left; *een* ~ *van drie verdiepingen* a three-storeyed house; *ik kom van* ~ I have come from home; *dan zijn we nog verder van* ~ then we will be even worse off; *(op kosten) van* ~ *uit* on the house; *het is niet om over naar* ~ *te schrijven* it is nothing to write home about; *van* ~ *uit* originally, by birth **2** House: *het Koninklijk* ~ the Royal Family ‖ [Belg] *daar komt niets van in* ~ **a)** that's not on; **b)** it won't work, nothing will come of it

het **huis-aan-huisblad** /hœysanhœyzblɑt/ (pl: -en) free local paper

het **huisarrest** /hœysarɛst/ house arrest: ~ *hebben* be under house arrest; be kept in

de **huisarts** /hœysɑrts/ (pl: -en) family doctor

de **huisartsenpost** (pl: -en) [roughly] doctor's surgery

de **huisbaas** /hœyzbas/ (pl: -bazen) landlord

het **huisbezoek** /hœyzbəzuk/ (pl: -en) house call

de **huisdeur** /hœyzdør/ (pl: -en) front door

het **huisdier** /hœyzdir/ (pl: -en) pet

huiselijk /hœysələk/ (adj) **1** domestic, home; family: *in de ~e kring* in the family circle **2** homelike, homey: *een* ~ *type* a home-loving type

de **huisgenoot** /hœysxənot/ (pl: -genoten) housemate; member of the family

het **huisgezin** /hœysxəzɪn/ (pl: -nen) family

huishoudelijk /hœyshɑudələk/ (adj) domestic, household

het ¹**huishouden** /hœyshɑudə(n)/ (pl: -s) **1** housekeeping: *het* ~ *doen* run the house, do the housekeeping **2** household: *woningen voor een- en tweepersoonshuishoudens* houses for single people and couples

²**huishouden** /hœyshɑudə(n)/ (hield huis, heeft huisgehouden) carry on, cause damage (or: havoc)

de **huishoudfolie** /hœyshɑutfoli/ cling film

het **huishoudgeld** /hœyshɑutxɛlt/ housekeeping (money)

de **huishouding** /hœyshɑudɪŋ/ (pl: -en) housekeeping: *een gemeenschappelijke* ~ *voeren* have a joint household

de **huishoudster** /hœyshɑutstər/ (pl: -s) housekeeper

het **huisje** /hœyʃə/ (pl: -s) bungalow, cottage, small house, little house

huisje-boompje-beestje /hœyʃəbompjə-beʃə/ (adj) suburban bliss

de **huisjesmelker** /hœyʃəsmɛlkər/ (pl: -s) rackrenter; [Am] slumlord

de **huiskamer** /hœyskamər/ (pl: -s) living room

de **huisman** /hœysmɑn/ (pl: -nen) househusband

de **huismeester** /hœysmestər/ (pl: -s) caretaker, warden

het **huismiddel** /hœysmɪdəl/ (pl: -en) home remedy

de **huismoeder** /hœysmudər/ (pl: -s) housewife

de **huismus** /hœysmʏs/ (pl: -sen) **1** house sparrow **2** stay-at-home

het **huisnummer** /hœysnʏmər/ (pl: -s) house number

de **huisraad** /hœysrat/ household effects

de **huisregels** /hœysreɣəls/ (pl) house rules

de **huisschilder** /hœysχɪldər/ (pl: -s) house painter

de **huissleutel** /hœysløtəl/ (pl: -s) latchkey, front-door key

de **huisstijl** /hœystɛɪl/ (pl: -en) house style

de **huisstofmijt** /hœystɔfmɛɪt/ (pl: -en) house dust mite

de **huisvader** /hœysfadər/ (pl: -s) family man, father (of the family)

huisvesten /hœysfɛstə(n)/ (huisvestte, heeft gehuisvest) house, accommodate

de **huisvesting** /hœysfɛstɪŋ/ **1** housing **2** accommodation: *ergens ~ vinden* find accommodation somewhere

de **huisvredebreuk** /hœysfredəbrøk/ unlawful entry, trespass (in s.o.'s house)

de **huisvriend** /hœysfrint/ (pl: -en) family friend, friend of the family

de **huisvrouw** /hœysfrɑu/ (pl: -en) housewife

het **huisvuil** /hœysfœyl/ household refuse

huiswaarts /hœyswarts/ (adv) homeward(s)

het **huiswerk** /hœyswɛrk/ homework: *~ maken* do one's homework

de **huiszoeking** /hœysukɪŋ/ (pl: -en) (house) search

huiveren /hœyvərə(n)/ (huiverde, heeft gehuiverd) **1** shiver; shudder; tremble: *~ van de kou* shiver with cold **2** recoil (from), shrink (from)

huiverig /hœyvərəχ/ (adj) hesitant, wary

de **huivering** /hœyvərɪŋ/ (pl: -en) shiver, shudder

huiveringwekkend /hœyvərɪŋwɛkənt/ (adj, adv) horrible, terrifying

het **huizenblok** /hœyzə(n)blɔk/ (pl: -ken) row of houses

huizenhoog /hœyzə(n)hoχ/ (adj, adv) towering: *huizenhoge golven* mountainous waves

de **huizenmarkt** /hœyzəmɑrkt/ housing market

de **hulde** /hʏldə/ homage, tribute

het **huldeblijk** /hʏldəblɛɪk/ tribute

huldigen /hʏldəɣə(n)/ (huldigde, heeft gehuldigd) honour, pay tribute (to)

de **huldiging** /hʏldəɣɪŋ/ (pl: -en) homage, tribute

¹**hullen** /hʏlə(n)/ (hulde, heeft gehuld) wrap up in; [fig also] veil (in), cloak (in)

zich ²**hullen** /hʏlə(n)/ (hulde zich, heeft zich gehuld) wrap o.s. (up); [fig also] veil (or: cloak, shroud) o.s. (in)

de **hulp** /hʏlp/ (pl: -en) **1** help, assistance: *om ~ roepen* call (out) for help; *iem. te ~ komen* come to s.o.'s aid; *eerste ~ (bij ongelukken)* first aid; *~ verlenen* render assistance, assist **2** helper, assistant: *~ in de huishouding* home help

hulpbehoevend /hʏlbəhuvənt/ (adj) in need of help; invalid; infirm; needy

de **hulpbron** /hʏlbrɔn/ (pl: -nen) resource

de **hulpdienst** /hʏlbdinst/ (pl: -en) auxiliary service(s); emergency service(s): *telefonische ~* helpline

hulpeloos /hʏlpəlos/ (adj, adv) helpless

het **hulpgeroep** /hʏlpχərup/ a cry (or: call) for help

het **hulpmiddel** /hʏlpmɪdəl/ (pl: -en) aid, help, means

de **hulppost** /hʏlpɔst/ (pl: -en) aid station; first-aid post

het **hulpstuk** /hʏlpstʏk/ (pl: -ken) accessory, attachment

de **hulptroepen** /hʏlptrupə(n)/ (pl) auxiliary troops (or: forces); reinforcements

hulpvaardig /hʏlpfardəχ/ (adj) helpful

de **hulpverlener** /hʏlpfərlenər/ (pl: -s) social worker

de **hulpverlening** /hʏlpfərlenɪŋ/ assistance, aid; relief

het **hulpwerkwoord** /hʏlpwɛrkwort/ (pl: -en) auxiliary

de **huls** /hʏls/ (pl: hulzen) **1** case, cover, container **2** cartridge case, shell

de **hulst** /hʏlst/ holly

humaan /hymɑn/ (adj, adv) humane

de **humaniora** /hymanijora/ [Belg] [roughly] grammar school education

het **humanisme** /hymanɪsmə/ humanism

de **humanist** /hymanɪst/ (pl: -en) humanist

humanitair /hymanitɛːr/ (adj, adv) humanitarian

het **humeur** /hymør/ (pl: -en) humour, temper, mood

humeurig /hymørəχ/ (adj, adv) moody

de **hummel** /hʏməl/ (pl: -s) toddler, (tiny) tot

de **hummus** /hʏmus/ hummus

de **humor** /hymɔr/ humour: *gevoel voor ~* sense of humour

de **humorist** /hymorɪst/ (pl: -en) humorist; comic

humoristisch /hymorɪstis/ (adj, adv) humorous: *een ~e* **opmerking** a humorous remark

de **humus** /hymys/ humus

¹**hun** /hyn/ (pers pron) them: *ik zal het ~ geven* I'll give it (to) them; *heb je ~ al geroepen?* have you already called them?

²**hun** /hyn/ (poss pron) their: *~ kinderen* their children; *die zoon van ~* that son of theirs

het **hunebed** /hynəbɛt/ (pl: -den) megalith(ic tomb, monument, grave)

hunkeren /hynkərə(n)/ (hunkerde, heeft gehunkerd) long for, yearn for

hup /hyp/ (int) **1** come on, go (to it): *~ Henk ~!* come on Henk! **2** hup, oops-a-daisy: *een, twee, …~!* one, two, … up you go!

de **huppeldepup** /hypəldəpyp/ what's-his-name, what's-her-name

huppelen /hypələ(n)/ (huppelde, heeft/is gehuppeld) hop, skip, frolic

huren /hyrə(n)/ (huurde, heeft gehuurd) **1** rent; charter: *een huis ~* rent a house; *kamers ~* live in rooms **2** hire, take on: *een kok ~* hire (*or:* take on) a cook

hurken /hyrkə(n)/ (hurkte, is gehurkt) squat: *zij zaten gehurkt op de grond* they were squatting on the ground ‖ *op zijn ~ (gaan) zitten* squat (on one's haunches)

het **hurktoilet** /hyrktwalɛt/ (pl: -ten) squat toilet

de **hut** /hyt/ (pl: -ten) **1** hut: *een lemen ~* a mud hut **2** cabin

de **hutkoffer** /hytkɔfər/ (pl: -s) cabin trunk

de **hutselen** /hytsələ(n)/ (hutselde, heeft gehutseld) mix (up), shake (up): *dominostenen door elkaar ~* shuffle dominoes

de **hutspot** /hytspɔt/ hot(ch)-pot(ch)

de **huur** /hyr/ (pl: huren) rent; lease: *achterstallige ~* rent in arrears, back rent; *kale ~* basic rent; *iem. de ~ opzeggen* give s.o. notice (to leave, quit); *dit huis is te ~* this house is to let; [Am] this house is for rent; *hij betaalt €800,- ~ voor dit huis* he pays 800 euros rent for this house

de **huurachterstand** /hyraχtərstɑnt/ (pl: -en) arrears of rent

de **huurauto** /hyrauto/ (pl: -'s) rented car, hire(d) car

het **huurcontract** /hyrkɔntrɑkt/ (pl: -en) rental agreement; lease: *een ~ aangaan* sign a lease; *een ~ opzeggen* terminate a lease

de **huurder** /hyrdər/ (pl: -s) renter; tenant; hirer: *de huidige ~s* the sitting tenants

het **huurhuis** /hyrhœys/ (pl: -huizen) rented house

de **huurkoop** /hyrkop/ instalment buying, hire purchase (system)

de **huurling** /hyrlɪŋ/ (pl: -en) hireling; mercenary

de **huurmoord** /hyrmort/ (pl: -en) assassination; hit

de **huurmoordenaar** /hyrmordənar/ (pl: -s)

(hired) assassin

de **huurovereenkomst** /hyrovəreŋkɔmst/ (pl: -en) *see* huurcontract

de **huurprijs** /hyrprɛis/ (pl: -prijzen) rent; rental (price)

de **huurschuld** /hyrsχγlt/ (pl: -en) rent arrears, arrears of rent: *de ~ bedraagt €5000,-* the rent arrears amount to €5000

de **huurtoeslag** /hyrtuslɑχ/ (pl: -en) rent subsidy, housing benefit

de **huurverhoging** /hyrvərhoγɪŋ/ rent increase

de **huurwoning** /hyrwonɪŋ/ (pl: -en) rented house (*or:* flat)

huwbaar /hywbar/ (adj) marriageable: *de huwbare leeftijd bereiken* reach marriageable age

het **huwelijk** /hywələk/ (pl: -en) **1** marriage, wedding: *ontbinding van een ~* dissolution of a marriage; *gemengd ~* mixed marriage; *een wettig ~* a lawful marriage; *een ~ inzegenen* perform a marriage service; *een ~ sluiten (aangaan) met* get married to; *een kind, buiten ~ geboren* a child born out of wedlock; *zijn ~ met* his marriage to; *een meisje ten ~ vragen* propose to a girl; *een ~ uit liefde* a love match; *een burgerlijk ~* a civil wedding; *een kerkelijk ~* a church wedding; *een ~ voltrekken* perform a marriage service, celebrate a marriage **2** matrimony: *na 25 jaar ~* after 25 years of matrimony

huwelijks /hywələks/ (adj) marital, married: *~e voorwaarden* marriage settlement (*or:* articles)

het **huwelijksaanzoek** /hywələksanzuk/ (pl: -en) proposal (of marriage): *een ~ doen* propose (to s.o.); *een ~ krijgen* receive a proposal (of marriage)

de **huwelijksakte** /hywələksɑktə/ (pl: -n, -s) marriage certificate

het **huwelijksgeschenk** /hywələksχəsχɛŋk/ (pl: -en) wedding present (*or:* gift)

de **huwelijksnacht** /hywələksnɑχt/ (pl: -en) wedding night: *de eerste ~* the wedding night

de **huwelijksplechtigheid** /hywələksplɛχtəχɛit/ (pl: -heden) wedding, marriage ceremony, wedding ceremony

de **huwelijksreis** /hywələksrɛis/ (pl: -reizen) honeymoon (trip): *zij zijn op ~* they are on (their) honeymoon (trip)

huwen /hywə(n)/ (huwde, heeft/is gehuwd) marry

de **huzaar** /hyzar/ (pl: huzaren) hussar

de **huzarensalade** /hyzarə(n)saladə/ (pl: -s) [roughly] Russian salad

de **hyacint** /hijasɪnt/ (pl: -en) hyacinth

de **hybride** /hibridə/ (pl: -n) hybrid, cross

de **hybrideauto** /hibridəauto/ (pl: -'s) hybrid car

hydraulisch /hidrɑulis/ (adj, adv) hydraulic:

~e pers (or: *remmen*) hydraulic press (*or:* brakes)

de **hyena** /hijena/ (pl: -'s) hy(a)ena

de **hygiëne** /hiɣ(i)jenə/ hygiene: **persoonlijke (intieme)** ~ personal hygiene

¹**hygiënisch** /hiɣ(i)jenis/ (adj) hygienic, sanitary: *~e omstandigheden* sanitary conditions; *~e voorschriften* hygienic (*or:* sanitary) regulations

²**hygiënisch** /hiɣ(i)jenis/ (adv) hygienically: ~ *verpakt* hygienically packed (*or:* wrapped)

de **hymne** /himnə/ (pl: -n) hymn

de **hype** /hɑjp/ (pl: -s) hype, fad, craze

hypen /hɑjpə(n)/ (hypete, heeft gehypet) hype

hyper- /hipər-/ hyper-, ultra-, super-

hyperactief /hipərɑktif/ (adj) hyperactive

de **hyperbool** /hipərbol/ (pl: hyperbolen) hyperbola

hypercorrect /hipərkorɛkt/ (adj) hypercorrect

de **hyperlink** /hɑjpərlɪŋk/ hyperlink

de **hypermarkt** /hipərmɑrkt/ (pl: -en) hypermarket

hypermodern /hipərmodɛrn/ (adj, adv) ultramodern; super-fashionable: *een* ~ *interieur* an ultramodern interior

de **hyperventilatie** /hipərvɛntila(t)si/ hyperventilation

hyperventileren /hipərvɛntilerə/ (hyperventileerde, heeft gehyperventileerd) hyperventilate

de **hypnose** /hipnozə/ hypnosis: *iem. onder ~ brengen* put s.o. under hypnosis

hypnotisch /hipnotis/ (adj, adv) hypnotic: *~e blik* hypnotic gaze

hypnotiseren /hipnotizerə(n)/ (hypnotiseerde, heeft gehypnotiseerd) hypnotize

de **hypnotiseur** /hipnotizør/ (pl: -s) hypnotist, hypnotherapist

de **hypochonder** /hipoxɔndər/ (pl: -s) hypochondriac

de ¹**hypocriet** /hipokrit/ (pl: -en) hypocrite

²**hypocriet** /hipokrit/ (adj) hypocritical, insincere

de **hypocrisie** /hipokrizi/ hypocrisy

de **hypotenusa** /hipotenyza/ (pl: -'s) hypotenuse

hypothecair /hipotekɛːr/ (adj) mortgage: *~e lening* mortgage (loan)

de **hypotheek** /hipotek/ (pl: hypotheken) mortgage: *een* ~ *aflossen* pay off a mortgage; *een* ~ *afsluiten* take out a mortgage; *een* ~ *nemen op een huis* take out a mortgage on a house

de **hypotheekrente** /hipotekrɛntə/ mortgage (interest)

de **hypothese** /hipotezə/ (pl: -n, -s) hypothesis: *een* ~ *opstellen* formulate a hypothesis

hypothetisch /hipotetis/ (adj, adv) hypothetical

de **hysterie** /hɪsteri/ hysteria

hysterisch /hɪsteris/ (adj, adv) hysterical: ~ *gekrijs* hysterical screams; *~e toevallen (aanvallen) krijgen* have (fits of) hysterics; *doe niet zo* ~*!* don't be so (*or:* get) hysterical!

I

de **i** /i/ (pl: i's) i, I

Iberisch /iberis/ (adj) Iberian: *het ~ Schiereiland* the Iberian Peninsula

de **ibis** /ibɪs/ (pl: -sen) ibis

de **icetea** /ɑjsti:/ ice tea

de **icoon** /ikon/ (pl: iconen) icon: *zij is een ~ van de jaren tachtig* she's an eighties icon

de **ICT** /isetə/ *informatie- en communicatietechnologie* ICT, information and communication technology

de **ICT'er** ICT specialist

het **¹ideaal** /idejal/ (pl: idealen) **1** ideal: *zich iem. tot ~ stellen* take s.o. as a model **2** ambition, ideal: *het ~ van zijn jeugd was arts te worden* the ambition of his youth was to become a doctor; *een ~ nastreven* pursue an ideal (*or:* ambition), follow a dream

²ideaal /idejal/ (adj, adv) ideal, perfect

idealiseren /idejalizerə(n)/ (idealiseerde, heeft geïdealiseerd) idealize, glamorize

het **idealisme** /idejalɪsmə/ idealism

de **idealist** /idejalɪst/ (pl: -en) idealist

idealistisch /idejalɪstis/ (adj) idealistic

idealiter /idejalitɛr/ (adv) ideally, theoretically, in theory

het/de **idee** /ide/ (pl: -ën) **1** idea: *zich een ~ vormen van iets* form an idea of sth. **2** idea, notion, concept(ion): *ik heb geen (flauw) ~* I haven't the faintest (*or:* foggiest) idea **3** idea, view || *ik heb een ~* I've got an idea; *op een ~ komen* think of sth., hit upon an idea; *zij kwam op het ~ om* she hit upon the idea of

ideëel /idejel/ (adj) idealistic

de **ideeënbus** /idejə(n)bʏs/ (pl: -sen) suggestion box

het/de **idee-fixe** /idefɪks/ (pl: -n) obsession

idem /idɛm/ (adv) ditto, idem

identiek /idɛntik/ (adj) identical (with, to)

de **identificatie** /idɛntifika(t)si/ (pl: -s) identification

de **identificatieplicht** /idɛntifika(t)siplɪxt/ obligation to carry identification

identificeren /idɛntifiserə(n)/ (identificeerde, heeft geïdentificeerd) identify

de **identiteit** /idɛntitɛit/ identity

het **identiteitsbewijs** /idɛntitɛitsbəwɛis/ (pl: -bewijzen) identity card, ID card

de **identiteitskaart** /idɛntitɛitskart/ (pl: -en) identity card; ID (card)

de **ideologie** /idejoloyi/ (pl: -ën) ideology

ideologisch /idejoloyis/ (adj, adv) ideological

het **idioom** /idijom/ (pl: idiomen) idiom

de **¹idioot** /idijot/ (pl: idioten) idiot; fool: *een volslagen ~* an absolute fool

²idioot /idijot/ (adj, adv) idiotic; foolish: *doe niet zo ~* don't be such a fool (*or:* an idiot)

idolaat /idolat/ (adj, adv): *~ van* infatuated with, mad about

het **idool** /idol/ (pl: idolen) idol

de **idylle** /idɪlə/ (pl: -n, -s) idyl(l)

idyllisch /idɪlis/ (adj, adv) idyllic

ieder /idər/ (ind pron) **1** every; each; any: *het kan ~e dag afgelopen zijn* it may be over any day (now); *werkelijk ~e dag* every single day; *ze komt ~e dag* she comes every day **2** everyone, everybody; each (one), anyone, anybody: *tot ~s verbazing* to everyone's surprise; *~ van ons* each of us, every one of us; *~ voor zich* every man for himself

iedereen /idəren/ (ind pron) everyone, everybody, all; anybody; anyone: *jij bent niet ~* you're not just anybody

het **iederwijs** [roughly] democratic school, democratic education system

iel /il/ (adj, adv) thin, puny

iemand /imɑnt/ (ind pron) someone, somebody; anyone; anybody: *is daar ~?* is anybody there?; *hij is niet zomaar ~* he's not just anybody; *hij wilde niet dat ~ het wist* he didn't want anyone to know; *zij maakte de indruk van ~ die* she gave the impression of being s.o. (*or:* a woman) who

de **iep** /ip/ (pl: -en) elm

de **Ier** /ir/ (pl: -en) Irishman: *tien ~en* ten Irishmen

Ierland /irlɑnt/ Ireland, Republic of Ireland

het **¹Iers** /irs/ Irish

²Iers /irs/ (adj) Irish

¹iets /its/ (ind pron) **1** anything: *hij heeft ~ wat ik niet begrijp* there is something about him which I don't understand **2** something; anything: *~ lekkers* (or: *moois*) something tasty (*or:* beautiful); *~ dergelijks* something like that **3** something, a little, a bit: *beter ~ dan niets* something is better than nothing; *een mysterieus ~* something mysterious, a mysterious something

²iets /its/ (adv) a bit, a little, slightly: *als zij er ~ om gaf* if she cared at all; *we moeten ~ vroeger weggaan* we must leave a bit (*or:* slightly) earlier

ietwat /itwɑt/ (adv) somewhat, slightly

de **iftar** /ɪftɑr/ (pl: -s) iftar

de **iglo** /iɣlo/ (pl: -'s) igloo

de **i-grec** /iɣrɛk/ (pl: -s) y

ijdel /ɛidəl/ (adj, adv) vain, conceited

de **ijdelheid** /ɛidəlhɛit/ (pl: -heden) vanity, conceit

de **ijdeltuit** /ɛidəltœyt/ (pl: -en) vain person

ijken /ɛikə(n)/ (ijkte, heeft geijkt) calibrate

het **ijkpunt** /ɛikpʏnt/ (pl: -en) benchmark (figure)

ijl /ɛil/ (adj) rarefied: *~e lucht* thin (*or:* rare-

fied) air
ijlen /ɛ͟ilə(n)/ (ijlde, heeft geijld) be delirious, ramble; rave
ijlings /ɛ͟ɪlɪŋs/ (adv) with all speed, in great haste
het **ijs** /ɛis/ **1** ice: *zich op glad ~ bevinden (begeven)* skate on thin ice; *het ~ breken* break the ice; *de haven was door ~ gesloten* the port was icebound **2** ice cream
de **ijsafzetting** /ɛ͟ɪsɑfsɛtɪŋ/ icing up; ice accretion
de **ijsbaan** /ɛ͟izban/ (pl: ijsbanen) skating rink, ice(-skating) rink
de **ijsbeer** /ɛ͟izber/ (pl: ijsberen) polar bear
ijsberen /ɛ͟izbərə(n)/ (ijsbeerde, heeft geijsbeerd) pace up and down
de **ijsberg** /ɛ͟izbɛrx/ (pl: -en) iceberg
de **ijsbergsla** /ɛ͟izbɛrxsla/ iceberg lettuce
de **ijsbloemen** /ɛ͟ɪzblumə(n)/ (pl) frostwork
het **ijsblokje** /ɛ͟izblɔkjə/ (pl: -s) ice cube
de **ijsbreker** /ɛ͟ɪzbrekər/ (pl: -s) icebreaker
de **ijscoman** /ɛ͟iskomɑn/ (pl: -nen) ice-cream man
ijselijk /ɛ͟isələk/ (adj, adv) hideous, dreadful
de **ijsemmer** /ɛ͟ɪsɛmər/ (pl: -s) ice bucket
het **ijshockey** /ɛ͟ishɔki/ ice hockey
het **ijsje** /ɛ͟ɪʃə/ (pl: -s) ice (cream)
de **ijskar** /ɛ͟iskɑr/ ice-cream cart
de **ijskast** /ɛ͟iskɑst/ (pl: -en) fridge, refrigerator: *iets in de ~ zetten* **a)** put sth. in the fridge; **b)** [fig] shelve sth., put sth. on ice
ijskoud /ɛiskɑu͟t/ (adj, adv) **1** ice-cold, icy(-cold) **2** [fig] icy, (as) cold as ice: *een ~e ontvangst* an icy welcome
IJsland /ɛ͟islɑnt/ Iceland
de **IJslander** /ɛ͟ɪslɑndər/ (pl: -s) Icelander
IJslands /ɛ͟islɑnts/ (adj) Icelandic
de **ijslolly** /ɛ͟isloli/ (pl: -'s) ice lolly; [Am] popsicle
de **ijsmuts** /ɛ͟ismʏts/ (pl: -en) [roughly] woolly hat
de **ijspegel** /ɛ͟ɪspeɣəl/ (pl: -s) icicle
de **ijssalon** /ɛ͟isalɔn/ (pl: -s) ice-cream parlour
de **ijsschots** /ɛ͟isxɔts/ (pl: -en) (ice) floe
de **ijstaart** /ɛ͟ɪstart/ (pl: -en) ice-cream cake
de **ijsthee** /ɛ͟iste/ ice(d) tea
de **ijstijd** /ɛ͟istɛit/ (pl: -en) ice age, glacial period (*or:* epoch)
de **ijsvogel** /ɛ͟isfoɣəl/ (pl: -s) kingfisher
ijsvrij /ɛisfrɛ͟i/ (adj) clear of ice ‖ *~ hebben* have a day off to go skating
de **ijver** /ɛ͟ivər/ diligence
de **ijveraar** /ɛ͟ɪvərar/ (pl: -s) advocate, zealot
ijveren /ɛ͟ɪvərə(n)/ (ijverde, heeft geijverd) devote o.s. (to), work (for)
ijverig /ɛ͟ivərəx/ (adj, adv) diligent: *een ~ scholier* an industrious (*or:* a diligent) pupil; *men deed ~ onderzoek* painstaking inquiries were made
de **ijzel** /ɛ͟izəl/ black ice
ijzelen /ɛ͟izələ(n)/ (ijzelde, heeft geijzeld) freeze over: *het ijzelt* it is freezing over

het **ijzer** /ɛ͟izər/ (pl: -s) iron: *~ smeden* (or: *gieten*) forge (*or:* cast) iron; *men moet het ~ smeden als het heet is* strike while the iron is hot
het/de **ijzerdraad** /ɛ͟izərdrat/ (iron) wire
ijzeren /ɛ͟izərə(n)/ (adj) iron: *een ~ gezondheid* an iron constitution
het **ijzererts** /ɛ͟izərɛrts/ (pl: -en) iron ore
de **ijzerhandel** /ɛ͟izərhɑndəl/ (pl: -s) **1** hardware store, ironmonger's shop **2** hardware trade, ironmongery
ijzerhoudend /ɛizərhɑu͟dənt/ (adj) ferriferous; ferrous
ijzersterk /ɛizərstɛ͟rk/ (adj) iron, cast-iron: *hij kwam met ~e argumenten* he produced very strong arguments; *een ~ geheugen* an excellent (*or:* infallible) memory
de **ijzertijd** /ɛ͟izərtɛit/ Iron Age
de **ijzerwaren** /ɛ͟izərwarə(n)/ (pl) hardware, ironmongery
de **ijzerzaag** /ɛ͟ɪzərzax/ (pl: -zagen) metal saw
ijzig /ɛ͟izəx/ (adj, adv) icy, freezing: *~e kalmte* steely composure
ijzingwekkend /ɛɪzɪŋwɛ͟kənt/ (adj, adv) horrifying, gruesome
ik /ɪk/ (pers pron) I: *ik ben het* it's me; *als ik er niet geweest was* … if it hadn't been for me …; *ze is beter dan ik* she's better than I am
de **ik-figuur** /ɪ͟kfiɣyr/ (pl: ik-figuren) first-person narrator
ikzelf /ɪksɛ͟lf/ (I) myself
illegaal /ileɣa͟l/ (adj, adv) **1** illegal **2** underground: *~ werk* underground work
de **illegaliteit** /ɪleɣalitɛ͟it/ (pl: -en) **1** illegality **2** resistance (movement)
de **illusie** /ɪly͟zi/ (pl: -s) illusion, (pipe)dream; delusion: *maakt u zich (daarover) geen ~s* you need have no illusions about that; *een ~ verstoren* (or: *wekken*) shatter (*or:* create) an illusion
de **illusionist** /ɪlyz(i)jonɪ͟st/ (pl: -en) conjurer
illuster /ɪly͟stər/ (adj) illustrious, distinguished
de **illustratie** /ɪlʏstra͟(t)si/ (pl: -s) illustration
illustratief /ɪlʏstrati͟f/ (adj) illustrative: *~ in dit verband is* … a case in point is …
de **illustrator** /ɪlʏstra͟tor/ (pl: -s, -en) illustrator
illustreren /ɪlʏstre͟rə(n)/ (illustreerde, heeft geïllustreerd) illustrate; exemplify
het/de **image** /ɪ͟mɪtʃ/ image
imaginair /imaʒinɛ͟ːr/ (adj, adv) imaginary: *een ~ getal* an imaginary number
het/de **imago** /ima͟yo/ (pl: -'s) image
de **imam** /i͟mɑm/ (pl: -s) imam
de **imbeciel** /ɪmbesi͟l/ (pl: -en) imbecile
het **IMF** /iɛmɛ͟f/ *Internationaal Monetair Fonds* IMF
de **imitatie** /imita͟(t)si/ (pl: -s) imitation, copy, copying; impersonation: *een slechte ~* a poor (*or:* bad) imitation
de **imitator** /imita͟tor/ (pl: -s, -en) imitator, impersonator

imiteren /imit̪ɛrə(n)/ (imiteerde, heeft
geïmiteerd) imitate, copy; impersonate

de **imker** /ɪmkər/ (pl: -s) bee-keeper

immens /ɪmɛns/ (adj, adv) immense

immer /ɪmər/ (adv) ever, always

immers /ɪmərs/ (adv) **1** after all: *hij komt ~
morgen* after all, he is coming tomorrow; he
is coming tomorrow, isn't he? **2** for, since

de **immigrant** /ɪmiɣrɑnt/ (pl: -en) immigrant

de **immigratie** /ɪmiɣra(t)si/ (pl: -s) immigration

immigreren /ɪmiɣrɛrə(n)/ (immigreerde, is
geïmmigreerd) immigrate

de **immobiliën** /ɪmobilijə(n)/ (pl) [Belg] property, real estate

immoreel /ɪmorɛl/ (adj, adv) immoral

de **immuniteit** /ɪmynɪtɛit/ (pl: -en) immunity

immuun /imyn/ (adj) immune: *~ voor kritiek*
immune to criticism

het **immuunsysteem** /ɪmynsistem/ immune
system

het/de **i-mode** /ɑimod/ i-mode

de **impact** /ɪmpɛkt/ impact, effect

de **impasse** /ɪmpɑsə/ (pl: -s, -n) impasse, deadlock

het/de **imperiaal** /ɪmperijal/ (pl: -s) roof-rack

het **imperialisme** /ɪmperijalɪsmə/ imperialism

de **imperialist** /ɪmperijalɪst/ (pl: -en) imperialist

imperialistisch /ɪmperijalɪstis/ (adj, adv)
imperialist(ic)

het **imperium** /ɪmperijʏm/ (pl: -s, imperia) empire

impertinent /ɪmpɛrtinɛnt/ (adj, adv) impertinent

het **implantaat** /ɪmplɑntat/ (pl: implantaten)
implant

implanteren /ɪmplɑntɛrə(n)/ (implanteer-
de, heeft geïmplanteerd) implant

implementeren /ɪmplɛmɛntɛrə(n)/ (im-
plementeerde, heeft geïmplementeerd) implement

de **implicatie** /ɪmplika(t)si/ (pl: -s) implication

impliceren /ɪmplisɛrə(n)/ (impliceerde,
heeft geïmpliceerd) imply

impliciet /ɪmplisit/ (adj, adv) implicit

imploderen /ɪmplodɛrə(n)/ (imlodeerde,
is geïmplodeerd) implode

de **implosie** /ɪmplozi/ (pl: -s) implosion

imponeren /ɪmponɛrə(n)/ (imponeerde,
heeft geïmponeerd) impress, overawe: *laat
je niet ~ door die deftige woorden* don't be
overawed by those posh words

impopulair /ɪmpopylɛːr/ (adj) unpopular:
~e maatregelen nemen take unpopular
measures

de **import** /ɪmport/ **1** import(ation) **2** import(s)

importeren /ɪmportɛrə(n)/ (importeerde,
heeft geïmporteerd) import

de **importeur** /ɪmportør/ (pl: -s) importer

imposant /ɪmpozɑnt/ (adj) impressive, im-

posing

impotent /ɪmpotɛnt/ (adj) impotent

impregneren /ɪmprɛɣnɛrə(n)/ (impreg-
neerde, heeft geïmpregneerd) impregnate

het **impresariaat** /ɪmprɛsarijat/ [roughly]
managership; agency

de **impresario** /ɪmprɛsarijo/ (pl: -'s) impresario

de **impressie** /ɪmprɛsi/ (pl: -s) impression

het **impressionisme** /ɪmprɛʃonɪsmə/ impres-
sionism

improductief /ɪmprodʏktif/ (adj) unproductive

de **improvisatie** /ɪmproviza(t)si/ (pl: -s) improvisation

improviseren /ɪmprovizɛrə(n)/ (improvi-
seerde, heeft geïmproviseerd) improvise

de **impuls** /ɪmpʏls/ (pl: -en) **1** impulse, impetus
2 impulse, urge: *hij handelde in een ~* he acted on (an) impulse

impulsief /ɪmpʏlsif/ (adj, adv) impulsive,
impetuous

¹**in** /ɪn/ (adj) in: *de bal was in* the ball was in

²**in** /ɪn/ (adv) **1** in, into, inside: *dat wil er bij mij
niet in* I find that hard to believe; *dag in dag
uit* day in (and) day out **2** in, inside: *tussen
twee huizen in* (in) between two houses ‖ *tegen alle verwachtingen in* contrary to all expectations

³**in** /ɪn/ (prep) **1** in, at: *een vertegenwoordiger
in het bestuur* a representative on the board;
puistjes in het gezicht pimples on one's face;
in heel het land throughout (or: all over) the
country; *hij is nog nooit in Londen geweest* he
has never been to London; *hij zat niet in dat
vliegtuig* he wasn't on that plane; *in slaap*
asleep **2** into: *in de hoogte kijken* look up; *in
het Japans vertalen* translate into Japanese
3 in, at; during: *in het begin* at the beginning; *een keer in de week* once a week **4** in: *er
gaan 100 cm in een meter* there are 100 cen-
timetres to a metre; *twee meter in omtrek*
two metres in circumference; *in een rustig
tempo* at an easy pace; *in tweeën snijden* cut
in two ‖ *professor in de natuurkunde* professor of physics; *zij is goed in wiskunde* she's
good at mathematics; *uitbarsten in gelach*
burst into laughter

inacceptabel /ɪnɑksɛptabəl/ (adj, adv) unacceptable

de **inachtneming** /ɪnɑxtnemɪŋ/ regard, consideration, observation: *met ~ van* having
regard to, considering, taking into account;
met ~ van de voorschriften in compliance with
the regulations

inademen /ɪnademə(n)/ (ademde in, heeft
ingeademd) inhale, breathe in

de **inauguratie** /ɪnɑuɣyra(t)si/ (pl: -s) inauguration

inaugureren /ɪnɑuɣyrɛrə(n)/ (inaugureer-
de, heeft geïnaugureerd) inaugurate

inbedden /ɪmbɛdə(n)/ (bedde in, heeft ingebed) bed, embed

zich **inbeelden** /ɪmbeldə(n)/ (beeldde zich in, heeft zich ingebeeld) imagine: *dat beeld je je maar in* that's just your imagination

de **inbeelding** /ɪmbeldɪŋ/ (pl: -en) imagination

inbegrepen /ɪmbəɣrepə(n)/ (adj) included, including

het **inbegrip** /ɪmbəɣrɪp/: *met ~ van* including

inbellen /ɪmbɛlə(n)/ (belde in, heeft ingebeld) [comp] dial up

inbinden /ɪmbɪndə(n)/ (bond in, heeft ingebonden) bind

inblazen /ɪmblazə(n)/ (blies in, heeft ingeblazen) blow into; [fig] breathe into: *iets nieuw leven ~* breathe new life into sth.

inblikken /ɪmblɪkə(n)/ (blikte in, heeft ingeblikt) can, tin

de **inboedel** /ɪmbudəl/ (pl: -s) moveables, furniture, furnishings: *een ~ verzekeren* [roughly] insure the contents of one's house against fire and theft

de **inboedelverzekering** /ɪmbudəlvərzekərɪŋ/ (pl: -en) [roughly] fire and theft insurance

inboeten /ɪmbutə(n)/ (boette in, heeft ingeboet) lose

inboezemen /ɪmbuzəmə(n)/ (boezemde in, heeft ingeboezemd) inspire

de **inboorling** /ɪmborlɪŋ/ (pl: -en) native

de **inborst** /ɪmbɔrst/ disposition, character

inbouwen /ɪmbɑuwə(n)/ (bouwde in, heeft ingebouwd) build in

de **inbouwkeuken** /ɪmbɑukøkə(n)/ (pl: -s) built-in kitchen

de **inbox** /ɪmbɔks/ in box

de **inbraak** /ɪmbrak/ (pl: inbraken) breaking in, burglary: *~ plegen* in break into, burgle

het **inbraakalarm** /ɪmbrakalɑrm/ burglar (*or:* intrusion) alarm

inbreken /ɪmbrekə(n)/ (brak in, heeft ingebroken) break in(to) (a house), burgle (a house): *~ in een computersysteem* break into a computer system; *er is alweer bij ons ingebroken* our house has been broken into (*or:* burgled) again

de **inbreker** /ɪmbrekər/ (pl: -s) burglar; [in computer] hacker

de **inbreng** /ɪmbrɛŋ/ (pl: -en) contribution

inbrengen /ɪmbrɛŋə(n)/ (bracht in, heeft ingebracht) **1** bring in(to); insert; inject **2** contribute **3** bring (forward): *daar valt niets tegen in te brengen* there is nothing to be said against this

de **inbreuk** /ɪmbrøk/ (pl: -en) infringement, violation

inburgeren /ɪmbʏrɣərə(n)/ (burgerde in, is ingeburgerd) naturalize, settle down, settle in

de **inbussleutel** /ɪmbʏsløtəl/ (pl: -s) Allen key

de **Inca** /ɪŋka/ Inca

incalculeren /ɪŋkɑlkylerə(n)/ (calculeerde

in, heeft ingecalculeerd) calculate in

de **incarnatie** /ɪŋkɑrna̱(t)si/ (pl: -s) incarnation

incasseren /ɪŋkɑse̱rə(n)/ (incasseerde, heeft geïncasseerd) **1** collect; cash (in) **2** accept, take

het **incasseringsvermogen** /ɪŋkɑse̱rɪŋsfərmoɣə(n)/ stamina, resilience: *hij heeft een groot ~* he can take a lot

het **incasso** /ɪŋka̱so/ collection: *automatische ~* direct debit

de **incest** /ɪnsɛst/ incest

incestueus /ɪnsɛstywø̱s/ (adj) incestuous

inchecken /ɪntʃɛkə(n)/ (checkte in, heeft ingecheckt) [airport] check in; [hotel] register

het **incident** /ɪnsidɛnt/ (pl: -en) incident

incidenteel /ɪnsidɛnte̱l/ (adj, adv) incidental, occasional: *dit verschijnsel doet zich ~ voor* this phenomenon occurs occasionally

inclusief /ɪŋklyzi̱f/ (adv) including; [abbr: incl.] inclusive (of): *45 euro ~ (bedieningsgeld)* 45 euros, including service

incognito /ɪŋko̱ɣnito/ (adv) incognito

incompetent /ɪŋkɔmpətɛnt/ (adj) incompetent, unqualified

incompleet /ɪŋkɔmple̱t/ (adj) incomplete

in concreto /ɪŋkɔŋkre̱to/ in the concrete, in this particular case

inconsequent /ɪŋkɔnsəkwɛnt/ (adj, adv) inconsistent

incontinent /ɪŋkɔntinɛnt/ (adj) incontinent

incorrect /ɪŋkɔrɛkt/ (adj, adv) incorrect

incourant /ɪŋkurɑnt/ (adj) unsaleable, unmarketable: *~e maten* off-sizes

de **incrowd** /ɪŋkrɑud/ (pl: -s) in-crowd

de **incubatietijd** /ɪŋkyba̱(t)sitɛit/ (pl: -en) incubation period

indammen /ɪndɑmə(n)/ (damde in, heeft ingedamd) dam (up): *een conflict ~* keep a conflict under control

zich **indekken** /ɪndɛkə(n)/ (dekte zich in, heeft zich ingedekt) cover o.s. (against)

indelen /ɪndelə(n)/ (deelde in, heeft ingedeeld) **1** divide, order, class(ify): *zijn dag ~* plan one's day **2** group, class(ify)

de **indeling** /ɪndelɪŋ/ (pl: -en) division, arrangement, classification; lay-out: *de ~ van een gebied in districten* the division of a region into districts

zich **indenken** /ɪndɛŋkə(n)/ (dacht zich in, heeft zich ingedacht) imagine: *zich in iemands situatie ~* put o.s. in s.o.'s place (*or:* shoes)

inderdaad /ɪndərda̱t/ (adv) indeed; really; sure enough: *ik heb dat ~ gezegd, maar ...* I did say that, but ...; *het lijkt er ~ op dat het helpt* it really does seem to help; *dat is ~ het geval* that is indeed the case; *~, dat dacht ik nu ook!* exactly, that's what I thought, too!

indertijd /ɪndərtɛi̱t/ (adv) at the time

¹**indeuken** /ɪndøkə(n)/ (deukte in, is ingedeukt) be dented

²**indeuken** /ɪndøkə(n)/ (deukte in, heeft in-

gedeukt) dent

de **index** /ˈɪndɛks/ (pl: -en) index

het **indexcijfer** /ˈɪndɛksɛɪfər/ (pl: -s) index (number)

indexeren /ɪndɛkseːrə(n)/ (indexeerde, heeft geïndexeerd) index

India /ˈɪndija/ India

de **indiaan** /ɪndijaːn/ (pl: indianen) (American) Indian

indiaans /ɪndijaːns/ (adj) Indian

Indiaas /ɪndijaːs/ (adj) Indian

het **indianenverhaal** /ɪndijaːnə(n)vərhaːl/ (pl: -verhalen) tall story

de **indicatie** /ɪndikaː(t)si/ (pl: -s) indication

Indië /ˈɪndijə/ the Dutch East Indies; India

indien /ɪndiːn/ (conj) if, in case; supposing

indienen /ɪndiːnə(n)/ (diende in, heeft ingediend) submit

de **indiensttreding** /ɪndiːnstreːdɪŋ/ taking up one's duties, commencement of employment

de **Indiër** /ˈɪndijər/ (pl: -s) Indian

de **indigestie** /ɪndiɣɛsti/ indigestion

indikken /ˈɪndɪkə(n)/ (dikte in, heeft/is ingedikt) thicken

indirect /ɪndirɛkt/ (adj, adv) indirect; roundabout: *op ~e manier* in an indirect way, in a roundabout way; *~e vrije trap* indirect free kick

Indisch /ˈɪndis/ (adj) (East) Indian

indiscreet /ɪndɪskreːt/ (adj, adv) indiscreet: *zonder ~ te zijn* without being indiscreet

het/de **individu** /ˈɪndividy/ (pl: -en) individual; person

het **individualisme** /ɪndividywalɪsmə/ individualism

de **individualist** /ɪndividywalɪst/ (pl: -en) individualist

¹**individueel** /ɪndividyweːl/ (adj) individual, particular

²**individueel** /ɪndividyweːl/ (adv) individually, singly

de **indoctrinatie** /ɪndɔktrinaː(t)si/ (pl: -s) indoctrination

indommelen /ˈɪndɔmələ(n)/ (dommelde in, is ingedommeld) doze off

Indonesië /ɪndoneːzijə/ Indonesia

de **Indonesiër** /ɪndoneːzijər/ (pl: -s) Indonesian

Indonesisch /ɪndoneːzis/ (adj) Indonesian

indoor- indoor

¹**indraaien** /ˈɪndraːjə(n)/ (draaide in, is ingedraaid) turn in(to): *de auto draaide de straat in* the car turned into the street

²**indraaien** /ˈɪndraːjə(n)/ (draaide in, heeft ingedraaid) screw in(to): *een schroef ~ drive (or: screw) in a screw*

indringen /ˈɪndrɪŋə(n)/ (drong in, is ingedrongen) penetrate (into), intrude (into); soak (into)

indringend /ˈɪndrɪŋənt/ (adj) penetrating: *een ~e blik* a penetrating gaze, a piercing

look

de **indringer** /ˈɪndrɪŋər/ (pl: -s) intruder, trespasser

indrinken /ˈɪndrɪŋkə(n)/ (dronk in, heeft ingedronken) drink in

indruisen /ˈɪndrœysə(n)/ (druiste in, heeft/is ingedruist) go against, conflict with

de **indruk** /ˈɪndrʏk/ (pl: -ken) **1** impression; air; idea: *diepe (grote) ~ maken* make a deep impression; *ik kon niet aan de ~ ontkomen dat* I could not escape the impression that; *dat geeft* (or: *wekt*) *de ~ ...* that gives (or: creates) the impression that ...; *ik kreeg de ~ dat* I got the impression that; *weinig ~ maken op iem.* make little impression on s.o. **2** impression, (im)print: *op de sneeuw waren ~ken van vogelpootjes zichtbaar* in the snow the prints (or: imprints) of birds' feet were visible

indrukken /ˈɪndrʏkə(n)/ (drukte in, heeft ingedrukt) push in, press

indrukwekkend /ɪndrʏkwɛkənt/ (adj, adv) impressive

induiken /ˈɪndœykə(n)/ (dook in, heeft/is ingedoken) **1** dive in(to): *zijn bed* (or: *de koffer*) *~* turn in, hit the sack **2** plunge in(to): *ergens dieper ~* delve deeper into sth.

industrialiseren /ɪndʏstrijalizeːrə(n)/ (industrialiseerde, heeft geïndustrialiseerd) industrialize

de **industrie** /ɪndʏstri/ (pl: -ën) (manufacturing) industry

industrieel /ɪndʏstrijeːl/ (adj) industrial

het **industriegebied** /ɪndʏstriɣəbit/ (pl: -en) industrial area; industrial estate (or: park); trading estate

het **industrieland** /ɪndʏstrilɑnt/ (pl: -en) industrialized nation (or: country)

het **industrieterrein** /ɪndʏstriteːrɛin/ (pl: -en) industrial zone (or: estate, park)

indutten /ˈɪndʏtə(n)/ (dutte in, is ingedut) doze off, nod off

induwen /ˈɪndywə(n)/ (duwde in, heeft ingeduwd) push in(to)

ineengedoken /ɪneːnɣədokə(n)/ (adj) crouched, hunched (up)

ineenkrimpen /ɪneːnkrɪmpə(n)/ (kromp ineen, is ineengekrompen) curl up, double up; [fig] flinch

ineens /ɪneːns/ (adv) **1** (all) at once: *bij betaling ~ krijg je korting* you get a discount for cash payment **2** all at once, all of a sudden, suddenly: *zomaar ~* just like that

ineenstorten /ɪneːnstɔrtə(n)/ (stortte ineen, is ineengestort) collapse

de **ineenstorting** /ɪneːnstɔrtɪŋ/ collapse

ineffectief /ɪnɛfɛktif/ (adj, adv) ineffective, inefficient

inefficiënt /ɪnɛfiʃɛnt/ (adj, adv) inefficient

inenten /ˈɪnɛntə(n)/ (entte in, heeft ingeënt) vaccinate, inoculate

de **inenting** /ˈɪnɛntɪŋ/ (pl: -en) vaccination, inoculation

het **inentingsbewijs** /ɪnɛntɪŋzbəwɛɪs/ (pl: -bewijzen) vaccination certificate

de **infanterie** /ɪnfɑntəri/ infantry

infantiel /ɪnfɑntil/ (adj, adv) infantile: *doe niet zo ~* don't be such a baby

het **infarct** /ɪnfɑrkt/ (pl: -en) infarct(ion); heart attack

infecteren /ɪnfɛkterə/ (infecteerde, heeft geïnfecteerd) infect

de **infectie** /ɪnfɛksi/ (pl: -s) infection

inferieur /ɪnferijør/ (adj) inferior, low-grade

het **inferno** /ɪnfɛrno/ (pl: -'s) inferno

de **infiltrant** /ɪnfɪltrɑnt/ (pl: -en) infiltrator

de **infiltratie** /ɪnfɪltra(t)si/ (pl: -s) infiltration

infiltreren /ɪnfɪltrerə(n)/ (infiltreerde, is geïnfiltreerd) infiltrate: *~ in* een beweging infiltrate (into) a movement

de **inflatie** /ɪnfla(t)si/ (pl: -s) inflation

inflatoir /ɪnflatwɑr/ (adj) inflationary

de **influenza** /ɪnflywɛnza/ influenza

influisteren /ɪnflœystərə(n)/ (fluisterde in, heeft ingefluisterd) whisper (in s.o.'s ear)

de **info** /ɪnfo/ (pl: -'s) info

de **informant** /ɪnfɔrmɑnt/ (pl: -en) informant

de **informateur** /ɪnfɔrmatør/ (pl: -s) politician who investigates whether a proposed cabinet formation will succeed

de **informatica** /ɪnfɔrmatika/ computer science, informatics

de **informaticus** /ɪnfɔrmatikʏs/ (pl: informatici) information scientist, computer scientist

de **informatie** /ɪnfɔrma(t)si/ (pl: -s) **1** information; data **2** information; intelligence: *om nadere ~ verzoeken* request further information; *~(s) inwinnen (bij …)* make inquiries (of …), obtain information (from …)

de **informatiedrager** /ɪnfɔrma(t)sidraɣər/ (pl: -s) data carrier

informatief /ɪnfɔrmatif/ (adj) informative

de **informatietechnologie** /ɪnfɔrma(t)sitɛxnoloɣi/ information technology *(IT)*

de **informatieverwerking** /ɪnfɔrma(t)sivərwɛrkɪŋ/ data processing (*or:* handling)

de **informatisering** /ɪnfɔrmatizerɪŋ/ (pl: -en) computerization

informeel /ɪnfɔrmel/ (adj, adv) informal, unofficial; casual

¹**informeren** /ɪnfɔrmerə(n)/ (informeerde, heeft geïnformeerd) inquire, enquire, ask: *ik heb ernaar geïnformeerd* I have made inquiries about it; *~ bij* iem. ask s.o.; *naar* de aanvangstijden *~* inquire about opening times

²**informeren** /ɪnfɔrmerə(n)/ (informeerde, heeft geïnformeerd) inform

de **infostress** /ɪnfostrɛs/ info-stress

infrarood /ɪnfrarot/ (adj) infra-red

de **infrastructuur** /ɪnfrastrʏktyr/ (pl: -structuren) infrastructure

het **infuus** /ɪnfys/ (pl: infusen) drip

de **ingaan** /ɪnɣan/ (ging in, is ingegaan) **1** go in(to): *een deur* ~ go through a door **2** go in(to), come in(to), enter: *een weg* ~ turn into a road **3** examine, go into: *uitgebreid ~ op* consider at length **4** agree with, agree to, comply with: *op* een aanbod ~ accept an offer **5** take effect: *de regeling gaat 1 juli in* the regulation is effective as from (*or:* of) July 1st || ~ *tegen* run counter to

de **ingang** /ɪnɣɑŋ/ (pl: -en) **1** entrance, entry, doorway; acceptance: *de nieuwe ideeën vonden* gemakkelijk ~ *bij het publiek* the new ideas found a ready reception with the public **2** commencement: *met* ~ *van 1 april* as from (*or:* of) April 1st; *met* onmiddellijke ~ to take effect at once, starting immediately

ingebed /ɪnɣəbɛt/ (adj) embedded

ingebeeld /ɪnɣəbelt/ (adj) imaginary

ingebonden /ɪnɣəbɔndə(n)/ (adj) bound

ingebouwd /ɪnɣəbaut/ (adj) built-in

de **ingebruikneming** /ɪnɣəbrœyknemɪŋ/ introduction; occupation

ingeburgerd /ɪnɣəbʏrɣərt/ (adj) **1** naturalized **2** established: *~ raken* take hold

ingehouden /ɪnɣəhaudə(n)/ (adj) **1** restrained **2** subdued; bated

ingelegd /ɪnɣəlɛxt/ (adj) inlaid

ingemaakt /ɪnɣəmakt/ (adj) preserved, bottled

ingenaaid /ɪnɣənajt/ (adj) stitched

de **ingenieur** /ɪnʒənør/ (pl: -s) engineer

ingenieus /ɪnɣenijøs/ (adj, adv) ingenious

ingenomen /ɪnɣənomə(n)/ (adj) (+ met) pleased (with), satisfied (with)

ingesloten /ɪnɣəslotə(n)/ (adj, adv) **1** enclosed **2** surrounded

ingespannen /ɪnɣəspɑnə(n)/ (adj, adv) **1** intensive, intense: *~ luisteren* listen intently **2** strenuous: *na drie dagen van ~ arbeid* after three strenuous days

de **ingesprektoon** /ɪnɣəsprɛkton/ engaged signal; [Am] busy signal

ingetogen /ɪnɣətoɣə(n)/ (adj, adv) modest

ingeval /ɪnɣəvɑl/ (conj) in case, in the event of

ingevallen /ɪnɣəvɑlə(n)/ (adj) hollow; sunken

ingeven /ɪnɣevə(n)/ (gaf in, heeft ingegeven) inspire: *doe wat uw hart u ingeeft* follow the dictates of your heart

de **ingeving** /ɪnɣevɪŋ/ (pl: -en) inspiration, intuition: *een ~ krijgen* have a flash of inspiration, have a brainwave

ingevolge /ɪnɣəvɔlɣə/ (prep) [form] in accordance with; under, by virtue of

ingevroren /ɪnɣəvrorə(n)/ (adj) icebound; frozen

de **ingewanden** /ɪnɣəwɑndə(n)/ (pl) intestines

de **ingewijde** /ɪnɣəwɛidə/ (pl: -n) initiate; [fig also] insider; adept

ingewikkeld /ɪnɣəwɪkəlt/ (adj, adv) complicated

ingeworteld /ɪŋɣəwɔrtəlt/ (adj) deep-rooted

de **ingezetene** /ɪŋɣəzetənə/ (pl: -n) resident, inhabitant

ingezonden /ɪŋɣəzɔndə(n)/ (adj) sent in: ~ *brieven* letters to the editor

de **ingooi** /ɪŋɣoj/ (pl: -en) throw-in

¹**ingooien** /ɪŋɣojə(n)/ (gooide in, heeft ingegooid) [sport] throw in

²**ingooien** /ɪŋɣojə(n)/ (gooide in, heeft ingegooid) **1** throw in(to) **2** smash

ingraven /ɪŋɣravə(n)/ (groef in, heeft ingegraven) bury: *zich (in de grond)* ~ dig (o.s.) in; burrow

het **ingrediënt** /ɪŋɣredijɛnt/ (pl: -en) ingredient

de **ingreep** /ɪŋɣrep/ (pl: ingrepen) intervention

ingrijpen /ɪŋɣrɛipə(n)/ (greep in, heeft ingegrepen) **1** interfere **2** intervene

ingrijpend /ɪŋɣrɛipənt/ (adj, adv) radical

ingroeien /ɪŋɣrujə(n)/ (groeide in, is ingegroeid) grow in(to): *een ingegroeide nagel* an ingrown nail

de **inhaalmanoeuvre** /ɪnhalmanœ:vrə/ (pl: -s) overtaking manoeuvre

de **inhaalrace** /ɪnhalres/ (pl: -s) race to recover lost ground, race to catch up

de **inhaalstrook** /ɪnhalstrok/ (pl: -stroken) fast lane

het **inhaalverbod** /ɪnhalvərbɔt/ overtaking prohibition; [Am] passing restriction

de **inhaalwedstrijd** /ɪnhalwɛtstrɛit/ (pl: -en) rearranged fixture, postponed match

inhaken /ɪnhakə(n)/ (haakte in, heeft/is ingehaakt) (+ op) take up

inhakken /ɪnhakə(n)/ (hakte in, heeft ingehakt) (+ op) pitch into

¹**inhalen** /ɪnhalə(n)/ (haalde in, heeft ingehaald) [traf] overtake, pass

²**inhalen** /ɪnhalə(n)/ (haalde in, heeft ingehaald) **1** draw in, take in; haul in **2** catch up with; outrun **3** make up (for); recover: *de verloren tijd* ~ make up for lost time **4** bring in

inhaleren /ɪnhalerə(n)/ (inhaleerde, heeft geïnhaleerd) inhale; [only with direct object] draw in

inhalig /ɪnhaləx/ (adj) greedy

de **inham** /ɪnhɑm/ (pl: -men) bay, cove, creek

inheems /ɪnhems/ (adj) native: *~e planten* indigenous plants

de **inhoud** /ɪnhɑut/ (pl: -en) **1** content, capacity **2** content **3** contents **4** import

¹**inhouden** /ɪnhɑudə(n)/ (hield in, heeft ingehouden) **1** restrain, hold (in, back): *de adem* ~ hold one's breath **2** deduct: *een zeker percentage van het loon* ~ withhold a certain percentage of the wages **3** contain, hold **4** involve, mean: *wat houdt dit in voor onze klanten?* what does this mean for our customers? **5** hold in

zich ²**inhouden** /ɪnhɑudə(n)/ (hield zich in, heeft zich ingehouden) control o.s.: *zich ~ om niet in lachen uit te barsten* keep a straight face

de **inhouding** /ɪnhɑudɪŋ/ (pl: -en) deduction; amount withheld

de **inhoudsmaat** /ɪnhɑutsmat/ (pl: -maten) measure of capacity (*or:* volume)

de **inhoudsopgave** /ɪnhɑutsɔpxavə/ (pl: -n) (table of) contents

inhuldigen /ɪnhʏldəɣə(n)/ (huldigde in, heeft ingehuldigd) inaugurate, install

de **inhuldiging** /ɪnhʏldəɣɪŋ/ (pl: -en) inauguration

inhuren /ɪnhyrə(n)/ (huurde in, heeft ingehuurd) engage

de **initiaal** /ini(t)ʃal/ (pl: initialen) initial

het **initiatief** /ini(t)ʃatif/ (pl: initiatieven) initiative; enterprise

de **initiatiefnemer** /ini(t)ʃatifnemər/ (pl: -s) initiator

de **initiator** /ini(t)ʃator/ (pl: -s, -en) initiator

initiëren /ini(t)ʃerə(n)/ (initieerde, heeft geïnitieerd) initiate (into)

injecteren /ɪnjɛktɛrə(n)/ (injecteerde, heeft geïnjecteerd) inject

de **injectie** /ɪnjɛksi/ (pl: -s) injection

de **injectienaald** /ɪnjɛksinalt/ (pl: -en) (hypodermic) needle

inkapselen /ɪnkɑpsələ(n)/ (kapselde in, heeft ingekapseld) encase

de **inkeer** /ɪŋker/ repentance

inkepen /ɪŋkepə(n)/ (keepte in, heeft ingekeept) notch; groove

de **inkeping** /ɪŋkepɪŋ/ (pl: -en) notch

de **inkijk** /ɪŋkɛik/ looking (in), view (of the inside); cleavage

inkijken /ɪŋkɛikə(n)/ (keek in, heeft ingekeken) take a look at

de **inkjet** /ɪŋkjɛt/ inkjet

inklappen /ɪŋklɑpə(n)/ (klapte in, heeft ingeklapt) fold in, fold up

inklaren /ɪŋklarə(n)/ (klaarde in, heeft ingeklaard) clear (inwards)

inkleden /ɪŋkledə(n)/ (kleedde in, heeft ingekleed) frame, express: *hoe zal ik mijn verzoek ~?* how shall I put my request?

inkleuren /ɪŋklørə(n)/ (kleurde in, heeft ingekleurd) colour

inklinken /ɪŋklɪŋkə(n)/ (klonk in, is ingeklonken) settle

de **inkom** /ɪŋkɔm/ [Belg] admission, entrance fee

het ¹**inkomen** /ɪŋkomə(n)/ (pl: -s) income; revenue

²**inkomen** /ɪŋkomə(n)/ (kwam in, is ingekomen) enter, come in(to): *ingekomen stukken* (*or: brieven*) incoming correspondence (*or:* letters) ‖ *daar kan ik ~* I (can) appreciate that, I quite understand that; *daar komt niets van in* that's out of the question, no way!

het **inkomgeld** /ɪŋkɔmɣɛlt/ (pl: -en) [Belg] admission (charge), entrance fee

de **inkomsten** /ɪŋkɔmstə(n)/ (pl) income; earnings; revenue(s)

de **inkomstenbelasting** /ɪŋkɔmstə(n)bəlɑstɪŋ/ (pl: -en) income tax

de **inkoop** /ɪŋkop/ (pl: inkopen) purchase, purchasing, buying

de **inkoopprijs** /ɪŋkoprɛis/ (pl: -prijzen) cost price

inkopen /ɪŋkopə(n)/ (kocht in, heeft ingekocht) buy, purchase

de **inkoper** /ɪŋkopər/ (pl: -s) buyer, purchasing agent

inkoppen /ɪŋkɔpə(n)/ (kopte in, heeft ingekopt) head (the ball) in(to the goal)

het **inkoppertje** easy score

inkorten /ɪŋkɔrtə(n)/ (kortte in, heeft ingekort) shorten, cut down

inkrimpen /ɪŋkrɪmpə(n)/ (kromp in, heeft ingekrompen) reduce, cut (down)

de **inkrimping** /ɪŋkrɪmpɪŋ/ (pl: -en) reduction; cut(s)

de **inkt** /ɪŋkt/ (pl: -en) ink: *met ~ schrijven* write in ink

de **inktvis** /ɪŋktfɪs/ (pl: -sen) octopus; squid

de **inktvlek** /ɪŋktflɛk/ (pl: -ken) ink blot

inladen /ɪnladə(n)/ (laadde in, heeft ingeladen) load

de **inlander** /ɪnlɑndər/ (pl: -s) native

inlands /ɪnlɑnts/ (adj) native; internal; domestic, home-grown

inlassen /ɪnlɑsə(n)/ (laste in, heeft ingelast) insert

zich **inlaten** /ɪnlatə(n)/ (liet zich in, heeft zich ingelaten) meddle (with, in), concern o.s. (with): *zich ~ met dergelijke mensen* associate with such people

de **inleg** /ɪnlɛx/ **1** deposit(ing); deposit **2** stake

inleggen /ɪnlɛɣə(n)/ (legde in, heeft ingelegd) **1** deposit; stake; invest **2** put, throw in (*or:* down) **3** preserve

het **inlegkruisje** /ɪnlɛxkrœysjə/ (pl: -s) panty shield

het **inlegvel** /ɪnlɛxfɛl/ (pl: -len) insert

inleiden /ɪnlɛidə(n)/ (leidde in, heeft ingeleid) introduce

inleidend /ɪnlɛidənt/ (adj) introductory; opening

de **inleider** /ɪnlɛidər/ (pl: -s) (opening) speaker

de **inleiding** /ɪnlɛidɪŋ/ (pl: -en) **1** introductory remarks, opening remarks, preamble **2** introduction, preface, foreword

zich **inleven** /ɪnlevə(n)/ (leefde zich in, heeft zich ingeleefd) put (*or:* imagine) o.s. (in), empathize (with)

inleveren /ɪnlevərə(n)/ (leverde in, heeft ingeleverd) hand in, turn in

inlezen /ɪnlezə(n)/ (las in, heeft ingelezen): *zich ~* read up (on), study the literature; *gegevens ~* read in data

inlichten /ɪnlɪxtə(n)/ (lichtte in, heeft inge-

licht) inform

de **inlichting** /ɪnlɪxtɪŋ/ (pl: -en) **1** (piece of) information: *~en inwinnen* make inquiries, ask for information **2** information (office); inquiries; intelligence (service)

de **inlichtingendienst** /ɪnlɪxtɪŋə(n)dinst/ (pl: -en) **1** information office, inquiries office **2** intelligence (service), secret service

inlijsten /ɪnlɛistə(n)/ (lijstte in, heeft ingelijst) frame

inlijven /ɪnlɛivə(n)/ (lijfde in, heeft ingelijfd) incorporate (in/with); annex

de **inlineskate** /ɪnlɑjnsket/ (pl: -s) in-line skate

inlineskaten /ɪnlɑjnsketə(n)/ inline skate

inloggen /ɪnlɔɣə(n)/ (logde in, heeft ingelogd) log on, log in (on)

¹**inlopen** /ɪnlopə(n)/ (liep in, is ingelopen) **1** walk into, step into; [bldg] enter; turn into **2** catch up: *op iem. ~* catch up on s.o.

²**inlopen** /ɪnlopə(n)/ (liep in, heeft ingelopen) **1** wear in **2** make up ‖ *zich ~* warm up

inlossen /ɪnlɔsə(n)/ (loste in, heeft ingelost) redeem

inluiden /ɪnlœydə(n)/ (luidde in, heeft ingeluid) herald

¹**inmaken** /ɪmakə(n)/ (maakte in, heeft ingemaakt) preserve; conserve

²**inmaken** /ɪmakə(n)/ (maakte in, heeft ingemaakt) [fig] slaughter

zich **inmengen** /ɪmɛŋə(n)/ (mengde zich in, heeft zich ingemengd) interfere (in, with)

de **inmenging** /ɪmɛŋɪŋ/ (pl: -en) interference (in, with)

inmiddels /ɪmɪdəls/ (adv) meanwhile, in the meantime: *dat is ~ bevestigd* this has since (*or:* now) been confirmed

in natura /ɪnatyra/ (adj) in kind

innemen /ɪnemə(n)/ (nam in, heeft ingenomen) **1** take **2** take (up); occupy: *zijn plaats ~* take one's seat **3** capture

innemend /ɪnemənt/ (adj, adv) captivating, engaging, winning

innen /ɪnə(n)/ (inde, heeft geïnd) collect; cash

het ¹**innerlijk** /ɪnərlək/ (pl: -en) inner self, inner nature

²**innerlijk** /ɪnərlək/ (adj, adv) inner

¹**innig** /ɪnəx/ (adj) **1** profound, deep(est) **2** ardent, fervent **3** close, deep, intimate

²**innig** /ɪnəx/ (adv) (most) deeply

de **inning** /ɪnɪŋ/ (pl: -en) **1** collection; cashing **2** innings; inning

de **innovatie** /ɪnova(t)si/ (pl: -s) innovation

innovatief /ɪnovatif/ (adj, adv) innovative

¹**inpakken** /ɪmpakə(n)/ (pakte in, heeft ingepakt) pack in: *~ en wegwezen* pack up and go

²**inpakken** /ɪmpakə(n)/ (pakte in, heeft ingepakt) **1** pack (up) **2** wrap (up) ‖ *zich laten ~* come off worst; be taken to the cleaners, be taken in

inpalmen /ɪmpɑlmə(n)/ (palmde in, heeft ingepalmd) charm, win over
inpassen /ɪmpɑsə(n)/ (paste in, heeft ingepast) fit in
inpeperen /ɪmpepərə(n)/ (peperde in, heeft ingepeperd) [fig] get even with (s.o.) (for)
inperken /ɪmpɛrkə(n)/ (perkte in, heeft ingeperkt) restrict, curtail
in petto /ɪmpɛto/ (adv) in reserve, in store
inpikken /ɪmpɪkə(n)/ (pikte in, heeft ingepikt) **1** grab, snap up; pinch **2** [Belg] take up
inplakken /ɪmplɑkə(n)/ (plakte in, heeft ingeplakt) stick (or: glue, paste) in
inpluggen /ɪmplʏɣə(n)/ (plugde in, heeft ingeplugd) plug in
inpolderen /ɪmpoldərə(n)/ (polderde in, heeft ingepolderd) drain, impolder
de **inpoldering** /ɪmpoldərɪŋ/ (pl: -en) (land) reclamation, impoldering
inpompen /ɪmpompə(n)/ pump in(to)
inpraten /ɪmprɑtə(n)/ (praatte in, heeft ingepraat) talk (s.o.) into (sth.): *op iem. ~ work on s.o.*
inprenten /ɪmprɛntə(n)/ (prentte in, heeft ingeprent) impress (on), instil (in(to)); imprint
de **input** /ɪmput/ (pl: -s) input
de **inquisitie** /ɪŋkwizi̱(t)si/ inquisition
inregenen /ɪnreɣənə(n)/ (regende in, heeft ingeregend) rain in: *het regent hier in* the rain's coming in (or: through)
inrekenen /ɪnrekənə(n)/ (rekende in, heeft ingerekend) pull in; round up
het **¹inrichten** /ɪnrɪχtə(n)/ [Belg] organize: *de ~de macht* the (school) administration (or: management)
²inrichten /ɪnrɪχtə(n)/ (richtte in, heeft ingericht) equip; furnish: *een compleet ingerichte keuken* a fully-equipped kitchen
de **inrichter** /ɪnrɪχtər/ [Belg] organizer
de **inrichting** /ɪnrɪχtɪŋ/ (pl: -en) **1** design; layout **2** institution
¹inrijden /ɪnrɛidə(n)/ (reed in, is ingereden) ride in(to); [car] drive in(to)
²inrijden /ɪnrɛidə(n)/ (reed in, heeft ingereden) run in; break in
de **inrit** /ɪnrɪt/ (pl: -ten) drive(way)
inroepen /ɪnrupə(n)/ (riep in, heeft ingeroepen) call in, call upon
inroosteren /ɪnrostərə(n)/ (roosterde in, heeft ingeroosterd) schedule
de **inruil** /ɪnrœyl/ exchange, trade-in, part exchange: *€2000,- bij ~ van* uw oude auto 2,000 euros in part exchange for your old car
inruilen /ɪnrœylə(n)/ (ruilde in, heeft ingeruild) **1** exchange **2** trade in, part-exchange
de **inruilwaarde** /ɪnrœylwardə/ (pl: -n) trade-in (or: part-exchange) value
inruimen /ɪnrœymə(n)/ (ruimde in, heeft ingeruimd) clear (out)

inrukken /ɪnrʏkə(n)/ (rukte in, is ingerukt) dismiss, withdraw: *ingerukt mars!* dismiss!
inschakelen /ɪnsχakələ(n)/ (schakelde in, heeft ingeschakeld) **1** switch on; connect **2** call in, bring in, involve
inschatten /ɪnsχɑtə(n)/ (schatte in, heeft ingeschat) estimate, assess
inschenken /ɪnsχɛŋkə(n)/ (schonk in, heeft ingeschonken) pour (out)
inschepen /ɪnsχepə(n)/ (scheepte in, heeft ingescheept) embark
inscheuren /ɪnsχørə(n)/ (scheurde in, is ingescheurd) tear
¹inschieten /ɪnsχitə(n)/ (schoot in, is ingeschoten) **1** fall through: *mijn lunch zal er wel bij ~* then I can say goodbye to my lunch **2** shoot in(to): *een zijstraat ~* shoot into a side street **3** score
²inschieten /ɪnsχitə(n)/ (schoot in, heeft ingeschoten) **1** lose **2** shoot into the net
inschikkelijk /ɪnsχi̱kələk/ (adj, adv) accommodating: *niet erg ~* rather uncompromising
inschikken /ɪnsχɪkə(n)/ (schikte in, heeft/is ingeschikt) move up: *als iedereen even wat inschikt* if everyone can just move up a bit
het **inschrijfgeld** /ɪnsχrɛifχɛlt/ (pl: -en) registration fee; entry fee; enrolment fee
¹inschrijven /ɪnsχrɛivə(n)/ (schreef in, heeft ingeschreven) bid, submit a bid
²inschrijven /ɪnsχrɛivə(n)/ (schreef in, heeft ingeschreven) register; enter; enrol; sign up: *zich (laten) ~* sign up, register (o.s.); *zich als student ~* enrol as a student
de **inschrijving** /ɪnsχrɛivɪŋ/ (pl: -en) **1** registration; entry; enrolment **2** [com] subscription; bid: *een ~ openen* call for bids (or: tenders)
het **inschrijvingsformulier** /ɪnsχrɛivɪŋsformylir/ (pl: -en) application form; enrolment form
inschuiven /ɪnsχœyvə(n)/ (schoof in, heeft ingeschoven) push in, slide in
de **inscriptie** /ɪnskrɪpsi/ (pl: -s) inscription; legend
het **insect** /ɪnsɛkt/ (pl: -en) insect
de **insectenbeet** /ɪnsɛktə(n)bet/ (pl: -beten) insect bite
het **insecticide** /ɪnsɛktisi̱də/ (pl: -n, -s) insecticide
inseinen /ɪnsɛinə(n)/ (seinde in, heeft ingeseind) tip off
de **inseminatie** /ɪnsemina̱(t)si/ insemination: *kunstmatige ~* artificial insemination
insgelijks /ɪnsχələ̱ɪks/ (adv) likewise; (and) the same to you
de **insider** /ɪnsɑjdər/ (pl: -s) insider
het **insigne** /ɪnsi̱nə/ (pl: -s) badge
de **insinuatie** /ɪnsinywa̱(t)si/ (pl: -s) insinuation
insinueren /ɪnsinywe̱rə(n)/ (insinueerde, heeft geïnsinueerd) insinuate
¹inslaan /ɪnslan/ (sloeg in, is ingeslagen)

1 take; turn into: [fig] *een verkeerde* **weg** ~ take the wrong path (*or:* turning), go the wrong way; [fig] *nieuwe* **wegen** ~ break new ground, blaze a (new) trail **2** strike, hit ‖ *het nieuws sloeg in* **als** *een bom* the news came as a bombshell

²**inslaan** /ɪnslan/ (sloeg in, heeft ingeslagen) **1** smash (in), beat (in) **2** stock (up on, with)

de **inslag** /ɪnslɑx/ (pl: -en) **1** impact **2** streak [pers]; slant; bias

inslapen /ɪnslapə(n)/ (sliep in, is ingeslapen) **1** fall asleep, drop off (*or:* go) to sleep **2** pass away, pass on

inslikken /ɪnslɪkə(n)/ (slikte in, heeft ingeslikt) swallow

de **insluiper** /ɪnslœypər/ (pl: -s) sneak-thief, intruder

insluiten /ɪnslœytə(n)/ (sloot in, heeft ingesloten) **1** enclose; surround: *een* **antwoordformulier** ~ enclose an answer form **2** shut in, lock in

¹**insmeren** /ɪnsmerə(n)/ (smeerde in, heeft ingesmeerd) rub (with); put … on

zich ²**insmeren** /ɪnsmerə(n)/ (smeerde zich in, heeft zich ingesmeerd) put oil on: *zich* ~ *met bodylotion* rub o.s. with body lotion

insneeuwen /ɪnsnewə(n)/ (sneeuwde in, is ingesneeuwd) snow in

insnijden /ɪnsnɛidə(n)/ (sneed in, heeft ingesneden) cut into; [med] lance: *een* **wond** ~ make an incision in a wound

inspannen /ɪnspɑnə(n)/ (spande in, heeft ingespannen) use; exert: *zich* ~ *voor iets* take a lot of trouble about sth.; *zich moeten* ~ *om wakker te blijven* have to struggle to stay awake

inspannend /ɪnspɑnənt/ (adj) strenuous, laborious; exacting

de **inspanning** /ɪnspɑnɪŋ/ (pl: -en) effort, exertion; strain: *met een laatste* ~ *van zijn* **krachten** with a final effort, with one last effort

inspecteren /ɪnspɛktɛrə(n)/ (inspecteerde, heeft geïnspecteerd) inspect, examine, survey

de **inspecteur** /ɪnspɛktør/ (pl: -s) inspector, examiner

de **inspectie** /ɪnspɛksi/ (pl: -s) **1** inspection, examination, survey **2** inspectorate

¹**inspelen** /ɪnspelə(n)/ (speelde in, heeft ingespeeld) **1** anticipate **2** go along with; capitalize on; take advantage of; feel for

²**inspelen** /ɪnspelə(n)/ (speelde in, heeft ingespeeld) [sport] practise, warm up

de **inspiratie** /ɪnspira(t)si/ (pl: -s) inspiration

inspireren /ɪnspirɛrə(n)/ (inspireerde, heeft geïnspireerd) inspire: *geïnspireerd worden door iets* **(iem.)** be inspired by sth. (s.o.)

inspirerend /ɪnspirɛrənt/ (adj, adv) inspiring

de **inspraak** /ɪnsprak/ participation, involvement; say (in sth.)

inspreken /ɪnsprekə(n)/ (sprak in, heeft ingesproken) record: *u kunt nu uw* **boodschap** ~ you may leave (*or:* record) your message now ‖ *iem.* **moed** ~ put heart into s.o.

inspringen /ɪnsprɪŋə/ (sprong in, is ingesprongen) **1** stand in: *voor een collega* ~ stand in for a colleague **2** jump on(to), leap on(to), seize (up)on ‖ *deze* **regel** *moet een beetje* ~ this line needs to be indented slightly

inspuiten /ɪnspœytə(n)/ (spoot in, heeft ingespoten) inject; fix

instaan /ɪnstan/ (stond in, heeft ingestaan) answer, be answerable (*or:* responsible); guarantee; vouch: *voor iem.* ~ vouch for s.o.

instabiel /ɪnstabil/ (adj) unstable

de **instabiliteit** /ɪnstabilitɛit/ instability

de **installateur** /ɪnstɑlatør/ (pl: -s) fitter, installer; electrician

de **installatie** /ɪnstɑla(t)si/ (pl: -s) **1** installation **2** installation, plant, equipment, machinery; fittings: *een nieuwe* **stereo-installatie** a new hifi-set **3** installation, inauguration

installeren /ɪnstɑlɛrə(n)/ (installeerde, heeft geïnstalleerd) install; inaugurate: *iem.* **als** *lid* ~ initiate s.o. as a member

de **instandhouding** /ɪnstɑnthɑudɪŋ/ maintenance, preservation

de **instantie** /ɪnstɑnsi/ (pl: -s) **1** body, authority: *de* **officiële** ~*s* the government agencies, the official bodies **2** [law] instance ‖ *in eerste* ~ *dachten we dat het waar was* initially we thought it was true

instappen /ɪnstɑpə(n)/ (stapte in, is ingestapt) get in; get on; board

insteken /ɪnstekə(n)/ (stak in, heeft ingestoken) put in: *de* **stekker** ~ plug in, put in the plug

instellen /ɪnstɛlə(n)/ (stelde in, heeft ingesteld) **1** establish, create **2** set up, start **3** adjust; focus; tune: *een* **camera** *(scherp)* ~ focus a camera; *zakelijk ingesteld zijn* have a businesslike attitude (*or:* mentality)

de **instelling** /ɪnstɛlɪŋ/ (pl: -en) **1** institute, institution **2** focus(s)ing; tuning **3** attitude, mentality: *een* **negatieve** ~ a negative attitude

instemmen /ɪnstɛmə(n)/ (stemde in, heeft ingestemd) agree (with, to)

de **instemming** /ɪnstɛmɪŋ/ approval

het **instinct** /ɪnstɪŋkt/ (pl: -en) instinct

instinctief /ɪnstɪŋktif/ (adj, adv) instinctive

instinctmatig /ɪnstɪŋktmatəx/ (adj, adv) instinctive: ~ **handelen** act on one's instinct(s)

de **instinker** /ɪnstɪŋkər/ tricky question

institutioneel /ɪnstity(t)ʃonel/ (adj) institutional

het **instituut** /ɪnstityt/ (pl: instituten) institution, institute

instoppen /ɪnstɔpə(n)/ (stopte in, heeft ingestopt) **1** put in **2** tuck in: *iem. lekker ~ tuck s.o.* in nice and warm

de **instorten** /ˈɪnstɔrtə(n)/ (stortte in, is ingestort) **1** collapse; fall down; cave in: *de zaak staat op ~* the business is at the point of collapse **2** collapse, break down

de **instorting** /ˈɪnstɔrtɪŋ/ (pl: -en) collapse [bldg]; breakdown; caving, cave-in

de **instroom** /ˈɪnstrom/ (pl: instromen) influx, inflow: *de ~ van eerstejaars studenten* the intake of first-year students

de **instructeur** /ɪnstrʏktø:r/ (pl: -s) instructor

de **instructie** /ɪnstrʏksi/ (pl: -s) instruction; order; directive

instructief /ɪnstrʏktif/ (adj, adv) instructive, informative

instrueren /ɪnstrywe:rə(n)/ (instrueerde, heeft geïnstrueerd) instruct

het **instrument** /ɪnstrymɛnt/ (pl: -en) **1** instrument: *~en aflezen* read instruments (*or:* dials) **2** tool **3** (musical) instrument: *een ~ bespelen* play an instrument

instrumentaal /ɪnstrymɛntal/ (adj) instrumental

instuderen /ˈɪnstyderə(n)/ (studeerde in, heeft ingestudeerd) practise, learn: *een muziekstuk ~* practise a piece of music

de **instuif** /ˈɪnstœyf/ (pl: instuiven) **1** (informal) party **2** youth centre

insturen /ˈɪnstyrə(n)/ (stuurde in, heeft ingestuurd) **1** send in, submit **2** steer into; sail into [ship]

de **insuline** /ɪnsylinə/ insulin

intact /ɪntɑkt/ (adj) intact

de **intake** /ˈɪntek/ (pl: -s) register

het **intakegesprek** /ˈɪntekχəsprɛk/ (pl: -ken) interview on admission

de **inteelt** /ˈɪntelt/ inbreeding

integendeel /ɪnteɣə(n)del/ (adv) on the contrary: *ik lui? ~!* me lazy? quite the contrary!

integer /ɪnteɣər/ (adj, adv) upright, honest

de **¹integraal** /ɪnteɣral/ (pl: integralen) [maths] integral

²integraal /ɪnteɣral/ (adj, adv) integral, complete

de **integraalhelm** /ɪnteɣralhɛlm/ (pl: -en) regulation (crash-)helmet

de **integratie** /ɪnteɣra(t)si/ integration

integreren /ɪnteɣre:rə(n)/ (integreerde, heeft/is geïntegreerd) integrate

de **integriteit** /ɪnteɣritɛit/ integrity

¹intekenen /ˈɪntekənə(n)/ (tekende in, heeft ingetekend) subscribe, sign up

²intekenen /ˈɪntekənə(n)/ (tekende in, heeft ingetekend) register, enter

de **intekenlijst** /ˈɪnteke(n)lɛist/ (pl: -en) subscription list

het **intellect** /ɪntɛlɛkt/ intellect

intellectueel /ɪntɛlɛktywel/ (adj, adv) intellectual

intelligent /ɪntɛliɣɛnt/ (adj, adv) intelligent, bright

het **intelligent design** /ɪntɛlɪdʒəndizɑjn/ intelligent design

de **intelligentie** /ɪntɛliɣɛnsi/ intelligence

het **intelligentiequotiënt** /ɪntɛliɣɛnsikoʃɛnt/ (pl: -en) intelligence quotient, IQ

de **intelligentietest** /ɪntɛliɣɛnsitɛst/ (pl: -s) intelligence test

de **intelligentsia** /ɪntɛliɣɛn(t)sija/ intelligentsia

intens /ɪntɛns/ (adj, adv) intense: *~ gelukkig* blissfully happy; *~ genieten* enjoy immensely

intensief /ɪntɛnzif/ (adj, adv) intensive

de **intensiteit** /ɪntɛnzitɛit/ intensity, intenseness

de **intensive care** /ɪntɛnsɪfkɛ:r/ intensive care: *op de ~ liggen* be in intensive care

intensiveren /ɪntɛnzive:rə(n)/ (intensiveerde, heeft geïntensiveerd) intensify

de **intentie** /ɪntɛnsi/ (pl: -s) intention, purpose: *de ~ hebben om* intend to

de **interactie** /ɪntərɑksi/ (pl: -s) interaction

interactief /ɪntərɑktif/ (adj, adv) interactive

de **intercedent** /ɪntərsedɛnt/ intermediary

de **intercity** /ɪntərsɪti/ (pl: -'s) intercity (train): *de ~ nemen* go by intercity (train)

de **intercom** /ɪntərkɔm/ (pl: -s) intercom: *iets over de ~ omroepen* announce sth. over (*or:* on) the intercom

de **intercommunale** /ɪntərkɔmynalə/ (pl: -s) [Belg] [roughly] intermunicipal (utility) company (with state and/or private participation)

intercontinentaal /ɪntərkɔntinɛntal/ (adj, adv) intercontinental

interdisciplinair /ɪntərdisiplinɛ:r/ (adj, adv) interdisciplinary

interen /ˈɪntərə(n)/ (teerde in, heeft/is ingeteerd) eat into (one's capital)

interessant /ɪntərɛsɑnt/ (adj, adv) **1** interesting: *~ willen zijn (doen)* show off **2** advantageous, profitable

het/de **interesse** /ɪntərɛsə/ (pl: -s) interest: *een brede ~ hebben* have wide interests

¹interesseren /ɪntərɛse:rə(n)/ (interesseerde, heeft geïnteresseerd) interest: *wie het gedaan heeft interesseert me niet* I am not interested in who did it

zich **²interesseren** /ɪntərɛse:rə(n)/ (interesseerde zich, heeft zich geïnteresseerd) be interested

de **interest** /ˈɪntərɛst/ (pl: -en) interest: *samengestelde ~* compound interest; *tegen 9 % ~* at the rate of 9 %

de **interface** /ˈɪntərfes/ (pl: -s) interface

het **interieur** /ɪnter(i)jø:r/ (pl: -s) interior, inside

het **interim** /ˈɪntərɪm/ (pl: -s) **1** interim: *de directeur ad ~* the acting manager **2** [Belg] temporary replacement (*or:* job)

het **interimbureau** /ˈɪntərɪmbyro/ (pl: -s) [Belg]

employment agency

de **interland** /ɪntərlɒnt/ (pl: -s) international (match); test match

interlokaal /ɪntərlokạl/ (adj, adv) trunk

intermenselijk /ɪntərmɛnsələk/ (adj) interpersonal: ~e **verhoudingen** human relations

het **intermezzo** /ɪntərmɛdzo/ (pl: -'s) intermezzo; [fig] interlude

intern /ɪntɛrn/ (adj, adv) **1** resident: ~e **patiënten** in-patients **2** internal, domestic: uitsluitend voor ~ **gebruik** confidential

het **internaat** /ɪntərnạt/ (pl: internaten) boarding school

internationaal /ɪntərnɑ(t)ʃonạl/ (adj, adv) international

de **international** /ɪntərnɛʃənəl/ (pl: -s) international

internationaliseren /ɪntərnɑ(t)ʃonalizẹrə(n)/ (internationaliseerde, heeft geïnternationaliseerd) internationalize

interneren /ɪntɛrnẹrə(n)/ (interneerde, heeft geïnterneerd) intern

het **internet** /ɪntərnɛt/ Internet

het **internetadres** /ɪntərnɛtadrɛs/ (pl: -sen) Internet address

internetbankieren (internetbankierde, heeft geïnternetbankierd) e-banking, Internet banking

internetbellen /ɪntərnɛtbɛlə(n)/ (internetbelde, heeft geïnternetbeld) Internet telephony

het **internetcafé** /ɪntərnɛtkɑfe/ (pl: -s) Internet café, cybercafé

de **internetprovider** /ɪntərnɛtprovɑjdər/ (pl: -s) Internet (service) provider

de **internettelefonie** internet telephony

de **internettelevisie** Internet television

internetten /ɪntərnɛtə(n)/ (internette, heeft geïnternet) surf the Net

de **internetter** /ɪntərnɛtər/ (pl: -s) netter, nettie, nethead

de **internetveiling** internet auction

de **internist** /ɪntərnɪst/ (pl: -en) internist

de **interpellatie** /ɪntərpɛlɑ(t)si/ (pl: -s) interpellation

interpelleren /ɪntərpɛlẹrə(n)/ (interpelleerde, heeft geïnterpelleerd) interpellate: de minister ~ **over** interpellate the minister about

de **interpretatie** /ɪntərpretɑ(t)si/ (pl: -s) interpretation, reading: **foute (verkeerde)** ~ misinterpretation

interpreteren /ɪntərpretẹrə(n)/ (interpreteerde, heeft geïnterpreteerd) interpret

de **interpunctie** /ɪntərpʏŋksi/ punctuation

interrumperen /ɪntərʏmpẹrə(n)/ (interrumpeerde, heeft geïnterrumpeerd) interrupt

de **interruptie** /ɪntərʏpsi/ (pl: -s) interruption

het **interval** /ɪntərvɑl/ (pl: -len) interval

de **interventie** /ɪntərvɛnsi/ (pl: -s) intervention

het **interview** /ɪntərvju/ (pl: -s) interview

interviewen /ɪntərvjuwə(n)/ (interviewde, heeft geïnterviewd) interview

intiem /ɪntịm/ (adj, adv) **1** intimate **2** cosy: een ~ gesprek a cosy chat

de **intifada** /ɪntifạda/ (pl: -'s) intifada

intikken /ɪntɪkə(n)/ (tikte in, heeft ingetikt) **1** smash, break **2** type in ‖ de **bal** ~ flick the ball in (or: home)

de **intimidatie** /ɪntimidạ(t)si/ (pl: -s) intimidation

intimideren /ɪntimidẹrə(n)/ (intimideerde, heeft geïntimideerd) intimidate

de **intimiteit** /ɪntimitɛit/ (pl: -en) **1** intimacy, familiarity **2** liberty: ongewenste ~en sexual harassment

de **intocht** /ɪntɔχt/ (pl: -en) entry: zijn ~ **houden** in make one's entry into

intoetsen /ɪntutsə(n)/ (toetste in, heeft ingetoetst) key in, enter

intolerant /ɪntolerɒnt/ (adj) intolerant

de **intolerantie** /ɪntolerɒn(t)si/ intolerance

intomen /ɪntomə(n)/ (toomde in, heeft ingetoomd) curb, restrain, check

de **intonatie** /ɪntonạ(t)si/ (pl: -s) intonation

het **intranet** /ɪntranɛt/ intranet

intrappen /ɪntrɑpə(n)/ (trapte in, heeft ingetrapt) kick in (or: down)

intraveneus /ɪntravenøs/ (adj, adv) intravenous

de **intrede** /ɪntredə/ entry: zijn ~ **doen** set in

intreden /ɪntredə(n)/ (trad in, is ingetreden) **1** enter a convent (or: monastery) **2** set in, occur, take effect

de **intrek** /ɪntrɛk/ residence: bij iem. zijn ~ **nemen** move in with s.o.

¹**intrekken** /ɪntrɛkə(n)/ (trok in, is ingetrokken) **1** move in (with): **bij** zijn vriendin ~ move in with one's girlfriend **2** be absorbed, soak in: de **verf** moet nog ~ the paint must soak in first

²**intrekken** /ɪntrɛkə(n)/ (trok in, heeft ingetrokken) **1** draw in, draw up, retract **2** withdraw; cancel; abolish; drop; repeal: een **verlof** ~ cancel leave

de **intrekking** /ɪntrɛkɪŋ/ (pl: -en) withdrawal; abolition; cancellation; repeal

de **intrigant** /ɪntriɣɒnt/ (pl: -en) intriguer, schemer

de **intrige** /ɪntriʒə/ (pl: -s) intrigue, plot

intrigeren /ɪntriɣẹrə(n)/ (intrigeerde, heeft geïntrigeerd) intrigue, fascinate

het/de **intro** /ɪntro/ (pl: -'s) intro

de **introducé** /ɪntrodyse/ (pl: -s) guest, friend

introduceren /ɪntrodysẹrə(n)/ (introduceerde, heeft geïntroduceerd) **1** introduce; initiate **2** introduce, phase in

de **introductie** /ɪntrodʏksi/ (pl: -s) **1** introduction, presentation **2** launch(ing)

de **introductieweek** /ɪntrodʏksiwek/ orientation week

introvert /ɪntrovɜrt/ (adj) introverted

intuinen /ɪntœynə(n)/ go for, fall for: *er* (or: *ergens*) ~ fall for it (or: sth.)

de **intuïtie** /ɪntywi(t)si/ (pl: -s) intuition, instinct: *op zijn* ~ *afgaan* act on one's intuition

intuïtief /ɪntywitif/ (adj, adv) intuitive, instinctive: ~ *aanvoelen* know intuitively

intussen /ɪntʏsə(n)/ (adv) meanwhile, in the meantime

intypen /ɪntipə(n)/ (typte in, heeft ingetypt) type in, enter

de **inval** /ɪnval/ (pl: -len) **1** raid, invasion: *een* ~ *doen in* raid [bldg]; invade **2** (bright) idea

invalide /ɪnvalidə/ (adj) invalid, handicapped

de **invalidenwagen** /ɪnvalidə(n)waɣə(n)/ (pl: -s) car for disabled; motorized quadricycle

invallen /ɪnvalə(n)/ (viel in, is ingevallen) **1** raid, invade **2** set in; fall; close in **3** stand in (for), (act as a) substitute (for) **4** fall down, come down, collapse: *ingevallen* **wangen** hollow (or: sunken) cheeks

de **invaller** /ɪnvalər/ (pl: -s) substitute; replacement

de **invalshoek** /ɪnvalshuk/ (pl: -en) **1** angle of incidence **2** approach, point of view

de **invalsweg** /ɪnvalswɛɣ/ (pl: -en) approach road

de **invasie** /ɪnvazi/ (pl: -s) invasion

de **inventaris** /ɪnvɛntarɪs/ (pl: -sen) **1** inventory, list (of contents) **2** stock (in trade), inventory; fittings; furniture

de **inventarisatie** /ɪnvɛntariza(t)si/ (pl: -s) stocktaking, making (or: drawing up) an inventory

inventariseren /ɪnvɛntarizerə(n)/ (inventariseerde, heeft geïnventariseerd) **1** (make an) inventory, take stock (of), draw up a statement of assets and liabilities **2** list

inventief /ɪnvɛntif/ (adj) inventive, ingenious

de **inventiviteit** /ɪnvɛntivitɛit/ inventiveness, ingenuity

de **investeerder** /ɪnvɛsterdər/ (pl: -s) investor

investeren /ɪnvɛsterə(n)/ (investeerde, heeft geïnvesteerd) invest

de **investering** /ɪnvɛsterɪŋ/ (pl: -en) investment

de **investeringsmaatschappij** /ɪnvɛsterɪŋsmatsχapɛi/ (pl: -en) investment company

invetten /ɪnvɛtə(n)/ (vette in, heeft ingevet) grease

de **invitatie** /ɪnvita(t)si/ (pl: -s) invitation

de **in-vitrofertilisatie** /ɪnvitrofɛrtiliza(t)si/ in vitro fertilization

invliegen /ɪnvliɣə(n)/ (vloog in, heeft ingevlogen) *er* ~ be had, be fooled

de **invloed** /ɪnvlut/ (pl: -en) influence: ~ *uitoefenen op iem.* influence s.o., exert/exercise (an) influence on s.o.; *zijn* ~ *gebruiken* exert

(or: use) one's influence; *rijden* **onder** ~ drive under the influence, drink and drive

invloedrijk /ɪnvlutrɛik/ (adj) influential

[1] **invoegen** /ɪnvuɣə(n)/ (voegde in, heeft ingevoegd) join the (stream of) traffic, merge

[2] **invoegen** /ɪnvuɣə(n)/ (voegde in, heeft ingevoegd) insert (into)

de **invoegstrook** /ɪnvuχstrok/ (pl: -stroken) acceleration lane

de **invoer** /ɪnvur/ (pl: -en) **1** import; [goods] imports **2** input

invoeren /ɪnvurə(n)/ (voerde in, heeft ingevoerd) **1** import **2** introduce **3** enter, input (to); read in(to)

de **invoerrechten** /ɪnvurɛχtə(n)/ (pl) import duty

het **invoerverbod** /ɪnvurvərbɔt/ import ban

invreten /ɪnvretə(n)/ (vrat in, heeft ingevreten) corrode

invriezen /ɪnvrizə(n)/ (vroor in, heeft ingevroren) freeze

het **invulformulier** /ɪnvʏlfɔrmylir/ (pl: -en) form (for completion)

invullen /ɪnvʏlə(n)/ (vulde in, heeft ingevuld) fill in: [fig] *iets* **voor** *iem.* ~ decide sth. for s.o., tell s.o. what to do (and think)

de **invulling** /ɪnvʏlɪŋ/ (pl: -en) interpretation

inweken /ɪnwekə(n)/ (weekte in, heeft/is ingeweekt) soak

inwendig /ɪnwɛndəχ/ (adj, adv) internal, inner; inside

[1] **inwerken** /ɪnwɛrkə(n)/ (werkte in, heeft ingewerkt) (+ op) act on, affect: *op elkaar* ~ interact

[2] **inwerken** /ɪnwɛrkə(n)/ (werkte in, heeft ingewerkt) show the ropes, break in

de **inwerking** /ɪnwɛrkɪŋ/ (pl: -en) action, effect

de **inwerkingtreding** /ɪnwɛrkɪŋtredɪŋ/ coming into force, taking effect

de **inwerktijd** /ɪnwɛrktɛit/ (pl: -en) training period

inwerpen /ɪnwɛrpə(n)/ (wierp in, heeft ingeworpen) throw in; insert

inwijden /ɪnwɛidə(n)/ (wijdde in, heeft ingewijd) **1** inaugurate, dedicate; consecrate **2** initiate

de **inwijding** /ɪnwɛidɪŋ/ (pl: -en) **1** inauguration, dedication; consecration **2** initiation

de **inwijkeling** /ɪnwɛikəlɪŋ/ (pl: -en) [Belg] immigrant

het **inwijken** /ɪnwɛikə(n)/ [Belg] immigrate

inwikkelen /ɪnwɪkələ(n)/ (wikkelde in, heeft ingewikkeld) wrap (up)

inwilligen /ɪnwɪləɣə(n)/ (willigde in, heeft ingewilligd) grant, comply with, agree to: *zijn* **eisen** ~ comply with (or: agree to) his demands

inwinnen /ɪnwɪnə(n)/ (won in, heeft ingewonnen) obtain, gather

inwisselbaar /ɪnwɪsəlbar/ (adj) exchangeable; convertible; redeemable

inwisselen /ɪnwɪsələ(n)/ (wisselde in, heeft ingewisseld) exchange; convert; cash; change; redeem

inwonen /ɪnwonə(n)/ (woonde in, heeft ingewoond) live; live in: *Gerard woont nog bij zijn ouders in* Gerard still lives with his parents

inwonend /ɪnwonənt/ (adj) resident, living in: *-e kinderen* children living at home

de **inwoner** /ɪnwonər/ (pl: -s) inhabitant, resident

de **inwoning** /ɪnwonɪŋ/ living together: *kost en ~* board and lodging, room and board

de **inworp** /ɪnwɔrp/ (pl: -en) throwing in; insertion

inwrijven /ɪnvrɛivə(n)/ (wreef in, heeft ingewreven) rub in(to): *dat zal ik hem eens ~* I'll rub his nose in it

inzaaien /ɪnzajə(n)/ (zaaide in, heeft ingezaaid) sow, seed

de **inzage** /ɪnzaɣə/ inspection: *een exemplaar ter ~* an inspection copy

inzake /ɪnzakə/ (prep) concerning, with regard to, in respect of, as far as ... is concerned

inzakken /ɪnzakə(n)/ (zakte in, is ingezakt) **1** collapse; give way **2** [com] collapse, slump

inzamelen /ɪnzamələ(n)/ (zamelde in, heeft ingezameld) collect; raise

de **inzameling** /ɪnzaməlɪŋ/ (pl: -en) collection

inzegenen /ɪnzeɣənə(n)/ (zegende in, heeft ingezegend) solemnize

de **inzegening** /ɪnzeɣənɪŋ/ (pl: -en) solemnization

inzenden /ɪnzɛndə(n)/ (zond in, heeft ingezonden) send in, submit; contribute

de **inzending** /ɪnzɛndɪŋ/ (pl: -en) **1** submission; contribution **2** entry, contribution; exhibit

inzepen /ɪnzepə(n)/ (zeepte in, heeft ingezeept) soap; lather

de **inzet** /ɪnzɛt/ (pl: -ten) **1** effort: *de spelers vochten met enorme ~* the players gave it all they'd got **2** stake, bet: *de ~ verhogen* raise one's bet (*or:* the stakes)

inzetbaar /ɪnzɛdbar/ (adj) usable; available

¹**inzetten** /ɪnzɛtə(n)/ (zette in, heeft ingezet) set in

²**inzetten** /ɪnzɛtə(n)/ (zette in, heeft ingezet) **1** stake, bet **2** start; strike up

³**inzetten** /ɪnzɛtə(n)/ (zette in, heeft ingezet) **1** put in; set **2** start, launch: *de aanval ~* go onto the attack; *de achtervolging ~* set off in pursuit **3** bring into action

zich ⁴**inzetten** /ɪnzɛtə(n)/ (zette zich in, heeft zich ingezet) do one's best: *zich voor een zaak ~* devote o.s. to a cause

het **inzicht** /ɪnzɪxt/ (pl: -en) **1** insight, understanding: *een beter ~ krijgen in* gain an insight into **2** view, opinion

inzichtelijk /ɪnzɪxtələk/ (adj): *een kwestie ~ maken* clarify an issue

inzien /ɪnzin/ (zag in, heeft ingezien)

1 have a look at: *stukken ~* examine documents; *een boek vluchtig ~* leaf through a book **2** see, recognize: *de noodzaak gaan ~ van* come to recognize the necessity of **3** take a ... view of, consider: *ik zie het somber in* I'm pessimistic about it ‖ *mijns ~s* in my view (*or:* opinion), to my mind

de **inzinking** /ɪnzɪŋkɪŋ/ (pl: -en) breakdown: *ik had een kleine ~* it was one of my off moments

inzitten /ɪnzɪtə(n)/ (zat in, heeft ingezeten) sit in: [fig] *dat zit er niet in* there's no chance of that ‖ *ergens over ~* be worried about sth.

de **inzittende** /ɪnzɪtəndə/ (pl: -n) occupant, passenger

inzoomen /ɪnzumə(n)/ (zoomde in, heeft ingezoomd) zoom in (on): *~ op een onderwerp* zoom in on a subject

het **ion** /ijɔn/ (pl: -en) ion

i.p.v. (abbrev) *in plaats van* instead of

het **IQ** /iky/ (pl: IQ's) *intelligentiequotiënt* IQ

Iraaks /iraks/ (adj) Iraqi

Iraans /irans/ (adj) Iranian

Irak /irɑk/ Iraq

de **Irakees** /irakes/ (pl: Irakezen) Iraqi

Iran /iran/ Iran

de **Iraniër** /iranijər/ (pl: -s) Iranian

de **iris** /irɪs/ (pl: -sen) iris

de **irisscan** /irɪskɛn/ (pl: -s) iris scan

de **ironie** /ironi/ irony

ironisch /ironis/ (adj, adv) ironic(al)

irrationeel /ira(t)ʃonel/ (adj, adv) irrational

irreëel /irejel/ (adj) unreal, imaginary

irrelevant /irelevɑnt/ (adj) irrelevant: *dat is ~* that's beside the point

de **irrigatie** /iriɣa(t)si/ (pl: -s) irrigation

irrigeren /iriɣerə(n)/ (irrigeerde, heeft geïrrigeerd) irrigate

irritant /iritɑnt/ (adj, adv) irritating, annoying

de **irritatie** /irita(t)si/ (pl: -s) irritation

irriteren /iriterə(n)/ (irriteerde, heeft geïrriteerd) irritate, annoy: *het irriteert mij* it is getting on my nerves

de **ischias** /ɪsxijɑs/ sciatica

de **islam** /ɪslɑm/ Islam

de **islamiet** /ɪslamit/ (pl: -en) Islamite

het **islamisme** /ɪslamɪsmə/ Islamism

islamitisch /ɪslamitis/ (adj) Islamic

de **isolatie** /izola(t)si/ (pl: -s) **1** insulation **2** isolation

de **isoleercel** /izolersɛl/ (pl: -len) isolation cell; padded cell

het **isolement** /izoləmɛnt/ isolation

¹**isoleren** /izolerə(n)/ (isoleerde, heeft geïsoleerd) [elec] insulate (from, against)

²**isoleren** /izolerə(n)/ (isoleerde, heeft geïsoleerd) isolate; quarantine; cut off

Israël /ɪsraɛl/ Israel

de **Israëli** /ɪsraeli/ (pl: -'s) Israeli

de **Israëliër** /ɪsraelijər/ (pl: -s) Israeli

Israëlisch /ˈɪsraelis/ (adj) Israeli

het/de **issue** /ɪʃu/ (pl: -s) issue: *een hot* ~ a burning issue

de **IT** /ite/ *informatietechnologie* IT, information technology

de **Italiaan** /italjan/ (pl: Italianen) Italian

het ¹**Italiaans** /italjans/ Italian

²**Italiaans** /italjans/ (adj) Italian

Italië /italijə/ Italy

het **item** /ajtəm/ (pl: -s) item, topic: *een hot* ~ a burning issue

de **IT'er** /itejər/ IT specialist

i.t.t. (abbrev) *in tegenstelling tot* in contrast with, as opposed to

de **ivf** /iveɛf/ *in-vitrofertilisatie* IVF

i.v.m. (abbrev) *in verband met* in connection with

het **ivoor** /ivor/ (pl: ivoren) ivory

de **Ivoorkust** /ivorkyst/ Ivory Coast

ivoren /ivorə(n)/ (adj) ivory

de **Ivoriaan** /ivorijan/ (pl: Ivorianen) Ivory Coaster

het **Ivriet** /ivrit/ (modern) Hebrew

j

de **j** /je/ (pl: j's) j, J

ja /ja/ (int) **1** yes; yeah; all right, OK: *ja knik-ken* nod (agreement); *en zo ja* and if so **2** really, indeed: *o ja?* oh yes?; (oh) really? ‖ *o ja, nu ik je toch spreek …* oh, yes, by the way …

de **jaap** /jap/ (pl: japen) cut, gash, slash

het **jaar** /jar/ (pl: jaren) year: *een half ~* half a year; *het hele ~ door* throughout the year; *~ in, ~ uit* year after year; *in de laatste paar ~, de laatste jaren* in the last few years, in recent years; *om de twee ~* every other year; *over vijf ~* five years from now; *per ~* yearly, a year; *de jaren tachtig, negentig, nul, tien* the eighties, nineties, noughties, (twenty-)tens; *een kind van zes ~* a six-year-old (child); *uit het ~ nul* from the year dot; *vorige week dinsdag is ze twaalf ~ geworden* she was twelve last Tuesday

de **jaarbeurs** /jarbørs/ (pl: -beurzen) **1** (annual) fair, trade fair **2** exhibition centre

het **jaarboek** /jarbuk/ (pl: -en) yearbook, annual

de **jaarcijfers** /jarsɛifərs/ (pl) annual returns

de **jaargang** /jarɣaŋ/ (pl: -en) volume, year (of publication)

de **jaargenoot** /jarɣənot/ (pl: -genoten) classmate

het **jaargetijde** /jarɣətɛidə/ (pl: -n) season

de **jaarkaart** /jarkart/ (pl: -en) annual season ticket

jaarlijks /jarləks/ (adj, adv) annual, yearly: *dit feest wordt ~ gevierd* this celebration takes place every year

de **jaarmarkt** /jarmarkt/ (pl: -en) (annual) fair

de **jaarring** /jarɪŋ/ (pl: -en) annual ring, growth (or: tree) ring

het **jaartal** /jartal/ (pl: -len) year, date

de **jaartelling** /jartɛlɪŋ/ (pl: -en) era: *de christelijke ~* the Christian era

de **jaarvergadering** /jarvərɣadərɪŋ/ (pl: -en) annual meeting

het **jaarverslag** /jarvərslax/ (pl: -en) annual report

de **jaarwisseling** /jarwɪsəlɪŋ/ (pl: -en) turn of the year: *goede (prettige) ~!* Happy New Year!

het **JAC** /jak/ *Jongerenadviescentrum* young people's advisory centre

de **¹jacht** /jaxt/ (pl: -en) **1** hunting; shooting: *op ~ gaan* **a)** go (out) hunting; **b)** go (out) shooting; **c)** go hunting, prowl **2** hunt; shoot **3** hunt, chase: *~ maken op oorlogsmisdadigers* hunt down war criminals

het **²jacht** /jaxt/ (pl: -en) yacht

jachten /jaxtə(n)/ (jachtte, heeft/is gejacht) hurry, rush

het **jachtgebied** /jaxtxəbit/ (pl: -en) hunt(ing ground); shoot(ing); shooting ground

het **jachtgeweer** /ja(xt)xəwer/ (pl: -geweren) shotgun

de **jachthaven** /jaxthavə(n)/ (pl: -s) yacht basin; marina

de **jachthond** /jaxthɔnt/ (pl: -en) hound

jachtig /jaxtəx/ (adj, adv) hurried, hectic

de **jachtluipaard** /jaxtlœypart/ (pl: -en) cheetah

de **jachtopziener** /jaxtopsinər/ (pl: -s) gamewarden

het **jachtseizoen** /jaxtsɛizun/ (pl: -en) hunting season, shooting season

de **jachtvergunning** /jaxtfərɣʏnɪŋ/ (pl: -en) hunting licence

het **jack** /jɛk/ (pl: -s) jacket, coat

de **jackpot** /dʒɛkpɔt/ (pl: -s) jackpot

het **jacquet** /ʒakɛt/ (pl: -ten) morning coat

de **jacuzzi**® /dʒakuzi/ (pl: -'s) jacuzzi

het/de **jade** /jadə/ jade

¹jagen /jaɣə(n)/ (jaagde/joeg, heeft gejaagd) hunt; shoot: *op patrijs ~* hunt partridge

²jagen /jaɣə(n)/ (jaagde/joeg, heeft gejaagd) **1** hunt, hunt for; shoot **2** drive; put; race; rush: *prijzen omhoog* (or: *omlaag*) *~* drive prices up (or: down)

de **jager** /jaɣər/ (pl: -s) hunter

de **jaguar** /dʒɛɡuwar/ (pl: -s) jaguar

Jahweh /jawɛ/ Yahweh

de **jakhals** /jɑkhɑls/ (pl: jakhalzen) jackal

jakkeren /jɑkərə(n)/ (jakkerde, heeft/is gejakkerd) ride hard, rush along

jakkes /jɑkəs/ (int) [inform] ugh!, bah!, pooh!

de **jaknikker** /jɑknɪkər/ (pl: -s) **1** yes-man **2** pumpjack; nodding donkey

Jakob /jakɔp/ James, Jacob: *de ware ~* Mr Right

de **jakobsschelp** /jakɔpsxɛlp/ (pl: -en) scallop

jaloers /jalurs/ (adj, adv) jealous (of), envious (of)

de **jaloezie** /ʒaluzi/ (pl: -ën) **1** envy; jealousy **2** (Venetian) blind

de **jam** /ʒɛm/ (pl: -s) jam

Jamaica /jamɑjka/ Jamaica

de **Jamaicaan** /jamajkan/ (pl: Jamaicanen) Jamaican

Jamaicaans /dʒamajkans/ (adj) Jamaican

jammen /dʒɛmə(n)/ (jamde, heeft gejamd) gig, jam

jammer /jamər/ (adj) a pity, a shame, too bad, bad luck: *het is ~ dat …* **a)** it's a pity (or: shame) that …; **b)** too bad that …; *wat ~!* what a pity! (or: shame!); *het is erg ~ voor hem* it's very hard on him; *~, hij is net weg* (a) pity (or: bad luck), he has just left

jammeren /jamərə(n)/ (jammerde, heeft

gejammerd) moan
jammerlijk /jɑmərlək/ (adj, adv) pitiful,
miserable: ~ *mislukken* fail miserably
de **jampot** /ʒɛmpɔt/ (pl: -ten) jam jar
Jan /jɑn/ John: ~ *Rap en zijn maat* ragtag and
bobtail; ~ *en* **alleman** every Tom, Dick and
Harry; ~ *met de pet* the (ordinary) man in the
street
de **janboel** /jɑmbul/ shambles, mess
janboerenfluitjes /jɑmburə(n)flœycəs/:
op zijn ~ anyhow, any old how
de **janet** /ʒanɛt/ (pl: -ten) [Belg] homo, poof-
(ter), pansy
janken /jɑŋkə(n)/ (jankte, heeft gejankt)
whine, howl; [inform] blubber
Jan Klaassen /jɑŋklɑːsə(n)/ Punch: ~ *en Ka-*
trijn Punch and Judy
de **januari** /jɑnywari/ January
de **jap** /jɑp/ (pl: -pen) Jap
Japan /jɑpɑn/ Japan
de **Japanner** /jɑpɑnər/ (pl: -s) Japanese
het **¹Japans** /jɑpɑns/ Japanese
²Japans /jɑpɑns/ (adj) Japanese
de **japon** /jɑpɔn/ (pl: -nen) dress; gown
¹jarenlang /jɑrə(n)lɑŋ/ (adj) many years': *een*
~e **vriendschap** a friendship of many years'
(standing)
²jarenlang /jɑrə(n)lɑŋ/ (adv) for years and
years
het **jargon** /jɑrɣɔn/ (pl: -s) jargon: *ambtelijk* ~
officialese
jarig /jɑrəx/ (adj): *de ~e* **Job** (or: **Jet**) the
birthday boy (or: girl); *ik* **ben** *vandaag* ~ it's
my birthday today
de **jarige** /jɑrəɣə/ (pl: -n) person celebrating his
(or: her) birthday, birthday boy (or: girl)
de **jarretelle** /ʒɑrətɛl/ (pl: -s) suspender; [Am]
garter
de **jas** /jɑs/ (pl: -sen) **1** coat **2** jacket ‖ *in een*
nieuw ~je steken give (or: get) a facelift
het **jasje** /jɑʃə/ (pl: -s) **1** (short, little) coat **2** jacket
de **jasmijn** /jɑsmɛin/ (pl: -en) jasmine
jasses /jɑsəs/ (int) [inform] ugh!
de **jat** /jɑt/ (pl: -ten) [inform] paw
jatten /jɑtə(n)/ (jatte, heeft gejat) [inform]
pinch, nick
Java /jɑva/ Java
de **Javaan** /jɑvɑn/ (pl: Javanen) Javan(ese)
jawel /jɑwɛl/ (int) (oh) yes; certainly: ~ *me-*
neer certainly sir
het **jawoord** /jɑwort/ consent; [roughly] 'I will'
jazeker /jɑzekər/ (int) yes, certainly, indeed
de **jazz** /dʒɛːz/ jazz
het **jazzballet** /dʒɛːsbɑlɛt/ jazz ballet
de **jazzband** /dʒɛːsbɛnt/ (pl: -s) jazz band
¹je /jə/ (pers pron) you: *jullie zouden je moeten*
schamen you ought to be ashamed of yourselves
²je /jə/ (poss pron) your: *één van je* **vrienden** a
friend of yours

³je /jə/ (ind pron) you: *zoiets* **doe** *je niet* you
don't do things like that
de **jeans** /dʒiːns/ jeans
jee /je/ (int) (oh) Lord!, dear me!
de **jeep** /dʒip/ (pl: -s) jeep
jegens /jeɣəns/ (prep) towards: *diep* **wan-**
trouwen *koesteren ~ iem.* have a deep distrust of s.o.
Jehova /jəhova/ Jehovah: ~*'s* **getuigen** Jehovah's Witnesses
Jemen /jemə(n)/ (the) Yemen
de **Jemeniet** /jemənit/ (pl: -en) Yemeni
Jemenitisch /jemənitis/ (adj) Yemenite
de **jenaplanschool** /jenaplɑnsχol/ (pl: -scho-
len) [roughly] Summerhill school
de **jenever** /jənevər/ (pl: -s) Dutch gin, jenever
de **jeneverbes** /jənevərbɛs/ (pl: -sen) juniper
berry
jengelen /jɛŋələ(n)/ (jengelde, heeft gejen-
geld) **1** whine, moan **2** drone: ~ *op een gitaar*
twang (away) on a guitar
jennen /jɛnə(n)/ (jende, heeft gejend)
badger, pester
de **jerrycan** /dʒɛrikɛn/ (pl: -s) jerrycan
Jeruzalem /jeryzalɛm/ Jerusalem
de **jet** /dʒɛt/ (pl: -s) jet (aircraft)
de **jetlag** /dʒɛtlɛːk/ (pl: -s) jet lag
de **jetset** /dʒɛtsɛt/ jet set
de **jetski**® /dʒɛtski/ (pl: -'s) jet-ski
het **jeu de boules** /ʒədəbul/ boule
de **jeugd** /jøχt/ **1** youth **2** young people: *de ~*
van tegenwoordig young people nowadays
de **jeugdbende** /jøχtbɛndə/ gang of youths
de **jeugdherberg** /jøχthɛrbɛrχ/ (pl: -en) youth
hostel
de **jeugdherinnering** /jøχthɛrɪnərɪŋ/ (pl: -en)
reminiscence of childhood, childhood memory
jeugdig /jøɣdəχ/ (adj) youthful, young(ish):
een programma voor ~e **kijkers** a programme
for younger viewers
het **jeugdjournaal** /jøχtʃurnal/ (pl: -s) news
broadcast for young people
de **jeugdliefde** /jøχtlivdə/ (pl: -s) youthful
love, adolescent love, calf-love; [pers] old
flame: *zij is een van zijn ~s* she's one of his old
loves
de **jeugdpuistjes** /jøχtpœyʃəs/ (pl) acne,
spots, pimples
de **jeugdrechter** /jøχtrɛχtər/ (pl: -s) [Belg] juvenile court magistrate
de **jeugdvriend** /jøχtfrint/ (pl: -en) old (girl)
friend
de **jeugdwerkloosheid** /jøχtwɛrkloshɛit/
youth unemployment
de **jeugdzonde** /jøχtsɔndə/ (pl: -n) sin of one's
youth
de **jeuk** /jøk/ itch(ing): *ik heb overal* ~ I'm itching
all over; [fig] *ergens ~ van* **krijgen** get hot under the collar about sth., get worked up
about sth.

jeuken /jøkə(n)/ (jeukte, heeft gejeukt) itch: *mijn* **handen** ~ *om hem een pak slaag te geven* I'm (just) itching to give him a good thrashing

jeukerig /jøkərəχ/ (adj) itchy

de **je-weet-wel** /jəweṯwɛl/ [of pers] what's-his-name; you know …

jezelf /jəzɛlf/ (ref pron) yourself: *kijk* **naar** ~ look at yourself

de **jezuïet** /jezywiṯ/ (pl: -en) Jesuit

Jezus /jezʏs/ Jesus

de **jicht** /jɪχt/ gout

het ¹**Jiddisch** /jɪdis/ Yiddish

²**Jiddisch** /jɪdis/ (adj) Yiddish

de **jihad** /dʒihaṯ/ jihad, jehad

jij /jɛi/ (pers pron) you: *zeg,* ~ **daar!** hey, you!; ~ **hier?** goodness, are you here?

jijen /jɛɪjə(n)/: ~ *en* **jouen** be on familiar (*or:* christian-name) terms (with s.o.)

de **jingle** /dʒɪŋgəl/ (pl: -s) jingle

jippie /jɪpi/ (int) yippee

het **jiujitsu** /jiujɪtsu/ ju-jitsu

jl. (abbrev) *jongstleden* ult; inst

de **job** /dʒɔp/ (pl: -s) job

Job /jɔp/ Job: *zo arm* **als** ~ as poor as a church mouse

de **jobdienst** /dʒɔbdinst/ (pl: -en) [Belg] (student) employment agency

de **jobstijding** /jɔpstɛidɪŋ/ (pl: -en) bad tidings; bad news

de **jobstudent** /dʒɔpstydɛnt/ (pl: -en) [Belg] student with part-time job

het **joch** /jɔχ/ lad

het **jochie** /jɔχi/ (pl: -s) (little) lad

de **jockey** /dʒɔki/ (pl: -s) jockey

jodelen /jodələ(n)/ (jodelde, heeft gejodeld) yodel

het **jodendom** /jodəndɔm/ Judaism

het **Jodendom** /jodəndɔm/ Jews, Jewry

de **Jodenvervolging** /jodə(n)vərvɔlχɪŋ/ persecution of the Jews

de **jodin** /jodɪn/ (pl: -nen) Jewess

de **Jodin** /jodɪn/ (pl: -nen) Jewess

het **jodium** /jodijʏm/ iodine

de **Joegoslaaf** /juχoslaf/ (pl: Joegoslaven) Yugoslav(ian)

Joegoslavië /juχoslavijə/ Yugoslavia

Joegoslavisch /juχoslavis/ (adj) Yugoslav(ian)

de **joekel** /jukəl/ (pl: -s) whopper: *wat een* ~ *van een* **huis!** what a whacking great house!

joelen /julə(n)/ (joelde, heeft gejoeld) whoop, roar: *een* ~*de* **menigte** a roaring crowd

joggen /dʒɔgə(n)/ (jogde, heeft/is gejogd) jog

de **jogger** /dʒɔgər/ (pl: -s) jogger

de **jogging** /dʒɔgɪŋ/ **1** jogging **2** [Belg] track suit

het **joggingpak** /dʒɔgɪŋpɑk/ (pl: -ken) tracksuit

joh /jɔ/ (int) [inform] you: *hé* ~, *kijk een beetje*

uit hey (you), watch out; *kop op,* ~ (come on) cheer up, (old boy, girl)

Johannes /johɑnəs/ John: ~ *de* **Doper** John the Baptist

de **joint** /dʒɔjnt/ (pl: -s) joint, stick

de **joint venture** /dʒɔjntvɛncər/ (pl: -s) joint venture

de **jojo** /jojo/ (pl: -'s) yo-yo

de **joker** /jokər/ (pl: -s) joker

de **jokkebrok** /jokəbrɔk/ (pl: -ken) (little) fibber

jokken /jokə(n)/ (jokte, heeft gejokt) fib, tell a fib

jolig /joləχ/ (adj, adv) jolly

het ¹**jong** /jɔŋ/ (pl: -en) **1** young (one); pup(py) **2** kid, child

²**jong** /jɔŋ/ (adj) **1** young: *op* ~*e* **leeftijd** at an early age; ~ *en* **oud** young and old **2** recent, late: *de* ~*ste* **berichten** the latest news **3** young, new, immature: ~*e* **kaas** unmatured (*or:* green) cheese

de **jongedame** /jɔŋədamə/ (pl: -s) young lady

de **jongeheer** /jɔŋəheːr/ (pl: -heren) young gentleman

de **jongelui** /jɔŋəlœy/ (pl) youngsters, young people

de **jongeman** /jɔŋəmɑn/ (pl: -nen) young man

de ¹**jongen** /jɔŋə(n)/ (pl: -s) **1** boy, youth, lad: *is het een* ~ *of een* **meisje?** is it a boy or a girl? **2** boy, lad, guy: *onze* ~*s hebben zich dapper geweerd* our boys put up a brave defence **3** kids; lads; chaps; folks; guys: *gaan jullie mee,* ~*s?* are you coming, you lot?

²**jongen** /jɔŋə(n)/ (jongde, heeft gejongd) give birth, drop (their) young, bear young; litter: *onze* **kat** *heeft vandaag gejongd* our cat has had kittens today

jongensachtig /jɔŋənsɑχtəχ/ (adj, adv) boyish: *zich* ~ **gedragen** behave like a boy

de **jongensdroom** /jɔŋə(n)zdrom/ (pl: -dromen) boyish dream; childhood dream

de **jongere** /jɔŋərə/ (pl: -n) young person, youngster

het **jongerencentrum** /jɔŋərə(n)sɛntrʏm/ (pl: -centra) [roughly] youth centre

het **jongerenwerk** /jɔŋərə(n)wɛrk/ youth work

jongleren /jɔŋlɛrə(n)/ (jongleerde, heeft gejongleerd) juggle

de **jongleur** /jɔŋlɶr/ (pl: -s) juggler, acrobat

jongstleden /jɔŋstledə(n)/ (adj) last: *de* **14e** ~ the 14th of this month

de **jonkheer** /jɔŋkheːr/ (pl: -heren) esquire

het **jonkie** /jɔŋki/ (pl: -s) [inform] young one

de **jonkvrouw** /jɔŋkfrɑu/ (pl: -en) [roughly] Lady

de **jood** /jot/ (pl: joden) Jew

de **Jood** /jot/ (pl: Joden) Jew

joods /jots/ (adj, adv) Jewish, Judaic

Joods /jots/ (adj, adv) Jewish, Judaic

Joost /jost/: ~ **mag** *het* **weten** God knows, search me, hanged if I know

de **Jordaan** /jɔrdan/ (the river) Jordan
Jordaans /jɔrdans/ (adj) Jordanian
Jordanië /jɔrdanijə/ Jordan
de **Jordaniër** /jɔrdanijər/ (pl: -s) Jordanian
de **jota** /jota/ (pl: -'s) iota
jou /jɑu/ (pers pron) you: ~ *moet ik* **hebben** you're just the person I need; *is dit boek van* ~? is this book yours?
jouen /jɑuwə(n)/: *jijen en* ~ be on familiar (*or:* christian-name) terms (with s.o.)
de **joule** /ʒul/ (pl: -s) joule
het **journaal** /ʒurnal/ (pl: journalen) news, newscast: *het* ~ *van 8 uur* the 8 o'clock news
de **journalist** /ʒurnalɪst/ (pl: -en) journalist
de **journalistiek** /ʒurnalɪstik/ journalism
jouw /jɑu/ (poss pron) your: *is dat* ~ **werk**? is that your work?; *dat potlood is* **het** ~e that pencil is yours
joviaal /jovijal/ (adj, adv) jovial
de **joypad** (pl: -s) joypad
het/de **joyriding** /dʒɔjrɑjdɪŋ/ joyriding
de **joystick** /dʒɔjstɪk/ (pl: -s) joystick
jr. (abbrev) *junior* Jr.
jubelen /jybələ(n)/ (jubelde, heeft gejubeld) shout with joy, be jubilant
de **jubelstemming** /jybəlstɛmɪŋ/ jubilant mood
de **jubilaris** /jybilarɪs/ (pl: -sen) [roughly] person celebrating his (*or:* her) jubilee
jubileren /jybilerə(n)/ (jubileerde, heeft gejubileerd) celebrate one's jubilee (*or:* anniversary)
het **jubileum** /jybilejvm/ (pl: jubilea) anniversary; jubilee: **gouden** ~ golden jubilee, 50th anniversary
het **judo** /jydo/ judo
de **judoka** /jydoka/ (pl: -'s) judoka, judoist
de **juf** /jyf/ (pl: -s, -fen) teacher; [form of address] Miss
het **juffershondje** /jyfərshɔncə/ (pl: -s) lapdog
de **juffrouw** /jyfrɑu/ (pl: -en) madam
juichen /jœyxə(n)/ (juichte, heeft gejuicht) shout with joy, be jubilant: *de* **menigte** *juichte toen het doelpunt werd gemaakt* the crowd cheered when the goal was scored
de **juichkreet** /jœyxkret/ (pl: -kreten) shout of joy (*or:* jubilation)
¹**juist** /jœyst/ (adj, adv) **1** right, correct: *de* ~*e tijd* the right (*or:* correct) time; *is dit de* ~*e spelling*? is this the right spelling? **2** right, proper: *precies op het* ~*e* **ogenblik** just at the right moment
²**juist** /jœyst/ (adv) **1** just, exactly, of all times (*or:* places, people); no, on the contrary: *ze bedoelde* ~ *het* **tegendeel** she meant just the opposite; *gelukkig? ik ben* ~ *diepbedroefd!* happy? no (*or:* on the contrary), I'm terribly sad!; **daarom** ~ *dat's exactly why;* ~ *op dat ogenblik kwam zij binnen* just at that very moment (*or:* right at that moment) she came in **2** just

de **juistheid** /jœysthɛit/ correctness, accuracy; truth; appropriateness
het **juk** /jyk/ (pl: -ken) yoke
het **jukbeen** /jygben/ (pl: -deren) cheekbone
de **jukebox** /dʒugbɔks/ (pl: -en) jukebox
de **juli** /jyli/ July
¹**jullie** /jyli/ (pers pron) you: ~ **hebben** *gelijk* you're right
²**jullie** /jyli/ (poss pron) your: *is die auto van* ~? is that car yours?
de **jumbojet** /dʒʏmbodʒɛt/ (pl: -s) jumbo jet
jumpen /dʒʏmpə(n)/ (jumpte, heeft gejumpt) jump
de **jungle** /dʒʏŋgəl/ (pl: -s) jungle
de **juni** /jyni/ June
de **junior** /jynijor/ (pl: -en) junior
de **junk** /dʒʏŋk/ (pl: -s) **1** junkie, junky **2** junk, smack
het **junkfood** /dʒʏŋkfuːt/ junk food
de **junta** /xʏnta/ (pl: -'s) junta
jureren /ʒyrerə(n)/ (jureerde, heeft gejureerd) adjudicate
de **jurering** /ʒyrerɪŋ/ (pl: -en) adjudication
juridisch /jyridis/ (adj, adv) legal, law
de **jurisdictie** /jyrɪzdɪksi/ (pl: -s) jurisdiction; competence
de **jurisprudentie** /jyrɪsprydɛnsi/ jurisprudence
de **jurist** /jyrɪst/ (pl: -en) jurist, lawyer
de **jurk** /jyrk/ (pl: -en) dress: *een* **blote** ~ a revealing dress
de **jury** /ʒyri/ (pl: -'s) jury
het **jurylid** /ʒyrilɪt/ (pl: -leden) **1** member of the jury **2** (panel of) judges
de **juryrechtspraak** /ʒyrirɛxtsprak/ trial by jury
de **jus** /ʒy/ gravy
de **jus d'orange** /ʒydorɑ̃ʃ/ orange juice
de **juskom** /ʒykɔm/ (pl: -men) gravy boat
de **justitie** /jysti(t)si/ **1** justice: *minister van* ~ Minister of Justice; *officier van* ~ public prosecutor **2** judiciary; the law; the police: *met* ~ *in aanraking komen* come into conflict with the law
justitieel /jysti(t)fel/ (adj) judicial: *een* ~ **onderzoek** a judicial inquiry (*or:* investigation)
het **justitiepaleis** /jysti(t)sipalɛis/ (pl: -paleizen) [Belg] Palace of Justice
de ¹**jute** /jytə/ jute
²**jute** /jytə/ (adj) jute
juten (adj) jute, burlap
Jutland /jytlɑnt/ Jutland
jutten /jytə(n)/ (jutte, heeft gejut) search beaches
de **jutter** /jytər/ (pl: -s) beachcomber
het **juweel** /jywel/ (pl: juwelen) **1** jewel, gem **2** jewellery
het **juwelenkistje** /jywelə(n)kɪʃə/ (pl: -s) jewel case
de **juwelier** /jywəlir/ (pl: -s) jeweller

k

de **k** /ka/ (pl: k's) k

K /ka/ (abbrev) *1024 bytes, kilobyte* K: *een bestand van 2506 K* a 2506K file

de **kaaiman** /kajmɑn/ (pl: -nen) cayman

de **kaak** /kak/ (pl: kaken) jaw

het **kaakbeen** /kagben/ (pl: -deren, -benen) jawbone

de **kaakchirurg** /kakʃiryrx/ (pl: -en) oral surgeon, dental surgeon

het **kaakje** /kakjə/ (pl: -s) biscuit

de **kaakslag** /kakslɑx/ (pl: -en) slap in the face; punch in the face: *iem. een ~ geven* slap (*or:* punch) s.o. in the face

kaal /kal/ (adj) **1** bald: *zo ~ als een biljartbal zijn* be (as) bald as a coot **2** (thread)bare: *een kale plek* a (thread)bare spot; *de kale huur* the basic rent **3** bare: *de bomen worden ~* the trees are losing their leaves

de **kaalkop** /kalkɔp/ (pl: -pen) [inform] baldy

kaalplukken /kalplykə(n)/ (plukte kaal, heeft kaalgeplukt) **1** squeeze dry, bleed white **2** seize the criminal assets of

kaalscheren /kalsxerə(n)/ (schoor kaal, heeft kaalgeschoren) shave

de **kaalslag** /kalslɑx/ deforestation

de **kaap** /kap/ (pl: kapen) cape: *~ de Goede Hoop* Cape of Good Hope

Kaapstad /kapstɑt/ Cape Town

Kaapverdië /kapfɛrdijə/ Cape Verde (Islands)

de **Kaapverdiër** /kapfɛrdijər/ (pl: -s) Cape Verdean

Kaapverdisch /kapfɛrdis/ (adj) Cape Verdean

de **Kaapverdische Eilanden** /kapfɛrdisə-ɛilɑndə(n)/ (pl) Cape Verde Islands

de **kaars** /kars/ (pl: -en) candle

het **kaarslicht** /karslɪxt/ candlelight

kaarsrecht /karsrɛxt/ (adj, adv) dead straight; bolt upright

het **kaarsvet** /karsfɛt/ candle-grease

de **kaart** /kart/ (pl: -en) **1** card: *de gele (or: rode) ~ krijgen* be shown the yellow (*or:* red) card **2** menu **3** cards, hand: *een spel ~en* a pack of cards **4** ticket **5** map; chart || *dat is geen haalbare ~* it's not a viable proposition; *open ~ spelen* put all one's cards on the table; *van de ~ zijn* be upset

kaarten /kartə(n)/ (kaartte, heeft gekaart) play cards

de **kaartenbak** /kartə(n)bɑk/ (pl: -ken) card-index box (*or:* drawer)

het **kaartenhuis** /kartə(n)hœys/ (pl: -huizen) house of cards: *instorten als een ~* collapse like a house of cards

de **kaarting** /kartɪŋ/ (pl: -en) [Belg] drive, bridge drive, whist drive

het **kaartje** /karcə/ (pl: -s) **1** (business) card **2** ticket

kaartlezen /kartlezə(n)/ read maps

het **kaartspel** /kartspɛl/ card playing, card game; cards: *geld verliezen bij het ~* lose money at cards

het **kaartsysteem** /kartsistem/ (pl: -systemen) card index

de **kaartverkoop** /kartfɛrkop/ ticket sales

de **kaas** /kas/ (pl: kazen) cheese: *jonge ~* unmatured (*or:* green) cheese; *belegen ~* matured cheese; *oude ~* fully mature cheese || *hij heeft er geen ~ van gegeten* he's not much good at it, he doesn't know the first thing about it

de **kaasboer** /kazbur/ (pl: -en) cheesemonger

de **kaasfondue** /kasfɔndy/ (pl: -s) cheese fondue

de **kaasschaaf** /kasxaf/ (pl: -schaven) cheese slicer

de **kaasstolp** /kasstɔlp/ (pl: -en) **1** cheese cover **2** ivory tower

kaatsen /katsə(n)/ (kaatste, heeft gekaatst) bounce

het **kabaal** /kabal/ racket, din

kabbelen /kɑbələ(n)/ (kabbelde, heeft gekabbeld) lap; [also fig] ripple; babble, murmur

de **kabel** /kabəl/ (pl: -s) **1** cable **2** wire; cable

de **kabelbaan** /kabəlban/ (pl: -banen) funicular (railway), cable-lift

de **kabelexploitant** /kabəlɛksplwatɑnt/ (pl: -en) operator of a cable TV system

de **kabeljauw** /kabəljɑu/ (pl: -en) cod(fish)

het **kabelnet** /kabəlnɛt/ (pl: -ten) cable television network: *aangesloten zijn op het ~* receive cable television

de **kabeltelevisie** /kabəltelevizi/ cable television

het **kabinet** /kabinɛt/ (pl: -ten) cabinet, government: *het ~ is gevallen* the government has fallen; *het ~-Rutte* the Rutte cabinet (*or:* government)

de **kabinetschef** /kabinɛtʃɛf/ (pl: -s) [roughly] principal private secretary

de **kabinetscrisis** /kabinɛtskrizɪs/ (pl: -crises) fall of the government

de **kabinetsformatie** /kabinɛtsfɔrma(t)si/ (pl: -s) formation of a (new) government (*or:* cabinet)

de **kabouter** /kabɑutər/ (pl: -s) **1** gnome, pixie; little people: *dat hebben de ~tjes gedaan* it must have been the fairies (*or:* the little people) **2** Brownie

de **kachel** /kɑxəl/ (pl: -s) stove; heater; fire; fire

het **kadaster** /kadɑstər/ **1** [roughly] land register **2** [roughly] land registry

het **kadaver** /kadavər/ (pl: -s) (dead) body;

corpse

de **kade** /k<u>a</u>də/ (pl: -n) quay, wharf: *het schip ligt
aan de ~* the ship lies by the quay(side)

het **kader** /k<u>a</u>dər/ (pl: -s) **1** frame(work): *in het ~
van* within the framework (*or:* scope) of, as
part of **2** executives

het **kadetje** /kad<u>ɛ</u>cə/ (pl: -s) (bread) roll

het **kaf** /kɑf/ chaff

de **kaffer** /k<u>ɑ</u>fər/ (pl: -s) boor, lout

de **Kaffer** /k<u>ɑ</u>fər/ (pl: -s) Kaffir

het/de **kaft** /kɑft/ (pl: -en) **1** cover **2** jacket

de **kaftan** /k<u>ɑ</u>ftɑn/ (pl: -s) kaftan
kaften /k<u>ɑ</u>ftə(n)/ (kaftte, heeft gekaft) cover

het **kaftpapier** /k<u>ɑ</u>ftpapir/ wrapping paper,
brown paper

de **kajak** /k<u>a</u>jɑk/ (pl: -s) kayak

de **kajotter** /kaj<u>ɔ</u>tər/ (pl: -s) [Belg] member of
KAJ

de **kajuit** /kaj<u>œy</u>t/ (pl: -en) saloon

de **kak** /kɑk/ **1** [inform] shit, crap **2** la-di-da
people, snooty people, snobs || *kale (kouwe)
~* swank, la-di-da behaviour
kakelbont /kakəlb<u>ɔ</u>nt/ (adj) gaudy
kakelen /k<u>a</u>kələ(n)/ (kakelde, heeft geka-
keld) cackle; [fig also] chatter
kakelvers /k<u>a</u>kəlvɛrs/ (adj) farm-fresh

de **kaketoe** /k<u>a</u>kətu/ (pl: -s) cockatoo

het **kaki** /k<u>a</u>ki/ khaki
kakken /k<u>ɑ</u>kə(n)/ (kakte, heeft gekakt) [in-
form] crap, shit

de **kakkerlak** /k<u>ɑ</u>kərlɑk/ (pl: -ken) cockroach

de **kalebas** /kaləb<u>ɑ</u>s/ (pl: -sen) gourd, calabash

de **kalender** /kal<u>ɛ</u>ndər/ (pl: -s) calendar

het **kalenderjaar** /kal<u>ɛ</u>ndərjar/ (pl: -jaren) calendar year

het **kalf** /kɑlf/ (pl: kalveren) calf: *de put dempen
als het ~ verdronken is* lock the stable door after the horse has bolted

het **kalfsleer** /k<u>ɑ</u>lfsler/ calf, calfskin

het **kalfsmedaillon** /k<u>ɑ</u>lfsmedɑjɔn/ (pl: -s) medallion of veal

de **kalfsoester** /k<u>ɑ</u>lfsustər/ (pl: -s) veal esca-
lope

het **kalfsvlees** /k<u>ɑ</u>lfsfles/ veal

het **kaliber** /kal<u>i</u>bər/ (pl: -s) calibre, bore

het **kalium** /k<u>a</u>lijʏm/ potassium, potash

de **kalk** /kɑlk/ **1** lime; (quick)lime; slaked lime
2 (lime) mortar **3** plaster; whitewash

de **kalkaanslag** /k<u>ɑ</u>lkanslɑχ/ scale, fur
kalken /k<u>ɑ</u>lkə(n)/ (kalkte, heeft gekalkt)
1 scribble **2** chalk

de **kalknagel** /k<u>ɑ</u>lknaɣəl/ fungal nail

de **kalkoen** /kɑlk<u>u</u>n/ (pl: -en) turkey

het/de **kalksteen** /k<u>ɑ</u>lksten/ (pl: -stenen) limestone
kalligraferen /kaliɣraf<u>e</u>rə(n)/ (kalligrafeer-
de, heeft gekalligrafeerd) write in calligraphy (*or:* fine handwriting)

de **kalligrafie** /kaliɣraf<u>i</u>/ (pl: -ën) calligraphy,
penmanship
kalm /kɑlm/ (adj, adv) **1** calm, cool, com-

posed **2** peaceful, quiet: *~ aan!* take it easy!,
easy does it!
kalmeren /kɑlm<u>e</u>rə(n)/ (kalmeerde, heeft
gekalmeerd) calm down, soothe, tranquillize: *een ~d effect* a calming (*or:* soothing,
tranquillizing) effect

het **kalmeringsmiddel** /kɑlm<u>e</u>rɪŋsmɪdəl/ (pl:
-en) sedative, tranquillizer
kalmpjes /k<u>ɑ</u>lmpjəs/ (adv) calmly

de **kalmte** /k<u>ɑ</u>lmtə/ **1** calm(ness), composure:
zijn ~ bewaren keep one's head/composure
(*or:* self-control, cool) **2** calm(ness), tranquillity, quietness
kalven /k<u>ɑ</u>lvə(n)/ (kalfde, heeft gekalfd)
calve

de **kalverliefde** /k<u>ɑ</u>lvərlivdə/ (pl: -s) calf love

de **kam** /kɑm/ (pl: -men) comb

de **kameel** /kam<u>e</u>l/ (pl: kamelen) camel

het/de **kameleon** /kamelej<u>ɔ</u>n/ (pl: -s) chameleon

de **kamer** /k<u>a</u>mər/ (pl: -s) **1** room, chamber
2 room, apartment: *~s verhuren* take in
lodgers; *~ met ontbijt* Bed and Breakfast, B &
B; *Renske woont op ~s* Renske is (*or:* lives) in
lodgings; *op ~s gaan wonen* move into lodgings **3** chamber, house: [Belg] *Kamer van
Volksvertegenwoordigers* Lower House (of
Parliament); *de Eerste Kamer* **a)** the Upper
Chamber (*or:* Upper House); **b)** the (House
of) Lords, the Upper House; **c)** [Am] the Senate; *de Tweede Kamer* **a)** the Lower Chamber
(*or:* Lower House); **b)** the (House of) Commons; **c)** [Am] the House (of Representatives)
4 chamber, board: *de Kamer van Koophandel
en Fabrieken* the Chamber of Commerce

de **kameraad** /kamər<u>a</u>t/ (pl: kameraden) comrade, companion, mate, pal, buddy

de **kameraadschap** /kamər<u>a</u>tsχɑp/ companionship, (good-)fellowship, camaraderie
kameraadschappelijk /kaməratsχ<u>ɑ</u>pələk/
(adj, adv) companionable, friendly: *~ met
iem. omgaan* fraternize with s.o.

de **kamerbewoner** /k<u>a</u>mərbəwonər/ (pl: -s)
lodger
kamerbreed /kamərbr<u>e</u>t/ (adj) wall-to-wall

het **kamerdebat** /k<u>a</u>mərdebɑt/ (pl: -ten) parliamentary debate; congressional debate

de **kamergenoot** /k<u>a</u>mərɣənot/ (pl: -genoten)
room-mate

de **kamerjas** /k<u>a</u>mərjɑs/ (pl: -sen) dressing
gown

het **kamerlid** /k<u>a</u>mərlɪt/ (pl: -leden) Member of
Parliament, MP

het **kamermeisje** /k<u>a</u>mərmɛiʃə/ (pl: -s) cham-
bermaid

de **kamermuziek** /k<u>a</u>mərmyzik/ chamber music
Kameroen /kamər<u>u</u>n/ Cameroon

de **Kameroener** /kamər<u>u</u>nər/ (pl: -s) Cameroonian
Kameroens /kamər<u>u</u>ns/ (adj) Cameroonian

het **kamerorkest** /k<u>a</u>mərɔrkɛst/ (pl: -en) chamber orchestra

de **kamerplant** /kɑmərplɑnt/ (pl: -en) house plant, indoor plant

de **kamertemperatuur** /kɑmərtɛmpəratyr/ room temperature

de **kamerverkiezing** /kɑmərvərkizɪŋ/ (pl: -en) parliamentary elections; [Am] congressional elections

de **kamerzetel** /kɑmərzetəl/ (pl: -s) seat

de **kamfer** /kɑmfər/ camphor

het **kamgaren** /kɑmɣarə(n)/ worsted (yarn)

de **kamikaze** /kamikazə/ (pl: -s) kamikaze, suicide pilot

de **kamille** /kamɪlə/ camomile

kammen /kɑmə(n)/ (kamde, heeft gekamd) comb

het **kamp** /kɑmp/ (pl: -en) camp

de **kampeerboerderij** /kɑmperburdərɛi/ (pl: -en) farm campsite

de **kampeerder** /kɑmperdər/ (pl: -s) camper

het **kampeerterrein** /kɑmpertɛrɛin/ (pl: -en) camp(ing) site; caravan park (or: site)

de **kampeerwagen** /kɑmperwaɣə(n)/ (pl: -s) **1** caravan **2** camper

het **kampement** /kɑmpəmɛnt/ (pl: -en) camp, encampment

kampen /kɑmpə(n)/ (kampte, heeft gekampt) contend (with), struggle (with), wrestle (with): _met tegenslag_ **te** ~ _hebben_ have to cope with setbacks

de **kamper** /kɑmpər/ mobile home resident

kamperen /kɑmperə(n)/ (kampeerde, heeft/is gekampeerd) camp (out), encamp, pitch (one's) tents, bivouac: _vrij_ (or: _bij de boer_) ~ camp wild (or: on a farm)

de **kamperfoelie** /kɑmpərfuli/ (pl: -s) honeysuckle

de **kampioen** /kɑmpijun/ (pl: -en) champion, titleholder

het **kampioenschap** /kɑmpijunsχɑp/ (pl: -pen) championship, contest, competition, tournament

het **kampvuur** /kɑmpfyr/ (pl: -vuren) campfire

de **kan** /kɑn/ (pl: -nen) jug: _de zaak is in ~nen en_ **kruiken** it's in the bag

het **kanaal** /kanal/ (pl: kanalen) **1** canal, channel: _Het Kanaal_ the (English) Channel **2** canal, duct

de **Kanaaleilanden** /kanalɛilɑndə(n)/ (pl) Channel Islands (or: Isles)

de **Kanaaltunnel** /kanaltʏnəl/ Channel Tunnel, Chunnel

kanaliseren /kanalizerə(n)/ (kanaliseerde, heeft gekanaliseerd) [fig] channel

de **kanarie** /kanari/ (pl: -s) canary (bird)

kanariegeel /kanariɣel/ (adj) canary yellow

de **kandelaar** /kɑndəlar/ (pl: -s) candlestick, candleholder

de **kandidaat** /kɑndidat/ (pl: kandidaten) **1** candidate; applicant: _zich_ ~ **stellen** (voor) run (for) **2** candidate, examinee

de **kandidatuur** /kɑndidatyr/ (pl: kandidaturen) candidature, nomination

kandideren /kɑndiderə(n)/ (kandideerde, heeft gekandideerd) nominate, put forward: _zich_ ~ put o.s. up (for); [esp Am] run (for)

de **kandij** /kɑndɛi/ candy

het/de **kaneel** /kanel/ cinnamon

de **kangoeroe** /kɑŋɣəru/ (pl: -s) kangaroo

de **kanjer** /kɑɲər/ (pl: -s) **1** wizard, humdinger, whizz kid; [sport] star (player) **2** whopper, colossus: _een_ ~ **van** _een vis_ (or: _appel_) a whopping fish (or: apple)

de **kanker** /kɑŋkər/ cancer; carcinoma: _aan_ ~ **doodgaan** die of cancer

de **kankeraar** /kɑŋkərar/ (pl: -s) grouser

de **kankerbestrijding** /kɑŋkərbəstrɛidɪŋ/ fight against cancer, cancer control; (anti-)cancer campaign

kankeren /kɑŋkərə(n)/ (kankerde, heeft gekankerd) grouse, grumble, gripe: ~ _op de maatschappij_ grouse about society

het **kankergezwel** /kɑŋkərɣəzwɛl/ (pl: -len) cancerous tumour

de **kankerpatiënt** /kɑŋkərpaʃɛnt/ (pl: -en) cancer patient

kankerverwekkend /kɑŋkərvərwɛkənt/ (adj) carcinogenic

de **kannibaal** /kɑnibal/ (pl: kannibalen) cannibal, man-eater

het **kannibalisme** /kɑnibalɪsmə/ cannibalism

de **kano** /kano/ (pl: -'s) canoe

het **kanon** /kɑnɔn/ (pl: -nen) **1** gun, cannon **2** big shot, big name

het **kanonschot** /kɑnɔnsχɔt/ (pl: -en) gunshot, cannonshot

de **kanonskogel** /kɑnɔnskoɣəl/ (pl: -s) cannonball

de **kanovaarder** /kanovardər/ (pl: -s) canoeist

de **kans** /kɑns/ (pl: -en) **1** chance, possibility, opportunity; liability; risk: _vijftig_ **procent** ~ equal chances, even odds; _(een)_ **grote** ~ _dat ..._ a good chance that ...; _hij_ **heeft** _een goede_ (or: _veel_) ~ _te winnen_ he stands (or: has) a good chance of winning; _de ~en_ **keren** the tide (or: his luck) is turning; _geen_ ~ **maken** _op_ stand no chance of (sth., doing sth.); _ik_ **zie** _er wel ~ toe_ I think I can manage it; ~ _zien te ontkomen_ manage to escape; _de ~ is honderd tegen één_ the odds (or: chances) are a hundred to one **2** opportunity, chance, break, opening: _zijn ~en_ **grijpen** seize the opportunity; _zijn ~ ~_ **afwachten** await one's chances; _een_ **gemiste** ~ a lost (or: missed) opportunity; _geen schijn van_ ~ not a chance in the world; _zijn ~_ **schoon** _zien_ see one's chance, see one's way clear (to)

KANS complaints of the arm, neck and/or shoulder

kansarm /kɑnsɑrm/ (adj) underprivileged, deprived

de **kansberekening** /kɑnzbərekənɪŋ/ (pl: -en)

theory of probability; calculation of probability

de **kansel** /kɑnsəl/ (pl: -s) pulpit

de **kanselier** /kɑnsəliːr/ (pl: -s) chancellor

de **kanshebber** /kɑnshɛbər/ (pl: -s) likely candidate (*or:* winner): *de grootste* ~ the favourite; ~ *zijn voor* … be in line for

kansloos /kɑnslos/ (adj, adv) prospectless: *hij was* ~ *tegen* hem he didn't stand a chance against him

kansrijk /kɑnsrɛik/ (adj) likely [candidate]; strong

het **kansspel** /kɑnspɛl/ (pl: -en) game of chance

de **kant** /kɑnt/ (pl: -en) **1** edge, side; margin: *aan de* ~! out of the way!; *aan de* ~ *gaan staan* stand (*or:* step) aside; *zijn auto aan de* ~ *zetten* pull up (*or:* over) **2** lace **3** bank, edge: *op de* ~ *klimmen* climb ashore **4** side, face, surface; [fig] aspect; [fig] facet; [fig] angle; [fig] view: *zich van zijn goede* ~ *laten zien* show one's good side; *iemands sterke* (or: *zwakke*) ~*en* s.o.'s strong (*or:* weak) points; *deze* ~ *boven* this side up **5** side, end, edge: *iets op zijn* ~ *zetten* put sth. on its side; *de scherpe* ~*en van iets afnemen* tone sth. down (a bit); *scherpe* ~ (cutting) edge **6** way, direction: *zij kan nog alle* ~*en op* she has kept her options open; *deze* ~ *op, alstublieft* this way, please; *van alle* ~*en on all sides; *geen* ~ *meer op kunnen* have nowhere (left) to go **7** side, part(y): *familie van vaders* (or: *moeders*) ~ relatives on one's father's (*or:* mother's) side; *ik sta aan jouw* ~ I'm on your side || *iem. van* ~ *maken* do s.o. in

de **kanteel** /kɑntel/ (pl: kantelen) merlon

¹**kantelen** /kɑntələ(n)/ (kantelde, is gekanteld) topple over, turn over

²**kantelen** /kɑntələ(n)/ (kantelde, heeft gekanteld) tilt, tip (over, to one side), turn over: *niet* ~! this side up!

het **kantelraam** /kɑntəlram/ (pl: -ramen) swing (*or:* cantilever) window

kanten /kɑntə(n)/ (adj) (of) lace, lacy

kant-en-klaar /kɑntɛŋklar/ (adj) ready-to-use, ready for use, ready-made; instant; ready-to-wear; off the peg: *geen kant-en-klare oplossing hebben* have no cut-and-dried solution

de **kant-en-klaarmaaltijd** /kɑntɛŋklar-maltɛit/ ready meal

de **kantine** /kɑntinə/ (pl: -s) canteen

het **kantje** /kɑncə/ (pl: -s) **1** edge, verge: *dat was op het* ~ *af, het was* ~ *boord* that was a near thing (*or:* close shave) **2** page, side: *een opstel van drie* ~*s* a three-page essay || *er de* ~*s aflopen* cut corners

de **kantlijn** /kɑntlɛin/ (pl: -en) margin

het **kanton** /kɑntɔn/ (pl: -s) canton, district

het **kantongerecht** /kɑntɔŋɣərɛxt/ (pl: -en) cantonal court; [England] [roughly] magistrates' court; [Am] [roughly] municipal (*or:* police, Justice) of the Peace court

de **kantonrechter** /kɑntɔnrɛxtər/ (pl: -s) cantonal judge, magistrate, JP; [Am] Justice of the Peace

het **kantoor** /kɑntor/ (pl: kantoren) office: *na* ~ *een borrel pakken* have a drink after office hours; *naar* ~ *gaan* go to the office; *hij is op* ~ he is in his office; *overdag ben ik op* (*mijn*) ~ I am at the office in the daytime; *op* ~ *werken* work in an office

de **kantoorbaan** /kɑntorban/ (pl: -banen) office job, clerical job

de **kantoorboekhandel** /kɑntorbukhɑndəl/ (pl: -s) (office) stationer's (shop)

het **kantoorgebouw** /kɑntorɣəbau/ (pl: -en) office block (*or:* building)

het **kantoorpersoneel** /kɑntorpɛrsonel/ office staff (*or:* employees, workers)

de **kantoortijd** /kɑntortɛit/ office (*or:* business) hours: *onder* ~ during office (*or:* business) hours

de **kanttekening** /kɑntekənɪŋ/ (pl: -en) (short, marginal) comment

de **kap** /kɑp/ (pl: -pen) **1** hood **2** cap **3** hood; bonnet; [Am] hood: *het* ~*je van het brood* the end slice, the crust; *twee (huizen) onder één* ~ two semi-detached houses; a semi-detached house || [Belg] *op iemands* ~ *zitten* pester s.o.

de **kapel** /kɑpɛl/ (pl: -len) **1** chapel **2** dormer (window) **3** band

de **kapelaan** /kɑpəlan/ (pl: -s) curate, assistant priest

kapen /kapə(n)/ (kaapte, heeft gekaapt) hijack

de **kaper** /kapər/ (pl: -s) hijacker: *er zijn* ~*s op de kust* we've got plenty of competitors (*or:* rivals)

de **kaping** /kapɪŋ/ (pl: -en) hijack(ing)

het **kapitaal** /kapital/ **1** fortune: *een* ~ *aan boeken* a (small) fortune in books **2** capital

de **kapitaalgoederen** /kapitalɣudərə(n)/ (pl) capital goods, investment goods

kapitaalkrachtig /kapitalkrɑxtəx/ (adj) wealthy, substantial

de **kapitaalmarkt** /kapitalmɑrkt/ capital market

de **kapitaalvernietiging** /kapitalvərnitəɣɪŋ/ (pl: -en) **1** destruction of capital **2** waste of talent

het **kapitalisme** /kapitalɪsmə/ capitalism

de **kapitalist** /kapitalɪst/ (pl: -en) capitalist

kapitalistisch /kapitalɪstis/ (adj) capitalist(ic)

de **kapitein** /kapitɛin/ (pl: -s) captain; skipper

het **kapittel** /kapɪtəl/ (pl: -s, -en) chapter

het **kapje** /kɑpjə/ (pl: -s) **1** cap; (face)mask **2** heel

de **kaplaars** /kaplars/ (pl: kaplaarzen) top boot, jackboot

het **kapmes** /kɑpmɛs/ (pl: -sen) chopping-knife; cleaver; machete

de **kapok** /kapɔk/ kapok

kapot /kapɔt/ (adj) **1** broken, in bits: *die jas is ~* that coat is torn **2** broken; broken down [car]: *de koffieautomaat is ~* the coffee machine is out of order **3** dead beat, worn out: *zich ~ werken* work one's fingers to the bone; *hij is niet ~ te krijgen* he's a tough one (*or:* cookie) **4** cut up, broken-hearted: *ergens ~ van zijn* be (all) cut up about sth.

kapotgaan /kapɔtχan/ (ging kapot, is kapotgegaan) **1** break, fall apart; break down **2** pop off, kick the bucket

het **kapotje** /kapɔcə/ (pl: -s) rubber, French letter

kapotmaken /kapɔtmakə(n)/ (maakte kapot, heeft kapotgemaakt) break (up), destroy, wreck, ruin

kapotvallen /kapɔtfalə(n)/ (viel kapot, is kapotgevallen) fall to pieces, fall and break, smash

¹**kappen** /kɑpə(n)/ (kapte, heeft gekapt) chop, cut ‖ *ik kap er mee* I'm knocking off

²**kappen** /kɑpə(n)/ (kapte, heeft gekapt) **1** cut down, chop down, fell **2** do one's (*or:* s.o.'s) hair: *zich laten ~* have one's hair done **3** cut, hew

de **kapper** /kɑpər/ (pl: -s) hairdresser, hairstylist; barber

de **kappertjes** /kɑpərcəs/ (pl) capers

het/de **kapsalon** /kɑpsalɔn/ (pl: -s) hairdresser's; barber's shop

kapseizen /kɑpsɛizə(n)/ (kapseisde, is gekapseisd) capsize, keel over

het **kapsel** /kɑpsəl/ (pl: -s) **1** hairstyle, haircut **2** hairdo

de **kapsones** /kɑpsɔnəs/ (pl): *~ hebben* be full of o.s.

de **kapstok** /kɑpstɔk/ (pl: -ken) hallstand; hatstand; hat rack; coat hooks

de **kaptafel** /kɑptafəl/ (pl: -s) dressing table

de **kapucijner** /kapysɛinər/ (pl: -s) [roughly] marrowfat (pea)

de **kar** /kɑr/ (pl: -ren) **1** cart, barrow: [fig] *de ~ trekken* do the dirty work **2** car

het **karaat** /karat/ (pl: -s, karaten) carat

de **karabijn** /karabɛin/ (pl: -en) carbine

de **karaf** /karɑf/ (pl: -fen) carafe, decanter

het **karakter** /karɑktər/ (pl: -s) **1** character, nature: *iem. met een sterk ~* s.o. with (great) strength of character **2** character, personality, spirit: *~ tonen* show character (*or:* spirit); *zonder ~* without character, spineless **3** character, symbol

de **karaktereigenschap** /karɑktərɛiγə(n)-sχɑp/ (pl: -pen) character trait

karakteriseren /karɑkterizerə(n)/ (karakteriseerde, heeft gekarakteriseerd) characterize

karakteristiek /karɑktərɪstik/ (adj) characteristic (of), typical (of)

karakterloos /karɑktərlos/ (adj) characterless, insipid

de **karaktertrek** /karɑktərtrɛk/ (pl: -ken) characteristic, feature, trait

de **karamel** /karamɛl/ (pl: -s) caramel, toffee

het **karaoke** /karaokə/ karaoke

het **karate** /karatə/ karate

de **karavaan** /karavan/ (pl: karavanen) caravan, train

de **karbonade** /karbonadə/ (pl: -s) chop, cutlet

de **kardinaal** /kardinal/ (pl: kardinalen) cardinal

Karel /karəl/ Charles: *~ de Grote* Charlemagne

de **kariboe** /karibu/ (pl: -s) caribou

karig /karəχ/ (adj) **1** sparing, mean, frugal **2** meagre, scant(y), frugal: *een ~ maal* a frugal meal

de **karikatuur** /karikatyr/ (pl: karikaturen) caricature

het/de **karkas** /karkɑs/ (pl: -sen) carcass

het **karma** /kɑrma/ karma

de **karnemelk** /kɑrnəmɛlk/ buttermilk

karnen /kɑrnə(n)/ (karnde, heeft gekarnd) churn

de **karper** /kɑrpər/ (pl: -s) carp

het **karpet** /kɑrpɛt/ (pl: -ten) rug

karren /kɑrə(n)/ (karde, heeft/is gekard) ride; bike

het **karrenspoor** /kɑrə(n)spor/ (pl: -sporen) cart track

de **karrenvracht** /kɑrə(n)vrɑχt/ (pl: -en) cartload

het **karretje** /kɑrəcə/ (pl: -s) (little) cart, car; trap; trolley; soapbox

het **kartel** /kɑrtɛl/ cartel, trust

kartelen /kɑrtələ(n)/ (kartelde, heeft gekarteld) serrate, notch; mill

het **kartelmes** /kɑrtəlmɛs/ (pl: -sen) serrated knife

de **kartelrand** /kɑrtəlrɑnt/ (pl: -en) milled edge

karten /kɑːrtə(n)/ (kartte, heeft/is gekart) (go-)kart

het **karting** /kɑːrtɪŋ/ karting

het **karton** /kɑrtɔn/ (pl: -s) **1** cardboard **2** carton, cardboard box

kartonnen /kɑrtɔnə(n)/ (adj) cardboard: *een ~ bekertje* a paper cup

de **karwats** /kɑrwɑts/ (pl: -en) (riding) crop, (riding) whip

het/de **karwei** /kɑrwɛi/ (pl: -en) **1** job, work: *een heidens ~* a hell of a job **2** odd job, chore **3** job, task, chore

de **karwij** /kɑrwɛi/ caraway (seed)

de **kas** /kɑs/ (pl: -sen) **1** greenhouse, hothouse **2** cashdesk, cashier's office **3** cash, fund(s): *de kleine ~* petty cash; *de ~ beheren* (*or:* *houden*) manage (*or:* keep) the cash; *krap (slecht) bij ~ zitten* be short of cash (*or:* money) **4** socket

het **kasboek** /kɑzbuk/ (pl: -en) cash book, account(s) book de **kasbon** /kɑzbɔn/ (pl: -nen) [Belg] (type of) savings certificate

de **kasgroente** /kɑsχruntə/ (pl: -n, -s) greenhouse vegetables

het **kasjmier** /kɑʃmir/ cashmere

de **Kaspische Zee** /kɑspisəze/ Caspian Sea

de **kasplant** /kɑsplɑnt/ (pl: -en) hothouse plant

de **kassa** /kɑsa/ (pl: -'s) **1** cash register, till **2** cash desk; checkout; box office, booking office

de **kassabon** /kɑsabɔn/ (pl: -nen) receipt, sales slip, docket

het **kassaldo** /kɑsɑldo/ (pl: -'s) cash balance

de **kassei** /kɑsɛi/ (pl: -en) cobble(stone), paving stone, sett

de **kassier** /kɑsir/ (pl: -s) cashier; teller

het **kassucces** /kɑsyksɛs/ (pl: -sen) box-office success, box-office hit

de **kast** /kɑst/ (pl: -en) **1** cupboard; wardrobe; chest of drawers; cabinet: *iem.* **op** *de ~ jagen (krijgen)* get a rise out of s.o.; *alles* **uit** *de ~ halen* pull out all the stops **2** barracks; barn: *een ~* **van** *een huis* a barn of a house

de **kastanje** /kɑstɑnə/ (Spanish, sweet) chestnut

de **kastanjeboom** /kɑstɑnəbom/ (pl: -bomen) chestnut (tree)

het **¹kastanjebruin** /kɑstɑnəbrœyn/ chestnut, auburn

²kastanjebruin /kɑstɑnəbrœyn/ (adj) chestnut, auburn

de **kaste** /kɑstə/ (pl: -n) caste

het **kasteel** /kɑstel/ (pl: kastelen) castle

de **kastelein** /kɑstəlɛin/ (pl: -s) innkeeper, publican, landlord

het **kastenstelsel** /kɑstəstɛlsəl/ caste system

het **kasticket** /kɑstikɛt/ (pl: -s) [Belg] receipt

kastijden /kɑstɛidə(n)/ (kastijdde, heeft gekastijd) chastise, castigate, punish

het **kastje** /kɑʃə/ (pl: -s) **1** cupboard, locker: *van het ~ naar de muur gestuurd worden* be sent (*or:* driven) from pillar to post **2** box

de **kat** /kɑt/ (pl: -ten) **1** cat: *leven als ~ en* **hond** be like cat and dog; *de* **Gelaarsde** *Kat* Puss-in-Boots **2** snarl: *iem. een ~ geven* snarl (*or:* snap) at s.o. ‖ *maak dat de ~ wijs* pull the other one, tell it to the marines

katachtig /kɑtɑχtəχ/ (adj) catlike

de **katalysator** /kɑtalizator/ (pl: -s, -en) (catalytic) converter [of car]

de **katapult** /kɑtapʏlt/ (pl: -en) catapult

de **kater** /kɑtər/ (pl: -s) **1** tomcat **2** hangover **3** disillusionment

het/de **katern** /kɑtɛrn/ (pl: -en) quire, gathering

de **katheder** /kɑtedər/ (pl: -s) lectern

de **kathedraal** /kɑtedral/ (pl: kathedralen) cathedral

de **katheter** /kɑtetər/ (pl: -s) catheter: *een ~* **inbrengen** *bij* catheterize

de **kathode** /kɑtodə/ (pl: -n, -s) cathode

het **katholicisme** /kɑtolisɪsmə/ (Roman) Catholicism

katholiek /kɑtolik/ (adj) (Roman) Catholic

het **katje** /kɑcə/ (pl: -s) **1** kitten **2** [bot] catkin

het/de **katoen** /kɑtun/ cotton

katoenen /kɑtunə(n)/ (adj) cotton

de **katoenplantage** /kɑtunplɑntaʒə/ cotton plantation

de **katrol** /kɑtrɔl/ (pl: -len) **1** (fishing) reel **2** pulley

het **kattebelletje** /kɑtəbɛləcə/ (pl: -s) (scribbled) note, memo

katten /kɑtə(n)/ (katte, heeft gekat) snap (at), snarl (at)

de **kattenbak** /kɑtə(n)bɑk/ (pl: -ken) **1** cat('s) box **2** dicky seat; [Am] rumble seat

de **kattenbakkorrels** /kɑtə(n)bɑkərəls/ (pl) cat litter

de **kattenkop** /kɑtə(n)kɔp/ (pl: -pen) **1** cat's head **2** cat, bitch

het **kattenkwaad** /kɑtə(n)kwat/ mischief: *~* **uithalen** get into mischief

het **kattenluik** /kɑtə(n)lœyk/ cat flap

de **kattenpis** /kɑtə(n)pɪs/: *dat is* **geen** *~* no kidding; that's not to be sneezed at

katterig /kɑtərəχ/ (adj) under the weather; hung over; disappointed, disillusioned

kattig /kɑtəχ/ (adj, adv) catty

de **katzwijm** /kɑtswɛim/: *in ~ vallen* faint

de **kauw** /kɑu/ (pl: -en) jackdaw

kauwen /kɑuwə(n)/ (kauwde, heeft gekauwd) chew: [fig] **op** *iets ~* chew sth. over

het/de **kauwgom** /kɑuɣɔm/ chewing gum

de **kavel** /kavəl/ (pl: -s) lot, parcel; share

de **kaviaar** /kavijar/ caviar

de **Kazach** /kazɑk/ Kazakh

het **¹Kazachs** /kazɑχs/ Kazakh

²Kazachs /kazɑχs/ (adj) Kazakh

Kazachstan /kazɑkstɑn/ Kazakhstan

de **kazerne** /kazɛrnə/ (pl: -s) barrack(s) [mil]; station

het **kazuifel** /kazœyfəl/ (pl: -s) chasuble

KB /kilobɑjt(s)/ *kilobyte* K, KB

de **kebab** /kebɑb/ kebab

de **keel** /kel/ (pl: kelen) throat: *het* **hangt** *me (mijlenver) de ~* **uit** I'm fed up with it; *zijn ~* **schrapen** clear one's throat; *een ~* **opzetten** start yelling

het **keelgat** /kelɣɑt/ (pl: -en) gullet: *in het* **verkeerde** *~ schieten* **a)** go down the wrong way; **b)** [fig] not go down very well (with s.o.)

de **keelholte** /kelhɔltə/ pharynx

de **keelontsteking** /kelɔntstekɪŋ/ (pl: -en) throat infection, laryngitis

de **keelpijn** /kelpɛin/ sore throat

keepen /kipə(n)/ (keepte, heeft gekeept) be in goal, keep goal

de **keeper** /kipər/ (pl: -s) (goal)keeper; goalie

de **keer** /ker/ (pl: keren) time: *een* **doodenkele** *~* once in a blue moon; *een* **enkele** *~* once or twice; *geen* **enkele** *~* not once; *een* **andere** *~* another time; *nou vooruit, voor* **deze** *~ dan!* all right then, but just this once!; *nog* een ~*(tje)* (once) again, once more; *(op)* **een** ~ one day; **één** enkele ~, slechts **één** ~ only once; *negen van de* **tien** ~ nine times out of ten; *dat heb ik nu al* **tien** (or: **honderd**) ~ *gehoord* I've already heard that dozens of times (or: a hundred times); **twee** ~ twice; **twee** ~ twee is vier twice two is four; ~ *op* ~ time after time, time and again; *binnen de* **kortste** keren in no time (at all)

de **keerkring** /kɛrkrɪŋ/ (pl: -en) tropic
het **keerpunt** /kɛrpʏnt/ (pl: -en) turning point
de **keerzijde** /kɛrzɛidə/ (pl: -n) other side; reverse
de **keet** /ket/ (pl: keten) **1** hut, shed **2** racket: ~ **trappen** (or: **schoppen**) horse about (around)
keffen /kɛfə(n)/ (kefte, heeft gekeft) yap
het **keffertje** /kɛfərcə/ (pl: -s) yapper
de **kegel** /keɣəl/ (pl: -s) **1** cone **2** ninepin; skittle
de **kegelbaan** /keɣəlban/ (pl: -banen) skittle alley
kegelen /keɣələ(n)/ (kegelde, heeft gekegeld) play skittles (or: ninepins)
de **kei** /kɛi/ (pl: -en) **1** boulder **2** cobble(stone); set(t) || *Eric* **is** een ~ in wiskunde Eric is brilliant at maths
keihard /kɛihɑrt/ (adj, adv) **1** rock-hard, hard; as hard as rock [after vb] **2** hard, tough || ~ *schreeuwen* shout at the top of one's voice; *de radio* **stond** ~ **aan** the radio was on full blast (or: was blaring away)
keilen /kɛilə(n)/ (keilde, heeft gekeild) throw, chuck, fling: *iem. de deur uit* ~ throw (or: chuck) s.o. out (of the door)
de **keizer** /kɛizər/ (pl: -s) emperor
de **keizerin** /kɛizərɪn/ (pl: -nen) empress
keizerlijk /kɛizərlək/ (adj, adv) imperial
het **keizerrijk** /kɛizərɛik/ (pl: -en) empire
de **keizersnede** /kɛizərsnedə/ (pl: -n) Caesarean (section)
de **kelder** /kɛldər/ (pl: -s) cellar, basement
kelderen /kɛldərə(n)/ (kelderde, is gekelderd) plummet, tumble
het **kelderluik** /kɛldərlœyk/ (pl: -en) trapdoor (to a cellar)
kelen /kelə(n)/ (keelde, heeft gekeeld) **1** cut (s.o.'s) throat **2** strangle, throttle
de **kelk** /kɛlk/ (pl: -en) **1** goblet **2** calyx
de **kelner** /kɛlnər/ (pl: -s) waiter
de **Kelten** /kɛltə(n)/ (pl) Celts
het **¹Keltisch** /kɛltis/ Celtic
²Keltisch /kɛltis/ (adj) Celtic
de **kemphaan** /kɛmphan/ (pl: -hanen) **1** ruff **2** fighting cock: *vechten* **als** kemphanen fight like fighting cocks
de **kenau** /kenɑu/ (pl: -s) battle-axe, virago
kenbaar /kɛmbar/ (adj) known
het **kengetal** /kɛnɣətɑl/ (pl: -len) dialling code; [Am] area code; prefix
Kenia /kenija/ Kenya
de **Keniaan** /kenijan/ (pl: Kenianen) Kenyan

Keniaans /kenijans/ (adj) Kenyan
het **kenmerk** /kɛmɛrk/ (pl: -en) (identifying) mark; hallmark [also fig]; reference [abbr: ref]
kenmerken /kɛmɛrkə(n)/ (kenmerkte, heeft gekenmerkt) characterize, mark, typify
kenmerkend /kɛmɛrkənt/ (adj, adv) (+ voor) characteristic (of), typical (of); specific (to): ~*e* **eigenschappen** distinctive characteristics
de **kennel** /kɛnəl/ (pl: -s) kennel
¹kennelijk /kɛnələk/ (adj) evident, apparent; clear; obvious; unmistakable
²kennelijk /kɛnələk/ (adv) evidently, clearly, obviously: *het* **is** ~ *zonder opzet* **gedaan** it was obviously done unintentionally
kennen /kɛnə(n)/ (kende, heeft gekend) know, be acquainted with: *iem.* **leren** ~ get to know s.o.; *elkaar (beter)* **leren** ~ get (better) acquainted; *ken je* **deze** *al?* have you heard this one?; *ik ken* **haar** *al jaren* I've known her for years; *sinds ik* **jou** *ken …* since I met you …; *iem.* **van** *naam* ~ know s.o. by name; *iem. door en door* ~ know s.o. inside out; *iets van buiten* ~, *iets uit zijn hoofd* ~ know sth. by heart; *ons* **kent** **ons** we know what to expect, we know each others ways; [fig] *laat je niet* ~*!* give 'em hell!
de **kenner** /kɛnər/ (pl: -s) **1** connoisseur **2** authority (on), expert (on)
de **kennersblik** /kɛnərzblɪk/ (pl: -ken) expert('s) eye
de **kennis** /kɛnɪs/ (pl: -sen) **1** knowledge (of); acquaintance (with): **met** ~ *van zaken* knowledgeably; ~ *is macht* knowledge is power **2** consciousness: *zij is weer* **bij** ~ *gekomen* she has regained consciousness, she has come round **3** knowledge, information; learning; know-how: *een* **grondige** ~ *van het Latijn hebben* have a thorough knowledge of Latin **4** acquaintance: *hij heeft veel* **vrienden** *en* ~*sen* he has a lot of friends and acquaintances
de **kennisgeving** /kɛnɪsxevɪŋ/ (pl: -en) notification, notice
de **kennismaatschappij** /kɛnɪsmatsxɑpɛi/ knowledge (or: information) society
kennismaken /kɛnɪsmakə(n)/ (maakte kennis, heeft kennisgemaakt) get acquainted (with), meet, get to know, be introduced: *aangenaam kennis te maken!* pleased to meet you
de **kennismaking** /kɛnɪsmakɪŋ/ (pl: -en) **1** acquaintance **2** introduction (to)
kennisnemen (nam kennis van, heeft heeft kennisgenomen van) take note (of)
de **kennisneming** /kɛnɪsnemɪŋ/ examination, inspection: *na* ~ *van de stukken* after examination of the documents; *ter* ~ for your information
de **kennissenkring** /kɛnɪsə(n)krɪŋ/ (pl: -en)

(circle of) acquaintances

kenschetsen /kɛnsxɛtsə(n)/ (kenschetste, heeft gekenschetst) characterize

het **kenteken** /kɛntekə(n)/ (pl: -s) registration number; [Am] license number

het **kentekenbewijs** /kɛntekə(n)bəwɛis/ (pl: -bewijzen) [roughly] vehicle registration document; logbook

de **kentekenplaat** /kɛntekə(n)plat/ (pl: -platen) number plate; [Am] license plate

kenteren /kɛntərə(n)/ (kenterde, heeft gekenterd) turn

de **kentering** /kɛntərɪŋ/ (pl: -en) turn: ~ *in de publieke opinie* turn (*or:* change) of public opinion

de **keper** /kepər/: *op de* ~ *beschouwd* on closer inspection; when all is said and done

het **keppeltje** /kɛpəlcə/ (pl: -s) yarmulka

de **keramiek** /keramik/ ceramics; pottery

keramisch /keramis/ (adj) ceramic, pottery: *een ~e kookplaat* a ceramic hob; [Am] a ceramic stove top

de **kerel** /kerəl/ (pl: -s) **1** (big) fellow, (big) guy, (big) chap (*or:* bloke) **2** he-man: *kom naar buiten als je een* ~ *bent* come outside if you're man enough

¹**keren** /kerə(n)/ (keerde, is gekeerd) turn (round); shift: ~ *verboden* no U-turns

²**keren** /kerə(n)/ (keerde, heeft gekeerd) **1** turn **2** turn (towards) **3** turn (back); stem: *het water* ~ stem the (flow of) water

zich ³**keren** /kerə(n)/ (keerde zich, heeft zich gekeerd) **1** turn (round): *zich ergens niet kunnen wenden* of ~ not have room to move **2** turn ‖ *in zichzelf gekeerd zijn* be introverted, keep to o.s.

de **kerf** /kɛrf/ (pl: kerven) notch, nick; groove

de **kerfstok** /kɛrfstɔk/ (pl: -ken): *heel wat op zijn* ~ *hebben* have a lot to answer for

de **kerk** /kɛrk/ (pl: -en) church

de **kerkbank** /kɛrgbaŋk/ pew

de **kerkdienst** /kɛrgdinst/ (pl: -en) (divine) service, church; mass

kerkelijk /kɛrkələk/ (adj) church, ecclesiastical

de **kerkenraad** /kɛrkə(n)rat/ (pl: -raden) **1** church council meeting **2** (parochial) church council

de **kerker** /kɛrkər/ (pl: -s) dungeon, prison, jail

de **kerkfabriek** /kɛrkfabrik/ (pl: -en) (church-)fabric

de **kerkganger** /kɛrkxaŋər/ (pl: -s) churchgoer

het **kerkgebouw** /kɛrkxəbau/ (pl: -en) church (building)

het **kerkgenootschap** /kɛrkxənotsxap/ (pl: -pen) (religious) denomination, (religious) community

het **kerkhof** /kɛrkhɔf/ (pl: -hoven) churchyard, graveyard

de **kerkklok** /kɛrklɔk/ (pl: -ken) **1** church bell **2** church clock

het **kerkkoor** /kɛrkkor/ (pl: -koren) **1** choir **2** church choir

de **kerkmuziek** /kɛrkmyzik/ church music, religious music

het **kerkplein** /kɛrkplɛin/ (pl: -en) [roughly] village square

de **kerktoren** /kɛrktorə(n)/ (pl: -s) church tower; steeple; spire

de **kerkuil** /kɛrkœyl/ (pl: -en) barn owl

kermen /kɛrmə(n)/ (kermde, heeft gekermd) moan; whine; wail

de **kermis** /kɛrməs/ (pl: -sen) fair

de **kermisexploitant** /kɛrmɪsɛksplwatant/ (pl: -en) showman

de **kern** /kɛrn/ (pl: -en) **1** core; heart; pith **2** [fig] core, heart, essence: *tot de* ~ *van een zaak doordringen* get (down) to the (very) heart of the matter **3** central

kernachtig /kɛrnaxtəx/ (adj, adv) pithy, concise, terse

het **kernafval** /kɛrnafɑl/ nuclear waste

de **kernbom** /kɛrmbɔm/ (pl: -men) nuclear bomb

de **kerncentrale** /kɛrnsɛntralə/ (pl: -s) nuclear (*or:* atomic) power station, nuclear plant, atomic plant

het **kerndoel** /kɛrndul/ (pl: -en) primary objective, chief aim

de **kernenergie** /kɛrnenɛrʒi/ nuclear energy

de **kernfusie** /kɛrnfyzi/ nuclear fusion

de **kernfysica** /kɛrnfizika/ nuclear physics

de **kernfysicus** /kɛrnfizikʏs/ (pl: -fysici) physicist, atomic physicist

kerngezond /kɛrnɣəzɔnt/ (adj) perfectly healthy, in perfect health; as fit as a fiddle

de **kernmacht** /kɛrnmaxt/ (pl: -en) nuclear power

de **kernoorlog** /kɛrnorlɔx/ (pl: -en) nuclear war

de **kernproef** /kɛrmpruf/ (pl: -proeven) nuclear test, atomic test

de **kernreactie** /kɛrnrejaksi/ (pl: -s) nuclear reaction

de **kernreactor** /kɛrnrejaktɔr/ (pl: -s, -en) (nuclear, atomic) reactor

de **kerntaak** /kɛrntak/ (pl: -taken) core task

het **kernwapen** /kɛrnwapə(n)/ (pl: -s) nuclear weapon, atomic weapon

de **kerosine** /kerozinə/ kerosene

de **kerrie** /kɛri/ curry

de **kers** /kɛrs/ cherry: [fig] *de* ~ *op de taart* the icing on the cake

de **kersenbonbon** /kɛrsə(n)bɔmbɔn/ (pl: -s) cherry liqueur chocolate

de **kerst** /kɛrst/ Christmas

de **kerstavond** /kɛrstavɔnt/ (pl: -en) evening of Christmas Eve

de **kerstboom** /kɛrstbom/ (pl: -bomen) Christmas tree

de **kerstdag** /kɛrstdax/ (pl: -en) Christmas Day: *prettige ~en!* Merry (*or:* Happy) Christmas!;

eerste ~ Christmas Day; *tweede* ~ Boxing Day

kerstenen /kɛrstənə(n)/ (kerstende, heeft gekerstend) christianize

het **kerstfeest** /kɛrstfest/ (pl: -en) (feast, festival of) Christmas: *zalig (gelukkig)* ~! Merry Christmas!

de **kerstkaart** /kɛrstkart/ Christmas card

de **kerstkrans** /kɛrstkrɑns/ (pl: -en) (almond) pastry ring

het **kerstlied** /kɛrstlit/ (pl: -eren) (Christmas) carol

de **Kerstman** /kɛrstmɑn/ (pl: -nen) Santa (Claus), Father Christmas

Kerstmis /kɛrstmɪs/ Christmas

de **kerstnacht** /kɛrstnɑxt/ (pl: -en) Christmas night

de **kerstomaat** /kɛrstomat/ (pl: -tomaten) cherry tomato

het **kerstpakket** /kɛrstpɑkɛt/ (pl: -ten) Christmas hamper (*or*: box)

de **kerststal** /kɛrstɑl/ (pl: -len) crib

de **Kerstster** /kɛr(st)stɛr/ Star of Bethlehem

de **kerststol** /kɛr(st)stɔl/ (pl: -len) (Christmas) stollen

de **kerstvakantie** /kɛrstfɑkɑn(t)si/ (pl: -s) Christmas holiday(s); [Am] Christmas vacation

kersvers /kɛrsfɛrs/ (adj) fresh, new: ~ *uit de winkel* fresh (*or*: straight) from the shop

de **kervel** /kɛrvəl/ chervil

¹**kerven** /kɛrvə(n)/ (kerfde, is gekerfd) gouge (out), cut

²**kerven** /kɛrvə(n)/ (kerfde, heeft gekerfd) **1** notch, nick, cut; score **2** carve (out), cut (out): *zij kerfden hun **naam** in de boom* they carved their names in the tree

de **ketchup** /kɛtʃʏp/ ketchup

de **ketel** /ketəl/ (pl: -s) **1** kettle; cauldron **2** boiler

het/de **ketelsteen** /ketəlsten/ (boiler) scale

de **keten** /ketə(n)/ (pl: -s) **1** chains **2** chain **3** chain, series

ketenen /ketə(n)nə(n)/ (ketende, heeft geketend) **1** chain (up) **2** chain **3** [fig] curb

de **ketjap** /kɛtjɑp/ soy sauce

ketsen /kɛtsə(n)/ (ketste, heeft/is geketst) **1** glance off, ricochet (off) **2** misfire, fail to go off: *het **geweer** ketste* the gun misfired

de **ketter** /kɛtər/ (pl: -s) heretic ‖ *roken **als** een* ~ smoke like a chimney

de **ketterij** /kɛtərɛi/ (pl: -en) heresy

ketters /kɛtərs/ (adj, adv) heretical

de **ketting** /kɛtɪŋ/ (pl: -en) chain: *aan de* ~ *leggen* chain up

de **kettingbotsing** /kɛtɪŋbɔtsɪŋ/ (pl: -en) multiple collision (*or*: crash), pile-up

de **kettingbrief** /kɛtɪŋbrif/ (pl: -brieven) chain letter

de **kettingkast** /kɛtɪŋkɑst/ (pl: -en) chain guard

de **kettingreactie** /kɛtɪŋrejɑksi/ (pl: -s) chain reaction

de **kettingroker** /kɛtɪŋrokər/ (pl: -s) chain smoker

het **kettingslot** /kɛtɪŋslɔt/ chain lock

de **kettingzaag** /kɛtɪŋzax/ (pl: -zagen) chainsaw

de **keu** /kø/ (pl: -s) (billiard) cue

de **keuken** /køkə(n)/ (pl: -s) **1** kitchen **2** (art of) cooking, cuisine: *de Franse* ~ French cooking (*or*: cuisine)

de **keukendoek** /køkə(n)duk/ (pl: -en) kitchen towel

de **keukenhulp** /køkə(n)hʏlp/ (pl: -en) food processor

de **keukenkast** /køkə(n)kɑst/ (pl: -en) kitchen cabinet (*or*: cupboard)

het **keukenkruid** /køkə(n)krœyt/ kitchen herb

de **keukenmachine** /køkə(n)maʃinə/ (pl: -s) food processor

de **keukenrol** /køkə(n)rɔl/ (pl: -len) kitchen roll

het **keukenschort** /køkə(n)sxɔrt/ apron

Keulen /kølə(n)/ Cologne

de **keur** /kør/ (pl: -en) **1** hallmark **2** choice (selection)

keuren /kørə(n)/ (keurde, heeft gekeurd) test; inspect; sample; taste; examine: *films* ~ censor films; *iem. geen **blik** waardig* ~ not deign to look at s.o.

¹**keurig** /kørəx/ (adj) **1** neat, tidy: *er* ~ *uitzien* look neat (and tidy), look smart **2** smart, nice: *een* ~ *handschrift* a neat hand **3** fine, choice: *een* ~ *rapport* (or: *opstel*) an excellent report (*or*: essay)

²**keurig** /kørəx/ (adv) nicely; neatly ‖ ~ *netjes gekleed* properly dressed

de **keuring** /kørɪŋ/ (pl: -en) **1** test; inspection; examination: *een medische* ~ a medical (examination) **2** testing; inspection; sampling; tasting; examination

de **keuringsarts** /kørɪŋsɑrts/ medical examiner

de **keuringsdienst** /kørɪŋzdinst/ (pl: -en) inspection service: *Keuringsdienst van Waren* commodity inspection department

het **keurkorps** /kørkɔrps/ (pl: -en) crack troops

de **keurmeester** /kørmestər/ (pl: -s) inspector; [gold and silver] assay-master

het **keurmerk** /kørmɛrk/ (pl: -en) hallmark; quality mark

het **keurslijf** /kørslɛif/ (pl: -lijven) straitjacket

de **keus** /køs/ (pl: keuzen) **1** choice, selection **2** choice, option, alternative: *er is **volop** ~* there's a lot to choose from; *aan u de* ~ the choice is yours **3** choice, assortment: *een grote* ~ a large choice (*or*: assortment), a wide range

de **keutel** /køtəl/ (pl: -s) droppings; pellet

keuvelen /køvələ(n)/ (keuvelde, heeft gekeuveld) (have a) chat, talk

de **keuze** /køzə/ (pl: -n) *see keus*

het **keuzemenu** /kǿzəmøny/ (pl: -'s) **1** set menu, fixed price menu **2** menu

het **keuzepakket** /kǿzəpɑkɛt/ (pl: -ten) options; choice of subjects (or: courses)

het **keuzevak** /kǿzəvɑk/ (pl: -ken) option, optional subject (or: course)

de **kever** /kévər/ (pl: -s) **1** beetle **2** Beetle

het **keyboard** /ki̠ːbɔːrd/ (pl: -s) keyboard

de **keycard** /ki̠ːkɑːrt/ keycard

de **keycord** /ki̠kɔːrt/ keycord

kg (abbrev) *kilogram* kg

de **ki** /kai/ *kunstmatige inseminatie* artificial insemination

kibbelen /kɪ̠bələ(n)/ (kibbelde, heeft gekibbeld) bicker, squabble

de **kibbeling** /kɪ̠bəlɪŋ/ cod parings

de **kibboets** /kɪbuts/ (pl: -en, kibboetsim) kibbutz

de **kick** /kɪk/ (pl: -s) kick

kickboksen /kɪ̠gbɔksə(n)/ kickboxing

kicken /kɪ̠kə(n)/ (kickte, heeft gekickt) get a kick (out of); [Am] get off (on), dig: *dat is ~!* that's cool!

kidnappen /kɪ̠tnɛpə(n)/ (kidnapte, heeft gekidnapt) kidnap

de **kidnapper** /kɪ̠tnɛpər/ (pl: -s) kidnapper

de **kids** /kɪts/ (pl) [inform] kids

kiekeboe /ki̠kəbu/ (int) peekaboo!

het **kiekje** /ki̠kjə/ (pl: -s) snap(shot)

de **kiel** /kil/ (pl: -en) **1** smock **2** [shipp] keel

kielekiele /kiləki̠lə/: *het was ~* it was touch and go, it was a close shave

kielhalen /ki̠lhalə(n)/ (kielhaalde, heeft gekielhaald) keelhaul

het **kielzog** /ki̠lzɔχ/ wake, wash

de **kiem** /kim/ (pl: -en) germ, seed

kiemen /ki̠mə(n)/ (kiemde, heeft/is gekiemd) germinate

kien /kin/ (adj, adv) sharp, keen

de **kiepauto** /ki̠pɑuto/ (pl: -'s) tip up truck

¹**kiepen** /ki̠pə(n)/ (kiepte, is gekiept) topple, tumble: *het glas is van de tafel gekiept* the glass toppled off the table

²**kiepen** /ki̠pə(n)/ (kiepte, heeft gekiept) tip over, topple (over)

¹**kieperen** /ki̠pərə(n)/ (kieperde, is gekieperd) tumble, topple

²**kieperen** /ki̠pərə(n)/ (kieperde, heeft gekieperd) [inform] dump

de **kier** /kir/ (pl: -en) chink, slit; crack: *door een ~ van de schutting* through a crack in the fence; *de deur staat op een ~* the door is ajar

kierewiet /ki̠rəwit/ (adj) [inform] mad, bananas: *het is om ~ van te worden!* it's enough to drive me mad (or: bananas)

de **kies** /kis/ (pl: kiezen) molar, back tooth: *een rotte ~* a bad (or: decayed) molar; [fig] a rotten apple (in the barrel)

de **kiesbrief** /ki̠zbrif/ (pl: -brieven) [Belg] polling card

het **kiesdistrict** /ki̠zdɪstrɪkt/ (pl: -en) electoral district, constituency

de **kiesdrempel** /ki̠zdrɛmpəl/ (pl: -s) electoral threshold

kieskeurig /kiskǿrəχ/ (adj) choosy, fussy

de **kieskring** /ki̠skrɪŋ/ (pl: -en) electoral district, constituency; ward

de **kiespijn** /ki̠spɛin/ toothache

het **kiesrecht** /ki̠srɛχt/ (pl: -en) suffrage, right to vote, (the) vote

het **kiesstelsel** /ki̠stɛlsəl/ (pl: -s) electoral (or: voting) system

de **kiestoon** /ki̠ston/ dialling tone

kietelen /ki̠tələ(n)/ (kietelde, heeft gekieteld) tickle

de **kieuw** /kiw/ (pl: -en) gill

de **kieviet** /ki̠vit/ (pl: -en) lapwing, peewit, plover

het **kiezel** /ki̠zəl/ (pl: -s) gravel; shingle

de **kiezelsteen** /ki̠zəlsten/ (pl: -stenen) pebble

¹**kiezen** /ki̠zə(n)/ (koos, heeft gekozen) **1** choose, decide: *zorgvuldig ~* pick and choose; *~ tussen* choose between; *je kunt uit drie kandidaten ~* you can choose from three candidates **2** vote: *voor een vrouwelijke kandidaat ~* vote for a woman candidate

²**kiezen** /ki̠zə(n)/ (koos, heeft gekozen) **1** choose, select, pick (out): *partij ~* take sides **2** vote (for); elect **3** choose, elect ‖ *een nummer ~* dial a number

de **kiezer** /ki̠zər/ (pl: -s) voter, constituent; electorate

de **kift** /kɪft/: *dat is de ~* sour grapes!

de **kijf** /kɛif/: *dat staat buiten ~* that is beyond dispute (or: question(ing))

de **kijk** /kɛik/ view, outlook, insight: *~ op iets hebben* have a good eye for sth.; [fig] *iem. te ~ zetten* expose s.o.

het **kijkcijfer** /kɛ̠iksɛifər/ (pl: -s) rating

de **kijkdichtheid** /kɛigdɪ̠χthɛit/ (pl: -heden) ratings

¹**kijken** /kɛ̠ikə(n)/ (keek, heeft gekeken) **1** look, see: *ga eens ~ wie er is* go and see who's there; *daar sta ik van te ~* well I'll be blowed; *kijk eens wie we daar hebben* look who's here!; *goed ~* watch closely; [fig] *naar iets ~* have a look at (or: see) about sth.; *zij ~ niet op geld (een paar euro)* money is no object with them; *uit het raam ~* look out (of) the window; *even de andere kant op ~* look the other way **2** look, search: *we zullen ~ of dat verhaal klopt* we shall see whether that story checks out **3** look, appear ‖ *laat eens ~, wat hebben we nodig* let's see, what do we need

²**kijken** /kɛ̠ikə(n)/ (keek, heeft gekeken) look at, watch: *kijk haar eens (lachen)* look at her (laughing)

de **kijker** /kɛ̠ikər/ (pl: -s) **1** spectator, onlooker; viewer **2** binoculars, opera-glass(es)

het **kijkje** /kɛ̠ikjə/ (pl: -s) (quick) look, glance: *de politie zal een ~ nemen* the police will have a look

de **kijkoperatie** /kɛɪkopəra(t)si/ (pl: -s) keyhole operation (*or:* surgery); exploratory operation (*or:* surgery)

de **kijkwoning** /kɛɪkwonɪŋ/ (pl: -en) [Belg] show house

kijven /kɛɪvə(n)/ (kijfde, heeft gekijfd) quarrel, wrangle, rail (at)

de **kik** /kɪk/ sound ‖ *zonder een ~ te* **geven** without a sound (*or:* peep)

kikken /kɪkə(n)/ (kikte, heeft gekikt) open one's mouth, give a sound (*or:* peep)

de **kikker** /kɪkər/ (pl: -s) frog

het **kikkerbad** /kɪkərbɑt/ paddling pool, wading pool

het **kikkerbilletje** /kɪkərbɪləcə/ (pl: -s) frog's leg

het **kikkerdril** /kɪkərdrɪl/ frogspawn, frogs' eggs

de **kikkererwt** /kɪkərɛrt/ (pl: -en) chickpea

het **kikkerland** /kɪkərlɑnt/ chilly country

het **kikkervisje** /kɪkərvɪʃə/ (pl: -s) tadpole

de **kikvors** /kɪkfɔrs/ (pl: -en) frog

de **kikvorsman** /kɪkfɔrsmɑn/ (pl: -nen) frogman

kil /kɪl/ (adj, adv) chilly, cold

de **killer** /kɪlər/ (pl: -s) killer

het/de **kilo** /kilo/ (pl: -'s) kilo

de **kilocalorie** /kilokalori/ (pl: -ën) kilocalorie

het/de **kilogram** /kiloɣrɑm/ (pl: -men) kilogram(me)

de **kilometer** /kilometər/ (pl: -s) kilometre: *op een ~ afstand* at a distance of one kilometre; *90 ~ per uur rijden* drive at 90 kilometres an hour

de **kilometerteller** /kilometərtɛlər/ (pl: -s) milometer; [Am] odometer

de **kilometervergoeding** /kilometərvərɣudɪŋ/ mileage (allowance)

de **kilowatt** /kilowɑt/ (pl: -s) kilowatt

het **kilowattuur** /kilowɑtyr/ kilowatt-hour

de **kilt** /kɪlt/ (pl: -s) kilt

de **kilte** /kɪltə/ chilliness

de **kim** /kɪm/ (pl: -men) horizon

de **kimono** /kimono/ (pl: -'s) kimono

de **kin** /kɪn/ (pl: -nen) chin ‖ [Belg] *op zijn ~ kloppen* get nothing to eat

het **kind** /kɪnt/ (pl: -eren) child, baby: *een ~ hebben van* have a child by; *een ~ krijgen* have a baby; *~eren opvoeden* bring up children; *een ~ van zes jaar* a six-year-old (child); [fig] *een ~ kan de was doen* that's child's play, it's as simple as ABC; *van ~ af aan, van ~s af* since (*or:* from) childhood, since I/he/… was a child

kinderachtig /kɪndərɑxtəx/ (adj, adv) **1** childlike; child(ren)'s **2** [depr] childish, infantile: *doe niet zo ~* grow up!, don't be such a baby!

de **kinderarbeid** /kɪndərɑrbɛit/ child labour

de **kinderarts** /kɪndərɑrts/ (pl: -en) paediatrician

de **kinderbescherming** /kɪndərbəsxɛrmɪŋ/ child welfare: *Raad voor de Kinderbescherming* child welfare council

de **kinderbijslag** /kɪndərbɛislɑx/ family allowance, child benefit

het **kinderboek** /kɪndərbuk/ (pl: -en) children's book

de **kinderboerderij** /kɪndərburdərɛi/ (pl: -en) children's farm

het **kinderdagverblijf** /kɪndərdɑxfərblɛif/ (pl: -verblijven) crèche, day-care centre

de **kinderhand** /kɪndərhɑnt/ (pl: -en) child(ren)'s hand

de **kinderjaren** /kɪndərjarə(n)/ (pl) childhood (years): *sinds mijn ~* since I was a child

de **kinderkamer** /kɪndərkamər/ (pl: -s) nursery

kinderlijk /kɪndərlək/ (adj, adv) childlike; childish

kinderloos /kɪndərlos/ (adj) childless

het **kindermeisje** /kɪndərmɛiʃə/ (pl: -s) nurse(maid), nanny

het **kindermenu** /kɪndərmənу/ (pl: -'s) children's menu

de **kindermishandeling** /kɪndərmɪshɑndəlɪŋ/ child abuse

de **kinderoppas** /kɪndərɔpɑs/ (pl: -sen) babysitter, childminder

de **kinderopvang** /kɪndərɔpfɑŋ/ (day) nursery, day-care centre, crèche

de **kinderporno** /kɪndərpɔrno/ child pornography

de **kinderrechter** /kɪndərɛxtər/ (pl: -s) [roughly] magistrate of (*or:* in) a juvenile court

kinderrijk /kɪndərɛik/ (adj) (blessed) with many children: *een ~ gezin* a large family

het **kinderslot** /kɪndərslɔt/ (pl: -en) childproof lock

het **kinderspel** /kɪndərspɛl/ (pl: -en) **1** children's games; [fig] child's play **2** children's game

de **kindersterfte** /kɪndərstɛrftə/ child mortality

de **kinderstoel** /kɪndərstul/ (pl: -en) high chair

het **kindertehuis** /kɪndərtəhœys/ (pl: -tehuizen) children's home

de **kindertelefoon**® /kɪndərteləfon/ (pl: -s) children's helpline, childline

de **kindertijd** /kɪndərtɛit/ childhood (days)

de **kinderverlamming** /kɪndərvərlɑmɪŋ/ polio

de **kinderwagen** /kɪndərwaɣə(n)/ (pl: -s) baby buggy, pram

de **kinderziekte** /kɪndərziktə/ (pl: -n, -s) childhood disease; [fig] teething troubles; growing pains: *de ~n (nog niet) te boven zijn* still have teething troubles

het **kinderzitje** /kɪndərzɪcə/ (pl: -s) baby seat, child's seat

kinds /kɪnts/ (adj) senile, in one's second childhood

kindsbeen /kɪn(t)sben/: *van ~ (af)* from

childhood (on), since childhood
de **kindsoldaat** /kɪntsɔldɑt/ child soldier
de **kinesist** /kinezɪst/ (pl: -en) [Belg] physiotherapist
de **kinesitherapie** /kinezɪterɑpi/ [Belg] physiotherapy
de **kinine** /kininə/ quinine
de **kink** /kɪŋk/ (pl: -en) kink, hitch
de **kinkhoest** /kɪŋkhust/ whooping cough
kinky /kɪŋki/ (adj, adv) kinky
de **kiosk** /kijɔsk/ (pl: -en) kiosk; newspaper stand, book stand
de **kip** /kɪp/ (pl: -pen) **1** chicken, hen: *er was geen ~ te zien* (or: *te bekennen*) there wasn't a soul to be seen **2** chickens, poultry
het/de **kipfilet** /kɪpfile/ (pl: -s) chicken breast(s)
kiplekker /kɪplɛkər/ (adj) as fit as a fiddle
de **kippenborst** /kɪpə(n)bɔrst/ (pl: -en) chicken breast
het **kippenboutje** /kɪpə(n)bɑucə/ (pl: -s) chicken leg
het **kippengaas** /kɪpə(n)ɣas/ chicken wire
het **kippenhok** /kɪpə(n)hɔk/ (pl: -ken) **1** chicken coop **2** [fig] pandemonium, chicken coop
de **kippenren** /kɪpə(n)rɛn/ (pl: -nen) chicken run
de **kippensoep** /kɪpə(n)sup/ chicken soup
het **kippenvel** /kɪpə(n)vɛl/ goose flesh (or: pimples)
kippig /kɪpəx/ (adj) short-sighted, nearsighted
de **Kirgies** /kɪrɣis/ (pl: Kirgiezen) Kyrgyz
Kirgizië /kɪrɣizijə/ Kirghizistan
het ¹**Kirgizisch** /kɪrɣizis/ Kyrgyz
²**Kirgizisch** /kɪrɣizis/ (adj) Kyrgyz
kirren /kɪrə(n)/ (kirde, heeft gekird) coo, gurgle
de **kirsch** /kirʃ/ kirsch
kissebissen /kɪsəbɪsə(n)/ (kissebiste, heeft gekissebist) squabble, bicker
de **kist** /kɪst/ (pl: -en) **1** chest **2** coffin **3** box; case; crate
kisten /kɪstə(n)/ (kistte, heeft gekist): [inform] *laat je niet ~* don't let them walk all over you
het/de **kit** /kɪt/ cement, glue, sealant
kitesurfen /kɑjtsʏrfə(n)/ (kitesurfte/kitesurfde, heeft gekitesurft/gekitesurfd) kite surf
kits /kɪts/ (adj): *alles ~?* how's things?, everything O.K.? (or: all right?)
de **kitsch** /kɪtʃ/ kitsch
de **kittelaar** /kɪtəlɑr/ (pl: -s) clitoris
kitten /kɪtə(n)/ (kitte, heeft gekit) seal (tight)
kittig /kɪtəx/ (adj, adv) spirited
de **kiwi** /kiwi/ (pl: -'s) kiwi
klaaglijk /klaxlək/ (adj, adv) plaintive
de **Klaagmuur** /klaxmyr/ Wailing Wall
de **klaagzang** /klaxsɑŋ/ (pl: -en) lament(ation): *een ~ aanheffen* raise one's voice in complaint

klaar /klar/ (adj, adv) **1** clear **2** pure **3** ready: *de boot is ~ voor vertrek* the boat is ready to sail; *~ voor de strijd* ready for action; *~ terwijl u wacht* ready while you wait; *~? af!* ready, get set, go! **4** finished, done: *ik ben zo ~* I won't be a minute (or: second); *we zijn ~ met eten* (or: *opruimen*) we've finished eating (or: clearing up)
klaarblijkelijk /klarblɛɪkələk/ (adv) evidently, obviously
klaarkomen /klarkomə(n)/ (kwam klaar, is klaargekomen) **1** (be) finish(ed), complete; settle things **2** come
klaarleggen /klarlɛɣə(n)/ (legde klaar, heeft klaargelegd) put ready; lay out
klaarlicht /klarlɪxt/ (adj): *op ~e dag* in broad daylight
klaarliggen /klarlɪɣə(n)/ (lag klaar, heeft klaargelegen) be ready: *iets hebben ~* have sth. ready
klaarmaken /klarmakə(n)/ (maakte klaar, heeft klaargemaakt) **1** get ready, prepare **2** make; get ready; prepare; cook: *het ontbijt ~* get breakfast ready
de **klaar-over** /klarovər/ member of the school crossing patrol, lollipop boy (or: girl)
klaarspelen /klarspelə(n)/ (speelde klaar, heeft klaargespeeld) manage (to do), pull off
klaarstaan /klarstan/ (stond klaar, heeft klaargestaan) be ready, be waiting; stand by: *zij moet altijd voor hem ~* he expects her to be at his beck and call
klaarstomen /klarstomə(n)/ (stoomde klaar, heeft klaargestoomd) cram: *iem. voor een examen ~* cram s.o. for an exam
klaarwakker /klarwɑkər/ (adj) wide awake; [fig] (on the) alert
klaarzetten /klarzɛtə(n)/ (zette klaar, heeft klaargezet) put ready, put out, set out
Klaas /klas/ Nick, Nicholas: *~ Vaak* the sandman, Wee Willie Winkie
de **klacht** /klɑxt/ (pl: -en) **1** complaint; symptom: *wat zijn de ~en van de patiënt?* what are the patient's symptoms?; *zijn ~en uiten* air one's grievances; *~en behandelen* deal with complaints **2** lament, complaint
het **klad** /klɑt/ (pl: -den) (rough) draft
het **kladblaadje** /klɑdblacə/ (pl: -s) (piece of) scrap paper
het **kladblok** /klɑdblɔk/ (pl: -ken) scribbling-pad
kladden /klɑdə(n)/ (kladde, heeft geklad) make stains (or: smudges, blots)
kladderen /klɑdərə(n)/ (kladderde, heeft gekladderd) make blots (or: smudges)
het **kladje** /klɑcə/ (rough) draft; (piece of) scrap paper
het **kladpapier** /klɑtpapir/ (pl: -en) scrap paper
de **kladversie** /klɑtfɛrzi/ (pl: -s) rough version

(or: copy)
klagen /klaɣə(n)/ (klaagde, heeft geklaagd) complain

de **klager** /klaɣər/ (pl: -s) complainer

klakkeloos /klɑkəlos/ (adj, adv) unthinking; indiscriminate; groundless: *iets ~ **aannemen*** accept sth. unthinkingly (or: uncritically)

klakken /klɑkə(n)/ (klakte, heeft geklakt) click, clack

klam /klɑm/ (adj, adv) clammy, damp

de **klamboe** /klɑmbu/ (pl: -s) mosquito net

de **klandizie** /klɑndizi/ clientele, customers

de **klank** /klɑŋk/ (pl: -en) sound

het **klankbord** /klɑŋkbɔrt/ (pl: -en) sounding board: [fig] *een ~ **vormen*** be, act as a sounding board (for)

de **klant** /klɑnt/ (pl: -en) customer, client; [in catering industry] guest: *een **vaste** ~* a regular (customer); a patron; a habitué; *de ~ is koning* the customer is always right

de **klantenbinding** /klɑntə(n)bɪndɪŋ/ customer relations

de **klantenkaart** /klɑntə(n)kart/ loyalty card

de **klantenkring** /klɑntə(n)krɪŋ/ (pl: -en) customers, clientele

de **klantenservice** /klɑntə(n)sɥrvɪs/ aftersales service; [Am] customer service; service department

klantvriendelijk /klɑntfrindələk/ (adj) customer-friendly

de **klap** /klɑp/ (pl: -pen) **1** bang, crash; crack: *met een ~ dichtslaan* slam (shut) **2** slap, smack; [fig] *iem. een ~ **geven*** hit s.o.; *iem. een ~ **om** de oren geven* box s.o.'s ears ‖ *als ~ op de **vuurpijl*** to crown (or: top, cap) it all, the crowning touch

de **klapband** /klɑpbɑnt/ (pl: -en) blow-out, flat

de **klapdeur** /klɑbdør/ (pl: -en) swing-door, self-closing door

de **klaplong** /klɑplɔŋ/ (pl: -en) pneumothorax

de **klaploper** /klɑplopər/ (pl: -s) sponger, scrounger

¹klappen /klɑpə(n)/ (klapte, heeft geklapt) clap; flap; slam: *in de handen ~* clap (one's hands)

²klappen /klɑpə(n)/ (klapte, is geklapt) burst: *de **voorband** is geklapt* the front tyre has burst; *in elkaar ~* collapse ‖ *uit de **school** ~, [Belg] uit de **biecht** klappen* tell tales

de **klapper** /klɑpər/ (pl: -s) **1** folder, file **2** smash, hit

klapperen /klɑpərə(n)/ (klapperde, heeft geklapperd) bang, rattle; chatter

klappertanden /klɑpərtɑndə(n)/ (klappertandde, heeft geklappertand) [roughly] shiver

de **klaproos** /klɑpros/ (pl: -rozen) poppy

de **klapschaats** /klɑpsxats/ (pl: -en) clap skate

de **klapstoel** /klɑpstul/ (pl: -en) folding chair; tip-up seat, theatre seat

het **klapstuk** /klɑpstʏk/ (pl: -ken) **1** rib of beef **2** highlight

de **klaptafel** /klɑptafəl/ (pl: -s) folding table

de **klapzoen** /klɑpsun/ (pl: -en) smacking kiss, smack(er)

de **klare** /klarə/ jenever, Dutch gin

klaren /klarə(n)/ (klaarde, heeft geklaard) **1** clarify **2** settle, manage: *kan hij dat klusje alleen ~?* can he manage that job alone?

de **klarinet** /klarinɛt/ (pl: -ten) clarinet

de **klas** /klɑs/ (pl: -sen) **1** classroom **2** class **3** form; [Am] grade: *in de **vierde** ~ zitten* be in the fourth form **4** class, grade; [sport] league; [sport] division

de **klasgenoot** /klɑsxənot/ (pl: -genoten) classmate

het **klaslokaal** /klɑslokal/ (pl: -lokalen) classroom

de **klasse** /klɑsə/ (pl: -n) class, league: *dat is **grote** ~!* that's first-rate!

het **klassement** /klɑsəmɛnt/ (pl: -en) list of rankings (or: ratings); [sport] league table: *hij staat **bovenaan (in)** het ~* he is (at the) top of the league (table)

het **klassenboek** /klɑsə(n)buk/ (pl: -en) class register, form register; [Am] roll book

de **klassenjustitie** /klɑsəjʏsti(t)si/ class justice

de **klassenleraar** /klɑsə(n)lerar/ (pl: -leraren) form teacher, class teacher; [Am] homeroom teacher

de **klassenstrijd** /klɑsə(n)strɛit/ class struggle

de **klassenvertegenwoordiger** /klɑsə(n)vərteɣə(n)wordəɣər/ (pl: -s) class representative (or: spokesman)

¹klasseren /klɑserə(n)/ (klasseerde, heeft geklasseerd) **1** classify **2** [Belg] list

zich **²klasseren** /klɑserə(n)/ (klasseerde zich, heeft zich geklasseerd) qualify, rank: *zich ~ voor de finale* qualify for the final(s)

de **klassering** /klɑserɪŋ/ (pl: -en) classification

klassiek /klɑsik/ (adj) classic(al), traditional: *de ~e **oudheid*** classical antiquity; *een ~ **voorbeeld*** a classic example

de **klassieker** /klɑsikər/ (pl: -s) classic

klassikaal /klɑsikal/ (adj, adv) class, group: *iets ~ **behandelen*** deal with sth. in class

de **klastitularis** /klɑstitylarɪs/ (pl: -sen) [Belg] class teacher

klateren /klatərə(n)/ (klaterde, heeft geklaterd) splash; gurgle

het **klatergoud** /klatərɣɑut/ tinsel, gilt

klauteren /klɑutərə(n)/ (klauterde, heeft/is geklauterd) clamber, scramble

de **klauw** /klɑu/ (pl: -en) claw; clutch(es); talon: *uit de ~en lopen* get out of hand (or: control)

het/de **klavecimbel** /klavəsɪmbəl/ (pl: -s) harpsichord, (clavi)cembalo

de **klaver** /klavər/ (pl: -s) clover

het **klaverblad** /klavərblɑt/ (pl: -en) cloverleaf

de **klaveren** /klavərə(n)/ clubs

klaverjassen /klavərjɑsə(n)/ (klaverjaste,

heeft geklaverjast) play (Klaber)jass

het **klavertjevier** /klavərcəvi̱r/ (pl: -en) four-leaf clover

het **klavier** /klavi̱r/ (pl: -en) keyboard

de **kledder** /klɛ̱dər/ (pl: -s) blob, dollop

kledderen /klɛ̱dərə(n)/ (kledderde, heeft gekledderd) slop

kleddernat /klɛ̱dərnɑt/ (adj) soaking (wet); soaked

kleden /kle̱də(n)/ (kleedde, heeft gekleed) dress, clothe

de **klederdracht** /kle̱dərdrɑχt/ (pl: -en) (traditional, national) costume (or: dress)

de **kledij** /kledɛ̱ɪ/ attire

de **kleding** /kle̱dɪŋ/ clothing, clothes, garments

het **kledingstuk** /kle̱dɪŋstvk/ (pl: -ken) garment, article of clothing

het **kleed** /klet/ (pl: kleden) **1** carpet; rug; (table)cloth **2** [Belg] dress

het **kleedgeld** /kle̱tχɛlt/ dress (or: clothing) allowance

het **kleedhokje** /kle̱thɔkjə/ (pl: -s) changing cubicle

de **kleedkamer** /kle̱tkamər/ (pl: -s) dressing room; [sport] changing room

de **kleefstof** /kle̱fstɔf/ (pl: -fen) adhesive

de **kleerborstel** /kle̱rbɔrstəl/ (pl: -s) clothes brush

de **kleerhanger** /kle̱rhɑŋər/ (pl: -s) coat-hanger, clothes hanger

de **kleerkast** /kle̱rkɑst/ (pl: -en) wardrobe

de **kleermaker** /kle̱rmakər/ (pl: -s) tailor

de **kleermakerszit** /kle̱rmakərzɪt/: *in* ~ *zitten* sit cross-legged

de **kleerscheuren** /kle̱rsχørə(n)/ (pl): *er zonder* ~ *afkomen* escape unscathed (or: unhurt); get off scot-free

klef /klɛf/ (adj) **1** sticky, clammy **2** sticky; gooey; doughy **3** clinging

de **klei** /klɛi/ clay

de **kleiduif** /klɛ̱idœyf/ (pl: -duiven) clay pigeon

kleien /klɛ̱ɪjə(n)/ (kleide, heeft gekleid) work with clay

klein /klɛin/ (adj) **1** small, little: *een* ~ *eindje* a short distance; a little way; *een* ~ *beetje* a little bit **2** little, young **3** small, minor: *hebt u het niet* ~*er?* have you got nothing smaller? || ~ *maar fijn* good things come in small packages

kleinburgerlijk /klɛimbY̱rɣərlək/ (adj) lower middle class, petty bourgeois; narrow-minded

de **kleindochter** /klɛ̱indɔχtər/ (pl: -s) granddaughter

Klein Duimpje /klɛindœy̱mpjə/ Tom Thumb

kleineren /klɛine̱rə(n)/ (kleineerde, heeft gekleineerd) belittle, disparage

kleingeestig /klɛiŋe̱stəχ/ (adj) narrow-minded, petty

het **kleingeld** /klɛ̱iŋɛlt/ (small) change

de **kleinigheid** /klɛ̱inəχhɛit/ (pl: -heden) **1** little thing: *ik heb een* ~*je meegebracht* I have brought you a little sth. **2** trivial matter, unimportant matter, trifle

het **kleinkind** /klɛ̱iŋkɪnt/ (pl: -eren) grandchild

kleinkrijgen /klɛ̱iŋkrɛɪɣə(n)/ (kreeg klein, heeft kleingekregen) subdue, bring (s.o.) to his knees

de **kleinkunst** /klɛ̱iŋkvnst/ cabaret

kleinmaken /klɛ̱imakə(n)/ (maakte klein, heeft kleingemaakt) cut small, cut up

het **kleinood** /klɛ̱inot/ (pl: kleinoden, kleinodiën) jewel, gem, bijou

kleinschalig /klɛɪnsχa̱ləχ/ (adj) small-scale

het **kleintje** /klɛ̱incə/ (pl: -s) **1** small one, short one; shorty **2** little one; baby

kleinzerig /klɛinze̱rəχ/ (adj): *hij is altijd* ~ he always makes a fuss about a little bit of pain

kleinzielig /klɛinzi̱ləχ/ (adj) petty, narrow-minded

de **kleinzoon** /klɛ̱inzon/ (pl: -s, -zonen) grandson

de ¹**klem** /klɛm/ (pl: -men) **1** grip **2** emphasis, stress: *met* ~ *beweren dat …* insist on the fact that … **3** trap **4** clip

²**klem** /klɛm/ (adj) jammed, stuck || *zich* ~ *zuipen* get smashed

¹**klemmen** /klɛ̱mə(n)/ (klemde, heeft geklemd) stick, jam

²**klemmen** /klɛ̱mə(n)/ (klemde, heeft geklemd) clasp, press

klemrijden /klɛ̱mrɛɪdə(n)/ (reed klem, heeft klemgereden): *een auto* ~ force a car to stop

de **klemtoon** /klɛ̱mton/ (pl: -tonen) stress, accent; [fig] emphasis: *de* ~ *ligt op de eerste lettergreep* the stress (or: accent) is on the first syllable

klemvast /klɛmvɑ̱st/ (adj) jammed, stuck: *de bal* ~ *hebben* have the ball safely in his hands

de **klep** /klɛp/ (pl: -pen) **1** lid; valve; key **2** flap; ramp **3** flap; fly **4** visor

de **klepel** /kle̱pəl/ (pl: -s) clapper

kleppen /klɛ̱pə(n)/ (klepte, heeft geklept) **1** clack **2** peal, toll

klepperen /klɛ̱pərə(n)/ (klepperde, heeft geklepperd) clatter, rattle

de **kleptomaan** /klɛptoma̱n/ (pl: -manen) kleptomaniac

de **kleren** /kle̱rə(n)/ (pl) clothes: *andere* (or: *schone*) ~ *aantrekken* change (into sth. else, into clean clothes); *zijn* ~ *uittrekken* undress

klerikaal /klerika̱l/ (adj) clerical

de **klerk** /klɛrk/ (pl: -en) clerk

de **klets** /klɛts/ **1** rubbish, twaddle **2** splash

kletsen /klɛ̱tsə(n)/ (kletste, heeft gekletst) **1** chatter, chat **2** gossip **3** talk nonsense (or: rubbish), babble

de **kletskoek** /klɛ̱tskuk/ [inform] nonsense, twaddle

de **kletskous** /klɛtskɑus/ (pl: -en) [inform] chatterbox, garrulous chap

de **kletsmajoor** /klɛtsmajor/ (pl: -s) [inform] twaddler, gossipmonger

kletsnat /klɛtsnɑt/ (adj) soaking (wet)

kletteren /klɛtərə(n)/ (kletterde, heeft gekletterd) clash; clang; patter; rattle: *de borden kletterden op de grond* the plates crashed to the floor

kleumen /klømə(n)/ (kleumde, heeft gekleumd) be half frozen

de **kleur** /klør/ (pl: -en) **1** colour: *wat voor ~ ogen heeft ze?* what colour are her eyes?; *primaire ~en* primary colours **2** complexion: *een ~ krijgen* flush, blush **3** [cards] suit

de **kleurdoos** /klørdos/ (pl: -dozen) paintbox

kleurecht /klørɛxt/ (adj) colour fast

kleuren /klørə(n)/ (kleurde, heeft gekleurd) colour, paint; dye; tint

kleurenblind /klørə(n)blɪnt/ (adj) colour-blind

de **kleurenfoto** /klørə(n)foto/ (pl: -'s) colour photo(graph), colour picture

het **kleurenspectrum** /klørə(n)spɛktrʏm/ (pl: -spectra) colour spectrum

de **kleurentelevisie** /klørə(n)teləvizi/ (pl: -s) colour television

kleurig /klørəx/ (adj, adv) colourful

de **kleurling** /klørlɪŋ/ (pl: -en) coloured person

kleurloos /klørlos/ (adj) **1** colourless; pale **2** colourless, dull

het **kleurpotlood** /klørpɔtlot/ (pl: -potloden) colour pencil, (coloured) crayon

kleurrijk /klørɛik/ (adj) colourful

de **kleurspoeling** /klørspulɪŋ/ (pl: -en) colour rinse

de **kleurstof** /klørstɔf/ (pl: -fen) **1** colour; dye; colouring (matter): *(chemische) ~fen toevoegen* add colouring matters **2** pigment

het **kleurtje** /klørcə/ (pl: -s) colour; flush; blush

de **kleuter** /kløtər/ (pl: -s) pre-schooler (in a nursery class); [Am] kindergartner

het **kleuterbad** /kløtərbɑt/ (pl: -en) paddling pool, wading pool

de **kleuterleidster** /kløtərlɛitstər/ (pl: -s) nursery school teacher; [Am] kindergarten teacher

het **kleuteronderwijs** /kløtərɔndərwɛis/ pre-school education, nursery education

de **kleuterschool** /kløtərsχol/ (pl: -scholen) nursery school; [Am] kindergarten

kleven /klevə(n)/ (kleefde, heeft gekleefd) **1** stick (to), cling (to): *zijn overhemd kleefde aan zijn rug* his shirt stuck (or: clung) to his back **2** be sticky: *mijn handen ~* my hands are sticky

kleverig /klevərəx/ (adj) sticky

kliederen /klidərə(n)/ (kliederde, heeft gekliederd) make a mess, mess about (or: around)

de **kliek** /klik/ (pl: -en) clique

het **kliekje** /klikjə/ (pl: -s) leftover(s)

de **klier** /klir/ **1** gland **2** pain in the neck

klieren /klirə(n)/ (klierde, heeft geklierd) [inform] be a pest, be a pain in the neck; [Am] be a pain in the ass

klieven /klivə(n)/ (kliefde, heeft gekliefd) cleave

de **klif** /klɪf/ (pl: -fen) cliff

de **klik** /klɪk/ (pl: -ken) click

klikken /klɪkə(n)/ (klikte, heeft geklikt) **1** click **2** tell (on s.o.), snitch (on), blab: *je mag niet ~* don't tell tales **3** click, hit it off: *het klikte meteen tussen hen* they hit it off immediately

de **klikspaan** /klɪkspan/ (pl: -spanen) tell-tale

de **klim** /klɪm/ climb

het **klimaat** /klimat/ (pl: klimaten) climate

de **klimaatbeheersing** /klimadbəhersɪŋ/ air conditioning

klimaatneutraal /klimatnøtral/ (adj) carbon-neutral: *~ produceren* produce in a carbon neutral way

de **klimaatverandering** /klimatfərɑndərɪŋ/ (pl: -en) climatic change

klimmen /klɪmə(n)/ (klom, heeft/is geklommen) climb (up, down), clamber (about): *met het ~ der jaren* with advancing years

de **klimmer** /klɪmər/ (pl: -s) climber

de **klimmuur** /klɪmyr/ climbing wall

het/de **klimop** /klɪmɔp/ ivy

de **klimplant** /klɪmplɑnt/ (pl: -en) climber, climbing plant, creeper

het **klimrek** /klɪmrɛk/ (pl: -ken) **1** climbing frame **2** wall bars

de **klimwand** /klɪmwɑnt/ climbing wall

de **kling** /klɪŋ/ (pl: -en): *iem. over de ~ jagen* put s.o. to the sword

klingelen /klɪŋələ(n)/ (klingelde, heeft geklingeld) tinkle, jingle

de **kliniek** /klinik/ (pl: -en) clinic

klinisch /klinis/ (adj, adv) clinical

de **klink** /klɪŋk/ (pl: -en) **1** (door)handle **2** latch

klinken /klɪŋkə(n)/ (klonk, heeft geklonken) sound, resound; clink; ring: *die naam klinkt me bekend (in de oren)* that name sounds familiar to me

de **klinker** /klɪŋkər/ (pl: -s) **1** vowel **2** clinker

klinkklaar /klɪŋklar/ (adj): *klinkklare onzin* plain (or: utter) nonsense

de **klinknagel** /klɪŋknaɣəl/ (pl: -s) rivet

de **klip** /klɪp/ (pl: -pen) rock; cliff

klip-en-klaar /klɪpɛŋklar/ (adv) crystal-clear: *iets ~ formuleren* say sth. in plain language (or: words)

de **klipper** /klɪpər/ (pl: -s) clipper

het **klissen** /klɪsə(n)/ [Belg] arrest, run in: *een inbreker ~* arrest a burglar

de **klit** /klɪt/ (pl: -ten) tangle

klitten /klɪtə(n)/ (klitte, heeft geklit) **1** stick: *aan elkaar ~* hang (or: stick) together **2** become entangled, get entangled

het **klittenband** /klɪtə(n)bɑnt/ (pl: -en) Velcro
de **klodder** /klɔdər/ (pl: -s) daub; clot; blob: *een
~ mayonaise* a dollop of mayonnaise
klodderen /klɔdərə(n)/ (klodderde, heeft
geklodderd) **1** mess (about, around) **2** daub
de ¹**kloek** /kluk/ (pl: -en) broody hen
²**kloek** /kluk/ (adj) stout, sturdy, robust
de **klojo** /klɔjo/ (pl: -'s) [inform] jerk
de **klok** /klɔk/ (pl: -ken) **1** clock: *hij kan nog geen
~ kijken* he can't tell (the) time yet; *de ~
loopt voor* (or: *achter, gelijk*) the clock is fast
(or: slow, on time); *met de ~ mee* clockwise;
tegen de ~ in anticlockwise; [Am] counter-
clockwise; [fig] *iets aan de grote ~ hangen*
make a fuss about sth., tell everyone about
sth.; [fig] *daar kun je de ~ op gelijkzetten* you
can set your watch by it **2** bell
het **klokgelui** /klɔkχəlœy/ (bell-)ringing, chim-
ing; bell tolling
het **klokhuis** /klɔkhœys/ (pl: -huizen) core
klokken /klɔkə(n)/ (klokte, heeft geklokt)
[sport] time, clock
de **klokkenluider** /klɔkə(n)lœydər/ **1** bell-
ringer **2** [fig] whistle-blower
het **klokkenspel** /klɔkə(n)spɛl/ (pl: -len) **1** carillon, chimes **2** glockenspiel
de **klokkentoren** /klɔkə(n)torə(n)/ (pl: -s) bell
tower, belfry
klokkijken /klɔkɛɪkə(n)/ tell (the) time
de **klokslag** /klɔkslɑχ/ (pl: -en): ~ *vier uur* on
(or: at) the stroke of four
klokvast /klɔkfɑst/ (adj) [Belg] punctual: *~e
treinen* punctual trains
de **klomp** /klɔmp/ (pl: -en) **1** clog; [Am] wood-
en shoe **2** clod, lump
de **klompvoet** /klɔmpfut/ (pl: -en) club-foot
klonen /klonə(n)/ (kloonde, heeft ge-
kloond) clone
de **klont** /klɔnt/ (pl: -en) **1** lump, dab: *de saus zit
vol ~en* the sauce is full of lumps (or: is lump-
y) **2** clot
klonteren /klɔntərə(n)/ (klonterde, heeft
geklonterd) become lumpy, get lumpy; clot;
curdle
klonterig /klɔntərəχ/ (adj) lumpy
het **klontje** /klɔncə/ (pl: -s) **1** lump, dab **2** sugar
lump (or: cube)
de **kloof** /klof/ (pl: kloven) **1** split **2** crevice,
chasm, cleft **3** [fig] gap, gulf
klooien /klojə(n)/ (klooide, heeft geklooid)
bungle, mess up
de **kloon** /klon/ (pl: klonen) clone
het **klooster** /klostər/ (pl: -s) monastery, convent; nunnery; cloister
de **kloosterling** /klostərlɪŋ/ (pl: -en) religious,
monk, nun
de **kloot** /klot/ (pl: kloten) [inform] ball ‖ *naar
de kloten zijn* be screwed up
de **klootzak** /klotsɑk/ (pl: -ken) [inform] bastard, son-of-a-bitch
de **klop** /klɔp/ (pl: -pen) **1** knock **2** lick(ing)

de **klopboor** /klɔbor/ (pl: -boren) hammer drill
de **klopgeest** /klɔpχest/ (pl: -en) poltergeist
de **klopjacht** /klɔpjɑχt/ (pl: -en) round-up;
drive
¹**kloppen** /klɔpə(n)/ (klopte, heeft geklopt)
1 knock (at, on); tap: *er wordt geklopt* there's
a knock at the door **2** beat, throb: *met ~d
hart* with one's heart racing (or: pounding)
3 agree: *dat klopt* that's right
²**kloppen** /klɔpə(n)/ (klopte, heeft geklopt)
knock; tap; beat: *eieren ~* beat (or: whisk)
eggs; *iem. op de schouder ~* pat s.o. on the
back
de **klopper** /klɔpər/ knocker
de **klos** /klɔs/ (pl: -sen) bobbin, reel ‖ *de ~ zijn*
be the fall guy
klossen /klɔsə(n)/ (kloste, heeft/is geklost)
clump, stump
klote /klotə/ (adj, adv) [vulg]: *een klotedag* a
bloody (or: fucking) awful day; *zich ~ voelen*
feel shitty (or: crappy); *~weer* bloody awful
weather, rotten weather; *een ~wijf* a (fucking) bitch; *dat is zwaar ~* that's really bloody
awful
klotsen /klɔtsə(n)/ (klotste, heeft/is ge-
klotst) slosh, splash
kloven /klovə(n)/ (kloofde, heeft gekloofd)
split, cleave; cut
de **klucht** /klʏχt/ (pl: -en) farce
de **kluif** /klœyf/ (pl: kluiven) knuckle(bone);
[fig] big job, tough job
de **kluis** /klœys/ (pl: kluizen) safe, safe-deposit
box
kluisteren /klœystərə(n)/ (kluisterde, heeft
gekluisterd): *aan het ziekbed gekluisterd zijn*
be bedridden, be confined to one's sickbed;
aan de televisie gekluisterd zitten be glued to
the television
de **kluit** /klœyt/ (pl: -en) **1** lump, clod: *zich niet
met een ~je in het riet laten sturen* not let o.s.
be fobbed off (or: be given the brush-off)
2 ball of earth (or: soil)
kluiven /klœyvə(n)/ (kloof, heeft gekloven)
gnaw
de **kluizenaar** /klœyzənar/ (pl: -s) hermit, recluse
klunen /klynə(n)/ (kluunde, heeft/is ge-
kluund) walk (on skates)
de **klungel** /klʏŋəl/ (pl: -s) clumsy oaf
klungelen /klʏŋələ(n)/ (klungelde, heeft
geklungeld) bungle, botch (up)
klungelig /klʏŋələχ/ (adj, adv) clumsy, bungling
de **kluns** /klʏns/ (pl: klunzen) dimwit, oaf, bungler
de **klus** /klʏs/ (pl: -sen) **1** big job, tough job
2 small job, chore: *~jes opknappen (klaren)*
do odd jobs
de **klusjesman** /klʏʃəsmɑn/ (pl: -nen) handyman, odd-job man
klussen /klʏsə(n)/ (kluste, heeft geklust)

1 do odd jobs **2** moonlight

de **kluts** /klʏts/: *de ~ kwijt zijn (raken)* be lost (*or:* confused); be shaken (*or:* rattled)

klutsen /klʏtsə(n)/ (klutste, heeft geklutst) beat (up)

het **kluwen** /klywə(n)/ (pl: -s) ball

het **klysma** /klɪsma/ (pl: -'s) enema

km (abbrev) *kilometer* km

het **KMI** /kaɛmi/ [Belg] *Koninklijk Meteorologisch Instituut* (Belgian) Royal Meteorological Institute

de **kmo** /kaɛmo/ *kleine of middelgrote onderneming* [Belg] SMB, small and medium-sized businesses

km/u (abbrev) *kilometer per uur* km/h, mph

het **knaagdier** /knaɣdir/ (pl: -en) rodent

de **knaagtand** /knaxtɑnt/ (pl: -en) (rodent) incisor

de **knaap** /knap/ (pl: knapen) boy, lad

knabbelen /knɑbələ(n)/ (knabbelde, heeft geknabbeld) nibble (on), munch (on)

het **knabbeltje** /knɑbəlcə/ (pl: -s) nibble(s), snack

het **knäckebröd** /knɛkəbrøt/ crispbread, knäckebröd

knagen /knaɣə(n)/ (knaagde, heeft geknaagd) gnaw, eat: *een ~d geweten* pangs of conscience

de **knak** /knɑk/ (pl: -ken) crack, snap

knakken /knɑkə(n)/ (knakte, heeft/is geknakt) snap, break; crack

de **knakker** /knɑkər/ (pl: -s) [inform] character, customer

de **knakworst** /knɑkwɔrst/ (pl: -en) [roughly] frankfurter

de **knal** /knɑl/ (pl: -len) bang, pop

knallen /knɑlə(n)/ (knalde, heeft geknald) **1** bang; crack; pop **2** go all-out

de **knalpot** /knɑlpɔt/ (pl: -ten) silencer; [Am] muffler

¹**knap** /knɑp/ (adj, adv) **1** good-looking; handsome; pretty **2** clever, bright: *een ~pe kop* a brain, a whizz kid **3** smart, capable, clever; handy: *een ~ stuk werk* a clever piece of work

²**knap** /knɑp/ (adv) cleverly, well

¹**knappen** /knɑpə(n)/ (knapte, heeft geknapt) crackle; crack

²**knappen** /knɑpə(n)/ (knapte, is geknapt) crack; snap

de **knapperd** /knɑpərt/ (pl: -s) brain, whiz(z) kid

knapperen /knɑpərə(n)/ (knapperde, heeft geknapperd) crackle; crack

knapperig /knɑpərəx/ (adj) crisp; crunchy; brittle; crusty

de **knapzak** /knɑpsɑk/ (pl: -ken) knapsack

knarsen /knɑrsə(n)/ (knarste, heeft geknarst) crunch: *de deur knarst in haar scharnieren* the door creaks (*or:* squeaks) on its hinges

knarsetanden /knɑrsətɑndə(n)/ (knarsetandde, heeft geknarsetand) grind one's teeth

de **knauw** /knɑu/ (pl: -en) **1** bite **2** [fig] blow

knauwen /knɑuwə(n)/ (knauwde, heeft geknauwd) gnaw (at), chew; crunch (on)

de **knecht** /knɛxt/ (pl: -en) servant; farmhand

kneden /knedə(n)/ (kneedde, heeft gekneed) knead, mould

kneedbaar /knedbar/ (adj) **1** kneadable, workable **2** [fig] pliable: *iem. ~ maken* make s.o. putty in one's hands

de **kneep** /knep/ (pl: knepen) **1** pinch (mark) **2** [fig] knack: *de ~jes van het vak kennen* know the tricks of the trade

de ¹**knel** /knɛl/ (pl: -len) **1** catch **2** fix, jam

²**knel** /knɛl/ (adj) stuck, caught: *~ komen te zitten* get stuck (*or:* caught)

¹**knellen** /knɛlə(n)/ (knelde, heeft gekneld) squeeze; pinch

²**knellen** /knɛlə(n)/ (knelde, heeft gekneld) squeeze, press

het **knelpunt** /knɛlpʏnt/ (pl: -en) bottleneck

knetteren /knɛtərə(n)/ (knetterde, heeft geknetterd) crackle; splutter

knettergek /knɛtərɣɛk/ (adj) nuts, (stark staring) mad; [Am] (raving) mad

de **kneus** /knøs/ (pl: kneuzen) **1** old crock (*or:* wreck) [esp cars] **2** [educ] drop-out

kneuterig /knøtərəx/ (adj, adv) snug, cosy

kneuzen /knøzə(n)/ (kneusde, heeft gekneusd) bruise

de **kneuzing** /knøzɪŋ/ (pl: -en) bruise, bruising

de **knevel** /knevəl/ (pl: -s) moustache

knevelen /knevələ(n)/ (knevelde, heeft gekneveld) tie down, tie up; gag

knibbelen /knɪbələ(n)/ (knibbelde, heeft geknibbeld) haggle, bargain

de **knie** /kni/ (pl: -ën) knee: *iets onder de ~ krijgen* master sth., get the hang (*or:* knack) of sth.

de **knieband** /knibɑnt/ (pl: -en) **1** knee protector (*or:* supporter) **2** hamstring

de **kniebeschermer** /knibəsxɛrmər/ (pl: -s) knee-pad

de **kniebroek** /knibruk/ (pl: -en) knee breeches

de **kniebuiging** /knibœyɣɪŋ/ (pl: -en) **1** kneeling **2** knee bend

het **kniegewricht** /kniɣəvrɪxt/ (pl: -en) knee joint

de **knieholte** /knihɔltə/ (pl: -s, -n) hollow (*or:* back) of the knee

knielen /knilə(n)/ (knielde, heeft/is gekniel d) kneel

de **knieschijf** /knisxɛif/ (pl: -schijven) kneecap

de **kniesoor** /knisor/ (pl: kniesoren) moper, moaner: *een ~ die daarop let* details, details, but that is a (mere) detail

de **knieval** /knival/ (pl: -len) genuflection: *een ~ doen voor iem.* fall to one's knees before s.o.

kniezen /knizə(n)/ (kniesde, heeft gekniesd) grumble (about), moan (about), mope

knijpen /knɛipə(n)/ (kneep, heeft geknepen) **1** pinch **2** press, squeeze ‖ *'m ~* have the wind up

de **knijper** /knɛipər/ (pl: -s) (clothes) peg, clip

de **knijpfles** /knɛipflɛs/ (pl: -sen) squeeze-bottle

de **knijpkat** /knɛipkɑt/ (pl: -ten) dynamo torch

de **knik** /knɪk/ (pl: -ken) **1** crack; kink **2** twist, kink **3** nod

knikkebollen /knɪkəbɔlə(n)/ (knikkebolde, heeft geknikkebold) nod

¹**knikken** /knɪkə(n)/ (knikte, is geknikt) **1** crack, snap **2** bend, buckle

²**knikken** /knɪkə(n)/ (knikte, heeft) nod

³**knikken** /knɪkə(n)/ (knikte, heeft geknikt) bend, twist

de **knikker** /knɪkər/ (pl: -s) marble

¹**knikkeren** /knɪkərə(n)/ (knikkerde, heeft geknikkerd) play marbles: [fig] *ik heb nog met hem geknikkerd* [roughly] I knew him when he was in short pants

²**knikkeren** /knɪkərə(n)/ (knikkerde, heeft geknikkerd) [inform] kick out, chuck out: *iem.* **eruit** *~* chuck s.o. out

de **knip** /knɪp/ (pl: -pen) **1** snap; (spring) catch; clasp **2** catch

het **knipmes** /knɪpmɛs/ (pl: -sen) clasp-knife: *buigen* **als** *een ~* bow and scrape, grovel

knipogen /knɪpoɣə(n)/ (knipoogde, heeft geknipoogd) wink

de **knipoog** /knɪpoːx/ (pl: -ogen) wink: *hij* **gaf** *mij een ~* he winked at me

¹**knippen** /knɪpə(n)/ (knipte, heeft geknipt) cut, snip

²**knippen** /knɪpə(n)/ (knipte, heeft geknipt) **1** cut (off, out): *de* **heg** *~* clip (or: trim) the hedge; *zijn* **nagels** *~* cut (or: clip) one's nails **2** cut: *~ en* **plakken** cut and paste

knipperen /knɪpərə(n)/ (knipperde, heeft geknipperd) **1** blink **2** flash

het **knipperlicht** /knɪpərlɪxt/ (pl: -en) indicator; flashing light

het **knipsel** /knɪpsəl/ (pl: -s) cutting

het **KNMI** /kaɛnɛmi/ *Koninklijk Nederlands Meteorologisch Instituut* Royal Dutch Meteorological Institute

de **kno-arts** /kaɛnoɑrts/ (pl: -en) ENT specialist

de **knobbel** /knɔbəl/ (pl: -s) **1** knob; knot; bump **2** [fig] gift, talent: *een* **wiskunde-knobbel** *hebben* have a gift for mathematics

de ¹**knock-out** /nɔkɑut/ (pl: -s) knock-out

²**knock-out** /nɔkɑut/ (adj) knock-out

de **knoei** /knuj/: *lelijk* **in** *de ~ zitten* be in a terrible mess (or: fix)

de **knoeiboel** /knujbul/ mess

knoeien /knujə(n)/ (knoeide, heeft geknoeid) **1** make a mess, spill **2** make a mess (of) **3** tinker (with), monkey about (with)

4 cheat, tamper (with)

de **knoeier** /knujər/ (pl: -s) **1** messy person **2** bungler **3** cheat

de **knoest** /knust/ (pl: -en) knot

de **knoet** /knut/ (pl: -en) cat-o'-nine-tails

het/de **knoflook** /knɔflok/ garlic

knokig /knokəx/ (adj) bony

de **knokkel** /knɔkəl/ (pl: -s) knuckle

knokken /knɔkə(n)/ (knokte, heeft geknokt) **1** fight **2** [fig] fight hard

de **knokpartij** /knɔkpɑrtɛi/ (pl: -en) fight, scuffle

de **knokploeg** /knɔkpluːx/ (pl: -en) (bunch, gang of) thugs; henchmen

de **knol** /knɔl/ (pl: -len) **1** tuber **2** turnip

het **knolgewas** /knɔlɣəwɑs/ (pl: -sen) tuberous plant

de **knolraap** /knɔlrap/ (pl: -rapen) swede, kohlrabi

de **knolselderij** /knɔlsɛldərɛi/ celeriac

de **knoop** /knop/ (pl: knopen) **1** button **2** knot: *een ~ leggen* (or: *maken*) tie (*or:* make) a knot; *(met zichzelf)* **in** *de ~ zitten* be at odds with o.s. ‖ *het schip* **voer** *negen knopen* the ship was doing nine knots; [fig] *de ~* **door-hakken** cut the (Gordian) knot, take the plunge

het **knooppunt** /knopʏnt/ (pl: -en) intersection; interchange

het **knoopsgat** /knopsxɑt/ (pl: -en) buttonhole

de **knop** /knɔp/ (pl: -pen) **1** button, switch: *met een druk* **op** *de ~* presto, with a press of the button; [fig] *de ~* **omzetten** switch over, turn the corner **2** button, handle: *de ~ van een* **deur** the handle of a door **3** bud: *de roos is nog* **in** *de ~* the rose bush is in bud (*or:* is not fully out yet)

knopen /knopə(n)/ (knoopte, heeft geknoopt) knot, make a knot, tie: *twee touwen* **aan** *elkaar ~* tie two ropes together

knorren /knɔrə(n)/ (knorde, heeft geknord) grunt

knorrig /knɔrəx/ (adj, adv) grumbling: *in een zeer ~e bui* **zijn** have the grumps, be grouchy

de **knot** /knɔt/ (pl: -ten) knot, ball; tuft

de ¹**knots** /knɔts/ (pl: -en) **1** club **2** whopper

²**knots** /knɔts/ (adj, adv) [inform] crazy, loony

knotten /knɔtə(n)/ (knotte, heeft geknot) top, head

de **knotwilg** /knɔtwɪlx/ (pl: -en) pollard willow

de **knowhow** /nohɑu/ know-how

knudde /knʏdə/ (adj) [inform] no good at all, rubbishy

de **knuffel** /knʏfəl/ (pl: -s) cuddle, hug

het **knuffeldier** /knʏfəldir/ (pl: -en) soft toy, cuddly toy, teddy (bear)

knuffelen /knʏfələ(n)/ (knuffelde, heeft geknuffeld) cuddle

de **knuist** /knœyst/ (pl: -en) fist

de **knul** /knʏl/ (pl: -len) fellow, guy, chap, bloke

kogel

knullig /kny̆ləx/ (adj, adv) awkward: *dat is ~ gedaan* that has been done clumsily

de **knuppel** /kny̆pəl/ (pl: -s) **1** club; truncheon **2** stick; joystick

knus /knʏs/ (adj, adv) cosy, homey

de **knutselaar** /kny̆tsəlar/ (pl: -s) handyman, do-it-yourselfer

knutselen /kny̆tsələ(n)/ (knutselde, heeft geknutseld) knock together, knock up

het **knutselwerk** /kny̆tsəlwɛrk/ **1** odd jobs, tinkering **2** handiwork, handicraft(s)

de **koala** /kowa̱la/ (pl: -'s) koala (bear)

het **kobalt** /kobɑlt/ cobalt

de **koe** /ku/ (pl: koeien) **1** cow: [fig] *over ~tjes en kalfjes praten* talk about one thing and another; [fig] *oude koeien uit de sloot halen* open old wounds (*or:* sores); *de ~ bij de hoorns vatten* [fig] take the bull by the horns **2** giant

de **koehandel** /ku̱hɑndəl/ horse trading

de **koeienletters** /ku̱jə(n)lɛtərs/ (pl) giant letters

koeioneren /kujone̱rə(n)/ (koeioneerde, heeft gekoeioneerd) bully

de **koek** /kuk/ (pl: -en) **1** cake: *dat is andere ~!* that is another (*or:* a different) kettle of fish; *dat gaat erin als (gesneden) ~* it is a huge success; it's selling like hot cakes **2** biscuit; [Am] cooky, cookie: *een ~je van eigen deeg krijgen* get a taste of one's own medicine

de **koekenpan** /ku̱kə(n)pɑn/ (pl: -nen) frying pan

de **koekoek** /ku̱kuk/ (pl: -en) cuckoo

de **koekoeksklok** /ku̱kuksklɔk/ (pl: -ken) cuckoo clock

de **koektrommel** /ku̱ktrɔməl/ (pl: -s) biscuit tin; [Am] cooky tin

koel /kul/ (adj) **1** cool; chilly **2** cool, calm

koelbloedig /kulblu̱dəx/ (adj, adv) cold-blooded, calm, cool

de **koelbox** /ku̱lbɔks/ (pl: -en) cool box, cooler

de **koelcel** /ku̱lsɛl/ (pl: -len) cold store

koelen /ku̱lə(n)/ (koelde, heeft gekoeld) cool (down, off); chill

de **koeler** /ku̱lər/ (pl: -s) cooler; ice bucket

het **koelhuis** /ku̱lhœys/ (pl: -huizen) cold store

de **koeling** /ku̱lɪŋ/ **1** cold store **2** cooling; refrigeration

de **koelkast** /ku̱lkɑst/ (pl: -en) fridge, refrigerator

de **koeltas** /ku̱ltɑs/ (pl: -sen) thermos bag

de **koelte** /ku̱ltə/ cool(ness)

koeltjes /ku̱ləs/ (adj) (a bit) chilly || *~ reageren* respond coolly

de **koeltoren** /ku̱ltorə(n)/ cooling tower

de **koelvloeistof** /ku̱lvlujstɔf/ (pl: -fen) coolant

het **koelwater** /ku̱lwatər/ cooling-water

koen /kun/ (adj, adv) [form] bold

de **koepel** /ku̱pəl/ (pl: -s) dome

de **koepelorganisatie** /ku̱pəlɔrɣaniza(t)si/ umbrella organisation

de **koepeltent** /ku̱pəltɛnt/ dome tent

de **Koerd** /kurt/ (pl: -en) Kurd

Koerdisch /ku̱rdis/ (adj) Kurdish

Koerdistan /ku̱rdistɑn/ Kurdistan

koeren /ku̱rə(n)/ (koerde, heeft gekoerd) coo

de **koerier** /kurir/ (pl: -s) courier

de **koers** /kurs/ **1** course: *van ~ veranderen* change course (*or:* tack) **2** route **3** price; (exchange) rate

de **koersdaling** /ku̱rzdalɪŋ/ (pl: -en) fall in prices; depreciation

koersen /ku̱rsə(n)/ (koerste, heeft/is gekoerst) (+ op) set course for

de **koersschommeling** /ku̱rsxɔmǝlɪŋ/ (pl: -en) price fluctuation (*or:* variation), market fluctuation

de **koerswijziging** /ku̱rswɛizəɣɪŋ/ (pl: -en) change in course (*or:* direction)

de **koerswinst** /ku̱rswɪnst/ (pl: -en) stock market profit, gain(s) (made by stock fluctuations)

koest /kust/ (adj): *zich ~ houden* keep quiet, keep a low profile

koesteren /ku̱stərə(n)/ (koesterde, heeft gekoesterd) cherish, foster: *hoop ~* nurse hopes

het **koeterwaals** /ku̱tərwals/ gibberish

de **koets** /kuts/ (pl: -en) coach, carriage

de **koetsier** /kutsi̱r/ (pl: -s) coachman

de **koevoet** /ku̱vut/ (pl: -en) crowbar

Koeweit /ku̱wɛit/ Kuwait

de **Koeweiter** /ku̱wɛitər/ (pl: -s) Kuwaiti

Koeweits /ku̱wɛits/ (adj) Kuwaiti

de **koffer** /kɔ̱fər/ (pl: -s) (suit)case, (hand)bag; trunk

de **kofferbak** /kɔ̱fərbɑk/ (pl: -ken) boot; [Am] trunk

de **koffie** /kɔ̱fi/ coffee: *~ drinken* have coffee; [fig] *dat is geen zuivere ~* there's sth. fishy about it, it looks suspicious

de **koffieboon** /kɔ̱fibon/ (pl: -bonen) coffee bean

het **koffiedik** /kɔ̱fidɪk/ coffee grounds: *het is zo helder als ~* it is as clear as mud; *ik kan geen ~ kijken* I can't read tea-leaves, I am not a crystal-gazer

de **koffiekan** /kɔ̱fikɑn/ (pl: -nen) coffeepot

het **koffiekopje** /kɔ̱fikɔpjə/ (pl: -s) coffee cup

de **koffiemelk** /kɔ̱fimɛlk/ evaporated milk

de **koffiepot** /kɔ̱fipɔt/ (pl: -ten) coffeepot

de **koffieshop** /kɔ̱fiʃɔp/ (pl: -s) **1** coffee shop **2** cannabis coffee shop

de **koffietafel** /kɔ̱fitafəl/ (pl: -s) (light) lunch

de **koffietijd** /kɔ̱fitɛit/ coffee time; lunch time

het **koffiezetapparaat** /kɔ̱fizɛtɑparat/ (pl: -apparaten) coffee-maker

koffiezetten /kɔ̱fizɛtə(n)/ (zette koffie, heeft koffiegezet) make coffee, put coffee on

de **kogel** /ko̱ɣəl/ (pl: -s) **1** bullet; ball: *een ver-*

dwaalde ~ a stray bullet **2** shot ‖ *de* ~ *is door de kerk* the die is cast

de **kogelbiefstuk** /koɣəlbifstʏk/ (pl: -ken) round steak

het **kogelgewricht** /koɣəlɣəvrɪ̩xt/ (pl: -en) ball(-and-socket) joint

het **kogellager** /koɣəlaɣər/ (pl: -s) ball-bearing

kogelslingeren /koɣəslɪŋərə(n)/ hammer (throw)

kogelstoten /koɣəlstotə(n)/ shot-put(ting)

kogelvrij /koɣəlvrɛi/ (adj) bulletproof

de **koikarper** /kɔikarpər/ koi (carp)

de **kok** /kɔk/ (pl: -s) cook: *de chef-*~ the chef

koken /kokə(n)/ (kookte, heeft gekookt) **1** boil: *water kookt bij 100° C* water boils at 100° C **2** cook, do the cooking ‖ ~ *van woede* boil (*or:* seethe) with rage

kokendheet /kokənhet/ (adj) piping (*or:* boiling, scalding) hot

de **koker** /kokər/ (pl: -s) **1** case **2** cylinder **3** shaft; chute

koket /kokɛt/ (adj) **1** coquettish **2** smart, stylish

kokhalzen /kɔkhalzə(n)/ (kokhalsde, heeft gekokhalsd) retch, heave

kokkerellen /kɔkərɛlə(n)/ (kokkerelde, heeft gekokkereld) cook

het **kokos** /kokɔs/ **1** coconut **2** coconut fibre

de **kokosmat** /kokɔsmat/ (pl: -ten) coconut matting

de **kokosnoot** /kokɔsnot/ coconut

de **kokospalm** /kokɔspalm/ (pl: -en) coconut palm

de **koksmuts** /kɔksmʏts/ (pl: -en) chef's hat

de **kolder** /kɔldər/ nonsense, rubbish

de **kolen** /kolə(n)/ (pl) coal: *op hete* ~ *zitten* be on tenterhooks

de **kolencentrale** /kolə(n)sɛntralə/ (pl: -s) coal-fired power station

de **kolenmijn** /kolə(n)mɛin/ (pl: -en) coal mine

de **kolere** /kolerə/: [vulg] *krijg de* ~! get stuffed!, drop dead!

de **kolf** /kɔlf/ (pl: kolven) **1** butt **2** flask; retort **3** cob

de **kolibrie** /kolibri/ (pl: -s) hummingbird

het/de **koliek** /kolik/ (pl: -en) colic

de **kolk** /kɔlk/ (pl: -en) eddy, whirlpool

kolken /kɔlkə(n)/ (kolkte, heeft gekolkt) swirl, eddy

de **kolom** /kolɔm/ (pl: -men) column

de **kolonel** /kolonɛl/ (pl: -s) colonel

koloniaal /kolonijal/ (adj) colonial

het **kolonialisme** /kolonijalɪsmə/ colonialism

de **kolonie** /koloni/ (pl: -s en koloniën) colony

de **kolonisatie** /koloniza(t)si/ colonization

koloniseren /kolonizerə(n)/ (koloniseerde, heeft gekoloniseerd) colonize

de **kolonist** /kolonɪst/ (pl: -en) colonist, settler

de **kolos** /kolɔs/ (pl: -sen) colossus

kolossaal /kolɔsal/ (adj, adv) colossal, immense

kolven /kɔlvə(n)/ (kolfde, heeft gekolfd) express milk

de **¹kom** /kɔm/ (pl: -men) **1** bowl; washbasin **2** basin, bowl **3** socket: *haar arm is uit de* ~ *geschoten* her arm is dislocated ‖ *de bebouwde* ~ the built-up area; [Am] the city limits

²kom /kɔm/ (int) come on!: ~ *nou*, *dat maak je me niet wijs* come on (now) (*or:* look), don't give me that; ~, *ik stap maar weer eens op* right, I'm off now!; ~ *op!* come on!

de **komaf** /kɔmɑf/ origin, birth: *van goede* ~ upper-crust, high-born ‖ [Belg] ~ *maken met iets* give short shrift to sth.

de **kombuis** /kɔmbœys/ (pl: kombuizen) galley

de **komediant** /komedijɑnt/ (pl: -en) comedy actor, comedian

de **komedie** /komedi/ (pl: -s) comedy; [fig also] (play-)acting

de **komeet** /komet/ (pl: kometen) comet

komen /komə(n)/ (kwam, is gekomen) **1** come, get: *er komt regen* it is going to rain; *er kwam bloed uit zijn mond* there was blood coming out of his mouth; *ergens bij kunnen* ~ be able to get at sth.; *de politie laten* ~ send for (*or:* call) the police; *ik kom eraan!* (*or:* *al!*) (I'm) coming!, I'm on my way!; *kom eens langs!* come round some time!; *ergens achter* ~ find out sth., get to know sth.; *hoe kom je erbij!* what(ever) gave you that idea?; *ergens overheen* ~ get over sth.; [fig] *we kwamen er niet uit* we couldn't work it out; *hoe kom je van hier naar het museum?* how do you get to the museum from here?; *hij komt uit Engeland* he's from England; *wie het eerst komt, het eerst maalt* first come, first served **2** come ((a)round, over), call: *er* ~ *mensen vanavond* we've got) people coming this evening **3** (+ aan) touch: *kom nergens aan!* don't touch (anything)! **4** come (about), happen: *hoe komt het?* how come?, how did that happen?; *daar komt niets van in* that's out of the question; *dat komt ervan als je niet luistert* that's what you get (*or:* what happens) if you don't listen **5** (+ aan) come (by), get (hold of): *aan geld zien te* ~ get hold of some money; *daar kom ik straks nog op* I'll come round to that in a moment ‖ *daar komt nog bij dat …* what's more …, besides …; *kom nou!* don't be silly!, come off it!

komend /komənt/ (adj) coming, to come; next: ~*e week* next week

de **komiek** /komik/ (pl: -en) comedian, comic

de **komijn** /komɛin/ cumin

komisch /komis/ (adj, adv) comic(al), funny

de **komkommer** /kɔmkɔmər/ (pl: -s) cucumber

de **komkommertijd** /kɔmkɔmərtɛit/ silly season

de **komma** /kɔma/ (pl: -'s) **1** comma **2** (decimal) point: *tot op vijf cijfers na de* ~ *uitrekenen* calculate to five decimal places; *nul* ~ *drie (0,3)* nought point three (0.3); [Am] zero point three (0.3)

de **kommer** /kɔmər/ sorrow: ~ en *kwel* sorrow and misery

het **kompas** /kɔmpɑs/ (pl: -sen) compass

de **kompasnaald** /kɔmpɑsnalt/ (pl: -en) compass needle

het **kompres** /kɔmprɛs/ (pl: -sen) compress

de **komst** /kɔmst/ coming, arrival: *er is storm op* ~ there is a storm brewing

het **konijn** /konɛin/ (pl: -en) rabbit; bunny

het **konijnenhok** /konɛinə(n)hɔk/ (pl: -ken) rabbit hutch

het **konijnenhol** /konɛinə(n)hɔl/ (pl: -en) rabbit hole (or: burrow)

de **koning** /konɪŋ/ (pl: -en) king

de **koningin** /konɪŋɪn/ (pl: -nen) queen

Koninginnedag /konɪŋɪnədɑχ/ (pl: -en) Queen's Birthday

Koningsdag /konɪŋzdɑχ/ King's Day

koningsgezind /konɪŋsχəzɪnt/ (adj) royalist(ic), monarchist

het **koningshuis** /konɪŋshœys/ (pl: -huizen) royal family (or: house)

koninklijk /konɪŋklək/ (adj) royal; regal

het **koninkrijk** /konɪŋkrɛik/ (pl: -en) kingdom

konkelen /kɔŋkələ(n)/ (konkelde, heeft gekonkeld) scheme, intrigue

de **kont** /kɔnt/ (pl: -en) [inform] bottom, behind, bum: *je kunt hier je ~ niet* **keren** you couldn't swing a cat here

het **konvooi** /kɔnvoj/ (pl: -en) convoy

de **kooi** /koj/ (pl: -en) **1** cage **2** pen; coop; fold; sty **3** berth, bunk

de **kook** /kok/ boil: *aan de ~ brengen* bring to the boil; *volkomen van de ~ raken* go to pieces

het **kookboek** /kogbuk/ (pl: -en) cookery book

de **kookgelegenheid** /kokχəleγə(n)hɛrt/ cooking facilities

de **kookkunst** /kokʏnst/ cookery, (the art of) cooking, culinary art

de **kookplaat** /kokplat/ (pl: -platen) hotplate, hob

het **kookpunt** /kokpʏnt/ (pl: -en) boiling point: *het ~* **bereiken** [also fig] reach boiling point

de **kookwekker** /kokwɛkər/ (pl: -s) kitchen timer

de **kool** /kol/ (pl: kolen) **1** cabbage **2** coal

het **kooldioxide** /koldijɔksidə/ carbon dioxide

het **koolhydraat** /kolhidrat/ (pl: -hydraten) carbohydrate

de **koolmees** /kolmes/ (pl: -mezen) great tit

het **koolmonoxide** /kolmɔnɔksidə/ carbon monoxide

de **koolraap** /kolrap/ (pl: -rapen) kohlrabi, turnip cabbage

de **koolrabi** /kolrabi/ kohlrabi

de **koolstof** /kolstɔf/ carbon

de **koolvis** /kolvɪs/ (pl: -sen) pollack

de **koolwaterstof** /kolwatərstɔf/ (pl: -fen) hydrocarbon

het **koolwitje** /kolwɪcə/ (pl: -s) cabbage white

(butterfly)

het **koolzaad** /kolzat/ (rape)seed, colza

het **koolzuur** /kolzyr/ carbon dioxide

koolzuurhoudend /kolzyrhɑudənt/ (adj) carbonated

de **koon** /kon/ (pl: konen) cheek

de **koop** /kop/ (pl: kopen) buy, sale, purchase: ~ en *verkoop* buying and selling; *de ~* **gaat** *door* the deal (or: sale) is going through; *op de ~ toe* into the bargain; *te ~ (zijn, staan)* (be) for sale; *te ~ of te huur* to buy or let; *te ~ gevraagd* wanted

de **koopakte** /kopɑktə/ (pl: -n, -s) deed of sale (or: purchase)

de **koopavond** /kopavɔnt/ (pl: -en) late-night shopping, late opening

het **koopcontract** /kopkɔntrɑkt/ (pl: -en) contract (or: bill) of sale; purchase deed, title deed; deed of purchase

koopgraag /kopχraχ/ (adj) acquisitive, eager to spend money

de **koophandel** /kophɑndəl/ commerce, trade: *Kamer van Koophandel* [roughly] Chamber of Commerce

het **koophuis** /kophœys/ owner-occupied house

het **koopje** /kopjə/ (pl: -s) bargain, good buy (or: deal)

de **koopjesjager** /kopjəsjaγər/ (pl: -s) bargain hunter, snapper-up

de **koopkracht** /kopkrɑχt/ buying power

de **koopman** /kopmɑn/ (pl: kooplieden) merchant, businessman

de **koopsom** /kopsɔm/ (pl: -men) purchase price

de **koopvaardij** /kopfardɛi/ merchant navy

de **koopwaar** /kopwar/ (pl: -waren) merchandise, wares

koopziek /kopsik/ (adj) shopaholic, addicted to buying

de **koopzondag** /kopsɔndɑχ/ shopping Sunday

het **koor** /kor/ (pl: koren) choir, chorus: *een* **gemengd** ~ a mixed (voice) choir

het/de **koord** /kort/ (pl: -en) cord, (thick) string, (light) rope

koorddansen /kordɑnsə(n)/ walk a tightrope

de **koorddanser** /kordɑnsər/ (pl: -s) tightrope walker, high wire walker

de **koorknaap** /korknap/ (pl: -knapen) choirboy: [fig] *hij is* **geen** ~ he's no choirboy (or: angel)

de **koorts** /korts/ fever: *bij iem. de ~* **opnemen** take s.o.'s temperature

koortsachtig /kortsɑχtəχ/ (adj, adv) feverish: *~e* **bedrijvigheid** frenzied activity

koortsig /kortsəχ/ (adj) feverish

de **koortslip** /kortslɪp/ (pl: -pen) cold sore

de **koortsthermometer** /kortstɛrmometər/ (pl: -s) clinical thermometer

de **koortsuitslag** /kↄrtsœytslɑχ/ cold sore
koortsvrij /kↄrtsfrɛɪ/ (adj) free of fever,
without fever

de **koorzang** /koːrzɑŋ/ choral singing

koosjer /koʃər/ (adj) kosher: [fig] *dat zaakje
is niet ~* that business doesn't look too kosher

de **koosnaam** /koːsnam/ pet name, term of endearment

het **kootje** /koːcə/ (pl: -s) phalanx

de **kop** /kↄp/ (pl: -pen) **1** head: *er zit ~ noch
staart aan* you can't make head or tail of it; *~
dicht!* shut up!; *een **mooie** ~ met haar* a
beautiful head of hair; *een **rooie** ~ krijgen* go
red, flush; *iem. op zijn ~ geven* give s.o. what
for; *dat zal je de ~ niet **kosten*** it's not going to
kill you **2** head, brain: *dat is een **knappe** ~* he
is a clever (*or:* smart) fellow **3** head, top: *de ~
van Overijssel* the north of Overijssel; *de ~
van een **spijker** (or: **hamer**)* the head of a nail
(*or:* hammer); *op ~ liggen* be in the lead; *over
de ~ slaan* overturn, somersault; *over de ~
gaan* go broke, fold **4** cup, mug **5** headline,
heading || *~ of **munt*** heads or tails; *het is vijf
uur op de ~ af* it is exactly five o'clock

de **kopbal** /kↄbɑl/ (pl: -len) header

kopen /koːpə(n)/ (kocht, heeft gekocht)
1 buy, purchase: *wat koop ik **ervoor?*** what
good will it do me? **2** buy (off)

de **kop-en-schotel** /kↄpɛnsχoːtəl/ (pl: -s) cup
and saucer

de **¹koper** /koːpər/ (pl: -s) buyer

het **²koper** /koːpər/ (pl: -s) **1** copper **2** brass
3 brass (section)

het/de **koperdraad** /koːpərdrat/ copper (*or:* brass)
wire

koperen /koːpərə(n)/ (adj) brass, copper

het **koperwerk** /koːpərwɛrk/ copper work,
brass work, brassware

de **kopgroep** /kↄpχrup/ (pl: -en) leading
group; break(away)

de **kopie** /kopiː/ (pl: -ën) **1** copy, duplicate
2 (photo)copy

het **kopieerapparaat** /kopijeːrɑparat/ (pl: -ap-
paraten) photocopier

kopiëren /kopijeːrə(n)/ (kopieerde, heeft
gekopieerd) **1** copy, make a copy (of); transcribe **2** (photo)copy, xerox

de **kopij** /kopɛi/ (pl: -en) copy, manuscript

het **kopje** /kↄpjə/ (pl: -s) (small, little) cup || *~
duikelen* turn somersaults; *de poes **gaf** haar
steeds ~s* the cat kept nuzzling (up) against
her

kopjeduikelen /kↄpjədœykələ(n)/ (duikelde kopje, heeft kopjegeduikeld) (turn, do a)
somersault

kopje-onder /kↄpjəↄndər/ (adv): *hij ging ~*
he got a ducking

de **koplamp** /kↄplɑmp/ (pl: -en) headlight

de **koploper** /kↄploːpər/ (pl: -s) leader, front
runner; trendsetter

de **¹koppel** /kↄpəl/ (sword) belt

het **²koppel** /kↄpəl/ **1** couple, pair; group;
bunch; set **2** couple: *een **aardig** ~* a nice couple

de **koppelaar** /kↄpəlar/ (pl: -s) matchmaker,
marriage broker

de **koppelbaas** /kↄpəlbas/ (pl: -bazen) (illegal)
labour subcontractor

koppelen /kↄpələ(n)/ (koppelde, heeft gekoppeld) **1** couple (with, to) **2** link, relate:
*twee mensen **proberen** te ~* try to pair two
people off

de **koppeling** /kↄpəlɪŋ/ (pl: -en) clutch (pedal):
*de ~ **intrappen*** let out the clutch

het **koppelteken** /kↄpəlteːkə(n)/ (pl: -s) hyphen

het **koppelwerkwoord** /kↄpəlwɛrkwort/ (pl:
-en) copula

koppen /kↄpə(n)/ (kopte, heeft gekopt)
head

koppensnellen /kↄpə(n)snɛlə(n)/ head-
hunt

koppig /kↄpəχ/ (adj, adv) **1** stubborn, headstrong: *(zo) ~ **als** een ezel* (as) stubborn as a
mule **2** heady

de **koppigaard** /kↄpəχart/ (pl: -s) [Belg] stubborn person, obstinate person

de **koppigheid** /kↄpəχhɛit/ stubbornness

de **koprol** /kↄprↄl/ (pl: -len) somersault

kopschuw /kↄpsχyw/ (adj) shy, withdrawn:
*iem. ~ **maken*** scare (*or:* frighten) s.o. off

de **kop-staartbotsing** /kↄpstartbↄtsɪŋ/ (pl:
-en) rear-end collision

de **kopstem** /kↄpstɛm/ (pl: -men) falsetto

de **kopstoot** /kↄpstoːt/ (pl: kopstoten) butt (of
the head): *iem. een ~ **geven*** headbutt s.o.

het **kopstuk** /kↄpstʏk/ (pl: -ken) head man, boss

de **koptelefoon** /kↄpteləfoːn/ (pl: -s) head-
phone(s), earphone(s), headset

de **kopzorg** /kↄpsↄrχ/ (pl: -en) worry, headache

het **koraal** /koral/ (pl: koralen) coral

het **koraaleiland** /koralɛilɑnt/ (pl: -en) coral island

het **koraalrif** /koralrɪf/ (pl: -fen) coral reef

de **Koran** /koran/ Koran

kordaat /kↄrdat/ (adj, adv) firm, plucky,
bold

het **kordon** /kↄrdↄn/ (pl: -s) cordon

Korea /koreːja/ Korea

de **Koreaan** /koreːjan/ (pl: Koreanen) Korean

het **¹Koreaans** /koreːjans/ Korean

²Koreaans /koreːjans/ (adj) Korean

het **koren** /koːrə(n)/ (pl: -s) corn; [Am] wheat;
grain

de **korenbloem** /koːrə(n)blum/ (pl: -en) corn-
flower

de **korenschuur** /koːrə(n)sχyr/ (pl: -schuren)
granary

de **korenwolf** /koːrə(n)wↄlf/ (pl: -wolven) European hamster

de **korf** /kↄrf/ (pl: korven) basket; hive

het **korfbal** /kↄrvbɑl/ korfball

korfballen /kↄrvbɑlə(n)/ (korfbalde, heeft

koud

gekorfbald) play korfball

het **korhoen** /kɔrhun/ (pl: -ders) black grouse

de **koriander** /korijɒndər/ coriander (seed)

de **kornuit** /kɔrnœyt/ (pl: -en) mate; [Am] buddy

de **korporaal** /kɔrporal/ (pl: -s) corporal

het **korps** /kɔrps/ (pl: -en) corps, body; staff; force

de **korpschef** /kɔrpʃɛf/ (pl: -s) superintendent

de **korrel** /kɔrəl/ (pl: -s) granule, grain: *iets met een ~(tje) zout nemen* take sth. with a pinch of salt

korrelig /kɔrələɣ/ (adj) granular

het **korset** /kɔrsɛt/ (pl: -ten) corset

de **korst** /kɔrst/ (pl: -en) crust; scab; rind

het **korstmos** /kɔrstmɔs/ (pl: -sen) lichen

kort /kɔrt/ (adj, adv) short; brief: *alles ~ en klein slaan* smash everything to pieces; *een ~ overzicht* a brief (*or:* short) summary; *~ daarvoor* shortly before; *tot voor ~* until recently; *iets in het ~ uiteenzetten* explain sth. briefly ‖ *we komen drie man te ~* we're three men short; *te ~ komen* run short (of)

kortaangebonden /kɔrtaŋɣəbɔndə(n)/ (adj) short-spoken, curt

kortademig /kɔrtadəməɣ/ (adj) short of breath; [also fig] short-winded

kortaf /kɔrtɑf/ (adj, adv) curt, abrupt

korten /kɔrtə(n)/ (kortte, heeft gekort) cut (back): *~ op de uitkeringen* cut back on social security

het **kortetermijngeheugen** short-term memory

de **korting** /kɔrtɪŋ/ (pl: -en) discount, concession; cut: *~ geven op de prijs* give a discount off the price

de **kortingskaart** /kɔrtɪŋskart/ (pl: -en) concession (*or:* reduced-fare) card/pass; discount card

kortom /kɔrtɔm/ (adv) in short, to put it briefly (*or:* shortly)

kortsluiten /kɔrtslœytə(n)/ (sloot kort, heeft kortgesloten) short-circuit: [fig] *de zaken ~ align* (*or:* fine-tune) matters

de **kortsluiting** /kɔrtslœytɪŋ/ (pl: -en) short circuit, short

kortstondig /kɔrtstɔndəɣ/ (adj) short-lived, brief

kortweg /kɔrtwɛɣ/ (adv) briefly, shortly

kortwieken /kɔrtwikə(n)/ (kortwiekte, heeft gekortwiekt) clip the wings of

kortzichtig /kɔrtsɪxtəɣ/ (adj, adv) short-sighted

kosmisch /kɔsmis/ (adj) cosmic

de **kosmonaut** /kɔsmonaut/ (pl: -en) cosmonaut

de **kosmos** /kɔsmɔs/ cosmos

de **kost** /kɔst/ (pl: -en) **1** cost, expense; outlay; charge: *de ~en dekken* cover the costs; *~en van levensonderhoud* cost of living; *op haar eigen ~en* at her own expense; *op ~en van* at the expense of **2** living: *wat doe jij voor de ~?* what do you do for a living?; *de ~ verdienen* make a living (as a ..., by ...-ing) **3** board(ing), keep: *~ en inwoning* board and lodging **4** fare, food: *dagelijkse ~* ordinary food

kostbaar /kɔstbar/ (adj) **1** expensive **2** valuable; [stronger] precious

de **kostbaarheden** /kɔstbarhedə(n)/ (pl) valuables

kostelijk /kɔstələk/ (adj, adv) precious; exquisite; delicious; excellent

¹**kosteloos** /kɔstəlos/ (adj) free

²**kosteloos** /kɔstəlos/ (adv) free of charge

kosten /kɔstə(n)/ (kostte, heeft gekost) cost, be, take: *het heeft ons maanden gekost om dit te regelen* it took us months to organize this; *het ongeluk kostte (aan) drie kinderen het leven* three children died (*or:* lost their lives) in the accident; *dit karwei zal heel wat tijd ~* this job will take (up) a great deal of time

de **kosten-batenanalyse** /kɔstə(n)batə(n)anali:zə/ (pl: -s) cost-benefit analysis

kostenbesparend /kɔstə(n)bəsparənt/ (adj) money-saving, cost-cutting

kostendekkend /kɔstə(n)dɛkənt/ (adj) cost-effective, self-supporting

de **kostenstijging** /kɔstə(n)stɛiɣɪŋ/ increase in costs

de **koster** /kɔstər/ (pl: -s) verger

de **kostganger** /kɔstxaŋər/ (pl: -s) boarder, lodger

het **kostgeld** /kɔstxɛlt/ (pl: -en) board (and lodging)

het **kostje** /kɔʃə/ (pl: -s): *zijn ~ is gekocht* he has it made

de **kostprijs** /kɔstprɛis/ cost price

de **kostschool** /kɔstsxol/ (pl: -scholen) boarding school; public school: *op een ~ zitten* attend a boarding school

het **kostuum** /kɔstym/ (pl: -s) **1** suit **2** costume, dress

de **kostwinner** /kɔstwɪnər/ (pl: -s) breadwinner

het **kot** /kɔt/ (pl: -ten) **1** hovel **2** [Belg] student apartment (*or:* room): *op ~ zitten* be in digs

de **kotbaas** /kɔdbas/ (pl: kotbazen) [Belg] landlord

de **kotelet** /kotəlɛt/ (pl: -ten) chop, cutlet

de **koter** /kotər/ (pl: -s) [inform] youngster, kid

de **kotmadam** /kɔtmadɑm/ (pl: -men, -s) [Belg] landlady

kotsbeu (adj): [Belg; inform] *iets ~ zijn* be sick and tired of sth.

kotsen /kɔtsə(n)/ (kotste, heeft gekotst) [inform] puke

kotsmisselijk /kɔtsmɪsələk/ (adj) [inform] sick as a dog (*or:* cat): [fig] *ik word er ~ van* I'm sick to death of it, it makes me sick

de **kotter** /kɔtər/ (pl: -s) cutter

de **kou** /kau/ cold(ness), chill

koud /kaut/ (adj) cold; chilly: *het laat mij ~* it

leaves me cold
koudbloedig /kɑudblu̱dəx/ (adj) cold-
blooded

het **koudvuur** /kɑu̱tfyr/ gangrene

de **koudwatervrees** /kɑutwa̱tərvres/ cold
feet

het **koufront** /kɑu̱frɔnt/ (pl: -en) cold front

de **koukleum** /kɑu̱kləm/ (pl: -en) shivery type

de **kous** /kɑus/ (pl: -en) stocking; sock

kouvatten /kɑu̱vətə(n)/ (vatte kou, heeft
kougevat) catch cold

kouwelijk /kɑu̱wələk/ (adj, adv) chilly, sensitive to cold

de **Kozak** /kozɑ̱k/ (pl: -ken) Cossack

de [1]**kozijn** /kozɛi̱n/ [Belg] cousin

het [2]**kozijn** /kozɛi̱n/ (window, door) frame

de **kraag** /krax/ (pl: kragen) **1** collar: *iem. bij (in)*
zijn ~ grijpen grab s.o. by the collar; collar s.o.
2 head

de **kraai** /krɑj/ (pl: -en) crow

kraaien /kra̱jə(n)/ (kraaide, heeft gekraaid)
crow

het **kraaiennest** /kra̱jənɛst/ (pl: -en) crow's-
nest

de **kraaienpootjes** /kra̱jə(n)pocəs/ (pl) crow's-
feet

de **kraak** /krak/ (pl: kraken) break-in

het **kraakbeen** /kra̱gben/ (pl: -deren) cartilage

het **kraakpand** /kra̱kpɑnt/ (pl: -en) squat

de **kraakstem** /kra̱kstɛm/ grating (*or*: rasping)
voice

de **kraal** /kral/ (pl: kralen) bead

de **kraam** /kram/ (pl: kramen) stall, booth

de **kraamafdeling** /kra̱mɑvdelɪŋ/ (pl: -en)
maternity ward

het **kraambed** /kra̱mbɛt/ childbed: *een lang ~ a*
long period of lying-in

de **kraamhulp** /kra̱mhʏlp/ (pl: -en) maternity
assistant

de **kraamkamer** /kra̱mkɑmər/ (pl: -s) delivery
room; [before delivery] labour room

de **kraamkliniek** /kra̱mklinik/ (pl: -en) maternity clinic

de **kraamverzorgster** /kra̱mvərzɔrxstər/ (pl:
-s) maternity nurse

het **kraamvisite** /kra̱mvizitə/ (pl: -s): *op ~ ko-*
men come to see the new mother and her
baby

de **kraamvrouw** /kra̱mvrɑu/ (pl: -en) woman
in childbed; mother of newly-born baby

de **kraamzorg** /kra̱mzɔrx/ maternity care

de **kraan** /kran/ (pl: kranen) **1** tap; [Am] faucet;
(stop)cock; valve **2** crane

de **kraandrijver** /kra̱ndrɛivər/ (pl: -s) crane
driver (*or*: operator)

de **kraanvogel** /kra̱nvoɣəl/ (pl: -s) (common)
crane

de **kraanwagen** /kra̱nwaɣə(n)/ (pl: -s) breakdown lorry (*or*: truck); [Am] tow truck

het **kraanwater** /kra̱nwatər/ tap water

de **krab** /krɑp/ (pl: -ben) crab

de **krabbel** /krɒ̱bəl/ (pl: -s) **1** scratch (mark)
2 scrawl

[1]**krabbelen** /krɒ̱bələ(n)/ (krabbelde, heeft
gekrabbeld) scratch || (*weer*) *overeind ~*
scramble to one's feet

[2]**krabbelen** /krɒ̱bələ(n)/ (krabbelde, heeft
gekrabbeld) scrawl

het **krabbeltje** /krɒ̱bəlcə/ (pl: -s) scrawl

[1]**krabben** /krɒ̱bə(n)/ (krabde, heeft gekrabd)
scratch: *zijn hoofd ~* scratch one's head

[2]**krabben** /krɒ̱bə(n)/ (krabde, heeft gekrabd)
scratch out, scratch off

de **krach** /krɑx/ (pl: -s) crash

de **kracht** /krɑxt/ (pl: -en) strength, power;
force: *drijvende ~ achter* moving force (*or*:
spirit) behind; *op eigen ~* on one's own, by
o.s.; *op volle* (or: *halve*) *~ (werken)* operate at
full (*or*: half) speed/power; *met zijn laatste*
~en with a final effort; *het vergt veel van mijn*
~en it's a great drain on my energy; *van ~ zijn*
be valid (*or*: effective); *zijn ~en meten met*
iem. measure one's strength with s.o., pit
one's strength against s.o.; *zijn woorden ~*
bijzetten reinforce his words, suit the action
to the word

de **krachtbron** /krɑ̱xtbrɔn/ (pl: -nen) source of
energy (*or*: power); power station

de **krachtcentrale** /krɒ̱xtsɛntralə/ (pl: -s) power station

krachtdadig /krɑxda̱dəx/ (adj, adv) energetic, vigorous

krachteloos /krɑ̱xtəlos/ (adj) weak; limp;
powerless

krachtens /krɒ̱xtəns/ (prep) by virtue of,
under

krachtig /krɒ̱xtəx/ (adj, adv) **1** strong, powerful: *een ~e motor* a powerful engine; *mati-*
ge tot ~e wind moderate to strong winds
2 powerful, forceful: *kort maar ~* **a)** brief and
to the point; **b)** [fig] short but (*or*: and) sweet
3 potent

de **krachtmeting** /krɒ̱xtmetɪŋ/ (pl: -en) contest, trial of strength

de **krachtpatser** /krɒ̱xtpɑtsər/ (pl: -s) muscleman, bruiser

de **krachtsinspanning** /krɒ̱xtsɪnspɑnɪŋ/ (pl:
-en) effort

de **krachtsport** /krɒ̱xtsport/ (pl: -en) strength
sport

de **krachtterm** /krɒ̱xtɛrm/ (pl: -en) swearword:
hij gebruikte nogal veel ~en he used a lot of
swearwords (*or*: strong language)

de **krachttraining** /krɒ̱xtrenɪŋ/ (pl: -en)
weight training

de **krak** /krɑk/ (pl: -ken) crack, snap

krakelen /krakḛlə(n)/ (krakeelde, heeft ge-
krakeeld) quarrel, row

de **krakeling** /kra̱kəlɪŋ/ (pl: -en) type of biscuit;
[Am] type of cookie: *zoute ~en* pretzels

[1]**kraken** /kra̱kə(n)/ (kraakte, heeft gekraakt)
crack; creak; crunch: *een ~de stem* a grating

voice
²**kraken** /krɑkə(n)/ (kraakte, heeft gekraakt)
1 crack **2** break into [bldg]; crack; hack
3 pan, slate || *het **pand** is gekraakt* the build-
ing has been broken into by squatters

de **kraker** /krɑkər/ (pl: -s) **1** squatter **2** [comp]
hacker

krakkemikkig /krɑkəmɪkəχ/ (adj, adv) [in-
form] rickety

de **kram** /krɑm/ (pl: -men) clamp; cramp (iron);
clasp || [Belg] *uit* zijn ~*men schieten* blow one's
top

de **kramiek** /krɑmik/ (pl: -en) [Belg] currant
loaf

de **kramp** /krɑmp/ (pl: -en) cramp

krampachtig /krɑmpɑχtəχ/ (adj, adv)
1 forced: *met een ~ **vertrokken** gezicht* gri-
macing **2** frenetic: *zich ~ aan iem. (iets) **vasthouden*** cling to s.o. (sth.) for dear life **3** con-
vulsive

kranig /krɑnəχ/ (adj) plucky, brave

krankjorum /krɑŋkjorʏm/ (adj, adv) [in-
form] bonkers, nuts

krankzinnig /krɑŋksɪnəχ/ (adj) **1** mentally
ill, insane, mad: ~ *worden* go insane, go out
of one's mind **2** crazy, mad

de **krankzinnige** /krɑŋksɪnəχə/ (pl: -n) madman, madwoman

de **krans** /krɑns/ (pl: -en) **1** wreath **2** ring: *een ~
om de zon* (or: *de maan*) a corona round the
sun (or: moon)

de **kransslagader** /krɑnslɑχɑdər/ (pl: -s) coronary artery

de **krant** /krɑnt/ (pl: -en) (news)paper

het **krantenartikel** /krɑntə(n)ɑrtikəl/ (pl: -en)
newspaper article

het **krantenbericht** /krɑntə(n)bərɪχt/ (pl: -en)
newspaper report

de **krantenbezorger** /krɑntə(n)bəzɔrɣər/ (pl:
-s) (news)paper boy (or: girl)

de **krantenkiosk** /krɑntə(n)kijɔsk/ (pl: -en)
newspaper kiosk (or: stand)

het **krantenknipsel** /krɑntə(n)knɪpsəl/ (pl: -s)
newspaper cutting, press cutting

de **krantenkop** /krɑntə(n)kɔp/ (pl: -pen)
(newspaper) headline

de **krantenwijk** /krɑntə(n)wɛik/ (pl: -en)
(news)paper round; [Am] (news)paper route

krap /krɑp/ (adj, adv) **1** tight; narrow
2 tight, scarce: *een ~pe **markt** a small market;
~ (bij kas) **zitten*** be short of money (or: cash) ||
*met een ~pe **meerderheid*** with a bare majority

de ¹**kras** /krɑs/ (pl: -sen) scratch

²**kras** /krɑs/ (adj, adv) **1** strong, vigorous; hale
and hearty **2** strong, drastic: *dat is een nogal
~se **opmerking*** that is a rather crass remark

het **kraslot** /krɑslɔt/ (pl: -en) scratch card

¹**krassen** /krɑsə(n)/ (kraste, heeft gekrast)
1 scrape: *zijn ring kraste **over** het glas* his ring
scraped across the glass **2** rasp; scrape; croak;

hoot; screech

²**krassen** /krɑsə(n)/ (kraste, heeft gekrast)
scratch; carve

het **krat** /krɑt/ (pl: -ten) crate

de **krater** /krɑtər/ (pl: -s) crater: *een ~ **slaan***
leave a crater

het **krediet** /krədit/ (pl: -en) **1** credit: *veel ~
hebben* enjoy great trust **2** credit, respect

de **kredietbank** /krədidbɑŋk/ (pl: -en) [rough-
ly] finance company

de **kredietcrisis** /krəditkrizɪs/ (pl: -crises) credit crunch, credit crisis

de **kredietinstelling** /krəditɪnstɛlɪŋ/ (pl: -en)
credit institution (*or:* company)

kredietwaardig /krəditwɑrdəχ/ (adj) cred-
itworthy

de **kreeft** /kreft/ (pl: -en) lobster

de **Kreeft** /kreft/ (pl: -en) [astrology] Cancer

de **Kreeftskeerkring** /kreftskerkrɪŋ/ tropic of
Cancer

de **kreek** /krek/ (pl: kreken) **1** creek, cove
2 stream

de **kreet** /kret/ (pl: kreten) **1** cry **2** slogan,
catchword

de **krekel** /krekəl/ (pl: -s) cricket

het **kreng** /krɛŋ/ (pl: -en) **1** beast, bastard; bitch
2 wretched thing **3** carrion

krenken /krɛŋkə(n)/ (krenkte, heeft gekrenkt) offend, hurt

de **krent** /krɛnt/ currant: *de ~en **uit** de pap* the
best bits

de **krentenbol** /krɛntə(n)bɔl/ (pl: -len) currant
bun

het **krentenbrood** /krɛntə(n)brot/ (pl: -bro-
den) currant loaf

krenterig /krɛntərəχ/ (adj, adv) stingy

Kreta /kretɑ/ Crete

de **kreukel** /krøkəl/ (pl: -s) crease

¹**kreukelen** /krøkələ(n)/ (kreukelde, is gekreukeld) get creased (*or:* rumpled)

²**kreukelen** /krøkələ(n)/ (kreukelde, heeft
gekreukeld) crease: *het zat in gekreukeld **papier*** it was wrapped in crumpled paper

kreukelig /krøkələχ/ (adj) crumpled,
creased

de **kreukelzone** /krøkəlzɔːnə/ (pl: -s) crumple
zone

¹**kreuken** /krøkə(n)/ (kreukte, is gekreukt)
get creased (*or:* rumpled)

²**kreuken** /krøkə(n)/ (kreukte, heeft gekreukt) crease, crumple

kreukvrij /krøkfrɛɪ/ (adj) crease-resistant

kreunen /krønə(n)/ (kreunde, heeft ge-
kreund) groan, moan

de **kreupel** /krøpəl/ (adj, adv) **1** lame **2** poor,
clumsy

het **kreupelhout** /krøpəlhɑut/ undergrowth

de **krib** /krɪp/ (pl: -ben) manger, crib

kribbig /krɪbəχ/ (adj, adv) grumpy, catty

de **kriebel** /kribəl/ (pl: -s) itch, tickle: *ik **krijg**
daar de ~s van* it gets on my nerves

kriebelen /kriˌbələ(n)/ (kriebelde, heeft gekriebeld) tickle; itch

de **kriebelhoest** /kriˌbəlhust/ tickling cough

kriebelig /kriˌbələχ/ (adj) crabbed ‖ ~ van iets **worden** get irritated by sth.

de **kriek** /krik/ (pl: -en) **1** black cherry **2** [Belg] cherry beer

krieken /kriˌkə(n)/: **met (bij)** het ~ van de dag at (the crack of) dawn

de **krielkip** /krilˌkɪp/ (pl: -pen) bantam hen

het **krieltje** /krilˌcə/ (pl: -s) (small) new potato

krijgen /krɛiˌɣə(n)/ (kreeg, heeft gekregen) get; receive; catch: **aandacht** ~ receive attention; je krijgt de **groeten** van … … sends (you) his regards; zij kreeg er **hoofdpijn** van it gave her a headache; **slaap** (or: **trek**) ~ feel sleepy (or: hungry); iets **af** ~ get sth. done (or: finished); dat goed **is** niet meer te ~ you can't get hold of that stuff any more; iem. te **pakken** ~ get (hold of) s.o.; ik krijg nog geld **van** je you (still) owe me some money; iets **voor** elkaar ~ manage sth.

de **krijger** /krɛiˌɣər/ (pl: -s) warrior

het **krijgertje** /krɛiˌɣərcə/: ~ **spelen** play tag (or: tig)

de **krijgsgevangene** /krɛiˌxsχəvɑŋənə/ (pl: -n) prisoner of war

krijgshaftig /krɛiˌxshɑftəχ/ (adj, adv) warlike

de **krijgsheer** /krɛiˌxsher/ warlord

het **Krijgshof** /krɛiˌxshɔf/ [Belg] military high court

de **krijgslist** /krɛiˌxslɪst/ (pl: -en) stratagem, ruse

de **krijgsmacht** /krɛiˌxsmɑχt/ (pl: -en) armed forces, army

de **krijgsraad** /krɛiˌxsrat/ (pl: -raden) court-martial

krijsen /krɛiˌsə(n)/ (krijste, heeft gekrijst) **1** shriek, screech **2** scream

het **krijt** /krɛit/ chalk; crayon ‖ bij iem. **in** het ~ staan owe s.o. sth.

krijten /krɛiˌtə(n)/ (krijtte, heeft gekrijt) chalk

het **krijtje** /krɛiˌcə/ (pl: -s) piece of chalk

de **krijtrots** /krɛiˌtrɔts/ (pl: -en) chalk cliff

krijtwit /krɛiˌtwɪt/ (adj) (as) white as chalk

de **krik** /krɪk/ (pl: -s) jack

de **Krim** /krɪm/: **de** ~ the Crimea

de **krimp** /krɪmp/ shrinkage: ~ van de **bevolking** demographic shrinkage; **economische** ~ economic shrinkage (or: contraction) ‖ geen ~ **geven** not flinch

krimpen /krɪmˌpə(n)/ (kromp, is gekrompen) shrink, contract

de **krimpfolie** /krɪmˌpfoli/ clingfilm, shrink-wrapping

krimpvrij /krɪmpfrɛi/ (adj) shrink-proof, shrink-resistant

de **kring** /krɪŋ/ (pl: -en) circle, ring; circuit: in **besloten** ~ in a closed (or: private) circle, private(ly); in **politieke** ~en in political circles; de **huiselijke** ~ the family (or: domestic) circle; ~en onder de ogen **hebben** have bags under one's eyes; ~en maken **op** een tafelblad make rings on a table top; **in** een ~ zitten sit in a ring (or: circle)

kringelen /krɪŋˌələ(n)/ (kringelde, heeft gekringeld) spiral

de **kringloop** /krɪŋˌlop/ cycle; circulation

het **kringlooppapier** /krɪŋˌlopapir/ recycled paper

de **kringloopwinkel** /krɪŋˌlopwɪŋkəl/ (pl: -s) shop specialized in recycled goods

de **kringspier** /krɪŋˌspir/ (pl: -en) orbicularis, sphincter(-muscle)

krioelen /krijuˌlə(n)/ (krioelde, heeft gekrioeld) swarm, teem

de **kriskras** /krɪsˌkrɑs/ (adv) criss-cross

het **kristal** /krɪsˌtɑl/ (pl: -len) crystal

kristalhelder /krɪsˌtɑlhɛldər/ (adj) crystal-clear; lucid

kristallen /krɪsˌtɑlə(n)/ (adj) crystal

de **kristalsuiker** /krɪsˌtɑlsœykər/ granulated sugar

de **¹kritiek** /kritik/ (pl: -en) **1** criticism: **opbouwende** (or: **afbrekende**) ~ constructive (or: destructive) criticism **2** (critical) review: **goede** (or: **slechte**) ~en krijgen get good (or: bad) reviews

²kritiek /kritik/ (adj) critical; crucial: de **toestand** van de patiënt was ~ the patient's condition was critical

kritiekloos /kritiˌklos/ (adj, adv) uncritical: iets ~ **aanvaarden** accept sth. without question

kritisch /kritis/ (adj, adv) **1** critical **2** fault-finding: een ~ **iem.** a fault-finder

kritiseren /kritizeˌrə(n)/ (kritiseerde, heeft gekritiseerd) criticize; review

de **Kroaat** /krowˌat/ (pl: Kroaten) Croat, Croatian

Kroatië /krowˌa(t)sijə/ Croatia

het **¹Kroatisch** /krowˌatis/ Croatian

²Kroatisch /krowˌatis/ (adj) Croatian

de **kroeg** /kruχ/ (pl: -en) pub: altijd **in** de ~ zitten always be in the pub

de **kroegbaas** /kruɣˌbas/ (pl: -bazen) publican

de **kroegentocht** /kruɣə(n)tɔχt/ (pl: -en) pub-crawl; [Am] bar-hopping

de **kroegloper** /kruχˌlopər/ (pl: -s) pub-crawler

de **kroepoek** /kruˌpuk/ prawn crackers, shrimp crackers

de **kroes** /krus/ (pl: kroezen) mug

het **kroeshaar** /kruˌshar/ (pl: -haren) frizzy hair, curly hair

kroezen /kruˌzə(n)/ (kroesde, heeft gekroesd) frizzle, curl (up)

krokant /krokˌɑnt/ (adj) crisp(y), crunchy

de **kroket** /krokˌɛt/ croquette

de **krokodil** /krokodˌɪl/ (pl: -len) crocodile

de **krokodillentranen** /krokodˌɪlə(n)tranə(n)/

(pl): ~ *huilen* shed crocodile tears

de **krokus** /krо̱kʏs/ (pl: -sen) crocus

de **krokusvakantie** /krо̱kʏsfakɑnsi/ [roughly] spring half-term; [Am] [roughly] semester break

krols /krɔls/ (adj) on heat

krom /krɔm/ (adj, adv) **1** bent, crooked; curved: ~*me benen* bow-legs **2** clumsy: ~ *Nederlands* bad Dutch

krombuigen /krɔmbœyɣə(n)/ (boog krom, heeft/is kromgebogen) bend

kromgroeien /krɔmɣrujə(n)/ (groeide krom, is kromgegroeid) grow crooked

kromliggen /krɔmlɪɣə(n)/ (lag krom, heeft kromgelegen) scrimp and save

de **kromme** /krо̱mə/ (pl: -n) **1** curve **2** graph

¹**krommen** /krо̱mə(n)/ (kromde, is gekromd) bend

²**krommen** /krо̱mə(n)/ (kromde, heeft gekromd) bend

de **krommenaas** /krɔmənа̱s/: [Belg] *zich van ~ gebaren* act dumb, pretend not to hear

de **kromming** /krɔmɪŋ/ (pl: -en) bend(ing), curving; curvature

kromtrekken /krɔmtrɛkə(n)/ (trok krom, is kromgetrokken) warp; buckle

kronen /krо̱nə(n)/ (kroonde, heeft gekroond) crown

de **kroniek** /kronі̱k/ (pl: -en) chronicle

de **kroning** /krо̱nɪŋ/ (pl: -en) crowning; coronation

de **kronkel** /krɔ̱ŋkəl/ (pl: -s) twist(ing); kink

kronkelen /krɔ̱ŋkələ(n)/ (kronkelde, heeft/is gekronkeld) twist, wind; wriggle: ~ *van pijn* writhe in agony

kronkelig /krɔ̱ŋkələχ/ (adj) twisting, winding

de **kronkelweg** /krɔ̱ŋkəlwɛχ/ (pl: -en) twisting road, winding road, crooked path

de **kroon** /kron/ (pl: kronen) **1** crown; [of flower] corolla **2** Crown: *een benoeming* **door** *de* ~ a Crown appointment ‖ *dat is de* ~ *op zijn werk* that is the crowning glory of his work; *dat* **spant** *de* ~ that takes the cake

de **kroongetuige** /krо̱nɣətœyɣə/ (pl: -n) crown witness

het **kroonjaar** /krо̱njar/ (pl: -jaren) jubilee year

het **kroonjuweel** /krо̱njywel/ [literally and fig] crown jewel

de **kroonkurk** /krо̱ŋkʏrk/ (pl: -en) crown cap

de **kroonlijst** /krо̱nlɛist/ (pl: -en) cornice

de **kroonluchter** /krо̱nlʏχtər/ (pl: -s) chandelier

de **kroonprins** /krо̱mprɪns/ (pl: -en) crown prince; [fig] heir-apparent

de **kroonprinses** /krо̱mprɪnsɛs/ (pl: -sen) crown princess

het **kroonsteentje** /krо̱nstencə/ (pl: -s) connector

het **kroos** /kros/ duckweed

het **kroost** /krost/ offspring

de **krop** /krɔp/ (pl: -pen) **1** head: *een* ~ *sla* a head of lettuce **2** crop, gizzard

het **krot** /krɔt/ (pl: -ten) slum (dwelling), hovel

de **krottenwijk** /krɔ̱tə(n)wɛik/ (pl: -en) slum(s)

het **kruid** /krœyt/ (pl: -en) **1** herb **2** herb, spice

kruiden /krœ̱ydə(n)/ (kruidde, heeft gekruid) season, flavour; [fig also] spice (up)

de **kruidenboter** /krœ̱ydə(n)botər/ herb butter

de **kruidenier** /krœydənі̱r/ (pl: -s) grocer

het **kruidenrekje** /krœ̱ydə(n)rɛkjə/ (pl: -s) spice rack

de **kruidenthee** /krœ̱ydə(n)te/ herb(al) tea

kruidig /krœ̱ydəχ/ (adj) spicy

het **kruidje-roer-mij-niet** /krœycəru̱rmənit/ (pl: kruidjes-roer-mij-niet) **1** [bot] touch-me-not **2** [fig] thin-skinned (*or:* touchy) person

de **kruidkoek** /krœ̱ytkuk/ [roughly] spiced gingerbread

de **kruidnagel** /krœ̱ytnaɣəl/ (pl: -s, -en) clove

¹**kruien** /krœ̱yə(n)/ (kruide, heeft gekruid) break up, drift

²**kruien** /krœ̱yə(n)/ (kruide, heeft gekruid) wheel

de **kruier** /krœ̱yər/ (pl: -s) porter

de **kruik** /krœyk/ (pl: -en) **1** jar, pitcher, crock **2** hot-water bottle

het **kruim** /krœym/ (pl: -en) **1** crumb **2** [Belg] the pick of the bunch, the very best

de **kruimel** /krœ̱yməl/ (pl: -s) crumb

het **kruimeldeeg** /krœ̱yməldeχ/ crumbly pastry; [Am] crumb crust

de ¹**kruimeldief** /krœ̱yməldif/ (pl: -dieven) petty thief

de ²**kruimeldief**® /krœ̱yməldif/ (pl: -dieven) crumb-sweeper, dustbuster

kruimelen /krœ̱ymələ(n)/ (kruimelde, heeft gekruimeld) crumble

het **kruimelwerk** /krœ̱yməlwɛrk/ **1** odd jobs **2** pottering (about)

kruimig /krœ̱yməχ/ (adj) mealy, floury

de **kruin** /krœyn/ (pl: -en) crown

kruipen /krœ̱ypə(n)/ (kroop, heeft/is gekropen) **1** creep, crawl **2** crawl (along); drag: *de uren kropen* **voorbij** time dragged (on)

kruiperig /krœ̱ypərəχ/ (adj, adv) cringing, slimy, servile

het **kruis** /krœys/ (pl: kruizen) **1** cross **2** crotch; seat **3** crotch, groin **4** head: ~ *of munt?* heads or tails? ‖ [Belg; fig] *een* ~ *over iets* **maken** put an end to sth.; *een* ~ **slaan** cross o.s.

de **kruisband** /krœ̱yzbɑnt/ (pl: -en) cruciate ligament

het **kruisbeeld** /krœ̱yzbelt/ (pl: -en) crucifix

de **kruisbes** /krœ̱yzbɛs/ (pl: -sen) gooseberry

de **kruisbestuiving** /krœ̱yzbəstœyvɪŋ/ (pl: -en) cross-pollination [also fig]

de **kruisboog** /krœ̱yzboχ/ (pl: -bogen) **1** ogive **2** crossbow

kruiselings /krœ̱ysəlɪŋs/ (adj, adv) crosswise, crossways

kruisen

kruisen /krœysə(n)/ (kruiste, heeft gekruist) cross, intersect: *patroon van elkaar ~de lijnen* pattern of intersecting lines

de **kruiser** /krœysər/ (pl: -s) **1** cruiser **2** cabin cruiser

kruisigen /krœysəɣə(n)/ (kruisigde, heeft gekruisigd) crucify

de **kruisiging** /krœysəɣɪŋ/ (pl: -en) crucifixion

de **kruising** /krœysɪŋ/ (pl: -en) **1** crossing, junction, intersection; crossroads **2** crossing, hybridization; cross-fertilization **3** cross, hybrid; cross-breed

het **kruisje** /krœyʃə/ (pl: -s) **1** cross; mark **2** sign of the cross

de **kruiskopschroevendraaier** /krœyskɔpsxruvə(n)drajər/ (pl: -s) Phillips screwdriver

het **kruispunt** /krœyspʏnt/ (pl: -en) crossing, junction, intersection; crossroad(s): [fig] *op een ~ staan* stand at the crossroads

de **kruisraket** /krœysrakɛt/ (pl: -ten) cruise missile

de **kruisridder** /krœysrɪdər/ (pl: -s) crusader

de **kruissnelheid** /krœysnɛlhɛɪt/ cruising speed

de **kruisspin** /krœyspɪn/ (pl: -nen) diadem spider

de **kruissteek** /krœystek/ (pl: -steken) cross-stitch

het **kruisteken** /krœystekə(n)/ (pl: -s) (sign of the) cross

de **kruistocht** /krœystɔxt/ (pl: -en) crusade

de **kruisvaarder** /krœysfardər/ (pl: -s) crusader

het **kruisverhoor** /krœysfərhor/ (pl: -verhoren) cross-examination: *iem. aan een ~ onderwerpen* cross-examine s.o.

de **kruiswoordpuzzel** /krœyswortpʏzəl/ (pl: -s) crossword (puzzle)

het **kruit** /krœyt/ (gun)powder

de **kruitdamp** /krœydɑmp/ (pl: -en) gunsmoke: [fig] *toen de ~ was opgetrokken* when the smoke (of battle) had cleared

het **kruitvat** /krœytfɑt/ (pl: -en) powder keg

de **kruiwagen** /krœywaɣə(n)/ (pl: -s) **1** (wheel)barrow **2** [fig] connections: *~s gebruiken* pull strings

de **kruk** /krʏk/ **1** stool **2** crutch **3** (door) handle

de **krukas** /krʏkɑs/ (pl: -sen) crankshaft

de **krul** /krʏl/ (pl: -len) curl; ringlet

krullen /krʏlə(n)/ (krulde, heeft gekruld) curl

de **krullenbol** /krʏlə(n)bɔl/ (pl: -len) curly (head)

de **krulspeld** /krʏlspɛlt/ (pl: -en) curler, roller

de **krultang** /krʏltɑŋ/ (pl: -en) curling iron

het **kso** /kɑɛso/ [Belg] *kunstsecundair onderwijs* secondary fine arts education

kubiek /kybik/ (adj) cubic

de **kubus** /kybʏs/ (pl: -sen) cube

kuchen /kʏxə(n)/ (kuchte, heeft gekucht) cough

de **kudde** /kʏdə/ (pl: -s) herd; flock

het **kuddedier** /kʏdədir/ (pl: -en) **1** herd animal **2** one of the herd (*or:* mob)

kuieren /kœyərə(n)/ (kuierde, heeft/is gekuierd) stroll, go for a walk

de **kuif** /kœyf/ (pl: kuiven) **1** forelock; quiff **2** (head of) hair **3** crest, tuft

het **kuiken** /kœykə(n)/ (pl: -s) chick(en)

de **kuil** /kœyl/ (pl: -en) pit, hole; hollow; pothole

het **kuiltje** /kœylcə/ (pl: -s) dimple; cleft

de **kuip** /kœyp/ (pl: -en) tub; barrel

het **kuipje** /kœypjə/ (pl: -s) tub

de ¹**kuis** /kœys/ (pl: kuizen) [Belg] (house)cleaning: *grote ~* spring-cleaning

²**kuis** /kœys/ (adj, adv) chaste, pure

kuisen /kœysə(n)/ (kuiste, heeft gekuist) [Belg] clean

de **kuisheid** /kœyshɛit/ chastity, purity

de **kuisheidsgordel** /kœyshɛitsxordəl/ (pl: -s) chastity belt

de **kuisvrouw** /kœysfrɑu/ (pl: -en) [Belg] cleaning lady (*or:* woman)

de **kuit** /kœyt/ (pl: -en) **1** [anatomy] calf **2** spawn

het **kuitbeen** /kœydben/ (pl: -benen) fibula

kukeleku /kykələky/ (int) cock-a-doodle-doo

kukelen /kykələ(n)/ (kukelde, is gekukeld) go flying, tumble

de **kul** /kʏl/ (pl: -len) [inform] rubbish

de **kummel** /kʏməl/ cum(m)in; caraway (seed)

de **kumquat** /kumkwɑt/ (pl: -s) cumquat

de **kunde** /kʏndə/ knowledge, learning

kundig /kʏndəx/ (adj, adv) able, capable, skilful: *iets ~ repareren* repair sth. skilfully

de **kunne** /kʏnə/ sex: *van beiderlei ~* of both sexes

¹**kunnen** /kʏnə(n)/ (kon, heeft gekund) may, might, could, it is possible that …: *het kan een vergissing zijn* it may be a mistake

²**kunnen** /kʏnə(n)/ (kon, heeft gekund) be acceptable: *zo kan het niet langer* it (*or:* things) can't go on like this; *die trui kán gewoon niet* that sweater's just impossible

³**kunnen** /kʏnə(n)/ (kon, heeft gekund) can, could, be able to; be possible: *hij kan goed zingen* he's a good singer; *een handige man kan alles* a handy man can do anything; *hij liep wat hij kon* he ran as fast as he could; *hij kan niet meer* he can't go on; *buiten iets ~ do* without sth.; *het deksel kan er niet af* the lid won't come off; *morgen kan ik niet* tomorrow's impossible for me

⁴**kunnen** /kʏnə(n)/ (aux vb, kon, heeft gekund) can, be allowed to; may; could; be allowed to, might: *zoiets kun je niet doen* you can't do that sort of thing; *je had het me wel ~ vertellen* you might (*or:* could) have told me; *de gevangene kon ontsnappen* the prisoner was able to (*or:* managed to) escape

kuub

de **kunst** /kʏnst/ (pl: -en) **1** art: *een handelaar in* ~ an art dealer **2** art, skill: *zwarte* ~ black magic; *dat is uit de* ~ that's amazing! **3** trick

de **kunstacademie** /kʏnstakademi/ (pl: -s) art academy

het **kunstbeen** /kʏnstben/ (pl: -benen) artificial leg

de **kunstbloem** /kʏnstblum/ (pl: -en) artificial flower

de **kunstcriticus** /kʏnstkritikʏs/ (pl: -critici) art critic

de **kunstenaar** /kʏnstənar/ (pl: -s) artist

het **kunst- en vliegwerk** /kʏnstɛnvliːxwɛrk/: *met veel* ~ by pulling out all the stops

de **kunstgalerij** /kʏns(t)xalərɛi/ (pl: -en) (art) gallery

het **kunstgebit** /kʏnstxəbɪt/ (pl: -ten) (set of) false teeth, (set of) dentures; (dental) plate

de **kunstgeschiedenis** /kʏnstxəsxidənɪs/ (pl: -sen) history of art; [subject] art history

het **kunstgras** /kʏnstxras/ (pl: -sen) artificial grass (*or:* turf)

de **kunstgreep** /kʏnstxrep/ (pl: -grepen) trick, manoeuvre

de **kunsthandelaar** /kʏnsthandəlar/ (pl: -s, -handelaren) art dealer

het/de **kunsthars** /kʏnsthars/ synthetic resin; phenolic resin

de **kunstheup** /kʏnsthøp/ (pl: -en) artificial hip

kunstig /kʏnstəx/ (adj, adv) ingenious, skilful

het **kunstijs** /kʏnstɛis/ artificial ice, man-made ice; (ice) rink

de **kunstijsbaan** /kʏnstɛizban/ (pl: -banen) ice rink, skating rink

het **kunstje** /kʏnʃə/ (pl: -s) **1** knack, trick: *dat is een koud* ~ that's child's play, there's nothing to it **2** trick: *geen* ~*s!* none of your tricks!

het **kunstleer** /kʏnstler/ imitation leather

het **kunstlicht** /kʏnstlɪxt/ artificial light

de **kunstliefhebber** /kʏnstlifhɛbər/ art lover

de **kunstmaan** /kʏnstman/ (pl: -manen) satellite

kunstmatig /kʏnstmatəx/ (adj, adv) artificial; synthetic; man-made; imitation

de **kunstmest** /kʏnstmɛst/ fertilizer

kunstrijden /kʏnstrɛidə(n)/ figure-skate

het **kunstschaatsen** /kʏn(st)sxatsə(n)/ figure-skating

de **kunstschat** /kʏn(st)sxɑt/ (pl: -ten) art treasure

de **kunstschilder** /kʏnstsxɪldər/ (pl: -s) artist, painter

de **kunststof** /kʏnstɔf/ (pl: -fen) synthetic (material, fibre), plastic: *van* ~ synthetic, plastic

het **kunststuk** /kʏnstʏk/ (pl: -ken) work of art; feat; stunt: *een journalistiek* ~*je* a masterpiece of journalism; *dat is een* ~ *dat ik je niet na zou doen* that's a feat I couldn't match

de **kunstverzameling** /kʏnstfərzaməlɪŋ/ (pl: -en) art collection

de **kunstvezel** /kʏnstfezəl/ (pl: -s) man-made fibre, synthetic fibre

het **kunstvoorwerp** /kʏnstforwɛrp/ (pl: -en) work of art; artefact

de **kunstvorm** /kʏnstfɔrm/ (pl: -en) art form, medium (of art)

het **kunstwerk** /kʏnstwɛrk/ (pl: -en) work of art, masterpiece: *dat is een klein* ~*je* it's a little gem (*or:* masterpiece)

kunstzinnig /kʏnstsɪnəx/ (adj) artistic(ally-minded): ~*e vorming* art(istic) training (*or:* education)

de **kür** /kyr/ (pl: -en) performance (to music)

de [1]**kuren** /kyrə(n)/ (pl) quirks; moods: *hij heeft altijd van die vreemde* ~ he's quirky (*or:* moody); *vol* ~ **a)** moody; **b)** awkward

[2]**kuren** /kyrə(n)/ (kuurde, heeft gekuurd) take a cure

de [1]**kurk** /kʏrk/ cork: *doe de* ~ *goed op de fles* cork the bottle properly

het/de [2]**kurk** /kʏrk/ cork: *wij hebben* ~ *in de gang* we've got cork flooring in the hall

kurkdroog /kʏrgdroːx/ (adj) (as) dry as a bone, bone-dry

de **kurkentrekker** /kʏrkə(n)trɛkər/ (pl: -s) corkscrew

de **kurkuma** /kʏrkuma/ turmeric

de **kus** /kʏs/ (pl: -sen) kiss: *geef me eens een* ~ give me a kiss; how about a kiss?; *een* ~ *krijgen van iem.* get a kiss from (*or:* be kissed by) s.o.; *iem. een* ~ *toewerpen* blow s.o. a kiss; ~*jes!* (lots of) love (and kisses)

het **kushandje** /kʏshɑncə/ (pl: -s) a blown kiss: ~*s geven* blow kisses (to s.o.)

het [1]**kussen** /kʏsə(n)/ (pl: -s) cushion; pillow; pad: *de* ~*s (op)schudden* plump up the pillows

[2]**kussen** /kʏsə(n)/ (kuste, heeft gekust) kiss: *iem. gedag (vaarwel)* ~ kiss s.o. goodbye; *elkaar* ~ kiss (each other)

het/de **kussensloop** /kʏsə(n)slop/ (pl: -slopen) pillowcase, pillowslip

de **kust** /kʏst/ (pl: -en) **1** coast, (sea)shore: *de* ~ *is veilig* the coast is clear; *een huisje aan de* ~ a cottage by the sea; *onder (voor) de* ~ off the coast, offshore; inshore; *vijftig kilometer uit de* ~ fifty kilometres offshore (*or:* off the coast) **2** seaside

het **kustgebied** /kʏstxəbit/ (pl: -en) coastal area (*or:* region)

de **kustlijn** /kʏstlɛin/ (pl: -en) coastline, shoreline

de **kustplaats** /kʏstplats/ (pl: -en) seaside town, coastal town

de **kuststreek** /kʏ(st)strek/ coastal region

de **kuststrook** /kʏ(st)strok/ coastal strip

de **kustvaarder** /kʏstfardər/ (pl: -s) coaster

de **kustwacht** /kʏstwɑxt/ coast guard (service)

de **kut** /kʏt/ (pl: -ten) [inform] cunt

de **kuub** /kyp/ cubic metre: *te koop voor een tientje de* ~ on sale for ten euros a cubic metre de **kuur** /kyr/ (pl: kuren) cure, course of treatment

het **kuuroord** /kyrort/ (pl: -en) health resort; spa

het **¹kwaad** /kwat/ (pl: kwaden) **1** wrong, harm: *een noodzakelijk ~* a necessary evil; *van ~ tot erger vervallen* go from bad to worse **2** harm, damage: *meer ~ dan goed* **doen** do more harm than good; *dat kan* **geen** *~* it can't do any harm

²kwaad /kwat/ (adj) bad; vicious: *~* **bloed** *zetten* breed (or: create) bad blood; *hij is* **de** *~ste niet* he's not a bad guy

³kwaad /kwat/ (adj, adv) **1** bad, wrong: *het te ~ krijgen* be overcome (by); break down **2** bad; evil: *ze* **bedoelde** *er niets ~s mee* she meant no harm (or: offence) **3** angry: *zich ~ maken, ~ worden* get angry; *iem. ~* **maken** make s.o. angry; *~ zijn* **op** *iem.* be angry at (or: with) s.o.; *~ zijn* **om** *iets* be angry at (or: about) sth.

kwaadaardig /kwatardəx/ (adj, adv) **1** malicious; vicious **2** pernicious; malignant

kwaaddenkend /kwadɛŋkənt/ (adj) suspicious

de **kwaadheid** /kwathɛit/ anger: *rood worden van ~* turn red with anger (or: fury)

kwaadschiks /kwatsxɪks/ (adv) unwillingly

kwaadspreken /kwatsprekə(n)/ (sprak kwaad, heeft kwaadgesproken) speak ill (or: badly): *~ van (iem.)* speak ill (or: badly) of (s.o.); slander (s.o.)

kwaadwillig /kwatwɪləx/ (adj) malevolent

de **kwaal** /kwal/ (pl: kwalen) **1** complaint, disease, illness: *een* **hartkwaal** a heart condition **2** trouble, problem

de **kwab** /kwap/ (pl: -ben) (roll of) fat (or: flab), jowl

het **kwadraat** /kwadrat/ (pl: kwadraten) square: *drie ~* three squared

kwadratisch /kwadratis/ (adj) quadratic

de **kwajongen** /kwajɔŋə(n)/ (pl: -s) **1** mischievous boy, naughty boy, brat **2** rascal

kwajongensachtig /kwajɔŋənsɑxtəx/ (adj, adv) boyish, mischievous

de **kwajongensstreek** /kwajɔŋə(n)strek/ (pl: -streken) (boyish) prank, practical joke: *een ~* **uithalen** play a practical joke

de **kwak** /kwak/ (pl: -ken) **1** dab; blob; dollop: *een ~* **eten** a dollop of food **2** thud, thump, smack

kwaken /kwakə(n)/ (kwaakte, heeft gekwaakt) quack; croak

de **kwakkel** /kwɑkəl/ (pl: -s) [Belg] canard, unfounded rumour (or: story)

kwakkelen /kwɑkələ(n)/ (kwakkelde, heeft gekwakkeld) drag on; linger; be fitful

het **kwakkelweer** /kwɑkəlwer/ unsteady weather, changeable weather

¹kwakken /kwɑkə(n)/ (kwakte, is gekwakt) bump, crash, fall with a thud: *hij kwakte te-*

gen de grond he landed with a thud on the floor

²kwakken /kwɑkə(n)/ (kwakte, heeft gekwakt) dump, chuck; dab: *zij kwakte haar tas* **op** *het bureau* she smacked her bag down on the desk

de **kwakzalver** /kwɑksɑlvər/ (pl: -s) quack (doctor)

de **kwakzalverij** /kwaksɑlvərɛi/ quackery

de **kwal** /kwal/ (pl: -len) **1** jellyfish **2** jerk

de **kwalificatie** /kwalifika(t)si/ (pl: -s) qualification(s)

de **kwalificatiewedstrijd** /kwalifika(t)siwɛtstrɛit/ (pl: -en) qualifying match

¹kwalificeren /kwalifiserə(n)/ (kwalificeerde, heeft gekwalificeerd) **1** call, describe as **2** qualify

zich **²kwalificeren** /kwalifiserə(n)/ (kwalificeerde zich, heeft zich gekwalificeerd) qualify (for)

kwalijk /kwalək/ (adj, adv) evil, vile, nasty; [adverb] vilely; nastily, badly: *de ~e* **gevolgen** *van het roken* the bad (or: detrimental) effects of smoking; *dat is een ~e* **zaak** that is a nasty business ‖ *neem me niet ~, dat ik te laat ben* excuse my being late, excuse me for being late; *neem(t) (u) mij niet ~* I beg your pardon; *je kunt hem dat toch niet ~* **nemen** you can hardly blame him

kwalitatief /kwalitatif/ (adj, adv) qualitative: *~ was het* **verschil** *groot* there was a large difference in quality

de **kwaliteit** /kwalitɛit/ (pl: -en) **1** quality: *~* **leveren** deliver a quality product; *hout van* **slechte** *~* low-quality wood; *van* **slechte** *~ (of)* poor quality **2** characteristic

de **kwaliteitsgarantie** /kwalitɛitsxɑran(t)si/ guarantee, warranty of quality

kwantificeren /kwantifiserə(n)/ (kwantificeerde, heeft gekwantificeerd) quantify

de **kwantiteit** /kwantitɛit/ (pl: -en) quantity, amount

het **kwantum** /kwɑntʏm/ (pl: -s) quantum

de **kwantumkorting** /kwɑntʏmkortɪŋ/ (pl: -en) quantity rebate

de **kwantumtheorie** /kwɑntʏmtejori/ quantum theory

de **kwark** /kwark/ fromage frais, curd cheese

de **kwarktaart** /kwɑrktart/ (pl: -en) [roughly] cheesecake

het **kwart** /kwart/ (pl: -en) quarter: *voor een ~ leeg* a quarter empty; *het is ~* **voor** *(or: over) elf* it is a quarter to (or: past) eleven; it is ten forty-five (or: eleven fifteen)

het **kwartaal** /kwartal/ (pl: kwartalen) quarter, trimester; [educ] term: *(eenmaal) per ~* quarterly

de **kwartaalcijfers** /kwartalsɛifərs/ (pl) quarterly balance

de **kwartel** /kwɑrtəl/ (pl: -s) quail: *zo doof* **als** *een ~* as deaf as a post het **kwartet** /kwɑrtɛt/ (pl: -ten) quartet: *een ~ voor strijkers* a string quartet

het **kwartetspel** /kwɑrtɛtspɛl/ (pl: -en) happy families; [Am] old maid
kwartetten /kwɑrtɛtə(n)/ (kwartette, heeft gekwartet) play happy families; [Am] play old maid

de **kwartfinale** /kwɑrtfinalə/ (pl: -s) quarter-finals: *de ~(s) halen* make the quarter-finals

de **kwartfinalist** /kwɑrtfinalɪst/ quarter-finalist

het **kwartier** /kwɑrtir/ (pl: -en) quarter (of an hour): *het duurde een* ~ **a)** it took a quarter of an hour; **b)** it lasted a quarter of an hour; *om het* ~ every quarter (of an hour) of an hour; *drie* ~ three-quarters of an hour

het **kwartje** /kwɑrcə/ (pl: -s) 25-cent piece; [Am] quarter: *het kost twee ~s* it costs fifty cents; *het ~ is gevallen* the penny has dropped, it's finally clicked

de **kwartnoot** /kwɑrtnot/ (pl: -noten) crotchet; [Am] quarter note

het **kwarts** /kwɑrts/ quartz

de **kwartslag** /kwɑrtslɑχ/ (pl: -en) quarter (of a) turn

de **kwast** /kwɑst/ (pl: -en) **1** brush **2** tassel; [small] tuft: *met ~en (versierd)* tasselled **3** (lemon) squash, lemonade

de **kwatong** /kwɑtɔŋ/ (pl: -en) [Belg] scandalmonger: *~en beweren …* it is rumoured that …

het **kwatrijn** /kwɑtrɛin/ (pl: -en) quatrain

de **kwebbel** /kwɛbəl/ chatterbox ‖ *houd je ~ dicht* shut your trap
kwebbelen /kwɛbələ(n)/ (kwebbelde, heeft gekwebbeld) chatter

de **kweek** /kwek/ **1** cultivation; culture; growing **2** culture, growth: *eigen ~* homegrown (players)

de **kweekplaats** /kwekplats/ (pl: -en) **1** nursery; [fig also] breeding ground **2** [fig] hotbed

de **kweekvijver** /kwekfɛivər/ (pl: -s) fish-breeding pond; [fig] breeding ground
kweken /kwekə(n)/ (kweekte, heeft gekweekt) **1** grow, cultivate: *gekweekte planten* cultivated plants; *zelf gekweekte tomaten* home-grown tomatoes **2** raise, breed: *oesters ~* breed oysters **3** [fig] breed, foster: *goodwill ~* foster goodwill

de **kweker** /kwekər/ (pl: -s) grower; (market) gardener; nurseryman

de **kwekerij** /kwekərɛi/ (pl: -en) nursery; market garden
kwekken /kwɛkə(n)/ (kwekte, heeft gekwekt) chatter, jabber

de **kwelgeest** /kwɛlɣest/ (pl: -en) tormentor, teaser, pest
kwellen /kwɛlə(n)/ (kwelde, heeft gekweld) **1** hurt; [stronger] torment; torture **2** torment: *gekweld worden door geldgebrek* be

troubled by lack of money; *een ~de pijn* an excruciating pain **3** trouble, worry: *die gedachte bleef hem* ~ the thought kept troubling him; *gekweld door wroeging* (or: *een obsessie*) haunted by remorse (or: by an obsession)

de **kwelling** /kwɛlɪŋ/ (pl: -en) **1** torture, torment **2** torment, agony: *een brief schrijven is een ware ~ voor hem* writing a letter is sheer torment for him

het **kwelwater** /kwɛlwatər/ seepage (water)

de **kwestie** /kwɛsti/ (pl: -s) question, matter; issue: *een slepende ~* a matter that drags on; *de persoon* (or: *de zaak*) *in ~* the person (or: matter) in question; *een ~ van smaak* a question (or: matter) of taste; *een ~ van vertrouwen* a matter of confidence
kwetsbaar /kwɛtsbar/ (adj) vulnerable: *dit is zijn kwetsbare plek* (or: *zijde*) this is his vulnerable spot (or: side)

de **kwetsbaarheid** /kwɛtsbarhɛit/ vulnerability
kwetsen /kwɛtsə(n)/ (kwetste, heeft gekwetst) injure, wound, hurt, bruise: *iemands gevoelens ~* hurt s.o.'s feelings; *gekwetste trots* wounded pride

de **kwetsuur** /kwɛtsyr/ (pl: kwetsuren) injury
kwetteren /kwɛtərə(n)/ (kwetterde, heeft gekwetterd) twitter

de **kwibus** /kwibʏs/ (pl: -sen) joker: *een rare ~* a weird chap (or: customer)
kwiek /kwik/ (adj, adv) alert, spry

het/de **kwijl** /kwɛil/ slobber
kwijlen /kwɛilə(n)/ (kwijlde, heeft gekwijld) slobber: *om van te ~* mouth-watering
kwijnen /kwɛinə(n)/ (kwijnde, heeft gekwijnd): *een ~d bestaan leiden* linger on
kwijt /kwɛit/ (adj) **1** lost: *ik ben mijn sleutels ~* I have lost my keys; *zijn verstand ~ zijn* have lost one's mind **2** rid (of): *ik ben mijn kiespijn ~* my toothache is gone (or: over); *hij is al die zorgen ~* he is rid of all those troubles; *die zijn we gelukkig ~* we are well rid of him, good riddance to him **3** deprived (of): *ik ben zijn naam ~* I've forgotten his name; [fig] *nu ben ik het ~* it has slipped my memory; *de weg ~ zijn* be lost, have lost one's way ‖ *ik kan mijn auto nergens ~* I can't park my car anywhere

zich **kwijten** /kwɛitə(n)/ (kweet zich, heeft zich gekweten): *zich van zijn taak ~* acquit o.s. of one's task
kwijtraken /kwɛitrakə(n)/ (raakte kwijt, is kwijtgeraakt) **1** lose: *zijn evenwicht ~* [also fig] lose one's balance (or: composure); *de weg ~* lose one's way **2** dispose of, sell: *die zul je makkelijk ~* you will easily dispose (or: get rid) of those
kwijtschelden /kwɛitsχɛldə(n)/ (schold kwijt, heeft kwijtgescholden) forgive, let off: *hij heeft mij de rest kwijtgescholden* he has let me off the rest; *van zijn straf is (hem) 2 jaar*

kwijtgescholden he had 2 years of his punishment remitted; *iem. een* **straf** ~ let s.o. off a punishment

het **kwik** /kwɪk/ mercury: *het* ~ **stijgt** (or: **daalt**) the thermometer is rising (*or:* falling)

de **kwikstaart** /kwɪkstart/ (pl: -en) wagtail

het **kwikzilver** /kwɪksɪlvər/ mercury

de **kwinkslag** /kwɪŋkslɑχ/ (pl: -en) witticism

het **kwintet** /kwɪntɛt/ (pl: -ten) quintet

kwispelen /kwɪspələ(n)/ (kwispelde, heeft gekwispeld) wag: *met de staart* ~ wag one's tail

kwistig /kwɪstəχ/ (adj, adv) lavish

de **kwitantie** /kwitɑnsi/ (pl: -s) receipt ‖ *een* ~ *innen* collect payment

l

l /ɛl/ (pl: l's) l, L
de **¹la** /la/ (pl: la's) [mus] la
de **²la** /la/ (pl: la's) drawer; till: *de la uittrekken* (or: *dichtschuiven*) open (or: shut) a drawer
de **laadbak** /lɑdbɑk/ (pl: -ken) (loading) platform
het **laadruim** /lɑtrœym/ (pl: -en) cargo hold; cargo compartment, freight compartment
het **laadvermogen** /lɑtfərmoɣə(n)/ carrying capacity
de **¹laag** /laχ/ (pl: lagen) **1** layer; coating; film; sheet; coat **2** stratum: *in brede lagen van de bevolking* in large sections of the population ‖ *de volle ~ krijgen* get the full blast (of s.o.'s disapproval)
²laag /laχ/ (adj, adv) **1** low: *een ~ bedrag* a small amount; *het gas ~ draaien* turn the gas down; *de barometer stond ~* the barometer was low **2** low, mean
laag-bij-de-gronds /laɣbɛidəɣrɔnts/ (adj, adv) commonplace: *~e opmerkingen* crude remarks
de **laagbouw** /laɣbɑu/ low-rise building
laagdrempelig /laɣdrɛmpələɣ/ (adj) **1** approachable, get-at-able, (easily) accessible **2** accessible
laaghartig /laχhɑrtəɣ/ (adj, adv) mean, low
het **laagseizoen** /laχsɛizun/ (pl: -en) low season, off season
de **laagte** /laχtə/ (pl: -n, -s) depression; hollow
de **laagvlakte** /laχflɑktə/ (pl: -n, -s) lowland plain, lowland(s)
laagvliegen /laχfliɣə(n)/ fly low, hedge-hop
het **laagwater** /laχwatər/ low tide
laaien /lajə(n)/ (laaide, heeft gelaaid) blaze
laaiend /lajənt/ (adj, adv) **1** wild: *~ enthousiast zijn over iets* be wildly enthusiastic about sth. **2** furious
laakbaar /lɑgbar/ (adj, adv) reprehensible
de **laan** /lan/ (pl: lanen) avenue: *iem. de ~ uitsturen* sack s.o., fire s.o.; send s.o. packing
de **laars** /lars/ (pl: laarzen) boot
laat /lat/ (adj, adv) late: *van de vroege morgen tot de late avond* from early in the morning till late at night; *een wat late reactie* a rather belated reaction; *is het nog ~ geworden gisteravond?* did the people stay late last night?; *~ opblijven* stay up late; *gisteravond ~* late last night; *hoe ~ is het?* what's the time?, what time is it?; *'s avonds ~ komen* late at night; *te ~ komen (op school, op kantoor, op je werk)* be late (for school, at the office, for work); *een*

dag te ~ a day late (or: overdue); *~ in de middag* (or: *het voorjaar*) in the late afternoon (or: spring); *beter ~ dan nooit* better late than never
de **laatbloeier** /lɑdblujər/ (pl: -s) late-bloomer
laatdunkend /lɑdʏŋkənt/ (adj, adv) conceited, condescending: *zich ~ uitlaten over iem.* be condescending about s.o.
de **laatkomer** /lɑtkomər/ (pl: -s) latecomer
¹laatst /latst/ (adj) **1** last: *dat zou het ~e zijn wat ik zou doen* that is the last thing I would do **2** latest, last: *in de ~e jaren* in the last few years, in recent years; *de ~e tijd* recently, lately **3** final, last: *voor de ~e keer optreden* make one's last (or: final) appearance **4** latter: *in de ~e helft van juli* in the latter (or: second) half of July; *ik heb voorkeur voor de ~e* I prefer the latter
²laatst /latst/ (adv) **1** recently, lately: *ik ben ~ nog bij hem geweest* I visited him recently **2** last: *morgen op ~ zijn* ~ tomorrow at the latest; *op het ~ waren ze allemaal dronken* they all ended up drunk; *voor het ~* for the last time; *toen zag hij haar voor het ~* that was the last time he saw her
de **laatstgenoemde** /lɑtstχənumdə/ last (named, mentioned); latter
laattijdig /latɛidəχ/ (adj, adv) [Belg] tardy, tardily
het **lab** /lɑp/ (pl: -s) lab
het/de **label** /lebəl/ (pl: -s) label; sticker; address tag
labelen /lebələ(n)/ (labelde, heeft gelabeld) label
het **labeur** /labør/ [Belg] labour, chore
labeuren /labørə(n)/ [Belg] slave away, toil
labiel /labil/ (adj) unstable
het **labo** /labo/ (pl: -'s) [Belg] lab
de **laborant** /laborɑnt/ (pl: -en) laboratory assistant (or: technician)
het **laboratorium** /laboratorijʏm/ (pl: laboratoria) lab(oratory)
de **labrador** /lɑbradɔr/ labrador
het **labyrint** /labirɪnt/ (pl: -en) labyrinth
de **lach** /lɑχ/ laugh, (burst of) laughter: *de slappe ~ hebben* have the giggles; *in de ~ schieten* burst out laughing; [Am also] crack up
de **lachbui** /lɑχbœy/ (pl: -en) fit of laughter
lachen /lɑχə(n)/ (lachte, heeft gelachen) **1** laugh; smile: *hij kon zijn ~ niet houden* he couldn't help laughing; *laat me niet ~* don't make me laugh; *er is (valt) niets te ~* this is no laughing matter; *om* (or: *over*) *iets ~* laugh about (or: at); *tegen iem. ~* laugh at s.o.; *wie het laatst lacht, lacht het best* he who laughs last laughs longest **2** (+ om) laugh at: *daar kun je nu wel om ~, maar …* it's all very well to laugh, but …
lachend /lɑχənt/ (adj) laughing, smiling
de **lacher** /lɑχər/ (pl: -s) laugher
lacherig /lɑχərəχ/ (adj) giggly
het **lachertje** /lɑχərcə/ (pl: -s) laugh, joke

de **lachfilm** /lɑxfɪlm/ (pl: -s) comedy

het **lachgas** /lɑxɑs/ laughing gas

het **lachsalvo** /lɑxsɑlvo/ (pl: -'s) burst of laughter

de **lachspiegel** /lɑxspiɣəl/ (pl: -s) carnival mirror

de **lachspier** /lɑxspir/ (pl: -en): *op de ~en werken* get s.o. laughing

lachwekkend /lɑxwɛkənt/ (adj) laughable; ridiculous

laconiek /lakonik/ (adj, adv) laconic

de **lacune** /lakynə/ (pl: -s) gap

de **ladder** /lɑdər/ (pl: -s) ladder, scale || *een ~ in je kous* a run (or: ladder) in your stocking

de **ladderwagen** /lɑdərwaɣə(n)/ (pl: -s) ladder truck

ladderzat /lɑdərzɑt/ (adj) smashed, blind drunk

de **lade** /lɑdə/ (pl: -n, -s) drawer; till

de **ladekast** /lɑdəkɑst/ (pl: -en) chest (of drawers); filing cabinet

laden /lɑdə(n)/ (laadde, heeft geladen) **1** load: *koffers uit de auto ~* unload the bags from the car **2** charge: *een geladen atmosfeer* a charged atmosphere

de **lading** /lɑdɪŋ/ (pl: -en) **1** cargo; [ship] load: *te zware ~* overload **2** charge

de **ladyshave** /lɛdiʃef/ (pl: -s) ladyshave, women's shaver

laf /lɑf/ (adj, adv) cowardly

de **lafaard** /lɑfart/ (pl: -s) coward

lafhartig /lɑfhɑrtəx/ (adj, adv) *see laf*

de **lafheid** /lɑfhɛit/ (pl: -heden) cowardice

het **lagedrukgebied** /laɣədrʏkxəbit/ (pl: -en) low-pressure area

het **lagelonenland** /laɣəlonə(n)lɑnt/ low-wage country

het **lager** /laɣər/ (pl: -s) bearing

het **Lagerhuis** /laɣərhœys/ Lower House; [Great Britain and Canada] House of Commons

de **lagerwal** /laɣərwɑl/ lee shore: *aan ~ geraken* come down in the world, go to seed

de **lagune** /laɣynə/ (pl: -s) lagoon

het/de **lak** /lɑk/ (pl: -ken) lacquer, varnish; polish: *de ~ is beschadigd* the paintwork is damaged || *daar heb ik ~ aan* I couldn't care less

de **lakei** /lakɛi/ (pl: -en) lackey

het **laken** /lɑkə(n)/ (pl: -s) **1** sheet; tablecloth: *~s uitdelen* rule the roost, run the show **2** cloth, worsted: *het ~ van een biljart* the cloth of a billiard table || *van hetzelfde ~ een pak krijgen*, [Belg] *van hetzelfde laken een broek krijgen* have a taste of one's own medicine

lakken /lɑkə(n)/ (lakte, heeft gelakt) **1** lacquer, varnish; polish **2** paint, enamel

de **lakmoesproef** /lɑkmuspruf/ (pl: -proeven) [also fig] litmus test

laks /lɑks/ (adj, adv) lax

het **lakwerk** /lɑkwɛrk/ paint(work)

lallen /lɑlə(n)/ (lalde, heeft gelald) slur one's words

het **¹lam** /lɑm/ (pl: lammeren) lamb

²lam /lɑm/ (adj, adv) **1** paralysed; [fig also] out of action **2** numb

de **lama** /lɑma/ (pl: -'s) llama

de **lambrisering** /lɑmbrizerɪŋ/ (pl: -en) wainscot(t)ing, panelling

de **lamel** /lamɛl/ (pl: -len) plate, (laminated) layer; strip

het **laminaat** /laminat/ (pl: laminaten) laminate

lamleggen /lɑmlɛɣə(n)/ (lei lam, heeft lamgelegd) paralyse: *het verkeer ~* bring the traffic to a standstill

lamlendig /lɑmlɛndəx/ (adj, adv) shiftless

de **lamp** /lɑmp/ (pl: -en) lamp, light; bulb: *er gaat een ~je bij mij branden* that rings a bell; *tegen de ~ lopen* get caught

de **lampion** /lɑmpijɔn/ (pl: -s, -nen) Chinese lantern

het **lamsvlees** /lɑmsfles/ lamb

het **lamswol** /lɑmswɔl/ lambswool

de **lanceerbasis** /lɑnseːrbazɪs/ (pl: -bases) launch site, launch pad

het **lanceerplatform** /lɑnseːrplɑtfɔrm/ (pl: -s) launching site

lanceren /lɑnseːrə(n)/ (lanceerde, heeft gelanceerd) launch; blast, lift off: *een bericht* (or: *een gerucht*) *~* spread a report (or: a rumour)

de **lancering** /lɑnseːrɪŋ/ (pl: -en) launch(ing); blast-off, lift-off

het **lancet** /lɑnsɛt/ (pl: -ten) lancet

het **land** /lɑnt/ (pl: -en) **1** land: *aan ~ gaan* go ashore; *te ~ en ter zee* on land and sea; *~ in zicht!* land ho! **2** country: *~ van herkomst* country of origin; *in ons ~* in this country; *de Lage Landen* the Low Countries || *er is met hem geen ~ te bezeilen* you won't get anywhere with him, you're wasting your time with him

de **landarbeider** /lɑntɑrbɛidər/ (pl: -s) farm worker, agricultural worker

de **landbouw** /lɑndbɑu/ farming: *~ en veeteelt* a) arable farming and stockbreeding; b) arable and dairy farming

het **landbouwbedrijf** /lɑndbɑubədrɛif/ (pl: -bedrijven) farm

het **landbouwbeleid** /lɑndbɑubəlɛit/ agricultural policy

de **landbouwer** /lɑndbɑuwər/ (pl: -s) farmer

de **landbouwgrond** /lɑndbɑuɣrɔnt/ (pl: -en) agricultural land, farming land, farmland

landbouwkundig /lɑndbɑukʏndəx/ (adj) agricultural

de **landbouwmachine** /lɑndbɑumaʃinə/ (pl: -s) agricultural machine, farming machine

de **landbouwuniversiteit** /lɑndbɑuwynivɛrzitɛit/ (pl: -universiteiten) agricultural university; [as a name] University of Agriculture

de **landeigenaar** /lɑntɛiɣənar/ (pl: -s, -eigenaren) landowner

landelijk /lɑndələk/ (adj, adv) **1** national

2 rural, country
landen /lɑndə(n)/ (landde, is geland) land: ~ *op Zaventem* land at Zaventem
de **landengte** /lɑntɛŋtə/ (pl: -n, -s) isthmus, neck of land
de **landenwedstrijd** /lɑndə(n)wɛtstrɛit/ (pl: -en) international match (*or:* contest)
landerig /lɑndərəχ/ (adj) down in the dumps, listless
de **landerijen** /lɑndərɛiə(n)/ (pl) (farm)land(s)
de **landgenoot** /lɑntχənot/ (pl: -genoten) (fellow) countryman
het **landgoed** /lɑntχut/ (pl: -eren) country estate
het **landhuis** /lɑnthœys/ (pl: -huizen) country house
de **landing** /lɑndɪŋ/ (pl: -en) landing: *een zachte* ~ a smooth landing
de **landingsbaan** /lɑndɪŋzban/ (pl: -banen) runway
het **landingsgestel** /lɑndɪŋsχəstɛl/ (pl: -len) landing gear, undercart
de **landingstroepen** /lɑndɪŋstrupə(n)/ (pl) landing force(s)
het **landingsvaartuig** /lɑndɪŋsfartœyχ/ (pl: -en) landing craft
landinwaarts /lɑntɪnwarts/ (adv) inland
de **landkaart** /lɑntkart/ (pl: -en) map
het **landklimaat** /lɑntklimat/ continental climate
de **landloper** /lɑntlopər/ (pl: -s) tramp, vagrant
de **landmacht** /lɑntmɑχt/ army, land forces
het **landmark** /lɛntmaːrk/ landmark
de **landmeter** /lɑntmetər/ (pl: -s) (land) surveyor
de **landmijn** /lɑntmɛin/ (pl: -en) landmine
het **landnummer** /lɑntnʏmər/ (pl: -s) international (dialling) code
de **landrot** /lɑntrɔt/ (pl: -ten) landlubber
het **landsbelang** /lɑn(t)sbəlɑŋ/ (pl: -en) national interest
het **landschap** /lɑntsχɑp/ (pl: -pen) landscape
de **landsgrens** /lɑn(t)sχrɛns/ (pl: -grenzen) border
de **landskampioen** /lɑn(t)skɑmpijun/ (pl: -en) national champion
de **landstreek** /lɑntstrek/ (pl: -streken) region, district
de **landsverdediging** /lɑntsfərdedəɣɪŋ/ [Belg] defence
de **landtong** /lɑntɔŋ/ (pl: -en) spit of land, headland
het **landverraad** /lɑntfərat/ (high) treason
de **landverrader** /lɑntfəradər/ (pl: -s) traitor (to one's country)
de **landweg** /lɑntwɛχ/ (pl: -en) country road lane; (country) track
de **landwijn** /lɑntwɛin/ (pl: -en) local wine
de **landwind** /lɑntwɪnt/ land wind
de **landwinning** /lɑntwɪnɪŋ/ (pl: -en) land reclamation

¹**lang** /lɑŋ/ (adj) long; tall: *de kamer is zes meter* ~ the room is six metres long; *een ~e vent* a tall guy
²**lang** /lɑŋ/ (adv) **1** long, (for) a long time: *ik blijf geen dag ~er* I won't stay another day, I won't stay a day longer; ~ *duren* take a long time, last long (*or:* a long time); *ze leefden ~ en gelukkig* they lived happily ever after; ~ *zal hij leven!* for he's a jolly good fellow!; ~ *meegaan* last (a long time); ~ *opblijven* stay up late; *ze kan niet ~er wachten* she can't wait any longer (*or:* more) **2** far (from), (not) nearly: *dat smaakt ~ niet slecht* it doesn't taste at all bad; *hij is nog ~ niet zover* he hasn't got nearly as far as that; *wij zijn er nog ~ niet* we've (still got) a long way to go; *bij ~e na niet* far from it
langdradig /lɑŋdradəχ/ (adj, adv) long-winded
langdurig /lɑŋdyrəχ/ (adj, adv) long(-lasting), lengthy; long-standing, long-established
de **langeafstandsraket** /lɑŋəɡfstɑn(t)srakɛt/ (pl: -ten) long-range missile
de **langeafstandsvlucht** /lɑŋəɡfstɑn(t)sflʏχt/ (pl: -en) long-distance flight
het **langetermijngeheugen** long-term memory
langgerekt /lɑŋɣərɛkt/ (adj) long-drawn-out, elongated
langlaufen /lɑŋlaufə(n)/ (langlaufte, heeft/ is gelanglauft) ski cross-country
langlopend /lɑŋlopənt/ (adj) long-term
de **langoustine** /lɑŋgustinə/ (pl: -s) langoustine
¹**langs** /lɑŋs/ (adv) **1** along: *in een boot de kust ~ varen* sail along the coast, skirt the coast **2** round, in, by: *ik kom nog weleens* ~ I'll drop in (*or:* round, by) sometime **3** past: *hij kwam net* ~ he just came past ‖ *ervan* ~ *krijgen* catch it
²**langs** /lɑŋs/ (prep) **1** along: ~ *de rivier wandelen* go for a walk along the river **2** via, by (way, means of): ~ *de regenpijp naar omlaag* down the drainpipe; *hier* (*or:* *daar*) ~ this (*or:* that) way **3** past: ~ *elkaar heen praten* talk at cross purposes **4** in at: *wil jij even* ~ *de bakker rijden?* could you just drop in at the bakery?
langsgaan /lɑŋsχan/ (ging langs, is langsgegaan) **1** pass (by) **2** call in (at)
langskomen /lɑŋskomə(n)/ (kwam langs, is langsgekomen) **1** come past, come by, pass by **2** come round (*or:* over), drop by, drop in
de **langslaper** /lɑŋslapər/ (pl: -s) late riser
de **langspeelplaat** /lɑŋspelplat/ (pl: -platen) long-playing record, LP
langsrijden /lɑŋsrɛidə(n)/ (reed langs, is langsgereden) ride past; drive past
de **langstlevende** /lɑŋstlevəndə/ (pl: -n) survivor
langszij /lɑŋsɛi/ (adv) alongside

languit /lɑŋœɛ̯t/ (adv) (at) full-length, stretched out

langverwacht /lɑŋvərwɑxt/ (adj) long-awaited

langwerpig /lɑŋwɛrpəx̯/ (adj, adv) elongated, long

langzaam /lɑŋzam/ (adj, adv) **1** slow: *een langzame **dood** sterven* die a slow (*or:* lingering) death; *~ aan!* slow down!, (take it) easy!; *het ~ aan doen* take things eas(il)y; *~ maar zeker* slowly but surely **2** gradual, bit by bit, little by little: *~ **werd** hij wat beter* he gradually got a bit better

langzaamaan /lɑŋzaman/ (adv) gradually: *het ~ **doen*** go slow

de **langzaamaanactie** /lɑŋzamanɑksi/ (pl: -s) go-slow

langzamerhand /lɑŋzamərhɑnt/ (adv) gradually, bit by bit, little by little: *ik **krijg** er ~ genoeg van* I'm beginning to get tired of it

lankmoedig /lɑŋkmu̯dəx̯/ (adj, adv) long-suffering

de **lans** /lɑns/ (pl: -en) lance

de **lantaarn** /lɑntarn/ (pl: -s) **1** street lamp, street light **2** lantern; torch; [Am] flashlight

de **lantaarnpaal** /lɑntarmpal/ (pl: -palen) lamp post

lanterfanten /lɑntərfɑntə(n)/ (lanterfantte, heeft gelanterfant) lounge (about), loaf (about); sit about (*or:* around)

Laos /la̯os/ Laos: *Democratische **volksrepubliek*** ~ People's Democratic Republic of Laos

de **Laotiaan** /lao(t)ʃan/ (pl: Laotianen) Laotian

Laotiaans /lao(t)ʃans/ (adj) Laotian

de **lap** /lɑp/ (pl: -pen) piece, length; rag

de **Lap** /lɑp/ (pl: -pen) Lapp

het **lapje** /lɑpjə/ (pl: -s): *iem. **voor** het ~ houden* have s.o. on, pull s.o.'s leg

de **lapjeskat** /lɑpjəskɑt/ (pl: -ten) tabby-and-white cat; [Am] calico cat

Lapland /lɑplɑnt/ Lapland

de **Laplander** /lɑplɑndər/ (pl: -s) Lapp, Laplander

Laplands /lɑplɑn(t)s/ (adj) Lapp(ish)

het **lapmiddel** /lɑpmɪdəl/ (pl: -en) makeshift (measure), stopgap

lappen /lɑpə(n)/ (lapte, heeft gelapt) patch, mend; cobble || *ramen ~* cobble the windows; *dat zou jij **mij** niet moeten ~* don't try that (one) on me; *iem. **erbij** ~* blow the whistle on s.o.

de **lappendeken** /lɑpə(n)dekə(n)/ (pl: -s) patchwork quilt

de **lappenmand** /lɑpəmɑnt/ (pl: -en): *in de ~ zijn* be laid up, be on the sick list

de **laptop** /lɛptɔp/ laptop (computer)

larderen /lɑrde̯rə(n)/ (lardeerde, heeft gelardeerd) lard; [fig] (inter)lard

de **larie** /la̯ri/ rubbish

de **lariekoek** /la̯rikuk/ (stuff and) nonsense, rubbish

de **¹lariks** /lɑrɪks/ (pl: -en) [tree] larch

het **²lariks** /lɑrɪks/ [wood] larch

de **larve** /lɑrvə/ (pl: -n) larva

de **las** /lɑs/ (pl: -sen) weld; joint; [film] splice

het **lasapparaat** /lɑsaparat/ (pl: lasapparaten) welding apparatus, welder; [film] splicer

de **lasbril** /lɑzbrɪl/ (pl: -len) welding goggles

de **laser** /le̯zər/ (pl: -s) laser

de **laserprinter** /le̯zərprɪntər/ (pl: -s) laser printer

de **lasershow** /le̯zərʃo/ laser show

de **laserstraal** /le̯zərstral/ (pl: -stralen) laser beam

het **laserwapen** /le̯zərwapə(n)/ laser weapon

de **lasnaad** /lɑsnat/ (pl: -naden) weld

¹lassen /lɑsə(n)/ (laste, heeft gelast) weld; join; [film] splice

²lassen /lɑsə(n)/ (laste, heeft gelast) put in; [also fig] insert

de **lasser** /lɑsər/ (pl: -s) welder

de **lasso** /lɑso/ (pl: -'s) lasso

de **last** /lɑst/ (pl: -en) **1** load; burden: *hij bezweek haast **onder** de ~* he nearly collapsed under the burden **2** cost(s), expense(s): *sociale ~en* National Insurance contributions; [Am] social security premiums **3** trouble; inconvenience: *iem. **tot** ~ zijn* bother s.o.; *wij hebben veel ~ **van** onze buren* our neighbours are a great nuisance to us **4** charge: *iem. iets **ten** ~e leggen* charge s.o. with sth.

het **lastdier** /lɑsdir/ (pl: -en) beast of burden

de **lastenverlichting** /lɑstə(n)vərlɪxtɪŋ/ (pl: -en) reduction in the tax burden

de **lastenverzwaring** /lɑstə(n)vərzwarɪŋ/ (pl: -en) increase in the tax burden

de **laster** /lɑstər/ slander; libel

de **lastercampagne** /lɑstərkɑmpaɲə/ (pl: -s) smear campaign

lasteren /lɑstərə(n)/ (lasterde, heeft gelasterd) slander; libel

de **lastgeving** /lɑstxevɪŋ/ (pl: -en) order, instruction(s)

lastig /lɑstəx̯/ (adj, adv) difficult: *een ~ **vraagstuk*** a tricky problem

lastigvallen (viel lastig, heeft lastiggevallen) bother, trouble; harass

de **¹last minute** /lɑːstmɪnɪt/ (pl: -s) last-minute holiday (*or:* break)

²last minute /lɑːstmɪnɪt/ (adj) last-minute

de **lastpost** /lɑstpɔst/ (pl: -en) nuisance, pest

de **lat** /lɑt/ (pl: -ten) slat: *de bal kwam **tegen** de ~* the ball hit the crossbar; *zo mager **als** een ~* (as) thin as a rake; [fig] *de ~ te hoog **leggen*** set the bar too high; [Belg] [fig] *de ~ gelijk **leggen*** give everyone the same odds

¹laten /la̯tə(n)/ (liet, heeft gelaten) **1** omit, keep from: *laat **dat!*** stop that!; *hij kan **het** niet ~* he can't help (doing) it; *laat **maar!*** never mind! **2** leave, let: *waar heb ik dat **potlood** gelaten?* where did I leave (*or:* put) that pencil?; *iem.* ~ *halen* **a)** send for s.o.; **b)** have s.o. fetched; *daar zullen we het bij* ~*!* let's leave it at that! **3** put: *waar moet ik het boek* ~*?* where shall I put (*or:* leave) the book? **4** show (into), let (into): *hij werd in de kamer gelaten* he was shown into the room **5** let, allow: *laat de kinderen maar* just let the kids be

²**laten** /lɑtə(n)/ (aux vb, liet, heeft gelaten) let: ~ *we niet vergeten, dat …* don't let us forget that …

latent /latɛnt/ (adj, adv) latent

¹**later** /lɑtər/ (adj) later, subsequent; future: *op* ~*e leeftijd* at an advanced age, late in life

²**later** /lɑtər/ (adv) later (on), afterwards; presently: *enige tijd* ~ after some time (*or:* a while), a little later (on); *even* ~ soon after, presently; *niet* ~ *dan twee uur* no later than two o'clock; ~ *op de dag* later that (same) day, later in the day

lateraal /laterɑl/ (adj) lateral

het **Latijn** /latɛin/ Latin

Latijns-Amerika /lɑtɛinsamerika/ Latin America

Latijns-Amerikaans /lɑtɛinsamerikans/ (adj) Latin-American

de **latrelatie** /lɑtrela(t)si/: *ze hebben een* ~ they are living apart together

de **laurier** /lɑurir/ (pl: -en) **1** laurel **2** bay [culinary]

lauw /lɑu/ (adj, adv) lukewarm

de **lauweren** /lɑuwərə(n)/ (pl) laurels: *op zijn* ~ *rusten* rest on one's laurels

lauwwarm /lɑuwɑrm/ (adj) lukewarm

de **lava** /lɑva/ (pl: -'s) lava

de **lavabo** /lavabo/ (pl: -'s) [Belg] washbasin

laveloos /lɑvelos/ (adj) [inform] sloshed, loaded

laven /lɑvə(n)/ (laafde, heeft gelaafd): *zich* ~ *aan* refresh o.s. at

de **lavendel** /lavɛndəl/ (pl: -s) lavender

laveren /lɑverə(n)/ (laveerde, heeft/is gelaveerd) tack; [fig] steer a middle course

het **lawaai** /lawaj/ noise, din; [stronger] racket

lawaaierig /lawajərəχ/ (adj, adv) noisy

de **lawaaimaker** /lawajmakər/ (pl: -s) noisemaker

de **lawine** /lawinə/ (pl: -s) avalanche; [fig also] barrage

het **lawinegevaar** /lawinəχəvar/ danger of avalanches

het **laxeermiddel** /lɑksermɪdəl/ (pl: -en) laxative

laxeren /lɑksera(n)/ (laxeerde, heeft gelaxeerd) purge: *dat werkt* ~*d* that is a laxative

het **lazarus** /lɑzərʏs/: *zich het* ~ *schrikken* get the shock of one's life

de **lazer** /lɑzər/ body: *iem. op zijn* ~ *geven* beat the crap out of s.o.; bawl (*or:* chew) s.o. out

het **lcd-scherm** /ɛlsedesχɛrm/ LCD display, screen

de **leaseauto** /lisɑuto/ (pl: -'s) leased car

leasen /lisə(n)/ (leasede/leasete, heeft geleased/geleaset) lease

de **lector** /lɛktɔr/ (pl: -en, -s) **1** lecturer **2** [Belg] lector

de **lectuur** /lɛktyr/ reading (matter)

de **ledematen** /ledəmatə(n)/ (pl) limbs

het **ledental** /ledə(n)tal/ (pl: -len) membership (figure)

lederen /ledərə(n)/ (adj) leather

de **lederwaren** /ledərwarə(n)/ (pl) leather goods (*or:* articles)

het **ledikant** /ledikɑnt/ (pl: -en) bed(stead)

de **ledlamp** /lɛtlɑmp/ (pl: -en) LED lamp, LED light

het **leed** /let/ sorrow, grief

het **leedvermaak** /letfərmak/ malicious pleasure

het **leedwezen** /letwezə(n)/ [form]: *tot mijn* ~ *…* I regret to say …

leefbaar /levbar/ (adj) liveable, bearable; endurable: *een huis* ~ *maken* make a house inhabitable

de **leefgemeenschap** /lefχəmensχɑp/ (pl: -pen) commune; community

het **leefklimaat** /lefklimat/ social climate

het **leefloon** /leflon/ (pl: -lonen) social security; welfare

het **leefmilieu** /lefmɪljø/ (pl: -s) environment

de **leeftijd** /leftɛit/ (pl: -en) age: *Gérard is op een moeilijke* ~ Gérard is at an awkward age; *hij bereikte de* ~ *van 65 jaar* he lived to be 65; *op vijftienjarige* ~ at the age of (*or:* aged) fifteen; *Eric ziet er jong uit voor zijn* ~ Eric looks young for his age; [Belg] *de derde* ~ the over sixty-fives

de **leeftijdgenoot** /leftɛitχənot/ (pl: -genoten) contemporary, peer

de **leeftijdsdiscriminatie** /leftɛitzdɪskrimina(t)si/ age discrimination

de **leeftijdsgrens** /leftɛitsχrɛns/ (pl: -grenzen) age limit

de **leefwijze** /lefwɛizə/ (pl: -n) lifestyle, way of life, manner of living

leeg /leχ/ (adj) **1** empty; vacant; flat; blank: *een lege accu* a flat battery; *met lege handen vertrekken* [fig] leave empty-handed **2** idle, empty **3** [fig] empty, hollow

leegeten /leχetə(n)/ (at leeg, heeft leeggegeten) finish, empty

het **leeggoed** /leχut/ [Belg] empties

leeghalen /leχhalə(n)/ (haalde leeg, heeft leeggehaald) empty; clear out [bldg]; turn out; ransack

het **leeghoofd** /leχhoft/ (pl: -en) nitwit, emptyheaded person

leeglopen /leχlopə(n)/ (liep leeg, is leeggelopen) (become) empty; become deflated; go flat; run down

leegmaken /leχmakə(n)/ (maakte leeg, heeft leeggemaakt) empty; finish; clear: *zijn zakken* ~ turn out one's pockets

leegstaan /lexstan/ (stond leeg, heeft leeg-gestaan) be empty (or: vacant)

de **leegstand** /lexstant/ vacancy

de **leegte** /lexta/ (pl: -s, -n) emptiness: *hij liet een grote ~ achter* he left a great void (behind him)

de **leek** /lek/ (pl: leken) layman

het/de **leem** /lem/ loam

de **leemte** /lemta/ (pl: -n, -s) gap, blank

het **leen** /len/ (pl: lenen) loan: *iets van iem. in (te) ~ hebben* have sth. on loan from s.o.

de **leenheer** /lenher/ (pl: -heren) liege (lord)

de **leenman** /leman/ (pl: -nen) vassal

het **leenstelsel** /lenstɛlsəl/ (pl: -s) feudal system

leep /lep/ (adj, adv) cunning, canny

de **¹leer** /ler/ apprenticeship: *in de ~ zijn (bij)* serve one's apprenticeship (with)

het **²leer** /ler/ leather

het **leerboek** /lerbuk/ (pl: -en) textbook

de **leergang** /leryɑn/ (pl: -en) (educational) method, methodology

het **leergeld** /leryɛlt/ (pl: -en) apprenticeship fee: [fig] *~ betalen* pay one's dues, learn one's lesson

leergierig /leryirəx/ (adj, adv) inquisitive, eager to learn

het **leerjaar** /lerjar/ (pl: -jaren) (school) year: *beroepsvoorbereidend ~* vocational training year

de **leerkracht** /lerkrɑxt/ (pl: -en) teacher, instructor

de **leerling** /lerlɪŋ/ (pl: -en) **1** student, pupil **2** disciple, follower **3** apprentice, trainee: *leerling-verpleegster* trainee nurse

leerlooien /lerlojə(n)/ tan

de **leerlooierij** /lerlojərɛi/ (pl: -en) **1** tanning **2** tannery

de **leermeester** /lermestər/ (pl: -s) master

de **leermethode** /lermetodə/ teaching method, training method

het **leermiddelen** /lermɪdələ(n)/ educational aids

het **leerplan** /lerplɑn/ (pl: -nen) syllabus, curriculum

de **leerplicht** /lerplɪxt/ compulsory education

leerplichtig /lerplɪxtəx/ (adj) of school age

leerrijk /lerɛik/ (adj) instructive, informative

de **leerschool** /lersxol/ (pl: -scholen) school

de **leerstoel** /lerstul/ (pl: -en) chair

de **leerstof** /lerstɔf/ subject matter, (subject) material

het **leertje** /lertʃə/ (pl: -s) washer

het **leervak** /lervɑk/ (pl: -ken) subject

de **leerweg** /lerwɛx/ (learning) track, study option: *de theoretische ~* the theoretical track; *de gemengde ~* the combined track; *de kader-beroepsgerichte ~* the advanced vocational track; *de basisberoepsgerichte ~* the basic vocational track

leerzaam /lerzam/ (adj, adv) instructive, informative: *een leerzame ervaring* a valuable experience

leesbaar /lezbar/ (adj, adv) **1** legible **2** readable

leesblind /lezblɪnt/ (adj) dyslexic

de **leesblindheid** /lezblɪnthɛit/ dyslexia

het **leesboek** /lezbuk/ (pl: -en) reader

de **leesbril** /lezbrɪl/ reading glasses

de **leeslamp** /leslɑmp/ (pl: -en) reading lamp

de **leesmoeder** /lesmudər/ (pl: -s) (parent) volunteer reading teacher

de **leest** /lest/ (pl: -en) last

het **leesteken** /lesteka(n)/ (pl: -s) punctuation mark

de **leesvaardigheid** /lesfɑrdəxhɛit/ reading proficiency (or: skill)

het **leesvoer** /lesfur/ something to read

de **leeszaal** /lesal/ (pl: -zalen) reading room; public library

de **leeuw** /lew/ (pl: -en) lion: *zo sterk als een ~* as strong as an ox

de **Leeuw** /lew/ (pl: -en) [astrology] Leo

het **leeuwendeel** /lewə(n)del/ lion's share

de **leeuwentemmer** /lewə(n)tɛmər/ (pl: -s) lion-tamer

de **leeuwerik** /lewərɪk/ (pl: -en) lark

de **leeuwin** /lewɪn/ (pl: -nen) lioness

het/de **lef** /lɛf/ guts, nerve: *heb het ~ niet om dat te doen* don't you dare do that

de **lefgozer** /lɛfxozər/ (pl: -s) [inform] hotshot; show-off

de **leg** /lɛx/: *van de ~ zijn* have stopped laying

legaal /leyal/ (adj, adv) legal

het **legaat** /leyat/ (pl: legaten) legacy

legaliseren /leyalizerə(n)/ (legaliseerde, heeft gelegaliseerd) legalize

de **legbatterij** /lɛxbɑtərɛi/ (pl: -en) battery (cage)

legen /leyə(n)/ (leegde, heeft geleegd) empty

de **legenda** /leyɛnda/ (pl: -'s) legend

legendarisch /leyɛndaris/ (adj) legendary

de **legende** /leyɛndə/ (pl: -n, -s) legend

het **leger** /leyər/ (pl: -s) **1** army; armed forces: *een ~ op de been brengen* raise an army; *in het ~ gaan* join the army **2** lair

de **legerbasis** /leyərbazɪs/ (pl: -bases) army base

legeren /leyərə(n)/ (legerde, heeft gelegerd) **1** encamp **2** quarter; billet

legergroen /leyəryrun/ (adj) olive drab (or: green)

de **legering** /leyərɪŋ/ alloy

de **legermacht** /leyərmɑxt/ (pl: -en) armed forces; army

de **leges** /leyɛs/ (pl) (legal) dues, fees

leggen /lɛyə(n)/ (legde, heeft gelegd) **1** lay (down); floor: *te ruste(n) ~* lay to rest **2** put, put aside

de **legging** /lɛgɪŋ/ (pl: -s) leggings

legio /leyijo/ (adj) countless: *hij maakte ~ fouten* the errors he made were legion

het **legioen** /leɣiju̯n/ (pl: -en) **1** legion **2** supporters

de **legionella** /leɣijonɛla/ **1** Legionella pneumophila **2** legionnaires' disease

de **legislatuur** /leɣɪslaty̯r/ (pl: legislaturen) **1** (exercise of) legislative power **2** [Belg] term

legitiem /leɣitim̩/ (adj, adv) legitimate

de **legitimatie** /leɣitima(t)si/ (pl: -s) identification, proof of identity, ID

het **legitimatiebewijs** /leɣitima(t)sibəwɛɪs/ (pl: -bewijzen) identity papers (or: card); ID

de **legitimatieplicht** /leɣitima(t)siplɪxt/ compulsory identification

zich **legitimeren** /leɣitimerə(n)/ (legitimeerde zich, heeft zich gelegitimeerd) identify o.s., prove one's identity

de **legkast** /lɛxkɑst/ (pl: -en) cupboard (with shelves)

de **legkip** /lɛxkɪp/ (pl: -pen) laying hen

de **legpuzzel** /lɛxpʏzəl/ (pl: -s) jigsaw (puzzle)

de **leguaan** /leɣywa̯n/ (pl: leguanen) iguana

de **lei** /lɛi/ slate: *(weer) met een **schone** ~ beginnen* start again with a clean slate

de **leiband** /lɛɪbɑnt/ (pl: -en) leash: [fig] *hij loopt **aan** de ~ van ...* he's spoonfed by ...

leiden /lɛidə(n)/ (leidde, heeft geleid) **1** lead, bring, guide: *iem. ~ **naar** lead (or: steer) s.o. towards; de nieuwe bezuinigingen zullen **ertoe** ~ dat ...* as a result of the new cutbacks, ...; *de weg leidde ons door het dorpje* the road took (or: led) us through the village; *zij leidde hem **door** de gangen* she led (or: guided) him through the corridors; *tot niets ~* lead nowhere **2** manage; conduct; direct: *zich **laten** ~ door* be guided (or: ruled) by **3** [sport] (be in the) lead || *een druk **leven** ~* lead a busy life

de **leider** /lɛidər/ (pl: -s) leader; [com] director; manager; guide

het **leiderschap** /lɛɪdərsxɑp/ leadership

de **leiding** /lɛidɪŋ/ (pl: -en) **1** guidance, direction: *onder zijn **bekwame** ~ under his (cap)able leadership; ~ **geven** (aan)* direct; lead; manage, run; govern; preside over, chair; *wie **heeft** er hier de ~?* who's in charge here? **2** direction; management; managers; (board of) directors; leadership: *de ~ **heeft** hier **gefaald*** the management is at fault here **3** pipe; wire; cable: *elektrische ~* electric wire (or: cable) **4** lead: *Ajax heeft de ~ **met** 2 tegen 1* Ajax leads 2-1

leidinggevend /lɛidɪŋɣevənt/ (adj) executive, managerial, management

het **leidingwater** /lɛidɪŋwatər/ tap water

de **leidraad** /lɛidra̯t/ (pl: leidraden) guide(line)

het **leidsel** /lɛitsəl/ (pl: -s) rein

de **leidsman** /lɛɪtsmɑn/ (pl: -nen, leidslieden) guide, leader

leien /lɛiə(n)/ (adj) slate

het/de **leisteen** /lɛɪsten/ slate

het **¹lek** /lɛk/ (pl: -ken) leak(age), puncture; flat: *een ~ **dichten*** stop a leak

²lek /lɛk/ (adj) leaky, punctured; flat: *een ~ke band krijgen* get a puncture

de **lekkage** /lɛkaʒə/ (pl: -s) leak(age)

¹lekken /lɛkə(n)/ (lekte, heeft gelekt) leak, be leaking; take in water; drip

²lekken /lɛkə(n)/ (lekte, is gelekt) leak, seep

¹lekker /lɛkər/ (adj) **1** nice, good, tasty; delicious: *ze weet wel wat ~ **is*** she knows a good thing when she sees it; *is het ~? ja, het **heeft** me ~ **gesmaakt*** do you like it? yes, I enjoyed it **2** nice, sweet **3** well, fine: *ik **ben** niet ~* I'm not feeling too well **4** nice, pleasant **5** nice; comfortable; lovely: *~ **rustig*** nice and quiet

²lekker /lɛkər/ (adv) **1** well, deliciously: *~ (kunnen) **koken*** be a good cook **2** nicely, fine: *slaap ~, **droom** maar ~* sleep tight, sweet dreams; *het ~ **vinden** om* like to || *~ **puh*** hard cheese, yah boo sucks to you

de **lekkerbek** /lɛkərbɛk/ (pl: -ken) gourmet, foodie

het **lekkerbekje** /lɛkərbɛkjə/ (pl: -s) fried fillet of haddock

de **lekkernij** /lɛkərnɛi/ (pl: -en) delicacy; sweet

het **lekkers** /lɛkərs/ sweet(s); snack

de **lel** /lɛl/ clout

de **lelie** /leli/ (pl: -s) (madonna) lily

het **lelietje-van-dalen** /lelicəvɑndalə(n)/ (pl: lelietjes-van-dalen) lily of the valley

¹lelijk /lɛlək/ (adj) **1** ugly: *een ~ **eendje** un* ugly duckling; *het was een ~ **gezicht*** it looked awful **2** bad, nasty: *een ~ **hoestje*** a bad cough

²lelijk /lɛlək/ (adv) badly, nastily: *zich ~ **vergissen** in iem. (iets)* be badly mistaken about s.o. (sth.)

de **lelijkerd** /lɛləkərt/ (pl: -s) **1** ugly man; hag, witch **2** rascal, ugly customer

lemen /lemə(n)/ (adj) loam

het **lemmet** /lɛmət/ (pl: -en) blade

de **lemming** /lɛmɪŋ/ (pl: -s, -en) lemming

de **lende** /lɛndə/ (pl: -nen) **1** lumbar region, small of the back **2** loin, haunch

de **lendenbiefstuk** /lɛndəbifstʏk/ (pl: -ken) sirloin

de **lendendoek** /lɛndə(n)duk/ (pl: -en) loincloth

lenen /lenə(n)/ (leende, heeft geleend) **1** lend (to): *ik heb hem **geld** geleend* I have lent him some money **2** borrow (of, from): *mag ik je **fiets** vandaag ~?* can I borrow your bike today?

de **lener** /lenər/ (pl: -s) **1** lender **2** borrower

lengen /lɛŋə(n)/: *de **dagen** ~* the days are growing longer (or: drawing) out

de **lengte** /lɛŋtə/ (pl: -n, -s) **1** length: *een plank in de ~ **doorzagen*** saw a board lengthways (or: lengthwise) **2** length, height: *hij lag in zijn **volle** ~ op de grond* he lay full-length on the ground || *over een ~ **van** 60 meter* for a distance of 60 metres

de **lengteas** /lɛ̃ŋtəɑs/ (pl: -sen) longitudinal axis

de **lengtecirkel** /lɛ̃ŋtəsɪrkəl/ (pl: -s) meridian

de **lengtemaat** /lɛ̃ŋtəmɑt/ (pl: -maten) linear (or: longitudinal) measurement

de **lengterichting** /lɛ̃ŋtərɪχtɪŋ/ longitudinal direction, linear direction

lenig /lenəχ/ (adj, adv) lithe

de **lenigheid** /lenəχhɛit/ litheness

de **lening** /lenɪŋ/ (pl: -en) loan: *iem. een ~ ver- strekken* grant s.o. a loan

de **lens** /lɛns/ (pl: lenzen) lens; [contact lenses also] contacts

de **lente** /lɛntə/ (pl: -s) spring: *in de ~* in (the) spring, in springtime; *één zwaluw* **maakt** *nog geen ~* one swallow doesn't make a summer

lenteachtig /lɛntəɑχtəχ/ (adj, adv) spring- like

het **lente-uitje** /lɛntəɶycə/ (pl: -s) spring onion

de **lepel** /lepəl/ (pl: -s) **1** spoon; ladle; teaspoon: *een baby* **met** *een ~ voeren* spoonfeed a baby **2** spoonful

de **lepelaar** /lepəlɑr/ (pl: -s) spoonbill

lepelen /lepələ(n)/ (lepelde, heeft gele- peld): *iets* **naar** *binnen ~ spoon sth. up

de **lepra** /lepra/ leprosy

de **leraar** /lerar/ (pl: leraren) teacher: *hij is ~ Engels* he's an English teacher

de **lerarenopleiding** /lerarə(n)ɔplɛidɪŋ/ (pl: -en) secondary teacher training (course): *de* **tweedefaselerarenopleiding** post-graduate teacher training (course)

de **lerares** /lerarɛs/ (pl: -sen) see *leraar*

¹**leren** /lerə(n)/ (adj) leather

²**leren** /lerə(n)/ (leerde, heeft geleerd) **1** learn ((how) to do): *een vak ~* learn a trade; *iem. ~* **kennen** get to know s.o.; *op dat gebied* **kun** *je nog heel wat van hem ~* he can still teach you a thing or two; *hij wil ~* **schaatsen** he wants to learn (how) to skate; *iets al doen- de ~* pick sth. up as you go along; *iets van bui- ten ~* learn sth. by heart **2** teach: *de* **ervaring** *leert ...* experience teaches ... **3** study, learn: *haar kinderen kunnen* **goed** (or: **niet**) *~ her* children are good (or: no good) at school

³**leren** /lerə(n)/ (leerde, heeft geleerd) **1** teach (s.o. (how) to do sth.): *iem. ~* **lezen en schrijven** teach s.o. to read and write **2** pick up, learn: *hij leert* **het** *al aardig* he is beginning to get the hang of it

de **lering** /lerɪŋ/ (pl: -en): *~ uit iets* **trekken** learn (a lesson) from sth.

de **les** /lɛs/ (pl: -sen) **1** lesson, class: *ik heb ~ van 9 tot 12* I have lessons (or: classes) from 9 to 12; *een ~ laten* **uitvallen** drop a class; *~ in tekenen* drawing (or: art) classes **2** [fig] lecture, les- son: *bij de ~ blijven* be alert; *dat is een* **goede** *~ voor hem* that's been a good lesson to him; *iem. de ~ lezen*, [Belg] *iem. de les* **spellen** give s.o. a talking-to; *een* **wijze** *~ a*

wise lesson

de **lesauto** /lɛsɑuto/ (pl: -'s) learner car; [Am] driver education car

de **lesbienne** /lɛzbi(j)jɛnə/ (pl: -s) lesbian

lesbisch /lɛzbis/ (adj) lesbian

het **lesgeld** /lɛsχɛlt/ tuition fee(s)

lesgeven /lɛsχevə(n)/ (gaf les, heeft lesge- geven) teach

het **leslokaal** /lɛslokɑl/ (pl: leslokalen) class- room

de **Lesothaan** /ləsotɑn/ (pl: Lesothanen) Mo- sotho

Lesothaans /ləsotɑns/ (adj) Lesotho

Lesotho /ləsoto/ Lesotho

het **lesrooster** /lɛsrostər/ (pl: -s) school timeta- ble; [Am] school schedule

lessen /lɛsə(n)/ (leste, heeft gelest) quench

de **lessenaar** /lɛsənɑr/ (pl: -s) (reading, writing) desk, lectern

lest /lɛst/ (adj, adv): *ten* **langen** *~e* at (long) last, finally

het **lesuur** /lɛsyr/ (pl: lesuren) lesson, period

de **Let** /lɛt/ (pl: -ten) Latvian

de **lethargie** /letarχi/ lethargy

Letland /lɛtlɑnt/ Latvia

de **Letlander** /lɛtlɑndər/ (pl: -s) see *Let*

Letlands /lɛtlɑn(t)s/ (adj) see ²*Lets*

het ¹**Lets** /lɛts/ Latvian

²**Lets** /lɛts/ (adj) Latvian

het **letsel** /lɛtsəl/ injury

letten /lɛtə(n)/ (lette, heeft gelet) **1** pay at- tention (to): *daar heb ik niet* **op** *gelet* I didn't notice; *op zijn* **gezondheid** *~* watch one's health; *let* **op** *mijn woorden* mark my words; *let maar niet* **op** *haar* don't pay any attention to her **2** take care of: *goed* **op** *iem. ~* take good care of s.o.; *er wordt ook* **op** *de uitspraak gelet* pronunciation is also taken into consid- eration (or: account) || *wat let je?* what's keeping (or: stopping) you?

de **letter** /lɛtər/ (pl: -s) letter; [pl, notice] letter- ing: *met* **grote** *~s* in capitals

de **letteren** /lɛtərə(n)/ (pl) language and liter- ature, arts: *~ studeren* be an arts student

de **lettergreep** /lɛtərχrep/ (pl: -grepen) sylla- ble

de **letterkunde** /lɛtərkʏndə/ literature

letterkundig /lɛtərkʏndəχ/ (adj, adv) liter- ary

letterlijk /lɛtərlək/ (adj, adv) literal: *iets al te ~ opvatten* take sth. too literally

het **letterteken** /lɛtərtekə(n)/ (pl: -s) character

het **lettertype** /lɛtərtipə/ (pl: -s) type(face), fount; [Am] font

de **leugen** /løɣə(n)/ (pl: -s) lie: *een ~tje* **om** *best- wil* a white lie

de **leugenaar** /løɣənɑr/ (pl: -s) liar

leugenachtig /løɣənɑχtəχ/ (adj) lying

de **leugendetector** /løɣə(n)detɛktɔr/ (pl: -s) lie detector

leuk /løk/ (adj, adv) **1** funny, amusing: *hij*

denkt zeker dat hij ~ *is* he seems to think he is funny; *ik zie niet in wat daar voor* ~*s aan is* I don't see the funny side of it **2** pretty, nice: *een* ~ *bedrag* quite a handsome sum; *echt een* ~*e vent (knul)* a really nice guy; *dat staat je* ~ that suits you **3** nice, pleasant: *ik vind het* ~ *werk* I enjoy the work; *iets* ~ *vinden* enjoy (*or:* like) sth.; *laten we iets* ~*s gaan doen* let's do sth. nice; ~ *dat je gebeld hebt* it was nice of you to call

de **leukemie** /lœykəmi̱/ leukaemia

de **leukerd** /lø̱kərt/ (pl: -s) funny man (*or:* guy)

het/de **leukoplast**® /lø̱koplɑst/ sticking plaster

leunen /lø̱nə(n)/ (leunde, heeft geleund) lean (on, against): *achterover* ~ lean back, recline

de **leuning** /lø̱nɪŋ/ (pl: -en) **1** (hand)rail **2** back, arm (rest) **3** rail(ing), guard rail

de **leunstoel** /lø̱nstul/ (pl: -en) armchair

leuren /lø̱rə(n)/ (leurde, heeft geleurd) peddle

de **leus** /løs/ (pl: leuzen) slogan, motto

de **leut** /løt/ fun

leuteren /lø̱tərə(n)/ (leuterde, heeft geleuterd) drivel

Leuven /lø̱və(n)/ Leuven, Louvain

het ¹**leven** /le̱və(n)/ (pl: -s) **1** life, existence: *de aanslag heeft aan twee mensen het* ~ *gekost* the attack cost the lives of two people; *het* ~ *schenken aan* give birth to; *zijn* ~ *wagen* risk one's life; *nog in* ~ *zijn* be still alive; *zijn* ~ *niet (meer) zeker zijn* be not safe here (any more) **2** life, reality: *een organisatie in het* ~ *roepen* set up an organization **3** life, lifetime: *zijn hele verdere* ~ for the rest of his life; *hun* ~ *lang hebben ze hard gewerkt* they worked hard all their lives **4** life, living: *het* ~ *wordt steeds duurder* the cost of living is going up all the time; *zijn* ~ *beteren* mend one's ways **5** life, liveliness: *er kwam* ~ *in de brouwerij* things were beginning to liven up

²**leven** /le̱və(n)/ (leefde, heeft geleefd) **1** live, be alive: *blijven* ~ stay alive; *en zij leefden nog lang en gelukkig* and they lived happily ever after; *leef je nog?* are you still alive?; *stil gaan* ~ retire; *naar iets toe* ~ look forward to sth. **2** [fig] live (on) **3** live (on, by); live off: *zij moet ervan* ~ she has to live on it

levend /le̱vənt/ (adj) living; live; alive

levendig /le̱vəndəχ/ (adj, adv) **1** lively **2** lively, vivacious: ~ *van aard zijn* have a vivacious nature **3** vivid, clear: *ik kan mij die dag nog* ~ *herinneren* I remember that day clearly **4** vivid, spirited: *over een* ~*e fantasie beschikken* have a vivid imagination

levenloos /le̱və(n)los/ (adj) lifeless, dead: *iem.* ~ *aantreffen* find s.o. dead

levensbedreigend /le̱vənzbədrɛ̱i̯ɣənt/ (adj) life-threatening

de **levensbehoefte** /le̱vənzbəhʊftə/ (pl: -n) **1** necessity of life **2** necessities (of life)

het **levensbelang** /le̱vənzbəlɑŋ/ (pl: -en) vital importance

de **levensbeschouwing** /le̱və(n)zbəsχɑuwɪŋ/ (pl: -en) philosophy of life

de **levensbeschrijving** /le̱vənzbəsχrɛivɪŋ/ (pl: -en) biography, curriculum vitae

de **levensduur** /le̱vənzdyr/ [fig] **1** lifespan: *de gemiddelde* ~ *van de Nederlander* the life expectancy of the Dutch **2** life

¹**levensecht** /le̱vənsɛχt/ (adj) lifelike

²**levensecht** /le̱vənsɛχt/ (adv) in a lifelike way (*or:* manner)

de **levenservaring** /le̱vənsɛrvarɪŋ/ (pl: -en) experience of life

de **levensfase** /le̱və(n)sfazə/ (pl: -s) stage of life

de **levensgenieter** /le̱və(n)sχənitər/ (pl: -s) [roughly] bon vivant, pleasure-lover

het **levensgevaar** /le̱vənsχəvar/ danger of life, peril to life: *buiten* ~ *zijn* be out of danger

levensgevaarlijk /le̱vənsχəva̱rlək/ (adj, adv) perilous

de **levensgezel** /le̱vənsχəzɛl/ (pl: -len) life partner (*or:* companion)

levensgroot /le̱vənsχro̱t/ (adj) **1** life-size(d) **2** huge, enormous

de **levenskunstenaar** /le̱və(n)skʏnstənar/ (pl: -s) master in the art of living

¹**levenslang** /le̱vənslɑŋ/ (adj) lifelong: ~*e herinneringen* lasting memories || *hij kreeg* ~ he was sentenced to life (imprisonment)

²**levenslang** /le̱vənslɑ̱ŋ/ (adv) all one's life

het **levenslied** /le̱və(n)slit/ (pl: -liederen) [roughly] sentimental song

de **levensloop** /le̱vənslop/ **1** course of life **2** curriculum vitae

de **levenslust** /le̱və(n)slʏst/ joy of living

levenslustig /le̱vənslʏ̱stəχ/ (adj) high-spirited

de **levensmiddelen** /le̱vənsmɪdələ(n)/ (pl) food(s)

de **levensomstandigheden** /le̱vənsɔmstandəχhedə(n)/ (pl) living conditions, circumstances (*or:* conditions) of life

het **levensonderhoud** /le̱vənsɔndərhaut/ support, means of sustaining life: *de kosten van* ~ *stijgen* (*or: dalen*) living costs are rising (*or:* falling)

de **levensovertuiging** /le̱və(n)sovərtœyɣɪŋ/ philosophy of life

de **levenspartner** /le̱vənspɑrtnər/ (pl: -s) life partner, life companion

de **levensstandaard** /le̱vənstɑndart/ standard of living

de **levensstijl** /le̱vənstɛil/ (pl: -en) lifestyle, style of living

het **levensteken** /le̱və(n)stekə(n)/ (pl: -s, -en) sign of life

levensvatbaar /le̱və(n)sfɑdbar/ (adj) viable; feasible

de **levensverwachting** /le̱vənsfərwɑχtɪŋ/

1 expectation of (*or:* from) life 2 life expectancy

de **levensverzekering** /l<u>e</u>vənsfərzekərɪŋ/ (pl: -en) life insurance (policy)

de **levensvreugde** /l<u>e</u>və(n)sfrøɣdə/ joy of living

de **levenswandel** /l<u>e</u>vənswɔndəl/ conduct (in life), life

het **levenswerk** /l<u>e</u>vənswɛrk/ life's work, lifework

de **levenswijsheid** /l<u>e</u>və(n)swɛɪshɛɪt/ wisdom

de **levenswijze** /l<u>e</u>vənswɛɪzə/ way of life

de **lever** /l<u>e</u>vər/ (pl: -s) liver: [Belg] *het ligt op zijn ~ it rankles him* ‖ *iets op zijn ~ hebben* have sth. on one's mind

de **leverancier** /levərɑns<u>i</u>r/ (pl: -s) supplier

de **leverantie** /levər<u>ɑ</u>nsi/ (pl: -s) delivery, supply(ing)

leverbaar /l<u>e</u>vərbar/ (adj) available, ready for delivery: *niet meer ~* out of stock

leveren /l<u>e</u>vərə(n)/ (leverde, heeft geleverd) 1 supply, deliver 2 furnish, provide: *iem. stof ~ voor een verhaal* provide s.o. with material for a story 3 fix, do, bring off: *ik weet niet hoe hij het hem geleverd heeft* I don't know how he pulled it off

de **levering** /l<u>e</u>vərɪŋ/ (pl: -en) delivery

de **leveringstermijn** /l<u>e</u>vərɪŋstɛrmɛɪn/ delivery period (*or:* time)

de **leverpastei** /l<u>e</u>vərpɑstɛi/ (pl: -en) liver paté

de **levertijd** /l<u>e</u>vərtɛit/ (pl: -en) delivery time

de **leverworst** /l<u>e</u>vərwɔrst/ (pl: -en) liver sausage

lezen /l<u>e</u>zə(n)/ (las, heeft gelezen) 1 read: *je handschrift is niet te ~* your (hand)writing is illegible; *veel ~ over een schrijver* (or: *een bepaald onderwerp*) read up on a writer (*or:* on a particular subject); *ik lees hier dat ...* it says here that ... 2 read (out, aloud) ‖ *de angst stond op zijn gezicht te ~* anxiety was written all over his face

de **lezer** /l<u>e</u>zər/ (pl: -s) reader: *het aantal ~s van deze krant neemt nog steeds toe* the readership of this newspaper is still increasing

de **lezing** /l<u>e</u>zɪŋ/ (pl: -en) 1 reading: *bij oppervlakkige* (or: *nauwkeurige*) *~ on* a cursory (*or:* a careful reading) 2 lecture

de **lhbt'er** (pl: -s) *lesbienne, homo, biseksueel, transgender* LGBT *(lesbian, gay, bisexual, transgendered)*

de **liaan** /lijan/ (pl: lianen) liana, liane

de **Libanees** /liban<u>e</u>s/ Lebanese

Libanon /l<u>i</u>banɔn/ (the) Lebanon

de **libel** /lib<u>ɛ</u>l/ (pl: -len) dragonfly

liberaal /liber<u>a</u>l/ (adj, adv) 1 liberal; [in the Netherlands also] conservative 2 liberal, broad-minded

liberaliseren /liberaliz<u>e</u>rə(n)/ (liberaliseerde, heeft geliberaliseerd) liberalize

het **liberalisme** /liberal<u>ɪ</u>smə/ liberalism

Liberia /lib<u>e</u>rija/ Liberia

de **Liberiaan** /liberij<u>a</u>n/ (pl: Liberianen) Liberian

Liberiaans /liberij<u>a</u>ns/ (adj) Liberian

de **libero** /l<u>i</u>bəro/ (pl: -'s) [sport] sweeper

de **libido** /l<u>i</u>bido/ libido, sex drive

Libië /l<u>i</u>bijə/ Libya

de **Libiër** /l<u>i</u>bijər/ (pl: -s) Libyan

Libisch /l<u>i</u>bis/ (adj) Libyan

de **licentiaat** /lisɛnsj<u>a</u>t/ [Belg] licentiate

het **² licentiaat** /lisɛnsj<u>a</u>t/ licentiate, licence

de **licentie** /lis<u>ɛ</u>nsi/ (pl: -s) 1 licence 2 permit

het **lichaam** /l<u>ɪ</u>χam/ (pl: lichamen) 1 body: *over zijn hele ~ beven* shake all over 2 trunk

de **lichaamsbeweging** /l<u>ɪ</u>χamzbəweɣɪŋ/ (pl: -en) (physical) exercise; gymnastics

de **lichaamsbouw** /l<u>ɪ</u>χamzbɑu/ build, figure

het **lichaamsdeel** /l<u>ɪ</u>χamzdel/ (pl: -delen) part of the body; limb

de **lichaamstaal** /l<u>ɪ</u>χamstal/ body language

de **lichaamsverzorging** /l<u>ɪ</u>χamsfərzɔrχɪŋ/ personal hygiene

lichamelijk /l<u>ɪ</u>χamələk/ (adj, adv) physical

het **¹ licht** /lɪχt/ (pl: -en) light: *tussen ~ en donker* in the twilight; *waar zit de knop van het ~?* where's the light switch?; *groot ~* full beam; *dat werpt een nieuw ~ op de zaak* that puts things in a different light; *het ~ aandoen* (or: *uitdoen*) put the light on (or: off); *toen ging er een ~je (bij me) op* then it dawned on me; *het ~ staat op rood* the light is red; *aan het ~ komen* come to light

² licht /lɪχt/ (adj) 1 light, delicate: *zij voelde zich ~ in het hoofd* she felt light in the head; *een kilo te ~* a kilogram underweight 2 light, bright: *het wordt al ~* it is getting light 3 light; pale 4 light, easy 5 light, slight: *een ~e afwijking hebben* be a bit odd; *een ~e blessure* a minor injury

³ licht /lɪχt/ (adv) 1 lightly; light: *~ slapen* sleep light 2 slightly 3 easily: *~ verteerbaar* (easily) digestible, light 4 highly: *~ ontvlambare stoffen* highly (in)flammable materials

de **lichtbak** /l<u>ɪ</u>χtbɔk/ (pl: -ken) 1 light box 2 illuminated sign

lichtbewolkt /l<u>ɪ</u>χtbəwɔlkt/ (adj) rather cloudy, with some clouds

lichtblauw /l<u>ɪ</u>χtbl<u>ɑu</u>/ (adj) light (*or:* pale) blue

de **lichtbron** /l<u>ɪ</u>χtbrɔn/ (pl: -nen) light source, source of light

de **lichtbundel** /l<u>ɪ</u>χtbʏndəl/ (pl: -s) beam of light

lichtelijk /l<u>ɪ</u>χtələk/ (adv) slightly

lichten /l<u>ɪ</u>χtə(n)/ (lichtte, heeft gelicht) 1 lift, raise 2 remove: *iem. van zijn bed ~* arrest s.o. in his bed

lichtend /l<u>ɪ</u>χtənt/ (adj) shining

lichterlaaie /lɪχtərl<u>a</u>jə/: *het gebouw stond in ~* the building was in flames (*or:* ablaze)

lichtgelovig /lɪχtɣəl<u>o</u>vəχ/ (adj) gullible

lichtgeraakt /l<u>ɪ</u>(χt)ɣər<u>a</u>kt/ (adj) touchy: *~*

zijn be quick to take offence

lichtgevend /lɪxtxevənt/ (adj) luminous

lichtgevoelig /lɪ(xt)xəvu̱lǝx/ (adj) (light) sensitive

het **lichtgewicht** /lɪ(xt)xəwɪxt/ (pl: -en) light-weight

lichtgewond /lɪ(xt)xəwɔnt/ (adj) slightly injured (*or:* wounded)

de **lichting** /lɪxtɪŋ/ (pl: -en) **1** levy, draft **2** collection

het **lichtjaar** /lɪxtjar/ (pl: -jaren) light year

het **lichtjesfeest** /lɪxjəsfest/ Diwali, Festival of Lights

de **lichtkogel** /lɪxtkoɣəl/ (pl: -s) (signal) flare

de **lichtkrans** /lɪxtkrɑns/ (pl: -en) halo; aureole

de **lichtkrant** /lɪxtkrɑnt/ (pl: -en) illuminated news trailer

de **lichtmast** /lɪxtmɑst/ (pl: -en) lamp-post, lamp standard

het **lichtnet** /lɪxtnɛt/ (pl: -ten) (electric) mains, lighting system: *een apparaat op het ~ aansluiten* connect an appliance to the mains; *op het ~ werken* run off the mains

de **lichtpen** /lɪxtpɛn/ (pl: -nen) light pen(cil)

het **lichtpunt** /lɪxtpʏnt/ (pl: -en) **1** point (*or:* spot) of light **2** [fig] ray of hope

de **lichtreclame** /lɪxtrəklamə/ illuminated advertising, neon signs (*or:* advertising)

de **lichtschakelaar** /lɪxtsxakəlar/ (pl: -s) light switch

de **lichtshow** /lɪxtʃo/ (pl: -s) light show

het **lichtsignaal** /lɪxtsɪɲal/ (pl: -signalen) light signal, flash: *een ~ geven* flash

de **lichtsterkte** /lɪxtstɛrktə/ brightness; luminous intensity

de **lichtstraal** /lɪxtstral/ (pl: -stralen) ray of light; beam (*or:* shaft) of light

lichtvaardig /lɪxtfardəx/ (adj, adv) rash

de **lichtval** /lɪxtfɑl/ light

lichtvoetig /lɪxtfu̱təx/ (adj, adv) light-footed

lichtzinnig /lɪxtsɪnəx/ (adj, adv) **1** frivolous: *~ omspringen met* trifle with **2** light, loose: *~ leven* live a loose life

de **lichtzinnigheid** /lɪxtsɪnəxhɛit/ frivolity

het **lid** /lɪt/ (pl: leden) **1** member: *het aantal leden bedraagt … * the membership is …; *~ van de gemeenteraad* (town) councillor; *~ van de Kamer* Member of Parliament, M.P.; *deze omroep heeft 500.000 leden* this broadcasting company has a membership of 500,000; *~ worden van* join, become a member of; *~ zijn van de bibliotheek* belong to the library; *~ zijn van* be a member of; be (*or:* serve) on; *zich als ~ opgeven* apply for membership **2** part, member; limb: *recht van lijf en leden* straight-limbed; *het (mannelijk) ~* the (male) member

het **lidgeld** /lɪtxɛlt/ [Belg] subscription

de **lidkaart** /lɪtkart/ (pl: -en) [Belg] membership card

het **lidmaatschap** /lɪtmatsxɑp/ (pl: -pen) membership: *bewijs van ~* membership card; *iem. van het ~ van een vereniging uitsluiten* exclude s.o. from membership of a club; *het ~ kost €25,-* the membership fee is 25 euros; *zijn ~ opzeggen* resign one's membership

de **lidmaatschapskaart** /lɪtmatsxɑpskart/ (pl: -en) membership card

de **lidstaat** /lɪtstat/ (pl: lidstaten) member state

het **lidwoord** /lɪtwort/ (pl: -en) article: *bepaald en onbepaald ~* definite and indefinite article

Liechtenstein /liːxtənstɛin/ Liechtenstein

de **Liechtensteiner** /liːxtənstɛinər/ (pl: -s) Liechtensteiner

Liechtensteins /liːxtənstɛins/ (adj) Liechtenstein

het **lied** /lit/ (pl: -eren) song: *het hoogste ~ zingen* be wild with joy

de **lieden** /lidə(n)/ (pl) folk, people: *dat kun je verwachten bij zulke ~* that's what you can expect from people like that

liederlijk /lidərlək/ (adj, adv) debauched

het **liedje** /licə/ (pl: -s) song: *het is altijd hetzelfde ~* it's the same old story

het **¹lief** /lif/ **1** girlfriend, boyfriend, beloved **2** joy: *~ en leed met iem. delen* share life's joys and sorrows with s.o.

²lief /lif/ (adj) **1** dear, beloved: *(maar) mijn lieve kind* (but) my dear; [in letters] *Lieve Maria* Dear Maria **2** nice, sweet: *een ~ karakter* a sweet nature, a kind heart; *zij zijn erg ~ voor elkaar* they are very devoted to each other; *dat was ~ van haar om jou mee te nemen* it was nice of her to take you along **3** dear, sweet: *er ~ uitzien* look sweet (*or:* lovely) **4** dear, treasured: *iets voor ~ nemen* put up with sth.; make do with sth.; *tegenslagen voor ~ nemen* take the rough with the smooth

³lief /lif/ (adv) sweetly, nicely: *iem. ~ aankijken* give s.o. an affectionate look ‖ *ik ga net zo ~ niet* I'd (just) as soon not go

liefdadig /livdadəx/ (adj) charitable: *een ~ doel* a good cause; *het is voor een ~ doel* it is for charity; *~e instellingen* charitable institutions

de **liefdadigheid** /livdadəxhɛit/ charity, benevolence, beneficence: *~ bedrijven* do charitable work

de **liefdadigheidsinstelling** /livdadəxhɛitsɪnstɛlɪŋ/ (pl: -en) charity, charitable institution

de **liefde** /livdə/ (pl: -s, -n) love: *haar grote ~* her great love; *kinderlijke ~* childish love (*or:* affection); filial love (*or:* affection); *een ongelukkige ~ achter de rug hebben* have suffered a disappointment in love; *vrije ~* free love; *de ware ~* true love; *iemands ~ beantwoorden* return s.o.'s love (*or:* affection); *de ~ bedrijven* make love; *geluk hebben in de ~* be fortunate (*or:* successful) in love; *~ op het eerste* *gezicht* love at first sight; *hij deed het **uit** ~* he did it for love; *trouwen **uit** ~* marry for love; *de ~ **voor** het vaderland* (the) love of one's country; *~ **voor** de kunst* love of art; *~ is blind* love is blind

liefdeloos /lịvdəlos/ (adj, adv) loveless

de **liefdesbrief** /lịvdəzbrif/ (pl: -brieven) love letter

het **liefdesleven** /lịvdəsleṿə(n)/ (pl: -s) love life

het **liefdesverdriet** /lịvdəsfərdrit/ pangs of love: *~ **hebben*** be disappointed in love

liefdevol /lịvdəvol/ (adj, adv) loving: *~le **verzorging*** tender loving care; *iem. ~ **aankijken*** give s.o. a loving look

het **liefdewerk** /lịvdəwɛrk/ (pl: -en) charity, charitable work: *het is ~ oud papier* it's for love only

liefhebben /lịfhɛbə(n)/ (had lief, heeft liefgehad) love

de **liefhebber** /lịfhɛbər/ (pl: -s) lover: *een ~ van chocola* a chocolate lover; *een ~ van **opera*** an opera lover (*or:* buff); *zijn er nog ~s?* (are there) any takers?; *daar zullen wel ~s **voor** zijn* there are sure to be customers for that

de **liefhebberij** /lifhɛbərɛị/ (pl: -en) hobby, pastime: *een dure ~* [fig] an expensive hobby; *tuinieren is zijn **grootste** ~* gardening is his favourite pastime

het **liefje** /lịfjə/ (pl: -s) sweetheart

liefkozen /lịfkozə(n)/ (liefkoosde, heeft geliefkoosd) caress, fondle, cuddle

de **liefkozing** /lịfkozɪŋ/ (pl: -en) caress

liefst /lifst/ (adv) **1** dearest, sweetest: *zij zag er van allen het ~ **uit*** she looked the sweetest (*or:* prettiest) of them all **2** rather, preferably: *men neme een banaan, ~ een **rijpe** …* take a banana, preferably a ripe one …; *wat zou je het ~ **doen?*** what would you rather do?, what would you really like to do?; *in welke auto rijd je het ~?* which car do you prefer to drive?

de **liefste** /lịfstə/ (pl: -n) sweetheart, darling: *mijn ~* my dear(est) (*or:* love)

liegen /lịɣə(n)/ (loog, heeft gelogen) lie, tell a lie: *hij **staat** gewoon te ~!* he's a downright liar!; *tegen iem. ~* lie to s.o.; *hij liegt **alsof** het gedrukt staat, hij liegt dat hij barst* he is telling barefaced lies; *dat is allemaal gelogen* that's a pack of lies

de **lier** /lir/ (pl: -en) lyre

de **lies** /lis/ (pl: liezen) groin

de **liesbreuk** /lịzbrøk/ (pl: -en) inguinal hernia

de **lieslaars** /lịslars/ (pl: -laarzen) wader

het **lieveheersbeestje** /livəhẹrzbefə/ (pl: -s) ladybird; [Am] ladybug

de **lieveling** /lịvəlɪŋ/ (pl: -en) **1** darling, sweetheart: *zij is de ~ van de **familie*** she's the darling of the family **2** favourite, darling: *de ~ van het **publiek*** the darling (*or:* favourite) of the public

liever /lịvər/ (adv) rather: *ik drink ~ **koffie***

dan thee I prefer coffee to tea; *ik zou ~ **gaan** (dan blijven)* I'd rather go than stay; *ik weet het, of ~ **gezegd**, ik denk het* I know, at least, I think so; *als je ~ **hebt** dat ik wegga, hoef je het maar te zeggen* if you'd sooner (*or:* rather) I'd leave, just say so; *ik **zie** hem ~ gaan dan komen* I'm glad to see the back of him; *hoe meer, **hoe** ~ the more the better; *hij ~ **dan** ik* rather him than me

de **lieverd** /lịvərt/ (pl: -s) darling: [iron] *het is me een ~je* he's (*or:* she's) a nice one

de **lift** /lɪft/ (pl: -en) **1** lift; [Am] elevator: *de ~ **nemen*** take the lift **2** lift, ride: *iem. een ~ **geven*** give s.o. a lift (*or:* ride); *een ~ **krijgen*** get (*or:* hitch) a lift; *een ~ **vragen*** thumb (*or:* hitch) a lift

liften /lɪftə(n)/ (liftte, heeft/is gelift) hitch(-hike)

de **lifter** /lɪftər/ (pl: -s) hitchhiker

de **liftkoker** /lɪftkokər/ (pl: -s) lift shaft; [Am] elevator shaft

de **liga** /lịɣa/ (pl: -'s) league

het **ligbad** /lɪɣbɑt/ (pl: -en) bath; [Am] (bath)tub

de **ligdag** /lɪɣdɑx/ (pl: -en) lay day

de **ligfiets** /lɪɣfits/ (pl: -en) recumbent bike

liggen /lɪɣə(n)/ (lag, heeft gelegen) **1** lie; be laid up: *er lag een halve meter **sneeuw*** there was half a metre of snow; *lekker tegen iem. aan **gaan*** ~ snuggle up to s.o.; *lig je **lekker? (goed?)*** are you comfortable?; *ik **blijf** morgen ~ tot half tien* I'm going to stay in bed till 9.30 tomorrow; *gaan ~* lie down; *hij ligt **in (op)** bed* he is (lying) in bed; *op sterven ~* lie (*or:* be) dying **2** (+ aan) depend (on); be caused by; be due to: *dat ligt **eraan*** it depends; *ik denk dat het **aan** je versterker ligt* I think that it's your amplifier that's causing the trouble; *aan mij zal het niet ~* it won't be my fault; *is het nu zo koud of ligt het **aan** mij?* is it really so cold, or is it just me?; *het ligt **aan** die rotfiets van me* it's that bloody bike of mine; *als het aan mij ligt niet* not if I can help it; *waar zou dat **aan** ~?* what could be the cause of that?; *het lag misschien ook een beetje **aan** mij* I may have had sth. to do with it; *het kan **aan** mij ~, maar …* it may be just me, but …; *als het **aan** mij ligt* if it is up to me **3** die down: *de wind ging ~* the wind died down ‖ *die zaak ligt nogal **gevoelig*** the matter is a bit delicate; *dat werk is voor ons **blijven** ~* that work has been left for us; *ik **heb** (nog) een paar flessen wijn ~* I have a few bottles of wine (left); [Belg] *iem. ~ **hebben*** take s.o. in; *ik heb dat boek **laten** ~* I left that book (behind); *dit bed ligt **lekker** (*or:* **hard**)* this bed is comfortable (*or:* hard); *de zaken ~ nu heel **anders*** things have changed a lot (since then); *het plan, zoals het **er** nu ligt, is onaanvaardbaar* as it stands, the plan is unacceptable; *uw bestelling ligt **klaar*** your order is ready (for dispatch, collection); *zo ~ de zaken nu eenmaal* I'm afraid

that's the way things are; *Antwerpen ligt **aan** de Schelde* Antwerp lies on the Scheldt; *de schuld ligt **bij** mij* the fault is mine; *onder het gemiddelde ~* be below average; *de bal ligt **op** de grond* the ball is on the ground; *op het zuiden ~* face (the) south; *ze ~ **voor** het grijpen* they're all over the place
liggend /lɪɣənt/ (adj) lying, horizontal: *een ~e **houding*** a lying (*or:* recumbent) posture
de **ligging** /lɪɣɪŋ/ (pl: -en) position, situation, location: *de ~ van de **heuvels*** the lie of the hills; *de **schilderachtige** ~ van dat kasteel* the picturesque location of the castle
light /lɑjt/ (adj) lite, diet: *cola ~* diet coke
de **lightrail** /lɑjtrel/ light rail
de **ligplaats** /lɪɣplats/ (pl: -en) berth, mooring (place)
de **ligstoel** /lɪɣstul/ (pl: -en) reclining chair (*or:* seat); deckchair
de **liguster** /liɣʏstər/ (pl: -s) privet
lijdelijk /lɛɪdələk/ (adj, adv) resigned ‖ *~ toezien* look on passively
het **¹lijden** /lɛidə(n)/ suffering; pain; agony; grief; misery: *nu is hij **uit** zijn ~ verlost* **a)** he is now released from his suffering; **b)** [fig] that's put him out of his misery; *een dier **uit** zijn ~ verlossen* put an animal out of its misery
²lijden /lɛidə(n)/ (leed, heeft geleden) suffer: *zij leed het **ergst** van al* she was (the) hardest hit of all; *aan een kwaal ~* suffer from a complaint; *zijn gezondheid leed er **onder*** his health suffered (from it)
³lijden /lɛidə(n)/ (leed, heeft geleden) suffer, undergo: *hevige **pijn** ~* suffer (*or:* be in) terrible pain; *een groot **verlies** ~* suffer (*or:* sustain) a great loss; *honger ~* starve ‖ *het leed **is** geleden* the suffering is over, what's done is done
lijdend /lɛidənt/ (adj) suffering
de **lijdensweg** /lɛidə(n)swɛx/ (pl: -en): *haar afstuderen werd een ~* she went through hell getting her degree
lijdzaam /lɛitsam/ (adj, adv) patient; passive: *~ **toezien*** stand by and watch
het **lijf** /lɛif/ (pl: lijven) body: *in **levenden** lijve* **a)** in person; **b)** alive and well; *bijna geen kleren **aan** zijn ~ hebben* have hardly a shirt to one's back; *iets **aan** den lijve ondervinden* experience (sth.) personally; *iem. **te** ~ gaan* go for (*or:* attack) s.o.; *iem. (toevallig) **tegen** het ~ lopen* run into s.o., stumble upon s.o.; *ik kon hem niet **van** het ~ houden* I couldn't keep him off me; *gezond **van** ~ en leden* able-bodied ‖ *dat heeft niets **om** het ~* there's nothing to it, that's nothing, it's a piece of cake
de **lijfarts** /lɛifarts/ (pl: -en) personal physician
de **lijfeigene** /lɛifɛiɣənə/ (pl: -n) serf
lijfelijk /lɛifələk/ (adj, adv) physical: *zij was ~ **aanwezig*** she was there in person
de **lijfrente** /lɛifrɛntə/ (pl: -n, -s) annuity
de **lijfspreuk** /lɛifsprøk/ (pl: -en) motto

de **lijfstraf** /lɛifstrɑf/ (pl: -fen) corporal punishment
de **lijfwacht** /lɛifwɑxt/ bodyguard
het **lijk** /lɛik/ (pl: -en) **1** corpse, (dead) body: *over mijn ~!* over my dead body!; *over ~en gaan* let nothing (*or:* no one) stand in one's way **2** [fig] carcass: *een **levend** ~* a walking corpse
lijkbleek /lɛiɣblek/ (adj) deathly pale, ashen
lijken /lɛikə(n)/ (leek, heeft geleken) **1** be like, look (a)like, resemble: *je lijkt je **vader** wel* you act (*or:* sound, are) just like your father; *het lijkt wel **wijn*** it's almost like wine; *zij lijkt **op** haar moeder* she looks like her mother; *ze ~ helemaal niet **op** elkaar* they're not a bit alike; *dat lijkt nergens **op (naar)*** it is absolutely hopeless (*or:* useless) **2** seem, appear, look: *hij lijkt **jonger** dan hij is* he looks younger than he is; *het lijkt me **vreemd*** it seems odd to me; *het lijkt maar **zo*** it only seems that way **3** suit, fit: *dat lijkt me wel wat* I like the sound (*or:* look) of that; *het lijkt **me** niets* I don't think much of it
de **lijkenpikker** /lɛikə(n)pɪkər/ (pl: -s) vulture
de **lijkkist** /lɛikɪst/ (pl: -en) coffin
de **lijkschouwer** /lɛiksxɑuwər/ (pl: -s) autopsist, medical examiner; [law] coroner
de **lijkschouwing** /lɛiksxɑuwɪŋ/ (pl: -en) autopsy
de **lijkwagen** /lɛikwaɣə(n)/ (pl: -s) hearse
de **lijm** /lɛim/ (pl: -en) glue
lijmen /lɛimə(n)/ (lijmde, heeft gelijmd) **1** glue (together); [also fig] patch up; [also fig] mend: [fig] *de **brokken** ~* pick up the pieces; *de scherven **aan** elkaar ~* glue (*or:* stick) the pieces together **2** talk round, win over: *zich niet **laten** ~* refuse to be roped in
de **lijmpoging** /lɛimpoɣɪŋ/ attempt to patch up
de **lijmsnuiver** /lɛimsnœyvər/ (pl: -s) glue sniffer
de **lijn** /lɛin/ (pl: -en) **1** line, rope; leash; lead: *~en **trekken** (or: **krassen**) op* draw (*or:* scratch) lines on; *een hond **aan** de ~ houden* keep a dog on the leash **2** line, crease: *de **scherpe** ~en om de neus* the deep lines around the nose **3** (out)line, contour: *iets in **grote** ~en aangeven* sketch sth. in broad outlines; *in **grote** ~en* broadly speaking, on the whole; *aan de (slanke) ~ **doen*** slim, be on a diet **4** line, rank: *op **dezelfde** lijn zitten* be on the same wavelength **5** line, route: *de ~ **Haarlem-Amsterdam*** the Haarlem-Amsterdam line; *die ~ **bestaat** niet meer* that service (*or:* route) no longer exists; *blijft u even **aan** de ~ a.u.b.* hold the line, please; *ik heb je moeder **aan** de ~* your mother is on the phone **6** [fig] line, course, trend: *de **grote** ~en uit het oog verliezen* lose o.s. in details ‖ *iem. **aan** het ~tje houden* keep s.o. dangling
de **lijndienst** /lɛindinst/ (pl: -en) regular service, scheduled service, line: *een ~ **onderhou-***

den *op* run a regular service on

lijnen /lɛinə(n)/ (lijnde, heeft gelijnd) slim, diet

de **lijnkaart** /lɛinkart/ [Belg] smart card for payment on public transport

de **lijnolie** /lɛinoli/ linseed oil

¹**lijnrecht** /lɛinrɛχt/ (adj) (dead) straight

²**lijnrecht** /lɛinrɛχt/ (adv) **1** straight, right: ~ *naar beneden* straight down **2** directly, flatly: ~ *staan* **tegenover** be diametrically (*or:* flatly) opposed to

de **lijnrechter** /lɛinrɛχtər/ (pl: -s) linesman

het **lijntoestel** /lɛintustɛl/ (pl: -len) airliner, scheduled plane

de **lijnvlucht** /lɛinvlyχt/ (pl: -en) scheduled flight

het **lijnzaad** /lɛinzat/ linseed

lijp /lɛip/ (adj, adv) [inform] silly, daft: *doe niet zo ~!* don't be silly! (*or:* daft!)

de **lijst** /lɛist/ (pl: -en) **1** list, record, inventory, register: *~en* **bijhouden** *van de uitgaven* keep records of the costs; *zijn naam staat* **bovenaan** *de ~* he is (at the) top of the list; *iem. (iets)* **op** *een ~ zetten* put s.o. (sth.) on a list **2** frame: *een* **vergulde** *~* a gilt frame

de **lijstaanvoerder** /lɛistanvurdər/ (pl: -s) (league) leader

de **lijster** /lɛistər/ (pl: -s) thrush

de **lijsterbes** /lɛistərbɛs/ rowan (tree), mountain ash

de **lijsttrekker** /lɛistrɛkər/ (pl: -s) [roughly] party leader (during election campaign)

lijvig /lɛivəχ/ (adj) corpulent, hefty

lijzig /lɛizəχ/ (adj, adv) drawling: *een ~e* **stem** a sing-song voice

de **lijzijde** /lɛizɛidə/ lee (side)

de **lik** /lɪk/ (pl: -ken) **1** lick; smack **2** lick, dab

de **likdoorn** /lɪgdorn/ (pl: -s) corn

de **likeur** /likør/ (pl: -en) liqueur

likkebaarden /lɪkəbardə(n)/ (likkebaardde, heeft gelikkebaard) lick one's lips

likken /lɪkə(n)/ (likte, heeft gelikt) lick

likmevestje /lɪkməvɛsʃə/: *een organisatie* **van** *~* crummy (*or:* lousy) organization

het **lik-op-stukbeleid** /lɪkɔpstʏgbəlɛit/ tit-for-tat policy (*or:* strategy)

lila /lila/ (adj) lilac; lavender

de **lilliputter** /lilipʏtər/ (pl: -s) midget, dwarf

Limburg /lɪmbʏrχ/ Limburg

de **Limburger** /lɪmbʏrɣər/ (pl: -s) Limburger

Limburgs /lɪmbʏrχs/ (adj) Limburg

de **limerick** /lɪmərɪk/ (pl: -s) limerick

de **limiet** /limit/ (pl: -en) limit

limiteren /limitərə(n)/ (limiteerde, heeft gelimiteerd) limit, confine

de **limo** /limo/ (pl: -'s) limo

de **limoen** /limun/ (pl: -en) lime

de **limonade** /limonadə/ (pl: -s) lemonade: *priklimonade, ~ gazeuse* fizzy (*or:* aerated, sparkling) lemonade

de **limonadesiroop** /limonadəsirop/ lemon syrup

de **limousine** /limuzinə/ (pl: -s) limousine, limo

de **linde** /lɪndə/ (pl: -n) lime (tree), linden

lineair /linejɛːr/ (adj) linear ‖ *~e* **hypotheek** level repayment mortgage

linea recta /linejarɛkta/ (adv) straight: ~ *gaan naar* go straight to

linedansen /lɑjndɑnsə(n)/ (linedanste, heeft gelinedanst) line dance

de **lingerie** /lɛ̃ʒəri/ lingerie, women's underwear, ladies' underwear

de **linguïst** /lɪŋɡwɪst/ (pl: -en) linguist

het/de **liniaal** /linijal/ (pl: linialen) ruler

de **linie** /lini/ (pl: -s) line, rank: *door de* **vijandelijke** *~ (heen)breken* break through the enemy lines ‖ *over de* **hele** *~* on all points, across the board

link /lɪŋk/ (adj) **1** risky, dicey: *~e* **jongens** a nasty bunch **2** sly, cunning

linken /lɪŋkə(n)/ (linkte, heeft gelinkt) (hyper)link

de **linker** /lɪŋkər/ (adj) left, left-hand; nearside: *~ rijbaan* left lane; *het ~* **voorwiel** the nearside wheel

de **linkerarm** /lɪŋkərɑrm/ left arm

het **linkerbeen** /lɪŋkərben/ (pl: -benen) left leg: *hij is* **met** *zijn ~ uit bed gestapt* he got out of bed on the wrong side

de **linkerhand** /lɪŋkərhɑnt/ (pl: -en) left hand: *twee ~en hebben* be all fingers and thumbs

de **linkerkant** /lɪŋkərkɑnt/ (pl: -en) left(-hand) side, left

de **linkervleugel** /lɪŋkərvløɣəl/ (pl: -s) **1** left wing: *de ~ van een* **gebouw** (or: *een* **voetbalelftal**) the left wing of a building (*or:* football team) **2** left (wing), Left

de **linkerzijde** /lɪŋkərzɛidə/ (pl: -n) left(-hand) side, left, nearside: *zij zat* **aan** *mijn ~* she was sitting on my left

links /lɪŋks/ (adj, adv) **1** left, to (*or:* on) the left: *de* **tweede** *straat ~* the second street on the left; ~ *en* **rechts** [also fig] right and left, on all sides; ~ **houden** keep (to the) left; *iem. ~* **laten liggen** ignore s.o., pass s.o. over, give s.o. the cold shoulder; *iets ~* **laten liggen** ignore sth., pass sth. over; ~ *van iem. zitten* sit to (*or:* on) s.o.'s left **2** left, left-handed, anticlockwise: ~ **afslaan** turn (to the) left; ~ *de bocht* **om** *rijden* take the left-hand bend (*or:* turn) **3** left-handed; left-footed: ~ **schrijven** write with one's left hand **4** left-wing, leftist, socialist

de **linksachter** /lɪŋksɑχtər/ (pl: -s) left back

linksaf /lɪŋksɑf/ (adv) (to the) left, leftwards: *bij de brug* **moet** *u ~* **(gaan)** turn left at the bridge

de **linksback** /lɪŋksbɛk/ (pl: -s) left back

de **linksbuiten** /lɪŋksbœytə(n)/ (pl: -s) outside left, left-wing(er)

linkshandig /lɪŋkshɑndəχ/ (adj) left-handed

linksom /lɪŋksɔm/ (adv) left: ~ *draaien* turn (to the) left

linnen /lɪnə(n)/ (adj) linen, flax: ~ *ondergoed* linen underwear, linen

het **linnengoed** /lɪnə(n)ɣut/ linen

de **linnenkast** /lɪnə(n)kɑst/ (pl: -en) linen cupboard

het/de ¹**linoleum** /linolejʏm/ linoleum

²**linoleum** /linolejʏm/ (adj) linoleum

het **linolzuur** /linolzyr/ (pl: -zuren) linoleic acid

het **lint** /lɪnt/ (pl: -en) ribbon, tape; (bias) binding; band: *het* ~ *van een schrijfmachine* a (typewriter) ribbon; *door het* ~ *gaan* blow one's top, fly off the handle

het **lintje** /lɪncə/ (pl: -s) decoration: *een* ~ *krijgen* be decorated, get a medal

de **lintmeter** /lɪntmetər/ (pl: -s) [Belg] tape measure

de **lintworm** /lɪntwɔrm/ (pl: -en) tapeworm

de **linze** /lɪnzə/ (pl: -n) lentil

de **lip** /lɪp/ (pl: -pen) lip: *dikke ~pen* thick (or: full) lips; *gesprongen ~pen* chapped (or: cracked) lips; *zijn ~pen ergens bij aflikken* lick (or: smack) one's lips; *aan iemands ~pen hangen* hang on s.o.'s lips (or: every word); [fig] *iem. op de* ~ *zitten* sit very close to s.o., be sticky

de **lipgloss** /lɪpglɔs/ lipgloss

het **lipje** /lɪpjə/ tab; lip

liplezen /lɪplezə(n)/ lip-read

de **liposuctie** /liposʏksi/ (pl: -s) liposuction

de **lippenstift** /lɪpə(n)stɪft/ (pl: -en) lipstick

de **liquidatie** /likwida(t)si/ (pl: -s) 1 liquidation, elimination 2 liquidation, winding-up, break-up, dissolution; settlement

liquide /likidə/ (adj) liquid, fluid: ~ *middelen* liquid (or: fluid) assets

liquideren /likwidɛrə(n)/ (liquideerde, heeft geliquideerd) 1 [com] wind up, liquidate 2 eliminate, dispose of

de **lire** /lɪrə/ (pl: -s) lira

de **lis** /lɪs/ (pl: -sen) [bot] flag, iris

de **lisdodde** /lɪzdɔdə/ (pl: -n) reed mace

lispelen /lɪspələ(n)/ (lispelde, heeft gelispeld) lisp, speak with a lisp

Lissabon /lɪsabɔn/ Lisbon

de **list** /lɪst/ (pl: -en) trick, ruse, stratagem; cunning; craft, deception: ~ *en bedrog* double-crossing, double-dealing

listig /lɪstəx/ (adj, adv) cunning, crafty, wily

de **litanie** /litani/ (pl: -ën) litany

de **liter** /litər/ (pl: -s) litre: *twee ~ melk* two litres of milk

literair /litərɛːr/ (adj, adv) literary: ~ *tijdschrift* literary journal

de **literatuur** /litəratyr/ literature

de **literatuurlijst** /litəratyrlɛist/ (pl: -en) reading list, bibliography

de **literfles** /litərflɛs/ (pl: -sen) litre bottle

de **litho** /lito/ (pl: -'s) litho

Litouwen /litɑuwə(n)/ Lithuania

de **Litouwer** /litɑuwər/ (pl: -s) Lithuanian

het ¹**Litouws** /litɑus/ Lithuanian

²**Litouws** /litɑus/ (adj) Lithuanian

het **lits-jumeaux** /liʒymo/ (pl: -) twin beds

het **litteken** /lɪtekə(n)/ (pl: -s) scar, mark: *met ~s op zijn gezicht* with a scarred face

de **liturgie** /litʏrɣi/ (pl: -ën) liturgy, rite

liturgisch /litʏrɣis/ (adj) liturgical

live /lɑjf/ (adj) live

de **living** /lɪvɪŋ/ (pl: -s) living room

de **livrei** /livrɛi/ (pl: -en) livery

de **lob** /lɔp/ (pl: -ben, -s) 1 seed leaf 2 [sport] lob

lobben /lɔbə(n)/ (lobde, heeft gelobd) lob

de **lobbes** /lɔbəs/ (pl: -en) 1 big, good-natured dog 2 kind soul, good-natured fellow, big softy

de **lobby** /lɔbi/ (pl: -'s) 1 lobby 2 [in hotel] lobby; lounge, foyer, hall

lobbyen /lɔbijə(n)/ (lobbyde, heeft gelobbyd) lobby

de **locatie** /loka(t)si/ (pl: -s) location

de **locoburgemeester** /lokobʏrɣəmestər/ (pl: -s) deputy mayor, acting mayor

de **locomotief** /lokomotif/ (pl: locomotieven) engine, locomotive

loden /lodə(n)/ (adj) 1 lead, leaden: ~ *pijp* lead pipe 2 [fig] leaden, heavy

het/de **loeder** /ludər/ (pl: -s) [inform] brute, bastard

de **loef** /luf/ [fig] *iem. de* ~ *afsteken* steal a march on s.o.

de **loefzijde** /lufsɛidə/ windward (side)

de **loei** /luj/ [inform] thump; bash; sizzler; cracker: *een* ~ *verkopen (uitdelen)* hit (or: lash) out (at s.o.)

loeien /lujə(n)/ (loeide, heeft geloeid) 1 moo; low; bellow 2 howl; whine; roar; blare; hoot; wail: *de motor laten* ~ race the engine; *met ~de sirenes* with blaring sirens

loeihard /lujhɑrt/ (adj, adv) [inform] 1 amazingly fast 2 blaring, deafening

de **loempia** /lumpija/ (pl: -'s) spring roll, egg roll

loensen /lunsə(n)/ (loenste, heeft geloenst) squint, be cross-eyed

de **loep** /lup/ (pl: -en) magnifying glass, lens: *iets onder de* ~ *nemen* scrutinize sth., take a close look at sth.

loepzuiver /lupsœyvər/ (adj, adv) flawless, perfect

de **loer** /lur/ 1 lurking: *op de* ~ *liggen* [also fig] lie in wait (for), lurk, be on the lookout (for) 2 trick: *iem. een* ~ *draaien* play a nasty (or: dirty) trick on s.o.

loeren /lurə(n)/ (loerde, heeft geloerd) leer (at); peer at; spy on: *het gevaar loert overal* there is danger lurking everywhere; *op iem. (iets)* ~ lie in wait for s.o. (sth.)

de ¹**lof** /lɔf/ 1 praise, commendation: *iem.* ~ *toezwaaien* give (high) praise to s.o., pay tribute to s.o.; ~ *oogsten* win praise; *vol* ~ *zijn over* speak highly of, be full of praise for **2** honour, credit

het **²lof** /lɔf/ chicory

loffelijk /lɔfələk/ (adj, adv) praiseworthy

het **loflied** /lɔflit/ (pl: -liederen) hymn, song of praise: *een ~ op de natuur* an ode to nature

de **loftrompet** /lɔftrɔmpɛt/: *de ~ over iem. steken* trumpet forth (*or:* sing) s.o.'s praises

de **loftuiting** /lɔftœytɪŋ/ (pl: -en) (words of) praise, eulogy

de **lofzang** /lɔfsɑŋ/ (pl: -en) ode

log /lɔx/ (adj, adv) unwieldy, cumbersome, ponderous, clumsy, heavy; sluggish; lumbering: *een ~ gevaarte* a cumbersome (*or:* an unwieldy) monster; *een ~ge olifant* a ponderous (*or:* an unwieldy) elephant; *met ~ge tred lopen* lumber (along), move with heavy gait

de **logaritme** /loɣɑrɪtmə/ (pl: -n) logarithm

het **logboek** /lɔɣbuk/ (pl: -en) log(book), journal: *in het ~ opschrijven* log

de **loge** /loːʒə/ (pl: -s) box, loge

de **logé** /loʒe/ (pl: -s) guest, visitor: *we krijgen een ~* we are having a visitor (*or:* s.o. to stay)

het **logeerbed** /loʒerbɛt/ (pl: -den) spare bed

de **logeerkamer** /loʒerkamər/ (pl: -s) guest room, spare (bed)room, visitor's room

de **logeerpartij** /loʒerpɑrtɛi/ (pl: -en) stay; [Am] slumber party, pyjama party

logen /loɣə(n)/ (loogde, heeft geloogd) soak in (*or:* treat with) lye

logenstraffen /loɣə(n)strɑfə(n)/ (logenstrafte, heeft gelogenstraft) belie

logeren /loʒerə(n)/ (logeerde, heeft/is gelogeerd) stay, put up; board; lodge: *blijven ~* stay the night, stay over; *ik logeer bij een vriend* I'm staying at a friend's (home) (*or:* with a friend); *kan ik bij jou ~?* could you put me up (for the night)?; *in een hotel ~* stay at a hotel; *iem. te ~ krijgen* have s.o. staying

de **logica** /loɣika/ logic: *er zit geen ~ in wat je zegt* there is no logic in what you're saying

het **logies** /loʒis/ accommodation, lodging(s): *~ met ontbijt* bed and breakfast

de **login** /loxɪn/ (pl: -s) login

de **loginnaam** /loxɪnam/ (pl: -s) log-in name

logisch /loɣis/ (adj, adv) logical, rational: *een ~e tegenstrijdigheid* a logical paradox; *~ denken* think logically (*or:* rationally); *dat is nogal ~* that's only logical, that figures

de **logistiek** /loɣɪstik/ logistics

het **logo** /loɣo/ (pl: -'s) logo

de **logopedie** /loɣopedi/ speech therapy

de **logopedist** /loɣopedɪst/ (pl: -en) speech therapist

de **loipe** /lɔjpə/ (pl: -s, -n) (ski) run

de **lok** /lɔk/ (pl: -ken) **1** lock, strand of hair; tress; curl; ringlet **2** locks, hair; tresses

het **¹lokaal** /lokal/ (pl: lokalen) (class)room

²lokaal /lokal/ (adj) local; topical: *om 10 uur lokale tijd* at 10 o'clock local time; *lokale verdoving* local anaesthesia

het **lokaas** /lokas/ (pl: lokazen) bait

lokaliseren /lokalizerə(n)/ (lokaliseerde, heeft gelokaliseerd) locate

het **loket** /lokɛt/ (pl: -ten) (office) window; booking office, ticket office; box-office (window); counter

de **lokettist** /lokɛtɪst/ (pl: -en) booking-clerk, ticket-clerk; box-office clerk; counter clerk

lokken /lɔkə(n)/ (lokte, heeft gelokt) **1** entice, lure: *in de val ~* lure into a trap **2** tempt, entice, attract

het **lokkertje** /lɔkərcə/ (pl: -s) bait, carrot; loss leader; special offer

de **lokroep** /lɔkrup/ (pl: -en) call (note)

de **lol** /lɔl/ [inform] laugh, fun, lark: *zeg, doe me een ~ (en hou op) de* do me a favour (and knock it off, will you); *voor de ~* for a laugh, for fun (*or:* a lark); *ik doe dit niet voor de ~* I'm not doing this for the good of my health; *de ~ was er gauw af* the fun was soon over

de **lolbroek** /lɔlbruk/ (pl: -en) [inform] clown, joker

het **lolletje** /lɔləcə/ (pl: -s) [inform]: *dat is geen ~* it's not exactly a laugh a minute

lollig /lɔləx/ (adj, adv) [inform] jolly, funny

de **lolly** /lɔli/ (pl: -'s) lollipop, lolly

de **lommerd** /lɔmərt/ (pl: -s) pawnshop

lommerrijk /lɔmərɛik/ (adj) shady

de **¹lomp** /lɔmp/ (pl: -en) [esp pl] rag; [esp pl] tatter

²lomp /lɔmp/ (adj, adv) **1** ponderous, unwieldy: *~e schoenen* clumsy shoes; *zich ~ bewegen* move clumsily, he got in an ungainly manner **2** clumsy, awkward, ungainly **3** rude, unmannerly, uncivil: *iem. ~ behandelen* treat s.o. rudely, be uncivil to s.o.

de **lomschool** /lɔmsxol/ (pl: -scholen) [Dutch] remedial school

Londen /lɔndə(n)/ London

Londens /lɔndə(n)s/ (adj) London

lonen /lonə(n)/ (loonde, heeft geloond) be worth: *dat loont de moeite niet* it is not worth one's while

lonend /lonənt/ (adj) paying, rewarding; profitable; remunerative: *dat is niet ~* that doesn't pay

de **long** /lɔŋ/ (pl: -en) lung

de **longarts** /lɔŋarts/ (pl: -en) lung specialist

de **longdrink** /lɔŋdrɪŋk/ (pl: -s) long drink

het **longemfyseem** /lɔŋɛmfizem/ (pl: -emfysemen) (pulmonary) emphysema

de **longkanker** /lɔŋkaŋkər/ lung cancer

de **longlist** /lɔŋlɪst/ longlist

de **longontsteking** /lɔŋɔntstekɪŋ/ (pl: -en) pneumonia

lonken /lɔŋkə(n)/ (lonkte, heeft gelonkt) make eyes at

de **lont** /lɔnt/ (pl: -en) fuse; touchpaper; [fig] *een kort ~je hebben* have a short fuse

loochenen /loxənə(n)/ (loochende, heeft geloochend) deny het **lood** /lot/ **1** lead: *met ~ in de schoenen* with a heavy heart **2** lead, shot, ammunition ‖ *uit het ~ (geslagen) zijn* be thrown off one's balance

de **loodgieter** /lotχitər/ (pl: -s) plumber

het **loodje** /locə/ (pl: -s) (lead) seal ‖ *de laatste ~s wegen het zwaarst* the last mile is the longest one; *het ~ leggen* **a)** come off badly, get the short end of the stick; **b)** kick the bucket

de **loodlijn** /lotlɛin/ (pl: -en) perpendicular (line), normal (line)

loodrecht /lotrɛχt/ (adj, adv) perpendicular (to), plumb; sheer: *~ op iets staan* be at right angles to sth.

de ¹**loods** /lots/ pilot

de ²**loods** /lots/ shed; hangar

loodsen /lotsə(n)/ (loodste, heeft geloodst) pilot, steer, conduct; shepherd

loodvrij /lotfrɛi/ (adj) lead-free, unleaded

loodzwaar /lotswar/ (adj, adv) heavy

het **loof** /lof/ foliage, leaves; green

de **loofboom** /lovbom/ (pl: -bomen) deciduous tree

het **Loofhuttenfeest** /lofhʏtə(n)fest/ Feast of Tabernacles

het/de **loog** /loχ/ (pl: logen) caustic (solution), lye

looien /lojə(n)/ (looide, heeft gelooid) tan

het **looizuur** /lojzyr/ tannic acid, tannin

de ¹**look** /luk/ (pl: -s) look

het/de ²**look** /lok/ allium

loom /lom/ (adj, adv) **1** heavy, leaden; slow; sluggish: *zich ~ bewegen* move heavily (*or:* sluggishly) **2** languid, listless

het **loon** /lon/ (pl: lonen) **1** pay, wage(s): *een hoog ~ verdienen* earn high wages **2** deserts, reward: *hij gaf hem zijn verdiende ~* he gave him his just deserts

de **loonadministratie** /lonɑtministra(t)si/ (pl: -s) wages administration (*or:* records)

de **loonbelasting** /lombəlɑstɪŋ/ (pl: -en) income tax

de **loondienst** /londinst/ (pl: -en) paid employment, salaried employment

de **loonlijst** /lonlɛist/ (pl: -en) payroll

de **loonmatiging** /lomatəχɪŋ/ wage restraint

het **loonstrookje** /lonstrokjə/ (pl: -s) payslip

de **loonsverhoging** /lonsfərhoχɪŋ/ (pl: -en) wage increase, pay increase, increase in wages (*or:* pay), rise; [Am] raise

de **loop** /lop/ (pl: lopen) **1** course, development: *de ~ van de Rijn* the course of the Rhine; *zijn gedachten de vrije ~ laten* give one's thoughts (*or:* imagination) free rein; *in de ~ der jaren* through the years **2** barrel **3** run, flight

de **loopafstand** /lopɑfstɑnt/ walking distance

de **loopbaan** /loban/ (pl: -banen) career

de **loopbrug** /lobrʏχ/ footbridge

de **loopgraaf** /lopχraf/ (pl: -graven) trench

de **loopgravenoorlog** /lopχravə(n)orlɔχ/ (pl: -en) trench war(fare) [also fig]

het **loopje** /lopjə/ (pl: -s) [mus] run, roulade

de **loopjongen** /lopjɔŋə(n)/ (pl: -s) errand boy, messenger boy

de **looplamp** /loplɑmp/ (pl: -en) portable inspection lamp

de **loopneus** /lopnøs/ (pl: -neuzen) runny nose, running nose

de **looppas** /lopɑs/ jog, run

de **loopplank** /loplɑŋk/ (pl: -en) gangplank, gangway

het **looprek** /loprɛk/ (pl: -ken) walking frame, walker

loops /lops/ (adj) on heat, in heat, in season

de **looptijd** /loptɛit/ (pl: -en) term, (period of) currency, duration

het **loopvlak** /lopflɑk/ tread

loos /los/ (adj) false, empty: *~ alarm* false alarm ‖ *er is iets ~* something's up (*or:* going on)

de **loot** /lot/ (pl: loten) shoot, cutting

het **lootje** /locə/ (pl: -s) lottery ticket, raffle ticket, lot: *~s trekken* draw lots

¹**lopen** /lopə(n)/ (liep, heeft/is gelopen) **1** walk, go: *iem. in de weg ~* get in s.o.'s way; *op handen en voeten ~* walk on one's hands and feet, walk on all fours **2** run: *het op een ~ zetten* take to one's heels **3** run, go: *het is anders gelopen* it worked out (*or:* turned out) otherwise ‖ *dit horloge loopt uitstekend* this watch keeps excellent time; *de kraan loopt niet meer* the tap's stopped running; *een motor die loopt op benzine* an engine that runs on petrol; *alles loopt gesmeerd* everything's running smoothly; *iets laten ~* **a)** let sth. go; **b)** let sth. slide (*or:* slip)

²**lopen** /lopə(n)/ (liep, heeft gelopen) go to, attend: *college ~* attend lectures

lopend /lopənt/ (adj) **1** running, moving: *~e band* conveyor belt; assembly line; [fig] *aan de ~e band* continually, ceaselessly **2** current, running: *het ~e jaar* the current year **3** running; streaming; runny

de **loper** /lopər/ (pl: -s) **1** walker; courier; messenger **2** carpet (strip); runner **3** bishop **4** pass-key, master key, skeleton key, picklock

het/de **lor** /lɔr/ (pl: -ren) rag

los /lɔs/ (adj, adv) **1** loose, free; undone; detachable; movable: *er is een schroef ~* a screw has come loose; *~! let go!* **2** loose, separate, odd, single: *thee wordt bijna niet meer ~ verkocht* tea is hardly sold loose any more **3** slack, loose ‖ *met ~se handen rijden* ride with no hands; *ze leven er maar op ~* they live from one day to the next

losbandig /lɔzbɑndəχ/ (adj, adv) lawless; loose; fast, dissipated

losbarsten /lɔzbɑrstə(n)/ (barstte los, is losgebarsten) break out, burst out, flare up, erupt; blow up

de **losbol** /lɔzbɔl/ (pl: -len) fast liver, rake

losbranden /lɔzbrɑndə(n)/ (brandde los, is losgebrand) fire (*or:* blaze) away: *brand maar los!* fire away!

¹losbreken /lɔzbrekə(n)/ (brak los, is losgebroken) **1** break out (*or:* free), escape: *de hond is losgebroken* the dog has torn itself free **2** burst out, blow up: *een hevig onweer brak los* a heavy thunderstorm broke

²losbreken /lɔzbrekə(n)/ (brak los, heeft losgebroken) break off, tear off (*or:* loose), separate

losdraaien /lɔzdrajə(n)/ (draaide los, heeft losgedraaid) **1** unscrew, untwist **2** take off, twist off, loosen

de **loser** /luːzər/ loser

losgaan /lɔsxan/ (ging los, is losgegaan) come loose, work loose, become untied (*or:* unstuck, detached)

het **losgeld** /lɔsxɛlt/ (pl: -en) ransom (money)

losjes /lɔʃəs/ (adv) **1** loosely **2** airily, casually

loskloppen /lɔsklɔpə(n)/ (klopte los, heeft losgeklopt) beat, knock loose (*or:* off)

losknopen /lɔsknopə(n)/ (knoopte los, heeft losgeknoopt) undo, untie

loskomen /lɔskomə(n)/ (kwam los, is losgekomen) **1** come loose, come off, break loose (*or:* free), come apart: *hij kan niet ~ van zijn verleden* he cannot forget his past **2** come out, unbend, relax

loskoppelen /lɔskɔpələ(n)/ (koppelde los, heeft losgekoppeld) detach, uncouple, disconnect, separate

loskrijgen /lɔskrɛiɣə(n)/ (kreeg los, heeft losgekregen) **1** get loose; get undone; get free (*or:* released): *een knoop ~* get a knot untied **2** secure, extract, (manage to) obtain; raise

¹loslaten /lɔslatə(n)/ (liet los, heeft losgelaten) come off, peel off, come loose (*or:* unstuck, untied), give way

²loslaten /lɔslatə(n)/ (liet los, heeft losgelaten) **1** release, set free, let off, let go, discharge; unleash: *laat me los!* let go of me!, let me go! **2** reveal, speak; release; leak: *geen woord ~ over iets* keep mum (*or:* close) about sth.

losliggend /lɔslɪɣənt/ (adj) loose

loslippig /lɔslɪpəx/ (adj) loose-lipped, loose-tongued

loslopen /lɔslopə(n)/ (liep los, heeft losgelopen) walk about (freely), run free; be at large; stray ‖ *het zal wel ~* it will be all right, it'll sort itself out

loslopend /lɔslopənt/ (adj) stray, unattached

losmaken /lɔsmakə(n)/ (maakte los, heeft losgemaakt) **1** release, set free; untie: *de hond ~* unleash the dog; *een knoop ~* untie a knot, undo a button **2** loosen (up); rake **3** stir up: *die tv-film heeft een hoop losgemaakt* that TV film has created quite a stir

de **losprijs** /lɔsprɛis/ (pl: -prijzen) ransom (money)

losraken /lɔsrakə(n)/ (raakte los, is losgeraakt) come loose (*or:* off, away), dislodge, become detached

losrukken /lɔsrʏkə(n)/ (rukte los, heeft losgerukt) tear loose, rip off, wrench, yank away (*or:* off)

de **löss** /lʏs/ loess

losscheuren /lɔsxørə(n)/ (scheurde los, heeft losgescheurd) tear loose, rip off (*or:* away)

losschroeven /lɔsxruvə(n)/ (schroefde los, heeft losgeschroefd) unscrew, loosen; screw off; disconnect

lossen /lɔsə(n)/ (loste, heeft gelost) **1** unload, discharge **2** discharge; shoot; fire: *een schot op (het) doel ~* shoot at goal

losslaan /lɔslan/ (sloeg los, is losgeslagen) **1** break away **2** [fig] go astray: *die jongen is helemaal losgeslagen* that boy has gone completely astray

losstaan /lɔstan/ (stond los, heeft losgestaan): *~ van* be unrelated to

losstaand /lɔstant/ (adj) detached; isolated; free-standing; disconnected

lostrekken /lɔstrɛkə(n)/ (trok los, heeft losgetrokken) pull loose, loosen, draw loose

los-vast /lɔsfɑst/ (adj) half-fastened; [fig] casual

¹losweken /lɔswekə(n)/ (weekte los, is losgeweekt) become unstuck

²losweken /lɔswekə(n)/ (weekte los, heeft losgeweekt) soak off; steam off (*or:* open)

loszitten /lɔstə(n)/ (zat los, heeft losgezeten) be loose; be slack: *die knoop zit los* that button is coming off

het **lot** /lɔt/ (pl: -en) **1** lottery ticket; raffle ticket **2** lot, share: [fig] *zij is een ~ uit de loterij* she is one in a thousand **3** fortune, chance **4** lot, fate, destiny: *iem. aan zijn ~ overlaten* leave s.o. to fend for himself, leave s.o. to his fate; *berusten in zijn ~* resign o.s. to one's fate

loten /lotə(n)/ (lootte, heeft geloot) draw lots

de **loterij** /lotərɛi/ (pl: -en) lottery

de **lotgenoot** /lɔtxənot/ (pl: lotgenoten) companion (in misfortune, adversity), fellow-sufferer

de **loting** /lotɪŋ/ (pl: -en) drawing lots

de **lotion** /loʃɔn/ (pl: -s) lotion, wash

de **lotto** /lɔto/ (pl: -'s) lottery

de **lotus** /lotʏs/ (pl: -sen) lotus

de **louche** /luʃ(ə)/ (adj) shady, suspicious(-looking)

de **lounge** /lɑundʒ/ (pl: -s) lounge

¹louter /lɑutər/ (adj) sheer, pure; mere; bare: *uit ~ medelijden* purely out of compassion; *door ~ toeval* by pure coincidence

²louter /lɑutər/ (adv) purely, merely, only: *het heeft ~ theoretische waarde* it has only theoretical value

loven /l<u>o</u>və(n)/ (loofde, heeft geloofd)
1 praise, commend, laud **2** [rel] praise, bless,
glorify: *looft de Heer* praise the Lord

lovend /l<u>o</u>vənt/ (adj, adv) laudatory, approving; full of praise

de **loverboy** /l<u>o</u>vərbɔj/ lover boy

het **lovertje** /l<u>o</u>vərcə/ (pl: -s) spangle, sequin

de **lowbudgetfilm** /lob<u>y</u>dʒɛtfɪlm/ (pl: -s) low-
budget film, film made on a shoestring

loyaal /loj<u>a</u>l/ (adj, adv) loyal, faithful, steadfast

de **loyaliteit** /lwajalit<u>ɛi</u>t/ loyalty

¹**lozen** /l<u>o</u>zə(n)/ (loosde, heeft geloosd)
drain, empty: ~ *in (op) de zee* discharge into
the sea

²**lozen** /l<u>o</u>zə(n)/ (loosde, heeft geloosd) get
rid of, send off, dump

de **lozing** /l<u>o</u>zɪŋ/ (pl: -en) drainage, discharge,
dumping

de **lp** /ɛlp<u>e</u>/ (pl: lp's) LP

het **lpg** /ɛlpeɣ<u>e</u>/ *liquefied petroleum gas* LPG, LP
gas

het **lso** /ɛlɛs<u>o</u>/ [Belg] *lager secundair onderwijs*
junior secondary general education

de **lucht** /lʏχt/ (pl: -en) **1** air: ~ *krijgen* **a)** breathe; **b)** [fig] get room to breathe; *in de ~ vliegen* blow up, explode; *die bewering is uit de ~
gegrepen* that statement is totally unfounded; *uit de ~ komen vallen* appear out of thin
air; [Belg] be dumbfounded **2** sky **3** smell,
scent, odour ‖ *gebakken* ~ hot air

de **luchtaanval** /lʏχtanval/ (pl: -len) air raid

de **luchtafweer** /lʏχtafwer/ anti-aircraft guns

het **luchtafweergeschut** /lʏχtafwerɣəsχʏt/
anti-aircraft guns

het **luchtalarm** /lʏχtalɑrm/ (pl: -en) air-raid
warning (*or:* siren), (air-raid) alert

de **luchtballon** /lʏχtbɑlɔn/ (pl: -nen) (hot-air)
balloon

het **luchtbed** /lʏχtbɛt/ (pl: -den) air-bed, Lilo,
inflatable bed

de **luchtbel** /lʏχtbɛl/ (pl: -len) air bubble (*or:*
bell)

de **luchtbevochtiger** /lʏχtbəvɔχtəɣər/ (pl: -s)
humidifier

de **luchtbrug** /lʏχtbrʏχ/ (pl: -gen) **1** overhead
bridge **2** airlift

luchtdicht /lʏɣdɪχt/ (adj, adv) airtight, hermetic

de **luchtdruk** /lʏɣdrʏk/ (atmospheric) pressure,
air pressure

het **luchtdrukpistool** /lʏɣdrʏkpistol/ (pl: -pis-
tolen) air pistol

luchten /lʏχtə(n)/ (luchtte, heeft gelucht)
air, ventilate

de **luchter** /lʏχtər/ (pl: -s) candelabrum, chandelier

het/de **luchtfilter** /lʏχtfɪltər/ (pl: -s) air filter (*or:*
cleaner)

de **luchtfoto** /lʏχtfoto/ (pl: -'s) aerial photo-

(graph), aerial view

luchtgekoeld /lʏ(χt)ɣək<u>u</u>lt/ (adj) air-cooled

het **luchtgevecht** /lʏ(χt)ɣəvɛχt/ (pl: -en) dog-
fight

luchthartig /lʏχth<u>ɑ</u>rtəχ/ (adj, adv) light-
hearted, carefree

de **luchthaven** /lʏχthavə(n)/ (pl: -s) airport

de **luchthavenbelasting** /lʏχthavə(n)-
bəlɑstɪŋ/ airport tax

luchtig /lʏχtəχ/ (adj) **1** light, airy **2** light,
cool, thin **3** airy, light-hearted: *iets op ~e
toon meedelen* announce sth. casually **4** airy,
vivacious, light ‖ ~ *gekleed* lightly dressed

het **luchtje** /lʏχjə/ (pl: -s) smell, scent, odour: *er
zit een ~ aan* [fig] there is sth. fishy about it ‖
een ~ scheppen take a breath of fresh air, get
a bit of fresh air

het **luchtkasteel** /lʏχtkɑstel/ (pl: -kastelen) castle in the air, daydream

de **luchtkoker** /lʏχtkokər/ (pl: -s) air (*or:* venti-
lating) shaft

het **luchtkussen** /lʏχtkʏsə(n)/ (pl: -s) air cushion
(*or:* pillow)

de **luchtlaag** /lʏχtlaχ/ (pl: -lagen) layer of air

de **luchtlandingstroepen** /lʏχtlɑndɪŋstru-
pə(n)/ (pl) airborne troops

luchtledig /lʏχtl<u>e</u>dəχ/ (adj) exhausted (*or:*
void) of air: *een ~e ruimte* a vacuum

de **luchtmacht** /lʏχtmɑχt/ (pl: -en) air force

de **luchtmachtbasis** /lʏχtmɑχtbazɪs/ (pl: -bas-
es) air(-force) base

luchtmobiel /lʏχtmobi<u>l</u>/ (adj) airborne

de **luchtpijp** /lʏχtpɛip/ (pl: -en) windpipe, tra-
chea

de **luchtpost** /lʏχtpɔst/ airmail

het **luchtruim** /lʏχtrœym/ atmosphere, airspace, air

het **luchtschip** /lʏχtsχɪp/ (pl: -schepen) airship,
dirigible

de **luchtspiegeling** /lʏχtspiɣəlɪŋ/ (pl: -en) mirage

de **luchtsprong** /lʏχtsprɔŋ/ (pl: -en) jump in
the air, caper

de **luchtstreek** /lʏχtstrek/ (pl: -streken) zone,
region

de **luchtstroom** /lʏχtstrom/ (pl: -stromen) air
current, flow of air

de **luchtvaart** /lʏχtfart/ aviation, flying

de **luchtvaartmaatschappij** /lʏχtfartmat-
sχɑpɛi/ (pl: -en) airline (company): *de Koninklijke Luchtvaartmaatschappij* Royal Dutch
Airlines, KLM

de **luchtverfrisser** /lʏχtfərfrɪsər/ (pl: -s) air
freshener

het **luchtverkeer** /lʏχtfərker/ air traffic

de **luchtverkeersleider** /lʏχtfərkerslɛidər/
(pl: -s) air traffic controller

de **luchtverversing** /lʏχtfərvɛrsɪŋ/ ventilation

de **luchtvervuiling** /lʏχtfərvœylɪŋ/ air pollution

de **luchtvochtigheid** /lʏχtf<u>ɔ</u>χtəχhɛit/ humidity

de **luchtweerstand** /lʏҳtwerstɑnt/ drag, air resistance

de **luchtwegen** /lʏҳtweɣə(n)/ (pl) bronchial tubes

de **luchtzak** /lʏҳtsɑk/ (pl: -ken) air pocket, air hole

luchtziek /lʏҳtsik/ (adj) airsick

de **luchtziekte** /lʏҳtsiktə/ airsickness

de **lucifer** /lysifɛr/ (pl: -s) match

het **lucifersdoosje** /lysifɛrzdoʃə/ (pl: -s) matchbox

het **lucifershoutje** /lysifɛrshɑucə/ (pl: -s) matchstick

lucky /lʏki/ (adj) lucky

lucratief /lykratif/ (adj, adv) lucrative, profitable

ludiek /lydik/ (adj, adv) playful: *~e protestacties* happenings

luguber /lyɣybər/ (adj, adv) lugubrious, sinister

de ¹**lui** /lœy/ (pl) people, folk: *zijn ouwe ~* his old folks (*or:* parents)

²**lui** /lœy/ (adj, adv) lazy, idle, indolent; slow; heavy: *een ~e stoel* an easy chair; *liever ~ dan moe zijn* be bone idle

de **luiaard** /lœyart/ (pl: -s) **1** lazybones **2** sloth

luid /lœyt/ (adj, adv) loud: *~ en duidelijk* loud and clear; *met ~e stem* in a loud voice

¹**luiden** /lœydə(n)/ (luidde, heeft geluid) **1** sound, ring; toll: *de klok luidt* the bell is ringing (*or:* tolling) **2** read, run: *het vonnis luidt …* the verdict is …

²**luiden** /lœydə(n)/ (luidde, heeft geluid) ring, sound

luidkeels /lœytkels/ (adv) loudly, at the top of one's voice

luidop /lœytɔp/ (adv) [Belg] aloud, out loud

luidruchtig /lœytrʏҳtəҳ/ (adj, adv) noisy, boisterous

de **luidspreker** /lœytsprekər/ (pl: -s) (loud)speaker

de **luier** /lœyər/ (pl: -s) nappy

luieren /lœyərə(n)/ (luierde, heeft geluierd) be idle (*or:* lazy), laze

de **luifel** /lœyfəl/ (pl: -s) awning

de **luiheid** /lœyhɛit/ laziness, idleness

het **luik** /lœyk/ (pl: -en) hatch; trapdoor; shutter

Luik /lœyk/ Liège

de **luilak** /lœylɑk/ (pl: -ken) lazybones, sluggard

Luilekkerland /lœylɛkərlɑnt/ (land of) Cockaigne, land of plenty

de **luim** /lœym/ (pl: -en) humour, mood, temper

de **luipaard** /lœypart/ (pl: -en) leopard

de **luis** /lœys/ (pl: luizen) louse; aphid

de **luister** /lœystər/ lustre, splendour: *een gebeurtenis ~ bijzetten* add lustre to an event

de **luisteraar** /lœystərar/ (pl: -s) listener

het **luisterboek** /lœystərbuk/ (pl: -en) audio book

luisteren /lœystərə(n)/ (luisterde, heeft geluisterd) **1** listen: *goed kunnen ~* be a good listener; *luister eens* listen …, say … **2** eavesdrop, listen (in) **3** listen, respond: *naar hem wordt toch niet geluisterd* nobody pays any attention to (*or:* listens to) him anyway || *dat luistert nauw* that requires precision, it's very precise work

luisterrijk /lœystərɛik/ (adj, adv) splendid, glorious, magnificent

de **luistertoets** /lœystərtuts/ (pl: -en) listening comprehension test

de **luistervaardigheid** /lœystərvardəҳhɛit/ listening (skill)

de **luistervink** /lœystərvɪŋk/ (pl: -en) eavesdropper

de **luit** /lœyt/ (pl: -en) lute

de **luitenant** /lœytənɑnt/ (pl: -s) lieutenant

de **luiwammes** /lœywɑməs/ (pl: -en) [inform] lazybones

luizen /lœyzə(n)/ (luisde, heeft geluisd): *iem. erin ~* take s.o. in, trick s.o. into sth.; trip s.o. up

de **luizenbaan** /lœyzə(n)ban/ (pl: -banen) soft job, cushy job

het **luizenleven** /lœyzə(n)levə(n)/ (pl: -s) cushy life

lukken /lʏkə(n)/ (lukte, is gelukt) succeed, be successful, work, manage, come off (*or:* through), gel: *het is niet gelukt* it didn't work, it didn't go through, it was no go; *het lukte hem te ontsnappen* he managed to escape; *die foto is goed gelukt* that photo has come out well

lukraak /lʏkrak/ (adj, adv) haphazard, random, wild, hit-or-miss

de **lul** /lʏl/ (pl: -len) [inform] **1** prick, cock **2** prick, drip

lullen /lʏlə(n)/ (lulde, heeft geluld) [inform] (talk) bullshit, drivel

lullig /lʏləҳ/ (adj, adv) [inform] shitty, (bloody) stupid, pathetic: *doe niet zo ~* don't be such a jerk (*or:* tit)

lumineus /lyminøs/ (adj) brilliant, bright

de **lummel** /lʏməl/ (pl: -s) [inform] clodhopper, gawk

lummelen /lʏmələ(n)/ (lummelde, heeft gelummeld) [inform] hang around, fool around

de **lunch** /lʏnʃ/ (pl: -es) lunch(eon)

het **lunchconcert** /lʏnʃkɔnsɛrt/ (pl: -en) lunch concert

lunchen /lʏnʃə(n)/ (lunchte, heeft geluncht) lunch, have (*or:* eat, take) lunch

het **lunchpakket** /lʏnʃpɑkɛt/ (pl: -ten) packed lunch

de **lunchpauze** /lʏnʃpauzə/ (pl: -s) lunch break

de **lunchroom** /lʏnʃru:m/ (pl: -s) tearoom; [Am] [roughly] coffee shop

de **luren** /lyrə(n)/ (pl): *iem. in de ~ leggen* take

s.o. in, take s.o. for a ride
lurken /lỵrkə(n)/ (lurkte, heeft gelurkt) suck
noisily
de **lurven** /lỵrvə(n)/ (pl): [inform] *iem.* **bij** *zijn ~
pakken* get s.o., grab s.o.
de **lus** /lʏs/ (pl: -sen) loop; noose
de **lust** /lʏst/ (pl: -en) **1** desire, interest: *tijd en ~
ontbreken me om …* I have neither the time
nor the energy to (*or:* for) … **2** lust, passion,
desire **3** delight, joy: *~en en **lasten*** joys and
burdens; *zwemmen is zijn ~ en zijn **leven***
swimming is all the world to him, swimming
is his ruling passion; *een ~ **voor** het oog* a
sight for sore eyes
lusteloos /lỵstəlos/ (adj, adv) listless, languid, apathetic
lusten /lỵstə(n)/ (lustte, heeft gelust) like,
enjoy, be fond of, have a taste for: *ik zou wel
een **pilsje** ~* I could do with a beer; [fig] *ik lust
hem **rauw*** let me get my hands on him
lustig /lỵstəx/ (adj, adv) cheerful, gay, merry
de **lustmoord** /lỵstmort/ (pl: -en) sex murder
(*or:* killing)
het **lustobject** /lỵstɔpjɛkt/ (pl: -en) sex object
het **lustrum** /lỵstrʏm/ (pl: lustra) lustrum
luthers /lỵtərs/ (adj) Lutheran
luttel /lỵtəl/ (adj) little, mere; few; inconsiderable
luwen /lỵwə(n)/ (luwde, is geluwd) subside,
die down
de **luwte** /lỵwtə/ (pl: -n) lee, shelter
de **luxaflex**® /lỵksaflɛks/ Venetian blinds
de ¹**luxe** /lỵksə/ luxury: *het zou **geen** (overbodige)
~ zijn* it would certainly be no luxury, it's
really necessary
²**luxe** /lỵksə/ (adj) luxury, fancy, de luxe: *een ~
tent* a posh (*or:* fancy) place
het **luxeartikel** /lỵksəɑrtikəl/ (pl: -en) luxury article; [pl] luxury goods
Luxemburg /lỵksəmbʏrx/ Luxembourg
de **Luxemburger** /lỵksəmbʏrɣər/ (pl: -s) Luxembourger
Luxemburgs /lỵksəmbʏrxs/ (adj) (of/from)
Luxembourg
luxueus /lyksywØs/ (adj, adv) luxurious, opulent, plush
het **lyceum** /lisejʏm/ (pl: lycea) [roughly] gram-
marschool; [Am] high school
de **lymf** /lɪmf/ lymph
de **lymfklier** /lɪmfklir/ (pl: -en) lymph node (*or:*
gland)
lynchen /lɪnʃə(n)/ (lynchte, heeft gelyncht)
lynch
de **lynx** /lɪŋks/ (pl: -en) lynx
de **lyriek** /lirịk/ lyric(al) (poetry)
lyrisch /lịris/ (adj, adv) lyric(al)

m

de **m** /ɛm/ (pl: m's) m, M

de **ma** /ma/ (pl: ma's) mum; [Am] mom: *pa en ma* Mum (*or:* Mom) and Dad

de **maag** /maχ/ (pl: magen) stomach: *ergens mee in zijn ~ zitten* be worried about sth., be troubled by sth.; *iem. iets in de ~ splitsen* unload sth. onto s.o.

de **maagband** /maχbɑnt/ (pl: -en) gastric band, lap band

de **maagd** /maχt/ (pl: -en) virgin

de **Maagd** /maχt/ (pl: -en) [astrology] Virgo

het **maag-darmkanaal** /maχdɑrmkanal/ (pl: -kanalen) gastrointestinal tract

maagdelijk /maχdələk/ (adj, adv) virginal: *~ wit* virgin white

de **maagdelijkheid** /maχdələkhɛit/ virginity

het **maagdenvlies** /maχdə(n)vlis/ (pl: -vliezen) hymen

de **maagklacht** /maχklɑχt/ (pl: -en) stomach disorder

de **maagkramp** /maχkrɑmp/ (pl: -en) stomach cramps

de **maagpijn** /maχpɛin/ (pl: -en) stomach-ache

het **maagsap** /maχsɑp/ gastric juice

het **maagzuur** /maχsyr/ heartburn

de **maagzweer** /maχswer/ (pl: -zweren) ulcer

maaien /majə(n)/ (maaide, heeft gemaaid) mow, cut

de **maaier** /majər/ (pl: -s) mower

de **maaimachine** /majmaʃinə/ (pl: -s) (lawn)-mower

de **maak** /mak/: *er zijn plannen in de ~ om ...* plans are being made to ...

het **¹maal** /mal/ meal: *een feestelijk ~* a festive meal

het/de **²maal** /mal/ **1** time: *een paar ~* once or twice, several times; *anderhalf ~ zoveel* half as much (*or:* many) (again) **2** times: *lengte ~ breedte ~ hoogte* length times width times height; *tweemaal drie is zes* two times three is six

de **maalstroom** /malstrom/ (pl: -stromen) whirlpool; [fig] vortex

het **maalteken** /maltekə(n)/ (pl: -s) multiplication sign

de **maaltijd** /maltɛit/ (pl: -en) meal, dinner

de **maaltijdcheque** /maltɛitʃɛk/ (pl: -s) [Belg] luncheon voucher

de **maan** /man/ (pl: manen) moon

de **maand** /mant/ (pl: -en) month: *de ~ januari* the month of January; *een ~ vakantie* a month's holiday; *drie ~en lang* for three months; *binnen een ~* within a month; *een baby van vier ~en* a four-month-old baby

het **maandabonnement** /mantabɔnəmɛnt/ (pl: -en) monthly subscription; monthly season ticket

de **maandag** /mandɑχ/ (pl: -en) Monday: *ik train altijd op ~* I always train on Mondays; *ik doe het ~ wel* I will do it on Monday; *'s ~s* on Mondays, every Monday

¹maandags /mandɑχs/ (adj) Monday

²maandags /mandɑχs/ (adv) on Mondays

het **maandblad** /mantblɑt/ (pl: -en) monthly (magazine)

maandelijks /mandələks/ (adj, adv) monthly, once a month, every month: *in ~e termijnen* in monthly instalments

maandenlang /mandə(n)lɑŋ/ (adj, adv) for months, months long

de **maandkaart** /mantkart/ (pl: -en) monthly (season) ticket

het **maandsalaris** /mantsalarɪs/ monthly salary

het **maandverband** /mantfərbɑnt/ (pl: -en) sanitary towel; [Am] sanitary napkin

de **maanfase** /manfazə/ phase (of the moon)

de **maanlanding** /manlɑndɪŋ/ (pl: -en) moon landing

het **maanlandschap** /manlɑntsχɑp/ (pl: -pen) moonscape, lunarscape

het **maanlicht** /manlɪχt/ moonlight

het **maanmannetje** /manmɑnəcə/ man in the moon

de **maansverduistering** /mansfərdœystərɪŋ/ (pl: -en) eclipse of the moon, lunar eclipse

het **maanzaad** /manzat/ poppy seed

¹maar /mar/ (adv) **1** but, only, just: *zeg het ~: koffie of thee?* which will it be: coffee or tea?; *kom ~ binnen* come on in; *dat komt ~ al te vaak voor* that happens only (*or:* all) too often; *het is ~ goed dat je gebeld hebt* it's a good thing you rang; *als ik ook ~ een minuut te lang wegblijf* if I stay away even a minute too long; *doe het nu ~* just do it; *let ~ niet op hem* don't pay any attention to him; *ik zou ~ uitkijken* you'd better be careful **2** only, as long as: *als het ~ klaar komt* as long as (*or:* so long as) it is finished **3** (if) only: *ik hoop ~ dat hij het vindt* I only hope he finds it || *wat je ~ wil* whatever you want; *ik vind het ~ niks* I'm none too happy about it; *zoveel als je ~ wilt* as much (*or:* many) as you like

²maar /mar/ (conj) but: *klein, ~ dapper* small but tough || *ja ~, als dat nu niet zo is* yes, but what if that isn't true?; *nee ~!* really!

de **maarschalk** /marsχɑlk/ (pl: -en) Field Marshal; [Am] General of the Army

de **maart** /mart/ March

de **maas** /mas/ (pl: mazen) mesh: *door de mazen (van het net) glippen* slip through the net

de **Maas** /mas/ Meuse

de **¹maat** /mat/ **1** size, measure; measurements: *in hoge mate* to a great degree, to a large extent; *in toenemende mate* increasingly, more and more; *welke ~ hebt u?* what size do

you take? **2** measure: *maten en **gewichten***
weights and measures **3** moderation **4** [mus]
time; beat: *(geen)* ~ *kunnen **houden*** be (un)a-
ble to keep time **5** [mus] bar, measure: *de*
eerste maten van het volkslied the first few
bars of the national anthem ‖ *de* ~ *is **vol***
that's the limit

de **²maat** /mɑt/ **1** pal, mate **2** (team)mate;
[cards] partner

de **maatbeker** /mɑdbekər/ (pl: -s) measuring
cup

maatgevend /mɑtχevənt/ (adj) normative;
indicative: *dat **is** toch niet ~?* that is not a criterion, is it?

het **maatgevoel** /mɑtχəvul/ sense of rhythm

het **maatglas** /mɑtχlɑs/ measuring glass; grad-
uated cylinder

maathouden /mɑthɑudə(n)/ (hield maat,
heeft maatgehouden) [mus] keep time

het **maatje** /mɑcə/ (pl: -s) chum, pal: *goede ~s*
zijn met iem. be the best of friends with s.o.;
goede ~s worden met iem. chum up with s.o.

de **maatjesharing** /mɑcəsharɪŋ/ (pl: -en)
[roughly] young herring

het **maatkostuum** /mɑtkɔstym/ (pl: -s) custom-
made suit, tailored suit

de **maatregel** /mɑtreɣəl/ (pl: -en) measure:
*~en **nemen*** (or: *treffen*) take steps

de **maatschap** /mɑtsχɑp/ (pl: -pen) partnership

maatschappelijk /mɑtsχɑpələk/ (adj, adv)
1 social: *hij zit in het* ~ *werk* he's a social
worker **2** joint: *het* ~ *kapitaal* nominal capital

de **maatschappij** /mɑtsχɑpɛi/ (pl: -en) **1** society, association **2** company

de **maatschappijleer** /mɑtsχɑpɛiler/ social
studies

de **maatstaf** /mɑtstɑf/ (pl: -staven) criterion,
standard(s)

het **maatwerk** /mɑtwɛrk/ custom-made clothes
(or: shoes)

macaber /mɑkɑbər/ (adj, adv) macabre

de **macaroni** /mɑkɑroni/ macaroni

Macedonië /mɑsədonijə/ Macedonia

de **Macedoniër** /mɑsədonijər/ Macedonian

het **¹Macedonisch** /mɑsədonis/ Macedonian

²Macedonisch /mɑsədonis/ (adj) Macedonian

de **machete** /mɑ(t)ʃetə/ (pl: -s) machete

¹machinaal /mɑʃinɑl/ (adj) mechanized, machine

²machinaal /mɑʃinɑl/ (adv) mechanically, by
machine

de **machine** /mɑʃinə/ (pl: -s) machine; machinery

de **machinebankwerker** /mɑʃinəbɑŋk-
wɛrkər/ (pl: -s) lathe operator

het **machinegeweer** /mɑʃinəɣəwer/ (pl: -ge-
weren) machine-gun

de **machinekamer** /mɑʃinəkɑmər/ (pl: -s) en-

gine room

de **machinist** /mɑʃinɪst/ (pl: -en) **1** [railways]
engine driver; [Am] engineer **2** [shipp] engineer

de **¹macho** /mɑtʃo/ (pl: -'s) macho

²macho /mɑtʃo/ (adj) macho

de **macht** /mɑχt/ (pl: -en) **1** power, force: *(naar)*
de ~ *grijpen* (attempt to) seize power; *aan de*
~ *zijn* be in power; *iem. in zijn* ~ *hebben* have
s.o. in one's power; *de* ~ *over het stuur verlie-*
zen lose control of the wheel **2** authority:
rechterlijke ~ the judicial branch, the judiciary; *de **uitvoerende*** (or: *wetgevende*) ~ the
executive (or: legislative) branch **3** power,
force: *dat gaat **boven** mijn* ~ that is beyond
my power; *met (uit) alle* ~ with all one's
strength ‖ [maths] *een getal **tot** de vierde* ~
verheffen raise a number to the fourth power; [maths] *drie tot de **derde*** ~ three cubed

machteloos /mɑχtəlos/ (adj, adv) powerless: *machteloze **woede*** impotent (or: helpless) anger

de **machteloosheid** /mɑχtəloshɛit/ powerlessness

de **machthebber** /mɑχthɛbər/ (pl: -s) ruler,
leader

machtig /mɑχtəχ/ (adj) **1** powerful, mighty:
*haar gevoelens werden haar **te*** ~ she was overcome by her emotions **2** rich, heavy **3** competent (in)

machtigen /mɑχtəɣə(n)/ (machtigde, heeft
gemachtigd) authorize

de **machtiging** /mɑχtəɣɪŋ/ (pl: -en) authorization

het **machtsblok** /mɑχ(t)sblɔk/ (pl: -ken) power
block

de **machtshonger** /mɑχ(t)shɔŋər/ lust for
power

het **machtsmiddel** /mɑχ(t)smɪdəl/ (pl: -en)
means of (exercising) power, weapon

het **machtsmisbruik** /mɑχ(t)smɪzbrœyk/
abuse of power

de **machtsovername** /mɑχ(t)sovərnamə/ (pl:
-s) assumption of power; take-over

de **machtspolitiek** /mɑχ(t)spolitik/ power
politics

de **machtspositie** /mɑχ(t)spozi(t)si/ (pl: -s) position of power

de **machtsstrijd** /mɑχtstrɛit/ (pl: -en) struggle
for power, power struggle

het **machtsvacuüm** /mɑχ(t)sfakywʏm/ power
vacuum

machtsverheffen /mɑχ(t)sfərhɛfə(n)/
raise to the power

het **machtsvertoon** /mɑχtsfərton/ display of
power, show of strength

het **macramé** /makrame/ macramé

macro /makro/ (adv) macro

macrobiotisch /makrobijotis/ (adj) macrobiotic

Madagaskar /madaɣɑskɑr/ Madagascar

de **madam** /madɑm/ (pl: -men) lady: *de ~ spelen (uithangen)* act the lady

de **made** /madə/ (pl: -n) maggot, grub

het **madeliefje** /madəlifjə/ (pl: -s) daisy

de **madonna** /madɔna/ (pl: -'s) Madonna

Madrileens /madrilens/ (adj) of/from Madrid; Madrid

maf /mɑf/ (adj, adv) [inform] crazy, nuts: *doe niet zo ~* don't be so daft, stop goofing around

maffen /mɑfə(n)/ (mafte, heeft gemaft) [inform] sleep, snooze, kip

de **maffia** /mɑfija/ mafia

de **maffioso** /mɑfijozo/ (pl: maffiosi) mafioso

de **mafkees** /mɑfkes/ (pl: mafkezen) [inform] goof(ball), nut

het **magazijn** /maɣazɛin/ (pl: -en) **1** warehouse; stockroom; supply room **2** magazine

de **magazijnbediende** /maɣazɛimbədində/ (pl: -n, -s) warehouseman; supply clerk

het **magazine** /mɛɡəzɪn/ (pl: -s) **1** magazine **2** current affairs programme

mager /maɣər/ (adj, adv) **1** thin; skinny **2** lean: *~e riblappen* lean beef (ribs) **3** feeble

de **magie** /maɣi/ magic

magisch /maɣis/ (adj) magic(al)

magistraal /maɣistral/ (adj) magisterial; [fig also] masterly

de **magistraat** /maɣistrat/ (pl: magistraten) magistrate

het **magma** /mɑɣma/ magma

de **magnaat** /mɑɣnat/ (pl: magnaten) magnate, tycoon

de **magneet** /mɑɣnet/ (pl: magneten) magnet

de **magneetkaart** /mɑɣnetkart/ swipe card

de **magneetzweeftrein** magnetic levitation train, maglev train

het **magnesium** /mɑɣnezijʏm/ magnesium

magnetisch /mɑɣnetis/ (adj) magnetic

de **magnetiseur** /mɑɣnetizør/ (pl: -s) magnetizer

het **magnetisme** /mɑɣnetɪsmə/ magnetism

de **magnetron** /mɑɣnetrɔn/ (pl: -s) microwave

magnifiek /mɑɣnifik/ (adj, adv) magnificent

de **magnolia** /mɑɣnolija/ (pl: -'s) magnolia

de **maharadja** /maharɑtja/ (pl: -'s) maharaja(h)

het **¹mahonie** /mahoni/ mahogany

²mahonie /mahoni/ (adj) mahogany

de **mail** /mel/ (pl: -s) (e-)mail

het **mailadres** mail address

de **mailbox** /mɛlbɔks/ mail box

mailen /melə(n)/ (mailde, heeft gemaild) **1** e-mail **2** do a mailshot

de **mailing** /melɪŋ/ (pl: -s) mailing

de **mailinglijst** /melɪŋlɛist/ (pl: -en) mailing list

de **mailinglist** /melɪŋlɪst/ (pl: -s) mailing list

de **maillot** /majo/ (pl: -s) tights

het **mailtje** /melcə/ e-mail

de **mainport** /menpɔːrt/ (pl: -s) transport hub

de **mais** /mɑjs/ maize; [Am] corn: *gepofte ~* popcorn

de **maiskolf** /mɑjskɔlf/ (pl: -kolven) corn-cob

de **maiskorrel** /mɑjskɔrəl/ (pl: -s) kernel of maize; [Am] kernel of corn

de **maîtresse** /mɛːtrɛsə/ (pl: -s) mistress

de **maizena** /mɑjzena/ cornflour; [Am] cornstarch

de **majesteit** /majəstɛit/ (pl: -en) Majesty

majestueus /majɛstywøs/ (adj, adv) majestic(al)

de **majeur** /maʒør/ major: *in ~ spelen* play in a major key

de **majoor** /major/ (pl: -s) major

de **majoraan** /majoran/ (sweet) marjoram

de **majorette** /majorɛtə/ (pl: -s) (drum) majorette

mak /mɑk/ (adj, adv) **1** tame(d) **2** [fig] meek, gentle

de **makelaar** /makəlar/ (pl: -s) **1** estate agent; [Am] real estate agent **2** broker, agent: *~ in assurantiën* insurance broker

de **makelaardij** /makəlardɛi/ brokerage, agency; estate agency

de **makelij** /makəlɛi/ make, produce: *van eigen ~* home-grown, home-produced

maken /makə(n)/ (maakte, heeft gemaakt) **1** repair, fix: *zijn auto kan niet meer gemaakt worden* his car is beyond repair; *zijn auto laten ~* have one's car repaired (*or:* fixed) **2** make, produce; manufacture: *fouten ~* make mistakes; *cider wordt van appels gemaakt* cider is made from apples **3** cause || *je hebt daar niets te ~* you have no business there; *dat heeft er niets mee te ~* that's got nothing to do with it; *ze wil niets meer met hem te ~ hebben* she doesn't want anything more to do with him; *het (helemaal) ~* make it (to the top); *hij zal het niet lang meer ~* he is not long for this world; *je hebt het ernaar gemaakt* you('ve) asked for it; *ik weet het goed gemaakt* I'll tell you what, I'll make you an offer; *hoe maakt u het?* how do you do?; *hoe maakt je broer het?* how is your brother?; *maak dat je wegkomt!* get out of here!

de **maker** /makər/ (pl: -s) maker, producer; artist

de **make-up** /mekʏp/ make-up

¹makkelijk /mɑkələk/ (adj) easy, simple

²makkelijk /mɑkələk/ (adv) easily, readily: *jij hebt ~ praten* it's easy (enough) for you to talk

de **makker** /mɑkər/ (pl: -s) pal, mate

het **makkie** /mɑki/ (pl: -s) piece of cake; cushy job, easy job

de **makreel** /makrel/ (pl: makrelen) mackerel

de **¹mal** /mɑl/ (pl: -len) mould, template || *iem. voor de ~ houden* make fun of s.o., pull s.o.'s leg

²mal /mɑl/ (adj, adv) silly, foolish: *nee, ~le meid (jongen)* no, silly!; *ben je ~?* of course not!, are you kidding?

malafide /malafi̱də/ (adj) fraudulent, crooked

de **Malagassiër** /malaɣɒsijər/ (pl: -s) Malagasy

Malagassisch /malaɣɒsis/ (adj) Malagasy

de **malaise** /malɛ̱:zə/ **1** malaise **2** depression, slump

de **malaria** /mala̱rija/ malaria

Malawi /mala̱wi/ Malawi

de **Malawiër** /mala̱wijər/ (pl: -s) Malawian

Malawisch /mala̱wis/ (adj) Malawian

de **Malediven** /maledi̱və(n)/ (pl) Maldive Islands, Maldives

Maleis /malɛ̱is/ (adj) Malay; [Am] Malayan

Maleisië /malɛ̱isijə/ Malaysia

de **Maleisiër** /malɛ̱isijər/ Malaysian

Maleisisch /malɛ̱izis/ (adj) Malaysian

¹**malen** /ma̱lə(n)/ (maalde, heeft gemaald) turn, grind

²**malen** /ma̱lə(n)/ (maalde, heeft gemalen) grind; crush

het **mali** /ma̱li/ [Belg] deficit, shortfall

Mali /ma̱li/ Mali

de **maliënkolder** /ma̱lijənkɔldər/ (pl: -s) coat of mail

de ¹**Malinees** /malinɛ̱s/ (pl: Malinezen) Malian

²**Malinees** /malinɛ̱s/ (adj) Malian

de **maling** /ma̱lɪŋ/ grind ‖ *daar heb ik ~ aan* I don't care two hoots (*or:* give a hoot); *~ aan iets (iem.) hebben* not care (*or:* not give a rap) about sth. (s.o.); *iem. in de ~ nemen* pull s.o.'s leg, fool s.o.

de **mallemoer** /maləmu̱r/: *dat gaat je geen ~ aan* that's none of your damn (*or:* bloody) business; *naar zijn ~* ruined, finished

de **malloot** /malo̱t/ (pl: malloten) idiot, fool

mals /mals/ (adj, adv) tender

het/de **malt** /malt/ low alcohol beer, non-alcoholic beer

Malta /ma̱lta/ Malta

Maltees /maltɛ̱s/ (adj) Maltese

Maltezer /maltɛ̱zər/ (adj) Maltese

de **malus** /ma̱lʏs/ (pl: -sen) (financial) penalty

de **malversatie** /malvɛrsa̱(t)si/ (pl: -s) malversation; embezzlement

de **mama** /ma̱ma/ (pl: -'s) mam(m)a

de **mammoet** /ma̱mut/ (pl: -en, -s) mammoth

de **mammoettanker** /ma̱mutɛŋkər/ (pl: -s) mammoth tanker, supertanker

de **man** /man/ (pl: -nen) **1** man: *op de ~ spelen* **a)** go for the man (*or:* player); **b)** [fig] get personal; *een ~ uit duizenden* a man in a million; *een ~ van weinig woorden* a man of few words; *hij is een ~ van zijn woord* he is as good as his word **2** man, human: *de gewone (kleine) ~* the man in the street, the common man; *vijf ~ sterk* five strong; *met hoeveel ~ zijn we?* how many are we?, how many of us are there? **3** husband

het **management** /mɛ̱nədʒmənt/ management

het **managementteam** /mɛ̱nədʒmənti:m/ (pl: -s) management team

managen /mɛ̱nədʒə(n)/ (managede, heeft gemanaged) manage

de **manager** /mɛ̱nədʒər/ (pl: -s) manager

de **manche** /mɑ̃ʃ(ə)/ (pl: -s) **1** heat **2** game

de **manchet** /mɑnʃɛ̱t/ (pl: -ten) cuff

de **manchetknoop** /mɑnʃɛ̱tknop/ (pl: -knopen) cuff link

het **manco** /mɑ̱ŋko/ (pl: -'s) **1** defect, shortcoming **2** shortage

de **mand** /mɑnt/ (pl: -en) basket ‖ *bij een verhoor door de ~ vallen* have to own up (*or:* come clean); *door de ~ vallen als coach* fail as a coach, be a failure as a coach

het **mandaat** /mɑnda̱t/ (pl: mandaten) mandate: [Belg] *een dubbel ~* a double mandate

de **mandarijn** /mɑndari̱n/ (pl: -en) mandarin; [small] tangerine

de **mandataris** /mɑndata̱rɪs/ (pl: -sen) **1** mandatary **2** [Belg] representative

de **mandekking** /mɑ̱ndɛkɪŋ/ man-to-man marking; [Am] man-on-man coverage

de **mandoline** /mɑndoli̱nə/ (pl: -s) mandolin

de **mandril** /mɑndrɪ̱l/ (pl: -s) mandrill

de **manege** /manɛ̱ʒə/ (pl: -s) riding school, manège

de ¹**manen** /ma̱nə(n)/ (pl) mane

²**manen** /ma̱nə(n)/ (maande, heeft gemaand) **1** remind; [stronger] demand: *iem. om geld ~* demand payment from s.o. **2** urge ‖ *iem. tot kalmte ~* calm s.o. down

de **maneschijn** /ma̱nəsxɛin/ moonlight

het **mangaan** /mɑŋɣa̱n/ manganese

het **mangat** /mɑ̱ŋɣɑt/ (pl: -en) manhole

de **mangel** /mɑ̱ŋəl/ (pl: -s): [fig] *door de ~ gehaald worden* be put through the wringer; be crucified

de **mango** /mɑ̱ŋo/ (pl: -'s) mango

de **mangrove** /mɑŋɣro̱və/ (pl: -n, -s) mangrove

manhaftig /mɑnha̱ftəx/ (adj, adv) manful, manly: *zich ~ gedragen* act manfully (*or:* bravely)

de **maniak** /manija̱k/ (pl: -ken) maniac; freak; buff; fan

maniakaal /manijaka̱l/ (adj, adv) maniacal

de **manicure** /maniky̱rə/ (pl: -n) manicurist

de **manie** /ma̱ni/ (pl: -s) mania

de **manier** /mani̱r/ (pl: -en) **1** way, manner: *daar is hij ook niet op een eerlijke ~ aangekomen* he didn't get that by fair means; *hun ~ van leven* their way of life; *op een fatsoenlijke ~* in a decent manner, decently; *op de een of andere ~* somehow or other; *op de gebruikelijke ~ (in)* the usual way; *dat is geen ~ (van doen)* that is no way to behave **2** manners: *wat zijn dat voor ~en!* what kind of behaviour is that!

het **manifest** /manifɛ̱st/ (pl: -en) manifesto

de **manifestatie** /manifɛsta̱(t)si/ (pl: -s) demonstration; happening; event

zich **manifesteren** /manifɛstɛrə(n)/ (manifes-
teerde zich, heeft zich gemanifesteerd)
manifest o.s.

de **manipulatie** /manipyla(t)si/ (pl: -s) manipulation: *genetische* ~ genetic engineering
manipuleren /manipylɛrə(n)/ (manipu-
leerde, heeft gemanipuleerd) manipulate
manisch-depressief /manizdeprɛsif/ (adj)
manic-depressive

het **manjaar** /mɑnjar/ (pl: manjaren) man-year
mank /mɑŋk/ (adj, adv) lame: ~ *lopen* (walk
with a) limp

het **mankement** /mɑŋkəmɛnt/ (pl: -en) defect;
bug
¹**mankeren** /mɑŋkɛrə(n)/ (mankeerde, heeft
gemankeerd) be wrong, be the matter: *wat
mankeert je toch?* what's wrong (or: the matter) with you?; *er mankeert nogal wat **aan***
there's a fair amount wrong with it
²**mankeren** /mɑŋkɛrə(n)/ (mankeerde, heeft
gemankeerd) have sth. the matter: *ik man-
keer **niets** I'm all right, there's nothing wrong
with me

de **mankracht** /mɑŋkrɑxt/ manpower

het **manna** /mɑna/ manna
mannelijk /mɑnələk/ (adj, adv) male, masculine: *een ~e **stem** a masculine voice

het **mannenkoor** /mɑnə(n)kor/ (pl: -koren)
male choir, men's chorus

de **mannenstem** /mɑnə(n)stɛm/ male voice,
man's voice

de **mannequin** /mɑnəkɛ̃/ (pl: -s) model

het **mannetje** /mɑnəcə/ **1** little fellow, little
guy **2** man: *daar heeft hij zijn ~s voor* he leaves
that to his underlings **3** male ‖ *zijn ~ **staan***
hold one's (own) ground, stick up for o.s.

de **mannetjesputter** /mɑnəcəspytər/ (pl: -s)
strapper, he-man, she man

de **manoeuvre** /manœːvrə/ (pl: -s) manoeuvre
manoeuvreren /manuvrɛrə(n)/ (manoeu-
vreerde, heeft gemanoeuvreerd) manoeuvre: *iem. **in** een onaangename positie ~* manoeuvre s.o. into an awkward position

de **manometer** /manometər/ (pl: -s) manometer, pressure gauge
mans /mɑns/ (adj): *zij is er ~ **genoeg** voor* she
can handle it

de **manschappen** /mɑnsxɑpə(n)/ men
manshoog /mɑnshox/ (adj) man-size(d), of
a man's height

de **mantel** /mɑntəl/ (pl: -s) **1** coat; [also fig]
cloak **2** [technology] casing, housing

de **mantelorganisatie** /mɑntələrɣaniza(t)si/
(pl: -s) umbrella organization

het **mantelpak** /mɑntəlpɑk/ (pl: -ken) suit

de **mantelzorg** /mɑntəlzɔrx/ volunteer aid

de **mantra** /mɑntra/ (pl: -'s) mantra

de **manufacturen** /manyfɑktyrə(n)/ (pl) drapery

het **manuscript** /manyskrɪpt/ (pl: -en) manuscript; typescript

het **manusje-van-alles** /manyʃəvɑnɑləs/ (pl:
manusjes-van-alles) jack-of-all-trades; (general) dogsbody

het **manuur** /mɑnyr/ (pl: manuren) man-hour

het **manwijf** /mɑnwɛɪf/ (pl: -wijven) mannish
woman, battle-axe

de **map** /mɑp/ (pl: -pen) file, folder

de **maquette** /mɑkɛtə/ (pl: -s) (scale-)model

de **maraboe** /marabu/ (pl: -s) marabou

de **marathon** /maratɔn/ (pl: -s) marathon: *halve* ~ half-marathon

de **marathonloop** /maratɔnlop/ (pl: -lopen)
marathon race
marchanderen /marʃɑndɛrə(n)/ (marchan-
deerde, heeft gemarchandeerd) bargain
marcheren /marʃɛrə(n)/ (marcheerde,
heeft/is gemarcheerd) march

de **marconist** /markonɪst/ (pl: -en) radio operator

de **marechaussee** /marəʃose/ (pl: -s) military
police, MP

de **maretak** /marətɑk/ (pl: -ken) mistletoe

de **margarine** /marɣarinə/ (pl: -s) margarine

de **marge** /mɑːrʒə/ (pl: -s) **1** margin: *gerommel
in de* ~ fiddling about **2** band
marginaal /marɣinal/ (adj) marginal

de **margriet** /marɣrit/ (pl: -en) marguerite, (ox-
eye) daisy
Maria-Hemelvaart /marijahɛməlvart/ Assumption (of the Virgin Mary)

de **marihuana** /marijuwana/ marijuana, marihuana

de **marine** /marinə/ navy

de **marinebasis** /marinəbazɪs/ (pl: -bases) naval base
marineren /marinɛrə(n)/ (marineerde,
heeft gemarineerd) marinate, marinade

de **marinier** /marinir/ (pl: -s) marine: *het **Korps**
Mariniers* the Marine Corps; the Marines

de **marionet** /marijonɛt/ puppet
maritiem /maritim/ (adj) maritime

de **marjolein** /marjolɛin/ marjoram

de **mark** /mɑrk/ (pl: -en) mark
markant /mɑrkɑnt/ (adj) striking

de **markeerstift** /markɛrstɪft/ (pl: -en) marker,
marking pen
markeren /markɛrə(n)/ (markeerde, heeft
gemarkeerd) mark

de **marketing** /mɑːrkətɪŋ/ marketing

de **markies** /mɑrkis/ (pl: markiezen) marquis

de **markiezin** /mɑrkizɪn/ (pl: -nen) marquise

de **markt** /mɑrkt/ (pl: -en) market: *een **dalende**
(or: **stijgende**)* ~ a bear (or: bull) market; *naar
de ~ gaan* go to market; *van alle ~en thuis zijn*
be able to turn one's hand to anything; *zichzelf **uit** de ~ prijzen* price o.s. out of the market ‖ [Belg] *het niet **onder** de ~ hebben* be
having a hard time

het **marktaandeel** /mɑrktandel/ (pl: -aande-
len) market share, share of the market

de **marktdag** /mɑrktdɑx/ (pl: -en) market day

de **markteconomie** /mɑrktekonomi/ (pl: -ën) market economy

de **markthal** /mɑrkthɑl/ (pl: -len) market hall, covered market

de **marktkoopman** /mɑrktkopmɑn/ (pl: -nen, marktkooplui) market vendor, stallholder

de **marktkraam** /mɑrktkram/ (pl: -kramen) market stall (or: booth)

het **marktonderzoek** /mɑrktɔndərzuk/ market research

de **marktwaarde** /mɑrktwardə/ market value

de **marktwerking** /mɑrktwɛrkɪŋ/ free-market system, free competition

de **marmelade** /mɑrməladə/ (pl: -s) marmalade

het **marmer** /mɑrmər/ (pl: -s) marble

marmeren /mɑrmərə(n)/ (adj) marble

de **marmot** /mɑrmɔt/ (pl: -ten) 1 marmot 2 guinea pig

de **Marokkaan** /mɑrɔkan/ (pl: Marokkanen) Moroccan

Marokkaans /mɑrɔkans/ (adj) Moroccan

Marokko /mɑrɔko/ Morocco

de **mars** /mɑrs/ (pl: -en) march ‖ *hij heeft niet veel in zijn ~* a) he hasn't got much about him; b) he is pretty ignorant; c) he isn't very bright; d) he's not up to much; *hij heeft heel wat in zijn ~* a) he has a lot to offer; b) he is pretty knowledgeable; c) he's a clever chap; *voorwaarts ~!* forward march!; *ingerukt ~!* dismiss!

Mars /mɑrs/ Mars

het/de **marsepein** /mɑrsəpɛin/ marzipan

de **marskramer** /mɑrskramər/ (pl: -s) hawker, pedlar

het **marsmannetje** /mɑrsmɑnəcə/ (pl: -s) Martian

de **martelaar** /mɑrtəlar/ (pl: martelaren) martyr

het **martelaarschap** /mɑrtəlarsχɑp/ martyrdom

de **marteldood** /mɑrtəldot/ death through torture

martelen /mɑrtələ(n)/ (martelde, heeft gemarteld) torture

de **martelgang** /mɑrtəlɣɑŋ/ (pl: -en) [also fig] calvary

de **marteling** /mɑrtəlɪŋ/ (pl: -en) torture

de **¹marter** /mɑrtər/ (pl: -s) [animal] marten

het **²marter** /mɑrtər/ [fur] marten

de **Martinikaan** /mɑrtinikan/ (pl: Martinikanen) inhabitant (or: native) of Martinique

Martinikaans /mɑrtinikans/ (adj) of/from Martinique

Martinique /mɑrtinik/ Martinique

het **marxisme** /mɑrksɪsmə/ Marxism

de **marxist** /mɑrksɪst/ (pl: -en) Marxist

de **mascara** /mɑskara/ mascara

de **mascotte** /mɑskɔtə/ (pl: -s) mascot

het **masker** /mɑskər/ (pl: -s) mask

de **maskerade** /mɑskəradə/ (pl: -s) 1 masked procession 2 masquerade

maskeren /mɑskɛrə(n)/ (maskeerde, heeft gemaskeerd) mask, hide: *hij maskeerde zijn slechte **bedoelingen*** he masked his evil intentions

het **masochisme** /mɑsoχɪsmə/ masochism

de **masochist** /mɑsoχɪst/ (pl: -en) masochist

de **massa** /mɑsa/ (pl: -'s) 1 mass, heaps: *hij heeft een ~ **vrienden*** he has heaps (or: loads) of friends; *~'s **mensen*** masses (or: swarms) of people 2 mass, crowd; [pol] masses: *met de ~ meedoen* go with (or: follow) the crowd

massaal /mɑsal/ (adj, adv) 1 massive: *~ **verzet*** massive resistance 2 mass, wholesale; bulk [goods]

de **massabijeenkomst** /mɑsabɛienkɔmst/ (pl: -en) mass meeting

de **massage** /mɑsaʒə/ massage

het **massagraf** /mɑsaɣrɑf/ (pl: -graven) mass grave

de **massamedia** /mɑsamedija/ (pl) mass media

de **massamoord** /mɑsamort/ (pl: -en) mass murder

de **massaproductie** /mɑsaprodʏksi/ mass production

de **massasprint** /mɑsasprɪnt/ (pl: -s) field sprint

het **massavernietigingswapen** /mɑsavərnitəɣɪŋswapə(n)/ weapon of mass destruction

masseren /mɑserə(n)/ (masseerde, heeft gemasseerd) massage, do a massage on

de **masseur** /mɑsør/ (pl: -s) masseur

massief /mɑsif/ (adj) solid, massive, heavy: *een ring van ~ **zilver*** a ring of solid silver

de **mast** /mɑst/ (pl: -en) 1 mast: *de ~ **strijken*** lower the mast 2 pylon

de **master** /mɑːstər/ Master: *zijn ~ **doen*** do one's MA/MSc/Master's, take one's finals

het **masterplan** /mɑːstərplɑn/ (pl: -nen) master plan

masturberen /mɑstʏrbɛrə(n)/ (masturbeerde, heeft gemasturbeerd) masturbate

de **¹mat** /mɑt/ (pl: -ten) mat: *~ten kloppen* beat (or: shake) mats

²mat /mɑt/ (adj) checkmate: *~ **staan*** be checkmated; *iem. ~ **zetten*** checkmate s.o.

³mat /mɑt/ (adj, adv) 1 mat(t); dull; dim [light]; pearl 2 mat(t); frosted

de **matador** /mɑtadɔr/ (pl: -s) matador

de **match** /mɛtʃ/ (pl: -es) match: *er was **geen** ~ tussen hen* they didn't click, they were not well-matched

het **matchpoint** /mɛtʃpɔjnt/ (pl: -s) match point: *op ~ staan* be at match point

de **mate** /matə/ (pl: -n) measure, extent, degree: *in **dezelfde** ~* equally, to the same extent; *in mindere ~* to a lesser degree; *in grote* (or: *hoge*) *~* to a great (or: large) extent, largely

mateloos /matəlos/ (adj, adv) immoderate,

excessive: ~ *rijk* immensely rich

de **matennaaier** /mɑtənajər/ rat

het **materiaal** /mater(i)jal/ (pl: materialen) material(s)

de **materialist** /materijalɪst/ (pl: -en) materialist

materialistisch /mater(i)jalɪstis/ (adj, adv) materialistic

de **materie** /matɛri/ (pl: -s) matter; (subject) matter

het ¹**materieel** /materijel/ material(s), equipment: *rollend* ~ rolling stock

²**materieel** /materijel/ (adj) material: *materiële schade* property (*or*: material) damage

de **materniteit** /matɛrnitɛit/ [Belg] maternity ward

het **matglas** /mɑtxlɑs/ frosted glass

de **mathematicus** /matematikʏs/ mathematician

mathematisch /matematis/ (adj, adv) mathematical

matig /matəx/ (adj, adv) **1** moderate **2** moderate, mediocre

matigen /matəɣə(n)/ (matigde, heeft gematigd) moderate, restrain: *matig uw snelheid* reduce your speed

de **matiging** /matəɣɪŋ/ moderation

de **matinee** /matine/ (pl: -s) matinee

matineus /matinøs/ (adj) early

het **matje** /mɑcə/ (pl: -s) mat: *op het ~ moeten komen* **a)** be put on the spot; **b)** be (put) on the carpet

de **matrak** /matrɑk/ (pl: -ken) [Belg] truncheon, baton

het/de **matras** /matrɑs/ (pl: -sen) mattress

de **matrijs** /matrɛis/ (pl: matrijzen) mould, matrix

de **matrix** /matrɪks/ (pl: matrices) matrix

de **matroos** /matros/ (pl: matrozen) sailor

de **matse** /mɑtsə/ (pl: -s) matzo

matsen /mɑtsə(n)/ (matste, heeft gematst) [inform] do a favour; wangle

de **mattenklopper** /mɑtə(n)klɔpər/ (pl: -s) carpet-beater

Mauritaans /mɑuritans/ (adj) Mauritanian

Mauritanië /mɑuritanijə/ Mauretania

de **Mauritaniër** /mɑuritanijər/ (pl: -s) Mauritanian

de **Mauritiaan** /mɑuri(t)ʃan/ (pl: Mauritianen) Mauritian

Mauritiaans /mɑuri(t)ʃans/ (adj) Mauritian

Mauritius /mɑurɪtsijʏs/ (island of) Mauritius

het **mausoleum** /mɑuzolɛjʏm/ (pl: -s, mausolea) mausoleum

mauwen /mɑuwə(n)/ (mauwde, heeft gemauwd) **1** miaow, mew **2** whine

de **mavo** /mavo/ (pl: -'s) school for lower general secondary education

m.a.w. (abbrev) *met andere woorden* in other words

het **maxi** /mɑksi/ maxi

¹**maximaal** /mɑksimal/ (adj) maximum, maximal

²**maximaal** /mɑksimal/ (adv) at (the) most: *dit werk duurt ~ een week* this work takes a week at most

het **maximum** /mɑksimʏm/ (pl: maxima) maximum

de **maximumsnelheid** /mɑksimʏmsnɛlhɛit/ (pl: -heden) speed limit; maximum speed

de **maximumtemperatuur** /mɑksimʏmtɛmpəratyr/ maximum temperature

de **mayonaise** /majonɛːzə/ mayonnaise: *patat met ~* chips with mayonnaise; [Am] French fries with mayonnaise

de **mazelen** /mazələ(n)/ (pl) measles

de **mazout** /mazʏt/ [Belg] (heating) oil

de **mazzel** /mɑzəl/ [inform] (good) luck: *de ~!* see you!; ~ *hebben* have (good) luck

mazzelen /mɑzələ(n)/ (mazzelde, heeft gemazzeld) [inform] have (good) luck

het **mbo** /ɛmbeo/ *middelbaar beroepsonderwijs* intermediate vocational education

m.b.v. (abbrev) *met behulp van* by means of

me /mə/ (pers pron) me

de **ME** /ɛmɛ/ (pl: ME's) *mobiele eenheid* anti-riot squad

de **meander** /mejɑndər/ (pl: -s) meander

het **meao** /meao/ (pl: -'s) *middelbaar economisch en administratief onderwijs* intermediate business education

de **mecanicien** /mekaniʃɛ/ (pl: -s) mechanic

de **meccano** /mɛkano/ (pl: -'s) meccano (set)

de **mechanica** /meхanika/ mechanics

het/de **mechaniek** /meхanik/ (pl: -en) mechanism

de **mechanisatie** /meхaniza(t)si/ mechanization

mechanisch /meхanis/ (adj, adv) mechanical: ~ *speelgoed* clockwork toys

mechaniseren /meхanizerə(n)/ (mechaniseerde, heeft gemechaniseerd) mechanize

het **mechanisme** /meхanɪsmə/ (pl: -n) mechanism; [fig also] machinery

de **medaille** /medɑjə/ (pl: -s) medal

het **medaillon** /medɑjɔn/ (pl: -s) medallion; locket

mede /medə/ (adv) [form] also: ~ *hierdoor* as a consequence of this and other factors; ~ *namens* also on behalf of; ~ *wegens* partly due to

de **medeburger** /medəbʏrɣər/ (pl: -s) fellow citizen

mededeelzaam /medədɛlzam/ (adj) communicative

de **mededeling** /medədelɪŋ/ (pl: -en) announcement, statement

het **mededelingenbord** /medədelɪŋə(n)bɔrt/ (pl: -en) notice board

de **mededinger** /medədɪŋər/ (pl: -s) rival; competitor

het **mededogen** /medədoɣə(n)/ compassion

de **mede-eigenaar** /mẹdəɛiɣənar/ (pl: -s, mede-eigenaren) joint owner

de **medeklinker** /mẹdəklɪŋkər/ (pl: -s) consonant

de **medeleerling** /mẹdəlerlɪŋ/ (pl: -en) fellow pupil

het **medeleven** /mẹdəlevə(n)/ sympathy: *op-recht* ~ sincere sympathy; *mijn* ~ *gaat uit naar* my sympathy lies with; *zijn* ~ *tonen* express one's sympathy

het **medelijden** /mẹdəlɛidə(n)/ pity, compassion: *heb* ~ *(met)* have mercy (upon); ~ *met zichzelf hebben* feel sorry for oneself

de **medemens** /mẹdəmɛns/ (pl: -en) fellow man

medeplichtig /medəplɪxtəɣ/ (adj) accessory

de **medeplichtige** /medəplɪxtəɣə/ (pl: -n) accessory (to), accomplice; partner

de **medereiziger** /mẹdərɛizəɣər/ (pl: -s) fellow traveller (*or:* passenger)

medeschuldig /medəsxʏldəx/ (adj) implicated (in), also guilty, also to blame

de **medestander** /mẹdəstandər/ (pl: -s) supporter

medeverantwoordelijk /mẹdəvərantwordələk/ (adj) jointly responsible (for), co-responsible (for)

de **medewerker** /mẹdəwɛrkər/ (pl: -s) **1** fellow worker, co-worker; collaborator; contributor, correspondent: *onze juridisch* (or: *economisch*) ~ our legal (*or:* economics) correspondent **2** employee, staff member

de **medewerking** /mẹdəwɛrkɪŋ/ cooperation, assistance: *de politie riep de* ~ *in van het publiek* the police made an appeal to the public for cooperation

het **medeweten** /mẹdəwetə(n)/ (fore)knowledge: *dit is buiten mijn* ~ *gebeurd* this occurred unknown to me (*or:* without my knowledge)

de **medezeggenschap** /medəzɛɣə(n)sxap/ say; participation

de **media** /mẹdija/ (pl) media

mediageniek /medijaʒənik/ (adj) mediagenic

de **mediaspeler** /mẹdijaspelər/ (pl: -s) **1** media player **2** (portable) media player

de **mediastilte** media silence

de **mediatheek** /medijatek/ (pl: mediatheken) multimedia centre (*or:* library)

de **mediator** /mịdijetɔr/ mediator

het **medicament** /medikamɛnt/ (pl: -en) medicament, medicine

de **medicijn** /medisɛin/ (pl: -en) medicine: *een student (in de)* ~*en* a medical student

het **medicijnkastje** /medisɛinkaʃə/ (pl: -s) medicine chest (*or:* cabinet)

de **medicus** /mẹdikʏs/ (pl: medici) doctor, medical practitioner

medio /mẹdijo/ (adv) in the middle of: ~

september in mid-September

medisch /mẹdis/ (adj, adv) medical: *op* ~ *advies* on the advice of one's doctor

de **meditatie** /medita(t)si/ (pl: -s) meditation

mediteren /meditẹrə(n)/ (mediteerde, heeft gemediteerd) meditate

mediterraan /meditɛran/ (adj) Mediterranean

het ¹**medium** /mẹdijʏm/ (pl: media) medium

²**medium** /mẹdijʏm/ (adj) medium(-sized)

mee /me/ (adv) with, along: *waarom ga je niet* ~*?* why don't you come along? ‖ *met de klok* ~ clockwise; *kan ik ook* ~*?* can I come too?; *hij heeft zijn uiterlijk* ~ he has his looks going for him; *dat kan nog jaren* ~ that will last for years; *het kan er* ~ *door* it's all right, it'll do; *ergens te vroeg* (or: *te laat*) ~ *komen* be too early (*or:* late) with sth.

meebrengen /mẹbrɛŋə(n)/ (bracht mee, heeft meegebracht) **1** bring (along) (with one): *wat zal ik voor je* ~*?* what shall I bring you? **2** involve: *de moeilijkheden die dit met zich heeft meegebracht* the difficulties which resulted from this

¹**meedelen** /mẹdelə(n)/ (deelde mee, heeft meegedeeld) share (in), participate (in): *alle erfgenamen delen mee* all heirs are entitled to a share

²**meedelen** /mẹdelə(n)/ (deelde mee, heeft meegedeeld) inform (of), let … know; notify, announce; report: *ik zal het haar voorzichtig* ~ I shall break it to her gently; *hierbij deel ik u mee, dat* … I am writing to inform you that …

meedingen /mẹdɪŋə(n)/ (dong mee, heeft meegedongen) compete

meedoen /mẹdun/ (deed mee, heeft meegedaan) join (in), take part (in): *mag ik* ~*?* can I join in (*or:* you)?; ~ *aan een wedstrijd* compete in a game; ~ *aan een project* (or: *staking*) take part in a project (*or:* strike); *oké, ik doe mee* okay, count me in

meedogenloos /medọɣə(n)los/ (adj, adv) merciless

mee-eten /mẹetə(n)/ (at mee, heeft meegegeten) eat with (s.o.)

de **mee-eter** /mẹetər/ (pl: -s) blackhead, whitehead

meegaan /mẹɣan/ (ging mee, is meegegaan) **1** go along (or: with), accompany, come along (or: with): *is er nog iem. die meegaat?* is anyone else coming (or: going)? **2** [fig] go (along) with, agree (with): *met de mode* ~ keep up with (the) fashion **3** last: *dit toestel gaat jaren mee* this machine will last for years

meegaand /mẹɣant/ (adj) compliant, pliable

¹**meegeven** /mẹɣevə(n)/ (gaf mee, heeft meegegeven) give (way), yield: *de planken geven niet mee* there is no give in the boards

²**meegeven** /meːɣeːvə(n)/ (gaf mee, heeft meegegeven) give: *iem. een **boodschap** ~* send a message with s.o.

meehelpen /meːhɛlpə(n)/ (hielp mee, heeft meegeholpen) help (in, with), assist (with)

¹**meekomen** /meːkomə(n)/ (kwam mee, is meegekomen) **1** come (also), come along **2** keep up (with)

²**meekomen** /meːkomə(n)/ (kwam mee, is meegekomen) **1** come (along, with, also): *ik heb er geen bezwaar tegen als **hij** meekomt* I don't object to his coming (along) **2** keep up (with)

meekrijgen /meːkrɛiɣə(n)/ (kreeg mee, heeft meegekregen) **1** get, receive: *kan ik het **geld** direct ~?* can I have the money immediately? **2** win over, get on one's side

het **meel** /meːl/ flour

de **meeldraad** /meːldraːt/ (pl: -draden) stamen

meeleven /meːleːvə(n)/ (leefde mee, heeft meegeleefd) sympathize

meelijwekkend /meːlɛiwɛkənt/ (adj) pitiful

meelopen /meːlopə(n)/ (liep mee, is meegelopen) walk along (with), accompany

de **meeloper** /meːlopər/ (pl: -s) hanger-on

meeluisteren /meːlœystərə(n)/ (luisterde mee, heeft meegeluisterd) listen (in)

meemaken /meːmakə(n)/ (maakte mee, heeft meegemaakt) experience; go through; live; see; take part (in): *had hij dit nog maar mee **mogen** maken* if he had only lived to see this; *ze heeft heel wat meegemaakt* she has seen (or: been through) a lot

meenemen /meːnemə(n)/ (nam mee, heeft meegenomen) take along (or: with): [in restaurant] *~ graag* to take away please ‖ *dat is meegenomen* that's a (welcome) bonus, that's (always) sth.

meepraten /meːpratə(n)/ (praatte mee, heeft meegepraat) take part (or: join) in a conversation: *daar kun je niet **over** ~* you don't know anything about it

het ¹**meer** /meːr/ (pl: meren) lake

²**meer** /meːr/ (num) **1** more: *~ **dood** dan levend* more dead than alive; *des **te** ~* all the more (so); *steeds ~* more and more; *hij heeft ~ **boeken** dan ik* he has got more books than I (have) **2** more, further: *wie waren er **nog** ~?* who else was there?; *wat kan ik **nog** ~ doen?* what else can I do? **3** any more, no more, (any) longer: *zij is **geen** kind ~* she is no longer a child; *hij had **geen** appels ~* he had no more apples, he was out of apples **4** more (often): *we moeten dit ~ **doen*** we must do this more often ‖ *onder ~* among other things; among others; *zonder ~* **a)** naturally, of course; **b)** right away

de **ME'er** /ɛmɛjər/ riot policeman

meerdaags /meːrdaxs/ (adj) of (or: for) more than one day: *~e **weerprognose*** weather forecast for the coming days

de ¹**meerdere** /meːrdərə/ (pl: -n) superior; superior officer

²**meerdere** /meːrdərə/ (num) several, a number of

de **meerderheid** /meːrdərhɛit/ majority

meerderjarig /meːrdərjaːrəx/ (adj) of age: *~ **worden*** come of age

de **meerderjarige** /meːrdərjaːrəɣə/ (pl: -n) adult

de **meerderjarigheid** /meːrdərjaːrəxhɛit/ adulthood, legal age

meerderlei /meːrdərlɛi/ (pron) multiple

meerekenen /meːrekənə(n)/ (rekende mee, heeft meegerekend) count (in)

meerijden /meːrɛidə(n)/ (reed mee, heeft/is meegereden) come (or: ride) (along) with: *ik vroeg of ik mee **mocht** rijden* I asked for a lift

meerjarig /meːrjaːrəx/ (adj) of more than one year; long-term

de **meerkeuzetoets** /meːrkøːzətuts/ (pl: -en) multiple-choice test

de **meerkeuzevraag** /meːrkøːzəvraːx/ (pl: -vragen) multiple-choice question

de **meerkoet** /meːrkut/ coot

meermaals /meːrmaːls/ (adv) several times, more than once

meeroken /meːrokə(n)/ (rookte mee, heeft meegerookt) be subjected to passive smoking

de **meerpaal** /meːrpaːl/ (pl: -palen) mooring post

meerstemmig /meːrstɛməx/ (adj, adv) many-voiced

het **meervoud** /meːrvɑut/ (pl: -en) plural: *in het ~* (in the) plural

¹**meervoudig** /meːrvɑudəx/ (adj) plural

²**meervoudig** /meːrvɑudəx/ (adv) poly-, multi-: *~ onverzadigde vetzuren* polyunsaturated fatty acids

de **meerwaarde** /meːrwaːrdə/ surplus (or: excess) value

het **meerwerk** /meːrwɛrk/ additional (or: extra) work

meerzijdig /meːrzɛidəx/ (adj) multilateral

de **mees** /meːs/ (pl: mezen) tit

meesjouwen /meːsjɑuwə(n)/ (sjouwde mee, heeft meegesjouwd) lug; [Am] tote

meeslepen /meːslepə(n)/ (sleepte mee, heeft meegesleept) **1** drag (along) **2** carry (with, away): *zich **laten** ~* get carried away

meeslepend /meːslepənt/ (adj, adv) compelling, moving

meesleuren /meːslørə(n)/ (sleurde mee, heeft meegesleurd) sweep away (or: along)

meesmuilen /meːsmœylə(n)/ (meesmuilde, heeft gemeesmuild) smirk

meespelen /meːspelə(n)/ (speelde mee, heeft meegespeeld) take part (or: join) in a game; play (along with); be a cast member

¹**meest** /meːst/ (adj) **1** most, the majority of: *op zijn ~* at (the) most **2** most, greatest

²**meest** /mest/ (adv) most, best: *de ~ gelezen krant* the most widely read newspaper
meestal /mestɑl/ (adv) mostly, usually
de **meester** /mestər/ (pl: -s) **1** master: *~ in de rechten* [roughly] Master of Laws **2** teacher, (school)master
het **meesterbrein** /mestərbrɛin/ (pl: -en) mastermind
de **meesteres** /mestərɛs/ (pl: -sen) mistress
de **meesterhand** /mestərhɑnt/ master-hand, touch of the master
meesterlijk /mestərlək/ (adj, adv) masterly
het **meesterschap** /mestərsxɑp/ mastery, skill
het **meesterstuk** /mestərstʏk/ (pl: -ken) masterpiece
het **meesterwerk** /mestərwɛrk/ (pl: -en) masterpiece, masterwork
de **meet** /met/ (pl: meten): *van ~ af aan* from the beginning
meetbaar /medbar/ (adj) measurable
¹**meetellen** /metɛlə(n)/ (telde mee, heeft meegeteld) count: *dat telt niet mee* that doesn't count
²**meetellen** /metɛlə(n)/ (telde mee, heeft meegeteld) count also, count in, include
de **meeting** /miːtɪŋ/ (pl: -s) meeting
het **meetinstrument** /metɪnstrymɛnt/ (pl: -en) measuring instrument
de **meetkunde** /metkʏndə/ geometry
de **meetlat** /metlɑt/ (pl: -ten) measuring rod: [fig] *iem. langs de ~ leggen* judge s.o.
het **meetlint** /metlɪnt/ (pl: -en) tape-measure
meetronen /metronə(n)/ (troonde mee, heeft meegetroond) coax along
de **meeuw** /mew/ (pl: -en) (sea)gull
meevallen /mevɑlə(n)/ (viel mee, is meegevallen) turn out (*or:* prove, be) better than expected: *dat zal wel ~* it won't be so bad
de **meevaller** /mevɑlər/ (pl: -s) piece (*or:* bit) of luck: *een financiële ~* a windfall
meevoelen /mevulə(n)/ (voelde mee, heeft meegevoeld) sympathize (with)
meevoeren /mevurə(n)/ (voerde mee, heeft meegevoerd) carry (along)
meewarig /mewarəx/ (adj, adv) pitying: *met een ~e blik keek ze hem aan* she looked at him pityingly
meewerken /mewɛrkə(n)/ (werkte mee, heeft meegewerkt) **1** cooperate, work together: *we werkten allemaal een beetje mee* we all pulled together, we all did our little bit **2** assist: *allen werkten mee om het concert te laten slagen* everyone assisted in making the concert a success ‖ *~d voorwerp* indirect object
meezingen /mezɪŋə(n)/ (zong mee, heeft meegezongen) sing along (with)
meezitten /mezɪtə(n)/ (zat mee, heeft meegezeten) be favourable: *het zat hem niet mee* luck was against him; *als alles meezit* if all goes well, if everything runs smoothly

de **megabioscoop** /meɣabijoskop/ multiplex
de **megabyte** /meɣabɑjt/ megabyte
de **megafoon** /meɣafon/ (pl: -s, megafonen) megaphone
de **megahertz** /meɣahɛrts/ megahertz
megalomaan /meɣaloman/ (adj) megalomaniac(al)
de **mei** /mɛi/ May
de **meid** /mɛit/ (pl: -en) girl, (young) woman: *je bent al een hele ~* you're quite a woman (*or:* girl)
de **meidengroep** /mɛidə(n)ɣrup/ (pl: -en) female band
de **meidoorn** /mɛidorn/ (pl: -s) hawthorn
de **meikever** /mɛikevər/ (pl: -s) May-bug, cockchafer
de **meineed** /mɛinet/ (pl: meineden) perjury
het **meisje** /mɛiʃə/ (pl: -s) **1** girl, daughter **2** girl, young woman (*or:* lady) **3** girlfriend **4** girl, maid
meisjesachtig /mɛiʃəsɑxtəx/ (adj, adv) girlish, girl-like
de **meisjesnaam** /mɛiʃəsnam/ (pl: -namen) maiden name
mej. (abbrev) *Mejuffrouw* Miss
de **mejuffrouw** /məjʏfrɑu/ (pl: -en) Miss; Ms
mekaar /məkar/ (ref pron) [inform] each other, one another ‖ *komt voor ~* OK, I'll see to it
het **mekka** /mɛka/ (pl: -'s) Mecca
mekkeren /mɛkərə(n)/ (mekkerde, heeft gemekkerd) **1** bleat **2** keep on (at s.o. about sth.), nag
melaats /melats/ (adj) leprous
de **melaatsheid** /melatshɛit/ leprosy
de **melancholie** /melɑnxoli/ melancholy
melancholiek /melɑnxolik/ (adj, adv) melancholy
de **melange** /melɑ̃ʒə/ (pl: -s) blend, mélange
¹**melden** /mɛldə(n)/ (meldde, heeft gemeld) report, inform (of); announce: *ze heeft zich ziek gemeld* she has reported (herself) sick; she called in sick; *niets te ~ hebben* [fig] have nothing (*or:* no news) to report
zich ²**melden** /mɛldə(n)/ (meldde zich, heeft zich gemeld) report, check in
de **melding** /mɛldɪŋ/ (pl: -en) mention(ing), report(ing)
de **meldkamer** /mɛltkamər/ (pl: -s) centre; emergency room
melig /meləx/ (adj, adv) corny
de **melk** /mɛlk/ milk: *halfvolle ~* low-fat milk; *koffie met ~* white coffee
de **melkboer** /mɛlgbur/ (pl: -en) milkman
de **melkbus** /mɛlgbʏs/ (pl: -sen) milk churn
melken /mɛlkə(n)/ (molk/melkte, heeft gemolken) milk
de **melkfles** /mɛlkflɛs/ (pl: -sen) milk bottle
het **melkgebit** /mɛlkxəbɪt/ (pl: -ten) milk teeth
de **melkkoe** /mɛlku/ **1** dairy cow **2** [fig] milch cow

het/de **melkpoeder** /mɛlkpudər/ powdered milk, dehydrated milk

de **melktand** /mɛlktɑnt/ (pl: -en) milk tooth

het **melkvee** /mɛlkfe/ dairy cattle

de **melkveehouder** /mɛlkfehɑudər/ (pl: -s) dairy farmer

de **Melkweg** /mɛlkwɛx/ (pl: -en) Milky Way

de **melodie** /melodi/ (pl: -ën) melody, tune

melodieus /melod(i)jøs/ (adj, adv) melodious

het **melodrama** /melodrɑma/ (pl: -'s) melodrama

melodramatisch /melodramɑtis/ (adj, adv) melodramatic(al)

de **meloen** /məlun/ (pl: -en) melon

het/de **membraan** /mɛmbran/ (pl: membranen) membrane

het/de **memo** /memo/ (pl: -'s) memo

de **memoires** /memwɑrəs/ (pl) memoirs

memorabel /memorabəl/ (adj) memorable

het **memorandum** /memorɑndym/ (pl: -s, memoranda) memorandum, note

memoreren /memorɛrə(n)/ (memoreerde, heeft gememoreerd) mention, remind

de **memorie** /memori/ (pl: -s) **1** memory: *kort van ~ zijn* have a short memory **2** memorandum: *~ van toelichting* explanatory memorandum

men /mɛn/ (ind pron) **1** one; people; they: *~ zegt* it is said, people (*or:* they) say; *~ zegt dat hij ziek is* he is said to be ill **2** one; you: *~ kan hen niet laten omkomen* they cannot be allowed to die; *~ zou zeggen dat …* by the look of it … **3** one; they: *~ had dat kunnen voorzien* that could have been foreseen; *~ hoopt dat …* it is hoped that …

de **meneer** /mənɛr/ (pl: meneren) gentleman; [before surname] Mr

menen /menə(n)/ (meende, heeft gemeend) **1** mean: *dat meen je niet!* you can't be serious!; *ik meen het!* I mean it! **2** intend, mean: *het goed met iem. ~* mean well towards s.o. **3** think: *ik meende dat …* I thought …

menens /menəns/ (adj): *het is ~* it's serious

de **mengeling** /mɛŋəlɪŋ/ (pl: -en) mixture

het **mengelmoes** /mɛŋəlmus/ mishmash, jumble

¹mengen /mɛŋə(n)/ (mengde, heeft gemengd) **1** mix, blend: *door elkaar ~* mix together **2** mix, bring in: *mijn naam wordt er ook in gemengd* my name was also brought in (*or:* dragged in)

zich **²mengen** /mɛŋə(n)/ (mengde zich, heeft zich gemengd) get (o.s.) involved (in), get (o.s.) mixed up (in): *zich in de discussie ~* join in the discussion

de **mengkleur** /mɛŋklør/ mixed (*or:* blended) colour

de **mengkraan** /mɛŋkran/ (pl: -kranen) mixer tap

het **mengpaneel** /mɛŋpanel/ (pl: -panelen) mixing console, mixer

het **mengsel** /mɛŋsəl/ (pl: -s) mixture, blend

de **menie** /meni/ red lead

meniën /menijə(n)/ (meniede, heeft gemenied) red-lead

menig /menəx/ (num) many; many a: *in ~ opzicht* in many respects

menigeen /menəxen/ (ind pron) many (people)

menigmaal /menəxmal/ (adv) many times, many a time

de **menigte** /menəxtə/ (pl: -n, -s) crowd

de **mening** /menɪŋ/ (pl: -en) opinion, view: *afwijkende ~* dissenting view (*or:* opinion); *zijn ~ geven* give one's opinion (*or:* view); *naar mijn ~* in my opinion (*or:* view), I think, I feel; *van ~ veranderen* change one's opinion (*or:* view); *voor zijn ~ durven uitkomen* stand up for one's opinion

de **meningsuiting** /menɪŋsœytɪŋ/ (expression of) opinion, speech: *vrije ~* freedom of speech

het **meningsverschil** /menɪŋsfərsxɪl/ (pl: -len) difference of opinion

de **meniscus** /menɪskys/ meniscus, kneecap

mennen /mɛnə(n)/ (mende, heeft gemend) drive

de **menopauze** /menopɑuzə/ menopause

de **¹mens** /mɛns/ **1** human (being), man; man(kind): *ik ben ook maar een ~* I'm only human; *dat doet een ~ goed* that does you good; *geen ~* not a soul **2** people: *de gewone ~en* ordinary people **3** person: *een onmogelijk ~ zijn* be impossible (to deal with)

het **²mens** /mɛns/ thing, creature: *het is een braaf (best) ~* she's a good (old) soul

de **mensa** /mɛnza/ (pl: -'s) refectory; (student) cafeteria

de **mensaap** /mɛnsap/ (pl: -apen) anthropoid (ape), man ape

het **mensbeeld** /mɛnzbelt/ (pl: -en) portrayal of man(kind)

menselijk /mɛnsələk/ (adj) **1** human: *vergissen is ~* to err is human **2** humane: *niet ~* inhumane, inhuman

de **menselijkheid** /mɛnsələkhɛit/ humanity: *misdaden tegen de ~* crimes against humanity

de **menseneter** /mɛnsə(n)etər/ (pl: -s) cannibal

de **mensengedaante** /mɛnsə(n)ɣədantə/ human form

de **mensenhandel** /mɛnsə(n)hɑndəl/ human trafficking

de **mensenhater** /mɛnsə(n)hatər/ (pl: -s) misanthrope

de **mensenheugenis** /mɛnsə(n)høɣənɪs/ human memory: *sinds ~* from (*or:* since) time immemorial

de **mensenkennis** /mɛnsə(n)kɛnɪs/ insight into (human) character (*or:* human nature) het **mensenleven** /mɛnsə(n)levə(n)/ (pl: -s) (human) life

de **mensenmassa** /mɛnsəmɑsa/ (pl: -'s) crowd

de **mensenrechten** /mɛnsə(n)rɛxtə(n)/ (pl) human rights

mensenschuw /mɛnsə(n)sxyw/ (adj) shy, afraid of people

de **mensensmokkel** /mɛnsə(n)smɔkəl/ frontier-running

de **mensenvriend** /mɛnsə(n)vrint/ philanthropist

het **mens-erger-je-niet** /mɛnsɛryərjənit/ ludo; [Am] sorry

de **mensheid** /mɛnshɛit/ human nature, humanity

menslievend /mɛnslivənt/ (adj, adv) charitable, humanitarian; philanthropic

mensonterend /mɛnsɔnterənt/ (adj) degrading, disgraceful

mensonwaardig /mɛnsɔnwardəx/ (adj) degrading

de **menstruatie** /mɛnstrywa(t)si/ menstruation, period

de **menstruatiepijn** /mɛnstrywa(t)sipɛin/ (pl: -en) menstrual pain

menstrueren /mɛnstrywerə(n)/ (menstrueerde, heeft gemenstrueerd) menstruate

menswaardig /mɛnswardəx/ (adj) decent, dignified

de **menswetenschappen** /mɛnswetə(n)sxɑpə(n)/ (pl) life sciences; social sciences

mentaal /mɛntal/ (adj, adv) mental

de **mental coach** /mɛntəlkotʃ/ mental coach

de **mentaliteit** /mɛntalitɛit/ mentality

de **menthol** /mɛntɔl/ menthol

de **mentor** /mɛntɔr/ (pl: -en) **1** tutor; [Am] student adviser **2** mentor

het/de **menu** /məny/ (pl: -'s) menu

de **menubalk** /mənybɑlk/ (pl: -en) menu bar, button bar

het/de **menuet** /menywɛt/ (pl: -ten) minuet

de **menukaart** /mənykart/ (pl: -en) menu

de **mep** /mɛp/ (pl: -pen) smack ǁ *de* **volle** ~ the full whack

meppen /mɛpə(n)/ (mepte, heeft gemept) smack

merci /mɛrsi/ (int) thanks

Mercurius /mɛrkyrijʏs/ Mercury

de **merel** /merəl/ (pl: -s) blackbird

meren /merə(n)/ (meerde, heeft gemeerd) moor

het **merendeel** /merə(n)del/ greater part; majority

merendeels /merə(n)dels/ (adv) **1** for the most part **2** mostly

het **merg** /mɛrx/ (bone) marrow: *die kreet ging door ~ en* **been** it was a harrowing (*or:* heart-rending) cry

de **mergel** /mɛryəl/ marl

de **meridiaan** /meridijan/ (pl: meridianen) meridian

het **merk** /mɛrk/ (pl: -en) **1** brand (name), trademark; make **2** mark; hallmark

het **merkartikel** /mɛrkartikəl/ proprietary brand

merkbaar /mɛrgbar/ (adj, adv) noticeable

merken /mɛrkə(n)/ (merkte, heeft gemerkt) **1** notice, see: *dat is (duidelijk) te* ~ it shows; *hij liet niets* ~ he gave nothing away; *je zult het* **wel** ~ you'll find out; *ik merkte het* **aan** *zijn gezicht* I could tell (*or:* see) by the look on his face **2** mark; brand

de **merkkleding** /mɛrkledɪŋ/ designer wear (*or:* clothes)

merkwaardig /mɛrkwardəx/ (adj, adv) peculiar: *het ~e van de zaak is ...* the curious (*or:* odd) thing (about it) is ...

de **merrie** /mɛri/ (pl: -s) mare

het **mes** /mɛs/ (pl: -sen) knife; blade: *het ~ snijdt aan twee kanten* it is doubly advantageous

mesjogge /məʃɔyə/ (adj) [inform] crazy, nutty

het **mespunt** /mɛspʏnt/ (pl: -en): *een ~je* **zout** *toe* a pinch of salt

de **mess** /mɛs/ (pl: -es) mess (hall), messroom

messcherp /mɛsxɛrp/ (adj) razor-sharp

de **Messias** /mɛsijɑs/ Messiah

het **messing** /mɛsɪŋ/ brass

de **messteek** /mɛstek/ (pl: messteken) stab (of a knife)

de **mest** /mɛst/ **1** manure **2** fertilizer

mesten /mɛstə(n)/ (mestte, heeft gemest) fertilize; fatten

de **mesthoop** /mɛsthop/ (pl: -hopen) dunghill

het **mestkalf** /mɛstkɑlf/ (pl: -kalveren) fatting calf

de **mestvaalt** /mɛstfalt/ (pl: -en) dunghill

het **mestvee** /mɛstfe/ beef cattle, store cattle, fatstock

de **mestvork** /mɛstfɔrk/ dung fork

met /mɛt/ (prep) **1** (along) with, of: *~ Janssen* [on the telephone] Janssen speaking (*or:* here); *~ wie* **spreek** *ik?* [on the telephone] who am I speaking to?; **spreken** *~ iem.* speak to s.o.; *~ (zijn)* **hoevelen** *zijn zij?* how many of them are there? **2** with, and; including: *~ rente* with interest; *~* **vijf** plus (*or:* and) five; *tot en ~ hoofdstuk drie* up to and including chapter three **3** (mixed) with, and **4** with, by, through, in: *~ de* **trein** *van acht uur* by the eight o'clock train **5** with, by, at: *ik kom ~* **Kerstmis** I'm coming at Christmas ǁ *een zak ~* **geld** a bag of money

de ¹**metaal** /metal/ metal industry; steel industry

het ²**metaal** /metal/ metal

metaalachtig /metalɑxtəx/ (adj, adv) metallic: *het* **klinkt** *~* it sounds metallic

de **metaalbewerking** /metalbəwɛrkɪŋ/ metalworking

de **metaaldetector** /metaldetɛktɔr/ (pl: -s, -en) metal detector

metaalindustrie

de **metaalindustrie** /metaːlɪndʏstri/ (pl: -ën) metallurgical industry

de **metaalmoeheid** /metaːlmuhɛɪt/ metal fatigue

de **metafoor** /metafoːr/ (pl: metaforen) metaphor: *om een ~ te* **gebruiken** metaphorically speaking

metafysisch /metafiːzis/ (adj, adv) metaphysical

metalen /metaːlə(n)/ (adj) **1** metal, metallic **2** metallic

metallic /metɛlɪk/ (adj) metallic

de **metamorfose** /metamɔrfoːzə/ (pl: -n, -s) metamorphosis

meteen /məteːn/ (adv) **1** immediately, at once, right (or: straight) away: *ze* **kwam** *~ toen ze het hoorde* she came as soon as she heard it; *dat* **zeg** *ik u zo ~* I'll tell you in (just) a minute; *ze was ~* **dood** she was killed instantly; **nu** *~* (right) now, this (very) minute **2** at the same time, too: *koop er ook ~ eentje voor mij* buy one for me (too) while you're about it

meten /meːtə(n)/ (mat/meette, heeft gemeten) measure; meter

de **meteoor** /metejoːr/ (pl: meteoren) meteor

de **meteoriet** /metejoriːt/ (pl: -en) meteorite

de **meteorologie** /metejoroloɣi/ meteorology

meteorologisch /metejoroloɣis/ (adj) meteorological

de **meteoroloog** /metejoroloːx/ (pl: -logen) meteorologist

de ¹**meter** /meːtər/ **1** metre: *méters* **boeken** yards of books; **vierkante** (or: **kubieke**) *~* square (or: cubic) metre **2** meter, gauge: *de ~* **opnemen** read the meter **3** indicator, (meter) needle ‖ **voor** *geen ~* not at all, no way

de ²**meter** /meːtər/ godmother

de **meterkast** /meːtərkɑst/ (pl: -en) meter cupboard

de **metgezel** /mɛtxəzɛl/ (pl: -len) companion

het **methaan** /metaːn/ methane

het **methadon** /metadɔn/ methadone

de **methode** /metoːdə/ (pl: -n, -s) method, system

de **methodiek** /metodiːk/ (pl: -en) methodology

de **meting** /meːtɪŋ/ (pl: -en) measuring, measurement

metriek /metriːk/ (adj) metric

de **metro** /meːtro/ (pl: -'s) underground (railway); [Am] subway; tube; metro

de **metronoom** /metronoːm/ (pl: -nomen) metronome

de **metropool** /metropoːl/ (pl: -polen) metropolis

het **metrostation** /meːtrostaˌ(t)ʃɔn/ (pl: -s) undergroundstation; [Am] subway station; tube station; metro station

het **metrum** /meːtrʏm/ (pl: -s, metra) metre

de **metselaar** /mɛtsəlar/ (pl: -s) bricklayer

metselen /mɛtsələ(n)/ (metselde, heeft gemetseld) build (in brick, with bricks); lay bricks

de **metten** /mɛtə(n)/ (pl): *korte ~ maken (met)* make short (or: quick) work (of)

metterdaad /mɛtərdaːt/ (adv) indeed, in fact

het **meubel** /møbəl/ (pl: -s, -en) piece of furniture; furniture

de **meubelboulevard** /møbəlbuləvar/ (pl: -s) furniture heaven (or: strip)

de **meubelmaker** /møbəlmakər/ (pl: -s) furniture maker

de **meubelzaak** /møbəlzak/ (pl: -zaken) furniture business (or: shop)

het **meubilair** /møbilɛːr/ furniture, furnishings

meubileren /møbilerə(n)/ (meubileerde, heeft gemeubileerd) furnish

de **meug** /møχ/: *iets tegen* **heug** *en ~ opeten* force down sth.

de **meute** /møtə/ (pl: -s) gang, crowd

de **mevrouw** /məvrɑu/ (pl: -en) **1** madam, ma'am, miss **2** Mrs; Ms

de **Mexicaan** /mɛksikaːn/ (pl: Mexicanen) Mexican

Mexicaans /mɛksikaːns/ (adj) Mexican

Mexico /mɛksiko/ Mexico

mezelf /məzɛlf/ (ref pron) myself, me: *ik* **vermaak** *~ wel* I'll look after myself

de **mezzosopraan** /mɛtsosopran/ (pl: -sopranen) mezzo-soprano

m.i. (abbrev) *mijns inziens* in my opinion

miauw /mijɑu/ (int) miaow, mew

miauwen /mijɑuwə(n)/ (miauwde, heeft gemiauwd) miaow, mew

de **micro** /miːkro/ (pl: -'s) [Belg] mike

de **microbe** /mikroːbə/ (pl: -n) microbe

de **microfilm** /miːkrofɪlm/ (pl: -s) microfilm

de **microfoon** /mikrofɔn/ (pl: -s) microphone; mike

de **microgolf** /miːkroɣɔlf/ (pl: -golven) [Belg] microwave

het **microkrediet** (pl: -en) microcredit

het **micro-organisme** /miːkrooˌrɣanɪsmə/ (pl: -n) micro-organism

de **microprocessor** /miːkroprosɛsɔr/ (pl: -s) microprocessor

de **microscoop** /mikroskoːp/ (pl: microscopen) microscope

microscopisch /mikroskoːpis/ (adj, adv) microscopic: *~* **klein** microscopic

de **middag** /mɪdɑχ/ (pl: -en) **1** afternoon: *'s ~s* in the afternoon; *om 5 uur* **'s** *~s* at 5 o'clock in the afternoon, at 5 p.m. **2** noon: *tussen de ~* at lunchtime

het **middagdutje** /mɪdɑɣdʏtcə/ (pl: -s) afternoon nap

het **middageten** /mɪdɑɣetə(n)/ lunch(eon)

de **middagpauze** /mɪdɑɣpɑuzə/ (pl: -s) lunch hour, lunchtime, lunch-hour break

de **middagtemperatuur** /mɪdɑχtɛmpəratyr/

                                               migratie

afternoon temperature

het **middaguur** /mɪdɑɣyr/ noon

het **middel** /mɪdəl/ (pl: -en) **1** waist **2** means: *het is een ~, geen doel* it's a means to an end; *door ~ van* by means of **3** remedy: *een ~tje tegen hoofdpijn* a headache remedy; *het ~ is soms erger dan de kwaal* the remedy may be worse than the disease

middelbaar /mɪdəlbar/ (adj) middle; [educ] secondary

de **middeleeuwen** /mɪdəlewə(n)/ (pl) Middle Ages

middeleeuws /mɪdəlews/ (adj) medi(a)eval: *~e geschriften* medi(a)eval documents; *~e opvattingen* medi(a)eval ideas

het **middelgebergte** /mɪdəlɣəbɛrχtə/ (pl: -n, -s) low mountain range

middelgroot /mɪdəlɣrot/ (adj) medium-size(d)

middellands /mɪdəlɑn(t)s/ (adj) Mediterranean: *de Middellandse Zee* the Mediterranean (Sea)

middellang /mɪdəlɑŋ/ (adj) **1** medium (length (*or:* range)) **2** medium length (*or:* term)

de **middellijn** /mɪdəlɛin/ (pl: -en) diameter

de **middelmaat** /mɪdəlmat/ average

middelmatig /mɪdəlmatəχ/ (adj, adv) average, mediocre: *ik vind het maar ~* I think it's pretty mediocre

de **middelmatigheid** /mɪdəlmatəχɦɛit/ mediocrity

het **middelpunt** /mɪdəlpʏnt/ (pl: -en) centre, middle

middelpuntvliedend /mɪdəlpʏntflidənt/ (adj) centrifugal

middels /mɪdəls/ (prep) by means of

middelst /mɪdəlst/ (adj) middle(most)

de **middelvinger** /mɪdəlvɪŋər/ (pl: -s) middle finger

het ¹**midden** /mɪdə(n)/ (pl: -s) **1** middle, centre: *dat laat ik in het ~* I won't go into that; *de waarheid ligt in het ~* the truth lies (somewhere) in between **2** middle, midst: *te ~ van* in the midst of, among

²**midden** /mɪdə(n)/ (adv) in the middle of: *~ in de zomer* in the middle of (the) summer; *hij is ~ (in de) veertig* he is in his middle forties (*or:* mid-forties)

Midden-Amerika /mɪdə(n)amerika/ Central America

de **middenberm** /mɪdə(n)bɛrm/ (pl: -en) central reservation

middendoor /mɪdə(n)dor/ (adv) in two

Midden-Europa /mɪdə(n)øropa/ Central Europe

Midden-Europees /mɪdə(n)øropes/ (adj) Central-European

de **middengolf** /mɪdə(n)ɣolf/ medium wave

middenin /mɪdə(n)ɪn/ (adv) in the middle (*or:* centre)

de **middenjury** /mɪdə(n)ʒyri/ [Belg] central examination committee

het **middenkader** /mɪdə(n)kadər/ middle management

de **middenklasse** /mɪdə(n)klɑsə/ medium range (*or:* size)

de **middenmoot** /mɪdə(n)mot/ middle bracket (*or:* group): *die sportclub hoort thuis in de ~* that's just an average club

de **middenmoter** /mɪdəmotər/ (pl: -s) [roughly] average joe; [Am] average guy

het **middenoor** /mɪdə(n)or/ (pl: -oren) middle ear

het **Midden-Oosten** /mɪdə(n)ostə(n)/ Middle East

het **middenpad** /mɪdə(n)pɑt/ (centre) aisle; gangway

het **middenrif** /mɪdə(n)rɪf/ midriff, diaphragm

het **middenschip** /mɪdə(n)sχɪp/ nave

de **middenstand** /mɪdə(n)stɑnt/ (the) self-employed, tradespeople

de **middenstander** /mɪdə(n)stɑndər/ (pl: -s) tradesman, shopkeeper

het **middenstandsdiploma** /mɪdə(n)stɑnts-diploma/ (pl: -'s) [roughly] retailer's certificate (*or:* diploma)

de **middenstip** /mɪdə(n)stɪp/ (pl: -pen) centre spot

het **middenveld** /mɪdə(n)vɛlt/ midfield

de **middenvelder** /mɪdə(n)vɛldər/ (pl: -s) midfielder, midfield player

de **middenweg** /mɪdə(n)wɛχ/ (pl: -en) middle course, medium: *de gulden ~* the golden mean, the happy medium

de **middernacht** /mɪdərnɑχt/ midnight

middernachtelijk /mɪdərnɑχtələk/ (adj) midnight

het **midgetgolf** /mɪdʒətɡolf/ miniature golf, midget golf

de **midlifecrisis** /mɪtlɑjfkrɑjsəs/ (pl: -crises) midlife crisis

de **midvoor** /mɪtfor/ centre forward

de **midweek** /mɪtwek/ (pl: -weken) midweek

de **midwinter** /mɪtwɪntər/ (pl: -s) midwinter

de **miep** /mip/ (pl: -en) bird; [Am] broad

de **mier** /mir/ (pl: -en) ant

de **miereneter** /mirə(n)etər/ (pl: -s) ant-eater

de **mierenhoop** /mirə(n)hop/ (pl: -hopen) ant-hill

de **mierenneuker** /mirənøkər/ (pl: -s) [inform] nitpicker

de **mierikswortel** /mirɪkswortəl/ horseradish

het **mietje** /micə/ (pl: -s) [inform] **1** gay, pansy **2** softy, wet; chicken

miezeren /mizərə(n)/ (miezerde, heeft gemiezerd) drizzle

miezerig /mizərəχ/ (adj) **1** drizzly **2** tiny, puny

de **migraine** /miɡrɛːnə/ migraine

de **migrant** /miɣrɑnt/ (pl: -en) migrant

de **migratie** /miɣra(t)si/ (pl: -s) migration

migreren /miɣreːrə(n)/ (migreerde, is gemigreerd) migrate

de **mihoen** /mihuːn/ (thin) Chinese noodles

mij /mɛi/ (pers pron) **1** me: *hij had het (aan)* ~ *gegeven* he had given it to me; *dat is van* ~ that's mine; *een vriend van* ~ a friend of mine; *dat is* ~ *te duur* that's too expensive for me **2** myself: *ik schaam* ~ *zeer* I am deeply ashamed

mijden /mɛɪdə(n)/ (meed, heeft gemeden) avoid

de **mijl** /mɛil/ (pl: -en) mile

mijlenver /mɛilə(n)vɛr/ (adj, adv) miles (away); [adverb also] for miles

de **mijlpaal** /mɛilpaːl/ (pl: mijlpalen) milestone

mijmeren /mɛimərə(n)/ (mijmerde, heeft gemijmerd) muse (on), (day)dream (about)

de **¹mijn** /mɛin/ (pl: -en) mine: *op een* ~ *lopen* strike (or: hit) a mine

²mijn /mɛin/ (poss pron) my ‖ *daar moet ik het* ~*e van weten* I must get to the bottom of this

de **mijnbouw** /mɛɪmbɑu/ mining (industry)

de **mijnenlegger** /mɛɪnə(n)lɛɣər/ minelayer; minecraft

de **mijnenveger** /mɛɪnə(n)veɣər/ (pl: -s) minesweeper

het **mijnenveld** /mɛɪnə(n)vɛlt/ (pl: -en) minefield

mijnerzijds /mɛɪnərzɛɪts/ (adv) on (or: for) my part

de **mijnheer** /mənɛr/ (pl: mijnheren) **1** sir: ~ *de voorzitter* Mr chairman; ~ *Jansen* Mr Jansen **2** gentleman

de **mijnschacht** /mɛinsxɑχt/ (pl: -en) mine shaft

de **mijnwerker** /mɛinwɛrkər/ (pl: -s) miner

de **mijt** /mɛit/ (pl: -en) mite

de **mijter** /mɛitər/ (pl: -s) mitre

mijzelf /mɛizɛlf/ (ref pron) myself

mikken /mɪkə(n)/ (mikte, heeft gemikt) (take) aim: ~ *op iets* (take) aim at sth.

de **mikmak** /mɪkmɑk/ [inform] caboodle

het **mikpunt** /mɪkpʏnt/ (pl: -en) butt, target

Milaan /milaːn/ Milan

mild /mɪlt/ (adj, adv) mild; soft; gentle

de **milicien** /miliʃɛ/ (pl: -s) [Belg; historical] conscript

het **milieu** /mɪljø/ (pl: -s) **1** milieu: *iem. uit een ander* ~ s.o. from a different social background (or: milieu) **2** environment

het **milieubeheer** /mɪljøbəheːr/ conservation (of nature), environmental protection

de **milieubescherming** /mɪljøbəsxɛrmɪŋ/ conservation, environmental protection

de **milieubeweging** /mɪljøbəweχɪŋ/ (pl: -en) ecology movement, environmental movement

milieubewust /mɪljøbəwʏst/ (adj) environment-minded, environmentally conscious

de **milieueffectrapportage** /mɪljøɛfɛktrapɔrtaʒə/ (pl: -s) environmental impact statement

de **milieuheffing** /mɪljøhɛfɪŋ/ (pl: -en) environmental tax (or: fee)

de **milieuramp** /mɪljørɑmp/ (pl: -en) environmental disaster

de **milieuvervuiling** /mɪljøvərvœylɪŋ/ environmental pollution

milieuvriendelijk /mɪljøvrɪndələk/ (adj, adv) ecologically sound, environmentally friendly (or: safe)

de **milieuwetgeving** /mɪljøwɛtχevɪŋ/ environmental legislation

de **milieuzone** /mɪljøzoːnə/ (pl: -s) low emission zone

de **¹militair** /militɛːr/ (pl: -en) soldier, serviceman

²militair /militɛːr/ (adj, adv) military: *in* ~*e dienst gaan* do one's military service, join the Army

de **militant** /militɑnt/ (pl: -en) [Belg] activist

militaristisch /militarɪstis/ (adj, adv) militarist(ic)

de **militie** /mili(t)si/ [Belg; historical] compulsory military service

de **miljard** /mɪljɑrt/ (num) billion, (a, one) thousand million: *de schade loopt in de* ~*en euro's* the damage runs into billions of euros

de **miljardair** /mɪljardɛːr/ (pl: -s) multimillionaire

miljardste /mɪljɑrtstə/ (num) billionth

het **miljoen** /mɪljun/ (pl: -en) million

de **miljoenennota** /mɪljunənota/ (pl: -'s) budget

de **miljoenenschade** /mɪljunə(n)sxadə/ damage amounting to millions

de **miljoenenstad** /mɪljunə(n)stɑt/ city with over a million inhabitants

de **miljoenste** /mɪljunstə/ millionth

de **miljonair** /mɪljɔnɛːr/ (pl: -s) millionaire

de **milkshake** /mɪlkʃek/ (pl: -s) milk shake

het **mille** /mil/ (one) thousand

het **millennium** /mɪlɛnijʏm/ (pl: millennia) millennium

de **millibar** /milibar/ (pl: -en, -s) millibar

het **milligram** /miliɣrɑm/ (pl: -men) milligram

de **milliliter** /mililitər/ (pl: -s) millilitre

de **millimeter** /milimetər/ (pl: -s) millimetre

millimeteren /milimetərə(n)/ (millimeterde, heeft gemillimeterd) crop

de **milt** /mɪlt/ (pl: -en) spleen

het **miltvuur** /mɪltfyr/ anthrax

de **mime** /mim/ mime

de **mimespeler** /mimspelər/ (pl: -s) mime artist

de **mimiek** /mimik/ facial expression

de **mimosa** /mimoza/ (pl: -'s) mimosa

de **¹min** /mɪn/ (pl: -nen) minus; minus (sign) ‖ *zij heeft op haar rapport een zeven* ~ she has a seven minus on her report; *de thermometer staat op* ~ *10°* the thermometer is at minus 10°; *tien* ~ *drie is zeven* ten minus three equals seven; ~ *of meer* more or less

²**min** /mɪn/ (adj) **1** poor: *arbeiders waren haar te* ~ workmen were beneath her **2** little, few: *zo* ~ *mogelijk fouten maken* make as few mistakes as possible

minachten /mɪnɑxtə(n)/ (minachtte, heeft geminacht) disdain, hold in contempt

minachtend /mɪnɑxtənt/ (adj, adv) disdainful, contemptuous: ~ *behandelen* treat with contempt

de **minachting** /mɪnɑxtɪŋ/ contempt, disdain: *uit* ~ *voor* in contempt of

de **minaret** /minarɛt/ (pl: -ten) minaret

de **minarine** /minarinə/ [Belg] low-fat margarine

minder /mɪndər/ (adj) **1** less, fewer; smaller: *hij heeft niet veel geld, maar nog* ~ *verstand* he has little money and even less intelligence; *dat was* ~ *geslaagd* that was less successful; *hoe* ~ *erover gezegd wordt, hoe beter* the less said about it the better; *vijf minuten meer of* ~ give or take five minutes; *groepen van negen en* ~ groups of nine and under **2** worse: *mijn ogen worden* ~ my eyes are not what they used to be

minderbedeeld (adj) less fortunate

de **mindere** /mɪndərə/ (pl: -n) inferior

minderen /mɪndərə(n)/ (minderde, heeft geminderd) decrease: *vaart* ~ slow down; ~ *met* (roken) cut down on (smoking)

de **minderheid** /mɪndərhɛit/ (pl: -heden) minority

de **mindering** /mɪndərɪŋ/ (pl: -en) decrease: *iets in* ~ *brengen (op)* deduct sth. (from)

minderjarig /mɪndərjarəx/ (adj) minor: ~ *zijn* be a minor

de **minderjarigheid** /mɪndərjarəxhɛit/ minority

minderwaardig /mɪndərwardəx/ (adj) inferior (to)

de **minderwaardigheid** /mɪndərwardəxhɛit/ inferiority

het **minderwaardigheidscomplex** /mɪndərwardəxhɛrtskɔmplɛks/ (pl: -en) inferiority complex

mineraal /minəral/ (adj) mineral || *rijk aan mineralen* rich in minerals

het **mineraalwater** /minəralwatər/ mineral water

de **mineur** /minør/ minor

het **mini** /mini/ mini

de **miniatuur** /minijatyr/ (pl: miniaturen) miniature

de **minibar** /miniba:r/ minibar

de ¹**miniem** /minim/ (pl: -en) [Belg] junior member (10, 11 years) of sports club

²**miniem** /minim/ (adj, adv) small, slight, negligible

de **minima** /minima/ (pl) minimum wage earners

minimaal /minimal/ (adj, adv) **1** minimal, minimum: ~ *presteren* perform very poorly

2 at least

minimaliseren /minimalizerə(n)/ (minimaliseerde, heeft geminimaliseerd) minimize

het **minimum** /minimʏm/ (pl: minima) minimum

de **minimumleeftijd** /minimʏmleftɛit/ (pl: -en) minimum age

het **minimumloon** /minimʏmlon/ (pl: -lonen) minimum wage

de **minimumtemperatuur** /minimʏmtɛmpəratyr/ minimum temperature

de **minirok** /minirɔk/ (pl: -ken) miniskirt

de **minister** /minɪstər/ (pl: -s) minister, secretary of state; [Am] secretary: ~ *van Binnenlandse Zaken* Minister of the Interior; Home Secretary; [Am] Secretary of the Interior; ~ *van Buitenlandse Zaken* Minister for Foreign Affairs; Secretary of State for Foreign and Commonwealth Affairs; Foreign Secretary; [Am] Secretary of State; ~ *van Defensie* Minister of Defence; Secretary of State for Defence; [Am] Secretary of Defense; Defense Secretary; ~ *van Economische Zaken* Minister for Economic Affairs; Secretary of State for Trade and Industry; [Am] [roughly] Secretary for Commerce; ~ *van Financiën* Minister of Finance; Chancellor of the Exchequer; [Am] Secretary of the Treasury; ~ *van Justitie* Minister of Justice; [roughly] Lord (High) Chancellor; [Am] [roughly] Attorney General; ~ *van Landbouw en Visserij* Minister of Agriculture and Fisheries; ~ *van Onderwijs en Wetenschappen* Minister of Education and Science; [Am] Secretary of Education; ~ *van Ontwikkelingssamenwerking* Minister for Overseas Development; ~ *van Sociale Zaken en Werkgelegenheid* Minister for Social Services and Employment; [Am] [roughly] Secretary of Labor; ~ *van Verkeer en Waterstaat* Minister of Transport and Public Works; [Am] Secretary of Transportation; ~ *van Volkshuisvesting, Ruimtelijke Ordening en Milieubeheer* Minister for Housing, Regional Development and the Environment; [Am] [roughly] Secretary for Housing and Urban Development; ~ *van Volksgezondheid, Welzijn en Sport* Minister of Health, Welfare and Sport; [Am] [roughly] Secretary of Health and Human Services; *eerste* ~ prime minister, premier

het **ministerie** /minɪsteri/ (pl: -s) ministry, department: ~ *van Buitenlandse Zaken* Ministry of Foreign Affairs; Foreign (and Commonwealth) Office; [Am] State Department; ~ *van Defensie* Ministry of Defence; [Am] Department of Defense; (the) Pentagon; ~ *van Financiën* Ministry of Finance; Treasury; [Am] Treasury Department || *het Openbaar Ministerie* the Public Prosecutor

ministerieel /minɪsterijel/ (adj) ministerial: *de ministeriële verantwoordelijkheid* ministerial responsibility

de **minister-president** /mɪnɪstərprezidɛnt/ (pl: -en) prime minister, premier

de **ministerraad** /minɪstərat/ (pl: -raden) council of ministers

de **ministerspost** /minɪstərspɔst/ ministerial post

de **minnaar** /mɪnar/ (pl: -s) lover, mistress

de **minne** /mɪnə/: *een zaak* **in** *der ~ schikken* settle something amicably/by mutual agreement

minnetjes /mɪnəcəs/ (adj, adv) poor

het **minpunt** /mɪmpʏnt/ (pl: -en) minus (point)

minst /mɪnst/ (adj, adv) **1** slightest, lowest: *niet* **de (het)** *~e … * not a shadow of …, not the slightest … **2** least: *op z'n ~* at the (very) least; *bij* **het** *~e of geringste* at the least little thing **3** least; fewest: *zij verdient het ~e* **geld** she earns the least money; *de ~e* **fouten** the fewest mistakes

minstens /mɪnstəns/ (adv) at least: *ik moet ~* **vijf** *euro hebben* I need five euros at least

de **minstreel** /mɪnstrel/ (pl: minstrelen) minstrel

het **minteken** /mɪntekə(n)/ (pl: -s) minus (sign)

minus /mɪnʏs/ (prep) minus

minuscuul /minʏskyl/ (adj, adv) tiny, minuscule, minute

de **minutenwijzer** /minʏtə(n)wɛizər/ (pl: -s) minute hand

minutieus /miny(t)ʃøs/ (adj, adv) meticulous: *iets ~* **beschrijven** describe sth. in meticulous (or: minute) detail

de **minuut** /minʏt/ (pl: minuten) **1** minute: *het is tien minuten* **lopen** it's a ten-minute walk **2** second, minute: *de situatie verslechterde* **met** *de ~* the situation was getting worse by the minute

het **mirakel** /mirakəl/ (pl: -s, -en) miracle, wonder

de **mirre** /mɪrə/ myrrh

de ¹**mis** /mɪs/ (pl: -sen) Mass

²**mis** /mɪs/ (adj, adv) **1** out, off target: *~* **poes!** tough (luck)!; *was het ~ of* **raak?** was it a hit or a miss? **2** wrong: *het* **liep** *~* it went wrong; *daar is niks ~* **mee** there's nothing wrong with that

het **misbaar** /mɪzbar/ uproar, hullabaloo

het **misbaksel** /mɪzbɑksəl/ (pl: -s) bastard, louse

het **misbruik** /mɪzbrœyk/ (pl: -en) abuse, misuse; excess: *~ van iem.* **maken** take advantage of s.o., use s.o., exploit s.o.; *seksueel ~* sexual abuse

misbruiken /mɪzbrœykə(n)/ (misbruikte, heeft misbruikt) **1** abuse, misuse; impose upon **2** violate

de **misdaad** /mɪzdat/ (pl: misdaden) crime

de **misdaadbestrijding** /mɪzdadbəstrɛidɪŋ/ crime prevention, fight against crime

misdadig /mɪzdadəχ/ (adj, adv) criminal

de **misdadiger** /mɪzdadəχər/ (pl: -s) criminal

de **misdadigheid** /mɪzdadəχhɛit/ crime, criminality

de **misdienaar** /mɪzdinar/ (pl: -s) acolyte; altar boy

misdoen /mɪzdun/ (misdeed, heeft misdaan) do wrong

zich **misdragen** /mɪzdraɣə(n)/ (misdroeg zich, heeft zich misdragen) misbehave; be (a) naughty (boy, girl)

het **misdrijf** /mɪzdrɛif/ (pl: misdrijven) criminal offence, criminal act, crime; [law] felony

de **misdruk** /mɪzdrʏk/ (pl: -ken) bad copy

miserabel /mizerabəl/ (adj, adv) miserable, wretched

de **misère** /mizɛːrə/ (pl: -s) misery

misgaan /mɪsχan/ (ging mis, is misgegaan) go wrong: *dit* **plan** *moet haast wel ~* this plan is almost sure to fail

misgrijpen /mɪsχrɛipə(n)/ (greep mis, heeft misgegrepen) miss one's hold

misgunnen /mɪsχʏnə(n)/ (misgunde, heeft misgund) (be)grudge, resent

mishandelen /mɪshɑndələ(n)/ (mishandelde, heeft mishandeld) ill-treat, maltreat, batter: *dieren ~* be cruel to (or: maltreat) animals

de **mishandeling** /mɪshɑndəlɪŋ/ (pl: -en) ill-treatment, maltreatment; [law] battery

miskennen /mɪskɛnə(n)/ (miskende, heeft miskend) misunderstand: *een miskend* **genie** (or: **talent**) a misunderstood genius (or: talent)

de **miskenning** /mɪskɛnɪŋ/ denial

de **miskleun** /mɪskløn/ (pl: -en) blunder, boob

de **miskoop** /mɪskop/ (pl: miskopen) bad bargain, bad buy

de **miskraam** /mɪskram/ (pl: miskramen) miscarriage

misleiden /mɪslɛidə(n)/ (misleidde, heeft misleid) mislead, deceive: *iem. ~* lead s.o. up the garden path

de **misleiding** /mɪslɛidɪŋ/ (pl: -en) deception

¹**mislopen** /mɪslopə(n)/ (liep mis, is misgelopen) go wrong, miscarry: *het* **plan** *liep mis* the plan miscarried (or: was a failure)

²**mislopen** /mɪslopə(n)/ (liep mis, heeft misgelopen) miss (out on): *hij is zijn* **carrière** *misgelopen* he missed his vocation, he's in the wrong business

de **mislukkeling** /mɪslʏkəlɪŋ/ (pl: -en) failure

mislukken /mɪslʏkə(n)/ (mislukte, is mislukt) fail, be unsuccessful, go wrong; fall through; break down: *een mislukte* **advocaat** (or: **schrijver**) a failed lawyer (or: writer); *een mislukte* **poging** an unsuccessful attempt

de **mislukking** /mɪslʏkɪŋ/ (pl: -en) failure

mismaakt /mɪsmakt/ (adj) deformed

de **mismaaktheid** /mɪsmakthɛit/ deformity

het **mismanagement** /mɪsmɛnədʒmənt/ mismanagement

mobilofoon

mismoedig /mɪsmudəχ/ (adj) dejected, dispirited, discouraged

misnoegd /mɪsnuχt/ (adj) displeased (with/at)

het **misnoegen** /mɪsnuɣə(n)/ displeasure

de **mispel** /mɪspəl/ (pl: -s, -en) medlar

mispeuteren /mɪspøtərə(n)/ (mispeuterde, heeft mispeuterd) [Belg] do sth. wrong, be up to

misplaatst /mɪsplatst/ (adj) out of place, misplaced; uncalled-for

misprijzen /mɪsprɛɪzə(n)/ (misprees, heeft misprezen) disapprove of: *een ~de blik* a look of disapproval, a disapproving look

het **mispunt** /mɪspʏnt/ (pl: -en) pain (in the neck), bastard, louse

zich **misrekenen** /mɪsrekənə(n)/ (misrekende zich, heeft zich misrekend) miscalculate

het **missaal** /mɪsal/ (pl: missalen) missal

misschien /mɪsχin/ (adv) perhaps, maybe: *bent u ~ mevrouw Hendriks?* are you Mrs Hendriks by any chance?; *heeft u ~ een paperclip voor me?* do you happen to have (*or:* could you possibly let me have) a paper clip?; *het is ~ beter als …* it may be better (*or:* perhaps it's better) if …; *~ vertrek ik morgen, ~ ook niet* maybe I'll leave tomorrow, maybe not; *zoals je ~ weet* as you may know; *wilt u ~ een kopje koffie?* would you care for some coffee?

misselijk /mɪsələk/ (adj, adv) **1** sick (in the stomach): *om ~ van te worden* sickening, nauseating, disgusting **2** nasty; disgusting; revolting: *een ~e grap* a sick joke

de **misselijkheid** /mɪsələkhɛit/ (feeling of) sickness, nausea

missen /mɪsə(n)/ (miste, heeft gemist) miss, go without; spare; afford; lack; lose: [fig] *zijn doel ~* miss the mark; *iem. zeer ~* miss s.o. badly; *ik kan mijn bril niet ~* I can't get along without my glasses; *kun je je fiets een paar uurtjes ~?* can you spare your bike for a couple of hours?; *ze kunnen elkaar niet ~* they can't get along without one another; *ik zou het voor geen geld willen ~* I wouldn't part with it (*or:* do without it) for all the world ‖ *dat kan niet ~* that can't fail (*or:* go wrong), that's bound to work (*or:* happen)

de **misser** /mɪsər/ (pl: -s) **1** failure, mistake, flop **2** miss; bad shot, poor shot; misthrow; bad throw; miscue

de **missie** /mɪsi/ (pl: -s) mission; missionary work

de **missionaris** /mɪʃonarɪs/ (pl: -sen) missionary

misslaan /mɪslan/ (sloeg mis, heeft misgeslagen) miss

misstaan /mɪstan/ (misstond, heeft misstaan) not suit ‖ *een verontschuldiging zou niet ~* an apology would not be out of place

de **misstand** /mɪstant/ (pl: -en) abuse, wrong

de **misstap** /mɪstap/ (pl: -pen) **1** false step, wrong step **2** slip: *een ~ begaan* make a slip; slip up

de **missverkiezing** /mɪsfərkizɪŋ/ (pl: -en) beauty contest

de **mist** /mɪst/ fog; mist: *dichte ~* (a) thick fog; *de ~ ingaan* **a)** go wrong (*or:* fail) completely; **b)** fall flat; **c)** go wrong, be all at sea

de **mistbank** /mɪstbaŋk/ (pl: -en) fog bank

misten /mɪstə(n)/ (mistte, heeft gemist) be foggy, be misty

het **mistgordijn** /mɪstχɔrdɛɪn/ curtain of fog

de **misthoorn** /mɪsthorn/ (pl: -s) foghorn

mistig /mɪstəχ/ (adj) foggy; misty

de **mistlamp** /mɪstlamp/ (pl: -en) fog lamp

de **mistletoe** /mɪsəlto/ mistletoe

mistroostig /mɪstrostəχ/ (adj) **1** dispirited, dejected **2** dismal, miserable

de **misvatting** /mɪsfatɪŋ/ (pl: -en) misconception, fallacy

het **misverstand** /mɪsfərstant/ (pl: -en) misunderstanding: *een ~ uit de weg ruimen* clear up a misunderstanding

misvormd /mɪsfɔrmt/ (adj) deformed, disfigured; [fig] distorted

de **misvorming** /mɪsfɔrmɪŋ/ (pl: -en) **1** deformation; [fig] distortion **2** deformity; [fig] distortion

de **mitella** /mitɛla/ (pl: -'s) sling

de **mitrailleur** /mitrajør/ (pl: -s) machine-gun

mits /mɪts/ (conj) if, provided that: *~ goed bewaard, kan het jaren meegaan* (if) stored well, it can last for years

de **mix** /mɪks/ (pl: -en, -es) mix

de **mixdrank** /mɪksdraŋk/ mix

mixen /mɪksə(n)/ (mixte, heeft gemixt) mix

de **mixer** /mɪksər/ (pl: -s) mixer; liquidizer; blender

het **mkb** /ɛmkabe/ *midden- en kleinbedrijf* small and medium-sized businesses

MKZ /ɛmkazɛt/ *mond-en-klauwzeer* foot and mouth (disease)

ml (abbrev) *milliliter* ml

de **mlk-school** /ɛmɛlkasχol/ school for children with learning problems

mm (abbrev) *millimeter* mm

m.m.v. (abbrev) *met medewerking van* with the cooperation of

mobiel /mobil/ (adj) mobile: *~e telefoon* mobile (phone); [Am] cellphone

het **mobieltje** /mobilcə/ (pl: -s) mobile (phone); [Am] cellphone

het/de **mobilhome** /mobəlhom/ [Belg] camper (van)

de **mobilisatie** /mobiliza(t)si/ (pl: -s) mobilization

mobiliseren /mobilizerə(n)/ (mobiliseerde, heeft gemobiliseerd) mobilize

de **mobiliteit** /mobilitɛit/ (pl: -en) mobility

de **mobilofoon** /mobilofon/ (pl: -s) radio-telephone

de **mocassin** /mɔkɑsɛ̃/ (pl: -s) moccasin
modaal /modal/ (adj) average
de **modaliteit** /modalitɛit/ **1** modality **2** term
de **modder** /mɔdər/ mud; sludge
het **modderbad** /mɔdərbɑt/ (pl: -en) mudbath
modderen /mɔdərə(n)/ (modderde, heeft gemodderd) muddle (along, through)
het/de **modderfiguur** /mɔdərfiɣyr/: een ~ **slaan** cut a sorry figure, look like a fool
modderig /mɔdərəx/ (adj) muddy
de **modderpoel** /mɔdərpul/ (pl: -en) quagmire; [fig] mire
de **modderschuit** /mɔdərsxœyt/ (pl: -en) mud boat (or: barge)
moddervet /mɔdərvɛt/ (adj) gross(ly fat)
de **mode** /modə/ (pl: -s) fashion: zich naar de **laatste** ~ kleden dress after the latest fashion; (in de) ~ **zijn** be fashionable
modebewust /modəbəwʏst/ (adj, adv) fashion-conscious
het **modeblad** /modəblɑt/ (pl: -en) fashion magazine
de **modegek** /modəɣɛk/ fashion plate
de **modegril** /modəɣrɪl/ (pl: -len) fashion fad
het **model** /modɛl/ (pl: -len) **1** model, type, style: ~ **staan** voor serve as a model (or: pattern) for; **als** ~ nemen voor iets model sth. (or: o.s.) on **2** model, design: het ~ van een **overhemd** the style of a shirt **3** model, style: goed **in** ~ blijven stay in shape
de **modelbouw** /modɛlbɑu/ model making, modelling (to scale)
het **modellenbureau** /modɛlə(n)byro/ (pl: -s) modelling agency
modelleren /modɛlɣrə(n)/ (modelleerde, heeft gemodelleerd) model: ~ **naar** fashion after, model on
de **modelwoning** /modɛlwonɪŋ/ (pl: -en) show house
het/de **modem** /modəm/ (pl: -s) modem
de **modeontwerper** /modəontwɛrpər/ (pl: -s) fashion designer
modern /modɛrn/ (adj, adv) modern: het huis **is** ~ **ingericht** the house has a modern interior; de ~ste technieken most modern (or: state-of-the-art) technology
moderniseren /modɛrnizərə(n)/ (moderniseerde, heeft gemoderniseerd) modernize
de **modernisering** /modɛrnizərɪŋ/ (pl: -en) modernization
de **modeshow** /modəʃow/ (pl: -s) fashion show
het **modewoord** /modəwort/ (pl: -en) vogue word
de **modezaak** /modəzak/ (pl: -zaken) clothes shop, clothes store; fashion store
modieus /modijøs/ (adj, adv) fashionable: een modieuze **dame** a lady of fashion
modificeren /modifisərə(n)/ (modificeerde, heeft gemodificeerd) modify
de **modulatie** /modyla(t)si/ modulation
de **module** /modylə/ (pl: -s) module

de **modus** /modʏs/ (pl: modi) mode
de **¹moe** /mu/ mum(my); [Am] mom ‖ **nou** ~! well I say!
²moe /mu/ (adj) **1** tired: ~ **van** het wandelen tired with walking **2** tired (of), weary (of): zij **is** het warme weer ~ she is (sick and) tired of the hot weather
de **moed** /mut/ **1** courage, nerve: al zijn ~ **bijeenrapen (verzamelen)** muster up (or: summon up, pluck up) one's courage **2** courage, heart: met **frisse** ~ beginnen begin with fresh courage; come up smiling; de ~ **opgeven** lose heart; ~ **putten** uit take heart from; de ~ **zonk** hem in de schoenen his heart sank into his boots
moedeloos /mudəlos/ (adj, adv) despondent, dejected
de **moedeloosheid** /mudəlosɦɛit/ despondency, dejection
de **moeder** /mudər/ (pl: -s) mother: een **alleenstaande** ~ a single mother; hij is niet bepaald ~s **mooiste** he's no oil-painting; bij ~s **pappot** (blijven) zitten be (or: remain) tied to one's mother's apron strings; **vadertje** en ~tje spelen play house
het **moederbedrijf** /mudərbədrɛif/ (pl: -bedrijven) parent company
Moederdag /mudərdɑx/ Mother's Day
het **moederhuis** /mudərɦœys/ (pl: -huizen) [Belg] maternity home
de **moederkoek** /mudərkuk/ (pl: -en) placenta
het **moederland** /mudərlɑnt/ motherland
moederlijk /mudərlək/ (adj, adv) **1** motherly **2** maternal
de **moedermaatschappij** /mudərmatsxɑpɛi/ (pl: -en) parent company
de **moedermelk** /mudərmɛlk/ mother's milk
het **moederschap** /mudərsxɑp/ motherhood
de **moederskant** /mudərskɑnt/ mother's side, maternal side: grootvader **van** ~ maternal grandfather
het **moederskindje** /mudərskɪncə/ (pl: -s) **1** mother's child **2** mummy's boy (or: girl)
de **moedertaal** /mudərtal/ (pl: -talen) mother tongue: iem. met Engels **als** ~ a native speaker of English
de **moedervlek** /mudərvlɛk/ (pl: -ken) birthmark, mole
de **moederziel** /mudərzil/: ~ **alleen** all alone
moedig /mudəx/ (adj, adv) brave; plucky
moedwillig /mutwɪləx/ (adj, adv) wilful, malicious
de **moeflon** /muflɔn/ (pl: -s) mouf(f)lon
de **moeheid** /muɦɛit/ tiredness, weariness
moeilijk /mujlək/ (adj, adv) **1** difficult: ~ **opvoedbare** kinderen problem children; **doe** niet zo ~ don't make such a fuss; het ~ **hebben** have a rough time, have a (hard (or: bad)) time of it **2** hard, difficult: het is ~ te **geloven** it's hard to believe; hij **maakte** het ons ~ he gave us a hard (or: difficult) time **3** hardly:

daar kan ik ~ iets over **zeggen** it's hard for me to say ‖ zij is een ~ **persoon** she is hard to please

de **moeilijkheid** /mu̲jləkhɛit/ (pl: -heden) difficulty, trouble, problem: om moeilijkheden **vragen** be asking for trouble; in moeilijkheden verkeren be in trouble; daar **zit (ligt)** de ~ there's the catch

de **moeite** /mu̲jtə/ **1** effort, trouble: **vergeefse** ~ wasted effort; **bespaar** je de ~ (you can) save yourself the trouble (or: bother); ~ **doen** take pains (or: trouble); u hoeft geen extra ~ te **doen** you need not bother, don't put yourself out; het **is** de ~ niet (waard) it's not worth it (or: the effort, the bother); het is de ~ **waard** om het te proberen it's worth a try (or: trying); het was zeer de ~ **waard** it was most rewarding; dank u wel **voor** de ~! thank you very much!, sorry to have troubled you!; dat is me te **veel** ~! that's too much trouble **2** trouble, difficulty; bother: ik **heb** ~ met zijn gedrag I find his behaviour hard to take (or: accept)

moeiteloos /mu̲jtəlos/ (adj, adv) effortless, easy: **leer** ~ Engels! learn English without tears!

moeizaam /mu̲jzam/ (adj) laborious ‖ zich ~ een weg **banen** (door) make one's way with difficulty (through)

de **moer** /mur/ **1** nut **2** mother **3** doe; queen (bee); vixen ‖ daar schiet je **geen** ~ mee op that doesn't get you anywhere; dat gaat je **geen** ~ aan that's none of your damn (or: bloody) business

het **moeras** /mura̲s/ (pl: -sen) swamp, marsh

het **moerasgebied** /mura̲sχəbit/ marshland

moerassig /mura̲səχ/ (adj) swampy

de **moersleutel** /mu̲rsløtəl/ (pl: -s) spanner; [Am] wrench

het **moes** /mus/ purée

de **moesson** /muso̲n/ (pl: -s) monsoon

de **moestuin** /mu̲stœyn/ (pl: -en) kitchen garden, vegetable garden

¹**moeten** /mu̲tə(n)/ (moest, heeft gemoeten) like

²**moeten** /mu̲tə(n)/ (aux vb, moest, heeft gemoeten) **1** must, have to, should, ought to: ik moet **zeggen,** dat ... I must say (or: have to say) that ...; ik moest wel **lachen** I couldn't help laughing; het hoeft zo ~ **zijn** it had to be (like that); **als** het moet if I (or: we) must **2** want, need: ik moet er niet aan **denken** wat het kost I hate to think (of) what it costs; ~ jullie niet **eten?** don't you want to eat?; dat moet ik nog **zien** I'll have to see; **wat** moet dat? what's all this about?; het huis moet **nodig** eens geschilderd worden the house badly needs a coat of paint **3** should, ought to: dat moet **gezegd (worden)** it has to be said; moet je eens **horen** listen (to this); de trein moet om vier uur **vertrekken** the train is due to leave at four o'clock; je moest eens **weten** ... if only you knew ...; dat moet jij (zelf) **weten** it's up to you; moet je nu al **weg?** are you off already?; ze moet er nodig eens uit she needs a day out **4** must; be supposed to, said to: zij moet vroeger een mooi meisje **geweest zijn** she must have been a pretty girl once **5** [Belg] need (to), have (to): u moet niet komen you needn't come

de **moezelwijn** /mu̲zəlwɛin/ (pl: -en) Moselle (wine)

de ¹**mof** /mɔf/ (pl: -fen) kraut

de ²**mof** /mɔf/ (pl: -fen) (coupling) sleeve, bush, socket

¹**mogelijk** /mo̲ɣələk/ (adj) possible, likely, potential: hoe **is** het ~ dat je je daarin vergist hebt? how could you possibly have been mistaken about this?; het **is** ~ dat hij wat later komt he may come a little later; het is **heel goed** ~ dat hij het niet gezien heeft he may very well not have seen it; het is **ons** niet ~ ... it's impossible for us, we cannot possibly ...; al **het** ~e doen do everything possible; **zoveel** ~ as far/often/much as possible

²**mogelijk** /mo̲ɣələk/ (adv) possibly, perhaps

mogelijkerwijs /moɣələkərwɛi̲s/ (adv) possibly, perhaps, conceivably

de **mogelijkheid** /mo̲ɣələkhɛit/ (pl: -heden) **1** possibility; chance; eventuality: zij **onderschat** haar mogelijkheden she underestimates herself **2** possibilities, prospects

¹**mogen** /mo̲ɣə(n)/ (mocht, heeft gemogen) like: ik mag hem **wel** I quite (or: rather) like him

²**mogen** /mo̲ɣə(n)/ (aux vb, mocht, heeft gemogen) **1** can, be allowed to, may, must, should, ought to: mag ik een **kilo** peren van u? (can I have) a kilo of pears, please; mag ik uw **naam** even? could (or: may) I have your name, please?; je mag **gaan spelen,** maar je mag je niet vuilmaken you can go out and play, but you're not to get dirty; als ik **vragen** mag if you don't mind my asking; mag ik **even?** do you mind?, may I?; mag ik er even **langs?** excuse me (please) **2** should, ought to: je **had** me weleens ~ **waarschuwen** you might (or: could) have warned me; hij mag blij **zijn** dat ... he ought to (or: should) be happy that ... **3** may, might ‖ het mocht niet **baten** it didn't help, it was to no avail; dat ik dit nog mag **meemaken!** that I should live to see this!; dat mocht je **willen** wouldn't you just like that; you'd like that, wouldn't you?; het heeft niet zo ~ **zijn** it was not to be; zo mag ik het **horen** (or: **zien**) that's what I like to hear (or: see)

de **mogendheid** /mo̲ɣənthɛit/ (pl: -heden) power

het ¹**mohair** /mohɛ̲ːr/ mohair

²**mohair** /mohɛ̲ːr/ (adj) mohair

Mohammed /moha̲mɛt/ Mohammed

de **mohammedaan** /mohaməda̲n/ (pl: mohammedanen) Mohammedan

mohammedaans /mohaməda̱ns/ (adj) Mohammedan

Mohikanen /mohika̱nə(n)/ (pl) Mohicans

de **mok** /mɔk/ (pl: -ken) mug

de **moker** /mo̱kər/ (pl: -s) sledgehammer

de **mokerslag** /mo̱kərslɑx/ (pl: -en) sledgehammer blow [also fig]

de **mokka** /mo̱ka/ mocha (coffee)

het/de **mokkel** /mɔ̱kəl/ [inform] chick, cracker

mokken /mɔ̱kə(n)/ (mokte, heeft gemokt) grouse, sulk

de ¹**mol** /mɔl/ [mus] **1** flat **2** minor

de ²**mol** /mɔl/ mole

Moldavië /mɔlda̱vijə/ Moldavia

de **Moldaviër** /mɔlda̱vijər/ (pl: -s) Moldavian

Moldavisch /mɔlda̱vis/ (adj) Moldovan

moleculair /molekylɛ̱ːr/ (adj) molecular

het/de **molecule** /molekyl(ə)/ (pl: -n) molecule

de **molen** /mo̱lə(n)/ (pl: -s) **1** (wind)mill **2** [angling] reel ‖ *het zit in de ~* it is in the pipeline

de **molenaar** /mo̱lənar/ (pl: -s) miller

de **molensteen** /mo̱lə(n)sten/ (pl: -stenen) millstone

de **molenwiek** /mo̱lə(n)wik/ (pl: -en) sail arm, wing

molesteren /molɛste̱rə(n)/ (molesteerde, heeft gemolesteerd) molest

mollen /mɔ̱lə(n)/ (molde, heeft gemold) wreck, bust (up)

mollig /mɔ̱ləx/ (adj) plump; chubby

het/de **molm** /mɔlm/ mouldered wood

de **molotovcocktail** /mo̱lotɔfkɔktel/ (pl: -s) Molotov cocktail

de **molshoop** /mɔ̱lshop/ (pl: -hopen) molehill

het **molton** /mɔ̱ltɔn/ flannel

de **Molukken** /moly̱kə(n)/ (pl) Moluccas, Molucca Islands

de **Molukker** /moly̱kər/ (pl: -s) Moluccan

Moluks /moly̱ks/ (adj) Molucca(n)

het/de **mom** /mɔm/: *onder het ~ van de weg te vragen* on (or: under) the pretext of asking the way

het **moment** /momɛ̱nt/ (pl: -en) moment, minute: *één ~, ik kom zó* one moment please, I'm coming; hang on a minute, I'm coming; *daar heb ik geen ~ aan gedacht* it never occurred to me

momenteel /momɛnte̱l/ (adv) at present, at the moment, currently

de **momentopname** /momɛ̱ntɔpnamə/ (pl: -n, -s) random indication (or: picture)

mompelen /mɔ̱mpələ(n)/ (mompelde, heeft gemompeld) mumble, mutter

Monaco /mo̱nako/ Monaco

de **monarch** /monɑ̱rx/ (pl: -en) monarch

de **monarchie** /monɑrxi̱/ (pl: -ën) monarchy

de **monarchist** /monɑrxɪ̱st/ (pl: -en) monarchist; royalist

de **mond** /mɔnt/ (pl: -en) mouth; muzzle: *een grote ~ hebben* **a)** be loud-mouthed; **b)** be cheeky, give s.o. lip; **c)** talk big; *iem. een grote ~ geven* talk back at (*or:* to) s.o., give s.o. lip; *hij kan zijn grote ~ niet houden* he can't keep his big mouth shut; *dat is een hele ~ vol* that's quite a mouthful; *zijn ~ houden* keep quiet; shut up; *zijn ~ opendoen* open one's mouth; speak up; *iem. de ~ snoeren* silence s.o.; *zijn ~ voorbijpraten* spill the beans; *met de ~ vol tanden staan* be at a loss for words, be tongue-tied

mondain /mɔndɛ̱/ (adj) fashionable: *een ~e badplaats* a sophisticated resort, a luxury resort

monddood /mɔndo̱t/ (adj): *~ maken* silence

mondeling /mɔ̱ndəlɪŋ/ (adj, adv) oral; verbal; by word of mouth: *een ~ examen* an oral (exam(ination)); *een ~e toezegging* (or: *afspraak*) a verbal agreement (*or:* arrangement)

het **mond-en-klauwzeer** /mɔntɛŋkla̱uzer/ foot-and-mouth disease

de **mondharmonica** /mɔ̱ntharmonika/ (pl: -'s) harmonica

de **mondhoek** /mɔ̱nthuk/ (pl: -en) corner of the mouth

mondiaal /mɔndija̱l/ (adj, adv) worldwide, global

de **mondialisering** /mɔndijalize̱rɪŋ/ globalization

mondig /mɔ̱ndəx/ (adj) of age; mature, independent

de **monding** /mɔ̱ndɪŋ/ (pl: -en) mouth; estuary

het **mondje** /mɔ̱ncə/ (pl: -s) mouthful; taste: *een ~ Turks spreken* have a smattering of Turkish; *(denk erom,) ~ dicht* mum's the word; *hij is niet op zijn ~ gevallen* **a)** he has a ready tongue; **b)** he gives as good as he gets

mondjesmaat /mɔ̱ncəsmat/ (adv) scantily, sparsely

het **mondkapje** /mɔ̱ntkɑpjə/ surgical mask

de **mond-op-mondbeademing** /mɔntɔpmɔ̱ntbəadəmɪŋ/ mouth-to-mouth (resuscitation, respiration), rescue breathing

het **mondstuk** /mɔ̱ntstʏk/ (pl: -ken) **1** mouthpiece; nozzle **2** filter

de **mond-tot-mondreclame** /mɔntɔtmɔ̱ntrəklamə/ advertisement by word of mouth, word-of-mouth advertising

de **mondvol** /mɔ̱ntfɔl/ mouthful

de **mondvoorraad** /mɔ̱ntforat/ provisions, supplies

de **Monegask** /moneyɑ̱sk/ (pl: -en) Monegasque

Monegaskisch /moneyɑ̱skis/ (adj) Monegasque

monetair /monetɛ̱ːr/ (adj, adv) monetary: *het Internationaal Monetair Fonds* the International Monetary Fund

de **moneybelt** /mɔ̱nibɛlt/ money belt

Mongolië /mɔŋyo̱lijə/ Mongolia

mongoloïde /mɔŋɣolowidə/ (adj) mongoloid

Mongoloïde /mɔŋɣolowidə/ (adj) Mongoloid

de **mongool** /mɔŋɣol/ (pl: mongolen) mongol

de **Mongool** /mɔŋɣol/ (pl: Mongolen) Mongol(ian)

het ¹**Mongools** /mɔŋɣols/ Mongolian

²**Mongools** /mɔŋɣols/ (adj) Mongolian: *de ~e volksrepubliek* the Mongolian People's Republic

de **monitor** /monitɔr/ (pl: -s) **1** monitor **2** [Belg] youth leader **3** [Belg] tutor

monitoren /monitɔrə(n)/ (monitorde, heeft gemonitord) monitor

de **monnik** /mɔnək/ (pl: -en) monk

het **monnikenwerk** /mɔnəkə(n)wɛrk/ drudgery, donkey work

mono /mono/ (adv) mono

de **monocle** /monɔklə/ (pl: -s) monocle

de **monocultuur** /monokʏltyr/ (pl: -culturen) monoculture

de ¹**monofoon** monophonic ringtone

²**monofoon** (adj) monophonic

monogaam /monoɣam/ (adj) monogamous

de **monogamie** /monoɣami/ monogamy

de **monografie** /monoɣrafi/ (pl: -ën) monograph

het **monogram** /monoɣrɔm/ (pl: -men) monogram

de **monoloog** /monolox/ (pl: -logen) monologue

monomaan /monoman/ (adj) monomaniac(al)

het **monopolie** /monopoli/ (pl: -s) monopoly

de **monopoliepositie** /monopolipozi(t)si/ monopoly position

de **monopolist** /monopolɪst/ (pl: -en) monopolist

monotoon /monoton/ (adj, adv) monotonous, in a monotone

de **monseigneur** /monsɛɲør/ (pl: -s) Monsignor

het **monster** /mɔnstər/ (pl: -s) **1** monster **2** sample, specimen **3** monster, giant

monsteren /mɔnstərə(n)/ (monsterde, heeft gemonsterd) **1** examine, inspect **2** review, inspect

monsterlijk /mɔnstərlək/ (adj, adv) monstrous, hideous

de **monsterzege** /mɔnstərzeɣə/ (pl: -s) mammoth victory

de **montage** /mɔntaʒə/ **1** assembly, mounting **2** [film] editing

de **montagefoto** /mɔntaʒəfoto/ (pl: -'s) **1** photomontage **2** Photofit (picture)

de **Montenegrijn** /mɔntəneɣrɛɪn/ (pl: -en) Montenegran

het **Montenegrijns** /mɔntəneɣrɛɪns/ Montenegran

Montenegro /mɔntəneɣro/ Montenegro

monter /mɔntər/ (adj, adv) lively, cheerful, vivacious

monteren /mɔntɛrə(n)/ (monteerde, heeft gemonteerd) **1** assemble; install **2** mount, fix **3** edit; cut [film]; assemble **4** fix; mount

de **montessorischool** /mɔntɛsorisxol/ (pl: -scholen) Montessori school

de **monteur** /mɔntør/ (pl: -s) mechanic; serviceman; repairman

het/de **montuur** /mɔntyr/ (pl: monturen) frame: *een bril zonder ~* rimless glasses

het **monument** /monymɛnt/ (pl: -en) monument: *een ~ ter herinnering aan de doden* a memorial to the dead

monumentaal /monymɛntal/ (adj, adv) monumental

de **monumentenlijst** /monymɛntə(n)lɛist/ (pl: -en) [roughly] list of national monuments and historic buildings

¹**mooi** /moj/ (adj) **1** beautiful: *iets ~ vinden* think sth. is nice **2** good-looking, handsome; pretty, beautiful **3** lovely, beautiful: *zij ziet er ~ uit* she looks lovely; *deze fiets is er niet ~er op worden* this bicycle isn't what it used to be **4** smart: *zich ~ maken* dress up **5** good; excellent: *~e cijfers halen* get good marks; [Am] get good grades **6** good, fine; nice, handsome: *het kon niet ~er* it couldn't have been better; *te ~ om waar te zijn* too good to be true **7** good, nice: *een ~ verhaal* a nice (*or:* good) story; *het is ~ (geweest)* zo! that's enough now!, all right, that'll do!

²**mooi** /moj/ (adv) well, nicely: *jij hebt ~ praten* it's all very well for you to talk; *dat is ~ meegenomen* that is so much to the good; *~ zo!* good!, well done!

het **moois** /mojs/ fine thing(s), sth. beautiful: [iron] *dat is ook wat ~!* a nice state of affairs!

de **moord** /mort/ (pl: -en) murder; assassination; [law] homicide: *een ~ plegen* commit murder, take a life; *~ en brand schreeuwen* scream blue murder

de **moordaanslag** /mortanslox/ (pl: -en) attempted murder

moorddadig /mordadəx/ (adj) murderous

moorden /mordə(n)/ (moordde, heeft gemoord) kill, murder

de **moordenaar** /mordənar/ (pl: -s) murderer, killer

moordend /mordənt/ (adj) murderous, deadly; fatal: *~e concurrentie* cut-throat competition

de **moordkuil** /mortkœyl/ *van zijn hart geen ~ maken* make no disguise of one's feelings

de **moordpartij** /mortpartɛɪ/ (wholesale) massacre, slaughter

de **moordzaak** /mortsak/ (pl: -zaken) murder case

de **moorkop** /morkɔp/ (pl: -pen) chocolate éclair

de **moot** /mot/ (pl: moten) piece

de **mop** /mɔp/ (pl: -pen) joke: *een schuine ~ a dirty joke*

de **mopperaar** /mɔpərar/ (pl: -s) grumbler

mopperen /mɔpərə(n)/ (mopperde, heeft gemopperd) grumble, grouch

de **moraal** /moral/ morality, moral(s)

moraliseren /moralizerə(n)/ (moraliseerde, heeft gemoraliseerd) moralize

moralistisch /moralɪstis/ (adj, adv) moralistic

het **moratorium** /moratorijʏm/ (pl: -s, moratoria) moratorium; ban

morbide /mɔrbidə/ (adj) morbid

mordicus /mɔrdikʏs/ (adv): *ergens ~ tegen zijn* be dead against sth.

het **¹moreel** /morel/ morale: *het ~ hoog houden* keep up morale

²moreel /morel/ (adj, adv) moral

de **mores** /mɔrɛs/ (pl) mores

de **morfine** /mɔrfinə/ morphine

morfologisch /mɔrfoloɣis/ (adj, adv) morphologic(al)

de **¹morgen** /mɔrɣə(n)/ (pl: -s) morning: *de hele ~ all morning; 's ~s in the morning; (goede) ~! (good) morning!; om 8 uur 's ~s at 8 a.m.*

²morgen /mɔrɣə(n)/ (adv) tomorrow: *vandaag of ~ one of these days; ~ over een week a week tomorrow; tot ~! see you tomorrow!, till tomorrow!; de krant van ~ tomorrow's (news)paper*

morgenavond /mɔrɣə(n)avɔnt/ (adv) tomorrow evening

morgenmiddag /mɔrɣə(n)mɪdax/ (adv) tomorrow afternoon

morgenochtend /mɔrɣə(n)ɔxtənt/ (adv) tomorrow morning

het **morgenrood** /mɔrɣə(n)rot/ aurora, red morning sky

morgenvroeg /mɔrɣə(n)vrux/ (adv) tomorrow morning

het **mormel** /mɔrməl/ (pl: -s) mutt: *een verwend ~ a spoilt brat*

de **mormoon** /mɔrmon/ (pl: mormonen) Mormon; Latter-day Saint

de **morning-afterpil** /mɔrnɪŋɑːftərpɪl/ (pl: -len) morning-after pill

morrelen /mɔrələ(n)/ (morrelde, heeft gemorreld) fiddle

morren /mɔrə(n)/ (morde, heeft gemord) grumble

morsdood /mɔrzdot/ (adj) (as) dead as a doornail

het **morse** /mɔrsə/ Morse (code)

morsen /mɔrsə(n)/ (morste, heeft gemorst) (make a) mess (on, of), spill: *het kind zit te ~ met zijn eten* the child is messing around with his food

het **morseteken** /mɔrsətekə(n)/ (pl: -s) Morse sign

morsig /mɔrsəx/ (adj, adv) dirty, messy

de **mortel** /mɔrtəl/ mortar

het/de **mortier** /mɔrtir/ (pl: -en) mortar

de **mortiergranaat** /mɔrtirɣranat/ mortar bomb

het **mortuarium** /mɔrtywarijʏm/ (pl: mortuaria) **1** mortuary **2** funeral parlour; [Am] funeral home

het **mos** /mɔs/ (pl: -sen) moss

de **moskee** /mɔske/ (pl: -ën) mosque

Moskou /mɔskɑu/ Moscow

de **moslim** /mɔslɪm/ (pl: -s) Muslim, Moslem

de **moslima** /mɔslɪma/ moslima

de **mossel** /mɔsəl/ (pl: -en) mussel

de **mosterd** /mɔstərt/ mustard: *hij weet waar Abraham de ~ haalt* he knows what's what

het **mosterdgas** /mɔstərtxɑs/ mustard gas

de **mot** /mɔt/ (pl: -ten) moth

het **motel** /motɛl/ (pl: -s) motel

de **motie** /mo(t)si/ (pl: -s) motion

het **motief** /motif/ (pl: motieven) **1** motive **2** motif, design

de **motivatie** /motiva(t)si/ motivation

motiveren /motiverə(n)/ (motiveerde, heeft gemotiveerd) **1** explain, account for; defend; justify **2** motivate

de **motor** /motər/ (pl: -en) **1** engine; motor: *de ~ starten* (or: *afzetten*) start (*or:* turn off) the engine **2** motorcycle **3** driving force

de **motoragent** /motərɑɣɛnt/ (pl: -en) motorcycle policeman

het **motorblok** /motərblɔk/ (pl: -ken) engine block

de **motorboot** /motərbot/ (pl: -boten) motorboat

de **motorcoureur** /motərkurør/ (pl: -s) motorcycle racer; rider

de **motorcross** /motərkrɔs/ (pl: -es) motocross

de **motorfiets** /motərfits/ (pl: -en) motorcycle, motorbike, bike: *~ met zijspan* sidecar motorcycle

de **motoriek** /motorik/ (loco)motor system, locomotion

motorisch /motoris/ (adj, adv) motor: *een ~ gehandicapte* a disabled person; *hij is ~ gestoord* he has a motor disability

het **motorjacht** /motərjɑxt/ (pl: -en) motor yacht

de **motorkap** /motərkɑp/ (pl: -pen) bonnet; [Am] hood

de **motorolie** /motəroli/ (engine) oil

de **motorpech** /motərpɛx/ engine trouble

de **motorrace** /motərɛs/ (pl: -s) motorcycle race

de **motorrijder** /motərɛɪdər/ (pl: -s) motorcyclist

de **motorrijtuigenbelasting** /motərɛitœyɣə(n)bəlɑstɪŋ/ [roughly] road tax

de **motorsport** /motərspɔrt/ motorcycle racing

het **motorvoertuig** /motərvurtœyx/ (pl: -en) motor vehicle; [Am] automobile

de **motregen** /mɔtreɣə(n)/ (pl: -s) drizzle
motregenen /mɔtreɣənə(n)/ (motregende, heeft gemotregend) drizzle
mottig /mɔtəx/ (adj) moth-eaten, scruffy
het **motto** /mɔto/ (pl: -'s) motto; slogan
de **mountainbike** /mauntənbɑjk/ (pl: -s) mountain bike
de **mousse** /mus/ (pl: -s) mousse
mousseren /musɛrə(n)/ (mousseerde, heeft gemousseerd) sparkle, fizz
het/de **mout** /mɑut/ malt
de **mouw** /mɑu/ (pl: -en) sleeve: *de ~en opstropen* roll up one's sleeves; *ergens een ~ aan weten te passen* find a way (a)round sth.
mouwloos /mɑulos/ (adj) sleeveless
het **mozaïek** /mozaik/ (pl: -en) mosaic
de **Mozambikaan** /mozɑmbikɑn/ (pl: Mozambikanen) Mozambican
Mozambikaans /mozɑmbikɑns/ (adj) Mozambican
Mozambique /mozɑmbik/ Mozambique
Mozes /mozəs/ Moses
de **mp3** MP3
de **mp3-speler** /ɛmpedrispelər/ MP3 player
de **MRI-scan** /ɛmɛriskɛn/ MRI scan
MS /ɛmɛs/ *multiple sclerose* MS
het **mt** *managementteam* management team
de **mts** /ɛmteɛs/ (pl: -'en) *middelbare technische school* intermediate technical school
de **muesli** /mysli/ muesli
de **muezzin** /muwɛdzɪn/ muezzin
muf /myf/ (adj) musty, stale; stuffy
de **mug** /myx/ (pl: -gen) mosquito; [small] gnat: *van een ~ een olifant maken* make a mountain out of a molehill
de **muggenbeet** /myɣə(n)bet/ (pl: -beten) mosquito bite
de **muggenbult** /myɣə(n)bylt/ mosquito bite
de **muggenolie** /myɣə(n)oli/ insect repellent
muggenziften /myɣə(n)zɪftə(n)/ (muggenziftte, heeft gemuggenzift) niggle, split hairs, nit-pick
de **muggenzifter** /myɣə(n)zɪftər/ (pl: -s) niggler, hairsplitter, nit-picker
de **muil** /mœyl/ mouth, muzzle
het **muildier** /mœyldir/ (pl: -en) mule
de **muilezel** /mœylezəl/ (pl: -s) hinny
de **muilkorf** /mœylkɔrf/ (pl: -korven) muzzle
muilkorven /mœylkɔrvə(n)/ (muilkorfde, heeft gemuilkorfd) muzzle
de **muis** /mœys/ (pl: muizen) mouse; ball
de **muisarm** /mœysɑrm/ (pl: -en) mouse arm
de **muiscursor** (pl: -s) mouse cursor
muisgrijs /mœysxrɛis/ (adj) dun(-coloured)
de **muisklik** /mœysklɪk/ mouse click
de **muismat** /mœysmɑt/ mousemat, mouse pad
muisstil /mœystɪl/ (adj) (as) still (*or:* quiet) as a mouse
de **muiten** /mœytə(n)/ (muitte, heeft gemuit) mutiny

de **muiterij** /mœytərɛi/ (pl: -en) mutiny: *er brak ~ uit* a mutiny broke out
de **muizenissen** /mœyzənɪsə(n)/ (pl) worries
de **muizenval** /mœyzə(n)vɑl/ (pl: -len) mousetrap
mul /myl/ (adj) loose, sandy
de **mulat** /mylɑt/ (pl: -ten) mulatto
multicultureel /myltikyltyrel/ (adj) multicultural
multifunctioneel /myltifynkʃonel/ (adj) multifunctional
de **multimedia** /myltimedija/ (pl) multimedia
de **multimiljonair** /myltimɪljonɛːr/ (pl: -s) multimillionaire
de **multinational** /myltinɛʃənəl/ (pl: -s) multinational
multiple /myltipəl/ (adj) multiple
de **multiplechoicetest** /myltɪpəltʃɔjstɛst/ (pl: -s) multiple choice test
het **multiplex** /myltiplɛks/ multi-ply (board)
multiresistent /myltirezistɛnt/ (adj) multiresistant: *~e bacteriën* multiresistant bacteria
de **multivitamine** /myltivitaminə/ multivitamin
het **mum** /mym/: *in een ~ (van tijd)* in a jiffy (*or:* trice)
de **mummie** /mymi/ (pl: -s) mummy
München /mynʃə(n)/ Munich
de **munitie** /myni(t)si/ (am)munition, ammo
de **munt** /mynt/ (pl: -en) **1** coin: *iem. met gelijke ~ terugbetalen* give s.o. a taste of their own medicine **2** token
de **munteenheid** /myntenhɛit/ (pl: -heden) monetary unit
munten /myntə(n)/ (muntte, heeft gemunt) **1** mint, coin **2** coin ‖ [fig] *het op iem. gemunt hebben* have it in for s.o., be down on s.o.; *zij hebben het op mijn leven gemunt* they're after my life
het **muntgeld** /myntxɛlt/ coin, coinage
het **muntstelsel** /myntstɛlsəl/ monetary system
het **muntstuk** /myntstyk/ (pl: -ken) coin
murmelen /myrmələ(n)/ (murmelde, heeft gemurmeld) mumble, murmur
murw /myrf/ (adj) tender, soft
de **mus** /mys/ (pl: -sen) sparrow
het **museum** /myzejym/ (pl: musea) museum; (art) gallery
de **musical** /mjuzɛkəl/ (pl: -s) musical
musiceren /myzisɛrə(n)/ (musiceerde, heeft gemusiceerd) make music
de **musicoloog** /myzikolox/ (pl: -logen) musicologist
de **musicus** /myzikys/ (pl: musici) musician
de **muskaatdruif** /myskɑdrœyf/ (pl: -druiven) muscadine
de **muskaatwijn** /myskɑtwɛin/ muscatel
de **musketier** /myskətir/ (pl: -s) musketeer
de **muskiet** /myskit/ (pl: -en) mosquito
het **muskietengaas** /myskitə(n)ɣas/ mosquito

net(ting)

de **muskusrat** /mỵskʏsrɑt/ (pl: -ten) muskrat

de **must** /mʏst/ must

de **mutant** /mytɑnt/ (pl: -en) mutant

de **mutatie** /myta(t)si/ (pl: -s) **1** mutation; transaction **2** mutation; turnover

muteren /mytₑrə(n)/ (muteerde, heeft gemuteerd) mutate

de **muts** /mʏts/ (pl: -en) hat, cap

de **mutualiteit** /mytywalitₑit/ [Belg] health insurance scheme

de **muur** /myr/ (pl: muren) wall: *een blinde ~ a blank wall; de muren komen op mij af the walls are closing in on me;* [sport] *een ~tje vormen (opstellen)* make a wall; *uit de ~ eten, iets uit de ~ trekken* [roughly] eat from a vending machine

het **muurbloempje** /myrblumpjə/ wallflower

de **muurkrant** /myrkrɑnt/ (pl: -en) wall poster

de **muurschildering** /myrsxɪldərɪŋ/ (pl: -en) mural

muurvast /myrvɑst/ (adj, adv) firm, solid; unyielding; unbending: *de besprekingen zitten ~* the talks have reached total deadlock

de **muurverf** /myrvɛrf/ masonry paint

de **muzak** /myzɑk/ muzak

de **muze** /myzə/ (pl: -n) **1** muse **2** (the) Muses: *zich aan de ~n wijden* devote o.s. to the arts

de **muziek** /myzik/ music: *op de maat van de ~ dansen* dance in time to the music; *op ~ dansen* dance to music; *dat klinkt mij als ~ in de oren* it's music to my ears

het **muziekinstrument** /myzikɪnstrymɛnt/ (pl: -en) musical instrument

het **muziekje** /myzikjə/ (pl: -s) bit (*or:* piece) of music: *een ~ opzetten* play a bit of music

de **muziekkapel** /myzikapɛl/ (pl: -len) band

de **muziekles** /myziklɛs/ music lesson

het **muziekmobieltje** /myzikmobilcə/ (pl: -s) music cellphone (*or:* mobile phone)

de **muzieknoot** /myziknot/ (pl: -noten) (musical) note

het **muziekpapier** /myzikpɑpir/ music paper

de **muziekschool** /myziksxol/ (pl: -scholen) school of music

de **muzieksleutel** /myziksløtəl/ (pl: -s) clef

de **muziekstandaard** /myzikstɑndart/ (pl: -en, -s) music stand

het **muziekstuk** /myzikstʏk/ (pl: -ken) piece of music, composition

de **muziekuitvoering** /myzikœytfurɪŋ/ (pl: -en) musical performance

muzikaal /myzikal/ (adj, adv) musical: *~ gevoel* feel for music

de **muzikant** /myzikɑnt/ (pl: -en) musician

mw. (abbrev) *mevrouw of mejuffrouw* Ms

Myanmar /mijɑnmɑr/ Myanmar

de **¹Myanmarees** /mijɑnmarₑs/ (pl: Myanmarezen) inhabitant (*or:* native) of Myanmar

²Myanmarees /mijɑnmarₑs/ (adj) Myanmar

het **mysterie** /mɪstₑri/ (pl: -s) mystery

mysterieus /mɪster(i)jøs/ (adj, adv) mysterious

mystiek /mɪstik/ (adj) **1** mystic, mysterious **2** mystical: *een ~e ervaring* a mystical experience

de **mythe** /mitə/ (pl: -n) myth; [pers] legend

mythisch /mitis/ (adj) mythic(al)

de **mythologie** /mitoloyi/ (pl: -ēn) mythology

mythologisch /mitoloyis/ (adj) mythological

n

de **n** /ɛn/ (pl: n's) n, N

na /na/ (prep) after: *de ene **blunder** na de andere maken* make one blunder after the other (or: another); *na u!* after you! ‖ *wat eten we na?* what's for dessert?; *op een paar uitzonderingen na* with a few exceptions; *de op één na grootste* (or: *sterkste*) the second biggest (or: strongest); *het op drie na grootste bedrijf* the fourth largest company

de **naad** /nat/ (pl: naden) seam; joint ‖ *zich uit de ~ werken* work o.s. to death

het **naadje** /naːcə/: *het ~ van de kous willen weten* want to know all the ins and outs

naadloos /naːtlos/ (adj) seamless

de **naaf** /naf/ (pl: naven) hub

de **naaidoos** /najdos/ (pl: -dozen) sewing box

naaien /najə(n)/ (naaide, heeft genaaid) sew

het **naaigaren** /najɣarə(n)/ (pl: -s) sewing thread (or: cotton): *een klosje ~* a reel of thread (or: cotton)

de **naaimachine** /najmaʃinə/ (pl: -s) sewing machine

de **naaister** /najstər/ (pl: -s) seamstress

naakt /nakt/ (adj, adv) **1** naked, nude: *~ slapen* sleep in the nude **2** bare

de **naaktloper** /naktlopər/ (pl: -s) nudist

de **naaktslak** /naktslak/ slug

het **naaktstrand** /naktstrant/ (pl: -en) nude beach

de **naald** /nalt/ (pl: -en) needle: *het oog van een ~* the eye of a needle

de **naaldboom** /naltbom/ (pl: -bomen) conifer

het **naaldbos** /naltbɔs/ (pl: -sen) coniferous forest

de **naaldhak** /nalthak/ (pl: -ken) stiletto(heel); [Am] spike heel

het **naaldhout** /nalthaut/ softwood, coniferous wood

de **naam** /nam/ (pl: namen) name; reputation: *een goede* (or: *slechte*) *~ hebben* have a good (or: bad) reputation; *zijn ~ eer aandoen* live up to one's reputation (or: name); *dat mag geen ~ hebben* that's not worth mentioning; *~ maken* make a name for o.s. (with, as); *de dingen bij de ~ noemen* call a spade a spade; *een cheque uitschrijven op ~ van* make out a cheque to; *ten name van, op ~ van* in the name of; *wat was uw ~ ook weer?* what did you say your name was?

het **naambordje** /nambɔrcə/ (pl: -s) nameplate

de **naamdag** /namdɑx/ (pl: -dagen) name day

de **naamgenoot** /namɣənot/ (pl: -genoten) namesake

het **naamkaartje** /namkarcə/ (pl: -s) calling-card, business card

naamloos /namlos/ (adj, adv) anonymous, unnamed

het **naamplaatje** /namplacə/ nameplate

de **naamval** /namvɑl/ (pl: -len) case

het **naamwoord** /namwort/ (pl: -en) noun: *een bijvoeglijk ~* an adjective; *een zelfstandig ~* a noun

naamwoordelijk /namwordələk/ (adj) nominal

na-apen /naːapə(n)/ (aapte na, heeft nageaapt) ape, mimic

de **na-aper** /naːapər/ (pl: -s) mimic, copycat

¹**naar** /nar/ (adj, adv) nasty, horrible

²**naar** /nar/ (prep) **1** to, for: *~ huis gaan* go home; *~ de weg vragen* ask the way; *op zoek ~* in search of; *~ iem. vragen* ask for (or: after) s.o. **2** (according) to: *ruiken* (or: *smaken*) *~* smell (or: taste) of

naargeestig /narɣestəx/ (adj, adv) gloomy, dismal

¹**naargelang** /narɣəlɑŋ/ (prep) according to, depending on: *al ~ de leeftijd* depending on (one's) age

²**naargelang** /narɣəlɑŋ/ (conj) as: *~ je ouder wordt...* as you get older

naarmate /narmatə/ (conj) as: *~ je meer verdient, ga je ook meer belasting betalen* the more you earn, the more tax you pay

naartoe /nartu/ (adv): *waar moet dit ~?* where will this lead us?

¹**naast** /nast/ (adj) **1** near(est), closest; immediate: *de ~e bloedverwanten* the next of kin **2** out, off (target): *hij schoot ~* he shot wide

²**naast** /nast/ (prep) **1** next to, beside; wide of: *~ iem. gaan zitten* sit down next to (or: beside) s.o. **2** alongside, next to: *~ elkaar* side by side, next to one another **3** after, next to

de **naaste** /nastə/ (pl: -n) neighbour

de **naastenliefde** /nastə(n)livdə/ charity

de **nabehandeling** /nabəhandəlɪŋ/ after-care

de **nabeschouwing** /nabəsxauwɪŋ/ (pl: -en) summing-up; recap, review

nabespreken /nabəsprekə(n)/ (besprak na, heeft nabesproken) discuss afterwards

de **nabestaande** /nabəstandə/ (pl: -n) (surviving) relative; next of kin

nabestellen /nabəstɛlə(n)/ (bestelde na, heeft nabesteld) reorder, have copies made of

¹**nabij** /nabɛi/ (adj) close, near: *de ~e omgeving* the immediate surroundings

²**nabij** /nabɛi/ (prep) near (to), close to: *om en ~ de duizend euro* roughly (or: around, about) a thousand euros

nabijgelegen /nabɛiɣələɣə(n)/ (adj) nearby

de **nabijheid** /nabɛihɛit/ neighbourhood, vi-

cinity
nablijven /n<u>a</u>blɛivə(n)/ (bleef na, is nage-
bleven) stay behind
nablussen /n<u>a</u>blʏsə(n)/ damp down
nabootsen /n<u>a</u>botsə(n)/ (bootste na, heeft
nagebootst) imitate, copy; mimic
de **nabootsing** /n<u>a</u>botsɪŋ/ (pl: -en) imitation,
copying; copy
naburig /nab<u>y</u>rəχ/ (adj) neighbouring,
nearby
de **nacht** /naχt/ (pl: -en) night: *de afgelopen ~*
last night; *de komende ~* tonight; *het werd ~*
night (*or:* darkness) fell; *tot laat in de ~* deep
into the night; *'s ~s* at night; *om drie uur 's ~s*
at three o'clock in the morning, at three a.m.
nachtblind /n<u>a</u>χtblɪnt/ (adj) night-blind
nachtbraken /n<u>a</u>χtbrakə(n)/ (nachtbraak-
te, heeft genachtbraakt) **1** stay out till the
early hours **2** work into the early hours
de **nachtbraker** /n<u>a</u>χtbrakər/ (pl: -s) **1** night-
reveller **2** night owl
de **nachtclub** /n<u>a</u>χtklʏp/ (pl: -s) nightclub
de **nachtdienst** /n<u>a</u>ɣdinst/ (pl: -en) night shift
het **nachtdier** /n<u>a</u>ɣdir/ (pl: -en) nocturnal animal
de **nachtegaal** /n<u>a</u>χtəɣal/ (pl: nachtegalen)
nightingale
nachtelijk /n<u>a</u>χtələk/ (adj, adv) **1** night
2 nocturnal, of night **3** night(time)
het **nachthemd** /n<u>a</u>χthɛmt/ (pl: -en) night-
gown
de **nachtjapon** /n<u>a</u>χtjapɔn/ (pl: -nen) night-
gown, nightdress, nightie
de **nachtkaars** /n<u>a</u>χtkars/ (pl: -en): *uitgaan als
een ~* peter out (like a damp squib)
het **nachtkastje** /n<u>a</u>χtkɑʃə/ (pl: -s) night table,
bedside table
het **nachtleven** /n<u>a</u>χtlevə(n)/ (pl: -s) nightlife
de **nachtmerrie** /n<u>a</u>χtmɛri/ (pl: -s) nightmare
de **nachtmis** /n<u>a</u>χtmɪs/ (pl: -sen) midnight
mass
de **nachtploeg** /n<u>a</u>χtpluχ/ (pl: -en) night shift
de **nachtrust** /n<u>a</u>χtrʏst/ night's rest
het **nachtslot** /n<u>a</u>χtslɔt/ (pl: -en) double lock
de **nachttrein** /n<u>a</u>χtrɛin/ (pl: -en) night train
het **nachtverblijf** /n<u>a</u>χtfərblɛɪf/ (pl: -verblij-
ven) night's lodging; night-quarters
de **nachtvlucht** /n<u>a</u>χtflʏχt/ (pl: -en) night
flight
de **nachtvoorstelling** /n<u>a</u>χtforstɛlɪŋ/ (pl: -en)
late-night performance
de **nachtvorst** /n<u>a</u>χtfɔrst/ night frost; ground
frost
de **nachtwake** /n<u>a</u>χtwakə/ (pl: -n) vigil, night
watch
de **nachtwaker** /n<u>a</u>χtwakər/ (pl: -s) night
watchman
het **nachtwerk** /n<u>a</u>χtwɛrk/ nightwork
de **nachtzoen** /n<u>a</u>χtsun/ (pl: -en) good-night
kiss: *iem. een ~ geven* kiss s.o. good night
de **nachtzuster** /n<u>a</u>χtsʏstər/ (pl: -s) night nurse

de **nacompetitie** /n<u>a</u>kɔmpəti(t)si/ (pl: -s) [socc]
play-offs
de **nadagen** /n<u>a</u>daɣə(n)/ (pl): *in de ~ van zijn
carrière* in the twilight (*or:* the latter days) of
one's career, towards the end of one's career
de **nadarafsluiting** /n<u>a</u>dɑrɑfslœytɪŋ/ (pl: -en)
[Belg] crush barrier
nadat /nad<u>ɑ</u>t/ (conj) after: *het moet gebeurd
zijn ~ ze vertrokken waren* it must have happened after they left
het **nadeel** /n<u>a</u>del/ (pl: nadelen) disadvantage;
damage; drawback: *zo zijn voor- en nadelen
hebben* have its pros and cons; *al het bewijsmateriaal spreekt in hun ~* all the evidence is
against them; *ten nadele van* to the detriment of
nadelig /nad<u>e</u>ləχ/ (adj, adv) adverse, harmful
nadenken /n<u>a</u>dɛŋkə(n)/ (dacht na, heeft
nagedacht) **1** think: *even ~* let me think; *ik
heb er niet bij nagedacht* I did it without
thinking; *ik moet er eens over ~* I'll think
about it **2** think, reflect (on, upon), consider:
zonder erbij na te denken without (even, so
much as) thinking; *stof tot ~* food for think
nadenkend /nad<u>ɛ</u>ŋkənt/ (adj, adv)
thoughtful
nader /n<u>a</u>dər/ (adj, adv) **1** closer, nearer:
partijen ~ tot elkaar proberen te brengen try to
bring parties closer together **2** closer; further; more detailed (*or:* specific): *bij ~e kennismaking* on further (*or:* closer) acquaintance
naderbij /nadərb<u>ɛ</u>i/ (adv) closer, nearer
naderen /n<u>a</u>dərə(n)/ (naderde, heeft gena-
derd) approach
naderhand /n<u>a</u>dərhɑnt/ (adv) afterwards
nadien /nad<u>i</u>n/ (adv) after(wards), later
nadoen /n<u>a</u>dun/ (deed na, heeft nagedaan)
1 copy **2** imitate, copy; mimic: *de scholier
deed zijn leraar na* the schoolboy mimicked
his teacher
de **nadruk** /n<u>a</u>drʏk/ (pl: -ken) emphasis, stress
nadrukkelijk /nadr<u>ʏ</u>kələk/ (adj, adv) em-
phatic, express
nagaan /n<u>a</u>ɣan/ (ging na, is nagegaan)
1 check (up): *we zullen die zaak zorgvuldig ~*
we will look carefully into the matter **2** work
out (for o.s.), examine: *voor zover we kunnen
~* as far as we can gather (*or:* ascertain)
3 imagine: *kun je ~!* just imagine!
de **nageboorte** /n<u>a</u>ɣəbortə/ (pl: -n) afterbirth
de **nagedachtenis** /n<u>a</u>ɣədɑχtənɪs/ memory:
ter ~ aan mijn moeder in memory of my
mother
de **nagel** /n<u>a</u>ɣəl/ (pl: -s) nail; claw
nagelbijten /n<u>a</u>ɣəlbɛitə(n)/ bite one's nails
het/de **nagellak** /n<u>a</u>ɣəlɑk/ (pl: -ken) nail polish (*or:*
varnish)
de **nagelriem** /n<u>a</u>ɣəlrim/ (pl: -en) cuticle
nagenoeg /n<u>a</u>ɣənuχ/ (adv) almost, nearly

het **nagerecht** /n<u>a</u>ɣərɛχt/ (pl: -en) dessert (course)

het **nageslacht** /n<u>a</u>ɣəslɑχt/ (pl: -en) offspring, descendants

nahouden /n<u>a</u>hɑudə(n)/ keep (in) (after hours), detain (after hours)

naïef /na<u>i</u>f/ (adj, adv) naive

de **na-ijver** /n<u>a</u>ɛɪvər/ envy, jealousy

de **naïviteit** /naivit<u>ɛ</u>ɪt/ naïveté

het **najaar** /n<u>a</u>jar/ autumn

de **najaarsmode** /n<u>a</u>jarsmodə/ autumn fashion(s)

najagen /n<u>a</u>jaɣə(n)/ (jaagde na/joeg na, heeft nagejaagd) **1** chase **2** go for (or: after), pursue: *een doel* ~ pursue a goal

nakaarten /n<u>a</u>kartə(n)/ (kaartte na, heeft nagekaart) have a chat afterwards

het **nakie** /n<u>a</u>ki/ [inform]: *in zijn* ~ *staan* stand naked (to the world)

nakijken /n<u>a</u>kɛikə(n)/ (keek na, heeft nagekeken) **1** watch, follow (with one's eyes): *zij keek de wegrijdende **auto** na* she watched the car drive off **2** check, have (or: take) a look at: *zich **laten** ~* have a check-up **3** correct: *veel proefwerken* ~ mark a lot of papers; [Am] grade a lot of papers || *hij **had** het* ~ he could whistle for it

de **nakomeling** /n<u>a</u>koməlɪŋ/ (pl: -en) descendant; offspring

¹**nakomen** /n<u>a</u>komə(n)/ (kwam na, is nagekomen) come later, arrive later, come after(wards)

²**nakomen** /n<u>a</u>komə(n)/ (kwam na, is nagekomen) observe; perform; fulfil: *een **belofte*** ~ keep a promise

het **nakomertje** /n<u>a</u>komərcə/ (pl: -s) afterthought

nalaten /n<u>a</u>latə(n)/ (liet na, heeft nagelaten) **1** leave (behind); bequeath (to) **2** refrain from (-ing): *hij **kan** het niet* ~ *een grapje te maken* he cannot resist making a joke

de **nalatenschap** /nal<u>a</u>tənsχɑp/ (pl: -pen) estate, inheritance

nalatig /nal<u>a</u>təχ/ (adj, adv) negligent

de **nalatigheid** /nal<u>a</u>təχhɛɪt/ negligence

naleven /n<u>a</u>levə(n)/ (leefde na, heeft nageleefd) observe; comply with

de **naleving** /n<u>a</u>levɪŋ/ observance, compliance (with)

nalezen /n<u>a</u>lezə(n)/ (las na, heeft nagelezen) read again

nalopen /n<u>a</u>lopə(n)/ (liep na, heeft nagelopen) **1** walk after, run after **2** check

de **namaak** /n<u>a</u>mak/ imitation, copy; fake; counterfeit

namaken /n<u>a</u>makə(n)/ (maakte na, heeft nagemaakt) **1** imitate, copy **2** fake, counterfeit

name /n<u>a</u>mə/: *met* ~ especially, particularly; *ze heeft je niet **met** ~ genoemd* she didn't mention your name (specifically)

namelijk /n<u>a</u>mələk/ (adv) **1** namely **2** you see, as it happens, it so happens (that): *ik **had** ~ **beloofd** dat …* it so happens I had promised that …

namens /n<u>a</u>məns/ (prep) on behalf of

nameten /n<u>a</u>metə(n)/ (mat na/meette na, heeft nagemeten) check (or: verify) (the measurements of)

Namibië /nam<u>i</u>bijə/ Namibia

de **Namibiër** /nam<u>i</u>bijər/ (pl: -s) Namibian

Namibisch /nam<u>i</u>bis/ (adj) Namibian

de **namiddag** /n<u>a</u>mɪdɑχ/ (pl: -en) afternoon

de **nanny** /nɛ̃ni/ (pl: -'s) nanny

naoorlogs /n<u>a</u>orlɔχs/ (adj) postwar

het **napalm** /n<u>a</u>pɑlm/ napalm

Napels /n<u>a</u>pəls/ Naples

napluizen /n<u>a</u>plœyzə(n)/ (ploos na, heeft nageplozen) examine closely, scrutinize, unravel

het ¹**nappa** /n<u>a</u>pa/ nap(p)a (leather), sheepskin

²**nappa** /n<u>a</u>pa/ (adj) nap(p)a (leather), sheepskin

napraten /n<u>a</u>pratə(n)/ (praatte na, heeft nagepraat) echo, parrot

de **nar** /nɑr/ (pl: -ren) fool, idiot

de **narcis** /nɑrsɪs/ (pl: -sen) [white] narcissus; [yellow] daffodil

de **narcose** /nɑrk<u>o</u>zə/ narcosis; anaesthetic

narekenen /n<u>a</u>rekənə(n)/ (rekende na, heeft nagerekend) go over (or: through) (again), check

de **narigheid** /n<u>a</u>rəχhɛɪt/ trouble

naroepen /n<u>a</u>rupə(n)/ (riep na, heeft nageroepen) **1** call after **2** jeer at

narrig /nɑrəχ/ (adj, adv) peevish: ~ *reageren* react peevishly

nasaal /nazal/ (adj, adv) nasal

de **naschok** /n<u>a</u>sχɔk/ (pl: -ken) aftershock

de **nascholing** /n<u>a</u>sχolɪŋ/ (pl: -en) refresher course, continuing education

de **nascholingscursus** /n<u>a</u>sχolɪŋskʏrzʏs/ continuing-education course; refresher course

het **naschrift** /n<u>a</u>sχrɪft/ (pl: -en) postscript

het **naseizoen** /n<u>a</u>sɛizun/ (pl: -en) late season

de **nasi** /n<u>a</u>si/ rice: ~ *goreng* fried rice

naslaan /n<u>a</u>slan/ (sloeg na, heeft nageslagen): *het woordenboek **erop*** ~ consult a dictionary

het **naslagwerk** /n<u>a</u>slɑχwɛrk/ (pl: -en) reference book (or: work)

de **nasleep** /n<u>a</u>slep/ aftermath, (after)effects, consequences

de **nasmaak** /n<u>a</u>smak/ (pl: nasmaken) aftertaste

naspelen /n<u>a</u>spelə(n)/ (speelde na, heeft nagespeeld) [mus] repeat (by ear); play (sth.) after (s.o.); represent; play (out), act (out)

nastaren /n<u>a</u>starə(n)/ (staarde na, heeft nagestaard) stare (or: gaze) after

nastreven /n<u>a</u>strevə(n)/ (streefde na, heeft nagestreefd) aim for, aim at, strive for (or:

after): *geluk* ~ seek happiness

nasynchroniseren /nɑsɪnxronizerə(n)/ (synchroniseerde na, heeft nagesynchroniseerd) dub

het **¹nat** /nɑt/ liquid; juice

²nat /nɑt/ (adj, adv) **1** wet; moist; damp: ~ *worden* get wet; *door* ~ *door* ~ drenched (*or:* soaked) (to the skin) **2** wet; rainy

natafelen /nɑtafələ(n)/ (tafelde na, heeft nagetafeld) linger at the table

natekenen /nɑtekənə(n)/ (tekende na, heeft nagetekend) draw

natellen /nɑtɛlə(n)/ (telde na, heeft nageteld) count again, check

de **natie** /nɑ(t)si/ (pl: -s) nation, country

nationaal /nɑ(t)ʃonɑl/ (adj, adv) national

het **nationaalsocialisme** /nɑ(t)ʃonɑlsoʃalɪsmə/ National Socialism; Nazism

de **nationaalsocialist** /nɑ(t)ʃonɑlsoʃalɪst/ (pl: -en) National Socialist, Nazi

de **nationalisatie** /nɑ(t)ʃonalizɑ(t)si/ (pl: -s) nationalization

nationaliseren /nɑ(t)ʃonalizerə(n)/ (nationaliseerde, heeft genationaliseerd) nationalize

het **nationalisme** /nɑ(t)ʃonalɪsmə/ nationalism

de **nationalist** /nɑ(t)ʃonalɪst/ (pl: -en) nationalist

nationalistisch /nɑ(t)ʃonalɪstis/ (adj, adv) nationalist(ic)

de **nationaliteit** /nɑ(t)ʃonalitɛit/ (pl: -en) nationality: *hij is van Britse* ~ he has the British nationality

natmaken /nɑtmakə(n)/ (maakte nat, heeft natgemaakt) wet; moisten

natrappen /nɑtrapə(n)/ (trapte na, heeft nagetrapt) kick s.o. when he is down

natrekken /nɑtrɛkə(n)/ (trok na, heeft nagetrokken) check (out); investigate

het **natrium** /nɑtrijʏm/ sodium

het **nattevingerwerk** /nɑtəvɪŋərwɛrk/ guesswork

de **nattigheid** /nɑtəxɛit/ damp: ~ *voelen* smell a rat, be uneasy (about sth.)

de **natura** /nɑtyra/: *in* ~ in kind

de **naturalisatie** /nɑtyralizɑ(t)si/ (pl: -s) naturalization

naturaliseren /nɑtyralizerə(n)/ (naturaliseerde, heeft genaturaliseerd) naturalize: *zich laten* ~ be naturalized

naturel /nɑtyrɛl/ (adj) **1** natural: ~ *leer* natural leather; ~ *linnen* unbleached linen **2** [sport] natural

het **naturisme** /nɑtyrɪsmə/ naturism, nudism

de **naturist** /nɑtyrɪst/ (pl: -en) naturist

de **natuur** /nɑtyr/ **1** nature; country(side); scenery: *wandelen in de vrije* ~ (take a) walk (out) in the country(side); *terug naar de* ~ back to nature **2** nature, character: *twee tegengestelde naturen* two opposite natures (*or:* characters); *dat is zijn tweede* ~ that's be-

come second nature (to him)

het **natuurbeheer** /nɑtyrbəher/ (nature) conservation

de **natuurbescherming** /nɑtyrbəsxɛrmɪŋ/ (nature) conservation, protection of nature

het **natuurgebied** /nɑtyrɣəbit/ (pl: -en) scenic area; nature reserve; wildlife area

de **natuurgenezer** /nɑtyrɣənezər/ (pl: -s) healer

natuurgetrouw /nɑtyrɣətrɑu/ (adj, adv) true to nature (*or:* life)

de **natuurkunde** /nɑtyrkyndə/ physics

natuurkundig /nɑtyrkyndəx/ (adj) physical, physics

de **natuurkundige** /nɑtyrkyndəɣə/ (pl: -n) physicist

de **natuurliefhebber** /nɑtyrlifhɛbər/ (pl: -s) nature lover, lover of nature

natuurlijk /nɑtyrlək/ (adj, adv) natural; true to nature (*or:* life): *maar* ~! why, of course! (*or:* naturally!)

het **natuurmonument** /nɑtyrmonymɛnt/ (pl: -en) nature reserve

het **natuurproduct** /nɑtyrprodʏkt/ (pl: -en) natural product

het **natuurreservaat** /nɑtyrezɛrvat/ (pl: -reservaten) nature reserve

het **natuurschoon** /nɑtyrsxon/ natural (*or:* scenic) beauty

het **natuurtalent** /nɑtyrtalɛnt/ (pl: -en) gift; natural talent, born talent; [pers] gifted (*or:* naturally talented) person

het **natuurverschijnsel** /nɑtyrvərsxɛinsəl/ (pl: -en, -s) natural phenomenon

de **natuurvoeding** /nɑtyrvudɪŋ/ (pl: -en) organic food, natural food, wholefood

de **natuurwetenschap** /nɑtyrwetənsxɑp/ (pl: -pen) (natural) science

het **¹nauw** /nɑu/ (tight) spot (*or:* corner): *iem. in het* ~ *drijven* drive s.o. into a corner, put s.o. in a (tight) spot

²nauw /nɑu/ (adj, adv) **1** narrow **2** close: *een* ~*e samenhang* a close connection **3** precise, particular: *wat geld betreft kijkt hij niet zo* ~ he's not so fussy (*or:* strict) when it comes to money **4** narrow, close-fitting; tight

nauwelijks /nɑuwələks/ (adv) hardly, scarcely, barely ‖ *ik was* ~ *thuis, of …* I'd only just got home when …

nauwgezet /nɑuɣəzɛt/ (adj, adv) painstaking, conscientious, scrupulous; punctual

nauwkeurig /nɑukørəx/ (adj, adv) accurate, precise; careful; close: *tot op de millimeter* ~ accurate to (within) a millimetre

de **nauwkeurigheid** /nɑukørəxɛit/ accuracy, precision, exactness: *met de grootste* ~ with clockwork precision

nauwlettend /nɑulɛtənt/ (adj, adv) close; conscientious; careful: ~ *toezien op* keep a close watch on

n.a.v. (abbrev) *naar aanleiding van* in connection with, with reference to

de **navel** /navəl/ (pl: -s) navel

de **navelsinaasappel** /navəlsinɑsɑpəl/ (pl: -s) navel orange

navelstaren /navəlstarə(n)/ indulgence in navel-gazing

de **navelstreng** /navəlstrɛŋ/ (pl: -en) umbilical cord, navel string

het **naveltruitje** /navəltrœycə/ (pl: -s) crop top

navenant /navənɑnt/ (adj, adv): *de prijzen zijn ~ hoog* the prices are correspondingly (*or:* proportionately) high; *de prijs is laag en de kwaliteit is ~* the price is low and so is the quality

navertellen /navərtɛlə(n)/ (vertelde na, heeft naverteld) repeat, retell: *hij zal het niet ~* he won't live to tell the tale

de **navigatie** /naviɣa(t)si/ navigation

navigeren /naviɣerə(n)/ (navigeerde, heeft genavigeerd) navigate

de **NAVO** /navo/ *Noord-Atlantische Verdragsorganisatie* NATO

navolgen /navɔlɣə(n)/ (volgde na, heeft nagevolgd) follow, imitate: *iemands voorbeeld ~* follow s.o.'s example

de **navolger** /navɔlɣər/ (pl: -s) follower, imitator, copier

de **navolging** /navɔlɣɪŋ/ (pl: -en) imitation, following

de **navraag** /navrax/ inquiry: *~ doen bij* inquire with

navragen /navraɣə(n)/ (vraagde na/vroeg na, heeft nagevraagd) inquire (about, into)

navrant /navrɑnt/ (adj, adv) distressing: *een ~ geval* a sad case

navulbaar /navʏlbar/ (adj) refillable

de **navulverpakking** /navʏlvərpɑkɪŋ/ (pl: -en) refillable packaging

de **naweeën** /nawejə(n)/ (pl) **1** afterpains, aftereffects **2** aftereffects; aftermath

de **nawerking** /nawɛrkɪŋ/ (pl: -en) aftereffect(s)

nawijzen /nawɛizə(n)/ (wees na, heeft nagewezen) point at (*or:* after): *iem. met de vinger ~* point the finger at s.o.

het **nawoord** /nawort/ (pl: -en) afterword, epilogue

de **nazaat** /nazat/ (pl: nazaten) descendant, offspring

nazeggen /nazɛɣə(n)/ (zegde na/zei na, heeft nagezegd) repeat: *zeg mij na* repeat after me

nazenden /nazɛndə(n)/ (zond na, heeft nagezonden) send on (*or:* after), forward

de **nazi** /natsi/ (pl: -'s) Nazi

nazien /nazin/ (zag na, heeft nagezien) look over (*or:* through), check

de **nazit** /nazɪt/ (pl: -ten) informal gathering after a meeting, performance, ...

de **nazomer** /nazomər/ (pl: -s) late summer

de **nazorg** /nazɔrx/ **1** aftercare **2** maintenance

NB /ɛnbe/ (abbrev) *nota bene* NB

n.Chr. (abbrev) *na Christus* AD (Anno Domini)

de **neanderthaler** /nejɑndərtalər/ (pl: -s) Neanderthal (man)

de **necropolis** /nekropɔlɪs/ (pl: -sen) necropolis

de **nectar** /nɛktɑr/ nectar

de **nectarine** /nɛktarinə/ (pl: -s) nectarine

nederig /nedərəx/ (adj, adv) humble, modest

de **nederlaag** /nedərlax/ (pl: -lagen) defeat; setback: *een ~ lijden* suffer a defeat, be defeated

Nederland /nedərlɑnt/ the Netherlands, Holland

de **Nederlander** /nedərlɑndər/ (pl: -s) Dutchman: *de ~s* the Dutch

het **Nederlanderschap** /nedərlɑndərsxɑp/ Dutch nationality: *het ~ verliezen* lose one's Dutch nationality

het **Nederlands** /nedərlɑnts/ Dutch: *het Algemeen Beschaafd ~* Standard Dutch

Nederlandstalig /nedərlɑntstaləx/ (adj) Dutch-speaking: *een ~ lied* a song in Dutch

de **nederzetting** /nedərzɛtɪŋ/ (pl: -en) settlement, post

nee /ne/ (int) **1** no: *geen ~ kunnen zeggen* not be able to say no; *daar zeg ik geen ~ tegen* I wouldn't say no (to that); *~ toch* you can't mean it; really?; surely not **2** really, you're joking (*or:* kidding)

de **neef** /nef/ (pl: neven) **1** nephew **2** cousin: *zij zijn ~ en nicht* they are cousins

neer /ner/ (adv) down

neerbuigend /nerbœyɣənt/ (adj) condescending, patronizing

neerdalen /nerdalə(n)/ (daalde neer, is neergedaald) come down, go down, descend

neergaan /nerɣan/ (ging neer, is neergegaan): *de straat* (*or:* trap) *op- en ~ go* up and down the street (*or:* stairs)

neergooien /nerɣojə(n)/ (gooide neer, heeft neergegooid) throw down, toss down: *het bijltje er bij ~* throw in the towel

neerhalen /nerhalə(n)/ (haalde neer, heeft neergehaald) **1** take down, pull down, lower **2** pull (*or:* take, knock) down, raze **3** take down, bring down

neerkijken /nerkɛikə(n)/ (keek neer, heeft neergekeken) look down (on), look down one's nose (at)

neerkomen /nerkomə(n)/ (kwam neer, is neergekomen) **1** come down, descend, fall, land: *waar is het vliegtuig neergekomen?* where did the aeroplane land? **2** fall (on): *alles komt op mij neer* it all falls on my shoulders **3** come (*or:* boil) down (to), amount (to): *dat komt op hetzelfde neer* it comes (*or:* boils down) to the same thing

de **neerlandicus** /nerlɑndikʏs/ (pl: neerlandici) Dutch specialist, student of (*or:* authority on) Dutch

neerleggen /nɛrlɛɣə(n)/ (legde neer, heeft neergelegd) **1** put (down), lay (down), set (down): *een bevel naast zich ~* disregard (*or:* ignore) a command **2** put aside, lay down: *zijn ambt ~* resign (from) one's office

neerploffen /nɛrplɔfə(n)/ (plofte neer, is neergeploft) flop down, plump down

neersabelen /nɛrsabələ(n)/ (sabelde neer, heeft neergesabeld) **1** put to the sword, cut down (with a sword) **2** [fig] tear apart, tear to pieces; torpedo

neerschieten /nɛrsxitə(n)/ (schoot neer, heeft neergeschoten) **1** shoot (down) **2** bring down, down

¹neerslaan /nɛrslan/ (sloeg neer, is neergeslagen) fall down; drop down: *een wolk van stof sloeg neer op het plein* a cloud of dust settled on the square

²neerslaan /nɛrslan/ (sloeg neer, heeft neergeslagen) **1** turn down; let down; lower: *de ogen ~* lower one's eyes **2** strike down, knock down; [sport] floor ‖ *een opstand ~* put down (*or:* crush) an insurrection (*or:* a rebellion)

neerslachtig /nɛrslɔxtəx/ (adj, adv) dejected, depressed

de **neerslag** /nɛrslɑx/ (pl: -en) **1** precipitation; rain; rainfall; layer; fall: *kans op ~* chance of rain **2** deposit

neersteken /nɛrstekə(n)/ (stak neer, heeft neergestoken) stab (to death)

neerstorten /nɛrstɔrtə(n)/ (stortte neer, is neergestort) crash down, thunder down; crash: *~d puin* falling rubble

neerstrijken /nɛrstrɛikə(n)/ (streek neer, is neergestreken) **1** alight, settle (on), perch (on) **2** descend (on); settle (on): *op een terrasje ~* descend on a terrace

neertellen /nɛrtɛlə(n)/ (telde neer, heeft neergeteld) pay (out), fork out

neervallen /nɛrvalə(n)/ (viel neer, is neergevallen) **1** fall down, drop down: *werken tot je erbij neervalt* work till you drop **2** drop (down), flop (down)

neerwaarts /nɛrwarts/ (adj, adv) downward(s), down

neerzetten /nɛrzɛtə(n)/ (zette neer, heeft neergezet) put down, lay down, place; set down; erect: *een goede tijd ~* record a good time

de **neet** /net/ (pl: neten) nit

het **¹negatief** /neɣatif/ (pl: negatieven) negative (plate, film)

²negatief /neɣatif/ (adj, adv) **1** negative; [esp maths, science] minus: *een ~ getal* a negative (*or:* minus) (number) **2** negative, critical

negen /neɣə(n)/ (num) nine: *~ op (van) de tien keer* nine times out of ten

negende /neɣəndə/ (num) ninth

negentien /neɣə(n)tin/ (num) nineteen

negentiende /neɣə(n)tində/ (num) nineteenth

negentiende-eeuws /neɣə(n)tindeɣws/ (adj) nineteenth-century

negentig /neɣəntəx/ (num) ninety: *hij was in de ~* he was in his nineties

de **neger** /neɣər/ (pl: -s) (African, American) black (person); [depr] Negro

negeren /nəɣerə(n)/ (negeerde, heeft genegeerd) ignore, take no notice of; [pers also] give the cold shoulder; disregard; brush aside: *iem. volkomen ~* cut s.o. dead

neigen /nɛiɣə(n)/ (neigde, heeft geneigd) incline (to, towards), be inclined (to, towards), tend (to, towards)

de **neiging** /nɛiɣɪŋ/ (pl: -en) inclination, tendency

de **nek** /nɛk/ (pl: -ken) nape (*or:* back) of the neck: *je ~ breken over de rommel* trip over the rubbish; *zijn ~ uitsteken* stick one's neck out; *tot aan zijn ~ in de schulden zitten* be up to one's ears in debt; *iem. in zijn ~ hijgen* be close on s.o.'s heels; *uit zijn ~ praten* talk out of the back of one's neck; *over zijn ~ gaan* heave, puke

de **nek-aan-nekrace** /nɛkanɛkres/ (pl: -s) neck-and-neck race

nekken /nɛkə(n)/ (nekte, heeft genekt) break (*or:* wring) s.o.'s neck

de **nekkramp** /nɛkrɑmp/ (pl: -en) spotted fever

het **nekvel** /nɛkfɛl/ scruff of the neck: *iem.* (or: *een hond) in zijn ~ pakken* take s.o. (*or:* a dog) by the scruff of the neck

nemen /nemə(n)/ (nam, heeft genomen) **1** take: *maatregelen ~* take steps (*or:* measures); *de moeite ~ om* take the trouble to; *ontslag ~* resign; *een kortere weg ~* take a short cut; *iem. iets kwalijk ~* take sth. ill of s.o.; *iem. (niet) serieus ~* (not) take s.o. seriously; *strikt genomen* strictly (speaking); *iem. (even) apart ~* take s.o. aside; *voor zijn rekening ~* deal with, account for **2** have: *wat neem jij?* what are you having?; *neem nog een koekje* (do) have another biscuit **3** take, get, have, take out: *een dag vrij ~* have (*or:* take) a day off **4** take, use: *de bus ~* catch (*or:* take) the bus, go by bus **5** take; seize; capture

het **neofascisme** /nejofaʃɪsmə/ neo-Fascism

het **neon** /nejɔn/ neon

de **neonazi** /nejonatsi/ (pl: -'s) neo-Nazi

de **neonreclame** /nejonrəklamə/ (pl: -s) neon sign(s)

de **nep** /nɛp/ sham, fake, swindle; rip-off: *het is allemaal ~* it's bogus (*or:* fake, a sham)

Nepal /nepɑl/ Nepal

de **Nepalees** /nepalɛs/ (pl: Nepalezen) Nepalese, Nepali

neppen /nɛpə(n)/ (nepte, heeft genept) [inform] humbug, bamboozle, cheat: *ze hebben* *me aardig genept **met** dit horloge* I've really been ripped off with this watch

de **nepper** /nɛpər/ [inform] fake

Neptunus /nɛptynʏs/ Neptune

de **nerd** /nʏ:rd/ (pl: -s) nerd

de **nerf** /nɛrf/ (pl: nerven) grain(ing), texture; vein; rib

nergens /nɛrɣəns/ (adv) **1** nowhere: *met onbeleefdheid **kom** je ~* being rude will get you nowhere; *ik kon ~ **naartoe*** I had nowhere to go **2** nothing: *~ **aan komen!*** don't touch!; *ik weet ~ **van*** I know nothing about it

de **nering** /nerɪŋ/ (pl: -en): *de tering naar de ~ zetten* cut one's coat according to one's cloth

de **¹nerts** /nɛrts/ (pl: -en) [animal] mink

het **²nerts** /nɛrts/ [fur] mink

nerveus /nɛrvøs/ (adj, adv) nervous, tense, high(ly)-strung

de **nervositeit** /nɛrvozitɛɪt/ nervousness

het **nest** /nɛst/ (pl: -en) **1** nest; eyrie; den; hole **2** litter, nest; brood **3** jam, spot, fix: *in de ~en zitten* be in a fix

nestelen /nɛstələ(n)/ (nestelde, heeft genesteld) nest

het **¹net** /nɛt/ (pl: -ten) **1** net: *achter het ~ vissen* miss out, miss the boat **2** network, system; net; mains; grid: *een ~ van **telefoonverbindingen*** a network of telephone connections

²net /nɛt/ (adj) **1** neat, tidy; trim: *iets in het ~ schrijven* copy out sth. **2** respectable, decent: *een ~te **buurt*** a respectable (*or:* genteel) neighbourhood

³net /nɛt/ (adv) just, exactly: *~ **goed*** serves you/him (*or:* her, them) right; *het **gaat** maar ~* it's a tight fit; *zij ging ~ **vertrekken*** she was about to leave; *~ **iets** voor hem* a) just the thing for him; **b)** just like him, him all over; *~ **wat** ik dacht* just as I thought; *dat is ~ **wat** ik nodig heb* that's exactly what I need; *ze is ~ **zo** goed als hij* she's every bit as good as he is; *zo is het maar ~* right you are!, just as you say!; *we hadden ~ zo goed niets kunnen doen* we might just as well have done nothing; *we kwamen ~ te laat* we came just too late; *~ **echt*** just like the real thing; *wij **zijn** ~ thuis* we've (only) just come home

de **netbal** /nɛdbɑl/ (pl: -len) netball

netelig /netələχ/ (adj) thorny, knotty, tricky

de **netelroos** /netəlros/ nettle rash

de **netheid** /nɛtheɪt/ neatness, tidiness; cleanliness; smartness

netjes /nɛɕəs/ (adj, adv) **1** neat, tidy, clean **2** neat, smart: *~ **gekleed*** all dressed up **3** decent, respectable, proper: *gedraag je ~* behave yourself

het **netnummer** /nɛtnʏmər/ (pl: -s) dialling code; [Am] area code

de **netspanning** /nɛtspɑnɪŋ/ mains voltage

de **nettiquette** /nɛtikɛtə/ netiquette

netto /nɛto/ (adj, adv) net, nett, clear, real: *het ~ **maandsalaris*** the take-home pay; *de*

*opbrengst **bedraagt** ~ €2000,-* the net(t) profit is €2,000

de **nettowinst** /nɛtowɪnst/ net profit

het **netvlies** /nɛtflis/ (pl: netvliezen) retina

het **netwerk** /nɛtwɛrk/ network, criss-cross pattern; [fig also] system: *een ~ **van** intriges* a web of intrigue

netwerken /nɛtwɛrkə(n)/ (netwerkte, heeft genetwerkt) network

neuken /nøkə(n)/ (neukte, heeft geneukt) [inform] screw, fuck

neuraal /nøyral/ (adj) neural

neuriën /nørijə(n)/ (neuriede, heeft geneuried) hum

de **neurochirurgie** /nøroʃɪrʏrɣi/ neurosurgery

de **neurologie** /nøroloɣi/ neurology, neuroscience

de **neuroloog** /nøroloχ/ (pl: -logen) neurologist

de **neuroot** /nørot/ (pl: neuroten) neurotic, psycho, nutcase

de **neurose** /nørozə/ (pl: -n, -s) neurosis

neurotisch /nørotis/ (adj) neurotic

de **neus** /nøs/ (pl: neuzen) **1** nose, scent; [fig also] flair: *een **fijne** ~ voor iets hebben* have a good nose for sth., have an eye for sth.; *een **frisse** ~ halen* get a breath of fresh air; *doen alsof zijn ~ **bloedt*** play (*or:* act) dumb; [Belg] *van zijn ~ **maken*** show off, make a fuss; *de ~ voor iem. (iets) **ophalen*** turn up one's nose at s.o. (sth.); look down one's nose at s.o. (sth.); *zijn ~ **snuiten*** blow one's nose; *zijn ~ in andermans zaken **steken*** stick one's nose into other people's affairs; *iem. **met** zijn ~ op de feiten drukken* make s.o. face the facts; *niet verder kijken dan zijn ~ lang is* be unable to see further than (the end of) one's nose; *dat ga ik jou niet **aan** je ~ hangen* that's none of your business **2** nose; nozzle; (toe)cap; toe ‖ *dat examen is een **wassen** ~* that exam is just a mere formality

de **neusdruppels** /nøzdrʏpəls/ (pl) nose drops

het **neusgat** /nøsχɑt/ (pl: -en) nostril

de **neushoorn** /nøshorn/ (pl: -s) rhinoceros, rhino

de **neuslengte** /nøslɛŋtə/ (pl: -n, -s) nose, hair('s breadth)

neuspeuteren /nøspøtərə(n)/ pick one's nose

de **neusvleugel** /nøsfløɣəl/ (pl: -s) nostril

de **neut** /nøt/ (pl: -en) drop, snort(er)

neutraal /nøtral/ (adj) neutral, impartial

neutraliseren /nøtralizɛrə(n)/ (neutraliseerde, heeft geneutraliseerd) neutralize, counteract

de **neutraliteit** /nøtralitɛɪt/ neutrality: *de ~ **schenden*** violate neutrality

de **neutronenbom** /nøytronə(n)bɔm/ (pl: -men) neutron bomb

neuzen /nøzə(n)/ (neusde, heeft geneusd) browse, nose around (*or:* about)

de **nevel** /nֶevəl/ (pl: -en) mist; [light] haze; spray

nevelig /nֶevələx/ (adj) misty, hazy

de **nevenactiviteit** /nֶevə(n)aktiviteit/ sideline

het **neveneffect** /nֶevə(n)ɛfɛkt/ (pl: -en) side effect

de **nevenfunctie** /nֶevə(n)fʏŋksi/ (pl: -s) additional job

de **neveninkomsten** /nֶevə(n)ɪŋkɔmstə(n)/ (pl) additional income

de **newfoundlander** /ɲufֶoundlɛndər/ (pl: -s) Newfoundland (dog)

de **ngo** /ɛŋɣeֶo/ (pl: -'s) NGO

het **Nicaragua** /nikarֶaɣuwa/ Nicaragua

de **Nicaraguaan** /nikarֶagwֶan/ (pl: Nicaraguanen) Nicaraguan

Nicaraguaans /nikaragwֶans/ (adj) Nicaraguan

de **nicht** /nɪxt/ **1** niece **2** cousin **3** fairy, queen, poofter; [Am] faggot

nichterig /nֶɪxtərəx/ (adj, adv) fairy, poofy

de **nicotine** /nikotֶinə/ nicotine

niemand /nֶimɑnt/ (ind pron) no one, nobody: **voor** ~ **onderdoen** be second to none; ~ **anders** dan none other than

het **niemandsland** /nֶimɑntslɑnt/ no-man's-land

de **nier** /nir/ (pl: -en) kidney: **gebakken** ~(tjes) fried kidney(s)

de **niersteen** /nֶirsten/ (pl: -stenen) kidney stone

de **niesbui** /nֶizbœy/ (pl: -en) attack (or: fit) of sneezing

¹**niet** /nit/ (ind pron) nothing, nought: dat is ~ **meer** dan een suggestie that's nothing more than a suggestion

²**niet** /nit/ (adv) not: ~ **geslaagd** (or: **gereed**) unsuccessful (or: unprepared); ik **hoop** van ~ I hope not; hoe vaak **heb** ik ~ **gedacht** … how often have I thought …; geloof jij dat verhaal ~? ik **ook** ~ don't you believe this story? neither (or: nor) do I; ~ **alleen** …, maar ook … not only … but also …; het betaalt goed, **daar** ~ **van** it's well-paid, that's not the point, but; **helemaal** ~ not at all; no way; denk dat **maar** ~ don't you believe it!; ik neem aan **van** ~ I don't suppose so, I suppose not; ze is ~ al te slim she is none too bright

nieten /nֶitə(n)/ (niette, heeft geniet) staple

nietes /nֶitəs/ (int) [inform] it isn't: het is jouw schuld! ~! welles! it's your fault! - oh no it isn't! - oh yes it is!

nietig /nֶitəx/ (adj) **1** invalid, null (and void) **2** puny

de **nietje** /nֶicə/ (pl: -s) staple

de **nietmachine** /nֶitmaʃinə/ (pl: -s) stapler

niet-roken /nitrֶokə(n)/ (adv) non-smoking

niets /nits/ (ind pron) **1** not at all: dat **bevalt** mij ~ I don't like that at all **2** nothing, not anything: weet je ~ **beters?** don't you know (of) anything better?; zij moet ~ van hem

hebben she will have nothing to do with him; **verder** ~? is that all?; ik geloof er ~ **van** I don't believe a word of it; **voor** ~ **a)** for nothing, gratis, free (of charge); **b)** for nothing; niet **voor** ~ not for nothing, for good reason; dat is ~ **voor** mij that's not my cup of tea; dit is ~ **dan** opschepperij that's just (or: mere) boasting ‖ in het ~ verdwijnen disappear into thin air

de **nietsnut** /nֶitsnʏt/ (pl: -ten) good-for-nothing

nietsontziend /nitsɔntsֶint/ (adj) unscrupulous, uncompromising

nietsvermoedend /nֶitsfərmudənt/ (adj, adv) unsuspecting

nietszeggend /nֶitsɣֶɛɣənt/ (adj) meaningless; empty: een ~e **opmerking** a triviality, a purposeless remark

niettegenstaande /nֶiteɣənstandə/ (prep) notwithstanding, despite, in spite of: ~ het **feit** dat … notwithstanding (or: despite, in spite of) the fact that …

niettemin /nitəmֶɪn/ (adv) nevertheless, nonetheless, even so, still: ~ **is** het waar dat … it is nevertheless true that …

nietwaar /nitwֶar/ (int) is(n't) it?, do(n't) you?, have(n't) we?: jij kent zijn pa, ~? you know his dad, don't you?; dat is mogelijk, ~? it's possible, isn't it?

nieuw /niw/ (adj) **1** new, recent: **het** ~ste op het gebied van the latest thing in **2** new; unworn; unused: zogoed als ~ as good as new **3** fresh; young: ~e **haring** early-season herring(s) **4** new, fresh; original; novel: een ~ **begin** maken make a fresh start; ik **ben** hier ~ I'm new here **5** new; modern

de **nieuwbouw** /nֶiwbɑu/ **1** construction of new buildings **2** new(ly built) houses

de **nieuwbouwwijk** /nֶiwbɑuwɛik/ (pl: -en) new housing estate (or: development)

de **nieuweling** /nֶiwəlɪŋ/ (pl: -en) **1** novice, beginner **2** new boy (or: girl, pupil)

de **nieuwemaan** /nֶiwəman/ new moon

Nieuw-Guinea /niwɣinֶeja/ New Guinea

Nieuwjaar /niwjֶar/ New Year, New Year's Day: **gelukkig (zalig)** nieuwjaar! Happy New Year!

de **nieuwjaarsdag** /niwjarzdֶɑx/ (pl: -en) New Year's Day

de **nieuwjaarswens** /niwjֶarswɛns/ (pl: -en) New Year's greeting(s)

de **nieuwkomer** /nֶiwkomər/ (pl: -s) newcomer; new boy (or: girl, pupil): een ~ in de top veertig a newcomer to the top twenty

het **nieuws** /niws/ news; piece of news: **buitenlands** (or: **binnenlands**) ~ foreign (or: domestic) news; ik heb **goed** ~ I have (some) good news; dat is **oud** ~ that's stale news; that's ancient history; het ~ van acht uur the eight o'clock news; is er nog ~? any news?, what's new?

het **nieuwsbericht** /ni̯wzbərɪxt/ (pl: -en) news report; news bulletin; news flash

de **nieuwsbrief** /ni̯wzbrif/ (pl: -brieven) newsletter

de **nieuwsdienst** /ni̯wzdinst/ (pl: -en) news service, press service

nieuwsgierig /niwsxi̯rəx/ (adj, adv) curious (about), inquisitive, nosy

de **nieuwsgierigheid** /niwsxi̯rəxhɛit/ curiosity, inquisitiveness: *branden van ~* be dying from curiosity

de **nieuwsgroep** /ni̯wsxrup/ (pl: -en) newsgroup

de **nieuwslezer** /ni̯wslezər/ (pl: -s) newsreader

het **nieuwsoverzicht** /ni̯wsovərzɪxt/ (pl: -en) news summary: *kort ~* rundown on the news

de **nieuwswaarde** /ni̯wswardə/ news value

de **nieuwszender** /ni̯wsɛndər/ (pl: -s) news network

het **nieuwtje** /ni̯wcə/ (pl: -s) piece (*or:* item, bit) of news

Nieuw-Zeeland /niwzе̄lɑnt/ New Zealand

de **Nieuw-Zeelander** /niwzēlɑndər/ (pl: -s) New Zealander

Nieuw-Zeelands /niwzēlɑn(t)s/ (adj) New Zealand; of, from New Zealand

niezen /ni̯zə(n)/ (niesde, heeft geniesd) sneeze

de [1]**Niger** /ni̯ɣər/ Niger

[2]**Niger** /ni̯ɣər/ Niger

de [1]**Nigerees** /niɣerе̄s/ (pl: Nigerezen) Nigerien

[2]**Nigerees** /niɣerе̄s/ (adj) Nigerien

Nigeria /niɣērija/ Nigeria

de **Nigeriaan** /niɣerija̯n/ (pl: Nigerianen) Nigerian

Nigeriaans /niɣerija̯ns/ (adj) Nigerian

nihil /nihi̯l/ (adj) nil, zero

de **nijd** /nɛit/ envy, jealousy: *groen en geel worden van ~ over iets* be green with envy at sth.; *haat en ~* hatred and malice

nijdig /nɛi̯dəx/ (adj, adv) angry, annoyed, cross

de **Nijl** /nɛil/ Nile

het **nijlpaard** /nɛi̯lpart/ (pl: -en) hippopotamus; hippo

nijpend /nɛi̯pənt/ (adj) pinching, biting: *het ~ tekort aan* the acute shortage of

de **nijptang** /nɛi̯ptɑŋ/ (pl: -en) (pair of) pincers

nijver /nɛi̯vər/ (adj, adv) industrious, hardworking

de **nijverheid** /nɛi̯vərhɛit/ industry

de **nikab** /nika̯p/ niqab, face veil

het **nikkel** /nɪ̯kəl/ nickel

nikkelen /nɪ̯kələ(n)/ (adj) **1** nickel **2** nickel-plated

niks /nɪks/ (ind pron) [inform] nothing; [Am] zilch: *dat wordt ~* that won't work; *nou, ik vind het maar ~!* well I don't think much of it

niksen /nɪ̯ksə(n)/ [inform] sit around, loaf about, laze about, do nothing

de **niksnut** /nɪ̯ksnʏt/ (pl: -ten) [inform] good-for-nothing, layabout

de **nimf** /nɪmf/ (pl: -en) nymph

nimmer /nɪ̯mər/ (adv) never

nippen /nɪ̯pə(n)/ (nipte, heeft genipt) sip (at), take a sip

het **nippertje** /nɪ̯pərcə/: *op het ~* at the very last moment (*or:* second), in the nick of time; *dat was op het ~* that was a close (*or:* near) thing; *de student haalde op het ~ zijn examen* the student only passed by the skin of his teeth

het **nirwana** /nɪrva̯na/ nirvana

de **nis** /nɪs/ (pl: -sen) niche, alcove

het **nitraat** /nitra̯t/ (pl: nitraten) nitrate

het **nitriet** /nitri̯t/ (pl: nitrieten) nitrite

het **niveau** /nivо̄/ (pl: -s) level, standard: *rugby op hoog ~* top-class rugby; *het ~ daalt* the tone (of the conversation) is dropping; *onder zijn ~ werken* work below one's capability

nivelleren /nivɛle̯rə(n)/ (nivelleerde, heeft genivelleerd) level (out)

de **nivellering** /nivɛle̯rɪŋ/ (pl: -en) levelling (out), evening out

nl. (abbrev) *namelijk* viz.

Noach /no̯wɑx/ Noah: *de ark van ~* Noah's ark

nobel /no̯bəl/ (adj, adv) noble(-minded), generous

de **Nobelprijs** /nobɛ̯lprɛis/ (pl: -prijzen) Nobel prize: *de ~ voor de vrede* the Nobel Peace prize

noch /nɔx/ (conj) neither, nor: *~ de een ~ de ander* neither the one nor the other

nochtans /nɔxtɑ̯ns/ (adv) [form] nevertheless, nonetheless

de **no-claimkorting** /noklɛ̯mkortɪŋ/ no claim(s) bonus

nodeloos /no̯dəlos/ (adj, adv) unnecessary: *zich ~ ongerust maken* worry over nothing

[1]**nodig** /no̯dəx/ (adj) **1** necessary, needful: *zij hadden al hun tijd ~* they had no time to waste (*or:* spare); *iets ~ hebben* need (*or:* require) sth.; *er is moed voor ~ om* it takes courage to; *dat is hard (dringend) ~* that is badly needed, that is vital; *zo (waar) ~* if need be, if necessary **2** usual, customary

[2]**nodig** /no̯dəx/ (adv) necessarily, needfully, urgently ‖ *dat moet jij ~ zeggen* look who's talking

noemen /nu̯mə(n)/ (noemde, heeft genoemd) **1** call, name: *noem jij dit een gezellige avond?* is this your idea of a pleasant evening?; *dat noem ik nog eens moed* that's what I call courage!; *iem. bij zijn voornaam ~* call s.o. by his first name; *een kind naar zijn vader ~* name a child after his father **2** mention, cite; name: *om maar eens iets te ~* to name (but) a few

noemenswaardig /numənswa̯rdəx/ (adj, adv) appreciable, considerable, noticeable, worthy of mention: *niet ~* inappreciable; nothing to speak of de **noemer** /numər/ (pl: -s) denominator

nog /nɔχ/ (adv) **1** still, so far: *niemand heeft dit ~ geprobeerd* no one has tried this (as) yet; *zelfs nu ~* even now; *tot ~ toe* so far, up to now **2** still **3** even, still: *~ groter* even larger, larger still **4** from now (on), more: *~ drie nachtjes slapen* three (more) nights **5** again, (once) more: *~ één woord en ik schiet* one more word and I'll shoot; *neem er ~ eentje!* have another (one)! ‖ *ik zag hem vorige week ~* I saw him only last week; *verder ~ iets?* anything else?; *ze zijn er ~ maar net* they've only just arrived; *~ geen maand geleden* less than a month ago

de **noga** /noɣa/ nougat

nogal /nɔχɑl/ (adv) rather, fairly, quite, pretty: *ik vind het ~ duur* I think it is rather (*or:* quite) expensive; *er waren er ~ wat* there were quite a few (of them)

nogmaals /nɔχmals/ (adv) once again (*or:* more)

de **no-goarea** /nogoɛːrijə/ no-go area

de **nok** /nɔk/ (pl: -ken) ridge, crest, peak

de **nomade** /nomadə/ (pl: -n) nomad

nominaal /nominal/ (adj) nominal

de **nominatie** /nomina(t)si/ (pl: -s) nomination (list)

nomineren /nominerə(n)/ (nomineerde, heeft genomineerd) nominate

de **non** /nɔn/ (pl: -nen) nun, sister

het **non-actief** /nɔnɑktif/: *(tijdelijk) op ~ staan* be suspended

de **nonchalance** /nɔnʃalãsə/ nonchalance, casualness

nonchalant /nɔnʃalɑnt/ (adj, adv) nonchalant, casual

de **nonnenschool** /nɔnə(n)sχol/ (pl: -scholen) convent (school)

non-profit /nɔmprɔfɪt/ (adj) nonprofit

de **nonsens** /nɔnsɛns/ nonsense, rubbish

non-stop /nɔnstɔp/ (adj) nonstop

de **nood** /not/ (pl: noden) distress; extremity; (time(s) of) emergency: *uiterste ~* dire need; *mensen in ~* people in distress (*or:* trouble); *in de ~ leert men zijn vrienden kennen* a friend in need is a friend indeed; *in geval van ~* in an emergency, in case of need

de **noodgang** /notχɑŋ/ breakneck speed

het **noodgebouw** /notχəbɑu/ temporary building, makeshift building

noodgedwongen /notχədwɔŋə(n)/ (adv) out of (*or:* from) (sheer) necessity: *wij moeten ~ andere maatregelen treffen* we are forced to take other measures

het **noodgeval** /notχəval/ (pl: -len) (case of) emergency

de **noodhulp** /notɦʏlp/ (pl: -en) **1** temporary help, worker **2** emergency relief, emergency aid

de **noodklok** /notklɔk/ (pl: -ken) alarm (bell)

de **noodkreet** /notkret/ (pl: -kreten) cry of dis-

tress, call for help

de **noodlanding** /notlɑndɪŋ/ (pl: -en) forced landing, emergency landing, belly landing, crash landing

noodlijdend /notlɛɪdənt/ (adj) destitute, indigent, needy

het **noodlot** /notlɔt/ fate

noodlottig /notlɔtəχ/ (adj, adv) fatal (to), disastrous (to), ill-fated: *een ~e reis* an ill-fated journey

de **noodmaatregel** /notmatreɣəl/ emergency measure

de **noodoplossing** /notɔplɔsɪŋ/ (pl: -en) temporary solution

de **noodrem** /notrɛm/ (pl: -men) emergency brake, safety brake

de **noodsituatie** /notsitywa(t)si/ (pl: -s) emergency (situation), difficult position, precarious position

de **noodsprong** /notsprɔŋ/ (pl: -en) desperate move (*or:* measure)

de **noodstop** /notstɔp/ (pl: -pen) emergency stop

de **noodtoestand** /notustɑnt/ (pl: -en) emergency (situation), crisis

de **nooduitgang** /notœytχɑŋ/ (pl: -en) emergency exit; fire-escape

de **noodvaart** /notfart/ breakneck speed

het **noodverband** /notfərbɑnt/ first-aid (*or:* emergency, temporary) dressing

de **¹noodweer** /notwer/ self-defence

het **²noodweer** /notwer/ heavy weather, storm, filthy weather

de **noodzaak** /notsak/ necessity, need: *ik zie de ~ daarvan niet in* I don't see the need for this

noodzakelijk /notsakələk/ (adj) necessary, imperative, essential, vital: *het hoogst ~e* the bare necessities

noodzakelijkerwijs /notsakələkərwɛis/ (adv) necessarily, inevitably, of necessity

noodzaken /notsakə(n)/ (noodzaakte, heeft genoodzaakt) force, oblige, compel

nooit /nojt/ (adv) **1** never: *bijna ~* hardly ever, almost never; *~ van mijn leven* never in my life; *~ van gehoord!* never heard of it (*or:* him) **2** never, certainly not, definitely not, no way: *je moet het ~ doen* you must never do that; *~ ofte nimmer* absolutely not, never ever; *dat ~!* never!

de **Noor** /nor/ (pl: Noren) Norwegian

noord /nort/ (adj, adv) north(erly), northern

Noord-Afrika /nortafrika/ North Africa

Noord-Amerika /nortamerika/ North America

Noord-Amerikaans /nortamerikans/ (adj) North American

Noord-Atlantisch /nortɑtlɑntis/ (adj) North Atlantic

Noord-Brabant /nordbrabɑnt/ North Brabant

Noord-Brabants /nordbraban(t)s/ (adj)

North Brabant

noordelijk /nordələk/ (adj, adv) north-(erly), northern, northerly, northward: *de wind is ~* the wind is northerly; *een ~e koers kiezen* steer a northerly course; *het ~ half-rond* the northern hemisphere

het **noorden** /nordə(n)/ north; North: *ten ~ van* (to the) north of

de **noordenwind** /nordə(n)wɪnt/ (pl: -en) north(erly) wind

de **noorderbreedte** /nordərbretə/ north latitude: *Madrid ligt op 40 graden ~* Madrid lies in 40° north latitude

de **noorderkeerkring** /nordərkerkrɪŋ/ Tropic of Cancer

het **noorderlicht** /nordərlɪxt/ aurora borealis, northern lights

de **noorderling** /nordərlɪŋ/ (pl: -en) northern-er

de **noorderzon** /nordərzɔn/: *met de ~ vertrekken* do a moonlight flit; abscond; skeddadle

Noord-Holland /northɔlɑnt/ North Holland

de **Noord-Ier** /nortir/ (pl: -en) inhabitant (*or:* native) of Northern Ireland

Noord-Ierland /nortirlɑnt/ Northern Ireland

Noord-Iers /nortirs/ (adj) (of) Northern Ireland

de **Noordkaap** /nortkap/ North Cape, Arctic Cape

Noord-Korea /nortkoreja/ North Korea

de **Noord-Koreaan** /nortkorejan/ (pl: Noord-Koreanen) North Korean

Noord-Koreaans /nortkorejans/ (adj) North Korean

de **noordkust** /nortkʏst/ north(ern) coast

noordoost /nortost/ (adj) northeast(erly)

het **noordoosten** /nortostə(n)/ north-east

de **noordpool** /nortpol/ North Pole

de **Noordpool** /nortpol/ Arctic

de **noordpoolcirkel** /nortpolsɪrkəl/ Arctic Circle

het **noordpoolgebied** /nortpolɣəbit/ Arctic (region)

noordwaarts /nortwarts/ (adj, adv) north-ward(s), northward

noordwest /nortwɛst/ (adj) northwest(erly)

het **noordwesten** /nortwɛstə(n)/ north-west

de **Noordzee** /nortse/ North Sea

de **Noorman** /norman/ (pl: -nen) Norseman, Viking

het **Noors** /nors/ Norwegian

Noorwegen /norweɣə(n)/ Norway

de **noot** /not/ (pl: noten) **1** nut: *een harde ~ (om te kraken)* a tough (*or:* hard) nut (to crack) **2** [mus] note: *hele* (or: *halve*) *noten spelen* play semibreves (*or:* minims); *een kwart ~* a crotchet; *een valse ~* a wrong note **3** (foot)note: *ergens een kritische ~ bij plaatsen* comment (critically) on sth.

de **nootmuskaat** /notmʏskat/ nutmeg

de **nop** /nɔp/ (pl: -pen) nix: *voor ~* for nothing, for free

nopen /nopə(n)/ (noopte, heeft genoopt) impel, compel

de **nopjes** /nɔpjəs/ (pl): *in zijn ~ zijn* be (as) pleased as Punch, be delighted

noppes /nɔpəs/ (ind pron): *je kunt er voor ~ naar binnen* you can go there for nothing (*or:* for free); *heb ik nou alles voor ~ gedaan?* has it all been an utter waste of time?

de **nor** /nɔr/ (pl: -ren) [inform] clink, nick

het **nordic walking** /nɔrdɪkwɔːkɪŋ/ Nordic Walking

de **noren** /norə(n)/ (pl) racing skates

de **norm** /nɔrm/ (pl: -en) standard, norm

normaal /nɔrmal/ (adj, adv) normal: *~ ben ik al thuis om deze tijd* I am normally (*or:* usually) home by this time

de **normaalschool** /nɔrmalsxol/ (pl: -scholen) [Belg] training college for primary school teachers

normaliseren /nɔrmalizerə(n)/ (normaliseerde, heeft genormaliseerd) normalize

normaliter /nɔrmalitər/ (adv) normally, usually, as a rule

Normandië /nɔrmɑndijə/ Normandy

de **Normandiër** /nɔrmɑndijər/ (pl: -s) Norman

Normandisch /nɔrmɑndis/ (adj) Norman

het **normbesef** /nɔrmbəsɛf/ sense of standards (*or:* values)

de **normering** /nɔrmerɪŋ/ (pl: -en) standard

de **normvervaging** /nɔrmvərvaɣɪŋ/ (pl: -en) blurring of (moral) standards

nors /nɔrs/ (adj, adv) surly, gruff, grumpy

de **nostalgie** /nɔstalɣi/ nostalgia

nostalgisch /nɔstalɣis/ (adj, adv) nostalgic

de **nota** /nota/ (pl: -'s) **1** account, bill **2** memorandum

de **notabele** /notabələ/ (pl: -n) dignitary, leading citizen

nota bene /notabenə/ nota bene, please note ‖ *ze heeft ~ alwéér een andere auto* she's got yet another new car, would you believe

het **notariaat** /notar(i)jat/ (pl: notariaten) **1** office of notary (public) **2** notary's practice

notarieel /notar(i)jel/ (adj, adv) notarial: *een notariële akte* a notarial act (*or:* deed)

de **notaris** /notarɪs/ (pl: -sen) notary (public)

het **notariskantoor** /notarɪskɑntor/ (pl: -kantoren) notary('s) office

de **notatie** /nota(t)si/ notation; notation system

het/de **notebook** /nodbuk/ (pl: -s) notebook (computer)

de **notenbalk** /notə(n)bɑlk/ (pl: -en) staff, stave

de **notenboom** /notə(n)bom/ (pl: -bomen) walnut (tree)

de **notendop** /notə(n)dɔp/ (pl: -pen) nutshell

het **notenhout** /notə(n)haut/ walnut

de **notenkraker** /nо̱tə(n)krakər/ (pl: -s) (pair of) nutcrackers

het **notenschrift** /nо̱tə(n)sχrɪft/ (pl: -en) (musical) notation; staff notation

¹**noteren** /notе̱rə(n)/ (noteerde, heeft genoteerd) list; quote

²**noteren** /notе̱rə(n)/ (noteerde, heeft genoteerd) **1** note (down), make a note of, record, register; book: *een telefoonnummer ~* jot down (*or:* make a note) of a telephone number **2** quote: *aan de beurs genoteerd zijn* be listed on the (stock) market

de **notering** /notе̱rɪŋ/ (pl: -en) quotation; quoted price; rate

de **notie** /nо̱(t)si/ (pl: -s) notion, idea: *geen flauwe ~* not the faintest notion

de **notitie** /notі̱(t)si/ (pl: -s) note; memo(randum)

het **notitieblok** /notі̱(t)siblɔk/ (pl: -ken) notepad, memo pad; scribbling pad

het **notitieboekje** /notі̱(t)sibukjə/ (pl: -s) notebook, memorandum book

notoir /notwа̱r/ (adj) notorious

de **notulen** /nо̱tylə(n)/ (pl) minutes

notuleren /notylе̱rə(n)/ (notuleerde, heeft genotuleerd) take (the) minutes

de **notulist** /notylі̱st/ minutes secretary

¹**nou** /nɑu/ (adv) [inform] **1** now: *wat moeten we ~ doen?* what do we (have to) do now? **2** now (that): *~ zij het zegt, geloof ik het* now that she says so I believe it

²**nou** /nɑu/ (int) [inform] **1** now, well: *kom je ~?* well, are you coming? **2** well, really: *meen je dat ~?* do you really mean it?; *hoe kan dat ~?* how on earth can that be? (*or:* have happened?); *~ dan!* exactly, couldn't agree more!; *~, en of!* you bet! **3** again: *wanneer ga je ~ ook weer weg?* when were you leaving again? **4** oh (very) well, never mind: *~ ja, zo erg is 't niet* never mind, it's not all that bad; *dat is ~ niet bepaald eenvoudig* well, that's not so easy **5** oh, now, … on earth, … ever: *waar bleef je ~?* where on earth have you been? ‖ *~ en?* so what?; *~, dat was het dan* well (*or:* so), that was that

Nova Zembla /novazе̱mbla/ Novaya Zemlya

de **novelle** /novе̱lə/ (pl: -n) short story, novella

de **november** /novе̱mbər/ November

nu /ny/ (adv) **1** now, at the moment: *nu en dan* now and then, at times, occasionally; *ik kan nu niet* I can't (right, just) now; *nu nog niet* not yet; *tot nu (toe)* up to now, so far **2** now(adays), these days ‖ *het hier en het nu* the here and now

de **nuance** /nywа̱sə/ (pl: -s) nuance

nuanceren /nywɑnsе̱rə(n)/ (nuanceerde, heeft genuanceerd) nuance, differentiate; qualify

nuchter /nʏχtər/ (adj) **1** fasting; newborn: *voor de operatie moet je ~ zijn* you must have

an empty stomach before surgery **2** sober: *~ worden* sober up **3** sober, plain: *de ~e waarheid* the plain (*or:* simple) truth **4** sober(-minded), sensible, level-headed

nucleair /nyklejɛ̱:r/ (adj, adv) nuclear

de **nudist** /nydі̱st/ (pl: -en) nudist, naturist

nuffig /nʏ̱fəχ/ (adj) prim, prissy

de **nuk** /nʏk/ (pl: -ken) mood, quirk

nukkig /nʏ̱kəχ/ (adj) quirky, moody, sullen

de **nul** /nʏl/ (pl: -len) nought; zero; 0: *tien graden onder ~* ten (degrees) below zero; *PSV heeft met 2-0 verloren* PSV lost two-nil ‖ *nul op het rekest krijgen* meet with a refusal; be turned down

de **nulmeridiaan** /nʏ̱lmeridijan/ (pl: -meridianen) prime meridian

het **nulpunt** /nʏ̱lpʏnt/ zero (point)

numeriek /nymerі̱k/ (adj) numerical, numeric

het **nummer** /nʏ̱mər/ (pl: -s) **1** number, figure: *~ één van de klas zijn* be top of one's class; *mobiel ~* mobile (phone) number; [Am] cellphone number; *vast ~* landline number **2** number, issue: *een ~ van een tijdschrift* a number (*or:* issue) of a periodical; *een oud ~* a back issue (*or:* number) **3** number; track: *een ~ draaien* play a track **4** act, routine, number: *een ~ brengen* do a routine (*or:* an act) ‖ *iem. op zijn ~ zetten* put s.o. in his (*or:* her) place

het **nummerbord** /nʏ̱mərbɔrt/ (pl: -en) number plate; [Am] license plate

nummeren /nʏ̱mərə(n)/ (nummerde, heeft genummerd) number

de **nummering** /nʏ̱mərɪŋ/ (pl: -en) numeration

de **nummermelder** /nʏ̱mərmɛldər/ caller ID

het **nummertje** /nʏ̱mərcə/ (pl: -s) **1** number **2** [inform] screw, fuck

de **nummerweergave** /nʏ̱mərwerγavə/ caller ID

nurks /nʏrks/ (adj, adv) gruff

het **nut** /nʏt/ use(fulness); benefit; point; value; purpose: *het heeft geen enkel ~ om …* it is useless (*or:* pointless) to …; *ik zie er het ~ niet van in* I don't see the point of it

het **nutsbedrijf** /nʏ̱tsbədrɛif/ (pl: -bedrijven): *openbare nutsbedrijven* public utilities

nutteloos /nʏ̱təlos/ (adj, adv) **1** useless: *een nutteloze vraag* a pointless question **2** fruitless

de **nutteloosheid** /nʏtəlо̱shɛit/ uselessness, futility

nuttig /nʏ̱təχ/ (adj, adv) **1** useful: *zich ~ maken* make o.s. useful **2** advantageous: *zijn tijd ~ besteden* make good use of one's time

nuttigen /nʏ̱təγə(n)/ (nuttigde, heeft genuttigd) consume, take, partake of

de **nv** /ɛnvе̱/ *naamloze vennootschap* plc (public limited company); [Am] Inc (incorporated)

n.v.t. (abbrev) *niet van toepassing* n/a

het/de **nylon** /nɛilɔn/ nylon

de **nymfomane** /nɪmfomanə/ (pl: -n, -s) nymphomaniac

O

o /o/ (int) O, oh, ah || *o zo* verleidelijk ever so tempting

o.a. (abbrev) *onder andere* among other things, for instance

de **oase** /owaze/ (pl: -s) oasis

de **obelisk** /obəlɪsk/ (pl: -en) obelisk

de **O-benen** /obenə(n)/ (pl) bandy legs, bow-legs: *met ~* bandy-legged, bow-legged

de **ober** /obər/ (pl: -s) waiter

de **obesitas** /obezitas/ obesity

het **object** /ɔpjɛkt/ (pl: -en) object

objectief /ɔpjɛktif/ (adj, adv) objective

de **objectiviteit** /ɔpjɛktivitɛit/ objectiveness, objectivity, impartiality

obligaat /obliɣat/ (adj, adv) obligatory: *obligate* **toespraken** standard speeches

de **obligatie** /obliɣa(t)si/ (pl: -s) bond, debenture

obsceen /ɔpsen/ (adj) obscene

obscuur /ɔpskyr/ (adj) **1** obscure, dark **2** shady, obscure: *een ~* **zaakje** a shady (*or:* doubtful) business

obsederen /ɔpsederə(n)/ (obsedeerde, heeft geobsedeerd) obsess

de **observatie** /ɔpsɛrva(t)si/ (pl: -s) observation

de **observatiepost** /ɔpsɛrva(t)sipost/ (pl: -en) observation post

de **observator** /ɔpsɛrvator/ (pl: -s, -en) observer

het **observatorium** /ɔpsɛrvatorijʏm/ (pl: observatoria) observatory

observeren /ɔpsɛrverə(n)/ (observeerde, heeft geobserveerd) observe, watch

de **obsessie** /ɔpsɛsi/ (pl: -s) obsession, hang-up

het **obstakel** /ɔpstakəl/ (pl: -s) obstacle, obstruction, impediment: *een belangrijk ~* **vormen** constitute a major obstacle

obstinaat /ɔpstinat/ (adj) obstinate, stubborn

de **obstipatie** /ɔpstipa(t)si/ constipation

de **obstructie** /ɔpstrʏksi/ (pl: -s) obstruction: ~ **plegen** commit obstruction

de **occasie** /ɔkazi/ (pl: -s) [Belg] bargain

de **occasion** /ɔkeʒən/ (pl: -s) used car

occult /ɔkʏlt/ (adj) occult

het **occultisme** /ɔkʏltɪsmə/ occultism

de **oceaan** /osejan/ (pl: oceanen) ocean, sea: *de* **Stille (Grote)** *Oceaan* the Pacific (Ocean)

Oceanië /osejanijə/ Oceania

och /ɔx/ (int) oh, o, ah: ~ *kom* oh, go on (with you)

de **ochtend** /ɔxtənt/ (pl: -en) morning; dawn; daybreak: *de* **hele** ~ all morning; *om 7 uur* **'s**

~*s at 7 o'clock in the morning, at 7 a.m.*

het **ochtendblad** /ɔxtəndblɑt/ (pl: -en) morning (news)paper

het **ochtendgloren** /ɔxtəntxlorə(n)/ [form] daybreak

het **ochtendhumeur** /ɔxtənthymør/ (pl: -en) (early) morning mood: *een ~* **hebben** have got up on the wrong side of the bed

de **ochtendjas** /ɔxtəntjas/ (pl: -sen) dressing gown; housecoat

de **ochtendkrant** /ɔxtəntkrɑnt/ (pl: -en) morning (news)paper

de **ochtendmens** /ɔxtəntmɛns/ (pl: -en) early bird (*or:* riser)

de **ochtendschemering** /ɔxtəntsxemərɪŋ/ dawn

de **ochtendspits** /ɔxtəntspɪts/ morning rush hour

het/de **octaaf** /ɔktaf/ (pl: octaven) octave, eighth

het **octaan** /ɔktan/ octane

de **octopus** /ɔktopʏs/ (pl: -sen) octopus

het **octrooi** /ɔktroj/ (pl: -en) patent: ~ *aanvragen* apply for a patent

de **ode** /odə/ (pl: -n, -s) ode: *een ~ brengen aan iem.* pay tribute to s.o.

oecumenisch /øykymenɪs/ (adj) ecumenical, interfaith

het **oedeem** /œydem/ (pl: oedemen) (o)edema

het **oedipuscomplex** /œydipuskomplɛks/ (pl: -en) Oedipus complex

oef /uf/ (int) phew, whew, oof

het **oefenboek** /ufənbuk/ (pl: -en) workbook, exercise book

¹**oefenen** /ufənə(n)/ (oefende, heeft geoefend) train, practise; rehearse; drill [mil]: ~ *voor een voorstelling* rehearse for a performance

²**oefenen** /ufənə(n)/ (oefende, heeft geoefend) train, coach; [mil] drill: *zich ~ in het zwemmen* practise swimming

de **oefening** /ufənɪŋ/ (pl: -en) **1** exercise: *dat is een* **goede** ~ *voor je* it is good practice for you **2** exercise, drill

het **oefenterrein** /ufə(n)tɛrɛin/ (pl: -en) practice ground, training ground

de **oefenwedstrijd** /ufə(n)wɛtstrɛit/ (pl: -en) training (*or:* practice, warm-up) match; sparring match

de **oehoe** /uhu/ (pl: -s) eagle owl

oei /uj/ (int) oops; ouch

het ¹**Oekraïens** /ukrains/ Ukrainian

²**Oekraïens** /ukrains/ (adj) Ukrainian

de **Oekraïne** /ukrainə/ Ukraine

de **Oekraïner** /ukrainər/ (pl: -s) Ukrainian

de **oen** /un/ (pl: -en) [inform] blockhead, dummy

oeps /ups/ (int) oops, whoops

de **Oeral** /ural/: *de ~* the Urals; the Ural Mountains

het **oerbos** /urbɔs/ (pl: -sen) primeval forest

oergezellig /urɣəzɛləx/ (adj, adv) [inform]

very pleasant; delightful

de **oerknal** /ˈurknɑl/ Big Bang

de **oermens** /ˈurmɛns/ (pl: -en) primitive (*or:* prehistoric) man

oeroud /urˈɑut/ (adj) ancient, prehistoric, primeval

oersaai /ursˈaj/ (adj, adv) [inform] deadly dull

de **oertijd** /ˈurtɛɪt/ (pl: -en) prehistoric times

het **oerwoud** /ˈurwɑut/ (pl: -en) **1** primeval forest, virgin forest; jungle **2** [fig] jungle, chaos, hotchpotch

de **OESO** /ˈuzo/ OECD

de **oester** /ˈustər/ (pl: -s) oyster

de **oesterbank** /ˈustərbɑŋk/ (pl: -en) oyster bank

de **oesterzwam** /ˈustərzwɑm/ (pl: -men) oyster mushroom

het **oestrogeen** /ˈœystroɣen/ (pl: oestrogenen) oestrogen

het **oeuvre** /ˈœːvrə/ oeuvre, works, body of work

de **oever** /ˈuvər/ (pl: -s) bank; shore: *de rivier is* ***buiten*** *haar ~s getreden* the river has burst its banks

oeverloos /ˈuvərlos/ (adj) endless, interminable: *~ gezwets* blather, claptrap

de **Oezbeek** /uzbˈek/ Uzbek

het **¹Oezbeeks** /uzbˈeks/ Uzbek

²Oezbeeks /uzbˈeks/ (adj) Uzbek

Oezbekistan /uzbˈekistɑn/ Uzbekistan

of /ɔf/ (conj) **1** (either …) or: *je krijgt of het* ***een*** *of het* ***ander*** you get either the one or the other; *het is óf het* ***een*** *óf het* ***ander*** you can't have it both ways; *Sepke zei weinig of* ***niets*** Sepke said little or nothing; ***min*** *of* ***meer*** more or less; *vroeg of* ***laat*** sooner or later, eventually **2** or: *de influenza of* ***griep*** influenza, or flu **3** (hardly …) when, (no sooner …) than: *ik weet* ***niet*** *beter of …* for all I know … **4** although, whether … or (not), no matter (how, what, where): *of je het nu leuk vindt of niet* whether you like it or not **5** as if, as though: *hij* ***doet*** *of er niets gebeurd is* he is behaving (*or:* acts) as if nothing has happened; *het is* ***net*** *of het regent* it looks just as though it were raining **6** whether, if: *ik* ***vraag*** *me af of hij komen zal* I wonder whether (*or:* if) he'll come ‖ *ik weet niet,* ***wie*** *of het gedaan heeft* I don't know who did it; ***wanneer*** *of ze komt, ik weet 't niet* when she is coming I don't know; *een dag of* ***tien*** about ten days, ten days or so

het **offensief** /ɔfɛnsˈif/ (pl: offensieven) offensive: *in het ~ gaan* go on the offensive

het **offer** /ˈɔfər/ (pl: -s) offering, sacrifice, gift, donation: *zware ~s eisen* take a heavy toll

de **offerande** /ˈɔfərɑndə/ (pl: -n, -s) offering, sacrifice; offertory

offeren /ˈɔfərə(n)/ (offerde, heeft geofferd) sacrifice, offer (up)

het **offerfeest** /ˈɔfərfest/ (pl: -en) ceremonial offering

het **Offerfeest** [Islam] Eid al-Adha, Celebration of Sacrifice

de **offerte** /ɔfˈɛrtə/ (pl: -s) offer; tender; quotation

de **official** /ɔfˈɪʃəl/ (pl: -s) official

officieel /ɔfiʃˈel/ (adj, adv) **1** official, formal: *iets ~* ***meedelen*** announce sth. officially **2** formal, ceremonial

de **officier** /ɔfisˈir/ (pl: -en) officer

officieus /ɔfiʃˈøs/ (adj, adv) unofficial, semi-official

offline /ɔfˈlɑjn/ (adj) off-line

offshore /ɔfˈʃoːr/ (adj) offshore

de **offshoring** /ˈɔfʃoːrɪŋ/ offshoring

ofschoon /ɔfsxˈon/ (conj) (al)though, even though

ofte /ˈɔftə/ (conj): *nooit ~ nimmer* not ever

oftewel /ɔftəwˈɛl/ (conj) *see ofwel*

ofwel /ɔfwˈɛl/ (conj) **1** either … or **2** or, that is, i.e.: *de cobra ~* ***brilslang*** the cobra, or hooded snake

het **ogenblik** /ˈoɣə(n)blɪk/ (pl: -ken) **1** moment, instant, minute, second: *een ~* ***rust*** a moment's peace; *in een ~* in a moment; *juist* ***op*** *dat ~* just at that very moment (*or:* instant); *(heeft u)* ***een*** *~je?* just a moment (*or:* minute); would you mind waiting a moment? **2** moment, time, minute

ogenblikkelijk /oɣə(n)blɪkˈələk/ (adv) immediately, at once, this instant: ***ga*** *~ de dokter* ***halen*** go and fetch the doctor immediately (*or:* at once)

ogenschijnlijk /oɣə(n)sxɛɪnlək/ (adj, adv) apparent, ostensible; at first sight

ogenschouw /oɣə(n)sxɑu/: *iets in ~* ***nemen*** take stock of sth.

o.g.v. (abbrev) *op grond van* on the basis of

het/de **ohm** /om/ (pl: -s) ohm

de **ok** /oka̯/ *operatiekamer* operating theatre

OK /okˈe/ (int) OK

de **okapi** /okˈapi/ (pl: -'s) okapi

oké /okˈej/ (int) OK

de **oker** /ˈokər/ (pl: -s) ochre

de **oksel** /ˈɔksəl/ (pl: -s) armpit

de **oktober** /ɔktˈobər/ (pl: -s) October

de **oldtimer** /ˈoltɑjmər/ vintage car

de **oleander** /oleˈɑndər/ (pl: -s) oleander

de **olie** /ˈoli/ (pl: oliën) oil

de **oliebol** /ˈolibɔl/ (pl: -len) **1** [roughly] doughnut ball **2** [fig] idiot, fathead

de **olieboycot** /ˈolibɔjkɔt/ (pl: -s) oil boycott

de **oliebron** /ˈolibrɔn/ (pl: -nen) oil well

de **oliecrisis** /ˈolikrɪzɪs/ oil crisis

oliedom /olidˈɔm/ (adj, adv) (as) dumb as an ox

de **oliekachel** /ˈolikɑxəl/ (pl: -s) oil heater

de **olielamp** /ˈolilɑmp/ (pl: -en) oil lamp

oliën /ˈolijə(n)/ (oliede, heeft geolied) oil, lubricate; grease

de **olieraffinaderij** /o̯lirɑfinɑdərɛi/ (pl: -en) oil refinery

het **oliesel** /o̯lisəl/ anointing, extreme unction, last rites: *het laatste (Heilig)* ~ *toedienen* administer extreme unction (*or:* the last rites)

de **olietanker** /o̯litɛŋkər/ (pl: -s) (oil) tanker

de **olieverf** /o̯livɛrf/ oil colour(s), oil paint

de **olievlek** /o̯livlɛk/ (pl: -ken) (oil-)slick: *zich als een ~ uitbreiden* spread unchecked

de **olifant** /o̯lifɑnt/ (pl: -en) elephant: *als een ~ in een porseleinkast* like a bull in a china shop

de **olifantshuid** /o̯lifɑn(t)shœyt/: [fig] *een ~ hebben* have a thick skin, have a hide like a rhinoceros

de **oligarchie** /oliɣɑrxi/ (pl: -ën) oligarchy

de **olijf** /o̯lɛif/ (pl: olijven) olive

de **Olijfberg** /o̯lɛivbɛrx/ Mount of Olives

de **olijfboom** /o̯lɛifbom/ (pl: -bomen) olive (tree)

de **olijfolie** /o̯lɛrfoli/ olive oil

olijk /o̯lək/ (adj, adv) [form] roguish, arch

de **olm** /ɔlm/ (pl: -en) elm (tree)

o.l.v. (abbrev) *onder leiding van* conducted by

O.L.V. (abbrev) *Onze-Lieve-Vrouw* BVM; Our (Blessed) Lady

de **olympiade** /olɪmpijɑdə/ (pl: -s) Olympiad, Olympics, Olympic Games

olympisch /o̯lɪmpis/ (adj) Olympic

¹**om** /ɔm/ (adj) **1** roundabout, circuitous: *een straatje (blokje) om* round the block **2** over, up, finished: *voor het jaar om is* before the year is out; *uw tijd is om* your time is up

²**om** /ɔm/ (adv) **1** (a)round, about; on: *doe je das om* put your scarf on; *toen zij de hoek om kwamen* when they came (a)round the corner **2** about: *waar gaat het om?* what's it about?; what's the matter?

³**om** /ɔm/ (prep) **1** (a)round, about: *om de hoek* (just) round the corner **2** at: *ik zie je vanavond om acht uur* I'll see you tonight at eight (o'clock); *om een uur of negen* around nine (o'clock) **3** every: *om beurten* in turn; *om de twee uur* every two hours **4** for (reasons of), on account of, because of: *om deze reden* for this reason **5** to, in order to, so as to: *niet om te eten* not fit to eat, inedible

het **OM** /oɛm/ *Openbaar Ministerie* Public Prosecutor

de **oma** /o̯ma/ (pl: -'s) gran(ny), grandma, grandmother

de **omafiets** /o̯mafits/ (pl: -en) [roughly] sit-up-and-beg type bicycle

Oman /o̯mɑn/ Oman

de **Omaniet** /omani̱t/ (pl: -en) Omani

Omanitisch /omani̱tis/ (adj) Omani

omarmen /ɔmɑrmə(n)/ (omarmde, heeft omarmd) embrace; hug: *een voorstel* ~ accept a proposal with open arms

ombinden /o̯mbɪndə(n)/ (ombond, heeft ombonden) tie on (*or:* round)

ombouwen /o̯mbɑuwə(n)/ (bouwde om, heeft omgebouwd) convert; reconstruct; rebuild; alter

ombrengen /o̯mbrɛŋə(n)/ (bracht om, heeft omgebracht) kill, murder

de **ombudsman** /o̯mbʏtsmɑn/ (pl: -nen) ombudsman

ombuigen /o̯mbœyɣə(n)/ (boog om, heeft is omgebogen) **1** restructure, adjust, change (the direction of) **2** bend (round, down, back)

omcirkelen /ɔmsɪrkələ(n)/ (omcirkelde, heeft omcirkeld) (en)circle, ring; [fig also] surround: *de politie omcirkelde het gebouw* the police surrounded the building

omdat /ɔmdɑt/ (conj) because, as: *juist* ~ … precisely because …; *waarom ga je niet mee?* ~ *ik er geen zin in heb* why don't you come along? because I don't feel like it

omdoen /o̯mdun/ (deed om, heeft omgedaan) put on: *zijn veiligheidsgordel* ~ fasten one's seat belt

omdopen /o̯mdopə(n)/ (doopte om, heeft omgedoopt) rename

¹**omdraaien** /o̯mdrajə(n)/ (draaide om, is omgedraaid) **1** turn (round): *de brandweerauto draaide de hoek om* the fire engine turned the corner **2** turn back (*or:* round)

²**omdraaien** /o̯mdrajə(n)/ (draaide om, heeft omgedraaid) **1** turn (round), turn over: *zich* ~ roll over (on one's side) **2** reverse, swing round

omduwen /o̯mdywə(n)/ (duwde om, heeft omgeduwd) push over; knock over

de **omega** /o̯meɣa/ (pl: -'s) omega

de **omelet** /o̯məlɛt/ (pl: -ten) omelette

omfloerst /ɔmflʏrst/ (adj) shrouded: *met ~e stem* in a muffled voice

omgaan /o̯mɣan/ (ging om, is omgegaan) **1** go round; turn; round: *de hoek* ~ turn the corner; *een blokje* ~ (go for a) walk around the block **2** go about (with), associate (with); handle; manage: *zo ga je niet met mensen om* that's no way to treat people

omgaand /o̯mɣant/ (adj, adv): *per ~e* antwoorden answer by return (of post, mail)

de **omgang** /o̯mɣɑŋ/ contact, association: *hij is gemakkelijk* (or: *lastig*) *in de* ~ he is easy (*or:* difficult) to get on with

de **omgangsregeling** /o̯mɣɑŋsreɣəlɪŋ/ (pl: -en) arrangement(s) concerning parental access

de **omgangstaal** /o̯mɣɑŋstal/ everyday speech

de **omgangsvormen** /o̯mɣɑŋsfɔrmə(n)/ (pl) manners, etiquette

¹**omgekeerd** /o̯mɣəkert/ (adj) **1** turned round; upside down; inside out; back to front: ~ *evenredig* inversely proportional (to) **2** opposite, reverse

²**omgekeerd** /o̯mɣəkert/ (adv) the other way round: *het is precies* ~ it's just the other

way round
omgeven (omgaf, heeft omgeven) surround, encircle: *geheel door land* ~ landlocked
de **omgeving** /ɔmɣevɪŋ/ neighbourhood, vicinity, surrounding area (*or:* districts)
omgooien /ɔmɣojə(n)/ (gooide om, heeft omgegooid) **1** knock over, upset **2** change round
de **omhaal** /ɔmhal/ (pl: omhalen) overhead kick || *met veel* ~ *van woorden* in a roundabout way
omhakken /ɔmhɑkə(n)/ (hakte om, heeft omgehakt) chop down, cut down, fell
het **omhalen** /ɔmhalə(n)/ [Belg] collect, make a collection
de **omhaling** /ɔmhalɪŋ/ (pl: -en) [Belg] collection
omhanden /ɔmhɑndə(n)/ (adv): *niets* ~ *hebben* have nothing to do; be at a loose end
omhangen /ɔmhɑŋə(n)/ (hing om, heeft omgehangen) hang over (*or:* round)
omheen /ɔmhen/ (adv) round (about), around: *ergens* ~ *draaien* talk round sth., beat about the bush
omheinen /ɔmhɛɪnə(n)/ (omheinde, heeft omheind) fence off (*or:* in)
de **omheining** /ɔmhɛɪnɪŋ/ (pl: -en) fence, enclosure
omhelzen /ɔmhɛlzə(n)/ (omhelsde, heeft omhelsd) embrace, hug: *iem.* *stevig* ~ give s.o. a good hug
de **omhelzing** /ɔmhɛlzɪŋ/ (pl: -en) embrace, hug
omhoog /ɔmhox/ (adv) **1** up (in the air) **2** up(wards); in(to) the air: *handen* ~! hands up!
omhooggaan /ɔmhoxan/ (ging omhoog, is omhooggegaan) go up(wards), rise: *de prijzen gaan omhoog* prices are going up (*or:* are rising)
omhooghouden /ɔmhoxhɑudə(n)/ (hield omhoog, heeft omhooggehouden) hold up
omhoogkomen /ɔmhoxkomə(n)/ (kwam omhoog, is omhooggekomen) **1** come (*or:* get) up **2** [fig] get on (*or:* ahead)
omhoogzitten /ɔmhoxsɪtə(n)/ (zat omhoog, heeft omhooggezeten): *met iets* ~ be stuck over (*or:* on) sth.; be stuck with sth.
omhullen /ɔmhylə(n)/ (omhulde, heeft omhuld) envelop, wrap
het **omhulsel** /ɔmhylsəl/ (pl: -s) covering, casing, envelope, shell; husk; hull; pod
de **omissie** /ɔmɪsi/ (pl: -s) omission
de **omkadering** /ɔmkɑdərɪŋ/ (pl: -en) [Belg] staff-pupil ratio
omkeerbaar /ɔmkerbar/ (adj) reversible
¹**omkeren** /ɔmkerə(n)/ (keerde om, is omgekeerd) turn back, turn round
²**omkeren** /ɔmkerə(n)/ (keerde om, heeft

omgekeerd) **1** turn (round); turn; invert: *zich* ~ turn (a)round **2** switch (round), change (round); twist (round)
omkijken /ɔmkɛikə(n)/ (keek om, heeft omgekeken) **1** look round: *hij keek niet op of om* he didn't even look up **2** look after; worry about, bother about: *niet naar iem.* ~ not worry (*or:* bother) about s.o.; leave s.o. to his own devices; *je hebt er geen* ~ *naar* it needs no looking after
omkleden /ɔmkledə(n)/ (kleedde om, heeft omgekleed) change, put other clothes on
omkomen /ɔmkomə(n)/ (kwam om, is omgekomen) **1** die; be killed: ~ *van honger* starve to death **2** come round, turn: *hij zag haar juist de hoek* ~ he saw her just (as she was) coming round (*or:* turning) the corner
omkoopbaar /ɔmkobar/ (adj) bribable, corruptible
omkopen /ɔmkopə(n)/ (kocht om, heeft omgekocht) bribe, buy (over), corrupt: *zich laten* ~ accept a bribe
de **omkoperij** /ɔmkopərɛi/ bribery, corruption
omlaag /ɔmlax/ (adv) down, below: *naar* ~ down(wards)
omlaaggaan /ɔmlaxan/ (ging omlaag, is omlaaggegaan) go down
omleggen /ɔmlɛɣə(n)/ (legde om, heeft omgelegd) **1** put round; [Am] put around; put on **2** kill
omleiden /ɔmlɛidə(n)/ (leidde om, heeft omgeleid) divert, re-route; train
de **omleiding** /ɔmlɛidɪŋ/ (pl: -en) [traf] (traffic) diversion, detour; relief route, alternative route
omliggend /ɔmlɪɣənt/ (adj) surrounding
omlijnen /ɔmlɛinə(n)/ (omlijnde, heeft omlijnd) outline
de **omlijsting** /ɔmlɛistɪŋ/ (pl: -en) frame; [fig] setting
de **omloop** /ɔmlop/ (pl: omlopen) circulation
de **omloopsnelheid** /ɔmlopsnɛlhɛit/ (pl: -heden) **1** rate of circulation **2** orbital velocity
¹**omlopen** /ɔmlopə(n)/ (liep om, is omgelopen) walk round, go round: *ik loop wel even om* I'll go round the back
²**omlopen** /ɔmlopə(n)/ (liep om, heeft omgelopen) (run into and) knock over
de **ommekeer** /ɔməker/ turn(about); about-turn; about-face, U-turn, revolution
het **ommetje** /ɔməcə/ (pl: -s) stroll, (little) walk
het **ommezien** /ɔməzin/: *in een* ~ *was hij terug* (*or: klaar*) he was back (*or:* finished) in a jiffy
de **ommezijde** /ɔməzɛidə/ (pl: -n) reverse (side), back, other side: *zie* ~ see overleaf
de **ommezwaai** /ɔməzwaj/ (pl: -en) revolution; reversal, U-turn: *een politieke* ~ a political U-turn
de **omnisport** /ɔmnisport/ (pl: -en) [Belg] multifaceted sports program at youth sport camps

de **omnivoor** /ɔmnivoːr/ (pl: omnivoren) omnivore

omploegen /ɔmpluɣə(n)/ (ploegde om, heeft omgeploegd) **1** plough (up) **2** plough in (or: under)

ompraten /ɔmpraːtə(n)/ (praatte om, heeft omgepraat) persuade, bring round, talk round; talk into; talk out of

de **omrastering** /ɔmrɑstərɪŋ/ (pl: -en) fencing, fence(s)

omrekenen /ɔmreːkənə(n)/ (rekende om, heeft omgerekend) convert (to), turn (into)

¹**omrijden** /ɔmrɛidə(n)/ (reed om, heeft/is omgereden) make a detour, take a roundabout route, take the long way round

²**omrijden** /ɔmrɛidə(n)/ (reed om, heeft omgereden) knock down, run down

omringen /ɔmrɪŋə(n)/ (omringde, heeft omringd) surround, enclose

de **omroep** /ɔmrup/ (pl: -en) broadcasting corporation (or: company), (broadcasting) network

omroepen /ɔmrupə(n)/ (riep om, heeft omgeroepen) **1** broadcast, announce (over the radio, on TV) **2** call (over the PA, intercom): *iemands naam laten* ~ have s.o. paged

de **omroeper** /ɔmrupər/ (pl: -s) announcer

de **omroepinstallatie** /ɔmrupɪnstɑla(t)si/ (pl: -s) sound system

omroeren /ɔmrurə(n)/ (roerde om, heeft omgeroerd) stir, churn

omruilen /ɔmrœylə(n)/ (ruilde om, heeft omgeruild) exchange, trade (in), change (over, round, places), swap

omschakelen /ɔmsχakələ(n)/ (schakelde om, heeft omgeschakeld) convert, change (or: switch) over (to)

de **omschakeling** /ɔmsχakəlɪŋ/ (pl: -en) switch, shift, changeover

omscholen /ɔmsχolə(n)/ (schoolde om, heeft omgeschoold) retrain, re-educate: *waarom laat je je niet* ~? why don't you get retrained?

de **omscholing** /ɔmsχolɪŋ/ retraining, re-education

omschoppen /ɔmsχɔpə(n)/ (schopte om, heeft omgeschopt) kick over

omschrijven /ɔmsχrɛivə(n)/ (omschreef, heeft omschreven) **1** describe, determine **2** define, specify, state: *iemands bevoegdheden nader* ~ define s.o.'s powers

de **omschrijving** /ɔmsχrɛivɪŋ/ (pl: -en) **1** description, paraphrase **2** definition, specification, characterization

omsingelen /ɔmsɪŋələ(n)/ (omsingelde, heeft omsingeld) surround, besiege

¹**omslaan** /ɔmslaːn/ (sloeg om, is omgeslagen) **1** turn; round **2** change; break; swing (round), veer (round): *het* **weer** *slaat om* the weather is breaking **3** overturn, topple, keel (over); capsize [ship]

²**omslaan** /ɔmslaːn/ (sloeg om, heeft omgeslagen) **1** fold over (or: back); turn down; turn back **2** turn (over)

omslachtig /ɔmslɑχtəχ/ (adj, adv) laborious; time-consuming; lengthy; wordy; longwinded; roundabout

het/de **omslag** /ɔmslɑχ/ **1** cuff **2** cover; dust jacket

de **omslagdoek** /ɔmslɑɣduk/ (pl: -en) shawl, wrap

het **omslagpunt** /ɔmslɑχpʏnt/ (pl: -en) turning point

omsluiten /ɔmslœytə(n)/ (omsloot, heeft omsloten) enclose, surround

omsmelten /ɔmsmɛltə(n)/ (smolt om, heeft omgesmolten) melt down, re-melt

omspitten /ɔmspɪtə(n)/ (spitte om, heeft omgespit) dig up, break up, turn over

omspoelen /ɔmspulə(n)/ (spoelde om, heeft omgespoeld) rinse (out), wash out, wash up

omspringen /ɔmsprɪŋə(n)/ (sprong om, heeft/is omgesprongen) deal (with): *slordig met andermans boeken* ~ be careless with s.o. else's books

de **omstander** /ɔmstɑndər/ (pl: -s) bystander, onlooker, spectator: *de* ~s bystanders

omstandig /ɔmstɑndəχ/ (adj, adv) elaborate: *iets* ~ *uitleggen* elaborate (or: amplify) on sth.

de **omstandigheid** /ɔmstɑndəχhɛit/ (pl: -heden) circumstance; situation; condition: *naar omstandigheden* considering (or: under) the circumstances; *in de* **gegeven** *omstandigheden* under (or: in) the circumstances

omstoten /ɔmstotə(n)/ (stootte om, heeft omgestoten) knock over

omstreden /ɔmstreːdə(n)/ (adj) controversial; debatable; contentious; contested; disputed: *een* ~ *boek* a controversial book

omstreeks /ɔmstreks/ (prep) (round) about, (a)round, towards, in the region (or: neighbourhood) of

de **omstreken** /ɔmstreːkə(n)/ (pl) neighbourhood, district; environs; surroundings: *de stad* **Brussel** *en* ~ the city of Brussels and (its) environs

omtoveren /ɔmtovərə(n)/ (toverde om, heeft omgetoverd) transform

de **omtrek** /ɔmtrɛk/ (pl: -ken) **1** [maths] perimeter; circumference; periphery **2** contour(s), outline(s), silhouette; skyline **3** surroundings, vicinity, environs, surrounding district (or: area): *in de* **wijde** ~ for miles around

omtrekken /ɔmtrɛkə(n)/ (omtrok, heeft omtrokken) pull down ‖ *een* ~*de* **beweging** *maken* **a)** make an enveloping (or: outflanking) movement; **b)** [fig] (try to) circumvent the issue

¹**omtrent** /ɔmtrɛnt/ (adv) about, approximately

²**omtrent** /ɔmtrɛnt/ (prep) **1** about, (a)round

2 concerning, with reference to, about

omturnen /ɔmtʏrnə(n)/ (turnde om, heeft omgeturnd) win over, bring round; [Am] bring around

omvallen /ɔmvalə(n)/ (viel om, is omgevallen) fall over (*or:* down); turn over (*or:* on its side): ~ *van de slaap* be dead tired

de **omvang** /ɔmvaŋ/ **1** girth, circumference, bulk(iness) **2** dimensions, size, volume, magnitude, scope: *de volle* ~ *van de schade* the full extent of the damage

omvangrijk /ɔmvɑŋrɛik/ (adj) sizeable; bulky; extensive

omvatten /ɔmvɑtə(n)/ (omvatte, heeft omvat) contain, comprise, include, cover

omver /ɔmvɛr/ (adv) over, down

omvergooien /ɔmvɛrɣojə(n)/ (gooide omver, heeft omvergegooid) knock over, bowl over, upset, overturn

omverlopen /ɔmvɛrlopə(n)/ (liep omver, heeft omvergelopen) knock, run down (*or:* over), bowl over: *omvergelopen worden* be knocked off one's feet

omverrijden /ɔmvɛrɛidə(n)/ (reed omver, heeft omvergereden) run, knock down (*or:* over)

omverwerpen /ɔmvɛrwɛrpə(n)/ (wierp omver, heeft omvergeworpen) **1** knock over (*or:* down), throw down **2** [fig] overthrow

omvliegen /ɔmvliɣə(n)/ (vloog om, is omgevlogen) **1** fly past, fly by, rush by: *een bocht* ~ tear round a corner **2** fly round, tear round, race round: *de tijd vloog om* the time flew by

omvormen /ɔmvɔrmə(n)/ (vormde om, heeft omgevormd) transform, convert (into)

omvouwen /ɔmvɑuwə(n)/ (vouwde om, heeft omgevouwen) fold down (*or:* over); turn down

omwaaien /ɔmwajə(n)/ (waaide/woei om, is omgewaaid) be (*or:* get) blown down, blow down; be blown off one's feet

de **omweg** /ɔmwɛx/ (pl: -en) detour, roundabout route, roundabout way: *langs een* ~ indirectly; *een* ~ *maken* make a detour, take a roundabout route

de **omwenteling** /ɔmwɛntəlɪŋ/ (pl: -en) **1** rotation, revolution, turn; orbit **2** [pol] revolution, upheaval

¹**omwisselen** /ɔmwɪsələ(n)/ (wisselde om, heeft omgewisseld) change places, swap places, change seats

²**omwisselen** /ɔmwɪsələ(n)/ (wisselde om, heeft omgewisseld) exchange (for), swap: *dollars* ~ *in euro* change dollars into euros

omzeilen /ɔmzɛilə(n)/ (omzeilde, heeft omzeild) skirt, get round; by-pass

de **omzendbrief** /ɔmzɛndbrif/ (pl: -brieven) [Belg] circular (letter)

de. **omzet** /ɔmzɛt/ (pl: -ten) **1** turnover, volume of trade (*or:* business) **2** returns, sales, business

de **omzetbelasting** /ɔmzɛdbəlɑstɪŋ/ sales tax, turnover tax

omzetten /ɔmzɛtə(n)/ (zette om, heeft omgezet) **1** turn over, sell: *goederen* ~ sell goods **2** convert (into), turn (into): *een terdoodveroordeling in levenslang* ~ commute a sentence from death to life imprisonment

omzichtig /ɔmzɪxtəx/ (adj, adv) cautious, circumspect, prudent

omzien /ɔmzin/ (zag om, heeft omgezien) look (after)

omzwaaien /ɔmzwajə(n)/ (zwaaide om, is omgezwaaid) change subject(s)

de **omzwerving** /ɔmzwɛrvɪŋ/ (pl: -en) wandering, ramble: *nachtelijke* ~*en* nocturnal rambles

onaangedaan /ɔnaŋədan/ (adj) unmoved: ~ *blijven* remain unmoved

onaangekondigd /ɔnaŋəkɔndəxt/ (adj) unannounced: *een* ~ *bezoek* a surprise visit

onaangenaam /ɔnaŋənam/ (adj, adv) unpleasant, disagreeable

onaangepast /ɔnaŋəpɑst/ (adj) maladjusted: ~ *gedrag vertonen* show maladjusted behaviour

onaangetast /ɔnaŋətɑst/ (adj) unaffected; intact

onaannemelijk /ɔnanemələk/ (adj) implausible, incredible, unbelievable

onaantastbaar /ɔnantɑstbar/ (adj) unassailable, impregnable

onaantrekkelijk /ɔnantrɛkələk/ (adj) unattractive, unprepossessing, unappealing

onaanvaardbaar /ɔnanvardbar/ (adj) unacceptable

onaardig /ɔnardəx/ (adj, adv) unpleasant, unfriendly, unkind

onachtzaam /ɔnɑxtsam/ (adj, adv) inattentive, careless; negligent

onaf /ɔnɑf/ (adj) unfinished, incomplete

onafgebroken /ɔnɑfxəbrokə(n)/ (adj, adv) **1** continuous, sustained: *40 jaar* ~ *dienst* 40 years continuous service **2** unbroken, uninterrupted: *we hebben drie dagen* ~ *regen gehad* the rain hasn't let up for three days

onafhankelijk /ɔnɑfhɑŋkələk/ (adj, adv) independent (of)

de **onafhankelijkheid** /ɔnɑfhɑŋkələkhɛit/ independence

onafscheidelijk /ɔnɑfsxɛidələk/ (adj, adv) inseparable (from)

onafzienbaar /ɔnɑfsimbar/ (adj, adv) immense, vast

onbaatzuchtig /ɔmbatsʏxtəx/ (adj, adv) unselfish

onbarmhartig /ɔmbɑrmhɑrtəx/ (adj, adv) merciless, unmerciful, ruthless

onbedaarlijk /ɔmbədarlək/ (adj, adv) uncontrollable

de **onbedachtzaamheid** /ɔmbədɔx(t)samhɛit/ thoughtlessness, rashness

onbedekt /ɔmbədɛ̱kt/ (adj, adv) uncovered, exposed

onbedoeld /ɔmbədu̱lt/ (adj, adv) unintentional, inadvertent: *iem. ~ kwetsen* hurt s.o. unintentionally

onbedorven /ɔmbədɔ̱rvə(n)/ (adj) unspoilt, untainted

onbeduidend /ɔmbədœydənt/ (adj) insignificant, trivial, inconsequential

onbegaanbaar /ɔmbəɣa̱mbar/ (adj) impassable

onbegonnen /ɔmbəɣɔ̱nə(n)/ (adj) hopeless, impossible

onbegrensd /ɔmbəɣrɛ̱nst/ (adj) unlimited, boundless, infinite

onbegrijpelijk /ɔmbəɣrɛi̱pələk/ (adj, adv) incomprehensible, unintelligible

het **onbegrip** /ɔ̱mbəɣrɪp/ incomprehension, lack of understanding, ignorance

onbehaaglijk /ɔmbəha̱xlək/ (adj) uncomfortable

het **onbehagen** /ɔ̱mbəha̱ɣə(n)/ discomfort (about)

onbeheerd /ɔmbəhe̱rt/ (adj) abandoned, unattended, ownerless: *laat uw bagage niet ~ achter* do not leave your baggage unattended

onbeheerst /ɔmbəhe̱rst/ (adj, adv) uncontrolled, unrestrained

onbeholpen /ɔmbəhɔ̱lpə(n)/ (adj, adv) awkward, clumsy, inept

onbehoorlijk /ɔmbəho̱rlək/ (adj, adv) unseemly; improper, indecent: *hij gedraagt zich ~* he behaves in an unseemly manner; *~e taal* indecent language; *het was nogal ~ van hem om ...* it was rather unbecoming of him to ...

onbehouwen /ɔmbəhɑ̱uwə(n)/ (adj) coarse, crude

onbekend /ɔmbəkɛ̱nt/ (adj) unknown, out-of-the-way, unfamiliar: *met ~e bestemming vertrekken* leave for an unknown destination

de **onbekende** /ɔmbəkɛ̱ndə/ (pl: -n) unknown (person), stranger

onbekommerd /ɔmbəkɔ̱mərt/ (adj, adv) carefree, unconcerned

onbekwaam /ɔmbəkwa̱m/ (adj) incompetent, incapable

onbelangrijk /ɔmbəlɑ̱nrɛik/ (adj, adv) unimportant, insignificant; inconsiderable: *iets ~s* sth. trivial

onbeleefd /ɔmbəle̱ft/ (adj, adv) impolite, rude

de **onbeleefdheid** /ɔmbəle̱fthɛit/ impoliteness, rudeness, incivility, discourtesy; insult

onbelemmerd /ɔmbəlɛ̱mərt/ (adj, adv) unobstructed

onbemand /ɔmbəmɑ̱nt/ (adj) unmanned

de **onbenul** /ɔ̱mbənʏl/ (pl: -len) fool, idiot

onbenullig /ɔmbənʏ̱ləx/ (adj, adv) inane, stupid, fatuous

onbepaald /ɔmbəpa̱lt/ (adj) **1** indefinite, unlimited **2** indefinite, indeterminate, undefined

onbeperkt /ɔmbəpɛ̱rkt/ (adj, adv) unlimited, unbounded

onbeproefd /ɔmbəpru̱ft/ (adj) untried: *geen middel ~ laten* leave no stone unturned

onbereikbaar /ɔmbərɛi̱gbar/ (adj) **1** inaccessible **2** unattainable, out of (*or:* beyond) reach: *een ~ ideaal* an unattainable ideal

onberekenbaar /ɔmbəre̱kəmbar/ (adj, adv) unpredictable

onberispelijk /ɔmbərɪ̱spələk/ (adj, adv) perfect; irreproachable

onbeschaafd /ɔmbəsxa̱ft/ (adj, adv) **1** uncivilized **2** uneducated, unrefined

onbeschadigd /ɔmbəsxa̱dəxt/ (adj) undamaged, intact

onbescheiden /ɔmbəsxɛi̱də(n)/ (adj, adv) **1** immodest, forward **2** indiscreet, indelicate **3** presumptuous, bold: *zo ~ zijn om ... be so bold as to ...

onbeschoft /ɔmbəsxɔ̱ft/ (adj, adv) rude, ill-mannered, boorish

onbeschreven /ɔmbəsxre̱və(n)/ (adj) blank

onbeschrijfelijk /ɔmbəsxrɛi̱fələk/ (adj, adv) indescribable; beyond description (*or:* words) [after vb]; [depr] unspeakable: *het is ~* it defies (*or:* beggars) description

onbeslist /ɔmbəslɪ̱st/ (adj) undecided, unresolved: *de wedstrijd eindigde ~* the match ended in a draw

onbespeelbaar /ɔmbəspe̱lbar/ (adj) unplayable; not fit (*or:* unfit) for play

onbespoten /ɔmbəspo̱tə(n)/ (adj) unsprayed

onbespreekbaar /ɔmbəspre̱gbar/ (adj) taboo

onbesproken /ɔmbəspro̱kə(n)/ (adj): *van ~ gedrag* of irreproachable (*or:* blameless) conduct

onbestaanbaar /ɔmbəsta̱mbar/ (adj) impossible

onbestelbaar /ɔmbəstɛ̱lbar/ (adj) undeliverable

onbestemd /ɔmbəstɛ̱mt/ (adj) vague

onbestendig /ɔmbəstɛ̱ndəx/ (adj) unsettled, variable: *het weer is ~* the weather is changeable (*or:* variable)

onbestuurbaar /ɔmbəstyrbar/ (adj) **1** uncontrollable, out of control; unmanageable **2** ungovernable

onbesuisd /ɔmbəsœy̱st/ (adj, adv) rash

onbetaalbaar /ɔmbəta̱lbar/ (adj) **1** prohibitive, impossibly dear **2** priceless, invaluable **3** priceless, hilarious

onbetaald /ɔmbəta̱lt/ (adj) unpaid (for); outstanding; unsettled; undischarged

onbetekenend /ɔmbəte̱kənənt/ (adj) insignificant

onbetrouwbaar /ɔmbətrɑ̱ubar/ (adj) unreliable; [pers also] untrustworthy; shady; shifty

onbetuigd /ɔmbətœyχt/ (adj): *zich niet ~ laten* keep one's end up

onbetwist /ɔmbətwɪst/ (adj) undisputed: *de ~e kampioen* the unrivalled champion

onbevangen /ɔmbəvɑŋə(n)/ (adj, adv) open(-minded)

onbevestigd /ɔmbəvɛstəχt/ (adj) unconfirmed

onbevlekt /ɔmbəvlɛkt/ (adj) immaculate

onbevoegd /ɔmbəvuχt/ (adj) unauthorized; unqualified

de **onbevoegde** /ɔmbəvuɣdə/ (pl: -n) unauthorized person; unqualified person

onbevooroordeeld /ɔmbəvorordelt/ (adj, adv) unprejudiced, open-minded

onbevredigend /ɔmbəvredəɣənt/ (adj) unsatisfactory

onbewaakt /ɔmbəwakt/ (adj) unguarded, unattended

onbeweeglijk /ɔmbəwexlək/ (adj, adv) motionless

onbewerkt /ɔmbəwɛrkt/ (adj) unprocessed, raw

onbewezen /ɔmbəwezə(n)/ (adj) unproved, unproven

onbewogen /ɔmbəwoɣə(n)/ (adj, adv) **1** immobile **2** unmoved

onbewolkt /ɔmbəwɔlkt/ (adj) cloudless, clear

onbewoonbaar /ɔmbəwombar/ (adj) uninhabitable

onbewoond /ɔmbəwont/ (adj) uninhabited: *een ~ eiland* a desert island

onbewust /ɔmbəwʏst/ (adj, adv) unconscious (of): *iets ~ doen* do sth. unconsciously

onbezoldigd /ɔmbəzɔldəχt/ (adj) unpaid

onbezonnen /ɔmbəzɔnə(n)/ (adj, adv) unthinking, rash, thoughtless

onbezorgd /ɔmbəzɔrχt/ (adj, adv) carefree, unconcerned: *een ~e oude dag* a carefree old age

onbillijk /ɔmbɪlək/ (adj, adv) unfair, unreasonable

onbrandbaar /ɔmbrɑndbar/ (adj) incombustible, non-flammable

onbreekbaar /ɔmbrebar/ (adj) unbreakable, non-breakable

het **onbruik** /ɔmbrœyk/: *in ~ raken* fall (or: pass) into disuse, go out of date

onbruikbaar /ɔmbrœygbar/ (adj) unusable; useless

onbuigzaam /ɔmbœyχsam/ (adj) inflexible

de **oncoloog** /ɔŋkoloɣ/ (pl: -logen) oncologist

oncomfortabel /ɔnkɔmfɔrtabəl/ (adj) uncomfortable

oncontroleerbaar /ɔŋkɔntrolerbar/ (adj) unverifiable

onconventioneel /ɔŋkɔnvɛn(t)ʃonel/ (adj, adv) unconventional

ondankbaar /ɔndɑŋbar/ (adj, adv) ungrateful: *een ondankbare taak* a thankless (or: an unrewarding) task

de **ondankbaarheid** /ɔndɑŋbarhɛit/ ingratitude

ondanks /ɔndɑŋks/ (prep) in spite of, contrary to: *~ haar inspanningen lukte het (haar) niet* for (or: despite) all her efforts, she didn't succeed

ondeelbaar /ɔndelbar/ (adj) indivisible: *een ~ getal* a prime number

ondefinieerbaar /ɔndefinijerbar/ (adj) indefinable

ondemocratisch /ɔndemokratis/ (adj) undemocratic

ondenkbaar /ɔndɛŋbar/ (adj) inconceivable, unthinkable

¹**onder** /ɔndər/ (adv) below, at the bottom: *~ aan de bladzijde* at the foot (or: bottom) of the page

²**onder** /ɔndər/ (prep) **1** under, below, underneath: *hij zat ~ de prut* he was covered with mud; *de tunnel gaat ~ de rivier door* the tunnel goes (or: passes) under(neath) the river; *zes graden ~ nul* six degrees below zero **2** among(st): *er was ruzie ~ de supporters* there was a fight among the supporters; *~ andere* among other things; *~ ons gezegd (en gezwegen)* between you and me (and the doorpost) ‖ *~ toezicht van de politie* under police surveillance; *zij leed erg ~ het verlies* she suffered greatly from the loss

onderaan /ɔndəran/ (adv) at the bottom, below: *~ op de bladzijde* at the bottom (or: foot) of the page

de **onderaannemer** /ɔndəranemər/ (pl: -s) subcontractor

onderaards /ɔndərarts/ (adj) subterranean

onderaf /ɔndərɑf/ (adv): *hij heeft zich van ~ opgewerkt* he has worked his way up from the bottom of the ladder

de **onderafdeling** /ɔndəravdelɪŋ/ (pl: -en) subdepartment

de **onderarm** /ɔndərɑrm/ (pl: -en) forearm

het **onderbeen** /ɔndərben/ (pl: -benen) (lower) leg; shin; calf

onderbelicht /ɔndərbəlɪχt/ (adj) **1** underexposed **2** [fig] neglected, give too little attention

onderbewust /ɔndərbəwʏst/ (adj, adv) subconscious

het **onderbewuste** /ɔndərbəwʏstə/ subconscious, unconscious

het **onderbewustzijn** /ɔndərbəwʏ(st)sɛin/ subconscious

de **onderbezetting** /ɔndərbəzɛtɪŋ/ undermanning, being short-handed

de **onderbouw** /ɔndərbɑu/ the lower classes of secondary school

onderbouwen /ɔndərbɑuwə(n)/ (onderbouwde, heeft onderbouwd) build, found;

[fig also] substantiate
onderbreken /ɔndərbrɛkə(n)/ (onderbrak, heeft onderbroken) **1** interrupt, break **2** interrupt, cut short; break in (on)

de **onderbreking** /ɔndərbrɛkɪŋ/ (pl: -en) **1** interruption **2** break

onderbrengen /ɔndərbrɛŋə(n)/ (bracht onder, heeft ondergebracht) **1** accommodate; lodge; house; put up: *zijn kinderen bij iem. ~ lodge* one's children with s.o. **2** class(ify) (with, under, in)

de **onderbroek** /ɔndərbruk/ (pl: -en) underpants; panties

de **onderbuik** /ɔndərbœyk/ (pl: -en) abdomen

het **onderbuikgevoel** (instinctive) envy, hate, rancour

de **onderdaan** /ɔndərdan/ (pl: onderdanen) subject

het **onderdak** /ɔndərdɑk/ accommodation; shelter; lodging: *iem. ~ geven* accommodate (*or:* lodge) s.o., get s.o. a place; *~ vinden* find accommodation

onderdanig /ɔndərdanəx/ (adj) submissive, humble

het **onderdeel** /ɔndərdel/ (pl: -delen) part, (sub)division; branch: *het volgend ~ van ons programma* the next item on our programme

de **onderdirecteur** /ɔndərdirɛktər/ (pl: -en) assistant manager: *~ van een school* deputy headmaster

onderdoen /ɔndərdun/ (deed onder, heeft ondergedaan) be inferior (to): *voor niemand ~ yield to no one, be second to none

onderdompelen /ɔndərdompələ(n)/ (dompelde onder, heeft ondergedompeld) immerse, submerge

onderdoor /ɔndərdor/ (adv) under

onderdrukken /ɔndərdrykə(n)/ (onderdrukte, heeft onderdrukt) **1** oppress **2** suppress, repress: *een glimlach ~* suppress a smile

de **onderdrukking** /ɔndərdrykɪŋ/ (pl: -en) oppression

onderduiken /ɔndərdœykə(n)/ (dook onder, is ondergedoken) **1** go into hiding, go underground **2** dive (in)

de **onderduiker** /ɔndərdœykər/ (pl: -s) person in hiding

onderen /ɔndərə(n)/ (adv) **1** (+ naar) down(wards); downstairs **2** (+ van) below, underneath **3** (+ van) from below; from downstairs: *van ~ af beginnen* start from scratch (*or:* the bottom)

¹**ondergaan** /ɔndərɣan/ (ging onder, is ondergegaan) go down; set: *de ~de zon* the setting sun

²**ondergaan** /ɔndərɣan/ (onderging, heeft ondergaan) undergo, go through

de **ondergang** /ɔndərɣɑŋ/ **1** ruin, (down)fall: *dat was zijn ~* that was his undoing **2** setting

ondergeschikt /ɔndərɣəsxɪkt/ (adj) **1** subordinate **2** minor, secondary

de **ondergeschikte** /ɔndərɣəsxɪktə/ (pl: -n) subordinate

ondergeschoven /ɔndərɣəsxovə(n)/ (adj): [fig] *een ~ kindje* an issue that deserves more attention, a neglected issue

de **ondergetekende** /ɔndərɣətekəndə/ (pl: -n) **1** undersigned: *ik, ~* I, the undersigned **2** yours truly

het **ondergoed** /ɔndərɣut/ underwear

de **ondergrens** /ɔndərɣrɛns/ (pl: -grenzen) lower limit

de **ondergrond** /ɔndərɣrɔnt/ (pl: -en) base; basis; foundation: *witte sterren op een blauwe ~* white stars on a blue background

ondergronds /ɔndərɣrɔnts/ (adj) underground

de **ondergrondse** /ɔndərɣrɔntsə/ (pl: -n, -s) **1** underground; [Am] subway **2** underground, resistance

onderhand /ɔndərhɑnt/ (adv) meanwhile

de **onderhandelaar** /ɔndərhɑndəlar/ (pl: -s, -handelaren) negotiator

onderhandelen /ɔndərhɑndələ(n)/ (onderhandelde, heeft onderhandeld) negotiate; bargain

de **onderhandeling** /ɔndərhɑndəlɪŋ/ (pl: -en) **1** negotiation; bargaining **2** negotiation; talks

onderhands /ɔndərhɑnts/ (adj, adv) **1** underhand(ed), backstairs, underhand: *iets ~ regelen* make hole-and-corner arrangements **2** private **3** [sport] underhand, underarm: *een bal ~ ingooien* throw in a ball underarm

onderhavig /ɔndərhavəx/ (adj) present, in question, in hand

onderhevig /ɔndərhevəx/ (adj) liable (to), subject (to)

het **onderhoud** /ɔndərhaut/ maintenance, upkeep

onderhouden /ɔndərhaudə(n)/ (onderhield, heeft onderhouden) **1** maintain, keep up; service: *het huis was slecht ~* the house was in bad repair; *betrekkingen ~ met* maintain (*or:* have) relations with; *een contact ~* keep in touch **2** maintain, support

onderhoudend /ɔndərhaudənt/ (adj, adv) entertaining, amusing

de **onderhoudsbeurt** /ɔndərhautsbørt/ (pl: -en) overhaul, service

de **onderhuur** /ɔndərhyr/ sublet: *iets in ~ hebben* have the subtenancy of sth.

de **onderhuurder** /ɔndərhyrdər/ (pl: -s) subtenant

¹**onderin** /ɔndərɪn/ (adv) below, at the bottom

²**onderin** /ɔndərɪn/ (prep) at the bottom of: *het ligt ~ die kast* it's at the bottom of that cupboard

de **onderjurk** /ɔndərjʏrk/ (pl: -en) slip

de **onderkaak** /ɔndərkak/ (pl: -kaken) lower

jaw; mandible

de **onderkant** /ɔndərkɑnt/ (pl: -en) underside, bottom

onderkennen /ɔndərkɛnə(n)/ (onderkende, heeft onderkend) recognize

de **onderkin** /ɔndərkɪn/ (pl: -nen) double chin

onderkoeld /ɔndərkult/ (adj) supercooled: *ernstig* ~ suffering from hypothermia; [fig] *een* ~*e reactie* an unemotional reaction, a cold reaction

het **onderkomen** /ɔndərkomə(n)/ (pl: -s) somewhere to go (or: sleep, stay), accommodation; shelter

de **onderkruiper** /ɔndərkrœypər/ (pl: -s) **1** scab **2** squirt, shrimp

de **onderlaag** /ɔndərlax/ (pl: -lagen) lower layer; foundation; undercoat: [fig] *de* ~ *van de maatschappij* the dregs of society

onderlangs /ɔndərlɑns/ (adv) along the bottom (or: foot), underneath

onderlegd /ɔndərlɛxt/ (adj) (well-)grounded: *zij is goed* ~ she's well educated

het **onderlichaam** /ɔndərlɪxam/ (pl: -lichamen) lower part of the body

het **onderlijf** /ɔndərlɛif/ (pl: -lijven) lower part of the body

onderling /ɔndərlɪŋ/ (adj, adv) mutual, among ourselves, among them(selves), together: *de partijen konden de kwestie* ~ *regelen* the parties were able to arrange the matter between (or: among) themselves

de **onderlip** /ɔndərlɪp/ (pl: -pen) lower lip: *de* ~ *laten hangen* [roughly] pout

onderlopen /ɔndərlopə(n)/ (liep onder, is ondergelopen) be flooded

ondermijnen /ɔndərmɛinə(n)/ (ondermijnde, heeft ondermijnd) undermine, subvert

ondernemen /ɔndərnemə(n)/ (ondernam, heeft ondernomen) undertake, take upon o.s.

ondernemend /ɔndərnemənt/ (adj) enterprising

de **ondernemer** /ɔndərnemər/ (pl: -s) entrepreneur, employer; operator; owner

de **onderneming** /ɔndərnemɪŋ/ (pl: -en) **1** undertaking, enterprise; venture: *het is een hele* ~ it's quite an undertaking **2** company, business; [large] concern: *een* ~ *drijven* carry on an enterprise

de **ondernemingsraad** /ɔndərnemɪŋsrat/ (pl: -raden) works council, employees council

de **onderofficier** /ɔndərofisir/ (pl: -en) NCO, non-commissioned officer

het **onderonsje** /ɔndərɔnʃə/ (pl: -s) private chat

onderontwikkeld /ɔndərɔntwɪkəlt/ (adj) underdeveloped, backward

onderop /ɔndərɔp/ (adv) at the bottom, below

het **onderpand** /ɔndərpɑnt/ (pl: -en) pledge, security, collateral: *tegen* ~ *lenen* borrow on security

de **onderpastoor** /ɔndərpɑstor/ (pl: -s) [Belg; Roman Catholicism] curate, priest in charge

het **onderricht** /ɔndərɪxt/ instruction, tuition

onderrichten /ɔndərɪxtə(n)/ (onderrichtte, heeft onderricht) instruct, teach

onderschatten /ɔndərsxɑtə(n)/ (onderschatte, heeft onderschat) underestimate

het **onderscheid** /ɔndərsxɛit/ difference, distinction: *een* ~ *maken tussen* ... distinguish ... from ... (or: between) ...

¹**onderscheiden** /ɔndərsxɛidə(n)/ (onderscheidde, heeft onderscheiden) **1** distinguish, discern: *niet te* ~ *zijn van* be indistinguishable from **2** decorate: ~ *worden met een medaille* be awarded a medal

zich ²**onderscheiden** /ɔndərsxɛidə(n)/ (onderscheidde zich, heeft zich onderscheiden) distinguish o.s. (for)

de **onderscheiding** /ɔndərsxɛidɪŋ/ (pl: -en) decoration, honour: [Belg] *met* ~ with distinction

onderscheppen /ɔndərsxɛpə(n)/ (onderschepte, heeft onderschept) intercept

het **onderschrift** /ɔndərsxrɪft/ (pl: -en) caption, legend

onderschrijven /ɔndərsxrɛivə(n)/ (onderschreef, heeft onderschreven) subscribe to, endorse

het **onderspit** /ɔndərspɪt/: *het* ~ *delven* get the worst (of it)

onderst /ɔndərst/ (adj) bottom(most), under(most)

onderstaand /ɔndərstant/ (adj) (mentioned) below

ondersteboven /ɔndərstəbovə(n)/ (adv) **1** upside down: *je houdt het* ~ you have it the wrong way up **2** upset: ~ *zijn van iets* be upset (or: cut up) about sth.

de **ondersteek** /ɔndərstek/ (pl: -steken) bedpan

het **onderstel** /ɔndərstɛl/ (pl: -len) chassis, undercarriage; landing gear

ondersteunen /ɔndərstønə(n)/ (ondersteunde, heeft ondersteund) support; back (up)

de **ondersteuning** /ɔndərstønɪŋ/ **1** support **2** support, (public) assistance

onderstrepen /ɔndərstrepə(n)/ (onderstreepte, heeft onderstreept) underline

het **onderstuk** /ɔndərstʏk/ (pl: -ken) base, lower part

ondertekenen /ɔndərtekənə(n)/ (ondertekende, heeft ondertekend) sign

de **ondertekening** /ɔndərtekənɪŋ/ (pl: -en) **1** signing **2** signature

ondertitelen /ɔndərtitələ(n)/ (ondertitelde, heeft ondertiteld) subtitle

de **ondertiteling** /ɔndərtitəlɪŋ/ (pl: -en) subtitles

de **ondertoon** /ɔndərton/ (pl: -tonen) undertone; [fig also] undercurrent, overtone

ondertussen

ondertussen /ɔndərtɣsə(n)/ (adv) meanwhile, in the meantime
onderuit /ɔndərœɣt/ (adv) **1** (out) from under: *je kunt er niet ~ haar ook te vragen* you can't avoid inviting her, too **2** down; flat; over **3** sprawled, sprawling
onderuitgaan /ɔndərœɣtxan/ (ging onderuit, is onderuitgegaan) topple over, be knocked off one's feet; trip; slip
onderuithalen /ɔndərœɣthalə(n)/ (haalde onderuit, heeft onderuitgehaald) **1** [sport] bring down, take down **2** trip up, floor: *hij werd volledig onderuitgehaald* they wiped the floor with him
ondervangen /ɔndərvɑŋə(n)/ (onderving, heeft ondervangen) overcome
onderverdelen /ɔndərvərdelə(n)/ (verdeelde onder, heeft onderverdeeld) (sub)divide; break down
de **onderverdeling** /ɔndərvərdelɪŋ/ (pl: -en) subdivision, breakdown
onderhuren /ɔndərvərhyrə(n)/ (onderverhuurde, heeft onderverhuurd) sublet, sublease
onderverzekerd /ɔndərvərzekərt/ (adj) underinsured
ondervinden /ɔndərvɪndə(n)/ (ondervond, heeft ondervonden) experience: *medeleven ~* meet with sympathy; *moeilijkheden* (or: *concurrentie*) *~* be faced with difficulties (or: competition)
de **ondervinding** /ɔndərvɪndɪŋ/ (pl: -en) experience
ondervoed /ɔndərvut/ (adj) undernourished
de **ondervoeding** /ɔndərvudɪŋ/ undernourishment; malnutrition
de **ondervraagde** /ɔndərvraɣdə/ (pl: -n) interviewee; person heard (or: questioned)
ondervragen /ɔndərvraɣə(n)/ (ondervroeg, heeft ondervraagd) **1** interrogate; question; examine; hear **2** interview
de **ondervraging** /ɔndərvraɣɪŋ/ (pl: -en) questioning, interrogation, examination, interview
onderwaarderen /ɔndərwardərə(n)/ (onderwaardeerde, heeft ondergewaardeerd) underestimate
onderweg /ɔndərwɛx/ (adv) **1** on (or: along) the way; in transit; en route: *we zijn het ~ verloren* we lost it on the way **2** on one's (or: its, the) way
de **onderwereld** /ɔndərwerəlt/ underworld
het **onderwerp** /ɔndərwɛrp/ (pl: -en) subject (matter)
onderwerpen /ɔndərwɛrpə(n)/ (onderwierp, heeft onderworpen) subject
onderwijl /ɔndərwɛil/ (adv) meanwhile
het **onderwijs** /ɔndərwɛis/ education, teaching: *academisch ~* university education; *bijzonder ~* private education; [Belg] special

needs education; *buitengewoon ~* special needs education; *hoger ~* higher education; *lager ~* primary education; *middelbaar (voortgezet) ~* secondary education; *openbaar ~* state education; *algemeen secundair ~* general secondary education; *speciaal ~* special needs education; [Belg] *technisch secundair ~* secondary technical education; [Belg] *vernieuwd secundair ~* comprehensive school system; *voortgezet ~* secondary education
de **onderwijsinspectie** /ɔndərwɛisɪnspɛksi/ (pl: -s) schools inspectorate
de **onderwijsinstelling** /ɔndərwɛisɪnstɛlɪŋ/ (pl: -en) educational institution
de **onderwijskunde** /ɔndərwɛiskʏndə/ didactics, theory of education
het **onderwijsprofiel** /ɔndərwɛisprofil/ educational profile
onderwijzen /ɔndərwɛizə(n)/ (onderwees, heeft onderwezen) teach, instruct: *iem. iets ~* instruct s.o. in sth., teach s.o. sth.
de **onderwijzer** /ɔndərwɛizər/ (pl: -s) (school)teacher, schoolmaster, schoolmistress
de **onderzeeër** /ɔndərzejər/ (pl: -s) submarine
de **onderzetter** /ɔndərzɛtər/ (pl: -s) **1** mat, coaster **2** mat, stand
de **onderzijde** /ɔndərzɛidə/ (pl: -n) underside
het **onderzoek** /ɔndərzuk/ **1** investigation, examination, study, research: *bij nader ~* on closer examination (or: inspection) **2** investigation; inquiry: *een ~ instellen naar* inquire into, examine, investigate **3** [med] examination, check-up
onderzoeken /ɔndərzukə(n)/ (onderzocht, heeft onderzocht) **1** examine, inspect, investigate; search; test (for): *de dokter onderzocht zijn ogen* the doctor examined his eyes **2** investigate, examine, inquire into: *mogelijkheden ~* examine (or: investigate) possibilities **3** inquire into, investigate, examine || *het bloed ~* carry out a blood test
de **onderzoeker** /ɔndərzukər/ (pl: -s) researcher, research worker (or: scientist), investigator
de **onderzoeksrechter** /ɔndərzuksrɛxtər/ (pl: -s) [Belg] [roughly] examining magistrate
ondeskundig /ɔndɛskʏndəx/ (adj, adv) incompetent: *~ gerepareerd* repaired amateurishly
de **ondeugd** /ɔndøxt/ vice
ondeugdelijk /ɔndøɣdələk/ (adj) inferior
ondeugend /ɔndøɣənt/ (adj, adv) naughty, mischievous
ondiep /ɔndip/ (adj) shallow; superficial: *een ~e tuin* a short garden
het **ondier** /ɔndir/ (pl: -en) monster, beast
het **onding** /ɔndɪŋ/ (pl: -en) rotten thing, useless thing
ondoelmatig /ɔndulmatəx/ (adj, adv) inefficient

349

ongekunsteld

ondoenlijk /ɔndu̱nlək/ (adj) unfeasible, impracticable
ondoordacht /ɔndordɑ̱xt/ (adj, adv) inadequately considered, rash
ondoordringbaar /ɔndordrɪ̱ŋbar/ (adj) impenetrable; impermeable (to): *ondoordringbare duisternis* (or: *wildernis*) impenetrable darkness (or: wilderness)
ondoorgrondelijk /ɔndorɣrɔ̱ndələk/ (adj) unfathomable; inscrutable
ondoorzichtig /ɔndorzɪ̱xtəɣ/ (adj) **1** nontransparent, opaque **2** [fig] obscure
ondraaglijk /ɔndra̱xlək/ (adj, adv) unbearable
ondrinkbaar /ɔndrɪ̱ŋbar/ (adj) undrinkable
ondubbelzinnig /ɔndʏbəlzɪ̱nəɣ/ (adj, adv) unambiguous; unmistakable
onduidelijk /ɔndœ̱ydələk/ (adj, adv) indistinct; obscure; unclear: *de situatie is* ~ the situation is obscure (or: unclear); ~ *spreken* speak indistinctly
de **onduidelijkheid** /ɔndœ̱ydələkhɛit/ (pl: -heden) indistinctness, lack of clarity; [stronger] obscurity
onecht /ɔnɛ̱xt/ (adj) **1** illegitimate **2** false **3** fake(d)
oneens /ɔne̱ns/ (adj) in disagreement, at odds: *het met iem.* ~ *zijn* over iets disagree with s.o. about sth.
oneerbaar /ɔne̱rbar/ (adj, adv) indecent, improper
oneerbiedig /ɔnerbi̱dəɣ/ (adj, adv) disrespectful
oneerlijk /ɔne̱rlək/ (adj, adv) dishonest, unfair
de **oneerlijkheid** /ɔne̱rləkhɛit/ (pl: -heden) dishonesty, unfairness
oneetbaar /ɔne̱dbar/ (adj) inedible; not fit to eat [after vb]: *dit oude brood is* ~ this stale bread is not fit to eat
oneffen /ɔnɛ̱fə(n)/ (adj) uneven
oneigenlijk /ɔnɛ̱iɣə(n)lək/ (adj, adv) improper: ~ *gebruik* improper use
oneindig /ɔnɛ̱indəɣ/ (adj, adv) infinite, endless: ~ *groot* (or: *klein*) infinite(ly large), infinitesimal(ly)
de **oneindigheid** /ɔnɛ̱indəɣhɛit/ infinity
de **onenigheid** /ɔne̱nəɣhɛit/ (pl: -heden) discord, disagreement
onervaren /ɔnɛrva̱rə(n)/ (adj, adv) inexperienced
de **onervarenheid** /ɔnɛrva̱rənhɛit/ inexperience, lack of experience (or: skill)
oneven /ɔne̱və(n)/ (adj, adv) odd, uneven
onevenredig /ɔnevə(n)re̱dəɣ/ (adj, adv) disproportionate
onevenwichtig /ɔnevə(n)wɪ̱xtəɣ/ (adj) unbalanced, unstable
onfatsoenlijk /ɔnfɑtsu̱nlək/ (adj, adv) ill-mannered, bad-mannered; offensive; improper; indecent
onfeilbaar /ɔnfɛ̱ilbar/ (adj, adv) infallible
onfortuinlijk /ɔnfɔrtœ̱ynlək/ (adj, adv) unfortunate, unlucky
onfris /ɔnfrɪ̱s/ (adj, adv) **1** unsavoury; stale; musty; stuffy: *er* ~ *uitzien* not look fresh; [of pers] look unsavoury **2** unsavoury, shady: *een* ~*se affaire* an unsavoury (or: a shady) business
ongeacht /ɔŋɣəɑ̱xt/ (prep) irrespective of, regardless of
ongeboren /ɔŋɣəbo̱rə(n)/ (adj) unborn
ongebreideld /ɔŋɣəbrɛ̱idəlt/ (adj) unbridled, unrestrained
ongebruikelijk /ɔŋɣəbrœ̱ykələk/ (adj) unusual
ongebruikt /ɔŋɣəbrœ̱ykt/ (adj) unused; new
ongecompliceerd /ɔŋɣəkɔmplise̱rt/ (adj, adv) uncomplicated
ongedaan /ɔŋɣəda̱n/ (adj) undone: *dat kun je niet meer* ~ *maken* you can't go back on it now
ongedeerd /ɔŋɣəde̱rt/ (adj) unhurt, uninjured, unharmed
ongedekt /ɔŋɣədɛ̱kt/ (adj, adv) uncovered
het **ongedierte** /ɔŋɣədi̱rtə/ vermin
het **ongeduld** /ɔŋɣədʏlt/ impatience
ongeduldig /ɔŋɣədʏ̱ldəɣ/ (adj, adv) impatient
ongedurig /ɔŋɣədy̱rəɣ/ (adj) restless, restive, fidgety
ongedwongen /ɔŋɣədwɔ̱ŋə(n)/ (adj, adv) relaxed, informal
ongeëvenaard /ɔŋɣəevəna̱rt/ (adj, adv) unequalled, unmatched
ongefrankeerd /ɔŋɣəfrɑŋke̱rt/ (adj) unstamped
ongegeneerd /ɔŋɣəʒəne̱rt/ (adj, adv) unashamed, impertinent
ongegrond /ɔŋɣəɣrɔ̱nt/ (adj, adv) unfounded, groundless: ~*e klachten* unfounded complaints
ongehinderd /ɔŋɣəhɪ̱ndərt/ (adj, adv) unhindered: ~ *werken* work undisturbed
ongehoord /ɔŋɣəho̱rt/ (adj, adv) outrageous: ~ *laat* outrageously late
ongehoorzaam /ɔŋɣəho̱rzam/ (adj) disobedient
de **ongehoorzaamheid** /ɔŋɣəho̱rzamhɛit/ disobedience
ongehuwd /ɔŋɣəhy̱wt/ (adj) single, unmarried
ongeïnteresseerd /ɔŋɣəɪntərɛse̱rt/ (adj, adv) uninterested: ~ *toekijken* watch with indifference
ongekend /ɔŋɣəkɛ̱nt/ (adj, adv) unprecedented
ongekroond /ɔŋɣəkro̱nt/ (adj) uncrowned
ongekunsteld /ɔŋɣəkʏ̱nstəlt/ (adj, adv) artless, unaffected

ongeldig /ɔnɣɛldəх/ (adj) invalid

ongelegen /ɔnɣəleɣə(n)/ (adj, adv) inconvenient, awkward

ongeletterd /ɔnɣəlɛtərt/ (adj) **1** unlettered **2** illiterate

het **¹ongelijk** /ɔnɣəlɛik/ wrong: *ik geef je geen ~ I don't blame you*

²ongelijk /ɔnɣəlɛik/ (adj, adv) **1** unequal: *het is ~ verdeeld in de wereld* there's a lot of injustice in the world; *een ~e strijd* an unequal (*or:* a one-sided) fight **2** uneven

de **ongelijkheid** /ɔnɣəlɛikhɛit/ **1** inequality; difference **2** unevenness

ongelijkmatig /ɔnɣəlɛikmatəх/ (adj, adv) uneven, unequal; irregular

ongelofelijk /ɔnɣəlofələk/ (adj, adv) incredible, unbelievable

het **ongeloof** /ɔnɣəlof/ disbelief

ongeloofwaardig /ɔnɣəlofwardəх/ (adj) incredible, implausible

ongelovig /ɔnɣəlovəх/ (adj, adv) **1** disbelieving, incredulous **2** unbelieving

het **ongeluk** /ɔnɣəlʏk/ (pl: -ken) accident: *een ~ krijgen* have an accident; *per ~ iets verklappen* inadvertently let sth. slip

het **ongelukje** /ɔnɣəlʏkjə/ (pl: -s) mishap: *een ~ hebben* have a little accident

ongelukkig /ɔnɣəlʏkəх/ (adj, adv) **1** unhappy: *iem. diep ~ maken* make s.o. deeply unhappy **2** unlucky **3** unfortunate: *hij is ~ terechtgekomen* he landed awkwardly

de **ongeluksdag** /ɔnɣəlʏksdɑх/ (pl: -en) unlucky day

het **ongeluksgetal** /ɔnɣəlʏksхətɑl/ (pl: -len) unlucky number

de **ongeluksvogel** /ɔnɣəlʏksfoɣəl/ (pl: -s) unlucky person

het **ongemak** /ɔnɣəmɑk/ (pl: -ken) inconvenience, discomfort

ongemakkelijk /ɔnɣəmɑkələk/ (adj, adv) uncomfortable

ongemanierd /ɔnɣəmanirt/ (adj, adv) ill-mannered

ongemerkt /ɔnɣəmɛrkt/ (adj, adv) unnoticed: *~ (weten te) ontsnappen* (manage to) escape without being noticed

ongemoeid /ɔnɣəmujt/ (adj) undisturbed: *iem. ~ laten* leave s.o. alone

ongemotiveerd /ɔnɣəmotivert/ (adj, adv) unmotivated, without motivation

ongenaakbaar /ɔnɣənagbar/ (adj) **1** unapproachable **2** indomitable

de **ongenade** /ɔnɣənadə/ **1** disgrace, disfavour: *in ~ vallen* fall into disfavour **2** displeasure

ongenadig /ɔnɣənadəх/ (adj, adv) merciless(ly): *het is ~ koud* it is bitterly cold; *hij kreeg een ~ pak voor zijn broek* he got a merciless thrashing

ongeneeslijk /ɔnɣəneslək/ (adj, adv) incurable: *~ ziek* incurably ill

ongenietbaar /ɔnɣənidbar/ (adj) disagreeable

het **ongenoegen** /ɔnɣənuɣə(n)/ (pl: -s) displeasure, dissatisfaction

ongenuanceerd /ɔnɣənywɑnsert/ (adj, adv) over-simplified: *~ denken* think simplistically; *een ~e uitlating* a blunt remark

ongeoorloofd /ɔnɣəorloft/ (adj) illegal, illicit, improper

ongepast /ɔnɣəpɑst/ (adj, adv) improper

de **ongerechtigheid** /ɔnɣərɛхtəхhɛit/ (pl: -heden) **1** injustice **2** flaw

het **ongerede** /ɔnɣəredə/: *in het ~ raken* break down; get lost; get mixed up

ongeregeld /ɔnɣəreɣəlt/ (adj, adv) **1** disorderly, disorganized **2** irregular: *op ~e tijden* at odd times || *een zootje ~* a mixed bag; a motley crew

de **ongeregeldheden** /ɔnɣəreɣəlthedə(n)/ (pl) disturbances, disorders

ongerept /ɔnɣərɛpt/ (adj) untouched, unspoilt

het **ongerief** /ɔnɣərif/ inconvenience

ongerijmd /ɔnɣərɛimt/ (adj, adv) absurd: *een bewijs uit het ~e* an indirect demonstration (*or:* proof)

ongerust /ɔnɣərʏst/ (adj, adv) worried, anxious (for): *ik begin ~ te worden* I'm beginning to get worried

de **ongerustheid** /ɔnɣərʏsthɛit/ concern, worry

ongeschikt /ɔnɣəsхɪkt/ (adj, adv) unsuitable

ongeschonden /ɔnɣəsхɔndə(n)/ (adj) intact, undamaged

ongeschoold /ɔnɣəsхolt/ (adj) unskilled, untrained

ongeslagen /ɔnɣəslaɣə(n)/ (adj) unbeaten

ongesteld /ɔnɣəstɛlt/ (adj): *zij is ~* she is having her period

ongestoord /ɔnɣəstort/ (adj, adv) **1** undisturbed **2** clear: *~e ontvangst* clear reception

ongestraft /ɔnɣəstrɑft/ (adj, adv) unpunished: *iets ~ doen* get away with sth.

ongetrouwd /ɔnɣətrɑut/ (adj) unmarried, single: *~e oom* bachelor uncle; *~e tante* maiden aunt

ongetwijfeld /ɔnɣətwɛifəlt/ (adv) no doubt, without a doubt, undoubtedly

ongevaarlijk /ɔnɣəvarlək/ (adj) harmless, safe

het **ongeval** /ɔnɣəvɑl/ (pl: -len) accident

de **ongevallenverzekering** /ɔnɣəvɑlə(n)vərzekərɪn/ (pl: -en) accident insurance

ongeveer /ɔnɣəver/ (adv) about, roughly, around: *dat is het ~* that's about it

ongevoelig /ɔnɣəvuləх/ (adj, adv) insensitive (to), insensible (to)

de **ongevoeligheid** /ɔnɣəvuləхhɛit/ insensitivity

ongevraagd /ɔnɣəvraхt/ (adj) unasked(-

for), uninvited

ongewapend /ɔŋɣəwapənt/ (adj) unarmed

ongewenst /ɔŋɣəwɛnst/ (adj) unwanted, undesired; undesirable

ongewerveld /ɔŋɣəwɛrvəlt/ (adj) invertebrate: *~e dieren* invertebrates

ongewijzigd /ɔŋɣəwɛɪzəxt/ (adj) unaltered, unchanged

ongewild /ɔŋɣəwɪlt/ (adj, adv) **1** unintentional, unintended **2** unwanted

ongewis /ɔŋɣəwɪs/ (adj) uncertain

ongewoon /ɔŋɣəwon/ (adj, adv) unusual

ongezellig /ɔŋɣəzɛləx/ (adj, adv) **1** unsociable **2** cheerless, comfortless **3** unenjoyable, dreary, no fun

ongezien /ɔŋɣəzin/ (adj, adv) **1** unseen, unnoticed **2** (sight) unseen: *hij kocht het huis ~* he bought the house (sight) unseen

ongezoet /ɔŋɣəzut/ (adj) unsweetened

ongezond /ɔŋɣəzɔnt/ (adj, adv) **1** unhealthy **2** unsound, unhealthy

ongezouten /ɔŋɣəzɑutə(n)/ (adj) **1** unsalted, saltless **2** unvarnished; strong, outspoken

ongrijpbaar /ɔŋɣrɛibar/ (adj) elusive

ongunstig /ɔŋɣʏnstəx/ (adj, adv) unfavourable: *in het ~ste geval* at (the) worst; *op een ~ moment* at an awkward moment

onguur /ɔŋɣyr/ (adj) **1** unsavoury **2** rough

onhaalbaar /ɔnhalbar/ (adj) unfeasible

onhandelbaar /ɔnhɑndəlbar/ (adj) unmanageable, unruly, intractable

onhandig /ɔnhɑndəx/ (adj, adv) clumsy, awkward: *zij is erg ~* she's all fingers and thumbs

de **onhandigheid** /ɔnhɑndəxhɛit/ (pl: -heden) clumsiness, awkwardness

onhebbelijk /ɔnhɛbələk/ (adj, adv) unmannerly: *de ~e gewoonte hebben om ...* have the objectionable habit of ...

het **onheil** /ɔnhɛil/ (pl: -en) calamity, disaster; doom

onheilspellend /ɔnhɛilspɛlənt/ (adj, adv) ominous

de **onheilsprofeet** /ɔnhɛilsprofet/ (pl: -profeten) prophet of doom

onherbergzaam /ɔnhɛrbɛrxsam/ (adj, adv) inhospitable

onherkenbaar /ɔnhɛrkɛmbar/ (adj, adv) unrecognizable

onherroepelijk /ɔnhɛrupələk/ (adj, adv) irrevocable

onherstelbaar /ɔnhɛrstɛlbar/ (adj, adv) irreparable: *~ beschadigd* damaged beyond repair

onheus /ɔnhøs/ (adj, adv) impolite

on hold /ɔnhoːlt/ (adv): *een project ~ zetten* put a project on hold

onhoorbaar /ɔnhorbar/ (adj, adv) inaudible

onhoudbaar /ɔnhɑudbar/ (adj) **1** unbeara-

ble, intolerable **2** unstoppable

onhygiënisch /ɔnhiɣ(i)jenis/ (adj, adv) unhygienic, insanitary

onjuist /ɔnjœyst/ (adj, adv) **1** inaccurate, false **2** incorrect, mistaken

onkerkelijk /ɔnkɛrkələk/ (adj) nondenominational; nonchurchgoing

onkies /ɔnkis/ (adj, adv) indelicate

onklaar /ɔnklar/ (adj): *iets ~ maken* put sth. out of order, inactivate sth.

de **onkosten** /ɔnkɔstə(n)/ (pl) **1** expense(s), expenditure: *~ vergoed* (all) expenses covered **2** extra expense(s)

de **onkostenvergoeding** /ɔnkɔstə(n)vərɣudɪŋ/ (pl: -en) payment (or: reimbursement) of expenses; mileage allowance

onkreukbaar /ɔnkrøgbar/ (adj) upright, unimpeachable

het **onkruid** /ɔnkrœyt/ weed(s): *~ vergaat niet* ill weeds grow apace

onkuis /ɔnkœys/ (adj, adv) **1** improper, indecent **2** unchaste, impure

de **onkunde** /ɔnkʏndə/ ignorance

onkwetsbaar /ɔnkwɛtsbar/ (adj, adv) invulnerable

onlangs /ɔnlɑŋs/ (adv) recently, lately: *ik heb hem ~ nog gezien* I saw him just the other day

onleesbaar /ɔnlezbar/ (adj, adv) **1** illegible **2** unreadable

online /ɔnlɑjn/ (adj) on-line

onlogisch /ɔnloɣis/ (adj, adv) illogical

de **onlusten** /ɔnlʏstə(n)/ (pl) riots, disturbances

de **onmacht** /ɔmɑxt/ impotence, powerlessness

onmatig /ɔmatəx/ (adj, adv) intemperate, immoderate, excessive

de **onmens** /ɔmɛns/ (pl: -en) brute, beast

onmenselijk /ɔmɛnsələk/ (adj, adv) inhuman

onmerkbaar /ɔmɛrgbar/ (adj, adv) unnoticeable, imperceptible

onmetelijk /ɔmetələk/ (adj) immense, immeasurable

onmiddellijk /ɔmɪdələk/ (adj, adv) immediate, immediately, directly, at once, straightaway: *ik kom ~ naar Utrecht* I'm coming to Utrecht straightaway (or: at once, immediately)

de **onmin** /ɔmɪn/: *met iem. in ~ leven* be at odds with s.o.

onmisbaar /ɔmɪzbar/ (adj, adv) indispensable, essential

onmiskenbaar /ɔmɪskɛmbar/ (adj, adv) unmistakable, indisputable: *hij lijkt ~ op zijn vader* he looks decidedly like his father

onmogelijk /ɔmoɣələk/ (adj, adv) impossible: *een ~ verhaal* a preposterous story; *ik kan ~ langer blijven* I can't possibly stay any longer; *iem. het leven ~ maken* pester the life out of s.o.

onmondig /ɔmˌɔndəx/ (adj) incapable (of self-government)

onnadenkend /ɔnadɛnkənt/ (adj, adv) unthinking: ~ *handelen* act without thinking

onnatuurlijk /ɔnatyrlək/ (adj, adv) unnatural

onnauwkeurig /ɔnaukørəx/ (adj, adv) inaccurate

de **onnauwkeurigheid** /ɔnaukørəxhɛit/ inaccuracy

onnavolgbaar /ɔnavɔlɣbar/ (adj, adv) inimitable

onnodig /ɔnodəx/ (adj, adv) unnecessary, needless, superfluous: ~ *te zeggen dat ...* needless to say ...

onnozel /ɔnozəl/ (adj, adv) foolish, silly: *met een ~e grijns* with a sheepish grin

de **onnozelaar** /ɔnozəlar/ (pl: -s) [Belg; depr] Simple Simon, birdbrain

onofficieel /ɔnɔfiˈfel/ (adj, adv) unofficial

onomstotelijk /ɔnɔmstotələk/ (adj, adv) indisputable, conclusive

onomwonden /ɔnɔmwɔndə(n)/ (adj, adv) frank, plain

ononderbroken /ɔnɔndərbrokə(n)/ (adj, adv) continuous, uninterrupted

onontbeerlijk /ɔnɔndbɛrlək/ (adj) indispensable

onontkoombaar /ɔnɔntkombar/ (adj, adv) inescapable, inevitable: *dat leidt ~ tot verlies* that inevitably leads to loss(es)

onooglijk /ɔnoxlək/ (adj, adv) unsightly, ugly

onopgemerkt /ɔnɔpxəmɛrkt/ (adj, adv) unnoticed, unobserved

onophoudelijk /ɔnɔphaudələk/ (adj, adv) continuous, ceaseless, incessant

onoplettend /ɔnɔplɛtənt/ (adj, adv) inattentive, inadvertent

onoplosbaar /ɔnɔplɔzbar/ (adj) **1** insoluble, indissoluble **2** unsolvable

onopvallend /ɔnɔpfɑlənt/ (adj, adv) inconspicuous, nondescript; unobtrusive; discreet: *~ te werk gaan* act discreetly

onopzettelijk /ɔnɔpsɛtələk/ (adj, adv) unintentional, inadvertent

onovergankelijk /ɔnovərɣɑnkələk/ (adj, adv) intransitive

onoverkomelijk /ɔnovərkɔmələk/ (adj) insurmountable

onovertroffen /ɔnovərtrɔfə(n)/ (adj) unsurpassed, unrivalled

onoverwinnelijk /ɔnovərwɪnələk/ (adj) invincible

onoverzichtelijk /ɔnovərzɪxtələk/ (adj, adv) cluttered, poorly organized (*or:* arranged)

onpaar /ɔmpar/ (adj) unpaired, odd

onparlementair /ɔmpɑrləmɛntɛːr/ (adj) unparliamentary

onpartijdig /ɔmpɑrtɛidəx/ (adj, adv) impartial, unbiased

de **onpartijdigheid** /ɔmpɑrtɛidəxhɛit/ impartiality

onpasselijk /ɔmpɑsələk/ (adj) sick

onpeilbaar /ɔmpɛɪlbar/ (adj) **1** unfathomable **2** unlimited

onpersoonlijk /ɔmpərsonlək/ (adj, adv) impersonal

onplezierig /ɔmpləzirəx/ (adj, adv) unpleasant, nasty

onpraktisch /ɔmprɑktis/ (adj, adv) impractical

onprettig /ɔmprɛtəx/ (adj, adv) unpleasant, disagreeable, nasty

onproductief /ɔmprodyktif/ (adj, adv) unproductive

het **onraad** /ɔnrat/ trouble, danger: *~ bespeuren* smell a rat

onrealistisch /ɔnrejalɪstis/ (adj) unrealistic

het **onrecht** /ɔnrɛxt/ injustice, wrong: *iem. ~ (aan)doen* do s.o. wrong; *ten ~e* a) erroneously, mistakenly; b) wrongfully, improperly

onrechtmatig /ɔnrɛxtmatəx/ (adj, adv) unlawful, illegal; wrongful; unjust

onrechtvaardig /ɔnrɛxtfardəx/ (adj, adv) unjust

de **onrechtvaardigheid** /ɔnrɛxtfardəxhɛit/ (pl: -heden) injustice, wrong

onredelijk /ɔnredələk/ (adj, adv) unreasonable, unfounded

onregelmatig /ɔnreɣəlmatəx/ (adj, adv) irregular

onreglementair /ɔnreɣləmɛntɛːr/ (adj) not regulatory

onrein /ɔnrɛɪn/ (adj, adv) unclean

onrendabel /ɔnrɛndabəl/ (adj) uneconomic

onrijp /ɔnrɛɪp/ (adj) **1** unripe, unseasoned **2** immature

onroerend /ɔnrurənt/ (adj) immovable: *makelaar in ~ goed* estate agent

de **onroerendezaakbelasting** /ɔnrurəndəzaɡbəlɑstɪŋ/ property tax(es)

de **onrust** /ɔnrʏst/ restlessness, agitation: *~ zaaien* stir up trouble

onrustbarend /ɔnrʏstbarənt/ (adj, adv) alarming

onrustig /ɔnrʏstəx/ (adj, adv) restless, turbulent

de **onruststoker** /ɔnrʏstokər/ (pl: -s) troublemaker, agitator

het **¹ons** /ɔns/ (pl: -en, onzen) quarter of a pound, four ounces: *een ~ ham* a quarter of ham

²ons /ɔns/ (pers pron) us: *het is ~ een genoegen* (it's) our pleasure; *onder ~ gezegd* (just) between ourselves; *dat is van ~* that's ours, that belongs to us

³ons /ɔns/ (poss pron) our: *~ huis* our house; *uw boeken en die van ~* your books and ours

onsamenhangend /ɔnsamə(n)hɑŋənt/ (adj, adv) incoherent, disconnected

onschadelijk /ɔnsxadələk/ (adj, adv) harmless; innocent; non-noxious: *een bom ~ ma-ken* defuse a bomb

onschatbaar /ɔnsχ*ǫ*dbar/ (adj, adv) invaluable: *van onschatbare* **waarde** *zijn* be invaluable

onschendbaar /ɔnsχ*ɛ*ndbar/ (adj) immune

onscherp /ɔnsχ*ɛ*rp/ (adj) out of focus, blurred

de **onschuld** /*ǫ*nsχʏlt/ innocence

onschuldig /ɔnsχʏldəχ/ (adj) **1** innocent, guiltless **2** innocent, harmless

onsmakelijk /ɔnsm*ạ*kələk/ (adj, adv) **1** distasteful, unpalatable **2** distasteful, disagreeable, unsavoury

onsportief /ɔnsp*ǫ*rtif/ (adj, adv) unsporting, unsportsmanlike: *hij* **heeft** *zich ~* **gedragen** he behaved unsportingly

onstabiel /ɔnstab*i*l/ (adj, adv) unstable

onsterfelijk /ɔnst*ɛ*rfələk/ (adj, adv) immortal

de **onsterfelijkheid** /ɔnst*ɛ*rfələkhɛit/ immortality

onstuimig /ɔnst*œy*məχ/ (adj) **1** turbulent **2** passionate, tempestuous

onstuitbaar /ɔnst*œy*dbar/ (adj, adv) unstoppable

onsympathiek /ɔnsɪmpat*i*k/ (adj, adv) uncongenial: *een ~e* **houding** an unengaging manner

onszelf /ɔns*ɛ*lf/ (ref pron) ourselves

ontaard /ɔnt*ạ*rt/ (adj) degenerate

ontaarden /ɔnt*ạ*rdə(n)/ (ontaardde, is ontaard) degenerate (into), deteriorate

ontactisch /ɔnt*ǫ*ktis/ (adj) impolitic

ontberen /ɔndb*e*rə(n)/ (ontbeerde, heeft ontbeerd) lack

de **ontbering** /ɔndb*e*rɪŋ/ (pl: -en) hardship, (de)privation

ontbieden /ɔndb*i*də(n)/ (ontbood, heeft ontboden) summon, send for

het **ontbijt** /ɔndb*ɛi*t/ breakfast: *een kamer met ~* bed and breakfast, B & B

ontbijten /ɔndb*ɛi*tə(n)/ (ontbeet, heeft ontbeten) (have) breakfast

de **ontbijtkoek** /ɔndb*ɛi*tkuk/ (pl: -en) [roughly] gingercake, gingerbread

ontbinden /ɔndb*ɪ*ndə(n)/ (ontbond, heeft ontbonden) dissolve; disband; annul

de **ontbinding** /ɔndb*ɪ*ndɪŋ/ (pl: -en) **1** annulment **2** decomposition, decay; corruption [also fig]: *tot ~* **overgaan** decompose, decay; *in* **staat** *van ~* in a state of decomposition

ontbloot /ɔndbl*ǫ*t/ (adj) bare, naked

ontbloten /ɔndbl*ǫ*tə(n)/ (ontblootte, heeft ontbloot) bare; expose

de **ontboezeming** /ɔndb*u*zəmɪŋ/ (pl: -en) outpouring

ontbossen /ɔndb*ǫ*sə(n)/ (ontboste, heeft ontbost) deforest

ontbranden /ɔndbr*ạ*ndə(n)/ (ontbrandde, is ontbrand) ignite

ontbreken /ɔndbr*e*kə(n)/ (ontbrak, heeft ontbroken) **1** be lacking (in): *waar het* **aan** *ontbreekt is ...* what's lacking is ...; *er ontbreekt nog* **veel** *aan* there's still much to be desired **2** be absent, be missing

ontcijferen /ɔntsɛifərə(n)/ (ontcijferde, heeft ontcijferd) decipher

ontdaan /ɔnd*ạ*n/ (adj) upset, disconcerted

ontdekken /ɔnd*ɛ*kə(n)/ (ontdekte, heeft ontdekt) discover: *iets bij toeval ~* hit upon (or: stumble on) sth.

de **ontdekker** /ɔnd*ɛ*kər/ (pl: -s) discoverer

de **ontdekking** /ɔnd*ɛ*kɪŋ/ (pl: -en) discovery, find: *een ~* **doen** make a discovery

de **ontdekkingsreiziger** /ɔnd*ɛ*kɪŋsrɛizəγər/ (pl: -s) explorer, discoverer

zich **ontdoen** /ɔnd*u*n/ (ontdeed zich, heeft zich ontdaan) (+ van) dispose of, get rid of, remove

ontdooien /ɔnd*oj*ə(n)/ (ontdooide, is ontdooid) thaw, defrost; melt

ontduiken /ɔnd*œy*kə(n)/ (ontdook, heeft ontdoken) evade, elude, dodge

ontegenzeglijk /ɔnteγənz*ɛ*χlək/ (adj) undeniable, incontestable

onteigenen /ɔnt*ɛi*γənə(n)/ (onteigende, heeft onteigend) **1** expropriate **2** dispossess

ontelbaar /ɔnt*ɛ*lbar/ (adj, adv) countless, innumerable

ontembaar /ɔnt*ɛ*mbar/ (adj) untameable, indomitable

onterecht /ɔntər*ɛ*χt/ (adj, adv) undeserved, unjust

onteren /ɔnt*e*rə(n)/ (onteerde, heeft onteerd) dishonour, violate

onterven /ɔnt*ɛ*rvə(n)/ (onterfde, heeft onterfd) disinherit

ontevreden /ɔntəvr*e*də(n)/ (adj, adv) dissatisfied (with): *je mag niet ~* **zijn** (you) mustn't grumble

de **ontevredenheid** /ɔntəvr*e*dənhɛit/ dissatisfaction (about, with)

zich **ontfermen** /ɔntf*ɛ*rmə(n)/ (ontfermde zich, heeft zich ontfermd) (+ over) take pity on

ontfutselen /ɔntf*ʏ*tsələ(n)/ (ontfutselde, heeft ontfutseld) filch, pilfer

ontgaan /ɔntχ*ạ*n/ (ontging, is ontgaan) **1** escape, pass (by): *de* **overwinning** *kon ons niet meer ~* victory was ours **2** escape, miss, fail to notice: *het kon niemand ~* **dat** no one could fail to notice that **3** escape, elude: *de* **logica** *daarvan ontgaat mij* the logic of it escapes me

ontgelden /ɔntχ*ɛ*ldə(n)/: *hij heeft het* **moeten** *~* he got it in the neck, he had to pay for it

ontginnen /ɔntχ*ɪ*nə(n)/ (ontgon, heeft ontgonnen) reclaim; cultivate

de **ontginning** /ɔntχ*ɪ*nɪŋ/ exploitation, development; reclamation

ontglippen /ɔntχl*ɪ*pə(n)/ (ontglipte, is ontglipt) slip, get away: *de bal ontglipte hem* the ball slipped out of his hands

de **ontgoocheling** /ɔntxoxəlɪŋ/ (pl: -en) disillusionment

ontgroeien /ɔntxrujə(n)/ (ontgroeide, is ontgroeid) outgrow: [fig] *de kinderschoenen* (or: *schoolbanken*) *ontgroeid zijn* have left one's childhood (or: schooldays) behind

de **ontgroening** /ɔntxrunɪŋ/ ragging; [Am] hazing

het **onthaal** /ɔnthal/ **1** welcome, reception **2** [Belg] reception

de **onthaalouder** /ɔnthaloudər/ [Belg] temporary host to (foreign) children

onthaasten /ɔnthastə(n)/ (onthaastte, heeft onthaast) de-stress, relax, calm down

onthalen /ɔnthalə(n)/ (onthaalde, heeft onthaald) entertain: *iem. warm ~* give s.o. a warm welcome

onthand /ɔnthɑnt/ (adj) inconvenienced

ontharen /ɔntharə(n)/ (onthaarde, heeft onthaard) depilate

ontheemd /ɔnthemt/ (adj) homeless; [fig] uprooted

ontheffen /ɔnthɛfə(n)/ (onthief, heeft ontheven) exempt, release

de **ontheffing** /ɔnthɛfɪŋ/ (pl: -en) exemption; release: *~ hebben van* be released from

onthoofden /ɔnthovdə(n)/ (onthoofdde, heeft onthoofd) behead, decapitate

de **onthoofding** /ɔnthovdɪŋ/ (pl: -en) decapitation, beheading

¹**onthouden** /ɔnthoudə(n)/ (onthield, heeft onthouden) remember: *goed gezichten kunnen ~* have a good memory for faces; *ik zal het je helpen ~* I'll remind you of it

zich ²**onthouden** /ɔnthoudə(n)/ (onthield zich, heeft zich onthouden) abstain (from), refrain (from)

de **onthouding** /ɔnthoudɪŋ/ **1** abstention **2** continence, abstinence

onthullen /ɔnthʏlə(n)/ (onthulde, heeft onthuld) **1** unveil **2** reveal, disclose, divulge

de **onthulling** /ɔnthʏlɪŋ/ (pl: -en) **1** unveiling **2** revelation, disclosure: *opzienbarende ~en* startling disclosures

onthutst /ɔnthʏtst/ (adj, adv) disconcerted, dismayed

¹**ontkennen** /ɔntkɛnə(n)/ (ontkende, heeft ontkend) plead not guilty

²**ontkennen** /ɔntkɛnə(n)/ (ontkende, heeft ontkend) deny, negate: *hij ontkende iets met de zaak te maken te hebben* he denied any involvement in the matter

ontkennend /ɔntkɛnənt/ (adj, adv) negative

de **ontkenning** /ɔntkɛnɪŋ/ (pl: -en) denial, negation

de **ontkerkelijking** /ɔntkɛrkələkɪŋ/ secularization

ontketenen /ɔntketənə(n)/ (ontketende,

heeft ontketend) let loose; unchain; unleash

ontkiemen /ɔntkimə(n)/ (ontkiemde, is ontkiemd) germinate; [fig also] bud

ontkleden /ɔntkledə(n)/ (ontkleedde, heeft ontkleed) undress: *zich ~* undress

de **ontknoping** /ɔntknopɪŋ/ (pl: -en) ending, dénouement: *zijn ~ naderen* reach a climax

ontkomen /ɔntkomə(n)/ (ontkwam, is ontkomen) **1** escape, get away **2** evade, get round

ontkoppelen /ɔntkɔpələ(n)/ (ontkoppelde, heeft ontkoppeld) uncouple; [fig] disconnect, unlink

ontkrachten /ɔntkrɑxtə(n)/ (ontkrachtte, heeft ontkracht) enfeeble: *een bewijs ~* take the edge off a piece of evidence

ontkurken /ɔntkʏrkə(n)/ (ontkurkte, heeft ontkurkt) uncork, unstop(per)

ontladen /ɔntladə(n)/ (ontlaadde, heeft ontladen) unload; discharge: [fig] *zich ~* be released

de **ontlading** /ɔntladɪŋ/ (pl: -en) **1** release **2** discharge

¹**ontlasten** /ɔntlɑstə(n)/ (ontlastte, heeft ontlast) unburden, relieve: *we moeten hem wat ~* we've got to take some of the weight off his shoulders

zich ²**ontlasten** /ɔntlɑstə(n)/ (ontlastte zich, heeft zich ontlast) empty (or: move, open) one's bowels

de **ontlasting** /ɔntlɑstɪŋ/ stools, (human) excrement; faeces

ontleden /ɔntledə(n)/ (ontleedde, heeft ontleed) **1** dissect, anatomize **2** analyse: *een zin ~* analyse (or: parse) a sentence

de **ontleding** /ɔntledɪŋ/ (pl: -en) **1** dissection **2** analysis

ontlenen /ɔntlenə(n)/ (ontleende, heeft ontleend) **1** (+ aan) derive (from), borrow (from), take **2** (+ aan) take (from), derive (from)

ontlokken /ɔntlɔkə(n)/ (ontlokte, heeft ontlokt) elicit (from)

ontlopen /ɔntlopə(n)/ (ontliep, is ontlopen) differ from: *die twee ~ elkaar niet veel* they don't differ greatly

ontluiken /ɔntlœykə(n)/ (ontlook, is ontloken) burgeon, bud: *een ~de liefde* an awakening love; *een ~d talent* a burgeoning (or: budding) talent

ontmaagden /ɔntmaɣdə(n)/ (ontmaagdde, heeft ontmaagd) deflower

ontmantelen /ɔntmɑntələ(n)/ (ontmantelde, heeft ontmanteld) dismantle, strip

ontmaskeren /ɔntmɑskərə(n)/ (ontmaskerde, heeft ontmaskerd) unmask, expose

ontmoedigen /ɔntmudəɣə(n)/ (ontmoedigde, heeft ontmoedigd) discourage, demoralize; deter: *we zullen ons niet laten ~ door ... we* won't let ... get us down

ontmoeten /ɔntmutə(n)/ (ontmoette,

heeft ontmoet) **1** meet, run into, bump into **2** meet, see

de **ontmoeting** /ɔntmutɪŋ/ (pl: -en) meeting, encounter: *een* **toevallige** ~ a chance meeting (*or:* encounter)

de **ontmoetingsplaats** /ɔntmutɪŋsplats/ (pl: -en) meeting place

ontnemen /ɔntnemə(n)/ (ontnam, heeft ontnomen) take away

de **ontnieter** /ɔntnitər/ staple extractor

de **ontnuchtering** /ɔntnʏxtərɪŋ/ disillusionment, disenchantment

ontoegankelijk /ɔntuɣɑŋkələk/ (adj) inaccessible, impervious (to)

ontoelaatbaar /ɔntuladbar/ (adj) inadmissible

ontoereikend /ɔnturɛɪkənt/ (adj, adv) inadequate

ontoerekeningsvatbaar /ɔnturekənɪŋsfɑdbar/ (adj) not responsible; [law] of unsound mind

ontoonbaar /ɔntombar/ (adj) unpresentable

ontploffen /ɔntplɔfə(n)/ (ontplofte, is ontploft) explode, blow up: *ik dacht dat hij zou* ~ I thought he'd explode

de **ontploffing** /ɔntplɔfɪŋ/ (pl: -en) explosion

ontplooien /ɔntplojə(n)/ (ontplooide, heeft ontplooid) develop

zich **ontpoppen** /ɔntpɔpə(n)/ (ontpopte zich, heeft zich ontpopt) reveal o.s. (as), turn out (to be)

ontrafelen /ɔntrafələ(n)/ (ontrafelde, heeft ontrafeld) unravel, disentangle

ontreddered /ɔntrɛdərt/ (adj) upset, broken down: *in* ~*e* **toestand** in a desperate situation

ontregeld /ɔntreɣəlt/ (adj) unsettled, disordered

ontregelen /ɔntreɣələ(n)/ (ontregelde, heeft ontregeld) disorder, disorganize, dislocate

ontroeren /ɔntrurə(n)/ (ontroerde, heeft ontroerd) move, touch

ontroerend /ɔntrurənt/ (adj) moving, touching; tear-jerking

de **ontroering** /ɔntrurɪŋ/ (pl: -en) emotion

ontroostbaar /ɔntrostbar/ (adj) inconsolable, broken-hearted

de **¹ontrouw** /ɔntrɑu/ **1** disloyalty, unfaithfulness **2** unfaithfulness, infidelity

²ontrouw /ɔntrɑu/ (adj) **1** disloyal (to), untrue (to) **2** unfaithful

ontruimen /ɔntrœymə(n)/ (ontruimde, heeft ontruimd) **1** clear, vacate **2** clear, evacuate: *de politie moest het* **pand** ~ the police had to clear the building

de **ontruiming** /ɔntrœymɪŋ/ (pl: -en) **1** evacuation **2** eviction

ontschepen /ɔntsxepə(n)/ (ontscheepte, is ontscheept) disembark

ontschieten /ɔntsxitə(n)/ (ontschoot, is

ontschoten) slip, elude

ontsieren /ɔntsirə(n)/ (ontsierde, heeft ontsierd) mar, blot

ontslaan /ɔntslan/ (ontsloeg, heeft ontslagen) **1** dismiss, discharge: *ontslagen* **worden** be dismissed; *iem. op staande voet* ~ dismiss s.o. on the spot **2** relieve, discharge: *een patiënt* ~ *uit een ziekenhuis* discharge a patient from hospital

het **ontslag** /ɔntslɑx/ (pl: -en) **1** dismissal, discharge: *eervol* ~ honourable discharge; *(zijn)* ~ *nemen* resign, hand in one's notice (*or:* resignation) **2** resignation, notice **3** exemption

de **ontslagbrief** /ɔntslɑɣbrif/ (pl: -brieven) notice; (letter of) resignation

de **ontslagvergoeding** /ɔntslɑxfərɣudɪŋ/ severance pay

de **ontsluiting** /ɔntslœytɪŋ/ **1** opening up: *de* ~ *van een* **gebied** the opening up of an area **2** dilat(at)ion

ontsmetten /ɔntsmɛtə(n)/ (ontsmette, heeft ontsmet) disinfect

de **ontsmetting** /ɔntsmɛtɪŋ/ disinfection, decontamination

het **ontsmettingsmiddel** /ɔntsmɛtɪŋsmɪdəl/ (pl: -en) disinfectant, antiseptic

ontsnappen /ɔntsnɑpə(n)/ (ontsnapte, is ontsnapt) **1** escape (from): *aan de dood* ~ escape death **2** escape, get away, get out: *weten te* ~ make one's getaway **3** escape, elude: *aan de aandacht* ~ escape notice **4** pull (*or:* break) away (from)

de **ontsnapping** /ɔntsnɑpɪŋ/ (pl: -en) escape

¹ontspannen /ɔntspɑnə(n)/ (adj) relaxed, easy: *zich* ~ **gedragen** have an easy manner

²ontspannen /ɔntspɑnə(n)/ (ontspande, heeft ontspannen) **1** slacken, unbend **2** relax: *zich* ~ relax

de **ontspanning** /ɔntspɑnɪŋ/ (pl: -en) relaxation, recreation

ontsporen /ɔntsporə(n)/ (ontspoorde, is ontspoord) **1** be derailed **2** [fig] go (*or:* run) off the rails

de **ontsporing** /ɔntsporɪŋ/ (pl: -en) derailment; [fig] lapse

ontspringen /ɔntsprɪŋə(n)/ (ontsprong, is ontsprongen) rise: *de rivier ontspringt in de bergen* the river rises in the mountains || [fig] *de* **dans** ~ have a lucky escape

ontspruiten /ɔntsprœytə(n)/ (ontsproot, is ontsproten) originate (from)

het **¹ontstaan** /ɔntstan/ origin; creation; development, coming into existence

²ontstaan /ɔntstan/ (ontstond, is ontstaan) **1** come into being, arise: *door haar vertrek ontstaat een* **vacature** her departure has created a vacancy **2** originate, start

ontsteken /ɔntstekə(n)/ (ontstak, is ontstoken) be(come) inflamed

de **ontsteking** /ɔntstekɪŋ/ (pl: -en) **1** inflam-

mation **2** ignition
ontsteld /ɔntstɛlt/ (adj, adv) dismayed
de **ontsteltenis** /ɔntstɛltənɪs/ **1** dismay, confusion **2** dismay; horror
ontstemd /ɔntstɛmt/ (adj) untuned, out of tune
de **ontstentenis** /ɔntstɛntənɪs/: *bij ~ van* in the absence of
ontstijgen /ɔntstɛɪɣə(n)/ (ontsteeg, is ontstegen) mount, rise (up)
ontstoken /ɔntstoːkə(n)/ (adj) inflamed
ontstoppen /ɔntstɔpə(n)/ (ontstopte, heeft ontstopt) **1** unblock, unclog **2** unstop(per), uncork
de **ontstopper** /ɔntstɔpər/ (pl: -s) plunger
zich **onttrekken** /ɔntrɛkə(n)/ (onttrok zich, heeft zich onttrokken) withdraw (from), back out of
onttronen /ɔntroːnə(n)/ (onttroonde, heeft onttroond) dethrone, depose
de **ontucht** /ɔntʏxt/ illicit sexual acts, sexual abuse
ontvangen /ɔntfɑŋə(n)/ (ontving, heeft ontvangen) **1** receive; collect; draw: *in dank ~ received* with thanks **2** receive; welcome: *iem. hartelijk* (or: *met open armen) ~ receive* s.o. with open arms, make s.o. very welcome
de **ontvanger** /ɔntfɑŋər/ (pl: -s) **1** receiver, recipient **2** receiver
de **ontvangst** /ɔntfɑŋst/ (pl: -en) **1** receipt: *betalen na ~ van de goederen* pay on receipt of goods; *na ~ van uw brief* on receipt of your letter; *tekenen voor ~* sign for receipt **2** collection **3** reception: *een hartelijke* (or: *gunstige) ~* a warm (*or:* favourable) reception
het **ontvangstbewijs** /ɔntfɑŋstbəwɛis/ (pl: -bewijzen) receipt
ontvankelijk /ɔntfɑŋkələɣ/ (adj) **1** susceptible (to): *~ voor* open to, receptive to **2** admissible, sustainable
ontvlambaar /ɔntflɑmbar/ (adj) inflammable
ontvlammen /ɔntflɑmə(n)/ (ontvlamde, is ontvlamd) inflame
ontvluchten /ɔntflʏxtə(n)/ (ontvluchtte, is ontvlucht) **1** escape (from), run away from **2** flee
de **ontvoerder** /ɔntfurdər/ (pl: -s) kidnapper
ontvoeren /ɔntfurə(n)/ (ontvoerde, heeft ontvoerd) kidnap
de **ontvoering** /ɔntfurɪŋ/ (pl: -en) kidnapping
ontvouwen /ɔntfɑuwə(n)/ (ontvouwde, heeft ontvouwd/ontvouwen) unfold
ontvreemden /ɔntfreːmdə(n)/ (ontvreemdde, heeft ontvreemd) steal
ontwaken /ɔntwaːkə(n)/ (ontwaakte, is ontwaakt) awake, (a)rouse
ontwapenen /ɔntwaːpənə(n)/ (ontwapende, heeft ontwapend) disarm: *een ~de glimlach* a disarming smile
de **ontwapening** /ɔntwaːpənɪŋ/ disarmament

ontwaren /ɔntwaːrə(n)/ (ontwaarde, heeft ontwaard) [form] descry
ontwarren /ɔntwɑrə(n)/ (ontwarde, heeft ontward) disentangle
ontwennen /ɔntwɛnə(n)/ (ontwende, is ontwend) get out of the habit
de **ontwenningskuur** /ɔntwɛnɪŋskyr/ (pl: -kuren) detoxification
de **ontwenningsverschijnselen** /ɔntwɛnɪŋsfərsxɛɪnsələ(n)/ (pl) withdrawal symptoms
het **ontwerp** /ɔntwɛrp/ (pl: -en) draft; design
ontwerpen /ɔntwɛrpə(n)/ (ontwierp, heeft ontworpen) **1** design; plan **2** devise, plan; formulate; draft; draw up
de **ontwerper** /ɔntwɛrpər/ (pl: -s) designer, planner
ontwijken /ɔntwɛikə(n)/ (ontweek, heeft ontweken) avoid
ontwijkend /ɔntwɛikənt/ (adj, adv) evasive
de **ontwikkelaar** /ɔntwɪkəlar/ (pl: -s) developer
ontwikkeld /ɔntwɪkəlt/ (adj) **1** developed, mature **2** educated, informed; cultivated; cultured
¹**ontwikkelen** /ɔntwɪkələ(n)/ (ontwikkelde, heeft ontwikkeld) **1** develop **2** educate: *zich ~* educate o.s. ‖ *foto's ~ en afdrukken* process a film
zich ²**ontwikkelen** /ɔntwɪkələ(n)/ (ontwikkelde zich, heeft zich ontwikkeld) develop (into): *we zullen zien hoe de zaken zich ~* we'll see how things develop
de **ontwikkeling** /ɔntwɪkəlɪŋ/ (pl: -en) **1** development, growth: *tot ~ komen* develop **2** education: *algemene ~* general knowledge
de **ontwikkelingshulp** /ɔntwɪkəlɪŋshʏlp/ foreign aid, development assistance
het **ontwikkelingsland** /ɔntwɪkəlɪŋslɑnt/ (pl: -en) developing country
de **ontwikkelingsmaatschappij** /ɔntwɪkəlɪŋsmatsxɑpɛɪ/ (pl: -en) development company
ontworstelen /ɔntwɔrstələ(n)/ (ontworstelde, heeft ontworsteld): *zij ontworstelde zich aan zijn greep* she struggled out of his grasp
ontwortelen /ɔntwɔrtələ(n)/ (ontwortelde, heeft ontworteld) uproot
ontwrichten /ɔntwrɪxtə(n)/ (ontwrichtte, heeft ontwricht) **1** disrupt **2** dislocate
het **ontzag** /ɔntsɑx/ awe, respect
ontzaglijk /ɔntsɑxlək/ (adj) tremendous, enormous: *~ veel* an awful lot, terribly much
¹**ontzeggen** /ɔntsɛɣə(n)/ (ontzegde/ontzei, heeft ontzegd) refuse, deny
zich ²**ontzeggen** /ɔntsɛɣə(n)/ (ontzegde zich/ontzei zich, heeft zich ontzegd) deny o.s.: *hij ontzegde zich veel om ... he* made many sacrifices to ...

onverstoorbaar

de **ontzegging** /ɔntsɛɣɪŋ/ (pl: -en) denial, refusal: ~ van de **rijbevoegdheid** disqualification from driving

ontzenuwen /ɔntsenywə(n)/ (ontzenuwde, heeft ontzenuwd) refute, disprove

ontzet /ɔntsɛt/ (adj) relief

ontzetten /ɔntsɛtə(n)/ (ontzette, heeft ontzet) **1** expel, remove **2** relieve; rescue **3** appal, horrify

¹ontzettend /ɔntsɛtənt/ (adj) **1** appalling **2** terrific, immense, tremendous

²ontzettend /ɔntsɛtənt/ (adv) awfully, tremendously: het **spijt** me ~ I'm terribly (or: awfully) sorry

de **ontzetting** /ɔntsɛtɪŋ/ (pl: -en) **1** deprivation; removal: ~ uit een recht disfranchisement **2** relief; rescue **3** horror, dismay: tot onze ~ to our dismay (or: horror)

ontzien /ɔntsin/ (ontzag, heeft ontzien) spare: iem. ~ spare s.o.

onuitputtelijk /ɔnœytpʏtələk/ (adj, adv) inexhaustible

onuitroeibaar /ɔnœytrujbar/ (adj) ineradicable; indestructible

onuitspreekbaar /ɔnœytspreɡbar/ (adj) unpronounceable

onuitsprekelijk /ɔnœytsprekələk/ (adj, adv) unspeakable

onuitstaanbaar /ɔnœytstambar/ (adj, adv) unbearable, insufferable: die kerel **vind** ik ~ I can't stand that guy

onvast /ɔnvɔst/ (adj, adv) unsteady, unstable

onveilig /ɔnvɛiləχ/ (adj, adv) unsafe, dangerous

de **onveiligheid** /ɔnvɛiləχhɛit/ danger(ousness)

onveranderd /ɔnvərɔndərt/ (adj) unchanged, unaltered

¹onveranderlijk /ɔnvərɔndərlək/ (adj) unchanging, unvarying

²onveranderlijk /ɔnvərɔndərlək/ (adv) invariably

onverantwoord /ɔnvərɔntwort/ (adj, adv) irresponsible

onverantwoordelijk /ɔnvərɔntwordələk/ (adj, adv) irresponsible; unjustifiable

onverbeterlijk /ɔnvərbetərlək/ (adj) incorrigible

onverbiddelijk /ɔnvərbɪdələk/ (adj, adv) unrelenting, implacable

onverdeeld /ɔnvərdelt/ (adj) undivided

onverdiend /ɔnvərdint/ (adj, adv) undeserved

onverdraagzaam /ɔnvərdraχsam/ (adj) intolerant (towards)

de **onverdraagzaamheid** /ɔnvərdraχsamhɛit/ intolerance

onverenigbaar /ɔnvərenəybar/ (adj) incompatible (with)

onvergeeflijk /ɔnvərɣeflək/ (adj, adv) unforgivable, inexcusable

onvergelijkbaar /ɔnvɛrɣəlɛiɡbar/ (adj, adv) incomparable

onvergetelijk /ɔnvərɣetələk/ (adj, adv) unforgettable

onverhard /ɔnvərhɔrt/ (adj) unpaved

onverhoeds /ɔnvərhuts/ (adj, adv) unexpected

¹onverholen /ɔnvərholə(n)/ (adj) unconcealed

²onverholen /ɔnvərholə(n)/ (adv) openly

onverhoopt /ɔnvərhopt/ (adj) unhoped-for, unexpected; in the unlikely event

onverklaarbaar /ɔnvərklarbar/ (adj, adv) inexplicable, unaccountable: op onverklaarbare **wijze** unaccountably

onverkoopbaar /ɔnvərkobar/ (adj) unsaleable

onverkort /ɔnvərkɔrt/ (adj, adv) **1** unabridged **2** unimpaired: ~ van **toepassing** fully applicable

onverkwikkelijk /ɔnvərkwɪkələk/ (adj) nasty

de **onverlaat** /ɔnvərlat/ (pl: onverlaten) miscreant

onverlet /ɔnvərlɛt/ (adj): dat **laat** ~ dat ... the fact remains that ...

onvermijdelijk /ɔnvərmɛidələk/ (adj, adv) inevitable: ~e **fouten** unavoidable mistakes

¹onverminderd /ɔnvərmɪndərt/ (adj, adv) undiminished: ~ van kracht blijven remain in full force

²onverminderd /ɔnvərmɪndərt/ (prep) without prejudice to

onvermoeibaar /ɔnvərmujbar/ (adj) indefatigable, tireless

het **onvermogen** /ɔnvərmoɣə(n)/ impotence, powerlessness; inability

onvermurwbaar /ɔnvərmʏrfbar/ (adj) unrelenting

onverricht /ɔnvərɪχt/ (adj): ~er **zake** terugkeren return without having achieved one's aim

¹onverschillig /ɔnvərsχɪləχ/ (adj) indifferent (to): hij zat daar met een ~ **gezicht** he sat there looking completely indifferent (or: unconcerned)

²onverschillig /ɔnvərsχɪləχ/ (adv) indifferently: iem. ~ **behandelen** treat s.o. with indifference

de **onverschilligheid** /ɔnvərsχɪləχhɛit/ indifference

onverschrokken /ɔnvərsχrɔkə(n)/ (adj, adv) fearless

onverslijtbaar /ɔnvərslɛidbar/ (adj) indestructible; durable [goods]

onverstaanbaar /ɔnvərstambar/ (adj) unintelligible; inarticulate; inaudible

onverstandig /ɔnvərstɔndəχ/ (adj, adv) foolish, unwise

onverstoorbaar /ɔnvərstorbar/ (adj, adv)

358

imperturbable, unflappable
onverteerbaar /ɔnvərtḙrbar/ (adj, adv) indigestible; [fig also] unacceptable
onvertogen /ɔnvərtoɣə(n)/ (adj) indecent: *er is geen ~ woord gevallen* there was no bad feeling
onvervalst /ɔnvərvɑlst/ (adj) pure, unadulterated; broad
onvervangbaar /ɔnvərvɑŋbar/ (adj) irreplaceable
onvervreemdbaar /ɔnvərvrḙmdbar/ (adj, adv) inalienable
onvervuld /ɔnvərvˠlt/ (adj) unfulfilled
onverwacht /ɔnvərwɑχt/ (adj, adv) unexpected, surprise: *dat soort dingen gebeurt altijd ~* that sort of thing always happens when you least expect it
onverwachts /ɔnvərwɑχts/ (adj, adv) unexpected, sudden, surprise
onverwarmd /ɔnvərwɑrmt/ (adj) unheated
onverwoestbaar /ɔnvərwˠstbar/ (adj) indestructible; tough; durable
onverzadigbaar /ɔnvərzadəɣbar/ (adj) insatiable
onverzadigd /ɔnvərzadəχt/ (adj) **1** insatiate(d) **2** unsaturated
onverzekerd /ɔnvərzekərt/ (adj) uninsured; uncovered
onverzettelijk /ɔnvərzɛtələk/ (adj, adv) unbending, intransigent
onverzoenlijk /ɔnvərzunlək/ (adj, adv) irreconcilable
onverzorgd /ɔnvərzɔrχt/ (adj) careless, untidy; uncared-for; untended: *zij ziet er ~ uit* she neglects her appearance
onvindbaar /ɔnvˠndbar/ (adj) untraceable; not to be found
onvoldaan /ɔnvɔldan/ (adj) **1** unpaid **2** unsatisfied
de ¹**onvoldoende** /ɔnvɔldundə/ (pl: -s) unsatisfactory mark; [Am] unsatisfactory grade; fail: *een ~ halen* fail (an exam, a test); *hij had twee ~s* he had two unsatisfactory marks
²**onvoldoende** /ɔnvɔldundə/ (adj, adv) insufficient, unsatisfactory: *een ~ hoeveelheid* an insufficient amount
onvolkomen /ɔnvɔlkomə(n)/ (adj) imperfect
onvolledig /ɔnvɔledəχ/ (adj, adv) incomplete
onvolprezen /ɔnvɔlprezə(n)/ (adj) unsurpassed
onvoltooid /ɔnvɔltɔjt/ (adj) unfinished: *~ verleden tijd* simple past (tense), imperfect (tense)
onvolwassen /ɔnvɔlwɑsə(n)/ (adj) immature: *~ reageren* react in an adolescent way
¹**onvoorbereid** /ɔnvorbərɛit/ (adj) unprepared
²**onvoorbereid** /ɔnvorbərɛit/ (adv) unaware(s), by surprise

onvoordelig /ɔnvordḙləχ/ (adj, adv) unprofitable, uneconomic(al): *~ uit zijn* pay too high a price
onvoorspelbaar /ɔnvorspɛlbar/ (adj, adv) unpredictable
onvoorstelbaar /ɔnvorstɛlbar/ (adj) inconceivable, unimaginable, unthinkable: *het is ~!* it's unbelievable!, it's incredible!
onvoorwaardelijk /ɔnvorwardələk/ (adj, adv) unconditional, unquestioning: *~e straf* non-suspended sentence
onvoorzichtig /ɔnvorzɪχtəχ/ (adj, adv) careless; [stronger] reckless: *je hebt zeer ~ gehandeld* you have acted most imprudently
de **onvoorzichtigheid** /ɔnvorzɪχtəχhɛit/ (pl: -heden) carelessness; [stronger] recklessness; lack of caution
¹**onvoorzien** /ɔnvorzin/ (adj) unforeseen: *~e uitgaven* incidental expenditure(s)
²**onvoorzien** /ɔnvorzin/ (adv) accidentally
de **onvrede** /ɔnvredə/ dissatisfaction (with)
onvriendelijk /ɔnvrɪndələk/ (adj, adv) unfriendly, hostile
onvrij /ɔnvrɛi/ (adj) unfree
onvrijwillig /ɔnvrɛiwɪləχ/ (adj, adv) involuntary
onvruchtbaar /ɔnvrˠχtbar/ (adj) infertile, barren
de **onvruchtbaarheid** /ɔnvrˠχ(t)barhɛit/ infertility
onwaar /ɔnwar/ (adj) untrue, false
onwaardig /ɔnwardəχ/ (adj) unworthy (of)
onwaarschijnlijk /ɔnwarsχɛinlək/ (adj) unlikely, improbable: *het is hoogst ~ dat* it is most (or: highly) unlikely that
de **onwaarschijnlijkheid** /ɔnwarsχɛinləkhɛit/ (pl: -heden) improbability, unlikelihood
het **onweer** /ɔnwer/ (pl: onweren) thunderstorm: *we krijgen ~* we're going to have a thunderstorm
onweerlegbaar /ɔnwerlɛɣbar/ (adj, adv) irrefutable
de **onweersbui** /ɔnwerzbœy/ (pl: -en) thunder(y) shower
onweerstaanbaar /ɔnwerstambar/ (adj, adv) irresistible, compelling
onwel /ɔnwɛl/ (adj) unwell, ill, indisposed
onwelkom /ɔnwɛlkɔm/ (adj) unwelcome
onwennig /ɔnwɛnəχ/ (adj) unaccustomed, ill at ease: *zij staat er nog wat ~ tegenover* she has not quite got used to the idea
onweren /ɔnwerə(n)/ (onweerde, heeft geonweerd) thunder: *het heeft geonweerd* there has been a thunderstorm
onwerkbaar /ɔnwɛrgbar/ (adj) unworkable: *een onwerkbare situatie* an impossible situation
onwerkelijk /ɔnwɛrkələk/ (adj) unreal
onwetend /ɔnwetənt/ (adj) **1** ignorant **2** unaware
de **onwetendheid** /ɔnwetənthɛit/ ignorance:

uit (or: *door*) ~ out of (*or:* through) ignorance

onwetenschappelijk /ɔnwetənsχɑpələk/ (adj, adv) unscientific, unscholarly

onwettig /ɔnwɛtəχ/ (adj, adv) **1** illegal; illicit; unlawful **2** illegitimate

onwezenlijk /ɔnweːzə(n)lək/ (adj) unreal

onwijs /ɔnwɛis/ (adv) awfully, fabulously, terrifically, ever so: ~ *gaaf* brill; ~ *hard werken* work like mad (*or:* crazy)

de **onwil** /ɔnwɪl/ unwillingness: *uit pure* ~ out of sheer stubbornness; *[Am]* out of sheer bloody-mindedness

onwillekeurig /ɔnwɪləkøːrəχ/ (adj) **1** involuntary **2** inadvertently, unconsciously || ~ *lachte hij* he laughed in spite of himself

onwillig /ɔnwɪləχ/ (adj, adv) unwilling

onwrikbaar /ɔnvrɪɡbaːr/ (adj, adv) irrefutable

onzalig /ɔnzaːləχ/ (adj, adv) unlucky: *wie kwam er op die* ~*e gedachte?* whose silly idea was it?

onzedelijk /ɔnzeːdələk/ (adj, adv) indecent, obscene

de **onzedelijkheid** /ɔnzeːdələkhɛit/ immorality, indecency, immodesty

onzeker /ɔnzeːkər/ (adj, adv) **1** insecure, unsure **2** uncertain, unsure; precarious: *het aantal gewonden is nog* ~ the number of injured is not yet known; *hij nam het zekere voor het* ~*e* he decided to play safe

de **onzekerheid** /ɔnzeːkərhɛit/ (pl: -heden) uncertainty, doubt: *in* ~ *laten* (or: *verkeren*) keep (*or:* be) in a state of suspense

onzelfstandig /ɔnzɛlfstɑndəχ/ (adj) dependent (on others)

Onze-Lieve-Heer /ɔnzəliːvəheːr/ Our Lord, (the good) God

Onze-Lieve-Vrouw /ɔnzəliːvəvrɑu/ Our Lady

het **onzevader** /ɔnzəvaːdər/ (pl: -s) Lord's Prayer: *het* ~ *bidden* say the Lord's Prayer

onzichtbaar /ɔnzɪχtbaːr/ (adj) invisible

onzijdig /ɔnzɛidəχ/ (adj) neutral

de **onzin** /ɔnzɪn/ nonsense: *klinkklare* ~ utter nonsense; ~ *verkopen* talk nonsense

onzindelijk /ɔnzɪndələk/ (adj, adv) not toilet-trained

onzinnig /ɔnzɪnəχ/ (adj, adv) absurd, senseless; nonsensical

onzorgvuldig /ɔnzɔrχfʏldəχ/ (adj, adv) careless, negligent

¹**onzuiver** /ɔnzœyvər/ (adj) **1** impure **2** gross **3** inaccurate, imperfect

²**onzuiver** /ɔnzœyvər/ (adv) out of tune

het **oog** /oːχ/ (pl: ogen) **1** eye: *een blauw* ~ a black eye; *dan kun je het met je eigen ogen zien* then you can see for yourself; *goede ogen hebben* have good eyesight; *geen* ~ *dichtdoen* not sleep a wink; *zijn ogen geloven* (or: *vertrouwen*) believe (*or:* trust) one's

eyes; *hij had alleen* ~ *voor haar* he only had eyes for her; *aan één* ~ *blind* blind in one eye; *iem. iets onder vier ogen zeggen* say sth. to s.o. in private; *goed uit zijn ogen kijken* keep one's eyes open; *kun je niet uit je ogen kijken?* can't you look where you're going?; *zijn ogen de kost geven* take it all in; ~ *om* ~, *tand om tand* an eye for an eye, a tooth for a tooth **2** look, glance, eye: *zij kon haar ogen niet van hem afhouden* she couldn't take (*or:* keep) her eyes off him; *(zo) op het* ~ on the face of it; *iem. op het* ~ *hebben* have s.o. in mind, have one's eye on s.o.; *wat mij voor ogen staat* what I have in mind **3** view, eye: *zo ver het* ~ *reikt* as far as the eye can see; *in het* ~ *lopend* conspicuous, noticeable; *iets uit het* ~ *verliezen* lose sight of sth.; *uit het* ~, *uit het hart* out of sight, out of mind || *in mijn ogen* in my opinion (*or:* view); *met het* ~ *op* with a view to; in view of

de **oogappel** /oːχɑpəl/ (pl: -s) apple of one's eye: *hij was zijn moeders* ~ he was the apple of his mother's eye

de **oogarts** /oːχɑrts/ (pl: -en) ophthalmologist, eye specialist

de **oogbol** /oːχbɔl/ (pl: -len) eyeball

de **ooggetuige** /oːχətœyɣə/ (pl: -n) eyewitness

het **ooggetuigenverslag** /oːχətœyɣə(n)vərslɑχ/ (pl: -en) eyewitness report

de **ooghoek** /oːχhuk/ (pl: -en) corner of the eye

de **ooghoogte** /oːχhoːχtə/ eye level

het **oogje** /oːχjə/ (pl: -s) **1** eye: *een* ~ *dichtknijpen* (or: *dichtdoen*) close (*or:* shut) one's eyes (to) **2** glance, look, peep: *een* ~ *in het zeil houden* keep a lookout || *een* ~ *hebben op* have one's eye on

de **oogklep** /oːχklɛp/ (pl: -pen) blinker; *[Am]* blinder; *[fig]* ~*pen voor hebben* be blind to, be blinkered

het **ooglid** /oːχlɪt/ (pl: oogleden) (eye)lid

oogluikend /oːχlœykənt/ (adj): *iets* ~ *toelaten (toestaan)* turn a blind eye to sth.

het **oogmerk** /oːχmɛrk/ (pl: -en): *met het* ~ *om* with a view to, with the object (*or:* intention) of

de **oogopslag** /oːχɔpslɑχ/ glance, look, glimpse

het **oogpunt** /oːχpʏnt/ (pl: -en) viewpoint, point of view

de **oogschaduw** /oːχsχaduw/ eyeshadow

de **oogst** /oːχst/ (pl: -en) **1** harvesting, reaping **2** harvest, crop: *de* ~ *binnenhalen* bring in the harvest

oogsten /oːχstə(n)/ (oogstte, heeft geoogst) harvest; pick

oogstrelend /oːχstreːlənt/ (adj) delightful

de **oogsttijd** /oːχstɛit/ (pl: -en) harvest(ing) time

oogverblindend /oːχfərblɪndənt/ (adj) blinding, dazzling: *een* ~*e schoonheid* a raving beauty

de **oogwenk** /oːχwɛŋk/ (pl: -en) moment, instant

de **oogwimper** /oxwɪmpər/ (pl: -s) (eye)lash

het **oogwit** /oxwɪt/ white of the eye

de **ooi** /oj/ (pl: -en) ewe

de **ooievaar** /ojəvar/ (pl: -s) stork

ooit /ojt/ (adv) ever, at any time: *Jan, die ~ een vriend van me was* John, who was once a friend of mine; *groter dan ~ tevoren* bigger than ever (before); *de beste prestatie ~* the best-ever performance

ook /ok/ (adv) **1** also, too: *zijn er ~ brieven?* are there any letters?; *morgen kan ~ nog* tomorrow will be all right too; *ik hou van tennis en hij ~* I like tennis and so does he; *ik ben er ~ nog* I'm here too; *hij kookte en heelgoed ~* he did the cooking and very well too; *hij heeft niet gewacht, en ik trouwens ~ niet* he didn't wait and neither did I; *zo vreselijk moeilijk is het nu ~ weer niet* it's not all that difficult (after all); *dat hebben we ~ weer gehad* so much for that, that's over and done with; *opa praatte ~ zo* grandpa used to talk like that (too); *dat is waar ~!* that's true, of course!; oh, I almost forgot! **2** even: *~ al is hij niet rijk* even though he's not rich **3** anyhow, anyway: *hoe jong ik ~ ben ...* (as) young as I may be (*or:* am) ...; *hoe het ~ zij,* laten we nu maar gaan anyway, let's go now; *wat je ~ doet* whatever you do; *wie (dan) ~* whoever; *hoe zeer zij zich ~ inspande* however she tried **4** again, too: *dat gezanik ~* all that fuss (too); *jij hebt ~ nooit tijd!* you never have any time!; *hoe heet hij ~ weer?* what was his name again?

de **oom** /om/ (pl: -s) uncle

het **oor** /or/ (pl: oren) **1** ear: *met een half ~ mee-luisteren* listen with only an ear; *dat gaat het ene ~ in,* het andere uit it goes (at) in one ear and out (at) the other; *zijn oren (niet) geloven* (not) believe one's ears; *een en al ~ zijn* be all ears; [Belg] *op zijn beide* (*or:* twee) *oren slapen* have no worries, sleep the sleep of the just; *doof aan één ~* deaf in one ear; *gaatjes in de oren hebben* have pierced ears; *iets in de oren knopen* get sth. into one's head; *ik stond wel even met mijn oren te klapperen* I couldn't believe my ears (*or:* what I was hearing); *iem. met iets om de oren slaan* blow s.o. up over sth.; *tot over de oren verliefd zijn* be head over heels in love; [fig] *het zit tussen je oren* it's all in your head **2** handle, ear ‖ *iem. een ~ aan-naaien* fool s.o., take s.o. for a ride

de **oorarts** /orarts/ (pl: -en) otologist, ear specialist

de **oorbel** /orbɛl/ (pl: -len) earring

het **oord** /ort/ (pl: -en) region, place; resort

het **oordeel** /ordel/ (pl: oordelen) judg(e)ment; verdict; sentence

oordelen /ordələ(n)/ (oordeelde, heeft geoordeeld) **1** judge, pass judgement; sentence **2** judge, make up one's mind

het **oordopje** /ordɔpjə/ (pl: -s) **1** earplug **2** earphone

de **oordruppels** /ordrʏpəls/ (pl) eardrops

de **oorkonde** /orkɔndə/ (pl: -n) document, charter, deed

de **oorlel** /orlɛl/ (pl: -len) lobe (of the ear)

de **oorlog** /orlɔx/ (pl: -en) war: *het is ~* there's a war on; *de ~ verklaren aan* declare war on; *~ voeren* wage war

de **oorlogsheld** /orlɔxshɛlt/ (pl: -en) war hero

de **oorlogsmisdadiger** /orlɔxsmɪzdadəɣər/ (pl: -s) war criminal

het **oorlogspad** /orlɔxspat/: *op het ~ zijn* be on the warpath

het **oorlogsschip** /orlɔxsxɪp/ (pl: -schepen) warship

de **oorlogssterkte** /orlɔxstɛrktə/: *op ~* at fighting strength

de **oorlogsverklaring** /orlɔxsfərklarɪŋ/ (pl: -en) declaration of war

oorlogszuchtig /orlɔxsʏxtəx/ (adj, adv) warlike, war-minded

de **oorlogvoering** /orlɔxfurɪŋ/ conduct (*or:* waging) of the war, warfare

oormerken /ormɛrkə(n)/ (oormerkte, heeft geoormerkt) earmark

de **oorontsteking** /orɔntstekɪŋ/ (pl: -en) inflammation of the ear

de **oorpijn** /orpɛin/ (pl: -en) earache

de **oorring** /orɪŋ/ (pl: -en) earring

de **oorschelp** /orsxɛlp/ (pl: -en) auricle

het/de **oorsmeer** /orsmer/ ear wax

de **oorsprong** /orsprɔŋ/ (pl: -en) origin, source: *van ~* originally

[1] **oorspronkelijk** /orsprɔŋkələk/ (adj) original, innovative: *een ~ kunstenaar* an original (*or:* innovative) artist

[2] **oorspronkelijk** /orsprɔŋkələk/ (adv) originally, initially

de **oorspronkelijkheid** /orsprɔŋkələkhɛit/ originality

het **oortje** /orcə/ earphone

oorverdovend /orvərdovənt/ (adj, adv) deafening

de **oorvijg** /orvɛix/ (pl: -en) box on the ear

de **oorworm** /orwɔrm/ earwig

de **oorzaak** /orzak/ (pl: oorzaken) cause, origin: *~ en gevolg* cause and effect

oorzakelijk /orzakələk/ (adj): *~ verband* causal connection, causality

oost /ost/ (adj) east: *~ west, thuis best* east, west, home's best

het **Oostblok** /ostblɔk/ Eastern bloc

Oost-Duitsland /ostdœytslant/ East Germany; German Democratic Republic

oostelijk /ostələk/ (adj, adv) **1** eastern **2** [to the east] easterly; eastward; [from the east] easter(ly) [wind]: *een ~e wind* an easterly wind

het **oosten** /ostə(n)/ east: *ten ~ van* (to the) east of; *het ~ van Frankrijk* eastern France

opdraaien

Oostende /ostɛndə/ Ostend
Oostenrijk /ostə(n)rɛik/ Austria
de **Oostenrijker** /ostə(n)rɛikər/ (pl: -s) Austrian
Oostenrijks /ostə(n)rɛiks/ (adj) Austrian
de **oostenwind** /ostə(n)wɪnt/ (pl: -en) east wind, easterly
de **oosterburen** /ostərbyrə(n)/ (pl) neighbours to the east
de **oosterlengte** /ostərlɛŋtə/ eastern longitude
oosters /ostərs/ (adj) oriental
Oost-Europa /ostøropa/ Eastern Europe
Oost-Europees /ostøropes/ (adj) East European
Oost-Indisch /ostɪndis/ (adj, adv) East Indian ‖ ~ *doof zijn* pretend not to hear
de **oostkust** /ostkʏst/ (pl: -en) east(ern) coast
oostwaarts /ostwarts/ (adv) eastward
de **Oostzee** /ostse/ Baltic (Sea)
het **ootje** /ocə/: *iem. in het ~ nemen* take s.o. for a ride, pull s.o.'s leg
ootmoedig /otmudəx/ (adj, adv) humble
¹**op** /ɔp/ (adj) used up, gone: *het geld* (or: *mijn geduld*) *is op* the money (or: my patience) has run out; *hij is op van de zenuwen* he is a nervous wreck
²**op** /ɔp/ (adv) up: *trap op en trap af* up and down the stairs; *de straat op en neer lopen* walk up and down the street; *zij had een nieuwe hoed op* she had a new hat on
³**op** /ɔp/ (prep) **1** in, on, at: *op een motor rijden* ride a motorcycle; *op de hoek wonen* live on the corner; *later op de dag* later in the day; *op negenjarige leeftijd* at the age of nine; *op maandag* (on) Monday; *op een maandag* on a Monday; *op vakantie* on holiday; *op zijn vroegst* at the earliest; *op haar eigen manier* in her own way; *op zijn minst* at (the very) least; *op zijn snelst* at the quickest **2** in, to: *op de eerste plaats* in the first place, first(ly); in first place; *de auto loopt 1 op 8* the car does 8 km to the litre; *één op de duizend* one in a thousand; *op één na de laatste* the last but one
de **opa** /opa/ (pl: -'s) grandpa, grandad
de ¹**opaal** /opal/ (pl: opalen) [stone] opal
het ²**opaal** /opal/ [mineral] opal
opbaren /obarə(n)/ (baarde op, heeft opgebaard) place on a bier: *opgebaard liggen* lie in state
opbellen /obɛlə(n)/ (belde op, heeft opgebeld) (tele)phone, call, ring (up): *ik zal je nog wel even ~* I'll give you a call (or: ring)
opbergen /obɛrɣə(n)/ (borg op, heeft opgeborgen) put away, store; file (away)
opbeuren /obørə(n)/ (beurde op, heeft opgebeurd) cheer up
opbiechten /obixtə(n)/ (biechtte op, heeft opgebiecht) confess: *alles eerlijk ~* make a clean breast of it

opbieden /obidə(n)/ (bood op, heeft opgeboden): *tegen iem. ~ bid against s.o.
opblaasbaar /oblazbar/ (adj) inflatable
de **opblaasboot** /oblazbot/ (pl: -boten) inflatable boat
opblazen /oblazə(n)/ (blies op, heeft opgeblazen) blow up, inflate
opblijven /oblɛivə(n)/ (bleef op, is opgebleven) stay up
opbloeien /oblujə(n)/ (bloeide op, is opgebloeid) **1** bloom **2** flourish, prosper
het **opbod** /obɔt/: *iets bij ~ verkopen* sell sth. by auction
opboksen /obɔksə(n)/ (bokste op, heeft opgebokst) compete
opborrelen /obɔrələ(n)/ (borrelde op, is opgeborreld) bubble up
de **opbouw** /obau/ **1** construction **2** structure
opbouwen /obauwə(n)/ (bouwde op, heeft opgebouwd) build up, set up: *het weefsel is uit cellen opgebouwd* the tissue is made up (or: composed) of cells
opbouwend /obauwənt/ (adj) constructive
opbranden /obrandə(n)/ (brandde op, is opgebrand) be burned up (or: down)
opbreken /obrekə(n)/ (brak op, heeft opgebroken) **1** break up, take down (or: apart) **2** break up, tear up: *de straat ~ dig* (or: break) up the street
opbrengen /obrɛŋə(n)/ (bracht op, heeft opgebracht) **1** bring in, yield **2** work up: *begrip* (or: *belangstelling*) *~ voor* show understanding for (or: an interest in) **3** apply
de **opbrengst** /obrɛŋst/ (pl: -en) yield, profit; revenue
opdagen /obdaɣə(n)/ (daagde op, is opgedaagd) turn up, show up
opdat /obdɑt/ (conj) so that
opdienen /obdinə(n)/ (diende op, heeft opgediend) serve (up), dish up
opdiepen /obdipə(n)/ (diepte op, heeft opgediept) dig up
zich **opdirken** /obdɪrkə(n)/ (dirkte zich op, heeft zich opgedirkt) [inform] doll (or: jazz) o.s. up
opdissen /obdɪsə(n)/ (diste op, heeft opgedist) serve up, dish up
opdoeken /obdukə(n)/ (doekte op, heeft opgedoekt) shut down
opdoemen /obdumə(n)/ (doemde op, is opgedoemd) loom (up), appear
opdoen /obdun/ (deed op, heeft opgedaan) **1** gain, get: *kennis ~* acquire knowledge; *inspiratie ~* gain inspiration **2** apply, put on
zich **opdoffen** /obdɔfə(n)/ (dofte zich op, heeft zich opgedoft) doll o.s. up
de **opdoffer** /obdɔfər/ (pl: -s) **1** punch **2** setback
de **opdonder** /obdɔndər/ (pl: -s) punch
opdonderen /obdɔndərə(n)/ (donderde op, is opgedonderd) get lost
opdraaien /obdrajə(n)/ (draaide op, heeft/

is opgedraaid): *ik wil **hier** niet **voor** ~* I don't want to take any blame for this; *voor de kosten ~* foot the bill; *iem. **voor** iets laten ~ land* (*or:* saddle) s.o. with sth.

de **opdracht** /ˈɔbdrɑχt/ (pl: -en) assignment, order: *we **kregen** ~ om …* we were told to …, given orders to …

de **opdrachtgever** /ˈɔbdrɑχtχevər/ (pl: -s) client, customer

opdragen /ˈɔbdraɣə(n)/ (droeg op, heeft opgedragen) charge, commission, assign

opdraven /ˈɔbdravə(n)/ (draafde op, is opgedraafd) show up, put in an appearance

opdreunen /ˈɔbdrønə(n)/ (dreunde op, heeft opgedreund) rattle off, reel off, drone

opdrijven /ˈɔbdrɛivə(n)/ (dreef op, heeft opgedreven) force up, drive up

¹**opdringen** /ˈɔbdrɪŋə(n)/ (drong op, is opgedrongen) push forward, press forward; press on, push on

²**opdringen** /ˈɔbdrɪŋə(n)/ (drong op, heeft opgedrongen) force on, press on; intrude on, impose on: *dat werd **ons** opgedrongen* that was forced on us

zich ³**opdringen** /ˈɔbdrɪŋə(n)/ (drong zich op, heeft zich opgedrongen) force o.s. on, impose o.s. (on), impose one's company (on): *ik **wil** me niet ~* I don't want to intrude

opdringerig /ˈɔbdrɪŋərəχ/ (adj, adv) obtrusive; pushy: *~e **reclameboodschappen*** aggressive advertising

opdrinken /ˈɔbdrɪŋkə(n)/ (dronk op, heeft opgedronken) drink (up)

opdrogen /ˈɔbdroɣə(n)/ (droogde op, is opgedroogd) dry (up); run dry

de **opdruk** /ˈɔbdrʏk/ (pl: -ken) (im)print

opdrukken /ˈɔbdrʏkə(n)/ (drukte op, heeft opgedrukt) **1** print on(to), impress on(to); stamp on(to) **2** push up, press up: *zich ~ do* press-ups

opduikelen /ˈɔbdœykələ(n)/ (duikelde op, heeft opgeduikeld) dig up

opduiken /ˈɔbdœykə(n)/ (dook op, is opgedoken) **1** surface, rise (*or:* come) to the surface **2** turn up

opduwen /ˈɔbdywə(n)/ (duwde op, heeft opgeduwd) push up, press up

opdweilen /ˈɔbdwɛilə(n)/ (dweilde op, heeft opgedweild) mop up

opeen /ɔˈpen/ (adv) together

opeens /ɔˈpens/ (adv) suddenly, all at once, all of a sudden

de **opeenstapeling** /ɔˈpenstapəlɪŋ/ (pl: -en) accumulation, build-up

opeenvolgend /ɔpenˈvɔlɣənt/ (adj) successive, consecutive

de **opeenvolging** /ɔˈpenvɔlɣɪŋ/ (pl: -en) succession

opeisen /ˈɔpɛisə(n)/ (eiste op, heeft opgeëist) claim, demand: *de **aandacht** ~* demand (*or:* compel) attention; *een **aanslag** ~*

claim responsibility for an attack

open /ˈopə(n)/ (adj, adv) open; unlocked; vacant: *de **deur** staat ~* the door is ajar (*or:* open); *met ~ **ogen*** with one's eyes open; *een ~ **plek** in het bos* a clearing in the woods; *tot hoe laat zijn de **winkels** ~?* what time do the shops close?; *~ en **bloot*** openly, for all (the world) to see

openbaar /ˈopə(n)bar/ (adj, adv) public, open: *de openbare **orde** verstoren* disturb the peace ‖ *in het ~* in public, publicly

de **openbaarheid** /opə(n)ˈbarhɛit/ publicity

de **openbaarmaking** /opə(n)ˈbarmakɪŋ/ publication, disclosure

¹**openbaren** /opəmˈbarə(n)/ (openbaarde, heeft geopenbaard) reveal

zich ²**openbaren** /opəmˈbarə(n)/ (openbaarde zich, heeft zich geopenbaard) manifest o.s.

de **openbaring** /opə(n)ˈbarɪŋ/ (pl: -en) revelation

openbarsten /ˈopə(n)bɑrstə(n)/ (barstte open, is opengebarsten) burst open

openbreken /ˈopə(n)brekə(n)/ (brak open, heeft opengebroken) break (open), force open, prise open: *een **slot** ~* force a lock

de **opendeurdag** /ˈopə(n)dørdɑχ/ (pl: -en) [Belg] open day

¹**opendoen** /ˈopə(n)dun/ (deed open, heeft opengedaan) open the door; answer the door (*or:* bell, ring): *er werd **niet** opengedaan* there was no answer

²**opendoen** /ˈopə(n)dun/ (deed open, heeft opengedaan) open

opendraaien /ˈopə(n)drajə(n)/ (draaide open, heeft opengedraaid) open; turn on; unscrew

openduwen /ˈopə(n)dywə(n)/ (duwde open, heeft opengeduwd) push open

¹**openen** /ˈopənə(n)/ (opende, heeft geopend) open, begin: [cards] *met schoppen ~* lead spades

²**openen** /ˈopənə(n)/ (opende, heeft geopend) **1** open; turn on; unscrew: *een **bestand** ~* open a file, get into a file **2** open, start

de **opener** /ˈopənər/ (pl: -s) opener

opengaan /ˈopə(n)ɣan/ (ging open, is opengegaan) open

openhalen /ˈopə(n)halə(n)/ (haalde open, heeft opengehaald) tear: *ik heb mijn jas opengehaald **aan** een spijker* I tore my coat on a nail

openhartig /opənˈhɑrtəχ/ (adj, adv) frank, candid; straightforward: *een ~ **gesprek*** a heart-to-heart (talk)

de **openhartigheid** /opə(n)ˈhɑrtəχhɛit/ frankness, candour

de **openheid** /ˈopənhɛit/ openness, sincerity: *in alle ~* in all candour

openhouden /ˈopə(n)hɑudə(n)/ (hield open, heeft opengehouden) keep open: *de*

deur *voor iem.* ~ hold the door (open) for s.o.

de **opening** /opənɪŋ/ (pl: -en) opening; gap

de **openingsplechtigheid** /opənɪŋsplɛxtəx‑hɛit/ (pl: -heden) opening ceremony, inauguration

openlaten /opə(n)latə(n)/ (liet open, heeft opengelaten) **1** leave open; leave on, leave running **2** leave blank; leave open

openlijk /opə(n)lək/ (adj, adv) **1** open, overt: ~ *voor iets* **uitkomen** openly admit sth. **2** public: *iets* ~ **verkondigen** declare sth. in public

de **openlucht** /opə(n)lʏxt/ open air: **in** *de* ~ *slapen* sleep in the open air

het **openluchtmuseum** /opə(n)lʏxtmyzejʏm/ (pl: -musea) open-air museum, historical village

het **openluchttheater** /opə(n)lʏxtejatər/ (pl: -s) open-air theatre

openmaken /opə(n)makə(n)/ (maakte open, heeft opengemaakt) open (up)

openslaan /opə(n)slan/ (sloeg open, heeft opengeslagen) open

openslaand /opə(n)slant/ (adj): *~e* **deuren** double doors

opensnijden /opə(n)snɛidə(n)/ (sneed open, heeft opengesneden) cut (open)

openstaan /opə(n)stan/ (stond open, heeft opengestaan) be open; be unlocked: *mijn* **huis** *staat altijd voor jou open* my door will always be open to (or: for) you; *de* **kraan** *staat open* the tap is on (or: is running)

openstellen /opə(n)stɛlə(n)/ (stelde open, heeft opengesteld) open

opentrekken /opə(n)trɛkə(n)/ (trok open, heeft opengetrokken) pull open, open: *een grote* **bek** ~ open one's big mouth

openvallen /opə(n)valə(n)/ (viel open, is opengevallen) fall open, drop open

openvouwen /opə(n)vɑuwə(n)/ (vouwde open, heeft opengevouwen) unfold, open (out)

openzetten /opə(n)zɛtə(n)/ (zette open, heeft opengezet) open; turn on

de **opera** /opera/ (pl: -'s) opera

de **operatie** /opera(t)si/ (pl: -s) operation, surgery: *een grote* (or: *kleine*) ~ **ondergaan** undergo major (or: minor) surgery

operatief /operatif/ (adj, adv) surgical, operative

de **operatiekamer** /opera(t)sikamər/ (pl: -s) operating room

de **operatietafel** /opera(t)sitafəl/ (pl: -s) operating table

operationeel /opera(t)ʃonel/ (adj) operational; in running (or: working) order

opereren /opererə(n)/ (opereerde, heeft geopereerd) **1** work; use **2** operate, perform surgery (or: an operation): *iem.* ~ operate on s.o.; *zij is geopereerd* **aan** *de longen* she has had an operation on the lungs

de **operette** /opərɛtə/ (pl: -s) light opera

opeten /opetə(n)/ (at op, heeft opgegeten) eat (up), finish

opfleuren /opflørə(n)/ (fleurde op, heeft/is opgefleurd) cheer up, brighten up

opflikkeren /opflɪkərə(n)/ (flikkerde op, is opgeflikkerd) flare up, flicker

opfokken /opfɔkə(n)/ (fokte op, heeft opgefokt) work up, whip up, stir up

opfrissen /opfrɪsə(n)/ (friste op, heeft/is opgefrist) freshen (up): *zijn* **Engels** ~ brush up (on) one's English; *zich* ~ freshen up; [Am] wash up

opgaan /opxan/ (ging op, is opgegaan) **1** go up; climb **2** come up, rise **3** go, be finished **4** hold good (or: true), apply: *dit gaat niet op* **voor** *arme mensen* this doesn't apply to (or: this is not true of) poor people ‖ *als het die kant opgaat* **met** *de maatschappij dan ...* if that is the way society is going ...

opgaand /opxant/ (adj) rising

de **opgang** /opxɑŋ/ (pl: -en): ~ **maken** catch on, take (on)

de **opgave** /opxavə/ (pl: -n) **1** statement, specification: *zonder* ~ *van redenen* without reason given **2** question: *schriftelijke ~n* written assignments **3** task, assignment

opgeblazen /opxəblazə(n)/ (adj) puffy, bloated, swollen

opgebrand /opxəbrɑnt/ (adj) burnt-out, worn-out

opgefokt /opxəfɔkt/ (adj) worked up

opgeilen /opxɛilə(n)/ (geilde op, heeft opgegeild) [inform] turn on

opgelaten /opxəlatə(n)/ (adj) embarrassed

het **opgeld** /opxɛlt/ (pl: -en): ~ **doen** catch on, take (on)

opgelucht /opxəlʏxt/ (adj) relieved: ~ **ademhalen** heave a sigh of relief

opgeruimd /opxərœymt/ (adj) tidy, neat: ~ *staat netjes* good riddance (to bad rubbish)

opgescheept /opxəsxept/ (adj): *met iem. (iets)* ~ *zitten* be stuck with s.o. (sth.)

opgeschoten /opxəsxotə(n)/ (adj) lanky

opgetogen /opxətoxə(n)/ (adj) delighted, overjoyed

opgeven /opxevə(n)/ (gaf op, heeft opgegeven) **1** give up, abandon: *(het)* **niet** ~ not give in (or: up), hang on; *je moet* **nooit (niet** *te gauw)* ~ never say die **2** give, state: *zijn* **inkomsten** ~ *aan de belasting* declare one's income to the tax inspector; *als reden* ~ give (or: state) as one's reason **3** give, assign **4** enter: *zich* ~ **voor** *een cursus* enrol (or: sign up) for a course; *als vermist* ~ report (as) missing **5** give (up), surrender

opgewassen /opxəwasə(n)/ (adj) equal (to); up (to): *hij bleek niet* ~ **tegen** *die taak* the task proved beyond him (or: too much for him)

opgewekt /opxəwɛkt/ (adj, adv) cheerful,

good-humoured: *hij is altijd heel ~* he is always in good spirits (*or*: bright and breezy)

opgewonden /ɔpxəwɔndə(n)/ (adj, adv) **1** excited **2** agitated, in a fluster

opgezet /ɔpxəzɛt/ (adj) **1** swollen, bloated **2** [Belg] happy, content: *~ zijn met iets* be pleased about sth.

opgooien /ɔpxojə(n)/ (gooide op, heeft opgegooid) throw up, toss up

opgraven /ɔpxravə(n)/ (groef op, heeft opgegraven) dig up, unearth; excavate; exhume

de **opgraving** /ɔpxravɪŋ/ (pl: -en) **1** dig(ging); excavation; exhumation: *~en vonden plaats in ...* excavations were carried out in ... **2** excavation, dig, (archaeological) site

opgroeien /ɔpxrujə(n)/ (groeide op, is opgegroeid) grow (up)

de **ophaalbrug** /ɔphalbrʏx/ (pl: -gen) lift bridge, drawbridge

de **ophaaldienst** /ɔphaldinst/ (pl: -en) collecting service, collection service

ophalen /ɔphalə(n)/ (haalde op, heeft opgehaald) **1** raise, draw up, pull up; hoist **2** collect: *een bestand ~* download a file; *vuilnis ~* collect refuse (*or*: rubbish); [Am] collect garbage, *kom je me vanavond ~?* are you coming round for me tonight? **3** bring up, bring back, recall: *herinneringen ~ aan de goede oude tijd* reminisce about the good old days **4** collect **5** brush up (on), polish up: *rapportcijfers ~* improve on one's (report) marks

ophanden /ɔphɑndə(n)/: *~ zijn* be imminent, be close at hand, be approaching

¹**ophangen** /ɔphɑŋə(n)/ (hing op, heeft opgehangen) hang up, ring off

²**ophangen** /ɔphɑŋə(n)/ (hing op, heeft opgehangen) hang (up); post: *de was ~* hang out the wash(ing) ‖ *zich ~* hang o.s.

ophebben /ɔphɛbə(n)/ (had op, heeft opgehad) **1** wear, have on **2** have finished, have had

de **ophef** /ɔphɛf/ fuss, noise, song (and dance): *~ maken over iets* kick up (*or*: make a fuss) about sth.; *zonder veel ~* without much ado

opheffen /ɔphɛfə(n)/ (hief op, heeft opgeheven) **1** raise, lift: *met opgeheven hoofd* with (one's) head held high **2** cancel (out), neutralize: *het effect ~ van iets* counteract sth. **3** remove; discontinue: *de club werd na een paar maanden opgeheven* the club was disbanded after a couple of months

de **opheffingsuitverkoop** /ɔphɛfɪŋsœytfərkop/ closing-down sale

ophefmakend /ɔphɛfmakənt/ (adj, adv) [Belg] sensational

ophelderen /ɔphɛldərə(n)/ (helderde op, heeft opgehelderd) clear up, clarify

de **opheldering** /ɔphɛldərɪŋ/ (pl: -en) explanation

ophemelen /ɔphemələ(n)/ (hemelde op, heeft opgehemeld) praise to the skies, extol

ophijsen /ɔphɛisə(n)/ (hees op, heeft opgehesen) pull up, hoist (up); raise

ophitsen /ɔphɪtsə(n)/ (hitste op, heeft opgehitst) **1** egg on, goad: *een hond ~* tease (*or*: bait) a dog; *iem. ~* get s.o.'s hackles up **2** incite, stir up: *de mensen tegen elkaar ~* set people at one another's throats

ophoepelen /ɔphupələ(n)/ (hoepelde op, is opgehoepeld) [inform] get lost, clear (*or*: push, buzz) off

ophogen /ɔphoɣə(n)/ (hoogde op, heeft opgehoogd) raise

ophokken /ɔphɔkə(n)/ (hokte op, heeft opgehokt): *pluimvee ~* keep poultry indoors

zich **ophopen** /ɔphopə(n)/ (hoopte zich op, heeft zich opgehoopt) pile up, accumulate: *de sneeuw heeft zich opgehoopt* the snow has banked up

¹**ophouden** /ɔphɑudə(n)/ (hield op, heeft/is opgehouden) stop; quit; (come to an) end: *de straat hield daar op* the street ended there; *dan houdt alles op* then there's nothing more to be said; *plotseling ~* break off; *ze hield maar niet op met huilen* she (just) went on crying (and crying); *~ met roken* give up (*or*: stop) smoking; *het is opgehouden met regenen* the rain has stopped; *even ~ met werken* have a short break in one's work; *hou op!* stop it!, cut it out!; *laten we erover ~* let's leave it at that

²**ophouden** /ɔphɑudə(n)/ (hield op, heeft opgehouden) **1** hold up, delay; [pers also] keep; [pers also] detain: *iem. niet langer ~* not take up any more of s.o.'s time; *dat houdt de zaak alleen maar op* that just slows things down; *ik werd opgehouden* I was delayed (*or*: held up) **2** keep on ‖ *de schijn ~* keep up appearances, go through the motions

de **opinie** /opini/ (pl: -s) opinion, view

het **opinieblad** /opiniblɑt/ (pl: -en) [roughly] news magazine

de **opiniepeiling** /opinipɛilɪŋ/ (pl: -en) (opinion) poll: *(een) ~(en) houden (over)* canvass opinion (on)

het/de **opium** /opijʏm/ opium

opjagen /ɔpjaɣə(n)/ (jaagde op/joeg op, heeft opgejaagd) hurry, rush; hound

opjutten /ɔpjʏtə(n)/ (jutte op, heeft opgejut) [inform] needle, give (s.o.) the jitters

opkalefateren /ɔpkaləfatərə(n)/ (kalefaterde op, heeft opgekalefaterd) patch (up), doctor (up)

opkijken /ɔpkɛikə(n)/ (keek op, heeft opgekeken) **1** look up: *~ tegen iem.* look up to s.o. **2** sit up, be surprised: *daar kijk ik van op* I'd never have thought it

opkikkeren /ɔpkɪkərə(n)/ (kikkerde op, is opgekikkerd): *daar zal je van ~* it'll pick you up, it'll do you good

het **opklapbed** /ɔpklɑbɛt/ (pl: -den) foldaway bed

opklappen /ɔpklɑpə(n)/ (klapte op, heeft opgeklapt) fold up

opklaren /ɔpklɑrə(n)/ (klaarde op, is opgeklaard) brighten up, clear up: *de lucht klaart op* the sky's clearing up

opklimmen /ɔpklɪmə(n)/ (klom op, is opgeklommen) climb

opkloppen /ɔpklɔpə(n)/ (klopte op, heeft opgeklopt) **1** beat up: *slagroom* ~ whip cream **2** exaggerate

de **opknapbeurt** /ɔpknɑbørt/ (pl: -en) redecoration, facelift

¹**opknappen** /ɔpknɑpə(n)/ (knapte op, is opgeknapt) pick up, revive: *het weer is opgeknapt* the weather has brightened up; *hij zal er erg van* ~ it'll do him all the good in the world

²**opknappen** /ɔpknɑpə(n)/ (knapte op, heeft opgeknapt) **1** tidy up, do up, redecorate; restore: *het dak moet nodig eens opgeknapt worden* the roof needs repairing (*or:* fixing) **2** fix, carry out: *dat zal zij zelf wel* ~ she'll take care of it herself

zich ³**opknappen** /ɔpknɑpə(n)/ (knapte zich op, heeft zich opgeknapt) freshen (o.s.) up

opknopen /ɔpknopə(n)/ (knoopte op, heeft opgeknoopt) string up

opkomen /ɔpkomə(n)/ (kwam op, is opgekomen) **1** come up; rise; come in: *spontaan* (*or: vanzelf*) ~ crop up **2** rise, ascend **3** occur; recur: *het komt niet bij hem op* it doesn't occur to him; *het eerste wat bij je opkomt* the first thing that comes into your mind **4** come on; set in; rise: *ik voel een verkoudheid* (*or: de koorts*) ~ I can feel a cold (*or:* the fever) coming on **5** enter, come on (stage) **6** fight (for), stand up (for): *steeds voor elkaar* ~ stick together || *kom op, we gaan* come on, let's go; *kom maar op als je durft!* come on if you dare!

de **opkomst** /ɔpkɔmst/ **1** rise **2** attendance; turnout **3** entrance **4** rise, boom

opkopen /ɔpkopə(n)/ (kocht op, heeft opgekocht) buy up

opkrabbelen /ɔpkrɑbələ(n)/ (krabbelde op, is opgekrabbeld) struggle up (*or:* to) one's feet

opkrikken /ɔpkrɪkə(n)/ (krikte op, heeft opgekrikt) **1** jack up **2** hype up, pep up: *het moreel* ~ boost morale

opkroppen /ɔpkrɔpə(n)/ (kropte op, heeft opgekropt) bottle up, hold back

opkuisen /ɔpkœysə(n)/ (kuiste op, heeft opgekuist) [Belg] clean (up), tidy (up)

oplaadbaar /ɔplɑdbar/ (adj) rechargeable

oplaaien /ɔplajə(n)/ (laaide op, is opgelaaid) flare (*or:* flame, blaze) up

opladen /ɔplɑdə(n)/ (laadde op, heeft opgeladen) charge

de **oplader** /ɔpladər/ (pl: -s) charger

de **oplage** /ɔplaɣə/ (pl: -n) edition, issue; circulation: *een krant met een grote* ~ a newspaper with a wide circulation

oplappen /ɔplɑpə(n)/ (lapte op, heeft opgelapt) patch up

oplaten /ɔplɑtə(n)/ (liet op, heeft opgelaten) fly; release; launch

de **oplawaai** /ɔplawaj/ (pl: -en) wallop

oplazeren /ɔplazərə(n)/ (lazerde op, is opgelazerd) [inform] bugger off, piss off, beat it

opleggen /ɔplɛɣə(n)/ (legde op, heeft opgelegd) enforce; impose: *wetten* ~ enforce (*or:* impose, lay down) laws; *iem. het zwijgen* ~ [also fig] silence s.o., put (*or:* reduce) s.o. to silence

de **oplegger** /ɔplɛɣər/ (pl: -s) semi-trailer, trailer: *truck met* ~ articulated lorry; [Am] articulated truck

opleiden /ɔplɛidə(n)/ (leidde op, heeft opgeleid) educate, instruct: *hij is tot advocaat opgeleid* he has been trained as a lawyer

de **opleiding** /ɔplɛidɪŋ/ (pl: -en) **1** education, training: *een wetenschappelijke* ~ an academic (*or:* a university) education; *een* ~ *volgen (krijgen)* receive training, train; *zij volgt een* ~ *voor secretaresse* she is doing a secretarial course **2** institute, (training) college; academy

het **opleidingscentrum** /ɔplɛidɪŋsɛntrʏm/ (pl: -centra) training centre

opletten /ɔplɛtə(n)/ (lette op, heeft opgelet) **1** watch, take care: *let op waar je loopt* look where you're going; *let maar eens op* mark my words; wait and see **2** pay attention: *opgelet!, let op!* attention please!, take care!

oplettend /ɔplɛtənt/ (adj, adv) **1** observant, observing: *zij sloeg hem* ~ *gade* she watched him carefully (*or:* closely) **2** attentive

de **oplettendheid** /ɔplɛtəntɦɛit/ attention, attentiveness

opleuken /ɔpløkə(n)/ (leukte op, heeft opgeleukt) liven up, brighten up

opleven /ɔplevə(n)/ (leefde op, is opgeleefd) revive

opleveren /ɔpleverə(n)/ (leverde op, heeft opgeleverd) **1** deliver; surrender: *tijdig* ~ deliver on time **2** yield: *wat levert dat baantje op?* what does (*or:* how much does) the job pay?; *voordeel* ~ yield profit; *het schrijven van boeken levert weinig op* writing (books) doesn't bring in much **3** produce: *het heeft me niets dan ellende opgeleverd* it brought me nothing but misery

de **oplevering** /ɔpleverɪŋ/ (pl: -en) delivery; [bldg] completion

de **opleving** /ɔplevɪŋ/ revival; recovery; upturn, pick-up: *een plotselinge* ~ an upsurge

oplezen /ɔplezə(n)/ (las op, heeft opgele-

oplichten

zen) read (out), call (out, off)

oplichten /ɔplɪxtə(n)/ (lichtte op, heeft opgelicht) swindle, cheat, con: *iem. ~ voor 2 ton* swindle (*or:* con) s.o. out of 200,000 euros

de **oplichter** /ɔplɪxtər/ (pl: -s) swindler, crook, con(fidence) man (woman)

de **oplichterij** /ɔplɪxtərɛi/ (pl: -en) swindle, con(-trick)

de **oplichting** /ɔplɪxtɪŋ/ fraud, con(-trick)

oplikken /ɔplɪkə(n)/ (likte op, heeft opgelikt) lick up, lap up

de **oploop** /ɔplop/ **1** crowd **2** riot, tumult

¹**oplopen** /ɔplopə(n)/ (liep op, is opgelopen) **1** go up, run up, walk up: *de trap ~* run (*or:* go, walk) up the stairs **2** increase, mount, rise: *de spanning laten ~* build up the tension **3** bump into, run into

²**oplopen** /ɔplopə(n)/ (liep op, heeft opgelopen) catch, get: *een verkoudheid ~* catch a cold || *achterstand ~* get behind, fall behind

oplopend /ɔplopənt/ (adj) **1** rising, sloping (upwards) **2** increasing, mounting: *een hoog ~e ruzie* a flaming row

oplosbaar /ɔplɔzbar/ (adj) solvable

de **oploskoffie** /ɔplɔskɔfi/ instant coffee

het **oplosmiddel** /ɔplɔsmɪdəl/ (pl: -en) solvent; thinner

¹**oplossen** /ɔplɔsə(n)/ (loste op, is opgelost) dissolve: *die vlekken lossen op als sneeuw voor de zon* those stains will vanish in no time

²**oplossen** /ɔplɔsə(n)/ (loste op, heeft opgelost) **1** solve **2** (re)solve: *dit zou het probleem moeten ~* this should settle (*or:* solve) the problem

de **oplossing** /ɔplɔsɪŋ/ (pl: -en) solution; answer

opluchten /ɔplʏxtə(n)/ (luchtte op, heeft opgelucht) relieve: *dat lucht op!* what a relief!; *opgelucht ademhalen* draw a breath of relief

de **opluchting** /ɔplʏxtɪŋ/ relief: *tot mijn grote ~* to my great relief, much to my relief

opluisteren /ɔplœystərə(n)/ (luisterde op, heeft opgeluisterd) grace, add lustre to

de **opmaak** /ɔpmak/ **1** layout, set-out, mock-up; format **2** embellishment; trimming

de **opmaat** /ɔpmat/ overture(s), prelude

opmaken /ɔpmakə(n)/ (maakte op, heeft opgemaakt) **1** finish (up), use up: *al zijn geld ~* spend all one's money **2** make up: *zich ~* make o.s. up **3** draw up: *de balans ~* weigh the pros and cons, take stock **4** lay out, make up **5** gather: *moet ik daaruit ~ dat ... * do I gather (*or:* conclude) from it that ...

de **opmars** /ɔpmars/ (pl: -en) [also fig] march, advance

opmerkelijk /ɔpmɛrkələk/ (adj, adv) remarkable, striking

opmerken /ɔpmɛrkə(n)/ (merkte op, heeft opgemerkt) **1** observe; note **2** note, notice **3** observe, remark: *mag ik misschien even iets*

~? may I make an observation?

de **opmerking** /ɔpmɛrkɪŋ/ (pl: -en) remark, observation, comment: *hou je brutale ~en voor je* keep your comments to yourself

opmerkzaam /ɔpmɛrksam/ (adj, adv) attentive, observant

opmeten /ɔpmetə(n)/ (mat op/meette op, heeft opgemeten) measure; survey

opnaaien /ɔpnajə(n)/ (naaide op, heeft opgenaaid) needle: *laat je toch niet zo ~* keep your hair (*or:* shirt) on

de **opname** /ɔpnamə/ (pl: -n, -s) **1** admission **2** shot; [film] shooting; take; recording **3** withdrawal

opnemen /ɔpnemə(n)/ (nam op, heeft opgenomen) **1** withdraw: *een snipperdag ~* take a day off **2** take: *iets (te) gemakkelijk ~* be (too) casual about sth. **3** record; [film] shoot: *een concert ~* record a concert **4** measure: *de gasmeter ~* read the (gas)meter; *de tijd ~ (van)* time a person **5** take down **6** admit, introduce, include: *laten ~ in een ziekenhuis* hospitalize; *in het ziekenhuis opgenomen worden* be admitted to hospital **7** admit, receive: *ze werd snel opgenomen in de groep* she was soon accepted as one of the group **8** answer: *er wordt niet opgenomen* there's no answer **9** absorb || *het tegen iem. ~* take s.o. on; *hij kan het tegen iedereen ~* he can hold his own against anyone; *het voor iem. ~* speak (*or:* stick) up for s.o.

opnieuw /ɔpniw/ (adv) **1** (once) again, once more: *telkens (steeds) ~* again and again; time and (time) again **2** (once) again, once more: *nu moet ik weer helemaal ~ beginnen* now I'm back to square one

opnoemen /ɔpnumə(n)/ (noemde op, heeft opgenoemd) name, call (out); enumerate: *te veel om op te noemen* too much (*or:* many) to mention

de **opoe** /opu/ (pl: -s) gran(ny), gran(d)ma

opofferen /ɔpɔfərə(n)/ (offerde op, heeft opgeofferd) sacrifice

de **opoffering** /ɔpɔfərɪŋ/ (pl: -en) sacrifice; [fig] expense

het **oponthoud** /ɔpɔnthaut/ stop(page), delay: *~ hebben* be delayed

oppakken /ɔpakə(n)/ (pakte op, heeft opgepakt) run in, pick up, round up

de **oppas** /ɔpas/ (pl: -sen) babysitter, childminder

oppassen /ɔpasə(n)/ (paste op, heeft opgepast) **1** look out, be careful: *pas op voor zakkenrollers* beware of pickpockets **2** babysit

de **oppasser** /ɔpasər/ (pl: -s) keeper

oppeppen /ɔpɛpə(n)/ (pepte op, heeft opgepept) pep (up)

opperbest /ɔpərbɛst/ (adj, adv) splendid, excellent: *in een ~ humeur* in high spirits

het **opperbevel** /ɔpərbəvɛl/ supreme command, high command de **opperbevelhebber** /ɔpərbəvɛlhɛbər/ (pl: -s) commander-in-chief, supreme commander

opperen /ɔpərə(n)/ (opperde, heeft geopperd) put forward, propose, suggest

het **opperhoofd** /ɔpərhoft/ (pl: -en) chief, chieftain

de **opperhuid** /ɔpərhœyt/ epidermis

oppermachtig /ɔpərmɑxtəx/ (adj, adv) supreme

opperst /ɔpərst/ (adj) supreme, complete

het **oppervlak** /ɔpərvlɑk/ (pl: -ken) **1** surface, face **2** (surface) area

oppervlakkig /ɔpərvlɑkəx/ (adj, adv) superficial, shallow: (zo) ~ *beschouwd* on the face of it; *iem.* ~ *kennen* have a nodding acquaintance with s.o., know s.o. slightly

de **oppervlakkigheid** /ɔpərvlɑkəxhɛit/ (pl: -heden) superficiality, shallowness

de **oppervlakte** /ɔpərvlɑktə/ (pl: -n, -s) **1** surface, face **2** surface (area)

het **oppervlaktewater** /ɔpərvlɑktəwatər/ (pl: -en) surface water

het **Opperwezen** /ɔpərwezə(n)/ Supreme Being

oppiepen /ɔpipə(n)/ (piepte op, heeft opgepiept) bleep

oppikken /ɔpɪkə(n)/ (pikte op, heeft opgepikt) pick up, collect: *ik pik je bij het station op* I will pick you up at the station

oppimpen /ɔpɪmpə(n)/ (pimpte op, heeft opgepimpt) pimp up, sex up

opplakken /ɔplɑkə(n)/ (plakte op, heeft opgeplakt) stick (on), glue (on), paste (on), affix

oppoetsen /ɔputsə(n)/ (poetste op, heeft opgepoetst) polish (up): [fig] *zijn Frans* ~ brush up one's French

oppompen /ɔpɔmpə(n)/ (pompte op, heeft opgepompt) pump up; blow up [socc]; inflate

de **opponent** /ɔponɛnt/ (pl: -en) opponent

de **opportunist** /ɔportynɪst/ (pl: -en) opportunist

opportunistisch /ɔportynɪstis/ (adj, adv) opportunistic

de **oppositie** /ɔpozi(t)si/ (pl: -s) opposition

de **oppositieleider** /ɔpozi(t)silɛidər/ (pl: -s) opposition leader, leader of the opposition

oppotten /ɔpɔtə(n)/ (potte op, heeft opgepot) hoard (up)

oprakelen /ɔprakələ(n)/ (rakelde op, heeft opgerakeld) rake up, drag up

opraken /ɔprakə(n)/ (raakte op, is opgeraakt) run out (or: short, low), be low; run out

oprapen /ɔprapə(n)/ (raapte op, heeft opgeraapt) pick up, gather

oprecht /ɔprɛxt/ (adj, adv) sincere, heartfelt

de **oprechtheid** /ɔprɛxthɛit/ sincerity: *in alle* ~ in all sincerity

oprichten /ɔprɪxtə(n)/ (richtte op, heeft opgericht) set up, establish; start; found: *een onderneming* ~ establish (or: start) a company

de **oprichter** /ɔprɪxtər/ (pl: -s) founder

de **oprichting** /ɔprɪxtɪŋ/ (pl: -en) foundation; establishment; formation

oprijden /ɔprɛidə(n)/ (reed op, is opgereden) ride along; drive along: *een oprijlaan* ~ turn into a drive; *tegen iets* ~ crash into (or: collide with) sth.

de **oprijlaan** /ɔprɛilan/ (pl: -lanen) drive(way)

oprijzen /ɔprɛizə(n)/ (rees op, is opgerezen) rise, tower

de **oprit** /ɔprɪt/ (pl: -ten) **1** drive, access **2** approach road, slip road

de **oproep** /ɔprup/ call, appeal

oproepen /ɔprupə(n)/ (riep op, heeft opgeroepen) **1** summon, call (up); page: *als getuige* ~ call as a witness; *opgeroepen voor militaire dienst* conscripted (or: drafted) into military service **2** call up, evoke, conjure up; arouse

de **oproepkracht** /ɔprupkrɑxt/ (pl: -en) standby employee (or: worker)

het **oproer** /ɔprur/ (pl: -en) revolt; insurrection

de **oproerkraaier** /ɔprurkrajər/ (pl: -s) agitator, insurgent

de **oproerpolitie** /ɔprurpoli(t)si/ riot police

oprollen /ɔprɔlə(n)/ (rolde op, heeft opgerold) **1** roll up, curl up; coil up; wind **2** round up

de **oprotpremie** /ɔprɔtpremi/ (pl: -s) [inform] **1** severance pay **2** repatriation bonus

oprotten /ɔprɔtə(n)/ (rotte op, is opgerot) [vulg] piss off, sod off, bugger off

opruien /ɔprœyjə(n)/ (ruide op, heeft opgeruid) incite, agitate

opruimen /ɔprœymə(n)/ (ruimde op, heeft opgeruimd) clean (out), clear (out), tidy (up), clear (up): *de rommel* ~ clear (or: tidy) away the mess; *opgeruimd staat netjes* a) that's things nice and tidy again; b) [iron] good riddance (to bad rubbish)

de **opruiming** /ɔprœymɪŋ/ (pl: -en) clearance; (clearance) sale; clear-out

de **opruimingsuitverkoop** /ɔprœymɪŋsœytfərkop/ (stock-)clearance sale

oprukken /ɔprʏkə(n)/ (rukte op, is opgerukt) advance

opscharrelen /ɔpsxɑrələ(n)/ (scharrelde op, heeft opgescharreld) rake up, dig up

opschepen /ɔpsxepə(n)/ (scheepte op, heeft opgescheept) saddle with, palm off on: *iem. met iets* ~ saddle s.o. with sth., plant sth. on s.o.

de **opscheplepel** /ɔpsxɛplepəl/ (pl: -s) tablespoon, server

¹**opscheppen** /ɔpsxɛpə(n)/ (schepte op, heeft opgeschept) brag, boast: ~ *met (over) zijn nieuwe auto* show off one's new car

²**opscheppen** /ɔpsχɛpə(n)/ (schepte op, heeft opgeschept) dish up, serve out, spoon out; ladle out: *mag ik je nog eens ~?* may I give you (*or:* will you have) another helping?

de **opschepper** /ɔpsχɛpər/ (pl: -s) boaster, braggart

opschepperig /ɔpsχɛpərəχ/ (adj, adv) boastful

de **opschepperij** /ɔpsχɛpərɛi/ (pl: -en) bragging; exhibitionism; show

opschieten /ɔpsχitə(n)/ (schoot op, is opgeschoten) **1** hurry up, push on (*or:* ahead) **2** get on, make progress (*or:* headway): *daar schiet je niks mee op* that's not going to get you anywhere **3** get on (*or:* along): *ze kunnen goed met elkaar ~* they get on very well (together)

opschorten /ɔpsχɔrtə(n)/ (schortte op, heeft opgeschort) adjourn; suspend; postpone, put on hold

het **opschrift** /ɔpsχrɪft/ (pl: -en) **1** legend; inscription; lettering **2** headline; heading; caption; direction

opschrijven /ɔpsχrɛivə(n)/ (schreef op, heeft opgeschreven) write/take/put (*or:* note, jot) down: *schrijf het maar voor mij op* charge it to (*or:* put it on) my account

opschrikken /ɔpsχrɪkə(n)/ (schrikte op, is opgeschrikt) start, startle, jump

opschudden /ɔpsχʏdə(n)/ (schudde op, heeft opgeschud) **1** shake up, fluff up, plump up: *de kussens ~* shake (*or:* plump, fluff) up the pillows **2** shake (up): *ze werd opgeschud uit haar dromen* she was shaken out of her dreams; *een ingeslapen organisatie ~* shake things up at a sleepy organization

de **opschudding** /ɔpsχʏdɪŋ/ (pl: -en) commotion, disturbance

opschuiven /ɔpsχœyvə(n)/ (schoof op, is opgeschoven) move up (*or:* over), shift up, shove up

opslaan /ɔpslan/ (sloeg op, heeft opgeslagen) **1** lay up, store **2** hit up; serve **3** lift, raise **4** save: *gegevens ~* store data

de **opslag** /ɔpslɑχ/ (pl: -en) **1** rise; [Am] raise; surcharge: *~ krijgen* get (*or:* receive) a rise **2** [sport] serve; service; ball **3** storage

de **opslagplaats** /ɔpslɑχplats/ (pl: -en) warehouse, (storage) depot; store; depository [goods]

de **opslagtank** /ɔpslɑχtɛŋk/ storage tank

opslokken /ɔpsləkə(n)/ (slokte op, heeft opgeslokt) swallow up (*or:* down)

¹**opsluiten** /ɔpslœytə(n)/ (sloot op, heeft opgesloten) shut up, lock up; confine; put (*or:* place) under restraint; cage; pound: *opgesloten in zijn kamertje zitten* be cooped up in one's room

zich ²**opsluiten** /ɔpslœytə(n)/ (sloot zich op, heeft zich opgesloten) shut o.s. in, lock o.s. up

de **opsluiting** /ɔpslœytɪŋ/ confinement, imprisonment: *eenzame ~* solitary confinement

de **opsmuk** /ɔpsmʏk/ finery, gaudery: *zonder ~* unadorned, plain

opsnorren /ɔpsnɔrə(n)/ (snorde op, heeft opgesnord) [inform] ferret out, rake out

opsnuiven /ɔpsnœyvə(n)/ (snoof op, heeft opgesnoven) sniff (up), snuff; inhale; snort

opsodemieteren /ɔpsodəmitərə(n)/ (sodemieterde op, is opgesodemieterd) [inform] piss off, fuck off

het **opsolferen** /ɔpsɔlfərə(n)/ [Belg] palm off (on): *iem. iets ~* palm sth. off on s.o.

opsommen /ɔpsɔmə(n)/ (somde op, heeft opgesomd) enumerate, recount

de **opsomming** /ɔpsɔmɪŋ/ (pl: -en) enumeration, list, run-down

opsouperen /ɔpsupərə(n)/ (soupeerde op, heeft opgesoupeerd) squander, spend

opsparen /ɔpsparə(n)/ (spaarde op, heeft opgespaard) save up; hoard (up)

opspelden /ɔpspɛldə(n)/ (speldde op, heeft opgespeld) pin up/on

opspelen /ɔpspelə(n)/ (speelde op, heeft opgespeeld) play up

opsplitsen /ɔpsplɪtsə(n)/ (splitste op, heeft opgesplitst) split up (into), break up (into)

opsporen /ɔpspɔrə(n)/ (spoorde op, heeft opgespoord) track, trace; detect; track down, hunt down

de **opsporing** /ɔpspɔrɪŋ/ (pl: -en) location, tracing

de **opsporingsdienst** /ɔpspɔrɪŋzdinst/ (pl: -en) investigation service (*or:* department)

de **opspraak** /ɔpsprak/ discredit: *in ~ komen* get o.s. talked about

opspringen /ɔpsprɪŋə(n)/ (sprong op, is opgesprongen) jump/leap (*or:* spring, start) up; spring (*or:* jump, start) to one's feet; bounce

opstaan /ɔpstan/ (stond op, is opgestaan) stand up, get up, get (*or:* rise) to one's feet, get on one's feet: *met vallen en ~* with ups and downs; *hij staat altijd vroeg op* he's an early riser (*or:* bird), he is always up early

de **opstand** /ɔpstɑnt/ (pl: -en) (up)rising, revolt, rebellion, insurrection

de **opstandeling** /ɔpstɑndəlɪŋ/ (pl: -en) rebel, insurgent

opstandig /ɔpstɑndəχ/ (adj) rebellious, mutinous, insurgent

de **opstanding** /ɔpstɑndɪŋ/ resurrection: *de ~ van Christus* the Resurrection of Christ

de **opstap** /ɔpstɑp/ (pl: -pen) step: *struikel niet over het ~je* don't stumble over the step, mind the step

¹**opstapelen** /ɔpstapələ(n)/ (stapelde op, heeft opgestapeld) pile up, heap up, stack (up); amass; accumulate

zich ²**opstapelen** /ɔpstapələ(n)/ (stapelde zich op, heeft zich opgestapeld) pile up, accumulate, mount up

opstappen /ˈɔpstɑpə(n)/ (stapte op, is opgestapt) go away, move on; be off; resign

opsteken /ˈɔpsteːkə(n)/ (stak op, heeft opgestoken) **1** put up, hold up, raise **2** learn; pick up: *zij hebben er niet veel **van** opgestoken* they have not taken much of it in **3** gather up, pin up

de **opsteker** /ˈɔpsteːkər/ (pl: -s) windfall, piece of (good) luck

het **opstel** /ˈɔpstɛl/ (pl: -len) (school) essay, composition: *een ~ **maken** over* write/do an essay (*or:* a paper) on

¹**opstellen** /ˈɔpstɛlə(n)/ (stelde op, heeft opgesteld) **1** set up (*or:* erect); post, place (sth., s.o.); arrange; dispose, line up; deploy: [sport] *opgesteld **staan*** be lined up **2** draw up, formulate; draft: *een **plan** ~* draw up a plan

zich ²**opstellen** /ˈɔpstɛlə(n)/ (stelde zich op, heeft zich opgesteld) **1** take up a position; form; line up, station o.s., post o.s. **2** take up a position (on), adopt an attitude (towards); pose (as): *zich **keihard** ~* take a hard line

de **opstelling** /ɔpˈstɛlɪŋ/ (pl: -en) **1** placing, erection; deployment; position; arrangement **2** position, attitude **3** [sport] line-up

opstijgen /ˈɔpstɛiɣə(n)/ (steeg op, is opgestegen) **1** ascend, rise; go up; take off; lift off **2** mount

opstoken /ˈɔpstoːkə(n)/ (stookte op, heeft opgestookt) incite (to), put up (to sth.)

het **opstootje** /ˈɔpstoːcə/ (pl: -s) disturbance, (street) row

de **opstopping** /ɔpˈstɔpɪŋ/ (pl: -en) stoppage, blockage; traffic jam; congestion

opstrijken /ˈɔpstrɛikə(n)/ (streek op, heeft opgestreken) pocket, rake in, scoop in, scoop up

opstropen /ˈɔpstroːpə(n)/ (stroopte op, heeft opgestroopt) roll up, turn up

opstuiven /ˈɔpstœyvə(n)/ (stoof op, is opgestoven) **1** fly up **2** dash up, tear up; flare out/up

opsturen /ˈɔpstyːrə(n)/ (stuurde op, heeft opgestuurd) send, post, mail

optekenen /ˈɔpteːkənə(n)/ (tekende op, heeft opgetekend) write, note, take down

optellen /ˈɔptɛlə(n)/ (telde op, heeft opgeteld) add (up), count up, total up: *twee **getallen** (bij elkaar) ~* add up two numbers

de **optelling** /ɔpˈtɛlɪŋ/ (pl: -en) **1** addition **2** (addition) sum

opteren /ɔpˈteːrə(n)/ (opteerde, heeft geopteerd): *~ **voor*** opt for, choose

de **opticien** /ɔptiˈʃɛ̃/ (pl: -s) optician

de **optie** /ˈɔpsi/ (pl: -s) **1** option; choice, alternative: *een ~ **op** een huis hebben* have an option on a house **2** [Belg] optional subject

de **optiebeurs** /ˈɔpsibørs/ (pl: -beurzen) options market

de **optiek** /ɔpˈtiːk/ point of view, angle

optillen /ɔpˈtɪlə(n)/ (tilde op, heeft opgetild) lift (up), raise

¹**optimaal** /ɔptiˈmaːl/ (adj) optimum

²**optimaal** /ɔptiˈmaːl/ (adv) optimal

optimaliseren /ɔptimaliˈzeːrə(n)/ (optimaliseerde, heeft geoptimaliseerd) optimize

het **optimisme** /ɔptiˈmɪsmə/ optimism

de **optimist** /ɔptiˈmɪst/ (pl: -en) optimist

optimistisch /ɔptiˈmɪstis/ (adj, adv) optimistic: *de zaak ~ **bekijken*** look on the bright side

optioneel /ɔpʃoˈneːl/ (adj) optional

optisch /ˈɔptis/ (adj) optic(al), visual

de **optocht** /ˈɔptɔxt/ (pl: -en) procession, parade; march

optornen /ˈɔptɔrnə(n)/ (tornde op, is opgetornd) battle (with), struggle (against)

het ¹**optreden** /ˈɔptreːdə(n)/ (pl: -s) **1** action; way of acting; behaviour; attitude; manner; bearing; demeanour: *het ~ van de **politie** werd fel bekritiseerd* the conduct of the police was strongly criticized **2** appearance, performance; show

²**optreden** /ˈɔptreːdə(n)/ (trad op, heeft opgetreden) **1** appear; perform: *in een film ~* appear in a film **2** act (as), serve (as) **3** act, take action: *streng ~* take firm action

het **optrekje** /ˈɔptrɛkjə/ (pl: -s) pied-à-terre

¹**optrekken** /ˈɔptrɛkə(n)/ (trok op, is opgetrokken) **1** accelerate **2** be busy (with); take care (of); hang around (with): *samen ~* hang around together **3** rise, lift

²**optrekken** /ˈɔptrɛkə(n)/ (trok op, heeft opgetrokken) pull up, haul up, raise; hoist (up): *met opgetrokken **knieën*** with one's knees pulled up

optrommelen /ˈɔptrɔmələ(n)/ (trommelde op, heeft opgetrommeld) drum up

optuigen /ˈɔptœyɣə(n)/ (tuigde op, heeft opgetuigd) dress up, tart up

opvallen /ˈɔpfɑlə(n)/ (viel op, is opgevallen) strike, be conspicuous, attract attention (*or:* notice): *~ **door** zijn kleding* attract attention because of (*or:* on account of) one's clothes

opvallend /ˈɔpfɑlənt/ (adj, adv) striking, conspicuous, marked: *het ~ste **kenmerk*** the most striking feature

de **opvang** /ˈɔpfɑŋ/ relief, emergency measures

opvangen /ˈɔpfɑŋə(n)/ (ving op, heeft opgevangen) **1** catch, receive **2** overhear, pick up, catch: *flarden van een gesprek ~* overhear scraps of conversation **3** take care of; receive: *de **kinderen** ~ als ze uit school komen* take care of (*or:* look after) the children after school **4** catch, collect

het **opvanghuis** /ˈɔpfɑŋhœys/ (pl: -huizen) reception centre, relief centre

opvatten /ˈɔpfɑtə(n)/ (vatte op, heeft opgevat) take, interpret: *iets **verkeerd** (fout) ~* misinterpret (*or:* misunderstand) sth.

de **opvatting** /ɔpfɑtɪŋ/ (pl: -en) view, notion, opinion

opvegen /ɔpfeɣə(n)/ (veegde op, heeft opgeveegd) sweep up

opvijzelen /ɔpfɛɪzələ(n)/ (vijzelde op, heeft opgevijzeld) boost

opvissen /ɔpfɪsə(n)/ (viste op, heeft opgevist) **1** dredge up **2** [fig] fish out/up, dig up

opvliegen /ɔpfliɣə(n)/ (vloog op, is opgevlogen) **1** fly up **2** jump to one's feet **3** flare out/up

opvliegend /ɔpfliɣənt/ (adj) short-tempered, quick-tempered

de **opvlieger** /ɔpfliɣər/ (pl: -s) flush

opvoeden /ɔpfudə(n)/ (voedde op, heeft opgevoed) bring up, raise: **goed** (or: **slecht**) *opgevoed* well-bred (or: ill-bred); well (or: badly) brought up

de **opvoeder** /ɔpfudər/ (pl: -s) educator, tutor, governess

de **opvoeding** /ɔpfudɪŋ/ (pl: -en) upbringing, education: *een* **strenge** ~ a strict upbringing

opvoedkundig /ɔpfutkʏndəx/ (adj, adv) educational, educative, pedagogic(al)

opvoeren /ɔpfurə(n)/ (voerde op, heeft opgevoerd) **1** increase; step up, speed up; accelerate: *een* **motor** ~ tune (up) an engine; *de* **snelheid** ~ raise (or: step up) the pace; increase speed **2** perform, put on, present

de **opvoering** /ɔpfurɪŋ/ (pl: -en) **1** production, presentation **2** performance

opvolgen /ɔpfɔlɣə(n)/ (volgde op, heeft opgevolgd) **1** succeed **2** follow up, observe; comply with; obey: *iemands* **advies** ~ follow (or: take) s.o.'s advice

de **opvolger** /ɔpfɔlɣər/ (pl: -s) successor (to)

opvouwbaar /ɔpfɑubar/ (adj) folding, fold-up, foldaway; collapsible

opvouwen /ɔpfɑuwə(n)/ (vouwde op, heeft opgevouwen) fold up; fold away

opvragen /ɔpfraɣə(n)/ (vraagde op/vroeg op, heeft opgevraagd) claim, ask for; reclaim; ask for (sth.) back

opvreten /ɔpfretə(n)/ (vrat op, heeft opgevreten) eat up, devour: *ik* **kan** *je wel* – I could just eat you up

opvrolijken /ɔpfroləkə(n)/ (vrolijkte op, heeft opgevrolijkt) cheer (s.o.) up, brighten (s.o., sth.) up

opvullen /ɔpfʏlə(n)/ (vulde op, heeft opgevuld) stuff, fill

opwaaien /ɔpwajə(n)/ (waaide op/woei op, is opgewaaid) (get) blow(n) up

opwaarderen /ɔpwardərə(n)/ (waardeerde op, heeft opgewaardeerd) revalue, upgrade, uprate

opwaarts /ɔpwarts/ (adj, adv) upward; upwards: ~e **druk** upward pressure, upthrust; [of a liquid] buoyancy

opwachten /ɔpwɑxtə(n)/ (wachtte op, heeft opgewacht) lie in wait for

de **opwachting** /ɔpwɑxtɪŋ/: *zijn* ~ **maken** **a)** pay (someone) a visit; **b)** arise, arrive; **c)** be ready to participate (or: for ...)

¹**opwarmen** /ɔpwɑrmə(n)/ (warmde op, is opgewarmd) **1** warm up, heat up **2** [sport] warm up, loosen up, limber up

²**opwarmen** /ɔpwɑrmə(n)/ (warmde op, heeft opgewarmd) warm up, heat up, reheat

opwegen /ɔpweɣə(n)/ (woog op, heeft opgewogen) be equal (to); make up (for); compensate (for)

opwekken /ɔpwɛkə(n)/ (wekte op, heeft opgewekt) **1** arouse; excite; stir: *de* **eetlust** *(van iem.)* ~ whet (s.o.'s) appetite **2** generate, create: **elektriciteit** ~ generate electricity

opwekkend /ɔpwɛkənt/ (adj, adv) **1** cheerful **2** tonic

opwellen /ɔpwɛlə(n)/ (welde op, is opgeweld) well up, rise

de **opwelling** /ɔpwɛlɪŋ/ (pl: -en) impulse: *in een* ~ *iets doen* do sth. on impulse

zich **opwerken** /ɔpwɛrkə(n)/ (werkte zich op, heeft zich opgewerkt) work one's way up, climb the ladder

opwerpen /ɔpwɛrpə(n)/ (wierp op, heeft opgeworpen) **1** throw up: *een* **muntstuk** ~ toss a coin **2** raise **3** raise, erect: **barricades** ~ raise (or: erect) barriers ‖ *zich* ~ *als* set o.s. up as

¹**opwinden** /ɔpwɪndə(n)/ (wond op, heeft opgewonden) **1** wind up **2** wind **3** excite, wind (or: key, tense) up

zich ²**opwinden** /ɔpwɪndə(n)/ (wond zich op, heeft zich opgewonden) become incensed, get excited, fume: *zich* ~ *over iets* get worked up about sth.

opwindend /ɔpwɪndənt/ (adj) **1** exciting, thrilling: *het* **was** *heel* ~ it was quite a thrill **2** sexy, suggestive

de **opwinding** /ɔpwɪndɪŋ/ (pl: -en) excitement; tension: *voor de* **nodige** ~ *zorgen* cause quite a stir

opzadelen /ɔpsadələ(n)/ (zadelde op, heeft opgezadeld) saddle

opzeggen /ɔpsɛɣə(n)/ (zegde op/zei op, heeft opgezegd) **1** cancel, terminate; resign; give notice: *zijn* **betrekking** ~ resign from one's job, resign one's post **2** read out; recite

de **opzegtermijn** /ɔpsɛxtɛrmɛɪn/ (pl: -en) (period, term of) notice

de ¹**opzet** /ɔpsɛt/ **1** organization; scheme; idea; layout; design, plan; set-up **2** intention, aim

het ²**opzet** /ɔpsɛt/ intention, purpose: *met* ~ on purpose

opzettelijk /ɔpsɛtələk/ (adj, adv) deliberate, intentional; on purpose: *hij deed het* ~ he did it on purpose

¹**opzetten** /ɔpsɛtə(n)/ (zette op, is opgezet) blow up; arise; gather; rise, set in

²**opzetten** /ɔpsɛtə(n)/ (zette op, heeft opgezet) **1** put up, raise; stand (sth., s.o.) up: *een*

tent ~ pitch (*or:* put up) a tent **2** put on: *zijn hoed* ~ put one's hat on; *theewater* ~ put the kettle on (for tea) **3** set up, start (off): *een* **zaak** ~ set up in business, set up shop **4** stuff

het **opzicht** /ɔpsɪχt/ (pl: -en) respect, aspect: *ten ~e van* a) compared with (*or:* to), in relation to; *b*) with respect (*or:* regard) to, as regards; *in* **geen** *enkel* ~ in no way, not in any sense

de **opzichter** /ɔpsɪχtər/ (pl: -s) **1** supervisor; overseer; superintendent **2** inspector; (site) foreman

opzichtig /ɔpsɪχtəχ/ (adj, adv) showy; blatant

het **¹opzien** /ɔpsin/ stir, fuss; amazement: *veel ~ baren* cause quite a stir (*or:* fuss)

²opzien /ɔpsin/ (zag op, heeft opgezien) **1** look up: *daar zullen ze van* ~ that'll make them sit up (and take notice) **2** (+ tegen) not be able to face, shrink from: *ergens* **als** *(tegen) een berg tegen* ~ dread sth.

opzienbarend /ɔpsimbarənt/ (adj) sensational, spectacular, stunning

de **opziener** /ɔpsinər/ (pl: -s) supervisor, inspector

opzij /ɔpsɛi/ (adv) **1** aside, out of the way **2** at (*or:* on) one side

opzijgaan /ɔpsɛiɣan/ (ging opzij, is opzijgegaan) give way to, make way for, go to one side

opzijleggen /ɔpsɛilɛɣə(n)/ (legde opzij, heeft opzijgelegd): *geld* ~ put money aside; *hij legde het boek opzij tot 's avonds* he put the book aside till the evening

opzijzetten /ɔpsɛisɛtə(n)/ (zette opzij, heeft opzijgezet) put (*or:* set) aside, table, discard, scrap

opzitten /ɔpsɪtə(n)/ (zat op, heeft opgezeten) sit up (and beg) ‖ *hij heeft er 20 jaar tropen* ~ he's been in the tropics 20 years

opzoeken /ɔpsukə(n)/ (zocht op, heeft opgezocht) **1** look up, find: *een* **adres** ~ look up an address **2** look up, call on

opzuigen /ɔpsœyɣə(n)/ (zoog op, heeft opgezogen) suck up; hoover up, vacuum up: *limonade door een rietje* ~ drink lemonade through a straw

opzwellen /ɔpswɛlə(n)/ (zwol op, is opgezwollen) swell (up, out), bulge; billow; balloon

opzwepen /ɔpswepə(n)/ (zweepte op, heeft opgezweept) whip up

oraal /oral/ (adj, adv) oral

het **orakel** /orakəl/ (pl: -s) oracle

de **orang-oetan** /oraŋutan/ (pl: -s) orang-utan

het **¹oranje** /orɑɲə/ (pl: -s) [color] orange; [traffic lights] amber

²oranje /orɑɲə/ (adj) orange; [traffic lights] amber

Oranje /orɑɲə/ (pl: -s) **1** (the house of) Orange **2** the Dutch team

de **oratie** /ora(t)si/ (pl: -s) oration

het **oratorium** /oratorijʏm/ (pl: -s, oratoria) **1** oratorio **2** oratory

de **orchidee** /ɔrxide/ (pl: -ën) orchid

de **orde** /ɔrdə/ (pl: -n, -s) **1** order: *voor de* **goede** ~ *wijs ik u erop dat …* for the record, I would like to remind you that …; *iem.* **tot** *de ~ roepen* call s.o. to order **2** order; discipline: *verstoring van de* **openbare** ~ disturbance of the peace; *dat komt (wel)* **in** ~ it will turn out all right (*or:* OK); *in ~!* all right!, fine!, OK! ‖ *iem. een ~* **verlenen** invest s.o. with a decoration, decorate s.o.; *dat is van een heel* **andere** ~ that is of an entirely different order; *aan de ~ van de* **dag** *zijn* be the order of the day

ordelijk /ɔrdələk/ (adj, adv) neat, tidy

ordeloos /ɔrdəlos/ (adj, adv) disorganized, disorderly

ordenen /ɔrdənə(n)/ (ordende, heeft geordend) arrange, sort (out)

de **ordening** /ɔrdənɪŋ/ (pl: -en) **1** arrangement, organization **2** regulation, structuring

ordentelijk /ɔrdɛntələk/ (adj, adv) respectable, decent

de **order** /ɔrdər/ (pl: -s) order, instruction, command: *uitstellen tot* **nader** ~ put off until further notice; *een* ~ *plaatsen voor twee vracht-auto's bij D.* order two lorries from D.

de **ordeverstoring** /ɔrdəvərstorɪŋ/ (pl: -en) disturbance, disturbance (*or:* breach) of the peace

ordinair /ɔrdinɛːr/ (adj, adv) **1** common, vulgar; coarse; crude **2** common, ordinary, normal

de **ordner** /ɔrtnər/ (pl: -s) (document) file

de **oregano** /oreɣano/ oregano

oreren /orerə(n)/ (oreerde, heeft georeerd) **1** deliver a speech **2** orate

het **orgaan** /ɔrɣan/ (pl: organen) organ

de **orgaandonatie** /ɔrɣandona(t)si/ (pl: -s) organ donation

de **orgaantransplantatie** /ɔrɣantrɑnsplɑnta(t)si/ organ transplant(ation)

de **organisatie** /ɔrɣaniza(t)si/ (pl: -s) **1** organization, arrangement **2** organization, society, association

de **organisatieadviseur** /ɔrɣaniza(t)siatfizør/ (pl: -s) organization consultant

de **organisator** /ɔrɣanizator/ (pl: -en) organizer

organisatorisch /ɔrɣanizatoris/ (adj, adv) organizational

organisch /ɔrɣanis/ (adj, adv) organic

organiseren /ɔrɣanizerə(n)/ (organiseerde, heeft georganiseerd) **1** organize, arrange **2** organize, fix up, stage

het **organisme** /ɔrɣanɪsmə/ (pl: -n) organism

de **organist** /ɔrɣanɪst/ (pl: -en) organist, organ player

het **orgasme** /ɔrɣɑsmə/ (pl: -n) orgasm, climax

het **orgel** /ɔrɣəl/ (pl: -s) (pipe) organ: *een* ~

orgelman

draaien grind an organ

de **orgelman** /ɔrɣəlman/ organ-grinder

de **orgie** /ɔrɣi/ (pl: -ën) orgy, revelry

de **Oriënt** /orijɛnt/ Orient

de **oriëntatie** /orijɛnta(t)si/ orientation, information: *zijn ~ kwijtraken* lose one's bearings

zich **oriënteren** /orijɛnterə(n)/ (oriënteerde zich, heeft zich georiënteerd) **1** orientate o.s. **2** look around

het **oriënteringsvermogen** /orijɛntɛrɪŋsfərmoɣə(n)/ sense of direction

de **originaliteit** /oriʒinalitɛit/ originality

de **origine** /oriʒinə/ origin: *zij zijn van Franse ~* they are of French origin (*or:* extraction)

origineel /oriʒinel/ (adj, adv) original

de **orka** /ɔrka/ (pl: -'s) orc(a)

de **orkaan** /ɔrkan/ (pl: orkanen) hurricane

de **orkaankracht** /ɔrkaŋkrɑχt/ hurricane force

het **orkest** /ɔrkɛst/ (pl: -en) orchestra

orkestreren /ɔrkɛstrerə(n)/ (orkestreerde, heeft georkestreerd) orchestrate

het **ornaat** /ɔrnat/ (pl: ornaten): *in vol ~* in best bib and tucker, dressed (up) to the nines

het **ornament** /ɔrnamɛnt/ (pl: -en) ornament

de **orthodontist** /ɔrtodɔntɪst/ (pl: -en) orthodontist

orthodox /ɔrtodɔks/ (adj) orthodox

de **orthopedie** /ɔrtopedi/ orthop(a)edics

orthopedisch /ɔrtopedis/ (adj) orthop(a)edic

de **os** /ɔs/ (pl: ossen) bullock, ox: *slapen als een os* sleep like a log

de **OS** /oɛs/ (pl) *Olympische Spelen* Olympic Games

de **ossenhaas** /ɔsə(n)has/ (pl: -hazen) tenderloin

de **ossenstaartsoep** /ɔsə(n)startsup/ oxtail soup

de **otter** /ɔtər/ (pl: -s) otter

oubollig /aubɔləχ/ (adj) corny, waggish

oud /aut/ (adj) **1** old: *zo'n veertig jaar ~* fortyish; *vijftien jaar ~* fifteen years old (*or:* of age), old fifteen; *hij werd honderd jaar ~* he lived to (be) a hundred; *de ~ste zoon* a) the elder son; b) the oldest son; *haar ~ere zusje* her elder (*or:* big) sister; *hoe ~ ben je?* how old are you?; *toen zij zo ~ was als jij* when she was your age; *zij zijn even ~* they are the same age; *hij is vier jaar ~er dan ik* he is four years older than me; *kinderen van zes jaar en ~er* children from six upwards **2** old, aged: *de ~e dag* old age; *men is nooit te ~ om te leren* you are never too old to learn **3** old, ancient; long-standing: *een ~e mop* a corny joke; *~ papier* waste paper; *~er in dienstjaren* senior **4** ancient; outdated; archaic: *~ nummer* back issue **5** ex-, former, old ‖ *~ en jong* young and old; *~ en nieuw vieren* see in the New Year

oudbakken /audbɑkə(n)/ (adj) stale

de **oudedagsvoorziening** /audədɑχsfor-

zinɪŋ/ (pl: -en) provision for old age

de **oudejaarsavond** /audəjarsavɔnt/ (pl: -en) New Year's Eve

de **ouder** /audər/ (pl: -s) parent: *mijn ~s* my parents; my folks

de **ouderavond** /audəravɔnt/ (pl: -en) parents' evening

de **ouderdom** /audərdɔm/ age, (old) age

de **ouderdomskwaal** /audərdɔmskwal/ (pl: -kwalen) old person's complaint

de **ouderejaars** /audərəjars/ older student, senior student

ouderlijk /audərlək/ (adj) parental

de **ouderling** /audərlɪŋ/ (pl: -en) church warden, elder

de **ouderraad** /audərat/ (pl: -raden) parents' council

het **ouderschapsverlof** /audərsχapsfərlɔf/ (pl: -verloven) maternity leave; parental leave

ouderwets /audərwɛts/ (adj, adv) old-fashioned; outmoded

de **oudgediende** /autχədində/ (pl: -n) old hand, veteran

de **oudheid** /authɛit/ antiquity, ancient times

de **oudheidkunde** /authɛitkʏndə/ arch(a)eology

het **oudjaar** /autjar/ New Year's Eve

het **oudje** /aucə/ (pl: -s) old person, old chap, old fellow, old dear, old girl

de **oud-leerling** /autlerlɪŋ/ (pl: -en) former pupil

de **oudoom** /autom/ (pl: -s) great-uncle

oudsher /autshɛr/ (adv): *van ~* of old, from way back

de **oudste** /autstə/ (pl: -n) **1** oldest, eldest: *wie is de ~, jij of je broer?* who is older, you or your brother? **2** (most) senior

de **oud-strijder** /autstrɛidər/ (pl: -s) war veteran

de **oudtante** /autantə/ (pl: -s) great-aunt

de **outbox** /audbɔks/ outbox

de **outcast** /autka:st/ outcast

de **outfit** /autfɪt/ (pl: -s) outfit

de **outlet** /autlɛt/ outlet

het/de **outplacement** /autplɛsmənt/ outplacement

de **output** /autput/ (pl: -s) output: *als ~ leveren* output

de **outsider** /autsajdər/ (pl: -s) outsider

de **outsourcing** /autso:rsɪŋ/ outsourcing

de **ouverture** /uvɛrtyrə/ (pl: -s, -n) overture, prelude

de **ouwe** /auwə/ (pl: -n) [inform] **1** chief, boss **2** old man ‖ *een gouwe ~* a golden oldie

de **ouwehoer** /auwəhur/ [inform] windbag

ouwehoeren /auwəhurə(n)/ (ouwehoerde, heeft geouwehoerd) [inform] go on

de **ouwel** /auwəl/ wafer

ouwelijk /auwələk/ (adj, adv) oldish, elderly

het **ov** /ove/ *openbaar vervoer* public transport

het **¹ovaal** /ov<u>a</u>l/ (pl: ovalen) oval
²ovaal /ov<u>a</u>l/ (adj) oval

de **ovatie** /ov<u>a</u>(t)si/ (pl: -s) ovation

de **ov-chipkaart** /ovetʃɪpkart/ (pl: -en) [Dutch] public transport pass

de **oven** /ovə(n)/ (pl: -s) oven

de **ovenschaal** /<u>o</u>və(n)sχal/ (pl: -schalen) baking dish, casserole

de **ovenschotel** /<u>o</u>və(n)sχotəl/ (pl: -s) oven dish

de **ovenwant** /<u>o</u>və(n)want/ oven glove; [Am] oven mitt

¹over /<u>o</u>vər/ (adj) over, finished: *de pijn is al ~* the pain has gone

²over /<u>o</u>vər/ (adv) **1** across, over: *zij zijn ~ uit Ankara* they are over from Ankara; *~ en weer* back and forth; from both sides **2** left, over: *als er genoeg tijd ~ is* if there is enough time left

³over /<u>o</u>vər/ (prep) **1** over, above: *~ een periode van … over* a period of … **2** across, over: *hij werkt ~ de grens* he works across (*or:* over) the border; *~ de heuvels* over (*or:* beyond) the hills; *~ straat lopen* walk around; *~ de hele lengte* all along **3** about: *de winst ~ het vierde kwartaal* the profit over the fourth quarter **4** by way of, via: *zij communiceren ~ de mobilofoon* they communicate by mobile telephone; *zij reed ~ Nijmegen naar Zwolle* she drove to Zwolle via Nijmegen; *een brug ~ de rivier* a bridge over (*or:* across) the river **5** about: *verheugd ~* delighted at (*or:* with) **6** over, across **7** after, in: *zaterdag ~ een week* a week on Saturday **8** past: *zij is twee maanden ~ tijd* she is two months overdue; *tot ~ zijn oren in de problemen zitten* be up to one's neck in trouble; *het is kwart ~ vijf* it is a quarter past five; *het is vijf ~ half zes* it is twenty-five to six

overal /<u>o</u>vəral/ (adv) **1** everywhere; anywhere: *~ bekend* widely known; *van ~* from everywhere, from all over the place **2** everything: *zij weet ~ van* she knows about everything

de **overall** /ovər<u>o</u>:l/ (pl: -s) overalls

overbekend /ovərbək<u>ɛ</u>nt/ (adj) very well-known

overbelast /ovərbəl<u>a</u>st/ (adj) overloaded, overburdened

overbelasten /<u>o</u>vərbəlastə(n)/ (overbelastte, heeft overbelast) overload, overburden, overtax

de **overbelasting** /<u>o</u>vərbəlastɪŋ/ stress, strain

overbelichten /<u>o</u>vərbəlɪχtə(n)/ (belichtte over, heeft overbelicht) overexpose

de **overbevolking** /<u>o</u>vərbəvɔlkɪŋ/ overpopulation

overbevolkt /ovərbəv<u>o</u>lkt/ (adj) overpopulated

overbezet /ovərbəz<u>ɛ</u>t/ (adj) overcrowded: *mijn agenda is al ~* my programme is already overbooked

het **overblijfsel** /<u>o</u>vərblɛifsəl/ (pl: -en) **1** relic; remnant; remains **2** remains; leftovers; remnant

overblijven /<u>o</u>vərblɛivə(n)/ (bleef over, is overgebleven) **1** be left, remain: *van al mijn goede voornemens blijft zo niets over* all my good intentions are coming to nothing now **2** be left (over)

de **overblijver** /<u>o</u>vərblɛivər/ (pl: -s) school-luncher

overbluffen /ovərbl<u>y</u>fə(n)/ (overblufte, heeft overbluft) confound, dumbfound: *laat je door hem niet ~* don't let him come it over (*or:* with) you

overbodig /ovərb<u>o</u>dəχ/ (adj, adv) superfluous, redundant; unnecessary: *~ te zeggen* needless to say; *het is geen ~e luxe* it would be no luxury, it's really necessary

¹overboeken /<u>o</u>vərbukə(n)/ (boekte over, heeft overgeboekt) transfer

²overboeken /ovərb<u>u</u>kə(n)/ (overboekte, heeft overboekt) overbook

de **overboeking** /<u>o</u>vərbukɪŋ/ (pl: -en) transfer (into, to)

overboord /ovərb<u>o</u>rt/ (adv) overboard: *man ~!* man overboard!

overbrengen /<u>o</u>vərbrɛŋə(n)/ (bracht over, heeft overgebracht) **1** take (*or:* bring, carry) (across), move, transfer **2** convey, communicate: *boodschappen* (or: *iemands groeten*) *~* convey messages (*or:* s.o.'s greetings) **3** pass (on)

overbruggen /ovərbr<u>y</u>ɣə(n)/ (overbrugde, heeft overbrugd) bridge; tide over

de **overbruggingsperiode** /ovərbr<u>y</u>ɣɪŋsperijodə/ (pl: -s) interim (period)

de **overcapaciteit** /<u>o</u>vərkapasitɛɪt/ overcapacity

de **overdaad** /<u>o</u>vərdat/ excess

overdadig /ovərd<u>a</u>dəχ/ (adj, adv) excessive, profuse; extravagant; lavish; wasteful

overdag /ovərd<u>a</u>χ/ (adv) by day, during the daytime

overdekken /ovərd<u>ɛ</u>kə(n)/ (overdekte, heeft overdekt) cover

overdekt /ovərd<u>ɛ</u>kt/ (adj) covered: *een ~ zwembad* an indoor swimming pool

overdenken /ovərd<u>ɛ</u>ŋkə(n)/ (overdacht, heeft overdacht) consider, think over

overdoen /<u>o</u>vərdun/ (deed over, heeft overgedaan) do again: *een examen ~* resit an examination; [fig] *iets (nog eens) dunnetjes ~* give a repeat performance, have another try (*or:* go) (at sth.)

overdonderen /ovərd<u>o</u>ndərə(n)/ (overdonderde, heeft overdonderd) overwhelm, confound: *een ~d succes* an overwhelming success

de **overdosis** /<u>o</u>vərdozɪs/ (pl: -doses) overdose

de **overdracht** /<u>o</u>vərdraχt/ (pl: -en) transfer,

overdrachtelijk

handing over

overdrachtelijk /ovərdrɑ̯xtələk/ (adj, adv) metaphorical

overdragen /o̯vərdraɣə(n)/ (droeg over, heeft overgedragen) hand over, assign; delegate

overdreven /o̯vərdre̯və(n)/ (adj, adv) exaggerated: hij **doet (is)** wel wat ~ he lays it on a bit thick; dat **is** sterk ~ that is highly (or: grossly) exaggerated; that's a bit thick

overdrijven /o̯vərdrɛ̯ivə(n)/ (overdreef, heeft overdreven) **1** overdo (it, sth.), go too far (with sth.): je moet (het) **niet** ~ you mustn't overdo it (or: things) **2** exaggerate

de **overdrijving** /o̯vərdrɛ̯ivɪŋ/ (pl: -en) exaggeration; overstatement

de **overdruk** /o̯vərdrʏk/ (pl: -ken) overpressure

overduidelijk /o̯vərdœ̯ydələk/ (adj, adv) patently obvious, evident

overdwars /o̯vərdwɑ̯rs/ (adv) crosswise, transversely

overeen /o̯vəre̯n/ (adv) **1** to the same thing **2** crossed ‖ [Belg] de armen ~ arms crossed

¹**overeenkomen** /o̯vəre̯ŋko̯mə(n)/ (kwam overeen, is overeengekomen) **1** correspond (to): ~ **met** de beschrijving fit the description **2** be similar (to): geheel ~ **met** fully correspond to (or: with)

²**overeenkomen** /o̯vəre̯ŋko̯mə(n)/ (kwam overeen, is overeengekomen) agree (on), arrange: **zoals** overeengekomen as agreed; iets **met** iem. ~ arrange sth. with s.o.

de **overeenkomst** /o̯vəre̯ŋkɔmst/ (pl: -en) **1** similarity, resemblance: ~ **vertonen** met show similarity to, resemble **2** agreement: een ~ **sluiten** met iem. make (or: enter into) an agreement with s.o.

overeenkomstig /o̯vəre̯ŋkɔ̯mstəx/ (prep) in accordance with, according to: ~ de **verwachtingen** in line with expectations

overeenstemmen /o̯vəre̯nste̯mə(n)/ (stemde overeen, heeft overeengestemd) see ¹overeenkomen

de **overeenstemming** /o̯vəre̯nste̯mɪŋ/ **1** harmony, conformity, agreement: niet **in** ~ met out of line (or: keeping) with, inconsistent with **2** agreement: **tot** (een) ~ komen come to terms, reach an agreement

overeind /o̯vərɛ̯int/ (adv) **1** upright; on end: ~ **gaan staan** stand up (straight), get to one's feet **2** standing: ~ **blijven** keep upright; keep one's footing

overgaan /o̯vərɣan/ (ging over, is overgegaan) **1** move over (or: across), go over, cross (over): de **brug** ~ go over the bridge, cross (over) the bridge **2** transfer, pass **3** move up: **van** de vierde **naar** de vijfde klas ~ move up from the fourth to the fifth form **4** change, convert, turn: de kleuren gingen in elkaar over the colours shaded into one another **5** move on to; proceed to, turn to; change (over) to;

switch (over) (to): ~ **tot** de aanschaf van (or: het gebruik van) ... start buying (or: using) ... **6** pass (over, away); wear off; blow over: de **pijn** zal wel ~ the pain will wear off **7** ring

de **overgang** /o̯vərɣɑŋ/ (pl: -en) **1** transitional stage, link **2** transition, change(over) **3** change of life, menopause: in de ~ zijn be at the change of life

de **overgangsperiode** /o̯vərɣɑ̯ŋsperijodə/ (pl: -n, -s) transition(al) period

overgankelijk /o̯vərɣɑ̯ŋkələk/ (adj) transitive

de **overgave** /o̯vərɣavə/ **1** surrender, capitulation **2** dedication, devotion, abandon(ment)

¹**overgeven** /o̯vərɣevə(n)/ (gaf over, heeft overgegeven) be sick, vomit, throw up

zich ²**overgeven** /o̯vərɣevə(n)/ (gaf zich over, heeft zich overgegeven) surrender

overgevoelig /o̯vərɣəvu̯ləx/ (adj, adv) hypersensitive, oversensitive

het **overgewicht** /o̯vərɣəwɪxt/ overweight, extra (weight)

¹**overgieten** /o̯vərɣi̯tə(n)/ (overgoot, heeft overgoten) bathe [light]; cover

²**overgieten** /o̯vərɣi̯tə(n)/ (goot over, heeft overgegoten) pour (into)

de **overgooier** /o̯vərɣojər/ (pl: -s) pinafore dress

het **overgordijn** /o̯vərɣɔrdɛin/ (pl: -en) (long, heavy, lined) curtain

overgroot /o̯vərɣro̯t/ (adj) vast, huge: met overgrote **meerderheid** by an overwhelming majority

de **overgrootmoeder** /o̯vərɣro̯tmudər/ (pl: -s) great-grandmother

de **overgrootvader** /o̯vərɣro̯tfadər/ (pl: -s) great-grandfather

overhaast /o̯vərha̯st/ (adj, adv) rash, hurried, (over)hasty

overhaasten /o̯vərha̯stə(n)/ (overhaastte, heeft overhaast) rush, hurry

overhalen /o̯vərhalə(n)/ (haalde over, heeft overgehaald) **1** persuade, talk (s.o.) into (sth.): iem. **tot** iets ~ talk s.o. into doing sth. **2** pull (on): de **trekker** ~ pull the trigger

de **overhand** /o̯vərhɑnt/ upper hand, advantage

overhandigen /o̯vərhɑ̯ndəɣə(n)/ (overhandigde, heeft overhandigd) hand (over), present: iem. **iets** ~ hand sth. over to s.o.

de **overheadkosten** /o̯vərhɛ̯ːtkɔstə(n)/ (pl) overhead cost (or: expenses)

de **overheadprojector** /o̯vərhɛ̯ːtprojɛktɔr/ (pl: -s) overhead projector

overhebben /o̯vərhɛbə(n)/ (had over, heeft overgehad) **1** have (for), be prepared to give (for); not begrudge (s.o. sth.): ik zou er **alles** voor ~ I would do (or: give) anything for it **2** have over, have left: geen **geld** meer ~ have no more money left

overheen /o̯vərhe̯n/ (adv) **1** over: daar

groeit hij wel ~ he will grow out of it **2** across, over: *er een doek* (or: *dweil*) ~ *halen* run a cloth (*or:* mop) over it **3** past ‖ *ergens ~ lezen* miss (*or:* overlook) sth.; *zich ergens ~ zetten* get the better of sth., overcome sth., get over it

overheerlijk /ovərh**ɛ**rlək/ (adj, adv) absolutely delicious

overheersen /ovərh**ɛ**rsə(n)/ (overheerste, heeft overheerst) dominate, predominate

de **overheerser** /ovərh**ɛ**rsər/ (pl: -s) oppressor, dictator

de **overheersing** /ovərh**ɛ**rsɪŋ/ (pl: -en) rule, oppression

de **overheid** /**o**vərhɛit/ (pl: -heden) **1** government **2** authority: *de* **plaatselijke** ~ the local authorities

het **overheidsbedrijf** /**o**vərhɛitsbədrɛif/ (pl: -bedrijven) public enterprise, state enterprise; a public utility company

de **overheidsdienst** /**o**vərhɛitsdinst/ (pl: -en) government service, public service, the civil service

de **overheidsinstelling** /**o**vərhɛitsɪnstɛlɪŋ/ (pl: -en) government institution (*or:* agency)

overheidswege /**o**vərhɛitsweɣə/: *van* ~ by the authorities, officially

overhellen /**o**vərhɛlə(n)/ (helde over, heeft overgeheld) lean (over), tilt (over)

het **overhemd** /**o**vərhɛmt/ (pl: -en) shirt

overhevelen /**o**vərhevələ(n)/ (hevelde over, heeft overgeheveld) transfer

overhoophalen /ovərh**o**phalə(n)/ (haalde overhoop, heeft overhoopgehaald) turn upside down

overhoopliggen /ovərh**o**plɪɣə(n)/ (lag overhoop, heeft overhoopgelegen) **1** be in a mess **2** be at loggerheads (with): *ze liggen altijd met elkaar overhoop* they're always at loggerheads (with one another)

overhoren /ovərh**o**rə/ (overhoorde, heeft overhoord) test

de **overhoring** /ovərh**o**rɪŋ/ (pl: -en) test

overhouden /**o**vərhaudə(n)/ (hield over, heeft overgehouden) have left, still have

overig /**o**vərəɣ/ (adj) remaining, other

overigens /**o**vərəɣəns/ (adv) anyway, for that matter, though

overjarig /ovərj**a**rəɣ/ (adj) more than one year old

de **overjas** /**o**vərjɑs/ (pl: -sen) overcoat

de **overkant** /**o**vərkɑnt/ other side, opposite side: *zij woont* **aan** *de* ~ she lives across the street

de **overkapping** /ovərk**ɑ**pɪŋ/ (pl: -en) covering, roof

overkijken /**o**vərkɛikə(n)/ (keek over, heeft overgekeken) look over: *zijn* **les** ~ look through one's lesson

overkoepelend /ovərk**u**pələnt/ (adj, adv) coordinating

overkoken /**o**vərkokə(n)/ (kookte over, is overgekookt) boil over

¹**overkomen** /**o**vərkomə(n)/ (kwam over, is overgekomen) **1** come over: *oma is* **uit** *Marokko overgekomen* granny has come over from Morocco **2** come across, get across

²**overkomen** /ovərk**o**mə(n)/ (overkwam, is overkomen) happen to, come over: *dat* **kan** *de beste* ~ that could happen to the best of us; *ik wist niet wat* **mij** *overkwam* I didn't know what was happening to me

¹**overladen** /ovərl**a**də(n)/ (adj) overloaded, overburdened

²**overladen** /ovərl**a**də(n)/ (overlaadde, heeft overladen) shower, heap on (*or:* upon): *hij werd ~* **met** *werk* he was overloaded with work

³**overladen** /**o**vərladə(n)/ (laadde over, heeft overgeladen) transfer; trans-ship

overlangs /ovərl**ɑ**ŋs/ (adj, adv) lengthwise; longitudinal: *iets ~* **doorsnijden** cut sth. lengthwise

overlappen /ovərl**ɑ**pə(n)/ (overlapte, heeft overlapt) overlap

de **overlast** /**o**vərlɑst/ inconvenience, nuisance: *~* **veroorzaken** cause trouble (*or:* annoyance)

overlaten /**o**vərlatə(n)/ (liet over, heeft overgelaten) **1** leave: *laat dat maar* **aan** *mij over!* just leave that to me! **2** leave (over): *veel* (or: *niets*) *te wensen ~* leave much (*or:* nothing) to be desired

overleden /ovərl**e**də(n)/ (adj) dead

de **overledene** /ovərl**e**dənə/ (pl: -n) deceased

het **overleg** /ovərl**ɛ**ɣ/ **1** thought, consideration **2** consultation, deliberation: *~* **voeren** *(over)* consult (on); *in (nauw) ~* **met** in (close) consultation with; *in onderling ~* by mutual agreement

¹**overleggen** /ovərl**ɛ**ɣə(n)/ (overlegde, heeft overlegd) **1** consider: *hij overlegt wat hem te doen staat* he is considering what he has to do **2** consult, confer: *iets* **met** *iem. ~* consult (with) s.o. on sth.

²**overleggen** /**o**vərlɛɣə(n)/ (legde over, heeft overgelegd) produce/submit (*or:* hand in) documents

overleven /ovərl**e**və(n)/ (overleefde, heeft overleefd) survive, outlive

de **overlevende** /ovərl**e**vəndə/ (pl: -n) survivor

overleveren /**o**vərlevərə(n)/ (leverde over, heeft overgeleverd) hand over, turn over, turn in

de **overlevering** /**o**vərlevərɪŋ/ (pl: -en) tradition: *via* **mondelinge** ~ via oral tradition

overlezen /**o**vərlezə(n)/ (las over, heeft overgelezen) read over (*or:* through): *een ar-tikel vluchtig ~* skim through an article

overlijden /ovərl**ɛ**idə(n)/ (overleed, is overleden) die

het **overlijdensbericht** /ovərl**ɛ**idə(n)zbərɪχt/

(pl: -en) death announcement: *de ~en* the obituaries; the deaths

de **overloop** /ˈoʋərlop/ (pl: -lopen) landing

overlopen /oʋərlopə(n)/ (liep over, is over-gelopen) **1** walk over (*or:* across) **2** go over, defect: ~ *naar de vijand* desert (*or:* defect) to the enemy **3** overflow ‖ ~ *van enthousiasme* be brimming (*or:* bubbling) (over) with en-thusiasm

de **overloper** /ˈoʋərlopər/ (pl: -s) deserter, de-fector

de **overmaat** /ˈoʋərmat/ excess: *tot* ~ *van ramp* to make matters worse

de **overmacht** /ˈoʋərmɑxt/ **1** superior numbers (*or:* strength, forces): *tegenover een geweldi-ge* ~ *staan* face fearful odds **2** circumstances beyond one's control, force majeure; Act of God

overmaken /ˈoʋərmakə(n)/ (maakte over, heeft overgemaakt) transfer, remit

overmannen /oʋərmɑnə(n)/ (overmande, heeft overmand) overcome, overpower, overwhelm

overmatig /oʋərmatəx/ (adj, adv) excessive

overmeesteren /oʋərmestərə(n)/ (over-meesterde, heeft overmeesterd) overpower, overcome

de **overmoed** /ˈoʋərmut/ overconfidence, recklessness

overmoedig /oʋərmudəx/ (adj, adv) over-confident, reckless

overmorgen /ˈoʋərmɔrɣə(n)/ (adv) the day after tomorrow

overnachten /oʋərnɑxtə(n)/ (overnachtte, heeft overnacht) stay (*or:* spend) the night, stay (over)

de **overnachting** /oʋərnɑxtɪŋ/ (pl: -en) **1** stay **2** night: *het aantal ~en* the number of nights (spent, slept)

de **overname** /ˈoʋərnamə/ takeover, purchase, taking-over

overnemen /ˈoʋərnemə(n)/ (nam over, heeft overgenomen) **1** receive **2** take (over): *de macht* ~ assume power **3** adopt: *de ge-woonten van een land* ~ adopt the customs of a country **4** take over, buy

de **overpeinzing** /oʋərpɛɪnzɪŋ/ (pl: -en) re-flection

overplaatsen /ˈoʋərplatsə(n)/ (plaatste over, heeft overgeplaatst) transfer

de **overplaatsing** /ˈoʋərplatsɪŋ/ (pl: -en) trans-fer, move

overplanten /ˈoʋərplɑntə(n)/ (plantte over, heeft overgeplant) **1** transplant **2** trans-plant, graft

de **overproductie** /ˈoʋərprodʏksi/ overproduc-tion

overreden /oʋərʁedə(n)/ (overreedde, heeft overreed) persuade

¹**overrijden** /ˈoʋərɛɪdə(n)/ (reed over, heeft overgereden) drive over; ride over

²**overrijden** /oʋərɛɪdə(n)/ (overreed, heeft overreden) run over, knock down

overrijp /oʋərɛɪp/ (adj) overripe

overrompelen /oʋərɔmpələ(n)/ (overrom-pelde, heeft overrompeld) (take by) surprise, catch off guard, catch napping

overrulen /oʋərulə(n)/ (overrulede, heeft overruled) overrule

overschaduwen /oʋərsxadywə(n)/ (over-schaduwde, heeft overschaduwd) overshad-ow, put in the shade

overschakelen /oʋərsxakələ(n)/ (schakel-de over, heeft/is overgeschakeld) **1** switch over **2** switch (*or:* change, go) over: *op de vierdaagse werkweek* ~ go over to a four-day week

de **overschakeling** /ˈoʋərsxakəlɪŋ/ switch-over, changeover

overschatten /oʋərsxɑtə(n)/ (overschatte, heeft overschat) overestimate, overrate

de **overschatting** /oʋərsxɑtɪŋ/ (pl: -en) overestimation; overrating

overschieten /ˈoʋərsxitə(n)/ (schoot over, is overgeschoten) be left (over)

het **overschot** /ˈoʋərsxɔt/ (pl: -ten) remainder; remains; residue; remnant(s): *het stoffelijk* ~ the (mortal) remains, the body ‖ [Belg] ~ *van* be absolutely right

overschreeuwen /oʋərsxrewə(n)/ (over-schreeuwde, heeft overschreeuwd) shout down: [fig] *zijn angst* ~ try to drown one's fear

overschrijden /oʋərsxrɛɪdə(n)/ (over-schreed, heeft overschreden) exceed, go be-yond

¹**overschrijven** /oʋərsxrɛɪvə(n)/ (over-schreef, heeft overschreven) overwrite

²**overschrijven** /ˈoʋərsxrɛɪvə(n)/ (schreef over, heeft overgeschreven) **1** copy; [depr] crib: *iets in het net* ~ copy sth. out neatly **2** transfer; put in (s.o.'s) name

de **overschrijving** /ˈoʋərsxrɛɪvɪŋ/ (pl: -en) **1** putting in s.o. (else)'s name; [sport] trans-fer **2** remittance

¹**overslaan** /ˈoʋərslan/ (sloeg over, is overge-slagen) **1** jump (over); be infectious; be catching **2** break, crack: *met ~de stem* with a catch in one's voice

²**overslaan** /ˈoʋərslan/ (sloeg over, heeft overgeslagen) miss (out), skip, leave out, omit: *één beurt* ~ miss one turn; *een bladzij-de* ~ skip a page; *een jaar* ~ skip a year

de **overslag** /ˈoʋərslɑx/ (pl: -en) transfer, trans-shipment

overspannen /oʋərspɑnə(n)/ (adj) **1** over-strained, overtense(d) **2** overwrought: *hij is erg* ~ he is suffering from severe (over)strain

het **overspel** /ˈoʋərspɛl/ adultery

overspelen /ˈoʋərspelə(n)/ (speelde over, heeft overgespeeld) **1** replay: *de wedstrijd moest overgespeeld worden* the match had to be replayed **2** [sport] play on (to), pass the ball on to

overspelig /ovərspe̱ləx/ (adj) adulterous

overspoelen /ovərspu̱lə(n)/ (overspoelde, heeft overspoeld) wash over; flood (across), inundate

het **overstaan** /o̱vərstan/: **ten ~ van** in the presence of, before

overstag /ovərsta̱x/ (adv): **~ gaan** tack; [fig] change one's mind

de **overstap** /o̱vərstɑp/ (pl: -pen) changeover, switch-over

overstappen /o̱vərstɑpə(n)/ (stapte over, is overgestapt) **1** step over, cross **2** change, transfer: **~ op de trein naar Groningen** change to the Groningen train

de **overste** /o̱vərstə/ (pl: -n) **1** lieutenant-colonel **2** (father, mother) superior, prior, prioress

de **oversteek** /o̱vərstek/ (pl: -steken) crossing

de **oversteekplaats** /o̱vərstekplats/ (pl: -en) crossing(-place); pedestrian crossing

oversteken /o̱vərstekə(n)/ (stak over, is overgestoken) cross (over), go across, come across

overstelpen /ovərste̱lpə(n)/ (overstelpte, heeft overstelpt) shower, swamp, inundate

overstemmen /ovərste̱mə(n)/ (overstemde, heeft overstemd) drown (out); shout down

[1]**overstromen** /o̱vərstromə(n)/ (stroomde over, is overgestroomd) **1** flow over, flood **2** overflow

[2]**overstromen** /ovərstro̱mə(n)/ (overstroomde, heeft overstroomd) **1** flood, inundate **2** flood, swamp: **de markt ~ met** flood the market with

de **overstroming** /ovərstro̱mɪŋ/ (pl: -en) flood

overstuur /ovərsty̱r/ (adj, adv) upset; shaken

de **overtocht** /o̱vərtɔxt/ (pl: -en) crossing; voyage

overtollig /ovərtɔ̱ləx/ (adj, adv) **1** surplus, excess **2** superfluous, redundant

overtreden /ovərtre̱də(n)/ (overtrad, heeft overtreden) break, violate

de **overtreder** /ovərtre̱dər/ (pl: -s) offender, wrongdoer

de **overtreding** /ovərtre̱dɪŋ/ (pl: -en) offence, violation (or: breach) (of the rules); [sport] foul: **een zware ~** a bad foul; **een ~ begaan tegenover een tegenspeler** foul an opponent

overtreffen /ovərtre̱fə(n)/ (overtrof, heeft overtroffen) exceed, surpass, excel

het/de **overtrek** /o̱vərtrɛk/ (pl: -ken) cover, case

[1]**overtrekken** /o̱vərtrɛkə(n)/ (trok over, is overgetrokken) pass (over)

[2]**overtrekken** /o̱vərtrɛkə(n)/ (trok over, heeft overgetrokken) trace: **met inkt ~** trace in ink

[3]**overtrekken** /ovərtrɛ̱kə(n)/ (overtrok,

heeft overtrokken) cover; upholster

overtuigd /ovərtœyxt/ (adj) confirmed, convinced: **hij was ervan ~ te zullen slagen** he was confident (or: sure) that he would succeed; **ik ben er (vast, heilig) van ~ dat ...** I'm (absolutely) convinced that ...

overtuigen /ovərtœyɣə(n)/ (overtuigde, heeft overtuigd) convince, persuade

overtuigend /ovərtœyɣənt/ (adj, adv) convincing; cogent; persuasive; conclusive

de **overtuiging** /ovərtœyɣɪŋ/ (pl: -en) conviction, belief, persuasion: **godsdienstige ~** religious persuasion (or: beliefs); **vol (met) ~** with conviction

overtypen /o̱vərtipə(n)/ (typte over, heeft overgetypt) retype; type out

het **overuur** /o̱vəryr/ (pl: -uren) overtime hour; overtime: **overuren maken** work overtime

de **overval** /o̱vərval/ (pl: -len) surprise attack; raid; hold-up; stick-up

overvallen /ovərva̱lə(n)/ (overviel, heeft overvallen) **1** raid; hold up; assault [pers]; surprise **2** surprise, take by surprise; overtake

de **overvaller** /o̱vərvalər/ (pl: -s) raider, attacker

[1]**overvaren** /o̱vərvarə(n)/ (voer over, is overgevaren) cross (over), sail across

[2]**overvaren** /o̱vərvarə(n)/ (voer over, heeft overgevaren) ferry, take across, put across

ooververhit /ovərvərhɪt/ (adj) overheated: **de gemoederen raakten ~** feelings ran high

ooververhitten /ovərvərhɪtə(n)/ (ooververhitte, heeft ooververhit) overheat

ooververmoeid /ovərvərmujt/ (adj) overtired, exhausted

de **ooververtegenwoordiging** /o̱vərvərteɣə(n)wordəɣɪŋ/ overrepresentation

de **ooververvzekering** /o̱vərvərzekərɪŋ/ overinsurance

ooovervleugelen /ovərvlø̱ɣələ(n)/ (oovervleugelde, heeft oovervleugeld) outstrip, eclipse

de **oovervvloed** /o̱vərvlut/ abundance

oovervloedig /ovərvlu̱dəx/ (adj, adv) abundant, plentiful, copious

oovervloeien /o̱vərvlujə(n)/ (vloeide over, heeft/is overgevloeid) **1** overflow, run over **2** (+ van) overflow (with): **~ van enthousiasme** bubble (over) with enthusiasm

oovervvoeren /ovərvu̱rə(n)/ (oovervoerde, heeft oovervoerd) glut, overstock, oversupply, surfeit

oovervol /ovərvɔ̱l/ (adj) overfull; overcrowded; packed

oovervragen /ovərvra̱ɣə(n)/ (oovervraagde/ oovervroeg, heeft oovervraagd) overcharge, ask too much

ooverwaaien /o̱vərwajə(n)/ (waaide over/ woei over, is overgewaaid) blow over

de **ooverwaarde** /o̱vərwardə/ surplus value: **de ~ van een huis** home equity

overwaarderen /o̯vərwardərə(n)/ (waardeerde over, heeft overgewaardeerd) overvalue, overrate

de ¹**overweg** /o̯vərwɛх/ level crossing; [Am] railroad crossing: *een bewaakte* ~ a guarded (*or:* manned) level crossing

²**overweg** /o̯vərwɛх/ (adv): *met een nieuwe machine* ~ *kunnen* know how to handle a new machine; *goed met elkaar* ~ *kunnen* get along well

overwegen /o̯vərwe̯ɣə(n)/ (overwoog, heeft overwogen) consider, think over, think out: *de nadelen (risico's)* ~ count the cost; *wij* ~ *een nieuwe auto te kopen* we are thinking of (*or:* considering) buying a new car

overwegend /o̯vərwe̯ɣənt/ (adv) predominantly, mainly, for the most part

de **overweging** /o̯vərwe̯ɣɪŋ/ (pl: -en) **1** consideration, thought **2** consideration, ground, reason

overweldigen /o̯vərwɛ̯ldəɣə(n)/ (overweldigde, heeft overweldigd) overwhelm, overcome

overweldigend /o̯vərwɛ̯ldəɣənt/ (adj) overwhelming, overpowering: *een ~e meerderheid halen* win a landslide victory

het **overwerk** /o̯vərwɛrk/ overtime (work)

overwerken /o̯vərwɛrkə(n)/ (werkte over, heeft overgewerkt) work overtime

overwerkt /o̯vərwɛ̯rkt/ (adj) overworked, overstrained

het **overwicht** /o̯vərwɪхt/ ascendancy, preponderance; authority

de **overwinnaar** /o̯vərwɪnar/ (pl: -s) victor, winner; conqueror

overwinnen /o̯vərwɪnə(n)/ (overwon, heeft overwonnen) **1** defeat, overcome **2** conquer, overcome **3** conquer, overcome, surmount: *moeilijkheden* ~ overcome/surmount (*or:* get over) difficulties

de **overwinning** /o̯vərwɪnɪŋ/ (pl: -en) victory, conquest, triumph; win: *een ~ behalen* win a victory, be victorious, win, triumph; *een verpletterende* ~ a sweeping victory

overwinteren /o̯vərwɪntərə(n)/ (overwinterde, heeft overwinterd) **1** (over)winter **2** hibernate

de **overwintering** /o̯vərwɪntərɪŋ/ (pl: -en) (over)wintering, hibernation

overwoekeren /o̯vərwu̯kərə(n)/ (overwoekerde, heeft overwoekerd) overgrow, overrun: *overwoekerd worden door onkruid* become overgrown with weeds

overzees /o̯vərze̯s/ (adj) oversea(s)

overzetten /o̯vərzɛtə(n)/ (zette over, heeft overgezet) take across (*or:* over); ferry (across, over): *iem. de grens* ~ deport s.o.

het **overzicht** /o̯vərzɪхt/ (pl: -en) **1** survey, view: ~ *vanuit de lucht* bird's-eye view; *ik heb geen enkel* ~ *meer* I have lost all track of the situation **2** survey, (over)view, summary; review

overzichtelijk /o̯vərzɪ̯хtələk/ (adj, adv) well-organized; clearly set out

overzien /o̯vərzi̯n/ (overzag, heeft overzien) survey; overlook; command (a view of); review: *de gevolgen zijn niet te* ~ the consequences are incalculable

de **overzijde** /o̯vərzɛidə/ other side, opposite side: *aan de* ~ *van het gebouw* opposite the building

overzwemmen /o̯vərzwɛmə(n)/ (zwom over, heeft/is overgezwommen) swim (across): *het Kanaal* ~ swim the Channel

de **ov-jaarkaart** /oveja̯rkart/ (pl: -en) annual season ticket, travel card

de **OVSE** /oveɛse̯/ Organisatie voor Veiligheid en Samenwerking in Europa OSCE

de **ovulatie** /ovyla̯(t)si/ (pl: -s) ovulation

de **oxidatie** /ɔksida̯(t)si/ (pl: -s) oxidation

het **oxide** /ɔksi̯də/ (pl: -n, -s) oxide

oxideren /ɔkside̯rə(n)/ (oxideerde, is geoxideerd) oxidize

de **ozb** /ozɛdbe̯/ onroerendezaakbelasting property tax(es)

het/de **ozon** /ozɔn/ ozone

de **ozonlaag** /o̯zɔnlax/ ozone layer

p

de **p** /pe/ (pl: p's) p, P

de **pa** /pa/ (pl: pa's) dad(dy), pa: *haar pa en* **ma** her mum and dad(dy)

p/a /pea̯/ (abbrev) *per adres* c/o

het **paadje** /pacə/ (pl: -s) path; trail

paaien /paɪə(n)/ (paaide, heeft gepaaid) placate, appease

de **paal** /pal/ (pl: palen) **1** post, stake, pole; pile **2** (goal)post: *hij schoot* **tegen (op)** *de ~* he hit the (goal)post || *voor ~ staan* look foolish (*or:* stupid)

paaldansen /paldansə(n)/ (paaldanste, heeft gepaaldanst) pole dancing

de **paalwoning** /palwonɪŋ/ (pl: -en) pile dwelling

het **paar** /par/ (pl: paren) **1** pair, couple: *twee ~ sokken* two pairs of socks **2** (a) few, (a) couple of

het **paard** /part/ (pl: -en) **1** horse: *op het* **verkeerde** *~ wedden* back the wrong horse; *men moet een gegeven ~ niet in de bek zien* never look a gift horse in the mouth; *over het ~ getild zijn* be swollen-headed, be puffed up; *het ~ achter de wagen* **spannen** a) make things difficult for o.s.; **b)** put the cart before the horse **2** (vaulting) horse **3** knight

de **paardenbloem** /pardə(n)blum/ (pl: -en) dandelion

de **paardenkastanje** /pardə(n)kastaɲə/ (pl: -s) horse chestnut

de **paardenkracht** /pardə(n)kraxt/ (pl: -en) horsepower

het **paardenmiddel** /pardəmɪdəl/ (pl: -en) rough remedy

de **paardenrennen** /pardə(n)rɛnə(n)/ (pl) horse races

de **paardensport** /pardə(n)sport/ equestrian sport(s); horse racing

de **paardensprong** /pardə(n)sprɔŋ/ (pl: -en) **1** jump **2** knight's move

de **paardenstaart** /pardə(n)start/ (pl: -en) **1** horsetail **2** ponytail

de **paardenstal** /pardə(n)stal/ (pl: -len) stable

de **paardenvijg** /pardə(n)vɛɪx/ (pl: -en) horse-droppings; horse-dung

paardrijden /partrɛɪdə(n)/ (reed paard, heeft paardgereden) ride (horseback): *zij zit* **op** *~* she is taking riding lessons

de **paardrijder** /partrɛɪdər/ (pl: -s) horseman, horsewoman; rider

het **paarlemoer** /parləmur/ mother-of-pearl

paars /pars/ (adj) purple

de **paartijd** /partɛɪt/ mating season; rut

het **paartje** /parcə/ (pl: -s) couple, pair: *een pas* **getrouwd** *~* a newly wed couple, newlyweds

paasbest /pazbɛst/ (adj): *op zijn ~ zijn* be all dressed up

de **paasdag** /pazdax/ (pl: -en) Easter Day: *Eerste ~* Easter Sunday

het **paasei** /pasɛɪ/ (pl: -eren) Easter egg

het **paasfeest** /pasfest/ (pl: -en) Easter

de **paashaas** /pashas/ (pl: -hazen) Easter bunny (*or:* rabbit)

de **paasvakantie** /pasfakansi/ (pl: -s) Easter holidays

de **pabo** /pabo/ (pl: -'s) [Dutch] teacher training college (for primary education)

de **pacemaker** /pesmekər/ (pl: -s) pacemaker

de **pacht** /paxt/ (pl: -en) lease: *in ~ nemen* lease, take on lease

pachten /paxtə(n)/ (pachtte, heeft gepacht) lease, rent

de **pachter** /paxtər/ (pl: -s) leaseholder, lessee; tenant (farmer)

de **pachtsom** /paxtsɔm/ (pl: -men) rent, rental

het **pacifisme** /pasifɪsmə/ pacifism

de **pacifist** /pasifɪst/ (pl: -en) pacifist

pacifistisch /pasifɪstis/ (adj, adv) pacifist(ic)

het **pact** /pakt/ (pl: -en) pact, treaty

de ¹**pad** /pat/ (pl: -den) toad || [Belg] *een ~ in iemands* **korf** *zetten* thwart s.o.; set off

het ²**pad** /pat/ (pl: -en) **1** path, walk; track; trail; gangway; aisle: *platgetreden ~en bewandelen* walk the beaten path (*or:* tracks) **2** path, way: *iem. op het* **slechte** *~ brengen* lead s.o. astray; *hij is het* **slechte** *~ opgegaan* he has taken to crime; *iemands ~ kruisen* cross s.o.'s path || *op ~ gaan* set off

de **paddenstoel** /padəstul/ (pl: -en) [general] fungus; [poisonous] toadstool; [edible] mushroom

de **paddo** /pado/ shroom, magic mushroom

de **padvinder** /patfɪndər/ (pl: -s) (boy) scout, girl guide

de **padvinderij** /patfɪndərɛɪ/ scouting

de **paella** /paɛlja/ paella

paf /paf/ (adj): *iem. ~ doen staan* make s.o. gasp, stagger s.o.; *ik sta ~* I'm flabbergasted!, well, blow me down!

paffen /pafə(n)/ (pafte, heeft gepaft) [inform] puff

pafferig /pafərəx/ (adj) doughy; puffy

pag. (abbrev) *pagina* p.

de **page** /paʒə/ (pl: -s) page

de **pagina** /paɣina/ (pl: -'s) page: *~ 2 en 3* pages 2 and 3

de **pagode** /paɣɔdə/ (pl: -n, -s) pagoda

paintballen /pɛndbɔlə(n)/ (paintballde, heeft gepaintballd) go paintballing

de **pais** /pajs/: *alles is weer ~ en* **vree** peace reigns once more

het **pak** /pak/ (pl: -ken) **1** pack(age); packet; parcel; carton: *een ~ melk* a carton of milk;

pakhuis

een ~ sneeuw a layer of snow **2** suit: *een nat ~ halen* get drenched, get a drenching **3** bale; batch; bundle; packet: *een ~ oud papier* a batch (*or:* bundle) of waste paper ‖ *een kind een ~ slaag geven* spank (*or:* wallop) a child, give a child a spanking; *dat is een ~ van mijn hart* that takes a load off my mind, that's a great relief

het **pakhuis** /pɑkhœys/ (pl: pakhuizen) warehouse, storehouse

het **pakijs** /pɑkɛɪs/ pack (ice)

de **Pakistaan** /pakistan/ (pl: Pakistani) Pakistani

Pakistaans /pakistans/ (adj) Pakistan(i), of Pakistan, from Pakistan

Pakistan /pakistɑn/ Pakistan

het **pakje** /pɑkjə/ (pl: -s) parcel, present

¹**pakken** /pɑkə(n)/ (pakte, heeft gepakt) hold; grip; bite; take

²**pakken** /pɑkə(n)/ (pakte, heeft gepakt) **1** get, take, fetch: *een pen ~* get a pen; *pak een stoel* grab a chair **2** catch, grasp, grab; seize: *een kind (eens lekker) ~* hug (*or:* cuddle) a child; *de daders zijn nooit gepakt* the offenders were never caught; *proberen iem. te ~ te krijgen* try to get hold of s.o.; *iets te ~ krijgen* lay one's hands on sth.; [fig] *iem. te ~ nemen* have a go at s.o.; *nou heb ik je te ~* got you!; *als ik hem te ~ krijg* if I catch him, if I lay hands on him; *iem. op iets ~* get s.o. on sth.; *pak me dan, als je kan!* catch me if you can! **3** pack; wrap up: *zijn boeltje bij elkaar ~* pack (one's bags)

pakkend /pɑkənt/ (adj) catching; catchy; fascinating, appealing; fetching; arresting; gripping; catching; attractive: *een ~e titel* a catchy (*or:* an arresting) title

de **pakkerd** /pɑkərt/ (pl: -s) hug and a kiss

het **pakket** /pɑkɛt/ (pl: -ten) **1** parcel **2** pack; kit; [fig] package

de **pakketpost** /pɑkɛtpɔst/ parcel post

pakkie-an /pɑkian/: *dat is niet mijn ~* that's not my department

de **pakking** /pɑkɪŋ/ (pl: -en) gasket, packing

het **pakpapier** /pɑkpapir/ packing paper, wrapping paper

de **paksoi** /pɑksɔj/ pak-choi cabbage

pakweg /pɑkwɛx/ (adv) roughly, approximately, about, around

de ¹**pal** /pɑl/ (pl: -len) catch

²**pal** /pɑl/ (adv) directly: *de wind staat ~ op het raam* the wind blows right on the window; *hij stond ~ voor mijn neus* he stood directly in front of me ‖ [fig] *~ staan voor iets* stand firm for sth.

het **paleis** /palɛis/ (pl: paleizen) **1** palace; court **2** hall

de **Palestijn** /paləstɛin/ (pl: -en) Palestinian

Palestijns /paləstɛins/ (adj) Palestinian, Palestine

Palestina /paləstina/ Palestine

het **palet** /palɛt/ (pl: -ten) palette

de **paling** /palɪŋ/ (pl: -en) eel, eels

de **palissade** /palisadə/ (pl: -n, -s) palisade, stockade

de **pallet** /pɛlət/ (pl: -s) pallet (board)

de **palm** /pɑlm/ (pl: -en) palm

de **palmboom** /pɑlmbom/ (pl: -bomen) palm

de **palmolie** /pɑlmoli/ palm oil

Palmpasen /pɑlmpasə(n)/ Palm Sunday

de **palmtak** /pɑlmtɑk/ (pl: -ken) palm

de **palmtop** /pɑlmtɔp/ palmtop

het **pamflet** /pɑmflɛt/ (pl: -ten) pamphlet; broadsheet

pamperen /pɛmpərə(n)/ (pamperde, heeft gepamperd) pamper

het **pampus** /pɑmpys/: *voor ~ liggen* be dead to the world, be out cold

de **pan** /pɑn/ (pl: -nen) **1** pan: [fig] *dat swingt de ~ uit* that's really far out; [fig] *de ~ uit rijzen* soar, snowball, rocket **2** (pan)tile ‖ *in de ~ hakken* cut to ribbons (*or:* pieces), make mincemeat of

Panama /panama/ Panama

de **Panamees** /panames/ Panamanian

het/de **pancreas** /pɑŋkrejɑs/ pancreas

het **pand** /pɑnt/ **1** premises, property, building, house **2** pawn, pledge, security

de **panda** /pɑnda/ (pl: -'s) panda

de **pandjesjas** /pɑncəsjɑs/ (pl: -sen) tailcoat

het **paneel** /panel/ (pl: panelen) panel

het **paneermeel** /panermel/ breadcrumbs

het **panel** /pɛnəl/ (pl: -s) panel

paneren /panerə(n)/ (paneerde, heeft gepaneerd) bread(crumb)

de **panfluit** /pɑnflœyt/ (pl: -en) pan pipe(s)

pang /pɑŋ/ (int) pow, bang

de **paniek** /panik/ panic, alarm; terror: *er ontstond ~* panic broke out; *~ zaaien* spread panic (*or:* alarm); *geen ~!* don't panic

paniekerig /panikərəx/ (adj, adv) panicky, panic-stricken: *~ reageren* panic (in reaction to)

het **paniekvoetbal** /panikfudbɑl/ **1** panicky play **2** [fig] panic measure(s) (*or:* behaviour): *~ spelen* be panicking

de **paniekzaaier** /paniksajər/ (pl: -s) panic-monger, alarmist

panisch /panis/ (adj, adv) panic, frantic: *een ~e angst hebben voor iets* (or: *om iets te doen*) be terrified (of doing) sth.

panklaar /pɑnklar/ (adj) **1** ready to cook **2** [fig] ready-made: *een panklare oplossing* an instant solution

de **panne** /pɑnə/ breakdown: *~ hebben* have a breakdown, have engine trouble

de **pannenkoek** /pɑnə(n)kuk/ (pl: -en) pancake

de **pannenlap** /pɑnə(n)lɑp/ (pl: -pen) oven cloth; oven glove

de **pannenset** /pɑnə(n)sɛt/ (pl: -s) set of (pots and) pans de **pannenspons** /pɑnə(n)spɔns/ (pl: -spon-zen) scourer, scouring pad

het **panorama** /panorɑma/ (pl: -'s) panorama

de **pantalon** /pɑntalɔn/ (pl: -s) (pair of) trou-sers; (pair of) slacks: *twee* ~s two pair(s) of trousers

de **panter** /pɑntər/ (pl: -s) panther; leopard

de **pantoffel** /pɑntɔfəl/ (pl: -s) (carpet) slipper

de **pantoffelheld** /pɑntɔfəlhɛlt/ (pl: -en) faint-heart

de **pantomime** /pɑntomim/ (pl: -s, -n) mime, dumbshow

het **pantser** /pɑntsər/ (pl: -s) **1** (plate) armour, armour-plating **2** (suit of) armour

de **pantserdivisie** /pɑn(t)sərdivizi/ (pl: -s) ar-moured division

pantseren /pɑntsərə(n)/ (pantserde, heeft gepantserd) armour(-plate)

de **pantserwagen** /pɑn(t)sərwaɣə(n)/ (pl: -s) armoured car

de **panty** /pɛnti/ (pl: -'s) (pair of) tights: *drie* ~'s three pairs of tights

de **pap** /pɑp/ (pl: -pen) porridge; pap: *ik lust er wel* ~ *van* this is meat and drink to me || *geen* ~ *meer kunnen zeggen* **a)** be (dead)beat; **b)** be whacked (out), be fagged (out); **c)** be full up

de **papa** /papa/ (pl: -'s) papa, dad(dy)

de **papaja** /papaja/ (pl: -'s) papaya, pawpaw

de **paparazzo** /paparɔtso/ (pl: paparazzi) pa-parazzo

de **papaver** /papavər/ (pl: -s) poppy

de **papegaai** /papəɣaj/ (pl: -en) parrot

de **paper** /pepər/ (pl: -s) paper

de **paperassen** /papərɑsə(n)/ (pl) papers, pa-perwork; bumf

de **paperback** /pepərbɛk/ (pl: -s) paperback

de **paperclip** /pepərklɪp/ (pl: -s) paperclip

het **Papiamento** /papijamɛnto/ Papiamento

het **papier** /papir/ (pl: -en) **1** paper: *zijn gedach-ten op* ~ *zetten* put one's thoughts down on paper **2** paper; document

papieren /papirə(n)/ (adj) paper

het **papiergeld** /papirɣɛlt/ paper money: €*100,- in* ~ 100 euros in notes

het **papier-maché** /pɑpirmɑʃe/ papier-mâché

het **papiertje** /papircə/ (pl: -s) piece of paper; wrapper

de **papierversnipperaar** /papirvərsnɪpərar/ (pl: -s) (paper) shredder

de **papierwinkel** /pɑpirwɪŋkəl/ mass of pa-perwork

de **papil** /papɪl/ (pl: -len) papilla

het **papkind** /pɑpkɪnt/ (pl: -eren) milksop, sissy

de **paplepel** /pɑpləpəl/ (pl: -s): *dat is hem met de* ~ *ingegeven* he learned it at his mother's knee

Papoea-Nieuw-Guinea /papuwaniw-ɣineja/ Papua New Guinea

de **pappa** /pɑpa/ (pl: -'s) papa, dad, daddy

de **pappenheimer** /pɑpə(n)hɛɪmər/ (pl: -s): *hij kent zijn* ~s he knows his people (*or:* custom-ers)

papperig /pɑpərəx/ (adj) **1** mushy **2** puffy

de **pappie** /pɑpi/ (pl: -s) daddy

de **paprika** /paprika/ (pl: -'s) (sweet) pepper

het **paprikapoeder** /paprikapudər/ paprika

de **paps** /pɑps/ dad, daddy

de **papyrus** /papirys/ (pl: -sen) papyrus

de **papzak** /pɑpsɑk/ (pl: -ken) potbelly

de **paraaf** /paraf/ (pl: parafen) initials

paraat /parat/ (adj) ready, prepared

de **parabel** /parabəl/ (pl: -s, -en) parable

de **parabool** /parabol/ (pl: parabolen) parabo-la

de **parachute** /paraʃyt/ (pl: -s) parachute

parachutespringen /paraʃytsprɪŋə(n)/ parachuting

de **parachutist** /paraʃytɪst/ (pl: -en) parachut-ist

de **parade** /paradə/ (pl: -s) parade

het **paradepaard** /paradəpart/ (pl: -en) show-piece

paraderen /paraderə(n)/ (paradeerde, heeft geparadeerd) parade

het **paradijs** /paradɛis/ (pl: paradijzen) paradise

paradijselijk /paradɛisələk/ (adj, adv) heavenly

de **paradox** /paradɔks/ (pl: -en) paradox

paradoxaal /paradɔksal/ (adj, adv) para-doxical

paraferen /paraferə(n)/ (parafeerde, heeft geparafeerd) initial

de **paraffine** /parɔfinə/ (pl: -n) paraffin wax

de **parafrase** /parafrazə/ (pl: -n, -s) paraphrase

de **paragnost** /paraɣnɔst/ (pl: -en) psychic

de **paragraaf** /paraɣraf/ (pl: -grafen) section

Paraguay /paraɣwɑj/ Paraguay

de **Paraguayaan** /paraɣwajan/ (pl: Para-guayanen) Paraguayan

Paraguayaans /paraɣwajans/ (adj) Para-guayan

de ¹**parallel** /paralɛl/ (pl: -len) parallel: *deze* ~ *kan nog verder doorgetrokken worden* this parallel (*or:* analogy) can be carried further

²**parallel** /paralɛl/ (adj, adv) **1** parallel (to, with): *die wegen lopen* ~ *aan (met)* elkaar those roads run parallel to each other; ~ *schakelen* shunt **2** parallel (to), analogous (to, with)

het **parallellogram** /paralɛloɣrɑm/ (pl: -men) parallelogram

de **parallelweg** /parɑlɛlwɛx/ (pl: -en) parallel road

paramedisch /paramedis/ (adj) paramedi-cal

de **parameter** /parametər/ (pl: -s) parameter

paramilitair /paramilitɛːr/ (adj) paramili-tary

de **paranoia** /paranɔja/ paranoia

paranoïde /paranowidə/ (adj) paranoid

paranormaal /paranɔrmal/ (adj, adv) para-normal, psychic de **paraplu** /paraplý/ (pl: -'s) umbrella

de **parapsychologie** /pˌarapsiˌxoloɣi/ parapsy-
chology, psychic research

de **parasiet** /parasít/ (pl: -en) **1** parasite **2** parasite, sponge(r)
  parasiteren /parasitérə(n)/ (parasiteerde,
  heeft geparasiteerd) parasitize; [fig] sponge
  (on, off)

de **parasol** /parasɔ́l/ (pl: -s) sunshade, parasol
  parastataal /parastatál/ (adj) [Belg] semi-
  governmental: *parastatale **instelling*** semi-
  governmental institution, [roughly] quango

de **paratroepen** /parátrupə(n)/ (pl) para-
troopers

de **paratyfus** /parátifʏs/ paratyphoid (fever)

het **parcours** /parkúr(s)/ (pl: -en) track
  pardoes /pardús/ (adv) bang, slap, smack

het **¹pardon** /pardɔ́n/ pardon, mercy: *generaal ~*
  amnesty; *zonder ~* without mercy, merciless-
  ly
  ²pardon /pardɔ́n/ (int) pardon (me), I beg
  your pardon, excuse me, (so) sorry: *stond ik
  op uw tenen? ~!* sorry, did I step on your toe?

de **parel** /parəl/ (pl: -s) pearl
  parelen /parélə(n)/ (parelde, heeft gepa-
  reld) pearl: *het **zweet** parelde op haar voorhoofd* her forehead was beaded with sweat

het **parelhoen** /parəlhun/ (pl: -ders) guinea
  fowl; guinea hen
  ¹paren /parə(n)/ (paarde, heeft gepaard)
  mate (with)
  ²paren /parə(n)/ (paarde, heeft gepaard)
  [fig] combine (with), couple (with): *gepaard
  gaan met* go (hand in hand) with
  pareren /parérə(n)/ (pareerde, heeft gepa-
  reerd) parry

het/de **parfum** /parfým/ (pl: -s) perfume, scent
  parfumeren /parfymérə(n)/ (parfumeerde,
  heeft geparfumeerd) scent, perfume

de **paria** /parija/ (pl: -'s) pariah, outcast
  Parijs /parɛis/ Paris

de **paring** /parɪŋ/ (pl: -en) **1** mating **2** pairing

de **Parisienne** /parizɛ́nə/ Parisian

de **pariteit** /paritɛ́it/ parity

het **park** /park/ (pl: -en) **1** park **2** fleet; plant

de **parka** /parka/ (pl: -'s) parka

de **parkeerautomaat** /parkérautomat/ (pl:
  -automaten) (car-park) ticket machine (*or:*
  dispenser); [Am] (parking lot) ticket machine

de **parkeerbon** /parkérbɔn/ (pl: -nen) parking
  ticket

de **parkeergarage** /parkérɣaraʒə/ (pl: -s) (underground) car park; [Am] (underground)
  parking garage

het **parkeergeld** /parkérɣɛlt/ parking fee

de **parkeergelegenheid** /parkérɣə-
  leɣə(n)hɛit/ parking facilities

de **parkeermeter** /parkérmetər/ parking meter

de **parkeerplaats** /parkérplats/ (pl: -en) parking place (*or:* space); car park; [Am] parking

lot

de **parkeerschijf** /parkérsxɛif/ (pl: -schijven)
  (parking) disc

het **parkeerterrein** /parkértɛrɛin/ (pl: -en) car
  park; [Am] parking lot

het **parkeerverbod** /parkérvərbɔt/ parking
  ban; [on notice] No Parking: *hier **geldt** een ~*
  this is a no-parking zone
  parkeren /parkérə(n)/ (parkeerde, heeft
  geparkeerd) park; pull in (*or:* over)

het **parket** /parkɛt/ (pl: -ten) **1** parquet (floor)
  2 public prosecutor ‖ *in een **lastig** ~ zitten*
  find o.s. in a difficult (*or:* an awkward) position

de **parketvloer** /parkɛtflur/ (pl: -en) parquet
  (floor)

de **parkiet** /parkit/ (pl: -en) parakeet

de **parking** /pɑːrkɪŋ/ (pl: -s) [Belg] car park;
  [Am] parking lot

de **parkinson** /parkɪnsɔn/ Parkinson's disease

het **parlement** /parləmɛ́nt/ (pl: -en) parliament: *in het ~* in parliament
  parlementair /parləmɛntɛ́ːr/ (adj) parliamentary

de **parlementariër** /parləmɛntarijər/ (pl: -s)
  member of (a) parliament, parliamentarian;
  representative

de **parlementsverkiezing** /parləmɛ́n(t)sfər-
  kizɪŋ/ (pl: -en) parliamentary election
  parmantig /parmɑ́ntəx/ (adj, adv) jaunty,
  dapper
  parochiaal /paroxijál/ (adj) parochial

de **parochiaan** /paroxiján/ (pl: parochianen)
  parishioner

de **parochie** /parɔ́xi/ (pl: -s) parish

de **parodie** /parodí/ (pl: -ën) parody (of, on);
  travesty (of)
  parodiëren /parodijérə(n)/ (parodieerde,
  heeft geparodieerd) parody

het **parool** /parɔ́l/ (pl: parolen) watchword, slogan: *oppletten **is** het ~* pay attention is the
  motto

het **part** /part/ share, portion ‖ *voor mijn ~* for all
  I care, as far as I'm concerned; *iem. ~en **spelen*** play tricks on s.o.

het/de **parterre** /partɛ́ːrə/ (pl: -s) ground floor; [Am
  also] first floor

de **participatie** /partisipá(t)si/ (pl: -s) participation
  participeren /partisipérə(n)/ (participeer-
  de, heeft geparticipeerd) participate (in),
  take part (in)

de **¹particulier** /partikylír/ (pl: -en) private individual (*or:* person): *geen **verkoop** aan ~en*
  trade (sales) only
  ²particulier /partikylír/ (adj, adv) private:
  *het ~ **initiatief*** private enterprise

de **partij** /partɛ́i/ (pl: -en) **1** party, side: *de **strijdende** ~en* the warring parties; *~ **kiezen*** take
  sides **2** set, batch, lot; consignment; shipment: *bij* (or: *in*) *~en verkopen* sell in lots

3 [mus] part **4** game

het **partijbestuur** /pɑrtɛɪbəstyr/ (pl: -besturen) party executive (committee)

het **partijcongres** /pɑrtɛɪkɔŋɣrɛs/ (pl: -sen) party congress; party conference; party convention

partijdig /pɑrtɛɪdəχ/ (adj, adv) bias(s)ed, partial

de **partijleider** /pɑrtɛɪlɛɪdər/ (pl: -s) party leader

de ¹**partijpolitiek** /pɑrtɛɪpolitik/ party politics
²**partijpolitiek** /pɑrtɛɪpolitik/ (adj) party political

de **partituur** /pɑrtityr/ (pl: partituren) score

de **partizaan** /pɑrtizan/ (pl: partizanen) partisan

de **partner** /pɑrtnər/ (pl: -s) **1** partner, companion **2** (co-)partner, associate

het **partnerregister** /pɑrtnərəɣɪstər/ register in which cohabitation contracts are officially recorded

het **partnerschap** /pɑrtnərsχɑp/ partnership: *een geregistreerd ~* a civil partnership

parttime /pɑːrtɑjm/ (adj) part-time

de **parttimebaan** /pɑːrtɑjmban/ part-time job

de **parttimer** /pɑːrtɑjmər/ (pl: -s) part-timer

de **party** /pɑːrti/ (pl: -'s) party

de **partydrug** /pɑːrtidryːɡ/ party drug

de **partytent** /pɑːrtitɛnt/ (pl: -en) party tent

de **parvenu** /pɑrvəny/ (pl: -'s) parvenu

de ¹**pas** /pɑs/ **1** step, pace; gait: *iem. de ~ afsnijden* cut (or: head) s.o. off **2** pass **3** pass; passport ‖ *het leger moest er aan te ~ komen* the army had to step in; *goed van ~ komen* come in handy (or: useful); *dat komt uitstekend van ~* that's just the thing; *altijd wel van ~ komen* always come in handy

²**pas** /pɑs/ (adv) **1** (only) just, recently: *hij begint ~* he is just beginning, he has only just started; *~ geplukt* freshly picked; *een ~ getrouwd stel* a newly-wed couple; *~ geverfd* wet paint; *ik werk hier nog maar ~* I'm new here (or: to this job) **2** only, just: *hij is ~ vijftig (jaar)* he's only fifty **3** only, not until: *~ toen vertelde hij het mij* it was only then that he told me; *~ toen hij weg was, begreep ik …* it was only after he had left that I understood …; *~ geleden, ~ een paar dagen terug* only recently, only the other day **4** really: *dat is ~ een vent* he's (what I call) a real man; *dat is ~ hard werken!* now, that really is hard work!

het **Pascha** /pɑsχɑ/ Pesach

Pasen /pɑsə(n)/ Easter

de **pasfoto** /pɑsfoto/ (pl: -'s) passport photo(graph)

pasgeboren /pɑsχəbↄrə(n)/ (adj) newborn, newly born

pasgetrouwd /pɑsχətrɑut/ (adj) newly married

het **pashokje** /pɑshↄkjə/ (pl: -s) fitting room

het **pasje** /pɑʃə/ (pl: -s) **1** step **2** pass

de **paskamer** /pɑskamər/ (pl: -s) fitting room

pasklaar /pɑsklar/ (adj) (made) to measure; fitted; [fig] ready-made

het **paspoort** /pɑspoːrt/ (pl: -en) passport

de **paspoortcontrole** /pɑspoːrtkↄntrↄːlə/ passport control

de **pass** /pɑːs/ (pl: -es) pass: *een goede ~ geven* make a good pass

de **passaat** /pɑsat/ (pl: passaten) trade wind

de **passage** /pɑsaʒə/ (pl: -s) passage, extract: *een ~ uit een gedicht voorlezen* read an extract from a poem

de **passagier** /pɑsaʒir/ (pl: -s) passenger

het **passagiersschip** /pɑsaʒirsχɪp/ (pl: -schepen) passenger ship

passant /pɑsɑnt/: *en ~ in passing*; [chess] *en ~ slaan* take (a pawn) en passant

¹**passen** /pɑsə(n)/ (paste, heeft gepast) **1** fit: *het past precies* it fits like a glove; *deze sleutel past op de meeste sloten* this key fits most locks **2** (+ bij) fit, go (with), match: *deze hoed past er goed bij* this hat is a good match; *ze ~ goed (or: slecht) bij elkaar* they are well-matched (or: ill-matched) **3** (+ op) look after, take care of: *op de kinderen ~* look after the children; *pas op het afstapje* (or: *je hoofd*) watch/mind the step (or: your head) **4** [cards] pass

²**passen** /pɑsə(n)/ (paste, heeft gepast) **1** fit: *~ en meten* try it in all different ways; *met wat ~ en meten komen we wel rond* with a bit of juggling we'll manage **2** pay with the exact money: *hebt u het niet gepast?* haven't you got the exact change? (or: money?) **3** try on

³**passen** /pɑsə(n)/ (passte, heeft gepasst) [socc] pass

passend /pɑsənt/ (adj, adv) **1** suitable (for), appropriate: *niet bij elkaar ~e partners* incompatible partners; *niet bij elkaar ~e sokken* odd socks; *slecht bij elkaar ~* ill-matched **2** proper, becoming: *een ~ gebruik maken van* make proper use of

de **passer** /pɑsər/ (pl: -s) compass

de **passerdoos** /pɑsərdos/ (pl: -dozen) compass case

¹**passeren** /pɑsɛrə(n)/ (passeerde, is gepasseerd) pass, overtake: *de auto passeerde (de fietser)* the car overtook (the cyclist); *een huis ~* pass (by) a house

²**passeren** /pɑsɛrə(n)/ (passeerde, heeft/is gepasseerd) **1** pass through; cross: *de grens* (or: *een brug*) *~* cross the border (or: a bridge); *de vijftig gepasseerd zijn* have turned fifty **2** pass over: *zich gepasseerd voelen* feel passed over

de **passie** /pɑsi/ (pl: -s) passion (for); zeal (for), enthusiasm (for)

passief /pɑsif/ (adj, adv) passive

het **passiespel** /pɑsispɛl/ (pl: -en) passion play

de **passievrucht** /pɑsivryχt/ (pl: -en) passion

fruit

de **passiva** /pɑsiva/ (pl) liabilities

het **password** /pɑːswʏːrt/ (pl: -s) password

de **pasta** /pɑsta/ (pl: -'s) **1** paste **2** pasta

de **pastei** /pɑstɛi/ (pl: -en) pasty, pie

het **pastel** /pɑstɛl/ (pl: -s) pastel

de **pasteltint** /pɑstɛltɪnt/ (pl: -en) pastel shade (*or*: tone)

pasteuriseren /pɑstørizerə(n)/ (pasteuriseerde, heeft gepasteuriseerd) pasteurize

de **pastille** /pɑstijə/ (pl: -s) pastille, lozenge

de **pastoor** /pɑstoːr/ (pl: -s) (parish) priest; padre: *Meneer Pastoor* Father

de **pastor** /pɑstoːr/ (pl: -s, pastores) pastor, minister; [Roman Catholicism] priest

pastoraal /pɑstoraːl/ (adj, adv) **1** pastoral: ~ *medewerker* church worker **2** pastoral, bucolic

het **pastoraat** /pɑstoraːt/ **1** pastoral care **2** priesthood

de **pastorie** /pɑstori/ (pl: -ën) parsonage; [Roman Catholicism] presbytery

de **pasvorm** /pɑsfɔrm/ (pl: -en) fit

pat /pɑt/ (adj) stalemate: *iem. ~ zetten* stalemate s.o.

de **patat** /pɑtɑt/ chips, French fries: *een zakje ~ a bag of chips; ~ met* chips with mayonnaise

het **patatje** /pɑtɑcə/ (pl: -s) (portion of) chips

de **patatkraam** /pɑtɑtkram/ (pl: -kramen) [roughly] fish and chips stand; [Am] [roughly] hot dog stand

de **patch** /pɛtʃ/ patch

de **paté** /pate/ (pl: -s) pâté

het **patent** /pɑtɛnt/ (pl: -en) patent

patenteren /pɑtɛnterə(n)/ (patenteerde, heeft gepatenteerd) (grant a) patent ǁ *een gepatenteerde leugenaar* a patent liar

de **pater** /pɑtər/ (pl: -s) father

de ¹**paternoster** /pɑtərnɔstər/ (pl: -s) rosary

het ²**paternoster** /pɑtərnɔstər/ paternoster, Our Father

pathetisch /patetis/ (adj, adv) pathetic

het **pathos** /pɑtɔs/ pathos; melodrama

het **patience** /paʃɑ̃s/ patience; [Am] solitaire

de **patiënt** /paʃɛnt/ (pl: -en) patient: *zijn ~en bezoeken* do one's rounds

de **patio** /pa(t)s(i)jo/ (pl: -'s) patio

de **patisserie** /patisəri/ (pl: -ën) **1** pastries **2** pastry shop

de **patriarch** /patrijɑrx/ (pl: -en) patriarch

de **patrijs** /patrɛis/ (pl: patrijzen) partridge

de **patrijspoort** /patrɛisport/ (pl: -en) porthole

de **patriot** /patrijɔt/ (pl: -ten) patriot

patriottisch /patrijɔtis/ (adj) patriotic

het **patronaat** /patronaːt/ (pl: patronaten) [Belg] employers

de **patrones** /patronɛs/ (pl: -sen) **1** patron (saint) **2** patron(ess)

de ¹**patroon** /patron/ **1** patron **2** boss

de ²**patroon** /patron/ cartridge: *een losse ~ a blank*

het ³**patroon** /patron/ **1** pattern, design: *volgens een vast ~* according to an established pattern **2** pattern, style

de **patrouille** /patrujə/ (pl: -s) patrol

patrouilleren /patrujerə(n)/ (patrouilleerde, heeft gepatrouilleerd) patrol

pats /pɑts/ (int) wham, bang: *pats-boem* wham bam

de **patser** /pɑtsər/ (pl: -s) show-off

patserig /pɑtsərəx/ (adj, adv) flashy

de **patstelling** /pɑtstɛlɪŋ/ stalemate [also fig]

de **pauk** /pauk/ (pl: -en) kettledrum; timpani

de **paukenist** /paukənɪst/ (pl: -en) kettledrummer

de **paus** /paus/ (pl: -en) pope

pauselijk /pousələk/ (adj) papal, pontifical: *~ gezag* papacy, papal authority

de **pauw** /pau/ (pl: -en) peacock; [female also] peahen

de **pauze** /pauzə/ (pl: -s) interval, break, intermission; [sport] (half-)time: *een kwartier ~ houden* take (*or*: have) a fifteen-minute break; *een ~ inlassen* introduce an extra break

pauzeren /pauzerə(n)/ (pauzeerde, heeft gepauzeerd) pause, take a break, have a rest

het **paviljoen** /pavɪljun/ (pl: -en, -s) pavilion

de **pavlovreactie** /pɑflɔfrejɑksi/ (pl: -s) Pavlovian response

het **pay-per-view** /pepərvjuː/ pay-per-view

de **pc** /pese/ *personal computer* pc

de **pech** /pɛx/ **1** bad (*or*: hard, tough) luck: *~ gehad* hard (*or*: tough) luck **2** breakdown ǁ *~ met de auto* car trouble

de **pechdienst** /pɛxdinst/ (pl: -en) [Belg] breakdown service

de **pechstrook** /pɛxstrok/ (pl: -stroken) [Belg] hard shoulder

de **pechvogel** /pɛxfoɣəl/ (pl: -s) unlucky person: *hij is een echte ~* he's a walking disaster area

het/de **pedaal** /pədaːl/ (pl: pedalen) treadle; pedal

de **pedaalemmer** /pədaːlɛmər/ (pl: -s) pedal bin

de **pedagogiek** /pedaɣoɣik/ (theory of) education, educational theory (*or*: science); pedagogy

pedagogisch /pedaɣoɣis/ (adj, adv) pedagogic(al): *~e academie* teacher(s') training college

de **pedagoog** /pedaɣox/ (pl: -gogen) education(al)ist

pedant /pədɑnt/ (adj, adv) pedantic

de **peddel** /pɛdəl/ (pl: -s) paddle

peddelen /pɛdələ(n)/ (peddelde, heeft/is gepeddeld) paddle

de **pedicure** /pedikyrə/ (pl: -s) chiropodist, pedicure

de ¹**pedofiel** /pedofil/ (pl: -en) paedophile

²**pedofiel** /pedofil/ (adj) paedophile

de **pee** /pe/ [inform]: *(ergens) de ~ (over) in heb-*

ben be annoyed about sth.

de **peen** /pen/ (pl: penen) carrot ‖ *~tjes zweten* be in a cold sweat

de **peer** /per/ (pl: peers) **1** pear **2** bulb

de **pees** /pes/ (pl: pezen) tendon, sinew

de **peetmoeder** /petmudər/ (pl: -s) godmother

de **peetoom** /petom/ (pl: -s) godfather

de **peettante** /petɑntə/ (pl: -s) godmother

de **peetvader** /petfadər/ (pl: -s) godfather

de **pegel** /peɣəl/ (pl: -s) icicle

de **peignoir** /pɛɲwar/ (pl: -s) dressing gown, housecoat

het **peil** /pɛil/ (pl: -en) **1** level, standard: *het ~ van de conversatie daalde* the level of conversation dropped **2** mark, level: *zijn conditie op ~ brengen* (or: *houden*) get o.s. into condition, keep fit (*or:* in shape) ‖ *dat is beneden ~* that is below the mark

de **peildatum** /pɛildatʏm/ (pl: -data) set day, reference date

peilen /pɛilə(n)/ (peilde, heeft gepeild) **1** sound, fathom **2** [fig] gauge; sound (out): *ik zal Bernard even ~, kijken wat die ervan vindt* I'll sound Bernard out, see what he thinks

het **peilglas** /pɛilɣlɑs/ (pl: -glazen) gaugeglass

de **peiling** /pɛilɪŋ/ (pl: -en) sounding

het **peillood** /pɛilot/ (pl: -loden) plumb (*or:* lead) line

peilloos /pɛilos/ (adj) unfathomable

de **peilstok** /pɛilstɔk/ (pl: -ken) sounding rod; gauging-rod; dipstick

peinzen /pɛinzə(n)/ (peinsde, heeft gepeinsd) (+ over) think about, contemplate: *hij peinst er niet over* he won't even contemplate (*or:* consider) it; *hij peinst zich suf over een oplossing* he is racking his brains to find a solution

het/de **pek** /pɛk/ pitch

de **pekel** /pekəl/ salt, grit

het **pekelvlees** /pekəlvles/ salted meat

de **pekinees** /pekines/ (pl: pekinezen) pekinese

de **pelgrim** /pɛlɣrɪm/ (pl: -s) pilgrim

de **pelgrimstocht** /pɛlɣrɪmstɔxt/ (pl: -en) pilgrimage

de **pelikaan** /pelikan/ (pl: pelikanen) pelican

pellen /pɛlə(n)/ (pelde, heeft gepeld) peel, skin; blanch; husk; hull; shell

het **peloton** /pelətɔn/ (pl: -s) **1** platoon **2** [sport] pack, (main)bunch

de **pels** /pɛls/ (pl: pelzen) fleece, fur

het **pelsdier** /pɛlzdir/ (pl: -en) furred animal, furbearing animal

de **pelsjager** /pɛlsjaɣər/ (pl: -s) trapper

de **pen** /pɛn/ (pl: -nen) **1** pen **2** pin; needle

de **penalty** /pɛnəlti/ (pl: -'s) penalty (kick, shot): *een ~ nemen* take a penalty

de **penaltystip** /pɛnəltistɪp/ penalty spot

het/de **pendant** /pɛndɑnt/ (pl: -en) counterpart

de **pendel** /pɛndəl/ (pl: -s) commuting

de **pendelaar** /pɛndəlar/ (pl: -s) commuter

de **pendeldienst** /pɛndəldinst/ (pl: -en) shuttle service

pendelen /pɛndələ(n)/ (pendelde, heeft gependeld) commute

het **pendelverkeer** /pɛndəlvərker/ commuter traffic

de **pendule** /pɛndylə/ (pl: -s) (mantel) clock (with pendulum)

penetrant /penətrɑnt/ (adj, adv) penetrating

de **penetratie** /penətra(t)si/ (pl: -s) penetration

penetreren /penətrerə(n)/ (penetreerde, heeft gepenetreerd) penetrate

penibel /penibəl/ (adj) painful, awkward

de **penicilline** /penisilinə/ penicillin

de **penis** /penɪs/ penis

penitentiair /penitɛn(t)ʃɛːr/ (adj) penitentiary: *een ~e inrichting* a penitentiary; a pen

de **penlight** /pɛnlɑjt/ **1** penlight **2** penlight battery

pennen /pɛnə(n)/ (pende, heeft gepend) scribble, pen

de **pennenstreek** /pɛnə(n)strek/ (pl: -streken) penstroke: *met één ~* with one stroke of the pen

de **pennenvrucht** /pɛnə(n)vrʏxt/ (pl: -en) product of one's pen

de **penning** /pɛnɪŋ/ (pl: -en) token

de **penningmeester** /pɛnɪŋmestər/ (pl: -s) treasurer

de **pens** /pɛns/ (pl: -en) paunch, belly, gut

het **penseel** /pɛnsel/ (pl: penselen) (paint)brush

de **pensioen** /pɛnʃun/ (pl: -en) pension, retirement (pay); superannuation: *~ aanvragen* apply for a pension; *met ~ gaan* retire

het **pensioenfonds** /pɛnʃunfɔn(t)s/ (pl: -en) pension fund

pensioengerechtigd /pɛnʃuŋɣərɛxtəxt/ (adj) pensionable: *de ~e leeftijd bereiken* reach retirement age

de **pensioenuitkering** /pɛnʃunœytkerɪŋ/ (pl: -en) pension, retirement pay

het **pension** /pɛnʃɔn/ (pl: -s) **1** guest house, boarding house **2** bed and board: *vol ~* full board; *in ~ zijn* be a lodger **3** kennel

het **pensionaat** /pɛnʃonat/ (pl: pensionaten) boarding school

de **pensionhouder** /pɛnʃɔnhaudər/ (pl: -s) landlord

de **pensionhoudster** /pɛnʃɔnhautstər/ landlady

de **penvriend** /pɛnvrint/ (pl: -en) pen-friend; [Am] pen pal

de **peper** /pepər/ (pl: -s) pepper: *een snufje ~* a dash of pepper

peperduur /pepərdyr/ (adj) very expensive, pricey

de **peperkoek** /pepərkuk/ (pl: -en) [roughly] gingerbread, gingercake

peperkorrel

de **peperkorrel** /pe̯pərkɔrəl/ (pl: -s) pepper-corn

de **pepermolen** /pe̯pərmolə(n)/ (pl: -s) pepper mill

de **pepermunt** /pepərmʏnt/ (pl: -en) pepper-mints: *een rolletje ~* a tube of peppermints

de **pepernoot** /pe̯pərnot/ (pl: -noten) [rough-ly] spiced ginger nut

het **pepmiddel** /pɛ̯pmɪdəl/ (pl: -en) pep pill

de **pepperspray** /pe̯pərspre/ (pl: -s) pepper spray

de **peptalk** /pɛ̯ptɔːk/ pep talk

per /pɛr/ (prep) **1** per, a, by: *iets ~ post ver-zenden* send sth. by post (or: mail); *het aantal inwoners ~ vierkante kilometer* the number of inhabitants per square kilometre; *iets ~ kilo* (or: *paar*) *verkopen* sell sth. by the kilo (or: in pairs); *ze kosten 3 euro ~ stuk* they cost 3 eu-ros apiece (or: each); *~ uur betaald worden* be paid by the hour **2** from, as of: *de nieuwe ta-rieven worden ~ 1 februari van kracht* the new rates will take effect on February 1

het **perceel** /pɛrse̯l/ (pl: percelen) **1** property **2** parcel, lot, section

het **percent** /pɛrsɛ̯nt/ (pl: -en) per cent

het **percentage** /pɛrsɛnta̯ʒə/ (pl: -s) percentage

de **percussie** /pɛrkʏ̯si/ (pl: -s) percussion

de **perenboom** /pe̯rə(n)bom/ (pl: -bomen) pear (tree)

perfect /pɛrfɛ̯kt/ (adj, adv) perfect: *hij gaf een ~ imitatie van die zangeres* he did a per-fect imitation of that singer; *in ~e staat* a) in mint condition; b) in perfect condition; *alles is ~ in orde* everything is perfect

de **perfectie** /pɛrfɛ̯ksi/ (pl: -s) perfection

perfectioneren /pɛrfɛkʃone̯rə(n)/ (perfec-tioneerde, heeft geperfectioneerd) perfect, bring to perfection

de **perfectionist** /pɛrfɛkʃonɪ̯st/ (pl: -en) per-fectionist

perfectionistisch /pɛrfɛkʃonɪ̯stis/ (adj) perfectionist

de **perforator** /pɛrfora̯tɔr/ (pl: -s) perforator, punch

perforeren /pɛrfore̯rə(n)/ (perforeerde, heeft geperforeerd) perforate: *een geperfo-reerde long* a perforated lung

de **pergola** /pɛ̯rɣola/ (pl: -'s) pergola

de **periferie** /periferi̯/ (pl: -ën) periphery

de **periode** /perijo̯də/ (pl: -s) period, time; phase; episode, chapter: *~n met zon* sunny periods; *verkozen voor een ~ van twee jaar* elected for a two-year term (of office)

het/de **1periodiek** /perijodi̯k/ (pl: -en) **1** periodical **2** increment

2periodiek /perijodi̯k/ (adj, adv) periodic(al): *het ~ systeem* the periodic table

de **periscoop** /perisko̯p/ (pl: periscopen) peri-scope

het **perk** /pɛrk/ (pl: -en) **1** bed; flower bed **2** bound, limit: *binnen de ~en houden* limit, contain; *dat gaat alle ~en te buiten* that's the very limit

het **perkament** /pɛrkamɛ̯nt/ (pl: -en) parch-ment

de **1permanent** /pɛrmanɛ̯nt/ (pl: -s) permanent (wave)

2permanent /pɛrmanɛ̯nt/ (adj) **1** perma-nent, perpetual **2** permanent, enduring; lasting; standing

3permanent /pɛrmanɛ̯nt/ (adv) permanent-ly, perpetually, all the time

permanenten /pɛrmanɛ̯ntə(n)/ (perma-nentte, heeft gepermanent) give a perma-nent wave, perm

de **permissie** /pɛrmɪ̯si/ (pl: -s) permission, leave

permitteren /pɛrmite̯rə(n)/ (permitteerde, zich, heeft zich gepermitteerd) permit, grant permission, allow: *ik kan me niet ~ dat te doen* I can't afford to do that

perplex /pɛrplɛ̯ks/ (adj) perplexed, baffled, flabbergasted

het **perron** /pɛrɔ̯n/ (pl: -s) platform

de **pers** /pɛrs/ (pl: -en) **1** press: *de ~ te woord staan* talk to the press **2** (printing) press: *ter ~e gaan* go to press

de **Pers** /pɛrs/ (pl: Perzen) Persian

het **persagentschap** /pɛ̯rsaɣɛntsχɑp/ (pl: -pen) press (or: news) agency

het **persbericht** /pɛ̯rzbərɪχt/ (pl: -en) press re-port, newspaper report

het **persbureau** /pɛ̯rsbyro/ (pl: -s) news agency, press agency, press bureau

de **persconferentie** /pɛ̯rskɔnferɛnsi/ (pl: -s) press conference, news conference

per se /pɛrse̯/ (adv) at any price, at all costs: *hij wilde haar ~ zien* he was set on seeing (or: determined to see) her

1persen /pɛ̯rsə(n)/ (perste, heeft geperst) press, compress: *je moet harder ~* you must press harder

2persen /pɛ̯rsə(n)/ (perste, heeft geperst) **1** press; stamp (out) **2** press (out), squeeze (out) **3** press, squeeze, push: *zich door een nauwe doorgang ~* squeeze (o.s.) through a narrow gap

de **persfotograaf** /pɛ̯rsfotoɣraf/ (pl: -grafen) press photographer, newspaper photogra-pher

de **persiflage** /pɛrsifla̯ʒə/ (pl: -s) (+ op) parody (of)

de **perskaart** /pɛ̯rskart/ (pl: -en) press card (or: pass)

het/de **personage** /pɛrsona̯ʒə/ (pl: -s) character, role

de **personalia** /pɛrsona̯lija/ (pl) personal par-ticulars (or: details)

het **personeel** /pɛrsone̯l/ personnel, staff; em-ployees; workforce; crew; (factory) hands: *tien man ~* a staff of ten; *wij hebben een groot tekort aan ~* we are badly understaffed (or:

short-staffed); *onderwijzend* ~ teaching staff

de **personeelschef** /pɛrsoneːlʃɛf/ (pl: -s) personnel manager, staff manager

de **personeelszaken** /pɛrsoneːlzakə(n)/ (pl) **1** personnel matters, staff matters **2** personnel department

de **personenauto** /pɛrsoːnə(n)ɑuto/ (pl: -'s) (private, passenger) car

de **personificatie** /pɛrsoːnifika(t)si/ (pl: -s) personification

de **persoon** /pɛrsoːn/ (pl: personen) person, individual; [pl mostly] people: *een tafel voor* **één** ~ a table for one || *ze kwam in* **(hoogst)eigen** ~ she came personally (*or:* in person)

¹**persoonlijk** /pɛrsoːnlək/ (adj) **1** personal, private: *om* ~*e* **redenen** for personal (*or:* private) reasons, for reasons of one's own; *een* ~ **onderhoud** a personal talk **2** personal, individual

²**persoonlijk** /pɛrsoːnlək/ (adv) personally || ~ **vind** *ik hem een kwal* personally, I think he's a pain

de **persoonlijkheid** /pɛrsoːnləkhɛit/ (pl: -heden) personality, character

de **persoonsbeschrijving** /pɛrsoːnzbəsχrɛivɪŋ/ (pl: -en) personal description

het **persoonsbewijs** /pɛrsoːnzbəwɛis/ (pl: -bewijzen) identity card

persoonsgebonden /pɛrsoːnsχəbondə(n)/ (adj) personal

de **persoonsvorm** /pɛrsoːnsfɔrm/ (pl: -en) finite verb

het **perspectief** /pɛrspɛktif/ (pl: perspectieven) **1** prospect, perspective **2** perspective, context: *iets in* **breder** ~ *zien* look at (*or:* see) sth. in a wider context || *in* ~ *tekenen* draw in perspective

de **perssinaasappel** /pɛrsinɑsɑpəl/ (pl: -s) juice orange

de **persvrijheid** /pɛrsfrɛihɛit/ freedom of the press

pertinent /pɛrtinɛnt/ (adj) definite(ly), emphatic(ally)

Peru /peru/ Peru

de **Peruaan** /peruwaːn/ (pl: Peruanen) Peruvian

Peruaans /peruwaːns/ (adj) Peruvian

pervers /pɛrvɛrs/ (adj, adv) perverted, degenerate; unnatural

Perzië /pɛrzijə/ Persia

de **perzik** /pɛrzɪk/ (pl: -en) peach

Perzisch /pɛrzis/ (adj) Persian: ~ *tapijt* Persian rug (*or:* carpet)

de **peseta** /peseta/ (pl: -'s) peseta

het **pessimisme** /pɛsimɪsmə/ pessimism

de **pessimist** /pɛsimɪst/ (pl: -en) pessimist

pessimistisch /pɛsimɪstis/ (adj, adv) pessimistic, gloomy

de **pest** /pɛst/ **1** (bubonic) plague, pestilence **2** miserable || *de* ~ *in* **hebben** be in a foul mood; *de* ~ **aan** *iets (iem.) hebben* loathe/de-

test sth. (s.o.)

pesten /pɛstə(n)/ (pestte, heeft gepest) pester, tease: *hij* **zit** *mij altijd* **te** ~ he is always on at me

het **pesticide** /pɛstisidə/ (pl: -n, -s) pesticide

de **pestkop** /pɛstkɔp/ (pl: -pen) [inform] pest, nuisance

de **pesto** /pɛsto/ pesto

de **pet** /pɛt/ (pl: -ten) **1** cap: *met de* ~ *naar iets gooien* make a half-hearted attempt at sth., have a shot at sth.; *met de* ~ *rondgaan* pass the hat round **2** [fig] upstairs: *dat gaat* **boven** *mijn* ~ that is beyond me; *ik kan er* **met** *mijn* ~ *niet bij* it beats me || *geen* **hoge** ~ *op hebben van* not think much of, have a low opinion of

het **petekind** /peːtəkɪnt/ (pl: -eren) godchild

de **peter** /peːtər/ (pl: -s) godfather

de **peterselie** /peːtərseli/ parsley

de **petfles** /pɛtflɛs/ (pl: -sen) PET-bottle, (reusable) plastic bottle

de **petitie** /pəti(t)si/ (pl: -s) petition: *een* ~ *indienen* file a petition

de **petroleum** /petroːlejʏm/ petroleum, mineral oil

petto /pɛto/ *iets in* ~ *hebben* have sth. in reserve (*or:* in hand)

de **petunia** /petynija/ (pl: -'s) petunia

de **peuk** /pøk/ (pl: -en) **1** butt, stub **2** fag

de **peul** /pøl/ (pl: -en) pod, capsule

de **peulenschil** /pølə(n)sχɪl/ (pl: -len) trifle: *dat is maar een* ~*(letje) voor hem* **a)** that's peanuts (*or:* chicken feed) to him; **b)** he can do it standing on his head

de **peulvrucht** /pølvrʏχt/ (pl: -en) dried legume

de **peuter** /pøtər/ (pl: -s) pre-schooler, toddler

peuteren /pøtərə(n)/ (peuterde, heeft gepeuterd) pick: *in zijn neus* ~ pick one's nose

de **peuterleidster** /pøtərlɛitstər/ (pl: -s) nursery-school teacher

de **peuterspeelzaal** /pøtərspelzal/ (pl: -zalen) playgroup

de **peutertuin** /pøtərtœyn/ (pl: -en) day nursery, crèche

pezen /peːzə(n)/ (peesde, heeft gepeesd) [inform] slave

pezig /peːzəχ/ (adj) sinewy, stringy

de **pfeiffer** /pfɑjfər/ glandular fever

het **pgb** /peːɣebeː/ (pl: -'s) [Dutch] *persoonsgebonden budget* personal budget

het **phishing** /fɪʃɪŋ/ phishing

de **pH-waarde** /pehawardə/ pH value

de **pi** /pi/ (pl: pi's) pi

de **pianist** /pijanɪst/ (pl: -en) pianist, piano player

de **piano** /pijano/ (pl: -'s) piano

het **pianoconcert** /pijanokɔnsɛrt/ (pl: -en) **1** piano recital: *een* ~ **geven** give a piano recital **2** piano concerto

de **pianoles** /pijanolɛs/ piano lesson

pianospelen /pijanospelə(n)/ play(ing) the

piano
de **pianostemmer** /pijanostɛmər/ (pl: -s) piano tuner
de **pias** /pijɑs/ (pl: -sen) clown, buffoon
de **piccalilly** /pɪkalɪli/ piccalilli
de **piccolo** /pɪkolo/ (pl: -'s) **1** bell-boy **2** piccolo
de **picknick** /pɪknɪk/ (pl: -s) picnic
picknicken /pɪknɪkə(n)/ (picknickte, heeft gepicknickt) picnic
de **picknickmand** /pɪknɪkmɑnt/ (pl: -en) picnic hamper (*or*: basket)
de **pick-up** /pɪkʏp/ (pl: -s) record player
pico bello /pikobɛlo/ (adj, adv) splendid, outstanding
het **pictogram** /pɪktoɣrɑm/ (pl: -men) pictogram
de **pief** /pif/ (pl: -en) [inform] type, sort: *zich een **hele** ~ voelen* think one is a big shot (*or*: cheese)
de **piek** /pik/ (pl: -en) **1** spike: *een ~ **haar*** a spike of hair **2** peak, summit **3** top
pieken /pikə(n)/ (piekte, heeft gepiekt) be spiky, stand out
de **piekeraar** /pikərar/ (pl: -s) worrier, brooder
piekeren /pikərə(n)/ (piekerde, heeft gepiekerd) worry, brood
piekfijn /pikfɛin/ (adj, adv) posh, smart
het **piekuur** /pikyr/ (pl: -uren) peak hour; rush hour
de **piemel** /pimǝl/ (pl: -s) willie
pienter /pintər/ (adj) bright, sharp, shrewd
piep /pip/ (int) squeak; peep; cheep
piepen /pipə(n)/ (piepte, heeft gepiept) squeak; peep; cheep; creak; pipe
de **pieper** /pipər/ (pl: -s) **1** b(l)eeper **2** spud
piepjong /pipjɔŋ/ (adj): *niet (zo) ~ **meer zijn*** be no chicken
piepklein /pipklɛin/ (adj) teeny(-weeny), teensy
het **piepschuim** /pipsχœym/ styrofoam, polystyrene foam
de **piepstem** /pipstɛm/ (pl: -men) squeaky voice
de **pieptoon** /pipton/ (pl: -tonen) bleep, beep
de **piepzak** /pipsɑk/ [inform]: *in de ~ zitten* have the wind up
de **pier** /pir/ (pl: -en) **1** worm, earthworm **2** pier
de **piercing** /pirsɪŋ/ piercing
het **pierenbad** /pirə(n)bɑt/ paddling pool
de **pies** /pis/ [inform] pee, wee
piesen /pisə(n)/ (pieste, heeft gepiest) [inform] pee, wee
de **piet** /pit/ (pl: -en) geezer, feller: *hij vindt zichzelf een **hele** ~* he thinks he's really s.o.
Piet /pit/: *Jan, ~ en Klaas* Tom, Dick and Harry; *er voor ~ **Snot** bijzitten* sit there like a fool
de **piëteit** /pijetɛit/ piety
pietepeuterig /pitəpøtərəχ/ (adj, adv) [inform] **1** finical, finicky **2** microscopic(al)
het **pietje-precies** /picəprəsis/: *een ~ zijn* be a fusspot

pietluttig /pitlʏtəχ/ (adj) meticulous, petty, niggling
het **pigment** /pɪɣmɛnt/ pigment
de **pigmentvlek** /pɪɣmɛntflɛk/ (pl: -ken) birthmark, mole
de **pij** /pɛi/ (pl: -en) (monk's) habit, frock
de **pijl** /pɛil/ (pl: -en) arrow: *nog **meer** ~en op zijn boog hebben* have more than one string to one's bow
de **pijl-en-boog** /pɛilɛmboχ/ (pl: pijl-en-bogen) bow and arrow
de **pijler** /pɛilər/ (pl: -s) pillar
pijlsnel /pɛilsnɛl/ (adj, adv) (as) swift as an arrow
het **pijltje** /pɛilcǝ/ (pl: -s) dart
de **pijltjestoets** /pɛilcǝstuts/ (pl: -en) scroll arrow
de **pijn** /pɛin/ (pl: -en) pain; ache: *~ **in** de buik hebben* have (a) stomach-ache, have a pain in one's stomach; *~ **in** de keel hebben* have a sore throat; *iem. ~ **doen*** hurt s.o., give s.o. pain ‖ *met veel ~ **en moeite** iets gedaan krijgen* get sth. accomplished with a great deal of trouble (*or*: a great effort)
de **pijnappel** /pɛinɑpəl/ (pl: -s) pine cone
de **pijnbank** /pɛimbɑŋk/ (pl: -en) rack
de **pijnboom** /pɛimbom/ (pl: -bomen) pine (tree)
de **pijngrens** /pɛiŋɣrɛns/ pain threshold
pijnigen /pɛinəɣə(n)/ (pijnigde, heeft gepijnigd) **1** torture **2** torment: *zijn **hersens*** beat one's brains out
¹**pijnlijk** /pɛinlǝk/ (adj) **1** painful, sore: *~ **aanvoelen*** hurt, be painful **2** painful, hurtful: *een ~e **opmerking*** an embarrassing remark **3** painful, awkward, embarrassing: *er viel een ~e **stilte*** there was an uncomfortable silence
²**pijnlijk** /pɛinlǝk/ (adv) painfully: *~ **getroffen** zijn* be pained
pijnloos /pɛinlos/ (adj) painless
de **pijnstiller** /pɛinstɪlər/ (pl: -s) painkiller
de **pijp** /pɛip/ (pl: -en) **1** pipe, tube **2** leg
pijpen /pɛipə(n)/ (pijpte, heeft gepijpt) [inform] blow; suck off: *gepijpt **worden*** be blown (*or*: sucked (off)) ‖ [fig] *~ **naar** iemands dansen* dance attendance (up)on s.o.
de **pijpenkrul** /pɛipə(n)krʏl/ (pl: -len) corkscrew curl
de **pijpensteel** /pɛipə(n)stel/ (pl: -stelen): *het regent pijpenstelen* it's raining cats and dogs
de **pijpleiding** /pɛiplɛidɪŋ/ (pl: -en) piping; pipeline
de **pik** /pɪk/ [inform] penis: *een stijve ~* a hard-on
pikant /pikɑnt/ (adj) piquant
pikdonker /pɪgdɔŋkər/ (adj) pitch-dark, pitch-black
het **pikhouweel** /pɪkhɑuwel/ (pl: -houwelen) pickaxe
¹**pikken** /pɪkə(n)/ (pikte, heeft gepikt) peck

²**pikken** /pɪkə(n)/ (pikte, heeft gepikt) [inform] **1** lift, pinch: *zij heeft dat geld gepikt* she stole that money **2** take, put up with: *pik jij dat allemaal maar?* do you just put up with all that?; *we ~ het niet langer* we won't take it any longer

pikzwart /pɪkswɑrt/ (adj) pitch-black: *~ haar* raven(-black) hair

de **pil** /pɪl/ (pl: -len) pill: *het is een bittere ~ voor hem* it is a bitter pill for him to swallow; *de ~ slikken* be on the pill

de **pilaar** /pilaːr/ (pl: pilaren) pillar

de **piloot** /piloːt/ (pl: piloten) pilot: *automatische ~* automatic pilot

de **pilot** /pɑjlət/ (pl: -s) pilot

het/de **pils** /pɪls/ beer, lager

pimpelen /pɪmpələ(n)/ (pimpelde, heeft gepimpeld) tipple, booze

de **pimpelmees** /pɪmpəlmeːs/ blue tit

pimpelpaars /pɪmpəlpaːrs/ (adj) (lurid) purple: *hij is ~ van de kou* he is blue with cold

pimpen /pɪmpə(n)/ (pimpte, heeft gepimpt) pimp

de **pin** /pɪn/ (pl: -nen) peg, pin

het **pinapparaat** /pɪnɑparat/ (pl: -apparaten) PIN-code reader

de **pinautomaat** /pɪnɑutomat/ [roughly] EFTPOS, Electronic Fund Transfer at Point Of Sale: *kan ik de ~ gebruiken?* can I use my direct debit card?, can I use Chip and PIN?

het/de **pincet** /pɪnsɛt/ (pl: -ten) (pair of) tweezers

de **pincode** /pɪŋkodə/ (pl: -s) PIN code

de **pinda** /pɪnda/ (pl: -'s) peanut

de **pindakaas** /pɪndakas/ peanut butter

de **pindasaus** /pɪndasaus/ (pl: -sauzen) peanut sauce

de **pineut** /pinøt/ dupe: *de ~ zijn* be the dupe

de **pingelaar** /pɪŋəlar/ (pl: -s) **1** [socc] player who holds on to the ball **2** haggler

pingelen /pɪŋələ(n)/ (pingelde, heeft gepingeld) **1** haggle (over, about) **2** hold on to the ball

het **pingpong** /pɪŋpɔŋ/ ping-pong

pingpongen /pɪŋpɔŋə(n)/ (pingpongde, heeft gepingpongd) play ping-pong

de **pinguïn** /pɪŋgwɪn/ (pl: -s) penguin

de **pink** /pɪŋk/ (pl: -en) little finger

de **pinksterbloem** /pɪŋkstərblum/ (pl: -en) cuckoo flower, lady's smock

de **pinksterdag** /pɪŋkstərdɑχ/ (pl: -en) Whit Sunday, Whit Monday

Pinksteren /pɪŋkstərə(n)/ Whitsun(tide)

de **pinkstergemeente** /pɪŋkstərɣeməntə/ (pl: -n, -s) Pentecostal church

pinnen /pɪnə(n)/ (pinde, heeft gepind) **1** pay by switch card **2** withdraw cash from a cashpoint

pinnig /pɪnəχ/ (adj, adv) tart; snappish

de **pinpas** /pɪmpɑs/ (pl: -sen) cash card; switch card

de **pint** /pɪnt/ (pl: -en) pint

het **pintje** /pɪncə/ (pl: -s) [Belg] pint (of beer)

de **pioen** /pijun/ (pl: -en) peony

de **pion** /pijɔn/ (pl: -nen) pawn

de **pionier** /pijonir/ (pl: -s) pioneer

het/de **pipet** /pipɛt/ (pl: -ten) pipette

pips /pɪps/ (adj) washed out, pale

de **piraat** /pirat/ (pl: piraten) pirate

de **piramide** /piramidə/ (pl: -n, -s) pyramid

het **piramidespel** /piramidəspɛl/ pyramid scheme

de **piranha** /pirɑna/ (pl: -'s) piranha

de **piratenzender** /piratə(n)zɛndər/ (pl: -s) pirate (radio station)

de **piraterij** /piratərɛɪ/ piracy: *~ op internet* Internet piracy

de **pirouette** /piruwɛt(ə)/ (pl: -n, -s) pirouette

de **pis** /pɪs/ [inform] piss

de **pisang** /pisɑŋ/ banana

pisnijdig /pɪsnɛɪdəχ/ (adj, adv) [inform] pissed off

de **pispaal** /pɪspal/ (pl: -palen) [inform] target

de **pispot** /pɪspɔt/ (pl: -ten) piss-pot

de **pissebed** /pɪsəbɛt/ (pl: -den) woodlouse

pissen /pɪsə(n)/ (piste, heeft gepist) [inform] piss

pissig /pɪsəχ/ (adj, adv) [inform] pissed off, bloody annoyed

de **pistache** /pistɑʃ/ (pl: -s) pistachio (nut)

de **piste** /pistə/ (pl: -s) **1** ring **2** [cycling] track **3** [skiing] piste

de **pistolet** /pistolɛt/ (pl: -s) bread roll

het **pistool** /pistoːl/ (pl: pistolen) pistol, gun: *nietpistool* staple gun

de ¹**pit** /pɪt/ (pl: -ten) **1** seed; pip; stone **2** wick **3** burner

het/de ²**pit** /pɪt/ spirit: *er zit ~ in die meid* she's a girl with spirit

het **pitabroodje** /pitabroːcə/ (pl: -s) pitta (bread)

de **pitbullterriër** /pɪtbultɛrijər/ (pl: -s) pit bull (terrier)

de **pits** /pɪts/ pit(s)

pitten /pɪtə(n)/ (pitte, heeft gepit) [inform] turn in, kip: *gaan ~* hit the sack

pittig /pɪtəχ/ (adj, adv) **1** lively, pithy; racy **2** [fig] stiff **3** spicy, hot, strong **4** tough

pittoresk /pitorɛsk/ (adj, adv) picturesque; scenic

de **pixel** /pɪksəl/ pixel

de **pizza** /pidza/ (pl: -'s) pizza

de **pizzakoerier** /pɪtsakurir/ (pl: -s) pizza deliverer, pizza delivery boy

de **pizzeria** /pidzərija/ (pl: -'s) pizzeria

de **pk** /peka/ *paardenkracht* h.p.

de **PKN** *Protestantse Kerk in Nederland* Dutch United Protestant Chruches

de **plaag** /plaχ/ (pl: plagen) plague

de **plaaggeest** /plaχest/ (pl: -en) tease(r)

de **plaat** /plat/ (pl: platen) **1** plate; sheet; slab **2** record **3** plate, print ‖ [inform] *uit zijn ~ gaan* be over the moon; hit the roof het **plaatje** /plɑcə/ (pl: -s) **1** plate; sheet; slab; identity disc **2** snapshot, photo **3** picture

de **plaats** /plats/ (pl: -en) **1** place, position: *de ~ van bestemming* the destination; *de juiste man op de juiste ~* the right man in the right place; *op uw ~en! klaar, af* on your marks, get set, go; *in (op) de eerste ~* in the first place; *op de eerste ~ komen* come first, take first place; *op de eerste ~ eindigen* be (placed) first; *ter ~e* on the spot; on the scene; [Belg] *ter ~e trappelen* be stuck **2** room, space; seat: *~ maken (voor iem.)* make room (for s.o.) **3** town **4** place; seat: *neemt u a.u.b. ~* please take your seats ‖ *in ~ van* instead of

de **plaatsbepaling** /platsbəpalɪŋ/ orientation

de **plaatsbespreking** /platsbəsprekɪŋ/ booking, reservation

het **plaatsbewijs** /platsbəwɛis/ (pl: -bewijzen) ticket

¹plaatselijk /platsələk/ (adj) local: *een ~e verdoving* a local anaesthetic

²plaatselijk /platsələk/ (adv) **1** locally, on the spot: *iets ~ onderzoeken* investigate sth. on the spot **2** in some places: *~ regen* local showers

¹plaatsen /platsə(n)/ (plaatste, heeft geplaatst) **1** place, put: *de ladder tegen het schuurtje ~* lean (*or:* put) the ladder against the shed; *iets niet kunnen ~* [also fig] not be able to place sth. **2** rank ‖ *een order ~* place an order

zich **²plaatsen** /platsə(n)/ (plaatste zich, heeft zich geplaatst) qualify (for)

het **plaatsgebrek** /platsxəbrɛk/ lack of space

plaatshebben /platshɛbə(n)/ (had plaats, heeft plaatsgehad) take place

de **plaatsing** /platsɪŋ/ (pl: -en) **1** placement, positioning **2** [sport] ranking; qualification

plaatsmaken /platsmakə(n)/ (maakte plaats, heeft plaatsgemaakt) make room (*or:* space) (for)

de **plaatsnaam** /platsnam/ (pl: -namen) place name

plaatsnemen /platsnemə(n)/ (nam plaats, heeft plaatsgenomen) take a seat

het **plaatstaal** /platstal/ sheet steel, steelplate

plaatsvervangend /platsfərvɑŋənt/ (adj) substitute; temporary: *~e schaamte* vicarious shame

de **plaatsvervanger** /platsfərvɑŋər/ (pl: -s) substitute, replacement; deputy

plaatsvinden /platsfɪndə(n)/ (vond plaats, heeft plaatsgevonden) take place, happen

de **placebo** /plasebo/ (pl: -'s) placebo

de **placemat** /plɛsmɛt/ (pl: -s) place mat

de **placenta** /plasɛnta/ (pl: -'s) placenta

de **pladijs** /pladɛis/ (pl: pladijzen) [Belg] plaice

het **plafond** /plafɔn/ (pl: -s) ceiling

de **plag** /plɑx/ (pl: -gen) sod, turf

plagen /playə(n)/ (plaagde, heeft geplaagd) tease: *iem. met iets ~* tease s.o. about sth.

plagerig /playərəx/ (adj, adv) teasing

de **plagerij** /playərɛi/ (pl: -en) teasing

het **plagiaat** /playijat/ (pl: plagiaten) plagiarism: *~ plegen* plagiarize

de **plaid** /plet/ (pl: -s) travelling rug; [Am] plaid blanket

de **plak** /plɑk/ (pl: -ken) **1** slice: *iets in ~ken snijden* slice sth. **2** (dental) plaque ‖ *onder de ~ zitten* be henpecked

het **plakband** /plɑgbɑnt/ adhesive tape

het **plakboek** /plɑgbuk/ (pl: -en) scrapbook

het **plakkaat** /plɑkat/ (pl: plakkaten) placard, poster

de **plakkaatverf** /plɑkatfɛrf/ poster paint

¹plakken /plɑkə(n)/ (plakte, heeft geplakt) stick; paste ‖ *ergens blijven ~* stick (*or:* hang) around somewhere; outstay one's welcome

²plakken /plɑkə(n)/ (plakte, heeft geplakt) **1** stick (to, on), glue (to, on) **2** repair: *een band ~* repair a puncture

de **plakker** /plɑkər/ (pl: -s) billsticker

plakkerig /plɑkərəx/ (adj) sticky

het **plakplaatje** /plɑkplacə/ (pl: -s) transfer

het **plaksel** /plɑksəl/ (pl: -s) paste

de **plakstift** /plɑkstɪft/ (pl: -en) Pritt stick

het **plakwerk** /plɑkwɛrk/ sticking, glueing

plamuren /plamyrə(n)/ (plamuurde, heeft geplamuurd) fill

de **plamuur** /plamyr/ filler

het **plamuurmes** /plamyrmɛs/ (pl: -sen) filling-knife

het **plan** /plɑn/ (pl: -nen) **1** plan: *een ~ uitvoeren* carry out a plan; *een ~ maken (voor ...)* draw up a plan for sth., plan sth.; *het ~ opvatten (om)* plan (to), intend (to), propose (to); *een ~ smeden (tegen)* scheme (against), plot (against); *zijn ~ trekken* [Belg] manage, cope; *wat ben je van ~?* what are you going to do?; *we waren net van ~ om ...* we were just about (*or:* going) to ... **2** plan, design

het **plan de campagne** /plɑndəkɑmpɑɲə/ plan (*or:* scheme) of action

de **planeconomie** /plɑnekonomi/ (pl: -ën) planned economy

de **planeet** /planet/ (pl: planeten) planet

het **planetarium** /planetarijʏm/ (pl: -s, planetaria) planetarium

de **plank** /plɑŋk/ (pl: -en) plank; board; shelf: *de ~ misslaan* be wide of the mark

de **plankenkoorts** /plɑŋkə(n)korts/ stage fright

het **plankgas** /plɑŋkxɑs/ [roughly] full throttle: *~ geven* step on the gas

de **plankton** /plɑŋkton/ plankton

plankzeilen /plɑŋksɛilə(n)/ windsurfing, boardsailing

planmatig /plɑmmatəx/ (adj, adv) systematic; according to plan

plannen /plɛnə(n)/ (plande, heeft gepland) plan

de **planning** /plɛnɪŋ/ plan, planning

de **planologie** /planoloɣi/ (town and country) planning

de **plant** /plɑnt/ (pl: -en) plant

plantaardig /plɑntardəx/ (adj) vegetable

de **plantage** /plɑntaʒə/ (pl: -s) plantation

planten /plɑntə(n)/ (plantte, heeft geplant) plant; plant out

de **plantenbak** /plɑntə(n)bɑk/ (pl: -ken) flower box

de **planteneter** /plɑntə(n)etər/ (pl: -s) herbivore

de **plantengroei** /plɑntə(n)ɣruj/ **1** plant growth **2** vegetation

de **plantenkas** /plɑntə(n)kɑs/ (pl: -sen) greenhouse

de **planter** /plɑntər/ (pl: -s) planter

de **plantkunde** /plɑntkʏndə/ botany

het **plantsoen** /plɑntsun/ (pl: -en) public garden(s), park

de **plaque** /plɑk/ (pl: -s) plaque

de **plas** /plɑs/ (pl: -sen) **1** puddle, pool **2** water, pee: *een ~je (moeten) doen* (have to) go (to the toilet, loo); (have to) do a wee(-wee) **3** pool, pond

het **plasma** /plɑsma/ (pl: -'s) plasma

¹**plassen** /plɑsə(n)/ (plaste, heeft geplast) **1** go (to the toilet, loo), (have a) pee: *ik moet nodig ~* I really have to go **2** splash

²**plassen** /plɑsə(n)/ (plaste, heeft geplast) pass: *bloed ~* pass blood (in one's urine)

het ¹**plastic** /plɛstɪk/ plastic

²**plastic** /plɛstɪk/ (adj) plastic

de ¹**plastiek** /plɑstik/ (pl: -en) **1** plastic art(s) **2** model

het ²**plastiek** /plɑstik/ [Belg] plastic

plastificeren /plɑstifisɛrə(n)/ (plastificeerde, heeft geplastificeerd) plasticize

plastisch /plɑstis/ (adj) plastic

¹**plat** /plɑt/ (adj) **1** flat **2** closed down, shut down: *de haven gaat morgen ~* tomorrow the port will be shut down

²**plat** /plɑt/ (adj, adv) broad ‖ *~ praten* speak in dialect; *~ uitgedrukt* to put it crudely (*or:* coarsely); *de zaal ~ krijgen* **a)** carry the audience with one; **b)** bring the house down

de ¹**plataan** /platan/ (pl: platanen) [tree] plane (tree)

het ²**plataan** /platan/ [wood] plane (tree)

platbranden /plɑdbrɑndə(n)/ (brandde plat, heeft platgebrand) burn to the ground

het **plateau** /plato/ (pl: -s) **1** dish, platter **2** plateau

de **plateauzool** /platozol/ (pl: -zolen) platform sole

de **platenspeler** /platə(n)spelər/ (pl: -s) record player

de **platenzaak** /platə(n)zak/ (pl: -zaken) record shop

het **platform** /plɑtfɔrm/ (pl: -s) platform

platgaan /plɑtxan/ (lag plat, heeft platgelegen) **1** be bowled over by (s.o.): *de zaal* ging plat the audience was rolling in the aisles **2** fail, go down

het ¹**platina** /platina/ platinum

²**platina** /platina/ (adj) platinum

platleggen /plɑtlɛɣə(n)/ (legde plat, heeft platgelegd) **1** lay flat **2** bring to a standstill

platliggen /plɑtlɪxə(n)/ (lag plat, heeft platgelegen) be at a standstill

platlopen /plɑtlopə(n)/ (liep plat, heeft platgelopen) trample down

platonisch /platonis/ (adj, adv) platonic

platspuiten /plɑtspœytə(n)/ (spoot plat, heeft platgespoten) [inform] knock out with sedatives

de **plattegrond** /platəɣrɔnt/ (pl: -en) **1** (street) map **2** floor plan

de **plattekaas** /platəkas/ [Belg] cottage cheese, cream cheese

het **platteland** /platəlɑnt/ country(side)

de **plattelandsbevolking** /platəlɑn(t)sbəvɔlkɪŋ/ rural population

plattrappen /plɑtrɑpə(n)/ (trapte plat, heeft platgetrapt) trample down

plattreden /plɑtredə(n)/ (trad plat, heeft platgetreden) trample down: *platgetreden paden* well-trodden paths

de **platvis** /plɑtfɪs/ (pl: -sen) flatfish

platvloers /plɑtflurs/ (adj) coarse, crude

de **platvoet** /plɑtfut/ (pl: -en) flatfoot

platzak /plɑtsɑk/ (adj) (flat) broke

plausibel /plɑuzibəl/ (adj) plausible

plaveien /plavɛrjə(n)/ (plaveide, heeft geplaveid) pave

het **plaveisel** /plavɛisəl/ (pl: -s) paving, pavement

de **plavuis** /plavœys/ (pl: plavuizen) (floor) tile; flag(stone)

het/de **playback** /plejbɛk/ (pl: -s) miming

playbacken /plejbɛkə(n)/ (playbackte, heeft geplaybackt) mime (to one's own, another person's voice)

de **playboy** /plejbɔj/ (pl: -s) playboy

het **plebs** /plɛps/ plebs

plechtig /plɛxtəx/ (adj, adv) solemn: *~ beloven (te)* solemnly promise (to)

de **plechtigheid** /plɛxtəxhɛit/ (pl: -heden) ceremony

plechtstatig /plɛxtstatəx/ (adj, adv) solemn

het **plectrum** /plɛktrʏm/ (pl: -s, plectra) plectrum

de **plee** /ple/ (pl: -s) [inform] loo; [Am] john: *op de ~ zitten* be in the loo

het **pleeggezin** /pleɣəzɪn/ (pl: -nen) foster home

het **pleegkind** /plexkɪnt/ (pl: -eren) foster-child: *(iem.) als ~ opnemen* take (s.o.) in as foster-child

de **pleegouders** /plexɑudərs/ (pl) foster-parents

plegen /pleɣə(n)/ (pleegde, heeft gepleegd) commit

het **pleidooi** /plɛidoj/ (pl: -en) **1** plea: *een ~ houden voor* make a plea for **2** counsel's speech (*or:* argument)

het **plein** /plɛin/ (pl: -en) square, plaza: *op (aan) het ~* in the square

de **pleinvrees** /plɛinvres/ agoraphobia

de ¹**pleister** /plɛistər/ (sticking) plaster

het ²**pleister** /plɛistər/ plaster

pleisteren /plɛistərə(n)/ (pleisterde, heeft gepleisterd) **1** plaster **2** put a plaster on

de **pleisterplaats** /plɛistərplats/ (pl: -en) stopping place

het **pleisterwerk** /plɛistərwɛrk/ plasterwork, plaster(ing)

het **pleit** /plɛit/ **1** (law)suit: *het ~ winnen* win one's suit **2** dispute: *het ~ beslechten* decide the argument

de **pleitbezorger** /plɛidbəzɔrɣər/ (pl: -s) advocate, champion, supporter

pleiten /plɛitə(n)/ (pleitte, heeft gepleit) plead: *dat pleit voor hem* that is to his credit

de **pleiter** /plɛitər/ (pl: -s) counsel

de **plek** /plɛk/ (pl: -ken) **1** spot: *een blauwe ~* a bruise; *iemands zwakke ~ raken* find s.o.'s weak spot **2** spot, place: *ter ~ke* on site, in situ

plenair /plenɛːr/ (adj) plenary

plengen /plɛŋə(n)/ (plengde, heeft geplengd): *tranen ~* shed tears, weep

de **plensbui** /plɛnzbœy/ (pl: -en) downpour

¹**plenzen** /plɛnzə(n)/ (plensde, heeft geplensd) pour

²**plenzen** /plɛnzə(n)/ (plensde, heeft geplensd) splash

het **pleonasme** /plejonɑsmə/ (pl: -n) pleonasm

pletten /plɛtə(n)/ (plette, heeft geplet) **1** crush **2** flatten; squash

pletter /plɛtər/: *te ~ slaan tegen de rotsen* be dashed against the rocks; *zich te ~ vervelen* be bored stiff (*or:* to death)

pleuren /plørə(n)/ (pleurde, heeft gepleurd) [inform] chuck: *hij pleurde zijn rommel in de kast* he chucked his junk in the closet

het/de **pleuris** /plørɪs/ [inform]: *de ~ breekt uit* the shit hits the fan; *ik schrok me de ~* I was frightened to death, I was scared out of my wits; *krijg de ~* go to hell

de **plevier** /pləviːr/ (pl: -en) plover

het **plexiglas** /plɛksiɣlɑs/ plexiglass

plezant /pləzɑnt/ (adj) [Belg] pleasant

het **plezier** /pləziːr/ **1** pleasure, fun: *iem. een ~ doen* do s.o. a favour; *~ hebben* have fun, enjoy o.s.; *veel ~!* enjoy yourself! **2** pleasure, enjoyment: *met alle ~* with pleasure; *ik heb hier altijd met ~ gewerkt* I have always enjoyed working here

plezieren /pləziːrə(n)/ (plezierde, heeft geplezierd): *als ik je ermee kan ~* if that's what makes you happy; *iem. met iets ~* oblige s.o. with sth.

plezierig /pləziːrəx/ (adj, adv) pleasant

het **plezierjacht** /pləziːrjɑxt/ (pl: -en) pleasure yacht

de **plezierreis** /pləziːrɛis/ (pl: -reizen) (pleasure) trip, outing

de **plicht** /plɪxt/ (pl: -en) duty: *het is niet meer dan je ~ (om ...)* you are in duty bound (to ...); *de ~ roept* duty calls; *zijn ~ doen* (*or: vervullen*) do one's duty, perform one's duty; *zijn ~ verzaken* neglect one's duty

plichtmatig /plɪxtmatəx/ (adj, adv) dutiful: *een ~ bezoekje* a duty call

de **plichtpleging** /plɪxtpleɣɪŋ/ (pl: -en) ceremony: *met veel ~en* with considerable ceremony; *zonder ~(en)* unceremonious(ly), without ceremony

het **plichtsbesef** /plɪxtsbəsɛf/ sense of duty

plichtsgetrouw /plɪxtsxətrɑu/ (adj, adv) dutiful

het **plichtsverzuim** /plɪx(t)sfərzœym/ neglect of duty

de **plint** /plɪnt/ (pl: -en) skirting board; [Am] baseboard

de **ploeg** /pluɣ/ (pl: -en) **1** gang; shift: *in ~en werken* work (in) shifts **2** [sport] team; side **3** plough

ploegen /pluɣə(n)/ (ploegde, heeft/is geploegd) plough: *een akker* (*or: het land*) *~* plough a field (*or:* the land)

de **ploegendienst** /pluɣə(n)dinst/ (pl: -en) shift work: *in ~ werken* work (in) shifts

de **ploegleider** /pluɣlɛidər/ (pl: -s) [sport] team manager; captain

het **ploegverband** /pluɣfərbɑnt/: [sport] *in ~* as a team

de **ploert** /plurt/ (pl: -en) cad, scab

de **ploeteraar** /plutərar/ (pl: -s) plodder, slogger

ploeteren /plutərə(n)/ (ploeterde, heeft geploeterd) plod (away, along)

de **plof** /plɔf/ (pl: -fen) thud, bump, plop

ploffen /plɔfə(n)/ (plofte, is geploft) **1** thud, flop **2** pop, bang ‖ *in een stoel ~* plump down (*or:* flop) into a chair

plomp /plɔmp/ (adj, adv) plump; squat; cumbersome

plompverloren /plɔmpfərlorə(n)/ (adv) bluntly

de **plons** /plɔns/ (pl: -en, plonzen) splash ‖ *~! daar viel de steen in het water* splash! went the stone into the water

plonzen /plɔnzə(n)/ (plonsde, heeft/is geplonsd) splash

de **plooi** /ploj/ (pl: -en) pleat, fold ‖ *zijn gezicht in de ~ houden* keep a straight face

plooibaar /plojbar/ (adj) pliable, flexible

plooien /plojə(n)/ (plooide, heeft geplooid) fold, pleat, crease

de **plooirok** /plojrɔk/ (pl: -ken) pleated skirt

de **plot** /plɔt/ (pl: -s) plot

¹**plotseling** /plɔtsəlɪŋ/ (adj) sudden, unexpected

²plotseling /plǫtsəlɪŋ/ (adv) suddenly, unexpectedly

het/de **¹pluche** /plyʃ(ə)/ plush

²pluche /plyʃ(ə)/ (adj) plush

pluchen /plyʃə(n)/ (adj) plush

de **plug** /plʏx/ (pl: -gen) plug

de **pluim** /plœym/ (pl: -en) **1** plume, feather **2** plume; [small] tuft: *een ~ van* **rook** a plume of smoke ‖ *iem. een ~ geven* pat s.o. on the back

de **pluimage** /plœymaʒə/ (pl: -s) plumage

het **pluimvee** /plœymve/ poultry

de **pluis** /plœys/ bit of fluff ‖ *het is daar* **niet** ~ there's sth. fishy there

pluizen /plœyzə(n)/ (pluisde, heeft geplozen/gepluisd) give off fluff; pill

de **pluk** /plʏk/ (pl: -ken) **1** tuft, wisp **2** crop

plukken /plʏkə(n)/ (plukte, heeft geplukt) **1** pick: *pluk de* **dag** live for the moment **2** pluck

de **plumeau** /plymo/ (pl: -s) feather duster

de **plumpudding** /plʏmpʏdɪŋ/ (pl: -en, -s) plum pudding

de **plunderaar** /plʏndərar/ (pl: -s) plunderer, looter

plunderen /plʏndərə(n)/ (plunderde, heeft geplunderd) **1** plunder, loot **2** plunder, raid; rifle through: *de* **koelkast** ~ raid the fridge

de **plundering** /plʏndərɪŋ/ (pl: -en) plundering, looting

de **plunje** /plʏɲə/ togs, duds

de **plunjezak** /plʏɲəzɑk/ (pl: -ken) kitbag

het/de **¹plus** /plʏs/ (pl: -sen) **1** plus (sign) **2** plus (pole)

²plus /plʏs/ (prep) plus: *twee ~* **drie** *is vijf* two plus (*or:* and) three is five ‖ *vijfenzestig ~* over-65

plusminus /plʏsmɪnʏs/ (adv) approximately, about: *~* **duizend** *euro* approximately (*or:* about) a thousand euros

het **pluspunt** /plʏspʏnt/ (pl: -en) plus, asset: *ervaring* **is** *bij sollicitaties een ~* experience is a plus (*or:* an asset) when applying for a job

het **plusteken** /plʏstekə(n)/ (pl: -s) plus (sign)

het **plutonium** /plytonijʏm/ plutonium

pneumatisch /pnœmatis/ (adj, adv) pneumatic

de **po** /po/ (pl: po's) chamber pot, po

pochen /poxə(n)/ (pochte, heeft gepocht) boast, brag

pocheren /poʃerə(n)/ (pocheerde, heeft gepocheerd) poach

de **pochet** /poʃɛt/ (pl: -ten) dress-pocket handkerchief, breast-pocket handkerchief

het **pocketboek** /pɔkədbuk/ (pl: -en) paperback

de **podcast** /pɔtka:st/ (pl: -s) podcast

het **podium** /podijʏm/ (pl: podia) **1** stage; apron **2** platform, podium

de **poedel** /pudəl/ (pl: -s) poodle

poedelnaakt /pudəlnakt/ (adj) stark naked, in one's birthday suit

de **poedelprijs** /pudəlprɛɪs/ (pl: -prijzen) booby prize

het **poeder** /pudər/ (pl: -s) powder

de **poederblusser** /pudərblʏsər/ (pl: -s) powder extinguisher

de **poederbrief** /pudərbrif/ powder letter

de **poederdoos** /pudərdos/ (pl: -dozen) compact

poederen /pudərə(n)/ (poederde, heeft gepoederd) powder: *zich (het gezicht) ~* powder one's face (*or:* nose)

de **poedermelk** /pudərmɛlk/ dried milk, powdered milk

de **poedersneeuw** /pudərsnew/ powder snow

de **poedersuiker** /pudərsœykər/ icing sugar

de **poedervorm** /pudərvɔrm/: *in ~* in powder form

de **poef** /puf/ (pl: -en) hassock

het/de **poeha** /puha/ hoo-ha, fuss

de **poel** /pul/ (pl: -en) pool; puddle

de **poelier** /pulir/ (pl: -s) poulterer('s)

de **poema** /puma/ (pl: -'s) puma

het/de **poen** /pun/ dough, dosh

de **¹poep** /pup/ [inform] crap, shit; dog-do; birddo

de **²poep** (pl: -en) [Belg; inform] bum; [Am] fanny: *op zijn ~* **krijgen** get (*or:* be) spanked

poepen /pupə(n)/ (poepte, heeft gepoept) [inform] **1** (have a) crap: *in zijn broek ~* do it in one's pants **2** [Belg] screw, fuck

de **poes** /pus/ (pl: poezen) (pussy)cat: *een* **jong** *~je* a kitten ‖ *mis ~!* wrong!

het **poesiealbum** /pusialbʏm/ (pl: -s) album (of verses)

poeslief /puslif/ (adj, adv) suave, bland, smooth; honeyed; sugary; silky: *iets ~* **vragen** purr a question, ask sth. in the silkiest tones

de **poespas** /puspas/ hoo-ha, song and dance: *laat die ~ maar achterwege* stop making such a song and dance about it

de **poesta** /pusta/ (pl: -'s) puszta

de **poet** /put/ [inform] loot

poëtisch /powetis/ (adj, adv) poetic

de **poets** /puts/ (pl: -en): *iem. een ~* **bakken** play a trick (*or:* hoax) on s.o.; [Belg] *~* **wederom** tit for tat

de **poetsdoek** /putsduk/ (pl: -en) cleaning cloth, cleaning rag

poetsen /putsə(n)/ (poetste, heeft gepoetst) clean; polish: *zijn* **tanden** *~* brush one's teeth

de **poetsvrouw** /putsfrau/ (pl: -en) cleaning woman

de **poëzie** /powezi/ poetry

de **pof** /pɔf/: *op de ~* on tick, on credit

de **pofbroek** /pɔvbruk/ (pl: -en) knickerbockers

poffen /pɔfə(n)/ (pofte, heeft gepoft) roast; pop

het **poffertje** /pɔfərcə/ (pl: -s) kind of small

pancake

pogen /pọɣə(n)/ (poogde, heeft gepoogd) [form] endeavour, attempt, seek

de **poging** /pọɣɪŋ/ (pl: -en) attempt, try; effort: *een ~ wagen* have a try at sth.; *~ tot moord* attempted murder; *een vergeefse ~* a vain (or: futile, useless) attempt

de **pogrom** /pọɣrɔm/ (pl: -s) pogrom

de **pointe** /pwɛ̃ːntə/ (pl: -s) point: *hij heeft de ~ niet begrepen* he missed the point

pokdalig /pɔɡdaləɣ/ (adj) pockmarked

poken /pọkə(n)/ (pookte, heeft gepookt) poke

het **poker** /pọkər/ poker

pokeren /pọkərə(n)/ (pokerde, heeft gepokerd) play poker

de **pokken** /pɔkə(n)/ smallpox

het **pokkenweer** /pɔkə(n)wer/ [inform] filthy (or: lousy) weather

de **pol** /pɔl/ (pl: -len) clump

polair /polɛːr/ (adj) polar

de **polarisatie** /polariza(t)si/ (pl: -s) polarization

polariseren /polarizerə(n)/ (polariseerde, heeft gepolariseerd) polarize

de **polder** /pɔldər/ (pl: -s) polder

het **poldermodel** /pɔldərmɔdɛl/ (pl: -len) polder model

de **polemiek** /polemik/ (pl: -en) polemic: *een ~ voeren* engage in a polemic (or: controversy)

Polen /pọlə(n)/ Poland

de **poli** /pọli/ (pl: -'s) outpatients'

de **poliep** /polip/ (pl: -en) polyp

polijsten /polɛistə(n)/ (polijstte, heeft gepolijst) polish (up); sand(paper)

de **polikliniek** /poliklinik/ (pl: -en) outpatient clinic

poliklinisch /poliklinis/ (adj): *~e patiënt* outpatient

de **polio** /pọlijo/ polio

de **polis** /pọlɪs/ (pl: -sen) (insurance) policy

de **polishouder** /pọlɪshaudər/ (pl: -s) policyholder

de **polisvoorwaarden** /pọlɪsforwardə(n)/ (pl) terms (or: conditions) of a policy

de **politicologie** /politikoloɣi/ political science

de **politicus** /pọlitikʏs/ (pl: politici) politician

de **politie** /poli(t)si/ (pl: -s) police (force)

de **politieagent** /poli(t)siaɣɛnt/ (pl: -en) police officer, policeman

de **politieauto** /poli(t)siauto/ (pl: -'s) police car, patrol car

het **politiebericht** /poli(t)sibərɪxt/ (pl: -en) police message

de **politiebewaking** /poli(t)sibəwakɪŋ/ police protection

het **politiebureau** /poli(t)sibyro/ (pl: -s) police station

de **politiecommissaris** /poli(t)sikɔmɪsarɪs/ (pl: -sen) Chief of Police

de **politiehond** /poli(t)sihɔnt/ (pl: -en) police dog

de **¹politiek** /politik/ **1** politics: *in de ~ zitten* be in politics, be a politician **2** policy: *binnenlandse* (or: *buitenlandse*) *~* internal (or: foreign) policy

²politiek /politik/ (adj, adv) political

de **politiemacht** /poli(t)simɑxt/ body of police, police presence: *er was een grote ~ op de been* the police were present in force

de **politieman** /poli(t)simɑn/ (pl: -nen) policeman, police officer

de **politierechter** /poli(t)sirɛxtər/ (pl: -s) magistrate

de **politiestaat** /poli(t)sistat/ (pl: -staten) police state

het **politietoezicht** /poli(t)situzɪxt/ police supervision

de **politieverordening** /poli(t)sivərɔrdənɪŋ/ (pl: -en) by-law; [Am] local ordinance

de **polka** /pɔlka/ (pl: -'s) polka

de **poll** /pɔl/ (pl: -s) poll

de **pollen** /pɔlə(n)/ pollen

de **pollepel** /pɔlepəl/ (pl: -s) wooden spoon

het **polo** /pọlo/ **1** polo **2** sports shirt

de **polonaise** /polonɛːzə/ (pl: -s) **1** conga: *een ~ houden* do the conga **2** polonaise

het **poloshirt** /pọloʃːrt/ (pl: -s) sports shirt, tennis shirt

de **pols** /pɔls/ (pl: -en) **1** wrist **2** pulse: *iem. de ~ voelen* feel (or: take) s.o.'s pulse

het **polsbandje** wrist band

polsen /pɔlsə(n)/ (polste, heeft gepolst): *iem. ~ over iets* sound s.o. out on (or: about) sth.

het **polsgewricht** /pɔlsxəvrɪxt/ wrist (joint)

het **polshorloge** /pɔlshɔrloʒə/ (pl: -s) wristwatch

de **polsslag** /pɔlslɑx/ (pl: -en) pulse

de **polsstok** /pɔlstɔk/ (pl: -ken) (jumping) pole

polsstokhoogspringen /pɔlstɔkhox-sprɪŋə(n)/ pole vaulting

de **polyester** /polijɛstər/ (pl: -s) polyester

de **polyether** /polietər/ polyether; foam rubber

de **¹polyfoon** /polifọn/ polyphonic ringtone

²polyfoon /polifọn/ (adj) polyphonic

de **polygamie** /poliɣami/ polygamy

Polynesisch /polinezis/ (adj) Polynesian

de **pomp** /pɔmp/ (pl: -en) pump

de **pompbediende** /pɔmbədində/ (pl: -n, -s) service (or: petrol) station attendant

de **pompelmoes** /pɔmpəlmus/ (pl: -moezen) grapefruit

pompen /pɔmpə(n)/ (pompte, heeft gepompt) pump

pompeus /pɔmpøs/ (adj, adv) pompous

de **pomphouder** /pɔmphaudər/ (pl: -s) petrol station owner; [Am] gas station owner

de **pompoen** /pɔmpun/ (pl: -en) pumpkin

het **pompstation** /pɔmpsta(t)ʃɔn/ (pl: -s) filling station, service station

395

portokosten

de **poncho** /pɔnʃo/ (pl: -'s) poncho
het **pond** /pɔnt/ (pl: -en) half a kilo(gram), 500 grams; [approx] pound; [currency] pound: *het weegt een ~* it weighs half a kilo ‖ *het volle ~ moeten betalen* have to pay the full price
  poneren /ponerə(n)/ (poneerde, heeft geponeerd) postulate, advance: *een stelling ~* advance a thesis
  ponsen /pɔnsə(n)/ (ponste, heeft geponst) punch
de **ponskaart** /pɔnskart/ (pl: -en) **1** punch(ed) card **2** embossed card
de **pont** /pɔnt/ (pl: -en) ferry(boat)
  pontificaal /pɔntifikal/ (adj, adv) pontifical
het/de **ponton** /pɔntɔn/ (pl: -s) pontoon
de **pontonbrug** /pɔntɔmbrʏχ/ (pl: -gen) pontoon bridge
de **pony** /pɔni/ **1** pony **2** fringe
de **pooier** /pojər/ (pl: -s) pimp
de **pook** /pok/ (pl: poken) **1** poker **2** gear lever, (gear)stick
de **pool** /pol/ (pl: polen) pole
de **Pool** /pol/ (pl: Polen) Pole
de **poolcirkel** /polsɪrkəl/ (pl: -s) polar circle
de **poolexpeditie** /polɛkspedi(t)si/ (pl: -s) polar expedition
het **poolgebied** /polɣəbit/ (pl: -en) polar region
het **poolijs** /polɛɪs/ polar ice
het **poollicht** /polɪχt/ polar lights; aurora polaris
het ¹**Pools** /pols/ Polish
  ²**Pools** /pols/ (adj) Polish
de **poolshoogte** /polshoχtə/ latitude, altitude of the pole: *~ nemen* a) [shipp] take one's bearings; b) [fig] size up the situation
de **Poolster** /polstɛr/ (the) Pole Star, Polaris
de **poon** /pon/ (pl: ponen) gurnard
de **poort** /port/ (pl: -en) gate, gateway
de **poos** /pos/ (pl: pozen) while, time: *een hele ~* a good while, a long time
de **poot** /pot/ (pl: poten) **1** paw, leg: *de poten van een tafel* the legs of a table; [fig] *zijn ~ stijf houden* stand firm, stick to one's guns; *geen ~ hebben om op te staan* not have a leg to stand on **2** queer, gay (man) ‖ *de ~ van een bril* the arms of a pair of glasses; [fig] *alles kwam op zijn ~jes terecht* everything turned out all right
het **pootgoed** /potχut/ seeds
  pootjebaden /pocəbadə(n)/ paddle
de **pop** /pɔp/ (pl: -pen) **1** doll **2** puppet: *daar heb je de ~pen aan het dansen* here we go, now we're in for it **3** dummy: *zij is net een aangeklede ~* she looks like a dressed-up doll
het **popcorn** /pɔpkɔːrn/ popcorn
  popelen /popələ(n)/ (popelde, heeft gepopeld) quiver: *zitten te ~ om weg te mogen* be raring (or: itching) to go
het **popfestival** /pɔpfɛstival/ pop festival, rock

festival
de **popgroep** /pɔpχrup/ (pl: -en) pop group, rock group, rock band
de **popmuziek** /pɔpmyzik/ rock music, pop music
het **poppenhuis** /pɔpə(n)hœys/ (pl: -huizen) doll's house
de **poppenkast** /pɔpə(n)kɑst/ (pl: -en) **1** puppet theatre **2** puppet show
de **poppenwagen** /pɔpə(n)waɣə(n)/ (pl: -s) doll's pram; [Am] baby carriage
  popperig /pɔpərəχ/ (adj) doll-like, pretty-pretty
de **popster** /pɔpstɛr/ (pl: -ren) pop star, rock star
  populair /popylɛːr/ (adj, adv) popular
  populairwetenschappelijk /popylɛːrwetə(n)sχɑpələk/ (adj, adv) popular-science
  populariseren /popylarizerə(n)/ (populariseerde, heeft gepopulariseerd) popularize
de **populariteit** /popylaritɛit/ popularity
de **populatie** /popyla(t)si/ (pl: -s) population
de **populier** /popylir/ (pl: -en) poplar
het **populisme** /popylɪsmə/ populism
de **pop-up** /pɔpʏp/ pop-up
de **por** /pɔr/ (pl: -ren) jab, prod, dig
  poreus /porøs/ (adj) porous
de **porie** /pori/ (pl: poriën) pore
de **porno** /pɔrno/ porn(o)
de **pornografie** /pɔrnoɣrafi/ pornography
  pornografisch /pɔrnoɣrafis/ (adj, adv) pornographic
  porren /pɔrə(n)/ (porde, heeft gepord) prod: *iem. in de zij ~* poke s.o. in the ribs ‖ *ergens wel voor te ~ zijn* not take much persuading
het **porselein** /pɔrsəlɛin/ china(ware), porcelain
  porseleinen /pɔrsəlɛinə(n)/ (adj) china, porcelain
de **porseleinkast** /pɔrsəlɛiŋkɑst/ (pl: -en) china cabinet
de ¹**port** /pɔrt/ (pl: -en) port (wine)
het/de ²**port** /pɔrt/ (pl: -en) **1** postage **2** surcharge
het **portaal** /pɔrtal/ (pl: portalen) porch, hall; portal
  portable /pɔːrtəbəl/ (adj) portable
de **portal** /pɔːrtal/ (pl: -s) portal
de **portefeuille** /pɔrtəfœyə/ (pl: -s) wallet
de **portemonnee** /pɔrtəmɔnɛ/ (pl: -s) purse, wallet
de **portie** /pɔrsi/ (pl: -s) **1** share, portion: *zijn ~ wel gehad hebben* have had one's fair share **2** portion; helping: *een grote (flinke) ~ geduld* a good deal of patience
het/de **portiek** /pɔrtik/ (pl: -en) porch; doorway
de ¹**portier** /pɔrtir/ doorkeeper, gatekeeper
het ²**portier** /pɔrtir/ door
het/de **porto** /pɔrto/ (pl: porti) postage
de **portofoon** /pɔrtofɔn/ (pl: -s) walkie-talkie
de **portokosten** /pɔrtokɔstə(n)/ (pl) postage charges (or: expenses)

de **Porto Ricaan** /pɔrtorikạn/ (pl: Porto Ricanen) Puerto Rican
Porto Ricaans /pɔrtorikạns/ (adj) Puerto Rican
Porto Rico /pɔrtorịko/ Puerto Rico
het **portret** /pɔrtrɛt̲/ (pl: -ten) portrait
de **portretschilder** /pɔrtrɛ̲tsxɪldər/ (pl: -s) portrait-painter
portretteren /pɔrtrɛterə(n)/ (portretteerde, heeft geportretteerd) portray
Portugal /pɔ̲rtyɣal/ Portugal
Portugees /pɔrtyɣẹs/ (adj) Portuguese
portvrij /pɔrtfrɛi̲/ (adj) post-paid, postage free
de **pose** /pọzə/ (pl: -s) pose, posture: *een ~ aannemen* assume a pose
poseren /pozerə(n)/ (poseerde, heeft geposeerd) pose, sit
de **positie** /pozi(t)si/ (pl: -s) **1** position, posture: *~ kiezen* (or: *innemen*) choose (or: take) up a position **2** position, attitude: *in een conflict ~ nemen* (or: *kiezen*) take (or: choose) sides in a conflict **3** position, situation **4** position, post **5** (social) position, status, (social) rank: *een hoge ~* a high position (or: rank) (in society)
positief /pozitị̲f/ (adj, adv) **1** positive, affirmative **2** positive, favourable: *positieve kritiek* constructive criticism; *iets ~ benaderen* approach sth. positively
de **positiekleding** /pozi(t)sikledɪŋ/ maternity clothes
de **positieven** /pozitivə(n)/ (pl): *weer bij zijn ~ komen* come to one's senses
de **¹post** /pɔst/ (pl: -en) **1** post office, postal services **2** post, mail: *aangetekende ~* registered mail; *elektronische ~* electronic mail, e-mail **3** post; post office; letterbox **4** post, jamb **5** item; entry: *de ~ salarissen* the salary item **6** post, position: *een ~ bekleden* hold a post, occupy a position
de **²post** (pl: -s) post
het **postadres** /pɔstadrɛs/ (pl: -sen) address
het **postagentschap** /pɔstaɣɛntsxap/ (pl: -pen) sub-post office
de **postbezorging** /pɔstbəzɔrɣɪŋ/ (pl: -en) postal delivery, delivery of the post; [Am] mail delivery, delivery of the mail
de **postbode** /pɔstbodə/ (pl: -s) postman; [Am] mailman
de **postbus** /pɔstbʏs/ (pl: -sen) postoffice box, PO Box
de **postcode** /pɔstkodə/ (pl: -s) postal code; [Am] ZIP code
de **¹postdoc** /pɔsdɔk/ (pl: -s) postdoc(toral); [Am also] postgraduate
²postdoc /pɔsdɔk/ (adj) postdoctoral; [Am also] postgraduate
de **postduif** /pɔzdœyf/ (pl: -duiven) carrier pigeon, homing pigeon
de **postelein** /pɔstəlɛi̲n/ purslane

¹posten /pɔstə(n)/ (postte, heeft gepost) stand guard
²posten /pɔstə(n)/ (postte, heeft gepost) post; [Am] mail; send off
de **poster** /pọstər/ (pl: -s) poster
posteren /posterə(n)/ (posteerde, heeft geposteerd) post
poste restante /postərɛstɑ̃ntə/ (adv) poste restante; [Am] general delivery: *De heer H. de Vries, ~ Hoofdpostkantoor* Brighton Mr H. de Vries, c/o Main Post Office, Brighton
de **posterijen** /pɔstərɛi̲ə(n)/ (pl) Post Office, Postal Services
de **posting** /pọstɪŋ/ (pl: -s) post
de **postkamer** /pɔstkamər/ (pl: -s) post room
het **postkantoor** /pɔstkɑntor/ (pl: -kantoren) post office
de **postkoets** /pɔstkuts/ (pl: -en) stagecoach
postmodern /postmodɛ̲rn/ (adj) postmodern
postnataal /postnatạl/ (adj) postnatal
het **postnummer** /pɔstnʏmər/ (pl: -s) [Belg] postcode, postal code
de **postorder** /pɔstɔrdər/ (pl: -s) mail order
het **postorderbedrijf** /pɔstɔrdərbədrɛif/ (pl: -bedrijven) mail-order firm (or: company), catalogue house
het **postpakket** /pɔstpɑkɛt/ (pl: -ten) parcel, parcel-post package
het **postpapier** /pɔstpapir/ writing paper, letter paper, notepaper: *~ en enveloppen* stationery
de **postrekening** /pɔstrekənɪŋ/ (pl: -en) giro bank account
het **poststempel** /pɔststɛmpəl/ postmark
postuum /pɔstym/ (adj, adv) posthumous
het **postuur** /pɔstyr/ (pl: posturen) figure, shape; build; stature
het **postvak** /pɔstfɑk/ (pl: -ken) pigeon-hole
postvatten /pɔstfɑtə(n)/ (vatte post, heeft postgevat) **1** take up one's station, post o.s. **2** take form
de **postwissel** /pɔstwɪsəl/ (pl: -s) postal order, money order
de **postzegel** /pɔstseɣəl/ (pl: -s) stamp: *voor een euro aan ~s bijplakken* stamp an excess amount of one euro; *voor drie euro aan ~s bijsluiten* enclose three euros in stamps
de **postzegelverzameling** /pɔ̲(st)seɣəlvərzaməlɪŋ/ (pl: -en) stamp collection
de **¹pot** /pɔt/ [inform] dyke, dike; gay
de **²pot** /pɔt/ **1** pot; jar: *een ~ jam* a jar of jam **2** pot, chamber pot: *hij kan (me) de ~ op* he can get stuffed **3** pot, saucepan: *eten wat de ~ schaft* eat whatever's going **4** kitty, pool ‖ *dat is één ~ nat* you can't really tell the difference; [of pers] they're birds of a feather
potdicht /pɔdɪxt/ (adj) tight, locked, sealed: *de deur is ~* the door is shut tight
poten /potə(n)/ (pootte, heeft gepoot) plant; set; put in

potent /potɛnt/ (adj) potent, virile

de **potentaat** /potɛntat/ (pl: potentaten) potentate

de **potentiaal** /potɛn(t)ʃal/ (pl: potentialen) potential

de **potentie** /potɛn(t)si/ (pl: -s) potence

het ¹**potentieel** /potɛnʃel/ potential; capacity

²**potentieel** /potɛnʃel/ (adj, adv) **1** potential: *potentiële* **koper** prospective (or: would-be) buyer **2** latent, potential

de **potgrond** /potxrɔnt/ potting compost (soil)

potig /potəx/ (adj) burly, sturdy, husky

het **potje** /pɔcə/ (pl: -s) **1** (little) pot; terrine: *zijn eigen ~ koken* [fig] fend for o.s. **2** game: *een ~ kaarten, biljarten* play a game of cards, billiards **3** fund ‖ *er een ~ van maken* mess (or: muck) things up

het **potjeslatijn** /pɔcəslatɛɪn/ gibberish; mumbo jumbo

het **potlood** /potlot/ (pl: potloden) pencil: *met ~ tekenen* draw in pencil

de **potloodslijper** /potlotslɛɪpər/ (pl: -s) pencil sharpener

de **potloodventer** /potlotfɛntər/ (pl: -s) flasher

de **potplant** /potplant/ (pl: -en) pot plant, potted plant

het/de **potpourri** /potpori/ (pl: -'s) potpourri, medley

potsierlijk /potsirlək/ (adj) clownish, ridiculous, grotesque

potten /pɔtə(n)/ (potte, heeft gepot) **1** hoard; stash (away) **2** pot

pottenbakken /pɔtə(n)bakə(n)/ pottery(-making), ceramics

de **pottenbakker** /pɔtə(n)bakər/ (pl: -s) potter

de **pottenbakkerij** /pɔtə(n)bakərɛi/ (pl: -en) pottery

de **pottenkijker** /pɔtə(n)kɛikər/ (pl: -s) Nosy Parker, snooper

potverteren /pɔtfərterə(n)/ squander

de **potvis** /pɔtfɪs/ (pl: -sen) sperm whale

de **poule** /pul/ (pl: -s) group

pover /povər/ (adj, adv) poor, meagre, miserable: *een ~ resultaat* a poor result

de **pr** /peɛr/ *public relations* PR

Praag /prax/ Prague

de **praal** /pral/ splendour, pomp: *met pracht en ~* with pomp and circumstance

het **praalgraf** /pralɣraf/ (pl: -graven) mausoleum

de **praat** /prat/ talk: *veel ~(s) hebben* be all talk; *met iem. aan de ~ raken* get talking to s.o. ‖ *een auto aan de ~ krijgen* get a car to start

de **praatgroep** /pratxrup/ (pl: -en) discussion group

het **praatje** /pracə/ (pl: -s) **1** chat, talk **2** talk, speech: *mooie ~s* fine words **3** airs: *~s krijgen* put on airs

de **praatjesmaker** /pracəsmakər/ (pl: -s) **1** boaster, braggart **2** windbag, gasbag

de **praatpaal** /pratpal/ (pl: -palen) emergency telephone

de **praatshow** /pratʃo/ (pl: -s) chat show, talk show

de **praatstoel** /pratstul/: *hij zit weer op zijn ~* he's on again

de **pracht** /praxt/ **1** magnificence, splendour **2** [fig] beauty, gem

prachtig /praxtəx/ (adj, adv) **1** splendid, magnificent **2** exquisite, gorgeous ‖ *~!* excellent!

de **prachtkerel** /praxtkerəl/ (pl: -s) a fine man; a great guy

het **practicum** /praktikʏm/ (pl: practica) practical, lab(oratory): *ik heb vanmiddag ~* I've got a practical this afternoon

de **pragmaticus** /praxmatikʏs/ (pl: pragmatici) pragmatist

pragmatisch /praxmatis/ (adj) pragmatic(al)

de **prairie** /prɛːri/ (pl: -s) prairie

de **prak** /prak/ mash, mush ‖ *een auto in de ~ rijden* smash (up) a car

prakken /prakə(n)/ (prakte, heeft geprakt) mash

prakkiseren /prakizerə(n)/ (prakkiseerde, heeft geprakkiseerd) [inform] **1** brood, worry: *zich suf ~* worry o.s. sick **2** muse, think

de **praktijk** /praktɛik/ (pl: -en) practice; experience: *echt een man van de ~* a doer (rather than a thinker); *een eigen ~ beginnen* start a practice of one's own; *in de ~* in (actual) practice; *iets in ~ brengen* put sth. into practice, apply (or: implement) sth.

de **praktijkervaring** /praktɛikɛrvarɪŋ/ practical experience

praktijkgericht /praktɛikxərɪxt/ (adj) practically-oriented

¹**praktisch** /praktis/ (adj, adv) **1** practical, handy, useful: *~e kennis* working knowledge **2** practical, realistic; businesslike

²**praktisch** /praktis/ (adv) practically, almost: *de was is ~ droog* the laundry's practically dry

praktiseren /praktizerə(n)/ (praktiseerde, heeft gepraktiseerd) practise

de **praline** /pralinə/ (pl: -s) chocolate (praline)

prat /prat/ (adj, adv) proud: *~ gaan op zijn intelligentie* boast (or: brag) about one's intelligence

praten /pratə(n)/ (praatte, heeft gepraat) talk, speak: *we ~ er niet meer over* let's forget it, let's leave it at that; *je hebt gemakkelijk ~* it's easy (or: it's all right) for you to talk; *daarover valt te ~* that's a matter for discussion; *iedereen praat erover* it's the talk of the town, everyone is talking about it; *langs iem. heen ~* talk across s.o.; *hij kan ~ als Brugman* he can talk the hind legs off a donkey

de **prater** /pratər/ (pl: -s) talker: *hij is geen grote ~* he isn't much of a talker

de **prauw** /prɑu/ (pl: -en) proa

het/de **pre** /pre/ (pl: -'s) preference: *een ~ hebben* have the preference

precair /prekɛ:r/ (adj, adv) precarious, delicate

het **precedent** /presədɛnt/ (pl: -en) precedent: *een ~ scheppen* establish (*or:* create) a precedent

¹**precies** /prəsis/ (adj, adv) precise, exact, accurate, specific: *~ een kilometer* one kilometre exactly; *dat is ~ hetzelfde* that is precisely (*or:* exactly) the same (thing); *om ~ te zijn* to be precise; *~ in het midden* right in the middle; *~ om twaalf uur* at twelve (o'clock) sharp, on the stroke of twelve; *~ op tijd* right on time; *~ drie jaar geleden* exactly (*or:* precisely) three years ago

²**precies** /prəsis/ (int) precisely, exactly

preciseren /presizerə(n)/ (preciseerde, heeft gepreciseerd) specify: *kunt u dat nader ~?* could you be more specific?

de **precisie** /presizi/ precision, accuracy

het **predicaat** /predikat/ **1** title **2** [linguistics] predicate

de **predikant** /predikɑnt/ (pl: -en) **1** minister, pastor; vicar, rector; parson [Anglican Church]; clergyman **2** [Roman Catholicism] preacher

prediken /predɪkə(n)/ (predikte, heeft gepredikt) preach

de **preek** /prek/ (pl: preken) **1** sermon, homily (on): *een ~ houden* deliver a sermon **2** sermon, lecture (on)

de **preekstoel** /prekstul/ (pl: -en) pulpit

prefabriceren /prefabriserə(n)/ (prefabriceerde, heeft geprefabriceerd) prefabricate

preferent /preferɛnt/ (adj) preferred, preferential

prefereren /prefererə(n)/ (prefereerde, heeft geprefereerd) prefer: *dit is te ~ boven dat* this is preferable to that

de **prehistorie** /prehɪstori/ prehistory

prehistorisch /prehɪstoris/ (adj) prehistoric

de **prei** /prɛi/ (pl: -en) leek

preken /prekə(n)/ (preekte, heeft gepreekt) **1** preach, deliver (*or:* preach) a sermon **2** preach, moralize

de **prelude** /prelydə/ (pl: -s) prelude

prematuur /prematyr/ (adj) premature

de **premie** /premi/ (pl: -s) **1** premium, bonus, gratuity **2** premium; (insurance) contribution: *de sociale ~s* social insurance (*or:* security) contributions

de **premier** /prəmje/ (pl: -s) prime minister, premier

de **première** /prəmjɛ:rə/ (pl: -s) première; first night; opening performance

de **preminiem** /preminim/ (pl: -en) [Belg] junior member (6-10 years) of sports club

prenataal /prenatal/ (adj) antenatal; [Am] prenatal

de **prent** /prɛnt/ (pl: -en) print, illustration; cartoon

de **prentbriefkaart** /prɛndbrifkart/ (pl: -en) (picture) postcard

het **prentenboek** /prɛntə(n)buk/ (pl: -en) picture book

prepaid /pri:pet/ (adj) pay-as-you-go, prepay: *~ beltegoed* prepaid phone credit

het **preparaat** /preparat/ (pl: preparaten) preparation

prepareren /preparerə(n)/ (prepareerde, heeft geprepareerd) prepare

het **prepensioen** /prepɛnʃun/ (pl: -en) pre-pension scheme; [Am] pre-pension plan

de **presbyteriaan** /prɛzbiterijan/ (pl: -rianen) Presbyterian

de **preselectie** /presəlɛksi/ [Belg] qualifying round

het ¹**present** /prezɛnt/ (pl: -en) present, gift

²**present** /prezɛnt/ (adj) present; in attendance: *ze waren allemaal ~* they were all present; *~! present!*, here!

de **presentatie** /prezɛnta(t)si/ (pl: -s) presentation, introduction: *de ~ is in handen van Joris* the programme is presented by Joris

de **presentator** /prezɛntator/ (pl: -en) presenter; host, hostess, anchorman

het **presenteerblaadje** /prəzɛnterblacə/ tray, platter: *de baan werd hem op een ~ aangeboden* the job was handed to him on a silver platter

presenteren /prezɛnterə(n)/ (presenteerde, heeft gepresenteerd) **1** present, introduce **2** present; offer **3** pass off (as) **4** present, host

de **presentie** /prezɛn(t)si/ presence

de **presentielijst** /prezɛnsilɛist/ (pl: -en) attendance list, (attendance) roll, (attendance) register

de **president** /prezidɛnt/ (pl: -en) President

de **president-directeur** /prezidɛndirɛktør/ (pl: -en) chairman (of the board)

presidentieel /prezidɛn(t)ʃel/ (adj) presidential

de **presidentsverkiezing** /prezidɛn(t)sfərkizɪŋ/ presidential election

pressen /prɛsə(n)/ (preste, heeft geprest) press, put pressure on

de **pressie** /prɛsi/ (pl: -s) pressure

de **prestatie** /prɛsta(t)si/ (pl: -s) performance, achievement, feat: *een hele ~* quite an achievement; *een ~ leveren* achieve sth., perform well, do well

het **prestatieloon** /prɛsta(t)silon/ (pl: -lonen) merit pay

presteren /prɛsterə(n)/ (presteerde, heeft gepresteerd) achieve, perform: *hij heeft nooit veel gepresteerd* he has never done anything to speak of

het **prestige** /prɛsti:ʒə/ prestige

prestigieus /prɛstiʒøs/ (adj) prestigious

de **pret** /prɛt/ **1** fun, hilarity: *~ hebben* (*or:* ma-

ken) have fun, have a good time; *dat was dolle* ~ it was great (*or:* glorious) fun; *dat mag de* ~ *niet drukken* never mind **2** fun, enjoyment **3** fun, entertainment: *(het is) uit met de* ~*!* the party is over

pretenderen /pretɛndɛrə(n)/ (pretendeerde, heeft gepretendeerd) profess (to be), make out, pretend (to be)

de **pretentie** /pretɛn(t)si/ (pl: -s) pretension: *ik heb niet de* ~ ... I make no pretension(s) to ..., I don't pretend to ...

pretentieus /pretɛn(t)jøs/ (adj, adv) pretentious

het **pretje** /prɛcə/ (pl: -s) bit of fun: *dat is geen* ~ that's no picnic

de **pretogen** /prɛtoɣə(n)/ (pl) twinkling eyes

het **pretpark** /prɛtpɑrk/ (pl: -en) amusement park

prettig /prɛtəɣ/ (adj, adv) pleasant, nice: ~ *weekend!* have a pleasant (*or:* nice) weekend; *deze krant leest* ~ this paper is nice to read

preuts /prøts/ (adj, adv) prudish, prim (and proper)

de **preutsheid** /prøtshɛit/ prudishness, primness

prevaleren /prevalɛrə(n)/ (prevaleerde, heeft geprevaleerd) prevail

prevelen /prevələ(n)/ (prevelde, heeft gepreveld) mumble, murmur

de **preventie** /prevɛnsi/ (pl: -s) prevention

preventief /prevɛntif/ (adj, adv) preven(ta)tive, precautionary

de **pr-functionaris** /peɛrfʏŋkʃonɑrɪs/ PR officer

het **prieel** /prijel/ (pl: priëlen) summerhouse, arbour

priegelen /priɣələ(n)/ (priegelde, heeft gepriegeld) do fine (*or:* delicate) (needle)work

het **priegelwerk** /priɣəlwɛrk/ close work, delicate work

de **priem** /prim/ (pl: -en) awl, bodkin

het **priemgetal** /primɣətɑl/ (pl: -len) prime (number)

de **priester** /pristər/ (pl: -s) priest

prijken /prɛikə(n)/ (prijkte, heeft geprijkt) be resplendent, adorn

de **prijs** /prɛis/ (pl: prijzen) **1** price; fare; charge: *voor een zacht* ~*je* at a bargain price; *tot elke* ~ at any price (*or:* cost), at all costs **2** price (tag): *het* ~*je hangt er nog aan* it has still got the price on **3** prize, award: *een* ~ *uitloven* put up a prize; *in de prijzen vallen* be among the winners **4** reward, prize || *iets op* ~ *stellen* appreciate sth.

prijsbewust /prɛizbəwʏst/ (adj) cost-conscious

de **prijsdaling** /prɛizdalɪŋ/ (pl: -en) fall (*or:* drop, decrease) in price

prijsgeven /prɛisxevə(n)/ (gaf prijs, heeft prijsgegeven) give up, abandon, consign

het **prijskaartje** /prɛiskarcə/ (pl: -s) price tag

de **prijsklasse** /prɛisklɑsə/ (pl: -n) price range, price bracket

de **prijslijst** /prɛislɛist/ (pl: -en) price list

de **prijsopgave** /prɛisɔpχavə/ (pl: -n) estimate; quotation; tender

de **prijsuitreiking** /prɛisœytrɛikɪŋ/ (pl: -en) distribution of prizes; prize-giving (ceremony)

de **prijsvechter** /prɛisfɛχtər/ **1** discounter **2** prize fighter

de **prijsverhoging** /prɛisfərhoɣɪŋ/ price increase, rise

de **prijsverlaging** /prɛisfərlaɣɪŋ/ price reduction, price cut

de **prijsvraag** /prɛisfraχ/ (pl: -vragen) competition, (prize) contest

de **prijswinnaar** /prɛiswɪnar/ (pl: -s) prizewinner

¹**prijzen** /prɛizə(n)/ (prees, heeft geprezen) praise, commend: *een veelgeprezen boek* a highly-praised book || *zich gelukkig* ~ *met* call (*or:* consider) o.s. lucky that

²**prijzen** /prɛizə(n)/ (prijsde, heeft geprijsd) price; ticket; mark: *vele artikelen zijn tijdelijk lager geprijsd* many articles have been temporarily marked down

prijzig /prɛizəχ/ (adj) expensive, pricey

de **prik** /prɪk/ (pl: -ken) **1** prick, prod **2** injection, shot **3** pop, fizz: *mineraalwater zonder* ~ still mineral water || *dat is vaste* ~ that happens all the time

de **prikactie** /prɪkɑksi/ (pl: -s) lightning strike

het **prikbord** /prɪgbɔrt/ (pl: -en) noticeboard; [Am] bulletin board

het **prikje** /prɪkjə/ (pl: -s): *iets voor een* ~ *kopen* buy sth. dirt cheap (*or:* for next to nothing)

de **prikkel** /prɪkəl/ (pl: -s) incentive, stimulant, stimulus

prikkelbaar /prɪkəlbar/ (adj) touchy, irritable

het/de **prikkeldraad** /prɪkəldrat/ barbed wire

¹**prikkelen** /prɪkələ(n)/ (prikkelde, heeft geprikkeld) prickle, tingle; sting: *mijn been prikkelt* my leg is tingling

²**prikkelen** /prɪkələ(n)/ (prikkelde, heeft geprikkeld) irritate, vex

¹**prikken** /prɪkə(n)/ (prikte, heeft geprikt) sting, tingle: *de rook prikt in mijn ogen* the smoke is making my eyes smart

²**prikken** /prɪkə(n)/ (prikte, heeft geprikt) **1** prick; prod: *een ballon lek* ~ pop a balloon **2** stick (to), affix (to): *een poster op de muur* ~ pin a poster on the wall **3** inject

de **prikklok** /prɪklɔk/ (pl: -ken) time clock

de **priklimonade** /prɪklimonadə/ (pl: -s) pop

pril /prɪl/ (adj) early, fresh, young

¹**prima** /prima/ (adj, adv) excellent, great, terrific, fine: *een* ~ *vent* a nice chap; [Am] a great guy

²**prima** /prima/ (int) great

primaat

het **primaat** /primat/ primacy, pre-eminance
¹**primair** /primɛːr/ (adj) primary, basic
²**primair** /primɛːr/ (adj, adv) **1** primary, initial, first **2** primary, principal, essential, chief
de **primeur** /primør/ (pl: -s) sth. new; scoop
primitief /primitif/ (adj, adv) **1** primitive, elemental **2** primitive, makeshift: *het ging er heel ~ toe* it was very rough and ready there
de **primula** /primyla/ (pl: -'s) primula, primrose
het **principe** /prɪnsipə/ (pl: -s) principle: *een man met hoogstaande ~s* a man of high principles; *uit ~ on* principle, as a matter of principle
principieel /prɪnsipjel/ (adj, adv) **1** fundamental, essential, basic **2** on principle, of principle: *een ~ dienstweigeraar* a conscientious objector (to military service)
de **prins** /prɪns/ (pl: -en) prince
prinselijk /prɪnsələk/ (adj) princely
de **prinses** /prɪnsɛs/ (pl: -sen) princess
Prinsjesdag /prɪnʃəzdɑx/ (pl: -en) [Dutch] [roughly] day of the Queen's (*or:* King's) speech
de **print** /prɪnt/ (pl: -s) **1** print-out **2** print
printen /prɪntə(n)/ (printte, heeft geprint) print
de **printer** /prɪntər/ (pl: -s) printer
de **prior** /prijor/ (pl: -s) prior
de **prioriteit** /prijoritɛit/ (pl: -en) priority: *~en stellen* establish priorities; get one's priorities right
het **prisma** /prɪsma/ (pl: -'s) prism
het **privaatrecht** /privatrɛxt/ private law
de **privacy** /prɑjvəsi/ privacy, seclusion: *iemands ~ schenden* infringe (on) s.o.'s privacy, invade s.o.'s privacy
privatiseren /privatizerə(n)/ (privatiseerde, heeft geprivatiseerd) privatize, denationalize
privé /prive/ (adj, adv) private, confidential, personal: *ik zou je graag even ~ willen spreken* I'd like to talk to you privately (*or:* in private) for a minute
de **privédetective** /privedɪtɛktɪf/ (pl: -s) private detective
het **privéleven** /privelevə(n)/ private life
de **privésfeer** /privesfer/: *in de ~* personal, private
het **privilege** /privilɛʒə/ (pl: -s) privilege
pro /pro/ (adj) pro(-) ‖ *het ~ en het contra* horen hear the pros and cons
probaat /probat/ (adj, adv) effective, efficacious: *een ~ middel* an efficacious remedy, a tried and tested remedy
het **probeersel** /probersəl/ (pl: -s) experiment, try-out
proberen /probɛrə(n)/ (probeerde, heeft geprobeerd) **1** try (out), test: *het met water en zeep ~* try soap and water **2** try, attempt: *dat hoef je niet eens te ~* you needn't bother (trying that)

het **probleem** /problem/ (pl: problemen) problem, difficulty, trouble: *in de problemen zitten* be in difficulties (*or:* trouble); *geen ~!* no problem!; *ergens geen ~ van maken* not make a problem of (*or:* about) sth., not make difficulties about sth.
het **probleemgeval** /problemɣəval/ (pl: -len) problematical case
probleemloos /problemlos/ (adj, adv) uncomplicated, smooth, trouble-free: *alles verliep ~* things went very smoothly (*or:* without a hitch)
de **probleemstelling** /problemstɛlɪŋ/ (pl: -en) definition (*or:* formulation) of a problem
de **problematiek** /problematik/ problem(s), issue
problematisch /problematis/ (adj) problematic(al)
het **procedé** /prosede/ (pl: -s) process, technique
procederen /prosədɛrə(n)/ (procedeerde, heeft geprocedeerd) litigate, take legal action, proceed (against); prosecute: *gaan ~* go to court
de **procedure** /prosədyrə/ (pl: -s) **1** procedure, method **2** (law)suit, action, legal proceedings (*or:* procedure): *een ~ tegen iem. aanspannen* start legal proceedings against s.o.
de **procedurefout** /prosədyrəfaut/ (pl: -en) procedural mistake, mistake in procedure
het **procent** /prosɛnt/ (pl: -en) per cent, percent: *honderd ~ zeker* dead certain (*or:* sure)
procentueel /prosɛntywel/ (adj) in terms of percentage
het **proces** /prosɛs/ (pl: -sen) **1** (law)suit; trial; action, legal proceedings: *iem. een ~ aandoen* take s.o. to court **2** process
de **proceskosten** /prosɛskostə(n)/ (pl) (legal) costs
de **processie** /prosɛsi/ (pl: -s) procession
de **processor** /prosɛsor/ (pl: -s, -en) processor
het **proces-verbaal** /prosɛsfərbal/ (pl: processen-verbaal) charge; summons; ticket: *een ~ aan zijn broek krijgen* be booked, get a ticket; *~ opmaken tegen iem.* take s.o.'s name and address, book s.o.
de **proclamatie** /proklama(t)si/ (pl: -s) **1** proclamation **2** [Belg] public announcement of the results (of a competition, exams, …)
proclameren /proklamɛrə(n)/ (proclameerde, heeft geproclameerd) proclaim
de **procuratiehouder** /prokyra(t)sihaudər/ (pl: -s) deputy manager
de **procureur** /prokyrør/ (pl: -s) [law] [roughly] solicitor; [Am] [roughly] attorney; [Belg] *~ des Konings* [roughly] public prosecutor
de **procureur-generaal** /prokyrørɣenəral/ (pl: procureurs-generaal) Procurator-General; [roughly] Attorney General
pro Deo /prodejo/ (adv) free (of charge), for nothing

de **producent** /prodysɛnt/ (pl: -en) producer

de **producer** /prodjuːsər/ (pl: -s) producer

produceren /prodyserə(n)/ (produceerde, heeft geproduceerd) produce, make, manufacture; generate

het **product** /prodʏkt/ (pl: -en) product, production; commodity: *het bruto* **nationaal** ~ the gross national product; the GNP

de **productie** /prodʏksi/ (pl: -s) **1** production: *uit de ~ nemen* stop producing (*or:* production) **2** production; output; yield; produce

productief /prodʏktif/ (adj) **1** productive, fruitful **2** productive, prolific: *een ~ dagje* a good day's work

de **productiekosten** /prodʏksikostə(n)/ (pl) cost(s) of production

de **productieleider** /prodʏksilɛidər/ (pl: -s) production manager; producer

de **productiemaatschappij** /prodʏksimatsχɑpɛi/ (pl: -en) film production company

het **productieproces** /prodʏksiprosɛs/ (pl: -sen) production process, manufacture

de **productiviteit** /prodʏktivitɛit/ productivity, productive capacity

het **productschap** /prodʏktsχɑp/ (pl: -pen) [roughly] Commodity Board

de **proef** /pruf/ (pl: proeven) **1** test, examination, trial: *op de ~ stellen* put to the test; *proeven nemen* carry out experiments **2** test, try, trial, probation: *iets een week op ~ krijgen* have sth. on a week's trial; *op ~ on probation* **3** proof ‖ *de ~ op de som nemen* test sth., put it to the test, try (out) sth.

de **proefballon** /pruvbɑlɔn/ trial balloon: [fig] *een ~netje* **oplaten** float a trial balloon, put out a feeler

het **proefdier** /pruvdir/ (pl: -en) laboratory animal

proefdraaien /pruvdrajə(n)/ (draaide proef, heeft proefgedraaid) trial run, test run

het **proefkonijn** /prufkonɛin/ (pl: -en) guinea pig

het **proeflokaal** /pruflokal/ (pl: -lokalen) public house

de **proefneming** /prufnemɪŋ/ (pl: -en) test(ing)

proefondervindelijk /prufɔndərvɪndələk/ (adj, adv) experimental, by experiment (*or:* experience)

de **proefperiode** /prufperijodə/ (pl: -n, -s) trial period; probationary period; probation

de **proefpersoon** /prufpɛrson/ (pl: -personen) (experimental, test) subject

het **proefproces** /prufprosɛs/ (pl: -sen) test case

de **proefrit** /prufrɪt/ (pl: -ten) test drive; trial run: *een ~ maken met de auto* test-drive the car

het **proefschrift** /prufsχrɪft/ (pl: -en) (doctoral, Ph D) thesis, dissertation

de **proeftijd** /pruftɛit/ probation, probation-ary period, trial period: [law] *voorwaardelijk veroordeeld* **met** *een ~ van twee jaar* a suspended sentence with two years' probation

de **proeftuin** /pruftœyn/ (pl: -en) experimental garden (*or:* field)

het **proefwerk** /prufwɛrk/ (pl: -en) test (paper): *een ~ opgeven* set a test

proesten /prustə(n)/ (proestte, heeft geproest) **1** sneeze **2** snort, splutter

proeven /pruvə(n)/ (proefde, heeft geproefd) taste, try, sample, test: *van het eten ~* try some of the food

de **proeverij** /pruvərɛi/ tasting

de **prof** /prɔf/ (pl: -s) **1** prof **2** pro

profaan /profan/ (adj) profane

de **profclub** /prɔfklʏp/ (pl: -s) professional club

de **profeet** /profet/ (pl: profeten) prophet, prophetess

professioneel /profɛʃonel/ (adj) professional ‖ *iets ~ aanpakken* approach sth. in a professional way

de **professor** /profɛsɔr/ (pl: -en) professor: *~ in de taalwetenschap* a professor of linguistics; *een* **verstrooide** *~* an absent-minded professor

de **profetie** /profe(t)si/ (pl: -ën) prophecy

profetisch /profetis/ (adj, adv) prophetic

proficiat /profisijɑt/ (int) congratulations: *~ met je verjaardag* happy birthday!

het **profiel** /profil/ (pl: -en) profile

de **profielschets** /profilsχɛts/ (pl: -en) profile

de **profielzool** /profilzol/ (pl: -zolen) grip sole, sole with a tread

het **profijt** /profɛit/ (pl: -en) profit, benefit

profileren /profilerə(n)/ (profileerde, heeft geprofileerd) **1** characterize, make known **2** profile, mould

profiteren /profiterə(n)/ (profiteerde, heeft geprofiteerd) profit (from, by), take advantage (of), exploit: *zoveel mogelijk ~ van* make the most of

de **profiteur** /profitør/ (pl: -s) profiteer

pro forma /proformɑ/ (adv) for form's sake, for appearance's sake

het **profvoetbal** /prɔfudbɑl/ professional football

de **prognose** /proɣnozə/ (pl: -s) prognosis, forecast

het **programma** /proɣrɑma/ (pl: -'s) **1** programme: *het hele ~ afwerken* go (*or:* get) through the whole programme **2** [comp] program

het **programmaboekje** /proɣrɑmabukjə/ programme

de **programmagids** /proɣrɑmaɣɪts/ listings; [Am] TV guide

de **programmamaker** /proɣrɑmamakər/ (pl: -s) programme maker (*or:* writer), producer

de **programmatuur** /proɣramatyr/ (pl: programmaturen) software; programs

de **programmeertaal** /proɣramertal/ (pl: -talen) computer language

¹programmeren /proɣramɛrə(n)/ (programmeerde, heeft geprogrammeerd) [comp] program

²programmeren /proɣramɛrə(n)/ (programmeerde, heeft geprogrammeerd) programme, schedule: *de uitzending is geprogrammeerd voor woensdag* the programme is to be broadcast on Wednesday

de **programmeur** /proɣramør/ (pl: -s) programmer

de **progressie** /proɣrɛsi/ (pl: -s) **1** progress **2** progression

progressief /proɣrɛsif/ (adj, adv) progressive; liberal

het **project** /projɛkt/ (pl: -en) project

projecteren /projɛktɛrə(n)/ (projecteerde, heeft geprojecteerd) project

de **projectie** /projɛksi/ (pl: -s) projection

het **projectiel** /projɛktil/ (pl: -en) missile, projectile

de **projectleider** /projɛktlɛɪdər/ (pl: -s) project manager

de **projectontwikkelaar** /projɛktɔntwɪkəlar/ (pl: -s) property developer; [Am] real estate developer

de **projector** /projɛktɔr/ (pl: -s) projector

de **proleet** /prolet/ (pl: proleten) plebeian

het **proletariaat** /proletarijat/ proletariat

de **proletariër** /proletarijər/ (pl: -s) proletarian

prolongeren /prolɔnɣɛrə(n)/ (prolongeerde, heeft geprolongeerd) prolong, extend: *zijn titel ~* retain one's (championship) title

de **proloog** /prolox/ (pl: prologen) prologue

de **promenade** /promənadə/ (pl: -s) shopping precinct, shopping mall

het **promillage** /promilaʒə/ (pl: -s) blood alcohol level

het **promille** /promil/ (pl: -n) per thousand, per mil(le): *acht ~* 0.8 percent

prominent /prominɛnt/ (adj) prominent

promoten /promotə(n)/ (promootte, heeft gepromoot) promote

de **promotie** /promo(t)si/ (pl: -s) promotion: *~ maken* get promotion

de **promotor** /promotər/ (pl: -s) **1** [roughly] tutor (*or:* supervisor) (of a PhD student) **2** promoter

de **promovendus** /promovɛndʏs/ (pl: promovendi) **1** doctoral (*or:* PhD) student **2** promoted player (*or:* team)

promoveren /promovɛrə(n)/ (promoveerde, is gepromoveerd) **1** take one's doctoral degree (*or:* one's Ph D): *hij is gepromoveerd op een onderzoek naar …* he obtained his doctorate with a thesis on … **2** [sport] be promoted, go up

prompt /prɔmt/ (adj, adv) **1** prompt, speedy **2** punctual, prompt: *~ op tijd* right (*or:* dead) on time

pronken /prɔnkə(n)/ (pronkte, heeft ge-

pronkt) flaunt (o.s., sth.); prance; strut: *zij loopt graag te ~ met haar zoon* she likes to show off her son

de **prooi** /proj/ (pl: -en) **1** prey; quarry **2** prey, victim: *ten ~ vallen aan* become prey to

proost /prost/ (int) cheers

proosten /prostə(n)/ (proostte, heeft geproost) toast, raise one's glass

de **prop** /prɔp/ (pl: -pen) ball: *een ~ watten* a wad of cotton wool ‖ *met iets op de ~pen komen* come up with sth.

de **propaganda** /propaɣɔnda/ propaganda

propageren /propaɣɛrə(n)/ (propageerde, heeft gepropageerd) propagate

de **propedeuse** /propədœyzə/ foundation course

propedeutisch /propədœytis/ (adj) preliminary, introductory

de **propeller** /propɛlər/ (pl: -s) (screw) propeller, (air)screw

proper /propər/ (adj) neat, tidy; clean

de **proportie** /propɔrsi/ (pl: -s) **1** proportion, relation: *iets in (de juiste) ~(s) zien* keep sth. in perspective **2** proportion, dimension

proportioneel /propɔrʃonel/ (adj, adv) proportional

proppen /prɔpə(n)/ (propte, heeft gepropt) shove, stuff, cram, pack: *iedereen werd in één auto gepropt* everyone was squeezed (*or:* packed) into one car

propvol /prɔpfɔl/ (adj) full to the brim (*or:* to bursting), chock-full, crammed; packed (tight): *een ~le bus* an overcrowded bus

het/de **prospectus** /prɔspɛktʏs/ (pl: -sen) prospectus

de **prostaat** /prostat/ (pl: prostaten) prostate (gland)

de **prostaatkanker** /prostatkɑnkər/ cancer of the prostate

de **prostituee** /prɔstitywe/ (pl: -s) prostitute

de **prostitutie** /prɔstity(t)si/ prostitution

het **protectionisme** /protɛkʃonɪsmə/ protectionism

het/de **proteïne** /protejinə/ protein

het **protest** /protɛst/ (pl: -en) protest: *uit ~ (tegen)* in protest (against); *~ aantekenen tegen* enter (*or:* lodge) a protest against, raise an objection against

de **protestant** /protɛstɑnt/ (pl: -en) Protestant

protestants /protɛstɑnts/ (adj, adv) Protestant; [non-Anglican] dissenting; Nonconformist

de **protestbeweging** /protɛstbəweɣɪŋ/ (pl: -en) protest movement

protesteren /protɛstɛrə(n)/ (protesteerde, heeft geprotesteerd) protest

de **protestmars** /protɛstmɑrs/ (pl: -en) protest march

de **prothese** /protezə/ (pl: -n, -s) prothesis, prosthesis; dentures; false teeth

het **protocol** /protokɔl/ (pl: -len) **1** protocol

2 record
protocollair /protokɔlɛːr/ (adj) required by protocol, according to protocol
het **proton** /prot̯ɔn/ (pl: -en) proton
de **protonkaart** /prot̯ɔnkart/ (pl: -en) [Belg] rechargeable smart card
het **prototype** /prot̯otipə/ (pl: -n, -s) prototype
protserig /prɔt̯sərəχ/ (adj, adv) flash(y)
het/de **proviand** /provijɑnt/ provisions: ~ *inslaan* stock (up) provisions, victual
de **provider** /provɑjdər/ provider
provinciaal /provɪnʃal/ (adj, adv) provincial: *een provinciale weg* [roughly] a secondary road
de **provincie** /provɪnsi/ (pl: -s) province, region: *de ~ Limburg* the Province of Limburg
de **provisie** /provizi/ (pl: -s) commission; brokerage
provisorisch /provizoris/ (adj, adv) provisional, temporary
provoceren /provosɛrə(n)/ (provoceerde, heeft geprovoceerd) provoke, incite
provocerend /provosɛrənt/ (adj, adv) provocative, provoking
het **proza** /proza/ prose
prozaïsch /prozais/ (adj, adv) prosaic
de **pruik** /prœyk/ (pl: -en) wig, toupee
pruilen /prœylə(n)/ (pruilde, heeft gepruild) pout, sulk
de **pruim** /prœym/ **1** plum; prune **2** plug, wad
pruimen /prœymə(n)/ (pruimde, heeft gepruimd) chew tobacco
de **pruimenboom** /prœymə(n)bom/ (pl: -bomen) plum (tree)
Pruisen /prœysə(n)/ Prussia
Pruisisch /prœysis/ (adj, adv) Prussian
het **prul** /prʏl/ (pl: -len) **1** piece of waste paper **2** (piece of) trash, piece of rubbish (or: junk)
de **prullaria** /prʏlarija/ (pl) nicknacks, knickknacks
de **prullenbak** /prʏlə(n)bɑk/ (pl: -ken) **1** waste paper basket, wastebasket **2** recycle bin, trash can
de **prullenmand** /prʏlə(n)mɑnt/ (pl: -en) wastepaperbasket; [esp Am] wastebasket: *dat gaat rechtstreeks de ~ in* that is going straight into the wastepaperbasket
de **prut** /prʏt/ **1** mud, ooze, sludge **2** mush **3** grounds
de **pruts** /prʏts/ (pl: -en) [Belg] trinket
prutsen /prʏtsə(n)/ (prutste, heeft geprutst) mess about (or: around), potter (about), tinker (about): *je moet niet zelf aan je tv gaan zitten ~* you shouldn't mess about with your TV-set yourself
de **prutser** /prʏtsər/ (pl: -s) botcher, bungler
het **prutswerk** /prʏtswɛrk/ botch(-up)
pruttelen /prʏtələ(n)/ (pruttelde, heeft gepruetteld) simmer, perk; percolate
het **PS** /pɛɛs/ *postscriptum* PS
de **psalm** /psɑlm/ (pl: -en) psalm

het **psalmboek** /psɑlmbuk/ (pl: -en) psalm-book, psalter
het **pseudoniem** /psœydonim/ (pl: -en) pseudonym
de **psoriasis** /psorijazɪs/ psoriasis
pst /pst/ (int) ps(s)t: *~! kom eens hier!* ps(s)t! come here!
de **psyche** /psiχə/ psyche
psychedelisch /psiχədelis/ (adj) psychedelic
de **psychiater** /psiχijatər/ (pl: -s) psychiatrist: *je moet naar een ~* you should see a psychiatrist
de **psychiatrie** /psiχijatri/ psychiatry
psychiatrisch /psiχijatris/ (adj) psychiatric: *een ~e inrichting* a mental hospital
psychisch /psiχis/ (adj, adv) psychological, mental: *~ gestoord* emotionally disturbed; *dat is ~, niet lichamelijk* that is psychological, not physical
de **psychoanalyse** /psiχoanalizə/ (pl: -n, -s) psychoanalysis
de **psychologie** /psiχoloɣi/ psychology
psychologisch /psiχoloɣis/ (adj, adv) psychological
de **psycholoog** /psiχoloχ/ (pl: -logen) psychologist
de **psychopaat** /psiχopat/ (pl: -paten) psychopath
de **psychose** /psiχozə/ (pl: -n, -s) psychosis
psychosomatisch /psiχosomatis/ (adj, adv) psychosomatic
de **psychotherapeut** /psiχoterapœyt/ (pl: -en) psychotherapist
de **psychotherapie** /psiχoterapi/ psychotherapy, psychotherapeutics
psychotisch /psiχotis/ (adj) psychotic
PTSS PTSD *(post-traumatic stress disorder)*
de **PTT** /petetɛ/ *Post, Telegrafie, Telefonie* Post Office
de **puber** /pybər/ (pl: -s) adolescent
puberaal /pybəral/ (adj, adv) adolescent
puberen /pybərə(n)/ (puberde, heeft gepuberd) reach puberty
de **puberteit** /pybərtɛit/ puberty, adolescence: *in de ~ zijn* be going through one's adolescence
de **publicatie** /pyblika(t)si/ (pl: -s) publication
publiceren /pyblisɛrə(n)/ (publiceerde, heeft gepubliceerd) publish
de **publiciteit** /pyblisitɛit/ publicity: *~ krijgen* attract attention, get publicity; *iets in de ~ brengen* bring sth. to public notice
de **public relations** /pʏblɪkrilɛʃəns/ (pl) public relations
het **¹publiek** /pyblik/ **1** public; [sport] crowd; audience; readership; clientele; visitors: *een breed ~ proberen te bereiken* try to cater for a broad public; *veel ~ trekken* (or: *draw*) a good crowd, be well attended; *het grote ~* the general public, the millions **2** (general) public: *toegankelijk voor (het) ~ ~*

open to the (general) public

²publiek /pyblik/ (adj, adv) public: *er was veel ~e belangstelling* it was well attended

de **publieksprijs** /pybliksprɛɪs/ prize awarded by the public

de **publiekstrekker** /pyblikstrɛkər/ (pl: -s) crowd-puller; (good) box-office draw; box-office success, box-office hit

de **publiekswissel** /pyblikswɪsəl/ (pl: -s) last-minute substitution

de **pudding** /pydɪŋ/ (pl: -en, -s) pudding

de **puf** /pyf/ (get up and) go, energy: *ergens de ~ niet meer voor hebben* not feel up to sth. any more

puffen /pyfə(n)/ (pufte, heeft gepuft) pant: *~ van* de warmte pant with the heat

het **pufje** (pl: -s) puff

de **pui** /pœy/ (pl: -en) (lower) front, (lower) façade; shopfront

puik /pœyk/ (adj, adv) **1** choice; top quality **2** great, first-rate

puilen /pœylə(n)/ bulge

het/de **puimsteen** /pœymsten/ pumice (stone)

het **puin** /pœyn/ rubble: *~ ruimen* a) clear up the rubble; b) [fig] pick up the pieces, sort sth. out; *in ~ liggen* lie (or: be) in ruins; be smashed (up, to bits)

de **puinhoop** /pœynhop/ (pl: -hopen) **1** heap of rubble (or: rubbish) **2** mess, shambles: *jij hebt er een ~ van gemaakt* you have made a mess of it

puinruimen /pœynrœymə(n)/ (ruimde puin, heeft puingeruimd) **1** clear up the debris **2** [fig] pick up the pieces

de **puist** /pœyst/ (pl: -en) pimple, spot: *~jes uitknijpen* squeeze spots

de **pukkel** /pykəl/ (pl: -s) pimple, spot

de **pul** /pyl/ (pl: -len) tankard, mug

pulken /pylkə(n)/ (pulkte, heeft gepulkt) pick: *zit niet zo in je neus te ~* stop picking your nose

de **pullover** /pylovər/ (pl: -s) pullover, sweater

de **pulp** /pylp/ **1** pulp: *tot ~ geslagen* beaten to a pulp **2** pulp, junk (reading)

pulseren /pylserə(n)/ (pulseerde, heeft gepulseerd) pulsate

de **pummel** /pyməl/ (pl: -s) lout, boor

de **pump** /pymp/ (pl: -s) pump

de **punaise** /pynɛːzə/ (pl: -s) drawing pin; [Am] thumbtack

de **punctie** /pyŋksi/ (pl: -s) puncture: *lumbale ~* lumbar puncture

punctueel /pyŋktywel/ (adj, adv) punctual

de **punk** /pyŋk/ punk

de **punker** /pyŋkər/ (pl: -s) punk

de **¹punt** /pynt/ (pl: -en) **1** point, tip; corner; angle: *het ligt op het ~je van mijn tong* it's on the tip of my tongue; *een ~ aan een potlood slijpen* sharpen a pencil; *op het ~je van zijn stoel zitten* be (sitting) on the edge of his seat **2** wedge ‖ [Belg] *op ~ stellen* arrange, fix up

het **²punt** /pynt/ (pl: -en) **1** point, place: *het laagste ~ bereiken* reach rock-bottom **2** point, moment: *hij stond op het ~ om te vertrekken* he was (just) about to leave **3** point; item; count; matter; question; issue: *zijn zwakke ~* his weak point; *tot in de ~jes verzorgd* a) impeccably dressed; b) shipshape; *geen ~!* no problem!

het/de **³punt** /pynt/ (pl: -en) **1** full stop; decimal (point): *~en en strepen* dots and dashes; *de dubbelepunt* the colon; *ik was gewoon kwaad, ~, uit!* I was just angry, full stop **2** point: *hoeveel ~en hebben jullie?* what's your score?; *op ~en winnen (verslaan)* win on points; *hij is twee ~en vooruitgegaan* he has gone up (by) two marks **3** mark

het **puntdak** /pyndɑk/ (pl: -en) gable(d) roof, peaked roof

punten /pyntə(n)/ (puntte, heeft gepunt) **1** sharpen, point **2** trim

de **puntendeling** /pyntə(n)delɪŋ/ (pl: -en) draw

de **puntenlijst** /pyntə(n)lɛɪst/ (pl: -en) scorecard; scoresheet; report

de **puntenslijper** /pyntə(n)slɛɪpər/ (pl: -s) (pencil) sharpener

de **puntentelling** /pyntə(n)tɛlɪŋ/ (pl: -en) scoring

de **punter** /pyntər/ (pl: -s) **1** punt **2** toe-kick, toe-shot

puntgaaf /pyntxaf/ (adj, adv) perfect, flawless

het **punthoofd** /pynthoft/ (pl: -en): *ik krijg er een ~ van* it is driving me crazy (or: up the wall)

puntig /pyntəx/ (adj, adv) pointed, sharp: *~e uitsteeksels* sharp points; *~e bladeren* pointed leaves

het **puntje** /pyncə/ (pl: -s) **1** (small, little) point, tip, dot: *de ~s op de i zetten* dot the i's and cross the t's **2** [roughly] roll **3** dot; spot ‖ *als ~ bij paaltje komt* when it comes to the crunch (or: point)

de **puntkomma** /pyntkoma/ (pl: -'s) semicolon

de **puntmuts** /pyntmyts/ (pl: -en) pointed cap, pointed hat

puntsgewijs /pyntsxəwɛɪs/ (adj, adv) point by point, step by step

de **puntzak** /pyntsɑk/ (pl: -ken) cornet, cone

de **pupil** /pypɪl/ **1** pupil, student **2** [sport] [roughly] junior

de **puppy** /pypi/ (pl: -'s) puppy

de **puree** /pyre/ puree; mashed potatoes ‖ *in de ~ zitten* be in hot water (or: the soup)

pureren /pyrerə(n)/ (pureerde, heeft gepureerd) puree, mash

purgeren /pyrɣerə(n)/ (purgeerde, heeft gepurgeerd) purge (of/from): *een ~d middel* a laxative

puriteins /pyritɛɪns/ (adj, adv) puritan(ic(al))

het **¹purper** /pʏrpər/ purple

²purper /pʏrpər/ (adj) purple

de **purser** /pʏːrsər/ (pl: -s) purser

het/de **pus** /pʏs/ pus

pushen /puʃə(n)/ (pushte, heeft gepusht) push (on), urge (on), drive (on)

de **put** /pʏt/ (pl: -ten) **1** well: *dat is een **bodemloze** ~* it's a bottomless pit; *diep **in** de ~ zitten* be down, feel low; *iem. **uit** de ~ halen* cheer s.o. up **2** drain ‖ *geld in een **bodemloze** ~ gooien* pour (*or:* throw) money down the drain

de **putsch** /putʃ/ (pl: -en) putsch

putten /pʏtə(n)/ (putte, heeft geput) draw (from, on)

puur /pyr/ (adj) **1** pure: *pure **chocola*** plain chocolate; *~ **goud*** solid gold; *een **whisky** ~ graag* a straight whisky, please **2** pure, absolute, sheer: *het was ~ **toeval** dat ik hem zag* it was pure chance that I saw him

de **puzzel** /pʏzəl/ (pl: -s) puzzle

puzzelen /pʏzələ(n)/ (puzzelde, heeft gepuzzeld) do puzzles, solve crossword, jigsaw puzzles

het **pvc** /pevese/ PVC

de **pygmee** /pɪɣmeː/ (pl: -ën) pygmy

de **pyjama** /pijama/ (pl: -'s) pyjamas: *twee ~'s* two pairs of pyjamas

de **pylon** /pilɔn/ (pl: -en) (traffic) cone

de **pyloon** /pilɔn/ (pl: pylonen) pylon

Pyreneeën /pirəneːjə(n)/ (adj) Pyrenees

de **pyromaan** /piromaːn/ (pl: pyromanen) pyromaniac, firebug

de **pyrrusoverwinning** /pɪrʏsovərwɪnɪŋ/ (pl: -en) Pyrrhic victory

Pythagoras /pitaɣorɑs/ Pythagoras: *stelling van ~* Pythagorean theorem

de **python** /pitɔn/ (pl: -s) python

q

de **q** /ky/ (pl: q's) q
Qatar /katɑr/ Qatar
de ¹**Qatarees** /katarēs/ (pl: Qatarezen) Qatari
²**Qatarees** /katarēs/ (adj) Qatari
qua /kwa/ (prep) as regards, as far as … goes
de **quarantaine** /karɑntɛːnə/ quarantine: *in* ~
gehouden worden be kept in quarantine
quartair /kwɑrtɛːr/ (adj) quaternary: *de* ~*e*
sector the government (*or:* public) sector
quasi /kwasi/ (adv) **1** quasi(-), pseudo-: *een*
quasi-intellectueel a pseudo-intellectual
2 [Belg] almost, nearly: *het is* ~ *onmogelijk* it
is scarcely (*or:* hardly) possible
het **quatre-mains** /kɑtrəmɛ̃/ (piano) duet,
composition for four hands
de **quatsch** /kwɑtʃ/ nonsense, rubbish: *ach,* ~*!*
nonsense!
de **querulant** /kwerylɑnt/ (pl: -en) quarrel-
monger, troublemaker
de **quiche** /kiʃ/ (pl: -s) quiche
de **quilt** /kwɪlt/ (pl: -s) quilt
quilten /kwɪltə(n)/ (quiltte, heeft gequilt)
quilt
quitte /kit/ (adj) quits, even: ~ *spelen* break
even; ~ *staan met* be quits with
het **qui-vive** /kiviːvə/: *op zijn* ~ *zijn* be on the qui
vive (*or:* the alert)
de **quiz** /kwɪs/ quiz
de **quizleider** /kwɪslɛidər/ (pl: -s) quizmaster
het **quorum** /kwɔrʏm/ (pl: -s) quorum
de **quota** /kwota/ quota, share
het **quotiënt** /koʃɛnt/ quotient
het **quotum** /kwɔtʏm/ (pl: -s, quota) quota

r

de **r** /ɛr/ (pl: r's) r, R

de **¹ra** /ra/ (pl: ra's) [shipp] yard

²ra /ra/ (int): *ra, ra, wie is dat?* guess who?

de **raad** /rat/ (pl: raden) **1** advice: *iem. ~ geven* advise s.o.; *luister naar mijn ~* take my advice **2** council, board: *de ~ van bestuur* (or: *van commissarissen*) the board (of directors, of management) || *met voorbedachten rade* intentionally, deliberately; *moord met voorbedachten rade* premeditated (or: *wilful*) murder; *hij weet overal ~ op* he's never at a loss; *geen ~ weten met iets* not know what to do with sth.; *not know how to cope with sth.*; *ten einde ~ zijn* be at one's wits' end

het **raadhuis** /rathœys/ (pl: -huizen) town hall, city hall

raadplegen /ratpleɣə(n)/ (raadpleegde, heeft geraadpleegd) consult, confer with

het **raadsbesluit** /ratsbəslœyt/ (pl: -en) decision (of the council)

het **raadsel** /ratsəl/ (pl: -s) **1** riddle: *een ~ opgeven* ask a riddle **2** mystery: *het is mij een ~ hoe dat zo gekomen is* it's a mystery to me how that could have happened; *voor een ~ staan* be mystified, puzzled, baffled

raadselachtig /ratsəlɑxtəx/ (adj, adv) mysterious, puzzling

het **raadslid** /ratslɪt/ (pl: -leden) councillor

de **raadsman** /ratsmɑn/ (pl: raadslieden) legal adviser

de **raadzaal** /ratsal/ (pl: -zalen) council chamber

raadzaam /ratsam/ (adj) advisable, wise

de **raaf** /raf/ (pl: raven) raven

raak /rak/ (adj, adv) home: *~ schieten* hit the mark; *ieder schot was ~* every shot went home; [iron] *het is weer ~* they're at it again || *maar ~* at random; *maar ~ slaan* hit right and left; *klets maar ~* say what you like

de **raaklijn** /raklɛin/ (pl: -en) tangent (line)

het **raakpunt** /rakpʏnt/ (pl: -en) point of contact: *ze hebben geen enkel ~* they have absolutely nothing in common

het **raakvlak** /rakflɑk/ (pl: -ken) **1** tangent plane **2** interface, common ground: *de taalkunde heeft ~ken met andere disciplines* linguistics has much ground in common with other disciplines; *het ~ tussen* the interface between

het **raam** /ram/ (pl: ramen) window, casement: *het ~pje omlaag draaien* wind down the car window

het **raamkozijn** /ramkozɛin/ (pl: -en) window frame

de **raamvertelling** /ramvərtɛlɪŋ/ (pl: -en) frame story

het **raamwerk** /ramwɛrk/ (pl: -en) framework; outline: *het Europese ~* the shared institutions of the EU; *het ~ van haar scriptie is af* the outline of her thesis is finished

de **raap** /rap/ (pl: rapen) turnip || *recht voor zijn ~* straight from the shoulder

de **raapstelen** /rapstelə(n)/ (pl) turnip tops (or: greens)

¹raar /rar/ (adj) odd, funny, strange: *een rare an odd fish, an oddball; een rare snuiter* a strange guy, a weirdo

²raar /rar/ (adv) oddly, strangely: *daar zul je ~ van opkijken* you'll be surprised

raaskallen /raskɑlə(n)/ (raaskalde, heeft geraaskald) rave, talk gibberish, talk rot

de **raat** /rat/ (pl: raten) (honey)comb

de **rabarber** /rabɑrbər/ rhubarb

het **rabat** /rabɑt/ discount

de **rabbi** /rɑbi/ (pl: -'s) rabbi

de **rabbijn** /rɑbɛin/ (pl: -en) rabbi

rabiaat /rabijat/ (adj, adv) rabid

de **rabiës** /rabijəs/ rabies

de **race** /res/ (pl: -s) race: *nog in de ~ zijn* still be in the running; *een ~ tegen de klok* a race against time; *het is een gelopen ~* it's a foregone conclusion

de **raceauto** /resauto/ (pl: -'s) racing car

de **racebaan** /rezban/ (pl: -banen) (race)track

de **racefiets** /resfits/ (pl: -en) racing bicycle (or: bike)

racen /resə(n)/ (racete, heeft/is geracet) race

het **racisme** /rasɪsmə/ racism

de **racist** /rasɪst/ (pl: -en) racist

racistisch /rasɪstis/ (adj, adv) racist

het **racket** /rɛkət/ (pl: -s) racket

het **rad** /rɑt/ (pl: -eren) (cog)wheel: *het ~ van avontuur* the wheel of Fortune; *iem. een ~ voor (de) ogen draaien* pull the wool over s.o.'s eyes

de **radar** /radɑr/ (pl: -s) radar

radeloos /radəlos/ (adj) desperate

raden /radə(n)/ (raadde, heeft geraden) guess: *raad eens wie daar komt* guess who's coming; *goed geraden* you've guessed it; *mis (fout) ~* guess wrong; *je raadt het toch niet* you'll never guess; *je mag driemaal ~ wie het gedaan heeft* you'll never guess who did it || *dat is je geraden* you'd better

het **radertje** /radərcə/ (pl: -s) cog(wheel): *een klein ~ in het geheel zijn* be just a cog in the machine

het **raderwerk** /radərwɛrk/ wheels, gear(s)

de **radiator** /radijatɔr/ (pl: -en) radiator

radicaal /radikal/ (adj) radical, drastic: *een ~ geneesmiddel* a radical cure; *een radicale partij* a radical party

radicaliseren /radikalizerə(n)/ (radicaliseerde, is geradicaliseerd) radicalize de **radijs** /rɑdɛis/ (pl: radijzen) radish

de **radio** /rɑdijo/ (pl: -'s) radio, radio set: *de ~ uitzetten* switch off (*or:* turn off) the radio

radioactief /radijoɑktif/ (adj) radioactive: *~ afval* radioactive waste

de **radioactiviteit** /radijoɑktivitɛit/ radioactivity

radiografisch /radijoɣrafis/ (adj, adv) radiographic ‖ *~ bestuurd* radio-controlled

de **radiologie** /radijoloɣi/ radiology

de **radioloog** /radijolox/ (pl: -logen) radiologist

de **radio-omroep** /rɑdijoomrup/ (pl: -en) broadcasting service

het **radioprogramma** /rɑdijoproɣrɑma/ (pl: -'s) radio programme

het **radiostation** /rɑdijosta(t)ʃɔn/ (pl: -s) radio (*or:* broadcasting) station

het **radiotoestel** /rɑdijotustɛl/ (pl: -len) radio (set)

de **radio-uitzending** /rɑdijoœytsɛndɪŋ/ (pl: -en) radio broadcast (*or:* transmission)

de **radiozender** /rɑdijozɛndər/ (pl: -s) radio transmitter

het **radium** /radijʏm/ radium

de **radius** /radijʏs/ (pl: -sen, radii) radius

de **radslag** /rɑtslɑx/ (pl: -en) cartwheel: *~en maken* turn cartwheels

de **rafel** /rafəl/ (pl: -s) frayed end, loose end: *de ~s hangen erbij* it is falling apart

rafelen /rafələ(n)/ (rafelde, heeft gerafeld) fray: *een gerafeld vloerkleed* a frayed carpet

rafelig /rafələx/ (adj) frayed

de **raffinaderij** /rɑfinadərɛi/ (pl: -en) refinery

het **raffinement** /rɑfinəmɛnt/ refinement, subtlety

raffineren /rɑfinerə(n)/ (raffineerde, heeft geraffineerd) refine

het **rag** /rɑx/ cobweb(s)

de **rage** /raʒə/ (pl: -s) craze, rage: *de nieuwste ~* the latest craze

de **ragebol** /raɣəbɔl/ (pl: -len) ceiling mop

ragfijn /rɑxfɛin/ (adj) as light (*or:* fine, thin) as gossamer

de **ragout** /raɣu/ (pl: -s) ragout: *~ van rundvlees* beef ragout (*or:* stew)

de **rail** /rel/ (pl: -s) **1** rail: *iets (iem.) weer op de ~s zetten* put sth. (s.o.) back on the rails **2** rail(way): *vervoer per ~* rail transport

de **raison** /rɛzɔ̃/ (pl: -s) **1** rail: *à ~ van ...* on payment of ...; *~ d'être* raison d'être

rakelings /rakəlɪŋs/ (adv) closely, narrowly: *de steen ging ~ langs zijn hoofd* the stone narrowly missed his head

¹**raken** /rakə(n)/ (raakte, is geraakt) get, become: *betrokken ~ bij* become involved in; *gewend ~ aan* get used to; [sport] *uit vorm ~* lose one's form

²**raken** /rakə(n)/ (raakte, heeft geraakt) **1** hit **2** affect, hit: *dat raakt me totaal niet* that leaves me cold **3** touch: *de auto raakte heel*

even het paaltje the car grazed the post

de **raket** /rakɛt/ (pl: -ten) missile, rocket: *een ~ lanceren* launch a missile (*or:* rocket)

de **raketbasis** /rakɛdbazɪs/ (pl: -bases) missile base, rocket base

het **raketschild** /rakɛtsxɪlt/ space shield, rocket shield

de **rakker** /rɑkər/ (pl: -s) rascal

de **rally** /rɛli/ (pl: -'s) rally

de **ram** /rɑm/ (pl: -men) ram

de **Ram** /rɑm/ (pl: -men) Aries, the Ram

de **ramadan** /rɑmadɑn/ Ramadan

ramen /ramə(n)/ (raamde, heeft geraamd) estimate

de **raming** /ramɪŋ/ (pl: -en) estimate

de **ramkoers** /rɑmkurs/: *op ~ liggen* be on a collision course, be heading for a direct confrontation

de **rammel** /rɑməl/ (pl: -s) beating: *een pak ~* a beating

de **rammelaar** /rɑməlar/ (pl: -s) rattle

¹**rammelen** /rɑmələ(n)/ (rammelde, heeft gerammeld) **1** rattle: *aan de deur ~* rattle the door; *met z'n sleutels ~* clink one's keys **2** be ramshackle: *dit plan rammelt aan alle kanten* this plan is totally unsound ‖ *ik rammelde van de honger* my stomach was rumbling with hunger

²**rammelen** /rɑmələ(n)/ (rammelde, heeft gerammeld) shake: *een kind door elkaar ~* give a child a shaking

rammen /rɑmə(n)/ (ramde, heeft geramd) ram, bash in (*or:* down): *de deur ~* bash the door down; *de auto ramde een muur* the car ran into a wall

de **rammenas** /ramənɑs/ (pl: -sen) winter radish

de **ramp** /rɑmp/ (pl: -en) disaster: *een ~ voor het milieu* an environmental disaster; *ik zou het geen ~ vinden als hij niet kwam* I wouldn't shed any tears if he didn't come; *tot overmaat van ~* to make matters worse

het **rampenplan** /rɑmpə(n)plɑn/ (pl: -nen) contingency plan

het **rampgebied** /rɑmpxəbit/ (pl: -en) disaster area

de **rampspoed** /rɑmpsput/ (pl: -en) misfortune, adversity

rampzalig /rɑmpsaləx/ (adj, adv) disastrous

de **rancune** /rɑŋkynə/ (pl: -s) rancour: *~ koesteren jegens iem.* hold a grudge against s.o.; *sans ~* no hard feelings

rancuneus /rɑŋkynøs/ (adj) vindictive

de **rand** /rɑnt/ (pl: -en) **1** edge, rim: *de ~ van een bord* (*or:* *schaal*) the rim of a plate (*or:* dish); *een opstaande ~* a raised edge; *een brief met een zwarte ~* a black-edged letter; *aan de ~ van de stad* on the outskirts of the town; *aan de ~ van de samenleving* on the fringes of society **2** border, edge: *een ~ langs het tafelkleed* a border on the tablecloth **3** frame, rim: *de ~ van een* **spiegel** the frame of a mirror; *een bril met* **gouden** *~en* gold-rimmed glasses **4** edge, brink, (b)rim, verge: *aan de ~ van de afgrond* **a)** on the brink of the precipice; **b)** [fig] on the verge of disaster; *tot de ~ gevuld* filled to the brim **5** rand ‖ *zwarte ~en onder zijn nagels hebben* have dirt under one's fingernails

de **randapparatuur** /rɑntɑparatyr/ peripheral equipment

de **randgemeente** /rɑntχəmentə/ (pl: -n, -s) suburb

de **randgroepjongere** /rɑntχrupjoŋərə/ (pl: -n) young drop-out

het **randje** /rɑncə/ (pl: -s) edge, border, rim; [fig] verge; [fig] brink ‖ *op het ~ (af)* on the borderline; *dat was* **op** *het ~* that was close (or: touch and go)

de **Randstad** /rɑntstɑt/: *de ~ (Holland)* the cities (or: conurbation) of western Holland

het **randverschijnsel** /rɑntfərsχɛinsəl/ (pl: -en) marginal phenomenon

de **randvoorwaarde** /rɑntforwardə/ (pl: -n) precondition

de **rang** /rɑŋ/ (pl: -en) **1** rank, position: *een ~* **hoger** *dan hij* one rank above him; *mensen van alle ~en en* **standen** people from all walks of life **2** circle: *we zaten* **op** *de tweede ~* we were in the upper circle

het **rangeerterrein** /rɑnʒertɛrɛin/ (pl: -en) marshalling yard

rangeren /rɑnʒerə(n)/ (rangeerde, heeft gerangeerd) shunt: *een* **trein** *op een zijspoor ~* shunt a train into a siding

de **ranglijst** /rɑŋlɛist/ (pl: -en) (priority) list, list (of candidates); (league) table: **bovenaan** *de ~ staan* be at the top of the list

het **rangnummer** /rɑŋnʏmər/ (pl: -s) number

de **rangorde** /rɑŋordə/ (pl: -n, -s) order

rangschikken /rɑŋsχɪkə(n)/ (rangschikte, heeft gerangschikt) **1** classify, order, class **2** order, arrange: *alfabetisch ~* arrange in alphabetical order

de **rangschikking** /rɑŋsχɪkɪŋ/ **1** classification **2** arrangement, order

het **rangtelwoord** /rɑŋtɛlwort/ (pl: -en) ordinal (number)

de **ranja**® /rɑnja/ orange squash, orangeade

de **rank** /rɑŋk/ (pl: -en) tendril

de **ransel** /rɑnsəl/ (pl: -s) knapsack

ranselen /rɑnsələ(n)/ (ranselde, heeft geranseld) flog, thrash

het **rantsoen** /rɑntsun/ (pl: -en) ration, allowance: *een ~* **boter** a ration (or: an allowance) of butter

rantsoeneren /rɑn(t)sunerə(n)/ (rantsoeneerde, heeft gerantsoeneerd) ration

ranzig /rɑnzəχ/ (adj) rancid

rap /rɑp/ (adj, adv) quick, swift: *iets ~* **doen** do sth. quickly

rapen /rapə(n)/ (raapte, heeft geraapt) pick up

de **rapmuziek** /rɛpmyzik/ rap music

rappen /rɛpə(n)/ (rapte, heeft gerapt) rap

de **rapper** /rɛpər/ (pl: -s) rapper

het **rapport** /rɑpɔrt/ (pl: -en) report, despatch: *~* **uitbrengen** (or: **opmaken**) *over* produce (or: make) a report on; *een onvoldoende* **op** *zijn ~ krijgen* get a fail mark in one's report

de **rapportage** /rɑpɔrtaʒə/ (pl: -s) report(ing)

het **rapportcijfer** /rɑpɔrtsɛifər/ (pl: -s) report mark

de **rapportenvergadering** /rɑpɔrtə(n)vərɣadərɪŋ/ meeting to discuss pupils' reports

rapporteren /rɑpɔrterə(n)/ (rapporteerde, heeft gerapporteerd) report; cover: *~ aan* report to

de **rapsodie** /rɑpsodi/ (pl: -ën) rhapsody

rara /rara/ (int): *~, wat is dat?* guess what this is; *~, wie ben ik?* guess who

de **rariteit** /rɑritɛit/ (pl: -en) curio(sity): *een handeltje* **in** *~en* an antique shop

het **¹ras** /rɑs/ (pl: -sen) race; breed; variety: *van* **gemengd** *~* of mixed race

²ras (adj, adv) swift; rapid, quick: *met ~se* **schreden** swiftly, rapidly

de **rasartiest** /rɑsɑrtist/ born artist

rasecht /rɑsɛχt/ (adj) (true) born

de **rashond** /rɑshont/ pedigree dog, pure-bred dog

de **rasp** /rɑsp/ (pl: -en) grater

het **raspaard** /rɑspart/ (pl: -en) thoroughbred

raspen /rɑspə(n)/ (raspte, heeft geraspt) grate: *kaas ~* grate cheese

de **rassendiscriminatie** /rɑsə(n)dɪskriminɑ(t)si/ racial discrimination

de **rassenhaat** /rɑsə(n)hat/ racial hatred

de **rasta** /rɑsta/ Rasta(farian)

de **raster** /rɑstər/ fence, lattice

raszuiver /rɑsœyvər/ (adj) pure-blooded; pure-bred

de **rat** /rɑt/ (pl: -ten) rat: *hij zat als een ~* **in** *de val* he was caught out

de **rataplan** /rɑtaplɑn/: *de* **hele** *~* the whole caboodle (or: lot)

de **ratel** /ratəl/ (pl: -s) rattle

ratelen /ratələ(n)/ (ratelde, heeft gerateld) rattle: *de* **wekker** *ratelt* the alarm clock is jangling

de **ratelslang** /ratəlslɑŋ/ (pl: -en) rattlesnake

ratificeren /ratifiserə(n)/ (ratificeerde, heeft geratificeerd) ratify

de **ratio** /ra(t)sijo/ **1** reason **2** ratio

rationeel /ra(t)ʃonel/ (adj, adv) rational

het/de **ratjetoe** /rɑcətu/ (pl: -s) hotchpotch, mishmash

rato /rato/: *naar ~* pro rata, in proportion

de **rats** /rɑts/: [inform] *in de ~ zitten (over)* have the wind up (about)

het **rattengif** /rɑtə(n)ɣɪf/ rat poison

het **rattenkruit** /rɑtə(n)krœyt/ arsenic

¹rauw /rɑu/ (adj) **1** raw: *~e* **biefstuk** raw

steak **2** sore: *een ~e plek* a raw spot **3** rough, tough ‖ *dat viel ~ op mijn dak* that was an unexpected blow; *ik laat hem ~* I let him do his worst

²rauw /rɑu/ (adv) rawly, sorely, roughly

de **rauwkost** /rɑukɔst/ vegetables eaten raw

de **ravage** /ravaʒə/ (pl: -s) **1** ravage(s), havoc: *die hevige storm heeft een ~ aangericht* that violent storm has wreaked havoc **2** debris

de **rave** /rev/ rave

het **ravijn** /ravɛin/ (pl: -en) ravine, gorge

de **ravioli** /ravijoli/ ravioli

ravotten /ravɔtə(n)/ (ravotte, heeft geravot) romp, horse around

het **rayon** /rɛjɔn/ (pl: -s) district; territory: *hij heeft Limburg als zijn ~* he works Limburg

de **rayonchef** /rɛjɔnʃɛf/ (pl: -s) area supervisor

de **razen** /razə(n)/ (raasde, heeft/is geraasd) race, tear: *de auto's ~ over de snelweg* the cars are racing along the motorway

razend /razənt/ (adj, adv) **1** furious: *iem. ~ maken* infuriate s.o.; *als een ~e tekeergaan* rave like a madman **2** terrific: *hij heeft het ~ druk* he's up to his neck in work; *~ snel, in ~e vaart* at a terrific pace, at breakneck speed

razendsnel /razəntsnɛl/ (adj, adv) superfast, high-speed

de **razernij** /razərnɛi/ frenzy, rage: *in blinde ~* in a blind rage; *iem. tot ~ brengen* infuriate s.o.

de **razzia** /razija/ (pl: -'s) razzia

de **r&b** /ɑrɛmbi/ R&B, rhythm and blues

de **re** /re/ (pl: re's) re, D

de **reactie** /rejɑksi/ (pl: -s) reaction, response: *als ~ op* in reaction to; *snelle ~s* sharp reflexes; *een ~ vertonen* respond

de **reactiesnelheid** /rejɑksisnɛlhɛit/ speed of reaction

reactionair /rejɑkʃonɛːr/ (adj, adv) reactionary

de **reactor** /rejɑktɔr/ (pl: -s) reactor: *snelle ~* fast reactor

de **reader** /riːdər/ (pl: -s) reader

de **reageerbuis** /rejaɣerbœys/ (pl: -buizen) test tube: *bevruchting in een ~* test-tube (or: in vitro) fertilization

de **reageerbuisbaby** /rejaɣerbœyzbebi/ (pl: -'s) test-tube baby

reageren /rejaɣerə(n)/ (reageerde, heeft gereageerd) react (to); respond: *te sterk ~* overreact; *moet je eens kijken hoe hij daarop reageert* look how he reacts to that; *ze reageerde positief op de behandeling* she responded to the treatment

realiseerbaar /rejalizerbar/ (adj) realizable, feasible

¹realiseren /rejalizerə(n)/ (realiseerde, heeft gerealiseerd) realize: *dat is niet te ~* that is impractical

zich **²realiseren** /rejalizerə(n)/ (realiseerde zich, heeft zich gerealiseerd) realize

het **realisme** /rejalɪsmə/ realism

de **realist** /rejalɪst/ (pl: -en) realist

realistisch /rejalɪstis/ (adj, adv) realistic: *~ beschrijven* (or: *schilderen*) describe (or: paint) realistically

de **realiteit** /rejalitɛit/ (pl: -en) reality: *we moeten de ~ onder ogen zien* we must face facts (or: reality)

de **realiteitszin** /rejalitɛitsɪn/ sense of reality

de **realitysoap** /rijɛlətisop/ reality soap

de **reallifesoap** /rilɑjfsop/ real-life soap

de **reanimatie** /reanima(t)si/ resuscitation, reanimation

reanimeren /reanimɛrə(n)/ (reanimeerde, heeft gereanimeerd) resuscitate, revive

de **rebel** /rəbɛl/ (pl: -len) rebel

rebelleren /rəbɛlɛrə(n)/ (rebelleerde, heeft gerebelleerd) rebel: *~ tegen ...* rebel against ...

de **rebellie** /rəbɛli/ rebellion

rebels /rəbɛls/ (adj, adv) rebellious

de **rebound** /ribaunt/ rebound

de **rebus** /rebys/ (pl: -sen) rebus

recalcitrant /rekɑlsitrɑnt/ (adj, adv) recalcitrant

recapituleren /rekɑpitylɛrə(n)/ (recapituleerde, heeft gerecapituleerd) recapitulate, summarize

de **recensent** /resɛnsɛnt/ (pl: -en) reviewer, critic

recenseren /resɛnsɛrə(n)/ (recenseerde, heeft gerecenseerd) review

de **recensie** /resɛnsi/ (pl: -s) review, notice: *lovende (juichende) ~s krijgen* get rave reviews

recent /rəsɛnt/ (adj) recent

het **recept** /rəsɛpt/ (pl: -en) **1** prescription: *alleen op ~ verkrijgbaar* available only on prescription **2** recipe

de **receptie** /resɛpsi/ (pl: -s) **1** reception: *staande ~* stand-up reception **2** reception (desk): *melden bij de ~* report to the reception (desk)

de **receptionist** /resɛpʃonɪst/ (pl: -en) receptionist

de **recessie** /rəsɛsi/ recession

de **recette** /rəsɛtə/ (pl: -s) receipts

de **recherche** /reʃɛrʒə/ (pl: -s) criminal investigation department

de **rechercheur** /reʃɛrʃør/ (pl: -s) detective

het **¹recht** /rɛxt/ (pl: -en) **1** justice, right: *iem. ~ doen* do s.o. justice; *iem. (iets) geen ~ doen* be unfair to s.o. (sth.); *het ~ handhaven* uphold the law; *het ~ aan zijn kant hebben* be in the right **2** law: *student (in de) ~en* law student; *burgerlijk ~* civil law; *het ~ in eigen handen nemen* take the law into one's own hands; *~en studeren* read (or: study) law; *volgens Engels ~* under English law **3** right: *~ van bestaan hebben* have a right to exist; *het ~ van de sterkste* the law of the jungle; *dat is mijn goed ~* that is my right; *het volste ~ hebben om ...* have every right to ...; *niet het ~ heb-*

ben *iets te doen* have no right to do sth.; *goed* **tot** *zijn* ~ **komen** show up well; *voor zijn* ~*(en)* opkomen defend one's right(s) **4** rights: *de* ~*en van de* **mens** human rights **5** right, claim: ~ *op* **uitkering** entitlement to a benefit; ~ hebben *op iets* have the right to sth. **6** (copy)-right(s): *alle* ~*en* **voorbehouden** all rights reserved ‖ *iets* **tot** *zijn* ~ *laten komen* do justice to sth., give sth. its due

²recht /rɛχt/ (adj, adv) **1** straight: *de auto* **kwam** ~ *op* **ons** *af* the car was coming straight at us; *iets* ~ **leggen** put sth. straight; ~ *op iem. (iets)* **afgaan** go straight for s.o. (sth.); *iem.* ~ *in* de ogen kijken look s.o. straight in the eye; ~ **voor** *zich uitkijken* look straight ahead; *hij woont* ~ **tegenover** *mij* he lives straight across from me; ~ **tegenover** *elkaar* face-to-face **2** straight (up), upright: ~ *zitten* (or: **staan**) sit (or: stand) up straight; ~ *overeind* straight up; bolt upright **3** right; direct; directly: *de* ~*e* **zijde** *van een voorwerp* the right side of an object **4** right; true: *op het* ~*e* **pad** *blijven* keep to the straight and narrow ‖ ~*e* **hoek** right angle

de **rechtbank** /rɛχtbɑŋk/ (pl: -en) **1** court (of law, justice), lawcourt: *voor de* ~ *moeten komen* have to appear in court (or: before the court) **2** court, law courts, magistrates' court; [Am] courthouse

rechtbreien /rɛχ(t)brɛijə(n)/ (breide recht, heeft rechtgebreid) put right, rectify

rechtbuigen /rɛχ(t)bœyɣə(n)/ (boog recht, heeft rechtgebogen) straighten (out), bend straight

rechtdoor /rɛχtdor/ (adv) straight on (or: ahead)

rechtdoorzee /rɛɣdorze/ (adj) straight, honest, sincere

de **¹rechter** /rɛχtər/ (pl: -s) judge, magistrate: *naar de* ~ *stappen* go to court; *voor de* ~ *moeten verschijnen* have to appear in court

²rechter /rɛχtər/ (adj) right; right(-hand): *de* ~ **deur** the door on the (or: your) right

de **rechterarm** /rɛχtərɑrm/ right arm

het **rechterbeen** /rɛχtərben/ right leg

de **rechter-commissaris** /rɛχtərkɔmɪsɑrɪs/ (pl: rechters-commissarissen) examining judge (or: magistrate)

de **rechterhand** /rɛχtərhɑnt/ (pl: -en) right hand: *de tweede straat* **aan** *uw* ~ the second street on your right

de **rechterkant** /rɛχtərkɑnt/ right(-hand) side: *aan de* ~ on the right(-hand) side

rechterlijk /rɛχtərlək/ (adj, adv) judicial, court: *de* ~*e* **macht** the judiciary

de **rechtervleugel** /rɛχtərvløɣəl/ (pl: -s) **1** right wing: *de* ~ *van een* **gebouw** (or: *een* **voetbalelftal**) the right wing of a building (or: football team) **2** right (wing), Right

de **rechtervoet** /rɛχtərvut/ right foot

de **rechterzijde** /rɛχtərzɛidə/ right(-hand)

side: *pijn* **in** *de* ~ *hebben* have a pain in one's right side; *aan de* ~ on the right(-hand side)

rechtgeaard /rɛ(χt)χəa̱rt/ (adj) right-minded: *iedere* ~*e* **Fransman** every true Frenchman

de **rechthoek** /rɛχthuk/ (pl: -en) rectangle, oblong

rechthoekig /rɛχthu̱kəχ/ (adj, adv) **1** right-angled, at right angles: *een* ~*e* **driehoek** a right-angled triangle **2** rectangular, oblong: *een* ~*e* **kamer** a rectangular room

rechtmatig /rɛχtma̱təχ/ (adj, adv) rightful; lawful; legitimate: *de* ~*e* **eigenaars** the rightful (or: legitimate) owners

rechtop /rɛχto̱p/ (adv) upright, straight (up); on end: ~ **lopen** walk upright; ~ *zitten* sit up straight

rechts /rɛχts/ (adj, adv) **1** right(-hand): *de eerste* **deur** ~ the first door on (or: to) the right; ~ **afslaan** turn (off to the) right; ~ **houden** keep (to the) right; ~ **rijden** drive on the right; ~ **boven** (or: **beneden**) top (or: bottom) right; *hij zat* ~ *van mij* he sat on my right(-hand side) **2** right-handed: ~ **schrijven** write with one's right hand **3** [pol] right-wing

de **rechtsachter** /rɛχtsɑ̱χtər/ (pl: -s) right back

rechtsaf /rɛχtsɑf/ (adv) (to the, one's) right: *bij de splitsing* **moet** *u* ~ you have to turn right at the junction

de **rechtsbescherming** /rɛχtsbəsχɛrmɪŋ/ legal protection

de **rechtsbijstand** /rɛχtsbɛistɑnt/ legal aid

de **rechtsbuiten** /rɛχtsbœytə(n)/ (pl: -s) right-winger, outside right

rechtschapen /rɛχtsχa̱pə(n)/ (adj, adv) righteous, honest

het **rechtsgebied** /rɛχ(t)sχəbit/ jurisdiction

rechtsgeldig /rɛχtsχɛ̱ldəχ/ (adj) (legally) valid, lawful

de **rechtsgeldigheid** /rɛχtsχɛ̱ldəχhɛit/ legality, legal force (or: validity)

de **rechtsgeleerde** /rɛχ(t)sχəlerdə/ (pl: -n) lawyer

de **rechtsgelijkheid** /rɛχtsχəlɛ̱ikhɛit/ equality before the law, equality of rights (or: status)

het **rechtsgevoel** /rɛχ(t)sχəvul/ sense of justice

rechtshandig /rɛχtshɑndəχ/ (adj) right-handed

de **rechtshulp** /rɛχtshʏlp/ legal aid: *bureau* **voor** ~ legal advice centre

rechtsom /rɛχ(t)so̱m/ (adv) (to the) right

rechtsomkeert /rɛχtsɔmkert/ (adv): ~ **maken** a) [mil] do an about-turn; b) [fig] make a U-turn

de **rechtsongelijkheid** /rɛχtsɔŋəlɛ̱ikhɛit/ inequality of status, legal inequality

de **rechtsorde** /rɛχtsɔrdə/ legal order, system of law(s)

de **rechtspersoon** /rɛχtspɛrsɔn/ (pl: -personen) legal body (or: entity, person)

de **rechtspositie** /rɛχtspozi(t)si/ legal position

de **rechtspraak** /rɛχtsprak/ **1** administration of justice (or: of the law) **2** jurisdiction: *de ~ in strafzaken* criminal jurisdiction

rechtspreken /rɛχtsprekə(n)/ (sprak recht, heeft rechtgesproken) administer justice: *de ~de macht* the judicature; the judiciary; *~ in een zaak* judge a case

de **rechtsstaat** /rɛχtstat/ (pl: -staten) constitutional state

rechtstreeks /rɛχtstreks/ (adj, adv) **1** direct, straight(forward): *een ~e verbinding* a direct connection; *~ naar huis gaan* go straight (or: right) home **2** direct, immediate: *een ~e uitzending* a direct broadcast; *hij wendde zich ~ tot de minister* he went straight to the minister

de **rechtsvervolging** /rɛχtsfərvolχɪŋ/ (pl: -en) legal proceedings, prosecution: *een ~ tegen iem. instellen* institute legal proceedings against s.o.; *ontslaan van ~* acquit

de **rechtsvordering** /rɛχ(t)sfordərɪŋ/ (pl: -en) **1** (legal) action **2** legal procedure

de **rechtswinkel** /rɛχtswɪŋkəl/ (pl: -s) law centre (or: clinic)

de **rechtszaak** /rɛχtsak/ (pl: -zaken) lawsuit: *ergens ~ van maken* take a matter to court

de **rechtszaal** /rɛχtsal/ (pl: -zalen) courtroom

de **rechtszitting** /rɛχtsɪtɪŋ/ (pl: -en) sitting (or: session) of the court

rechttoe /rɛχtu/ (adv): *~, rechtaan* straightforward; *het was allemaal ~ rechtaan* it was plain sailing all the way

rechttrekken /rɛχtrɛkə(n)/ (trok recht, heeft rechtgetrokken) set right, put right

rechtuit /rɛχtœyt/ (adv) straight on (or: ahead): *~ lopen* walk straight on

rechtvaardig /rɛχtfardəχ/ (adj, adv) just, fair: *een ~ oordeel* a fair judg(e)ment; *iem. ~ behandelen* treat s.o. fairly

rechtvaardigen /rɛχtfardəɣə(n)/ (rechtvaardigde, heeft gerechtvaardigd) justify; warrant: *zich tegenover iem. ~ justify o.s. to s.o.

de **rechtvaardigheid** /rɛχtfardəχhɛit/ justice

de **rechtvaardiging** /rɛχtfardəɣɪŋ/ justification

rechtzetten /rɛχtsɛtə(n)/ (zette recht, heeft rechtgezet) **1** put right, set right, rectify **2** adjust **3** set up, put up, raise

rechtzinnig /rɛχtsɪnəχ/ (adj, adv) orthodox; [Protestantism] Reformed

de **recidivist** /residivɪst/ (pl: -en) recidivist, repeated offender

het **recital** /risɑjtəl/ (pl: -s) recital

de **reclamatie** /reklama(t)si/ **1** reclamation **2** claim

de **reclame** /rəklamə/ (pl: -s) **1** advertising, publicity: *~ maken (voor iets)* advertise (sth.) **2** ad(vertisement), sign

de **reclameaanbieding** /rəklaməambidɪŋ/ (pl: -en) special offer

de **reclameboodschap** /rəklaməbotsχɑp/ (pl: -pen) commercial

het **reclamebureau** /rəklaməbyro/ advertising agency

de **reclamecampagne** /rəklaməkɑmpɑɲə/ (pl: -s) advertising campaign: *een ~ voeren* run (or: conduct) an advertising campaign

de **reclamefolder** /rəklaməfoldər/ (pl: -s) advertising brochure (or: pamphlet)

reclameren /reklamɣrə(n)/ (reclameerde, heeft gereclameerd) complain, put in a claim

de **reclamespot** /rəklaməspot/ (pl: -s) commercial, (advertising) spot

de **reclamestunt** /rəklaməstʏnt/ (pl: -s) advertising stunt, publicity stunt

de **reclassering** /reklɑsɣrɪŋ/ after-care and rehabilitation

de **reclasseringsambtenaar** /reklɑsɣrɪŋsɑmtənar/ probation officer

de **reconstructie** /rekɔnstrʏksi/ (pl: -s) reconstruction

reconstrueren /rekɔnstrywɣrə(n)/ (reconstrueerde, heeft gereconstrueerd) reconstruct

de **reconversie** /rekɔnvɣrsi/ (pl: -s) [Belg] switch

het **record** /rəkɔːr/ (pl: -s) record: *een ~ breken* (or: *vestigen*) break (or: establish) a record

de **recorder** /rikɔːrdər/ (pl: -s) recorder

de **recordhouder** /rəkɔːrhɑudər/ (pl: -s) record-holder

de **recordpoging** /rəkɔːrpoχɪŋ/ (pl: -en) attempt on a record

de **recreant** /rekrejɑnt/ (pl: -en) [roughly] holiday-maker; [Am] vacationer

de **recreatie** /rekreja(t)si/ (pl: -s) recreation, leisure

recreatief /rekrejatif/ (adj) recreational

recreëren /rekrejɣrə(n)/ (recreëerde, heeft gerecreëerd) relax

rectaal /rɛktal/ (adj, adv) rectal

de **rectificatie** /rɛktifika(t)si/ (pl: -s) rectification

rectificeren /rɛktifisɣrə(n)/ (rectificeerde, heeft gerectificeerd) rectify

de **rector** /rɛktɔr/ (pl: -en, -s) **1** headmaster; [esp Am] principal **2** rector

het **reçu** /rəsy/ (pl: -'s) receipt

recyclen /risɑjk(ə)lə(n)/ (recyclede, heeft gerecycled) recycle

recycleren /resiklɣrə(n)/ (recycleerde, heeft gerecycleerd) [Belg] recycle

de **recycling** /risɑjklɪŋ/ recycling

de **redacteur** /redaktɣr/ (pl: -en, -s) editor

de **redactie** /redɑksi/ (pl: -s) editors, editorial staff

redactioneel /redɑkʃonɣl/ (adj) editorial: *een ~ artikel* an editorial

reddeloos /rɛdəlos/ (adv): *~ verloren* irretrievably lost, beyond redemption

¹redden /rɛdə(n)/ (redde, heeft gered)

1 save, rescue; salvage: *de ~de* **hand** *toeste-ken* be the saving of a person; *we moeten* **zien te** ~ *wat er te* ~ *valt* we must make the best of a bad job; *gered* **zijn** be helped; *een ~de* **engel** a ministering angel **2** (+ het) manage: *de zie-ke zal* **het** *niet* ~ the patient won't pull through ‖ *Jezus redt* Jesus saves

zich **²redden** /rɛdə(n)/ (redde zich, heeft zich ge-red) manage, cope: *ik red me* **best!** I can manage all right!

de **redder** /rɛdər/ (pl: -s) rescuer, saviour
de **redding** /rɛdɪŋ/ (pl: -en) rescue, salvation
de **reddingsactie** /rɛdɪŋsɑksi/ (pl: -s) rescue operation
de **reddingsboot** /rɛdɪŋzbot/ (pl: -boten) life-boat
de **reddingsbrigade** /rɛdɪŋzbriɣadə/ (pl: -s, -n) rescue party (*or:* team)
de **reddingsoperatie** /rɛdɪŋsopəra(t)si/ rescue operation
de **reddingspoging** /rɛdɪŋspoɣɪŋ/ (pl: -en) rescue attempt (*or:* bid, effort): *hun ~en* **mochten** *hem niet* **baten** their attempts (*or:* efforts) to rescue him were in vain
het **reddingswerk** /rɛdɪŋswɛrk/ rescue work (*or:* operations)
de **rede** /redə/ (pl: -s) **1** reason, sense: *hij is niet* **voor** ~ *vatbaar* he won't listen to (*or:* see) reason **2** speech; address: *een* ~ **houden** make a speech **3** reason, intelligence, intellect ‖ *iem.* **in** *de* ~ *vallen* interrupt s.o.; *directe, indirecte* ~ direct, indirect speech
¹redelijk /redələk/ (adj) **1** rational, sensible **2** reasonable, fair: *binnen ~e* **grenzen** within (reasonable) limits; *een ~e* **prijs** a reasonable price; *een ~e* **kans** *maken* stand a reasonable chance
²redelijk /redələk/ (adv) **1** rationally: ~ **denken** think rationally **2** reasonably, fairly: *ik ben* ~ **gezond** I am in reasonably good health
redelijkerwijs /redələkərwɛis/ (adv) in fairness: ~ **kunt** *u niet meer* **verlangen** in all fairness you cannot expect more
de **redelijkheid** /redələkhɛit/: *dat kan* **in** ~ *niet van ons gevraagd worden* that cannot in reasonableness (*or:* fairness) be asked of us
redeloos /redəlos/ (adj, adv) **1** irrational **2** unreasonable
de **reden** /redə(n)/ (pl: -en) **1** reason, cause, occasion: *om* **persoonlijke** *~en* for personal reasons; *ik* **heb** *er mijn* ~ *voor* I have my reasons; *om* **die** ~ for that reason; *geen* ~ **tot** *klagen hebben* have no cause (*or:* ground) for complaint; *een* ~ *te meer om ...* all the more reason why ... **2** reason, motive: *zonder* **opgaaf** *van ~en* without reason; ~ **geven** *tot* give cause for
de **redenaar** /redənar/ (pl: -s) speaker, orator
redeneren /redənerə(n)/ (redeneerde, heeft geredeneerd) reason, argue (about): *daartegen* **is (valt)** *niet te* ~ there is no arguing with that
de **redenering** /redənerɪŋ/ (pl: -en) reasoning, argumentation: *een* **fout** *in de* ~ a flaw in the reasoning; *een* **logische** ~ a logical line of argument
de **reder** /redər/ (pl: -s) shipowner
de **rederij** /redərɛi/ (pl: -en) shipping company, shipowner(s)
redetwisten /redətwɪstə(n)/ (redetwistte, heeft geredetwist) argue
de **redevoering** /redəvurɪŋ/ (pl: -en) speech, address: *een* ~ **houden** make (*or:* deliver) a speech
redigeren /rediɣərə(n)/ (redigeerde, heeft geredigeerd) edit
het **redmiddel** /rɛtmɪdəl/ (pl: -en) remedy: *een* **laatste** ~ a last resort
reduceren /redyserə(n)/ (reduceerde, heeft gereduceerd) reduce, decrease: *gereduceerd* **tarief** reduced rate
de **reductie** /redyksi/ (pl: -s) reduction, decrease; cut; cutback: ~ **geven** give a discount
het/de **ree** /re/ (pl: -ën) roe(deer)
de **reebok** /rebɔk/ (pl: -ken) roebuck
reeds /rets/ (adv) [form] already: ~ **bij** *het begin* already from the (very) beginning; ~ **lang** for a long time
reëel /rejel/ (adj, adv) **1** real, actual: *reële* **groei** *van het inkomen* growth of real income **2** realistic, reasonable: *een reële* **kijk** *op het leven hebben* have a realistic outlook on life
de **reeks** /reks/ (pl: -en) **1** series, row; string **2** series, succession, sequence: *een* ~ **ongelukken** a string (*or:* succession) of accidents
de **reep** /rep/ (pl: repen) **1** strip; thong; band; sliver: *de komkommer* **in** *~jes snijden* slice the cucumber thinly **2** (chocolate) bar
de **reet** /ret/ (pl: reten) **1** crack, chink **2** [vulg] arse; [Am] ass; backside
het **referaat** /refərat/ (pl: referaten) lecture, paper: *een* ~ **houden** *over iets* read a paper on sth.
het **referendum** /refərɛndʏm/ (pl: -s, referenda) referendum: *een* **bindend** ~ a binding referendum
de **referentie** /refərɛnsi/ (pl: -s) reference; [pers also] referee: *mag ik u* **als** ~ *opgeven?* may I use you as a reference?
het **referentiekader** /refərɛn(t)sikadər/ (pl: -s) frame of reference
refereren /refərerə(n)/ (refereerde, heeft gerefereerd) refer (to)
reflecteren /reflɛktərə(n)/ (reflecteerde, heeft gereflecteerd) reflect, mirror
de **reflectie** /reflɛksi/ (pl: -s) reflection
de **reflector** /reflɛktɔr/ (pl: -en) reflector; Cats-eye
de **reflex** /reflɛks/ (pl: -en) reflex: *een* **aangeboren** ~ an innate reflex
de **reformwinkel** /refɔrmwɪŋkəl/ (pl: -s) health food shop, wholefood shop

refrein

het **refrein** /rəfrɛin/ (pl: -en) refrain, chorus: *iedereen zong het ~ mee* everybody joined in the chorus

de **refter** /rɛftər/ (pl: -s) refectory

de **regatta** /reɣɑta/ (pl: -'s) regatta

het **regeerakkoord** /rəɣerɑkort/ (pl: -en) coalition agreement

de **regeerperiode** /rəɣɛrperijodə/ period of office, period of government

de **regel** /reɣəl/ (pl: -s) **1** line: *een ~ overslaan* skip a line; leave a line blank; *tussen de ~s door lezen* read between the lines **2** rule: *het is ~ dat ...* it is a (general) rule that ...; *in de ~ as a rule, ordinarily* **3** rule, regulation; law: *tegen alle ~s in* contrary to (*or:* against) all the rules

de **regelafstand** /reɣəlɑfstɑnt/ (pl: -en) line space, spacing: *op enkele ~ single-spaced*

regelbaar /reɣəlbar/ (adj) regulable; adjustable

regelen /reɣələ(n)/ (regelde, heeft geregeld) **1** regulate; arrange; fix (up); settle; control [traf]; adjust; order: *de geluidssterkte ~ adjust the volume; de temperatuur ~ regulate (or: control) the temperature; het verkeer ~ direct the traffic; ik zal dat wel even ~ I'll take care of that* **2** regulate, lay down rules for

de **regelgeving** /reɣəlɣevɪŋ/ rules; instructions

de **regeling** /reɣəlɪŋ/ (pl: -en) **1** regulation, arrangement, settlement, ordering; control [traf]; adjustment: *de ~ van de geldzaken* the settling of money matters; *een ~ treffen* make an arrangement (*or:* a settlement) **2** arrangement, settlement; scheme

de **regelmaat** /reɣəlmat/ regularity: *met de ~ van de klok* as regular as clockwork

regelmatig /reɣəlmatəx/ (adj, adv) **1** regular, orderly: *een ~e ademhaling* regular (*or:* even) breathing; *een ~ leven leiden* lead a regular (*or:* an orderly) life **2** regular; frequent: *~ naar de kerk gaan* be a regular churchgoer; *dat komt ~ voor* that happens regularly

de **regelneef** /reɣəlnef/ (pl: -neven) busybody, organizer

regelrecht /reɣəlrɛxt/ (adj, adv) straight, direct; [adverb also] right: *de kinderen kwamen ~ naar huis* the children came straight home

de **regen** /reɣə(n)/ (pl: -s) **1** rain: *aanhoudende ~ persistent rain; in de stromende ~ in the pouring rain; zure ~ acid rain* **2** rain; shower

regenachtig /reɣənɑxtəx/ (adj) rainy, showery: *een ~e dag* a rainy day

de **regenboog** /reɣə(n)box/ (pl: -bogen) rainbow

de **regenboogtrui** /reɣə(n)boxtrœy/ (pl: -en) [sport] rainbow jersey

het **regenboogvlies** /reɣə(n)boxflis/ (pl: -vliezen) iris

de **regenbui** /reɣə(n)bœy/ (pl: -en) shower (of rain); downpour

de **regendruppel** /reɣə(n)drʏpəl/ (pl: -s, -en) raindrop

regenen /reɣənə(n)/ (regende, heeft geregend) rain; [light] shower; drizzle: *het heeft flink geregend* there was quite a downpour; *het regent dat het giet* it is pouring

de **regenjas** /reɣə(n)jɑs/ (pl: -sen) raincoat, mackintosh

de **regenkleding** /reɣə(n)kledɪŋ/ rainproof clothing, rainwear

de **regenmeter** /reɣə(n)metər/ (pl: -s) rain gauge

het **regenpak** /reɣə(n)pɑk/ (pl: -ken) waterproof suit

de **regenpijp** /reɣə(n)pɛip/ (pl: -en) drainpipe

de **regent** /reɣɛnt/ (pl: -en) **1** regent **2** [Belg] teacher for lower classes in secondary school

de **regentijd** /reɣə(n)tɛit/ (pl: -en) rainy season, rains: *in de ~ during the rainy season*

de **regenton** /reɣə(n)tɔn/ (pl: -nen) water butt

de **regenval** /reɣə(n)vɑl/ rain(fall); shower

de **regenvlaag** /reɣə(n)vlax/ (pl: -vlagen) scud, rainy squall

het **regenwater** /reɣə(n)watər/ rainwater

de **regenworm** /reɣə(n)wɔrm/ (pl: -en) earthworm

het **regenwoud** /reɣə(n)wɑut/ (pl: -en) rainforest

regeren /rəɣerə(n)/ (regeerde, heeft geregeerd) rule (over); reign; govern, control: *de ~de partij* the party in power

de **regering** /rəɣerɪŋ/ (pl: -en) government: *de ~ is afgetreden* the government has resigned

het **regeringsbeleid** /rəɣerɪŋzbəlɛit/ government policy

het **regeringsbesluit** /rəɣerɪŋzbəslœyt/ (pl: -en) government decision

de **regeringsleider** /rəɣerɪŋslɛidər/ (pl: -s) leader of the government

de **regeringspartij** /rəɣerɪŋspɑrtɛi/ (pl: -en) party in office (*or:* power), government party

de **regeringsverklaring** /rəɣerɪŋsfərklarɪŋ/ (pl: -en) government policy statement

de **regie** /reʒi/ (pl: -s) direction, production

het **regime** /reʒim/ (pl: -s) regime

het **regiment** /reʒimɛnt/ (pl: -en) regiment

de **regio** /reɣijo/ (pl: -'s) region, area

het **regiokorps** /reɣijokɔrps/ (pl: -en) regional police force

regionaal /reɣ(i)jonal/ (adj, adv) regional

regisseren /reʒiserə(n)/ (regisseerde, heeft geregisseerd) direct, produce

de **regisseur** /reʒisør/ (pl: -s) director, producer

het **register** /rəɣɪstər/ (pl: -s) **1** register, record: *de ~s van de burgerlijke stand* the register of births, deaths and marriages; *een alfabetisch ~ an alphabetical register* **2** index, table of contents de **registeraccountant** /rəɣɪstərɑkɑuntənt/ (pl: -s) chartered accountant, certified public accountant

de **registratie** /reɣɪstra(t)si/ (pl: -s) registration

registreren /reɣɪstrɇrə(n)/ (registreerde, heeft geregistreerd) register, record

het **reglement** /reɣləmɛnt/ (pl: -en) regulation(s), rule(s); rule book; rules and regulations: *huishoudelijk* ~ regulations

reglementair /reɣləmɛntɇːr/ (adj, adv) regulation, prescribed, official: *iets* ~ *vaststellen* prescribe sth.; ~ *winnen* be declared the winner(s)

regressief /reɣrɛsif/ (adj, adv) regressive

reguleren /reɣylɇrə(n)/ (reguleerde, heeft gereguleerd) regulate, control, adjust

regulier /reɣylir/ (adj) regular, normal

de **rehabilitatie** /rehabilita(t)si/ (pl: -s) rehabilitation, vindication

rehabiliteren /rehabilitɇrə(n)/ (rehabiliteerde, heeft gerehabiliteerd) rehabilitate, vindicate

de **rei** /rɛi/ (pl: -en) [Belg] town canal, city canal

de **reiger** /rɛiɣər/ (pl: -s) heron

reiken /rɛikə(n)/ (reikte, heeft gereikt) reach, extend: *zo ver het* **oog** *reikt* as far as the eye can see

reikhalzend /rɛikhɑlzənt/ (adj) longingly, anxiously

de **reikwijdte** /rɛikwɛitə/ range, scope

reilen /rɛilə(n)/: *het* ~ *en* **zeilen** *van de politiek* the ins and outs of politics; *zoals het nu reilt en* **zeilt** as things are at the moment

rein /rɛin/ (adj, adv) clean ‖ *~e* **dieren** clean animals

de **reïncarnatie** /rɛinkɑrna(t)si/ (pl: -s) reincarnation

reinigen /rɛinəɣə(n)/ (reinigde, heeft gereinigd) clean (up), wash; cleanse: **chemisch** ~ dry-clean

de **reiniging** /rɛinəɣɪŋ/ cleaning, cleansing, washing, purification: **chemische** ~ dry-cleaning

de **reinigingsdienst** /rɛinəɣɪŋzdinst/ (pl: -en) cleaning service (*or:* department)

het **reinigingsmiddel** /rɛinəɣɪŋsmɪdəl/ (pl: -en) cleansing agent, clean(s)er; detergent

de **reis** /rɛis/ (pl: reizen) **1** trip, journey; voyage; passage; flight: **enkele** ~ single (journey); [Am] one-way; **goede** ~ have a good (*or:* pleasant) journey; *een* ~ *om de wereld* **maken** go round the world; *op* ~ *gaan* go on a journey **2** trip, tour: *een geheel* **verzorgde** ~ a package tour (*or:* holiday)

het **reisbureau** /rɛizbyro/ (pl: -s) travel agency; travel agent's

de **reischeque** /rɛisʃɛk/ (pl: -s) traveller's cheque

het **reisgezelschap** /rɛisɣəzɛlsχɑp/ (pl: -pen) tour(ing) group (*or:* party); coach party

de **reisgids** /rɛisχɪts/ (pl: -en) **1** travel brochure

(*or:* leaflet) **2** guidebook, (travel) guide **3** (travel) guide, courier

de **reiskosten** /rɛiskɔstə(n)/ (pl) travelling expenses: *reis- en* **verblijfkosten** travel and living expenses

de **reiskostenvergoeding** /rɛiskɔstə(n)vərɣudɪŋ/ (pl: -en) travelling allowance

de **reisleider** /rɛislɛidər/ (pl: -s) (travel, tour) guide, courier

de **reisorganisatie** /rɛisɔrɣaniza(t)si/ (pl: -s) travel organization (*or:* company), tour operator

de **reisorganisator** /rɛisɔrɣanizatɔr/ (pl: -en) tour operator

de **reisplanner** /rɛisplɛnər/ (pl: -s) journey planner

de **reisverzekering** /rɛisfərzekərɪŋ/ (pl: -en) travel insurance

de **reiswieg** /rɛiswiχ/ (pl: -en) carrycot, portable crib

reizen /rɛizə(n)/ (reisde, heeft/is gereisd) travel, go on a trip (*or:* journey): *op en neer* ~ travel up and down; *per spoor* ~ travel by train

de **reiziger** /rɛizəɣər/ (pl: -s) **1** traveller, tourist; passenger: *~s naar Sheffield hier overstappen* passengers for Sheffield change here **2** travelling salesman

de **¹rek** /rɛk/ elasticity, give, flexibility: *de* ~ *is er uit* the party is over

het **²rek** /rɛk/ rack; shelves

rekbaar /rɛgbar/ (adj) elastic: *een* ~ **begrip** an elastic concept, a broad notion

¹rekenen /rɇkənə(n)/ (rekende, heeft gerekend) **1** calculate, do sums (*or:* figures), reckon: *goed* **kunnen** ~ be good at figures; *in euro's* ~ calculate (*or:* think) in euros **2** consider, include, take into consideration (*or:* account): *daar had ik niet* **op** *gerekend* I hadn't counted on (*or:* expected) that; *daar mag je wel* **op** ~ you'd better allow for that **3** (+ op) rely, count on, trust: *kan ik* **op** *je* ~? can I count (*or:* depend) on you?; *reken maar niet* **op** *ons* count us out **4** (+ op) expect: *je kunt* **op** *40 gasten* ~ you can expect 40 guests

²rekenen /rɇkənə(n)/ (rekende, heeft gerekend) **1** count: *alles* *bij elkaar gerekend* all told; in all **2** charge, ask: **hoeveel** *rekent u daarvoor?* how much do you charge for that? **3** count, number: *zich ~ tot* count o.s. as (*or:* among) **4** bear in mind, remember, allow for: *reken* **maar!** you bet!

de **rekenfout** /rɇkənfɑut/ (pl: -en) miscalculation

het **Rekenhof** /rɇkənhɔf/ [Belg] (the) Treasury

de **rekening** /rɇkənɪŋ/ (pl: -en) **1** bill; [Am also] check; invoice: *een* **hoge** ~ a stiff bill; *een* ~ **betalen** (*or:* **voldoen**) pay/settle an account (*or:* a bill); *ober,* **mag** *ik de ~?* waiter, may I have the bill please? **2** account: *een* ~ **openen** *(bij een bank)* open an account (at a bank); *op ~ van* at the expense of; *dat is* **voor** *mijn ~* I'll take care of that, leave that to me; *kosten* **voor** *zijn ~ nemen* pay the costs **3** (+ voor) expense: *voor* **eigen** *~* at one's own expense ‖ *~* **houden** *met iets* take sth. into account; *je* **moet** *een beetje ~* **houden** *met je ouders* you should show some consideration for your parents

de **rekening-courant** /rekənɪŋkurɑnt/ (pl: rekeningen-courant) current account

de **rekeninghouder** /rekənɪŋhɑudər/ (pl: -s) account holder

het **rekeningnummer** /rekənɪŋnʏmər/ account number

de **Rekenkamer** /rekə(n)kamər/ audit office, auditor's office

de **rekenkunde** /rekə(n)kʏndə/ arithmetic, maths

rekenkundig /rekə(n)kʏndəx/ (adj, adv) arithmetic(al)

de **rekenliniaal** /rekə(n)linijal/ (pl: -linialen) slide rule

de **rekenmachine** /rekə(n)maʃinə/ (pl: -s) calculator

de **rekenschap** /rekənsxɑp/ account, explanation: *ik* **ben** *u geen ~* **verschuldigd** I don't owe you any explanation ‖ *zich ~ van iets* **geven** realise; give account of sth.

de **rekensom** /rekə(n)sɔm/ (pl: -men) **1** sum; number work **2** [fig] problem, question: *het is een* **eenvoudig** *~metje* it's just a matter of adding two and two; *een* **eenvoudige** *~ leert dat …* it is easy to calculate that …

het **rekest** /rekɛst/ (pl: -en) petition

¹**rekken** /rɛkə(n)/ (rekte, heeft/is gerekt) stretch: *dat* **elastiek** *rekt niet goed meer* that elastic has lost its stretch

²**rekken** /rɛkə(n)/ (rekte, heeft gerekt) **1** stretch (out) **2** drag out, draw out; prolong: *het* **leven** *van een stervende ~* prolong a dying person's life; [socc] *tijd ~* use delaying tactics

rekruteren /rekryterə(n)/ (rekruteerde, heeft gerekruteerd) recruit

de **rekruut** /rekryt/ (pl: rekruten) recruit

de **rekstok** /rɛkstɔk/ (pl: -ken) horizontal bar, high bar

het **rekwisiet** /rekwizit/ (pl: -en) (stage-)property, prop

de **rel** /rɛl/ (pl: -len) disturbance, riot: *een ~* **schoppen** kick up (*or:* cause) a row

het **relaas** /relas/ (pl: relazen) account: *zijn ~* **doen** tell one's story

het **relais** /rəlɛ:/ relay

relateren /relaterə(n)/ (relateerde, heeft gerelateerd) relate

de **relatie** /rela(t)si/ (pl: -s) **1** relation(s), connection, relationship, contact: *~s* **onderhouden** *(met)* maintain relations (with); *in ~ staan tot* have relations with **2** affair, relationship: *een ~* **hebben** *met iem.* have a relationship

with s.o.

het **relatiebureau** /rela(t)sibyro/ (pl: -s) dating agency

relatief /relatif/ (adj, adv) relative, comparative

het **relatiegeschenk** /rela(t)siɣəsxɛŋk/ (pl: -en) business gift

relativeren /relativerə(n)/ (relativeerde, heeft gerelativeerd) put into perspective

relaxed /rilɛkst/ (adj, adv) relaxed, cool, laid-back

relaxen /rilɛksə(n)/ (relaxte, heeft gerelaxt) relax

relevant /reləvɑnt/ (adj) relevant: *die* **vraag** *is niet ~* that question is irrelevant

de **relevantie** /reləvɑnsi/ relevance

het **reliëf** /reljɛf/ relief

de **religie** /reliɣi/ (pl: -s) religion

religieus /reliɣjøs/ (adj, adv) religious

de **relikwie** /relikwi/ relic

de **reling** /relɪŋ/ (pl: -en) rail

de **relschopper** /rɛlsxɔpər/ (pl: -s) rioter, hooligan

de **rem** /rɛm/ (pl: -men) brake: *op de ~* **gaan** *staan* slam (*or:* jam) on the brakes

de **rembekrachtiging** /rɛmbəkrɑxtəɣɪŋ/ power(-assisted) brakes

het **remblok** /rɛmblɔk/ (pl: -ken) brake block

het **rembours** /rɑmbu̱rs/ (pl: -en) cash on delivery, COD: *onder ~ versturen* send (sth.) COD

het/de **remedie** /rəmedi/ (pl: -s) remedy: *dat is de* **aangewezen** *~* that is the obvious remedy

de **remise** /rəmizə/ (pl: -s) draw, tie, drawn game

het **remlicht** /rɛmlɪxt/ (pl: -en) brake light

remmen /rɛmə(n)/ (remde, heeft geremd) brake; [fig also] curb; check; inhibit: *geremd in zijn ontwikkeling* curbed in its development

de **remming** /rɛmɪŋ/ (pl: -en) check; [fig] inhibition

het/de **rempedaal** /rɛmpədal/ (pl: -pedalen) brake pedal

het **remspoor** /rɛmspor/ (pl: remsporen) skid mark

de **remweg** /rɛmwɛx/ braking distance

de **ren** /rɛn/ run

de **renaissance** /renɛsãsə/ renaissance

de **renbaan** /rɛmban/ (pl: renbanen) (race)track, (race)course

rendabel /rɛndabəl/ (adj) profitable, cost-effective

het **rendement** /rɛndəmɛnt/ (pl: -en) **1** return, yield, output: *het ~ van* **obligaties** the return (*or:* yield) on bonds **2** efficiency, output, performance: *het ~ van een elektrische* **lamp** the efficiency (*or:* output) of an electric lamp

renderen /rɛnderə(n)/ (rendeerde, heeft gerendeerd) pay (a profit): *niet ~d* not commercially viable

het **rendier** /rɛndir/ (pl: -en) reindeer

rennen /rɛnə(n)/ (rende, heeft/is gerend)

run, race: *we zijn laat, we* **moeten** ~ we're late; we must dash (off) (*or:* must fly)

de **renner** /rɛnər/ (pl: -s) rider

de **renovatie** /renova(t)si/ (pl: -s) renovation, redevelopment

renoveren /renovɛrə(n)/ (renoveerde, heeft gerenoveerd) renovate; redevelop

het **renpaard** /rɛmpart/ (pl: -en) racehorse, thoroughbred

de **rentabiliteit** /rɛntabilitɛit/ productivity, cost-effectiveness, profitability

de **rente** /rɛntə/ (pl: -n, -s) interest: ~ **opbrengen** yield interest; ~ **op** ~ compound interest; *een lening* **tegen** *vijf procent* ~ a loan at five per cent interest

renteloos /rɛntəlos/ (adj) **1** interest-free **2** non-productive

de **rentenier** /rɛntənir/ (pl: -s) person of independent (*or:* private) means

rentenieren /rɛntənirə(n)/ (rentenierde, heeft gerentenierd) **1** live off one's investments **2** lead a life of leisure

het **rentepercentage** /rɛntəpɛrsɛntaʒə/ interest rate

de **rentestand** /rɛntəstɑnt/ (pl: -en) interest rate

de **renteverhoging** /rɛntəvərhoɣɪŋ/ rise in interest rates

de **renteverlaging** /rɛntəvərlaɣɪŋ/ fall in interest rates

de **rentevoet** /rɛntəvut/ interest rate, rate of interest

de **rentmeester** /rɛntmestər/ (pl: -s) steward, manager

de **rentree** /rãtre/ (pl: -s) comeback, re-entry: *zijn* ~ **maken** make one's comeback

de **reorganisatie** /reɔrɣaniza(t)si/ (pl: -s) reorganization

reorganiseren /reɔrɣanizɛrə(n)/ (reorganiseerde, heeft gereorganiseerd) reorganize: *het* **onderwijs** ~ reorganize the educational system

rep /rɛp/: *het hele land was* **in** ~ *en roer* the entire country was in (an) uproar

de **reparateur** /reparatør/ (pl: -s) repairer, repairman; service engineer

de **reparatie** /repara(t)si/ (pl: -s) repair: *mijn horloge is* **in** *(de)* ~ my watch is being repaired

repareren /reparɛrə(n)/ (repareerde, heeft gerepareerd) repair, mend, fix: *dat* **is** *niet meer* **te** ~ it's beyond repair

repatriëren /repatrijɛrə(n)/ (repatrieerde, heeft gerepatrieerd) repatriate

het **repertoire** /repɛrtwar/ (pl: -s) repertoire, repertory: *het* **klassieke** ~ the classics; *zijn* ~ **afwerken** do one's repertoire

[1]**repeteren** /repətɛrə(n)/ (repeteerde, heeft gerepeteerd) **1** rehearse **2** repeat, circulate

[2]**repeteren** /repətɛrə(n)/ (repeteerde, heeft gerepeteerd) rehearse; run through, go through

de **repetitie** /repəti(t)si/ (pl: -s) rehearsal; run-through; practice: **generale** ~ dress rehearsal; final (*or:* last) rehearsal

de **replica** /rɛplika/ (pl: -'s) replica, copy

de **repliek** /replik/ (pl: -en) retort, response: *iem.* **van** ~ *dienen* put s.o. in his place

de **reportage** /repɔrtaʒə/ (pl: -s) report, coverage; commentary: *de* ~ *van een* **voetbalwedstrijd** the coverage of a football match

de **reporter** /ripɔːrtər/ (pl: -s) reporter

reppen /rɛpə(n)/ (repte, heeft gerept) **1** mention **2** hurry, rush

de **represaille** /reprɛzɑjə/ (pl: -s) reprisal, retaliation: ~*s* **nemen** *(tegen)* retaliate (*or:* take reprisals) (against)

representatief /reprezɛntatif/ (adj) **1** representative (of), typical (of): *een representatieve* **groep** *van de bevolking* a cross-section of the population; *een representatieve* **steekproef** a representative sample **2** representative, presentable: *een representatieve* **functie** a representative position

representeren /reprezɛntɛrə(n)/ (representeerde, heeft gerepresenteerd) represent

de **repressie** /reprɛsi/ (pl: -s) repression

repressief /reprɛsif/ (adj, adv) repressive

de **reprimande** /reprimɑndə/ (pl: -s) reprimand; rebuke; talking-to

reproduceren /reprodysɛrə(n)/ (reproduceerde, heeft gereproduceerd) reproduce, copy

de **reproductie** /reprodʏksi/ (pl: -s) reproduction, copy

het **reptiel** /rɛptil/ (pl: -en) reptile

de **republiek** /repyblik/ (pl: -en) republic

de **republikein** /repyblikɛin/ (pl: -en) republican

republikeins /repyblikɛins/ (adj, adv) republican

de **reputatie** /repyta(t)si/ (pl: -s) reputation, name; fame: *een* **goede** (or: **slechte**) ~ *hebben* have a good (*or:* bad) reputation; *iemands* ~ **schaden**, *slecht zijn voor iemands* ~ damage s.o.'s reputation

het **requiem** /rekwijɛm/ (pl: -s) requiem (mass)

de **research** /risʏːrtʃ/ research

het **reservaat** /rezɛrvat/ (pl: reservaten) reserve, preserve: **indianenreservaat** Indian reservation; **natuurreservaat** nature reserve

de **reserve** /rezɛrvə/ (pl: -s) **1** reserve(s): *zijn* ~*s* **aanspreken** draw on one's reserves **2** reserve, reservation: *zonder* **enige** ~ without reservations

de **reservebank** /rezɛrvəbɑŋk/ (pl: -en) reserve(s') bench, sub bench

het **reserveonderdeel** /rezɛrvəɔndərdel/ (pl: -onderdelen) spare part

reserveren /rezɛrvɛrə(n)/ (reserveerde, heeft gereserveerd) **1** reserve, put aside (*or:* away, by): *1000* **euro** ~ *voor* set aside 1000 euros for; *een artikel* **voor** *iem.* ~ put aside an article for s.o. **2** book, reserve: *een* **tafel** *~ re-serve (or: book) a table*

de **reservering** /rezɛrvɛrɪŋ/ (pl: -en) booking, reservation

de **reservesleutel** /rəzɛrvəsløtəl/ (pl: -s) spare key

het **reservewiel** /rəzɛrvəwil/ (pl: -en) spare wheel

het **reservoir** /rezɛrvwar/ (pl: -s) reservoir, tank

resetten /risɛtə(n)/ (resette, heeft gereset) reset

resistent /rezistɛnt/ (adj) resistant (to): *~ worden* **tegen** *antibiotica* become resistant (or: immune) to antibiotics

de **resolutie** /rezoly(t)si/ (pl: -s) resolution

resoluut /rezolyt/ (adj, adv) resolute, determined

resoneren /rezonɛrə(n)/ (resoneerde, heeft geresoneerd) resonate

het **resort** (pl: -s) resort

het **respect** /rɛspɛkt/ respect; regard; deference: *~* **afdwingen** *command respect; voor iets (iem.) ~* **tonen** *show respect for sth. (s.o.);* **met** *alle ~* with all (due) respect

respectabel /rɛspɛktabəl/ (adj, adv) respectable; considerable

respecteren /rɛspɛktɛrə(n)/ (respecteerde, heeft gerespecteerd) respect, appreciate: *zichzelf ~d* self-respecting; *iemands* **opvattingen** *~* respect s.o.'s views

respectievelijk /rɛspɛktivələk/ (adj, adv) respective: *bedragen van ~ 10, 20 en 30 euro* sums of 10, 20 and 30 euros respectively

respectloos /rɛspɛktlos/ (adj) disrespectful: *iem. ~* **behandelen** *treat s.o. disrespectfully*

het **respijt** /rɛspɛit/ respite, grace, delay

het/de **respons** /rɛspɔns/ response, reaction

het **ressentiment** /rɛsɛntimɛnt/ (pl: -en) resentment

het **ressort** /rɛsɔrt/ (pl: -en) jurisdiction

ressorteren /rɛsortɛrə(n)/ (ressorteerde, heeft geressorteerd): *~* **onder** *come under*

de **rest** /rɛst/ (pl: -en) rest, remainder: *de ~ van het* **materiaal** *the remainder of the material;* **voor** *de ~ geen nieuws* otherwise no news

het **restant** /rɛstɑnt/ (pl: -en) remainder, remnant

het **restaurant** /rɛstorɑnt/ (pl: -s) restaurant

de **restauratie** /rɛstora(t)si/ (pl: -s) restoration

restaureren /rɛstorɛrə(n)/ (restaureerde, heeft gerestaureerd) restore

resten /rɛstə(n)/ (restte, heeft/is gerest) remain, be left: *hem restte niets meer dan ... there was nothing left for him but to ...; nu rest* **mij** *nog te verklaren ... now it only remains for me to say ...*

resteren /rɛstɛrə(n)/ (resteerde, is geresteerd) be left, remain

restitueren /rɛstitywɛrə(n)/ (restitueerde, heeft gerestitueerd) refund, pay back

de **restitutie** /rɛstity(t)si/ (pl: -s) refund

het **restje** /rɛʃə/ (pl: -s): *ik heb nog een ~ van gisteren* I've got a few scraps (left over) from yesterday

de **restrictie** /rɛstrɪksi/ (pl: -s) restriction

de **restwarmte** /rɛstwɑrmtə/ residual heat (or: warmth)

restylen /ristɑjlə(n)/ give sth./s.o. a makeover

het **resultaat** /rezʏltat/ (pl: resultaten) **1** result, effect, outcome: *het plan had het* **beoogde** *~ the plan had the desired effect; resultaten* **behalen** *achieve results;* **met** *het ~ dat ... with the result that ...;* **zonder** *~ with no result* **2** result; returns

resulteren /rezʏltɛrə(n)/ (resulteerde, heeft geresulteerd) result: *het* **daaruit** *~de verlies* the loss resulting from it, the resulting loss; *~* **in** *result in, lead up to; dit heeft geresulteerd* **in** *zijn ontslag* this has resulted in his dismissal; *wanneer het signaal sterk is dan zal dat ~* **in** *een goede ontvangst* if the signal is strong, high quality reception will be the result; *wat resulteert is ...* the result (or: outcome, upshot) is ...

het **resumé** /rezymɛ/ (pl: -s) summary, abstract

resumeren /rezymɛrə(n)/ (resumeerde, heeft geresumeerd) **1** summarize **2** recapitulate

de **resusfactor** /rezʏsfɑktor/ (pl: -en) Rhesus factor

rete- very

de **retoriek** /retorik/ rhetoric: *holle ~* empty rhetoric

retorisch /retoris/ (adj, adv) rhetorical: *een ~e* **vraag** *a rhetorical question*

de **retort** /rətɔrt/ (pl: -en) retort

retoucheren /rətuʃɛrə(n)/ (retoucheerde, heeft geretoucheerd) retouch, touch up

het ¹**retour** /rətur/ (pl: -s) return (ticket); [Am] round-trip (ticket): *een ~ eerste* **klas** *Utrecht a first-class return (ticket) to Utrecht; op zijn ~ past his (or: its) best*

²**retour** /rətur/ (adv) back || *~* **afzender** *return to sender; drie* **euro** *~ three euros change*

het **retourbiljet** /rəturbɪljɛt/ (pl: -ten) return ticket; [Am] round-trip ticket

de **retourenveloppe** /rəturɛnvəlɔp/ (pl: -n) self-addressed envelope

retourneren /rəturnɛrə(n)/ (retourneerde, heeft geretourneerd) return

het **retourtje** /rəturcə/ return; [Am] round-trip

de **retourvlucht** /rəturvlʏχt/ (pl: -en) **1** return flight **2** return flight; [Am] round-trip flight

het **retrospectief** /retrospɛktif/ (pl: retrospectieven) retrospective: *in ~* in retrospect

de **return** /rity:rn/ (pl: -s) **1** return **2** return match, return game **3** return: *een* **harde** *~ a hard return; een* **zachte** *~ a soft return*

de **reu** /rø/ (pl: -en) male dog

de **reuk** /røk/ (pl: -en) **1** smell, odour: *een onaangename ~* **verspreiden** *give off an un-*

pleasant smell **2** smell; scent: *op de ~ afgaan* hunt by scent

reukloos /rø̞klos/ (adj, adv) odourless; scentless

de **reukzin** /rø̞ksɪn/ (sense of) smell

het **reuma** /rø̞ma/ rheumatism

reumatisch /rø̞ma̱tis/ (adj) rheumatic

de **reünie** /rejyni/ (pl: -s) reunion

de **reuring** /rø̞rɪŋ/ **1** buzz, hum **2** stir: *voor ~ zorgen* cause a stir (*or*: an uproar), rock the boat

de **reus** /rø̞s/ (pl: reuzen) giant

reusachtig /rø̞zɑ̱xtəx/ (adj) **1** gigantic, huge **2** great, terrific

reuze /rø̞zə/ (adv) [inform] enormously: *~ veel* an awful lot; *~ bedankt* thanks awfully

de **reuzel** /rø̞zəl/ (pl: -s) lard

het **reuzenrad** /rø̞zə(n)rɑt/ (pl: -eren) Ferris wheel

de **revalidatie** /revalida̱(t)si/ rehabilitation

het **revalidatiecentrum** /revalida̱(t)sisɛntrʏm/ (pl: -centra) rehabilitation centre

revalideren /revalide̱rə(n)/ (revalideerde, heeft/is gerevalideerd) recover, convalesce

de **revaluatie** /revalywa̱(t)si/ revaluation

revalueren /revalywe̱rə(n)/ (revalueerde, heeft gerevalueerd) revalue

de **revanche** /revɑ̃ʃ/ **1** revenge: *~ nemen op iem.* take revenge on s.o. **2** [sport] return (game, match); return bout: *iem. ~ geven* give s.o. a return game

zich **revancheren** /rəvɑ̃ʃe̱rə(n)/ (revancheerde zich, heeft zich gerevancheerd) revenge (o.s.), be revenged

de **revers** /rəvɛːr/ lapel

reviseren /revize̱rə(n)/ (reviseerde, heeft gereviseerd) overhaul

de **revisie** /revi̱zi/ (pl: -s) **1** revision; review **2** overhaul, going-over

de **revolte** /revo̞ltə/ (pl: -s) revolt, insurgence

de **revolutie** /revoly̱(t)si/ (pl: -s) revolution: *de Amerikaanse Revolutie* the American War of Independence

revolutionair /revoly(t)ʃonɛːr/ (adj, adv) revolutionary: *een ~e ontdekking* a revolutionary discovery

de **revolver** /revo̞lvər/ (pl: -s) revolver

de **revue** /rəvy̱/ (pl: -s) **1** revue, show **2** review

Rhodos /rodɔs/ Rhodes

het/de **Riagg** /rijɑx/ *Regionale Instelling voor Ambulante Geestelijke Gezondheidszorg* regional institute for mental welfare

riant /rijɑ̱nt/ (adj, adv) ample, spacious: *een ~e villa* a spacious villa

de **rib** /rɪp/ (pl: -ben) rib: *de zwevende ~ben* the floating ribs; *je kunt zijn ~ben tellen* he is a bag of bones; *dat is een ~ uit je lijf* that costs an arm and a leg

de **ribbel** /rɪ̱bəl/ (pl: -s) rib, ridge; ripple

de **ribbenkast** /rɪ̱bə(n)kɑst/ (pl: -en) rib cage

de **ribbroek** /rɪ̱bruk/ (pl: -en) cord(uroy) trou-

sers

de **ribeye** /rɪpɑj/ ribeye

het **ribfluweel** /rɪ̱pflywel/ cord(uroy)

de **ribkarbonade** /rɪ̱pkɑrbonadə/ (pl: -s) rib chop

de **richel** /rɪ̱xəl/ (pl: -s) ledge, ridge

¹**richten** /rɪ̱xtə(n)/ (richtte, heeft gericht) **1** direct, aim, orient: *gericht op* aimed at, directed at, oriented towards; *zijn ogen op iets ~* focus one's eyes on sth.; *het geweer op iem. ~* aim a gun at s.o. **2** direct, address; extend: *een brief, aan mij gericht* a letter addressed to me; *een vraag ~ tot de voorzitter* direct a question to the chairman **3** align: *naar het oosten gericht* facing east

zich ²**richten** /rɪ̱xtə(n)/ (richtte zich, heeft zich gericht) **1** (+ tot) address (o.s. to): *richt u met klachten tot ons bureau* address any complaints to our office **2** (+ naar) conform to: *zich ~ naar de omstandigheden* be guided by circumstances

de **richting** /rɪ̱xtɪŋ/ (pl: -en) direction: *zij gingen ~ Amsterdam* they went in the direction of (*or*: they headed for) Amsterdam; *iem. een zetje in de goede ~ geven* give s.o. a push in the right direction; [traf] *~ aangeven* indicate direction, signal; *dat komt aardig in de ~* that's looks sth. like it; *van ~ veranderen* change direction

de **richtingaanwijzer** /rɪ̱xtɪŋanwɛizər/ (pl: -s) (direction) indicator

het **richtingsgevoel** /rɪ̱xtɪŋsɣəvul/ sense of direction

de **richtlijn** /rɪ̱xtlɛin/ (pl: -en) guideline; directions: *iets volgens de ~en uitvoeren* do sth. in the prescribed way

de **richtmicrofoon** /rɪ̱xtmikrofon/ (pl: -s) directional microphone

het **richtsnoer** /rɪ̱xtsnur/ (pl: -en) guideline; directions

de **ridder** /rɪ̱dər/ (pl: -s) knight: *iem. tot ~ slaan* dub s.o. a knight; knight s.o.

ridderen /rɪ̱dərə(n)/ (ridderde, heeft geridderd) knight: *geridderd worden* be knighted, receive a knighthood

ridderlijk /rɪ̱dərlək/ (adj) chivalrous ‖ *hij kwam er ~ voor uit* he frankly (*or*: openly) admitted it

de **ridderorde** /rɪ̱dərɔrdə/ (pl: -n, -s) knighthood, order

de **ridderzaal** /rɪ̱dərzal/ (pl: -zalen) great hall

ridicuul /ridiky̱l/ (adj, adv) ridiculous

de **riedel** /ri̱dəl/ (pl: -s) tune, jingle

de **riek** /rik/ (pl: -en) (three-pronged) fork

rieken /ri̱kə(n)/ (rook/riekte, heeft geroken) smack (of), smell (of), reek (of): *die riekt naar verraad* this smacks of treason

de **riem** /rim/ (pl: -en) **1** belt **2** strap; belt; sling; leash **3** seat belts

het **riet** /rit/ reed; cane

rieten /ri̱tə(n)/ (adj) reed; rush; cane; wicker(work): ~ *stoel* cane (*or:* wicker) chair; ~ *dak* thatched roof

het **rietje** /rícə/ (pl: -s) **1** straw **2** [mus] reed

de **rietsuiker** /rítsœykər/ cane sugar

het **rif** /rɪf/ (pl: -fen) reef

rigoureus /riɣorǿs/ (adj, adv) rigorous

de **rij** /rɛi/ (pl: -en) **1** row, line: *~en auto's* rows of cars; queues of cars; *een ~ bomen* a line of trees; *een ~ mensen* **a)** a row of people; **b)** a line (*or:* queue) of people; *in de eerste* (*or:* *voorste*) *~en* in the front seats (*or:* rows); *in de ~ staan* queue; [Am] stand in line **2** row; string: *een ~ getallen* **a)** a column of figures; **b)** a row of figures; *ze niet allemaal op een ~tje hebben* have a screw loose

de **rijbaan** /rɛiban/ (pl: rijbanen) roadway; lane: *weg met gescheiden rijbanen* dual carriageway

het **rijbewijs** /rɛibəwɛis/ (pl: rijbewijzen) driving licence; [Am] driver's license: *z'n ~ halen* pass one's driving test

de **rijbroek** /rɛibruk/ (pl: -en) jodhpurs, riding breeches

rijden /rɛidə(n)/ (reed, heeft/is gereden) **1** drive; ride: *honderd kilometer per uur ~* drive (*or:* do) a hundred kilometres an hour; *het is twee uur ~* it's a two-hour drive; *hij werd bekeurd omdat hij te hard reed* he was fined for speeding; *door het rode licht ~* go through a red light; *in een auto ~* drive (in) a car; *op een (te) paard ~* ride a horse (*or:* on horseback) **2** drive [car]; ride; move; run; do: *hoeveel heeft je auto al gereden?* how many miles (*or:* kilometres) has your car done?; *(te) dicht op elkaar ~* not keep one's distance; *de tractor rijdt op dieselolie* the tractor runs (*or:* operates) on diesel oil; *die auto rijdt lekker* that car is pleasant to drive **3** skate

rijdend /rɛidənt/ (adj) **1** mobile: *~e bibliotheek* mobile (*or:* travelling) library; [Am] bookmobile **2** moving

de **rijder** /rɛidər/ (pl: -s) rider; driver [car]; cyclist

het **rijdier** /rɛidir/ (pl: -en) riding animal, mount

rijendik (adj) packed

het **rijexamen** /rɛiɛksamə(n)/ (pl: -s) driving test: *~ doen* take one's driving test

het **rijgedrag** /rɛiɣədraχ/ driving (behaviour), motoring performance

rijgen /rɛiɣə(n)/ (reeg, heeft geregen) thread, string

de **rijglaars** /rɛiχlars/ (pl: -laarzen) lace-up boot

de **rijinstructeur** /rɛiɪnstrʏktør/ (pl: -s) driving instructor

het ¹**rijk** /rɛik/ (pl: -en) **1** realm: *het ~ der hemelen* the Kingdom of Heaven; *het Britse Rijk* the British Empire; *het Derde Rijk* the Third Reich **2** state, kingdom, empire **3** government, State: *door het Rijk gefinancierd* State-financed ‖ *het ~ alleen hebben* have the place (all) to o.s.

²**rijk** /rɛik/ (adj) **1** rich, wealthy: *stinkend ~ zijn* be filthy rich **2** rich; fertile; generous: *hij heeft een ~e verbeelding* he has a fertile imagination ‖ *ik ben je liever kwijt dan ~* I'd rather see the back of you

de **rijkaard** /rɛikart/ (pl: -s) rich person; moneybags

de **rijkdom** /rɛiɣdɔm/ (pl: -men) **1** wealth, affluence **2** resource: *natuurlijke ~men* natural resources

rijkelijk /rɛikələk/ (adj, adv) lavish, liberal

de **rijkelui** /rɛikəlœy/ (pl) [inform] rich people

het **rijkeluiskind** /rɛikəlœyskɪnt/ (pl: -eren) [inform] rich man's son, rich man's daughter

de **rijksambtenaar** /rɛiksɑmtənar/ (pl: -ambtenaren) public servant

de **rijksbegroting** /rɛiksbəɣrotɪŋ/ (pl: -en) (national) budget

de **rijksdaalder** /rɛiksdaldər/ (pl: -s) two-and-a-half guilder coin

de **rijksdienst** /rɛiksdinst/ (pl: -en) national agency

de **rijksinstelling** /rɛiksɪnstɛlɪŋ/ government institution (*or:* institute)

het **rijksinstituut** /rɛiksɪnstityt/ national institute

het **rijksmuseum** /rɛiksmyzejʏm/ (pl: -musea) national museum; national gallery

de **rijksoverheid** /rɛiksoːvərhɛit/ (pl: -heden) central government, national government

de **rijkspolitie** /rɛikspoli(t)si/ national police (force)

het **rijksregisternummer** /rɛiksrəɣɪstər-nʏmər/ [Belg] Citizen Service Number (CSN)

de **rijksuniversiteit** /rɛiksynivɛrzitɛit/ (pl: -en) state university

de **Rijksvoorlichtingsdienst** /rɛiks-forlɪχtɪŋzdinst/ government information service

de **Rijkswacht** /rɛikswɑχt/ [Belg] state police

de **rijkswachter** /rɛikswɑχtər/ (pl: -s) [Belg] state policeman

Rijkswaterstaat /rɛikswatərstat/ [roughly] Department (*or:* Ministry) of Waterways and Public Works

de **rijksweg** /rɛikswɛχ/ (pl: -en) national trunk road; [Am] state highway

de **rijlaars** /rɛɪlars/ (pl: -laarzen) riding boot

de **rijles** /rɛilɛs/ (pl: -sen) driving lesson; riding lesson: *~ nemen* take driving (*or:* riding) lessons

het **rijm** /rɛim/ (pl: -en) rhyme; verse: *op ~* rhyming, in rhyme

de **rijmelarij** /rɛɪmelarɛɪ/ (pl: -en) doggerel (verse)

rijmen /rɛimə(n)/ (rijmde, heeft gerijmd) **1** be in rhyme (*or:* verse), rhyme (with): *deze woorden ~ op elkaar* these words rhyme (with each other) **2** rhyme, versify ‖ *dat viel niet te ~ met ...* that could not be reconciled with ...

het **rijmpje** /rɛimpjə/ (pl: -s) rhyme, short verse

de **Rijn** /rɛin/ Rhine

de **rijnaak** /rɛinak/ (pl: rijnaken) Rhine barge

de ¹**rijp** /rɛip/ (white) frost, hoarfrost

²**rijp** /rɛip/ (adj) **1** ripe: ~ *maken (worden)* ripen, mature **2** mature: *op ~ere leeftijd* at a ripe age **3** (+ voor) ripe (for), ready (for): ~ *voor de sloop* ready for the scrap heap **4** serious: *na* ~ *beraad* after careful consideration

het **rijpaard** /rɛipart/ (pl: -en) saddle horse

rijpen /rɛipə(n)/ (rijpte, heeft/is gerijpt) ripen; mature

de **rijpheid** /rɛiphɛit/ ripeness, maturity: *tot* ~ *komen* ripen, mature

de **rijschool** /rɛisχol/ (pl: rijscholen) driving school; riding school (*or:* academy)

het **rijshout** /rɛishɑut/ osier, brush(wood)

de **rijst** /rɛist/ rice

de **rijstebrij** /rɛistəbrɛi/ rice pudding

de **rijstijl** /rɛistɛil/ (pl: -en) driving style

de **rijstkorrel** /rɛistkɔrəl/ (pl: -s) grain of rice

de **rijstrook** /rɛistrok/ (traffic) lane

de **rijsttafel** /rɛistafəl/ (pl: -s) (Indonesian) rice meal

de **rijtijd** /rɛitɛit/ (pl: -en) driving time; travel time

het **rijtjeshuis** /rɛicəshœys/ (pl: -huizen) terrace(d) house; [Am] row house

het **rijtuig** /rɛitœyχ/ (pl: -en) **1** carriage **2** carriage; [Am] car

de **rijvaardigheid** /rɛivardəχhɛit/ driving ability (*or:* proficiency)

het **rijverbod** /rɛivərbɔt/ (pl: -en) driving ban

de **rijweg** /rɛiwɛχ/ (pl: -en) road(way)

het **rijwiel** /rɛiwil/ (pl: -en) (bi)cycle

het **rijwielpad** /rɛiwilpɑt/ (pl: -en) cycle path, cycle track

de **rijwielstalling** /rɛiwilstɑlɪŋ/ (pl: -en) (bi)cycle lock-up

rijzen /rɛizə(n)/ (rees, is gerezen) rise: *laat het deeg* ~ leave the dough to rise; *de prijzen* ~ *de pan***uit** prices are soaring

rijzig /rɛizəχ/ (adj, adv) tall: ~ *van gestalte* tall in build (*or:* stature)

de **rikketik** /rɪkətɪk/ (pl: -ken) ticker

de **riksja** /rɪkʃa/ (pl: -'s) rickshaw

rillen /rɪlə(n)/ (rilde, heeft gerild) shiver, shudder, tremble: *hij rilde van de kou* he shivered with cold

rillerig /rɪlərəχ/ (adj) shivery

de **rilling** /rɪlɪŋ/ (pl: -en) shiver, shudder, tremble: *koude ~en hebben* have the shakes (*or:* shivers); *er liep een ~ over mijn rug* a shiver ran down my spine

de **rimboe** /rɪmbu/ (pl: -s) jungle

de **rimpel** /rɪmpəl/ (pl: -s) wrinkle: *een gezicht vol ~s* a wrinkled face

rimpelen /rɪmpələ(n)/ (rimpelde, heeft/is gerimpeld) **1** wrinkle (up): *het voorhoofd* ~ wrinkle one's forehead **2** crinkle (up)

rimpelig /rɪmpələχ/ (adj) wrinkled: *een ~e*

appel a wizened apple

de **ring** /rɪŋ/ (pl: -en) ring

de **ringbaard** /rɪŋbart/ (pl: -en) fringe of beard

de **ringband** /rɪŋbɑnt/ (pl: -en) ring-binder

ringeloren /rɪŋəlorə(n)/: *zich laten* ~ let o.s. be bullied (*or:* browbeat)

ringen /rɪŋə(n)/ (ringde, heeft geringd) ring

de **ringmap** /rɪŋmɑp/ (pl: -pen) ring-binder

de **ringslang** /rɪŋslɑŋ/ (pl: -en) grass snake, ring(ed) snake

de **ringtone** /rɪŋton/ ring tone

de **ringvaart** /rɪŋvart/ (pl: -en) ring canal, belt canal

de **ringvinger** /rɪŋvɪŋər/ (pl: -s) ring finger

de **ringweg** /rɪŋwɛχ/ (pl: -en) ring road

de **ringworm** /rɪŋwɔrm/ (pl: -en) ringworm

rinkelen /rɪŋkələ(n)/ (rinkelde, heeft gerinkeld) jingle, tinkle; ring; chink: *~de ruiten* rattling panes of glass; *de ~de tamboerijn* the jingling tambourine

de **rinoceros** /rinosərɔs/ (pl: -sen) rhinoceros, rhino

de **riolering** /rijolɛrɪŋ/ (pl: -en) sewerage, sewer system

het **riool** /rijol/ (pl: riolen) sewer: *een open* ~ an open sewer

de **riooljournalistiek** /rijolʒurnalɪstik/ gutter journalism

het **risico** /riziko/ (pl: -'s) risk: *dat behoort tot de ~'s van het vak* that's an occupational hazard; *het* ~ *lopen (van)* run the risk (of); *te veel ~'s nemen* run (*or:* take) too many risks; *op eigen* ~ at one's own risk; *voor* ~ *van de eigenaar* at the owner's risk; *geen* ~ *willen nemen* not want to take any chances

risicodragend /rizikodraɣənt/ (adj) risk-bearing

de **risicogroep** /rizikoɣrup/ (pl: -en) high-risk group

de **risicowedstrijd** /rizikowɛtstrɛit/ high-risk match

riskant /rɪskɑnt/ (adj) risky: *een ~e onderneming* a risky enterprise

riskeren /rɪskɛrə(n)/ (riskeerde, heeft geriskeerd) risk

de **rit** /rɪt/ (pl: -ten) **1** ride, run; drive: *een ~je maken* go for a ride **2** [cycling] stage, ride: [fig] *de zaak weer op de* ~ *krijgen* get things back on track (*or:* the rails)

het **ritme** /rɪtmə/ (pl: -s) rhythm: *uit zijn* ~ *raken* lose one's rhythm

ritmisch /rɪtmis/ (adj, adv) rhythmic(al): ~ *bewegen* move rhythmically

de **rits** /rɪts/ (pl: -en) **1** zipper, zip **2** bunch; string; batch; battery: *een* ~ *kinderen* a whole string of children

ritselen /rɪtsələ(n)/ (ritselde, heeft geritseld) rustle: *ik hoor een muis* ~ *achter het behang* I can hear a mouse scuffling behind the wallpaper; ~ *met een papiertje* rustle a paper

ritsen /rɪtsə(n)/ (ritste, heeft geritst) zipper

merge, merge alternately

de **ritssluiting** /rɪtslœytɪŋ/ (pl: -en) zipper, zip: *kun je me even helpen met mijn ~? can you help zip me up? (or: unzip me?)*

het **¹ritueel** /ritywe̱l/ (pl: rituelen) ritual

²ritueel /ritywe̱l/ (adj) ritual

de **ritzege** /rɪtseɣə/ (pl: -s) stage victory: *een ~ behalen* win a stage

de **rivaal** /riva̱l/ (pl: rivalen) rival

de **rivaliteit** /rivalite̱it/ rivalry

de **rivier** /rivi̱r/ (pl: -en) river: *een ~ oversteken* cross a river; *een huis aan de ~* a house on the river

de **Rivièra** /rivjɛ̱ːra/ Riviera

de **rivierarm** /rivi̱rɑrm/ (pl: -en) arm of a river

de **riviermond** /rivi̱rmɔnt/ (pl: -en) river mouth; estuary

de **rob** /rɔp/ (pl: -ben) seal

de **robbenjacht** /rɔbə(n)jɑχt/ seal hunting

de **¹robijn** /robɛ̱in/ [gem] ruby

het **²robijn** /robɛ̱in/ [mineral] ruby

de **robot** /ro̱bɔt/ (pl: -s) robot: *hij lijkt wel een ~* he is like a robot

robuust /robyst/ (adj, adv) robust; solid: *een ~e gezondheid* robust health

de **rochel** /rɔχəl/ (pl: -s) **1** lump of spit **2** hawk

rochelen /rɔχələ(n)/ (rochelde, heeft gerocheld) hawk (up)

de **rock-'n-roll** /rɔkənrɔ̱l/ rock 'n' roll

de **rockzanger** /rɔ̱ksɑŋər/ (pl: -s) rock singer

het **rococo** /rokoko̱/ rococo

de **roddel** /rɔ̱dəl/ (pl: -s) gossip: *de nieuwste ~s uit de showwereld* the latest gossip in show business; *~ en achterklap* gossip

de **roddelaar** /rɔ̱dəlar/ (pl: -s) gossip

het **roddelblad** /rɔ̱dəlblɑt/ (pl: -en) gossip magazine

roddelen /rɔ̱dələ(n)/ (roddelde, heeft geroddeld) gossip (about)

de **roddelpers** /rɔ̱dəlpɛrs/ gutter press, gossip papers

de **rodehond** /ro̱dəhɔnt/ German measles, rubella

de **rodekool** /ro̱dəko̱l/ (pl: -kolen) red cabbage

het **Rode Kruis** /ro̱dəkrœys/ Red Cross

de **rodelbaan** /ro̱dəlban/ (pl: -banen) toboggan run; luge run

rodelen /ro̱dələ(n)/ (rodelde, heeft/is geroddeld) toboggan; luge run

de **rodeo** /ro̱dejo/ (pl: -'s) rodeo

de **rododendron** /rododɛ̱ndrɔn/ (pl: -s) rhododendron

de **roe** /ru/ (pl: -s) rod

de **roebel** /ru̱bəl/ (pl: -s) rouble

de **roede** /ru̱də/ (pl: -n, -s) rod

het **roedel** /ru̱dəl/ (pl: -s) herd; pack

de **roeibaan** /ru̱iban/ (pl: -banen) rowing course

de **roeiboot** /ru̱ibot/ (pl: -boten) rowing boat

roeien /ru̱iə(n)/ (roeide, heeft/is geroeid) row: *met grote slagen ~* take big strokes

de **roeier** /ru̱iər/ (pl: -s) rower, oarsman

de **roeispaan** /ru̱ispan/ (pl: -spanen) oar; scull; paddle

de **roeiwedstrijd** /ru̱iwɛtstrɛit/ (pl: -en) boat race, rowing race; regatta

roekeloos /ru̱kəlos/ (adj, adv) reckless: *~ rijden* drive recklessly

de **roem** /rum/ glory, fame, renown: *op zijn ~ teren* rest on one's laurels

de **Roemeen** /rume̱n/ (pl: Roemenen) Romanian

het **Roemeens** /rume̱ns/ Romanian

roemen /ru̱mə(n)/ (roemde, heeft geroemd) praise, speak highly of

Roemenië /rume̱nijə/ Romania

de **roemer** /ru̱mər/ (pl: -s) rummer

roemloos /ru̱mlos/ (adj) inglorious

roemrijk /ru̱mrɛik/ (adj, adv) glorious: *een ~ verleden* a glorious past

roemrucht /rumrʏ̱χt/ (adj) illustrious, renowned

de **roep** /rup/ call; cry; shout

¹roepen /ru̱pə(n)/ (riep, heeft geroepen) call, cry, shout; clamour: *om hulp ~* call (or: cry) out for help; *een ~de in de woestijn* a voice (crying) in the wilderness

²roepen /ru̱pə(n)/ (riep, heeft geroepen) call, summon: *de ober ~* call the waiter; *iem. op het matje ~* carpet s.o.; *de plicht roept (mij)* duty calls; *ik zal je om zeven uur ~* I'll call you at seven; *je komt als geroepen* (you're) just the person we need; *daar voel ik mij niet toe geroepen* I don't quite feel like it

de **roepia** /ru̱pija/ (pl: -'s) rupiah

de **roeping** /ru̱pɪŋ/ (pl: -en) vocation, mission, calling

de **roepnaam** /ru̱pnam/ (pl: -namen) nickname

het **roer** /rur/ (pl: -en) **1** rudder **2** helm; tiller: *het ~ niet uit handen geven* remain at the helm; *het ~ omgooien* [fig] change course (or: tack)

roerbakken /ru̱rbɑkə(n)/ (roerbakte, heeft geroerbakt/roergebakken) stir-fry

het **roerei** /ru̱rɛi/ (pl: -eren) scrambled eggs

roeren /ru̱rə(n)/ (roerde, heeft geroerd) stir, mix: *de soep ~* stir the soup; *door elkaar ~* mix together

roerend /ru̱rənt/ (adj, adv) moving, touching

de **roerganger** /ru̱rɣɑŋər/ (pl: -s) helmsman, steersman: *de grote ~* the Great Helmsman

roerig /ru̱rəχ/ (adj) lively, active, restless

roerloos /ru̱rlos/ (adj, adv) motionless, immovable, immobile

het **roerstaafje** /ru̱rstafjə/ coffee stirrer

de **roes** /rus/ (pl: roezen) **1** flush; high: *in een ~* in a whirl (of excitement) **2** fuddle, intoxication; high: *zijn ~ uitslapen* sleep it off

het/de **roest** /rust/ (pl: -en) rust: *een laag ~* a layer of rust ‖ *oud ~* scrap iron

roestbruin /rustbrœyn/ (adj) rust, rust-co-

loured
roesten /r<u>u</u>stə(n)/ (roestte, heeft/is geroest) rust, get rusty

roestig /r<u>u</u>stəχ/ (adj) rusty

roestvrij /rustfr<u>ɛi</u>/ (adj) rustproof, rust-resistant: ~ *staal* stainless steel

het **roet** /rut/ soot: *zo zwart als* ~ as black as soot

het/de **roetfilter** /r<u>u</u>tfɪltər/ (pl: -s) soot filter, particle filter

roetsjen /r<u>u</u>tʃə(n)/ (roetsjte, heeft/is geroetsjt) slide

roetzwart /rutsw<u>ɔ</u>rt/ (adj) black, pitch-black

de **roffel** /r<u>ɔ</u>fəl/ (pl: -s) roll; ruffle

roffelen /r<u>ɔ</u>fələ(n)/ (roffelde, heeft geroffeld) roll: *met de vingers op de tafel* ~ drum (one's fingers) on the table

de **rog** /rɔχ/ (pl: -gen) ray

de **rogge** /r<u>ɔ</u>ɣə/ rye: *brood van* ~ bread made from rye

het **roggebrood** /r<u>ɔ</u>ɣəbrot/ (pl: -broden) rye bread, pumpernickel

de **rok** /rɔk/ (pl: -ken) **1** skirt; petticoat: *Schotse* ~ kilt; *een wijde* ~ a full skirt **2** tail coat, tails: *de heren waren in* ~ the men wore evening dress

de **rokade** /rok<u>a</u>də/ (pl: -s) castling: *de korte* (or: *lange*) ~ castling on the king's side (or: queen's side)

roken /r<u>o</u>kə(n)/ (rookte, heeft gerookt) **1** smoke, puff (at): *stoppen met* ~ stop (or: give up) smoking; *verboden te* ~ no smoking; *minder gaan* ~ cut down on smoking; *de schoorsteen rookt* the chimney is smoking **2** smoke, cure

de **roker** /r<u>o</u>kər/ (pl: -s) smoker

rokerig /r<u>o</u>kərəχ/ (adj) smoky

de **rokkenjager** /r<u>ɔ</u>kə(n)jaɣər/ (pl: -s) womanizer

het **rokkostuum** /r<u>ɔ</u>kostym/ (pl: -s) dress suit

de **rol** /rɔl/ (pl: -len) **1** part, role: *zijn* ~ *instuderen* learn one's part; *de* ~*len omkeren* reverse roles; turn the tables **2** roll; cylinder; coil; scroll; reel; spool: *een* ~ *behang* a roll of wallpaper; *een* ~ *beschuit* a packet of rusks **3** roller; rolling pin || *een* ~ *spelen* a) play a part, play-act; b) play a part (in), enter in(to)

het/de **rolgordijn** /r<u>ɔ</u>lɣordɛin/ (pl: -en) (roller) blind: *een* ~ *ophalen* (or: *laten zakken*) let up (or: down) a blind

de **rolkoffer** /r<u>ɔ</u>lkɔfər/ (pl: -s) wheeled suitcase

de **rollade** /rol<u>a</u>də/ (pl: -s) rolled meat

de **rollator** /rol<u>a</u>tɔr/ Zimmer frame, rollator

rollebollen /r<u>ɔ</u>ləbɔlə(n)/ (rollebolde, heeft gerollebold) **1** turn (or: go) head over heels **2** tumble, roll

¹**rollen** /r<u>ɔ</u>lə(n)/ (rolde, heeft/is gerold) roll: *er gaan koppen* ~ heads will roll; *de zaak aan het* ~ *brengen* set the ball rolling

²**rollen** /r<u>ɔ</u>lə(n)/ (rolde, heeft gerold) **1** roll (up): *een sigaret* ~ roll a cigarette **2** wrap,

roll (up): *zich in een deken* ~ wrap o.s. up in a blanket **3** lift: *zakken* ~ pick pockets

het **rollenpatroon** /r<u>ɔ</u>lə(n)patron/ (pl: -patronen) sex role

het **rollenspel** /r<u>ɔ</u>lə(n)spɛl/ role-playing

de **roller** /r<u>ɔ</u>lər/ (pl: -s) roller

het **rolletje** /r<u>ɔ</u>ləcə/ (pl: -s) (small) roll; roller: *een* ~ *drop* a packet of liquorice; *alles liep op* ~*s* everything went like clockwork (or: went smoothly)

het **rolluik** /r<u>ɔ</u>llœyk/ (pl: -en) roll-down shutter

het **rolmodel** /r<u>ɔ</u>lmodɛl/ (pl: -len) role model

de **rolschaats** /r<u>ɔ</u>lsχats/ (pl: -en) roller skate

rolschaatsen /r<u>ɔ</u>lsχatsə(n)/ (rolschaatste, heeft/is gerolschaatst) roller skate

de **rolschaatser** /r<u>ɔ</u>lsχatsər/ (pl: -s) roller skater

de **rolstoel** /r<u>ɔ</u>lstul/ (pl: -en) wheelchair: *toegankelijk voor* ~*en* with access for wheelchairs

de **roltrap** /r<u>ɔ</u>ltrɑp/ (pl: -pen) escalator, moving staircase

de **rolverdeling** /r<u>ɔ</u>lvərdelɪŋ/ (pl: -en) cast(ing); [fig] division of roles

de **Roma** /r<u>o</u>ma/ (pl) Roma (gypsies)

Romaans /rom<u>a</u>ns/ (adj) **1** Latin: *de* ~*e volken* the Latin peoples **2** Romance, Latin

de **roman** /rom<u>ɑ</u>n/ (pl: -s) novel

de **romance** /rom<u>ɑ</u>sə/ (pl: -s) romance

de **romanschrijver** /rom<u>ɑ</u>nsχrɛivər/ (pl: -s) novelist, fiction writer

de **romanticus** /rom<u>ɑ</u>ntikʏs/ (pl: romantici) romantic

de **romantiek** /rom<u>ɑ</u>ntik/ romance: *een vleugje* ~ a touch of romance

romantisch /rom<u>ɑ</u>ntis/ (adj, adv) romantic

romantiseren /romɑntiz<u>e</u>rə(n)/ (romantiseerde, heeft geromantiseerd) romanticize

Rome /r<u>o</u>mə/ Rome: *het oude* ~ Ancient Rome; *zo oud als de weg naar* ~ as old as the hills

de **Romein** /rom<u>ɛi</u>n/ (pl: -en) Roman

Romeins /rom<u>ɛi</u>ns/ (adj) Roman: *uit de* ~*e oudheid* from Ancient Rome; *het* ~ *recht* Roman law

romig /r<u>o</u>məχ/ (adj) creamy

de **rommel** /r<u>ɔ</u>məl/ **1** mess, shambles: ~ *maken* make a mess **2** junk, rubbish, trash

rommelen /r<u>ɔ</u>mələ(n)/ (rommelde, heeft gerommeld) **1** rumble, roll: *de donder rommelt in de verte* the thunder is rumbling in the distance **2** rummage: *in zijn papieren* ~ shuffle one's papers

rommelig /r<u>ɔ</u>mələχ/ (adj, adv) messy, untidy

de **rommelmarkt** /r<u>ɔ</u>məlmɑrkt/ (pl: -en) flea market, jumble sale

de **romp** /rɔmp/ (pl: -en) **1** trunk; torso **2** shell; hull

de **romper** /r<u>ɔ</u>mpər/ (pl: -s) rompers

de **rompslomp** /r<u>ɔ</u>mpslɔmp/ fuss, bother:

ambtelijke ~ red tape, bureaucracy; *papieren* ~ paperwork

¹**rond** /rɔnt/ (adj, adv) **1** round, circular **2** arranged, fixed (up): *de zaak is* ~ everything is arranged (*or:* fixed) **3** around, about || *een mooi* ~ *bedrag* a nice round figure

²**rond** /rɔnt/ (prep) **1** round; [fig] surrounding: *in de berichtgeving* ~ *de affaire* in the reporting of the affair **2** around, about: ~ *de middag* around midday; ~ *de 2000 betogers* approximately (*or:* about, some) 2000 demonstrators

rondbazuinen /rɔndbazœynə(n)/ (bazuinde rond, heeft rondgebazuind) broadcast, trumpet (around)

rondbrengen /rɔndbrɛŋə(n)/ (bracht rond, heeft rondgebracht) bring round

ronddelen /rɔndelə(n)/ (deelde rond, heeft rondgedeeld) hand round (*or:* around); deal: *wie moet de kaarten* ~? whose deal is it?, who's dealing?

ronddraaien /rɔndrajə(n)/ (draaide rond, heeft/is rondgedraaid) turn (round); spin (round): ~ *in* een cirkel, kringetje go round in circles

ronddwalen /rɔndwalə(n)/ (dwaalde rond, heeft rondgedwaald) wander, wander around

de **ronde** /rɔndə/ (pl: -n) **1** rounds; beat: *de* ~ *doen* go on one's rounds **2** round(s): *de eerste* ~ *van onderhandelingen* the first round of talks; *de praatjes doen de* ~ stories are going around **3** lap, circuit: *laatste* ~ bell lap; *twee* ~*n voor* (*or:* *achter*) *liggen* be two laps ahead (*or:* behind) **4** tour; race: *de* ~ *van Frankrijk* the Tour de France

de **rondetafelconferentie** /rɔndətafəlkɔnfɛrɛn(t)si/ (pl: -s) round-table conference

rondgaan /rɔntxan/ (ging rond, is rondgegaan) **1** go round: ~ *als* een lopend vuurtje spread like wildfire **2** go round, pass round: *laat de schaal nog maar eens* ~ pass the plate round again

de **rondgang** /rɔntxaŋ/ (pl: -en) **1** circuit **2** tour

rondhangen /rɔnthaŋə(n)/ (hing rond, heeft rondgehangen) hang around (*or:* about)

de **ronding** /rɔndɪŋ/ (pl: -en) curve

het **rondje** /rɔncə/ (pl: -s) **1** round: *een* ~ *van de zaak* (a round of) drinks on the house; *hij gaf een* ~ he stood a round (of drinks) **2** [sport] lap; circuit

rondkijken /rɔntkɛikə(n)/ (keek rond, heeft rondgekeken) look round: *goed* ~ *voor je iets koopt* shop around

rondkomen /rɔntkomə(n)/ (kwam rond, is rondgekomen) manage, get by; live: *hij kan er net mee* ~ he can just manage (*or:* get by) on it

rondleiden /rɔntlɛidə(n)/ (leidde rond,

heeft rondgeleid) **1** lead round **2** show round, take round: *mensen in een museum* ~ show (*or:* take) people round a museum

de **rondleiding** /rɔntlɛidɪŋ/ (pl: -en) (guided, conducted) tour

rondlopen /rɔntlopə(n)/ (liep rond, heeft/is rondgelopen) go around, walk around: *je moet daar niet mee blijven* ~ you shouldn't let that weigh (*or:* prey) on your mind

rondneuzen /rɔntnøzə(n)/ (neusde rond, heeft rondgeneusd) nose about, prowl

¹**rondom** /rɔntɔm/ (adv) all round, on all sides: *het plein met de huizen* ~ the square with houses round it

²**rondom** /rɔntɔm/ (prep) (a)round

het **rondpunt** /rɔntpʏnt/ (pl: -en) [Belg] roundabout

de **rondreis** /rɔntrɛis/ (pl: -reizen) tour, circular tour: *op haar* ~ *door de Verenigde Staten* on her tour of America

rondreizen /rɔntrɛizə(n)/ (reisde rond, heeft/is rondgereisd) travel around (*or:* about): *de wereld* ~ travel round the globe (*or:* world)

rondrennen /rɔntrɛnə(n)/ (rende rond, heeft rondgerend) run around, chase about

rondrijden /rɔntrɛidə(n)/ (reed rond, heeft/is rondgereden) go for a drive (*or:* run, ride)

de **rondrit** /rɔntrɪt/ (pl: -ten) tour

rondslingeren /rɔntslɪŋərə(n)/ (slingerde rond, heeft rondgeslingerd) lie about (*or:* around): *zijn boeken laten* ~ leave his books lying around (*or:* about)

rondsturen /rɔntstyrə(n)/ (stuurde rond, heeft rondgestuurd) send round: *circulaires* ~ distribute circulars

de **rondte** /rɔntə/ (pl: -n, -s) circle, round(ness): *in de* ~ *zitten* sit in a circle

rondtrekken /rɔntrɛkə(n)/ (trok rond, heeft/is rondgetrokken) travel (a)round: ~*de seizoenarbeiders* migrant seasonal workers

ronduit /rɔntœyt/ (adv) plain, straight(forward), frank: *het is* ~ *belachelijk* absolutely (*or:* simply) ridiculous; *iem.* ~ *de waarheid zeggen* tell s.o. the plain truth

de **rondvaart** /rɔntfart/ (pl: -en) round trip, circular trip (*or:* tour); cruise: *een* ~ *door de grachten maken* make (*or:* go) for a tour of the canals

de **rondvaartboot** /rɔntfardbot/ (pl: -boten) boat for canal trips

rondvertellen /rɔntfɛrtɛlə(n)/ (vertelde rond, heeft rondverteld) put about, spread about: *hij heeft dat overal rondverteld* he spread (*or:* put) that about everywhere

rondvliegen /rɔntfliɣə(n)/ (vloog rond, heeft/is rondgevlogen) fly about (*or:* around): *geraakt worden door* ~*de kogels* be hit by flying bullets

de **rondvlucht** /rɔntflʏxt/ (pl: -en) round trip (by plane/helicopter): *een* ~ *boven de stad* *maken* go for a round trip over the town

de **rondvraag** /rɔntfraχ/: *iets voor de* ~ *hebben* have sth. for any other business

de **rondweg** /rɔntwɛχ/ (pl: -en) ring road, bypass, relief road: *een* ~ *aanleggen om L.* bypass L.

rondzwerven /rɔntswɛrvə(n)/ (zwierf rond, heeft rondgezworven) roam about, wander about: *op straat* ~ **a)** hang about the streets; **b)** roam the streets

ronken /rɔŋkə(n)/ (ronkte, heeft geronkt) **1** snore **2** throb

ronselen /rɔnsələ(n)/ (ronselde, heeft geronseld) recruit

de **röntgenfoto** /rʏntχə(n)foto/ (pl: -'s) X-ray, roentgenogram, roentgenograph: *een* ~ *laten maken* have an X-ray taken

het **röntgenonderzoek** /rʏntχənɔndərzuk/ X-ray

de **röntgenstralen** /rʏntχə(n)stralə(n)/ (pl) X-rays, roentgen rays

rood /rot/ (adj) red; ginger; ruddy; copper(y); ginger: *met een* ~ *hoofd van de inspanning* flushed with exertion; *iem. de rode kaart tonen* show s.o. the red card; *door* ~ *(licht) rijden* jump the lights; ~ *worden* go red (or: scarlet), flush, blush; *het licht sprong op* ~ the light changed to red; *over de rooie gaan* flip one's lid, lose one's cool ‖ ~ *staan* be in the red; *in het* ~ *(gekleed)* dressed in red

roodbont /rodbɔnt/ (adj) red and white; skewbald

het **roodborstje** /rodbɔrʃə/ (pl: -s) robin (redbreast)

roodbruin /rodbrœyn/ (adj) reddish brown, russet; sorrel: *het* ~ *van herfstbladeren* the russet (colour) of autumn leaves

roodgloeiend /rotχlujənt/ (adj) red-hot: *de telefoon staat* ~ the telephone hasn't stopped ringing

roodharig /rodharəχ/ (adj) red-haired, red-headed

de **roodhuid** /rodhœyt/ (pl: -en) redskin

Roodkapje /rotkɑpjə/ Little Red Riding Hood

de **roodvonk** /rotfɔŋk/ scarlet fever

de **roof** /rof/ (pl: roven) **1** robbery: *op* ~ *uitgaan* commit robbery **2** preying, hunting

de **roofbouw** /rovbɑu/ exhaustion, overuse: ~ *plegen op zijn gezondheid* undermine one's health; ~ *plegen op zijn lichaam* wear o.s. out

het **roofdier** /rovdir/ (pl: -en) animal (or: beast) of prey, predator

de **roofmoord** /rofmort/ (pl: -en) robbery with murder

de **roofoverval** /rofovərvɑl/ (pl: -len) robbery, hold-up: *een* ~ *plegen op een juwelierszaak* rob a jeweller's

de **rooftocht** /roftɔχt/ (pl: -en) raid

de **roofvogel** /rofoɣəl/ (pl: -s) bird of prey

rooien /rojə(n)/ (rooide, heeft gerooid) dig

up; lift, raise; uproot: *een bos* ~ clear a wood (or: forest)

de **rook** /rok/ smoke; fume(s): *men kan er de* ~ *snijden* it's thick with smoke in here; *in* ~ *opgaan* go up in smoke; *onder de* ~ *van de stad wonen* live a stone's throw from the town; *waar* ~ *is, is vuur* there's no smoke without fire

de **rookbom** /rogbɔm/ (pl: -men) smoke bomb

het **rookgordijn** /rokχɔrdɛin/ (pl: -en) smoke-screen: *een* ~ *leggen* put up (or: lay) a smokescreen

het **rookkanaal** /rokanal/ (pl: -kanalen) flue

de **rooklucht** /roklʏχt/ smell of smoke

de **rookmelder** /rokmɛldər/ (pl: -s) smoke alarm, smoke detector

de **rookpaal** [roughly] pillar indicating 'smoking zone' on a railway platform

de **rookpauze** /rokpɑuzə/ (pl: -s) cigarette break: *een* ~ *inlassen* take a break for a cigarette

de **rookschade** /roksχadə/ smoke damage

het **rooksignaal** /roksɪnal/ (pl: -signalen) smoke signal

het **rookverbod** /rokfɛrbɔt/ ban on smoking

het **rookvlees** /rokfles/ [roughly] smoke-dried beef (or: meat)

rookvrij /rokfrɛi/ (adj) no(n)-smoking: *een* ~ *gebouw* a non-smoking building, a smoke-free building

de **rookwolk** /rokwɔlk/ (pl: -en) cloud (or: pall) of smoke

de **rookworst** /rokwɔrst/ (pl: -en) [roughly] smoked sausage

de **room** /rom/ cream: *dikke* ~ double cream; *zure* ~ sour cream

de **roomboter** /rombotər/ butter

het **roomijs** /romɛis/ ice cream

de **roomkaas** /romkas/ (pl: -kazen) cream cheese

rooms /roms/ (adj) Roman Catholic

Rooms /roms/ (adj) Roman

de **roomsaus** /romsɑus/ (pl: -sauzen) cream sauce

het **rooms-katholicisme** /romskɑtolisɪsmə/ Roman Catholicism

rooms-katholiek /romskɑtolik/ (adj) Roman Catholic

de **roomsoes** /romsus/ (pl: -soezen) cream puff

de **roos** /ros/ (pl: rozen) **1** rose: [fig] *op rozen zitten* lie on a bed of roses **2** bull's-eye: *in de* ~ *schieten* score a bull's-eye; *(midden) in de* ~ bang in the middle **3** dandruff

rooskleurig /rosklørəχ/ (adj, adv) rosy, rose-coloured: *een* ~*e toekomst* a rosy (or: bright) future

het/de **rooster** /rostər/ (pl: -s) **1** grid, grating, grate; grille; gridiron: *het* ~ *van de kachel* the stove grate; [Belg] *iem. op het* ~ *leggen* grill s.o. **2** grid **3** schedule; timetable, roster: *een* ~ *opstellen (opmaken)* draw up a roster (or:

roosteren

426

rota)
roosteren /r̪o̪stərə(n)/ (roosterde, heeft geroosterd) **1** grill, roast, broil **2** toast
het **ros** /rɔs/ (pl: -sen) steed
de **rosbief** /rɔzbif/ roast beef
de **rosé** /roze̪/ rosé (wine)
rossig /rɔsəx/ (adj) reddish, ruddy; sandy
rot /rɔt/ (adj) **1** rotten, bad; decayed; putrid: *door en door ~, zo ~ als een mispel* rotten to the core **2** rotten, lousy, wretched: *zich ~ lachen* split one's sides laughing; *zij schrok zich ~* she got the fright of her life, she was scared out of her wits; *zich ~ vervelen* be bored to tears
het/de **rotan** /ro̪tɑn/ rattan
de **rotatie** /rota̪(t)si/ (pl: -s) rotation, revolution
het **rotding** /rɔdɪŋ/ [inform] damn thing, bloody thing
roteren /rote̪rə(n)/ (roteerde, heeft geroteerd) rotate: *een ~de beweging* a rotary motion
het **rotje** /rɔcə/ (pl: -s) (fire)cracker, squib, banger
het **rotjong** /rɔtjɔŋ/ [inform] brat, little pest
de **rotonde** /rotɔndə/ (pl: -s) roundabout
de **rotopmerking** /rɔtopmɛrkɪŋ/ (pl: -en) nasty remark
de **rotor** /ro̪tɔr/ (pl: -s) rotor
de **rots** /rɔts/ (pl: -en) rock, cliff; crag: *als een ~ in de branding* as steady as a rock; *het schip liep op de ~en* the ship struck the rocks
rotsachtig /rɔtsɑxtəx/ (adj) rocky, rugged
het **rotsblok** /rɔtsblɔk/ (pl: -ken) boulder
de **rotskust** /rɔtskʏst/ rocky coast
de **rotstreek** /rɔtstrek/ (pl: rotstreken) dirty trick, mean trick: *iem. een ~ leveren* play a dirty trick on s.o.
de **rotstuin** /rɔtstœyn/ (pl: -en) rock garden, rockery
rotsvast /rɔtsfɑst/ (adj, adv) rock-solid, rocklike: *een ~e overtuiging* a deep-rooted conviction
de **rotswand** /rɔtswɑnt/ (pl: -en) rock face, cliff face
rotten /rɔtə(n)/ (rotte, heeft/is gerot) rot, decay: *~d hout* rotting wood
rottig /rɔtəx/ (adj, adv) [inform] rotten, nasty
de **rottigheid** /rɔtəxhɛit/ [inform] misery, wretchedness
de **rottweiler** /rɔtwɑjlər/ (pl: -s) Rottweiler
de **rotvent** /rɔtfɛnt/ (pl: -en) [inform] bastard, jerk
het **rotweer** /rɔtwer/ [inform] awful weather
de **rotzak** /rɔtsɑk/ (pl: -ken) [inform] bastard, jerk
de **rotzooi** /rɔtsoj/ [inform] **1** (piece of) junk, trash **2** mess, shambles
rotzooien /rɔtsojə(n)/ (rotzooide, heeft gerotzooid) [inform] **1** mess about: *~ met de boekhouding* tamper with the accounts, cook

the books **2** fool around
het/de **rouge** /ruːʒə/ rouge, blusher
de **roulatie** /rula(t)si/ circulation: *in ~ brengen* bring into circulation [film]
rouleren /rule̪rə(n)/ (rouleerde, heeft gerouleerd) **1** circulate, be in circulation **2** rotate, take turns; work in shifts
de **roulette** /rulɛtə/ (pl: -s) roulette (table)
de **route** /rutə/ (pl: -s) route, way; round
de **routekaart** /rutəkart/ (pl: -en) **1** key map **2** road-map
de **routeplanner** /rutəplɛnər/ (pl: -s) route planner
de **routine** /rutinə/ **1** practice, skill, knack **2** routine, grind: *de dagelijkse ~* the daily grind
de **routineklus** /rutinəklʏs/ routine job
routinematig /rutinəmatəx/ (adj) routine
het **routineonderzoek** /rutinəondərzuk/ (pl: -en) routine check-up
routineus /rutinøs/ (adj) routine
de **rouw** /rau/ mourning; sorrow; grief: *in de ~ zijn* be in mourning; *in ~ dompelen* plunge into mourning
de **rouwadvertentie** /rɑuɑtfərtɛn(t)si/ (pl: -s) death announcement
de **rouwband** /rɑubɑnt/ (pl: -en) mourning band, black armband
rouwen /rɑuwə(n)/ (rouwde, heeft gerouwd) mourn, grieve
rouwig /rɑuwəx/ (adj) regretful, sorry: *ergens niet ~ om zijn* not regret sth.
de **rouwkrans** /rɑukrɑns/ funeral wreath
de **rouwstoet** /rɑustut/ (pl: -en) funeral procession
roven /rovə(n)/ (roofde, heeft geroofd) steal, rob
de **rover** /rovər/ (pl: -s) robber
royaal /rojal/ (adj, adv) **1** generous, open-handed: *een royale beloning* a handsome (*or:* generous) reward **2** spacious, ample: *een royale meerderheid* a comfortable majority
royeren /rwɑjerə(n)/ (royeerde, heeft geroyeerd) expel (from)
roze /rɔːzə/ (adj) pink, rose
de **rozemarijn** /rozəmɑrɛin/ rosemary
de **rozenbottel** /rozə(n)bɔtəl/ (pl: -s) rose hip
de **rozengeur** /rozə(n)ɣør/ smell (*or:* scent) of roses: *het is er niet alleen ~ en maneschijn* it's not all sweetness and light there
de **rozenkrans** /rozə(n)krɑns/ (pl: -en) rosary: *de ~ bidden* say the rosary
de **rozenstruik** /rozə(n)strœyk/ (pl: -en) rose bush
rozig /rozəx/ (adj) languid
de **rozijn** /rozɛin/ (pl: -en) raisin
RSI /ɛrɛsi/ RSI
het/de **rubber** /rʏbər/ rubber
de **rubberboot** /rʏbərbot/ (pl: -boten) (rubber) dinghy
rubberen /rʏbərə(n)/ (adj) rubber

de **rubberlaars** /rʏbərlars/ rubber boot, wellington

rubriceren /rybrisẹrə(n)/ (rubriceerde, heeft gerubriceerd) class, classify

de **rubriek** /rybrik/ (pl: -en) **1** column, feature, section: *de advertentierubriek(en)* the advertising columns **2** section, group

de **ruchtbaarheid** /rʏχtbarhɛɪt/ publicity: *~ aan iets geven* give publicity to sth.

rücksichtslos /rʏksɪχ(t)slos/ (adj, adv) unscrupulous, thoughtless

de **rucola** /rykola/ (pl: -'s) rocket; [Am] arugula

rudimentair /rydimɛntɛːr/ (adj, adv) rudimentary

de **rug** /rʏχ/ (pl: -gen) back: *iem. de ~ toekeren* turn one's back on s.o.; *achter de ~ van iem. kwaadspreken* talk about s.o. behind his back; *ik zal blij zijn als het achter de ~ is* I'll be glad to get it over and done with; *hij heeft een moeilijke tijd achter de ~* he had a difficult time; *het (geld) groeit mij niet op de ~* I am not made of money; *een duwtje* (or: *steuntje*) *in de ~* a bit of encouragement (or: support), a helping hand, a leg up; *met de ~ tegen de muur* with one's back to the wall

het **rugby** /rʏgbi/ rugby

rugbyen /rʏɣbijə(n)/ (rugbyde, heeft gerugbyd) play rugby (or: rugger)

de **rugdekking** /rʏɣdɛkɪŋ/ backing: *iem. ~ geven* [sport] cover a team-mate; [fig] back s.o.

ruggelings /rʏɣəlɪŋs/ (adv) **1** back to back **2** backward(s)

de **ruggengraat** /rʏɣə(n)ɣrat/ (pl: -graten) backbone, spine

het **ruggenmerg** /rʏɣə(n)mɛrχ/ spinal marrow (or: cord)

de **ruggensteun** /rʏɣə(n)støn/ (pl: -en) **1** back support **2** backing, support: *iem. ~ geven* give s.o. backing

de **ruggespraak** /rʏɣəsprak/ consultation: *~ met iem. houden* consult s.o.

de **rugklachten** /rʏχklaχtə(n)/ (pl) back trouble, backache

de **rugleuning** /rʏχlønɪŋ/ (pl: -en) back (of a chair)

het **rugnummer** /rʏχnʏmər/ (pl: -s) (player's) number

de **rugpijn** /rʏχpɛɪn/ pain in the back, backache

de **rugslag** /rʏχslɑχ/ backstroke, back-crawl

de **rugwind** /rʏχwɪnt/ (pl: -en) tail wind, following wind

de **rugzak** /rʏχsɑk/ (pl: -ken) rucksack, backpack

rugzwemmen /rʏχswɛmə(n)/ swim backstroke

de **rui** /rœy/ **1** moult(ing) **2** [Belg] covered canal, roofed-over canal

ruien /rœyə(n)/ (ruide, heeft geruid) moult, shed one's feathers

de **ruif** /rœyf/ (pl: ruiven) rack

ruig /rœyχ/ (adj) **1** rough: *een ~ feest* a rowdy party **2** shaggy, hairy

¹**ruiken** /rœykə(n)/ (rook, heeft geroken) **1** smell: *aan iets ~* have a smell (or: sniff) at sth. **2** smell, stink, reek

²**ruiken** /rœykə(n)/ (rook, heeft geroken) [also fig] smell, scent: *onraad ~* scent (or: sense) danger; *hoe kon ik dat nu ~!* how could I possibly know!

de **ruiker** /rœykər/ (pl: -s) posy, bouquet

de **ruil** /rœyl/ (pl: -en) exchange, swap

¹**ruilen** /rœylə(n)/ (ruilde, heeft geruild) change: *ik zou niet met hem willen ~* I would not change places with him

²**ruilen** /rœylə(n)/ (ruilde, heeft geruild) exchange, swap

de **ruilhandel** /rœylhɑndəl/ barter (trade): *~ drijven* barter

het **ruilmiddel** /rœylmɪdəl/ (pl: -en) means (or: medium) of exchange

de **ruilverkaveling** /rœylvərkavəlɪŋ/ (pl: -en) land consolidation

het ¹**ruim** /rœym/ (pl: -en) hold

²**ruim** /rœym/ (adj, adv) **1** spacious, large; roomy: *een ~ assortiment* a large assortment; *~ wonen* live spaciously **2** free: *~ baan maken* make way; *in de ~ste zin* in the broadest sense **3** wide, roomy, loose: *die jas zit ~* that coat is loose-fitting **4** ample, liberal: *een ~e meerderheid* a big majority

³**ruim** /rœym/ (adv) (rather) more than, sth. over, well over: *~ een uur* well over an hour; *dat is ~ voldoende* that is amply sufficient

ruimdenkend /rœymdɛŋkənt/ (adj) broad(-minded)

ruimen /rœymə(n)/ (ruimde, heeft geruimd) **1** clear out **2** clear away

ruimhartig /rœymhɑrtəχ/ (adj) generous, warm-hearted

ruimschoots /rœymsχots/ (adv) amply, plentifully: *~ de tijd* (or: *gelegenheid*) *hebben* have ample time (or: opportunity); *~ op tijd aankomen* arrive in ample time

de **ruimte** /rœymtə/ (pl: -n, -s) room; space: *wegens gebrek aan ~* for lack of room (or: space); *de begrippen ~ en tijd* the concepts of time and space; *te weinig ~ hebben* be cramped for space; *~ uitsparen* save space; *iem. de ~ geven* give s.o. elbow room

het **ruimtegebrek** /rœymtəɣəbrɛk/ lack (or: shortage) of space

het **ruimtelaboratorium** /rœymtəlaboratorijʏm/ (pl: -laboratoria) spacelab

ruimtelijk /rœymtələk/ (adj, adv) **1** spatial, spacial, space: *~e ordening* environmental (or: town and country) planning **2** three-dimensional: *~ inzicht hebben* have good spatial skills

het **ruimtepak** /rœymtəpɑk/ (pl: -ken) space suit

het **ruimteschip** /rœymtəsχɪp/ (pl: -schepen) spacecraft

het **ruimtestation** /rœymtəsta(t)ʃɔn/ (pl: -s)
space station

de **ruimtevaarder** /rœymtəvardər/ (pl: -s)
spaceman, astronaut

de **ruimtevaart** /rœymtəvart/ space travel

het **ruimtevaartuig** /rœymtəvartœyχ/ (pl: -en)
spacecraft

het **ruimteveer** /rœymtəver/ (pl: -veren)
(space) shuttle

de **ruin** /rœyn/ (pl: -en) gelding

de **ruïne** /rywinə/ (pl: -s) ruins, ruin; [pers]
wreck

ruïneren /rywinɣrə(n)/ (ruïneerde, heeft
geruïneerd) ruin

de **ruis** /rœys/ noise; murmur

ruisen /rœysə(n)/ (ruiste, heeft geruist) rustle; gurgle

de **ruit** /rœyt/ (pl: -en) **1** (window)pane, window **2** diamond; check

de ¹**ruiten** /rœytə(n)/ diamonds: *ruitenvrouw*
queen of diamonds; *ruitenboer* jack (*or:*
knave) of diamonds; ~ *is troef* diamonds are
trumps

²**ruiten** /rœytə(n)/ (adj) check(ed), chequered

de **ruitensproeier** /rœytə(n)sprujər/ (pl: -s)
screenwasher; [Am] windshield washer

de **ruitenwisser** /rœytə(n)wɪsər/ (pl: -s) windscreen wiper, wiper

de **ruiter** /rœytər/ (pl: -s) horseman, rider

de **ruiterij** /rœytərɛi/ cavalry, horse

ruiterlijk /rœytərlək/ (adj, adv) frank: *iets ~
toegeven* admit sth. frankly

het **ruiterpad** /rœytərpat/ (pl: -en) bridle path

de **ruitersport** /rœytərsport/ equestrian
sport(s), riding

het **ruitjespapier** /rœycəspapir/ squared paper

de ¹**ruk** /rʏk/ (pl: -ken) **1** jerk, tug **2** gust (of
wind) **3** distance, way **4** time, spell: *in één ~
doorwerken* work on at one stretch; [inform]
dat kan me geen ~ schelen I don't give a damn

²**ruk** (adj) [inform] the pits, crappy

¹**rukken** /rʏkə(n)/ (rukte, heeft gerukt) jerk
(at), tug (at)

²**rukken** /rʏkə(n)/ (rukte, heeft gerukt) tear,
wrench: *iem. de kleren van het lijf ~* tear the
clothes from s.o.'s body

de **rukwind** /rʏkwɪnt/ (pl: -en) squall, gust (of
wind)

rul /rʏl/ (adj) loose, sandy

de **rum** /rʏm/ rum

de **rumboon** /rʏmbon/ (pl: rumbonen) rum
bonbon

de **rum-cola** /rʏmkola/ rum and coke

het **rumoer** /rymur/ (pl: -en) noise; din; racket;
row: ~ *maken* make a noise

rumoerig /rymurəχ/ (adj) noisy

de **run** /rʏn/ (pl: -s) run: *er was een ~ op die bank*
there was a run on that bank

het **rund** /rʏnt/ (pl: -eren) **1** cow; cattle; ox
2 cow; bull; cattle **3** idiot, fool: *een ~ van een
vent* a prize idiot ‖ *bloeden als een ~* bleed like

a pig

het **rundergehakt** /rʏndərɣəhakt/ minced
beef, mince

de **runderlap** /rʏndərlap/ (pl: -pen) braising
steak

de **runderrollade** /rʏndərɔladə/ collared beef,
rolled beef

het **rundvee** /rʏntfe/ cattle: *twintig stuks ~*
twenty head of cattle

het **rundvlees** /rʏntfles/ beef

de **rune** /rynə/ (pl: -n) rune

runnen /rʏnə(n)/ (runde, heeft gerund) run,
manage: *hij runt het bedrijf in z'n eentje* he
runs the company all by himself

de **running** /rʏnɪŋ/: *in de ~ zijn voor …* be in the
running for …; *uit de ~ zijn* be out of the
running

de **rups** /rʏps/ (pl: -en) caterpillar

de **rupsband** /rʏpsbant/ (pl: -en) caterpillar
(track)

het **rupsvoertuig** /rʏpsfurtœyχ/ (pl: -en) caterpillar

de **Rus** /rʏs/ (pl: -sen) Russian

Rusland /rʏslant/ Russia

de **Russin** /rʏsɪn/ (pl: -nen) *see Rus*

Russisch /rʏsis/ (adj) Russian ‖ *een ~ ei* egg
mayonnaise; ~ *roulette* Russian roulette

de **rust** /rʏst/ **1** rest; relaxation **2** rest; lie-down
3 quiet: *gun hem wat ~* give him a break;
nooit (geen ogenblik) ~ hebben never have a
moment's peace; *wat ~ nemen* take a break;
laat me met ~! leave me alone!; *tot ~ komen*
settle (*or:* calm) (down) **4** (peace and) quiet;
still(ness): *alles was in diepe ~* all was quiet
5 [sport] half-time, interval

de **rustdag** /rʏzdaχ/ (pl: -en) rest day; day off;
holiday

rusteloos /rʏstəlos/ (adj, adv) restless

rusten /rʏstə(n)/ (rustte, heeft gerust)
1 rest, relax, take (*or:* have) a rest: *even ~
have* (*or:* take) a break **2** rest, sleep: *hij ligt te
~* he is resting **3** rest, pause **4** weigh; be burdened (*or:* encumbered) with: *op hem rust
een zware verdenking* he is under strong suspicion ‖ *we moeten het verleden laten ~* we've
got to let bygones be bygones

rustgevend /rʏstχevənt/ (adj) **1** comfort-
ing **2** restful, calming

het **rusthuis** /rʏsthœys/ (pl: -huizen) rest home

rustiek /rʏstik/ (adj) rural; pastoral

¹**rustig** /rʏstəχ/ (adj, adv) **1** peaceful, quiet
2 calm, still: *het water is ~* the water's calm
3 steady: *een ~e ademhaling* even breathing
4 calm: ~ *weer* calm weather; ~ *antwoorden*
answer calmly; *zich ~ houden* keep calm; *hij
komt ~ een uur te laat* he quite happily (*or:*
cheerfully) comes an hour late; *ze zat ~ te lezen* she sat quietly reading; *het ~ aan doen*
take it easy **5** quiet; smooth; uneventful:
daar kan ik ~ studeren I can study there in
peace; *het is hier lekker ~* it's nice and quiet

here

²rustig /rʏstəχ/ (adv) safely: *je kunt me ~ bellen* feel free to call me; *dat mag je ~ weten* I don't mind if you know that

de **rustplaats** /rʏstplats/ (pl: -en) resting place: *de laatste ~* the final resting place; *naar zijn laatste ~ brengen* lay to rest

het **rustpunt** /rʏstpʏnt/ (pl: -en) pause; period

de **ruststand** /rʏstɑnt/ (pl: -en) [sport] half-time score

de **rustverstoring** /rʏstfərstorɪŋ/ disturbance

ruw /ryw/ (adj, adv) **1** rough: *een ~e plank* a rough plank; *een ~e schets* a rough draft; *een ~ spel* a rough game; *iets ~ afbreken* break sth. off abruptly; *iem. ~ behandelen* treat s.o. roughly **2** raw, crude; rough-hewn: *~e olie* crude oil

ruwweg /rywɛχ/ (adv) roughly: *~ geschat* at a rough estimate (*or:* guess)

de **ruzie** /ryzi/ (pl: -s) quarrel, argument: *slaande ~ hebben* have a blazing row; *een ~ bijleggen* patch up a quarrel; *~ krijgen met iem.* have an argument with s.o.; *~ zoeken* look for trouble (*or:* a fight); *~ hebben met iem.* (or: *om iets*) quarrel with s.o. (*or:* over sth.)

ruziën /ryzijə(n)/ (ruziede, heeft geruzied) quarrel

de **ruziezoeker** /ryzizukər/ (pl: -s) quarrelsome person

Rwanda /ruwɑnda/ Rwanda

de **¹Rwandees** /ruwɑndes/ (pl: Rwandezen) Rwandan

²Rwandees /ruwɑndes/ (adj) Rwandan

S

de **s** /ɛs/ (pl: s'en) s, S
saai /saj/ (adj, adv) boring, dull
de **saamhorigheid** /samhorəxhɛɪt/ solidarity
de **sabbat** /sɑbɑt/ (pl: -ten) sabbath
het **sabbatical year** /səbɛtɪkəljɪr/ sabbatical year
sabbelen /sɑbələ(n)/ (sabbelde, heeft gesabbeld) suck: ~ *aan een lolly* suck a lollipop
de **sabel** /sabəl/ sabre
de **sabotage** /sabotaʒə/ sabotage
saboteren /sabotɛrə(n)/ (saboteerde, heeft gesaboteerd) **1** commit sabotage (on) **2** sabotage, undermine
de **saboteur** /sabotør/ (pl: -s) saboteur
het **sacrament** /sɑkramɛnt/ (pl: -en) sacrament
de **sacristie** /sɑkrɪsti/ (pl: -ën) sacristy
het **sadisme** /sadɪsmə/ sadism
de **sadist** /sadɪst/ (pl: -en) sadist
sadistisch /sadɪstis/ (adj, adv) sadistic
het **sadomasochisme** /sadomasoχɪsmə/ sadomasochism
de **safari** /safari/ (pl: -'s) safari: *op ~ gaan* go on safari
de **safe** /sef/ (pl: -s) safe, safe-deposit box
de **¹saffier** /sɑfir/ (pl: -en) [gem] sapphire
het **²saffier** /sɑfir/ [mineral] sapphire
de **saffraan** /sɑfran/ saffron
de **sage** /saɣə/ (pl: -n) legend
de **Sahara** /sahara/ Sahara
saillant /sɑjɑnt/ (adj, adv) salient
Saksisch /sɑksis/ (adj) Saxon
de **salade** /saladə/ (pl: -s) salad
de **salamander** /salamɑndər/ (pl: -s) salamander
de **salami** /salami/ salami
de **salariëring** /salarijerɪŋ/ payment
het **salaris** /salɑrɪs/ (pl: -sen) salary, pay
de **salarisschaal** /salɑrɪsχal/ (pl: -schalen) salary scale
de **salarisverhoging** /salɑrɪsfərhoɣɪŋ/ (pl: -en) (salary) increase, (pay) rise
het **saldo** /sɑldo/ (pl: -'s, saldi) balance: *een positief ~* a credit balance; *een negatief ~* a deficit; *per ~* on balance
het **saldotekort** /sɑldotəkɔrt/ (pl: -en) deficit; overdraft
de **salesmanager** /sɛlsmɛnədʒər/ (pl: -s) sales manager
de **salie** /sali/ sage
de **salmiak** /sɑlmijɑk/ salty liquorice powder
de **salmonella** /sɑlmonɛla/ salmonella
het **salomonsoordeel** /salomɔnsordel/ (pl: -oordelen) judgment of Solomon

het/de **salon** /salɔn/ (pl: -s) drawing room, salon
salonfähig /salɔnfɛjiχ/ (adj) socially acceptable
de **salontafel** /salɔntafəl/ (pl: -s) coffee table
het **salpeterzuur** /sɑlpetərzyr/ nitric acid
de **salto** /sɑlto/ (pl: -'s) somersault
salueren /salywɛrə(n)/ (salueerde, heeft gesalueerd) salute
het **saluut** /salyt/ salute
het **saluutschot** /salytsχɔt/ (pl: -schoten) salute
het **salvo** /sɑlvo/ (pl: -'s) salvo, volley
Samaritaan /samaritan/ (pl: Samaritanen) Samaritan ‖ *de barmhartige ~* the good Samaritan
de **samba** /sɑmba/ (pl: -'s) samba
de **sambal** /sɑmbɑl/ sambal
samen /samə(n)/ (adv) **1** together; in chorus: *zij hebben ~ een kamer* they share a room **2** with each other, with one another: *het ~ goed kunnen vinden* get on well (together) **3** in all, altogether: *~ is dat 21 euro* that makes 21 euros altogether (*or:* in all)
samenbrengen /samə(n)brɛŋə(n)/ (bracht samen, heeft samengebracht) bring together
samendrukken /samə(n)drʏkə(n)/ (drukte samen, heeft samengedrukt) compress
samengaan /samə(n)ɣan/ (ging samen, is samengegaan) go together, go hand in hand: *niet ~ met* not go (together) with
samengesteld /samə(n)ɣəstɛlt/ (adj) compound
de **samenhang** /samə(n)hɑŋ/ connection
samenhangen /samə(n)hɑŋə(n)/ (hing samen, heeft samengehangen) be connected, be linked: *dat hangt samen met het klimaat* that has to do with the climate
samenhangend /samə(n)hɑŋənt/ (adj, adv) related, connected: *een hiermee ~ probleem* a related problem
samenknijpen /samə(n)knɛɪpə(n)/ (kneep samen, heeft samengeknepen) squeeze together; screw up
samenkomen /samə(n)komə(n)/ (kwam samen, is samengekomen) come together, meet (together); converge (on)
de **samenkomst** /samə(n)kɔmst/ (pl: -en) meeting
samenleven /samə(n)levə(n)/ (leefde samen, heeft samengeleefd) live together
de **samenleving** /samə(n)levɪŋ/ society: *de huidige ~* modern society
het **samenlevingscontract** /samə(n)levɪŋskɔntrɑkt/ (pl: -en) cohabitation agreement
de **samenloop** /samə(n)lop/ concurrence, conjunction: *een ~ van omstandigheden* a combination of circumstances
samenpersen /samə(n)pɛrsə(n)/ (perste samen, heeft samengeperst) compress, press together

het **samenraapsel** /s<u>a</u>mə(n)rapsəl/ (pl: -s) pack; ragbag

samenscholen /s<u>a</u>mə(n)sχolə(n)/ (schoolde samen, heeft/is samengeschoold) assemble

de **samenscholing** /s<u>a</u>mə(n)sχolɪŋ/ (pl: -en) gathering, assembly

samensmelten /s<u>a</u>mə(n)smɛltə(n)/ (smolt samen, is samengesmolten) fuse (together)

samenspannen /s<u>a</u>mə(n)spɑnə(n)/ (spande samen, heeft/is samengespannen) conspire, plot (together)

het **samenspel** /s<u>a</u>mə(n)spɛl/ combined action (or: play); teamwork

het **samenstel** /s<u>a</u>mə(n)stɛl/ composition, system

samenstellen /s<u>a</u>mə(n)stɛlə(n)/ (stelde samen, heeft samengesteld) **1** put together, make up, compose: *samengesteld zijn uit* be made up (or: composed) of **2** draw up, compose; compile

de **samensteller** /s<u>a</u>mə(n)stɛlər/ (pl: -s) compiler; composer

de **samenstelling** /s<u>a</u>mə(n)stɛlɪŋ/ (pl: -en) **1** composition, make-up **2** [linguistics] compound

samentrekken /s<u>a</u>mə(n)trɛkə(n)/ (trok samen, is samengetrokken) contract, shrink

samenvallen /s<u>a</u>mə(n)vɑlə(n)/ (viel samen, is samengevallen) coincide (with); correspond: *gedeeltelijk* ~ overlap

samenvatten /s<u>a</u>mə(n)vɑtə(n)/ (vatte samen, heeft samengevat) summarize, sum up: *kort samengevat* (to put it) in a nutshell; *iets in een paar woorden* ~ sum sth. up in a few words

de **samenvatting** /s<u>a</u>mə(n)vɑtɪŋ/ (pl: -en) summary; highlights

samenvoegen /s<u>a</u>mə(n)vuχə(n)/ (voegde samen, heeft samengevoegd) join (together)

samenwerken /s<u>a</u>mə(n)wɛrkə(n)/ (werkte samen, heeft samengewerkt) cooperate, work together: *gaan* ~ join forces (with); *nauw* ~ cooperate closely

de **samenwerking** /s<u>a</u>mə(n)wɛrkɪŋ/ cooperation, teamwork: *in nauwe* ~ *met* in close collaboration with

samenwonen /s<u>a</u>mə(n)wonə(n)/ (woonde samen, heeft samengewoond) **1** live together, cohabit **2** live (together) with, share a house (or: flat)

het **samenzijn** /s<u>a</u>mə(n)zɛɪn/ gathering

de **samenzweerder** /s<u>a</u>mə(n)zwerdər/ (pl: -s) conspirator

samenzweren /s<u>a</u>mə(n)zwerə(n)/ (zwoer samen, heeft samengezworen) conspire, plot: *tegen iem.* ~ conspire (or: plot) against s.o.

de **samenzwering** /s<u>a</u>mə(n)zwerɪŋ/ (pl: -en) conspiracy, plot

samsam /sɑmsɑm/ (adv) [inform] fifty-fifty: ~ *doen* go halves (with s.o.)

het **sanatorium** /sanat<u>o</u>rijʏm/ (pl: sanatoria) sanatorium

de **sanctie** /s<u>ɑ</u>ŋksi/ (pl: -s) sanction: ~*s opleggen aan* impose sanctions against (or: on); ~*s verbinden aan* apply sanctions to

sanctioneren /sɑŋkʃonᵉrə(n)/ (sanctioneerde, heeft gesanctioneerd) sanction

de **sandaal** /sɑnd<u>a</u>l/ (pl: sandalen) sandal

de **sandwich** /s<u>ɛ</u>ntwɪtʃ/ (pl: -es) **1** sandwich **2** [Belg] bridge roll

saneren /san<u>e</u>rə(n)/ (saneerde, heeft gesaneerd) **1** put in order, see to: *zijn gebit laten* ~ have one's teeth seen to **2** reorganize, redevelop: *de binnenstad* ~ redevelop the town centre

de **sanering** /san<u>e</u>rɪŋ/ **1** [roughly] course of dental treatment **2** reorganization; redevelopment; clean-up (operation)

het ¹**sanitair** /sanit<u>ɛ</u>r/ sanitary fittings, bathroom fixtures

²**sanitair** /sanit<u>ɛ</u>r/ (adj) sanitary: ~*e artikelen* bathroom equipment; ~*e voorzieningen* toilet facilities

het **Sanskriet** /sɑnskr<u>i</u>t/ Sanskrit: *dat is* ~ *voor hem* that is Greek to him

de **santenkraam** /s<u>ɑ</u>ntə(n)kram/: *de hele* ~ the whole lot (or: caboodle); [Am] the whole shebang (or: enchilada)

het **sap** /sɑp/ (pl: -pen) juice; sap; fluid: *het* ~ *uit een citroen knijpen* squeeze the juice from a lemon

de **sapcentrifuge** /s<u>ɑ</u>psɛntrify:ʒə/ (pl: -s) juice extractor, juicer

het **sapje** /s<u>ɑ</u>pjə/ (pl: -s) (fruit) juice

de **sappel** /s<u>ɑ</u>pəl/ [inform]: *zich (te)* ~ *maken over iets* worry about sth.

sappelen /s<u>ɑ</u>pələ(n)/ (sappelde, heeft gesappeld) slave (or: slog) (away), drudge

sappig /s<u>ɑ</u>pəχ/ (adj) juicy: ~ *vlees* juicy (or: succulent) meat

het **sarcasme** /sɑrk<u>ɑ</u>smə/ (pl: -n) sarcasm

sarcastisch /sɑrk<u>ɑ</u>stis/ (adj, adv) sarcastic: ~*e opmerkingen* snide remarks

de **sarcofaag** /sɑrkof<u>a</u>χ/ (pl: -fagen) sarcophagus

de **sardine** /sɑrd<u>i</u>nə/ (pl: -s) sardine

Sardinië /sɑrd<u>i</u>nijə/ Sardinia

de **sarong** /s<u>a</u>rɔŋ/ (pl: -s) sarong

sarren /s<u>ɑ</u>rə(n)/ (sarde, heeft gesard) bait, (deliberately) provoke, needle

de **sas** /sɑs/: *hij is zeer in zijn* ~ *met zijn nieuwe auto* he's delighted (or: over the moon, very pleased) with his new car

de **satan** /s<u>a</u>tɑn/ (pl: -s) devil, fiend

Satan /s<u>a</u>tɑn/ Satan

satanisch /sat<u>a</u>nis/ (adj, adv) satanic(al), diabolic: *een* ~*e blik* (or: *lach*) a fiendish look (or: laugh)

de **saté** /sat<u>e</u>/ satay

de **satelliet** /satəl<u>i</u>t/ (pl: -en) satellite

de **satellietschotel** /satəlitsχotəl/ satellite dish

de **satellietstaat** /satəlitstat/ (pl: -staten) satellite (state)

de **satellietverbinding** /satəlitfərbɪndɪŋ/ (pl: -en) satellite link(-up)

de **satésaus** /satesaus/ (pl: -sauzen) satay sauce

het **satéstokje** /satestɔkjə/ (pl: -s) skewer

het **satijn** /satɛin/ (pl: -en) satin

satijnen /satɛinə(n)/ (adj) satin

de **satire** /satirə/ (pl: -s) satire: *een ~ schrijven op* satirize, write a satire on

satirisch /satiris/ (adj, adv) satiric(al)

Saturnus /satʏrnʏs/ Saturn

de **saucijs** /sosɛis/ (pl: saucijzen) sausage

het **saucijzenbroodje** /sosɛizə(n)brocə/ (pl: -s) sausage roll

Saudi-Arabië /saudiarabijə/ Saudi Arabia

Saudi-Arabisch /saudiarabis/ (adj) Saudi (Arabian)

de **Saudiër** /saudijər/ (pl: -s) Saudi (Arabian)

Saudisch /saudis/ (adj) Saudi (Arabian)

de **sauna** /sauna/ (pl: -'s) sauna (bath)

de **saus** /saus/ (pl: sauzen) sauce; gravy; (salad) dressing: *zoetzure* ~ sweet and sour (sauce)

de **sauskom** /sauskɔm/ (pl: -men) sauce boat

de **sauslepel** /sauslepəl/ (pl: -s) sauce spoon (*or*: ladle)

sauteren /soterə(n)/ (sauteerde, heeft gesauteerd) sauté

¹**sauzen** /sauzə(n)/ (sausde, heeft gesausd) distemper, colour-wash

²**sauzen** /sauzə(n)/ (sausde, heeft gesausd): *het saust* it's pouring

de **savanne** /savɑnə/ (pl: -n) savannah

saven /sevə(n)/ (savede, heeft gesaved) save

de **savooiekool** /savojəkol/ (pl: -kolen) savoy (cabbage)

de **sax** /saks/ (pl: -en) sax(ophone)

de **saxofonist** /saksofonɪst/ (pl: -en) saxophonist, saxophone player

de **saxofoon** /saksofon/ (pl: -s) saxophone

de **S-bocht** /ɛzbɔχt/ (pl: -en) S-bend

het **scala** /skala/ (pl: -'s) scale, range: *een breed ~ van artikelen* a wide range of items

de **scalp** /skɑlp/ (pl: -en) scalp

het **scalpel** /skɑlpɛl/ (pl: -s) scalpel

scalperen /skɑlperə(n)/ (scalpeerde, heeft gescalpeerd) scalp

de **scan** /skɛn/ (pl: -s) scan

scanderen /skɑnderə(n)/ (scandeerde, heeft gescandeerd) chant

Scandinavië /skɑndinavijə/ Scandinavia

de **Scandinaviër** /skɑndinavijər/ (pl: -s) Scandinavian

Scandinavisch /skɑndinavis/ (adj) Scandinavian

scannen /skɛnə(n)/ (scande, heeft gescand) scan

de **scanner** /skɛnər/ (pl: -s) scanner

het **scenario** /sənario/ (pl: -'s) scenario; screen-play [film]; script

de **scene** /si:n/ (pl: -s) scene

de **scène** /sɛːnə/ scene: *hij had de overval zelf in ~ gezet* he had faked the robbery himself

de **scepsis** /skɛpsɪs/ scepticism

de **scepter** /skɛptər/ (pl: -s) sceptre: *de ~ voeren (zwaaien)* hold sway (over)

sceptisch /skɛptis/ (adj, adv) sceptical

de **schaaf** /sχaf/ (pl: schaven) **1** plane **2** slicer

de **schaafwond** /sχafwɔnt/ (pl: -en) graze, scrape

het ¹**schaak** /sχak/ chess: *een partij* ~ a game of chess

²**schaak** /sχak/ (adj) in check: ~ *staan* be in check; *iem.* ~ *zetten* put s.o. in check

het **schaakbord** /sχagbɔrt/ (pl: -en) chessboard

schaakmat /sχakmɑt/ (adj) checkmate: ~ *staan* be checkmated; *iem.* ~ *zetten* checkmate s.o.

de **schaakpartij** /sχakpɑrtɛi/ (pl: -en) game of chess

het **schaakspel** /sχakspɛl/ (pl: -len) **1** chess **2** chess set

het **schaakstuk** /sχakstʏk/ (pl: -ken) chessman, piece

het **schaaktoernooi** /sχakturnoj/ (pl: -en) chess tournament

de **schaal** /sχal/ (pl: schalen) **1** scale: *er wordt op grote ~ misbruik van gemaakt* it is misused on a large scale; *op ~ tekenen* draw to scale; ~ *4:1* a scale of four to one **2** dish; plate: *een ~ met fruit* a bowl of fruit

het **schaaldier** /sχaldir/ (pl: -en) crustacean

het **schaalmodel** /sχalmodɛl/ (pl: -len) scale model

de **schaalverdeling** /sχalvərdelɪŋ/ (pl: -en) graduation, scale division: *een ~ op iets aanbrengen* graduate sth.

de **schaalvergroting** /sχalvərɣrotɪŋ/ (pl: -en) increase (in scale), expansion

het **schaambeen** /sχamben/ (pl: -deren) pubis, pubic bone

het **schaamdeel** /sχamdel/ (pl: -delen) genital(s), private part(s): *de vrouwelijke* (*or*: *mannelijke*) *schaamdelen* the female (*or*: male) genitals

het **schaamhaar** /sχamhar/ (pl: -haren) pubic hair

de **schaamlippen** /sχamlɪpə(n)/ (pl) labia: *de grote* (or: *de kleine*) ~ the labia majora (*or*: minora)

het **schaamrood** /sχamrot/: *iem. het ~ naar de kaken jagen* bring a blush (of shame) to s.o.'s cheeks

de **schaamte** /sχamtə/ shame: *blozen* (or: *rood worden*) *van* ~ blush (*or*: go red) with shame; *plaatsvervangende* ~ *voelen* be ashamed for s.o. (else)

schaamteloos /sχamtəlos/ (adj, adv) shameless

het **schaap** /sχap/ (pl: schapen) sheep: *een kud-*

de schapen a flock of sheep; *het zwarte ~ (van de familie) zijn* be the black sheep (of the family); *~jes tellen* count sheep

schaapachtig /sχapɑχtəχ/ (adj, adv) silly: *iem. ~ aankijken* look stupidly at s.o.; *~ lachen* grin sheepishly

de **schaapherder** /sχaphɛrdər/ (pl: -s) shepherd

de **schaar** /sχar/ (pl: scharen) **1** (pair of) scissors: *de ~ in iets zetten* take the scissors (*or:* a pair of scissors) to sth.; *één ~* one pair of scissors; *twee scharen* two (pairs of) scissors **2** pincers; claws

¹**schaars** /sχars/ (adj) scarce: *mijn ~e vrije ogenblikken* my rare free moments

²**schaars** /sχars/ (adv) sparingly, sparsely; scantily: *~ verlicht* dimly lit

de **schaarste** /sχarstə/ scarcity, shortage

de **schaats** /sχats/ (pl: -en) skate: *de ~en onderbinden* put on one's skates

de **schaatsbaan** /sχatsban/ (pl: -banen) (skating) rink

schaatsen /sχatsə(n)/ (schaatste, heeft/is geschaatst) skate

de **schaatser** /sχatsər/ (pl: -s) skater

schabouwelijk /sχabɒuwələk/ (adj) [Belg] wretched, dismal

de **schacht** /sχɑχt/ (pl: -en) **1** shaft; shank; [bot] stem **2** [Belg] fresher, first-year student

de **schade** /sχadə/ (pl: -n) **1** loss(es): *de ~ inhalen* recoup one's losses; *~ lijden* suffer a loss **2** damage; [pers also] harm: *~ aanrichten* damage sth.; *~ aan iets toebrengen* (*or:* **berokkenen**) do (*or:* cause) damage to sth.; *zijn auto heeft heel wat ~ opgelopen* his car has suffered quite a lot of damage; *de ~ loopt in de miljoenen* the damage runs into millions ‖ *door ~ en schande* wijs worden live and learn, learn the hard way

de **schadeclaim** /sχadəklem/ (pl: -s) insurance claim (for damage): *een ~ afhandelen* settle a claim

de **schade-expert** /sχadɛkspɛːr/ (pl: -s) loss adjuster; [Am] insurance adjuster

het **schadeformulier** /sχadəfɔrmylir/ (pl: -en) claim form

schadelijk /sχadələk/ (adj, adv) harmful, damaging: *~e dieren* pests, vermin; *~e gewoonten* pernicious habits

schadeloosstellen /sχadəlostɛlə(n)/ (stelde schadeloos, heeft schadeloosgesteld) compensate; repay; reimburse: *zich ergens voor ~* compensate (o.s.) for sth.

de **schadeloosstelling** /sχadəlostɛlɪŋ/ (pl: -en) compensation: *volledige ~ betalen* pay full damages

schaden /sχadə(n)/ (schaadde, heeft geschaad) damage, harm: *roken schaadt de gezondheid* smoking damages your health; *baat het niet, het schaadt ook niet* it can't do any harm and it may do some good

de **schadepost** /sχadəpɔst/ (pl: -en) loss, (financial) setback

de **schadevergoeding** /sχadəvərɣudɪŋ/ (pl: -en) compensation; damages: *volledige ~ betalen* pay full damages; *~ eisen voor* claim compensation (*or:* damages) for; *€1000,- ~ krijgen* receive 1000 euros in damages

de **schaduw** /sχadyw/ (pl: -en) shade, shadow: *in iemands ~ staan* be outshone (*or:* overshadowed) by s.o.; *uit de ~ treden* come out of the shadows

schaduwen /sχadywə(n)/ (schaduwde, heeft geschaduwd) shadow, tail: *iem. laten ~* have s.o. shadowed (*or:* tailed)

het **schaduwkabinet** /sχadywkabinɛt/ (pl: -ten) shadow cabinet

de **schaduwzijde** /sχadywzɛidə/ (pl: -n) **1** shady side **2** drawback: *de ~ van een overigens nuttige maatregel* the drawback to an otherwise useful measure

schaften /sχɑftə(n)/ (schaftte, heeft geschaft) break (for lunch, dinner)

de **schakel** /sχakəl/ (pl: -s) link: *een belangrijke ~* a vital link; *de ontbrekende ~* the missing link

de **schakelaar** /sχakəlar/ (pl: -s) switch

de **schakelarmband** /sχakəlɑrmbɑnt/ (pl: -en) chain bracelet

schakelen /sχakələ(n)/ (schakelde, heeft geschakeld) **1** connect: *parallel* (*or:* *in serie*) *~* connect in parallel (*or:* in series) **2** change, change gear(s): *naar de tweede versnelling ~* change to second (gear)

de **schakeling** /sχakəlɪŋ/ (pl: -en) **1** connection, circuit **2** gear change: *automatische ~* automatic gear change

de **schakelkast** /sχakəlkɑst/ (pl: -en) switch box, switch cupboard

schaken /sχakə(n)/ (schaakte, heeft geschaakt) play chess: *een partijtje ~* play a game of chess; *simultaan ~* play simultaneous chess

de **schaker** /sχakər/ (pl: -s) chess player

de **schakering** /sχakerɪŋ/ (pl: -en) **1** diversity **2** pattern(ing)

het **schaliegas** /sχaliɣɑs/ shale gas

schalks /sχɑlks/ (adj) mischievous, sly

schallen /sχɒlə(n)/ (schalde, heeft geschald) (re)sound; peal

schamel /sχaməl/ (adj, adv) poor, shabby: *een ~ pensioentje* a meagre (*or:* miserable) pension

zich **schamen** /sχamə(n)/ (schaamde zich, heeft zich geschaamd) be ashamed (of), be embarrassed: *zich dood* (*or:* *rot*) *~* die with shame; *daar hoef je je niet voor te ~* there's no need to be ashamed of that; *zich nergens voor ~* not be ashamed of anything

schamper /sχɒmpər/ (adj) scornful, sarcastic, sneering

schamperen /sχɒmpərə(n)/ (schamperde,

schampschot

heeft geschamperd) sneer

het **schampschot** /sχɑmpsχɔt/ (pl: -schoten)
grazing shot

het **schandaal** /sχɑndaːl/ (pl: schandalen)
1 scandal, outrage: *een* **publiek** (or: *een poli-*
tiek) ~ a public outrage, a political scandal
2 shame, disgrace: *een grof* ~ a crying shame

de **schandaalpers** /sχɑndaːlpɛrs/ gutter press
schandalig /sχɑndaːləχ/ (adj, adv) scandalous, outrageous, disgraceful: ~ **duur** outrageously expensive; *het* **is** ~ *zoals hij ons be-*
handelt it's disgraceful the way he treats us

de **schande** /sχɑndə/ disgrace, shame: *het* **is**
(een) ~ it's a disgrace; ~ *van iets* **spreken** cry
out against sth.
schandelijk /sχɑndələk/ (adj, adv) scandalous, outrageous: *een* ~ **boek** an infamous
book

de **schandpaal** /sχɑntpaːl/ (pl: -palen): *iem.* **aan**
de ~ *nagelen* pillory s.o.

de **schandvlek** /sχɑntflɛk/ (pl: -ken) **1** blot
2 disgrace

de **schans** /sχɑns/ (pl: -en) ski jump
schansspringen /sχɑnsprɪŋə(n)/ ski jump

het/de **schap** /sχɑp/ (pl: -pen) shelf: *de* ~*pen* **bijvul-**
len re-stock the shelves

de **schapenkaas** /sχaːpə(n)kaːs/ sheep's (or:
ewe's) cheese

de **schapenscheerder** /sχaːpə(n)sχeːrdər/ (pl:
-s) sheepshearer

de **schapenvacht** /sχaːpə(n)vɑχt/ (pl: -en)
sheepskin, fleece

het **schapenvlees** /sχaːpə(n)vleːs/ mutton, lamb

de **schapenwol** /sχaːpə(n)wɔl/ sheep's wool

de **schapenwolkjes** /sχaːpə(n)wɔlkjəs/ (pl)
fleecy clouds
schappelijk /sχɑpələk/ (adj, adv) reasonable, fair

de **schar** /sχɑr/ (pl: -ren) dab, sheepdog

¹**scharen** /sχaːrə(n)/ (schaarde, is geschaard)
jackknife

²**scharen** /sχaːrə(n)/ (schaarde, heeft geschaard) range: *zich* **om** *het vuur* ~ gather
round the fire; [fig] *zich* **achter** *iem.* ~ side
with s.o.

het/de **scharminkel** /sχɑrmɪŋkəl/ (pl: -s) scrag(gy
person): *een* **mager** ~ a bag of bones

het **scharnier** /sχɑrniːr/ (pl: -en) hinge: *om een* ~
draaien hinge
scharnieren /sχɑrniːrə(n)/ (scharnierde,
heeft gescharnierd) hinge

de **scharrel** /sχɑrəl/ (pl: -s) [inform] **1** flirt
2 flirtation: *aan de* ~ *zijn* fool around

de **scharrelaar** /sχɑrəlaːr/ (pl: -s) odd-jobber

het **scharrelei** /sχɑrəlɛi/ (pl: -eren) free-range
egg
scharrelen /sχɑrələ(n)/ (scharrelde, heeft
gescharreld) **1** rummage (about): *hij scharrelt*
de hele dag **in** *de tuin* he potters about in the
garden all day (long) **2** scratch

de **scharrelkip** /sχɑrəlkɪp/ (pl: -pen) free-

range chicken

de **schat** /sχɑt/ (pl: -ten) **1** treasure: *een* **ver-**
borgen ~ a hidden treasure **2** treasure, riches: ~*ten aan iets* **verdienen** make a fortune
out of sth.; *een* ~ **aan** *gegevens* (or: *materiaal*)
a wealth of data (*or:* material) **3** darling,
dear, honey: *zijn het geen* ~*jes?* aren't they
sweet?

de **schatbewaarder** /sχɑdbəwaːrdər/ (pl: -s)
[Belg] treasurer
schateren /sχaːtərə(n)/ (schaterde, heeft
geschaterd) roar (with laughter): *de kinderen*
~ *van plezier* the children shouted with
pleasure

de **schaterlach** /sχaːtərlɑχ/ loud laughter

de **schatgraver** /sχɑtχraːvər/ (pl: -s) treasure
digger

de **schatkamer** /sχɑtkaːmər/ (pl: -s) treasury,
treasure house

de **schatkist** /sχɑtkɪst/ (pl: -en) **1** treasure
chest **2** treasury, (the) Exchequer
schatplichtig /sχɑtplɪχtəχ/ (adj) tributary:
~ *zijn* **aan** *iem.* be indebted to s.o.
schatrijk /sχɑtrɛik/ (adj) wealthy: *ze* **zijn**
schat- en ~ they are fabulously wealthy

de **schattebout** /sχɑtəbɑut/ (pl: -en) dear,
darling
schatten /sχɑtə(n)/ (schatte, heeft geschat)
value; estimate; assess; appraise: *de* **afstand**
~ estimate the distance; *hoe oud schat je*
hem? how old do you take him to be?; *de*
schade ~ **op** assess the damage at
schattig /sχɑtəχ/ (adj, adv) sweet, lovely: *zij*
ziet er ~ **uit** she looks lovely

de **schatting** /sχɑtɪŋ/ (pl: -en) estimate, assessment: *een* **voorzichtige** ~ a conservative estimate; **naar** ~ *drie miljoen* an estimated three
million
schaven /sχaːvə(n)/ (schaafde, heeft ge-
schaafd) **1** plane: *planken* ~ plane boards
2 graze, scrape **3** slice, shred: **komkommers**
~ slice cucumbers

het **schavot** /sχavɔt/ (pl: -ten) scaffold: *iem.* **op**
het ~ *brengen* **a)** condemn s.o. to the scaffold;
b) [fig] cause s.o.'s downfall

de **schavuit** /sχavœyt/ (pl: -en) rascal

de **schede** /sχeːdə/ (pl: -n, -s) **1** sheath **2** vagina

de **schedel** /sχeːdəl/ (pl: -s) skull

de **schedelbasisfractuur** /sχeːdəlbaːzɪsfrɑk-
tyːr/ (pl: -fracturen) fracture of the base of
the skull
scheef /sχeːf/ (adj, adv) **1** crooked; oblique;
leaning; slanting; sloping: *scheve* **hoeken**
oblique angles; *een* ~ **gezicht** *trekken* pull a
wry face; *een scheve* **neus** *hebben* have a
crooked nose; *het schilderij* **hangt** ~ the picture is crooked **2** wrong, distorted: *de zaak*
gaat **(loopt)** ~ things are going wrong

de **scheefgroei** /sχeːfχruj/ [fig] adverse development
scheel /sχeːl/ (adj, adv) cross-eyed

scheelzien /sx̲e̲lzin/ (zag scheel, heeft scheelgezien) squint

de **scheen** /sx̲en/ (pl: schenen) shin: *iem.* **tegen** *de schenen schoppen* tread on s.o.'s toes

het **scheenbeen** /sx̲e̲mben/ (pl: -deren, -benen) shinbone

de **scheenbeschermer** /sx̲e̲mbəsx̲ɛrmər/ (pl: -s) shinguard

de **scheepsbouw** /sx̲e̲psbɑu/ shipbuilding (industry)

de **scheepsbouwer** /sx̲e̲psbɑuwər/ (pl: -s) shipbuilder

de **scheepshut** /sx̲e̲pshʏt/ (pl: -ten) (ship's) cabin

de **scheepslading** /sx̲e̲psladɪŋ/ (pl: -en) shipload, (ship's) cargo

de **scheepsramp** /sx̲e̲psrɑmp/ (pl: -en) shipping disaster

het **scheepsrecht** /sx̲e̲psrɛxt/: *driemaal is ~* third time lucky

het **scheepsruim** /sx̲e̲psrœym/ (pl: -en) (ship's) hold

de **scheepswerf** /sx̲e̲pswɛrf/ (pl: -werven) shipyard

de **scheepvaart** /sx̲e̲pfart/ shipping (traffic), navigation

het **scheepvaartverkeer** /sx̲e̲pfartførker/ shipping (traffic)

het **scheerapparaat** /sx̲e̲rɑparɑt/ (pl: -apparaten) shaver

de **scheerkwast** /sx̲e̲rkwɑst/ (pl: -en) shaving brush

de **scheerlijn** /sx̲e̲rlɛɪn/ (pl: -en) **1** stretching wire **2** guy (rope)

het **scheermes** /sx̲e̲rmɛs/ (pl: -sen) razor

het **scheermesje** /sx̲e̲rmɛʃə/ (pl: -s) razor blade

de **scheerwol** /sx̲e̲rwɔl/ (virgin) wool: *zuiver ~* pure new wool

de **scheerzeep** /sx̲e̲rzep/ shaving soap

de **scheet** /sx̲et/ (pl: scheten) [inform] fart: *een ~ laten* fart

scheidbaar /sx̲ɛɪdbar/ (adj, adv) separable

¹**scheiden** /sx̲ɛɪdə(n)/ (scheidde, is gescheiden) **1** part (company), separate: *hier ~ onze* **wegen** here our ways part; *~ van* part (or: separate) from; *als vrienden ~* part (as) friends **2** divorce; separate: *zij gaan ~* they are getting divorced

²**scheiden** /sx̲ɛɪdə(n)/ (scheidde, heeft gescheiden) **1** separate, divide: *dooier en eiwit ~* separate the yolk from the (egg) white; *het* **hoofd** *van de romp ~* sever the head from the body; *twee* **vechtende** *jongens ~* separate two fighting boys; *huisvuil ~* sort the household waste **2** divorce; separate: *zich* **laten** *~* get a divorce

de **scheiding** /sx̲ɛɪdɪŋ/ (pl: -en) **1** separation, detachment: *een ~ maken (veroorzaken) (in)* rupture, disrupt **2** divorce: *~ van tafel en bed* legal separation, separation from bed and board **3** parting

de **scheidingswand** /sx̲ɛɪdɪŋswɑnt/ dividing wall

de **scheidslijn** /sx̲ɛɪtslɛin/ (pl: -en) dividing line; [fig] borderline

de **scheidsmuur** /sx̲ɛɪtsmyr/ (pl: -muren) partition; [fig] barrier

de **scheidsrechter** /sx̲ɛɪtsrɛxtər/ (pl: -s) umpire; referee: *als ~ optreden bij een wedstrijd* umpire (or: referee) a match

de **scheikunde** /sx̲ɛikʏndə/ chemistry

scheikundig /sx̲ɛikʏndəx/ (adj, adv) chemical

schel /sx̲ɛl/ (adj, adv) shrill: *een ~le stem* a shrill (or: piercing) voice

de **Schelde** /sx̲ɛldə/ Scheldt

schelden /sx̲ɛldə(n)/ (schold, heeft gescholden) curse, swear: *vloeken en ~* curse and swear; *op iem. ~* scold s.o., call s.o. names

de **scheldnaam** /sx̲ɛltnam/ (pl: -namen) term of abuse

het **scheldwoord** /sx̲ɛltwort/ (pl: -en) term of abuse

schelen /sx̲elə(n)/ (scheelde, heeft gescheeld) **1** differ: *ze ~ twee maanden* they are two months apart **2** concern, matter: *het kan mij niets* (or: *geen bal*) *~* I don't give a hoot (or: care two hoots); *het kan me niet ~* I don't care; I don't mind; *kan mij wat ~!* why should I care! ‖ *het scheelde geen haar* it was a close shave; *het scheelde weinig, of hij was verdronken* he narrowly escaped being drowned; *dat scheelt (me) weer een ritje* that saves (me) another trip

de **schelm** /sx̲ɛlm/ (pl: -en) crook

de **schelp** /sx̲ɛlp/ (pl: -en) **1** shell **2** auricle

de **schelpdieren** /sx̲ɛlbdirə(n)/ (pl) shellfish

de **schelvis** /sx̲ɛlvɪs/ (pl: -sen) haddock

het **schema** /sx̲ema/ (pl: -'s) **1** diagram, plan **2** plan, outline **3** schedule: *we liggen weer op ~* we're back on schedule; *achter* (or: *voor*) *op het ~* behind (or: ahead of) schedule

schematisch /sx̲emɑtis/ (adj, adv) schematic, diagrammatic: *iets ~ voorstellen (aangeven)* represent sth. in diagram form

de **schemer** /sx̲emər/ twilight: *de ~ valt* evening is falling

het **schemerdonker** /sx̲emərdɔŋkər/ twilight, half-light; dusk

schemeren /sx̲emərə(n)/ (schemerde, heeft geschemerd) grow dark; become light: *het begint te ~* it is getting dark (or: light); twilight is setting in

schemerig /sx̲emərəx/ (adj, adv) dusky

de **schemering** /sx̲emərɪŋ/ twilight, dusk, dawn

de **schemerlamp** /sx̲emərlɑmp/ (pl: -en) floor lamp, standard lamp

de **schemertoestand** /sx̲emərtustɑnt/ twilight state

schenden /sx̲ɛndə(n)/ (schond, heeft geschonden) **1** damage **2** break, violate: *een* *verdrag* (or: *mensenrechten*) ~ violate a treaty (or: human rights)

de **schending** /sχɛndɪŋ/ (pl: -en) violation; breach

de **schenkel** /sχɛŋkəl/ (pl: -s) shank

schenken /sχɛŋkə(n)/ (schonk, heeft geschonken) **1** pour (out) **2** give: *zijn hart* ~ *aan* give one's heart to ‖ *geen aandacht* ~ *aan iem.* take no notice (or: account) of s.o., pay no attention to s.o.

de **schenking** /sχɛŋkɪŋ/ (pl: -en) gift, donation: *een* ~ *doen* make a gift (or: donation)

de **schennis** /sχɛnɪs/ (pl: -sen) violation: ~ *plegen* commit indecent exposure

de **schep** /sχɛp/ **1** scoop; shovel **2** (table)-spoon(ful), scoop(ful): *drie* ~*pen ijs* three scoops of ice cream

de **schepen** /sχepə(n)/ (pl: -en) [Belg] alderman

het **schepencollege** /sχepə(n)kɔleʒə/ (pl: -s) [Belg] bench of (Mayor and) Aldermen

het **schepijs** /sχɛpɛis/ (easy-scoop) ice cream

het **schepje** /sχɛpjə/ (pl: -s) **1** (small) spoon **2** spoon(ful): *een* ~ *suiker* a spoonful of sugar ‖ *er een* ~ *(boven)op doen* a) add a little extra; b) heighten (the effect)

het **schepnet** /sχɛpnɛt/ (pl: -ten) dip (or: landing) net

¹**scheppen** /sχɛpə(n)/ (schepte, heeft geschept) scoop, shovel: *een emmer water* ~ draw a bucket of water; *leeg* ~ empty; *vol* ~ fill; *zand op een kruiwagen* ~ shovel sand into a wheelbarrow

²**scheppen** /sχɛpə(n)/ (schiep, heeft geschapen) create: *God schiep de hemel en de aarde* God created heaven and earth

de **schepper** /sχɛpər/ (pl: -s) creator

de **schepping** /sχɛpɪŋ/ (pl: -en) creation

het **scheppingsverhaal** /sχɛpɪŋsfərhal/ story of the Creation

het **schepsel** /sχɛpsəl/ (pl: -en, -s) creature

¹**scheren** /sχerə(n)/ (schoor, heeft geschoren) shave; shear: *zich* ~ shave; *geschoren schapen* shorn sheep

²**scheren** /sχerə(n)/ (scheerde, heeft/is gescheerd): *scheer je weg!* get away!, buzz off!

de **scherf** /sχɛrf/ (pl: scherven) fragment; splinter: *in scherven (uiteen)vallen* fall to pieces; *scherven brengen geluk* [roughly] no good crying over spilt milk

de **schering** /sχerɪŋ/ (pl: -en): *dat is* ~ *en inslag* that is the order of the day

het **scherm** /sχɛrm/ (pl: -en) **1** screen, shade **2** curtain: *de man achter de* ~*en* the man behind the scenes **3** screen, display

schermen /sχɛrmə(n)/ (schermde, heeft geschermd) fence

de **schermutseling** /sχɛrmʏtsəlɪŋ/ (pl: -en) skirmish, clash

het ¹**scherp** /sχɛrp/ **1** edge: *op het* ~ *van de snede balanceren* be on a knife-edge **2** ball: *met* ~ *schieten* fire (with) live ammunition; *op* ~

staan be on edge

²**scherp** /sχɛrp/ (adj) **1** sharp, pointed; [maths] acute: *een* ~*e kin* a pointed chin **2** sharp, pungent, hot; spicy; cutting; biting: ~*e mosterd* (or: *kerrie*) hot mustard (or: curry) **3** strict, severe: ~ *toezicht* close control **4** sharp, harsh: ~*e kritiek* sharp criticism **5** sharp, clear-cut: *een* ~ *contrast vormen* be in sharp contrast with; ~ *stellen* focus **6** live; armed

scherpen /sχɛrpə(n)/ (scherpte, heeft gescherpt) sharpen

scherpomlijnd /sχɛrpɔmlɛint/ (adj) clear-cut, well-defined

de **scherpschutter** /sχɛrpsχʏtər/ (pl: -s) sharpshooter; sniper

de **scherpslijper** /sχɛrpslɛipər/ (pl: -s) quibbler

de **scherpte** /sχɛrptə/ (pl: -n, -s) sharpness, keenness: *de* ~ *van het beeld* the sharpness of the picture; *de* ~ *van een foto* the focus of a picture

scherpzinnig /sχɛrpsɪnəχ/ (adj, adv) **1** acute, discerning, sharp(-witted): *een* ~*e geest* a subtle mind **2** shrewd, clever: ~ *antwoorden* give a shrewd answer

de **scherts** /sχɛrts/ joke, jest

schertsen /sχɛrtsə(n)/ (schertste, heeft geschertst) joke, jest

de **schertsfiguur** /sχɛrtsfiɣyr/ (pl: -figuren) joke, nonentity

de **schertsvertoning** /sχɛrtsfərtonɪŋ/ (pl: -en) joke

de **schets** /sχɛts/ (pl: -en) sketch: *een eerste* ~ a first draft; *een ruwe* (or: *korte*) ~ *van mijn leven* a rough (or: brief) outline of my life

het **schetsboek** /sχɛtsbuk/ (pl: -en) sketchbook

schetsen /sχɛtsə(n)/ (schetste, heeft geschetst) sketch: *een beeld* ~ *van* paint a picture of; *ruw (in grote lijnen)* ~ give a rough sketch (of)

schetteren /sχɛtərə(n)/ (schetterde, heeft geschetterd) blare

de **scheur** /sχør/ (pl: -en) **1** crack, crevice; split: *een* ~ *in een muur* a crack in a wall **2** tear: *hij heeft een* ~ *in mijn nieuwe boek gemaakt* he has torn my new book ‖ *zijn* ~ *opentrekken* open one's big mouth

de **scheurbuik** /sχørbœyk/ scurvy: *aan* ~ *lijdend* scorbutic

¹**scheuren** /sχørə(n)/ (scheurde, is gescheurd) tear (apart); crack; split: *pas op, het papier zal* ~ be careful, the paper will tear; *de auto scheurde door de bocht* the car came screeching round the corner

²**scheuren** /sχørə(n)/ (scheurde, heeft gescheurd) tear: *zijn kleren* ~ tear one's clothes

de **scheuring** /sχørɪŋ/ (pl: -en) rift, split; schism

de **scheurkalender** /sχørkalɛndər/ (pl: -s) block-calendar

de **scheut** /sχøt/ (pl: -en) **1** shoot, sprout **2** twinge, stab (of pain) **3** dash; shot: *een* ~

melk a dash of milk

scheutig /sx̯ø̯tǝɣ/ (adj) generous

schichtig /sx̯ɪx̯tǝɣ/ (adj, adv) nervous, timid; skittish

schielijk /sx̯ilǝk/ (adv) quickly, rapidly

het **schiereiland** /sx̯irɛilɑnt/ (pl: -en) peninsula

de **schietbaan** /sx̯idbɑn/ (pl: -banen) shooting range

¹**schieten** /sx̯itǝ(n)/ (schoot, heeft geschoten) **1** shoot; fire: *op iem.* ~ shoot (*or:* take a shot) at s.o. **2** (+ laten) let go, release; drop [pers]; forget [pers]: *laat hem ~ forget (about) him

²**schieten** /sx̯itǝ(n)/ (schoot, is geschoten) shoot, dash: *de prijzen ~ omhoog* prices are soaring; *het kind was plotseling de **weg** over geschoten* the child had suddenly dashed (out) across the road ‖ *de tranen schoten haar in de ogen* tears rushed to her eyes; *weer te binnen ~* come back (to mind); *iem. te hulp ~* rush to s.o.'s aid (*or:* assistance)

³**schieten** /sx̯itǝ(n)/ (schoot, heeft geschoten) shoot: *hij **kon** haar wel ~* he could (cheerfully) have murdered her; *zich een kogel door het hoofd ~* blow out one's brains; *naast ~* miss; *in het doel ~* net (the ball)

het **schietgebed** /sx̯itx̯ǝbɛt/ (pl: -en) short prayer, quick prayer: *een ~je **doen*** say a quick prayer

de **schietpartij** /sx̯itpɑrtɛi/ (pl: -en) shoot-out

de **schietschijf** /sx̯itsx̯ɛif/ (pl: -schijven) target

de **schietstoel** /sx̯itstul/ (pl: -en) ejector seat, ejection seat

de **schiettent** /sx̯itɛnt/ (pl: -en) rifle gallery, shooting gallery

¹**schiften** /sx̯ɪftǝ(n)/ (schiftte, is geschift) curdle, turn

²**schiften** /sx̯ɪftǝ(n)/ (schiftte, heeft geschift) sort (out), sift (through)

de **schifting** /sx̯ɪftɪŋ/ (pl: -en) **1** sifting: *Jan is **bij** de eerste ~ afgevallen* Jan was weeded out in the first round **2** curdling

de **schijf** /sx̯ɛif/ (pl: schijven) **1** disc **2** disc, plate; (potter's) wheel **3** slice: *een ~je citroen* a slice of lemon **4** disk

de **schijfrem** /sx̯ɛifrɛm/ (pl: -men) disc brake

de **schijn** /sx̯ɛin/ **1** appearance, semblance: *op de uiterlijke ~ afgaan* judge by (outward) appearances; *~ bedriegt* appearances are deceptive; *de ~ ophouden tegenover de familie* keep up appearances in front of the family **2** show, appearances: *schone ~* glamour, cosmetics, gloss **3** shadow, gleam: *geen ~ van kans hebben* not have the ghost of a chance

schijnbaar /sx̯ɛimbar/ (adj, adv) seeming, apparent: *~ oprecht* seemingly sincere

de **schijnbeweging** /sx̯ɛimbǝweɣɪŋ/ (pl: -en) feint, dummy (movement, pass): *een ~ **maken*** (make a) feint

de ¹**schijndood** /sx̯ɛindot/ apparent death, suspended animation

²**schijndood** /sx̯ɛindot/ (adj) apparently dead, in a state of suspended animation

schijnen /sx̯ɛinǝ(n)/ (scheen, heeft geschenen) **1** shine: *de zon schijnt* the sun is shining; *met een zaklantaarn in iemands gezicht ~* flash a torch in s.o.'s face **2** seem, appear: *het schijnt zo* it looks like it; *hij schijnt erg rijk te zijn* apparently he is very rich

schijnheilig /sx̯ɛinhɛilǝɣ/ (adj, adv) hypocritical, sanctimonious: *met een ~ gezicht* sanctimoniously

het **schijnhuwelijk** /sx̯ɛinhywǝlǝk/ (pl: -en) marriage of convenience

het **schijnsel** /sx̯ɛinsǝl/ (pl: -s) shine, light

het **schijntje** /sx̯ɛincǝ/ (pl: -s): *ik kocht het **voor** een ~* I bought it for a song

de **schijnvertoning** /sx̯ɛinvǝrtonɪŋ/ (pl: -en) diversion

de **schijnwerper** /sx̯ɛinwɛrpǝr/ (pl: -s) floodlight; spotlight: *iem. **in** de ~s zetten* spotlight s.o.; *in de ~s staan* be in the limelight

het/de **schijt** /sx̯ɛit/ [inform] shit, crap

schijten /sx̯ɛitǝ(n)/ (scheet, heeft gescheten) [inform] shit, crap

de **schijterd** /sx̯ɛitǝrt/ (pl: -s) [inform] funk, scaredy-cat

schijterig /sx̯ɛitǝrǝɣ/ (adj, adv) [inform] chicken-hearted

de **schijterij** /sx̯ɛitǝrɛi/ [inform] shits; trots; runs: *aan de ~ zijn* have the shits (*or:* trots, runs)

de **schik** /sx̯ɪk/ contentment, fun: *~ **hebben** in zijn werk* enjoy one's work

schikken /sx̯ɪkǝ(n)/ (schikte, heeft geschikt) arrange, order: *de **boeken** in volgorde ~* put the books in order

de **schikking** /sx̯ɪkɪŋ/ (pl: -en) arrangement, ordering ‖ *een ~ **treffen** (met)* reach an understanding (with)

de **schil** /sx̯ɪl/ (pl: -len) skin; rind; peel

het **schild** /sx̯ɪlt/ (pl: -en) **1** shield; shell **2** sign

de **schilder** /sx̯ɪldǝr/ (pl: -s) **1** (house-)painter; (house-)decorator **2** painter

schilderachtig /sx̯ɪldǝrɑx̯tǝɣ/ (adj, adv) picturesque; scenic

schilderen /sx̯ɪldǝrǝ(n)/ (schilderde, heeft geschilderd) paint, decorate: *zijn huis laten ~* have one's house painted

het **schilderij** /sx̯ɪldǝrɛi/ (pl: -en) painting, picture: *een ~ **in** olieverf* an oil painting

de **schildering** /sx̯ɪldǝrɪŋ/ (pl: -en) painting, picture: *~en **op** een wand* murals

de **schilderkunst** /sx̯ɪldǝrkʏnst/ (art of) painting

het **schildersbedrijf** /sx̯ɪldǝrzbǝdrɛif/ (pl: -bedrijven) painter and decorator's business

de **schildersezel** /sx̯ɪldǝrsezǝl/ (pl: -s) (painter's) easel

het **schilderstuk** /sx̯ɪldǝrstʏk/ (pl: -ken) painting, picture

het **schilderwerk** /sx̯ɪldǝrwɛrk/ **1** painting: *het*

~ *op de wand* the mural (painting) **2** paint-work: *het ~ **aanbesteden*** give out the paint-work by contract

de **schildklier** /sxɪltklir/ (pl: -en) thyroid gland

de **schildknaap** /sxɪltknap/ (pl: -knapen) shield-bearer, squire

de **schildpad** /sxɪltpɑt/ (pl: -den) tortoise; turtle

de **schildwacht** /sxɪltwɑxt/ (pl: -en) sentry, guard: *~en **aflossen*** change the guard

de **schilfer** /sxɪlfər/ (pl: -s) scale; flake; chip; sliver

schilferen /sxɪlfərə(n)/ (schilferde, heeft/is geschilferd) flake (off), peel (off)

schillen /sxɪlə(n)/ (schilde, heeft geschild) peel: *aardappels ~* peel potatoes

de **schim** /sxɪm/ (pl: -men) shadow: *~men in het donker* shadows in the dark

de **schimmel** /sxɪməl/ (pl: -s) **1** mould, mildew: *de ~ van kaas **afhalen*** scrape the mould off cheese; *er zit ~ **op** die muur* there is mildew on the wall **2** [bot] fungus **3** grey

schimmelen /sxɪmələ(n)/ (schimmelde, is geschimmeld) mould, become mouldy (*or:* mildewed)

schimmelig /sxɪmələx/ (adj) mouldy

de **schimmelinfectie** /sxɪmməlɪnfɛksi/ (pl: -s) fungal infection

het **schimmenspel** /sxɪmə(n)spɛl/ shadow theatre, shadow play

schimmig /sxɪməx/ (adj) shadowy

schimpen /sxɪmpə(n)/ (schimpte, heeft geschimpt) scoff, jeer, sneer

het **schip** /sxɪp/ (pl: schepen) ship; vessel; barge; boat: *per ~* by ship (*or:* boat); [fig] *zijn schepen achter zich **verbranden*** burn one's boats; [fig] *het zinkende ~ **verlaten*** leave the sinking ship; [fig] *schoon ~ maken* make a clean sweep, clean things up

de **schipbreuk** /sxɪpbrøk/ (pl: -en) shipwreck, wreck: *~ **lijden** a)* founder, be wrecked; *b)* be shipwrecked

de **schipbreukeling** /sxɪpbrøkəlɪŋ/ (pl: -en) shipwrecked person

de **schipper** /sxɪpər/ (pl: -s) **1** master (of a ship), captain, skipper **2** captain of a barge

schipperen /sxɪpərə(n)/ (schipperde, heeft geschipperd) give and take: *je moet een beetje **weten** te ~* you've got to give and take (a bit)

de **schipperstrui** /sxɪpərstrœy/ (pl: -en) seaman's pullover

het **schisma** /sxɪsma/ (pl: -'s, -ta) schism

schitteren /sxɪtərə(n)/ (schitterde, heeft geschitterd) **1** glitter, shine, twinkle: *zijn ogen schitterden **van** plezier* his eyes twinkled with amusement **2** shine (in, at), excel (in, at): *~ in gezelschap* be a social success

schitterend /sxɪtərənt/ (adj, adv) **1** brilliant, sparkling: *het **weer** was ~* the weather was gorgeous **2** splendid, magnificent: *een ~*

doelpunt a marvellous goal

de **schittering** /sxɪtərɪŋ/ (pl: -en) brilliance, radiance

schizofreen /sxidzofren/ (adj) schizophrenic

de **schizofrenie** /sxidzofreni/ schizophrenia

de **schlager** /ʃlagər/ (pl: -s) (schmalzy) pop(ular) song

de **schlemiel** /ʃləmil/ (pl: -en) [inform] wally

de **schmink** /ʃmɪŋk/ greasepaint, make-up

schminken /ʃmɪŋkə(n)/ (schminkte, heeft geschminkt) make (s.o.) up: *zich ~* make (o.s.) up

de **schnabbel** /ʃnɑbəl/ (pl: -s) (bit of a) job on the side: *daar **heb** ik een leuke ~ aan* it brings in a bit extra for me

de **schnitzel** /ʃnɪtsəl/ (pl: -s) (veal, pork) cutlet, schnitzel

het **schoeisel** /sxujsəl/ footwear

de **schoen** /sxun/ (pl: -en) shoe: *twee **paar** ~en* two pairs of shoes; *hoge ~en* boots; [Belg] *in nauwe ~tjes zitten* be in dire straits; *zijn ~en **aantrekken*** put on one's shoes; *zijn ~en **uittrekken*** take off one's shoes; [fig] *de **stoute** ~en aantrekken* take the plunge; *ik zou niet graag **in** zijn ~en willen staan* I wouldn't like to be in his shoes

de **schoenenzaak** /sxunə(n)zak/ (pl: -zaken) shoe shop

de **schoener** /sxunər/ (pl: -s) schooner

de **schoenlepel** /sxunlepəl/ (pl: -s) shoehorn

de **schoenmaat** /sxunmat/ (pl: -maten) shoe size

de **schoenmaker** /sxunmakər/ (pl: -s) cobbler, shoemaker: *die schoenen moeten **naar** de ~* those shoes need repairing

het/de **schoensmeer** /sxunsmer/ shoe polish, shoe cream

de **schoenveter** /sxunvetər/ (pl: -s) shoelace: *zijn ~s **strikken** (or: **vastmaken**)* lace up (*or:* tie) one's shoes

de **schoenzool** /sxunzol/ (pl: -zolen) sole

de **schoep** /sxup/ (pl: -en) blade

de **schoffel** /sxɔfəl/ (pl: -s) hoe

schoffelen /sxɔfələ(n)/ (schoffelde, heeft geschoffeld) weed

schofferen /sxɔferə(n)/ (schoffeerde, heeft geschoffeerd) treat with contempt

het **schoffie** /sxɔfi/ (pl: -s) rascal

de **schoft** /sxɔft/ **1** bastard **2** shoulder; withers

schofterig /sxɔftərəx/ (adj, adv) rascally

de **schok** /sxɔk/ (pl: -ken) **1** shock: *dat nieuws zal een ~ **geven*** that news will come as quite a shock; *de ~ te boven komen* get over the shock **2** jolt: *een ~ **krijgen*** receive a shock; *de ~ken van een **aardbeving*** earthquake tremors; *de ~ was zo **hevig** dat ...* the (force of the) impact was so great that ...

het **schokbeton** /sxɔgbətɔn/ vibrated concrete

de **schokbreker** /sxɔgbrekər/ (pl: -s) shock absorber

de **schokdemper** /sxɔgdɛmpər/ (pl: -s) shock absorber

het **schokeffect** /sxɔkɛfɛkt/ (pl: -en) shock, impact: *voor een ~ zorgen* create a shock

¹**schokken** /sxɔkə(n)/ (schokte, heeft geschokt) shake, jolt

²**schokken** /sxɔkə(n)/ (schokte, heeft geschokt) shock: *~de beelden* shocking scenes

de ¹**schol** /sxɔl/ (pl: -len) plaice

²**schol** /sxɔl/ (int) [Belg] cheers!

de **scholekster** /sxɔlɛkstər/ (pl: -s) oystercatcher

scholen /sxɔlə(n)/ (schoolde, heeft geschoold) school, train

de **scholengemeenschap** /sxɔlə(n)ɣəmensxɑp/ (pl: -pen) [roughly] comprehensive school

de **scholier** /sxolir/ (pl: -en) **1** pupil; [Am] student **2** [Belg] junior member (14, 15 years) of sports club

de **scholing** /sxolɪŋ/ training, schooling: *een man met weinig ~* a man of little schooling (*or:* education)

de **schommel** /sxɔməl/ (pl: -s) swing

schommelen /sxɔmələ(n)/ (schommelde, heeft/is geschommeld) **1** swing; rock; roll **2** swing, rock: *ze zijn aan het ~* they are playing on the swings **3** fluctuate

de **schommeling** /sxɔməlɪŋ/ (pl: -en) fluctuation, swing

de **schommelstoel** /sxɔməlstul/ (pl: -en) rocking chair

de **schoof** /sxof/ (pl: schoven) sheaf

schooien /sxojə(n)/ (schooide, heeft geschooid) beg: *die hond schooit bij iedereen om een stukje vlees* that dog begs a piece of meat from everybody

de **schooier** /sxojər/ (pl: -s) tramp, vagrant; [Am] bum

de **school** /sxol/ (pl: scholen) school: *een ~ haringen* a school of herring; *een bijzondere ~* a denominational school; *hogere ~* college for higher education; *de lagere ~* primary school; *de middelbare ~* secondary school; [Am] high school; *een neutrale ~* a non-denominational school; *een openbare ~* a state school; [Am] a public school; *Vrije School* Rudolf Steiner School; *een witte ~* a predominantly white school; *naar ~ gaan* go to school; *de kinderen zijn naar ~* the children are at school; *op de middelbare ~ zitten* go to (*or:* attend) secondary school; *uit ~ komen* come home from school; *als de kinderen van ~ zijn* when the children have finished school; *zij werd van ~ gestuurd* she was expelled from school; *een ~ voor voortgezet onderwijs* a secondary school

de **schoolagenda** /sxolaɣɛnda/ (pl: -'s) school diary

de **schoolarts** /sxolarts/ (pl: -en) school doctor

de **schoolbank** /sxolbɑŋk/ (pl: -en) school desk: *ik heb met hem in de ~en gezeten* we went to school together, we were schoolmates

de **schoolbel** /sxolbɛl/ (pl: -len) school bell

het **schoolbestuur** /sxolbəstyr/ (pl: -besturen) board of governors

schoolblijven /sxolblɛiva(n)/ (bleef school, is schoolgebleven) stay in (after school), be kept in (after school)

het **schoolboek** /sxolbuk/ (pl: -en) school book, textbook

het **schoolbord** /sxolbɔrt/ (pl: -en) blackboard

de **schoolbus** /sxolbʏs/ (pl: -sen) school bus

de **schooldag** /sxoldɑx/ (pl: -en) school day: *de eerste ~* the first day of school

het **schoolfeest** /sxolfest/ (pl: -en) school party

schoolgaand /sxolɣant/ (adj) schoolgoing

het **schoolgebouw** /sxolɣəbau/ (pl: -en) school (building)

het **schoolgeld** /sxolɣɛlt/ (pl: -en) tuition, fee(s)

het **schoolhoofd** /sxolhoft/ (pl: -en) principal, headmaster, headmistress

het **schooljaar** /sxoljar/ (pl: -jaren) school year: *het eerste ~ over moeten doen* have to repeat the first year

de **schooljeugd** /sxoljøxt/ school-age children, school-agers

de **schooljongen** /sxoljɔŋə(n)/ (pl: -s) schoolboy

de **schooljuffrouw** /sxoljʏfrau/ (pl: -en) (school)teacher

de **schoolkeuze** /sxolkøzə/ choice of school

de **schoolklas** /sxolklɑs/ (pl: -sen) class, form

de **schoolkrant** /sxolkrɑnt/ (pl: -en) school (news)paper

het **schoollokaal** /sxolokal/ (pl: -lokalen) schoolroom

de **schoolmeester** /sxolmestər/ (pl: -s) **1** schoolteacher **2** pedant, prig: *de ~ spelen (uithangen)* be a pedant

het **schoolmeisje** /sxolmɛiʃə/ (pl: -s) schoolgirl

het **schoolonderzoek** /sxolɔndərzuk/ (pl: -en) exam(ination)

de **schoolopleiding** /sxoloplɛidɪŋ/ (pl: -en) education: *een goede ~ genoten hebben* have had the advantage of a good education

het **schoolplein** /sxolplɛin/ (pl: -en) (school) playground: *de kinderen spelen op het ~* the children were playing in the playground

de **schoolreis** /sxolrɛis/ (pl: -reizen) school trip

de **schoolreünie** school reunion

schools /sxols/ (adj, adv) **1** school, schoolish **2** scholastic

het **schoolschrift** /sxolsxrɪft/ (pl: -en) school notebook

de **schoolslag** /sxolslɑx/ breaststroke

de **schooltas** /sxoltɑs/ (pl: -sen) schoolbag; satchel

de **schooltelevisie** /sxolteləvizi/ educational television

de **schooltijd** /sxoltɛit/ (pl: -en) school time

(*or:* hours): *de ~en* **variëren** *soms van school tot school* school hours can vary from school to school; **buiten** (or: *na*) ~ outside (*or:* after) school; **gedurende** *de ~*, **onder** ~ during school (time)

het **schoolvak** /sx̲olvɑk/ (pl: -ken) school subject

de **schoolvakantie** /sx̲olvakɑnsi/ (pl: -s) school holidays

de **schoolverlater** /sx̲olvərlatər/ (pl: -s) school leaver; [Am] recent graduate; drop-out

het **schoolverzuim** /sx̲olvərzœym/ school absenteeism

het **schoolvoorbeeld** /sx̲olvorbelt/ (pl: -en) classic example: *dit is een ~* **van** *hoe het niet moet* this is a classic example of how it shouldn't be done

de **schoolvriend** /sx̲olvrint/ (pl: -en) school friend

schoolziek /sx̲olzik/ (adj) shamming, malingering

schoolzwemmen /sx̲olzwɛmə(n)/ swimming (in school)

het ¹**schoon** /sx̲on/ beauty: *het vrouwelijk* ~ female beauty

²**schoon** /sx̲on/ (adj) **1** clean; neat: ~ *water* clean (*or:* fresh) water **2** beautiful, fine: *de schone* **kunsten** the fine arts **3** clear; after tax: *50 pond* ~ *per week* **verdienen** make 50 pounds a week net (*or:* after tax) **4** [Belg] fine, pretty ‖ *tachtig kilo* ~ *aan de* **haak** eighty kilo's net (weight); eighty kilo's without clothes; *zijn* **kans** ~ *zien* see one's chance (*or:* opportunity)

de **schoonbroer** /sx̲ombrur/ (pl: -s) brother-in-law

de **schoondochter** /sx̲ondɔxtər/ (pl: -s) daughter-in-law

de **schoonfamilie** /sx̲onfamili/ (pl: -s) in-laws

de **schoonheid** /sx̲onhɛit/ (pl: -heden) beauty

de **schoonheidsfoutje** /sx̲onhɛitsfɑucə/ little slip, flaw

het/de **schoonheidssalon** /sx̲onhɛitsalɔn/ (pl: -s) beauty salon (*or:* parlour)

de **schoonheidsspecialiste** /sx̲onhɛitspeʃalɪstə/ (pl: -s) beautician; cosmetician

het **schoonheidsvlekje** /sx̲onhɛitsflɛkjə/ (pl: -s) beauty spot

de **schoonheidswedstrijd** /sx̲onhɛitswɛtstrɛit/ (pl: -en) beauty contest

schoonhouden /sx̲onhɑudə(n)/ (hield schoon, heeft schoongehouden) clean: *een* **kantoor** ~ clean an office

de **schoonmaak** /sx̲omak/ (house) cleaning, clean-up: *de* **grote** ~ the spring-cleaning; *grote* ~ **houden** spring-clean; make a clean sweep

de **schoonmaakartikelen** /sx̲omakɑrtikələ(n)/ (pl) cleaning products, cleanser(s)

schoonmaken /sx̲omakə(n)/ (maakte schoon, heeft schoongemaakt) clean

de **schoonmaker** /sx̲omakər/ (pl: -s) cleaner

de **schoonmoeder** /sx̲omudər/ (pl: -s) mother-in-law

de **schoonouders** /sx̲onɑudərs/ (pl) in-laws

het **schoonschrift** /sx̲onsx̲rɪft/ (pl: -en) calligraphy

schoonspoelen /sx̲onspulə(n)/ (spoelde schoon, heeft schoongespoeld) rinse (out)

schoonspringen /sx̲onsprɪŋə(n)/ platform diving

de **schoonvader** /sx̲onvadər/ (pl: -s) father-in-law

de **schoonzoon** /sx̲onzon/ (pl: -s, -zonen) son-in-law

de **schoonzus** /sx̲onzʏs/ (pl: -sen) sister-in-law

schoonzwemmen /sx̲onzwɛmə(n)/ synchronized swimming

de **schoorsteen** /sx̲orsten/ (pl: -stenen) chimney: *de ~* **trekt** *niet goed* the chimney doesn't draw well; *de ~* **vegen** sweep the chimney

de **schoorsteenmantel** /sx̲orstemɑntəl/ (pl: -s) mantelpiece

de **schoorsteenveger** /sx̲orstenveɣər/ (pl: -s) chimney sweep

schoorvoetend /sx̲orvutənt/ (adj) reluctantly

de **schoot** /sx̲ot/ (pl: schoten) lap: *bij iem.* **op** ~ *kruipen* clamber onto s.o.'s lap

het **schoothondje** /sx̲othɔncə/ (pl: -s) lapdog

de **schop** /sx̲ɔp/ **1** kick: *een* **vrije** ~ a free kick; *iem. een ~ onder zijn kont* **geven** kick s.o. (*or:* up) the behind **2** shovel; spade

de ¹**schoppen** /sx̲ɔpə(n)/ (pl: -) spades: ~ *is* **troef** spades are trump; *één* ~ one spade

²**schoppen** /sx̲ɔpə(n)/ (schopte, heeft geschopt) kick: **tegen** *een bal* ~ kick a ball ‖ *het* **ver** ~ go far (in the world)

het/de **schoppenaas** /sx̲ɔpə(n)a̲s/ ace of spades

schor /sx̲ɔr/ (adj, adv) hoarse, husky

het **schorem** /sx̲orəm/ riff-raff, scum

de **schorpioen** /sx̲ɔrpijun/ (pl: -en) scorpion

de **Schorpioen** /sx̲ɔrpijun/ (pl: -en) Scorpio

de **schors** /sx̲ɔrs/ (pl: -en) bark

schorsen /sx̲ɔrsə(n)/ (schorste, heeft geschorst) **1** adjourn **2** suspend: *een speler* **voor** *drie wedstrijden* ~ suspend a player for three games; *als lid* ~ suspend s.o. from membership

de **schorseneer** /sx̲ɔrsəne̲r/ (pl: schorseneren) scorzonera

de **schorsing** /sx̲ɔrsɪŋ/ (pl: -en) suspension: *door zijn gedrag een* ~ **oplopen** be suspended for bad conduct

het/de **schort** /sx̲ɔrt/ (pl: -en) apron: *een ~* **voordoen** put on an apron

schorten /sx̲ɔrtə(n)/ (schortte, heeft geschort): *het schort* **aan** ... the trouble is ...; *wat schort eraan?* what's wrong?, what's the matter?

het **schot** /sx̲ɔt/ (pl: -en) **1** shot: *een ~* **in** *de roos* a bull's-eye; *een ~* **op** *goal* a shot at goal

2 range: *buiten* ~ *blijven, zich buiten* ~ *houden* keep out of range; *iem. (iets) onder* ~ *hebben* have s.o. (sth.) within range; *onder* ~ *houden* keep covered; *onder* ~ *nemen* cover **3** movement: *er komt (zit)* ~ *in de zaak* things are beginning to get going (*or:* to move) **4** partition

de **Schot** /sχɔt/ (pl: -ten) Scot

de **schotel** /sχotəl/ (pl: -s) **1** dish; [small] saucer: *een vuurvaste* ~ an ovenproof dish **2** dish: *een warme* ~ a hot dish ‖ *een vliegende* ~ a flying saucer

de **schotelantenne** /sχotəlantɛnə/ (satellite) dish, dish aerial, saucer aerial

Schotland /sχɔtlɑnt/ Scotland

de **schots** /sχɔts/ (pl: -en) (ice) floe ‖ ~ *en scheef* higgledy-piggledy, topsy-turvy

Schots /sχɔts/ (adj) Scottish, Scots; Scotch: ~*e whisky* Scotch (whisky)

de **schotwond** /sχɔtwɔnt/ (pl: -en) bullet wound, gunshot wound

de **schouder** /sχɑudər/ (pl: -s) shoulder: *de* ~*s ophalen* shrug one's shoulders; *iem. op zijn* ~ *kloppen* pat s.o. on the back; *een last van iemands* ~*s nemen* [fig] take a weight off s.o.'s shoulders

de **schouderband** /sχɑudərbɑnt/ (pl: -en) shoulder strap: *zonder* ~*jes* strapless

het **schouderblad** /sχɑudərblɑt/ (pl: -en) shoulder blade (*or:* bone)

het **schouderklopje** /sχɑudərklɔpjə/ (pl: -s) pat on the back

de **schoudertas** /sχɑudərtɑs/ (pl: -sen) shoulder bag

de **schoudervulling** /sχɑudərvʏlɪŋ/ (pl: -en) shoulder pad

de **schouw** /sχɑu/ (pl: -en) mantel(piece)

de **schouwburg** /sχɑubʏrχ/ (pl: -en) theatre: *naar de* ~ *gaan* go to the theatre

het **schouwspel** /sχɑuspɛl/ (pl: -en) spectacle; sight; show: *een aangrijpend* ~ a touching sight

schraal /sχral/ (adj, adv) **1** lean **2** poor; arid **3** bleak; cutting **4** dry: *schrale handen* chapped hands

schragen /sχraɣə(n)/ (schraagde, heeft geschraagd) **1** prop (up) **2** [fig] support, buoy (up)

de **schram** /sχrɑm/ (pl: -men) scratch, scrape: *geen* ~*metje hebben* not have a scratch; *vol* ~*men zitten* be all scratched

schrander /sχrɑndər/ (adj, adv) clever, sharp

schranzen /sχrɑnzə(n)/ (schransde, heeft geschransd) gormandize, stuff o.s.

schrap /sχrɑp/ (adv) braced: *zich* ~ *zetten* brace o.s.; dig (one's heels) in

schrapen /sχrapə(n)/ (schraapte, heeft geschraapt) **1** clear: *de keel* ~ clear one's throat **2** scrape: *geld bij elkaar* ~ scrape money together

schrappen /sχrɑpə(n)/ (schrapte, heeft geschrapt) **1** scrape; scale **2** strike off, strike out, delete: *iem. als lid* ~ drop s.o. from membership

de **schrede** /sχredə/ (pl: -n) pace, step

de **schreef** /sχref/ (pl: schreven): *over de* ~ *gaan* overstep the mark

de **schreeuw** /sχrew/ (pl: -en) shout, cry: *een* ~ *geven* (let out a) yell, give a cry

¹**schreeuwen** /sχrewə(n)/ (schreeuwde, heeft geschreeuwd) **1** scream, cry (out), yell (out) **2** cry out (for): *deze problemen* ~ *om een snelle oplossing* these problems are crying out for a quick solution **3** scream, shout: *hij schreeuwt tegen iedereen* he shouts at everyone **4** cry; screech; squeal

²**schreeuwen** /sχrewə(n)/ (schreeuwde, heeft geschreeuwd) shout (out), yell (out): *een bevel* ~ shout (*or:* yell) (out) an order

de **schreeuwlelijk** /sχrewlelək/ (pl: -en) **1** loudmouth, bigmouth **2** squaller, screamer

schreien /sχrɛiə(n)/ (schreide, heeft geschreid) weep, cry (out) ‖ *bittere* (or: *hete*) *tranen* ~ weep bitter (*or:* hot) tears

schriel /sχril/ (adj) thin, meagre

het **schrift** /sχrɪft/ (pl: -en) **1** writing: *iets op* ~ *stellen* put sth. in writing; *ik heb het op* ~ I have it in writing **2** (hand)writing: *duidelijk leesbaar* ~ legible handwriting **3** exercise book, notebook

de **Schrift** /sχrɪft/ Scripture(s): *de Heilige* ~ (Holy) Scripture, the Scriptures

schriftelijk /sχrɪftələk/ (adj, adv) written, in writing: *een* ~*e cursus* a correspondence course; ~ *bevestigen* confirm in writing; *iets* ~ *vastleggen* put sth. in writing ‖ *voor het* ~ *zakken* fail one's written exams

schrijden /sχrɛidə(n)/ (schreed, heeft/is geschreden) stride, stalk

de **schrijfbenodigdheden** /sχrɛivbənodəχthedə(n)/ (pl) stationery, writing materials

het **schrijfblok** /sχrɛivblɔk/ (pl: -ken) writing pad, (note)pad

de **schrijffout** /sχrɛifɑut/ (pl: -en) writing error, slip of the pen

het **schrijfgerei** /sχrɛifχərɛi/ stationery

de **schrijfmachine** /sχrɛifmɑʃinə/ (pl: -s) typewriter

het **schrijfpapier** /sχrɛifpɑpir/ writing paper

de **schrijfster** /sχrɛifstər/ (pl: -s) writer

de **schrijftaal** /sχrɛiftal/ written language

de **schrijfvaardigheid** /sχrɛifardəχhɛit/ writing skill

schrijlings /sχrɛilɪŋs/ (adj, adv) straddling, astride: ~ *op een paard zitten* sit astride a horse

schrijnen /sχrɛinə(n)/ (schrijnde, heeft geschrijnd) **1** chafe **2** smart

schrijven /sχrɛivə(n)/ (schreef, heeft geschreven) write: *een vriend* ~ write to a friend; **voluit** ~ write (out) in full; **op** een advertentie ~ answer an advertisement; op het moment waarop ik dit schrijf at the time of writing

de **schrijver** /sxrɛivər/ (pl: -s) writer, author

de **schrik** /sxrɪk/ (pl: -ken) **1** terror, shock, fright: iem. ~ aanjagen give s.o. a fright; **van de ~ bekomen** get over the shock; **met de ~ vrijkomen** have a lucky escape; **tot mijn** ~ to my alarm (or: horror); **tot hun grote** ~ to their horror **2** fright, fear **3** terror: hij is de ~ van de **buurt** he is the terror of the neighbourhood

schrikaanjagend /sxrɪkaɲaxənt/ (adj) terrifying, frightening

schrikbarend /sxrɪgbaːrənt/ (adj, adv) alarming, shocking: ~ **hoge** prijzen staggering prices

het **schrikbeeld** /sxrɪgbelt/ (pl: -en) phantom, spectre, bogey: het ~ van de **werkloosheid** the spectre of unemployment

het **schrikbewind** /sxrɪgbəwɪnt/ (pl: -en) reign of terror: [fig] een ~ **voeren** terrorize the place, conduct a reign of terror

de **schrikdraad** /sxrɪgdraːt/ (pl: -draden) electric fence

de **schrikkeldag** /sxrɪkəldɑx/ (pl: -en) leap day

het **schrikkeljaar** /sxrɪkəljaːr/ (pl: -jaren) leap year

de **schrikkelmaand** /sxrɪkəlmaːnt/ (pl: -en) February

schrikken /sxrɪkə(n)/ (schrok, is geschrokken) be shocked (or: scared, frightened): ik schrik me **kapot (dood)** I'm scared stiff (or: to death); **wakker** ~ wake with a start; iem. **laten** ~ frighten s.o.; hij schrok **ervan** it frightened him; **van iets** ~ be frightened by sth.; iem. aan **het** ~ maken give s.o. a fright

schril /sxrɪl/ (adj, adv) **1** shrill; squeaky: een ~le **stem** a shrill voice **2** sharp; glaring

schrobben /sxrɔbə(n)/ (schrobde, heeft geschrobd) scrub

de **schroef** /sxruf/ (pl: schroeven) **1** screw: alles staat weer op **losse** schroeven everything's unsettled (or: up in the air) again; [fig] de schroeven **aandraaien** put the screws on; een ~ **vastdraaien** (or: losdraaien) tighten (or: loosen) a screw; er **zit** een ~je bij hem **los** he has a screw loose **2** screw propeller

het **schroefdeksel** /sxruvdɛksəl/ (pl: -s) screw cap, screw-on lid

de **schroefdop** /sxruvdɔp/ (pl: -pen) screw cap, screw top: de ~ van een **fles** losdraaien screw the top off a bottle

de **schroefdraad** /sxruvdraːt/ (pl: -draden) (screw) thread

schroeien /sxrujə(n)/ (schroeide, heeft geschroeid) **1** singe; sear: zijn **kleren** ~ singe one's clothes **2** scorch: de zon schroeide het **gras** the sun scorched the grass

schroeven /sxruvə(n)/ (schroefde, heeft geschroefd) screw: iets **in** elkaar ~ screw sth.

together; iets **uit** elkaar ~ unscrew sth.

de **schroevendraaier** /sxruvə(n)draːjər/ (pl: -s) screwdriver

schrokken /sxrɔkə(n)/ (schrokte, heeft geschrokt) cram down, gobble: zit niet zo te ~ don't bolt your food like that

schromelijk /sxroːmələk/ (adj, adv) gross: ~ **overdreven** grossly exaggerated

schromen /sxroːmə(n)/ (schroomde, heeft geschroomd) hesitate

schrompelen /sxrɔmpələ(n)/ (schrompelde, is geschrompeld) shrivel

de **schroom** /sxroːm/ hesitation, diffidence

de ¹**schroot** /sxroːt/ lath: een muur **met** ~jes betimmeren lath a wall

het ²**schroot** /sxroːt/ **1** scrap (iron, metal) **2** lumps

de **schroothoop** /sxroːthoːp/ (pl: -hopen) scrap heap: deze auto is rijp **voor** de ~ this car is fit for the scrap heap

de **schub** /sxʏp/ (pl: -ben) scale

schuchter /sxʏxtər/ (adj, adv) shy, timid: een ~e **poging** a timid attempt

schudden /sxʏdə(n)/ (schudde, heeft geschud) shake; shuffle: ~ **voor gebruik** shake before use; iem. flink de **hand** ~ pump s.o.'s hand; **nee** ~ (met het hoofd) shake one's head; iem. **van** zich af ~ shake s.o. off; iem. door elkaar ~ shake s.o. up || dat **kun** je wel ~! forget it!, nothing doing!

de **schuier** /sxœyər/ (pl: -s) brush

de **schuif** /sxœyf/ (pl: schuiven) **1** bolt **2** [Belg] drawer

de **schuifbalk** [comp] scroll bar

het **schuifdak** /sxœyvdɑk/ (pl: -en) sunroof

de **schuifdeur** /sxœyvdør/ (pl: -en) sliding door

schuifelen /sxœyfələ(n)/ (schuifelde, heeft geschuifeld) shuffle: **met** de voeten ~ shuffle one's feet

het **schuifje** /sxœyfjə/ (pl: -s) (small) bolt

de **schuifladder** /sxœyfladər/ (pl: -s) extension ladder

de **schuifpui** /sxœyfpœy/ (pl: -en) sliding patio doors, sliding French window; [Am] sliding French door

het **schuifraam** /sxœyfraːm/ (pl: -ramen) sash window; sliding window

de **schuiftrombone** /sxœyftrɔmbɔːnə/ (pl: -s) slide trombone

de **schuiftrompet** /sxœyftrɔmpɛt/ (pl: -ten) trombone

de **schuifwand** /sxœyfwɑnt/ (pl: -en) sliding wall

schuilen /sxœylə(n)/ (schuilde, heeft gescholen/geschuild) **1** hide: daarin schuilt een groot **gevaar** that carries a great risk (with it) **2** shelter (from)

schuilgaan /sxœylɣaːn/ (ging schuil, is schuilgegaan) be hidden: de zon ging schuil **achter** donkere wolken the sun was hidden (or: went) behind dark clouds

zich **schuilhouden** /sχœɐ̯lhɑudə(n)/ (hield zich schuil, heeft zich schuilgehouden) be in hiding, hide o.s. away

de **schuilkelder** /sχœɐ̯lkɛldər/ (pl: -s) air-raid shelter

de **schuilnaam** /sχœɐ̯lnam/ (pl: -namen) pseudonym, pen-name

de **schuilplaats** /sχœɐ̯lplats/ (pl: -en) **1** hiding place, (place of) shelter; hideout: *iem. een ~ verlenen* give shelter to s.o. **2** shelter: *een ~ zoeken* take shelter

het **schuim** /sχœym/ foam; froth; lather

het **schuimbad** /sχœymbɑt/ (pl: -en) bubble bath

schuimbekken /sχœymbɛkə(n)/ (schuimbekte, heeft geschuimbekt) foam: *~ van woede* foam with rage

het **schuimblusapparaat** /sχœymblʏsɑparat/ (pl: -apparaten) foam extinguisher

schuimen /sχœymə(n)/ (schuimde, heeft geschuimd) foam, froth; lather: *die zeep schuimt niet* that soap does not lather

de **schuimkraag** /sχœymkraχ/ (pl: -kragen) head

het **schuimpje** /sχœympjə/ (pl: -s) meringue

het **¹schuimplastic** /sχœymplɛstɪk/ foam plastic
²schuimplastic /sχœymplɛstɪk/ (adj) foam plastic

de **¹schuimrubber** /sχœymrʏbər/ foam rubber
²schuimrubber /sχœymrʏbər/ (adj) foam rubber

de **schuimspaan** /sχœymspan/ (pl: -spanen) skimmer

de **schuimwijn** /sχœymwɛin/ (pl: -en) sparkling wine

schuin /sχœyn/ (adj, adv) **1** slanting, sloping: *~e rand* bevelled edge; *een ~e streep* a slash; *een stuk hout ~ afzagen* saw a piece of wood slantwise; *iets ~ houden* slant sth.; *~ oversteken* cross diagonally; *~ schrijven* write in italics; *hier ~ tegenover* diagonally across from here **2** smutty, dirty ‖ *met een ~ oog kijken naar* look at … with envious eyes, cast envious looks at

de **schuinsmarcheerder** /sχœynsmɑrʃerdər/ (pl: -s) debauchee

de **schuit** /sχœyt/ (pl: -en) barge, boat

het **schuitje** /sχœycə/ (pl: -s) boat: *in hetzelfde ~ zitten* be in the same boat

¹schuiven /sχœyvə(n)/ (schoof, heeft/is geschoven) **1** slide: *de lading ging ~* the cargo shifted; *in elkaar ~* slide into one another, telescope **2** move (*or:* bring) one's chair: *dichterbij ~* bring one's chair closer ‖ *laat hem maar ~* let him get on with it; *met data ~* rearrange dates

²schuiven /sχœyvə(n)/ (schoof, heeft geschoven) push, shove: *een stoel bij de tafel ~* pull up a chair; *iets (iem.) terzijde ~* brush sth. (s.o.) aside; *iets voor zich uit ~* put sth. off, postpone sth.

de **schuiver** /sχœyvər/ (pl: -s) skid, lurch: *een ~ maken* skid, lurch

de **schuld** /sχʏlt/ (pl: -en) **1** debt: *zijn ~en afbetalen* pay off (*or:* settle) one's debts; *~en hebben* have debts, be in debt; *zich in de ~en steken* incur debts, get into debt **2** guilt, blame: *iem. de ~ van iets geven* blame s.o. for sth.; *het is mijn eigen ~* it is my own fault; *eigen ~ dikke bult* it's your own fault

de **schuldbekentenis** /sχʏldbəkɛntənɪs/ (pl: -sen) **1** bond; IOU **2** admission (*or:* confession) of guilt: *een volledige ~ afleggen* make a full confession

schuldbewust /sχʏldbəwʏst/ (adj) conscious of guilt, contrite

de **schuldeiser** /sχʏltɛisər/ (pl: -s) creditor

de **schuldenaar** /sχʏldənar/ (pl: -s, schuldenaren) debtor

het **schuldgevoel** /sχʏltχəvul/ (pl: -ens) feeling of guilt, guilty conscience

schuldig /sχʏldəχ/ (adj) **1** owing: *hoeveel ben ik u ~?* how much do I owe you? **2** guilty: *zich ~ voelen* feel guilty; *de rechter heeft hem ~ verklaard* the judge has declared him guilty

de **schuldige** /sχʏldəɣə/ (pl: -n) culprit, guilty party; offender

de **schuldsanering** /sχʏltsanerɪŋ/ (pl: -en) debt restructuring

de **schuldvraag** /sχʏltfraχ/ (pl: -vragen) the question of guilt

de **schulp** /sχʏlp/ (pl: -en) shell: *in zijn ~ kruipen* withdraw (*or:* retire) into one's shell

schunnig /sχʏnəχ/ (adj) shabby; filthy

schuren /sχyrə(n)/ (schuurde, heeft/is geschuurd) **1** grate, scour **2** sand(paper)

de **schurft** /sχʏrft/ scabies; mange: *de ~ aan iem. hebben* hate s.o.'s guts

de **schurk** /sχʏrk/ (pl: -en) scoundrel, villain

de **schurkenstaat** /sχʏrkə(n)stat/ (pl: -staten) rogue state

de **schurkenstreek** /sχʏrkə(n)strek/ (pl: -streken) piece of villainy

het **schut** /sχʏt/ (pl: -ten) shelter, cover ‖ *iem. voor ~ zetten* make s.o. look a fool; *voor ~ staan* look a fool (*or:* an idiot)

het **schutblad** /sχʏdblɑt/ (pl: -en) endpaper, end leaf

de **schutkleur** /sχʏtklør/ (pl: -en) camouflage

de **schutsluis** /sχʏtslœys/ (pl: -sluizen) lock

de **schutspatroon** /sχʏtspatron/ (pl: -patronen) patron (saint)

schutten /sχʏtə(n)/ (schutte, heeft geschut) lock

de **schutter** /sχʏtər/ (pl: -s) rifleman; marksman ‖ *hij is een goede ~* he is a crack shot

schutteren /sχʏtərə(n)/ (schutterde, heeft geschutterd) **1** fumble **2** falter, stammer

de **schutting** /sχʏtɪŋ/ (pl: -en) fence: *een ~ om een bouwterrein zetten* fence off a construction site

schuttingtaal

de **schuttingtaal** /sχɣtɪntal/ foul language, obscene language: ~ *uitslaan* use foul (*or:* obscene) language

het **schuttingwoord** /sχɣtɪŋwɔrt/ (pl: -en) four-letter word, obscenity

de **schuur** /sχyr/ (pl: schuren) shed; barn: *de oogst in de ~ brengen* bring in the harvest

de **schuurmachine** /sχyrmaʃinə/ (pl: -s) sander, sanding machine

het **schuurmiddel** /sχyrmɪdəl/ (pl: -en) abrasive

het **schuurpapier** /sχyrpapir/ sandpaper

het/de **schuurpoeder** /sχyrpudər/ scouring powder

de **schuurspons** /sχyrspɔns/ (pl: -sponzen) scourer

schuw /sχyw/ (adj, adv) shy, timid

schuwen /sχywə(n)/ (schuwde, heeft geschuwd) shun, shrink from

de **schwalbe** /ʃwɑlbə/ (pl: -s) deliberate dive to draw a penalty

de **schwung** /ʃwuŋ/ verve, dash

de **sciencefiction** /sɑjənsfɪkʃən/ science fiction, sci-fi

de **sclerose** /sklerozə/ (pl: -n, -s) sclerosis: *multiple ~* multiple sclerosis

de **scooter** /skutər/ (pl: -s) (motor) scooter

de **scootmobiel** /skutmobil/ miniscooter, mobility scooter

de **score** /skorə/ (pl: -s) score: *een gelijke ~ a* draw (*or:* tie); *een ~ behalen van ...* make a score of ...

het **scorebord** /skorəbɔrt/ (pl: -en) scoreboard

scoren /skorə(n)/ (scoorde, heeft gescoord) score: *een doelpunt ~* score (a goal)

de **scout** /skɑut/ (pl: -s) **1** Scout **2** talent-scout

de **scouting** /skɑutɪŋ/ Scouting

scrabbelen® /skrɛbələ(n)/ (scrabbelde, heeft gescrabbeld) play Scrabble

screenen /skriːnə(n)/ (screende, heeft gescreend) screen; vet

de **screensaver** /skriːnsevər/ screensaver

het **script** /skrɪpt/ (pl: -s) script

de **scriptie** /skrɪpsi/ (pl: -s) thesis, term paper: *een ~ schrijven over* write a thesis about (*or:* on)

scrollen /skrɔlə(n)/ (scrolde, heeft gescrold) scroll

het **scrotum** /skrotʏm/ (pl: -s) scrotum

de **scrupule** /skrypylə/ (pl: -s) scruple, qualm

scrupuleus /skrypyløs/ (adj, adv) scrupulous

de **sculptuur** /skʏlptyr/ (pl: sculpturen) sculpture

de **seance** /sejãsə/ (pl: -s) seance

sec /sɛk/ (adj) *seconde* sec

de **seconde** /səkɔndə/ (pl: -n) **1** second: *in een onderdeel van een ~* in a split second **2** second, moment: *hij houdt geen ~ zijn mond* he never stops talking

de **secondelijm** /səkɔndəlɛim/ superglue

de **secondewijzer** /səkɔndəwɛizər/ (pl: -s) second hand

het **secreet** /səkret/ (pl: secreten) (dirty) swine, sod; bitch

de **secretaire** /sɪkrətɛːr(ə)/ (pl: -s) writing desk

de **secretaresse** /sɪkrətarɛsə/ (pl: -s) secretary

het **secretariaat** /sɪkrətarijat/ (pl: secretariaten) secretariat; secretary's office

de **secretaris** /sɪkrətarɪs/ (pl: -sen) secretary; clerk

de **secretaris-generaal** /sɪkrətarɪsχenəral/ (pl: secretarissen-generaal) secretary-general

de **sectie** /sɛksi/ (pl: -s) **1** autopsy; post-mortem (examination); dissection: *~ verrichten* carry out a post-mortem (*or:* an autopsy) **2** section; department: *de ~ betaald voetbal* the Football League; *de ~ Frans* the French department

de **sector** /sɛktor/ (pl: -en) sector: *de agrarische ~* the agricultural sector; *de zachte ~* the social sector

de **secularisatie** /sekylariza(t)si/ secularization

seculier /sekylir/ (adj) secular

secundair /sekyndɛːr/ (adj, adv) secondary, minor: *van ~ belang* of minor importance

secuur /səkyr/ (adj, adv) precise, meticulous

sedert /sedərt/ (prep) since; for: *~ enige tijd* for some time

seffens /sɛfə(n)s/ (adv) [Belg] at once, straightaway

het **segment** /sɛɣmɛnt/ (pl: -en) segment: *de ~en van een tunnel* the sections of a tunnel

het **sein** /sɛin/ (pl: -en) **1** signal, sign: *het ~ op veilig zetten* set the sign at clear **2** tip, hint: *geef me even een ~tje als je hulp nodig hebt* just let me know if you need any help

seinen /sɛinə(n)/ (seinde, heeft geseind) **1** signal; flash **2** telegraph; radio

de **seinwachter** /sɛinwɑχtər/ (pl: -s) signalman

seismisch /sɛismis/ (adj) seismic

de **seismograaf** /sɛismoɣraf/ (pl: -grafen) seismograph

het **seizoen** /sɛizun/ (pl: -en) season: *weer dat past bij het ~* seasonable weather; *buiten het ~* in the off-season, out of season; off-season

de **seizoenarbeid** /sɛizunɑrbɛit/ seasonal work (*or:* employment)

de **seizoenarbeider** /sɛizunɑrbɛidər/ (pl: -s) seasonal worker

de **seizoenopruiming** /sɛizunɔprœymɪŋ/ end-of-season sale

de **seizoenkaart** /sɛizunkart/ (pl: -en) season ticket

de **seizoenwerkloosheid** /sɛizunwɛrkloshɛit/ seasonal unemployment

de **seks** /sɛks/ sex: *~ hebben* have sex; *onveilige ~* unprotected sex

de **sekse** /sɛksə/ (pl: -n) sex: *iem. van de andere ~* s.o. of the opposite sex

de **seksfilm** /sɛksfɪlm/ (pl: -s) sex film; skin-flick

de **seksist** /sɛksɪst/ (pl: -en) sexist; male chauvinist

seksistisch /sɛksɪstis/ (adj, adv) sexist, like a sexist: *een ~e* **opmerking** a sexist remark

het **seksleven** /sɛkslevə(n)/ sex life

de **seksshop** /sɛkʃɔp/ (pl: -s) sex shop, porn shop

het **sekssymbool** /sɛksɪmbol/ (pl: -symbolen) sex symbol

de **seksualiteit** /sɛksywalitɛit/ sexuality

seksueel /sɛksywel/ (adj, adv) sexual: *seksuele* **voorlichting** sex education; *~ overdraagbare* aandoeningen sexually transmitted disease(s)

de **seksuoloog** /sɛksywolox/ (pl: -logen) sexologist

de **sekte** /sɛktə/ (pl: -n, -s) sect

de **selderij** /sɛldərɛi/ celery

select /selɛkt/ (adj) select

selecteren /selɛktərə(n)/ (selecteerde, heeft geselecteerd) select, pick (out): *hij werd niet geselecteerd* **voor** *die wedstrijd* he was not picked (or: selected) for that match

de **selectie** /selɛksi/ (pl: -s) selection: [sport] *de ~ bekendmaken* announce the selection, name the squad

selectief /selɛktif/ (adj, adv) selective

de **selectieprocedure** /selɛksiprosedyrə/ (pl: -s) selection procedure

de **selectiewedstrijd** /selɛksiwɛtstrɛit/ (pl: -en) selection match; preliminary match

de **semafoon** /semafon/ (pl: -s) [roughly] radio(tele)phone

het **semester** /semɛstər/ (pl: -s) six months, semester, term (of six months)

de **semieten** /semitə(n)/ (pl) Semites

het **seminarie** /seminari/ (pl: -s) seminary: *op het ~ zitten* be at a seminary

het **semioverheidsbedrijf** /semiovərhɛitsbədrɛif/ (pl: -bedrijven) semi state-controlled company

de **senaat** /senat/ (pl: senaten) senate

de **senator** /senator/ (pl: -en) senator: *tot ~ gekozen worden* be elected (as) senator

Senegal /senɛɣal/ Senegal

de ¹**Senegalees** /seneɣales/ (pl: Senegalezen) Senegalese

²**Senegalees** /seneɣales/ (adj) Senegalese

seniel /senil/ (adj) senile

de **seniliteit** /senilitɛit/ senility

de **senior** /senijor/ (pl: -en) senior

de **seniorenpas** /senijorə(n)pɑs/ (pl: -sen) pensioner's ticket (or: pass), senior citizen's pass (or: reduction card)

de **sensatie** /sɛnsa(t)si/ (pl: -s) sensation, feeling; thrill; stir: *op ~ belust zijn* be looking for sensation

de **sensatiepers** /sɛnsa(t)sipɛrs/ gutter press

de **sensatiezucht** /sɛnsa(t)sizyxt/ sensationalism

sensationeel /sɛnsa(t)ʃonel/ (adj, adv) sensational; spectacular

sensibel /sɛnsibəl/ (adj) sensitive (to)

sensitief /sɛnsitif/ (adj) sensitive

de **sensor** /sɛnsor/ (pl: -s, -en) sensor

sensueel /sɛnsywel/ (adj, adv) sensual

het **sentiment** /sɛntimɛnt/ (pl: -en) sentiment: *vals ~* cheap sentiment

sentimenteel /sɛntimɛntel/ (adj, adv) sentimental: *een sentimentele* **film** a sentimental film; *a tear-jerker*

separaat /separat/ (adj) separate

de **separatist** /separatɪst/ (pl: -en) separatist

seponeren /seponerə(n)/ (seponeerde, heeft geseponeerd) dismiss, drop

de **september** /sɛptɛmbər/ September

septisch /sɛptis/ (adj) septic: *~e* **put** septic tank

sereen /seren/ (adj, adv) serene

de **serenade** /serenadə/ (pl: -s) serenade: *iem. een ~* **brengen** serenade s.o.

de **sergeant** /sɛrʒɑnt/ (pl: -s) sergeant

de **sergeant-majoor** /sɛrʒɑntmajor/ (pl: -s) sergeant major

de **serie** /seri/ (pl: -s) series; serial: *een* **Amerikaanse** *~ op de tv* an American serial on TV

de **seriemoordenaar** /serimordənar/ (pl: -s) serial killer

het **serienummer** /serinymər/ (pl: -s) serial number

de **serieproductie** /seriprodyksi/ serial production, series production

serieus /serijøs/ (adj, adv) serious; straight: *een serieuze* **zaak** no laughing matter; *~? se-riously?, really?*

de **sering** /serɪŋ/ (pl: -en) lilac: *een* **boeket** *~en* a bouquet of lilac

seropositief /seropozitif/ (adj) HIV-positive

het **serpent** /sɛrpɛnt/ (pl: -en) **1** serpent **2** shrew, bitch

de **serpentine** /sɛrpɛntinə/ (pl: -s) streamer

de **serre** /sɛːrə/ (pl: -s) **1** sunroom **2** conservatory

het **serum** /serym/ (pl: sera) serum

de **serveerster** /sɛrverstər/ waitress

de **server** /syːrvər/ (pl: -s) server

serveren /sɛrverə(n)/ (serveerde, heeft geserveerd) serve: *koel ~* serve chilled; *onderhands* (or: *bovenhands*) *~* serve underarm (or: overarm)

het **servet** /sɛrvɛt/ (pl: -ten) napkin

de **service** /syːrvɪs/ **1** service: *dat* **is** *nog eens ~!* that is what I call service! **2** service charge: *~* **inbegrepen** service charges included

de **servicebeurt** /syːrvɪzbørt/ (pl: -en) service: *met je auto naar de garage gaan* **voor** *een ~* take the car to be serviced

de **serviceflat** /syːrvɪsflɛt/ (pl: -s) service flat

de **servicekosten** /syːrvɪskɔstə(n)/ (pl) service charge(s)

Servië /sɛrvijə/ Serbia

de **Serviër** /sɛrvijər/ (pl: -s) Serb(ian)

het **servies** /sɛrvis/ (pl: serviezen) service: *thee-servies* tea service (*or:* set); *30-delig* ~ 30-piece service

het **serviesgoed** /sɛrvisxut/ (pl: -eren) crockery

het **¹Servisch** /sɛrvis/ Serbian

²Servisch /sɛrvis/ (adj) Serbian

het **sesamzaad** /sezɑmzat/ (pl: -zaden) sesame seed(s)

de **sessie** /sɛsi/ (pl: -s) session, sitting; jam session

de **set** /sɛt/ (pl: -s) set

het **setpoint** /sɛtpɔjnt/ (pl: -s) set point

de **setter** /sɛtər/ (pl: -s) setter: *Ierse* ~ Irish setter

het/de **sexappeal** /sɛksəpi:l/ sex appeal

de **sextant** /sɛkstɑnt/ (pl: -en) sextant

het **sextet** /sɛkstɛt/ (pl: -ten) sextet(te)

sexy /sɛksi/ (adj) sexy

de **Seychellen** /seʃɛlə(n)/ (pl) the Seychelles

de **sfeer** /sfer/ (pl: sferen) **1** atmosphere **2** atmosphere; character; ambience: *een huis met een heel eigen* ~ a house with a distinctive character **3** sphere: *in hogere sferen zijn* have one's head in the clouds

sfeervol /sfervɔl/ (adj) attractive

de **sfinx** /sfɪŋks/ (pl: -en) sphinx

de **shag** /ʃɛk/ hand-rolling tobacco: ~ *roken* roll one's own

de **shampoo** /ʃɑmpo/ (pl: -s) shampoo

het **shantykoor** /ʃɛntikor/ (pl: -koren) shanty choir

de **sharia** /ʃɑrija/ sharia(h)

de **sheet** /ʃi:t/ (pl: -s) sheet

de **sheriff** /ʃɛrɪf/ (pl: -s) sheriff

de **sherry** /ʃɛri/ (pl: -'s) sherry

de **shetlander** /ʃɛtlɑndər/ (pl: -s) Shetland (pony)

het **shirt** /ʃy:rt/ (pl: -s) shirt; blouse

de **shirtreclame** /ʃy:rtrəklamə/ (pl: -s) shirt advertising

shit /ʃɪt/ (int) [inform] shit

de **shoarma** /ʃwɑrma/ doner kebab: *een broodje* ~ a doner kebab

de **shock** /ʃɔk/ (pl: -s) shock

de **shocktherapie** /ʃɔkterapi/ shock treatment (*or:* therapy)

de **shocktoestand** /ʃɔktustɑnt/ (pl: -en) state of shock: *hij is in* ~ he is in (a state of) shock

shoppen /ʃɔpə(n)/ (shopte, heeft geshopt) shop; shop around

de **short** /ʃɔ:rt/ shorts

de **shortlist** /ʃɔ:rtlɪst/ (pl: -s) shortlist

het **shorttrack** /ʃɔ:rtrɛk/ short-track speed skating

de **shot** /ʃɔt/ (pl: -s) shot: *een* ~ *nemen* take a shot; jack up

het **shotten** /ʃɔtə(n)/ [Belg] play football

de **shovel** /ʃovəl/ (pl: -s) shovel

de **show** /ʃow/ (pl: -s) show, display

de **showbusiness** /ʃobɪznɪs/ show business

showen /ʃowə(n)/ (showde, heeft geshowd) show, display

de **showroom** /ʃoru:m/ (pl: -s) show room

de **shredder** /ʃrɛdər/ (pl: -s) shredder

de **shuttle** /ʃytəl/ (pl: -s) shuttle

de **si** /si/ (pl: si's) [mus] ti, si

de **siamees** /sijames/ (pl: siamezen) Siamese (cat)

Siamees /sijames/ (adj) Siamese

Siberië /siberijə/ Siberia

Siberisch /siberis/ (adj, adv) Siberian

de **Siciliaan** /sisilijɑn/ (pl: Sicilianen) Sicilian

Sicilië /sisilijə/ Sicily

sidderen /sɪdərə(n)/ (sidderde, heeft gesidderd) tremble, shiver: *ik sidderde bij de gedachte alleen al* the very thought of it made me shudder

de **siddering** /sɪdərɪŋ/ (pl: -en) shudder, shiver: *er ging een* ~ *door de menigte* a shudder (*or:* shiver) went through the crowd

de **sier** /sir/ show: *dat is alleen maar voor de* ~ it's only for show ‖ *goede* ~ *maken (met iets)* try to cut a dash (with sth.), show off (sth.)

het **sieraad** /sirat/ (pl: sieraden) jewel; jewellery

sieren /sirə(n)/ (sierde, heeft gesierd) adorn: *dat siert hem* it is to his credit

sierlijk /sirlək/ (adj, adv) elegant, graceful

de **sierlijkheid** /sirləkhɛit/ elegance, grace(fulness)

de **sierplant** /sirplɑnt/ (pl: -en) ornamental plant

Sierra Leone /ʃɛralejonə/ Sierra Leone

de **Sierra Leoner** /ʃɛralejonər/ (pl: -s) Sierra Leonean

Sierra Leoons /ʃɛralejons/ (adj) Sierra Leonian

de **sierstrip** /sirstrɪp/ (pl: -s) trim

de **siësta** /sijɛsta/ (pl: -'s) siesta: ~ *houden* have a siesta

de **sigaar** /siɣar/ (pl: sigaren) cigar: *een* ~ *opsteken* light a cigar ‖ *de* ~ *zijn* have had it; get the blame

het **sigarenbandje** /siɣarə(n)bɑncə/ (pl: -s) cigar band

de **sigarenwinkel** /siɣarə(n)wɪŋkəl/ cigar shop, tobacconist's

de **sigaret** /siɣarɛt/ (pl: -ten) cigarette: *een pakje ~ten* a packet of cigarettes; [Am] a pack of cigarettes; *een* ~ *opsteken* (*or: uitmaken*) light (*or:* put out) a cigarette

de **sigarettenautomaat** /siɣarɛtə(n)automat/ (pl: -automaten) cigarette (vending) machine

het **signaal** /sɪnal/ (pl: signalen) **1** signal, sign: *het* ~ *voor de aftocht geven* sound the retreat **2** signal: *het* ~ *stond op rood* the signal was red

het **signalement** /sɪnaləmɛnt/ (pl: -en) description: *hij beantwoordt niet aan het* ~ he doesn't fit the description

signaleren /sɪnalerə(n)/ (signaleerde, heeft

gesignaleerd) **1** see, spot: *hij was in een nachtclub gesignaleerd* he had been seen in a nightclub **2** point out: *problemen* (or: *misstanden*) ~ point out problems (*or:* evils)

de **signalisatie** /sɪnaliza(t)si/ [Belg] traffic signs, road signs

de **signatuur** /sɪnatyr/ (pl: signaturen) **1** signature **2** nature, character

signeren /sɪnerə(n)/ (signeerde, heeft gesigneerd) sign, autograph: *een door de auteur gesigneerd exemplaar* a signed (an autographed) copy

significant /sɪɣnifikɑnt/ (adj, adv) significant

sijpelen /sɛipələ(n)/ (sijpelde, heeft/is gesijpeld) trickle, ooze, seep

de **sik** /sɪk/ (pl: -ken) goatee

de **sikh** /sɪk/ (pl: -s) Sikh

de **sikkel** /sɪkəl/ (pl: -s) sickle

sikkeneurig /sɪkənørəx/ (adj, adv) peevish, grouchy

sikkepit /sɪkəpɪt/ whit, bit

het/de **silhouet** /siluwɛt/ (pl: -ten) silhouette

het **silicium** /silisijʏm/ silicon

het/de **siliconenkit** /silikonə(n)kɪt/ silicone paste, fibre-glass paste

de **silo** /silo/ (pl: -'s) silo

de **simkaart** /sɪmkart/ (pl: -en) SIM card

simpel /sɪmpəl/ (adj, adv) simple: *~e kost* simple (*or:* modest) fare; *zo ~ ligt dat!* it's as simple as that!

de **simulant** /simylɑnt/ (pl: -en) simulator

simuleren /simylerə(n)/ (simuleerde, heeft gesimuleerd) simulate, sham

simultaan /simyltan/ (adj, adv) simultaneous: [sport] *~ spelen* give a simultaneous display

de **simultaanpartij** /simyltampɑrtɛi/ (pl: -en) simultaneous game

simultaanschaken play simultaneous chess

de **sinaasappel** /sinasapəl/ (pl: -en, -s) orange

de **sinaasappelkist** /sinasapəlkɪst/ orange crate, orange box

het **sinaasappelsap** /sinasapəlsap/ orange juice

de **sinas** /sinas/ orangeade, orange soda

¹**sinds** /sɪnts/ (prep) since; for: *ik ben hier al ~ jaren* niet meer geweest I haven't been here for years; *ik heb hem ~ maandag niet meer gezien* I haven't seen him since Monday; *~ kort* recently; for a short time now

²**sinds** /sɪnts/ (conj) since; ever since: *~ ik Jan ken* since I met (*or:* have known) Jan

sindsdien /sɪn(t)sdin/ (adv) since: *~ is er van hen niets meer vernomen* they have not been heard of (ever) since; *~ werkt hij niet meer* he hasn't worked since (then)

Singapore /sɪŋapur/ Singapore

de ¹**Singaporees** /sɪŋaporeːs/ (pl: Singaporezen) Singaporean

²**Singaporees** /sɪŋaporeːs/ (adj) Singaporean

de **singel** /sɪŋəl/ (pl: -s) **1** canal **2** webbing

de **singer-songwriter** /sɪŋərsɔŋrajtər/ singer-song writer

de **single** /sɪŋɡəl/ (pl: -s) single

de **singlet** /sɪŋɡlɛt/ (pl: -s) singlet; [Am] undershirt

sinister /sinɪstər/ (adj, adv) sinister: *~e plannen* sinister designs

de **sint** /sɪnt/ (pl: -en) **1** saint **2** St Nicholas

de **sint-bernardshond** /sɪndbɛrnartshɔnt/ (pl: -en) St Bernard (dog)

de **sintel** /sɪntəl/ (pl: -s) cinder: *gloeiende ~s* glowing embers

de **sintelbaan** /sɪntəlban/ (pl: -banen) cinder track

Sinterklaas /sɪntərklas/ see Sint-Nicolaas

de **sinterklaasavond** /sɪntərklasavɔnt/ (pl: -en) St Nicholas' Eve

het **sinterklaasgedicht** /sɪntərklasxədɪxt/ (pl: -en) St Nicholas' poem

de **sint-juttemis** /sɪntjʏtəmɪs/: *wachten tot ~* wait till the cows come home

Sint-Nicolaas /sɪntnikolas/ **1** St Nicholas **2** feast of St Nicholas

de **sinus** /sinʏs/ (pl: -sen) sine (of angle)

sip /sɪp/ (adj) glum, crestfallen

Sire /sirə/ your Majesty, Sire

de **sirene** /sirenə/ (pl: -s) siren: *met loeiende ~* with wailing sirens

de **siroop** /sirop/ (pl: siropen) syrup: *vruchten op lichte* (or: *zware*) *~* fruit in light (*or:* heavy) syrup

de **sisklank** /sɪsklɑŋk/ (pl: -en) sibilant

sissen /sɪsə(n)/ (siste, heeft gesist) **1** hiss: *een ~d geluid maken* make a hissing noise **2** sizzle: *het spek siste in de pan* the bacon was sizzling in the pan

de **sisser** /sɪsər/ (pl: -s): *met een ~ aflopen* blow over; fizzle out

de **sisyfusarbeid** /sizifʏsarbɛit/ Sisyphean task

de ¹**site** /sajt/ site, website

de ²**site** /sitə/ [Belg] (archaeological) site/dig

de **situatie** /sitywa(t)si/ (pl: -s) situation, position: *een moeilijke ~* a difficult situation; *in de huidige ~* as things stand, in the present situation

situeren /sitywerə(n)/ (situeerde, heeft gesitueerd) place, locate, set: *waar is de handeling van het verhaal gesitueerd?* where is the story set?, where does the action of the story take place?

de **sjaak** /ʃak/: [inform] *de ~ zijn* be the sucker, be muggins

de **sjaal** /ʃal/ (pl: -s) scarf: *een ~ omslaan* put on a scarf

de **sjabloon** /ʃablon/ (pl: sjablonen) stencil (plate); template; [fig] stereotype

de **sjacheraar** /ʃɑxərar/ (pl: -s) haggler, horsetrader

de **sjah** /ʃa/ (pl: -s) shah

de **sjalot** /ʃalɔt/ (pl: -ten) shallot

sjansen /ʃɑnsə(n)/ (sjanste, heeft gesjanst) [inform] flirt, make eyes at s.o.: ~ **met** *de buurman* flirt with the neighbour

de **sjasliek** /ʃɑslik/ shashlik

de **sjeik** /ʃɛik/ (pl: -s) sheik(h)

het **sjekkie** /ʃɛki/ (pl: -s) [inform] (hand-rolled) cigarette, roll-up: *een* ~ *draaien* roll a cigarette

de **sjerp** /ʃɛrp/ (pl: -en) sash

¹**sjezen** /ʃezə(n)/ (sjeesde, is gesjeesd) drop out

²**sjezen** /ʃezə(n)/ (sjeesde, heeft/is gesjeesd) race, scream

de **sjiiet** /ʃiit/ (pl: -en) Shiite

de **sjoege** /ʃuɣə/: [inform] *hij* **gaf** *geen* ~ he didn't react

de **sjoelbak** /ʃulbɑk/ (pl: -ken) shovelboard

sjoelen /ʃulə(n)/ (sjoelde, heeft gesjoeld) play at shovelboard

sjoemelen /ʃumələ(n)/ (sjoemelde, heeft gesjoemeld) [inform] cheat

sjofel /ʃofəl/ (adj, adv) shabby

sjokken /ʃɔkə(n)/ (sjokte, heeft/is gesjokt) trudge

de **sjonnie** /ʃɔni/ (pl: -s) greaser

sjorren /ʃɔrə(n)/ (sjorde, heeft gesjord) lug, heave

sjotten (sjotte, heeft gesjot) [Belg] **1** play soccer **2** shoot, kick

sjouwen /ʃɑuwə(n)/ (sjouwde, heeft/is gesjouwd) lug, drag: *lopen* ~ trudge; traipse

de **sjouwer** /ʃɑuwər/ (pl: -s) porter; docker

het ¹**skai** /skɑj/ imitation leather

²**skai** /skɑj/ (adj) imitation leather

het **skateboard** /skedbɔːrd/ (pl: -s) skateboard

skaten /sketə(n)/ (skatete, heeft/is geskatet) skateboard

de **skeeler** /skilər/ (pl: -s) skeeler

skeeleren /skilərə(n)/ (skeelerde, heeft/is geskeelerd) rollerblade

het **skelet** /skəlɛt/ (pl: -ten) skeleton; frame

de **skelter** /skɛltər/ (pl: -s) (go-)kart

skelteren /skɛltərə(n)/ (skelterde, heeft/is geskelterd) go-kart: **het** ~ go-karting

de **sketch** /skɛtʃ/ (pl: -es) sketch

de **ski** /ski/ (pl: -'s) ski

het **skicentrum** /skisɛntrʏm/ (pl: skicentra) ski resort

skiën /skijə(n)/ (skiede, heeft/is geskied) ski: *gaan* ~ go skiing

de **skiër** /skijər/ (pl: -s) skier

de **skiff** /skɪf/ (pl: -s) skiff

het **skigebied** /skiɣəbit/ (pl: -en) skiing area (or: centre)

de **skileraar** /skilerar/ (pl: skileraren) ski instructor

de **skilift** /skilɪft/ (pl: -en) ski lift

de **skipiste** /skipistə/ (pl: -s, -n) ski run

de **skischans** /skisχɑns/ (pl: -en) ski jump

de **skischoen** /skisχun/ (pl: -en) ski boot

skispringen /skisprɪŋə(n)/ ski-jumping

de **skistok** /skistɔk/ (pl: -ken) ski stick; [Am] ski pole

de **sla** /sla/ lettuce; salad: *een* **krop** ~ a head of lettuce; *de* ~ *aanmaken* dress the salad

de **slaaf** /slaf/ (pl: slaven) slave

slaafs /slafs/ (adj, adv) slavish, servile: *~e gehoorzaamheid* servile obedience

de **slaag** /slaχ/: [also fig] *iem. (een pak)* ~ *geven* give s.o. a beating

slaags /slaχs/ (adv): ~ *raken met iem.* come to blows (*or:* grips) with s.o.

slaan /slan/ (sloeg, heeft geslagen) **1** hit, strike; slap; beat: *de* **klok** *slaat ieder kwartier* the clock strikes the quarters; *zich* **ergens** *doorheen* ~ pull through; *zijn hart ging* **sneller** ~ his heart beat faster; *een paal* **in** *de grond* ~ drive a stake into the ground; *met de* **vleugels** ~ flap one's wings; *met de deur* ~ slam the door; *iem.* **in** *elkaar* ~ beat s.o. up; *hij is er niet (bij) weg te* ~ wild horses couldn't drag him away **2** take, capture **3** (+ op) refer to: *waar slaat dat nu weer* **op**? what do you mean by that?; *dat slaat* **op** *mij* that is meant for (*or:* aimed at) me; *dat slaat nergens* **op** that makes no sense at all ‖ *over de kop* ~ overturn; *een mantel om iem. heen* ~ wrap a coat round s.o.; *de armen* **om** *de hals van iem.* ~ fling one's arms around s.o.'s neck; *de benen* **over** *elkaar* ~ cross one's legs

de **slaap** /slap/ **1** sleep: *in* ~ *vallen* fall asleep **2** sleepiness: ~ *hebben* be (*or:* feel) sleepy; ~ *krijgen* get sleepy **3** temple

de **slaapbank** /slabɑŋk/ (pl: -en) sofa bed

slaapdronken /slabdrɔŋkə(n)/ (adj) half asleep, drowsy

het **slaapgebrek** /slapχəbrɛk/ lack of sleep

de **slaapgelegenheid** /slapχələɣənhɛit/ (pl: -heden) sleeping accommodation, place to sleep

de **slaapkamer** /slapkamər/ (pl: -s) bedroom

de **slaapkop** /slapkɔp/ (pl: -pen) **1** sleepyhead **2** dope

het **slaapliedje** /slaplicə/ (pl: -s) lullaby

het **slaapmiddel** /slapmɪdəl/ (pl: -en) sleeping pill

de **slaapmuts** /slapmʏts/ (pl: -en) nightcap

het **slaapmutsje** /slapmʏtʃə/ (pl: -s) nightcap

de **slaappil** /slapɪl/ (pl: -len) sleeping pill

de **slaapplaats** /slaplats/ (pl: -en) place to sleep, bed

de **slaapstad** /slapstɑt/ (pl: -steden) dormitory suburb; dormitory town

de **slaapster** /slapstər/ (pl: -s): *de* **Schone** *Slaapster* Sleeping Beauty

de **slaaptrein** /slaptrɛin/ (pl: -en) sleeper, overnight train

slaapverwekkend /slapfərwɛkənt/ (adj) sleep-inducing; [fig] soporific: *een* ~ *boek* a tedious book

de **slaapwandelaar** /sl<u>a</u>pwɑndəlar/ (pl: -s) sleepwalker

slaapwandelen /sl<u>a</u>pwɑndələ(n)/ (slaapwandelde, heeft geslaapwandeld) walk in one's sleep: *het* ~ sleepwalking

de **slaapzaal** /sl<u>a</u>psal/ (pl: -zalen) dormitory, dorm

de **slaapzak** /sl<u>a</u>psɑk/ (pl: -ken) sleeping bag

het **slaatje** /sl<u>a</u>cə/ (pl: -s) salad || *hij wil overal een ~ uit slaan* he tries to cash in on everything

de **slab** /slɑp/ (pl: -ben) bib: *een kind een ~ voordoen* put a child's bib on

de **slabak** /sl<u>a</u>bɑk/ (pl: -ken) salad bowl

slabakken /slab<u>ɑ</u>kə(n)/ (slabakte, heeft geslabakt) [Belg] hang fire, do badly: *de ~de economie* the stagnating economy

de **slacht** /slɑxt/ slaughter(ing)

het **slachtafval** /sl<u>ɑ</u>xtɑfɑl/ offal

de **slachtbank** /sl<u>ɑ</u>xtbɑŋk/ (pl: -en): *naar de ~ geleid worden* be led to the slaughter

slachten /sl<u>ɑ</u>xtə(n)/ (slachtte, heeft geslacht) slaughter, butcher: *geslachte koeien* slaughtered cows

het **slachthuis** /sl<u>ɑ</u>xthœys/ (pl: -huizen) slaughterhouse

de **slachting** /sl<u>ɑ</u>xtɪŋ/ (pl: -en) slaughter(ing); massacre

het **slachtoffer** /sl<u>ɑ</u>xtɔfər/ (pl: -s) victim; casualty: ~ *worden van* fall victim (*or:* prey) to

de **slachtofferhulp** /sl<u>ɑ</u>xtɔfərhʏlp/ help (*or:* aid) to victims

de **slachtpartij** /sl<u>ɑ</u>xtpɑrtɛi/ (pl: -en) slaughter, massacre

het **slachtvee** /sl<u>ɑ</u>xtfe/ stock (*or:* cattle) for slaughter(ing), beef cattle

de ¹**slag** /slɑx/ **1** blow; punch; lash: *iem. een (zware) ~ toebrengen* deal s.o. a heavy blow **2** stroke; drive: *een ~ in de lucht* a shot in the dark **3** [mil] battle: *in de ~ bij Nieuwpoort* at the Battle of Nieuwpoort; [Belg] *zich uit de ~ trekken* get out of a difficult situation **4** bang, bump **5** wave: *hij heeft een mooie ~ in zijn haar* he has a nice wave in his hair **6** stroke; beat: *(totaal) van ~ zijn* be (completely) thrown out **7** knack: *de ~ van iets te pakken krijgen* get the knack (*or:* hang) of sth. **8** [cards] trick: *iem. een voor zijn* be one up on s.o. **9** take, capture **10** stroke: *vrije ~* freestyle || *een ~ naar iets slaan* have a shot (*or:* stab) at sth.; *een goede ~ slaan* make a good deal; *aan de ~ gaan* get to work; *hij was op ~ dood* he was killed instantly; *zonder ~ of stoot* [fig] without striking a blow, without any resistance

het ²**slag** /slɑx/ sort, kind: *dat is niet voor ons ~ mensen* that's not for the likes of us; *iem. van jouw ~* s.o. like you

de **slagader** /sl<u>ɑ</u>xadər/ (pl: -s) artery: *grote ~* aorta

de **slagboom** /sl<u>ɑ</u>xbom/ (pl: -bomen) barrier

slagen /sl<u>a</u>ɣə(n)/ (slaagde, is geslaagd) **1** (+ in, met) succeed (in); be successful (in): *ben je erin geslaagd?* did you pull it off, did you manage? **2** succeed in (-ing), manage (to): *ik slaagde er niet in de top te bereiken* I failed to make it to the top **3** (+ voor) pass; qualify (as, for): *hij is voor zijn Frans geslaagd* he has passed (his) French **4** be successful: *de operatie is geslaagd* the operation was successful; *de tekening is goed geslaagd* the drawing has turned out well

de **slager** /sl<u>a</u>ɣər/ (pl: -s) butcher

de **slagerij** /slaɣər<u>ɛi</u>/ (pl: -en) butcher's (shop)

het **slaghout** /sl<u>ɑ</u>xhɑut/ (pl: -en) bat

het **slaginstrument** /sl<u>ɑ</u>xɪnstrymɛnt/ (pl: -en) percussion instrument

de **slagpen** /sl<u>ɑ</u>xpɛn/ (pl: -nen) **1** flight feather **2** firing pin

de **slagregen** /sl<u>ɑ</u>xreɣə(n)/ (pl: -s) driving (*or:* torrential) rain

de **slagroom** /sl<u>ɑ</u>xrom/: *aardbeien met ~* strawberries and whipped cream

het **slagschip** /sl<u>ɑ</u>xsxɪp/ (pl: -schepen) battleship

de **slagtand** /sl<u>ɑ</u>xtɑnt/ (pl: -en) **1** tusk **2** fang

slagvaardig /slɑxf<u>a</u>rdəx/ (adj) decisive

het **slagveld** /sl<u>ɑ</u>xfɛlt/ (pl: -en) battlefield

het **slagwerk** /sl<u>ɑ</u>xwɛrk/ (pl: -en) percussion (section); rhythm section

de **slagwerker** /sl<u>ɑ</u>xwɛrkər/ (pl: -s) percussionist; drummer

de **slagzij** /sl<u>ɑ</u>xsɛi/ list [ship]; bank: *dat schip maakt zware ~* that ship is listing heavily

de **slagzin** /sl<u>ɑ</u>xsɪn/ (pl: -nen) slogan, catchphrase

de **slak** /slɑk/ (pl: -ken) **1** snail; slug **2** slag, dross

slaken /sl<u>a</u>kə(n)/ (slaakte, heeft geslaakt) give, utter: *een kreet ~* give a cry, shriek; *een zucht ~* give (*or:* heave) a sigh

de **slakkengang** /sl<u>ɑ</u>kə(n)ɣɑŋ/ snail's pace

het **slakkenhuis** /sl<u>ɑ</u>kə(n)hœys/ (pl: -huizen) **1** snail's shell **2** [med] cochlea

de **slalom** /sl<u>a</u>lɔm/ (pl: -s) slalom

de **slamix** /sl<u>a</u>mɪks/ (pl: -en) salad dressing

de **slang** /slɑŋ/ (pl: -en) **1** snake: *giftige ~en* poisonous snakes **2** hose

de **slangenbeet** /sl<u>ɑ</u>ŋə(n)bet/ (pl: -beten) snakebite

het **slangengif** /sl<u>ɑ</u>ŋə(n)ɣɪf/ snake poison

de **slangenmens** /sl<u>ɑ</u>ŋəmɛns/ (pl: -en) contortionist

slank /slɑŋk/ (adj) slender; slim: *aan de ~e lijn doen* be slimming (*or:* dieting)

de **slaolie** /sl<u>a</u>oli/ salad oil

slap /slɑp/ (adj) **1** slack: [fig] *een ~pe tijd* a slack season; *het touw hangt ~* the rope is slack **2** soft, limp **3** weak, flabby: *~pe spieren* flabby muscles; *we lagen ~ van het lachen* we were in stitches **4** empty, feeble: *een ~ excuus* a lame (*or:* feeble) excuse; *~ geklets* empty talk, slip-slop

slapeloos /slapələs/ (adj, adv) sleepless
de **slapeloosheid** /slapələshɛit/ insomnia, sleeplessness: *aan ~ lijden* suffer from insomnia
slapen /slapə(n)/ (sliep, heeft geslapen) **1** sleep: *gaan ~* go to bed; go to sleep; *hij kon er niet van ~* it kept him awake; *slaap lekker* sleep well; *bij iem. blijven ~* spend the night at s.o.'s house (*or:* place); spend the night with s.o.; *ik wil er een nachtje over ~* I'd like to sleep on it; *hij slaapt als een os (een roos)* he sleeps like a log **2** sleep (with) || *mijn been slaapt* I've got pins and needles in my leg
slapend /slapənt/ (adj) sleeping: *~e rijk worden* make money without any effort
slaperig /slapərəχ/ (adj, adv) sleepy; drowsy
de **slapjanus** /slapjanʏs/ (pl: -sen) [inform] wimp, weed
de **slappeling** /slapəlɪŋ/ (pl: -en) weakling, softie
de **slapte** /slaptə/ slackness
de **slasaus** /slasaus/ (pl: -sauzen) salad dressing
de **slash** /slɛʃ/ (pl: -es) slash
de **slavenarbeid** /slavə(n)arbɛit/ slave labour
de **slavenhandel** /slavə(n)handəl/ slave trade
de **slavernij** /slavərnɛi/ slavery: *afschaffing van de ~* abolition of slavery
de **slavin** /slavɪn/ (pl: -nen) (female) slave
slecht /slɛχt/ (adj, adv) **1** bad; poor: *een ~ gebit* bad teeth; *~ betaald* badly (*or:* low) paid; *~ worden* worsen, deteriorate; *~ ter been zijn* have difficulty (in) walking **2** bad, unfavourable: *hij heeft het ~ getroffen* he has been unlucky; *het er ~ afbrengen* come off badly, be badly off **3** bad, wrong: *zich op het ~e pad begeven* go astray **4** bad, ill: *het loopt nog eens ~ met je af* you will come to no good
de **slechterik** /slɛχtərɪk/ (pl: -en) baddie, bad guy, villain
slechtgehumeurd /slɛχtχəhymørt/ (adj) bad-tempered
slechtgemanierd /slɛ(χt)χəmanirt/ (adj) bad-mannered, ill-mannered
slechthorend /slɛχthorənt/ (adj) hard of hearing
slechts /slɛχts/ (adv) only, merely, just: *in ~ enkele gevallen* in only (*or:* just) a few cases
slechtziend /slɛχtsint/ (adj) visually handicapped: *~ zijn* have bad eyesight
de **sledehond** /sledəhont/ (pl: -en) husky
de **slee** /sle/ (pl: -ën) sledge; [Am] sled
sleeën /slejə(n)/ (sleede, heeft/is gesleed) sledge; [Am] sled; sleigh
de **sleep** /slep/ (pl: slepen) **1** train **2** train: *een ~ kinderen* an army of kids **3** tow: *iem. een ~(je) geven,* *iem. op ~ nemen* give s.o. a tow, take s.o. in tow
de **sleepboot** /slebot/ (pl: -boten) tug(boat)
de **sleepkabel** /slepkabəl/ (pl: -s) tow rope
het **sleepnet** /slepnɛt/ (pl: -ten) trawl (net), dragnet
het **sleeptouw** /sleptɑu/ (pl: -en) tow rope: *iem. op ~ nemen* take s.o. in tow
de **sleepwagen** /slepwaɣə(n)/ (pl: -s) breakdown truck, breakdown van; [Am] tow truck
sleets /slets/ (adj) worn
slenteren /slɛntərə(n)/ (slenterde, heeft/is geslenterd) stroll, amble: *op straat ~* loaf about the streets
slepen /slepə(n)/ (sleepte, heeft gesleept) **1** drag, haul: *iem. door een examen ~* pull s.o. through an exam; *iem. voor de rechter ~* take s.o. to court **2** tow
slepend /slepənt/ (adj) **1** dragging: *een ~e gang hebben* drag (*or:* shuffle) one's feet **2** lingering, long-drawn-out
de **slet** /slɛt/ (pl: -ten) slut
de **sleuf** /sløf/ (pl: sleuven) **1** slot; slit: *de ~ van een spaarpot* the slot in a piggybank **2** groove; trench
de **sleur** /slør/ rut, grind: *de alledaagse ~* the daily grind
sleuren /slørə(n)/ (sleurde, heeft gesleurd) drag, haul
de **sleutel** /sløtəl/ (pl: -s) **1** key **2** [fig] key, clue **3** spanner; [Am] wrench: *een Engelse ~* a monkey wrench **4** [mus] clef
het **sleutelbeen** /sløtəlben/ (pl: -deren) collarbone, clavicle
de **sleutelbos** /sløtəlbɔs/ (pl: -sen) bunch of keys
sleutelen /sløtələ(n)/ (sleutelde, heeft gesleuteld) **1** work (on), repair **2** [fig] fiddle (with), tinker (with): *er moet nog wel wat aan de tekst gesleuteld worden* the text needs a certain amount of touching up
de **sleutelfiguur** /sløtəlfiɣyr/ (pl: -figuren) key figure
het **sleutelgat** /sløtəlɣat/ (pl: -en) keyhole: *aan het ~ luisteren* listen (*or:* eavesdrop) at the keyhole; *door het ~ kijken* peep through the keyhole
de **sleutelhanger** /sløtəlhaŋər/ (pl: -s) keyring
de **sleutelpositie** /sløtəlpozi(t)si/ (pl: -s) key position
de **sleutelring** /sløtəlrɪŋ/ (pl: -en) keyring
het **slib** /slɪp/ silt; sludge
de **sliding** /slajdɪŋ/ (pl: -s) sliding tackle
de **sliert** /slirt/ (pl: -en) **1** string, thread; wisp: *~en rook* wisps of smoke **2** pack, bunch: *een hele ~* a whole bunch
het **slijk** /slɛik/ mud, mire: *iem. (or: iemands naam) door het ~ sleuren* drag s.o. (*or:* s.o.'s name) through the mud/mire
het/de **slijm** /slɛim/ (pl: -en) mucus; phlegm
de **slijmbal** /slɛimbɑl/ (pl: -len) [inform] toady, bootlicker
de **slijmbeurs** /slɛimbørs/ (pl: -beurzen) bursa
slijmen /slɛimə(n)/ (slijmde, heeft geslijmd) butter up, soft-soap: *~ tegen iem.* butter s.o. up

slijmerig /slɛimərəχ/ (adj, adv) slimy

het **slijmvlies** /slɛimvlis/ (pl: -vliezen) mucous membrane

slijpen /slɛipə(n)/ (sleep, heeft geslepen) **1** sharpen **2** grind, polish; cut: *diamant ~ cut diamonds* **3** cut

de **slijpsteen** /slɛipsten/ (pl: -stenen) grindstone

de **slijtage** /slɛitaʒə/ wear (and tear): *tekenen van ~ vertonen* show signs of wear; *aan ~ onderhevig zijn* be subject to wear

slijten /slɛitə(n)/ (sleet, heeft/is gesleten) **1** wear (out): *die jas is kaal gesleten* that coat is worn bare **2** wear away, wear off; waste (away) **3** spend, pass: *zijn leven in eenzaamheid ~* spend one's days in solitude

de **slijter** /slɛitər/ (pl: -s) wine merchant; [Am] liquor dealer ‖ *ik ga naar de ~* I'm going to the wine shop

de **slijterij** /slɛitərɛi/ (pl: -en) wine shop; [Am] liquor store

slijtvast /slɛitfɑst/ (adj) hard-wearing, wear-resistant

slikken /slɪkə(n)/ (slikte, heeft geslikt) **1** swallow; gulp (down) **2** swallow, put up with: *je hebt het maar te ~* you just have to put up with it

slim /slɪm/ (adj, adv) clever, smart: *~me oogjes* shrewd eyes; *een ~me zet* a clever move; *iem. te ~ af zijn* be too clever for s.o.

de **slimheid** /slɪmhɛit/ cleverness

de **slimmigheid** /slɪməχhɛit/ dodge, trick: *hij wist zich door een ~je eruit te redden* he weaseled his way out of it

de **slinger** /slɪŋər/ (pl: -s) **1** festoon, streamer; garland **2** swing, sway **3** pendulum

de **slingerbeweging** /slɪŋərbəweɣɪŋ/ (pl: -en) **1** swing **2** swerve

[1]**slingeren** /slɪŋərə(n)/ (slingerde, heeft/is geslingerd) **1** swing, sway: *~ op zijn benen* sway on one's legs **2** sway, lurch; yaw [ship] **3** lie about (or: around): *laat je boeken niet altijd op mijn bureau ~!* don't always leave your books lying around on my desk! **4** wind

[2]**slingeren** /slɪŋərə(n)/ (slingerde, heeft geslingerd) **1** sling, fling: *bij de botsing werd de bestuurder uit de auto geslingerd* in the crash the driver was flung out of the car **2** swing, sway

zich [3]**slingeren** /slɪŋərə(n)/ (slingerde zich, heeft zich geslingerd) wind; wind (o.s.)

de **slingerplant** /slɪŋərplɑnt/ (pl: -en) creeper, runner

slinken /slɪŋkə(n)/ (slonk, is geslonken) shrink: *de voorraad slinkt* the supply is dwindling

slinks /slɪŋks/ (adj, adv) cunning, devious: *op ~e wijze* by devious means

de **slip** /slɪp/ skid: *in een ~ raken* go into a skid

het **slipgevaar** /slɪpχəvar/ risk of skidding

het **slipje** /slɪpjə/ (pl: -s) (pair of) briefs (or:

panties), (pair of) knickers

slippen /slɪpə(n)/ (slipte, is geslipt) slip; skid

de **slipper** /slɪpər/ (pl: -s) mule; slipper

het **slippertje** /slɪpərcə/ (pl: -s): *een ~ maken* have a bit on the side

de **sliptong** /slɪptɔŋ/ (pl: -en) slip, sole

slissen /slɪsə(n)/ (sliste, heeft geslist) lisp

slobberen /slɔbərə(n)/ (slobberde, heeft geslobberd) **1** bag, sag: *zijn jasje slobbert om zijn lijf* his baggy coat hangs around his body **2** slobber, slurp

de **slobbertrui** /slɔbərtrœy/ (pl: -en) baggy sweater

de **sloddervos** /slɔdərvɔs/ (pl: -sen) slob

de **sloeber** /slubər/ (pl: -s): *een arme ~* a poor wretch (or: devil)

de **sloep** /slup/ (pl: -en) cutter: *de ~ strijken* lower the boat

de **sloerie** /sluri/ (pl: -s) slut

de **slof** /slɔf/ (pl: -fen) **1** slipper, mule: *zij kan het op haar ~fen af* she can do it with her eyes shut (or: with one hand tied behind her back) **2** carton ‖ *uit zijn ~ schieten* hit the roof

sloffen /slɔfə(n)/ (slofte, heeft/is gesloft) shuffle: *loop niet zo te ~!* don't shuffle (or: drag) your feet!

de **slogan** /slogən/ (pl: -s) slogan

de **slok** /slɔk/ (pl: -ken) **1** drink; sip [small]: *grote ~ken nemen* gulp **2** swallow, gulp ‖ *een ~ op hebben* have had one too many

de **slokdarm** /slɔkdɑrm/ (pl: -en) gullet

de **slokop** /slɔkɔp/ (pl: -pen) glutton

de **slons** /slɔns/ (pl: slonzen) slattern, sloven, slut

slonzig /slɔnzəχ/ (adj, adv) slovenly, sloppy

de **sloof** /slof/ (pl: sloven) (household) drudge

sloom /slom/ (adj, adv) listless, slow: *doe niet zo ~* come on, I haven't got all day

de [1]**sloop** /slop/ (pl: slopen) **1** demolition **2** demolition firm; scrapyard: *rijp voor de ~* on its last legs, fit for the scrap heap

het/de [2]**sloop** /slop/ (pl: slopen) pillowcase: *lakens en slopen* bedlinen

de **sloopauto** /slopɑuto/ (pl: -'s) scrap car, wreck

het **slooppand** /slopɑnt/ (pl: -en) building due for demolition

de **sloot** /slot/ (pl: sloten) ditch; [sport] water jump

slootjespringen /slocəsprɪŋə(n)/ leap (over) ditches

het **slootwater** /slotwatər/ ditchwater; [fig] dishwater

het **slop** /slɔp/ (pl: -pen) alley(way); blind alley: *in het ~ raken* come to a dead end

slopen /slopə(n)/ (sloopte, heeft gesloopt) **1** demolish **2** break up; scrap **3** undermine: *~d werk* exhausting (or: back-breaking) work; *een ~de ziekte* a wasting disease

de **sloper** /slopər/ (pl: -s) demolition contractor

de **sloperij** /slopərɛi/ (pl: -en) demolition firm

(*or:* contractors); scrapyard

de **sloppenwijk** /slɔpə(n)wɛik/ (pl: -en) slums, slum area

slordig /slɔrdəχ/ (adj, adv) careless; untidy; sloppy: *wat zit je haar* ~ how untidy your hair is; ~ *schrijven* scribble

de **slordigheid** /slɔrdəχhɛit/ (pl: -heden) carelessness, sloppiness

het **slot** /slɔt/ (pl: -en) **1** lock; fastening: *iem. achter* ~ *en grendel zetten* put s.o. behind bars; *achter* ~ *en grendel* under lock and key; *een deur op* ~ *doen* lock a door; *alles op* ~ *doen* lock up **2** end, conclusion: *ten* ~*te* finally, eventually, at last; ~ *volgt* to be concluded **3** castle ‖ *per* ~ *van rekening* after all, on balance; all things considered

het **slotakkoord** /slɔtakort/ (pl: -en) final chord

de **slotenmaker** /slɔtə(n)makər/ (pl: -s) locksmith

de **slotfase** /slɔtfazə/ (pl: -s, -n) final stage

de **slotgracht** /slɔtχraχt/ (pl: -en) (castle) moat

de **slotkoers** /slɔtkurs/ (pl: -en) closing price(s)

de **slotscène** /slɔtsɛːnə/ final scene

de **slotsom** /slɔtsɔm/ conclusion

het **slotwoord** /slɔtwort/ closing word(s)

de **Sloveen** /slovẹn/ (pl: Slovenen) Slovene, Slovenian

het **¹Sloveens** /slovẹns/ Slovene

²Sloveens /slovẹns/ (adj) Slovenian

sloven /slọvə(n)/ (sloofde, heeft gesloofd) drudge

Slovenië /slovẹnijə/ Slovenia

de **Slowaak** /slowak/ Slovak

het **¹Slowaaks** /slowaks/ Slovak

²Slowaaks /slowaks/ (adj) Slovak(ian)

Slowakije /slowakɛiə/ Slovakia

de **slow motion** /slomọʃən/ (pl: -s) slow motion

de **sluier** /slœyər/ (pl: -s) veil

sluik /slœyk/ (adj) straight, lank

de **sluikreclame** /slœykrəklamə/ (pl: -s) clandestine advertising

sluikstorten /slœykstɔrtə(n)/ [Belg] dump (illegally)

sluimeren /slœymərə(n)/ (sluimerde, heeft gesluimerd) slumber

sluipen /slœypə(n)/ (sloop, is geslopen) **1** steal, sneak; stalk: *naar boven* ~ steal (*or:* sneak) upstairs **2** creep

de **sluipmoord** /slœypmort/ (pl: -en) assassination

de **sluipmoordenaar** /slœypmordənar/ (pl: -s) assassin ‖ *overgewicht is een* ~ overweight is an unseen killer

de **sluiproute** /slœyprutə/ (pl: -s) short cut

de **sluipschutter** /slœypsχytər/ (pl: -s) sniper

het **sluipverkeer** /slœypfərker/ cut-through traffic

de **sluipweg** /slœypwɛχ/ (pl: -en) secret route

de **sluis** /slœys/ (pl: sluizen) lock; sluice: *door een* ~ *varen* pass through a lock

de **sluiswachter** /slœyswɑχtər/ (pl: -s) lockkeeper

¹sluiten /slœytə(n)/ (sloot, heeft gesloten) balance: *de begroting* ~*d maken* balance the budget ‖ *over en* ~ over and out

²sluiten /slœytə(n)/ (sloot, heeft gesloten) **1** shut, close; close down: *de grenzen* ~ close the frontiers; *het raam* ~ shut (*or:* close) the window; *de winkel (zaak)* ~ **a)** close (the shop) down; **b)** shut up shop; *dinsdagmiddag zijn alle winkels gesloten* it is early closing day on Tuesday **2** conclude, enter into: *een verbond* ~ *(met)* enter into an alliance (with); *vrede* ~ make peace; make up (with s.o.) **3** close, conclude

de **sluiting** /slœytɪŋ/ (pl: -en) **1** shutting (off); closure; conclusion: ~ *van de rekening* balancing of the account **2** fastening, fastener; lock; clasp: *de* ~ *van deze jurk zit op de rug* this dress does up at the back

de **sluitingsdatum** /slœytɪŋzdatʏm/ (pl: -data) closing date

de **sluitingstijd** /slœytɪŋstɛit/ (pl: -en) closing time: *na* ~ after hours

de **sluitpost** /slœytpɔst/ (pl: -en): *als* ~ *op de begroting dienen* be considered unimportant, come at the bottom of the list

de **sluitspier** /slœytspir/ (pl: -en) sphincter

het **sluitstuk** /slœytstʏk/ (pl: -ken) final piece

sluizen /slœyzə(n)/ (sluisde, heeft gesluisd) channel, transfer

de **slungel** /slʏŋəl/ (pl: -s) beanpole

slungelig /slʏŋələχ/ (adj, adv) lanky

de **slurf** /slʏrf/ (pl: slurven) trunk

slurpen /slʏrpə(n)/ (slurpte, heeft geslurpt) slurp

sluw /slyw/ (adj, adv) sly, crafty, cunning: *de* ~*e vos* the sly (*or:* cunning) old fox

de **sluwheid** /slywhɛit/ (pl: -heden) slyness, cunning

sm (abbrev) SM, S and M

de **smaad** /smat/ defamation (of character), libel

de **smaak** /smak/ (pl: smaken) taste; flavour: *een goede* ~ *hebben* have good taste; *van goede* (or: *slechte*) ~ *getuigen* be in good (*or:* bad) taste; *de* ~ *van iets te pakken hebben* have acquired a taste for; *in de* ~ *vallen bij …* appeal to …, find favour with …; *over* ~ *valt niet te twisten* there is no accounting for taste(s)

het **smaakje** /smakjə/ (pl: -s) taste: *er zit een* ~ *aan dat vlees* that meat has a funny taste

de **smaakmaker** /smakmakər/ (pl: -s) **1** seasoning **2** trendsetter

de **smaakpapil** /smakpapɪl/ (pl: -len) taste bud

de **smaakstof** /smakstɔf/ (pl: -fen) flavour(ing), seasoning

smaakvol /smakfɔl/ (adj, adv) tasteful; in good taste: ~ *gekleed zijn* be tastefully dressed

smachten /smɔχtə(n)/ (smachtte, heeft ge-smacht) **1** languish: *iem. ~de blikken toewerpen* look longingly at s.o. **2** (+ naar) long (for), yearn (for)

smadelijk /smɑdələk/ (adj, adv) humiliating; scornful

de **smak** /smɑk/ (pl: -ken) **1** fall: *een ~ maken* fall with a bang **2** crash, smack: *met een ~ neerzetten* slam (*or:* slap) down **3** heap, pile: *dat kost een ~ geld* that costs a load of money

smakelijk /smɑkələk/ (adj, adv) tasty, appetizing: *eet ~!* enjoy your meal

smakeloos /smɑkəlos/ (adj, adv) tasteless; lacking in taste

smaken /smakə(n)/ (smaakte, heeft ge-smaakt) taste: *hoe smaakt het?* how does it taste?; *heeft het gesmaakt, meneer?* (or: *mevrouw?*) did you enjoy your meal, sir? (or: madam?); *naar iets ~* taste of sth.; *dat smaakt naar meer* that's very moreish

¹**smakken** /smɑkə(n)/ (smakte, heeft ge-smakt) smack one's lips: *smak niet zo!* don't make so much noise (when you're eating)

²**smakken** /smɑkə(n)/ (smakte, is gesmakt) crash: *tegen de grond ~* crash to the ground

smal /smɑl/ (adj) narrow: *~le opening* small opening; *een ~ gezichtje* a pinched face; *de ~le weg* [fig] the straight and narrow (path)

het **smaldeel** /smɑldel/ (pl: -delen) squadron; [fig] contingent

smalend /smalənt/ (adj, adv) scornful

het **smalspoor** /smɑlspor/ narrow-gauge railway

de ¹**smaragd** /smarɑχt/ (pl: -en) [gem] emerald

het ²**smaragd** /smarɑχt/ [mineral] emerald

de **smart** /smɑrt/ (pl: -en) **1** sorrow, grief, pain: *gedeelde ~ is halve ~* a sorrow shared is a sorrow halved **2** yearning, longing: *met ~ op iets (iem.) wachten* wait anxiously for sth. (s.o.)

het **smartboard** /smɑːrdbɔːrt/ (pl: -s) SMART board

smartelijk /smɑrtələk/ (adj, adv) grievous, painful

het **smartengeld** /smɑrtəɣɛlt/ (pl: -en) damages; (financial, monetary) compensation

de **smartlap** /smɑrtlɑp/ (pl: -pen) tear-jerker

de **smash** /smɛʃ/ (pl: -es) (overhead) smash

smashen /smɛʃə(n)/ (smashte, heeft ge-smasht) smash

smeden /smedə(n)/ (smeedde, heeft ge-smeed) forge: *twee stukken ijzer aan elkaar ~* weld two pieces of iron (together); *uit één stuk gesmeed* forged in one piece || *plannen ~* make (or: lay) plans

de **smederij** /smedərɛi/ (pl: -en) forge

het **smeedijzer** /smetɛizər/ (pl: -s) wrought iron

de **smeekbede** /smekbedə/ (pl: -s, -n) plea (for), cry (for)

het/de **smeer** /smer/ grease, oil; polish

smeerbaar /smerbar/ (adj) spreadable

de **smeerboel** /smerbul/ mess

het **smeergeld** /smerɣɛlt/ (pl: -en) bribe(s)

de **smeerkaas** /smerkas/ (pl: -kazen) cheese spread

de **smeerlap** /smerlɑp/ (pl: -pen) **1** skunk, bastard **2** pervert; dirty old man

het **smeermiddel** /smermɪdəl/ (pl: -en) lubricant

de **smeerolie** /smeroli/ lubricant

smeken /smekə(n)/ (smeekte, heeft ge-smeekt) implore, beg: *iem. om hulp ~* beg (for) s.o.'s help

smelten /smɛltə(n)/ (smolt, heeft/is gesmol-ten) melt; melt down: *de sneeuw smelt* the snow is melting (or: thawing); *deze reep chocolade smelt op de tong* this bar of chocolate melts in the mouth

de **smeltkroes** /smɛltkrus/ (pl: -kroezen) melt-ingpot [also fig]

het **smeltpunt** /smɛltpʏnt/ (pl: -en) melting point, point of fusion

smeren /smerə(n)/ (smeerde, heeft ge-smeerd) **1** grease, oil; lubricate **2** smear: *crème op zijn huid ~* rub cream on one's skin **3** butter: *brood ~* butter bread, make sandwiches || *'m ~* clear off; make tracks

de **smering** /smerɪŋ/ (pl: -en) lubrication

de **smeris** /smerɪs/ (pl: -sen) cop

de **smet** /smɛt/ (pl: -ten) blemish, taint, stain

smetteloos /smɛtəlos/ (adj, adv) [also fig] spotless, immaculate: *~ wit* immaculate(ly) white

smeuïg /smøjəχ/ (adj, adv) **1** smooth, creamy **2** vivid

smeulen /smølə(n)/ (smeulde, heeft ge-smeuld) smoulder

de **smid** /smɪt/ (pl: smeden) smith

de **smiezen** /smizə(n)/ (pl) [inform]: *iets in de ~ hebben* be on to sth., see the way the land lies; *iem. in de ~ hebben* have s.o. taped; [Am] be wise to s.o.

smijten /smɛitə(n)/ (smeet, heeft gesme-ten) throw, fling: *met de deuren ~* slam the doors; [fig] *iem. iets naar het hoofd ~* throw sth. in s.o.'s teeth

smikkelen /smɪkələ(n)/ (smikkelde, heeft gesmikkeld) tuck in

de **smiley** /smɑjli/ (adj) smiley

de **smoel** /smul/ [inform] **1** trap: *houd je ~!* shut your trap! **2** face: *~en trekken* pull faces

het **smoelenboek** /smulə(n)buk/ almanac, year book, web page with photos, staff pages

de **smoes** /smus/ (pl: smoezen) excuse: *een ~je bedenken* think up a story (or: an excuse)

smoezelig /smuzələχ/ (adj) grubby, dingy

smoezen /smuzə(n)/ (smoesde, heeft ge-smoesd) **1** invent (or: cook up) excuses **2** whisper de **smog** /smɔg/ smog

de **smoking** /smo̱kɪŋ/ (pl: -s) dinner jacket

de **smokkel** /smo̱kəl/ smuggling

de **smokkelaar** /smo̱kəlar/ (pl: -s) smuggler

de **smokkelarij** /smɔkəlare̱i̱/ (pl: -en) smuggling

smokkelen /smo̱kələ(n)/ (smokkelde, heeft gesmokkeld) smuggle

de **smokkelwaar** /smo̱kəlwar/ contraband

de ¹**smoor** /smor/: (er) de ~ **inhebben** be peeved, be pissed off at sth.

²**smoor** /smor/ (adj): ~ **op** iem. zijn have a crush on s.o.

smoorheet /smorhe̱t/ (adj) stifling

smoorverliefd /smorvərli̱ft/ (adj) smitten (with s.o.)

de **smoothie** /smu̱:θi/ (pl: -s) smoothie

smoren /smo̱rə(n)/ (smoorde, heeft gesmoord) **1** smother, choke **2** braise

de **smos** /smɔs/ [Belg]: een **broodje** ~ a salad roll

het **smout** /smɑut/ [Belg] lard

de **sms 1** short message service **2** text message

de **sms-alert** (pl: -s) text-message alert

sms'en /ɛsɛmɡsə(n)/ (sms'te, heeft gesms't) text: ik heb haar ge-sms't I texted her, I sent her a text (message)

smullen /smy̱lə(n)/ (smulde, heeft gesmuld) feast (on): dat **wordt** ~! yum-yum!; om **van te** ~ finger-lickin' good

de **smulpaap** /smy̱lpap/ (pl: -papen) [inform] gourmet

de **smurf** /smʏrf/ (pl: -en) smurf

de **smurrie** /smʏri/ gunge; sludge

snaaien /sna̱jə(n)/ (snaaide, heeft gesnaaid) snitch, snatch

de **snaar** /snar/ (pl: snaren) string, chord; snare: een **gevoelige** ~ raken touch a tender spot; de snaren **spannen** string; snare

het **snaarinstrument** /sna̱rɪnstrymɛnt/ (pl: -en) stringed instrument

de **snack** /snɛk/ (pl: -s) snack

de **snackbar** /snɛɡbar/ (pl: -s) snack bar

snakken /sna̱kə(n)/ (snakte, heeft gesnakt) **1** gasp, pant: naar adem ~ gasp for breath **2** crave: ~ **naar** aandacht be craving (for) attention

snappen /sna̱pə(n)/ (snapte, heeft gesnapt) get: snap **je?** (you) see?; ik snap **'m** I get it; ik snap **niet** waar het om gaat I don't see it; ik snap er niets **van** I don't get it, it beats me

de **snars** /snars/: **geen** ~ not a bit; hij weet er **geen** ~ **van** he doesn't know a thing about it; ik begrijp er **geen** ~ van I haven't got a clue

de **snater** /sna̱tər/ [inform] trap: hou je ~! shut your trap (or: face)!

snateren /sna̱tərə(n)/ (snaterde, heeft gesnaterd) honk

de **snauw** /snɑu/ (pl: -en) growl, snarl

snauwen /sna̱uwə(n)/ (snauwde, heeft gesnauwd) snarl, growl, snap

snauwerig /sna̱uwərəx/ (adj, adv) snappish; gruff

de **snavel** /sna̱vəl/ (pl: -s) bill; beak: hou je ~! shut up!

snedig /sne̱dəx/ (adj, adv) witty

de **snee** /sne/ (pl: -ën) **1** slice: een **dun** ~tje koek a thin slice of cake **2** cut; gash **3** [med] incision

de **sneer** /sner/ (pl: sneren) gibe, taunt

de **sneeuw** /snew/ snow: een dik **pak** ~ (a) thick (layer of) snow; **natte** ~ sleet; [Belg] **zwarte** ~ zien be destitute, live in poverty; **smeltende** ~ slush; het verdwijnt **als** ~ voor de zon it vanishes into thin air; **vastzitten** in de ~ be snowbound

de **sneeuwbal** /sne̱wbal/ (pl: -len) snowball

het **sneeuwbaleffect** /sne̱wbalɛfɛkt/ (pl: -en) domino theory, snowball

sneeuwblind /sne̱wblɪnt/ (adj) snow-blind

de **sneeuwbril** /sne̱wbrɪl/ (pl: -len) (pair of) snow goggles

de **sneeuwbui** /sne̱wbœy/ (pl: -en) snow (shower)

sneeuwen /sne̱wə(n)/ (sneeuwde, heeft gesneeuwd) snow: het sneeuwt **hard** (or: **licht**) it is snowing heavily (or: lightly)

de **sneeuwgrens** /sne̱wɡrɛns/ snowline

de **sneeuwjacht** /sne̱wjɑxt/ blizzard

de **sneeuwketting** /sne̱wkɛtɪŋ/ (pl: -en) (snow) chain

het **sneeuwklokje** /sne̱wklɔkjə/ (pl: -s) snowdrop

de **sneeuwman** /sne̱wman/ (pl: -nen) snowman

de **sneeuwpop** /sne̱wpɔp/ (pl: -pen) snowman

sneeuwruimen /sne̱wrœymə(n)/ (ruimde sneeuw, heeft sneeuwgeruimd) clear snow, shovel (away) snow

de **sneeuwschoen** /sne̱wsxun/ (pl: -en) snowshoe

de **sneeuwschuiver** /sne̱wsxœyvər/ (pl: -s) **1** snow shovel **2** snowplough

de **sneeuwstorm** /sne̱wstɔrm/ (pl: -en) snowstorm

de **sneeuwval** /sne̱wval/ (pl: -len) snowfall

de **sneeuwvlok** /sne̱wvlɔk/ (pl: -ken) snowflake

sneeuwvrij /snewvre̱i̱/ (adj) clear of snow: de wegen ~ **maken** clear the roads of snow

sneeuwwit /snewwɪ̱t/ (adj) snowy; niveous

Sneeuwwitje /snewɪ̱cə/ Snow White

snel /snɛl/ (adj) **1** fast, rapid **2** quick, swift; fast; speedy: een ~ **besluit** a quick decision; ~ **achteruitgaan** decline rapidly; ~ van begrip **zijn** be quick (on the uptake) ‖ iem. te ~ **af** zijn steal a march on s.o., beat s.o. to the punch

de **snelbinder** /sne̱lbɪndər/ (pl: -s) carrier straps

de **snelheid** /sne̱lhɛit/ (pl: -heden) speed, pace, tempo; velocity: bij **hoge** snelheden at high speeds; de **maximum** ~ the speed limit; op **volle** ~ (at) full speed; ~ **minderen** reduce speed, slow down

de **snelheidsbegrenzer** /snɛlhɛitsbəɣrɛnzər/ (pl: -s) governor, speed limiting device

de **snelheidscontrole** /snɛlhɛitskɔntrɔːlə/ (pl: -s) speed(ing) check

de **snelheidsmaniak** /snɛlhɛitsmanijɑk/ (pl: -ken) speeder, speed merchant

de **snelkoker** /snɛlkokər/ (pl: -s) pressure cooker

de **snelkookpan** /snɛlkokpɑn/ (pl: -nen) pressure cooker

de **snelkoppeling** /snɛlkɔpəlɪŋ/ (pl: -en) link
snelladen /snɛladə(n)/ fast-charge, quick-charge

de **snellader** /snɛladər/ (pl: -s) fast-charger, quick-charger

het **snelrecht** /snɛlrɛχt/ summary justice (or: proceedings)

de **sneltoets** /snɛltuts/ (pl: -en) hotkey

de **sneltrein** /snɛltrɛin/ (pl: -en) express (train), intercity (train)

de **sneltreinvaart** /snɛltrɛinvart/ tearing rush (or: hurry): hij kwam **in** een ~ de hoek om he came tearing round the corner

het **snelverkeer** /snɛlvərker/ fast (or: through) traffic
snelwandelen /snɛlwɑndələ(n)/ race walking

de **snelweg** /snɛlwɛχ/ (pl: -en) motorway; [Am] freeway ‖ elektronische (or: digitale) ~ electronic (or: digital) highway
snerpen /snɛrpə(n)/ **1** bite, cut: een ~de kou cutting (or: piercing) cold **2** squeal, shriek

de **snert** /snɛrt/ pea soup
sneu /snø/ (adj, adv) unfortunate
sneuvelen /snøvələ(n)/ (sneuvelde, is gesneuveld) **1** fall (in battle), be killed (in action): ~ in de strijd be killed in action **2** break, get smashed
snibbig /snɪbəχ/ (adj) snappy, snappish

de **snijbloem** /snɛiblum/ (pl: -en) cut flower

de **snijboon** /snɛibon/ (pl: -bonen) French bean; [Am] string bean

de **snijbrander** /snɛibrɑndər/ (pl: -s) oxyacetylene burner, cutting torch

¹**snijden** /snɛidə(n)/ (sneed, heeft gesneden) **1** cut, carve; slice **2** [traf] cut in (on s.o.)

²**snijden** /snɛidə(n)/ (sneed, heeft gesneden) **1** cut: uit hout een **figuur** ~ carve a figure out of wood **2** cross, intersect
snijdend /snɛidənt/ (adj) cutting: een ~e **wind** a piercing (or: biting) wind

de **snijmachine** /snɛimɑʃinə/ (pl: -s) cutter, cutting machine; slicer; shredder

de **snijmais** /snɛimɑjs/ green maize (fodder)

de **snijplank** /snɛiplɑŋk/ (pl: -en) breadboard; chopping board; carving board

het **snijpunt** /snɛipʏnt/ (pl: -en) crossing; intersection

de **snijtand** /snɛitɑnt/ (pl: -en) incisor

de **snijwond** /snɛiwɔnt/ (pl: -en) cut

de **snik** /snɪk/ (pl: -ken) gasp: de **laatste** ~ geven breathe one's last; tot aan zijn **laatste** ~ to his dying day ‖ niet goed ~ cracked, off one's rocker
snikheet /snɪkhet/ (adj) sizzling (hot), scorching (hot)
snikken /snɪkə(n)/ (snikte, heeft gesnikt) sob

de **snip** /snɪp/ (pl: -pen) snipe

de **snipper** /snɪpər/ (pl: -s) snip, shred; clipping: in ~s scheuren tear (in)to shreds

de **snipperdag** /snɪpərdɑχ/ (pl: -en) day off
snipperen /snɪpərə(n)/ (snipperde, heeft gesnipperd) shred, cut up (fine)
snipverkouden /snɪpfərkɑudə(n)/ (adj) (all) stuffed up: ~ zijn have a streaming cold

de **snit** /snɪt/ (pl: -ten): het is naar de **laatste** ~ it's the latest thing (in fashion)

de **snob** /snɔp/ (pl: -s) snob
snoeien /snujə(n)/ (snoeide, heeft gesnoeid) **1** trim; prune **2** cut back, prune: in een begroting ~ prune a budget

de **snoeischaar** /snujsχar/ (pl: -scharen) pruning shears

de **snoek** /snuk/ (pl: -en) pike

de **snoekbaars** /snukbars/ (pl: -baarzen) pikeperch

de **snoep** /snup/ sweets; [Am] candy
snoepen /snupə(n)/ (snoepte, heeft gesnoept) eat sweets; [Am] eat candy

de **snoeper** /snupər/ (pl: -s) s.o. with a sweet tooth ‖ een ouwe ~ an old goat, a dirty old man

het **snoepgoed** /snupχut/ confectionery, sweets; [Am also] candy

het **snoepje** /snupjə/ (pl: -s) sweet; [Am] candy

het **snoepreisje** /snuprɛiʃə/ (pl: -s) facility trip; [Am] junket

de **snoepwinkel** /snupwɪŋkəl/ (pl: -s) sweetshop; [Am] candy store

het **snoer** /snur/ (pl: -en) **1** string, rope: kralen **aan** een ~ rijgen string beads **2** flex, lead; [Am] cord

de **snoes** /snus/ (pl: snoezen) sweetie, pet, poppet

de **snoeshaan** /snushan/ (pl: -hanen) queer customer (or: fellow)

de **snoet** /snut/ (pl: -en) **1** snout **2** face, mug: een **aardig** ~je a pretty little face
snoeven /snuvə(n)/ (snoefde, heeft gesnoefd) swagger, brag
snoezig /snuzəχ/ (adj, adv) cute, sweet

de **snol** /snɔl/ (pl: -len) [inform] tart
snood /snot/ (adj, adv): snode **plannen** hebben be scheming

de **snor** /snɔr/ (pl: -ren) **1** moustache: zijn ~ laten staan grow a moustache **2** whiskers ‖ dat zit wel ~ that's fine, all right, okay, Bob's your uncle!

de **snorfiets** /snɔrfits/ (pl: -en) moped

het **snorhaar** /snɔrhar/ (pl: -haren) **1** (hair of a)

moustache **2** whisker

de **snorkel** /snɔrkəl/ (pl: -s) snorkel

snorkelen /snɔrkələ(n)/ (snorkelde, heeft/is gesnorkeld) snorkel

snorren /snɔrə(n)/ (snorde, heeft gesnord) whirr, buzz, hum: *een ~de kat* a purring cat

de **snorscooter** /snɔrskutər/ (pl: -s) (motor) scooter

het/de **snot** /snɔt/ (nasal) mucus (*or:* discharge); snot

de **snotaap** /snɔtap/ (pl: -apen) brat, whippersnapper

de **snotneus** /snɔtnøs/ (pl: -neuzen) **1** runny nose **2** (tiny) tot, (little) kid **3** brat

snotteren /snɔtərə(n)/ (snotterde, heeft gesnotterd) **1** sniff(le) **2** blubber

snowboarden /snoːbɔːrdə(n)/ (snowboardde, heeft/is gesnowboard) go snowboarding

snuffelen /snʏfələ(n)/ (snuffelde, heeft gesnuffeld) **1** sniff (at) **2** nose (about), pry (into): *in laden ~* rummage in drawers

de **snufferd** /snʏfərt/ (pl: -s) [inform] hooter ‖ *ik gaf hem een klap op zijn ~* I gave him one on the kisser

het **snufje** /snʏfjə/ (pl: -s) **1** novelty; newest device (*or:* gadget): *het nieuwste ~* the latest thing **2** dash: *een ~ zout* a pinch of salt

snugger /snʏɣər/ (adj, adv) [inform] bright, clever

de **snuisterij** /snœystərɛi/ (pl: -en) bauble, trinket

de **snuit** /snœyt/ (pl: -en) snout: *de ~ van een varken* a pig's snout

snuiten /snœytə(n)/ (snoot, heeft gesnoten) blow (one's nose)

de **snuiter** /snœytər/ (pl: -s): *een rare ~* a strange guy, a weirdo

snuiven /snœyvə(n)/ (snoof, heeft gesnoven) **1** sniff(le), snort: *cocaïne ~* sniff cocaine; *~ als een paard* snort like a horse **2** sniff (at)

snurken /snʏrkə(n)/ (snurkte, heeft gesnurkt) snore

so (abbrev) **1** *schriftelijke overhoring* [Dutch] quiz, written test **2** *secundair onderwijs* [Belg] secondary education

de **soa** /soːwa/ *seksueel overdraagbare aandoening* VD, venereal disease

de **soap** /sop/ (pl: -s) soap

de **soapie** /sopi/ soap star

de **soapster** /sopstɛr/ soap star

sober /sobər/ (adj, adv) austere, frugal: *in ~e bewoordingen* in plain words (*or:* language); *hij leeft zeer ~* he lives very austerely (*or:* frugally)

de **soberheid** /sobərhɛit/ austerity, frugality

¹**sociaal** /soʃal/ (adj) social: *hoog op de sociale ladder* high up on the social scale; *iemands sociale positie* s.o.'s social position

²**sociaal** /soʃal/ (adv) **1** socially **2** socially-minded: *~ denkend* humanitarian, socially aware

de **sociaaldemocraat** /soʃaldemokrat/ (pl: -democraten) social democrat

sociaaldemocratisch /soʃaldemokratis/ (adj) social democratic

het **socialisme** /soʃalɪsmə/ socialism

de **socialist** /soʃalɪst/ (pl: -en) socialist

socialistisch /soʃalɪstis/ (adj, adv) socialist(ic)

de **sociëteit** /soʃetɛit/ (pl: -en) **1** association, club: *lid van een ~ worden* become a member of (*or:* join) an association **2** association (building), club(house) **3** society

de **sociologie** /soʃoloɣi/ sociology

sociologisch /soʃoloɣis/ (adj, adv) sociological

de **socioloog** /soʃolox/ (pl: -logen) sociologist

de **soda** /soda/ **1** (washing) soda **2** soda (water): *een whisky-soda* a whisky and soda

de **sodemieter** /sodəmitər/: *als de ~!* like crazy; *iem. op z'n ~ geven* beat the hell out of someone; *dat gaat je geen ~ aan* that's none of your bloody business; that's none of your fucking business

¹**sodemieteren** /sodəmitərə(n)/ (sodemieterde, is gesodemieterd) [inform] tumble

²**sodemieteren** /sodəmitərə(n)/ (sodemieterde, heeft gesodemieterd) [inform] chuck

soebatten /subɑtə(n)/ (soebatte, heeft gesoebat) [inform] pester, implore: *na lang ~* after pestering (*or:* imploring) long enough

het **soelaas** /sulas/: *dat biedt ~* that is a consolation

de **soenniet** /sunɪt/ (pl: -en) Sunni

de **soep** /sup/ (pl: -en) soup; consommé: *een ~ laten trekken* make a stock (*or:* broth) ‖ *het is niet veel ~s* it's not up to much; *in de ~ lopen* come badly unstuck; *dat is linke ~* that's a risky business

het **soepballetje** /subɑləcə/ (pl: -s) meatball

het **soepbord** /subɔrt/ (pl: -en) soup bowl

soepel /supəl/ (adj, adv) **1** supple, pliable **2** supple; flexible; (com)pliant: *een ~e regeling* a flexible arrangement **3** supple: *~e bewegingen* supple (*or:* lithe) movements

de **soepelheid** /supəlhɛit/ suppleness, flexibility

de **soepgroente** /supxruntə/ (pl: -n) vegetables for soup

de **soepkop** /supkɔp/ (pl: -pen) soup cup

de **soeplepel** /suplepəl/ (pl: -s) **1** soup ladle **2** soup spoon

de **soepstengel** /supstɛŋəl/ (pl: -s) breadstick

het **soepzootje** /supsocə/ mess, shambles

de **soesa** /suza/ fuss, to-do, bother

soeverein /suvərɛin/ (adj, adv) sovereign

de **soevereiniteit** /suvərɛinitɛit/ sovereignty

soezen /suzə(n)/ (soesde, heeft gesoesd) doze, drowse

soezerig /suzərəx/ (adj) drowsy, dozy

de **sof** /sɔf/ flop, washout

de **sofa** /sofa/ (pl: -'s) sofa, couch

het **sofinummer** /sofinʏmər/ (pl: -s) [roughly] National Insurance Number; [Am] [roughly] Social Security Number

het **softbal** /sɔftbɑl/ softball

softballen /sɔf(t)bɑlə(n)/ (softbalde, heeft gesoftbald) play softball

het **softijs** /sɔftɛis/ soft ice-cream, Mr. Softy

de **softporno** /sɔftpɔrno/ soft porn(ography)

de **software** /sɔftwɛːr/ software

de **soigneur** /swaɲør/ (pl: -s) helper; [boxing] [roughly] second

de **soja** /soja/ (sweet) soy (sauce)

de **sojaboon** /sojabon/ (pl: -bonen) soya bean

de **sojaolie** /sojaoli/ soya bean oil

de **sojasaus** /sojasaus/ soy sauce

het **sojavlees** /sojavles/ soya meat

de **sok** /sɔk/ sock: *hij haalde het **op** zijn ~ken* he did it effortlessly || *iem. **van** de ~ken rijden* bowl s.o. over, knock s.o. down

de **sokkel** /sɔkəl/ (pl: -s) pedestal

de **sol** /sɔl/ (pl: -len) [mus] so(h), sol, G

het **solarium** /solarijʏm/ (pl: solaria) solarium

de **soldaat** /sɔldat/ (pl: soldaten) **1** (common) soldier, private: *de **gewone** soldaten* the ranks **2** soldier; troops: *de **Onbekende** Soldaat* the Unknown Soldier

het **soldaatje** /sɔldacə/ (pl: -s) toy soldier, tin soldier: *~ **spelen** play (at) soldiers

het/de **soldeer** /sɔldeːr/ solder

de **soldeerbout** /sɔldeːrbaut/ (pl: -en) soldering iron

het **soldeersel** /sɔldeːrsəl/ (pl: -s) solder

de **solden** /sɔldə(n)/ [Belg] sale

solderen /sɔldeːrə(n)/ (soldeerde, heeft gesoldeerd) solder

de **soldij** /sɔldɛi/ pay(ment)

solidair /solidɛːr/ (adj, adv) sympathetic: *~ zijn* show solidarity (with)

de **solidariteit** /solidaritɛit/ solidarity: *uit ~ met* in sympathy with

solide /solidə/ (adj, adv) **1** solid; hard-wearing **2** steady

de **solist** /solɪst/ (pl: -en) soloist

solitair /solitɛːr/ (adj, adv) solitary

sollen /sɔlə(n)/ (solde, heeft gesold) (+ met) trifle with: *hij **laat** niet met zich ~* he won't be trifled with

de **sollicitant** /sɔlisitɑnt/ (pl: -en) applicant

de **sollicitatie** /sɔlisita(t)si/ (pl: -s) application

de **sollicitatiebrief** /sɔlisita(t)sibrif/ (pl: -brieven) (letter of) application

het **sollicitatiegesprek** /sɔlisita(t)siɣəsprɛk/ (pl: -ken) interview (for a position, job)

solliciteren /sɔlisiteːrə(n)/ (solliciteerde, heeft gesolliciteerd) apply (for)

het/de **solo** /solo/ (pl: -'s, soli) solo

de **solocarrière** /solokɑrijɛːrə/ (pl: -s) solo career

het **soloconcert** /solokɔnsɛrt/ solo concert

de **solutie** /soly(t)si/ (pl: -s) (rubber) solution

de **som** /sɔm/ (pl: -men) sum: *een ~ **geld** a sum of money; ~men **maken** do sums

Somalië /somalijə/ Somalia

de **Somaliër** /somalijər/ (pl: -s) Somali

Somalisch /somalis/ (adj) Somali

somber /sɔmbər/ (adj, adv) **1** dejected, gloomy: *het ~ **inzien** take a sombre (or: gloomy) view (of things) **2** gloomy; dark: *~ **weer** gloomy weather

de **somma** /sɔma/ sum

sommeren /sɔmeːrə(n)/ (sommeerde, heeft gesommeerd) summon(s), call (up)on

sommige /sɔməɣə/ (ind pron) some, certain: *~n* some (people)

soms /sɔms/ (adv) **1** sometimes **2** perhaps, by any chance: *heb* je Jan *~ **gezien**?* have you seen John by any chance?; *dat is toch mijn zaak, of **niet** ~?* that's my business, or am I mistaken?

de **sonar** /sonar/ (pl: -s) sonar

de **sonate** /sonatə/ (pl: -s) sonata

de **sonde** /sɔndə/ (pl: -s) **1** probe **2** [med] catheter

de **sondevoeding** /sɔndəvudɪŋ/ (pl: -en) dripfeed

het **songfestival** /sɔŋfɛstival/ (pl: -s) song contest: *het Eurovisie ~* the Eurovision Song Contest

de **songtekst** /sɔŋtɛkst/ lyric(s)

het **sonnet** /sɔnɛt/ (pl: -ten) sonnet

de **¹soort** /sort/ (pl: -en) species: *de **menselijke** ~* the human species

het/de **²soort** /sort/ (pl: -en) **1** sort, kind, type: *ik ken dat ~* I know the type; *in zijn ~* in its way, of its kind; *in alle ~en en maten* in all shapes and sizes **2** sort (of), kind (of): *als een ~ **vis** (rather) like some kind of a fish || *~ **zoekt** ~* like will to like; birds of a feather flock together

soortelijk /sortələk/ (adj, adv) specific

het **soortement** /sortəmɛnt/ [inform] a sort of, a kind of

soortgelijk /sortxəlɛik/ (adj) similar; of the same kind

de **soos** /sos/ club

het **sop** /sɔp/ (pl: -pen) (soap)suds

het **sopje** /sɔpjə/ (soap)suds: *zal ik de keuken nog een ~ **geven**?* shall I give the kitchen a(nother) wash?

soppen /sɔpə(n)/ (sopte, heeft gesopt) dunk

de **¹sopraan** /sopran/ [singer] soprano

de **²sopraan** /sopran/ [voice] soprano

de **sorbet** /sɔrbɛt/ (pl: -s) sorbet

sorry /sɔri/ (int) sorry

sorteren /sɔrteːrə(n)/ (sorteerde, heeft gesorteerd) sort (out): *op maat ~* sort according to size

de **sortering** /sɔrteːrɪŋ/ (pl: -en) selection, range, assortment

SOS /ɛsoɛs/ *Save our Souls* SOS: *een ~(-signaal)* **uitzenden** broadcast an SOS (message)

de **soufflé** /sufle/ (pl: -s) soufflé

souffleren /sufleːrə(n)/ (souffleerde, heeft

gesouffleerd) prompt

de **souffleur** /suflø̞r/ (pl: -s) prompter

de **soul** /sol/ soul (music)

de **sound** /saunt/ (pl: -s) sound

de **soundbite** /saundbɑjt/ (pl: -s) sound bite

de **soundcheck** /sauntʃɛk/ (pl: -s) soundcheck

de **soundtrack** /sauntrɛk/ (pl: -s) soundtrack

het **souper** /supe/ (pl: -s) supper, dinner

de **souteneur** /sutənø̞r/ (pl: -s) pimp

het **souterrain** /sutərɛ̃/ (pl: -s) basement

het **souvenir** /suvənir/ (pl: -s) souvenir

de **sovjet** /sɔvjɛt/ (pl: -s) soviet: *de* **Opperste** *Sovjet* the Supreme Soviet

de **Sovjet-Unie** /sɔvjɛtyni/ Soviet Union

sowieso /zowizo/ (adv) in any case, anyhow: *het wordt ~ laat op dat feest* that party will in any case go on until late

de ¹**spa**® /spa/ mineral water

de ²**spa** /spa/ spade

de **spaak** /spak/ (pl: spaken) spoke: *iem. een ~ in het wiel* **steken** put a spoke in s.o.'s wheel ‖ *~ lopen* go wrong

de **spaan** /span/ (pl: spanen) **1** chip (of wood): *er bleef* **geen** *~ van heel* there was nothing left of it **2** skimmer

de **spaander** /spandər/ (pl: -s) chip, splinter

de **spaanplaat** /spamplat/ (pl: -platen) chipboard

Spaans /spans/ (adj) Spanish ‖ *zeg het eens op z'n ~* say it in Spanish

de **spaarbank** /sparbɑŋk/ (pl: -en) savings bank: *geld op de ~ hebben* have money in a savings bank (*or:* savings account)

het **spaarbankboekje** /sparbɑŋbukjə/ (pl: -s) deposit book

de **spaarcenten** /sparsɛntə(n)/ (pl) savings

de **spaarder** /spardər/ (pl: -s) saver

het **spaargeld** /sparɣɛlt/ (pl: -en) savings

de **spaarlamp** /sparlɑmp/ (pl: -en) low-energy light bulb

de **spaarpot** /sparpɔt/ (pl: -ten) **1** money box, piggy bank **2** savings, nest egg: *een ~je* **aanleggen** start saving for a rainy day; *zijn ~ aanspreken* draw on one's savings

de **spaarrekening** /sparekənɪŋ/ (pl: -en) savings account

het **spaartegoed** /spartəɣut/ (pl: -en) savings balance

het **spaarvarken** /sparvɑrkə(n)/ (pl: -s) piggy bank

spaarzaam /sparzam/ (adj, adv) **1** thrifty, economical: *hij* **is** *erg ~ met zijn lof* he's very sparing in (*or:* with) his praise; *~* **zijn** *met zijn woorden* not waste words **2** scanty, sparse: *de doodstraf* **wordt** *~ toegepast* the death penalty is seldom imposed

de **spaarzegel** /sparzeɣəl/ (pl: -s) trading stamp

de **spade** /spadə/ (pl: spaden) spade

de **spagaat** /spaɣat/ (pl: spagaten) splits

de **spaghetti** /spaɣɛti/ (pl: -'s) spaghetti: *een sliert ~* a strand of spaghetti

de **spalk** /spɑlk/ (pl: -en) splint

spalken /spɑlkə(n)/ (spalkte, heeft gespalkt) put in splints

de **spam** /spɛm/ spam

het **spamfilter** /spɛmfɪltər/ spam filter

spammen /spɛmə(n)/ (spamde, heeft gespamd) spam

het **span** /spɑn/ (pl: -nen) team; [of pers] couple: *een ~* **paarden** a team of horses

het **spandoek** /spɑnduk/ (pl: -en) banner: *een ~ met zich* **meedragen** carry a banner

de **spaniël** /spɛnjəl/ (pl: -s) spaniel

de **Spanjaard** /spɑnjart/ (pl: -en) Spaniard

Spanje /spɑnjə/ Spain

de **spankracht** /spɑnkrɑxt/ tension; muscle tone

spannen /spɑnə(n)/ (spande, heeft gespannen) **1** stretch, tighten **2** harness ‖ *het zal erom ~ wie er wint* it will be a close match (*or:* race); *dat spant de* **kroon** that takes the cake

spannend /spɑnənt/ (adj) exciting, thrilling: *een ~* **ogenblik** a tense moment; *een ~* **verhaal** an exciting story

de **spanning** /spɑnɪŋ/ (pl: -en) **1** tension; [fig also] suspense: *~ en* **sensatie** excitement and suspense; *de ~* **stijgt** the tension mounts; *de ~ viel van haar* **af** that was a load off her shoulders; *ze zaten* **vol** *~ te wachten* they were waiting anxiously; *in ~ zitten* be in suspense **2** tension: *een ~ van 10.000* **volt** a charge of 10,000 volts

de **spanningsboog** /spɑnɪŋzbox/ (pl: -bogen) voltage curve: [fig] *een* **korte** *~ hebben* have a short attention span

het **spanningsveld** /spɑnɪŋsfɛlt/ (pl: -en) [esp fig] area of tension

het **spant** /spɑnt/ (pl: -en) rafter, truss

de **spanwijdte** /spɑnwɛitə/ (pl: -n, -s) wingspan; wingspread

de **spar** /spɑr/ (pl: -ren) spruce

de **sparappel** /spɑrɑpəl/ (pl: -s, -en) fir cone

¹**sparen** /sparə(n)/ (spaarde, heeft gespaard) save (up): *voor een nieuwe auto ~* save up for a new car

²**sparen** /sparə(n)/ (spaarde, heeft gespaard) **1** save, spare **2** collect ‖ *spaar me de* **details** spare me the details, all right?

de **spareribs** /spɛːrɪps/ (pl) spareribs

sparren /spɛrə(n)/ (sparde, heeft gespard) work out; spar

de **sparringpartner** /spɛrɪŋpɑːrtnər/ (pl: -s) sparring-partner

spartelen /spɑrtələ(n)/ (spartelde, heeft gesparteld) flounder, thrash about: *het kleine kind spartelde* **in** *het water* the little child splashed about in the water

spastisch /spɑstis/ (adj, adv) spastic

de **spat** /spɑt/ (pl: -ten) **1** splash **2** speck, spot

de **spatader** /spɑtadər/ (pl: -en) varicose vein

het **spatbord** /spɑdbɔrt/ (pl: -en) mudguard;

[Am] fender

de **spatel** /spɑtəl/ (pl: -s) spatula

de **spatie** /spa(t)si/ (pl: -s) space, spacing, interspace: *iets typen* **met** *een* ~ type sth. with interspacing

de **spatiebalk** /spa(t)sibɑlk/ (pl: -en) space bar

de **spatlap** /spɑtlɑp/ (pl: -pen) mud flap

spatten /spɑtə(n)/ (spatte, heeft/is gespat) splash, sp(l)atter: *vonken* ~ *in het rond* sparks flew all around; *er is verf* **op** *mijn kleren gespat* some paint has splashed on my clothes; *zij spatte (mij)* **met** *water in mijn gezicht* she spattered water in my face; *uit elkaar* ~ burst

de **speaker** /spikər/ (pl: -s) speaker

de **specerij** /spesərɛi/ (pl: -en) spice, seasoning

de **specht** /spɛxt/ (pl: -en) woodpecker

¹**speciaal** /speʃal/ (adj) special: *in dit speciale* **geval** in this particular case

²**speciaal** /speʃal/ (adv) especially, particularly, specially: *ik* **doel** ~ *op hem* I mean him in particular; ~ **gemaakt** specially made

de **speciaalzaak** /speʃalzak/ (pl: -zaken) specialist shop

de **special** /spɛʃəl/ (pl: -s) special (issue): *een* ~ *over de Kinks* a special on the Kinks

de **specialisatie** /speʃaliza(t)si/ (pl: -s) specialization

zich **specialiseren** /speʃalizerə(n)/ (specialiseerde zich, heeft zich gespecialiseerd) (+ in) specialize (in)

het **specialisme** /speʃalɪsmə/ (pl: -n) specialism

de **specialist** /speʃalɪst/ (pl: -en) specialist

specialistisch /speʃalɪstis/ (adj, adv) specialist(ic)

de **specialiteit** /speʃalitɛit/ (pl: -en) speciality

de **specie** /spesi/ (pl: -s) cement, mortar

de **specificatie** /spesifika(t)si/ (pl: -s) specification: ~ *van een* **nota** *vragen* request an itemized bill

specificeren /spesifiserə(n)/ (specificeerde, heeft gespecificeerd) specify, itemize

specifiek /spesifik/ (adj, adv) specific

het **specimen** /spesimɛn/ (pl: -s) specimen, exemplar

spectaculair /spɛktakylɛːr/ (adj) spectacular

het **spectrum** /spɛktrəm/ (pl: spectra) spectrum

het/de **speculaas** /spekylas/: *gevulde* ~ [roughly] spiced cake filled with almond paste

de **speculaaspop** /spekylaspɔp/ (pl: -pen) [roughly] gingerbread man

de **speculant** /spekylɑnt/ (pl: -en) speculator

de **speculatie** /spekyla(t)si/ (pl: -s) speculation

speculeren /spekylerə(n)/ (speculeerde, heeft gespeculeerd) 1 (+ op) speculate (on) 2 speculate

de **speech** /spiːtʃ/ (pl: -es) speech: *een* ~ *afsteken* deliver a speech

speechen /spiːtʃə(n)/ (speechte, heeft gespeecht) give (*or:* make) a speech

de **speed** /spiːd/ speed

de **speedboot** /spiːdbot/ (pl: -boten) speedboat

het **speeksel** /speksəl/ saliva

de **speelautomaat** /spelɑutomat/ (pl: -automaten) slot machine

de **speelbal** /spelbɑl/ (pl: -len): *het schip was een* ~ *van de* **golven** the ship was the waves' plaything

de **speeldoos** /speldos/ (pl: -dozen) 1 music box 2 toybox

de **speelfilm** /spelfɪlm/ (pl: -s) (feature) film

het **speelgoed** /spelɣut/ toy(s): *een* **stuk** ~ a toy

de **speelhal** /spelhɑl/ (pl: -len) amusement arcade

de **speelhelft** /spelhɛlft/ (pl: -en) half

de **speelkaart** /spelkart/ (pl: -en) playing card

de **speelkameraad** /spelkamərat/ (pl: -kameraden) playfellow, playmate

het **speelkwartier** /spelkwartir/ (pl: -en) playtime; break

de **speelplaats** /spelplats/ (pl: -en) playground, play area: *op de* ~ in the playground

de **speelruimte** /spelrœymtə/ (pl: -n, -s) 1 play, latitude: ~ **hebben** have some play; *iem.* ~ **geven** leave s.o. a bit of elbow room 2 play area, room to play

speels /spels/ (adj) 1 playful; [esp animal] frisky 2 playful, light

de **speelsheid** /spelshɛit/ playfulness

de **speeltafel** /speltafəl/ (pl: -s) gaming table

het **speeltje** /speltʃə/ (pl: -s) (little) toy

het **speeltoestel** /speltustɛl/ (pl: -len) playground (*or:* outdoor) equipment

de **speeltuin** /speltœyn/ (pl: -en) playground

het **speelveld** /spelvɛlt/ (pl: -en) (sports, playing) field

de **speen** /spen/ (pl: spenen) 1 (rubber) teat; [Am] nipple 2 teat

de **speer** /sper/ (pl: speren) spear; javelin ‖ *als een* ~ like a rocket

de **speerpunt** /sperpʏnt/ (pl: -en) spearhead: *de* ~*en van een* **beleid** the spearheads of a policy

speerwerpen /sperwɛrpə(n)/ throw(ing) the javelin: *het* ~ **winnen** win the javelin (event)

het **spek** /spɛk/ bacon; fat

spekglad /spɛkxlɑt/ (adj) (very) slippery

spekken /spɛkə(n)/ (spekte, heeft gespekt) lard: *zijn verhaal* **met** *anekdotes* ~ spice one's story with anecdotes

het **spekkie** /spɛki/ (pl: -s) [roughly] marshmallow

de **speklap** /spɛklɑp/ (pl: -pen) thick slice of fatty bacon

het **spektakel** /spɛktakəl/ (pl: -s) 1 spectacle, show: *het* ~ **is afgelopen** the show is over 2 uproar, fuss: *het* **was** *me een* ~ it was a tremendous fuss

het **spel** /spɛl/ (pl: -en, -len) 1 game; gambling 2 game, match: [cards] *een* **goed** (*or:* **sterk**) ~

in handen hebben have a good hand; *doe je ook een ~letje mee?* do you want to join in? (*or:* play?); *het ~ meespelen* play the game, play along (with s.o.); *zijn ~ slim spelen* play one's cards well **3** play: *hoog ~ spelen* play for high stakes, play high; *vals ~* cheating; *vuil* (or: *onsportief*) *~* foul play **4** acting, performance || *een ~ kaarten* a pack (*or:* deck) of cards; *buiten ~ blijven* stay (*or:* keep) out of it; *in het ~ zijn* be involved; be in question, be at stake; *er is een vergissing in het ~* there is an error somewhere; *zijn leven* (or: *alles*) *op het ~ zetten* risk/stake one's life (*or:* everything); *vrij ~ hebben* have free play, have an open field

de **spelbreker** /spɛlbrekər/ (pl: -s) spoilsport

de **spelcomputer** /spɛlkɔmpjutər/ (pl: -s) games computer

de **speld** /spɛlt/ (pl: -en) pin: *men kon er een ~ horen vallen* you could have heard a pin drop; *daar is geen ~ tussen te krijgen* there's no flaw in that argument

spelden /spɛldə(n)/ (speldde, heeft gespeld) pin

het **speldenkussen** /spɛldə(n)kʏsə(n)/ (pl: -s) pincushion

de **speldenprik** /spɛldə(n)prɪk/ (pl: -ken) pinprick: *~ken uitdelen* needle (s.o.), hit out

het **speldje** /spɛlcə/ (pl: -s) **1** pin **2** pin, badge

¹**spelen** /spelə(n)/ (speelde, heeft gespeeld) **1** be set (in), take place (in): *de film speelt in New York* the film is set in New York **2** play: *de wind speelde met haar haren* the wind played (*or:* was playing) with her hair

²**spelen** /spelə(n)/ (speelde, heeft gespeeld) **1** play: *al ~d leren* learn through play; *vals ~* **a)** cheat; **b)** [mus] play out of tune; [sport] *voor ~* play up front **2** act, play: *piano ~* play the piano **4** play, perform **5** be of importance, count: *dat speelt geen rol* that is of no account; *die kwestie speelt nog steeds* that is still an (important) issue

spelenderwijs /speləndərwɛis/ (adv) without effort, with (the greatest of) ease

de **speleoloog** /spelejolox/ (pl: -logen) speleologist

de **speler** /spelər/ (pl: -s) player; gambler

de **spelfout** /spɛlfɑut/ (pl: -en) spelling mistake (*or:* error)

de **speling** /spelɪŋ/ (pl: -en) **1** play: *een ~ van de natuur* a freak of nature **2** play; slack; margin

de **spelleider** /spɛlɛɪdər/ (pl: -s) instructor; emcee

spellen /spɛlə(n)/ (spelde, heeft gespeld) spell: *hoe spelt hij zijn naam?* how does he spell his name?; *een woord verkeerd ~* misspell a word

het **spelletje** /spɛləcə/ (pl: -s) game

de **spelling** /spɛlɪŋ/ (pl: -en) spelling

het **spelonk** /spelɔŋk/ (pl: -en) cave, cavern

de **spelregel** /spɛlreɣəl/ (pl: -s) rule of play (*or:* the game): *je moet je aan de ~s houden* you must stick to the rules; *de ~s overtreden* break the rules

de **spelshow** /spɛlʃo/ game show

de **spelt** /spɛlt/ spelt

de **spelverdeler** /spɛlvərdelər/ (pl: -s) playmaker

de **spencer** /spɛnsər/ (pl: -s) spencer

spenderen /spɛndərə(n)/ (spendeerde, heeft gespendeerd) spend

het **sperma** /spɛrma/ sperm

de **spermabank** /spɛrmabɑŋk/ (pl: -en) sperm bank

de **spertijd** /spɛrtɛɪt/ (pl: -en) curfew

het **spervuur** /spɛrvyr/ barrage, curtain fire: *een ~ van vragen* a barrage of questions

de **sperwer** /spɛrwər/ (pl: -s) sparrowhawk

de **sperzieboon** /spɛrzibon/ (pl: -bonen) green bean

de **spetter** /spɛtər/ (pl: -s) **1** spatter **2** hunk

spetteren /spɛtərə(n)/ (spetterde, heeft gespetterd) sp(l)atter; crackle

de **speurder** /spørdər/ (pl: -s) detective, sleuth

speuren /spørə(n)/ (speurde, heeft gespeurd) investigate, hunt: *naar iets ~ hunt* (*or:* search) for sth.

de **speurhond** /spørhɔnt/ (pl: -en) tracker (dog), bloodhound

de **speurtocht** /spørtɔxt/ (pl: -en) search

het **speurwerk** /spørwɛrk/ investigation, detective work

spichtig /spɪxtəx/ (adj, adv) lanky, spindly: *een ~ meisje* a skinny girl

de **spie** /spi/ (pl: -ën) pin; wedge

spieden /spidə(n)/ (spiedde, heeft gespied): *~d om zich heen kijken* look furtively around

de **spiegel** /spiɣəl/ (pl: -s) mirror: *vlakke* (or: *holle, bolle*) *~s* flat (*or:* concave, convex) mirrors; *in de ~ kijken* look at o.s. (in the mirror)

het **spiegelbeeld** /spiɣəlbelt/ (pl: -en) **1** reflection **2** mirror image

het **spiegelei** /spiɣəlɛi/ (pl: -eren) fried egg

spiegelen /spiɣələ(n)/ (spiegelde, heeft gespiegeld) reflect, mirror

spiegelglad /spiɣəlɣlɑt/ (adj) as smooth as glass; icy; slippery

de **spiegeling** /spiɣəlɪŋ/ (pl: -en) reflection

de **spiegelruit** /spiɣəlrœyt/ (pl: -en) plate-glass window

het **spiegelschrift** /spiɣəlsxrɪft/ mirror writing

het **spiekbriefje** /spigbrifjə/ (pl: -s) crib (sheet)

spieken /spikə(n)/ (spiekte, heeft gespiekt) copy, use a crib: *bij iem. ~* copy from s.o.

de **spier** /spir/ (pl: -en) muscle: *de ~en losmaken* loosen up the muscles, limber up, warm up; *hij vertrok geen ~* (*van zijn gezicht*) he didn't bat an eyelid

de **spierbal** /spirbɑl/ (pl: -len): *zijn ~len gebruiken* flex one's muscle(s)

de **spierkracht** /spirkrɑxt/ muscle (power),

muscular strength

spiernaakt /spirnakt/ (adj) stark naked

de **spierpijn** /spirpɛin/ (pl: -en) sore muscles, aching muscles, muscular pain

het **spierweefsel** /spirwefsəl/ (pl: -s) muscular tissue

spierwit /spirwɪt/ (adj) (as) white as a sheet

de **spies** /spis/ (pl: spiezen) skewer

de **spijbelaar** /spɛibəlar/ (pl: -s) truant

spijbelen /spɛibələ(n)/ (spijbelde, heeft gespijbeld) play truant

de **spijker** /spɛikər/ (pl: -s) nail: *de ~ op de kop slaan* hit the nail on the head; *~s met koppen slaan* get down to business

de **spijkerbroek** /spɛikərbruk/ (pl: -en) (pair of) jeans: *ik heb een nieuwe ~* I've got a new pair of jeans; *waar is mijn ~?* where are my jeans?

¹**spijkeren** /spɛikərə(n)/ (spijkerde, heeft gespijkerd) drive in nails

²**spijkeren** /spɛikərə(n)/ (spijkerde, heeft gespijkerd) nail

spijkerhard /spɛikərhɑrt/ (adj) (as) hard as a rock; [fig] (as) hard as nails: *~e journalisten* hard-boiled journalists

het **spijkerjasje** /spɛikərjɑʃə/ denim jacket, jeans jacket

het **spijkerschrift** /spɛikərsxrɪft/ cuneiform script

de **spijkerstof** /spɛikərstɔf/ (pl: -fen) denim

de **spijl** /spɛil/ (pl: -en) bar; rail(ing)

de **spijs** /spɛis/ (pl: spijzen) foods, victuals

de **spijskaart** /spɛiskart/ (pl: -en) menu

de **spijsvertering** /spɛisfərterɪŋ/ digestion: *een slechte ~ hebben* suffer from indigestion

de **spijt** /spɛit/ regret: *daar zul je geen ~ van hebben* you won't regret that; *geen ~ hebben* have no regrets; *daar zul je ~ van krijgen* you'll regret that; you'll be sorry; *tot mijn (grote) ~* (much) to my regret

spijten /spɛitə(n)/ (speet, heeft gespeten) regret, be sorry: *het spijt me dat ik u stoor* I'm sorry to disturb you; *het spijt me u te moeten zeggen …* I'm sorry (to have) to tell you …

spijtig /spɛitəx/ (adj, adv) regrettable

de **spike** /spɑjk/ (pl: -s) spikes

de **spikkel** /spɪkəl/ (pl: -s) fleck, speck

spiksplinternieuw /spɪksplɪntərniw/ (adj) spanking new, brand new

de **spil** /spɪl/ (pl: -len) **1** pivot: *om een ~ draaien* pivot, swivel **2** pivot, key figure; playmaker [socc]

de **spillebeen** /spɪləben/ spindleshanks

de **spin** /spɪn/ (pl: -nen, -s) **1** spider: *nijdig als een ~* furious, absolutely wild **2** [on bike] spider **3** spin: *een bal veel ~ geven* give a ball a lot of spin

de **spinazie** /spinazi/ spinach: *~ à la crème* creamed spinach

het **spinet** /spinɛt/ (pl: -ten) spinet

spinnen /spɪnə(n)/ (spinde/spon, heeft ge-

spind) **1** spin: *garen ~* spin thread (*or:* yarn) **2** purr

het **spinnenweb** /spɪnə(n)wɛp/ (pl: -ben) cobweb, spider('s) web

het **spinnewiel** /spɪnəwil/ (pl: -en) spinning wheel

het **spinrag** /spɪnrɑx/ cobweb, spider('s) web: *zo fijn* (*or:* zo dun, zo teer) *als ~* as fine (*or:* thin, delicate) as gossamer

de **spion** /spijɔn/ (pl: -nen) spy

de **spionage** /spijonaʒə/ espionage, spying

spioneren /spijonɛrə(n)/ (spioneerde, heeft gespioneerd) spy

de **spiraal** /spiral/ (pl: spiralen) spiral

het/de **spiraalmatras** /spiralmatrɑs/ (pl: -sen) spring mattress

het **spiraaltje** /spiralcə/ (pl: -s) IUD, coil

de **spirit** /spɪrɪt/ spirit, guts

het **spiritisme** /spiritɪsmə/ spiritualism

spiritueel /spiritywel/ (adj, adv) spiritual

de **spiritus** /spiritʏs/ methylated spirits, alcohol

het ¹**spit** /spɪt/ (pl: -ten) spit: *aan het ~ gebraden* broiled on the spit; *kip van 't ~* barbecued chicken

het/de ²**spit** /spɪt/ (pl: -ten) lumbago

het/de ¹**spits** /spɪts/ **1** peak, point: *de ~ van een toren* the spire **2** rush line **3** [sport] forward line **4** striker ‖ *de (het) ~ afbijten* open the batting; *iets op de ~ drijven* bring sth. to a head

²**spits** /spɪts/ (adj, adv) pointed, sharp: *~ toelopen* taper (off), end in a point

de **spitsboog** /spɪtsbox/ (pl: -bogen) pointed arch

spitsen /spɪtsə(n)/ (spitste, heeft gespitst) prick

de **spitskool** /spɪtskol/ (pl: -kolen) pointed cabbage, hearted cabbage

de **spitsstrook** /spɪtstrok/ hard shoulder used as running lane during rush hour, hard shoulder running

de **spitstechnologie** /spɪtstɛxnoloɣi/ (pl: -ën) [Belg] state-of-the-art technology

het **spitsuur** /spɪtsyr/ (pl: -uren) rush hour: *buiten de spitsuren* outside the rush hour; *in het ~* during the rush hour

spitsvondig /spɪtsfɔndəx/ (adj, adv) clever

spitten /spɪtə(n)/ (spitte, heeft gespit) dig: *land ~* turn the soil over

de **spitzen** /ʃpɪtsən/ (pl) point shoes, ballet shoes

de **spleet** /splet/ (pl: spleten) crack

het **spleetoog** /spletox/ (pl: -ogen) slit-eye, slant-eye

splijten /splɛitə(n)/ (spleet, heeft/is gespleten) split

de **splijtstof** /splɛitstɔf/ (pl: -fen) nuclear fuel, fissionable material

de **splijtzwam** /splɛitswɑm/ (pl: -men) divisive element

de **splinter** /splɪntər/ (pl: -s) splinter

splinternieuw /splɪntərniw/ (adj) brand-

splinterpartij

new

de **splinterpartij** /splɪntərpɑrtɛɪ/ (pl: -en) splinter group

het **split** /splɪt/ slit; placket

de **spliterwt** /splɪtɛrt/ (pl: -en) split pea

de **splitpen** /splɪtpɛn/ (pl: -nen) split pin

¹**splitsen** /splɪtsə(n)/ (splitste, heeft gesplitst) **1** divide, split **2** separate, split up

zich ²**splitsen** /splɪtsə(n)/ (splitste zich, heeft zich gesplitst) split (up), divide: *daar splitst de weg zich* the road forks there

de **splitsing** /splɪtsɪŋ/ (pl: -en) **1** splitting (up), division **2** fork, branch(ing): *bij de ~ links afslaan* turn left at the fork

de **spoed** /sput/ speed: *op ~ aandringen* stress the urgency of the matter; *met ~* with haste, urgently; *~!* [on letters] urgent

de **spoedbehandeling** /spudbəhandəlɪŋ/ (pl: -en) emergency treatment

de **spoedcursus** /sputkʏrzʏs/ (pl: -sen) intensive course, crash course

het **spoeddebat** /spudəbɑt/ (pl: -ten) emergency debate

spoedeisend /sputɛɪsənt/ (adj) urgent: *de afdeling ~e hulp* the accident and emergency department; [Am] the emergency room

spoeden /spudə(n)/ (spoedde zich, heeft zich gespoed) [form] speed

het **spoedgeval** /sputxəval/ (pl: -len) emergency (case), urgent matter

¹**spoedig** /spudəx/ (adj) **1** near: *~e levering* prompt (*or:* swift) delivery **2** speedy, quick: *een ~ antwoord* a quick answer

²**spoedig** /spudəx/ (adv) shortly, soon: *zo ~ mogelijk* as soon as possible

de **spoel** /spul/ (pl: -en) **1** reel; [Am] spool; bobbin **2** shuttle

de **spoelbak** /spulbɑk/ (pl: -ken) washbasin

¹**spoelen** /spulə(n)/ (spoelde, is gespoeld) wash: *naar zee* (or: *aan land) ~* wash out to sea (*or:* ashore)

²**spoelen** /spulə(n)/ (spoelde, heeft gespoeld) rinse (out): *de mond ~* rinse one's mouth (out)

de **spoeling** /spulɪŋ/ (pl: -en) rinse; rinsing: *een ~ geven* rinse (out)

de **spoiler** /spɔɪlər/ (pl: -s) spoiler

spoken /spokə(n)/ (spookte, heeft gespookt) **1** prowl (round, about): *nog laat door het huis ~* prowl about in the house late at night **2** be haunted: *in dat bos spookt het* that forest is haunted

de **sponning** /spɔnɪŋ/ (pl: -en) groove, rebate

de **spons** /spɔns/ (pl: sponzen) sponge

de **sponsor** /spɔnsɔr/ (pl: -s) sponsor

sponsoren /spɔnsɔrə(n)/ (sponsorde, heeft gesponsord) sponsor

de **sponsoring** /spɔnsərɪŋ/ sponsoring

spontaan /spɔntan/ (adj, adv) spontaneous

de **spontaniteit** /spɔntanitɛit/ (pl: -en) spontaneity

het **spook** /spok/ (pl: spoken) ghost; phantom: *overal spoken zien* see ghosts everywhere

spookachtig /spokɑxtəx/ (adj, adv) ghostly

het **spookhuis** /spokhœys/ (pl: -huizen) haunted house

de **spookrijder** /spokrɛidər/ (pl: -s) ghostrider

de **spookverschijning** /spokfərsχɛinɪŋ/ (pl: -en) spectre, ghost

de ¹**spoor** /spor/ spur: *een paard de sporen geven* spur a horse

het ²**spoor** /spor/ **1** track, trail: *ik ben het ~ bijster (kwijt)* I've lost track of things; *op het goede ~ zijn* be on the right track (*or:* trail); *de politie heeft een ~ gevonden* the police have found a clue; *iem. op het ~ komen* track s.o. down, trace s.o.; *iem. op het ~ zijn* be on s.o.'s track **2** track **3** trace: *sporen van geweld(pleging)* marks of violence **4** track, trail: *op een dood ~ komen (raken)* get into a blind alley; *uit het ~ raken* run off the rails

de **spoorbaan** /sporban/ (pl: -banen) railway

het **spoorboekje** /sporbukjə/ (pl: -s) (train, railway) timetable

de **spoorboom** /sporbom/ (pl: -bomen) level-crossing barrier

de **spoorbreedte** /sporbretə/ (pl: -s) (railway) gauge

de **spoorbrug** /sporbrʏχ/ (pl: -gen) railway bridge

de **spoorlijn** /sporlɛin/ (pl: -en) railway line

spoorloos /sporlos/ (adj) without a trace: *mijn bril is ~* my glasses have vanished

spoorslags /sporslɑxs/ (adv) at full speed

de **spoorverbinding** /sporvərbɪndɪŋ/ (pl: -en) (railway) connection

de **spoorvorming** /sporvɔrmɪŋ/ **1** (road) rutting **2** ruts

de **spoorweg** /sporwɛχ/ (pl: -en) railway (line)

de **spoorwegmaatschappij** /sporwɛχmatsχɑpɛɪ/ (pl: -en) railway (company)

het **spoorwegnet** /sporwɛχnɛt/ (pl: -ten) railway network

de **spoorwegovergang** /sporwɛχovərɣɑŋ/ (pl: -en) level crossing: *bewaakte ~* guarded level crossing

spoorzoeken /sporzukə(n)/ tracking

sporadisch /sporadis/ (adj, adv) sporadic: *maar ~ voorkomen* be few and far between

de **spore** /sporə/ [bot] spore, sporule

¹**sporen** /sporə(n)/ (spoorde, heeft/is gespoord) travel by rail (*or:* train)

²**sporen** /sporə(n)/ (spoorde, heeft gespoord) (+ met) be consistent with, be in line with ‖ *hij spoort niet* he's not all there

de **sporenplant** /sporə(n)plɑnt/ cryptogam

de **sport** /spɔrt/ (pl: -en) **1** sport(s): *een ~ beoefenen* practise (*or:* play) a sport; *veel* (or: *weinig) aan ~ doen* go in for (*or:* not go in for) sports **2** rung: *de hoogste ~ bereiken* reach the highest rung (of the ladder)

de **sportartikelen** /spɔrtɑrtikələ(n)/ (pl) sports

equipment

de **sportarts** /spɔrtɑrts/ (pl: -en) sports doctor (or: physician)

de **sportclub** /spɔrtklʏp/ (pl: -s) sports club

de **sportdag** /spɔrdɑx/ (pl: -en) sports day

de **sportdrank** /spɔrdrɑŋk/ (pl: -en) sports drink, energy drink

sporten /spɔrtə(n)/ (sportte, heeft gesport): *Jaap sport veel* Jaap does a lot of sport

de **sporter** /spɔrtər/ (pl: -s) sportsman

de **sportfiets** /spɔrtfits/ (pl: -en) sports bicycle, racing bicycle

de **sporthal** /spɔrthɑl/ (pl: -len) sports hall (or: centre)

sportief /spɔrtif/ (adj, adv) **1** sports, sporty: *een ~ evenement* a sports event; *een ~ jasje* a casual (or: sporty) jacket **2** sport(s)-loving, sporty **3** sportsmanlike: *~ zijn* be sporting (or: a good sport) (about sth.); *iets ~ opvatten* take sth. well

de **sportiviteit** /spɔrtivitɛit/ sportsmanship

de **sportkleding** /spɔrtkledɪŋ/ sportswear

de **sportliefhebber** /spɔrtlifhɛbər/ (pl: -s) sports enthusiast

de **sportman** /spɔrtmɑn/ (pl: -nen) sportsman

het **sportpark** /spɔrtpɑrk/ (pl: -en) sports park

de **sportschoen** /spɔrtsxun/ (pl: -en) sport(s) shoe

de **sportschool** /spɔrtsxol/ (pl: -scholen) **1** school for martial arts **2** fitness centre; gym

de **sporttas** /spɔrtɑs/ (pl: -sen) sports bag, kitbag

het **sportterrein** /spɔrtɛrɛin/ (pl: -en) sports field, playing field

de **sportuitslagen** /spɔrtœytslaɣə(n)/ (pl) sports results

het **sportveld** /spɔrtfɛlt/ (pl: -en) sports field, playing field

de **sportvereniging** /spɔrtfərenəɣɪŋ/ (pl: -en) sports club

het **sportvliegtuig** /spɔrtflixtœyx/ (pl: -en) private pleasure aircraft

de **sportvrouw** /spɔrtfrɑu/ (pl: -en) sportswoman

de **sportwagen** /spɔrtwaɣə(n)/ (pl: -s) sport(s) car

de **sportzaal** /spɔrtsal/ (pl: -zalen) fitness centre, gym

de **spot** /spɔt/ (pl: -s) **1** mockery: *de ~ drijven met* poke fun at, mock **2** (advertising) spot **3** spot(light)

spotgoedkoop /spɔtxutkop/ (adj, adv) dirt cheap

het **spotlight** /spɔtlɑjt/ (pl: -s) spotlight

de **spotprent** /spɔtprɛnt/ (pl: -en) cartoon

de **spotprijs** /spɔtprɛis/ (pl: -prijzen) bargain price, giveaway price

spotten /spɔtə(n)/ (spotte, heeft gespot) **1** joke, jest **2** mock: *hij laat niet met zich ~* he is not to be trifled with ‖ *daar moet je niet*

mee ~ that is no laughing matter

de **spotter** /spɔtər/ (pl: -s) **1** mocker, scoffer **2** spotter, observer

de **spouwmuur** /spɑumyr/ (pl: -muren) cavity wall

de **spraak** /sprak/ speech

het **spraakgebrek** /sprakxəbrɛk/ (pl: -en) speech defect

de **spraakherkenning** /sprakhɛrkɛnɪŋ/ speech recognition

de **spraakles** /spraklɛs/ (pl: -sen) speech training; speech therapy

spraakmakend /sprakmakənt/ (adj) talked-about, discussed

de **spraakverwarring** /sprakvərwɑrɪŋ/ (pl: -en) babel, confusion of tongues

spraakzaam /spraksam/ (adj) talkative

de **sprake** /sprakə/: *er is geen ~ van* that is (absolutely) out of the question; *er is hier ~ van … it* it is a matter (or: question) of …; *iets ter ~ brengen* bring sth. up; *ter ~ komen* come up; *geen ~ van!* certainly not!

sprakeloos /sprakəlos/ (adj, adv) speechless: *iem. ~ doen staan* leave s.o. speechless

sprankelen /sprɑŋkələ(n)/ (sprankelde, heeft gesprankeld) sparkle

het **sprankje** /sprɑŋkjə/ (pl: -s) spark: *er is nog een ~ hoop* there is still a glimmer of hope

de **spray** /sprej/ (pl: -s) spray

sprayen /sprejə(n)/ (sprayde, heeft gesprayd) spray

de **spreadsheet** /sprɛtʃi:t/ (pl: -s) spreadsheet

de **spreekbeurt** /spregbørt/ (pl: -en) talk

de **spreekbuis** /spregbœys/ (pl: -buizen) spokesman, spokesperson

de **spreekkamer** /sprekamər/ (pl: -s) consulting room, surgery

het **spreekkoor** /sprekor/ (pl: -koren) chant(ing): *spreekkoren aanheffen* break into chants

de **spreektaal** /sprektal/ spoken language

het **spreekuur** /sprekyr/ (pl: -uren) office hours; [med] surgery (hours): *~ houden* have office hours, have surgery; *op het ~ komen* come during office hours

de **spreekvaardigheid** /sprekfardəxhɛit/ fluency, speaking ability

het **spreekverbod** /sprekfərbɔt/ (pl: -en) ban on public speaking

het **spreekwoord** /sprekwort/ (pl: -en) proverb, saying: *zoals het ~ zegt* as the saying goes

spreekwoordelijk /sprekwordələk/ (adj, adv) proverbial

de **spreeuw** /sprew/ (pl: -en) starling

de **sprei** /sprɛi/ (pl: -en) (bed)spread

spreiden /sprɛidə(n)/ (spreidde, heeft gespreid) **1** spread (out): *het risico ~* spread the risk; *de vakanties ~* stagger holidays **2** spread (out), space

de **spreiding** /sprɛidɪŋ/ **1** spread(ing), disper-

464

sal **2** spacing; spread: *de ~ van de **macht*** the distribution of power

¹spreken /spr<u>e</u>kə(n)/ (sprak, heeft gesproken) speak, talk: *de **feiten** ~ voor zich* the facts speak for themselves; *het spreekt **vanzelf*** it goes without saying; *daar spreekt u **mee!*** speaking; *spreek ik **met** Jan?* is that Jan?

²spreken /spr<u>e</u>kə(n)/ (sprak, heeft gesproken) **1** speak, tell: *een vreemde **taal** ~* speak a foreign language **2** speak, talk to (*or:* with): *iem. niet **te** ~ krijgen* not be able to get in touch with s.o. ‖ *niet **te** ~ zijn over iets* be unhappy (*or:* be not too pleased) about sth.

¹sprekend /spr<u>e</u>kənt/ (adj) **1** speaking, talking: *een ~e **film*** a talking film; *een ~e **papegaai*** a talking parrot **2** strong, striking: *een ~e **gelijkenis*** a striking resemblance **3** expressive

²sprekend /spr<u>e</u>kənt/ (adv) exactly: *zij **lijkt** ~ op haar moeder* she looks exactly (*or:* just) like her mother; *dat portret **lijkt** ~ op Karin* that picture captures Karin perfectly

de **spreker** /spr<u>e</u>kər/ (pl: -s) speaker

sprenkelen /spr<u>e</u>ŋkələ(n)/ (sprenkelde, heeft gesprenkeld) sprinkle

de **spreuk** /sprøk/ (pl: -en) maxim, saying: *oude ~* old saying

de **spriet** /sprit/ (pl: -en) blade

het/de **springconcours** /spr<u>ɪ</u>ŋkɔŋkur/ (pl: -en) jumping competition

springen /spr<u>ɪ</u>ŋə(n)/ (sprong, heeft/is gesprongen) **1** jump, leap, spring; vault: *hoog* (*or: **ver, omlaag***) ~ jump high (*or:* far, down); *over een sloot ~* leap a ditch; *staan **te** ~ om weg te komen* be dying to leave; *zitten **te** ~ om iets* be bursting (*or:* dying) for sth. **2** burst; explode; blast; pop: *mijn **band** is gesprongen* my tyre has burst; *een **snaar** is gesprongen* a string has snapped; *op ~ staan* a) be about to explode; b) be bursting ‖ *op groen ~* change to green

het **springkasteel** /spr<u>ɪ</u>ŋkɑstel/ bouncy castle

de **springlading** /spr<u>ɪ</u>ŋladɪŋ/ (pl: -en) explosive charge

springlevend /spr<u>ɪ</u>ŋl<u>e</u>vənt/ (adj) alive (and kicking)

de **springplank** /spr<u>ɪ</u>ŋplɑŋk/ (pl: -en) springboard

de **springstof** /spr<u>ɪ</u>ŋstɔf/ (pl: -fen) explosive

het **springtij** /spr<u>ɪ</u>ŋtɛɪ/ (pl: -en) spring tide

het **springtouw** /spr<u>ɪ</u>ŋtɑu/ (pl: -en) skipping rope

het **springuur** /spr<u>ɪ</u>ŋyr/ (pl: -uren) [Belg; educ] free period

de **springveer** /spr<u>ɪ</u>ŋver/ (pl: -veren) box spring

de **springvloed** /spr<u>ɪ</u>ŋvlut/ (pl: -en) spring tide

de **sprinkhaan** /spr<u>ɪ</u>ŋkhan/ (pl: -hanen) grasshopper; [Africa and Asia] locust

de **sprinklerinstallatie** /spr<u>ɪ</u>ŋklərɪnstɑla(t)si/ (pl: -s) sprinkler system

de **sprint** /sprɪnt/ (pl: -s) sprint

sprinten /spr<u>ɪ</u>ntə(n)/ (sprintte, heeft/is gesprint) sprint

de **sprinter** /spr<u>ɪ</u>ntər/ (pl: -s) sprinter

de **sprits** /sprɪts/ (pl: -en) (Dutch) short biscuit

sproeien /spr<u>u</u>jə(n)/ (sproeide, heeft gesproeid) spray, water; sprinkle; irrigate

de **sproeier** /spr<u>u</u>jər/ (pl: -s) sprinkler; jet; spray nozzle; irrigator

de **sproet** /sprut/ (pl: -en) freckle: *~en **in** het gezicht hebben* have a freckled face

sprokkelen /spr<u>ɔ</u>kələ(n)/ (sprokkelde, heeft gesprokkeld) gather wood (*or:* kindling): *hout ~* gather wood

de **sprong** /sprɔŋ/ (pl: -en) leap, jump; vault: *hij gaat **met** ~en vooruit* he's coming along by leaps and bounds

het **sprookje** /spr<u>o</u>kjə/ (pl: -s) fairy tale ‖ *iem. ~s vertellen* lead s.o. up the garden path

sprookjesachtig /spr<u>o</u>kjəsɑxtəx/ (adj, adv) fairy-tale; [fig] fairy-like: *de grachten waren ~ **verlicht*** the canals were romantically illuminated

de **sprot** /sprɔt/ (pl: -ten) sprat

de **spruit** /sprœyt/ **1** shoot **2** sprig, sprout

spruiten /spr<u>œy</u>tə(n)/ (sproot, is gesproten) **1** sprout **2** result from

de **spruitjes** /spr<u>œy</u>cəs/ (pl) (Brussels) sprouts

de **spruw** /spryw/ thrush

spugen /sp<u>y</u>ɣə(n)/ (spuugde, heeft gespogen/gespuugd) **1** spit **2** throw up: *de boel **onder** ~* be sick all over the place

spuien /sp<u>œy</u>ə(n)/ (spuide, heeft gespuid) spout, unload: *kritiek ~* pour forth criticism

het **spuigat** /sp<u>œy</u>ɣɑt/ (pl: -en) scupper

de **spuit** /spœyt/ (pl: -en) **1** syringe, squirt **2** needle; shot

de **spuitbus** /sp<u>œy</u>dbʏs/ (pl: -sen) spray (can)

¹spuiten /sp<u>œy</u>tə(n)/ (spoot, is gespoten) squirt, spurt; gush

²spuiten /sp<u>œy</u>tə(n)/ (spoot, heeft gespoten) **1** squirt, spurt; erupt: *lak **op** iets ~* spray lacquer on sth. **2** spray(-paint) **3** inject: *hij spuit* he's a junkie; *iem. **plat** ~* knock s.o. out (with an injection)

de **spuiter** /sp<u>œy</u>tər/ (pl: -s) junkie

de **spuitgast** /sp<u>œy</u>txɑst/ (pl: -en) hoseman

het **spuitje** /sp<u>œy</u>cə/ (pl: -s) **1** needle **2** shot

het **spuitwater** /sp<u>œy</u>twatər/ seltzer, soda water

het **spul** /spʏl/ (pl: -len) **1** gear, things; togs; belongings **2** stuff, things

de **spurt** /spʏrt/ (pl: -s) spurt: *er de ~ **in** zetten* step on it

spurten /sp<u>ʏ</u>rtə(n)/ (spurtte, heeft/is gespurt) spurt, sprint

sputteren /sp<u>ʏ</u>tərə(n)/ (sputterde, heeft gesputterd) sputter, cough

het **spuug** /spyx/ spittle, spit

spuugzat /sp<u>yx</u>sɑt/ (adj): *iets ~ **zijn*** be sick and tired of sth.

spuwen /spy̲wə(n)/ (spuwde, heeft ge-
spuwd) **1** spit, spew **2** spew (up), throw up
de **spyware** /spɔ̲jwɛːr/ spyware
het **squadron** /skwo̲drən/ (pl: -s) squadron
het **squash** /skwɔʃ/ squash
de **squashbaan** /skwɔ̲ʒban/ (pl: -banen)
squash court
squashen /skwɔ̲ʃə(n)/ (squashte, heeft ge-
squasht) play squash
sr. (abbrev) *senior* Sr.
Sri Lanka /srilo̲ŋka/ Sri Lanka
de **Sri Lankaan** /srilo̲ŋka̲n/ (pl: Sri Lankanen)
Sri Lankan
Sri Lankaans /srilo̲ŋka̲ns/ (adj) Sri Lankan
sst /st/ (int) (s)sh, hush
de **staaf** /staf/ (pl: staven) bar
de **staafmixer** /sta̲fmɪksər/ (pl: -s) hand blender
de **staak** /stak/ (pl: staken) stake, pole, post
het **staakt-het-vuren** /staktətfy̲rə(n)/ cease-
fire
het **staal** /stal/ **1** steel: *zo hard **als** ~* as hard as
iron **2** sample: *een (mooi) ~tje van zijn soort
humor* a fine example of his sense of humour
de **staalborstel** /sta̲lbɔrstəl/ (pl: -s) wire brush
de **staalindustrie** /sta̲lɪndystri/ (pl: -ën) steel
industry
de **staalkaart** /sta̲lkart/ (pl: -en) sampling
de **staalwol** /sta̲lwɔl/ steel wool
staan /stan/ (stond, heeft gestaan) **1** stand:
gaan ~ stand up; *achter* (or: *naast*) *elkaar **gaan**
~* queue (or: line) up; *die gebeurtenis staat geheel **op** zichzelf* that is an isolated incident;
*zich ~de **houden*** a) stay (or: remain) standing; b) [fig] not succumb, hold firm **2** stand,
be: *hoe ~ de **zaken?*** how are things?; *er goed
voor ~* look good; *zij ~ **sterk*** they are in a
strong position; *buiten iets ~* not be involved
in sth.; *de snelheidsmeter stond **op** 80 km/uur*
the speedometer showed 80 km/h; *zij staat
derde in het algemeen klassement* she is third
in the overall ranking **3** look **4** say, be written: *er staat niet **bij** wanneer* it doesn't say
when; *in de tekst staat daar niets over* the text
doesn't say anything about it; *wat staat er **op**
het programma?* what's on the programme?
5 stand still: *blijven ~* stand still **6** leave,
stand: *hij kon nauwelijks spreken, **laat** ~ zingen*
he could barely speak, let alone sing; *laat ~
dat ... not to mention (that) ...*, let alone
(that) ...; *zijn baard **laten** ~* grow a beard
7 insist (on) ‖ *er staat hem wat te **wachten***
there is sth. in store for him; *ergens van ~ (te)
kijken be flabbergasted; *ze staat al een uur te
wachten* she has been waiting (for) an hour
staand /stant/ (adj) standing: *~e **passagier***
standing passenger ‖ *iem. ~e **houden*** stop
s.o.; *zich ~e **houden*** keep going, carry on; *~e
houden (dat)* maintain (that)
de **staanplaats** /sta̲mplats/ (pl: -en) standing
room; terrace

de **staar** /star/ cataract, stare; film
de **staart** /start/ (pl: -en) **1** tail: *met de ~ kwispelen* wag its tail **2** pigtail; ponytail
het **staartbeen** /sta̲rtben/ (pl: -deren, -benen)
tail-bone, coccyx
de **staartdeling** /sta̲rtdelɪŋ/ (pl: -en) long division
de **staartster** /sta̲rtstɛr/ (pl: -ren) comet
de **staartvin** /sta̲rtfɪn/ (pl: -nen) tail fin
de **staat** /stat/ (pl: staten) **1** state, condition,
status: *burgerlijke ~* marital status; *in **goede**
~ verkeren* be in good condition; *in prima ~
van onderhoud* in an excellent state of repair
2 condition: *tot alles **in** ~ zijn* be capable of
anything **3** state, country, nation, power;
the body politic: *de ~ der **Nederlanden*** the
kingdom of the Netherlands **4** council,
board: *de **Provinciale** Staten* the Provincial
Council **5** statement, record, report, survey ‖
in alle staten zijn be frenzied (or: agitated), be
beside o.s.
de **staatkunde** /sta̲tkʏndə/ politics, political
science
staatkundig /statkʏ̲ndəx/ (adj, adv) political
het **staatsbedrijf** /sta̲tsbədrɛɪf/ (pl: -bedrijven)
state enterprise
het **staatsbelang** /sta̲tsbəlɑŋ/ state (or: national) interest
het **staatsbestel** /sta̲tsbəstɛl/ system of government, polity
het **staatsbezoek** /sta̲tsbəzuk/ (pl: -en) state
visit
het **Staatsblad** /sta̲tsblɑt/ (pl: -en) law gazette
Staatsbosbeheer /statsbo̲zbəher/ Forestry
Commission
de **staatsburger** /sta̲tsbʏrɣər/ (pl: -s) citizen;
subject
het **staatsburgerschap** /sta̲tsbʏrɣərsxɑp/ citizenship, nationality
de **Staatscourant** /sta̲tskurɑnt/ Government
Gazette
het **staatsexamen** /sta̲tsɛksamə(n)/ (pl: -s)
state exam(ination), university entrance examination
het **staatsgeheim** /sta̲tsxəhɛim/ (pl: -en) official secret, state secret
de **staatsgreep** /sta̲tsxrep/ (pl: -grepen) coup
(d'état)
het **staatshoofd** /sta̲tshoft/ (pl: -en) head of
state
het **staatsieportret** /sta̲tsiportrɛt/ (pl: -ten) official portrait
de **staatsinrichting** /sta̲tsɪnrɪxtɪŋ/ (pl: -en)
civics
de **staatslening** /sta̲tslenɪŋ/ (pl: -en) national
loan
de **staatsloterij** /statslotərɛ̲i/ (pl: -en) state
lottery, national lottery
de **staatsman** /sta̲tsmɑn/ (pl: -lieden) statesman

het **staatsrecht** /stɑtsrɛχt/ constitutional law

de **staatsschuld** /stɑtsχγlt/ (pl: -en) government debt

de **staatssecretaris** /stɑtsɪkrətɑrɪs/ (pl: -sen) [Belg] State Secretary

stabiel /stabil/ (adj) stable; firm

de **stabilisatie** /stabiliza(t)si/ stabilization

stabiliseren /stabilizerə(n)/ (stabiliseerde, heeft gestabiliseerd) stabilize, steady; firm (up)

de **stabiliteit** /stabilitɛit/ stability; balance; steadiness

het **stabiliteitspact** /stabilitɛitspɑkt/ stability pact

de **stacaravan** /stakɛrəvɛn/ (pl: -s) caravan

staccato /stɑkato/ (adv) staccato

de **stad** /stɑt/ (pl: steden) town; city; borough: ~ en land aflopen search high and low, look everywhere (for); de ~ uit zijn be out of town

het **stadhuis** /stɑthœys/ (pl: -huizen) town hall, city hall

het **stadion** /stadijɔn/ (pl: -s) stadium

het **stadium** /stadijγm/ (pl: stadia) stage, phase

het **stadsbestuur** /stɑtsbəstyr/ (pl: -besturen) town council, city council, municipality

de **stadsbus** /stɑtsbγs/ (pl: -sen) local bus

het **stadsdeel** /stɑtsdel/ (pl: -delen) quarter, area, part of town; district; [roughly] borough

het **stadslicht** /stɑtslɪχt/ (pl: -en) parking light

de **stadsmens** /stɑtsmɛns/ (pl: -en) city dweller, townsman

de **stadsmuur** /stɑtsmyr/ (pl: -muren) town wall, city wall

de **stadstaat** /stɑtstat/ (pl: -staten) city-state

de **stadsvernieuwing** /stɑtsfərniwɪŋ/ (pl: -en) urban renewal

de **stadswijk** /stɑtswɛik/ (pl: -en) ward, district, area

de **staf** /stɑf/ (pl: staven) **1** staff, (walking) stick; wand **2** staff; [Am] faculty **3** [mil] staff, corps

de **stafchef** /stɑfʃɛf/ (pl: -s) chief of staff

de **stafhouder** /stɑfhɑudər/ (pl: -s) [Belg] president of the Bar Council

de **stafkaart** /stɑfkart/ (pl: -en) topographic map, ordnance survey map

het **staflid** /stɑflɪt/ (pl: -leden) staff member

de **stage** /staʒə/ (pl: -s) work placement; teaching practice; [med] housemanship; [Am] intern(e)ship: ~ lopen do a work placement practice

de **stageplaats** /staʒəplats/ (pl: -en) trainee post

de **stagiair** /staʒɛːrə/ (pl: -s) student on work placement; student teacher

de **stagnatie** /stɑɣna(t)si/ (pl: -s) stagnation

stagneren /stɑɣnerə(n)/ (stagneerde, is gestagneerd) stagnate, come to a standstill

de **sta-in-de-weg** /staɪndəwɛχ/ (pl: -s) obstacle

¹**staken** /stakə(n)/ (staakte, heeft gestaakt) **1** strike, go on strike: gaan ~ go (or: come out) on strike **2** tie

²**staken** /stakə(n)/ (staakte, heeft gestaakt) cease, stop, discontinue; suspend: zijn pogingen ~ cease one's efforts; het verzet ~ cease resistance

de **staker** /stakər/ (pl: -s) striker

de **staking** /stakɪŋ/ (pl: -en) strike (action), walkout: in ~ zijn (or: gaan) be (or: come out) on strike

de **stakingsbreker** /stakɪŋzbrekər/ (pl: -s) strike-breaker; [depr] scab

de **stakker** /stɑkər/ (pl: -s) wretch, poor soul (or: creature, thing): een arme ~ a poor beggar

de **stal** /stɑl/ (pl: -len) stable; cowshed; sty; fold: iets van ~ halen dig sth. out (or: up) (again)

de **stalactiet** /stalɑktit/ (pl: -en) stalactite

de **stalagmiet** /stalɑɣmit/ (pl: -en) stalagmite

stalen /stalə(n)/ (adj) steel, steely: met een ~ gezicht stony-faced

stalken /stɑlkə(n)/ (stalkte, heeft gestalkt) stalk

de **stalker** /stɑlkər/ stalker

de **stalking** /stɑlkɪŋ/ stalking

de **stalknecht** /stɑlknɛχt/ (pl: -en, -s) stableman, stable hand, groom

stallen /stɑlə(n)/ (stalde, heeft gestald) store, put up (or: away); garage

het **stalletje** /stɑləcə/ (pl: -s) stall, stand, booth

de **stalling** /stɑlɪŋ/ (pl: -en) garage; shelter

de **stam** /stɑm/ (pl: -men) **1** trunk, stem, stock **2** stock, clan **3** tribe, race

het **stamboek** /stɑmbuk/ (pl: -en) pedigree; studbook; herdbook

het **stamboekvee** /stɑmbukfe/ pedigree(d) cattle

de **stamboom** /stɑmbom/ (pl: -bomen) family tree, genealogical tree; genealogy; pedigree

het **stamcafé** /stɑmkafe/ (pl: -s) favourite pub; [Am] favorite bar; [British] local; [Am] hangout

de **stamcel** /stɑmsɛl/ (pl: -len) stem cell

stamelen /stamələ(n)/ (stamelde, heeft gestameld) stammer, stutter, sp(l)utter

de **stamgast** /stɑmɣɑst/ (pl: -en) regular (customer)

het **stamhoofd** /stɑmhoft/ (pl: -en) chieftain, tribal chief, headman

de **stamhouder** /stɑmhɑudər/ (pl: -s) son and heir, family heir

de **staminee** /staminé/ (pl: -s) [Belg] pub

stammen /stɑmə(n)/ (stamde, is gestamd) descend (from), stem (from); date (back to, from)

de **stammenstrijd** /stɑmə(n)strɛit/ (inter)tribal dispute, tribal war

¹**stampen** /stɑmpə(n)/ (stampte, heeft gestampt) stamp: met zijn voet ~ stamp one's foot

²**stampen** /stɑmpə(n)/ (stampte, heeft ge-

stampt) pound, crush, pulverize: *gestampte aardappelen* mashed potatoes

de **stamper** /stɑmpər/ (pl: -s) **1** stamp(er), pounder; masher **2** [bot] pistil

de **stampij** /stɑmpɛi̯/ hullabal(l)oo, hubbub, uproar: ~ *maken* raise hell, kick up a row (*or:* fuss)

de **stamppot** /stɑmpɔt/ (pl: -ten) [roughly] stew, hotchpotch; mashed potatoes and cabbage

stampvoeten /stɑmpfutə(n)/ (stampvoette, heeft gestampvoet) stamp one's feet

stampvol /stɑmpfɔl/ (adj) packed; full to the brim; full up

de **stamtafel** /stɑmtafəl/ (pl: -s) table (reserved) for regulars

de **stamvader** /stɑmvadər/ (pl: -s) ancestor, forefather

de **stand** /stɑnt/ (pl: -en) **1** posture, bearing: *een ~ aannemen* assume a position **2** position: *de ~ van de dollar* the dollar rate; *de ~ van de zon* the position of the sun **3** state, condition: *de burgerlijke ~* the registry office **4** score: *de ~ is 2-1* the score is 2-1 **5** estate, class, station, order: *mensen van alle rangen en ~en* people from all walks of life **6** existence, being: *tot ~ brengen* bring about, achieve **7** stand

de ¹**standaard** /stɑndart/ (pl: -s) **1** stand, standard **2** standard, prototype

²**standaard** /stɑndart/ (adj, adv) standard

de **standaardisatie** /stɑndardiza(t)si/ standardization

standaardiseren /stɑndardizerə(n)/ (standaardiseerde, heeft gestandaardiseerd) standardize: *het gestandaardiseerde type* the standard model

de **standaarduitvoering** /stɑndartœy̯tfurɪŋ/ (pl: -en) standard type (*or:* model, design)

het **standaardwerk** /stɑndartwɛrk/ (pl: -en) standard work (*or:* book)

het **standbeeld** /stɑndbelt/ (pl: -en) statue

stand-by /stɛndbɑi̯/ (adj) standby

standhouden /stɑnthɑu̯də(n)/ (hield stand, heeft standgehouden) hold out, stand up

de **stand-in** /stɛntɪn/ (pl: -s) stand-in

het **standje** /stɑncə/ (pl: -s) **1** position, posture **2** rebuke

het **standlicht** /stɑntlɪχt/ (pl: -en) [Belg] sidelight, parking light

de **standplaats** /stɑntplats/ (pl: -en) stand: *~ voor taxi's* taxi rank; [Am] taxi stand

het **standpunt** /stɑntpʏnt/ (pl: -en) standpoint, point of view: *bij zijn ~ blijven* hold one's ground

standrechtelijk /stɑntrɛχtələk/ (adj, adv) summary

het **standsverschil** /stɑn(t)sfərsχɪl/ (pl: -len) class difference, social difference

de **stand-upcomedian** /stɛndʏpkɔmidijən/

stand-up comedian

standvastig /stɑntfɑstəχ/ (adj, adv) firm, perseverant, persistent

de **standwerker** /stɑntwɛrkər/ (pl: -s) hawker, (market, street) vendor

de **stang** /stɑŋ/ (pl: -en) stave, bar, rod; crossbar || *iem. op ~ jagen* needle s.o.

de **stank** /stɑŋk/ (pl: -en) stench, bad (*or:* foul, nasty) smell

het **stanleymes** /stɛnlimɛs/ (pl: -sen) Stanley knife

stansen /stɑnsə(n)/ (stanste, heeft gestanst) punch

stante pede /stɑntəpedə/ (adv) on the spot, this minute

de **stap** /stɑp/ (pl: -pen) **1** step, footstep, pace, stride: *een ~ in de goede richting doen* take a step in the right direction; *~(je) voor ~(je)* inch by inch, little by little; *een ~(je) terug doen* take a step down (in pay) **2** [fig] step, move; grade: *~pen ondernemen tegen* take steps against **3** step, tread || *op ~ gaan* set out (*or:* off)

de **stapel** /stapəl/ (pl: -s) **1** pile, heap, stack **2** stock || *te hard van ~ lopen* go too fast

het **stapelbed** /stapəlbɛt/ (pl: -den) bunk beds

stapelen /stapələ(n)/ (stapelde, heeft gestapeld) pile up, heap up, stack

stapelgek /stapəlɣɛk/ (adj, adv) **1** crazy, (as) mad as a hatter, (raving) mad **2** mad, crazy

het **stapelhuis** /stapəlhœy̯s/ (pl: -huizen) [Belg] warehouse

de **stapelwolk** /stapəlwɔlk/ (pl: -en) cumulus, woolpack

stappen /stɑpə(n)/ (stapte, heeft/is gestapt) **1** step, walk: *eruit ~* quit, get/step out; do o.s. in, catch the bus **2** go out, go for a drink

het **stappenplan** /stɑpə(n)plɑn/ (pl: -nen) step-by-step plan

stapvoets /stɑpfuts/ (adv) at a walk; at walking pace

star /stɑr/ (adj, adv) **1** frozen, stiff; glassy **2** rigid, inflexible, uncompromising

staren /starə(n)/ (staarde, heeft gestaard) **1** stare, gaze **2** peer: *zich blind ~ op iets* be fixated on sth.

de **start** /stɑrt/ (pl: -s) start: [car] *de koude ~* the cold start; *een vliegende ~ maken* get off to (*or:* make) a flying start

de **startbaan** /stɑrdban/ (pl: -banen) runway; airstrip

het **startblok** /stɑrdblɔk/ (pl: -ken) starting block

starten /stɑrtə(n)/ (startte, heeft/is gestart) start, begin; take off; [sport] be off

de **starter** /stɑrtər/ (pl: -s) starter

het **startgeld** /stɑrtχɛlt/ (pl: -en) entry fee

de **startkabel** /stɑrtkabəl/ (pl: -s) jump lead; [Am] jumper cable

startklaar /stɑrtklar/ (adj) ready to start (*or:*

startmotor

de **startmotor** /stɑrtmotər/ (pl: -en) starter, starting motor

de **startpagina**® /stɑrtpaɣina/ start page

het **startpunt** /stɑrtpʏnt/ (pl: -en) starting point

het **startschot** /stɑrtsxɔt/ (pl: -en) starting shot

het **startsein** /stɑrtsɛɪn/ starting signal: *iem. het ~ geven* give s.o. the green light

stateloos /statələs/ (adj) stateless

de **Staten** /statə(n)/ (pl) (Dutch) Provincial Council

de **Statenbijbel** /statə(n)bɛibəl/ (Dutch) Authorized Version (of the Bible)

de **Staten-Generaal** /statə(n)ɣenəral/ (pl) States General, Dutch parliament

het **statief** /statif/ (pl: statieven) tripod, stand

het **statiegeld** /sta(t)siɣɛlt/ deposit: *geen ~* non-returnable

statig /statəx/ (adj, adv) **1** stately, grand: *een ~e dame* a queenly woman, a woman of regal bearing **2** solemn

het **station** /sta(t)ʃɔn/ (pl: -s) (railway) station; [Am] depot

stationair /staʃɔnɛːr/ (adj) stationary: *een motor ~ laten draaien* let an engine idle

de **stationcar** /steʃənkaːr/ (pl: -s) estate (car); [Am] station wagon

stationeren /sta(t)ʃɔnerə(n)/ (stationeerde, heeft gestationeerd) station, post

de **stationschef** /sta(t)ʃɔnʃɛf/ (pl: -s) stationmaster

de **stationshal** /sta(t)ʃɔnshɑl/ (pl: -len) station concourse

de **stationsrestauratie** /sta(t)ʃɔnsrɛstora(t)si/ (pl: -s) station buffet

statisch /statis/ (adj) static

de **statistiek** /statɪstik/ (pl: -en) statistics

statistisch /statɪstis/ (adj, adv) statistical

de **status** /statʏs/ **1** (social) status, standing **2** (legal) status

de **statusregel** /statʏsreɣəl/ (pl: -s) status line

het **statussymbool** /statʏsɪmbol/ (pl: -symbolen) status symbol

statutair /statytɛːr/ (adj, adv) statutory

de **statuur** /statyr/ stature: *hij heeft onvoldoende ~ voor die functie* he has insufficient stature for this position; *iem. van zijn ~* s.o. of his stature

het **statuut** /statyt/ (pl: statuten) statute, regulation

staven /stavə(n)/ (staafde, heeft gestaafd) substantiate, prove

de **steak** /stek/ (pl: -s) (beef)steak

het/de **steaming** [Belg] [roughly] racketeering

stedelijk /stedələk/ (adj) municipal, urban: *de ~e bevolking* the urban population

de **stedeling** /stedəlɪŋ/ (pl: -en) town-dweller; townspeople

de **stedenbouwkunde** /stedə(n)bɑukʏndə/ urban development

steeds /stets/ (adv) **1** always, constantly: *iem. ~ aankijken* keep looking at s.o.; *~ weer* time after time, repeatedly **2** increasingly, more and more: *~ groter* bigger and bigger; *~ slechter worden* go from bad to worse; *het regent nog ~* it is still raining

de **steeg** /stex/ (pl: stegen) alley(way)

de **steek** /stek/ (pl: steken) **1** stab; thrust; prick; stab wound **2** sting; bite **3** shooting pain, stabbing pain; twinge: *een ~ in de borst* a twinge in the chest **4** stitch: *een ~ laten vallen* a) drop a stitch; b) [fig] make a gaffe, make a mistake || *iem. in de ~ laten* let s.o. down; *ik zie geen ~* I can't see a (blind) thing

steekhoudend /stekhɑudənt/ (adj) convincing, valid

de **steekpartij** /stekpɑrtɛi/ (pl: -en) knifing

de **steekpenningen** /stekpɛnɪŋə(n)/ (pl) bribe(s); kickback(s)

de **steekproef** /stekpruf/ (pl: -proeven) random check, spot check, (random) sample survey

de **steeksleutel** /steksløtəl/ (pl: -s) (open-end, fork) spanner (*or:* wrench)

de **steekvlam** /stekflɑm/ (pl: -men) (jet, burst of) flame, flash

de **steekwagen** /stekwaɣə(n)/ (pl: -s) handtruck

het **steekwapen** /stekwapə(n)/ (pl: -s) stabbing weapon

de **steekwond** /stekwɔnt/ (pl: -en) stab wound

de **steel** /stel/ (pl: stelen) **1** stalk, stem **2** handle; stem

de **steelpan** /stelpɑn/ (pl: -nen) saucepan

steels /stels/ (adj) stealthy

de ¹**steen** /sten/ **1** stone; [Am] rock; [large] rock; pebble **2** stone; brick; cobble(stone): *ergens een ~tje toe bijdragen* do one's bit towards sth.; chip in with **3** [sport] man; piece || *de onderste ~ moet boven komen* we must get to the bottom of this

het/de ²**steen** /sten/ stone || *~ en been klagen* complain bitterly

de **steenarend** /stenarənt/ (pl: -en) golden eagle

de **steenbok** /stembɔk/ (pl: -ken) ibex, wild goat

de **Steenbok** /stembɔk/ (pl: -ken) [astrology] Capricorn

de **Steenbokskeerkring** /stembɔkskerkrɪŋ/ tropic of Capricorn

steengrillen /stenɣrɪlə(n)/ (steengrilde, heeft gesteengrild) stone grill

de **steengroeve** /stenɣruvə/ (pl: -n) (stone) quarry

het **steenkolenengels** /stenkolə(n)ɛŋəls/ broken English

de **steenkool** /stenkol/ coal

steenkoud /stenkɑut/ (adj) freezing (cold), ice-cold: *ik heb het ~* I am freezing

de **steenpuist** /stempœyst/ (pl: -en) boil

steenrijk /stenrɛɪk/ (adj) immensely rich

het **steenslag** /stenslɑx/ road-metal; chippings

de **steentijd** /stentɛit/ Stone Age

het **steentje** /stencə/ (pl: -s) small stone; pebble: *een ~ bijdragen* do one's bit

de **steenweg** /stenwɛx/ (pl: -en) [Belg] (paved) road

de **steenworp** /stenwɔrp/ (pl: -en): *hij woont op een ~ afstand* he lives within a stone's throw

steevast /stevɑst/ (adj, adv) invariable, regular

de **steiger** /stɛiɣər/ (pl: -s) **1** landing (stage, place) **2** scaffold(ing)

steigeren /stɛiɣərə(n)/ (steigerde, heeft gesteigerd) rear (up)

steil /stɛil/ (adj, adv) steep; precipitous: *een ~e afgrond* a sharp drop; *~ haar* straight hair; *ergens ~ van achterover slaan* be flabbergasted by sth.

steilen /stɛilə(n)/ (steilde, heeft gesteild) straighten, flat-iron

de **steiltang** /stɛiltɑŋ/ (pl: -en) flat-iron

de **stek** /stɛk/ (pl: -ken) **1** cutting, slip **2** niche, den: *dat is zijn liefste ~* that is his favourite spot

stekeblind /stekəblɪnt/ (adj) (as) blind as a bat

de **stekel** /stekəl/ (pl: -s) prickle, thorn; spine

de **stekelbaars** /stekəlbars/ (pl: -baarzen) stickleback

stekelig /stekələx/ (adj) **1** prickly, spiny, bristly **2** [fig] sharp, cutting

het **stekelvarken** /stekəlvɑrkə(n)/ (pl: -s) porcupine; hedgehog

¹**steken** /stekə(n)/ (stak, heeft gestoken) **1** stick: *ergens in blijven ~* get stuck (*or:* bogged) (down) in sth. **2** sting: *de zon steekt* there is a burning sun **3** thrust, stab ‖ *daar steekt iets achter* there is sth. behind it

²**steken** /stekə(n)/ (stak, heeft gestoken) **1** stab: *alle banden waren lek gestoken* all the tyres had been punctured **2** sting, cut **3** sting, prick **4** stick **5** put, place: *veel tijd in iets ~* spend a lot of time on sth.; *zijn geld in een zaak ~* put one's money in(to) an undertaking

stekend /stekənt/ (adj, adv) stinging, sharp

stekken /stɛkə(n)/ (stekte, heeft gestekt) slip, strike: *planten ~* take (*or:* strike) cuttings of plants

de **stekker** /stɛkər/ (pl: -s) plug

de **stekkerdoos** /stɛkərdos/ (pl: -dozen) multiple socket

het **stel** /stɛl/ (pl: -len) **1** set: *ik neem drie ~ kleren mee* I'll take three sets of clothes with me **2** couple: *een pasgetrouwd ~* newly-weds **3** couple, lot ‖ *het hoeft niet op ~ en sprong* there's no rush

stelen /stelə(n)/ (steelde, heeft gesteeld) steal: *uit ~ gaan* go thieving; *dat kan me gestolen worden* I'd be well shot of it, I'd be better off without that

de **stellage** /stɛlaʒə/ (pl: -s) stand, stage, platform

stellen /stɛlə(n)/ (stelde, heeft gesteld) **1** put, set: *iem. iets beschikbaar ~* put sth. at s.o.'s disposal **2** set, adjust: *een machine ~* adjust (*or:* regulate) a machine **3** suppose: *stel het geval van een leraar die …* take the case of a teacher who … **4** manage, (make) do: *we zullen het met minder moeten ~* we'll have to make do with less

het **stelletje** /stɛlɛcə/ (pl: -s) **1** bunch: *een ~ ongeregeld* a disorderly bunch **2** couple, pair

stellig /stɛləx/ (adj, adv) definite, certain

de **stelling** /stɛlɪŋ/ (pl: -en) **1** scaffold(ing) **2** rack **3** proposition **4** theorem, proposition: *de ~ van Pythagoras* the Pythagorean theorem ‖ *~ nemen tegen* make a stand against, set one's face against

de **stellingname** /stɛlɪŋnamə/ (pl: -s, -n) position, stand

stelpen /stɛlpə(n)/ (stelpte, heeft gestelpt) staunch, stem

de **stelplaats** /stɛlplats/ (pl: -en) [Belg] depot

de **stelregel** /stɛlreɣəl/ (pl: -s) principle: *een goede ~* a good rule to go by

de **stelschroef** /stɛlsxruf/ (pl: -schroeven) setscrew

het **stelsel** /stɛlsəl/ (pl: -s) system

stelselmatig /stɛlsəlmatəx/ (adj, adv) systematic

de **stelt** /stɛlt/ (pl: -en) stilt ‖ *de boel op ~en zetten* raise hell

de **steltloper** /stɛltlopər/ (pl: -s) grallatorial bird

de **stem** /stɛm/ (pl: -men) **1** voice: *zijn ~ verliezen* lose one's voice; *met luide ~* out loud; *een ~ van binnen* an inner voice **2** part, voice **3** vote: *beiden behaalden een gelijk aantal ~men* it was a tie between the two; *de meeste ~men gelden* the majority decides; *de ~men staken* there is a tie; *de ~men tellen* count the votes; *zijn ~ uitbrengen* cast one's vote, vote

de **stemband** /stɛmbɑnt/ (pl: -en) vocal cord

het **stembiljet** /stɛmbɪljɛt/ (pl: -ten) ballot (paper)

het **stembureau** /stɛmbyro/ (pl: -s) **1** polling station; [Am] polling place **2** polling committee

de **stembus** /stɛmbʏs/ (pl: -sen) ballot box: *naar de ~ gaan* go to the polls

de **stemcomputer** /stɛmkɔmpjutər/ (pl: -s) voting computer

het **stemdistrict** /stɛmdɪstrɪkt/ (pl: -en) constituency; borough; ward

het **stemgeluid** /stɛmɣəlœyt/ (pl: -en) voice

stemgerechtigd /stɛmɣərɣxtəxt/ (adj) entitled to vote

stemhebbend /stɛmhɛbənt/ (adj) voiced

het **stemhokje** /stɛmhɔkjə/ (pl: -s) (voting)

booth
stemloos /stɛmlos/ (adj) voiceless, unvoiced
stemmen /stɛmə(n)/ (stemde, heeft gestemd) **1** vote: *ik stem* **voor** (or: **tegen**) I vote in favour (*or:* against) **2** [mus] tune; tune up || *iem.* **gunstig** ~ put s.o. in the right mood, get in s.o.'s good books
de **stemmer** /stɛmər/ (pl: -s) tuner
stemmig /stɛməx/ (adj, adv) sober, subdued
de **stemming** /stɛmɪn/ (pl: -en) **1** mood: *in een* **slechte** (or: **goede**) ~ *zijn* be in a bad (*or:* good) mood; *de* ~ *zit erin* there's a general mood of cheerfulness **2** feeling: *er heerst een* **vijandige** ~ feelings are hostile **3** vote: *een* **geheime** ~ a secret ballot; *een voorstel* **in** ~ *brengen* put a proposal to the vote **4** [mus] tuning
de **stempel** /stɛmpəl/ **1** seal **2** stamp; postmark
de **stempelautomaat** /stɛmpəlɑutomat/ (pl: -automaten) stamping machine
¹**stempelen** /stɛmpələ(n)/ (stempelde, heeft gestempeld) [Belg] be unemployed (*or:* on the dole)
²**stempelen** /stɛmpələ(n)/ (stempelde, heeft gestempeld) stamp; postmark
het **stempelgeld** /stɛmpəlxɛlt/ [Belg] unemployment benefit, the dole
het **stempelkussen** /stɛmpəlkysə(n)/ (pl: -s) inkpad
de **stemplicht** /stɛmplɪxt/ compulsory voting
het **stemrecht** /stɛmrɛxt/ (right to) vote, voting right; franchise; suffrage
de **stemverheffing** /stɛmvərhɛfɪn/ (pl: -en) raising of one's voice: *zij sprak* **met** ~ she raised her voice as she spoke
de **stemvork** /stɛmvɔrk/ (pl: -en) tuning fork
de **stemwijzer**® voting aid
het/de **stencil** /stɛnsəl/ (pl: -s) stencil, handout
stencilen /stɛnsələ(n)/ (stencilde, heeft gestencild) duplicate, stencil
stenen /stenə(n)/ (adj) stone; brick
de **stengel** /stɛnəl/ (pl: -s) **1** stalk, stem **2** stick
de **stengun** /stɛnɡyn/ (pl: -s) sten gun
stenigen /stenəyə(n)/ (stenigde, heeft gestenigd) stone
de **stennis** /stɛnɪs/ [inform] commotion: ~ *ma-ken* kick up a row
het/de **steno** /steno/ stenography, shorthand
de **stenograaf** /stenoyraf/ (pl: -grafen) shorthand writer; [Am] stenographer
de **stenografie** /stenoyrafi/ stenography
de **step** /stɛp/ (pl: -pen) scooter
de **steppe** /stɛpə/ (pl: -n) steppe
de **ster** /stɛr/ (pl: -ren) star: *een* **vallende** ~ a shooting star; [fig] *hij speelt de ~ren van de* **hemel** his playing is out of this world
de **stereo** /sterejo/ stereo(phony)
stereotiep /sterejotip/ (adj, adv) stock, stereotypic(al): *een ~e* **uitdrukking** a cliché

de **stereotoren** /sterejotorə(n)/ (pl: -s) music centre
het **stereotype** /sterejotipə/ stereotype
het **sterfbed** /stɛrvbɛt/ (pl: -den) deathbed: *op* *zijn* ~ *zal hij er nog berouw over hebben* he'll regret it to his dying day
sterfelijk /stɛrfələk/ (adj) mortal
het **sterfgeval** /stɛrfxəval/ (pl: -len) death
de **sterfte** /stɛrftə/ (pl: -n, -s) **1** death **2** mortality
het **sterftecijfer** /stɛrftəsɛifər/ (pl: -s) mortality rate
steriel /steril/ (adj) **1** sterile **2** sterile, infertile
de **sterilisatie** /steriliza(t)si/ (pl: -s) sterilization
steriliseren /sterilizɛrə(n)/ (steriliseerde, heeft gesteriliseerd) sterilize; fix
de **steriliteit** /sterilitɛit/ sterility
¹**sterk** /stɛrk/ (adj) **1** strong, powerful, tough: *~e* **thee** strong tea **2** strong, sharp: *een ~e* **stijging** a sharp rise; *een ~e* **wind** a strong wind || *~er nog* indeed, more than that
²**sterk** /stɛrk/ (adv) **1** strongly, greatly, highly: *een* ~ **vergrote** *foto* a much enlarged photograph; *iets* ~ **overdrijven** greatly exaggerate sth. **2** well || *zij staat* (*nogal*) ~ she has a strong case; *dat* **lijkt** *me* ~ I doubt it, I wouldn't count on it
de **sterkedrank** /stɛrkədrɑnk/ strong drink, liquor
sterken /stɛrkə(n)/ (sterkte, heeft gesterkt) strengthen: *in zijn mening gesterkt worden* be confirmed in one's views
de **sterkte** /stɛrktə/ (pl: -n, -s) **1** strength, power, intensity; volume; loudness: *de* ~ *van een* **geluid** (or: *van het* **licht**) the intensity of a noise (*or:* the light); *op* **volle** (or: **halve**) ~ at full (*or:* half) strength **2** fortitude, courage: ~ (*gewenst*)! all the best!, good luck! **3** strength, potency
de **stern** /stɛrn/ (pl: -en) tern
het **sterrenbeeld** /stɛrə(n)belt/ (pl: -en) sign of the zodiac
de **sterrenhemel** /stɛrə(n)heməl/ starry sky
de **sterrenkijker** /stɛrə(n)kɛikər/ (pl: -s) telescope
de **sterrenkunde** /stɛrə(n)kyndə/ astronomy
de **sterrenkundige** /stɛrə(n)kyndəyə/ (pl: -n) astronomer
het **sterrenstelsel** /stɛrə(n)stɛlsəl/ (pl: -s) stellar system
de **sterrenwacht** /stɛrə(n)wɑxt/ (pl: -en) observatory
het **sterretje** /stɛrəcə/ (pl: -s) **1** sparkler **2** star, asterisk
de **sterveling** /stɛrvəlɪn/ (pl: -en) mortal: *er was* **geen** ~ *te bekennen* there wasn't a (living) soul in sight
sterven /stɛrvə(n)/ (stierf, is gestorven) die: ~ *aan een ziekte* die of an illness; ~ *aan zijn*

verwondingen die from one's injuries; *op ~ na dood zijn* be as good as dead

de **stethoscoop** /stetosk<u>o</u>p/ (pl: stethoscopen) stethoscope

de **steun** /st<u>ø</u>n/ (pl: -en) **1** support, prop: *een ~tje in de rug* a bit of encouragement (*or:* support), a helping hand **2** support, assistance: *dat zal een grote ~ voor ons zijn* that will be a great help to us **3** support, aid, assistance

de **steunbeer** /st<u>ø</u>mber/ (pl: -beren) buttress

[1]**steunen** /st<u>ø</u>nə(n)/ (steunde, heeft gesteund) lean (on), rest (on)

[2]**steunen** /st<u>ø</u>nə(n)/ (steunde, heeft gesteund) **1** support, prop (up): *een muur ~* support (*or:* prop up) a wall **2** [fig] support, back up: *iem. ergens in ~* back up s.o. in sth.

de **steunfraude** /st<u>ø</u>nfrɑudə/ (pl: -s) social security fraud

de **steunkous** /st<u>ø</u>ŋkɑus/ (pl: -en) support stocking

de **steunpilaar** /st<u>ø</u>mpilar/ (pl: -pilaren) pillar [also fig]

het **steunpunt** /st<u>ø</u>mpʏnt/ (pl: -en) (point of) support

de **steuntrekker** /st<u>ø</u>ntrɛkər/ (pl: -s) person on the dole; [Am] person on welfare (benefit)

de **steunzool** /st<u>ø</u>nzol/ (pl: -zolen) arch support

de **steur** /st<u>ø</u>r/ (pl: -en) sturgeon

de **steven** /st<u>e</u>və(n)/ (pl: -s) [shipp] stem; stern

[1]**stevig** /st<u>e</u>vəχ/ (adj) **1** substantial, hearty **2** robust, hefty; [fig] stiff; [fig] heavy: *een ~e hoofdpijn* a splitting headache **3** solid, strong, sturdy **4** tight, firm: *een ~ pak slaag* a good hiding **5** substantial, considerable

[2]**stevig** /st<u>e</u>vəχ/ (adv) **1** solidly, strongly: *die ladder staat niet ~* that ladder is a bit wobbly **2** tightly, firmly: *we moeten er ~ tegenaan gaan* we really need to get (*or:* buckle) down to it

de **stevigheid** /st<u>e</u>vəχhɛit/ sturdiness, strength, solidity

de **steward** /sc<u>u</u>wərt/ (pl: -s) steward; flight attendant

de **stewardess** /scuwɑrd<u>ɛ</u>s/ (pl: -en) stewardess, (air) hostess

stichtelijk /st<u>ɪ</u>χtələk/ (adj, adv) devotional, pious

stichten /st<u>ɪ</u>χtə(n)/ (stichtte, heeft gesticht) found, establish: *een gezin ~* start a family

de **stichter** /st<u>ɪ</u>χtər/ (pl: -s) founder

de **stichting** /st<u>ɪ</u>χtɪŋ/ (pl: -en) foundation, establishment

de **stick** /st<u>ɪ</u>k/ (pl: -s) stick

de **sticker** /st<u>ɪ</u>kɛr/ (pl: -s) sticker

het **stickie** /st<u>ɪ</u>ki/ (pl: -s) joint, stick

de **stiefbroer** /st<u>i</u>vbrur/ (pl: -s) stepbrother

de **stiefdochter** /st<u>i</u>vdɔχtər/ (pl: -s) stepdaughter

het **stiefkind** /st<u>i</u>fkɪnt/ (pl: -eren) stepchild

de **stiefmoeder** /st<u>i</u>fmudər/ (pl: -s) stepmother

de **stiefvader** /st<u>i</u>fadər/ (pl: -s) stepfather

de **stiefzoon** /st<u>i</u>fson/ (pl: -s, -zonen) stepson

de **stiefzuster** /st<u>i</u>fsʏstər/ (pl: -s) stepsister

[1]**stiekem** /st<u>i</u>kəm/ (adj) **1** sneaky **2** secret

[2]**stiekem** /st<u>i</u>kəm/ (adv) **1** in an underhand way, on the sly **2** in secret: *iets ~ doen* do sth. on the sly; *~ weggaan* steal (*or:* sneak) away

de **stiekemerd** /st<u>i</u>kəmərt/ (pl: -s) sneak, sly dog

de **stielman** /st<u>i</u>lmɑn/ (pl: -nen) [Belg] craftsman, skilled worker

de **stier** /st<u>i</u>r/ (pl: -en) bull

de **Stier** /st<u>i</u>r/ (pl: -en) [astrology] Taurus

het **stierengevecht** /st<u>i</u>rə(n)χəvɛχt/ (pl: -en) bullfight

de **stierenvechter** /st<u>i</u>rə(n)vɛχtər/ (pl: -s) bullfighter

stierlijk /st<u>i</u>rlək/ (adv): [inform] *ik verveel me ~* I'm bored stiff (*or:* to tears)

de **stift** /st<u>ɪ</u>ft/ (pl: -en) **1** cartridge **2** felt-tip (pen)

de **stifttand** /st<u>ɪ</u>ftɑnt/ (pl: -en) crowned tooth

het **stigma** /st<u>ɪ</u>χma/ (pl: -'s, -ta) stigma

stigmatiseren /stɪχmatiz<u>e</u>rə(n)/ (stigmatiseerde, heeft gestigmatiseerd) stigmatize

[1]**stijf** /st<u>ɛi</u>f/ (adj) **1** stiff, rigid: *~ van de kou* numb with cold **2** stiff, wooden

[2]**stijf** /st<u>ɛi</u>f/ (adv) **1** stiffly, rigidly: *zij hield het pak ~ vast* she held on to the package with all her might **2** stiffly, formally

de **stijfheid** /st<u>ɛi</u>fhɛit/ (pl: -heden) stiffness

stijfjes /st<u>ɛi</u>fjəs/ (adj, adv) stiff, formal

de **stijfkop** /st<u>ɛi</u>fkɔp/ (pl: -pen) stubborn person, pigheaded person

het/de **stijfsel** /st<u>ɛi</u>fsəl/ paste

de **stijgbeugel** /st<u>ɛi</u>ɣbøɣəl/ (pl: -s) stirrup

stijgen /st<u>ɛi</u>ɣə(n)/ (steeg, is gestegen) **1** rise; climb: *een ~de lijn* an upward trend **2** increase, rise: *de prijzen* (*or:* *lonen*) *~* prices (*or:* wages) are rising

de **stijging** /st<u>ɛi</u>ɣɪŋ/ (pl: -en) rise, increase

de **stijl** /st<u>ɛi</u>l/ (pl: -en) **1** style; register: *ambtelijke ~* officialese; *journalistieke ~* journalese; *het onderwijs nieuwe ~* the new style of education; *in de ~ van* after the fashion of **2** post ‖ *dat is geen ~* that's no way to behave

het **stijldansen** /st<u>ɛi</u>ldɑnsə(n)/ ballroom dancing

de **stijlfiguur** /st<u>ɛi</u>lfiɣyr/ (pl: -figuren) figure of speech, trope

stijlloos /st<u>ɛi</u>los/ (adj, adv) **1** tasteless, lacking in style **2** ill-mannered

stijlvol /st<u>ɛi</u>lvɔl/ (adj, adv) stylish, fashionable

de **stik** /st<u>ɪ</u>k/ (int) [inform] oh heck, oh damn; nuts (to you); get lost

stikdonker /st<u>ɪ</u>ɣdɔnkər/ (adj) [inform] pitch-dark, pitch-black

stikken /st<u>ɪ</u>kə(n)/ (stikte, is gestikt) **1** suffocate, choke; be stifled: *in iets ~* choke on sth.; *~ van het lachen* be in stitches **2** (+ in) be bursting (with); be up to one's ears (in) **3** drop dead: *iem. laten ~* leave s.o. in the lurch; stand up **4** stitch **5** be full (of), swarm (with): *dit opstel stikt van de fouten* this essay is riddled with errors

de **stikstof** /stɪkstɔf/ nitrogen

¹stil /stɪl/ (adj) **1** quiet, silent **2** still, motionless **3** quiet, calm: *de ~le tijd* the slack season, the off season ‖ *Stille Nacht* Silent Night

²stil /stɪl/ (adv) **1** quietly **2** still **3** quietly, calmly

de **stiletto** /stilɛto/ (pl: -'s) flick knife; [Am] switchblade

¹stilhouden /stɪlhɑudə(n)/ (hield stil, heeft stilgehouden) stop, pull up

²stilhouden /stɪlhɑudə(n)/ (hield stil, heeft stilgehouden) **1** keep quiet, hold still **2** keep quiet, hush up: *zij hielden hun huwelijk stil* they got married in secret

de **stille** /stɪlə/ (pl: -n) plain-clothes policeman

stilleggen /stɪlɛɣə(n)/ (legde stil, heeft stilgelegd) stop, shut down, close down

stillen /stɪlə(n)/ (stilde, heeft gestild) satisfy

stilletjes /stɪləcəs/ (adv) **1** quietly **2** secretly, on the sly

het **stilleven** /stɪlevə(n)/ (pl: -s) still life

stilliggen /stɪlɪɣə(n)/ (lag stil, heeft stilgelegen) **1** lie still (*or:* quiet) **2** lie idle, be idle: *het werk ligt stil* work is at a standstill

stilstaan /stɪlstan/ (stond stil, heeft stilgestaan) **1** stand still, pause, come to a standstill: *heb je er ooit bij stilgestaan dat …* has it ever occurred to you that … **2** stand still, stop, be at a standstill

de **stilstand** /stɪlstɑnt/ **1** standstill, stagnation: *tot ~ brengen* bring to a standstill (*or:* halt) **2** [Belg] stop: *deze trein heeft ~en te Lokeren en te Gent* this train stops at Lokeren and Ghent

de **stilte** /stɪltə/ **1** silence, quiet: *een minuut ~* a minute's silence; *de ~ verbreken* break the silence **2** quiet, privacy, secrecy

stilzetten /stɪlzɛtə(n)/ (zette stil, heeft stilgezet) (bring to a) stop

stilzitten /stɪlzɪtə(n)/ (zat stil, heeft stilgezeten) sit still, stand still

het **stilzwijgen** /stɪlzwɛɪɣə(n)/ silence

stilzwijgend /stɪlzwɛɪɣənt/ (adj, adv) tacit, understood: *~ aannemen (veronderstellen) dat …* take (it) for granted that …; *een contract ~ verlengen* automatically renew a contract

de **stimulans** /stimylɑns/ (pl: -en) stimulus

stimuleren /stimylerə(n)/ (stimuleerde, heeft gestimuleerd) stimulate, encourage; boost [com]

de **stimulus** /stimylʏs/ (pl: stimuli) stimulus, incentive

de **stinkbom** /stɪŋbɔm/ (pl: -men) stink bomb

het **stinkdier** /stɪŋdir/ (pl: -en) skunk

stinken /stɪŋkə(n)/ (stonk, heeft gestonken) stink, smell: *uit de mond ~* have bad breath; [fig] *die zaak stinkt* there's sth. fishy about that, that business stinks ‖ [inform] *erin ~* a) walk right into it (*or:* the trap); b) fall for sth., rise to the bait, be fooled

stinkend /stɪŋkənt/ (adj) stinking, smelly

de **stip** /stɪp/ (pl: -pen) **1** dot; speck **2** [sport] (penalty) spot (*or:* mark)

stippelen /stɪpələ(n)/ (stippelde, heeft gestippeld) dot, speckle

de **stippellijn** /stɪpəlɛin/ (pl: -en) dotted line

stipt /stɪpt/ (adj, adv) exact, punctual; prompt; strict: *~ om drie uur* at three o'clock sharp; *~ op tijd* right on time

de **stiptheid** /stɪptɛit/ accuracy; punctuality; promptness; strictness

de **stiptheidsactie** /stɪptɛitsɑksi/ (pl: -s) work-to-rule, go-slow; [Am] slow-down (strike)

stockeren /stɔkərə(n)/ (stockeerde, heeft gestockeerd) [Belg] stock

stoeien /stujə(n)/ (stoeide, heeft gestoeid) play around: *met het idee ~* toy with the idea (of)

de **stoel** /stul/ (pl: -en) chair; seat: *een luie (gemakkelijke) ~* an easy chair; *pak ~* take a seat; *de poten onder iemands ~ wegzagen* cut the ground from under s.o.'s feet; pull the rug from under s.o.

stoelen /stulə(n)/ (stoelde, heeft gestoeld) be based (on)

de **stoelendans** /stulə(n)dɑns/ (pl: -en) musical chairs

de **stoelgang** /stulɣɑŋ/ (bowel) movement, stool(s)

de **stoeltjeslift** /stulcəslɪft/ (pl: -en) chairlift

de **stoemp** /stump/ [Belg] [roughly] stew, hotchpotch

de **stoep** /stup/ (pl: -en) **1** pavement; [Am] sidewalk **2** (door)step: *onverwachts op de ~ staan bij iem.* turn up on s.o.'s doorstep

de **stoeprand** /stuprɑnt/ (pl: -en) kerb; [Am] curb

de **stoeptegel** /stupteɣəl/ paving stone

stoer /stur/ (adj, adv) **1** sturdy, powerful(ly built) **2** tough

de **stoet** /stut/ (pl: -en) procession, parade

de **stoethaspel** /stuthɑspəl/ (pl: -s) clumsy person, bungler

de **¹stof** /stɔf/ (pl: -fen) **1** substance; matter **2** material, cloth, fabric **3** (subject) matter, material: *~ tot nadenken hebben* have food for thought

het **²stof** /stɔf/ (pl: -fen) dust: *~ afnemen* dust; *in het ~ bijten* bite the dust; *iem. in het ~ bijten* make s.o. grovel, make s.o. eat dirt; *veel ~ doen opwaaien* kick up (*or:* raise) a dust, cause a great deal of controversy

de **stofdoek** /stɔvduk/ (pl: -en) duster, (dust)-

cloth
stoffelijk /stɔfələk/ (adj) material
¹**stoffen** /stɔfə(n)/ (adj) cloth, fabric
²**stoffen** /stɔfə(n)/ (stofte, heeft gestoft)
dust
de **stoffer** /stɔfər/ (pl: -s) brush: ~ *en blik* dustpan and brush
stofferen /stɔferə(n)/ (stoffeerde, heeft gestoffeerd) **1** upholster **2** [roughly] decorate;
furnish with carpets and curtains
de **stoffering** /stɔferɪŋ/ (pl: -en) soft furnishings; [Am] fabrics; cloth; upholstery
stoffig /stɔfəx/ (adj) dusty; [fig also] mouldy
de **stofjas** /stɔfjɑs/ (pl: -sen) dustcoat, duster
de **stofwisseling** /stɔfwɪsəlɪŋ/ metabolism
stofzuigen /stɔfsœyɣə(n)/ (stofzuigde,
heeft gestofzuigd) vacuum, hoover
de **stofzuiger** /stɔfsœyɣər/ (pl: -s) vacuum
(cleaner), hoover
de **stok** /stɔk/ (pl: -ken) stick; cane: *zij kregen het
aan* de ~ *over de prijs* they fell out over the
price; [fig] *een* ~ *achter de deur* the big stick
het **stokbrood** /stɔgbrot/ (pl: -broden) ba-
guette, French bread
stokdoof /stɔgdof/ (adj) stone-deaf, (as)
deaf as a post
¹**stoken** /stokə(n)/ (stookte, heeft gestookt)
1 heat **2** make trouble
²**stoken** /stokə(n)/ (stookte, heeft gestookt)
1 stoke (up); feed; light; kindle: *het vuur* ~
stoke up the fire **2** burn **3** stir up: *ruzie* ~ stir
up strife **4** distil
de **stoker** /stokər/ (pl: -s) **1** fireman, stoker;
[fig] firebrand; troublemaker **2** distiller
het **stokje** /stɔkjə/ (pl: -s) stick; perch: *ergens een
~ voor steken* put a stop to sth.; *van zijn ~
gaan* pass out, faint
stokken /stɔkə(n)/ (stokte, is gestokt) catch,
halt: *de aanvoer van voedsel stokt* food supplies have broken down; *zijn adem stokte* his
breath caught in his throat, his breath stopped short
stokoud /stɔkɑut/ (adj) ancient
het **stokpaardje** /stɔkparcə/ (pl: -s) hobby-
horse: *iedereen heeft wel zijn* ~ everyone has
his fads and fancies
stokstijf /stɔkstɛif/ (adj, adv) (as) stiff as a
rod; stock-still
de **stokvis** /stɔkfɪs/ (pl: -sen) stockfish
de **stol** /stɔl/ (pl: -len) stollen
de **stola** /stola/ (pl: -'s) stole
stollen /stɔlə(n)/ (stolde, is gestold) solidify;
coagulate; congeal; set; clot
de **stolp** /stɔlp/ (pl: -en) (bell-)glass
het **stolsel** /stɔlsəl/ (pl: -s) coagulum; clot
stom /stɔm/ (adj) **1** dumb, mute **2** stupid,
dumb: *ik voelde me zo* ~ I felt such a fool; *iets
~s doen* do sth. stupid
de **stoma** /stoma/ (pl: -'s) fistula; colostomy
stomdronken /stɔmdrɔŋkə(n)/ (adj) dead
drunk

¹**stomen** /stomə(n)/ (stoomde, heeft/is ge-
stoomd) steam
²**stomen** /stomə(n)/ (stoomde, heeft ge-
stoomd) dry-clean: *een pak laten* ~ have a suit
cleaned
de **stomerij** /stomərɛi/ (pl: -en) dry cleaner's
de **stomheid** /stɔmhɛit/ dumbness, muteness;
speechlessness: *met* ~ *geslagen zijn* be dumbfounded
stommelen /stɔmələ(n)/ (stommelde,
heeft/is gestommeld) stumble
de **stommeling** /stɔməlɪŋ/ (pl: -en) fool, idiot
het **stommetje** /stɔmɑcə/: ~ *spelen* keep one's
mouth shut
de **stommiteit** /stɔmitɛit/ (pl: -en) stupidity:
~*en begaan* make stupid mistakes
de ¹**stomp** /stɔmp/ (pl: -en) **1** stump, stub
2 thump; punch
²**stomp** /stɔmp/ (adj) blunt: *een* ~*e neus* a
snub nose
stompen /stɔmpə(n)/ (stompte, heeft ge-
stompt) thump; punch
stompzinnig /stɔmpsɪnəx/ (adj, adv) obtuse, dense, stupid: ~ *werk* monotonous (or:
stupid) work
stomtoevallig /stɔmtuvɑləx/ (adv) accidentally, by a (mere) fluke
stomverbaasd /stɔmvərbast/ (adj, adv)
astonished, amazed, flabbergasted
stomvervelend /stɔmvərvelənt/ (adj)
deadly dull, boring; really annoying: ~ *werk
moeten doen* have to do deadly boring work
stomweg /stɔmwɛx/ (adv) simply, just
stoned /stont/ (adj) high, stoned
de **stoof** /stof/ (pl: stoven) footwarmer
de **stoofpeer** /stofper/ (pl: -peren) cooking
pear
de **stoofschotel** /stofsxotəl/ (pl: -s) stew, casserole
de **stookolie** /stokoli/ fuel oil
de **stoom** /stom/ steam: ~ *afblazen* let off
steam
het **stoombad** /stombɑt/ (pl: -en) steam bath,
Turkish bath
de **stoomboot** /stombot/ (pl: -boten) steamboat, steamer
de **stoomcursus** /stomkyrzys/ (pl: -sen) crash
course, intensive course
de **stoommachine** /stomɑʃinə/ (pl: -s) steam
engine
het **stoomstrijkijzer** /stomstrɛikɛizər/ (pl: -s)
steam iron
de **stoomtrein** /stomtrɛin/ (pl: -en) steam
train
de **stoomwals** /stomwɑls/ (pl: -en) steamroller
de **stoornis** /stornɪs/ (pl: -sen) disturbance, disorder
de **stoorzender** /storzɛndər/ (pl: -s) jammer,
jamming station
de **stoot** /stot/ thrust; punch; stab; gust: *een* ~
onder de gordel a blow below the belt

het **stootblok** /stodblɔk/ (pl: -ken) buffer (stop)
het **stootje** /stoːcə/ (pl: -s) thrust; push; nudge: *wel tegen* een ~ *kunnen* stand rough handling (*or:* hard wear); be thick-skinned
het **stootkussen** /stoːtkʏsə(n)/ (pl: -s) **1** buffer, pad **2** buffer, fender
de ¹**stop** /stɔp/ (pl: -pen) **1** fuse: *alle ~pen sloegen bij hem door* he blew a fuse **2** stop, break: *een sanitaire ~ maken* stop to go to the bathroom
²**stop** /stɔp/ (int) **1** stop! **2** stop (it)
het **stopbord** /stɔbɔrt/ (pl: -en) stop sign
het **stopcontact** /stɔpkɔntɑkt/ (pl: -en) (plug-)socket, power point, electric point, outlet
het **stoplicht** /stɔplɪxt/ (pl: -en) traffic light(s)
de **stopnaald** /stɔpnaːlt/ (pl: -en) darning needle
de **stoppel** /stɔpəl/ (pl: -s) stubble, bristle
de **stoppelbaard** /stɔpəlbaːrt/ (pl: -en) stubbly beard, stubble; five o'clock shadow
¹**stoppen** /stɔpə(n)/ (stopte, is gestopt) stop: *stop!* stop!
²**stoppen** /stɔpə(n)/ (stopte, heeft gestopt) **1** fill (up); stuff: *een gat* ~ fill a hole **2** put (in(to)): *iets in zijn mond* ~ put sth. in(to) one's mouth **3** stop: *de keeper kon de bal niet* ~ the goalkeeper couldn't save the ball **4** darn, mend
de **stopplaats** /stɔplaːts/ (pl: -en) stop, stopping place
het **stopsein** /stɔpsɛɪn/ (pl: -en) stop sign, halt sign
de **stopstreep** /stɔpstreːp/ (pl: -strepen) halt line
de **stoptrein** /stɔptrɛɪn/ (pl: -en) slow train
het **stopverbod** /stɔpfərbɔt/ (pl: -en) stopping prohibition; no stopping, clearway
de **stopverf** /stɔpfɛrf/ putty
de **stopwatch** /stɔpwɔtʃ/ (pl: -es) stopwatch
het **stopwoord** /stɔpwoːrt/ (pl: -en) stopgap
stopzetten /stɔpsɛtə(n)/ (zette stop, heeft stopgezet) stop, bring to a standstill (*or:* halt); discontinue; suspend
storen /stoːrə(n)/ (stoorde, heeft gestoord) **1** disturb; intrude; interrupt; interfere: *de lijn is gestoord* there is a breakdown on the line; *stoor ik u?* am I in your way?; am I interrupting (you)?, am I intruding?; *niet ~!* do not disturb!; *iem. in zijn werk* ~ disturb s.o. at his work **2** take notice (of), mind: *zij stoorde er zich niet aan* she took no notice of it
storend /stoːrənt/ (adj, adv) interfering; annoying: *~e bijgeluiden* irritating background noise; *~e fouten* annoying errors; *ik vind het niet ~* it doesn't bother me
de **storing** /stoːrɪŋ/ (pl: -en) **1** disturbance; interruption; trouble; failure; breakdown **2** interference, static **3** [meteorology] disturbance; depression
de **storm** /stɔrm/ (pl: -en) gale, storm: *een ~ in een glas water* a storm in a teacup; *het loopt* ~

there is a real run on it
stormachtig /stɔrmɑxtəx/ (adj, adv) **1** stormy, blustery **2** stormy; tumultuous
stormen /stɔrmə(n)/ (stormde, is gestormd) storm, rush: *naar voren* ~ rush forward (*or:* ahead)
de **stormloop** /stɔrmloːp/ rush, run
stormlopen /stɔrmloːpə(n)/ (liep storm, heeft stormgelopen): *het loopt storm* there's quite a rush, there's a run on it
de **stormram** /stɔrmrɑm/ (pl: -men) battering-ram
de **stormvloed** /stɔrmvluːt/ (pl: -en) storm tide, storm flood (*or:* surge)
de **stormvloedkering** /stɔrmvluːtkerɪŋ/ (pl: -en) storm surge barrier, flood barrier
het **stort** /stɔrt/ (pl: -en) dump, tip
de **stortbak** /stɔrdbɑk/ (pl: -ken) cistern, tank
de **stortbui** /stɔrdbœy/ (pl: -en) downpour, cloudburst
¹**storten** /stɔrtə(n)/ (stortte, is gestort) fall, crash: *in elkaar* ~ **a)** collapse, cave in [bldg]; **b)** collapse, crack up
²**storten** /stɔrtə(n)/ (stortte, heeft gestort) **1** throw, dump **2** pay, deposit: *het gestorte bedrag is* … the sum paid is …
zich ³**storten** /stɔrtə(n)/ (stortte zich, heeft zich gestort) **1** throw o.s.: *zich in de politiek* ~ dive into politics **2** (+ op) throw o.s. (into), dive (into), plunge (into)
de **storting** /stɔrtɪŋ/ (pl: -en) payment, deposit
de **stortkoker** /stɔrtkokər/ (pl: -s) (garbage) chute (*or:* shoot)
de **stortplaats** /stɔrtplaːts/ (pl: -en) dump, dumping ground (*or:* site)
de **stortregen** /stɔrtreɣə(n)/ (pl: -s) downpour
stortregenen /stɔrtreɣənə(n)/ (stortregende, heeft gestortregend) pour (with rain, down)
de **stortvloed** /stɔrtflut/ (pl: -en) torrent, deluge, flood
¹**stoten** /stoːtə(n)/ (stootte, heeft/is gestoten) bump, knock, hit: *pas op, stoot je hoofd niet* mind your head; *op moeilijkheden* ~ run into difficulties; *iem. van zijn voetstuk* ~ knock s.o. off his pedestal
²**stoten** /stoːtə(n)/ (stootte, heeft gestoten) **1** thrust, push: *niet ~!* handle with care!; *een vaas van de kast* ~ knock a vase off the sideboard **2** play (*or:* shoot) (a ball)
zich ³**stoten** /stoːtə(n)/ (stootte zich, heeft zich gestoten) bump (o.s.): *we stootten ons aan de tafel* we bumped into the table
de **stotteraar** /stɔtəraːr/ (pl: -s) stutterer, stammerer
stotteren /stɔtərə(n)/ (stotterde, heeft gestotterd) stutter, stammer
stout /staut/ (adj, adv) naughty: ~ *zijn* misbehave
stoutmoedig /stautmuːdəx/ (adj, adv) bold, audacious

stouwen /stɑuwə(n)/ (stouwde, heeft gestouwd) stow, cram

stoven /stovə(n)/ (stoofde, heeft gestoofd) stew, simmer

de **stoverij** /stovərɛi/ (pl: -en) [Belg] stew

de **straal** /stral/ (pl: stralen) **1** beam, ray **2** jet; trickle **3** radius: *binnen* een ~ *van 10 kilometer* within a radius of 10 km ‖ *iem.* ~ *voorbijlopen* walk right past s.o.

de **straaljager** /straljaɣər/ (pl: -s) fighter jet

de **straalkachel** /stralkɑχəl/ (pl: -s) electric heater

het **straalvliegtuig** /stralvliχtœyχ/ (pl: -en) jet

de **straat** /strat/ (pl: straten) street: *een doodlopende* ~ dead end street; *de volgende* ~ *rechts* the next turning to the right; *de* ~ *opbreken* dig up the street; *op* ~ *staan* be (out) on the street(s); *drie* straten verderop three streets away

straatarm /stratɑrm/ (adj) penniless

de **straatbende** /stradbɛndə/ street gang

het **straatgevecht** /stratχəvɛχt/ (pl: -en) street fight, riot

de **straathond** /strathont/ (pl: -en) cur, mutt

het **straatje** /stracə/ (pl: -s) alley, lane

de **straatjongen** /stratjɔŋə(n)/ (pl: -s) street urchin

de **straatlantaarn** /stratlɑntarn/ (pl: -s) street lamp

de **straatlengte** /stratlɛŋtə/ (pl: -n, -s): *met een* ~ *winnen* win by a mile

het **straatmeubilair** /stratmøbilɛːr/ street furniture

de **straatmuzikant** /stratmyzikɑnt/ busker

Straatsburg /stratsbyrχ/ Strasbourg

de **straatsteen** /stratsten/ (pl: -stenen) paving brick

de **straattaal** /stratal/ bad language

de **straatventer** /stratfɛntər/ (pl: -s) vendor

de **straatverlichting** /stratfərlɪχtɪŋ/ street lighting

het **straatvuil** /stratfœyl/ street refuse; [Am] street garbage

de **straatwaarde** /stratwardə/ street value

de **¹straf** /straf/ (pl: -fen) punishment; penalty: *een zware* (or: *lichte*) ~ a heavy (or: light) punishment; *een* ~ *ondergaan* pay the penalty; *zijn* ~ *ontlopen* get off scot-free; *voor* ~ for punishment

²straf /straf/ (adj, adv) stiff, severe: *~fe taal* hard words

strafbaar /strɑvbar/ (adj) punishable: *een* ~ *feit* an offence, a punishable (or: penal) act; *dat is* ~ that's an offence; *iets* ~ *stellen* attach a penalty to sth., make sth. punishable

de **strafbal** /strɑvbɑl/ (pl: -len) penalty (shot)

de **strafbank** /strɑvbɑŋk/ **1** dock: *op het ~je zitten* be in the dock **2** [sport] penalty box (or: bench)

het **strafblad** /strɑvblɑt/ police record, record of convictions (or: offences)

de **strafcorner** /strɑfkɔːrnər/ (pl: -s) penalty corner

de **strafexpeditie** /strɑfɛkspedi(t)si/ (pl: -s) punitive expedition

straffeloos /strɑfəlos/ (adj, adv) unpunished

straffen /strɑfə(n)/ (strafte, heeft gestraft) punish, penalize

het **strafhof** (pl: -hoven) criminal court

het **strafkamp** /strɑfkɑmp/ (pl: -en) prison camp, penal colony

de **strafmaat** /strɑfmat/ (pl: -maten) sentence, penalty

de **strafpleiter** /strɑfplɛitər/ (pl: -s) criminal lawyer, advocate, counsellor

het/de **strafport** /strɑfpɔrt/ surcharge

het **strafproces** /strɑfprosɛs/ (pl: -sen) criminal action, criminal proceedings

het **strafpunt** /strɑfpʏnt/ (pl: -en) penalty point: *een* ~ *geven* award a penalty point

het **strafrecht** /strɑfrɛχt/ criminal law, criminal justice

strafrechtelijk /strɑfrɛχtələk/ (adj, adv) criminal: *iem.* ~ *vervolgen* prosecute s.o.

de **strafschop** /strɑfsχɔp/ (pl: -pen) penalty (kick), spot kick

het **strafschopgebied** /strɑfsχɔpχəbit/ (pl: -en) penalty area, penalty box

de **strafvermindering** /strɑfərmɪndərɪŋ/ reduction of (one's) sentence, remission

de **strafvervolging** /strɑfərvɔlɣɪŋ/ (criminal) prosecution, criminal proceedings: *tot* ~ *overgaan* prosecute, institute criminal proceedings

de **strafvordering** /strɑfɔrdərɪŋ/ criminal proceedings: *wetboek van* ~ Code of Criminal Procedure

het **strafwerk** /strɑfwɛrk/ lines, (school) punishment: ~ *maken* do (or: write) lines; do impositions (or: an imposition)

de **strafworp** /strɑfwɔrp/ (pl: -en) penalty throw; foul shot

de **strafzaak** /strɑfsak/ (pl: -zaken) criminal case, criminal trial

strak /strɑk/ (adj, adv) **1** tight; taut: *iem.* ~ *houden* keep s.o. on a tight rein; ~ *trekken* stretch, pull tight **2** fixed, set, intent: ~ *voor zich uit kijken* sit staring (fixedly) **3** fixed, set; stern; tense

strakblauw /strɑgblɑu/ (adj) clear blue, sheer blue, cloudless

straks /strɑks/ (adv) later, soon, next: ~ *meer hierover* I'll return to this later; *tot* ~ so long, see you later (or: soon)

stralen /stralə(n)/ (straalde, heeft gestraald) **1** radiate, beam **2** shine, beam, radiate

stralend /stralənt/ (adj, adv) **1** radiant, brilliant; [stronger] dazzling **2** radiant, beaming **3** glorious, splendid

de **straling** /stralɪŋ/ (pl: -en) radiation

stram /strɑm/ (adj, adv) stiff, rigid

het **stramien** /stramin/ pattern

het **strand** /strɑnt/ (pl: -en) beach, seaside

stranden /strɑndə(n)/ (strandde, is ge-strand) **1** be cast (*or:* washed) ashore; run aground (*or:* ashore); be stranded **2** fail: *een plan laten ~* wreck a project **3** be stranded

het **strandhuisje** /strɑnthœyʃə/ (pl: -s) beach cabin

de **strandjutter** /strɑntjʏtər/ (pl: -s) beach-comber; wrecker

de **strandstoel** /strɑntstul/ (pl: -en) deck chair

de **strateeg** /stratex/ (pl: strategen) strategist

de **strategie** /strateɣi/ (pl: -ën) strategy

strategisch /strateɣis/ (adj, adv) strategic

de **stratenmaker** /stratə(n)makər/ (pl: -s) paviour, road worker; road mender

de **stratosfeer** /stratosfer/ stratosphere

de **stream** /striːm/ (pl: -s) stream

de **streber** /strebər/ (pl: -s) careerist, (social) climber

de **streefdatum** /strevdatʏm/ (pl: -data) target date

de **streek** /strek/ (pl: streken) **1** trick; prank; antic; caper: *een stomme ~ uithalen* do sth. silly **2** region, area: *in deze ~* in these parts (*or:* this part) of the country **3** stroke ‖ *van ~ zijn* **a)** be out of sorts; **b)** be upset, be in a dither; **c)** be upset, be out of order

de **streekbus** /strebʏs/ (pl: -sen) regional (*or:* county, country) bus

de **streekroman** /strekromɑn/ (pl: -s) regional novel

het **streekvervoer** /strekfərvur/ regional transport

de **streep** /strep/ (pl: strepen) **1** line, score; mark(ing): [fig] *daar hebben we een ~ onder gezet* that's a closed book (*or:* issue) now **2** tripe, line; band; bar; streak: *iem. over de ~ trekken* win s.o. over **3** stripe, chevron

het **streepje** /strepjə/ (pl: -s) thin line, narrow line; hyphen; dash; slash ‖ *een ~ voor hebben* be privileged, be in s.o.'s favour (*or:* good books)

de **streepjescode** /strepjəskodə/ (pl: -s) bar code

¹strekken /strekə(n)/ (strekte, heeft ge-strekt) **1** extend, stretch, go **2** last, go

²strekken /strekə(n)/ (strekte, heeft ge-strekt) stretch, unbend, extend, straighten

de **strekking** /strekɪŋ/ (pl: -en) import; tenor; purport; purpose; intent; effect: *de ~ van het verhaal* the drift of the story

strelen /strelə(n)/ (streelde, heeft gestreeld) caress, stroke, fondle

de **streling** /strelɪŋ/ (pl: -en) caress

stremmen /stremə(n)/ (stremde, heeft ge-stremd) block, obstruct

de **stremming** /stremɪŋ/ (pl: -en) **1** blocking: *~ van het verkeer* traffic jam, blocking of the traffic **2** coagulation

het **stremsel** /stremsəl/ (pl: -s) coagulant

de **¹streng** /strɛŋ/ (pl: -en) **1** twist, twine, skein, hank **2** strand

²streng /strɛŋ/ (adj, adv) **1** severe, hard: *het vriest ~* there's a sharp frost **2** severe, strict; stringent; rigid; harsh: *~ eisen* stern de-mands; *een ~e onderwijzer* a stern (*or:* strict) teacher

strepen /strepə(n)/ (streepte, heeft ge-streept) line, streak, stripe

de **stress** /strɛs/ stress, strain

stressbestendig /strɛzbəstɛndəx/ (adj) im-mune to stress

stressen /strɛsə(n)/ (streste, heeft gestrest) work under stress

het **stretch** /strɛtʃ/ stretchy material (*or:* fabric), elastic

de **stretcher** /strɛtʃər/ (pl: -s) stretcher

het **¹streven** /strevə(n)/ **1** striving (for), pursuit (of); endeavour: *het ~ naar onafhankelijkheid* the pursuit of independence **2** ambition, as-piration, aim: *een nobel ~* a noble ambition

²streven /strevə(n)/ (streefde, heeft ge-streefd) strive (for, after), aspire (after, to), aim (at): *je doel voorbij ~* defeat your object

de **striem** /strim/ (pl: -en) slash, score; weal; welt

striemen /strimə(n)/ (striemde, heeft ge-striemd) slash, score

de **strijd** /strɛit/ **1** fight, struggle; combat; bat-tle: *de ~ aanbinden* engage (*or:* enter) into combat, join battle; *hevige (zware) ~* fierce battle (*or:* struggle, fighting), battle royal; *leveren* wage a fight, put up a fight (*or:* struggle); *de ~ om het bestaan* the struggle for life **2** strife, dispute, controversy, conflict: *innerlijke ~* inner struggle (*or:* conflict); *in ~ met de wet* against the law

strijdbaar /strɛidbar/ (adj) militant, warlike

de **strijdbijl** /strɛidbɛil/ (pl: -en) battle-axe; tomahawk: *de ~ begraven* bury the hatchet

strijden /strɛidə(n)/ (streed, heeft gestre-den) **1** struggle, fight, wage war (against, on); battle **2** compete, contend

de **strijder** /strɛidər/ (pl: -s) fighter; warrior; combatant

strijdig /strɛidəx/ (adj) **1** contrary (to), ad-verse (to), inconsistent (with) **2** conflicting; incompatible (with)

de **strijdkrachten** /strɛitkrɑxtə(n)/ (pl) (arm-ed) forces (*or:* services)

de **strijdkreet** /strɛitkret/ (pl: -kreten) battle cry, war cry

strijdlustig /strɛitlʏstəx/ (adj) pugnacious, combative; militant

het **strijdperk** /strɛitpɛrk/ (pl: -en) arena

de **strijkbout** /strɛikbɑut/ (pl: -en) iron

¹strijken /strɛikə(n)/ (streek, heeft gestre-ken) brush, sweep ‖ *met de eer gaan ~* carry off the palm (for), take the credit (for)

²strijken /strɛikə(n)/ (streek, heeft gestre-ken) **1** smooth, spread, brush **2** stroke, brush

3 iron || *de* **zeilen** ~ lower (*or:* strike) the sails

het **strijkgoed** /str<u>ɛ</u>ɪkχut/ clothes that need to be ironed; ironed clothes

het **strijkijzer** /str<u>ɛ</u>ɪkɛɪzər/ (pl: -s) iron, flat-iron

het **strijkinstrument** /str<u>ɛ</u>ɪkɪnstrymɛnt/ (pl: -en) stringed instrument: *de* ~*en* the strings

het **strijkorkest** /str<u>ɛ</u>ɪkɔrkɛst/ (pl: -en) string orchestra

de **strijkplank** /str<u>ɛ</u>ɪkplɑŋk/ (pl: -en) ironing board

de **strijkstok** /str<u>ɛ</u>ɪkstɔk/ (pl: -ken) bow || *er blijft veel* **aan** *de* ~ *hangen* the rake-off is considerable

de **strik** /strɪk/ (pl: -ken) **1** bow **2** snare, trap

het **strikje** /str<u>ɪ</u>kjə/ (pl: -s) bow tie

strikken /str<u>ɪ</u>kə(n)/ (strikte, heeft gestrikt) **1** tie in a bow: *zijn* **das** ~ knot a tie **2** snare **3** trap (into)

strikt /strɪkt/ (adj, adv) strict; stringent; rigorous: ~ **vertrouwelijk** strictly confidential

de **strikvraag** /str<u>ɪ</u>kfraχ/ (pl: -vragen) catch question, trick question

de **string** /strɪŋ/ **1** thong **2** (character) string

stringent /strɪnχɛnt/ (adj) stringent

de **strip** /strɪp/ (pl: -s, -pen) **1** strip; slip; band **2** comic strip, (strip) cartoon

het **stripboek** /str<u>ɪ</u>buk/ (pl: -en) comic (book)

de **stripfiguur** /str<u>ɪ</u>pfiɣyr/ (pl: -figuren) comic(-strip) character

strippen /str<u>ɪ</u>pə(n)/ (stripte, heeft gestript) strip

de **strippenkaart** /str<u>ɪ</u>pə(n)kart/ (pl: -en) [roughly] bus and tram card

de **stripper** /str<u>ɪ</u>pər/ (pl: -s) (male/female) stripper

de **striptease** /str<u>ɪ</u>pti:s/ striptease

de **striptekenaar** /str<u>ɪ</u>ptekənar/ (pl: -s) strip cartoonist

het **stripverhaal** /str<u>ɪ</u>pfərhal/ (pl: -verhalen) comic (strip)

het **stro** /stro/ straw

de **strobloem** /str<u>o</u>blum/ (pl: -bloemen) strawflower, everlasting (flower)

het **strobreed** /str<u>o</u>bret/: *iem.* **geen** ~ *in de weg leggen* not put the slightest obstacle in s.o.'s way

stroef /struf/ (adj, adv) **1** rough, uneven **2** stiff, difficult, awkward; jerky; brusque; tight **3** stiff, staid; awkward; stern; difficult (to get on with); remote; reserved; stand-offish

de **strofe** /str<u>o</u>fə/ (pl: -n) stanza, strophe

de **strohalm** /str<u>o</u>hɑlm/ (pl: -en) (stalk of) straw: *zich* **aan** *een (laatste)* ~ *vastklampen* clutch at a straw (*or:* at straws)

de **strohoed** /str<u>o</u>hut/ (pl: -en) straw (hat)

stroken /str<u>o</u>kə(n)/ (strookte, heeft gestrookt) tally, agree, square: *dat strookt niet* **met** *elkaar* these things do not match; *dat strookt niet* **met** *mijn plannen* that does not fit my plans

de **stroman** /str<u>o</u>mɑn/ (pl: -nen) straw man, man of straw, puppet, figurehead

stromen /str<u>o</u>mə(n)/ (stroomde, heeft/is gestroomd) **1** stream, pour, flow: *een* **snel** ~*de rivier* a fast-flowing river; *het* **water** *stroomde de dijk over* the water flooded over the dike **2** pour, flock || ~*de* **regen** pouring rain

de **stroming** /str<u>o</u>mɪŋ/ (pl: -en) **1** current, flow **2** movement, trend, tendency

strompelen /str<u>ɔ</u>mpələ(n)/ (strompelde, is gestrompeld) stumble, totter, limp

de **stronk** /strɔŋk/ (pl: -en) **1** stump, stub **2** stalk

de **stront** /strɔnt/ [inform] shit, dung, filth: *er is* ~ *aan de* **knikker** the shit has hit the fan, we're in the shit

het **strontje** /str<u>ɔ</u>ncə/ (pl: -s) sty(e)

het **strooibiljet** /str<u>o</u>jbɪljɛt/ (pl: -ten) handbill, pamphlet, leaflet

¹strooien /str<u>o</u>jə(n)/ (adj) straw: *een* ~ **dak** a thatched roof, a thatch

²strooien /str<u>o</u>jə(n)/ (strooide, heeft gestrooid) scatter; strew; sow; sprinkle; dredge: **zand (pekel)** ~ *bij gladheid* grit icy roads

het **strooizout** /str<u>o</u>jzout/ road salt

de **strook** /strok/ (pl: stroken) **1** strip; band **2** strip, slip; label; tag; stub; counterfoil

de **stroom** /strom/ (pl: stromen) **1** stream, flow; current; flood: *de zwemmer* **werd** *door de* ~ **meegesleurd** the swimmer was swept away by the current (*or:* tide) **2** stream, flood: *een* ~ **goederen** a flow of goods; *er kwam een* ~ *van* **klachten** *binnen* complaints came pouring in **3** (electric) power, (electric) current: *er* **staat** ~ *op die draad* that is a live wire; **onder** ~ *staan* be live (*or:* charged)

stroomafwaarts /strom<u>a</u>fwarts/ (adj, adv) downstream, downriver

de **stroomdraad** /str<u>o</u>mdrat/ live wire, contact wire, electric wire

stroomlijnen /str<u>o</u>mlɛɪnə(n)/ (stroomlijnde, heeft gestroomlijnd) streamline

stroomopwaarts /strom<u>ɔ</u>pwarts/ (adj, adv) upstream, upriver

het **stroomschema** /str<u>o</u>msχema/ flow chart (*or:* sheet, diagram)

de **stroomsterkte** /str<u>o</u>mstɛrktə/ **1** current intensity **2** force of the current

de **stroomstoot** /str<u>o</u>mstot/ (pl: -stoten) (current) surge; pulse; transient

de **stroomstoring** /str<u>o</u>mstorɪŋ/ (pl: -en) electricity failure, power failure

het **stroomverbruik** /str<u>o</u>mvərbrœyk/ electricity consumption, power consumption

de **stroomversnelling** /str<u>o</u>mvərsnɛlɪŋ/ (pl: -en) rapid: *in een* ~ *geraken* gain momentum, develop (*or:* move) rapidly; be accelerated

de **stroomvoorziening** /str<u>o</u>mvorzinɪŋ/ electricity (*or:* power) supply

de **stroop** /strop/ (pl: stropen) syrup; treacle: ~

(om iemands mond) **smeren** butter s.o. up, softsoap s.o.

de **strooptocht** /strˈɔptɔχt/ (pl: -en) (predatory) raid

de **stroopwafel** /strˈopwafəl/ (pl: -s) treacle waffle

de **strop** /strɔp/ (pl: -pen) **1** halter, (hangman's) rope; noose; snare; trap **2** bad luck, tough luck; raw deal; financial blow (or: setback); loss

de **stropdas** /strˈɔbdɑs/ (pl: -sen) tie

stropen /strˈopə(n)/ (stroopte, heeft gestroopt) **1** skin **2** poach

de **stroper** /strˈopər/ (pl: -s) poacher

stroperig /strˈopərəχ/ (adj) **1** syrupy **2** [fig] smooth(-talking)

de **stroperij** /stropərˈɛi/ (pl: -en) poaching

de **strot** /strɔt/ (pl: -ten) throat; gullet: het **komt** me de ~ **uit** I'm sick of it; ik krijg het niet **door** mijn ~ I couldn't eat it to save my life; the words stick in my throat

het **strottenhoofd** /strˈɔtə(n)hoft/ (pl: -en) larynx

de **strubbelingen** /strˈʏbəlɪŋə(n)/ (pl) difficulties; trouble; frictions

structureel /strʏktyrˈel/ (adj, adv) structural; constructional

structureren /strʏktyrˈerə(n)/ (structureerde, heeft gestructureerd) structure, structuralize

de **structuur** /strʏktˈyr/ (pl: structuren) structure, texture, fabric

de **structuurverf** /strʏktˈyrvɛrf/ (pl: -verven) cement paint

de **struif** /strœyf/ (pl: struiven) (contents of an) egg

de **struik** /strœyk/ (pl: -en) **1** bush, shrub **2** bunch; head

het **struikelblok** /strˈœykəlblɔk/ (pl: -ken) stumbling block, obstacle

struikelen /strˈœykələ(n)/ (struikelde, is gestruikeld) stumble (over), trip (over)

het **struikgewas** /strˈœykχəwɑs/ (pl: -sen) bushes, shrubs, brushwood

de **struikrover** /strˈœykrovər/ (pl: -s) highwayman, footpad

struinen /strˈœynə(n)/ (struinde, heeft gestruind) forage (about/around)

struis /strœys/ (adj) robust

de **struisvogel** /strˈœysfoɣəl/ (pl: -s) ostrich

de **struisvogelpolitiek** /strˈœysfoɣəlpolitik/ ostrich policy: een ~ **volgen** refuse to face facts, bury one's head in the sand

het **stucwerk** /stˈʏkwɛrk/ stucco(work)

de **stud** /stʏt/ (pl: -s) egghead

de **studeerkamer** /stydˈerkamər/ (pl: -s) study

de **student** /stydˈɛnt/ (pl: -en) student; undergraduate; (post)graduate: ~ **Turks** student of Turkish

de **studentenbeweging** /stydˈɛntə(n)bəweɣɪŋ/ student movement

het **studentencorps** /stydˈɛntə(n)kɔːr/ (pl: -corpora) [roughly] student(s') union

het **studentenhuis** /stydˈɛntə(n)hœys/ (pl: -huizen) student(s') house

de **studentenstop** /stydˈɛntə(n)stɔp/ (pl: -s) (student) quota

de **studentitijd** /stydˈɛntə(n)tɛit/ (pl: -en) college days, student days

de **studentenvereniging** /stydˈɛntə(n)vərenəɣɪŋ/ (pl: -en) [roughly] student union

studentikoos /stydɛntikˈos/ (adj, adv) typical of a student, student-like

studeren /stydˈerə(n)/ (studeerde, heeft gestudeerd) **1** study; go to (or: be at) university/college: **Marijke** studeert Marijke is at university (or: college); oude talen ~ read classics; hij studeert **nog** he is still studying (or: at college); **verder** ~ continue one's studies; ~ **voor** een examen study (or: revise) for an exam **2** practise (music): **piano** ~ practise the piano

de **studie** /stˈydi/ (pl: -s) study: **met** een ~ beginnen take up a (course of) study

de **studieadviseur** /stˈydiɑtfizər/ (pl: -s) supervisor; [Am] adviser

de **studiebegeleiding** /stˈydibəɣəlɛidɪŋ/ (pl: -en) tutoring, coaching

de **studiebeurs** /stˈydibørs/ (pl: -beurzen) grant

het **studieboek** /stˈydibuk/ (pl: -en) textbook, manual

de **studiebol** /stˈydibɔl/ (pl: -len) bookworm, scholar

de **studiefinanciering** /stˈydifinɑnsirɪŋ/ student grant(s)

de **studiegenoot** /stˈydiɣənot/ (pl: -genoten) fellow student

de **studiegids** /stˈydiɣɪts/ (pl: -en) prospectus; [Am] catalog

het **studiehuis** /stˈydihœys/ (pl: -huizen) **1** space in secondary school for private study **2** educational reform stimulating private study

het **studiejaar** /stˈydijar/ (pl: -jaren) (school) year; university year, academic year

de **studiemeester** /stˈydimestər/ (pl: -s) [Belg] [roughly] supervisor

het **studieprogramma** /stˈydiproɣrɑma/ (pl: -'s) course programme, study programme, syllabus

het/de **studiepunt** /stˈydipʏnt/ (pl: -en) credit

de **studiereis** /stˈydirɛis/ (pl: -reizen) study tour (or: trip)

de **studierichting** /stˈydirɪχtɪŋ/ (pl: -en) subject, course(s), discipline, branch of study (or: studies)

de **studieschuld** /stˈydisχʏlt/ (pl: -en) student loan

de **studietoelage** /stˈyditulaɣə/ (pl: -n) scholarship, (study) grant

de **studiezaal** /stˈydizal/ (pl: -zalen) reading room

de **studio** /stу̲dijo/ (pl: -'s) studio

het **stuf** /stʏf/ eraser

de **stuff** /stʏf/ dope, stuff; pot; grass; weed

stug /stʏx/ (adj, adv) **1** stiff, tough **2** surly, dour, stiff ‖ ~ **doorwerken** work (or: slog) away; dat **lijkt** me ~ that seems pretty stiff (or: tall, steep) to me

het **stuifmeel** /stœ̲yfmel/ pollen

de **stuifsneeuw** /stœ̲yfsnew/ powder (or: drifting) snow

de **stuip** /stœyp/ (pl: -en) convulsion; [small] twitch; fit; spasm: iem. de ~en op het lijf **jagen** scare s.o. stiff, scare the (living) daylights out of s.o.

stuiptrekken /stœ̲yptrɛkə(n)/ (stuiptrekte, heeft gestuiptrekt) convulse, be convulsed, become convulsed

de **stuiptrekking** /stœ̲yptrɛkɪŋ/ (pl: -en) convulsion, spasm; [small] twitch

het **stuitbeen** /stœ̲ydben/ (pl: -deren) tailbone, coccyx

stuiten /stœ̲ytə(n)/ (stuitte, heeft/is gestuit) **1** encounter, happen upon, chance upon, stumble across **2** meet with, run up against **3** bounce, bound

stuitend /stœ̲ytənt/ (adj, adv) revolting, shocking

de **stuiter** /stœ̲ytər/ (pl: -s) big marble, taw, bonce

stuiteren /stœ̲ytərə(n)/ (stuiterde, heeft/is gestuiterd) play at marbles

het **stuitje** /stœ̲ycə/ tail bone

stuiven /stœ̲yvə(n)/ (stoof, heeft/is gestoven) **1** blow, fly about, fly up **2** dash, rush, whiz ‖ [Belg] het zal er ~ there'll be a proper dust-up

de **stuiver** /stœ̲yvər/ (pl: -s) five-cent piece

stuivertje-wisselen /stœ̲yvərcəwɪsələ(n)/ change (or: trade) places

het **¹stuk** /stʏk/ (pl: -ken) **1** piece, part, fragment; lot; length: iets in ~ken **snijden** cut sth. up (into pieces); uit één ~ vervaardigd made in (or: of) one piece **2** piece, item: een ~ **gereedschap** a piece of equipment, a tool; per ~ verkopen sell by the piece, sell singly; **twintig** ~s vee twenty head of cattle; een ~ **of** tien appels about ten apples, ten or so apples **3** (postal) article, (postal) item **4** piece, article **5** document, paper **6** piece, picture **7** piece, play **8** piece; chessman; draughtsman ‖ iem. van zijn ~ brengen unsettle (or: unnerve, disconcert) s.o.; klein **van** ~ small, of small stature, short; [Belg] op het ~ van ... as far as ... is concerned, as for ...

²stuk /stʏk/ (adj) **1** apart, to pieces **2** out of order, broken down, bust: iets ~ **maken** break (or: ruin) sth.

de **stukadoor** /stykado̲r/ (pl: -s) plasterer

stuken /stу̲kə(n)/ (stuukte, heeft gestuukt) plaster

stukgaan /stу̲kxan/ (ging stuk, is stukge-

gaan) break down, fail; break to pieces

het **stukgoed** /stу̲kxut/ (pl: -eren) general cargo; (load of) packed goods

het **stukje** /stу̲kjə/ (pl: -s) **1** small piece, little bit: ~ bij beetje bit by bit, inch by inch **2** short piece

het **stukloon** /stу̲klon/: tegen ~ werken work at piece rate, be paid by the piece

¹stuklopen /stу̲klopə(n)/ (liep stuk, is stukgelopen) go wrong, break down: een stukgelopen **huwelijk** a broken marriage

²stuklopen /stу̲klopə(n)/ (liep stuk, heeft stukgelopen) wear out

stukmaken /stу̲kmakə(n)/ (maakte stuk, heeft stukgemaakt) break (to pieces)

de **stukprijs** /stу̲kprɛis/ (pl: -prijzen) unit price

de **stulp** /stʏlp/ (pl: -en) **1** hovel, hut **2** bell-glass

de **stumper** /stʏmpər/ (pl: -s) wretch

de **stunt** /stʏnt/ (pl: -s) stunt, tour de force, feat

stuntelen /stʏntələ(n)/ (stuntelde, heeft gestunteld) bungle, flounder

stuntelig /stʏntələx/ (adj, adv) clumsy

stunten /stʏntə(n)/ (stuntte, heeft gestunt) stunt

de **stuntman** /stʏntmɑn/ (pl: -nen) stunt man

de **stuntprijs** /stʏntprɛis/ (pl: -prijzen) incredibly (or: record) low price; price breakers

stuntvliegen /stʏntfliɣə(n)/ stunt flying, aerobatics

het **stuntwerk** /stʏntwɛrk/ stuntwork

sturen /stу̲rə(n)/ (stuurde, heeft gestuurd) **1** steer; drive; guide **2** send; forward [goods]; dispatch; address: van school ~ expel (from school)

de **stut** /stʏt/ (pl: -ten) prop, stay, support

stutten /stʏtə(n)/ (stutte, heeft gestut) prop (up), support

het **stuur** /styr/ (pl: sturen) steering wheel; [car] wheel; [shipp] helm; rudder; controls; handlebars: **aan** het ~ zitten be at (or: behind) the wheel; de macht over het ~ verliezen lose control of one's car, bike)

de **stuurbekrachtiging** /stу̲rbəkrɑxtəɣɪŋ/ power steering

het **stuurboord** /stу̲rbort/ starboard

de **stuurgroep** /stу̲rɣrup/ (pl: -en) steering committee

de **stuurhut** /stу̲rhʏt/ (pl: -ten) pilothouse, wheel house

de **stuurinrichting** /stу̲rɪnrɪxtɪŋ/ steerage, steering-gear

de **stuurknuppel** /stу̲rknʏpəl/ (pl: -s) control stick (or: lever), (joy) stick

stuurloos /stу̲rlos/ (adj, adv) out of control, rudderless, adrift

de **stuurman** /stу̲rmɑn/ (pl: stuurlui) **1** mate: de beste stuurlui staan aan **wal** the best coaches are in the sands **2** [sport] helmsman; cox-(swain)

stuurs /styrs/ (adj, adv) surly, sullen

het **stuurslot** /stʏrslɔt/ (pl: -en) steering wheel lock

het **stuurwiel** /stʏrwil/ (pl: -en) (steering) wheel; control wheel; [shipp] helm

de **stuw** /styw/ (pl: -en) dam, barrage, flood-control dam

de **stuwdam** /stywdɑm/ (pl: -men) dam, barrage, flood-control dam

stuwen /stywə(n)/ (stuwde, heeft gestuwd) **1** drive, push, force, propel, impel **2** stow, pack, load

de **stuwkracht** /stywkrɑχt/ (pl: -en) force, drive; thrust

het **stuwmeer** /stywmer/ (pl: -meren) (storage) reservoir

de **stylist** /stilɪst/ (pl: -en) stylist

de **subcultuur** /sʏpkʏltyr/ (pl: subculturen) subculture; (the) underground

subiet /sybit/ (adv) immediately, at once

het **subject** /sʏpjɛkt/ (pl: -en) subject

subjectief /sʏpjɛktif/ (adj, adv) subjective, personal

de **subjectiviteit** /sʏpjɛktivitɛit/ subjectivity

subliem /syblim/ (adj, adv) sublime, fantastic, super

het **submenu** /sʏpməny/ (pl: -'s) submenu; cascading menu

de **subsidie** /sʏpsidi/ (pl: -s) subsidy; (financial) aid; grant; allowance: *een ~ geven voor* grant a subsidy for

subsidiëren /sʏpsidijerə(n)/ (subsidieerde, heeft gesubsidieerd) subsidize, grant (an amount)

de **substantie** /sʏpstɑnsi/ (pl: -s) substance, matter

substantieel /sʏpstɑn(t)ʃel/ (adj, adv) substantial

het **substantief** /sʏpstɑntif/ (pl: substantieven) noun

substitueren /sʏpstitywerə(n)/ (substitueerde, heeft gesubstitueerd) substitute

de **substitutie** /sʏpstity(t)si/ (pl: -s) substitution

de **¹substituut** /sʏpstityt/ (pl: substituten) substitute

het **²substituut** /sʏpstityt/ (pl: substituten) substitute

subtiel /sʏptil/ (adj, adv) subtle, sophisticated; delicate

de **subtop** /sʏptɔp/ (pl: -pen) second rank

het **subtotaal** /sʏptotal/ (pl: subtotalen) subtotal

subtropisch /sʏptropis/ (adj) subtropical

subversief /sʏpfɛrsif/ (adj) subversive

het **succes** /sʏksɛs/ (pl: -sen) success, luck: *een goedkoop ~je boeken* score a cheap success; *veel ~ toegewenst!* good luck!; *~ met je rijexamen!* good luck with your driving test!; *een groot ~ zijn* be a big success, be a hit

de **succesformule** /sʏksɛsfɔrmylə/ (pl: -s) formula for success

het **succesnummer** /sʏksɛsnʏmər/ (pl: -s) hit

de **successie** /sʏksɛsi/ (pl: -s) succession: *voor de vierde maal in ~* for the fourth time in succession (*or:* a row)

het **successierecht** /sʏksɛsirɛχt/ (pl: -en) inheritance tax

successievelijk /sʏksɛsivələk/ (adv) successively, one by one

succesvol /sʏksɛsfɔl/ (adj, adv) successful

Sudan /sudɑn/ (the) Sudan

de **¹Sudanees** /sudanes/ (pl: Sudanezen) Sudanese

²Sudanees /sudanes/ (adj) Sudanese

sudderen /sʏdərə(n)/ (sudderde, heeft gesudderd) simmer

de **sudoku** /sudoku/ sudoku

het/de **¹suède** /sywɛːdə/ suede

²suède /sywɛːdə/ (adj) suede

het **Suezkanaal** /sywɛskanal/ Suez Canal

suf /sʏf/ (adj, adv) drowsy, dozy; dopey; groggy

suffen /sʏfə(n)/ (sufte, heeft gesuft) nod, (day)dream

de **sufferd** /sʏfərt/ (pl: -s) dope, fathead

suggereren /sʏɣərerə(n)/ (suggereerde, heeft gesuggereerd) suggest, imply

de **suggestie** /sʏɣɛsti/ (pl: -s) suggestion; proposal: *een ~ doen* make a suggestion (*or:* proposal)

suggestief /sʏɣɛstif/ (adj, adv) suggestive, insinuating

suïcidaal /sywisidal/ (adj) suicidal

de **suïcide** /sywisidə/ (pl: -s, -n) suicide: *~ plegen* commit suicide

de **suiker** /sœykər/ (pl: -s) sugar: *~ doen in* put sugar in

de **suikerbiet** /sœykərbit/ (pl: -en) sugar beet

de **suikerfabriek** /sœykərfabrik/ (pl: -en) sugar refinery

het **Suikerfeest** /sœykərfest/ Sugar feast, Eid al-Fitr

het **suikerklontje** /sœykərklɔncə/ (pl: -s) lump of sugar, sugar cube

de **suikeroom** /sœykərom/ (pl: -s) rich uncle

de **suikerpatiënt** /sœykərpaʃɛnt/ (pl: -en) diabetic

de **suikerpot** /sœykərpɔt/ (pl: -ten) sugar bowl

het **suikerriet** /sœykərit/ sugar cane

de **suikerspin** /sœykərspɪn/ (pl: -nen) candy floss; [Am] cotton candy

de **suikertante** /sœykərtɑntə/ (pl: -s) rich aunt

suikervrij /sœykərvrɛi/ (adj) sugarless, diabetic; low-sugar

het **suikerzakje** /sœykərzɑkjə/ (pl: -s) sugar bag

de **suikerziekte** /sœykərziktə/ diabetes

de **suite** /switə/ (pl: -s) suite (of rooms)

suizen /sœyzə(n)/ (suisde, heeft gesuisd) rustle; sing; whisper

de **sukade** /sykadə/ candied peel

de **sukkel** /sʏkəl/ (pl: -s) dope, idiot, twerp

de **sukkelaar** /sʏkəlar/ (pl: -s) wretch, poor soul

(*or:* beggar)
sukkelen /sɣkələ(n)/ (sukkelde, heeft/is gesukkeld) be ailing, be sickly, suffer (from sth.): *hij sukkelt* **met** *zijn gezondheid* he is in bad health ‖ *in slaap* ~ doze off, drop off
het **sukkelgangetje** /sɣkəlɣaŋəcə/ jog(trot), shambling gait
de **sul** /sʏl/ (pl: -len) softy, sucker
het **sulfaat** /sʏlfa̱t/ (pl: sulfaten) sulphat; [Am] sulfate
het **sulfiet** /sʏlfi̱t/ sulphite; [Am] sulfite
de **sulky** /sɣlki/ (pl: -'s) sulky
  sullig /sɣləχ/ (adj, adv) **1** soft **2** dopey, silly
de **sultan** /sɣltɑn/ (pl: -s) sultan
  summier /sʏmi̱r/ (adj, adv) summary, brief
het **summum** /sɣmʏm/ the height (of)
  super /sypər/ (adj, adv) super, great, first class
de **superbenzine** /sypərbɛnzinə/ 4 star petrol; [Am] high octane gas(oline)
de **superette** /sypərɛ̱tə/ (pl: -s) [Belg] small self-service shop
de **supergeleiding** /sypərɣəlɛidɪŋ/ (pl: -en) superconductivity
de **superieur** /syperijø̱r/ (pl: -en) superior
de **superioriteit** /syperijoritɛ̱rt/ superiority
de **superlatief** /sypərlati̱f/ (pl: superlatieven) superlative (degree)
de **supermacht** /sypərmɑχt/ (pl: -en) superpower
de **supermarkt** /sypərmɑrkt/ (pl: -en) supermarket
de **supermens** /sypərmɛns/ superman, superwoman
  supersonisch /sypərso̱nis/ (adj) supersonic
de **supertanker** /sypərtɛ̱ŋkər/ (pl: -s) supertanker
de **supervisie** /sypərvi̱zi/ supervision
de **supervisor** /sypərvi̱zɔr/ (pl: -s) supervisor
het **supplement** /sʏpləmɛ̱nt/ (pl: -en) supplement
de **suppoost** /sypo̱st/ (pl: -en) attendant
de **supporter** /sypɔ̱:rtər/ (pl: -s) supporter
de **suprematie** /syprema(t)si̱/ supremacy
  surfen /sɣ:rfə(n)/ (surfte/surfde, heeft/is gesurft/gesurfd) **1** be surfing (*or:* surfboarding); windsurfing **2** [comp] surf
de **surfer** /sɣ:rfər/ (pl: -s) surfer; windsurfer
het **surfpak** /sɣrfpɑk/ (pl: -ken) surfer's wetsuit
de **surfplank** /sɣ:rfplɑŋk/ (pl: -en) surfboard; sailboard
  Surinaams /syrina̱ms/ (adj) Surinamese; Surinam
  Suriname /syrina̱mə/ Surinam
de **Surinamer** /syrina̱mər/ (pl: -s) Surinamese
de **surprise** /sʏrpri̱zə/ (pl: -s) surprise (gift)
het **surrealisme** /sʏrejalɪ̱smə/ surrealism
  surrealistisch /sʏrejalɪ̱stis/ (adj, adv) surrealist(ic)
het **surrogaat** /sʏroɣa̱t/ (pl: surrogaten) surrogate

de **surseance** /sʏrsejã̱sə/ (pl: -s): ~ *van* **betaling** moratorium, suspension of payment
de **surveillance** /sʏrvɛi̱ɡ̃sə/ surveillance; supervision; duty
de **surveillancewagen** /sʏrvɛi̱ɡ̃səwaɣə(n)/ (pl: -s) patrol car
de **surveillant** /sʏrvɛi̱ɡnt/ (pl: -en) supervisor, observer; invigilator
  surveilleren /sʏrvɛi̱erə(n)/ (surveilleerde, heeft gesurveilleerd) supervise; invigilate; (be on) patrol
de **survivaltocht** /sʏrvɑjvəltɔχt/ (pl: -en) survival trip
de **sushi** /su̱ʃi/ (pl: -'s) sushi
  sussen /sɣsə(n)/ (suste, heeft gesust) soothe; pacify [pers]; ease; hush up
de **SUV** *sports utility vehicle* SUV
  s.v.p. /ɛsfepe̱/ (abbrev) *s'il vous plaît* please
de **swastika** /swɑ̱stika/ (pl: -'s) swastika
de **Swaziër** /swa̱zijər/ (pl: -s) Swazi
  Swaziland /swa̱zilɑnt/ Swaziland
  Swazisch /swa̱zis/ (adj) Swazi
de **sweater** /swɛ̱tər/ (pl: -s) sweater, jersey
het **sweatshirt** /swɛ̱tʃʏ:rt/ (pl: -s) sweatshirt
  swingen /swɪ̱ŋə(n)/ (swingde, heeft geswingd) swing
  switchen /swɪ̱tʃə(n)/ (switchte, heeft/is geswitcht) switch; change (*or:* swop) over
de **syfilis** /si̱filɪs/ syphilis
de **syllabe** /sɪla̱bə/ (pl: -n) syllable
de **syllabus** /sɪ̱labʏs/ (pl: -sen, syllabi) syllabus
de **symbiose** /sɪmbijo̱zə/ symbiosis
de **symboliek** /sɪmboli̱k/ (pl: -en) symbolism
  symbolisch /sɪmbo̱lis/ (adj, adv) symbolic(al): *een* ~ *bedrag* a nominal amount
  symboliseren /sɪmbolize̱rə(n)/ (symboliseerde, heeft gesymboliseerd) symbolize, represent
het **symbool** /sɪmbo̱l/ (pl: symbolen) symbol
de **symfonie** /sɪmfoni̱/ (pl: -ën) symphony
het **symfonieorkest** /sɪmfoni̱ɔrkɛst/ (pl: -en) symphony orchestra
de **symmetrie** /sɪmetri̱/ symmetry
  symmetrisch /sɪmɛ̱tris/ (adj, adv) symmetrical
de **sympathie** /sɪmpati̱/ (pl: -ën) sympathy, feeling: *zijn* ~ **betuigen** express one's sympathy
  sympathiek /sɪmpati̱k/ (adj, adv) sympathetic, likable, congenial: *ik* **vind** *hem erg* ~ I like him very much; ~ **staan** *tegenover iem.* (*iets*) be sympathetic to(wards) s.o. (sth.)
  sympathiseren /sɪmpatize̱rə(n)/ (sympathiseerde, heeft gesympathiseerd) sympathize (with)
het **symposium** /sɪmpo̱zijʏm/ (pl: symposia, -s) symposium, conference
  symptomatisch /sɪmtoma̱tis/ (adj, adv) symptomatic
het **symptoom** /sɪmto̱m/ (pl: symptomen) symptom, sign: *een* ~ *zijn van* be symptomat-

ic (*or:* a symptom) of

de **symptoombestrijding** /sɪmtombəstrɛɪdɪŋ/ treatment of (the) symptoms

de **synagoge** /sinaɣoɣə/ (pl: -n) synagogue

de **synchronisatie** /sɪŋxroniza(t)si/ (pl: -s) synchronization

synchroon /sɪŋxron/ (adj, adv) synchronous, synchronic

syndicaal /sɪndikal/ (adj, adv) [Belg] (trade) union

het **syndicaat** /sɪndikat/ (pl: syndicaten) syndicate

het **syndroom** /sɪndrom/ (pl: syndromen) syndrome

de **synode** /sinodə/ (pl: -n, -s) synod

het ¹**synoniem** /sinonim/ (pl: -en) synonym

²**synoniem** /sinonim/ (adj) synonymous (with)

syntactisch /sɪntɑktis/ (adj, adv) syntactic(al)

de **syntaxis** /sɪntɑksɪs/ syntax

de **synthese** /sɪntezə/ (pl: -n, -s) synthesis

de **synthesizer** /sɪntəsɑjzər/ (pl: -s) synthesizer

synthetisch /sɪntetis/ (adj, adv) synthetic, man-made

Syrië /sirijə/ Syria

de **Syriër** /sirijər/ (pl: -s) Syrian

het ¹**Syrisch** /siris/ Syrian

²**Syrisch** /siris/ (adj) Syrian

het **systeem** /sistem/ (pl: systemen) system; method: *daar zit geen ~ in* there is no system (*or:* method) in it; [socc] *spelen volgens het 4-3-3-systeem* play in the 4-3-3 line-up

de **systeembeheerder** /sistembəherdər/ (pl: -s) system manager

de **systematiek** /sɪstematik/ system

systematisch /sistematis/ (adj, adv) systematic; methodical: *een ~ overzicht* a systematic survey; *~ te werk gaan* proceed systematically (*or:* methodically)

t

de **t** /te/ (pl: t's) t, T

taai /taj/ (adj, adv) tough, hardy: ~ *vlees* tough meat; *houd je* ~ **a)** take care (of yourself); **b)** [Am] hang in there; **c)** chin up

het/de **taaitaai** /tajtaj/ gingerbread

de **taak** /tak/ (pl: taken) **1** task, job, duty; responsibility; assignment: *een zware* ~ *op zich nemen* undertake an arduous task; *het is niet mijn* ~ *dat te doen* it is not my place to do that; *iem. een* ~ *opgeven (opleggen)* set s.o. a task; *tot* ~ *hebben* have as one's duty; *niet voor zijn* ~ *berekend zijn* be unequal to one's task **2** [educ] assignment

de **taakbalk** /tagbɑlk/ (pl: -en) taskbar

de **taakleerkracht** /taklerkrɑχt/ (pl: -en) remedial teacher

de **taakleraar** /taklerar/ (pl: -leraren) [Belg] remedial teacher

de **taakomschrijving** /takɔmsχrɛivɪŋ/ (pl: -en) job description

de **taakstraf** /takstrɑf/ (pl: -fen) community service

het **taakuur** /takyr/ (pl: -uren) non-teaching period, free period

de **taakverdeling** /takfərdelɪŋ/ division of tasks (or: labour)

de **taal** /tal/ (pl: talen) **1** language; speech; language skills: *vreemde talen* foreign languages; *zich een* ~ *eigen maken* master a language **2** language: *gore* ~ *uitslaan* use foul language || *de* ~ *van het lichaam* body language

de **taalbarrière** /talbɑr(i)jɛːrə/ (pl: -s) language barrier

de **taalbeheersing** /talbəhersɪŋ/ **1** mastery of a language **2** applied linguistics

de **taalcursus** /talkʏrsʏs/ (pl: -sen) language course

de **taalfout** /talfɑut/ (pl: -en) language error

het **taalgebied** /talɣəbit/ (pl: -en): *het Franse* ~ French-speaking regions

het **taalgebruik** /talɣəbrœyk/ (linguistic) usage, language

het **taalgevoel** /talɣəvul/ linguistic feeling

de **taalgrens** /talɣrɛns/ (pl: -grenzen) language boundary

de **taalkunde** /talkʏndə/ linguistics

taalkundig /talkʏndəχ/ (adj, adv) linguistic: ~ *ontleden* parse

het **taallab** /talɑp/ (pl: -s) [Belg] language laboratory

de **taalstrijd** /talstrɛit/ linguistic conflict

de **taalvaardigheid** /talvardəχhɛit/ language proficiency; [as school subject] (Dutch) language skills

de **taalwetenschap** /talwetə(n)sχɑp/ linguistics

de **taart** /tart/ (pl: -en) cake; pie; tart

het **taartje** /tarcə/ (pl: -s) a (piece of) cake; a tart (or: pie)

de **taartschep** /tartsχɛp/ (pl: -pen) cake-slice, cake-server

het **taartvorkje** /tartforkjə/ (pl: -s) cake-fork

de **tab** tab: *een* ~ *geven* insert a tab, press tab

de **tabak** /tabɑk/ tobacco

de **tabaksaccijns** /tabɑksɑksɛins/ (pl: -accijnzen) tobacco duty (excise, tax)

de **tabaksplant** /tabɑksplɑnt/ (pl: -en) tobacco plant

het **tabblad** /tɑblɑt/ (pl: -en) **1** file tab **2** tab

de **tabel** /tabɛl/ (pl: -len) table

het/de **tabernakel** /tabərnakəl/ (pl: -s) tabernacle

het/de **¹tablet** /tablɛt/ (pl: -ten) tablet; bar: *een ~je innemen tegen de hoofdpijn* take a pill for one's headache

de **²tablet** (pl: -s) tablet (computer)

de **tabloid** /tɛblɔjt/ tabloid

het **tabloidformaat** /tɛblɔjtfɔrmat/ tabloid size

het **¹taboe** /tabu/ (pl: -s) taboo: *een* ~ *doorbreken* break a taboo

²taboe /tabu/ (adj) taboo: *iets* ~ *verklaren* pronounce sth. taboo

het **taboeret** /taburɛt/ (pl: -ten) tabouret

de **taboesfeer** /tabusfer/ taboo: *iets uit de* ~ *halen* stop sth. being taboo, legitimize sth.

de **tachograaf** /taχoɣraf/ (pl: -grafen) **1** tachometer **2** tachograph

tachtig /tɑχtəχ/ (num) eighty: *mijn oma is* ~ *(jaar oud)* my grandmother is eighty (years old); *de jaren* ~ the eighties; *in de* ~ *zijn* be in one's eighties

tachtigjarig /tɑχtəχjarəχ/ (adj) **1** eighty-year-old: *een* ~*e* an eighty-year-old **2** eighty years'

tachtigste /tɑχtəχstə/ (num) eightieth

tackelen /tɛkələ(n)/ (tackelde, heeft getackeld) [sport] tackle

de **tackle** /tɛkəl/ (pl: -s) tackle

de **tact** /tɑkt/ tact: *iets met* ~ *regelen* use tact in dealing with sth.

de **tacticus** /tɑktikʏs/ (pl: tactici) tactician

de **tactiek** /tɑktik/ tactics; strategy: *dat is niet de juiste* ~ *om zoiets te regelen* that is not the way to go about such a thing; *van* ~ *veranderen* change (or: alter) one's tactics

tactisch /tɑktis/ (adj, adv) tactical; tactful: *iets* ~ *aanpakken* set about sth. tactically (or: shrewdly)

tactloos /tɑktlos/ (adj, adv) tactless: ~ *optreden* show no tact

tactvol /tɑktfɔl/ (adj, adv) tactful

de **Tadzjiek** /tadʒik/ (pl: -en) Tajik

het **¹Tadzjieks** /tadʒiks/ Tajiki

²Tadzjieks /tadʒiks/ (adj) Tajiki

Tadzjikistan /tɑdʒikistɑn/ Tadzhikistan

het **taekwondo** /tɑjkwɔndo/ taekwondo

de **tafel** /tɑfəl/ (pl: -s) table: *de ~s van vermenigvuldiging* the multiplication tables; *de ~ afruimen* (or: *dekken*) clear (or: lay) the table; *aan ~ gaan* sit down to dinner; *om de ~ gaan zitten* sit down at the table (and start talking); *iem. onder ~ drinken* drink s.o. under the table; *het ontbijt staat op ~* breakfast is on the table; *ter ~ komen* come up (for discussion); *van ~ gaan* leave the table

het **tafelkleed** /tɑfəlklet/ (pl: -kleden) tablecloth

het **tafellaken** /tɑfəlakə(n)/ (pl: -s) table-cloth

de **tafelpoot** /tɑfəlpot/ (pl: -poten) table-leg

het **tafeltennis** /tɑfəltɛnɪs/ table tennis

tafeltennissen /tɑfəltɛnɪsə(n)/ (tafeltenniste, heeft getafeltennist) play table tennis

de **tafeltennisser** /tɑfəltɛnɪsər/ (pl: -s) table-tennis player

het **tafelvoetbal** /tɑfəlvudbɑl/ table football

de **tafelwijn** /tɑfəlwɛin/ (pl: -en) table wine

het **tafelzilver** /tɑfəlzɪlvər/ silver cutlery, silverware

het **tafereel** /tɑfərel/ (pl: taferelen) tableau, scene

de **tag** /tɛːk/ (pl: -s) tag

taggen /tɛɡə(n)/ (tagde, heeft getagd) tag

de **tahoe** /tahu/ tofu

het **tai chi** /tɑjtʃi/ tai chi, t'ai chi (ch'uan)

de **taiga** /tɑjɡɑ/ (pl: -'s) taiga

de **taille** /tɑjə/ (pl: -s) waist: *een dunne ~ hebben* have a slender waist

Taiwan /tɑjwɑn/ Taiwan

de ¹**Taiwanees** /tɑjwanes/ (pl: Taiwanezen) Taiwanese

²**Taiwanees** /tɑjwanes/ (adj) Taiwanese

de **tak** /tɑk/ (pl: -ken) branch; fork; section: *een ~ van sport* a branch of sports; *de wandelende ~* the stick insect; [Am] the walking stick

het/de **takel** /takəl/ (pl: -s) tackle: *in de ~s hangen* be in the sling

takelen /takələ(n)/ (takelde, heeft getakeld) hoist: *een auto uit de sloot ~* hoist a car (up) out of the ditch

de **takelwagen** /takəlwaɣə(n)/ (pl: -s) breakdown lorry; [Am] tow truck

het **takenpakket** /takə(n)pɑkɛt/ job responsibilities (in a job)

het **takkewijf** /tɑkəwɛif/ (pl: -wijven) [vulg] bitch

de **taks** /tɑks/ (pl: -en) regular (or: usual) amount, share

het **tal** /tɑl/ number: *~ van voorbeelden* numbers of (or: numerous) examples

talen /talə(n)/ (taalde, heeft getaald) care (about/for)

de **talenknobbel** /talə(n)knɔbəl/ linguistic talent, gift (or: feel) for languages

het **talenpracticum** /talə(n)prɑktikʏm/ (pl: -practica) language lab(oratory)

het **talent** /talɛnt/ (pl: -en) **1** talent; gift; ability: *ze heeft ~* she is talented; *verborgen ~en* hidden talents **2** talent(ed person): *aanstormend ~* raging talent, up-and-coming talent

de **talentenjacht** /talɛntə(n)jɑχt/ (pl: -en) talent scouting

¹**talentvol** /talɛntfɔl/ (adj) talented, gifted

²**talentvol** /talɛntfɔl/ (adv) ably, with great talent

het **talenwonder** /talə(n)wɔndər/ (pl: -en) linguistic genius

de **talg** /tɑlχ/ **1** sebum **2** tallow

de **talisman** /talɪsmɑn/ (pl: -s) talisman

de **talk** /tɑlk/ **1** talc **2** tallow

het/de **talkpoeder** /tɑlkpudər/ talcum powder

de **talkshow** /tɔːkʃo/ (pl: -s) talk show

talloos /tɑlos/ (adj, adv) innumerable, countless

talmen /tɑlmə(n)/ (talmde, heeft getalmd) tarry, put off

talrijk /tɑlrɛik/ (adj) numerous, many

het **talud** /talʏt/ incline, slope; bank

tam /tɑm/ (adj) **1** tame, tamed; domestic: *een ~me vos* a tame fox; *~ maken* domesticate; tame **2** tame, gentle: *een ~ paard* a gentle (or: tame) horse

de **tamboer** /tɑmbur/ (pl: -s) drummer

de **tamboerijn** /tɑmburɛin/ (pl: -en) tambourine

tamelijk /tamələk/ (adv) fairly, rather: *~ veel bezoekers* quite a lot of visitors

de **Tamil** /tamil/ Tamil

de **tampon** /tɑmpɔn/ (pl: -s) tampon

de **tamtam** /tɑmtɑm/ (pl: -s) **1** tom-tom **2** fanfare: *~ maken over iets* make a fuss about (or: a big thing) of sth.

de **tand** /tɑnt/ (pl: -en) **1** tooth: *er breekt een ~ door* he/she is cutting a tooth (or: teething); *een ~ laten vullen* (or: *trekken*) have a tooth filled (or: extracted); *zijn ~en laten zien* show (or: bare) one's teeth; *zijn ~en poetsen* brush one's teeth; *iem. aan de ~ voelen* grill s.o.; *tot de ~en gewapend zijn* be armed to the teeth; [fig] *de ~ des tijds* the ravages of time **2** tooth; prong; cog: *de ~en van een kam* (or: *hark, zaag*) the teeth of a comb (or: rake, saw)

de **tandarts** /tɑndɑrts/ (pl: -en) dentist

de **tandartsassistente** /tɑndɑrtsɑsistɛntə/ (pl: -s) dentist's assistant

het **tandbederf** /tɑndbədɛrf/ caries, tooth decay, dental decay

tandeloos /tɑndəlos/ (adj) toothless

de **tandem** /tɛndəm/ (pl: -s) tandem

de **tandenborstel** /tɑndə(n)bɔrstəl/ (pl: -s) toothbrush

tandenknarsen /tɑndə(n)knɑrsə(n)/ (tandenknarste, heeft getandenknarst) gnash (or: grind) one's teeth

de **tandenstoker** /tɑndə(n)stokər/ (pl: -s) toothpick

het **tandglazuur** /tɑntχlazyr/ (dental) enamel

de **tandheelkunde** /tɑnthelky͟ndə/ dentistry

tandheelkundig /tɑnthelky͟ndəχ/ (adj) dental

de **tandpasta** /tɑntpɑsta/ (pl: -'s) toothpaste

de **tandplak** /tɑntplɑk/ (dental) plaque

het **tandrad** /tɑntrɑt/ (pl: -raderen) gear (wheel)

de **tandradbaan** /tɑntrɑdban/ (pl: -banen) rack railway, cog railway

het/de **tandsteen** /tɑntsten/ tartar

de **tandtechnicus** /tɑntɛχnikʏs/ (pl: -technici) dental technician

het **tandvlees** /tɑntfles/ gums

het **tandwiel** /tɑntwil/ (pl: -en) gearwheel, cogwheel; chainwheel; sprocket wheel

de **tandzijde** /tɑntsɛɪdə/ dental floss

tanen /tanə(n)/ (taande, is getaand) wane, fade

de **tang** /tɑŋ/ (pl: -en) **1** tongs; (pair of) pliers; (pair of) pincers **2** shrew, bitch

de **tangens** /tɑŋəns/ (pl: -en, tangenten) tangent

de **tango** /tɑŋgo/ (pl: -'s) tango

tanig /tanəχ/ (adj) tawny

de **tank** /tɛŋk/ (pl: -s) tank: *een volle ~ benzine* a full (or: whole) tank of petrol; [Am] a full (or: whole) tank of gas; *de ~ volgooien* fill up (the tank)

de **tankauto** /tɛŋkauto/ (pl: -'s) tank lorry; [Am] tank truck

tanken /tɛŋkə(n)/ (tankte, heeft getankt) fill up (with): *ik heb 25 liter getankt* I put 25 litres in (the tank); *ik tank meestal super* I usually take four star; [Am] I usually take super

de **tanker** /tɛŋkər/ (pl: -s) tanker

het **tankstation** /tɛŋksta(t)ʃɔn/ (pl: -s) filling station

de **tankwagen** /tɛŋkwaɣə(n)/ (pl: -s) tank lorry; [Am] tank truck

het/de **tannine** /taninə/ (pl: -s, -n) tannin

de **tantaluskwelling** /tɑntalʏskwɛlɪŋ/ (pl: -en) (sheer) torment

de **tante** /tɑntə/ (pl: -s) **1** aunt, auntie **2** woman, female: *een lastige ~, geen gemakkelijke ~* a fussy (or: difficult) lady/woman

Tanzania /tɑnzanija/ Tanzania

de **Tanzaniaan** /tɑnzanijan/ (pl: Tanzanianen) Tanzanian

Tanzaniaans /tɑnzanijans/ (adj) Tanzanian

de **tap** /tɑp/ (pl: -pen) **1** plug; bung; stopper; tap **2** tap; spigot: *bier uit de ~* beer on tap (or: draught) **3** bar: *achter de ~ staan* serve at the bar

de **tapas** /tɑpas/ (pl) tapas

de **tapasbar** (pl: -s) tapas bar

het **tapbier** /tɑbir/ draught beer; [Am] draft beer

tapdansen /tɛbdɑnsə(n)/ (tapdanste, heeft getapdanst) tap-dance

de **tapdanser** /tɛbdɑnsər/ (pl: -s) tap-dancer

de **tape** /tep/ (pl: -s) tape

de **tapenade** /tapənada/ tapenade

de **taperecorder** /teprikɔːrdər/ (pl: -s) tape recorder

het **tapijt** /tapɛit/ (pl: -en) carpet; [small] rug: *een vliegend ~* a magic carpet

de **tapijttegel** /tapɛiteɣəl/ (pl: -s) carpet tile (or: square)

de **tapir** /tapir/ (pl: -s) tapir

de **tapkast** /tɑpkɑst/ (pl: -en) bar

de **tapkraan** /tɑpkran/ (pl: tapkranen) tap

tappen /tɑpə(n)/ (tapte, heeft getapt) **1** tap, draw (off); serve: *hier wordt bier getapt* they sell beer here; *bier ~* tap beer **2** crack: *moppen ~* crack (or: tell) jokes

taps /tɑps/ (adj, adv) tapering, conical; conically

de **taptoe** /tɑptu/ (pl: -s) tattoo

de **tapvergunning** /tɑpfərɣʏnɪŋ/ (pl: -en) licence to sell spirits; [Am] liquor license

de **tarbot** /tɑrbɔt/ (pl: -ten) turbot

het **tarief** /tarif/ (pl: tarieven) tariff, rate; fare: *het gewone ~ betalen* pay the standard charge (or: rate); *vast ~* fixed (or: flat) rate; *tegen verlaagd ~* at a reduced tariff (or: rate); *het volle ~ berekenen* charge the full rate

de **tarra** /tɑra/ tare (weight)

de **tartaar** /tɑrtar/ steak tartare

de **Tartaar** /tɑrtar/ Tartar

tarten /tɑrtə(n)/ (tartte, heeft getart) defy, flout: *de dood ~* brave death; *het noodlot ~* tempt fate

de **tarwe** /tɑrwə/ wheat

de **tarwebloem** /tɑrwəblum/ wheat flour

het **tarwebrood** /tɑrwəbrot/ (pl: -broden) wheat bread

de **tas** /tɑs/ (pl: -sen) **1** bag; satchel; (brief)case; (hand)bag: *een plastic ~* a plastic bag **2** [Belg] cup

de **tasjesdief** /tɑʃəzdif/ (pl: -dieven) bag snatcher, purse snatcher

Tasmanië /tɑsmanijə/ Tasmania

de **tast** /tɑst/ **1** touch **2** groping, feeling: *hij greep op de ~ naar de lamp* he groped (or: felt) for the lamp; *iets op de ~ vinden* find sth. by touch

tastbaar /tɑstbar/ (adj, adv) tangible

tasten /tɑstə(n)/ (tastte, heeft getast) **1** grope **2** dip: *in zijn beurs ~* dip into one's purse

de **tastzin** /tɑ(st)sɪn/ touch; feeling

de **tatoeage** /tatuwaʒə/ (pl: -s) tattoo

tatoeëren /tatuwerə(n)/ (tatoeëerde, heeft getatoeëerd) tattoo: *zich laten ~* have o.s. tattooed

de **taugé** /tauge/ bean sprouts

de **tautologie** /tautoloɣi/ (pl: -ën) tautology, tautologism

t.a.v. (abbrev) **1** *ten aanzien van* with regard to **2** *ter attentie van* attn., (for the) attention (of)

de **taxateur** /taksat̯ør/ (pl: -s) appraiser; assessor

de **taxatie** /taksa(t)si/ (pl: -s) **1** assessment, appraisal: *een ~ verrichten* make an assessment **2** estimation **3** valuation

taxeren /taks̯erə(n)/ (taxeerde, heeft getaxeerd) evaluate, value (at): *de schade ~ assess* the damage

de **taxfreeshop** /tɛksfri̯ʃɔp/ (pl: -s) duty free (shop)

de **taxi** /taksi/ (pl: -'s) taxi, cab: *een ~ bestellen* call a cab

de **taxichauffeur** /taksiʃofør/ (pl: -s) taxi driver

taxiën /taksijə(n)/ (taxiede, heeft/is getaxied) taxi

de **taxistandplaats** /taksistantplats/ (pl: -en) taxi rank; [Am] taxi stand

de **taxus** /taksʏs/ (pl: -sen) yew (tree)

de **tbc** /tebese̯/ TB

de **T-bonesteak** /ti̯bonstek/ (pl: -s) T-bonesteak

de **tbs** /tebe̯ɛs/: *~ krijgen* be detained under a hospital order

t.b.v. (abbrev) **1** *ten behoeve van* on behalf of **2** *ten bate van* in favour of

¹**te** /tə/ (adv) too: *te laat* too late; late, overdue; *dat is een beetje te* that's a bit much; *te veel om op te noemen* too much (*or:* many) to mention

²**te** /tə/ (prep) **1** to: *dreigen te vertrekken* threaten to leave; *zij ligt te slapen* she is sleeping (*or:* asleep); *een dag om nooit te vergeten* a day never to be forgotten **2** in: *te Parijs aankomen* arrive in Paris **3** to, for: *te koop* for sale || *te voet* on foot

het **teakhout** /ti̯khaut/ teak

het **team** /tim/ (pl: -s) team: *een ~ samenstellen* put together a team; *samen een ~ vormen* team up together

de **teamgeest** /ti̯mɣest/ team spirit

het **teamverband** /ti̯mvərbant/ team: *in ~ werken* work in (*or:* as) a team

de **techneut** /tɛxnøt/ (pl: -en) boffin

de **technicus** /tɛxnikʏs/ (pl: technici) engineer, technician

de **techniek** /tɛxnik̯/ (pl: -en) **1** technique, skill: *over onvoldoende ~ beschikken* possess insufficient skills **2** engineering, technology

technisch /tɛxnis/ (adj) technical, technological, engineering: *de ~e dienst* the technical department; *een ~e storing* a technical hitch; *een ~e term* a technical term; *hij is niet erg ~* he is not very technical(ly-minded); *een Lagere* (*or:* *Middelbare) Technische School* a junior (*or:* senior) secondary technical school; *een Hogere Technische School* (*or:* *Technische Universiteit*) a college (*or:* university) of technology

de **technologie** /tɛxnoloɣi̯/ technology

technologisch /tɛxnolo̯ɣis/ (adj, adv) technological

de **teckel** /tɛk̯kəl/ (pl: -s) dachshund

de **teddybeer** /tɛ̯diber/ (pl: -beren) teddy bear

teder /te̯dər/ (adj, adv) tender

de **tederheid** /te̯dərhɛit/ tenderness

de **teef** /tef/ (pl: teven) bitch: *een loopse ~* a bitch on (*or:* in) heat

de **teek** /tek/ (pl: teken) tick

de **teelaarde** /te̯lardə/ humus, leaf mould

de **teelbal** /te̯lbal/ (pl: -len) testicle

de **teelt** /telt/ (pl: -en) **1** culture, cultivation, production: *de ~ van druiven* the cultivation of grapes **2** culture; crop; harvest: *eigen ~* home-grown

de **teen** /ten/ (pl: tenen) toe; [garlic] clove: *de grote* (*or:* *kleine*) ~ the big (*or:* little) toe; *op zijn tenen lopen* [fig] push o.s. to the limit; *van top tot ~* from head to foot; *gauw op zijn ~tjes getrapt zijn* be quick to take offence, be touchy

de **teenslipper** /te̯nslɪpər/ (pl: -s) flip-flop

het ¹**teer** /ter/ tar

²**teer** /ter/ (adj, adv) delicate: *een tere huid* delicate skin

de **teerling** /te̯rlɪŋ/ (pl: -en): [fig] *de ~ is geworpen* the die is cast

de **tegel** /te̯ɣəl/ (pl: -s) tile; paving stone: *~s zetten* tile

tegelijk /təɣəlɛi̯k/ (adv) at the same time (*or:* moment), also, as well: *~ met* at the same time as; *hij is dokter en ~ apotheker* he is a doctor as well as a pharmacist

tegelijkertijd /təɣəlɛikərtɛi̯t/ (adv) at the same time (*or:* moment), simultaneously

het **tegelpad** /te̯ɣəlpat/ tile, path; flagstone path

de **tegelvloer** /te̯ɣəlvlur/ (pl: -en) tiled floor

de **tegelwand** /te̯ɣəlwant/ (pl: -en) tiled wall

de **tegelzetter** /te̯ɣəlzɛtər/ (pl: -s) tiler

tegemoet /təɣəmu̯t/ (adv): *iem. ~ gaan* (*or:* *komen, lopen*) go to meet s.o.; go (*or:* come, walk) towards s.o.; *aan iemands wensen ~ komen* meet s.o.'s wishes; *iem. een heel eind ~ komen* meet s.o. (more than) half way; *iets ~ zien* await (*or:* face) sth., look forward to sth.

tegemoetkomen (kwam tegemoet, heeft/is tegemoetgekomen) meet, come towards: *aan bezwaren ~ meet* (*or:* give in to) objections

tegemoetkomend /təɣəmu̯tkomənt/ (adj) oncoming, approaching: *~ verkeer* oncoming traffic

de **tegemoetkoming** /təɣəmu̯tkomɪŋ/ (pl: -en) subsidy, contribution: *een ~ in* a contribution towards, a grant for

het ¹**tegen** /te̯ɣə(n)/ (pl: -s) con(tra), disadvantage: *alles heeft zijn voor en ~* everything has its advantages and disadvantages; *de voors en ~s op een rij zetten* weigh the pros and cons; *de argumenten voor en ~* the arguments for and against

²**tegen** /te̯ɣə(n)/ (adv) against: *zijn stem ~ uit-brengen* vote against (*or:* no); *ergens iets (op) ~ hebben* mind sth., have sth. against sth.; be opposed to sth., object to sth.; *iedereen was ~* everybody was against it; *hij was fel ~* he was dead set against it

³**tegen** /te̯ɣə(n)/ (prep) **1** against: *~ de stroom in* against the current **2** (up) to, against: *iets ~ iem. zeggen* say sth. to s.o. **3** against, to, with: *vriendelijk* (*or:* lomp) *~ iem. zijn* be friendly towards (*or:* rude to) s.o.; *daar kun je niets op ~ hebben* you cannot object to that; *zij heeft iets ~ hem* she has a grudge against him; *daar is toch niets op ~?* nothing wrong with that, is there?; *hij kan niet ~ vliegen* flying doesn't agree with him; *ergens niet ~ kunnen* not be able to stand (*or:* take) sth.; *er is niets ~ te doen* it can't be helped; *zich ~ brand verzekeren* take out fire insurance **4** against, counter to; in contravention of: *dat is ~ de wet* that is illegal (*or:* against the law) **5** towards, by, come: *~ elf uur* towards eleven (o'clock), just before eleven o'clock; *by* eleven; *een man van ~ de zestig* a man getting (*or:* going) on for sixty **6** (up) against **7** against, for, at: *~ elke prijs* whatever the cost; *een lening ~ 7,5 % rente* a loan at 7.5 % interest **8** to, (as) against: *tien ~ één* ten to one

tegenaan /te̯ɣə(n)a̯n/ (adv) (up) against: *er flink ~ gaan* go hard at it; *ergens (toevallig) ~ lopen* hit (*or:* chance) upon sth., run into sth.

de **tegenaanval** /te̯ɣə(n)a̯nval/ (pl: -len) counter-attack: *in de ~ gaan* counter-attack, strike (*or:* hit) back

het **tegenargument** /te̯ɣə(n)arɣymɛnt/ (pl: -en) counter-argument

het **tegenbericht** /te̯ɣə(n)bərɪxt/ (pl: -en) notice (*or:* message) to the contrary: *zonder ~ reken ik op uw komst* if I don't hear otherwise, I'll be expecting you

het **tegenbod** /te̯ɣə(n)bɔt/ counter-offer

het **tegendeel** /te̯ɣə(n)del/ opposite: *het bewijs van het ~ leveren* provide proof (*or:* evidence) to the contrary

het **tegendoelpunt** /te̯ɣə(n)dulpʏnt/ (pl: -en) goal against one('s team): *twee ~en krijgen* concede two goals; *een ~ maken* score in reply

tegendraads /te̯ɣə(n)dra̯ts/ (adj, adv) contrary, awkward

het **tegeneffect** /te̯ɣə(n)ɛfɛkt/ **1** counter-effect **2** backspin

tegengaan /te̯ɣə(n)ɣan/ (ging tegen, is tegengegaan) combat, fight

het **tegengas** /te̯ɣə(n)ɣas/: *~ geven* resist, put up a fight

tegengesteld /te̯ɣə(n)ɣəstɛlt/ (adj, adv) opposite: *in ~e richting* in the opposite direction

het **tegengestelde** /te̯ɣə(n)ɣəstɛldə/ opposite

het **tegengif** /te̯ɣə(n)ɣɪf/ antidote

de **tegenhanger** /te̯ɣə(n)haŋər/ (pl: -s) counterpart

tegenhouden /te̯ɣə(n)haudə(n)/ (hield tegen, heeft tegengehouden) **1** stop: *ik laat me door niemand ~* I won't be stopped by anyone **2** prevent, stop

tegenin /te̯ɣə(n)ɪn/ (adv) opposed to, against: *ergens ~ gaan* oppose sth.

de **tegenkandidaat** /te̯ɣə(n)kandidat/ (pl: -kandidaten) opponent, rival (candidate)

tegenkomen /te̯ɣə(n)komə(n)/ (kwam tegen, is tegengekomen) **1** meet: *iem. op straat ~* run (*or:* bump) into s.o. on the street **2** stumble across (*or:* upon); run across

het **tegenlicht** /te̯ɣə(n)lɪxt/ backlight(ing)

de **tegenligger** /te̯ɣə(n)lɪɣər/ (pl: -s) oncoming vehicle, approaching vehicle

de **tegenmaatregel** /te̯ɣəmatreɣəl/ (pl: -en) countermeasure

tegennatuurlijk /te̯ɣənaty̯rlək/ (adj, adv) unnatural, abnormal

het **tegenoffensief** /te̯ɣə(n)ɔfɛnsif/ (pl: -offensieven) counter-offensive

tegenop /te̯ɣə(n)ɔp/ (adv) up: *er ~ zien om … not look forward to …* ‖ *daar kan ik niet ~* that's too much for me; *niemand kon tegen hem op* nobody could match (*or:* beat) him

tegenover /te̯ɣə(n)o̯vər/ (prep) **1** across, facing, opposite: *~ elkaar zitten* sit opposite (*or:* facing) each other; *de huizen hier ~* the houses across from here (*or:* opposite) **2** against, as opposed to: *daar staat ~ dat je … on the other hand you …* **3** towards; before: *hoe sta je ~ die kwestie?* how do you feel about that matter? ‖ *staat er nog iets ~?* what's in it (for me)?

tegenovergesteld /te̯ɣə(n)o̯vərɣəstɛlt/ (adj) opposite; reverse

tegenoverstellen /te̯ɣə(n)o̯vərstɛlə(n)/ (stelde tegenover, heeft tegenovergesteld) provide (*or:* offer) (sth.) in exchange; set (sth.) against: *ergens een financiële vergoeding ~* offer compensation for sth.

de **tegenpartij** /te̯ɣə(n)partɛi/ (pl: -en) opposition; (the) other side: *een speler van de ~* a player from the opposing team

de **tegenpool** /te̯ɣə(n)pol/ (pl: -polen) opposite

de **tegenprestatie** /te̯ɣə(n)prɛsta(t)si/ (pl: -s) sth. done in return (*or:* exchange): *een ~ leveren* do sth. in return

de **tegenslag** /te̯ɣə(n)slɑx/ (pl: -en) setback, reverse: *~ hebben* (or: *ondervinden*) meet with (*or:* experience) adversity

tegenspartelen /te̯ɣə(n)spartələ(n)/ (spartelde tegen, heeft tegengesparteld) **1** struggle **2** grumble (at, over, about), protest

het **tegenspel** /te̯ɣə(n)spɛl/ (pl: -en) defence; response: *~ bieden* offer resistance

de **tegenspeler** /te̯ɣə(n)spelər/ (pl: -s) co-star

de **tegenspoed** /teɣə(n)sput/ adversity, misfortune

de **tegenspraak** /teɣə(n)sprak/ **1** objection, protest, argument: *geen ~ duldend* peremptory, pontifical **2** contradiction: *dat is in flagrante ~ met* that is in flagrant contradiction to (*or:* with)

tegenspreken /teɣə(n)sprekə(n)/ (sprak tegen, heeft tegengesproken) **1** object, protest, argue (with); answer back, talk back **2** deny, contradict: *dat gerucht is door niemand tegengesproken* nobody disputed (*or:* refuted) the rumour; *zichzelf ~* contradict o.s.

tegensputteren /teɣə(n)spʏtərə(n)/ (sputterde tegen, heeft tegengesputterd) protest, grumble

tegenstaan /teɣə(n)stan/ (stond tegen, heeft tegengestaan): *dat eten staat hem tegen* he can't stomach that food; *zijn manieren staan me tegen* I can't stand his manners

de **tegenstand** /teɣə(n)stɑnt/ opposition; resistance: *~ bieden (aan)* offer resistance (to)

de **tegenstander** /teɣə(n)stɑndər/ (pl: -s) opponent: *~ van iets zijn* be opposed to sth.

de **tegenstelling** /teɣə(n)stɛlɪŋ/ (pl: -en) contrast: *in ~ met* (or: *tot*) in contrast with (*or:* to), contrary to

tegenstemmen /teɣə(n)stɛmə(n)/ (stemde tegen, heeft tegengestemd) vote against

de **tegenstrever** /teɣə(n)strevər/ (pl: -s) opponent

tegenstribbelen /teɣə(n)strɪbələ(n)/ (stribbelde tegen, heeft tegengestribbeld) struggle (against), resist

tegenstrijdig /teɣə(n)strɛidəx/ (adj, adv) contradictory, conflicting

de **tegenstrijdigheid** /teɣə(n)strɛidəxhɛit/ (pl: -heden) contradiction, inconsistency

tegenvallen /teɣə(n)vɑlə(n)/ (viel tegen, is tegengevallen) disappoint: *dat valt mij van je tegen* you disappoint me

de **tegenvaller** /teɣə(n)vɑlər/ (pl: -s) disappointment: *een financiële ~* a financial setback

de **tegenvoeter** /teɣə(n)vutər/ (pl: -s) antipode

het **tegenvoorstel** /teɣə(n)vorstɛl/ (pl: -len) counter-proposal

tegenwerken /teɣə(n)wɛrkə(n)/ (werkte tegen, heeft tegengewerkt) work against (one, s.o.), cross, oppose

de **tegenwerking** /teɣə(n)wɛrkɪŋ/ (pl: -en) opposition

tegenwerpen /teɣə(n)wɛrpə(n)/ (wierp tegen, heeft tegengeworpen) object, argue

de **tegenwerping** /teɣə(n)wɛrpɪŋ/ (pl: -en) objection

het **tegenwicht** /teɣə(n)wɪxt/ (pl: -en) counterbalance

de **tegenwind** /teɣə(n)wɪnt/ (pl: -en) headwind; [fig] opposition: *wij hadden ~* we had the wind against us

¹**tegenwoordig** /teɣə(n)wordəx/ (adj) present, current: *de ~e tijd* the present (tense)

²**tegenwoordig** /teɣə(n)wordəx/ (adv) now(adays), these days: *de jeugd van ~* today's youth

de **tegenwoordigheid** /teɣə(n)wordəxhɛit/ presence: *~ van geest* presence of mind

de **tegenzet** /teɣə(n)zɛt/ (pl: -ten) countermove, response

de **tegenzin** /teɣə(n)zɪn/ dislike; [stronger] aversion: *hij doet alles met ~* he does everything reluctantly

tegenzitten /teɣə(n)zɪtə(n)/ (zat tegen, heeft tegengezeten) be against, go against

het **tegoed** /təɣut/ (pl: -en) balance

de **tegoedbon** /təɣudbɔn/ (pl: -nen) credit note

het **tehuis** /təhœys/ (pl: tehuizen) home; hostel; shelter: *~ voor ouden van dagen* old people's home

de **teil** /tɛil/ (pl: -en) (wash)tub; washing-up bowl

het/de **teint** /tɛːnt/ complexion

teisteren /tɛistərə(n)/ (teisterde, heeft geteisterd) ravage; sweep: *door de oorlog geteisterd* war-stricken

tekeergaan /təkerɣan/ (ging tekeer, is tekeergegaan) rant (and rave), storm, carry on (about sth.): *tegen iem. ~* rant and rave at s.o.

het **teken** /tekə(n)/ (pl: -s) **1** sign; indication: *het is een veeg ~* it promises no good; *een ~ van leven* a sign of life **2** sign; symbol; signal: *een ~ geven om te beginnen* (or: *vertrekken*) give a signal to start (*or:* leave); *het is een ~ aan de wand* the writing is on the wall **3** mark ‖ *het congres staat in het ~ van ...* the theme of the conference will be ...

de **tekenaar** /tekənar/ (pl: -s) artist; draughtsman

de **tekendoos** /tekə(n)dos/ (pl: -dozen) set (*or:* box) of drawing instruments

tekenen /tekənə(n)/ (tekende, heeft getekend) **1** draw; [fig] portray; depict: *figuurtjes ~* doodle; *met potlood* (or: *houtskool, krijt*) *~* draw in pencil (*or:* charcoal, crayon) **2** sign: *hij tekende voor vier jaar* he signed on for four years

tekenend /tekənənt/ (adj) characteristic (of), typical (of)

de **tekenfilm** /tekə(n)fɪlm/ (pl: -s) (animated) cartoon

de **tekening** /tekənɪŋ/ (pl: -en) **1** drawing; design; plan: *een ~ op schaal* a scale drawing **2** pattern; marking

de **tekenles** /tekənlɛs/ (pl: -sen) drawing lesson

het **tekenpapier** /tekəmpɑpir/ drawing-paper

het **tekenpotlood** /tekəmpɔtlot/ (pl: -potloden) drawing pencil de **tekentafel** /t<u>e</u>kə(n)tafəl/ (pl: -s) drawing table (*or:* stand)

het **tekort** /tək<u>o</u>rt/ (pl: -en) **1** deficit, shortfall **2** shortage, deficiency: *een ~ aan vitamines* a vitamin deficiency

tekortdoen (deed tekort, heeft tekortgedaan): *iem. ~* wrong s.o.; *de waarheid ~* not be quite truthful, squeeze the truth

tekortkomen /tək<u>o</u>rtkomə(n)/ (kwam tekort, is tekortgekomen) run short (of): *hij komt drie euro tekort* he's three euros short; *we komen handen tekort* we're short-handed (*or:* short of staff, short-staffed); *niets ~* lack for nothing, not go short; *zij kwam ogen en oren tekort* [roughly] her eyes were popping out of her head, [roughly] she didn't know where to start

de **tekortkoming** /tək<u>o</u>rtkomɪŋ/ (pl: -en) shortcoming, failing

tekortschieten /tək<u>o</u>rtsxitə(n)/ (schoot tekort, heeft tekortgeschoten) not come up to the mark, not be up to scratch: *woorden schieten tekort om ...* there are no words to (describe, express, say ...)

de **tekst** /tɛkst/ (pl: -en) **1** text; lines **2** words, lyrics

de **tekstballon** /t<u>ɛ</u>kstbalɔn/ (pl: -nen) balloon

het **tekstbestand** /t<u>ɛ</u>kstbəstɑnt/ (pl: -en) text file

de **tekstschrijver** /t<u>ɛ</u>kstsxrɛivər/ (pl: -s) scriptwriter; copywriter; songwriter

de **tekstverklaring** /t<u>ɛ</u>kstfərklarɪŋ/ (pl: -en) close reading

de **tekstverwerker** /t<u>ɛ</u>kstfərwɛrkər/ (pl: -s) word processor

de **tekstverwerking** /t<u>ɛ</u>kstfərwɛrkɪŋ/ word processing

de **tel** /tɛl/ **1** count: *ik ben de ~ kwijt* I've lost count **2** moment, second: *in twee ~len ben ik klaar* I'll be ready in two ticks (*or:* a jiffy) **3** account: *weinig in ~ zijn* not count for much ‖ *op zijn ~len passen* watch one's step, mind one's p's and q's; [Belg] *van geen ~ zijn* be of little (*or:* no) account

telbaar /t<u>ɛ</u>lbar/ (adj) countable: *~ naamwoord* count(able) noun

telebankieren /t<u>e</u>ləbɑŋkirə(n)/ (telebankierde, heeft getelebankierd) computerized banking

de **telecommunicatie** /t<u>e</u>ləkɔmynika(t)si/ telecommunication

de **telefax** /t<u>e</u>ləfɑks/ (pl: -en) **1** (tele)fax **2** (tele)fax (machine)

telefoneren /teləfon<u>e</u>rə(n)/ (telefoneerde, heeft getelefoneerd) telephone, phone, call: *hij zit te ~* he's on the phone; *met iem. ~* telephone s.o.

de **telefonie** /teləfon<u>i</u>/ **1** telephony **2** telephone system

telefonisch /teləf<u>o</u>nis/ (adj, adv) by telephone: *ben je ~ bereikbaar?* can you be

reached by phone?; *we hebben ~ contact met elkaar gehad* we have talked to each other on the phone

de **telefonist** /teləfon<u>ɪ</u>st/ (pl: -en) telephonist, (switchboard) operator

de **telefoon** /teləf<u>o</u>n/ (pl: -s) **1** telephone, phone: *draagbare (draadloze) ~* cellular (tele)phone, cellphone, mobile phone; *de ~ gaat* the phone is ringing; *blijft u even aan de ~?* would you hold on for a moment please?; *per ~* by telephone **2** receiver: *de ~ neerleggen* put down the receiver (*or:* phone); *de ~ opnemen* answer the phone **3** (telephone) call: *er is ~ voor u* there's a (phone) call for you

de **telefoonaansluiting** /teləf<u>o</u>nanslœytɪŋ/ (pl: -en) (telephone) connection

de **telefoonbeantwoorder** /teləf<u>o</u>mbəɑntwordər/ (pl: -s) answering machine

het **telefoonboek** /teləf<u>o</u>mbuk/ (pl: -en) (telephone) directory, phone book

de **telefooncel** /teləf<u>o</u>nsɛl/ (pl: -len) telephone box (*or:* booth)

de **telefooncentrale** /teləf<u>o</u>nsɛntralə/ (pl: -s) (telephone) exchange; switchboard

het **telefoongesprek** /teləf<u>o</u>ŋɡəsprɛk/ (pl: -ken) **1** telephone conversation **2** phone call

de **telefoongids** /teləf<u>o</u>ŋɡɪts/ (pl: -en) (telephone) directory, phone book

de **telefoonkaart** /teləf<u>o</u>ŋkart/ (pl: -en) phonecard

de **telefoonlijn** /teləf<u>o</u>nlɛin/ telephone line

het **telefoonnummer** /teləf<u>o</u>nymər/ (pl: -s) (phone) number: *geheim ~* ex-directory number

de **telefoonrekening** /teləf<u>o</u>nrekənɪŋ/ (pl: -en) telephone bill

de **telefoonseks** /teləf<u>o</u>nsɛks/ telephone sex

de **telefoontik** /teləf<u>o</u>ntɪk/ (telephone) unit

het **telefoontoestel** /teləf<u>o</u>ntustɛl/ (pl: -len) telephone

de **telegraaf** /teləɣr<u>a</u>f/ (pl: -grafen) telegraph

telegraferen /teləɣraf<u>e</u>rə(n)/ (telegrafeerde, heeft getelegrafeerd) telegraph: *hij telegrafeerde naar Parijs* he telegraphed (*or:* cabled) Paris

de **telegrafie** /teləɣraf<u>i</u>/ telegraphy

het **telegram** /teləɣr<u>a</u>m/ (pl: -men) telegram: *iem. een ~ sturen* telegraph (*or:* cable) s.o.; *per ~* by telegram (*or:* cable)

de **telegramstijl** /teləɣr<u>a</u>mstɛil/ telegram style

de **telelens** /t<u>e</u>lelɛns/ (pl: -lenzen) telephoto lens

de **telemarketeer** /t<u>e</u>ləma:rkəti:r/ (pl: -s) telemarketer

de **telemarketing** /t<u>e</u>ləma:rkətɪŋ/ telemarketing

telen /t<u>e</u>lə(n)/ (teelde, heeft geteeld) grow, cultivate

het **teleonthaal** /t<u>e</u>ləonthal/ [Belg] helpline

de **telepathie** /teləpati/ telepathy
telepathisch /teləpatis/ (adj, adv) telepathic

de **teler** /tɛlər/ (pl: -s) grower

de **telescoop** /teləskop/ (pl: -scopen) telescope

teleshoppen /teləʃɔpə(n)/ (teleshopte, heeft geteleshopt) teleshopping

de **teletekst** /tɛlətɛkst/ teletext

teleurstellen /teləʏrstɛlə(n)/ (stelde teleur, heeft teleurgesteld) disappoint, let down, be disappointing: *zich teleurgesteld **voelen*** feel disappointed; *stel **mij** niet teleur* don't let me down; *teleurgesteld zijn **over** iets (iem.)* be disappointed with sth. (in s.o.)

teleurstellend /teləʏrstɛlənt/ (adj) disappointing

de **teleurstelling** /teləʏrstɛlɪŋ/ (pl: -en) disappointment

televergaderen /teləvərɣadərə(n)/ teleconferencing

de **televisie** /teləvizi/ (pl: -s) television; television set: *(naar de)* ~ *kijken* watch television

de **televisiefilm** /teləvizifɪlm/ (pl: -s) TV film

de **televisiekijker** /teləvizikɛikər/ (pl: -s) (television) viewer

de **televisieomroep** /teləviziɔmrup/ (pl: -en) television company

het **televisieprogramma** /teləviziproɣrama/ television programme

de **televisieserie** /teləviziseri/ (pl: -s) television series

het **televisietoestel** /teləvizitustɛl/ (pl: -len) television set, TV set

de **televisie-uitzending** /teləviziœytsɛndɪŋ/ (pl: -en) television broadcast (*or:* programme)

de **televisiezender** /teləvizizɛndər/ (pl: -s) **1** television channel; [Am] television station **2** television transmitter (*or:* mast)

het **telewerken** /teləwɛrkə(n)/ teleworking

de **telex** /tɛlɛks/ telex: *per* ~ by telex

de **telg** /tɛlx/ (pl: -en) descendant

de **telganger** /tɛlɣaŋər/ (pl: -s) ambler

telkens /tɛlkəns/ (adv) **1** every time, in each case: ~ *en* ~ *weer*, ~ *maar weer* again and again, time and (time) again **2** repeatedly

¹**tellen** /tɛlə(n)/ (telde, heeft geteld) **1** count: *tot tien* ~ count (up) to ten **2** count, matter: *het enige dat telt **bij** hem* the only thing that matters to him

²**tellen** /tɛlə(n)/ (telde, heeft geteld) **1** count: *wel **(goed)** geteld zijn er dertig* there are thirty all told **2** number, have; consist of: *het huis telde 20 **kamers*** the house had 20 rooms

de **teller** /tɛlər/ (pl: -s) **1** [maths] numerator: *de* ~ *en de **noemer*** the numerator and the denominator **2** counter, meter

de **telling** /tɛlɪŋ/ (pl: -en) count(ing): *de* ~ *bijhouden* keep count (*or:* score)

het **telraam** /tɛlram/ (pl: telramen) abacus

het **telwoord** /tɛlwort/ (pl: -en) numeral

temeer /təmeːr/ (adv) all the more

temmen /tɛmə(n)/ (temde, heeft getemd) **1** tame, domesticate: *zijn **driften*** (*or:* ***hartstochten***) ~ control one's urges (*or:* passions) **2** tame; break

de **temmer** /tɛmər/ (pl: -s) tamer

de **tempel** /tɛmpəl/ (pl: -s) temple

het **temperament** /tɛmpəramɛnt/ (pl: -en) **1** temperament, disposition **2** spirit

de **temperatuur** /tɛmpəratyr/ (pl: temperaturen) temperature: *iemands* ~ *opnemen* take s.o.'s temperature; *op* ~ *moeten komen* have to warm up

de **temperatuurstijging** /tɛmpəratyrstɛiɣɪŋ/ rise (*or:* increase) in temperature

temperen /tɛmpərə(n)/ (temperde, heeft getemperd) temper, mitigate

het **tempo** /tɛmpo/ (pl: -'s) **1** tempo, pace: *het **jachtige** ~ van het moderne leven* the feverish pace of modern life; *het* ~ ***aangeven*** set the pace; *het* ~ ***opvoeren*** increase the pace **2** [mus] tempo, time **3** speed: ~ ***maken*** make good time

temporiseren /tɛmporizeːrə(n)/ (temporiseerde, heeft getemporiseerd) stall, play for time

ten /tɛn/ (prep) at, in, to, on: ~ *huize van* at the house/home of, at …'s place; ~ ***westen** van* (to the) west of; ~ ***tweede*** secondly, in the second place

de **tendens** /tɛndɛns/ (pl: -en) tendency, trend

tendentieus /tɛndɛnʃøs/ (adj, adv) tendentious, biased

tenderen /tɛndərə(n)/ (tenderde, heeft getenderd) tend (towards/to)

teneinde /tɛnɛində/ (conj) so that, in order to

tenenkrommend /tenə(n)krɔmənt/ (adj) cringe-making

de **teneur** /tənøːr/ tenor

de **tengel** /tɛŋəl/ (pl: -s) paw

tenger /tɛŋər/ (adj) slight, delicate: ~ ***gebouwd*** slightly built

tenietdoen /tənidun/ (deed teniet, heeft tenietgedaan) annul, nullify, undo

tenietgaan /tənitxan/ (ging teniet, is tenietgegaan) perish

de **tenlastelegging** /tɛnlɒstələɣɪŋ/ (pl: -en) charge, indictment

tenminste /tɛmɪnstə/ (adv) at least: *ik doe het liever niet,* ~ ***niet** dadelijk* I'd rather not, at least not right away; *dat is* ~ *iets* that is sth. at any rate

het **tennis** /tɛnɪs/ tennis

de **tennisarm** /tɛnɪsɑrm/ tennis elbow

de **tennisbaan** /tɛnɪzban/ (pl: -banen) tennis court: *verharde* ~ hard court

de **tennisbal** /tɛnɪzbɑl/ (pl: -len) tennis ball

de **tennishal** /tɛnɪshɑl/ (pl: -len) indoor tennis court(s)

het/de **tennisracket** /tɛnɪsrɛkət/ (pl: -s) tennis

racket
tennissen /tɛnɪsə(n)/ (tenniste, heeft getennist) play tennis
de **tennisser** /tɛnɪsər/ (pl: -s) tennis player
de **tenor** /tənor/ (pl: -en) tenor
tenslotte /tɛnslɔtə/ (adv) after all: ~ *is zij nog maar een kind* after all she's only a child
de **tent** /tɛnt/ (pl: -en) **1** tent; stand: *een ~ opslaan* (or: *opzetten, afbreken*) pitch (*or:* put up, take down) a tent; *iem. uit zijn ~ lokken* draw s.o. out **2** place, joint ‖ *ze braken de ~ bijna af* you could hardly keep them in their seats
de **tentakel** /tɛntakəl/ (pl: -s) tentacle
het **tentamen** /tɛntamə(n)/ (pl: -s) exam: ~ *doen* take an exam
het **tentenkamp** /tɛntə(n)kɑmp/ (pl: -en) (en)camp(ment), campsite
de **tentharing** /tɛntharɪŋ/ (pl: -en) tent peg
tentoonspreiden /tɛntonsprɛidə(n)/ (spreidde tentoon, heeft tentoongespreid) display; show (off)
tentoonstellen /tɛntonstɛlə(n)/ (stelde tentoon, heeft tentoongesteld) exhibit, display: *tentoongestelde voorwerpen* exhibits, articles on display
de **tentoonstelling** /tɛntonstɛlɪŋ/ (pl: -en) exhibition, show, display
de **tentstok** /tɛntstɔk/ (pl: -ken) tent pole
het **tentzeil** /tɛntsɛil/ (pl: -en) canvas
het/de **tenue** /təny/ (pl: -s) dress, uniform
de **tenuitvoerlegging** /tənœytfurlɛɣɪŋ/ (pl: -en) execution
tenzij /tɛnzɛi/ (conj) unless, except(ing)
de **tepel** /tepəl/ (pl: -s) nipple; teat
ter /tɛr/ (prep) at, to, in, on: ~ *plaatse* on the spot, locally
de **teraardebestelling** /tɛrardəbəstɛlɪŋ/ (pl: -en) [form] burial, funeral
terdege /tɛrdeɣə/ (adv) thoroughly, properly
¹**terecht** /tərɛxt/ (adj) correct, appropriate
²**terecht** /tərɛxt/ (adv) **1** found (again): *haar horloge is* ~ her watch has been found **2** rightly: *hij is voor zijn examen gezakt, en* ~ he failed his examination and rightly so
terechtbrengen /tərɛxtbrɛŋə(n)/ (bracht terecht, heeft terechtgebracht): *niet veel ~ van iets* not make much of sth., not have much success with sth.
terechtkomen /tərɛxtkomə(n)/ (kwam terecht, is terechtgekomen) **1** fall, land, end up (in, on, at): *lelijk* ~ have (*or:* take) a nasty fall **2** turn out all right: *wat is er van hem terechtgekomen?* what has happened to him?
terechtkunnen /tərɛxtkʏnə(n)/ (kon terecht, heeft terechtgekund) **1** go into, enter **2** (get) help (from): *daarmee kun je overal terecht* that will do (*or:* be acceptable) everywhere
terechtstaan /tərɛxtstan/ (stond terecht,

heeft terechtgestaan) stand trial, be tried: ~ *wegens diefstal* be tried for theft
terechtstellen /tərɛxtstɛlə(n)/ (stelde terecht, heeft terechtgesteld) execute, put to death
de **terechtstelling** /tərɛxtstɛlɪŋ/ (pl: -en) execution
terechtwijzen /tərɛxtwɛizə(n)/ (wees terecht, heeft terechtgewezen) reprimand, reprove, put s.o. in one's place
de **terechtwijzing** /tərɛxtwɛizɪŋ/ (pl: -en) reprimand
teren /terə(n)/ (teerde, heeft geteerd) live (on, off)
tergen /tɛrɣə(n)/ (tergde, heeft getergd) provoke (deliberately), badger, bait: *iem. zo ~ dat hij iets doet* provoke s.o. into (doing) sth.
tergend /tɛrɣənt/ (adj, adv) provocative: ~ *langzaam* exasperatingly slow
de **tering** /terɪŋ/ (pl: -en) consumption, tuberculosis
terloops /tɛrlops/ (adj, adv) casual, passing
de **term** /tɛrm/ (pl: -en) term, expression: *in bedekte ~en iets meedelen* speak about sth. in guarded terms
de **termiet** /tɛrmit/ (pl: -en) termite, white ant
de **termijn** /tɛrmɛin/ (pl: -en) **1** term, period: *op korte* (or: *op lange*) ~ in the short (*or:* long) term; *op kortst mogelijke* ~ as soon as possible **2** deadline: *een ~ vaststellen* set a deadline **3** instalment
de **termijnmarkt** /tɛrmɛinmɑrkt/ (pl: -en) forward market, futures market: *de ~ voor goud* the forward market in gold, gold futures
terminaal /tɛrminal/ (adj) terminal, final: *terminale zorg* terminal care
de **terminal** /tʏrminəl/ (pl: -s) terminal
de **terminologie** /tɛrminoloɣi/ (pl: -ën) terminology, jargon
de **terminus** /tɛrminʏs/ (pl: termini) [Belg] terminus
ternauwernood /tɛrnɑuwərnot/ (adv) hardly, scarcely, barely
terneergeslagen /tɛrneərɣəslaɣə(n)/ (adj) depressed, downcast: *een ~ indruk maken* seem down
de **terp** /tɛrp/ (pl: -en) mound, terp
de **terpentijn** /tɛrpəntɛin/ turpentine
het ¹**terracotta** /tɛrakɔta/ terra cotta
²**terracotta** /tɛrakɔta/ (adj) terracotta
het **terrarium** /tɛrarijʏm/ (pl: -s, terraria) terrarium
het **terras** /tɛrɑs/ (pl: -sen) **1** pavement café; [Am] sidewalk café; outdoor café: *op een ~je zitten* sit in an outdoor café **2** terrace, patio **3** terrace, sunroof
het **terrein** /tɛrɛin/ (pl: -en) **1** ground(s), territory; terrain: *de voetbalclub speelde op eigen* ~ the football team played on home turf; *eigen* ~ (or: *privéterrein*) private property; *het*

~ *verkennen* a) [literally] explore the area; b) [fig] scout (out) the territory; ~ *winnen* gain ground 2 [fig] field, ground: *zich op **bekend*** ~ *bevinden* be on familiar ground; *zich op **gevaarlijk** ~ begeven* be on slippery ground, be on thin ice; *onderzoek doen **op** een bepaald* ~ do research in a particular area (*or*: field)

de **terreinwagen** /tərɛɪnwaɣə(n)/ (pl: -s) all-terrain vehicle

de **terreinwinst** /tərɛɪnwɪnst/ territorial gain: ~ ***boeken*** gain ground

de **terreur** /tɛrør/ terror

het **terreuralarm** terror alert, terror alarm

de **terriër** /tɛrijər/ (pl: -s) terrier

de **terrine** /tɛrinə/ (pl: -s) tureen

territoriaal /tɛritor(i)jal/ (adj) territorial

het **territorium** /tɛritor(i)jʏm/ (pl: territoria) territory

terroriseren /tɛrorizerə(n)/ (terroriseerde, heeft geterroriseerd) terrorize

het **terrorisme** /tɛrorɪsmə/ terrorism

de **terrorist** /tɛrorɪst/ (pl: -en) terrorist

terroristisch /tɛrorɪstis/ (adj, adv) terrorist(ic): *een ~e **aanslag*** a terrorist attack

terstond /tɛrstɔnt/ (adv) 1 at once, immediately 2 presently, shortly

tertiair /tɛr(t)ʃɛːr/ (adj) tertiary: ~ *onderwijs* higher education

de **terts** /tɛrts/ (pl: -en) [mus] tierce, third

terug /tərʏχ/ (adv) 1 back: *hij wil zijn **fiets** ~* he wants his bike back; *ik **ben** zo* ~ I'll be back in a minute; *heb je ~ van 20 euro?* do you have change for 20 euros?; *wij **moeten** ~ we* have to go back; *heen en ~* back and forth; *~ naar af* back to square one; *~ **uit** het buitenland* back from abroad; *~ **van** weg geweest* a) be back again; b) [fig] have made a comeback 2 [Belg] again ǁ *daar **heeft** hij niet van ~* that's too much for him

terugbellen /tərʏɣbɛlə(n)/ (belde terug, heeft teruggebeld) call back

terugbetalen /tərʏɣbətalə(n)/ (betaalde terug, heeft terugbetaald) pay back, refund

de **terugbetaling** /tərʏɣbətalɪŋ/ (pl: -en) repayment, reimbursement

de **terugblik** /tərʏɣblɪk/ review, retrospect(ive)

terugblikken /tərʏɣblɪkə(n)/ (blikte terug, heeft teruggeblikt) look back

terugbrengen /tərʏɣbrɛŋə(n)/ (bracht terug, heeft teruggebracht) 1 bring back, take back, return: *een geleend **boek** ~* return a borrowed book 2 restore: *iets **in** de oorspronkelijke staat* ~ restore sth. to its original state 3 reduce, cut back: *de **werkloosheid** (or: **inflatie***) ~ reduce unemployment (*or*: inflation)

terugdeinzen /tərʏɣdɛinzə(n)/ (deinsde terug, is teruggedeinsd) shrink, recoil: *voor niets* ~ stop at nothing

terugdenken /tərʏɣdɛŋkə(n)/ (dacht terug, heeft teruggedacht) think back to: *met ple-*

*zier **aan** iets ~* remember sth. with pleasure

terugdoen /tərʏɣdun/ (deed terug, heeft teruggedaan) 1 put back 2 return, do in return: *doe hem de **groeten** terug* return the compliments to him

terugdraaien /tərʏɣdrajə(n)/ (draaide terug, heeft teruggedraaid) reverse, change, undo: *een **maatregel** ~* reverse a measure

terugfluiten /tərʏɣflœytə(n)/ (floot terug, heeft teruggefloten) call back

teruggaan /tərʏɣan/ (ging terug, is teruggegaan) go back, return: *~ **in** de geschiedenis* (*or*: *tijd*) go back in history (*or*: time); *naar huis* ~ go back home

de **teruggang** /tərʏɣɑŋ/ decline, decrease: *economische* ~ economic recession

de **teruggave** /tərʏɣavə/ restoration, return, restitution: *~ van de **belasting*** income tax refund

teruggetrokken /tərʏɣətrɔkə(n)/ (adj) retired, withdrawn: *een ~ **leven** leiden* lead a retired (*or*: secluded) life

teruggeven /tərʏɣevə(n)/ (gaf terug, heeft teruggegeven) 1 give back, return: *ik zal je het boek morgen* ~ I'll return the book (to you) tomorrow 2 give (back), refund: *hij kon niet ~ **van** vijftig euro* he couldn't change a fifty-euro note

terughoudend /tərʏɣhɑudənt/ (adj) reserved, reticent

de **terugkeer** /tərʏɣker/ return, comeback, recurrence

terugkeren /tərʏɣkerə(n)/ (keerde terug, is teruggekeerd) return, come back, go back; recur: *naar huis* ~ return home; *een **jaarlijks** ~d festival* a recurring yearly festival

terugkijken /tərʏɣkɛikə(n)/ (keek terug, heeft teruggekeken) look back (on, upon)

terugkomen /tərʏɣkomə(n)/ (kwam terug, is teruggekomen) return, come back; recur: *ze **kan** elk moment ~* she may be back (at) any moment; *weer ~ **bij** het begin* come full circle; *daar kom ik nog **op** terug* I'll come back to that; *op een beslissing ~* reconsider a decision; *hij is er **van** teruggekomen* he changed his mind

de **terugkomst** /tərʏɣkɔmst/ return: *bij zijn ~* on his return

terugkoppelen /tərʏɣkɔpələ(n)/ (koppelde terug, heeft teruggekoppeld) give feedback (information) (to); submit (to)

terugkrabbelen /tərʏɣkrɑbələ(n)/ (krabbelde terug, is teruggekrabbeld) back out; go back on; cop out, opt out

terugkrijgen /tərʏɣkrɛiɣə(n)/ (kreeg terug, heeft teruggekregen) 1 get back, recover, regain: *zijn **goederen** ~* get one's goods (*or*: things) back 2 get in return: *te weinig (**wissel**)geld ~* be short-changed

terugleggen /tərʏɣlɛɣə(n)/ (legde terug, heeft teruggelegd) put back

de **terugloop** /tərᵪlop/ fall(ing-off), decrease
teruglopen /tərᵪlopə(n)/ (liep terug, is te-
ruggelopen) **1** walk back; flow back **2** drop,
fall, decline: *de dollar liep nog verder terug* the
dollar suffered a further setback
terugnemen /tərᵪnemə(n)/ (nam terug,
heeft teruggenomen) take back; retract:
[fig] *gas* ~ ease up (*or:* off), take things easy;
zijn woorden ~ retract (*or:* take back) one's
words

de **terugreis** /tərᵪrɛis/ (pl: -reizen) return trip
terugrijden /tərᵪrɛidə(n)/ (reed terug,
heeft/is teruggereden) drive back; ride back
terugroepen /tərᵪrupə(n)/ (riep terug,
heeft teruggeroepen) call back, recall; call
off: *de acteurs werden tot driemaal toe teruggeroepen* the actors had three curtain calls
terugschakelen /tərᵪsχakələ(n)/ (schakelde terug, heeft/is teruggeschakeld)
change down, shift down
terugschrijven /tərᵪsχrɛivə(n)/ (schreef
terug, heeft teruggeschreven) write back
terugschrikken /tərᵪsχrɪkə(n)/ (schrok
terug, is teruggeschrikt) **1** recoil; shy **2** [fig]
recoil, baulk: ~ *van de hoge bouwkosten* baulk
at the high construction costs; *nergens voor* ~
be afraid of nothing
¹**terugslaan** /tərᵪslan/ (sloeg terug, heeft
teruggeslagen) **1** hit back **2** backfire: *de motor slaat terug* the engine backfires **3** blow
back, move back
²**terugslaan** /tərᵪslan/ (sloeg terug, heeft
teruggeslagen) hit back, strike back

de **terugslag** /tərᵪslɑχ/ **1** recoil(ing); backfire:
het geweer had een ontzettende ~ the gun had
a terrible kick (*or:* recoil) **2** reaction, backlash: *een* ~ *krijgen* be set back, experience a
backlash
terugspelen /tərᵪspelə(n)/ (speelde terug, heeft teruggespeeld) play back
terugspoelen /tərᵪspulə(n)/ (spoelde terug, heeft teruggespoeld) rewind
terugsturen /tərᵪstyrə(n)/ (stuurde terug,
heeft teruggestuurd) send back, return

de **terugtocht** /tərᵪtɔχt/ (pl: -en) journey
back, journey home

de **terugtraprem** /tərᵪtraprɛm/ (pl: -men)
hub brake, back-pedalling brake
terugtreden /tərᵪtredə(n)/ (trad terug, is
teruggetreden) withdraw (from)
¹**terugtrekken** /tərᵪtrɛkə(n)/ (trok terug,
heeft teruggetrokken) **1** withdraw: *troepen*
~ withdraw (*or:* pull back) troops **2** draw
back, pull back
zich ²**terugtrekken** /tərᵪtrɛkə(n)/ (trok zich terug, heeft zich teruggetrokken) **1** retire, retreat: *zich* ~ *op het platteland* retreat to the
country **2** withdraw (from): *zich voor een
examen* ~ withdraw from an exam

de **terugval** /tərᵪfɑl/ reversion, relapse; [com]
spin

terugvallen /tərᵪfɑlə(n)/ (viel terug, is te-
ruggevallen) (+ op) fall back on
terugverlangen /tərᵪfərlɑŋə(n)/ (verlangde terug, heeft terugverlangd) recall
longingly: *naar huis* ~ long to go back home
terugvinden /tərᵪfɪndə(n)/ (vond terug,
heeft teruggevonden) find again, recover
terugvragen /tərᵪfraɣə(n)/ (vroeg terug,
heeft teruggevraagd) ask back

de **terugwedstrijd** /tərᵪwɛtstrɛit/ (pl: -en)
[Belg] return match

de **terugweg** /tərᵪwɛχ/ (pl: -en) way back: *op
de* ~ *gaan we bij oma langs* on the way back
we shall drop in on grandma
terugwerken /tərᵪwɛrkə(n)/ (werkte terug, heeft teruggewerkt) be retrospective,
be retroactive: *met* ~*de kracht* retrospective-
ly
terugzetten /tərᵪsɛtə(n)/ (zette terug,
heeft teruggezet) put back, set back, replace: *de wijzers* ~ put (*or:* move) back the
hands; *de teller* ~ *op nul* reset the counter (to
zero)
terugzien /tərᵪsin/ (zag terug, heeft te-
ruggezien) see again
terwijl /tɛrwɛil/ (conj) **1** while: ~ *hij omkeek,
ontsnapte de dief* while he looked round, the
thief escaped **2** whereas, while: *hij werkt
over,* ~ *zijn vrouw vandaag jarig is* he is working
overtime even though his wife has her birthday today
terzijde /tɛrzɛidə/ (adv) aside: ~ *leggen* put
aside; *iem.* ~ *staan* assist s.o., stand by s.o.

de **test** /tɛst/ (pl: -s) test: *een schriftelijke* ~ a
written test

het **testament** /tɛstamɛnt/ (pl: -en) **1** will: *een* ~
maken (or: *herroepen*) make (*or:* revoke) a
will **2** Testament
testamentair /tɛstamɛntɛːr/ (adj, adv) tes-
tamentary

het **testbeeld** /tɛstbelt/ (pl: -en) test card

de **testcase** /tɛstkes/ (pl: -s) test (case), experiment
testen /tɛstə(n)/ (testte, heeft getest) test

de **testikel** /tɛstikəl/ (pl: -s) testicle

het **testosteron** /tɛstɔsterɔn/ testosterone

de **testpiloot** /tɛstpilot/ (pl: -piloten) test pilot

de **tetanus** /tetanʏs/ tetanus

de **teug** /tøχ/ (pl: -en) draught; [Am] draft; pull:
met volle ~*en van iets genieten* enjoy sth.
thoroughly (*or:* to the full)

de **teugel** /tøɣəl/ (pl: -s) rein: *de* ~*s in handen
nemen* take (up) the reins, assume control
teut /tøt/ (adj) [inform] **1** dawdler **2** bore
teuten /tøtə(n)/ (teutte, heeft geteut) [in-
form] **1** dilly-dally, dawdle **2** drivel, chatter

het **teveel** /təvel/ surplus
tevens /tevəns/ (adv) **1** also, besides, as well
as **2** at the same time: *hij was voorzitter en* ~
penningmeester he was chairman and treasurer at the same time

tevergeefs /təvərɣe̯efs/ (adj, adv) in vain, vainly

tevoorschijn /təvo̯rsχɛin/ (adv): *tevoorschijn komen* appear; come out; *tevoorschijn brengen* produce; *zijn zakdoek tevoorschijn halen* take out one's handkerchief

tevoren /təvo̯rə(n)/ (adv) before, previously: *van* ~ before(hand), in advance

tevreden /təvre̯də(n)/ (adj) satisfied, contented

de **tevredenheid** /təvre̯dənhɛit/ satisfaction: *werk naar* ~ *verrichten* work satisfactorily; *tot volle* ~ *van* to the complete satisfaction of

tevredenstellen /təvre̯də(n)stɛlə(n)/ (stelde tevreden, heeft tevredengesteld) satisfy

tevree (adj) satisfied, happy

de **tewaterlating** /təwa̯tərlatɪŋ/ (pl: -en) launching

teweegbrengen /təwe̯ɣbrɛŋə(n)/ (bracht teweeg, heeft teweeggebracht) bring about; bring on; produce

tewerkstellen /təwɛrkstɛlə(n)/ (stelde tewerk, heeft tewerkgesteld) employ; hire

het/de **textiel** /tɛkstil/ textile

de **textielindustrie** /tɛkstilɪndʏstri/ textile industry

tezamen /təza̯mə(n)/ (adv) together

de **tgv** High Speed Train

t.g.v. (abbrev) **1** *ten gevolge van* as a result of, resulting from **2** *ter gelegenheid van* on the occasion of

het **Thai** /tɑj/ Thai

Thailand /tɑjlɑnt/ Thailand

de **Thailander** /tɑjlɑndər/ (pl: -s) Thai

Thais /tɑjs/ (adj) Thai

thans /tɑns/ (adv) at present, now

het **theater** /teja̯tər/ (pl: -s) **1** theatre; cinema; [Am] movie theater **2** dramatic arts, performing arts, (the) stage

de **theatervoorstelling** /teja̯tərvorstɛlɪŋ/ (pl: -en) theatre performance

theatraal /tejatra̯l/ (adj, adv) theatrical

de **thee** /te/ tea: *een kopje* ~ a cup of tea; *slappe* ~ weak tea; ~ *drinken* drink (*or:* have) tea; ~ *inschenken* pour out tea; ~ *zetten* make tea

de **theedoek** /te̯duk/ (pl: -en) tea towel

theedrinken /te̯drɪŋkə(n)/ (dronk thee, heeft theegedronken) have tea

het **theelepeltje** /te̯lepəlcə/ (pl: -s) teaspoon; teaspoonful

het **theelichtje** /te̯lɪxjə/ (pl: -s) hot plate (for tea); tea-warmer

de **Theems** /tems/ Thames

de **theemuts** /te̯mʏts/ (pl: -en) (tea-)cosy

de **theepauze** /te̯pauzə/ (pl: -s) tea break

de **theepot** /te̯pɔt/ (pl: -ten) teapot

het **theeservies** /te̯sɛrvis/ (pl: -serviezen) tea service

het **theewater** /te̯watər/ tea-water: ~ *opzetten* put the kettle on (for tea)

het **theezakje** /te̯zɑkjə/ (pl: -s) tea bag

het **theezeefje** /te̯zefjə/ (pl: -s) tea strainer

het **thema** /te̯ma/ (pl: -'s) theme, subject (matter): *een* ~ *aansnijden* broach a subject

het **themapark** /te̯mapɑrk/ (pl: -en) theme park

de **thematiek** /tematik/ theme(s)

thematisch /tema̯tis/ (adj, adv) thematic

de **theologie** /tejolo̯ɣi/ theology, divinity

theologisch /tejolo̯ɣis/ (adj, adv) theological

de **theoloog** /tejolo̯x/ (pl: -logen) theologian

de **theoreticus** /tejore̯tikʏs/ (pl: theoretici) theoretician, theorist

¹**theoretisch** /tejore̯tis/ (adj) theoretic(al)

²**theoretisch** /tejore̯tis/ (adv) theoretically, in theory

de **theorie** /tejori/ (pl: -ën) theory, hypothesis: ~ *en praktijk* theory and practice; *in* ~ *is dat mogelijk* theoretically (speaking) that's possible

de **therapeut** /terapø̯yt/ (pl: -en) therapist

therapeutisch /terapø̯ytis/ (adj, adv) therapeutic(al)

de **therapie** /terapi/ (pl: -ën) **1** therapy **2** (psycho)therapy: *in* ~ *zijn* be having (*or:* undergoing) therapy

de **thermiek** /tɛrmik/ thermals, up-currents

de **thermometer** /tɛrmo̯metər/ (pl: -s) thermometer: *de* ~ *daalt* (or: *stijgt*) the thermometer is falling (*or:* rising); *de* ~ *stond op twintig graden Celsius* the thermometer read (*or:* stood at) twenty degrees centigrade

de **thermosfles**® /tɛrmɔsflɛs/ (pl: -sen) thermos (flask)

de **thermoskan**® /tɛrmɔskɑn/ (pl: -nen) thermos (jug)

de **thermostaat** /tɛrmosta̯t/ (pl: -staten) thermostat

de **these** /te̯zə/ (pl: -n, -s) thesis

de **thesis** /te̯zɪs/ (pl: theses) [Belg] dissertation, thesis

thomas /to̯mas/: *een ongelovige* ~ a doubting Thomas

de **Thora** /to̯ra/ Torah

de **thriller** /θrɪlər/ (pl: -s) thriller

het ¹**thuis** /tœys/ home, hearth: *hij heeft geen* ~ he has no home; *mijn* ~ my home; *bericht van* ~ *krijgen* receive news from home

²**thuis** /tœys/ (adv) **1** home: *de artikelen worden kosteloos* ~ *bezorgd* the articles are delivered free; *wel* ~! safe journey! **2** at home: *verzorging* ~ home nursing; *doe maar of je* ~ *bent* make yourself at home; *zich ergens* ~ *gaan voelen* settle down (*or:* in); [sport] *spelen we zondag* ~? are we playing at home this Sunday?; *iem. (bij zich)* ~ *uitnodigen* ask s.o. round (*or:* to one's house); *zich ergens* ~ *voelen* feel at home (*or:* ease) somewhere; *hij was niet* ~ he wasn't in (*or:* at home), he was out; *bij ons* ~ at our place, at home, back

home; *bij jou* ~ (over) at your place ‖ *samen uit*, **samen** ~ we stick together, we're in this together

thuisbankieren /tœyzbɑŋkirə(n)/ (thuisbankierde, heeft thuisgebankierd) home banking

thuisbezorgen /tœyzbəzɔrɣə(n)/ (bezorgde thuis, heeft thuisbezorgd) deliver (to the house, door)

de **thuisbioscoop** /tœyzbijɔskop/ home cinema

thuisblijven /tœyzblɛivə(n)/ (bleef thuis, is thuisgebleven) stay at home, stay in

thuisbrengen /tœyzbrɛŋə(n)/ (bracht thuis, heeft thuisgebracht) **1** bring home, see home; take home: *de* **man** *werd ziek thuisgebracht* the man was brought home sick **2** place: *iets (iem.) niet thuis* **kunnen** *brengen* not be able to place sth. (s.o.)

de **thuisclub** /tœysklʏp/ (pl: -s) home team

het **thuisfront** /tœysfrɔnt/ home front

de **thuishaven** /tœyshavə(n)/ (pl: -s) home port, port of register (or: registry); home base, haven

thuishoren /tœyshorə(n)/ (hoorde thuis, heeft thuisgehoord) **1** belong, go: *dat speelgoed hoort* **hier** *niet thuis* those toys don't belong here; *waar hoort dat thuis?* where does that go? **2** be from, come from: *waar (or: in welke haven) hoort dat* **schip** *thuis?* what is that ship's home port? (or: port of registry?)

thuishouden /tœyshaudə(n)/ (hield thuis, heeft thuisgehouden) keep at home ‖ *hou je* **handen** *thuis!* keep (or: lay) off me!, (keep your) hands off (me)!

thuiskomen /tœyskomə(n)/ (kwam thuis, is thuisgekomen) come home, come back, get back: *je* **moet** ~ you're wanted at home; *ik kom vanavond* **niet** *thuis* I won't be in tonight

de **thuiskomst** /tœyskɔmst/ homecoming, return: **behouden** ~ safe return

het **thuisland** /tœyslɑnt/ (pl: -en) homeland

thuisloos /tœyslos/ (adj) homeless

de **thuismarkt** /tœysmɑrkt/ (pl: -en) domestic market

de **thuisreis** /tœysrɛis/ (pl: -reizen) homeward journey: *hij is* **op** *de* ~ he is bound for home

de **thuisverpleging** /tœysfərplexɪŋ/ home nursing, home care

de **thuiswedstrijd** /tœyswɛtstrɛit/ (pl: -en) home game (or: match)

het **thuiswerk** /tœyswɛrk/ outwork; cottage industry: ~ **doen** take in outwork

de **thuiswerker** /tœyswɛrkər/ (pl: -s) outworker

de **thuiszorg** /tœysɔrɣ/ home care

de **ti** /ti/ (pl: ti's) [mus] te, ti

de **TIA** /tija/ transient ischaemic attack TIA

Tibet /tibɛt/ Tibet

de **Tibetaan** /tibetan/ (pl: Tibetanen) Tibetan

Tibetaans /tibetans/ (adj) Tibetan

de **tic** /tɪk/ (pl: -s) **1** trick, quirk: *zij* **heeft** *een* ~ *om alles te bewaren* she's got a quirk of hoarding things **2** tic, jerk **3** [roughly] shot: *een* **tonic** *met een* ~ a tonic with a shot (of gin), a gin and tonic

het **ticket** /tɪkət/ (pl: -s) ticket

de **tiebreak** /tɑjbrek/ (pl: -s) tie break(er)

tien /tin/ (num) ten; [in dates] tenth: *zij is* ~ *jaar* she is ten years old (or: of age); *een* **man** *of* ~ about ten people; ~ **tegen** *één dat … ten to one that …* ‖ *een* ~ **voor** *Engels* top marks for English; an A+ for English

tiende /tində/ (adj) tenth, tithe: **een** ~ *gedeelte*, **een** ~ a tenth (part), a tithe

tienduizend /tindœyzənt/ (num) ten thousand ‖ **enige** ~*en* some tens of thousands

de **tiener** /tinər/ (pl: -s) teenager

tienjarig /tinjarəx/ (adj) decennial, ten-year

de **tienkamp** /tiŋkɑmp/ (pl: -en) decathlon

tiens /tćɛ̃/ (int) [Belg] well, well

het **tiental** /tintɑl/ (pl: -len) ten: *na enkele* ~*len* **jaren** after a few decades

tientallig /tintɑləx/ (adj) decimal, denary

het **tientje** /tincə/ (pl: -s) ten euros; ten-euro note

het **tienvoud** /tinvɑut/ (pl: -en) tenfold

tieren /tirə(n)/ (tierde, heeft getierd) rage

de **tiet** /tit/ (pl: -en) [inform] boob, knocker

tig /tɪx/ (num) umpteen; zillions: *ik heb het al* ~ **keer** *gezegd* I've already said it umpteen times

het **tij** /tɛi/ (pl: -en) tide: *het is* **hoog** (or: **laag**) ~ it's high (or: low) tide, the tide is in (or: out); [fig] *het* ~ *proberen te* **keren** try to stem (or: turn) the tide

de **tijd** /tɛit/ (pl: -en) **1** time: *in de* **helft** *van de* ~ in half the time; *in een* **jaar** ~ (with)in a year; *na bepaalde* ~ after some (or: a) time, eventually; *een* **hele** ~ *geleden* a long time ago; *een* ~ **lang** for a while (or: time); **vrije** ~ spare (or: free) time, time off, leisure (time); *het duurde een* ~*je voor ze eraan gewend was* it took a while before (or: until) she got used to it; *ik* **geef** *je vijf seconden de* ~ I'm giving you five seconds; **heb** *je even* ~? have you got a moment? (or: a sec?); ~ **genoeg** **hebben** have plenty of time; have time enough; ~ **kosten** take time; *de* ~ **nemen** *voor iets* take one's time over sth.; ~ **opnemen** record the time; *dat* **was** *me nog eens een* ~*!* those were the days!; ~ **winnen** gain time; play for time; *uw* ~ *is* **om** your time is up; **binnen** *de kortst mogelijke* ~ in (next to) no time; *het heeft* **in** *een niet zo geregend* it hasn't rained like this for ages; **sinds** *enige* ~ for some time (past); *de* ~ *zal het leren* time will tell; *de* ~ *van* **aankomst** the time of arrival; *vorig jaar om* **dezelfde** ~ (at) the same time last year; *het* **is** ~ it's time; time's up; *zijn* ~ *uitzitten* serve (or: do) one's time; **eindelijk!** *het* **werd** ~ at last! it was about time (too)!; *het* **wordt** ~ *dat … it is* (high) time that ...; *morgen* **om** *deze* ~ (about, around) this time tomorrow; *op vaste* ~*en* at set (*or:* fixed) times; *de brandweer kwam net* **op** ~ the fire brigade arrived just in time; *stipt* **op** ~ punctual; on the dot; **op** ~ *naar bed gaan* go to bed in good time; **te** *zijner* ~ in due course, when appropriate; **tegen** *die* ~ by that time, by then; *van* ~ **tot** ~ from time to time; *van* ~ **af** from that time (on, onwards), ever since, since then; *veel* ~ *in beslag nemen* take up a lot of time; ~ *te kort komen* run out (*or:* run short) of time **2** time(s), period, age: *de* **laatste** ~ lately, recently; *hij heeft een* **moeilijke** ~ *gehad* he has been through (*or:* had) a hard time; *de goede* **oude** ~ the good old days; *zijn (beste)* ~ **gehad hebben** be past one's best (*or:* prime); *de* ~*en* **zijn veranderd** times have changed; *in deze* ~ *van het jaar* at this time of (the) year; *met zijn* ~ *meegaan* keep up with (*or:* move with) the times; *dat was* **voor** *mijn* ~ that was before my time (*or:* day); *dat was* **voor** *die* ~ *heel ongebruikelijk* in (*or:* for) those days it was most unusual; *je moet de* **eerste** ~ *nog rustig aandoen* to begin with (*or:* at first) you must take it easy; *een* ~*je* a while **3** season, time **4** tense: *de* **tegenwoordige** (or: **verleden**) ~ the present (*or:* past) tense; *toekomende* ~ future tense

de **tijdbom** /tɛidbɔm/ (pl: -men) time bomb

¹**tijdelijk** /tɛidələk/ (adj) temporary, provisional, interim: ~ **personeel** temporary staff

²**tijdelijk** /tɛidələk/ (adv) temporarily

tijdens /tɛidəns/ (prep) during

het **tijdgebrek** /tɛitxəbrɛk/ lack of time

de **tijdgeest** /tɛitxest/ spirit of the age (*or:* times)

de **tijdgenoot** /tɛitxənot/ (pl: -genoten) contemporary

¹**tijdig** /tɛidəx/ (adj) timely: ~*e* **hulp** *is veel waard* timely help is of great value

²**tijdig** /tɛidəx/ (adv) in time; on time

de **tijding** /tɛidɪŋ/ (pl: -en) news

tijdlang /tɛitlɑŋ/ (adv) while; for a while

tijdloos /tɛitlos/ (adj, adv) timeless, ageless

de **tijdnood** /tɛitnot/ lack (*or:* shortage) of time: *in* ~ *zitten* be pressed for time

het **tijdpad** /tɛitpɑt/ (pl: -en) time schedule

het **tijdperk** /tɛitpɛrk/ (pl: -en) period, age, era: *het* ~ *van de* **computer** the age of the computer; *het* **stenen** ~ the Stone Age

tijdrekken /tɛitrɛkə(n)/ time wasting; playing for time

de **tijdrit** /tɛitrɪt/ (pl: -ten) time trial

tijdrovend /tɛitrovənt/ (adj) time-consuming: *dit* **is** *zeer* ~ this takes up a lot of time

het **tijdsbestek** /tɛrtsbəstɛk/ (period of) time: *binnen een* ~ *van* within (the period of)

het **tijdschema** /tɛitsxema/ (pl: -'s) schedule, timetable: *we lopen achter* **op** *het* ~ we're (running) behind schedule

het **tijdschrift** /tɛitsxrɪft/ (pl: -en) periodical, journal; magazine

de **tijdsdruk** /tɛitsdrʏk/ pressure of time

de **tijdslimiet** /tɛitslimit/ (pl: -en) time limit, deadline: *de* ~ **overschrijden** exceed (*or:* go over) the time limit

het **tijdstip** /tɛitstɪp/ (pl: -pen) (point of, in) time; moment

het **tijdsverschil** /tɛitsfərsxɪl/ (pl: -len) time difference

het **tijdvak** /tɛitfɑk/ (pl: -ken) period

het **tijdverdrijf** /tɛitfərdrɛif/ pastime

de **tijdverspilling** /tɛitfərspɪlɪŋ/ waste of time

de **tijdwinst** /tɛitwɪnst/ gain in time: *enige* ~ **boeken** gain some time

de **tijdzone** /tɛitsɔːnə/ (pl: -s) time-zone

de **tijger** /tɛiɣər/ (pl: -s) tiger

de **tijm** /tɛim/ thyme

de **tik** /tɪk/ (pl: -ken) tap; slap; tick: *iem. een* ~ *om de oren* (or: **op** *de vingers*) *geven* give s.o. a cuff on the ear (*or:* a rap on the knuckles)

de **tikfout** /tɪkfɑut/ (pl: -en) typing error (*or:* mistake)

het **tikje** /tɪkjə/ (pl: -s) **1** touch, clip: *de bal een* ~ *geven* clip the ball **2** touch, shade: *zich een* ~ **beter** *voelen* feel slightly better

het **tikkeltje** /tɪkəltʃə/ touch, shade

¹**tikken** /tɪkə(n)/ (tikte, heeft getikt) tap; tick: *de* **wekker** *tikte niet meer* the alarmclock had stopped ticking; **tegen** *het raam* ~ tap at (*or:* on) the window

²**tikken** /tɪkə(n)/ (tikte, heeft getikt) **1** tap: *de* **maat** ~ tap (out) the beat **2** type: *een brief* ~ type a letter

het **tikkertje** /tɪkərtʃə/ tag: ~ **spelen** play tag

til /tɪl/: *er zijn grote veranderingen* **op** ~ there are big changes on the way

de **tilapia** /tilapija/ tilapia

¹**tillen** /tɪlə(n)/ (tilde, heeft getild) lift (a weight): *ergens niet (zo)* **zwaar** *aan* ~ not feel strongly about

²**tillen** /tɪlə(n)/ (tilde, heeft getild) lift, raise: *iem. in de hoogte* ~ lift s.o. up (in the air)

de **tillift** /tɪlɪft/ hoist, lift

de **tilt** /tɪlt/: *op* ~ *slaan* hit the roof

het **timbre** /tɛbrə/ (pl: -s) [mus] timbre

timen /tɑjmə(n)/ (timede, heeft getimed) time

de **time-out** /tɑjmɑut/ (pl: -s) time-out

timide /timidə/ (adj) timid, shy

de **timing** /tɑjmɪŋ/ timing

¹**timmeren** /tɪmərə(n)/ (timmerde, heeft getimmerd) hammer: **goed** *kunnen* ~ be good at carpentry; *de hele boel in elkaar* ~ smash the whole place up

²**timmeren** /tɪmərə(n)/ (timmerde, heeft getimmerd) build, put together: *een* **boekenkast** ~ build a bookcase

de **timmerman** /tɪmərmɑn/ (pl: timmerlieden, timmerlui) carpenter

het **timmerwerk** /tɪmərwɛrk/ carpentry,

woodwork

het **tin** /tɪn/ tin

tingelen /tɪŋələ(n)/ (tingelde, heeft getin-geld) tinkle, jingle: *op de piano* ~ tinkle away at the piano

tinnen /tɪnə(n)/ (adj) tin, pewter: ~ *soldaat-jes* tin soldiers

de **tint** /tɪnt/ (pl: -en) tint, hue: *iets een **feestelijk** ~je geven* give sth. a festive touch; *Mary had een **frisse** (or: **gelige**) ~* Mary had a fresh (or: sallow) complexion; *warme ~en* warm tones

tintelen /tɪntələ(n)/ (tintelde, heeft getin-teld) tingle

de **tinteling** /tɪntəlɪŋ/ (pl: -en) tingle, tingling

tinten /tɪntə(n)/ (tintte, heeft getint) tint, tinge

de **tip** /tɪp/ (pl: -s) **1** tip; corner: *een ~je van de **sluier** oplichten* lift (or: raise) (a corner of) the veil **2** tip, lead, clue; tip-off: *iem. een ~ **geven*** tip s.o. off, give s.o. a tip-off

het **tipgeld** /tɪpxɛlt/ tip-off money

de **tipgever** /tɪpxevər/ (pl: -s) (police) informer; tipster

de **tippel** /tɪpəl/ (pl: -s) toddle, walk: *een **hele** ~* quite a walk

de **tippelaarster** /tɪpəlarstər/ (pl: -s) street-walker

tippelen /tɪpələ(n)/ (tippelde, heeft getip-peld) be on (or: walk) the streets, solicit

de **tippelzone** /tɪpəlzɔːnə/ (pl: -s) streetwalk-ers' district

tippen /tɪpə(n)/ (tipte, heeft getipt) **1** tip (s.o.) off; [Am; to police also] finger **2** tip (as) **3** tip, touch lightly, finger lightly: *aan iets (iem.) niet kunnen ~* have nothing on sth. (s.o.)

tipsy /tɪpsi/ (adj) tipsy

tiptop /tɪptɔp/ (adj, adv) tip-top, A 1: ~ *in orde* in apple-pie order, in tip-top (or: A 1) condition

de **tirade** /tiraːdə/ (pl: -s) tirade

de **tiran** /tirɑn/ (pl: -nen) tyrant

de **tirannie** /tirɑni/ (pl: -ën) tyranny

tiranniek /tirɑnik/ (adj, adv) tyrannical

tiranniseren /tirɑnizeːrə(n)/ (tiranniseerde, heeft getiranniseerd) tyrannize (over)

de **Tiroler** /tiroːlər/ (pl: -s) Tyrolean

het **tissue** /tɪʃu/ (pl: -s) paper handkerchief

de **titel** /tiːtəl/ (pl: -s) **1** title; heading **2** title; (university) degree: *een ~ **behalen*** get a de-gree; win a title; *de ~ **veroveren** (or: **verde-digen**)* win (or: defend) the title

de **titelhouder** /tiːtəlhɑudər/ (pl: -s) title-hold-er

de **titelpagina** /tiːtəlpaɣinaː/ (pl: -'s) title-page, title

de **titelrol** /tiːtəlrɔl/ (pl: -len) title role

de **titelsong** /tiːtəlsɔŋ/ (pl: -s) title track

de **titelverdediger** /tiːtəlvərdedəɣər/ (pl: -s) titleholder, defender

de **titularis** /titylɑrɪs/ (pl: -sen) [Belg] class teacher

tja /ca/ (int) well

de **tjalk** /calk/ (pl: -en) Dutch sailing vessel

de **tjaptjoi** /cɑpcɔj/ chop suey

tjilpen /cɪlpə(n)/ (tjilpte, heeft getjilpt) chirp; peep; tweet

tjirpen /cɪrpə(n)/ (tjirpte, heeft getjirpt) chirp, chirrup; chirr

tjokvol /cɔkfɔl/ (adj) chock-a-block, chock-full: *de zaal **was** ~* the hall was jam-packed (or: chock-a-block)

tjonge /cɔŋə/ (int) dear me

de **tl-buis** /teɛlbœys/ (pl: tl-buizen) strip light, neon light (or: tube, lamp)

t.n.v. (abbrev) *ten name van* in the name of

de **toa** /toːwa/ *technisch onderwijsassistent* school laboratory assistant

de **toast** /tost/ (pl: -s) (piece, slice of) toast

de **tobbe** /tɔbə/ (pl: -s) (wash)tub

tobben /tɔbə(n)/ (tobde, heeft getobd) **1** worry, fret **2** struggle: *opa tobt met zijn been* grandpa is troubled by his leg

toch /tɔχ/ (adv) **1** nevertheless, still, yet, all the same: *ik **doe** het (lekker) ~* I'll do it any-way; *maar ~* (but) still, even so **2** rather, ac-tually **3** indeed **4** anyway, anyhow: *het wordt ~ **niks*** it won't work anyway; *nu je hier ~ **bent*** since you're here || *dat kunnen ze ~ **niet** me-nen?* surely they can't be serious?; *we hebben het ~ **al** zo moeilijk* it's difficult enough for us as it is

de **tocht** /tɔχt/ (pl: -en) **1** draught; breeze: *op de ~ zitten* sit in a draught; *~ **voelen*** feel a draught **2** journey, trip: *een ~ **maken** met de auto* go for a drive in the car

tochten /tɔχtə(n)/ (tochtte, heeft getocht) be draughty

tochtig /tɔχtəχ/ (adj) draughty; breezy

het **tochtje** /tɔχjə/ (pl: -s) trip, ride, drive

de **tochtstrip** /tɔχtstrɪp/ (pl: -s) draught ex-cluder, weather strip(ping)

¹**toe** /tu/ (adv) **1** to(wards) **2** too, as well: *dat **doet** er niet(s) ~* that doesn't matter **3** to, for: *aan iets ~ **komen*** get round to sth. **4** shut, closed || *er slecht aan ~ **zijn*** be in a bad way; *tot nu ~* so far, up to now; *dat was nog **tot** daaraan ~* there's no great harm in that, that doesn't matter so much

²**toe** /tu/ (int) **1** come on **2** please, do **3** come on, go on **4** there now

het ¹**toebehoren** /tubəhorə(n)/ accessories; at-tachments

²**toebehoren** /tubəhorə(n)/ (behoorde toe, heeft toebehoord) belong to

toebereiden /tubərɛɪdə(n)/ (bereidde toe, heeft toebereid) prepare

toebrengen /tubrɛŋə(n)/ (bracht toe, heeft toegebracht) deal, inflict, give: *iem. een **wond** ~* inflict a wound on s.o.

toedekken /tudɛkə(n)/ (dekte toe, heeft toegedekt) cover up; tuck in, tuck up: *iem. **warm** ~* tuck s.o. in nice and warm

toedichten /tudɪxtə(n)/ (dichtte toe, heeft toegedicht) attribute (to)

toedienen /tudinə(n)/ (diende toe, heeft toegediend) administer, apply: *medicijnen* ~ administer medicine

het **¹toedoen** /tudun/ agency, doing: *dit is allemaal door jouw ~ gebeurd* this is all your doing

²toedoen /tudun/ (deed toe, heeft toegedaan) add: *wat doet het er toe?* what does it matter?, what difference does it make?; *wat jij vindt, doet er niet toe* your opinion is of no consequence

de **toedracht** /tudraxt/ facts, circumstances: *de ware ~ van de zaak* what actually happened

toedragen /tudrayə(n)/ (droeg toe, heeft toegedragen) bear

zich **toe-eigenen** /tuɛiɣənə(n)/ (eigende zich toe, heeft zich toegeëigend) appropriate

de **toef** /tuf/ (pl: -en) tuft: *een ~ slagroom* a blob of cream

toegaan /tuɣan/ (ging toe, is toegegaan) happen, go on: *het gaat er daar ruig aan toe* there are wild goings-on there

de **toegang** /tuɣaŋ/ (pl: -en) **1** entrance, entry, access: *iem. de ~ ontzeggen* refuse s.o. admittance (*or:* access), bar s.o.; *verboden ~* no admittance **2** access; admittance; admission: *bewijs van ~* ticket (of admission); *~ hebben tot een vergadering* be admitted to a meeting; *zich ~ verschaffen* gain access (to)

het **toegangsbewijs** /tuɣaŋzbəwɛis/ (pl: -bewijzen) (admission) ticket, pass

de **toegangscode** /tuɣaŋskodə/ (pl: -s) access code

de **toegangsprijs** /tuɣaŋsprɛis/ (pl: -prijzen) entrance fee, price of admission

de **toegangsweg** /tuɣaŋswɛx/ (pl: -en) access (road), approach

toegankelijk /tuɣaŋkələk/ (adj) accessible, approachable: *moeilijk* (*or:* *gemakkelijk*) ~ difficult (*or:* easy) of access; *~ voor het publiek* open to the public

de **toegankelijkheid** /tuɣaŋkələkhɛit/ accessibility, approachability

toegedaan /tuɣədan/ (adj) dedicated

toegeeflijk /tuɣeflək/ (adj) indulgent, lenient: *~ zijn tegenover een kind* indulge a child

de **toegeeflijkheid** /tuɣefləkhɛit/ indulgence, lenience

toegepast /tuɣəpast/ (adj) applied

¹toegeven /tuɣevə(n)/ (gaf toe, heeft toegegeven) **1** yield, give in; give way: *onder druk ~* submit under pressure **2** admit, own: *hij wou maar niet ~* he wouldn't own up

²toegeven /tuɣevə(n)/ (gaf toe, heeft toegegeven) **1** indulge, humour; pamper; spoil, allow (for), take into account: *over en weer wat ~* give and take **2** admit, grant: *zijn nederlaag ~* admit defeat **3** throw in, add: *op de koop ~* include in the bargain

toegewijd /tuɣəwɛit/ (adj) devoted, dedicated: *een ~e verpleegster* a dedicated nurse

de **toegift** /tuɣɪft/ (pl: -en) encore: *een ~ geven* do an encore

de **toehoorder** /tuhordər/ (pl: -s) listener

toejuichen /tujœiɣxə(n)/ (juichte toe, heeft toegejuicht) **1** cheer; clap; applaud **2** applaud: *een besluit ~* welcome a decision

de **toejuiching** /tujœiɣxɪŋ/ (pl: -en) **1** applause **2** acclaim

toekennen /tukɛnə(n)/ (kende toe, heeft toegekend) **1** ascribe to, attribute to **2** award, grant: *macht ~ aan* assign authority to

de **toekenning** /tukɛnɪŋ/ award, grant

toekeren /tukerə(n)/ (keerde toe, heeft toegekeerd) turn to

toekijken /tukɛikə(n)/ (keek toe, heeft toegekeken) **1** look on, watch **2** sit by (and watch)

toekomen /tukomə(n)/ (kwam toe, is toegekomen) **1** belong to, be due: *iem. de eer geven die hem toekomt* do s.o. justice **2** approach: *daar ben ik nog niet aan toegekomen* I haven't got round to that yet

toekomend /tukomənt/ (adj) future

de **toekomst** /tukomst/ future: *in de nabije* (*or:* *verre*) ~ in the near (*or:* distant) future; *de ~ voorspellen* tell fortunes; *de ~ lacht hem toe* the future looks rosy for him

toekomstig /tukomstəx/ (adj) future, coming ‖ *zijn ~e echtgenote* his bride-to-be; *de ~e eigenaar* the prospective owner

de **toekomstmuziek** /tukomstmyzik/: *dat is nog ~* that's still in the future

toelaatbaar /tuladbar/ (adj) permissible, permitted

toelachen /tulaxə(n)/ (lachte toe, heeft toegelachen) smile at ‖ *het geluk lacht ons toe* fortune smiles on us

de **toelage** /tulaɣə/ (pl: -n) allowance; grant

toelaten /tulatə(n)/ (liet toe, heeft toegelaten) **1** permit, allow: *als het weer het toelaat* weather permitting **2** admit, receive: *zij werd niet in Nederland toegelaten* she was refused entry to the Netherlands

het **toelatingsexamen** /tulatɪŋsɛksamə(n)/ (pl: -s) entrance exam(ination)

toeleggen /tulɛɣə(n)/ (legde toe, heeft toegelegd) add (to)

het **toeleveringsbedrijf** /tulevərɪŋzbədrɛif/ (pl: -bedrijven) supplier, supply company

toelichten /tulɪxtə(n)/ (lichtte toe, heeft toegelicht) explain, throw light on, clarify: *zijn standpunt ~* explain one's point of view; *als ik dat even mag ~* if I may go into that briefly

de **toelichting** /tulɪxtɪŋ/ (pl: -en) explanation, clarification: *dat vereist enige ~* that requires some explanation

de **toeloop** /tulop/ onrush, rush; flood

toelopen /tulopə(n)/ (liep toe, is toegelopen) taper (off), come (*or:* run) to a point

toeluisteren /tuloeystərə(n)/ (luisterde toe, heeft toegeluisterd) listen (to): *aandachtig* ~ listen carefully

het **toemaatje** /tumacə/ (pl: -s) [Belg] extra, bonus

¹**toen** /tun/ (adv) **1** then, in those days, at the (*or:* that) time: *er stond hier* ~ *een kerk* there used to be a church here **2** then, next: *en* ~? (and) then what?, what happened next?

²**toen** /tun/ (conj) when, as: ~ *hij binnenkwam* when he came in

de **toenaam** /tunam/ surname: *iem. met naam en* ~ *noemen* mention s.o. by name

de **toenadering** /tunadərɪŋ/ (pl: -en) [oft pl] advance; approach

de **toename** /tunamə/ (pl: -n) increase, growth: *een* ~ *van het verbruik* an increase in consumption

de **toendra** /tundra/ (pl: -'s) tundra

toenemen /tunemə(n)/ (nam toe, is toegenomen) increase, grow; expand: *in* ~*de mate* increasingly, to an increasing extent; *in kracht* ~ grow (*or:* increase) in strength

toenmalig /tumalǝɣ/ (adj) then: *de* ~*e koning* the king at the (*or:* that) time

toentertijd /tuntərtɛɪt/ (adv) then, at the time

toepasselijk /tupɑsələk/ (adj) appropriate, suitable

toepassen /tupɑsə(n)/ (paste toe, heeft toegepast) **1** use, employ **2** apply, adopt; enforce: *een methode* ~ use a method; *in de praktijk* ~ use in (actual) practice

de **toepassing** /tupɑsɪŋ/ (pl: -en) **1** use, employment: *niet van* ~ *(n.v.t.)* not applicable (n/a); *van* ~ *zijn op* apply to **2** application: *in* ~ *brengen* put into practice

de **toer** /tur/ (pl: -en) **1** trip, tour; ride; drive **2** revolution: *op volle* ~*en draaien* go at full speed, be in top gear; *hij is een beetje over zijn* ~*en* he's in a bit of a state **3** job, business ‖ *op de lollige* ~ *gaan* act the clown

de **toerbeurt** /turbørt/ (pl: -en) turn: *bij* ~ in rotation, by turns; *we doen dat bij* ~ we take turns at it

toereikend /turɛɪkənt/ (adj) sufficient; adequate

toerekeningsvatbaar /turekənɪŋsfɑdbar/ (adj) accountable, responsible

toeren /turə(n)/ (toerde, heeft/is getoerd) go for a ride; go for a drive

het **toerental** /turə(n)tɑl/ (pl: -len) rpm *(revolutions per minute)*

de **toerenteller** /turə(n)tɛlər/ (pl: -s) revolution counter

de **toerfiets** /turfits/ (pl: -en) touring bicycle, sports bicycle

het **toerisme** /turɪsmə/ tourism

de **toerist** /turɪst/ (pl: -en) tourist

de **toeristenbelasting** /turɪstə(n)bəlɑstɪŋ/ tourist tax

het **toeristenseizoen** /turɪstə(n)sɛizun/ (pl: -en) tourist season

toeristisch /turɪstis/ (adj) tourist: *een* ~*e trekpleister* a tourist attraction

het **toernooi** /turnoj/ (pl: -en) tournament

toerusten /turvstə(n)/ (rustte toe, heeft toegerust) equip; furnish: *een leger* ~ equip an army; *toegerust met* equipped (*or:* fitted) (out) with

toeschietelijk /tusxitələk/ (adj) accommodating, obliging

toeschieten /tusxitə(n)/ (schoot toe, is toegeschoten) rush forward

de **toeschouwer** /tusxɑuwər/ (pl: -s) **1** spectator; viewer; audience: *veel* ~*s trekken* draw a large audience **2** onlooker, bystander

toeschrijven /tusxrɛivə(n)/ (schreef toe, heeft toegeschreven) **1** blame, attribute: *een ongeluk* ~ *aan het slechte weer* blame an accident on the weather **2** attribute, ascribe: *dit schilderij schrijft men toe aan Vermeer* this painting is attributed to Vermeer

toeslaan /tuslan/ (sloeg toe, heeft toegeslagen) **1** hit home, strike home **2** strike: *inbreker slaat opnieuw toe!* burglar strikes again!

de **toeslag** /tuslɑx/ (pl: -en) **1** surcharge **2** bonus: *een* ~ *voor vuil werk* a bonus for dirty work

toespelen /tuspelə(n)/ (speelde toe, heeft toegespeeld) pass (to); slip (to)

de **toespeling** /tuspelɪŋ/ (pl: -en) allusion, reference: ~*en maken* drop hints, make insinuations

de **toespijs** /tuspɛis/ (pl: toespijzen) **1** dessert, sweet, pudding **2** side dish

toespitsen /tuspɪtsə(n)/ (spitste toe, heeft toegespitst) intensify

de **toespraak** /tusprak/ (pl: toespraken) speech; address: *een* ~ *houden* make a speech

toespreken /tusprekə(n)/ (sprak toe, heeft toegesproken) speak to, address

toestaan /tustan/ (stond toe, heeft toegestaan) allow, permit: *uitstel* (or: *een verzoek*) ~ grant a respite (*or:* a request)

de **toestand** /tustɑnt/ (pl: -en) state, condition, situation: *de* ~ *van de patiënt is kritiek* the patient is in a critical condition; *de* ~ *in de wereld* the state of world affairs

toesteken /tustekə(n)/ (stak toe, heeft toegestoken) extend, put out, hold out: *de helpende hand* ~ extend (*or:* lend) a helping hand

het **toestel** /tustɛl/ (pl: -len) **1** apparatus, appliance; set: *vraag om* ~ *212* ask for extension 212 **2** plane

het **toestelnummer** /tustɛlnʏmər/ (pl: -s) extension (number)

toestemmen /tˈustɛmə(n)/ (stemde toe, heeft toegestemd) agree (to), consent (to): *erin ~ dat … agree that …,* agree to (…ing)

de **toestemming** /tˈustɛmɪŋ/ (pl: -en) agreement, consent, approval (of); permission: *zijn ~ geven* (or: *verlenen, weigeren*) *aan iem.* give (or: grant, refuse) permission to s.o.

toestoppen /tˈustɔpə(n)/ (stopte toe, heeft toegestopt) slip

toestromen /tˈustromə(n)/ (stroomde toe, is toegestroomd) stream to(wards), flow (or: flock, crowd) towards

toesturen /tˈustyrə(n)/ (stuurde toe, heeft toegestuurd) send; remit

de **toet** /tut/ (pl: -en) face

toetakelen /tˈutakələ(n)/ (takelde toe, heeft toegetakeld) **1** beat (up), knock about: *hij is lelijk toegetakeld* he has been badly beaten (up) **2** rig out

toetasten /tˈutastə(n)/ (tastte toe, heeft toegetast) take, seize; help o.s.

de **toeter** /tˈutər/ (pl: -s) **1** tooter **2** horn

¹**toeteren** /tˈutərə(n)/ (toeterde, heeft getoeterd) hoot, honk

²**toeteren** /tˈutərə(n)/ (toeterde, heeft getoeterd) bellow

het **toetje** /tˈucə/ (pl: -s) dessert: *als ~ is er fruit* there is fruit for dessert

toetreden /tˈutredə(n)/ (trad toe, is toegetreden) join

de **toetreding** /tˈutredɪŋ/ (pl: -en) joining, entry (into)

de **toets** /tuts/ (pl: -en) **1** test, check: *een schriftelijke ~* a written test, a test paper **2** key: *een ~ aanslaan* strike a key

toetsen /tˈutsə(n)/ (toetste, heeft getoetst) test, check: *iets aan de praktijk ~* test sth. out in practice

het **toetsenbord** /tˈutsə(n)bɔrt/ (pl: -en) keyboard; console

het **toeval** /tˈuval/ coincidence, accident, chance: *door een ongelukkig ~* by mischance; *stom ~* by sheer accident; (by) a (mere) fluke; *niets aan het ~ overlaten* leave nothing to chance

toevallen /tˈuvalə(n)/ (viel toe, is toegevallen) fall to; accrue to

¹**toevallig** /tuvˈɑləx/ (adj) accidental: *een ~e ontmoeting* a chance meeting; *een ~e voorbijganger* a passer-by

²**toevallig** /tuvˈɑləx/ (adv) by (any) chance: *elkaar ~ treffen* meet by chance

de **toevalligheid** /tuvˈɑləxɛit/ (pl: -heden) coincidence

de **toevalstreffer** /tˈuvalstrɛfər/ (pl: -s) chance hit, stroke of luck

toeven /tˈuvə(n)/ (toefde, heeft getoefd) [form] stay: *het is daar goed ~* it is a nice place to stay

de **toeverlaat** /tˈuvərlat/ support: *hij was hun steun en ~* he was their help and stay

toevertrouwen /tˈuvərtrɑuwə(n)/ (vertrouwde toe, heeft toevertrouwd) **1** entrust: *dat is hem wel toevertrouwd* leave that to him, trust him for that **2** confide (to): *iets aan het papier ~* commit sth. to paper

de **toevloed** /tˈuvlut/ flow

de **toevlucht** /tˈuvlʏxt/ refuge, shelter: *dit middel was zijn laatste ~* this (expedient) was his last resort; *~ zoeken bij* take refuge with

het **toevluchtsoord** /tˈuvlʏxtsort/ (pl: -en) (port, house, haven of) refuge

toevoegen /tˈuvuɣə(n)/ (voegde toe, heeft toegevoegd) add: *suiker naar smaak ~* add sugar to taste

de **toevoeging** /tˈuvuɣɪŋ/ (pl: -en) addition; additive

de **toevoer** /tˈuvur/ supply

toewensen /tˈuwɛnsə(n)/ (wenste toe, heeft toegewenst) wish: *iem. veel geluk ~* wish s.o. all the best (or: every happiness)

de **toewijding** /tˈuwɛidɪŋ/ devotion

toewijzen /tˈuwɛizə(n)/ (wees toe, heeft toegewezen) assign, grant: *het kind werd aan de vader toegewezen* the father was awarded (or: granted, given) custody of the child; *een prijs ~* award a prize

toezeggen /tˈuzɛɣə(n)/ (zegde toe/zei toe, heeft toegezegd) promise

de **toezegging** /tˈuzɛɣɪŋ/ (pl: -en) promise: *~en doen* make promises

toezenden /tˈuzɛndə(n)/ (zond toe, heeft toegezonden) send (to)

het **toezicht** /tˈuzɪxt/ supervision: *~ houden op* supervise, oversee; look after; *onder ~ staan van* be supervised by

de **toezichthouder** /tˈuzɪxthɑudər/ (pl: -s) supervisor

toezien /tˈuzin/ (zag toe, heeft toegezien) **1** look on, watch: *machteloos ~* stand by helplessly **2** see, take care: *hij moest er op ~ dat alles goed ging* he had to see to it that everything went all right

toezwaaien /tˈuzwajə(n)/ (zwaaide toe, heeft toegezwaaid) wave to

tof /tɔf/ (adj, adv) **1** decent, O.K.: *een ~fe meid* a decent girl, an O.K. girl **2** great

de **toffee** /tˈɔfe/ (pl: -s) toffee

de **tofoe** /tˈofu/ tofu

de **toga** /tˈoɣa/ (pl: -'s) gown, robe: *een advocaat in ~* a robed lawyer

Togo /tˈoɣo/ Togo

de ¹**Togolees** /toɣolˈes/ (pl: Togolezen) Togolese

²**Togolees** /toɣolˈes/ (adj) Togolese

het **toilet** /twalˈɛt/ (pl: -ten) toilet, lavatory: *een openbaar ~* a public convenience; [Am] a restroom; *naar het ~ gaan* go to the toilet

het **toiletartikel** /twalˈɛtɑrtikəl/ (pl: -en) toiletry; toilet requisites (or: things)

de **toiletjuffrouw** /twalˈɛtjʏfrɑu/ (pl: -en) lavatory attendant

het **toiletpapier** /twalˈɛtpapir/ toilet paper (or: tissue) de **toiletrol** /twalɛtrɔl/ (pl: -len) toilet paper

de **toilettafel** /twalɛtafəl/ (pl: -s) dressing table

de **toilettas** /twalɛtɑs/ (pl: -sen) toilet bag

de **toiletverfrisser** /twalɛtfərfrɪsər/ (pl: -s) toilet freshener, lavatory freshener

tokkelen /tɔkələ(n)/ (tokkelde, heeft/is getokkeld) strum

het **tokkelinstrument** /tɔkəlɪnstrymɛnt/ (pl: -en) plucked instrument

de **toko** /toko/ (pl: -'s) general shop; Indonesian shop: [fig] alleen oog hebben voor je eigen ~ only be interested in one's own patch

de **tol** /tɔl/ (pl: -len) **1** top: mijn hoofd draait **als** een ~ my head is spinning **2** toll: ergens ~ voor moeten **betalen** [fig] have to pay the price for sth.; ~ **heffen** levy (or: take) (a) toll (on)

tolerant /tolerɑnt/ (adj, adv) tolerant

de **tolerantie** /tolerɑn(t)si/ tolerance

tolereren /tolerɛrə(n)/ (tolereerde, heeft getolereerd) tolerate, put up with

de **tolk** /tɔlk/ (pl: -en) interpreter

tolken /tɔlkə(n)/ (tolkte, heeft getolkt) interpret

tollen /tɔlə(n)/ (tolde, heeft getold) **1** play with (or: spin) a top **2** spin, whirl: zij stond te ~ van de slaap she was reeling with sleep

de **tolweg** /tɔlwɛx/ (pl: -en) toll road; turnpike

de **tomaat** /tomat/ (pl: tomaten) tomato

de **tomatenketchup** /tomatə(n)kɛtʃʏp/ (pl: -s) (tomato) ketchup

de **tomatenpuree** /tomatə(n)pyre/ tomato purée

het **tomatensap** /tomatə(n)sɑp/ tomato juice

de **tomatensoep** /tomatə(n)sup/ tomato soup

de **tombe** /tɔmbə/ (pl: -s, -n) tomb

tomeloos /toməlos/ (adj, adv) unbridled, uncontrolled

de **tompoes** /tɔmpus/ (pl: tompoezen, -en) vanilla slice

de **tomtom** /tɔmtɔm/ (pl: -s) sat nav, GPS

de **ton** /tɔn/ (pl: -nen) **1** cask, barrel **2** a hundred thousand euros **3** (metric) ton

de **tondeuse** /tɔndøzə/ (pl: -s) (pair of) clippers, trimmers; shears

het **toneel** /tonel/ (pl: tonelen) **1** stage: op het ~ verschijnen enter the stage, appear on the stage; iets ten tonele voeren stage sth., put sth. on the scene **2** scene, spectacle **3** theatre

het **toneelgezelschap** /tonelɣəzɛlsxɑp/ (pl: -pen) theatrical company, theatre company

de **toneelkijker** /tonelkɛɪkər/ (pl: -s) (pair of) (opera) glasses

de **toneelschool** /tonelsxol/ (pl: -scholen) drama school

de **toneelschrijver** /tonelsxrɛɪvər/ (pl: -s) playwright

het **toneelspel** /tonelspɛl/ (pl: -en) **1** play **2** play-acting

toneelspelen /tonelspelə(n)/ (speelde to-

neel, heeft toneelgespeeld) **1** act, play **2** play-act, dramatize: wat **kun** jij ~! what a play-actor you are!

de **toneelspeler** /tonelspelər/ (pl: -s) **1** actor, player **2** play-actor

het **toneelstuk** /tonelstʏk/ (pl: -ken) play: een ~ **opvoeren** perform a play

de **toneelvereniging** /tonelvərenəxɪŋ/ (pl: -en) drama club

de **toneelvoorstelling** /tonelvorstɛlɪŋ/ (pl: -en) theatrical performance

tonen /tonə(n)/ (toonde, heeft getoond) show; display

de **toner** /tonər/ (pl: -s) toner

de **tong** /tɔŋ/ (pl: -en) **1** tongue: met **dubbele (dikke)** ~ spreken speak thickly, speak with a thick tongue; de ~en **kwamen los** the tongues were loosened, tongues were wagging; zijn ~ **uitsteken** tegen iem. put out one's tongue at s.o.; het ligt vóór **op** mijn ~ it's on the tip of my tongue **2** sole

de **tongval** /tɔŋval/ (pl: -len) accent

de **tongzoen** /tɔŋzun/ (pl: -en) French kiss

tongzoenen /tɔŋzunə(n)/ (tongzoende, heeft getongzoend) French kiss

de **tonic** /tɔnɪk/ (pl: -s) tonic

de **tonijn** /tonɛin/ (pl: -en) tunny(fish), tuna (fish)

de **tonnage** /tɔnaʒə/ tonnage: **bruto** ~ gross tonnage

de **tonsil** /tɔnsɪl/ (pl: -len) tonsil

de **toog** /tox/ (pl: togen) **1** cassock, soutane **2** bar **3** counter

de **tooi** /toj/ (pl: -en) decoration(s), ornament(s); plumage

tooien /tojə(n)/ (tooide, heeft getooid) adorn

de **toom** /tom/ (pl: tomen) bridle, reins: **in** ~ houden (keep in) check, keep under control

de **toon** /ton/ (pl: tonen) **1** tone; note: een **halve** ~ a semitone, a half step; de ~ **aangeven** a) give the key; b) [fig] lead (or: set) the tone; c) set the fashion; een ~tje lager **zingen** change one's tune; **uit** de ~ vallen not be in keeping, not be incongruous; be the odd man out; [fig] de **juiste** ~ aanslaan strike the right note **2** tone (colour), timbre

toonaangevend /tonaŋɣevənt/ (adj) authoritative, leading

de **toonaard** /tonart/ (pl: -en): in **alle** ~en in every possible way

toonbaar /tombar/ (adj) presentable

de **toonbank** /tombɑŋk/ (pl: -en) counter: illegale cd's **onder** de ~ verkopen sell bootleg CDs under the counter; [fig] **over** de ~ vliegen sell like hot cakes

het **toonbeeld** /tombelt/ (pl: -en) model, paragon, example

de **toonder** /tondər/ (pl: -s) bearer: een cheque **aan** ~ a cheque (payable) to bearer

de **toonhoogte** /tonhoxtə/ (pl: -n, -s) pitch: de

juiste ~ *hebben* be at the right pitch

de **toonladder** /tonlodər/ (pl: -s) scale: ~*s spelen* play (*or:* practise) scales

toonloos /tonlos/ (adj) toneless, flat

de **toonsoort** /tonsort/ (pl: -en) [mus] key

de **toonzaal** /tonzal/ (pl: -zalen) showroom

de **toorn** /torn/ wrath, anger

de **toorts** /torts/ (pl: -en) torch

de **toost** /tost/ toast: *een ~ (op iem.) uitbrengen* propose a toast (to s.o.)

toosten /tostə(n)/ (tooste, heeft getoost) toast: ~ *op* drink (a toast) to

de **top** /top/ (pl: -pen) **1** top, tip; peak: *aan (op) de ~ staan* be at the top; *van ~ tot teen* from head to foot **2** top, peak, height || ~ *tien* top ten; [Belg] *hoge ~pen scheren* be successful

de **topaas** /topas/ topaz

de **topambtenaar** /topamtənar/ (pl: -ambtenaren) key official

de **topconditie** /topkondi(t)si/ (tip-)top condition (*or:* form)

de **topconferentie** /topkonferɛnsi/ (pl: -s) summit (conference, meeting); summit talks, top-level talks

de **topdrukte** /tobdrvktə/ rush hour

de **topfunctie** /topfvŋksi/ (pl: -s) top position, leading position

de **topfunctionaris** /topfvŋkʃonarɪs/ (pl: -sen) key official

de **tophit** /tophɪt/ (pl: -s) smash hit

het **topje** /topjə/ (pl: -s) **1** tip: *het ~ van de ijsberg* the tip of the iceberg **2** top

de **topklasse** /topklasə/ (pl: -n) top class

topless /topləs/ (adj) topless

de **topman** /topman/ (pl: -nen) senior man (*or:* executive), top-ranking official, senior official: ~ *in het bedrijfsleven* captain of industry

de **topografie** /topoɣrafi/ (pl: -ën) topography

het **topoverleg** /topoverlɛɣ/ top-level talks, summit talks

toppen /topə(n)/ (topte, heeft getopt) top, head

de **topper** /topər/ (pl: -s) **1** top **2** (smash) hit **3** top match **4** ace **5** leading figure

de **topprestatie** /toprɛsta(t)si/ (pl: -s) top performance, record performance: *een ~ leveren* turn in a top performance

het **toppunt** /topʏnt/ (pl: -en) **1** height, top: *dat is het ~!* that's the limit!, that beats everything! **2** top, highest point; summit

de **topscorer** /topskorər/ (pl: -s) top scorer

de **topsnelheid** /topsnɛlhɛit/ (pl: -heden) top speed: *op ~ rijden* drive at top speed

de **topspin** /topspɪn/ topspin

de **topsport** /topsport/ top-class sport

de **topvorm** /topform/ top(-notch) form

topzwaar /topswar/ (adj) top-heavy

de **tor** /tor/ (pl: -ren) beetle

de **toreador** /torejadɔr/ (pl: -s) toreador

de **toren** /torə(n)/ (pl: -s) **1** tower; steeple; spire: *in een ivoren ~ zitten* live in an ivory

tower **2** rook, castle

de **torenflat** /torə(n)flɛt/ (pl: -s) high-rise flat(s); [Am] high-rise apartment(s)

torenhoog /torə(n)hoɣ/ (adj) towering; sky-high

de **torenspits** /torə(n)spɪts/ (pl: -en) steeple, spire

de **torenvalk** /torə(n)vɑlk/ (pl: -en) kestrel, windhover

de **tornado** /tornado/ (pl: -'s) tornado

tornen /tornə(n)/ (tornde, heeft getornd) unsew, unstitch: *er valt aan deze beslissing niet te ~* there's no going back on this decision

torpederen /torpədɛrə(n)/ (torpedeerde, heeft getorpedeerd) torpedo

de **torpedo** /torpedo/ (pl: -'s) torpedo

torsen /torsə(n)/ (torste, heeft getorst) bear, suffer

de **torsie** /torsi/ torsion

de **torso** /torso/ (pl: -'s) torso

de **tortelduif** /tortəldœyf/ (pl: -duiven) turtledove

tossen /tosə(n)/ (toste, heeft getost) toss (up, for)

de **tosti** /tosti/ (pl: -'s) toasted ham and cheese sandwich

het **tostiapparaat** /tostiaparat/ (pl: -apparaten) (sandwich) toaster

tot /tot/ (prep) **1** (up) to, as far as: *de trein rijdt ~ Amsterdam* the train goes as far as Amsterdam; ~ *hoever,* ~ *waar?* how far?; ~ *bladzijde drie* up to page three **2** to, until: *van dag ~ dag* from day to day; ~ *zaterdag!* see you on Saturday!; ~ *de volgende keer* until (the) next time; ~ *nog (nu) toe* so far; ~ *en met 31 december* up to and including 31 December; *van 3 ~ 12 uur* from 3 to (*or:* till) 12 o'clock; *van maandag ~ en met zaterdag* from Monday to Saturday; [Am also] Monday through Saturday **3** at: ~ *elke prijs* at any price || *iem.* ~ *president kiezen* elect s.o. president

totaal /total/ (adj, adv) total, complete: *een totale ommekeer (ommezwaai)* an about-turn, an about-face; *totale uitverkoop* clearance sale; *iets ~ anders* sth. completely different; *het is €33,- ~* it's 33 euros in all; *in ~* in all (*or:* total)

het **totaalbedrag** /totalbədrɑɣ/ (pl: -en) total (sum, amount)

totalitair /totalitɛːr/ (adj, adv) totalitarian

de **totaliteit** /totalitɛit/ (pl: -en) totality

total loss /totɑllɔs/ (adj): *een auto ~ rijden* smash (up) a car, wreck a car

totdat /todɑt/ (conj) until

de **totempaal** /totəmpal/ (pl: -palen) totem pole

de **toto** /toto/ tote; [socc] (football) pools: *in de ~ geld winnen* win money on the pools

de **totstandkoming** /totstɑntkomɪŋ/ coming about, realization

toucheren /tuʃerə(n)/ (toucheerde, heeft getoucheerd) **1** receive **2** hit

het/de **touchscreen** /tɑtʃskri:n/ touch screen

de **toupet** /tupɛt/ (pl: -ten) toupee

de **tour** /tur/ (pl: -s) **1** outing, trip **2** tour

de **touringcar** /turɪŋkɑ:r/ (pl: -s) (motor) coach; [Am] bus

de **tournee** /turne/ (pl: -s) tour: *op ~ zijn* be on tour

het/de **tourniquet** /turnikɛt/ (pl: -s) turnstile; revolving door(s)

de **touroperator** /turɔpəretər/ (pl: -s) tour operator

het **touw** /tɑu/ (pl: -en) rope, (piece of) string: *ik kan er geen ~ aan vastknopen* I can't make head or tail of it; *iets met een ~ vastbinden (dichtbinden)* tie sth. (up) ‖ *in ~ zijn* be busy, be hard at it; *iets op ~ zetten* set sth. on foot, start sth.

de **touwladder** /tɑulɑdər/ (pl: -s) rope ladder

het **touwtje** /tɑucə/ (pl: -s) (piece of) string: *de ~s in handen hebben* be pulling the strings, be running the show

touwtjespringen /tɑucəsprɪŋə(n)/ (sprong touwtje, heeft touwtjegesprongen) skipping

touwtrekken /tɑutrɛkə(n)/ tug-of-war

t.o.v. (abbrev) *ten opzichte van* with respect to, with regard to

de **tovenaar** /tovənar/ (pl: -s) magician, sorcerer, wizard

de **toverdrank** /tovərdrɑŋk/ (pl: -en) magic potion

¹**toveren** /tovərə(n)/ (toverde, heeft getoverd) work magic; do conjuring tricks

²**toveren** /tovərə(n)/ (toverde, heeft getoverd) conjure (up): *iets tevoorschijn ~* conjure up sth.

de **toverheks** /tovərhɛks/ (pl: -en) sorceress, magician

de **toverij** /tovərɛi/ (pl: -en) magic, sorcery

de **toverslag** /tovərslɑx/: *als bij ~* like magic

de **toverspreuk** /tovərsprøk/ (pl: -en) (magic) spell, (magic) charm

de **toverstaf** /tovərstaf/ (pl: -staven) magic wand

toxisch /tɔksis/ (adj) toxic, poisonous

traag /trax/ (adj, adv) slow: *hij is nogal ~ van begrip* he isn't very quick in the uptake; *~ op gang komen* get off to a slow start

de **traagheid** /traxhɛit/ slowness: *de ~ van geest* slowness (of mind)

de **traan** /tran/ (pl: tranen) tear; teardrop: *in tranen uitbarsten* burst into tears, burst out crying; *tranen met tuiten huilen* cry buckets, cry one's eyes out

het **traangas** /tranɣɑs/ tear-gas

de **traanklier** /traŋklir/ (pl: -en) tear gland

het **tracé** /trase/ (pl: -s) (planned) route

traceren /traserə(n)/ (traceerde, heeft getraceerd) trace

trachten /trɑxtə(n)/ (trachtte, heeft getracht) attempt, try

de **tractor** /trɑktɔr/ (pl: -s) tractor

de **traditie** /tradi(t)si/ (pl: -s) tradition: *een ~ in ere houden* uphold a tradition

traditiegetrouw /tradi(t)siɣətrɑu/ (adj, adv) traditional; true to tradition

traditioneel /tradi(t)ʃonel/ (adj, adv) traditional

de **tragedie** /traɣedi/ (pl: -s) tragedy

de **tragiek** /traɣik/ tragedy

tragikomisch /traɣikomis/ (adj) tragicomic

tragisch /traɣis/ (adj, adv) tragic: *het ~e is* the tragedy of it is …

de **trailer** /trelər/ (pl: -s) trailer

¹**trainen** /trenə(n)/ (trainde, heeft getraind) train; work out: *(weer) gaan ~* go into training (again)

²**trainen** /trenə(n)/ (trainde, heeft getraind) train: *een elftal ~* train (or: coach) a team; *zijn geheugen ~* train one's memory; *zich ~ in iets* train for sth.

de **trainer** /trenər/ (pl: -s) trainer, coach

traineren /trɛnerə(n)/ (traineerde, heeft getraineerd) delay: *hij probeert de zaak alleen maar te ~* he's just dragging his feet

de **training** /trenɪŋ/ (pl: -en) training, practice; workout: *een zware ~* a heavy workout

het **trainingspak** /trenɪŋspak/ (pl: -ken) tracksuit, jogging suit

het **traject** /trajɛkt/ (pl: -en) route, stretch; section

het **traktaat** /trɑktat/ (pl: traktaten) **1** treaty **2** tract

de **traktatie** /trɑkta(t)si/ (pl: -s) treat

trakteren /trɑkterə(n)/ (trakteerde, heeft getrakteerd) treat: *~ op gebakjes* treat s.o. to cake; *ik trakteer* this is my treat

de **tralie** /trali/ (pl: -s) bar: *achter de ~s zitten* be behind bars

de **tram** /trɛm/ (pl: -s) tram: *met de ~ gaan* take the (or: go by) tram

de **tramhalte** /trɛmhɑltə/ (pl: -s) tramstop

het **trammelant** /trɑmələnt/ [inform] trouble

de **trampoline** /trɑmpolinə/ (pl: -s) trampoline

trampolinespringen /trɑmpolinəsprɪŋə(n)/ trampolining

de **trance** /trãs/ (pl: -s) trance: *iem. in ~ brengen* send s.o. into a trance

tranen /tranə(n)/ (traande, heeft getraand) run, water: *~de ogen* running (or: watering) eyes

de **transactie** /trɑnsɑksi/ (pl: -s) transaction, deal

trans-Atlantisch /trɑnsɑtlɑntis/ (adj) transatlantic

het/de **transfer** /trɑnsfy:r/ (pl: -s) transfer

het **transferium** /trɑnsferijʏm/ [roughly] Park and Ride

de **transfermarkt** /trɑnsfy:rmɑrkt/ transfer market

de **transfersom** /trɑnsfy:rsɔm/ (pl: -men)

transfer fee
de **transformatie** /trɑnsfɔrmɑ(t)si/ (pl: -s) transformation
de **transformator** /trɑnsfɔrmɑtor/ (pl: -en, -s) transformer
transformeren /trɑnsfɔrmerə(n)/ (transformeerde, heeft getransformeerd) transform in(to)
de **transfusie** /trɑnsfyzi/ (pl: -s) transfusion
de **transistor** /trɑnzɪstor/ (pl: -s) transistor
de **transistorradio** /trɑnzɪstoradijo/ (pl: -'s) transistor (radio)
de **transit** /trɑnzit/ transit
transitief /trɑnzitif/ (adj) transitive
het/de **transito** /trɑnzito/ transit
de **transmissie** /trɑnsmɪsi/ (pl: -s) transmission
het ¹**transparant** /trɑnspɑrɑnt/ (pl: -en) transparency, overhead sheet
²**transparant** /trɑnspɑrɑnt/ (adj) transparent
de **transpiratie** /trɑnspira(t)si/ (pl: -s) perspiration
transpireren /trɑnspirerə(n)/ (transpireerde, heeft getranspireerd) perspire
de **transplantatie** /trɑnsplɑnta(t)si/ (pl: -s) transplant(ation)
transplanteren /trɑnsplɑnterə(n)/ (transplanteerde, heeft getransplanteerd) transplant
het **transport** /trɑnspɔrt/ (pl: -en) transport; [esp Am] transportation: *tijdens* het ~ in (or: during) transit
de **transportband** /trɑnspɔrdbɑnt/ (pl: -en) conveyer (belt)
het **transportbedrijf** /trɑnspɔrdbədrɛif/ (pl: -bedrijven) transport company, haulier
¹**transporteren** /trɑnspɔrterə(n)/ (transporteerde, heeft getransporteerd) transport
²**transporteren** /trɑnspɔrterə(n)/ (transporteerde, heeft getransporteerd) wind (the film) (on)
de **transporteur** /trɑnspɔrtør/ (pl: -s) carrier
de **transportkosten** /trɑnspɔrtkostə(n)/ (pl) transport costs (or: charges)
de **transportonderneming** /trɑnspɔrtondərnemɪŋ/ (pl: -en) see *transportbedrijf*
de **transseksualiteit** /trɑnsɛksywalitɛit/ transsexualism
de ¹**transseksueel** /trɑnsɛksywel/ (pl: -seksuelen) transsexual
²**transseksueel** /trɑnsɛksywel/ (adj) transsexual
de **trant** /trɑnt/ **1** style, manner: *in dezelfde* ~ (all) in the same key **2** kind: *iets in die* ~ sth. of the kind (or: sort)
de **trap** /trɑp/ (pl: -pen) **1** (flight of) stairs; (flight of) steps: *een steile* ~ steep stairs; *de* ~ *afgaan* go down(stairs); *de* ~ *opgaan* go upstairs; *boven* (or: *onder, beneden*) *aan de* ~ at the head (or: at the foot, at the bottom) of the stairs **2** kick: *vrije* ~ free kick; *iem. een* ~

nageven [fig] hit s.o. when he is down **3** step **4** [linguistics] degree: *de* ~*pen van vergelijking* the degrees of comparison; *overtreffende* ~ superlative; *vergrotende* ~ comparative
de **trapeze** /trapezə/ (pl: -s) trapeze
het **trapezium** /trapezijʏm/ (pl: -s) trapezium; [Am] trapezoid
de **trapgevel** /trɑpxevəl/ (pl: -s) (crow-)stepped gable
de **trapleuning** /trɑplønɪŋ/ (pl: -en) (stair) handrail; banister
traploos /trɑplos/ (adj) stepless
de **traploper** /trɑplopər/ (pl: -s) stair carpet
trappelen /trɑpələ(n)/ (trappelde, heeft getrappeld) stamp: ~*de paarden* stamping (and pawing) horses; ~ *van ongeduld* strain at the leash; be dying (to do sth., go somewhere)
de **trappelzak** /trɑpəlzɑk/ (pl: -ken) infant's sleeping bag
¹**trappen** /trɑpə(n)/ (trapte, heeft/is getrapt) step, stamp: *ergens in* ~ fall for sth., rise to the bait, buy sth.
²**trappen** /trɑpə(n)/ (trapte, heeft getrapt) kick, boot: *tegen* een bal ~ kick a ball; *eruit getrapt zijn* have got the boot (or: sack); have been kicked out || *lol* ~ horse about (or: around), lark about (or: around)
het **trappenhuis** /trɑpə(n)hœys/ (pl: -huizen) (stair)well
de **trapper** /trɑpər/ (pl: -s) pedal: *op de* ~*s gaan staan* throw one's weight on the pedals
de **trappist** /trɑpɪst/ (pl: -en) Trappist
het **trappistenbier** /trɑpɪstə(n)bir/ Trappist beer
het **trapportaal** /trɑportal/ (pl: -portalen) landing
trapsgewijs /trɑpsxəwɛis/ (adj, adv) gradual, step-by-step
het **trapveldje** /trɑpfɛlcə/ (pl: -s) grassplot
het/de **trauma** /trauma/ (pl: -'s) trauma
de **traumahelikopter** /traumahelikɔptər/ trauma helicopter
het **traumateam** /traumati:m/ (pl: -s) medical emergency team
traumatisch /traumatis/ (adj) traumatic
de **travestie** /travɛsti/ (pl: -ën) transvestism
de **travestiet** /travɛstit/ (pl: -en) transvestite
de **trawler** /trɔːlər/ (pl: -s) trawler
de **trechter** /trɛxtər/ (pl: -s) funnel
de **tred** /trɛt/ (pl: -en) step, pace: *gelijke* ~ *houden met* keep pace with
de **trede** /tredə/ (pl: -n) step; rung
treden /tredə(n)/ (trad, is getreden) step: *in bijzonderheden* ~ go into detail(s); *in contact* ~ *met iem.* contact s.o.; *in het huwelijk* ~ (*met*) get married (to s.o.); *naar buiten* ~ *met iets* come out, make sth. public
de **tredmolen** /trɛtmolə(n)/ (pl: -s) treadmill
de **tree** /tre/ (pl: -ën, -s) see *trede*

de **treeplank** /treplɑŋk/ (pl: -en) footboard
treffen /trɛfə(n)/ (trof, heeft getroffen) **1** hit: *getroffen door de bliksem* struck by lightning **2** meet: *niemand thuis ~* find nobody (at) home **3** hit, strike: *getroffen worden door* meet with; be stricken by **4** make: *voorbereidingen ~* make preparations || *je treft het (goed)* you're lucky (*or:* in luck); *zij hebben het met elkaar getroffen* they are happy with one another, they get on like a house on fire
treffend /trɛfənt/ (adj, adv) striking; apt: *een ~e gelijkenis* a striking similarity
de **treffer** /trɛfər/ (pl: -s) hit; goal
het **trefpunt** /trɛfpʏnt/ (pl: -en) meeting place; crossroads
het **trefwoord** /trɛfwort/ (pl: -en) headword; reference
trefzeker /trɛfsekər/ (adj, adv) accurate
de **trein** /trɛin/ (pl: -en) train: *per ~ reizen* go by train; *iem. van de ~ halen* meet s.o. at the station || *dat loopt als een ~* it's going like a bomb, there's no stopping it
de **treinbestuurder** /trɛimbəstyrdər/ (pl: -s) train driver
de **treinconducteur** /trɛinkɔndʏktør/ (pl: -s) guard; [Am] conductor
het **treinkaartje** /trɛiŋkarcə/ (pl: -s) train ticket
het **treinongeluk** /trɛinɔŋɣəlʏk/ train accident
de **treinramp** /trɛinrɑmp/ (pl: -en) train disaster
de **treinreis** /trɛinrɛis/ (pl: -reizen) train journey
de **treinreiziger** /trɛinrɛizəɣər/ (pl: -s) rail(way) passenger
het **treinstel** /trɛinstɛl/ (pl: -len) train unit
het **treinverkeer** /trɛinvərker/ train traffic, rail traffic
de **treiteraar** /trɛitərar/ (pl: -s) tormentor
treiteren /trɛitərə(n)/ (treiterde, heeft getreiterd) torment
de **trek** /trɛk/ (pl: -ken) **1** pull **2** stroke **3** feature, line **4** (characteristic) feature, trait: *dat is een akelig ~je van haar* that is a nasty trait of hers **5** appetite: *~ hebben* feel (*or:* be) hungry; *heeft u ~ in een kopje koffie?* do you feel like a cup of coffee, would you care for a cup of coffee? **6** popularity: *in ~ zijn* be popular, be in demand **7** migration || *een ~ aan een sigaar doen* take a puff at a cigar; *niet aan zijn ~ken komen* come into one's own
de **trekhaak** /trɛkhak/ (pl: -haken) drawbar; tow bar
de **trekharmonica** /trɛkharmonika/ (pl: -'s) accordion; concertina
¹**trekken** /trɛkə(n)/ (trok, heeft/is getrokken) **1** pull: *aan een sigaar ~* puff at (*or:* draw) a cigar **2** go, move; travel; migrate: *de verkiezingskaravaan trekt het hele land door* the election caravan is touring the whole country; *in een huis ~* move into a house **3** stretch: *met*

zijn been ~ walk with a stiff leg || *deze planken zijn krom getrokken* these planks are warped; *thee laten ~* brew tea
²**trekken** /trɛkə(n)/ (trok, heeft getrokken) **1** draw; extract; pull (out) **2** draw, attract: *publiek* (or: *kopers*) ~ draw an audience (*or:* customers); *volle zalen ~* play to (*or:* draw) full houses **3** pull: *iem. aan zijn haar ~* pull s.o.'s hair; *iem. aan zijn mouw ~* pull (at) s.o.'s sleeve **4** pull, draw, tow: *de aandacht ~* attract attention **5** draw; [maths] extract: *een conclusie ~* draw a conclusion || *gezichten ~* make (*or:* pull) (silly) faces
de **trekker** /trɛkər/ (pl: -s) **1** hiker **2** trigger: *de ~ overhalen* pull the trigger **3** truck, lorry: *~ met oplegger* truck and trailer **4** tractor
de **trekking** /trɛkɪŋ/ (pl: -en) draw
de **trekkracht** /trɛkrɑxt/ (pl: -en) tractive power, pulling power
de **trekpleister** /trɛkplɛistər/ (pl: -s) draw, attraction: *een toeristische ~* a tourist attraction
de **trekschuit** /trɛksχœyt/ (pl: -en) tow barge
de **trektocht** /trɛktɔxt/ (pl: -en) hike, hiking tour
de **trekvogel** /trɛkfoɣəl/ (pl: -s) migratory bird, bird of passage
het **trema** /trema/ (pl: -'s) diaeresis
de **trend** /trɛnt/ (pl: -s) trend
de **trendbreuk** /trɛndbrøk/ (pl: -en) deviation from a trend
trendgevoelig /trɛntχəvuləχ/ (adj, adv) subject to trends
de **trendsetter** /trɛntsɛtər/ (pl: -s) trendsetter
trendy /trɛndi/ (adj) trendy: *~ zijn* be (really) in, be the in-thing
treuren /trørə(n)/ (treurde, heeft getreurd) **1** sorrow, mourn, grieve: *~ om een verlies* mourn a loss **2** be sorrowful, be mournful
treurig /trørəχ/ (adj, adv) sad, tragic, unhappy: *een ~ gezicht* a sorry (*or:* gloomy) sight; a sad (*or:* dejected) face
de **treurigheid** /trørəχhɛit/ sorrow, sadness
de **treurmars** /trørmɑrs/ (pl: -en) funeral march
het **treurspel** /trørspɛl/ (pl: -en) tragedy
de **treurwilg** /trørwɪlχ/ (pl: -en) weeping willow
treuzelen /trøzələ(n)/ (treuzelde, heeft getreuzeld) dawdle: *~ met zijn werk* dawdle over one's work
de **triangel** /trijɑŋəl/ (pl: -s) triangle
de **triatlon** /trijɑtlɔn/ (pl: -s) triathlon
het **tribunaal** /tribynal/ (pl: tribunalen) tribunal
de **tribune** /tribynə/ (pl: -s) stand; gallery
het **tricot** /triko/ (pl: -s) tricot
triest /trist/ (adj, adv) **1** sad **2** melancholy, depressing, dreary
het **triktrak** /trɪktrak/ backgammon
het **triljard** /trɪljɑrt/ (pl: -en) a thousand quadrillions; [Am] octillion

het **triljoen** /trɪljun/ (pl: -en) trillion; [Am] quintillion

trillen /trɪlə(n)/ (trilde, heeft getrild) vibrate; tremble; shake: *met ~de stem* in a trembling voice

de **trilling** /trɪlɪŋ/ (pl: -en) **1** vibration; tremor **2** trembling, shaking

de **trilogie** /triloɣi/ (pl: -ën) trilogy

de **trimbaan** /trɪmban/ (pl: -banen) keep-fit trail

het **trimester** /trimɛstər/ (pl: -s) trimester; term: *midden in het ~* (in) mid-term

¹trimmen /trɪmə(n)/ (trimde, heeft/is getrimd) do keep-fit (exercises); jog; work out

²trimmen /trɪmə(n)/ (trimde, heeft getrimd) trim

de **trimmer** /trɪmər/ (pl: -s) jogger

het **trimpak** /trɪmpɑk/ tracksuit

de **trimschoen** /trɪmsχun/ (pl: -en) training shoe, jogging shoe

het **trio** /trijo/ (pl: -'s) trio

de **triomf** /trijɔmf/ (pl: -en) triumph

triomfantelijk /trijɔmfɑntələk/ (adj, adv) triumphant

triomferen /trijɔmferə(n)/ (triomfeerde, heeft getriomfeerd) triumph

de **triomftocht** /trijɔmftɔχt/ (pl: -en) triumphal procession

de **trip** /trɪp/ (pl: -s) **1** trip **2** (acid) trip

het **triplex** /triplɛks/ plywood

triplo /triplo/: *in ~* in triplicate

trippelen /trɪpələ(n)/ (trippelde, heeft/is getrippeld) trip, patter

trippen /trɪpə(n)/ (tripte, heeft getript) trip (out): *hij tript op hardrockmuziek* he gets off on hard rock (music)

de **trits** /trɪts/ (pl: -en): *een hele ~* a battery (of); [Am] a bunch (of)

triviaal /trivijal/ (adj) trivial

troebel /trubəl/ (adj) turbid, cloudy: *in ~ water vissen* fish in troubled waters

de **troef** /truf/ (pl: troeven) trumps, trump (card): *welke kleur is ~?* what suit is trumps?; *zijn laatste ~ uitspelen* play one's trump card

de **troep** /trup/ (pl: -en) **1** troop; pack **2** mess: *gooi de hele ~ maar weg* just get rid of the whole lot; *~ maken* make a mess **3** [mil] troop: [fig] *voor de ~ en uit lopen* jump the gun, chafe at the bit **4** company

de **troepenmacht** /trupə(n)mɑχt/ (pl: -en) (military) force

het **troeteldier** /trutəldir/ (pl: -en) cuddly toy, soft toy

het **troetelkind** /trutəlkɪnt/ (pl: -kinderen) darling, pet; spoiled child

de **troetelnaam** /trutəlnam/ (pl: -namen) pet name

troeven /truvə(n)/ (troefde, heeft getroefd) [cards] trump, play trumps

de **trofee** /trofe/ (pl: -ën) trophy

de **troffel** /trɔfəl/ (pl: -s) trowel

de **trog** /trɔχ/ (pl: -gen) trough

Trojaans /trojans/ (adj) Trojan

Troje /troje/ Troy

de **trojka** /trɔjka/ (pl: -'s) troika, triumvirate

de **trol** /trɔl/ (pl: -len) troll

de **trolleybus** /trɔlibʏs/ (pl: -sen) trolleybus

de **trom** /trɔm/ (pl: -men) drum

de **trombone** /trɔmboːnə/ (pl: -s) trombone

de **trombonist** /trɔmbonɪst/ (pl: -en) trombonist

de **trombose** /trɔmboːzə/ thrombosis

de **trommel** /trɔməl/ (pl: -s) **1** drum: *de ~ slaan* beat the drum **2** box

trommelen /trɔmələ(n)/ (trommelde, heeft getrommeld) drum: *op de tafel ~* drum (on) the table ‖ *een groep mensen bij elkaar ~* drum up a group of people

de **trommelrem** /trɔməlrɛm/ (pl: -men) drum brake

het **trommelvlies** /trɔməlvlis/ (pl: -vliezen) eardrum, tympanum

de **trompet** /trɔmpɛt/ (pl: -ten) trumpet

trompetten /trɔmpɛtə(n)/ (trompette, heeft getrompet) trumpet

de **trompettist** /trɔmpɛtɪst/ (pl: -en) trumpet player

de **tronie** /troni/ (pl: -s) mug

de **troon** /tron/ (pl: tronen) throne: *de ~ beklimmen (bestijgen)* come to (or: ascend) the throne; *afstand doen van de ~* abdicate (or: renounce) the throne; *iem. van de ~ stoten* dethrone s.o.

de **troonopvolger** /tronɔpfɔlɣər/ (pl: -s) heir (to the throne)

de **troonrede** /tronredə/ (pl: -s) Queen's speech, King's speech

de **troonsafstand** /tronsɑfstɑnt/ abdication (of the throne)

de **troonsbestijging** /tronzbəstɛɪɣɪŋ/ accession (to the throne)

de **troost** /trost/ comfort, consolation: *een bakje ~* a) [Dutch] a cup of coffee; b) [British] a cuppa; *een schrale ~* cold (or: scant) comfort/consolation; *~ putten uit de gedachte* find comfort in the idea

troosteloos /trostəlos/ (adj, adv) disconsolate; cheerless: *een ~ landschap* a dreary (or: desolate) landscape/scene

troosten /trostə(n)/ (troostte, heeft getroost) comfort, console: *zij was niet te ~* she was beyond (all) consolation

de **troostprijs** /trostprɛis/ (pl: -prijzen) consolation prize

de **tropen** /tropə(n)/ (pl) tropics

het **tropenrooster** /tropə(n)rostər/ (pl: -s) work schedule suited to a tropical climate

tropisch /tropis/ (adj, adv) tropical: *het is hier ~ (warm)* it is sweltering here

de **tros** /trɔs/ (pl: -sen) **1** cluster; bunch **2** hawser: *de ~sen losgooien* cast off, unmoor

de **trostomaat** /trostomat/ (pl: -tomaten) vine

tomato

de **¹trots** /trɔts/ pride, glory: *ze is de ~ van haar ouders* she is her parents' pride and joy; *met gepaste ~* with justifiable pride

²trots /trɔts/ (adj, adv) proud

trotseren /trɔtserə(n)/ (trotseerde, heeft getrotseerd) **1** defy; brave: *de blik(ken) ~ (van)* outface, outstare **2** stand up (to)

het **trottoir** /trɔtwar/ (pl: -s) pavement; [Am] sidewalk

de **troubadour** /trubadur/ (pl: -s) troubadour

de **¹trouw** /trɑu/ fidelity, loyalty, faith(fulness); allegiance: *te goeder ~ zijn* be bona fide, be in good faith; *te kwader ~* mala fide, in bad faith

²trouw /trɑu/ (adj, adv) faithful: *~e onderdanen* loyal subjects; *elkaar ~ blijven* be (or: remain) faithful/true to each other

het **trouwboekje** /trɑubukjə/ (pl: -s) [roughly] marriage certificate

de **trouwdag** /trɑudɑx/ (pl: -en) wedding day

trouweloos /trɑuwəlos/ (adj, adv) perfidious, disloyal

¹trouwen /trɑuwə(n)/ (trouwde, is getrouwd) get married: *ik ben er niet mee getrouwd* I'm not wedded (or: tied) to it; *ze trouwde met een arts* she married a doctor; *voor de wet ~* get married in a registry office

²trouwen /trɑuwə(n)/ (trouwde, heeft getrouwd) marry

trouwens /trɑuwəns/ (adv) **1** mind you: *ik vind haar ~ wel heel aardig* mind you, I do think she's very nice; *hij komt niet; ik ~ ook niet* he isn't coming; neither am I for that matter **2** by the way: *~, was Jan er ook?* by the way, was Jan there as well?

de **trouwerij** /trɑuwərɛi/ (pl: -en) wedding

de **trouwjurk** /trɑujʏrk/ (pl: -en) wedding dress

de **trouwpartij** /trɑupɑrtɛi/ (pl: -en) **1** wedding (party) **2** wedding ceremony, marriage ceremony

de **trouwplannen** /trɑuplɑnə(n)/ (pl): *~ hebben* be going (or: planning) to get married

de **trouwring** /trɑurɪŋ/ (pl: -en) wedding ring

de **truc** /trʏk/ (pl: -s) trick: *een ~ met kaarten* a card trick; *dat is de ~* that's the secret

de **trucage** /trykaʒə/ (pl: -s) trickery

de **truck** /trʏk/ (pl: -s) articulated lorry; [Am] trailer truck; truck

de **trucker** /trʏkər/ (pl: -s) lorry-driver; [Am] trucker

de **truffel** /trʏfəl/ (pl: -s) truffle

de **trui** /trœy/ (pl: -en) **1** jumper; sweater **2** jersey, shirt: *de gele ~* the yellow jersey

de **trukendoos** /trykə(n)dos/ box of tricks

de **trust** /trʏst/ (pl: -s) trust, cartel

de **trut** /trʏt/ (pl: -ten) [inform] cow: *stomme ~!* silly cow!

truttig /trʏtəx/ (adj, adv) [inform] frumpy

de **try-out** /trɑjɑut/ (pl: -s) tryout; public rehearsal

de **tsaar** /tsar/ (pl: tsaren) tsar, czar

het **T-shirt** /tiʃʏːrt/ (pl: -s) T-shirt, tee shirt

Tsjaad /tʃat/ Chad

de **Tsjadiër** /tʃadijər/ (pl: -s) Chadian

Tsjadisch /tʃadis/ (adj) Chadian

de **Tsjech** /tʃɛx/ (pl: -en) Czech

Tsjechië /tʃɛxijə/ Czech Republic

het **¹Tsjechisch** /tʃɛxis/ Czech

²Tsjechisch /tʃɛxis/ (adj) Czech

Tsjecho-Slowakije /tʃɛxoslowakɛijə/ Czechoslovakia

de **Tsjetsjeen** /tʃetʃen/ (pl: Tsjetsjenen) Chechen

het **¹Tsjetsjeens** /tʃetʃens/ Chechen

²Tsjetsjeens /tʃetʃens/ (adj) Chechen

Tsjetsjenië /tʃetʃenijə/ Chech(e)nia

het **tso** /teɛso/ [Belg] secondary technical education

de **tsunami** /tsunami/ tsunami

de **tuba** /tyba/ (pl: -'s) tuba

de **tube** /tybə/ (pl: -s) tube

de **tuberculose** /tybɛrkyloze/ tuberculosis

de **tucht** /tʏxt/ discipline: *de ~ handhaven* maintain (or: keep) discipline

het **tuchtcollege** /tʏxtkɔleʒə/ (pl: -s) disciplinary tribunal

het **tuchtrecht** /tʏxtrɛxt/ disciplinary rules

de **tuchtschool** /tʏxtsxol/ (pl: -scholen) youth custody centre

tuffen /tʏfə(n)/ (tufte, heeft/is getuft) chug; drive

de **tuibrug** /tœybrʏx/ (pl: -gen) rope bridge, cable bridge

het **tuig** /tœyx/ (pl: -en) **1** harness **2** riff-raff: *langharig werkschuw ~* long-haired workshy layabouts **3** tackle

tuigen /tœyɣə(n)/ (tuigde, heeft getuigd) harness; tackle (up); bridle

het **tuigje** /tœyxjə/ (pl: -s) safety harness

de **tuimelaar** /tœyməlar/ (pl: -s) tumbler, wobbly clown, wobbly man

tuimelen /tœymələ(n)/ (tuimelde, is getuimeld) tumble, topple

de **tuimeling** /tœymɪŋ/ (pl: -en) tumble, fall

het **tuimelraam** /tœymⱥram/ (pl: -ramen) pivot(al) window

de **tuin** /tœyn/ (pl: -en) garden || *iem. om de ~ leiden* lead s.o. up the garden path

de **tuinbank** /tœymbɑŋk/ (pl: -en) garden bench

de **tuinboon** /tœymbon/ (pl: -bonen) broad bean

de **tuinbouw** /tœymbɑu/ horticulture, market gardening

het **tuinbouwbedrijf** /tœymbɑubədrɛif/ (pl: -bedrijven) market garden

de **tuinbouwschool** /tœymbɑusxol/ (pl: -scholen) horticultural school (or: college)

de **tuinbroek** /tœymbruk/ (pl: -en) dungarees, overalls

het **tuincentrum** /tœynsɛntrʏm/ (pl: -centra) garden centre

de **tuinder** /tœyndər/ (pl: -s) market gardener
tuinen /tœynə(n)/ (tuinde, is getuind): *erin* ~ fall for it

het **tuinfeest** /tœynfest/ (pl: -en) garden party

het **tuingereedschap** /tœynɣəretsχɑp/ garden(ing) tools

het **tuinhuisje** /tœynhœyʃə/ (pl: -s) garden house

de **tuinier** /tœynir/ (pl: -s) gardener
tuinieren /tœynirə(n)/ (tuinierde, heeft getuinierd) garden

de **tuinkabouter** /tœynkɑbɑutər/ (pl: -s) garden gnome

de **tuinkers** /tœynkɛrs/ (garden) cress

de **tuinman** /tœymɑn/ (pl: tuinlieden) gardener

de **tuinslang** /tœynslɑŋ/ (pl: -en) (garden) hose

de **tuinstoel** /tœynstul/ (pl: -en) garden chair

de **tuit** /tœyt/ (pl: -en) **1** spout **2** nozzle
¹tuiten /tœytə(n)/ (tuitte, heeft getuit) tingle, ring: *mijn oren* ~ my ears are ringing
²tuiten /tœytə(n)/ (tuitte, heeft getuit) purse: *de lippen* ~ purse one's lips

tuk /tʏk/ (adj) keen (on): *daar ben ik* ~ *op* I'm keen on (or: mad about) that ‖ *ik had je lekker* ~ *gisteren, hè?* I really had you fooled yesterday, didn't I?; *iem.* ~ *hebben* pull s.o.'s leg

het **tukje** /tʏkjə/ (pl: -s) nap: *een* ~ *doen* take a nap
tukken /tʏkə(n)/ (tukte, heeft getukt) nap, doze

de **tulband** /tʏlbɑnt/ (pl: -en) turban

de **tulp** /tʏlp/ (pl: -en) tulip

de **tulpenbol** /tʏlpə(n)bɔl/ (pl: -len) tulip bulb

de **tulpvakantie** /tʏlpfɑkɑn(t)si/ (pl: -s) half-term holiday, spring holiday

de **tumor** /tymɔr/ (pl: -en) tumour: *kwaadaardige* (or: *goedaardige*) ~ malignant (or: benign) tumour

het **tumult** /tymʏlt/ (pl: -en) tumult, uproar
tumultueus /tymʏltywøs/ (adj) tumultuous

de **tune** /cu:n/ (pl: -s) tune

de **tuner** /cu:nər/ (pl: -s) tuner
Tunesië /tynezijə/ Tunisia

de **Tunesiër** /tunezijər/ (pl: -s) Tunisian
Tunesisch /tynezis/ (adj) Tunisian

de **tunnel** /tʏnəl/ (pl: -s) tunnel

de **tunnelvisie** /tʏnəlvizi/ tunnel vision

de **turbine** /tʏrbinə/ (pl: -s) turbine

de **turbo** /tʏrbo/ (pl: -'s) **1** turbo((super)charger) **2** turbo(-car) ‖ *turbostofzuiger* high-powered vacuum cleaner
turbulent /tʏrbylɛnt/ (adj) turbulent; tempestuous

de **turbulentie** /tʏrbylɛn(t)si/ (pl: -s) turbulence
tureluurs /tyrəlyrs/ (adj) mad, whacky, crazy: *het is om* ~ *(van) te worden* it's enough to drive anybody mad (or: up the wall)

turen /tyrə(n)/ (tuurde, heeft getuurd) peer, gaze, stare: *in de verte* ~ gaze into the distance

de **turf** /tʏrf/ (pl: turven) **1** peat **2** tally **3** tome

het/de **turfmolm** /tʏrfmɔlm/ peat dust
Turijn /tyrɛin/ Turin

de **Turk** /tʏrk/ (pl: -en) Turk
Turkije /tʏrkɛiə/ Turkey

de **Turkmeen** /tʏrkmen/ (pl: Turkmenen) Turkmen
Turkmeens /tʏrkmens/ (adj) Turkoman, Turkman
Turkmenistan /tʏrkmenistɑn/ Turkmenistan

de **¹turkoois** /tʏrkɔjs/ [gem] turquoise

het **²turkoois** /tʏrkɔjs/ [mineral] turquoise
Turks /tʏrks/ (adj) Turkish: ~ *bad* Turkish bath
turnen /tʏrnə(n)/ (turnde, heeft geturnd) practise gymnastics, perform gymnastics

de **turner** /tʏrnər/ (pl: -s) gymnast
turquoise /tʏrkwazə/ (adj) turquoise
turven /tʏrvə(n)/ (turfde, heeft geturfd) tally

tussen /tʏsə(n)/ (prep) **1** between: ~ *de middag* at lunchtime; *dat blijft* ~ *ons (tweeën)* that's between you and me **2** among: *het huis stond* ~ *de bomen* in the house stood among(st) the trees; ~ *vier muren* within four walls ‖ *iem. er (mooi)* ~ *nemen* have s.o. on, take s.o. in; *als er niets* ~ *komt, dan …* unless sth. unforeseen should occur
tussenbeide /tʏsə(n)bɛidə/ (adv) between, in: ~ *komen* interrupt, butt in; step in, intervene; intercede

de **tussendeur** /tʏsə(n)dør/ (pl: -en) communicating door, dividing door
tussendoor /tʏsə(n)dor/ (adv) **1** through; between them **2** between times: *proberen* ~ *wat te slapen* try to snatch some sleep

het **tussendoortje** /tʏsə(n)dorcə/ (pl: -s) snack

de **tussenhandel** /tʏsə(n)hɑndəl/ distributive trade(s)

de **tussenhandelaar** /tʏsə(n)hɑndəlar/ (pl: -s, -handelaren) middleman
tussenin /tʏsə(n)ɪn/ (adv) in between, between the two, in the middle

de **tussenkomst** /tʏsə(n)kɔmst/ **1** intervention **2** mediation

de **tussenlanding** /tʏsə(n)lɑndɪŋ/ (pl: -en) stop(over)
tussenliggend /tʏsə(n)lɪχənt/ (adj) intervening

de **tussenmuur** /tʏsə(n)myr/ (pl: -muren) partition; dividing wall

de **tussenpaus** /tʏsə(n)pɑus/ (pl: -en) [fig] transitory figure

de **tussenpersoon** /tʏsə(n)pɛrson/ (pl: -personen) go-between, intermediary: *als* ~ *fungeren* act as an intermediary

de **tussenpoos** /tʏsə(n)pos/ (pl: -pozen): *met*

de **tussenruimte** /tʏsə(n)rœymtə/ (pl: -n, -s) space: *met gelijke ~n plaatsen* space evenly

de **tussenstand** /tʏsə(n)stɑnt/ (pl: -en) [roughly] score (so far); half-time score

de **tussenstop** /tʏsə(n)stɔp/ (pl: -s) stop(over)

de **tussentijd** /tʏsə(n)tɛit/ (pl: -en) interim: *in de ~* in the meantime, meanwhile

tussentijds /tʏsə(n)tɛits/ (adj) interim: *~e verkiezingen* by-elections

tussenuit /tʏsə(n)œyt/ (adv) out (from between two things) ‖ *er ~ knijpen* do a bunk, cut and run

het **tussenuur** /tʏsə(n)yr/ (pl: -uren) **1** free hour **2** free period

tussenvoegen /tʏsə(n)vuɣə(n)/ (voegde tussen, heeft tussengevoegd) insert

de **tussenwand** /tʏsə(n)wɑnt/ (pl: -en) partition

de **tussenweg** /tʏsə(n)wɛx/ (pl: -en) middle course

de **tussenwoning** /tʏsə(n)wonɪŋ/ (pl: -en) terraced house, town house

de **tut** /tʏt/ (pl: -ten) [inform] frump

tutoyeren /tytwajeːrə(n)/ (tutoyeerde, heeft getutoyeerd) be on first-name terms

de **tutu** /tyty/ (pl: -'s) tutu

de **tv** /teveː/ (pl: tv's) TV, television: *tv kijken* watch TV; *wat komt er vanavond op (de) tv?* what's on (TV) tonight?

de **tv-serie** /teveːseri/ (pl: -s) TV series

t.w. (abbrev) *te weten* namely; viz

twaalf /twalf/ (num) twelve; [in dates] twelfth: *~ dozijn* gross; *om ~ uur 's nachts* at midnight; *om ~ uur 's middags* at (twelve) noon ‖ *de grote wijzer staat al bijna op de ~* the big hand is nearly on the twelve

twaalfde /twalvdə/ (num) twelfth

het **twaalftal** /twalftɑl/ (pl: -len) dozen, twelve

het **twaalfuurtje** /twalfyrcə/ (pl: -s) midday snack, lunch

twee /tweː/ (num) two; [in dates] second: *~ keer per week* twice a week; *een stuk of ~ a* couple of; *~ weken* a fortnight, two weeks; *in ~ën delen* divide in two; halve; *zij waren met hun ~ën* there were two of them ‖ *hij eet en drinkt voor ~* he eats and drinks (enough) for two; *~ aan ~* in twos

de **tweebaansweg** /twebanswɛx/ (pl: -en) **1** two-lane road **2** dual carriageway; [Am] divided highway

het **tweed** /twiːd/ (pl: -s) tweed

tweedaags /twedaxs/ (adj) two-day

de ¹**tweede** /twedə/ (pl: -n) half: *anderhalf is gelijk aan drie ~n* one and a half is the same as three halves

²**tweede** /twedə/ (num) second: *de ~ Kamer* the Lower House (*or:* Chamber); *~ keus* second rate, seconds; *als ~ eindigen* **a)** finish second; **b)** be runner-up; **c)** [fig] come off sec-

ond best; *ten ~* in the second place

tweedegraads /twedeɣrats/ (adj) second-degree: *tweedegraadsbevoegdheid* lower secondary school teaching qualification; *tweedegraadsverbranding* second-degree burn

tweedehands /twedəhɑnts/ (adj, adv) second-hand

tweedejaars /twedəjars/ (adj) second-year

het **Tweede Kamerlid** /twedəkɑmərlɪt/ (pl: -leden) member of the Lower House

het **tweedekansonderwijs** /twedəkɑnsɔndərwɛis/ secondary education for adults

tweedelig /twedeləx/ (adj) two-piece: *een ~ badpak* a two-piece (bathing-suit)

de **tweedelijnszorg** /twedəlɛinsɔrx/ secondary health care

de **tweedeling** /twedelɪŋ/ (pl: -en) split: *sociale ~* social divide

tweederangs /twedərɑŋs/ (adj) second-class

de **tweedracht** /twedrɑxt/ discord

tweeduizend /twedœyzənt/ (num) two thousand

twee-eiig /tweˌɛiəx/ (adj) fraternal

het **tweegevecht** /tweɣəvɛxt/ (pl: -en) man-to-man fight, duel

tweehandig /twehɑndəx/ (adj, adv) ambidext(e)rous

tweehonderd /twehɔndərt/ (num) two hundred

tweehoog /twehox/ (adv) on the second floor; [Am] on the third floor

tweejarig /twejarəx/ (adj) **1** two-year(-old) **2** biennial

de **tweekamerwoning** /twekɑmərwonɪŋ/ (pl: -en) two-room flat

de **tweekamp** /twekɑmp/ (pl: -en) twosome

de **tweekwartsmaat** /twekwɑrtsmat/ (pl: -maten) two-four time

tweeledig /tweledəx/ (adj, adv) double, twofold

de **tweeling** /twelɪŋ/ (pl: -en) **1** twins: *eeneiige* (or: *twee-eiige*) *~en* identical (*or:* fraternal) twins **2** twin

de **tweelingbroer** /twelɪŋbrur/ (pl: -s) twin brother

de **Tweelingen** /twelɪŋə(n)/ (pl) [astrology] Gemini, Twins

de **tweelingzus** /twelɪŋzʏs/ (pl: -sen) twin sister

tweemaal /twemal/ (adv) twice: *zich wel ~ bedenken* think twice

tweemaandelijks /twemandələks/ (adj) **1** bimonthly: *een ~ tijdschrift* a bimonthly **2** two-month

tweemotorig /twemotorəx/ (adj) twin-engined

de **twee-onder-een-kapwoning** /tweɔndərenkɑpwonɪŋ/ (pl: -en) semi-detached house; [Am] (one side of a) duplex

het tweepersoonsbed /tweˈpɛrsonzbɛt/ (pl: -den) double bed

de tweepersoonskamer /tweˈpɛrsonskamər/ (pl: -s) double(-bedded) room; twin-bedded room

tweeslachtig /tweslɑxtəx/ (adj) bisexual

de tweespalt /tweˈspɑlt/ discord

de tweesprong /tweˈsprɔŋ/ (pl: -en) fork, crossroads

tweestemmig /twestɛməx/ (adj, adv) in two voices; two part

de tweestrijd /tweˈstrɛit/ internal conflict: *in ~ staan* be torn between (two things)

de tweet /twiːt/ (pl: -s) tweet

het tweetal /tweˈtɑl/ (pl: -len) pair, couple

tweetalig /twetɑləx/ (adj) bilingual

tweetallig /twetɑləx/ (adj) binary

tweeten /twiːtə(n)/ (tweette, heeft getweet) tweet

tweetjes /tweˈcəs/ (num): *wij ~* we two; *zij waren met hun ~* there were two of them

de tweeverdiener /tweˈvərdinər/ (pl: -s) two-earner; two-earner family, double-income family

het tweevoud /tweˈvɑut/ (pl: -en) **1** double, duplicate: *in ~* in duplicate **2** binary, double (of a number)

tweevoudig /twevɑudəx/ (adj, adv) double, twofold

de tweewieler /tweˈwilər/ (pl: -s) two-wheeler

tweezijdig /twezɛidəx/ (adj) two-sided

de tweezitsbank /tweˈzɪtsbɑŋk/ (pl: -en) two-person settee, two-seater settee

de twijfel /twɛifəl/ (pl: -s) doubt: *het voordeel van de ~* the benefit of the doubt; *boven (alle) ~ verheven zijn* be beyond all doubt; *iets in ~ trekken* cast doubt on sth., question sth.; *zonder ~* no doubt, doubtless, undoubtedly

de twijfelaar /twɛifəlar/ (pl: -s) doubter; sceptic

twijfelachtig /twɛifəlɑxtəx/ (adj, adv) **1** doubtful **2** dubious: *de ~e eer hebben om … have* the dubious honour of (doing sth.)

twijfelen /twɛifələ(n)/ (twijfelde, heeft getwijfeld) doubt: *daar valt niet aan te ~* that is beyond (all) doubt

het twijfelgeval /twɛifəlɣəval/ (pl: -len) dubious case, doubtful case

de twijg /twɛix/ (pl: -en) twig

twinkelen /twɪŋkələ(n)/ (twinkelde, heeft getwinkeld) twinkle

de twinkeling /twɪŋkəlɪŋ/ (pl: -en) twinkling

twintig /twɪntəx/ (num) twenty; [in dates] twentieth: *de jaren ~* the Twenties, the 1920s; *zij was in de ~* she was in her twenties; *er waren er in de ~* there were twenty odd

de twintiger /twɪntəɣər/ (pl: -s) person in his (*or*: her) twenties

twintigste /twɪntəxstə/ (num) twentieth: *een shilling was een ~ pond* a shilling was a twentieth of a pound

de twist /twɪst/ (pl: -en) quarrel: *een ~ bijleggen* settle a quarrel (*or*: dispute)

de twistappel /twɪstɑpəl/ (pl: -s) apple of discord

twisten /twɪstə(n)/ (twistte, heeft getwist) **1** dispute: *daarover wordt nog getwist* that is still a moot point (*or*: in dispute); *over deze vraag valt te ~* this is a debatable (*or*: an arguable) question **2** quarrel: *de ~de partijen* the contending parties

het twitterbericht /twɪtərbərɪxt/ (pl: -en) tweet

twitteren /twɪtərə(n)/ (twitterde, heeft getwitterd) twitter

de tycoon /tɑjkuːn/ (pl: -s) tycoon

de tyfoon /tɑjfuːn/ (pl: -s) typhoon

de tyfus /tifʏs/ typhoid

het/de type /tipə/ (pl: -s) type, character: *een onguur ~* a shady customer; *hij is mijn ~ niet* he's not my type

de typefout /tipfɑut/ (pl: -en) typing error, typo

de typemachine /tipmɑʃinə/ (pl: -s) typewriter

typen /tipə(n)/ (typte, heeft getypt) type: *een getypte brief* a typed (*or*: typewritten) letter; *blind ~* touch-type

typeren /tipərə(n)/ (typeerde, heeft getypeerd) typify, characterize: *dat typeert haar* that is typical of her

typerend /tipərənt/ (adj) typical (of)

typisch /tipis/ (adj, adv) **1** typical: *dat is ~ mijn vader* that's typical of my father; *~ Amerikaans* typically American; *het ~e van een zaak* the curious part of the matter **2** peculiar

de typist /tipɪst/ (pl: -en) typist

typografisch /tipoɣrɑfis/ (adj) typographic(al)

t.z.t. (abbrev) *te zijner tijd* in due time, in due course

u

u /y/ (pers pron) you: *als ik u **was*** if I were you || *een machine waar je u tegen **zegt*** an impressive (*or:* awesome) machine

de **ufo** /ẏfo/ (pl: -'s) *unidentified flying object* UFO

Uganda /uɣɑndɑ/ Uganda

de **Ugandees** /uɣɑnde̱s/ Ugandan

de **ui** /œy/ (pl: uien) onion

de **uiensoep** /œ̱yə(n)sup/ onion soup

de **uier** /œ̱yər/ (pl: -s) udder

de **uil** /œyl/ (pl: -en) owl

de **uilenbal** /œ̱ylə(n)bɑl/ (pl: -len) **1** (owl's) pellet **2** dimwit, nincompoop

het **uilskuiken** /œ̱ylskœykə(n)/ (pl: -s) [fig, inform] ninny, nitwit

¹**uit** /œyt/ (adj) **1** out, away: *de bal **is*** ~ the ball is out; *die vlek gaat **er** niet* ~ that stain won't come out **2** over: *de school gaat* ~ school is over; school is out; *het **is** ~ tussen hen* it is finished between them; *het is ~ **met** de pret* the game (*or:* party) is over now **3** (gone) out: *de lamp **is*** ~ the light is out (*or:* off) **4** out, after: *op iets* ~ *zijn* be out for (*or:* after) sth. || *dit boek **is** pas* ~ this book has just been published

²**uit** /œyt/ (adv) out: *hij liep de **kamer*** ~ he walked out of the room; *Ajax **speelt** volgende week* ~ Ajax are playing away next week || *moet je ook die **kant** ~?* are you going that way, too?; *voor zich* ~ *zitten kijken* sit staring into space; *ik zou **er** graag eens* ~ *willen* I would like to get away sometime; *de aankoop heb je **er** na een jaar* ~ the purchase will save its cost in a year

³**uit** /œyt/ (prep) **1** out (of), from: ~ *het **raam** kijken* look out of the window; *een speler* ~ *het **veld** sturen* order a player off (the field) **2** off: *2 km ~ de **kust*** 2 kilometres off the coast **3** (out) of: *iets ~ **ervaring** kennen* know sth. from experience; ~ *zichzelf* of itself; of one's own accord [pers] **4** out of, from: ~ *bewondering* out of (*or:* in) admiration; *zij trouwden ~ **liefde*** they married for love

uitademen /œ̱ytadəmə(n)/ (ademde uit, heeft uitgeademd) breathe out, exhale

uitbaggeren /œ̱ydbɑɣərə(n)/ (baggerde uit, heeft uitgebaggerd) dredge

uitbalanceren /œydbalɑnserə(n)/ (balanceerde uit, heeft uitgebalanceerd) balance

uitbannen /œ̱ydbɑnə(n)/ (bande uit, heeft uitgebannen) banish; ban

uitbarsten /œ̱ydbɑrstə(n)/ (barstte uit, is uitgebarsten) **1** burst out: *in lachen* ~ burst out laughing; *in tranen* ~ burst into tears **2** erupt

de **uitbarsting** /œ̱ydbɑrstɪŋ/ (pl: -en) **1** outburst; eruption **2** bursting out: *tot een ~ **komen*** come to a head

uitbaten /œ̱ydbatə(n)/ (baatte uit, heeft uitgebaat) [Belg] run

de **uitbater** /œ̱ydbatər/ (pl: -s) manager

uitbeelden /œ̱ydbeldə(n)/ (beeldde uit, heeft uitgebeeld) portray, represent: *een **verhaal*** ~ act out a story

de **uitbeelding** /œ̱ydbeldɪŋ/ (pl: -en) portrayal, representation

uitbesteden /œ̱ydbəstedə(n)/ (besteedde uit, heeft uitbesteed) **1** board out: *de **kinderen** een week* ~ board the children out for a week **2** farm out, contract (out)

uitbetalen /œ̱ydbətalə(n)/ (betaalde uit, heeft uitbetaald) pay (out); cash

de **uitbetaling** /œ̱ydbətalɪŋ/ (pl: -en) payment

uitbijten /œ̱ydbɛitə(n)/ (beet uit, heeft uitgebeten) **1** bite (out) **2** eat away: *dat **zuur** bijt uit* that acid is corrosive

¹**uitblazen** /œ̱ydblazə(n)/ (blies uit, heeft uitgeblazen) take a breather, catch one's breath

²**uitblazen** /œ̱ydblazə(n)/ (blies uit, heeft uitgeblazen) **1** blow (out); breathe out: *de laatste **adem*** ~ breathe one's last **2** blow out

uitblijven /œ̱ydblɛivə(n)/ (bleef uit, is uitgebleven) **1** stay away; stay out **2** fail to occur (*or:* appear, materialize): *de **gevolgen** bleven niet uit* the consequences (soon) became apparent

uitblinken /œ̱ydblɪŋkə(n)/ (blonk uit, heeft uitgeblonken) excel: ~ *in* excel in

de **uitblinker** /œ̱ydblɪŋkər/ (pl: -s) brilliant person (*or:* student): *in sport was hij **geen*** ~ he did not shine in sports

uitbloeien /œ̱ydblujə(n)/ (bloeide uit, is uitgebloeid) leave off flowering: *de **rozen** zijn uitgebloeid* the roses have finished flowering

de **uitbouw** /œ̱ydbɑu/ (pl: -en) extension, addition

uitbouwen /œ̱ydbɑuwə(n)/ (bouwde uit, heeft uitgebouwd) **1** build out; add on to **2** develop, expand

de **uitbraak** /œ̱ydbrak/ break, jailbreak

uitbraken /œ̱ydbrakə(n)/ (braakte uit, heeft uitgebraakt) vomit

¹**uitbranden** /œ̱ydbrɑndə(n)/ (brandde uit, is uitgebrand) **1** burn up **2** be burnt down (*or:* out)

²**uitbranden** /œ̱ydbrɑndə(n)/ (brandde uit, heeft uitgebrand) burn down, burn out

de **uitbrander** /œ̱ydbrɑndər/ (pl: -s) dressing down, telling-off

¹**uitbreiden** /œ̱ydbrɛidə(n)/ (breidde uit, heeft uitgebreid) extend, expand: *zijn **kennis*** ~ extend one's knowledge

zich **²uitbreiden** /ˈœydbrɛidə(n)/ (breidde zich uit, heeft zich uitgebreid) extend, expand; spread

de **uitbreiding** /ˈœydbrɛidɪŋ/ (pl: -en) **1** extension, expansion **2** extension, addition; development

uitbreken /ˈœydbrekə(n)/ (brak uit, heeft/is uitgebroken) break out: *er is **brand*** (or: *een **epidemie***) *uitgebroken* a fire (or: an epidemic) has broken out; *een **muur*** ~ knock down (a part of) a wall

uitbrengen /ˈœydbrɛŋə(n)/ (bracht uit, heeft uitgebracht) **1** bring out, say: *een **toost*** ~ propose a toast to s.o.; *hij kon geen **woord*** ~ he couldn't bring out (or: utter) a word, the words stuck in his throat **2** make, give: ***verslag*** ~ *van een vergadering* give an account of a meeting **3** bring out; release; publish: *een nieuw **merk** auto* ~ put a new make of car on the market

uitbroeden /ˈœydbrudə(n)/ (broedde uit, heeft uitgebroed) hatch (out): ***eieren*** ~ hatch (out) eggs; *hij zit een **idee** uit te broeden* he is brooding over an idea

uitbuiten /ˈœydbœytə(n)/ (buitte uit, heeft uitgebuit) exploit, use: *een **gelegenheid*** ~ make the most of an opportunity

de **uitbuiter** /ˈœydbœytər/ (pl: -s) exploiter

de **uitbuiting** /ˈœydbœytɪŋ/ (pl: -en) exploitation

uitbundig /ˈœydbʏndəx/ (adj, adv) exuberant

uitchecken /ˈœytʃɛkə(n)/ (checkte uit, heeft uitgecheckt) check out

uitdagen /ˈœydaɣə(n)/ (daagde uit, heeft uitgedaagd) challenge: ***tot** een duel* ~ challenge s.o. to a duel

uitdagend /ˈœydaɣənt/ (adj, adv) defiant: ~ *gekleed gaan* dress provocatively

de **uitdager** /ˈœydaɣər/ (pl: -s) challenger

de **uitdaging** /ˈœydaɣɪŋ/ (pl: -en) challenge, provocation

uitdelen /ˈœydelə(n)/ (deelde uit, heeft uitgedeeld) distribute, hand out

uitdenken /ˈœydɛŋkə(n)/ (dacht uit, heeft uitgedacht) invent, devise, think up

uitdeuken /ˈœydøkə(n)/ (deukte uit, heeft uitgedeukt) beat out (a dent, dents)

uitdiepen /ˈœydipə(n)/ (diepte uit, heeft uitgediept) **1** deepen **2** explore (or: study) in depth

uitdijen /ˈœydɛiə(n)/ (dijde uit, is uitgedijd) expand, swell, grow

uitdoen /ˈœydun/ (deed uit, heeft uitgedaan) **1** take off, remove: *zijn **kleren*** ~ take off one's clothes **2** turn off, switch off

uitdokteren /ˈœydoktərə(n)/ (dokterde uit, heeft uitgedokterd) work out, figure out

uitdossen /ˈœydosə(n)/ (doste uit, heeft uitgedost) dress up, deck out

uitdoven /ˈœydovə(n)/ (doofde uit, heeft uitgedoofd) extinguish; stub out

de **uitdraai** /ˈœydraj/ (pl: -en) print-out

uitdraaien /ˈœydrajə(n)/ (draaide uit, heeft uitgedraaid) **1** turn off, switch off; turn out, put out **2** print out

uitdragen /ˈœydraɣə(n)/ (droeg uit, heeft uitgedragen) propagate, spread

uitdrijven /ˈœydrɛivə(n)/ (dreef uit, heeft uitgedreven) drive out, expel; exorcize

uitdrogen /ˈœydroɣə(n)/ (droogde uit, is uitgedroogd) dry out; dry up

uitdrukkelijk /ˈœydrʏkələk/ (adj, adv) express, distinct: *iets* ~ ***verbieden*** expressly forbid sth.

uitdrukken /ˈœydrʏkə(n)/ (drukte uit, heeft uitgedrukt) **1** express, put: *zijn **gedachten*** ~ express (or: convey, voice) one's thoughts; *om het **eenvoudig** uit te drukken* in plain terms, to put it plainly (or: simply) **2** stub out, put out ‖ *de waarde van iets **in** geld* ~ express the value of sth. in terms of money

de **uitdrukking** /ˈœydrʏkɪŋ/ (pl: -en) **1** expression, idiom; term: *een **vaste*** ~ a fixed expression **2** expression, look: *een **verwilderde*** ~ *in zijn ogen* a wild (or: haggard) look in his eyes ‖ ~ ***geven*** *aan* express, voice

uitdunnen /ˈœydʏnə(n)/ (dunde uit, heeft/is uitgedund) thin (out), deplete: *het deelnemersveld is flink uitgedund* the number of participants has thinned out

uiteendrijven /œytˈɛndrɛivə(n)/ (dreef uiteen, heeft uiteengedreven) scatter, disperse

uiteenlopen /œytˈɛnlopə(n)/ (liep uiteen, is uiteengelopen) vary, differ, diverge: *de **meningen** liepen zeer uiteen* opinions were sharply (or: much) divided; ***sterk*** ~ vary (or: differ) widely

uiteenlopend /œytˈɛnlopənt/ (adj) various, varied

uiteenvallen /œytˈɛnvalə(n)/ (viel uiteen, is uiteengevallen) fall apart, collapse; break up

uiteenzetten /œytˈɛnzɛtə(n)/ (zette uiteen, heeft uiteengezet) explain, set out

de **uiteenzetting** /œytˈɛnzɛtɪŋ/ (pl: -en) explanation, account: *een* ~ ***houden*** *over een kwestie* give an account of sth.

het **uiteinde** /ˈœytɛində/ (pl: -n) **1** extremity, tip, (far) end **2** end, close; end of the year: *iem. een **zalig*** ~ *wensen* wish s.o. a happy New Year

¹uiteindelijk /œytˈɛindələk/ (adj, adv) final, ultimate, last: *de ~e **beslissing*** the final decision

²uiteindelijk /œytˈɛindələk/ (adv) finally, eventually, in the end: ~ ***belandde** ik in Rome* eventually I ended (or: landed) up in Rome

uiten /ˈœytə(n)/ (uitte, heeft geuit) utter, express, speak

uit-en-ter-na /œytɛntɛrˈna/ (adv) **1** endlessly **2** down to the finest detail, thoroughly

uitentreuren /œytəntrɶrə(n)/ (adv) over

and over again, continually

uiteraard /œytəra̱rt/ (adv) of course; naturally

het ¹**uiterlijk** /œytərlək/ **1** appearance, looks: *hij heeft zijn ~ niet mee* his looks are against him; *mensen op hun ~ beoordelen* judge people by their looks **2** (outward) appearance, show: *dat is alleen maar voor het ~* that's just for appearance's sake (*or:* for show)

²**uiterlijk** /œytərlək/ (adj) outward, external: *op de ~e schijn afgaan* judge by appearances

³**uiterlijk** /œytərlək/ (adv) **1** outwardly, from the outside, externally: *~ scheen hij kalm* outwardly he seemed calm enough **2** at the (very) latest, not later than: *~ (op)* 1 november not later than November 1; *tot ~* 10 juli until July 10 at the latest

uitermate /œytərma̱tə/ (adv) extremely

¹**uiterst** /œytərst/ (adj) **1** far(thest), extreme, utmost: *het ~e puntje* the (extreme) tip, the far end; *~ rechts* (the) far right **2** greatest, utmost: *zijn ~e best doen om te helpen* do one's level best to help, bend over backwards to help **3** final, last: *een ~e poging* a last-ditch effort

²**uiterst** /œytərst/ (adv) extremely, most

het **uiterste** /œytərstə/ (pl: -n) **1** extreme, utmost, limit: *tot ~n vervallen* go to extremes; *van het ene ~ in het andere (vervallen)* go from one extreme to the other **2** utmost, extreme, last: *bereid zijn tot het ~ te gaan* be prepared to go to any length **3** extremity, end

de **uiterwaard** /œytərwart/ (pl: -en) (river) foreland, water meadow

uitfluiten /œytflœytə(n)/ (floot uit, heeft uitgefloten) hiss (at), give (s.o.) the bird: *uitgefloten worden* receive catcalls; get the bird

uitfoeteren /œytfutərə(n)/ (foeterde uit, heeft uitgefoeterd) [inform] storm at; [Am] bawl out

uitgaan /œytχan/ (ging uit, is uitgegaan) **1** go out, leave: *het huis (de deur) ~* leave the house; *een avondje ~* have a night out; *met een meisje ~* go out with a girl, take a girl out, date a girl **2** be over, be out; break up; go out: *de school* (or: *de bioscoop*) *gaat uit* school (or: the film) is over **3** (+ van) start (from), depart (from), take for granted, assume: *men is ervan uitgegaan dat …* it has been assumed (or: taken for granted) that … ‖ *die vlekken gaan er niet uit* these spots won't come out

uitgaand /œytχant/ (adj) outgoing, outward; outbound; outward bound: *~e brieven* (or: *post*) outgoing letters (or: post)

de **uitgaansavond** /œytχansavɔnt/ (pl: -en) (regular) night out

de **uitgaansgelegenheid** /œytχansχəleɣə(n)hɛit/ (pl: -heden) place of entertainment

het **uitgaansleven** /œytχanslevə(n)/ nightlife:

een bruisend ~ a bustling nightlife

het **uitgaansverbod** /œytχansfərbɔt/ (pl: -verboden) curfew

de **uitgang** /œytχɑŋ/ (pl: -en) exit, way out

de **uitgangspositie** /œytχɑŋspozi(t)si/ (pl: -s) point of departure: *zich in een goede* (or: *slechte*) *~ bevinden om …* be in a good (or: bad) position for sth.

het **uitgangspunt** /œytχɑŋspʏnt/ (pl: -en) point of departure, starting point

de **uitgave** /œytχavə/ (pl: -n) **1** outlay; spending; expenditure, costs: *de ~n voor defensie* defence expenditure **2** edition; issue **3** publication, production

het **uitgavenpatroon** /œytχavəpatron/ pattern of spending

uitgeblust /œytχəblʏst/ (adj) washed out: *een ~e indruk maken* look washed out

uitgebreid /œytχəbrɛit/ (adj, adv) extensive, comprehensive; detailed

uitgehongerd /œytχəhɔŋərt/ (adj) famished, starving

uitgekiend /œytχəkint/ (adj) sophisticated, cunning

uitgekookt /œytχəkokt/ (adj) sly, shrewd

uitgelaten /œytχəlatə(n)/ (adj, adv) elated, exuberant

het **uitgeleide** /œytχəlɛidə/ send-off, escort

uitgelezen /œytχəlezə(n)/ (adj) exquisite; superior; select

uitgemaakt /œytχəmakt/ (adj) established, settled

uitgemergeld /œytχəmɛrɣəlt/ (adj) emaciated, gaunt

uitgeprocedeerd /œytχəprosədərt/ (adj) exhausted of all legal procedures

uitgeput /œytχəpʏt/ (adj) **1** exhausted, worn out: *~ van pijn* exhausted with pain **2** empty; flat **3** exhausted, at an end: *onze voorraden zijn ~* our supplies have run out (or: are exhausted)

uitgerekend /œytχərekənt/ (adv) precisely, of all (people, things), very: *~ jij!* you of all people!; *~ vandaag* today of all days

uitgeslapen /œytχəslapə(n)/ (adj) wide awake, rested

uitgesloten /œytχəslotə(n)/ (adj) out of the question, impossible

uitgesproken /œytχəsprokə(n)/ (adj, adv) marked, clear(-cut): *een ~ voorkeur* a marked preference; *met de ~ bedoeling (om) te …* with the explicit aim to …; *~ lelijk* undeniably ugly

uitgestorven /œytχəstɔrvə(n)/ (adj) **1** deserted, desolate **2** extinct

uitgestrekt /œytχəstrɛkt/ (adj) vast, extensive

uitgeteld /œytχətɛlt/ (adj) exhausted, deadbeat; [sport] (counted) out: *~ op de bank liggen* lie on the couch, dead to the world; *ze is in september ~* she is due in September

uitgeven /œytχevə(n)/ (gaf uit, heeft uit-
gegeven) **1** spend, pay: *geld aan boeken* (or:
als water) ~ spend money on books (or: like
water) **2** issue, emit: *vals geld* ~ pass counterfeit money **3** publish **4** pass off (as): *zich
voor iem. anders* ~ impersonate s.o., pose as
s.o. else

de **uitgever** /œytχevər/ (pl: -s) publisher

de **uitgeverij** /œytχevərɛi/ (pl: -en) publishing
house (or: company), publisher('s)

uitgewerkt /œytχəwɛrkt/ (adj) elaborate,
detailed

uitgewoond /œytχəwont/ (adj) run-down,
dilapidated

¹**uitgezonderd** /œytχəzɔndərt/ (prep) except for, apart from: *niemand* ~ with no exceptions, bar none

²**uitgezonderd** /œytχəzɔndərt/ (conj)
except(ing), apart from, but, except for the
fact that: *iedereen ging mee,* ~ *hij* everyone
came (along), except for him, everybody but
him came (along)

de **uitgifte** /œytχɪftə/ (pl: -n) issue, distribution

uitgillen /œytχɪlə(n)/ (gilde uit, heeft uit-
gegild) scream (out), shriek (out): *hij gilde het
uit van de pijn* he screamed with pain

uitglijden /œytχlɛidə(n)/ (gleed uit, is uit-
gegleden) **1** slip, slide **2** slip (and fall): ~ *over
een bananenschil* slip on a banana peel

de **uitglijder** /œytχlɛidər/ (pl: -s) blunder, slip(-
up)

uitgraven /œytχravə(n)/ (groef uit, heeft
uitgegraven) **1** dig up, excavate **2** dig out:
een sloot ~ deepen (or: dig out) a ditch

uitgroeien /œytχrujə(n)/ (groeide uit, is
uitgegroeid) grow (into), develop (into)

de **uithaal** /œythal/ (pl: uithalen) hard shot,
sizzler

uithakken /œythakə(n)/ (hakte uit, heeft
uitgehakt) **1** chop (or: cut, hack) away **2** cut
out

¹**uithalen** /œythalə(n)/ (haalde uit, heeft
uitgehaald) (take a) swing: ~ *in de richting van
de bal* take a swing (or: swipe) at the ball

²**uithalen** /œythalə(n)/ (haalde uit, heeft
uitgehaald) **1** take out, pull out, remove;
unpick, undo; extract **2** empty, clear out,
clean out; draw: *een vogelnest* ~ take the
eggs from a bird's nest **3** play, do: *een grap
met iem.* ~ play a joke on s.o.; *wat heb je nu
weer uitgehaald!* what have you been up to
now! **4** be of use, help: *het haalt niets uit* it is
no use (or: all in vain)

het **uithangbord** /œythɑŋbɔrt/ (pl: -en) sign-
(board): *mijn arm is geen* ~ I can't hold this
forever

¹**uithangen** /œythɑŋə(n)/ (hing uit, heeft
uitgehangen) **1** hang out **2** be, hang out

²**uithangen** /œythɑŋə(n)/ (hing uit, heeft
uitgehangen) **1** hang out, put out **2** play, act

uitheems /œythems/ (adj) exotic, foreign

de **uithoek** /œythuk/ (pl: -en) remote corner,
outpost: *tot in de verste* ~*en van het land* to
the farthest corners of the country; *in een* ~
wonen live in the back of beyond

uithollen /œythɔlə(n)/ (holde uit, heeft uit-
gehold) **1** scoop out, hollow out **2** erode: *de
democratie* ~ undermine (or: erode) democracy

uithongeren /œythɔŋərə(n)/ (hongerde
uit, heeft uitgehongerd) starve (out): *de vij-
and* ~ starve the enemy out (or: into submission)

uithoren /œythorə(n)/ (hoorde uit, heeft
uitgehoord) interrogate, question

uithouden /œythaudə(n)/ (hield uit, heeft
uitgehouden) **1** stand, endure: *hij kon het
niet langer* ~ he could not take (or: stand) it
any longer **2** stick (it) out: *het ergens lang* ~
stay (or: stick it out) somewhere for a long
time

het **uithoudingsvermogen** /œythaudɪŋsfər-
moɣə(n)/ staying power, endurance: *geen* ~
hebben lack stamina

uithuilen /œythœylə(n)/ (huilde uit, heeft
uitgehuild) cry to one's heart's content

uithuwelijken /œythywələkə(n)/ (huwe-
lijkte uit, heeft uitgehuwelijkt) marry off,
give in marriage

de **uiting** /œytɪŋ/ (pl: -en) utterance, expression, word(s): ~ *geven aan zijn gevoelens* express (or: vent, air) one's feelings; *tot* ~ *komen in* manifest (or: reveal) itself in

het **uitje** /œycə/ (pl: -s) **1** outing, (pleasure) trip,
excursion **2** cocktail onion

uitjoelen /œytjulə(n)/ (joelde uit, heeft uit-
gejoeld) see *uitjouwen*

uitjouwen /œytjauwə(n)/ (jouwde uit,
heeft uitgejouwd) boo, hoot at, jeer at

uitkafferen /œytkɑfərə(n)/ (kafferde uit,
heeft uitgekafferd) [inform] give (s.o.) a
bawling, bite (s.o.'s) head off

uitkammen /œytkɑmə(n)/ (kamde uit,
heeft uitgekamd) comb (out), search

uitkauwen /œytkɑuwə(n)/ (kauwde uit,
heeft uitgekauwd) chew (up)

uitkeren /œytkerə(n)/ (keerde uit, heeft
uitgekeerd) pay (out), remit

de **uitkering** /œytkerɪŋ/ (pl: -en) payment, remittance; benefit; allowance, pension: *recht
hebben op een* ~ be entitled to benefit; *een
maandelijkse* ~ a monthly allowance; *van
een* ~ *leven* live on social security; be on the
dole

de **uitkeringstrekker** /œytkerɪŋstrɛkər/ (pl:
-s) social security recipient, benefit claimant

uitkienen /œytkinə(n)/ (kiende uit, heeft
uitgekiend) [inform] figure out

uitkiezen /œytkizə(n)/ (koos uit, heeft uitgekozen) choose, select: *je hebt het maar voor
het* ~ (you can) take your pick

de **uitkijk** /œytkɛik/ (pl: -en) lookout, watch:

op de ~ *staan* be on the watch (*or:* lookout) (for), keep watch (for)

¹**uitkijken** /ˈœytkɛikə(n)/ (keek uit, heeft uitgekeken) **1** watch out, look out, be careful: ~ *met* *oversteken* take care crossing the street **2** overlook, look out on: *dit raam kijkt uit op de zee* this window overlooks the sea **3** look out (for), watch (for): *naar* een andere baan ~ watch (*or:* look) out for a new job **4** look forward (to): *naar* de vakantie ~ look forward to the holidays

²**uitkijken** /ˈœytkɛikə(n)/ (keek uit, is uitgekeken) tire (of sth.): *gauw uitgekeken zijn op iets* quickly tire (*or:* get tired) of sth.

de **uitkijkpost** /ˈœytkɛikpɔst/ (pl: -en) lookout; observation post

de **uitkijktoren** /ˈœytkɛiktorə(n)/ (pl: -s) watchtower

uitklapbaar /ˈœytklɑbar/ (adj) folding, collapsible: *deze* **stoel** *is* ~ *tot een bed* this chair converts into a bed

uitklappen /ˈœytklɑpə(n)/ (klapte uit, heeft/is uitgeklapt) fold (out)

uitklaren /ˈœytklarə(n)/ (klaarde uit, heeft uitgeklaard) clear (through customs)

uitkleden /ˈœytkledə(n)/ (kleedde uit, heeft uitgekleed) undress, strip (off): *zich* ~ undress, strip (off)

uitkloppen /ˈœytklɔpə(n)/ (klopte uit, heeft uitgeklopt) beat (out), shake (out): *een* **kleed** ~ beat a carpet

uitknijpen /ˈœytknɛipə(n)/ (kneep uit, heeft uitgeknepen) squeeze (out, dry): *een* **puistje** ~ squeeze out a pimple

uitknippen /ˈœytknɪpə(n)/ (knipte uit, heeft uitgeknipt) cut, clip: **prentjes** ~ cut out pictures

uitkomen /ˈœytkomə(n)/ (kwam uit, is uitgekomen) **1** end up, arrive at: *op de hoofdweg* ~ join (onto) the main road **2** lead (to), give out (into, on to): *die deur komt uit op de straat* ~ this door opens (out) on to the street **3** come out, sprout **4** hatch (out) **5** be revealed (*or:* disclosed): *het kwam uit* it was revealed, it transpired **6** (+ voor) admit: *voor zijn mening durven* ~ stand up for one's opinion; *eerlijk* ~ **voor** admit openly, be honest about **7** prove to be true (*or:* correct), come true; come out, work out; be right: *die* **som** *komt niet uit* that sum doesn't add up; *mijn* **voorspelling** *kwam uit* my prediction proved correct (*or:* came true) **8** [sport] play; [cards] lead: **met** *klaveren* (*or:* *troef*) ~ lead clubs (*or:* trumps) **9** appear, be published: *een nieuw tijdschrift* **laten** ~ publish a new magazine **10** turn out, work out: **bedrogen** ~ be deceived; *dat komt (me)* **goed** *uit* that suits me fine, that's very timely (*or:* convenient) **11** show up, stand out, come out, be apparent: *iets goed* **laten** ~ show sth. to advantage; **tegen** *de lichte achtergrond komen de kleuren*

goed uit the colours show up (*or:* stand out) well against the light background

de **uitkomst** /ˈœytkɔmst/ (pl: -en) (final, net) result, outcome

uitkopen /ˈœytkopə(n)/ (kocht uit, heeft uitgekocht) buy out

uitkotsen /ˈœytkɔtsə(n)/ (kotste uit, heeft uitgekotst) [inform] throw up, spew up

uitkramen /ˈœytkramə(n)/ (kraamde uit, heeft uitgekraamd): **onzin** ~ talk nonsense

uitkrijgen /ˈœytkrɛiɣə(n)/ (kreeg uit, heeft uitgekregen) **1** get off, get out of: *zijn* **laarzen** *niet* ~ not be able to get one's boots off **2** finish, get to the end of

de **uitlaat** /ˈœytlat/ (pl: uitlaten) exhaust (pipe); [Am] muffler; funnel

de **uitlaatgassen** /ˈœytlatχɑsə(n)/ (pl) exhaust fumes

de **uitlaatklep** /ˈœytlatklɛp/ (pl: -pen) **1** outlet valve; exhaust valve, escape valve **2** [fig] outlet

de **uitlaatpijp** /ˈœytlatpɛip/ (pl: -en) [car] exhaust pipe

uitlachen /ˈœytlɑχə(n)/ (lachte uit, heeft uitgelachen) laugh at, deride, scoff (at), ridicule: *iem. in zijn gezicht* ~ laugh in s.o.'s face

uitladen /ˈœytladə(n)/ (laadde uit, heeft uitgeladen) unload; discharge [ship]

uitlaten /ˈœytlatə(n)/ (liet uit, heeft uitgelaten) show out (*or:* to the door), see out (*or:* to the door), let out; discharge: *een* **bezoeker** ~ show a visitor out (*or:* to the door); *de* **hond** ~ take the dog out (for a walk)

de **uitlating** /ˈœytlatɪŋ/ (pl: -en) utterance, statement, comment

de **uitleg** /ˈœytlɛχ/ explanation, account: *haar* ~ *van wat er gebeurd was* her account of what had happened

uitleggen /ˈœytlɛɣə(n)/ (legde uit, heeft uitgelegd) explain, interpret: **dromen** ~ interpret dreams; **verkeerd** ~ misinterpret, misconstrue

uitlekken /ˈœytlɛkə(n)/ (lekte uit, is uitgelekt) **1** drain; drip dry: *groente* **laten** ~ drain vegetables **2** get out, leak out: *het* **plan** *is uitgelekt* the plan has got (*or:* leaked) out

uitlenen /ˈœytlenə(n)/ (leende uit, heeft uitgeleend) lend (out), loan

zich **uitleven** /ˈœytlevə(n)/ (leefde zich uit, heeft zich uitgeleefd) live it up, let o.s. go

uitleveren /ˈœytleverə(n)/ (leverde uit, heeft uitgeleverd) extradite; hand over: *iem. aan de politie* ~ hand s.o. over (*or:* turn s.o. in) to the police

de **uitlevering** /ˈœytleverɪŋ/ (pl: -en) extradition

uitlezen /ˈœytlezə(n)/ (las uit, heeft uitgelezen) **1** read to the end, read through, finish (reading) **2** [comp] read out

uitlijnen /ˈœytlɛinə(n)/ (lijnde uit, heeft uitgelijnd) **1** align **2** align, line up

uitloggen /œytlɔɣə(n)/ (logde uit, heeft uitgelogd) log off, log out

uitlokken /œytlɔkə(n)/ (lokte uit, heeft uitgelokt) provoke, elicit, stimulate: *een discussie* ~ provoke a discussion; *hij lokt het zelf uit* he is asking for it (*or:* trouble)

de **uitloop** /œytlop/ extension: *een* ~ *tot vier jaar* an extension to four years

uitlopen /œytlopə(n)/ (liep uit, is uitgelopen) **1** run out (of), walk out (of), leave: *de straat* ~ walk down the street **2** sprout, shoot, come out **3** result in, end in: *dat loopt op niets* (or: *een mislukking*) *uit* that will come to nothing (*or:* end in failure); *die ruzie liep uit op een gevecht* the quarrel ended in a fight **4** draw ahead (of): *hij is al 20 seconden uitgelopen* he's already in the lead by 20 seconds **5** overrun its (*or:* one's) time: *de receptie liep uit* the reception went on longer than expected **6** run: *uitgelopen oogschaduw* smeared (*or:* smudged) eyeshadow; *de verf is uitgelopen* the paint has run

de **uitloper** /œytlopər/ (pl: -s) runner, stolon; foothill; tail end

uitloten /œytlotə(n)/ (lootte uit, heeft uitgeloot) **1** eliminate by lottery **2** draw, select

uitloven /œytlovə(n)/ (loofde uit, heeft uitgeloofd) offer, put up: *een beloning* ~ offer (*or:* put up) a reward

uitmaken /œytmakə(n)/ (maakte uit, heeft uitgemaakt) **1** break off; finish; terminate: *het* ~ break (or: split) up **2** constitute, make up: *deel* ~ *van* be (a) part of; *een belangrijk deel van de kosten* ~ form (or: represent) a large part of the cost **3** matter, be of importance: *het maakt mij niet(s) uit* it is all the same to me, I don't care; *wat maakt dat uit?* what does that matter?; *weinig* ~ make little difference **4** determine, establish; make out: *dat maakt hij toch niet uit* that's not for him to decide; *dat maak ik zelf nog wel uit* I'll be the judge of that **5** (+ voor) call, brand: *iem. voor dief* ~ call s.o. a thief

uitmelken /œytmɛlkə(n)/ (molk uit, heeft uitgemolken) bleed dry (*or:* white), strip bare: *een onderwerp* ~ flog a subject to death

uitmesten /œytmɛstə(n)/ (mestte uit, heeft uitgemest) **1** clean out, muck out: *een stal* ~ muck out a stable **2** clean up, tidy up: *een kast* ~ tidy up (*or:* clear out) a cupboard

uitmeten /œytmetə(n)/ (mat uit/meette uit, heeft uitgemeten) **1** measure (out) **2** [fig] make much of, enlarge

uitmonden /œytmɔndə(n)/ (mondde uit, heeft/is uitgemond) **1** flow (out), discharge, run into **2** lead to, end in: *het gesprek mondde uit in een enorme ruzie* the conversation ended in a fierce quarrel

uitmoorden /œytmordə(n)/ (moordde uit, heeft uitgemoord) massacre, butcher

uitmunten /œytmʏntə(n)/ (muntte uit, heeft uitgemunt) stand out, excel

uitmuntend /œytmʏntənt/ (adj, adv) excellent, first-rate

uitnodigen /œytnodəɣə(n)/ (nodigde uit, heeft uitgenodigd) invite, ask: *iem. op een feestje* ~ invite (*or:* ask) s.o. to a party

de **uitnodiging** /œytnodəɣɪŋ/ (pl: -en) invitation: *een* ~ *voor de lunch* an invitation to lunch

uitoefenen /œytufənə(n)/ (oefende uit, heeft uitgeoefend) **1** practise, pursue, be engaged in **2** exert; exercise; wield: *kritiek* ~ *op* criticize, censure

de **uitoefening** /œytufənɪŋ/ exercise; exertion; practice: *in de* ~ *van zijn ambt* in the performance (*or:* discharge, exercise) of his duties

uitpakken /œytpakə(n)/ (pakte uit, heeft uitgepakt) unwrap, unpack

uitpersen /œytpɛrsə(n)/ (perste uit, heeft uitgeperst) squeeze; crush

uitpluizen /œytplœyzə(n)/ (ploos uit, heeft uitgeplozen) unravel; sift (out, through): *iets helemaal* ~ get to the bottom of sth.

¹**uitpraten** /œytpratə(n)/ (praatte uit, is uitgepraat) finish (talking), have one's say: *iem. laten* ~ let s.o. finish, hear s.o. out

²**uitpraten** /œytpratə(n)/ (praatte uit, heeft uitgepraat) talk out (*or:* over), have out: *we moeten het* ~ we'll have to talk this out (*or:* over)

uitprinten /œytprɪntə(n)/ (printte uit, heeft uitgeprint) print (out)

uitproberen /œytprobərə(n)/ (probeerde uit, heeft uitgeprobeerd) try (out), test

uitpuilen /œytpœylə(n)/ (puilde uit, heeft/is uitgepuild) bulge (out), protrude: *~de ogen* bulging (*or:* protruding) eyes

uitputten /œytpʏtə(n)/ (putte uit, heeft uitgeput) **1** exhaust, finish (up): *de voorraad raakt uitgeput* the supply is running out **2** exhaust, wear out

de **uitputting** /œytpʏtɪŋ/ (pl: -en) exhaustion, fatigue: *de* ~ *van de olievoorraden* the exhaustion of oil supplies

uitrangeren /œytrɑnʒerə(n)/ (rangeerde uit, heeft uitgerangeerd) sidetrack, shunt

uitrazen /œytrazə(n)/ (raasde uit, heeft/is uitgeraasd) let (*or:* blow) off steam; blow out: *de kinderen laten* ~ let the children have their fling

uitreiken /œytrɛikə(n)/ (reikte uit, heeft uitgereikt) distribute, give out; present: *diploma's* ~ present diplomas; *iem. een onderscheiding* ~ confer a distinction on s.o.

de **uitreiking** /œytrɛikɪŋ/ (pl: -en) distribution; presentation

het **uitreisvisum** /œytrɛisfizʏm/ (pl: -visa) exit visa

uitrekenen /œytrekənə(n)/ (rekende uit,

heeft uitgerekend) calculate, compute || *zij is begin* **maart** *uitgerekend* the baby is due at the beginning of March

¹uitrekken /œytrɛkə(n)/ (rekte uit, is uitgerekt) stretch: *de* **trui** *is in de was uitgerekt* the sweater has stretched in the wash

²uitrekken /œytrɛkə(n)/ (rekte uit, heeft uitgerekt) stretch (out); elongate: *een* **elastiek** ~ stretch out a rubber band; *zich* ~ stretch o.s. (out)

uitrichten /œytrɪχtə(n)/ (richtte uit, heeft uitgericht) do, accomplish: *dat zal niet* **veel** ~ that won't help much

uitrijden /œytrɛidə(n)/ (reed uit, is uitgereden) drive to the end (of); ride to the end (of) || **mest** ~ spread manure (*or:* fertilizer)

de **uitrit** /œytrɪt/ (pl: -ten) exit: ~ **vrijhouden** *s.v.p.* please keep (the) exit clear

uitroeien /œytrujə(n)/ (roeide uit, heeft uitgeroeid) exterminate, wipe out

de **uitroeiing** /œytrujɪŋ/ (pl: -en) extermination

de **uitroep** /œytrup/ (pl: -en) exclamation, cry

uitroepen /œytrupə(n)/ (riep uit, heeft uitgeroepen) **1** exclaim, shout, cry (out), call (out) **2** call, declare: *een* **staking** ~ call a strike; *hij werd* **tot** *winnaar uitgeroepen* he was declared (*or:* voted) the winner

het **uitroepteken** /œytruptekə(n)/ (pl: -s) exclamation mark

uitroken /œytrokə(n)/ (rookte uit, heeft uitgerookt) smoke out: **vossen** ~ smoke out foxes

uitrollen /œytrɔlə(n)/ (rolde uit, heeft uitgerold) unroll: *de* **tuinslang** ~ unreel the garden hose

¹uitrukken /œytrʏkə(n)/ (rukte uit, is uitgerukt) turn out: *de* **brandweer** *rukte uit* the fire brigade turned out

²uitrukken /œytrʏkə(n)/ (rukte uit, heeft uitgerukt) tear out, pull out: **planten** ~ root up (*or:* uproot) plants

¹uitrusten /œytrʏstə(n)/ (rustte uit, heeft/is uitgerust) rest

²uitrusten /œytrʏstə(n)/ (rustte uit, heeft uitgerust) equip, fit out: *uitgerust* **met** *16 kleppen* fitted with 16 valves

de **uitrusting** /œytrʏstɪŋ/ (pl: -en) equipment, kit, outfit, gear: *zijn* **intellectuele** ~ his intellectual baggage; *ze waren* **voorzien van** *de modernste* ~ they were fitted out with the latest equipment

uitschakelen /œytsχakələ(n)/ (schakelde uit, heeft uitgeschakeld) **1** switch off: *de* **motor** ~ cut (*or:* stop) the engine **2** [fig] eliminate; knock out: *door ziekte uitgeschakeld zijn* be out of circulation through ill health

uitscheiden /œytsχɛidə(n)/ (scheidde uit/schee uit, is uitgescheiden/uitgescheden) [inform] (+ met) stop (-ing), cease (to, -ing): *ik*

schei uit met werken als ik zestig word I'll stop working when I turn sixty; *schei uit!* cut it out!; knock it off!

uitschelden /œytsχɛldə(n)/ (schold uit, heeft uitgescholden) abuse, call names: *iem.* ~ **voor** *dief* call s.o. a thief

¹uitscheuren /œytsχørə(n)/ (scheurde uit, is uitgescheurd) tear: *het* **knoopsgat** *is uitgescheurd* the buttonhole is torn

²uitscheuren /œytsχørə(n)/ (scheurde uit, heeft uitgescheurd) tear out

uitschieten /œytsχitə(n)/ (schoot uit, is uitgeschoten) shoot out, dart out: *het* **mes** *schoot uit* the knife slipped

de **uitschieter** /œytsχitər/ (pl: -s) peak, highlight

uitschijnen /œytsχɛinə(n)/: [Belg] *iets laten* ~ let it be understood, hint at sth.

het **uitschot** /œytsχɔt/ **1** refuse **2** scum, dregs

uitschreeuwen /œytsχrewə(n)/ (schreeuwde uit, heeft uitgeschreeuwd) cry out: **het** ~ *van pijn* cry out (*or:* yell, bellow) with pain

uitschrijven /œytsχrɛivə(n)/ (schreef uit, heeft uitgeschreven) **1** write out, copy out: **aantekeningen** ~ write out notes **2** call; hold; organize **3** write out: *een* **recept** ~ write out a prescription; **rekeningen** ~ make out accounts || *iem.* **als** *lid* ~ strike s.o.'s name off the membership list

uitschudden /œytsχʏdə(n)/ (schudde uit, heeft uitgeschud) shake (out)

uitschuifbaar /œytsχœyvbar/ (adj) extending

uitschuiven /œytsχœyvə(n)/ (schoof uit, heeft uitgeschoven) **1** slide out, pull out **2** extend: *een* **tafel** ~ extend (*or:* pull out) a table

¹uitslaan /œytslan/ (sloeg uit, is uitgeslagen) grow mouldy, become mouldy; sweat || *een* ~*de* **brand** a blaze

²uitslaan /œytslan/ (sloeg uit, heeft uitgeslagen) **1** beat out, strike out: *het* **stof** ~ beat (*or:* shake) out the dust **2** shake out, beat out: *een* **stofdoek** ~ shake out a duster **3** utter, talk: **onzin** ~ talk rot

de **uitslag** /œytslɑχ/ (pl: -en) **1** rash; damp: *daar* **krijg** *ik* ~ *van* that brings out (*or:* gives me) a rash **2** result, outcome: *de* ~ *van de* **verkiezingen** (or: *van het* **examen**) the results of the elections (*or:* examination)

uitslapen /œytslapə(n)/ (sliep uit, heeft/is uitgeslapen) have a good lie-in, sleep late: *goed uitgeslapen zijn* [fig] be pretty astute (*or:* shrewd); *tot* *10 uur* ~ stay in bed until 10 o'clock

uitsloven /œytslovə(n)/ (sloofde zich uit, heeft zich uitgesloofd) slave away, work o.s. to death

de **uitslover** /œytslovər/ (pl: -s) eager beaver, show-off

uitsluiten /œytslœytə(n)/ (sloot uit, heeft uitgesloten) **1** shut out, lock out: *zij wordt van verdere deelname uitgesloten* she has been disqualified **2** exclude, rule out: *die mogelijkheid kunnen we niet* ~ that is a possibility we can't rule out (*or:* ignore); *dat is uitgesloten* that is out of the question

uitsluitend /œytslœytənt/ (adj, adv) only; exclusively: ~ *volwassenen* adults only

de **uitsluiting** /œytslœytɪŋ/ (pl: -en) **1** exclusion; [sport] disqualification **2** exception: *met* ~ *van* exclusive of, to the exclusion of

het **uitsluitsel** /œytslœytsəl/ (pl: -s) definite answer

de **uitsmijter** /œytsmɛitər/ (pl: -s) **1** bouncer **2** fried bacon and eggs served on slices of bread **3** final number of a show

uitsnijden /œytsnɛidə(n)/ (sneed uit, heeft uitgesneden) cut (out); carve (out): *een laag uitgesneden japon* a low-cut (*or:* low-necked) dress

de **uitspanning** /œytspanɪŋ/ (pl: -en) café, pub

het **uitspansel** /œytspansəl/ firmament, welkin

uitsparen /œytsparə(n)/ (spaarde uit, heeft uitgespaard) **1** save (on), economize (on): *dertig euro* ~ save thirty euros **2** leave blank (*or:* open): *openingen* ~ leave spaces

de **uitsparing** /œytsparɪŋ/ (pl: -en) cutaway; notch

de **uitspatting** /œytspatɪŋ/ (pl: -en) splurge; extravagance: *zich overgeven aan ~en* indulge in excesses

uitspelen /œytspelə(n)/ (speelde uit, heeft uitgespeeld) **1** finish, play out **2** play, lead: *mensen tegen elkaar* ~ play people off against one another

uitsplitsen /œytsplɪtsə(n)/ (splitste uit, heeft uitgesplitst) itemize, break down

uitspoelen /œytspulə(n)/ (spoelde uit, heeft uitgespoeld) rinse (out), wash (out)

uitspoken /œytspokə(n)/ (spookte uit, heeft uitgespookt) [inform] be (*or:* get) up to

de **uitspraak** /œytsprak/ (pl: uitspraken) **1** pronunciation, accent: *de* ~ *van het Chinees* the pronunciation of Chinese **2** pronouncement, judgement **3** [law] judg(e)ment, sentence; verdict: ~ *doen* pass judg(e)ment, pass (*or:* pronounce) sentence

uitspreiden /œytsprɛidə(n)/ (spreidde uit, heeft uitgespreid) spread (out), stretch (out)

uitspreken /œytsprekə(n)/ (sprak uit, heeft/is uitgesproken) **1** pronounce; articulate: *hoe moet je dit woord ~?* how do you pronounce this word? **2** say, express: *iem. laten* ~ let s.o. have his say, hear s.o. out **3** declare, pronounce: *een vonnis* ~ pronounce judgement

uitspringen /œytsprɪŋə(n)/ (sprong uit, is uitgesprongen) stand out

uitspugen /œytspyɣə(n)/ (spoog uit/spuug-

de uit, heeft uitgespogen/uitgespuugd) spit out

¹**uitstaan** /œytstan/ (stond uit, heeft uitgestaan) stand (*or:* stick, jut) out, protrude

²**uitstaan** /œytstan/ (stond uit, heeft uitgestaan) stand, endure, bear: *hitte* (or: *lawaai*) *niet kunnen* ~ not be able to endure the heat (*or:* noise); *iem. niet kunnen* ~ hate s.o.'s guts || *ik heb nog veel geld* ~ I have a lot of money out (at interest)

uitstallen /œytstalə(n)/ (stalde uit, heeft uitgestald) display, expose (for sale); [fig] show off

het **uitstalraam** /œytstalram/ (pl: -ramen) [Belg] shop window, display window

het **uitstapje** /œytstapjə/ (pl: -s) trip, outing, excursion: *een* ~ *maken* take (*or:* make) a trip, go on an outing

uitstappen /œytstapə(n)/ (stapte uit, is uitgestapt) get off (*or:* down), step out, get out

het **uitsteeksel** /œytsteksəl/ (pl: -s) projection, protuberance

het **uitstek** /œytstɛk/: *bij* ~ pre-eminently

¹**uitsteken** /œytstekə(n)/ (stak uit, heeft uitgestoken) **1** stick out, jut out, project, protrude **2** stand out: *de toren steekt boven de huizen uit* the tower rises (high) above the houses; *boven alle anderen* ~ tower above all the others

²**uitsteken** /œytstekə(n)/ (stak uit, heeft uitgestoken) **1** hold out, put out **2** reach out, stretch out: *zijn hand naar iem.* ~ extend one's hand to s.o.

uitstekend /œytstekənt/ (adj, adv) excellent, first-rate: *van ~e kwaliteit* of high quality

het **uitstel** /œytstɛl/ delay, postponement, deferment: ~ *van betaling* postponement (*or:* extension) of payment; *zonder* ~ without delay || [Belg; law] *met* ~ suspended; *van* ~ *komt afstel* tomorrow never comes; *one of these days is none of these days*

uitstellen /œytstɛlə(n)/ (stelde uit, heeft uitgesteld) put off, postpone, defer: *voor onbepaalde tijd* ~ postpone indefinitely

uitsterven /œytstɛrvə(n)/ (stierf uit, is uitgestorven) die (out); become extinct: *het dorp was uitgestorven* the village was deserted

uitstijgen /œytstɛiɣə(n)/ (steeg uit, is uitgestegen) surpass

uitstippelen /œytstɪpələ(n)/ (stippelde uit, heeft uitgestippeld) outline, map out, trace out; work out: *een route* ~ map out a route

de **uitstoot** /œytstot/ (pl: uitstoten) discharge, emissions

uitstorten /œytstɔrtə(n)/ (stortte uit, heeft uitgestort) **1** pour out (*or:* forth), empty (out): *zijn hart* ~ *bij iem.* pour out (*or:* unburden, open) one's heart (to s.o.) **2** pour out: *zijn woede* ~ *over iem.* vent one's rage upon s.o.

uitstoten /œytstotə(n)/ (stootte uit, heeft uitgestoten) **1** expel, cast out: *iem.* ~ *uit de groep* expel (*or:* banish) s.o. from the group **2** emit, utter: *onverstaanbare klanken* ~ emit (*or:* utter) unintelligible sounds **3** eject; emit

¹**uitstralen** /œytstralə(n)/ (straalde uit, heeft/is uitgestraald) radiate, emanate

²**uitstralen** /œytstralə(n)/ (straalde uit, heeft uitgestraald) [also fig] radiate, give off, exude: *zelfvertrouwen* ~ radiate (*or:* exude, ooze) self-confidence

de **uitstraling** /œytstralɪŋ/ (pl: -en) radiation, emission; [fig] aura: *een enorme* ~ *hebben* [roughly] possess charisma, have a certain magic

¹**uitstrekken** /œytstrɛkə(n)/ (strekte uit, heeft uitgestrekt) **1** stretch (out), reach (out), extend: *met uitgestrekte armen* with outstretched arms **2** extend

zich ²**uitstrekken** /œytstrɛkə(n)/ (strekte zich uit, heeft zich uitgestrekt) extend, stretch (out): *zich* ~ *over* extend over

uitstrijken /œytstrɛikə(n)/ (streek uit, heeft uitgestreken) spread, smear

het **uitstrijkje** /œytstrɛikjə/ (pl: -s) (cervical) smear, swab

uitstrooien /œytstrojə(n)/ (strooide uit, heeft uitgestrooid) scatter, spread

de **uitstroom** /œytstrom/ (out)flow

de **uitstulping** /œytstʏlpɪŋ/ (pl: -en) bulge

uitsturen /œytstyrə(n)/ (stuurde uit, heeft uitgestuurd) send out; [sport] send off (the field): *iem. op iets* ~ send s.o. for sth.

uittekenen /œytekənə(n)/ (tekende uit, heeft uitgetekend) draw, trace out: *ik kan die plaats wel* ~ I know every detail of that place

uittesten /œytɛstə(n)/ (testte uit, heeft uitgetest) test (out), try (out), put to the test

uittikken /œytɪkə(n)/ (tikte uit, heeft uitgetikt) type out

de **uittocht** /œytɔχt/ (pl: -en) exodus, trek

de **uittrap** /œytrɑp/ (pl: -pen) goal kick

uittrappen /œytrɑpə(n)/ (trapte uit, heeft uitgetrapt) **1** kick (the ball) into play, take a goal kick **2** put out of play (*or:* into touch, over the line) **3** kick off

uittreden /œytredə(n)/ (trad uit, is uitgetreden) resign (from): *vervroegd* ~ retire early, take early retirement

de **uittreding** /œytredɪŋ/ (pl: -en) **1** resignation, retirement **2** leaving

¹**uittrekken** /œytrɛkə(n)/ (trok uit, zijn uitgetrokken) go out, march out: *erop* ~ *om* set out to

²**uittrekken** /œytrɛkə(n)/ (trok uit, heeft uitgetrokken) **1** take off; pull off: *zijn kleren* ~ take off one's clothes; undress **2** put aside, set aside, reserve: *een bedrag voor iets* ~ put (*or:* set) aside a sum (of money) for sth.

het **uittreksel** /œytrɛksəl/ (pl: -s) excerpt, extract

uittypen /œytipə(n)/ (typte uit, heeft uitgetypt) type out

uitvaardigen /œytfardəɣə(n)/ (vaardigde uit, heeft uitgevaardigd) issue, put out; [law also] make

de **uitvaart** /œytfart/ (pl: -en) funeral (service), burial (service)

het **uitvaartcentrum** /œytfartsɛntrʏm/ (pl: -centra) funeral parlour, mortuary

de **uitvaartdienst** /œytfardinst/ (pl: -en) funeral service, burial service

de **uitval** /œytfɑl/ (pl: -len) **1** outburst, explosion **2** (hair) loss

uitvallen /œytfɑlə(n)/ (viel uit, is uitgevallen) **1** burst out, explode, blow up **2** fall (*or:* drop, come) out: *zijn haren vallen uit* he is losing his hair **3** drop out, fall out; break down: *de stroom is uitgevallen* there's a power failure **4** turn out, work out: *we weten niet hoe de stemming zal* ~ we don't know how (*or:* which way) the vote will go

de **uitvaller** /œytfɑlər/ (pl: -s) person who drops out, casualty

de **uitvalsbasis** /œytfɑlzbazɪs/ operating base

de **uitvalsweg** /œytfɑlswɛχ/ (pl: -en) main traffic road (out of a town)

uitvaren /œytfarə(n)/ (voer uit, is uitgevaren) sail, put (out) to sea, leave port

uitvechten /œytfɛχtə(n)/ (vocht uit, heeft uitgevochten) fight out: *iets met iem.* ~ fight (*or:* have) sth. out with s.o.

uitvegen /œytfeɣə(n)/ (veegde uit, heeft uitgeveegd) **1** sweep out, clean out **2** wipe out; erase: *een woord op het schoolbord* ~ wipe (*or:* rub) out a word on the blackboard

uitvergroten /œytfərɣrotə(n)/ (vergrootte uit, heeft uitvergroot) enlarge, magnify, blow up

de **uitvergroting** /œytfərɣrotɪŋ/ (pl: -en) enlargement, blow-up

uitverkocht /œytfərkɔχt/ (adj) **1** sold out: *onze kousen zijn* ~ we have run out of stockings **2** sold out, booked out, fully booked: *voor een ~e zaal spelen* play to a full house

de **uitverkoop** /œytfərkop/ (clearance, bargain) sale

uitverkoren /œytfərkorə(n)/ (adj) chosen; elect

uitvinden /œytfɪndə(n)/ (vond uit, heeft uitgevonden) **1** invent **2** find out, discover

de **uitvinder** /œytfɪndər/ (pl: -s) inventor

de **uitvinding** /œytfɪndɪŋ/ (pl: -en) invention; gadget: *een* ~ *doen* invent sth.

uitvissen /œytfɪsə(n)/ (viste uit, heeft uitgevist) dig (*or:* fish, ferret) out

uitvlakken /œytflɑkə(n)/ (vlakte uit, heeft uitgevlakt) wipe out: [fig] *dat moet je niet* ~ that's not to be sneezed at

het **uitvloeisel** /œytflujsəl/ (pl: -s, -en) consequence

de **uitvlucht** /ɶytflʏχt/ (pl: -en) excuse, pretext: *~en zoeken* make excuses; dodge (*or:* evade) the question

uitvoegen /ɶytfuɣə(n)/ (voegde uit, heeft uitgevoegd) exit

de **uitvoegstrook** /ɶytfuχstrok/ (pl: -stroken) deceleration lane

de **uitvoer** /ɶytfur/ (pl: -en) **1** export: *de in- en ~ van goederen* the import and export of goods **2** exports **3** execution: *een opdracht ten ~ brengen* carry out an instruction (*or:* order)

uitvoerbaar /ɶytfurbar/ (adj) feasible, workable, practicable

de **uitvoerder** /ɶytfurdər/ (pl: -s) works foreman

uitvoeren /ɶytfurə(n)/ (voerde uit, heeft uitgevoerd) **1** export **2** do: *hij voert niets uit* he doesn't do a stroke (of work) **3** perform, carry out: *plannen ~* carry out (*or:* execute) plans

uitvoerend /ɶytfurənt/ (adj) executive: *~ personeel* staff carrying out the work

uitvoerig /ɶytfurəχ/ (adj, adv) comprehensive, full; elaborate; detailed: *iets ~ beschrijven* (or: *bespreken*) describe (*or:* discuss) sth. at great/some length

de **uitvoering** /ɶytfurɪŋ/ (pl: -en) **1** carrying out, performance: *werk in ~* road works (ahead), men at work; work in progress **2** performance; execution **3** design, construction; workmanship: *wij hebben dit model in twee ~en* we have two versions of this model

de **uitvoerrechten** /ɶytfurɛχtə(n)/ (pl) export duty

uitvouwen /ɶytfɑuwə(n)/ (vouwde uit, heeft uitgevouwen) unfold, fold out, spread out

uitvreten /ɶytfretə(n)/ (vrat uit, heeft uitgevreten) be up to: *wat heeft hij nou weer uitgevreten?* what has he been up to now?

de **uitvreter** /ɶytfretər/ (pl: -s) sponger, parasite

uitwaaien /ɶytwajə(n)/ (waaide uit/woei uit, is uitgewaaid) **1** blow out, be blown out **2** get a breath of (fresh) air

het/de **uitwas** /ɶytwɑs/ (pl: -sen) excrescence, morbid growth; excesses

uitwasemen /ɶytwasəmə(n)/ (wasemde uit, heeft uitgewasemd) **1** evaporate **2** steam; perspire

uitwassen /ɶytwɑsə(n)/ (waste uit, heeft uitgewassen) **1** wash (out); swab (out) **2** wash out (*or:* away)

de **uitwedstrijd** /ɶytwɛtstrɛit/ (pl: -en) away match (*or:* game)

de **uitweg** /ɶytwɛχ/ (pl: -en) way out; answer: *hij zag geen andere ~ meer dan onder te duiken* he had no choice but to go into hiding

uitweiden /ɶytwɛidə(n)/ (weidde uit, heeft uitgeweid) expatiate (on), hold forth

uitwendig /ɶytwɛndəχ/ (adj, adv) external, outward, exterior: *een geneesmiddel voor ~ gebruik* a medicine for external use

¹**uitwerken** /ɶytwɛrkə(n)/ (werkte uit, is uitgewerkt) wear off; have spent one's force: *de verdoving is uitgewerkt* (the effect of) the anaesthetic has worn off

²**uitwerken** /ɶytwɛrkə(n)/ (werkte uit, heeft uitgewerkt) **1** work out, elaborate: *zijn aantekeningen ~* work up one's notes; *een idee ~* develop an idea; *uitgewerkte plannen* detailed plans **2** work out, compute: *sommen ~* work out sums

de **uitwerking** /ɶytwɛrkɪŋ/ (pl: -en) **1** effect, result: *de beoogde ~ hebben* have the desired (*or:* intended) effect, be effective; *de medicijnen hadden geen ~* the medicines had no effect (*or:* didn't work) **2** working out, elaboration **3** working out, computation

de **uitwerpselen** /ɶytwɛrpsələ(n)/ (pl) excrement; droppings

uitwijken /ɶytwɛikə(n)/ (week uit, is uitgeweken) get out of the way (of); make way (for): *rechts ~* swerve to the right; *men liet het luchtverkeer naar Oostende ~* air traffic was diverted to Ostend

uitwijzen /ɶytwɛizə(n)/ (wees uit, heeft uitgewezen) **1** show, reveal: *de tijd zal het ~* time will tell **2** deport; expel

de **uitwijzing** /ɶytwɛizɪŋ/ (pl: -en) deportation; expulsion

uitwisselbaar /ɶytwɪsəlbar/ (adj) interchangeable, exchangeable

uitwisselen /ɶytwɪsələ(n)/ (wisselde uit, heeft uitgewisseld) exchange; swap: *ervaringen ~* compare notes

de **uitwisseling** /ɶytwɪsəlɪŋ/ (pl: -en) exchange, swap

uitwissen /ɶytwɪsə(n)/ (wiste uit, heeft uitgewist) wipe out, erase; efface: *een opname ~* wipe (*or:* erase) a recording; *sporen ~* cover up one's tracks

uitwonend /ɶytwonənt/ (adj) (living) away from home: *een ~e dochter* one daughter living away from home

de **uitworp** /ɶytwɔrp/ (pl: -en) throw(-out)

uitwrijven /ɶytfrɛivə(n)/ (wreef uit, heeft uitgewreven) **1** rub; polish (up): *zijn ogen ~* rub one's eyes **2** spread, rub over

uitwringen /ɶytfrɪŋə(n)/ (wrong uit, heeft uitgewrongen) wring out

¹**uitzaaien** /ɶytsajə(n)/ (zaaide uit, heeft uitgezaaid) sow, disseminate

zich ²**uitzaaien** /ɶytsajə(n)/ (zaaide zich uit, heeft zich uitgezaaid) [med] metastasize; spread: *de kanker had zich uitgezaaid* the cancer had spread (*or:* formed secondaries)

de **uitzaaiing** /ɶytsajɪŋ/ (pl: -en) [med] spread, dissemination

uitzakken /ɶytsɑkə(n)/ (zakte uit, is uitgezakt) sag, give way: *een uitgezakt lichaam* a sagging body

het **uitzendbureau** /œytsɛndbyro/ (pl: -s) (temporary) employment agency, temp(ing) agency: *voor een ~ werken* temp, do temping

uitzenden /œytsɛndə(n)/ (zond uit, heeft uitgezonden) broadcast, transmit: *de tv zendt de wedstrijd uit* the match will be televised (*or:* be broadcast)

de **uitzending** /œytsɛndɪŋ/ (pl: -en) broadcast, transmission: *een rechtstreekse ~* a direct (*or:* live) broadcast; *u bent nu in de ~* you're on the air now

de **uitzendkracht** /œytsɛntkrɑχt/ (pl: -en) temporary worker (*or:* employee), temp

het **uitzendwerk** /œytsɛntwɛrk/ work as a temp(orary)

het/de **uitzet** /œytsɛt/ (pl: -ten) outfit; trousseau

uitzetten /œytsɛtə(n)/ (zette uit, heeft uitgezet) **1** throw out, put out, expel; deport: *ongewenste vreemdelingen ~* deport (*or:* expel) undesirable aliens **2** switch off, turn off: *het gas ~* turn the gas off **3** expand, enlarge; extend

de **uitzetting** /œytsɛtɪŋ/ (pl: -en) ejection, expulsion; deportation; eviction

het **uitzicht** /œytsɪχt/ (pl: -en) **1** view, prospect, panorama: *vrij ~* unobstructed view; *met ~ op* with a view of, overlooking, looking (out) onto **2** prospect, outlook: *~ geven* op *promotie* hold out prospects (*or:* the prospect) of promotion

uitzichtloos /œytsɪχtlos/ (adj) hopeless, dead-end

uitzieken /œytsikə(n)/ (ziekte uit, heeft/is uitgeziekt) fully recover

uitzien /œytsin/ (zag uit, heeft uitgezien) face, front, look out on: *een kamer die op zee uitziet* a room with a view of the sea, a room facing the sea

uitzingen /œytsɪŋə(n)/ (zong uit, heeft uitgezongen) hold out, manage

uitzinnig /œytsɪnəχ/ (adj, adv) delirious, wild: *een ~e menigte* a frenzied (*or:* hysterical) crowd

uitzitten /œytsɪtə(n)/ (zat uit, heeft uitgezeten) sit out, stay until the end of: *zijn tijd ~* sit out (*or:* wait out) one's time

uitzoeken /œytsukə(n)/ (zocht uit, heeft uitgezocht) **1** select, choose, pick out **2** sort (out) **3** sort out, figure out

uitzonderen /œytsɔndərə(n)/ (zonderde uit, heeft uitgezonderd) except, exclude

de **uitzondering** /œytsɔndərɪŋ/ (pl: -en) exception: *een ~ maken voor* make an exception for; *een ~ op de regel* an exception to the rule; *met ~ van* with the exception of, excepting, save

uitzonderlijk /œytsɔndərlək/ (adj, adv) exceptional, unique

uitzuigen /œytsœyɣə(n)/ (zoog uit, heeft uitgezogen) **1** squeeze dry, bleed dry, exploit **2** vacuum (out)

de **uitzuiger** /œytsœyɣər/ (pl: -s) bloodsucker, extortionist

uitzwaaien /œytswajə(n)/ (zwaaide uit, heeft uitgezwaaid) send off, wave goodbye to

uitzwermen /œytswɛrmə(n)/ (zwermde uit, is uitgezwermd) swarm out, swarm off

uitzweten /œytswetə(n)/ (zweette uit, heeft uitgezweet) sweat out

de **uk** /ʏk/ (pl: ukken) toddler, kiddy

ultiem /ʏltim/ (adj) ultimate, last-minute

het **ultimatum** /ʏltimatʏm/ (pl: -s) ultimatum: *een ~ stellen* give (s.o.) an ultimatum

ultralinks /ʏltralɪŋks/ (adj, adv) extreme left

ultramodern /ʏltramodɛrn/ (adj) ultramodern

ultrarechts /ʏltrarɛχ(t)s/ (adj, adv) extreme right

ultraviolet /ʏltravijolɛt/ (adj) ultraviolet

de **umlaut** /ʏmlɑut/ (pl: -en) umlaut (mark)

unaniem /ynanim/ (adj, adv) unanimous: *~ aangenomen* adopted unanimously

undercover /ʏndərkɔvər/ (adv) undercover

de **underdog** /ʏndərdɔːk/ (pl: -s) underdog

het **understatement** /ʏndərstetmənt/ (pl: -s) understatement

de ¹**uni** /yni/ (pl: -'s) uni

²**uni** /yni/ (adj) unicolour(ed)

het **unicum** /ynikʏm/ (pl: -s): *dit is een ~* this is unique, this is a unique event

de **unie** /yni/ (pl: -s) union, association: *Europese Unie* European Union

de **unief** /ynif/ (pl: -s) [Belg] university

uniek /ynik/ (adj, adv) unique

het **uniform** /ynifɔrm/ (pl: -en) uniform: *een ~ dragen* wear a uniform

uniformeren /ynifɔrmerə(n)/ (uniformeerde, heeft geüniformeerd) make uniform

uniseks /ynisɛks/ (adj) unisex

de **unit** /junɪt/ (pl: -s) unit

universeel /ynivɛrzel/ (adj, adv) universal: *de universele rechten van de mens* the universal rights of man

universitair /ynivɛrzitɛːr/ (adj) university: *iem. met een ~e opleiding* s.o. with a university education

de **universiteit** /ynivɛrzitɛit/ (pl: -en) university: *hoogleraar aan de ~ van Oxford* professor at Oxford University; *naar de ~ gaan* go to the university; [Am also] go to college

het **universum** /ynivɛrzʏm/ universe

unzippen /ʏnzɪpə(n)/ (unzipte, heeft geünzipt) unzip, decompress, unpack

de **update** /ʏbdet/ (pl: -s) update

updaten /ʏbdetə(n)/ (updatete, heeft geüpdatet) update

de **upgrade** /ʏpɡret/ (pl: -s) upgrade

upgraden /ʏpɡredə(n)/ (upgradede, heeft

geüpgraded) upgrade

uploaden /ˈyplodə(n)/ (uploadde, heeft geüpload) upload

het **uppie** /ˈypi/ [inform]: *in z'n* ~ on (*or:* by) one's lonesome

up-to-date /ʌptuˈdɛt/ (adj) up-to-date

het **uranium** /yˈranijʏm/ uranium: *verrijkt* ~ enriched uranium

het/de **urban** /ˈyːrbən/ urban music

urenlang /yrə(n)ˈlɑŋ/ (adj, adv) interminable, endless: *er werd* ~ *vergaderd* the meeting went on for hours

urgent /ʏrˈɣɛnt/ (adj) urgent

de **urgentie** /ʏrˈɣɛnsi/ urgency

de **urgentieverklaring** /ʏrˈɣɛnsivərklariŋ/ (pl: -en) certificate of urgency (*or:* need)

de **urine** /yˈrinə/ urine

urineren /yrinˈerə(n)/ (urineerde, heeft geürineerd) urinate

het **urinoir** /yrinˈwaːr/ (pl: -s) urinal

de **URL** /yɛrˈɛl/ *uniform resource locator* URL

de **urn** /ʏrn/ (pl: -en) urn

de **urologie** /yroloˈɣi/ urology

de **uroloog** /yroˈlox/ (pl: urologen) urologist

Uruguay /urugwaˈj/ Uruguay

de **Uruguayaan** /urugwajˈan/ (pl: Uruguayanen) Uruguayan

Uruguayaans /urugwajˈans/ (adj) Uruguayan

de **USA** /juˈɛsˈe/ (pl) *United States of America* USA

de **usance** /yˈzɑ̃sə/ (pl: -s) custom, common practice

de **USB-stick** /yˈɛzbˈɛstɪk/ (pl: -s) USB flash drive, USB stick

de **user** /ˈjuːzər/ (pl: -s) user

de **utiliteitsbouw** /ytilitˈɛɪtsbɑu/ commercial and industrial building

de **utopie** /ytoˈpi/ (pl: -ën) utopia, utopian dream

utopisch /yˈtopis/ (adj) utopian

het **uur** /yr/ (pl: uren) **1** hour: *lange uren maken* put in (*or:* work) long hours; *verloren* ~*(tje)* spare time (*or:* hour); *het duurde uren* it went on for hours, it took hours; *over een* ~ in an hour; *€25 per* ~ *verdienen* earn 25 euros an hour; *100 kilometer per* ~ 100 kilometres per (*or:* an) hour; *per* ~ *betaald worden* be paid by the hour; *kun je hier binnen twee* ~ *zijn?* can you be here within two hours?; *het is een* ~ *rijden* it is an hour's drive; *een* ~ *in de wind stinken* stink to high heaven **2** hour, period, lesson: *we hebben het derde* ~ *wiskunde* we have mathematics for the third lesson **3** o'clock: *op het hele* ~ on the hour; *op het halve* ~ on the half hour; *hij kwam tegen drie* ~ he came around three o'clock; *om ongeveer acht* ~ round about eight (o'clock); *om negen* ~ *precies* at nine o'clock sharp **4** hour, moment: *het* ~ *van de waarheid is aangebroken* the moment of truth is upon us; *zijn laatste* ~

heeft geslagen his final hour has come; his number is up

het **uurloon** /ˈyrlon/ (pl: uurlonen) hourly wage, hourly pay: *zij werkt op* ~ she is paid by the hour

het **uurtarief** /ˈyrtarif/ (pl: -tarieven) hourly rate

het **uurtje** /ˈyrcə/ (pl: -s) hour: *in de kleine ~s thuiskomen* come home in the small hours

het **uurwerk** /ˈyrwɛrk/ (pl: -en) clock, timepiece

de **uurwijzer** /ˈyrwɛizər/ (pl: -s) hour hand

uw /yw/ (poss pron) your: *het uwe* yours

uwerzijds /ywərˈzɛɪts/ (adv) on your part

uzelf /yˈzɛlf/ (ref pron) yourself, yourselves

V

de **v** /ve/ (pl: v's) v, V
vaag /vaχ/ (adj, adv) vague, faint, dim: *ik heb zo'n ~ vermoeden dat …* I have a hunch (or: a sneaking suspicion) that …
de **vaagheid** /vaχhɛit/ (pl: -heden) vagueness
vaak /vak/ (adv) often, frequently: *dat gebeurt niet ~* that doesn't happen very often; *steeds vaker* more and more (frequently)
vaal /val/ (adj) faded
de **vaan** /van/ (pl: vaans) flag, standard
het **vaandel** /vandəl/ (pl: -s) banner, flag
de **vaandrig** /vandrɪχ/ (pl: -s) reserve officer candidate
het **vaantje** /vancə/ (pl: -s) (small) flag, pennant
het **vaarbewijs** /varbəwɛis/ (pl: -bewijzen) navigation licence
vaardig /vardəχ/ (adj) skilful, proficient
de **vaardigheid** /vardəχhɛit/ (pl: -heden) skill, skilfulness; proficiency: *sociale vaardigheden* social skills; *~ in het schrijven* writing skill
de **vaargeul** /varχøl/ (pl: -en) channel, waterway
de **vaarroute** /varutə/ (pl: -s) sea lane
de **vaars** /vars/ (pl: vaarzen) heifer
de **vaart** /vart/ (pl: -en) **1** speed; [also fig] pace: *in volle ~* at full speed (or: tilt); *de ~ erin houden* keep up the pace; *het zal zo'n ~ niet lopen* it won't come to that (or: get that bad); *~ minderen* reduce speed, slow down; *ergens ~ achter zetten* hurry (or: speed) things up, get a move on **2** navigation, (sea) trade: *de wilde ~* tramp shipping
de **vaartijd** /vartɛit/ sailing time
het **vaartuig** /vartœyχ/ (pl: -en) vessel, craft
het **vaarwater** /varwatər/ (pl: -s, -en) water(s): *in rustig ~* in smooth water(s)
de **vaarweg** /varwɛχ/ (pl: -en) waterway
het **vaarwel** /varwɛl/ farewell: *iem. ~ zeggen* bid s.o. farewell
de **vaas** /vas/ (pl: vazen) vase
de **vaat** /vat/ washing-up, dishes
de **vaatdoek** /vaduk/ (pl: -en) dishcloth
de **vaatwasmachine** /vatwasmaʃinə/ (pl: -s) dishwasher
de **vaatwasser** /vatwasər/ (pl: -s) dishwasher
vacant /vakɑnt/ (adj) vacant, free, open: *een ~e betrekking* a vacancy, an opening
de **vacature** /vakatyrə/ (pl: -s) vacancy, opening: *voorzien in een ~* fill a vacancy
de **vacaturebank** /vakatyrəbɑŋk/ (pl: -en) job vacancy department
het **vaccin** /vaksɛ̃/ (pl: -s) vaccine
de **vaccinatie** /vaksina(t)si/ (pl: -s) vaccination

vaccineren /vaksinerə(n)/ (vaccineerde, heeft gevaccineerd) vaccinate
de **vacht** /vaχt/ (pl: -en) **1** fleece; fur; coat **2** sheepskin **3** fur, pelt: *de ~ van een beer* a bearskin
het **vacuüm** /vakywʏm/ (pl: -s) vacuum
vacuümverpakt /vakywʏmvərpɑkt/ (adj) vacuum-packed, vacuum-sealed
de **vader** /vadər/ (pl: -s) father: *~tje en moedertje spelen* play house; *het Onze Vader* the Lord's Prayer; *natuurlijke* (or: *wettelijke*) *~* natural (or: legal) father; *hij zou haar ~ wel kunnen zijn* he is old enough to be her father; *van ~ op zoon* from father to son; *zo ~, zo zoon* like father, like son
Vaderdag /vadərdɑχ/ Father's Day
het **vaderland** /vadərlɑnt/ (pl: -en) (native) country: *voor het ~ sterven* die for one's country; *een tweede ~* a second home
vaderlands /vadərlɑnts/ (adj) national, native: *de ~e geschiedenis* national history
de **vaderlandsliefde** /vadərlɑntslivdə/ patriotism, love of (one's) country
¹**vaderlijk** /vadərlək/ (adj) **1** paternal **2** fatherly
²**vaderlijk** /vadərlək/ (adv) in a fatherly way, like a father
het **vaderschap** /vadərsχɑp/ paternity, fatherhood
de **vaderskant** /vadərskɑnt/ father's side, paternal side: *familie van ~* paternal relatives, relatives on one's father's side
vadsig /vɑtsəχ/ (adj, adv) (fat and) lazy
de **vagebond** /vaχəbɔnt/ (pl: -en) vagabond, tramp
vagelijk /vaχələk/ (adv) vaguely, faintly
het **vagevuur** /vaχəvyr/ purgatory
de **vagina** /vaχina/ (pl: -'s) vagina
vaginaal /vaχinal/ (adj) vaginal
het **vak** /vak/ (pl: -ken) **1** section, square, space; box **2** compartment; pigeon-hole; shelf: *de ~ken bijvullen* fill the shelves **3** trade; profession: *een ~ leren* learn a trade; *een ~ uitoefenen* practise a trade, be in a trade (or: business); *zijn ~ verstaan* understand one's business, know what one is about **4** subject; course: *exacte ~ken* (exact) sciences; science and maths
de **vakantie** /vakɑnsi/ (pl: -s) holiday(s); [esp Am] vacation: *een week ~* a week's holiday; *de grote ~* the summer holidays; *prettige ~!* have a nice holiday!; *een geheel verzorgde ~* a package tour; *~ hebben* have a holiday; *~ nemen* take a holiday; *met ~ gaan* go on holiday
het **vakantieadres** /vakɑn(t)siadrɛs/ (pl: -sen) holiday address
de **vakantiedag** /vakɑnsidɑχ/ (pl: -en) (day of one's) holiday
de **vakantieganger** /vakɑnsiɣaŋər/ (pl: -s) holidaymaker

het **vakantiegeld** /vakɑnsiɣɛlt/ (pl: -en) holiday pay

het **vakantiehuis** /vakɑnsihœys/ (pl: -huizen) holiday cottage

de **vakantiespreiding** /vakɑn(t)sisprɛɪdɪŋ/ staggering of holidays; [Am] staggering of vacation

de **vakantietijd** /vakɑnsitɛit/ (pl: -en) holiday period (or: season)

de **vakantietoeslag** /vakɑn(t)situslɑχ/ (pl: -toeslagen) holiday pay

het **vakantiewerk** /vakɑnsiwɛrk/ holiday job, summer job

vakbekwaam /vɑgbəkwɑm/ (adj) skilled

de **vakbekwaamheid** /vɑgbəkwɑmhɛit/ (professional) skill

de **vakbeurs** /vɑgbørs/ (pl: vakbeurzen) trade fair

de **vakbeweging** /vɑgbəweɣɪŋ/ trade unions

het **vakblad** /vɑgblɑt/ (pl: -en) trade journal

de **vakbond** /vɑgbɔnt/ (pl: -en) (trade) union

de **vakbondsleider** /vɑgbɔntslɛidər/ (pl: -s) (trade) union leader

de **vakcentrale** /vɑksɛntralə/ (pl: -s) trade union federation

het **vakdiploma** /vɑgdiploma/ (pl: -'s) (professional) diploma

het **vakgebied** /vɑkχəbit/ (pl: -en) field (of study)

de **vakgroep** /vɑkχrup/ (pl: -en) [roughly] department

de **vakidioot** /vɑkidijot/ (pl: -idioten) narrow-minded specialist, … freak

het **vakjargon** /vɑkjɑrɣɔn/ (pl: -s) (technical) jargon

het **vakje** /vɑkjə/ **1** compartment **2** box **3** pigeon-hole

de **vakkennis** /vɑkɛnɪs/ professional knowledge, expert knowledge; know-how

het **vakkenpakket** /vɑkə(n)pɑkɛt/ (pl: -ten) chosen set of course options

de **vakkenvuller** /vɑkə(n)vᵛlər/ (pl: -s) stock clerk, grocery clerk

¹**vakkundig** /vakᵧndəχ/ (adj) skilled, competent

²**vakkundig** /vakᵧndəχ/ (adv) competently, with great skill: *het is ~ gerepareerd* it has been expertly done

de **vakliteratuur** /vɑklitərɑtyr/ professional literature

de **vakman** /vɑkmɑn/ (pl: vaklui, vaklieden, -nen, vakmensen) expert, professional; skilled worker

het **vakmanschap** /vɑkmɑnsχɑp/ skill; craftsmanship: *het ontbreekt hem aan ~* he lacks skill

de **vaktaal** /vɑktal/ jargon

de **vakterm** /vɑktɛrm/ (pl: -en) technical term

de **vakvereniging** /vɑkfərenəɣɪŋ/ (pl: -en) (trade) union

het **vakwerk** /vɑkwɛrk/ craftmanship, work-

manship: *~ afleveren* produce excellent work

de **val** /vɑl/ (pl: -len, -len) **1** fall (off, from); trip: *een vrije ~ maken* skydive; *hij maakte een lelijke ~* he had a nasty fall; *ten ~ komen* fall (down), have a fall; *iem. ten ~ brengen* bring s.o. down **2** (down)fall, collapse: *de regering ten ~ brengen* overthrow (or: bring down) the government **3** trap; snare: *een ~ opzetten* set (or: lay) a trap **4** trap, frame-up: *in de ~ lopen* walk (or: fall) into a trap; *rise to* (or: swallow) the bait

de **valavond** /vɑlavɔnt/ [Belg] dusk, twilight

Valentijnsdag /vɑləntɛinzdɑχ/ St Valentine's Day

de **valhelm** /vɑlhɛlm/ (pl: -en) (crash) helmet

valide /validə/ (adj) **1** able-bodied **2** valid

het **valies** /valis/ (pl: valiezen) (suit)case

het **valium®** /valijʏm/ Valium

de **valk** /vɑlk/ (pl: -en) falcon

de **valkuil** /vɑlkœyl/ (pl: -en) pitfall, trap

de **vallei** /vɑlɛi/ (pl: -en) valley

vallen /vɑlə(n)/ (viel, is gevallen) **1** fall, drop: *er valt sneeuw* (or: *hagel*) it is snowing (or: hailing); *uit elkaar ~* fall apart, drop to bits; *zijn blik laten ~ op* let one's eye fall on **2** fall (over); trip (up): *iem. doen ~* make s.o. fall; trip s.o. up; *zij kwam lelijk te ~* she had a bad fall; *met ~ en opstaan* by trial and error; *van de trap ~* fall (or: tumble) down the stairs **3** come, fall: *dat valt buiten zijn bevoegdheid* that falls outside his jurisdiction **4** drop: *iem. laten ~* drop (or: ditch) s.o.; *hij liet de aanklacht ~* he dropped the charge **5** go (for), take (to): *zij valt op donkere mannen* she goes for dark men ‖ *Kerstmis valt op een woensdag* Christmas (Day) is on a Wednesday; *het ~ van de avond* nightfall; *er vielen doden* (or: *gewonden*) there were fatalities (or: casualties); *er viel een stilte* there was a hush, silence fell; *met haar valt niet te praten* there is no talking to her; *er valt wel iets voor te zeggen om …* there is sth. to be said for …

het **valluik** /vɑlœyk/ (pl: -en) trapdoor

de **valpartij** /vɑlpɑrtɛi/ (pl: -en) spill, fall

de **valreep** /vɑlrep/ (pl: valrepen) gangway, gangplank ‖ *op de ~* right at the end, at the final (or: last) moment

¹**vals** /vɑls/ (adj) **1** false, fake, phoney; pseudo- **2** wrong, false: *een ~ spoor* a false trail **3** [mus] flat; sharp; false **4** mean, vicious: *een ~ beest* a vicious animal **5** forged, fake, false, counterfeit: *een ~e Vermeer* a forged (or: fake) Vermeer **6** false, artificial; mock; imitation: *~ haar* false hair

²**vals** /vɑls/ (adv) falsely: *~ spelen* play out of tune; cheat (at cards); *~ zingen* sing out of tune, sing off key

het **valscherm** /vɑlsχɛrm/ (pl: -en) parachute

valselijk /vɑlsələk/ (adv) falsely, wrongly

de **valsemunter** /vɑlsəmᵧntər/ (pl: -s) counterfeiter, forger

de **valsheid** /vɑlshɛit/ **1** spuriousness: *overtuigd van de ~ van het schilderij* convinced that the painting is a fake **2** forgery, fraud, counterfeiting: *~ in geschrifte* forgery

de **valstrik** /vɑlstrɪk/ (pl: -ken) snare, trap: *iem. in een ~ lokken* lead (*or:* lure) s.o. into a trap

de **valuta** /valyta/ (pl: -'s) currency

de **valutahandel** /valytahɑndəl/ (foreign) exchange dealings

de **vampier** /vɑmpir/ (pl: -s) vampire

¹**van** /vɑn/ (adv) of, from: *je kunt er wel een paar ~ nemen* you can have some (of those)

²**van** /vɑn/ (prep) **1** from: *hij is ~ Amsterdam* he's from Amsterdam; *~ dorp tot dorp* from one village to another; *~ een bord eten* eat from (*or:* off) a plate **2** from: *~ de vroege morgen tot de late avond* from (the) early morning till late at night; *~ tevoren* beforehand, in advance; *~ toen af* from then on, from that day (*or:* time) (on) **3** of: *het hoofd ~ de school* the head(master) of the school; *de trein ~ 9.30 uur* the 9.30 train; *een foto ~ mijn vader* a) a picture of my father's; b) a picture of my father; *~ wie is dit boek?* whose book is this? it's mine **4** (made, out) of: *een tafel ~ hout* a wooden table **5** by, of: *dat was niet slim ~ Jan* that was not such a clever move of Jan's; *het volgende nummer is ~ Van Morrison* the next number is by Van Morrison; *een plaat ~ de Stones* a Stones record, a record by the Stones || *drie ~ de vier* three out of four; *een jas met ~ die koperen knopen* a coat with those brass buttons; *~ dat geld kon hij een auto kopen* he was able to buy a car with that money; *daar niet ~* that's not the point; *ik geloof ~ niet* I don't think so; *ik verzeker u ~ wel* I assure you I do; *het lijkt ~ wel* it seems (*or:* looks) like it

vanaf /vɑnɑf/ (prep) **1** from, as from; [Am] as of; beginning; since: *~ de 16e eeuw* from the 16th century onward(s); *~ vandaag* as from today; [Am] as of today **2** from, over: *prijzen ~ …* prices (range) from …

vanavond /vɑnavɔnt/ (adv) tonight, this evening

vanbinnen /vɑmbɪnə(n)/ (adv) (on the) inside

vanboven /vɑmbovə(n)/ (adv) **1** on the top, on the upper surface, above **2** from above

vanbuiten /vɑmbœytə(n)/ (adv) **1** from the outside **2** on the outside **3** by heart: *iets ~ kennen* (or: *leren*) know (*or:* learn) sth. by heart

vandaag /vɑndax/ (adv) today: *~ de dag* nowadays, these days, currently; *tot op de dag van ~* to this very day, to date; *~ is het maandag* today is Monday; *~ over een week* a week from today, in a week's time, a week from now; *de krant van ~* today's paper; *liever ~ dan morgen* the sooner the better || *~ of*

morgen one of these days, soon

de **vandaal** /vɑndal/ (pl: vandalen) vandal

vandaan /vɑndan/ (adv) **1** away, from: *we moeten hier ~!* let's go away! **2** out of, from: *waar heb je die oude klok ~?* where did you pick up (*or:* get) that old clock?; *waar kom (ben) jij ~?* where are you from?, where do you come from? || *hij woont overal ver ~* he lives miles from anywhere

vandaar /vɑndar/ (adv) therefore, that's why

het **vandalisme** /vɑndalɪsmə/ vandalism

vandoor /vɑndor/ (adv) off, away: *ik moet er weer ~* I have to be off; *hij is er met het geld ~* he has run off with the money

vaneen /vɑnen/ (adv) separated, split up

vangen /vɑŋə(n)/ (ving, heeft gevangen) **1** catch; capture; (en)trap: *een dief ~* catch a thief **2** catch **3** make: *twintig piek per uur ~* make five quid an hour; [Am] make ten bucks an hour

het **vangnet** /vɑŋnɛt/ (pl: -ten) **1** (trap-)net **2** safety net

de **vangrail** /vɑŋrel/ (pl: -s) crash barrier

de **vangst** /vɑŋst/ (pl: -en) catch, capture; haul: *de politie deed een goede ~* the police made a good catch (*or:* haul)

de **vanille** /vanijə/ vanilla

het **vanille-ijs** /vanijɛis/ vanilla ice cream

vanjewelste /vɑnjəwɛlstə/ (adj): *een succes ~* a howling success; *een klap ~* a huge (*or:* tremendous) blow

vanmiddag /vɑmɪdɑx/ (adv) this afternoon

vanmorgen /vɑmɔrɣə(n)/ (adv) this morning; in the morning: *~ vroeg* early this morning

vannacht /vɑnɑxt/ (adv) tonight; last night: *je kunt ~ blijven slapen, als je wil* you can stay the night, if you like; *hij kwam ~ om twee uur thuis* he came home at two o'clock in the morning

vanouds /vɑnɑuts/ (adv): *het was weer als ~* it was just like old times again

vanuit /vɑnœyt/ (prep) **1** from; out of: *ik keek ~ mijn raam naar beneden* I looked down from (*or:* out of) my window **2** starting from

vanwaar /vɑnwar/ (adv) **1** from where **2** why: *~ die haast?* what's the hurry?

vanwege /vɑnweɣə/ (prep) because of, owing to, due to, on account of

vanzelf /vɑnzɛlf/ (adv) **1** by o.s., of o.s., of one's own accord **2** as a matter of course, automatically: *alles ging (liep) als ~* everything went smoothly; *dat spreekt ~* that goes without saying

¹**vanzelfsprekend** /vɑnzɛlfsprekənt/ (adj) obvious, natural, self-evident

²**vanzelfsprekend** /vɑnzɛlfsprekənt/ (adv) obviously, naturally, of course: *als ~ aannemen* take sth. for granted

de ¹**varen** /varə(n)/ (pl: -s) fern

²**varen** /vₐrə(n)/ (voer, heeft/is gevaren) sail: *het schip vaart 10* **knopen** the ship sails at 10 knots; *hij wil* **gaan** ~ he wants to go to sea (*or:* be a sailor); *alle voorzichtigheid* **laten** ~ throw (*or:* fling) all caution to the wind(s)

de **varia** /vₐrija/ (pl) miscellany

variabel /varijₐbəl/ (adj) variable, flexible: *~e* **werktijden** flexible working hours

de **variabele** /varijabələ/ (pl: -n) variable

de **variant** /varijₐnt/ (pl: -en) variant, variation: *een ~* **op** a variant of, a variation on

de **variatie** /varija(t)si/ (pl: -s) variation, change: **voor** *de ~* for a change

variëren /varijₑrə(n)/ (varieerde, heeft gevarieerd) vary, differ: *sterk ~de* **prijzen** widely differing prices

het **variété** /varijetₑ/ (pl: -s) variety, music hall

de **variëteit** /varijetₑit/ (pl: -en) variety, diversity

het **varken** /vₐrkə(n)/ (pl: -s) pig; hog; swine: *zo lui* **als** *een* ~ bone idle (*or:* lazy)

de **varkensfokkerij** /vₐrkənsfokərₑi/ (pl: -en) pig farm

de **varkenshaas** /vₐrkənshas/ (pl: -hazen) pork tenderloin (*or:* steak)

de **varkenspest** /vₐrkə(n)spₑst/ swine fever

de **varkensstal** /vₐrkə(n)stɑl/ (pl: -len) pigsty; pig house

het **varkensvlees** /vₐrkənsfles/ pork

het **varkensvoer** /vₐrkə(n)sfur/ pigfeed, pigfood; (pig)swill

de **vaseline** /vazəlinə/ vaseline

¹**vast** /vɑst/ (adj) **1** fixed, immovable: *~e* **vloerbedekking** wall-to-wall carpet(ing) **2** fixed, stationary: *~* **raken** get stuck (*or:* caught, jammed); *~e* **datum** fixed date; *~e* **inkomsten** a fixed (*or:* regular) income; *~e* **kosten** fixed (*or:* standing) charges; *een ~e* **prijs** a fixed (*or:* set) price; *een ~e* **telefoon** a landline (telephone), a fixed line telephone **3** firm, steady: *met ~e* **hand** with a steady (*or:* sure) hand; *~e* **overtuiging** firm conviction **4** permanent; regular; steady: *~* **adres** fixed address; *een ~e* **betrekking** a permanent position; *~e* **klanten** regular costumers; regulars **5** solid: *~* **voedsel** solid food **6** firm: *~e* **vorm** geven shape **7** tight, firm **8** established, standing: *een ~* **gebruik** a (set) custom; *een ~e* **regel** a fixed (*or:* set) rule

²**vast** /vɑst/ (adv) **1** fixedly, firmly **2** certainly, for certain (*or:* sure): *hij* **is** *het ~* **vergeten** he must have forgotten (it); *~ en* **zeker** definitely, certainly **3** for the time being, for the present: **begin** *maar ~ met eten* go ahead and eat (*or:* start eating)

vastberaden /vɑstbərₐdə(n)/ (adj) resolute, firm, determined

vastbesloten /vɑstbəslₒtə(n)/ (adj) determined

zich **vastbijten** /vₐstbɛitə(n)/ (beet zich vast, heeft zich vastgebeten) [fig] cling to: *zich* **in**

een onderwerp ~ get (*or:* sink) one's teeth into a subject

vastbinden /vₐstbɪndə(n)/ (bond vast, heeft vastgebonden) tie (up, down), bind (up), fasten: *zijn* **armen** *werden vastgebonden* his arms were tied (*or:* bound) (up)

het **vasteland** /vɑstəlɑnt/ **1** continent **2** mainland; Continent

de ¹**vasten** /vₐstə(n)/ fast(ing)

²**vasten** /vₐstə(n)/ (vastte, heeft gevast) fast

Vastenavond /vɑstə(n)ₐvɔnt/ Shrove Tuesday

de **vastentijd** /vₐstə(n)tɛit/ **1** Lent **2** fast, time of fasting

het **vastgoed** /vₐstxut/ real estate (*or:* property)

vastgrijpen /vₐstxrɛipə(n)/ (greep vast, heeft vastgegrepen) grasp, clasp

de **vastheid** /vₐsthɛit/ **1** firmness **2** fixity **3** invariability **4** solidity **5** consistency

vasthouden /vₐsthaudə(n)/ (hield vast, heeft vastgehouden) hold (fast); grip; detain: *iemands* **hand** ~ hold s.o.'s hand; *hou je vast!* brace yourself (for the shock)!

vasthoudend /vɑsthₐudənt/ (adj) tenacious; persistent; persevering

zich **vastklampen** /vₐstklɑmpə(n)/ (klampte zich vast, heeft zich vastgeklampt) cling, clutch, hang on

vastklemmen /vₐstklɛmə(n)/ (klemde vast, heeft vastgeklemd) clip (on), tighten: *de* **deur** *zat vastgeklemd* the door was jammed

vastleggen /vₐstlɛɣə(n)/ (legde vast, heeft vastgelegd) **1** tie up: *zich niet ~* **op** *iets, zich nergens* **op** ~ refuse to commit o.s., leave one's options open; be non-committal **2** set down, record: *iets* **schriftelijk** *~* put sth. down in writing

vastliggen /vₐstlɪɣə(n)/ (lag vast, heeft vastgelegen) be tied up, be fixed: *die voorwaarden liggen vast* **in** *het contract* those conditions have been laid down in the contract

vastlijmen /vₐstlɛimə(n)/ (lijmde vast, heeft vastgelijmd) glue (together), stick (together)

vastlopen /vₐstlopə(n)/ (liep vast, is vastgelopen) **1** jam, get jammed: *het* **schip** *is vastgelopen* the ship has run aground **2** [fig] get stuck, be bogged down: *de* **onderhandelingen** *zijn vastgelopen* negotiations have reached a deadlock

vastmaken /vₐstmakə(n)/ (maakte vast, heeft vastgemaakt) fasten; tie up; do up, button up; secure

vastpakken /vₐstpakə(n)/ (pakte vast, heeft vastgepakt) grip, grasp; grab

vastpinnen /vₐstpɪnə(n)/ (pinde vast, heeft vastgepind) pin down, peg down

vastplakken /vₐstplakə(n)/ (plakte vast, heeft vastgeplakt) stick together, glue together

vastroesten /vɑstrustə(n)/ (roestte vast, is vastgeroest) rust

vastspijkeren /vɑ(st)spɛikərə(n)/ (spijkerde vast, heeft vastgespijkerd) nail (down); tack

vaststaan /vɑstan/ (stond vast, heeft vastgestaan) **1** be certain: *het* staat nu vast, dat it is now definite (*or:* certain) that; *de datum stond nog* ***niet*** *vast* the date was still uncertain (yet) **2** be fixed: *zijn* ***besluit*** *staat vast* his mind is made up

vaststaand /vɑ(st)stant/ (adj) certain; final: *een ~* ***feit*** an established (*or:* a recognized) fact

vaststellen /vɑstɛlə(n)/ (stelde vast, heeft vastgesteld) **1** fix, determine, settle, arrange: *een* ***datum*** *~* settle on (*or:* fix) a date; *een* ***prijs*** *~* fix a price **2** decide (on), specify; lay down: *op vastgestelde* ***tijden*** at stated times (*or:* intervals) **3** find, conclude **4** determine, establish: *de* ***doodsoorzaak*** *~* establish (*or:* determine) the cause of death; *de* ***schade*** *~* assess the damage

de **vaststelling** /vɑ(st)stɛlɪŋ/ (pl: -en) **1** arrangement **2** conclusion **3** decree, assessment

vastvriezen /vɑstfrizə(n)/ (vroor vast, is vastgevroren) freeze (in)

vastzetten /vɑstsɛtə(n)/ (zette vast, heeft vastgezet) **1** fix, fasten; secure **2** tie up, lock up, settle (on): *zijn* ***spaargeld*** *voor vijf jaar ~* tie up one's savings for five years

vastzitten /vɑstsɪtə(n)/ (zat vast, heeft vastgezeten) **1** be stuck; be jammed: *~* ***in*** *de file* be stuck in a tailback **2** be stuck (*or:* fixed): *daar zit heel wat* ***aan*** *vast* there is (a lot) more to it (than meets the eye) **3** be locked up, be behind bars: *hij heeft een* ***jaar*** *vastgezeten* he has been inside for a year **4** be in a fix **5** be tied (down) (to), be committed (to): *hij heeft het beloofd; nu zit hij* ***eraan*** *vast* he made that promise, he can't get out of it now

de **¹vat** /vɑt/ hold, grip; handle: *geen ~* ***op*** *iem. hebben* have no hold over s.o.

het **²vat** /vɑt/ barrel; cask; drum: *een ~* ***petroleum*** an oil drum; *bier* ***van*** *het ~* draught beer

vatbaar /vɑdbar/ (adj) **1** susceptible to, liable to: *hij is zeer ~* ***voor*** *kou* he is very prone to catching colds **2** amenable (to), open to: *hij is niet* ***voor*** *rede ~* he's impervious (*or:* not open) to reason

het **Vaticaan** /vatikan/ Vatican

Vaticaanstad /vatikanstɑt/ Vatican City

vatten /vɑtə(n)/ (vatte, heeft gevat) catch

de **vazal** /vazɑl/ (pl: -len) vassal

v.Chr. (abbrev) *voor Christus* BC

vechten /vɛxtə(n)/ (vocht, heeft gevochten) **1** fight; combat: *wij moesten ~* ***om*** *in de trein te komen* we had to fight our way into the train **2** fight (for, against): *tegen de slaap ~* fight off sleep

de **vechter** /vɛxtər/ (pl: -s) fighter, combatant

de **vechtersbaas** /vɛxtərzbas/ (pl: -bazen) hooligan, hoodlum

de **vechtlust** /vɛxtlʏst/ fight, fighting spirit

de **vechtpartij** /vɛxtpɑrtɛi/ (pl: -en) fight, brawl

de **vechtsport** /vɛxtspɔrt/ (pl: -en) combat sport

de **vector** /vɛktɔr/ (pl: -en) vector

de **¹vedergewicht** /vedərɣəwɪxt/ [boxer] featherweight

het **²vedergewicht** /vedərɣəwɪxt/ featherweight

vederlicht /vedərlɪxt/ (adj, adv) feathery

de **vedette** /vədɛtə/ (pl: -s, -n) star, celebrity

het **vee** /ve/ cattle: *een* ***stuk*** *~* a head of cattle

de **veearts** /vearts/ (pl: -en) veterinary (surgeon); [Am] veterinarian; vet

de **¹veeg** /vex/ (pl: vegen) **1** wipe; lick **2** streak; smudge: *er zit een* ***zwarte*** *~ op je gezicht* there's a black smudge on your face

²veeg /vex/ (adj) **1** fatal **2** ominous, fateful: *een ~* ***teken*** a bad sign (*or:* omen)

de **veehandel** /vehandəl/ cattle trade

de **veehouder** /vehaudər/ (pl: -s) cattle breeder, cattle farmer; [Am] rancher

de **veehouderij** /vehaudərɛi/ (pl: -en) cattle farm; [Am] cattle ranch

de **veejay** /viːdʒe/ veejay, VJ

¹veel /vel/ (ind pron) much, many, a lot, lots: *~* ***geluk!*** good luck!; *weet ik ~* how should I know?; *~* ***te*** *~* far too much (*or:* many); *één keer* ***te*** *~* (just) once too often

²veel /vel/ (adv) much, a lot: *hij was kwaad, maar zij was nog ~* ***kwader*** he was angry, but she was even more so; *ze* ***lijken*** *~ op elkaar* they are very much alike

³veel /vel/ (num) many, a lot ‖ *het zijn er ~* there's a lot of them

veelal /velɑl/ (adv) **1** usually **2** mostly

veelbelovend /velbəlovənt/ (adj, adv) promising: *~* ***zijn*** show great promise

veelbetekenend /velbətəkənənt/ (adj, adv) meaning(ful): *iem. ~* ***aankijken*** give s.o. a meaning look

veelbewogen /velbəwoɣə(n)/ (adj) eventful; hectic, turbulent; chequered

veeleer /veler/ (adv) [form] rather

veeleisend /velɛisənt/ (adj) demanding, particular (about)

de **veelheid** /velhɛit/ multitude

de **veelhoek** /velhuk/ (pl: -en) polygon

veelomvattend /velomvɑtənt/ (adj) comprehensive, extensive

de **veelpleger** /velpleɣər/ multiple offender

veelsoortig /velsɔrtəx/ (adj) multifarious, varied

veelstemmig /velstɛməx/ (adj) polyphonic

het **veelvoud** /velvɑut/ (pl: -en) multiple: *zijn salaris bedraagt een ~* ***van*** *het hare* his salary is many times larger than hers

de **veelvraat** /vˈelvrat/ (pl: -vraten) glutton
veelvuldig /velvˈyldəχ/ (adj) frequently, often
veelzeggend /velzˈɛχənt/ (adj) telling, revealing: *dat is* ~ that is saying a lot
veelzijdig /velzˈɛidəχ/ (adj) many-sided, versatile: *haar ~e belangstelling* her varied interests; *een ~e geest* a versatile mind
de **veemarkt** /vˈemɑrkt/ (pl: -en) cattle market
het **veen** /ven/ (pl: venen) peat
de **veenbes** /vˈembɛs/ (pl: -sen) cranberry
de **¹veer** /ver/ **1** feather **2** spring
het **²veer** /ver/ ferry
de **veerboot** /vˈerbot/ (pl: -boten) ferry(boat)
de **veerdienst** /vˈerdinst/ (pl: -en) ferry (service, line)
de **veerkracht** /vˈerkrɑχt/ elasticity, resilience
veerkrachtig /verkrˈɑχtəχ/ (adj) elastic, springy, resilient
de **veerman** /vˈermɑn/ (pl: veerlieden, veerlui) ferryman
de **veerpont** /vˈerpɔnt/ (pl: -en) ferry(boat)
veertien /vˈertin/ (num) fourteen: *vandaag over ~ dagen* in a fortnight('s time), two weeks from today; *~ dagen* fourteen days; a fortnight; *het zijn er ~* there are fourteen (of them)
veertiende /vˈertində/ (num) fourteenth
veertig /fˈertəχ/ (num) forty: *in de jaren ~* in the forties; *hij loopt tegen de ~* he is pushing forty; *~ plus* more than 40 % fat
de **veertiger** /fˈertəɣər/ (pl: -s) man of forty: *hij is een goede ~* he is somewhere in his forties
veertigjarig /fertəχjˈarəχ/ (adj) **1** forty years', fortieth: *~e bruiloft* fortieth wedding anniversary **2** forty-year-old
veertigste /fˈertəχstə/ (num) fortieth
veertigurig /fertəɣˈyrəχ/ (adj) forty-hour: *de ~e werkweek* the forty-hour week
de **veestal** /vˈestɑl/ (pl: -len) cowshed
de **veestapel** /vˈestapəl/ (pl: -s) (live)stock
de **veeteelt** /vˈetelt/ stock breeding, cattle breeding
het **veevervoer** /vˈevərvur/ transport of livestock (*or:* cattle)
het **veevoer** /vˈevur/ feed
de **veewagen** /vˈewaɣə(n)/ (pl: -s) cattle truck; cattle lorry
de **vegaburger** /vˈeɣabyrɣər/ (pl: -s) veggie burger
vegen /vˈeɣə(n)/ (veegde, heeft geveegd) **1** sweep, brush: *de schoorsteen ~* sweep the chimney **2** wipe: *voeten ~ a.u.b.* wipe your feet please
de **veger** /vˈeɣər/ (pl: -s) (sweeping) brush: *~ en blik* dustpan and brush
de **vegetariër** /veɣetˈarijər/ (pl: -s) vegetarian
vegetarisch /veɣetˈaris/ (adj) vegetarian: *ik eet altijd ~* I'm a vegetarian
de **vegetatie** /veɣetˈa(t)si/ (pl: -s) vegetation
vegeteren /veɣetˈerə(n)/ (vegeteerde, heeft

gevegeteerd) vegetate
het **vehikel** /vehˈikəl/ (pl: -s) vehicle
veilen /vˈɛilə(n)/ (veilde, heeft geveild) sell by auction: *antiek* (*or:* *huizen*) ~ auction antiques (*or:* houses)
veilig /vˈɛiləχ/ (adj, adv) safe, secure; (all-)clear: ~ *verkeer* [roughly] road safety; *iets ~ opbergen* put sth. in a safe place; ~ *thuiskomen* return home safe(ly); ~ *en wel* safe and sound
de **veiligheid** /vˈɛiləχɦɛit/ safety, security: *de openbare* ~ public security; *iets in* ~ *brengen* bring sth. to (a place of) safety
de **veiligheidsagent** /vˈɛiləχɦɛitsaɣɛnt/ (pl: -en) security officer
de **veiligheidsbril** /vˈɛiləχɦɛitsbrɪl/ (pl: -len) safety goggles, protective goggles
de **veiligheidsdienst** /vˈɛiləχɦɛitsdinst/ (pl: -en) security forces: *binnenlandse* ~ (counter)intelligence
het **veiligheidsglas** /vˈɛiləχɦɛitsχlɑs/ safety (*or:* shatterproof) glass
de **veiligheidsgordel** /vˈɛiləχɦɛitsχɔrdəl/ (pl: -s) safety belt; seat belt
veiligheidshalve /vɛiləχɦɛrtshɑlvə/ (adv) for reasons of safety (*or:* security)
de **veiligheidsmaatregel** /vˈɛiləχɦɛitsmatreɣəl/ (pl: -en, -s) security measure
de **Veiligheidsraad** /vˈɛiləχɦɛitsrat/ Security Council
het **veiligheidsslot** /vˈɛiləχɦɛitslɔt/ (pl: -en) safety lock
de **veiligheidsspeld** /vˈɛiləχɦɛitspɛlt/ (pl: -en) safety pin
veiligstellen /vˈɛiləχstɛlə(n)/ (stelde veilig, heeft veiliggesteld) safeguard, secure: *zijn toekomst* ~ provide for the future
de **veiling** /vˈɛilɪŋ/ (pl: -en) auction
het **veilinghuis** /vˈɛilɪŋɦœys/ (pl: -huizen) auctioneering firm
de **veilingmeester** /vˈɛilɪŋmestər/ (pl: -s) auctioneer
de **veilingsite** /vˈɛilɪŋsɑjt/ auction site
veinzen /vˈɛinzə(n)/ (veinsde, heeft geveinsd) pretend, feign
het **vel** /vɛl/ (pl: -len) **1** skin: *het is om uit je ~ te springen* it is enough to drive you up the wall; *~ over been zijn* be all skin and bone; *lekker in zijn ~ zitten* feel good **2** sheet
het **veld** /vɛlt/ (pl: -en) field; open country (*or:* fields); pitch; square: *in geen ~en of wegen was er iem. te zien* there was no sign of anyone anywhere; *een speler uit het ~ sturen* send a player off (the field) ‖ *uit het ~ geslagen zijn* be confused, be taken aback
het **veldbed** /vˈɛldbɛt/ (pl: -den) camp bed
het **veldboeket** /vˈɛldbukɛt/ (pl: -ten) bouquet of wild flowers
de **veldfles** /vˈɛltflɛs/ (pl: -sen) water bottle
de **veldheer** /vˈɛlther/ (pl: -heren) general
het **veldhospitaal** /vˈɛlthɔspital/ (pl: -hospita-

len) field hospital

de **veldloop** /vɛltlop/ (pl: -lopen) cross-country (race)

de **veldmaarschalk** /vɛltmarsxɑlk/ (pl: -en) Field Marshal; [Am] General of the Army

de **veldmuis** /vɛltmœys/ (pl: -muizen) field vole, field mouse

veldrijden /vɛltrɛɪdə(n)/ cyclo-cross (racing)

de **veldsla** /vɛltsla/ lamb's lettuce

de **veldslag** /vɛltslɑx/ (pl: -en) (pitched) battle

de **veldspeler** /vɛltspelər/ (pl: -s) fielder

de **veldtocht** /vɛltɔxt/ (pl: -en) campaign

het **veldwerk** /vɛltwɛrk/ fieldwork: *het ~ ver-richten* do the donkey work, do the spade-work

de **veldwerker** /vɛltwɛrkər/ (pl: -s) field work-er

velen /velə(n)/ stand, bear

velerlei /velərlɛɪ/ (adj) many, multifarious: *op ~ gebied* in many fields; *~ oorzaken* a va-riety of causes

de **velg** /vɛlx/ (pl: -en) rim

vellen /vɛlə(n)/ (velde, heeft geveld) cut down, fell: *bomen ~* cut down trees

de **velo** /velo/ [Belg] bike

het/de **velours** /vəlur/ velour(s)

het **ven** /vɛn/ (pl: -nen) pool; hollow

de **vendetta** /vɛndɛta/ (pl: -'s) vendetta, blood feud

Venetië /vene(t)sijə/ Venice

de **Venezolaan** /venezolan/ (pl: Venezolanen) Venezuelan

Venezolaans /venezolans/ (adj) Venezue-lan

Venezuela /venezywela/ Venezuela

het **venijn** /vənɛɪn/ poison, venom: *het ~ zit in de staart* the sting is in the tail

venijnig /vənɛɪnəx/ (adj, adv) vicious; ven-omous: *~e blikken* malicious looks

de **venkel** /vɛŋkəl/ fennel

de **vennoot** /vɛnot/ (pl: vennoten) partner

de **vennootschap** /vɛnotsxɑp/ (pl: -pen) **1** partnership, firm; [Am also] company **2** trading partnership: *besloten ~* private limited company; *naamloze ~* public limited company

de **vennootschapsbelasting** /vɛnotsxɑps-bəlɑstɪŋ/ corporation tax

het **venster** /vɛnstər/ (pl: -s) window

de **vensterbank** /vɛnstərbɑŋk/ (pl: -en) win-dowsill

de **vensterenveloppe** /vɛnstərɛnvəlɔp/ (pl: -n) window envelope

het **vensterglas** /vɛnstərɣlas/ (pl: -glazen) win-dow glass; window-pane

de **vent** /vɛnt/ (pl: -en) **1** fellow, guy, bloke: *een leuke ~* a dishy bloke (*or:* guy) **2** son(ny), lad(die)

venten /vɛntə(n)/ (ventte, heeft gevent) hawk, peddle

de **venter** /vɛntər/ (pl: -s) street trader, hawker,

pedlar

het **ventiel** /vɛntil/ (pl: -en) valve

de **ventilatie** /vɛntila(t)si/ ventilation

de **ventilator** /vɛntilatɔr/ (pl: -s, -en) fan, ven-tilator

¹**ventileren** /vɛntilerə(n)/ (ventileerde, heeft geventileerd) air

²**ventileren** /vɛntilerə(n)/ (ventileerde, heeft geventileerd) ventilate, air: *zijn me-ning ~* ventilate (*or:* air) one's opinion

de **ventweg** /vɛntwɛx/ (pl: -en) service road

¹**ver** /vɛr/ (adj) distant, far; far-off; [after vb] far off; a long way: *~re landen* distant (*or:* far-off) countries; *de ~re toekomst* the dis-tant future; *in een ~ verleden* in some distant (*or:* remote) past; *een ~re reis* a long journey

²**ver** /vɛr/ (adv) **1** far; a long way: *hij sprong zeven meter ~* he jumped a distance of seven metres; *~ gevorderd zijn* be well advanced; *het zou te ~ voeren om …* it would be going too far to …; *~ vooruitzien* look well (*or:* way) ahead; *hoe ~ is het nog?* how much fur-ther is it?; *hoe ~ ben je met je huiswerk?* how far have you got with your homework?; *dat gaat te ~!* that is the limit!; *~ weg* a long way off, far away; *het is zo ~!* here we go, this is it; *ben je zo ~?* (are you) ready?; *van ~ komen* come a long way, come from distant parts; *~ te zoeken zijn* be miles away; [fig] not be about (*or:* around) **2** (by) far, way: *~ heen zijn* be far gone; *zijn tijd ~ vooruit zijn* be way ahead of one's time

veraangenamen /vəranənama(n)/ (ver-aangenaamde, heeft veraangenaamd) sweeten, make more pleasant

verachtelijk /vərɑxtələk/ (adj, adv) despi-cable

verachten /vərɑxtə(n)/ (verachtte, heeft veracht) despise, scorn

de **verachting** /vərɑxtɪŋ/ contempt

de **verademing** /vəradəmɪŋ/ relief

veraf /vɛrɑf/ (adv) far away, far off, a long way away (*or:* off)

verafgelegen /vɛrɑfxələleɣə(n)/ (adj) far-away; [after vb] far away; remote

verafgoden /vərɑfɣodə(n)/ (verafgoodde, heeft verafgood) idolize

verafschuwen /vərɑfsxywə(n)/ (veraf-schuwde, heeft verafschuwd) loathe, detest

de **veranda** /vərɑnda/ (pl: -'s) veranda

¹**veranderen** /vərɑndərə(n)/ (veranderde, is veranderd) **1** change: *de tijden ~* times are changing **2** change, switch: *van huisarts ~* change one's doctor; *van onderwerp ~* change the subject

²**veranderen** /vərɑndərə(n)/ (veranderde, heeft veranderd) **1** alter, change: *een jurkje ~* alter a dress; *dat verandert de zaak* that changes things; *daar is niets meer aan te ~* nothing can be done about that **2** change, turn (into): *Jezus veranderde water in wijn* Je-

de **verandering** /vərɔndərɪŋ/ (pl: -en)
1 change; variation: ~ *van* **omgeving** change of scene(ry); *voor* de ~ for a change **2** alteration: *een* ~ **aanbrengen** *in* make an alteration (*or*: a change) to

veranderlijk /vərɔndərlək/ (adj) changeable, variable; unsettled; fickle

verankeren /vərɑnkərə(n)/ (verankerde, heeft verankerd) anchor; [fig] embed

verantwoord /vərɑntwort/ (adj) **1** safe; sensible **2** well-considered, sound: *~e* **voeding** a well-balanced (*or*: sensible) diet

verantwoordelijk /vərɑntwordələk/ (adj) responsible: *de ~e* **minister** the minister responsible; *iem. voor iets ~* **stellen** hold s.o. responsible for sth.

de **verantwoordelijkheid** /vərɑntwordələkhɛit/ (pl: -heden) responsibility: *de ~ voor iets op zich* **nemen** take (*or*: assume) responsibility for sth.; *de ~ voor een aanslag* **opeisen** claim responsibility for an attack

¹verantwoorden /vərɑntwordə(n)/ (verantwoordde, heeft verantwoord) justify, account for: *ik kan dit niet* **tegenover** *mijzelf ~* I cannot square this with my conscience

zich **²verantwoorden** /vərɑntwordə(n)/ (verantwoordde zich, heeft zich verantwoord) justify, answer (to s.o. for sth.)

de **verantwoording** /vərɑntwordɪŋ/ (pl: -en) **1** account: ~ *afleggen* render account; *aan iem. ~* **verschuldigd zijn** be accountable (*or*: answerable) to s.o.; *iem.* **ter** ~ *roepen* call s.o. to account **2** responsibility: *op jouw ~* you take the responsibility

¹verarmen /vərɑrmə(n)/ (verarmde, is verarmd) become impoverished, be reduced to poverty

²verarmen /vərɑrmə(n)/ (verarmde, heeft verarmd) impoverish ‖ *verarmd* **uranium** depleted uranium

verassen /vərɔsə(n)/ (veraste, heeft verast) incinerate, cremate

het **¹verbaal** /vɛrbal/ (pl: verbalen) booking, ticket

²verbaal /vɛrbal/ (adj) verbal

verbaasd /vərbast/ (adj) surprised, astonished, amazed: ~ *zijn* **over** *iets* be surprised (*or*: amazed) at sth.

verbaliseren /vɛrbalizɛrə(n)/ (verbaliseerde, heeft geverbaliseerd) book

het **verband** /vərbɑnt/ (pl: -en) **1** bandage: *een* ~ *aanleggen* put on a bandage **2** connection; context; relation(ship): *in* **landelijk** (*or*: **Europees**) ~ at a national (*or*: European) level; *in* **ruimer** ~ in a wider context; ~ **houden** *met iets* be connected with sth.; *dit* **houdt** ~ *met het feit dat* this has to do with the fact that; *de woorden* **uit** *hun* ~ *rukken* take words out of context

de **verbanddoos** /vərbɑndoos/ (pl: -dozen)

verbannen /vərbɑnə(n)/ (verbande, heeft verbannen) banish, exile: ~ *zijn* be banished, be under a ban

de **verbanning** /vərbɑnɪŋ/ (pl: -en) banishment, exile

verbasteren /vərbɑstərə(n)/ (verbasterde, heeft verbasterd) corrupt

¹verbazen /vərbazə(n)/ (verbaasde, heeft verbaasd) amaze, surprise, astonish: *dat verbaast me* **niets** that doesn't surprise me in the least

zich **²verbazen** /vərbazə(n)/ (verbaasde zich, heeft zich verbaasd) be surprised (*or*: amazed) (at)

de **verbazing** /vərbazɪŋ/ surprise, amazement, astonishment: *wie* **schetst** *mijn ~* imagine my surprise; *dat* **wekte** ~ that came as a surprise; *tot mijn ~ hoorde ik …* I was surprised to hear …

verbazingwekkend /vərbazɪŋwɛkənt/ (adj, adv) astonishing, surprising; amazing

¹verbeelden /vərbɛldə(n)/ (verbeeldde, heeft verbeeld) represent, be meant (*or*: supposed) to be: *dat* **moet** *een badkamer ~!* that is supposed to be a bathroom!

zich **²verbeelden** /vərbɛldə(n)/ (verbeeldde zich, heeft zich verbeeld) imagine, fancy: *dat verbeeld je je* **maar** you are just imagining it (*or*: things); *hij verbeeldt zich heel wat* he has a high opinion of himself; *verbeeld je maar niets!* don't go getting ideas (into your head)!

de **verbeelding** /vərbɛldɪŋ/ **1** imagination: *dat* **spreekt tot** *de ~* that appeals to one's imagination **2** conceit(edness), vanity: ~ **hebben** be conceited, think a lot of o.s.

verbergen /vərbɛrɣə(n)/ (verborg, heeft verborgen) hide, conceal: *zij* **hield** *iets voor hem verborgen* she was holding sth. back from him

verbeten /vərbɛtə(n)/ (adj) grim, dogged

¹verbeteren /vərbɛtərə(n)/ (verbeterde, is verbeterd) improve, get better: *verbeterde* **werkomstandigheden** improved working conditions

²verbeteren /vərbɛtərə(n)/ (verbeterde, heeft verbeterd) **1** improve: *zijn* **Engels** *~* improve (*or*: brush up) one's English **2** correct **3** beat, improve on: *een* **record** *~* break a record

de **verbetering** /vərbɛtərɪŋ/ (pl: -en) **1** improvement: *het* **is** *een hele ~ vergeleken met …* it's a great improvement on … **2** correction; rectification; marking

verbeurdverklaren /vərbɔrtfərklarə(n)/ (verklaarde verbeurd, heeft verbeurdverklaard) seize, confiscate

verbieden /vərbidə(n)/ (verbood, heeft verboden) forbid; ban; suppress: *verboden* **toegang** no admittance; *verboden* **in** *te* **rijden**

no entry (*or*: access); *verboden te **roken*** no smoking; *verboden **voor** onbevoegden* no unauthorized entry; no trespassing

verbijsterd /vərbɛistərt/ (adj) bewildered, amazed, baffled

verbijsteren /vərbɛistərə(n)/ (verbijsterde, heeft verbijsterd) bewilder, amaze

de **verbijstering** /vərbɛistərɪŋ/ bewilderment, amazement

zich **verbijten** /vərbɛitə(n)/ (verbeet zich, heeft zich verbeten) be (almost) bursting; bite one's lips

verbinden /vərbɪndə(n)/ (verbond, heeft verbonden) **1** join (together), connect (to, with): ~ *met* join to, link up to (*or*: with) **2** connect, link **3** bandage **4** connect, attach, join (up): *er zijn geen kosten **aan** verbonden* there are no expenses involved **5** connect (with), put through (to): *ik ben **verkeerd** verbonden* I have got a wrong number; *kunt u mij **met** de heer Jefferson ~?* could you put me through to Mr Jefferson?

de **verbinding** /vərbɪndɪŋ/ (pl: -en) **1** connection, link: *een ~ tot stand brengen* establish (*or*: make) a connection **2** connection: *een **directe** ~* a direct connection; *a through train*; *de ~en **met** de stad zijn uitstekend* connections with the city are excellent **3** connection: *geen ~ **kunnen krijgen*** not be able to get through; *de ~ **werd verbroken*** the connection was broken, we (*or*: they) were cut off

de **verbintenis** /vərbɪntənɪs/ (pl: -sen) **1** obligation, commitment **2** agreement, contract **3** association; relationship

verbitterd /vərbɪtərt/ (adj, adv) bitter (at, by), embittered (at, by)

de **verbittering** /vərbɪtərɪŋ/ bitterness

verbleken /vərblekə(n)/ (verbleekte, is verbleekt) **1** (turn, go) pale, turn white, go white **2** fade

verblijden /vərblɛidə(n)/ (verblijdde, heeft verblijd): *iem. **met** iets ~* make s.o. happy with sth.

het **verblijf** /vərblɛif/ (pl: verblijven) **1** stay **2** residence; accommodation: *de verblijven **voor** de bemanning* (*or*: *het personeel*) the crew's (*or*: servants') quarters

de **verblijfkosten** /vərblɛifkɔstə(n)/ (pl) accommodation expenses, living expenses

de **verblijfplaats** /vərblɛifplats/ (pl: -en) (place of) residence, address: *iem. zonder vaste **woon-** of ~* s.o. with no permanent home or address

de **verblijfsstatus** /vərblɛifstatʏs/ asylum status

de **verblijfsvergunning** /vərblɛifsfərɣʏnɪŋ/ (pl: -en) residence permit

verblijven /vərblɛivə(n)/ (verbleef, heeft/is verbleven) **1** stay: *hij verbleef enkele maanden **in** Japan* he stayed in Japan for several

months **2** live

verblinden /vərblɪndə(n)/ (verblindde, heeft verblind) dazzle, blind: *een ~de **schoonheid*** a dazzling (*or*: stunning) beauty

verbloemen /vərblumə(n)/ (verbloemde, heeft verbloemd) disguise, gloss over, cover up

verbluffend /vərblʏfənt/ (adj, adv) staggering, astounding: ~ *snel handelen* act amazingly (*or*: incredibly) quickly

verbluft /vərblʏft/ (adj) staggered, stunned: ~ *staan kijken* be dumbfounded

het **verbod** /vərbɔt/ (pl: -en) ban, prohibition; embargo: *een ~ **uitvaardigen*** impose (*or*: declare) a ban

verboden /vərbodə(n)/ (adj) forbidden, banned, prohibited: *tot ~ **gebied** verklaren* declare (*or*: put) out of bounds; ~ *wapenbezit* illegal possession of arms

het **verbodsbord** /vərbɔtsbɔrt/ (pl: -en) prohibition sign

verbolgen /vərbɔlɣə(n)/ (adj) enraged (by, at)

het **verbond** /vərbɔnt/ (pl: -en) **1** treaty, pact: *een ~ **sluiten** (or: **aangaan**) met* make (*or*: enter) into a treaty with **2** union

verbonden /vərbɔndə(n)/ (adj) **1** committed, bound **2** allied, joined (together) **3** bandaged, dressed **4** joined (to), united (with); bound (to), wedded (to): *zich **met** iem. ~ voelen* feel a bond with s.o. ‖ *verkeerd ~* wrong number

verborgen /vərbɔrɣə(n)/ (adj) hidden, concealed

verbouwen /vərbɑuwə(n)/ (verbouwde, heeft verbouwd) **1** cultivate, grow **2** carry out alterations, renovate

verbouwereerd /vərbɑuwərert/ (adj) dumbfounded, flabbergasted

de **verbouwing** /vərbɑuwɪŋ/ (pl: -en) alteration, renovation: *gesloten **wegens** ~* closed for repairs (*or*: alterations)

¹**verbranden** /vərbrɑndə(n)/ (verbrandde, is verbrand) **1** burn down, burn up: *hij is bij dat ongeluk **levend** verbrand* he was burnt alive in that accident **2** burn; scorch: *het **vlees** staat te ~* the meat is burning

²**verbranden** /vərbrɑndə(n)/ (verbrandde, heeft verbrand) **1** burn (down), incinerate **2** burn; scald: *zijn **gezicht** is door de zon verbrand* his face is sunburnt

de **verbranding** /vərbrɑndɪŋ/ (pl: -en) **1** burning, incineration **2** burn; scald

de **verbrandingsmotor** /vərbrɑndɪŋsmotər/ (pl: -en) (internal-)combustion engine

verbrassen /vərbrɑsə(n)/ (verbraste, heeft verbrast) squander, dissipate

¹**verbreden** /vərbredə(n)/ (verbreedde, heeft verbreed) broaden, widen

zich ²**verbreden** /vərbredə(n)/ (verbreedde zich, heeft zich verbreed) broaden (out): *de **weg***

verbreedt zich daar the road broadens (out)
there
verbreiden /vǝrbrɛɪdǝ(n)/ (verbreidde,
heeft verbreid) spread
verbreken /vǝrbrekǝ(n)/ (verbrak, heeft
verbroken) **1** break (up): *een zegel* ~ break a
seal **2** break (off), sever: *een relatie* ~ break
off a relationship
verbrijzelen /vǝrbrɛɪzǝlǝ(n)/ (verbrijzelde,
heeft verbrijzeld) shatter, crush
verbroederen /vǝrbrudǝrǝ(n)/ (verbroe-
derde, heeft verbroederd) fraternize (with)
verbrokkelen /vǝrbrɔkǝlǝ(n)/ (verbrokkel-
de, heeft/is verbrokkeld) crumble
verbruien /vǝrbrœyjǝ(n)/ (verbruide, heeft
verbruid): *hij heeft **het** bij mij verbruid* I wash
my hands of him now
het **verbruik** /vǝrbrœyk/ consumption
verbruiken /vǝrbrœykǝ(n)/ (verbruikte,
heeft verbruikt) consume, use up
de **verbruiker** /vǝrbrœykǝr/ (pl: -s) consumer,
user
de **verbruikzaal** /vǝrbrœyksal/ (pl: -zalen)
dining area
verbuigen /vǝrbœyɣǝ(n)/ (verboog, heeft
verbogen) bend, twist
de **verbuiging** /vǝrbœyɣɪŋ/ (pl: -en) declen-
sion
¹verdacht /vǝrdɑxt/ (adj) **1** suspected: *iem. ~
maken* cast a slur on s.o., smear s.o. **2** suspicious, questionable: *een ~ zaakje* a questionable (*or:* shady) business
²verdacht /vǝrdɑxt/ (adv) suspiciously: *dat
lijkt ~ veel op* ... that looks suspiciously like ...
de **verdachte** /vǝrdɑxtǝ/ (pl: -n) suspect
de **verdachtenbank** /vǝrdɑxtǝ(n)bɑŋk/ dock,
witness box; [Am] witness stand
de **verdachtmaking** /vǝrdɑxtmakɪŋ/ (pl: -en)
imputation; insinuation; slur
verdagen /vǝrdaɣǝ(n)/ (verdaagde, heeft
verdaagd) adjourn: *een zitting* ~ adjourn a
session
de **verdaging** /vǝrdaxɪŋ/ (pl: -en) postponement; adjournment
verdampen /vǝrdɑmpǝ(n)/ (verdampte,
heeft/is verdampt) evaporate, vaporize
de **verdamping** /vǝrdɑmpɪŋ/ evaporation, va-
porization
verdedigbaar /vǝrdedǝybar/ (adj) **1** defensible **2** defensible, justifiable
verdedigen /vǝrdedǝɣǝ(n)/ (verdedigde,
heeft verdedigd) **1** defend: *een ~de houding
aannemen* be on the defensive **2** defend,
support: *zijn belangen* ~ stand up for (*or:* defend) one's interests; *zich* ~ defend (*or:* justify) o.s.
de **verdediger** /vǝrdedǝɣǝr/ (pl: -s) **1** defender, advocate **2** counsel (for the defence)
3 [sport] defender, back: *centrale* ~ central
defender; *vrije* ~ libero
de **verdediging** /vǝrdedǝɣɪŋ/ (pl: -en) **1** de-

fence: [sport] *in de* ~ *gaan* go on the defensive; [fig] *in de* ~ *schieten* be on the defensive
2 counsel (for the defence), defence
verdeeld /vǝrdelt/ (adj) divided: *hierover zijn
de meningen* ~ opinions are divided on this
(problem, issue, question)
de **verdeeldheid** /vǝrdelthɛit/ discord, dissension: *er heerst* ~ *binnen de partij* the party is
divided (*or:* split); ~ *zaaien* spread discord
de **verdeelsleutel** /vǝrdelsløtǝl/ (pl: -s) key,
ratio, formula
de **verdeelstekker** /vǝrdelstɛkǝr/ (pl: -s)
adapter
verdekt /vǝrdɛkt/ (adj) concealed, hidden:
zich ~ opstellen conceal o.s., take cover
¹verdelen /vǝrdelǝ(n)/ (verdeelde, heeft
verdeeld) **1** divide, split (up) **2** divide (up),
distribute: *de buit* ~ divide the loot **3** spread:
de taken ~ allocate (*or:* share) (out) the tasks
zich **²verdelen** /vǝrdelǝ(n)/ (verdeelde zich, heeft
zich verdeeld) divide, split (up): *de rivier ver-
deelt zich hier in twee takken* the river divides
(*or:* forks) here
verdelgen /vǝrdɛlɣǝ(n)/ (verdelgde, heeft
verdelgd) eradicate
het **verdelgingsmiddel** /vǝrdɛlɣɪŋsmɪdǝl/
pesticide; insecticide; weedkiller
de **verdeling** /vǝrdelɪŋ/ (pl: -en) **1** division
2 distribution
verdenken /vǝrdɛŋkǝ(n)/ (verdacht, heeft
verdacht) suspect (of): *zij wordt ervan verdacht, dat* ... she is under the suspicion of ...;
iem. van diefstal ~ suspect s.o. of theft
de **verdenking** /vǝrdɛŋkɪŋ/ (pl: -en) suspicion:
onder ~ staan be suspected (*or:* under suspicion); *iem. in hechtenis nemen op ~ van moord*
arrest s.o. on suspicion of murder
¹verder /vɛrdǝr/ (adj) **1** (the) rest of **2** further, subsequent
²verder /vɛrdǝr/ (adv) **1** farther, further:
twee regels ~ two lines (further) down; *hoe
ging het* ~? how did it go on?; ~ *lezen* go on
(*or:* continue) reading, read on **2** further,
furthermore, in addition, moreover: ~ *verklaarde zij* ... she went on (*or:* proceeded) to
say ... **3** for the rest, apart from that: *is er ~
nog iets?* anything else?
het **verderf** /vǝrdɛrf/ ruin, destruction: *iem. in
het ~ storten* ruin s.o., bring ruin upon s.o.
verderfelijk /vǝrdɛrfǝlǝk/ (adj) pernicious:
~*e invloeden* baneful influences
verderop /vɛrdǝrɔp/ (adv) further on, farther on: *zij woont vier huizen* ~ she lives four
houses (further) down; ~ *in de straat* down
(*or:* up) the street
verderven /vǝrdɛrvǝ(n)/ deprave, corrupt
verdichten /vǝrdɪxtǝ(n)/ (verdichtte, heeft
verdicht) condense
de **verdichting** /vǝrdɪxtɪŋ/ **1** condensation
2 [fig] condensing
het **verdichtsel** /vǝrdɪxtsǝl/ (pl: -s) fabrication,

invention
¹verdiend /vərdiːnt/ (adj) deserved: *volko-men* ~ richly deserved; *dat is zijn ~e loon* it serves him right, he had it coming to him
²verdiend /vərdiːnt/ (adv) deservedly: *de thuisclub won ~ met 3-1* the home team won deservedly by 3 to 1
¹verdienen /vərdiːnə(n)/ (verdiende, heeft verdiend) **1** earn, make money: *zij verdient uitstekend* she is very well paid **2** pay: *dat baantje verdient slecht* that job does not pay well
²verdienen /vərdiːnə(n)/ (verdiende, heeft verdiend) **1** earn, make, be paid: *een goed salaris ~* earn a good salary; *zuur verdiend* hard-earned, hard-won **2** deserve, merit: *dat voorbeeld verdient geen navolging* that example ought not to be followed
de **verdienste** /vərdiːnstə/ (pl: -n) **1** wages, pay, earnings; profit: *zonder ~n zijn* be out of a job, earn no money **2** merit: *een man van ~* a man of (great) merit
verdienstelijk /vərdiːnstələk/ (adj, adv) deserving, (praise)worthy: *zich ~ maken* make o.s. useful
¹verdiepen /vərdiːpə(n)/ (verdiepte, heeft verdiept) deepen, broaden: *zijn kennis ~* gain more in-depth knowledge
zich **²verdiepen** /vərdiːpə(n)/ (verdiepte zich, heeft zich verdiept) (+ in) go (deeply) into, be absorbed in: *verdiept zijn in* be engrossed (*or:* absorbed) in
de **verdieping** /vərdiːpɪŋ/ (pl: -en) floor, storey: *een huis met zes ~en* a six-storeyed house; *op de tweede ~* on the second floor; [Am] on the third floor
de **verdikking** /vərdɪkɪŋ/ (pl: -en) thickening, bulge
verdisconteren /vərdɪskɔntɛrə(n)/ (verdisconteerde, heeft verdisconteerd) discount
verdoen /vərduːn/ (verdeed, heeft verdaan) waste (away), fritter (away), squander: *ik zit hier mijn tijd te ~* I am wasting my time here
verdoezelen /vərduːzələ(n)/ (verdoezelde, heeft verdoezeld) blur, disguise: *de ware toedracht ~* fudge (*or:* disguise) the real facts
verdonkeremanen /vərdɔŋkərəmaːnə(n)/ (verdonkeremaande, heeft verdonkeremaand) embezzle; suppress
verdoofd /vərdoːft/ (adj) stunned, stupefied, numb
verdord /vərdɔrt/ (adj) shrivelled; withered; parched: *~e bladeren* withered leaves
verdorie /vərdoːri/ (int) [inform] darned
verdorren /vərdɔrə(n)/ (verdorde, is verdord) shrivel (up), parch; wither (up); wilt
verdorven /vərdɔrvə(n)/ (adj) depraved, perverted: *een ~ mens* a wicked person, a pervert
verdoven /vərdoːvə(n)/ (verdoofde, heeft verdoofd) stun, stupefy; benumb: *~de mid-*

delen drugs, narcotic(s); *de patiënt wordt plaatselijk verdoofd* the patient receives a local anaesthetic
de **verdoving** /vərdoːvɪŋ/ (pl: -en) **1** anaesthesia, anaesthetic **2** stupor
verdraagzaam /vərdraːxsam/ (adj) tolerant: *~ jegens elkaar zijn* be tolerant of each other
de **verdraagzaamheid** /vərdraːxsamhɛit/ tolerance
verdraaid /vərdraːit/ (adj) **1** darn(ed) **2** distorted, twisted
verdraaien /vərdraːjə(n)/ (verdraaide, heeft verdraaid) **1** turn **2** distort; twist: *de waarheid ~* distort the truth **3** disguise: *zijn stem ~* disguise (*or:* mask) one's voice
de **verdraaiing** /vərdraːjɪŋ/ (pl: -en) distortion, twist
het **verdrag** /vərdrɔx/ (pl: -en) treaty, agreement: *een ~ sluiten* enter into (*or:* make) a treaty
verdragen /vərdraːɣə(n)/ (verdroeg, heeft verdragen) **1** bear, endure, stand: *hij kan de gedachte niet ~, dat …* he cannot bear (*or:* stand) the idea that … **2** bear, stand, put up with, take: *ik kan veel ~, maar nu is 't genoeg* I can stand (*or:* take) a lot, but enough is enough
het **verdriet** /vərdriːt/ grief (*or:* distress) (at, over), sorrow (at): *iem. ~ doen (aandoen)* distress s.o., give s.o. pain (*or:* sorrow); *~ hebben* be in distress; grieve
verdrietig /vərdriːtəx/ (adj) sad, grieved: *~ maken* sadden
verdrievoudigen /vərdrivoudəɣə(n)/ (verdrievoudigde, heeft/is verdrievoudigd) triple, treble: *de winst is verdrievoudigd* profit has tripled
verdrijven /vərdrɛivə(n)/ (verdreef, heeft verdreven) drive away, chase away, dispel: *de pijn ~* dispel the pain
¹verdringen /vərdrɪŋə(n)/ (verdrong, heeft verdrongen) **1** push away (*or:* aside) **2** shut out; repress; suppress
zich **²verdringen** /vərdrɪŋə(n)/ (verdrong zich, heeft zich verdrongen) crowd (round): *de menigte verdrong zich voor de etalage* people crowded round the shop window
¹verdrinken /vərdrɪŋkə(n)/ (verdronk, is verdronken) drown: *~ in het huiswerk* be swamped by homework
²verdrinken /vərdrɪŋkə(n)/ (verdronk, heeft verdronken) drink away; drown
de **verdrinkingsdood** /vərdrɪŋkɪŋzdoːt/ death by drowning
verdrogen /vərdroːɣə(n)/ (verdroogde, is verdroogd) **1** dry out, dry up, dehydrate: *dat brood is helemaal verdroogd* that loaf (of bread) has completely dried out **2** shrivel (up), wither (away, up)
verdrukken /vərdrʏkə(n)/ (verdrukte, heeft

verdrukt) oppress, repress

de **verdrukking** /vərdrʏ̱kɪŋ/ (pl: -en): *in de ~ raken (komen)* get into hot water (*or:* a scrape)

verdubbelen /vərdʏ̱bələ(n)/ (verdubbelde, heeft/is verdubbeld) double: *met verdubbelde energie* with redoubled energy

verduidelijken /vərdœ̱ydələkə(n)/ (verduidelijkte, heeft verduidelijkt) explain, make (more) clear, clarify

de **verduidelijking** /vərdœ̱ydələkɪŋ/ (pl: -en) explanation: *ter ~* by way of illustration

verduisteren /vərdœ̱ystərə(n)/ (verduisterde, heeft verduisterd) **1** darken, dim: *de zon ~* blot out the sun **2** embezzle

de **verduistering** /vərdœ̱ystərɪŋ/ (pl: -en) **1** darkening **2** eclipse **3** embezzlement

verdunnen /vərdʏ̱nə(n)/ (verdunde, heeft verdund) **1** thin; dilute: *melk met water ~* dilute milk with water **2** thin (out)

de **verdunning** /vərdʏ̱nɪŋ/ (pl: -en) thinning, dilution

verduren /vərdy̱rə(n)/ (verduurde, heeft verduurd) bear, endure, suffer: *heel wat moeten ~* have to put up with a great deal; *het zwaar te ~ hebben* a) have a hard (*or:* rough) time of it; b) suffer great hardship(s)

verduurzamen /vərdy̱rzamə(n)/ (verduurzaamde, heeft verduurzaamd) preserve, cure

verdwaald /vərdwa̱lt/ (adj) lost; stray: *een ~e kogel* a stray bullet; *~ raken* lose one's way

verdwaasd /vərdwa̱st/ (adj) foolish; groggy: *~ voor zich uit staren* stare vacantly into space

verdwalen /vərdwa̱lə(n)/ (verdwaalde, is verdwaald) lose one's way, get lost, go astray

verdwijnen /vərdwɛ̱inə(n)/ (verdween, is verdwenen) disappear; vanish: *een verdwenen boek* a missing (*or:* lost) book; *mijn kiespijn is verdwenen* my toothache has worn off (*or:* disappeared); *geleidelijk ~* fade out (*or:* away), melt away; *spoorloos ~* vanish without (leaving) a trace

de **verdwijning** /vərdwɛ̱inɪŋ/ (pl: -en) disappearance

de **verdwijntruc** /vərdwɛ̱intrʏk/ (pl: -s) disappearing act, vanishing trick

veredelen /vəre̱dələ(n)/ (veredelde, heeft veredeld) ennoble, elevate, refine

de **veredeling** /vəre̱dəlɪŋ/ refinement; improvement; upgrading

vereenvoudigen /vərɛnvɑ̱udəɣə(n)/ (vereenvoudigde, heeft vereenvoudigd) simplify: *de vereenvoudigde spelling* simplified spelling

de **vereenvoudiging** /vərɛnvɑ̱udəxɪŋ/ (pl: -en) simplification; reduction [fraction]

vereenzamen /vərɛ̱nzamə(n)/ (vereenzaamde, is vereenzaamd) grow lonely, become lonely

vereenzelvigen /vərɛnzɛ̱lvəɣə(n)/ (vereenzelvigde, heeft vereenzelvigd) identify: *zij vereenzelvigde zich met Julia Roberts* she identified (herself) with Julia Roberts

de **vereerder** /vəre̱rdər/ (pl: -s) worshipper, admirer

vereeuwigen /vəre̱wəɣə(n)/ (vereeuwigde, heeft vereeuwigd) immortalize

vereffenen /vərɛ̱fənə(n)/ (vereffende, heeft vereffend) settle, square; smooth out: *iets* (or: *een rekening) met iem. te ~ hebben* have to settle an account

de **vereffening** /vərɛ̱fənɪŋ/ (pl: -en) settlement, payment

vereisen /vərɛ̱isə(n)/ (vereiste, heeft vereist) require, demand: *ervaring vereist* experience required; *de vereiste zorg aan iets besteden* give the necessary care (*or:* attention) to sth.

het/de **vereiste** /vərɛ̱istə/ (pl: -n) requirement: *aan de ~n voldoen* meet (*or:* fulfil) the requirements; *dat is een eerste ~* that is a prerequisite (*or:* a must)

¹**veren** /ve̱rə(n)/ (adj) feather: *een ~ pen* a quill (pen)

²**veren** /ve̱rə(n)/ (veerde, heeft geveerd) **1** be springy: *het veert niet meer* it has lost its spring (*or:* bounce) **2** spring: *overeind ~* spring to one's feet

verend /ve̱rənt/ (adj) springy, elastic: *een ~ matras* a springy (*or:* bouncy) mattress

verenigbaar /vəre̱nəɣbar/ (adj) compatible (with), consistent (with)

verenigd /vəre̱nəxt/ (adj) united, allied

de **Verenigde Arabische Emiraten** /vəre̱nəɣdəarabisəemira̱tə(n)/ (pl) United Arab Emirates

de **Verenigde Staten** /vəre̱nəɣdəsta̱tə(n)/ (pl) United States (of America)

het **Verenigd Koninkrijk** /vəre̱nəxtko̱nɪŋkrɛik/ United Kingdom

verenigen /vəre̱nəɣə(n)/ (verenigde, heeft verenigd) unite (with), combine, join (to, with): *zich ~ in een organisatie* form an organisation; *het nuttige met het aangename ~* mix (*or:* combine) business with pleasure

de **vereniging** /vəre̱nəɣɪŋ/ (pl: -en) club, association, society: *een ~ oprichten* found an association

vereren /vəre̱rə(n)/ (vereerde, heeft vereerd) worship, adore

¹**verergeren** /vərɛ̱rɣərə(n)/ (verergerde, is verergerd) worsen, become worse, grow worse, deteriorate: *de toestand verergert* the situation is deteriorating (*or:* growing worse)

²**verergeren** /vərɛ̱rɣərə(n)/ (verergerde, heeft verergerd) worsen, make worse, aggravate

de **verering** /vəre̱rɪŋ/ (pl: -en) **1** worship, veneration **2** [rel] devotion, cult: *de ~ van Maria* the devotion to Maria, the Maria cult

de **verf** /vɛrf/ (pl: verven) paint; dye: *pas op voor de ~!* (watch out,) fresh (*or:* wet) paint!; *het huis zit nog goed in de ~* the paintwork (on the house) is still good ‖ *niet uit de ~ komen* not live up to its promise, not come into its own

de **verfbom** /vɛrvbɔm/ (pl: -men) paint bomb

de **verfdoos** /vɛrvdos/ (pl: -dozen) paint box, (box of) paints

verfijnen /vərfɛinə(n)/ (verfijnde, heeft verfijnd) refine: *zijn techniek ~* refine (*or:* polish (up)) one's technique

de **verfijning** /vərfɛinɪŋ/ (pl: -en) refinement, sophistication

verfilmen /vərfɪlmə(n)/ (verfilmde, heeft verfilmd) film, turn (*or:* make) into a film: *een roman ~* film a novel, adapt a novel for the screen

de **verfilming** /vərfɪlmɪŋ/ (pl: -en) film version, screen version

de **verfkwast** /vɛrfkwɑst/ (pl: -en) paintbrush

de **verflaag** /vɛrflax/ (pl: -lagen) coat (*or:* layer) of paint: *bovenste ~* topcoat

verflauwen /vərflɑuwə(n)/ (verflauwde, is verflauwd) fade

verfoeien /vərfujə(n)/ (verfoeide, heeft verfoeid) detest, loathe

verfomfaaid /vərfɔmfajt/ (adj) dishevelled, tousled

verfraaien /vərfrajə(n)/ (verfraaide, heeft verfraaid) embellish (with)

de **verfraaiing** /vərfrajɪŋ/ (pl: -en) embellishment

verfrissen /vərfrɪsə(n)/ (verfriste, heeft verfrist) refresh, freshen up: *zich ~* freshen up, refresh (o.s.)

verfrissend /vərfrɪsənt/ (adj) refreshing, invigorating

de **verfrissing** /vərfrɪsɪŋ/ (pl: -en) refreshment: *enige ~en gebruiken* take (*or:* have) some refreshments

de **verfroller** /vɛrfrɔlər/ (pl: -s) paint roller

verfrommelen /vərfrɔmələ(n)/ (verfrommelde, heeft verfrommeld) crumple (up), rumple (up)

de **verfspuit** /vɛrfspœyt/ (pl: -en) paint spray(er), spray gun

de **verfstof** /vɛrfstɔf/ (pl: -fen) paint; dye (base); pigment

de **verfverdunner** /vɛrfərdynər/ (pl: -s) thinner

vergaan /vərɣan/ (verging, is vergaan) **1** fare: *vergane glorie* lost (*or:* faded) glory **2** perish, pass away: *horen en zien vergaat je erbij* the noise is enough to waken the dead **3** perish, decay, rot **4** perish; [fig] be consumed with; be wrecked (*or:* lost); founder: *ik verga van de kou* I am freezing to death; *~ van de honger* be starving to death; *~ van de dorst* be dying of thirst ‖ *ik weet niet hoe het*

hem is ~ I don't know what has become of him

vergaand /vɛrɣant/ (adj) far-reaching, drastic

de **vergaarbak** /vərɣarbɑk/ (pl: -ken) reservoir

vergaderen /vərɣadərə(n)/ (vergaderde, is vergaderd) meet, assemble: *hij heeft al de hele ochtend vergaderd* he has been in conference all morning; *de raad vergaderde twee uur lang* the council sat for two hours

de **vergadering** /vərɣadərɪŋ/ (pl: -en) meeting, assembly: *het verslag van een ~* the minutes of a meeting; *gewone (algemene) ~* general meeting (*or:* assembly); *een ~ bijwonen* (or: *houden*) attend (*or:* hold) a meeting; *de ~ sluiten* close (*or:* conclude) the meeting; *een ~ leiden* chair a meeting

de **vergaderzaal** /vərɣadərzal/ (pl: -zalen) meeting hall, assembly room, conference room

vergallen /vərɣɑlə(n)/ (vergalde, heeft vergald) embitter, spoil

vergankelijk /vərɣɑŋkələk/ (adj) transitory, transient; fleeting

zich **vergapen** /vərɣapə(n)/ (vergaapte zich, heeft zich vergaapt) gaze at, gape at: *zich ~ aan een motor* gape (in admiration) at a motorbike

vergaren /vərɣarə(n)/ (vergaarde, heeft vergaard) gather

vergassen /vərɣɑsə(n)/ (vergaste, heeft vergast) **1** gas **2** gasify

de **vergassing** /vərɣɑsɪŋ/ **1** gasification **2** gassing

¹**vergeefs** /vərɣefs/ (adj) vain, futile; in vain: *een ~e reis* a futile (*or:* useless) journey; *~e pogingen* vain (*or:* futile, useless) attempts

²**vergeefs** /vərɣefs/ (adv) in vain: *~ zoeken* look in vain

vergeetachtig /vərɣetɑxtəx/ (adj) forgetful

het **vergeetboek** /vərɣedbuk/: *in het ~ raken* be(come) forgotten, sink into oblivion

het **vergeet-mij-nietje** /vərɣetmɛinicə/ (pl: -s) forget-me-not

vergelden /vərɣɛldə(n)/ (vergold, heeft vergolden) repay; reward; take revenge on: *kwaad met kwaad ~* pay back (*or:* repay) evil with evil

de **vergelding** /vərɣɛldɪŋ/ (pl: -en) repayment; reward; revenge; retaliation: *ter ~ werden krijgsgevangenen doodgeschoten* prisoners of war were shot in retaliation (*or:* reprisal)

de **vergeldingsmaatregel** /vərɣɛldɪŋsmatreɣəl/ (pl: -en) reprisal

vergelen /vərɣelə(n)/ (vergeelde, is vergeeld) yellow, go yellow, turn yellow

het **vergelijk** /vɛrɣələɛik/ (pl: -en) agreement; settlement

vergelijkbaar /vɛrɣələɛigbar/ (adj) comparable: *meel en vergelijkbare producten* flour and similar products; *~ zijn met* be compara-

ble to
vergelijken /vɛrɣəlɛikə(n)/ (vergeleek, heeft vergeleken) compare; compare with sth.; compare to sth.: *vergelijk artikel 12, tweede lid* see (*or:* cf.) article 12, subsection two; *niet te ~ zijn met* be (*or:* bear) no comparison with, not be comparable to; *vergeleken met vroeger is er veel veranderd* compared with (*or:* by contrast with) the past a lot has changed

de **vergelijking** /vɛrɣəlɛikɪŋ/ (pl: -en) **1** comparison; analogy: *de trappen van ~* the degrees of comparison; *in ~ met* in (*or:* by) comparison with; *ter ~* by way of comparison, for comparison **2** [maths] equation

vergemakkelijken /vɛrɣəmɔkələkə(n)/ (vergemakkelijkte, heeft vergemakkelijkt) simplify, facilitate: *dat dient om het leven te ~* that serves to make life easier

vergen /vɛrɣə(n)/ (vergde, heeft gevergd) demand, require; tax: *het uiterste ~ van iem.* strain (*or:* try) s.o. to the limit

de **vergetelheid** /vərɣɛtəlhɛɪt/ oblivion: *in de ~ geraken* be(come) forgotten, fall into oblivion

¹**vergeten** /vərɣɛtə(n)/ (adj) forgotten; neglected: *~ schrijvers* forgotten (*or:* obscure) writers

²**vergeten** /vərɣɛtə(n)/ (vergat, is vergeten) **1** forget, slip one's mind: *alles is ~ en vergeven* everything is forgiven and forgotten, (there are) no hard feelings; *dat ben ik glad ~* clean forgot(ten); *dat kun je wel ~* you can kiss that goodbye! **2** forget, overlook; leave behind: *ze waren ~ zijn naam op de lijst te zetten* they had forgotten to put his name on the list; *niet te ~* not forgetting (*or:* omitting) **3** forget, put out of one's mind: *zijn zorgen ~* forget one's worries; *vergeet het maar!* forget it!, no way!

vergeven /vərɣɛvə(n)/ (vergaf, heeft vergeven) **1** forgive: *ik kan mezelf nooit ~, dat ik … I* can never forgive myself for (…ing) **2** poison: *het huis is ~ van de stank* the house is pervaded by the stench; *~ van de luizen* lice-ridden, crawling with lice **3** give (away): *zij heeft zes vrijkaartjes te ~* she has six free tickets to give away

vergevensgezind /vərɣɛvə(n)sxəzɪnt/ (adj) forgiving

de **vergeving** /vərɣɛvɪŋ/ forgiveness; pardon; absolution: *iem. om ~ vragen voor iets* ask s.o.'s forgiveness for sth.

vergevorderd /vɛrɣəvɔrdərt/ (adj) (far) advanced

zich **vergewissen** /vɛrɣəwɪsə(n)/ (vergewiste zich, heeft zich vergewist) ascertain, make certain, make sure

vergezellen /vɛrɣəzɛlə(n)/ (vergezelde, heeft vergezeld) accompany; attend (on): *iem. op (de) reis ~* accompany s.o. on a jour-

ney
het **vergezicht** /vɛrɣəzɪxt/ (pl: -en) (panoramic, wide) view, vista

vergezocht /vɛrɣəzɔxt/ (adj) far-fetched

het/de **vergiet** /vərɣit/ (pl: -en) colander; strainer: *zo lek als een ~* leak like a sieve

vergieten /vərɣitə(n)/ (vergoot, heeft vergoten) shed

het **vergif** /vərɣɪf/ (pl: -fen) poison; venom: *dodelijk ~* lethal (*or:* deadly) poison

de **vergiffenis** /vərɣɪfənɪs/ forgiveness; pardon; absolution

vergiftig /vərɣɪftəx/ (adj) poisonous; venomous

vergiftigen /vərɣɪftəɣə(n)/ (vergiftigde, heeft vergiftigd) poison

de **vergiftiging** /vərɣɪftəɣɪŋ/ (pl: -en) poisoning: *hij stierf door ~* he died of poisoning

zich **vergissen** /vərɣɪsə(n)/ (vergiste zich, heeft zich vergist) be mistaken (*or:* wrong), make a mistake: *zich lelijk ~* be greatly mistaken; *vergis je niet* make no mistake; *als ik mij niet vergis* if I'm not wrong (*or:* mistaken); *zich in de persoon ~* mistake s.o.; *zich in iem. ~* be mistaken (*or:* wrong) about s.o.; *als hij dat denkt, vergist hij zich* if he thinks that he'll have to think again; *~ is menselijk* to err is human

de **vergissing** /vərɣɪsɪŋ/ (pl: -en) mistake, error: *iets per ~ doen* do sth. by mistake (*or:* inadvertently); *een ~ maken* (or: *begaan*) make (*or:* commit) a mistake (*or:* an error)

vergoeden /vərɣudə(n)/ (vergoedde, heeft vergoed) **1** make good, compensate for, refund: *onkosten ~* pay expenses; *iem. de schade ~* compensate (*or:* pay) s.o. for the damage **2** compensate, make up (for): *dat vergoedt veel* that makes up for a lot

de **vergoeding** /vərɣudɪŋ/ (pl: -en) **1** compensation, reimbursement: *~ eisen* claim damages; *een ~ vragen voor* charge for **2** allowance, fee; expenses: *tegen een geringe ~* for a small fee

vergoelijken /vərɣuləkə(n)/ (vergoelijkte, heeft vergoelijkt) smooth over

vergokken /vərɣɔkə(n)/ (vergokte, heeft vergokt) gamble away

vergooien /vərɣojə(n)/ (vergooide, heeft vergooid) throw away, waste: *zijn leven ~* throw (*or:* fritter) away one's life

vergrendelen /vərɣrɛndələ(n)/ (vergrendelde, heeft vergrendeld) bolt, (double) lock

het **vergrijp** /vərɣrɛip/ (pl: -en) offence: *een licht ~* a minor offence

zich **vergrijpen** /vərɣrɛipə(n)/ (vergreep zich, heeft zich vergrepen) assault; violate: *zich aan iem. ~* assault s.o.

vergrijzen /vərɣrɛizə(n)/ (vergrijsde, is vergrijsd) age, get old: *Nederland vergrijst* the population of the Netherlands is ageing

de **vergrijzing** /vərɣrɛizɪŋ/ ageing

vergroeien /vərɣrujə(n)/ (vergroeide, is

vergroeid) grow crooked; grow deformed, become deformed

het **vergrootglas** /vərɣro̱txlɑs/ (pl: -glazen) magnifying glass

vergroten /vərɣro̱tə(n)/ (vergrootte, heeft vergroot) **1** increase: *de kansen* (or: *risico's*) ~ increase the chances (or: risks) **2** enlarge: *de kamer* ~ extend (or: enlarge) the room **3** magnify, enlarge; blow up

de **vergroting** /vərɣro̱tɪŋ/ (pl: -en) **1** increase: ~ *van de omzet* increase in the turnover **2** enlargement

vergruizen /vərɣrœyzə(n)/ (vergruisde, heeft vergruisd) pulverize, crush

verguizen /vərɣœyzə(n)/ (verguisde, heeft verguisd) abuse

verguld /vərɣʏlt/ (adj) **1** gilded, gilt, gold-plated **2** pleased, flattered: *Laurette was er vreselijk mee* ~ Laurette was absolutely delighted with it

vergulden /vərɣʏldə(n)/ (verguldde, heeft verguld) gild, gold-plate

de **vergunning** /vərɣʏnɪŋ/ (pl: -en) **1** permission **2** permit; licence: *een restaurant met volledige* ~ a fully licensed restaurant; *een ~ verlenen* (or: *intrekken*) grant (or: suspend) a licence

het **verhaal** /vərha̱l/ (pl: verhalen) story: *de kern van het* ~ the point of the story; *om een lang ~ kort te maken* to cut a long story short; *sterke verhalen* tall stories; *zijn ~ doen* tell (or: relate) one's story; *~tjes vertellen* tell tales || *het is weer het bekende* ~ it's the same old story; *iem. op ~ laten komen* let s.o. get one's breath back

verhalen /vərha̱lə(n)/ (verhaalde, heeft verhaald) recover, recoup: *de schade op iem.* ~ recover the damage from s.o.

verhandelen /vərhɑndələ(n)/ (verhandelde, heeft verhandeld) trade (in), sell

de **verhandeling** /vərhɑndəlɪŋ/ (pl: -en) [Belg] (mini-)dissertation

zich **verhangen** /vərhɑŋə(n)/ (verhing zich, heeft zich verhangen) hang o.s.

verhapstukken /vərhɑpstʏkə(n)/ [inform] settle; do, finish (off)

verhard /vərhɑrt/ (adj) **1** hard; paved: *~e wegen* metalled roads; [Am] paved roads **2** [fig] hardened, callous

¹**verharden** /vərhɑrdə(n)/ (verhardde, is verhard) harden: *in het kwaad* ~ become set in evil ways

²**verharden** /vərhɑrdə(n)/ (verhardde, heeft verhard) harden; metal; pave: *een tuinpad* ~ pave a garden path

de **verharding** /vərhɑrdɪŋ/ (pl: -en) hardening; metalling; paving: *een ~ van standpunten* a hardening of points of view

verharen /vərha̱rə(n)/ (verhaarde, is verhaard) moult; shed (hair): *de kat is aan het ~* the cat is moulting

verheerlijken /vərhe̱rləkə(n)/ (verheerlijkte, heeft verheerlijkt) idolize, glamourize

¹**verheffen** /vərhɛfə(n)/ (verhief, heeft verheven) **1** raise, lift **2** [fig] raise, elevate; uplift; lift up: *iets tot regel* ~ make sth. the rule

zich ²**verheffen** /vərhɛfə(n)/ (verhief zich, heeft zich verheven) rise: *zich hoog ~ boven de stad* rise (or: tower) above the city

verheffend /vərhɛfənt/ (adj) elevating: *een weinig ~ schouwspel* an unedifying spectacle

¹**verhelderen** /vərhɛldərə(n)/ (verhelderde, is verhelderd) clear (up)

²**verhelderen** /vərhɛldərə(n)/ (verhelderde, heeft verhelderd) clarify: *een ~d antwoord* an illuminating answer

verhelen /vərhe̱lə(n)/ (verheelde, heeft verheeld) conceal, hide

verhelpen /vərhɛlpə(n)/ (verhielp, heeft verholpen) put right, remedy

het **verhemelte** /vərhe̱məltə/ (pl: -n, -s) palate, roof of the mouth: *een gespleten* ~ a cleft palate

verheugd /vərhøxt/ (adj) glad, pleased: *zich bijzonder ~ tonen* (over iets) take great pleasure in sth.

zich **verheugen** /vərhøɣə(n)/ (verheugde zich, heeft zich verheugd) be glad, be pleased (or: happy): *zich ~ op* look forward to

verheugend /vərhøɣənt/ (adj) joyful: *~ nieuws* good news

verheven /vərhe̱və(n)/ (adj) elevated; [fig] above (to), superior (to): *boven iedere verdenking* ~ above (or: beyond) all suspicion

verhevigen /vərhe̱vəɣə(n)/ (verhevigde, heeft/is verhevigd) intensify

verhinderen /vərhɪndərə(n)/ (verhinderde, heeft verhinderd) prevent: *iemands plannen* ~ obstruct (or: foil) s.o.'s plans; *dat zal mij niet ~ om tegen dit voorstel te stemmen* that won't prevent me from voting against this proposal; *verhinderd zijn* be unable to come (or: attend)

de **verhindering** /vərhɪndərɪŋ/ (pl: -en) absence, inability to come: *bij* ~ in case of absence

verhit /vərhɪt/ (adj) **1** hot; flushed **2** heated: *~te discussies* heated discussions

verhitten /vərhɪtə(n)/ (verhitte, heeft verhit) **1** heat **2** inflame, stir up: *dat verhitte de gemoederen* that made feelings run high

de **verhitting** /vərhɪtɪŋ/ heating(-up)

verhoeden /vərhudə(n)/ (verhoedde, heeft verhoed) prevent, forbid: *God verhoede dat je ziek wordt* God forbid that you should be ill

verhogen /vərho̱ɣə(n)/ (verhoogde, heeft verhoogd) **1** raise: *een dijk* ~ raise a dike **2** increase: *de prijzen* ~ raise (or: increase) prices

de **verhoging** /vərho̱ɣɪŋ/ (pl: -en) **1** raising **2** elevation, platform; rise: *de spreker stond op een* ~ the speaker stood on a (raised) platform **3** increase, rise **4** temperature, fever: *ik **had** wat* ~ I had a slight temperature

verhongeren /vərhɔ̞ŋərə(n)/ (verhongerde, is verhongerd) **1** starve (to death), die of starvation: *de kinderen waren **half** verhongerd* the children were famished (*or:* half starved) **2** starve, go hungry

het **verhoor** /vərhor/ (pl: verhoren) interrogation, examination

verhoren /vərhor̞ə(n)/ (verhoorde, heeft verhoord) **1** interrogate, question; cross-examine: *getuigen* ~ hear witnesses **2** hear, answer; grant: *een **gebed*** ~ answer (*or:* hear) a prayer

zich **verhouden** /vərhɑu̯də(n)/ (verhield zich, heeft zich verhouden) be as, be in the proportion of: *60 verhoudt zich **tot** 12 als 5 tot 1* 60 is to 12 as 5 to 1

de **verhouding** /vərhɑu̯dɪŋ/ (pl: -en) **1** relation(ship), proportion: *in* ~ *tot* in proportion to; *naar* ~ *is dat duur* that is comparatively expensive **2** affair, relationship **3** proportions: *gevoel **voor** ~en bezitten* have a sense of proportion

verhoudingsgewijs /vərhɑu̯dɪŋsxəwɛi̯s/ (adv) comparatively, relatively

het **verhuisbericht** /vərhœy̯zbərɪxt/ (pl: -en) change of address card

de **verhuiswagen** /vərhœy̯swaɣə(n)/ (pl: -s) removal van

verhuizen /vərhœy̯zə(n)/ (verhuisde, is verhuisd) move (house), relocate ‖ *iem.* ~ move s.o.

de **verhuizer** /vərhœy̯zər/ (pl: -s) remover

de **verhuizing** /vərhœy̯zɪŋ/ (pl: -en) move, moving

verhullen /vərhʏlə(n)/ (verhulde, heeft verhuld) veil, conceal (from): *niets ~de foto's* revealing photos

verhuren /vərhyrə(n)/ (verhuurde, heeft verhuurd) let; [Am] rent; lease out

de **verhuur** /vərhyr/ letting; [Am] rental

het **verhuurbedrijf** /vərhyrbədrɛi̯f/ leasing company, hire company (*or:* firm); [esp Am also] rental company (*or:* agency)

de **verhuurder** /vərhyrdər/ (pl: -s) letter; [Am] renter; landlord; landlady

verifiëren /verifijɛr̞ə(n)/ (verifieerde, heeft geverifieerd) verify, examine, audit, prove

verijdelen /vərɛi̯dələ(n)/ (verijdelde, heeft verijdeld) frustrate, defeat: *een **aanslag*** ~ foil an attempt on s.o.'s life

de **vering** /ver̞ɪŋ/ (pl: -en) springs; [car] suspension

verjaard /vərjɑrt/ (adj) time-barred, superannuated

de **verjaardag** /vərjɑrdɑx/ (pl: -en) birthday: *vandaag **is** het mijn* ~ today is my birthday

het **verjaardagscadeau** /vərjɑrdɑxskado/ birthday present

het **verjaardagsfeest** /vərjɑrdɑxsfest/ (pl: -en) birthday party

de **verjaardagskalender** /vərjɑrdɑxskalɛndər/ (pl: -s) birthday calendar

verjagen /vərjaɣə(n)/ (verjaagde/verjoeg, heeft verjaagd) drive away, chase away

verjaren /vərjar̞ə(n)/ (verjaarde, is verjaard) become prescribed, become (statute-)barred, become out-of-date

de **verjaring** /vərjar̞ɪŋ/ (pl: -en) prescription; limitation

de **verjaringstermijn** /vərjar̞ɪŋstɛrmɛi̯n/ period of limitation

verjongen /vərjɔ̞ŋə(n)/ (verjongde, heeft verjongd) rejuvenate, make young

de **verjonging** /vərjɔ̞ŋɪŋ/ (pl: -en) rejuvenation

de **verjongingskuur** /vərjɔ̞ŋɪŋskyr/ (pl: -kuren) rejuvenation cure: *een* ~ *ondergaan hebben* [fig] have undergone rejuvenation, be revitalized

verkapt /vərkɑpt/ (adj) veiled, disguised; in disguise

verkassen /vərkɑsə(n)/ (verkaste, is verkast) [inform] move (house)

verkavelen /vərkavələ(n)/ (verkavelde, heeft verkaveld) parcel out, (sub)divide

de **verkaveling** /vərkavəlɪŋ/ (pl: -en) allotment, subdivision

het **verkeer** /vərker/ **1** traffic: *handel en* ~ trade (*or:* traffic) and commerce; *druk* ~ heavy traffic; *veilig* ~ road safety; *het overige* ~ *in gevaar brengen* be a danger to other road-users **2** association: *in het **maatschappelijk*** ~ in society; *in het **dagelijks*** ~ in everyday life **3** movement: *er bestaat **vrij*** ~ *tussen die twee landen* there is freedom of movement between the two countries

verkeerd /vərker̞t/ (adj, adv) **1** wrong: *een verdediger op het ~e **been** zetten* wrong-foot a defender; *een ~e **diagnose*** a faulty diagnosis; *de ~e **dingen** zeggen* say the wrong things; *het eten kwam in mijn ~e **keelgat*** the food went down the wrong way; *op een* ~ *spoor zitten* be on the wrong track; *iets* ~ *aanpakken* go about sth. the wrong way; *hij **doet** alles* ~ he can't do a thing right; *pardon, u **loopt*** ~ pardon me, but you're going the wrong way (*or:* in the wrong direction); *het liep* ~ *met hem **af*** he came to grief (*or:* to a bad end); *iets* ~ *spellen* (or: *uitspreken, vertalen*) misspell (*or:* mispronounce, mistranslate) sth.; ~ *verbonden zijn* have dialled a wrong number; *we zitten* ~ we must be wrong; *hij had **iets** ~s gegeten* sth. he had eaten had upset him; *je hebt **de** ~e voor* you've mistaken your man **2** wrong; inside out: *zijn handen **staan*** ~ he's all thumbs; ~ *om* the other way round; upside down

de **verkeersagent** /vərker̞sɑɣɛnt/ traffic policeman (*or:* policewoman)

het **verkeersbord** /vərker̞zbɔrt/ (pl: -en) road sign, traffic sign de **verkeersbrigadier** /vərkɛrzbriɣadir/ (pl: -s) lollipop man (or: lady)

de **verkeerschaos** /vərkɛrsxaɔs/ traffic chaos

de **verkeersdrempel** /vərkɛrzdrɛmpəl/ (pl: -s) speed ramp

de **verkeersleider** /vərkɛrslɛidər/ (pl: -s) air-traffic controller

de **verkeersleiding** /vərkɛrslɛidɪŋ/ (pl: -en) traffic department; [aviation] air-traffic control, ground control

het **verkeerslicht** /vərkɛrslɪχt/ (pl: -en) traffic lights: *het ~ sprong op groen* the traffic lights changed to green

het **verkeersongeval** /vərkɛrsɔŋɣəval/ (pl: -len) road accident, traffic accident

de **verkeersopstopping** /vərkɛrsɔpstɔpɪŋ/ (pl: -en) traffic jam

de **verkeersovertreding** /vərkɛrsovərtredɪŋ/ (pl: -en) traffic offence

het **verkeersplein** /vərkɛrsplɛin/ (pl: -en) roundabout; [Am] rotary (intersection)

de **verkeerspolitie** /vərkɛrspoli(t)si/ traffic police

de **verkeersregel** /vərkɛrsreɣəl/ (pl: -s) traffic rule

het **verkeersslachtoffer** /vərkɛrslaχtɔfər/ (pl: -s) road casualty, road victim: *het aantal ~s* the toll on the road(s)

de **verkeerstoren** /vərkɛrstorə(n)/ (pl: -s) control tower

de **verkeersveiligheid** /vərkɛrsfɛiləχhɛit/ road safety, traffic safety

de **verkeersvlieger** /vərkɛrsfliɣər/ (pl: -s) airline pilot

de **verkeerswisselaar** /vərkɛrswɪsəlar/ (pl: -s) [Belg] cloverleaf junction

verkennen /vərkɛnə(n)/ (verkende, heeft verkend) explore, scout (out); [mil] reconnoitre: *de boel ~* explore the place; *de markt ~* feel out the market

de **verkenner** /vərkɛnər/ (pl: -s) **1** scout **2** (Boy) Scout, Girl Scout

de **verkenning** /vərkɛnɪŋ/ (pl: -en) exploration, scout(ing)

verkeren /vərkɛrə(n)/ (verkeerde, heeft verkeerd) be (in): *in de hoogste kringen ~* move in the best circles

de **verkering** /vərkɛrɪŋ/ (pl: -en) courtship: *vaste ~ hebben* go steady; *~ krijgen met iem.* start going out with s.o.

verketteren /vərkɛtərə(n)/ (verketterde, heeft verketterd) execrate, decry, denounce

verkiesbaar /vərkizbar/ (adj) eligible (for election): *zich ~ stellen als president* run for president; *zich ~ stellen* stand for office

verkieslijk /vərkislək/ (adj) preferable

verkiezen /vərkizə(n)/ (verkoos, heeft verkozen) prefer (to): *lopen boven fietsen ~* prefer walking to cycling

de **verkiezing** /vərkizɪŋ/ (pl: -en) election: *algemene ~en* general elections; *tussentijdse*

~en [roughly] by-elections; *~en uitschrijven* call (for) an election

de **verkiezingscampagne** /vərkizɪŋskampaɲə/ (pl: -s) election campaign

het **verkiezingsdebat** /vərkizɪŋzdəbat/ (pl: -ten) election debate

het **verkiezingsprogramma** /vərkizɪŋsproɣrama/ (pl: -'s) (electoral) platform: *iets als punt in het ~ opnemen* make sth. a plank in one's platform

de **verkiezingsstrijd** /vərkizɪŋstrɛit/ electoral struggle

de **verkiezingsuitslag** /vərkizɪŋsœytslaχ/ (pl: -en) election result: *de ~ bekendmaken* declare the poll

¹**verkijken** /vərkɛikə(n)/ give away, let go by: *die kans is verkeken* that chance has gone by

zich ²**verkijken** /vərkɛikə(n)/ (verkeek zich, heeft zich verkeken) make a mistake, be mistaken: *ik heb me op hem verkeken* I have been mistaken in him

verkikkerd /vərkɪkərt/ (adj) [inform] nuts (on, about), gone (on)

verklaarbaar /vərklarbar/ (adj) explicable, explainable; understandable: *om verklaarbare redenen* for obvious reasons

verklappen /vərklɑpə(n)/ (verklapte, heeft verklapt) give away, let out: *een geheim ~* tell a secret

¹**verklaren** /vərklarə(n)/ (verklaarde, heeft verklaard) **1** explain, elucidate: *iemands gedrag ~* account for s.o.'s conduct **2** declare; certify: *iem. krankzinnig ~* certify s.o. insane; *iets ongeldig ~* declare sth. invalid; *een huis onbewoonbaar ~* condemn a house

zich ²**verklaren** /vərklarə(n)/ (verklaarde zich, heeft zich verklaard) explain o.s.: *verklaar je nader* explain yourself

de **verklaring** /vərklarɪŋ/ (pl: -en) **1** explanation: *dat behoeft geen nadere ~* that needs no further explanation **2** statement; testimony: *een beëdigde ~* a sworn statement; *een ~ afleggen* make a statement

zich **verkleden** /vərklɛdə(n)/ (verkleedde zich, heeft zich verkleed) **1** change (one's clothes): *ik ga me ~* I'm going to change (my clothes); *zich ~ voor het eten* dress for dinner **2** dress up

verkleinen /vərklɛinə(n)/ (verkleinde, heeft verkleind) **1** reduce, make smaller: *op verkleinde schaal* on a reduced scale **2** reduce, diminish, lessen

de **verkleining** /vərklɛinɪŋ/ (pl: -en) reduction

het **verkleinwoord** /vərklɛinwort/ (pl: -en) diminutive

verkleumd /vərklømt/ (adj) numb (with cold)

verkleumen /vərklømə(n)/ (verkleumde, is verkleumd) grow numb: *we staan hier te ~* we are freezing in (or: out) here

verkleuren /vərklø̞rə(n)/ (verkleurde, is verkleurd) discolour, lose colour; fade: *deze trui verkleurt **niet*** this sweater will keep its colour

de **verkleuring** /vərklø̞rɪŋ/ (pl: -en) fading; discoloration

verklikken /vərklɪkə(n)/ (verklikte, heeft verklikt) give away; squeal on: *iets* ~ blab sth., spill the beans

de **verklikker** /vərklɪkər/ (pl: -s) telltale, tattler; informer; grass

verklooien (verklooide, heeft verklooid) fuck up

verknallen /vərknɑlə(n)/ (verknalde, heeft verknald) blow, spoil: *je hebt het **mooi** verknald* you've made a hash of it

zich **verkneukelen** /vərknø̞kələ(n)/ (verkneukelde zich, heeft zich verkneukeld) exult (over), gloat (over)

verknippen /vərknɪpə(n)/ (verknipte, heeft verknipt) **1** cut up **2** spoil in cutting

verknipt /vərknɪpt/ (adj) hung-up, kooky, nutty: *een ~e **figuur*** a weirdo, a nut(case)

verknocht /vərknɔxt/ (adj) devoted (to), attached (to)

verknoeien /vərknujə(n)/ (verknoeide, heeft verknoeid) botch (up), spoil, mess up: *de boel **lelijk** ~* make a fine mess of things

verkoelend /vərkulənt/ (adj) cooling, refreshing

de **verkoeling** /vərkulɪŋ/ (pl: -en) cooling

de **verkoeverkamer** /vərkuvərkamər/ recovery room

de **verkokering** /vərkokərɪŋ/ compartmentalization

verkommeren /vərkɔmərə(n)/ (verkommerde, is verkommerd) sink into poverty, pine away

verkondigen /vərkɔndəγə(n)/ (verkondigde, heeft verkondigd) proclaim, put forward

de **verkondiging** /vərkɔndəγɪŋ/ (pl: -en) proclamation; preaching

de **verkoop** /vɛrkop/ (pl: verkopen) sale(s): *~ bij **opbod*** (sale by) auction; *iets **in** de ~ brengen* put sth. up for sale (*or:* on the market)

verkoopbaar /vərkobar/ (adj) saleable, marketable

de **verkoopcijfers** /vɛrkopsɛifərs/ (pl) sales figures

de **verkoopleider** /vɛrkoplɛidər/ (pl: -s) sales manager

het **verkooppraatje** /vɛrkopracə/ (pl: -s) sales pitch

de **verkoopprijs** /vɛrkoprɛis/ (pl: -prijzen) selling price

het **verkooppunt** /vɛrkopʏnt/ (pl: -en) (sales) outlet, point of sale

de **verkoopster** /vɛrkopstər/ (pl: -s) saleswoman; shop assistant

de **verkoopvoorwaarden** /vɛrkopforwardə(n)/ (pl) terms and conditions of sale

verkopen /vərkopə(n)/ (verkocht, heeft verkocht) **1** sell: *~ **nee** ~* give (s.o.) no for an answer; *met winst* (*or: verlies*) ~ sell at a profit (*or:* loss); *éénmaal! andermaal! verkocht!* going! going! gone! **2** give: *iem. een **dreun** ~* clobber s.o.

de **verkoper** /vərkopər/ (pl: -s) salesman; shop assistant

de **verkoping** /vərkopɪŋ/ (pl: -en) (public) sale, auction: *bij **openbare** ~* by auction

verkorten /vərkɔrtə(n)/ (verkortte, heeft verkort) shorten, abridge, condense; reduce

verkouden /vərkaudə(n)/ (adj): *~ **worden*** catch (a) cold; *~ **zijn*** have a cold

de **verkoudheid** /vərkauthɛit/ (common) cold: *een ~ **opdoen*** catch (a) cold

verkrachten /vərkrɑxtə(n)/ (verkrachtte, heeft verkracht) rape, (sexually) assault

de **verkrachter** /vərkrɑxtər/ (pl: -s) rapist

de **verkrachting** /vərkrɑxtɪŋ/ (pl: -en) rape

verkrampen /vərkrɑmpə(n)/ (verkrampte, is verkrampt) go tense, tense up

verkrampt /vərkrɑmt/ (adj) contorted; [fig] constrained

¹**verkreukelen** /vərkrø̞kələ(n)/ (verkreukelde, is verkreukeld) crumple: *een verkreukeld **pak*** a creased suit

²**verkreukelen** /vərkrø̞kələ(n)/ (verkreukelde, heeft verkreukeld) rumple (up), crumple (up): *papier* ~ crumple up paper

verkrijgbaar /vərkrɛiγbar/ (adj) available: *het formulier is ~ **bij** de administratie* the form can be obtained from the administration; *zonder recept* ~ over-the-counter

verkrijgen /vərkrɛiγə(n)/ (verkreeg, heeft verkregen) **1** receive, get **2** obtain, come by, secure: *een betere **positie*** ~ secure a better position; *moeilijk te* ~ hard to come by

verkroppen /vərkrɔpə(n)/: *iets niet **kunnen** ~* be unable to take sth.

verkrotten /vərkrɔtə(n)/ (verkrotte, is verkrot) decay, become run-down: *verkrotte **huizen*** slummy (*or:* dilapidated) houses

verkruimelen /vərkrœymələ(n)/ (verkruimelde, heeft verkruimeld) crumble

verkwanselen /vərkwɑnsələ(n)/ (verkwanselde, heeft verkwanseld) bargain away, fritter away, squander

verkwikken /vərkwɪkə(n)/ (verkwikte, heeft verkwikt) refresh

verkwikkend /vərkwɪkənt/ (adj) refreshing, invigorating, stimulating

verkwisten /vərkwɪstə(n)/ (verkwistte, heeft verkwist) waste; squander

verkwistend /vərkwɪstənt/ (adj) prodigal; wasteful

de **verkwister** /vərkwɪstər/ (pl: -s) squanderer, waster

de **verkwisting** /vərkwɪstɪŋ/ (pl: -en) waste(fulness), squandering: *het is **pure** ~* it's an utter waste

verlagen /vərl<u>a</u>ɣə(n)/ (verlaagde, heeft verlaagd) lower; reduce: *(met)* **30** % ~ lower (*or:* reduce) by 30 % ‖ *zich* ~ *tot* stoop to, lower o.s. to

de **verlaging** /vərl<u>a</u>ɣɪŋ/ (pl: -en) lowering; reduction

¹**verlammen** /vərl<u>ɑ</u>mə(n)/ (verlamde, is verlamd) become paralysed (*or:* numb)

²**verlammen** /vərl<u>ɑ</u>mə(n)/ (verlamde, heeft verlamd) paralyse: *de* **schrik** *verlamde mij* I was paralysed with fear

verlammend /vərl<u>ɑ</u>mənt/ (adj, adv) paralysing

de **verlamming** /vərl<u>ɑ</u>mɪŋ/ (pl: -en) paralysis

het ¹**verlangen** /vərl<u>ɑ</u>ŋə(n)/ (pl: -s) longing, desire; craving: *aan iemands* ~ **voldoen** comply with s.o.'s wish

²**verlangen** /vərl<u>ɑ</u>ŋə(n)/ (verlangde, heeft verlangd) (+ naar) long (for), crave: *ik verlang* **ernaar** *je te zien* I long to see you; [stronger] I'm dying to see you

³**verlangen** /vərl<u>ɑ</u>ŋə(n)/ (verlangde, heeft verlangd) want, wish for; demand: *wat kun je nog* **meer** ~ what more can you ask for?; *dat kunt u niet* **van** *mij* ~ you can't expect me to do that

het **verlanglijstje** /vərl<u>ɑ</u>ŋlɛiscə/ (pl: -s) list of gifts wanted

¹**verlaten** /vərl<u>a</u>tə(n)/ (adj) **1** deserted: *een* ~ **huis** an abandoned house **2** desolate, lonely **3** abandoned

²**verlaten** /vərl<u>a</u>tə(n)/ (verliet, heeft verlaten) **1** leave: *het* **land** ~ leave the country; *de* **school** ~ leave school **2** abandon, leave: **vrouw** *en* **kinderen** ~ leave (*or:* abandon) one's wife and children

de **verlatenheid** /vərl<u>a</u>tənhɛit/ desolation, abandonment: *een* **gevoel** *van* ~ a feeling of desolation

het ¹**verleden** /vərl<u>e</u>də(n)/ past: *het* ~ **laten rusten** let bygones be bygones; *teruggaan* **in** *het* ~ go back in time

²**verleden** /vərl<u>e</u>də(n)/ (adj) past: *het* ~ **deelwoord** the past (*or:* perfect) participle; ~ **tijd** past tense; *voltooid* ~ **tijd** past perfect (*or:* pluperfect) (tense); ~ **week** last week

verlegen /vərl<u>e</u>ɣə(n)/ (adj, adv) **1** shy: ~ *zijn* **tegenover** *meisjes* be shy with girls **2** (+ om) in need of, at a loss for, pressed for: *ik zit niet* **om** *werk* ~ I have my work cut out as it is

de **verlegenheid** /vərl<u>e</u>ɣə(n)hɛit/ **1** shyness **2** embarrassment, trouble: *iem.* **in** ~ *brengen* embarrass s.o.

verleggen /vərl<u>ɛ</u>ɣə(n)/ (verlegde, heeft verlegd) move, shift; push back

verleidelijk /vərl<u>ɛi</u>dələk/ (adj, adv) tempting, inviting, seductive: *een* ~ **aanbod** a tempting offer

verleiden /vərl<u>ɛi</u>də(n)/ (verleidde, heeft verleid) **1** tempt, invite, entice: *iem.* **ertoe** ~ *om iets te doen* tempt s.o. into doing sth.

2 seduce

de **verleider** /vərl<u>ɛi</u>dər/ (pl: -s) seducer, tempter

de **verleiding** /vərl<u>ɛi</u>dɪŋ/ (pl: -en) temptation; seduction: *de* ~ *niet* **kunnen weerstaan** be unable to resist (the) temptation; *in de* ~ *komen om* feel (*or:* be) tempted to

de **verleidster** /vərl<u>ɛi</u>tstər/ seducer, temptress

verlenen /vərl<u>e</u>nə(n)/ (verleende, heeft verleend) grant, confer: *iem.* **onderdak** ~ take s.o. in; harbour s.o.; **voorrang** ~ give way (*or:* priority); [traf] give right of way; [Am] yield

het **verlengde** /vərl<u>ɛ</u>ŋdə/ extension: *in elkaars* ~ *liggen* be in line

verlengen /vərl<u>ɛ</u>ŋə(n)/ (verlengde, heeft verlengd) **1** extend, lengthen **2** extend, prolong: *een* **(huur)contract** ~ renew a lease; *zijn* **verblijf** ~ prolong one's stay; *verlengd* **worden** go into extra (*or:* injury) time; [Am] go (into) overtime

de **verlenging** /vərl<u>ɛ</u>ŋɪŋ/ (pl: -en) **1** extension; [sport] extra time, injury time; [Am] overtime **2** lengthening, extension

het **verlengsnoer** /vərl<u>ɛ</u>ŋsnur/ (pl: -en) extension lead

het **verlengstuk** /vərl<u>ɛ</u>ŋstʏk/ (pl: -ken) extension (piece): [fig] *het* ~ *zijn van* be a continuation of

verlept /vərl<u>ɛ</u>pt/ (adj) withered, wilted

verleren /vərl<u>e</u>rə(n)/ (verleerde, heeft verleerd) forget (how to); unlearn: *je bent het* **schaken** *blijkbaar een beetje verleerd* your chess seems a bit rusty; *om het* **niet** *(helemaal) te* ~ just to keep one's hand in

verlevendigen /vərl<u>e</u>vəndəɣə(n)/ (verlevendigde, heeft verlevendigd) revive; enliven

verlicht /vərl<u>ɪ</u>xt/ (adj) **1** lit (up), lighted, illuminated: **helder** ~ well-lit, brightly lit **2** relieved, lightened: *met* ~ **gemoed** with (a) light heart

verlichten /vərl<u>ɪ</u>xtə(n)/ (verlichtte, heeft verlicht) **1** light, illuminate **2** relieve, lighten: *dat verlicht de* **pijn** that relieves (*or:* eases) the pain

de **verlichting** /vərl<u>ɪ</u>xtɪŋ/ (pl: -en) **1** light(ing), illumination **2** lightening: ~ *van* **straf** mitigation of punishment

verliefd /vərl<u>i</u>ft/ (adj) in love (with), amorous, loving: **zwaar** ~ *zijn* be madly (*or:* deeply) in love ‖ *hij keek haar* ~ **aan** he gave her a fond (*or:* loving) look

de **verliefdheid** /vərl<u>i</u>fthɛit/ (pl: -heden) being in love, love

het **verlies** /vərl<u>i</u>s/ (pl: verliezen) loss: ~ **lijden** suffer a loss; make a loss; *met* ~ *verkopen* sell at a loss; *met* ~ *draaien* make a loss (*or:* losses); *niet tegen (zijn)* ~ *kunnen* be a bad loser

verliesgevend /vərlisx<u>e</u>vənt/ (adj) loss-making

de **verliespost** /vərl<u>i</u>spɔst/ (pl: -en) loss-making activity

verliezen /vərl<u>i</u>zə(n)/ (verloor, heeft/is verloren) **1** lose: *zijn **bladeren** ~* defoliate; *de **macht** ~* fall from power; ***terrein** ~* lose ground **2** lose, miss: *er is geen **tijd** te ~* there is no time to lose (*or:* to be lost)

de **verliezer** /vərl<u>i</u>zər/ (pl: -s) loser

verlinken /vərl<u>ɪ</u>ŋkə(n)/ (verlinkte, heeft verlinkt) [inform] tell on, grass on

verloederen /vərl<u>u</u>dərə(n)/ (verloederde, is verloederd) degenerate

de **verloedering** /vərl<u>u</u>dərɪŋ/ corruption

het **verlof** /vərl<u>ɔ</u>f/ (pl: verloven) **1** leave, permission: *~ **krijgen** om ...* obtain permission to ... **2** leave (of absence); furlough: ***buitengewoon** ~* special leave; *met ~ zijn* be on leave

verlokkelijk /vərl<u>ɔ</u>kələk/ (adj, adv) tempting

de **verlokking** /vərl<u>ɔ</u>kɪŋ/ (pl: -en) temptation

verloochenen /vərl<u>o</u>xənə(n)/ (verloochende, heeft verloochend) renounce

verloofd /vərl<u>ɔ</u>ft/ (adj) engaged (to)

de **verloofde** /vərl<u>ɔ</u>fdə/ (pl: -n, -s) fiancé; fiancée

het **verloop** /vərl<u>o</u>p/ **1** course, passage: *na ~ van tijd* in time, after some time **2** course, progress, development: *voor een vlot ~ van de **besprekingen*** for smooth progress in the talks **3** turnover, wastage: ***natuurlijk** ~* natural wastage

de **verloopstekker** /vərl<u>o</u>pstɛkər/ (pl: -s) adapter

verlopen /vərl<u>o</u>pə(n)/ (verliep, is verlopen) **1** (e)lapse, go by, pass **2** expire: *mijn **rijbewijs** is ~* my driving licence has expired **3** go (off): *vlot ~* go smoothly **4** drop off, fall off, go down(hill)

verloren /vərl<u>o</u>rə(n)/ (adj) lost: *~ **moeite*** wasted effort; *een ~ **ogenblik*** an odd moment; *voor een ~ **zaak** vechten* fight a losing battle

de **verloskamer** /vərl<u>ɔ</u>skamər/ (pl: -s) delivery room

de **verloskunde** /vərl<u>ɔ</u>skʏndə/ obstetrics

verloskundig /vərl<u>ɔ</u>skʏndəχ/ (adj) obstetric

de **verloskundige** /vərl<u>ɔ</u>skʏndəɣə/ (pl: -n) midwife; obstetrician

verlossen /vərl<u>ɔ</u>sə(n)/ (verloste, heeft verlost) **1** deliver (from), release (from), save (from): *een dier **uit** zijn lijden ~* put an animal out of its misery **2** deliver (of)

de **verlosser** /vərl<u>ɔ</u>sər/ (pl: -s) saviour, rescuer: *de Verlosser* our Saviour, the Redeemer

de **verlossing** /vərl<u>ɔ</u>sɪŋ/ (pl: -en) deliverance, release

verloten /vərl<u>o</u>tə(n)/ (verlootte, heeft verloot) raffle (off)

zich **verloven** /vərl<u>o</u>və(n)/ (verloofde zich, heeft zich verloofd) get engaged (to)

de **verloving** /vərl<u>o</u>vɪŋ/ (pl: -en) engagement: *zijn ~ **verbreken*** break off one's (*or:* the) engagement

verluiden /vərl<u>œy</u>də(n)/ (verluidde, heeft verluid): *naar verluidt* it is reported that, it is understood that, allegedly

verlummelen /vərl<u>ʏ</u>mələ(n)/ (verlummelde, heeft verlummeld) fritter away

het **vermaak** /vərm<u>a</u>k/ (pl: vermaken) amusement, enjoyment, pleasure: *onschuldig ~* good clean fun

vermaard /vərm<u>a</u>rt/ (adj) renowned (for), celebrated (for), famous (for)

vermageren /vərm<u>a</u>ɣərə(n)/ (vermagerde, is vermagerd) lose weight, become thin(ner), get thin(ner); slim: *sterk vermagerd* emaciated, wasted

de **vermageringskuur** /vərm<u>a</u>ɣərɪŋskyr/ (pl: -kuren) slimming diet: *een ~ **ondergaan*** be (*or:* go) on a (slimming, reducing) diet

vermakelijk /vərm<u>a</u>kələk/ (adj, adv) amusing

vermaken /vərm<u>a</u>kə(n)/ (vermaakte, heeft vermaakt) **1** amuse, entertain: *zich ~* enjoy (*or:* amuse) o.s., have fun **2** bequeath, make over

vermalen /vərm<u>a</u>lə(n)/ (vermaalde, heeft vermalen) grind

vermanen /vərm<u>a</u>nə(n)/ (vermaande, heeft vermaand) admonish, warn

de **vermaning** /vərm<u>a</u>nɪŋ/ (pl: -en) admonition

zich **vermannen** /vərm<u>ɑ</u>nə(n)/ (vermande zich, heeft zich vermand) screw up one's courage, take heart

vermeend /vərm<u>e</u>nt/ (adj) supposed, alleged

vermeerderen /vərm<u>e</u>rdərə(n)/ (vermeerderde, heeft/is vermeerderd) increase, enlarge, grow: *~ **met** 25 %* increase by 25 per cent

vermelden /vərm<u>ɛ</u>ldə(n)/ (vermeldde, heeft vermeld) **1** mention **2** state, give

vermeldenswaard /vərm<u>ɛ</u>ldə(n)swart/ (adj) worth mentioning, worthy of mention

de **vermelding** /vərm<u>ɛ</u>ldɪŋ/ (pl: -en) mention, statement: *eervolle ~* honourable mention; *onder ~ van ...* giving (*or:* stating, mentioning) ...

vermengen /vərm<u>ɛ</u>ŋə(n)/ (vermengde, heeft vermengd) mix; blend

de **vermenging** /vərm<u>ɛ</u>ŋɪŋ/ (pl: -en) mix(ture), mixing, blend(ing)

[1] **vermenigvuldigen** /vərmenəχf<u>ʏ</u>ldəɣə(n)/ (vermenigvuldigde, heeft vermenigvuldigd) **1** duplicate **2** [maths] multiply: *vermenigvuldig dat getal **met** 8* multiply that number by 8

zich [2] **vermenigvuldigen** /vərmenəχf<u>ʏ</u>ldəɣə(n)/ (vermenigvuldigde zich, heeft zich vermenigvuldigd) multiply, increase; reproduce

de **vermenigvuldiging** /vərmenəχf<u>ʏ</u>ldəɣɪŋ/

(pl: -en) multiplication: *tafel van* ~ multiplication table

de **vermicelli** /vɛrmisɛli/ vermicelli

vermijden /vərmɛidə(n)/ (vermeed, heeft vermeden) avoid: *angstvallig* ~ shun, fight shy of

verminderd /vərmɪndərt/ (adj, adv) diminished, reduced: ~ *toerekeningsvatbaar* not fully accountable for one's actions

verminderen /vərmɪndərə(n)/ (verminderde, heeft verminderd) decrease, reduce: *de uitgaven* ~ cut (back on) expenses

de **vermindering** /vərmɪndərɪŋ/ (pl: -en) decrease, reduction: ~ *van straf* reduction of (a) sentence

verminken /vərmɪŋkə(n)/ (verminkte, heeft verminkt) mutilate

de **verminking** /vərmɪŋkɪŋ/ (pl: -en) mutilation

de **vermissing** /vərmɪsɪŋ/ (pl: -en) loss; absence

vermist /vərmɪst/ (adj): *iem. (iets) als ~ opgeven* report s.o. missing, report sth. lost

de **vermiste** /vərmɪstə/ (pl: -n) missing person

vermits /vərmɪts/ (adv) [Belg] since, as, because

vermoedelijk /vərmudələk/ (adj, adv) supposed: *de ~e dader* the suspect; *de ~e oorzaak* the probable cause

het ¹**vermoeden** /vərmudə(n)/ (pl: -s) **1** conjecture, surmise **2** suspicion: *ik had er geen flauw ~ van* I didn't have the slightest suspicion (*or:* the faintest idea); *ik had al zo'n ~, ik had er al een ~ van* I had my suspicions (all along)

²**vermoeden** /vərmudə(n)/ (vermoedde, heeft vermoed) suspect, suppose: *dit heb ik nooit kunnen* ~ this is the last thing I expected

vermoeid /vərmujt/ (adj) tired (with), weary (of): *dodelijk* ~ dead tired, completely worn-out

de **vermoeidheid** /vərmujthɛit/ tiredness; weariness; fatigue: ~ *van de ogen* eye strain

vermoeien /vərmujə(n)/ (vermoeide, heeft vermoeid) tire (out), weary, fatigue; exhaust

vermoeiend /vərmujənt/ (adj) tiring; wearisome; tiresome

het **vermogen** /vərmoɣə(n)/ (pl: -s) **1** fortune; property; capital **2** power, capacity **3** power, ability: *naar mijn beste* ~ to the best of my ability

vermogend /vərmoɣənt/ (adj) rich, wealthy: *~e mensen* people of substance

de **vermogensaanwas** /vərmoɣə(n)sanwɑs/ capital gain

de **vermogensbelasting** /vərmoɣə(n)zbəlɑstɪŋ/ wealth tax

vermolmd /vərmɔlmt/ (adj) mouldered, decayed, rotten

vermommen /vərmɔmə(n)/ (vermomde,

heeft vermomd) disguise, dress up: *vermomd als* disguised as

de **vermomming** /vərmɔmɪŋ/ (pl: -en) disguise

vermoorden /vərmordə(n)/ (vermoordde, heeft vermoord) murder; assassinate: [Belg] *zwijgen als vermoord* be silent as the grave

vermorzelen /vərmɔrzələ(n)/ (vermorzelde, heeft vermorzeld) crush, smash up

de **vermout** /vɛrmut/ vermouth

vermurwen /vərmʏrwə(n)/ (vermurwde, heeft vermurwd) mollify

vernauwen /vərnɑuwə(n)/ (vernauwde, heeft vernauwd) narrow (down), constrict, contract || *zich* ~ narrow

de **vernauwing** /vərnɑuwɪŋ/ (pl: -en) narrowing, constriction: ~ *van de bloedvaten* stricture (*or:* stenosis) of the blood vessels

vernederen /vərnedərə(n)/ (vernederde, heeft vernederd) humble; humiliate

vernederend /vərnedərənt/ (adj) humiliating; degrading

de **vernedering** /vərnedərɪŋ/ (pl: -en) humiliation: *een ~ ondergaan* suffer a humiliation (*or:* an indignity)

vernederlandsen /vərnedərlɑntsə(n)/ (vernederlandste, is vernederlandst) become Dutch, turn Dutch

vernemen /vərnemə(n)/ (vernam, heeft vernomen) learn, be told (*or:* informed) (of)

verneuken /vərnøkə(n)/ (verneukte, heeft verneukt) [vulg] shaft, screw, con: *laat je niet ~* don't let them fuck you about (*or:* shit on you); *je wordt verneukt waar je bij staat* it's a rip-off (*or:* con)

vernielen /vərnilə(n)/ (vernielde, heeft vernield) destroy, wreck

de **vernieling** /vərnilɪŋ/ (pl: -en) destruction, devastation: *~en aanrichten* go on the rampage; *zij ligt helemaal in de* ~ she's a complete wreck

de **vernielzucht** /vərnilzʏχt/ destructiveness, vandalism

vernietigen /vərnitəɣə(n)/ (vernietigde, heeft vernietigd) destroy, ruin; annihilate: *iemands verwachtingen* ~ dash s.o.'s expectations

vernietigend /vərnitəɣənt/ (adj, adv) destructive, devastating: *een ~ oordeel* a scathing judgment

de **vernietiging** /vərnitəɣɪŋ/ (pl: -en) destruction; annihilation

vernieuwen /vərniwə(n)/ (vernieuwde, heeft vernieuwd) **1** renew, modernize; renovate **2** renew, restore

de **vernieuwer** /vərniwər/ (pl: -s) **1** renewer; renovator **2** innovator

de **vernieuwing** /vərniwɪŋ/ (pl: -en) **1** renewal, modernization; renovation; rebuilding **2** modernization, renovation; reform: *allerlei ~en aanbrengen* carry out all sorts of renovations

het/de **vernis** /vɛrnɪs/ (pl: -sen) varnish

vernissen /vɛrnɪsə(n)/ (verniste, heeft gevernist) varnish

vernoemen /vɛrnumə(n)/ (vernoemde, heeft vernoemd) name after, call after

het **vernuft** /vɛrnʏft/ ingenuity, genius

vernuftig /vɛrnʏftəx/ (adj) ingenious, witty

veronachtzamen /vɛrɔnɑxtsamə(n)/ (veronachtzaamde, heeft veronachtzaamd) neglect

veronderstellen /vɛrɔndərstɛlə(n)/ (veronderstelde, heeft verondersteld) suppose, assume: *ik veronderstel van wel* I suppose so

de **veronderstelling** /vɛrɔndərstɛlɪŋ/ (pl: -en) assumption, supposition: *in de ~ verkeren dat … be under the impression that …*

verongelijkt /vɛrɔŋɣəlɛɪkt/ (adj, adv) aggrieved, wronged

verongelukken /vɛrɔŋɣəlʏkə(n)/ (verongelukte, is verongelukt) **1** have an accident; be lost, be killed **2** (have a) crash; be wrecked, be lost [ship]: *het vliegtuig verongelukte* the plane crashed

verontreinigen /vɛrɔntrɛɪnəɣə(n)/ (verontreinigde, heeft verontreinigd) pollute, contaminate

de **verontreiniging** /vɛrɔntrɛɪnəɣɪŋ/ (pl: -en) pollution, contamination: *de ~ van het milieu* environmental pollution

verontrust /vɛrɔntrʏst/ (adj) alarmed, worried, concerned

verontrusten /vɛrɔntrʏstə(n)/ (verontrustte, heeft verontrust) alarm, worry: *zich ~ over iets* be disturbed (*or:* worried) about sth., to worry about sth.

verontrustend /vɛrɔntrʏstənt/ (adj) alarming, worrying, disturbing

[1]**verontschuldigen** /vɛrɔntsxʏldəɣə(n)/ (verontschuldigde, heeft verontschuldigd) excuse, pardon: *iem. ~ excuse s.o.*

zich [2]**verontschuldigen** /vɛrɔntsxʏldəɣə(n)/ (verontschuldigde zich, heeft zich verontschuldigd) apologize, excuse: *zich laten ~ beg to be excused; zich vanwege ziekte ~ excuse o.s. on account of illness*

de **verontschuldiging** /vɛrɔntsxʏldəɣɪŋ/ (pl: -en) **1** excuse, apology: *~en aanbieden* apologize, offer one's apologies **2** excuse, defence: *hij voerde als ~ aan dat* he offered the excuse that

verontwaardigd /vɛrɔntwardəxt/ (adj, adv) indignant (about, at)

de **verontwaardiging** /vɛrɔntwardəɣɪŋ/ indignation, outrage: *tot grote ~ van* to the great indignation of

de **veroordeelde** /vɛrɔrdeldə/ (pl: -n) condemned man (*or:* woman), convict

veroordelen /vɛrɔrdelə(n)/ (veroordeelde, heeft veroordeeld) **1** condemn; [law] sentence; find guilty: *~ tot de betaling van de*

kosten order (s.o.) to pay costs **2** condemn; denounce

de **veroordeling** /vɛrɔrdelɪŋ/ (pl: -en) **1** [law] conviction; sentence: *voorwaardelijke ~* suspended sentence **2** condemnation; denunciation

veroorloven /vɛrɔrlovə(n)/ (veroorloofde, heeft veroorloofd) permit, allow; afford: *zo'n dure auto kunnen wij ons niet ~* we can't afford such an expensive car

veroorzaken /vɛrɔrzakə(n)/ (veroorzaakte, heeft veroorzaakt) cause, bring about: *schade ~* cause damage

verorberen /vɛrɔrbərə(n)/ (verorberde, heeft verorberd) consume

verordenen /vɛrɔrdenə(n)/ (verordende, heeft verordend) **1** decree **2** order

de **verordening** /vɛrɔrdenɪŋ/ (pl: -en) regulation(s), ordinance, statute

verouderd /vɛrɑudərt/ (adj) old-fashioned, (out)dated

verouderen /vɛrɑudərə(n)/ (verouderde, is verouderd) become obsolete (*or:* antiquated), date, go out of date

de **veroudering** /vɛrɑudərɪŋ/ obsolescence, getting (*or:* becoming) out of date

de **veroveraar** /vɛrovərar/ (pl: -s) conqueror: *Willem de Veroveraar* William the Conqueror

veroveren /vɛrovərə(n)/ (veroverde, heeft veroverd) conquer, capture, win: *de eerste plaats ~ in de wedstrijd* take the lead

de **verovering** /vɛrovərɪŋ/ (pl: -en) conquest, capture

verpachten /vɛrpɑxtə(n)/ (verpachtte, heeft verpacht) lease (out): *verpachte grond* land on lease

verpakken /vɛrpɑkə(n)/ (verpakte, heeft verpakt) pack (up), package: *een cadeau in papier ~* wrap a present in paper

de **verpakking** /vɛrpɑkɪŋ/ (pl: -en) packing, wrapping, paper

het **verpakkingsmateriaal** /vɛrpɑkɪŋsmaterijal/ (pl: -materialen) packing material

verpatsen /vɛrpɑtsə(n)/ (verpatste, heeft verpatst) [inform] flog

verpauperen /vɛrpɑupərə(n)/ (verpauperde, is verpauperd) impoverish, go down (in the world), be reduced to poverty: *een verpauperde stad* a run-down town

de **verpaupering** /vɛrpɑupərɪŋ/ deterioration, impoverishment

verpesten /vɛrpɛstə(n)/ (verpestte, heeft verpest) [inform] poison, contaminate, spoil: *de sfeer ~* spoil the atmosphere

het **verpinken** /vɛrpɪŋkə(n)/: [Belg] *zonder (te) ~* without batting an eyelid

[1]**verplaatsen** /vɛrplatsə(n)/ (verplaatste, heeft verplaatst) move; shift: *zijn activiteiten ~* shift one's activities

zich [2]**verplaatsen** /vɛrplatsə(n)/ (verplaatste zich, heeft zich verplaatst) **1** move, shift, change places **2** project o.s., put o.s. in s.o. else's shoes: *zich **in** iemands positie* ~ imagine o.s. in s.o. else's position

de **verplaatsingskosten** /vərplatsɪŋskɔstə(n)/ (pl) [Belg] call out charge

verplanten /vərplɑntə(n)/ (verplantte, heeft verplant) transplant

het **verpleeghuis** /vərpleɣhœys/ (pl: -huizen) nursing home, convalescent home

de **verpleeghulp** /vərpleɣhʏlp/ (pl: -en) nurse's aide, nursing auxiliary, medical orderly

de **verpleegkundige** /vərpleɣkʏndəɣə/ (pl: -n) nurse: *gediplomeerd* ~ trained (*or:* qualified) nurse

de **verpleegster** /vərpleɣstər/ (pl: -s) nurse

verplegen /vərpleɣə(n)/ (verpleegde, heeft verpleegd) nurse, care for: *~d **personeel*** nursing staff

de **verpleger** /vərpleɣər/ (pl: -s) (male) nurse

de **verpleging** /vərpleɣɪŋ/ nursing, care: *zij gaat **in** de* ~ she is going into nursing

verpletteren /vərplɛtərə(n)/ (verpletterde, heeft verpletterd) **1** crush, smash **2** [fig] shatter: *dit **bericht** verpletterde haar* the news shattered her

verpletterend /vərplɛtərənt/ (adj, adv) crushing: *een ~e **nederlaag*** a crushing defeat

verplicht /vərplɪχt/ (adj, adv) **1** compelled, obliged: *zich* ~ **voelen** *om* feel compelled to **2** compulsory, obligatory: *~e **lectuur*** required reading (matter); ~ **verzekerd** *zijn* be compulsorily insured; *iets* ~ **stellen** make sth. compulsory

verplichten /vərplɪχtə(n)/ (verplichtte, heeft verplicht) oblige, compel: *de wet verplicht **ons** daartoe* the law obliges us to do that

de **verplichting** /vərplɪχtɪŋ/ (pl: -en) obligation, commitment; liability: *financiële ~en* financial liabilities (*or:* obligations); *sociale ~en* social duties; *~en **aangaan*** enter into obligations (*or:* a contract); *zijn ~en **nakomen*** fulfil one's obligations

verpoten /vərpotə(n)/ (verpootte, heeft verpoot) transplant

verprutsen /vərprʏtsə(n)/ (verprutste, heeft verprutst) bungle, botch

verpulveren /vərpʏlvərə(n)/ (verpulverde, heeft verpulverd) pulverize; [+ direct object also] crush

het **verraad** /vərat/ treason, treachery, betrayal: *~ **plegen*** commit treason

verraden /vəradə(n)/ (verraadde, heeft verraden) **1** betray, commit treason: *iem. **aan** de politie* ~ squeak (*or:* rat) on s.o. **2** betray: *een **geheim*** ~ betray (*or:* let out) a secret; *niets ~, hoor!* don't breathe a word!

de **verrader** /vəradər/ (pl: -s) traitor, betrayer; squealer

verraderlijk /vəradərlək/ (adj, adv) treach-

erous

verrassen /vərɑsə(n)/ (verraste, heeft verrast) (take by) surprise: *door noodweer verrast* caught in a thunderstorm; *onaangenaam verrast zijn* be startled, be taken aback

de **verrassing** /vərɑsɪŋ/ (pl: -en) **1** surprise; shock: *voor iem. een* ~ *in petto **hebben*** have a surprise in store for s.o.; *het **was** voor ons geen* ~ *meer* it didn't come as a surprise to us **2** surprise, amazement: *tot mijn* ~ *bemerkte ik …* I was surprised to see that …

verrast /vərɑst/ (adj, adv) surprised; amazed: ~ **keek** *hij* **op** he looked up in surprise

verregaand /vɛrəɣant/ (adj, adv) far-reaching, outrageous; radical: *in ~e **staat** van ontbinding* in an advanced state of decomposition

verregenen /vəreɣənə(n)/ (verregende, is verregend) spoil by rain; rain off; drench

verrek /vərɛk/ (int) [inform] gosh, (good) gracious

verrekenen /vərekənə(n)/ (verrekende, heeft verrekend) settle, deduct, adjust; pay out: *iets **met** iets* ~ balance sth. with sth.

de **verrekening** /vərekənɪŋ/ (pl: -en) settlement

de **verrekijker** /vɛrəkɛikər/ (pl: -s) binoculars; telescope

¹**verrekken** /vərɛkə(n)/ (verrekte, is verrekt) [inform] die, kick the bucket: ~ **van** de honger starve; ~ **van** de pijn be groaning with pain; ~ **van** de kou perish with cold

²**verrekken** /vərɛkə(n)/ (verrekte, heeft verrekt) strain; pull; twist, wrench; sprain: *een **pees*** ~ stretch a tendon; *zich* ~ strain o.s.

verrekt /vərɛkt/ (adj, adv) [inform] strained

verreweg /vɛrəwɛχ/ (adv) (by) far, much; easily: *dat **is** ~ het beste* that's easily (*or:* much) the best; *hij **is** ~ de sterkste* he's far and away the strongest

verrichten /vərɪχtə(n)/ (verrichtte, heeft verricht) perform; conduct; carry out: *wonderen* ~ work wonders, perform miracles

de **verrichting** /vərɪχtɪŋ/ (pl: -en) **1** performance **2** action; operation

verrijden /vərɛidə(n)/ (verreed, heeft verreden) **1** move; wheel; drive **2** compete in, compete for: *een **kampioenschap*** ~ organize (*or:* hold) a championship; *een wedstrijd **laten*** ~ run off a race

verrijken /vərɛikə(n)/ (verrijkte, heeft verrijkt) enrich: *zijn **kennis*** ~ improve one's knowledge; *zich* ~ *ten koste van een ander* get rich at the expense of s.o. else; *verrijkt **voedsel*** fortified food

de **verrijking** /vərɛikɪŋ/ enrichment

verrijzen /vərɛizə(n)/ (verrees, is verrezen) (a)rise; spring up [bldg]; shoot up

de **verrijzenis** /vərɛizənɪs/ resurrection

zich **verroeren** /vərurə(n)/ (verroerde zich,

heeft zich verroerd) move: *je **kunt** je hier nauwelijks ~* you can hardly move in here; *verroer je niet* don't move

verroest /vərʊ̆st/ (adj) rusty

verroesten /vərʊ̆stə(n)/ (verroestte, is verroest) rust, get rusty: *verroest **ijzer*** rusty iron

verrot /vərɔ̆t/ (adj) rotten; bad; putrid, wretched: *iem. ~ **slaan*** knock the living daylights out of s.o.; ***door en door** ~* rotten to the core

verrotten /vərɔ̆tə(n)/ (verrotte, is verrot) rot, decay: ***doen** ~* rot (down); decay

de **verrotting** /vərɔ̆tɪŋ/ rot(ting), decay: *dit hout is **tegen** ~ bestand* this wood is treated for rot

verruilen /vərœylə(n)/ (verruilde, heeft verruild) (ex)change, swap

verruimen /vərœymə(n)/ (verruimde, heeft/is verruimd) widen, broaden; liberalize: *zijn **blik** ~* widen (or: broaden) one's outlook; ***mogelijkheden** ~* create more possibilities

de **verruiming** /vərœymɪŋ/ widening, broadening; liberalization

verrukkelijk /vərʏkələk/ (adj, adv) delightful, gorgeous; delicious

de **verrukking** /vərʏkɪŋ/ (pl: -en) delight

verrukt /vərʏkt/ (adj) delighted, overjoyed

verruwen /vərywə(n)/ (verruwde, is verruwd) coarsen; become vulgar; become brutalized

de **verruwing** /vərywɪŋ/ coarsening, vulgarization

het **¹vers** /vɛrs/ (pl: verzen) **1** verse: *Lucas 6, ~ **10*** St Luke, chapter 6, verse 10 **2** verse, stanza; couplet: *dat is ~ **twee*** that's another story **3** verse, poem; rhyme

²vers /vɛrs/ (adj, adv) fresh, new: *~ **bloed*** fresh (or: young, new) blood; *~e **eieren*** new-laid eggs; *~e **sneeuw*** fresh (or: new-fallen) snow; *~ **blijven*** keep fresh (or: good); *~ **van** de pers* hot from the press

verschaald /vərsxălt/ (adj): *~ **bier*** stale (or: flat) beer

verschaffen /vərsxɑ̆fə(n)/ (verschafte, heeft verschaft) provide (with), supply (with): *het leger verschafte hem een complete **uitrusting*** the army issued him with a complete kit

verschalken /vərsxɑ̆lkə(n)/ (verschalkte, heeft verschalkt) outwit, (out)fox: *de **keeper** ~* outmanoeuvre the keeper

zich **verschansen** /vərsxɑ̆nsə(n)/ (verschanste zich, heeft zich verschanst) entrench o.s., barricade o.s., take cover: *zich **in** zijn kamer ~* barricade o.s. in one's room

het **verscheiden** /vərsxɛɪdə(n)/ [form] departure

verscheidene /vərsxɛɪdənə/ (num) several, various

de **verscheidenheid** /vərsxɛɪdənhɛit/ variety, diversity; assortment; range: *een **grote** ~ aan gerechten* a wide variety of dishes

verschepen /vərsxɛ̆pə(n)/ (verscheepte, heeft verscheept) ship (off, out)

de **verscheping** /vərsxɛ̆pɪŋ/ (pl: -en) shipping

verscherpen /vərsxɛ̆rpə(n)/ (verscherpte, heeft verscherpt) tighten (up): *het **toezicht** ~* tighten up control

verscheuren /vərsxø̆rə(n)/ (verscheurde, heeft verscheurd) **1** tear (up); shred; rip (up) **2** maul, tear to pieces (or: apart)

het **verschiet** /vərsxĭt/: *dat ligt nog **in** het ~* that's still in store

verschieten /vərsxĭtə(n)/ (verschoot, is verschoten) fade: *de **gordijnen** zijn verschoten* the curtains are (or: have) faded ‖ *van **kleur** ~* a) blush, go red; b) rapidly become multicultural

verschijnen /vərsxɛ̆ɪnə(n)/ (verscheen, is verschenen) **1** appear, surface; emerge **2** appear, turn up **3** appear, come out, be published

de **verschijning** /vərsxɛ̆ɪnɪŋ/ (pl: -en) **1** appearance; publication **2** figure, presence: *een **indrukwekkende** ~* an imposing presence

het **verschijnsel** /vərsxɛ̆ɪnsəl/ (pl: -en) phenomenon; symptom; sign: *een **eigenaardig** ~* a strange phenomenon

het **verschil** /vərsxɪl/ (pl: -len) **1** difference, dissimilarity, distinction: *~ van **mening*** a difference of opinion; *een **groot** ~ maken* make all the difference; *~ **maken** tussen* draw a distinction between, differentiate between; *~ **maken*** make a difference; *met dit ~, dat ...* with one difference, namely that ...; *een ~ van dag en nacht* a world of difference **2** difference, remainder: *het ~ **delen*** split the difference

verschillen /vərsxɪlə(n)/ (verschilde, heeft verschild) differ (from), be different (from); vary: *van mening ~ met iem.* disagree with s.o., differ with s.o.; *smaken ~* tastes differ; everyone to his taste

verschillend /vərsxɪlənt/ (adj, adv) **1** different (from), various: *wij **denken** daar ~ over* we don't see eye to eye on that **2** several, various, different: *bij ~e **gelegenheden*** on various occasions

verscholen /vərsxŏlə(n)/ (adj) hidden; secluded: *het huis **lag** ~ achter de bomen* the house was tucked away behind the trees

verschonen /vərsxŏnə(n)/ (verschoonde, heeft verschoond) change: *de **baby** ~* change the baby's nappy; *de **bedden** ~* put clean sheets on the beds; *zich ~* put on clean clothes

de **verschoning** /vərsxŏnɪŋ/ (pl: -en) change of underwear

de **verschoppeling** /vərsxɔ̆pəlɪŋ/ (pl: -en) outcast

verschralen /vərsxra̲lə(n)/ (verschraalde, is verschraald) decrease

[1]**verschrikkelijk** /vərsxri̲kələk/ (adj) terrible; devastating; excruciating: *een ~e hongersnood* a devastating famine; *~e sneeuwman* Abominable Snowman, yeti; *een ~ kabaal* an infernal racket

[2]**verschrikkelijk** /vərsxri̲kələk/ (adv) terribly, awfully; terrifically: *Sander maakte een ~ mooi doelpunt* Sander scored a terrific goal

de **verschrikking** /vərsxri̲kɪŋ/ (pl: -en) terror, horror: *de ~en van de oorlog* the horrors of war

verschroeien /vərsxru̲jə(n)/ (verschroeide, heeft verschroeid) scorch; singe; sear: *de tactiek van de verschroeide aarde* scorched earth policy

verschrompelen /vərsxro̲mpələ(n)/ (verschrompelde, heeft/is verschrompeld) shrivel (up); atrophy: *een verschrompeld gezicht* a wizened face

zich **verschuilen** /vərsxœy̲lə(n)/ (verschool zich/ verschuilde zich, heeft zich verscholen) hide (o.s.), lurk: *zich in een hoek ~* hide (o.s.) in a corner

verschuiven /vərsxœy̲və(n)/ (verschoof, heeft verschoven) **1** move, shift; shove aside **2** postpone

de **verschuiving** /vərsxœy̲vɪŋ/ (pl: -en) **1** shift **2** postponement

verschuldigd /vərsxʏ̲ldəxt/ (adj) due; indebted: *het ~e geld* the money due; *iem. iets ~ zijn* be indebted to s.o., owe s.o. sth.

de **versheid** /vɛ̲rshɛit/ freshness

het/de **vershoudfolie** cling film

de **versie** /vɛ̲rzi/ (pl: -s) version

de **versierder** /vərsi̲rdər/ (pl: -s) womanizer, ladykiller

versieren /vərsi̲rə(n)/ (versierde, heeft versierd) **1** decorate: *de kerstboom ~* trim the Christmas tree; *straten ~* decorate the streets **2** pick up, get off with

de **versiering** /vərsi̲rɪŋ/ (pl: -en) decoration

de **versiertoer** /vərsi̲rtur/: *op de ~ gaan* try to pick up s.o., try to make s.o.

versimpelen /vərsɪ̲mpələ(n)/ (versimpelde, heeft versimpeld) (over)simplify

versjacheren /vərfɑ̲xərə(n)/ (versjacherde, heeft versjacherd) squander

versjouwen /vərfɑu̲wə(n)/ (versjouwde, heeft versjouwd) drag away

verslaafd /vərsla̲ft/ (adj) addicted (to), hooked (on): *~ raken aan drugs* contract the drug habit; *aan de drank* (or: *het spel*) *~ zijn* be addicted to drink (*or:* gambling)

de **verslaafde** /vərsla̲vdə/ (pl: -n) alcoholic; (drug) addict; junkie

verslaan /vərsla̲n/ (versloeg, heeft verslagen) defeat; beat [sport]: *iem. ~ met schaken* defeat s.o. at chess

het **verslag** /vərslɑ̲x/ (pl: -en) report; commentary: *een direct ~ van de wedstrijd* a live commentary on the match; *~ uitbrengen* report on, give an account of

verslagen /vərsla̲ɣə(n)/ (adj) **1** defeated, beaten **2** dismayed

de **verslagenheid** /vərsla̲ɣənhɛit/ dismay (at), consternation (at)

de **verslaggever** /vərslɑ̲xevər/ (pl: -s) reporter; commentator

de **verslaggeving** /vərslɑ̲xevɪŋ/ (pl: -en) (press) coverage

zich **verslapen** /vərsla̲pə(n)/ (versliep zich, heeft zich verslapen) oversleep: *hij had zich drie uur ~* he overslept and was three hours late

verslappen /vərslɑ̲pə(n)/ (verslapte, is verslapt) slacken; flag; wane: *de pols verslapt* the pulse is getting weaker

verslavend /vərsla̲vənt/ (adj, adv) addictive

de **verslaving** /vərsla̲vɪŋ/ addiction, (drug-)dependence

verslechteren /vərslɛ̲xtərə(n)/ (verslechterde, is verslechterd) get worse, worsen, deteriorate

verslepen /vərsle̲pə(n)/ (versleepte, heeft versleept) drag (off, away); tow (away)

versleten /vərsle̲tə(n)/ (adj) **1** worn(-out), shabby: *tot op de draad ~* threadbare **2** worn-out; burnt-out: *een ~ paard* an old nag

de **versleuteling** [comp] encryption

verslijten /vərsli̲itə(n)/ (versleet, heeft versleten) wear out: *hij had al drie echtgenotes versleten* he had already got through three wives

zich **verslikken** /vərsli̲kə(n)/ (verslikte zich, heeft zich verslikt) **1** choke: *pas op, hij verslikt zich* watch out, it has gone down the wrong way; *zich in een graat ~* choke on a bone **2** underrate, underestimate

verslinden /vərsli̲ndə(n)/ (verslond, heeft verslonden) devour; eat up; eat: *die auto verslindt benzine* that car drinks petrol; *een boek ~* devour a book

verslingerd /vərsli̲ŋərt/ (adj): *zij is ~ aan slagroomgebakjes* she is mad about cream cakes

versloffen /vərslo̲fə(n)/ (verslofte, is versloft): *de boel laten ~* let things go

verslonzen /vərslo̲nzə(n)/ (verslonsde, is verslonsd) degrade

versmaden /vərsma̲də(n)/ (versmaadde, heeft versmaad): *dat is niet te ~* that's not to be sneezed at (*or:* despised)

[1]**versmallen** /vərsmɑ̲lə(n)/ (versmalde, heeft/is versmald) narrow

zich [2]**versmallen** /vərsmɑ̲lə(n)/ (versmalde zich, heeft zich versmald) narrow, become narrow(er): *ginds versmalt de weg zich* the road gets narrow(er) there

versmelten /vərsmɛ̲ltə(n)/ (versmolt, is versmolten) blend, merge

de **versnapering** /vərsnɑ̲pərɪŋ/ (pl: -en) snack,

titbit

versnellen /vərsnɛlə(n)/ (versnelde, heeft/is versneld) quicken, accelerate, speed up

de **versnelling** /vərsnɛlɪŋ/ (pl: -en) **1** acceleration; increase (in) **2** gear: *in* de eerste ~ zetten put into first gear; *in* een hogere ~ schakelen change up; move into gear; een auto met *automatische* ~ a car with automatic transmission; een fiets *met* tien ~*en* a ten-speed bike

de **versnellingsbak** /vərsnɛlɪŋzbɑk/ (pl: -ken) gearbox

versnijden /vərsnɛɪdə(n)/ (versneed, heeft versneden) **1** cut up **2** adulterate

versnipperen /vərsnɪpərə(n)/ (versnipperde, heeft versnipperd) **1** cut up (into pieces) **2** fragment; fritter away

versoberen /vərsobərə(n)/ (versoberde, heeft versoberd) economize, cut down (on expenses)

versoepelen /vərsupələ(n)/ (versoepelde, heeft/is versoepeld) relax; liberalize

verspelen /vərspɛlə(n)/ (verspeelde, heeft verspeeld) forfeit, lose: een *kans* ~ throw away a chance; zijn *rechten* ~ forfeit one's rights

versperren /vərspɛrə(n)/ (versperde, heeft versperd) block; barricade: iem. de *weg* ~ bar s.o.'s way; de *weg* ~ block the road

de **versperring** /vərspɛrɪŋ/ (pl: -en) barrier, barricade

verspillen /vərspɪlə(n)/ (verspilde, heeft verspild) waste; fritter away

de **verspilling** /vərspɪlɪŋ/ (pl: -en) **1** wasting: ~ van *energie* wasting energy **2** waste: *wat* een ~*!* what a waste!

versplinteren /vərsplɪntərə(n)/ (versplinterde, heeft/is versplinterd) smash; splinter: die *plank* is versplinterd that plank has splintered

verspreid /vərsprɛɪt/ (adj, adv) scattered: een over het hele land ~*e organisatie* a nationwide organization; haar speelgoed *lag* ~ over de vloer the floor was strewn with her toys; *wijd* ~ widespread; widely (or: commonly) held

¹**verspreiden** /vərsprɛɪdə(n)/ (verspreidde, heeft verspreid) **1** spread, disperse, distribute; circulate: een kwalijke *geur* ~ give off a ghastly smell; *licht* ~ shed light; *warmte* ~ give off heat **2** disperse

zich ²**verspreiden** /vərsprɛɪdə(n)/ (verspreidde zich, heeft zich verspreid) spread (out): de menigte verspreidde *zich* the crowd dispersed

de **verspreiding** /vərsprɛɪdɪŋ/ spread, distribution

zich **verspreken** /vərsprɛkə(n)/ (versprak zich, heeft zich versproken) make a slip (or: mistake)

de **verspreking** /vərsprɛkɪŋ/ (pl: -en) slip of the tongue, mistake

¹**verspringen** /vɛrsprɪŋə(n)/ (sprong ver, heeft vergesprongen) do the long jump: zij sprong zes *meter* ver she jumped six metres

²**verspringen** /vərsprɪŋə(n)/ (versprong, is versprongen) **1** jump **2** stagger: ~de *naden* staggered seams

de **verspringer** /vɛrsprɪŋər/ long jumper; [Am] broad-jumper

de **versregel** /vɛrsreɣəl/ (pl: -s) line (of poetry)

verst /vɛrst/ (adj, adv) furthest, farthest: het ~*e* punt the farthest point; dat is in de ~*e verte* niet mijn bedoeling that's the last thing I intended

verstaan /vərstan/ (verstond, heeft verstaan) **1** (be able to) hear: helaas verstond ik zijn *naam* niet unfortunately I didn't catch his name; ik versta geen *woord!* I can't hear a word that is being said; hij kon *zichzelf* nauwelijks ~ he could hardly hear himself speak **2** understand: heb ik *goed* ~ dat … did I hear you right …; *te* ~ geven give (s.o.) to understand (that) **3** understand, mean: wat versta jij *daaronder?* what do you understand by that? **4** know: zijn *vak* ~ know one's trade

verstaanbaar /vərstambar/ (adj, adv) **1** audible **2** understandable: zich ~ *maken* make o.s. understood

het **verstand** /vərstɑnt/ **1** (power of) reason, (powers of) comprehension; brain(s): *gezond* ~ common sense; een goed ~ *hebben* have a good head on one's shoulders; iem. iets *aan* het ~ brengen drive sth. home to s.o.; *bij* zijn (volle) ~ in full possession of one's faculties **2** knowledge, understanding: ~ *hebben* van know about, understand, be a good judge of; daar heb ik *geen* ~ van I don't know the first thing about that

¹**verstandelijk** /vərstɑndələk/ (adj) intellectual: ~*e vermogens* intellect, intellectual powers

²**verstandelijk** /vərstɑndələk/ (adv) rationally

de **verstandhouding** /vərstɑnthɑudɪŋ/ (pl: -en) understanding; relations: een *blik* van ~ an understanding look; een *goede* ~ hebben met be on good terms with

verstandig /vərstɑndəɣ/ (adj, adv) sensible: iets ~ *aanpakken* go about sth. in a sensible way

het **verstandshuwelijk** /vərstɑn(t)shywələk/ (pl: -en) **1** marriage of convenience **2** alliance of convenience

de **verstandskies** /vərstɑntskis/ (pl: -kiezen) wisdom tooth

de **verstandsverbijstering** /vərstɑntsfərbɛɪstərɪŋ/ madness: handelen in een *vlaag* van ~ act in a fit of madness (or: insanity)

verstarren /vərstɑrə(n)/ (verstarde, is verstard) become rigid, freeze: verstarde *tradities* fossilized traditions

verstedelijken /vərstedələkə(n)/ (verstedelijkte, is verstedelijkt) urbanize de **verstedelijking** /vərstedələkɪŋ/ urbanization

versteend /vərstent/ (adj) petrified; [also fig] fossilized

het **verstek** /vərstɛk/ (pl: -ken) default (of appearance): ~ *laten gaan* be absent, fail to appear

de **verstekeling** /vərstekəlɪŋ/ (pl: -en) stowaway

verstelbaar /vərstɛlbar/ (adj) adjustable

versteld /vərstɛlt/ (adj) stunned: *iem.* ~ *doen staan* astonish s.o.; ~ *staan (van iets)* be dumbfounded

verstellen /vərstɛlə(n)/ (verstelde, heeft versteld) **1** adjust **2** mend, repair

versterken /vərstɛrkə(n)/ (versterkte, heeft versterkt) **1** strengthen; intensify: *geluid* ~ amplify sound **2** fortify

de **versterker** /vərstɛrkər/ (pl: -s) amplifier

de **versterking** /vərstɛrkɪŋ/ (pl: -en) strengthening, reinforcement; amplification: *het leger kreeg* ~ the army was reinforced

versterven /vərstɛrvə(n)/ (verstierf, is verstorven) **1** mortify o.s. **2** starve

verstevigen /vərstevəɣə(n)/ (verstevigde, heeft verstevigd) strengthen, consolidate; prop up: *zijn positie* ~ consolidate one's position

verstijven /vərstɛivə(n)/ (verstijfde, is verstijfd) stiffen: ~ *van* kou grow numb with cold; ~ *van* schrik be petrified with fear

verstikken /vərstɪkə(n)/ (verstikte, heeft verstikt) smother, choke

verstikkend /vərstɪkənt/ (adj) suffocating: ~*e hitte* stifling heat

de **verstikking** /vərstɪkɪŋ/ (pl: -en) suffocation

¹**verstoken** /vərstokə(n)/ (adj) deprived (of)

²**verstoken** /vərstokə(n)/ (verstookte, heeft verstookt) spend on heating

verstokt /vərstɔkt/ (adj) hardened, confirmed: *een* ~*e vrijgezel* a confirmed bachelor

verstomd /vərstɔmt/ (adj): ~ *doen staan* strike dumb, astound; ~ *staan* be dumbfounded (*or:* flabbergasted)

verstommen /vərstɔmə(n)/ (verstomde, is verstomd) become silent: *het lawaai* verstom-de the noise died down

verstoord /vərstort/ (adj) annoyed, upset

verstoppen /vərstɔpə(n)/ (verstopte, heeft verstopt) hide: *zijn geld* ~ hide (*or:* stash) away one's money

het **verstoppertje** /vərstɔpərcə/ hide-and-seek: ~ *spelen* play (at) hide-and-seek

de **verstopping** /vərstɔpɪŋ/ (pl: -en) **1** blockage **2** constipation

verstopt /vərstɔpt/ (adj) blocked (up): *mijn neus is* ~ my nose is all stuffed up; *het riool is* ~ the sewer is clogged

verstoren /vərstorə(n)/ (verstoorde, heeft verstoord) disturb: *het evenwicht* ~ upset the

balance; *de stilte* ~ break the silence

de **verstoring** /vərstorɪŋ/ (pl: -en) disruption: ~ *van de openbare orde* disorderly conduct

verstoten /vərstotə(n)/ (verstootte, heeft verstoten) cast off, cast out: *een kind* ~ disown a child

verstrekken /vərstrɛkə(n)/ (verstrekte, heeft verstrekt) supply with, provide with; distribute: *de bank zal hem een lening* ~ the bank will grant him a loan

verstrekkend /vɛrstrɛkənt/ (adj) far-reaching

de **verstrekking** /vərstrɛkɪŋ/ (pl: -en) supply, provision

verstrijken /vərstrɛikə(n)/ (verstreek, is verstreken) go by; elapse; expire: *de termijn verstrijkt op* 1 juli the term expires on the 1st of July

verstrikken /vərstrɪkə(n)/ (verstrikte, heeft verstrikt) entangle: *in iets verstrikt raken* get entangled in sth.

verstrooid /vərstrojt/ (adj) absent-minded

de **verstrooidheid** /vərstrojthɛit/ absent-mindedness: *uit* ~ *iets doen* do sth. from absent-mindedness

verstrooien /vərstrojə(n)/ (verstrooide, heeft verstrooid) scatter, spread: *de as van een overledene* ~ scatter a deceased person's ashes

de **verstrooiing** /vərstrojɪŋ/ (pl: -en) **1** entertainment, diversion **2** scattering, dispersion

verstuiken /vərstœykə(n)/ (verstuikte, heeft verstuikt) sprain

de **verstuiver** /vərstœyvər/ (pl: -s) spray, atomizer

versturen /vərstyrə(n)/ (verstuurde, heeft verstuurd) send (off): *iets naar iem.* ~ send sth. to s.o.; *per post* ~ mail

versuft /vərsyft/ (adj) dizzy, dazed; stunned

de **versukkeling** /vərsʏkəlɪŋ/: *in de* ~ *raken* be ailing, fall into a decline

versus /vɛrsʏs/ (prep) versus

het **vertaalbureau** /vərtalbyro/ (pl: -s) translation agency

de **vertaalslag** /vərtalslɔx/ (pl: -en) applying an idea, rule, etc. from one situation to another

zich **vertakken** /vərtɑkə(n)/ (vertakte zich, heeft zich vertakt) branch (off)

de **vertakking** /vərtɑkɪŋ/ (pl: -en) **1** branching (off) **2** ramification, branch

vertalen /vərtalə(n)/ (vertaalde, heeft vertaald) translate; interpret: *vrij* ~ give a free translation; *uit het Engels in het Frans* ~ translate from English into French

de **vertaler** /vərtalər/ (pl: -s) translator: *beëdigd* ~ sworn translator

de **vertaling** /vərtalɪŋ/ (pl: -en) translation: *een* ~ *maken* do a translation

de **verte** /vɛrtə/ (pl: -n, -s) distance: *in de verste* ~ *niet* not remotely; *het lijkt er in de* ~ *op* there is a slight resemblance; *uit de* ~ from a distance

vertederen /vərt<u>e</u>dərə(n)/ (vertederde, heeft vertederd) soften, move: *zij keek het kind vertederd aan* she gave the child a tender look

de **vertedering** /vərt<u>e</u>dərɪŋ/ **1** endearment, softening **2** tenderness

verteerbaar /vərt<u>e</u>rbar/ (adj) digestible; [fig also] palatable; acceptable: *licht* ~ *voedsel* light food

vertegenwoordigen /vərteɣə(n)-w<u>o</u>rdəɣə(n)/ (vertegenwoordigde, heeft vertegenwoordigd) represent

de **vertegenwoordiger** /vərteɣə(n)-w<u>o</u>rdəɣər/ (pl: -s) **1** representative **2** (sales) representative

de **vertegenwoordiging** /vərteɣə(n)-w<u>o</u>rdəɣɪŋ/ (pl: -en) **1** representation **2** delegation

vertekend /vərt<u>e</u>kənt/ (adj) distorted
vertekenen /vərt<u>e</u>kənə(n)/ (vertekende, heeft vertekend) distort

vertellen /vərt<u>ɛ</u>lə(n)/ (vertelde, heeft verteld) tell: *een mop* ~ crack a joke; *moet je mij* ~*!* you're telling me!; *dat wordt verteld* so they say; *zal ik je eens wat* ~*?* you know what?; let me tell you sth.; *wat vertel je me nou?* I can't believe it!; *je kunt me nog meer* ~ tell me another (one); *iets verder* ~ *aan anderen* pass sth. on to others; *vertel het maar niet verder* this is just between us

de **verteller** /vərt<u>ɛ</u>lər/ (pl: -s) narrator

de **vertelling** /vərt<u>ɛ</u>lɪŋ/ (pl: -en) story, tale

¹**verteren** /vərt<u>e</u>rə(n)/ (verteerde, heeft verteerd) be consumed (*or:* eaten away): *dat laken verteert door het vocht* that sheet is mouldering away with the damp; *door verdriet verteerd worden* be eaten up (*or:* eat one's heart out) with grief

²**verteren** /vərt<u>e</u>rə(n)/ (verteerde, heeft verteerd) digest: *niet te* ~ indigestible

verticaal /vɛrtik<u>a</u>l/ (adj, adv) vertical: *in verticale stand* in (an) upright position

het **vertier** /vərt<u>i</u>r/ entertainment, diversion

vertikken /vərt<u>ɪ</u>kə(n)/ (vertikte, heeft vertikt) refuse (flatly)

zich **vertillen** /vərt<u>ɪ</u>lə(n)/ (vertilde zich, heeft zich vertild) strain o.s. (in) lifting: [fig] *zich aan iets* ~ bite off more than one can chew

vertimmeren /vərt<u>ɪ</u>mərə(n)/ (vertimmerde, heeft vertimmerd) alter, renovate

vertoeven /vərt<u>u</u>və(n)/ (vertoefde, heeft vertoefd) sojourn, stay

vertolken /vərt<u>ɔ</u>lkə(n)/ (vertolkte, heeft vertolkt) **1** express, voice **2** play, interpret

de **vertolker** /vərt<u>ɔ</u>lkər/ (pl: -s) interpreter, performer; exponent, mouthpiece: *een* ~ *van het levenslied* a performer of the popular ballad

de **vertolking** /vərt<u>ɔ</u>lkɪŋ/ (pl: -en) interpreta-tion

¹**vertonen** /vərt<u>o</u>nə(n)/ (vertoonde, heeft vertoond) **1** show: *geen gelijkenis* ~ *met* bear no resemblance to; *tekenen* ~ *van* show signs of **2** show, present: *kunsten* ~ do tricks

zich ²**vertonen** /vərt<u>o</u>nə(n)/ (vertoonde zich, heeft zich vertoond) show one's face, turn up: *je kunt je zo niet* ~ *in het openbaar* you're not fit to be seen in public (like this); *ik durf me daar niet meer te* ~ I'm afraid to show my face there now

de **vertoning** /vərt<u>o</u>nɪŋ/ (pl: -en) **1** show(ing), presentation **2** show, production: *het was een grappige* ~ it was a curious spectacle

het **vertoon** /vərt<u>o</u>n/ showing, producing: *met veel* ~ with great ostentation, with a lot of showing off; *op* ~ *van een identiteitsbewijs* on presentation of an ID

vertragen /vərtr<u>a</u>ɣə(n)/ (vertraagde, heeft/is vertraagd) slow down; be delayed: *een vertraagde filmopname* a slow-motion film scene

de **vertraging** /vərtr<u>a</u>ɣɪŋ/ (pl: -en) delay: ~ *ondervinden* be delayed

vertrappen /vərtr<u>ɑ</u>pə(n)/ (vertrapte, heeft vertrapt) tread on, trample underfoot

het **vertrek** /vərtr<u>ɛ</u>k/ (pl: -ken) **1** departure; sailing: *bij zijn* ~ on his departure; *op het punt van* ~ *staan* be about to leave **2** room

de **vertrekhal** /vərtr<u>ɛ</u>khɑl/ (pl: -len) departure hall

¹**vertrekken** /vərtr<u>ɛ</u>kə(n)/ (vertrok, is vertrokken) leave: *wij* ~ *morgen naar Londen* we are off to (*or:* leave for) London tomorrow

²**vertrekken** /vərtr<u>ɛ</u>kə(n)/ (vertrok, heeft vertrokken) pull, distort: *zonder een spier te* ~ without batting an eyelid; *een van angst vertrokken gezicht* a face contorted (*or:* distorted, twisted) with fear

het **vertrekpunt** /vərtr<u>ɛ</u>kpʏnt/ (pl: -en) start-(ing point); point of departure

het **vertreksein** /vərtr<u>ɛ</u>ksɛin/ departure signal, green light

de **vertrektijd** /vərtr<u>ɛ</u>ktɛit/ (pl: -en) time of departure

¹**vertroebelen** /vərtr<u>u</u>bələ(n)/ (vertroebelde, is vertroebeld) become clouded

²**vertroebelen** /vərtr<u>u</u>bələ(n)/ (vertroebelde, heeft vertroebeld) cloud; obscure: *dat vertroebelt de zaak* that confuses (*or:* obscures) the issue

vertroetelen /vərtr<u>u</u>tələ(n)/ (vertroetelde, heeft vertroeteld) pamper

vertrouwd /vərtr<u>ɑu</u>t/ (adj) **1** reliable, trustworthy: *een* ~ *persoon* a trusted person **2** familiar (with): *zich* ~ *maken met die technieken* familiarize o.s. with those techniques

de **vertrouwdheid** /vərtr<u>ɑu</u>thɛit/ familiarity

vertrouwelijk /vərtr<u>ɑu</u>wələk/ (adj, adv) intimate, confidential: ~ *met iem. omgaan* be close to s.o.; ~ *met elkaar praten* have a heart-to-heart talk; *een ~e* **mededeling** a confidential communication

de **vertrouwelijkheid** /vərtrɑuwələkhɛit/ confidentiality

de **vertrouweling** /vərtrɑuwəlɪŋ/ (pl: -en) confidant(e)

het ¹**vertrouwen** /vərtrɑuwə(n)/ confidence, trust: *op* **goed** ~ on trust; *ik* **heb** *er weinig ~ in* I'm not very optimistic; *~* **hebben** *in de toekomst* have faith in the future; *~* **wekken** inspire confidence; *vol ~ zijn* be confident; *iem. in ~ nemen* take s.o. into one's confidence; *goed* **van** *~ zijn* be (too) trusting

²**vertrouwen** /vərtrɑuwə(n)/ (vertrouwde, heeft vertrouwd) trust: *hij* **is** *niet* **te** *~* he is not to be trusted; *ik vertrouw* **erop** *dat … I trust that …; op God ~* trust in God; *iem.* **voor** *geen cent ~* not trust s.o. an inch

de **vertrouwensarts** /vərtrɑuwə(n)sɑrts/ (pl: -en) doctor at an advice centre

de **vertrouwenskwestie** /vərtrɑuwə(n)skwɛsti/ (pl: -s) matter of confidence || *de ~* **stellen** ask for a vote of confidence

de **vertrouwenspersoon** /vərtrɑuwə(n)spɛrson/ (pl: -personen) confidential advisor

vertrouwenwekkend /vərtrɑuwə(n)wɛkənt/ (adj) inspiring confidence

vertwijfeld /vərtwɛifəlt/ (adj, adv) despairing: *~* **raken** (be driven to) despair

de **vertwijfeling** /vərtwɛifəlɪŋ/ (pl: -en) despair, desperation

veruit /vɛrœyt/ (adv) by far: *~ de* **beste** *zijn* by far and away the best

vervaardigen /vərvɑrdəɣə(n)/ (vervaardigde, heeft vervaardigd) make: *met de hand vervaardigd* made by hand; *deze tafel is* **van** *hout vervaardigd* this table is made of wood

de **vervaardiging** /vərvɑrdəχɪŋ/ manufacture, construction

vervaarlijk /vərvɑrlək/ (adj, adv) tremendous

¹**vervagen** /vərvaɣə(n)/ (vervaagde, is vervaagd) become faint (*or:* blurred); dim; fade (away)

²**vervagen** /vərvaɣə(n)/ (vervaagde, heeft vervaagd) blur, dim: *de tijd heeft die* **herinneringen** *vervaagd* time has dimmed those memories

het **verval** /vərvɑl/ **1** decline: *het ~ van de goede* **zeden** the deterioration of morals; *dit gebouw is flink* **in** *~ geraakt* this building has fallen into disrepair **2** fall

de **vervaldatum** /vərvɑldatʏm/ (pl: -data) expiry date

¹**vervallen** /vərvɑlə(n)/ (adj) **1** dilapidated **2** bedraggled

²**vervallen** /vərvɑlə(n)/ (verviel, is vervallen) **1** fall into disrepair **2** lapse: *in oude fouten ~* relapse into old errors; *tot armoede ~* be reduced to poverty **3** expire: *400* **arbeidsplaatsen** *komen te ~* 400 jobs are to go (*or:* disap-

pear); *die* **mogelijkheid** *vervalt* that possibility is no longer open; *de* **vergadering** *vervalt* the meeting has been cancelled

vervalsen /vərvɑlsə(n)/ (vervalste, heeft vervalst) **1** forge, counterfeit **2** tamper (with): *een* **cheque** *~* forge a cheque

de **vervalser** /vərvɑlsər/ (pl: -s) forger, counterfeiter

de **vervalsing** /vərvɑlsɪŋ/ (pl: -en) forgery, counterfeit

vervangen /vərvɑŋə(n)/ (verving, heeft vervangen) replace, take the place of, substitute: *niet* **te** *~* irreplaceable

de **vervanger** /vərvɑŋər/ (pl: -s) replacement, substitute: *de ~ van de* **minister** the substitute minister

de **vervanging** /vərvɑŋɪŋ/ (pl: -en) replacement, substitution

het **vervangingsinkomen** /vərvɑŋɪŋsɪŋkomə(n)/ (pl: -s) [Belg] payment, remittance

de **verve** /vɛrvə/ verve: *met veel ~* with a great deal of verve, with animation

verveeld /vərvelt/ (adj) bored, weary: [Belg] *~ zitten met iets* not know what to do about sth.; *~* **toekijken** watch indifferently

verveelvoudigen /vərvelvɑudəɣə(n)/ (verveelvoudigde, heeft verveelvoudigd) multiply

¹**vervelen** /vərvelə(n)/ (verveelde, heeft verveeld) bore, annoy: *tot ~s toe* ad nauseam, over and over again

zich ²**vervelen** /vərvelə(n)/ (verveelde zich, heeft zich verveeld) be(come) bored: *ik verveel me* **dood** I am bored stiff

vervelend /vərvelənt/ (adj, adv) **1** boring **2** annoying: *een ~* **karwei** a chore; *wat een ~e* **vent** what a tiresome fellow; *doe nu niet zo ~* don't be such a nuisance; *wat ~!* what a nuisance!

de **verveling** /vərvelɪŋ/ boredom: *louter* **uit** *~* out of pure boredom

vervellen /vərvɛlə(n)/ (vervelde, is verveld) peel

verven /vɛrvə(n)/ (verfde, heeft geverfd) **1** paint **2** dye

verversen /vərvɛrsə(n)/ (ververste, heeft ververst) **1** refresh **2** change, freshen

de **verversing** /vərvɛrsɪŋ/ (pl: -en) replacement

¹**vervlaamsen** /vərvlamsə(n)/ (vervlaamste, is vervlaamst) become Flemish

²**vervlaamsen** /vərvlamsə(n)/ (vervlaamste, heeft vervlaamst) make Flemish

vervliegen /vərvliɣə(n)/ (vervloog, is vervlogen) **1** fly **2** evaporate

vervloeken /vərvlukə(n)/ (vervloekte, heeft vervloekt) curse: *hij zal die* **dag** *~!* he will rue the day!

vervoegen /vərvuɣə(n)/ (vervoegde, heeft vervoegd) inflect || *zich ~* **bij** apply at

de **vervoeging** /vərvuɣɪŋ/ (pl: -en) conjuga-

tion

het **vervoer** /vərvur/ transport, transportation: *met het* **openbaar** ~ by public transport; *tijdens het* ~ *beschadigde goederen* goods damaged in transit

het **vervoerbedrijf** /vərvurbədrɛif/ (pl: -bedrijven) [goods] haulier; haulage firm; passenger transport company: *gemeentelijk* ~ municipal (*or:* city) transport company

de **vervoerder** /vərvurdər/ (pl: -s) transporter, carry

vervoeren /vərvurə(n)/ (vervoerde, heeft vervoerd) transport

de **vervoering** /vərvurɪŋ/ (pl: -en): *in* ~ *raken* be transported, be carried away (by)

het **vervoermiddel** /vərvurmɪdəl/ (pl: -en) (means of) transport: *openbare* ~*en* public service vehicles

het **vervolg** /vərvɔlx/ (pl: -en) **1** future **2** continuation (of), sequel (to) **3** continuation: ~ *op blz. 10* continued on page 10

vervolgen /vərvɔlɣə(n)/ (vervolgde, heeft vervolgd) **1** continue: *wordt vervolgd* to be continued **2** pursue; persecute **3** [law] sue; prosecute: *iem.* **gerechtelijk** ~ take legal action against s.o.

vervolgens /vərvɔlɣəns/ (adv) then: ~ *zei hij … he went on to say …*

de **vervolging** /vərvɔlɣɪŋ/ (pl: -en) **1** persecution **2** [law] legal action (*or:* proceedings), prosecution: *tot* ~ *overgaan* (decide to) prosecute

het **vervolgonderwijs** /vərvɔlxɔndərwɛis/ secondary education

de **vervolgopleiding** /vərvɔlxɔplɛidɪŋ/ (pl: -en) continuation course; [Am] continuing education (course); advanced training

het **vervolgverhaal** /vərvɔlxfərhal/ (pl: -verhalen) serial (story)

vervolmaken /vərvɔlmakə(n)/ (vervolmaakte, heeft vervolmaakt) (make) perfect

vervormen /vərvɔrmə(n)/ (vervormde, heeft vervormd) **1** transform; deform; disfigure **2** distort: *geluid vervormd* **weergeven** distort a sound

de **vervorming** /vərvɔrmɪŋ/ (pl: -en) transformation; disfiguring; deforming

¹**vervreemden** /vərvremdə(n)/ (vervreemdde, is vervreemd) become estranged (*or:* alienated): *van zijn werk vervreemd* **raken** lose touch with one's work; *van elkaar* ~ drift apart

²**vervreemden** /vərvremdə(n)/ (vervreemdde, heeft vervreemd) alienate, estrange: *zich* ~ *van* alienate o.s. from

de **vervreemding** /vərvremdɪŋ/ (pl: -en) alienation, estrangement

vervroegen /vərvruɣə(n)/ (vervroegde, heeft vervroegd) advance, (move) forward: *vervroegde* **uittreding** early retirement

vervuilen /vərvœylə(n)/ (vervuilde, heeft vervuild) pollute, make filthy, contaminate

de **vervuiler** /vərvœylər/ (pl: -s) polluter, contaminator: *de* ~ **betaalt** the polluter pays

de **vervuiling** /vərvœylɪŋ/ pollution, contamination: *de* ~ *van het* **milieu** environmental pollution

vervullen /vərvylə(n)/ (vervulde, heeft vervuld) **1** fill: *dat vervult ons* **met** *zorg* that fills us with concern; *van iets vervuld zijn* be full of sth. **2** fulfil; perform: *tijdens* **het** ~ *van zijn plicht* in the discharge of his duty **3** fulfil, realize: *iemands* **wensen** ~ comply with s.o.'s wishes

de **vervulling** /vərvylɪŋ/ fulfilment; discharge; realization: *een droom ging* **in** ~ a dream came true

verwaaid /vərwajt/ (adj) windblown

verwaand /vərwant/ (adj, adv) conceited, stuck-up

de **verwaandheid** /vərwanthɛit/ conceit(edness), arrogance: *naast zijn schoenen lopen van* ~ be too big for one's boots

verwaardigen /vərwardəɣə(n)/ (verwaardigde zich, heeft zich verwaardigd) condescend

verwaarloosbaar /vərwarlozbar/ (adj) negligible

verwaarloosd /vərwarlost/ (adj) neglected

verwaarlozen /vərwarlozə(n)/ (verwaarloosde, heeft verwaarloosd) neglect

de **verwaarlozing** /vərwarlozɪŋ/ neglect; negligence

verwachten /vərwaxtə(n)/ (verwachtte, heeft verwacht) **1** expect: *daar moet je ook niet* **alles** *van* ~ don't set your hopes too high; *lang verwacht* long-awaited; *dat had ik* **wel** *verwacht* that was just what I had expected **2** expect, be expecting: *ze verwacht een* **baby** she is expecting (a baby), she is in the family way

de **verwachting** /vərwaxtɪŋ/ (pl: -en) **1** anticipation: *in* ~ *zijn* be expecting, be an expectant mother **2** expectation; outlook: *de* ~*en waren* **hoog gespannen** expectations ran high; *het overtrof haar* **stoutste** ~*en* it surpassed her wildest expectations; ~*en* **wekken** arouse (one's) hopes; **beneden** *de* ~*en blijven* fall short of expectations, disappoint; *aan de* ~ *beantwoorden* come up to one's expectations

de ¹**verwant** /vərwant/ (pl: -en) relative, relation

²**verwant** /vərwant/ (adj) **1** related (to) **2** kindred: *daar* **voel** *ik* **me** *niet mee* ~ I feel no affinity for (*or:* with) that

de **verwantschap** /vərwantsxɑp/ (pl: -pen) relationship, affinity, connection

verward /vərwɑrt/ (adj, adv) **1** confused; (en)tangled **2** confused, muddled, incoherent

verwarmen /vərwɑrmə(n)/ (verwarmde,

heeft verwarmd) warm, heat: *de **kamer** was niet verwarmd* the room was unheated; *een glas hete **melk** zal je wat* ~ a glass of hot milk will warm you up

de **verwarming** /vərwɑrmɪŋ/ (pl: -en) heating (system): ***centrale*** ~ *aanleggen* put in central heating; *de* ~ *hoger* (or: *lager*) *zetten* turn the heat up (or: down)

de **verwarmingsinstallatie** /vərwɑrmɪŋs-ɪnstɑla(t)si/ (pl: -s) heating system

de **verwarmingsketel** /vərwɑrmɪŋsketəl/ (pl: -s) (central heating) boiler

verwarren /vərwɑrə(n)/ (verwarde, heeft verward) **1** tangle (up), confuse: *~d **werken*** lead to confusion **2** (+ met) confuse, mistake: *u verwart hem **met** zijn broer* you mistake him for his brother; *niet **te** ~ **met*** not to be confused with

de **verwarring** /vərwɑrɪŋ/ (pl: -en) entanglement, confusion; muddle: *er **ontstond** enige* ~ *over zijn identiteit* some confusion arose concerning (or: as to) his identity; ~ *stichten* cause confusion; *in* ~ *raken* become confused

verwateren /vərwatərə(n)/ (verwaterde, is verwaterd) become diluted (or: watered down), peter out: *de **vriendschap** tussen hen is verwaterd* their friendship has cooled off

verwedden /vərwɛdə(n)/ (verwedde, heeft verwed) bet: *ik wil er **alles** om* ~ *dat …* I'll bet you anything that …

het **verweer** /vərwer/ (pl: verweren) defence

verweerd /vərwert/ (adj) weather-beaten

het **verweerschrift** /vərwersxrɪft/ (pl: -en) (written) defence; pleading

verwekken /vərwɛkə(n)/ (verwekte, heeft verwekt) beget, father: ***kinderen*** ~ beget (or: father) children

de **verwekker** /vərwɛkər/ (pl: -s) begetter, father: *de* ~ *van het **kind*** the child's natural father

verwelken /vərwɛlkə(n)/ (verwelkte, is verwelkt) **1** wilt, wither **2** [fig] fade: *~de **schoonheid*** fading beauty

verwelkomen /vərwɛlkomə(n)/ (verwelkomde, heeft verwelkomd) welcome, greet; salute: *iem. **hartelijk** ~* give s.o. a hearty welcome

verwend /vərwɛnt/ (adj) **1** spoilt, pampered: *zij is een ~ **kreng*** she is a spoilt brat **2** discriminating: *een ~ **publiek*** a discriminating public (or: audience)

verwennen /vərwɛnə(n)/ (verwende, heeft verwend) spoil, indulge: ***zichzelf** ~* indulge (or: pamper) o.s.

verwensen /vərwɛnsə(n)/ (verwenste, heeft verwenst) curse

de **verwensing** /vərwɛnsɪŋ/ (pl: -en) curse

¹**verweren** /vərwerə(n)/ (verweerde, is verweerd) weather; erode; become weather-beaten

zich ²**verweren** /vərwerə(n)/ (verweerde zich,

heeft zich verweerd) defend o.s.; put up a fight: *voor hij zich **kon** ~ before* he could defend himself

verwerkelijken /vərwɛrkələkə(n)/ (verwerkelijkte, heeft verwerkelijkt) realize: *een **droom** (or: **wens**) ~* make a dream (or: wish) come true

verwerken /vərwɛrkə(n)/ (verwerkte, heeft verwerkt) **1** process, handle, convert: *zijn **maag** kon het niet ~* his stomach couldn't digest it; *huisvuil **tot** compost ~* convert household waste into compost **2** incorporate: *de nieuwste **gegevens** zijn erin verwerkt* the latest data are incorporated (in it) **3** cope with: *ze heeft haar **verdriet** nooit echt goed verwerkt* she has never really come to terms with her sorrow **4** absorb, cope with: *stadscentra kunnen zoveel **verkeer** niet ~* city centres cannot absorb so much traffic

de **verwerking** /vərwɛrkɪŋ/ processing, handling, assimilation, incorporation: *bij de* ~ *van deze gegevens* in processing (or: handling) these data

verwerpelijk /vərwɛrpələk/ (adj) reprehensible, objectionable

verwerpen /vərwɛrpə(n)/ (verwierp, heeft verworpen) reject, vote down, turn down

verwerven /vərwɛrvə(n)/ (verwierf, heeft verworven) obtain, acquire; achieve

de **verwerving** /vərwɛrvɪŋ/ acquisition, obtaining

verweven /vərwevə(n)/ (inter)weave: *hun belangen zijn **nauw** ~* their interests are closely knit; *met elkaar ~ zijn* be interwoven

verwezenlijken /vərwezə(n)ləkə(n)/ (verwezenlijkte, heeft verwezenlijkt) realize; fulfil; achieve: ***plannen*** (or: ***voornemens***) ~ realize one's plans (or: intentions)

de **verwezenlijking** /vərwezə(n)ləkɪŋ/ realization, fulfilment

verwijderd /vərwɛidərt/ (adj) remote, distant: *(steeds verder) van elkaar ~ **raken*** drift (further and further) apart; *een kilometer **van** het dorp ~* a kilometre out of the village

verwijderen /vərwɛidərə(n)/ (verwijderde, heeft verwijderd) remove: *iem. **uit** zijn huis ~* evict s.o.; *iem. **van** het veld ~* send s.o. off (the field)

de **verwijdering** /vərwɛidərɪŋ/ (pl: -en) **1** removal: ~ *van school* expulsion from school **2** estrangement: *er **ontstond** een ~ tussen hen* they drifted apart

verwijfd /vərwɛift/ (adj) effeminate, sissy

het **verwijsbriefje** /vərwɛizbrifjə/ (pl: -s) (doctor's) referral (letter)

het **verwijt** /vərwɛit/ (pl: -en) reproach, blame: *elkaar ~en **maken*** blame one another; *iem. ~en **maken*** reproach s.o.

verwijten /vərwɛitə(n)/ (verweet, heeft verweten) reproach, blame: *iem. iets ~* reproach s.o. with sth., blame s.o. for sth.

verwijtend /vərwɛitənt/ (adj, adv) reproachful: *iem.* ~ *aankijken* look at s.o. reproachfully

verwijzen /vərwɛizə(n)/ (verwees, heeft verwezen) refer: *een patiënt naar een specialist* ~ refer a patient to a specialist

de **verwijzing** /vərwɛizɪŋ/ (pl: -en) reference; referral

verwikkelen /vərwɪkələ(n)/ (verwikkelde, heeft verwikkeld) involve, implicate, mix up

de **verwikkeling** /vərwɪkəlɪŋ/ (pl: -en) complication

verwilderd /vərwɪldərt/ (adj) **1** wild, neglected: *een ~e boomgaard* a neglected (*or:* an overgrown) orchard **2** wild, unkempt, dishevelled **3** wild, mad: *er ~ uitzien* look wild (*or:* haggard)

verwisselbaar /vərwɪsəlbar/ (adj) exchangeable, convertible: *onderling ~* interchangeable

verwisselen /vərwɪsələ(n)/ (verwisselde, heeft verwisseld) **1** (ex)change, swap **2** mistake, confuse: *ik had u met uw broer verwisseld* I had mistaken you for your brother

de **verwisseling** /vərwɪsəlɪŋ/ (pl: -en) (ex)change, interchange, swap

verwittigen /vərwɪtəɣə(n)/ (verwittigde, heeft verwittigd) inform, advise, notify

verwoed /vərwut/ (adj, adv) passionate, ardent, impassioned: *~e pogingen doen* make frantic efforts

verwoest /vərwust/ (adj) destroyed, devastated, ravaged

verwoesten /vərwustə(n)/ (verwoestte, heeft verwoest) destroy, devastate, lay waste

verwoestend /vərwustənt/ (adj, adv) devastating, destructive

de **verwoestijning** /vərwustɛinɪŋ/ desertification

de **verwoesting** /vərwustɪŋ/ (pl: -en) devastation; ravages; destruction

verwonden /vərwɔndə(n)/ (verwondde, heeft verwond) wound; injure

verwonderd /vərwɔndərt/ (adj) surprised; [stronger] amazed; astonished

verwonderen /vərwɔndərə(n)/ (verwonderde, heeft verwonderd) amaze, astonish

de **verwondering** /vərwɔndərɪŋ/ surprise; [stronger] amazement; astonishment: *het hoeft geen ~ te wekken dat ...* it comes as no surprise that ...

verwonderlijk /vərwɔndərlək/ (adj) surprising

de **verwonding** /vərwɔndɪŋ/ (pl: -en) injury; wounding; wound: *~en oplopen* sustain injuries, be injured

verwoorden /vərwɔrdə(n)/ (verwoordde, heeft verwoord) put (in(to) words), express

verworden /vərwɔrdə(n)/ (verwerd, is verworden) degenerate, deteriorate

de **verworvenheid** /vərwɔrvənhɛit/ (pl: -heden) attainment, achievement

verwringen /vərwrɪŋə(n)/ twist; distort; contort: *een van pijn verwrongen gezicht* a face contorted with pain

verzachten /vərzɑxtə(n)/ (verzachtte, heeft verzacht) soften; ease: *pijn ~* relieve (*or:* alleviate) pain

verzachtend /vərzɑxtənt/ (adj) mitigating, extenuating

verzadigd /vərzadəxt/ (adj) **1** satisfied, full (up) **2** saturated: *een ~e arbeidsmarkt* a saturated labour market

verzadigen /vərzadəɣə(n)/ (verzadigde, heeft verzadigd) saturate

de **verzadiging** /vərzadəɣɪŋ/ satisfaction, saturation

het **verzadigingspunt** /vərzadəɣɪŋspʏnt/ saturation point

verzaken /vərzakə(n)/ (verzaakte, heeft verzaakt) **1** fail: *zijn plicht ~* neglect one's duty, fail in one's duty **2** revoke: *ze heeft verzaakt!* she revoked!

verzakken /vərzɑkə(n)/ (verzakte, is verzakt) subside; settle; sink; sag: *de grond verzakt* the ground has subsided (*or:* is subsiding)

de **verzakking** /vərzɑkɪŋ/ (pl: -en) subsidence, collapse

de **verzamelaar** /vərzamələr/ (pl: -s) collector

de **verzamel-cd** /vərzaməlsede/ compilation CD

¹**verzamelen** /vərzamələ(n)/ (verzamelde, heeft verzameld) gather (together), assemble; meet: *zich ~* gather, assemble; congregate; *we verzamelden (ons) op het plein* we assembled (*or:* met) in the square

²**verzamelen** /vərzamələ(n)/ (verzamelde, heeft verzameld) **1** collect; gather; compile: *krachten ~* summon up (one's) strength; *de verzamelde werken van ...* the collected works of ... **2** collect, save

de **verzameling** /vərzamələɪŋ/ (pl: -en) **1** collection; gathering; assembly; compilation: *een bonte ~ aanhangers* a motley collection of followers; *een ~ aanleggen* build up (*or:* put together) a collection **2** [maths] set

de **verzamelnaam** /vərzaməlnam/ (pl: -namen) collective term, generic term, umbrella term

de **verzamelplaats** /vərzaməlplats/ (pl: -en) meeting place (*or:* point); assembly point

de **verzamelstaat** /vərzaməlstat/ (pl: -staten) summary (list, table)

de **verzamelwoede** /vərzaməlwudə/ mania for collecting things

verzanden /vərzɑndə(n)/ (verzandde, is verzand) get bogged down

verzegelen /vərzeɣələ(n)/ (verzegelde, heeft verzegeld) seal, put (*or:* set) a seal on: *een woning ~* put a house under seal

555 **verzorgen**

de **verzegeling** /vərzeɣəlɪŋ/ (pl: -en) sealing, seal: *een ~ aanbrengen* (or: *verbreken*) affix (or: break) a seal
verzeild /vərzɛilt/ (adj): *hoe kom jij hier ~?* what brings you here?; *in moeilijkheden ~ raken* run into (or: hit) trouble, run into difficulties
de **verzekeraar** /vərzekərar/ (pl: -s) insurer; assurer
verzekerd /vərzekərt/ (adj) **1** assured (of), confident (of): *succes ~!* success guaranteed!; *u kunt ervan ~ zijn dat* you may rest assured that **2** insured: *het ~e bedrag* the sum insured
de **verzekerde** /vərzekərdə/ (pl: -n) policyholder; insured party
verzekeren /vərzekərə(n)/ (verzekerde, heeft verzekerd) **1** ensure; assure: *iem. van iets ~* assure s.o. of sth. **2** guarantee, assure **3** insure; assure: *zich ~ (tegen)* insure o.s. (against)
de **verzekering** /vərzekərɪŋ/ (pl: -en) **1** assurance, guarantee: *ik kan u de ~ geven, dat ...* I can give you an assurance that ... **2** insurance; assurance: *sociale ~* national insurance, social security; *een ~ aangaan (afsluiten)* take out insurance (or: an insurance policy) **3** insurance company, assurance company
de **verzekeringsagent** /vərzekərɪŋsaɣɛnt/ (pl: -en) insurance agent
de **verzekeringsmaatschappij** /vərzekərɪŋsmatsxɑpɛi/ (pl: -en) insurance company, assurance company
de **verzekeringspolis** /vərzekərɪŋspolɪs/ (pl: -sen) insurance policy
de **verzekeringspremie** /vərzekərɪŋspremi/ (pl: -s) insurance premium
de **verzekeringsvoorwaarden** (pl) policy conditions
verzelfstandigen /vərzɛlfstɑndəɣə(n)/ (verzelfstandigde, heeft verzelfstandigd) make independent; privatize
verzenden /vərzɛndə(n)/ (verzond, heeft verzonden) send, mail, dispatch; [goods] ship: *per schip ~* ship
de **verzender** /vərzɛndər/ (pl: -s) sender, shipper, consignor
de **verzending** /vərzɛndɪŋ/ (pl: -en) dispatch, mailing, shipping, forwarding
de **verzendkosten** /vərzɛntkɔstə(n)/ (pl) shipping (or: mailing, postage) costs
verzengen /vərzɛŋə(n)/ (verzengde, heeft/is verzengd) scorch: *een ~de hitte* a blistering heat
het **verzet** /vərzɛt/ resistance: *in ~ komen (tegen)* offer resistance (to)
het **verzetje** /vərzɛcə/ (pl: -s) diversion, distraction: *hij heeft een ~ nodig* he needs a bit of variety (or: a break)
de **verzetsbeweging** /vərzɛtsbəweɣɪŋ/ (pl: -en) resistance (movement), underground

de **verzetsstrijder** /vərzɛtstrɛidər/ (pl: -s) resistance fighter, member of the resistance (or: underground)
¹**verzetten** /vərzɛtə(n)/ (verzette, heeft verzet) move (around), shift: *een vergadering ~* put off (or: reschedule) a meeting; *heel wat werk ~* be able to take on (or: do, shift) a lot of work
zich ²**verzetten** /vərzɛtə(n)/ (verzette zich, heeft zich verzet) resist, offer resistance (or: opposition)
verzieken /vərzikə(n)/ (verziekte, heeft verziekt) spoil, ruin: *de sfeer ~* spoil the atmosphere
verziend /vɛrzint/ (adj) long-sighted
de **verziendheid** /vɛrzinthɛit/ long-sightedness
de **verzilting** /vərzɪltɪŋ/ salinization, salinity
verzilveren /vərzɪlvərə(n)/ (verzilverde, heeft verzilverd) **1** (plate with) silver, silverplate: *verzilverde lepels* plate(d) spoons **2** cash, convert into (or: redeem for) cash
verzinken /vərzɪŋkə(n)/ (verzonk, is verzonken) sink (down, away), submerge: *in gedachten verzonken zijn* be lost (or: deep) in thought
verzinnen /vərzɪnə(n)/ (verzon, heeft verzonnen) invent, think/make (or: dream, cook) up, devise: *een smoesje ~* think up (or: cook up) an excuse
het **verzinsel** /vərzɪnsəl/ (pl: -s) fabrication, invention, figment of one's imagination
het **verzoek** /vərzuk/ (pl: -en) **1** request, appeal, petition: *dringend ~* urgent request, entreaty; *aan een ~ voldoen* comply with a request; *op ~ van mijn broer* at my brother's request **2** petition, appeal: *een ~ indienen* petition, appeal, make a petition (or: an appeal)
verzoeken /vərzukə(n)/ (verzocht, heeft verzocht) request; petition; ask, beg: *mag ik om stilte ~* silence please, may I have a moment's silence
de **verzoeking** /vərzukɪŋ/ (pl: -en) temptation
het **verzoeknummer** /vərzuknʏmər/ (pl: -s) request
het **verzoekschrift** /vərzuksxrɪft/ (pl: -en) petition, appeal
verzoenen /vərzunə(n)/ (verzoende, heeft verzoend) reconcile, appease: *zich met iem. ~* become reconciled with s.o.
verzoenend /vərzunənt/ (adj, adv) conciliatory, expiatory
de **verzoening** /vərzunɪŋ/ (pl: -en) reconciliation
verzorgd /vərzɔrxt/ (adj) well cared-for, carefully kept (or: tended): *een goed ~ gazon* a well-tended lawn; *er ~ uitzien* be well dressed (or: groomed)
verzorgen /vərzɔrɣə(n)/ (verzorgde, heeft verzorgd) look after, (at)tend to, care for: *tot*

in de puntjes verzorgd taken care of down to the last detail

de **verzorgende** /vərz<u>o</u>rɣəndə/ care giver, carer

de **verzorger** /vərz<u>o</u>rɣər/ (pl: -s) attendant, caretaker: *ouders, voogden of ~s* parents or guardians

de **verzorging** /vərz<u>o</u>rɣɪŋ/ care, maintenance, nursing: *medische ~* medical care

de **verzorgingsflat** /vərz<u>o</u>rɣɪŋsflɛt/ (pl: -s) warden-assisted flat; [Am] retirement home with nursing care

de **verzorgingsstaat** /vərz<u>o</u>rɣɪŋstat/ welfare state

het **verzorgingstehuis** /vərz<u>o</u>rɣɪŋstəhœys/ (pl: -tehuizen) home; home for the elderly; old people's home, rest home

verzot /vərz<u>o</u>t/ (adj) crazy (about), mad (about, for): *ik ben ~ op kersen* I love cherries, I adore cherries

verzuchten /vərz<u>y</u>xtə(n)/ (verzuchtte, heeft verzucht) sigh

het **verzuim** /vərz<u>œy</u>m/ (pl: -en) omission; non-attendance; absence: *~ wegens ziekte* absence due to illness

verzuimen /vərz<u>œy</u>mə(n)/ (verzuimde, heeft verzuimd) be absent, fail to attend: *een les ~* cut (*or:* skip) (a) class

verzuipen /vərz<u>œy</u>pə(n)/ (verzoop, is verzopen) [inform] **1** drown, be drowned **2** be flooded

verzuren /vərz<u>y</u>rə(n)/ (verzuurde, is verzuurd) sour, turn sour, go sour; go off; acidify: *verzuurde grond* acid soil

verzwakken /vərzw<u>a</u>kə(n)/ (verzwakte, heeft/is verzwakt) weaken, grow weak; enfeeble; impair

verzwaren /vərzw<u>a</u>rə(n)/ (verzwaarde, heeft verzwaard) make heavier; [fig also] increase; strengthen: *de dijken ~* strengthen the dykes; *exameneisen ~* make an examination stiffer

verzwarend /vərzw<u>a</u>rənt/ (adj) aggravating

verzwelgen /vərzw<u>ɛ</u>lɣə(n)/ (verzwolg/verzwelgde, heeft verzwolgen) devour; engulf

verzwijgen /vərzw<u>ɛi</u>ɣə(n)/ (verzweeg, heeft verzwegen) keep silent about; withhold; suppress; conceal: *iets voor iem. ~* keep (*or:* conceal) sth. from s.o.; *een schandaal ~* hush up a scandal

verzwikken /vərzw<u>ɪ</u>kə(n)/ (verzwikte, heeft verzwikt) sprain, twist: *zijn enkel ~* sprain one's ankle

het **vest** /vɛst/ (pl: -en) waistcoat, vest; cardigan: *een pak met ~* a three-piece suit

de **vestiaire** /vɛstij<u>ɛː</u>rə/ (pl: -s) cloakroom

de **vestibule** /vɛstib<u>y</u>lə/ (pl: -s) hall(way), entrance hall, vestibule

¹vestigen /vɛstəɣə(n)/ (vestigde, heeft gevestigd) direct, focus: *ik heb mijn hoop op jou*

gevestigd I'm putting (all) my hopes in you

zich **²vestigen** /vɛstəɣə(n)/ (vestigde zich, heeft zich gevestigd) settle: *zich ergens ~* establish o.s., settle somewhere

de **vestiging** /vɛstəɣɪŋ/ (pl: -en) branch, office; outlet

de **vestigingsplaats** /vɛstəɣɪŋsplats/ (pl: -en) place of business, registered office, seat; [pers] place of residence

de **vesting** /vɛstɪŋ/ (pl: -en) fortress, fort, stronghold

het **vestingwerk** /vɛstɪŋwɛrk/ (pl: -en) fortification

de **vestzak** /vɛ(st)sɑk/ (pl: -ken) waistcoat pocket, watch pocket: [fig] *dat is vestzak-broekzak* that's just a shifting of funds

het **¹vet** /vɛt/ (pl: -ten) fat; oil; grease; dripping; lard: *iets in het ~ zetten* grease sth.

²vet /vɛt/ (adj, adv) **1** fat; rich; creamy **2** fatty, greasy, rich **3** fat; plum(my): *een ~te buit* rich spoils **4** greasy, oily: *een ~te huid* a greasy (*or:* an oily) skin **5** bold: *~te letters* bold (*or:* heavy) type, boldface; *~ gedrukt* in bold (*or:* heavy) type || *~ saai* really boring, mega boring

vetarm /vɛtɑrm/ (adj) low-fat

de **vete** /v<u>e</u>tə/ (pl: -s) feud, vendetta

de **veter** /v<u>e</u>tər/ (pl: -s) lace: *zijn ~s vastmaken (strikken)* do up (*or:* tie) one's shoelaces; *je ~ zit los!* your shoelace is undone!

de **veteraan** /vetər<u>a</u>n/ (pl: veteranen) veteran

de **veteranenziekte** /vetər<u>a</u>nə(n)ziktə/ Legionnaire's disease

de **¹veterinair** /vetərinɛ<u>ː</u>r/ (pl: -s) veterinary surgeon

²veterinair /vetərinɛ<u>ː</u>r/ (adj) veterinary

het **vetgehalte** /vɛtxəhɑltə/ (pl: -s, -n) fat content, percentage of fat

de **vetkuif** /vɛtkœyf/ (pl: vetkuiven) greased quiff

vetmesten /vɛtmɛstə(n)/ (mestte vet, heeft vetgemest) fatten (up), feed up

het **veto** /v<u>e</u>to/ (pl: -'s) veto: *het recht van ~ hebben* have the right (*or:* power) of veto; *zijn ~ over iets uitspreken* veto sth., exercise one's veto against sth.

het **vetoogje** /v<u>e</u>toxjə/ (pl: -s) drop of fat, fat globule

het **vetorecht** /v<u>e</u>torɛxt/ veto

de **vetplant** /vɛtplɑnt/ (pl: -en) succulent

de **vetpot** /vɛtpot/: *dat is geen ~* you won't exactly make a fortune

de **vetrol** /vɛtrol/ (pl: -len) roll of fat; spare tyre

vettig /vɛtəx/ (adj, adv) **1** fatty; greasy: *een ~e glans* an oily sheen **2** greasy; oily

de **vetvlek** /vɛtflɛk/ (pl: -ken) grease stain, greasy spot (*or:* mark): *vol ~ken* grease-stained

vetvrij /vɛtfr<u>ɛi</u>/ (adj) **1** greaseproof: *~ papier* greaseproof paper **2** fat-free, non-fat

de **vetzak** /vɛtsɑk/ (pl: -ken) fatso, fatty

de **vetzucht** /vɛtsʏχt/ fatty degeneration, (morbid) obesity

het **vetzuur** /vɛtsyr/ (pl: -zuren) fatty acid

het **veulen** /vø̜lə(n)/ (pl: -s) foal; colt; filly

de **vezel** /ve̯zəl/ (pl: -s) fibre; thread; filament

vezelrijk /ve̯zəlrɛik/ (adj) high-fibre

vgl. (abbrev) *vergelijk* cf., cp.

de **V-hals** /ve̯hɑls/ (pl: V-halzen) V-neck

via /vi̯ja/ (prep) via, by way of, by, through; by means of: ~ *de snelweg komen* take the motorway; [Am] take the expressway; *ik hoorde ~ mijn zuster, dat …* I heard from (*or:* through) my sister that …; *iets ~ ~ horen* learn (*or:* hear) of sth. in a roundabout way, hear sth. on the grapevine

het **viaduct** /vijadʏkt/ (pl: -en) viaduct, flyover, crossover; [Am] overpass

de **viagra** /vija̯gra/ viagra

de **vibrafoon** /vibrafo̯n/ (pl: -s) vibraphone, vibes

de **vibratie** /vibra̯(t)si/ (pl: -s) vibration

de **vibrator** /vibra̯tor/ (pl: -s) vibrator

vibreren /vibre̯rə(n)/ (vibreerde, heeft gevibreerd) vibrate

de **vicaris** /vika̯rəs/ (pl: -sen) vicar

de **vicepremier** /vi̯səprəmje/ vice-premier

de **vicepresident** /vi̯səprezidɛnt/ vice-president; vice-chairman

vice versa /visəvɛ̯rza/ (adv) vice versa

de **vicevoorzitter** /vi̯səvorzɪtər/ vice-chairman, deputy chairman

vicieus /visi̯jøs/ (adj) vicious

victoriaans /vɪktorijans/ (adj) Victorian

de **victorie** /vɪkto̯ri/ (pl: -s) victory: *~ kraaien* shout victory

de **video** /vi̯dejo/ (pl: -'s) video (tape, recorder): *iets op ~ zetten* record sth. on video

de **videoband** /vi̯dejobɑnt/ (pl: -en) videotape

de **videobewaking** /vi̯dejobəwakɪŋ/ closed circuit TV

de **videocamera** /vi̯dejokaməra/ (pl: -'s) video camera

de **videocassette** /vi̯dejokasɛtə/ (pl: -s) video cassette

de **videoclip** /vi̯dejoklɪp/ (pl: -s) videoclip

de **videofilm** /vi̯dejofɪlm/ (pl: -s) video (film, recording)

de **videojockey** /vi̯dejodʒɔki/ (pl: -s) video-jockey

de **videorecorder** /vi̯dejorikɔːrdər/ (pl: -s) video (recorder), VCR, video cassette recorder

het **videospel** /vi̯dejospɛl/ (pl: -en) video game

de **videotheek** /vi̯dejote̯k/ (pl: videotheken) video shop

vief /vif/ (adj, adv) lively, energetic

vier /vir/ (num) four; [in dates] fourth: *~ mei* the fourth of May; *een gesprek onder ~ ogen* a private conversation, a tête-à-tête; *zo zeker als tweemaal twee ~ is* as sure as I'm standing here; *half ~* half past three; *ze waren met z'n ~en* there were four of them; *hij kreeg een ~*

voor wiskunde he got four out of ten for maths

de **vierbaansweg** /vi̯rbanswɛχ/ (pl: -en) four-lane motorway; dual carriageway; [Am] divided highway

vierde /vi̯rdə/ (num) fourth: *de ~ klas* the fourth form; [Am] The fourth grade; *ten ~* fourthly, in the fourth place; *het is vandaag de ~* today is the fourth; *drie ~* three fourths, three-quarters; *als ~ eindigen* come in fourth

vierdelig /virde̯ləχ/ (adj) four-part; four-piece

vieren /vi̯rə(n)/ (vierde, heeft gevierd) 1 celebrate; observe; commemorate: *dat gaan we ~* this calls for a celebration 2 pay out, slacken: *een touw (laten) ~* pay out a rope

de **vierhoek** /vi̯rhuk/ (pl: -en) quadrangle, rectangle, square

de **viering** /vi̯rɪŋ/ (pl: -en) celebration; observance; commemoration; [rel] service: *ter ~ van* in celebration of

vierjarig /virja̯rəχ/ (adj) four-year-old; four-year(s'); four-yearly

het ¹**vierkant** /vi̯rkɑnt/ (pl: -en) square; quadrangle

²**vierkant** /vi̯rkɑnt/ (adj) square: *de kamer meet drie meter in het ~* the room is three metres square, the room is three by three (metres) ‖ *iem. ~ uitlachen* laugh at s.o. outright

de **vierkwartsmaat** /vi̯rkwartsmat/ (pl: -maten) four-four time, quadruple time, common time (*or:* measure)

de **vierling** /vi̯rlɪŋ/ (pl: -en) quadruplets, quads

viermaal /vi̯rmal/ (adv) four times

het **vierspan** /vi̯rspɑn/ (pl: -nen) four-in-hand

de **viersprong** /vi̯rsprɔŋ/ (pl: -en) crossroads

het **viertal** /vi̯rtɑl/ (pl: -len) (set of) four; foursome

het **vieruurtje** /viryrcə/ (pl: -s) [Belg] tea break, mid-afternoon snack

de **viervoeter** /vi̯rvutər/ (pl: -s) quadruped, four-footed animal

het **viervoud** /vi̯rvɑut/ (pl: -en) quadruple

de **vierwielaandrijving** /vi̯rwilandrɛivɪŋ/ four-wheel drive

vies /vis/ (adj, adv) 1 dirty, filthy 2 nasty, foul: *een ~ drankje* a nasty (*or:* vile) mixture ‖ *bij een ~ zaakje betrokken zijn* be involved in dirty (*or:* funny) business; *ergens niet ~ van zijn* not be averse to sth.; *die film viel ~ tegen* that film was a real let-down

de **viespeuk** /vi̯spøk/ (pl: -en) pig: *een oude ~* a dirty old man

Vietnam /vi̯ɛtnɑm/ Vietnam

de **Vietnamees** /vi̯ɛtname̯s/ Vietnamese

de **viewer** /vi̯juwər/ (pl: -s) viewer

de **viezerik** /vi̯zərɪk/ (pl: -en) pig, slob, dirty sod

de **viezigheid** /vi̯zəχhɛit/ dirt, grime

het **vignet** /vɪɲɛt/ (pl: -ten) 1 device, logo, emblem 2 sticker

de **vijand** /vɛi̯ɑnt/ (pl: -en) enemy: *dat zou je je*
ergste ~ nog niet toewensen you wouldn't
wish that on your worst enemy; *gezworen*
~en sworn (*or:* mortal) enemies
vijandelijk /vɛi̯ɣndələk/ (adj, adv) enemy,
hostile
de **vijandelijkheid** /vɛi̯ɣndələkhɛit/ (pl: -he-
den) hostility, act of war
vijandig /vɛi̯ɣndəχ/ (adj, adv) hostile, inimical: *een ~e daad* a hostile act; *iem. ~ gezind*
zijn be hostile towards s.o.
de **vijandigheid** /vɛi̯ɣndəχhɛit/ (pl: -heden)
hostility, animosity, enmity
de **vijandschap** /vɛi̯ɑntsχɑp/ (pl: -pen) enmity,
hostility, animosity: *in ~ leven* be at odds
(with)
vijf /vɛi̯f/ (num) five; [in dates] fifth: *~ juni*
the fifth of June; *om de ~ minuten* every five
minutes; *het is over vijven* it is past (*or:* gone)
five; *een stuk of ~* about five, five or so, five-
odd; *een briefje van ~* a five-pound note
vijfde /vɛi̯vdə/ (num) fifth: *auto met ~ deur*
hatchback; *ten ~* fifthly, in the fifth place; *als*
~ eindigen come in fifth
de **vijfenzestigpluskaart** /vɛi̯fə(n)sɛstəχ-
plʏskart/ (pl: -en) senior citizen's ticket (*or:*
pass)
de **vijfenzestigplusser** /vɛi̯fə(n)sɛstəχplʏsər/
(pl: -s) senior citizen, pensioner
de **vijfhoek** /vɛi̯fhuk/ (pl: -en) pentagon
het **vijfjarenplan** /vɛi̯fjarə(n)plɑn/ (pl: -nen)
five-year plan
vijfjarig /vɛi̯fjarəχ/ (adj) five-year-old; five-
year(s'); five-yearly
de **vijfling** /vɛi̯flɪŋ/ (pl: -en) quintuplets, quins:
zij kreeg een ~ she had quintuplets (*or:* quins)
het **vijftal** /vɛi̯ftɑl/ (pl: -len) (set of) five: *een ~*
jaren (about) five years, five (or so) years; *een*
vrolijk ~ a merry fivesome
vijftien /vɛi̯ftin/ (num) fifteen; [in dates]
fifteenth: *~ maart* the fifteenth of March;
rugnummer ~ number fifteen; *een man of ~*
about fifteen people, fifteen or so people
vijftig /fɛi̯ftəχ/ (num) fifty: *de jaren ~* the
fifties; *hij is in de ~* he is in his fifties; *tegen de*
~ lopen be getting on for (*or:* be pushing) fifty
de **vijftiger** /fɛi̯ftəɣər/ (pl: -s) s.o. in his fifties
de **vijg** /vɛi̯χ/ fig (tree) ‖ [Belg] *dat zijn ~en na*
Pasen that is (*or:* comes) too late to be of use
het **vijgenblad** /vɛi̯ɣə(n)blɑt/ (pl: -eren, -en) fig
leaf
de **vijgenboom** /vɛi̯ɣə(n)bom/ (pl: -bomen)
fig (tree)
de **vijl** /vɛi̯l/ (pl: -en) file
vijlen /vɛi̯lə(n)/ (vijlde, heeft gevijld) file
de **vijs** /vɛi̯s/ (pl: vijzen) [Belg] screw
de **vijver** /vɛi̯vər/ (pl: -s) pond
de **vijzel** /vɛi̯zəl/ **1** jack **2** Archimedean screw
de **Viking** /vikɪŋ/ (pl: -en) Viking
de **villa** /vila/ (pl: -'s) villa: *halve ~* semi-de-

tached house
de **villawijk** /vilawɛik/ (pl: -en) (exclusive) residential area
villen /vɪlə(n)/ (vilde, heeft gevild) skin, flay
het **vilt** /vɪlt/ felt
vilten /vɪltə(n)/ (adj) felt
het **viltje** /vɪlcə/ (pl: -s) beer mat
de **viltstift** /vɪltstɪft/ (pl: -en) felt-tip (pen)
de **vin** /vɪn/ (pl: -nen) **1** fin; flipper: *geen ~ ver-*
roeren not raise (*or:* lift) a finger, not move a
muscle **2** fin; vane
vinden /vɪndə(n)/ (vond, heeft gevonden)
1 find, discover, come across; strike: *dat boek*
is nergens te ~ that book is nowhere to be
found; *ergens voor te ~ zijn* be (very) ready to
do sth., be game for sth.; *iem. (iets) toevallig*
~ happen (*or:* chance) upon s.o. (sth.) **2** find,
think of **3** think, find: *ik vind het vandaag*
koud I think it's (*or:* I find it) cold today; *ik*
zou het prettig ~ als ... I'd appreciate it if ...;
hoe vind je dat? what do you think of that?;
zou je het erg ~ als ...? would you mind if ...?;
ik vind het goed that's fine by me, it suits me
fine; *vind je ook niet?* don't you agree?; *daar*
vind ik niets aan it doesn't do a thing for me ‖
het met iem. kunnen ~ get on (*or:* along) with
s.o.; *zich ergens in kunnen ~* agree with sth.;
zij hebben elkaar gevonden **a)** they have come
to terms (over it); **b)** they have found each
other
de **vinder** /vɪndər/ (pl: -s) finder, discoverer
de **vinding** /vɪndɪŋ/ (pl: -en) idea, invention
vindingrijk /vɪndɪŋrɛik/ (adj) ingenious, inventive: *een ~e geest* a fertile (*or:* creative)
mind
de **vindingrijkheid** /vɪndɪŋrɛikhɛit/ ingenuity, inventiveness, resourcefulness
de **vindplaats** /vɪntplats/ (pl: -en) place where
sth. is found, site, location
de **vinger** /vɪŋər/ (pl: -s) finger: *groene ~s heb-*
ben have green fingers; [Am] have a green
thumb; *lange ~s hebben* have sticky fingers;
met een natte ~ roughly, approximately; *als*
men hem een ~ geeft, neemt hij de hele hand
give him an inch and he'll take a mile; *hij*
heeft zich in de ~s gesneden [fig] he got (his
fingers) burned; *de ~ opsteken* put up (*or:*
raise) one's hand; *iets door de ~s zien* turn a
blind eye to sth., overlook sth.; *iets in de ~s*
hebben be a natural at sth.; *een ~ in de pap*
hebben have a finger in the pie; *met de ~s*
knippen snap one's fingers; *hij had haar nog*
met geen ~ aangeraakt he hadn't put (*or:* laid)
a finger on her; *op de ~s van één hand te tellen*
zijn be few and far between; *iem. op de ~s*
tikken rap s.o. over the knuckles; *iem. op de*
~s kijken breathe down s.o.'s neck; *dat had je*
op je ~s kunnen natellen that was to be expected
de **vingerafdruk** /vɪŋəravdrʏk/ (pl: -ken) fingerprint: *~ken nemen (van)* fingerprint s.o.,

take s.o.'s fingerprints

de **vingerhoed** /vɪŋərhut/ (pl: -en) thimble

de **vingertop** /vɪŋərtɔp/ (pl: -pen) fingertip

de **vingerverf** /vɪŋərvɛrf/ finger paint

vingervlug /vɪŋərvlʏx/ (adj) sticky-fingered

de **vingerwijzing** /vɪŋərwɛɪzɪŋ/ (pl: -en) hint, clue

de **vingerzetting** /vɪŋərzɛtɪŋ/ (pl: -en) fingering

de **vink** /vɪŋk/ (pl: -en) **1** finch; chaffinch **2** check (mark), tick

vinnig /vɪnəx/ (adj, adv) sharp, caustic

het **vinyl** /vinil/ vinyl

violet /vijolɛt/ (adj) violet

de **violist** /vijolɪst/ (pl: -en) violinist

de **viool** /vijol/ (pl: violen) violin, fiddle: (op de) ~ **spelen** play the violin (or: fiddle); **eerste** ~ first violin; hij speelt de **eerste** ~ he is (or: plays) first fiddle

het **vioolconcert** /vijolkɔnsɛrt/ (pl: -en) violin concerto

de **vioolsleutel** /vijolsløtəl/ G clef, violin clef

het **viooltje** /vijolcə/ (pl: -s) violet: **Kaaps** ~ African violet

de **vip** /vɪp/ (pl: -s) VIP

viraal /viral/ (adj) viral

viriel /viril/ (adj) virile

de **viroloog** /virolox/ (pl: -logen) virologist

virtueel /vɪrtywel/ (adj, adv) virtual, potential: een ~ **winkelcentrum** a virtual shopping centre

virtuoos /vɪrtywos/ (adj, adv) virtuoso

de **virtuositeit** /vɪrtywozitɛɪt/ virtuosity

virulent /virylɛnt/ (adj) virulent

het **virus** /virʏs/ (pl: -sen) virus

de **virusinfectie** /virʏsɪnfɛksi/ (pl: -s) virus infection, viral infection

de **virusscanner** /virʏskɛnər/ (pl: -s) virus scanner

de **virusziekte** /virʏsiktə/ (pl: -n, -s) viral disease

de **vis** /vɪs/ (pl: -sen) fish: een **mand** ~ a basket of fish; er **zit** hier veel ~ the fishing's good here; zo gezond **als** een ~ fit as a fiddle; zich voelen **als** een ~ in het water feel like a fish in water; zich voelen **als** een ~ op het droge feel like a fish out of water

de **Vis** /vɪs/ (pl: -sen) Pisces, Piscean

de **visagist** /vizaʒɪst/ (pl: -en) cosmetician, beauty specialist, beautician

de **visakte** /vɪsɑktə/ (pl: -n, -s) fishing licence

de **visboer** /vɪzbur/ (pl: -en) fishmonger

viseren /vizerə(n)/ (viseerde, heeft geviseerd) **1** aim at, have in view **2** [Belg] criticise

de **visgraat** /vɪsxrat/ (pl: visgraten) fish bone

de **vishandel** /vɪshɑndəl/ fish trade; fish shop; [Am] fish dealer

de **visie** /vizi/ (pl: -s) view, outlook, point of view: een man **met** ~ a man of vision

het **visioen** /vizjun/ (pl: -en) vision: een ~ **hebben** see (or: have) a vision

de **¹visionair** /viʒonɛːr/ (pl: -s) visionary

²visionair /viʒonɛːr/ (adj) visionary

de **visitatie** /vizita(t)si/ (pl: -s) **1** search **2** visitation

de **visite** /vizitə/ (pl: -s) **1** visit; call: bij iem. **op** ~ gaan pay s.o. a visit, call on s.o., visit **2** visitors, guests, company

het **visitekaartje** /vizitəkarcə/ (pl: -s) visiting card; (business) card: zijn ~ **achterlaten** make one's mark, establish one's presence

visiteren /vizi̇terə(n)/ (visiteerde, heeft gevisiteerd) examine, inspect; search

de **viskom** /vɪskɔm/ (pl: -men) fishbowl

de **vismarkt** /vɪsmɑrkt/ (pl: -en) fish market

het **visnet** /vɪsnɛt/ (pl: -ten) fish net, fishing net

de **visschotel** /vɪsxotəl/ (pl: -s) fish dish

vissen /vɪsə(n)/ (viste, heeft gevist) **1** fish; angle: **op** haring ~ fish for herring; **parels** ~ dive (or: fish) for pearls **2** drag, dredge || **naar** een complimentje ~ fish (or: angle) for a compliment

de **Vissen** /vɪsə(n)/ (pl) Pisces

de **visser** /vɪsər/ (pl: -s) fisherman; angler

de **visserij** /vɪsərɛɪ/ (pl: -en) fishing, fisheries, fishery

de **vissersboot** /vɪsərzbot/ (pl: -boten) fishing boat

de **vissersvloot** /vɪsərsflot/ fishing fleet

de **vissoep** /vɪsup/ fish soup

de **visstand** /vɪstɑnt/ fish stock

de **visstick** /vɪstɪk/ (pl: -s) fish finger

visualiseren /vizywalizerə(n)/ (visualiseerde, heeft gevisualiseerd) visualize

visueel /vizywel/ (adj, adv) visual: ~ **gehandicapt** visually handicapped

het **visum** /vizʏm/ (pl: visa) visa: een ~ **aanvragen** apply for a visa

de **visumplicht** /vizʏmplɪxt/ visa requirement

de **visvangst** /vɪsfɑŋst/ fishing, catching of fish: **van** de ~ leven fish for one's living

de **visvergunning** /vɪsfərɣʏnɪŋ/ (pl: -en) fishing licence (or: permit)

de **visvijver** /vɪsfɛivər/ (pl: -s) fishpond

het **viswater** /vɪswatər/ (pl: -s, -en) fishing ground(s)

het **viswijf** /vɪswɛɪf/ (pl: -wijven) fishwife

de **viswinkel** /vɪswɪŋkəl/ (pl: -s) fish shop, fishmonger's (shop); [Am] fish dealer

vitaal /vital/ (adj) vital: hij is nog erg ~ **voor** zijn leeftijd he's still very active for his age

de **vitaliteit** /vitalitɛɪt/ vitality, vigour

de **vitamine** /vitaminə/ (pl: -s) vitamin: rijk **aan** ~ rich in vitamins, vitamin-rich

het **vitaminegebrek** /vitaminəɣəbrɛk/ lack (or: deficiency) of vitamins, vitamin deficiency

het/de **vitrage** /vitraʒə/ (pl: -s) net curtain

de **vitrine** /vitrinə/ (pl: -s) **1** (glass, display) case, showcase **2** shop window, show window

vitten /vɪtə(n)/ (vitte, heeft gevit) find fault, carp

de **vivisectie** /vivisɛksi/ (pl: -s) vivisection

het **vizier** /vizir/ (pl: -s) **1** sight: *iem. in het ~ krijgen* spot s.o., catch sight of s.o. **2** visor

de **vj** /viːdʒe/ VJ, veejay

de **vla** /vla/ (pl: -'s) **1** [roughly] custard **2** flan; [Am] (open-faced) pie

de **vlaag** /vlax/ (pl: vlagen) **1** gust, squall **2** fit, flurry: *in een ~ van verstandsverbijstering* in a frenzy, in a fit of insanity; *bij vlagen* in fits and starts, in spurts (*or:* bursts)

de **vlaai** /vlaj/ (pl: -en) flan; [Am] (open-faced) pie

het **¹Vlaams** /vlams/ Flemish

²Vlaams /vlams/ (adj) Flemish ‖ *~e gaai* jay

de **Vlaamse** /vlamsə/ Flemish woman

Vlaanderen /vlandərə(n)/ Flanders

de **vlag** /vlax/ (pl: -gen) flag; colours; ensign: *met ~ en wimpel slagen* pass with (*or:* come through with) flying colours; *de Britse ~* the Union Jack

vlaggen /vlaɣə(n)/ (vlagde, heeft gevlagd) put out the flag

de **vlaggenmast** /vlaɣə(n)mɑst/ (pl: -en) flagpole, flagstaff

het **vlaggenschip** /vlaɣə(n)sxɪp/ (pl: -schepen) flagship

de **vlaggenstok** /vlaɣə(n)stɔk/ (pl: -ken) flagpole, flagstaff

het **¹vlak** /vlɑk/ (pl: -ken) **1** surface, face; facet: *het voorste* (or: *achterste*) *~* the front (*or:* rear) face **2** sphere, area, field: *op het menselijke ~* in the human sphere

²vlak /vlɑk/ (adj) **1** flat, level, even: *iets ~ strijken* level off sth., level sth. out **2** flat, shallow

³vlak /vlɑk/ (adv) **1** flat **2** right, immediately, directly: *~ tegenover elkaar* right (*or:* straight) opposite each other **3** close: *~ achter je* right (*or:* just) behind you; *~ bij de school* close to the school, right by the school; *het is ~ bij* it's no distance at all; *het is hier ~ in de buurt* it's just round the corner; [Am] it's just around the corner; *het ligt ~ voor je neus* it is staring you in the face, it's right under your nose

vlakaf /vlɑkɑf/ (adv) [Belg] plainly, bluntly

vlakbij /vlɑgbɛi/ (adv) nearby: *ik woon hier ~* I live nearby (*or:* close by)

de **vlakgom** /vlɑkxɔm/ rubber, eraser

de **vlakte** /vlɑktə/ (pl: -n, -s) plain: *een golvende ~* a rolling plain; *zich op de ~ houden* not commit o.s., leave (*or:* keep) one's options open; *na twee klappen ging hij tegen de ~* a couple of blows laid him flat

de **vlaktemaat** /vlɑktəmat/ (pl: -maten) surface measurement

de **vlam** /vlɑm/ (pl: -men) **1** flame: *~ vatten* catch fire; burst into flames; *in ~men opgaan* go up in flames; *de ~ sloeg in de pan* **a)** the pan caught fire; **b)** [fig] the fat was in the fire **2** flame: *een oude ~* an old flame

de **Vlaming** /vlamɪŋ/ (pl: -en) Fleming

vlammen /vlɑmə(n)/ (vlamde, heeft gevlamd) flame

vlammend /vlɑmənt/ (adj) fiery, burning: *een ~ protest* a burning protest

de **vlammenwerper** /vlɑmə(n)wɛrpər/ (pl: -s) flame-thrower

de **vlammenzee** /vlɑmə(n)ze/ sea of flame(s)

de **vlamverdeler** /vlɑmvərdelər/ (pl: -s) stove mat

het **vlas** /vlɑs/ flax

vlassen /vlɑsə(n)/ (vlaste, heeft gevlast) (+ op) be eager for

de **vlecht** /vlɛxt/ (pl: -en) braid, plait, tress: *een valse ~* a switch, a tress of false hair

vlechten /vlɛxtə(n)/ (vlocht, heeft gevlochten) braid, plait, twine

het **vlechtwerk** /vlɛxtwɛrk/ plaiting

de **vleermuis** /vlermœys/ (pl: -muizen) bat

het **vlees** /vles/ **1** flesh; meat: *dat is ~ noch vis* that is neither fish, flesh, nor good red herring; *in eigen ~ snijden* queer one's own pitch; *mijn eigen ~ en bloed* my own flesh and blood **2** flesh, pulp

de **vleesboom** /vlezbom/ (pl: -bomen) myoma, fibroid

vleesetend /vlesetənt/ (adj) carnivorous

de **vleeseter** /vlesetər/ (pl: -s) meat-eater; carnivore

vleesgeworden /vlesxəwordə(n)/ (adj) the incarnation of

het **vleesmes** /vlesmɛs/ (pl: -sen) carving knife

de **vleesschotel** /vlesxotəl/ (pl: -s) meat course (*or:* dish)

de **vleestomaat** /vlestomat/ (pl: -tomaten) beefsteak tomato

de **vleesvork** /vlesfɔrk/ (pl: -en) carving fork

de **vleeswaren** /vleswarə(n)/ (pl) meat products, meats: *fijne ~* (assorted) sliced cold meat; cold cuts

de **vleeswond** /vleswɔnt/ (pl: -en) flesh wound

de **vleet** /vlet/: *hij heeft boeken bij de ~* he has (got) lots of books

de **vlegel** /vleɣəl/ (pl: -s) brat, lout

vleien /vlɛiə(n)/ (vleide, heeft gevleid) flatter, butter up: *ik voelde me gevleid door haar antwoord* I was (*or:* felt) flattered by her answer

vleiend /vlɛiənt/ (adj, adv) flattering, coaxing

de **vleierij** /vlɛiərɛi/ (pl: -en) flattery: *met ~ kom je nergens* flattery will get you nowhere

de **vlek** /vlɛk/ (pl: -ken) **1** spot, mark, stain; blemish; blotch: *die ~ gaat er in de was wel uit* that spot will come out in the wash **2** [fig] blot, blemish ‖ *blinde ~ (in het oog)* blind spot (in the eye); [fig] *een blinde ~ voor iets hebben* have a blind spot for sth.

vlekkeloos /vlɛkələos/ (adj) spotless, immaculate

vlekken /vlɛkə(n)/ (vlekte, heeft gevlekt)

spot, stain

de **vlerk** /vlɛrk/ boor, lout

de **vleugel** /vlØɣəl/ (pl: -s) **1** wing: *zijn ~s uit-slaan* [also fig] spread (*or:* stretch) one's wings; [sport] *over de ~s spelen* play up and down the wings **2** grand piano
vleugellam /vløɣəlɑm/ (adj) broken-winged: *iem. ~ maken* paralyze s.o., render s.o. powerless

de **vleugelmoer** /vløɣəlmur/ (pl: -en) wing nut, butterfly nut

de **vleugelspeler** /vløɣəlspelər/ (pl: -s) [sport] (left, right) winger

het **vleugje** /vløxjə/ (pl: -s) breath, touch: *een ~ ironie* a tinge of irony; *een ~ romantiek* a romantic touch
vlezig /vlezəx/ (adj) **1** fleshy **2** plump

de **vlieg** /vlix/ (pl: -en) fly: *twee ~en in één klap (slaan)* kill two birds with one stone; *hij doet geen ~ kwaad* he wouldn't harm (*or:* hurt) a fly

de **vliegangst** /vlixɑŋst/ fear of flying

de **vliegbasis** /vliɣbazɪs/ (pl: -bases) airbase

het **vliegbrevet** /vliɣbrəvɛt/ (pl: -ten) pilot's licence, flying licence: *zijn ~ halen* qualify as a pilot, get one's wings

het **vliegdekschip** /vliɣdɛksxɪp/ (pl: -schepen) (aircraft) carrier
vliegen /vliɣə(n)/ (vloog, heeft/is gevlogen) fly; race: *de dagen ~ (om)* the days are simply flying; *hij ziet ze ~* he has got bats in the belfry; *eruit ~* get sacked; *met KLM ~* fly KLM ‖ *erin ~* fall for sth.

de **vliegenier** /vliɣənir/ (pl: -s) airman, aviator

de **vliegenmepper** /vliɣə(n)mɛpər/ (pl: -s) (fly) swatter

¹**vliegensvlug** /vliɣənsflʏx/ (adj) lightning

²**vliegensvlug** /vliɣənsflʏx/ (adv) as quick as lightning, like lightning (*or:* a shot)

de **vliegenzwam** /vliɣə(n)zwɑm/ (pl: -men) fly agaric

de **vlieger** /vliɣər/ (pl: -s) kite: *een ~ oplaten* fly a kite
vliegeren /vliɣərə(n)/ (vliegerde, heeft gevliegerd) fly kites (*or:* a kite)

het **vlieggewicht** /vlixəwɪxt/ flyweight

de **vlieghoogte** /vlixhoxtə/ (pl: -n) altitude

de **vlieginstructeur** /vlixɪnstrʏktør/ (pl: -s) flying instructor

de **vliegmaatschappij** (pl: -en) airline

de **vliegramp** /vlixrɑmp/ (pl: -en) plane crash

het/de **vliegticket** /vlixtɪkət/ airline ticket

het **vliegtuig** /vlixtœyx/ (pl: -en) aeroplane; [Am] airplane; aircraft, plane: *~jes vouwen* make paper aeroplanes (*or:* airplanes); *met het ~ reizen* fly, travel by air (*or:* plane)

de **vliegtuigkaper** /vlixtœyxkapər/ (pl: -s) (aircraft) hijacker

de **vliegtuigkaping** /vlixtœyxkapɪŋ/ (pl: -en) (aircraft) hijack(ing)

het **vliegveld** /vlixfɛlt/ (pl: -en) airport

het **vliegverbod** /vlixfərbɔt/ grounding; flight restriction

het **vliegwiel** /vlixwil/ (pl: -en) fly(wheel), driving wheel

de **vlier** /vlir/ (pl: -en) elder(berry)

de **vliering** /vlirɪŋ/ (pl: -en) attic, loft

het **vlies** /vlis/ (pl: vliezen) film; skin
vlijen /vlɛiə(n)/ (vlijde, heeft gevlijd) lay down, nestle
vlijmscherp /vlɛimsxɛrp/ (adj) razor-sharp

de **vlijt** /vlɛit/ diligence, application
vlijtig /vlɛitəx/ (adj, adv) diligent, industrious

de **vlinder** /vlɪndər/ (pl: -s) butterfly: *~s in mijn buik* butterflies in my stomach

de **vlinderdas** /vlɪndərdɑs/ (pl: -sen) bow tie

de **vlinderslag** /vlɪndərslɑx/ butterfly stroke

de **vlo** /vlo/ (pl: vlooien) flea: *onder de ~oien zitten* be flea-ridden

de **vloed** /vlut/ (pl: -en) (high) tide, flood (tide), rising tide: *het is nu ~* the tide is in; *bij ~* at high tide; *een ~ van klachten* a flood (*or:* deluge) of complaints

de **vloedgolf** /vlutxɔlf/ (pl: -golven) **1** groundswell **2** tidal wave

de **vloedlijn** /vlutlɛin/ (pl: -en) high-water line

het **vloei** /vluj/ tissue paper: *een pakje shag met ~* (a packet of) rolling tobacco and cigarette papers
vloeibaar /vlujbar/ (adj) liquid, fluid: *~ voedsel* liquid food
vloeien /vlujə(n)/ (vloeide, heeft/is gevloeid) **1** flow, stream: *in de kas ~* flow in **2** blot, smudge
vloeiend /vlujənt/ (adj, adv) flowing, liquid: *~e kleuren* blending colours; *een ~e lijn* a flowing line; *hij spreekt ~ Engels* he speaks English fluently

het **vloeipapier** /vlujpapir/ **1** blotting paper **2** tissue paper; cigarette paper

de **vloeistof** /vlujstɔf/ (pl: -fen) liquid, fluid

het **vloeitje** /vlujcə/ (pl: -s) cigarette paper

de **vloek** /vluk/ (pl: -en) curse: *er ligt een ~ op dat huis* a curse rests on that house; *een ~ uit-spreken (over iem., iets)* curse s.o. (sth.)
vloeken /vlukə(n)/ (vloekte, heeft gevloekt) curse, swear (at): *op iets ~* curse (*or:* swear) at sth.

de **vloer** /vlur/ (pl: -en) floor: *planken ~* planking; strip flooring; *met iem. de ~ aanvegen* mop (*or:* wipe) the floor with s.o.; *ik dacht dat ik door de ~ ging* I didn't know where to put myself; *veel mensen over de ~ hebben* have a lot of visitors; *hij komt daar over de ~* he is a regular visitor there

de **vloerbedekking** /vlurbədɛkɪŋ/ (pl: -en) floor covering: *vaste ~* wall-to-wall carpet(-ting)
vloeren /vlurə(n)/ (vloerde, heeft gevloerd) floor

het **vloerkleed** /vlurklet/ (pl: -kleden) carpet;

[small] rug

de **vloermat** /vlurmɑt/ (pl: -ten) floor mat

de **vloertegel** /vlurteɣəl/ (pl: -s) (paving) tile (*or:* stone): ~*s leggen* pave, lay (paving) tiles

de **vloerverwarming** /vlurvərwɑrmɪŋ/ (pl: -en) underfloor heating

de **vlok** /vlɔk/ (pl: -ken) **1** flock; tuft: ~*ken stof* whirls of dust **2** flake: ~*ken op brood* bread with chocolate flakes

de **vlonder** /vlɔndər/ (pl: -s) **1** (wooden) platform, planking **2** pallet

vlooien /vloːjə(n)/ (vlooide, heeft gevlooid) groom

de **vlooienband** /vloːjə(n)bɑnt/ (pl: -en) flea collar

de **vlooienmarkt** /vloːjə(n)mɑrkt/ (pl: -en) flea market

de **vloot** /vloːt/ (pl: vloten) fleet

het **vlos** /vlɔs/ floss (silk)

het ¹**vlot** /vlɔt/ (pl: -ten) raft: *op* een ~ *de rivier oversteken* raft across the river

²**vlot** /vlɔt/ (adj, adv) **1** facile; fluent; smooth: *een* ~*te pen* a ready pen; ~ *spreken* speak fluently **2** smooth; ready; prompt: *een zaak* ~ *afwikkelen* settle a matter promptly; *het ging heel* ~ it went off without a hitch; ~ *van begrip zijn* be quick-witted **3** sociable, easy to talk to: *hij is wat* ~*ter geworden* he has loosened up a little **4** easy, comfortable: *hij kleedt zich heel* ~ he is a sharp dresser **5** afloat

vlotjes /vlɔcəs/ (adv) smoothly, easily; promptly: *alles* ~ *laten verlopen* have things run smoothly

vlotten /vlɔtə(n)/ (vlotte, heeft/is gevlot) go smoothly: *het werk wil niet* ~ we are not making any progress (*or:* headway)

de **vlucht** /vlʏxt/ (pl: -en) flight, escape: *wij wensen u een aangename* ~ we wish you a pleasant flight; *iem. de* ~ *beletten* prevent s.o. from escaping; *op de* ~ *slaan* flee, run (for it); *iem. op de* ~ *jagen (drijven)* put s.o. to flight; *voor de politie op de* ~ *zijn* be on the run from the police

de **vluchteling** /vlʏxtəlɪŋ/ (pl: -en) fugitive; [pol] refugee

het **vluchtelingenkamp** /vlʏxtəlɪŋə(n)kɑmp/ (pl: -en) refugee camp

vluchten /vlʏxtə(n)/ (vluchtte, is gevlucht) flee, escape, run away: *uit het land* ~ flee (from) the country; *een bos in* ~ take refuge in the woods

het **vluchtgedrag** /vlʏxtxədrɑx/ flight

de **vluchtheuvel** /vlʏxthøvəl/ (pl: -s) traffic island

het **vluchthuis** /vlʏxthœys/ (pl: -huizen) [Belg] refuge (*or:* shelter) for battered women

vluchtig /vlʏxtəx/ (adj, adv) **1** brief; [depr] cursory; quick: ~*e kennismaking* casual acquaintance; *iets* ~ *doorlezen* glance over (*or:* through) sth., skim through sth. **2** volatile

de **vluchtleider** /vlʏxtlɛidər/ (pl: -s) flight controller

de **vluchtleiding** /vlʏxtlɛidɪŋ/ (pl: -en) flight (*or:* mission) control (team), ground control

het **vluchtmisdrijf** /vlʏxtmɪzdrɛif/ [Belg] offence of failing to stop

de **vluchtpoging** /vlʏxtpoɣɪŋ/ (pl: -en) attempted escape

de **vluchtrecorder** /vlʏxtrikɔːrdər/ (pl: -s) flight recorder, black box

de **vluchtstrook** /vlʏxtstrok/ (pl: -stroken) hard shoulder; [Am] shoulder

de **vluchtweg** /vlʏxtwɛx/ (pl: -en) escape route

vlug /vlʏx/ (adj, adv) **1** fast, quick: ~ *lopen* run fast; ~ *ter been zijn* be quick on one's feet; *iem. te* ~ *af zijn* be too quick for s.o. **2** quick; nimble; agile **3** quick, fast, prompt: *hij was* ~ *klaar* he was soon ready; *iets* ~ *doornemen* (or: *bekijken*) glance over (*or:* through) sth.; ~ *iets eten* have a quick snack **4** quick, sharp: *hij behoort niet tot de* ~*sten* he's none too quick; *hij was er al* ~ *bij* he was quick at everything; ~ *in* rekenen quick at sums

het **vmbo** /veːmbeoː/ *voorbereidend middelbaar beroepsonderwijs* lower vocational professional education

het **vmbo-b** [Dutch; educ] pre-vocational secondary education (block or day release)

het **vmbo-g** [Dutch; educ] pre-vocational secondary education (combined programme)

het **vmbo-k** [Dutch; educ] pre-vocational secondary education (middle management vocational programme)

het **vmbo-t** [Dutch; educ] pre-vocational secondary education (theoretical programme)

de **VN** /veːɛn/ (pl) *Verenigde Naties* UN

de **VN-vredesmacht** /veːɛnvredəsmɑxt/ UN peace-keeping force

het **vo** /veoː/ *voortgezet onderwijs* secondary education

vocaal /vokaːl/ (adj) vocal

het **vocabulaire** /vokabylɛːr(ə)/ vocabulary

het **vocht** /vɔxt/ **1** liquid; fluid: ~ *afscheiden* discharge fluid; secrete fluid **2** moisture, damp(ness): *de hoeveelheid* ~ *in de lucht* the humidity in the air

vochtig /vɔxtəx/ (adj) damp, moist: *een* ~ *klimaat* a damp climate; *de lucht is* ~ the air is damp; *zijn ogen werden* ~ his eyes became moist

de **vochtigheid** /vɔxtəxhɛit/ **1** moistness, dampness **2** moisture; humidity

het/de **vod** /vɔt/ (pl: -den) **1** rag: *een* ~*je papier* a scrap of paper **2** trash, rubbish: *dit is een* ~ this is trash || *iem. achter de* ~*den zitten* keep s.o. (hard) at it

¹**voeden** /vudə(n)/ (voedde, heeft gevoed) be nourishing (*or:* nutritious)

²**voeden** /vudə(n)/ (voedde, heeft gevoed) feed: *die vogels* ~ *zich met insecten* (or: *met*

zaden) these birds feed on insects (*or:* seeds); *zij voedt haar **kind** zelf* she breast-feeds her baby

het **voeder** /v<u>u</u>dər/ (pl: -s) fodder, feed
voederen /v<u>u</u>dərə(n)/ (voederde, heeft gevoederd) feed

de **voeding** /v<u>u</u>dɪŋ/ (pl: -en) **1** feeding, nutrition: *kunstmatige ~* artificial (*or:* forced) feeding **2** food; feed: *eenzijdige ~* an unbalanced diet; *gezonde* (*or: natuurlijke*) *~* health (*or:* natural) food **3** power supply

de **voedingsbodem** /v<u>u</u>dɪŋzbodəm/ (pl: -s) breeding ground

de **voedingsindustrie** /v<u>u</u>dɪŋsɪndʏstri/ (pl: -ēn) food industry

het **voedingsmiddel** /v<u>u</u>dɪŋsmɪdəl/ (pl: -en) food; [oft pl] foodstuff: *gezonde ~en* healthy (*or:* wholesome) foods

de **voedingsstof** /v<u>u</u>dɪŋstɔf/ (pl: -fen) nutrient

de **voedingsvezels** (pl) nutritional fibre

de **voedingswaarde** /v<u>u</u>dɪŋswardə/ nutritional value

het **voedsel** /v<u>u</u>tsəl/ food: *plantaardig ~* vegetable food; *~ tot zich **nemen*** take food (*or:* nourishment)

de **voedselbank** /v<u>u</u>tsəlbaŋk/ (pl: -en) food bank

de **voedselhulp** /v<u>u</u>tsəlhʏlp/ food aid

de **voedselketen** /v<u>u</u>tsəlketə(n)/ food chain

het **voedselpakket** /v<u>u</u>tsəlpakɛt/ (pl: -ten) food parcel

de **voedselvergiftiging** /v<u>u</u>tsəlvərɣɪftəɣɪŋ/ food poisoning

voedzaam /v<u>u</u>tsam/ (adj) nutritious, nourishing

de **voeg** /vuχ/ (pl: -en) joint; seam: *de ~en van een **muur** dichtmaken (aanstrijken)* point (the brickwork of) a wall; *uit zijn ~en **barsten*** come apart at the seams

de **voege** /v<u>u</u>ɣə/: [Belg] *in ~ treden* take effect, come into force
voegen /v<u>u</u>ɣə(n)/ (voegde, heeft gevoegd) **1** join (up): *hierbij voeg ik een **biljet** van €100,-* I enclose a 100-euro note; *zich bij iem. ~* join s.o. **2** add: *stukken **bij** een dossier ~* add documents to a file **3** point

het **voegwoord** /v<u>u</u>χwort/ (pl: -en) conjunction
voelbaar /v<u>u</u>lbar/ (adj, adv) tangible, perceptible: *het ijzer wordt ~ **warmer*** the iron is getting perceptibly hotter

¹**voelen** /v<u>u</u>lə(n)/ (voelde, heeft gevoeld) **1** feel: *het voelt **hard*** (*or: **ruw, zacht***) it feels hard (*or:* rough, soft) **2** be fond (of), like: *iets gaan ~ **voor** iem.* grow fond of s.o. **3** feel (like), like the idea (of): *veel **voor** de verpleging ~* like the idea of nursing; *ik voel wel iets **voor** dat plan* I rather like that plan; *ik voel er niet veel **voor** (om) te komen* I don't feel like coming

²**voelen** /v<u>u</u>lə(n)/ (voelde, heeft gevoeld) **1** feel: *leven ~* feel the baby move; *dat voel*

ik! that hurts!; *zijn invloed **doen** ~* make one's influence felt; *als je niet wil luisteren, **moet** je maar ~* (you'd better) do it or else!; *voel je (hem)?* get it? **2** feel (for, after): *laat mij eens ~* let me (have a) feel

zich ³**voelen** /v<u>u</u>lə(n)/ (voelde zich, heeft zich gevoeld) feel: *zich **lekker** ~* feel fine, feel on top of the world

de **voeling** /v<u>u</u>lɪŋ/ touch, contact: *~ **houden** met* maintain contact with, keep in touch with

de **voelspriet** /v<u>u</u>lsprit/ (pl: -en) feeler, antenna

het **voer** /vur/ feed; [also fig] food: *~ **geven*** feed; *~ **voor** psychologen* a fit subject for a psychologist

de **voerbak** /v<u>u</u>rbak/ (pl: -ken) (feeding) trough, manger

¹**voeren** /v<u>u</u>rə(n)/ (voerde, heeft gevoerd) lead, guide: *dat zou (mij, ons) te **ver** ~* that would be getting too far off the subject; *de reis voert **naar** Rome* the trip goes to Rome

²**voeren** /v<u>u</u>rə(n)/ (voerde, heeft gevoerd) **1** line **2** feed ‖ *een harde **politiek** ~* pursue a tough policy; *een **proces** ~* go to court (over); *iem. **dronken** ~* get (*or:* make) s.o. drunk

de **voering** /v<u>u</u>rɪŋ/ (pl: -en) lining

de **voertaal** /v<u>u</u>rtal/ (pl: -talen) language of instruction [educ]; [at conferences etc] official language

het **voertuig** /v<u>u</u>rtœyχ/ (pl: -en) vehicle

de **voet** /vut/ (pl: -en) **1** foot: *op **blote** ~en* barefoot; *iem. op **staande** ~ ontslaan* dismiss s.o. on the spot; *iem. op **vrije** ~en stellen* set s.o. free; [Belg] *met iemands ~en **spelen*** make a fool of s.o.; [Belg] *ergens zijn ~en aan **vegen*** drag one's feet; *de ~en **vegen*** wipe one's feet; *dat heeft heel wat ~en **in** de aarde* that'll take some doing; *onder de ~ gelopen worden* be overrun; *iem. **op** de ~ volgen* follow in s.o.'s footsteps; *de gebeurtenissen* (*or: de ontwikkelingen*) *op de ~ volgen* keep a close track of events (*or:* developments); *te ~ gaan* walk, go on foot; *zich **uit** de ~en maken* take to one's heels; *iem. **voor** de ~en lopen* hamper s.o., get in s.o.'s way (*or:* under s.o.'s feet); *geen ~ aan de grond krijgen* have no success; *~ bij stuk houden* stick to one's guns **2** foot, base: *de ~ van een **glas*** the stem (*or:* base) of a glass **3** footing; terms: *zij staan op **goede*** (*or: vertrouwelijke*) *~ met elkaar* they are on good (*or:* familiar) terms (with each other); *op ~ van oorlog leven* be on a war footing ‖ *dat is hem **ten** ~en uit* that's (so) typical of him, that's him all over

de **voetafdruk** /v<u>u</u>tavdrʏk/ (pl: -ken) footmark, footprint: *ecologische ~* ecological footprint

het **voetbad** /v<u>u</u>dbɑt/ (pl: -en) footbath

de ¹**voetbal** /v<u>u</u>dbal/ (pl: -len) [ball] football

het ²**voetbal** /v<u>u</u>dbal/ [sport] football: *Ameri-*

kaans ~ American football; *betaald* ~ professional football

de **voetbalbond** /vu̱dbɑlbɔnt/ football association

de **voetbalclub** /vu̱dbɑlklʏp/ football club

de **voetbalcompetitie** /vu̱dbɑlkɔmpəti(t)si/ (pl: -s) football competition

het **voetbalelftal** /vu̱dbɑlɛlftɑl/ football team: *het* ~ *van Ajax* the Ajax team

de **voetbalfan** /vu̱dbɑlfɛn/ (pl: -s) football fan

de **voetbalknie** /vu̱dbɑlkni/ (pl: -ën) cartilage trouble

voetballen /vu̱dbɑlə(n)/ (voetbalde, heeft gevoetbald) play football

de **voetballer** /vu̱dbɑlər/ (pl: -s) football player

het **voetbalpasje** /vu̱dbɑlpɑʃə/ (pl: -s) football identity card

de **voetbalschoen** /vu̱dbɑlsχun/ football boot

het **voetbalstadion** /vu̱dbɑlstɑdijɔn/ football stadium, soccer stadium

de **voetbalsupporter** /vu̱dbɑlsʏpɔrtər/ (pl: -s) football supporter

de **voetbaluitslagen** /vu̱dbɑlœytslaɣə(n)/ (pl) football results

het **voetbalvandalisme** /vu̱dbɑlvɑndɑlɪsmə/ football hooliganism

het **voetbalveld** /vu̱dbɑlvɛlt/ football pitch

de **voetbalwedstrijd** /vu̱dbɑlwɛtstrɛit/ football match

het **voeteneind** /vu̱tə(n)ɛint/ (pl: -en) foot

de **voetfout** /vu̱tfɑut/ (pl: -en) foot-fault

de **voetganger** /vu̱tχɑŋər/ (pl: -s) pedestrian

de **voetgangersbrug** /vu̱tχɑŋərzbrʏχ/ (pl: -gen) footbridge, pedestrian bridge

het **voetgangersgebied** /vu̱tχɑŋərsχəbit/ (pl: -en) pedestrian precinct (*or:* area)

de **voetgangersoversteekplaats** /vu̱tχɑŋərsovərstekplats/ (pl: -en) pedestrian crossing, zebra crossing

het **voetje** /vu̱cə/ (pl: -s) (little, small) foot: ~ *voor* ~ inch by inch

het **voetlicht** /vu̱tlɪχt/ (pl: -en) footlights: *iets voor het* ~ *brengen* bring sth. out into the open

de **voetnoot** /vu̱tnot/ (pl: -noten) **1** footnote **2** note in the margin, critical remark (*or:* comment)

het **voetpad** /vu̱tpɑt/ (pl: -en) footpath

de **voetreis** /vu̱trɛis/ (pl: -reizen) walking-trip, walking-tour, hike

het **voetspoor** /vu̱tspor/ (pl: -sporen) footprint; track; trail

de **voetstap** /vu̱tstɑp/ (pl: -pen) (foot)step

voetstoots /vu̱tstots/ (adv) without further ado, just like that

het **voetstuk** /vu̱tstʏk/ (pl: -ken) base; pedestal: *iem. op een* ~ *plaatsen* put (*or:* place) s.o. on a pedestal; [fig] *iem. van zijn* ~ *stoten* knock s.o. off his pedestal

de **voettocht** /vu̱tɔχt/ (pl: -en) walking tour, hiking tour

het **voetvolk** /vu̱tfɔlk/ foot soldiers; infantry

de **voetzoeker** /vu̱tsukər/ (pl: -s) jumping jack; [roughly] firecracker

de **voetzool** /vu̱tsol/ (pl: -zolen) sole (of the, one's foot)

de **vogel** /vo̱ɣəl/ (pl: -s) **1** bird: [Belg] *een* ~ *voor de kat zijn* be irretrievably lost; *de* ~ *is gevlogen* the bird has flown **2** customer, character: *het is een rare* ~ he's an odd character; *Joe is een vroege* ~ Joe's an early bird

de **vogelgriep** /vo̱ɣəlɣrip/ bird flu, avian influenza

het **vogelhuis** /vo̱ɣəlhœys/ (pl: -huizen) aviary; nesting box

de **vogelkooi** /vo̱ɣəlkoj/ (pl: -en) birdcage

het **vogelnest** /vo̱ɣəlnɛst/ (pl: -en) bird's nest: ~*en uithalen* go (bird-)nesting

de **vogelpest** /vo̱ɣəlpɛst/ bird flu, avian influenza, fowl pest

de **vogelpik** /vo̱ɣəlpɪk/ [Belg] darts

de **vogelspin** /vo̱ɣəlspɪn/ (pl: -nen) bird spider

de **vogeltrek** /vo̱ɣəltrɛk/ bird migration

de **vogelverschrikker** /vo̱ɣəlvərsχrɪkər/ (pl: -s) scarecrow

de **vogelvlucht** /vo̱ɣəlvlʏχt/ (pl: -en) bird's-eye view: *iets in* ~ *behandelen* sketch sth. briefly; *iets in* ~ *tekenen* draw a bird's-eye view of sth.

vogelvrij /vo̱ɣəlvrɛi/ (adj) outlawed

de **voicemail** /vɔismel/ [telecom] voice mail

vol /vɔl/ (adj, adv) **1** full (of), filled (with): *nieuwe ideeën* full of new ideas; *een huis* ~ *mensen* a house full of people; *met* ~*le mond praten* talk with one's mouth full; *iets* ~ *maken (gieten, stoppen)* fill sth. up; *helemaal* ~ full up, packed; ~ *van iets zijn* be full of sth.; *een* ~ *gezicht* a full (*or:* chubby) face; *zij is een* ~*le nicht van me* she's my first cousin **2** full (of), covered (with, in): *de tafel ligt* ~ *boeken* the table is covered with books; *de kranten staan er* ~ *van* the papers are full of it **3** complete, whole: *een* ~*le dagtaak* a full day's work; [fig also] a full-time job; *het kostte hem acht* ~*le maanden* it took me a good (*or:* all of) eight months; *in het* ~*ste vertrouwen* in complete confidence; *een* ~*le week de tijd hebben* have a full (*or:* whole) week ‖ *iem. voor* ~ *aanzien* take s.o. seriously

volautomatisch /vɔlautomati̱s/ (adj) fully automatic

de ¹**volbloed** /vɔ̱lblut/ (pl: -s, -en) thoroughbred: *Arabische* ~ Arab (thoroughbred)

²**volbloed** /vɔ̱lblut/ (adj) **1** full-blood(ed); pedigree: ~ *rundvee* pedigree cattle **2** thoroughbred

volbrengen /vɔlbrɛ̱ŋə(n)/ (volbracht, heeft volbracht) complete, accomplish

voldaan /vɔldaːn/ (adj) **1** satisfied, content(ed): *een* ~ *gevoel* a sense of satisfaction; ~ *zijn over iets* be satisfied (*or:* content) with sth. **2** paid: *voor* ~ *tekenen* receipt, sign for receipt

¹voldoen /vɔldun/ (voldeed, heeft voldaan) (+ aan) satisfy; meet; carry out; comply with: *aan de behoeften van de markt* ~ meet the needs of the market; *niet* ~ *aan* fall short of

²voldoen /vɔldun/ (voldeed, heeft voldaan) pay, settle: *een rekening* (or: *de kosten*) ~ pay a bill (or: the costs)

de **¹voldoende** /vɔldundə/ (pl: -s, -n) pass (mark); a bare pass: *een* ~ *halen voor wiskunde* pass (one's) maths

²voldoende /vɔldundə/ (adj) sufficient, satisfactory: *één blik op hem is* ~ *om …* one look at him is enough to …; *jouw examen was net* ~ you only just scraped through your exam; *het is niet* ~ *om van te leven* it is not enough to live on; *ruimschoots* ~ ample, more than enough

³voldoende /vɔldundə/ (adv) sufficiently, enough: *heb je je* ~ *voorbereid?* have you done enough preparation?

de **voldoening** /vɔldunɪŋ/ satisfaction

voldongen /vɔldɔŋə(n)/ (adj): *voor een* ~ *feit geplaatst worden* be presented with a fait accompli

voldragen /vɔldraɣə(n)/ (adj) full-term

volgeboekt /vɔlɣəbukt/ (adj) fully booked, booked up

de **volgeling** /vɔlɣəlɪŋ/ (pl: -en) follower; [rel also] disciple

¹volgen /vɔlɣə(n)/ (volgde, heeft/is gevolgd) **1** follow; be next: *nadere instructies* ~ further instructions will follow; *hier* ~ *de namen van de winnaars* the names of the winners are as follows; *op elkaar* ~ follow one another; *als volgt* as follows **2** follow (on): *daaruit volgt dat …* it follows that …

²volgen /vɔlɣə(n)/ (volgde, heeft gevolgd) **1** follow: *een spoor* (or: *de weg*) ~ follow a trail (or: the road) **2** follow, attend **3** follow; pursue: *zijn hart* ~ follow the dictates of one's heart || *ik kan je niet* ~ I don't follow you

volgend /vɔlɣənt/ (adj) following, next: *de ~e keer* next time (round); *wie is de ~e?* who's next?; *het gaat om het ~e* the problem is (or: the facts are) as follows

volgens /vɔlɣəns/ (prep) according to; in accordance with: ~ *mijn horloge is het drie uur* it's three o'clock by my watch; ~ *mij …* I think …, in my opinion …

het **volgnummer** /vɔlɣnʏmər/ (pl: -s) serial number

volgooien /vɔlɣojə(n)/ (gooide vol, heeft volgegooid) fill (up): *de tank* ~ fill (up) the tank, fill her up

de **volgorde** /vɔlɣɔrdə/ (pl: -n, -s) order; sequence: *in de juiste* ~ *leggen* put in the right order; *in willekeurige* ~ at random; *niet op* ~ out of order, not in order

volgroeid /vɔlɣrujt/ (adj) full(y)-grown

de **volgwagen** /vɔlɣwaɣə(n)/ (pl: -s) **1** car in a (funeral, wedding) procession **2** (official) following car

volgzaam /vɔlɣsam/ (adj) docile, obedient

volharden /vɔlhɑrdə(n)/ (volhardde, heeft volhard) persevere, persist

de **volharding** /vɔlhɑrdɪŋ/ perseverance, persistence

¹volhouden /vɔlhɑudə(n)/ (hield vol, heeft volgehouden) persevere, keep on: *we zijn ermee begonnen, nu moeten we* ~ now we've started we must see it through; ~*!* keep it up!, keep going!

²volhouden /vɔlhɑudə(n)/ (hield vol, heeft volgehouden) **1** carry on, keep up: *dit tempo is niet vol te houden* we can't keep up this pace **2** maintain, insist: *zijn onschuld* ~ insist on one's innocence; *iets hardnekkig* ~ stubbornly maintain sth.

de **volhouder** /vɔlhɑudər/ (pl: -s) stayer

de **volière** /vɔljɛːrə/ (pl: -s) aviary; birdhouse

het **volk** /vɔlk/ (pl: -en, -eren) **1** people, nation, race **2** people, populace, folk: *een man uit het* ~ a working(-class) man; *het gewone* ~ the common people **3** people: *het circus trekt altijd veel* ~ the circus always draws a crowd

de **Volkenbond** /vɔlkə(n)bɔnt/ League of Nations

de **volkenkunde** /vɔlkə(n)kʏndə/ cultural anthropology

de **volkenmoord** /vɔlkəmort/ (pl: -en) genocide

het **volkenrecht** /vɔlkə(n)rɛxt/ international law

¹volkomen /vɔlkomə(n)/ (adj) complete, total

²volkomen /vɔlkomə(n)/ (adv) completely: *dat is* ~ *juist* that's perfectly true

het **volkorenbrood** /vɔlkorə(n)brot/ wholemeal bread; [Am] whole-wheat bread

de **volksbuurt** /vɔlksbyrt/ (pl: -en) working-class area (or: district)

de **volksdans** /vɔlksdɑns/ (pl: -en) folk dance

het **volksdansen** /vɔlksdɑnsə(n)/ folk dancing

de **volksgezondheid** /vɔlksxəzɔnthɛit/ public health, national health

de **volksheld** /vɔlkshɛlt/ (pl: -en) popular hero, national hero

de **volkshuisvesting** /vɔlkshœysfɛstɪŋ/ **1** public housing **2** (public) housing department

het **volkslied** /vɔlkslit/ (pl: -eren) **1** national anthem **2** folk song

de **volksmenner** /vɔlksmɛnər/ (pl: -s) demagogue, agitator

de **volksmond** /vɔlksmɔnt/: *in de* ~ in popular speech (or: parlance); *in de* ~ *heet dit* this is popularly called

de **volksmuziek** /vɔlksmyzik/ folk music

de **volkspartij** /vɔlkspɑrtɛi/ (pl: -en) people's party

de **volksraadpleging** /vɔlksratpleɣɪŋ/ (pl: -en) referendum, plebiscite de **volksrepubliek** /vɔlksrepyblik/ (pl: -en) people's republic: *de ~ China* the People's Republic of China

de **volksstam** /vɔlkstɑm/ (pl: -men) crowd, horde

de **volkstaal** /vɔlkstal/ (pl: -talen) vernacular, everyday language

de **volkstelling** /vɔlkstɛlɪŋ/ (pl: -en) census: *er werd een ~ gehouden* a census was taken

de **volkstuin** /vɔlkstœyn/ (pl: -en) allotment (garden)

de **volksuniversiteit** /vɔlksynivɛrzitɛit/ (pl: -en) [roughly] adult education centre

de **volksverhuizing** /vɔlksfərhœyzɪŋ/ (pl: -en) 1 migrations of a nation 2 (mass) migration

de **volksverlakkerij** /vɔlksfərlɑkərɛi/ deception (of the public)

het **volksvermaak** /vɔlksfərmak/ (pl: -vermaken) popular amusement (or: entertainment)

de **volksvertegenwoordiger** /vɔlksfərteɣə(n)wordəɣər/ (pl: -s) representative (of the people), member of parliament, MP; [Am] Congressman

de **volksvertegenwoordiging** /vɔlksfərteɣə(n)wordəɣɪŋ/ (pl: -en) house (or: chamber) of representatives, parliament

de **volksverzekering** /vɔlksfərzekərɪŋ/ (pl: -en) national insurance, social insurance

de **volksvijand** /vɔlksfɛiɑnt/ (pl: -en) public enemy, enemy of the people: *roken is ~ nummer één* smoking is public enemy number one

de **volkswoede** /vɔlkswudə/ popular fury (or: anger)

volledig /vɔledəɣ/ (adj, adv) 1 full, complete: *~e betaling* payment in full; *het schip is ~ uitgebrand* the ship was completely burnt out; *ik lees u de titel ~ voor* I'll read you the title in full 2 full, full-time: *~e (dienst)betrekking* full-time job

de **volledigheid** /vɔledəɣhɛit/ completeness

volledigheidshalve /vɔledəɣhɛitshɑlvə/ (adv) for the sake of completeness

volleerd /vɔlert/ (adj) fully-qualified

de **vollemaan** /vɔləman/ full moon: *het is ~* there is a full moon; *bij ~* when the moon is full, at full moon

volleren /vɔlerə(n)/ (volleerde, heeft gevolleerd) volley

de ¹**volleybal** /vɔlibal/ (pl: -len) [ball] volleyball

het ²**volleybal** /vɔlibal/ [sport] volleyball

volleyballen /vɔlibalə(n)/ (volleyballde, heeft gevolleybald) play volleyball

vollopen /vɔlopə(n)/ (liep vol, is volgelopen) fill up, be filled: *de zaal begon vol te lopen* the hall was getting crowded; *het bad laten ~* run the bath

¹**volmaakt** /vɔlmakt/ (adj) perfect, consummate

²**volmaakt** /vɔlmakt/ (adv) perfectly: *ik ben ~ gezond* I am in perfect health

de **volmacht** /vɔlmɑxt/ (pl: -en) 1 power (of attorney), mandate, authority 2 warrant, authorization

volmondig /vɔlmɔndəɣ/ (adj, adv) wholehearted, frank: *~ iets bekennen* (or: *toegeven*) confess (or: admit) sth. frankly; *een ~ ja* a straightforward (or: heartfelt) 'yes'

volop /vɔlɔp/ (adv) in abundance, plenty, a lot of: *~ ruimte* ample room; *het is ~ zomer* it is the height of summer; *er was ~ te eten* there was food in abundance

het **volpension** /vɔlpɛnʃɔn/ full board

volproppen /vɔlprɔpə(n)/ (propte vol, heeft volgepropt) cram; stuff: *volgepropte trams* overcrowded (or: jam-packed) trams; *zich ~* stuff o.s.

volslagen /vɔlslaɣə(n)/ (adj, adv) complete, utter: *een ~ onbekende* a total stranger; *~ belachelijk* utterly ridiculous

volslank /vɔlslɑŋk/ (adj) plump; well-rounded

volstaan /vɔlstan/ (volstond, heeft volstaan) 1 be enough, be sufficient, do: *dat volstaat* that will do 2 limit o.s. (to)

volstoppen /vɔlstɔpə(n)/ (stopte vol, heeft volgestopt) stuff (full), fill to the brim (or: top)

volstrekt /vɔlstrɛkt/ (adj, adv) total, complete: *ik ben het ~ niet met hem eens* I disagree entirely with him

de **volt** /vɔlt/ (pl: -s) volt

het/de **voltage** /vɔltaʒə/ (pl: -s) voltage

voltallig /vɔltɑləɣ/ (adj) complete, full, entire: *het ~e bestuur* the entire committee; *de ~e vergadering* the plenary assembly (or: meeting)

voltijds /vɔltɛits/ (adj) full-time

voltooid /vɔltojt/ (adj) complete, finished: *een ~ deelwoord* a past (or: perfect) participle; *de ~ tegenwoordige* (or: *verleden*) *tijd* the perfect (or: pluperfect)

voltooien /vɔltojə(n)/ (voltooide, heeft voltooid) complete, finish

de **voltooiing** /vɔltojɪŋ/ (pl: -en) completion

de **voltreffer** /vɔltrɛfər/ (pl: -s) direct hit

voltrekken /vɔltrɛkə(n)/ (voltrok, heeft voltrokken) execute; celebrate; perform

de **voltrekking** /vɔltrɛkɪŋ/ (pl: -en) celebration; performing

voluit /vɔlœyt/ (adv) in full

het **volume** /vɔlymə/ (pl: -n, -s) volume, loudness

de **volumeknop** /vɔlyməknɔp/ (pl: -pen) volume control (or: knob)

volumineus /vɔlyminøs/ (adj) voluminous

volvet /vɔlvɛt/ (adj) full-cream

volwaardig /vɔlwardəɣ/ (adj) full; able(-bodied): *een ~ lid* a full member

¹**volwassen** /vɔlwɑsə(n)/ (adj) adult, grown-up; mature; full-grown; ripe: *~ gedrag* ma-

ture (*or:* adult) behaviour; *ik ben een ~ vrouw!* I'm a grown woman!; *toen zij ~ werd* on reaching womanhood; *~ worden* grow to maturity, grow up

² **volwassen** /vɔlwɑsə(n)/ (adv) in an adult (*or:* a mature) way: *zich ~ gedragen* behave like an adult

de **volwassene** /vɔlwɑsənə/ (pl: -n) adult, grown-up

het **volwassenenonderwijs** /vɔlwɑsənə(n)-ɔndərwɛis/ adult education

de **volwassenheid** /vɔlwɑsənhɛit/ adulthood, maturity

de **volzin** /vɔlzɪn/ (pl: -nen) sentence

de **vondeling** /vɔndəlɪŋ/ (pl: -en) abandoned child: *een kind te ~ leggen* abandon a child

de **vondst** /vɔnst/ (pl: -en) invention, discovery: *een ~ doen* make a (real) find; *een gelukkige ~* a lucky strike

de **vonk** /vɔŋk/ (pl: -en) spark || *de ~ sloeg over* the audience caught on

vonken /vɔŋkə(n)/ (vonkte, heeft gevonkt) spark(le), shoot sparks

het **vonnis** /vɔnɪs/ (pl: -sen) judgement; sentence; verdict: *een ~ vellen (uitspreken) over* pass (*or:* pronounce, give) judgement on

vonnissen /vɔnɪsə(n)/ (vonniste, heeft gevonnist) sentence, convict; pass judgement (*or:* sentence) (on)

de **voodoo** /vudu/ voodoo

de **voogd** /voxt/ (pl: -en) guardian: *toeziend ~* co-guardian, joint guardian; *~ zijn over iem.* be s.o.'s guardian

de **voogdij** /voɣdɛi/ (pl: -en) guardianship: *onder ~ staan* (or: *plaatsen*) be (*or:* place) under guardianship

de **voogdijminister** /voɣdɛimɪnɪstər/ (pl: -s) [Belg] minister in charge

de **voogdijraad** /voɣdɛirat/ (pl: -raden) guardianship board

de ¹ **voor** /vor/ (pl: voren) **1** furrow **2** wrinkle, furrow

het ² **voor** /vor/ (pl: -s) pro, advantage: *~ en tegen van een voorstel* the pros and cons of a proposition

³ **voor** /vor/ (adv) **1** in (the) front: *een kind met een slab ~* a child wearing a bib; *de auto staat ~* the car is at the door; *hij is ~ in de dertig* he is in his early thirties; *~ in het boek* near the beginning of the book **2** ahead, in the lead: *vier punten ~* four points ahead; *zij zijn ons ~ geweest* they got (t)here before (*or:* ahead of) us **3** for, in favour of: *ik ben er niet ~* I'm not in favour of that

⁴ **voor** /vor/ (prep) **1** for: *zij is een goede moeder ~ haar kinderen* she is a good mother to her children; *dat is net iets ~ hem* a) that is just the thing for him; b) that is just like him; *dat is niets ~ mij* that is not my kind of thing (*or:* my cup of tea) **2** before, in front of: *de dagen die ~ ons liggen* the days (that lie) ahead of

us **3** before, for **4** before, ahead of: *~ zondag* before Sunday; *tien ~ zeven* ten to seven **5** for, instead of: *ik zal ~ mijn zoon betalen* I'll pay for my son **6** for, in favour of: *ik ben ~ FC Utrecht* I'm a supporter of FC Utrecht || *wat zijn het ~ mensen?* what sort of people are they?

⁵ **voor** /vor/ (conj) before: *~ hij vertrok, was ik al weg* I was already gone before he left

vooraan /voran/ (adv) in (the) front: *~ lopen* walk at the front; *iets ~ zetten* put sth. (up) in front

vooraanstaand /voranstant/ (adj) prominent, leading

vooraf /voraf/ (adv) beforehand, in advance: *een verklaring ~* an explanation in advance; *je moet ~ goed bedenken wat je gaat doen* you need to think ahead about what you're going to do

voorafgaan /vorafxan/ (ging vooraf, is voorafgegaan) precede, go before, go in front (of): *de weken ~de aan het feest* the weeks preceding the celebration

voorafgaand /vorafxant/ (adj) preceding, foregoing: *~e toestemming* prior permission

het **voorafje** /vorafjə/ (pl: -s) appetizer, hors d'oeuvre

vooral /voral/ (adv) especially, particularly: *dat moet je ~ doen* do that (or: go ahead) by all means; *ga ~ vroeg naar bed* be sure to go to bed early; *maak haar ~ niet wakker* don't wake her up whatever you do; *vergeet het ~ niet* whatever you do, don't forget it; *~ omdat* especially because

vooraleer /voraler/ (conj) [form] afore, before

vooralsnog /voralsnɔx/ (adv) as yet, for the time being

het **voorarrest** /vorarɛst/ remand, custody, detention: *in ~ zitten* be on remand, be in custody; *in ~ gehouden worden* be taken into custody

de **vooravond** /voravɔnt/ (pl: -en) eve

de **voorbaat** /vorbat/: *bij ~ dank* thank (*or:* thanking) you in advance; *bij ~ kansloos zijn* not stand a chance from the very start

de **voorbank** /vorbɑŋk/ (pl: -en) front seats

voorbarig /vorbarəx/ (adj, adv) premature: *~ spreken* (or: *antwoorden*) speak (*or:* answer) too soon

voorbedacht /vorbədɑxt/ (adj): *met ~en rade* intentionally; with premeditation

het **voorbeeld** /vorbelt/ (pl: -en) example, model; instance: *een afschrikwekkend ~* a warning; *een ~ stellen* make an example of s.o.; *iemands ~ volgen* follow s.o.'s lead (*or:* example); *tot ~ dienen* serve as an example (*or:* a model) for

de **voorbeeldfunctie** /vorbeltfʏŋksi/ exemplary function: *een ~ vervullen* serve as an example to others

voorbeeldig /vorbeldəχ/ (adj, adv) exemplary, model: *een ~ gedrag* exemplary conduct

het **voorbehoedmiddel** /vorbəhutmɪdəl/ (pl: -en) contraceptive

het **voorbehoud** /vorbəhaut/ restriction, reservation; condition: *iets onder ~ beloven* make a conditional promise; *zonder ~* without reservations

het **voorbehouden** /vorbəhaudə(n)/ reserve

voorbereiden /vorbərɛidə(n)/ (bereidde voor, heeft voorbereid) prepare, get ready: *zich ~ op een examen* prepare for an exam; *op alles voorbereid zijn* be ready for anything

voorbereidend /vorbərɛidənt/ (adj) preparatory: *~ wetenschappelijk onderwijs* pre-university education; *-e werkzaamheden* groundwork

de **voorbereiding** /vorbərɛidɪŋ/ (pl: -en) preparation: *-en treffen* make preparations

de **voorbeschouwing** /vorbəsχauwɪŋ/ (pl: -en) preview

de **voorbespreking** /vorbəsprekɪŋ/ (pl: -en) preliminary talk

voorbestemmen /vorbəstɛmə(n)/ (bestemde voor, heeft voorbestemd) predestine, predetermine: *voorbestemd zijn om te …* predestined (*or:* fated) to …

¹**voorbij** /vorbɛi/ (adj) past; [after vb] over: *die tijd is ~* those days are gone; *-e tijden* bygone times

²**voorbij** /vorbɛi/ (adv) **1** past, by: *wacht tot de trein ~ is* wait until the train has passed **2** beyond, past: *hij is die leeftijd allang ~* he is way past that age; *je bent er al ~* you have already passed it

³**voorbij** /vorbɛi/ (prep) beyond, past: *we zijn al ~ Amsterdam* we've already passed Amsterdam; *hij ging ~ het huis* he went past the house

voorbijgaan /vorbɛiɣan/ (ging voorbij, is voorbijgegaan) pass by, go by: *de jaren gingen voorbij* the years passed by; *een kans voorbij laten gaan* pass up a chance; *er gaat praktisch geen week voorbij of …* hardly a week goes by when (*or:* that) … || *in het ~* incidentally, by the way, in passing

voorbijgaand /vorbɛiɣant/ (adj) transitory, passing: *van -e aard* of a temporary nature

de **voorbijganger** /vorbɛiɣaŋər/ (pl: -s) passer-by

voorbijkomen /vorbɛikomə(n)/ (kwam voorbij, is voorbijgekomen) come past, come by, pass (by)

voorbijrijden /vorbɛirɛidə(n)/ (reed voorbij, is voorbijgereden) drive past; ride past

voorbijschieten /vorbɛisχitə(n)/ (schoot voorbij, is voorbijgeschoten) whizz by || *zijn doel ~* overshoot the mark

voorbijtrekken /vorbɛitrɛkə(n)/ (trok voorbij, is voorbijgetrokken) pass: *hij zag zijn leven aan zijn oog ~* he saw his life pass before his eyes

voorbijvliegen /vorbɛivliɣə(n)/ (vloog voorbij, is voorbijgevlogen) fly (by): *de weken vlogen voorbij* the weeks just flew (by)

de **voorbode** /vorbodə/ (pl: -s) forerunner, herald; [fig] omen: *de zwaluwen zijn de ~n van de lente* the swallows are the heralds of spring

voordat /vordat/ (conj) **1** before; until: *alles was gemakkelijker ~ hij kwam* things were easier before he came; *~ ik je brief kreeg, wist ik er niets van* I knew nothing about it until I got your letter **2** before (that)

het **voordeel** /vordel/ (pl: -delen) **1** advantage, benefit: *Agassi staat op ~* advantage Agassi; *zijn ~ met iets doen* take advantage of sth.; *~ hebben bij* profit (*or:* benefit) from; *hij is in zijn ~ veranderd* he has changed for the better; *3-0 in het ~ van Nederland* 3-0 for the Dutch side (*or:* team); *iem. het ~ van de twijfel gunnen* give s.o. the benefit of the doubt **2** advantage, plus point: *de voor- en nadelen* the advantages and disadvantages; *een ~ behalen* gain an advantage

de **voordeelregel** /vordelreɣəl/ advantage rule

voordelig /vordeləχ/ (adj, adv) **1** profitable, lucrative: *~ kopen* get a bargain **2** economical, inexpensive: *-er zijn* be cheaper; *~ in het gebruik* be economical in use, go a long way

de **voordeur** /vordør/ (pl: -en) front door

¹**voordoen** /vordun/ (deed voor, heeft voorgedaan) show, demonstrate

zich ²**voordoen** /vordun/ (deed zich voor, heeft zich voorgedaan) act, appear, pose: *zich flink ~* put on a bold front; *zich ~ als politieagent* pose as a policeman

de **voordracht** /vordraχt/ (pl: -en) lecture: *een ~ houden over* read a paper on, give a lecture on

voordragen /vordraɣə(n)/ (droeg voor, heeft voorgedragen) **1** recite **2** nominate, recommend

voordringen /vordrɪŋə(n)/ (drong voor, is voorgedrongen) push forward (*or:* past, ahead), jump the queue

de **voorfilm** /vorfɪlm/ (pl: -s) short

voorgaan /vorɣan/ (ging voor, is voorgegaan) **1** go ahead (*or:* before), lead (the way): *dames gaan voor* ladies first; *iem. laten ~* let s.o. go first; *gaat u voor!* after you!, lead the way **2** take precedence, come first: *het belangrijkste moet ~* the most important has to come first

voorgaand /vorɣant/ (adj) preceding, former, last, previous: *op de -e bladzijde* on the preceding page

de **voorganger** /vorɣaŋər/ (pl: -s) predecessor

het **voorgebergte** /vorɣəbɛrχtə/ promontory,

headland
voorgekookt /v<u>o</u>rɣəkokt/ (adj) pre-
cooked, parboiled: *~e aardappelen* pre-
cooked potatoes; *~e rijst* parboiled rice
voorgeleiden /v<u>o</u>rɣəlɛidə(n)/ (geleidde
voor, heeft voorgeleid) bring in
voorgenomen /v<u>o</u>rɣənomə(n)/ (adj) intended, proposed: *de ~ maatregelen* the
proposed measures
het **voorgerecht** /v<u>o</u>rɣərɛχt/ (pl: -en) first
course, starter
de **voorgeschiedenis** /v<u>o</u>rɣəsχidənɪs/ previous history; [of pers] ancestry; past history
voorgeschreven /v<u>o</u>rɣəsχrevə(n)/ (adj)
prescribed, required
de **voorgevel** /v<u>o</u>rɣevəl/ (pl: -s) face
voorgeven /v<u>o</u>rɣevə(n)/ (gaf voor, heeft
voorgegeven) pretend
het **voorgevoel** /v<u>o</u>rɣəvul/ (pl: -ens) premonition; foreboding: *een angstig ~* an anxious
foreboding; *ergens een ~ van hebben* have a
premonition about sth.
voorgoed /v<u>o</u>rɣut/ (adv) for good, once
and for all: *dat is nu ~ voorbij* that is over and
done with now
de **voorgrond** /v<u>o</u>rɣront/ (pl: -en) foreground:
op de ~ treden, zich op de ~ plaatsen come to
prominence; *iets op de ~ plaatsen* place sth. in
the forefront; *hij dringt zich altijd op de ~* he
always pushes himself forward
de **voorhamer** /v<u>o</u>rhamər/ (pl: -s) sledge(hammer)
de **voorhand** /v<u>o</u>rhant/: *op ~* beforehand, in
advance
voorhanden /vorh<u>a</u>ndə(n)/ (adj) on hand,
in stock: *niet meer ~* unavailable
voorhebben /v<u>o</u>rhɛbə(n)/ (had voor, heeft
voorgehad) **1** have on, wear: *een schort ~*
have on (*or:* wear) an apron **2** have in front
of: *de verkeerde ~* have got the wrong one
(in mind) ‖ *het goed met iem. ~* mean well by
a person, wish a person well
voorheen /vorh<u>e</u>n/ (adv) formerly, in the
past
de **voorheffing** /v<u>o</u>rhɛfɪŋ/ (pl: -en) advance
tax payment
de **voorhoede** /v<u>o</u>rhudə/ (pl: -s) forward line,
forwards
de **voorhoedespeler** /v<u>o</u>rhudəspelər/ (pl: -s)
forward
het **voorhoofd** /v<u>o</u>rhoft/ (pl: -en) forehead
de **voorhoofdsholteontsteking** /v<u>o</u>r-
hoftsholtəontstekɪŋ/ (pl: -en) sinusitis
voorhouden /v<u>o</u>rhaudə(n)/ (hield voor,
heeft voorgehouden) represent, confront:
iem. zijn slechte gedrag ~ confront s.o. with
his bad conduct
de **voorhuid** /v<u>o</u>rhœyt/ (pl: -en) foreskin
voorin /vor<u>ɪ</u>n/ (adv) in (the) front; at the
beginning
vooringenomen /vor<u>ɪ</u>nɣənomə(n)/ (adj)

biased, prejudiced
het **voorjaar** /v<u>o</u>rjar/ (pl: -jaren) spring, springtime
de **voorjaarsmoeheid** /v<u>o</u>rjarsmuhɛit/
springtime fatigue
de **voorjaarsvakantie** /v<u>o</u>rjarsfakɑn(t)si/ (pl:
-s) spring holidays; [Am] spring vacation
de **voorkamer** /v<u>o</u>rkamər/ (pl: -s) front room
de **voorkant** /v<u>o</u>rkɑnt/ (pl: -en) front: *de ~ van
een auto* the front of a car
voorkauwen /v<u>o</u>rkɑuwə(n)/ (kauwde voor,
heeft voorgekauwd) repeat over and over
de **voorkennis** /v<u>o</u>rkɛnɪs/ foreknowledge; inside knowledge: *~ hebben van* have prior
knowledge of; *handel met ~* insider trading
(*or:* dealing)
de **voorkeur** /v<u>o</u>rkør/ preference: *mijn ~ gaat
uit naar* I (would) prefer; *de ~ geven aan* give
preference to; *bij ~* preferably
de **voorkeursbehandeling** /v<u>o</u>rkørz-
bəhandəlɪŋ/ (pl: -en) preferential treatment
de **voorkeurstem** /v<u>o</u>rkørstɛm/ (pl: -men)
preference vote
het ¹**voorkomen** /v<u>o</u>rkomə(n)/ **1** appearance,
bearing: *nu krijgt de zaak een geheel ander ~*
things are now looking a lot different **2** occurrence, incidence: *het regelmatig ~ van ongeregeldheden* the recurrence of disturbances
²**voorkomen** /v<u>o</u>rkomə(n)/ (kwam voor, is
voorgekomen) **1** occur, happen **2** occur, be
found: *die planten komen overal voor* those
plants grow everywhere **3** appear: *hij moet ~*
he has to appear in court **4** seem, appear: *dat
komt mij bekend voor* that rings a bell, that
sounds familiar
³**voorkomen** /vork<u>o</u>mə(n)/ (voorkwam,
heeft voorkomen) prevent: *om misverstan-
den te ~* to prevent (any) misunderstandings;
we moeten ~ dat hij hier weggaat we must
prevent him from leaving; *~ is beter dan genezen* prevention is better than cure
voorkomend /vork<u>o</u>mənt/ (adj) occurring:
dagelijks ~e zaken everyday events, recurrent
matters; *een veel ~ probleem* a common
problem; *zelden ~* unusual, rare
de **voorkoming** /vork<u>o</u>mɪŋ/ prevention: *ter ~
van ongelukken* to prevent accidents
voorlaatst /vorl<u>a</u>tst/ (adj) last but one
het **voorland** /v<u>o</u>rlɑnt/ (pl: -en) future: *dat is
ook haar ~* that's also in store for her
voorlaten /v<u>o</u>rlatə(n)/ (liet voor, heeft
voorgelaten) allow to go first, give precedence to
voorleggen /v<u>o</u>rlɛɣə(n)/ (legde voor, heeft
voorgelegd) present: *iem. een plan ~* present
s.o. with a plan; *een zaak aan de rechter ~*
bring a case before the court
de **voorletter** /v<u>o</u>rlɛtər/ (pl: -s) initial (letter):
wat zijn uw ~s? what are your initials?
voorlezen /v<u>o</u>rlezə(n)/ (las voor, heeft
voorgelezen) read aloud, read out loud: *iem.*

een **brief** (or: *de* **krant**) ~ read aloud a letter (or: the newspaper) to s.o.; *kinderen* **houden van** ~ children like to be read to; ~ **uit** *een boek* read aloud from a book

voorlichten /voːrlɪχtə(n)/ (lichtte voor, heeft voorgelicht) **1** inform: *zich goed* **laten** ~ seek good advice; *we zijn* **verkeerd** *voorgelicht* we were misinformed **2** tell (s.o.) the facts of life

de **voorlichter** /voːrlɪχtər/ (pl: -s) press officer, information officer

de **voorlichting** /voːrlɪχtɪŋ/ (pl: -en) information: *de* **afdeling** ~ public relations department; **seksuele** ~ sex education; *goede* ~ **geven** give good advice

de **voorlichtingsdienst** /voːrlɪχtɪŋzdinst/ (pl: -en) (public) information service

de **voorliefde** /voːrlivdə/ predilection, preference, fondness

voorliegen /voːrliɣə(n)/ (loog voor, heeft voorgelogen) lie to

voorlopen /voːrlopə(n)/ (liep voor, heeft voorgelopen) **1** walk (or: go) in front **2** be fast: *de* **klok** *loopt vijf minuten voor* the clock is five minutes fast

de **voorloper** /voːrlopər/ (pl: -s) precursor, forerunner

¹**voorlopig** /voːrlopəχ/ (adj) temporary, provisional: *een* ~e *aanstelling* a temporary appointment; ~ *verslag* interim report

²**voorlopig** /voːrlopəχ/ (adv) for the time being: *hij zal het* ~ *accepteren* he will accept it provisionally; ~ *niet* not for the time being; ~ *voor een maand* for a month to begin with

voormalig /voːrmaləχ/ (adj) former

de **voorman** /voːrman/ (pl: -nen) foreman

de **voormiddag** /voːrmɪdaχ/ (pl: -en) **1** morning **2** early afternoon

de **voorn** /voːrn/ (pl: -s) roach

de ¹**voornaam** /voːrnam/ first name: *iem.* **bij** *zijn* ~ *noemen* call s.o. by his first name

²**voornaam** /voːrnam/ (adj, adv) **1** distinguished, prominent: *een* ~ *voorkomen* a dignified (or: distinguished) appearance **2** main, important: *de* ~*ste* *dagbladen* the leading dailies; *de* ~*ste* *feiten* the main facts

het **voornaamwoord** /voːrnamwort/ (pl: -en) pronoun: *aanwijzend* ~ demonstrative pronoun; *bezittelijk* ~ possessive pronoun; *betrekkelijk* ~ relative pronoun; *persoonlijk* ~ personal pronoun

voornamelijk /voːrnaməlǝk/ (adv) mainly, chiefly

het ¹**voornemen** /voːrnemə(n)/ (pl: -s) intention; resolution: *zij is vol* **goede** ~*s* she is full of good intentions; *het* **vaste** ~ *iets te bereiken* the determination to achieve sth.

zich ²**voornemen** /voːrnemə(n)/ (nam zich voor, heeft zich voorgenomen) resolve: *hij had het zich* **heilig** *voorgenomen* he had firmly resolved to do so; *zij bereikte wat ze zich voorgeno-*

men had she achieved what she had set out (or: planned) to do

voornoemd /voːrnumt/ (adj) above-mentioned

de **vooronderstelling** /voːrɔndərstɛlɪŋ/ (pl: -en) presupposition

het **vooronderzoek** /voːrɔndərzuk/ (pl: -en) preliminary investigation: *gerechtelijk* ~ hearing

het **vooroordeel** /voːrordel/ (pl: -oordelen) prejudice: *een* ~ **hebben** *over* be prejudiced against; *zonder* *vooroordelen* unbiased, unprejudiced

vooroorlogs /voːrorlɔχs/ (adj) pre-war

voorop /voːrɔp/ (adv) in front, in the lead, first: *het nummer* **staat** ~ *het bankbiljet* the number is on the front of the banknote; ~ **staat**, *dat …* the main thing is that …

vooropgaan /voːrɔpχan/ (ging voorop, is vooropgegaan) lead (the way)

de **vooropleiding** /voːrɔplɛidɪŋ/ (pl: -en) (preliminary, preparatory) training

vooroplopen /voːrɔplopə(n)/ (liep voorop, heeft vooropgelopen) **1** walk (or: run) in front **2** lead (the way): ~ *in de modewereld* be a trendsetter in the fashion world

vooropstaan /voːrɔpstan/ (stond voorop, heeft vooropgestaan): *wat vooropstaat, is …* the main thing is that …

vooropstellen /voːrɔpstɛlə(n)/ (stelde voorop, heeft vooropgesteld) **1** assume: *laten we dit* ~: *…* let's get one thing straight right away: …; *ik stel voorop* **dat** *hij altijd eerlijk is geweest* to begin with, I maintain that he has always been honest **2** put first (and foremost): *de* **volksgezondheid** ~ put public health first (and foremost)

de **voorouders** /voːrauders/ (pl) ancestors, forefathers

voorover /voːrovər/ (adv) headfirst, face down: *met het gezicht* ~ **liggen** lie face down(ward); ~ **tuimelen** tumble headfirst (or: forward)

de **voorpagina** /voːrpaɣina/ (pl: -'s) front page: *de* ~'s **halen** make the front pages

de **voorpoot** /voːrpot/ (pl: -poten) foreleg, forepaw

de **voorpret** /voːrprɛt/ pleasurable anticipation

het **voorproefje** /voːrprufjə/ (pl: -s) (fore)taste

het **voorprogramma** /voːrproɣrama/ (pl: -'s) curtain-raiser; supporting programme; shorts: *een concert van Doe Maar met Frans Bauer* **in** *het* ~ a Doe Maar concert with Frans Bauer as supporting act

de **voorraad** /voːrat/ (pl: voorraden) **1** stock, supply: *de* ~ **goud** the gold reserve(s); *de* ~ **opnemen** take stock; *zolang de* ~ **strekt** as long as (or: while) supplies/stocks last; *niet meer in* ~ *zijn* not be in stock anymore; *uit* ~ *leverbaar* available from stock **2** supplies, stock(s): ~ **inslaan** *voor de winter* lay in supplies for the winter; *we zijn* **door** *onze ~ heen* we have gone through our supplies

de **voorraadkast** /vo̲ratkɑst/ (pl: -en) store cupboard; [Am] supply closet

voorradig /vora̲dəɣ/ (adj) in stock (*or:* store), on hand: *in alle kleuren ~* available in all colours

de **voorrang** /vo̲rɑŋ/ right of way, priority: *~* **hebben** *op* have (the) right of way over; *verkeer van rechts* **heeft** *~* traffic from the right has (the) right of way; *geen ~* **verlenen** fail to yield, fail to give (right of) way; *~* **verlenen** *aan verkeer van rechts* give way (*or:* yield) to the right; *(de) ~* **hebben** *(boven)* have (*or:* take) priority (over); *met ~ behandelen* give preferential treatment

de **voorrangsweg** /vo̲rɑŋswɛɣ/ (pl: -en) major road

het **voorrecht** /vo̲rɛɣt/ (pl: -en) privilege: *ik* **had** *het ~ hem te verwelkomen* I had the honour (*or:* privilege) of welcoming him

voorrekenen /vo̲rekənə(n)/ (rekende voor, heeft voorgerekend) figure out, work out

voorrijden /vo̲rɛidə(n)/ (reed voor, heeft/is voorgereden) drive up to the front (*or:* entrance, door)

de **voorrijkosten** /vo̲rɛikɔstə(n)/ (pl) call-out charge

de **voorronde** /vo̲rɔndə/ (pl: -n, -s) qualifying round, preliminary round

de **voorruit** /vo̲rœyt/ (pl: -en) windscreen; [Am] windshield

voorschieten /vo̲rsxitə(n)/ (schoot voor, heeft voorgeschoten) advance, lend: *ik zal het even ~* I'll lend you the money

de **voorschoot** /vo̲rsxot/ (pl: -schoten) apron, pinafore

het **voorschot** /vo̲rsxɔt/ (pl: -ten) advance, loan

voorschotelen /vo̲rsxotələ(n)/ (schotelde voor, heeft voorgeschoteld) dish up, serve up

het **voorschrift** /vo̲rsxrɪft/ (pl: -en) **1** prescription, order: *op ~ van de dokter* on doctor's orders **2** regulation, rule: *aan de ~en* **voldoen** satisfy (*or:* meet) the requirements; *volgens ~* as prescribed (*or:* directed)

voorschrijven /vo̲rsxrɛivə(n)/ (schreef voor, heeft voorgeschreven) prescribe: *rust ~* prescribe rest; *op de voorgeschreven* **tijd** at the appointed time

het **voorseizoen** /vo̲rsɛizun/ (pl: -en) pre-season

de **voorselectie** /vo̲rselɛksi/ (pl: -s) pre-selection

voorsorteren /vo̲rsɔrterə(n)/ (sorteerde voor, heeft voorgesorteerd) get in lane: *rechts ~* get in the right-hand lane

het **voorspel** /vo̲rspɛl/ (pl: -en) **1** prelude, prologue: *het ~ van de* **oorlog** the prelude to the war **2** foreplay

voorspelbaar /vorspɛlbar/ (adj) predictable

voorspelen /vo̲rspelə(n)/ (speelde voor, heeft voorgespeeld) play

voorspellen /vorspɛlə(n)/ (voorspelde, heeft voorspeld) **1** predict, forecast: *iem. een gouden* **toekomst** *~* predict a rosy future for s.o.; *ik heb het u wel voorspeld* I told you so **2** promise: *dat voorspelt niet veel* **goeds** that doesn't bode well

de **voorspelling** /vorspɛlɪŋ/ (pl: -en) **1** prophecy **2** prediction: *de ~en voor morgen* the (weather) forecast for tomorrow

voorspiegelen /vo̲rspiɣələ(n)/ (spiegelde voor, heeft voorgespiegeld) delude (with images of …)

de **voorspoed** /vo̲rsput/ prosperity: *in voor- en* **tegenspoed** for better or for worse; *voor- en* **tegenspoed** ups and downs

voorspoedig /vorspu̲dəɣ/ (adj, adv) successful, prosperous: *alles* **verliep** *~* it all went off well

de **voorspraak** /vo̲rsprak/ intercession

de **voorsprong** /vo̲rsprɔŋ/ (pl: -en) (head) start, lead: *hij won met* **grote** *~* he won by a large margin; *iem. een ~* **geven** give s.o. a head start; *een ~* **hebben** *op iem.* have the jump (*or:* lead) on s.o.

voorst /vorst/ (adj) first, front: *op de ~e* **bank** *zitten* be (*or:* sit) in the front row

voorstaan /vo̲rstan/ (stond voor, heeft voorgestaan) stand (*or:* be) in front: *de* **auto** *staat voor* the car is (out) at the front

de **voorstad** /vo̲rstɑt/ (pl: -steden) suburb

de **voorstander** /vo̲rstɑndər/ (pl: -s) supporter, advocate: *ik ben er een* **groot** *~ van* I'm all for it

het **voorstel** /vo̲rstɛl/ (pl: -len) proposal, suggestion: *iem. een ~* **doen** make s.o. a proposal (*or:* proposition)

voorstelbaar /vorstɛlbar/ (adj) imaginable, conceivable

¹**voorstellen** /vo̲rstɛlə(n)/ (stelde voor, heeft voorgesteld) **1** introduce: *zich ~* **aan** introduce o.s. to **2** suggest, propose **3** represent, play **4** represent, depict: *het schilderij stelt een* **huis** *voor* the painting depicts a house || *dat stelt* **niets** *voor* that doesn't amount to anything

zich ²**voorstellen** /vo̲rstɛlə(n)/ (stelde zich voor, heeft zich voorgesteld) imagine, conceive: *ik kan mij zijn* **gezicht** *niet meer ~* I can't recall his face; *dat kan ik me* **best** *~* I can imagine (that); *stel je voor!* just imagine!

de **voorstelling** /vo̲rstɛlɪŋ/ (pl: -en) **1** show(ing), performance: *doorlopende ~* non-stop (*or:* continuous) performance **2** representation, depiction **3** impression, idea: *dat is een* **verkeerde** *~ van zaken* that is a misrepresentation; *zich een ~ van iets* **maken** picture sth., form an idea of sth.

het **voorstellingsvermogen** /vo̲rstɛlɪŋsfərmoɣə(n)/ (power(s) of) imagination

voorstemmen /vọrstɛmə(n)/ (stemde voor, heeft voorgestemd) vote for

de **voorsteven** /vọrstevə(n)/ (pl: -s) stem, prow

de **voorstopper** /vọrstɔpər/ (pl: -s) centre back

voort /vort/ (adv) on(wards), forward

voortaan /vọrtan/ (adv) from now on

de **voortand** /vọrtɑnt/ (pl: -en) front tooth

het **voortbestaan** /vọrdbəstan/ continued existence (or: life), survival

¹**voortbewegen** /vọrdbəweɣə(n)/ (bewoog voort, heeft voortbewogen) drive, move on (or: forward): *het karretje werd* **door** *stroom voortbewogen* the buggy was driven by electricity

zich ²**voortbewegen** /vọrdbəweɣə(n)/ (bewoog zich voort, heeft zich voortbewogen) move on (or: forward)

voortborduren /vọrdbɔrdyrə(n)/ (borduurde voort, heeft voortgeborduurd) embroider, elaborate: **op** *een thema* ~ elaborate (or: embroider) on a theme

voortbrengen /vọrdbrɛŋə(n)/ (bracht voort, heeft voortgebracht) produce, create, bring forth: **kinderen** ~ produce children

het **voortbrengsel** /vọrdbrɛŋsəl/ (pl: -en) product

voortduren /vọrdyrə(n)/ (duurde voort, heeft voortgeduurd) continue, go on, wear on

voortdurend /vọrdyrənt/ (adj, adv) constant, continual; continuous: *een ~e* **dreiging** a constant threat (or: menace); *haar naam* **duikt** ~ **op** *in de krant* her name keeps cropping up in the (news)papers

het **voorteken** /vọrtekə(n)/ (pl: -s, -en) omen, sign

de **voortent** /vọrtɛnt/ (pl: -en) front bell (end), (front) extension; awning

voortgaan /vọrtxan/ (ging voort, is voortgegaan) continue

de **voortgang** /vọrtxɑŋ/ progress

voortgezet /vọrtxəzɛt/ (adj) continued, further: ~ **onderwijs** secondary education

voortijdig /vọrtɛ̣idəx/ (adj, adv) premature, untimely: *de les* **werd** ~ **afgebroken** the lesson was cut short; ~ *klaar zijn* be finished ahead of time

voortkomen /vọrtkomə(n)/ (kwam voort, is voortgekomen) (+ uit) stem (from), flow (from): *de* **daaruit** *~de misstanden* the resulting (or: consequent) abuses

voortleven /vọrtlevə(n)/ (leefde voort, heeft voortgeleefd) live on: *zij leeft voort* **in** *onze herinnering* she lives on in our memory

voortmaken /vọrtmakə(n)/ (maakte voort, heeft voortgemaakt) hurry up, make haste

het **voortouw** /vọrtɑu/: *het* ~ **nemen** take the lead

zich **voortplanten** /vọrtplɑntə(n)/ (plantte zich voort, heeft zich voortgeplant) **1** reproduce, multiply **2** propagate, be transmitted: *geluid plant zich voort* **in** *golven* sound is transmitted (or: travels) in waves

de **voortplanting** /vọrtplɑntɪŋ/ reproduction, multiplication, breeding: *geslachtelijke* ~ sexual reproduction

het **voortplantingsorgaan** /vọrtplɑntɪŋsɔrɣan/ (pl: -organen) reproductive organ

voortreffelijk /vortrɛ̣fələk/ (adj, adv) excellent, superb: *hij* **danst** ~ he dances superbly (or: exquisitely)

voortrekken /vọrtrɛkə(n)/ (trok voor, heeft voorgetrokken) favour, give preference to: *de een* **boven** *de ander* ~ favour one person above another

de **voortrekker** /vọrtrɛkər/ (pl: -s) **1** pioneer **2** Venture Scout; [Am] Explorer

voorts /vorts/ (adv) furthermore, moreover, besides

zich **voortslepen** /vọrtslepə(n)/ (sleepte zich voort, heeft zich voortgesleept) drag on, linger: *een trots al* **jarenlang** *~de kwestie* a lingering question

de **voortuin** /vọrtœyn/ (pl: -en) front garden; [Am] front yard

voortvarend /vortfạrənt/ (adj, adv) energetic, dynamic

voortvloeien /vọrtflujə(n)/ (vloeide voort, is voortgevloeid) result (from), arise (from)

voortvluchtig /vortflỵxtəx/ (adj) fugitive: *hij* **is** ~ he is on the run

voortzetten /vọrtsɛtə(n)/ (zette voort, heeft voortgezet) continue, carry on (or: forward): *de* **kennismaking** ~ pursue the acquaintance; *iemands* **werk** ~ carry on s.o.'s work

¹**vooruit** /vorœ̣yt/ (adv) **1** ahead, further: *hiermee* **kan** *ik weer een tijdje* ~ this will keep me going for a while **2** before(hand), in advance: *zijn tijd* ~ **zijn** be ahead of one's time; **ver** ~ well in advance

²**vooruit** /vorœ̣yt/ (int) get going, let's go, come on, go on: *~! aan je werk* come on, time for work

vooruitbetalen /vorœ̣ydbətalə(n)/ (betaalde vooruit, heeft vooruitbetaald) prepay, pay in advance

de **vooruitblik** /vorœ̣ydblɪk/ (pl: -ken) preview, look ahead: *een* ~ **op** *het volgende seizoen* a preview of (or: look ahead at) the coming season

vooruitdenken /vorœ̣ydɛŋkə(n)/ (dacht vooruit, heeft vooruitgedacht) think ahead

vooruitgaan /vorœ̣ytxan/ (ging vooruit, is vooruitgegaan) progress, improve: *zijn* **gezondheid** *gaat vooruit* his health is improving; *er financieel* **op** ~ be better off (financially); profit (financially)

de **vooruitgang** /vorœ̣ytxɑŋ/ (pl: -en) progress; improvement

vooruitkijken /vorœ̣ytkɛikə(n)/ (keek vooruit, heeft vooruitgekeken) look ahead

vooruitkomen /vorœytkomə(n)/ (kwam vooruit, is vooruitgekomen) get on (*or:* ahead), get somewhere, make headway: *moeizaam* ~ progress with difficulty

vooruitlopen /vorœytlopə(n)/ (liep vooruit, is vooruitgelopen) anticipate, be ahead (of): *~d op* in advance of; *op de gebeurtenissen* ~ anticipate events

vooruitstrevend /vorœytstrevənt/ (adj) progressive

het **vooruitzicht** /vorœytsɪχt/ (pl: -en) prospect, outlook: *goede ~en hebben* have good prospects; *iem. iets in het* ~ *stellen* hold out the prospect of sth. to s.o.

vooruitzien /vorœytsin/ (zag vooruit, heeft vooruitgezien) look ahead (*or:* forward): *regeren is* ~ foresight is the essence of government

vooruitziend /vorœytsint/ (adj) far-sighted; visionary

de **voorvader** /vorvadər/ (pl: -en) ancestor, forefather

het **voorval** /vorval/ (pl: -len) incident, event

voorvallen /vorvalə(n)/ (viel voor, is voorgevallen) occur, happen

de **voorvechter** /vorvɛχtər/ (pl: -s) champion, advocate

de **voorverkiezing** /vorvərkizɪŋ/ (pl: -en) preliminary election; [Am] primary (election)

de **voorverkoop** /vorvərkop/ advance booking (*or:* sale(s)): *de kaarten in de* ~ *zijn goedkoper* the tickets are cheaper if you buy them in advance

voorverpakt /vorvərpakt/ (adj) pre-packed

voorverwarmen /vorvərwarmə(n)/ (verwarmde voor, heeft voorverwarmd) preheat

het **voorvoegsel** /vorvuχsəl/ (pl: -s) prefix

voorwaar /vorwar/ (adv) indeed, truly

de **voorwaarde** /vorwardə/ (pl: -n) **1** condition, provision: *onder* ~ *dat …* provided that …, on condition that …; *onder geen enkele* ~ on no account, under no circumstances; *iets als* ~ *stellen* state (*or:* stipulate) sth. as a condition **2** [com] condition; terms: *wat zijn uw ~n?* what are your terms?

voorwaardelijk /vorwardələk/ (adj, adv) conditional, provisional: *~e invrijheidstelling* (release on) parole; *hij is* ~ *overgegaan* he has been put in the next class on probation, [Am] he has been put in the next grade on probation; ~ *veroordelen* give a suspended sentence; put on probation

[1]**voorwaarts** /vorwarts/ (adj, adv) forward(s), onward(s): *een stap* ~ a step forward(s)

[2]**voorwaarts** /vorwarts/ (int) forward: ~ *mars!* forward march!

de **voorwas** /vorwɑs/ pre-wash

de **voorwedstrijd** /vorwɛtstrɛit/ (pl: -en) preliminary competition (*or:* game)

voorwenden /vorwɛndə(n)/ (wendde voor, heeft voorgewend) pretend, feign

het **voorwendsel** /vorwɛntsəl/ (pl: -s) pretext, pretence: *onder valse ~s* under false pretences; *onder* ~ *van* under the pretext of

het **voorwerk** /vorwɛrk/ (pl: -en) preliminary work

het **voorwerp** /vorwɛrp/ (pl: -en) object: *het lijdend* ~ the direct object; *meewerkend* ~ indirect object; *gevonden ~en* lost property

het **voorwiel** /vorwil/ (pl: -en) front wheel

de **voorwielaandrijving** /vorwilandrɛivɪŋ/ front-wheel drive

het **voorwoord** /vorwort/ (pl: -en) foreword, preface

voorzeggen /vorzɛɣə(n)/ (zei/zegde voor, heeft voorgezegd) prompt: *het antwoord* ~ whisper the answer; *niet ~!* no prompting!

de **voorzet** /vorzɛt/ (pl: -ten) cross, centre; ball into the area: *een goede* ~ *geven* cross the ball well, send in a good cross

het **voorzetsel** /vorzɛtsəl/ (pl: -s) preposition

voorzetten /vorzɛtə(n)/ (zette voor, heeft voorgezet) **1** put (*or:* place) in front (of) **2** put forward, set forward; put ahead **3** cross; hit the ball into the area

voorzichtig /vorzɪχtəχ/ (adj, adv) **1** careful, cautious: *~! breekbaar!* fragile! handle with care!; *wees ~!* be careful!; *iem. het nieuws* ~ *vertellen* break the news gently to s.o.; ~ *te werk gaan* proceed cautiously (*or:* with caution) **2** cautious; discreet: ~ *naar iets informeren* make discreet inquiries (about sth.)

de **voorzichtigheid** /vorzɪχtəχhɛit/ caution, care

voorzichtigheidshalve /vorzɪχtəχhɛitshɑlvə/ (adv) as a precaution

[1]**voorzien** /vorzin/ (adj) provided: *wij zijn al* ~ we have been taken care of (*or:* seen to); *het gebouw is* ~ *van videobewaking* the buildiing is equipped with CCTV; *de deur is* ~ *van een slot* the door is fitted with a lock

[2]**voorzien** /vorzin/ (voorzag, heeft voorzien) **1** foresee, anticipate: *dat was te* ~ that was to be expected **2** (+ in) provide (for), see to: *in een behoefte* ~ fill a need; *in zijn onderhoud kunnen* ~ be able to support o.s. (*or:* to provide for o.s.) **3** (+ van) provide (with), equip (with): *het huis is* ~ *van centrale verwarming* the house has central heating

de **voorzienigheid** /vorzinəχhɛit/ providence: *Gods* ~ divine providence

de **voorziening** /vorzinɪŋ/ (pl: -en) provision, service: *sociale ~en* social services; *sanitaire ~en* sanitary facilities; *~en treffen* make arrangements

de **voorzijde** /vorzɛidə/ (pl: -n) front (side)

voorzitten /vorzɪtə(n)/ (zat voor, heeft voorgezeten) chair

de **voorzitter** /vorzɪtər/ (pl: -s) chairman: *mijnheer* (or: *mevrouw) de* ~ Mr Chairman, Madam Chairman (or: Chairwoman); ~ *zijn* chair a (or: the) meeting

het **voorzitterschap** /vˈorzɪtərsχɑp/ chairmanship

de **voorzorg** /vˈorzɔrχ/ (pl: -en) precaution: *uit ~ iets doen* do sth. as a precaution(ary measure)

de **voorzorgsmaatregel** /vˈorzɔrχsmatreɣəl/ (pl: -en) precaution, precautionary measure: *~en nemen (treffen) tegen* take precautions against

voos /vos/ (adj) **1** dried-out **2** hollow **3** rotten

¹**vorderen** /vˈordərə(n)/ (vorderde, is gevorderd) (make) progress, move forward, make headway: *naarmate de dag vorderde* as the day progressed (or: wore on)

²**vorderen** /vˈordərə(n)/ (vorderde, heeft gevorderd) **1** demand, claim: *het te ~ bedrag is … the amount due is …; geld ~ van iem.* demand money from s.o. **2** requisition

de **vordering** /vˈordərɪŋ/ (pl: -en) **1** progress, headway: *~en maken* (make) progress, make headway **2** demand, claim: *een ~ instellen tegen iem.* put in (or: submit) a claim against s.o.; *~ op iem.* claim against s.o.

voren /vˈorə(n)/ (adv): *kom wat naar ~* come closer (or: up here) a bit; *naar ~ komen* a) come forward; b) [fig] come up, come to the fore; *van ~* from (or: on) the front (side); *van ~ af aan* from the beginning

vorig /vˈorəχ/ (adj) **1** last, previous: *de ~e avond* the night before, the previous night; *in het ~e hoofdstuk* in the preceding (or: last) chapter; *de ~e keer* (the) last time **2** earlier, former: *haar ~e man* her former husband

de **vork** /vɔrk/ (pl: -en) fork

de **vorkheftruck** /vˈorkhɛftryk/ (pl: -s) forklift (truck)

de **vorm** /vɔrm/ (pl: -en) **1** form, shape, outline: *naar ~ en inhoud* in form and content; *de lijdende ~ van een werkwoord* the passive voice (or: form) of a verb **2** mould, form **3** (proper) form; shape; build: *in goede ~ zijn* be in good shape (or: condition)

vormelijk /vˈormələk/ (adj, adv) **1** formal **2** formalistic

vormen /vˈormə(n)/ (vormde, heeft gevormd) **1** shape, form, mould **2** form, make (up), build (up): *die delen ~ een geheel* those parts make up a whole; *zich een oordeel ~* form an opinion

vormend /vˈormənt/ (adj) formative: *algemeen ~ onderwijs* general (or: non-vocational) education

de **vormfout** /vˈormfaut/ (pl: -en) technicality
vormgeven /vˈormɣevə(n)/ (gaf vorm, heeft vormgegeven) design

de **vormgever** /vˈormɣevər/ (pl: -s) designer, stylist

de **vormgeving** /vˈormɣevɪŋ/ design, style, styling: *een heel eigen ~* a very personal (or:

individual) style

de **vorming** /vˈormɪŋ/ (pl: -en) **1** formation **2** education, training

het **vormsel** /vˈormsəl/ confirmation

de **vorst** /vɔrst/ (pl: -en) **1** frost, freeze: *vier graden ~* four degrees below freezing; *strenge ~* hard (or: sharp) frost; *we krijgen ~* there's (a) frost coming; *bij ~* in frosty weather, in case of frost **2** sovereign, monarch: *iem. als een ~ onthalen* entertain s.o. like a prince

vorstelijk /vˈorstələk/ (adj, adv) princely, royal, regal, lordly: *een ~ salaris* a princely salary; *iem. ~ belonen* reward s.o. generously

het **vorstendom** /vˈorstə(n)dom/ (pl: -men) principality, princedom

het **vorstenhuis** /vˈorstə(n)hœys/ (pl: -huizen) dynasty, royal house

de **vorstin** /vɔrstˈɪn/ (pl: -nen) queen, princess, sovereign's wife, ruler's wife

de **vorstschade** /vɔr(st)sχadə/ frost damage

het **vorstverlet** /vˈorstfərlɛt/ hold-ups due to frost

vorstvrij /vˈorstfrɛɪ/ (adj) frost-free

de **vos** /vɔs/ (pl: -sen) fox: *een troep ~sen* a pack of foxes; *een sluwe ~* a sly old fox; *een ~ verliest wel zijn haren, maar niet zijn streken* the leopard cannot change his spots

de **vossenjacht** /vˈosə(n)jɑχt/ (pl: -en) **1** treasure hunt **2** fox hunt: *op ~ gaan (zijn)* go fox-hunting, ride to (or: follow) the hounds

de **vouw** /vau/ (pl: -en) crease, fold: *een scherpe ~* a sharp crease; *zo gaat je broek uit de ~* that will take the crease out of your trousers

vouwbaar /vˈaubar/ (adj) foldable

de **vouwcaravan** /vˈaukɛrɑvɛn/ (pl: -s) folding caravan; [Am] folding trailer

de **vouwdeur** /vˈaudər/ (pl: -en) folding door
vouwen /vˈauwə(n)/ (vouwde, heeft gevouwen) fold: *de handen ~* fold one's hands (in prayer); *naar binnen ~* fold in(wards); turn in

de **vouwfiets** /vˈaufits/ (pl: -en) folding bike, collapsible bike

de **voyeur** /vwajˈør/ (pl: -s) voyeur, peeping Tom

de **vraag** /vraχ/ (pl: vragen) **1** question; request: *een pijnlijke ~ stellen* ask an embarrassing (or: a delicate) question; *de ~ brandde mij op de lippen* the question was on the tip of my tongue; *vragen stellen* (or: *beantwoorden*) ask (or: answer) questions; *veelgestelde vragen* FAQ *(frequently asked questions)* **2** demand, call: *~ en aanbod* supply and demand; *niet aan de ~ kunnen voldoen* be unable to meet the demand; *er is veel ~ naar tulpen* there's great demand (or: call) for tulips **3** question, problem, assignment **4** question, issue, problem, topic: *dat is zeer de ~* that is highly debatable (or: questionable); *het is nog de ~, of …* it remains to be seen whether …

de **vraagbaak** /vraɣbak/ (pl: vraagbaken)
1 oracle **2** handbook, encyclopedia **3** FAQ
(frequently asked questions)

het **vraaggesprek** /vraxəsprɛk/ (pl: -ken) interview

de **vraagprijs** /vraxprɛis/ (pl: -prijzen) asking price

het **vraagstuk** /vraxstʏk/ (pl: -ken) problem, question

het **vraagteken** /vraxtekə(n)/ (pl: -s) question mark; [fig also] mystery: *de toekomst is een* **groot** ~ the future is one big question mark

de **vraatzucht** /vratsʏxt/ gluttony

vraatzuchtig /vratsʏxtəx/ (adj, adv) gluttonous, greedy

de **vracht** /vraxt/ (pl: -en) **1** freight(age), cargo; load: ~ *innemen* take in cargo (*or:* freight(-age)) **2** load, burden, weight: *onder de* ~ *bezwijken* succumb under the burden **3** load, shipment **4** (cart)load, ton(s)

de **vrachtbrief** /vraxtbrif/ (pl: -brieven) waybill; consignment note; delivery note, forwarding note

het **vrachtschip** /vraxtsxɪp/ (pl: -schepen) freighter, cargo ship

het **vrachtverkeer** /vraxtfərker/ cargo trade, goods transport(ation); lorry traffic; [Am] truck traffic

het **vrachtvervoer** /vraxtfərvur/ goods carriage, cargo transport(ation)

het **vrachtvliegtuig** /vraxtflixtœyx/ (pl: -en) cargo plane (*or:* aircraft)

de **vrachtwagen** /vraxtwaɣə(n)/ (pl: -s) lorry; [Am] truck; van

de **vrachtwagenchauffeur** /vraxtwaɣə(n)ʃofør/ lorry driver; [Am] truck driver; [Am] trucker

¹**vragen** /vraɣə(n)/ (vroeg, heeft gevraagd) **1** ask (after, about), inquire (after, about): *daar wordt niet* *naar* gevraagd that's beside the point; *naar de bekende weg* ~ ask what one already knows (*or:* for the sake of asking) **2** ask (for), call (for): *erom* ~ ask for it; *dat is* *om* moeilijkheden ~ that's asking for trouble

²**vragen** /vraɣə(n)/ (vroeg, heeft gevraagd) **1** ask (for): *een politieagent de* *weg* ~ ask a policeman for (*or:* to show one) the way; *zou ik u iets* *mogen* ~? would you mind if I asked you a question?, can I ask you sth.?; ~ *hoe laat het is* ask (for) the time **2** ask, demand, request: *de* *rekening* ~ ask (*or:* call) for the bill

³**vragen** /vraɣə(n)/ (vroeg, heeft gevraagd) **1** ask, invite **2** ask, request: *hoeveel vraagt hij voor zijn* *huis?* how much does he want for his house?; *gevraagd:* *typiste* wanted: typist; *je vraagt* *te veel* van jezelf you're asking (*or:* demanding) too much of yourself; *veel* *aandacht* ~ demand a great deal of attention

¹**vragend** /vraɣənt/ (adj) interrogative: *een* ~ **voornaamwoord** an interrogative (pronoun)

²**vragend** /vraɣənt/ (adj, adv) questioning

de **vragenlijst** /vraɣə(n)lɛist/ (pl: -en) list of questions; questionnaire; inquiry form

de **vragensteller** /vraɣə(n)stɛlər/ questioner, inquirer, interviewer

de **vrede** /vredə/ **1** peace: ~ *sluiten* met conclude the peace with; ~ *stichten* make peace **2** peace, quiet(ude): ~ *met iets* **hebben** be resigned (*or:* reconciled) to sth.; accept sth.

vredelievend /vredəlivənt/ (adj, adv) peaceful, peace-loving

de **vrederechter** /vredərɛxtər/ (pl: -s) [Belg] justice of the peace

de **vredesactivist** /vredəsɑktivɪst/ (pl: -en) peace activist

het **vredesakkoord** /vredəsɑkort/ (pl: -en) peace agreement (*or:* treaty)

de **vredesbeweging** /vredəzbəweɣɪŋ/ (pl: -en) peace movement

de **vredesconferentie** /vredəskɔnferɛnsi/ (pl: -s) peace conference

de **vredesduif** /vredəzdœyf/ (pl: -duiven) dove of peace

de **vredesmacht** /vredəsmɑxt/ peacekeeping force

vredesnaam /vredəsnam/: *hoe is het* *in* ~ *mogelijk?* how on earth is that possible?, for crying out loud, how is that possible?

de **vredesonderhandelingen** /vredəsɔndərhɑndəlɪŋə(n)/ (pl) peace negotiations (*or:* talks)

de **vredesoperatie** /vredəsopəra(t)si/ (pl: -s) peace operation

het **Vredespaleis** /vredəspalɛis/ Peace Palace

de **vredespijp** /vredəspɛip/ (pl: -en) pipe of peace: *de* ~ *roken* smoke the pipe of peace, keep the (*or:* make) peace

het **vredesproces** /vredəsprosɛs/ peace process

de **vredestichter** /vredəstɪxtər/ (pl: -s) peacemaker

de **vredestijd** /vredəstɛit/ peacetime

het **vredesverdrag** /vredəsfərdrɑx/ (pl: -en) peace treaty

vredig /vredəx/ (adj) peaceful, quiet

vreedzaam /vretsam/ (adj, adv) peaceful, non-violent

¹**vreemd** /vremt/ (adj) **1** strange, odd, unfamiliar, unusual: *een* ~*e* **gewoonte** an odd (*or:* a strange) habit; *het* ~*e is, dat* ... the odd (*or:* strange, funny) thing is that ... **2** foreign, strange, imported: *zij* *is* hier ~ she is a stranger here **3** foreign, exotic: ~ *geld* foreign currency; ~*e* *talen* foreign languages **4** strange, outside: ~ *gaan* have an (extra-marital) affair

²**vreemd** /vremt/ (adv) strangely, oddly, unusually: ~ *doen* behave in an unusual way; ~ *genoeg* strangely enough, strange to say

de **vreemde** /vremdə/ **1** foreigner, stranger **2** stranger, outsider: *dat hebben ze* *van* geen ~ it's obvious who they got that from (*or:*

where they learnt that)

de **vreemdeling** /vr<u>e</u>mdəlɪŋ/ (pl: -en) foreigner, stranger: *ongewenste ~en* undesirable aliens; *hij is een ~ in zijn eigen land* he is a stranger in his own country

het **vreemdelingenbeleid** immigration policy

de **vreemdelingendienst** /vr<u>e</u>mdəlɪŋə(n)dinst/ aliens (registration) office

de **vreemdelingenhaat** /vr<u>e</u>mdəlɪŋə(n)hat/ xenophobia

het **vreemdelingenlegioen** /vr<u>e</u>mdəlɪŋə(n)leɣijun/ foreign legion

vreemdgaan /vr<u>e</u>mtxan/ (ging vreemd, heeft/is vreemdgegaan) cheat, sleep around, have extramarital relations

vreemdsoortig /vremts<u>o</u>rtəx/ (adj) peculiar, strange, odd

de **vrees** /vres/ (pl: vrezen) fear, fright: *hij greep haar vast uit ~ dat hij zou vallen* he grabbed hold of her for fear he should fall

de **vreetpartij** /vr<u>e</u>tpartɛi/ (pl: -en) blow-out

de **vreetzak** /vr<u>e</u>tsak/ (pl: -ken) glutton, pig

de **vrek** /vrɛk/ (pl: -ken) miser, skinflint, Scrooge

vrekkig /vr<u>e</u>kəx/ (adj, adv) miserly, stingy

¹**vreselijk** /vr<u>e</u>sələk/ (adj, adv) **1** terrible, awful: *~e honger hebben* have a ravenous appetite; *we hebben ~ gelachen* we nearly died (of) laughing **2** terrifying, horrible: *een ~e moord* a shocking (or: horrible) murder

²**vreselijk** /vr<u>e</u>sələk/ (adv) terribly, awfully, frightfully: *~ gezellig* awfully nice

het ¹**vreten** /vr<u>e</u>tə(n)/ **1** fodder; food; forage; slops **2** grub, nosh

²**vreten** /vr<u>e</u>tə(n)/ (vrat, heeft gevreten) eat (away), gnaw (at), prey (on): *het schuldbesef vrat aan haar* the sense of guilt gnawed at her (heart)

³**vreten** /vr<u>e</u>tə(n)/ (vrat, heeft gevreten) **1** feed: *dat is niet te ~!* that's not fit for pigs! **2** stuff (or: cram, gorge) (o.s.): *zich te barsten ~* stuff o.s. to the gullet (or: sick) **3** feed, eat **4** eat (up), devour: *kilometers ~* burn up the road; *dat toestel vréét stroom* this apparatus simply eats up electricity

de **vreugde** /vr<u>ø</u>ɣdə/ (pl: -n) joy, delight, pleasure: *tot mijn ~ hoor ik* I am delighted to hear

de **vreugdekreet** /vr<u>ø</u>ɣdəkret/ cry (or: shout) of joy

vreugdeloos /vr<u>ø</u>ɣdəlos/ (adj, adv) joyless, cheerless

vreugdevol /vr<u>ø</u>ɣdəvɔl/ (adj, adv) joyful

het **vreugdevuur** /vr<u>ø</u>ɣdəvyr/ (pl: -vuren) bonfire

vrezen /vr<u>e</u>zə(n)/ (vreesde, heeft gevreesd) fear, dread, be afraid (of, that): *ik vrees het ergste* I fear the worst; *God ~* fear God; *ik vrees van niet* (or: *wel*) I'm afraid not (or: so); *ik vrees dat hij niet komt* I'm afraid he won't come (or: show up)

de **vriend** /vrint/ (pl: -en) **1** friend: *~en en*

vriendinnen! friends!; *dikke ~en zijn* be (very) close friends; *even goede ~en* no hard feelings, no offence; *van je ~en moet je het maar hebben* with friends like that who needs enemies **2** (boy)friend: *ze heeft een ~(je)* she has a boyfriend ‖ *iem. te ~ houden* remain on good terms with s.o.

vriendelijk /vr<u>i</u>ndələk/ (adj, adv) **1** friendly, kind, amiable: *~ lachen* give a friendly smile; *zou u zo ~ willen zijn om ...* would you be kind enough (or: so kind) as to ...; *dat is erg ~ van u* that's very (or: most) kind of you **2** pleasant

de **vriendelijkheid** /vr<u>i</u>ndələkhɛit/ (pl: -heden) friendliness, kindness, amiability

de **vriendendienst** /vr<u>i</u>ndə(n)dinst/ (pl: -en) friendly turn, kind turn, act of friendship

de **vriendenkring** /vr<u>i</u>ndə(n)krɪŋ/ (pl: -en) circle of friends

het **vriendenprijsje** /vr<u>i</u>ndə(n)prɛiʃə/ (pl: -s) give-away: *voor een ~* for next to nothing

de **vriendin** /vrind<u>ɪ</u>n/ (pl: -nen) **1** (girl)friend, (lady) friend: *zij zijn dikke ~nen* they're the best of friends **2** girl(friend): *een vaste ~ hebben* have a steady girl(friend), go steady

de **vriendjespolitiek** /vr<u>i</u>ncəspolitik/ favouritism, nepotism

de **vriendschap** /vr<u>i</u>ntsxap/ (pl: -pen) friendship: *~ sluiten* make (or: become) friends, strike up a friendship; *uit ~ iets doen* do sth. out of friendship

vriendschappelijk /vrintsx<u>a</u>pələk/ (adj, adv) friendly, amicable; in a friendly way: *~e wedstrijd* friendly match; *~ met elkaar omgaan* be on friendly terms

vriesdrogen /vr<u>i</u>zdroɣə(n)/ (vriesdroogde, heeft gevriesdroogd) freeze-dry, lyophilize

de **vrieskist** /vr<u>i</u>skɪst/ (pl: -en) (chest-type) freezer, deep-freeze

de **vrieskou** /vr<u>i</u>skʊu/ frost

het **vriespunt** /vr<u>i</u>spʏnt/ freezing (point): *temperaturen boven* (or: *onder, rond*) *het ~* temperatures above (or: below, about) freezing (point)

het **vriesvak** /vr<u>i</u>sfak/ (pl: -ken) freezing compartment, freezer

het **vriesweer** /vr<u>i</u>swer/ freezing weather, frosty weather

vriezen /vr<u>i</u>zə(n)/ (vroor, heeft gevroren) freeze: *het vriest vijf graden* it's five (degrees) below freezing; *het vriest dat het kraakt* there's a sharp frost in the air

de **vriezer** /vr<u>i</u>zər/ (pl: -s) freezer, deep-freeze

¹**vrij** /vrɛi/ (adj) **1** free, open, unrestricted: *~e handel* free trade; *de ~e slag* freestyle; *een ~ uitzicht hebben* have a clear (or: an open) view; *de weg is ~* the road is clear; *weer op ~e voeten zijn* be outside again **2** free, complimentary **3** free, vacant: *die wc is ~* that lavatory is free (or: vacant, unoccupied); *de handen ~ hebben* have a free hand, have one's

hands free; *een stoel ~ **houden*** reserve a seat
²**vrij** /vrɛi/ (adv) quite, fairly, rather, pretty: *het komt ~ **vaak** voor* it occurs quite (*or:* fairly) often

vrijaf /vrɛiɑf/ (adj) off: *een halve **dag** ~* a half-holiday, half a day off; *~ **nemen*** take a holiday (*or:* some time off)

vrijblijvend /vrɛiblɛivənt/ (adj, adv) without (*or:* free of) obligations

de **vrijbrief** /vrɛibrif/ (pl: -brieven) [fig] licence

de **vrijbuiter** /vrɛibœytər/ (pl: -s) freebooter

de **vrijdag** /vrɛidɑx/ (pl: -en) Friday: *Goede Vrijdag* Good Friday

¹**vrijdags** /vrɛidɑxs/ (adj) Friday

²**vrijdags** /vrɛidɑxs/ (adv) on Fridays

de **vrijdenker** /vrɛidɛŋkər/ (pl: -s) freethinker

vrijelijk /vrɛijələk/ (adv) freely, without restraint

de **vrijemarkteconomie** /vrɛijəmɑrktekonomi/ free market economy

vrijen /vrɛiə(n)/ (vrijde/vree, heeft gevrijd/gevreeën) **1** neck, pet: *die twee **zitten** lekker te ~* those two are having a nice cuddle **2** make love, go to bed: *veilig ~* have safe sex

de **vrijer** /vrɛiər/ (pl: -s) boyfriend, lover, sweetheart, (young) man

de **vrijetijdsbesteding** /vrɛiətɛitsbəstedɪŋ/ leisure activities, recreation

de **vrijetijdskleding** /vrɛiətɛitskledɪŋ/ casual clothes (*or:* wear)

het **vrijgeleide** /vrɛiɣəlɛidə/ (pl: -n, -s) (letter of) safe-conduct, safeguard, pass(port), permit

¹**vrijgeven** /vrɛiɣevə(n)/ (gaf vrij, heeft vrijgegeven) give time off, give a holiday

²**vrijgeven** /vrɛiɣevə(n)/ (gaf vrij, heeft vrijgegeven) release: *de **handel** ~* decontrol the trade; *iets **voor** publicatie ~* release sth. for publication

vrijgevig /vrɛiɣevəx/ (adj, adv) generous, free with, liberal with

de **vrijgevigheid** /vrɛiɣevəxhɛit/ generosity, liberality

de **vrijgezel** /vrɛiɣəzɛl/ (pl: -len) bachelor, single: *een **verstokte** ~* a confirmed bachelor

de **vrijgezellenavond** /vrɛiɣəzɛlə(n)avɔnt/ (pl: -en) **1** stag-night; hen-party **2** singles night

de **vrijhandel** /vrɛihɑndəl/ free trade

de **vrijhaven** /vrɛihavə(n)/ (pl: -s) free port

de **vrijheid** /vrɛihɛit/ freedom, liberty: *het is hier ~, **blijheid*** it's Liberty Hall here; *~ van godsdienst* (*or:* *meningsuiting*) freedom of religion (*or:* speech); *persoonlijke ~* personal freedom (*or:* liberty); *kinderen veel ~ **geven*** give (*or:* allow) children a lot of freedom; *iem. **in** ~ stellen* set s.o. free (*or:* at liberty), free/release s.o.

het **vrijheidsbeeld** /vrɛihɛitsbelt/: *het Vrijheidsbeeld* the Statue of Liberty

de **vrijheidsberoving** /vrɛihɛitsbərovɪŋ/ deprivation of liberty (*or:* freedom)

de **vrijheidsstraf** /vrɛihɛrtstrɑf/ (pl: -fen) imprisonment, detention

de **vrijheidsstrijder** /vrɛihɛitstrɛidər/ (pl: -s) freedom fighter

vrijhouden /vrɛihaudə(n)/ (hield vrij, heeft vrijgehouden) **1** keep (free), reserve; set aside: *een **plaats** ~* keep a place (*or:* seat) free; *de **weg** ~* keep the road open (*or:* clear) **2** pay (for), stand (s.o. sth.)

het **vrijkaartje** /vrɛikarcə/ (pl: -s) free ticket

vrijkomen /vrɛikomə(n)/ (kwam vrij, is vrijgekomen) **1** come out; be set free, be released **2** be released; be set free **3** become free (*or:* available): *zodra er een **plaats** vrijkomt* as soon as there is a vacancy (*or:* place)

vrijlaten /vrɛilatə(n)/ (liet vrij, heeft vrijgelaten) **1** release, set free (*or:* at liberty); liberate; emancipate **2** leave free (*or:* vacant); leave clear: *deze **ruimte** ~ s.v.p.* please leave this space clear

de **vrijlating** /vrɛilatɪŋ/ release

vrijmaken /vrɛimakə(n)/ (maakte vrij, heeft vrijgemaakt) reserve, keep (free): *tijd ~* make time (for)

de **vrijmarkt** /vrɛimɑrkt/ (pl: -en) unregulated street market

de **vrijmetselaar** /vrɛimɛtsəlar/ (pl: -s) freemason, Mason

de **vrijmetselarij** /vrɛimɛtsəlarɛi/ Freemasonry, Masonry

vrijmoedig /vrɛimudəx/ (adj) frank, outspoken

de **vrijplaats** /vrɛiplats/ (pl: -en) refuge

vrijpleiten /vrɛiplɛitə(n)/ (pleitte vrij, heeft vrijgepleit) clear (of), exonerate (from)

vrijpostig /vrɛipɔstəx/ (adj) impertinent, impudent, saucy

de **vrijspraak** /vrɛisprak/ acquittal

vrijspreken /vrɛisprekə(n)/ (sprak vrij, heeft vrijgesproken) acquit (from), clear: *vrijgesproken worden **van** een beschuldiging* be cleared of (*or:* be acquitted on) a charge

vrijstaan /vrɛistan/ (stond vrij, heeft vrijgestaan) be free (to), be allowed (to), be permitted (to), be at liberty (to)

vrijstaand /vrɛistant/ (adj) apart, free; detached: *een ~ **huis*** a detached house

vrijstellen /vrɛistɛlə(n)/ (stelde vrij, heeft vrijgesteld) exempt; excuse; release: *vrijgesteld **van** militaire dienst* exempt from military service

de **vrijstelling** /vrɛistɛlɪŋ/ (pl: -en) exemption, release, freedom: *~ **verlenen** van* exempt from; *een ~ hebben **voor** wiskunde* be exempted from the maths exam

de **vrijster** /vrɛistər/ (pl: -s) spinster: *een **oude** ~* an old maid

vrijuit /vrɛiœyt/ (adv) freely: *u kunt ~ **spreken*** you can speak freely || *~ **gaan** a)* not be to blame; *b)* get off (*or:* go) scot-free, go clear/free

vrijwaren /vrɛiwarə(n)/ (vrijwaarde, heeft gevrijwaard) (safe)guard (against): *gevrij-waard tegen* protected from; *gevrijwaard blij-ven van blessures* remain free from injury

vrijwel /vrɛiwɛl/ (adv) nearly, almost, practically: *dat is ~ hetzelfde* that's nearly (*or:* almost) the same; *~ niets* hardly anything, next to nothing; *~ tegelijk aankomen* arrive almost simultaneously (*or:* at the same time); *het komt ~ op hetzelfde neer* it boils down to pretty well the same thing

vrijwillig /vrɛiwɪləχ/ (adj, adv) voluntary; volunteer; of one's own free will, of one's own volition: *~ iets op zich nemen* volunteer to do sth., take on sth. voluntarily

de **vrijwilliger** /vrɛiwɪləʏər/ (pl: -s) volunteer: *er hebben zich nog geen ~s gemeld* so far nobody has volunteered

het **vrijwilligerswerk** /vrɛiwɪləʏərswɛrk/ voluntary work, volunteer work

vrijzinnig /vrɛizɪnəχ/ (adj, adv) **1** liberal **2** [Belg] unbelieving

de **vroedvrouw** /vrutfrɑu/ (pl: -en) midwife

vroeg /vruχ/ (adj, adv) **1** early: *van ~ tot laat* from dawn till dusk (*or:* dark); *je moet er ~ bij zijn* you've got to get in quickly; *hij toonde al ~ tekentalent* he showed artistic talent at an early age; *volgende week is ~ genoeg* next week is soon enough; *niet ~er dan ...* not before ..., ... at the earliest; *het is nog ~* a) the day is still young; b) the night is still young; *'s morgens ~* early in the morning **2** early; young; premature: *een te ~ geboren kind* a premature baby

¹vroeger /vruʏər/ (adj) previous, former: *zijn ~e verloofde* his former (*or:* ex-fiancée)

²vroeger /vruʏər/ (adv) formerly, before, previously: *~ heb ik ook wel gerookt* I used to smoke; *~ stond hier een kerk* there used to be a church here; *het Londen van ~* London as it used to be (*or:* once was)

het **vroegpensioen** /vruχpɛnʃun/ early retirement

vroegrijp /vruχrɛip/ (adj) precocious; forward; early-ripening: *~e kinderen* precocious (*or:* forward) children

de **vroegte** /vruχtə/: *in alle ~* at (the) crack of dawn, bright and early

vroegtijdig /vruχtɛidəχ/ (adj, adv) early, premature

vrolijk /vrolək/ (adj, adv) cheerful, merry: *~ behang* cheerful (*or:* bright) wallpaper; *het was er een ~e boel* they were a merry crowd; *een ~e frans* quite a lad, a happy-go-lucky fellow; *~ worden* get (a bit, rather) merry; *een ~ leventje leiden* lead a merry life

vroom /vrom/ (adj, adv) pious, devout

de **vrouw** /vrɑu/ (pl: -en) **1** woman: *een alleenstaande ~* a single (*or:* an unattached) woman; *achter de ~en aanzitten* chase (after)

women, womanize; *de werkende ~* working women; *career women*; *een ~ achter het stuur* a woman driver; *Vrouw Holle* Mother Carey **2** wife: *man en ~* husband (*or:* man) and wife; *hoe gaat het met je ~?* how's your wife?; *een dochter van zijn eerste ~* a daughter by his first wife **3** queen **4** mistress, lady: *de ~ des huizes* lady (*or:* mistress) of the house

vrouwelijk /vrɑuwələk/ (adj) **1** female; woman: *een ~e arts* a woman doctor; *de ~e hoofdrol* the leading lady role (*or:* part) **2** feminine, womanly: *~e charme* feminine charm; *de ~e intuïtie* woman's intuition

de **vrouwenarts** /vrɑuwə(n)ɑrts/ (pl: -en) gynaecologist

de **vrouwenbesnijdenis** /vrɑuwə(n)bəsnɛidənɪs/ female genital mutilation *(FGM)*

de **vrouwenbeweging** /vrɑuwə(n)bəweʏɪŋ/ feminist movement, women's (rights) movement

het **vrouwenblad** /vrɑuwə(n)blɑt/ (pl: -en) women's magazine

de **vrouwengek** /vrɑuwə(n)ʏɛk/ (pl: -ken) ladies' man, womanizer

de **vrouwenhandel** /vrɑuwə(n)hɑndəl/ trade (*or:* traffic) in women; white slave trade

de **vrouwenjager** /vrɑuwə(n)jaʏər/ (pl: -s) womanizer, ladykiller

de **vrouwenstem** /vrɑuwə(n)stɛm/ (pl: -men) female voice, woman's voice

vrouwonvriendelijk /vrɑuɔnvrindələk/ (adj) disadvantageous to women

het **vrouwtje** /vrɑucə/ (pl: -s) **1** woman; wife(y): *een oud ~* a little old woman, a granny; *hij kijkt te veel naar de ~s* he's too keen on women (*or:* the ladies) **2** mistress **3** female

vrouwvriendelijk /vrɑuvrindələk/ (adj, adv) women-friendly

de **vrucht** /vrʏχt/ (pl: -en) **1** fruit: *~en op sap* fruit in syrup; *verboden ~en* forbidden fruit **2** foetus, embryo: *een onvoldragen ~* a foetus that has not been carried to term **3** [fig] fruit(s), reward(s): *zijn werk heeft weinig ~en afgeworpen* he has little to show for his work; *~en afwerpen* bear fruit; *de ~en van iets plukken* reap the fruit(s) (*or:* rewards) of sth.

vruchtbaar /vrʏχtbar/ (adj) **1** fruitful, productive **2** fertile; fruitful: *de vruchtbare periode van de vrouw* a woman's fertile period; *een vruchtbare bodem vinden* find fertile soil

de **vruchtbaarheid** /vrʏχtbarhɛit/ fertility, fruitfulness

het **vruchtbeginsel** /vrʏχtbəʏɪnsəl/ (pl: -s) ovary

vruchteloos /vrʏχtəlos/ (adj, adv) fruitless, futile

de **vruchtenpers** /vrʏχtə(n)pɛrs/ (pl: -en) fruit press

het **vruchtensap** /vrʏχtə(n)sɑp/ (pl: -pen) fruit juice

de **vruchtentaart** /vrʏχtə(n)tart/ (pl: -en) fruit

tart

het **vruchtgebruik** /vrɤ(ɤt)ɤəbrœyk/ usufruct

het **vruchtvlees** /vrɤɤtfles/ flesh (of a, the fruit), (fruit) pulp

het **vruchtwater** /vrɤɤtwatər/ amniotic fluid, water(s)

de **vruchtwateronderzoek** /vrɤɤtwatər-ɔndərzuk/ (pl: -en) amniocentesis

de **VS** /veɛs/ (pl) *Verenigde Staten* US, USA

de **V-snaar** /vesnar/ (pl: V-snaren) V-belt

het **vso** /veɛsɔ/ [Belg; educ] comprehensive school system

het **V-teken** /veɪtekə(n)/ V-sign

vuig /vœyɤ/ (adj, adv) foul; mean, low: *~e laster* foul slander

het ¹**vuil** /vœyl/ **1** refuse, rubbish; [Am esp] garbage: *iem. behandelen als een stuk ~* treat s.o. like dirt; *~ storten* tip (*or:* dump, shoot) rubbish; *verboden ~ te storten* dumping prohibited, no tipping (*or:* dumping) **2** dirt, filth

²**vuil** /vœyl/ (adj, adv) **1** dirty, filthy; polluted: *de ~e kopjes* the dirty (*or:* used) cups; *een ~e rivier* a dirty (*or:* polluted) river **2** dirty, foul: *iem. een ~e streek leveren* play a dirty (*or:* nasty trick) on s.o.; *~e viezerik* (*or: leugenaar*) dirty (*or:* filthy) swine/liar **3** dirty, nasty: *iem. ~ aankijken* give s.o. a dirty (*or:* filthy, nasty) look

de **vuilak** /vœylak/ (pl: -ken) [inform] pig, rotter, nasty piece of work, skunk

de **vuiligheid** /vœyləɤhɛit/ dirt, filth

vuilmaken /vœylmakə(n)/ (maakte vuil, heeft vuilgemaakt) make dirty, dirty, soil

het **vuilnis** /vœylnɪs/ refuse, rubbish; [Am esp] garbage

de **vuilnisauto** /vœylnɪsauto/ (pl: -'s) dustcart; [Am] garbage truck, trash truck

de **vuilnisbak** /vœylnɪzbak/ (pl: -ken) dustbin, rubbish bin; [Am] garbage can, trash can

het **vuilnisbakkenras** /vœylnɪzbakə(n)ras/ (pl: -sen) mongrel

de **vuilnisbelt** /vœylnɪzbɛlt/ (pl: -en) rubbish dump

de **vuilnishoop** /vœylnɪshop/ (pl: -hopen) rubbish dump; [Am] garbage heap

de **vuilniskoker** /vœylnɪskokər/ (pl: -s) rubbish chute

de **vuilnisman** /vœylnɪsman/ (pl: -nen) binman; [Am esp] garbage collector

de **vuilniszak** /vœylnɪsak/ (pl: -ken) rubbish bag, refuse bag

de **vuilophaaldienst** /vœylɔphaldinst/ (pl: -en) refuse collection

de **vuilstortplaats** /vœylstɔrtplats/ (pl: -en) rubbish dump

het **vuiltje** /vœylcə/ (pl: -s) smut, speck of dirt (*or:* dust, grit): *een ~ in het oog hebben* have sth. (*or:* a smut) in one's eye ‖ *er is geen ~ aan de lucht* everything is absolutely fine; [Am] everything is peachy keen

de **vuilverbranding** /vœylvərbrandɪŋ/ (pl:

-en) (waste, refuse, garbage) incinerator

de **vuilverwerking** /vœylvərwɛrkɪŋ/ waste processing

de **vuist** /vœyst/ (pl: -en) fist: *met gebalde ~en* with clenched fists; *een ~ maken* take a stand (*or:* hard line); *met de ~ op tafel slaan* bang one's fist on the table; take a hard line; *op de ~ gaan* come to blows; *uit het ~je eten* eat with one's fingers ‖ *voor de ~ (weg)* off the cuff, ad lib

de **vuistregel** /vœystreɤəl/ (pl: -s) rule of thumb

de **vuistslag** /vœystslaɤ/ (pl: -en) punch

vulgair /vʏlɤɛːr/ (adj, adv) vulgar, common; rude

de **vulkaan** /vʏlkan/ (pl: vulkanen) volcano

de **vulkaanuitbarsting** /vʏlkanœydbarstɪŋ/ volcanic eruption

vulkanisch /vʏlkanis/ (adj) volcanic: *~e stenen* volcanic rocks

vullen /vʏlə(n)/ (vulde, heeft gevuld) **1** fill (up); inflate: *het eten vult ontzettend* the meal is very filling **2** fill (up); stuff; pad: *een gat ~* fill (up) a hole; *een kip met gehakt ~* stuff a chicken with mince

de **vulling** /vʏlɪŋ/ (pl: -en) **1** filling; stuffing **2** cartridge, refill

de **vulpen** /vʏlpɛn/ (pl: -nen) fountain pen

het **vulpotlood** /vʏlpɔtlot/ (pl: vulpotloden) propelling pencil; [Am] refillable lead pencil

vunzig /vʏnzəɤ/ (adj) dirty, filthy

¹**vuren** /vyrə(n)/ (adj) pine, deal

²**vuren** /vyrə(n)/ (vuurde, heeft gevuurd) fire: *staakt het ~* cease fire

het **vurenhout** /vyrə(n)haut/ pine(wood), deal

vurenhouten /vyrə(n)hautə(n)/ (adj) pine, deal

vurig /vyrəɤ/ (adj, adv) **1** fiery, (red-)hot: *~e kolen* coals of fire **2** fiery, ardent, fervent; devout; burning: *~e paarden* fiery (*or:* high-spirited) horses; *een ~ voorstander van iets* a strong (*or:* fervent) supporter of sth.; *daarmee was zijn ~ste wens vervuld* it fulfilled his most ardent wish

de **VUT** /vʏt/ *vervroegde uittreding* early retirement: *in de ~ gaan* retire early, take early retirement

de **VUT-regeling** /vʏtreɤəlɪŋ/ (pl: -en) [roughly] early-retirement scheme

het **vuur** /vyr/ (pl: vuren) **1** fire: *voor iem. door het ~ gaan* go through fire (and water) for s.o.; *het huis staat in ~ en vlam* the house is in flames; *ik zou er mijn hand voor in het ~ durven steken* I'd stake my life on it; *in ~ en vlam zetten* set ablaze (*or:* on fire); *met ~ spelen* play with fire; *een ~ aansteken* light a fire; *iem. het ~ na aan de schenen leggen* make it (*or:* things) hot for s.o.; *een ~ uitdoven* put out (*or:* extinguish) a fire; *een pan op het ~ zetten* put a pan on the stove; *iem. zwaar onder ~ nemen* let fly at s.o.; *tussen twee vuren zitten* get caught in the middle (*or:* in the firing line) **2** fire, ardour, fervour: *in het ~ van zijn betoog* in the heat of his argument ‖ *eigen ~* friendly fire

de **vuurbal** /vy̱rbɑl/ (pl: -len) fireball, ball of fire

de **vuurdoop** /vy̱rdop/ baptism of fire

het **vuurgevecht** /vy̱rɣəvɛχt/ (pl: -en) gunfight

de **vuurhaard** /vy̱rhart/ (pl: -en) seat of the fire
Vuurland /vy̱rlɑnt/ Tierra del Fuego

de **vuurlinie** /vy̱rlini/ (pl: -s) firing line, line of fire

het **vuurpeloton** /vy̱rpelətɔn/ (pl: -s) firing squad

de **vuurpijl** /vy̱rpɛil/ (pl: -en) rocket

de **vuurproef** /vy̱rpruf/ (pl: -proeven) trial by fire; [fig] ordeal; acid test: *de ~ doorstaan* stand the test; *de ~ ondergaan* undergo a severe ordeal
vuurrood /vyro̱t/ (adj) crimson, scarlet: *~ aanlopen* turn crimson (*or:* scarlet)
vuurspuwend /vy̱rspywənt/ (adj) erupting; fire-breathing; fire-spitting

de **vuurspuwer** /vy̱rspywər/ (pl: -s) [roughly] fire-eater

de **vuursteen** /vy̱rsten/ flint

het **vuurtje** /vy̱rcə/ (pl: -s) **1** (small) fire: *het nieuws ging als een lopend ~ door de stad* the news spread through the town like wildfire **2** light: *iem. een ~ geven* give s.o. a light

de **vuurtoren** /vy̱rtorə(n)/ (pl: -s) lighthouse
vuurvast /vy̱rvɑst/ (adj) fireproof, flame-resistant, heat-resistant: *een ~ schaaltje* an ovenproof (*or:* a heat-resistant) dish

het **vuurvliegje** /vy̱rvliχjə/ (pl: -s) firefly

het **vuurwapen** /vy̱rwapə(n)/ (pl: -s) firearm, gun; arm

het **vuurwerk** /vy̱rwɛrk/ **1** firework **2** (display of) fireworks

de **vuurzee** /vy̱rze/ (pl: -ën) blaze, sea of fire (*or:* flame(s))

de **VVV**® /vevev e/ *Vereniging voor Vreemdelingenverkeer* Tourist Information Office
v.w.b. (abbrev) *voor wat betreft* as far as … is concerned

het **vwo** /veweo̱/ *voorbereidend wetenschappelijk onderwijs* pre-university education

W

de **w** /we/ (pl: w's) w, W
de **WA** /wea/ wettelijke aansprakelijkheid third-party liability
de **waadvogel** /wa̲tfoɣəl/ wader
de **waaghals** /wa̲xhɑls/ (pl: -halzen) daredevil
de **waagschaal** /wa̲xsxɑl/: zijn leven in de ~ stellen take one's life in one's (own) hands
het **waagstuk** /wa̲xstʏk/ (pl: -ken) risky enterprise
waaien /wa̲jə(n)/ (waaide/woei, heeft gewaaid) **1** blow; be blown: er woei een harde **storm** a storm was blowing **2** wave, fly ‖ **laat** maar ~ let it rip
de **waaier** /wa̲jər/ (pl: -s) fan
waaiervormig /wa̲jərvɔ̲rməx/ (adj, adv) fan-shaped
de **waakhond** /wa̲khɔnt/ (pl: -en) watchdog
waaks /waks/ (adj) watchful
de **waakvlam** /wa̲kflɑm/ (pl: -men) pilot light (or: flame)
waakzaam /wa̲ksam/ (adj, adv) watchful
de **waakzaamheid** /wa̲ksamhɛit/ watchfulness
de **Waal** /wal/ (pl: Walen) [pers] Walloon
het **¹Waals** /wals/ Walloon
²Waals /wals/ (adj) Walloon
de **waan** /wan/ delusion: iem. in de ~ laten not spoil s.o.'s illusions
de **waanzin** /wa̲nzɪn/ madness: dat is je **reinste** ~ that is pure nonsense (or: sheer madness)
waanzinnig /wanzɪ̲nəx/ (adj, adv) mad: ~ **populair** zijn be wildly popular
de **waanzinnige** /wanzɪ̲nəɣə/ (pl: -n) madman, maniac; madwoman
de **¹waar** /war/ (pl: waren) goods, ware(s): iem. ~ voor zijn geld **geven** give value for money
²waar /war/ (adj) **1** true, real, actual: de ware **oorzaak** the real (or: actual) cause; 't is toch niet ~! you don't say!, not really!; het is te mooi om ~ te **zijn** it's too good to be true; echt ~? is that really true?, really?; **eerlijk** ~! honest! **2** true; actual; real: een ~ **genot** a regular (or: real) treat; hij is **de** ware (jakob) he's Mr Right **3** true, correct ‖ dat is ~ ook ... that reminds me ..., by the way ...
³waar /war/ (adv) **1** where; what: ~ gaat het nu eigenlijk **om?** what is it really all about? **2** where; that; which: de **boodschap** ~ hij niet aan gedacht had the message (that, which) he hadn't remembered; het **dorp** ~ hij geboren is the village where (or: in which) he was born **3** wherever; everywhere; anywhere: meer welvaart dan ~ ook more prosperity than any-

where else **4** really, actually: dat **is** ~ gebeurd it really (or: actually) happened
waaraan /waran̲/ (adv) **1** what ... to: ~ **ligt** dit? what is the reason for it?; ~ heb ik dit te danken? what do I owe this to?, to what do I owe this? **2** what (or: which) ... to/of: het huis ~ **dacht** the house (which) I was thinking of **3** whatever ... to (or: of): ~ je ook **denkt** whatever you're thinking of (or: about)
waarachter /warɔ̲xtər/ (adv) **1** behind which **2** behind what (or: which)
waarachtig /warɔ̲xtəx/ (adj, adv) truly, really
waarbij /warbɛi̲/ (adv) at (or: by, near) ... which: een **ongeluk** ~ veel gewonden vielen an accident in which many people were injured
de **waarborg** /wa̲rbɔrx/ (pl: -en) guarantee; security
waarborgen /wa̲rbɔrɣə(n)/ (waarborgde, heeft gewaarborgd) guarantee
de **waarborgsom** /wa̲rbɔrxsɔm/ (pl: -men) deposit; [law] bail
de **¹waard** /wart/ (pl: -en) landlord
²waard /wart/ (adj) worth, worthy (of sth., s.o.): laten zien wat je ~ **bent** show s.o. what you're made of; hij **is** haar niet ~ he's not worthy of her; na een dag werken ben ik 's avonds **niets** (meer) ~ after a day's work I'm no good for anything; **veel** ~ zijn be worth a lot
de **waarde** /wa̲rdə/ (pl: -n) **1** value: ter ~ **van** ... at (the value of), worth ...; voorwerpen **van** ~ objects of value, valuables; iem. **in** zijn ~ laten accept s.o. as he is; iem. niet op zijn **juiste** ~ schatten underestimate s.o.; (zeer) veel ~ aan iets **hechten** value sth. highly; weinig ~ aan iets **hechten** attach little value to sth.; **van** ~ zijn, ~ hebben be valuable, be of value **2** value, reading: **in** ~ dalen depreciate, decrease (or: diminish) in value; de **gemiddelde** ~n van de zomertemperaturen the average summer temperature ‖ een **vaste** ~ a stalwart friend/ supporter
de **waardebon** /wa̲rdəbɔn/ (pl: -nen) voucher, coupon; gift voucher (or: coupon)
waardeloos /wa̲rdəlos/ (adj) worthless: dat **is** ~ that's useless (or: hopeless)
het **waardeoordeel** /wa̲rdəordel/ (pl: -oordelen) value judg(e)ment
waarderen /wardeːrə(n)/ (waardeerde, heeft gewaardeerd) appreciate, value: hij **weet** een goed glas wijn wel **te** ~ he likes (or: appreciates) a good glass of wine
waarderend /wardeːrənt/ (adj, adv) appreciative: zich (zeer) ~ over iem. **uitlaten** speak (very) highly of s.o.
de **waardering** /wardeːrɪŋ/ (pl: -en) appreciation, esteem: ~ **ondervinden** (van) win the esteem (or: regard) (of); als **blijk** van ~ as a tribute of one's appreciation (or: esteem)
waardevast /wa̲rdəvɑst/ (adj) stable (in

value); index-linked; inflation-proof

waardevol /wˈardəvɔl/ (adj) valuable, useful: *~le voorwerpen* valuables, objects of value

waardig /wˈardəx/ (adj, adv) dignified, worthy

de **waardigheid** /wˈardəxhɛit/ (pl: -heden) dignity, worth: *iets beneden zijn ~ achten* think sth. beneath one's dignity (*or:* beneath one)

de **waardin** /wardˈɪn/ (pl: -nen) landlady

waardoor /wardˈor/ (adv) **1** (as a result of) what, how: *~ ben je van gedachten veranderd?* what made you change your mind?; *ik weet ~ het komt* I know how it happened, I know what caused it **2** through which, by which, (which, that) ... through (*or:* by); (as a result of) which: *de buis ~ het gas stroomt* the tube through which the gas flows; *het begon te regenen, ~ de weg nog gladder werd* it started to rain, which made the road even more slippery

[1]**waargebeurd** (adj) true

[2]**waargebeurd** /wˈarɣəbørt/ (adj): *een waargebeurd verhaal* a true story

waarheen /warhˈen/ (adv) **1** where, where ... to: *~ zullen wij vandaag gaan?* where shall we go today? **2** where, to which, (which, that) ... to: *de plaats ~ ze me stuurden* the place to which they directed me **3** wherever: *~ u ook gaat* wherever you (may) go

de **waarheid** /wˈarhɛit/ (pl: -heden) truth, fact: *de ~ achterhalen* get at (*or:* find out) the truth; *om (u) de ~ te zeggen* to be honest (with you), to tell (you) the truth; *de ~ ligt in het midden* the truth lies (somewhere) in between; *een ~ als een koe* a truism; *ver bezijden de ~ zijn* be far removed from the truth; *de naakte ~* the naked truth

waarheidsgetrouw /wˈarhɛitsxətrɑu/ (adj, adv) truthful, true

waarin /warˈɪn/ (adv) **1** where, in what: *~ schuilt de fout?* where's the mistake? **2** in which, where, (which, that) ... in: *in de tijd ~ wij leven* the age (that, which) we live in **3** wherever, in whatever: *~ de fout ook gemaakt is* wherever the mistake was made

waarlangs /warlˈɑŋs/ (adv) **1** what ... past (*or:* along) **2** past which, along which, (which, that) ... past (*or:* along): *de weg ~ hij gaat* the way he is going, the road along which he is going **3** past whatever, along whatever: *~ zij ook kwamen* whatever way they came along

waarlijk /wˈarlək/ (adv) truly, really

[1]**waarmaken** /wˈarmakə(n)/ (maakte waar, heeft waargemaakt) **1** prove **2** fulfil: *de gewekte verwachtingen (niet) ~* (fail to) live up to expectations

zich [2]**waarmaken** /wˈarmakə(n)/ (maakte zich waar, heeft zich waargemaakt) prove o.s.

waarmee /warmˈe/ (adv) **1** what ... with (*or:* by): *~ sloeg hij je?* what did he hit you with? **2** with which, by which; which; (which) ... with (*or:* by): *de boot ~ ik vertrek* the boat on which I leave **3** (with, by) whatever: *~ hij ook dreigde, zij werd niet bang* whatever he threatened her with she didn't get scared

het **waarmerk** /wˈarmɛrk/ (pl: -en) stamp

waarmerken /wˈarmɛrkə(n)/ (waarmerkte, heeft gewaarmerkt) stamp: *een gewaarmerkt afschrift* a certified (*or:* an authenticated) copy

waarna /warnˈa/ (adv) after which: *~ Paul als spreker optrad* after which Paul spoke (*or:* took the floor)

waarnaar /warnˈar/ (adv) **1** what ... at (*or:* of, for): *~ smaakt dat?* what does it taste of? **2** to which; after (*or:* for, according to) which, (which, that) ... to (*or:* after, for): *het hoofdstuk ~ ze verwees* the chapter (that, which) she referred to **3** whatever ... to (*or:* at, for), wherever: *~ ik hier ook zoek, ik vind nooit wat* whatever I look for here, I never find anything

waarnaast /warnˈast/ (adv) **1** what ... next to (*or:* beside) **2** (which, that) ... next to (*or:* beside) **3** whatever ... next to (*or:* beside): *~ je dit schilderij ook hangt* whatever you hang this picture next to

waarneembaar /warnˈembar/ (adj, adv) perceptible: *niet ~* imperceptible

[1]**waarnemen** /wˈarnemə(n)/ (nam waar, heeft waargenomen) replace (temporarily), fill in, take over (temporarily), act: *de zaken voor iem. ~* fill in for (*or:* replace) s.o.

[2]**waarnemen** /wˈarnemə(n)/ (nam waar, heeft waargenomen) observe, perceive

waarnemend /wˈarnemənt/ (adj) temporary, acting

de **waarnemer** /wˈarnemər/ (pl: -s) **1** observer **2** representative, deputy, substitute

de **waarneming** /wˈarnemɪŋ/ (pl: -en) **1** observation, perception **2** substitution

waarom /warˈɔm/ (adv) **1** why, what ... for: *~ denk je dat?* why do you (*or:* what makes you) think so?; *~ in vredesnaam?* why on earth?, why for goodness' sake? **2** why, (which, that) ... for: *de reden ~ hij het deed* the reason (why, that) he did it **3** for whatever, whatever ... for: *~ hij het ook doet, hij moet ermee ophouden!* whatever he does it for, he has to stop it!

waaromheen /warɔmhˈen/ (adv) **1** what ... (a)round **2** (a)round which: *het huis ~ een tuin lag* the house which was surrounded by a garden

waaronder /warˈɔndər/ (adv) **1** what ... under (*or:* among), among what **2** under which; among which [inform]: *de boom ~ wij zaten* the tree under which we were sitting; *hij had een schat aan boeken, ~ heel zeldzame* he had a wealth of books, including some very rare ones **3** under whatever, whatever … under: ~ *hij ook* **keek,** *hij vond het niet* whatever he looked under, he couldn't find it

waarop /waˈrɔp/ (adv) **1** what … on (*or:* for), where **2** (which, that) … on/in (*or:* by, to): *de* **dag** ~ *hij aankwam* the day (on which) he arrived; *de* **manier** ~ *beviel me niet* I didn't like the way (in which) it was done; *op het* **tijdstip** ~ at the time that **3** whatever … on: ~ *je nu ook staat,.ik wil dat je naar beneden komt* whatever you are standing on now, I want you to get down

waarover /waˈroːvər/ (adv) **1** what … over (*or:* about, across): ~ **gaat** *het?* what is it about? **2** (which, that) … over (*or:* about, across): *de* **auto** ~ *ik met je vader gesproken heb* the car of (*or:* about) which I've spoken with your dad **3** whatever … about: ~ *de discussie dan ook* **gaat,** … whatever the discussion is about, …

waarschijnlijk /waːrsˈxɛinlək/ (adj, adv) probable, likely: *dat* **lijkt** *mij heel* ~ that seems quite likely to me; ~ **niet** I suppose not; *meer dan* ~ more than likely

de **waarschijnlijkheid** /waːrsˈxɛinləkhɛit/ probability, likelihood, odds: **naar** *alle* ~ in all probability (*or:* likelihood)

waarschuwen /ˈwaːrsxywə(n)/ (waarschuwde, heeft gewaarschuwd) **1** warn, alert: *ik heb je gewaarschuwd* I gave you fair warning, I told you so **2** warn, notify: *een* **dokter** *laten* ~ call a doctor **3** warn, caution: *ik waarschuw je voor de laatste maal* I'm telling you for the last time; *wees gewaarschuwd* you've been warned

de **waarschuwing** /ˈwaːrsxywɪŋ/ (pl: -en) warning; caution; reminder; notice: [sport] *een* **officiële** ~ *krijgen* be booked (*or:* cautioned); *Waarschuwing! Zeer brandbaar!* Caution! Highly flammable!

het **waarschuwingsbord** /ˈwaːrsxywɪŋzbɔrt/ (pl: -en) warning sign

waartegen /waːrˈteːɣə(n)/ (adv) **1** what … against (*or:* to): ~ **helpt** *dit middel?* what is this medicine for? **2** against which, to which, (which, that) … against (*or:* to): *de* **muur** ~ *een ladder staat* the wall against which a ladder is standing; *een* **raad** ~ *niets in te brengen valt* a piece of advice to which no objections can be made **3** whatever … against (*or:* to)

waartoe /waːrˈtu/ (adv) **1** what … for (*or:* to), why **2** (which, that) … for (*or:* to) **3** whatever … for (*or:* to): ~ *dit ook moge leiden* whatever this may lead to

waartussen /waːrˈtʏsə(n)/ (adv) **1** what … between (*or:* among, from): ~ **moeten** *wij* **kiezen?** a) what are we (supposed) to choose between; b) what are the alternatives? **2** between (*or:* among, from) which, (which,

that) … between (*or:* among, from) **3** whatever … between (*or:* among, from)

waaruit /waːˈrœyt/ (adv) **1** from what: ~ **bestaat** *de opdracht?* what does the assignment consist of? **2** from which: *het boek* ~ *u ons net voorlas* the book from which you read to us just now

waarvan /waːrˈvɑn/ (adv) **1** what … from (*or:* of): ~ **maakt** *hij dat?* what does he make that of? (*or:* from?); of (*or:* from) what does he make that? **2** (which, that) … from; of whom [of pers]; whose: *100* **studenten,** ~ *ongeveer de helft chemici* 100 students, of whom about half are chemists; *op* **grond** ~ on the basis of which; *dat is een* **onderwerp** ~ *hij veel verstand heeft* that is a subject he knows a lot about **3** whatever … from

waarvandaan /waːrvɑnˈdaːn/ (adv) **1** where … from **2** (which, that) … from **3** wherever … from: ~ *je ook belt, draai altijd eerst een 0* wherever you call from, always dial an 0 first

waarvoor /waːrˈvoːr/ (adv) **1** what … for (*or:* about): ~ **dient** *dat?* what's that for? **2** what … for: ~ **doe** *je dat?* what are you doing that for? **3** (which, that) … for: *een gevaar* ~ *ik u* **gewaarschuwd heb** a danger I warned you about **4** whatever … for: ~ *hij het ook doet, het is in elk geval niet het geld* whatever he does it for, it's not the money, that's for sure

waarzeggen /ˈwaːrzɛɣə(n)/ (waarzegde, heeft waargezegd) tell fortunes, divine the future

de **waarzegger** /ˈwaːrzɛɣər/ (pl: -s) fortune-teller; crystal-gazer

de **waarzegster** /ˈwaːrzɛxstər/ fortune-teller

het **waas** /waːs/ haze; [fig] air; aura, film: *een* ~ *van* **geheimzinnigheid** a shroud of secrecy; *een* ~ **voor** *de ogen krijgen* get a mist (*or:* haze) before one's eyes

de **wacht** /wɑxt/ (pl: -en) **1** watchman **2** watch; lookout: *(de)* ~ **houden** be on (*or:* stand) guard; [Belg] *van* ~ *zijn* be on night (*or:* weekend) duty, be on call **3** watch, guard ‖ *iets* **in** *de* ~ *slepen* carry off sth., pocket (*or:* bag) sth.

wachten /ˈwɑxtə(n)/ (wachtte, heeft gewacht) **1** wait, stay: *op de bus* ~ wait for the bus **2** wait, await: *iem.* **laten** ~ keep s.o. waiting; *waar wacht je nog* **op?** what are you waiting for?; *op zijn beurt* ~ await one's turn; *er zijn nog drie ~den voor u* hold the line, there are three callers before you; *je moet* **er** *niet te lang* **mee** ~ don't put it off too long **3** wait, await (s.o.), be in store for (s.o.): *er wachtte hem een onaangename* **verrassing** there was an unpleasant surprise in store for him; *er* **staan** *ons moeilijke tijden te* ~ difficult times lie ahead of us

de **wachter** /ˈwɑxtər/ (pl: -s) guard(sman), watchman

het **wachtgeld** /ˈwɑxtxɛlt/ (pl: -en) reduced pay

de **wachtkamer** /wɑxtkamər/ (pl: -s) waiting room

de **wachtlijst** /wɑxtlɛist/ (pl: -en) waiting list

wachtlopen /wɑxtlopə(n)/ (liep wacht, heeft wachtgelopen) be on patrol, be on (guard) duty

de **wachtpost** /wɑxtpɔst/ (pl: -en) watch (*or:* sentry, guard) post

de **wachtstand** /wɑx(t)stɑnt/ (pl: -en) suspension mode, suspended mode

de **wachttijd** /wɑxtɛit/ (pl: -en) wait, waiting period

het **wachtwoord** /wɑxtwort/ (pl: -en) password

het **wad** /wɑt/ (pl: -den) (mud) flat(s), shallow(s) || *de Wadden* the (Dutch) Wadden

waden /wadə(n)/ (waadde, heeft/is gewaad) wade

waf /wɑf/ (int) woof

de **wafel** /wafəl/ (pl: -s) waffle; wafer

het **wafelijzer** /wafəlɛizər/ (pl: -s) waffle iron

de **waffel** /wɑfəl/ (pl: -s) [inform] trap, gob

de ¹**wagen** /waɣə(n)/ (pl: -s) **1** wagon; cart; van; pram **2** car: *met de ~ komen* come by car

²**wagen** /waɣə(n)/ (waagde, heeft gewaagd) **1** risk: *het erop ~* chance (*or:* risk) it; *wie niet waagt, die niet wint* nothing ventured, nothing gained **2** venture, dare: *zijn kans ~* try one's luck; *waag het eens!* just you dare! || *aan elkaar gewaagd zijn* be well (*or:* evenly) matched

het **wagenpark** /waɣə(n)pɑrk/ (pl: -en) fleet (of cars, vans, taxis, buses)

wagenwijd /waɣə(n)wɛit/ (adv) wide open

wagenziek /waɣə(n)zik/ (adj) carsick

waggelen /wɑɣələ(n)/ (waggelde, heeft/is gewaggeld) totter, stagger; waddle; toddle

de **wagon** /waɣɔn/ (pl: -s) (railway) carriage; coach; wagon; van

de **wagonlading** /waɣɔnladɪŋ/ (pl: -en) wagonload

het **wak** /wɑk/ (pl: -ken) hole: *hij zakte in een ~ en verdronk* he fell through the thin ice and (was) drowned

de **wake** /wakə/ (pl: -n) watch; wake

waken /wakə(n)/ (waakte, heeft gewaakt) **1** watch, keep watch, stay awake: *bij een zieke ~* sit up with a sick person **2** watch, guard

wakker /wɑkər/ (adj, adv) awake: *daar lig ik niet van ~* I'm not going to lose any sleep over it; *~ schrikken* wake up with a start; *iem. ~ schudden* shake s.o. awake

de **wal** /wɑl/ (pl: -len) **1** bank, embankment; wall **2** quay(side), waterside: *aan de ~ on shore; van ~ steken* push off, go ahead, proceed; *iem. van de ~ in de sloot helpen* bring s.o. from bad to worse **3** shore: *aan ~ brengen* land, bring (sth., s.o.) ashore **4** bag || *van twee ~letjes eten* butter one's bread on both sides, play a double game

walgelijk /wɑlɣələk/ (adj, adv) disgusting, revolting: *een ~e stank* a nauseating stench

walgen /wɑlɣə(n)/ (walgde, heeft gewalgd) be nauseated, be disgusted, be revolted: *ik walg ervan* it turns my stomach

de **walging** /wɑlɣɪŋ/ disgust, revulsion, nausea

het **Walhalla** /wɑlhɑla/ Valhalla

de **walkietalkie** /wɔ:kitɔ:ki/ (pl: -s) walkietalkie

de **walkman**® /wɔ:kmɛ:n/ (pl: -s) walkman

Wallonië /wɑlonijə/ the Walloon provinces in Belgium

de **walm** /wɑlm/ (pl: -en) (thick, dense) smoke

walmen /wɑlmə(n)/ (walmde, heeft gewalmd) smoke

de **walnoot** /wɑlnot/ walnut

de **walrus** /wɑlrʏs/ (pl: -sen) walrus

de **wals** /wɑls/ (pl: -en) **1** roller **2** steamroller, roadroller; (rolling) mill **3** waltz

¹**walsen** /wɑlsə(n)/ (walste, heeft gewalst) waltz

²**walsen** /wɑlsə(n)/ (walste, heeft gewalst) roll, steamroller; roll

de **walvis** /wɑlvɪs/ (pl: -sen) whale

het **wanbedrijf** /wɑmbədrɛif/ (pl: -bedrijven) [Belg] criminal offence

het **wanbegrip** /wɑmbəɣrɪp/ (pl: -pen) fallacy, misconception, wrong idea, false idea

het **wanbeheer** /wɑmbəher/ mismanagement

het **wanbeleid** /wɑmbəlɛit/ mismanagement

de **wanbetaler** /wɑmbətalər/ (pl: -s) defaulter

de **wanbetaling** /wɑmbətalɪŋ/ (pl: -en) default, non-payment

de **wand** /wɑnt/ (pl: -en) wall; face; side; skin: *een buis met dikke ~en* a thick-walled tube

de **wandaad** /wɑndat/ (pl: -daden) outrage, misdeed

de **wandel** /wɑndəl/ walk

de **wandelaar** /wɑndəlar/ (pl: -s) walker; hiker

wandelen /wɑndələ(n)/ (wandelde, heeft/is gewandeld) walk; ramble; hike: *met de kinderen gaan ~* take the children for a walk

wandelend /wɑndələnt/ (adj) walking

de **wandelgang** /wɑndəlɣɑŋ/ (pl: -en): *ik hoorde het in de ~en* I just picked up some gossip

de **wandeling** /wɑndəlɪŋ/ (pl: -en) walk; ramble; [sport] hike

het **wandelpad** /wɑndəlpɑt/ (pl: -en) footpath

de **wandelstok** /wɑndəlstɔk/ (pl: -ken) walking stick

de **wandeltocht** /wɑndəltɔxt/ (pl: -en) walking tour

de **wandelwagen** /wɑndəlwaɣə(n)/ (pl: -s) buggy, pushchair; [Am] stroller

het **wandkleed** /wɑntklet/ (pl: -kleden) tapestry, wall hanging(s)

de **wandluis** /wɑntlœys/ (pl: -luizen) bedbug

het **wandmeubel** /wɑntmøbəl/ (pl: -s) wall unit

het **wandrek** /wɑntrɛk/ (pl: -ken) wall bars

de **wang** /wɑŋ/ (pl: -en) cheek: *bolle ~en* round (*or:* chubby) cheeks het **wangedrag** /wɑŋɣədrɑχ/ misbehaviour, bad conduct

de **wanhoop** /wɑnhop/ despair, desperation: *de ~ nabij zijn* be on the verge of despair

de **wanhoopsdaad** /wɑnhopsdat/ (pl: -daden) act of despair, desperate act

wanhopen /wɑnhopə(n)/ (wanhoopte, heeft gewanhoopt) despair

wanhopig /wɑnhopəχ/ (adj, adv) desperate, despondent, despairing: *iem. ~ maken* drive s.o. to despair; *zich ergens ~ aan vastklampen* hang on to sth. like grim death

wankel /wɑŋkəl/ (adj, adv) shaky, unstable: *~ evenwicht* shaky balance; *~e stoelen* rickety chairs

wankelen /wɑŋkələ(n)/ (wankelde, heeft gewankeld) stagger, wobble

wankelmoedig /wɑŋkəlmudəχ/ (adj, adv) unstable, irresolute, wavering

de **wanklank** /wɑŋklɑŋk/ (pl: -en) dissonance

¹**wanneer** /wɑneːr/ (adv) when: *~ dan ook* whenever

²**wanneer** /wɑneːr/ (conj) **1** when: *~ de zon ondergaat, wordt het koeler* when the sun sets it gets cooler **2** if: *hij zou beter opschieten, ~ hij meer zijn best deed* he would make more progress if he worked harder **3** whenever, if: *(altijd) ~ ik oesters eet, word ik ziek* whenever I eat oysters I get ill

de **wanorde** /wɑnɔrdə/ disorder, disarray: *de keuken was in de grootste ~* the kitchen was in a colossal mess

wanordelijk /wɑnɔrdələk/ (adj, adv) disorderly

de **wanprestatie** /wɑmprɛsta(t)si/ (pl: -s) failure

de **wansmaak** /wɑnsmak/ bad taste

wanstaltig /wɑnstɑltəχ/ (adj) misshapen, deformed

de ¹**want** /wɑnt/ (pl: -en) mitt(en)

²**want** /wɑnt/ (conj) because, as, for

wanten /wɑntə(n)/: *hij weet van ~* he knows the ropes (or: what's what)

de **wantoestand** /wɑntustɑnt/ (pl: -en) disgraceful state of affairs

het ¹**wantrouwen** /wɑntrɑuwə(n)/ distrust, suspicion

²**wantrouwen** /wɑntrɑuwə(n)/ (wantrouwde, heeft gewantrouwd) distrust, mistrust

wantrouwend /wɑntrɑuwənt/ (adj, adv) suspicious (of), distrustful

wantrouwig /wɑntrɑuwəχ/ (adj, adv) suspicious: *van aard* have a suspicious nature

de **wanverhouding** /wɑnvərhɑudɪŋ/ (pl: -en) disproportion, imbalance

de **WAO** /weao/ *Wet op de Arbeidsongeschiktheidsverzekering* disability insurance act

de **WAO'er** /weaoər/ recipient of disablement insurance benefits

het **wapen** /wɑpə(n)/ (pl: -s) **1** weapon; arms: *de ~s neerleggen* lay down arms **2** (coat of)

arms: *een leeuw in zijn ~ voeren* bear a lion in one's coat of arms

het **wapenbezit** /wɑpə(n)bəzɪt/ possession of firearms (or: weapons)

wapenen /wɑpənə(n)/ (wapende, heeft gewapend) arm; armour; reinforce

het **wapenfeit** /wɑpə(n)fɛɪt/ (pl: -en) **1** feat of arms **2** feat, exploit

de **wapenkunde** /wɑpə(n)kʏndə/ heraldry

de **wapenstilstand** /wɑpə(n)stɪlstɑnt/ (pl: -en) **1** armistice; suspension of arms (or: hostilities); ceasefire **2** [fig] truce

de **wapenstok** /wɑpə(n)stɔk/ (pl: -ken) [roughly] baton

het **wapentuig** /wɑpə(n)tœyχ/ armaments

de **wapenvergunning** /wɑpə(n)vərɣʏnɪŋ/ (pl: -en) firearms licence, gun licence

de **wapenwedloop** /wɑpə(n)wɛtlop/ arms race

wapperen /wɑpərə(n)/ (wapperde, heeft gewapperd) blow, fly, stream; flap; flutter: *laten ~* fly, blow, stream, wave ‖ *de handjes laten ~* get busy, buckle down

de **war** /wɑr/ tangle, muddle, confusion: *in de ~ zijn* be confused; *iem. in de ~ brengen* confuse s.o.; *plannen in de ~ sturen* upset s.o.'s plans; *iets in de ~ schoppen* make havoc of (or: foul up) sth.

de **warboel** /wɑrbul/ muddle, mess; tangle

warempel /wɑrɛmpəl/ (int) [inform] truly, really

de **waren** /wɑrə(n)/ (pl) goods, commodities

het **warenhuis** /wɑrə(n)hœys/ (pl: -huizen) (department) store

het **warhoofd** /wɑrhoft/ (pl: -en) scatterbrain

¹**warm** /wɑrm/ (adj) **1** warm, hot: *het ~ hebben* be warm (or: hot); *het begon (lekker) ~ te worden in de kamer* the room was warming up; *iets ~s* sth. warm (or: hot) (to eat, drink) **2** enthusiastically: *~ lopen voor iets* feel enthusiasm for sth. **3** warmly, pleasantly **4** warm, warm-hearted, ardent: *een ~ voorstander van iets zijn* be an ardent (or: a fervent) supporter of sth. **5** warmed up, enthusiastic **6** warm, pleasant ‖ *je bent ~!* you are (getting) warm! (or: hot!); *niet ~ of koud van iets worden* blow neither hot nor cold, be quite indifferent to sth.

²**warm** /wɑrm/ (adv) warmly: *iem. iets ~ aanbevelen* recommend sth. warmly to s.o.

warmbloedig /wɑrmbludəχ/ (adj) warmblooded

warmdraaien /wɑrmdrajə(n)/ (draaide warm, heeft/is warmgedraaid) warm up

warmen /wɑrmə(n)/ (warmde, heeft gewarmd) warm (up), heat (up)

de **warming-up** /wɔrmɪŋʏp/ (pl: -s) warm-up (exercise)

warmlopen /wɑrmlopə(n)/ (liep warm, is warmgelopen) **1** have warmed to, feel (great) enthusiasm for (s.o., sth.): *hij loopt niet*

warmpjes

586

*erg warm **voor** het plan* he has not really warmed to the plan **2** [sport] warm up, limber up

warmpjes /wɑrmpjəs/ (adv) warmly ‖ [fig] *er ~ **bij** zitten* be comfortably off, be well off

de **warmte** /wɑrmtə/ warmth, heat: *~ **(af)geven*** give off (*or:* emit) heat

de **warmtebron** /wɑrmtəbrɔn/ (pl: -nen) source of heat

het **warmtefront** /wɑrmtəfrɔnt/ (pl: -en) warm front

de **warmwaterkraan** /wɑrmwatərkran/ (pl: -kranen) hot(-water) tap

warrig /wɑrəx/ (adj) knotty, tangled; [fig] confused; muddled

wars /wɑrs/ (adj) averse (to)

Warschau /wɑrʃɑu/ Warsaw

de **wartaal** /wɑrtal/ gibberish, nonsense: *(er) ~ uitslaan* talk double Dutch (*or:* gibberish)

de **warwinkel** /wɑrwɪŋkəl/ mess, muddle

de **¹was** /wɑs/ (pl: -sen) wash, washing; laundry; linen: *de **fijne** ~* the fine (*or:* delicate) fabrics; *de **vuile** ~ buiten hangen* wash one's dirty linen in public; *iets **in** de ~ doen* put sth. in the wash

het/de **²was** /wɑs/ (pl: -sen) wax: *meubels **in** de ~ zetten* wax furniture ‖ *goed in de **slappe** ~ zitten* have plenty of dough

de **wasautomaat** /wɑsɑutomat/ (pl: wasautomaten) (automatic) washing machine

wasbaar /wɑzbar/ (adj) washable

de **wasbak** /wɑzbɑk/ (pl: -ken) washbasin, sink

de **wasbeer** /wɑzber/ (pl: wasberen) racoon

de **wasbenzine** /wɑzbɛnzinə/ benzine

de **wasdroger** /wɑzdroɣər/ (pl: -s) (tumble-)dryer

de **wasem** /wɑsəm/ (pl: -s) steam, vapour

wasemen /wɑsəmə(n)/ (wasemde, heeft gewasemd) steam

het **wasgoed** /wɑsxut/ wash, laundry, linen

het **washandje** /wɑshɑncə/ face cloth; [Am] wash rag

de **wasknijper** /wɑskɛipər/ (pl: -s) clothespeg

het **waskrijt** /wɑskrɛit/ grease pencil

de **waslijn** /wɑslɛin/ (pl: -en) clothes line

de **waslijst** /wɑslɛist/ (pl: -en) shopping list, catalogue

de **wasmachine** /wɑsmaʃinə/ (pl: -s) (automatic) washing machine

de **wasmand** /wɑsmɑnt/ (pl: -en) (dirty) clothes basket

het **wasmiddel** /wɑsmɪdəl/ (pl: -en) detergent

het/de **waspoeder** /wɑspudər/ (pl: -s) washingpowder, soap powder

het **wasrek** /wɑsrɛk/ (pl: -ken) drying rack

¹wassen /wɑsə(n)/ (adj) wax: *een ~ **beeld*** a wax figure

²wassen (wies, is gewassen) **1** grow **2** rise ‖ *bij **de** maan* while the moon is waxing

³wassen /wɑsə(n)/ (waste, heeft gewassen) **1** wash; launder; clean: *waar kan ik hier mijn **handen** ~?* where can I wash my hands?; *zich ~* **a)** wash, have a wash; **b)** have (*or:* take) a bath; **c)** wash o.s.; *iets op de hand ~* wash sth. by hand **2** wash, do the wash(ing)

het **wassenbeeldenmuseum** /wɑsə(n)bɛldə(n)myzejym/ waxworks

de **wasserette** /wɑsərɛtə/ (pl: -s) launderette

de **wasserij** /wɑsərɛi/ (pl: -en) laundry

de **wasstraat** /wɑstrat/ (pl: -straten) (automatic) car wash

de **wastafel** /wɑstafəl/ (pl: -s) washbasin

de **wasverzachter** /wɑsfərzɑxtər/ (pl: -s) fabric softener

¹wat /wɑt/ (ind pron) **1** sth.; anything; whatever: *ze **heeft** wel ~* she has got a certain sth.; *wil je ~ **drinken?*** would you like sth. to drink?; *zie jij ~?* do (*or:* can) you see anything?; *het is **altijd** ~ met hem* there is always sth. up with him **2** some, a bit (of); a little; a few: *geef me ~ **suiker*** (*or:* **geld**) give me some sugar (*or:* money); *geef mij ook ~* let me have some too; *~ **meer*** a bit (*or:* little) more; *~ **minder*** a bit (*or:* little) less ‖ *heel ~ boeken* quite a few books; a whole lot of books; *dat scheelt **nogal** ~* that makes quite a (bit of a) difference; *~ **kun** jij mooi **tekenen*** how well you draw!; *~ een onzin* what (absolute) nonsense; *~! komt hij niet?* what! isn't he coming?

²wat /wɑt/ (pron) what; which; whatever: *~ **bedoel** je daar nou mee?* just what do you mean by that?; [stronger] just what is that supposed to mean?; *wát **ga** je **doen?*** what are you going to do what?; *~ **heb** je 't liefste, koffie of thee?* which do you prefer, coffee or tea?; *~ **zeg** je?* (I beg your) pardon?; *~ is het **voor** iem.?* what's he (*or:* she) like?

³wat /wɑt/ (pron) that; which: *geef hem ~ hij nodig heeft* give him what he needs; *alles ~ je zegt, klopt* everything you say is true; *en ~ nog **belangrijker** is* and what's (even) more (important); *doe nou maar ~ ik zeg* just do as I say; *je kunt **doen** en **laten** ~ je wilt* you can do what (*or:* as you) please ‖ *ze zag eruit als een verpleegster, ~ ze ook was* she looked like a nurse, which in fact she was (too)

⁴wat /wɑt/ (adv) **1** somewhat, rather; a little, a bit: *hij is ~ **traag*** he is a little slow, he is on the slow side **2** very, extremely: *hij is er ~ **blij** mee* (or: **trots** op) he is extremely pleased with it (*or:* proud of it) **3** isn't it (*or:* that, he) …, …, aren't they (*or:* those) …: *~ **mooi** hè, die bloemen* aren't they beautiful, those flowers; *~ **lief** van je!* how nice of you!; [iron] *~ **ben** je weer vriendelijk* I see you're your usual friendly self again; *~ ze niet **verzinnen** tegenwoordig* the things they come up with these days; *~ **wil** je nog meer?* what more do (*or:* can) you want?; *~ **zal** hij blij **zijn!*** how happy (*or:* pleased) he will be!

het **water** /watər/ (pl: -en) **1** water: *de bloemen*

~ *geven* water the flowers; *bij* **laag** ~ at low water (*or:* tide); **stromend** ~ running water; *een schip* **te** ~ *laten* launch a ship; *iets* **boven** ~ *halen* [fig] unearth (*or:* dig up) sth. **2** water; waterway

waterafstotend /wɑtərɑfsto̱tənt/ (adj) water-repellent; waterproof

de **waterafvoer** /wɑ̱tərɑfur/ drainage (of water); sewage disposal

het **waterballet** /wɑ̱tərbɑlɛt/ (pl: -ten) wet affair

het **waterbed** /wɑ̱tərbɛt/ (pl: -den) waterbed

de **waterbouwkunde** /wɑ̱tərbɑukʏndə/ hydraulic engineering: **weg-** *en* ~ civil engineering

waterbouwkundig /wɑtərbɑukʏ̱ndəx/ (adj) hydraulic

de **waterbron** /wɑ̱tərbrɔn/ (pl: -nen) spring

de **waterdamp** /wɑ̱tərdɑmp/ (water) vapour

waterdicht /wɑ̱tərdɪxt/ (adj) waterproof; watertight: *een* ~ **alibi** a watertight alibi

waterdoorlatend /wɑtərdorlɑ̱tənt/ (adj) porous

de **waterdruppel** /wɑ̱tərdrʏpəl/ (pl: -s) drop of water

wateren /wɑ̱tərə(n)/ (waterde, heeft gewaterd) urinate

de **waterfiets** /wɑ̱tərfits/ (pl: -en) pedalo, pedal boat

de **watergolf** /wɑ̱tərɣɔlf/ (pl: -golven) **1** wave **2** set

watergolven /wɑ̱tərɣɔlvə(n)/ (watergolfde, heeft gewatergolfd) set: *zijn haar* **laten** ~ have one's hair set

het **waterhoen** /wɑ̱tərhun/ moorhen

het **waterhoofd** /wɑ̱tərhoft/ (pl: -en) hydrocephalus

de **waterhoogte** /wɑ̱tərhoxtə/ water level

de **waterhuishouding** /wɑ̱tərhœyshɑudɪŋ/ **1** soil hydrology **2** water management

waterig /wɑ̱tərəx/ (adj) **1** watery; slushy: *~e* **soep** thin soup **2** watery; [fig] wishy-washy: *een* ~ **zonnetje** a watery sun

het **waterijsje** /wɑ̱tərɛɨsə/ ice lolly; [Am] popsicle

het **waterkanon** /wɑ̱tərkanɔn/ (pl: -nen) water cannon

de **waterkans** /wɑ̱tərkɑns/ (pl: -en) [Belg] remote chance

de **waterkant** /wɑ̱tərkɑnt/ (pl: -en) waterside, waterfront: *aan de* ~ on the waterfront

de **waterkering** /wɑ̱tərkerɪŋ/ (pl: -en) dam, dike

de **waterkers** /wɑ̱tərkɛrs/ (water)cress

de **waterkoker** /wɑ̱tərkokər/ (pl: -s) electric kettle

waterkoud /wɑ̱tərkɑut/ (adj) clammy

de **waterkracht** /wɑ̱tərkrɑxt/ hydropower

de **waterlanders** /wɑ̱tərlɑndərs/ (pl) waterworks

de **waterleiding** /wɑ̱tərlɛidɪŋ/ (pl: -en) **1** wa-

ter pipe (*or:* supply): *een huis* **op** *de* ~ *aansluiten* to connect a house to the water main(s) **2** waterworks, water pipes: *een* **bevroren** ~ a frozen water pipe

het **waterleidingbedrijf** /wɑ̱tərlɛidɪŋbədrɛif/ (pl: -bedrijven) waterworks

de **waterlelie** /wɑ̱tərleli/ (pl: -s) water lily

de **waterloop** /wɑ̱tərlop/ (pl: -lopen) watercourse

de **Waterman** /wɑ̱tərmɑn/ (pl: -nen) [astrology] Aquarius

de **watermeloen** /wɑ̱tərməlun/ (pl: -en) watermelon

het **watermerk** /wɑ̱tərmɛrk/ (pl: -en) watermark

de **watermeter** /wɑ̱tərmetər/ (pl: -s) water meter

de **watermolen** /wɑ̱tərmolə(n)/ (pl: -s) watermill

de **waterontharder** /wɑ̱tərɔnthɑrdər/ (pl: -s) water softener

de **wateroverlast** /wɑ̱tərovərlɑst/ flooding

de ¹**waterpas** /wɑ̱tərpɑs/ (pl: -sen) spirit level; [Am] level

²**waterpas** /wɑ̱tərpɑs/ (adj) level

het **waterpeil** /wɑ̱tərpɛil/ water level

de **waterpijp** /wɑ̱tərpɛip/ (pl: -en) water pipe, hookah

het **waterpistool** /wɑ̱tərpistol/ (pl: -pistolen) water pistol

de **waterplant** /wɑ̱tərplɑnt/ (pl: -en) water plant

de **waterpokken** /wɑ̱tərpɔkə(n)/ (pl) chickenpox

de **waterpolitie** /wɑ̱tərpoli(t)si/ river police; harbour police

het **waterpolo** /wɑ̱tərpolo/ water polo

de **waterpomp** /wɑ̱tərpɔmp/ (pl: -en) water pump

de **waterpomptang** /wɑ̱tərpɔmptɑŋ/ (pl: -en) adjustable-joint pliers; [large] (adjustable) pipe wrench

de **waterput** /wɑ̱tərpʏt/ (pl: -ten) well

het **waterrad** /wɑ̱tərɑt/ (pl: -eren) water wheel

waterrijk /wɑ̱tərɛik/ (adj) watery, full of water

de **waterschade** /wɑ̱tərsxadə/ water damage

het **waterschap** /wɑ̱tərsxɑp/ (pl: -pen) **1** district water board **2** water board district

de **waterscheiding** /wɑ̱tərsxɛidɪŋ/ (pl: -en) watershed [also fig]

de **waterscooter** /wɑ̱tərskutər/ (pl: -s) aquascooter

de **waterski** /wɑ̱tərski/ (pl: -'s) water-ski

waterskiën /wɑ̱tərskijə(n)/ water-skiing

de **waterslang** /wɑ̱tərslɑŋ/ (pl: -en) hose(pipe)

de **watersnood** /wɑ̱tərsnot/ flood(ing)

de **watersnoodramp** /wɑ̱tərsnotramp/ (pl: -en) flood (disaster)

de **waterspiegel** /wɑ̱tərspiɣəl/ water surface; water level

watersport 588

de **watersport** /wa̱tərspɔrt/ (pl: -en) water sport, aquatic sport
de **waterstaat** /wa̱tərstat/ *see* minister
de **waterstand** /wa̱tərstɑnt/ (pl: -en) water level: *bij hoge* (or: *lage*) ~ at high (or: low) water
de **waterstof** /wa̱tərstɔf/ hydrogen
de **waterstofbom** /wa̱tərstɔvbɔm/ (pl: -men) hydrogen bomb, fusion bomb, H-bomb
het **waterstofperoxide** /wa̱tərstɔfpɛrɔksidə/ hydrogen peroxide
de **waterstraal** /wa̱tərstral/ (pl: -stralen) jet of water
watertanden /wa̱tərtɑndə(n)/ (watertandde, heeft gewatertand): *deze chocolaatjes **doen** mij* ~ these chocolates make my mouth water
de **watertoren** /wa̱tərtorə(n)/ (pl: -s) water tower
watertrappelen /wa̱tərtrɑpələ(n)/ tread water
de **waterval** /wa̱tərval/ (pl: -len) waterfall; fall: *de Niagara ~len* Niagara Falls
de **waterverf** /wa̱tərvɛrf/ watercolour
het **waterliegtuig** /wa̱tərvliχtœyχ/ (pl: -en) seaplane, water plane
de **watervogel** /wa̱tərvoɣəl/ (pl: -s) waterbird
de **watervrees** /wa̱tərvres/ hydrophobia: ~ *hebben* be hydrophobic
de **waterweg** /wa̱tərwɛχ/ (pl: -en) waterway
het **waterwingebied** /wa̱tərwɪnɣəbit/ (pl: -en) water-collection area
de **waterzuivering** /wa̱tərzœyvərɪn/ **1** water treatment **2** water treatment plant
het **watje** /wɒcə/ (pl: -s) **1** wad of cotton wool; [Am] wad of absorbent cotton **2** wally
de **watt** /wɑt/ (pl: -s) watt
de **watten** /wɑtə(n)/ (pl) cotton wadding, cotton wool; [Am] absorbent cotton: *een **prop** (dot)* ~ a plug (or: wad) of cottonwool; *iem. in de* ~ *leggen* pamper (or: mollycoddle) s.o.
het **wattenstaafje** /wɑtə(n)stafjə/ (pl: -s) cotton bud; [Am] cotton swab
wauwelen /wɒuwələ(n)/ (wauwelde, heeft gewauweld) [inform] chatter; jabber; drone (on)
de **WA-verzekering** /wea̱vərzekərɪn/ third-party insurance
de **wax** /wɑks/ wax
waxen /wɒksə(n)/ (waxte, heeft gewaxt) wax
het **waxinelichtje** /wɑksi̱nəlɪχjə/ (pl: -s) tea-light
wazig /wa̱zəχ/ (adj, adv) **1** hazy; blurred: *alles ~ zien* see everything (as if) through a haze (or: in a blur) **2** muzzy, drowsy: *met een ~e blik in de ogen* with a dazed look in the eyes
de **wc** /wese̱/ (pl: wc's) **1** *watercloset* WC, toilet, lavatory: *ik moet naar de wc* I have to go to the toilet **2** toilet(bowl)

de **wc-bril** /wese̱brɪl/ (pl: -len) toilet seat
het **wc-papier** /wese̱papir/ toilet paper
we /wə/ (pers pron) we, us: *laten we gaan* (or: *ophouden*) let's go (or: stop)
het **web** /wɛp/ (pl: -ben) web
de **webbrowser** /wɛbrɑuzər/ (pl: -s) web browser
de **webcam** /wɛpkɛm/ webcam
de **weblink** (pl: -s) weblink
het/de **weblog** /wɛplɔχ/ weblog
de **webmaster** /wɛpmɑːstər/ web master
de **webpagina** /wɛpaɣina/ (pl: -'s) web page
de **webserver** /wɛpsɪːrvər/ (pl: -s) web server
de **website** /wɛpsɑjt/ (pl: -s) website
de **webwinkel** /wɛpwɪnkəl/ (pl: -s) web shop, web store
wecken /wɛkə(n)/ (weckte, heeft geweckt) can, preserve
de **weckfles** /wɛkflɛs/ (pl: -sen) preserving jar
de **wedde** /wɛdə/ (pl: -n) pay, salary
wedden /wɛdə(n)/ (wedde, heeft gewed) bet (on): *met iem.* ~ *om* een tientje dat bet s.o. ten euros that; *denk jij dat Ron vandaag komt? - ik wed van wel* you think Ron will come today? - I bet he will
de **weddenschap** /wɛdə(n)sχap/ (pl: -pen) bet: *een ~ verliezen* lose a bet
de **weddeschaal** /wɛdəsχal/ (pl: -schalen) [Belg] salary scale
de **wederdienst** /we̱dərdinst/ (pl: -en) favour in return
de **wedergeboorte** /we̱dərɣəbortə/ (pl: -n) rebirth
de **wederhelft** /we̱dərhɛlft/ (pl: -en) consort; other half
de **wederhoor** /we̱dərhor/: *hoor en ~ toepassen* listen to both sides, listen to the other side
wederkerend /wedərke̱rənt/ (adj) reflexive
wederkerig /wedərke̱rəχ/ (adj, adv) mutual, reciprocal
wederom /wedərɔ̱m/ (adv) (once) again, once more
de **wederopbouw** /wedərɔ̱bɑu/ reconstruction, rebuilding
de **wederopstanding** /wedərɔ̱pstɑndɪn/ resurrection
wederrechtelijk /wedərɛ̱χtələk/ (adj, adv) unlawful, illegal
¹**wederzijds** /wedərzɛ̱its/ (adj) mutual, reciprocal: *de liefde was* ~ their love was mutual
²**wederzijds** /wedərzɛ̱its/ (adv) mutually
de **wedijver** /wɛtɛivər/ competition, rivalry
wedijveren /wɛtɛivərə(n)/ (wedijverde, heeft gewedijverd) strive (for)
de **wedloop** /wɛtlop/ (pl: wedlopen) race
de **wedren** /wɛtrɛn/ (pl: -nen) race
de **wedstrijd** /wɛtstrɛit/ (pl: -en) match, competition, game: *een ~ bijwonen* attend a

match; *een ~ fluiten* referee a match; *met nog drie ~en te spelen* with three games (still) to go

de **weduwe** /wedywə/ (pl: -n) widow: *groene ~* housebound wife

het **weduwepensioen** /wedywə(n)pɛnʃun/ (pl: -en) widows' benefit (*or:* pension)

de **weduwnaar** /wedywnar/ (pl: -s, weduwnaren) widower

de ¹**wee** /we/ labour pain, contraction: *de ~ën zijn begonnen* labour has started

²**wee** /we/ (adj) sickly

³**wee** /we/ (int) woe: *o ~ als je het nog eens doet* woe betide you if you do it again

de **weeffout** /wefaut/ (pl: -en) flaw, weaving fault

het **weefgetouw** /wefxətau/ (pl: -en) loom

het **weefsel** /wefsəl/ (pl: -s) **1** fabric, textile; weave **2** tissue, web

de **weegbree** /weybre/ plantain

de **weegbrug** /weybryx/ (pl: -gen) weighbridge

de **weegschaal** /wexsxal/ (pl: -schalen) (pair of) scales, balance: *twee weegschalen* two pairs of scales, two balances

de **Weegschaal** /wexsxal/ (pl: -schalen) [astrology] Libra

de ¹**week** /wek/ (pl: weken) week: *een ~ rust* a week's rest; *volgende ~ dinsdag* next Tuesday; *een ~ weggaan* go away for a week; *door de ~* on weekdays; *over een ~* in a week from now; *dinsdag over een ~* Tuesday week, a week from Tuesday; *morgen over twee weken* two weeks from tomorrow; *vandaag een ~ geleden* a week ago today

de ²**week** /wek/ (pl: weken) soak: *de was in de ~ zetten* put the laundry in (to) soak

³**week** /wek/ (adj) **1** soft: *~ worden* soften; *een ~ gestel* a weak constitution **2** weak, soft-hearted

het **weekblad** /wekblɑt/ (pl: -en) weekly, (news) magazine

het **weekdier** /wegdir/ (pl: -en) mollusc

het **weekeinde** /wekɛində/ (pl: -n) weekend: *in het ~* at the weekend; [Am] on the weekend

de **weekenddienst** /wikɛndinst/ (pl: -en) weekend duty

de **weekendtas** /wikɛntɑs/ holdall; [Am] carryall

weekhartig /wekhɑrtəx/ (adj) tender-hearted, softhearted

weeklagen /weklayə(n)/ (weeklaagde, heeft geweeklaagd) lament

het **weekoverzicht** /wekovərzɪxt/ (pl: -en) review of the week

de **weelde** /weldə/ luxury, over-abundance, wealth

weelderig /weldərəx/ (adj, adv) luxuriant; lush; sumptuous

de **weemoed** /wemut/ melancholy, sadness

weemoedig /wemudəx/ (adj, adv) melancholic, sad

Weens /wens/ (adj) Viennese

het ¹**weer** /wer/ **1** weather: *mooi ~ spelen (tegen iem.)* put on a show of friendliness; *~ of geen ~* come rain or shine **2** weathering: *het ~ zit in het tentdoek* the tent is weather-stained || *hij is altijd in de ~* he is always on the go

²**weer** /wer/ (adv) **1** again: *morgen komt er ~ een dag* tomorrow is another day; *het komt wel ~ goed* it will all turn out all right; *nu ik ~* now it's my turn; *wat moest hij nu ~?* what did he want now?; *wat nu ~?* now what? **2** back: *heen en ~ gaan* (or: *reizen*) go (or: travel) back and forth; *heen en ~ lopen* pace up and down || *zo moeilijk is het nou ook ~ niet* it's not all that hard

weerbaar /werbar/ (adj) able-bodied: *~ zijn* have spirit

weerbarstig /werbɑrstəx/ (adj, adv) stubborn, unruly

het **weerbericht** /werbərɪxt/ (pl: -en) weather forecast (*or:* report)

de **weerga** /werya/: *zonder ~* unparalleled

weergalmen /weryɑlmə(n)/ (weergalmde, heeft weergalmd) echo, resound: *de straten weergalmden van het gejuich* the streets resounded with the cheers

weergaloos /weryalos/ (adj, adv) unequalled, unparalleled

de **weergave** /weryavə/ (pl: -n) reproduction; account

weergeven /weryevə(n)/ (gaf weer, heeft weergegeven) **1** reproduce, render, represent; recite; convey **2** reproduce, repeat, report: *dit onderzoek geeft de feiten juist weer* this study presents the facts accurately **3** reflect

de **weergod** /weryɔt/ (pl: -en) weather god

de **weerhaak** /werhak/ (pl: -haken) barb, beard

de **weerhaan** /werhan/ (pl: -hanen) weathercock, weathervane

weerhouden /werhaudə(n)/ (weerhield, heeft weerhouden) **1** hold back, restrain: *iem. ervan ~ om iets te doen* stop (or: keep) s.o. from doing sth. **2** [Belg] retain, keep: *de beslissing is ~* the decision is upheld

de **weerkaart** /werkart/ (pl: -en) weather chart, weather map

weerkaatsen /werkɑtsə(n)/ (weerkaatste, heeft/is weerkaatst) reflect; reverberate; (re-)echo: *de muur weerkaatst het geluid* the wall echoes the sound; *het geluid weerkaatst tegen de muur* the sound reflects off (or: from) the wall

de **weerklank** /werklɑŋk/ echo: *geen ~ vinden* find no response

weerklinken /werklɪŋkə(n)/ (weerklonk, heeft weerklonken) **1** resound, ring out: *een schot weerklonk* a shot rang out **2** resound, reverberate

de **weerkunde** /wɛrkʏndə/ meteorology
weerkundig /werkʏndəχ/ (adj) meteorological

de **weerkundige** /werkʏndəɣə/ (pl: -n) meteorologist, weather expert
weerlegbaar /werlɛɣbar/ (adj) refutable
weerleggen /werlɛɣə(n)/ (weerlegde, heeft weerlegd) refute

de **weerlegging** /werlɛɣɪŋ/ refutation

het/de **weerlicht** /werlɪχt/ (heat, sheet) lightning
weerlichten /werlɪχtə(n)/ (weerlichtte, heeft geweerlicht) lighten
weerloos /werlos/ (adj) defenceless

de **weerman** /werman/ (pl: -nen) weatherman

de **weeromstuit** /werɔmstœyt/: *van de ~* on the rebound; *ik moest van de ~ ook lachen* I had to laugh too

het **weeroverzicht** /werovərzɪχt/ (pl: -en) weather survey: *en nu het ~* and now for a look at the weather

het **weerpraatje** /werpracə/ (pl: -s) (the) weather in brief, weather report

de **weerschijn** /wersχɛɪn/ reflection

de **weersgesteldheid** /wersχəstɛlthɛɪt/ weather situation: *bij elke ~* in all weathers

de **weerskanten** /werskantə(n)/ (pl): *aan ~ van de tafel* (or: *het raam*) on both sides of the table (or: window); *van* (or: *aan*) *~* from (or: on) both sides

de **weerslag** /werslaχ/ repercussion: *zijn ~ hebben op* have repercussions on

de **weersomstandigheden** /wersɔmstandəχhedə(n)/ (pl) weather conditions
weerspannig /werspɒnəχ/ (adj, adv) recalcitrant, rebellious, refractory
weerspiegelen /werspiɣələ(n)/ (weerspiegelde, heeft weerspiegeld) reflect

de **weerspiegeling** /werspiɣəlɪŋ/ (pl: -en) reflection: *een getrouwe ~ van iets* a true reflection (or: mirror) of sth.
weerstaan /werstan/ (weerstond, heeft weerstaan) resist, stand up to

de **weerstand** /werstant/ (pl: -en) **1** resistance, opposition: *~ bieden* offer resistance **2** aversion

het **weerstandsvermogen** /werstan(t)sfərmoɣə(n)/ resistance

het **weerstation** /wersta(t)ʃɔn/ (pl: -s) weather station

de **weersverwachting** /wersfərwaχtɪŋ/ (pl: -en) weather forecast

de **weerwil** /werwɪl/: *in ~ van* despite, in spite of, notwithstanding

de **weerwolf** /werwɔlf/ (pl: -wolven) werewolf

het **weerwoord** /werwort/ (pl: -en) answer, reply

het ¹**weerzien** /werzin/ reunion; meeting: *tot ~s* goodbye, until the next time

²**weerzien** /werzin/ (zag weer, heeft weergezien) meet again, see again

de **weerzin** /werzɪn/ disgust, reluctance, aversion, distaste: *iets met ~ doen* do sth. with great reluctance
weerzinwekkend /werzɪnwɛkənt/ (adj, adv) disgusting, revolting

de **wees** /wes/ (pl: wezen) orphan

het **weesgegroetje** /wesɣəχrucə/ (pl: -s) Hail Mary: *tien ~s bidden* say ten Hail Marys

het **weeshuis** /weshœys/ (pl: -huizen) orphanage

het **weeskind** /weskɪnt/ (pl: -eren) orphan (child)

de **weet** /wet/: *iets aan de ~ komen* find out sth.; *ergens geen ~ van hebben* have no knowledge of sth., be unaware of sth.

de **weetal** /wetal/ (pl: -len) know(-it)-all; [Am also] wise guy
weetgierig /wetχirəχ/ (adj, adv) inquisitive

het **weetje** /wecə/ (pl: -s): *allerlei ~s* all kinds of trivia

de ¹**weg** /wɛχ/ (pl: -en) **1** road, way, track: *zich een ~ banen* work (or: edge) one's way through; *(iem.) in de ~ staan* stand in s.o.'s (or: the) way; *(voor) iem. uit de ~ gaan* keep (or: get) out of s.o.'s way, avoid s.o.; *een misverstand uit de ~ helpen* clear up a misunderstanding; *een kortere ~ nemen* take a short cut; *op de goede* (or: *verkeerde*) *~ zijn* be on the right (or: wrong) track; *op ~ gaan* set off (on a trip), set out (for), go; *iem. op ~ helpen* set s.o. up **2** way, channel, means: *de ~ van de minste weerstand* the line (or: road) of least resistance **3** way, journey: *nog een lange ~ voor zich hebben* have a long way to go ‖ *zijns weegs gaan* go one's way

²**weg** /wɛχ/ (adv) **1** gone: *een mooie pen is nooit ~* a nice pen always comes in useful; *~ wezen!* (let's) get away from here!; (let's) get out of here!; *~ met ...* away (or: down) with ... **2** crazy **3** away ‖ *ze heeft veel ~ van haar zus* she takes after her sister, she is very like her sister

de **wegbereider** /wɛɣbərɛɪdər/ (pl: -s) pioneer
wegblazen /wɛɣblazə(n)/ (blies weg, heeft weggeblazen) blow away, blow off
wegblijven /wɛɣblɛɪvə(n)/ (bleef weg, is weggebleven) stay away
wegbranden /wɛɣbrandə(n)/ (brandde weg, heeft weggebrand): *die man is niet weg te bránden* there's no getting rid of that man
wegbrengen /wɛɣbrɛŋə(n)/ (bracht weg, heeft weggebracht) **1** take (away), deliver **2** see (off)
wegcijferen /wɛχsɛɪfərə(n)/ ignore: *zichzelf ~* efface o.s.

de **wegcode** /wɛχkodə/ (pl: -s) [Belg] traffic regulations; [roughly] Highway Code

het **wegdek** /wɛɣdɛk/ (pl: -ken) road (surface)
wegdenken /wɛɣdɛŋkə(n)/ (dacht weg, heeft weggedacht) think away: *internet is niet meer uit onze maatschappij weg te denken* it's impossible to imagine life today without the

Internet

wegdoen /wɛɣdun/ (deed weg, heeft weggedaan) **1** dispose of, part with, get rid of **2** put away

wegdragen /wɛɣdraɣə(n)/ (droeg weg, heeft weggedragen) carry away, carry off

wegdrijven /wɛɣdrɛivə(n)/ (dreef weg, is weggedreven) float away, drift away

wegduiken /wɛɣdœykə(n)/ (dook weg, is weggedoken) duck (away); dive away

wegduwen /wɛɣdywə(n)/ (duwde weg, heeft weggeduwd) push away, push aside

wegen /weɣə(n)/ (woog, heeft gewogen) weigh: *zwaarder ~ dan* outweigh; *zich laten ~* have o.s. weighed, be weighed

de **wegenbelasting** /weɣə(n)bəlɑstɪŋ/ road tax

de **wegenbouw** /weɣə(n)bau/ road building (*or:* construction)

de **wegenkaart** /weɣə(n)kart/ (pl: -en) road map

het **wegennet** /weɣənɛt/ (pl: -ten) road network (*or:* system)

wegens /weɣəns/ (prep) because of, on account of, due to: *terechtstaan ~ …* be tried on a charge of …

de **wegenwacht**® /weɣə(n)wɑxt/ (pl: -en) (AA) patrolman; AAA attendant

de **Wegenwacht**® /weɣə(n)wɑxt/ road-service; [roughly] AA-patrol, RAC-patrol; [Am] AAA road service

weggaan /wɛɣan/ (ging weg, is weggegaan) **1** go away, leave: *Joe is bij zijn vrouw weggegaan* Joe has left his wife; *~ zonder te betalen* leave without paying; *ga weg!* go away!, get lost!; get away!, you're kidding! **2** go away: *de pijn gaat al weg* the pain is already getting less

de **weggebruiker** /wɛɣəbrœykər/ (pl: -s) road user

weggeven /wɛɣevə(n)/ (gaf weg, heeft weggegeven) give away

het **weggevertje** /wɛɣevərcə/ (pl: -s) giveaway; dead giveaway

wegglijden /wɛɣlɛidə(n)/ (gleed weg, is weggegleden) slip (away): *de auto gleed weg in de modder* the car slipped in the mud

weggooien /wɛɣojə(n)/ (gooide weg, heeft weggegooid) throw away, throw out, discard: *dat is weggegooid geld* that is money down the drain

de **weggooiverpakking** /wɛɣojvərpɑkɪŋ/ disposable container (*or:* packaging, package)

weghalen /wɛɣhalə(n)/ (haalde weg, heeft weggehaald) remove; take away: *alle huisraad werd uit het huis weggehaald* the house was stripped (bare)

de **weghelft** /wɛɣhɛlft/ (pl: -en) side of the road

wegjagen /wɛɣjaɣə(n)/ (jaagde weg/joeg

weg, heeft weggejaagd) chase away: *klanten ~ door de hoge prijzen* frighten customers off by high prices

wegkijken /wɛɣkɛikə(n)/ (keek weg, heeft weggekeken) frown away: *hij werd weggekeken* they stared at him coldly until he left

wegkomen /wɛɣkomə(n)/ (kwam weg, is weggekomen) get away: *de meeste favorieten zijn goed weggekomen bij de start* the favourites got (off to) a good start; *slecht* (or: *goed*) *~ bij iets* come off badly (or: well) with sth.; *maakte dat ik wegkwam* I got out of there

wegkruipen /wɛɣkrœypə(n)/ (kroop weg, is weggekropen) crawl away, creep away

wegkwijnen /wɛɣkwɛinə(n)/ (kwijnde weg, is weggekwijnd) pine away, waste away

weglaten /wɛɣlatə(n)/ (liet weg, heeft weggelaten) leave out, omit

wegleggen /wɛɣlɛɣə(n)/ (legde weg, heeft weggelegd) **1** put aside, put away **2** lay aside, set aside, save

de **wegligging** /wɛɣlɪɣɪŋ/ road-holding

weglopen /wɛɣlopə(n)/ (liep weg, is weggelopen) **1** walk away, walk off: *dat loopt niet weg* that can wait; *~ voor een hond* run away from a dog **2** run away, walk out; run off: *een weggelopen kind* a runaway (child) **3** run off, run out

wegmaken /wɛɣmakə(n)/ (maakte weg, heeft weggemaakt) lose

de **wegmarkering** /wɛɣmɑrkerɪŋ/ (pl: -en) road marking

wegmoffelen /wɛɣmɔfələ(n)/ (moffelde weg, heeft weggemoffeld) quickly hide; cover up

wegnemen /wɛɣnemə(n)/ (nam weg, heeft weggenomen) remove, take away; dispel || *dat neemt niet weg, dat ik hem aardig vind* all the same I like him; *dat neemt niet weg, dat het geld verdwenen is* that doesn't alter the fact that the money has disappeared

de **wegomlegging** /wɛɣɔmlɛɣɪŋ/ (pl: -en) diversion; [Am] detour

wegpesten /wɛɣpɛstə(n)/ (pestte weg, heeft weggepest) harass (*or:* pester) (s.o.) until he leaves

wegpinken /wɛɣpɪŋkə(n)/ (pinkte weg, heeft weggepinkt): *een traantje ~* wipe away a tear

de **wegpiraat** /wɛɣpirat/ (pl: wegpiraten) road hog

wegpoetsen /wɛɣputsə(n)/ (poetste weg, heeft weggepoetst) gloss over

wegpromoveren /wɛɣpromoverə(n)/ (promoveerde weg, heeft weggepromoveerd) kick upstairs

wegraken /wɛɣrakə(n)/ (raakte weg, is weggeraakt) **1** faint **2** get lost

wegrennen /wɛɣrɛnə(n)/ (rende weg, is weggerend) run off (*or:* away)

wegrestaurant /wɛxrɛstorɑnt/ (pl: -s) transport cafe, wayside restaurant

wegrijden /wɛxrɛidə(n)/ (reed weg, is weggereden) drive off (*or:* away); ride off (*or:* away): *de auto reed met grote vaart weg* the car drove off at high speed

wegroepen /wɛxrupə(n)/ (riep weg, heeft weggeroepen) call off (*or:* away)

wegschoppen /wɛxsxɔpə(n)/ (schopte weg, heeft weggeschopt) kick away

wegslaan /wɛxslan/ (sloeg weg, heeft weggeslagen) knock off (*or:* away): *de golven hebben een **stuk** van de duinen weggeslagen* the waves have washed away part of the dunes; [fig] *zij is er niet **(van)** weg te slaan* she can hardly be dragged away (from it)

wegslepen /wɛxslepə(n)/ (sleepte weg, heeft weggesleept) tow away; drag away

wegslikken /wɛxslɪkə(n)/ (slikte weg, heeft weggeslikt) swallow (down): *ik moest even **iets** ~* I had to swallow hard

wegsluipen /wɛxslœypə(n)/ (sloop weg, is weggeslopen) sneak away, sneak off

wegsmelten /wɛxsmɛltə(n)/ (smolt weg, is weggesmolten) melt away

¹**wegspoelen** /wɛxspulə(n)/ (spoelde weg, is weggespoeld) be washed (*or:* carried, swept) away

²**wegspoelen** /wɛxspulə(n)/ (spoelde weg, heeft weggespoeld) **1** wash away, carry away; flush down **2** wash down

wegstemmen /wɛxstɛmə(n)/ (stemde weg, heeft weggestemd) vote out (of office), vote down

wegsterven /wɛxstɛrvə(n)/ (stierf weg, is weggestorven) die away (*or:* down), fade away

wegstoppen /wɛxstɔpə(n)/ (stopte weg, heeft weggestopt) hide away, stash away: *weggestopt **zitten** be hidden (*or:* tucked) away

wegstrepen /wɛxstrepə(n)/ (streepte weg, heeft weggestreept) cross off, cross out, delete

wegsturen /wɛxstyrə(n)/ (stuurde weg, heeft weggestuurd) send away

wegtrappen /wɛxtrɑpə(n)/ (trapte weg, heeft weggetrapt) kick away

wegtrekken /wɛxtrɛkə(n)/ (trok weg, is weggetrokken) draw off, move away, withdraw: *mijn **hoofdpijn** trekt weg* my headache is going (*or:* disappearing) ‖ *met een wit weggetrokken **gezicht*** white-faced

wegvagen /wɛxfaɣə(n)/ (vaagde weg, heeft weggevaagd) wipe out, sweep away

wegvallen /wɛxfɑlə(n)/ (viel weg, is weggevallen) **1** be omitted (*or:* dropped): *er is een **regel** (or: **letter**) weggevallen* a line (*or:* letter) has been left out **2** fall away

wegvegen /wɛxfeɣə(n)/ (veegde weg, heeft weggeveegd) wipe (*or:* sweep, brush)

away

wegverkeer /wɛxfərker/ road traffic

de **wegversmalling** /wɛxfərsmɑlɪŋ/ (pl: -en) narrowing of the road; road narrows

de **wegversperring** /wɛxfərspɛrɪŋ/ (pl: -en) roadblock

het **wegvervoer** /wɛxfərvur/ road transport

wegvliegen /wɛxfliɣə(n)/ (vloog weg, is weggevlogen) **1** fly away (*or:* off, out) **2** sell like hot cakes

wegvoeren /wɛxfurə(n)/ (voerde weg, heeft weggevoerd) carry away, carry off

wegwaaien /wɛxwajə(n)/ (waaide weg/ woei weg, is weggewaaid) be blown away, fly away, fly off

wegwerken /wɛxwɛrkə(n)/ (werkte weg, heeft weggewerkt) get rid of; polish off; put away; smoothe away: *iets **op** een foto* ~ block out sth. on a photo

de **wegwerker** /wɛxwɛrkər/ (pl: -s) roadmender; [Am] road worker

het **wegwerpartikel** /wɛxwɛrpɑrtikəl/ disposable article; disposables

de **wegwerpbeker** /wɛxwɛrbekər/ disposable cup

wegwerpen /wɛxwɛrpə(n)/ (wierp weg, heeft weggeworpen) throw away, throw out

de **wegwerpmaatschappij** /wɛxwɛrpmatsxɑpɛi/ consumer society

de **wegwerpverpakking** /wɛxwɛrpfərpɑkɪŋ/ (pl: -en) disposable container

wegwezen /wɛxwezə(n)/ clear off, clear out, push off, buzz off, scram: *jongens, ~!* let's get out of here!; *hé, jij daar, ~!* buzz off!, scram!

wegwijs /wɛxwɛis/ (adj) familiar, informed

de **wegwijzer** /wɛxwɛizər/ (pl: -s) signpost

wegzakken /wɛxsɑkə(n)/ (zakte weg, is weggezakt) sink

wegzetten /wɛxsɛtə(n)/ (zette weg, heeft weggezet) set aside, put aside, put away (*or:* aside): *ik **kon** mijn auto nergens* ~ I couldn't find anywhere to park

wegzinken /wɛxsɪŋkə(n)/ (zonk weg, is weggezonken) sink, go under, subside

de **wei** /wɛi/ (pl: -den) *see* **weide**

de **weide** /wɛidə/ (pl: -n) **1** meadow; pasture; grasslands **2** playground, playing field

weiden /wɛidə(n)/ (weidde, heeft geweid) graze, pasture

weids /wɛits/ (adj) grand

de **weifelaar** /wɛifəlar/ (pl: -s) waverer

weifelen /wɛifələ(n)/ (weifelde, heeft geweifeld) waver, hesitate, be undecided: *na enig* ~ *koos ik het groene jasje* after some hesitation I opted for the green jacket

de **weigeraar** /wɛiɣərar/ (pl: -s) refuser

weigerachtig /wɛiɣərɑxtəx/ (adj) unwilling, reluctant; uncooperative

¹**weigeren** /wɛiɣərə(n)/ (weigerde, heeft geweigerd) fail; jam; be jammed: *de **motor**

weigert the engine won't start

²weigeren /wɛiɣərə(n)/ (weigerde, heeft geweigerd) refuse, reject; turn down: *een visum* ~ withhold a visa; *iem.* **iets** ~ deny s.o. sth.

de **weigering** /wɛiɣərɪŋ/ (pl: -en) refusal; denial

het **weiland** /wɛilɑnt/ (pl: -en) pasture (land), grazing (land), meadow

¹weinig /wɛinəɣ/ (ind pron) little, not much, not a lot: ~ *Engels kennen* not know much English; ~ *of (tot) geen* **geld** little or no money; *er* ~ *van* **weten** not know a lot about it; *dat is veel* **te** ~ that's insufficient (*or:* quite inadequate); *twintig pond* **te** ~ *hebben* be twenty pounds short

²weinig /wɛinəɣ/ (adv) **1** little: ~ *bekende feiten* little-known facts; *er* ~ *om* **geven** care little about it; *dat* **scheelt** *maar* ~ it's a close thing **2** hardly ever: ~ *thuis* **zijn** not be in often

³weinig /wɛinəɣ/ (num) few, not many: *slechts* ~ **huizen** *staan leeg* there are only a few unoccupied houses; ~ *of (tot) geen* **mensen** few if any people

¹wekelijks /wekələks/ (adj) weekly: *onze* ~*e* **vergadering** our weekly meeting

²wekelijks /wekələks/ (adv) **1** weekly, once a week, every week: ~ *samenkomen* meet once a week **2** a week, per week: *hij* **verdient** ~ *500 euro* he earns 500 euros a week

weken /wekə(n)/ (weekte, heeft/is geweekt) soak

¹wekenlang /wekə(n)lɑŋ/ (adj, adv) lasting several weeks

²wekenlang /wekə(n)lɑŋ/ (adv) for weeks (on end)

wekken /wɛkə(n)/ (wekte, heeft gewekt) **1** wake (up); call: *tot leven* ~ bring into being **2** awaken, arouse, stir, excite; create: *iemands* **belangstelling** ~ arouse (*or:* excite) s.o.'s interest; *vertrouwen* ~ inspire confidence

de **wekker** /wɛkər/ (pl: -s) alarm (clock): *de* ~ *op zes uur* **zetten** set the alarm for six (o'clock)

de **wekkerradio** /wɛkəradijo/ (pl: -'s) radio alarm (clock), clock radio

het **¹wel** /wɛl/ (pl: -len) welfare, well-being: *zijn* ~ *en* **wee** his fortunes

²wel /wɛl/ (adv) **1** well: *en (dat)* **nog** ~ *op zondag* and on a Sunday, too! **2** rather, quite: *het was* ~ **aardig** it was all right; *'hoe is het ermee?' 'het* **gaat** ~*'* 'how are you?' 'all right'; *ik* **mag** *dat* ~ I quite like that; *het kan er* ~ *mee door* it'll do **3** probably: *het zal* ~ *lukken* it'll work out (all right); *dat zal* ~ *niet* I suppose not; *je zult* ~ *denken* what will you think?; *hij zal het* ~ *niet geweest zijn* I don't think it was him; *dat kan* ~ *(zijn)* that may be (so); *hij zal nu* ~ *in bed liggen* he'll be in bed by now **4** as much as; as many as; as often as: *dat kost* ~

100 euro it'll cost as much as 100 euros; *wat moet dat* ~ *niet kosten* I hate to think (of) what that costs **5** at least, just as: *dat is* ~ *zo makkelijk* it would be a lot easier that way; *het lijkt me* ~ *zo verstandig* it seems sensible to me **6** completely, all: *we zijn gezond en* ~ *aangekomen* we arrived safe and sound || *och, ik* **mag** *hem* ~ oh, I think he's all right; *dat* **dacht** *ik* ~ I thought as much; *wat zullen de mensen er* ~ *van zeggen?* what'll people say?; **heeft** *hij het* ~ **gedaan?** did he really do it?; *hij* **komt** ~ he will come (all right); *kom jij?* **misschien** ~! will you come?, I might!; *het is* **wél** **waar** but it is true; *'ik doe het niet', 'je* **doet** *het* ~!' 'I won't do it', 'oh yes you will!'; *jij wil niet?* **ik** ~! you don't want to? well I do!; *liever* ~ *dan* **niet** as soon as not; *nietes! wélles!* **a)** 'tisn't! 'tis!; **b)** [Am] it isn't, it is so! (*or:* too!); **c)** [depending on verb in previous sentence] didn't! did!; ~ *eens* once in a while; ever; *dat komt* ~ **eens** *voor* it happens at times; *heb je* ~ **eens** *Japans gegeten?* have you ever eaten Japanese food?; **dát** ~ granted, agreed; *hij* **wou** ~ he was all for it

³wel /wɛl/ (int) well, why: ~*? wat zeg je daarvan?* well? what do you say to that? || ~ **allemachtig!** well I'll be damned!; ~ *nee!* of course not!

het **welbehagen** /wɛlbəhaɣə(n)/ pleasure: *een* **gevoel** *van* ~ a sense of well-being

welbekend /wɛlbəkɛnt/ (adj) well-known, famous; familiar

welbeschouwd /wɛlbəsχɑut/ (adj, adv) all things considered, all in all

welbespraakt /wɛlbəsprakt/ (adj) eloquent

welbesteed /wɛlbəstet/ (adj) well-spent

het **welbevinden** /wɛlbəvɪndə(n)/ well-being

welbewust /wɛlbəwʏst/ (adj, adv) deliberate, well-considered

de **weldaad** /wɛldat/ (pl: weldaden) benefaction, charity

weldadig /wɛldadəɣ/ (adj) benevolent

weldenkend /wɛldɛŋkənt/ (adj) right-minded, right-thinking

de **weldoener** /wɛldunər/ (pl: -s) benefactor

weldra /wɛldra/ (adv) presently

weleens /welens/ (adv) once in a while, sometimes: *wil je* ~ *luisteren!* will you just listen (to me)!

het **weleer** /wɛler/ olden days (*or:* times)

welgemanierd /wɛlɣəmanirt/ (adj, adv) well-mannered

welgemeend /wɛlɣəment/ (adj) well-meaning, well-meant

welgesteld /wɛlɣəstɛlt/ (adj) well-to-do, well-off

welgeteld /wɛlɣətɛlt/ (adv) all-in-all, all told

welgevallen /wɛlɣəvalə(n)/: *zich iets* **laten** ~ put up with sth., submit to

welgezind /wɛlɣəzɪnt/ (adj) well-disposed (towards)

welig /wͤeləɣ/ (adj) luxuriant, abundant

welingelicht /wɛlɪnɣəlɪχt/ (adj) well-informed

weliswaar /wɛlɪswar/ (adv) it's true, to be sure: *ik* **heb** ~ **beloofd,** *maar ik kan het nu niet doen* I did promise (, it's true), but I cannot do it now

welja /wɛlja/ (int) yes of course: ~, **lach** *er maar om* go on, laugh; ~, **spot** *er maar mee* that's right, make fun of it

¹welk /wɛlk/ (ind pron) whatever, any (… what(so)ever); whichever; any: ~e **kleur** *je ook (maar) wilt, om het even* ~e **kleur** *je wilt* take any colour whatsoever; *om* ~e **reden** *ook* for any reason whatsoever; ~e *van de twee je ook* **kiest** whichever of the two you choose; *(geef me er maar een,) het geeft niet* ~e any (of them) will do; either (of them) will do

²welk /wɛlk/ (pron) which, what; which one: *om* ~e **reden?,** *met* ~e **bedoeling?** what for?; ~e **van** *die twee is van jou?* which of those two is yours?

³welk /wɛlk/ (pron) **1** who; whom; which: *de* **man** ~e *u gezien hebt, is hier* the man (whom) you saw is here **2** which: *wij verkopen koffie en thee,* ~e **artikelen** *veel aftrek vinden* we sell coffee and tea, (articles) which are much in demand; *… vanuit* ~e **overtuiging** *hij ertoe overging om … …* from which conviction he proceeded to …

welkom /wͤelkɔm/ (adj) welcome: *je* **bent** *altijd* ~ you're always welcome; *iem. hartelijk* ~ **heten** give s.o. a hearty (*or:* cordial) welcome ‖ ~ **thuis** welcome home

¹wellen /wͤelə(n)/ (welde, is geweld) well (up)

²wellen /wͤelə(n)/ (welde, heeft geweld) **1** simmer **2** steep

welles /wͤeləs/ (int) [inform] yes, it is (*or:* does): **nietes!** ~! it isn't! it is!

welletjes /wͤelətʃəs/ (adj) [inform] quite enough: *'t* **is** *zo* ~ that will do

wellicht /wɛlɪχt/ (adv) perhaps, possibly

welluidend /wɛlœydənt/ (adj, adv) melodious

de **wellust** /wͤelʏst/ voluptuousness, sensuality

wellustig /wɛlʏstəχ/ (adj, adv) sensual, voluptuous

welnee /wɛlne/ (int) of course not, certainly not

het **welnemen** /wͤelneme(n)/: **met** *uw* ~ by your leave

welnu /wͤelnʏ/ (int) well then: ~, *laat eens horen* well then, tell me (your story)

welopgevoed /wͤelɔpχəvut/ (adj) well-bred: ~e **kinderen** well brought up children

weloverwogen /wͤeloverwoɣə(n)/ (adj, adv) **1** (well-)considered: *in* ~ **woorden** in measured words **2** deliberate: *iets* ~ **doen** do

sth. deliberately

de **welp** /wͤelp/ **1** cub **2** Cub Scout

het **welslagen** /wͤelslaɣə(n)/ success

welsprekend /wͤelsprekənt/ (adj) eloquent

de **welsprekendheid** /wͤelsprekəntheɪt/ eloquence

de **welstand** /wͤelstant/ **1** good health **2** well-being

de **¹weltergewicht** /wͤeltərɣəwɪχt/ welterweight

het **²weltergewicht** /wͤeltərɣəwɪχt/ welterweight

welterusten /wͤeltərʏstə(n)/ (int) goodnight, sleep well

welteverstaan /wͤeltəvərstan/ (adv) that is, if you ask my meaning

de **welvaart** /wͤelvart/ prosperity

de **welvaartsmaatschappij** /wͤelvartsmatsχɑpeɪ/ affluent society

de **welvaartsstaat** /wͤelvartstat/ welfare state

welvarend /wͤelvarənt/ (adj) thriving; well-to-do

welverdiend /wͤelvərdɪnt/ (adj) well-deserved; well-earned; just

de **welving** /wͤelvɪŋ/ (pl: -en) curve, curvature

welwillend /wͤelwɪlənt/ (adj, adv) kind, sympathetic; favourable: ~ **staan** *tegenover iets* be favourably disposed towards sth.

de **welwillendheid** /wͤelwɪləntheɪt/ benevolence, kindness: *dankzij de* ~ *van* by (*or:* through) the courtesy of

het **welzijn** /wͤelzeɪn/ welfare, well-being

het **welzijnswerk** /wͤelzeɪnswɛrk/ welfare work, social work

de **welzijnswerker** /wͤelzeɪnswɛrkər/ (pl: -s) social worker

wemelen /wͤemələ(n)/ (wemelde, heeft gewemeld) teem (with), swarm (with): *zijn opstel wemelt* **van** *de fouten* his essay is full of mistakes

wendbaar /wͤendbar/ (adj) manoeuvrable

¹wenden /wͤendə(n)/ (wendde, heeft gewend) turn (about): *hoe je het ook wendt of* **keert** whichever way you look at it

zich **²wenden** /wͤendə(n)/ (wendde zich, heeft zich gewend) (+ tot) turn (to), apply (to)

de **wending** /wͤendɪŋ/ (pl: -en) turn: *het verhaal een andere* ~ *geven* give the story a twist

wenen /wͤenə(n)/ (weende, heeft geweend) weep

Wenen /wͤenə(n)/ Vienna

de **wenk** /wͤeŋk/ (pl: -en) sign, wink, nod

de **wenkbrauw** /wͤeŋkbrau/ (pl: -en) (eye)brow: *de* ~en **fronsen** frown; *de* ~en **optrekken** raise one's eyebrows

het **wenkbrauwpotlood** /wͤeŋkbraupɔtlot/ eyebrow pencil

wenken /wͤeŋkə(n)/ (wenkte, heeft gewenkt) beckon, signal, motion

wennen /wͤenə(n)/ (wende, is gewend) **1** get (*or:* become) used (to), get (*or:* become) accustomed (to): *dat zal wel* ~ you'll get used to it **2** adjust, settle in (*or:* down)

de **wens** /wɛns/ (pl: -en) **1** wish, desire: *zijn laatste* ~ his dying wish; *mijn* ~ **is vervuld** my wish has come true; *het gaat naar* ~ it is going as we hoped it would; *is alles naar* ~*?* is everything to your liking? **2** wish, greeting: *de beste* ~*en voor het nieuwe jaar* best wishes for the new year ‖ *de* ~ *is de vader van de gedachte* the wish is father to the thought

de **wensdroom** /wɛnzdrom/ (pl: -dromen) fantasy, pipe dream

wenselijk /wɛnsələk/ (adj, adv) desirable; advisable: *ik vind het* ~ *dat …* I find it advisable to …

wensen /wɛnsə(n)/ (wenste, heeft gewenst) wish, desire: *dat laat aan duidelijkheid niets te* ~ *over* that is perfectly clear; *nog veel* **te** ~ *overlaten* leave a lot to be desired; *ik wens met rust gelaten te worden* I want to be left alone; *iem. goede morgen* (or: *een prettige vakantie*) ~ wish s.o. good morning (*or:* a nice holiday)

de **wenskaart** /wɛnskart/ (pl: -en) greetings card

wentelen /wɛntələ(n)/ (wentelde, heeft/is gewenteld) roll, turn (round), revolve

de **wenteltrap** /wɛntəltrap/ (pl: -pen) spiral staircase, winding stairs (*or:* staircase)

de **wereld** /werəlt/ (pl: -en) world, earth: *zij komen uit alle delen van de* ~ they come from the four corners (*or:* from every corner) of the world; *aan het andere eind van de* ~ on the other side of the world; *wat is de* ~ *toch klein!* isn't it a small world!; *de* ~ *staat op zijn kop* it's a mad (*or:* topsy-turvy) world; *een kind ter* ~ *brengen (helpen)* bring a child into the world; *de rijkste man ter* ~ the richest man in the world; *er ging een* ~ *voor hem open* a new world opened up for him; *de derde* ~ the Third World; *dat is de omgekeerde* ~ that's putting things on their heads

de **Wereldbank** /werəldbaŋk/ World Bank
het **wereldbeeld** /werəldbelt/ world-view
de **wereldbeker** /werəldbekər/ (pl: -s) World Cup

wereldberoemd /werəldbərumt/ (adj) world-famous

de **wereldbol** /werəldbɔl/ (pl: -len) (terrestrial) globe

de **wereldburger** /werəldbʏrɣər/ (pl: -s) cosmopolitan, world citizen

het **werelddeel** /werəldel/ (pl: -delen) continent

Werelddierendag /werəldirə(n)dax/ World Animal Day

het **werelderfgoed** world heritage
de **wereldhaven** /werəlthavə(n)/ (pl: -s) international (sea)port

de **wereldkaart** /werəltkart/ (pl: -en) map of the world

de **wereldkampioen** /werəltkampijun/ (pl:

-en) world champion

het **wereldkampioenschap** /werəltkampijunsxap/ (pl: -pen) world championship; [Am] world's championship

wereldkundig /werəltkʏndəx/ (adj) public: *iets* ~ **maken** make sth. public

de **wereldleider** /werəltlɛidər/ world leader
wereldlijk /werəltlək/ (adj) worldly, secular

de **wereldmacht** /werəltmaxt/ (pl: -en) world power

het **Wereldnatuurfonds** /werəltnatyrfɔn(t)s/ World Wildlife Fund

de **wereldomroep** /werəltɔmrup/ (pl: -en) world service

de **wereldoorlog** /werəltorlɔx/ (pl: -en) world war: *de Tweede Wereldoorlog* the second World War, World War II

de **wereldpremière** /werəltprəmjɛːrə/ (pl: -s) world première

het **wereldrecord** /werəltrəkɔːr/ (pl: -s) world record

de **wereldreis** /werəltrɛis/ (pl: -reizen) journey around the world, world tour

de **wereldreiziger** /werəltrɛizəɣər/ (pl: -s) globe-trotter

werelds /werəlts/ (adj) worldly, secular
wereldschokkend /werəltsxɔkənt/ (adj) earth-shaking

de **wereldstad** /werəltstat/ (pl: -steden) metropolis

de **wereldtentoonstelling** /werəltɛntonstɛlɪŋ/ (pl: -en) world fair

de **wereldtitel** /werəltitəl/ (pl: -s) world title
de **wereldvrede** /werəltfredə/ world peace
wereldvreemd /werəltfrɛmt/ (adj) unworldly; other-worldly

wereldwijd /werəltwɛit/ (adj) worldwide
de **wereldwinkel** /werəltwɪŋkəl/ (pl: -s) thirdworld (aid) shop

het **wereldwonder** /werəltwɔndər/ (pl: -en): *de zeven* ~*en* the Seven Wonders of the World

de **wereldzee** /werəltse/ (pl: -ën) ocean
weren /werə(n)/ (weerde, heeft geweerd) avert, prevent, keep out

de **werf** /wɛrf/ (pl: werven) **1** shipyard; dockyard: *een schip van de* ~ *laten lopen* launch a ship **2** yard **3** [Belg] (building) site

het **werk** /wɛrk/ (pl: -en) work, job, task: *het verzamelde* ~ *van W.F. Hermans* W.F. Hermans' (collected) works; *ze houden hier niet van half* ~ they don't do things by halves here; *dat is een heel* ~ it's quite a job; *het is onbegonnen* ~ it's a hopeless task; *aangenomen* ~ contract work; *(vast)* ~ *hebben* have a regular job; *aan het* ~ *gaan* set to work; *aan het* ~ *houden* keep going; *iedereen aan het* ~*!* everybody to their work!; *iem. aan het* ~ *zetten* put (*or:* set) s.o. to work; *er is* ~ *aan de winkel* there is work to be done; ~ *in uitvoering* roadworks; *ieder ging op zijn eigen manier te* ~

everyone set about it in their own way; *het
vuile* ~ *opknappen* do the dirty work || *ze wil-
den er geen* ~ *van maken* they didn't want to
take the matter in hand; *alles in het* ~ *stellen*
make every effort to; *een goed begin is het
halve* ~ well begun is half done; the first
blow is half the battle; *vele handen maken
licht* ~ many hands make light work
werkbaar /wɛrgbar/ (adj) workable, feasible

de **werkbalk** /wɛrgbalk/ tool bar

de **werkbank** /wɛrgbaŋk/ (pl: -en) bench;
(work)bench

de **werkbespreking** /wɛrgbəsprekɪŋ/ (pl: -en)
[roughly] discussion of progress

het **werkbezoek** /wɛrgbəzuk/ (pl: -en) working
visit

het **werkcollege** /wɛrkɔleʒə/ (pl: -s) seminar,
tutorial

de **werkdag** /wɛrgdɑx/ (pl: -en) working day,
workday, weekday

de **werkdruk** /wɛrgdrʏk/ pressure of work
werkelijk /wɛrkələk/ (adj) real; true

de **werkelijkheid** /wɛrkələkhɛit/ reality: *de
alledaagse* ~ everyday reality; ~ *worden*
come true; *in* ~ actually; *dat is in strijd met de* ~
that conflicts with the facts
werkeloos /wɛrkəlos/ (adj) idle: ~ *toezien*
stand by and do nothing, stand by and
watch; *see werkloos*
werken /wɛrkə(n)/ (werkte, heeft gewerkt)
1 work; operate: *de tijd werkt in ons voordeel*
time is on our side; *iem. hard laten* ~ work s.o.
hard; *hard* ~ work hard; *aan iets* ~ work at
(*or:* on) sth.; ~ *op het land* work the soil (*or:*
land) **2** work, function: *dit apparaat werkt heel
eenvoudig* this apparatus is simple to operate; *zo werkt dat niet* that's not the way it
works **3** work, take effect: *de pillen begon-
nen te* ~ the pills began to take effect || *zich
kapot* ~ work one's fingers to the bone; *een
ongewenst persoon eruit* ~ get rid of an unwanted person; *zich omhoog* ~ work one's
way up (*or:* to the top); *zich in de nesten* ~ get
into trouble (*or:* a scrape), tie o.s. up
werkend /wɛrkənt/ (adj) working; employed: *snel ~e medicijnen* fast-acting medicines

de **werker** /wɛrkər/ (pl: -s) worker

de **werkervaring** /wɛrkɛrvarɪŋ/ work experience

het **werkgeheugen** /wɛrkxəhøyə(n)/ (pl: -s)
main memory

de **werkgelegenheid** /wɛrkxəleyənhɛit/ employment

de **werkgever** /wɛrkxevər/ (pl: -s) employer

de **werkgeversorganisatie** /wɛrkxevərs-
ɔryaniza(t)si/ (pl: -s) employers' organization
(*or:* federation)

de **werkgroep** /wɛrkxrup/ (pl: -en) study
group, working party

de **werking** /wɛrkɪŋ/ (pl: -en) **1** working, action, functioning: *buiten* ~ out of order; *in* ~
stellen put into action; activate; *de wet treedt
1 januari in* ~ the law will come into force (*or:*
effect) on January 1st **2** effect(s)

het **werkje** /wɛrkjə/ (pl: -s) pattern

de **werkkamer** /wɛrkamər/ (pl: -s) study

het **werkkamp** /wɛrkamp/ (pl: -en) **1** project
week **2** (hard) labour camp

de **werkkleding** /wɛrkledɪŋ/ workclothes,
working clothes

het **werkklimaat** /wɛrklimat/ (pl: -klimaten)
work climate, work atmosphere

de **werkkracht** /wɛrkraxt/ (pl: -en) worker,
employee

de **werkkring** /wɛrkrɪŋ/ (pl: -en) post, job;
working environment
werkloos /wɛrklos/ (adj) unemployed, out
of work (*or:* a job)

de **werkloosheid** /wɛrklosheit/ unemployment

het **werkloosheidscijfer** /wɛrklosheɪtsɛɪfər/
(pl: -s) unemployment figure

de **werkloosheidsuitkering** /wɛrklosheɪts-
œytkerɪŋ/ (pl: -en) unemployment benefit;
[Am] unemployment compensation

de **werkloze** /wɛrklozə/ (pl: -n) unemployed
person

de **werklust** /wɛrklʏst/ zest for work, willingness to work

de **werkmaatschappij** /wɛrkmatsxapɛi/ (pl:
-en) subsidiary (company)

de **werknemer** /wɛrknemər/ (pl: -s) employee

de **werknemersorganisatie** /wɛrknemərs-
ɔryaniza(t)si/ (pl: -s) (trade) union

de **werkonderbreking** /wɛrkondərbrekɪŋ/
(pl: -en) (work) stoppage, walkout

het **werkpaard** /wɛrkpart/ (pl: -en) workhorse

de **werkplaats** /wɛrkplats/ (pl: -en) workshop,
workplace: *sociale* ~ sheltered workshop

de **werkplek** /wɛrkplɛk/ (pl: -ken) workplace;
workstation

het **werkstation** /wɛrksta(t)ʃɔn/ (pl: -s) workstation

de **werkster** /wɛrkstər/ (pl: -s) **1** (woman, female) worker **2** cleaning lady

de **werkstraf** /wɛrkstraf/ (pl: -fen) community
service

de **werkstudent** /wɛrkstydɛnt/ (pl: -en) student working his way through college with a
(part-time) job

het **werkstuk** /wɛrkstʏk/ (pl: -ken) **1** piece of
work **2** [educ] paper, project

de **werktafel** /wɛrktafəl/ (pl: -s) work table,
desk

het **werkterrein** /wɛrktɛrɛin/ (pl: -en) working
space, work area

de **werktijd** /wɛrktɛit/ (pl: -en) working hours;
office hours: *na* ~ after hours

het **werktuig** /wɛrktœyx/ (pl: -en) tool; piece of
equipment, machine

de **werktuigbouwkunde** /wɛrktœyɣ-
bɑukʏndə/ mechanical engineering
werktuiglijk /wɛrktœyχlək/ (adj, adv) mechanical, automatic

het **werkuur** /wɛrkyr/ (pl: -uren) working hour,
hour of work

de **werkvergunning** /wɛrkfərɣʏnɪŋ/ (pl: -en)
work permit

de **werkverschaffing** /wɛrkfərsχɑfɪŋ/ (unemployment) relief work(s); [fig] work for the
sake of it

de **werkvloer** /wɛrkflur/ shop floor

de **werkweek** /wɛrkwek/ (pl: -weken)
1 (working) week **2** study week, project
week: **op** ~ *zijn* have a study week (*or:* project
week)

de **werkwijze** /wɛrkwɛizə/ (pl: -n) method (of
working); procedure; (manufacturing) process; routine: *dit is de* **normale** ~ this is (the)
standard (operating) procedure

de **werkwillige** /wɛrkwɪləɣə/ (pl: -n) non-
striker

het **werkwoord** /wɛrkwort/ (pl: -en) verb: **onregelmatig** ~ irregular verb; **sterke** (or:
zwakke) ~*en* strong (*or:* weak) verbs
werkzaam /wɛrksam/ (adj, adv) **1** working,
active; employed; engaged **2** active, industrious: *hij blijft* **als** *adviseur* ~ he will continue
to act as (an) adviser

de **werkzaamheden** /wɛrksamhedə(n)/ (pl)
activities; duties; operations; proceedings,
business: ~ **aan** *de metro* work on the underground

de **werkzoekende** /wɛrksukəndə/ (pl: -n) job-
seeker, person in search of employment
werpen /wɛrpə(n)/ (wierp, heeft geworpen) have puppies (*or:* kittens): *onze hond
heeft (drie jongen) geworpen* our dog has had
(three) pups

de **werper** /wɛrpər/ (pl: -s) pitcher

de **werphengel** /wɛrphɛŋəl/ (pl: -s) casting rod

de **wervel** /wɛrvəl/ (pl: -s) vertebra
wervelend /wɛrvələnt/ (adj) sparkling: *een
~e* **show** a spectacular show

de **wervelkolom** /wɛrvəlkolɔm/ (pl: -men)
vertebral column, spinal column, spine,
backbone

de **wervelstorm** /wɛrvəlstɔrm/ (pl: -en) cyclone, tornado, hurricane

de **wervelwind** /wɛrvəlwɪnt/ (pl: -en) whirlwind, tornado: *als een* ~ like a whirlwind
werven /wɛrvə(n)/ (wierf, heeft geworven)
1 recruit **2** [Belg] appoint
wervend (adj) attractive, compelling: *een
~e tekst* an attractive text

de **werving** /wɛrvɪŋ/ (pl: -en) recruitment; enlistment; enrolment: ~ *en* **selectie** recruitment and selection

de **wesp** /wɛsp/ (pl: -en) wasp

het **wespennest** /wɛspənɛst/ (pl: -en) wasps'
nest

de **wespentaille** /wɛspə(n)tɑjə/ (pl: -s) wasp
waist
west /wɛst/ (adj, adv) **1** west(erly), westward; to the west **2** west(erly); from the west

de **West-Duitser** /wɛsdœytsər/ (pl: -s) West
German
West-Duitsland /wɛsdœytslɑnt/ West Germany
westelijk /wɛstələk/ (adj, adv) west, westerly, western, westward: ~ **van** (to the) west
of; *de ~e* **Jordaanoever** the West Bank

het **westen** /wɛstə(n)/ west: *het ~ van* **Nederland** the west(ern part) of the Netherlands;
het **wilde** ~ the (Wild) West, the Frontier ‖
buiten ~ *raken* pass out; *iem.* **buiten** ~ *slaan*
knock s.o. out (cold); **buiten** ~ *zijn* be out
(cold)

de **westenwind** /wɛstə(n)wɪnt/ (pl: -en) west-
(erly) wind

de **westerlengte** /wɛstərlɛŋtə/ longitude
west: **op** *15°* ~ at 15° longitude west

de **westerling** /wɛstərlɪŋ/ (pl: -en) Westerner;
westerner

de **western** /wɛstərn/ (pl: -s) western
¹**westers** /wɛstərs/ (adj) western
²**westers** /wɛstərs/ (adv) in a western fashion
(*or:* manner)
West-Europa /wɛstøropa/ Western Europe
West-Europees /wɛstøropes/ (adj) West-
(ern) European
West-Indië /wɛstɪndijə/ (the) West Indies

de **westkust** /wɛstkʏst/ (pl: -en) west coast

de **wet** /wɛt/ (pl: -ten) **1** law, statute: *een* **ongeschreven** ~ an unwritten rule; *de* ~ **naleven**
(or: **overtreden**) abide by (*or:* break) the law;
de ~ **schrijft voor** *dat …* the law prescribes
that …; *de* ~ **toepassen** enforce the law; **volgens** *de* ~ *is het een misdaad* it's a crime before the law; *volgens de* **Engelse** ~ under
English law; **bij** *de* ~ *bepaald* regulated by
law; *in strijd* **met** *de* ~ unlawful; against the
law; **voor** *de* ~ *trouwen* marry at a registry office; *de* ~ *van* **Archimedes** Archimedes' principle **2** law, rule: *iem. de* ~ **voorschrijven** lay
down the law to s.o.

het **wetboek** /wɛdbuk/ (pl: -en) code, lawbook

het ¹**weten** /wetə(n)/ knowledge: **buiten** *mijn* ~
without my knowledge; **naar** *mijn beste* ~ to
the best of my knowledge
²**weten** /wetə(n)/ (wist, heeft geweten)
know, manage: *dat weet zelfs een* **kind!** even
a fool knows that!; *ik had het* **kunnen** ~ I
might have known; *ik zal het u* **laten** ~ I'll let
you know; ~ *te ontkomen* manage to escape;
ik zou weleens **willen** ~ *waarom hij dat zei* I'd
like to know why he said that; *daar weet ik*
alles *van* I know all about it; *ik weet* **het!** I've
got it!; *voor je* **het** *weet, ben je er* you're there
before you know it; *ze hebben* **het** *geweten*
they found out (to their cost); *hij wou er* **niets**
van ~ he wouldn't hear of it; *nu weet ik* **nóg**

niets! I'm no wiser than I was (before)!; *je weet **wie** het zegt* look who is talking; *je moet het **zelf** (maar)* ~ it's your decision; *je zou **beter** moeten* ~ you should know better (than that); *hij wist **niet** hoe gauw hij weg moest komen* he couldn't get away fast enough; *als dat geen zwendel is dan weet ik het **niet** (meer)* if that isn't a fraud I don't know what is; *ik zou **niet** ~ waarom (niet)* I don't see why (not); *weet je **wel**, je weet **wel** you know; *iets **zeker** ~ be* sure about sth.; *voor **zover** ik weet* as far as I know; *iets **te** ~ komen* find out sth.; *als je dat maar weet!* keep it in mind!; *niet **dat** ik weet* not that I know; *weet ik **veel**?* (do you) remember?; *weet ik veel!* search me! ‖ *ik wist **niet** wat ik zag!* I couldn't believe my eyes!; *je weet ('t) maar **nooit*** you never know

de **wetenschap** /wetə(n)sχαp/ (pl: -pen) **1** knowledge **2** learning; science; scholarship; learning

wetenschappelijk /wetə(n)sχαpələk/ (adj, adv) scholarly; scientific: *voorbereidend ~ **onderwijs*** pre-university education; *~ **personeel*** academic staff; [Am] faculty

de **wetenschapper** /wetənsχαpər/ (pl: -s) scholar; scientist; academic

wetenswaardig /wetə(n)swαrdəχ/ (adj) interesting; informative

de **wetenswaardigheid** /wetə(n)swαrdəχhεɪt/ (pl: -heden) piece of information

wetgevend /wεtχevənt/ (adj) legislative

de **wetgever** /wεtχevər/ (pl: -s) legislator

de **wetgeving** /wεtχevɪŋ/ (pl: -en) legislation

de **wethouder** /wεthαudər/ (pl: -s) alderman, (city, town) councillor: *de ~ van **volkshuisvesting*** the alderman for housing

wetmatig /wεtmαtəχ/ (adj, adv) systematic

het **wetsartikel** /wεtsαrtikəl/ (pl: -en, -s) section of a (*or:* the) law

de **wetsbepaling** /wεtsbəpαlɪŋ/ (pl: -en) statutory provision, legal provision

de **wetsdokter** /wεtsdɔktər/ (pl: -s, wetsdoktoren) [Belg] police physician

het **wetsontwerp** /wεtsɔntwεrp/ (pl: -en) bill: *een ~ **aannemen*** pass (*or:* adopt) a bill

de **wetsovertreding** /wεtsovərtredɪŋ/ (pl: -en) violation of a (*or:* the) law

het **wetsvoorstel** /wεtsforstεl/ (pl: -len) bill

de **wetswijziging** /wεtswεɪzəɣɪŋ/ (pl: -en) amendment: *een ~ **invoeren*** amend the law, make a statutory change

de **wetswinkel** /wεtswɪŋkəl/ (pl: -s) law centre

wettelijk /wεtələk/ (adj, adv) legal, statutory: *~e **aansprakelijkheid*** legal liability; *wettelijke-aansprakelijkheidsverzekering* third-party insurance

wetteloos /wεtəlos/ (adj, adv) lawless

wetten /wεtə(n)/ (wette, heeft gewet) whet

wettig /wεtəχ/ (adj, adv) legal; legitimate; valid: *de ~e **eigenaar*** the rightful owner

wettigen /wεtəɣə(n)/ (wettigde, heeft gewettigd) legalize

weven /wevə(n)/ (weefde, heeft geweven) weave

de **wever** /wevər/ (pl: -s) weaver

de **wezel** /wezəl/ (pl: -s) weasel: *zo bang **als** een* ~ as timid as a hare

het **¹wezen** /wezə(n)/ (pl: -s) **1** being, creature: *geen **levend** ~ te bespeuren* not a living soul in sight **2** being, nature; essence; substance: *haar **hele** ~ kwam ertegen in opstand* her whole soul rose against it

²wezen /wezə(n)/ be: *dat zal wel **waar** ~!* I bet!; *kan ~, maar ik mag hem niet* be that as it may, I don't like him; *wij zijn daar ~ **kijken*** we've been there to have a look; *laten we wel ~* (let's) be fair (*or:* honest) (now); *een studie die er ~ **mag*** a substantial study; *weg ~!* off with you!

wezenlijk /wezənlək/ (adj, adv) essential: *van ~ **belang*** essential, of vital importance; *een ~ **verschil*** a substantial difference

wezenloos /wezə(n)los/ (adj, adv) vacant: *zich ~ **schrijven*** write o.s. silly; *zich ~ **schrikken*** be scared out of one's wits

de **whiplash** /wɪplεʃ/ (pl: -es) whiplash (injury)

de **whirlpool** /wʏːlpuːl/ (pl: -s) whirlpool, jacuzzi

de **whisky** /wɪski/ whisky: ***Amerikaanse** whiskey* bourbon; *Ierse whiskey* Irish whiskey; ***Schotse** ~* Scotch (whisky); *~ **puur*** a straight (*or:* neat) whisky

de **whisky-soda** /wɪskisodα/ (pl: -'s) whisky and soda

de **whizzkid** /wɪskɪt/ (pl: -s) whizzkid

de **wichelroede** /wɪχəlrudə/ (pl: -n) divining rod, dowsing rod

het **wicht** /wɪχt/ (pl: -en) child

wie /wi/ (pron) **1** who; whose; which: *van ~ is dit boek?* whose book is this?; *~ **heb** je gezien?* who have you seen?; *met ~ (spreek ik)?* who is this? (*or:* that?); *~ **van** jullie?* which of you?; *~ er ook komt, zeg maar dat ik niet thuis ben* whoever comes, tell them I'm out **2** who; whose: *de **man** ~ns dood door ieder betreurd wordt* the man whose death is generally mourned; *het **meisje** (aan) ~ ik het boek gaf* the girl to whom I gave the book **3** whoever: *~ **anders** dan Jan?* who (else) but John?; *~ **dan ook** anybody, anyone, whoever* ‖ *~ niet akkoord gaat …* anyone who disagrees …

wiebelen /wibələ(n)/ (wiebelde, heeft gewiebeld) **1** wobble **2** rock: *ze **zat te** ~ op haar stoel* she was wiggling about on her chair

wieden /widə(n)/ (wiedde, heeft gewied) weed

wiedes /widəs/ (adj) [inform]: *dat is **nogal** ~* don't I know it, I should think so

de **wiedeweerga** /widəwεrɣα/: *als de ~* like greased lightning; on the double

de **wieg** /wiχ/ (pl: -en) cradle: *van de ~ tot het*

graf verzorgd looked after from the cradle to the grave || *in* de ~ *gelegd zijn voor …* be cut out (*or:* shaped) for, be fitted (*or:* born) by nature to

de **wiegen** /wiɣə(n)/ (wiegde, heeft gewiegd) rock

de **wiegendood** /wiɣə(n)dot/ cot death; [Am] crib death; SIDS *(sudden infant death syndrome)*

de **wiek** /wik/ (pl: -en) **1** sail, vane **2** wing

het **wiel** /wil/ (pl: -en) wheel: *het ~ weer uitvinden* re-invent the wheel; *iem. in* de *~en rijden* put a spoke in s.o.'s wheel || [fig] *het vijfde ~ aan de wagen zijn* be the odd man out

de **wielbasis** /wilbazɪs/ wheelbase

de **wieldop** /wildɔp/ (pl: -pen) hubcap

de **wielerbaan** /wilərban/ (pl: -banen) bicycle track, cycling track

de **wielerploeg** /wilərpluχ/ (pl: -en) (bi)cycling team

de **wielersport** /wilərspɔrt/ (bi)cycling

de **wielklem** /wilklɛm/ (pl: -men) wheel clamp

de **wielrennen** /wilrɛnə(n)/ (bi)cycle racing

de **wielrenner** /wilrɛnər/ (pl: -s) (racing) cyclist, bicyclist, cycler

het **wieltje** /wilcə/ (pl: -s) (little) wheel; castor: *dat loopt op ~s* that's running smoothly

de **wienerschnitzel** /winərʃnɪtsəl/ (pl: -s) Wiener schnitzel

wiens /wins/ (pron) whose

het **wier** /wir/ **1** alga **2** seaweed

de **wierook** /wirok/ incense: *~ branden* burn incense

de **wiet** /wit/ weed, grass

de **wig** /wɪχ/ (pl: -gen) wedge

de **wigwam** /wɪχwɑm/ (pl: -s) wigwam

wij /wɛi/ (pers pron) we: *(beter) dan ~* (better) than we are; *~ allemaal* all of us, we all

wijd /wɛit/ (adj, adv) **1** wide: *een ~e blik* a broad view; *met ~ open ogen* wide-eyed **2** wide, loose: *~er maken* let out, enlarge **3** wide, broad: *de ~e zee* the open sea

wijdbeens /wɛidbens/ (adv) with legs wide apart

wijden /wɛidə(n)/ (wijdde, heeft gewijd) **1** devote: *zijn aandacht aan iets ~* devote o.s. to sth. **2** [rel] consecrate; ordain: *gewijde muziek* sacred music

de **wijding** /wɛidɪŋ/ (pl: -en) consecration

wijdlopig /wɛitlopəχ/ (adj, adv) verbose; windy, long-winded: *een ~ verhaal* a long-winded story

de **wijdte** /wɛitə/ (pl: -n, -s) breadth, distance: *de ~ tussen de banken* the space between the benches

wijdverbreid /wɛitfərbrɛit/ (adj) widespread

wijdverspreid /wɛitfərsprɛit/ (adj) widespread; rife; rampant

wijdvertakt /wɛitfərtɑkt/ (adj) many-branched, ramified

het **wijf** /wɛif/ [inform] bitch: *een oud ~* an old bag; *stom ~!* stupid bitch (*or:* cow)!; *een lekker ~* a bit of all right, a looker, a cracker

het **wijfje** /wɛifjə/ female

het **wij-gevoel** /wɛiɣəvul/ (feeling of) solidarity, team spirit

de **wijk** /wɛik/ (pl: -en) district, area: *de deftige ~en* the fashionable areas

de **wijkagent** /wɛikaɣɛnt/ (pl: -en) policeman on the beat, local bobby

het **wijkcentrum** /wɛiksɛntrʏm/ (pl: wijkcentra) community centre

wijken /wɛikə(n)/ (week, is geweken) give in (to), give way (to), yield (to): *hij weet van geen ~* he sticks to his guns; *het gevaar is geweken* the danger is over

het **wijkgebouw** /wɛikχəbɑu/ (pl: -en) **1** community centre **2** local branch

de **wijkverpleegkundige** /wɛikfərpleχkʏndəɣə/ (pl: -n) district nurse

wijlen /wɛilə(n)/ (adj) late, deceased: *~ de heer Smit* the late Mr Smit

de **wijn** /wɛin/ (pl: -en) wine: *oude ~ in nieuwe zakken* old wine in new bottles

de **wijnazijn** /wɛinazɛin/ wine vinegar

de **wijnboer** /wɛinbur/ (pl: -en) winegrower

de **wijnbouw** /wɛinbɑu/ winegrowing, viniculture

de **wijnfles** /wɛinflɛs/ (pl: -sen) wine bottle

de **wijngaard** /wɛinɣart/ (pl: -en) vineyard

het **wijnglas** /wɛinɣlɑs/ (pl: -glazen) wineglass; rummer

de **wijnhandelaar** /wɛinhɑndəlar/ (pl: -s, wijnhandelaren) wine merchant

het **wijnjaar** /wɛinjar/ (pl: -jaren) wine-year

de **wijnkaart** /wɛinkart/ (pl: -en) wine list

de **wijnkelder** /wɛinkɛldər/ (pl: -s) (wine) cellar

de **wijnkenner** /wɛinkɛnər/ (pl: -s) connoisseur of wine

de **wijnkoeler** /wɛinkulər/ (pl: -s) wine cooler

de **wijnoogst** /wɛinoχst/ (pl: -en) vintage, grape harvest

de **wijnrank** /wɛinrɑŋk/ (pl: -en) (branch of a) vine

de **wijnstok** /wɛinstɔk/ (pl: -ken) (grape)vine

de **wijnstreek** /wɛinstrek/ (pl: -streken) wine(-growing) region

de **wijnvlek** /wɛinvlɛk/ (pl: -ken) birthmark

de ¹**wijs** /wɛis/ (pl: wijzen) **1** way, manner: *bij wijze van spreken* so to speak, as it were; *bij wijze van uitzondering* as an exception **2** tune: *hij kan geen ~ houden* he sings (*or:* plays) out of tune; *van de ~ raken* get in a muddle; *iem. van de ~ brengen* put s.o. out (*or:* off) his stroke; *hij liet zich niet van de ~ brengen* he kept a level head (*or:* his cool) || *onbepaalde ~* infinitive

²**wijs** /wɛis/ (adj, adv) wise: *ben je niet (goed) ~?* are you mad? (*or:* crazy?); *ik werd er niet wijzer van* I was none the wiser for it; *ik kan er*

niet ~ uit **worden** I can't make head or tail of it

de **wijsbegeerte** /wɛizbəɣertə/ (pl: -n) philosophy

wijselijk /wɛɪsələk/ (adv) wisely, sensibly: *hij hield ~ zijn mond* wisely, he kept silent

de **wijsgeer** /wɛisxer/ (pl: -geren) philosopher

wijsgerig /wɛɪsxerəx/ (adj, adv) philosophic(al)

de **wijsheid** /wɛishɛit/ (pl: -heden) wisdom; piece of wisdom: *hij meent de ~ in pacht te hebben* he thinks he knows it all; *waar heb je die ~ vandaan?* my, aren't you (or: we) clever?

de **wijsheidstand** /wɛishɛitstɑnt/ (pl: -en) [Belg] wisdom tooth

het **wijsje** /wɛiʃə/ (pl: -s) tune

wijsmaken /wɛismakə(n)/ (maakte wijs, heeft wijsgemaakt) fool, kid: *laat je niks ~!* don't buy that nonsense!; *maak dat je grootje* (or: *de kat*) *wijs* tell that to the marines!, tell me another one!

de **wijsneus** /wɛisnøs/ (pl: -neuzen) know(-it)-all

de **wijsvinger** /wɛisfɪŋər/ (pl: -s) forefinger

wijten /wɛitə(n)/ (weet, heeft geweten) blame (s.o. for sth.)

de **wijting** /wɛrtɪŋ/ (pl: -en) whiting

het **wijwater** /wɛiwatər/ holy water

de **wijze** /wɛizə/ (pl: -n) **1** manner, way **2** wise man (or: woman); learned man (or: woman)

¹**wijzen** /wɛizə(n)/ (wees, heeft gewezen) **1** point: *naar een punt ~* point to a spot; [fig] *met de vinger naar iem. ~* point the finger at s.o.; *er moet op worden gewezen dat ...* it should be pointed out that ... **2** indicate: *alles wijst erop dat ...* everything seems to indicate that ...

²**wijzen** /wɛizə(n)/ (wees, heeft gewezen) show, point out: *de weg ~* lead (or: show) the way

zich ³**wijzen** /wɛizə(n)/ (wees zich, heeft zich gewezen) show: *dat wijst zich vanzelf* that is self-evident

de **wijzer** /wɛizər/ (pl: -s) indicator; hand; pointer: *met de ~s van de klok mee* clockwise; *de grote* (or: *de kleine*) *~* the minute (or: hour) hand

de **wijzerplaat** /wɛizərplat/ (pl: -platen) dial

wijzigen /wɛizəɣə(n)/ (wijzigde, heeft gewijzigd) alter, change

de **wijziging** /wɛizəɣɪŋ/ (pl: -en) alteration, change: *~en aanbrengen in* make changes in

de **wikkel** /wɪkəl/ (pl: -s) wrapper

wikkelen /wɪkələ(n)/ (wikkelde, heeft gewikkeld) wind; wrap (up); enfold

wikken /wɪkə(n)/ weigh (up): *na lang ~ en wegen* after much deliberation, after mature consideration

de **wil** /wɪl/ will; wish: *geen eigen ~ hebben* have no mind of one's own; *met een beetje goeie ~ gaat het best* with a little good will it'll all

work out; *een sterke ~ hebben* be strong-willed; *zijn ~ is wet* his word is law; *tegen ~ en dank* willy-nilly, reluctantly; *ter ~le van* for the sake of

het ¹**wild** /wɪlt/ **1** game: ~, *vis en gevogelte* fish, flesh and fowl **2** wild: *in het ~ leven* (or: *groeien*) live (or: grow) (in the) wild

²**wild** /wɪlt/ (adj, adv) wild: *~e dieren* wild animals; ~ *enthousiast* zijn over iets go overboard about sth.; *in het ~e* (weg) at random

de **wilde** /wɪldə/ (pl: -n) savage

de **wildebras** /wɪldəbrɑs/ (pl: -sen) (young) tearaway

de **wildernis** /wɪldərnɪs/ (pl: -sen) wilderness

de **wildgroei** /wɪltxruj/ proliferation

wildkamperen /wɪltkɑmperə(n)/ (kampeerde wild, heeft wildgekampeerd) camp wild

het **wildpark** /wɪltpɑrk/ (pl: -en) wildlife park; game park (or: reserve)

wildplassen /wɪltplɑsə(n)/ (plaste wild, heeft wildgeplast) urinate in public

de **wildstand** /wɪltstɑnt/ wildlife population

het **wildviaduct** /wɪltfijadʏkt/ (pl: -en) wildlife viaduct

wildvreemd /wɪltfremt/ (adj) completely strange, utterly strange: *een ~ iem.* a perfect stranger

wildwatervaren /wɪltwatərvarə(n)/ white-water rafting

de **wildwestfilm** /wɪltwɛstfɪlm/ (pl: -s) western

het **wildwesttafereel** /wɪltwɛstafərel/ (pl: -taferelen): *het was een ~* it was bedlam, it was like sth. out of a Western

de **wilg** /wɪlx/ (pl: -en) willow (tree)

wilgen /wɪlɣə(n)/ (adj) willow

het **wilgenhout** /wɪlɣə(n)haut/ willow (wood)

de **willekeur** /wɪləkør/ **1** will; discretion: *naar ~* at will, at one's (own) discretion **2** arbitrariness, unfairness; capriciousness

willekeurig /wɪləkørəx/ (adj, adv) **1** arbitrary; random; indiscriminate: *neem een ~e steen* take any stone (you like) **2** arbitrary, high-handed; capricious

¹**willen** /wɪlə(n)/ (wilde/wou, heeft gewild) want, wish, desire: *het is (maar) een kwestie van ~* it's (only) a matter of will; *ik wil wel een pilsje* I wouldn't mind a beer; *wil je wat pinda's?* would you like some peanuts?; *ik wil het niet hebben* I won't have (or: allow) it; *niet ~ luisteren* refuse to listen; *ik wil niets meer met hem te maken hebben* I've done with him; *ik wil wel toegeven dat ...* I'm willing to admit that ...; *ik wou net vertrekken toen ...* I was just about (or: going) to leave when ...; *dat had ik best eens ~ zien!* I would have liked to have seen it!; *ja, wat wil je?* what else can you expect?; *wat wil je nog meer?* what more do you want?; *wilt u dat ik het raam openzet?* shall I open the window

(for you)?; *ik wou **dat** ik een fiets had* I wish I had a bike; *of je wilt of niet* whether you want to or not; *we moesten wel glimlachen, of we wilden of niet* we could not help but smile (*or:* help smiling); *dat **ding** wil niet* the thing won't (*or:* refuses to) go; *de motor wil niet **starten*** the engine won't start ‖ *men wil **er** niet **aan*** people are not buying (it), nobody is interested

²**willen** /wɪlə(n)/ (aux vb, wilde/wou, heeft gewild) will, would: *wil je me de melk even **(aan)geven?*** could (*or:* would) you pass me the milk, please?; *wil je me even **helpen?*** would you mind helping me?

willens /wɪlə(n)s/ (adv): ~ *en **wetens*** knowingly

willoos /wɪlos/ (adj, adv) unresisting: ~ *liet de jongen zich **meevoeren*** the boy went along without a struggle

de **wilsbeschikking** /wɪlzbəsxɪkɪŋ/ (pl: -en) will, testament

de **wilskracht** /wɪlskrɑχt/ will-power, will, backbone

de **wilsverklaring** /wɪlsfərklarɪŋ/ (pl: -en) living will

de **wimpel** /wɪmpəl/ (pl: -s) pennon, pennant

de **wimper** /wɪmpər/ (pl: -s) (eye)lash

de **wind** /wɪnt/ (pl: -en) wind; breeze; gale: *bestand zijn tegen **weer** en* ~ be wind and weatherproof; *geen **zuchtje*** ~ not a breath of wind, dead calm; *een **harde** (*or:* **krachtige**)* ~ a high (*or:* strong) wind; *de* ~ **gaat liggen** the wind is dropping; *de* ~ *van voren **krijgen*** get lectured at; *kijken uit welke hoek de* ~ **waait** see which way the wind blows; *de* ~ **mee** *hebben* **a)** have the wind behind one; **b)** [fig] have everything going for one; [fig] *een waarschuwing **in** de* ~ *slaan* disregard a warning; ***tegen** de* ~ *in* against the wind, into the teeth of the wind; *het gaat hem **voor** de* ~ he is doing well, he is flying high ‖ *~en **laten*** break wind

de **windbuil** /wɪndbœyl/ (pl: -en) windbag, gasbag

de **windbuks** /wɪndbʏks/ (pl: -en) air rifle, airgun

het **windei** /wɪntɛi/ (pl: -eren): *dat zal hem geen ~eren **leggen*** he'll do well out of it

winden /wɪndə(n)/ (wond, heeft gewonden) wind, twist, entwine; wrap

de **windenergie** /wɪntenɛrʒi/ wind energy

winderig /wɪndərəχ/ (adj) **1** windy, blowy; breezy; stormy; windswept **2** windy, flatulent

de **windhaan** /wɪnthan/ (pl: -hanen) weathercock

de **windhond** /wɪnthɔnt/ (pl: -en) greyhound; whippet

de **windhoos** /wɪnthos/ (pl: -hozen) whirlwind

het **windjack** /wɪntjɛk/ (pl: -s) windcheater; [Am] windbreaker

het **windjak** /wɪntjak/ (pl: -ken, -s) windcheater

de **windkracht** /wɪntkrɑχt/ wind-force: *wind met* ~ **7** force 7 wind(s)

de **windmolen** /wɪntmolə(n)/ (pl: -s) windmill: *tegen ~s vechten* tilt at windmills, fight windmills

het **windmolenpark** /wɪntmolə(n)park/ (pl: -en) wind park (*or:* farm)

de **windowdressing** /wɪndodrɛsɪŋ/ window dressing

de **windrichting** /wɪntrɪχtɪŋ/ (pl: -en) wind direction; points of the compass

de **windroos** /wɪntros/ (pl: -rozen) compass card

het **windscherm** /wɪntsχɛrm/ (pl: -en) windbreak

de **windsnelheid** /wɪntsnɛlhɛit/ (pl: -heden) wind speed

de **windsterkte** /wɪntstɛrktə/ wind-force

windstil /wɪntstɪl/ (adj) calm, windless, still

de **windstoot** /wɪntstot/ (pl: -stoten) gust (of wind); squall

de **windstreek** /wɪntstrek/ (pl: -streken) quarter, point of the compass

windsurfen /wɪntsʏːrfə(n)/ (windsurfte/windsurfde, heeft/is gewindsurft/gewindsurfd) go windsurfing

de **windsurfer** /wɪntsʏːrfər/ (pl: -s) windsurfer

de **windtunnel** /wɪntʏnəl/ (pl: -s) wind tunnel

de **windvaan** /wɪntfan/ (pl: -vanen) (wind)vane

de **windvlaag** /wɪntflaχ/ (pl: -vlagen) gust (of wind); blast; squall

de **windwijzer** /wɪntwɛizər/ (pl: -s) weathercock, weathervane

de **windzak** /wɪntsak/ windsock, air sock

de **wingerd** /wɪŋərt/ (pl: -s, -en) (grape)vine

het **wingewest** /wɪŋəwɛst/ (pl: -en) conquered land, colony

de **winkel** /wɪŋkəl/ (pl: -s) shop, store: *een* ~ *in **modeartikelen*** a boutique, a fashion store; *~s **kijken*** go window-shopping

de **winkelbediende** /wɪŋkəlbədɪndə/ shopassistant, counter-assistant, salesman, saleswoman

het **winkelcentrum** /wɪŋkəlsɛntrʏm/ (pl: -centra) shopping centre (*or:* precinct)

de **winkeldief** /wɪŋkəldif/ (pl: -dieven) shoplifter

de **winkeldiefstal** /wɪŋkəldifstal/ (pl: -len) shoplifting

winkelen /wɪŋkələ(n)/ (winkelde, heeft gewinkeld) shop, go shopping, do some (*or:* the) shopping

de **winkelgalerij** /wɪŋkəlχalərɛi/ (pl: -en) (shopping-)arcade

de **winkelhaak** /wɪŋkəlhak/ (pl: -haken) **1** three-cornered tear, right-angled tear **2** (carpenter's) square

de **winkelier** /wɪŋkəliːr/ (pl: -s) shopkeeper, retailer, tradesman de **winkeljuffrouw** /wɪŋkəljʏfrɑu/ (pl: -en) saleswoman, salesgirl

de **winkelketen** /wɪŋkəlketə(n)/ (pl: -s) chain of shops (or: stores), store chain

het **winkelpersoneel** /wɪŋkəlpɛrsonel/ shopworkers, shop staff (or: personnel)

de **winkelprijs** /wɪŋkəlprɛis/ (pl: -prijzen) retail price, shop price; [Am] store price

de **winkelstraat** /wɪŋkəlstrat/ (pl: -straten) shopping street

de **winkelwagen** /wɪŋkəlwaɣə(n)/ (pl: -s) (shopping) trolley; [Am] pushcart: [online shopping] *in* ~ add to cart

de **winnaar** /wɪnar/ (pl: -s) winner, victor; winning team

¹winnen /wɪnə(n)/ (won, heeft gewonnen) win: *het ~de doelpunt* the winning goal; *je kan niet altijd* ~ you can't win them all; *~ bij het kaarten* win at cards; *~ met 7-2* win 7-2, win by 7 goals (or: points) to 2; *(het)* ~ *van iem.* beat s.o., have the better of s.o.

²winnen /wɪnə(n)/ (won, heeft gewonnen) **1** win, gain; mine; extract: *zout uit zeewater ~* obtain salt from sea water **2** win, gain; enlist; secure: *iem. voor zich ~* win s.o. over

de **winning** /wɪnɪŋ/ winning, extraction; reclamation

de **winst** /wɪnst/ (pl: -en) **1** profit; return; earning(s); winning: *netto ~* net returns (or: gain, profit); *~ behalen* (or: *opleveren*) gain (or: make, yield) a profit; *tel uit je* ~ it can't go wrong; *op ~ spelen* play to win **2** gain, benefit, advantage: *een ~ van drie zetels in de Kamer behalen* gain three seats in Parliament

het **winstbejag** /wɪnstbəjɑx/ pursuit of profit: *iets uit ~ doen* do sth. for money (or: profit)

de **winstdeling** /wɪnzdelɪŋ/ (pl: -en) profit-sharing, participation

de **winst-en-verliesrekening** /wɪnstɛnvərlisrekənɪŋ/ (pl: -en) profit-and-loss account

winstgevend /wɪnstxevənt/ (adj) profitable, lucrative; remunerative; [fig] fruitful; economic

de **winstmarge** /wɪnstmɑːrʒə/ (pl: -s) profit margin, margin of profit

het **winstoogmerk** /wɪnstoxmɛrk/ (pl: -en) profit motive: *instelling zonder ~* non-profit institution

het **winstpunt** /wɪnstpʏnt/ (pl: -en) point (scored)

de **winstuitkering** /wɪnstœytkerɪŋ/ (pl: -en) (payment of a) dividend

de **winter** /wɪntər/ (pl: -s) winter: *hartje ~* the dead (or: depths) of winter; *we hebben nog niet veel ~ gehad* we haven't had much wintry weather (or: much of a winter) yet; *'s ~s* in (the) winter, in (the) wintertime

de **winteravond** /wɪntəraavɔnt/ (pl: -en) winter evening

de **winterdag** /wɪntərdɑx/ (pl: -en) winter('s) day

de **winterdepressie** /wɪntərdeprɛsi/ seasonal affective disorder, SAD

de **winterhanden** /wɪntərhandə(n)/ (pl) chilblained hands

de **winterjas** /wɪntərjɑs/ (pl: -sen) winter coat

het **winterkoninkje** /wɪntərkonɪŋkjə/ (pl: -s) wren

de **wintermaanden** /wɪntərmandə(n)/ (pl) winter months

de **winterpeen** /wɪntərpen/ (pl: -penen) winter carrot

winters /wɪntərs/ (adj, adv) wintery: *zich ~ aankleden* dress for winter

de **winterslaap** /wɪntərslap/ hibernation, winter sleep: *een ~ houden* hibernate

de **winterspelen** /wɪntərspelə(n)/ (pl) winter Olympics

de **wintersport** /wɪntərspɔrt/ (pl: -en) winter sports: *met ~ gaan* go skiing, go on a winter sports holiday

de **wintertijd** /wɪntərtɛit/ wintertime, winter season

het **winterweer** /wɪntərwer/ winter weather, wintry weather

de **win-winsituatie** /wɪnwɪnsitywa(t)si/ (pl: -s) win-win situation

de **wip** /wɪp/ (pl: -pen) **1** seesaw: *op de ~ zitten* have one's job on the line **2** skip, hop: *in een ~* in a flash (or: jiffy, tick), in no time; *met een ~ was hij bij de deur* he was at the door in one bound **3** [vulg] lay, screw

de **wipneus** /wɪpnøs/ (pl: wipneuzen) turned-up nose, snub nose

¹wippen /wɪpə(n)/ (wipte, heeft gewipt) **1** hop, bound; skip **2** whip, pop: *er even tussenuit ~* nip (or: pop) out for a while; *zij zat met haar stoel te ~ van ongeduld* she sat tilting her chair with impatience **3** play on a seesaw

²wippen /wɪpə(n)/ (wipte, heeft gewipt) topple, overthrow, unseat

de **wirwar** /wɪrwɑr/ criss-cross, jumble, tangle; snarl; maze: *een ~ van steegjes* a rabbit warren

wis /wɪs/ (adj, adv) certain, sure: *iem. van een ~se dood redden* save s.o. from certain death; *~ en waarachtig* upon my word

de **wisent** /wizɛnt/ (pl: -en) wisent, European bison

de **wiskunde** /wɪskʏndə/ mathematics; maths; [Am] math

de **wiskundeknobbel** /wɪskʏndəknɔbəl/ gift (or: head) for mathematics

de **wiskundeleraar** /wɪskʏndəlerar/ (pl: -leraren) mathematics teacher

wiskundig /wɪskʏndəx/ (adj, adv) mathematic(al)

wispelturig /wɪspəltʏrəx/ (adj, adv) inconstant, fickle, capricious

de **¹wissel** /wɪsəl/ (pl: -s) **1** substitute, sub: *een ~ inzetten* put in a substitute **2** change, switch

het/de **²wissel** /wɪsəl/ (pl: -s) points, switch: *een ~*

overhalen (or: *verzetten*) change (*or:* shift) the points

de **wisselautomaat** /wɪsəlɑutomat/ (pl: -automaten) (automatic) money changer, change machine

de **wisselbeker** /wɪsəlbekər/ (pl: -s) challenge cup

de **wisselbouw** /wɪsəlbɑu/ rotation of crops

¹**wisselen** /wɪsələ(n)/ (wisselde, heeft gewisseld) change, vary

²**wisselen** /wɪsələ(n)/ (wisselde, heeft gewisseld) **1** change, exchange: *van plaats ~* change places **2** change, give change: *kunt u ~?* can you change this? **3** exchange; bandy: *van gedachten ~ over* exchange views (*or:* ideas) about

het **wisselgeld** /wɪsəlɣɛlt/ change, (small, loose) change: *te weinig ~ terugkrijgen* be short-changed

het **wisselgesprek** /wɪsəlɣəsprɛk/ (pl: -ken) call waiting

de **wisseling** /wɪsəlɪŋ/ (pl: -en) **1** change, exchange **2** change, changing, turn(ing)

het **wisselkantoor** /wɪsəlkɑntor/ (pl: -kantoren) exchange office

de **wisselkoers** /wɪsəlkurs/ (pl: -en) exchangerate, rate of exchange

de **wisseloplossing** /wɪsəlɔplɔsɪŋ/ (pl: -en) [Belg] alternative solution

de **wisselslag** /wɪsəlslɑɣ/ (individual) medley

de **wisselspeler** /wɪsəlspelər/ (pl: -s) substitute, reserve; sub

de **wisselstroom** /wɪsəlstrom/ alternating current, AC

het **wisselstuk** /wɪsəlstʏk/ (pl: -ken) [Belg] (spare) part

de **wisseltruc** /wɪsəltrʏk/ (pl: -s) fast-change trick

wisselvallig /wɪsəlvɑləɣ/ (adj) changeable, unstable; uncertain; precarious

de **wisselwerking** /wɪsəlwɛrkɪŋ/ (pl: -en) interaction, interplay

wissen /wɪsə(n)/ (wiste, heeft gewist) **1** wipe **2** erase; [comp] delete

de **wisser** /wɪsər/ (pl: -s) wiper

het **wissewasje** /wɪsəwɑʃə/ (pl: -s) trifle

het **wit** /wɪt/ **1** white **2** cut-price

het **witbrood** /wɪtbrot/ (pl: -broden) white bread

het **witgoed** /wɪtɣut/ [roughly] white goods

witheet /wɪthet/ (adj): *~ van woede* boiling (over) with anger, fuming with anger

witjes /wɪcəs/ (adj) pale, white: *~ om de neus zien* look white about the gills

de **witkalk** /wɪtkɑlk/ whitewash, whit(en)ing

het **witlof** /wɪtlɔf/ chicory

de **witregel** /wɪtreɣəl/ (pl: -s) extra space (between the lines)

de **Wit-Rus** /wɪtrʏs/ (pl: -sen) White Russian, Belorussian

Wit-Rusland /wɪtrʏslɑnt/ White Russia, Belorussia

het ¹**Wit-Russisch** /wɪtrʏsis/ Belarusian

²**Wit-Russisch** /wɪtrʏsis/ (adj) Belarusian

het **witsel** /wɪtsəl/ whitewash, whit(en)ing

de **witteboordencriminaliteit** /wɪtəbordə(n)kriminalitɛit/ white-collar crime

de **wittebroodsweken** /wɪtəbrotswekə(n)/ (pl) honeymoon

de **wittekool** /wɪtəkol/ (pl: -kolen) white cabbage

witten /wɪtə(n)/ (witte, heeft gewit) whitewash

de **witvis** /wɪtfɪs/ (pl: -sen) catfish

witwassen /wɪtwɑsə(n)/ (waste wit, heeft witgewassen) launder

het **WK** /weka/ *wereldkampioenschap* World Championship

de **wodka** /wɔtka/ vodka

de **woede** /wudə/ **1** rage, fury, anger: *buiten zichzelf van ~ zijn* be beside o.s. with rage (*or:* anger) **2** mania

de **woedeaanval** /wudəanval/ (pl: -len) tantrum, fit (of anger)

woeden /wudə(n)/ (woedde, heeft gewoed) rage, rave

woedend /wudənt/ (adj, adv) furious, infuriated

de **woede-uitbarsting** /wudəœydbɑrstɪŋ/ (pl: -en) outburst of anger

woef /wuf/ (int) bow-wow, woof

de **woeker** /wukər/ usury

de **woekeraar** /wukərar/ (pl: -s) usurer; profiteer

woekeren /wukərə(n)/ (woekerde, heeft gewoekerd) **1** practise usury; profiteer **2** make the most (of): *met de ruimte ~* use (*or:* utilize) every inch of space **3** grow rank (*or:* rampant)

de **woekering** /wukərɪŋ/ (pl: -en) uncontrolled growth; rampant growth

de **woekerprijs** /wukərprɛis/ (pl: -prijzen) usurious price, exorbitant price

¹**woelen** /wulə(n)/ (woelde, heeft gewoeld) **1** toss about: *zij lag maar te ~* she was tossing and turning **2** churn (about, around)

²**woelen** /wulə(n)/ (woelde, heeft gewoeld) **1** turn up (the soil) **2** grub (up), root (out): *de varkens ~ de wortels bloot* the pigs are grubbing up the roots

woelig /wuləɣ/ (adj, adv) restless: *~e tijden* turbulent times

de **woensdag** /wunzdɑɣ/ (pl: -en) Wednesday: *'s ~s* Wednesday; on Wednesdays

¹**woensdags** /wunzdɑɣs/ (adj) Wednesday

²**woensdags** /wunzdɑɣs/ (adv) on Wednesdays

de **woerd** /wurt/ (pl: -en) drake

woest /wust/ (adj, adv) **1** savage, wild: *een ~ voorkomen hebben* have a fierce countenance **2** rude, rough **3** furious, infuriated: *in een ~e bui* in a fit of rage **4** waste; desolate

de **woesteling** /wˈustəlɪŋ/ (pl: -en) brute

de **woestenij** /wustənˈɛɪ̯/ (pl: -en) wilderness, waste(land)

de **woestijn** /wustˈɛin/ (pl: -en) desert

de **wok** /wɔk/ (pl: -ken) wok
wokken (wokte, heeft gewokt) stir fry

de **wol** /wɔl/ wool: *zuiver* ~ 100 % (*or:* pure) wool

de **wolf** /wɔlf/ (pl: wolven) wolf

het **wolfraam** /wˈɔlfram/ tungsten

de **wolk** /wɔlk/ (pl: -en) cloud ‖ *een* ~ *van een baby* a bouncing baby; [fig] *in de ~en zijn* (over iets) be over the moon about sth., tread (*or:* walk) on air

de **wolkbreuk** /wˈɔlɣbrøk/ (pl: -en) cloudburst
wolkeloos /wˈɔlkələos/ (adj) cloudless, unclouded: *een wolkeloze **hemel*** a clear sky

het **wolkendek** /wˈɔlkə(n)dɛk/ blanket (*or:* layer) of clouds

de **wolkenkrabber** /wˈɔlkə(n)krabər/ (pl: -s) skyscraper

het **wolkenveld** /wˈɔlkə(n)vɛlt/ (pl: -en) mass of cloud(s)

het **wolkje** cloudlet, little cloud, small cloud: *er is geen* ~ *aan de lucht* there isn't a cloud in the sky
wollen /wˈɔlə(n)/ (adj) woollen, wool
wollig /wˈɔləɣ/ (adj, adv) woolly: ~ *taalgebruik* woolly language

de **wolvin** /wɔlvˈɪn/ (pl: -nen) she-wolf

de **wond** /wɔnt/ (pl: -en) wound; injury: *een **gapende*** ~ a gaping wound, a gash; *Joris had een ~je **aan** zijn vinger* Joris had a cut (*or:* scratch) on his finger

het **wonder** /wˈɔndər/ (pl: -en) **1** wonder, miracle: *het **is** een* ~ *dat …* it is a miracle that …; *geen* ~ no (*or:* small) wonder, not surprising **2** wonder, marvel: *de ~en van de **natuur*** the wonders (*or:* marvels) of nature ‖ ~ *boven* ~ by amazing good fortune
wonderbaarlijk /wɔndərbˈarlək/ (adj, adv) miraculous; strange; curious

het **wonderkind** /wˈɔndərkɪnt/ (pl: -eren) (child) prodigy
wonderlijk /wˈɔndərlək/ (adj) strange, surprising

het **wondermiddel** /wˈɔndərmɪdəl/ (pl: -en) panacea; miracle drug

de **wonderolie** /wˈɔndəroli/ castor oil
wonderschoon /wɔndərsxˈon/ (adj, adv) wonderful, exceptionally beautiful
wonderwel /wɔndərwˈɛl/ (adv) wonderfully well: *hij **voelde** zich er* ~ *thuis* he felt wonderfully at home
wonen /wˈonə(n)/ (woonde, heeft gewoond) live: *op zichzelf gaan* ~ set up house, go and live on one's own

de **woning** /wˈonɪŋ/ (pl: -en) house; home: *iem. uit zijn* ~ *zetten* evict s.o.

de **woningbouw** /wˈonɪŋbɑu/ house-building, house-construction: *sociale* ~ council housing; [Am] public housing

de **woningbouwvereniging** /wˈonɪŋbɑuvərenəɣɪŋ/ (pl: -en) housing association (*or:* corporation)

de **woninginrichting** /wˈonɪŋɪnrɪxtɪŋ/ home furnishing(s)

de **woningmarkt** /wˈonɪŋmɑrkt/ (pl: -en) housing market

de **woningnood** /wˈonɪŋnot/ housing shortage
woonachtig /wonˈɑxtəɣ/ (adj): *hij **is** ~ in Leiden* he is a resident of Leiden

het **woonblok** /wˈomblɔk/ (pl: -ken) block

de **woonboot** /wˈombot/ (pl: -boten) houseboat

het **woonerf** /wˈonɛrf/ (pl: -erven) residential area (with restrictions to slow down traffic)

de **woongroep** /wˈonɣrup/ (pl: -en) commune

het **woonhuis** /wˈonhœys/ (pl: -huizen) (private) house; home

de **woonkamer** /wˈonkamər/ (pl: -s) living room

de **woonkeuken** /wˈonkøkə(n)/ (pl: -s) open kitchen, kitchen-dining room

de **woonomgeving** /wˈonɔmɣevɪŋ/ environment

de **woonplaats** /wˈomplats/ (pl: -en) (place of) residence, address; city; town

de **woonruimte** /wˈonrœymtə/ (pl: -n, -s) (housing, living) accommodation

de **woonst** /wonst/ (pl: -en) [Belg] **1** house **2** (place of) residence

de **woonwagen** /wˈonwaɣə(n)/ (pl: -s) caravan; [Am] (house) trailer

de **woonwagenbewoner** /wˈonwaɣə(n)bəwonər/ (pl: -s) caravan dweller; [Am] trailer park resident

het **woonwagenkamp** /wˈonwaɣə(n)kɑmp/ caravan camp; [Am] trailer camp

het **woon-werkverkeer** /wonwˈɛrkfərker/ commuter traffic

de **woonwijk** /wˈonwɛik/ (pl: -en) residential area; housing estate; district; quarter

het **woon-zorgcomplex** /wonzˈɔrɣkɔmplɛks/ sheltered accommodation

het **woord** /wort/ (pl: -en) word: *in* ~ *en **beeld*** in pictures and text; *met **andere** ~en* in other words; *geen **goed*** ~ *voor iets over hebben* not have a good word to say about sth.; *het **hoogste** ~ voeren* do most of the talking; *hij moet altijd het **laatste** ~ hebben* he always has to have the last word; *iem. **aan** zijn ~ **houden*** keep (*or:* hold) s.o. to his promise; *het ~ **geven** aan* give the floor to; *zijn* ~ *geven* give one's word; *het* ~ *tot iem. **richten*** address (*or:* speak to) s.o.; *iem. **aan** het ~ laten* allow s.o. to finish (speaking); *in **één*** ~ in a word, in sum (*or:* short); *op zijn ~en letten* be careful about what one says; *iem. **te** ~ staan* speak to (*or:* see) s.o.; *niet **uit** zijn ~en kunnen komen* not be able to express o.s., fumble for words;

met **twee** *~en spreken* [roughly] be polite; *te* **gek** *voor ~en* too crazy (*or:* ridiculous, absurd) for words

woordblind /wordblInt/ (adj) dyslexic

de **woordblindheid** /wordblInthɛit/ dyslexia

de **woordbreuk** /wordbrøk/ breaking of one's word (*or:* promise)

woordelijk /wordələk/ (adj, adv) word for word; literal(ly)

het **woordenboek** /wordə(n)buk/ (pl: -en) dictionary: *een ~ raadplegen* consult a dictionary; *refer to a dictionary*

de **woordenlijst** /wordə(n)lɛist/ (pl: -en) list of words; vocabulary

de **woordenschat** /wordə(n)sχat/ **1** lexicon **2** vocabulary

de **woordenstrijd** /wordə(n)strɛit/ (verbal) dispute

de **woordenwisseling** /wordə(n)wIsəlIŋ/ (pl: -en) **1** exchange of words, discussion **2** argument

het **woordgebruik** /wortχəbrœyk/ use of words

het **woordje** /worcə/ (pl: -s) word: *een goed ~ doen voor iem.* put in (*or:* say) a (good) word for s.o.; *een hartig ~ met iem. spreken* give s.o. a (good) talking-to; *ook een ~ meespreken* say one's piece

de **woordkeus** /wortkøs/ choice of words, wording

de **woordsoort** /wortsort/ (pl: -en) part of speech

de **woordspeling** /wortspelIŋ/ (pl: -en) pun, play on words

de **woordvoerder** /wortfurdər/ (pl: -s) **1** speaker **2** spokesman

1worden /wordə(n)/ (werd, is geworden) will be, come to, amount to: *dat wordt dan €2,00 per vel* that will be 2.00 euros per sheet

2worden /wordə(n)/ (aux vb, werd, is geworden) be: *er werd gedanst* there was dancing; *de bus wordt om zes uur gelicht* the post will be collected at six o'clock

3worden /wordə(n)/ (werd, is geworden) **1** be, get: *het wordt laat* (or: *kouder*) it is getting late (*or:* colder); *hij wordt morgen vijftig* he'll be fifty tomorrow **2** become: *dat wordt niets* it won't work, it'll come to nothing; *wat is er van hem geworden?* whatever became of him?

de **wording** /wordIŋ/ genesis, origin: *een stad in ~* a town in the making

de **workaholic** /wʏːrkəhɔlIk/ (pl: -s) workaholic

de **work-out** /wʏːrkaut/ work-out

de **workshop** /wʏːrkʃɔp/ (pl: -s) workshop

de **worm** /worm/ (pl: -en) worm

de **worp** /worp/ (pl: -en) throw(ing); shot

de **worst** /worst/ (pl: -en) sausage: *dat zal mij ~ wezen* I couldn't care less

de **worstelaar** /worstəlar/ (pl: -s) wrestler

worstelen /worstələ(n)/ (worstelde, heeft geworsteld) struggle; wrestle [sport]: *zich door een lijvig rapport heen ~* struggle (*or:* plough) (one's way) through a bulky report

de **worsteling** /worstəlIŋ/ (pl: -en) struggle, wrestle

het **worstenbroodje** /worstə(n)brocə/ (pl: -s) [roughly] sausage roll

de **wortel** /wortəl/ (pl: -s) root; carrot: *3 is de ~ van 9* 3 is the square root of 9; *~ schieten* take root

wortelen /wortələ(n)/ (wortelde, heeft/is geworteld) be rooted, root: [fig] *een diepgeworteld wantrouwen* a deep distrust, an instinctive distrust

het **wortelkanaal** /wortəlkanal/ (pl: -kanalen) root canal

het **wortelteken** /wortəltekə(n)/ (pl: -s) radical sign

het **worteltje** /wortəlcə/ carrot

het **worteltrekken** /wortəltrɛkə(n)/ extraction of the root(s)

het **woud** /waut/ (pl: -en) forest

de **woudloper** /wautlopər/ (pl: -s) trapper

would-be /wudbi/ (adj) would-be

de **wraak** /vrak/ revenge, vengeance: *~ nemen op iem.* take revenge on s.o.

de **wraakactie** /vrakaksi/ (pl: -s) act of revenge (*or:* vengeance, retaliation)

wraakzuchtig /vraksʏχtəχ/ (adj) (re)vengeful, vindictive

het **wrak** /vrak/ (pl: -ken) wreck: *zich een ~ voelen* feel a wreck

wraken /vrakə(n)/ (wraakte, heeft gewraakt) **1** object to: *de gewraakte passage* the passage objected to **2** challenge

het **wrakhout** /vrakhaut/ (pieces of) wreckage; driftwood

het **wrakstuk** /vrakstʏk/ (pl: -ken) piece of wreckage; wreckage

wrang /vraŋ/ (adj, adv) **1** sour, acid **2** unpleasant, nasty; wry

de **wrap** /vrɛp/ wrap

de **wrat** /vrat/ (pl: -ten) wart

wreed /vret/ (adj, adv) cruel

de **wreedheid** /vrethɛit/ (pl: -heden) cruelty

de **wreef** /vref/ (pl: wreven) instep

wreken /vrekə(n)/ (wreekte, heeft gewroken) revenge; avenge: *zich voor iets op iem. ~* revenge o.s. on s.o. for sth.

de **wreker** /vrekər/ (pl: -s) avenger, revenger

de **wrevel** /vrevəl/ resentment; [stronger] rancour

wrevelig /vrevələχ/ (adj) **1** peevish, tetchy, grumpy **2** resentful

wriemelen /vrimələ(n)/ (wriemelde, heeft gewriemeld) fiddle (with)

wrijven /vrɛivə(n)/ (wreef, heeft gewreven) **1** rub: *neuzen tegen elkaar ~* rub noses; *wrijf het er maar in* go on, rub it in **2** polish: *de meubels ~* polish the furniture

de **wrijving** /vrɛ̱ivɪŋ/ (pl: -en) friction
    wrikken /vrɪ̱kə(n)/ (wrikte, heeft gewrikt)
    lever, prize
    ¹wringen /vrɪ̱ŋə(n)/ (wrong, heeft gewron-
    gen) pinch
    ²wringen /vrɪ̱ŋə(n)/ (wrong, heeft gewron-
    gen) **1** wring: *zich in allerlei bochten* ~ wrig-
    gle; squirm **2** wring; press
de **wringer** /vrɪ̱ŋər/ (pl: -s) wringer, mangle
de **wroeging** /vru̱ɣɪŋ/ (pl: -en) remorse
    ¹wroeten /vru̱tə(n)/ (wroette, heeft ge-
    wroet) root, rout: *in iemands verleden* ~ pry
    into s.o.'s past
    ²wroeten /vru̱tə(n)/ (wroette, heeft ge-
    wroet) burrow, root (up): *de grond **onderste-
    boven*** ~ root up the earth
de **wrok** /vrɔk/ resentment, grudge; [stronger]
    rancour
de **wrong** /vrɔŋ/ (pl: -en) roll, wreath; chignon;
    bun
    wuft /wʏft/ (adj, adv) frivolous
    wuiven /wœy̯və(n)/ (wuifde, heeft ge-
    wuifd) wave
    wulps /wʏlps/ (adj, adv) voluptuous
    wurgen /wʏ̱rɣə(n)/ (wurgde, heeft ge-
    wurgd) strangle
de **wurgslang** /wʏ̱rɣslɑŋ/ (pl: -en) constrictor
    (snake)
de **¹wurm** /wʏrm/ worm
het **²wurm** /wʏrm/ mite: *het* ~ *kan nog niet **pra-
    ten*** the poor mite can't talk yet
    wurmen /wʏ̱rmə(n)/ (wurmde, heeft ge-
    wurmd) squeeze, worm
de **WW** /wewe̱/ *Werkloosheidswet* Unemploy-
    ment Insurance Act: *in de WW lopen (zitten)*
    be on unemployment (benefit), be on the
    dole
de **WW-uitkering** /wewe̱œytkerɪŋ/ (pl: -en)
    unemployment benefit(s)

X

de **x** /ɪks/ (pl: x'en) x, X

het **x-aantal** /ɪksantal/ (pl: -len) n: *een ~ kamers* n rooms

de **xantippe** /ksɑntɪpə/ (pl: -s) Xanthippe

de **x-as** /ɪksɑs/ (pl: -sen) x-axis

de **X-benen** /ɪkzbenə(n)/ knock knees: *~ hebben* be knock-kneed, have knock knees

het **X-chromosoom** /ɪksχromozom/ (pl: X-chromosomen) X chromosome

de **xenofobie** /ksenofobi/ xenophobia

de **xtc** /ɛkstəsi/ xtc

de **xylofoon** /ksilofon/ (pl: -s) xylophone

y

de **y** /igrɛk/ (pl: y's) y, Y

het **yang** /jɑŋ/ yang

de **y-as** /ɛiɑs/ (pl: -sen) y-axis

het **Y-chromosoom** /ɛixromozom/ (pl: Y-chro-
mosomen) Y chromosome

de **yen** /jɛn/ (pl: -s) yen

yes /jɛs/ (int): *reken maar van ~!* you bet!

de **yeti** /jeti/ (pl: -'s) yeti

het **yin** /jɪn/ yin

de **yoga** /joɣa/ yoga

de **yoghurt** /joɣʏrt/ yogurt

de **ypsilon** /ɪpsilɔn/ (pl: -s) upsilon

Z

de **z** /zɛt/ (pl: z's) z, Z

het **zaad** /zat/ (pl: zaden) **1** seed **2** sperm, semen

de **zaadbal** /zadbɑl/ (pl: -len) testicle

de **zaadcel** /zatsɛl/ (pl: -len) germ cell; sperm
cell

zaaddodend /zadodənt/ (adj) spermicidal

de **zaadlozing** /zatlozɪŋ/ (pl: -en) seminal discharge, ejaculation

de **zaag** /zaχ/ (pl: zagen) saw

het **zaagblad** /zaɣblɑt/ **1** saw (blade) **2** saw-
wort

de **zaagmachine** /zaχmaʃinə/ (pl: -s) saw

het **zaagsel** /zaχsəl/ sawdust

zaaien /zajə(n)/ (zaaide, heeft gezaaid)
sow: *onrust* ~ create unrest; *interessante banen zijn dun gezaaid* interesting jobs are few
and far between

de **zaaier** /zajər/ (pl: -s) sower

het **zaaigoed** /zajɣut/ sowing seed

de **zaak** /zak/ (pl: zaken) **1** thing; object **2** matter, affair, business: *de normale gang van zaken* the normal course of events; *zich met zijn
eigen zaken bemoeien* mind one's own business; *dat is jouw* ~ that is your concern; *de* ~ *in
kwestie* the matter in hand **3** business, deal:
goede zaken doen (met iem.) do good business
(with s.o.); *er worden goede zaken gedaan in
… trade* is good in …; *zaken zijn zaken* business is business; *hij is hier voor zaken* he is
here on business **4** business; shop: *op kosten
van de* ~ on the house; *een* ~ *hebben* run a
business; *een auto van de* ~ a company car
5 case, things: *weten hoe de zaken ervoor
staan* know how things stand, know what
the score is **6** point, issue: *dat doet hier niet(s)
ter zake* that is irrelevant, that is beside the
point; *kennis van zaken hebben* know one's
facts; be well-informed (on the matter)
7 case, lawsuit: *Maria's* ~ *komt vanmiddag
voor* Maria's case comes up this afternoon
8 affair: *Binnenlandse Zaken* Home (or: Internal) Affairs; *Buitenlandse Zaken* Foreign
Affairs **9** cause

de **zaakgelastigde** /zakχəlɑstəɣdə/ (pl: -n)
agent

het **zaakje** /zakjə/ (pl: -s) little matter/business
(or: affair, thing); small deal; job: *ik vertrouw
het* ~ *niet* I don't trust the set-up

de **zaakvoerder** /zakfurdər/ (pl: -s) [Belg]
manager

de **zaakwaarnemer** /zakwarnemər/ (pl: -s)
(business) minder

de **zaal** /zal/ (pl: zalen) **1** room; hall **2** hall;
ward; auditorium **3** hall, house: *een stamp-
volle* ~ a crowded (or: packed) hall, a full
house; *de* ~ *lag plat* it brought the house
down

de **zaalhuur** /zalhyr/ hall rent

de **zaalsport** /zalspɔrt/ (pl: -en) indoor sport

het **zaalvoetbal** /zalvudbɑl/ indoor football

zacht /zɑχt/ (adj, adv) **1** soft; smooth: *een ~e
landing* a smooth landing; *~e sector* social
sector **2** mild **3** kind, gentle: *op zijn ~st gezegd* to put it mildly **4** quiet, soft: *met ~e
stem* in a quiet voice

zachtaardig /zɑχtardəχ/ (adj, adv) good-
natured, gentle

zachtgekookt /zɑχtχəkokt/ (adj) soft-
boiled

de **zachtheid** /zɒχthɛɪt/ softness

zachtjes /zɑχjəs/ (adv) softly; quietly; gently: ~ *doen* be quiet; ~ *rijden* drive slowly; ~
aan! easy does it!, take it easy!; ~*!* hush!,
quiet!

zachtjesaan /zɑχjəsan/ (adv): *we moeten zo
~ vertrekken* we must be going soon

zachtmoedig /zɑχtmudəχ/ (adj, adv) mild(-
mannered)

zachtzinnig /zɑχtsɪnəχ/ (adj, adv) **1** good-
natured, mild(-mannered) **2** gentle, kind(ly);
tender

het **zadel** /zadəl/ (pl: -s) saddle

zadelen /zadələ(n)/ (zadelde, heeft geza-
deld) saddle (up)

de **zadelpijn** /zadəlpɛɪn/ saddle-soreness: ~
hebben be saddlesore

zagen /zaɣə(n)/ (zaagde, heeft gezaagd)
1 saw (up) **2** saw, cut: *planken* (or: *figuren*) ~
saw into planks (or: shapes)

de **zagerij** /zaɣərɛi/ (pl: -en) sawmill

de **zak** /zɑk/ (pl: -ken) **1** bag; [large] sack: *een ~
patat* a bag (or: packet) of chips; [fig] *iem. de
~ geven* give s.o. the sack, sack s.o.; [fig] *in ~
en as zitten* be in sackcloth and ashes **2** pocket: *geld op* ~ *hebben* have some money in
one's pockets (or: on one) **3** purse: *uit eigen
~ betalen* pay out of one's own purse; *een duit
in het ~je doen* put in one's pennyworth;
[Am] put in one's two cents **4** [inform] bore,
jerk; [stronger] bastard

de **zakagenda** /zɑkaɣɛnda/ pocket diary; [Am]
(small) agenda

het **zakboekje** /zɑgbukjə/ (pl: -s) (pocket) notebook

het **zakcentje** /zɑksɛncə/ (pl: -s) pocket money

de **zakdoek** /zɑgduk/ (pl: -en) handkerchief

zakelijk /zakələk/ (adj, adv) **1** business-
(like), commercial **2** business(like), objective
3 compact, concise: *een ~e stijl van schrijven* a
terse style of writing **4** practical, real(istic);
down-to-earth

de **zakelijkheid** /zakələkhɛɪt/ professionalism

het **zakencentrum** /zakə(n)sɛntrym/ (pl: -centra) business centre

het **zakendoen** /zɑkə(n)dun/ business

het **zakenkabinet** /zɑkə(n)kabinɛt/ (pl: -ten) government which is not supported by a parliamentary majority

het **zakenleven** /zɑkə(n)levə(n)/ business (life), commerce

de **zakenman** /zɑkə(n)mɑn/ (pl: zakenlui, zakenlieden) businessman: *een* **gewiekst** ~ a shrewd (*or:* an astute) businessman

de **zakenreis** /zɑkə(n)rɛis/ (pl: -reizen) business trip

de **zakenrelatie** /zɑkə(n)rela(t)si/ (pl: -s) business relation

de **zakenvriend** /zɑkə(n)vrint/ (pl: -en) business associate

de **zakenvrouw** /zɑkə(n)vrɑu/ (pl: -en) businesswoman

de **zakenwereld** /zɑkə(n)werəlt/ business world

het **zakformaat** /zɑkfɔrmat/ (pl: zakformaten) pocket size

het **zakgeld** /zɑkχɛlt/ pocket money, spending money, allowance

zakken /zɑkə(n)/ (zakte, is gezakt) **1** fall, drop; sink: *in elkaar* ~ collapse **2** fall (off), drop, come down, go down; sink: *de* **hoofdpijn** *is gezakt* the headache has eased; *het* **water** *is gezakt* the water has gone down (*or:* subsided) **3** fail, go down

zakkenrollen /zɑkə(n)rɔlə(n)/ pick pockets

de **zakkenroller** /zɑkə(n)rɔlər/ (pl: -s) pickpocket: *pas op voor ~s!* beware of pickpockets!

de **zakkenvuller** /zɑkə(n)vʏlər/ (pl: -s) [inform] profiteer

de **zaklamp** /zɑklɑmp/ (pl: -en) (pocket) torch; [Am] flashlight

de **zaklantaarn** /zɑklɑntarn/ (pl: -s) (pocket) torch, flashlight

zaklopen /zɑklopə(n)/ (run a) sack race

het **zakmes** /zɑkmɛs/ (pl: -sen) pocket knife

het **zakwoordenboek** /zɑkwordə(n)buk/ (pl: -en) pocket dictionary

het **zalencentrum** /zɑlə(n)sɛntrʏm/ function rooms

de **zalf** /zɑlf/ (pl: zalven) ointment, salve: *met* ~ *insmeren* rub ointment (*or:* salve) on

zalig /zɑləχ/ (adj, adv) gorgeous, glorious, divine

zaligmakend /zaləχmakənt/ (adj): *dat is ook niet* ~ that won't bring universal happiness either

de **zaligverklaring** /zɑləχfərklarɪŋ/ (pl: -en) beatification

de **zalm** /zɑlm/ (pl: -en) salmon

de **zalmforel** /zɑlmforɛl/ (pl: -len) salmon trout

zalmkleurig /zɑlmklørəχ/ (adj) salmon, salmon-coloured

zalven /zɑlvə(n)/ (zalfde, heeft gezalfd) put

(*or:* rub) ointment on

zalvend /zɑlvənt/ (adj, adv) unctuous, suave

de **zalving** /zɑlvɪŋ/ (pl: -en) anointment (with)

Zambia /zɑmbija/ Zambia

de **Zambiaan** /zambijan/ (pl: Zambianen) Zambian

Zambiaans /zambijans/ (adj) Zambian

het **zand** /zɑnt/ sand: ~ *erover* let's forget it, let bygones be bygones

de **zandafgraving** /zɑntɑfχravɪŋ/ (pl: -en) sandpit

de **zandbak** /zɑndbɑk/ (pl: -ken) sandbox

de **zandbank** /zɑndbɑŋk/ (pl: -en) sandbank

zanderig /zɑndərəχ/ (adj) sandy

de **zandgrond** /zɑntχrɔnt/ (pl: -en) sandy soil

het **zandkasteel** /zɑntkɑstel/ (pl: -kastelen) sandcastle

de **zandkorrel** /zɑntkɔrəl/ (pl: -s) grain of sand

de **zandloper** /zɑntlopər/ (pl: -s) hourglass; egg-timer

het **zandpad** /zɑntpɑt/ (pl: -en) sandy path

het/de **zandsteen** /zɑntsten/ sandstone

de **zandstorm** /zɑntstɔrm/ (pl: -en) sandstorm

zandstralen /zɑntstralə(n)/ (zandstraalde, heeft gezandstraald) sandblast

het **zandstrand** /zɑntstrɑnt/ (pl: -en) sandy beach

de **zandverstuiving** /zɑntfərstœyvɪŋ/ (pl: -en) sand drift, drifting sand

de **zandvlakte** /zɑntflɑktə/ (pl: -n, -s) sand flat, sand(y) plain

de **zandweg** /zɑntwɛχ/ (pl: -en) sand track (*or:* road), dirt track

de **zandzak** /zɑntsɑk/ (pl: -ken) sandbag

de **zang** /zɑŋ/ (pl: -en) song, singing; warbling

de **zanger** /zɑŋər/ (pl: -s) singer; vocalist

zangerig /zɑŋərəχ/ (adj) melodious; singsong

het **zangkoor** /zɑŋkor/ (pl: -koren) choir

de **zangleraar** /zɑŋlerar/ (pl: -leraren, -s) singing teacher

de **zangvereniging** /zɑŋvərenəχɪŋ/ (pl: -en) choir, choral society

de **zangvogel** /zɑŋvoɣəl/ (pl: -s) songbird

zaniken /zɑnəkə(n)/ (zanikte, heeft gezanikt) nag; moan; whine

zappen /zɛpə(n)/ (zapte, heeft/is gezapt) zap

¹**zat** /zɑt/ (adj) **1** drunken; [after vb] drunk **2** fed up: *'t* ~ *zijn* be fed up (with it)

²**zat** /zɑt/ (adv) plenty; to spare: *zij hebben* **geld** ~ they have plenty (*or:* oodles) of money; *tijd* ~ time to spare, plenty of time

de **zaterdag** /zɑtərdɑχ/ (pl: -en) Saturday

¹**zaterdags** /zɑtərdɑχs/ (adj) Saturday

²**zaterdags** /zɑtərdɑχs/ (adv) on Saturdays

de **zatlap** /zɑtlɑp/ (pl: -pen) boozer

ze /zə/ (pers pron) **1** she, her: *ze* **komt** *zo* she is just coming **2** they, them: *roep ze eens* just call them; *daar* **moesten** *ze eens iets aan* **doen** they ought to do sth. about that

de **zebra** /zebra/ (pl: -'s) zebra

het **zebrapad** /zebrapat/ (pl: -en) pedestrian crossing, zebra crossing

de **zede** /zedə/ (pl: -n) **1** custom; usage: ~*n en gewoonten* customs and traditions **2** morals, manners || *een meisje van lichte ~n* a girl of easy virtue
zedelijk /zedələk/ (adj, adv) moral
zedeloos /zedəlos/ (adj, adv) immoral, corrupt

het **zedendelict** /zedə(n)delɪkt/ (pl: -en) sexual offence

de **zedenleer** /zedə(n)ler/ [Belg; educ] ethics

het **zedenmisdrijf** /zedəmɪzdrɛɪf/ (pl: -misdrijven) sexual offence

de **zedenpolitie** /zedə(n)poli(t)si/ vice squad

de **zedenpreek** /zedə(n)prek/ (pl: -preken) sermon

de **zedenzaak** vice case
zedig /zedəx/ (adj, adv) modest

de **zee** /ze/ (pl: -ën) sea: *een ~ van tijd* oceans (or: heaps) of time; *aan ~* by the sea, on the coast; *met iem. in ~ gaan* join in with s.o., throw in one's lot with s.o.

de **zeearend** /zearənt/ (pl: -en) white-tailed eagle

de **zeearm** /zearm/ (pl: -en) arm of the sea, inlet

het **zeebanket** /zebɑŋkɛt/ seafood

de **zeebenen** /zebenə(n)/ (pl): *~ hebben* have got one's sea legs, be a good sailor

de **zeebeving** /zebevɪŋ/ (pl: -en) seaquake

de **zeebodem** /zebodəm/ (pl: -s) ocean floor, seabed, bottom of the sea

de **zeebonk** /zebɔŋk/ (pl: -en) sea dog

de **zeeduivel** /zedœyvəl/ (pl: -s) angler, anglerfish

de **zee-egel** /zeeɣəl/ (pl: -s) sea urchin

de **zee-engte** /zeɛŋtə/ (pl: -n, -s) strait

de **zeef** /zef/ (pl: zeven) sieve; strainer: *zo lek als een ~ zijn* leak like a sieve

de **zeefdruk** /zevdrʏk/ (pl: -ken) silk-screen (print)

het **zeegat** /zeɣat/ (pl: -en) tidal inlet (or: outlet)

het **zeegezicht** /zeɣəzɪxt/ (pl: -en) seascape

de **zeehaven** /zehavə(n)/ (pl: -s) harbour, seaport

de **zeeheld** /zehɛlt/ (pl: -en) sea hero

de **zeehond** /zehɔnt/ (pl: -en) seal

het **zeeklimaat** /zeklimat/ maritime climate, oceanic climate

de **zeekoe** /zeku/ (pl: zeekoeien) sea cow

de **zeekreeft** /zekreft/ (pl: zeekreeften) lobster
Zeeland /zelɑnt/ Zeeland

de **zeeleeuw** /zelew/ (pl: -en) sea lion

de **zeelieden** /zelidə(n)/ (pl) seamen, sailors

de **zeelucht** /zelʏxt/ sea air

het **¹zeem** /zem/ shammy, chamois

het/de **²zeem** /zem/ shammy, chamois

de **zeemacht** /zemɑxt/ navy; naval forces

de **zeeman** /zeman/ (pl: zeelieden, zeelui) sailor

de **zeemeermin** /zemermɪn/ (pl: -nen) mermaid

de **zeemeeuw** /zemew/ (pl: -en) (sea)gull

de **zeemijl** /zemɛil/ (pl: -en) nautical mile

het **zeemleer** /zemler/ chamois (or: shammy) leather, washleather
zeemleren /zemlerə(n)/ (adj) chamois, shammy

de **zeemogendheid** /zemoɣənthɛɪt/ (pl: -heden) maritime power, naval power

het **zeeniveau** /zenivo/ (pl: -s) sea level

de **zeeolifant** /zeolifant/ (pl: -en) elephant seal, sea elephant

de **zeep** /zep/ (pl: zepen) **1** soap **2** (soap)suds || *iem. om ~ brengen* kill s.o.; do s.o. in

het **zeepaardje** /zeparcə/ (pl: -s) sea horse

het **zeepbakje** /zebɑkjə/ (pl: -s) soap dish

de **zeepbel** /zebɛl/ (pl: -len) (soap) bubble

de **zeepkist** /zepkɪst/ (pl: -en) soapbox

het/de **zeeppoeder** /zepudər/ washing powder, detergent

het **zeepsop** /zepsɔp/ (soap)suds

het **¹zeer** /zer/ pain, ache; sore: *dat doet ~* that hurts
²zeer /zer/ (adj) sore, painful, aching: *een ~ hoofd* an aching head
³zeer /zer/ (adv) very, extremely, greatly: *~ tot mijn verbazing* (very) much to my amazement

de **zeereis** /zerɛis/ (pl: zeereizen) (sea) voyage; passage

de **zeerob** /zerɔp/ (pl: -ben) seal

de **zeerover** /zerovər/ (pl: -s) pirate

het **zeeschip** /zesxɪp/ (pl: zeeschepen) seagoing vessel, ocean-going vessel

de **zeeslag** /zeslɑx/ (pl: -en) sea battle, naval battle; [game] battleships

de **zeespiegel** /zespiɣəl/ (pl: -s) sea level

de **zeestraat** /zestrat/ (pl: -straten) strait
Zeeuws /zews/ (adj) Zeeland
Zeeuws-Vlaanderen /zewsflɑndərə(n)/ Zeeland Flanders

de **zeevaart** /zevart/ seagoing; shipping

de **zeevaartschool** /zevartsxol/ (pl: -scholen) nautical college
zeevarend /zevarənt/ (adj) maritime, seagoing

de **zeevis** /zevɪs/ (pl: -sen) saltwater fish, sea fish
zeewaardig /zewardəx/ (adj) seaworthy

het **zeewater** /zewatər/ seawater, salt water

de **zeewering** /zewerɪŋ/ (pl: -en) seawall

het **zeewier** /zewir/ seaweed

de **zeewind** /zewɪnt/ (pl: -en) sea breeze, sea wind
zeeziek /zezik/ (adj) seasick

het **zeezout** /zezaut/ sea salt

de **zege** /zeɣə/ (pl: -s) victory, triumph; win

de **¹zegel** /zeɣəl/ stamp

het ²**zegel** /ze̞ɣəl/ seal: *zijn ~ ergens op* **drukken,** *zijn ~* **hechten** *aan iets* set one's seal on sth.; give one's blessing to sth.

de **zegelring** /ze̞ɣəlrɪŋ/ (pl: -en) signet ring

de **zegen** /ze̞ɣə(n)/ **1** blessing; benediction: [iron] *mijn ~* **heb** *je (voor wat het waard is)* you've got my blessing(, for what it's worth) **2** blessing, boon: *dat is een ~* **voor** *de mensheid* that is a blessing (*or:* boon) to mankind

zegenen /ze̞ɣənə(n)/ (zegende, heeft gezegend) bless

zegerijk /ze̞ɣərɛik/ (adj) victorious, triumphant

de **zegetocht** /ze̞ɣətɔχt/ (pl: -en) triumphal march, victory march

zegevieren /ze̞ɣəvirə(n)/ (zegevierde, heeft gezegevierd) triumph

zeggen /ze̞ɣə(n)/ (zei, heeft gezegd) **1** say, tell: *wat* **wil** *je daarmee ~?* what are you trying to say?, what are you driving at?; *wat ik ~* **wou** by the way; *wat zegt u?* (I beg your) pardon?, sorry?; *wie zal het ~?* who can say? (*or:* tell?); *zegt u het* **maar** yes, please?; *zeg dat* **wel** you can say that again; *men zegt* **dat** *hij heel rijk is* he is said (*or:* reputed) to be very rich; *wat zeg je me daarvan!* how about that!, well I never!; *dat is toch zo, zeg nou* **zelf** it is true, admit it; *hoe zal ik* **het** *~?* how shall I put it?; *nou je* **het** *zegt* now (that) you mention it; *zo gezegd, zo gedaan* no sooner said than done; *zonder iets te ~* without (saying) a word; *zeg* **maar** *'Tom'* call me 'Tom'; *niets* **te** *~ hebben* have no authority; have no say **2** say, mean: *dat* **wil** *~* that means, i.e.; that is (to say) **3** say, prove **4** say, state ‖ *laten we ~ dat … let's say that …*

de **zeggenschap** /ze̞ɣənsχap/ say, voice: *~* **over** *iets krijgen* get control (*or:* authority) over sth.

de **zeggingskracht** /ze̞ɣɪŋskraχt/ power of expression, eloquence

het **zegje** /ze̞χjə/: *ieder wil zijn ~* **doen** everyone wants to have their say

de **zegsman** /ze̞χsman/ (pl: zegslieden, zegslui) informant, authority

de **zegswijze** /ze̞χswɛizə/ (pl: -n) phrase, saying

de **zeik** /zɛik/ [inform] piss **zeiken** /ze̞ikə(n)/ (zeikte, heeft gezeikt/gezeken) [inform] **1** piss **2** go on, harp (*or:* carry) on

de **zeikerd** /ze̞ikərt/ (pl: -s) [inform] bugger **zeikerig** /ze̞ikərəχ/ (adj, adv) [inform] fretful, whiny **zeiknat** /ze̞iknat/ (adj) [inform] sopping (wet)

het **zeil** /zɛil/ (pl: -en) **1** sail: *alle ~en* **bijzetten** employ full sail; pull out all the stops; *onder ~ gaan* **a)** set sail; **b)** [fig] doze off **2** floor covering **3** canvas, sailcloth; tarpaulin

de **zeilboot** /ze̞ilbot/ (pl: -boten) sailing boat

het/de **zeildoek** /zɛilduk/ canvas **zeilen** /ze̞ilə(n)/ (zeilde, heeft/is gezeild) sail

de **zeiler** /ze̞ilər/ (pl: -s) yachtsman, yachtswoman, sailor

het **zeiljacht** /ze̞iljaχt/ (pl: -en) yacht

de **zeilplank** /ze̞ilplaŋk/ (pl: -en) sailboard

het **zeilschip** /zɛilsχɪp/ (pl: -schepen) sailing ship

de **zeilsport** /zɛilsport/ sailing

de **zeiltocht** /zɛiltɔχt/ (pl: -en) sailing trip, sailing voyage

de **zeilwedstrijd** /zɛilwɛtstrɛit/ (pl: -en) sailing match; regatta

de **zeis** /zɛis/ (pl: -en) scythe **zeker** /ze̞kər/ (adj, adv) **1** safe: *(op) ~* **spelen** play safe; *hij heeft het ~e* **voor** *het onzekere genomen* he did it to be on the safe side **2** sure, certain: *iets ~* **weten** know sth. for sure; *om ~ te* **zijn** to be sure; *vast en ~!,* [Belg] *zeker en* **vast!** definitely; *~* **weten!** to be sure!, sure is (*or:* are)...! **3** probably: *je* **wou** *haar ~* **verrassen** I suppose you wanted to surprise her; *je hebt het ~ al af* you must have finished it by now **4** at least: *~* **dertig** *gewonden* at least thirty (people) injured ‖ *~* **niet** certainly not; *op ~e* **dag** one day; *een ~e* **meneer** *Pietersen* a (certain) Mr Pietersen

de **zekerheid** /ze̞kərhɛit/ (pl: zekerheden) **1** safety; safe keeping: *iem. een* **gevoel** *van ~ geven* give s.o. a sense of security; *voor alle ~* for safety's sake, to make quite sure **2** certainty; confidence ‖ **sociale** *~* social security

de **zekering** /ze̞kərɪŋ/ (pl: -en) (safety) fuse: *de ~en* **zijn doorgeslagen** the fuses have blown **zelden** /zɛldə(n)/ (adv) rarely, seldom: *~ of* **nooit** rarely if ever **zeldzaam** /zɛltsam/ (adj, adv) rare

de **zeldzaamheid** /zɛltsamhɛit/ (pl: -heden) rarity **zelf** /zɛlf/ (dem pron) self, myself, yourself, himself, herself, itself, ourselves, yourselves, themselves, oneself: *~ een zaak* **beginnen** start one's own business; *~* **gebakken** *brood* home-made bread; *ik* **kook** *~* I do my own cooking; *al* **zeg** *ik het ~* although I say it myself; *het* **huis** *~ is onbeschadigd* the house itself is undamaged

de **zelfbediening** /zɛlvbədinɪŋ/ self-service

het **zelfbedieningsrestaurant** /zɛlvbədinɪŋsrɛstorant/ (pl: -s) self-service restaurant

het **zelfbedrog** /zɛlvbədrɔχ/ self-deception

het **zelfbeeld** /zɛlvbelt/ self-image

de **zelfbeheersing** /zɛlvbəhersɪŋ/ self-control: *zijn ~* **verliezen** lose control of o.s.

het **zelfbeklag** /zɛlvbəklaχ/ self-pity

de **zelfbeschikking** /zɛlvbəsχɪkɪŋ/ self-determination

het **zelfbestuur** /zɛlvbəstyr/ self-government

de **zelfbevrediging** /zɛlvbəvredəɣɪŋ/ masturbation **zelfbewust** /zɛlvbəwʏst/ (adj, adv) self-

zenuwtrekje

confident, self-assured

het **zelfbewustzijn** /zɛlvbəwɣ(st)sɛɪn/ self-awareness

zelfde /zɛlvdə/ (adj) similar, very (same): *in deze ~ kamer* in this very room

de **zelfdiscipline** /zɛlvdisiplinə/ self-discipline

de **zelfdoding** /zɛlvdodɪŋ/ (pl: -en) suicide

zelfgenoegzaam /zɛlfxənuxsam/ (adj) conceited

zelfingenomen /zɛlfɪŋɣənomə(n)/ (adj) conceited

de **zelfkant** /zɛlfkɑnt/ (pl: -en): *aan de ~ van de maatschappij leven* live on the fringe(s) (*or:* border(s)) of society

de **zelfkennis** /zɛlfkɛnɪs/ self-knowledge

de **zelfkritiek** /zɛlfkritik/ self-criticism

het **zelfmedelijden** /zɛlfmedəlɛidə(n)/ self-pity

de **zelfmoord** /zɛlfmort/ (pl: -en) suicide: *~ plegen* commit suicide

de **zelfmoordaanslag** /zɛlfmortanslɑx/ (pl: -en) suicide attack

de **zelfmoordterrorist** /zɛlfmortɛrorɪst/ suicide bomber (*or:* terrorist)

de **zelfontplooiing** /zɛlfontplojɪŋ/ self-development; self-realization

de **zelfontspanner** /zɛlfontspɑnər/ (pl: -s) self-timer

de **zelfoverschatting** /zɛlfovərsxɑtɪŋ/ overestimation of o.s.: *aan ~ lijden* overestimate o.s.

het **zelfportret** /zɛlfportrɛt/ (pl: -ten) self-portrait

het **zelfrespect** /zɛlfrɛspɛkt/ self-respect

zelfrijzend /zɛlfrɛizənt/ (adj) self-raising

zelfs /zɛlfs/ (adv) even: *~ zijn vrienden vertrouwde hij niet* he did not even trust his friends; *~ in dat geval* even then so

de **zelfspot** /zɛlfspot/ self-mockery

zelfstandig /zɛlfstɑndəx/ (adj, adv) independent; self-employed: *een kleine ~e* a self-employed person

de **zelfstandigheid** /zɛlfstɑndəxhɛit/ independence

de **zelfstudie** /zɛlfstydi/ (pl: -s) private study, home study

de **zelfverdediging** /zɛlfərdedəɣɪŋ/ self-defence: *uit ~ handelen* act in self-defence

de **zelfverloochening** /zɛlfərloxənɪŋ/ self-denial

het **zelfvertrouwen** /zɛlfərtrɑuwə(n)/ (self-)confidence

het **zelfverwijt** /zɛlfərwɛrt/ self-reproach

zelfverzekerd /zɛlfərzekərt/ (adj, adv) (self-)assured

zelfvoldaan /zɛlfoldan/ (adj) self-satisfied

de **zelfwerkzaamheid** /zɛlfwɛrksamhɛit/ self-activation; self-motivation; independence

zelfzuchtig /zɛlfsyxtəx/ (adj, adv) selfish

de ¹**zemel** /zeməl/ (pl: -en, -s) bran

de ²**zemel** /zeməl/ (pl: -s) twaddler

de **zemelen** /zemələ(n)/ (pl) bran

zemen /zemə(n)/ (zeemde, heeft gezeemd) leather

het **zenboeddhisme** /zɛmbudɪsmə/ Zen (Buddhism)

de **zendamateur** /zɛntamatør/ (pl: -s) (radio) ham, amateur radio operator; CB-er

de **zendeling** /zɛndəlɪŋ/ (pl: -en) missionary

¹**zenden** /zɛndə(n)/ (zond, heeft gezonden) broadcast, transmit

²**zenden** /zɛndə(n)/ (zond, heeft gezonden) send: *iem. om de dokter ~* send for the doctor

de **zender** /zɛndər/ (pl: -s) **1** broadcasting station, transmitting station **2** sender **3** emitter, transmitter

de **zendgemachtigde** /zɛntxəmɑxtəɣdə/ (pl: -n) broadcasting licence-holder

de **zending** /zɛndɪŋ/ (pl: -en) supply; parcel; package

het **zendingswerk** /zɛndɪŋswɛrk/ missionary work

de **zendinstallatie** /zɛntɪnstɑla(t)si/ (pl: -s) transmitting station (*or:* equipment)

de **zendmast** /zɛntmɑst/ (pl: -en) (radio, TV) mast; radio tower, TV tower

de **zendpiraat** /zɛntpirat/ (pl: -piraten) radio pirate

het **zendstation** /zɛntsta(t)ʃon/ (pl: -s) broadcasting station, transmitting station

de **zendtijd** /zɛntɛit/ (pl: -en) broadcast(ing) time

de **zenuw** /zenyw/ (pl: -en) nerve; nerves: *stalen ~en* nerves of steel; *de ~en hebben* have the jitters; *ze was óp van de ~en* she was a nervous wreck; *op iemands ~en werken* get (*or:* grate) on s.o.'s nerves

de **zenuwaandoening** /zenywandunɪŋ/ (pl: -en) nervous disorder

zenuwachtig /zenywɑxtəx/ (adj, adv) nervous: *~ zijn voor het examen* be jittery before the exam

de **zenuwachtigheid** /zenywɑxtəxhɛit/ nervousness

de **zenuwbehandeling** /zenywbəhɑndəlɪŋ/ (pl: -en) root treatment, root-canal therapy

de **zenuwcel** /zenywsɛl/ (pl: -len) neuron

het **zenuwgas** /zenywɣɑs/ (pl: -sen) nerve gas

het **zenuwgestel** /zenywɣəstɛl/ nervous system

de **zenuwinzinking** /zenywɪnzɪŋkɪŋ/ (pl: -en) nervous breakdown

de **zenuwlijder** /zenywlɛidər/ (pl: -s) [inform] neurotic

de **zenuwontsteking** /zenywontstekɪŋ/ (pl: -en) neuritis

zenuwslopend /zenywslopənt/ (adj) nerve-racking; [Am] nerve-wracking

het **zenuwstelsel** /zenywstɛlsəl/ (pl: -s) nervous system

het **zenuwtrekje** /zenywtrɛkjə/ (pl: -s) (nerv-

de **zenuwziekte** /ze̱nywziktə/ (pl: -n, -s) nervous disease

de **zeperd** /ze̱pərt/ (pl: -s) [inform] fizzle, flop: *een ~ halen* fall flat (on one's face)

de **zeppelin** /zɛ̱pəlɪn/ (pl: -s) Zeppelin

de **zerk** /zɛrk/ (pl: -en) tombstone

de **zero tolerance** /ziroto̱lərəns/ zero tolerance

zes /zɛs/ (num) six; [in dates] sixth: *hoofdstuk ~* chapter six; *iets in ~sen delen* divide sth. into six (parts); *wij zijn met z'n ~sen* there are six of us; *met ~ tegelijk* in sixes; *~ min* barely a six; *voor dat proefwerk kreeg hij een ~* he got six for that test; *een ~je* six (out of ten), a mere pass mark

zesde /zɛ̱zdə/ (num) sixth

de **zeshoek** /zɛ̱shuk/ (pl: -en) hexagon

de **zesjescultuur** /zɛ̱ʃəskʏltyr/ culture of mediocrity

het **zestal** /zɛ̱stɑl/ (pl: -len) six

zestien /zɛ̱stin/ (num) sixteen; [in dates] sixteenth

zestiende /zɛ̱stində/ (num) sixteenth

zestig /sɛ̱stəx/ (num) sixty: *in de jaren ~* in the sixties; *voor in de ~ zijn* be just over sixty; *hij loopt tegen de ~* he is close on sixty; he is pushing sixty

de **zestiger** /sɛ̱stəxər/ (pl: -s) sixty-year-old, sexagenarian

de **zet** /zɛt/ (pl: -ten) **1** move: *een ~ doen* make a move; *jij bent aan ~* (it's) your move **2** push: *geef me eens een ~je* give me a boost, will you

de **zetbaas** /zɛ̱dbas/ (pl: zetbazen) manager

de **zetel** /ze̱təl/ (pl: -s) seat; [Belg] armchair

zetelen /ze̱tələ(n)/ (zetelde, heeft/is gezeteld) be established, have one's seat; reside

de **zetfout** /zɛ̱tfɑut/ (pl: -en) misprint

het **zetmeel** /zɛ̱tmel/ starch

de **zetpil** /zɛ̱tpɪl/ (pl: -len) suppository

zetten /zɛ̱tə(n)/ (zette, heeft gezet) **1** set, put; move: *enkele stappen ~* take a few steps; *iem. eruit ~* eject, evict s.o.; throw s.o. out; *een apparaat in elkaar ~* fit together, assemble a machine; contrive, think up **2** make || *zet de muziek harder* (or: *zachter*) turn up (or: down) the music; *zich ergens toe ~* put one's mind to sth.

de **zetter** /zɛ̱tər/ (pl: -s) compositor

de **zeug** /zøx/ (pl: -en) sow

zeulen /zø̱lə(n)/ (zeulde, heeft gezeuld) [inform] lug, drag

de **zeur** /zør/ (pl: -en) bore, nag

zeuren /zø̱rə(n)/ (zeurde, heeft gezeurd) nag, harp; whine: *wil je niet zo aan mijn kop ~* stop badgering me; *iem. aan het hoofd ~ (om, over)* nag s.o. (into, about)

¹**zeven** /ze̱və(n)/ (zeefde, heeft gezeefd) sieve, sift; strain

²**zeven** /ze̱və(n)/ (num) seven; [in dates] seventh: *morgen wordt ze ~* tomorrow she'll be

seven || *een ~ voor Nederlands* (a) seven for Dutch

zevende /ze̱vəndə/ (num) seventh

zeventien /ze̱və(n)tin/ (num) seventeen; [in dates] seventeenth

zeventiende /ze̱vəntində/ (num) seventeenth

zeventig /se̱vəntəx/ (num) seventy

de **zever** /ze̱vər/ (pl: -s) drivel

zeveren /ze̱vərə(n)/ (zeverde, heeft gezeverd) **1** slobber, slaver **2** drivel

z.g.a.n. (abbrev) *zogoed als nieuw* as good as new, virtually new

zgn. (abbrev) *zogenaamd* so-called

zich /zɪx/ (ref pron) **1** himself, herself, itself, oneself, themselves; him(self); her(self), it(self), one(self), them(selves): *geld bij ~ hebben* have money on one; *iem. bij ~ hebben* have s.o. with one **2** yourself, yourselves: *vergist u ~ niet?* aren't you mistaken?

het **zicht** /zɪxt/ **1** sight, view: *iem. het ~ belemmeren* block s.o.'s view; *het einde is in ~* the end is in sight (or: view); *uit het ~ verdwijnen* disappear from view **2** insight

zichtbaar /zɪ̱xtbar/ (adj, adv) visible: *~ opgelucht* visibly relieved; *niet ~ met het blote oog* not visible to the naked eye

de **zichtrekening** /zɪ̱xtrekənɪŋ/ (pl: -en) [Belg] current account

zichzelf /zɪxsɛ̱lf/ (ref pron) himself, herself, itself, oneself, themselves, self: *niet ~ zijn* not be oneself; *op ~ wonen* live on one's own; *tot ~ komen* come to oneself; *uit ~ of* one's own accord; *voor ~ beginnen* start a business of one's own

ziedend /zi̱dənt/ (adj) seething, furious, livid

ziek /zik/ (adj) ill, sick: *~ van iemands gezeur worden* get sick of s.o.'s moaning; *~ worden* fall ill (or: sick); *zich ~ melden* report sick

het **ziekbed** /zi̱gbɛt/ (pl: -den) **1** sickbed: *aan het ~ gekluisterd zijn* be confined to one's (sick)bed **2** illness: *na een kort ~* after a short illness

de **zieke** /zi̱kə/ (pl: -n) patient, sick person

ziekelijk /zi̱kələk/ (adj) **1** sickly **2** morbid, sick

de **ziekenauto** /zi̱kə(n)ɑuto/ (pl: -'s) ambulance

het **ziekenbezoek** /zi̱kə(n)bəzuk/ (pl: -en) visit to a (or: the) patient

de **ziekenboeg** /zi̱kə(n)bux/ (pl: -en) sickbay

de **ziekenbroeder** /zi̱kə(n)brudər/ (pl: -s) male nurse

het **ziekenfonds** /zi̱kə(n)fɔnts/ (pl: -en) [roughly] (Dutch) National Health Service: *ik zit in het ~* I'm covered by the National Health Service

het **ziekenhuis** /zi̱kə(n)hœys/ (pl: -huizen) hospital

de **ziekenhuisopname** /zi̱kə(n)hœysɔpnamə/ (pl: -n, -s) hospitalization

de **ziekenverpleger** /zi̯kə(n)vərpleɣər/ (pl: -s) nurse

de **ziekenwagen** /zi̯kə(n)waɣə(n)/ (pl: -s) ambulance

de **ziekte** /zi̯ktə/ (pl: -n, -s) **1** illness, sickness **2** disease, illness: *de ~ van Weil* Weil's disease; *een ernstige ~* a serious disease (*or:* illness); *een ~ oplopen* develop a disease (*or:* an illness)

het **ziektebeeld** /zi̯ktəbelt/ (pl: -en) syndrome

de **ziektekiem** /zi̯ktəkim/ (pl: -en) germ (of a, the disease)

de **ziektekosten** /zi̯ktəkɔstə(n)/ (pl) medical expenses

de **ziektekostenverzekering** /zi̯ktəkɔstə(n)vərzekərɪŋ/ (pl: -en) medical insurance, health insurance

het **ziekteverlof** /zi̯ktəvərlɔf/ sick leave

het **ziekteverloop** /zi̯ktəvərlop/ course of a disease

de **ziekteverwekker** /zi̯ktəvərwɛkər/ (pl: -s) pathogen

het **ziekteverzuim** /zi̯ktəvərzœym/ absence through illness; absenteeism

de **ziektewet** /zi̯ktəwɛt/ (Dutch) Health Law: *in de ~ lopen* be on sickness benefit (*or:* sick pay); [Am] be (out) on sick leave

de **ziel** /zil/ (pl: -en) soul: *zijn ~ en zaligheid voor iets over hebben* sell one's soul for sth.; *zijn ~ ergens in leggen* put one's heart and soul into sth.; *hoe meer ~en, hoe meer vreugd* the more the merrier

het **zielenheil** /zi̯lə(n)hɛil/ salvation (of one's soul)

de **zielenpiet** /zi̯ləpit/ (pl: -en) [inform] poor soul

zielig /zi̯ləɣ/ (adj, adv) **1** pitiful, pathetic: *ik vind hem echt ~* I think he's really pathetic; *wat ~!* how sad! **2** petty

zielloos /zi̯los/ (adj) **1** lifeless, inanimate **2** soulless

zielsbedroefd /zilzbədru̯ft/ (adj) brokenhearted, heart-broken

zielsgelukkig /zilsɣəlʏkəɣ/ (adj) ecstatic, blissfully happy

zielsveel /zi̯lsfel/ (adv) deeply, dearly: *~ van iem. houden* love s.o. (with) heart and soul

zieltogend /zi̯ltoɣənt/ (adj) moribund

¹**zien** /zin/ (zag, heeft gezien) **1** see: *ik zie het al voor me* I can just see it **2** look: *Bernard zag zo bleek als een doek* Bernard was (*or:* looked) as white as a sheet **3** look (out)

²**zien** /zin/ (zag, heeft gezien) **1** see: [fig] *iem. niet kunnen ~* not be able to stand (the sight of) s.o.; *zich ergens laten ~* show one's face somewhere; *waar zie je dat aan?* how can you tell?; *ik zie aan je gezicht dat je liegt* I can tell by the look on your face that you are lying; *tot ~s* goodbye; *het niet meer ~ zitten* have had enough (of it); not be able to see

one's way out (of a situation); *zie je, ziet u?* you see?; see? **2** see (to it): *je moet maar ~ hoe je het doet* you'll just have to manage ‖ *dat ~ we dán wel weer* we'll cross that bridge when we come to it

zienderogen /zindəro̯ɣə(n)/ (adv) visibly

de **ziener** /zi̯nər/ (pl: -s) seer

de **zienswijze** /zi̯nswɛizə/ (pl: -n) view

de **zier** /zir/ [inform] the least bit: *het kan mij geen ~ schelen* I couldn't care less

ziezo /zizo̯/ (int) there (we, you are)

de **zigeuner** /siɣønər/ (pl: -s) Gypsy

zigzag /zɪɣsɑɣ/ (adv) zigzag

zigzaggen /zɪɣsɑɣə(n)/ (zigzagde, heeft/is gezigzagd) zigzag

de ¹**zij** /zɛi/ (pl: zijden) side: *~ aan ~* side by side

het ²**zij** /zɛi/ (pl: zijden) silk

³**zij** /zɛi/ (pers pron) **1** she **2** they [pl]

de **zijaanzicht** /zɛi̯anzɪɣt/ (pl: -en) side-view

de **zijde** /zɛi̯də/ (pl: zijden) **1** side: *op zijn andere ~ gaan liggen* turn over; *van vaders ~* from one's father's side **2** silk

zijdeachtig /zɛi̯dəɑɣtəɣ/ (adj) silky

zijdelings /zɛi̯dəlɪŋs/ (adj, adv) indirect

zijden /zɛi̯də(n)/ (adj) silk

de **zijderups** /zɛi̯dərʏps/ (pl: -en) silkworm

de **zijdeur** /zɛi̯dør/ (pl: -en) side door

zijig /zɛi̯əɣ/ (adj) silky

de **zijinstromer** /zɛi̯ɪnstromər/ (pl: -s) **1** lateral entry teacher **2** [Belg] s.o. receiving further education

de **zijkamer** /zɛi̯kamər/ (pl: -s) room at (*or:* to) the side

de **zijkant** /zɛi̯kɑnt/ (pl: -en) side

de **zijlijn** /zɛi̯lɛin/ (pl: -en) **1** branch (line) **2** sideline; touchline

het ¹**zijn** /zɛin/ being, existence

²**zijn** /zɛin/ (was, is geweest) be: *er ~ mensen die …* there are people who …; *wat is er?* what's the matter?; what is it?; *we ~ er* here we are; *dat ~ mijn ouders* those are my parents; *dát is nog eens lopen* (now) that's what I call walking; *die beker is van tin* that cup is made of pewter; *als ik jou was, zou ik …* if I were you, I would …; *er was eens een koning …* once (upon a time) there was a king … ‖ *hij is voetballen* he is (out) playing football; *als het ware* as it were, so to speak

³**zijn** /zɛin/ (aux vb, was, is geweest) **1** have: *er waren gunstige berichten binnengekomen* favourable reports had come in **2** be: *hij is ontslagen* he has been fired

⁴**zijn** /zɛin/ (poss pron) his, its, one's: *vader ~ hoed* father's hat; *dit is ~ huis* this is his house; *ieder het ~e geven* give every man his due

het **zijpad** /zɛi̯pɑt/ (pl: -en) side path

de **zijrivier** /zɛi̯rivir/ (pl: -en) tributary

het/de **zijspan** /zɛi̯spɑn/ (pl: -nen) sidecar

de **zijspiegel** /zɛi̯spiɣəl/ (pl: -s) wing mirror

het **zijspoor** /zɛi̯spor/ (pl: zijsporen) siding: *iem. op een ~ brengen (zetten)* put s.o. on the sidelines; sideline s.o.

de **zijstraat** /zɛɪstrat/ (pl: -straten) side street: *ik noem maar een* ~ just to give an example

de **zijtak** /zɛɪtɑk/ (pl: -ken) **1** side branch **2** branch

zijwaarts /zɛɪwarts/ (adj, adv) sideward, sideways

de **zijweg** /zɛɪwɛx/ (pl: -en) side road

de **zijwind** /zɛɪwɪnt/ (pl: -en) side wind, crosswind

zilt /zɪlt/ (adj) [form] salt(y); briny

het **zilver** /zɪlvər/ silver

het/de **zilverdraad** /zɪlvərdrat/ **1** silver wire **2** silver thread

zilveren /zɪlvərə(n)/ (adj) **1** silver **2** silver(y)

zilverkleurig /zɪlvərklørəx/ (adj) silver(y)(-coloured)

de **zilvermeeuw** /zɪlvərmew/ (pl: -en) herring gull

het **zilverpapier** /zɪlvərpapir/ silver paper, silver foil

de **zilversmid** /zɪlvərsmɪt/ (pl: -smeden) silversmith

de **zilverspar** /zɪlvərspar/ (pl: -ren) silver fir

het **zilveruitje** /zɪlvərœycə/ (pl: -s) pearl onion, cocktail onion

de **zilvervliesrijst** /zɪlvərvlisrɛɪst/ brown rice

de **Zimbabwaan** /zɪmbɑpwan/ (pl: Zimbabwanen) Zimbabwean

Zimbabwaans /zɪmbɑpwans/ (adj) Zimbabwean

Zimbabwe /zɪmbɑpwə/ Zimbabwe

de **zin** /zɪn/ (pl: -nen) **1** sentence **2** senses: *bij ~nen komen* come to; come to one's senses **3** mind: *zijn eigen ~ doen* do as one pleases; *zijn ~nen op iets zetten* set one's heart on sth. **4** liking: *ergens (geen) ~ in hebben* (not) feel like sth.; *het naar de ~ hebben* find sth. to one's liking; *~ of geen ~* whether you like it or not **5** sense, meaning: *in de letterlijke ~ van het woord* in the literal sense of the word **6** sense, point || *kwaad in de ~ hebben* be up to no good

zindelijk /zɪndələk/ (adj) toilet-trained; clean; house-trained

zingen /zɪŋə(n)/ (zong, heeft gezongen) sing: *zuiver* (or: *vals*) ~ sing in (or: out) of tune

de **zingeving** /zɪnɣevɪŋ/ giving meaning (to)

het **zink** /zɪŋk/ zinc

¹**zinken** /zɪŋkə(n)/ (adj) zinc

²**zinken** /zɪŋkə(n)/ (zonk, is gezonken) sink: *diep gezonken zijn* have fallen low

de **zinkput** /zɪŋkpʏt/ (pl: -ten) cesspit, cesspool

zinloos /zɪnlos/ (adj, adv) **1** meaningless **2** useless, futile: *er is ~ om ...* there's no sense (or: point) (in) ...(-ing)

de **zinloosheid** /zɪnloshɛit/ **1** meaninglessness **2** uselessness

het **zinnebeeld** /zɪnəbelt/ (pl: -en) symbol

zinnelijk /zɪnələk/ (adj, adv) sensual

zinnen /zɪnə(n)/ (zinde, heeft gezind): *dat zinde haar helemaal niet* she did not like that at all; *op wraak* ~ be intent (or: bent) on revenge

zinnenprikkelend /zɪnə(n)prɪkələnt/ (adj) titillating

zinnig /zɪnəx/ (adj) sensible: *het is moeilijk daar iets ~s over te zeggen* it's hard to say anything meaningful about that

de **zinsbegoocheling** /zɪnzbəɣoxəlɪŋ/ (pl: -en) illusion

de **zinsbouw** /zɪnzbɑu/ sentence structure

het **zinsdeel** /zɪnzdel/ (pl: -delen) part (of a, the sentence); tag

de **zinsnede** /zɪnsnedə/ (pl: -n) phrase

de **zinsontleding** /zɪnsontledɪŋ/ (pl: -en) parsing (down to the level of the clause)

zinspelen /zɪnspelə(n)/ (zinspeelde, heeft gezinspeeld) allude (to), hint (at)

de **zinspeling** /zɪnspelɪŋ/ (pl: -en) allusion (to), hint

het **zinsverband** /zɪnsfərbɑnt/ context

het **zintuig** /zɪntœyx/ (pl: -en) sense

zintuiglijk /zɪntœyɣlək/ (adj, adv) sensual, sensory

zinvol /zɪnvol/ (adj) significant; advisable; a good idea

het **zionisme** /zijonɪsmə/ Zionism

het **zipbestand** (pl: -en) zip file

zippen /zɪpə(n)/ (zipte, heeft gezipt) zip, pack, compress

de **zit** /zɪt/ sit

het **zitbad** /zɪdbɑt/ (pl: -en) hip bath

de **zitbank** /zɪdbɑŋk/ (pl: -en) sofa, settee

de **zithoek** /zɪthuk/ (pl: -en) sitting area

het **zitje** /zɪcə/ (pl: -s) **1** sit(-down); seat **2** table and chairs

de **zitkamer** /zɪtkamər/ (pl: -s) living room

de **zitplaats** /zɪtplats/ (pl: -en) seat

de **zit-slaapkamer** /zɪtslapkamər/ (pl: -s) bedsitting-room; [Am] one-room apartment, studio apartment

zitten /zɪtə(n)/ (zat, heeft gezeten) **1** sit: *blijf* ~ a) stay sitting (down); b) remain seated; ~ *blijven* repeat a year; *gaan* ~ a) sit down; b) take a seat; *zit je goed? (lekker?)* are you comfortable?; *aan de koffie* ~ be having coffee; *waar zit hij toch?* where can he be?; *ernaast* ~ be wrong, be out; be off (target); *wij* ~ *nog midden in de examens* we are still in the middle of the exams; *zonder benzine* ~ be out of petrol; *(bijna) zonder geld* ~ have run short of money **2** be: *op een kantoor* ~ be (or: work) in an office **3** fit: *goed* ~ be a good fit **4** be (... -ing), sit (... -ing): *we* ~ *te eten* we are having dinner (or: lunch); *in zijn eentje* ~ *zingen* sit singing to o.s. || *met iets blijven* ~ be left (or: stuck) with sth.; *laat maar* ~ that's all right; (let's) forget it; *hij heeft zijn vrouw laten* ~ he has left his wife (in the lurch); *met iets* ~ be at a loss (what to do) about sth.; *hoe zit het (dan)* **met** *…?* what about … (then)?; [sport] *de* **bal** *zit* it's a goal!, it has (gone) in!, it's in the back of the net!; *het* **blijft** *niet ~* it won't stay put; *hoe zit* **dat** *in elkaar?* how does it (all) fit together?; how does that work?; *daar zit wat* **in** you (may) have sth. there; there's sth. in that; *onder de modder ~* be covered with mud; *het zit* **er** *(dik)* **in** there's a good chance (of that (happening)); *eruit halen wat* **erin** *zit* make the most (out) of sth.; *dat zit wel* **goed (snor)** that will be all right; *alles zit hem* **mee** (or: **tegen**) everything is going his way (*or*: against him); *hij zit overal* **aan** he cannot leave anything alone; *achter de meisjes* **aan** *~* chase ((around) after) girls; *mijn taak zit* **er** *weer* **op** that's my job out of the way

de **zittenblijver** /zɪ̱tə(n)blɛivər/ (pl: -s) repeater, pupil who stays down a class

zittend /zɪ̱tənt/ (adj) **1** sitting, seated **2** sedentary **3** incumbent

de **zitting** /zɪ̱tɪŋ/ (pl: -en) **1** seat **2** session, meeting

het **zitvlak** /zɪ̱tflɑk/ (pl: -ken) seat, bottom

het **zitvlees** /zɪ̱tfles/: *geen ~* **hebben** not be able to sit still

¹**zo** /zo/ (adv) **1** so, like this (*or*: that), this way, that way: *zó* **doe** *je dat!* that's the way you do it!; *zó* **is** *het!* that's the way it is!; *als dat zo* **is** *…* if that's the case …; *zo* **zijn** *er niet veel* there aren't many like that; *zo* **iets** *geks heb ik nog nooit gezien* I've never seen anything so crazy; *zij heeft er toch zo een hekel aan* she really hates it; *een jaar* **of** *zo* a year or so **2** as, so: *het is allemaal niet zo* **eenvoudig** it's not as simple as it seems (*or*: as all that); *half zo* **lang** (or: **groot**) half as long (*or*: big); *hij is niet zo* **oud** *als ik* he is not as old as I am; *zo* **goed** *als ie kon* as well as he could; *zo* **maar** just like that; without so much as a by-your-leave; *zo* **nu** *en dan* every now and then **3** right away: *ik* **ben** *zo terug* I'll be back right away; *zo* **juist** just now ‖ *het* **was** *maar zo zo* it was just so-so

²**zo** /zo/ (conj) if: *zo* **ja**, *waarom; zo* **nee**, *waarom niet* if so, why; if not, why not; *je zult je huiswerk maken, zo* **niet**, *dan krijg je een aantekening* you must do your homework, otherwise you'll get a bad mark

³**zo** /zo/ (int) well, so: *goed zo, Jan!* well done, John!; *o zo!* so there; *zo, dat is dat* well (then), that's that; *mijn vrouw heeft een nieuwe computer aangeschaft! zo!* my wife has bought herself a new computer. Really?

het **zoab** /zo̱ɑp/ porous asphalt

zoal /zo̱ɑl/ (adv): *wat* **heeft** *hij ~* **meegebracht?** what (kind of things) did he bring with him?

zoals /zo̱ɑls/ (conj) **1** like: *~* **gewoonlijk** as usual **2** as: *~ je* **wilt** as (*or*: whatever) you like

¹**zodanig** /zodɑ̱nəx/ (dem pron) such: *als ~ as*

²**zodanig** /zo̱dɑnəx/ (adv) so (much)

zodat /zodɑ̱t/ (conj) so (that), (so as) to: *ik zal het eens tekenen, ~ je kunt zien wat ik bedoel* I'll draw it so (that) you can see what I mean

de **zode** /zo̱də/ (pl: -n) turf: *dat* **zet** *geen ~n aan de dijk* that's no use, that won't get us anywhere

zodoende /zodu̱ndə/ (adv) (in) this, (in) that way; that's why, that's the reason

zodra /zodra̱/ (conj) as soon as: *~ ik geld heb, betaal ik u* I'll pay you as soon as I have the money; *~ hij opdaagt* the moment he shows up

zoek /zuk/ (adj) missing, gone: *~* **raken** get lost ‖ *op ~ gaan (zijn) naar iets* look for sth.; *op ~ naar het geluk* in pursuit of happiness; *het eind is ~* then there is no way out, then it's hopeless

de **zoekactie** /zu̱kɑksi/ (pl: -s) search (operation)

zoeken /zu̱kə(n)/ (zocht, heeft gezocht) **1** look for, search for: *we moeten een* **uitweg** *~* we've got to find a way out; *zoek je* **iets?** have you lost sth.?; *hij wordt gezocht (wegens diefstal)* he is wanted (for theft) **2** look for, search for, be after: *jij hebt hier* **niets** *te ~* you have no business (being) here; *zoiets had ik* **achter** *haar niet gezocht* I hadn't expected that of her

het **zoeklicht** /zu̱klɪxt/ (pl: -en) searchlight, spotlight

de **zoekmachine** /zu̱kmɑʃinə/ (pl: -s) search engine

zoekmaken /zu̱kmakə(n)/ (maakte zoek, heeft zoekgemaakt) **1** mislay, lose **2** waste (on)

het **zoekplaatje** /zu̱kplacə/ (pl: -s) [roughly] (picture) puzzle

zoekraken /zu̱krakə(n)/ (raakte zoek, is zoekgeraakt) get mislaid, be misplaced

de **zoektocht** /zu̱ktɔxt/ (pl: -en) search (for), quest (for)

de **Zoeloe** /zu̱lu/ (pl: -s) Zulu

zoemen /zu̱mə(n)/ (zoemde, heeft gezoemd) buzz

de **zoemer** /zu̱mər/ (pl: -s) buzzer

de **zoemtoon** /zu̱mton/ (pl: -tonen) buzz; hum; tone; signal

de **zoen** /zun/ (pl: -en) kiss

zoenen /zu̱nə(n)/ (zoende, heeft gezoend) kiss

zoet /zut/ (adj) **1** sweet: *lekker ~* nice and sweet **2** sweet, good: *iem. ~* **houden** keep s.o. happy (*or*: quiet)

de **zoetekauw** /zu̱təkɑu/ (pl: -en) sugar lover, s.o. with a sweet tooth

zoeten /zu̱tə(n)/ (zoette, heeft gezoet) sweeten

het **zoethoudertje** /zu̱thɑudərcə/ (pl: -s) sop

het **zoethout** /zu̱thɑut/ liquorice

zoetig /zutəx/ (adj) sweetish

de **zoetigheid** /zutəxhɛit/ (pl: -heden) sweet(s)

het **zoetje** /zucə/ (pl: -s) sweetener

zoetsappig /zutsɑpəx/ (adj, adv) namby-pamby, sugary

de **zoetstof** /zutstɔf/ (pl: -fen) sweetener

het **¹zoetzuur** /zutsyr/ (sweet) pickles

²zoetzuur /zutsyr/ (adj) **1** slightly sour (or: sharp) **2** pickled; sweet-and-sour

zoeven /zuvə(n)/ (zoefde, heeft/is gezoefd) whizz (past)

zo-even /zoevə(n)/ (adv) see zojuist

zogeheten /zoɣəhetə(n)/ (adj, adv) so-called

zogen /zoɣə(n)/ (zoogde, heeft gezoogd) breastfeed

zogenaamd /zoɣənamt/ (adj, adv) so-called, would-be: ze **was ~ verhinderd** sth. supposedly came up (to prevent her from coming)

zogezegd /zoɣəzɛxt/ (adv) as it were, so to speak: het **is ~ een kwajongen** he's what you'd call a young brat

zoiets /zoits/ (adv): ~ heb ik nog nooit gezien I have never seen anything like it; er is ook nog ~ als there is such a thing as

zojuist /zojœyst/ (adv) just (now)

¹zolang /zolɑŋ/ (adv) meanwhile, meantime

²zolang /zolɑŋ/ (conj) as long as: (voor) ~ het **duurt** [iron] as long as it lasts

de **zolder** /zɔldər/ (pl: -s) attic, loft

de **zoldering** /zɔldərɪŋ/ (pl: -en) see zolder

de **zolderkamer** /zɔldərkamər/ (pl: -s) attic room, room in the loft

de **zoldertrap** /zɔldərtrap/ (pl: -pen) attic stairs (or: ladder)

zomaar /zomar/ (adv) just (like that), without (any) warning: ~ **ineens** suddenly; **waarom** doe je dat? ~ why do you do that? just for the fun of it

de **zombie** /zɔmbi/ (pl: -s) zombie

de **zomer** /zomər/ (pl: -s) summer: **van (in)** de ~ in the summer

de **zomeravond** /zoməravɔnt/ (pl: -en) summer('s) evening

de **zomerdag** /zomərdɑx/ (pl: -en) summer('s) day

zomers /zomərs/ (adj) summery

de **zomerspelen** /zomərspelə(n)/ (pl) summer games, Summer Olympics

de **zomertijd** /zomərtɛit/ summer(time); summer time

de **zomervakantie** /zomərvakɑnsi/ (pl: -s) summer holiday

de **zon** /zɔn/ (pl: -nen) sun: de ~ **gaat op** (or: **gaat onder**) the sun is rising (or: setting); er is niets nieuws **onder** de ~ there is nothing new under the sun; af en toe ~ sunny periods

zo'n /zon/ (dem pron) **1** such (a): in ~ **geval** zou ik niet gaan I wouldn't go if that were the case **2** such (a): ik heb ~ **slaap** I am so sleepy

3 just like **4** about **5** one of those ‖ ~ **beetje** more or less; ik vind haar ~ **meid** I think she's a terrific girl

de **zonaanbidder** /zɔnambɪdər/ (pl: -s) sun-worshipper

de **zondaar** /zɔndar/ (pl: -s) sinner

de **zondag** /zɔndɑx/ (pl: -en) Sunday

¹zondags /zɔndɑxs/ (adj) Sunday

²zondags /zɔndɑxs/ (adv) on Sundays

het **zondagskind** /zɔndɑxskɪnt/ (pl: -eren) Sunday's child

de **zondagsrust** /zɔndɑxsrʏst/ Sunday('s) rest

de **zondagsschool** /zɔndɑxsxol/ (pl: -scholen) Sunday school

de **zonde** /zɔndə/ (pl: -n) **1** sin **2** shame: het zou ~ **van** je tijd zijn it would be a waste of time

de **zondebok** /zɔndəbɔk/ (pl: -ken) scapegoat, whipping boy

zonder /zɔndər/ (prep) without ‖ ~ **meer** just like that; of course; without delay

de **zonderling** /zɔndərlɪŋ/ (pl: -en) strange character, odd character

de **zondeval** /zɔndəval/ fall

zondig /zɔndəx/ (adj, adv) sinful

zondigen /zɔndəɣə(n)/ (zondigde, heeft gezondigd) sin

de **zondvloed** /zɔntflut/ Flood

de **zone** /zɔ:nə/ (pl: -s) zone; belt

het **zonenummer** /zɔ:nənʏmər/ (pl: -s) [Belg] area code

zonet /zonɛt/ (adv) [inform] just (now): hij **is ~ thuisgekomen** he('s) just got home (now)

de **zonkracht** /zɔnkrɑxt/ sunpower

het **zonlicht** /zɔnlɪxt/ sunlight

zonnebaden /zɔnəbadə(n)/ (zonnebaadde, heeft gezonnebaad) sunbathe

de **zonnebank** /zɔnəbɑŋk/ (pl: -en) sunbed, solarium

de **zonnebloem** /zɔnəblum/ (pl: -en) sunflower

de **zonnebrand** /zɔnəbrɑnt/ sunburn

de **zonnebrandolie** /zɔnəbrɑntoli/ sun(tan) oil

de **zonnebril** /zɔnəbrɪl/ (pl: -len) sunglasses

de **zonnecel** /zɔnəsɛl/ (pl: -len) solar cell

de **zonnecollector** /zɔnəkɔlɛktɔr/ (pl: -s, -en) solar collector

de **zonne-energie** /zɔnəenɛrʒi/ solar energy

de **zonnehemel** /zɔnəhemɘl/ (pl: -s) sunbed

zonneklaar /zɔnəklar/ (adj) obvious

de **zonneklep** /zɔnəklɛp/ (pl: -pen) (sun) visor

zonnen /zɔnə(n)/ (zonde, heeft gezond) sunbathe

het **zonnepaneel** /zɔnəpanel/ (pl: -panelen) solar panel

het **zonnescherm** /zɔnəsxɛrm/ (pl: -en) (sun)blind; parasol

de **zonneschijn** /zɔnəsxɛin/ sunshine

de **zonneslag** /zɔnəslɑx/ (pl: -en) sunstroke

de **zonnesteek** /zɔnəstek/ (pl: -steken) sunstroke: een ~ **krijgen** get sunstroke het **zonnestelsel** /zɔnəstɛlsəl/ (pl: -s) solar system

de **zonnestraal** /zɔnəstral/ (pl: -stralen) ray of sun(shine)

het **zonnetje** /zɔnəcə/ (pl: -s) **1** little sun; [fig] little sunshine: [fig] *ze **is** het ~ in huis* she is our little sunshine **2** sun(shine): *iem. in het ~ zetten* make s.o. the centre of attention

de **zonnewijzer** /zɔnəwɛizər/ (pl: -s) sundial

zonnig /zɔnəx/ (adj) sunny: *een ~e **toekomst*** a bright future

de **zonsondergang** /zɔnsɔndərɣaŋ/ (pl: -en) sunset

de **zonsopgang** /zɔnsɔpxaŋ/ (pl: -en) sunrise

de **zonsverduistering** /zɔnsfərdœystərɪŋ/ (pl: -en) eclipse of the sun

de **zonwering** /zɔnwerɪŋ/ awning, sunblind; (venetian) blind

de **zoo** /zo/ (pl: -s) zoo

het **zoogdier** /zoɣdir/ (pl: -en) mammal

de **zooi** /zoj/ (pl: -en) [inform] **1** mess **2** heap, load

de **zool** /zol/ (pl: zolen) **1** sole **2** insole

de **zoölogie** /zooloɣi/ zoology

zoölogisch /zooloɣis/ (adj) zoological

de **zoom** /zom/ (pl: zomen) **1** hem **2** edge

de **zoomlens** /zumlɛns/ (pl: -lenzen) zoom lens

de **zoon** /zon/ (pl: zonen, -s) son: *Angelo is de jongste* ~ Angelo is the youngest (*or:* younger) son; *de oudste* ~ **a)** the oldest son; **b)** the elder son; **c)** the eldest son

het **zootje** /zocə/ (pl: -s) [inform] **1** heap, load: *het hele* ~ the whole lot; *een ~ ongeregeld* a mixed bag; a motley crew **2** mess

de **zorg** /zɔrx/ (pl: -en) **1** care, concern: *iets met ~ behandelen* handle sth. carefully **2** concern, worry: *geen ~en hebben* have no worries; *dat is een (hele) ~ minder* that's (quite) a relief; *zich ~en maken over* worry about; *'t zal mij een ~ wezen, mij een ~* I couldn't care less

zorgelijk /zɔrɣələk/ (adj) worrisome, alarming

zorgeloos /zɔrɣəlos/ (adj, adv) carefree

de **zorgeloosheid** /zɔrxələshɛit/ freedom from care (*or:* worry)

zorgen /zɔrɣə(n)/ (zorgde, heeft gezorgd) **1** see to, take care of; provide; supply: *voor het eten* ~ see to the food; *daar moet jij voor* ~ that's your job **2** care for, look after, take care of **3** see (to), take care (to)

het **zorgenkind** /zɔrɣə(n)kɪnt/ (pl: -eren) problem child; source of concern

de **zorgplicht** /zɔrxplɪxt/ duty to provide for

de **zorgsector** /zɔrxsɛktɔr/ (pl: -s, -en) social service sector

de **zorgtoeslag** /zɔrxtuslax/ health care allowance

het **zorgverlof** /zɔrxfərlɔf/ care leave

de **zorgverzekeraar** /zɔrxfərzekərar/ (pl: -s) health insurer, health insurance company

de **zorgverzekering** /zɔrxfərzekərɪŋ/ (pl: -en) health insurance, medical insurance

zorgvuldig /zɔrxfʏldəx/ (adj, adv) careful, meticulous, painstaking: *een ~ onderzoek* a careful (*or:* thorough) examination

de **zorgvuldigheid** /zɔrxfʏldəxhɛit/ care, carefulness, precision

zorgwekkend /zɔrxwɛkənt/ (adj) worrisome, alarming

zorgzaam /zɔrxsam/ (adj, adv) careful, considerate: *een ~ huisvader* a caring father

de **¹zot** /zɔt/ fool, idiot

²zot /zɔt/ (adj, adv) crazy, idiotic; silly

het **¹zout** /zaut/ (pl: -en) (common) salt

²zout /zaut/ (adj) **1** salty **2** salted

zoutarm /zautarm/ (adj) low-salt

zouteloos /zautəlos/ (adj) insipid, flat, dull

zouten /zautə(n)/ (zoutte, heeft gezouten) salt

het **zoutje** /zaucə/ (pl: -s) salt(y) biscuit, cocktail biscuit: *Japanse ~s* Japanese rice crackers, senbei

zoutloos /zautlos/ (adj) salt-free

de **zoutzak** /zautsak/ (pl: -ken) salt-bag: *hij zakte als een ~ in elkaar* he collapsed (like a burst balloon)

het **zoutzuur** /zautsyr/ hydrochloric acid

zoveel /zovel/ (num) **1** as much, as many: *net ~* just as much (*or:* many); *dat is twee-maal ~* that's twice as much (*or:* many) **2** so, so that much (*or:* many): *om de ~ dagen* every so many days; *niet zóveel* not (as much as) that

zoveelste /zovelstə/ (num) such-and-such; umpteenth

¹zover /zovɛr/ (adv) so far, this far, that far: *ben je* ~? (are you) ready?; *het is* ~ the time has come, here we go!

²zover /zovɛr/ (conj) as far: *voor ~ ik weet niet* not to my knowledge, not that I know of; *in ~re* insofar, insomuch

zowaar /zowar/ (adv) actually

zowat /zowat/ (adv) [inform] almost: *ze zijn ~ even groot* they're about the same height

zowel /zowɛl/ (adv) both, as well as: *~ de mannen als de vrouwen* both the men and the women; the men as well as the women

z.o.z. /zɛtozɛt/ (abbrev) *zie ommezijde* p.t.o., please turn over

zozeer /zozer/ (adv) so much (so): *dat niet ~* not that so much, not so much that; *~ dat …* so much so that …

zozo /zozo/ (adv) so-so

z.s.m. (abbrev) *zo spoedig mogelijk* asap, as soon as possible

de **zucht** /zʏxt/ (pl: -en) **1** desire, longing, craving **2** sigh: *een diepe ~ slaken* heave a deep sigh; *een ~ van verlichting slaken* breathe (*or:* heave) a sigh of relief

zuchten /zʏxtə(n)/ (zuchtte, heeft gezucht) sigh

zuid /zœyt/ (adj, adv) south, south(ern);

southerly

Zuid-Afrika /zœyta̱frika/ South Africa

de **Zuid-Afrikaan** /zœytafrika̱n/ (pl: Zuid-Afrikanen) South African

het ¹**Zuid-Afrikaans** /zœytafrika̱ns/ Afrikaans

²**Zuid-Afrikaans** /zœytafrika̱ns/ (adj)
1 South African **2** Afrikaans

Zuid-Amerika /zœytame̱rika/ South America

de **Zuid-Amerikaan** /zœytamerika̱n/ (pl: Zuid-Amerikanen) South American

Zuid-Amerikaans /zœytamerika̱ns/ (adj) South American

¹**zuidelijk** /zœy̱dələk/ (adj) **1** southern **2** south(ern); southerly

²**zuidelijk** /zœy̱dələk/ (adv) (to the) south, southerly, southwards

het **zuiden** /zœy̱də(n)/ south: **ten** ~ (van) (to the) south (of)

de **zuidenwind** /zœy̱də(n)wɪnt/ (pl: -en) south (or: southern, southerly) wind

de **zuiderbreedte** /zœy̱dərbretə/ southern latitude: **op** *4°* ~ at a latitude of 4° South

de **zuiderburen** /zœy̱dərbyrə(n)/ (pl) neighbours to the south

de **zuiderkeerkring** /zœy̱dərkerkrɪŋ/ tropic of Capricorn

Zuid-Europa /zœytøro̱pa/ Southern Europe

Zuid-Europees /zœytørope̱s/ (adj) Southern European

Zuid-Holland /zœytho̱lɑnt/ South Holland

Zuid-Hollands /zœytho̱lɑnts/ (adj) South Holland

Zuid-Korea /zœytkore̱ja/ South Korea

de **Zuid-Koreaan** /zœytkoreja̱n/ (pl: Zuid-Koreanen) South Korean

Zuid-Koreaans /zœytkoreja̱ns/ (adj) South Korean

de **zuidkust** /zœy̱tkʏst/ (pl: -en) south(ern) coast

¹**zuidoost** /zœyto̱st/ (adj) south-east(ern); south-easterly

²**zuidoost** /zœyto̱st/ (adv) south-east(wards), to the south-east

Zuidoost-Azië /zœytosta̱zijə/ South-East Asia

¹**zuidoostelijk** /zœyto̱stələk/ (adj) south-east(ern); south-easterly

²**zuidoostelijk** /zœyto̱stələk/ (adv) (to the) south-east, south-easterly

het **zuidoosten** /zœyto̱stə(n)/ south-east; South-East

de **zuidpool** /zœy̱tpol/ South Pole

de **Zuidpool** /zœy̱tpol/ Antarctic

de **zuidpoolcirkel** /zœytpo̱lsɪrkəl/ Antarctic Circle

het **zuidpoolgebied** /zœytpo̱lɣəbit/ Antarctic, South Pole

Zuid-Sudan South Sudan

de ¹**Zuid-Sudanees** (pl: Zuid-Sudanezen)

South Sudanese

²**Zuid-Sudanees** (adj) South Sudanese

de **zuidvrucht** /zœy̱tfrʏχt/ (pl: -en) subtropical fruit

¹**zuidwaarts** /zœy̱twarts/ (adj) southward, southerly

²**zuidwaarts** /zœy̱twarts/ (adv) south-(wards)

¹**zuidwest** /zœytwɛ̱st/ (adj) south-west(ern); south-westerly

²**zuidwest** /zœytwɛ̱st/ (adv) south-west(-wards), to the south-west

¹**zuidwestelijk** /zœytwɛ̱stələk/ (adj) south-west(ern); south-westerly

²**zuidwestelijk** /zœytwɛ̱stələk/ (adv) (to the) south-west, south-westerly, south-west-wards

het **zuidwesten** /zœytwɛ̱stə(n)/ south-west; South-West

de **zuidwester** /zœytwɛ̱stər/ (pl: -s) **1** south-wester **2** sou'wester

de **zuigeling** /zœy̱ɣəlɪŋ/ (pl: -en) infant, baby

¹**zuigen** /zœy̱ɣə(n)/ (zoog, heeft gezogen) suck (on, away at)

²**zuigen** /zœy̱ɣə(n)/ (zoog, heeft gezogen) **1** suck; nurse **2** vacuum, hoover

de **zuiger** /zœy̱ɣər/ (pl: -s) piston

de **zuigfles** /zœy̱χflɛs/ (pl: -sen) feeding bottle

de **zuiging** /zœy̱ɣɪŋ/ (pl: -en) suction

de **zuigkracht** /zœy̱χkrɑχt/ **1** suction (power, force) **2** attraction

de **zuignap** /zœy̱χnɑp/ (pl: -pen) sucker

het/de **zuigtablet** /zœy̱χtablɛt/ (pl: -ten) lozenge

de **zuil** /zœyl/ (pl: -en) pillar, column, pile

zuinig /zœy̱nəχ/ (adj, adv) **1** economical, frugal, thrifty; sparing: ~ **op** *iets zijn* be careful about sth. **2** economical; efficient: *een motor* ~ **afstellen** tune (up) an engine to run efficiently

de **zuinigheid** /zœy̱nəχhɛit/ economy, frugality, thrift(iness)

¹**zuipen** /zœy̱pə(n)/ (zoop, heeft gezopen) [inform] booze ‖ *zich* **zat** ~ get sloshed (or: plastered)

²**zuipen** /zœy̱pə(n)/ (zoop, heeft gezopen) [inform] drink: *die auto zuipt* **benzine** that car just eats up petrol

de **zuiplap** /zœy̱plɑp/ (pl: -pen) [inform] boozer, drunk(ard)

de **zuippartij** /zœy̱pɑrtɛi/ (pl: -en) [inform] drinking bout (or: spree)

het/de **zuivel** /zœy̱vəl/ dairy produce, dairy products

de **zuivelfabriek** /zœy̱vəlfabrik/ (pl: -en) dairy factory, creamery

het **zuivelproduct** /zœy̱vəlprodʏkt/ (pl: -en) dairy product

¹**zuiver** /zœy̱vər/ (adj) **1** pure: *van* ~ *leer* genuine leather **2** clear, clean, pure **3** correct, true, accurate: *een* ~ *schot* an accurate shot

²**zuiver** /zœy̱vər/ (adv) **1** purely **2** [mus] in

tune

zuiveren /zœyvərə(n)/ (zuiverde, heeft gezuiverd) clean, purify; clear; cleanse: *de lucht ~* clear the air; *zich ~ van een verdenking* clear o.s. of a suspicion

de **zuiverheid** /zœyvərhɛit/ purity; soundness; accuracy

de **zuivering** /zœyvərɪŋ/ (pl: -en) purification

de **zuiveringsinstallatie** /zœyvərɪŋsɪnstala(t)si/ (pl: -s) purification plant; sewage-treatment plant

¹**zulk** /zʏlk/ (dem pron) such: *~e zijn* er ook that kind also exists

²**zulk** /zʏlk/ (adv) such: *het zijn ~e lieve mensen* they're such nice people

zullen /zʏlə(n)/ (aux vb, zou) **1** shall; will; should; would: *maar het zou nog erger worden* but worse was yet to come; *dat zul je nu altijd zien!* isn't that (just) typical!; *wat zou dat?* so what?, what's that to you? **2** will, would, be going (*or:* about) to: *zou je denken?* do you think (so)?; *als ik het kon, zou ik het doen* I would (do it) if I could; *hij zou fraude gepleegd hebben* he is said to have committed fraud; *dat zal vorig jaar geweest zijn* that would be (*or:* must have been) last year; *wie zal het zeggen?* who's to say?, who can say?; *zou hij ziek zijn?* can he be ill? (*or:* sick?); *dat zal wel* I bet it is; I suppose it will; I dare say

de **zult** /zʏlt/ brawn; [Am] headcheese

de **zuring** /zyrɪŋ/ sorrel

de ¹**zus** /zʏs/ (pl: -sen) sister; sis

²**zus** /zʏs/ (adv) so: *mijnheer ~ of zo* Mr so-and-so, Mr something-or-other

het **zusje** /zʏʃə/ (pl: -s) sister, sis; little sister

de **zuster** /zʏstər/ (pl: -s) **1** sister **2** nurse

de **zusterstad** /zʏstərstɑt/ (pl: -steden) twin town

het ¹**zuur** /zyr/ (pl: zuren) **1** acid **2** [roughly] pickles; pickled vegetables (*or:* onions) **3** heartburn, acidity (of the stomach)

²**zuur** /zyr/ (adj, adv) **1** sour: *de melk is ~* the milk has turned sour **2** acid

de **zuurkool** /zyrkol/ sauerkraut

de **zuurpruim** /zyrprœym/ (pl: -en) sourpuss, crab (apple)

de **zuurstof** /zyrstɔf/ oxygen

het **zuurstofmasker** /zyrstɔfmɑskər/ (pl: -s) oxygen mask

de **zuurstok** /zyrstɔk/ (pl: -ken) stick of rock

het **zuurtje** /zyrcə/ (pl: -s) acid drop

zuurverdiend /zyrvərdint/ (adj) hard-earned

de **zwaai** /zwaj/ (pl: -en) swing, sweep; sway; wave

de **zwaaideur** /zwajdør/ (pl: -en) swing-door

zwaaien /zwajə(n)/ (zwaaide, heeft/is gezwaaid) swing, sway; wave; flourish; brandish; wield: *met zijn armen ~* wave one's arms ǁ *er zal wat ~* there'll be the devil to pay

het **zwaailicht** /zwajlɪxt/ (pl: -en) flashing light

de **zwaan** /zwan/ (pl: zwanen) swan

het **zwaantje** /zwancə/ [Belg] motorcycle policeman

¹**zwaar** /zwar/ (adj, adv) **1** heavy, rough; full-bodied; strong: *dat is tien kilo ~* that weighs ten kilos; *~der worden* put on (*or:* gain) weight; *twee pond te ~* two pounds overweight (*or:* too heavy) **2** difficult, hard: *zware ademhaling* hard breathing, wheezing; *een zware bevalling* a difficult delivery; *een ~ examen* a stiff (*or:* difficult) exam; *hij heeft het ~* he is having a hard time of it **3** heavy, serious: *~ verlies* a heavy loss **4** heavy; deep

²**zwaar** /zwar/ (adv) heavily, heavy, hard, seriously, badly: *~ gewond* badly (*or:* seriously, severely) wounded ǁ *ergens te ~ aan tillen* attach too much importance to sth., make heavy weather of sth.; *het ~ te pakken hebben* **a)** have it bad(ly); **b)** have a bad case

zwaarbeladen /zwarbəladə(n)/ (adj) heavy laden, heavily laden

zwaarbewolkt /zwarbəwɔlkt/ (adj) overcast

het **zwaard** /zwart/ (pl: -en) sword

de **zwaardvis** /zwartfɪs/ (pl: -sen) swordfish

zwaargebouwd /zwarɣəbɑut/ (adj) heavily built; heavy-set; large-boned, thickset

zwaargewapend /zwarɣəwapənt/ (adj) heavily armed

de ¹**zwaargewicht** /zwarɣəwɪxt/ [boxer] heavyweight

het ²**zwaargewicht** /zwarɣəwɪxt/ heavyweight

zwaargewond /zwarɣəwɔnt/ (adj) badly, seriously wounded (*or:* injured)

zwaarmoedig /zwarmudəx/ (adj) melancholy, depressed: *~ kijken* look melancholy (*or:* depressed)

de **zwaarmoedigheid** /zwarmudəxhɛit/ **1** depressiveness, melancholy **2** melancholia; depression **3** melancholy, gloom, dejection

de **zwaarte** /zwartə/ **1** heaviness, weight **2** weight, size, strength

de **zwaartekracht** /zwartəkrɑxt/ gravity, gravitation

het **zwaartepunt** /zwartəpʏnt/ centre, central point, main point

zwaarwegend /zwarweɣənt/ (adj) weighty, important

zwaarwichtig /zwarwɪxtəx/ (adj, adv) weighty, ponderous

de **zwabber** /zwɑbər/ (pl: -s) mop

zwabberen /zwɑbərə(n)/ (zwabberde, heeft gezwabberd) mop

de **zwachtel** /zwɑxtəl/ (pl: -s) bandage

de **zwager** /zwaɣər/ (pl: -s) brother-in-law

zwak /zwɑk/ (adj, adv) **1** weak, feeble: *de zieke is nog ~ op zijn benen* the patient is still shaky on his legs **2** weak; delicate: *een ~ke gezondheid hebben* be in poor health **3** weak, poor, bad: *~ zijn in iets* be bad (*or:*

poor) at sth., be weak in sth. **4** weak, vulnerable **5** weak, insubstantial; poor **6** weak, faint || *een ~ voor iem. hebben* have a soft (*or:* tender) spot for s.o.

zwakbegaafd /zwɑgbəɣɑft/ (adj) retarded

de **zwakheid** /zwɑkhɛit/ (pl: -heden) weakness, failing

de **zwakkeling** /zwɑkəlɪŋ/ (pl: -en) weakling

de **zwakstroom** /zwɑkstrom/ low-voltage current, weak current

de **zwakte** /zwɑktə/ (pl: -s, -n) *see* zwakheid

zwakzinnig /zwɑksɪnəɣ/ (adj) mentally handicapped

de **zwakzinnigheid** /zwɑksɪnəɣhɛit/ mental defectiveness (*or:* deficiency)

zwalken /zwɑlkə(n)/ (zwalkte, heeft gezwalkt) drift about, wander

de **zwaluw** /zwɑlyw/ (pl: -en) swallow: *één ~ maakt nog geen zomer* one swallow does not make a summer

de **zwam** /zwɑm/ (pl: -men) fungus

zwammen /zwɑmə(n)/ (zwamde, heeft gezwamd) [inform] drivel, jabber

de **zwamneus** /zwɑmnøs/ (pl: -neuzen) [inform] gasbag, windbag

de **zwanenhals** /zwanə(n)hɑls/ (pl: -halzen) U-trap, gooseneck

de **zwanenzang** /zwanə(n)zɑŋ/ swan song

de **zwang** /zwɑŋ/: *in ~ zijn* be in vogue, be fashionable, be in fashion

zwanger /zwɑŋər/ (adj) pregnant, expecting

de **zwangerschap** /zwɑŋərsxɑp/ (pl: -pen) pregnancy

de **zwangerschapsgymnastiek** /zwɑŋərsxɑpsɣɪmnɑstik/ antenatal exercises

de **zwangerschapsonderbreking** /zwɑŋərsxɑpsɔndərbrekɪŋ/ (pl: -en) termination of pregnancy, abortion

de **zwangerschapstest** /zwɑŋərsxɑpstɛst/ (pl: -s) pregnancy test

het **zwangerschapsverlof** /zwɑŋərsxɑpsfərlɔf/ maternity leave

zwart /zwɑrt/ (adj, adv) **1** black, dark: *een ~e bladzijde in de geschiedenis* a black page in history; *~e goederen* black-market goods **2** black, dirty: *iem. ~ maken* blacken s.o.'s reputation || *~ op wit* in writing, in black and white

het **zwartboek** /zwɑrdbuk/ (pl: -en) black book

de **zwartepiet** /zwɑrtəpit/ (pl: -en) knave (*or:* jack) of spades

zwartgallig /zwɑrtxɑləɣ/ (adj) melancholic, morbid

de **zwarthandelaar** /zwɑrthɑndəlar/ (pl: -s, -handelaren) black marketeer, profiteer

de **zwartkijker** /zwɑrtkɛikər/ (pl: -s) **1** pessimist, worrywart **2** TV licence dodger

zwartmaken /zwɑrtmakə(n)/ (maakte zwart, heeft zwartgemaakt): *iem. ~* blacken s.o.'s good name (*or:* someone's character)

zwart-op-wit /zwɑrtɔpwɪt/ (adv) in black and white, in writing

zwartrijden /zwɑrtrɛidə(n)/ (reed zwart, heeft zwartgereden) **1** evade paying road tax; [Am] evade paying highway tax **2** dodge paying the fare

de **zwartrijder** /zwɑrtrɛidər/ (pl: -s) **1** road-tax dodger **2** fare-dodger

het **zwartwerk** /zwɑrtwɛrk/ moonlighting

zwartwerken /zwɑrtwɛrkə(n)/ (werkte zwart, heeft zwartgewerkt) moonlight, work on the side

zwart-wit /zwɑrtwɪt/ (adv) black-and-white

de **zwavel** /zwavəl/ sulphur

het **zwaveldioxide** /zwavəldijɔksidə/ sulphur dioxide

het **¹zwavelzuur** /zwavəlzyr/ sulphuric acid

²zwavelzuur /zwavəlzyr/ (adj) sulphuric acid

Zweden /zwedə(n)/ Sweden

de **Zweed** /zwet/ (pl: Zweden) Swede, Swedish woman

Zweeds /zwets/ (adj) Swedish

de **zweefduik** /zwevdœyk/ (pl: -en) [sport] swallow dive; [Am] swan dive

de **zweefmolen** /zwefmolə(n)/ (pl: -s) whirligig

de **zweeftrein** /zweftrɛin/ levitation train, maglev train

zweefvliegen /zwefliɣə(n)/ (zweefvliegde, heeft gezweefvliegd) glide

de **zweefvlieger** /zwefliɣər/ (pl: -s) glider pilot

het **zweefvliegtuig** /zwefliɣtœyx/ (pl: -en) glider

de **zweefvlucht** /zweflyxt/ (pl: -en) glide

de **zweem** /zwem/ trace, hint: *zonder een ~ van twijfel* without a shadow of a doubt

de **zweep** /zwep/ (pl: zwepen) whip, lash; crop

de **zweepslag** /zwepslɑɣ/ (pl: -en) **1** lash, whip(lash) **2** whiplash (injury)

de **zweer** /zwer/ (pl: zweren) ulcer; abscess; boil

het **zweet** /zwet/ sweat: *het ~ breekt hem uit* he's in a (cold) sweat; *baden in het ~* swelter

de **zweetband** /zwedbɑnt/ (pl: -en) sweatband

de **zweetdruppel** /zwedrɥpəl/ (pl: -s) drop (*or:* bead) of sweat

de **zweethanden** /zwethɑndə(n)/ (pl) sweaty hands

de **zweetlucht** /zwetlyxt/ body odour

de **zweetvoeten** /zwetfutə(n)/ (pl) sweaty feet

zwelgen /zwɛlɣə(n)/ (zwolg/zwelgde, heeft gezwolgen) wallow

zwellen /zwɛlə(n)/ (zwol, is gezwollen) swell: *doen ~* a) swell; b) belly, billow; c) bulge

de **zwelling** /zwɛlɪŋ/ (pl: -en) swell(ing)

het **zwembad** /zwɛmbɑt/ (pl: -en) (swimming) pool

de **zwemband** /zwɛmbɑnt/ (pl: -en) water ring

het **zwembandje** /zwɛmbɑncə/ (pl: -s) spare tyre, love handles

de **zwembroek** /zwɛmbruk/ (pl: -en) bathing trunks, swimming trunks

het **zwemdiploma** /zwɛmdiploma/ swimming certificate

zwemen /zwemə(n)/ (zweemde, heeft gezweemd) incline to, tend to

de **zwemles** /zwɛmlɛs/ swimming lesson: *op ~ zitten* take swimming lessons

zwemmen /zwɛmə(n)/ (zwom, heeft/is gezwommen) swim: *verboden te ~* no swimming allowed; *gaan ~* go for a swim

de **zwemmer** /zwɛmər/ (pl: -s) swimmer

het **zwempak** /zwɛmpɑk/ (pl: -ken) swimming suit, swimsuit

het **zwemvest** /zwɛmvɛst/ (pl: -en) life jacket (*or:* vest)

het **zwemvlies** /zwɛmvlis/ (pl: -vliezen) **1** web **2** flipper

de **zwemvogel** /zwɛmvoɣəl/ (pl: -s) web-footed bird

de **zwemwedstrijd** /zwɛmwɛtstrɛit/ (pl: -en) swimming competition (*or:* contest)

de **zwendel** /zwɛndəl/ swindle, fraud

de **zwendelaar** /zwɛndəlɑr/ (pl: -s) swindler, fraud

zwendelen /zwɛndələ(n)/ (zwendelde, heeft gezwendeld) swindle

de **zwengel** /zwɛŋəl/ (pl: -s) handle; crank

zwenken /zwɛŋkə(n)/ (zwenkte, is gezwenkt) swerve; [shipp] sheer: *naar rechts ~* swerve to the right

¹**zweren** /zwerə(n)/ (zwoor/zweerde, heeft gezworen) ulcerate; fester

²**zweren** /zwerə(n)/ (zwoer, heeft gezworen) swear; vow: *ik zou er niet op durven ~* I wouldn't take an oath on it; *ik zweer het (je)* I swear (to you)

de **zwerfkat** /zwɛrfkɑt/ (pl: -ten) stray cat

het **zwerfkind** /zwɛrfkɪnt/ (pl: -eren) young vagrant, vagrant child, runaway

de **zwerftocht** /zwɛrftɔχt/ (pl: -en) ramble; wandering

het **zwerfvuil** /zwɛrfœyl/ (street) litter

de **zwerm** /zwɛrm/ (pl: -en) swarm; flock

zwermen /zwɛrmə(n)/ (zwermde, heeft gezwermd) swarm

zwerven /zwɛrvə(n)/ (zwierf, heeft gezworven) **1** wander, roam, rove **2** tramp (about), knock about **3** lie about

de **zwerver** /zwɛrvər/ (pl: -s) **1** wanderer, drifter **2** tramp, vagabond

zweten /zwetə(n)/ (zweette, heeft gezweet) sweat

zweterig /zwetərəχ/ (adj) sweaty

zwetsen /zwɛtsə(n)/ (zwetste, heeft gezwetst) blather; boast; brag: *hij kan enorm ~* he talks a lot of hot air

de **zwetser** /zwɛtsər/ (pl: -s) boaster, bragger

zweven /zwevə(n)/ (zweefde, heeft gezweefd) **1** be suspended: *boven een afgrond ~* hang over an abyss **2** float; glide **3** hover

zwevend /zwevənt/ (adj) **1** floating: *een ~ plafond* a false ceiling **2** floating: *~e kiezer* floating voter

zweverig /zwevərəχ/ (adj) **1** woolly, free-floating **2** dizzy

zwichten /zwɪχtə(n)/ (zwichtte, is gezwicht) yield, submit; give in: *voor de verleiding ~* yield to the temptation

zwiepen /zwipə(n)/ (zwiepte, heeft gezwiept) bend: *de takken zwiepten in de wind* the branches swayed in the wind

de **zwier** /zwir/: *aan de ~ gaan* go on a spree

zwieren /zwirə(n)/ (zwierde, heeft/is gezwierd) sway, reel; whirl

zwierig /zwirəχ/ (adj, adv) elegant, graceful; dashing; flamboyant

het ¹**zwijgen** /zwɛiɣə(n)/ silence: *het ~ verbreken* break the silence; *er het ~ toe doen* let sth. pass

²**zwijgen** /zwɛiɣə(n)/ (zweeg, heeft gezwegen) be silent: *~ als het graf* be silent as the grave; *zwijg!* hold your tongue!, be quiet!

het **zwijggeld** /zwɛiɣɛlt/ (pl: -en) hush money

de **zwijgplicht** /zwɛiɣplɪχt/ oath of secrecy

zwijgzaam /zwɛiɣsam/ (adj) silent, incommunicative, reticent

de **zwijm** /zwɛim/: *in ~ liggen* be in a dead faint; *in ~ vallen* go off in a swoon

zwijmelen /zwɛimələ(n)/ (zwijmelde, heeft gezwijmeld) swoon

het **zwijn** /zwɛin/ (pl: -en) swine: *een wild ~* a wild boar

zwijnen /zwɛinə(n)/ (zwijnde, heeft gezwijnd) [inform] be lucky

de **zwijnenstal** /zwɛinə(n)stɑl/ (pl: -len) pigsty

zwikken /zwɪkə(n)/ (zwikte, is gezwikt) sprain, wrench

de **Zwitser** /zwɪtsər/ (pl: -s) Swiss

Zwitserland /zwɪtsərlɑnt/ Switzerland

Zwitsers /zwɪtsərs/ (adj) Swiss

zwoegen /zwuɣə(n)/ (zwoegde, heeft gezwoegd) **1** plod; drudge, slave (away); toil; labour **2** heave, pant

zwoel /zwul/ (adj) sultry; muggy

het **zwoerd** /zwurt/ (pl: -en) rind

English–Dutch

a

411 [Am; inform] info, gegevens: *the ~ on s.o.* (or: *sth.*) de gegevens van, over iem. (or: iets)

¹**a** (n) **1** a, A **2** de eerste, de hoogste (rang/graad), eersteklas ‖ *A-1* prima, eersteklas

²**a** (art) **1** een **2** per: *five times a day* vijf keer per dag **3** dezelfde, hetzelfde: *all of an age* allemaal even oud

AA 1 *Automobile Association* [roughly] ANWB **2** [Am] *Alcoholics Anonymous* AA

AA-patrol wegenwacht

ab [inform] *abdominal muscle* buikspier

¹**abandon** (n) ongedwongenheid, vrijheid: *with ~* uitbundig

²**abandon** (vb) **1** in de steek laten, aan zijn lot overlaten: *~ a baby* een baby te vondeling leggen; *the order to ~ ship* het bevel het schip te verlaten **2** opgeven, afstand doen van: *~ all hope* alle hoop laten varen **3** [sport] afgelasten

abandoned 1 verlaten, opgegeven **2** verdorven, losbandig, schaamteloos **3** ongedwongen, ongeremd, uitbundig

abandonment 1 achterlating; het in de steek laten **2** het prijsgeven

abate verminderen, afnemen: *the wind ~d* de wind ging liggen

abattoir slachthuisʰ, abattoirʰ

abbey 1 abdij **2** abdijkerk

abbot abt

abbreviate 1 inkorten, verkorten **2** afkorten

abbreviation 1 inkorting, verkorting **2** afkorting

ABC 1 abcʰ; alfabetʰ **2** eerste beginselen

abdicate afstand doen: *~ from the throne* troonsafstand doen

abdomen buik

abdominal buik-, onderbuik-

abduct ontvoeren, wegvoeren

abduction ontvoering, kidnapping

aberrant afwijkend, abnormaal

aberration 1 afwijking **2** afdwaling; misstap ‖ *in a moment of ~* in een vlaag van verstandsverbijstering

abhor verafschuwen, walgen van

abhorrent weerzinwekkend: *that's ~ to him* zoiets verafschuwt hij

abide blijven ‖ *~ by* a) zich neerleggen bij, zich houden aan; b) trouw blijven aan

ability bekwaamheid, vermogenʰ, bevoegdheid

abject 1 rampzalig, ellendig, miserabel: *~*

poverty troosteloze armoede **2** verachtelijk, laag

ablaze 1 in lichterlaaie: *set ~* in vuur en vlam zetten **2** schitterend, stralend

able 1 bekwaam, competent **2** in staat, de macht/mogelijkheid hebbend: *be ~ to* kunnen

able-bodied gezond van lijf en leden

ably see *able*

abnormal 1 abnormaal, afwijkend **2** uitzonderlijk

abnormality abnormaliteit; afwijking

¹**aboard** (adv) aan boord: *all ~!* instappen!

²**aboard** (prep) aan boord van

abolish afschaffen, een eind maken aan: *~ the death penalty* de doodstraf afschaffen

abolition afschaffing

abominable afschuwelijk, walgelijk: *Abominable Snowman* verschrikkelijke sneeuwman

abominate verfoeien, verafschuwen

abomination walgelijk iets, gruwel

aboriginal inheems, autochtoon, oorspronkelijk

abort [comp] afbreken

abortion 1 abortus **2** miskraam

abortive vruchteloos, mislukt

abound overvloedig aanwezig zijn, in overvloed voorkomen, wemelen (van)

¹**about** (adv) **1** ongeveer, bijna: *that's ~ it* moet het zo ongeveer zijn; *~ twenty* pence ongeveer twintig pence **2** [indicating place and direction] rond, rondom, in het rond, in de buurt: *there's a lot of flu ~* er heerst griep **3** om(gekeerd) [also fig]: *the wrong way ~* omgekeerd; *~ turn!* rechtsomkeert!; [Am] *~ face!* rechtsomkeert!

²**about** (prep) **1** rond, om … heen **2** rondom; in (de buurt van) [also fig]: *there was an air of mystery ~ the boy* de jongen had iets geheimzinnigs over zich **3** door … heen, over: *travel ~ the country* in het land rondreizen **4** over, met betrekking tot: *be quick ~ it* schiet eens wat op **5** omstreeks, omtrent, ongeveer: *~ midnight* rond middernacht ‖ *while you are ~ it* als je toch bezig bent; *what ~ it?* nou, so what?, wat wil je nu zeggen?; *what* (or: *how*) *~ a cup of coffee?* zin in een kop koffie?

about-face [Am] [also fig] totale ommekeer; draai van 180°: [mil] *~!* rechtsom(keert)!

about-turn [also fig] totale ommekeer; draai van 180°: [mil] *~!* rechtsom(keert)!

¹**above** (adv) **1** boven, hoger: *from ~* a) van boven; b) [fig] uit de hemel; *the ~* a) het bovengenoemde; b) de bovengenoemde personen **2** hoger, meer: *twenty and ~* twintig en meer; *imposed from ~* van hogerhand opgelegd

²**above** (prep) **1** boven **2** hoger dan, meer dan: *~ fifty* meer dan vijftig ‖ *~ all* vooral

aboveboard eerlijk, openlijk, rechtuit
abrasion schaafwond
¹**abrasive** (n) schuurmiddel^h
²**abrasive** (adj) **1** schurend, krassend **2** ruw, kwetsend: ~ *character* irritant karakter
abreast 1 zij aan zij, naast elkaar, op een rij: *two* ~ twee aan twee **2** in gelijke tred, gelijk, op dezelfde hoogte: *keep wages ~ of* de lonen gelijke tred doen houden met
abridge verkorten, inkorten
abroad in/naar het buitenland: *(back) from* ~ (terug) uit het buitenland
abrupt 1 abrupt, plotseling **2** kortaf
abs [inform] absoluut, echt: ~ *gorgeous* echt geweldig
ABS *Anti-lock Braking System* ABS *(anti-blokkeersysteem)*
abscess abces^h, ettergezwel^h
absence 1 afwezigheid, absentie: *he was condemned in his* ~ hij werd bij verstek veroordeeld **2** gebrek^h: *in the* ~ *of proof* bij gebrek aan bewijs
absent afwezig, absent: [mil] ~ *without leave* weggebleven zonder verlof
absentee afwezige; [educ] absent
absent-minded verstrooid, afwezig
absolute 1 absoluut, geheel, totaal: ~ *proof* onweerlegbaar bewijs **2** onvoorwaardelijk: ~ *promise* onvoorwaardelijke belofte
absolution absolutie, vergiffenis
absolve 1 vergeven, de absolutie geven **2** ontheffen, kwijtschelden: ~ *s.o. from a promise* iem. ontslaan van een belofte
absorb absorberen, (in zich) opnemen, opzuigen
absorbed geabsorbeerd: ~ *in a book* verdiept in een boek; ~ *in thought* in gedachten verzonken
absorption absorptie: *complete* ~ *in sport* volledig opgaan in sport
abstain (+ from) zich onthouden (van)
abstinence onthouding
¹**abstract** (n) **1** samenvatting, uittreksel^h **2** abstract kunstwerk^h
²**abstract** (adj) abstract, theoretisch, algemeen
³**abstract** (vb) **1** onttrekken, ontvreemden **2** afleiden **3** samenvatten
absurd absurd, dwaas, belachelijk
absurdity absurditeit; dwaasheid
abundance overvloed, weelde, menigte
abundant 1 overvloedig **2** rijk: *a river ~ in fish* een rivier rijk aan vis
¹**abuse** (n) **1** misbruik^h, verkeerd gebruik^h **2** scheldwoorden **3** mishandeling: *child* ~ kindermishandeling
²**abuse** (vb) **1** misbruiken **2** mishandelen **3** schelden, uitschelden
abusive beledigend: *become* ~ beginnen te schelden
abyss afgrond, peilloze diepte

AC *alternating current* wisselstroom
¹**academic** (n) academicus, wetenschapper
²**academic** (adj) academisch; [fig] abstract; theoretisch
academy academie, genootschap^h, school voor speciale opleiding
accede [form] **1** toestemmen: ~ *to his request* zijn verzoek inwilligen **2** aanvaarden: ~ *to the throne* de troon bestijgen **3** toetreden
¹**accelerate** (vb) sneller gaan, het tempo opvoeren, optrekken
²**accelerate** (vb) versnellen
acceleration 1 versnelling; acceleratie [car] **2** bespoediging
accelerator gaspedaal^h
¹**accent** (n) accent^h [also fig]; klemtoon, uitspraak: *the* ~ *is on exotic flowers* de nadruk ligt op exotische bloemen
²**accent** (vb) accentueren [also fig]; de klemtoon leggen op, (sterk) doen uitkomen
accept 1 aannemen, aanvaarden, accepteren: *an ~ed fact* een (algemeen) aanvaard feit; *be ~ed practice* algemeen gebruikelijk zijn **2** aanvaarden, tolereren, verdragen **3** goedvinden, goedkeuren, erkennen: *all members ~ed the proposal* alle leden namen het voorstel aan
acceptable 1 aanvaardbaar, aannemelijk **2** redelijk
acceptance 1 aanvaarding, overneming **2** gunstige ontvangst, bijval **3** instemming, goedkeuring **4** [com] accept, acceptatie
access (+ to) toegang (tot), toegangsrecht^h, toelating: *no (public)* ~ verboden toegang
accessibility toegankelijkheid
accessible (+ to) toegankelijk (voor), bereikbaar (voor); [fig] begrijpelijk (voor)
accessory 1 medeplichtige **2** accessoire
access provider internetaanbieder; internetprovider
accident 1 toeval^h, toevalligheid, toevallige omstandigheid: *by* ~ bij toeval, toevallig **2** ongeluk^h, ongeval^h: *by* ~ per ongeluk
accidental toevallig, onvoorzien, niet bedoeld: *~(ly) on purpose* per ongeluk expres
accident-prone gemakkelijk ongelukken krijgend
acclaim toejuiching, bijval, gejuich^h: *receive (critical)* ~ (door de critici) toegejuicht worden
acclamation toejuiching; gejuich^h ‖ *by* ~ bij acclamatie
acclimatize acclimatiseren
accommodate 1 huisvesten, onderbrengen **2** plaats hebben voor **3** aanpassen; (met elkaar) in overeenstemming brengen [plans, ideas]: ~ *o.s. (to)* zich aanpassen (aan)
accommodating inschikkelijk, meegaand, plooibaar
accommodation 1 logies^h; onderdak^h,

woonruimte **2** schikking: *come* to an ~ tot een vergelijk komen

accommodations [Am] **1** onderdak, verblijfplaats, logies **2** plaats, ruimte

accompaniment 1 bijkomstig verschijnsel, iets **2** [mus] begeleiding

accompany 1 begeleiden, vergezellen: *~ing letter* bijgaande brief **2** [mus] begeleiden

accomplice medeplichtige

accomplish 1 volbrengen, voltooien **2** tot stand brengen, bereiken

accomplished 1 volleerd; talentvol **2** volbracht; voltooid: ~ *fact* voldongen feit

accomplishment 1 prestatie **2** bekwaamheid, vaardigheid **3** voltooiing, vervulling

accord akkoord[h], schikking, overeenkomst, verdrag[h]: *of* one's own ~ uit eigen beweging

accordance: *in ~ with* overeenkomstig, in overeenstemming met

accordingly 1 dienovereenkomstig **2** dus

according to volgens, naar … beweert

accost aanklampen; lastigvallen

account 1 verslag[h], beschrijving, verklaring; uitleg [of behaviour]: *by all* ~s naar alles wat men hoort; *annual* ~ jaarverslag; *give* (or: *render*) *an* ~ *of* verslag uitbrengen over **2** rekening; factuur [also fig]: *settle* an ~ *with s.o.* de rekening vereffenen met iem. **3** rekenschap, verantwoording: *bring* (or: *call*) *s.o. to* ~ *for sth.* iem. ter verantwoording roepen voor iets; *give* (or: *render*) ~ *of* rekenschap afleggen over **4** beschouwing, aandacht: *take sth. into ~, take ~ of sth.* rekening houden met iets **5** belang[h], waarde, gewicht[h]: *of no ~* van geen belang **6** voordeel[h]: *put* (or: *turn*) *sth. to* (good) ~ zijn voordeel met iets doen ‖ *do* (or: *keep*) *(the) ~s* boekhouden; *on ~ of* wegens; *on no* ~ in geen geval

accountability verantwoordelijkheid, aansprakelijkheid

accountable 1 verantwoordelijk **2** verklaarbaar

accountancy accountancy, boekhouding

accountant accountant, (hoofd)boekhouder

account for 1 rekenschap geven van, verslag uitbrengen over **2** verklaren, uitleggen, veroorzaken: *his disease accounts for his strange behaviour* zijn ziekte verklaart zijn vreemde gedrag **3** vormen, uitmaken: *computer games accounted for two-thirds of his spending* computerspelletjes vormden twee derde van zijn uitgaven **4** bekend zijn: *the rest of the passengers still have to be accounted for* de overige passagiers worden nog steeds vermist

accounting period boekhoudkundige periode

accredit 1 toeschrijven; toekennen **2** accrediteren

accumulate (zich) opstapelen, (zich) ophopen: ~ *a fortune* een fortuin vergaren

accumulation 1 opeenstapeling, opeenhoping, accumulatie **2** aangroei

accumulative 1 opeenstapelend; ophopend **2** aangroeiend; vermeerderend

accuracy nauwkeurigheid, correctheid, exactheid

accurate nauwkeurig, correct

accusation beschuldiging, aanklacht

accuse beschuldigen, aanklagen

accused beschuldigd, aangeklaagd

accuser aanklager

accustom (ge)wennen, gewoon maken: *~ed to* gewend aan

ace 1 [cards] aas[+h], één; [fig] troef **2** [sport, esp tennis] ace **3** [inform] uitblinker: *an ~ at arithmetic* een hele piet in het rekenen

acerbity wrangheid, zuurheid, bitterheid

acetate acetaat[h]

[1]**ache** (n) (voortdurende) pijn: *~s and pains* pijntjes

[2]**ache** (vb) **1** (pijn) lijden [also fig] **2** pijn doen, zeer doen **3** [inform] (hevig) verlangen, hunkeren: *be aching to do sth.* staan te popelen om iets te doen; *~ for* hunkeren naar

achieve 1 volbrengen, voltooien, tot stand brengen **2** bereiken [goal etc]; presteren: ~ *success* succes behalen

achievement 1 prestatie **2** voltooiing **3** het bereiken

achiever iem. die goed presteert: *low* ~ iem. die minder presteert

Achilles heel achilleshiel; zwak punt

[1]**acid** (n) **1** zuur[h], zure vloeistof/drank **2** [inform] acid, lsd

[2]**acid** (adj) **1** zuur, zuurhoudend: ~ *rain* zure regen **2** bits, bijtend

acid test vuurproef [fig]

acknowledge 1 erkennen, accepteren **2** toegeven: ~ *sth. to s.o.* ten opzichte van iem. iets toegeven **3** ontvangst bevestigen van: *I herewith ~ (receipt of) your letter* hierbij bevestig ik de ontvangst van uw brief **4** een teken van herkenning geven aan [by means of a nod, greeting]

acknowledgement 1 erkenning, acceptatie **2** dank, bewijs[h] van dank: *in ~ of* als dank voor **3** ontvangstbevestiging, kwitantie

acne acne, jeugdpuistjes

acorn eikel

acoustic akoestisch

acoustics 1 geluidsleer **2** akoestiek [in concert hall etc]

acquaint op de hoogte brengen, in kennis stellen, vertrouwd maken: ~ *s.o. of* (or: *with*) *the facts* iem. op de hoogte stellen van de feiten

acquaintance 1 kennis, bekende **2** kennissenkring **3** bekendheid, vertrouwdheid, kennis: *have a nodding ~ with s.o.* iem. oppervlakkig kennen **4** kennismaking: *make s.o.'s ~* kennismaken met iem.

acquainted bekend; op de hoogte: *be ~ with sth.* iets kennen

acquiesce [form] (zwijgend) instemmen; zich schikken

acquiescence instemming, berusting

acquire 1 verwerven, verkrijgen, aanleren: *~d characteristics* aangeleerde eigenschappen; *it's an ~d taste* je moet het leren waarderen [food, drink, etc] **2** aanschaffen, (aan)kopen

acquisition aanwinst, verworven bezit^h, aankoop

acquisitive hebzuchtig, hebberig

acquit vrijspreken: *be ~ed (on a charge) of murder* vrijgesproken worden van moord || [form] *~ o.s. well* a) zich goed van zijn taak kwijten; b) zich goed gedragen

acquittal vrijspraak

acre 1 acre [4,047 square metres] **2** (-s) landerijen, grondgebied^h, groot gebied^h

acrid bijtend [also fig]; scherp, bitter

acrimonious bitter, scherp, venijnig

acrobat acrobaat

acrobatic 1 acrobatisch **2** soepel, lenig

acronym acroniem^h; letterwoord^h

¹across (adv) **1** [place] overdwars, gekruist: *it measured fifty yards ~* het had een doorsnede van vijftig yards **2** [place] aan de overkant **3** [direction; also fig] over, naar de overkant: *the actor came ~ well* de acteur kwam goed over (bij het publiek); *put a message ~* een boodschap overbrengen **4** [in crossword] horizontaal

²across (prep) (tegen)over [also fig]; dwars, gekruist, aan (naar) de overkant van: *look ~ the hedge* kijk over de haag; *from ~ the sea* van overzee; *the people ~ the street* a) de overburen; b) de mensen aan de overkant (van de straat)

across-the-board algemeen (geldend) [taxes etc]; voor iedereen

acrylic acryl

¹act (n) **1** handeling, daad, werk^h **2** besluit^h, bepaling, wet: *~ of Parliament* wet van het Parlement; [Am] *~ of Congress* wet van het Congres **3** akte, (proces)stuk^h **4** [theatre] bedrijf^h, akte **5** [circus] nummer^h, act **6** [inform; depr] komedie: *put on an ~* komedie spelen || [rel] *Acts* (or: *Acts of the Apostles*) Handelingen (van de Apostelen); *~ of God* overmacht, force majeure [force of nature]; *catch* (or: *take*) *s.o. in the (very) ~* iem. op heterdaad betrappen; [inform] *get in on the ~, get into the ~* meedoen (om zijn deel van de koek te hebben); [inform] *get one's ~ together* orde op zaken stellen, zijn zaakjes voor elkaar krijgen

²act (vb) **1** zich voordoen, zich gedragen: *he ~s like a madman* hij gedraagt zich als een krankzinnige **2** handelen, optreden, iets doen **3** fungeren, optreden: *~ as chairman* het voorzitterschap waarnemen **4** werken, functioneren **5** acteren, spelen **6** komedie spelen, zich aanstellen

³act (vb) **1** uitbeelden, spelen, uitspelen: *~ out one's emotions* zijn gevoelens naar buiten brengen **2** [theatre] spelen, opvoeren, acteren **3** spelen, zich voordoen als: *~ the fool* de idioot uithangen || *she doesn't ~ her age* zij gedraagt zich niet naar haar leeftijd

acting waarnemend, plaatsvervangend, tijdelijk

action 1 actie, daad, handeling, activiteit: *a man of ~* een man van de daad; *take ~* maatregelen nemen, tot handelen overgaan; *~s speak louder than words* geen woorden maar daden **2** gevechtsactie, strijd: *be killed in ~* in de strijd sneuvelen **3** proces^h, klacht, eis || *the ~ of the novel takes place in London* de roman speelt zich af in Londen

activate activeren, actief maken, in werking brengen

active 1 actief, werkend, in werking: *an ~ remedy* een werkzaam middel; *an ~ volcano* een werkende vulkaan **2** actief, bedrijvig: *lead an ~ life* een actief leven leiden **3** [econ] actief, productief || *be under ~ consideration* (ernstig) overwogen worden; [com] *~ securities* (or: *stocks*) actieve fondsen, druk verhandelde fondsen; [mil] *on ~ service* aan het front; [Am] in actieve (or: feitelijke) dienst

activity 1 activiteit, bedrijvigheid, drukte: *economic ~* conjunctuur, economische bedrijvigheid **2** werking, functie

act on 1 inwerken op, beïnvloeden **2** opvolgen, zich laten leiden door: *she acted on his advice* zij volgde zijn raad op

actor acteur [also fig]; toneelspeler

actress actrice [also fig]; toneelspeelster

actual werkelijk, feitelijk, eigenlijk: *~ figures* reële cijfers; *~ size* ware grootte; *what were his ~ words?* wat zei hij nou precies?

actuality werkelijkheid; feit^h, realiteit || *in ~* eigenlijk; in werkelijkheid

actually 1 eigenlijk, feitelijk, werkelijk **2** zowaar, werkelijk, echt: *they've ~ paid me!* ze hebben me zowaar betaald! || *You've met John, haven't you? - Actually, I haven't* Je kent John, hè? - Nee, ik ken hem niet

act up [inform] last bezorgen; haperen [of machine]; zich slecht gedragen [of children]

acumen [form] scherpzinnigheid

acupuncture acupunctuur

acute 1 acuut, ernstig, hevig **2** scherp(zinnig), fijn; gevoelig [wit, senses] || *an ~ angle* een scherpe hoek; *~ accent* accent aigu [on letter: é]

ad [inform] *advertisement* advertentie
AD *Anno Domini* n.Chr., na Christus ‖ *AD 79*
79 n.Chr.
adage adagium[h]; spreuk
adamant vastbesloten, onbuigzaam
[1]**adapt** (vb) (+ to) zich aanpassen (aan)
[2]**adapt** (vb) aanpassen, bewerken, geschikt
maken: *~ a novel* **for** *TV* een roman voor de tv
bewerken
adaptability aanpassingsvermogen[h]
adaptable buigzaam, soepel, flexibel
adaptation 1 aanpassing(sproces[h]) **2** bewerking: *an ~ of a novel by Minette Walters*
een bewerking van een roman van Minette
Walters
adapter 1 adapter; verloopstekker **2** verdeelstekker
[1]**add** (vb) **1** bijdragen **2** (op)tellen, (een) optelling maken
[2]**add** (vb) **1** toevoegen, erbij doen: *value ~ed*
tax belasting op de toegevoegde waarde,
btw **2** optellen: *~ five* **to** *three* tel vijf bij drie
op
ADD *attention deficit disorder* ADD, aan-
dachtstekortstoornis
addendum addendum[h]; aanvulling
adder adder
addict verslaafde; [fig] fanaat; enthousias-
teling
addicted verslaafd: *~ to alcohol* alcoholver-
slaafd; *~ to gambling* gokverslaafd
addiction verslaving, verslaafdheid
addictive verslavend
addition 1 toevoeging, aanwinst, bijvoegsel[h] **2** optelling: *in ~* bovendien, daarbij; *in ~*
to behalve, naast
additional bijkomend, aanvullend, extra
additive additief[h]; toevoeging
add-on 1 uitbreidingspakket[h]; aanvulling
2 randapparaat[h]
[1]**address** (n) **1** adres[h] [also comp] **2** toespraak **3** aanspreekvorm, aanspreektitel
[2]**address** (vb) **1** richten, sturen: *~ complaints*
to our office richt u met klachten tot ons bureau; *~ o.s. to* **a)** zich richten tot; **b)** zich bezighouden met, zich toeleggen op **2** adresseren **3** toespreken, een rede houden voor:
the teacher ~ed the pupils de onderwijzer
sprak tegen de leerlingen **4** aanspreken: *you*
have to ~ the judge **as** *'Your Honour'* je moet
de rechter met 'Edelachtbare' aanspreken
address bar adresbalk
address book adresboek[h]
addressee geadresseerde
[1]**add up** (vb) [inform] **1** steek houden, kloppen: *the evidence does not ~* het bewijsmateriaal deugt niet **2** (+ to) als uitkomst geven;
[fig] neerkomen (op); inhouden: *this so-called*
invention does not ~ **to** *much* deze zogenaam-
de uitvinding stelt weinig voor
[2]**add up** (vb) optellen

[1]**adept** (n) expert
[2]**adept** (adj) (+ at, in) bedreven (in), deskundig, ingewijd
adequacy geschiktheid, bekwaamheid
adequate 1 voldoende, net (goed) genoeg
2 geschikt, bekwaam
adhere 1 kleven, aankleven, vastkleven,
hechten **2** (+ to) zich houden (aan), vasthouden (aan), blijven bij
adherence het vasthouden
adherent aanhanger, voorstander, volgeling
[1]**adhesive** (n) kleefstof, plakmiddel[h], lijm
[2]**adhesive** (adj) klevend, plakkend: *~ plaster*
hechtpleister; *~ tape* plakband
adjacent 1 aangrenzend **2** nabijgelegen
adjective bijvoeglijk naamwoord[h]
[1]**adjoin** (vb) aaneengrenzen
[2]**adjoin** (vb) grenzen aan
adjourn 1 verdagen, uitstellen **2** schorsen,
onderbreken: *the court ~ed at six* het hof
ging om zes uur uiteen
adjudicate oordelen, arbitreren, jureren: *~*
(up)on a matter over een zaak oordelen
adjunct 1 toevoegsel[h], aanhangsel[h] **2** adjunct [employee, civil servant]
adjust 1 regelen, in orde brengen, rechtzetten **2** afstellen, instellen, bijstellen: *use*
button A to ~ the **volume** gebruik knop A om
de geluidssterkte in te stellen **3** taxeren;
vaststellen [damage] **4** (zich) aanpassen, in
overeenstemming brengen, harmoniseren: *~*
(o.s.) to new circumstances (zich) aan nieuwe
omstandigheden aanpassen
adjustable regelbaar, verstelbaar
adjustment 1 aanpassing **2** regeling;
schikking
[1]**ad lib** (adj) onvoorbereid, geïmproviseerd
[2]**ad lib** (vb) improviseren
[3]**ad lib** (adv) **1** ad libitum, naar believen
2 onvoorbereid, geïmproviseerd
administer 1 beheren, besturen **2** toepassen, uitvoeren: *~ justice* rechtspreken **3** toedienen, verschaffen ‖ *~ to s.o.'s needs* in iemands behoeften voorzien
administration beheer[h], administratie,
bestuur[h] ‖ *~ of an oath* afneming van een eed
Administration [Am] regering, bestuur[h],
ambtsperiode
administrative administratief, beheers-,
bestuurs-
administrator bestuurder, beheerder
admirable 1 bewonderenswaard(ig)
2 voortreffelijk, uitstekend
admiral admiraal: *Admiral of the* **Fleet** op-
peradmiraal [British Navy]
Admiralty mile zeemijl
admiration bewondering, eerbied
admire bewonderen
admirer bewonderaar, aanbidder
admissible 1 aannemelijk, aanvaardbaar,

acceptabel **2** geoorloofd [also law]; toelaatbaar

admission 1 erkenning, bekentenis, toegeving: *an ~ of guilt* een schuldbekentenis **2** toegang, toegangsprijs, entree **3** opname

¹admit (vb) **1** toelaten, ruimte laten: *these facts ~ of one interpretation only* deze feiten zijn maar voor één interpretatie vatbaar **2** toegang geven **3** erkennen, toegeven, bekennen

²admit (vb) **1** binnenlaten, toelaten: *he was ~ted to hospital* hij werd in het ziekenhuis opgenomen **2** toelaten, mogelijk maken: *his statement ~s more than one interpretation* zijn verklaring is voor meer dan één interpretatie vatbaar **3** erkennen, toegeven, bekennen: *he ~ted having lied* hij gaf toe dat hij gelogen had

admittance toegang: *no ~* geen toegang

admittedly 1 toegegeven **2** weliswaar

admonish waarschuwen, berispen

admonition waarschuwing, berisping

ad nauseam tot vervelens toe

adolescence puberteit, adolescentie

¹adolescent (n) puber, tiener, adolescent

²adolescent (adj) **1** opgroeiend **2** puberachtig, puberaal, jeugd-

adopt 1 adopteren, aannemen, (uit)kiezen **2** overnemen, aannemen: *~ an idea* een idee overnemen **3** aannemen, gebruiken, toepassen: *~ modern techniques* nieuwe technieken in gebruik nemen **4** aannemen, aanvaarden, goedkeuren: *~ a proposal* een voorstel aanvaarden

adoption 1 adoptie, aanneming **2** aanneming, het aannemen **3** gebruikʰ, toepassing **4** aanvaarding, goedkeuring, aanneming

adoptive adoptief, aangenomen, pleeg-: *an ~ child* een geadopteerd kind; *~ parents* pleegouders, adoptiefouders

adorable schattig, lief

adoration aanbidding, verering

adorbs [inform] schattig

adore 1 aanbidden, bewonderen **2** [rel] aanbidden, vereren **3** [inform] dol zijn op

adorn versieren, mooi maken

adrenaline adrenaline

adrenalized vol adrenaline

adrift 1 op drift **2** stuurloos; losgeslagen [also lit]; hulpeloos, doelloos

adroit handig: *be ~ at* (or: *in*) *carpentering* goed kunnen timmeren

adulation ophemeling; bewieroking

¹adult (n) volwassene [also animal]

²adult (adj) **1** volwassen, volgroeid, rijp **2** voor volwassenen: *~ education* volwassenenonderwijs; [euph] *~ movie* pornofilm

adulterate vervalsen, versnijden

adulterer overspelige man

adulteress overspelige vrouw

adulterous overspelig

adultery overspelʰ

adulthood volwassenheid; meerderjarigheid

¹advance (n) **1** voorschotʰ, vooruitbetaling **2** avance, eerste stappen, toenadering **3** vooruitgang [also fig]; vordering, ontwikkeling, verbetering: *in ~* a) vooraf, van tevoren [time]; b) vooruit, voorop [space]; *to be paid in ~* vooraf te voldoen

²advance (adj) vooraf, van tevoren, bij voorbaat: *~ booking* reservering (vooraf); *~ notice* vooraankondiging

³advance (vb) vooruitgaan, voortbewegen, vorderen, vooruitgang boeken: *the troops ~d against* (or: *on*) *the enemy* de troepen naderden de vijand

⁴advance (vb) **1** vooruitbewegen, vooruitbrengen, vooruitschuiven, vooruitzetten **2** promoveren, bevorderen (in rang): *~ s.o. to a higher position* iem. bevorderen **3** bevorderen; steunen [plan] **4** naar voren brengen, ter sprake brengen: *~ one's opinion* zijn mening naar voren brengen **5** voorschieten, vooruitbetalen

advanced 1 (ver)gevorderd **2** geavanceerd, modern, vooruitstrevend: *~ ideas* progressieve ideeën

advancement 1 vordering **2** bevordering, verbetering, vooruitgang

advantage 1 voordeelʰ, gunstige omstandigheid: *have the ~ of* (or: *over*) *s.o.* iets voorhebben op iem. **2** voordeelʰ, nutʰ, profijtʰ: *take (full) ~ of sth.* (gretig) gebruik (or: misbruik) maken van iets **3** overwichtʰ: *get the ~* de bovenhand krijgen **4** [tennis] voordeelʰ

advantageous 1 voordelig, nuttig, gunstig **2** winstgevend

advent aankomst, komst; nadering [of sth. or s.o. important]

Advent [rel] advent

adventure avontuurʰ, riskante onderneming

adventurer avonturier, gelukzoeker, huurling, speculant

adventurous 1 avontuurlijk, ondernemend **2** avontuurlijk, gewaagd, gedurfd

adverb bijwoordʰ

adverbial bijwoordelijke bepaling

advergame gamecommercial, advergame

adversary tegenstander, vijand

adverse 1 vijandig; *~ criticism* afbrekende kritiek **2** ongunstig, nadelig

adversity tegenslag, tegenspoed: *in (time of) ~* in (tijden van) tegenspoed

advert [inform] *advertisement* advertentie

advertise 1 adverteren, reclame maken (voor), bekendmaken, aankondigen **2** (+ for) een advertentie plaatsen (voor)

advertisement advertentie: *classified ~s* rubrieksadvertenties

advertising reclame

advice 1 raad, advies^h; *give s.o. a piece* (or: *bit*) *of* ~ iem. een advies geven; *act on* (or: *follow, take*) *s.o.'s* ~ iemands advies opvolgen; *on the doctor's* ~ op doktersadvies **2** [com] verzendadvies^h, verzendbericht^h

advisability raadzaamheid, wenselijkheid

advisable raadzaam, wenselijk

¹**advise** (vb) informeren, inlichten

²**advise** (vb) adviseren, (aan)raden: ~ *(s.o.) against* sth. (iem.) iets afraden; ~ *(s.o.) on* sth. (iem.) advies geven omtrent iets || *be well* ~*d to …* er verstandig aan doen om …

adviser adviseur, raadsman

advocacy 1 verdediging; voorspraak **2** advocatuur

¹**advocate** (n) verdediger, voorstander

²**advocate** (vb) bepleiten, verdedigen, voorstaan: *he* ~*s strong measures against truants* hij bepleit maatregelen tegen spijbelaars

¹**aerial** (n) antenne

²**aerial** (adj) lucht-, in de lucht, bovengronds

aerobatics stuntvliegen

aerobic 1 aerobic: ~ *dancing* aerobic(dansen) **2** [biology] aeroob

aerodrome vliegveld^h, (kleine) luchthaven

aeronautics luchtvaart(kunde)

aeroplane vliegtuig^h

aerosol can spuitbus

aerospace 1 ruimte; kosmos, heelal^h **2** ruimtevaartindustrie

aesthetics esthetica, schoonheidsleer, esthetiek

afar (van) ver(re), veraf, ver weg: *from* ~ van verre

affable vriendelijk; innemend

affair 1 zaak, aangelegenheid: *current* ~*s* lopende zaken, actualiteiten; *foreign* ~*s* buitenlandse zaken; *that is my* ~ dat zijn mijn zaken, dat gaat je niets aan **2** [inform] affaire, kwestie, ding^h, zaak(je^h) **3** verhouding

affect 1 voorwenden, doen alsof **2** zich voordoen als, spelen: ~ *the grieving widow* de diepbedroefde weduwe uithangen **3** (ont)roeren, aangrijpen: *his death* ~*ed me deeply* ik was diep getroffen door zijn dood **4** beïnvloeden, treffen: *how will the new law* ~ *us?* welke invloed zal de nieuwe wet op ons hebben? **5** aantasten, aanvallen: *smoking* ~*s your health* roken is slecht voor de gezondheid

affected 1 voorgewend, hypocriet: ~ *politeness* niet gemeende beleefdheid **2** gemaakt **3** ontroerd, aangedaan **4** getroffen, betrokken: *the* ~ *area* het getroffen gebied **5** aangetast: ~ *by pollution* aangetast door vervuiling

affection genegenheid: ~ *for* (or: *toward(s)*) genegenheid tot, liefde tot (or: voor)

affectionate hartelijk, warm, lief(hebbend): ~*ly (yours)* veel liefs [in letters]

affiliate (zich) aansluiten, opnemen, aannemen

affiliation connectie; band, verwantschap || *what is your religious* ~? tot welke kerk behoor je?

affinity 1 (aan)verwantschap^h **2** affiniteit, overeenkomst, sympathie: *feel* ~ *with* (or: *for*) sympathie voelen voor

affinity group belangengroep

affirm bevestigen, beamen, verzekeren

affirmation 1 bevestiging, verzekering **2** [law] belofte

¹**affirmative** (n) bevestiging: *answer in the* ~ bevestigend (*or:* met ja) antwoorden

²**affirmative** (adj) bevestigend; positief || [Am] ~ *action* voorkeursbehandeling, positieve discriminatie

¹**affix** (n) toevoegsel^h, aanhangsel^h

²**affix** (vb) toevoegen, (aan)hechten, kleven; vastmaken [also fig]: ~ *one's name to a letter* een brief ondertekenen

afflict kwellen, treffen, teisteren: *be* ~*ed with leprosy* lijden aan lepra

affliction 1 aandoening: ~*s of old age* ouderdomskwalen **2** nood; onheil^h, ramp

affluence overvloed; rijkdom, welvaart

affluent rijk, overvloedig, welvarend: *the* ~ *society* de welvaartsstaat

afford zich veroorloven, zich permitteren, riskeren: *I cannot* ~ *a holiday* ik kan me geen vakantie veroorloven

¹**affront** (n) belediging

²**affront** (vb) (openlijk) beledigen

Afghan Afghaan(se)

Afghanistan Afghanistan

afield ver (van huis); ver weg [also fig]

aflame in brand; in vuur en vlam; gloeiend [also fig]: ~ *with autumn colours* met vlammende herfstkleuren

afloat 1 vlot(tend), drijvend, varend **2** aan boord, op zee || *nasty rumours are* ~ er zijn gemene roddels in omloop

afoot [oft depr] op gang, in voorbereiding, in aantocht: *there is trouble* ~ er zijn moeilijkheden op til

aforesaid bovengenoemd

afraid bang, angstig, bezorgd: *she was* ~ *to wake her grandfather* ze durfde haar grootvader niet wakker te maken; ~ *of* sth. bang voor iets; *don't be* ~ *of asking for help* vraag gerust om hulp; *I'm* ~ *I'm late* het spijt me, maar ik ben te laat; *I'm* ~ *not* helaas niet, ik ben bang van niet; *I'm* ~ *I can't help you* ik kan u helaas niet helpen

afresh opnieuw, andermaal: *start* ~ van voren af aan beginnen

Africa Afrika

¹**African** (n) Afrikaan(se) || ~ *violet* Kaaps viooltje

²**African** (adj) Afrikaans

Afro afrokapsel^h; afrolook

¹after (adj) later, volgend

²after (adv) na, nadien, erachter: *five years ~* vijf jaar later; *shortly ~* spoedig daarna; *they lived happily ever ~* zij leefden nog lang en gelukkig

³after (prep) **1** achter, na: *cloud ~ cloud* de ene wolk na de andere; *Jack ran ~ Jill* Jack liep Jill achterna; *~ you* na u, ga je gang **2** [time] na: *day ~ day* dag in dag uit; *it's ~ two o'clock* het is over tweeën; *time ~ time* keer op keer **3** na, met uitzondering van: *the greatest (composer) ~ Beethoven* op Beethoven na de grootste (componist) **4** naar, volgens, in navolging van: *Jack takes ~ his father* Jack lijkt op zijn vader ‖ *~ all* toch, per slot (van rekening); *be ~ sth.* uit zijn op iets, iets najagen

⁴after (conj) nadat, als, toen, wanneer: *come back ~ finishing that job* kom terug als je met die klus klaar bent

aftercare nazorg

afterlife leven na de dood; hiernamaals^h

aftermath nasleep, naspel^h

afternoon middag; [Belg] namiddag [also fig]: *in* (or: *during*) *the ~* 's middags

afters toetje^h

afterthought 1 latere overweging **2** latere toevoeging, postscriptum^h

afterwards later, naderhand

again 1 opnieuw, weer, nog eens: *time and (time) ~* telkens opnieuw; *(the) same ~!* schenk nog eens in!, hetzelfde nog eens!; *be o.s. ~* hersteld zijn, er weer bovenop zijn; *back* (or: *home*) *~* weer terug (*or:* thuis); *never ~* nooit meer; *once ~* nog een keer, voor de zoveelste keer; *now and ~* nu en dan; *~ and again* telkens opnieuw **2** nogmaals ‖ *what is his name ~?* hoe heet hij ook (al) weer?

against 1 [place or direction; also fig] tegen, tegen ... aan, in strijd met: *a race ~ the clock* een race tegen de klok; *~ the current* tegen de stroom in; *evidence ~ John* bewijs-(materiaal) tegen John; *vaccination ~ the measles* inenting tegen de mazelen **2** tegenover, in tegenstelling met: *18, as ~ the 30 sold last year* 18, tegenover de 30 die vorig jaar zijn verkocht

¹age (n) **1** leeftijd, ouderdom: *be your ~!* doe niet zo kinderachtig!; *be* (or: *come*) *of ~* meerderjarig zijn (*or:* worden); *look one's ~* er zo oud uitzien als men is; *what is your ~?* hoe oud ben je?; *at the ~ of ten* op tienjarige leeftijd; *in his (old) ~* op zijn oude dag; *ten years of ~* tien jaar oud; *under ~* minderjarig, te jong **2** mensenleven^h, levensduur **3** eeuw, tijdperk^h: *the Stone Age* het stenen tijdperk, de steentijd **4** (-s) [inform] eeuwigheid: *wait for ~s* een eeuwigheid wachten; *you've been ~s* je bent vreselijk lang weggebleven

²age (vb) verouderen, ouder worden: *he has*

~d a lot hij is erg oud geworden

age bracket leeftijdsgroep

¹aged (adj) oud: *~ ten* tien jaar oud

²aged (adj) oud, (hoog)bejaard ‖ *the ~* de bejaarden

ageing veroudering(sproces)

ageism leeftijdsdiscriminatie

ageless leeftijdloos, nooit verouderend, eeuwig (jong)

agency 1 bureau^h, instantie, instelling: *travel ~* reisbureau **2** agentuur, agentschap^h, vertegenwoordiging **3** bemiddeling, tussenkomst, toedoen^h: *through* (or: *by*) *the ~ of friends* door toedoen van vrienden

agenda agenda: *the main point on the ~* het belangrijkste punt op de agenda

agent 1 agent, tussenpersoon, bemiddelaar, vertegenwoordiger: *secret ~* geheim agent **2** middel^h: *cleansing ~* reinigingsmiddel

age-old eeuwenoud

agglomeration opeenhoping, (chaotische) verzameling

aggravate 1 verergeren: *~ an illness* een ziekte verergeren **2** [inform] ergeren, irriteren

aggravation 1 verergering **2** ergernis

aggregate totaal^h: *in (the) ~* alles bij elkaar genomen, alles bij elkaar opgeteld

aggregation samenvoeging; verzameling, aggregatie: *state of ~* aggregatietoestand

aggression agressie

aggressive 1 agressief, aanvallend: *~ salesmen* opdringerige verkopers **2** ondernemend, ambitieus

aggressor aanvaller

aggrieved gekrenkt, gekwetst: *feel (o.s.) ~ at* (or: *by, over*) *sth.* zich gekrenkt voelen door iets

aghast (+ at) ontzet (door), verbijsterd, verslagen

agile lenig, beweeglijk, soepel

agility 1 behendigheid, vlugheid **2** alertheid

agitate optreden, strijden (voor/tegen): *~ for* (or: *against*) actie voeren voor (*or:* tegen)

agitated geërgerd; geagiteerd

agitation 1 actie, strijd **2** opschudding, opgewondenheid, spanning

agitator oproerkraaier

aglow gloeiend; stralend [also fig]

agnostic agnost, agnosticus

ago geleden: *ten years ~* tien jaar geleden; *not long ~* kort geleden

agog opgewonden; vol verwachting

agonize vreselijk lijden; worstelen [fig]: *~ over* zich het hoofd breken over

agonizing kwellend, hartverscheurend: *an ~ decision* een moeilijke beslissing

agony (ondraaglijke) pijn, kwelling, foltering

agony aunt [inform] Lieve Lita

agony column rubriek voor persoonlijke problemen

agrarian agrarisch; landbouw-

¹**agree** (vb) **1** akkoord gaan, het eens zijn, het eens worden, afspreken: ~ *to do sth.* afspreken iets te zullen doen; ~ *on sth.* het ergens over eens zijn; ~ *to sth.* met iets instemmen, in iets toestemmen; ~ *with s.o. about sth.* het met iem. over iets eens zijn; ~*d!* akkoord! **2** overeenstemmen, goed opschieten, passen: ~ *with* kloppen met

²**agree** (vb) **1** bepalen, overeenkomen, afspreken: ~ *a price* een prijs afspreken **2** goedkeuren, aanvaarden: ~ *a plan* een plan goedkeuren

agreeable prettig, aangenaam: *the terms are not* ~ *to us* de voorwaarden staan ons niet aan

agreement 1 overeenkomst, overeenstemming, afspraak, contract[h]: *be in* ~ *about* (or: *on, with*) 't eens zijn over, akkoord gaan met **2** instemming, goedkeuring

agriculture landbouw

agritourism agrotoerisme[h]

aground aan de grond, vast

ahead 1 voorop: [sport] *be* ~ leiden, voorstaan; *go* ~ voorop gaan **2** vooruit, voorwaarts, van tevoren, op voorhand: *full speed* ~*!* met volle kracht vooruit!; *look* (or: *plan*) ~ vooruitzien; *straight* ~ rechtdoor

ahead of voor: *the days* ~ *us* de komende dagen; ~ *his time* zijn tijd vooruit; *straight* ~ *you* recht voor je

ahoy ahoi

¹**aid** (n) **1** hulp, bijstand, assistentie: *come* (or: *go*) *to s.o.'s* ~ iem. te hulp komen; *in* ~ *of* ten dienste van; *first* ~ eerste hulp (bij ongelukken), EHBO **2** hulpmiddel[h], apparaat[h], toestel[h]: *audiovisual* ~*s* audiovisuele hulpmiddelen **3** helper, assistent

²**aid** (vb) helpen, steunen, bijstaan

aide 1 aide de camp, adjudant **2** assistent, naaste medewerker, helper

AIDS *Acquired Immune Deficiency Syndrome* aids

AIDS inhibitor aidsremmer

¹**ail** (vb) ziek(elijk) zijn, sukkelen; iets mankeren [also fig]

²**ail** (vb) schelen, mankeren

ailment kwaal, ziekte, aandoening

¹**aim** (n) **1** (streef)doel[h], bedoeling, plan[h] **2** aanleg: *take* ~ *(at)* aanleggen (op), richten (op)

²**aim** (vb) proberen, willen: ~ *to be an artist* kunstenaar willen worden; ~ *at doing sth.* iets willen doen, van plan zijn iets te doen; *what are you* ~*ing at?* wat wil je nu eigenlijk?

³**aim** (vb) richten, mikken, aanleggen: ~ *high* hoog mikken; [fig] ambitieus zijn; ~ *(a gun) at* (een vuurwapen) richten op

aimless doelloos, zinloos

¹**air** (n) **1** lucht, atmosfeer, dampkring, luchtruim[h], hemel: *in the open* ~ in de openlucht; *get some (fresh)* ~ een frisse neus halen; *by* ~ met het vliegtuig, per luchtpost **2** [radio, TV] ether: *be on the* ~ in de ether zijn, uitzenden, uitgezonden worden **3** bries(je[h]), lichte wind **4** voorkomen[h], sfeer, aanzicht[h]: *have an* ~ *of superiority* (or: *loneliness*) een superieure (or: eenzame) indruk maken **5** houding, manier van doen, aanstellerij: *give o.s.* ~*s*, *put on* ~*s* zich aanstellen, indruk proberen te maken ‖ *rumours are in the* ~ het gerucht doet de ronde; *my plans are still (up) in the* ~ mijn plannen staan nog niet vast

²**air** (vb) **1** drogen, te drogen hangen **2** luchten, ventileren **3** bekendmaken, luchten, ventileren: ~ *one's grievances* (or: *ideas*) uiting geven aan zijn klachten (or: ideeën)

air base luchtmachtbasis

airborne 1 in de lucht, door de lucht vervoerd **2** per vliegtuig getransporteerd: ~ *troops* luchtlandingstroepen

airbrush 1 spuitlakken **2** retoucheren [photo]

air corridor luchtweg; luchtcorridor

aircraft vliegtuig[h]

aircraft carrier vliegdekschip[h]

aircrew vliegtuigbemanning

airfield vliegveld[h], luchthaven

air force luchtmacht, luchtstrijdkrachten

air gun 1 luchtbuks; windbuks **2** verfspuit

air hostess stewardess

air kiss kus in de lucht

airlift luchtbrug

airline luchtvaartmaatschappij

airliner passagiersvliegtuig[h]

airmail luchtpost: *by* ~ per luchtpost

airplane [Am] vliegtuig[h]

air pollution luchtvervuiling

airport luchthaven, vliegveld[h]

air quotes luchthaakjes

air rage agressie in het vliegtuig

air raid luchtaanval

airship luchtschip[h], zeppelin

airsick luchtziek

airspace luchtruim[h] [of country]

airstrip landingsstrook

airtight luchtdicht; [fig] sluitend; onweerlegbaar: *his alibi is* ~ hij heeft een waterdicht alibi

air time 1 zendtijd **2** beltijd

airy 1 luchtig; fris **2** luchthartig, zorgeloos **3** vluchtig: ~ *promises* loze beloften

aisle 1 zijbeuk [of church] **2** gang(pad[h]); middenpad[h] [in church, train, theatre, etc] ‖ *we had them rolling in the* ~*s* het publiek lag in een deuk

aitch h: *drop one's* ~*es* de h's inslikken

ajar op een kier

akimbo (met de handen) in de zij

akin (+ to) verwant (aan), gelijk(soortig)

alabaster albast[h]: ~ *skin* albasten huid

alacrity monterheid, bereidwilligheid, enthousiasme[h]

[1]**alarm** (n) **1** alarm[h], schrik, paniek: *take* ~ *at* opschrikken van, in paniek raken bij **2** alarm[h], waarschuwing, alarmsignaal[h]: *raise* (or: *sound*) *the* ~ alarm geven **3** wekker **4** alarmsysteem[h], alarminstallatie

[2]**alarm** (vb) alarm slaan

[3]**alarm** (vb) alarmeren, opschrikken, verontrusten

alarm clock wekker: *he set the* ~ *for 6 o'clock* hij zette de wekker op zes uur

alarming alarmerend, onrustbarend, verontrustend

alas helaas

Albania Albanië

[1]**Albanian** (n) Albanees, Albanese

[2]**Albanian** (adj) Albanees

albatross albatros ‖ *an* ~ *around one's neck* een blok aan zijn been

albeit zij het: *a small difference,* ~ *an important one* een klein verschil, zij het een belangrijk verschil

album 1 album[h], fotoalbum[h], poëziealbum[h] **2** grammofoonplaat, cd

albumen eiwit[h]

alchemy alchemie

alcohol alcohol

[1]**alcoholic** (n) alcoholicus

[2]**alcoholic** (adj) alcoholisch, alcoholhoudend

alcolock alcoholslot[h]

alcopop alcopop

alder els, elzenboom

alderman [roughly] wethouder, [roughly] gedeputeerde; [Belg] [roughly] schepen

ale ale, (licht, sterk gehopt) bier[h]

[1]**alert** (n) alarm(signaal)[h], luchtalarm[h]: *on the* ~ *(for)* op zijn hoede (voor)

[2]**alert** (adj) **1** alert, waakzaam, op zijn hoede: ~ *to danger* op gevaar bedacht **2** levendig, vlug

[3]**alert** (vb) alarmeren, waarschuwen, attent maken: ~ *s.o. to the danger* iem. wijzen op het gevaar

A level *advanced level* Brits (examenvak[h] op) eindexamenniveau[h]: *pass one's* ~*s* zijn eindexamen halen, [roughly] slagen voor vwo

alga alg; zeewier[h]

algebra algebra

algebraic algebraïsch

Algeria Algerije

[1]**Algerian** (n) Algerijn(se)

[2]**Algerian** (adj) Algerijns

algorithm algoritme[h], handelingsvoorschrift[h]

[1]**alias** (n) alias, bijnaam, schuilnaam

[2]**alias** (adv) alias, anders genoemd

alibi 1 alibi[h] **2** [inform] excuus[h], uitvlucht

Alice band haarband; diadeem[+h]

[1]**alien** (n) vreemdeling, buitenlander, buitenaards wezen[h]

[2]**alien** (adj) **1** vreemd, buitenlands **2** afwijkend: ~ *to his nature* strijdig met zijn aard

alienate vervreemden; doen bekoelen [friendship]

alienation vervreemding

[1]**alight** (adj) brandend, in brand: *set* ~ aansteken

[2]**alight** (vb) afstappen, uitstappen, afstijgen: ~ *from a horse* van een paard stijgen

align 1 zich richten, op één lijn liggen **2** (+ with) zich aansluiten (bij)

alignment het op één lijn brengen, het in één lijn liggen: *out of* ~ ontzet, uit zijn verband

[1]**alike** (adj) gelijk(soortig), gelijkend: *they are very much* ~ ze lijken heel erg op elkaar

[2]**alike** (adv) gelijk, op dezelfde manier: *treat all children* ~ alle kinderen gelijk behandelen

alimony alimentatie

alive 1 levend, in leven **2** levendig, actief: ~ *and kicking* springlevend ‖ ~ *to* bewust van, op de hoogte van [a fact etc]

alkaline alkalisch; basisch

[1]**all** (n) gehele bezit[h]: *her jewels are her* ~ haar juwelen zijn haar gehele bezit

[2]**all** (pron) **1** alle(n), allemaal, iedereen: [tennis] *thirty* ~ dertig gelijk; *one* and ~, ~ *and sundry* alles en iedereen, jan en alleman; *they have* ~ *left,* ~ *of them have left* ze zijn allemaal weg **2** alles, al, allemaal: *when* ~ *is (said and) done* uiteindelijk; *it's* ~ *one* (or: *the same) to me* het kan me (allemaal) niet schelen; *above* ~ bovenal, voor alles **3** de grootst mogelijke: *with* ~ *speed* zo snel mogelijk; [inform] *of* ~ ...*!* nota bene!; *today of* ~ *days* uitgerekend vandaag **4** enig(e): *beyond* ~ *doubt* zonder enige twijfel **5** één en al; [Am] puur; zuiver: *he was* ~ *ears* hij was één en al oor; [Am] *it's* ~ *wool* het is zuivere wol **6** al(le), geheel: ~ *(the) angles (taken together) are 180°* alle hoeken van een driehoek (samen) zijn 180°; *with* ~ *my heart* van ganser harte; ~ *(the) morning* de hele morgen **7** al(le), ieder, elk: ~ *(the) angles are 60°* alle hoeken zijn 60° ‖ *once and for* ~ voorgoed, voor eens en altijd; *after* ~ per slot van rekening, toch, tenslotte; *he can't walk at* ~ hij kan helemaal niet lopen; *if I could do it at* ~ als ik het maar enigszins kon doen; [after thank you] *not at* ~ niets te danken, graag gedaan; *for* ~ *I know* voor zover ik weet; *in* ~ in 't geheel, in totaal; ~ *in* ~ al met al

[3]**all** (adv) helemaal, geheel, volledig; [inform] heel; erg: ~ *right* in orde, oké; *if it's* ~ *the same to him* als het hem niets uitmaakt; *I've known it* ~ *along* ik heb het altijd al geweten; ~ *at once* plotseling; ~ *over again* van voren

af aan; [Am] *books lay scattered* ~ **over** *(the place)* er lagen overal boeken; ~ **round** overal; [fig] in alle opzichten; ~ **too** *soon* (maar) al te gauw; *I'm* ~ **for** *it* ik ben er helemaal voor || ~ *the* **same** toch, desondanks; [inform] *it's not* ~ *that difficult* zo (vreselijk) moeilijk is het nu ook weer niet; ~ **out a)** uit alle macht; **b)** op volle snelheid; *that's Jack* ~ **over a)** [inform] dat is nou typisch Jack; **b)** hij lijkt precies op Jack

all<u>ay</u> [form] **1** verminderen, verlichten, verkleinen **2** kalmeren, (tot) bedaren (brengen): ~ *all fears* alle angst wegnemen

all but bijna, vrijwel: *he was* ~ *dead* hij was bijna dood; ~ *impossible* vrijwel onmogelijk

alleg<u>a</u>tion bewering, (onbewezen) beschuldiging

all<u>e</u>ge [form] beweren, aanvoeren: *the ~d* **thief** de vermeende dief

all<u>e</u>giance trouw, loyaliteit: *pledge* ~ *to the flag* trouw zweren aan de vlag

all<u>e</u>gory symbolische voorstelling

allel<u>u</u>ia halleluja[h]

all<u>e</u>rgic (+ to) allergisch (voor); [inform, fig] afkerig

all<u>e</u>rgy (+ to) allergie (voor)

all<u>e</u>viate verlichten, verzachten

alleви<u>a</u>tion verlichting, verzachtend middel[h]

all<u>e</u>y 1 steeg(je[h]), (door)gang **2** laan(tje[h]), pad[h] **3** kegelbaan || *blind* ~ doodlopende steeg

all<u>e</u>y cat [Am] zwerfkat

alli<u>a</u>nce 1 verdrag[h], overeenkomst, verbintenis **2** bond, verbond[h], vereniging, (bond)genootschap[h]

all<u>ie</u>d verbonden [also fig]; verenigd: *the Allied* **Forces** de geallieerden; *(closely)* ~ *to* (nauw) verwant met

all<u>i</u>gator alligator

all-<u>i</u>n [inform] *all-inclusive* all-in, alles inbegrepen, inclusief

all<u>o</u>cate toewijzen, toekennen

alloc<u>a</u>tion toewijzing

all<u>o</u>t toewijzen, toebedelen

all<u>o</u>tment 1 toegewezen deel[h], aandeel[h] **2** toewijzing, toekenning **3** perceel[h] [rented from government]; volkstuintje[h]

all-<u>ou</u>t [inform] volledig, intensief: *go* ~ alles op alles zetten

all<u>o</u>w 1 toestaan, (toe)laten, veroorloven: *no dogs ~ed* honden niet toegelaten; ~ *o.s.* zich veroorloven **2** voorzien in, mogelijk maken, zorgen voor: *the plan ~s one hour for lunch* het plan voorziet in één uur voor de lunch **3** toestaan, toestaan, toewijzen: ~ *twenty per cent* **off** *(for)* twintig procent korting geven (op) **4** toegeven, erkennen: *we must* ~ *that he is clever* we moeten toegeven dat hij slim is

all<u>o</u>wance 1 toelage, uitkering, subsidie

2 deel[h], portie, rantsoen[h] **3** vergoeding, toeslag **4** korting, aftrek || *make (an)* ~ **for,** *make* ~*(s)* **for** rekening houden met

all<u>o</u>w for rekening houden met: *allowing for his young age* gezien zijn jeugdige leeftijd

all<u>o</u>y legering, metaalmengsel[h]

all-purpose voor alle doeleinden; universeel

[1]**all r<u>i</u>ght** (adj) **1** gezond, goed, veilig, ongedeerd **2** goed (genoeg), aanvaardbaar, in orde: *his work is* ~ zijn werk is acceptabel; *it's* ~ **by** *me* van mij mag je; *if that's* ~ *with you* als jij dat goed vindt

[2]**all r<u>i</u>ght** (adv) **1** in orde, voldoende: *he's doing* ~ hij doet het aardig **2** inderdaad, zonder twijfel: *he's crazy* ~ hij is inderdaad écht gek **3** begrepen, in orde, (dat is) afgesproken

all-r<u>ou</u>nd allround, veelzijdig

All S<u>ai</u>nts' Day Allerheiligen [1 November]

All S<u>ou</u>ls' Day Allerzielen [2 November]

all-terrain geschikt voor elk terrein: ~ *bike* mountainbike; ~ *vehicle* terreinwagen

all-time van alle tijden: *an* ~ *record* een (langdurig) ongebroken record; *an* ~ *high* (or: *low*) een absoluut hoogtepunt (or: dieptepunt)

all<u>u</u>de to zinspelen op, toespelingen maken op

all<u>u</u>re aantrekkingskracht, charme

all<u>u</u>sion (+ to) zinspeling (op), toespeling

[1]**<u>a</u>lly** (n) bondgenoot, medestander, geallieerde: *the Allies* de geallieerden

[2]**all<u>y</u>** (vb) (zich) verenigen, (zich) verbinden: ~ *o.s.* **with** een verbond sluiten met

<u>a</u>lmanac almanak

alm<u>i</u>ghty 1 almachtig: *the Almighty* de Almachtige **2** [inform] allemachtig, geweldig: *an* ~ *din* een oorverdovend lawaai

<u>a</u>lmond amandel [fruit]

<u>a</u>lmost bijna, praktisch, haast: ~ *all of them* haast iedereen

alms aalmoes

<u>a</u>lmshouse hofje[h], armenhuis[h]

al<u>o</u>ft 1 omhoog; opwaarts [also fig]: *smoke kept rising* ~ er bleef maar rook opstijgen **2** [shipp] in de mast, in 't want

[1]**al<u>o</u>ne** (adj) alleen, afzonderlijk, in zijn eentje

[2]**al<u>o</u>ne** (adv) **1** slechts, enkel, alleen **2** alleen, in zijn eentje: *go it* ~ het op zijn eentje opknappen; *leave* (or: *let*) ~ met rust laten, afblijven van; *he cannot walk, let* ~ *run* hij kan niet eens lopen, laat staan rennen

[1]**al<u>o</u>ng** (adv) **1** door, verder, voort: *he brought his dog* ~ hij had zijn hond bij zich; *come* ~ kom mee; *go* ~ *(with)* meegaan (met); *I suspected it all* ~ ik heb het altijd wel vermoed; ~ *with* samen met **2** langs: *come* ~ *anytime* (je bent) altijd welkom

[2]**al<u>o</u>ng** (prep) langs, door: *flowers* ~ *the path*

bloemen langs het pad
alongside naast: ~ *the road* aan de kant van de weg
¹aloof (adj) afstandelijk, koel
²aloof (adv) op een afstand, ver: *keep* (or: *hold, stand*) ~ *(from)* zich afzijdig houden (van)
aloud hardop, hoorbaar
alp berg; alp
alphabet alfabetʰ; abcʰ [also fig]
alphabetical alfabetisch
alpha geek [inform] topnerd
alpha male alfaman; [fig] leider
alpine alpien; berg-: ~ *skiing* het alpineskiën
the **Alps** Alpen
already reeds, al (eerder)
¹Alsatian (n) **1** Elzasser, Elzassische **2** Duitse herder(shond)
²Alsatian (adj) Elzassisch
also ook, bovendien, eveneens
altar altaarʰ
altar boy misdienaar
alter 1 (zich) veranderen, (zich) wijzigen **2** [Am; inform; euph] helpen [pet]; castreren, steriliseren
alteration 1 wijziging, verandering **2** [Am; inform; euph] castratie, sterilisatie
altercation onenigheid, twist, ruzie, geruzieʰ
¹alternate (adj) afwisselend, beurtelings: *on* ~ *days* om de (andere) dag
²alternate (vb) afwisselen, verwisselen: *alternating current* wisselstroom
alternation (af)wisseling
¹alternative (n) alternatiefʰ, keuze, optie
²alternative (adj) alternatief
although hoewel, ofschoon
altitude hoogte
alto 1 altpartij, altinstrumentʰ, altstem **2** alt, altzanger(es)
altogether 1 totaal, geheel, helemaal: *at 50 he stopped working* ~ met 50 hield hij helemaal op met werken **2** in totaal, alles bij elkaar: *there were 30 people* ~ er waren in totaal 30 mensen
altruism altruïsmeʰ
aluminium aluminiumʰ
alumnus oud-student; oud-leerling, alumnus
always 1 altijd, steeds, voorgoed: *he's* ~ *complaining* hij loopt voortdurend te klagen **2** in elk geval, altijd nog: *we can* ~ *sell the boat* we kunnen altijd nog de boot verkopen
always-on: ~ *internet access* permanente internetverbinding
a.m. *ante meridiem* vm., voor de middag: *at 5* ~ om vijf uur 's ochtends
Am *America(n)*
amalgamate (doen) samensmelten, (zich) verbinden, annexeren, in zich opnemen

amass vergaren, opstapelen
¹amateur (n) amateur, liefhebber
²amateur (adj) [oft depr] amateur(s)-, amateuristisch
amaze verbazen, verwonderen, versteld doen staan
amazement verbazing, verwondering
amazing verbazingwekkend, verbazend
ambassador ambassadeur, vertegenwoordiger, (af)gezant
amber 1 amber(steen), barnsteen **2** amber(kleur); [traffic light] geelʰ, oranjeʰ
ambience sfeer, stemming, ambiance
ambiguity dubbelzinnigheid
ambiguous dubbelzinnig, onduidelijk
ambition ambitie, eerzucht
ambitious ambitieus, eerzuchtig
ambivalence ambivalentie: *feel some* ~ gemengde gevoelens hebben
ambivalent ambivalent, tegenstrijdig
¹amble (n) **1** telgang; pasgang [of horse] **2** kuierpas, kalme gang
²amble (vb) **1** in de telgang lopen **2** kuieren, op zijn gemak wandelen
ambulance ziekenwagen, ambulance
ambulant ambulant, in beweging, rondtrekkend
ambush hinderlaag, val(strik): *lie* (or: *wait*) *in* ~ in een hinderlaag liggen
amen amen, het zij zo: [fig] *say* ~ *to sth.* volledig met iets instemmen
amenable 1 handelbaar, plooibaar **2** ontvankelijk (voor): ~ *to reason* voor rede vatbaar
amend verbeteren [eg text, bill]; (bij amendement) wijzigen
amendment 1 amendementʰ **2** verbetering, rectificatie
amends genoegdoening, schadeloosstelling, compensatie: *make* ~ *for sth. to s.o.* iets weer goedmaken bij iem., iem. schadevergoeding betalen voor iets
amenity (sociale) voorziening, gemakʰ: *this house has all the amenities* dit huis is van alle gemakken voorzien
America Amerika
¹American (n) **1** Amerikaan(se): *Latin* ~ iem. uit Latijns-Amerika, Latijns-Amerikaan(se) **2** Amerikaans(-Engels)ʰ
²American (adj) Amerikaans: ~ *Indian* (Amerikaanse) indiaan
amethyst 1 amethist **2** violetʰ, violetkleur, purpervioletʰ
amiable beminnelijk, vriendelijk
amicable amicaal, vriend(schapp)elijk: *come to an* ~ *agreement* een minnelijke schikking treffen
amidst te midden van, tussen, onder
¹amiss (adj) **1** verkeerd, gebrekkig: *there is nothing* ~ *with her* ze mankeert niets **2** misplaatst, ongelegen: *an apology would not be* ~

een verontschuldiging zou niet misstaan
²**amiss** (adv) verkeerd, gebrekkig, fout(ief):
take sth. ~ iets kwalijk nemen
ammonia ammoniak
ammunition (am)munitie
amnesia amnesie, geheugenverlies^h
amnesty amnestie, generaal pardon^h
amoeba amoebe
amok: *run* ~ amok maken, als een bezetene
tekeergaan
among(st) onder, te midden van, tussen:
customs among(st) the Indians gebruiken bij de
indianen; *among(st)* **themselves** onder elkaar; *we have ten copies among(st) us* we hebben samen tien exemplaren
amoral amoreel, immoreel
amorous amoureus, verliefd
amount 1 hoeveelheid, grootte: *any* ~ *of
money* een berg geld **2** totaal^h, som, waarde:
to the ~ *of* ten bedrage van
amount to 1 bedragen, oplopen tot, bereiken: *it does not* ~ *much* het heeft niet veel
te betekenen **2** neerkomen op, gelijk staan
met: *his reply amounted to a* **refusal** zijn antwoord kwam neer op een weigering
amp [inform] **1** ampere ampère **2** *amplifier*
versterker
ampere ampère
ampersand en-teken^h [the & sign]
ample 1 ruim, groot, uitgestrekt **2** rij-
k(elijk), overvloedig: *have* ~ *resources* bemiddeld zijn
amplifier versterker
amplify 1 vergroten, vermeerderen
2 [elec] versterken
amputate amputeren, afzetten
amuse amuseren, vermaken, bezighouden:
be ~d at (or: *by, with*) sth. iets amusant vinden
amusement 1 amusement^h, vermaak^h
2 plezier^h, pret, genot^h: *watch in* ~ geamuseerd toekijken
amusement arcade automatenhal
amusing vermakelijk, amusant
an see ²*a*
anachronism anachronisme^h
anachronistic 1 anachronistisch **2** ouderwets
anaemia bloedarmoede
¹**anaesthetic** (n) verdovingsmiddel^h
²**anaesthetic** (adj) verdovend, narcotisch
anaesthetist anesthesist
anaesthetize verdoven, onder narcose
brengen
anagram anagram^h
anal anaal, aars-
analogous (+ to, with) analoog (aan),
overeenkomstig (met), parallel
analogue analoog: ~ *watch* horloge met
wijzerplaat
analogy analogie, overeenkomst: *on the* ~
of, by ~ *with* naar analogie van

analyse analyseren, ontleden, ontbinden
analysis analyse [also maths]; onderzoek^h,
ontleding
analyst analist(e), scheikundige
analytical analytisch
anarchist anarchist
anarchy anarchie
anatomy 1 (anatomische) bouw **2** anatomie, ontleding, analyse
ancestor 1 voorouder, voorvader **2** oerty-
pe^h, voorloper, prototype^h
ancestral voorouderlijk, voorvaderlijk
ancestry 1 voorgeslacht^h, voorouders,
voorvaderen **2** afkomst, afstamming
anchor anker^h: ~ *man* vaste presentator [of
news and current affairs programmes]
anchorage 1 verankering **2** ankerplaats
anchovy ansjovis
ancient antiek, klassiek, uit de oudheid: ~
history de oude geschiedenis
the **Ancients** de antieken
ancillary 1 ondergeschikt, bijkomstig: ~ *industry* toeleveringsbedrijf **2** helpend, aanvullend
and 1 en, (samen) met, en toen, dan: *children come* ~ *go* kinderen lopen in en uit; ~ *so
forth,* ~ *so* **on** enzovoort(s); ~/*or* en/of **2** [in-
tensifying or repetition] en (nog), (en) maar:
thousands ~ *thousands of people* duizenden en
nog eens duizenden mensen **3** [between
two verbs] te, om te: *try* ~ *finish it* probeer het
af te maken || *nice* ~ *quiet* lekker rustig
Andorra Andorra
¹**Andorran** (n) Andorrees, Andorrese
²**Andorran** (adj) Andorrees
androgynous 1 androgyn, hermafrodiet
2 [bot] tweeslachtig
anecdotal anekdotisch
anecdote anekdote
anemone anemoon, zeeanemoon
anew 1 opnieuw, nogmaals, weer **2** anders
angel 1 engel, beschermengel, engelbewaarder **2** schat, lieverd
angelic 1 engelachtig; hemels **2** [inform]
lief
¹**anger** (n) woede, boosheid: *be filled with* ~
at sth. woedend zijn om iets
²**anger** (vb) boos maken
anger management agressiebeheersing
¹**angle** (n) **1** hoek [also maths]; kant, uitstekende punt^h: *at an* ~ *(with)* schuin (op) **2** ge-
zichtshoek, perspectief^h; [fig] gezichtspunt^h;
standpunt^h: *look at* sth. *from a different* (or:
another) ~ iets van een andere kant bekijken
²**angle** (vb) (+ for) vissen (naar) [also fig];
hengelen (naar)
angle bracket punthaak
angler visser, hengelaar
Anglican anglicaans
anglicism anglicisme^h
angling hengelsport

Anglo-American Engels-Amerikaans; Anglo-Amerikaans

¹**Anglo-Saxon** (n) **1** Oudengels[h] **2** Angelsakser **3** (typische) Engelsman

²**Anglo-Saxon** (adj) **1** Angelsaksisch **2** [Am] Engels

³**Anglo-Saxon** (adv) Oudengels

Angola Angola

¹**Angolan** (n) Angolees, Angolese

²**Angolan** (adj) Angolees

angry boos, kwaad: be ~ about (or: at) sth. boos zijn over iets; be ~ at (or: with) s.o. boos zijn op iem.

anguish leed[h], pijn

anguished gekweld; vol angst; vol smart

angular 1 hoekig, hoekvormig, hoek- **2** kantig, met scherpe kanten

¹**animal** (n) dier[h], beest[h]

²**animal** (adj) **1** dierlijk: ~ husbandry veeteelt **2** vleselijk, zinnelijk: ~ desires vleselijke lusten

animal ambulance dierenambulance

the **animal kingdom** dierenrijk[h]

¹**animate** (adj) **1** levend, bezield **2** levendig, opgewekt

²**animate** (vb) **1** leven geven, bezielen **2** verlevendigen, opwekken **3** animeren, aanmoedigen, inspireren

animated levend(ig), bezield, geanimeerd || ~ cartoon tekenfilm

animation 1 animatiefilm, tekenfilm, poppenfilm **2** het maken van animatiefilms, animatie **3** levendigheid, opgewektheid, animo[h]

animosity vijandigheid, haat, wrok

aniseed anijszaad(je[h]), anijs

ankle enkel

anklet 1 enkelring **2** [Am] enkelsok, halve sok

annals annalen [also fig]; kronieken, jaarboeken

¹**annex** (n) **1** aanhangsel[h], addendum[h], bijlage **2** aanbouw, bijgebouw[h], dependance

²**annex** (vb) **1** aanhechten, (bij)voegen **2** annexeren, inlijven; [inform; iron] zich toe-eigenen

annexation 1 aanhechting **2** annexatie, inlijving

annihilate vernietigen; tenietdoen [also fig]

annihilation vernietiging

anniversary 1 verjaardag, jaardag, gedenkdag **2** verjaarsfeest[h], jaarfeest[h]

¹**annotate** (vb) (+ (up)on) aantekeningen maken (bij), commentaar schrijven (op)

²**annotate** (vb) annoteren

announce 1 aankondigen, bekendmaken, melden **2** omroepen

announcement aankondiging, bekendmaking, mededeling

announcer 1 omroeper **2** aankondiger

annoy 1 ergeren, kwellen, irriteren: be ~ed at sth. zich over iets ergeren; be ~ed with s.o. boos zijn op iem. **2** lastigvallen, hinderen, plagen

annoyance 1 ergernis, kwelling **2** last, hinder, plaag

¹**annual** (n) **1** eenjarige plant **2** jaarboek[h]

²**annual** (adj) **1** jaarlijks: [bookkeeping] ~ accounts jaarrekening; ~ income jaarinkomen **2** eenjarig

annuity jaargeld[h], jaarrente

annul 1 vernietigen, tenietdoen, schrappen **2** ongeldig verklaren, herroepen, annuleren

annunciation aankondiging, afkondiging

the **Annunciation** Maria-Boodschap

anoint 1 [rel] zalven **2** inwrijven, insmeren

anomaly anomalie, onregelmatigheid

anonymity anonimiteit

anonymous anoniem

anorak 1 anorak, parka **2** watje[h], nerd, studiebol, kluns

anorexic anorexiapatiënt

another 1 een ander(e), nog één **2** andere, verschillende: that's ~ matter dat is een heel andere zaak; for one reason or ~ om een of andere reden; in one way or ~ op een of andere wijze **3** nog een, een tweede, een andere: have ~ biscuit neem nog een koekje

¹**answer** (n) antwoord[h], reactie, oplossing, resultaat[h]: he gave (or: made) no ~ hij gaf geen antwoord; no ~ er wordt niet opgenomen, ik krijg geen gehoor; my only ~ to that mijn enige reactie daarop

²**answer** (vb) **1** antwoorden, een antwoord geven **2** voldoende zijn, aan het doel beantwoorden: one word would ~ één woord zou volstaan

³**answer** (vb) **1** antwoorden (op), beantwoorden, een antwoord geven op: ~ your father! geef je vader antwoord! **2** reageren op: ~ the telephone de telefoon opnemen; ~ the door de deur opendoen (als er gebeld wordt) **3** beantwoorden aan, voldoen aan: ~ the description aan het signalement beantwoorden

answerable 1 verantwoordelijk, aansprakelijk: be ~ to s.o. for sth. bij iem. voor iets verantwoording moeten afleggen **2** beantwoordbaar

¹**answer back** (vb) zich verdedigen

²**answer back** (vb) brutaal antwoorden, (schaamteloos) wat terugzeggen, tegenspreken

answer for verantwoorden, verantwoordelijk zijn voor: I can't answer for the consequences ik kan niet voor de gevolgen instaan

answering machine antwoordapparaat[h]

answerphone antwoordapparaat[h]

answer to 1 gehoorzamen: my dog answers to the name of Dixie mijn hond luistert naar de naam Dixie **2** zich verantwoorden tegen-

over: ~ the **headmaster** for your behaviour je
bij de directeur voor je gedrag verantwoorden **3** beantwoorden aan
ant mier
antagonist tegenstander; antagonist
antagonistic vijandig
antagonize zich in het harnas jagen
the **¹Antarctic** (n) **1** Antarctica, zuidpool, zuid-
poolgebiedʰ **2** Zuidelijke IJszee
²Antarctic (adj) antarctisch, zuidpool-: ~
Circle zuidpoolcirkel
antecedent iets voorafgaands, voorafgaand feitʰ: ~s antecedenten
antedate voorafgaan aan
antelope antilope
antenatal prenataal: ~ **care** zwanger-
schapszorg
antenna 1 [Am] antenne **2** voelhoorn,
(voel)spriet, antenne
anterior 1 voorste, eerste, voor- **2** voorafgaand: ~ **to** vroeger dan, voorafgaand aan
anthem lofzang: **national** ~ volkslied
anthology anthologie, bloemlezing
anthracite antracietʰ
anthropology antropologie, studie van de
mens
anti tegen, anti, tegenstander van, strijdig
met
anti-aircraft luchtdoel-; luchtafweer-
¹antibiotic (n) antibioticumʰ
²antibiotic (adj) antibiotisch
antibody antistof, antilichaamʰ
antic capriool, gekke streek
anticipate 1 vóór zijn, voorkomen, ondervangen, de wind uit de zeilen nemen **2** verwachten, tegemoet zien, hopen op: trouble is
~d men rekent op moeilijkheden **3** een
voorgevoel hebben van **4** anticiperen, vooruitlopen (op): I won't ~ ik wil niet op mijn
verhaal vooruitlopen
anticipation 1 verwachting; afwachting:
thanking you **in** ~ bij voorbaat dank **2** voorgevoelʰ, voorpret
anticlimax anticlimax
anticlockwise linksomdraaiend, tegen de
wijzers van de klok (in)
antidepressant kalmeringsmiddelʰ
antidote tegengifʰ
antifreeze antivries(middel)ʰ
antipathetic antipathiek: ~ **to** any new idea
voor geen enkel nieuw idee te vinden
antipathy antipathie, vooringenomenheid, afkeer
¹antiquarian (n) **1** oudheidkundige, oud-
heidkenner **2** antiquair **3** antiquaar, handelaar in oude boeken, prenten, enz.
²antiquarian (adj) **1** oudheidkundig **2** anti-
quarisch
antiquated ouderwets, verouderd, achterhaald
antique 1 antiek, oud **2** ouderwets

antiquities antiquiteiten, overblijfselen,
oudheden
antiquity 1 ouderdom **2** oudheid
anti-Semite antisemiet
anti-Semitism antisemitismeʰ
antiseptic antiseptisch, ontsmettend
antiskid antislip
antisocial 1 asociaal **2** ongezellig
anti-terrorist antiterreur-
antithesis antithese, tegenstelling, tegenstrijdigheid, tegengesteldeʰ
antithetic tegengesteld, tegenstrijdig
antitoxin tegengifʰ
antitrade: ~ **wind** antipassaatwind
antler geweitak: ~s geweiʰ
antsy ongedurig
anus anus, aars
anvil aambeeldʰ
anxiety bezorgdheid, ongerustheid, vrees
anxious 1 bezorgd, ongerust: you needn't
be ~ **about** me je hoeft je over mij geen zorgen te maken **2** verontrustend, zorgwekkend, beangstigend **3** [inform] verlangend:
he **was** ~ to leave hij stond te popelen om te
mogen vertrekken
¹any (pron) **1** [number or amount] enig(e),
enkele, wat: I cannot see ~ **houses** ik zie geen
huizen; have you got ~ **paper?** heb je papier?;
~ **child** can tell you that elk kind kan je dat
vertellen; I didn't get ~ ik heb er geen enkele
gehad; few, if ~ weinig of geen, zogoed als
geen **2** iem., iets, om het even wie (wat), wie
(wat) ook: ~ will **do** geef me er maar een, het
geeft niet welke
²any (adv) [in negative and interrogative
sentences] enigszins, in enig opzicht: are you
~ **happier** here? ben je hier gelukkiger?; I
cannot stand it ~ **longer** ik kan er niet meer
tegen
anybody om het even wie, wie dan ook,
iem., iedereen: she 's not just ~ ze is niet de
eerste de beste
anyhow 1 toch (maar) [at the end of a sen-
tence]: it's probably not worth it but let me see it
~ het heeft waarschijnlijk geen zin, maar laat
me het toch maar zien **2** hoe dan ook [at the
beginning of a sentence, after a pause]: ~, I
have to go now, sorry hoe dan ook, ik moet nu
gaan, het spijt me **3** ongeordend, slordig,
kriskras: he threw his clothes down just ~ hij
gooide zijn kleren zomaar ergens neer
anymore nog, meer, opnieuw, langer: it's
not hurting ~ het doet geen pijn meer
anyone see anybody
anyplace [Am; inform] waar dan ook: **sleep**
~ you like slaap waar je wilt
¹anything (n) alles, wat dan ook, wat het
ook zij
²anything (pron) om het even wat, wat dan
ook, iets, (van) alles: she didn't eat ~ ze at
niets; ~ **but** safe allesbehalve veilig; if ~ this

food is even worse dit eten is zo mogelijk nog slechter

³**anything** (adv) enigszins, in enige mate; [+ negation] bijlange na (niet): *it isn't ~ much* het heeft niet veel om het lijf

anytime [inform] wanneer (dan) ook, om het even wanneer: *he can come ~ now* hij kan nu elk ogenblik komen; *come ~ you like* kom wanneer je maar wilt

anyway 1 toch (maar): *he had no time but helped us ~* hij had geen tijd maar toch hielp hij ons **2** hoe dan ook, in ieder geval: *~, I must be off now* in ieder geval, ik moet er nu vandoor **3** eigenlijk: *why did he come ~?* waarom kwam hij eigenlijk?

¹**anywhere** (adv) **1** overal, ergens, om het even waar **2** in enigerlei mate, ergens: *she isn't ~ near as tall as me* ze is lang niet zo groot als ik

²**anywhere** (conj) waar … maar …: *go ~ you like* ga waar je maar naartoe wilt

aorta aorta

apart 1 los, onafhankelijk, op zichzelf **2** van elkaar (verwijderd), op … afstand, met … verschil: *five miles ~* op vijf mijlen (afstand) van elkaar **3** uit elkaar, aan stukken, kapot: *take ~ uit elkaar halen, demonteren || ~ from* behalve, afgezien van

apartheid apartheid

apartment 1 kamer, vertrek^h **2** appartement^h, appartementen, reeks kamers **3** [Am] flat, etage

apathetic apathisch; lusteloos

apathy apathie, lusteloosheid, onverschilligheid

¹**ape** (n) (mens)aap; [fig] na-aper

²**ape** (vb) na-apen

aperture 1 opening, spleet **2** lensopening

apex top, tip, hoogste punt^h; [fig] toppunt^h; hoogtepunt^h

apiarist imker, bijenhouder

apiculture bijenteelt

apiece elk, per stuk: *she gave us £10 ~* ze gaf ons elk £10

aplomb aplomb^h, zelfverzekerdheid

apocalyptic apocalyptisch

apogee hoogste punt^h, toppunt^h

apologetic verontschuldigend, schuldbewust

apologize zich verontschuldigen, zijn excuses aanbieden

apology verontschuldiging; *~ for absence* bericht van verhindering; *offer an ~ to s.o. for sth.* zich bij iem. voor iets verontschuldigen

apoplexy beroerte

apostle apostel

apostrophe apostrof, weglatingsteken^h

app *application* app

appal met schrik vervullen: *they were ~led at* (or: *by*) *it* ze waren er ontsteld over

appalling verschrikkelijk

apparatus apparaat^h, toestel^h, machine || *the men set up their ~* de mannen stelden hun apparatuur op

apparel [form] kleding; gewaad^h

apparent duidelijk, blijkbaar, kennelijk; *~ly he never got your letter* blijkbaar heeft hij je brief nooit ontvangen

apparition verschijning, spook^h, geest

¹**appeal** (n) **1** verzoek^h, smeekbede **2** [law] appel^h, (recht^h van) beroep^h: *lodge an ~* beroep aantekenen **3** aantrekkingskracht

²**appeal** (vb) **1** verzoeken, smeken **2** aantrekkelijk zijn voor, aanspreken, aantrekken **3** in beroep gaan, appelleren: *~ against that decision* tegen die beslissing beroep aantekenen

appealing 1 smekend, meelijwekkend **2** aantrekkelijk, aanlokkelijk

appeal to een beroep doen op; appelleren aan [feelings, common sense]: *may we ~ your generosity?* mogen wij een beroep doen op uw vrijgevigheid?

¹**appear** (vb) **1** verschijnen, voorkomen: *he had to ~ before court* hij moest voorkomen **2** opdagen **3** optreden

²**appear** (vb) **1** schijnen, lijken: *so it ~s* 't schijnt zo te zijn **2** blijken: *he ~ed to be honest* hij bleek eerlijk te zijn

appearance 1 verschijning, optreden^h: *he put in* (or: *made*) *an ~ at the party* hij liet zich even zien op het feest **2** uiterlijk^h, voorkomen^h: *~s schijn; ~s are deceptive* schijn bedriegt; *keep up ~s* de schijn ophouden

appease kalmeren, bedaren, sussen, verzoenen

appendicitis blindedarmontsteking

appendix 1 aanhangsel^h **2** [med] appendix $^{+h}$

appetite 1 eetlust, honger, trek: *lack of ~* gebrek aan eetlust **2** begeerte, zin: *whet s.o.'s ~* iem. lekker maken

appetizer 1 aperitief^h **2** voorgerecht(je)^h, hapje^h vooraf

appetizing eetlust opwekkend, smakelijk; appetijtelijk

¹**applaud** (vb) applaudisseren

²**applaud** (vb) toejuichen [also fig]; prijzen, loven

applause applaus^h, toejuiching

apple appel || *the ~ of his eye* zijn oogappel; *Big Apple* New York

applecart: *upset the ~* een streep door de rekening halen

apple-pie order: *everything is in ~* alles is volmaakt in orde

appliance 1 middel^h, hulpmiddel^h **2** toestel^h, gereedschap^h, apparaat^h

applicable 1 toepasselijk, van toepassing, bruikbaar: *not ~* niet van toepassing **2** geschikt, passend, doelmatig

applicant sollicitant, aanvrager

application 1 sollicitatie: *letter of* ~ sollicitatiebrief **2** aanvraag(formulier^h) **3** toepassing, gebruik^h: *for external* ~ *only* alleen voor
uitwendig gebruik **4** het aanbrengen [eg
unction on wound] **5** aanvraag, verzoek^h: *on*
~ op aanvraag **6** ijver, vlijt, toewijding
application software toepassingspro-
grammatuur
applied toegepast: ~ *physics* toegepaste
natuurkunde
¹**apply** (vb) **1** van toepassing zijn, betrekking
hebben (op), gelden: *these rules don't* ~ *to you*
dit reglement geldt niet voor u **2** zich richten, zich wenden: ~ *within* (or: *next door*) hier
(or: hiernaast) te bevragen **3** (+ for) solliciteren (naar), inschrijven (voor), aanvragen
²**apply** (vb) **1** aanbrengen, (op)leggen, toedienen **2** toepassen, aanwenden, gebruiken:
~ *the brakes* remmen ‖ ~ *o.s.* *(to)* zich inspannen (voor), zich toeleggen (op)
appoint 1 vaststellen, bepalen, vastleggen:
at the ~ed time op de vastgestelde tijd **2** benoemen, aanstellen
appointment 1 afspraak: *by* ~ volgens afspraak **2** aanstelling, benoeming
appraisal schatting, waardering, evaluatie
appraise schatten, waarderen, evalueren
¹**appreciate** (vb) stijgen [in price, value]
²**appreciate** (vb) **1** waarderen, (naar waarde) schatten **2** zich bewust zijn van, zich realiseren, erkennen: *you should* ~ *the risks* je
moet je bewust zijn van de risico's **3** dankbaar zijn voor, dankbaarheid tonen voor
appreciation 1 waardering, beoordeling
2 waardering, erkenning
apprehend aanhouden, in hechtenis nemen
apprehension 1 vrees, bezorgdheid: *she
had ~s for her safety and about her future* ze
maakte zich zorgen over haar veiligheid en
haar toekomst **2** aanhouding, arrestatie
apprehensive ongerust, bezorgd
apprentice leerjongen, leerling
¹**approach** (n) **1** toegang(sweg), oprit; aanvliegroute [of aeroplane] **2** aanpak, (wijze
van) benadering **3** contact^h, toenadering:
make ~es to s.o. bij iem. avances maken, met
iem. contact zoeken **4** benadering: *it's the
nearest* ~ *to …* het is bijna …, het lijkt het
meeste op …
²**approach** (vb) naderen, (naderbij) komen
³**approach** (vb) **1** naderen, komen bij
2 contact opnemen met, aanspreken, benaderen **3** aanpakken [of problem]
approbation officiële goedkeuring
¹**appropriate** (adj) geschikt, passend, toepasselijk: *where* ~ waar nodig, waar van
toepassing, in voorkomende gevallen; ~ *for,*
~ *to* geschikt voor
²**appropriate** (vb) **1** bestemmen, toewijzen
2 (zich) toe-eigenen: *he had ~d large sums to*

himself hij had zich grote bedragen toegeëigend
approval goedkeuring, toestemming: *on* ~
op zicht
¹**approve** (vb) akkoord gaan, zijn goedkeuring geven
²**approve** (vb) goedkeuren, toestemmen in,
akkoord gaan met: *an ~d contractor* een erkend aannemer
approximate bij benadering (aangegeven), naar schatting: *~ly three hours* ongeveer
drie uur
apricot abrikoos
April april
April Fools' Day één april
a priori van tevoren, vooraf
apron 1 schort^h, voorschoot^h **2** platform^h
[at airport]
apron string: *he is tied to his wife's ~s* hij
loopt aan de leiband van zijn vrouw
apt 1 geschikt, passend **2** geneigd **3** begaafd: ~ *at* goed in
aptitude 1 geschiktheid **2** neiging **3** aanleg, talent^h, begaafdheid
aquaplaning 1 het waterskiën **2** [traf]
aquaplaning^h
aquarium aquarium^h
Aquarius [astrology] (de) Waterman
aquascooter waterscooter
aquatic water-
aqueduct aquaduct^h
¹**Arab** (n) **1** Arabier, Arabische **2** Arabische
volbloed
²**Arab** (adj) Arabisch
Arabia Arabië
Arabian Arabisch
Arabic Arabisch: ~ *numerals* Arabische cijfers
¹**arable** (n) bouwland^h, landbouwgrond, ak-
kerland^h
²**arable** (adj) bebouwbaar, akker-
arbiter 1 leidende figuur, toonaangevend
iem. **2** scheidsrechter
arbitrary 1 willekeurig, grillig **2** eigenmachtig **3** scheidsrechterlijk
¹**arbitrate** (vb) arbitreren, als bemiddelaar
optreden
²**arbitrate** (vb) aan arbitrage onderwerpen,
scheidsrechterlijk (laten) regelen
arbitration arbitrage; scheidsrechterlijke
beslissing: *go to* ~ het geschil aan arbitrage
onderwerpen
arbour prieel^h
arc 1 (cirkel)boog **2** [elec] lichtboog, vlam-
boog
arcade 1 arcade, zuilengang **2** winkelgalerij
arcade game videospel^h
¹**arch** (n) **1** boog, gewelf^h, arcade: *triumphal*
~ triomfboog **2** voetholte
²**arch** (adj) ondeugend, schalks, guitig: *an* ~

glance (or: *smile*) een schalkse blik (*or:* guitig lachje)

³**arch** (vb) (+ across, over) (zich) welven (over), zich uitspannen

⁴**arch** (vb) **1** (over)welven, overspannen **2** krommen, buigen: *the cat ~ed its back* de kat zette een hoge rug op

archaeologist archeoloog, oudheidkundige

archaeology archeologie, oudheidkunde

archaic verouderd, ouderwets

archangel aartsengel

archbishop aartsbisschop

archenemy aartsvijand

archer boogschutter

archetype archetype^h; [fig] schoolvoorbeeld^h

archipelago archipel, eilandengroep

architect 1 architect **2** ontwerper **3** [fig] maker, schepper, grondlegger

architecture architectuur, bouwkunst, bouwstijl

archives 1 archief [storage location] **2** archieven [documents stored]

archivist archivaris

archway overwelfde doorgang; poort

arctic 1 (noord)pool-: *Arctic Circle* noordpoolcirkel **2** ijskoud

the **Arctic** noordpoolgebied, Arctica

ardent vurig, hevig, hartstochtelijk

ardour vurigheid, hartstocht

arduous moeilijk, zwaar, lastig

area 1 oppervlakte: *a farm of 60 square kilometres in* ~ een boerderij met een oppervlakte van 60 vierkante kilometer **2** gebied^h [also fig]; streek, domein^h **3** ruimte, plaats

area code [Am] netnummer^h

arena arena; strijdperk^h [also fig]

Argentina Argentinië

the **Argentine** Argentinië

¹**Argentinian** (n) Argentijn(se)

²**Argentinian** (adj) Argentijns

argot jargon^h

arguable 1 betwistbaar, aanvechtbaar **2** aantoonbaar, aanwijsbaar

¹**argue** (vb) **1** argumenteren, pleiten: *they were ~ing against* (or: *for*) zij pleitten tegen (*or:* voor) **2** (+ about, over) redetwisten (over), debatteren **3** twisten, ruziën, kibbelen: *don't ~ with me!* spreek me niet tegen!

²**argue** (vb) **1** doorpraten, bespreken **2** stellen, aanvoeren, bepleiten **3** overreden, overhalen: *I managed to ~ him into coming* ik kon hem overreden om te komen

argument 1 argument^h, bewijs^h, bewijsgrond: *a strong ~ for* (or: *against*) een sterk argument voor (*or:* tegen) **2** ruzie, onenigheid, woordenwisseling **3** hoofdinhoud; korte inhoud [of book] **4** bewijsvoering, betoog^h, redenering: *let us, for the sake of ~, suppose ...* stel nu eens (het hypothetische

geval) dat ... **5** discussie, gedachtewisseling

argumentation argumentatie, bewijsvoering

arid dor, droog, schraal, onvruchtbaar

Aries (de) Ram

arise 1 zich voordoen, gebeuren, optreden: *difficulties have ~n* er zijn moeilijkheden ontstaan **2** voortkomen, ontstaan: ~ *from* voortkomen uit, het gevolg zijn van

aristocracy [also fig] **1** aristocratie **2** aristocraten, aristocratie, adel

aristocrat aristocraat

¹**arithmetic** (n) **1** rekenkunde **2** berekening

²**arithmetic** (adj) rekenkundig: ~ *progression* rekenkundige reeks

ark ark: *Noah's* ~ ark van Noach

¹**arm** (n) **1** arm [of human being, animal; also fig]: ~ *in arm* arm in arm, gearmd; *at ~'s length* op een afstand, op gepaste afstand; *within ~'s reach* binnen handbereik; *a list as long as your* ~ een ellenlange lijst; *twist s.o.'s* ~ iemands arm omdraaien; [fig] forceren, het mes op de keel zetten **2** mouw **3** armleuning **4** afdeling, tak **5** (-s) wapen, (oorlogs)wapens, bewapening: *lay down (one's)* ~*s* de wapens neerleggen; *present* ~*s* het geweer presenteren **6** (-s) oorlogvoering, strijd **7** (-s) wapen^h, familiewapen^h || *be up in* ~*s about* (or: *over, against*) *sth.* verontwaardigd zijn over iets

²**arm** (vb) zich (be)wapenen [also fig]

³**arm** (vb) (be)wapenen [also fig]; uitrusten: ~*ed with a lot of information* voorzien van een boel informatie

armada armada, oorlogsvloot: *the (Spanish) Armada* de (Spaanse) Armada [of 1588]

armadillo gordeldier^h

armament 1 wapentuig^h [of tank, ship, aeroplane] **2** bewapening

armchair leunstoel: ~ *critics* stuurlui aan wal; ~ *shopping* thuiswinkelen

Armenia Armenië

¹**Armenian** (n) Armeniër, Armeense

²**Armenian** (adj) Armeens

armistice wapenstilstand, bestand^h

armlock armklem

armour 1 wapenrusting, harnas^h **2** pantser^h, pantsering, pantserbekleding **3** beschutting, dekking, schuilplaats

armoured 1 gepantserd: ~ *car* pantserwagen **2** gewapend [glass, concrete etc] **3** geharnast

armoury 1 wapenkamer, wapenmagazijn^h **2** wapens, wapensysteem^h **3** arsenaal^h [also fig]

armpit oksel

armrest (stoel)leuning

arms race bewapeningswedloop

arm-wrestling het armworstelen; het armdrukken

army leger^h [also fig]; massa, menigte: *join*

the ~ in dienst gaan; *an* ~ *of* **locusts** een grote zwerm sprinkhanen

ar<u>o</u>ma aroma^h, geur

arom<u>a</u>tic aromatisch, geurig

¹**ar<u>ou</u>nd** (adv) **1** rond [also fig]; in de vorm van een cirkel: *the other* **way** ~ andersom; *a* **way** ~ een omweg; **bring** ~ tot een andere mening brengen, overreden; *people* **gathered** ~ *to see* mensen verzamelden zich om te kijken; **pass** *it* ~ geef het rond; **turn** ~ (zich) omdraaien **2** in het rond, aan alle kanten, verspreid: *news* **gets** ~ *fast* nieuws verspreidt zich snel **3** [proximity] in de buurt: *for* **miles** ~ kilometers in de omtrek; **stay** ~ blijf in de buurt **4** [approximation] ongeveer, omstreeks: *he's* ~ **sixty** hij is rond de zestig; ~ **fifty** *people* om en nabij de vijftig mensen

²**ar<u>ou</u>nd** (prep) **1** rond, rondom, om … heen: ~ *the* **corner** om de hoek; *a chain* ~ *his neck* een ketting om zijn hals **2** [proximity] in het rond, rondom, om … heen: *only those* ~ **him** alleen zijn naaste medewerkers **3** [in all directions] door, rond, her en der in: *all* ~ *the country* door het hele land

ar<u>ou</u>sal 1 opwinding, prikkeling, ophitsing **2** het (op)wekken, uitlokking

ar<u>ou</u>se 1 wekken [also fig]; uitlokken, doen ontstaan: ~ **suspicion** wantrouwen wekken **2** opwekken, prikkelen, ophitsen

¹**arr<u>a</u>nge** (vb) **1** maatregelen nemen, in orde brengen: ~ **for** *sth.* iets regelen, ergens voor zorgen **2** overeenkomen, het eens zijn: ~ **with** *s.o.* **about** *sth.* iets overeenkomen met iem.

²**arr<u>a</u>nge** (vb) **1** (rang)schikken, ordenen, opstellen **2** bijleggen, rechtzetten, rechttrekken **3** regelen, organiseren, arrangeren, zorgen voor: ~ *a* **meeting** een vergadering beleggen **4** [mus] arrangeren

arr<u>a</u>ngement 1 ordening, (rang)schikking, opstelling **2** afspraak, regeling, overeenkomst **3** maatregel, voorzorg **4** [mus] arrangement^h, bewerking **5** plan^h

¹**arr<u>a</u>y** (n) **1** serie, collectie, reeks **2** gelid^h, marsorde, slagorde

²**arr<u>a</u>y** (vb) (in slagorde) opstellen, verzamelen, (in het gelid) schikken

arr<u>e</u>ars 1 achterstand: *in* ~ *with* **one's work** (*or: rent*) achter met zijn werk (*or:* huur) **2** (geld)schuld: *be in* ~ achter(op) zijn [payment]

¹**arr<u>e</u>st** (n) **1** stilstand [of growth, movement]: [med] **cardiac** ~ hartstilstand **2** bedwinging; beteugeling [of disease, decay etc] **3** arrestatie, aanhouding, (voorlopige) hechtenis: *place* ~ (or: *put*) **under** ~ in arrest nemen; **under** ~ in arrest

²**arr<u>e</u>st** (vb) **1** tegenhouden, bedwingen **2** arresteren, aanhouden **3** boeien, fascineren

arr<u>e</u>sting boeiend, fascinerend

arr<u>i</u>val 1 (aan)komst: **on** ~ bij aankomst **2** binnengevaren schip^h, binnengekomen trein (vliegtuig^h): [fig] **new** ~ pasgeborene **3** nieuwkomer, nieuweling

arr<u>i</u>ve 1 arriveren; aankomen [of persons, things] **2** arriveren, het (waar) maken **3** aanbreken; komen [of time]

arr<u>i</u>ve at bereiken [also fig]; komen tot: ~ *a* **conclusion** tot een besluit komen, een conclusie trekken

<u>a</u>rrogance arrogantie; aanmatiging

<u>a</u>rrogant arrogant, verwaand

<u>a</u>rrow pijl

arse [vulg] **1** reet **2** klootzak, lul

<u>a</u>rsenal [mil] arsenaal^h, (wapen)arsenaal^h

<u>a</u>rsenic 1 arsenicum^h, arseen^h **2** rattenkruit^h

<u>a</u>rson brandstichting

<u>a</u>rsonist brandstichter, pyromaan

art 1 kunst, bekwaamheid, vaardigheid: ~*s and* **crafts** kunst en ambacht; **work** *of* ~ kunstwerk; *the* **black** ~ zwarte kunst **2** kunst(greep), truc, list **3** kunst(richting): *the* **fine** ~*s* de schone kunsten

<u>a</u>rtefact kunstvoorwerp^h

art<u>e</u>rial slagaderlijk; arterieel: ~ **road** verkeersader

<u>a</u>rtery slagader; [fig] verkeersader; handelsader

<u>a</u>rtful listig, spitsvondig

art gallery kunstgalerie

arthr<u>i</u>tis artritis, jicht, gewrichtsontsteking

<u>a</u>rtichoke artisjok

<u>a</u>rticle 1 artikel^h, stuk^h, tekstfragment^h: *a* **newspaper** ~ een krantenartikel **2** [law] (wets)artikel^h, bepaling **3** [com] artikel^h, koopwaar, handelswaar: ~ *of* **clothing** kledingstuk **4** [linguistics] lidwoord^h: **definite** (*or:* **indefinite**) ~ bepaald (*or:* onbepaald) lidwoord **5** (-s) contract^h, statuten, akten

¹**art<u>i</u>culate** (adj) **1** zich duidelijk uitdrukkend [pers] **2** duidelijk; helder (uitgedrukt/verwoord) [thought etc]

²**art<u>i</u>culate** (vb) duidelijk spreken, articuleren

³**art<u>i</u>culate** (vb) **1** articuleren, duidelijk uitspreken **2** (helder) verwoorden, onder woorden brengen

art<u>i</u>culated geleed: ~ **bus** gelede bus, harmonicabus; ~ **lorry** vrachtwagen met aanhanger

articul<u>a</u>tion articulatie

<u>a</u>rtifice 1 truc, kunstgreep, list **2** handigheid **3** listigheid

artif<u>i</u>cial 1 kunstmatig: ~ **intelligence** kunstmatige intelligentie **2** kunst-, namaak-: ~ **flowers** kunstbloemen **3** gekunsteld, gemaakt: *an* ~ **smile** een gemaakte glimlach

art<u>i</u>llery [mil] **1** artillerie, geschut^h **2** artillerie [part of army]

<u>a</u>rtisan handwerksman, vakman, am-

bachtsman
artist artiest, (beeldend) kunstenaar (kunstenares)
artiste (variété)artiest(e)
artistic artistiek
artist's impression 1 robotfoto **2** schetsontwerp
artless argeloos, onschuldig
the **Arts** letteren
artwork 1 kunst **2** illustraties
arty [oft depr] **1** kitscherig **2** artistiekerig
Aruba Aruba
¹as (pron) die, dat: *the same as **he** had seen* dezelfde die hij gezien had
²as (adv) even, zo: *as fast as John* zo snel als John ‖ *as **well** as* zowel … als, niet alleen … maar ook; *as **from** now* van nu af
³as (prep) **1** [nature, role, function etc] als, in de rol van, in de hoedanigheid van: *Mary starring as Juliet* Mary in de rol van Julia **2** [comparison] als, gelijk: *as light as a feather* vederlicht ‖ *as **such*** als zodanig
⁴as (conj) **1** [agreement or comparison] (zo)als, naarmate, naargelang: *he lived as a **hermit** (would)* hij leefde als een kluizenaar; *cheap as cars **go*** goedkoop voor een wagen; *it's bad enough as it is* het is zo al erg genoeg; *as he later **realized*** zoals hij later besefte; *as it **were*** als het ware, om zo te zeggen; *such as* zoals; *he was so kind as to tell me all about it* hij was zo vriendelijk om mij alles daarover te vertellen, toen: *Jim sang as he scrubbed* Jim zong onder het schrobben **3** aangezien, daar, omdat: *as he was poor* daar hij arm was ‖ *as **for**, as to* wat betreft; *as **from** today* vanaf vandaag, met ingang van heden
asap *as soon as possible* z.s.m., zo spoedig mogelijk
asbestos asbestʰ
ASBO *anti-social behavior order* [roughly] rechterlijk doenormaalbevel
¹ascend (vb) **1** (op)stijgen, omhooggaan **2** oplopen [of slope, terrain]
²ascend (vb) **1** opgaan, naar boven gaan, beklimmen **2** bestijgen [throne]
ascendancy overwichtʰ, overhand: *have (or: **gain**) (the) ~ **over*** overwicht hebben (*or:* behalen) op
Ascension Hemelvaart: *~ **Day*** Hemelvaartsdag
ascent bestijging, opstijging, (be)klim(ming), het omhooggaan
ascertain vaststellen, bepalen, te weten komen, ontdekken
¹ascetic (n) asceet, iem. die zich onthoudt van weelde en genoegens
²ascetic (adj) ascetisch, zich onthoudend van weelde en genoegens
ASCII *American Standard Code for Information Interchange* ASCII
ascribe (+ to) toeschrijven (aan)

ASD *autistic spectrum disorder* ASS *(autismespectrumstoornis)*
ash 1 es, essenhoutʰ **2** (-es) as [after burning of corpse etc]
ashamed beschaamd: *feel ~* zich schamen; *be ~ of* zich schamen over
ashen 1 asgrauw; vaal **2** (lijk)bleek
ashore 1 kustwaarts, landwaarts **2** aan land, aan wal, op het strand
ashtray asbak
Ash Wednesday Aswoensdag
Asia Azië: *~ **Minor*** Klein-Azië
¹Asian (n) Aziaat, Aziatische
²Asian (adj) Aziatisch
¹aside (n) terloopse opmerking
²aside (adv) terzijde, opzij, zijwaarts: [fig] *brush ~ protests* protesten naast zich neerleggen; *set ~* a) opzijzetten; b) sparen [money] ‖ [Am] *~ **from*** afgezien van, behalve
asinine ezelachtig [also fig]; dwaas
¹ask (vb) vragen, informeren, navraag doen: *~ **for** advice* om raad vragen; [inform] *~ **for** it* erom vragen, het uitlokken
²ask (vb) **1** vragen, verzoeken: *~ s.o. a **question*** iem. een vraag stellen; *~ a favour of s.o.* iem. om een gunst vragen **2** eisen, verlangen: *that's too much to ~* dat is te veel gevraagd **3** vragen, uitnodigen ‖ [inform] *if you ~ **me*** volgens mij, als je het mij vraagt
askance achterdochtig, wantrouwend: *look ~ at s.o. (sth.)* iem. (iets) wantrouwend aankijken (bekijken)
askew scheef, schuin
aslant schuin; naar één kant
asleep in slaap, slapend: *fall ~* in slaap vallen; *fast* (or: *sound*) *~* in een diepe slaap
A/S level *Advanced Supplementary level* A/S-(examen)niveauʰ
asparagus asperge
aspect 1 gezichtspuntʰ, oogpuntʰ **2** zijde, kant, facetʰ
aspen esp(enboom), ratelpopulier: *tremble like an ~ **leaf*** trillen als een espenblad
asperity ruwheid, scherpheid
¹asphalt (n) asfaltʰ
²asphalt (vb) asfalteren
asphyxia verstikking(sdood)
asphyxiate doen stikken
aspirant kandidaat
aspirate 1 opzuigen, door zuigen verwijderen **2** [linguistics] aspireren
aspiration 1 aspiratie, strevenʰ, ambitie **2** inademing **3** aspiratie, opzuiging, wegzuiging, afzuiging **4** [linguistics] aspiratie
aspire sterk verlangen, streven: *~ **after**, ~ to sth.* naar iets streven
aspirin aspirine, aspirientjeʰ
ass 1 ezel [also fig]; domoor: *make an ~ of o.s.* zichzelf belachelijk maken **2** [Am; vulg] reet
assail [form] aanvallen [also fig]; overval-

len: *be ~ed* **with** (or: **by**) *doubt* overmand zijn door twijfel
ass<u>ai</u>lant aanvaller, belager
ass<u>a</u>ssin moordenaar, sluipmoordenaar, huurmoordenaar
ass<u>a</u>ssinate 1 vermoorden **2** vernietigen [character, reputation]
assassin<u>a</u>tion (sluip)moord
¹ass<u>au</u>lt (n) **1** aanval [also fig] **2** [mil] bestorming **3** daadwerkelijke bedreiging: ~ *and* **battery** mishandeling, geweldpleging
²ass<u>au</u>lt (vb) **1** aanvallen [also fig] **2** [mil] bestormen
ass<u>ay</u> analyseren; keuren [metal, ore]
¹ass<u>e</u>mble (vb) zich verzamelen, samenkomen
²ass<u>e</u>mble (vb) **1** assembleren, samenbrengen, verenigen; [techn] in elkaar zetten; monteren **2** ordenen
ass<u>e</u>mbler assembleerprogramma[h]
ass<u>e</u>mbly 1 samenkomst, vergadering, verzameling **2** assemblage, samenvoeging, montage **3** assemblee
ass<u>e</u>mbly language assembleertaal
ass<u>e</u>mbly line montageband; lopende band
¹ass<u>e</u>nt (n) toestemming, aanvaarding
²ass<u>e</u>nt (vb) toestemmen, aanvaarden: ~ *to sth.* met iets instemmen
ass<u>e</u>rt 1 beweren, verklaren **2** handhaven, laten gelden; opkomen voor [rights]: ~ *o.s.* op zijn recht staan, zich laten gelden
ass<u>e</u>rtion 1 bewering; verklaring **2** handhaving
ass<u>e</u>rtive 1 stellig, uitdrukkelijk, beslist **2** zelfbewust, zelfverzekerd, assertief
ass<u>e</u>ss 1 bepalen; vaststellen [value, amount, damage] **2** belasten; aanslaan [person, estate] **3** taxeren, schatten, ramen, beoordelen: ~ *the* **situation** de situatie beoordelen
ass<u>e</u>ssment 1 belasting, aanslag **2** schatting, taxatie, raming **3** vaststelling, bepaling **4** beoordeling
ass<u>e</u>ssor taxateur, schade-expert
<u>a</u>sset 1 goed[h], bezit[h]; [fig also] waardevolle eigenschap; pluspunt[h], aanwinst: *health is the* **greatest** ~ gezondheid is het grootste goed **2** [econ] creditpost **3** (-s) activa, baten, bedrijfsmiddelen: *~s and* **liabilities** activa en passiva, baten en lasten
ass<u>i</u>duous volhardend, vlijtig
ass<u>i</u>gn 1 toewijzen, toekennen, aanwijzen: ~ *s.o. a* **task** iem. een taak toebedelen **2** bepalen; vaststellen [day, date]; opgeven, aanwijzen **3** aanwijzen, aanstellen, benoemen: ~ *s.o.* **to** *a post in Berlin* iem. voor een functie in Berlijn aanwijzen
ass<u>i</u>gnment 1 taak, opdracht; [Am; educ] huiswerk[h] **2** toewijzing, toekenning, bestemming

ass<u>i</u>milate zich assimileren, opgenomen worden, gelijk worden: ~ *into*, ~ *with sth.* opgenomen worden in iets
ass<u>i</u>st helpen, bijstaan, assisteren
ass<u>i</u>stance hulp, bijstand, assistentie
¹ass<u>i</u>stant (n) **1** helper, assistent, adjunct **2** bediende, hulp
²ass<u>i</u>stant (adj) assistent-, hulp-, ondergeschikt
ass<u>i</u>sted-living: ~ *facility* verzorgingshuis; woon-zorgcomplex
¹ass<u>o</u>ciate (n) **1** partner, compagnon **2** (met)gezel, kameraad, makker
²ass<u>o</u>ciate (adj) toegevoegd, bijgevoegd, mede-: ~ *member* buitengewoon lid
³ass<u>o</u>ciate (vb) **1** zich verenigen, zich associëren **2** (+ with) omgaan (met)
⁴ass<u>o</u>ciate (vb) verenigen, verbinden; [also fig] associëren; in verband brengen: *closely ~d* **with** nauw betrokken bij
associ<u>a</u>tion 1 vereniging, genootschap[h], gezelschap[h], bond **2** associatie, verband[h], verbinding **3** samenwerking, connectie: *in ~* **with** samen met, in samenwerking met **4** omgang, vriendschap
Associ<u>a</u>tion f<u>oo</u>tball voetbal
ass<u>o</u>rt sorteren, ordenen, classificeren: ~ **with** indelen bij
ass<u>o</u>rted 1 gemengd, gevarieerd **2** bij elkaar passend: *ill-~* slecht bij elkaar passend
ass<u>o</u>rtment 1 assortiment[h], collectie, ruime keuze **2** sortering, ordening
ass<u>ua</u>ge 1 kalmeren, verzachten, verlichten, (tot) bedaren (brengen) **2** bevredigen; stillen [hunger, desire]; lessen [thirst]
ass<u>u</u>me 1 aannemen, vermoeden, veronderstellen **2** overnemen, nemen, grijpen **3** op zich nemen: *he ~d the* **role** *of benefactor* hij speelde de weldoener **4** voorwenden: *~d* **name** aangenomen naam, schuilnaam
ass<u>u</u>ming ervan uitgaande dat
ass<u>u</u>mption vermoeden[h], veronderstelling
ass<u>u</u>rance 1 zekerheid, vertrouwen[h] **2** zelfvertrouwen[h] **3** verzekering, levensverzekering **4** verzekering, belofte, garantie
ass<u>u</u>re verzekeren: ~ *s.o.* **of** *one's support* iem. van zijn steun verzekeren
<u>a</u>sterisk asterisk, sterretje[h]
<u>a</u>steroid asteroïde, kleine planeet
<u>a</u>sthma astma
ast<u>o</u>nish verbazen, versteld doen staan: *be ~d* **at** *sth.* zich over iets verbazen, stomverbaasd zijn over iets
ast<u>o</u>nishment verbazing
ast<u>ou</u>nd ontzetten, verbazen, schokken
ast<u>ou</u>nding verbazingwekkend
astr<u>a</u>y verdwaald: *go* ~ verdwalen, de verkeerde weg op gaan; *lead s.o.* ~ iem. op een dwaalspoor brengen
astr<u>i</u>de schrijlings, wijdbeens, dwars ‖ *she sat* ~ *her* **horse** ze zat schrijlings op haar

paard
astrology astrologie
astronaut astronaut, ruimtevaarder
astronomer astronoom, sterrenkundige
astronomical astronomisch [also fig]; sterrenkundig
astronomy astronomie, sterrenkunde
astute scherpzinnig, slim, sluw
asylum 1 asiel[h], toevlucht(soord[h]): *political ~* politiek asiel **2** (krankzinnigen)inrichting
asylum seeker asielzoeker; vluchteling
asymmetric asymmetrisch: *~ bars* brug met ongelijke leggers
at 1 [place, time, point on a scale] aan, te, in, op, bij: *at my aunt's* bij mijn tante; *at Christmas* met Kerstmis; *at the corner* op de hoek; *cheap at 10p* goedkoop voor 10 pence; *at that time* toen, in die tijd; *we'll leave it at that* we zullen het daarbij laten **2** [activity or profession] bezig met: *at work* aan het werk; *they're at it again* ze zijn weer bezig **3** [skill] op het gebied van: *my mother is an expert at wallpapering* mijn moeder kan geweldig goed behangen **4** door, naar aanleiding van, als gevolg van, door middel van, via: *at my command* op mijn bevel; *at a glance* in één oogopslag
atheism atheïsme[h], godloochening
atheist atheïst, godloochenaar
athlete atleet
athletic 1 atletisch **2** atletiek-
athletics atletiek
the **¹Atlantic** (n) Atlantische Oceaan
²Atlantic (adj): *the ~ Ocean* de Atlantische Oceaan
atlas atlas
ATM [Am] *automatic teller machine* geldautomaat, pinautomaat
atmosphere 1 dampkring; atmosfeer [also unit of pressure] **2** (atmo)sfeer, stemming
atmospheric atmosferisch, lucht-, dampkrings-
atoll atol[h], ringvormig koraaleiland[h]
atom 1 [science] atoom[h] **2** zeer kleine hoeveelheid, greintje[h]
atomic atoom-, kern-, nucleair: *~ power* atoomkracht; atoommogendheid; *~ power station* kerncentrale
atomize verstuiven, vernevelen
atomizer verstuiver
atone for goedmaken
atonement vergoeding, boetedoening: *make ~ for* goedmaken
atop boven op, bovenaan
atrocious 1 wreed, monsterachtig **2** afschuwelijk slecht
atrocity 1 wreedheid **2** afschuwelijkheid
atrophy [also fig] wegkwijnen
at-sign [comp] apenstaartje[h]
attach (aan)hechten, vastmaken, verbinden: *~ too much importance to sth.* ergens te zwaar aan tillen
attaché attaché
attaché case diplomatenkoffertje[h]
attachment 1 hulpstuk[h]: *~s* toebehoren[h], accessoires **2** aanhechting, verbinding **3** gehechtheid, genegenheid, trouw **4** [comp] attachment[h], bijlage
¹attack (n) **1** aanval, (scherpe) kritiek: *be under ~* aangevallen worden **2** aanpak
²attack (vb) **1** aantasten, aanvreten **2** aanpakken [eg a problem]
³attack (vb) aanvallen [also fig]; overvallen
attain bereiken, verkrijgen: *~ old age* een hoge leeftijd bereiken
attainment 1 verworvenheid, kundigheid **2** het bereiken, verwerving
¹attempt (n) **1** (+ to) poging (tot): *~ at conciliation* toenaderingspoging **2** aanval, aanslag: *~ on s.o.'s life* aanslag op iemands leven
²attempt (vb) proberen, wagen
¹attend (vb) **1** aanwezig zijn: *~ at church* de dienst bijwonen **2** opletten, (aandachtig) luisteren
²attend (vb) **1** bijwonen, aanwezig zijn bij, zitten op [school]: *will you be ~ing his lecture?* ga je naar zijn lezing? **2** zorgen voor, verplegen **3** letten op, bedienen **4** begeleiden, vergezellen; [fig] gepaard gaan met
attendance 1 opkomst, aantal aanwezigen **2** aanwezigheid: *compulsory ~* verschijningsplicht, verplichte aanwezigheid **3** dienst, toezicht[h]: *doctor in ~* dienstdoende arts
attendant 1 bediende, knecht **2** begeleider, volgeling: *~s* gevolg[h] **3** bewaker, suppoost
attend to 1 aandacht schenken aan, luisteren naar **2** zich inzetten voor, zorgen voor, bedienen: *attend to s.o.'s interests* iemands belangen behartigen; *are you being attended to?* wordt u al geholpen?
attention 1 aandacht, zorg: *this plant needs a lot of ~* deze plant vraagt veel zorg; *pay ~* opletten; *have a short ~ span* een korte spanningsboog hebben; *for the ~ of* ter attentie van **2** belangstelling, erkenning **3** attentie, hoffelijkheid || *be* (or: *stand*) *at ~* in de houding staan
attentive 1 aandachtig, oplettend **2** attent, hoffelijk
attenuate 1 verdunnen, dunner worden, versmallen **2** verzwakken, verminderen, dempen [sound]: *with old age memories ~* met de oude dag vervagen de herinneringen
¹attest (vb) (+ to) getuigen (van), getuigenis afleggen (van)
²attest (vb) **1** plechtig verklaren, officieel bevestigen **2** getuigen van, betuigen
attic vliering, zolder(kamer)
attire gewaad[h], kledij
attitude 1 houding, stand, attitude **2** hou-

ding, gedrag[h]: ~ *of mind* instelling **3** stand-punt[h], opvatting

attorney 1 procureur, gevolmachtigde: *power of* ~ volmacht **2** [Am] advocaat

Attorney General 1 procureur-generaal **2** [Am] minister van Justitie

attract aantrekken [also fig]; lokken, boeien

attraction 1 aantrekkelijkheid, aantrekking(skracht) **2** attractie, bezienswaardigheid

attractive aantrekkelijk, attractief

[1]**attribute** (n) **1** eigenschap, (essentieel) kenmerk[h] **2** attribuut[h], symbool[h]

[2]**attribute** (vb) toeschrijven, toekennen

attribution toeschrijving

attune doen overeenstemmen, afstemmen: *my ears are not ~d to modern jazz* mijn oren zijn niet gewend aan moderne jazz

aubergine aubergine

auburn kastanjebruin

[1]**auction** (n) veiling, verkoop bij opbod: *put up for* ~ veilen, bij opbod verkopen

[2]**auction** (vb) veilen, verkopen bij opbod

audacious 1 dapper, moedig **2** roekeloos **3** brutaal

audacity 1 dappere daad, waagstuk[h] **2** dapperheid **3** roekeloosheid **4** brutaliteit, onbeschoftheid

audible hoorbaar, verstaanbaar

audience 1 publiek[h], toehoorders, toeschouwers **2** (+ with) audiëntie (bij)

[1]**audit** (n) **1** accountantsonderzoek[h], accountantscontrole **2** accountantsverslag[h] **3** balans, afrekening

[2]**audit** (vb) (de boeken/rekeningen) controleren

audition auditie, proefoptreden[h]

auditor 1 toehoorder, luisteraar **2** (register)accountant; [Belg] bedrijfsrevisor

auditorium gehoorzaal, auditorium[h], aula

auditory auditief; gehoor-: ~ *nerve* gehoorzenuw

augment vergroten, (doen) toenemen, vermeerderen

augur: [form] ~ *well* (or: *ill*) *for* goeds (or: kwaads) voorspellen voor

augury voorspelling, voorteken[h]: *a hopeful* ~ een gunstig voorteken

august verheven, groots

August augustus

aunt tante

auntie [inform] tantetje[h]

aura aura, sfeer, waas[h]: *he has an ~ of respectability* hij heeft iets waardigs over zich

aural oor-; van het oor

auspices auspiciën, bescherming: *under the ~ of Her Majesty* onder de bescherming van Hare Majesteit

auspicious 1 gunstig, voorspoedig **2** veelbelovend

[1]**Aussie** (n) [inform] Australiër

[2]**Aussie** (adj) [inform] Australisch

austere 1 streng, onvriendelijk, ernstig **2** matig, sober, eenvoudig

austerity 1 soberheid, matiging **2** (strenge) eenvoud, soberheid **3** beperking, bezuiniging(smaatregel), inlevering: ~ *drive* bezuinigingscampagne

[1]**Australasian** (n) bewoner van Australaal-Azië [Oceania]

[2]**Australasian** (adj) Austraal-Aziatisch

Australia Australië

[1]**Australian** (n) Australiër, Australische

[2]**Australian** (adj) Australisch

Austria Oostenrijk

[1]**Austrian** (n) Oostenrijker, Oostenrijkse

[2]**Austrian** (adj) Oostenrijks

authentic authentiek, onvervalst, origineel

authenticate (voor) echt verklaren: ~ *a will* een testament bekrachtigen

authenticity 1 authenticiteit; echtheid **2** oprechtheid

author auteur, schrijver, maker, schepper

[1]**authoritarian** (n) autoritair iem., eigenmachtig individu[h]

[2]**authoritarian** (adj) autoritair, eigenmachtig

authoritative 1 gebiedend, autoritair: *he has an ~ manner* hij dwingt respect af **2** gezaghebbend

authority 1 autoriteit, overheidsinstantie, overheidspersoon: *the competent authorities* de bevoegde overheden, het bevoegd gezag **2** recht[h], toestemming **3** autoriteit, deskundige: *an ~ on the subject* een autoriteit op dit gebied **4** autoriteit, gezag[h], wettige macht: *abuse of* ~ machtsmisbruik **5** autoriteit, (moreel) gezag[h], invloed: *you cannot deny his* ~ je kunt niet ontkennen dat hij iem. van aanzien is **6** volmacht, machtiging

authority figure gezagdrager, gezagdraagster

authorization 1 autorisatie, machtiging, volmacht **2** vergunning, goedkeuring

authorize 1 machtigen, recht geven tot, volmacht verlenen: ~ *d agent* gevolmachtigd vertegenwoordiger, gevolmachtigde **2** goedkeuren, inwilligen, toelaten

autism autisme[h]

autistic autistisch

auto [Am; inform] auto

autobiographical autobiografisch

autobiography autobiografie

autocracy autocratie

autogas LPG, autogas[h]

autograph handschrift[h]; handtekening [of celebrity]

autoimmunity auto-immuniteit

automate automatiseren

[1]**automatic** (n) automatisch wapen[h]

[2]**automatic** (adj) automatisch, zelfwerkend,

zonder na te denken: *he ~ally thought of her* hij dacht onwillekeurig aan haar

automobile [Am] auto

autonomous autonoom, met zelfbestuur: *~ state* autonome staat

autonomy autonomie, zelfbestuurʰ, onafhankelijkheid: *~ of the individual* onafhankelijkheid van het individu

autopilot *automatic pilot* automatische piloot

autopsy [med] autopsie, lijkschouwing, sectie

autumn [also fig] herfst, najaarʰ, nadagen: *in (the) ~* in het najaar (*or:* de herfst)

¹**auxiliary** (n) **1** helper, hulpkracht, assistent **2** hulpmiddelʰ **3** hulpwerkwoordʰ

²**auxiliary** (adj) **1** hulp-, behulpzaam, helpend: *~ troops* hulptroepen; *~ verb* hulpwerkwoord **2** aanvullend, supplementair, reserve-

¹**avail** (n) nutʰ, voordeelʰ, baat: *to no ~* nutteloos, vergeefs

²**avail** (vb) baten, helpen, van nut zijn ‖ *Joe ~ed himself of the opportunity* Joe maakte van de gelegenheid gebruik

availability beschikbaarheid, verkrijgbaarheid, leverbaarheid, aanwezigheid

available beschikbaar, verkrijgbaar, leverbaar: *Mr Jones was not ~ for comment* meneer Jones was niet beschikbaar voor commentaar

avalanche lawine; [fig] vloed(golf); stortvloed

avarice gierigheid, hebzucht

avaricious hebzuchtig, gierig

avatar 1 incarnatie; belichaming **2** [comp] avatar

Ave *avenue* ln, laan

avenge wreken, wraak nemen (voor)

avenger wreker

avenue 1 avenue; (brede) laan **2** oprijlaan [to castle, estate] **3** weg [only fig]; toegang, middelʰ: *explore every ~* alle middelen proberen

¹**average** (n) gemiddeldeʰ, middelmaat; [also fig] doorsnee: *eight is the ~ of ten and six* acht is het gemiddelde van tien en zes; *above (the) ~* boven het gemiddelde; *below (the) ~* onder het gemiddelde ‖ *on (the) ~* gemiddeld, door de bank genomen

²**average** (adj) gemiddeld, midden-, doorsnee-: *~ man* de gewone man

³**average** (vb) het gemiddelde berekenen

¹**average out** (vb) [inform] gemiddeld op hetzelfde neerkomen: *the profits averaged out at fifty pounds a day* de winst kwam gemiddeld neer op vijftig pond per dag

²**average out** (vb) [inform] een gemiddelde berekenen van

averse (+ to) afkerig (van), tegen, afwijzend

aversion 1 (+ to) afkeer (van): *take an ~ to* een afkeer krijgen van **2** persoon (iets) waar men een hekel aan heeft

avert 1 (+ from) afwenden (van) [eyes]; afkeren **2** voorkomen, vermijden, afwenden: *~ danger* het gevaar keren

avian vogel-, ornithologisch

avian flu vogelgriep

aviary vogelhuisʰ, vogelverblijfʰ

aviation 1 luchtvaart, vliegkunst **2** vliegtuigbouw

avid 1 gretig, enthousiast: *an ~ reader* een grage lezer **2** verlangend

avocet kluut

avoid (ver)mijden, ontwijken: *they couldn't ~ doing it* zij moesten het wel doen

avoidance vermijding, het vermijden

avow 1 toegeven, erkennen **2** (openlijk) bekennen; belijden [belief etc]: *they are ~ed enemies* het zijn gezworen vijanden

avuncular als een (vriendelijke) oom, vaderlijk

await opwachten, verwachten, tegemoet zien ‖ *a warm welcome ~s them* er wacht hen een warm welkom

¹**awake** (adj) **1** wakker: *wide ~* klaarwakker [also fig] **2** waakzaam, alert: *~ to* zich bewust van

²**awake** (vb) **1** ontwaken [also fig]; wakker worden **2** (+ to) zich bewust worden (van), gaan beseffen

³**awake** (vb) **1** wekken, wakker maken **2** bewust maken

awakening 1 het ontwaken **2** bewustwording

¹**award** (n) **1** beloning, prijs **2** toekenning [of reward, prize, damages]

²**award** (vb) **1** toekennen [prize]; toewijzen **2** belonen

aware zich bewust, gewaar: *politically ~* politiek bewust; *be ~ of* zich bewust zijn van

awareness bewustzijnʰ: *lack of ~* onwetendheid

¹**away** (adj) uit-: *~ match* uitwedstrijd

²**away** (adv) **1** weg [also fig]; afwezig, op (een) afstand, uit: *give ~* weggeven **2** voortdurend, onophoudelijk: *she was chatting ~* ze zat aan één stuk door te kletsen ‖ *I'll do it right ~* ik zal het meteen doen

awe ontzagʰ, eerbied: *hold* (or: *keep*) *s.o. in ~* ontzag hebben voor iem.; *stand in ~ of* groot ontzag hebben voor

awe-inspiring ontzagwekkend

awesome ontzagwekkend, ontzag inboezemend

awful [inform] afschuwelijk, enorm: *an ~ lot* ontzettend veel

awfully [inform] erg, vreselijk, ontzettend: *thanks ~* reuze bedankt; *~ nice* vreselijk aardig

awhile korte tijd, een tijdje

awkward 1 onhandig, onbeholpen **2** onpraktisch **3** ongelegen; ongunstig [date,
time] **4** gênant: ~ *situation* pijnlijke situatie
5 opgelaten, niet op zijn gemak
awning luifel, kap, markies, zonnescherm[h]
awry scheef [also fig]; schuin, fout: *go* ~
mislukken
[1]**axe** (n) bijl: [fig] *have an* ~ *to grind* ergens
zelf een bijbedoeling mee hebben
[2]**axe** (vb) **1** ontslaan, aan de dijk zetten **2** afschaffen, wegbezuinigen
axis as(lijn), spil
axle [techn] (draag)as, spil
Azerbaijan Azerbeidzjan
[1]**Azerbaijani** (n) Azerbeidzjaan(se)
[2]**Azerbaijani** (adj) Azerbeidzjaans
azure hemelsblauw, azuurblauw; [fig] wol-
keloos

b

b *born* geb., geboren

B2B *business to business* b2b; business-to-business

BA *Bachelor of Arts* Bachelor of Arts [university degree]

¹babble (n) gebabbel[h], gewauwel[h], gekletsh

²babble (vb) babbelen

babe 1 [dated] kindje[h], baby **2** [inform] liefje[h], schatje[h] **3** [inform] mooie meid ‖ *~ in the woods* naïeveling

babel 1 spraakverwarring **2** wanorde; chaos

baboon baviaan [also fig; depr]; lomperd

baby 1 baby, zuigeling, kleuter **2** jongste, benjamin **3** [fig] klein kind[h], kinderachtig persoon **4** jong[h] [of animal] **5** schatje[h] **6** [inform] persoon, zaak: *that's your ~* dat is jouw zaak ‖ [fig] *be left carrying* (or: *holding*) *the ~* met de gebakken peren blijven zitten

baby boomer babyboomer, geboortegolver

baby grand [mus] kleine vleugel

baby minder babysitter, oppas

baby shower babyshower

baby sit babysitten

babysitter babysitter, oppas

bachelor 1 vrijgezel **2** bachelor [lowest university degree]: *Bachelor of Arts* bachelor in de letteren; *Bachelor of Science* bachelor in de exacte wetenschappen

¹back (n) **1** rug, achterkant: *behind* s.o.'s ~ achter iemands rug [also fig] **2** achter(hoede)speler, verdediger, back **3** achterkant, achterzijde, keerzijde, rug: *back to back* a) ruggelings, rug tegen rug; b) achtereenvolgens **4** (rug)leuning **5** achterste deel[h]: [fig] *at the ~ of one's mind* in zijn achterhoofd; *at the ~* achterin **6** [sport] achter[h] ‖ *know like the ~ of one's hand* als zijn broekzak kennen; [fig] *with one's ~ to the wall* met zijn rug tegen de muur; [inform] *get* (or: *put*) s.o.'s ~ *up* iem. irriteren; [inform] *get off* s.o.'s ~ iem. met rust laten; *pat o.s. on the ~* tevreden zijn over zichzelf; *put one's ~ into sth.* ergens de schouders onder zetten; *glad to see the ~ of s.o.* iem. liever zien gaan dan komen; *stab s.o. in the ~* iem. een dolk in de rug steken, iem. verraden; *turn one's ~ on* de rug toekeren

²back (adj) **1** achter(-): *~ room* a) achterkamer(tje); b) [also fig] ergens achteraf; *~ seat* a) achterbank [of car]; b) [fig] tweede plaats **2** terug- **3** ver (weg), (achter)afgelegen

4 achterstallig **5** oud [of edition]: *~ issue* (or: *number*) oud nummer [of magazine]

³back (vb) krimpen [of wind]

⁴back (vb) **1** (onder)steunen [also fin]; schragen, bijstaan **2** [inform] wedden (op), gokken op: [fig] *~ the wrong horse* op het verkeerde paard wedden

⁵back (vb) achteruit bewegen, achteruitrijden, (doen) achteruitgaan: *~ out* achteruit wegrijden

⁶back (adv) **1** achter(op), aan de achterkant: [Am] *~ of* achter **2** achteruit, terug **3** terug [also fig]; weer thuis **4** [inform] in het verleden, geleden, terug: *~ in 1975* al in 1975 **5** op (enige) afstand: *a few miles ~* een paar mijl terug **6** achterom ‖ *~ and forward* (or: *forth*) heen en weer

backache rugpijn

back away (also + from) achteruit weglopen (van), zich terugtrekken

backbencher gewoon Lagerhuislid[h]

backbite kwaadspreken (over), roddelen (over)

backbone ruggengraat [also fig]; wervelkolom, wilskracht, pit

backbreaking slopend, zwaar

back-burner [inform] op een laag pitje zetten

backchat [inform] tegenspraak; brutale opmerking

backcountry 1 afgelegen (berg)streek **2** [Austr] binnenland[h]

backdate 1 met terugwerkende kracht in doen gaan **2** antidateren

back door achterdeur

back down terugkrabbelen, toegeven

backdrop 1 [theatre] achterdoek[h] **2** achtergrond

backfire 1 terugslaan [of engine]; naontsteking hebben **2** mislopen, verkeerd aflopen

background achtergrond [also fig]

backhanded: *~ compliment* dubieus compliment

backing 1 (ruggen)steun, ondersteuning **2** achterban, medestanders **3** [mus] begeleiding

backlash tegenstroom, verzet[h], reactie

backlog achterstand

back off terugdeinzen, achteruitwijken

back out (+ of) zich terugtrekken (uit), afzien (van)

backpack rugzak

backpacking [inform] rugzaktoerisme[h]

backroom politics achterkamertjespolitiek

back-seat driver passagier die 'meerijdt'; [Am; fig] stuurman aan de wal

backside 1 [inform] achterwerk[h], zitvlak[h] **2** achtereinde[h]

backslash backslash

balance

backslide 1 terugvallen [in bad behaviour]; vervallen **2** afvallig worden

¹backspace (n) terugtoets, backspacetoets

²backspace (vb) met de cursor een positie teruggaan

backstage achter het podium, achter de schermen, in het geheim

backstair(s) 1 privé-, heimelijk: *backstair gossip* achterklap **2** achterbaks, onderhands

back street achterbuurt(en)

back-street clandestien: ~ *abortion* illegale abortus

backstroke rugslag

backtrack 1 terugkeren **2** terugkrabbelen

¹back up (vb) **1** [Am] een file vormen **2** [Am] achteruitrijden [of car]

²back up (vb) **1** (onder)steunen, staan achter, bijstaan **2** bevestigen [story]

back-up 1 (ruggen)steun, ondersteuning **2** reserve, voorraad **3** reservekopie (van computerbestandʰ) **4** [Am] file

backward 1 achter(lijk); achtergebleven [in development]; traag, niet bij **2** achteruit(-), ruggelings: *a ~ glance* een blik achterom

backwards 1 achteruit [also fig]; achterwaarts, ruggelings: ~ *and forward(s)* heen en weer **2** naar het verleden, terug

backwater 1 (stil) binnenwaterʰ; [fig] gatʰ; afgelegen stadjeʰ; [fig] impasse; (geestelijke) stagnatie **2** achterwaterʰ

backwoods binnenlanden

backyard 1 plaatsjeʰ, achterplaats; [fig] achtertuin: *in one's own* ~ in zijn eigen achtertuin **2** [Am] achtertuin

bacon baconʰ, spekʰ ‖ [inform] *bring home the* ~ de kost verdienen; [inform] *save one's* ~ zijn hachje redden, er zonder kleerscheuren afkomen

bacterial bacterieel; bacterie-

bacterium bacterie

¹bad (n) **1** het slechte, het kwade: *go to the* ~ de verkeerde kant opgaan **2** debetʰ, schuld: *be £ 100 to the* ~ voor 100 pond in het krijt staan

²bad (adj) **1** slecht, minderwaardig, verkeerd: *a ~ conscience* een slecht geweten; [inform] *make the best of a ~ job* het beste er van (zien te) maken; *go ~* bederven; *bad-mannered* ongemanierd; *not half, not so* ~ niet zo gek **2** kwaad, kwaadaardig, stout: *in ~ faith* te kwader trouw; *from ~ to worse* van kwaad tot erger **3** ziek, naar, pijnlijk **4** erg, ernstig, lelijk: ~ *debt* oninbare schuld; *be in a ~ way* er slecht aan toe zijn **5** ongunstig: *make the best of a ~ bargain* er het beste van maken; *that looks* ~ dat voorspelt niet veel goeds **6** schadelijk: ~ *for* your liver slecht voor je lever **7** vol spijt: *I feel ~ about* that dat spijt me

bad ass [Am; inform] rotzak; ruziezoeker

bad-ass [Am; inform] **1** retegoed, steen-

goed, keigaaf **2** stoer; eigenwijs

baddie slechterik

badge badge, insigneʰ, politiepenning

¹badger (n) das [animal]

²badger (vb) lastigvallen: *I ~ed him into working for me* ik drong zolang aan dat hij toch maar besloot voor mij te gaan werken

badly 1 slecht: *do* ~ een slecht resultaat behalen, het er slecht van afbrengen **2** erg, zeer, hard: *I need it* ~ ik heb het hard nodig; ~ *wounded* zwaar gewond

baffle verbijsteren, van zijn stuk brengen: *a problem that has ~d biologists for years* een probleem dat biologen al jaren voor raadsels stelt

bafflement verbijstering

¹bag (n) **1** zak, baal: *~s under the eyes* wallen onder de ogen **2** zak, tas, koffer **3** zak vol; [fig] grote hoeveelheid: *the whole ~ of tricks* de hele santenkraam; [inform] *~s of money* hopen geld **4** vangst [game] ‖ *a mixed ~* een allegaartje; [inform] *it's in the* ~ het is in kannen en kruiken

²bag (vb) vangen; schieten [game, fowl]

baggage bagage

baggy zakachtig, flodderig: ~ *cheeks* hangwangen

bag lady zwerfster

bagpipes doedelzak

the **Bahamas** Bahama's

Bahrain Bahrein

¹Bahraini (n) Bahreiner, Bahreinse

²Bahraini (adj) Bahreins

¹bail (n) borg(stelling), borgtocht, borgsom: *out on* ~ vrijgelaten op borgtocht

²bail (vb) hozen

³bail (vb) **1** vrijlaten tegen borgstelling **2** leeghozen

Bailey bridge baileybrug

bailiff 1 [law] deurwaarder **2** [Am; law] gerechtsdienaar

¹bail out (vb) hozen

²bail out (vb) **1** door borgtocht in vrijheid stellen, vrijkopen **2** [inform] uit de penarie helpen **3** leeghozen

¹bait (n) aasʰ, lokaasʰ; [fig] verleiding: *swallow* (or: *take*) *the* ~ toebijten, toehappen; [fig also] erin trappen

²bait (vb) **1** van lokaas voorzien **2** ophitsen [animal, esp dogs] **3** treiteren, boos maken

bake bakken (in een oven): *~d beans* witte bonen in tomatensaus

baked beans witte bonen in tomatensaus

baker bakker: [fig] *~'s dozen* dertien

baker's dozen dertien

bakery 1 bakkerij **2** bakkerswinkel

baking tin bakvorm

balaclava bivakmuts

¹balance (n) **1** balans, weegschaal: [fig] *his fate is* (or: *hangs*) *in the* ~ zijn lot is onbeslist **2** [com] balans: ~ *of payments* betalingsbalans; *strike* a ~ [fig] een compromis (*or:* het juiste evenwicht) vinden **3** [fin, com] saldo[h], tegoed[h], overschot[h]: ~ *in hand* kasvoorraad; ~ *due* debetsaldo **4** evenwicht[h], balans: ~ *of power* machtsevenwicht; *redress the* ~ het evenwicht herstellen || *on* ~ alles in aanmerking genomen

²**balance** (vb) **1** schommelen, balanceren, slingeren **2** [com] sluiten [of balance sheet]; gelijk uitkomen, kloppen: *of balance sheet* gelijk uitkomen, kloppen: ~ *de boeken kloppen*, de administratie klopt

³**balance** (vb) **1** wegen; [fig] overwegen; tegen elkaar afwegen **2** in evenwicht brengen, balanceren **3** [com] opmaken, laten kloppen; sluitend maken [balance sheet]: ~ *the books* het boekjaar afsluiten

balanced evenwichtig, harmonisch: ~ *diet* uitgebalanceerd dieet

balance sheet balans

balcony balkon[h], galerij

bald 1 kaal; [fig also] sober; saai: ~ *as a coot* kaal als een biljartbal; ~ *tyre* gladde band **2** naakt, bloot

balderdash onzin

baldly gewoonweg, zonder omwegen, regelrecht

bale baal

baleful 1 noodlottig **2** onheilspellend [eg glance]

¹**bale out** (vb) **1** hozen **2** het vliegtuig uitspringen [with parachute]

²**bale out** (vb) uithozen, leeghozen

¹**balk** (n) balk

²**balk** (vb) **1** weigeren, stokken, blijven steken: *the horse* ~*ed at the fence* het paard weigerde de hindernis **2** (+ at) terugschrikken (van/voor), bezwaar maken (tegen)

³**balk** (vb) verhinderen: ~ *s.o.'s plans* iemands plannen in de weg staan

Balkan Balkan-

Balkans Balkan

¹**ball** (n) **1** bal; [sport only] worp; schop, slag: *the* ~ *is in your court* nu is het jouw beurt [also fig]; *set* (or: *start*) *the* ~ *rolling* de zaak aan het rollen brengen **2** bol, bolvormig voorwerp[h], bal **3** prop, kluwen, bol **4** rond lichaamsdeel[h]; bal [of foot]; muis [of hand]; oogbol, oogappel **5** kogel **6** bal[h], dansfeest[h] **7** [inform] plezier[h], leut, lol

²**ball** (n) balspel[h]; [Am] honkbal[h]: *play* ~ met de bal spelen; [Am] honkbal spelen; [fig] meewerken

ballad ballade

ballast ballast; [fig] bagage

ballet 1 ballet[h], balletkunst **2** stuk balletmuziek

ball game balspel[h]; [Am esp] honkbalwedstrijd || *we are now in a whole* **new** ~ de zaak staat er nu heel anders voor

ballistic ballistisch || [Am; inform] *go* ~ in woede uitbarsten, ontploffen

¹**balloon** (n) **1** (lucht)ballon: *the* ~ *goes up* de ballon stijgt op; [fig] de pret begint; de moeilijkheden beginnen **2** ballon(netje[h]) [in cartoon]

²**balloon** (vb) **1** per luchtballon reizen **2** opzwellen, bol gaan staan

ballot 1 stem, stembiljet[h], stembriefje[h]: ~ *box* stembus; *cast one's* ~ zijn stem uitbrengen **2** stemming, stemronde: *let's take* (or: *have*) *a* ~ laten we erover stemmen

ballot screen keuzescherm[h]

ballpark [Am] honkbalveld[h] || *in the* ~ ongeveer juist, raak

ball-park ongeveer juist

ball pit ballenbak

ballroom balzaal, danszaal

balm balsem [also fig]; troost

balmy zacht; mild

balsam 1 [also fig] balsem **2** balsemboom

Baltic Baltisch: ~ *Sea* Oostzee

balustrade balustrade

bamboo bamboe[+h]

bamboozle [inform] **1** bedriegen, beetnemen: ~ *s.o.* **out of** *his money* iem. zijn geld afhandig maken **2** in de war brengen

¹**ban** (n) verbod[h]: ~ *on smoking* rookverbod; *impose a* ~ een verbod instellen

²**ban** (vb) **1** verbieden, verbannen, uitsluiten: *he was* ~*ned from driving* hij mocht geen auto meer rijden **2** verwerpen, afwijzen: ~ *the bomb* weg met de atoombom

banal [oft depr] banaal, gewoon, alledaags

banana banaan: *a hand of* ~*s* een kam bananen

bananas [inform] knettergek: *go* ~ stapelgek worden

¹**band** (n) **1** band [also fig]; riem, ring; (dwars)streep [on animal]; reep, rand, boord[h]: *a rubber* ~ een elastiekje **2** bende, groep, troep **3** band, orkest[h], (dans)orkestje[h], fanfare, popgroep

²**band** (vb) zich verenigen: ~ *together against* zich als één man verzetten tegen

¹**bandage** (n) verband[h]

²**bandage** (vb) verbinden

band-aid [Am; inform] **1** pleister **2** lapmiddel[h], tijdelijke oplossing

b and b *bed and breakfast* logies[h] met ontbijt

bandit bandiet

bandsman muzikant

bandstand muziektent

bandwagon 1 muziekwagen **2** [fig] iets dat algemene bijval vindt: *climb* (or: *jump*) *on the* ~ **a)** met de massa meedoen; **b)** aan de kant van de winnaar gaan staan

band width bandbreedte

bandy heen en weer doen bewegen || ~ *words with s.o.* ruzie maken met iem.; ~ *about* **a)** te pas en te onpas noemen; **b)** verspreiden, rondbazuinen; *have one's name* *bandied* **about** voortdurend genoemd worden

bandy-legged met O-benen

bane 1 last, pest, kruis[h]: *the* ~ *of my existence* (or: *life*) een nagel aan mijn doodskist **2** vloek, verderf[h]

[1]**bang** (n) **1** klap, dreun, slag **2** knal, ontploffing, schot[h] **3** plotselinge inspanning: *start* off with a ~ hard aan het werk gaan, hard van stapel lopen || [inform] *go* off with a ~ een reuzesucces oogsten

[2]**bang** (vb) **1** knallen, dreunen **2** (+ on) bonzen (op), kloppen, slaan || ~ *about* lawaai maken

[3]**bang** (vb) **1** stoten, bonzen, botsen **2** dichtgooien, dichtsmijten **3** smijten, (neer)smakken

[4]**bang** (adv) **1** precies, pats, vlak: ~ *in the face* precies in zijn gezicht; [inform] ~ *on* precies goed, raak; ~ *on* time precies op tijd **2** plof, boem, paf: *go* ~ uiteenbarsten, in elkaar klappen

[5]**bang** (int) boem!, pats!, pang!

bang away 1 [inform] hard werken, ploeteren **2** ratelen; er op los knallen [firearms]

banger 1 worstje[h] **2** stuk[h] (knal)vuurwerk

Bangladesh Bangladesh

[1]**Bangladeshi** (n) Bengalees, Bengalese

[2]**Bangladeshi** (adj) Bengalees

bangle armband

banish verbannen, uitwijzen, toegang ontzeggen, verwijderen: ~ *those thoughts from your mind* zet die gedachten maar uit je hoofd

banishment ballingschap, verbanning

banister 1 (trap)spijl **2** (trap)leuning

[1]**bank** (n) **1** bank, mistbank, wolkenbank, sneeuwbank, zandbank, ophoging, aardwal **2** oever, glooiing **3** bank [money, also in games]: *break* the ~ de bank doen springen

[2]**bank** (vb) **1** (also + up) zich opstapelen, een bank vormen: ~ *up* zich ophopen **2** (over)-hellen [in a bend] **3** een bankrekening hebben: *who(m) do you* ~ *with?* welke bank heb jij? || [inform] ~ *on* vertrouwen op

[3]**bank** (vb) **1** opstapelen, ophopen **2** doen hellen [eg an aeroplane, road]; doen glooien **3** (+ up) opbanken, afdekken; inrekenen [fire]

bank account bankrekening

banker bankier

bank holiday nationale feestdag

banking bankwezen[h]

banknote bankbiljet[h]

bankrupt failliet

bankruptcy bankroet[h], faillissement[h]

banner banier [also fig]; vaandel[h]: *under the* ~ *of* onder de vlag van

banner ad banner

banner headline krantenkop over hele pagina

banns geboden; (kerkelijke) huwelijksaankondiging: *call the* ~ een huwelijk (kerkelijk) afkondigen, in ondertrouw gaan

banquet banket[h], feestmaal[h], smulpartij

[1]**banter** (n) geplaag[h], scherts

[2]**banter** (vb) schertsen

[3]**banter** (vb) plagen, pesten

baptism doop: ~ *of fire* vuurdoop

Baptist 1 doper: *John* the ~ Johannes de Doper **2** doopsgezinde

baptize dopen

[1]**bar** (n) **1** langwerpig stuk[h] [of hard material]; staaf, stang, baar, reep; [sport] lat: ~ *of chocolate* reep chocola; ~ *of gold* baar goud; ~ *of soap* stuk zeep **2** afgrendelend iets, tralie, grendel, slagboom, afsluitboom; [fig] obstakel[h]; hindernis: *put behind* ~s achter (de) tralies zetten **3** streep; balk [on weapon, as mark of distinction] **4** bar [also as part of pub]; buffet[h] **5** balie [in courthouse]; gerecht[h], rechtbank: *be tried at (the)* ~ in openbare terechtzitting berecht worden

[2]**bar** (vb) **1** vergrendelen, afsluiten, opsluiten, insluiten: ~ *o.s. in* (or: *out*) zichzelf binnensluiten (*or:* buitensluiten) **2** versperren [also fig]; verhinderen **3** verbieden: ~ *s.o. from participation* iem. verbieden deel te nemen

[3]**bar** (prep) behalve, uitgezonderd

the **Bar** advocatuur, balie, advocatenstand; [Am] orde der juristen: *read* (or: *study*) *for the* ~ voor advocaat studeren

barb 1 weerhaak, prikkel **2** steek [fig]; hatelijkheid

[1]**barbarian** (n) **1** barbaar [also hist]; onbeschaafd iem., primitieveling **2** woesteling

[2]**barbarian** (adj) barbaars

barbaric barbaars, ruw, onbeschaafd, wreed

barbarity barbaarsheid; wreedheid

barbarous barbaars, onbeschaafd, wreed

barbecue barbecue, barbecuefeest[h]

barbed 1 met weerhaken **2** [fig] scherp; bijtend [remarks, words] || ~ *wire* prikkeldraad

barber herenkapper: *the* ~'s de kapper(szaak)

bar-code streepjescode, barcode

bard bard, dichter

[1]**bare** (adj) **1** naakt: *in his* ~ *skin* in zijn blootje; *lay* ~ blootleggen **2** kaal, leeg: *the* ~ *facts* de naakte feiten **3** enkel, zonder meer: *the* ~ *necessities (of life)* het strikt noodzakelijke

[2]**bare** (vb) **1** ontbloten: ~ *one's teeth* zijn tanden laten zien **2** blootleggen, onthullen: ~ *one's soul* zijn gevoelens luchten

barebacked met blote rug; ongezadeld

barefaced onbeschaamd, brutaal

barefoot blootsvoets: *walk* ~ op blote voeten lopen

barely nauwelijks, amper: ~ *enough* to eat

nauwelijks genoeg te eten
¹bargain (n) **1** afspraak, akkoord^h, transactie: *make* (or: *strike*) *a* ~ tot een akkoord komen **2** koopje^h ‖ *into the* ~ op de koop toe
²bargain (vb) onderhandelen, dingen ‖ *more than he ~ed for* meer dan waar hij op rekende

bargaining chip onderhandelingstroef
¹barge (n) schuit, aak, sloep
²barge (vb) [inform] stommelen: ~ *into* (or: *against*) *sth.* ergens tegenaan botsen ‖ ~ *in* a) binnenvallen; b) zich bemoeien

barge-pole vaarboom ‖ [inform] *I wouldn't touch* him *with a* ~ ik wil helemaal niets met hem te maken hebben

baritone bariton
¹bark (n) **1** blaffend geluid^h, geblaf^h, ruw stemgeluid^h: *his* ~ *is worse* than his *bite* (het is bij hem) veel geschreeuw en weinig wol **2** schors, bast

²bark (vb) (+ at) blaffen (tegen): [fig] ~ *at* s.o. iem. afblaffen
³bark (vb) (uit)brullen, aanblaffen, luid aanprijzen: ~ *(out) an order* een bevel schreeuwen

barley gerst
barman barman
barn 1 schuur **2** [Am] stal, loods: *a* ~ *of a house* een kast van een huis

barnacle goose brandgans
barn owl kerkuil
barnstorm op tournee gaan
barnyard boerenerf^h, hof
barometer barometer [also fig]; maatstaf
baron 1 baron **2** [Am] magnaat
baroness barones
baronet baronet
baroque barok
barrack 1 barak, keet **2** (-s) kazerne
barrage 1 stuwdam **2** versperring **3** spervuur^h [also fig]; barrage
barrel ton, vat^h ‖ *scrape the* ~ zijn laatste duiten bijeenschrapen, de laatste reserves gebruiken; *over a* ~ hulpeloos
barrel organ draaiorgel^h
barren 1 onvruchtbaar, steriel; [also fig] nutteloos **2** dor, bar, kaal
¹barricade (n) barricade, versperring
²barricade (vb) barricaderen, versperren, afzetten: ~ *o.s. in one's room* zich opsluiten in zijn kamer
barrier barrière, hek^h, slagboom, hindernis
barring behalve, uitgezonderd: ~ *very bad weather* tenzij het zeer slecht weer is; *he's the greatest singer,* ~ *none* hij is de allerbeste zanger, niemand uitgezonderd
barrister 1 advocaat **2** [Am] jurist
barrow 1 kruiwagen **2** draagbaar **3** handkar
bartender [Am] barman
¹barter (n) ruilhandel

²barter (vb) **1** ruilhandel drijven **2** loven en bieden
³barter (vb) **1** (+ for) ruilen (voor/tegen) **2** opgeven [in exchange for sth.]: ~ *away one's freedom* zijn vrijheid prijsgeven
¹base (n) **1** basis, voetstuk^h, grondlijn, grondvlak^h: *the* ~ *of the mountain* de voet van de berg **2** grondslag, fundament^h; [fig] uitgangspunt^h **3** hoofdbestanddeel^h **4** basiskamp^h, basis, hoofdkwartier^h **5** [sport] honk^h: *catch s.o. off* ~ iem. onverwacht treffen
²base (adj) **1** laag, minderwaardig: *a* ~ *action* een laffe daad **2** onedel [metal]; onecht [coin]
³base (vb) **1** (+ (up)on) baseren (op); gronden (op) [also fig]: ~ *o.s. on* uitgaan van; ~*d (up)on* mere *gossip* slechts op roddel berustend **2** vestigen
baseball honkbal^h
baseless ongegrond, ongefundeerd
basement souterrain^h, kelder
¹bash (n) **1** dreun, stoot, mep **2** [inform] fuif ‖ [inform] *have a* ~ *(at sth.)* iets eens proberen
²bash (vb) botsen, bonken
³bash (vb) slaan, beuken: ~ *the door down* de deur inbeuken
bashful verlegen
-bashing [inform] het afranselen; [fig] het fel bekritiseren: *union-bashing* zwaar uithalen naar de vakbond ‖ *bible-bashing* het fanatiek verkondigen van de Bijbel
basic basis-, fundamenteel, minimum-: ~ *data* hoofdgegevens; ~ *pay* (or: *salary*) basisloon
basically eigenlijk, voornamelijk
basics [oft inform] grondbeginselen, basiskennis
basil basilicum^h
basin 1 kom, schaal, schotel **2** waterbekken^h, bak **3** bekken^h, stroomgebied^h **4** wasbak, waskom, fonteintje^h **5** bassin^h, (haven)dok^h
basis basis, fundament^h; [fig] grondslag; hoofdbestanddeel^h: *on the* ~ *of* op grond van
bask [also fig] zich koesteren
basket mand, korf, schuitje^h, gondel; [basketball] basket: *make* (or: *shoot*) *a* ~ scoren
¹basketball (n) basketbal^h [sport]
²basketball (n) basketbal [ball]
¹Basque (n) Bask, Baskische
²Basque (adj) Baskisch
¹bass (n) baars, zeebaars
²bass (n) bas ‖ ~ *guitar* basgitaar
bass clef bassleutel, f-sleutel
bass drum grote trom; bassdrum
bassoon fagot, basson
bastard 1 bastaard, onecht kind^h **2** [inform; depr] smeerlap, schoft **3** [inform] vent: *you lucky* ~! geluksvogel die je bent!
baste bedruipen [with fat]

b̲a̲stion bastion[h] [also fig]; bolwerk[h]
¹bat (n) **1** vleermuis **2** knuppel; [cricket, table tennis] bat[h]; [baseball] slaghout[h], knuppel; [tennis] racket[h] ‖ [inform] *have ~s in the belfry* een klap van de molen gehad hebben; [inform] *off one's own ~* uit eigen beweging, op eigen houtje; [Am; inform] *(right) off the ~* direct
²bat (vb) **1** batten **2** knipp(er)en [eyes]: *without ~ting an eye(lid)* zonder een spier te vertrekken
b̲a̲tch partij, groep, troep: *a ~ of letters* een stapel brieven
b̲a̲tch processing batchverwerking
¹bath (n) **1** bad[h]: *have* (or: *take*) *a ~* een bad nemen **2** zwembad[h] **3** (-s) badhuis[h], kuuroord[h]
²bath (vb) een bad nemen
¹bathe (n) bad[h], zwempartij
²bathe (vb) **1** zich baden, zwemmen **2** [Am] een bad nemen, zich wassen **3** (+ in) baden (in) [fig]; opgaan
³bathe (vb) **1** baden, onderdompelen: *~d in sunshine* met zon overgoten **2** betten [eg wound]
b̲a̲throbe 1 badjas **2** [Am] kamerjas
b̲a̲throom 1 badkamer **2** [euph] toilet[h], wc
b̲a̲thtub badkuip
b̲a̲ton stok, wapenstok, gummistok, dirigeerstok; [sport] estafettestokje[h]: *under the ~ of* onder leiding van, gedirigeerd door
battalion bataljon[h]
¹b̲a̲tten (n) lat, plank
²b̲a̲tten (vb) **1** (+ (up)on) zich vetmesten (met) **2** (+ (up)on) parasiteren (op)
¹b̲a̲tter (n) beslag[h]
²b̲a̲tter (vb) beuken, timmeren: *~ (away) at* inbeuken op
³b̲a̲tter (vb) slaan, timmeren op, havenen
b̲a̲ttery 1 batterij [also mil]; reeks: *a ~ of questions* een spervuur van vragen **2** (elektrische) batterij, accu(mulator) **3** [law] aanranding
b̲a̲ttery charger batterijoplader
¹b̲a̲ttle (n) **1** (veld)slag, gevecht[h], competitie: *fight a losing ~* een hopeloze strijd voeren **2** overwinning: *youth is half the ~* als je maar jong bent
²b̲a̲ttle (vb) slag leveren [also fig]; strijden: *~ through the crowd* zich een weg banen door de menigte
b̲a̲ttle-axe 1 strijdbijl **2** [inform] dragonder; kenau
b̲a̲ttlefield slagveld[h] [also fig]
b̲a̲ttleground gevechtsterrein[h] [also fig]; slagveld[h]
b̲a̲ttleship slagschip[h]
b̲a̲tty [inform] getikt
b̲a̲uble snuisterij, prul[h]
b̲a̲uxite bauxiet[h]
Bav̲a̲ria Beieren

Bav̲a̲rian Beiers
¹b̲a̲wdy (n) schuine praat, schuine grap
²b̲a̲wdy (adj) schuin, vies
bawl schreeuwen: *~ at s.o.* iem. toebrullen ‖ *~ out* uitfoeteren
¹bay (n) **1** baai, zeearm, golf **2** (muur)vak[h] **3** nis, erker **4** afdeling, vleugel; ruimte [in bldg etc] **5** laurier(boom): *~ leaf* laurierblad **6** luid geblaf[h] ‖ *hold* (or: *keep*) *at ~* op een afstand houden
²bay (adj) voskleurig [horse]
³bay (vb) (aan)blaffen, huilen
b̲a̲yonet bajonet, bajonetsluiting
bay w̲i̲ndow erker
bay wreath lauwerkrans
baz̲a̲ar bazaar
BBC *British Broadcasting Corporation* BBC
BBQ *barbecue* BBQ
BC *before Christ* v.Chr., voor Christus
bcc *blind carbon copy* bcc
¹be (vb) **1** zijn, bestaan, voorkomen, plaatshebben **2** geweest (gekomen) zijn: *has the postman been?* is de postbode al geweest?
²be (aux vb) **1** aan het … zijn: *they were reading* ze waren aan het lezen, ze lazen **2** worden, zijn: *he has been murdered* hij is vermoord **3** mocht, zou: *if this were to happen, were this to happen* als dit zou gebeuren
³be (vb) **1** zijn: *she is a teacher* zij is lerares; *the bride-to-be* de aanstaande bruid; *be that as it may* hoe het ook zij **2** [+ indication of size or quantity] (waard/groot/oud) zijn, kosten, meten, duren: *it's three pounds* het kost drie pond; *it is three minutes* het duurt drie minuten **3** zijn, zich bevinden; plaatshebben [also fig]: *it was in 1953* het gebeurde in 1953; *what's behind this?* wat steekt hier achter? **4** zijn, betekenen: *what's it to you?* wat gaat jou dat aan? **5** bedoeld zijn, dienen: *an axe is to fell trees with* een bijl dient om bomen om te hakken ‖ [inform] *be nowhere* ver achterliggen; *as is* zoals hij is
be ab̲o̲ut 1 rondhangen, rondslingeren **2** er zijn, beschikbaar zijn: *there is a lot of flu about* er is heel wat griep onder de mensen **3** op het punt staan: *he was about to leave* hij ging net vertrekken
beach strand[h], oever
b̲e̲achcomber strandjutter
b̲e̲achhead bruggenhoofd[h] [on beach]
b̲e̲acon 1 (vuur)baken[h], vuurtoren, lichtbaken[h] **2** bakenzender, radiobaken[h]
bead 1 kraal **2** (-s) kralen halssnoer[h] **3** druppel, kraal: *~s of sweat* zweetdruppels
b̲e̲adle bode, ceremoniemeester; pedel [at university]
b̲e̲ady kraalvormig: *black ~ eyes* zwarte kraaloogjes ‖ *keep a ~ eye on s.o.* iem. scherp in de gaten houden
b̲e̲agle brak, kleine jachthond
beak snavel, bek, snuit, mondstuk[h]

beaker beker(glas)

the **be-all** essentie: *the ~ and **end-all** of sth.* de alfa en omega van iets

¹**beam** (n) **1** balk **2** boom, disselboom, ploegboom **3** straal, stralenbundel **4** geleide straal, bakenstraal: *be **off** ~* [inform] ernaast zitten, fout zijn **5** stralende blik (glimlach)

²**beam** (vb) stralen, schijnen

bean 1 boon **2** [Am; inform] knikker, kop, hersens ‖ [inform] *spill the ~s* zijn mond voorbijpraten

bean counter [mockingly] boekhouder-(tje)

bean sprouts taugé

¹**bear** (n) **1** beer **2** ongelikte beer, bullebak

²**bear** (vb) **1** houden [of ice] **2** dragen [of wall] **3** vruchten voortbrengen, vruchtbaar zijn **4** (aan)houden [of direction]; (voort)-gaan, lopen: *~ (to the) **left*** links afslaan **5** druk uitoefenen, duwen, leunen: *~ hard* (or: *heavily, severely*) *(up)on* zwaar drukken op [fig] **6** (+ (up)on) invloed hebben (op), van invloed zijn (op), betrekking hebben (op)

³**bear** (vb) **1** dragen: *~ **fruit*** vruchten voort-brengen; [fig] vruchten afwerpen; *~ **away*** *a prize, ~ **off** a price* een prijs in de wacht slepen **2** (over)brengen **3** vertonen, hebben: *~ **signs*** (or: ***traces***) *of* tekenen (or: sporen) ver-tonen van **4** hebben (voelen) voor, toedra-gen, koesteren **5** verdragen, uitstaan: *his words won't ~ repeating* zijn woorden zijn niet voor herhaling vatbaar **6** voortbrengen, ba-ren: *borne **by*** geboren uit

bearable draaglijk, te dragen

beard 1 baard **2** weerhaak

bear down persen, druk uitoefenen ‖ *~ (up)on* zwaar drukken op

bearer 1 drager: *the ~ of a **passport*** de houder van een paspoort **2** bode, bood-schapper: *the ~ of this **letter*** de brenger dezes **3** toonder [of cheque etc]: *pay to ~* betaal aan toonder

bear-hug [inform] houdgreep, onstuimige omhelzing

bearing 1 verband^h, betrekking: *have no ~ on* los staan van **2** betekenis, strekking **3** (-s) positie, ligging, plaats: *get* (or: *take*) *one's ~s* zich oriënteren, poolshoogte nemen **4** het dragen **5** houding, voorkomen^h, gedrag^h, optreden^h

be around even aanlopen, bezoeken

bear out (onder)steunen, bekrachtigen, staven: *bear **s.o.** out* iemands verklaring be-vestigen

bear up zich (goed) houden, zich redden: *~ **against** sth.* ergens tegen opgewassen zijn

bear with geduld hebben met

beast 1 beest^h [also fig]: *~ of **prey*** roofdier **2** rund^h

beastly beestachtig: *~ **stench*** walgelijke

stank; *~ **drunk*** stomdronken

¹**beat** (n) **1** slag **2** (vaste) ronde, (vaste) rou-te: *be **on** one's ~* zijn ronde doen **3** [mus] rit-me^h, beat

²**beat** (vb) **1** slaan, bonzen, beuken, woeden; kloppen [of heart, blood]; fladderen [of wing] **2** een klopjacht houden **3** zich (moei-zaam) een weg banen

³**beat** (vb) **1** slaan (op), klutsen; kloppen [rug]; fladderen met [wing]: [inform] *~ s.o.'s brains **out*** iem. de hersens inslaan; *the **recipe** to ~ all recipes* het recept dat alles slaat; *~ **back*** terugslaan, terugdrijven **2** (uit)smeden [door] **3** banen [path] **4** verslaan, eronder krijgen; breken [record]: [inform] *can you ~ **that?*** heb je ooit zoiets gehoord? **5** uitput-ten: *he was **dead** ~* hij was (dood)op **6** afzoe-ken **7** [Am; inform] ontlopen [punishment] ‖ [inform] *~ **it!*** smeer 'm!

¹**beat down** (vb) branden [of sun]

²**beat down** (vb) **1** neerslaan **2** intrappen [door] **3** naar beneden brengen; drukken [price] **4** afdingen (bij/op)

beaten 1 veel betreden; gebaand [of road, track; also fig]: *be off the ~ **track*** verafgele-gen zijn **2** gesmeed, geplet: *~ **gold*** bladgoud **3** verslagen

beater 1 klopper [of egg, carpet] **2** [hunt-ing] drijver

beating afstraffing [also fig]: *take some* (or: *a lot of*) *~* moeilijk te overtreffen zijn

beatitude 1 zaligverklaring **2** (geluk)zalig-heid

beat off afslaan, terugdrijven, afweren

beat up 1 [inform] in elkaar slaan **2** (op)-kloppen, klutsen **3** [inform] optrommelen, werven

beautician schoonheidsspecialist(e)

beautiful 1 mooi, fraai, prachtig **2** heer-lijk; verrukkelijk [of weather]

beautify verfraaien, (ver)sieren, mooi ma-ken

beauty 1 schoonheid: *that is the ~ of it* dat is het mooie ervan **2** [inform] pracht(exem-plaar^h), juweeltje^h

beauty parlour schoonheidssalon

beaver bever

beaver away [inform] zwoegen, ploeteren

because 1 omdat, want **2** (het feit) dat

because of wegens, vanwege

beck teken^h, knik, gebaar^h: *be at s.o.'s ~ and call* iem. op zijn wenken bedienen

beckon wenken, gebaren, een teken geven

¹**become** (vb) (+ of) gebeuren (met), worden (van), aflopen (met)

²**become** (vb) **1** passen: *it **ill** ~s you* het siert je niet **2** eer aandoen **3** (goed) staan [of clothes]

³**become** (vb) worden, (ge)raken: *~ mayor* burgemeester worden

becoming gepast, behoorlijk: *as is ~* zoals

het hoort

¹bed (n) **1** bed^h, slaapplaats, huwelijk^h; leger^h [of animal]; bloembed^h, tuinbed^h: ~ *and board* kost en inwoning; ~ *and breakfast* logies met ontbijt; *double* (or: *single*) ~ tweepersoonsbed, eenpersoonsbed; *spare* ~ logeerbed; *wet one's* ~ bedwateren **2** (rivier)bedding **3** bed(ding), grondslag, onderlaag, (bodem)laag

²bed (vb) **1** [inform] naar bed gaan met **2** planten: ~ *out* uitplanten

bedbug bedwants

bedding 1 beddengoed^h **2** onderlaag, grondslag, bedding **3** gelaagdheid

bedevil treiteren, dwarszitten, achtervolgen, (ernstig) bemoeilijken

bedfellow bedgenoot, bedgenote ‖ *adversity makes strange ~s* tegenspoed maakt vijanden tot vrienden

bedlam gekkenhuis^h [also fig]; gesticht^h; [inform] heksenketel

Bedouin bedoeïen

be down 1 beneden zijn; minder, gezakt zijn [lit and fig] **2** uitgeteld zijn; [fig] somber zijn: [inform] ~ *with the flu* geveld zijn door griep **3** buiten bedrijf zijn; plat liggen [of computer] ‖ [inform] ~ *on* s.o. iem. aanpakken, iem. fel bekritiseren; *he is down to his last pound* hij heeft nog maar één pond over

bedpan (onder)steek

bedraggled 1 doorweekt **2** verfomfaaid, toegetakeld, sjofel

bedridden bedlegerig

bedroom slaapkamer

bedside manner [roughly] optreden van dokter aan het ziekbed

bedspread sprei

bedstead ledikant^h

bedtime bedtijd

bedtime story verhaaltje voor het slapen gaan

bee 1 bij **2** [inform] gril ‖ [inform] *have a ~ in one's bonnet (about sth.)* **a)** door iets geobsedeerd worden; **b)** niet helemaal normaal zijn (op een bepaald punt)

beech beuk, beukenhout^h

¹beef (n) **1** rundvlees^h: *corned* ~ cornedbeef **2** [inform] kracht, spierballen

²beef (vb) [inform] kankeren, mopperen, zeuren

beefcake [inform] (foto's van) gespierde kerels; krachtpatsers

beefeater 1 koninklijke lijfwacht **2** hellebaardier van de Tower **3** [Am; inform] Engelsman

beefsteak biefstuk, runderlap(je^h)

beef up [inform] versterken, opvoeren

beehive 1 bijenkorf [also fig] **2** suikerbrood^h [hairdo]

beekeeper bijenhouder, imker

beeline rechte lijn: [inform] *make a ~ for*

(or: *to*) regelrecht afstevenen op

¹beep (n) **1** getoeter^h, toet **2** fluittoon, pieptoon; piep(je^h) [indicating time]

²beep (vb) **1** toeteren **2** piepen

beeper pieper, portofoon, semafoon

beer bier^h, glas^h bier

beeswax (bijen)was

beet 1 biet **2** [Am] (bieten)kroot, rode biet

beetle kever, tor

beetroot 1 (bieten)kroot, rode biet **2** beetwortel, suikerbiet

befall [form] overkomen, gebeuren (met)

befit [form] passen

be for zijn voor, voorstander zijn van ‖ *you're for it!* er zwaait wat voor je!

¹before (adv) **1** voorop, vooraan, ervoor **2** vroeger, eerder, vooraf: *three weeks* ~ drie weken geleden

²before (prep) **1** [time] vóór, vroeger dan, alvorens: ~ *Christmas* voor Kerstmis; ~ *long* binnenkort **2** [place] voor, voor ... uit, tegenover: *put a bill* ~ *parliament* een wetsontwerp bij het parlement indienen ‖ *put friendship* ~ *love* vriendschap hoger achten dan liefde; ~ *all else* bovenal

³before (conj) alvorens, voor

beforehand vooraf, van tevoren, vooruit

befriend een vriend zijn voor, bijstaan

¹beg (vb) **1** opzitten [of dog] **2** de vrijheid nemen, zo vrij zijn: *I* ~ *to differ* ik ben zo vrij daar anders over te denken

²beg (vb) **1** bedelen: ~ *for* bedelen om, smeken om **2** (dringend/met klem) verzoeken, smeken, (nederig) vragen

beget 1 verwekken **2** [form] voortbrengen; veroorzaken

¹beggar (n) bedelaar(ster), schooier ‖ *~s can't be choosers* [roughly] lieverkoekjes worden niet gebakken

²beggar (vb) te boven gaan: ~ *(all) description* alle beschrijving tarten

begin beginnen, aanvangen, starten: *life ~s at sixty* met zestig begint het echte leven ‖ *~ with* om te beginnen, in de eerste plaats

beginning 1 begin^h, aanvang: *from* ~ *to end* van begin tot einde; *in the* ~ aanvankelijk **2** (-s) (prille) begin^h

begrudge misgunnen, benijden, niet gunnen

beguile 1 bedriegen, verleiden: ~ *into* ertoe verleiden (te) **2** korten, verdrijven: *we ~d the time by playing cards* we kortten de tijd met kaartspelen **3** charmeren, betoveren

beguiling verleidelijk

behalf: *on* ~ *of my father* namens mijn vader; *in my* ~ voor mij

behave zich gedragen, zich goed gedragen: ~ *(yourself)!* gedraag je!

behaviour gedrag^h, houding, optreden^h: *be on one's best* ~ zichzelf van zijn beste kant laten zien

beh<u>ea</u>d onthoofden
¹beh<u>i</u>nd (n) [inform; euph] achterste[h]
²beh<u>i</u>nd (adv) **1** [movement, place or space] erachter, achteraan, achterop, achterin, achterom, voorbij **2** [delay or arrears] achterop, achter, achterstallig: *they fell ~* ze raakten achter [also fig]
³beh<u>i</u>nd (prep) **1** [place, direction or time; also fig] achter, voorbij, verder dan, om: *the house ~ the church* het huis achter de kerk; *put one's problems ~* one zijn problemen van zich afzetten **2** [delay or arrears] achter op, later dan, onder: *the bus is ~ schedule* de bus heeft vertraging **3** achter, aan de oorsprong van: *the real reasons ~ the quarrel* de echte redenen voor de ruzie **4** achter, ter ondersteuning van: *we are* (or: *stand*) *~ you* wij staan achter je, steunen je
beh<u>i</u>ndhand 1 achter(stallig) **2** achter, achterop: *be ~ with one's work* achter zijn met zijn werk
beh<u>o</u>ld [form] aanschouwen: [mockingly] *lo and ~!* welwel!, en ziedaar!
beh<u>o</u>lder aanschouwer; toeschouwer
beige beige[h]
be <u>i</u>n 1 binnen zijn, er zijn, aanwezig zijn: *the new fabrics aren't in yet* de nieuwe stoffen zijn nog niet binnen **2** geaccepteerd zijn, erbij, aanvaard, opgenomen zijn; in de mode zijn, in zijn [of things]: *~ on* meedoen aan ‖ [inform] *we're in for a nasty surprise* er staat ons een onaangename verrassing te wachten
b<u>ei</u>ng 1 wezen[h], schepsel[h], bestaan[h], zijn[h], existentie: *bring* (or: *call*) *into ~* creëren, doen ontstaan; *come into ~* ontstaan **2** wezen[h], essentie, aard, het wezenlijke
Belar<u>u</u>s Wit-Rusland
bel<u>a</u>ted laat
¹belch (n) boer, oprisping
²belch (vb) **1** boeren **2** (uit)braken, uitbarsten: *the volcano ~ed out rocks* de vulkaan spuwde stenen (uit)
bel<u>ea</u>guer 1 belegeren **2** zwaar bekritiseren
¹Belgian (n) Belg, Belgische
²Belgian (adj) Belgisch
Belgium België
bel<u>ie</u> 1 een valse indruk geven van, tegenspreken **2** logenstraffen: *the attack ~d our hopes for peace* de aanval logenstrafte onze hoop op vrede **3** niet nakomen
bel<u>ie</u>f 1 (geloofs)overtuiging **2** geloof[h], vertrouwen[h]: *beyond ~* ongelofelijk, niet te geloven **3** geloof[h], mening: *to the best of my ~* naar mijn beste weten
bel<u>ie</u>ve 1 geloven, gelovig zijn **2** (+ in) geloven (in), vertrouwen hebben (in) **3** geloven, menen, veronderstellen **4** geloven, voor waar aannemen: *I'll ~ anything of James* James acht ik tot alles in staat

bel<u>ie</u>ver 1 gelover; iem. die gelooft **2** gelovige
bel<u>i</u>ttle onbelangrijk(er) doen lijken, kleineren
Bel<u>i</u>ze Belize
¹Bel<u>i</u>zean (n) Belizaan(se)
²Bel<u>i</u>zean (adj) Belizaans
bell klok, bel, belsignaal[h] ‖ *that rings a ~* dat komt me ergens bekend voor
b<u>e</u>ll-boy piccolo
b<u>e</u>llhop [Am] piccolo
b<u>e</u>llicose strijdlustig, oorlogszuchtig, agressief
bell<u>i</u>gerent 1 oorlogvoerend **2** strijdlustig, uitdagend, agressief
¹b<u>e</u>llow (n) gebrul[h], geloei[h]
²b<u>e</u>llow (vb) loeien, brullen
b<u>e</u>llows blaasbalg: *a (pair of) ~* een blaasbalg
b<u>e</u>ll pepper paprika
b<u>e</u>lly 1 [inform] buik, maag, schoot **2** ronding [as of a stomach]; uitstulping, onderkant: *the ~ of an aeroplane* de buik van een vliegtuig
b<u>e</u>llyache buikpijn
b<u>e</u>lly button navel
belly-<u>u</u>p: [inform] *go ~* failliet gaan
bel<u>o</u>ng 1 passen, (thuis)horen: *it doesn't ~ here* dat hoort hier niet (thuis) **2** [inform] thuishoren, zich thuis voelen, op z'n plaats zijn: *a sense of ~ing* het gevoel erbij te horen
bel<u>o</u>ngings persoonlijke eigendommen, bagage
bel<u>o</u>ng to 1 toebehoren aan, (eigendom) zijn van **2** horen bij, lid zijn van: *which group do you ~?* bij welke groep zit jij?
Belor<u>u</u>ssia Wit-Rusland
bel<u>o</u>ved bemind, geliefd
¹bel<u>o</u>w (adv) beneden, eronder, onderaan: *she lives in the flat ~* ze woont in de flat hieronder; *see ~* zie verder
²bel<u>o</u>w (prep) **1** onder, beneden, lager (gelegen) dan; [fig] (verscholen/verborgen) achter: *the flat ~ ours* de flat onder de onze **2** ondergeschikt, lager dan, minder dan: *~ average* minderwaardig, slecht; *~ the average* onder het gemiddelde
¹belt (n) **1** gordel, (broek)riem, ceintuur **2** drijfriem: *fan ~* ventilatorriem **3** (transport)band, lopende band **4** [esp as second part of compound] zone, klimaatstreek, klimaatgebied[h]: *a ~ of low pressure* een lagedrukgebied ‖ *hit below the ~* onder de gordel slaan; *tighten one's ~,* [Am also] *pull one's ~ in* de buikriem aanhalen; *under one's ~* in zijn bezit, binnen
²belt (vb) **1** omgorden **2** een pak slaag geven (met een riem) ‖ *~ out* brullen, bulken
belt <u>u</u>p zijn veiligheidsgordel aandoen
bem<u>oa</u>n [form] beklagen
bem<u>u</u>sed 1 verbijsterd, verdwaasd **2** ver-

strooid
bench 1 bank, zitbank **2** (parlements)zetel; bank [in House of Commons] **3** rechterstoel **4** werkbank **5** [sport] reservebank, strafbank(je^h) **6** rechtbank, de rechters **7** [sport] de reservebank, de reservespelers
benchmark standaard, maatstaf
¹**bend** (n) **1** buiging, kromming, knik **2** bocht, draai: *a sharp ~ in the road* een scherpe bocht in de weg || *(go) (a)round the ~* knettergek (worden)
²**bend** (vb) buigen, zwenken: *~ down* zich bukken, vooroverbuigen || *~ over backwards* zich vreselijk uitsloven
³**bend** (vb) **1** buigen, krommen, verbuigen: [fig] *~ the rules* de regels naar zijn hand zetten; *~ down* (or: *up*) naar beneden (*or*: boven) buigen **2** onderwerpen, (doen) buigen, plooien: *~ s.o. to one's will* iem. naar zijn hand zetten
bender 1 [inform] feest^h; zuippartij: *on a ~* aan het zuipen, aan de drugs **2** [vulg] homo
¹**beneath** (adv) eronder, daaronder, onderaan
²**beneath** (prep) **1** onder, beneden, lager dan **2** achter, verborgen achter **3** onder, onder de invloed van: *bent ~ his burden* onder zijn last gebukt **4** beneden, onder, beneden de waardigheid van: *he thinks manual labour is ~ him* hij vindt zichzelf te goed voor handenarbeid
benediction [rel] zegening
benefactor weldoener
beneficent weldadig
beneficial voordelig, nuttig, heilzaam
beneficiary begunstigde
¹**benefit** (n) **1** voordeel^h, profijt^h, hulp: *give s.o. the ~ of the doubt* iem. het voordeel van de twijfel geven **2** uitkering, steun, steungeld^h: *be on ~s* in de bijstand zitten **3** benefiet^h, liefdadigheidsvoorstelling, benefiet-
²**benefit** (vb) voordeel halen, baat vinden
³**benefit** (vb) ten goede komen aan, goed doen voor
benevolent 1 welwillend, goedgunstig **2** liefdadig, vrijgevig
Bengal Bengaals
¹**Bengali** (n) Bengaal(se)
²**Bengali** (adj) Bengaals
benign 1 vriendelijk **2** zacht, gunstig, heilzaam: *a ~ climate* een zacht klimaat **3** goedaardig: *a ~ tumour* een goedaardig gezwel
benignant 1 beminnelijk, welwillend **2** goedaardig
Benin Benin
¹**Beninese** (n) Beniner, Beninse
²**Beninese** (adj) Benins
¹**bent** (n) neiging, aanleg, voorliefde, zwak^h
²**bent** (adj) **1** afwijkend, krom, illegaal **2** [inform] omkoopbaar **3** [vulg] homoseksueel **4** vastbesloten: *~ on* uit op

be off 1 [inform] ervandoor gaan [also fig]; vertrekken, weg zijn, wegwezen; [sport] starten; weg zijn; beginnen [talking]: *~ to a bad start* slecht van start gaan **2** verwijderd zijn [also fig]: *Easter was two weeks off* het was nog twee weken vóór Pasen **3** afgelast zijn, niet doorgaan **4** [inform] bedorven zijn [of food] **5** afgesloten zijn [of water, gas, electricity] || [inform] *be badly off* er slecht voorstaan
¹**be on** (vb) [inform] op kosten zijn van; betaald worden door: *the drinks are on John* John trakteert
²**be on** (vb) **1** aan (de gang) zijn; aan staan [of light, radio etc]: *the match is on* de wedstrijd is bezig **2** gevorderd zijn: *it was well on into the night* het was al diep in de nacht **3** doorgaan, gehandhaafd worden: *the party is on* het feest gaat door **4** [inform] toegestaan zijn: *that's not on!* dat doe je niet! **5** op het toneel staan; spelen [of actor] **6** op het programma staan [radio, TV, play] || [inform] *~ about sth.* het hebben over iets; [depr] altijd maar zeuren over iets; [inform] *~ to sth.* iets in de gaten hebben
be out 1 (er)uit zijn, (er)buiten zijn, weg zijn, er niet (meer) zijn **2** [inform] uit zijn, voorbij zijn: *before the year is out* voor het jaar voorbij is **3** uit(gedoofd) zijn **4** openbaar (gemaakt) zijn, gepubliceerd zijn: *the results are out* de resultaten zijn bekend **5** [inform] onmogelijk zijn, niet mogen: *rough games are out!* geen ruwe spelletjes! **6** ernaast zitten: *his forecast was well out* zijn voorspelling was er helemaal naast **7** in staking zijn **8** laag zijn [of tide]: *the tide is out* het is laagtij **9** [cricket, baseball] uit zijn || [inform] *~ to do sth.* van plan zijn iets te doen; *~ for o.s.* zijn eigen belangen dienen
be out of 1 uit zijn, buiten zijn: *~ it* er niet bij horen **2** zonder zitten: *he is out of a job* hij zit zonder werk; *we're out of sugar* we hebben geen suiker meer || [inform] *be well out of it* er mooi van af (gekomen) zijn
¹**be over** (vb) [with 'all'; inform] **1** overal bekend zijn in: *it's all over the office* het hele kantoor weet ervan **2** niet kunnen afblijven van, (overdreven) enthousiast begroeten
²**be over** (vb) **1** voorbij, over zijn: [inform] *that's over and done with* dat is voor eens en altijd voorbij **2** overschieten, overblijven: *there's a bit of fabric over* er schiet een beetje stof over **3** op bezoek zijn [from a distant country]: *Henk is over from Australia* Henk is over uit Australië
bequeath [form] vermaken, nalaten
bequest legaat^h
berate [form] uitschelden; een fikse uitbrander geven
bereave beroven, doen verliezen || *the ~d* de nabestaanden

ber<u>ea</u>vement 1 sterfgeval^h, overlijden^h **2** verlies^h: *we* **sympathize** *with you in your ~* wij betuigen onze oprechte deelneming met uw verlies

b<u>e</u>ret baret

b<u>e</u>rry bes

bers<u>e</u>rk woest, razend: *go ~* razend worden

¹**berth** (n) **1** kooi, hut **2** ligplaats, ankerplaats, aanlegplaats

²**berth** (vb) aanleggen, ankeren

bes<u>ee</u>ch smeken, dringend verzoeken

bes<u>e</u>t 1 [esp passive] belegeren [also fig]; overvallen, omsingelen: *young people, ~ by doubts* door twijfel overvallen jongeren **2** insluiten, versperren, bezetten

bes<u>i</u>de naast, bij, langs, dichtbij, vergeleken bij: *it's ~ the* **point** het doet hier niet ter zake || *be ~ o.s.* **with** *joy* buiten zichzelf van vreugde zijn

¹**bes<u>i</u>des** (adv) **1** bovendien, daarenboven: *Tina bought a new suit and a blouse ~* Tina kocht een nieuw pak en ook nog een bloes **2** anders, daarnaast, behalve dat **3** trouwens

²**bes<u>i</u>des** (prep) behalve, buiten, naast: *I can do nothing ~ wait* ik kan alleen maar wachten

bes<u>ie</u>ge 1 belegeren **2** bestormen: *~ s.o.* **with** *questions* **about** iem. bestormen met vragen over

besm<u>i</u>rch 1 bevuilen; besmeuren **2** [fig] bekladden; schaden

besp<u>a</u>tter 1 bespatten **2** bekladden [also fig]; belasteren, uitschelden

¹**best** (n) (de/het) beste: *with the ~ of* **intentions** met de beste bedoelingen; *to the ~ of my* **knowledge** *(and belief)* voor zover ik weet; *at ~* op z'n best (genomen), hoogstens; *at the ~ of times* onder de gunstigste omstandigheden || **get** (or: **have**) *the ~ of it* de overhand krijgen (or: hebben); *it is (all)* **for** *the ~* het komt allemaal wel goed

²**best** (adj) best(e) || *~ man* getuige [of bridegroom]; bruidsjonker; *the ~* **part** *of* het merendeel van

³**best** (adv) **1** het best: *~* **before** *10 February* ten minste houdbaar tot 10 februari **2** meest: *those ~* **able** *to pay* zij die het gemakkelijkste kunnen betalen

best-bef<u>o</u>re date houdbaarheidsdatum

b<u>e</u>stial [also fig] beestachtig, dierlijk

best<u>o</u>w verlenen, schenken

best s<u>e</u>ller 1 bestseller, succesartikel^h, succesproduct^h **2** successchrijver

b<u>e</u>sty [inform] hartsvriend(in), beste vriend(in)

¹**bet** (n) **1** weddenschap: *lay* (or: *make, place*) *a ~ (on sth.)* wedden (op iets) **2** inzet **3** iets waarop men wedt, kans, keuze: *your best ~ is* je maakt de meeste kans met

²**bet** (vb) **1** wedden, verwedden: *~ on sth.* op iets wedden **2** [inform] wedden, zeker (kun-

nen) zijn van

be thr<u>ou</u>gh 1 klaar zijn, er doorheen zijn: *I'm through* **with** *my work* ik ben klaar met mijn werk **2** [inform] erdoor zitten, er de brui aan geven; afgedaan hebben [of things]: *~* **with** *sth.* iets beu zijn; *I'm through* **with** *you* ik trek m'n handen van je af **3** verbonden zijn, verbinding hebben

be to 1 moeten: *what am I to* **do** wat moet ik doen? **2** [+ negation] mogen: *visitors are not to* **feed** *the animals* bezoekers mogen de dieren niet voeren **3** gaan, zullen: *we are to be* **married** *next year* we gaan volgend jaar trouwen **4** zijn te: *Molly is nowhere to be* **found** Molly is nergens te vinden

betr<u>a</u>y 1 verraden, in de steek laten **2** verraden, uitbrengen, verklappen: *his eyes ~ed his* **thoughts** zijn ogen verraadden zijn gedachten

betr<u>a</u>yal (daad van) verraad^h

betr<u>a</u>yer verrader

betr<u>o</u>thal verloving

betr<u>o</u>thed 1 verloofde, aanstaande (bruid/bruidegom) **2** verloofden, aanstaande bruid en bruidegom

¹**b<u>e</u>tter** (n) **1** (-s) beteren^h, meerderen, superieuren **2** iets beters **3** verbetering: *change for the ~* ten goede veranderen || *his emotions* **got** *the ~ of him* hij werd door zijn emoties overmand

²**b<u>e</u>tter** (adj) **1** beter: *~* **luck** *next time!* volgende keer beter!; *he is* **little** *~ than a thief* hij is nauwelijks beter dan een dief **2** groter; grootste [part]: *the ~* **part** *of the day* het grootste gedeelte van de dag **3** hersteld, genezen || *I'm none the ~* **for** *it* ik ben er niet beter van geworden

³**b<u>e</u>tter** (adv) **1** beter **2** meer: *I like prunes ~ than figs* ik hou meer van pruimen dan van vijgen

b<u>e</u>tterment verbetering

¹**betw<u>ee</u>n** (adv) ertussen, tussendoor: *two gardens with a* **fence** *~* twee tuinen met een schutting ertussen

²**betw<u>ee</u>n** (prep) tussen [two]; onder: *~* **school,** *her music and her friends she led a busy life* met de school, haar muziek en haar vrienden, had ze alles bij elkaar een druk leven; *they wrote the book ~* **them** ze schreven het boek samen; *~ you and me, ~ ourselves* onder ons (gezegd); *I was sitting ~ my two sisters* ik zat tussen mijn twee zussen in

betw<u>i</u>xt (er)tussen

be <u>u</u>p 1 in een hoge(re) positie zijn [also fig]: *petrol's up again* de benzine is weer duurder geworden **2** op zijn, opstaan, wakker zijn **3** op zijn, over zijn: [inform] *it's all up with him* het is met hem gedaan **4** ter discussie staan, in aanmerking komen: *~* **for** *discussion* ter discussie staan **5** zijn, wonen, studeren **6** aan de gang zijn, gaande zijn: *what's* up **with** you? wat is er met jou aan de hand? ‖ ~ **against** a problem op een probleem gestoten zijn; [inform] ~ **against** it in de puree zitten; be well up **in** sth. goed op de hoogte zijn van iets

be up to **1** komen tot: I'm up to my ears in work ik zit tot over m'n oren in het werk **2** in z'n schild voeren, uit zijn op: **what** are you up to now? wat voer je nu weer in je schild?

3 [esp with negation] voldoen aan, beantwoorden aan: it wasn't up to our expectations het beantwoordde niet aan onze verwachtingen **4** [with negation or interrogative] aankunnen, berekend zijn op, aandurven: he isn't up to this job hij kan deze klus niet aan ‖ it's up to you het is jouw zaak

beverage drank: **alcoholic** ~s alcoholhoudende dranken

bevvy [inform] drankje[h]

bewail betreuren

beware oppassen, op zijn hoede zijn, voorzichtig zijn: ~ **of** the dog pas op voor de hond

bewilder verbijsteren, van zijn stuk brengen

bewitch beheksen, betoveren, bekoren

be with [inform] **1** (kunnen) volgen, (nog) snappen: are you still with **me?** volg je me nog? **2** aan de kant staan van, op de hand zijn van, partij kiezen voor **3** horen bij: we are with the coach party wij horen bij het busgezelschap

1beyond (n) het onbekende, het hiernamaals: the **great** ~ het grote onbekende

2beyond (adv) **1** verder, daarachter, aan de overzijde, daarna **2** daarenboven, meer, daarbuiten

3beyond (prep) **1** voorbij, achter, verder dan: the hills ~ the **city** de heuvels achter de stad **2** naast, buiten, behalve, meer dan ‖ ~ **hope** er is geen hoop meer; it is ~ **me** dat gaat mijn verstand te boven

BFF [inform] best friend forever hartsvriend(in), allerbeste vriend(in)

Bhutan Bhutan

1Bhutanese (n) Bhutaan(se)

2Bhutanese (adj) Bhutaans

1bias (n) **1** neiging, tendens, vooroordeel[h], vooringenomenheid: **without** ~ onbevooroordeeld **2** [one-sided weighting] eenzijdige verzwaring [of ball]; afwijking [in shape or movement of ball]; effect[h]

2bias (vb) bevooroordeeld maken, beïnvloeden: he was ~ed **against** foreigners hij zat vol vooroordelen tegen buitenlanders

biased 1 vooringenomen, bevooroordeeld **2** tendentieus, in een bepaalde richting sturend

bib slab, slabbetje[h]

Bible 1 Bijbel **2** [fig] bijbel

biblical Bijbels

bibliographer bibliograaf

bibliography bibliografie, literatuurlijst

bicameral tweekamer-: a ~ **legislature** een wetgevend lichaam met twee kamers

bicarbonate bicarbonaat[h], zuiveringszout[h]: ~ of **soda** natriumbicarbonaat, zuiveringszout

bicentenary tweehonderdjarig jubileum[h]

bicentennial [Am] tweehonderdjarig jubileum[h]

bicker ruziën

1bicycle (n) fiets

2bicycle (vb) fietsen

1bid (n) **1** bod[h] **2** prijsopgave, offerte **3** [cards] bod[h], beurt (om te bieden) **4** poging [to obtain sth.]; gooi: a ~ **for** the presidency een gooi naar het presidentschap

2bid (vb) **1** bevelen, gelasten **2** heten, zeggen: ~ s.o. **farewell** iem. vaarwel zeggen **3** (uit)nodigen

3bid (vb) **1** bieden, een bod doen (van) **2** een prijsopgave indienen **3** dingen: ~ **for** the public's favour naar de gunst van het publiek dingen

bidder bieder: the **highest** ~ de meestbiedende

bidding 1 het bieden **2** gebod[h], bevel[h]: **do** s.o.'s ~ iemands bevelen uitvoeren; [depr] naar iemands pijpen dansen

bide: ~ one's **time** zijn tijd afwachten

biennial tweejarig

bifocals dubbelfocusbril

bifurcate zich splitsen; zich vertakken

1big (adj) **1** groot, omvangrijk, dik, zwaar: ~ **game** grof wild; ~ **money** grof geld, het grote geld; ~ **with** child (hoog)zwanger **2** belangrijk, invloedrijk, voornaam; [inform] langverwacht: ~ **business** het groot kapitaal, de grote zakenwereld **3** groot, ouder, volwassen: my ~ **sister** mijn grote zus **4** [inform] groot(s), hoogdravend, ambitieus: [inform] have ~ **ideas** ambitieus zijn, het hoog in de bol hebben ‖ be too ~ for one's **boots** het hoog in de bol hebben; [iron] ~ **deal!** reusachtig!, nou, geweldig!; what's the ~ **hurry?** vanwaar die haast?; what's the ~ **idea?** wat is hier aan de hand?

2big (adv) [inform] veel, duur, ruim: **pay** ~ for sth. veel voor iets betalen

bigamy bigamie, met twee personen gelijktijdig gehuwd zijn

the **big bang theory** oerknaltheorie

bigheaded [inform] verwaand

bigot dweper, fanaticus

bigoted onverdraagzaam

bigotry onverdraagzaamheid

big-time top-, eersteklas(-)

bigwig [inform; oft iron] hoge ome, hoge piet, bobo

1bike (n) [inform] **1** fiets **2** [Am] motorfiets

2bike (vb) [inform] **1** fietsen **2** [Am] motorrijden

bilateral 1 tweezijdig, tweevoudig **2** bilateraal, wederzijds (bindend), tussen twee landen (partijen)
bilberry bosbes
bile 1 gal **2** galstoornis **3** [fig] zwartgalligheid, humeurigheid
bilingual tweetalig
bilious 1 misselijk **2** afschuwelijk **3** [form] zwartgallig, humeurig
¹bill (n) **1** rekening, factuur, nota: *foot the ~ (for)* de hele rekening betalen (voor) **2** lijst, aanplakbiljetʰ, (strooi)biljetʰ, programmaʰ: *~ of fare* menu; *stick no ~s* verboden aan te plakken **3** certificaatʰ, bewijsʰ, brief, rapportʰ **4** bek, snavel, neus **5** [Am] (bank)biljetʰ **6** [fin] wissel, schuldbekentenis **7** wetsvoorstelʰ, wetsontwerpʰ ‖ *fill* (or: *fit*) *the ~* geschikt zijn, aan iemands wensen tegemoetkomen
²bill (vb) **1** aankondigen, aanplakken **2** op de rekening zetten, de rekening sturen
billboard [Am] aanplakbordʰ, reclamebordʰ
¹billet (n) **1** kwartierʰ, bestemming, verblijfplaats **2** inkwartieringsbevelʰ
²billet (vb) inkwartieren, onderbrengen: *the troops were ~ed at our school* de troepen werden ondergebracht in onze school
billiards (Engels) biljartʰ, het biljartspel
billion miljard, duizend miljoen; [fig] talloos
¹billow (n) **1** (zware) golf, hoge deining **2** [fig] golf, vloedgolf, zee
²billow (vb) deinen, golven, bol staan: *the ~ing sea* de golvende zee
billy goat (geiten)bok
bimonthly tweemaandelijks
bin vergaarbak, bak, mand, trommel, vuilnisbak, broodtrommel
binary binair, tweevoudig, dubbel(-)
¹bind (vb) (aaneen)plakken, zich (ver)binden, vast worden
²bind (vb) **1** (vast)binden, bijeenbinden, boeien **2** bedwingen, aan banden leggen, hinderen: *be snow-bound* vastzitten in de sneeuw **3** verplichten, verbinden, dwingen: *she is bound to come* ze moet komen, ze zal zeker komen; *~ s.o. to secrecy* iem. tot geheimhouding verplichten **4** (in)binden [book]; van een band voorzien ‖ *~ (up) a wound* een wond verbinden; *I'll be bound* ik ben er absoluut zeker van; *he is bound up in his job* hij gaat helemaal op in zijn werk
binder 1 binder [also agriculture; also machine]; boekbinder **2** band, snoerʰ, touwʰ, windselʰ **3** map, omslag⁺ʰ, ringband **4** bindmiddelʰ
bindery (boek)binderij
bindi bindi
¹binding (n) band, boekband, verbandʰ
²binding (adj) bindend

bindweed winde
binge [inform] feestʰ, braspartij: *~ eating* feesten, gaan stappen; *go on the ~* feesten, gaan stappen
binge drinking comazuipenʰ
bin liner vuilniszak
binoculars (verre)kijker, veldkijker, toneelkijker
biochemistry biochemie
biodegradable (biologisch) afbreekbaar
biodiversity biodiversiteit
bioengineering biotechniek
biofuel biobrandstof
biographer biograaf, biografe
biographical biografisch
biography biografie, levensbeschrijving
biological biologisch
biologist bioloog
biology biologie
bionic 1 bionisch **2** [inform] supervlug, supersterk
biopic [inform] *biographic picture* filmbiografie
biosphere biosfeer
biowaste bioafval
bipartisan tweepartijen-
bipartite tweedelig, tweeledig, tweezijdig: *a ~ contract* een tweezijdig contract
biplane tweedekker
¹bipolar (n) [inform] bipolaire stoornis
²bipolar (adj) **1** tweepolig **2** bipolair; manisch-depressief: *~ disorder* bipolaire stoornis
birch 1 berk(enboom) **2** berkenhoutʰ
bird 1 vogel: *~ of passage* trekvogel; [fig] passant, doortrekkend reiziger; *~ of prey* roofvogel **2** [inform] vogel, kerel **3** [inform] stukʰ, meisjeʰ ‖ *they are ~s of a feather* ze hebben veel gemeen; *kill two ~s with one stone* twee vliegen in één klap slaan; *the ~ is* (or: *has*) *flown* de vogel is gevlogen; [inform] *give s.o. the ~* iem. uitfluiten; *a ~ in the hand (is worth two in the bush)* beter één vogel in de hand dan tien in de lucht; *~s of a feather flock together* soort zoekt soort
bird-brained [inform] stompzinnig; onnozel
bird flu vogelgriep
bird's-eye panoramisch, in vogelvlucht: *a ~ view of the town* een panoramisch gezicht op de stad
bird watcher vogelaar
biro balpen
birth 1 geboorte; [fig] ontstaanʰ; beginʰ, oorsprong: *give ~ to* het leven schenken aan **2** afkomst, afstamming: *of noble ~* van adellijke afkomst; *he is French by ~* hij is Fransman van geboorte
birth certificate geboorteakte
birthday verjaardag: *happy ~!* gefeliciteerd!

birthday suit [mockingly] adamskostuum^h
birthmark moedervlek
birthplace 1 geboorteplaats; geboorte-
huis^h **2** bakermat
birth rate geboortecijfer^h
birthright 1 geboorterecht^h **2** eerstge-
boorterecht^h
biscuit 1 biscuit^h, cracker **2** [Am] zacht rond
koekje^h
bisect in tweeën delen, splitsen, halveren
bisexual biseksueel
bishop 1 bisschop **2** [chess] loper
bit 1 beetje^h, stukje^h, kleinigheid: *~s and
pieces, ~s and bobs* stukken en brokken; [in-
form] *do* one's *~* zijn steen(tje) bijdragen;
[inform] *~ by* bij beetjes, stukje voor stukje;
not a ~ better geen haar beter; *not a ~ (of it)*
helemaal niet(s), geen zier **2** ogenblikje^h,
momentje^h: *wait a ~!* wacht even! **3** (ge)bit^h
[mouthpiece for horse]: *take the ~ between its
teeth* **a)** op hol slaan [of horse]; **b)** (te) hard
van stapel lopen **4** boorijzer^h **5** schaafijzer^h,
schaafbeitel, schaafmes^h **6** bit^h [smallest unit
of information]
bitch 1 teef; wijfje^h [of dog, fox] **2** [depr]
teef, kreng (van een wijf), trut
¹bite (n) **1** beet, hap **2** hap(je^h); beetje^h
[food]: *have a ~ to eat* iets eten **3** beet [when
fishing] **4** vinnigheid, bits(ig)heid, scherpte:
there was a ~ in the air er hing een vinnige
kou in de lucht
²bite (vb) **1** bijten, toebijten; (toe)happen
[also fig]; zich (gemakkelijk) laten beetnemen, steken; prikken [of insects]: [fig] *~ one's
lip(s)* zich verbijten **2** bijten; inwerken [of
acids; also fig] **3** voelbaar worden; effect
hebben [esp with sth. negative] || *~ off more
than one can chew* te veel hooi op zijn vork
nemen; *once bitten, twice shy* [roughly] door
schade en schande wordt men wijs
¹bitter (n) **1** bitter^h (bier) **2** bitterheid, het
bittere || *take the ~ with the sweet* het nemen
zoals het valt
²bitter (adj) bitter [also fig]; bijtend, scherp,
venijnig, verbitterd
bittern roerdomp
bitumen bitumen^h
bivouac bivak^h
biweekly veertiendaags, tweewekelijks,
om de veertien dagen
bizarre bizar, zonderling
bizjet [inform] zakenvliegtuig^h
¹blab (vb) zijn mond voorbij praten, loslippig
zijn
²blab (vb) (er)uit flappen
blabbermouth [depr] kletskous
¹black (n) **1** zwart: *~ and white* zwart-wit
[film; also fig] **2** (roet)zwart^h, zwarte kleurstof **3** zwarte, neger(in) **4** zwart schaakstuk^h,
zwarte damsteen
²black (adj) **1** zwart, (zeer) donker; [fig also]

duister: *be in s.o.'s ~ book(s)* bij iem. slecht
aangeschreven staan; *Black Death* de Zwarte
Dood [plague epidemic]; *~ eye* donker oog,
blauw oog [after blow]; *~ market* zwarte
markt; *~ sheep* zwart schaap [fig]; *~ spot*
zwarte plek, rampenplek [where many accidents happen]; *~ tie* **a)** zwart strikje; **b)** smoking **2** zwart, vuil, besmeurd **3** zwart, (zeer)
slecht, somber, onvriendelijk: *give s.o. a ~
look* iem. onvriendelijk aankijken || *~ and
blue* bont en blauw [beaten]
³black (vb) **1** zwart maken; poetsen [(black)
shoes] **2** bevuilen **3** besmet verklaren [ship's
cargo, by strikers] || *~ s.o.'s eye* iem. een
blauw oog slaan
blackball deballoteren; als lid afwijzen
blackberry 1 braam(struik) **2** braam(bes)
blackbird merel
blackboard (school)bord^h
blackcurrant [bot] zwarte bes
blacken 1 zwart maken, bekladden **2** [fig]
zwartmaken: *~ s.o.'s reputation* iem. zwart
maken
blackguard schurk, bandiet
black-hat hacker criminele hacker, cracker
black-hat hacking cracking
blackhead mee-eter, vetpuistje^h
¹blackjack (n) [Am] ploertendoder
²blackjack (n) blackjack^h
¹blacklist (n) zwarte lijst
²blacklist (vb) op de zwarte lijst plaatsen
¹blackmail (n) afpersing, chantage
²blackmail (vb) chanteren, (geld) afpersen
van, afdwingen (onder dreiging): *~ s.o. into
sth.* iem. iets afdwingen
blackmailer afperser; chanteur
blackout 1 verduistering **2** black-out, tijdelijke bewusteloosheid, tijdelijk geheugen-
verlies^h, tijdelijk blindheid
blacksmith smid, hoefsmid
black-tie avondkleding: *~ dinner* diner in
avondkleding
bladder blaas
blade 1 lemmet^h [of knife]; blad^h [of axe,
saw]; kling [of sword]; (scheer)mesje^h, dunne
snijplaat; ijzer^h [of skate] **2** blaadje^h [eg of
grass]; halm: *a ~ of grass* een grassprietje
blader [inform] skater (op rollerblades)
¹blame (n) schuld, blaam; verantwoording
[for sth. bad]: *bear* (or: *take*) *the ~* de schuld
op zich nemen
²blame (vb) **1** de schuld geven aan, verwijten, iets kwalijk nemen: *I don't ~ Jane* ik geef
Jane geen ongelijk; *he is to ~* het is zijn
schuld **2** afkeuren, veroordelen
blameless onberispelijk, vlekkeloos, onschuldig
¹blanch (vb) bleek worden, wit wegtrekken:
~ at that remark verbleken bij die opmerking
²blanch (vb) [cooking] blancheren

bland 1 (zacht)aardig, vriendelijk **2** mild, niet te gekruid, zacht **3** neutraal, nietszeggend **4** flauw, saai **5** nuchter, koel

¹blank (n) **1** leegte, leemte: *his memory* is a ~ hij weet zich niets meer te herinneren **2** blanco formulierʰ **3** losse patroon [of gun]; losse flodder **4** niet, niet in de prijzen vallend lotʰ: *draw* a ~ niet in de prijzen vallen; [fig] bot vangen

²blank (adj) **1** leeg, blanco, onbeschreven: *a* ~ *cartridge* een losse patroon; *a* ~ *cheque* een blanco cheque **2** uitdrukkingsloos, onbegrijpend, ongeïnteresseerd: *a* ~ *look* een wezenloze blik ‖ *a* ~ *refusal* een botte weigering

¹blanket (n) (wollen) deken, bedekking; [fig] (dikke) laag

²blanket (adj) allesomvattend, algemeen geldig: *a* ~ *insurance* een pakketverzekering; *a* ~ *rule* een algemene regel

blare schallen, lawaai maken, luid klinken

blasphemous godslasterlijk

blasphemy (gods)lastering, blasfemie

¹blast (n) **1** (wind)vlaag, rukwind **2** sterke luchtstroom [eg with explosion] **3** explosie [also fig]; uitbarsting **4** stoot [eg on trumpet]; (claxon)signaalʰ ‖ *he was working at full* ~ hij werkte op volle toeren

²blast (vb) **1** opblazen, doen exploderen, bombarderen **2** vernietigen, verijdelen, ruïneren **3** [euph] verwensen, vervloeken: ~ *him!* laat hem naar de maan lopen!

blasted [inform] **1** getroffen [by lightning etc] **2** verschrompeld, verdwenen

blast furnace hoogoven

blast-off lancering [of rocket]

blatant 1 schaamteloos, onbeschaamd **2** overduidelijk, opvallend: *a* ~ *lie* een regelrechte leugen **3** hinderlijk, ergerlijk

¹blather (n) gekletsʰ, onzin, nonsens

²blather (vb) dom kletsen

¹blaze (n) **1** vlammen(zee), (verwoestend) vuurʰ, brand **2** uitbarsting, plotselinge uitval: *a* ~ *of anger* een uitbarsting van woede **3** felle gloed [of light, colour]; vol lichtʰ, schittering

²blaze (vb) **1** (fel) branden, gloeien, in lichterlaaie staan; [also fig] in vuur en vlam staan [of rage, excitement]: *the quarrel* ~d *up* de ruzie laaide op **2** (fel) schijnen, verlicht zijn, schitteren

³blaze (vb) [also fig] banen [road, trail]; aangeven, merken: ~ *a trail* een pad banen, een nieuwe weg inslaan

blaze away 1 oplaaien [of fire]; oplichten, opvlammen **2** erop los schieten

¹bleach (n) bleekmiddelʰ

²bleach (vb) bleken, bleek worden (maken), (doen) verbleken

bleak 1 guur [eg of weather]; troosteloos, grauw **2** ontmoedigend, deprimerend, somber: ~ *prospects* sombere vooruitzichten **3** onbeschut, aan weer en wind blootgesteld, kaal

bleary-eyed met wazige blik

¹bleat (n) blatend geluidʰ, geblaatʰ; [fig] gezanikʰ

²bleat (vb) blaten, blèren, mekkeren; [fig] zeuren; zaniken

¹bleed (vb) **1** bloeden, bloed verliezen: [fig] *her heart* ~s *for the poor* ze heeft diep medelijden met de armen **2** uitlopen; doorlopen [of colour] **3** (vloeistof) afgeven, bloeden; afscheiden [eg of plant] **4** uitgezogen worden, bloeden, afgezet worden

²bleed (vb) **1** doen bloeden, bloed afnemen van, aderlaten **2** uitzuigen, laten bloeden **3** onttrekken [eg liquid]

bleeding [inform] verdomd

bleeding-edge allermodernst; allernieuwst

¹bleep (n) piep, hoge pieptoon

²bleep (vb) (op)piepen, oproepen met piepsignaal

bleeper pieper [of paging system]

blemish vlek [also fig]; smet, onvolkomenheid

¹blend (n) mengselʰ [eg of tea, coffee, whisky]; melange, mengeling

²blend (vb) zich vermengen, bij elkaar passen: ~ *in with* harmoniëren met

³blend (vb) mengen, combineren

blender mengbeker, mixer

bless 1 zegenen, (in)wijden: ~ *o.s.* een kruis slaan; [fig] zich gelukkig prijzen **2** Gods zegen vragen voor **3** begunstigen, zegenen **4** vereren [eg God]; aanbidden, loven

blessed 1 heilig, (door God) gezegend **2** gelukkig, (geluk)zalig, gezegend: *the whole* ~ *day* de godganse dag; *every* ~ *thing* alles, maar dan ook alles

blessing 1 zegen(ing): *a* ~ *in disguise* een geluk bij een ongeluk; *count your* ~! wees blij met wat je hebt! **2** goedkeuring, aanmoediging, zegen

¹blight (n) **1** plantenziekte, meeldauw; soort bladluis **2** afzichtelijkheid, afschuwelijkheid **3** vloek

²blight (vb) **1** aantasten [with plant disease]; doen verdorren **2** een vernietigende uitwerking hebben op, zwaar schaden, verwoesten: *a life* ~ed *by worries* een leven dat vergald werd door de zorgen

blimey [vulg] verdikkeme

¹blind (n) **1** schermʰ, jaloezie, zonneschermʰ, rolgordijnʰ **2** voorwendselʰ, uitvlucht, dekmantel

²blind (adj) **1** blind; [fig] ondoordacht; roekeloos: ~ *fury* blinde woede; *as* ~ *as a bat* zo blind als een mol, stekeblind; *the* ~ de blinden **2** blind, zonder begrip, ongevoelig: *be* ~ *to s.o.'s faults* geen oog hebben voor de fou-

ten van iem. **3** doodlopend; [fig] zonder vooruitzichten ‖ *turn a* ~ *eye to sth.* iets door de vingers zien, een oogje dichtknijpen voor iets
³blind (vb) **1** verblinden, blind maken, misleiden **2** verduisteren, overschaduwen **3** blinddoeken
⁴blind (adv) blind(elings), roekeloos ‖ ~ *drunk* stomdronken
¹blindfold (adj) geblinddoekt: ~ *chess* blindschaken
²blindfold (vb) blinddoeken; [fig] misleiden
blindman's buff blindemannetje^h
blind spot 1 blinde vlek [in eye] **2** blinde hoek **3** zwakke plek: *I have a ~ where politics is concerned* van politiek heb ik geen kaas gegeten
bling bling
blini blini
¹blink (n) **1** knipoog, (oog)wenk **2** glimp, oogopslag **3** flikkering, schijnsel^h ‖ [inform] *on the* ~ niet in orde, defect
²blink (vb) **1** met half toegeknepen ogen kijken, knipogen **2** knipperen, flikkeren, schitteren
³blink (vb) knippe(re)n met
blink at een oogje dichtdoen voor: ~ *illegal practices* illegale praktijken door de vingers zien
blinkered [depr] met oogkleppen; bekrompen
blinkers oogkleppen; [fig] kortzichtigheid
blip 1 piep, bliep **2** [radar] echo
blipvert flitsreclame
bliss (geluk)zaligheid, het einde, puur genot^h
bliss out [inform] uit zijn dak gaan
B-list tot de subtop behorend; tweederangs
¹blister (n) **1** (brand)blaar **2** bladder, blaas
²blister (vb) **1** blaren krijgen **2** (af)bladderen, blazen vormen
³blister (vb) doen bladderen, verschroeien, blaren veroorzaken op
blistering 1 verschroeiend, verzengend: *the ~ sun* de gloeiend hete zon **2** vernietigend
blithe [form] **1** vreugdevol, blij **2** zorgeloos, onbezorgd
blithering stom, getikt: *you ~ idiot!* stomme idioot die je bent!
¹blitz (n) **1** blitzkrieg; bliksemoorlog **2** Duitse bomaanvallen op Londen in 1940 **3** (intensieve) campagne
²blitz (vb) bombarderen
blizzard (hevige) sneeuwstorm
bloated opgezwollen, opgezet, opgeblazen
blob klodder, druppel, spat
bloc [pol] blok^h, groep, coalitie
¹block (n) **1** blok^h [also pol]; stronk, (hak)-blok^h, kapblok^h, steenblok^h, beulsblok^h

2 blok^h [of buildings]; huizenblok^h; (groot) gebouw^h: ~ *of flats* flatgebouw; *walk around the* ~ een straatje omlopen **3** versperring, stremming; [psychology, sport] blokkering; obstructie
²block (vb) [sport] blokkeren, blokken, obstructie plegen
³block (vb) **1** versperren, blokkeren: ~ *off* afsluiten, blokkeren **2** belemmeren, verhinderen, tegenhouden: *he ~ed my plans* hij reed mij in de wielen **3** [sport, psychology] blokkeren, obstructie plegen tegen ‖ ~ *in* (or: *out*) ontwerpen, schetsen
¹blockade (n) blokkade, afsluiting, versperring
²blockade (vb) blokkeren, afsluiten, belemmeren, verhinderen
blockage 1 verstopping, opstopping, obstakel^h **2** stagnatie, stremming
blockbuster kassucces^h
blockhead domkop, stommerik
blog blog
blogger blogger
bloke kerel, gozer, vent
¹blond (n) **1** blond iem.; [woman] blondje^h; blondine **2** iem. met een lichte huidkleur **3** blond^h
²blond (adj) **1** blond **2** met een lichte huidkleur
blood 1 bloed^h: *in cold ~* in koelen bloede; *it makes your ~ boil* het maakt je razend; *let ~* aderlaten **2** temperament^h, aard, hartstocht **3** bloedverwantschap^h, afstamming, afkomst: *blue ~* blauw bloed; *bring in fresh ~* vers bloed inbrengen; *be* (or: *run*) *in one's ~* in het bloed zitten; ~ *is thicker than water* het hemd is nader dan de rok
bloodbath bloedbad^h; slachtpartij
blood clot bloedstolsel^h
bloodcurdling ijzingwekkend, huiveringwekkend, bloedstollend
bloodhound bloedhond; [fig] speurder; detective
bloodless 1 bloedeloos **2** bleek, kleurloos **3** saai, duf
blood relation bloedverwant(e)
blood revenge eerwraak
bloodshed bloedvergieten^h
bloodshot bloeddoorlopen
blood sport [depr] jacht^h; bloedige sport
bloodstream bloedstroom, bloedbaan
bloodthirsty bloeddorstig, moorddadig
blood vessel bloedvat^h, ader
¹bloody (adj) **1** bloed-, bloedrood, bebloed: ~ *nose* bloedneus **2** bloed(er)ig **3** bloeddorstig, wreed **4** verdraaid: *he's a ~ fool* hij is een domme idioot
²bloody (adv) [inform] erg: *you're ~ well right* je hebt nog gelijk ook
bloody-minded [inform] dwars, koppig
¹bloom (n) **1** bloem [esp of cultivated

plants]; bloesem **2** bloei(tijd), kracht, hoogste ontwikkeling: *in de* ~ *of one's youth* in de
kracht van zijn jeugd **3** waas^h, dauw **4** blos,
gloed
²**bloom** (vb) **1** bloeien, in bloei zijn **2** in volle
bloei komen [also fig]; tot volle ontplooiing
komen **3** floreren, gedijen **4** blozen; stralen
[esp of woman] **5** zich ontwikkelen, (op)-
bloeien, uitgroeien
bloomer [inform] blunder, flater, miskleun
blooming verdraaid
¹**blossom** (n) [also fig] bloesem, bloei: *be in*
~ in bloesem staan
²**blossom** (vb) **1** ontbloeien; tot bloei komen [of fruit trees] **2** zich ontwikkelen, opbloeien, zich ontpoppen
¹**blot** (n) vlek [also fig]: *the building was a* ~ *on
the landscape* het gebouw ontsierde het
landschap
²**blot** (vb) vlekken maken, knoeien, kliederen, vlekken (krijgen); vloeien [of paper]
³**blot** (vb) **1** bevlekken, bekladden **2** ontsieren **3** (af)vloeien, drogen met vloeipapier
blotch vlek, puist, smet
blot out 1 (weg)schrappen, doorhalen
2 verbergen, aan het gezicht onttrekken,
bedekken: *clouds* ~ *the sun* wolken schuiven
voor de zon **3** vernietigen, uitroeien
blotting paper vloei(papier)^h
blouse bloes [worn by women]; blauwe
(werk)kiel
¹**blow** (n) **1** wind(vlaag), rukwind, storm,
stevige bries **2** slag, klap, mep: *come to* (or:
exchange) ~*s* slaags raken; ~ *by* ~ *account*
gedetailleerd verslag; *without* (*striking*) *a* ~
zonder slag of stoot, zonder geweld **3** (tegen)slag, ramp, schok
²**blow** (vb) **1** (uit)blazen, fluiten, weerklinken, (uit)waaien, wapperen: ~ *down* neer-
geblazen worden, omwaaien; [inform] ~ *in*
a) (komen) binnenvallen, (komen) aanwaai-
en; **b)** inwaaien; *the scandal will* ~ *over* het
schandaal zal wel overwaaien **2** hijgen, blazen, puffen **3** stormen, hard waaien **4** [elec]
doorsmelten, doorbranden; doorslaan [of
fuse] ‖ [inform] ~ *hot and cold* (*about*) veranderen als het weer
³**blow** (vb) **1** blazen (op/door), aanblazen,
afblazen, opblazen, rondblazen, uitblazen,
wegblazen; snuiten [nose]; doen wapperen,
doen dwarrelen: *the door was* ~*n open* de
deur waaide open; *the wind blew her hair* de
wind waaide door haar haar; ~ *away* wegblazen, wegjagen; *the wind blew the trees
down* de wind blies de bomen om(ver); ~ *in*
a) doen binnenwaaien; **b)** doen springen
[window-pane]; ~ *off* **a)** wegblazen, doen
wegwaaien; **b)** laten ontsnappen [steam]; ~
over om(ver)blazen, doen omwaaien; ~ *sky-
high* in de lucht laten vliegen; [fig] geen
spaan heel laten van **2** doen doorslaan, doen

doorbranden **3** bespelen, blazen op, spelen
op **4** [inform] verprutsen, verknoeien
5 [vulg] pijpen, afzuigen
blow-dry föhnen
blow-dryer föhn, haardroger
blower 1 aanjager, blower, ventilator
2 [inform] telefoon
blowfly vleesvlieg
blowjob [vulg] pijpbeurt
blowout 1 klapband, lekke band **2** lek^h
3 uitbarsting [of oil well, gas well]; eruptie
4 [inform] eetfestijn^h, vreetpartij
¹**blow out** (vb) **1** uitwaaien, uitgaan
2 springen, klappen, barsten **3** ophouden te
werken [of electrical appliances]; uitvallen,
doorbranden
²**blow out** (vb) **1** uitblazen, uitdoen **2** doen
springen, doen klappen **3** buiten bedrijf
stellen [electrical appliances] ‖ ~ *one's brains*
zich voor de kop schieten
¹**blow up** (vb) **1** ontploffen, exploderen,
springen **2** [inform] in rook opgaan, verijdeld worden **3** opzwellen, opgeblazen
worden **4** (in woede) uitbarsten, ontploffen
5 sterker worden [of wind, storm]; komen
opzetten; [fig] uitbreken; losbarsten
²**blow up** (vb) **1** opblazen, laten ontploffen;
vullen [with air] **2** opblazen, overdrijven
3 aanblazen [fire]; aanwakkeren, (op)stoken
4 doen opwaaien, opjagen, opdwarrelen
5 [photo] (uit)vergroten
blow-up 1 explosie, ontploffing **2** uitbarsting, ruzie, herrie **3** [photo] (uit)vergroting
blowy winderig
¹**blubber** (n) **1** blubber **2** [inform] gejank^h,
gegrien^h
²**blubber** (vb) grienen, snotteren, janken
blubbery dik; vet
bludgeon (gummi)knuppel, knots
¹**blue** (n) **1** blauw **2** blauwsel^h [to dye linen
blue] **3** [the] blauwe lucht: *out of the* ~ plotseling, als een donderslag bij heldere hemel
4 blauwtje^h [butterfly] **5** lid^h (kleur) van een
conservatieve politieke partij; tory; conser-
vatief
²**blue** (adj) **1** blauw, azuur: ~ *blooded* van
adellijke afkomst; ~ *with* cold blauw van de
kou **2** gedeprimeerd, triest, somber **3** conservatief; tory **4** [inform] obsceen, porno-
gewaagd: ~ *film* (or: *movie*) pornofilm, seksfilm ‖ *wait till one is* ~ *in the face* wachten tot je
een ons weegt; *once in a* ~ *moon* (hoogst)
zelden, zelden of nooit; *cry* (or: *scream, shout*)
~ *murder* moord en brand schreeuwen
blueberry bosbes
bluebottle aasvlieg, bromvlieg
blue-collar hand-; fabrieks- [worker(s)]
blueprint blauwdruk, ontwerp^h, schets
blue ribbon hoogste onderscheiding, eerste prijs
blue-rinse met een blauwe kleurspoeling

blues 1 blues: *play a* ~ een blues spelen **2** [inform] zwaarmoedigheid, melancholie **bluestocking** [oft depr] geleerde vrouw **blue tit** pimpelmees
¹**bluff** (n) **1** hoge, steile oever, steile rotswand, klifʰ **2** bluf: *call one's* ~ **a)** iem. uitdagen; **b)** iemands uitdaging aannemen
²**bluff** (adj) kortaf maar oprecht, plompverloren maar eerlijk
³**bluff** (vb) **1** bluffen [also in poker]; brutaal optreden **2** doen alsof, voorwenden
⁴**bluff** (vb) **1** overbluffen, overdonderen **2** misleiden, bedriegen, doen alsof: ~ *one's way out of a situation* zich uit een situatie redden
¹**blunder** (n) blunder, miskleun
²**blunder** (vb) **1** blunderen, een stomme fout maken, een flater slaan **2** strompelen, (voort)sukkelen, zich onhandig voortbewegen: ~ *into a tree* tegen een boom op knallen
blunt 1 bot, stomp **2** afgestompt, ongevoelig, koud **3** (p)lomp, ongezouten, onomwonden: *tell s.o. sth.* ~*ly* iem. iets botweg vertellen
¹**blur** (n) onduidelijke plek, wazig beeldʰ, verflauwde indruk
²**blur** (vb) **1** vervagen, vaag worden **2** vlekken
³**blur** (vb) **1** bevlekken, besmeren; [fig] bekladden **2** onscherp maken, troebel maken: ~*red photographs* onscherpe foto's
blurb flaptekst
blurry onduidelijk, onscherp, vaag
blurt eruit flappen; eruit gooien: ~ *out* eruit flappen
¹**blush** (n) (schaamte)blos, (rode) kleur, schaamroodʰ
²**blush** (vb) blozen, een kleur krijgen, rood worden
¹**bluster** (n) **1** tumultʰ, drukte, geloeiʰ; gebulderʰ [of storm]; geraasʰ; getierʰ [of angry voices] **2** gebralʰ, opschepperij
²**bluster** (vb) **1** razen, bulderen, tieren **2** bulderen, loeien; huilen [of wind] **3** brallen, opscheppen
blvd *boulevard*
boar 1 beer [male pig] **2** wild zwijnʰ, everzwijnʰ
¹**board** (n) **1** plank, (vloer)deelʰ **2** (aanplak)bordʰ, scorebordʰ, schildʰ, plaat; bordʰ [basketball and korfball]; (schaak)bordʰ, (speel)bordʰ **3** [shipp] boordʰ: *go by the* ~ **a)** overboord slaan; **b)** volledig mislukken [of plans etc]; *on* ~ aan boord van **4** kost, kostgeldʰ, onderhoudʰ, pensionʰ: ~ *and lodging* kost en inwoning; *full* ~ vol pension **5** raad, bestuur(slichaam)ʰ: ~ *of directors* raad van bestuur; *editorial* ~ redactie; *be on the* ~ in het bestuur zitten, bestuurslid zijn ‖ *sweep the* ~ grote winst(en) boeken, zegevieren; [inform] *take on* ~ begrijpen, accepteren, aan-

nemen [of new ideas etc]; *above* ~ open, eerlijk; *across the* ~ over de hele linie, iedereen, niemand uitgezonderd
²**board** (vb) in de kost zijn
³**board** (vb) **1** beplanken, beschieten, betimmeren, bevloeren **2** in de kost hebben **3** uit huis doen, in de kost doen **4** aan boord gaan van; instappen [aeroplane]; opstappen [motorcycle]: ~ *a ship* zich inschepen **5** [shipp] enteren
boarder pensiongast, kostganger, kostleerling, intern
boarding beplanking, betimmering, schutting
boarding card instapkaart
boarding-house kosthuisʰ, pensionʰ
boarding pass instapkaart
boarding school kostschool, internaatʰ
boardroom bestuurskamer, directiekamer
boardsailing [sport] het plankzeilen, het (wind)surfen
¹**boast** (n) **1** [depr] bluf, grootspraak **2** trots, roem, glorie
²**boast** (vb) opscheppen, overdrijven, sterke verhalen vertellen: ~ *about*, ~ *of* opscheppen over, zich laten voorstaan op
³**boast** (vb) **1** in het (trotse) bezit zijn van, (kunnen) bogen op (het bezit van) **2** [depr] opscheppen
boaster opschepper, praatjesmaker
boat 1 (open) boot, vaartuigʰ, (dek)schuit, sloep: [fig] *be (all) in the same* ~ (allen) in hetzelfde schuitje zitten **2** [Am] (zeewaardig) schipʰ; (stoom)boot [used esp by non-sailors] **3** (jus)kom, sauskom ‖ *burn one's* ~*s* z'n schepen achter zich verbranden; *miss the* ~ de boot missen, zijn kans voorbij laten gaan; [inform] *push the* ~ *out* de bloemetjes buiten zetten; [inform] *rock the* ~ de boel in het honderd sturen, spelbreker zijn
boatswain bootsman, boots
¹**bob** (n) **1** hangend voorwerpʰ, (slinger)gewichtʰ; lens [of timepiece]; gewichtʰ; strik [of kite]; loodʰ [of plumb line]; dobber, waker **2** bob(slee) **3** gecoupeerde staart **4** plotselinge (korte) beweging, sprong, (knie)buiging, knicks **5** bob(bed kapselʰ), kortgeknipte kop, jongenskop ‖ [inform] *Bob's your uncle* klaar is Kees, voor mekaar
²**bob** (vb) **1** bobben, rodelen, bobsleeën **2** (zich) op en neer (heen en weer) bewegen, (op)springen, dobberen: ~ *up* (plotseling) tevoorschijn komen, komen boven drijven, opduiken **3** buigen, een (knie)buiging maken
³**bob** (vb) **1** (kort) knippen [hair] **2** couperen, kortstaarten **3** heen en weer (op en neer) bewegen, doen dansen, laten dobberen, knikken
bobbin spoel, klos, bobine
bobby [inform] bobby, oom agent, politieman

bobcat rode lynx
¹**bobsleigh** (n) bob(slee)
²**bobsleigh** (vb) bobsleeën, bobben
¹**bodily** (adj) lichamelijk: ~ *harm* lichamelijk letsel
²**bodily** (adv) **1** met geweld **2** lichamelijk, in levende lijve **3** in z'n geheel, met huid en haar
body 1 lichaam^h, romp, lijk^h: *just enough to keep ~ and* **soul** *together* net genoeg om je te redden **2** persoon; [law] rechtspersoon; [inform] mens; ziel **3** grote hoeveelheid, massa **4** voornaamste deel^h, grootste (centrale) deel^h, kern, meerderheid; schip^h [of church]; casco^h; carrosserie [of car]; romp [of aeroplane]; klankkast [of musical instrument]: *the ~ of a* **letter** de kern van een brief **5** lichaam^h, groep, korps^h: *the* **Governing** *Body is* (or: are) *meeting today* het bestuur vergadert vandaag; *they left* **in** *a ~* ze vertrokken als één man **6** voorwerp^h, object^h, lichaam^h: *heavenly bodies* hemellichamen **7** bodystocking
body bag lijkzak
body count aantal gesneuvelden
bodyguard lijfwacht
body search fouillering
bodywork carrosserie
boffin [inform] expert
bog 1 (veen)moeras^h **2** [inform] plee, wc
bog down 1 gehinderd worden, vastlopen **2** vast komen te zitten (in de modder) ‖ *get bogged down* **in** *details* in details verzanden
bogey 1 boeman, (kwel)duivel, kwade geest **2** spookbeeld^h, schrikbeeld^h **3** [golf] bogey, score van 1 slag boven par voor een hole **4** snotje^h
boggle 1 terugschrikken, terugdeinzen **2** duizelen: *the* **mind** *~s* het duizelt me
boggy moerassig, drassig
bogus vals, onecht, nep-, vervalst
¹**boil** (n) **1** steenpuist **2** kookpunt^h, kook
²**boil** (vb) **1** (staan te) koken, het kookpunt bereiken, gekookt worden: *~ing* **hot** kokend heet; *~* **down** inkoken; *~* **over a)** overkoken; **b)** [fig] uitbarsten (in woede), tot uitbarsting komen **2** (inwendig) koken: *~ing* **with** *anger* ziedend van woede ‖ [inform] *~* **down to** neerkomen op, in het kort, in grote lijnen
³**boil** (vb) koken, aan de kook brengen ‖ [inform] *~* **down** kort samenvatten, de hoofdlijnen aangeven
boiler boiler, stoomketel
boisterous 1 onstuimig, luid(ruchtig) **2** ruw, heftig; stormachtig [of wind, weather etc]
bold 1 (stout)moedig, doortastend **2** [oft depr] brutaal: *as ~ as* **brass** (honds)brutaal **3** krachtig, goed uitkomend **4** vet (gedrukt) ‖ *put a ~* **face** *on the matter* zich goedhouden
boldface vette letter
bold-faced 1 brutaal, schaamteloos **2** vet

gedrukt
Bolivia Bolivia
¹**Bolivian** (n) Boliviaan(se)
²**Bolivian** (adj) Boliviaans
bollard korte paal, bolder; meerpaal [shipp]; verkeerszuiltje^h, verkeerspaaltje^h
bollocks [vulg] **1** gelul^h **2** kloten
boloney [inform] onzin, (flauwe)kul, gelul^h
Bolshevism bolsjewisme^h
bolster 1 (onder)kussen^h, hoofdmatras^{+h} **2** steun, ondersteuning, stut
bolster up 1 met kussen(s) (onder)steunen **2** schragen, ondersteunen; opkrikken [also fig]: *~ s.o.'s* **morale** iem. moed inspreken
¹**bolt** (n) **1** bout **2** grendel, schuif **3** bliksemstraal, bliksemflits **4** sprong, duik: *make a ~ for it* er vandoor gaan ‖ *a ~ from the* **blue** een complete verrassing
²**bolt** (vb) **1** [inform] op de loop gaan, de bennen nemen; op hol slaan [of horse] **2** (plotseling/verschrikt) op(zij)springen, wegspringen **3** doorschieten, (vroegtijdig, te vroeg) in het zaad schieten **4** met bouten bevestigd zitten **5** sluiten, een grendel hebben
³**bolt** (vb) **1** (snel) verorberen: *~* **down** *food* eten opschrokken **2** vergrendelen, op slot doen **3** met bout(en) bevestigen
⁴**bolt** (adv) recht: *~* **upright** kaarsrecht
¹**bomb** (n) **1** bom **2** [inform] bom geld: *cost a ~* kapitalen kosten **3** [inform] hit, klapper, daverend succes^h: *go like a ~* **a)** als een trein lopen; **b)** scheuren [of car]
²**bomb** (vb) **1** bommen werpen **2** razen, racen
³**bomb** (vb) bombarderen
bombard bombarderen, met bommen, granaten bestoken; [fig] bestoken; lastigvallen: *~ s.o.* **with** *questions* vragen afvuren op iem.
bombardment bombardement^h, bomaanval
bombastic hoogdravend, gezwollen
bomber 1 bommenwerper **2** bommengooier [pers]
bomb scare bommelding
bombshell granaat^h, bom; [inform, fig] donderslag; (onaangename) verrassing: *drop a ~* een sensationele mededeling doen
bona fide te goeder trouw, bonafide, betrouwbaar
bonanza 1 rijke (erts)vindplaats [esp of gold, silver, oil]; rijke oliebron, mijn; [fig] goudmijn **2** grote (winst)opbrengst
bond 1 band, verbond^h, verbondenheid, binding **2** verbintenis, contract^h, verplichting **3** obligatie, schuldbekentenis **4** verbinding, hechting; [chem] verbinding **5** (-s) boeien, ketenen, gevangenschap
bondage 1 slavernij **2** onderworpenheid, het gebonden zijn, gebondenheid
bonded 1 in douaneopslag (geplaatst)

2 aan elkaar gelijmd, gelaagd

¹bone (n) **1** bot^h, been^h, graat: *I can feel it* (or: *it is*) *in my ~s* ik weet het zeker, ik voel het aankomen **2** kluif, stuk^h been, bot^h ‖ *~ of contention* twistappel; *make no ~s about* niet aarzelen om; *have a ~ to pick with s.o.* met iem. een appeltje te schillen hebben

²bone (adj) benen, van been, ivoren

³bone (vb) uitbenen, ontgraten

⁴bone (adv) extreem, uitermate: *~ dry* kurkdroog; *~ idle* (or: *lazy*) aartslui

boneheaded stom, achterlijk, idioot

bonfire vuur^h in de openlucht, vreugdevuur^h, vuur^h om dode bladeren (afval) te verbranden

bonkers gek, maf, getikt

bonnet **1** bonnet, hoed **2** beschermkap, schoorsteenkap; motorkap

bonus **1** bonus, premie, gratificatie **2** bijslag, toelage **3** [inform] meevaller, extraatje^h

bony **1** benig, mager **2** met veel botten (graten)

¹boo (n) boe, kreet van afkeuring, gejouw^h, boegeroep^h ‖ *wouldn't* (or: *couldn't*) *say ~ to a goose* **a)** dodelijk verlegen zijn; **b)** zo bang als een wezel zijn

²boo (vb) boe roepen, (weg)joelen, (uit)jouwen

boob [inform] **1** flater, blunder **2** [inform] tiet

boo-boo [inform] flater; blunder

booby [inform] stommerd, domkop, idioot

booby prize poedelprijs

¹booby trap (n) boobytrap, valstrikbom

²booby trap (vb) een boobytrap plaatsen bij

boodle **1** omkoopgeld^h, smeergeld^h **2** (smak) geld

boohoo geblèr^h, huiltje^h

¹book (n) **1** boek^h, boekdeel^h, boekwerk^h; [inform] telefoonboek^h **2** boek^h [chapter of bible, poem etc] **3** tekstboekje^h; libretto^h [of opera etc]; manuscript^h; script [of play] **4** (schrijf)boek^h, schrift^h, blocnote **5** boekje^h [cards, matches, stamps] **6** register^h, lijst, boek^h; lijst van aangegane weddenschappen [at races]: *make* (or: *keep*) *(a) ~* wedmakelen, bookmaker zijn **7** (-s) boek, kasboek^h, kantoorboek^h, journaal^h **8** (-s) boek^h, register^h, (leden)lijst ‖ *bring s.o. to ~ for sth.* iem. voor iets rekenschap laten afleggen, iem. zijn gerechte straf doen ondergaan; *read s.o. like a ~* iem. volkomen door hebben; [inform] *throw the ~ (of rules) at s.o.* **a)** iem. maximum straf toebedelen; **b)** iem. de les lezen; *by the ~* volgens het boekje; *in my ~* volgens mij, mijns inziens

²book (vb) een plaats bespreken, een kaartje nemen, reserveren ‖ *~ in* **a)** zich laten inschrijven [in hotel register]; **b)** inchecken [at airport]

³book (vb) **1** boeken, reserveren, bestellen: *~ a passage* passage boeken; *~ed up* volgeboekt, uitverkocht; [of person] bezet **2** inschrijven, registreren, noteren **3** bekeuren, een proces-verbaal opmaken tegen: *I was ~ed for speeding* ik werd wegens te hard rijden op de bon geslingerd **4** [sport] een gele kaart geven

the **Book** het Boek (der Boeken), de Heilige Schrift, de Bijbel

book debt vordering; uitstaande schuld

book end boekensteun

bookie [inform] bookmaker

booking **1** bespreking, reservering, boeking **2** verbalisering **3** [sport] gele kaart

booking office bespreekbureau^h, plaats(kaarten)bureau^h, loket^h

bookish **1** leesgraag, verslaafd aan boeken, geleerd: *~ person* boekenwurm, kamergeleerde **2** stijf

bookkeeper boekhouder

bookkeeping boekhouding, het boekhouden

booklet boekje^h

bookmaker bookmaker

bookmark boekenlegger

bookshop boekwinkel, boekhandel

bookstore [Am] boekwinkel; boekhandel

book token boekenbon

book up een plaats bespreken, reserveren

bookworm boekenwurm

¹boom (n) **1** (dof/hol) gedreun^h, gebulder^h, gedaver^h **2** hausse, (periode van) economische vooruitgang **3** (hoge) vlucht, grote stijging, bloei, opkomst **4** [shipp] giek, spriet **5** [shipp] (laad)boom **6** galg; statief^h [of microphone etc] **7** (haven)boom; versperring [of harbour entrance]

²boom (vb) **1** een dof geluid maken, dreunen, bulderen; rollen [of thunder] **2** een (hoge) vlucht nemen, zich snel ontwikkelen, bloeien; sterk stijgen [of price]: *business is ~ing* het gaat ons voor de wind **3** (snel) in aanzien stijgen

³boom (vb) (also + out) bulderend uiten

¹boomerang (n) boemerang [also fig]

²boomerang (vb) als een boemerang terugkeren, 'n boemerangeffect hebben

boom town explosief gegroeide stad

¹boon (n) **1** zegen, weldaad, gemak^h **2** gunst, wens

²boon (adj) monter, vrolijk: *~ companion* goede kameraad, boezemvriend(in), hartsvriend(in)

boor [depr] lomperd; vlegel

boorish lomp, boers, onbehouwen

¹boost (n) **1** duw (omhoog), zetje^h, (onder)steun(ing) **2** verhoging, (prijs)opdrijving **3** stimulans, aanmoediging, versterking: *a ~ to one's spirits* een opkikker(tje)

²boost (vb) **1** (omhoog)duwen, een zetje

geven, ondersteunen: ~ *s.o.* **up** iem. een duwtje (omhoog) geven **2** verhogen, opdrijven; opvoeren [price, production etc] **3** [Am] aanprijzen, reclame maken voor **4** stimuleren, aanmoedigen, bevorderen: ~ *one's **spirits*** iem. opvrolijken **5** verhogen [pressure]; versterken [radio signal]

booster 1 hulpkrachtbron, hulpversterker, aanjager, aanjaagpomp, startmotor **2** verbetering, opkikker

¹**boot** (n) **1** laars; hoge schoen **2** schop, trap **3** ontslagʰ **4** kofferbak, bagageruimte || *put the ~ in* in elkaar trappen, erop inhakken

²**boot** (vb) **1** schoppen, trappen **2** (also + up) [comp] opstarten, booten

bootee kort laarsjeʰ, gebreid babysokjeʰ

booth 1 kraam, marktkraam, stalletjeʰ, (feest)tent **2** hokjeʰ, stemhokjeʰ, telefooncel; (luister)cabine [in record shop etc]: ***polling*** ~ stemhokje

bootlace 1 veter voor laars **2** schoenveter

¹**bootleg** (n) illegale kopie [of record, CD]

²**bootleg** (adj) illegaal (geproduceerd) [liquor, records, CDs]

³**bootleg** (vb) smokkelen, clandestien (drank) stoken (verkopen)

bootlegger (drank)smokkelaar, illegale drankstoker (drankverkoper)

bootless [form] vergeefs; vruchteloos

booty 1 buit, roof **2** winst, prijs, beloning

¹**booze** (n) **1** sterkedrank: *on the* ~ aan de drank **2** zuippartij

²**booze** (vb) zuipen

boozer 1 kroeg **2** zuiplap, dronkaard

boozy [inform] **1** drankzuchtig **2** dronken **3** met alcohol: *a ~ **lunch*** een lunch met veel drank

¹**border** (n) **1** grens, grenslijn, afscheiding **2** rand, band, bies, lijst

²**border** (vb) begrenzen, omzomen, omranden

¹**borderline** (n) grens(lijn), scheidingslijn

²**borderline** (adj) **1** grens-, twijfelachtig: ~ *case* grensgeval **2** net (niet) acceptabel, op het kantje

border (up)on grenzen aan, liggen naast, belenden

¹**bore** (n) **1** vervelend persoon **2** vervelend iets **3** boorgatʰ **4** kaliberʰ, diameter; boring [of a cylinder, firearm] **5** boor

²**bore** (vb) vervelen: *I'm ~d stiff* ik verveel mij kapot

³**bore** (vb) **1** (een gat) boren, drillen, een put slaan **2** boren, doorboren, uitboren; kalibreren [weapons]; een gat boren in **3** doordringen, zich (een weg) banen, moeizaam vooruitkomen

boredom verveling

boring vervelend, saai, langdradig

born 1 geboren, van geboorte: ~ *and **bred*** geboren en getogen; ~ *again* herboren; *not*

~ *yesterday* niet op z'n achterhoofd gevallen **2** geboren, voorbestemd: ~ *to **be** a leader* voor het leiderschap in de wieg gelegd **3** geboren, van nature: *he is a* ~ ***actor*** hij is een rastoneelspeler **4** geboren, ontstaan, voortgekomen

borough 1 stad, (stedelijke) gemeente: *municipal* ~ (stedelijke) gemeente **2** kiesdistrictʰ

borrow 1 lenen, ontlenen **2** pikken

Borstal jeugdgevangenis; opvoedingsgestichtʰ

Bosnia and Herzegovina Bosnië en Herzegovina

¹**Bosnian** (n) Bosniër, Bosnische

²**Bosnian** (adj) Bosnisch

bosom 1 borst, boezem **2** borststukʰ [of piece of clothing] **3** ruimte tussen borst en kleding, boezem

¹**boss** (n) baas, chef, voorman

²**boss** (vb) commanderen, de baas spelen (over): ~ *s.o.* ***around*** iem. lopen te commanderen

botanic(al) 1 botanisch, plantkundig **2** plantaardig, uit planten verkregen

botany plantkunde, botanica

¹**botch** (n) knoeiwerkʰ, knoeiboel, puinhoop

²**botch** (vb) **1** verknoeien: ~ *it up* het verknallen **2** oplappen, slecht repareren

¹**both** (num) beide(n), allebei, alle twee: *I saw them* ~ ik heb ze allebei gezien; ~ *of them* alle twee

²**both** (conj) [with 'and'] zowel, beide: ~ *Jack and Jill got hurt* Jack en Jill raakten gewond; *he was* ~ *tall **and** fat* hij was lang én dik

¹**bother** (n) **1** last, lastpost: *I hope I'm not **being** a* ~ *to you* ik hoop dat ik u niet tot last ben **2** moeite, probleemʰ, moeilijkheid: *we had a lot of* ~ *finding the house* het heeft ons veel moeite gekost om het huis te vinden

²**bother** (vb) **1** de moeite nemen, zich de moeite geven: *don't* ~ ***about** that* maak je daar nu maar niet druk om; *don't* ~ doe maar geen moeite **2** lastigvallen, dwarszitten, irriteren: *his leg ~s him a **lot*** hij heeft veel last van zijn been; *I can't **be** ~ed* dat is me te veel moeite; *that **doesn't** ~ me* daar zit ik niet mee

bothersome vervelend, lastig

botnet botnetʰ, zombienetwerkʰ

Botswana Botswana

¹**Botswanan** (n) Botswaan(se)

²**Botswanan** (adj) Botswaans

¹**bottle** (n) fles; [fig] drank: *a ~ **of** rum* een fles rum; *our baby is brought up **on** the* ~ onze baby wordt met de fles grootgebracht

²**bottle** (vb) **1** bottelen, in flessen doen **2** inmaken

bottle bank glasbak

bottleneck flessenhals [also fig]; knelpuntʰ

bottle up opkroppen: ~ *your anger* je woe-

de opkroppen
¹bottom (n) **1** bodem, grond, het diepst: *from the ~ of my **heart** uit de grond van mijn hart* **2** onderste deel[h], voet, basis: *from the ~ up* van bij het begin, helemaal (opnieuw) **3** het laagste punt: *the ~ of the **garden*** achterin de tuin **4** achterste[h], gat[h] **5** kiel; [fig] schip[h]; bodem ‖ *I'll get **to** the ~ of this* ik ga dit helemaal uitzoeken
²bottom (adj) onderste, laatste, laagste
bottom line 1 saldo[h] **2** einduitkomst; resultaat[h], kern: *the ~ of the **lesson*** de moraal van het verhaal **3** bodemprijs; grens
bough tak
boulder kei, zwerfkei, rotsblok[h]
¹bounce (n) **1** vermogen tot stuit(er)en **2** stuit; terugsprong [of ball] **3** levendigheid, beweeglijkheid **4** opschepperij
²bounce (vb) **1** stuit(er)en, terugkaatsen: *~ **back** after a setback* er na een tegenslag weer bovenop komen **2** (op)springen, wippen **3** ongedekt zijn; geweigerd worden [of cheque]
³bounce (vb) **1** laten stuit(er)en, kaatsen, stuit(er)en **2** [inform] eruit gooien, ontslaan
bouncer 1 uitsmijter **2** iem. die (iets dat) stuit
bouncing gezond, levendig, flink
bouncy 1 levendig, levenslustig **2** die kan stuiten: *a ~ **mattress*** een goed verende matras
bouncy castle springkussen[h], springkasteel[h]
¹bound (n) **1** (-s) grens; [maths] limiet: *out of ~s* verboden terrein, taboe [also fig] **2** sprong **3** stuit; terugsprong [of ball] ‖ *keep within the ~s of reason* redelijk blijven
²bound (adj) **1** zeker: *he is ~ **to** pass his exam* hij haalt zijn examen beslist **2** op weg, onderweg: *this train is ~ **for** Poland* deze trein gaat naar Polen **3** gebonden, vast: *she is completely ~ **up in** her research* ze gaat helemaal op in haar onderzoek
³bound (vb) **1** springen **2** stuit(er)en, terugkaatsen
⁴bound (vb) begrenzen, beperken
-bound 1 [roughly] gehinderd door, [roughly] vastzittend aan: *be **snowbound*** vastzitten in de sneeuw **2** gebonden in: *leather~ books* in leer gebonden boeken
boundary grens, grenslijn
boundless grenzeloos
bountiful 1 vrijgevig, gul, royaal **2** overvloedig, rijk
bounty 1 gulheid, vrijgevigheid **2** (gulle) gift, donatie **3** premie, bonus
bounty hunter premiejager
bouquet 1 boeket[h], bos bloemen, ruiker **2** bouquet[h]; geur en smaak [of wine]
bourgeois (klein)burgerlijk; bourgeois
bout 1 vlaag, tijdje[h], periode; aanval [of ill-

ness]: *~s of **activity*** vlagen van activiteit; *~s of migraine* migraineaanvallen **2** wedstrijd [of boxing, wrestling]
boutique boetiek
bovine runderachtig, runder-
¹bow (n) **1** buiging: *take a ~* applaus in ontvangst nemen **2** boeg [foremost part of ship]
²bow (n) **1** boog, kromming **2** boog, handboog **3** strijkstok **4** strik
³bow (vb) **1** buigen, een buiging maken **2** buigen, zich gewonnen geven: *he ~ed **to** the inevitable* hij legde zich bij het onvermijdelijke neer
⁴bow (vb) **1** buigen, krommen **2** strijken [of violinist]
bowel 1 darm; *~s ingewanden **2** binnenste[h]: *deep in the ~s of the earth* in de diepste diepten van de aarde
bower tuinhuisje[h], prieel(tje)[h]
¹bowl (n) **1** kom, schaal, bekken[h] **2** [Am; geography] kom, komvormig gebied[h], bekken[h] **3** kop [of pipe] **4** [Am] amfitheater[h], stadion[h]
²bowl (n) [sport] bowl
³bowl (vb) **1** [cricket] bowlen **2** voortrollen, rollen ‖ *the batsman was ~ed **(out)*** de slagman werd uitgegooid
bowl along 1 vlot rijden; rollen [of car] **2** vlotten; lekker gaan [of work]
bowlegged met O-benen
bowler hat bolhoed
bowling alley kegelbaan, bowlingbaan, bowlingcentrum[h]
bowl over 1 omverlopen **2** van z'n stuk brengen
bow out officieel afscheid nemen; zich terugtrekken [from a high position]
bow tie strikje[h], vlinderdas
¹box (n) **1** doos, kist, bak, trommel, bus **2** loge, hokje[h]; cel e.d. [in theatre]: *telephone ~,* [Am] *call ~* telefooncel; *witness ~* getuigenbank **3** beschermhoes **4** kader[h], omlijning, omlijnd gebied[h] **5** mep, draai om de oren, oorveeg: *give s.o. a ~ on the ears* iem. een draai om de oren geven **6** buis, tv, televisie
²box (vb) **1** boksen (tegen/met) **2** in dozen doen **3** een draai om de oren geven: *~ s.o.'s ears* iem. een draai om z'n oren geven
boxer 1 bokser **2** boxer [dog]
box in opsluiten, insluiten: *feel boxed in* zich gekooid voelen
boxing het boksen, bokssport
Boxing Day tweede kerstdag
box junction [roughly] kruispunt dat te allen tijde vrijgelaten moet worden
box number (antwoord)nummer[h]
box office bespreekbureau[h], loket[h]; kassa [of cinema]: *be **bad** ~* geen publiek trekken
boxwood palmhout[h]; bukshout[h]
¹boy (n) **1** jongen, knul, zoon(tje)[h]: *that's my

~ grote jongen, bravo knul; ~s will be **boys** zo zijn jongens nu eenmaal **2** [Am] man, jongen, vent: come on, **old** ~ vooruit, ouwe jongen || jobs **for** the ~s vriendjespolitiek
²boy (int) [Am] (t)jonge jonge
¹boycott (n) boycot
²boycott (vb) boycotten
boyfriend vriend(jeʰ), vrijer
boyhood jongenstijd, jongensjaren
boy scout padvinder
bps bits per second bps
bra brassière beha
¹brace (n) **1** klamp, (draag)beugel, (muur)anker **2** steun, stut **3** booromslag: ~ and **bit** boor **4** band, riem **5** [dentistry] beugel **6** (-s) bretels **7** koppelʰ, paarʰ, stelʰ: three ~ of **partridge** drie koppel patrijzen
²brace (vb) **1** vastbinden, aantrekken, aanhalen **2** versterken, verstevigen, ondersteunen **3** schrap zetten: ~ **o.s.** for a shock zich op een schok voorbereiden
bracelet armband
bracing verkwikkend, opwekkend, versterkend
bracken varenvegetatie; varens
¹bracket (n) **1** steun, plankdrager **2** haakjeʰ, accolade: **in** ~s, **between** ~s tussen haakjes **3** klasse, groep: the lower **income** ~ de lagere inkomensgroep
²bracket (vb) **1** tussen haakjes zetten **2** (also + together) koppelen, in een adem noemen, in dezelfde categorie plaatsen **3** (onder)steunen [with a brace]
brackish brak; niet zuiver
brag (+ about, of) opscheppen (over)
braggart opschepper
braid 1 vlecht **2** galon, boordselʰ, tres
braille brailleʰ, blindenschriftʰ
¹brain (n) **1** hersenen, hersens; breinʰ [as organ] **2** [inform] knappe kop, breinʰ, genieʰ **3** breinʰ, intelligentie, hoofdʰ: she **has** (a lot of) ~s ze heeft (een goed stel) hersens; **pick** s.o.'s ~(s) iemands ideeën stelen
²brain (vb) de hersens inslaan
brain drain uittocht van het intellect
brainiac [esp Am; inform] knappe kop; nerd
brainpower intelligentie, intellectueel vermogen
brainteaser hersenkraker; puzzel, moeilijke vraag
brainwash hersenspoelen
brainwave ingeving, (goede) inval, goed ideeʰ
brainy slim, knap, intelligent
braise [cooking] smoren
¹brake (n) **1** rem: **apply** (or: **put on**) the ~s remmen; [fig] matigen, temperen **2** stationcar, combi
²brake (vb) (af)remmen
brake pad remblokjeʰ

bramble 1 braamstruik **2** doornstruik **3** braam
bran zemelen
¹branch (n) **1** tak, loot **2** vertakking; arm [of river, road etc] **3** tak, filiaalʰ, bijkantoorʰ, plaatselijke afdeling
²branch (vb) zich vertakken, zich splitsen: ~ **off** zich splitsen, afbuigen
branch out zijn zaken uitbreiden, zich ontwikkelen
¹brand (n) **1** merkʰ, merknaam, soort, typeʰ **2** brandmerkʰ
²brand (vb) **1** (brand)merken, markeren: ~ed **goods** merkartikelen **2** brandmerken
brandish zwaaien met: ~ a **sword** (dreigend) zwaaien met een zwaard
brandy 1 cognac **2** brandewijn
¹brass (n) **1** messingʰ, geelkoperʰ **2** koperʰ, koperen instrumenten **3** [inform] duiten, centen
²brass (adj) koperen || [inform] get down to ~ **tacks** spijkers met koppen slaan
brassy 1 (geel)koperen, koperkleurig **2** brutaal **3** blikkerig [sound]; schel
brat snotaap, rotkindʰ
¹brave (adj) dapper, moedig: put a ~ **face** on zich sterk houden
²brave (vb) trotseren, weerstaan
bravery moed, dapperheid
¹brawl (n) vechtpartij, knokpartij
²brawl (vb) knokken, op de vuist gaan
brawn spierkracht, spieren
¹bray (n) schreeuw [of donkey]; gebalkʰ
²bray (vb) balken [of donkey]
brazen brutaal
brazen out [inform] brazen **it** out zich er brutaal doorheen slaan
Brazil Brazilië
¹Brazilian (n) Braziliaan(se)
²Brazilian (adj) Braziliaans
¹breach (n) **1** breuk, bres, gatʰ **2** breuk, schending: ~ of **contract** contractbreuk; ~ of **the** peace ordeverstoring
²breach (vb) **1** doorbreken, een gat maken in **2** verbreken, inbreuk maken op
bread 1 broodʰ: ~ and **butter** boterham-(men); [fig] dagelijkse levensbehoeften, levensonderhoud; a **loaf** of ~ een brood; **slice** of ~ boterham **2** broodʰ, kost, levensonderhoudʰ: **daily** ~ dagelijks brood, dagelijkse levensbehoeften
bread-and-butter fundamenteel, basis-
breadth 1 breedte [of dimensions] **2** breedte, strook; baan [of material, wallpaper etc] **3** ruimte, uitgestrektheid
breadwinner broodwinner; kostwinner
¹break (n) **1** onderbreking, verandering, breuk, stroomstoring: a ~ for **lunch** een lunchpauze; there was a ~ in the **weather** het weer sloeg om **2** uitbraak, ontsnapping; [cycle racing] demarrage: **make** a ~ for it probe-

ren te ontsnappen **3** [tennis] servicedoorbraak **4** [inform] kans, geluk^h: *lucky* ~ geluk, meevaller; *give* s.o. a ~ iem. een kans geven, iem. een plezier doen **5** begin^h; het aanbreken [of day]: ~ *of day* dageraad

²**break** (vb) **1** breken, kapot gaan, het begeven: *his voice* broke hij kreeg de baard in zijn keel; ~ *with* breken met [eg tradition, family] **2** ontsnappen, uitbreken; [cycle racing] demarreren: ~ *free* (or: *loose*) ontsnappen, losbreken **3** ophouden, tot een einde komen; omslaan [of weather] **4** plotseling beginnen; aanbreken [of day]; losbreken; losbarsten [of storm] **5** bekendgemaakt worden [of news] **6** plotseling dalen, kelderen; ineenstorten [of prices on stock exchange] ‖ [inform; also com] ~ *even* quitte spelen

³**break** (vb) **1** breken [also fig]; kapot maken, (financieel) ruïneren; laten springen [bank]: ~ *cover* uit de schuilplaats komen; ~ *the law* de wet overtreden; ~ *a record* een record verbeteren **2** onderbreken [eg trip] **3** temmen; dresseren [horse] **4** (voorzichtig) vertellen [(bad) news]; tactvol vertellen **5** schaven; bezeren [skin] **6** ontcijferen; breken [code] **7** [tennis] doorbreken [service]

breakable breekbaar

breakage breuk, het breken, barst ‖ *£10 for* ~ £10 voor breukschade

¹**breakaway** (n) **1** afgescheiden groep **2** uitval, demarrage, aanval^h

²**breakaway** (adj) afgescheiden

break away (+ from) wegrennen (van), ontsnappen (aan); [fig] zich losmaken (van)

breakdown 1 defect^h, mankement^h **2** instorting, zenuwinstorting **3** uitsplitsing, specificatie: ~ *of costs* kostenverdeling, uitsplitsing van de kosten

¹**break down** (vb) **1** kapot gaan; defect raken [of machine]; verbroken raken [of connections] **2** mislukken [of talks, marriage etc] **3** instorten [of human being] **4** zich laten uitsplitsen: *the procedure can be broken down into five easy steps* de werkwijze kan onderverdeeld worden in vijf eenvoudige stappen, de werkwijze valt uiteen in vijf eenvoudige stappen

²**break down** (vb) **1** afbreken [wall; also fig]; vernietigen, slopen; inslaan, intrappen [door] **2** uitsplitsen, analyseren; [chem] afbreken

breaker 1 sloper **2** breker, brandingsgolf

break-even break-even, evenwichts-: ~ *point* (punt van) evenwicht tussen inkomsten en uitgaven

¹**breakfast** (n) ontbijt^h

²**breakfast** (vb) ontbijten

¹**break in** (vb) **1** interrumperen: ~ *on* interrumperen, verstoren **2** inbreken

²**break in** (vb) **1** africhten, dresseren **2** inlopen [shoes]

break-in inbraak

breakneck halsbrekend: *at (a)* ~ *speed* in razende vaart

¹**break off** (vb) **1** afbreken [eg of branch] **2** pauzeren **3** ophouden met praten, zijn mond houden

²**break off** (vb) **1** afbreken [eg branch; also fig: negotiations etc] **2** verbreken [relationship with s.o.]; ophouden met

breakout uitbraak, ontsnapping

break out 1 uitbreken **2** (also + of) ontsnappen (uit), uitbreken, ontkomen (aan) ‖ ~ *in* bedekt raken met, onder komen te zitten [eg small stains]

breakthrough doorbraak

¹**break through** (vb) doorbreken; [fig] een doorbraak maken

²**break through** (vb) doorbreken [also fig]

¹**break up** (vb) **1** uit elkaar vallen, in stukken breken; [fig] ten einde komen; ontbonden worden [of meeting]: *their marriage* broke up hun huwelijk ging kapot **2** uit elkaar gaan [of (marriage) partners, group of people etc]

²**break up** (vb) **1** uit elkaar doen vallen, in stukken breken; [fig] onderbreken, doorbreken [routine, part of text] **2** kapot maken [marriage] **3** verspreiden; uiteenjagen [group of people] **4** beëindigen; een eind maken aan [quarrel, fight, meeting]: *break it up!* hou ermee op! **5** doen instorten, in elkaar doen klappen

break-up 1 opheffing; beëindiging [business] **2** scheiding [of lovers]

breakwater golfbreker

bream brasem

breast 1 borst, voorzijde, borststuk^h **2** hart^h, boezem ‖ *beat one's* ~ groot misbaar van verdriet maken

breast stroke schoolslag

breath 1 adem(haling), lucht, het ademen: *get one's* ~ *(back) (again)* weer op adem komen; *out of* ~ buiten adem **2** zuchtje^h (wind), licht briesje^h **3** vleugje^h: *not a* ~ *of suspicion* geen greintje argwaan ‖ *take one's* ~ *away* perplex doen staan

breathalyser blaaspijpje^h

¹**breathe** (vb) **1** ademen, ademhalen; [form] leven: ~ *in* inademen; ~ *out* uitademen **2** op adem komen, uitblazen, bijkomen

²**breathe** (vb) **1** inademen **2** uitblazen, uitademen **3** inblazen, ingeven: ~ *new life into* nieuw leven inblazen

breather 1 pauze, adempauze **2** beetje beweging, wandeling

breathing space pauze; rustperiode

breathless 1 buiten adem, hijgend, ademloos **2** ademloos, gespannen

breath test blaasproef, blaastest

breech delivery stuitbevalling

breeches kniebroek; [inform] lange broek

¹**breed** (n) ras^h, aard, soort

²**breed** (vb) zich voortplanten, jongen

³**breed** 1 kweken, telen, fokken; [fig] voortbrengen 2 kweken, opvoeden, opleiden: *well bred* goed opgevoed, welgemanierd

breeder fokker

breeding 1 het fokken, het kweken, fokkerij, kwekerij 2 voortplanting, het jongen 3 opvoeding, goede manieren

breeding ground 1 broedgebiedʰ 2 [fig] broedplaats; kweekplaats

¹**breeze** (n) bries, wind

²**breeze** (vb) [inform] (zich) vlot bewegen: ~ *in* (vrolijk) binnen komen waaien

breezy 1 winderig, tochtig 2 opgewekt, levendig, vrolijk

brevity 1 kortheid 2 beknoptheid, bondigheid

¹**brew** (n) brouwselʰ, bierʰ

²**brew** (vb) 1 bierbrouwen 2 trekken [of tea] 3 broeien, dreigen, op komst zijn || ~ *up* thee zetten

³**brew** (vb) 1 brouwen [beer]; zetten [tea] 2 brouwen, uitbroeden

brewer brouwer

brewery brouwerij

¹**bribe** (n) 1 steekpenning, smeergeldʰ 2 lokmiddelʰ

²**bribe** (vb) (om)kopen, steekpenningen geven, smeergeld betalen

bribery omkoperij

¹**brick** (n) 1 baksteen 2 blokʰ [toy] || *drop* a ~ iets verkeerds zeggen, een blunder begaan

²**brick** (vb) metselen: ~ *up,* ~ *in* dichtmetselen, inmetselen

bricklayer metselaar

brickwork metselwerkʰ

bridal bruids-, huwelijks-, bruilofts-

bride bruid

bridegroom bruidegom

bridesmaid bruidsmeisjeʰ

¹**bridge** (n) 1 brug: [fig] *burn* one's ~s zijn schepen achter zich verbranden 2 neusrug 3 brug [of glasses frame] 4 kam [of string instrument]

²**bridge** (n) bridgeʰ [cards]

³**bridge** (vb) overbruggen, een brug slaan over

bridgehead bruggenhoofdʰ [also fig]

¹**bridle** (n) hoofdstelʰ; [fig] breidel; toom

²**bridle** (vb) (verontwaardigd) het hoofd in de nek gooien

³**bridle** (vb) 1 (een paard) het hoofdstel aandoen 2 breidelen, in toom houden

bridle path ruiterpadʰ

¹**brief** (n) 1 stukken, bescheiden, dossierʰ 2 (-s) (dames)slip, herenslip

²**brief** (adj) kort, beknopt, vluchtig: *a ~ look at the newspaper* een vluchtige blik in de krant; ~ *and to the point* kort en krachtig; *in ~* om kort te gaan, kortom

³**brief** (vb) instrueren, aanwijzingen geven

briefcase aktetas, diplomatenkoffertjeʰ

briefing (laatste) instructies, briefing, instruering

brigade brigade, korpsʰ

brigadier brigadegeneraal [in British army]; brigadecommandant

brigand (struik)rover, bandiet

bright 1 hel(der) [also fig]; licht, stralend: *always look on the ~ side of things* de dingen altijd van de zonnige kant bekijken; ~ *red* helderrood 2 opgewekt, vrolijk 3 slim, pienter: *a ~ idea* een slim idee

brighten 1 (doen) opklaren; ophelderen [also fig]: *the sky is ~ing up* de lucht klaart op 2 oppoetsen, opvrolijken: *she has ~ed up his whole life* dankzij haar is hij helemaal opgeleefd

brill [inform] fantastisch

brilliance 1 schittering 2 virtuositeit; genialiteit

brilliant 1 stralend, fonkelend, glinsterend: ~ *stars* fonkelende sterren; ~ *red* hoogrood 2 briljant, geniaal 3 geweldig, fantastisch, gaaf

¹**brim** (n) 1 (boven)rand, boordʰ: *full to the ~* tot de rand toe vol, boordevol [of a glass] 2 rand [of a hat]

²**brim** (vb) boordevol zijn, tot barstens toe gevuld zijn: *her eyes ~med with tears* haar ogen schoten vol tranen

brine 1 pekel(nat)ʰ 2 het zilte nat

bring 1 (mee)brengen, (mee)nemen, aandragen: *his cries brought his neighbours running* op zijn kreten kwamen zijn buren aangesneld; ~ *a case before the court* een zaak aan de rechter voorleggen 2 opleveren, opbrengen: ~ *a good price* een goede prijs opbrengen 3 teweegbrengen, leiden tot, voortbrengen: *I can't ~ myself to kill an animal* ik kan me(zelf) er niet toe brengen een dier te doden; *you've brought this problem (up)on yourself* je hebt je dit probleem zelf op de hals gehaald || ~ *home to* duidelijk maken, aan het verstand brengen

bring about veroorzaken, teweegbrengen, aanrichten: ~ *changes* veranderingen teweegbrengen

bring along 1 meenemen, meebrengen 2 opkweken, in de ontwikkeling stimuleren 3 doen gedijen

bring (a)round overhalen, ompraten, overreden

bring back 1 terugbrengen, retourneren, mee terugbrengen 2 in de herinnering terugbrengen, doen herleven, oproepen: *this song brings back memories* dit liedje brengt (goede) herinneringen boven 3 herinvoeren, herintroduceren: ~ *capital punishment* de doodstraf weer invoeren

bring down 1 neerhalen; neerschieten

[aeroplane, bird] **2** aan de grond zetten **3** [sport] neerleggen, onderuithalen; ten val brengen [opponent] **4** ten val brengen; omverwerpen [government] **5** drukken, verlagen; terugschroeven [costs]
bring forth [form] voortbrengen; [fig] veroorzaken; oproepen [protest, criticism]
bring in 1 binnenhalen [harvest] **2** opleveren, afwerpen, inbrengen **3** bijhalen, opnemen in, aanwerven: ~ *experts* to advise deskundigen in de arm nemen **4** inrekenen [detainee] **5** komen aanzetten met; introduceren [new fashion]; indienen [bill]
bring off 1 in veiligheid brengen, redden uit **2** [inform] voor elkaar krijgen, fiksen: we've brought it off we hebben het voor elkaar gekregen
bring on veroorzaken, teweegbrengen
bring out 1 naar buiten brengen, voor de dag komen met; [fig also] uitbrengen **2** op de markt brengen; uitbrengen [product] **3** duidelijk doen uitkomen: this photo brings out all the details op deze foto zijn alle details goed te zien
bring round bij bewustzijn brengen, bijbrengen || ~ *to* (het gesprek) in de richting sturen van
bring up 1 naar boven brengen **2** grootbrengen, opvoeden **3** ter sprake brengen, naar voren brengen **4** [inform] uitbraken, overgeven, uitkotsen
brink (steile) rand, (steile) oever: *on* (or: to) the ~ *of war* op de rand van oorlog
the **briny deep** [form] het zilte nat; het ruime sop
brisk 1 kwiek, vlot: ~ *trade* levendige handel **2** verkwikkend; fris [of wind]
brisket borststuk[h] [beef]
[1]**bristle** (n) stoppel(haar[h])
[2]**bristle** (vb) recht overeind staan [of hair]: ~ *(up)* zijn stekels opzetten, nijdig worden; ~ *with* anger opvliegen van woede; ~ *with* wemelen van
Brit Briton Brit(se)
Britain Groot-Brittannië
Britannia (Vrouwe) Brittannia
Britannic [form] Brits
British Brits, Engels: the ~ *Empire* het Britse Rijk; *the* ~ de Britten
Briton Brit(se)
Brittany Bretagne
brittle broos, breekbaar, onbestendig, wankel
broach 1 aanspreken; openmaken [bottle etc] **2** aansnijden, ter sprake brengen; beginnen over [topic]
[1]**broad** (n) **1** brede (ge)deel(te)[h] **2** [Am; inform] wijf[h], mokkel[h] || the Norfolk Broads de Norfolkse plassen
[2]**broad** (adj) **1** breed, uitgestrekt, in de breedte: ~ *bean* tuinboon; ~ *shoulders* brede

schouders; ~ly *speaking* in zijn algemeenheid **2** ruim(denkend) **3** gedurfd, onbekrompen, royaal **4** duidelijk, direct: a ~ *hint* een overduidelijke wenk **5** grof, plat, lomp: ~ *Scots* met een sterk Schots accent **6** ruim, globaal, ruw **7** helder, duidelijk: in ~ *daylight* op klaarlichte dag
broadband breedband
broadband internet access breedbandinternet[h]
[1]**broadcast** (n) (radio-)uitzending, tv-uitzending
[2]**broadcast** (vb) **1** uitzenden, in de lucht zijn **2** op de radio (or: televisie) zijn
[3]**broadcast** (vb) **1** breedwerpig zaaien; [fig] rondbazuinen; rondstrooien **2** uitzenden: a ~ing *station* een zendstation
broaden (zich) verbreden, breder worden (maken): reading ~s the *mind* lezen verruimt de blik
broad-minded ruimdenkend, tolerant
broadsheet serieuze krant (op groot formaat)
broccoli broccoli
brochure brochure, folder, prospectus: *advertising* ~s reclamefolders
brogue 1 gaatjesschoen **2** zwaar accent; [esp] Iers, Schots accent
[1]**broil** (vb) (liggen) bakken
[2]**broil** (vb) [esp Am] **1** grillen, roosteren **2** stoven: ~ing *hot* smoorheet, bloedheet
broiler 1 grill, braadrooster[h] **2** braadkuiken[h], slachtkuiken[h]
broke [inform] platzak, blut, aan de grond, bankroet: *stony* (or: flat) ~ finaal aan de grond, zonder een rooie cent
broken 1 gebroken, kapot, stuk: ~ *colours* gebroken kleuren; ~ *English* gebrekkig Engels; ~ *home* ontwricht gezin; a ~ *marriage* een stukgelopen huwelijk **2** oneffen [of terrain]; ruw, geaccidenteerd **3** onderbroken, verbrokkeld: a ~ *journey* een reis met veel onderbrekingen
broken-down versleten, vervallen
[1]**broker** (n) (effecten)makelaar
[2]**broker** (vb) als makelaar optreden
[3]**broker** (vb) (als makelaar) regelen
brokerage 1 makelaardij **2** courtage; makelaarsloon[h]
brolly [inform] paraplu
bronchitis bronchitis
[1]**bronze** (n) **1** bronzen (kunst)voorwerp[h] **2** bronzen medaille, brons[h], derde plaats **3** brons[h], bronskleur
[2]**bronze** (vb) bronsachtig worden, bruinen
[3]**bronze** (vb) bronzen, bruinen
Bronze Age bronstijd, bronsperiode
brooch broche
[1]**brood** (n) gebroed[h], broed(sel[h]); kroost[h] [also fig]
[2]**brood** (vb) **1** broeden **2** tobben, piekeren,

peinzen: *she just sits there ~ing* ze zit daar maar te piekeren; *~ about* (or: *on, over*) tobben over, piekeren over; *~ over* *one's future* inzitten over zijn toekomst

broody 1 broeds **2** bedrukt, somber

¹brook (n) beek, stroompje[h]

²brook (vb) dulden: *this matter ~s no delay* deze kwestie kan geen uitstel lijden

broom 1 bezem, schrobber **2** [bot] brem

broomstick bezemsteel

Bros Brothers Gebr. [Gebroeders]: *Jones ~* Gebr. Jones

broth bouillon, vleesnat[h], soep

brothel bordeel[h]

brother 1 broer: *he has been like a ~ to me* hij is als een broer voor me geweest **2** broeder, kloosterbroeder **3** [inform] makker, gast

brotherhood broederschap

brother-in-law zwager

brow 1 wenkbrauw: *knit one's brows* (de wenkbrauwen) fronsen **2** voorhoofd[h] **3** bovenrand, (overhangende) rotsrand, top, kruin

browbeat overdonderen, intimideren

brown bruin: *~ bread* bruinbrood, volkorenbrood; *~ paper* pakpapier

brownie goede fee, nachtelfje[h]

Brownie padvindster; kabouter [from 7 to 11 years of age]

brownie point [inform] schouderklopje[h], wit voetje[h]

¹browse (n) **1** [esp singular] het grasduinen, het neuzen: *have a good ~ through* flink grasduinen in **2** (jonge) scheuten [as food for animals]

²browse (vb) **1** grasduinen, (in boeken) snuffelen, (rond)neuzen **2** weiden, (af)grazen

browser zoekprogramma[h]

¹bruise (n) kneuzing [also of fruit]; blauwe plek

²bruise (vb) blauwe plek(ken) vertonen, gekneusd zijn

³bruise (vb) kneuzen, bezeren

bruiser krachtpatser, rouwdouwer

Brunei Brunei

¹Bruneian (n) Bruneier, Bruneise

²Bruneian (adj) Bruneis

brunt eerste stoot, zwaartepunt[h], toppunt[h]: *she bore the (full) ~ of his anger* zij kreeg de volle laag

¹brush (n) **1** borstel, kwast; penseel[h] [of artist, painter]; brushes: [fig] *tarred with the same ~* uit hetzelfde (slechte) hout gesneden **2** (af)borsteling **3** lichte aanraking, beroering **4** schermutseling, kort treffen[h] **5** kreupelhout[h], onderhout[h] **6** kreupelbos[h], met dicht struikgewas begroeid gebied[h]

²brush (vb) **1** afborstelen, opborstelen, uitborstelen, afvegen, wegvegen, uitvegen

2 strijken (langs/over), rakelings gaan (langs): *the cat's whiskers ~ed my cheek* de snorharen van de kat streken langs mijn wang

brush aside 1 opzijschuiven, wegschuiven [resistance, opposition etc]; uit de weg ruimen **2** terzijde schuiven, naast zich neerleggen: *brush complaints aside* klachten wegwuiven

¹brush off (vb) zich laten wegborstelen, (door borstelen) loslaten

²brush off (vb) **1** wegborstelen, afborstelen **2** (zich van) iem. afhouden, afschepen: *I won't be brushed off* ik laat me niet afschepen

brush-off [inform] afscheping, afpoeiering, de bons: *give s.o. the ~* a) iem. met een kluitje in het riet sturen; b) iem. de bons geven

brush up opfrissen, ophalen, bijspijkeren: *~ (on) your English* je Engels ophalen

brushwood onderhout[h], kreupelhout[h], sprokkelhout[h]

brusque bruusk, abrupt, kort aangebonden

Brussels sprouts spruitjes

brutal bruut, beestachtig, meedogenloos: *~ frankness* genadeloze openhartigheid

brutality bruutheid, wreedheid, onmenselijkheid

¹brute (n) **1** beest[h], dier[h] **2** bruut, woesteling

²brute (adj) bruut, grof: *~ force* grof geweld

B Sc Bachelor of Science [roughly] Bachelor (of Science)

BSE bovine spongiform encephalopathy BSE; gekkekoeienziekte

BSI British Standards Institution [roughly] NNI; Nederlands Normalisatie-instituut

BST British Summer Time

btw by the way T2H [tussen haakjes]; trouwens

¹bubble (n) **1** (lucht)bel(letje[h]): *blow ~s* bellen blazen **2** glaskoepel **3** [fig] zeepbel, ballonnetje[h]

²bubble (vb) **1** borrelen, bruisen, pruttelen **2** glimmen, stralen: *~ over with enthusiasm* overlopen van enthousiasme

bubble gum klapkauwgom

bubble wrap noppenfolie; bubbeltjesplastic[h]

¹bubbly (n) champagne

²bubbly (adj) **1** bruisend, sprankelend **2** jolig

bubonic: *~ plague* builenpest

buccaneer boekanier, zeerover, vrijbuiter

¹buck (n) **1** mannetjesdier[h]; bok [of deer]; ram(melaar) [of rabbit, hare] **2** dollar || [inform] *pass the ~ (to s.o.)* de verantwoordelijkheid afschuiven (op iem.), (iem.) de zwartepiet toespelen

²buck (vb) bokken [of horse]; bokkensprongen maken

³**buck** (vb) **1** afwerpen [horseman, horsewoman]; afgooien **2** [Am; inform] tegenwerken: *you can't go on ~ing the system* je kunt je niet blijven verzetten tegen het systeem

¹**bucket** (n) emmer: [inform, fig] *it came down in ~s* het regende dat het goot ‖ [inform] *kick the ~* het hoekje omgaan, de pijp uitgaan

²**bucket** (vb) [inform] gieten, plenzen; bij bakken neervallen [of rain also]

bucket seat kuipstoel [in car or aeroplane]

¹**buckle** (n) gesp

²**buckle** (vb) **1** met een gesp sluiten, aangegespt (kunnen) worden **2** kromtrekken, ontzetten, ontwricht raken **3** wankelen, wijken, bezwijken

³**buckle** (vb) (vast)gespen: *~ up a belt* een riem omdoen

¹**buck up** (vb) [inform] opschieten

²**buck up** (vb) [inform] opvrolijken: *~, things will be all right* kop op, het komt wel weer goed

buckwheat 1 boekweit **2** boekweitmeelʰ

bucolic landelijk, bucolisch

¹**bud** (n) knop, kiem: *nip in the ~* in de kiem smoren; [fig] *in the ~* in de dop

²**bud** (vb) knoppen, uitlopen

Buddha 1 Boeddha **2** Boeddhabeeld, boeddha

Buddhism boeddhismeʰ

budding ontluikend, aankomend, in de dop

buddy [inform] **1** maat, vriend, kameraad **2** buddy [of AIDS patient] **3** [as form of address; Am] maatjeʰ, makker

¹**budge** (vb) **1** zich (ver)roeren, (zich) bewegen, zich verplaatsen: *the screw won't ~* ik krijg geen beweging in die schroef **2** veranderen: *not ~ from one's opinion* aan zijn mening vasthouden

²**budge** (vb) (een klein stukje) verplaatsen, verschuiven, verschikken: *not ~ one inch* geen duimbreed wijken

budgerigar (gras)parkiet

¹**budget** (n) begroting, budgetʰ

²**budget** (adj) voordelig, goedkoop: *~ prices* speciale aanbiedingen

³**budget** (vb) **1** budgetteren, de begroting opstellen **2** huishouden

⁴**budget** (vb) in een begroting opnemen, reserveren, ramen

¹**buff** (n) **1** [inform] enthousiast, liefhebber, fanaat **2** rundleerʰ, buffelleerʰ **3** vaalgeelʰ, bruingeelʰ, buff: *~ yellow* vaalgeel **4** [inform] nakieʰ, blootjeʰ: *in the ~* naakt

²**buff** (vb) polijsten, opwrijven

buffalo buffel, karbouw, bizon

buffed [Am; inform] (goed) gespierd: *get ~* (meer) spieren kweken

¹**buffer** (n) buffer, stootkussenʰ, stootblokʰ

²**buffer** (vb) als buffer optreden voor, beschermen, behoeden

¹**buffet** (n) slag [also fig]; klap, dreun

²**buffet** (n) **1** dressoirʰ, buffetʰ **2** buffetʰ, schenktafel **3** niet-uitgeserveerde maaltijd: *cold ~* koud buffet

³**buffet** (vb) **1** meppen, slaan, beuken **2** teisteren, kwellen, treffen: *~ed by misfortunes* geteisterd door tegenslag

buffoon hansworst, potsenmaker, clown

¹**buff up** (vb) trainen

²**buff up** (vb) [leather] opwrijven, doen glanzen

¹**bug** (n) **1** halfvleugelig insectʰ, wants, bedwants **2** [Am] insectʰ, beestjeʰ, ongedierteʰ **3** [inform] virusʰ [also fig]; bacil, bacterie **4** [inform] obsessie **5** [inform] mankementʰ, storing, defectʰ **6** [inform] afluisterapparaatjeʰ, verborgen microfoontjeʰ

²**bug** (vb) [inform] **1** afluisterapparatuur plaatsen in **2** [Am] irriteren, ergeren, lastigvallen: *what is ~ging him?* wat zit hem dwars?

bugger 1 [vulg] lul(hannes), zak(kenwasser) **2** [vulg] pedo(fiel), homo(fiel) **3** (arme) drommel, (arme) donder, kerel ‖ *~ him!* hij kan de tering krijgen

bugger off ophoepelen

bugger up verpesten, verzieken

buggy 1 licht rijtuigjeʰ, open autootjeʰ **2** [Am] kinderwagen **3** wandelwagen

bugle bugel [for military signals]; signaalhoorn

¹**build** (n) (lichaams)bouw, gestalte, vorm

²**build** (vb) **1** bouwen **2** (in kracht) toenemen, aanwakkeren, verhevigen, groeien, aanzwellen: *tension built within her* de spanning in haar nam toe

³**build** (vb) **1** (op)bouwen, maken: *~ a fire* een vuur maken **2** vormen, ontwikkelen, ontplooien **3** samenstellen, vormen, opbouwen **4** (+ on) baseren (op), grondvesten, onderbouwen: *~ one's hopes on* zijn hoop vestigen op **5** inbouwen [also fig]; opnemen: *this clause was not built into my contract* deze clausule was niet in mijn contract opgenomen

builder aannemer, bouwer

building 1 gebouwʰ, bouwwerkʰ, pandʰ **2** bouw, het bouwen, bouwkunst

¹**build up** (vb) **1** aangroeien, toenemen, zich opstapelen: *tension was building up* de spanning nam toe **2** (geleidelijk) toewerken (naar)

²**build up** (vb) **1** opbouwen, ontwikkelen, tot bloei brengen: *~ a firm from scratch* een bedrijf van de grond af opbouwen **2** ophemelen, loven, prijzen

build-up 1 opstopping, opeenhoping, opeenstapeling: *a ~ of traffic* een verkeersopstopping **2** ontwikkeling, opbouw, vorming **3** (troepen)concentratie

built-in ingebouwd [also fig]; aangeboren:

~ *cupboard* muurkast
built-up 1 samengesteld, geconstrueerd
2 bebouwd, volgebouwd
bulb 1 bol(letje[h]), bloembol; [by extension] bolgewas[h]: ~ *fields* bollenvelden **2** (gloei)-lamp
bulbous bolvormig: ~ *nose* stompe neus
Bulgaria Bulgarije
1Bulgarian (n) Bulgaar(se)
2Bulgarian (adj) Bulgaars
1bulge (n) bobbel
2bulge (vb) **1** (op)zwellen, uitdijen **2** bol staan, opbollen, uitpuilen: ~ *out* uitpuilen
bulk 1 (grote) massa, omvang, volume[h]: ~ *buying* in het groot inkopen; *in* ~ **a)** onverpakt, los; **b)** in het groot **2** (scheeps)lading, vracht **3** grootste deel[h], merendeel[h], gros[h]: *the* ~ *of the books have already been sold* het merendeel van de boeken is al verkocht **4** kolos, gevaarte[h], massa **5** (scheeps)ruim[h]
bulkhead (waterdicht) schot[h], scheidingswand, afscheiding
bulky lijvig, log, dik, omvangrijk
bull 1 stier, bul; mannetje[h] [of whale, elephant etc]: *like a* ~ *in a china shop* als een olifant in een porseleinkast; *take the* ~ *by the horns* de koe bij de hoorns vatten **2** (pauselijke) bul **3** [vulg] kletspraat, gekletsh, gezeik[h]
bulldog buldog
bulldoze 1 met een bulldozer bewerken **2** [inform] (plat)walsen, doordrukken, zijn zin doordrijven
bulldozer bulldozer
bullet (geweer)kogel, patroon[h] ‖ *bite* (on) *the* ~ door de zure appel heen bijten
bulletin (nieuws)bulletin[h], dienstmededeling
bulletin board [Am] mededelingenbord[h], prikbord[h]
bullfight stierengevecht[h]
bullfrog brulkikvors
bullish 1 optimistisch **2** [fin] oplopend, stijgend
bull market stijgende markt [at stock exchange]
bullock 1 os **2** jonge stier, stiertje[h]
bullring arena [for bull fights]
bull's-eye 1 roos [target] **2** schot[h] in de roos [also fig]; rake opmerking **3** [type] toverbal [peppermint]
1bullshit (n) [vulg] gekletsh, kletspraat, gezeik[h]
2bullshit (vb) [vulg] lullen, zeiken: *don't* ~ *me* neem me niet in de zeik, lul niet
bull terrier bulterriër
1bully (n) **1** bullebak, beul, kwelgeest **2** [hockey] afslag
2bully (adj) [oft iron] prima: ~ *for you* bravo!, wat geweldig van jou!
3bully (vb) koeioneren, intimideren: ~ *s.o.*

into doing sth. iem. met bedreigingen dwingen tot iets
bullyboy [inform] (gehuurde) zware jongen, vechtersbaas
bully off [hockey] de afslag verrichten
bulrush 1 bies, mattenbies, stoelbies **2** lisdodde **3** [rel] papyrus(plant)
bulwark 1 (verdedigings)muur, wal, schans **2** bolwerk[h] [also fig]; bastion[h] **3** [shipp] verschansing
1bum (n) [vulg] **1** kont, gat[h], achterste[h] **2** [Am, Austr; depr] zwerver, schooier, landloper, bedelaar **3** (kloot)zak, mislukkeling, nietsnut
2bum (adj) [vulg] waardeloos, rottig
bum along [inform] toeren, rustig rijden
bum around [inform] lanterfanten, lummelen, rondhangen
bumble 1 mompelen, brabbelen, bazelen: *to keep bumbling* *on* *about sth.* blijven doorzeuren over iets **2** stuntelen, klungelen
bumblebee hommel
bumf [inform] [depr] papierrommel, papiertroep, papierwinkel
1bump (n) **1** bons, schok, stoot **2** buil, bult; hobbel [in road, terrein]
2bump (vb) **1** bonzen, stoten, botsen **2** hobbelen, schokken: *we* ~*ed along* *in our old car* we denderden voort in onze oude auto
3bump (vb) stoten tegen, botsen tegen, rammen: *don't* ~ *your head* stoot je hoofd niet
4bump (adv) pats-boem, pardoes
bumper 1 (auto)bumper, stootkussen[h], stootrand; [Am] buffer; stootb(l)ok **2** iets vols, iets groots, overvloed: ~ *crop* (or: *harvest*) recordoogst
bumph see bumf
bump into [inform] tegen het lijf lopen, toevallig tegenkomen
bump off [inform] koud maken, vermoorden
bumptious opdringerig, verwaand
bump up [inform] opprikken, opschroeven
bumpy hobbelig, bobbelig
bun 1 (krenten)bolletje[h], broodje[h]: [mockingly] *have a* ~ *in the* *oven* in verwachting zijn **2** (haar)knot(je[h])
1bunch (n) **1** bos(je)[h], bundel, tros: *a* ~ *of grapes* een tros(je) druiven; *a* ~ *of keys* een sleutelbos **2** [inform] troep(je[h]), groep(je[h]), stel(letje)[h]: *the* *best* *of the* ~ de beste van het stel
2bunch (vb) samendringen, samendrommen
1bundle (n) bundel, bos[h], pak(ket)[h], zenuwbundel, spierbundel: *he is a* ~ *of* *nerves* hij is één bonk zenuwen
2bundle (vb) **1** bundelen, samenbinden, samenpakken, samenvouwen: ~ *up old newspapers* een touwtje om oude kranten doen **2** proppen, (weg)stouwen, (weg)stoppen,

induwen, inproppen
¹bung (n) stop, kurk, afsluiter
²bung (vb) keilen, gooien, smijten
bungalow bungalow
bungee jumping bungeejumping
bungle (ver)knoeien, (ver)prutsen
bung up [inform] verstoppen, dichtstoppen: *my nose is bunged up* mijn neus zit verstopt
bunion (eelt)knobbel
bunk (stapel)bedʰ, kooi || [inform] *do a ~* ertussenuit knijpen, 'm smeren
bunk-bed stapelbedʰ
bunker [mil, sport] bunker
bunk-up duwtjeʰ
bunny (ko)nijntjeʰ
bunting 1 [zoology] gors, vink **2** dundoekʰ, vlaggetjes
¹buoy (n) **1** boei, ton(boei) **2** redding(s)boei
²buoy (vb) **1** drijvend houden: *~ed (up) by the sea* drijvend op de zee **2** schragen, ondersteunen, dragen
buoyant 1 drijvend **2** opgewekt, vrolijk, luchthartig
buoy up opvrolijken, opbeuren
bur klis, klit
burble 1 kabbelen **2** leuteren, ratelen, kwekken
¹burden (n) **1** last, vracht, verplichting: *beast of ~* lastdier, pakdier, pakezel, pakpaard; *~ of proof* bewijslast; *be a ~ to s.o.* iem. tot last zijn **2** leidmotiefʰ, grondthemaʰ, hoofdthemaʰ, kern
²burden (vb) belasten, beladen, overladen, (zwaar) drukken op
burdensome (lood)zwaar, bezwarend, drukkend
bureau 1 schrijftafel **2** [Am] ladekast **3** dienst, bureauʰ, kantoorʰ, departementʰ, ministerieʰ
bureaucracy bureaucratie
bureaucrat [oft depr] bureaucraat
bureaucratic bureaucratisch
burgeon [form; bot] uitbotten; uitlopen; [fig] snel groeien
burgh 1 stad, (stedelijke) gemeente **2** kiesdistrictʰ
burglar inbreker
burglary inbraak
burgle inbreken (in), inbraak plegen (bij), stelen (bij)
Burgundy 1 Bourgondië **2** bourgogne-(wijn), Bourgondische wijn **3** bordeauxrood
burial begrafenis
burka boerka
Burkina Faso Burkina Faso
¹Burkinese (n) Burkinees, Burkinese
²Burkinese (adj) Burkinees
burkini boerkini
burlap jute
burlesque koddig, kluchtig

burly potig, zwaar, flink
Burma Birma
¹Burmese (n) Birmaan(se)
²Burmese (adj) Birmaans
¹burn (n) brandwond, brandgaatjeʰ
²burn (vb) **1** branden, gloeien: *~ low* uitgaan, uitdoven; *~ing for an ideal* in vuur en vlam voor een ideaal; *~ with anger* koken van woede **2** branden, afbranden, verbranden, ontbranden, in brand staan (steken): *the soup ~t my mouth* ik heb mijn mond aan de soep gebrand; *~ away* opbranden, wegbranden; [fig] verteren; *~ off* wegbranden, afbranden, schoonbranden, leegbranden; *~ to death* door verbranding om het leven brengen
³burn (vb) **1** verteren **2** werken op, gebruiken als brandstof **3** in brand steken
burn down (tot de grond toe) afbranden, platbranden
burner brander; pit [of cooking apparatus etc]
burning brandend, gloeiend, dringend: *a ~ issue* een brandend vraagstuk
burnish (op)glanzen, gaan glanzen, polijsten
¹burn out (vb) **1** uitbranden; opbranden [also fig] **2** doorbranden [of electrical appliance etc]; doorslaan
²burn out (vb) **1** uitbranden: *the shed was completely burnt out* de schuur was volledig uitgebrand **2** door brand verdrijven uit, door brand dakloos maken **3** [inform] overwerken, over de kop werken: *burn o.s. out* zich over de kop werken **4** doen doorbranden
burnt gebrand, geschroeid, gebakken: *~ offering* (or: *sacrifice*) brandoffer
burnt-out 1 opgebrand, uitgeblust, versleten **2** uitgebrand **3** dakloos [because of fire] **4** [inform] doodmoe, uitgeput, afgepeigerd
¹burn up (vb) **1** oplaaien, feller gaan branden **2** [inform] scheuren, jakkeren, hard rijden **3** [Am; inform] laaiend (van woede) zijn
²burn up (vb) verstoken, opbranden
¹burp (n) [inform] boer(tjeʰ), oprisping
²burp (vb) [inform] (laten) boeren; een boertje laten doen [baby]
burqa boerka
¹burrow (n) legerʰ [of rabbit etc]; hol(letjeʰ), tunnel(tjeʰ)
²burrow (vb) **1** een leger graven; [fig] zich nestelen; beschutting zoeken **2** wroeten, graven, zich (een weg) banen: [fig] *~ into somebody's secrets* in iemands geheimen wroeten
bursar thesaurier, penningmeester
¹burst (n) uitbarsting, ontploffing; demarrage: *~ of anger* woede-uitbarsting; *~ of laughter* lachsalvo
²burst (vb) **1** losbarsten, uitbarsten, door-

breken, uit elkaar springen: ~ **forth,** ~ **out** uitroepen, uitbarsten; ~ **out** *crying* in huilen uitbarsten; ~ **into** *tears* in tranen uitbarsten **2** op barsten, springen staan, barstensvol zitten: *be ~ing to* **come** staan te popelen om te komen

³**burst** (vb) doorbreken, openbreken, verbreken, forceren, inslaan, intrappen: *the river will ~ its* **banks** de rivier zal buiten haar oevers treden; [fig] ~ *one's* **sides** *(with) laughing* schudden van het lachen

burst in komen binnenvallen, binnenstormen, (ruw) onderbreken

Burundi Burundi

¹**Burundian** (n) Burundiër, Burundische

²**Burundian** (adj) Burundisch

bury 1 begraven **2** verbergen, verstoppen: ~ *one's* **hands** *in one's pockets* zijn handen (diep) in zijn zakken steken **3** verzinken [also fig]: *buried* **in** *thoughts* in gedachten verzonken; ~ *o.s.* **in** *one's books* (or: *studies*) zich in zijn boeken (or: studie) verdiepen

¹**bus** (n) **1** (auto)bus: [fig] *miss the* ~ de boot missen; *go* **by** ~ de bus nemen **2** [inform] bak, kar **3** [inform] kist, vliegtuigʰ

²**bus** (vb) met de bus gaan (vervoeren), de bus nemen, per bus reizen, op de bus zetten

busby kolbak, berenmuts

bush 1 struik, bosjeʰ **2** struikgewasʰ, kreupelhoutʰ **3** rimboe, woestenij, wildernis ‖ *beat about the* ~ ergens omheen draaien, niet ter zake komen

bushed [inform] bekaf, doodop, uitgeput

Bushman Bosjesman

business 1 handel, zaken: *get* down to ~ ter zake komen, spijkers met koppen slaan; *mean* ~ het serieus menen; *be* **in** ~ (bezig met) handel drijven; [fig] startklaar staan; *on* ~ voor zaken **2** iets afdoends, ruwe behandeling, standjeʰ **3** (ver)plicht(ing), taak, verantwoordelijkheid, werkʰ: [inform] *my af-fairs* are no ~ *of yours* (or: *none of your* ~) mijn zaken gaan jou niets aan; *have* **no** ~ *to do sth.* ergens niet het recht toe hebben; *I will* **make** *it my* ~ *to see that …* ik zal het op me nemen ervoor te zorgen dat …; [inform] *mind your own* ~ bemoei je met je eigen (zaken) **4** agenda, programmaʰ: [inform] *like no-body's* ~ als geen ander; [on agenda of meeting] *any other* ~ rondvraag, wat verder ter tafel komt **5** aangelegenheid, affaire, zaak, kwestie: *I'm sick and tired of this* **whole** ~ ik ben dit hele gedoe meer dan zat **6** moeilijke taak, hele kluif **7** zaak, winkel, bedrijfʰ

business card adreskaartjeʰ, kaartjeʰ, visitekaartjeʰ

business hours kantooruren; openingstijden

businessman zakenman

busker (bedelend) straatmuzikant

bus shelter bushokjeʰ; abri

bus stop bushalte

¹**bust** (n) **1** buste, borstbeeldʰ **2** boezem, buste, borsten

²**bust** (adj) [inform] kapot, stuk, naar de knoppen: *go* ~ op de fles gaan

³**bust** (vb) [inform] **1** barsten, breken, kapotgaan **2** op de fles gaan, bankroet gaan

⁴**bust** (vb) [inform] **1** breken, mollen, kapotmaken **2** laten springen, doorbreken, verbreken, bankroet laten gaan, platzak maken **3** arresteren, aanhouden **4** een inval doen in; huiszoeking doen bij [by police]

busted [Am; inform] betrapt, gesnapt; er gloeiend bij

¹**bustle** (n) drukte, bedrijvigheid

²**bustle** (vb) druk in de weer zijn, jachten, zich haasten: ~ **with** bruisen van

bust-up [inform] **1** stennis, herrie **2** [Am] mislukking [of marriage]; het stuklopen

¹**busy** (adj) **1** bezig, druk bezet, bedrijvig: *she is* ~ **at** (or: *with*) *her work* ze is druk aan het werk **2** [Am] bezet; in gesprek [of telephone]

²**busy** (vb) bezighouden, zoet houden: ~ *o.s.* **with** *collecting stamps* postzegels verzamelen om iets omhanden te hebben

busybody bemoeial

¹**but** (adv) **1** slechts, enkel, alleen, maar, pas: *I* **could** ~ *feel sorry for her* ik kon enkel medelijden hebben met haar; *I know* ~ *one* ik ken er maar één **2** (en) toch, echter, anderzijds

²**but** (prep) behalve, buiten, uitgezonderd: *he wanted nothing* ~ **peace** hij wilde slechts rust; *the last* ~ **one** op één na de laatste

³**but** (conj) **1** [exception] behalve, buiten, uitgezonderd: *what could I do* ~ *surrender?* wat kon ik doen behalve me overgeven? **2** [contrast] maar (toch), niettemin, desondanks: *not a man* ~ *an* **animal** geen mens maar een dier; ~ **then** *(again)* (maar) anderzijds, maar ja; ~ **yet** niettemin

butane butaanʰ; butagasʰ

butch [inform] **1** manwijfʰ, pot **2** ruwe klant, vechtersbaas

¹**butcher** (n) slager, slachter: *the* ~'*s* de slager(ij)

²**butcher** (vb) **1** slachten **2** afslachten, uitmoorden

butchery 1 slachting, bloedbadʰ **2** het slachten [for consumption]

but for ware het niet voor, als niet

¹**butt** (n) **1** mikpuntʰ [of mockery] **2** doelwitʰ, roos **3** (dik) uiteindeʰ, kolf, handvatʰ, restantʰ, eindjeʰ, peuk; [inform] achtersteʰ; krent; [Am] romp; tors: [Am; inform] *kiss s.o.'s* ~ iem. in zijn kont kruipen, vreselijk slijmen bij iem. **4** [Am] sigaret, peuk **5** (bier)vatʰ, wijnvatʰ, (regen)ton **6** ram, kopstoot; stoot [with head or horns]

²**butt** (vb) rammen [with head or horns]; stoten, een kopstoot geven

byword

butter boter ‖ *(he looks as if)* ~ *wouldn't melt in his mouth* hij lijkt van de prins geen kwaad te weten
buttercup boterbloem
butterfingers [inform] stuntel, stoethaspel; [ball game] slecht vanger
butterfly 1 vlinder **2** vlinderslag
buttermilk karnemelk, botermelk
butter up [inform] vleien, stroop om de mond smeren, slijmen
butt in [inform] tussenbeide komen, onderbreken
buttock 1 bil **2** (-s) achterste[h], achterwerk[h]
button 1 knoop(je[h]) **2** (druk)knop, knopje[h] **3** [Am] button, rond insigne[h] ‖ [Am; inform] *on the* ~ **a)** precies, de spijker op z'n kop; **b)** in de roos
button bar knoppenbalk
[1]**buttonhole** (n) knoopsgat[h]
[2]**buttonhole** (vb) in zijn kraag grijpen, staande houden
[1]**button up** (vb) [inform] zijn kop houden
[2]**button up** (vb) dichtknopen, dichtdoen: [Am; inform] ~ *your lip* hou je kop ‖ *that job is buttoned up* dat is voor elkaar
[1]**buttress** (n) steunbeer; [fig] steunpilaar
[2]**buttress** (vb) (also + up) versterken met steun(beer); [fig] (onder)steunen
buxom weelderig; mollig
[1]**buy** (n) **1** aankoop, aanschaf, koop **2** koopje[h], voordeeltje[h]
[2]**buy** (vb) [inform] geloven, accepteren, (voor waar) aannemen: *don't* ~ *that nonsense* laat je niks wijsmaken
[3]**buy** (vb) aankopen, inkopen, opkopen, aanschaffen: *peace was dearly bought* de vrede werd duur betaald; ~ *time* tijd winnen; ~ *back* terugkopen; ~ *up* opkopen, overnemen ‖ [inform] ~ *it* gedood worden; *rent to* ~ huurkopen
buyer 1 koper, klant **2** inkoper [of department store etc]
[1]**buzz** (n) **1** bromgeluid, gonsgeluid, zoemgeluid[h], geroezemoes[h] **2** [inform] belletje[h], telefoontje[h]: *give mother a* ~ bel moeder even
[2]**buzz** (vb) **1** zoemen, brommen, gonzen; roezemoezen **2** druk in de weer zijn **3** op een zoemer drukken, (aan)bellen ‖ [Am; inform] ~ *along* opstappen [after visit]
buzzard buizerd
buzz cut [Am] stekeltjes, gemillimeterd haar
buzzer zoemer
buzz word modewoord[h]
[1]**by** (adv) langs, voorbij: *in years gone by* in vervlogen jaren ‖ *by and by* straks; *by and large* over 't algemeen
[2]**by** (prep) **1** [nearness] bij, dichtbij, vlakbij, naast; [on compass card] ten: *sit by my side* kom naast mij zitten; *by o.s.* alleen **2** [way,

medium etc] door, langs, via, voorbij: *travel by air* vliegen; *taught by radio* via de radio geleerd **3** [time] tegen, vóór, niet later dan; [by extension] op; om [certain time]; in [certain year]: *finished by Sunday* klaar tegen zondag; *by now* nu (al) **4** [instrument, means etc] door, door middel van, per, als gevolg van: *by accident* per ongeluk; *he missed by an inch* hij miste op een paar centimeter; *I did it all by myself* ik heb het helemaal alleen gedaan **5** ten opzichte van, wat ... betreft: *paid by the hour* per uur betaald; *play by the rules* volgens de regels spelen; *that is fine by me* ik vind het best, wat mij betreft is het goed **6** [time or circumstance] bij, tijdens: *by day* overdag **7** [sequence] na, per: *he got worse by the hour* hij ging van uur tot uur achteruit ‖ *swear by the Bible* (or: *Koran*) op de Bijbel (or: Koran) zweren
bye [inform] tot ziens, dag
by-election tussentijdse verkiezing
bygone voorbij, vroeger
bygones: *let* ~ *be* ~ men moet geen oude koeien uit de sloot halen
by-law 1 (plaatselijke) verordening, gemeenteverordening **2** [Am] (bedrijfs)voorschrift[h], (huis)regel: ~*s* huishoudelijk reglement[h]
[1]**bypass** (n) **1** [traf] rondweg, ringweg **2** [techn] omloopkanaal[h], omloopleiding, omloopverbinding **3** [med] bypass
[2]**bypass** (vb) om ... heen gaan, mijden
by-product 1 bijproduct[h] **2** bijverschijnsel[h]; neveneffect[h]
bystander omstander, toeschouwer
byte byte
byway zijweg ‖ [fig] *the* ~*s of literature* de minder bekende paden van de letterkunde
byword 1 spreekwoord[h], gezegde[h], zegswijze **2** belichaming, synoniem[h], prototype[h]: *Joe is a* ~ *for laziness* Joe is het prototype van de luilak

C

C 1 *Celsius* 2 *cent* 3 *centigrade* 4 *circa* ca.
cab 1 [Am] taxi **2** [inform; traf] cabine, bok, cockpit
c<u>a</u>baret 1 variétérestaurant^h **2** show; variété^h
c<u>a</u>bbage 1 kool **2** [inform] slome duikelaar^h, druiloor
cabby [inform] taxichauffeur
c<u>a</u>bdriver [esp Am] taxichauffeur
c<u>a</u>bin 1 (houten) optrek, huisje^h, hut, kleedhokje^h, badhokje^h; [railways] seinhuis^h **2** cabine; (slaap)hut [on ship]; laadruimte; bagageruim^h [in aeroplane]
c<u>a</u>bin cruiser motorjacht^h
c<u>a</u>binet 1 kast, porseleinkast, televisiemeubel^h, dossierkast **2** kabinet^h, ministerraad **3** kabinetsberaad^h, kabinetsvergadering
¹c<u>a</u>ble (n) **1** kabel, sleepkabel, trekkabel **2** (elektriciteits)kabel, televisiekabel **3** kabel, kabelvormig ornament^h; [knitting] kabelsteek
²c<u>a</u>ble (vb) telegraferen
c<u>a</u>ble car kabelwagen, gondel, cabine van een kabelbaan
c<u>a</u>ble television kabeltelevisie
c<u>a</u>bleway kabelbaan
cab<u>oo</u>dle [inform] troep, zwik, bups: *the whole* ~ de hele bups
cab rank taxistandplaats
cache 1 (geheime) bergplaats **2** (geheime/verborgen) voorraad **3** [comp] tijdelijk geheugen, cache(geheugen)
c<u>a</u>chet distinctie; cachet^h, allure
¹c<u>a</u>ckle (n) **1** kakelgeluid^h **2** giechel(lachje^h), gekraai^h: ~*s of excitement* opgewonden gilletjes **3** gekakel^h; [fig] gekwebbel^h; geklets^h: [inform] *cut the* ~ genoeg gekletst
²c<u>a</u>ckle (vb) **1** kakelen; [fig] kwebbelen; kletsen **2** giechelen, kraaien
cac<u>o</u>phonous kakofonisch
cac<u>o</u>phony kakofonie
c<u>a</u>ctus cactus
cad [depr] schoft
CAD *computer-aided design* CAD
cad<u>a</u>verous lijkachtig, lijkkleurig
c<u>a</u>ddie [golf] caddie
c<u>a</u>ddish schofterig, ploerterig
c<u>a</u>ddy theeblikje^h, theebusje^h
c<u>a</u>dence 1 stembuiging, toonval, intonatie **2** [mus] cadens **3** cadans, vloeiend ritme^h
cad<u>e</u>t cadet
¹c<u>a</u>dge (vb) [inform; depr] klaplopen, schooien

²c<u>a</u>dge (vb) [inform; depr] bietsen, aftroggelen
c<u>a</u>dre 1 kader^h **2** kaderlid^h
Caes<u>a</u>rean section keizersnede
caf<u>é</u> 1 eethuisje^h, café-restaurant^h, snackbar **2** theesalon, tearoom **3** koffiehuis^h
cafet<u>e</u>ria kantine, zelfbedieningsrestaurant^h
caff [inform] *see café*
¹cage (n) **1** kooi(constructie) **2** liftkooi, liftbak **3** gevangenis, (krijgs)gevangenkamp^h **4** [ice hockey] kooi, doel^h
²cage (vb) kooien, in een kooi opsluiten
cage fighting kooivechten^h
c<u>a</u>gey [inform] **1** gesloten, behoedzaam, teruggetrokken **2** argwanend, achterdochtig
caj<u>o</u>le (door vleierij) bepraten, ompraten, overhalen: ~ *s.o.* *into* *giving money* iem. geld aftroggelen
cake 1 cake, taart, (pannen)koek, gebak^h: *go* (or: *sell*) *like hot* ~*s* verkopen als warme broodjes, lopen als een trein **2** blok^h [of compact material]; koek ‖ [inform] *you can't have your* ~ *and eat it* je kunt niet alles willen
Cal 1 *California* **2** *(large) calorie*
cal<u>a</u>mity onheil^h, calamiteit, ramp(spoed)
c<u>a</u>lcify verkalken [also fig]
c<u>a</u>lcium calcium^h
¹c<u>a</u>lculate (vb) **1** rekenen, een berekening maken **2** schatten, een schatting maken
²c<u>a</u>lculate (vb) **1** (wiskundig) berekenen, (vooraf) uitrekenen **2** beramen, bewust plannen: ~*d to attract the attention* bedoeld om de aandacht te trekken **3** incalculeren: ~*d risk* ingecalculeerd risico
c<u>a</u>lculating berekenend
calcul<u>a</u>tion 1 berekening [also fig] **2** voorspelling, schatting **3** bedachtzaamheid
c<u>a</u>lculator rekenmachine, calculator
c<u>a</u>lculus calculus; analyse: ~ *of probabilities* kansrekening
c<u>a</u>lendar 1 kalender **2** [Am] agenda
calf 1 kalf^h: *the cow is in* (or: *with*) ~ de koe is drachtig, de koe moet kalven **2** [anatomy] kuit
c<u>a</u>libre kaliber^h, gehalte^h, niveau^h, klasse
¹call (n) **1** kreet, roep van dier, roep van vogel: *we heard a* ~ *for help* we hoorden hulpgeroep; *within* ~ binnen gehoorsafstand **2** (kort, formeel, zakelijk) bezoek^h: *pay a* ~ een visite afleggen; [inform; euph] naar een zekere plaats (or: nummer 100) gaan **3** beroep^h, aanspraak, claim **4** oproep(ing), roep(ing), appel^h, voorlezing van presentielijst; [fin] oproep tot aflossing van een schuld; aanmaning: *the actors received a* ~ *for eight o'clock* de acteurs moesten om acht uur op; *at* ~, *on* ~ (onmiddellijk) beschikbaar, op afroep; *the doctor was on* ~ de dokter had bereikbaarheidsdienst **5** reden, aanleiding,

noodzaak, behoefte: *there's no ~ for you to worry* je hoeft je niet ongerust te maken **6** telefoontje[h], (telefoon)gesprek[h] || *~ to the bar* toelating als advocaat; [euph] *~ of nature* aandrang [to go to the toilet]; natuurlijke behoefte

²call (vb) (even) langsgaan (langskomen), (kort) op bezoek gaan; stoppen [at a station]: *the ship ~s at numerous ports* het schip doet talrijke havens aan

³call (vb) **1** afroepen, oplezen, opsommen: *~ out numbers* nummers afroepen **2** (op)roepen, aanroepen; terugroepen [actor]; tot het priesterschap roepen: *~ a witness* een getuige oproepen **3** afkondigen, bijeenroepen, proclameren: *~ a meeting* een vergadering bijeenroepen **4** wakker maken, wekken, roepen **5** (be)noemen, aanduiden als: *~ s.o. a liar* iem. uitmaken voor leugenaar; [inform] *what-d'you-call-it* hoe-heet-het-ook-weer?, dinges; *Peter is ~ed after his grandfather* Peter is vernoemd naar zijn grootvader **6** vinden, beschouwen als: *I ~ it nonsense* ik vind het onzin **7** het houden op, zeggen, (een bedrag) afmaken op: *let's ~ it ten euros* laten we het op tien euro houden **8** [cards] bieden || *~ into being* in het leven roepen; *~ away* wegroepen; *~ forth* oproepen, (naar) boven brengen

⁴call (vb) **1** (uit)roepen: *~ for help* om hulp roepen **2** (op)bellen **3** [cards] bieden

call-back terugroeping

call-box telefooncel

call centre callcenter[h]; telefonische helpdesk

call charges voorrijkosten

caller 1 bezoeker **2** beller, iem. die belt

caller display nummerweergave; nummerherkenning

caller ID [techn] nummermelding

call for 1 komen om, (komen) afhalen **2** wensen, verlangen, vragen: *~ the bill* de rekening vragen **3** vereisen: *this situation calls for immediate action* in deze toestand is onmiddellijk handelen geboden

call-girl callgirl

call in 1 laten komen, de hulp inroepen van, consulteren: *~ a specialist* er een specialist bij halen **2** terugroepen, terugvorderen, uit de circulatie nemen: *some cars had to be called in* een aantal auto's moest terug naar de fabriek

calling 1 roeping **2** beroep[h]

call off afzeggen, afgelasten: *~ one's engagement* het afmaken

callous 1 vereelt, verhard **2** ongevoelig, gevoelloos

¹call out (vb) **1** uitroepen, een gil geven **2** roepen, hardop praten

²call out (vb) **1** afroepen, opnoemen **2** te hulp roepen [fire bridage etc]

callow 1 kaal [of birds]; zonder veren **2** groen, jong, onervaren

calltime gesprekstijd

call up 1 opbellen **2** in het geheugen roepen, zich (weer) voor de geest halen **3** [mil] oproepen, te hulp roepen, inschakelen: *~ reserves* reserves inzetten

call (up)on 1 (even) langsgaan bij, (kort) bezoeken: *we'll call (up)on you tomorrow* we komen morgen bij u langs **2** een beroep doen op, aanspreken

call waiting wisselgesprek[h]

¹calm (n) **1** (wind)stilte [also fig]; kalmte **2** windstilte [wind-force 0]

²calm (adj) kalm, (wind)stil, vredig, rustig

³calm (vb) kalmeren: *the gale ~ed (down)* de storm ging liggen

calorie calorie

calumny laster(praat), roddel, geroddel[h]

Cambodia Cambodja

¹Cambodian (n) Cambodjaan(se)

²Cambodian (adj) Cambodjaans

camel kameel, dromedaris

camera fototoestel[h], (film)camera || [law] *in ~* achter gesloten deuren

Cameroon Kameroen

¹Cameroonian (n) Kameroener, Kameroense

²Cameroonian (adj) Kameroens

camisole (mouwloos) hemdje[h]

camomile kamille

¹camouflage (n) camouflage

²camouflage (vb) camoufleren, wegmoffelen

¹camp (n) **1** kamp[h], legerplaats; [fig] aanhang van partij: *break (or: strike) ~, break up ~* (zijn tenten) opbreken **2** kitsch

²camp (adj) **1** verwijfd **2** homoseksueel **3** overdreven, theatraal, bizar **4** kitscherig

³camp (vb) kamperen, zijn kamp opslaan

campaign campagne, manoeuvre: *advertising ~* reclamecampagne

campaigner 1 campagnevoerder; activist: [fig] *old ~* oude rot in het vak **2** [Am] campagnemedewerker [in elections]

campground [Am] kampeerterrein[h]; camping

camphor kamfer

campsite kampeerterrein[h], camping

campus campus [university or school grounds]

¹can (n) **1** houder [usually of metal]; kroes, kan **2** blik[h], conservenblikje[h], filmblik[h]: *in the ~* gereed **3** [Am; inform] plee **4** [inform] bak, bajes, lik || [Am; inform] *~ of worms* een moeilijke kwestie; [inform] *carry (or: take) the ~ (back)* ergens voor opdraaien

²can (vb) inblikken, conserveren, inmaken || [Am; inform] *~ it!* hou op!

³can (aux vb) **1** kunnen, in staat zijn te: *I ~ readily understand that* ik kan dat best begrijpen; *could you **help** me please?* zou u mij alstublieft kunnen helpen? **2** kunnen, zou kunnen: *~ this **be** true?* zou dit waar kunnen zijn?; *I could go to the baker's if you like* ik zou naar de bakker kunnen gaan als je wilt **3** mogen, kunnen, bevoegd zijn te: *you ~ **go** now* je mag nu gaan

Canada Canada
¹Canadian (n) Canadees, Canadese
²Canadian (adj) Canadees
canal kanaalʰ, vaart, gracht, (water)leiding
canalization kanalisatie, het in banen leiden
canary kanarie(piet)
¹cancel (vb) tegen elkaar wegvallen, elkaar compenseren, tegen elkaar opwegen: *the **arguments** ~ (each other)* de argumenten wegen tegen elkaar op
²cancel (vb) **1** doorstrepen, doorhalen, (door)schrappen **2** opheffen, ongedaan maken, vernietigen **3** annuleren, afzeggen, opzeggen; intrekken [order]; herroepen, afgelasten **4** ongeldig maken; afstempelen [stamp]
cancellation annulering; ontbinding; afgelasting
¹cancel out (vb) elkaar compenseren, tegen elkaar opwegen
²cancel out (vb) compenseren, goedmaken, neutraliseren: *the **pros** and cons cancel each other out* de voor- en nadelen heffen elkaar op
cancer kanker, kwaadaardige tumor; [fig] (verderfelijk, woekerend) kwaadʰ
Cancer [astrology] (de) Kreeft: *tropic of ~* Kreeftskeerkring
candelabra armkandelaar
candid open(hartig), rechtuit, eerlijk: *~ **picture*** spontane foto
candidate kandidaat, gegadigde
candidature kandidatuur, kandidaatschapʰ
candle kaars ‖ *burn the ~ at both ends* te veel hooi op zijn vork nemen; *he can't **hold** a ~ to her* hij doet voor haar onder
candlelight kaarslichtʰ
candlestick kandelaar, kaarsenstandaard
candlewick kaarsenpit
can-do [inform] ondernemend: *people with a ~ **attitude*** mensen die van aanpakken weten
candour open(hartig)heid, eerlijkheid, oprechtheid
candy 1 (stukjeʰ) kandijʰ, suikergoedʰ **2** [Am] snoepjeʰ, snoepjes, zuurtjeʰ, zuurtjes, chocola(atjeʰ)
candyfloss suikerspin
¹cane (n) **1** dikke stengel, rietstengel, bamboestengel, rotan(stok) **2** rotting, wandelstok, plantensteun **3** [bot] stam, stengel, scheut **4** rietʰ, rotanʰ, bamboe⁺ʰ, suikerrietʰ:

get the ~ met het rietje krijgen
²cane (vb) **1** met het rietje geven, afranselen **2** matten [of furniture]
canine hondachtig, honds-
canine tooth hoektand
canister bus, trommel, blikʰ
cannabis (Indische) hennep, cannabis, marihuana, wiet
cannabis coffee shop koffieshop
canned ingeblikt, in blik ‖ *~ **music*** ingeblikte muziek, muzak
cannibal kannibaal, menseneter
cannibalism kannibalismeʰ
¹cannon (n) **1** kanonʰ, (stukʰ) geschutʰ, boordkanonʰ **2** [billiards] carambole
²cannon (vb) (op)botsen: *she ~ed **into** me* ze vloog tegen me op
cannonade kanonnade, bombardementʰ
cannon fodder kanonnenvoerʰ
canny 1 slim, uitgekookt **2** zuinig, spaarzaam
¹canoe (n) kano
²canoe (vb) kanoën, kanovaren
canon 1 kerkelijke leerstelling; (algemene) regel [also fig]: *the **Shakespeare** ~* (lijst van) aan Shakespeare toegeschreven werken **2** kanunnik
canonize heilig verklaren
canon law canoniek recht; kerkrechtʰ
canoodle [inform] knuffelen, scharrelen
can opener blikopener
canopy baldakijn; [fig] gewelfʰ; kap, dakʰ
cant 1 jargonʰ, boeventaal: *thieves' ~* dieventaal **2** schijnheilige praat
cantankerous ruzieachtig
canteen kantine
¹canter (n) handgalopʰ, rit(jeʰ) in handgalop
²canter (vb) in handgalop gaan (brengen)
¹Cantonese (n) Kantonees, Kantonese
²Cantonese (adj) Kantonees
canvas 1 canvas, zeildoek, tentdoek **2** schilderslinnen **3** borduurgaas **4** [shipp] zeilvoering: *under ~* onder vol zeil **5** doekʰ, stukʰ schilderslinnen, (olieverf)schilderij
canvass 1 diepgaand (be)discussiëren, grondig onderzoek doen **2** stemmen werven (in) **3** klanten werven, colporteren: *~ **for** a magazine* colporteren voor een weekblad **4** opiniepeiling houden (over)
canyon cañon, ravijnʰ
¹cap (n) **1** hoofddekselʰ; kapjeʰ [of nurse, domestic servant etc]; muts, pet, baret; [sport] cap [as a sign of selection; also fig]; selectie als international: *take the ~ round* met de pet rondgaan **2** kapvormig voorwerpʰ; hoed [of mushroom]; kniekap, flessendop, vulpendop, afsluitdop, beschermkapjeʰ **3** slaghoedjeʰ **4** klappertjeʰ ‖ *~ in hand* onderdanig, nederig; *if the ~ **fits,** wear it* wie de schoen past, trekke hem aan
²cap (vb) **1** een cap opzetten; [sport; fig] in

de nationale ploeg opstellen **2** verbeteren, overtroeven: *to ~ it all* als klap op de vuurpijl, tot overmaat van ramp
capability 1 vermogenʰ, capaciteit, bekwaamheid **2** vatbaarheid, ontvankelijkheid **3** (capabilities) talenten, capaciteiten
capable 1 in staat: *he is ~ of anything* hij is tot alles in staat **2** vatbaar: *~ of improvement* voor verbetering vatbaar **3** capabel, bekwaam
capacious ruim: *a ~ memory* een goed geheugen
capacity 1 hoedanigheid: *in my ~ of chairman* als voorzitter **2** vermogenʰ, capaciteit, aanleg **3** capaciteit, inhoud, volumeʰ: *seating ~* aantal zitplaatsen; *filled to ~* tot de laatste plaats bezet
capacity crowd volle zaal, bak
cape 1 cape **2** kaap, voorgebergteʰ
¹caper (n) **1** [fig] bokkensprong, capriool: *cut ~s* capriolen uithalen, zich idioot gedragen **2** [inform] (ondeugende) streek, kwajongensstreek **3** [inform] karweiʰ, klus
²caper (vb) (rond)dartelen, capriolen maken
the **Cape Verde Islands** Kaapverdische Eilanden
¹capital (n) **1** kapitaalʰ: [fig] *make ~ (out) of* munt slaan uit **2** [architecture] kapiteelʰ **3** hoofdletter, kapitaalʰ **4** hoofdstad
²capital (adj) **1** kapitaal, hoofd-: *~ city* (or: *town*) hoofdstad; *~ letters* hoofdletters **2** dood-, dodelijk: *~ punishment* doodstraf
capital gain vermogensaanwas: *~s tax* vermogens(aanwas)belasting
capitalism kapitalismeʰ
¹capitalist (n) kapitalist
²capitalist (adj) kapitalistisch
capitalization 1 kapitalisatie **2** [printing] gebruik van hoofdletters
capitalize kapitaliseren: [fig] *~ (up)on* uitbuiten, munt slaan uit
Capitol Hill 1 Capitol Hill **2** het (Amerikaanse) Congres
capitulate capituleren, zich overgeven
capitulation overgave
caprice gril, kuur, wispelturigheid
Capricorn [astrology] (de) Steenbok: *tropic of ~* Steenbokskeerkring
caps 1 *capital letters* **2** *capsule*
capsize (doen) kapseizen, (doen) omslaan
capsule 1 capsule **2** neuskegel [of rocket]; cabine [of spacecraft]
captain 1 kapitein [also mil]; bevelhebber, (scheeps)gezagvoerder; [mil] kapitein-ter-zee: *~ of industry* grootindustrieel **2** [aviation] gezagvoerder **3** [Am] korpscommandant, districtscommandant [of police] **4** voorman, ploegbaas **5** [sport] aanvoerder, captain
captcha captcha
caption 1 titel, kop, hoofdʰ **2** onderschriftʰ;

bijschriftʰ [of illustration]; ondertitel(ing) [film, TV]
captivate boeien, fascineren: *he was ~d by Geraldine* hij was helemaal weg van Geraldine
¹captive (n) gevangene [also fig]; krijgsgevangene
²captive (adj) **1** (krijgs)gevangen (genomen); [fig] geketend: *~ audience* een aan hun stoelen gekluisterd publiek; *be taken ~* gevangengenomen worden **2** geboeid, gecharmeerd
captivity gevangenschap [also fig]; krijgsgevangenschapʰ
¹capture (n) **1** gevangene, vangst, buit, prijs **2** vangst, gevangenneming
²capture (vb) **1** vangen, gevangennemen, gevangen houden; [fig] boeien; fascineren: *~ the imagination* tot de verbeelding spreken **2** buitmaken, bemachtigen, veroveren **3** [chess, draughts etc] slaan [piece, man etc]
car 1 auto(mobiel), motorrijtuigʰ, wagen: *by ~* met de auto **2** rijtuigʰ; [Am] (spoorweg)wagon; tram(wagen) **3** gondel [of airship, cable-lift]
carafe karaf
caramel karamel
carat karaatʰ: *pure gold is 24 ~s* zuiver goud is 24 karaat
caravan 1 karavaan **2** woonwagen, kermiswagen **3** caravan, kampeerwagen
carbine karabijn
carbohydrate koolhydraatʰ
carbon 1 koolstofʰ **2** carbon(papier)ʰ
carbonated koolzuurhoudend: *~ water* sodawater, spuitwater
carbon copy 1 doorslag **2** duplicaatʰ, getrouwe kopie
carbon footprint CO₂-voetafdruk
carbon monoxide koolmonoxideʰ, kolendamp
carbs [inform] *carbohydrates* koolhydraten; koolhydraatrijk voedselʰ
carbuncle 1 karbonkel **2** steenpuist
carburettor carburator
carcass 1 karkasʰ; romp [of slaughtered animal] **2** geraamteʰ, skeletʰ || *~ of a car* autowrak
carcinogen carcinogeenʰ; kankerverwekkende stof
carcinogenic kankerverwekkend
card 1 kaart: *house of ~s* kaartenhuis; *keep* (or: *play*) *one's ~s close to one's chest* zich niet in de kaart laten kijken, terughoudend zijn **2** programmaʰ [of sport event] **3** scorestaat, scorekaart [eg of cricket, golf] || *have a ~ up one's sleeve* (nog) iets achter de hand hebben; *he played his ~s right* (or: *well*) hij heeft zijn kansen goed benut; *put (all) one's ~s on the table* open kaart spelen; [inform] *it is on the ~s* het zit er in; *see cards*

¹**cardboard** (n) karton^h, bordpapier^h
²**cardboard** (adj) **1** kartonnen, bordpapieren **2** onecht, clichématig: ~ *characters* stereotiepe figuren
card-carrying 1 officieel **2** actief, geëngageerd
card-embedded met ingebouwde kaart
cardholder bezitter van creditcard; kaarthouder
cardiac hart-: ~ *arrest* hartstilstand
cardigan gebreid vestje^h
¹**cardinal** (n) **1** hoofdtelwoord^h **2** [Roman Catholicism] kardinaal
²**cardinal** (adj) **1** kardinaal, fundamenteel, vitaal: ~ *idea* centrale gedachte; ~ *number* hoofdtelwoord
cardiologist cardioloog; hartspecialist
cardiovascular cardiovasculair; hart- en vaat-
cards kaartspel^h: *play* ~ kaarten
¹**care** (n) **1** zorg, ongerustheid: *free* from ~(s) zonder zorgen **2** zorg(vuldigheid), voorzichtigheid: *take* ~ opletten; *handle* with ~ (pas op,) breekbaar! **3** verantwoordelijkheid, zorg, toezicht^h: *take* ~ of zorgen voor, onder zijn hoede nemen; *take* ~ to ervoor zorgen dat; ~ of per adres; *under* doctor's ~ onder doktersbehandeling **4** kinderzorg, kleuterzorg: *take into* ~ opnemen in een kindertehuis
²**care** (vb) **1** erom geven, zich erom bekommeren: *well, who* ~s? nou, en?, wat zou het?; *for all I* ~ wat mij betreft **2** bezwaar hebben: *I don't* ~ *if you do* mij best
³**care** (vb) **1** (graag) willen, zin hebben (in), bereid zijn te: *if only they would* ~ *to listen* als ze maar eens de moeite namen om te luisteren **2** zich bekommeren om, geven om, zich aantrekken van: *I couldn't* ~ *less* het zal me een zorg zijn; *Paul doesn't seem to* ~ *very much* zo te zien kan het Paul weinig schelen
¹**career** (n) **1** carrière, (succesvolle) loopbaan **2** (levens)loop, geschiedenis **3** beroep^h: ~s *master* (or: *mistress*) schooldecaan **4** (grote) vaart, (hoge) snelheid: *at* (or: *in*) *full* ~ in volle vaart
²**career** (vb) voortdaveren: ~ *about* rondrazen
care for 1 verzorgen, letten op, passen op, onderhouden **2** zin hebben in, (graag) willen: *would you care for a cup of coffee?* heb je zin in een kopje koffie? **3** houden van, belangstelling hebben voor: *more* than I ~ meer dan me lief is
carefree 1 onbekommerd, zonder zorgen **2** [depr] onverantwoordelijk, zorgeloos
careful 1 zorgzaam, met veel zorg **2** angstvallig **3** voorzichtig, omzichtig, oplettend: *be* ~ (about) what you say let op je woorden **4** zorgvuldig, nauwkeurig: ~ *examination* zorgvuldig onderzoek **5** nauwgezet

careless 1 onverschillig, onvoorzichtig **2** onoplettend **3** onzorgvuldig, slordig, nonchalant
carer thuisverzorger, verzorger, verzorgende
¹**caress** (n) teder gebaar^h, streling
²**caress** (vb) liefkozen, kussen, aanhalen
caretaker 1 conciërge, huismeester **2** huisbewaarder **3** toezichthouder, zaakwaarnemer
careworn afgetobd, (door zorgen) getekend
car ferry autoveer^h, autoveerboot, autoveerdienst, ferry(boot)
cargo lading, vracht, cargo
the ¹**Caribbean** (n) Caribisch gebied^h, Caribische zee
²**Caribbean** (adj) Caribisch
caribou kariboe
caricature karikatuur, spotprent
¹**caring** (n) **1** zorg, verzorging **2** hartelijkheid, warmte
²**caring** (adj) **1** zorgzaam, vol zorg, meelevend, attent: *a* ~ *society* een zorgzame maatschappij **2** verzorgend: *a* ~ *job* een verzorgend beroep
car kit carkit
carnage slachting [among people]; bloedbad^h
carnal [oft depr] vleselijk, lichamelijk
carnation anjer, anjelier
carnival 1 carnaval^h, carnavalstijd, carnavalsviering **2** [Am] circus, kermis **3** festival^h, beurs, jaarmarkt
carnivore carnivoor; vleeseter
carnivorous vleesetend
carol lofzang, kerstlied^h
carousel 1 [Am] carrousel^+h **2** [aviation] bagagecarrousel; bagageband
¹**carp** (n) karper(achtige)
²**carp** (vb) [oft depr] zeuren, vitten
car park 1 parkeerterrein^h **2** parkeergarage
carpenter timmerman
carpentry timmerwerk^h, timmerkunst
¹**carpet** (n) (vloer)tapijt^h, (vloer)kleed^h, karpet^h, (trap)loper: ~ *of flowers* bloemenkleed; *fitted* ~ vast tapijt ‖ *sweep under the* ~ in de doofpot stoppen
²**carpet** (vb) **1** tapijt leggen, bekleden: ~ *the stairs* een loper op de trap leggen **2** [inform] een uitbrander geven
carpetbag reistas, valies^h
carpeting 1 tapijt^h **2** [inform] uitbrander
carping 1 muggenzifterig, vitterig: ~ *criticism* kinderachtige kritiek **2** klagerig, zeurderig
carpool carpool, autopool
carport carport
carriage 1 rijtuig^h, koets; [railways] (personen)wagon **2** slee; onderstel^h [of car-

riage] **3** (lichaams)houding, gang **4** vervoer^h,
transport^h, verzending **5** vracht(prijs), ver-
voerskosten, verzendkosten
carriageway verkeersweg, rijweg, rijbaan
carrier 1 vervoerder van goederen of reizi-
gers, expediteur, transporteur, vrachtvaar-
der, expeditiebedrijf^h, transportbedrijf^h, ver-
voerbedrijf^h, luchtvaartmaatschappij, spoorwegmaatschappij, rederij **2** [med, science,
chem] drager **3** bagagedrager **4** [mil] ver-
voermiddel^h voor mensen en materieel,
vliegdekschip^h **5** (boodschappen)tas
carrier pigeon postduif
carrion aas^h [putrid flesh]; kadaver^h
carrot 1 peen, wortel(tje^h) **2** [fig, inform]
lokmiddel^h: **hold out** (or: **offer**) a ~ to s.o.
iem. een worst voorhouden
^1**carry** (vb) **1** dragen; reiken [eg of voice] **2** in
verwachting zijn, drachtig zijn **3** aangenomen worden [eg of bill]; erdoor komen
^2**carry** (vb) **1** vervoeren, transporteren,
(mee)dragen, steunen, (met zich) (mee)voe-
ren, bij zich hebben, afvoeren; [science] (ge)-
leiden; (binnen)halen [harvest etc]; drijven:
such a **crime** carries a severe punishment op
zo'n misdaad staat een strenge straf; diseases
carried by insects ziekten door insecten overgebracht; ~ to **excess** te ver doordrijven; the
loan carries an **interest** de lening is rentedra-
gend; write 3 and ~ **2** 3 opschrijven, 2 onthouden; Joan carries **herself** like a model Joan
beweegt zich als een mannequin; ~ **into** effect ten uitvoer brengen **2** in verwachting
zijn van **3** veroveren, in de wacht slepen: ~
one's **motion** (or: **bill**) zijn motie (or: wetsontwerp) erdoor krijgen **4** met zich meebrengen, impliceren **5** uitzenden, publiceren
‖ ~ all (or: everything) before one in ieder opzicht slagen; ~ too **far** overdrijven
carryall [Am] weekendtas, reistas
carry along stimuleren, aansporen,
(voort)drijven
carry away 1 meesleuren, meeslepen, opzwepen **2** wegdragen
carry back doen (terug)denken aan; terugvoeren
carrycot reiswieg
carry forward 1 [bookkeeping] transporteren **2** vorderen met [eg work]; voortzetten
3 in mindering brengen, overbrengen naar
volgend boekjaar
carryings-on [inform] **1** (dolle) streken,
handel en wandel **2** geflirt
carry off 1 winnen, veroveren, in de wacht
slepen **2** wegvoeren, ontvoeren, er vandoor
gaan met **3** trotseren, tarten ‖ I managed to
carry **it** off ik heb me eruit weten te redden
^1**carry on** (vb) **1** doorgaan, zijn gang gaan,
doorzetten **2** [inform] tekeergaan, stennis
maken, zich aanstellen: it is a shame how he
carried on in there het is een schande zoals hij

daarbinnen tekeer ging **3** [inform; oft depr]
scharrelen, het houden met (elkaar)
^2**carry on** (vb) **1** voortzetten, volhouden: ~
the good **work!** hou vol!, ga zo door! **2** (uit)-
voeren, drijven, gaande houden **3** voeren
[war, lawsuit]
carry out uitvoeren, vervullen, volbrengen
carry-out [Am] om mee te nemen: ~ **res-**
taurant afhaalrestaurant
^1**carry through** (vb) voortbestaan, voortduren
^2**carry through** (vb) erdoor helpen: his **faith**
carried him through zijn geloof hield hem op
de been
carsick wagenziek
^1**cart** (n) kar ‖ **put** (or: **set**) the ~ before the
horse het paard achter de wagen spannen
^2**cart** (vb) vervoeren in een kar: ~ **off** a prisoner een gevangene (hardhandig) afvoeren
cartilage kraakbeen^h
carton kartonnen doos: a ~ of **cigarettes**
een slof sigaretten; a ~ of **milk** een pak melk
cartoon 1 (politieke) spotprent, cartoon
2 strip(verhaal^h): **animated** ~ tekenfilm, animatiefilm **3** tekenfilm, animatiefilm
cartoonist cartoonist
cartridge 1 patroon(huls) **2** (kant-en-klare) vulling, cassette, inktpatroon, gasvulling
cartwheel 1 karrenwiel^h [also fig]; wagen-
wiel^h **2** radslag: **do** ~s, **turn** ~s radslagen maken
^1**carve** (vb) beeldhouwen
^2**carve** (vb) kerven, houwen, beitelen, graveren in: ~ wood **into** a figure uit hout een figuur snijden
^3**carve** (vb) voorsnijden [meat, poultry etc]
carve out 1 uitsnijden, afsnijden, (uit)hou-
wen **2** bevechten, zich veroveren: she has
carved out a successful career for herself zij
heeft een succesvolle carrière voor zichzelf
opgebouwd
carve up 1 [inform] opdelen, aan stukken
snijden **2** [inform] een jaap bezorgen
carving sculptuur, beeld(houwwerk)^h,
houtsnede, gravure, reliëf^h
car-wash autowasserette, carwash
^1**cascade** (n) kleine waterval
^2**cascade** (vb) (doen) vallen (als) in een waterval
^1**case** (n) **1** geval^h, kwestie, zaak, stand van
zaken, voorbeeld^h, patiënt, ziektegeval^h: former Yugoslavia is a ~ in **point** het voormalige
Joegoslavië is goed voorbeeld (hiervan); **in** ~
voor het geval dat; [Am] indien; (just) **in** ~
voor het geval dat; **in** ~ **of** in geval van, voor
het geval dat; **in** the ~ **of** met betrekking tot;
in **any** (or: **no**) ~ in elk (or: geen) geval **2** argumenten, bewijs(materiaal)^h, pleidooi^h:
have a **strong** ~ er sterk voor staan; make (out)
one's ~ aantonen dat men gelijk heeft
3 [law] (rechts)zaak, geding^h, proces^h

4 doos, kist, koffer, zak, tas(je^h), schede, koker, huls, mantel, sloop, overtrek, cassette, etui^h, omslag^{+h}, band, uitstalkast, vitrine; kast [of watch, piano; for books etc] **5** kozijn^h, raamwerk^h, deurlijst **6** [linguistics] naamval
²case (vb) voorzien van een omhulsel, insluiten, vatten
c̲a̲sebook example schoolvoorbeeld^h; model^h
c̲a̲se h̲i̲story voorgeschiedenis; ziektegeschiedenis
c̲a̲se law jurisprudentie; precedentenrecht^h
¹cash (n) contant geld^h, contanten, cash; [inform] geld^h; centen: ~ on *delivery* (onder) rembours, betaling bij levering; *hard* ~ munten; [inform] contant geld; *ready* ~ baar geld, klinkende munt; *(be) short of* ~ krap (bij kas) (zitten); *pay in* ~ contant betalen; ~ *down* (à) contant
²cash (vb) omwisselen in contanten [cheques etc]; verzilveren, innen
c̲a̲shcard betaalpas, pinpas
c̲a̲sh cow melkkoe [fig]
c̲a̲sh desk kassa
c̲a̲sh dispenser geldautomaat, flappentap
c̲a̲shew cashewnoot
c̲a̲shier 1 kassier **2** caissière, kassabediende
cash i̲n 1 het loodje leggen **2** zijn slag slaan: ~ *on* profiteren van
c̲a̲shless: ~ *society* plasticgeldmaatschappij
c̲a̲sh machine geldautomaat, pinautomaat
c̲a̲shmere 1 kasjmieren sjaal **2** kasjmier^h [wool]
c̲a̲shpoint geldautomaat, flappentap
c̲a̲sh register kasregister^h, kassa
c̲a̲sing 1 omhulsel^h, doos **2** kozijn^h, raamwerk^h, deurlijst
cas̲i̲no casino^h, gokpaleis^h
cask vat^h, fust^h
c̲a̲sket 1 (juwelen)kistje^h, cassette, doosje^h **2** [Am] dood(s)kist
cass̲a̲va maniok; cassave
c̲a̲sserole braadschotel, ovenschotel, stoofschotel, eenpansgerecht^h
cass̲e̲tte cassette
¹cast (n) **1** worp, gooi **2** iets wat geworpen wordt; lijn [with a fishing-fly for bait] **3** gietvorm, model^h, afdruk **4** gips(verband)^h **5** hoedanigheid, kwaliteit, aard, uitdrukking; uiterlijk^h [of face]: ~ *of mind* geestesgesteldheid **6** bezetting [of film, play etc]; cast, rolverdeling
²cast (vb) **1** zijn hengel uitwerpen **2** de doorslag geven, beslissend zijn: ~*ing vote* beslissende stem [of chairman, when votes are equally divided]
³cast (vb) **1** werpen, (van zich) afwerpen, uitgooien, laten vallen: [shipp] ~ *adrift* losgooien; ~ *ashore* op de kust werpen **2** kie-

zen [actors]; (de) rol(len) toedelen aan, casten **3** gieten [metals; also fig]; een afgietsel maken van
⁴cast (vb) (be)rekenen, uitrekenen, (be)cijferen, calculeren, optellen; trekken [horoscope]: ~ *(up) accounts* rekeningen optellen
cast ab̲o̲ut (koortsachtig) zoeken: ~ *for* an *excuse* koortsachtig naar een excuus zoeken
cast̲a̲net castagnet
cast as̲i̲de afdanken, aan de kant schuiven, laten vallen
c̲a̲staway 1 schipbreukeling **2** aan land gezette schepeling
cast aw̲a̲y 1 verwerpen, afwijzen **2** weggooien: ~ *one's life* zijn leven vergooien
cast d̲o̲wn 1 terneerslaan, droevig stemmen: [past participle] ~ terneergeslagen **2** neerslaan [eyes] **3** buigen [head]
caste kaste
c̲a̲stellated kasteelachtig
c̲a̲stigate [form] **1** kastijden, tuchtigen **2** hekelen **3** corrigeren; herzien [text]
c̲a̲sting gietstuk^h, gietsel^h
cast i̲ron gietijzer^h
cast-i̲ron 1 gietijzeren **2** ijzersterk: *a* ~ *will* een ijzeren wil
¹c̲a̲stle (n) **1** kasteel^h, slot^h; burcht [also fig] **2** [chess] toren, kasteel^h ‖ *build* ~*s in the air* luchtkastelen bouwen, dagdromen
²c̲a̲stle (vb): [chess] ~ *(the king)* rokeren, de rokade uitvoeren
¹cast o̲ff (vb) **1** van zich werpen; weggooien [clothes] **2** afdanken, aan de kant zetten
²cast o̲ff (vb) **1** [shipp] (de trossen) losgooien **2** [knitting] minderen, afhechten
cast-o̲ff afgedankt, weggegooid: ~ *clothes* afdankertjes, oude kleren
c̲a̲stor 1 strooier, strooibus: *a set of* ~*s* peper-en-zoutstelletje, olie-en-azijnstelletje **2** zwenkwieltje^h; rolletje^h [of furniture]
c̲a̲stor o̲il wonderolie
c̲a̲stor sugar poedersuiker
cast o̲ut verstoten, verjagen, uitdrijven
c̲a̲strate 1 castreren **2** ontzielen, beroven van energie **3** kuisen, zuiveren
castr̲a̲tion 1 castratie **2** ontzieling **3** kuising, zuivering
cast u̲p 1 doen aanspoelen, aan land werpen **2** optellen, berekenen
¹c̲a̲sual (n) **1** (-s) gemakkelijk zittende kleding **2** tijdelijke (arbeids)kracht
²c̲a̲sual (adj) **1** toevallig **2** ongeregeld, onsystematisch: ~ *labour* tijdelijk werk; ~ *labourer* los werkman **3** terloops, onwillekeurig: *a* ~ *glance* een vluchtige blik **4** nonchalant, ongeïnteresseerd **5** informeel: ~ *clothes* (or: *wear*) vrijetijdskleding, gemakkelijke kleren **6** oppervlakkig: *a* ~ *acquaintance* een oppervlakkige kennis
c̲a̲sualty 1 (dodelijk) ongeval^h, ongeluk^h, ramp: ~ *ward* (afdeling) eerste hulp [of hos-

pital] **2** slachtoffer[h], gesneuvelde, gewonde: *suffer heavy casualties* zware verliezen lijden

casuistry drogreden

cat kat ‖ *let the ~ out of the bag* uit de school klappen [esp unintentionally]; *it is raining ~s and dogs* het regent bakstenen; *play ~ and mouse (with s.o.)* kat en muis (met iem.) spelen; *(put) a ~ among the pigeons* een knuppel in het hoenderhok (werpen); *like sth. the ~ brought in* verfomfaaid; *when the ~'s away (the mice will play)* als de kat van huis is, dansen de muizen op tafel

cataclysm catastrofe; grote ramp

catacomb catacombe, (graf)kelder

[1]**catalogue** (n) **1** catalogus **2** (was)lijst, rits, opsomming: *a whole ~ of crimes* een hele rits misdaden

[2]**catalogue** (vb) catalogiseren

catalyst katalysator [also fig]

catamaran catamaran

[1]**catapult** (n) katapult

[2]**catapult** (vb) met een katapult (be)schieten ‖ *the driver was ~ed through the window* de chauffeur werd door de ruit geslingerd

cataract 1 waterval **2** sterke stroomversnelling [in river] **3** grauwe staar, cataract

catastrophe catastrofe, ramp

[1]**catcall** (n) fluitconcert[h], (afkeurend) gejoel[h]

[2]**catcall** (vb) een fluitconcert aanheffen

[3]**catcall** (vb) uitfluiten

[1]**catch** (n) **1** het vangen, vangst, buit, aanwinst, visvangst **2** houvast[h], greep **3** hapering [of voice, breath, machine etc]; het stokken **4** [inform] addertje[h] onder het gras, luchtje[h], valstrik **5** vergrendeling, pal, klink

[2]**catch** (n) overgooien [ball game]

[3]**catch** (vb) **1** vlam vatten, ontbranden **2** pakken, aanslaan: *the engine failed to ~* de motor sloeg niet aan **3** besmettelijk zijn; zich verspreiden [of disease] **4** [baseball] achtervangen, achtervanger zijn **5** klem komen te zitten, blijven haken ‖ *~ at any opportunity* iedere gelegenheid aangrijpen

[4]**catch** (vb) **1** (op)vangen, pakken, grijpen: *~ fish* (or: *thieves*) vis (or: dieven) vangen; *I caught my thumb in the car door* ik ben met mijn duim tussen het portier gekomen **2** (plotseling) stuiten op, tegen het lijf lopen **3** betrappen, verrassen: *caught in the act* op heterdaad betrapt; [iron] *~ me!* ik kijk wel uit! **4** inhalen **5** halen [eg train, bus]; (nog) op tijd zijn voor **6** oplopen, krijgen; opdoen [illness]: *~ (a) cold* kouvatten **7** trekken [attention etc]; wekken, vangen: *~ s.o.'s attention* (or: *interest*) iemands aandacht trekken (or: belangstelling wekken) **8** opvangen: *~ a glimpse of* een glimp opvangen van **9** stuiten, (plotseling) inhouden: *he caught his breath from fear* van angst stokte zijn adem **10** bevangen, overweldigen: [inform] *~ it* de wind van voren krijgen **11** verstaan, (kun-

nen) volgen: *I didn't quite ~ what you said* ik verstond je niet goed

catcher vanger; [esp baseball] achtervanger

catching 1 besmettelijk **2** boeiend

catch on [inform] **1** aanslaan, het doen, ingang vinden **2** doorhebben; snappen [idea, joke]

catch out 1 betrappen **2** vangen, erin laten lopen

[1]**catch up** (vb) **1** [inform] een achterstand wegwerken: *John had to ~ on* (or: *in*) *geography* John moest zijn aardrijkskunde ophalen **2** (weer) bij raken, (weer) op de hoogte raken

[2]**catch up** (vb) **1** oppakken, opnemen **2** ophouden, opsteken, omhoog houden

[3]**catch up** (vb) inhalen, bijkomen, gelijk komen: *~ to s.o.*, *~ with s.o.* iem. inhalen ‖ *be caught up in* verwikkeld zijn in

catchword kreet, slogan

catchy 1 pakkend, boeiend **2** gemakkelijk te onthouden; goed in het gehoor liggend [of music etc]

catechism 1 catechismus **2** (godsdienst)onderwijs[h] [in the form of question and answer]; catechese

categorical categorisch, onvoorwaardelijk, absoluut

categorize categoriseren

category categorie, groep

cater maaltijden verzorgen (bij), cateren

caterer 1 cateringbedrijf[h] **2** restaurateur, cateraar, hoteleigenaar, restauranteigenaar

cater for 1 maaltijden verzorgen, cateren: *weddings and parties catered for* wij verzorgen bruiloften en partijen [of dinners etc] **2** in aanmerking nemen, overwegen, rekening houden met **3** zich richten op, bedienen, inspelen op: *a play centre catering for children* een speeltuin die vertier biedt aan kinderen

catering catering, receptieverzorging, dinerverzorging

caterpillar 1 rups **2** rupsband **3** rupsbaan [fairground attraction]

cater to [depr] zich richten op, bedienen, inspelen op, tegemoetkomen aan: *politicians often ~ the whims of the voters* politici volgen vaak de grillen van de kiezers

caterwaul janken (als een krolse kat)

cat flap kattenluik[h]

cathedral kathedraal

cathode-ray tube kathodestraalbuis, beeldbuis

catholic universeel, algemeen: *a man of ~ tastes* een man met een brede belangstelling

Catholic katholiek

Catholicism katholicisme[h]

catnap hazenslaapje[h]; dutje[h]

cat's-eye kat(ten)oog[h] [reflector]

cat suit jumpsuit, bodystocking

cattle (rund)vee[h]: *the ~ are grazing* het vee graast

catwalk 1 richel, smal looppad[h]; [shipp] loopbrug **2** lang; smal podium[h] [for fashion parades etc]; lichtbrug [in theatre]

[1]**Caucasian** (n) **1** Kaukasiër, Kaukasische **2** blanke, lid[h] van het Indo-Europese ras

[2]**Caucasian** (adj) **1** Kaukasisch **2** blank, van het Indo-Europese ras

caucus [esp Am] **1** (besloten) partijbijeenkomst **2** (besloten) vergadering van de partijleiding

cauldron ketel, kookpot

cauliflower bloemkool

causal oorzakelijk

causality causaliteit

[1]**cause** (n) **1** oorzaak, reden: *give ~ for* reden geven tot; *there is no ~ for alarm* er is geen reden voor ongerustheid **2** zaak, doel[h]: *make common ~ with s.o.* gemene zaak maken met iem. [in politics etc]; *work for a good ~* voor een goed doel werken

[2]**cause** (vb) veroorzaken, ertoe brengen

'cause [inform] *because*

caustic 1 brandend: *~ soda* natronloog, caustische soda **2** bijtend [also fig]; sarcastisch

[1]**caution** (n) **1** waarschuwing **2** berisping **3** voorzichtigheid ‖ *throw* (or: *fling*) *~ to the winds* alle voorzichtigheid laten varen; *~!* voorzichtig!; [traf] let op!

[2]**caution** (vb) waarschuwen, tot voorzichtigheid manen

cautionary waarschuwend

cautious voorzichtig, op zijn hoede

cavalier 1 nonchalant, onnadenkend **2** hooghartig

cavalry 1 cavalerie; [originally] ruiterij **2** [Am] bereden strijdkrachten, lichte pantsers

[1]**cave** (n) hol[h], grot, spelonk

[2]**cave** (vb) een holte vormen, instorten, inzakken

[3]**cave** (vb) uithollen, uithakken, indeuken

cave-dweller holbewoner

cave in 1 instorten, invallen, inzakken **2** [inform] zwichten, (onder druk) toegeven

caveman holbewoner

cavern spelonk, diepe grot, hol[h]

caviar kaviaar

cavity 1 holte, gat[h] **2** gaatje[h]: *dental ~* gaatje in tand

cavity wall spouwmuur

caw gekras[h] [of raven]

cayman kaaiman

cc *cubic centimetre(s)* cc, kubieke centimeter

CD 1 *Corps Diplomatique* CD **2** *compact disc* cd

CD-ROM *compact disc read-only memory*

cd-rom

[1]**cease** (n): *without ~* onophoudelijk

[2]**cease** (vb) ophouden, tot een eind komen, stoppen

[3]**cease** (vb) beëindigen, uitscheiden met: *~ fire!* staakt het vuren!; *~ to exist* ophouden te bestaan

cease-fire 1 order om het vuren te staken **2** wapenstilstand

ceaseless [form] onafgebroken; aanhoudend

cedar ceder [tree and wood]

Ceefax teletekst

ceiling 1 plafond[h] **2** bovengrens [of wages, prices etc]; plafond[h]: *~ price* maximum prijs **3** [aviation] hoogtegrens [of aeroplane]; plafond[h]

celebrate 1 vieren **2** opdragen: *~ mass* de mis opdragen

celebration viering, festiviteit

celebrity 1 beroemdheid, beroemd persoon **2** roem, faam

celerity [form] snelheid

celery selderie, bleekselderij

celestial 1 goddelijk, hemels mooi **2** hemels: *~ body* hemellichaam

celibate ongehuwd

cell cel, batterijcel ‖ *solar ~* zonnecel

cellar 1 kelder **2** wijnkelder

cellist cellist; cellospeler

cellophane cellofaan[h]

cellphone mobiele telefoon, gsm

cellular 1 cellulair, cellig, met cellen: *~ tissue* celweefsel **2** celvormig **3** poreus

celluloid celluloid[h]

Celt Kelt [inhabitant of Ireland, Wales, Cornwall, Scotland, Brittany]

[1]**Celtic** (n) Keltisch[h] [language]

[2]**Celtic** (adj) Keltisch

[1]**cement** (n) cement[h]; mortel [also fig]; band, bindende kracht

[2]**cement** (vb) cement(er)en, met cement bestrijken ‖ *~ a union* een verbond versterken

cemetery begraafplaats, kerkhof[h]

censer wierookvat[h]

[1]**censor** (n) **1** censor **2** zedenmeester

[2]**censor** (vb) **1** censureren **2** schrappen

censorship censuur

[1]**censure** (n) afkeuring, terechtwijzing: *a vote of ~* een motie van wantrouwen

[2]**censure** (vb) afkeuren, bekritiseren

census 1 volkstelling **2** (officiële) telling

[1]**cent** (n) **1** cent **2** kleine munt ‖ *per ~* percent

[2]**cent** (abbrev) **1** *centigrade* **2** *century*

centenarian honderdjarig

[1]**centenary** (n) **1** eeuwfeest[h] **2** periode van honderd jaar

[2]**centenary** (adj) honderdjarig

[1]**centennial** (n) [Am] eeuwfeest[h]

[2]**centennial** (adj) **1** honderdste, honderdja-

rig: ~ **anniversary** eeuwfeest **2** honderd jaar
durend
center [Am] see ¹**centre**
centigrade Celsius
centimetre centimeter
centipede duizendpoot
central 1 centraal, midden-: ~ **government**
centrale regering **2** belangrijkst, voornaamst: the ~ **issue** de hoofdzaak
¹**centralize** (vb) zich concentreren, samenkomen
²**centralize** (vb) centraliseren, in één punt
samenbrengen
¹**centre** (n) **1** midden[h], centrum[h]; middelpunt[h] [also fig]; spil, as; [pol] centrumpartij;
(zenuw)centrum[h]; haard [of storm, rebel-
lion]: ~ of **attraction** zwaartepunt; [fig] middelpunt van de belangstelling; ~ of **gravity**
zwaartepunt **2** centrum[h], instelling, bureau[h]
²**centre** (adj) middel-, centraal
³**centre** (vb) zich concentreren, zich richten:
~ **(a)round** als middelpunt hebben
⁴**centre** (vb) **1** in het midden plaatsen **2** concentreren, (in het midden) samenbrengen
3 [techn] centreren
centrefold (meisje[h] op) uitklapplaat [in
magazine]
centrepiece 1 middenstuk[h] [on table]
2 belangrijkste onderdeel[h]
centrifugal centrifugaal, middelpuntvliedend
centrifuge centrifuge
century 1 eeuw **2** honderdtal[h]
ceramic keramisch
ceramics keramiek, pottenbakkerskunst
cereal 1 graan(gewas)[h] [edible] **2** graan-
product[h] [at breakfast]; cornflakes
cerebral hersen-: ~ **person** verstandsmens,
cerebraal iem.
¹**ceremonial** (n) **1** plechtigheid **2** ritueel[h]
3 ceremonieel[h], het geheel der ceremoniën
²**ceremonial** (adj) ceremonieel, plechtig
ceremony 1 ceremonie; [rel] rite: **master** of
ceremonies ceremoniemeester **2** formaliteit,
vorm: **stand** (up)on ~ hechten aan de vormen;
without ~ informeel
certain 1 zeker, overtuigd: **are** you ~? weet
je het zeker?; **make** ~ (that) zich ervan vergewissen (dat) **2** zeker, vaststaand: he **is** ~ to
come hij komt beslist; **for** ~ (vast en) zeker
3 zeker, bepaald, een of ander: a ~ **Mr** Jones
ene meneer Jones **4** enig, zeker **5** sommi-
ge(n): ~ **of** his friends enkele van zijn vrienden
certainly zeker, ongetwijfeld, beslist ‖ ~
not! nee!, onder geen beding!
certainty zekerheid, (vaststaand) feit[h], vaste overtuiging: I can't say **with** any ~ if it will
work ik weet (absoluut) niet zeker of het
werkt
certificate certificaat[h] [law]; getuigschrift[h],
legitimatiebewijs[h]: ~ of **birth** geboorteakte;

Certificate of Secondary **Education** (CSE) middelbareschooldiploma; [roughly] mavodiplo-
ma; General Certificate of **Education** (GCE)
middelbareschooldiploma; [roughly] havodiploma, [roughly] vwo-diploma; [since 1987]
General Certificate of Secondary **Education**
(GCSE) middelbareschooldiploma [roughly
combination of diplomas of higher general
secondary education and lower general secondary education]; ~ of **marriage** (afschrift
van) huwelijksakte; [roughly] trouwboekje
certificated gediplomeerd, bevoegd
¹**certify** (vb) **1** (+ to) getuigen (over/betref-
fende) **2** [Am] een diploma uitreiken
²**certify** (vb) **1** (officieel) verklaren: the **bank**
certified the accounts (as) correct de bank heeft
de rekening gefiatteerd **2** [Am] een certificaat verlenen aan, diplomeren **3** [inform]
officieel krankzinnig verklaren: **John** should
be certified ze zouden John moeten opbergen
certitude zekerheid, (vaste) overtuiging
cervical 1 hals-, nek- **2** baarmoederhals-: ~
smear uitstrijkje
cervix 1 hals **2** baarmoederhals
cessation beëindiging; het staken
cesspit beerput [also fig]; poel
cf confer vergl., vergelijk
ch chapter hfst., hoofdstuk
Chad Tsjaad
¹**Chadian** (n) Tsjadiër, Tsjadische
²**Chadian** (adj) Tsjadisch
chador gezichtssluier
¹**chafe** (vb) **1** schuren **2** zich ergeren, ongeduldig zijn: ~ **at**, ~ **under** zich opwinden over
3 tekeergaan
²**chafe** (vb) **1** warm wrijven **2** schuren,
(open)schaven: his collar ~d his **neck** zijn
boord schuurde om zijn nek **3** ergeren, irriteren
chaff 1 kaf[h] [also fig] **2** namaak, nep, prullaria **3** (goedmoedige) plagerij
chaffinch vink
chagrin verdriet[h], boosheid, ergernis
¹**chain** (n) **1** keting; keten [also chem]: a ~ of
office een ambtsketen **2** reeks, serie: a ~ of
coincidences een reeks van toevalligheden
3 groep, maatschappij, keten: a ~ **of** hotels
(or: shops) een hotelketen (or: winkelketen)
4 bergketen **5** kordon[h] **6** (-s) boeien, ketenen: **in** ~s geketend [also fig]
²**chain** (vb) ketenen, in de boeien slaan
chain lock kettingslot[h]
chain smoker kettingroker
chain store filiaal (van een winkelketen)
¹**chair** (n) **1** stoel, zetel, zitplaats; [fig] positie; functie: **take** a ~ ga zitten **2** voorzitters-
stoel, voorzitter(schap): **be in** (or: **take**) the ~
voorzitten **3** leerstoel **4** [inform] elektrische
stoel
²**chair** (vb) voorzitten, voorzitter zijn van: ~ a

meeting een vergadering voorzitten
ch<u>ai</u>rman voorzitter
ch<u>ai</u>rperson voorzitter, voorzitster
ch<u>a</u>lice kelk
¹chalk (n) **1** krijt(je)ʰ, kleurkrijt(je)ʰ: *a piece of ~, a stick of ~* een krijtje; [inform] *they are as different as ~ and cheese* ze verschillen als dag en nacht **2** krijtstreep **3** krijttekening, crayon
²chalk (vb) krijten, met krijt schrijven
chalk <u>up</u> 1 opschrijven [on blackboard, slate] **2** optellen (bij de score), noteren: *~ success* (or: *many points*) een overwinning (or: veel punten) boeken **3** op iemands rekening schrijven: *chalk it up, please!* wilt u het op mijn rekening zetten?
¹ch<u>a</u>llenge (n) uitdaging, moeilijke taak, test: *rise to the ~* de uitdaging aandurven
²ch<u>a</u>llenge (vb) **1** uitdagen, tarten, op de proef stellen: *~ s.o. to a duel* iem. uitdagen tot een duel **2** uitlokken, opwekken: *~ the imagination* de verbeelding prikkelen; *~ thought* tot nadenken stemmen **3** aanroepen, aanhouden: *~ a stranger* een vreemde staande houden **4** betwisten, in twijfel trekken **5** opeisen, vragen: *~ attention* de aandacht opeisen
ch<u>a</u>llenged [euph] gehandicapt
ch<u>a</u>llenger 1 uitdager **2** betwister, bestrijder **3** eiser, vrager **4** mededinger [eg for position]
ch<u>a</u>mber 1 [dated] kamer, vertrekʰ, slaapkamer: *~ of horrors* gruwelkamer **2** raad, collegeʰ, groep: *Chamber of Deputies* huis van afgevaardigden; *house of commerce* kamer van koophandel **3** afdeling van een rechtbank, kamer **4** (-s) ambtsvertrekken, kantoorʰ, kabinetʰ
ch<u>a</u>mberlain 1 kamerheer **2** penningmeester
cham<u>e</u>leon kameleon [also fig]
¹cham<u>o</u>is (n) gems
²cham<u>o</u>is (n) zeemlerenlap
champ [inform] *champion* kampioen
champ<u>a</u>gne champagne
¹ch<u>a</u>mpion (n) **1** kampioen, winnaar **2** voorvechter
²ch<u>a</u>mpion (vb) verdedigen, pleiten voor, voorstander zijn van
ch<u>a</u>mpionship kampioenschapʰ, kampioenswedstrijd
¹ch<u>a</u>nce (n) **1** kans, mogelijkheid, waarschijnlijkheid: *fat ~!* weinig kans!; *stand a fair ~* een redelijke kans maken; *are you Mr Buckett by (any) ~?* bent u toevallig de heer Buckett?; *(the) ~s are that* het is waarschijnlijk dat **2** toevallige gebeurtenis **3** kans, gelegenheid: *a ~ in a million* een kans van één op duizend **4** risicoʰ: *take ~s, take a ~* risico's nemen **5** het lot, de fortuin: *a game of ~* een kansspel; *leave to ~* aan het toeval overlaten

²chance (adj) toevallig: *a ~ meeting* een toevallige ontmoeting
³chance (vb) (toevallig) gebeuren: *I ~d to be on the same boat* ik zat toevallig op dezelfde boot || *~ (up)on* (toevallig) vinden
ch<u>a</u>ncel koorʰ [of church]
ch<u>a</u>ncellery 1 kanselarij **2** kanseliersambtʰ
ch<u>a</u>ncellor 1 kanselier, hoofd van een kanselarij; hoofd van een universiteit [in England as title of honour] **2** [Am; law] president; voorzitter [of some courts of law] **3** minister van financiën || *Chancellor of the Exchequer* minister van financiën
ch<u>a</u>ncy [inform] gewaagd, riskant, onzeker
chand<u>e</u>lier kroonluchter
¹change (n) **1** verandering, afwisseling, variatie: *a ~ for the better* (or: *worse*) een verandering ten goede (or: kwade); *she has had a ~ of heart* ze is van gedachten veranderd; *for a ~* voor de afwisseling **2** verversing: *a ~ of oil* nieuwe olie **3** [traf] het overstappen **4** wisselgeldʰ: *keep the ~!* laat maar zitten! **5** kleingeldʰ: *give ~ for a banknote* een briefje wisselen || *~ of life* overgang(sjaren); [inform] *get no ~ out of s.o.* geen cent wijzer worden van iem.
²change (vb) **1** veranderen, anders worden, wisselen **2** zich verkleden, andere kleren aantrekken **3** overstappen: *you have to ~ at Boxtel* u moet in Boxtel overstappen **4** [techn] schakelen: *~ down* terugschakelen; *~ into second gear* in zijn twee zetten
³change (vb) **1** veranderen, anders maken **2** (ver)ruilen, omruilen, (ver)wisselen: *~ one's clothes* zich omkleden; *~ gear* (over)schakelen; *~ oil* olie verversen **3** [fin] (om)wisselen **4** verschonen: *~ a baby* een baby een schone luier aandoen
ch<u>a</u>ngeable veranderlijk; wisselvallig
ch<u>a</u>ngeover 1 omschakeling, overschakeling, overgang **2** [sport] het wisselen
change <u>o</u>ver 1 veranderen, overgaan, omschakelen **2** ruilen (van plaats) **3** omzwaaien: *he changed over from gas to electricity* hij is overgestapt van gas naar elektriciteit
ch<u>a</u>nging room kleedkamer
¹ch<u>a</u>nnel (n) **1** kanaalʰ, zee-engte: *the Channel* het Kanaal **2** (vaar)geul, bedding **3** kanaalʰ, buis, pijp, goot **4** [radio, TV] kanaalʰ; [fig] netʰ; programmaʰ
²ch<u>a</u>nnel (vb) **1** kanaliseren, voorzien van kanalen **2** leiden, sturen, in bepaalde banen leiden
ch<u>a</u>nnel-hop [inform] **1** [TV] zappen; kanaalzwemmen **2** tripje(s) over het Kanaal maken
the **Ch<u>a</u>nnel Islands** Kanaaleilanden
ch<u>a</u>nnel-surf [esp Am; inform] zappen; kanaalzwemmen
¹chant (n) **1** liedʰ, (eenvoudige) melodie, psalm **2** zangerige intonatie

²**chant** (vb) **1** zingen, op één toon zingen **2** roepen, herhalen

chaos chaos, verwarring, wanorde

chaotic chaotisch, verward, ongeordend

¹**chap** (n) **1** [inform] vent, kerel, knul **2** kloof(je[h]); barst(je[n]) [in lip or skin]; scheur [in soil]

²**chap** (vb) splijten, (doen) barsten, kloven

chapel kapel ‖ *are you church or ~?* bent u anglicaans of protestants?

chaplain 1 kapelaan, huisgeestelijke **2** veldprediker, aalmoezenier

chapter 1 hoofdstuk[h]: *give ~ and verse* [inform, fig] alle details geven, tekst en uitleg geven **2** episode, periode: *a whole ~ of accidents* een hele reeks tegenslagen **3** [rel] kapittel[h], kapittelvergadering

chapter house kapittelzaal

¹**char** (n) **1** *charlady, charwoman* werkster **2** klus(je[h]), taak, (huishoudelijk) karwei(tje)[h]

²**char** (vb) werkster zijn

³**char** (vb) verbranden, verkolen, schroeien

character 1 (ken)teken[h], merkteken[h], kenmerk[h], (karakter)trek **2** teken[h], symbool[h], letter, cijfer[h] **3** persoon, type[h]; individu[n] [also depr]: *a suspicious ~* een louche figuur; *he is quite a ~* hij is me d'r eentje **4** personage[h], rol, figuur[+h] **5** [inform] excentriek figuur[+h] **6** karakter[h], aard, natuur: *out of ~* **a)** niet typisch; **b)** ongepast **7** schrift[h], handschrift[h], (druk)letters **8** moed

¹**characteristic** (n) kenmerk[h], (kenmerkende) eigenschap

²**characteristic** (adj) kenmerkend, tekenend

characterize kenmerken, typeren

character set tekenset

charade 1 schertsvertoning **2** (-s) lettergreepraadsel[h]; hints

charcoal 1 houtskool **2** donkergrijs[h], antraciet[h], antracietkleur

¹**charge** (n) **1** lading [also elec]; belasting **2** lading springstof, bom **3** prijs, kost(en), schuld **4** pupil, beschermeling **5** instructie, opdracht; [mil] (bevel tot de) aanval **6** [law] telastlegging, beschuldiging, aanklacht: *face a ~ of theft* terechtstaan wegens diefstal; *press ~s* een aanklacht indienen **7** zorg, hoede, leiding: *officer in ~* dienstdoend officier; *take ~ of* de leiding nemen over, zich belasten met; *in ~ of* verantwoordelijk voor

²**charge** (vb) **1** (aan)rekenen, in rekening brengen: *he ~d me five pounds* hij rekende mij vijf pond **2** beschuldigen, aanklagen: *~ s.o. with theft* iem. van diefstal beschuldigen **3** bevelen, opdragen

³**charge** (vb) **1** aanvallen, losstormen op **2** opladen, laden, vullen

charge card klantenkaart; klantenpas

charged 1 emotioneel, sterk voelend **2** geladen, omstreden: *a ~ atmosphere* een geladen atmosfeer

chariot triomfwagen, (strijd)wagen

charisma charisma[h]; uitstraling

charismatic charismatisch, inspirerend

charitable 1 menslievend, welwillend **2** liefdadig, vrijgevig **3** van een liefdadig doel: *~ institutions* liefdadige instellingen **4** mild in zijn oordeel, vergevensgezind

charity liefdadigheidsinstelling, liefdadigheid, (naasten)liefde ‖ *~ begins at home* [roughly] het hemd is nader dan de rok

charlatan charlatan, kwakzalver

¹**charm** (n) **1** charme, bekoorlijke eigenschap, aantrekkelijkheid **2** tovermiddel[h], toverspreuk: [inform] *it works like a ~* het werkt perfect **3** amulet **4** bedeltje[h] [on bracelet]

²**charm** (vb) **1** betoveren, charmeren **2** bezweren: *~ snakes* slangen bezweren

charming charmant, aantrekkelijk

¹**chart** (n) **1** kaart, zeekaart, weerkaart **2** grafiek, curve, tabel **3** (-s) hitparade

²**chart** (vb) in kaart brengen, een kaart maken van: *~ a course* een koers uitzetten

¹**charter** (n) **1** oorkonde, (voor)recht[h] **2** handvest[h]: *the ~ of the United Nations* het handvest van de Verenigde Naties **3** (firma)contract[h], statuten **4** het charteren, huur

²**charter** (vb) **1** een octrooi verlenen aan: *~ed accountant* (beëdigd) accountant **2** charteren, (af)huren

charwoman werkster

chary 1 voorzichtig **2** verlegen **3** zuinig, karig, spaarzaam **4** kieskeurig

¹**chase** (n) **1** achtervolging; jacht [also sport]: *give ~ (to)* achternazitten **2** park[h], jachtveld[h] **3** (nagejaagde) prooi **4** steeplechase, wedren met hindernissen

²**chase** (vb) jagen, zich haasten

³**chase** (vb) **1** achtervolgen, achternazitten; [fig] najagen: *~ up* opsporen **2** verjagen, verdrijven: *~ away* (or: *out, off*) wegjagen

chasm kloof, afgrond; [fig also] verschil[h]; tegenstelling

chassis chassis[h], onderstel[h], landingsgestel[h]

chaste kuis

chasten 1 kuisen, zuiveren **2** matigen

chastise kastijden, (streng) straffen

chastity kuisheid

¹**chat** (n) **1** babbeltje[h], praatje[h] **2** gekletsh], gebabbel[h]

²**chat** (vb) babbelen, kletsen, praten: *~ away* erop los kletsen

chatline babbellijn

chat room chatroom, babbelbox

chatshow talkshow, praatprogramma[h]

¹**chatter** (n) **1** geklets[h] **2** geklapper[h] [of teeth]

²**chatter** (vb) **1** kwebbelen, (druk) praten: *~ away* (erop los) praten **2** klapperen [of teeth]

chatterbox kletskous

chat up [inform] proberen te versieren; flirten met

¹chauffeur (n) chauffeur

²chauffeur (vb) vervoeren

chav [inform] aso, asociaal

¹cheap (adj) **1** goedkoop, voordelig: *on the* ~ voor een prikje **2** gemakkelijk **3** ordinair, grof: *a* ~ *kind of humour* flauwe grappen **4** onoprecht, oppervlakkig

²cheap (adv) **1** goedkoop, voordelig **2** vulgair, ordinair

¹cheapen (vb) goedkoop worden, in prijs dalen

²cheapen (vb) **1** goedkoop maken, goedkoper maken, in waarde doen dalen, verlagen; [fig] afbreuk doen aan **2** afdingen op

¹cheat (n) **1** bedrogʰ, afzetterij **2** bedrieger, valsspeler

²cheat (vb) **1** bedrog plegen, vals spelen **2** [inform] ontrouw zijn

³cheat (vb) **1** bedriegen, oplichten, afzetten: ~ *at exams* spieken; ~ *s.o. out of sth.* iem. iets afhandig maken **2** ontglippen (aan), ontsnappen aan

cheater bedrieger, oplichter, afzetter

¹check (n) **1** belemmering, oponthoudʰ: *keep a* ~ *on s.o.*, [Am] *have one's* ~*s upon s.o.* iem. in de gaten houden **2** proef, test, controle **3** [Am] rekening [in restaurant] **4** kaartjeʰ, reçuʰ, bonnetjeʰ **5** ruit(jeʰ), ruitpatroonʰ, geruite stof **6** controle, bedwangʰ: *without* ~ ongehinderd **7** schaakʰ: ~*!* schaak!

²check (vb) **1** controleren, testen: ~ *(up) on sth.* iets controleren **2** (doen) stoppen, tegenhouden, afremmen **3** schaak zetten, bedreigen **4** [Am] afgeven [for safekeeping] **5** kloppen, punt voor punt overeenstemmen ‖ ~ *into a hotel* zich inschrijven in een hotel

³check [Am] see **cheque**

check card [Am] betaalpas

checked geruit, geblokt

checker 1 [Am] caissière **2** [comp] controle, checker **3** controleur

checkers [Am] damspelʰ, dammen

¹check in (vb) zich inschrijven, inchecken

²check in (vb) [Am] **1** registreren, inschrijven **2** terugbrengen

checking account [Am] lopende rekening

checklist checklist, controlelijst

¹checkmate (n) schaakmatʰ

²checkmate (vb) schaakmat zetten

checkout kassa [at supermarket and the like]

check out vertrekken, zich uitschrijven: ~ *of a hotel* vertrekken uit een hotel

checkpoint controlepost

checkroom [Am] **1** bagagedepotʰ **2** garderobe [in hotel, theatre etc]

check-up (algemeen medisch) onderzoekʰ

cheddar kaas

cheek 1 wang: *turn the other* ~ de andere wang toekeren; ~ *by jowl (with)* **a)** dicht bijeen; **b)** (als) twee handen op een buik **2** brutaliteit, lefʰ

cheekbone jukbeenʰ

cheeky brutaal

cheep gefluitʰ; getjilpʰ [of birds]

¹cheer (n) **1** (juich)kreet, schreeuw: ~*s* hoerageroepʰ; gejuichʰ **2** aanmoediging **3** stemming, humeurʰ: *of* (or: *with*) *good* ~ welgemoed, vrolijk **4** vrolijkheid

²cheer (vb) juichen, schreeuwen, roepen ‖ ~ *up!* kop op!

³cheer (vb) **1** toejuichen, aanmoedigen: ~ *on* aanmoedigen **2** bemoedigen: ~ *up* opvrolijken

cheerful vrolijk, blij, opgewekt

cheerio [inform] **1** dag!, tot ziens! **2** proost!

cheerleader [Am] cheerleader

cheerless troosteloos; somber

cheers 1 proost! **2** [inform] dag!, tot ziens! **3** [inform] bedankt!

cheery vrolijk; opgewekt

cheese kaas

cheeseburger hamburger met kaas

cheesecake kwarktaart

cheesy 1 kaasachtig **2** [Am; inform] goedkoop; waardeloos

cheetah jachtluipaardʰ

chef chef-kok

¹chemical (n) chemisch productʰ

²chemical (adj) chemisch, scheikundig

chemist 1 chemicus, scheikundige **2** apotheker **3** drogist

chemistry 1 scheikunde **2** scheikundige eigenschappen; [fig] geheimzinnige werking: *the* ~ *of love* de mysterieuze werking van de liefde

chemotherapy chemotherapie

cheque cheque

cheque card betaalpas(jeʰ), bankkaart

chequer schakeren, afwisseling brengen in; [fig] kenmerken door wisselend succes: *a* ~*ed life* een leven met voor- en tegenspoed

cherish koesteren, liefhebben: ~ *hopes* hoop koesteren

cherry 1 kers **2** kersenboom: *flowering* ~ Japanse sierkers **3** kersenhoutʰ **4** kersroodʰ

chess schaakʰ, schaakspelʰ

chessman schaakstukʰ

chest 1 borst(kas): *get sth. off one's* ~ over iets zijn hart luchten **2** kist, kast, bak, doos: ~ *of drawers* ladekast

chestnut 1 kastanjeʰ, kastanjeboom **2** vos(paardʰ) **3** [inform] ouwe mop, bekend verhaalʰ **4** kastanjebruinʰ: ~ *mare* kastanjebruine merrie

¹chew (n) (tabaks)pruimʰ: *a* ~ *of tobacco* een tabakspruim

²chew (vb) **1** kauwen, pruimen **2** [inform,

also fig] herkauwen, (over)denken, bepraten: ~ sth. over ergens over nadenken; ~ over
sth. iets bespreken; ~ over (or: on) sth. nadenken over iets
chewing gum kauwgom
¹**chic** (n) chic, verfijning, stijl
²**chic** (adj) chic, stijlvol, elegant
chick 1 kuikenʰ, (jong) vogeltjeʰ **2** [inform]
meisjeʰ, grietjeʰ, stukʰ **3** kindʰ
¹**chicken** (n) **1** kuikenʰ, (jong) vogeltjeʰ **2** kip
3 kindʰ: Mary is no ~ Mary is niet meer zo
piep **4** [inform; depr] lafaard, bangerik
5 [inform] lekker stukʰ, grietjeʰ ‖ count one's
~s before they are hatched de huid verkopen
voordat men de beer geschoten heeft
²**chicken** (adj) [inform] laf, bang
chicken out [inform] ertussenuit knijpen,
bang worden
chickenpox waterpokken
chickpea kikkererwt
chicory 1 Brussels lofʰ, witlofʰ **2** [Am] andijvie
chide [form] berispen; afkeuren
¹**chief** (n) leider, aanvoerder, opperhoofdʰ
²**chief** (adj) belangrijkst, voornaamst, hoofd-
: ~ accountant hoofdaccountant; ~ constable
hoofd van politie in graafschap
chiefly voornamelijk, hoofdzakelijk, vooral
chieftain 1 hoofdman [of tribe etc] **2** ben-
deleider
chilblain winterhanden, wintervoeten
child 1 kindʰ [also fig]: from a ~ van jongs af
(aan); with ~ zwanger, in verwachting **2** nakomeling **3** volgeling, aanhanger **4** (gees-
tes)kindʰ, productʰ, resultaatʰ
child abuse kindermishandeling
childbirth bevalling, kraambedʰ
childhood jeugd, kinderjaren: second ~
kindsheid
childish kinderachtig; kinderlijk
childminding kinderoppas, kinderopvang
child molester kinderlokker
Chile Chili
¹**Chilean** (n) Chileen(se)
²**Chilean** (adj) Chileens
¹**chill** (n) **1** verkoudheid, koude rilling **2** kilte, koelte, frisheid; [fig] onhartelijkheid: cast
a ~ over sth. een domper zetten op iets
²**chill** (vb) **1** afkoelen, koud worden **2** chillen
‖ ~ed meat gekoeld vlees
chilli Spaanse peper; chilipeper
chilling angstaanjagend; beangstigend
chill room ontspanningsruimte
chilly 1 koel, kil, koud **2** huiverig **3** onvriendelijk, ongevoelig
chimaera hersenschim; schrikbeeldʰ
¹**chime** (n) **1** klok, klokkenspelʰ: a ~ of bells
een klokkenspel; ring the ~s de klokken luiden **2** klokgeluiʰ **3** harmonie, overeenstemming
²**chime** (vb) **1** luiden, slaan: ~ with in over-

eenstemming zijn met **2** in harmonie zijn,
overeenstemmen
chime in 1 overeenstemmen, instemmen:
~ with overeenstemmen met **2** opmerken;
invallen [with a remark]; bijvallen: ~ with invallen met [remark]
chimney schoorsteen, rookkanaalʰ
chimney-piece schoorsteenmantel
chimney sweep(er) schoorsteenveger
chimp [inform] chimpanzee chimpansee
chimpanzee chimpansee
chin kin ‖ [inform] (keep your) ~ up! kop op!
China 1 China: the People's Republic of ~ de
volksrepubliek China **2** porselein
¹**Chinese** (n) Chinees, Chinese
²**Chinese** (adj) Chinees, uit China ‖ ~ lantern
lampion, papieren lantaarn; ~ wall Chinese
Muur; [fig] onoverkomelijke hindernis
¹**chink** (n) **1** spleet, opening, gatʰ: [fig] that is
the ~ in his armour dat is zijn zwakke plek
2 lichtstraal [as if through a crack]; straaltjeʰ
licht: a ~ of light een lichtstraal **3** kling, het
rinkelen
²**chink** (vb) rinkelen [(as if) of metal, glass]
³**chink** (vb) **1** doen rinkelen [(like) metal,
glass] **2** dichten, (op)vullen
chin-wag [inform] gekletsʰ; praatjeʰ
¹**chip** (n) **1** splintertjeʰ, scherf **2** ficheʰ: [in-
form] when the ~s are down als het erop aan-
komt, als het menens wordt **3** friet, patat
4 (-s) [Am, Austr] chips **5** [techn] chip ‖ have a
~ on one's shoulder prikkelbaar zijn, lichtgeraakt zijn
²**chip** (vb) afbrokkelen: ~ away at a piece of
wood hout vorm geven
³**chip** (vb) **1** (af)kappen, afsnijden, onderbreken, in de rede vallen: ~ off afbikken, afbreken **2** beitelen, beeldhouwen
chip and PIN betalen met chipkaart of
pinpas, chippen en pinnen
chip in 1 (zijn steentje) bijdragen, lappen
2 opperen, onderbreken
chipmunk aardeekhoorn; wangzakeek-
hoorn
chipping 1 scherfjeʰ, stukjeʰ **2** bik, losse
stukjes steen
chirp tjirpen, tjilpen, piepen
chirpy vrolijk; levendig [inform]; spraakzaam
¹**chisel** (n) beitel
²**chisel** (vb) beitelen: [fig] ~led features
scherpe gelaatstrekken
chit 1 jong kindʰ, hummel **2** [oft depr; for
woman] jong dingʰ **3** briefjeʰ, memoʰ **4** rekening, bon(netjeʰ), cheque
chivalrous ridderlijk, galant
chivalry ridderschapʰ, ridderlijkheid
chives bieslookʰ
chivvy achterna zitten, (op)jagen
chlorine chloor⁺ʰ
chlorophyl(l) bladgroenʰ

chock-full propvol; tjokvol
¹chocolate (n) **1** chocolaatje*, bonbon, praline **2** chocolade: *a bar of* ~ een reep chocolade
²chocolate (adj) **1** chocoladekleurig **2** chocolade, naar chocolade smakend
¹choice (n) **1** keus, keuze, alternatief*, voorkeur: *the colour of your* ~ de kleur van uw keuze; *John has no* ~ *but to come* John moet wel komen; *by* ~, *for* ~ bij voorkeur; *from* ~ graag, gewillig **2** keuzemogelijkheid, optie
²choice (adj) **1** uitgelezen: ~ *meat* kwaliteitsvlees **2** zorgvuldig gekozen [of words]
choir koor*
choirboy koorknaap
¹choke (n) choke, gasklep
²choke (vb) (ver)stikken, naar adem snakken, zich verslikken
³choke (vb) **1** verstikken, doen stikken: ~ *a fire* een vuur doven **2** verstoppen **3** onderdrukken, inslikken, bedwingen
choker choker; nauwsluitende halsketting
cholera cholera
choleric zwartgallig
cholesterol cholesterol
choose 1 (uit)kiezen, selecteren: *a lot to* ~ *from* veel om uit te kiezen **2** beslissen, besluiten: *George chose not to come* George besloot niet te komen, George kwam liever niet **3** (ver)kiezen, willen, wensen
choos(e)y kieskeurig
¹chop (n) **1** houw, hak, slag **2** karbonade, kotelet **3** (karate)slag **4** (-s) kaken; lippen [of animals] **5** ontslag*: *get the* ~ ontslagen worden
²chop (vb) **1** hakken, kappen, houwen **2** voortdurend veranderen [also fig]: ~ *and change* erg veranderlijk zijn, vaak van mening veranderen
³chop (vb) **1** hakken, kappen, houwen: ~ *down trees* bomen omhakken **2** fijnhakken, fijnsnijden: ~*ped liver* (fijn)gehakte lever
chopper 1 hakker, houwer **2** hakmes*, kapmes* **3** bijl **4** [inform] helikopter
choppy 1 met korte golfslag: ~ *sea* ruwe zee **2** veranderlijk [of wind] **3** [Am; inform] onsamenhangend [of style]; hortend
chopstick (eet)stokje*
chop suey tjaptjoi [Chinese dish]
choral 1 koor- **2** gezongen
chord 1 snaar [also fig]: [fig] *that strikes a* ~ dat herinnert me aan iets **2** [mus] akkoord*
chore karwei(tje)*: *do the* ~*s* het huishouden doen
choreography choreografie
chorister koorknaap
chortle luidruchtig gegrinnik*
chorus 1 koor*: *answer in* ~ in koor antwoorden **2** refrein*
chow 1 chowchow [dog] **2** [inform] eten*, voer*

chow-chow chowchow [dog]
chowder [esp Am] dikke (vis)soep
¹chow down (n) [inform] voer*, vreten*
²chow down (vb) [inform] vreten, bikken
Christ Christus
christen 1 dopen **2** als (doop)naam geven, noemen, dopen
Christendom christenheid
christening doop
¹Christian (n) christen, christenmens
²Christian (adj) christelijk
Christianity 1 christendom* **2** christelijkheid
Christian name doopnaam, voornaam
Christmas Kerstmis, kerst(tijd): *the* ~ *season* het kerstseizoen
Christmas cracker knalbonbon
Christmas Eve kerstavond, avond (dag) voor Kerstmis
chrome chroom*, chromium*
chromium chromium*, chroom*
chromosome chromosoom*
chronic 1 chronisch, slepend, langdurend; [of disease also] ongeneeslijk **2** [inform] erg, slecht, vreselijk
chronicle kroniek
chronology chronologie
chrysanth(emum) chrysant
chubby [inform] mollig; gevuld [of face]
¹chuck (n) **1** aaitje* [under one's chin]; tikje*, klopje* **2** klem [on a lathe]
²chuck (vb) **1** [inform] gooien **2** [inform] de bons geven, laten zitten **3** [inform] ophouden met, laten, opgeven: ~ *it (in)* er de brui aan geven, ermee ophouden
¹chuckle (n) lachje*, gegrinnik*, binnenpretje*
²chuckle (vb) **1** grinniken, een binnenpretje hebben **2** leedvermaak hebben
chuffed blij, tevreden
¹chug (n) puf, geronk*
²chug (vb) (also + along) (voort)puffen
chum 1 makker, gabber; maat [esp among boys] **2** [Am] kamergenoot
chump [inform] sukkel ‖ *go off one's* ~ stapelgek worden
chunk brok*, stuk*; homp [also fig]: *a* ~ *of cheese* (or: *bread*) een brok kaas, een homp brood
chunky 1 in brokken, met stukjes **2** kort en dik, gedrongen [of animals, persons]
church 1 kerk(gebouw*): *established* ~ staatskerk **2** kerk(genootschap*): *the Church of England* de anglicaanse kerk **3** kerk(dienst)
churchgoer kerkgang(st)er
churchyard kerkhof*, begraafplaats
churlish boers, lomp
¹churn (n) **1** karn(ton) **2** melkbus
²churn (vb) **1** roeren [milk or cream] **2** karnen **3** omroeren, laten schuimen ‖ [inform] ~

out (in grote hoeveelheden tegelijk) produceren, (in grote hoeveelheden tegelijk) afdraaien [of text]
chute 1 helling, stortkoker **2** stroomversnelling **3** [inform] parachute
chutney chutney
chutzpah gotspe, schaamteloze brutaliteit
CIA [Am] *Central Intelligence Agency* CIA
cider cider, appelwijn
cigar sigaar
cigarette sigaret
C-in-C *Commander-in-chief* opperbevelhebber
cinch [Am] [inform] makkie^h, kinderspel^h || *it's a* ~ dat is een makkie
cinder sintel: ~s as
Cinderella Assepoester
cinema bioscoop, cinema
cinematic film-
cinnamon kaneel^h
cipher 1 nul **2** cijfer^h **3** sleutel [of code] **4** code, geheimschrift^h: *the message was in* ~ de boodschap was in geheimschrift
circa circa, omstreeks
¹circle (n) **1** cirkel **2** kring, ring; [archeology] kring stenen; rotonde, ringlijn, rondweg; balkon^h [in theatre]; [hockey] slagcirkel: *run round in* ~s nodeloos druk in de weer zijn **3** groep, clubje^h, kring || *vicious* ~ vicieuze cirkel
²circle (vb) rondcirkelen, ronddraaien, rondgaan
³circle (vb) omcirkelen
circuit 1 kring, omtrek, ronde **2** (race)baan, circuit^h **3** stroomkring, schakeling **4** [sport] circuit^h || *closed* ~ gesloten circuit
circuit board printplaat
circuitous omslachtig; met een omweg
¹circular (n) **1** rondschrijven^h, circulaire **2** rondweg
²circular (adj) **1** rond, cirkelvormig: ~ *saw* cirkelzaag **2** rondlopend, rondgaand, (k)ring-: ~ *road* rondweg **3** ontwijkend, indirect || ~ *letter* circulaire, rondschrijven
circulate (laten) circuleren, (zich) verspreiden
circulation 1 oplage **2** omloop, circulatie, distributie: *in* (or: *out of*) ~ in (or: uit) de roulatie **3** bloedsomloop
circumcision besnijdenis
circumference cirkelomtrek
circumflex accent^h circonflexe, dakje^h, kapje^h
circumscribe 1 begrenzen; beperken **2** omcirkelen **3** [geometry] omschrijven
circumspect omzichtig, op zijn hoede, voorzichtig
circumstance 1 omstandigheid, (materiële) positie, (financiële) situatie: *straitened* (or: *reduced*) ~s behoeftige omstandigheden; *in* (or: *under*) *the* ~s onder de gegeven

omstandigheden **2** feit^h, geval^h, gebeurtenis **3** praal, drukte, omhaal: *pomp and* ~ pracht en praal
circumstantial 1 (afhankelijk) van de omstandigheden: ~ *evidence* indirect bewijs **2** bijkomstig, niet essentieel **3** uitvoerig, omstandig
circumvent ontwijken, omzeilen
circus 1 circus **2** (rond) plein^h
CIS *Commonwealth of Independent States* GOS, Gemenebest van Onafhankelijke Staten
citadel fort^h, citadel, bolwerk^h
citation aanhaling, citaat^h
cite aanhalen, citeren: ~ *examples* voorbeelden aanhalen
citizen 1 burger, stedeling, inwoner **2** staatsburger, onderdaan: *Jeffrey is a British* ~ Jeffrey is Brits onderdaan **3** [Am] niet-militair, burger
citizenship (staats)burgerschap^h
citizenship course inburgeringscursus
citric citroen-: ~ *acid* citroenzuur
citrus citrus-
city (grote) stad; [fig] financieel centrum^h: *the City* de oude binnenstad van Londen
city break stedentrip
city council gemeenteraad
city hall [Am] **1** gemeentehuis^h, stadhuis^h **2** stadsbestuur^h
civic 1 burger-, burgerlijk **2** stedelijk, gemeente-: ~ *centre* bestuurscentrum, openbaar centrum
civics leer van burgerrechten en -plichten; [educ] [roughly] maatschappijleer
civil 1 burger-, burgerlijk, civiel: ~ *disobedience* burgerlijke ongehoorzaamheid; ~ *law* Romeins recht; ~ *marriage* burgerlijk huwelijk; ~ *war* burgeroorlog **2** beschaafd, beleefd **3** niet-militair, burger-: ~ *service* civiele dienst, ambtenarij || ~ *engineering* weg- en waterbouwkunde
¹civilian (n) burger, niet-militair
²civilian (adj) burger-, civiel, burgerlijk
civility beleefde opmerking, beleefdheid
civilization 1 beschaving, cultuur, ontwikkeling **2** de beschaafde wereld
civilize 1 beschaven, ontwikkelen, civiliseren **2** opvoeden
civilized 1 beschaafd; ontwikkeld **2** comfortabel **3** beleefd
clad [form] gekleed; bedekt
¹claim (n) **1** aanspraak, recht^h, claim, eis: *lay* ~ *to*, *make a* ~ *to* aanspraak maken op **2** vordering, claim **3** bewering, stelling
²claim (vb) een vordering indienen, een eis instellen, schadevergoeding eisen
³claim (vb) **1** opeisen, aanspraak maken op: ~ *damages* schadevergoeding eisen **2** beweren, verkondigen, stellen
¹clairvoyant (n) helderziende

²**clairvoyant** (adj) helderziend
¹**clam** (n) schelpdier[h] || *shut* up like a ~ geen mond open doen
²**clam** (vb): ~ *up* weigeren iets te zeggen
clamber opklimmen tegen, beklimmen
clammy klam, vochtig
clamorous lawaaierig, luidruchtig
¹**clamour** (n) **1** geschreeuw[h], getier[h] **2** herrie, lawaai[h]
²**clamour** (vb) **1** schreeuwen, lawaai maken **2** protesteren, zijn stem verheffen, aandringen: ~ *for* aandringen op
¹**clamp** (n) **1** klem, klamp, (klem)beugel **2** kram, (muur)anker
²**clamp** (vb) klampen, vastklemmen
clamp down (+ on) een eind maken (aan), de kop indrukken: *we're clamping down on overspending* we willen een eind maken aan de te hoge uitgaven
clam up dichtslaan, dichtklappen, weigeren iets te zeggen
clan geslacht[h], stam, familie, clan
clandestine clandestien, geheim
¹**clang** (n) metalige klank, galm; luiden [bell]; gekletter[h], gerinkel[h]
²**clang** (vb) (metalig) (doen) klinken, (metalig) (doen) luiden, (metalig) (doen) rinkelen, (doen) galmen
clanger miskleun, blunder, flater: *to drop a* ~ een flater slaan, een blunder begaan
¹**clap** (n) klap, slag, tik, applaus[h]: ~ *of thunder* donderslag
²**clap** (vb) **1** klappen, slaan, kloppen **2** applaudisseren
³**clap** (vb) **1** (stevig) plaatsen, zetten, planten, poten: ~ *s.o. in jail* iem. achter de tralies zetten **2** slaan: ~ *s.o. on the back* iem. op de rug slaan **3** klappen in, slaan in: ~ *one's hands* in de handen klappen
clapped-out 1 uitgeteld, afgedraaid **2** gammel, wrakkig
clapper 1 klepel **2** ratel
claptrap 1 holle frasen, goedkope trucs **2** onzin
clarification 1 zuivering; filtrering [liquid, air] **2** opheldering, verklaring, uitleg
¹**clarify** (vb) helder worden [liquid, fat, air]; [fig] verhelderen; duidelijk worden
²**clarify** (vb) **1** zuiveren, klaren, doen bezinken **2** ophelderen, duidelijk maken, toelichten
clarinet klarinet
clarion 1 klaroen, signaalhoorn: ~ *call* klaroengeschal **2** (klaroen)geschal[h]
clarity helderheid, duidelijkheid
¹**clash** (n) **1** gevecht[h], botsing, conflict[h] **2** (wapen)gekletter[h]
²**clash** (vb) **1** slaags raken, botsen **2** tegenstrijdig zijn, botsen, in conflict zijn (raken) || *the party ~es with my exam* het feest valt samen met mijn examen

¹**clasp** (n) gesp, haak, knip
²**clasp** (vb) **1** vastmaken, dichthaken, vastgespen **2** vastgrijpen, vasthouden: ~ *hands* elkaars hand grijpen **3** omvatten, omhelzen
clasp knife zakmes[h], knipmes[h]
¹**class** (n) **1** stand, (maatschappelijke) klasse **2** rang, klas(se), soort, kwaliteit **3** klas, klasgenoten **4** les, lesuur[h], college[h], cursus **5** categorie, groep, verzameling; [also maths, biology] klasse: *in a* ~ *of its* (or: *his*) *own* een klasse apart **6** stijl, distinctie
²**class** (vb) plaatsen, indelen, classificeren: ~ *as* beschouwen als
¹**classic** (n) **1** een van de klassieken: *that film is a real* ~ die film is een echte klassieker **2** (-s) klassieke talen
²**classic** (adj) **1** klassiek, tijdloos, traditioneel **2** kenmerkend, typisch, klassiek: *a* ~ *example* een schoolvoorbeeld
²**classical 1** klassiek, traditioneel **2** antiek, uit de klassieke oudheid
classification 1 categorie, classificatie, klasse **2** rangschikking, indeling
classified 1 geheim **2** gerubriceerd: ~ *ads* rubrieksadvertenties
classify 1 indelen, rubriceren, classificeren **2** geheim verklaren, als geheim aanmerken
classmate klasgenoot, klasgenote
classroom klas(lokaal[h])
classy sjiek, deftig, elegant
¹**clatter** (n) gekletter[h], gerammel[h], geklepper[h]
²**clatter** (vb) kletteren, klepperen
clause clausule, bepaling, beding[h] || [linguistics] *main* ~ hoofdzin; [linguistics] *subordinate* ~ bijzin
claustrophobic claustrofobisch
¹**claw** (n) **1** klauw **2** poot **3** schaar [of crab etc]
²**claw** (vb) klauwen, grissen, graaien
clay klei, leem[+h], aarde, modder
¹**clean** (n) schoonmaakbeurt: *give* the room a ~ de kamer een (goede) beurt geven
²**clean** (adj) **1** schoon, helder; zuiver [air] **2** sierlijk, regelmatig, duidelijk; helder [style] **3** compleet, helemaal: *a* ~ *break* een radicale breuk **4** oprecht, eerlijk, sportief: *come* ~ voor de draad komen (met), eerlijk bekennen **5** onschuldig, netjes, fatsoenlijk, kuis || *make a* ~ *breast of sth.* iets bekennen, ergens schoon schip mee maken; *wipe the slate* ~ met een schone lei beginnen
³**clean** (vb) schoon(gemaakt) worden, zich laten reinigen
⁴**clean** (vb) schoonmaken, reinigen, zuiveren: *have a* ~*ed* een jas laten stomen; ~ *down* schoonborstelen, schoonwassen
⁵**clean** (adv) **1** volkomen, helemaal, compleet: ~ *forgotten* glad vergeten **2** eerlijk, fair
clean-cut duidelijk, helder: *a* ~ *decision* een

ondubbelzinnige beslissing
cl<u>ea</u>ner 1 schoonmaker, schoonmaakster,
werkster **2** schoonmaakmiddel^h, reinigings-
middel^h **3** (-'s) stomerij ‖ [fig] *take s.o. to the*
~*'s* **a)** iem. uitkleden; **b)** de vloer met iem.
aanvegen
cl<u>ea</u>ning lady schoonmaakster, hulp in de
huishouding
cl<u>ea</u>nly proper, zindelijk, netjes
clean <u>ou</u>t 1 schoonvegen, uitvegen, uitmesten **2** [inform] kaal plukken, uitschudden; opkopen [stock]; afhandig maken
[money]
cl<u>ea</u>nse reinigen, zuiveren; desinfecteren
[wound]
cl<u>ea</u>n-sh<u>a</u>ven gladgeschoren
¹**cl<u>ea</u>n <u>u</u>p** (vb) de boel opruimen, schoon-
maken
²**cl<u>ea</u>n <u>u</u>p** (vb) **1** opruimen **2** (goed) schoon-
maken, opknappen: *clean o.s.* up zich op-
knappen **3** zuiveren; [fig] uitmesten; saneren: ~ *the* **town** de stad (van misdaad) zuiveren
cl<u>ea</u>n-up schoonmaakbeurt [also fig]; sanering
¹**cl<u>ea</u>r** (n): *be in the* ~ buiten gevaar zijn, vrij-
uit gaan
²**cl<u>ea</u>r** (adj) **1** helder, schoon, doorzichtig,
klaar **2** duidelijk, ondubbelzinnig, uitge-
sproken: **make** *o.s.* ~ duidelijk maken wat je
bedoelt; *do I* **make** *myself* ~? is dat duidelijk
begrepen? **3** netto; schoon [wages, profit
etc] **4** compleet, volkomen, absoluut: *a* ~
majority een duidelijke meerderheid **5** vrij,
open, op een afstand, veilig, onbelemmerd:
the **coast** *is* ~ de kust is veilig ‖ ~ **conscience**
zuiver geweten
³**cl<u>ea</u>r** (vb) **1** helder worden; opklaren [of air]
2 weggaan, wegtrekken; optrekken [of
fog]: ~ *away* optrekken
⁴**cl<u>ea</u>r** (vb) **1** helder maken, schoonmaken,
verhelderen **2** vrijmaken; ontruimen [bldg,
street]: ~ *the* **table** de tafel afruimen **3** verwijderen, opruimen **4** zuiveren, onschuldig
verklaren: ~ *s.o.* **of** *suspicion* iem. van verdenking zuiveren **5** (ruim) passeren; springen
over [gate]; erlangs kunnen **6** (laten) passeren [Customs]; inklaren, klaren, uitklaren
7 verrekenen; vereffenen [debt]; clearen
[cheque]
⁵**cl<u>ea</u>r** (adv) **1** duidelijk, helder: *his voice* **came**
through loud and ~ zijn stem kwam luid en
helder door **2** op voldoende afstand, een
eindje, vrij: **keep** (or: **stay, steer**) ~ *of* uit de
weg gaan, (proberen te) vermijden
cl<u>ea</u>rance 1 opheldering, verheldering,
verduidelijking **2** ontruiming, opruiming,
uitverkoop **3** vergunning, toestemming;
(akte van) inklaring [ships]; [aviation] toestemming tot landen (opstijgen) **4** speling,
vrije ruimte, tussenruimte: *there was only 2 ft*

~ *between the two ships* er zat maar twee
voet speling tussen de twee schepen
clear-c<u>u</u>t scherp omlijnd [also fig]; duidelijk, uitgesproken
clear-h<u>ea</u>ded helder denkend, scherpzinnig
cl<u>ea</u>ring 1 open(gekapte) plek [in forest]
2 verrekening, vereffening
cl<u>ea</u>rly 1 duidelijk: *understand sth.* ~ iets
goed begrijpen **2** ongetwijfeld
¹**cl<u>ea</u>r <u>o</u>ff** (vb) [inform] de benen nemen, 'm
smeren, afdruipen: ~*!* opgehoepeld!
²**cl<u>ea</u>r <u>o</u>ff** (vb) **1** afmaken, een eind maken
aan; uit de weg ruimen [arrears] **2** aflossen,
afbetalen
¹**cl<u>ea</u>r <u>ou</u>t** (vb) [inform] de benen nemen,
ophoepelen
²**cl<u>ea</u>r <u>ou</u>t** (vb) **1** uitruimen, leeghalen; uit-
halen [cupboard, drain]; opruimen [room]
2 [inform] uitputten; leeghalen [stocks]
clear-s<u>igh</u>ted 1 met scherpe blik [oft fig];
scherpzinnig **2** vooruitziend
¹**cl<u>ea</u>r <u>u</u>p** (vb) **1** opklaren [weather] **2** op-
houden; bijtrekken [difficulties] **3** (rommel)
opruimen
²**cl<u>ea</u>r <u>u</u>p** (vb) **1** opruimen; uit de weg rui-
men [mess]; afmaken [work] **2** verklaren,
uitleggen, ophelderen
cl<u>ea</u>rway autoweg [where there is no stop-
ping]
cl<u>ea</u>vage 1 scheiding, kloof; breuk [also
fig] **2** gleuf; gootje^h [between breasts]; de-
colleté^h, inkijk
cl<u>ea</u>ve kloven, splijten, hakken, (door)klie-
ven
cl<u>ea</u>ve to [form] hangen aan: ~ *old customs*
oude gewoonten trouw blijven
clef [mus] sleutel
¹**cl<u>e</u>ft** (n) **1** spleet, barst, scheur; kloof [also
fig] **2** gleuf; kuiltje^h [in chin]
²**cl<u>e</u>ft** (adj) gespleten; gekloofd [of hoof]: ~
palate gespleten gehemelte
cl<u>e</u>matis clematis, bosrank
cl<u>e</u>ment 1 mild, weldadig, zacht **2** genadig, welwillend
cl<u>e</u>nch dichtklemmen; op elkaar klemmen [jaws, teeth]; dichtknijpen: *with* ~*ed*
fists met gebalde vuisten **2** vastklemmen,
vastgrijpen
cl<u>e</u>rgy geestelijkheid, geestelijken
cl<u>e</u>rgyman geestelijke, predikant, priester
cl<u>e</u>ric geestelijke
cl<u>e</u>rical 1 geestelijk, kerkelijk **2** administratief, schrijf-: *a* ~ **job** een kantoorbaan
clerk 1 (kantoor)beambte, kantoorbedien-
de, klerk **2** secretaris, griffier, (hoofd)admi-
nistrateur **3** [Am] (winkel)bediende **4** [Am]
receptionist
cl<u>e</u>ver 1 knap, slim, intelligent, vernuftig: ~
at sth. goed in iets **2** handig
cliché gemeenplaats; cliché^h

click

¹**click** (n) klik, tik, klak
²**click** (vb) **1** klikken, tikken, ratelen: [comp]
~ *on* aanklikken; doorklikken **2** [inform] het
(samen) kunnen vinden, bij elkaar passen
3 [inform] op z'n plaats vallen; plotseling
duidelijk worden [joke, remark]
³**click** (vb) klikken met, laten klikken
clicks-and-mortar met winkel en website
click through doorklikken
client 1 cliënt **2** klant, afnemer, opdrachtgever
clientele 1 klantenkring **2** praktijk [of law-
yer] **3** vaste bezoekers [of theatre, restaurant etc]
cliff steile rots, klip, klifʰ
cliff-hanger spannende wedstrijd, spannend verhaalʰ
climactic leidend tot een climax
climate 1 klimaatʰ **2** (lucht)streek **3** sfeer,
stemming, klimaatʰ: *the present economic ~*
het huidige economische klimaat
climatic klimaat-
climax 1 hoogtepuntʰ, climax, toppuntʰ
2 orgasmeʰ
¹**climb** (n) **1** klim, beklimming **2** helling,
klim, weg omhoog
²**climb** (vb) **1** omhoog gaan, klimmen, stijgen, toenemen **2** oplopen; omhooggaan [of
road] **3** zich opwerken; opklimmen [rank,
position]
³**climb** (vb) klimmen in (op), beklimmen, bestijgen
climber 1 klimmer, klauteraar, bergbeklimmer **2** klimplant
¹**clinch** (n) **1** vaste greep, omklemming
2 [boxing] clinch **3** omarming, omhelzing
²**clinch** (vb) **1** [boxing] (met elkaar) in de
clinch gaan, lijf aan lijf staan **2** [inform] elkaar omhelzen
³**clinch** (vb) beklinken, sluiten; afmaken
[agreement, transaction]: *that ~ed the **matter***
dat gaf de doorslag
cling 1 kleven, zich vasthouden, zich vastklemmen **2** dicht blijven bij, hangen, hechten **3** zich vastklampen aan, vasthouden
clinging 1 aanhankelijk, plakkerig
2 nauwsluitend [clothing etc]
clinic 1 kliniek; privékliniek **2** adviesbu-
reauʰ, consultatiebureauʰ **3** groepspraktijk
4 spreekuurʰ
clinical klinisch, onbewogen; zakelijk [atti-
tude]
¹**clink** (n) gerinkelʰ, geklinkʰ
²**clink** (vb) klinken, rinkelen, rammelen
³**clink** (vb) laten rinkelen; klinken met [eg
glasses]
¹**clip** (n) **1** knippende beweging, scheerbeurt, trimbeurt **2** klem, knijper, clip **3** fragmentʰ, stukʰ; gedeelteʰ [from film]; (video)-
clip
²**clip** (vb) knippen, snoeien

³**clip** (vb) **1** (vast)klemmen, vastzetten: ~ *together* samenklemmen **2** (bij)knippen, afknippen, kort knippen, trimmen; scheren
[sheep]; uitknippen [from newspaper, film]
3 afbijten [words]; inslikken [letter(s), sylla-
ble]
clip out uitknippen
clipper 1 knipper, scheerder, (be)snoeier
2 klipper(schipʰ) **3** (-s) kniptang [of guard]
4 (-s) nagelkniptang **5** (-s) tondeuse
clipping krantenknipselʰ
clique kliek, club(jeʰ)
clitoris clitoris
¹**cloak** (n) **1** cape, mantel **2** bedekking, laag
3 dekmantel, verhulling
²**cloak** (vb) verhullen, verbergen, vermommen
cloakroom 1 garderobe **2** [euph] toiletʰ
¹**clobber** (n) **1** boeltjeʰ, spullen **2** plunje,
kloffieʰ
²**clobber** (vb) **1** aftuigen, een pak rammel
geven **2** in de pan hakken
¹**clock** (n) **1** klok, uurwerkʰ **2** [inform] meter,
teller, taximeter, prikklok, snelheidsmeter,
kilometerteller: *the car had 100,000 miles **on**
the* ~ de auto had 160.000 kilometer op de
teller
²**clock** (vb) klokken [time clock]: ~ *in*, ~ *on*
inklokken; *we have to* ~ *at 8 o'clock* wij moeten om 8 uur inklokken; ~ *off*, ~ *out* uitklok-
ken
clockwise met de (wijzers van de) klok mee
clockwork uurwerkʰ, opwindmechaniekʰ:
like ~ op rolletjes, gesmeerd
clockwork orange gerobotiseerde mens,
robot
clod kluit (aarde), klomp (klei), klont
¹**clog** (n) klomp
²**clog** (vb) **1** verstopt raken, dicht gaan zitten: ~ *up* a) verstopt raken [drain pipe];
b) vastlopen [machinery] **2** stollen, samen-
klonteren
³**clog** (vb) (doen) verstoppen: ~ *up* doen verstoppen, vast laten draaien [machines]; ~*ged
with dirt* totaal vervuild
cloister 1 kloostergang; kruisgang **2** kloos-
terlevenʰ
¹**clone** (n) kloon, kopie
²**clone** (vb) klonen: ~*d mobile **phone*** mobiel
met een gekloonde simkaart
¹**close** (n) **1** eindeʰ, slotʰ, besluitʰ: ***bring** to a ~*
tot een eind brengen, afsluiten **2** binnen-
plaats, hof(jeʰ) **3** terreinʰ [around church,
school etc]
²**close** (adj) **1** dicht, gesloten, nauw; benauwd [space]; drukkend [weather, air]
2 bedekt, verborgen, geheim, zwijgzaam
3 beperkt, select; besloten [partnership]
4 nabij; naast [relative(s)]; intiem; dik
[friend(ship)]; onmiddellijk; direct [vicinity];
getrouw; letterlijk [copy, translation]; gelijk

clutter

opgaand [contest, struggle]; kort [hair, grass]: ~ *at hand* (vlak) bij de hand, dicht in de buurt; *at* ~ *range* van dichtbij; [pol, sport] *it's too* ~ *to call* de uitslag is onvoorspelbaar, het wordt een fotofinish **5** grondig; diepgaand [attention]: *keep a* ~ *watch on s.o.* iem. scherp in de gaten houden ‖ *a* ~ *shave* (or: *thing, call*) op het nippertje
³close (vb) aflopen, eindigen; besluiten [of speaker]
⁴close (vb) **1** dichtmaken, (af)sluiten; hechten [wound]; dichten [hole] **2** besluiten, beëindigen; (af)sluiten [argument, plea] **3** dichter bij elkaar brengen, aaneensluiten **4** afmaken, rond maken; sluiten [agreement, business]
⁵close (adv) **1** dicht, stevig **2** dicht(bij), vlak, tegen: ~ *on sixty years* bijna zestig jaar
closed 1 dicht, gesloten **2** besloten, select, exclusief
closed-circuit via een gesloten circuit: ~ *television, CCTV* videobewaking, bewaking d.m.v. camera's
closed-door politics achterkamertjespolitiek
close down 1 sluiten, opheffen; dichtgaan, dichtdoen [of a business] **2** sluiten [of radio and TV programmes]
closefisted gierig; vrekkig
close in 1 korter worden; korten [of days] **2** naderen, dichterbij komen: ~ *(up)on* omsingelen, insluiten **3** (in)vallen [of darkness]
close-knit hecht
¹closet (n) **1** (ingebouwde) kast, bergruimte **2** privévertrek^h
²closet (vb) in een privévertrek opsluiten: [fig] *he was ~ed with the headmaster* hij had een privéonderhoud met het schoolhoofd
¹close up (vb) dichtgaan [of flowers]
²close up (vb) afsluiten, blokkeren, sluiten
close-up close-up; [fig] indringende beschrijving
closure 1 het sluiten, sluiting **2** slot^h, einde^h, besluit^h
¹clot (n) **1** klonter, klont **2** [inform] stommeling, idioot, ezel
²clot (vb) (doen) klonteren, (doen) stollen: ~*ted cream* dikke room
cloth 1 stuk^h stof, doek^h, lap **2** tafellaken^h **3** stof, materiaal^h, geweven stof **4** beroepskledij [of clergymen]; [fig] de geestelijkheid
clothe kleden, aankleden, van kleren voorzien
clothes kleding, kleren, (was)goed
clothes horse droogrek^h
clothing kleding, kledij
¹cloud (n) **1** wolk; [fig] schaduw; probleem^h: *under a* ~ uit de gratie **2** massa, menigte; zwerm [of insects] ‖ *every* ~ *has a silver lining* achter de wolken schijnt de zon
²cloud (vb) bewolken, verduisteren; betrek-

ken [also fig]: *the sky ~ed over* (or: *up*) het werd bewolkt
³cloud (vb) (zoals) met wolken bedekken, verduisteren; vertroebelen [also fig]: ~ *the issue* de zaak vertroebelen
cloudburst wolkbreuk
cloudy bewolkt, betrokken, duister; troebel [of liquid]; beslagen; dof [of glass]; onduidelijk; verward [of memory]
¹clout (n) **1** [inform] mep, klap **2** (politieke) invloed, (politieke) macht
²clout (vb) een klap geven
clove 1 teen(tje^h): *a* ~ *of garlic* een teentje knoflook **2** kruidnagel
clover klaver ‖ *be* (or: *live*) *in* ~ leven als God in Frankrijk
cloverleaf klaverblad^h; [also fig] verkeersknooppunt^h
clown clown, grappenmaker, moppentapper
cloy tegenstaan: *cream ~s if you have too much of it* room gaat tegenstaan als je er te veel van eet
¹club (n) **1** knuppel, knots **2** golfstok **3** klaveren [one card] **4** clubgebouw^h, clubhuis^h **5** club, sociëteit, vereniging: [inform] *'I've lost my money.' 'Join the* ~*!'* 'Ik heb mijn geld verloren.' 'Jij ook al!'
²club (vb) een bijdrage leveren ‖ *his friends ~bed together to buy a present* zijn vrienden hebben een potje gemaakt om een cadeautje te kopen
³club (vb) knuppelen
clubbing uitgaan^h (naar nachtclubs): *she goes ~ every Friday* ze gaat vrijdags altijd uit
clubfoot klompvoet
club sandwich [Am] clubsandwich
clue aanwijzing, spoor^h, hint: [inform] *I haven't (got) a* ~ ik heb geen idee
clueless stom, dom, idioot
¹clump (n) **1** groep; bosje^h [of trees or plants] **2** klont, brok^h: *a* ~ *of mud* een modderkluit
²clump (vb) stommelen, zwaar lopen
clumsy 1 onhandig, lomp, log **2** tactloos, lomp
¹cluster (n) bos(je)^h, groep(je^h)
²cluster (vb) **1** zich groeperen **2** in bosjes groeien, in een groep groeien
³cluster (vb) bundelen, groeperen
¹clutch (n) **1** greep, klauw; [fig also] macht; controle, bezit^h: *be in the ~es of a chanteur* zijn [fig] stel^h; greep, reeks **3** [techn] koppeling(spedaal^h): *let the* ~ *in* koppelen
²clutch (vb) grijpen, beetgrijpen, vastgrijpen, stevig vasthouden
clutch bag enveloptasje^h; damestas [without handle]
¹clutter (n) rommel, warboel

²clutter (vb) **1** rommelig maken, onoverzichtelijk maken, in wanorde brengen **2** (op)vullen, volstoppen: *a sink ~ed (up) with dishes* een aanrecht bedolven onder de borden
c/o *care of* p/a, per adres
Co 1 *company* **2** *county*
CO *commanding officer* bevelvoerend officier
¹coach (n) **1** koets, staatsiekoets **2** diligence **3** spoorrijtuigʰ, spoorwagon **4** bus, reisbus: *go* (or: *travel) by ~* met de bus reizen **5** trainer, coach
²coach (vb) **1** in een koets vervoeren **2** trainen, coachen
coachwork koetswerkʰ, carrosserie
coagulate stremmen; stollen
coal 1 steenkool **2** houtskool || *carry* (or: *take) ~s to Newcastle* water naar de zee dragen; *haul s.o. over the ~s* iem. de les lezen
coalescence samensmelting, samenvoeging
coalition [pol] coalitie, unie, verbondʰ
coalmine kolenmijn
coal pit kolenmijn
coal tit zwarte mees
coarse grof, ruw, ordinair, plat
¹coast (n) kust
²coast (vb) **1** freewheelen, met de motor in de vrijloop rijden **2** [fig] zonder inspanning vooruitkomen, zich (doelloos) laten voortdrijven, zich niet inspannen: *~ to victory* op zijn sloffen winnen
coastal kust-
coaster 1 kustbewoner **2** kustvaarder, coaster **3** onderzetter, bierviltjeʰ
coastguard 1 kustwachter **2** kustwacht
coastline kustlijn
¹coat (n) **1** (over)jas, mantel, jasjeʰ **2** vacht, beharing, verenkleedʰ **3** schil, dop, rok **4** laag, deklaag: *~ of paint* (or: *dust)* verflaag, stoflaag || *~ of arms* wapenschild, familiewapen; *~ of mail* maliënkolder
²coat (vb) een laag geven, met een laag bedekken
coating laag, deklaag
coat-tails slippenʰ || *ride on the ~ of* meerijden op het succes van
co-author medeauteur
coax vleien, overreden, overhalen: *the police ~ed the public away from the place of the accident* de politie verwijderde het publiek met zachte hand van de plaats van het ongeluk
coaxial: *~ cable* coaxiale kabel; coaxkabel
cob 1 mannetjeszwaan **2** maiskolf [without the corn]
cobalt 1 kobaltʰ **2** kobaltblauwʰ, ultramarijnʰ
¹cobble (n) kei, kinderkopjeʰ, kassei
²cobble (vb) bestraten (met keien), plaveien || *~ together* in elkaar flansen

cobbler schoenmaker
cobra cobra, brilslang
cobweb 1 spinnenwebʰ; webʰ [also fig] **2** spinragʰ **3** ragfijn weefselʰ [also fig] || *blow the ~s away* de dufheid verdrijven
cocaine cocaïne
cochineal cochenille [red paint]
¹cock (n) **1** haan; [fig] kemphaan **2** mannetjeʰ [of birds]; mannetjes- **3** [inform] makker, maat, ouwe jongen **4** kraan, tap **5** [vulg] lul, pik **6** haan [of firearms]: *go off at half ~* a) voortijdig beginnen; b) mislukken (door overijld handelen)
²cock (vb) **1** overeind (doen) staan: *~ the ears* de oren spitsen **2** spannen [cock of firearm] **3** scheef (op)zetten
cock-a-doodle-doo kukelekuʰ
cock-and-bull story sterk verhaalʰ, kletsverhaalʰ
cockeyed [inform] **1** scheef; schuin **2** onzinnig
cockle kokkel || *it warms the ~s of my heart* dat doet mijn hart goed
Cockney 1 cockney [inhabitant] **2** Cockneydialectʰ
cockpit 1 cockpit, stuurhut **2** vechtplaats voor hanen; [fig] slagveldʰ **3** [shipp] kuip
cockroach kakkerlak
cocktail cocktail
cock up 1 oprichten, spitsen: *~ one's ears* de oren spitsen **2** [inform] in de war sturen, in het honderd laten lopen
cock-up [inform] puinhoop, klerezooi
cocky brutaal en verwaand
cocoa 1 warme chocola **2** cacao(poederʰ)
coconut 1 kokosnoot **2** kokos(vleesʰ)
¹cocoon (n) **1** cocon, pop **2** overtrek, (beschermend) omhulselʰ
²cocoon (vb) (zich) verpoppen: *~ed from the outside world* afgeschermd van de buitenwereld; *be ~ed* in een beschermd leven leiden in
cod kabeljauw
COD *cash on delivery, (Am) collect on delivery* betaling bij aflevering, levering onder rembours
coddle 1 zacht koken **2** vertroetelen, verwennen
code 1 code **2** gedragslijn: *~ of honour* erecode **3** wetboekʰ
codify codificeren, schriftelijk vastleggen
co-driver bijrijder
codswallop nonsens, onzin
coed [Am; inform] studente
coeducation gemengd onderwijsʰ
coerce dwingen: *~ s.o. into doing sth.* iem. dwingen iets te doen **2** afdwingen **3** onderdrukken
coercion dwang
coexist co-existeren; (vreedzaam) naast elkaar bestaan
coexistence co-existentie, het (vreed-

zaam) naast elkaar bestaan
C of E *Church of England* anglicaanse kerk
coffee koffie
coffee shop coffeeshop: *Dutch* ~ coffee-shop
coffer 1 koffer, (geld)kist, brandkast **2** (-s) schatkist; [inform] fondsen
coffin (dood)kist
cog tand(je[h]) [of wheel] || [fig, inform] *a* ~ *in the **machine*** (or: **wheel**) een klein radertje in een grote onderneming
cogent overtuigend
cognac cognac
cognition 1 kenvermogen[h]; het kennen **2** waarneming
cognizance 1 kennis(neming), nota **2** gerechtelijk onderzoek[h]
cogwheel tandrad[h]
cohabit samenwonen: *~ing **agreement*** samenlevingscontract
cohere 1 nauw samenwerken **2** (logisch) samenhangen; coherent zijn
coherence samenhang
coherent samenhangend, begrijpelijk
cohesion (onderlinge) samenhang
[1]**coil** (n) **1** tros [of rope, cable] **2** winding, wikkeling **3** vlecht **4** [elec] spoel **5** [med] spiraaltje[h] || *this **mortal** ~* dit aardse ongerief
[2]**coil** (vb) (zich) kronkelen, (op)rollen
[1]**coin** (n) **1** munt(stuk[h]), geldstuk[h]: **toss** (or: **flip**) *a* ~ kruis of munt gooien, tossen **2** gemunt geld[h]
[2]**coin** (vb) **1** munten; slaan [money] **2** verzinnen, uitvinden: *~ a **word*** een woord verzinnen
coinage 1 munt(stelsel) **2** munten **3** neologisme[h]
coincide 1 (+ with) samenvallen (met) **2** (+ with) overeenstemmen (met), identiek zijn
coincidence 1 het samenvallen, samenloop (van omstandigheden): *a **mere** ~* puur toeval **2** overeenstemming
coitus [form] coïtus; geslachtsdaad
coke 1 cokes **2** coca-cola **3** [inform] cocaïne
Col *Colonel* kol., kolonel
colander vergiet[h]
[1]**cold** (n) **1** verkoudheid: *catch (a)* ~ kouvatten **2** kou || *she was **left** out in the* ~ ze was aan haar lot overgelaten
[2]**cold** (adj) koud, koel; [fig] onvriendelijk: *a ~ **fish*** een kouwe kikker; [inform] *~ **sweat*** het angstzweet; *it **leaves** me* ~ het laat me koud || *~ **comfort*** schrale troost; *get* (or: *have*) *~ **feet*** bang worden (or: zijn); [fig] *put sth. in(to)* ~ *storage* iets in de ijskast zetten; *make s.o.'s blood **run*** ~ iem. het bloed in de aderen doen stollen
[3]**cold** (adv) **1** in koude toestand **2** [inform] volledig, compleet: *~ **sober*** broodnuchter; *be **turned down*** ~ zonder meer afgewezen worden

cold call verkopen via telefoon; telemarketing bedrijven
coldshoulder [inform] de rug toekeren; negeren
cold sore koortslip
coleslaw koolsalade
colic koliek
collaborate 1 samenwerken, medewerken **2** collaboreren; heulen [with enemy]
collaboration 1 samenwerking **2** collaboratie [with the occupier(s)]
collagen collageen[h]
[1]**collapse** (n) **1** in(een)storting, in(een)-zakking **2** val, ondergang **3** inzinking, verval[h] van krachten **4** mislukking, fiasco[h]
[2]**collapse** (vb) **1** in(een)storten, in(een)vallen, in elkaar zakken **2** opvouwbaar zijn **3** bezwijken **4** mislukken
[3]**collapse** (vb) **1** in(een) doen storten, in-(een) doen vallen, in elkaar doen zakken **2** opvouwen, samenvouwen
collapsible opvouwbaar, inschuifbaar, inklapbaar, opklapbaar
[1]**collar** (n) **1** kraag, halskraag **2** boord(je[h]), halsboord[h] **3** halsband, halsring **4** halsketting, halssnoer[h] **5** gareel[h]; haam [of horse]
[2]**collar** (vb) [inform] in de kraag grijpen, inrekenen
collarbone sleutelbeen[h]
[1]**collateral** (n) zakelijk onderpand[h]
[2]**collateral** (adj) **1** bijkomstig; ondergeschikt **2** samengaand; bijkomend: *~ **damage*** nevenschade
colleague collega
[1]**collect** (adj) [Am] te betalen door opgeroepene [telephone]: *a ~ **call*** een telefoongesprek voor rekening van de opgeroepene; **call** *me* ~ bel me maar op mijn kosten
[2]**collect** (vb) **1** zich verzamelen **2** [inform] geld ontvangen
[3]**collect** (vb) **1** verzamelen **2** innen, incasseren, collecteren **3** (weer) onder controle krijgen: *~ **one's thoughts*** (or: **ideas**) zijn gedachten bijeenrapen; *~ **o.s.*** zijn zelfbeheersing terugkrijgen **4** afhalen, ophalen
collectable verzamelobject[h]
collected kalm, bedaard, beheerst
collection 1 verzameling, collectie **2** collecte, inzameling **3** buslichting **4** het verzamelen, het inzamelen, de incassering **5** incasso[h], inning
[1]**collective** (n) **1** groep, gemeenschap, collectief[h] **2** gemeenschappelijke onderneming, collectief landbouwbedrijf[h]
[2]**collective** (adj) gezamenlijk, gemeenschappelijk, collectief
collector 1 verzamelaar **2** collecteur [of public funds]; ontvanger (der belasting), inzamelaar **3** collectant
college 1 hogere beroepsschool, academie; instituut[h] **2** college[h] **3** [Am] (kleine) universi-

teit **4** grote kostschool **5** universiteitsge-
bouw[h], universiteitsgebouwen, schoolgebouw[h], schoolgebouwen **6** raad
coll_egiate 1 behorend tot een college,
universiteit **2** bestaande uit verschillende
autonome afdelingen [of university]
coll_ide botsen, aanrijden, aanvaren; [fig] in
botsing komen
coll_ision botsing, aanrijding, aanvaring;
[fig also] conflict[h]
coll_ision course ramkoers [also fig]
coll_oquial tot de spreektaal behorend, informeel
coll_oquialism 1 alledaagse uitdrukking
2 informele stijl
coll_ude samenzweren; samenspannen
the **coll_ywobbles** [inform] buikpijn [also fig]
Col_ogne Keulen
Col_ombia Colombia
1Col_ombian (n) Colombiaan(se)
2Col_ombian (adj) Colombiaans
col_on 1 dubbelepunt **2** karteldarm
col_onel kolonel
1col_onial (n) koloniaal
2col_onial (adj) koloniaal, van de koloniën
col_onialism kolonialisme[h], koloniaal stelsel[h]
col_onist kolonist
1col_onize (vb) een kolonie vormen
2col_onize (vb) koloniseren
col_onnade zuilenrij, zuilengalerij
col_ony kolonie [also biology]
col_ossal 1 kolossaal, reusachtig, enorm
2 [inform] geweldig, prachtig, groots
col_ossus kolos [also fig]
1col_our (n) **1** kleur; [fig] schilderachtigheid;
levendigheid, bloemrijke stijl: [fig] *paint in
glowing ~s* zeer enthousiast beschrijven
2 verf(stof), kleurstof, pigment[h] **3** kleurtje[h],
gelaatskleur: *have little* ~ er bleekjes uitzien
4 donkere huidkleur **5** schijn (van werkelijkheid), uiterlijk[h]: *give* (or: *lend*) ~ *to* geloof-
waardiger maken **6** soort, aard, slag **7** (-s)
nationale vlag, vaandel[h] **8** clubkleuren, insigne[h], lint[h] **9** gevoelens, positie, opvatting:
[inform] *show* one's *(true)* ~s zijn ware ge-
daante tonen || *with flying* ~s met vlag en
wimpel; *feel* (or: *look*) *off* ~ zich niet lekker
voelen
2col_our (vb) kleur krijgen, kleuren **2** blozen, rood worden: ~ *up* blozen
3col_our (vb) **1** kleuren, verven **2** vermommen **3** verkeerd voorstellen, verdraaien
4 beïnvloeden
col_our-blind kleurenblind
col_oured 1 gekleurd **2** niet-blank, zwart: *a
~ person* een niet-blanke; [esp] een zwarte;
[South Af] een kleurling
col_ouring 1 verf(stof), kleur(stof) **2** kleuring **3** (gezonde) gelaatskleur
col_t 1 veulen[h], jonge hengst **2** [inform;

sport] beginneling, jonge speler
col_umn 1 zuil, pilaar, pijler: ~ *of smoke*
rookzuil **2** kolom: *the advertising ~s* de ad-
vertentiekolommen **3** [mil] colonne
col_umnist columnist(e)
com_a coma[h]
1comb (n) **1** kam [also of cock etc] **2** honingraat
2comb (vb) **1** kammen **2** [inform] doorzoeken, uitkammen
1com_bat (n) strijd, gevecht[h]
2com_bat (vb) vechten (tegen), (be)strijden
com_bats combatbroek
com_bination 1 combinatie, vereniging,
verbinding: *in ~ with* samen met, in combinatie met **2** (geheime letter)combinatie
3 samenstelling
1com_bine (n) maaidorser, combine
2com_bine (vb) **1** zich verenigen, zich verbinden **2** samenwerken **3** [chem] zich verbinden
3com_bine (vb) **1** combineren, verenigen,
verbinden, samenvoegen: *~d operations* (or:
exercises) legeroefeningen waarbij land-,
lucht- en zeemacht samenwerken **2** in zich
verenigen
comb _out [inform] **1** uitkammen, doorzoeken **2** zuiveren, schiften **3** verwijderen; afvoeren [redundant staff]
1com_bustible (n) brandstof, brandbare stof
2com_bustible (adj) **1** (ver)brandbaar, ontvlambaar **2** opvliegend, lichtgeraakt
com_bustion verbranding: *spontaneous ~*
zelfontbranding
come 1 komen, naderen: *in the years to* ~ in
de komende jaren; *she came running* ze
kwam aanrennen; ~ *and go* heen en weer lopen; [fig] komen en gaan **2** aankomen, arriveren: *the goods have* ~ de goederen zijn
aangekomen; *the train is coming* de trein
komt eraan; *I'm coming!* ik kom eraan!; *first
~, first served* die eerst komt, eerst maalt
3 beschikbaar zijn, verkrijgbaar zijn, aangeboden worden: *this suit ~s in two sizes* dit pak
is verkrijgbaar in twee maten **4** verschijnen:
that news came as a surprise dat nieuws
kwam als een verrassing **5** meegaan: *are you
coming?* kom je mee? **6** gebeuren: ~ *what
may* wat er ook moge gebeuren; *(now that I)
~ to think of it* nu ik eraan denk; [inform]
how ~? hoe komt dat?, waarom? **7** staan,
komen, gaan: *my job ~s before everything else*
mijn baan gaat vóór alles **8** zijn: *it ~s cheaper
by the dozen* het is goedkoper per dozijn
9 beginnen, gaan, worden: *the buttons came
unfastened* de knopen raakten los; ~ *to* be-
lieve tot de overtuiging komen; ~ *to know*
s.o. better iem. beter leren kennen **10** (een
bepaalde) vorm aannemen || *the life to* ~ het
leven in het hiernamaals; [inform] *he'll be
eighteen* ~ *September* hij wordt achttien in

september; *she doesn't know whether she is coming or going* ze is de kluts kwijt; ~ *now!* komkom!, zachtjes aan!

come ab<u>ou</u>t gebeuren: *how did the accident ~?* hoe is het ongeluk gebeurd?

[1]**come acr<u>o</u>ss** (vb) **1** overkomen [of intention, joke etc]; begrepen worden: *his speech didn't ~ very well* zijn toespraak sloeg niet erg aan **2** [inform] lijken te zijn, overkomen (als): *he comes across to me as quite a nice fellow* hij lijkt me wel een aardige kerel

[2]**come acr<u>o</u>ss** (vb) aantreffen, vinden, stoten op: *I came across an old friend* ik liep een oude vriend tegen het lijf

come <u>a</u>fter 1 volgen, komen na, later komen **2** [inform] (achter iem.) aanzitten

come ag<u>ai</u>n 1 terugkomen, teruggaan **2** [inform] iets herhalen, iets nog eens zeggen: *~?* zeg 't nog eens

come al<u>o</u>ng 1 meekomen, meegaan **2** opschieten, vooruitkomen: *how is your work coming along?* schiet je op met je werk?; *~!* vooruit! schiet op! **3** zich voordoen, gebeuren: *take every opportunity that comes along* elke kans grijpen die zich voordoet **4** zijn best doen: *~!* komaan!

come ap<u>a</u>rt uit elkaar vallen, losgaan, uit elkaar gaan

come <u>a</u>t 1 komen bij, er bij kunnen, te pakken krijgen **2** bereiken, toegang krijgen tot: *the truth is often difficult to ~* het is vaak moeilijk de waarheid te achterhalen **3** er op losgaan, aanvallen: *he came at me with a knife* hij viel me aan met een mes

come aw<u>a</u>y 1 losgaan, loslaten **2** heengaan, weggaan, ervandaan komen

c<u>o</u>meback comeback, terugkeer: *stage* (or: *make, attempt*) *a ~* een comeback (proberen te) maken

come b<u>a</u>ck 1 terugkomen, terugkeren, een comeback maken **2** weer in de mode komen, weer populair worden **3** weer te binnen schieten: *it'll ~ to me in a minute* het schiet me zo wel weer te binnen

come betw<u>ee</u>n tussenbeide komen, zich bemoeien met

come b<u>y</u> 1 krijgen, komen aan: *jobs are hard to ~* werk is moeilijk te vinden **2** oplopen [disease, wound etc]; vinden, tegen het lijf lopen **3** voorbijkomen, passeren

com<u>e</u>dian 1 (blijspel)acteur; komediant [also fig] **2** blijspelauteur **3** komiek

c<u>o</u>medown [inform] **1** val, vernedering, achteruitgang **2** tegenvaller

come d<u>o</u>wn 1 neerkomen, naar beneden komen; [fig] *~ in the world* aan lagerwal raken **2** overgeleverd worden [of tradition etc] **3** dalen [also of aeroplane]; zakken; lager worden [of price] **4** <u>o</u>verkomen

come d<u>o</u>wn on 1 neerkomen op, toespringen (op), overvallen **2** straffen **3** [in-

form] krachtig eisen **4** [inform] berispen, uitschelden, uitvaren tegen: *he came down on me like a ton of bricks* hij verpletterde me onder zijn kritiek

come d<u>o</u>wn to [inform, fig] neerkomen op: *the problem comes down to this* het probleem komt hierop neer

c<u>o</u>medy 1 blijspel, komedie **2** humor

come fr<u>o</u>m 1 komen uit, afstammen van **2** het resultaat zijn van: *that's what comes from lying to people* dat komt ervan als je liegt tegen mensen

come <u>i</u>n 1 binnenkomen **2** aankomen: *he came in second* hij kwam als tweede binnen **3** in de mode komen, de mode worden **4** deelnemen, een plaats vinden: *this is where you ~* hier kom jij aan de beurt, hier begint jouw rol **5** voordeel hebben: *where do I ~?* wat levert het voor mij op? **6** beginnen, aan de beurt komen: *this is where we ~* hier begint voor ons het verhaal **7** opkomen; rijzen [of tide] **8** binnenkomen, in ontvangst genomen worden; verkregen worden [of money] **9** dienen, nut hebben: *~ handy* (or: *useful*) goed van pas komen

come <u>i</u>n for 1 krijgen, ontvangen: *~ a fortune* een fortuin krijgen **2** het voorwerp zijn van, uitlokken: *~ a great deal of criticism* heel wat kritiek uitlokken

come <u>i</u>nto 1 (ver)krijgen, verwerven, in het bezit komen van: *~ a fortune* een fortuin erven; *~ s.o.'s possession* in iemands bezit komen **2** komen in: *~ blossom* (or: *flower*) beginnen te bloeien; *~ fashion* in de mode komen **3** binnenkomen

c<u>o</u>mely aantrekkelijk, knap

come <u>o</u>f 1 komen uit, afstammen van: *he comes of noble ancestors* hij stamt uit een nobel geslacht **2** het resultaat zijn van: *that's what comes of being late* dat komt ervan als je te laat bent; *nothing came of it* er kwam niets van terecht, het is nooit iets geworden

come <u>o</u>ff 1 loslaten [eg of wallpaper from the wall]; losgaan **2** er afkomen, er afbrengen: *~ badly* het er slecht van afbrengen **3** lukken, goed aflopen **4** plaatshebben: *Henry's birthday party didn't ~* Henry's verjaardagsfeestje ging niet door **5** afkomen van, loslaten, verlaten: *has this button ~ your coat?* komt deze knoop van jouw jas? **6** afgaan [of price]: *that'll ~ your paycheck* dat zal van jouw salaris worden afgetrokken || [inform] *oh, ~ it!* schei uit!

come <u>o</u>n 1 naderbij komen, oprukken, (blijven) komen: *I'll ~ later* ik kom je wel achterna **2** opschieten, vooruitkomen **3** beginnen; opkomen [of thunderstorm]; vallen [of night]; aangaan [of light]; beginnen (te ontstaan) [of disease etc]: *I've got a cold coming on* ik heb een opkomende verkoudheid **4** op de tv komen **5** opkomen [of actor] **6** beter

worden, herstellen; opknappen [of disease]
7 [Am] een grote indruk maken; <u>o</u>verkomen
[on TV, radio] **8** aantreffen, stoten op
9 treffen [of sth. undesirable]; overvallen:
the disease came on her suddenly de ziekte trof
haar plotseling
c<u>o</u>me-on [inform] **1** lokmiddel^h, verlokking
2 [Am; inform] uitnodiging, invitatie ‖ [in-
form] *she gave me the ~ as soon as her husband had left* zodra haar man weg was, begon ze avances te maken
come <u>out</u> 1 uitkomen, naar buiten komen:
Lucy came out in the top three Lucy eindigde
bij de eerste drie **2** staken, in staking gaan
3 verschijnen, tevoorschijn komen; gepubliceerd worden [of book]; uitlopen, bloeien
[of plants, trees]; doorkomen [of sun]: *~ with
the truth* met de waarheid voor de dag komen **4** ontdekt worden **5** duidelijk worden,
goed uitkomen; er goed op staan [photo]
6 verdwijnen, verschieten; verbleken [of col-
our]; uitvallen [of hair, teeth] **7** zich voor
(tegen) iets verklaren: *the Government came
out strong(ly) against the invasion* de regering
protesteerde krachtig tegen de invasie
8 verwijderd worden; er uitgaan [of stain]
9 uitkomen, kloppen; juist zijn [of bill]
10 openlijk uitkomen voor [sexual inclina-
tion] ‖ *~ badly* (or: *well*) het er slecht (*or:*
goed) afbrengen; *~ right* (or: *wrong*) goed
(*or:* slecht) aflopen; *~ for s.o.* (*sth.*) iem. (iets)
zijn steun toezeggen
come <u>o</u>ver 1 <u>o</u>verkomen, komen over,
oversteken **2** (naar een andere partij) overlopen **3** langskomen, bezoeken **4** inslaan,
<u>o</u>verkomen, aanslaan **5** worden, zich voelen:
~ dizzy zich duizelig voelen **6** overk<u>o</u>men,
bekruipen: *a strange feeling came over her* een
vreemd gevoel bekroop haar; *what has ~
you?* wat bezielt je?
come r<u>ou</u>nd [Am] **1** aanlopen, langskomen, bezoeken **2** bijkomen, weer bij zijn
positieven komen **3** overgaan, bijdraaien:
Jim has ~ Jim heeft het geaccepteerd **4** terugkomen, (regelmatig) terugkeren **5** een
geschil bijleggen **6** een omweg maken **7** bijtrekken [after angry mood]: *Sue'll soon ~* Sue
komt vast gauw in een beter humeur
come<u>s</u>tible eetbaar
c<u>o</u>met komeet
come thr<u>ou</u>gh 1 doorkomen, overkomen:
the message isn't coming through clearly het
bericht komt niet goed door **2** overleven, te
boven komen; doorstaan [disease etc]
3 [Am] slagen, lukken, de bestemming bereiken **4** [inform] doen als verwacht, over de
brug komen
c<u>o</u>me to 1 bijkomen, weer bij zijn positieven komen **2** betreffen, aankomen op: *when
it comes to speaking clearly* wat duidelijk spreken betreft **3** komen tot (aan), komen bij: *~*

an agreement het eens worden; *~ s.o.'s aid*
iem. te hulp komen **4** bedragen, (neer)ko-
men op: *~ the same thing* op hetzelfde neerkomen **5** te binnen schieten, komen op
6 toekomen, ten deel vallen, gegeven worden: *it comes naturally to him,* [inform] *it
comes natural to him* het gaat hem makkelijk
af **7** overk<u>o</u>men: *I hope no harm will ~ you* ik
hoop dat je niets kwaads overkomt ‖ *he'll
never ~ anything* er zal nooit iets van hem
worden; *he had it coming to him* hij kreeg zijn
verdiende loon; *~ nothing* op niets uitdraai-
en; *we never thought things would ~ this!* we
hadden nooit gedacht dat het zo ver zou
komen!
come <u>u</u>p 1 uitkomen, kiemen **2** aan de
orde komen, ter sprake komen **3** gebeuren,
v<u>oo</u>rkomen, zich voordoen **4** vooruitkomen:
~ in the world vooruitkomen in de wereld
5 [inform] uitkomen, getrokken worden: *I
hope my number will ~ this time* ik hoop dat
mijn lotnummer deze keer wint ‖ *~ against*
in conflict komen met; *our holiday didn't ~ to
our expectations* onze vakantie viel tegen;
[inform] *you'll have to ~ with sth.* better je zult
met iets beters moeten komen
come upon 1 overvallen, overrompelen,
komen over **2** aantreffen, stoten op, tegen
het lijf lopen
come<u>u</u>ppance [inform] verdiende loon:
get one's ~ zijn verdiende loon krijgen
¹c<u>o</u>mfort (n) **1** troost, steun, bemoediging:
derive (or: *take*) *~ from sth.* troost putten uit
iets **2** comfort^h, gemak^h **3** welstand, welge-
steldheid: *live in ~* welgesteld zijn
²c<u>o</u>mfort (vb) troosten, bemoedigen
c<u>o</u>mfortable 1 aangenaam, gemakkelijk:
feel ~ zich goed voelen **2** royaal, vorstelijk
3 rustig, zonder pijn: *have a ~ night* een rustige nacht hebben **4** welgesteld: *live in ~ circumstances* in goeden doen zijn
c<u>o</u>mforter 1 trooster, steun **2** fopspeen
c<u>o</u>mfortless 1 troosteloos; somber **2** on-
gerieflijk
c<u>o</u>mfort z<u>o</u>ne: *to be out of one's ~* zich ongemakkelijk voelen
c<u>o</u>mfy [inform] aangenaam; behaaglijk
¹c<u>o</u>mic (n) **1** komiek, grappenmaker **2** (-s)
stripboek^h, strippagina
²c<u>o</u>mic (adj) **1** grappig, komisch: *~ relief* vro-
lijke noot **2** blijspel-
c<u>o</u>mical [inform] **1** grappig, komisch **2** blij-
spel-
comic str<u>i</u>p strip(verhaal^h)
¹c<u>o</u>ming (n) komst: *the ~s and goings* het
komen en gaan
²c<u>o</u>ming (adj) **1** toekomstig, komend, aanstaand: *the ~ week* volgende week **2** [in-
form] veelbelovend, in opkomst
c<u>o</u>mma 1 komma **2** cesuur ‖ *inverted ~s*
aanhalingstekens

¹command (n) **1** commando[h], leiding, militair gezag[h]: *be in ~ of the situation* de zaak onder controle hebben **2** bevel[h], order, gebod[h], opdracht **3** legeronderdeel[h], commando[h], legerdistrict[h] **4** beheersing, controle, meesterschap[h]: *have (a) good ~ of a language* een taal goed beheersen

²command (vb) **1** bevelen geven **2** het bevel voeren

³command (vb) **1** bevelen, commanderen **2** het bevel voeren over **3** beheersen: *~ o.s.* zich beheersen **4** bestrijken, overzien: *this hill ~s a fine **view*** vanaf deze heuvel heeft men een prachtig uitzicht **5** afdwingen: *~ **respect*** eerbied afdwingen

commandant commandant, bevelvoerend officier

commander 1 bevelhebber, commandant; [shipp] gezagvoerder: *~ in **chief*** opperbevelhebber **2** [shipp] kapitein-luitenant-ter-zee **3** commandeur [of knighthood]

commanding 1 bevelvoerend, bevelend **2** indrukwekkend, imponerend

commandment 1 bevel[h], order, gebod[h] **2** bevelschrift[h] **3** [rel] gebod[h]: *the **Ten** Commandments* de tien geboden

commando [mil] commando[h], stoottroep, stoottroeper

commemorate herdenken, gedenken, vieren

commence beginnen

commencement begin[h], aanvang

commend 1 toevertrouwen, opdragen: *~ sth. to s.o.'s care* iets aan iemands zorg toevertrouwen **2** prijzen: *highly ~ed* met eervolle vermelding **3** aanbevelen

commendation 1 prijs, eerbewijs[h], eervolle vermelding **2** lof, bijval **3** aanbeveling

¹comment (n) **1** (verklarende/kritische) aantekening, commentaar[h], toelichting: [inform] *no ~* geen commentaar **2** bemerking, opmerking **3** gepraat[h], praatjes

²comment (vb) **1** (+ (up)on) commentaar leveren (op) **2** opmerkingen maken, kritiek leveren

commentary 1 commentaar[h], opmerking **2** uitleg, verklaring **3** reportage: *a **running** ~* een doorlopende reportage

commentate verslag geven; commentaar leveren

commentator 1 commentator **2** verslaggever

commerce handel, (handels)verkeer[h]

¹commercial (n) reclame, spot

²commercial (adj) commercieel [also depr]: *~ **traveller*** vertegenwoordiger, handelsreiziger

commiserate (+ with) medelijden hebben (met), medeleven betuigen

¹commission (n) **1** opdracht **2** benoeming; aanstelling [of officer]; benoemingsbrief

3 commissie, comité[h] **4** commissie; verlening [of power, position etc]; machtiging, instructie **5** provisie, commissieloon[h] **6** het begaan [of crime, sin]

²commission (vb) **1** opdragen **2** bestellen

commissioner 1 commissaris **2** (hoofd)commissaris [of police] **3** (hoofd)ambtenaar

commit 1 toevertrouwen: *~ to memory* uit het hoofd leren **2** in (voorlopige) hechtenis nemen, opsluiten: *~ to prison* in hechtenis nemen **3** plegen, begaan, bedrijven: *~ **murder** (or: an **offence**)* een moord (or: misdrijf) plegen **4** beschikbaar stellen, toewijzen: *~ money to a new project* geld uittrekken voor een nieuw project ‖ *~ **oneself*** a) zich verplichten; b) zich uitspreken

commitment 1 verplichting, belofte **2** overtuiging **3** inzet, betrokkenheid **4** (bevel[h] tot) inhechtenisneming, (bevel[h] tot) aanhouding

committal 1 inhechtenisneming, opsluiting, opname **2** toezegging, belofte **3** verwijzing, toewijzing

committed 1 toegewijd, overtuigd **2** betrokken

committee commissie, bestuur[h], comité[h]: *~ of **inquiry*** onderzoekscommissie

commode 1 ladekast, commode **2** toilet[h]

commodious ruim

commodity 1 (handels)artikel[h], product[h], nuttig voorwerp[h] **2** basisproduct[h]; [roughly] grondstof

¹common (n) **1** gemeenschapsgrond **2** het gewone: *out of the ~* ongewoon, ongebruikelijk **3** (-s) burgerstand, (gewone) burgerij ‖ *in ~* gemeenschappelijk, gezamenlijk; *in ~ with* evenals, op dezelfde manier als

²common (adj) **1** gemeenschappelijk, gemeen: *by ~ **consent*** met algemene instemming; *it **is** very ~* het komt heel vaak voor **2** openbaar, publiek: *for the ~ **good*** in het algemeen belang **3** gewoon, algemeen, gebruikelijk, gangbaar: *the ~ **man*** de gewone man, Jan met de pet **4** ordinair: *as ~ **as** muck* (or: *dirt*) vreselijk ordinair ‖ *make ~ **cause** with* onder één hoedje spelen met; *~ **law*** gewoonterecht, ongeschreven recht; *~ **sense*** gezond verstand

commoner burger, gewone man

common-law (volgens het) gewoonterecht: *they are ~ **husband** and wife* ze zijn zonder boterbriefje getrouwd

commonly gewoonlijk; gebruikelijk, vaak

common-or-garden [inform] huis-tuin-en-keuken-; doodgewoon

¹commonplace (n) **1** cliché[h] **2** alledaags iets

²commonplace (adj) **1** afgezaagd, clichématig **2** alledaags, gewoon, doorsnee

common-room 1 docentenkamer **2** studentenvertrek[h], leerlingenkamer

the **Commons** (leden van het) Lagerhuis
Commonwealth Britse Gemenebest
commotion 1 beroering, onrust, opschudding **2** rumoer^h, lawaai^h, herrie
communal gemeenschappelijk: ~ *life* gemeenschapsleven
commune in nauw contact staan, gevoelens uitwisselen, zich één voelen: ~ *with friends* een intiem gesprek met vrienden hebben; ~ *with nature* zich één voelen met de natuur
communicable 1 besmettelijk **2** overdraagbaar [of ideas]
¹**communicate** (vb) **1** communiceren, contact hebben **2** in verbinding staan: *our living room ~s with the kitchen* onze woonkamer staat in verbinding met de keuken
²**communicate** (vb) overbrengen, bekendmaken, doorgeven
communication 1 mededeling, boodschap, bericht^h **2** verbinding, contact^h, communicatie **3** het overbrengen [of ideas, diseases] **4** (-s) verbindingen, communicatiemiddelen
communion 1 kerkgenootschap^h, gemeente, gemeenschap **2** gemeenschappelijkheid
Communion [Roman Catholicism] communie; [Protestant] avondmaal^h
communiqué bekendmaking, bericht^h, communiqué^h
communism communisme^h
¹**communist** (n) communist
²**communist** (adj) communistisch
community 1 gemeenschap, bevolkingsgroep **2** overeenkomst(igheid), gemeenschappelijkheid: *a ~ of interests* gemeenschappelijke belangen **3** [Roman Catholicism] congregatie, broederschap **4** bevolking, publiek^h, gemeenschap
community centre buurtcentrum^h, wijkcentrum^h
community service taakstraf
commutation 1 omzetting [of punishment]; vermindering **2** afkoopsom, het afkopen **3** het pendelen
¹**commute** (vb) pendelen
²**commute** (vb) **1** verlichten, verminderen, omzetten: ~ *a sentence from death to life imprisonment* een vonnis van doodstraf in levenslang omzetten **2** veranderen, omzetten, afkopen: ~ *an insurance policy into* (or: *for*) *a lump sum* een verzekeringspolis afkopen voor een uitkering ineens
commuter forens, pendelaar
¹**compact** (n) **1** overeenkomst, verbond^h, verdrag^h **2** poederdoos **3** [Am] middelgrote auto, compact car
²**compact** (adj) **1** compact, samengeperst **2** compact, bondig, beknopt
³**compact** (vb) een overeenkomst aangaan

⁴**compact** (vb) samenpakken, samenpersen
companion 1 metgezel, kameraad **2** vennoot, partner **3** handboek^h, gids, wegwijzer **4** één van twee bij elkaar horende exemplaren
companionship kameraadschap; gezelschap^h
company 1 gezelschap^h: *in ~ with* samen met; *request the ~ of* uitnodigen; *keep ~ with* omgaan met, verkering hebben met **2** bezoek^h, gasten: *have* (or: *expect*) ~ bezoek hebben (*or:* krijgen) **3** compagnonschap^h, compagnon(s) **4** gezelschap^h: *theatre* ~ toneelgezelschap **5** onderneming, firma, bedrijf^h: [econ] *limited* ~ naamloze vennootschap **6** gilde^h, genootschap^h **7** [mil] compagnie **8** [shipp] (gehele) bemanning
comparable vergelijkbaar: *my car is not ~ with* (or: *to*) *yours* mijn auto is niet met die van jou te vergelijken
¹**comparative** (n) vergrotende trap
²**comparative** (adj) betrekkelijk, relatief: *they live in ~ comfort now* het gaat ze nu verhoudingsgewijs beter
¹**compare** (n): [form] *beyond* (or: *past, without*) ~ onvergelijkbaar, weergaloos
²**compare** (vb) vergelijkbaar zijn, de vergelijking kunnen doorstaan: *our results ~ poorly with theirs* onze resultaten steken mager bij de hunne af
³**compare** (vb) vergelijken: *I'm tall ~d to him* vergeleken bij hem ben ik lang; ~ *down* jezelf vergelijken met minder bevoordeelden en daardoor beseffen dat je het zelf zo slecht nog niet hebt
comparison vergelijking: *bear* (or: *stand*) ~ *with* de vergelijking kunnen doorstaan met; *by* (or: *in*) ~ *with* in vergelijking met
compartment compartiment^h, vakje^h, (trein)coupé, (gescheiden) ruimte
compass 1 kompas^h: *the points of the* ~ de kompasrichtingen, de windstreken **2** (-es) passer: *a pair of ~es* een passer
compassion medelijden^h
compassionate medelevend, medelijdend: ~ *leave* verlof wegens familieomstandigheden
compatible verenigbaar, bij elkaar passend, aansluitbaar; bruikbaar in combinatie [of technical appliances]: ~ *systems* onderling verenigbare systemen; ~ *with* aangepast aan; *drinking is not ~ with driving* drinken en autorijden verdragen elkaar niet
compatriot landgenoot, landgenote
compel (af)dwingen, verplichten, noodzaken
compelling fascinerend, onweerstaanbaar, meeslepend
¹**compensate** (vb) **1** (+ for) dienen als tegenwicht (voor), opwegen (tegen) **2** compenseren, goedmaken

²**compensate** (vb) vergoeden, vereffenen, goedmaken
compensation compensatie, (onkosten)vergoeding, schadevergoeding, schadeloosstelling
compere conferencier, ceremoniemeester, presentator
compete concurreren, strijden, wedijveren: *competing interests* (tegen)strijdige belangen
competence (vak)bekwaamheid, vaardigheid, (des)kundigheid
competent 1 competent, (vak)bekwaam, (des)kundig **2** voldoende, toereikend, adequaat
competition 1 wedstrijd, toernooiʰ, concursʰ, competitie **2** rivaliteit, concurrentie
competitive concurrerend: ~ *examination* vergelijkend examen
competitor concurrent, (wedstrijd)deelnemer, rivaal
compilation samenstelling, bundel(ing), verzameling
compile samenstellen, bijeenbrengen, bijeengaren, verzamelen
complacency [depr] zelfgenoegzaamheid
complacent [oft depr] zelfvoldaan, zelfingenomen
complain klagen, zich beklagen, een klacht indienen: ~ *about* sth. *to* s.o. bij iem. ergens over klagen
complaint 1 klacht [also law]; grief, kwaal: *lodge* a ~ *against* s.o. een aanklacht tegen iem. indienen **2** beklagʰ, het klagen: *no cause* (or: *ground*) *for* ~ geen reden tot klagen
¹**complement** (n) **1** aanvulling **2** vereiste hoeveelheid, voltallige bemanning
²**complement** (vb) aanvullen, afronden
complementary aanvullend
¹**complete** (adj) **1** compleet, volkomen, totaal **2** klaar, voltooid
²**complete** (vb) vervolledigen, afmaken; invullen [a form]
completion voltooiing, afwerking, afronding
¹**complex** (n) **1** complexʰ [eg for sports]; samengesteld geheelʰ **2** [psychology] complexʰ; [inform, fig] obsessie
²**complex** (adj) gecompliceerd, samengesteld, ingewikkeld
complexion 1 huidskleur, uiterlijkʰ **2** aanzienʰ, voorkomenʰ, aard: *that changed the ~ of the matter* dat gaf de kwestie een heel ander aanzien
complexity 1 complicatie, moeilijkheid, probleemʰ **2** gecompliceerdheid, complexiteit
compliance 1 volgzaamheid, meegaandheid: *in ~ with* your wish overeenkomstig uw wens; ~ *with* the law naleving van de wet **2** onderdanigheid, onderworpenheid

compliant volgzaam, onderdanig
complicate 1 ingewikkeld(er) worden (maken) **2** verergeren
complicated gecompliceerd; ingewikkeld
complication complicatie, (extra, onvoorziene) moeilijkheid
complicity medeplichtigheid: ~ *in* medeplichtigheid aan
¹**compliment** (n) complimentʰ: *the ~s of the season* prettige feestdagen [at Christmas, New Year]; *pay* s.o. *a ~, pay* a ~ *to* s.o. *(on* sth.*)* iem. een complimentje (over iets) maken; *my ~s to* your wife de groeten aan uw vrouw
²**compliment** (vb) (+ on) complimenteren (met/over), een compliment maken, gelukwensen
complimentary 1 vleiend **2** gratis, bij wijze van geste gegeven: ~ *copy* presentexemplaar; ~ *tickets* vrijkaartjes
comply zich schikken, gehoorzamen: *refuse to* ~ weigeren mee te werken; ~ *with* a) zich neerleggen bij, gehoor geven aan; b) naleven [law]
¹**component** (n) component, onderdeelʰ, elementʰ
²**component** (adj) samenstellend: ~ *parts* onderdelen
comport [form] zich gedragen: *he ~ed himself with dignity* hij gedroeg zich waardig
compose 1 schrijven [literary or musical work]; componeren **2** zetten [printed matter] **3** samenstellen, vormen, in elkaar zetten: ~*d of* bestaande uit **4** tot bedaren brengen, bedaren, kalmeren: ~ *yourself* kalm nou maar **5** bijleggen [difference of opinion]
composed kalm, rustig, beheerst
composer 1 componist **2** auteur; schrijver [of letter, poem]
¹**composite** (n) samengesteld geheelʰ, samenstelling
²**composite** (adj) samengesteld: ~ *photograph* montagefoto, compositiefoto
composition 1 samenstelling, compositie, opbouw: *a piece* of his own ~ een stuk van eigen hand **2** het componeren, het (op)stellen **3** kunstwerkʰ, muziekstukʰ, compositie, dichtwerkʰ, tekst **4** opstelʰ, verhandeling **5** mengselʰ, samengesteld materiaalʰ, kunststof: *chemical* ~*s* chemische mengsels **6** het letterzetten
compost compost
composure (zelf)beheersing
¹**compound 1** samenstelʰ, mengselʰ, (chemische) verbinding **2** omheinde groep gebouwen, (krijgs)gevangenkampʰ; omheind gebiedʰ [for cattle]
²**compound** (adj) samengesteld, gemengd, vermengd, gecombineerd: ~ *fracture* gecompliceerde breuk; ~ *interest* samengestelde interest, rente op rente
³**compound** (vb) **1** dooreenmengen, ver-

mengen, samenstellen, opbouwen: ~ *a reci-pe* een recept klaarmaken **2** vergroten, verergeren: *the situation was ~ed by his absence* door zijn afwezigheid werd de zaak bemoeilijk
comprehend 1 (be)vatten, begrijpen, doorgronden **2** omvatten
comprehension 1 begrip^h, bevattingsvermogen^h **2** [educ] begripstest, leestoets, luistertoets, tekstbegrip^h **3** (toepassings)bereik^h
¹comprehensive (n) scholengemeenschap
²comprehensive (adj) allesomvattend, veelomvattend, uitvoerig, uitgebreid: ~ *insurance* allriskverzekering; ~ *school* middenschool
¹compress (n) kompres^h, drukverband^h
²compress (vb) samendrukken, samenpersen: *~ed air* perslucht
compression 1 samenpersing **2** dichtheid, compactheid
compressor compressor, perspomp
comprise bestaan uit, bevatten: *the house ~s five rooms* het huis telt vijf kamers
¹compromise (n) compromis^h, tussenoplossing, middenweg, tussenweg
²compromise (vb) een compromis sluiten
³compromise (vb) **1** door een compromis regelen **2** in opspraak brengen, de goede naam aantasten: *you ~d yourself by accepting that money* door dat geld aan te nemen heb je je gecompromitteerd **3** in gevaar brengen
compulsion dwang, verplichting, druk
compulsive dwingend, gedwongen, verplicht: *a ~ smoker* een verslaafd roker
compulsory 1 verplicht: ~ *military service* dienstplicht; [educ] ~ *subject* verplicht vak **2** noodzakelijk
compunction schuldgevoel^h, (gewetens)bezwaar^h, wroeging
compute berekenen, uitrekenen
computer computer
computerate computervaardig
computer dummy digibeet
computer game computerspel^h: *play a ~* gamen
¹computerize (vb) verwerken met een computer [information]; opslaan in een computer
²computerize (vb) computeriseren, overschakelen op computers
computer-literate vaardig in het gebruik van de computer, goed overweg kunnend met computers
computer moron digibeet
computing computerisering, het werken met computers, computerwerk^h
comrade kameraad, vriend, makker: *~s in arms* wapenbroeders
comradeship kameraadschap(pelijkheid), vriendschap

¹con (n) **1** *contra* tegenargument^h, nadeel^h, bezwaar^h: *the pros and ~s of this proposal* de voors en tegens van dit voorstel **2** tegenstem(mer) **3** [inform] oplichterij **4** [inform] *convict* veroordeelde, (oud-)gevangene
²con (vb) **1** [inform] oplichten, afzetten, bezwendelen: ~ *s.o. out of his money* iem. zijn geld afhandig maken **2** [inform] ompraten, bewerken, overhalen: *he ~ned me into signing* hij heeft me mijn handtekening weten te ontfutselen
con-artist [inform] oplichter
concave hol(rond)
conceal verbergen, verstoppen, achterhouden, geheimhouden: *~ed turning* let op, bocht [as a traffic sign]
concealment geheimhouding, verzwijging
¹concede (vb) zich gewonnen geven, opgeven
²concede (vb) **1** toegeven: ~ *defeat* zijn nederlaag erkennen **2** opgeven, prijsgeven
conceit verwaandheid, ijdelheid, verbeelding
conceited verwaand, ijdel, zelfingenomen
conceivable voorstelbaar, denkbaar, mogelijk
¹conceive (vb) **1** bedenken, ontwerpen: *she ~d a dislike for me* ze kreeg een hekel aan mij **2** opvatten, begrijpen
²conceive (vb) ontvangen [child]; zwanger worden (van)
conceive of zich voorstellen, zich indenken
¹concentrate (vb) (+ (up)on) zich concentreren (op), zich toeleggen
²concentrate (vb) concentreren: ~ *one's attention on* zijn aandacht richten op
concentrated 1 geconcentreerd, van sterk gehalte **2** krachtig, intens
concentration concentratie: *power of ~* concentratievermogen
concept idee^h, voorstelling, denkbeeld^h
conception 1 ontstaan^h [of idea etc]; ontwerp^h, vinding **2** voorstelling, opvatting, begrip^h: *I have no ~ of what he meant* ik heb er geen idee van wat hij bedoelde **3** bevruchting [also fig]
conceptual conceptueel: ~ *art* conceptuele kunst; ideeënkunst
¹concern (n) **1** aangelegenheid, belang^h, interesse: *your drinking habits are no ~ of mine* uw drinkgewoonten zijn mijn zaak niet **2** (be)zorg(dheid), begaanheid, (gevoel^h van) betrokkenheid: *no cause for ~* geen reden tot ongerustheid **3** bedrijf^h, onderneming, firma: *going ~* bloeiende onderneming **4** (aan)deel^h, belang^h
²concern (vb) **1** aangaan, van belang zijn voor: *where money is ~ed* als het om geld gaat; *to whom it may ~* aan wie dit leest [salutation of open letter]; *as far as I'm ~ed* wat

mij betreft, voor mijn part **2** betreffen, gaan over **3** zich aantrekken, zich interesseren: ~ *o.s.* **about** (or: *with*) *sth.* zich ergens voor inzetten, zorgen om maken
concerned 1 bezorgd, ongerust **2** geïnteresseerd, betrokken: *all the people* ~ alle (erbij) betrokkenen, alle geïnteresseerden; ~ *in* betrokken bij ‖ *be* ~ *with* betreffen, gaan over
concerning betreffende, in verband met, over
concert concert[h], muziekuitvoering ‖ *in* ~ in onderlinge samenwerking, in harmonie
concerted gecombineerd, gezamenlijk
concession 1 concessie(verlening), vergunning, tegemoetkoming **2** korting; (prijs)-reductie [with discount card]
conciliate 1 tot bedaren brengen, kalmeren **2** verzoenen, in overeenstemming brengen
conciliation verzoening
concise beknopt, kort maar krachtig
¹conclude (vb) **1** eindigen, aflopen **2** tot een conclusie (besluit/akkoord) komen
²conclude (vb) **1** beëindigen, (af)sluiten, afronden **2** (af)sluiten, tot stand brengen: *conclude an agreement* een overeenkomst sluiten **3** concluderen, vaststellen
conclusion 1 besluit[h], beëindiging, slot[h]: *in* ~ samenvattend, tot besluit **2** conclusie, gevolgtrekking: *come* to (or: *draw*, *reach*) ~s conclusies trekken; *a* *foregone* ~ een bij voorbaat uitgemaakte zaak; *jump* to ~s (or: *to a* ~) te snel conclusies trekken
conclusive afdoend, overtuigend, beslissend: ~ *evidence* overtuigend bewijs
concoct 1 samenstellen, bereiden, brouwen **2** [depr] verzinnen, bedenken, bekokstoven: ~ *an* *excuse* een smoes verzinnen
concord 1 verdrag[h], overeenkomst, akkoord[h] **2** harmonie, eendracht, overeenstemming **3** [linguistics] congruentie, overeenkomst
concourse 1 menigte **2** samenkomst, samenloop, bijeenkomst: *a fortunate* ~ *of* *circumstances* een gelukkige samenloop van omstandigheden **3** plein[h], promenade, (stations)hal
¹concrete (n) beton[h]
²concrete (adj) **1** concreet, echt, tastbaar **2** betonnen, beton-: ~ *jungle* betonwoestijn
concrete mixer betonmolen
concubine concubine, bijzit
concur samenvallen, overeenstemmen ‖ ~ *with* *s.o.* (or: *in* *sth.*) het eens zijn met iem. (iets)
concurrent samenvallend; gelijktijdig (optredend, voorkomend)
concussion 1 schok, stoot, klap **2** hersenschudding
condemn 1 veroordelen, schuldig verkla-

ren: ~*ed* *to* *spend one's life in poverty* gedoemd zijn leven lang armoede te lijden **2** afkeuren, verwerpen
condemnation veroordeling, afkeuring, verwerping
condensation condensatie, condens, condenswater[h]
condense condenseren [also fig]; indampen, bekorten, inkorten, verkorten: ~*d* *milk* gecondenseerde melk
condescend 1 zich verlagen, zich verwaardigen **2** neerbuigend doen, neerkijken
condescension neerbuigendheid
condiment kruiderij, specerij
¹condition (n) **1** (lichamelijke) toestand, (lichamelijke) staat, (lichamelijke) conditie: *she is in no* ~ *to work* ze is niet in staat om te werken; *in* (or: *out of*) ~ in (or: niet in) conditie **2** voorwaarde, conditie, beding[h]: *on* ~ *that* op voorwaarde dat **3** omstandigheid: *favourable* ~s gunstige omstandigheden **4** [med] afwijking, aandoening, kwaal
²condition (vb) bepalen, vaststellen, afhangen (van): *a nation's expenditure is* ~*ed* *by* *its income* de bestedingsmogelijkheden van een land worden bepaald door het nationale inkomen
conditional voorwaardelijk, conditioneel: [linguistics] ~ *mood* conditionalis, voorwaardelijke wijs
conditioner crèmespoeling
condolence 1 deelneming, sympathie, medeleven[h] **2** (-s) condoleantie, rouwbeklag[h]: *please accept my* ~s *on* … mag ik mijn deelneming betuigen met …
condom condoom[h], kapotje[h]
condominium [Am] **1** flatgebouw met koopflats **2** koopflat
condone vergeven
conducive [form] bevorderlijk; gunstig
¹conduct (n) gedrag[h], houding, handelwijze
²conduct (vb) **1** leiden, rondleiden, begeleiden: ~*ed* *tour* verzorgde reis, rondleiding **2** [mus] dirigeren, dirigent zijn (van) **3** (zich) gedragen: ~ *o.s.* zich gedragen **4** [science, elec] geleiden
conduction [science] geleiding, conductie
conductor 1 conducteur **2** [mus] dirigent, orkestleider **3** [science, elec] geleider
cone 1 kegel **2** (ijs)hoorntje[h] **3** dennenappel
confabulation 1 verzinsel[h] **2** praatje[h], babbeltje[h]
confectionery 1 banketbakkerij, banketbakkerswinkel **2** gebak[h], zoetigheid, suikergoed[h]
confederation (con)federatie, bond, verbond[h]
¹confer (vb) confereren, beraadslagen
²confer (vb) verlenen, uitreiken, schenken: ~ *a knighthood on s.o.* iem. een ridderorde ver-

lenen
conference conferentie, congres[h]
confess 1 bekennen, erkennen, toegeven: / *must ~ I like it* ik moet zeggen dat ik het wel prettig vind **2** [rel] (op)biechten, belijden
confession 1 bekentenis, erkenning, toegeving: *on his own ~* naar hij zelf toegeeft **2** [rel] biecht **3** [rel] (geloofs)belijdenis
confessor [rel] **1** biechtvader **2** belijder
confetti confetti
confidant vertrouweling, vertrouwensman
confide toevertrouwen, in vertrouwen mededelen
confide in vertrouwen, in vertrouwen nemen
confidence 1 (zelf)vertrouwen[h], geloof[h]: *in ~* in vertrouwen, vertrouwelijk **2** vertrouwelijke mededeling, geheim[h]
confidence trick oplichterij
confident (tref)zeker, zelfverzekerd, overtuigd
confidential 1 vertrouwelijk **2** vertrouwens-, privé-, vertrouwd
confine 1 beperken **2** opsluiten, insluiten: *be ~d to bed* het bed moeten houden
confined krap; eng, nauw
confinement opsluiting: *solitary ~* eenzame opsluiting
confirm 1 bevestigen, bekrachtigen: *~ by letter* (or: *in writing*) schriftelijk bevestigen **2** bevestigen, goedkeuren: *he hasn't been ~ed in office yet* zijn benoeming moet nog bevestigd worden **3** [Protestantism] confirmeren, (als lidmaat) aannemen **4** [Roman Catholicism] vormen, het vormsel toedienen
confirmation 1 bevestiging, bekrachtiging, goedkeuring: *evidence in ~ of your statement* bewijzen die uw bewering staven **2** [Protestantism] confirmatie, bevestiging als lidmaat **3** [Roman Catholicism] (heilig) vormsel[h]
confiscate in beslag nemen, verbeurd verklaren, afnemen
conflagration grote brand [of forests, buildings]; vuurzee
[1]**conflict** (n) strijd, conflict(situatie), onenigheid
[2]**conflict** (vb) **1** onverenigbaar zijn, in tegenspraak zijn, botsen: *~ing interests* (tegen)strijdige belangen **2** strijden, botsen, in conflict komen
confluence 1 toeloop, menigte **2** samenvloeiing
conform zich conformeren, zich aanpassen
conformity 1 overeenkomst, gelijkvormigheid: *in ~ with* in overeenstemming met, overeenkomstig **2** aanpassing, naleving
confound 1 verbazen, in verwarring brengen, versteld doen staan **2** verwarren, door elkaar halen
confront confronteren, tegenover elkaar

plaatsen; [fig] het hoofd bieden aan
confrontation 1 confrontatie **2** het tegenover (elkaar) stellen
confuse in de war brengen, door elkaar halen, verwarren
confused verward, wanordelijk, rommelig
confusion verwarring, wanorde
congeal (doen) stollen
congenial 1 (geest)verwant, gelijkgestemd, sympathiek **2** passend, geschikt, aangenaam
congenital 1 aangeboren **2** [fig] geboren: *a ~ thief* een aartsdief
congestion op(een)hoping, opstopping, verstopping
congestion charging rekeningrijden[h]
conglomeration bundeling, verzameling
Congo Congo
[1]**Congolese** (n) Congolees, Congolese
[2]**Congolese** (adj) Congolees
congratulate gelukwensen, feliciteren: *~ o.s. on* zichzelf gelukkig prijzen met
congratulation gelukwens, felicitatie: *~s!* gefeliciteerd!
congregation 1 bijeenkomst, verzameling **2** verzamelde groep mensen, menigte, groep **3** [rel] gemeente, congregatie
congress congres[h], vergadering, bijeenkomst
Congress [Am] het Congres
congruity gepastheid, overeenstemming, overeenkomst
conic(al) m.b.t. een kegel, kegelvormig, conisch
conifer naaldboom, conifeer
conjecture 1 gis(sing), (vage) schatting, vermoeden[h] **2** giswerk[h], speculatie, gokwerk[h]
conjugation 1 [linguistics] vervoeging **2** vereniging, verbinding, koppeling
conjunction 1 verbinding; combinatie, het samengaan: *in ~ with* samen met **2** [linguistics] voegwoord[h]
conjuncture (kritieke) toestand, samenloop van omstandigheden, (crisis)situatie
[1]**conjure** (vb) toveren, goochelen, manipuleren
[2]**conjure** (vb) (te voorschijn) toveren, oproepen, voor de geest roepen
conjurer goochelaar, illusionist
conk [inform] een oplawaai geven
conker (wilde) kastanje, paardenkastanje
con man [inform] *confidence man* oplichter; zwendelaar
[1]**connect** (vb) **1** in verbinding komen, in verband staan: *~ up* in verbinding komen **2** aansluiten, aansluiting hebben
[2]**connect** (vb) **1** verbinden, aaneensluiten, aaneenschakelen; doorverbinden [telephone]: *the islands are ~ed by a bridge* de eilanden staan via een brug met elkaar in ver-

binding; ~ *up* verbinden **2** (+ with) in verband brengen (met), een verbinding leggen tussen
connection 1 verbinding, verband^h, aansluiting: *miss* one's ~ zijn aansluiting missen [of bus, train]; *in* ~ *with* in verband met **2** samenhang, coherentie **3** connectie, betrekking, relatie **4** verwant, familielid^h **5** verbindingsstuk^h **6** [elec] lichtpunt^h, stopcontact^h, (wand)contactdoos
connive 1 oogluikend toelaten, (even) de andere kant opkijken: ~ *at* oogluikend toelaten, door de vingers zien **2** samenspannen, samenzweren
connotation (bij)betekenis, connotatie
¹conquer (vb) overwinnen, de (over)winnaar zijn
²conquer (vb) **1** veroveren, innemen; bemachtigen [also fig] **2** verslaan, overwinnen, bedwingen: ~ *mountains* bergen bedwingen
conqueror veroveraar, overwinnaar: *William the* Conqueror Willem de Veroveraar
conquest verovering, overwinning; het bedwingen [of a mountain]: *the* Norman Conquest de Normandische verovering
conscience geweten^h: *in all* ~ met een gerust geweten, waarachtig, werkelijk
conscientious plichtsgetrouw, zorgvuldig: ~ *objector* gewetensbezwaarde, principiële dienstweigeraar
conscious 1 bewust, denkend **2** welbewust, opzettelijk **3** (zich) bewust **4** bewust, bij kennis
consciousness 1 bewustzijn^h: *lose* ~ het bewustzijn verliezen **2** gevoel^h, besef^h
¹conscript (n) dienstplichtige
²conscript (vb) oproepen: ~*ed into* the army ingelijfd bij het leger
conscription dienstplicht
consecutive opeenvolgend: *on two* ~ *days* twee dagen achter elkaar
consensus algemene opvatting, overeenstemming
¹consent (n) toestemming, instemming, goedkeuring: *by* **common** (or: **general**) ~ met algemene stemmen
²consent (vb) toestemmen, zijn goedkeuring geven, zich bereid verklaren: ~ *to* sth. iets toestaan
consequence 1 consequentie, gevolg^h, gevolgtrekking, resultaat^h **2** belang^h, gewicht^h: *of no* ~ van geen belang
consequently dus; derhalve
conservation 1 behoud^h, instandhouding: ~ *of* **energy** behoud van energie **2** milieubeheer^h, milieubescherming, natuurbescherming, monumentenzorg
conservation area 1 (beschermd) natuurgebied^h **2** beschermd stads-, dorpsgezicht
conservationist milieubeschermer, natuurbeschermer

conservatism conservatisme^h, behoudzucht
¹conservative (n) conservatief, behoudend persoon; [pol] lid^h van de Conservatieve Partij
²conservative (adj) **1** conservatief, behoudend, traditioneel (ingesteld) **2** voorzichtig, gematigd, bescheiden: *a* ~ **estimate** een voorzichtige schatting
conservatory 1 serre, (planten)kas, broeikas **2** conservatorium^h, muziekacademie, toneelschool
¹conserve (n) jam, ingemaakte vruchten
²conserve (vb) **1** behouden, bewaren, goed houden **2** inmaken
consider 1 overwegen, nadenken over **2** beschouwen, zien: *we* ~ *him (to be) a* **man** *of* genius we beschouwen hem als een genie **3** in aanmerking nemen, rekening houden met, letten op
considerable aanzienlijk, behoorlijk: *a* ~ *time* geruime tijd
considerate attent, voorkomend, vriendelijk
consideration 1 overweging, aandacht: *take* sth. *into* ~ ergens rekening mee houden **2** (punt^h van) overweging, (beweeg)reden **3** voorkomendheid, attentheid, begrip^h
¹considering (adv) [at the end of a sentence] alles bij elkaar (genomen): *she has been very successful*, ~ eigenlijk heeft ze het ver gebracht
²considering (prep) gezien, rekening houdend met
consign 1 [com] verzenden, versturen, leveren **2** overdragen, toevertrouwen, in handen stellen: ~ *one's child* **to** s.o.'s care zijn kind aan iemands zorg toevertrouwen
consignment (ver)zending
consistency 1 consequentheid, samenhang **2** dikte, stroperigheid
consistent 1 consequent, samenhangend **2** overeenkomend, kloppend, verenigbaar: *be* ~ *with* kloppen met
consist in bestaan in, gevormd worden door: *my duties mainly* ~ *word processing and filing* mijn werkzaamheden bestaan voornamelijk in tekstverwerken en archiveren
consist of bestaan uit, opgebouwd zijn uit: *the convoy consisted of sixteen ships* het konvooi bestond uit zestien schepen
consolation troost, troostrijke gedachte
¹console (n) **1** steunstuk^h, draagsteen **2** toetsenbord^h, (bedienings)paneel^h, controlebord, schakelbord^h; [comp] console **3** radio-, televisie-, grammofoonmeubel^h
²console (vb) troosten, bemoedigen(d toespreken), opbeuren
¹consolidate (vb) **1** hechter, steviger worden **2** zich aaneensluiten, samengaan, fuseren

²**consolidate** (vb) **1** verstevigen, stabiliseren **2** (tot een geheel) verenigen
consonant medeklinker
¹**consort** (n) gade, gemaalʰ, gemalin
²**consort** (vb) omgaan, optrekken: ~ *with criminals* omgaan met misdadigers
consortium consortiumʰ; syndicaatʰ
conspicuous opvallend, in het oog lopend, opmerkelijk: *be ~ by one's absence* schitteren door afwezigheid
conspiracy samenzwering, complotʰ; [law] samenspanning
conspirator samenzweerder
conspire samenzweren; samenspannen
constable 1 agent, politieman **2** [Am] (ongeüniformeerde) politiefunctionaris onder sheriff; [roughly] vrederechter
constabulary politie(korpsʰ), politiemacht
constancy 1 standvastigheid, onveranderlijkheid **2** trouw
constant 1 constant, voortdurend, onveranderlijk **2** trouw, loyaal
constellation sterrenbeeldʰ; constellatie [also fig]
consternation opschudding
constipation constipatie, verstopping
constituency 1 kiesdistrictʰ **2** achterban, kiezers
¹**constituent** (n) **1** kiezer, ingezetene van een kiesdistrict **2** onderdeelʰ, bestanddeelʰ
²**constituent** (adj): ~ *body* kiescollege
constitute vormen, (samen) uitmaken, vertegenwoordigen
constitution 1 grondwet **2** conditie, gesteldheid
constitutional grondwettig, grondwettelijk
constrain (af)dwingen, verplichten, noodzaken: *feel ~ed to do sth.* zich ergens toe verplicht voelen
constraint 1 beperking, restrictie **2** dwang, verplichting **3** gedwongenheid, geforceerde stemming, geremdheid
constrict vernauwen, versmallen, beperken
construct construeren, in elkaar zetten, bouwen
construction 1 interpretatie, voorstelling van zaken, uitleg **2** constructie, aanbouw, aanleg, (huizen)bouw, bouwwerkʰ: *under ~* in aanbouw
constructive constructief, opbouwend, positief
construe interpreteren, opvatten, verklaren: *giving in now will be ~d as a weakness* nu toegeven zal als zwakheid worden uitgelegd
consul consul
consular consulair
consulate consulaatʰ
¹**consult** (vb) overleggen, beraadslagen: ~ *about* (or: *upon*) beraadslagen over

²**consult** (vb) raadplegen
consultancy 1 baan als consulterend geneesheer **2** baan als (bedrijfs)adviseur
consultant 1 consulterend geneesheer **2** consulent, (bedrijfs)adviseur, deskundige
consultation 1 vergadering, bespreking **2** overlegʰ, raadpleging, consultʰ: *in ~ with* in overleg met
consume 1 consumeren, verorberen **2** verbruiken, gebruiken **3** verteren, wegvreten, verwoesten: ~*d by* (or: *with*) *hate* verteerd door haat
consumer consument, verbruiker, koper
consumer goods consumptiegoederen
consumerism [Am] consumentismeʰ; overdreven consumptiedrang
consumer society consumptiemaatschappij
consummation 1 (eind)doelʰ **2** voltooiing, bekroning **3** huwelijksgemeenschap
consumption 1 consumptie, verbruikʰ, (ver)tering: *these oranges are unfit for ~* deze sinaasappelen zijn niet geschikt voor consumptie **2** verwoesting, aantasting
¹**contact** (n) **1** contactʰ, contactpersoon **2** contactlens **3** contactʰ [also elec]; aanraking
²**contact** (vb) **1** in contact brengen, een contact leggen tussen **2** contact opnemen met
contagion 1 besmetting **2** besmettelijke invloed; [fig] virusʰ
contagious besmet(telijk); [fig] aanstekelijk
contain 1 bevatten, tellen, inhouden **2** beheersen, onder controle houden, bedwingen: ~ *yourself!* beheers je!, hou je in!
container 1 houder, vatʰ, bak, doosjeʰ, bus, verpakking **2** container
contamination vervuiling, besmetting
¹**contemplate** (vb) nadenken, peinzen, in gedachten verzonken zijn
²**contemplate** (vb) **1** beschouwen **2** nadenken over, overdenken, zich verdiepen in **3** overwegen, zich bezinnen op
contemplation overpeinzing, bezinning, overdenking: *lost in ~* in gepeins verzonken
contemplative bedachtzaam, beschouwend
contemporaneous gelijktijdig, in de tijd samenvallend
¹**contemporary** (n) **1** tijdgenoot **2** leeftijdgenoot, jaargenoot
²**contemporary** (adj) **1** gelijktijdig, uit dezelfde tijd **2** even oud **3** eigentijds, hedendaags
contempt minachting, verachting: *beneath ~* beneden alle peil
contemptuous minachtend, verachtend
¹**contend** (vb) wedijveren, strijden: ~ *with difficulties* met problemen (te) kampen (hebben)

²**contend** (vb) betogen, (met klem) beweren
contender **1** [sport] uitdager **2** mededinger
¹**content** (n) **1** capaciteit, volumeʰ, omvang, inhoud(smaat) **2** inhoud, onderwerpʰ **3** gehalteʰ: *sugar* ~ suikergehalte, hoeveelheid suiker; *nutritional* ~ voedingswaarde **4** (-s) inhoud [of bottle, bag] **5** (-s) inhoud(sopgave) [of book]: *table of* ~s inhoudsopgave
²**content** (adj) tevreden, blij, content
content curation [Am] contentbeheerʰ
contented tevreden, blij
contention **1** standpuntʰ, stellingname, opvatting **2** geschilʰ, conflictʰ
contentious **1** ruzieachtig **2** controversieel; aanvechtbaar
contentment tevredenheid, voldoening
content provider informatieleverancier, dienstenaanbieder
¹**contest** (n) **1** krachtmeting, strijd, (kracht)proef **2** (wed)strijd, prijsvraag, concoursʰ
²**contest** (vb) twisten, strijden: ~ *against* (or: *with*) strijden met
³**contest** (vb) betwisten, aanvechten
contestant **1** kandidaat, deelnemer (aan wedstrijd), strijdende partij **2** betwister, aanvechter
context context [also fig]; verbandʰ, samenhang: *my words were quoted out of* ~ mijn woorden zijn uit hun verband gerukt
contiguity **1** aangrenzing, naburigheid **2** opeenvolging, aan(een)sluiting
continence zelfbeheersing, matigheid
continent continentʰ, werelddeelʰ
the **Continent** vastelandʰ (van Europa) [opposite Great Britain]
¹**continental** (n) vastelander, bewoner van het Europese vasteland; [Am also] Europeaan
²**continental** (adj) continentaal, het vasteland van Europa betreffende: ~ *breakfast* ontbijt met koffie en croissants enz.
contingency eventualiteit, onvoorziene gebeurtenis (uitgave)
contingency plan rampenplanʰ
¹**contingent** (n) **1** afvaardiging, vertegenwoordiging **2** [mil] (troepen)contingentʰ
²**contingent** (adj) **1** toevallig, onvoorzien **2** mogelijk, eventueel **3** bijkomend, incidenteel **4** voorwaardelijk, afhankelijk: *our success is* ~ *(up)on his cooperation* ons slagen hangt van zijn medewerking af
continual [depr] aanhoudend, voortdurend, onophoudelijk
continuation voortzetting, vervolgʰ, continuering
¹**continue** (vb) **1** doorgaan, voortgaan, verder gaan, volhouden, zich voortzetten **2** (in stand) blijven, voortduren, continueren: *the weather* ~s *fine* het mooie weer houdt aan **3** vervolgen, verder gaan: ~d *on page 106*

lees verder op bladzijde 106
²**continue** (vb) **1** voortzetten, (weer) doorgaan, voortgaan, verder gaan met, volhouden, vervolgen: *to be* ~d wordt vervolgd **2** handhaven, aanhouden, continueren **3** verlengen
continuity **1** tijdsmatig verloop, samenhang **2** [film] draaiboekʰ **3** [radio, TV] tekstboekʰ, draaiboekʰ, verbindende teksten
continuous ononderbroken, continu: ~ *performance* doorlopende voorstelling
contort verwringen
contortion **1** kronkeling, bocht **2** verwringing, ontwrichting
contour contour [also fig]; omtrek(lijn), vorm
contraband **1** smokkelwaar, smokkelgoedʰ **2** smokkel(handel)
contraception anticonceptie
contraceptive voorbehoed(s)middelʰ
¹**contract** (n) contractʰ, (bindende) overeenkomst, verdragʰ
²**contract** (vb) een overeenkomst, verdrag sluiten, een verbintenis aangaan, contracteren: ~*ing* **parties** contracterende partijen; ~ *out* zich terugtrekken
³**contract** (vb) bij contract regelen, contracteren, aangaan: ~ *out* uitbesteden
⁴**contract** (vb) samentrekken, inkrimpen, slinken
contraction samentrekking, inkorting, verkorting, (barens)wee
contractor **1** aannemer, aannemersbedrijfʰ, handelaar in bouwmaterialen **2** contractant, iem. die een contract aangaat
contradict tegenspreken, in tegenspraak zijn met, ontkennen
contradiction **1** tegenspraak, tegenstrijdigheid: ~ *in* **terms** contradictio in terminis, innerlijke tegenspraak **2** weerlegging
contradictory **1** tegenstrijdig, in tegenspraak: ~ *to* strijdig met **2** ontkennend
contraflow tweerichtingsverkeerʰ op één rijbaan
contrail *condensation trail* condensstreep
contralto alt
contraption gevalʰ, toestand, dingʰ, apparaatʰ
¹**contrary** (n) tegendeelʰ, tegen(over)gesteldeʰ: *on the* ~ integendeel, juist niet; *if I don't hear anything to the* ~ … zonder tegenbericht …
²**contrary** (adj) **1** tegen(over)gesteld, strijdig: ~ *to* tegen … in, ondanks **2** ongunstig, tegenwerkend, averechts: ~ *winds* tegenwind
³**contrary** (adj) tegendraads, weerbarstig, eigenwijs
¹**contrast** (n) contrastʰ, contrastwerking; [fig also] tegenbeeldʰ; verschilʰ: *in* ~ *to* (or: *with*) in tegenstelling tot

contrast · 718

²contrast (vb) contrasteren, (tegen elkaar) afsteken, (een) verschil(len) vertonen: ~ *with* afsteken bij
³contrast (vb) tegenover elkaar stellen, vergelijken
contravene [form] in strijd zijn met; overtreden
contribute een bijdrage leveren, bevorderen: ~ *to* bijdragen tot, medewerken aan
contribution bijdrage, inbreng, contributie
contributor bijdrager
contrite berouwvol, schuldbewust
contrivance 1 apparaat[h], toestel[h], (handig) ding[h] **2** (-s) list, truc, slimmigheid(je[h]) **3** vernuft[h], vernuftigheid, vindingrijkheid
contrive 1 voor elkaar boksen, kans zien om te: *he had ~d to meet her* hij had het zo gepland dat hij haar zou ontmoeten **2** bedenken, uitvinden, ontwerpen **3** beramen, smeden
contrived geforceerd, onnatuurlijk, gemaakt
¹control (n) **1** (-s) bedieningspaneel[h], controlepaneel[h] **2** (-s) controlemiddel[h], beheersingsmechanisme[h] **3** beheersing, controle, zeggenschap: *keep under* ~ bedwingen, in toom houden; *get* (or: *go*) *out of* ~ uit de hand lopen **4** bestuur[h], opzicht[h], toezicht[h], leiding: *be in* ~ de leiding hebben, het voor het zeggen hebben
²control (vb) **1** controleren, leiden, toezicht uitoefenen op, beheren **2** besturen, aan het roer zitten **3** in toom houden, beheersen, onder controle houden
control key controltoets
controller 1 controleur, controlemechanisme[h] **2** afdelingschef, afdelingshoofd[h]
control tower verkeerstoren
controversial 1 controversieel, aanvechtbaar, omstreden **2** tegendraads
controversy 1 strijdpunt[h] **2** onenigheid, verdeeldheid
conundrum 1 raadselachtige kwestie; vraag **2** strikvraag
convalesce herstellen; herstellende zijn [from a disease]; genezen
convalescence herstel(periode), genezing(speriode)
convalescent herstellend, genezend, herstellings-: ~ *hospital* (or: *nursing home*) herstellingsoord
convector warmtewisselaar, kachel
¹convene (vb) bijeenkomen, samenkomen, (zich) vergaderen
²convene (vb) **1** bijeenroepen, samenroepen **2** (voor het gerecht) dagen, dagvaarden
convenience 1 (openbaar) toilet[h], wc, urinoir[h]: *public* ~s openbare toiletten **2** gemak[h], comfort[h]: *his house has all the modern* ~s zijn huis is van alle moderne gemakken

voorzien; *at your earliest* ~ zodra het u gelegen komt
convenience food gemaksvoedsel[h], kant-en-klaarmaaltijd
convenience goods kant-en-klare consumptiegoederen
convenience store buurtwinkel
convenient 1 geschikt, handig: *they were* ~*ly forgotten* zij werden gemakshalve vergeten **2** gunstig gelegen, gemakkelijk bereikbaar
convent (nonnen)klooster[h], kloostergebouw[h], kloostergemeenschap
convention 1 overeenkomst, verdrag[h] **2** bijeenkomst, congres[h], conferentie **3** gewoonte, gebruik[h]
conventional gebruikelijk, traditioneel: ~ *wisdom* algemene opinie
¹converge (vb) samenkomen, samenlopen, samenvallen
²converge (vb) naar één punt leiden, doen samenkomen
conversation gesprek[h], conversatie, praatje[h]: *make* ~ converseren, een gesprek gaande houden
¹converse (n) tegendeel[h], omgekeerde
²converse (adj) tegenovergesteld, omgekeerd
³converse (vb) spreken, converseren
conversion 1 omzetting, overschakeling, omschakeling, omrekening, verbouwing **2** [rel] bekering **3** [rugby, Am football] conversie
¹convert (n) bekeerling
²convert (vb) (een) verandering(en) ondergaan, veranderen, overgaan
³convert (vb) **1** bekeren [also fig]; overhalen **2** omschakelen, overschakelen, omzetten, veranderen, ombouwen, verbouwen, omwisselen, inwisselen, omrekenen: ~ *a loan* een lening converteren
¹convertible (n) cabriolet
²convertible (adj) **1** inwisselbaar, omwisselbaar **2** met vouwdak, met open dak
convex convex, bol(rond)
convey 1 (ver)voeren, transporteren, (ge)leiden **2** meedelen, duidelijk maken, uitdrukken: *his tone* ~*ed his real intention* uit zijn toon bleek zijn werkelijke bedoeling
conveyor vervoerder, transporteur: ~ *belt* transportband, lopende band
¹convict (n) **1** veroordeelde **2** gedetineerde, gevangene
²convict (vb) veroordelen, schuldig bevinden: ~*ed of murder* wegens moord veroordeeld
conviction 1 veroordeling **2** (innerlijke) overtuiging, overtuigdheid, (vaste) mening: *carry* ~ overtuigend zijn
convince overtuigen, overreden, overhalen

convivial 1 (levens)lustig, joviaal, uitgelaten **2** vrolijk
convocation 1 vergadering **2** bijeenroeping
convoluted 1 ingewikkeld; ondoorzichtig **2** [form] (in elkaar) gedraaid; gekronkeld
convoy 1 konvooi^h, geleide^h, escorte^h **2** escortering
convulsion 1 (-s) stuip(trekking), convulsie **2** uitbarsting, verstoring **3** lachsalvo^h, onbedaarlijk gelach^h
^{1}coo (n) roekoe(geluid)^h, gekoer^h
^{2}coo (vb) koeren, kirren, lispelen
^{1}cook (n) kok(kin)
^{2}cook (vb) op het vuur staan, (af)koken, sudderen
^{3}cook (vb) [inform] knoeien met, vervalsen ‖ ~ up verzinnen
^{4}cook (vb) koken, (eten) bereiden
cookbook [Am] kookboek^h
cooker kooktoestel^h, kookplaat, kookstel^h
cookery book kookboek^h
cookie 1 koekje^h; biscuitje^h, kaakje^h **2** [comp] cookie^h
cooky 1 [Am] koekje^h, biscuitje^h **2** [Am; inform] figuur^{+h}, type^h, persoon
^{1}cool (n) **1** koelte, koelheid **2** kalmte, zelfbeheersing, onverstoorbaarheid: *keep your ~ hou je in*
^{2}cool (adj) **1** koel, fris **2** koel, luchtig; licht [of clothing] **3** kalm, rustig, beheerst: *(as) ~ as a cucumber* ijskoud, doodbedaard **4** kil, koel, afstandelijk **5** [inform] koel, ongeëmotioneerd: *a ~ card* (or: *customer, hand*) een gehaaid figuur, sluwe vos
^{3}cool (vb) (af)koelen [also fig]; verkoelen ‖ ~ *it* rustig maar, kalm aan
cooler koeler, koelcel, koeltas; [Am] ijskast
^{1}coop (n) kippenren, kippenhok^h
^{2}coop (vb) opsluiten (in een hok); kooien [of chickens]: ~ *up* (or: *in*) opsluiten, kooien
co-op co-operative coöperatieve onderneming
co-operate samenwerken, meewerken
co-operation 1 coöperatie, samenwerkingsverband^h **2** medewerking, samenwerking, hulp
^{1}co-operative (n) coöperatie, collectief^h, coöperatief bedrijf^h
^{2}co-operative (adj) **1** behulpzaam, meewerkend, bereidwillig **2** coöperatief, op coöperatieve grondslag
^{1}co-ordinate (n) **1** standgenoot, klassengenoot, soortgenoot, gelijke **2** [maths] coördinaat, waarde, grootheid
^{2}co-ordinate (adj) gelijkwaardig, gelijk in rang
^{3}co-ordinate (vb) (harmonieus) samenwerken
^{4}co-ordinate (vb) coördineren, rangschikken (in onderling verband), ordenen

co-ordinator coördinator
coot meerkoet
^{1}cop (n) **1** [inform] smeris **2** [inform] arrestatie, vangst
^{2}cop (vb) [inform] **1** betrappen, grijpen, vangen **2** raken, treffen ‖ ~ *it* last krijgen
cope het aankunnen, zich weten te redden: ~ *with* het hoofd bieden (aan), bestrijden
copier kopieerapparaat^h
co-pilot tweede piloot
copious 1 overvloedig **2** productief; vruchtbaar [author etc]
cop out [inform] terugkrabbelen; afhaken
copper 1 (rood) koper^h **2** koperkleur **3** koperen muntje^h, koper(geld)^h **4** [inform] smeris
copulation geslachtsgemeenschap
^{1}copy (n) **1** kopie, reproductie, imitatie, fotokopie **2** exemplaar^h, nummer^h **3** kopij, (reclame)tekst
^{2}copy (vb) een kopie maken, overschrijven
^{3}copy (vb) **1** kopiëren, een afdruk maken van, overschrijven: ~ *from s.o.* van iem. overschrijven, bij iem. afkijken; ~ *me in on your email* stuur mij een cc'tje; ~ *and paste* a) [comp] kopiëren en plakken, copy-pasten; b) copy-pasten [plagiarism] **2** navolgen, imiteren, overnemen
^{1}copybook (n) voorbeeldenboek^h, schrijfboek^h ‖ [inform] *blot one's ~* zijn reputatie verspelen, een slechte beurt maken
^{2}copybook (adj) perfect, (helemaal) volgens het boekje
copycat [inform] **1** na-aper, navolger **2** afkijker, spieker
copyleft copyleft^h
copyright auteursrecht^h
coral 1 koraal^h, kraal(tje^h) **2** koraalrood^h, koraalkleur^h
cord 1 [anatomy] streng, band: *umbilical ~* navelstreng **2** koord^h, streng, touw^h, snaar **3** (elektrisch) snoer^h, kabel, draad **4** ribfluweel^h, corduroy^h
cordial hartelijk
cordiality hartelijkheid, vriendelijkheid
cordon kordon^h, ring
corduroy (fijn) ribfluweel^h
core binnenste^h, kern, klokhuis^h; [nuclear energy] reactorkern; [fig] wezen^h; essentie, hart^h: *rotten to the ~* door en door rot
^{1}cork (n) kurk; drijver [of fishnet, fishing line]; flessenkurk, (rubber) stop
^{2}cork (vb) kurken: ~ *up* *a bottle* een fles kurken
corkscrew kurkentrekker
corm (stengel)knol
cormorant aalscholver
corn 1 likdoorn, eksteroog^h **2** korrel, graankorrel, maiskorrel, tarwekorrel, zaadje^h, graantje^h **3** graan^h, koren^h, tarwe; [Am] mais: ~ *on the cob* maiskolf, mais aan de kolf

[as cooked food] **4** [inform] sentimenteel gedoe^h
corned 1 gezouten: ~ *beef* cornedbeef **2** [Am; inform] teut; zat, dronken
¹corner (n) **1** hoek, bocht, hoekje^h: *in a remote* ~ *of the country* in een uithoek van het land; *cut* ~*s* **a)** bochten afsnijden; **b)** het niet zo nauw (meer) nemen **2** [sport] hoekschop || *cut* ~*s* **a)** de uitgaven besnoeien; **b)** formaliteiten omzeilen
²corner (vb) een bocht nemen, door de bocht gaan, de hoek omgaan
³corner (vb) in het nauw drijven, insluiten, klemzetten
cornerstone hoeksteen [also fig]; steunpilaar
cornet 1 [mus] kornet **2** (ijs)hoorn, cornetto
cornflour maizena, maismeel^h
corn flower korenbloem
corny [inform] afgezaagd, clichématig, flauw
corollary uitvloeisel^h; logisch gevolg^h
¹coronary (n) hartinfarct, hartaanval
²coronary (adj) m.b.t. de krans(slag)ader: ~ *arteries* krans(slag)aderen
coronation kroning
coroner 1 lijkschouwer **2** rechter van instructie
coronet 1 (adellijk) kroontje^h, prinsenkroon, prinsessenkroon **2** diadeem^+h, (haar)-kransje^h
¹corporal (n) korporaal
²corporal (adj) lichamelijk, lijfelijk, lichaams-: ~ *punishment* lijfstraf
corporate 1 gezamenlijk, collectief, verenigd: ~ *body, body corporate* lichaam, rechtspersoon **2** m.b.t. een gemeentebestuur, gemeente-, gemeentelijk **3** m.b.t. een naamloze vennootschap, bedrijfs-, ondernemings-: ~ *identity* bedrijfsidentiteit, huisstijl; ~ *lawyer* bedrijfsjurist
corporation 1 gemeenteraad, gemeentebestuur^h **2** rechtspersoon, lichaam^h; [Am] naamloze vennootschap; onderneming: ~ *tax* vennootschapsbelasting
corps 1 [mil] (leger)korps^h, wapen^h, staf **2** korps^h, staf: ~ *de ballet* (corps de) ballet; *diplomatic* ~ corps diplomatique
corpse lijk^h
corpulent dik, zwaarlijvig
corral [Am] (vee)kraal, omheining voor paarden
¹correct (adj) **1** correct, juist: *politically* ~ politiek correct **2** onberispelijk, beleefd
²correct (vb) **1** verbeteren, corrigeren, nakijken **2** terechtwijzen **3** rechtzetten, rectificeren **4** verhelpen, repareren, tegengaan
correction correctie, verbetering, rectificatie: ~ *fluid* correctievloeistof, blunderlak
corrective verbeterend, correctief

correlation correlatie [also statistics]; wisselwerking, wederzijdse betrekking
correspond 1 (+ to, with) overeenkomen, overeenstemmen (met), kloppen, corresponderen **2** corresponderen, een briefwisseling voeren, schrijven
correspondence 1 overeenkomst, overeenstemming, gelijkenis **2** correspondentie, briefwisseling: *commercial* ~ handelscorrespondentie
¹correspondent (n) correspondent; verslaggever
²correspondent (adj) [form] **1** overeenkomend **2** overeenkomstig
corridor 1 gang [also pol]; corridor, galerij **2** luchtweg, corridor, luchtvaartroute, vliegtuigroute
corroboration bevestiging, bekrachtiging
¹corrode (vb) vergaan, verteren, verroesten, (weg)roesten
²corrode (vb) aantasten, aanvreten, wegvreten
corrosion verroesting, aantasting, roest
corrugate plooien, golven: ~*d (card)board* golfkarton; *sheets of* ~*d iron* golfplaten
¹corrupt (adj) **1** verdorven, immoreel **2** corrupt, omkoopbaar **3** verbasterd, onbetrouwbaar: *a* ~ *form of Latin* verbasterd Latijn
²corrupt (vb) slecht worden, (zeden)bederf veroorzaken
³corrupt (vb) **1** omkopen, corrupt maken **2** verbasteren, vervalsen, verknoeien
corruption 1 corruptie, omkoperij **2** verbastering **3** bederf^h, verderf^h
corset korset^h, keurslijfje^h, rijglijfje^h
cortex cortex
¹cosh (n) (gummi)knuppel, ploertendoder
²cosh (vb) slaan met een gummiknuppel, aftuigen, neerknuppelen
cosine cosinus
¹cosmetic (n) cosmetisch middel^h, schoonheidsmiddel^h: ~*s* cosmetica
²cosmetic (adj) **1** cosmetisch, schoonheids-: ~ *surgery* cosmetische chirurgie **2** [depr] verfraaiend, voor de schone schijn, oppervlakkig
cosmic kosmisch, van het heelal
cosmonaut kosmonaut
cosmopolitan kosmopolitisch
cosset vertroetelen, verwennen
¹cost (n) kost(en), prijs, uitgave: *the* ~ *of living* de kosten van levensonderhoud; *at all* ~*s, at any* ~ koste wat het kost, tot elke prijs; *at the* ~ *of* ten koste van; *charged at* ~ in rekening gebracht || *count the* ~ de nadelen overwegen [before acting]
²cost (vb) kostbaar zijn, in de papieren lopen
³cost (vb) kosten, komen (te staan) op, vergen
¹co-star (n) tegenspeler, tegenspeelster
²co-star (vb) als tegenspeler optreden

Costa Rica Costa Rica
¹**Costa Rican** (n) Costa Ricaan(se)
²**Costa Rican** (adj) Costa Ricaans
cost-cutting kostenbesparend: ~ *measures* bezuinigingsmaatregelen
cost-effective rendabel
costing kostprijsberekening; raming
costly kostbaar, duur
costume kostuumʰ, pakʰ, (kleder)dracht
costume jewellery namaakbijouterie
¹**cosy** (n) **1** theemuts **2** eierwarmer
²**cosy** (adj) knus, behaaglijk, gezellig
cosy up [Am] dicht(er) aankruipen [to s.o.]; [fig] in de gunst proberen te komen [with s.o.]
cot 1 ledikantjeʰ, kinderbed(jeʰ), wieg **2** [Am] veldbedʰ, stretcher
cot death wiegendood
cottage 1 (plattelands)huisjeʰ **2** vakantiehuisjeʰ, zomerhuisjeʰ
cottage cheese [roughly] kwark; [Belg] [roughly] plattekaas
cotton 1 katoenʰ, katoenplant, katoendraad, katoenvezel **2** katoenen stof, katoenweefselʰ
cotton candy [Am] suikerspin
cotton on [inform] het snappen; doorkrijgen
¹**couch** (n) (rust)bank, sofa, divan
²**couch** (vb) **1** inkleden, formuleren, verwoorden: *the instructions were ~ed in simple language* de instructies waren in eenvoudige bewoordingen gesteld **2** vellen [spear, lance]
couch surfing het gratis verblijven bij particulieren
cougar 1 poema **2** oudere vrouw met jonge vriend
¹**cough** (n) **1** hoest: *have a bad ~* erg hoesten **2** kuch(jeʰ), hoestbui, hoestaanval
²**cough** (vb) **1** hoesten, kuchen **2** sputteren; blaffen [of firearm]: *the engine ~s and misfires* de motor sputtert en hapert
cough up 1 opbiechten, bekennen **2** dokken; ophoesten [money]
council 1 raad, (advies)collegeʰ, bestuurʰ: *municipal ~* gemeenteraad **2** kerkvergadering
council estate woningwetwijk, woningwetbuurt
councillor raadslidʰ
¹**counsel** (n) **1** raad, (deskundig) adviesʰ **2** overlegʰ **3** raadslieden, advocaat, verdediging ‖ *keep one's own ~* zijn motieven voor zich houden, zich niet blootgeven
²**counsel** (vb) advies geven, adviseren, aanraden
counselling het adviseren, adviseurschapʰ
counsellor 1 adviseur, consulent(e); [Am] (studenten)decaan; beroepskeuzeadviseur **2** [Am] raadsman, raadsvrouw, advocaat

¹**count** (n) **1** het uittellen [of a boxer]: *be out for the ~* uitgeteld zijn [also fig] **2** (niet-Engelse) graaf **3** telling, tel, getalʰ: *keep ~* de tel(ling) bijhouden, (mee)tellen; *lose ~* de tel kwijtraken
²**count** (vb) tellen, meetellen, gelden: *~ for little* (or: *nothing*) weinig (or: niets) voorstellen ‖ *~ against* pleiten tegen
³**count** (vb) **1** meetellen, meerekenen: *there were 80 victims, not ~ing the crew* er waren 80 slachtoffers, de bemanning niet meegerekend **2** rekenen tot, beschouwen (als), achten: *~ o.s. lucky* zich gelukkig prijzen ‖ *they'll ~ it against you ...* ze zullen het je kwalijk nemen ...
⁴**count** (vb) tellen, optellen, tellen tot: *~ down* aftellen
countdown het aftellen
¹**countenance** (n) **1** gelaatʰ, gelaatstrekken, gelaatsuitdrukking **2** aanzichtʰ, aanzienʰ **3** welwillende blik **4** kalmte, gemoedsrust, zelfbeheersing: *lose ~* van zijn stuk raken **5** (morele) steun, instemming, goedkeuring: *we won't give* (or: *lend*) *~ to such plans* we zullen dergelijke plannen niet steunen
²**countenance** (vb) goedkeuren, (stilzwijgend) toestaan, oogluikend toestaan, dulden
¹**counter** (n) **1** toonbank, balie, bar, loketʰ, kassa **2** ficheʰ **3** tegenzet, tegenmaatregel, tegenwichtʰ ‖ *over the ~* zonder recept (verkrijgbaar) [of drugs]; *under the ~* onder de toonbank
²**counter** (adj) **1** tegen(over)gesteld, tegenwerkend, contra- **2** duplicaat-, dubbel
³**counter** (vb) een tegenzet doen, zich verweren, terugvechten; [boxing] counteren
⁴**counter** (vb) **1** zich verzetten tegen, tegenwerken, (ver)hinderen **2** beantwoorden, reageren op **3** tenietdoen, weerleggen
⁵**counter** (adv) **1** in tegenovergestelde richting **2** op tegengestelde wijze: *act* (or: *go*) *~ to* niet opvolgen, ingaan tegen
counteract tegengaan, neutraliseren, tenietdoen
¹**counter-attack** (n) tegenaanval
²**counter-attack** (vb) in de tegenaanval gaan
³**counter-attack** (vb) een tegenaanval uitvoeren op
counterbalance tegenwichtʰ
counter-clockwise [Am] linksdraaiend, tegen de wijzers van de klok in (draaiend)
¹**counterfeit** (n) vervalsing, falsificatie
²**counterfeit** (adj) **1** vals, vervalst, onecht **2** voorgewend, niet gemeend
³**counterfeit** (vb) **1** vervalsen, namaken **2** doen alsof
counterfeiter vervalser, valsemunter
counterfoil controlestrookjeʰ, kwitantiestrook

counterpart tegenhanger
¹counterpoise (n) **1** tegenwicht^h, tegendruk **2** evenwicht^h
²counterpoise (vb) in evenwicht brengen, opwegen tegen, compenseren
counterproductive averechts; contraproductief
countersign medeondertekenen
counterweight tegen(ge)wicht^h, contragewicht^h
countess gravin, echtgenote van een graaf
countless talloos, ontelbaar
count out [inform] **1** niet meetellen, afschrijven, terzijde schuiven: *if it rains tonight you can count me out* als het vanavond regent moet je niet op me rekenen **2** [sport] uittellen [boxer] **3** neertellen
country 1 land^h, geboorteland^h, vaderland^h **2** volk^h, natie: *the ~ doesn't support this decision* het land staat niet achter deze beslissing **3** (land)streek, terrein^h **4** platteland^h, provincie: *go for a day in the ~* een dagje naar buiten gaan
country cousin provinciaal
countryfolk plattelanders, buitenlui
country house landhuis^h, buitenverblijf^h
countryman 1 landgenoot **2** plattelander
countryside platteland^h
count (up)on rekenen (vertrouwen) op
county graafschap^h, provincie
county council graafschapsbestuur^h, provinciaal bestuur^h; [roughly] Provinciale Staten
county court districtsrechtbank; [roughly] kantongerecht^h
county hall provinciehuis^h
coup 1 slimme zet, prestatie, succes^h: *make* (or: *pull off*) *a ~* zijn slag slaan **2** staatsgreep, coup
¹couple (n) **1** koppel^h, paar^h, span^h: *a ~ of* a) twee; b) [inform] een paar, een stuk of twee [not more than three] **2** (echt)paar^h, stel^h: *a married ~* een getrouwd stel, een echtpaar
²couple (vb) **1** paren vormen **2** paren, geslachtsgemeenschap hebben
³couple (vb) **1** (aaneen)koppelen, verbinden, aanhaken: *~ up* aan elkaar koppelen **2** (met elkaar) in verband brengen, gepaard laten gaan
coupling koppeling, verbinding, koppelstuk^h
coupon 1 bon, kaartje^h, zegel, kortingsbon **2** (toto)formulier^h
courage moed, dapperheid, durf: *muster up* (or: *pluck up, summon up*) *~* moed vatten
courageous moedig, dapper, onverschrokken
courgette courgette
courier 1 koerier, bode **2** reisgids, reisleider

course 1 loop, (voort)gang, duur: *the ~ of events* de loop der gebeurtenissen; *run* (or: *take*) *its ~* zijn beloop hebben, (natuurlijk) verlopen **2** koers, richting, route: *stay the ~* tot het eind toe volhouden; *on ~* op koers **3** manier, weg, (gedrags)lijn **4** cursus, curriculum^h: *an English ~* een cursus Engels **5** cyclus, reeks, serie: *~ of lectures* lezingencyclus **6** [sport] baan **7** [culinary] gang: *a three-~ dinner* een diner van drie gangen; *the main ~* het hoofdgerecht || *of ~* natuurlijk, vanzelfsprekend
courseware educatieve software
coursing hazen- of konijnenjacht met windhonden
¹court (n) **1** rechtbank, gerechtsgebouw^h, gerechtszaal, (gerechts)hof^h: *Court of Appeal(s)* hof van beroep; *Court of Claims* bestuursrechtelijk hof [Am]; *~ of inquiry* gerechtelijke commissie van onderzoek; *go to ~* naar de rechter stappen; *settle out of ~* buiten de rechter om schikken **2** hof^h, koninklijk paleis^h, hofhouding **3** [sport] (tennis)baan **4** omsloten ruimte, (licht)hal, binnenhof^h, binnenplaats || *laugh s.o. out of ~* iem. (iets) weghonen; *rule* (or: *put*) *out of ~* a) uitsluiten [witness, evidence; also fig]; b) (iets/iem.) totaal geen kans geven
²court (vb) verkering hebben
³court (vb) **1** vleien, in de gunst trachten te komen bij **2** flirten met, het hof maken, dingen naar de hand van, vragen om, uitlokken: *~ disaster* om moeilijkheden vragen **3** (trachten te) winnen, streven naar
courteous beleefd, welgemanierd
courtesy beleefdheid, welgemanierdheid, beleefdheidsbetuiging: *(by) ~ of* welwillend ter beschikking gesteld door, met toestemming van
court-house gerechtsgebouw^h
courtly 1 hoofs, verfijnd, elegant **2** welgemanierd, beleefd, hoffelijk
¹court martial (n) krijgsraad, (hoog) militair gerechtshof^h
²court martial (vb) voor een krijgsraad brengen
courtship 1 verkering(stijd) **2** het hof maken **3** [zoology] balts
courtyard binnenhof, binnenplaats, plein^h
cousin neef, nicht, dochter of zoon van tante of oom: *first ~* volle neef/nicht; [fig] nauwe verwante; *second ~* achterneef, achternicht, verre neef/nicht
cove 1 inham, kleine baai, kreek **2** beschutte plek, (beschutte) inham
covenant overeenkomst **2** [rel] verbond^h
¹cover (n) **1** bedekking, hoes: *~s* dekens; dekbed^h **2** deksel^+h, klep **3** omslag^+h, stofomslag^+h, boekband: *read a book from ~ to ~* een boek van begin tot eind lezen **4** enveloppe **5** mes en vork **6** invaller, vervanger **7** dek-

mantel, voorwendsel[h]: **under ~** *of friendship* onder het mom van vriendschap **8** dekking [also sport]; beschutting, schuilplaats: **take ~** dekking zoeken, (gaan) schuilen; **under ~** heimelijk, in het geheim, verborgen **9** dekking [insurance]
²cover (vb) [inform] (+ **for**) invallen (voor), vervangen
³cover (vb) **1** bedekken, overtrekken: *he was ~ed in* (or: *with*) *blood* hij zat onder het bloed; **~ over** bedekken **2** beslaan, omvatten, bestrijken **3** afleggen [distance] **4** bewaken [eg access roads] **5** verslaan, verslag uitbrengen over **6** dekken, verzekeren: *we aren't ~ed against fire* we zijn niet tegen brand verzekerd **7** onder schot houden, in bedwang houden **8** beheersen, controleren, bestrijken **9** [sport] dekken, bewaken || *a ~ing letter* (or: *note*) een begeleidend schrijven
coverage 1 dekking [also insurance]; verzekerd bedrag (risico) **2** berichtgeving, verslag[h], verslaggeving, publiciteit **3** bereik[h]
cover charge couvert(kosten)
covering bedekking, dekzeil[h]
cover story 1 omslagartikel[h]; coverstory **2** dekmantel
¹covert (n) **1** beschutte plaats, schuilplaats **2** kreupelhout[h]
²covert (adj) bedekt, heimelijk, illegaal
¹cover up (vb) dekking geven, een alibi verstrekken
²cover up (vb) **1** verdoezelen, wegmoffelen, verhullen: *~ one's tracks* zijn sporen uitwissen **2** toedekken, inwikkelen
cover-up 1 doofpotaffaire **2** dekmantel, alibi[h]
covet begeren
cow koe, wijfje[h]: [fig] *sacred ~* heilige koe || *till the ~s come home* tot je een ons weegt, eindeloos
coward lafaard
cowardice lafheid
cowboy 1 [Am] cowboy, veedrijver **2** beunhaas, knoeier **3** [inform] gewetenloos zakenman: *~ employers* gewetenloze werkgevers
cower in elkaar duiken, ineenkrimpen
cowl 1 monnikskap, kap **2** monnikspij **3** schoorsteenkap
co-worker collega, medewerker
cow pat koeienvlaai
cowslip 1 sleutelbloem **2** [Am] dotterbloem
cox stuurman; stuur[h] [of rowing boat]
coxcomb ijdeltuit
coy 1 koket **2** ingetogen; terughoudend: *a politician ~ about his plans* een politicus die zijn plannen voor zich houdt
cozy see ¹*cosy*
cps *characters, cycles per second*
CPU *Central Processing Unit* CVE

¹crab (n) **1** krab **2** [inform] schaamluis
²crab (vb) **1** krabben vangen **2** [inform] kankeren, mopperen
crab apple wilde appel
crabbed 1 chagrijnig, prikkelbaar **2** kriebelig, gekrabbeld; onduidelijk [of handwriting] **3** ingewikkeld
¹crack (n) **1** barst(je[h]), breuk, scheur(tje[h]) **2** kier, spleet **3** knal(geluid[h]), knak, kraak **4** klap, pets **5** [inform] gooi, poging: *have a ~ at* een gooi doen naar, proberen **6** grap(je[h]), geintje[h] **7** [inform] kraan, kei, uitblinker **8** [inform] (zuivere vorm van) cocaïne || *at the ~ of dawn* bij het krieken van de dag
²crack (adj) [inform] prima, keur-, uitgelezen: *a ~ shot* (or: *marksman*) een eersteklas schutter
³crack (vb) **1** in(een)storten, het begeven, knakken **2** knallen, kraken **3** barsten, splijten, scheuren **4** breken, schor worden; overslaan [of voice]
⁴crack (vb) **1** laten knallen, laten kraken: *~ a whip* klappen met een zweep **2** doen barsten, splijten, scheuren **3** meppen, slaan **4** de oplossing vinden van: *~ a code* een code ontcijferen **5** [inform] vertellen: *~ a joke* een mop vertellen
⁵crack (vb) **1** (open)breken, stukbreken, knappen: *~ a safe* een kluis openbreken **2** [chem] kraken
crack-brained onzinnig, getikt, dwaas
crackdown (straf)campagne, (politie)optreden[h], actie
crack down on met harde hand optreden tegen
cracker cracker(tje[h]), knäckebröd[h]
crackers [inform] gek
cracking [inform] **1** schitterend, uitstekend **2** snel: *~ pace* stevige vaart || *get ~* aan de slag gaan
¹crackle (n) geknetter[h], geknap(per)[h], geknisper[h]
²crackle (vb) knapp(er)en, knetteren, knisperen; kraken [of telephone]
crackpot [inform] zonderling
¹crack up (vb) [inform] bezwijken, instorten, eronderdoor gaan
²crack up (vb) [inform] **1** ophemelen, roemen, prijzen: *he isn't everything he's cracked up to be* hij is niet zo goed als iedereen zegt **2** in de lach schieten, in een deuk liggen
crack-up [inform] in(een)storting, inzinking
¹cradle (n) **1** wieg [also fig]; bakermat: *from the ~ to the grave* van de wieg tot het graf **2** stellage; [shipp] (constructie)bok; haak [of telephone]
²cradle (vb) **1** wiegen, vasthouden **2** in een wieg leggen **3** op de haak leggen [telephone]
¹craft (n) **1** vak[h], ambacht[h] **2** (kunst)vaardig-

heid, kunstnijverheid **3** bedrijfstak, branche, (ambachts)gilde[h]
²**craft** (n) **1** boot(je[h]), vaartuig[h] **2** vliegtuig[h] **3** ruimtevaartuig[h]
craftsman handwerksman; vakman [also fig]
crafty geslepen, doortrapt, geraffineerd
crag steile rots
¹**cram** (vb) **1** zich volproppen, schrokken **2** blokken, stampen
²**cram** (vb) **1** (vol)proppen, aanstampen, (vol)stouwen **2** klaarstomen [pupil] **3** erin stampen [subject matter]
cramp kramp(scheut): ~s maagkramp; buikkramp
cramped 1 benauwd, krap, kleinbehuisd **2** kriebelig [of handwriting] **3** gewrongen
cranberry veenbes
¹**crane** (n) **1** kraanvogel **2** kraan, hijskraan
²**crane** (vb) de hals uitstrekken, reikhalzen
³**crane** (vb) (reikhalzend) uitstrekken, vooruitsteken
¹**crank** (n) **1** krukas, autoslinger; crank [of bicycle] **2** [inform] zonderling, excentrikeling **3** [Am; inform] mopperkont
²**crank** (vb) aanzwengelen, aanslingeren: ~ up a car een auto aanslingeren
crankshaft krukas, trapas
cranky 1 [inform] zonderling, bizar **2** [Am; inform] chagrijnig
cranny spleet; scheur
¹**crap** (n) [vulg] **1** stront: have a ~ een drol leggen **2** kletspraat, gekletsʰ: a load of ~ een hoop gezever **3** troep, rotzooi
²**crap** (vb) [vulg] schijten, kakken
crap on [fig] doorzagen; tot vervelens toe blijven praten
¹**crash** (n) **1** klap, dreun **2** botsing, neerstorting, ongeluk[h] **3** krach, ineenstorting
²**crash** (adj) spoed-: ~ course stoomcursus, spoedcursus
³**crash** (vb) **1** te pletter slaan, verongelukken, botsen, (neer)storten: the plates ~ed to the floor de borden kletterden op de grond **2** stormen **3** dreunen, knallen **4** ineenstorten, failliet gaan; [comp] crashen; down gaan **5** [inform] (blijven) pitten, de nacht doorbrengen
⁴**crash** (vb) te pletter laten vallen
crash barrier vangrail
crash landing buiklanding, noodlanding
crass bot, onbehouwen, lomp: ~ stupidity peilloze domheid
crate 1 krat[h], kist **2** [inform] brik, bak **3** [inform] kist, wrakkig vliegtuig[h]
crater krater
crave hunkeren (naar), smachten (naar)
craving hunkering; verlangen[h]
¹**crawl** (n) **1** slakkengang **2** crawl(slag)
²**crawl** (vb) **1** kruipen, sluipen, moeizaam vooruitkomen **2** krioelen, wemelen: the

place was ~ing **with** vermin het krioelde er van ongedierte **3** kruipen, kruiperig doen, slijmen: ~ **to** one's boss de hielen likken van zijn baas
craze rage, manie, gril
crazy 1 gek, krankzinnig, dol, waanzinnig: go ~ gek worden; [inform] ~ **about** fishing gek van vissen **2** [inform] te gek, fantastisch
creak geknars[h], gekraak[h]
¹**cream** (n) **1** (slag)room[h] **2** crème [for use on skin] **3** crème(kleurig)
²**cream** (vb) **1** room toevoegen aan, in room e.d. bereiden: ~ed **potatoes** aardappelpuree **2** inwrijven; insmeren [skin]
³**cream** (vb) romen; afromen [also fig]: ~ **off** afromen
cream puff 1 roomsoesje[h] **2** [inform] slapjanus
cream tea aangeklede thee
¹**crease** (n) vouw, plooi, kreukel: ~ **resistant** kreukvrij
²**crease** (vb) persen, een vouw maken in
³**crease** (vb) kreuke(le)n, vouwen, plooien
¹**create** (vb) [inform] tekeergaan, leven maken
²**create** (vb) **1** scheppen, creëren, ontwerpen **2** veroorzaken, teweegbrengen
creation 1 schepping, instelling, oprichting: **the** Creation de schepping **2** creatie, (mode)ontwerp[h]
creative creatief, scheppend, vindingrijk: ~ **accounting** creatief boekhouden
creativity creativiteit, scheppingsdrang, scheppingsvermogen[h]
creator schepper
creature 1 schepsel[h], schepping, voortbrengsel[h]: ~ **of habit** gewoontedier, gewoontemens **2** dier[h], beest[h] **3** (levend) wezen[h] **4** stakker, mens(je[h]), creatuur[h]
crèche 1 crèche, kinderdagverblijf[h] **2** [Am] kerststal, krib
credence geloof[h]: attach (or: **give**) no ~ to geen geloof hechten aan
credentials introductiebrieven, geloofsbrieven, legitimatiebewijs
credibility geloofwaardigheid
credible geloofwaardig, betrouwbaar **2** overtuigend
¹**credit** (n) **1** krediet[h]: buy **on** ~ op krediet kopen; ~ **on** a prepaid phone card beltegoed **2** credit[h], creditzijde, creditpost **3** tegoed[h], spaarbanktegoed[h], positief saldo[h] **4** geloof[h], vertrouwen[h]: lend ~ to bevestigen, geloofwaardig maken **5** krediet[h], kredietwaardigheid, goede naam **6** krediet[h], krediettermijn **7** eer, lof, verdienste: it **does** you ~, it **is** to your ~, it reflects ~ **on** you het siert je, het strekt je tot eer **8** [Am] studiepunt[h], examenbriefje[h], tentamenbriefje[h] **9** sieraad[h]: she's a ~ **to** our family ze is een sieraad voor onze familie **10** (-s) titelrol, aftiteling

²credit (vb) **1** geloven, geloof hechten aan **2** crediteren, op iemands tegoed bijschrijven **3** toedenken, toeschrijven: *he is ~ed* **with** *the invention* de uitvinding staat op zijn naam
creditable 1 loffelijk, eervol, prijzenswaardig **2** te geloven
credit card credit card; [roughly] betaalkaart
credit crunch kredietcrisis
creditor crediteur, schuldeiser
credo credoʰ; geloofsbelijdenis
credulity lichtgelovigheid, goedgelovigheid
creed 1 geloofsbelijdenis; credoʰ [also fig] **2** (geloofs)overtuiging, gezindte
creek kreek; inham; bocht, kleine rivier ‖ [inform] *up the ~* in een lastig parket, in de penarie
¹creep (n) **1** [inform] gluiperd, griezel, engerd, slijmerd **2** (the creeps) kriebels, kippenvelʰ, koude rillingen
²creep (vb) kruipen, sluipen: *~ in* binnensluipen; *~ up on* bekruipen, besluipen
creeper 1 kruiper **2** kruipend gewasʰ, klimplant **3** (-s) [Am] kruippakʰ **4** (-s) bordeelsluipers, schoenen met crêpe zolen
creep out [inform] (iem.) schrik aanjagen, de stuipen op het lijf jagen
creepy griezelig, eng, huiveringwekkend
creepy-crawly [inform] beestjeʰ, (kruipend) insect (ongedierte)
cremate cremeren, verassen
cremation crematie
crematorium crematorium(gebouw)ʰ
crescent 1 halvemaan, afnemende maan **2** halvemaanvormig iets, halvemaantjeʰ
cress kers, gewone kers, tuinkers, sterrenkers
¹crest (n) **1** kam, pluim, kuif **2** helmbos, helmpluim, vederbos **3** top, berg-, heuveltop, golfkam: [fig] *he is riding the ~ (of the waves)* hij is op het hoogtepunt van zijn carrière/succes
²crest (vb) de top bereiken van; bedwingen [mountain]
crestfallen terneergeslagen, teleurgesteld
¹Cretan (n) Kretenzer, Kretenzische
²Cretan (adj) Kretenzisch, Kretenzer
Crete Kreta
crevice spleet; scheur, kloof
crew 1 bemanning: *several ~ are ill* verscheidene bemanningsleden zijn ziek **2** personeelʰ **3** ploeg, roeibootbemanning, roeiploeg
crew cut stekeltjes(haar); crewcut
¹crib (n) **1** [Am] ledikantjeʰ, bedjeʰ, wieg **2** krib, voederbak, ruif **3** kerststal **4** [inform] afgekeken antwoord, spiekwerkʰ, plagiaatʰ **5** [inform] spiekbriefjeʰ
²crib (vb) [inform] **1** spieken, afkijken, overschrijven **2** jatten, pikken

¹crick (n) stijfheid, spitʰ: *a ~ in the neck* een stijve nek
²crick (vb) verrekken, verdraaien, ontwrichten
¹cricket (n) cricketʰ: *that's not ~* dat is onsportief, zoiets doe je niet
²cricket (n) krekel
crier 1 schreeuwer **2** huilebalk **3** [hist] omroeper, stadsomroeper
crime 1 misdaad, misdrijfʰ **2** criminaliteit, (de) misdaad **3** schandaalʰ, schande: *it's a ~ the way he treats us* het is schandalig zoals hij ons behandelt
¹criminal (n) misdadiger
²criminal (adj) **1** misdadig, crimineel: *~ act* misdrijf, strafbare handeling **2** [inform] schandalig **3** strafrechtelijk, crimineel: *~ libel* smaad
crimson karmozijn(rood): *turn ~* (vuur)rood aanlopen, (diep) kleuren/blozen
cringe 1 ineenkrimpen, terugdeinzen, terugschrikken **2** (+ to) kruipen (voor), door het stof gaan (voor), zich vernederen **3** [inform] de kriebel(s) krijgen: *his foolish talk makes me ~* zijn gezwets hangt me mijlenver de keel uit
¹crinkle (n) kreuk, (valse/ongewenste) vouw
²crinkle (vb) (doen) kreuke(le)n, (doen) rimpelen, verfrommelen
crinkly 1 gekreukt; gekreukeld, verfrommeld **2** gekruld; kroezig
¹cripple (n) invalide, (gedeeltelijk) verlamde, kreupele
²cripple (vb) verlammen, invalide maken; [fig] (ernstig) beschadigen: *~d with gout* krom van de jicht
crisis crisis, kritiek stadiumʰ, keerpuntʰ
¹crisp (n) (aardappel)chip
²crisp (adj) **1** knapperig, krokant: *a ~ pound note* een kraaknieuw biljet van een pond **2** stevig; vers [vegetable etc] **3** fris, helder, verfrissend: *the ~ autumn wind* de frisse herfstwind **4** helder, ter zake, kernachtig
crispbread knäckebrödʰ
crisper groentelade, groentevakʰ [in refrigerator]
crispy knapperig, krokant
¹criss-cross (adj) kruiselings, kruis-
²criss-cross (vb) **1** (kriskras) (door)kruisen **2** doorsnijden: *train tracks ~ the country* spoorlijnen doorsnijden het land **3** krassen maken op, bekrassen
³criss-cross (adv) kriskras, door elkaar
criterion criteriumʰ
critic criticus, recensent
critical 1 kritisch; streng: *be ~ of sth.* ergens kritisch tegenover staan; *~ thinker* kritisch (or: onafhankelijk) denker **2** kritiek; cruciaal: *the patient's condition is ~* de toestand van de patiënt is kritiek; *of ~ importance* van cruciaal belang ‖ *~ writings* kritieken

criticism 1 kritiek, recensie, bespreking **2** afkeuring, afwijzing
criticize 1 kritiek hebben (op) **2** (be)kritiseren, beoordelen, recenseren **3** afkeuren
critique kritiek; recensie; kunstkritiek
¹croak (vb) **1** kwaken [of frogs]; krassen [of ravens and crows]; hees zijn, (ontevreden) grommen, brommen **2** [inform] het loodje leggen
²croak (n): *speak with a ~* hees zijn, spreken met schorre stem
Croat Kroaat, Kroatische
Croatia Kroatië
Croatian Kroatisch
crochet haakwerkʰ
crock 1 aardewerk(en) pot, kruik **2** potscherf **3** [inform] (oud) wrakʰ, kneusjeʰ, ouwe knol
crockery aardewerkʰ, vaatwerkʰ, serviesgoedʰ
crock up [inform] in elkaar klappen, instorten
crocodile 1 krokodil: *~ tears* krokodillentranen **2** rij (kinderen, 2 aan 2)
crocus krokus
crony makker, maat(jeʰ), gabber
crook 1 herdersstaf **2** bisschopsstaf, kromstaf **3** bocht, kronkel, buiging: *the ~ of one's arm* de elleboogholte **4** haak, hoek, luikʰ **5** [inform] oplichter, zwendelaar, flessentrekker
crooked 1 bochtig, slingerend, kronkelig **2** misvormd; krom(gegroeid) [also with age]; gebocheld **3** oneerlijk, onbetrouwbaar, achterbaks
crooner sentimenteel zanger; crooner
crop 1 krop [of bird] **2** rijzweep(jeʰ), karwats, rijstokjeʰ **3** gewasʰ, landbouwproductʰ, landbouwproducten **4** oogst [also fig]; graanoogst, lading, lichting: *a whole new ~ of students* een hele nieuwe lichting studenten || *a fine ~ of hair* een mooie bos haar
cropper [inform] smak: *come a ~* een (dood)smak maken; [fig] op z'n bek vallen, afgaan
crop spraying gewasbespuiting
crop up [inform] opduiken, de kop opsteken, plotseling ter sprake komen: *her name keeps cropping up in the papers* haar naam duikt voortdurend op in de krant
¹cross (n) **1** kruis(jeʰ), crucifixʰ, kruistekenʰ: *make the sign of the ~* een kruisje slaan (*or:* maken) **2** kruisʰ, beproeving, lijdenʰ **3** kruising, bastaard **4** [socc] voorzet
²cross (adj) boos, kwaad, uit zijn humeur: *be ~ with s.o.* kwaad op iem. zijn
³cross (vb) (elkaar) kruisen
⁴cross (vb) **1** kruisen, over elkaar slaan: *~ one's arms* (*or:* *legs*) zijn armen (*or:* benen) over elkaar slaan **2** een kruisteken maken boven: *~ o.s.* een kruis slaan **3** (door)strepen,

een streep trekken door: *~ out* (*or:* *off*) doorstrepen, doorhalen, schrappen [also fig] **4** dwarsbomen; doorkruisen [plan] **5** [biology] kruisen
⁵cross (vb) **1** oversteken, overtrekken, doortrekken **2** kruisen, (elkaar) passeren
the **Cross** (Heilige) Kruisʰ; kruisiging [of Christ]; christendomʰ
crossbow kruisboog
crossbreed 1 kruising, bastaard **2** gekruist rasʰ, bastaardrasʰ
¹cross-country (n) cross(country), terreinwedstrijd; [athletics] veldloop; [cycle racing] veldrit
²cross-country (adj) **1** terrein- **2** over het hele land, van kust tot kust: *~ concert tour* landelijke concerttournee
cross-examine aan een kruisverhoor onderwerpen [also fig]; scherp ondervragen
cross-eyed scheel(ogig): *he is slightly ~* hij loenst een beetje
crossfire [mil] kruisvuurʰ: [fig] *caught in the ~* tussen twee vuren zitten
crossing 1 oversteek, overtocht, overvaart **2** kruising, snijpuntʰ, kruispuntʰ **3** oversteekplaats, zebra, overweg
cross-legged met gekruiste benen; in kleermakerszit
crossover 1 overstap **2** oversteekplaats **3** [mus] cross-over
cross-purpose: *talk at ~s* langs elkaar heen praten
cross-reference verwijzing, referentie
crossroads wegkruising, tweesprong, driesprong, viersprong, kruispunt; [fig] tweesprong; beslissend moment, keerpunt
cross section dwarsdoorsnede [also fig]; kenmerkende steekproef
cross-stitch kruissteek
crossword kruiswoord(raadsel)ʰ
crotch 1 vertakking, vork **2** kruisʰ [of person or article of clothing]
crotchet [mus] kwartʰ, kwartnoot
crotchety chagrijnig; knorrig
crouch zich (laag) bukken, ineenduiken, zich buigen: *~ down* ineengehurkt zitten
¹crow (n) **1** kraai, roek **2** gekraaiʰ [of cock] **3** kreetjeʰ, geluidjeʰ; gekraaiʰ [of baby] || *as the ~ flies* hemelsbreed
²crow (vb) **1** kraaien [of cock, child]: *the baby ~ed with pleasure* het kindje kraaide van plezier **2** [inform] opscheppen, snoeven || *~ over* (triomfantelijk) juichen over, uitbundig leedvermaak hebben over
crowbar koevoet, breekijzerʰ
¹crowd (n) **1** (mensen)menigte, massa **2** [inform] volkjeʰ, kliek(jeʰ) || *follow* (*or:* *move with, go with*) *the ~* in de pas lopen, zich conformeren aan de massa
²crowd (vb) elkaar verdringen: *people ~ed round* mensen dromden samen

³**crowd** (vb) **1** (over)bevolken, (meer dan) volledig vullen: *shoppers ~ed the stores* de winkels waren vol winkelende mensen **2** proppen, persen, (dicht) op elkaar drukken ‖ ~ *out* buitensluiten, verdringen

crowded vol, druk

crowdfunding crowdfunding

crowdsourcing crowdsourcing

¹**crown** (n) **1** krans **2** kroon; [fig] vorstelijke macht; regering; [law] openbare aanklager: *minister of the Crown* zittend minister [in England] **3** hoogste punt^h, bovenste gedeelte^h, (hoofd)kruin, boomkruin; kroon [of tooth, molar] **4** [sport] kampioen(schap)stitel

²**crown** (vb) **1** kronen: *~ed heads* gekroonde hoofden, regerende vorsten **2** bekronen, belonen, eren **3** kronen, de top vormen van, sieren **4** voltooien, (met succes) bekronen, de kroon op het werk vormen: *to ~ (it) all* als klap op de vuurpijl; [iron] tot overmaat van ramp

crow's-foot kraaienpootje^h [wrinkle near corner of the eye]

crucial 1 cruciaal, (alles)beslissend; [inform] zeer belangrijk: ~ *point* keerpunt **2** kritiek

crucifix kruisbeeld^h

crucifixion kruisiging

crucify 1 kruisigen **2** tuchtigen

crude 1 ruw, onbewerkt, ongezuiverd, primitief: ~ *oil* ruwe olie, aardolie; *a ~ log cabin* een primitieve blokhut **2** rauw, bot, onbehouwen: ~ *behaviour* lomp gedrag

cruel wreed, hard(vochtig), gemeen; [fig] guur; bar

cruelty wreedheid: ~ *to animals* dierenmishandeling

cruise 1 een cruise maken **2** kruisen [of aeroplane, car etc]; zich met kruissnelheid voortbewegen, (langzaam) rondrijden, patrouilleren, surveilleren

crumb 1 kruimel, kruim(pje^h) **2** klein beetje^h, fractie, zweem(pje^h)

crumble ten onder gaan, vergaan, vervallen, afbrokkelen: *crumbling walls* bouwvallige muren ‖ ~ *away* a) afbrokkelen; b) verschrompelen

crumpet warm broodje^h [at breakfast] ‖ [inform] *a nice piece of* ~ een lekkere meid

¹**crumple** (vb) (also + up) verschrompelen, ineenstorten, ineenklappen

²**crumple** (vb) (also + up) kreuk(el)en, rimpelen, verfrommelen

¹**crunch** (n) **1** knerpend geluid^h, geknars^h **2** beslissend moment^h, beslissende confrontatie: *if* (or: *when*) *it comes to the* ~ als puntje bij paaltje komt

²**crunch** (vb) **1** (doen) knarsen **2** knauwen (op), (luidruchtig) kluiven, knagen (aan)

crusade kruistocht, felle campagne

¹**crush** (n) **1** drom, (samengepakte) mensen-

menigte **2** [always singular] gedrang^h: *avoid the* ~ de drukte vermijden **3** [inform] overmatig drukke bijeenkomst **4** [inform] (hevige) verliefdheid: *have a ~ on* smoorverliefd zijn op

²**crush** (vb) **1** in elkaar drukken, indeuken: *be ~ed to death in a crowd* doodgedrukt worden in een mensenmenigte **2** vernietigen, de kop indrukken

³**crush** (vb) dringen, (zich) persen

crush barrier dranghek^h

crushing vernietigend, verpletterend

¹**crust** (n) **1** korst, broodkorst, kapje^h, korstdeeg^h, bladerdeeg^h: *the earth's* ~ de aardkorst **2** aardkorst **3** (wond)korst **4** [inform] lef^h, brutaliteit ‖ [inform] *off one's* ~ getikt

²**crust** (vb) met een korst bedekt worden

crusty 1 knapperig **2** chagrijnig, humeurig

crutch kruk [for disabled person]

crux essentie, kern(punt^h)

¹**cry** (n) **1** kreet, (uit)roep, geschreeuw^h, schreeuw, strijdkreet **2** huilpartij, gehuil^h **3** diergeluid^h, schreeuw, (vogel)roep **4** roep, smeekbede, appel^h

²**cry** (vb) **1** schreeuwen, jammeren: *he cried (out) with pain* hij schreeuwde het uit van de pijn **2** een geluid geven [of animals, esp birds]; roepen

³**cry** (vb) **1** huilen, janken: ~ *for sth.* om iets jengelen, om iets huilen; ~ *for joy* huilen van blijdschap **2** roepen, schreeuwen: *the fields are ~ing out for rain* het land schreeuwt om regen ‖ ~ *sth. down* iets kleineren, iets afbreken; ~ *off* terugkrabbelen, er(gens) van afzien

crybaby huilebalk

crying hemeltergend, schreeuwend: *a ~ shame* een grof schandaal

crypt crypt(e), grafkelder, ondergrondse kapel

cryptic cryptisch, verborgen, geheimzinnig: ~ *crossword* cryptogram

¹**crystal** (n) **1** kristal **2** [Am] horlogeglas^h

²**crystal** (adj) **1** kristal(len): ~ *ball* kristallen bol [of fortune-teller] **2** (kristal)helder

crystal clear glashelder [also fig]

ct *cent* c

cub welp, jong^h, vossenjong^h

Cuba Cuba

¹**Cuban** (n) Cubaan(se)

²**Cuban** (adj) Cubaans

¹**cube** (n) **1** kubus, klontje^h, blokje^h: [Am] *a ~ of sugar* een suikerklontje **2** derde macht: ~ *root* derdemachtswortel

²**cube** (vb) tot de derde macht verheffen: *two ~d is eight* twee tot de derde is acht

cube root derdemachtswortel

cubic 1 kubiek, driedimensionaal: ~ *metre* kubieke meter **2** kubusvormig, rechthoekig **3** kubisch, derdemachts-

cubicle 1 kleedhokje^h **2** slaapho(e)kje^h

3 werkplek
¹cuckold (n) bedrogen echtgenoot
²cuckold (vb) bedriegen, ontrouw zijn
¹cuckoo (n) **1** koekoek **2** koekoeksroep
3 [fig] uilskuikenʰ, sul ‖ ~ *in the nest* ongewenste indringer
²cuckoo (adj) [inform] achterlijk, idioot
cucumber komkommer
cud herkauwmassa [from rumen]: *chew the* ~ herkauwen; [fig] prakkeseren, tobben
¹cuddle (vb) dicht tegen elkaar aan (genesteld) liggen: ~ *up* dicht tegen elkaar aankruipen; ~ *up to* s.o. zich bij iem. nestelen
²cuddle (vb) knuffelen, liefkozen
cuddly snoezig, aanhalig: *a* ~ *toy* een knuffelbeest
¹cudgel (n) knuppel ‖ *take* up the ~s *for* in de bres springen voor
²cudgel (vb) neerknuppelen
cue 1 aansporing, wenk, hint **2** richtsnoerʰ, voorbeeldʰ, leidraad: *take* one's ~ *from* een voorbeeld nemen aan **3** (biljart)keu
¹cuff (n) **1** manchet **2** [Am] (broek)omslagʰ **3** klap [with a flat hand]; draai om de oren, pets ‖ [inform] *off the* ~ voor de vuist (weg)
²cuff (vb) een draai om de oren geven
cuff link manchetknoop
cul-de-sac 1 doodlopende straat **2** dood puntʰ
¹cull (n) selectie
²cull (vb) **1** plukken [flowers etc] **2** verzamelen, vergaren **3** selecteren, uitkammen, uitziften: ~ *from* selecteren uit
culminate culmineren, zijn hoogtepunt bereiken
culpable 1 afkeurenswaardig, verwerpelijk **2** verwijtbaar: ~ *homicide* dood door schuld **3** aansprakelijk, schuldig
culprit 1 beklaagde, verdachte, beschuldigde **2** schuldige, dader, boosdoener
cult 1 rage; [depr] ziekelijke verering **2** sekte, kliek: ~ *book* cultboek, exclusief boek **3** cultus, eredienst: ~ *figure* cultfiguur
cultivate 1 cultiveren, aanbouwen, bebouwen, ontginnen **2** kweken [eg bacteria] **3** voor zich proberen te winnen, vleien
cultivation 1 [agriculture] cultuur, ontginning, verbouw: *under* ~ in cultuur **2** beschaafdheid, welgemanierdheid
cultural cultureel, cultuur-
culture 1 cultuur, beschaving(stoestand), ontwikkeling(niveauʰ) **2** (bacterie)kweek **3** algemene ontwikkeling **4** kweek, cultuur, teelt
cum met, plus, inclusief, annex, zowel als, tevens: *bed-cum-sitting room* zit-slaapkamer
cumbersome 1 onhandelbaar, log, (p)lomp **2** hinderlijk, lastig, zwaar
cumin komijn
cumulus stapelwolk
cunnilingus het beffen

¹cunning (n) sluwheid, listigheid, slimheid
²cunning (adj) sluw, listig, slim
cunt [vulg] kut
cup 1 kop(jeʰ), mok, beker **2** [sport] (wissel)beker, cup, bokaal ‖ *between* ~ *and lip* op de valreep; *my* ~ *of tea* (echt) iets voor mij
cupboard kast
cup final [sport] bekerfinale
cup-tie [sport] bekerwedstrijd
curable geneesbaar
curate hulppredikant; [Roman Catholicism] kapelaan
curative heilzaam; geneeskrachtig
curator beheerder, curator, conservator
¹curb (n) **1** rem, beteugeling **2** [Am] stoeprand
²curb (vb) intomen [also fig]; beteugelen, in bedwang houden ‖ [Am] ~ *your dog!* (hond) in de goot!
curd wrongel; gestremde melk: ~s *and whey* wrongel en wei
curd cheese kwark; [Belg] platte kaas
curdle stremmen, (doen) stollen: *her blood* ~d *at the spectacle* het schouwspel deed haar bloed stollen
¹cure (n) **1** (medische) behandeling, kuur **2** (genees)middelʰ, medicamentʰ; remedie [also fig] **3** genezing, herstelʰ
²cure (vb) **1** kuren, een kuur doen **2** een heilzame werking hebben **3** verduurzaamd worden, roken, drogen
³cure (vb) verduurzamen, conserveren; zouten, roken [fish, meat]; drogen [tobacco]
⁴cure (vb) genezen, beter maken, (doen) herstellen: ~ o.s. *of bad habits* zijn slechte gewoonten afleren
cure-all wondermiddelʰ; panacee
curfew 1 avondklok, uitgaansverbodʰ **2** spertijd
curiosity 1 curiositeit, rariteit **2** nieuwsgierigheid, benieuwdheid: ~ *killed the cat* [roughly] de duivel heeft het vragen uitgevonden **3** leergierigheid
curious 1 nieuwsgierig, benieuwd **2** leergierig **3** curieus, merkwaardig: ~*ly (enough)* merkwaardigerwijs, vreemd genoeg
¹curl (n) **1** (haar)krul, pijpenkrul **2** krul, spiraal
²curl (vb) **1** spiralen; zich winden [of plant]: *smoke* ~ed *from the chimney* uit de schoorsteen kringelde rook **2** (om)krullen
³curl (vb) **1** met krullen versieren **2** doen (om)krullen **3** kronkelen om, winden om ‖ *he* ~ed *his lip* hij keek smalend
⁴curl (vb) krullen [of hair]; in de krul zetten, kroezen
curler krulspeld, roller, kruller
curlew wulp
curl up 1 [inform] (doen) ineenkrimpen [in horror, of shame, with joy etc] **2** omkrullen **3** [inform] neergaan, neerhalen, in elkaar

(doen) klappen, tegen de vlakte (doen) gaan **4** zich (behaaglijk) oprollen, in elkaar kruipen

currant 1 krent **2** aalbes: *red* (or: *white*) ~ rode (*or:* witte) bes

currency 1 valuta, munt, (papier)geld[h]: *foreign* currencies vreemde valuta's **2** munt-, geldstelsel[h] **3** (geld)circulatie, (geld)omloop **4** gangbaarheid: *gain* ~ ingang vinden, zich verspreiden

[1]**current** (n) **1** stroom; stroming [in gas, liquid] **2** loop, gang, tendens **3** (elektrische) stroom: *alternating* ~ wisselstroom; *direct* ~ gelijkstroom

[2]**current** (adj) **1** huidig, actueel **2** gangbaar, geldend, heersend **3** [fin] in omloop

current account rekening-courant, (bank)girorekening, lopende rekening

current affairs actualiteiten, nieuws[h]

currently momenteel, tegenwoordig

curriculum onderwijsprogramma[h], leerplan[h]

curry 1 kerrie(poeder[h]) **2** Indiaas gerecht, curry: *go for a* ~ uit eten gaan in een Indiaas restaurant; Indiaas halen

[1]**curse** (n) **1** vloek(woord[h]), verwensing, doem: *lay* s.o. under a ~ een vloek op iem. leggen **2** bezoeking, ramp, plaag

[2]**curse** (vb) **1** vervloeken, verwensen, een vloek uitspreken over: [inform] ~ *it!* (or: *you!*) verdraaid! **2** [esp passive] straffen, bezoeken, kwellen: *be* ~*d with* gebukt gaan onder

[3]**curse** (vb) (uit)vloeken, vloeken (op), (uit)schelden

cursive aaneengeschreven

cursory vluchtig, oppervlakkig

curt kortaf, kortaangebonden: *a* ~ *manner* een botte manier van doen

curtail 1 inkorten, bekorten, verkorten **2** verkleinen, verminderen, beperken

[1]**curtain** (n) **1** gordijn[h], voorhang(sel[h]); [fig] barrière: ~ *of smoke* rookgordijn **2** [theatre] doek[h], (toneel)gordijn[h], scherm[h]

[2]**curtain** (vb) voorzien van gordijnen: ~ *off* afschermen [by means of a curtain]

curts(e)y reverence, korte buiging

[1]**curve** (n) **1** gebogen lijn, kromme, curve, boog **2** bocht [in road] **3** ronding; welving [of woman] ‖ [Am; inform, fig] *throw* s.o. a ~ iem. op het verkeerde been zetten

[2]**curve** (vb) buigen, een bocht (doen) maken, (zich) krommen

[1]**cushion** (n) **1** kussen[h], (lucht)kussen[h] **2** stootkussen[h], buffer, schokdemper **3** [billiards] band

[2]**cushion** (vb) **1** voorzien van kussen(s) **2** dempen, verzachten; opvangen [bang, shock, effect] **3** in de watten leggen, beschermen: *a* ~*ed life* een beschermd leventje

cushy [inform] makkelijk, comfortabel: *a* ~

job een luizenbaantje, een makkie

custodian 1 beheerder, conservator, bewaarder **2** voogd **3** [Am] conciërge, beheerder

custody 1 voogdij, zorg **2** beheer[h], hoede, bewaring **3** hechtenis, voorarrest[h], verzekerde bewaring: *take* s.o. *into* ~ iem. aanhouden

custom 1 gewoonte, gebruik[h] **2** klandizie **3** (-s) douaneheffing, invoerrechten **4** (-s) douane(dienst)

customary 1 gebruikelijk, gewoonlijk, normaal **2** gewoonte-, gebruik(s)-

custom-built op bestelling gebouwd, gebouwd (gemaakt) volgens de wensen van de koper

customer 1 klant, (regelmatige) afnemer **2** [inform] klant, gast: *awkward* ~ rare snijboon, vreemde vogel; *he is a tough* ~ het is een taaie

[1]**cut** (n) **1** slag (snee) met scherp voorwerp, (mes)sne(d)e, snijwond, houw, (zweep)slag **2** afgesneden, afgehakt, afgeknipt stuk[h], lap; bout [meat] **3** (haar)knipbeurt **4** vermindering, verlaging **5** coupure, weglating, verkorting **6** snit, coupe **7** doorsnijding, geul, kloof, kanaal[h], doorgraving, kortere weg: *take a short* ~ een kortere weg nemen **8** [inform] (aan)deel[h], provisie, commissie **9** [film] scherpe overgang ‖ ~ *and thrust* (woorden)steekspel, vinnig debat; [inform] *be a* ~ *above* beter zijn dan

[2]**cut** (vb) **1** (zich laten) snijden, knippen: *the butter* ~*s easily* de boter snijdt gemakkelijk **2** een inkeping (scheiding) maken, snijden, knippen, hakken, kappen, kerven, maaien ‖ ~ *and run* de benen nemen, 'm smeren; ~ *both ways* a) tweesnijdend zijn; b) voor- en nadelen hebben

[3]**cut** (vb) **1** snijden in, verwonden, stuksnijden: ~ *one's finger* zich in zijn vinger snijden **2** afsnijden, doorsnijden, lossnijden, wegsnijden, (af)knippen, (om)hakken, (om)kappen, (om)zagen: ~ *open* openhalen; ~ *away* wegsnijden, weghakken, wegknippen, snoeien; ~ *in half* doormidden snijden, knippen **3** maken met scherp voorwerp, kerven, slijpen, bijsnijden, bijknippen, bijhakken, boren, graveren, opnemen; maken [CD, record]: ~ *one's initials into sth.* zijn initialen ergens in kerven **4** maaien, oogsten; binnenhalen [crop] **5** inkorten; snijden (in) [book, film etc]; afsnijden [route, corner]; besnoeien (op), inkrimpen, bezuinigen: ~ *the travelling time by a third* de reistijd met een derde terugbrengen **6** stopzetten, ophouden met, afsluiten; afsnijden [water, energy]; uitschakelen, afzetten **7** krijgen [tooth]: *I'm* ~*ting my wisdom tooth* mijn verstandskies komt door **8** (diep) raken; pijn doen [of remark etc] **9** negeren, veronachtzamen, links laten liggen: ~ s.o. *dead* (or: *cold*) iem. niet zien

staan, iem. straal negeren
⁴cut (vb) **1** snijden, kruisen **2** [cards] couperen, afnemen **3** [inform] verzuimen, spijbelen, overslaan
cut across 1 afsnijden, doorsteken, een kortere weg nemen **2** strijdig zijn met, ingaan tegen **3** doorbreken, uitstijgen boven: ~ *traditional party loyalties* de aloude partijbindingen doorbreken
¹cut back (vb) snoeien [plants]
²cut back (vb) inkrimpen, besnoeien, bezuinigen
¹cut down (vb) minderen: *you work too much, try to* ~ *a bit* je werkt te veel, probeer wat te minderen
²cut down (vb) **1** kappen, omhakken, omhouwen, vellen **2** inperken, beperken, verminderen: ~ *one's expenses* zijn bestedingen beperken **3** inkorten, korter maken: ~ *an article* een artikel inkorten
cut down on minderen met, het verbruik beperken van: ~ *smoking* minder gaan roken
cute schattig, snoezig, leuk
cuticle 1 opperhuid **2** nagelriem
cutie leuk iem., mooie meid (jongen)
cut in 1 er(gens) tussen komen, in de rede vallen, onderbreken **2** gevaarlijk invoegen [with a vehicle]; snijden: ~ *on* s.o. iem. snijden
cut into 1 aansnijden: ~ *a cake* een taart aansnijden **2** onderbreken, tussenbeide komen, in de rede vallen: ~ *a conversation* zich (plotseling) mengen in een gesprek **3** storend werken op, een aanslag doen op: *this job cuts into my evenings off* deze baan kost me een groot deel van mijn vrije avonden
cutlery bestekʰ, eetgereiʰ, couvertʰ
cutlet [culinary] lapje vleesʰ, (lams)koteletjeʰ, kalfskoteletjeʰ
cut off 1 afsnijden, afhakken, afknippen **2** afsluiten, stopzetten, blokkeren **3** (van de buitenwereld) afsluiten, isoleren: *villages ~ by floods* door overstromingen geïsoleerde dorpen **4** onderbreken; verbreken [telephone connection]
cut-off scheiding, grens, afsluiting: ~ *date* sluitingsdatum
¹cut out (vb) **1** uitvallen, defect raken, het begeven: *the engine* ~ de motor sloeg af **2** afslaan: *the boiler cuts out at 90 degrees* de boiler slaat af bij 90 graden
²cut out (vb) **1** uitsnijden, uitknippen, uithakken, modelleren, vormen **2** knippen [dress, pattern]: *cut it out!* hou ermee op! **3** [inform] weglaten, verwijderen, schrappen **4** uitschakelen, elimineren; [inform] het nakijken geven **5** uitschakelen, afzetten || [inform] *be ~ for* geknipt zijn voor
cut-out 1 uitgeknipte, uitgesneden, uitgehakte figuur⁺ʰ, knipselʰ **2** [techn] afslag, (stroom)onderbreker: *automatic* ~ automa-

tische afslag, thermostaat
cut-price 1 met korting; goedkoop **2** discount-: ~ *shop* discountzaak
cutter 1 iem. die snijdt, gebruiker van scherp voorwerp, knipper, snijder, hakker, houwer, slijper **2** snijwerktuigʰ, snijmachine, schaar, tang, mesʰ; [in butcher's shop] cutter **3** sloep (van oorlogsschipʰ) **4** (motor)barkasʰ [for transport between ship and coast] **5** kotter **6** kustwachter, kustbewakingsschipʰ **7** [film] filmmonteerder
cut through zich worstelen door, doorbreken, zich heen werken door
¹cutting (n) **1** (afgesneden/afgeknipt/uitgeknipt) stuk(je)ʰ **2** stek [of plant] **3** (kranten)knipselʰ
²cutting (adj) **1** scherp, bijtend: ~ *remark* grievende opmerking **2** bijtend, snijdend; guur [of wind]
cutting edge 1 absolute voorhoede; (spraakmakende) avant-garde **2** voorsprong
cutting-edge allermodernst; allernieuwst, geavanceerd
cutting room montageruimte
cuttlefish inktvis
¹cut up (vb) zich (in stukken) laten snijden, zich (in stukken) laten knippen || [inform] ~ *rough* tekeergaan
²cut up (vb) **1** (in stukken) snijden, knippen **2** in de pan hakken, (vernietigend) verslaan **3** [inform] niets heel laten van, afkraken **4** [inform] (ernstig) aangrijpen: *be ~ about* sth. zich iets vreselijk aantrekken, ergens ondersteboven van zijn
cyanide cyanideʰ
cyberbullying het cyberpesten, het digipesten
cybercafé internetcaféʰ
cybercrime computercriminaliteit
cyclamen cyclaam
¹cycle (n) **1** cyclus **2** kringloop; [fig also] spiraal **3** [elec] trilling, trilling per seconde, hertz **4** *bicycle* fiets: *go by* ~ met de fiets gaan **5** *motorbicycle* motorfiets: *go by* ~ met de motorfiets gaan
²cycle (vb) **1** cirkelen, ronddraaien, kringen beschrijven **2** fietsen
cyclist fietser, wielrenner
cyclone cycloon, wervelstorm, tyfoon, tornado
cyder *see* cider
cygnet jonge zwaan
cylinder 1 cilinder **2** magazijnʰ [of revolver]; rol, wals, trommel, buis, pijp, (gas)fles
cynical cynisch
cynicism cynisme, cynische uitlating
¹Cypriot (n) Cyprioot, Cypriotische
²Cypriot (adj) Cypriotisch
Cyprus Cyprus
czar tsaar; [Am; inform] koning
¹Czech (n) Tsjech(ische)

²**Czech** (adj) Tsjechisch

d

d *died* gest.

, gestorven

¹**dab** (n) **1** tik(je^h), klopje^h lik(je^h), kwast(je^h), hoopje^h: *a ~ of paint* (or: *butter*) een likje verf (*or:* boter) **3** veegje^h: *a ~ with a sponge* (even) een sponsje eroverheen **4** kei, kraan: *he is a ~ (hand) at squash* hij kan ontzettend goed squashen **5** (-s) vingerafdrukken

²**dab** (vb) opbrengen [paint]: *~ on* (zachtjes) aanbrengen

³**dab** (vb) **1** (aan)tikken, (be)kloppen **2** betten, deppen

dabble 1 plassen, ploeteren **2** liefhebberen: *~ at* (or: *in*) *arts* (wat) rommelen in de kunst **3** (in water) rondscharrelen [across bottom]

dabbler liefhebber, amateur

dachshund teckel, taks, dashond

dad [inform] pa

daddy papa, pappie

daddy longlegs langpoot(mug); [Am] hooiwagen(achtige); langbeen

daffodil (gele) narcis

daft 1 halfgaar, niet goed snik **2** idioot, belachelijk, maf

dagger dolk || *at ~s drawn with s.o.* op voet van oorlog met iem.

¹**daily** (n) **1** dagblad^h, krant **2** werkster, schoonmaakster

²**daily** (adj) **1** dagelijks: *~ newspaper* dagblad **2** geregeld, vaak, constant || *the ~ grind* de dagelijkse sleur

³**daily** (adv) dagelijks, per dag

dainty 1 sierlijk, verfijnd **2** teer, gevoelig **3** kostelijk, verrukkelijk: *~ food* uitgelezen voedsel **4** kieskeurig, veeleisend

dairy 1 zuivelbedrijf^h, zuivelproducent **2** melkboer, melkman **3** melkvee(stapel)^h

dais podium^h, verhoging

daisy 1 madelief(je^h) **2** margriet, grote madelief || *be pushing up the daisies* onder de groene zoden liggen

dally 1 lanterfanten, (rond)lummelen, klungelen **2** treuzelen || *~ with* a) flirten met; b) spelen (or: stoeien) met [an idea]

¹**dam** (n) **1** (stuw)dam **2** barrière, belemmering, hinderpaal **3** moederdier^h [quadruped]

²**dam** (vb) **1** van een dam voorzien, afdammen **2** indammen, beteugelen

¹**damage** (n) **1** schade, beschadiging, averij **2** (-s) schadevergoeding, schadeloosstelling: *we will claim ~ from them* we zullen schadevergoeding van hen eisen

²**damage** (vb) beschadigen, schade toebrengen, aantasten

¹**damn** (n) [vulg] zak, (malle)moer: *not be worth a (tuppenny) ~* geen ene moer waard zijn; *not give a ~* het geen (ene) moer kunnen schelen

²**damn** (adj) godvergeten: *a ~ fool* een stomme idioot

³**damn** (vb) **1** [inform] vervloeken, verwensen: *I'll be ~ed if I go* ik vertik het (mooi) om te gaan **2** te gronde richten, ruïneren **3** (af)kraken, afbreken: *the play was ~ed by the critics* het stuk werd door de recensenten de grond in geboord **4** vloeken (tegen), uitvloeken

damning belastend, (ernstig) bezwarend, vernietigend

¹**damp** (n) **1** vocht^h, vochtigheid **2** nevel, damp

²**damp** (adj) vochtig, nattig, klam || *~ squib* sof, fiasco

³**damp** (vb) **1** bevochtigen **2** smoren, doven, temperen: *~ down* afdekken **3** temperen, doen bekoelen: *~ down s.o.'s enthusiasm* iemands enthousiasme temperen

dampen 1 bevochtigen **2** temperen, ontmoedigen

damper 1 sleutel [of stove]; regelschuif, demper **2** schokdemper, schokbreker **3** (trillings)demper **4** domper, teleurstelling

damsel [mockingly] jongedame: *a ~ in distress* een jonkvrouw in nood

¹**dance** (n) **1** dans, dansnummer^h **2** dansfeest^h, bal^h, dansavond || *lead s.o. a pretty ~* iem. het leven zuur maken

²**dance** (vb) (doen/laten) dansen, springen, (staan te) trappelen: *the leaves were dancing in the wind* de blaren dwarrelden in de wind; *her eyes ~d for* (or: *with*) *joy* haar ogen tintelden van vreugde; *~ a baby on one's knee* een kindje op zijn knie laten rijden

dancer danser(es), ballerina

dancing het dansen; danskunst, gedans^h

dandelion paardenbloem

dandle wiege(le)n [child]; laten dansen: *~ a baby on one's knee* een kindje op zijn knie laten rijden

dandruff (hoofd)roos

¹**dandy** (n) **1** fat, dandy, modegek **2** juweel(tje)^h, prachtstuk^h, prachtfiguur^h

²**dandy** (adj) **1** fatterig, dandyachtig **2** [Am] tiptop, puik, prima

Dane Deen || *Great ~* Deense dog

danger gevaar^h, risico^h: *be in ~ of* het gevaar lopen te; *out of ~* buiten (levens)gevaar

dangerous gevaarlijk, riskant

¹**dangle** (vb) bengelen, bungelen, slingeren

²**dangle** (vb) laten bengelen, slingeren: [fig] *~ sth. before* (or: *in front of*) *s.o.* iem. met iets trachten te paaien

¹**Danish** (n) Deen(se)

²**Danish** (adj) Deens
dank klam
Danube Donau
dapper 1 keurig, netjes, goed verzorgd **2** zwierig
dapple (be)spikkelen, met vlekken bedekken
¹**dare** (n) **1** uitdaging: *do sth. for a* ~ iets doen omdat men wordt uitgedaagd **2** gedurfde handeling, moedige daad
²**dare** (vb) uitdagen, tarten: *she ~d Bill to hit her* ze daagde Bill uit haar te slaan
³**dare** (aux vb) (aan)durven, het wagen, het lef hebben te: *he does not* ~ *to answer back, he* ~ *not answer back* hij durft niet tegen te spreken; *how* ~ *(you say such things)?* hoe durf je zoiets te zeggen? ‖ *I* ~ *say* ik veronderstel, ik neem aan, misschien
daredevil waaghals, durfal
¹**daring** (n) **1** moed, durf, lefʰ **2** gedurfdheid
²**daring** (adj) **1** brutaal, moedig, gedurfd **2** gewaagd
¹**dark** (n) **1** donkere kleur **2** donkere plaats **3** duisterʰ, duisternis: *in the* ~ in het donker; [fig] in het geniep **4** vallen van de avond: *after* (or: *before*) ~ na (or: voor) het donker ‖ *keep s.o. in the* ~ *about sth.* iem. ergens niets over laten weten; *be in the* ~ *(about sth.)* in het duister tasten (omtrent iets)
²**dark** (adj) **1** donker, duister, onverlicht: ~ *brown* donkerbruin **2** somber: *the* ~ *side of things* de schaduwzijde der dingen **3** verborgen, geheimzinnig ~ donker; laag en vol [of voice] ‖ ~ *horse* a) outsider [in race]; b) onbekende mededinger [at elections]
darkness duisternis, verdorvenheid: *powers of* ~ kwade machten
¹**darling** (n) schat(jeʰ), lieveling
²**darling** (adj) geliefd, (aller)lief(st)
¹**darn** (n) stop, gestopt gatʰ, stopselʰ
²**darn** (vb) stoppen, mazen
³**darn** (vb) (ver)vloeken, verwensen: ~ *(it)!* verdorie!, verdraaid!
darned [inform] verdraaid, vervloekt
¹**dart** (n) **1** pijl(tjeʰ) **2** (plotselinge, scherpe) uitval [also fig]; steek, sprong: *make a ~ for the door* naar de deur springen
²**dart** (vb) toesnellen, wegsnellen, toeschieten, wegschieten, toestuiven, wegstuiven
dartboard dartbordʰ
darts dartsʰ, vogelpik
¹**dash** (n) **1** ietsjeʰ, tik(kelt)jeʰ: ~ *of brandy* scheutje cognac **2** (snelle, krachtige) slag, dreun **3** spurt, sprint, uitval **4** streep [in Morse code]: *dots and ~es* punten en strepen **5** kastlijn, gedachtestreep(jeʰ)
²**dash** (vb) **1** (vooruit)stormen, (zich) storten, denderen: *I'm afraid I must ~ now* en nu moet ik er als de bliksem vandoor; ~ *away* wegstormen; ~ *off* er (als de gesmeerde bliksem) vandoor gaan **2** (rond)banjeren, (met veel

vertoon) rondspringen: ~ *about* rondbanjeren
³**dash** (vb) **1** verbrijzelen, verpletteren; [fig] verijdelen: *all my expectations were ~ed* al mijn verwachtingen werden de bodem ingeslagen **2** snel doen: ~ *sth. down* (or: *off*) iets nog even gauw opschrijven **3** vervloeken, verwensen: [inform] ~ *it (all)!* verdraaid! **4** doorspekken, larderen
⁴**dash** (vb) (met grote kracht) slaan, smijten, beuken: ~ *down* neersmijten; *the waves ~ed against the rocks* de golven beukten tegen de rotsen
dashboard dashboardʰ
dashed verdraaid, verduiveld
dashing 1 levendig, wilskrachtig, vlot **2** opzichtig
data 1 feitʰ, gegevenʰ **2** gegevens, data, informatie: *insufficient* ~ onvoldoende gegevens; *the* ~ *is* (or: *are*) *being prepared for processing* de informatie wordt gereedgemaakt voor verwerking
database database
data manager gegevensbeheerder
data stick USB-stick, datastick, geheugenstick
¹**date** (n) **1** dadel **2** datum, dagtekening **3** afspraak(jeʰ) **4** [Am] vriend(innet)jeʰ, partner, 'afspraakjeʰ', dateʰ **5** tijd(perkʰ), periode: *of early* ~, *of an early* ~ uit een vroege periode ‖ *out of* ~ verouderd, ouderwets; *to* ~ tot op heden; *up to* a) bij (de tijd), modern, geavanceerd; b) volledig bijgewerkt; *bring up to* ~ bijwerken, moderniseren
²**date** (vb) **1** verouderen, uit de tijd raken **2** dateren: ~ *back to* stammen uit **3** [Am] afspraakjes hebben, uitgaan, daten
³**date** (vb) **1** dateren, dagtekenen **2** dateren, de ouderdom vaststellen van: ~ *a painting* een schilderij dateren **3** uitgaan met, afspraakjes hebben met, vrijen met
dated ouderwets, gedateerd, verouderd
dating agency bemiddelingsbureauʰ
dative derde naamval
datum nulpuntʰ [of scale etc]; (gemiddeld laag)waterpeilʰ
¹**daub** (n) **1** lik, klodder, smeerʰ **2** kladschilderij, kladderwerkʰ **3** (muur)pleister, pleisterkalk
²**daub** (vb) besmeren, bekladden, besmeuren
daughter dochter
daughter-in-law schoondochter
daunt ontmoedigen, intimideren, afschrikken: *a ~ing prospect* een afschrikwekkend vooruitzicht
dauntless 1 onbevreesd **2** volhardend, vasthoudend
dawdle treuzelen, teuten ‖ ~ *over one's food* met lange tanden eten
¹**dawn** (n) dageraad [also fig]; zonsopgang:

the ~ of **civilization** de ochtendstond der beschaving; *at* ~ bij het krieken van de dag
²**dawn** (vb) dagen [also fig]; licht worden,
aanbreken, duidelijk worden: *it ~ed on me*
het drong tot me door
day 1 dag, etmaalʰ: *this* ~ **fortnight** (or:
week) vandaag over veertien dagen (*or:* een
week); ~ *and* **night, night** *and* ~ dag en nacht;
the ~ *after* **tomorrow** overmorgen; *the* ~ *before* **yesterday** eergisteren; *from* ~ **one** meteen, vanaf de eerste dag; ~ *in,* ~ *out* dag in,
dag uit; ~ *after* ~ dag in, dag uit; ~ *by* ~, *from*
~ *to* ~ dagelijks, van dag tot dag **2** werkdag:
an **8-hour** ~ een achturige werkdag; ~ *off*
vrije dag **3** [in compounds] (hoogtij)dag
4 tijdstipʰ, gelegenheid: *some* ~ a) eens,
eenmaal, op een keer; b) bij gelegenheid
5 dag, daglichtʰ: [form] *by* ~ overdag **6** tijd,
periode, dag(en): *(in)* ~*s of* **old** (or: **yore**) (in)
vroeger tijden; *he has* **had** *his* ~ hij heeft zijn
tijd gehad; *those* were *the* ~*s* dat waren nog
eens tijden; *these* ~*s* tegenwoordig, vandaag
de dag; *(in) this* ~ *and age* vandaag de dag
7 slag, strijd: *carry* (or: *save, win*) *the* ~ de
slag winnen **8** (-s) levensdagen, levenʰ || *that
will be the* ~ dat wil ik zien; *all in a* ~'*s work* de
normale gang van zaken; *call it a* ~ a) het
voor gezien houden; b) sterven; *make s.o.'s* ~
iemands dag goedmaken; *one of those* ~*s*
zo'n dag waarop alles tegenzit; *to the* ~ op
de dag af; *to this* ~ tot op de dag van vandaag, tot op heden; *from one* ~ *to* the next
van vandaag op morgen; [inform] *every* oth-
er ~ om de haverklap; *the other* ~ onlangs,
pas geleden; *she is thirty if she is a* ~ ze is op
zijn minst dertig
daybreak dageraad, zonsopgang
day-care dagopvang, kinderopvang: ~ *centre* crèche, kinderdagverblijf
¹**daydream** (n) dagdroom
²**daydream** (vb) dagdromen; mijmeren
daylight 1 daglichtʰ **2** dageraad || *see* ~ iets
in de gaten krijgen
daylight robbery 1 beroving op klaarlichte dag **2** schaamteloze oplichting
day-to-day 1 dagelijks **2** van dag tot dag
daytrip uitjeʰ, uitstapjeʰ, dagjeʰ uit
¹**daze** (n) verbijstering: *in a* ~ verbluft, ontsteld
²**daze** (vb) verbijsteren, verbluffen
¹**dazzle** (vb) **1** verblinden **2** verbijsteren
²**dazzle** (vb) imponeren, indruk maken (op)
DC *direct current* gelijkstroom
D-day *Decision day* D-day, D-dag, kritische
begindag
¹**dead** (n) hoogte-, dieptepuntʰ: *in the* (or: *at*)
~ *of night* in het holst van de nacht
²**dead** (adj) **1** dood, overleden, gestorven:
over my ~ **body** over mijn lijk; *rise from* **the** ~
uit de dood opstaan **2** verouderd **3** onwerk-
zaam, leeg, uit, op: ~ *battery* lege accu; *cut*

out (the) ~ **wood** verwijderen van overbodige
franje; ~ *and* **gone** dood (en begraven); [fig]
voorgoed voorbij **4** uitgestorven: *the place is*
~ het is er een dooie boel **5** gevoelloos, ongevoelig **6** [sport] uit (het spel) [of ball]
7 volkomen, absoluut: ~ *certainty* absolute
zekerheid; ~ *loss* a) puur verlies; b) tijdverspilling; c) [inform] miskleun, fiasco **8** abrupt, plotseling: *come to a* ~ *stop* (plotseling)
stokstijf stil (blijven) staan **9** exact, precies: ~
centre precieze midden || ~ *as a* **doornail**
morsdood; ~ *duck* mislukk(el)ing, verliezer; ~
end a) doodlopende straat; b) impasse, dood
punt; *come to a* ~ *end* op niets uitlopen;
[sport] ~ *heat* gedeelde eerste (tweede enz.)
plaats; *flog a* ~ *horse* achter de feiten aanlopen; ~ *letter* a) dode letter [of law]; b) onbe-
stelbare brief; *wait for a* ~ *man's* *shoes* op iemands bezit azen; *make a* ~ *set at* a) te lijf
gaan [fig]; b) (vastberaden) avances maken;
~ *to the* **world** a) in diepe slaap; b) bewusteloos; *I wouldn't be seen* ~ *in that dress* voor
geen goud zou ik me in die jurk vertonen
³**dead** (adv) **1** volkomen, absoluut: ~ *straight*
kaarsrecht; *stop* ~ stokstijf blijven staan; ~
tired (or: *exhausted*) doodop, bekaf **2** pal,
onmiddellijk: ~ *ahead of you* pal voor je; ~
against a) pal tegen [of wind]; b) fel tegen
[plan etc]
deadbeat nietsnut
dead beat doodop, bekaf
¹**deaden** (vb) de kracht verliezen, de helderheid verliezen, verflauwen, verzwakken
²**deaden** (vb) **1** verzwakken; dempen
[sound]; verzachten, dof maken [colour]
2 ongevoelig maken, verdoven: *drugs to* ~
the pain medicijnen om de pijn te stillen
dead-end 1 doodlopend **2** uitzichtloos
deadline (tijds)limiet, uiterste (in)leverda-
tum: *meet the* ~ binnen de tijdslimiet blijven;
miss the ~ de tijdslimiet overschrijden
deadlock patstelling
deadly 1 dodelijk [also fig]; fataal **2** [depr]
doods, dodelijk (saai) **3** doods-, aarts- **4** [in-
form] enorm **5** oer-, uiterst: ~ *dull* oersaai ||
the seven ~ **sins** de zeven hoofdzonden
deaf doof [also fig] || *as* ~ *as a* **(door)post**
stokdoof; *fall on* ~ **ears** geen gehoor vinden;
turn a ~ *ear* *to* doof zijn voor
deaf-aid (ge)hoorapparaatʰ
deafen verdoven, doof maken, overstemmen
deafening oorverdovend
deaf-mute doofstom
¹**deal** (n) **1** transactie, overeenkomst, handel
2 (grote) hoeveelheid, mate: *a great* ~ *of
money* heel wat geld **3** [depr] (koe)handel-
tjeʰ, deal **4** [cards] gift, het geven, beurt om
te geven: *it's your* ~ jij moet geven || *it's a* ~*!*
afgesproken!, akkoord!
²**deal** (vb) zaken doen, handelen

³**deal** (vb) geven, (uit)delen: ~ *(out)* *fairly* eerlijk verdelen
dealer 1 handelaar, koopman, dealer **2** effectenhandelaar
dealing 1 manier van zaken doen, aanpak **2** (-s) transacties, affaires; relaties [business] **3** (-s) betrekkingen, omgang
deal with 1 zaken doen met, handel drijven met, kopen bij **2** behandelen, afhandelen: ~ *complaints* klachten behandelen **3** aanpakken, een oplossing zoeken voor **4** optreden tegen **5** behandelen, omgaan met: *be* **impossible** *to* ~ onmogelijk in de omgang zijn **6** gaan over: *the book deals with racism* het boek gaat over racisme
dean 1 deken **2** oudste, overste **3** [university] decaan, faculteitsvoorzitter, (studenten)-decaan
¹**dear** (n) schat, lieverd
²**dear** (adj) **1** dierbaar, lief **2** lief, schattig **3** duur, prijzig **4** beste, lieve; geachte [eg in salutation]: ~ *Julia* beste Julia; *my* ~ *lady* mevrouw; ~ *sir* geachte heer; ~ *sirs* mijne heren, geachte heren **5** dierbaar, lief: *I* **hold** *her very* ~ ze ligt me na aan het hart ‖ *for* ~ *life* of zijn leven ervan afhangt
³**dear** (adv) **1** duur (betaald) [also fig] **2** innig, vurig
dearest liefste
dearly 1 innig, vurig: *wish* ~ vurig wensen **2** duur(betaald) [also fig]: *pay* ~ *for sth.* iets duur betalen **3** vurig
dearth schaarste, tekortʰ: *a* ~ *of talent* te weinig talent
death 1 sterfgevalʰ, slachtofferʰ **2** dood, overlijdenʰ; [fig] eindeʰ: *assisted* ~ hulp bij zelfdoding; [fig] *be in at the* ~ een onderneming zien stranden; *be the* ~ *of s.o.* iemands dood zijn [also fig]; *bore s.o. to* ~ iem. stierlijk vervelen; *war to the* ~ oorlog op leven en dood **3** de Dood, Magere Hein ‖ *at* ~*'s* **door** op sterven, de dood nabij; *dice with* ~ met vuur spelen; *flog to* ~ uitentreuren herhalen; *worked to* ~ afgezaagd, uitgemolken
death certificate overlijdensakte
death duty successierechtʰ
deathly doods, lijk-: ~ *pale* doodsbleek
death penalty doodstraf
death row [Am] dodencel(len): *be* **on** ~*(s)* ter dood veroordeeld zijn
death warrant 1 executiebevelʰ **2** [fig] doodvonnisʰ, genadeslag
debase 1 degraderen **2** vervalsen **3** verlagen, vernederen
¹**debate** (n) **1** (+ on, about) debatʰ (over), discussie, dispuutʰ: *that question is* **open** *to* ~ dat staat nog ter discussie **2** twist, conflictʰ, strijd **3** overweging, beraadʰ
²**debate** (vb) **1** (+ about, upon) debatteren (over), discussiëren, een debat houden **2** beraadslagen

³**debate** (vb) bespreken, beraadslagen over, in debat treden over
debauched liederlijk; verdorven
debauchery losbandigheid
¹**debit** (n) **1** schuldpost, debitering, debetboeking **2** debetsaldoʰ
²**debit** (vb) debiteren, als debet boeken
debit card bankpas, pinpas
debris puinʰ, brokstukken
debt schuld, (terugbetalings)verplichting: *owe s.o. a* ~ *of* **gratitude** iem. dank verschuldigd zijn; *get* (or: *run*) *into* ~ schulden maken
debtor 1 schuldenaar **2** debiteur
debug 1 [roughly] ontluizen, [roughly] van insecten ontdoen **2** (van mankementen) zuiveren, kinderziekten verhelpen bij **3** (van fouten) zuiveren, debuggen
debut debuutʰ
decade decenniumʰ, periode van tien jaar
decadence decadentie; vervalʰ [in art]
decadent decadent, genotzuchtig
decaf *decaffeinated coffee* cafeïnevrij(e koffie)
decanter decanteerfles; karaf
decapitate onthoofden
decathlon [athletics] tienkamp
¹**decay** (n) **1** vervalʰ, (geleidelijke) achteruitgang **2** bederfʰ, rotting
²**decay** (vb) **1** vervallen, in verval raken **2** (ver)rotten, bederven, verteren: *sugar may* ~ *the* **teeth** suiker kan tot tandbederf leiden
deceased overleden, pas gestorven
deceit bedrogʰ, oneerlijkheid
deceive bedriegen, misleiden, om de tuin leiden: *if my* **ears** *do not* ~ *me* als mijn oren me niet bedriegen
decelerate vertragen, afremmen, vaart minderen
December december
decency fatsoenʰ, fatsoenlijkheid
decent 1 fatsoenlijk **2** wellevend **3** behoorlijk: *a* ~ *wage* een redelijk loon **4** geschikt: *a* ~ *guy* een geschikte kerel
deception 1 misleiding, list, bedrogʰ **2** (valse) kunstgreep, (smerige) truc, kunstjeʰ
deceptive bedrieglijk, misleidend: *appearances are often* ~ schijn bedriegt
decibel decibel
¹**decide** (vb) **1** beslissen, een beslissing nemen, een keuze maken **2** besluiten, een besluit nemen: ~ *against* afzien van; *we have* ~*d against* it we hebben besloten het niet te doen
²**decide** (vb) **1** beslissen, uitmaken: ~ *a* **question** een knoop doorhakken **2** een uitspraak doen in
deciduous loof-: ~ *tree* loofboom
¹**decimal** (n) **1** decimale breuk: *recurring* ~ repeterende breuk **2** decimaal getalʰ
²**decimal** (adj) decimaal: ~ *point* decimaalteken, komma

decipher ontcijferen, decoderen
decision beslissing, besluit^h, uitspraak: *arrive at* (or: *take*) a ~ een beslissing nemen
decision maker beleidsvormer
decisive 1 beslissend, doorslaggevend **2** beslist, gedecideerd, zelfverzekerd
deck 1 (scheeps)dek^h, tussendekse ruimte: *clear the* ~*s (for action)* [fig] zich opmaken voor de strijd; *below* ~*(s)* benedendeks; *on* ~ aan dek **2** verdieping van bus **3** [Am] spel^h (kaarten) **4** (tape)deck^h, cassettedeck^h || *hit the* ~ op je bek vallen; [boxing] neergaan
deck-chair ligstoel, dekstoel
¹declaim (vb) **1** uitvaren, schelden: ~ *against* uitvaren tegen **2** retorisch spreken
²declaim (vb) declameren, voordragen
declaration 1 (openbare/formele) verklaring, afkondiging: *Declaration of Independence* Amerikaanse onafhankelijkheidsverklaring **2** geschreven verklaring: ~ *of income* aangifte inkomstenbelasting
¹declare (vb) **1** een verklaring afleggen, een aankondiging doen **2** (+ against, for) stelling nemen (tegen/voor), zich (openlijk) uitspreken (tegen/voor)
²declare (vb) **1** bekendmaken, aankondigen, afkondigen **2** bestempelen als, uitroepen tot: ~ *s.o. the* **winner** iem. tot winnaar uitroepen **3** aangeven [goods at Customs, income etc]: *nothing to* ~ niets aan te geven
declination 1 (voorover)helling **2** buiging **3** verval^h, achteruitgang **4** [Am] afwijzing **5** declinatie; [compass] afwijking(shoek)
¹decline (n) **1** verval^h, achteruitgang, aftakeling: *fall* (or: *go*) *into a* ~ beginnen af te takelen, in verval raken **2** daling, afname, vermindering: *on the* ~ tanend **3** slotfase, ondergang
²decline (vb) **1** (af)hellen, aflopen, dalen **2** ten einde lopen, aftakelen: *declining* **years** oude dag, laatste jaren **3** afnemen, achteruitgaan
³decline (vb) (beleefd) weigeren, afslaan, van de hand wijzen: ~ *an* **invitation** niet op een uitnodiging ingaan
declutter opruimen, van rommel ontdoen
decode decoderen, ontcijferen
¹decompose (vb) **1** desintegreren, uiteenvallen **2** (ver)rotten, bederven
²decompose (vb) **1** ontleden, ontbinden, afbreken **2** doen rotten
decompress 1 de druk verlagen in, op **2** [comp] uitpakken; decomprimeren
decontaminate ontsmetten, desinfecteren
decorate 1 afwerken, verven, schilderen, behangen **2** versieren, verfraaien: ~ *the* **Christmas tree** de kerstboom optuigen **3** decoreren, onderscheiden, een onderscheiding geven
decoration 1 versiering, decoratie, op-

smuk **2** inrichting (en stoffering), aankleding: *interior* ~ binnenhuisarchitectuur **3** onderscheiding(steken^h), decoratie, ordeteken^h, lintje^h
decorator afwerker (van huis), (huis)schilder, stukadoor, behanger
decorous correct, fatsoenlijk
decoy 1 lokvogel, lokeend **2** lokaas^h, lokmiddel^h
¹decrease (n) vermindering, afneming, daling
²decrease (vb) (geleidelijk) afnemen, (geleidelijk) teruglopen, (geleidelijk) achteruitgaan
³decrease (vb) verminderen, beperken, verkleinen
¹decree (n) verordening, besluit^h: *by* ~ bij decreet
²decree (vb) verordenen, bevelen
decrepit 1 versleten, afgeleefd, op **2** vervallen, bouwvallig, uitgewoond
decry 1 kleineren, openlijk afkeuren **2** kwaadspreken over, afgeven op
decryption ontcijfering; decodering, decryptie
dedicate 1 wijden, toewijden, in dienst stellen van **2** opdragen, toewijden: ~ *a book* *to s.o.* een boek aan iem. opdragen
dedicated toegewijd, trouw
dedication 1 opdracht **2** (in)wijding, inzegening **3** [singular] toewijding, trouw, toegedaanheid
deduce (logisch) afleiden: *and what do you* ~ *from that?* en wat maak je daaruit op?
deduct (+ from) aftrekken (van), in mindering brengen (op)
deductible [fin] aftrekbaar
deduction 1 conclusie, gevolgtrekking, slotsom **2** inhouding, korting, (ver)mindering
deed 1 daad, handeling: *in word and in* ~ met woord en daad **2** wapenfeit^h, (helden)daad **3** akte, document^h
deem [form] achten: ~ *sth. an* **honour** iets als een eer beschouwen
¹deep (n) diepte, afgrond
²deep (adj) **1** diep, diepgelegen, ver(afgelegen): *the* ~ **end** het diepe [in swimming pool]; ~ *in the* forest diep in het bos **2** diep(zinnig), moeilijk, duister, ontoegankelijk **3** diep(gaand); intens [of feelings]; donker [of colours]: ~ *in conversation* diep in gesprek **4** dik, achter elkaar: *the people were standing* **ten** ~ de mensen stonden tien rijen dik || *thrown in at the* ~ **end** in het diepe gegooid, meteen met het moeilijkste (moeten) beginnen; *in* ~ **water(s)** in grote moeilijkheden
³deep (adv) diep, tot op grote diepte: ~ *into* *the* **night** tot diep in de nacht
¹deepen (vb) **1** dieper worden **2** toenemen
²deepen (vb) vergroten; versterken

deep-freeze diepvriezen
deep fry frituren
deep-seated diepliggend; ingeworteld
deer hert[h]
def [inform] gaaf, vet, cool
deface 1 beschadigen, verminken **2** onleesbaar maken, bekladden
defamation laster
default 1 afwezigheid: *by* ~ bij gebrek aan beter; *in ~ of* bij gebrek aan, bij ontstentenis van **2** verzuim[h]; niet-nakoming [of obligation to pay]; wanbetaling
¹defeat (n) **1** nederlaag **2** mislukking **3** verijdeling, dwarsboming
²defeat (vb) **1** verslaan, overwinnen, winnen van **2** verijdelen, dwarsbomen: *be ~ed in an attempt* een poging zien mislukken **3** verwerpen, afstemmen **4** tenietdoen, vernietigen: *her expectations were ~ed* haar verwachtingen werden de bodem ingeslagen
defeatism moedeloosheid
¹defect (n) mankement[h], gebrek[h]: *a hearing ~* een gehoorstoornis
²defect (vb) **1** overlopen, afvallig worden **2** uitwijken [by seeking asylum]
defective 1 onvolkomen, gebrekkig, onvolmaakt **2** te kort komend, onvolledig
defector overloper, afvallige
defence 1 verdediging, afweer, defensief[h], bescherming; [law] verweer[h]: *~s* verdedigingswerken; *in ~ of* ter verdediging van **2** verdediging(srede), verweer[h] **3** [sport; also chess] verdediging **4** defensie, (lands)verdediging
defenceless weerloos; machteloos
defend 1 verdedigen, afweren, verweren, als verdediger optreden (voor) **2** beschermen, beveiligen: *~ from* behoeden voor, beschermen tegen
defendant gedaagde, beschuldigde
defender 1 verdediger; [sport] achterspeler **2** titelverdediger
defensive defensief, verdedigend, afwerend: *be on the ~* een defensieve houding aannemen
¹defer (vb) zich onderwerpen, het hoofd buigen: *~ to* eerbiedigen, respecteren, in acht nemen
²defer (vb) opschorten, uitstellen: *~red payment* uitgestelde betaling
deference achting, eerbied, respect[h]
defiance 1 trotsering, uitdagende houding: *in ~ of* in weerwil van, ondanks **2** openlijk verzet[h], opstandigheid: *in ~ of* a) met minachting voor; b) in strijd met
deficiency 1 tekort[h]; gebrek[h]: *~ of food* voedseltekort **2** onvolkomenheid; defect[h]
deficient 1 incompleet, onvolledig **2** ontoereikend, onvoldoende: *~ in iron* ijzerarm **3** onvolwaardig, zwakzinnig
deficit 1 tekort[h], nadelig saldo[h] **2** tekort[h],

gebrek[h] **3** [sport] achterstand
defile 1 bevuilen, verontreinigen, vervuilen **2** schenden, ontheiligen
define 1 definiëren, een definitie geven (van) **2** afbakenen, bepalen, begrenzen **3** aftekenen
definite 1 welomlijnd, scherp begrensd **2** ondubbelzinnig, duidelijk **3** uitgesproken, onbetwistbaar **4** beslist, vastberaden **5** [linguistics] bepaald: *~ article* bepaald lidwoord
definitely absoluut, beslist: *~ not* geen sprake van
definition 1 definitie, omschrijving **2** afbakening, bepaling, begrenzing **3** karakteristiek **4** scherpte; beeldscherpte [of TV]: *lack ~* onscherp zijn [eg photo]
definitive 1 definitief, blijvend, onherroepelijk **2** beslissend, afdoend **3** (meest) gezaghebbend, onbetwist **4** ondubbelzinnig
deflate 1 leeg laten lopen; [fig] doorprikken [conceitedness] **2** kleineren, minder belangrijk maken: *feel utterly ~d* zich geheel ontmoedigd voelen **3** [econ] aan deflatie onderwerpen, inkrimpen
deflation deflatie, waardevermeerdering van geld
deflect 1 (doen) afbuigen, (doen) afwijken, uitwijken **2** (+ from) afbrengen (van), afleiden (van)
defoliate ontbladeren
deforest [Am] ontbossen
deformed 1 misvormd, mismaakt **2** verknipt, pervers
deformity misvorming; vergroeiing
defraud bedriegen, bezwendelen: *~ s.o. of his money* iem. (door bedrog) zijn geld afhandig maken
defray financieren, betalen, voor zijn rekening nemen: *~ the cost(s)* de kosten dragen
defriend ontvrienden
defrost ontdooien
deft behendig, handig, bedreven
defunct verdwenen, in onbruik
defuse onschadelijk maken [also fig]; demonteren [explosives]: *~ a crisis* een crisis bezweren
defy 1 tarten, uitdagen: *I ~ anyone to prove I'm wrong* ik daag iedereen uit om te bewijzen dat ik ongelijk heb **2** trotseren, weerstaan: *~ definition* (or: *description*) elke beschrijving tarten
degenerate 1 degenereren, ontaarden, verloederen **2** verslechteren, achteruitgaan
degradation 1 degradatie; achteruitgang **2** vernedering
degrade 1 degraderen, achteruitzetten, terugzetten: *~ o.s.* zich verlagen **2** vernederen, onteren
degree 1 graad: *an angle of 45 degrees* een hoek van 45 graden; *~ of latitude* (or: *longitude*) breedtegraad, lengtegraad **2** (univer-

sitaire) graad, academische titel; [also] lesbevoegdheid **3** mate, hoogte, graad, trap: *to a high* (or: *certain*) ~ tot op grote (or: zekere) hoogte; *by* ~*s* stukje bij beetje, gaandeweg
¹dehydrate (vb) **1** vocht verliezen **2** opdrogen, uitdrogen, verdrogen, verdorren
²dehydrate (vb) vocht onttrekken aan
deice het ijs verwijderen van; ontdooien
deify vergoddelijken
deign zich verwaardigen, zich niet te goed achten: *not* ~ *to look at* geen blik waardig keuren
deity 1 god(in), godheid **2** (af)god, verafgode figuur
dejected 1 terneergeslagen, somber **2** bedroefd, verdrietig
dejection 1 neerslachtigheid **2** bedroefdheid, verdriet[h]
¹delay (n) **1** vertraging, oponthoud[h] **2** uitstel[h], verschuiving: *without (any)* ~ zonder uitstel
²delay (vb) treuzelen, tijd rekken (winnen)
³delay (vb) **1** uitstellen, verschuiven **2** ophouden, vertragen, hinderen
¹delegate (n) afgevaardigde, gedelegeerde, ge(vol)machtigde
²delegate (vb) **1** afvaardigen, delegeren **2** machtigen **3** delegeren, overdragen
delegation 1 delegatie, afvaardiging **2** machtiging
delete verwijderen, wissen, doorhalen, wegstrepen: ~ *from* schrappen uit; ~ *as applicable* doorhalen wat niet van toepassing is
deletion 1 (weg)schrapping, doorhaling **2** verwijderde passage
deli *delicatessen* delicatessenwinkel
¹deliberate (adj) **1** doelbewust, opzettelijk **2** voorzichtig, weloverwogen, bedachtzaam
²deliberate (vb) **1** wikken en wegen, beraadslagen **2** raad inwinnen, te rade gaan
³deliberate (vb) **1** (zorgvuldig) afwegen **2** beraadslagen, zich beraden over
deliberation 1 (zorgvuldige) afweging, overleg[h]: *after much* ~ na lang wikken en wegen **2** omzichtigheid, bedachtzaamheid
delicacy 1 delicatesse, lekkernij **2** (fijn)gevoeligheid, verfijndheid **3** tact
delicate 1 fijn, verfijnd **2** lekker [of foods] **3** teer, zwak, tenger: *a* ~ *constitution* een teer gestel **4** (fijn)gevoelig **5** tactvol **6** kieskeurig, kritisch **7** netelig
delicious (over)heerlijk, verrukkelijk, kostelijk
¹delight (n) **1** verrukking, groot genoegen[h] **2** genot[h], vreugde: *take* ~ *in* genot vinden in
²delight (vb) genot vinden
³delight (vb) in verrukking brengen: *she* ~*ed them with her play* haar spel bracht hen in verrukking
delighted verrukt, opgetogen: *I shall be* ~ het zal me een groot genoegen zijn; ~ *at* (or:

with) opgetogen over
delineate 1 omlijnen, afbakenen **2** schetsen, tekenen, afbeelden
delinquency 1 vergrijp[h], delict[h] **2** criminaliteit, misdadigheid, misdaad
delinquent wetsovertreder, jeugdige misdadiger: *juvenile* ~ jeugddelinquent
delirious 1 ijlend: *become* ~ gaan ijlen **2** dol(zinnig): ~ *with joy* dol(zinnig) van vreugde
¹deliver (vb) afkomen, over de brug komen: *he will* ~ *on his promise* hij zal doen wat hij beloofd heeft
²deliver (vb) **1** verlossen, bevrijden: *be* ~*ed of* verlost worden van, bevallen van **2** ter wereld helpen: ~ *a child* een kind ter wereld helpen **3** bezorgen, (af)leveren **4** voordragen, uitspreken: ~ *a lecture* (or: *paper*) een lezing houden
deliverance verlossing, bevrijding, redding
delivery 1 bevalling, verlossing, geboorte **2** bestelling, levering **3** bevrijding, verlossing, redding **4** bezorging, (post)bestelling **5** voordracht, redevoering ‖ *take* ~ *of* in ontvangst nemen
delivery room verloskamer
delouse ontluizen
delude misleiden, op een dwaalspoor brengen, bedriegen: ~ *o.s.* *into* zichzelf wijsmaken dat
deluge 1 zondvloed **2** overstroming, watervloed **3** wolkbreuk, stortbui **4** stortvloed, stroom; waterval [of words etc]
delusion waanidee[h], waanvoorstelling: ~*s of grandeur* grootheidswaan
demagogue demagoog, oproerstoker
¹demand (n) **1** eis, verzoek[h], verlangen[h] **2** aanspraak, claim, vordering: *make great* (or: *many*) ~*s on* veel vergen van **3** vraag, behoefte: *supply and* ~ vraag en aanbod; *meet the* ~ aan de vraag voldoen; *be in great* ~ erg in trek zijn
²demand (vb) **1** eisen, verlangen, vorderen: *I* ~ *a written apology* ik eis een schriftelijke verontschuldiging **2** vergen, vragen, (ver)eisen: *this job will* ~ *much of you* deze baan zal veel van u vragen
demanding veeleisend
demarcation afbakening, grens(lijn)
demean verlagen, vernederen: ~ *o.s.* zich verlagen; *such language* ~*s you* dergelijke taal is beneden je waardigheid
demeanour gedrag[h], houding, optreden[h]
demented 1 krankzinnig, gek, gestoord **2** dement, kinds
demerara bruine (riet)suiker
demerge weer uiteengaan
demise 1 het ter ziele gaan **2** [form; euph] overlijden[h], dood
demo 1 *demonstration* betoging, demon-

stratie, protestmars **2** *demonstration* proefopname

demobilize demobiliseren, uit de krijgsdienst ontslaan

democracy 1 democratie **2** medezeggenschap

democrat democraat

democratic democratisch

demolish 1 slopen, vernielen, afbreken, vernietigen **2** omverwerpen, te gronde richten **3** ontzenuwen, weerleggen

demolition vernieling, afbraak, sloop

demon 1 demon, boze geest, duivel; [fig] duivel(s mens) **2** bezetene, fanaat: *he is a ~ chessplayer* hij schaakt als een bezetene

¹demonstrate (vb) demonstreren, betogen

²demonstrate (vb) **1** demonstreren, een demonstratie geven van **2** aantonen, bewijzen **3** uiten, openbaren

demonstration 1 demonstratie, betoging, manifestatie **2** demonstratie, vertoning van de werking **3** bewijsʰ **4** uiting, manifestatie, vertoonʰ

demonstrative 1 (aan)tonend **2** open, extravert **3** [linguistics] aanwijzend: *~ pronoun* aanwijzend voornaamwoord

demonstrator 1 demonstrateur **2** demonstrant, betoger

demoralization 1 demoralisatie, ontmoediging **2** zedelijk bederfʰ

demoralize demoraliseren, ontmoedigen

demote degraderen, in rang verlagen

demotivate demotiveren, ontmoedigen

demure ingetogen; zedig

demystification ontsluiering, opheldering

den 1 holʰ, schuilplaats; legerʰ [of animal] **2** holʰ, (misdadigers)verblijfʰ **3** kamertjeʰ, hokʰ

denial 1 ontzegging, weigering **2** ontkenning **3** verwerping

denigrate kleineren, belasteren

denim 1 spijkerstof **2** (-s) spijkerbroek

denizen inwoner; bewoner

Denmark Denemarken

denomination 1 (eenheids)klasse, munteenheid, muntsoort, getalsoort, gewichtsklasse: *coin of the lowest ~* kleinste munteenheid **2** noemer: *reduce fractions to the same ~* breuken onder een noemer brengen **3** gezindte, kerk(genootschapʰ)

denominational confessioneel; bijzonder

denominator noemer, deler

denote 1 aanduiden, verwijzen naar, omschrijven **2** aangeven, duiden op **3** betekenen, als naam dienen voor

dénouement ontknoping; afloop

denounce 1 hekelen, afkeuren **2** aan de kaak stellen, openlijk beschuldigen

dense 1 dicht, compact, samengepakt: *~ly populated* dichtbevolkt **2** dom, hersenloos

density 1 dichtheid, compactheid, concentratie **2** bevolkingsdichtheid

¹dent (n) **1** deuk **2** [fig] deuk, knauw ‖ *that made a big ~ in our savings* dat kostte ons flink wat van ons spaargeld

²dent (vb) **1** deuken, een deuk maken (krijgen) in **2** [fig] deuken, een knauw geven

dental 1 dentaal, m.b.t. het gebit, tand- **2** tandheelkundig: *~ floss* tandzijde

dentist tandarts

dentistry tandheelkunde

denture 1 gebitʰ **2** (-s) kunstgebitʰ, vals gebitʰ

denunciation 1 openlijke veroordeling **2** beschuldiging, aangifte, aanklacht **3** opzegging [of pact etc]

deny 1 ontkennen: *there is no ~ing that* het valt niet te ontkennen dat **2** ontzeggen, weigeren

deodorant deodorant

¹depart (vb) heengaan, weggaan, vertrekken: *~ for* vertrekken naar, afreizen naar

²depart (vb) verlaten: *~ this life* sterven

department 1 afdeling, departementʰ; [education] vakgroep; sectie; instituutʰ [at university] **2** ministerieʰ, departementʰ: *Department of Environment* [roughly] Ministerie van Milieuzaken

department store warenhuisʰ

departure 1 vertrekʰ, vertrektijd **2** afwijking: *new ~* nieuwe koers; *a ~ from the agreed policy* een afwijking van het afgesproken beleid

depend afhangen: *it all ~s* het hangt er nog maar van af

dependable betrouwbaar

dependant afhankelijke [eg for sustenance]

dependence 1 afhankelijkheid: *~ on luxury* afhankelijkheid van luxe **2** vertrouwenʰ **3** verslaving

dependent afhankelijk: *~ (up)on* afhankelijk van

depend (up)on 1 afhangen van, afhankelijk zijn van **2** vertrouwen op, bouwen op, zich verlaten op: *can I depend (up)on on that?* kan ik daar op rekenen?

depict (af)schilderen, beschrijven, afbeelden: *in that book his father is ~ed as an alcoholic* in dat boek wordt zijn vader afgeschilderd als een alcoholist

depiction afbeelding; afschildering

deplete leeghalen, uitputten

deplorable betreurenswaardig, zeer slecht

deplore betreuren, bedroefd zijn over

deploy inzetten **2** [mil] opstellen

depopulate ontvolken

deport 1 (zich) gedragen, (zich) houden: *~ o.s.* zich gedragen **2** verbannen, uitzetten

deportation deportatie; verbanning

deportee gedeporteerde, banneling

deportment 1 (lichaams)houding, postuur[h] **2** gedrag[h], manieren, houding
depose 1 afzetten, onttronen **2** getuigen; onder ede verklaren [in writing]
¹deposit (n) **1** onderpand[h], waarborgsom, aanbetaling, statiegeld[h] **2** storting **3** deposito[h]; depositogeld[h] [with period of notice] **4** afzetting, ertslaag, bezinksel[h]
²deposit (vb) **1** afzetten, bezinken **2** neerleggen, plaatsen **3** deponeren, in bewaring geven, storten
depository opslagruimte, bewaarplaats
depot 1 depot[h], magazijn[h], opslagruimte **2** (leger)depot[h], militair magazijn[h] **3** [Am] spoorwegstation[h], busstation[h]
depravation verdorvenheid, bederf[h]
deprave bederven, doen ontaarden
depravity verdorvenheid
deprecation 1 afkeuring, protest[h] **2** geringschatting
depreciate 1 (doen) devalueren, in waarde (doen) dalen **2** kleineren
depreciation 1 devaluatie, waardevermindering, afschrijving **2** geringschatting
depredation plundering
depressed 1 gedeprimeerd, ontmoedigd **2** noodlijdend, onderdrukt: ~ *area* a) noodlijdend gebied; b) streek met aanhoudend hoge werkloosheid
depressing deprimerend, ontmoedigend
depression 1 laagte, holte, indruk **2** depressie, lagedrukgebied[h], lage luchtdruk **3** depressie, crisis(tijd) **4** depressiviteit, neerslachtigheid
deprivation 1 ontbering, verlies[h], gemis[h] **2** beroving, ontneming
deprive beroven: *the old man was ~d of his wallet* de oude man werd beroofd van zijn portefeuille; *they ~ those people of clean water* ze onthouden deze mensen schoon water
deprived misdeeld, achtergesteld, arm: ~ *children* kansarme kinderen
dept 1 *department* **2** *deputy*
depth 1 diepte: *he was beyond* (or: *out of*) *his ~* hij verloor de grond onder z'n voeten; *in ~* diepgaand, grondig **2** diepzinnigheid, scherpzinnigheid **3** het diepst, het holst: *in the ~s of Asia* in het hart van Azië; *in the ~(s) of winter* midden in de winter
deputation afvaardiging, delegatie
¹deputy (n) **1** (plaats)vervanger, waarnemer **2** afgevaardigde, kamerlid[h] **3** hulpsheriff; [roughly] plaatsvervangend commissaris
²deputy (adj) onder-, vice-, plaatsvervangend: ~ *director* onderdirecteur
derail (doen) ontsporen
derange verwarren, krankzinnig maken: *mentally ~d* geestelijk gestoord, krankzinnig
derelict verwaarloosd, verlaten
deride uitlachen, bespotten, belachelijk maken: ~ *as* uitmaken voor

derision spot: *be/become an object of ~* bespot worden
derisive spottend; honend
derivation afleiding, afkomst, etymologie
¹derivative (n) afleiding
²derivative (adj) afgeleid, niet oorspronkelijk
¹derive (vb) afstammen: ~ *from* ontleend zijn aan, (voort)komen uit
²derive (vb) afleiden, krijgen, halen: ~ *pleasure from* plezier ontlenen aan
dermatologist huidarts; dermatoloog
derogatory geringschattend, minachtend, kleinerend
descale ontkalken
descant [mus] discant, sopraan
¹descend (vb) **1** (af)dalen, naar beneden gaan, neerkomen **2** afstammen: *be ~ed from* afstammen van
²descend (vb) afdalen, naar beneden gaan langs; afzakken [river]
descendant afstammeling, nakomeling
descent 1 afkomst, afstamming: *Charles claims ~ from a Scottish king* Charles beweert af te stammen van een Schotse koning **2** overdracht, overerving **3** afdaling, landing, val **4** helling
describe 1 beschrijven, karakteriseren: *you can hardly ~ his ideas as original* je kunt zijn ideeën toch moeilijk oorspronkelijk noemen **2** beschrijven, trekken: ~ *a circle* een cirkel tekenen
description 1 beschrijving, omschrijving: *fit the ~* aan de beschrijving voldoen **2** soort, type[h]: *weapons of all ~s* (or: *every ~*) allerlei (soorten) wapens
descriptive beschrijvend
desecrate ontheiligen; schenden
¹desert (n) woestijn
²desert (vb) deserteren
³desert (vb) verlaten, in de steek laten: ~*ed streets* uitgestorven straten
desertion desertie
deserts: *give s.o. his (just) ~* iem. zijn verdiende loon geven
deserve verdienen, recht hebben op: *one good turn ~s another* de ene dienst is de andere waard
¹design (n) **1** ontwerp[h], tekening, blauwdruk, constructie, vormgeving **2** dessin[h], patroon[h] **3** opzet, bedoeling, doel[h]: *have ~s against* boze plannen hebben met; *by ~* met opzet
²design (vb) **1** ontwerpen **2** uitdenken, bedenken, beramen: *who ~ed this bank-robbery?* wie beraamde deze bankroof? **3** bedoelen, ontwikkelen, bestemmen: ~*ed for children* bedoeld voor kinderen
¹designate (adj) [form] aangesteld
²designate (vb) **1** aanduiden; markeren **2** noemen; bestempelen **3** aanstellen, be-

noemen: [inform] *the ~d* **driver** de bob
designer designer, ontwerper, tekenaar: *~
clothes* designerkleding
designing listig, berekenend, sluw
desirable 1 wenselijk **2** aantrekkelijk
¹desire (n) **1** (+ for) wens, verlangen (naar),
wil **2** begeerte, hartstocht
²desire (vb) wensen, verlangen, begeren:
leave much/nothing to be *~d* veel/niets te
wensen overlaten
desist (+ from) ophouden (met), uitscheiden (met), afzien (van)
desk 1 werktafel, (schrijf)bureauʰ **2** balie,
receptie, kas
desk job kantoorbaan
desktop [comp] desktop
desolate 1 verlaten, uitgestorven, troosteloos **2** diepbedroefd, eenzaam: *at 30 he was
already ~ and helpless* op zijn dertigste was hij
al zo eenzaam en hulpeloos
desolation 1 verwoesting, ontvolking
2 verlatenheid **3** eenzaamheid
¹despair (n) wanhoop, vertwijfeling: *drive
s.o. to ~*, *fill* s.o. *with ~* iem. tot wanhoop drijven; *be the ~ of* s.o. iem. wanhopig maken
²despair (vb) wanhopen
desperate wanhopig, hopeloos; uitzichtloos [of situation]; vertwijfeld; radeloos [of
deeds, people]: *a ~ action* een wanhoopsac-
tie; *she was ~ for a cup of tea* ze verlangde
verschrikkelijk naar een kopje thee
despicable verachtelijk
despise verachten, versmaden
despite ondanks: *~ the fact that* ondanks
het feit dat
despondent wanhopig; vertwijfeld
despot despoot; tiran
dessert dessertʰ
destination (plaats van) bestemming,
doelʰ, eindpuntʰ
destine bestemmen, (voor)beschikken: *be
~d for* bestemd zijn voor
destiny lotʰ, bestemming, beschikking
Destiny (nood)lotʰ
destitute arm, behoeftig
destroy vernielen, vernietigen, ruïneren:
*thousands of houses were ~ed by the earth-
quakes* door de aardbevingen zijn duizenden
huizen vernield
destruction 1 vernietiging, afbraak **2** ondergang
destructive vernietigend; destructief: *~
criticism* afbrekende kritiek
detach (+ from) losmaken (van), scheiden,
uit elkaar halen
detached 1 los; vrijstaand [of house]; niet
verbonden, geïsoleerd **2** onbevooroordeeld:
~ view of sth. objectieve kijk op iets **3** afstandelijk, gereserveerd
detachment 1 detachering, detachementʰ
2 scheiding **3** afstandelijkheid, gereser-

veerdheid **4** onpartijdigheid
detail 1 detailʰ, bijzonderheid, kleinigheid:
enter (or: *go*) *into ~(s)* op bijzonderheden ingaan **2** kleine versiering
detailed uitvoerig: *~ information available on
request* uitgebreide informatie op aanvraag
verkrijgbaar
detain 1 aanhouden, laten nablijven, gevangen houden **2** laten schoolblijven: *Henry
was ~ed for half an hour* Henry moest een
halfuur nablijven **3** ophouden, vertragen: *I
don't want to ~ you any longer* ik wil u niet
langer ophouden
detainee (politieke) gevangene, gedetineerde
detect ontdekken, bespeuren
detective detective, speurder, rechercheur
detention 1 opsluiting, (militaire) detentie, hechtenis **2** het schoolblijven: *keep a pupil in ~* een leerling laten nablijven **3** vertraging, oponthoudʰ
deter (+ from) afschrikken (van), ontmoedigen, afhouden (van)
detergent wasmiddelʰ, afwasmiddelʰ, rei-
nigingsmiddelʰ
deteriorate verslechteren, achteruitgaan
deterioration achteruitgang; verslechtering
determination 1 vast voornemenʰ, bedoeling, planʰ **2** vastberadenheid, vastbeslotenheid
determine 1 besluiten, beslissen: *Sheila ~d
to dye her hair green* Sheila besloot haar haar
groen te verven **2** doen besluiten, drijven tot
determined beslist, vastberaden, vastbesloten
deterrence afschrikking
deterrent afschrikwekkend middelʰ, af-
schrikmiddelʰ, atoombom: *the cameras are a ~
for shoplifters* de camera's hebben een pre-
ventieve werking tegen winkeldieven
detest verafschuwen, walgen van
dethrone afzetten, onttronen
¹detonate (vb) ontploffen, exploderen
²detonate (vb) tot ontploffing brengen, laten exploderen
detour 1 omweg, bocht, (rivier)kronkel
2 omleiding
¹detox (n) **1** ontwenning(skuur) **2** ontslak-
king
²detox (vb) **1** afkicken; ontwennen **2** ont-
slakken
detoxification centre ontwenningskliniek; afkickcentrumʰ
detract: *~ from* kleineren, afbreuk doen
aan, verminderen
detriment (oorzaak van) schade, kwaadʰ,
nadeelʰ: *to the ~ of* ten nadele van
detrimental schadelijk; slecht, nadelig
detritus resten, afval: *he waded through the
~ of the party* hij waadde door de resten van

het feest
deuce 1 twee [on dice] **2** [tennis] veertig gelijk || *a ~ of a fight* een vreselijke knokpartij
devaluation devaluatie, waardevermindering
devalue devalueren, in waarde (doen) dalen
devastate verwoesten, ruïneren, vernietigen
devastation verwoesting
¹develop (vb) **1** ontwikkelen, uitwerken, ontginnen: *~ing country* ontwikkelingsland; *~ a film* een film(pje) ontwikkelen **2** ontvouwen, uiteenzetten
²develop (vb) (zich) ontwikkelen, (doen) ontstaan, (doen) uitbreiden
developer 1 projectontwikkelaar **2** [photo] ontwikkelaar
development 1 ontwikkeling, verloop[h], evolutie, ontplooiing, groei, verdere uitwerking: *await further ~s* afwachten wat er verder komt **2** gebeurtenis **3** (nieuw)bouwproject[h]
deviant 1 afwijkend, tegen de norm **2** abnormaal
deviate (+ from) afwijken (van), afdwalen
deviation afwijking [from current norm]; deviatie: *~ from* afwijking van
device 1 apparaat[h], toestel[h]: *a new ~ for squeezing lemons* een nieuw apparaat om citroenen te persen **2** middel[h], kunstgreep, truc **3** devies[h], motto[h], leus **4** embleem[h] [on coat of arms] || *left to his own ~s* op zichzelf aangewezen
devil 1 duivel **2** man, jongen, donder, kerel || *give the ~ his due* ere wie ere toekomt, het iem. nageven; *~ take the hindmost* ieder voor zich en God voor ons allen; *be a ~* kom op, spring eens uit de band; *there'll be the ~ to pay* dan krijgen we de poppen aan het dansen; *the ~ of an undertaking* een helse klus
devil-may-care roekeloos; wie-dan-leeft-die-dan-zorgt
devious 1 kronkelend, slingerend; [fig] omslachtig: *~ route* omweg **2** onoprecht, onbetrouwbaar, sluw
devise bedenken, beramen
devoid (+ of) verstoken (van), ontbloot (van), gespeend (van)
¹devolve (vb) [form] terechtkomen: *his duties ~d on* (or: *to, upon*) *his secretary* zijn taken werden overgenomen door zijn secretaris || [form] *the property ~d to his son* het land viel toe aan zijn zoon
²devolve (vb) [form] afwentelen; delegeren, overdragen
devote (+ to) wijden (aan), besteden (aan): *~ o.s. to* zich overgeven aan
devotee 1 (+ of) liefhebber (van), aanbidder, enthousiast **2** aanhanger; volgeling [of religious sect] **3** dweper, fanaticus

devotion 1 toewijding, liefde, overgave: *~ to duty* plichtsbetrachting **2** het besteden **3** vroomheid
devour 1 verslinden [also fig]; verzwelgen **2** verteren: *(be) ~ed by jealousy* verteerd (worden) door jaloezie
devout 1 vroom **2** vurig, oprecht
dew dauw
dexterity handigheid, behendigheid, (hand)vaardigheid
diabetes diabetes, suikerziekte
¹diabetic (n) suikerzieke
²diabetic (adj) voor suikerzieken, diabetes-
diabolic(al) afschuwelijk, afgrijselijk, ontzettend
diadem diadeem[h]
diagnose een diagnose stellen (van)
diagnosis diagnose
¹diagonal (n) diagonaal
²diagonal (adj) diagonaal
diagram diagram[h], schets, schema[h], grafiek
¹dial (n) **1** wijzerplaat **2** schaal(verdeling); (afstem)schaal [of radio etc]; zonnewijzer **3** kiesschijf [of telephone] **4** afstemknop [of radio etc]
²dial (vb) draaien; bellen [of telephone]
dialect dialect[h]
dialling code 1 netnummer[h] **2** landnummer[h]
dialogue dialoog
dialogue box dialoogvenster[h]
dial-up kies-, geschakeld: *a ~ connection* kiesverbinding; *~line* geschakelde telefoonverbinding
diameter diameter, middellijn, doorsne(de)
diamond 1 diamant, diamanten sieraad[h] **2** ruit(vormige figuur) **3** ruiten(kaart) **4** (-s) ruiten [cards]: *Queen of ~s* ruitenvrouw || *it was ~ cut ~* het ging hard tegen hard
diaper [Am] luier
diaphragm diafragma[h], middenrif[h]
diarist dagboekschrijver
diarrhoea diarree [also fig]; buikloop
diary 1 dagboek[h] **2** agenda
diatribe scherpe kritiek; schimprede
¹dice (n) dobbelsteen; [also fig] kans; geluk[h]: *the ~ are loaded against him* het lot is hem niet gunstig gezind || [Am; inform] *no ~* tevergeefs
²dice (vb) in dobbelsteentjes snijden
³dice (vb) dobbelen
dices dobbelspel[h]
dicey link, riskant
dickhead idioot, stommeling
dicky wankel, wiebelig: *a ~ heart* een zwak hart
¹dictate (n) ingeving, bevel[h]
²dictate (vb) **1** dicteren **2** commanderen, opleggen
dictator dictator

diction 1 voordracht **2** taalgebruik[h], woordkeus
dictionary woordenboek[h]
didactic didactisch
diddle ontfutselen, bedriegen: *he ~d me out of £5* hij heeft me voor £5 afgezet
¹die (n) matrijs, stempel[h], gietvorm
²die (vb) **1** sterven, overlijden, omkomen: ~ *from* (or: *of*) *an illness* sterven aan een ziekte **2** ophouden te bestaan, verloren gaan: *the mystery ~d with him* hij nam het geheim mee in zijn graf **3** uitsterven, wegsterven **4** verzwakken, verminderen, bedaren ‖ ~ *away* **a)** wegsterven [of sound]; **b)** uitgaan [of fire]; **c)** gaan liggen [of wind]; ~ *down* **a)** bedaren, afnemen [of wind]; **b)** uitgaan [of fire]; ~ *off* **a)** een voor een sterven; **b)** uitsterven; *be dying for a cigarette* snakken naar een sigaret; ~ *of anxiety* doodsangsten uitstaan
die-cast gegoten
diehard 1 taaie[h], volhouder **2** aartsconservatief **3** onverzoenlijke
diesel diesel
¹diet (n) **1** dieet[h], leefregel; [attributive] light, dieet-: ~ *soda* frisdrank light; *on a ~ op dieet* **2** voedsel[h], voeding, kost: *her ~ consisted of bread and lentils* haar voedsel bestond uit brood en linzen
²diet (vb) op dieet zijn; [fig] lijnen
dietary dieet-; eet-: ~ *rules* voedselvoorschriften
dietician diëtist(e), voedingsspecialist(e)
differ 1 (van elkaar) verschillen, afwijken: *those twin sisters ~ from one another* die tweelingzusjes verschillen van elkaar **2** van mening verschillen: ~ *from s.o.* het met iem. oneens zijn
difference 1 verschil[h], onderscheid[h]: *that makes all the ~* dat maakt veel uit **2** verschil[h], rest: *split the ~* het verschil (samen) delen **3** meningsverschil[h], geschil(punt)[h]
different 1 verschillend, ongelijk, afwijkend: *as ~ as chalk and* (or: *from*) *cheese* verschillend als dag en nacht; [fig] *strike a ~ note* een ander geluid laten horen; ~ *from*, ~ *to* anders dan **2** ongewoon, speciaal ‖ *a horse of a ~ colour* een geheel andere kwestie
¹differential (n) **1** verschil in loon[h] **2** koersverschil[h] **3** [techn] differentieel[h]
²differential (adj) onderscheidend ‖ [maths] ~ *calculus* differentiaalrekening
¹differentiate (vb) **1** zich onderscheiden **2** een verschil maken: ~ *between* ongelijk behandelen
²differentiate (vb) onderscheiden, onderkennen
difficult moeilijk [also of character]; lastig
difficulty 1 moeilijkheid, probleem[h] **2** moeite: *with ~* met moeite
diffident bedeesd, terughoudend
¹diffuse (adj) diffuus; wijdlopig [also style]

²diffuse (vb) zich verspreiden; verstrooid worden [of light]
diffusion 1 verspreiding **2** [physics] diffusie
¹dig (n) **1** por; [fig] steek (onder water): *have a ~ at s.o.* iets hatelijks over iem. zeggen **2** (archeologische) opgraving **3** (-s) kamer(s)
²dig (vb) **1** doordringen **2** zwoegen, ploeteren **3** graven, delven, opgraven **4** uitgraven, rooien **5** uitzoeken, voor de dag halen **6** porren **7** vatten, snappen
¹digest (n) samenvatting, (periodiek) overzicht[h]
²digest (vb) verteren
³digest (vb) verteren [also fig]; slikken, verwerken, in zich opnemen
digestion spijsvertering, digestie
¹digestive (n) **1** digestief[h] **2** volkorenbiscuit[h]
²digestive (adj) **1** spijsverterings- **2** goed voor de spijsvertering
digger 1 graver, gouddelver **2** graafmachine **3** Australiër
digicam digitale camera
¹dig in (vb) **1** zich ingraven **2** aanvallen [food] **3** van geen wijken weten
²dig in (vb) **1** ingraven: *dig o.s. in* zich ingraven; [fig] zijn positie verstevigen **2** onderspitten
dig into 1 graven in: *dig sth. into the soil* iets ondergraven, iets onderspitten **2** prikken, slaan, boren in **3** zijn tanden zetten in, diepgaand onderzoeken: *the journalist dug into the scandal* de journalist beet zich vast in het schandaal
digit cijfer[h]; getal[h] [0 up to and including 9]
digital digitaal
digital money elektronisch geld[h], digitaal geld[h], e-geld[h]
dignified waardig, deftig, statig
dignitary (kerkelijk) hoogwaardigheidsbekleder: *the local dignitaries* de dorpsnotabelen
dignity waardigheid: *that is beneath his ~* dat is beneden zijn waardigheid
dig out 1 uitgraven **2** opdiepen, voor de dag halen **3** blootleggen
digress uitweiden: ~ *from one's subject* afdwalen van zijn onderwerp
digression (+ on) uitweiding (over)
¹dig up (vb) [Am] bijdrage leveren, betalen
²dig up (vb) **1** opgraven, uitgraven; omspitten [road] **2** blootleggen, opsporen **3** bij elkaar scharrelen **4** opscharrelen
dike *see* dyke
dilapidated vervallen, bouwvallig
¹dilate (vb) uitzetten; zich verwijden
²dilate (vb) **1** verwijden; opensperren [eyes] **2** doen uitzetten
dilatory 1 traag, langzaam, laks **2** vertragend

dilemma dilemma[h], netelig vraagstuk[h]
diligence ijver, vlijt, toewijding
diligent ijverig, vlijtig
dilly-dally [inform] **1** treuzelen **2** dubben; weifelen
dilute 1 verdunnen, aanlengen: ~ *the syrup with water or milk* de siroop met water of melk aanlengen **2** doen verbleken, doen vervalen **3** afzwakken, doen verwateren
¹dim (adj) **1** schemerig, (half)duister **2** vaag, flauw: *I have a ~ **understanding** of botany* ik heb een beetje verstand van plantkunde **3** stom ‖ *take a ~ **view** of sth.* iets afkeuren, niets ophebben met iets
²dim (vb) **1** verduisteren, versomberen **2** temperen, dimmen: ~ *the **headlights*** dimmen
dime dime; 10 centstuk[h] [Am]; cent, stuiver ‖ *a ~ a **dozen*** dertien in een dozijn
dimension 1 afmeting, grootte, omvang; [fig] kaliber[h]; formaat[h] **2** dimensie, aspect[h], kwaliteit
diminish verminderen, verkleinen, afnemen, z'n waarde verliezen, aantasten
diminutive 1 verklein- **2** nietig: *a ~ **kitten*** een piepklein poesje
dimple kuiltje[h]
dimwit sufferd, onbenul[h]
¹din (n) kabaal[h], lawaai[h]: *kick up* (or: *make) a* ~ herrie schoppen
²din (vb) **1** verdoven [of noise] **2** inprenten: ~ *sth.* **into** *s.o.* iets er bij iem. in stampen
dine dineren: ~ **out** buitenshuis dineren
diner 1 iem. die dineert, eter, gast **2** restauratiewagen **3** [Am] klein (weg)restaurant[h]
ding-dong 1 gebimbam[h]; gebeier[h] **2** [inform] herrieschopperij; felle discussie
dinghy 1 jol **2** kleine boot, (opblaasbaar) reddingsvlot[h], rubberboot
dingy 1 smerig, smoezelig **2** sjofel, armoedig
dining car restauratiewagen
dining room eetkamer; [in hotel] restaurant[h]
dinky 1 snoezig **2** [Am] armzalig
dinner eten[h], avondeten[h], (warm) middagmaal[h]: ~ *is **served*** er is opgediend
dinner jacket smoking(jasje)
dinner suit smoking
dinosaur dinosaurus
dint deuk; indruk [also fig]
dioxide dioxide[h]
¹dip (n) **1** indoping, onderdompeling, wasbeurt; [inform] duik **2** schepje[h] **3** helling, daling; dal[h] [landscape] **4** (kleine) daling, vermindering **5** dipsaus
²dip (vb) **1** duiken, plonzen, kopje-onder gaan **2** ondergaan, vallen, zinken **3** hellen, dalen **4** tasten, reiken, grijpen: ~ **in** toetasten; ~ **into** *one's financial resources* aanspraak

doen op zijn geldelijke middelen ‖ ~ **into** vluchtig bekijken
³dip (vb) **1** (onder)dompelen, (in)dopen; galvaniseren [in bath]; wassen [animals in a bathtub with insecticide] **2** verven, in verfbad dopen **3** dimmen [headlights]
diploma diploma[h]
diplomacy diplomatie [also fig]; (politieke) tact, diplomatiek optreden[h]
diplomat diplomaat
diplomatic 1 diplomatiek, m.b.t. diplomatieke dienst; [fig] met diplomatie: ~ *bag* diplomatieke post(zak) [for embassy etc] **2** subtiel, berekend, sluw
the **Dipper 1** [Am] Grote Beer: *Big* ~ Grote Beer; *Little* ~ Kleine Beer **2** waterspreeuw
dipsomaniac (periodiek) alcoholist, kwartaaldrinker
dipstick peilstok, meetstok
dire ijselijk, uiterst (dringend): *be in ~ **need** of water* snakken naar water; ~ *poverty* bittere armoede
¹direct (adj) **1** direct, rechtstreeks, onmiddellijk, openhartig: *be a ~ **descendant*** in een rechte lijn van iem. afstammen; *a ~ **hit*** een voltreffer **2** absoluut, exact, precies: ~ *opposites* absolute tegenpolen ‖ ~ *current* gelijkstroom; ~ *object* lijdend voorwerp
²direct (vb) **1** richten: *these measures are ~ed against abuse* deze maatregelen zijn gericht tegen misbruik **2** de weg wijzen, leiden: ~ *s.o.* **to** *the post office* iem. de weg wijzen naar het postkantoor **3** bestemmen, toewijzen **4** leiden, de leiding hebben over, besturen **5** geleiden, als richtlijn dienen voor **6** opdracht geven, bevelen; [law] instrueren
³direct (vb) regisseren, dirigeren
⁴direct (adv) rechtstreeks: *broadcast* ~ rechtstreeks uitzenden
direction 1 opzicht[h], kant, tendens, richting; [fig also] gebied[h]; terrein[h]: *progress in all ~s* vooruitgang op alle gebieden **2** instructie, bevel[h], aanwijzing: *at the ~ **of**, **by** ~ **of*** op last van **3** oogmerk[h], doel[h] **4** leiding, directie, supervisie: *in the ~ **of** London* in de richting van Londen **5** geleiding, het geleiden **6** directie, regie
directive instructie, bevel[h]
directly 1 rechtstreeks, openhartig **2** dadelijk, zo **3** precies, direct: ~ *opposite the door* precies tegenover de deur
director 1 directeur, manager, directielid[h]: *the **board** of ~s* de raad van bestuur **2** [Am] dirigent **3** regisseur, spelleider
directory 1 adresboek[h], gids, adressenbestand[h] **2** telefoonboek[h]
dirge lijkzang, treurzang, klaagzang
dirt 1 vuil[h], modder, drek, viezigheid: *treat s.o. like ~* iem. als oud vuil behandelen **2** lasterpraat, geroddel[h] **3** grond, aarde
dirt bike (cross)motor

dirt road [Am] onverharde weg; zandweg
dirty 1 vies, vuil, smerig **2** laag, gemeen: *give s.o. a ~ look* iem. vuil aankijken; *play a ~ trick on s.o.* iem. een gemene streek leveren **3** [inform] slecht; ruw [of weather] ‖ *wash one's ~ linen in public* de vuile was buiten hangen
disability 1 onbekwaamheid, onvermogen[h] **2** belemmering, nadeel[h], handicap **3** invaliditeit, lichamelijke ongeschiktheid
disable 1 onmogelijk maken, onbruikbaar, ongeschikt maken **2** invalide maken, arbeidsongeschikt maken: *~d persons* (lichamelijk) gehandicapte mensen; *the ~d* de invaliden
disadvantage nadeel[h], ongunstige situatie: *at a ~* in het nadeel
disadvantaged minder bevoorrecht
disagree 1 het oneens zijn, verschillen van mening, ruziën **2** verschillen, niet kloppen, niet overeenkomen: *the two statements ~* de twee beweringen stemmen niet overeen
disagreeable 1 onaangenaam **2** slecht gehumeurd, onvriendelijk
disagreement 1 onenigheid, meningsverschil[h], ruzie **2** verschil[h], afwijking
disagree with 1 niet liggen; ziek maken: *Italian wine disagrees with me* ik kan niet tegen Italiaanse wijn **2** afkeuren
disallow 1 niet toestaan, verbieden **2** ongeldig verklaren, verwerpen, afkeuren: *~ a goal* een doelpunt afkeuren
disappear verdwijnen
disappoint 1 teleurstellen, niet aan de verwachtingen voldoen, tegenvallen **2** verijdelen [plan]; doen mislukken, tenietdoen
disappointed teleurgesteld: *she was ~ in him* hij viel haar tegen
disappointment teleurstelling
disapproval afkeuring: *the teacher shook her head in ~* de docente schudde afkeurend haar hoofd
disapprove afkeuren, veroordelen: *he wanted to stay on but his parents ~d* hij wilde nog even blijven, maar zijn ouders vonden dat niet goed
¹disarm (vb) de kracht ontnemen, vriendelijk stemmen: *his quiet manners ~ed all opposition* zijn rustige manier van doen nam alle tegenstand weg; *a ~ing smile* een ontwapenende glimlach
²disarm (vb) ontwapenen, onschadelijk maken
disarmament ontwapening
disarrange in de war brengen, verstoren
disarray wanorde, verwarring
disaster ramp, catastrofe; [fig] totale mislukking: *court ~* om moeilijkheden vragen
disastrous rampzalig, noodlottig
disavowal 1 ontkenning, loochening **2** afwijzing

disband uiteengaan, ontbonden worden
disbelief ongeloof[h]: *he stared at us in ~* hij keek ons vol ongeloof aan
disbelieve niet geloven, betwijfelen, verwerpen
disc 1 schijf, parkeerschijf **2** discus **3** (grammofoon)plaat, cd, cd-rom **4** [med] schijf, tussenwervelschijf: *a slipped ~* een hernia **5** [comp] schijf
¹discard (vb) zich ontdoen van, weggooien, afdanken
²discard (vb) [cards] afgooien, ecarteren, niet bekennen
discern 1 waarnemen, onderscheiden, bespeuren: *I could hardly ~ the words on the traffic sign* ik kon de woorden op het verkeersbord nauwelijks onderscheiden **2** onderscheiden, verschil zien, onderscheid maken
discerning scherpzinnig, opmerkzaam, kritisch
¹discharge (n) **1** bewijs[h] van ontslag **2** lossing, ontlading, het uitladen **3** uitstorting, afvoer, uitstroming; [of gas etc; also fig] uiting **4** schot[h], het afvuren **5** aflossing, vervulling **6** ontslag[h] van rechtsvervolging, vrijspraak
²discharge (vb) **1** zich ontladen, zich uitstorten; etteren [of wound]: *the river ~s into the sea* de rivier mondt in zee uit **2** [elec] zich ontladen
³discharge (vb) **1** ontladen, uitladen, lossen **2** afvuren, afschieten, lossen **3** ontladen, van elektrische lading ontdoen **4** wegsturen, ontslaan, ontheffen van, vrijspreken, in vrijheid stellen: *~ the jury* de jury van zijn plichten ontslaan; *~ a patient* een patiënt ontslaan **5** uitstorten, uitstoten, afgeven **6** vervullen, voldoen, zich kwijten van: *~ one's duties* zijn taak vervullen
disciple discipel, leerling, volgeling
¹discipline (n) **1** methode, systeem[h] **2** vak[h], discipline, tak van wetenschap **3** discipline, tucht, orde, controle: *maintain ~* orde houden
²discipline (vb) **1** disciplineren, onder tucht brengen, drillen **2** straffen, disciplinaire maatregelen nemen tegen
disc jockey diskjockey
disclaim ontkennen, afwijzen, verwerpen, van de hand wijzen
disclaimer 1 ontkenning; afwijzing **2** [law] bewijs[h] van afstand
disclose onthullen [also fig]; bekendmaken, tonen
disco disco, discotheek
discomfit verwarren; in verlegenheid brengen
discomfort 1 ongemak[h], ontbering, moeilijkheid **2** ongemakkelijkheid, gebrek[h] aan comfort
disconcert 1 verontrusten, in verlegenheid

brengen **2** verijdelen [plans]
disconcerting verontrustend
disconnect losmaken, scheiden, loskoppelen; afsluiten [s.o., from gas supply etc]: *we were suddenly ~ed* de (telefoon)verbinding werd plotseling verbroken
disconsolate ontroostbaar; wanhopig
¹**discontent** (n) **1** grief, bezwaarʰ **2** ontevredenheid
²**discontent** (adj) (+ with) ontevreden (over/ met), teleurgesteld
¹**discontinue** (vb) tot een einde komen, ophouden
²**discontinue** (vb) **1** beëindigen, een eind maken aan, ophouden met **2** opzeggen [newspaper etc]
discord 1 onenigheid, twist, ruzie **2** lawaaiʰ
discotheque disco, discotheek
¹**discount** (n) **1** reductie, korting: *at a ~ of £3* met een korting van drie pond **2** discontoʰ, wisseldiscontoʰ
²**discount** (vb) **1** disconto geven (nemen); disconteren [Bill of Exchange] **2** korting geven (op) **3** buiten beschouwing laten, niet serieus nemen
discounter discountzaak
discourage 1 ontmoedigen, de moed ontnemen **2** weerhouden, afhouden, afbrengen
discouragement 1 tegenslag **2** ontmoediging **3** moedeloosheid
discourse 1 gesprekʰ, dialoog, conversatie **2** verhandeling, lezing
discourteous onbeleefd, onhoffelijk
discover 1 ontdekken, (uit)vinden: *Tasman ~ed New Zealand* Tasman heeft Nieuw-Zeeland ontdekt **2** onthullen, blootleggen; [fig] aan het licht brengen; bekendmaken **3** aantreffen, bemerken, te weten komen
discovery ontdekking: *a voyage of ~* een ontdekkingsreis
¹**discredit** (n) schande, diskredietʰ, opspraak: *bring ~ (up)on o.s., bring o.s. into ~* zich te schande maken
²**discredit** (vb) **1** te schande maken, in diskrediet brengen **2** wantrouwen, verdenken
discreditable schandelijk, verwerpelijk
discreet 1 discreet **2** bescheiden, onopvallend
discrepancy discrepantie, afwijking, verschilʰ
discrete afzonderlijk
discretion 1 oordeelkundigheid, tact, verstandʰ: *the age* (or: *years) of ~* de jaren des onderscheids **2** discretie, oordeelʰ, vrijheid (van handelen): *use one's ~* naar eigen goeddunken handelen
¹**discriminate** (vb) **1** onderscheid maken: *~ between* verschil maken tussen **2** discrimineren: *~ against* discrimineren; *she felt ~d*

²**discriminate** (vb) onderscheiden, herkennen
discriminating 1 opmerkzaam, scherpzinnig **2** onderscheidend, kenmerkend **3** kieskeurig, overkritisch **4** discriminerend
discrimination 1 onderscheidʰ, het maken van onderscheid **2** discriminatie **3** oordeelsvermogenʰ, kritische smaak
discus discus
discuss bespreken, behandelen, praten over: *okay, let's now ~ my pay rise* goed, laten we het nu eens over mijn loonsverhoging hebben
discussion 1 bespreking, discussie, gesprekʰ: *be under ~* in behandeling zijn **2** uiteenzetting, verhandeling, bespreking
disdain minachting
disease ziekte, aandoening, kwaal: *wasting ~* kwijnende ziekte
¹**disembark** (vb) van boord gaan, aan wal gaan, uitstappen
²**disembark** (vb) ontschepen, aan land brengen, lossen
disembodied zonder lichaam; onstoffelijk, niet tastbaar
disembowel 1 van de ingewanden ontdoen; ontweien [fish, game] **2** de buik openrijten van
disenchant ontgoochelen, ontnuchteren, uit de droom helpen
disenchantment desillusie
¹**disengage** (vb) losraken, zich losmaken
²**disengage** (vb) losmaken, vrij maken, bevrijden
disengagement 1 bevrijding **2** vrijheid; ongebondenheid, onafhankelijkheid **3** ongedwongenheid **4** verbreking van verloving **5** [mil] terugtrekking
¹**disentangle** (vb) zich ontwarren
²**disentangle** (vb) ontwarren, ontrafelen, oplossen
disfavour 1 afkeuring, lage dunk: *look upon* (or: *regard, view) s.o. with ~* iem. niet mogen **2** ongenade, ongunst
disfigurement misvorming, wanstaltigheid
¹**disgorge** (vb) leegstromen, zich legen, zich uitstorten
²**disgorge** (vb) **1** uitbraken, uitstoten **2** uitstorten, uitstromen
¹**disgrace** (n) schande, ongenade: *be in ~* uit de gratie zijn
²**disgrace** (vb) te schande maken, een slechte naam bezorgen
disgruntled ontevreden: *~ at sth.* (or: *with s.o.*) ontstemd over iets (iem.)
¹**disguise** (n) **1** vermomming: *in ~* vermomd, in het verborgene; *a blessing in ~* een geluk bij een ongeluk **2** voorwendselʰ,

schijn, dekmantel
²disguise (vb) **1** vermommen **2** een valse
voorstelling geven van **3** verbergen, maskeren, verhullen
¹disgust (n) afschuw, afkeer, walging
²disgust (vb) doen walgen, afkeer opwekken: *she was suddenly ~ed at* (or: *by, with*) *him*
plotseling vond ze hem weerzinwekkend
disgusting weerzinwekkend, walgelijk
¹dish (n) **1** schaal, schotel **2** gerecht[h], schotel
3 schotelvormig voorwerp[h], schotelantenne:
~ aerial schotelantenne **4** lekker stuk[h], lekkere meid
²dish (vb) ruïneren, naar de maan helpen,
verknallen || *~ out* a) uitdelen [papers, pre-
sents etc]; b) rondgeven, rondstrooien [ad-
vice]
dishcloth vaatdoek
dishearten ontmoedigen
dishevelled slonzig, slordig, onverzorgd
dishonest oneerlijk, bedrieglijk, vals
dishonesty leugenachtigheid; oneerlijkheid
dishonour schande, eerverlies[h], smaad
dish up 1 opdienen, serveren; [fig] presenteren; opdissen [facts etc] **2** het eten opdienen
dishwasher 1 afwasser, bordenwasser
2 afwasmachine, vaatwasmachine
disillusion desillusioneren, uit de droom
helpen: *be ~ed at* (or: *about, with*) teleurgesteld zijn over
disinclination tegenzin, onwil, afkeer: *feel
a ~ to meet s.o.* geen (echte) zin hebben om
iem. te ontmoeten
disinfect desinfecteren, ontsmetten
¹disinfectant (n) desinfecterend middel[h],
ontsmettingsmiddel[h]
²disinfectant (adj) desinfecterend, ontsmettend
disinherit onterven
disintegrate 1 uiteenvallen, uit elkaar
vallen, vergaan **2** [chem] afbreken
disinterested 1 belangeloos **2** [fig] ongeïnteresseerd, onverschillig
disjointed onsamenhangend; verward [of
story, ideas]
disk *see disc*
diskette diskette, floppy(disk)
disk storage schijfgeheugen[h]
¹dislike (n) afkeer, tegenzin: *likes and ~s*
sympathieën en antipathieën
²dislike (vb) niet houden van, een afkeer
hebben van, een hekel hebben aan
dislocate 1 verplaatsen **2** onklaar maken,
ontregelen; [fig] verstoren; in de war brengen **3** [med] ontwrichten
disloyal ontrouw, trouweloos, niet loyaal
dismal 1 ellendig, troosteloos, somber
2 zwak, armzalig
¹dismantle (vb) uitneembaar zijn [eg of ap-

pliance]
²dismantle (vb) **1** ontmantelen, van de bedekking ontdoen **2** leeghalen, van meubilair
(uitrusting) ontdoen, onttakelen **3** slopen,
afbreken, uit elkaar halen
¹dismay (n) wanhoop, verbijstering, ontzetting
²dismay (vb) verbijsteren, ontzetten, met
wanhoop vervullen: *be ~ed at* (or: *by) the
sight* de moed verliezen door de aanblik
dismember 1 uiteenrijten: *the body was
~ed by wolves* het lijk werd door wolven verscheurd **2** in stukken snijden **3** in stukken
verdelen
dismiss 1 laten gaan, wegsturen **2** ontslaan, opzeggen **3** van zich afzetten, uit zijn
gedachten zetten **4** afdoen, zich (kort) afmaken van, verwerpen: *they ~ed the suggestion* ze verwierpen het voorstel **5** afdanken,
laten inrukken
dismissal 1 verlof[h] om te gaan **2** ontslag[h]
3 verdringing, het uit zijn gedachten zetten
4 het terzijde schuiven, verwerping, het afdoen
dismissive minachtend, afwijzend
disobedient ongehoorzaam, opstandig
disobey niet gehoorzamen, ongehoorzaam zijn; negeren [order]; overtreden
[rules]
disorder 1 oproer[h], opstootje[h], ordeverstoring **2** stoornis, kwaal, ziekte, aandoening:
Boris suffered from a kidney ~ Boris leed aan
een nierkwaal **3** wanorde, verwarring, ordeloosheid
disorientate het gevoel voor richting ontnemen; desoriënteren
disown 1 verwerpen, afwijzen, ontkennen
2 verstoten, niet meer willen kennen
disparage 1 kleineren, geringschatten **2** in
diskrediet brengen, verdacht maken, vernederen
disparity ongelijkheid, ongelijksoortig-
heid, ongelijkwaardigheid: *(a) great ~ of* (or:
in) age between them een groot leeftijdsver-
schil tussen hen
¹dispatch (n) **1** bericht[h] **2** het wegsturen
3 doeltreffendheid, snelle afhandeling: *with
great ~* met grote doeltreffendheid
²dispatch (vb) **1** (ver)zenden, (weg)sturen
2 de genadeslag geven, doden **3** doeltreffend afhandelen **4** wegwerken [food etc];
soldaat maken
dispel verjagen, verdrijven
dispensary 1 apotheek; huisapotheek [in
school etc] **2** consultatiebureau[h], medische
hulppost
¹dispense (vb) ontheffing geven, vrijstelling
verlenen
²dispense (vb) **1** uitreiken, distribueren, geven: *~ justice* het recht toepassen, gerechtigheid doen geschieden **2** klaarmaken en le-

veren [drugs]: *dispensing* **chemist** apotheker
dispenser 1 apotheker **2** automaat, houder
dispense with 1 afzien van, het zonder stellen, niet nodig hebben **2** overbodig maken, terzijde zetten
¹disperse (vb) zich verspreiden, uiteengaan
²disperse (vb) **1** uiteen drijven, verspreiden, spreiden, uiteenplaatsen **2** verspreiden, overal bekendmaken **3** verjagen
dispirited moedeloos, somber, mistroostig
displace 1 verplaatsen, verschuiven: *~d people* ontheemden **2** vervangen, verdringen
displacement 1 verplaatsing **2** vervanging **3** waterverplaatsing [of ship]
¹display (n) **1** tentoonstelling, uitstalling, weergave: *the more expensive models are on ~ in our showroom* de duurdere modellen zijn uitgestald in onze toonzaal **2** vertoning, tentoonspreiding **3** demonstratie, vertoonʰ, druktemakerij
²display (vb) **1** tonen, exposeren, uitstallen **2** tentoonspreiden, tonen, aan de dag leggen: *a touching ~ of friendship and affection* een ontroerende blijk van vriendschap en genegenheid **3** te koop lopen met, demonstreren
displease ergeren, irriteren: *be ~d at sth.* (or: *with s.o.*) boos zijn over iets (or: op iem.)
displeasure afkeuring; ergernis: *incur s.o.'s ~* zich iemands ongenoegen op de hals halen
disposable 1 beschikbaar: *~ income* besteedbaar inkomen **2** wegwerp-, weggooi-
disposal 1 het wegdoen, verwijdering **2** overdracht, verkoop, schenking **3** beschikking: *I am entirely at your ~* ik sta geheel tot uw beschikking
dispose 1 plaatsen, ordenen, rangschikken, regelen **2** brengen tot, bewegen: *~ s.o. to do sth.* iem. er toe brengen iets te doen
disposed geneigd, bereid: *they seemed favourably ~ to(wards) that idea* zij schenen welwillend tegenover dat idee te staan
dispose of 1 van de hand doen, verkopen, wegdoen **2** afhandelen; uit de weg ruimen [questions, problems etc]
disposition 1 plaatsing, rangschikking, opstelling **2** aard, karakterʰ, neiging: *she has a* (or: *is of a) happy ~* zij heeft een opgewekt karakter
dispossess onteigenen, ontnemen: *~ s.o. of sth.* iem. iets ontnemen
disproportionate onevenredig, niet naar verhouding
disprove weerleggen, de onjuistheid aantonen van
¹dispute (n) **1** twistgesprekʰ, discussie, woordenstrijd: *the matter in ~* de zaak in kwestie **2** geschilʰ, twist: *beyond* (or: *past,*

without) ~ buiten kijf
²dispute (vb) redetwisten, discussiëren
³dispute (vb) **1** heftig bespreken, heftig discussiëren over **2** aanvechten, in twijfel trekken **3** betwisten, strijd voeren over **4** weerstand bieden aan
disqualification diskwalificatie; uitsluiting
disqualify 1 ongeschikt maken **2** onbevoegd verklaren **3** diskwalificeren, uitsluiten
disquieting onrustbarend; zorgwekkend, verontrustend
disregard 1 geen acht slaan op, negeren: *~ a warning* een waarschuwing in de wind slaan **2** geringschatten
disrepair vervalʰ, bouwvalligheid: *the house had fallen into ~* (or: *was in ~*) het huis was vervallen
disrepute slechte naam, diskredietʰ: *bring into ~* in diskrediet brengen
disrespect oneerbiedigheid; gebrek aan respect
disrespectful oneerbiedig; onbeleefd
disrupt 1 uiteen doen vallen, verscheuren **2** ontwrichten, verstoren: *communications were ~ed* de verbindingen waren verbroken
disruption ontwrichting; verstoring
diss [Am; inform] beledigen, dissen
dissatisfaction ontevredenheid
dissatisfy niet tevreden stellen: *dissatisfied with the results* ontevreden over de resultaten
dissect 1 in stukken snijden, verdelen **2** ontleden, grondig analyseren
dissection 1 ontleed deelʰ van dier of plant **2** ontleding, analyse
¹dissemble (vb) huichelen
²dissemble (vb) **1** veinzen; voorwenden **2** verhullen
disseminate uitzaaien, verspreiden
dissemination verspreiding: *the free ~ of information* de vrije verspreiding van informatie
dissension 1 meningsverschilʰ **2** tweedracht, verdeeldheid, onenigheid
dissent verschilʰ van mening
dissertation 1 verhandeling, dissertatie, proefschriftʰ **2** scriptie
dissident 1 dissident, andersdenkend **2** dissident, andersdenkende
dissimilar ongelijk, verschillend: *~ in character* verschillend van aard
dissimulation veinzerij
¹dissipate (vb) **1** verdrijven, verjagen, doen verdwijnen **2** verspillen [eg money, forces]; verkwisten
²dissipate (vb) zich verspreiden: *the mob rapidly ~d* de menigte ging snel uiteen
dissociate scheiden, afscheiden: *it is very hard to ~ the man from what he did* het is erg moeilijk om de man los te zien van wat hij

heeft gedaan; ~ *o.s.* *from* zich distantiëren van

dissolute 1 losbandig **2** verdorven

¹dissolve (vb) oplossen, smelten: [fig] ~ *in(to)* tears in tranen wegsmelten

²dissolve (vb) **1** oplossen **2** ontbinden [of parliament]; opheffen

dissonance 1 wanklank **2** onenigheid

dissuade ontraden, afraden

distance 1 afstand, tussenruimte, eind(je)[h]; [fig] afstand(elijkheid); terughoudendheid: *keep one's* ~ afstand bewaren; *within* ***walk-ing*** ~ op loopafstand; *in the* ~ in de verte **2** (tijds)afstand, tijdsverloop[h], tijdruimte

distant 1 ver, afgelegen, verwijderd: ~ *re-lations* verre bloedverwanten **2** afstandelijk: *a* ~ *smile* een gereserveerde glimlach

distaste (+ for) afkeer (van), aversie (van), weerzin: *for once he managed to overcome his* ~ *hard work* eenmaal wist hij zijn afkeer van hard werken te overwinnen

distasteful onaangenaam; akelig: *such a way of life is* ~ *to* me zo'n manier van leven staat mij (vreselijk) tegen

distil 1 distilleren: ~ *water* water distilleren **2** via distillatie vervaardigen, branden, stoken **3** [form] afleiden, de essentie weergeven van

distillery distilleerderij, stokerij

distinct 1 onderscheiden, verschillend, apart: *four* ~ *meanings* vier afzonderlijke betekenissen **2** duidelijk, goed waarneembaar, onmiskenbaar: *a* ~ *possibility* een stellige mogelijkheid

distinction 1 onderscheiding, ereteken[h] **2** onderscheid[h], onderscheiding, verschil[h]: *draw a sharp* ~ *between* een scherp onderscheid maken tussen **3** voortreffelijkheid, aanzien[h], gedistingeerdheid

distinctive onderscheidend, kenmerkend

distinguish 1 indelen, rangschikken **2** onderscheiden, onderkennen: ~ *cause and effect* oorzaak en gevolg onderscheiden **3** zien, onderscheiden: *I could* ~ *the tower in the dis-tance* in de verte kon ik de toren onderscheiden **4** kenmerken, karakteriseren || ~ *be-tween* onderscheid maken tussen, uit elkaar houden

distinguished 1 voornaam, aanzienlijk: ***distinguished-looking*** *ladies* voornaam uitziende dames **2** beroemd, befaamd **3** gedistingeerd

distort 1 vervormen, verwringen: *the frame of my bike was* ***completely*** *~ed* het frame van mijn fiets was helemaal vervormd **2** verdraaien, vertekenen: *a ~ed* ***version*** *of the facts* een verdraaide versie van de feiten

distract 1 afleiden **2** verwarren, verbijsteren

distraction 1 vermakelijkheid, ontspanning, vermaak[h] **2** afleiding, ontspanning,

vermaak[h] **3** gebrek[h] aan aandacht **4** verwarring, gekheid: *those children are driving me* **to** ~ ik word stapelgek van die kinderen

distraught radeloos: ~ *with* grief radeloos van verdriet

distress 1 leed[h], verdriet[h], zorg **2** nood, armoede **3** gevaar[h], nood: *a ship in* ~ een schip in nood

distressed 1 (diep) bedroefd **2** bang **3** overstuur, van streek **4** noodlijdend, behoeftig

distress signal noodsein[h]; noodsignaal[h]

distribute distribueren, verdelen: *the rain-fall is* ***evenly*** *~d throughout the year* de regenval is gelijkmatig over het jaar verdeeld

distribution verdeling, (ver)spreiding, distributie

district 1 district[h], regio **2** streek, gebied[h] **3** wijk, buurt: *a* ***residential*** ~ een woonwijk

district attorney [Am] officier van justitie

¹distrust (n) wantrouwen[h], argwaan, achterdocht

²distrust (vb) wantrouwen, geen vertrouwen stellen in

disturb 1 in beroering brengen [also fig]; verontrusten: *~ing* ***facts*** verontrustende feiten **2** storen: *be* ***mentally*** *~ed* geestelijk gestoord zijn; *please do not* ~! a.u.b. niet storen! **3** verstoren: ~ *the* ***peace*** de openbare orde verstoren

disturbance 1 opschudding, relletje[h] **2** stoornis, verstoring: *a* ~ *of the* ***peace*** een ordeverstoring **3** storing

disunity verdeeldheid, onenigheid

disuse onbruik[h]: ***fall into*** ~ in onbruik (ge)raken

¹ditch (n) sloot, greppel

²ditch (vb) [inform] afdanken, verlaten: *when did she* ~ ***Brian?*** wanneer heeft zij Brian de bons gegeven?

¹dither (n) zenuwachtigheid, nerveuze opwinding: *all* ***of*** *a* ~ zenuwachtig, opgewonden

²dither (vb) **1** aarzelen **2** zenuwachtig doen

ditto 1 dito[h], idem, hetzelfde **2** duplicaat[h]

ditty liedje[h], deuntje[h]

divan 1 divan; sofa **2** springbox

¹dive (n) **1** duik, duikvlucht **2** plotselinge snelle beweging, greep, duik: *he* ***made*** *a* ~ *for the ball* hij dook naar de bal **3** kroeg, tent

²dive (vb) **1** duiken [also fig]; onderduiken, een duikvlucht maken: ~ ***into*** *one's studies* zich werpen op zijn studie **2** wegduiken **3** tasten, de hand steken (in): *she ~d* ***into*** *her handbag* zij stak haar hand diep in haar tasje

diver duiker

diverge 1 uiteenlopen, uiteenwijken **2** afwijken, verschillen: *his account ~s* ***from*** *the official version* zijn verslag wijkt af van de officiële versie **3** afdwalen

diverse 1 divers, verschillend **2** afwisse-

lend, gevarieerd
div_ersify 1 diversifiëren; verscheidenheid
aanbrengen **2** afwisselen; variëren
div_ersion 1 afleidingsactie, schijnbeweging **2** afleiding, ontspanning **3** omleiding
div_ersity 1 ongelijkheid: *their ~ of interests*
hun uiteenlopende belangen **2** verscheidenheid, diversiteit
div_ert 1 een andere richting geven, verleggen, omleiden: *why was their plane ~ed to Vienna?* waarom moest hun toestel uitwijken
naar Wenen? **2** afleiden [attention] **3** amuseren, vermaken
div_est of [form] ontdoen van; beroven van:
~ parental power uit de ouderlijke macht
ontzetten
¹div_ide (n) **1** waterscheiding **2** scheidslijn
²div_ide (vb) **1** verdeeld worden **2** onenigheid krijgen **3** zich delen, zich vertakken
³div_ide (vb) **1** delen, in delen splitsen, indelen **2** scheiden: *~d highway* weg met gescheiden dubbele rijbanen **3** onderling verdelen [also fig]; distribueren, verkavelen: *~d
against itself* onderling verdeeld **4** delen:
how much is 18 ~d by 3? hoeveel is 18 gedeeld door 3?
div_idend dividend[h], winstaandeel[h], uitkering (van winst)
div_ination 1 profetie, voorspelling
2 waarzeggerij
¹div_ine (adj) **1** goddelijk **2** aan God gewijd:
~ service godsdienstoefening **3** hemels, verrukkelijk
²div_ine (vb) **1** waarzeggen **2** (met wichelroede) vaststellen
³div_ine (vb) **1** gissen, raden, inzien, een voorgevoel hebben van
div_iner 1 waarzegger **2** (wichel)roedelo-
per
div_ining rod wichelroede
div_inity 1 godheid, goddelijkheid, god,
goddelijk wezen[h]: *the Divinity* de Godheid
2 theologie
div_isible deelbaar
div_ision 1 (ver)deling, het delen: *a ~ of labour* een arbeidsverdeling **2** afdeling [orga-
nisation, bureau] **3** [mil] divisie **4** scheiding,
scheidslijn, afscheiding **5** verschil[h], ongelijkheid, onenigheid: *a ~ of opinion* uiteenlopende meningen
div_isive tot ongelijkheid leidend, onenigheid brengend
¹div_orce (n) (echt)scheiding
²div_orce (vb) scheiden (van), zich laten
scheiden van
div_orcee gescheiden vrouw
div_ot graszode, divot
div_ulge onthullen, openbaar maken, bekendmaken
DIY *do-it-yourself* d.h.z., doe-het-zelf
diz_zy 1 duizelig, draaierig **2** verward, ver-

suft **3** duizelingwekkend [of height, speed
etc]
DJ *disc jockey* deejay, dj
Djib_outi Djibouti
¹Djib_outian (n) Djiboutiaan(se)
²Djib_outian (adj) Djiboutiaans
DNA *deoxyribonucleic acid* DNA[h]
¹do (n) partij, feest[h] ‖ *do's and don'ts* wat wel
en wat niet mag
²do (vb) **1** doen, handelen, zich gedragen: *he
did well to refuse that offer* hij deed er goed
aan dat aanbod te weigeren; *she was hard
done by* zij was oneerlijk behandeld **2** het
stellen, maken, zich voelen: *how do you do*
hoe maakt u het?; *he is doing well* het gaat
goed met hem **3** aan de hand zijn, gebeuren: *nothing doing* a) er gebeurt (hier) niets;
b) daar komt niets van in **4** klaar zijn, opgehouden zijn (hebben): *be done with s.o.* niets
meer te maken (willen) hebben met iem.;
have done with sth. ergens een punt achter
zetten **5** geschikt zijn, voldoen, volstaan: *this
copy won't do* deze kopie is niet goed genoeg; *it doesn't do to say such things* zoiets
hoor je niet te zeggen; *that will do!* en nou is
't uit! **6** het (moeten) doen, het (moeten)
stellen met: *they'll have to do with what
they've got* ze zullen het moeten doen met
wat ze hebben ‖ *do away with* a) wegdoen,
weggooien, een eind maken aan; b) afschaffen [death penalty, institution etc]; *do for
s.o.* het huishouden doen voor iem., werkster
zijn bij iem.; *I could do with a few quid* ik zou
best een paar pond kunnen gebruiken; *it has
got nothing to do with you* jij staat erbuiten
³do (vb) **1** doen [sth. abstract]: *do one's best*
zijn best doen; *it isn't done* zoiets doet men
niet; *what can I do for you?* wat kan ik voor je
doen?; [in shop] wat mag het zijn? **2** bezig
zijn met [sth. concrete, existing]; doen, opknappen, in orde brengen, herstellen; oplossen [puzzles etc]; studeren: *do one's duty* zijn
plicht doen; *do psychology* psychologie studeren; *have one's teeth done* zijn tanden laten nakijken; *do up the kitchen* de keuken
opknappen **3** maken, doen ontstaan: *the
storm did a lot of damage* de storm richtte
heel wat schade aan; *do wonders* wonderen
verrichten **4** (aan)doen, geven, veroorzaken:
do s.o. a favour iem. een dienst bewijzen
5 beëindigen, afhandelen, afmaken; [in-
form, fig] uitputten; kapotmaken: *I have
done cleaning,* [inform] *I am done cleaning* ik
ben klaar met de schoonmaak; *done in* bekaf, afgepeigerd; [inform] *do s.o. in* iem. van
kant maken **6** [culinary] bereiden, klaarmaken: *well done* goed doorbakken [of meat]
7 rijden, afleggen: *do 50 mph.* 80 km/u rijden
8 [inform] beetnemen, afzetten, neppen: *do
s.o. for $100* iem. voor honderd dollar afzet-
ten **9** ontvangen, onthalen: *he does himself*

well hij zorgt wel dat hij niets te kort komt **10** [inform] uitzitten [a sentence]: *he has done time in Attica* hij zat vast in Attica ‖ *I've done it again* ik heb het weer verknoeid; *a boiled egg will do* **me** ik heb genoeg aan een gekookt ei; **over** *and done with* voltooid verleden tijd; *do* **up** *a zip* (or: *a coat*) een rits (or: jas) dichtdoen
⁴**do** (aux vb): [often untranslated] *do you know him?* ken je hem?; [in negative sentence] *I don't know him* ik ken hem niet; [replacing verb] *he laughed and so did she* hij lachte, en zij ook; *I treat my friends as he does his enemies: badly* ik behandel mijn vrienden zoals hij zijn vijanden: slecht; [to ask for consent] *he writes well, doesn't he?* hij schrijft goed, nietwaar?; [with emphasis, in imperative mood] *do come in!* kom toch binnen!; *oh, do be quiet!* o, houd alsjeblieft eens je mond!
doc *doctor* dokter
docile meegaand, volgzaam: *a ~ horse* een mak paard
¹**dock** (n) **1** dokᵇ, droogdokᵇ, havendokᵇ, kade: *floating ~* drijvend dok **2** (-s) haven(s) **3** werf **4** beklaagdenbank: *be in the ~* terechtstaan ‖ *in ~* **a)** in reparatie; **b)** in het ziekenhuis; **c)** op de helling
²**dock** (vb) **1** dokken, de haven binnenlopen, in het dok gaan **2** gekoppeld worden [spacecraft]
³**dock** (vb) **1** couperen [tail etc]; afsnijden, afknippen **2** korten, (gedeeltelijk) inhouden, achterhouden **3** dokken, in het dok brengen **4** koppelen [spacecraft]
docker dokwerker, havenarbeider, stuwadoor
docket 1 bon, kassabon, bewijsstukᵇ, reçuᵇ **2** korte inhoud [of document, report]
dockland havenbuurt; havenkwartierᵇ
dockyard werf
¹**doctor** (n) **1** dokter, arts; [Am] tandarts; veearts: *that is just what the ~ ordered* dat is net wat je nodig hebt **2** doctor [somebody holding the highest university degree]
²**doctor** (vb) **1** [euph] helpen, steriliseren, castreren **2** knoeien met, rommelen met, vervalsen: *~ the* **accounts** de boeken vervalsen
doctorate doctoraatᵇ; doctorstitel
doctrine 1 doctrine, leer **2** dogmaᵇ, beginselᵇ
¹**document** (n) documentᵇ, bewijsstukᵇ
²**document** (vb) documenteren, vastleggen
documentary documentaire
documentation 1 documentatie **2** bewijsmateriaalᵇ
dodder 1 beven [with old age, weakness] **2** schuifelen, strompelen
doddle eitjeᵇ: *it's a ~* het is een eitje, het is heel makkelijk
¹**dodge** (n) **1** (zij)sprong, ontwijkende be-

weging **2** foefjeᵇ, trucjeᵇ, slimmigheidjeᵇ: *a* **tax** *~* een belastingtruc
²**dodge** (vb) **1** (opzij) springen, snel bewegen, rennen: *the woman ~d* **behind** *the chair* de vrouw dook weg achter de stoel **2** uitvluchten zoeken, (eromheen) draaien
³**dodge** (vb) ontwijken, vermijden, ontduiken: *he kept dodging the* **question** hij bleef de vraag ontwijken
dodgem botsautootjeᵇ
dodger ontduiker; ontwijker
dodgy 1 slim, gewiekst **2** netelig: *~ situation* netelige situatie
dodo 1 dodo **2** [Am] sukkel ‖ [inform] *as* **dead** *as a ~* zo dood als een pier
doe wijfjeᵇ van een konijn
¹**dog** (n) **1** hond **2** [inform] kerel: *lucky ~* geluksvogel, mazzelaar ‖ *not a ~'s* **chance** geen schijn van kans; *he is a ~ in the* **manger** hij kan de zon niet in het water zien schijnen; *go to the ~s* naar de bliksem gaan; *the ~s* (wind)hondenrennen
²**dog** (vb) (achter)volgen, (achter)nazitten
dog collar 1 halsband **2** [mockingly] boord van een geestelijke
dog-eared met ezelsoren
dogged vasthoudend, volhardend: *it is ~ that does it* de aanhouder wint
doggerel 1 rijmelarij **2** kreupelrijmᵇ
doggy hondjeᵇ
dogma dogmaᵇ
dogmatic 1 dogmatisch **2** autoritair
dogsbody duvelstoejager, sloof: *a* **general** *~* een manusje-van-alles
doing 1 handeling, het handelen, het (toe)doen: *it is all* **their** *~* het is allemaal hun schuld **2** (-s) daden, handelingen
doldrums 1 neerslachtigheid: *be in the ~* in de put zitten **2** het stilliggen van een schip **3** [fig] stilstand
the **dole** werkloosheidsuitkering, steun: *be on the ~* steun trekken
doll 1 pop **2** meisjeᵇ, meid ‖ *Will you do it? You are* **a** *~!* Doe je het? Je bent een schat!
dollar dollar
dollop (klein) beetjeᵇ, kwak, scheut
doll up zich optutten: *doll o.s. up* zich uitdossen
dolly [child language] pop(jeᵇ)
dolphin dolfijn
dolt domoor, uilskuikenᵇ
domain 1 gebiedᵇ, (land)goedᵇ **2** gebiedᵇ [fig]; veldᵇ, terreinᵇ: *the garden is my wife's ~* de tuin is het domein van mijn vrouw
dome 1 koepel **2** gewelfᵇ **3** ronde top: *the ~ of a* **hill** de ronde top van een heuvel
¹**domestic** (n) bediende, dienstbode
²**domestic** (adj) **1** huishoudelijk, het huishouden betreffend: *~ economy* (or: *science*) huishoudkunde **2** huiselijk **3** binnenlands: *~ trade* binnenlandse handel **4** tam: *~ animals*

domesticate

huisdieren

domesticate 1 aan het huiselijk leven doen wennen **2** aan zich onderwerpen, temmen, beteugelen, tot huisdier maken
domicile verblijfplaats, woning
dominance overheersing
dominant dominant [also biology]; (over)heersend
dominate domineren, overheersen: *~ the conversation* het hoogste woord voeren
domination overheersing, heerschappij
¹Dominican (n) Dominicaan(se)
²Dominican (adj) Dominicaans
dominion 1 domein[h], (grond)gebied[h], rijk[h] **2** heerschappij, macht
domino dominosteen
dominoes domino(spel)[h]
¹don (n) docent aan een universiteit
²don (vb) [form] aandoen: *she ~ned her hat and coat* zij zette haar hoed op en trok haar jas aan
donate schenken, geven: *~ money towards sth.* geld schenken voor iets
donation schenking; donatie, bijdrage
done 1 netjes, gepast: *it is not ~* zoiets doet men niet **2** klaar, gereed, af: *be ~ with* klaar zijn met; *have ~ with* niets meer te maken (willen) hebben met **3** doodmoe, uitgeput || *hard ~ by* oneerlijk behandeld; *she seemed completely ~ in* (or: *up*) zij leek volkomen uitgeteld; *~!* akkoord!, afgesproken!
dongle dongel
donkey ezel [also fig]; domoor, sufferd || [inform] *nodding ~* jaknikker
donkey's years [inform] eeuwigheid; lange tijd; eeuwigheid: *I haven't heard from her for ~* het is eeuwen geleden dat ik iets van haar gehoord heb
donor 1 gever, schenker **2** donor
don't verbod[h]: *do's and ~s* wat wel en niet mag, geboden en verboden
donut [Am] *see* **doughnut**
doodah [inform] je-weet-wel; ding(etje)[h]
¹doodle (n) krabbel, figuurtje[h], poppetje[h]
²doodle (vb) krabbelen, figuurtjes tekenen
¹doom (n) **1** noodlot[h], lot[h]: *a sense of ~ and foreboding* een gevoel van naderend onheil **2** ondergang, verderf[h]: *meet one's ~* de ondergang vinden **3** laatste oordeel[h]
²doom (vb) **1** veroordelen, (ver)doemen **2** [esp as part participle] ten ondergang doemen: *the undertaking was ~ed from the start* de onderneming was vanaf het begin tot mislukken gedoemd
doomsday dag des oordeels [also fig]; doemdag: *till ~* eeuwig
door 1 deur, (auto)portier[h]: *answer the ~* (de deur) opendoen (voor iem. die aangebeld heeft); *show s.o. the ~* iem. de deur wijzen; *show s.o. to the ~* iem. uitlaten; *out of ~s* buiten(shuis) **2** toegang, mogelijkheid:

leave the ~ open de mogelijkheid openlaten || *lay the blame at s.o.'s ~* iem. de schuld geven
doorbell (voor)deurbel
doorknob deurknop
doorstep 1 stoep: *on the* (or: *your*) *~* vlakbij **2** [inform] dikke boterham; pil
doorway deuropening, ingang, deurgat[h]
¹dope (n) **1** sufferd, domoor **2** drugs, verdovende middelen **3** doping, stimulerende middelen **4** info(rmatie), nieuws[h] **5** smeermiddel[h], smeersel[h]
²dope (vb) verdovende middelen/doping toedienen aan: *they must have ~d his drink* zij moeten iets in zijn drankje gedaan hebben
dopey [inform] **1** suf **2** dom
dormant 1 slapend, sluimerend; [biology] in winterslaap **2** latent, verborgen **3** inactief: *a ~ volcano* een slapende vulkaan
dormitory 1 slaapzaal **2** [Am] studentenhuis[h]
dormouse slaapmuis
dosage dosering, dosis
¹dose (n) dosis [also fig]; hoeveelheid, stralingsdosis || *like a ~ of salts* razend vlug
²dose (vb) doseren, medicijn toedienen aan
¹doss (n) dutje[h]
²doss (vb) maffen
dosser dakloze
dosshouse logement[h], goedkoop hotelletje[h]
¹dot (n) punt[h] [also music, Morse; on letter]; spikkel, stip || *on the ~* stipt (op tijd)
²dot (vb) **1** een punt zetten op [also music]; [fig] *~ the i's (and cross the t's)* de puntjes op de i zetten **2** stippelen, (be)spikkelen: *~ted line* stippellijn || *sign on the ~ted line* (een contract) ondertekenen
dotage kindsheid, dementie: *be in his ~* oud en dement zijn
dot-com dotcombedrijf[h], internetbedrijf[h]
dote (up)on dol zijn op, verzot zijn op; [fig] aanbidden; verafgoden
dotty 1 gespikkeld, gestippeld **2** getikt, niet goed snik **3** (+ about) dol (op), gek (op)
¹double (n) **1** dubbel, dubbelt[h]: *~ or quits* quitte of dubbel **2** het dubbele, dubbele (hoeveelheid/snelheid e.d.) **3** dubbelganger **4** [film etc] dublure, vervanger, stuntman **5** verdubbeling [of score, board, stake etc in various sports] **6** (-s) [tennis] dubbel(spel)[h]: *mixed ~s* gemengd dubbel || *at* (or: *on*) *the ~* in looppas; [fig] meteen, onmiddellijk
²double (adj) **1** dubbel, tweemaal (zo groot/veel): *~ the amount* tweemaal zoveel; *~ bed* tweepersoonsbed; *~ chin* onderkin, dubbele kin; *~ cream* dikke room; *~ entry* (bookkeeping) dubbele boekhouding; *~ exposure* dubbele belichting; *~ glazing* (or: *windows*) dubbele beglazing (or: ramen); *~ standard* het meten met twee maten [fig] **2** oneerlijk, dubbelhartig, vals: *~ agent* dubbelagent,

dubbelspion ‖ ~ *Dutch* koeterwaals, onzin
³**double** (vb) **1** (zich) verdubbelen, doubleren **2** terugkeren, plotseling omkeren: ~
(back) **on** *one's tracks* op zijn schreden terugkeren **3** een dubbele rol spelen **4** [film etc]
als vervanger optreden: ~ *for an actor* een
(toneel)speler vervangen
⁴**double** (vb) **1** verdubbelen, doubleren,
tweemaal zo groot maken **2** [film etc] als
vervanger optreden van **3** [bridge] doubleren
⁵**double** (adv) dubbel, tweemaal (zoveel als),
samen
¹**double back** (vb) terugkeren
²**double back** (vb) terugslaan, terugvou-
wen
double-barrelled 1 dubbelloops **2** tweeledig; met twee oogmerken ‖ *a ~ name* een
dubbele naam
double-bass contrabas
double-breasted met twee rijen knopen,
dubbelrijs
double-cross bedriegen, dubbel spel spelen met, oplichten
¹**double-dealing** (n) oplichterij, bedrogʰ
²**double-dealing** (adj) oneerlijk, vals
double-digit in tientallen: ~ *inflation* inflatie van 10% en meer
double-edged tweesnijdend [also fig]: *a ~
argument* een argument dat zowel vóór als
tegen kan worden gebruikt
double-quick vliegensvlug, razendsnel, zo
snel je kunt
double-talk 1 onzin **2** dubbelzinnigheid,
dubbelzinnige opmerking(en)
double-time 1 looppas **2** overwerkgeldʰ;
onregelmatigheidstoeslag [of employee]
¹**double up** (vb) ineenkrimpen [with laughter, in pain]
²**double up** (vb) **1** buigen, doen ineenkrimpen: ~ *one's legs* zijn benen intrekken **2** opvouwen, omslaan, terugslaan
doubly dubbel (zo), tweemaal (zo): ~ *careful* extra voorzichtig
¹**doubt** (n) twijfel, onzekerheid, aarzeling:
the **benefit** *of the* ~ het voordeel van de twijfel; *be in no* ~ *about sth.* ergens zeker van zijn;
have one's ~s about sth. ergens aan twijfelen;
without (a) ~ ongetwijfeld; *no* ~ ongetwijfeld, zonder (enige) twijfel
²**doubt** (vb) twijfelen (aan), onzeker zijn, betwijfelen: ~ *that* (or: *whether*) (be)twijfelen
of
doubtless zeker; ongetwijfeld
douche irrigatie [of vagina]
dough 1 deegʰ **2** [inform] poen, centen
doughnut donut
dour streng, stug
dove duif [also fig]; aanhanger van vredes-
politiek
dovecot(e) duiventil

dovetail precies passen [also fig]; overeenkomen: *my plans ~ed with his* mijn plannen
sloten aan bij de zijne
dowager douairière
dowdy slonzig, slordig gekleed
¹**down** (n) donsʰ, haartjes, veertjes ‖ *have a ~
on s.o.* een hekel hebben aan iem.
²**down** (adj) **1** neergaand, naar onder leidend **2** beneden **3** depressief, verdrietig: *be
~ and out* berooid zijn, aan de grond zitten ‖
cash ~ contante betaling, handje contantje;
~ *payment* contante betaling; aanbetaling
³**down** (adv) neer, (naar) beneden, omlaag,
onder: *bend* ~ bukken, vooroverbuigen; *the
sun goes* ~ de zon gaat onder; *up and* ~ op en
neer; ~ *with the president!* weg met de president! ‖ *come* (or: *go*) ~ de universiteit verlaten [because of holidays or graduation]; *be
sent* ~ weggezonden worden van de universiteit; *eight ~ and two to go* acht gespeeld en
nog twee te gaan; ~ *under* in Australië en
Nieuw-Zeeland
⁴**down** (prep) **1** vanaf, langs: ~ *the coast*
langs de kust; ~ *(the)* **river** de rivier af, verder
stroomafwaarts; *he went* ~ *the* **street** hij liep
de straat door **2** neer, af ‖ ~ **town** de stad in,
in het centrum
down-and-out [inform] zwerver
down-at-heel [inform] haveloos; sjofel
downbeat [inform] pessimistisch; somber
downcast 1 terneergeslagen, somber,
neerslachtig **2** neergeslagen [eyes]: ~ *eyes*
neergeslagen ogen
downer [inform] **1** kalmerend middelʰ;
tranquillizer **2** teleurstelling: *be on a* ~ depri
zijn
downfall 1 stortbui **2** val; ondergang
downgrade 1 degraderen, in rang verlagen **2** de waarde naar beneden halen van
downhearted ontmoedigd, terneergeslagen, in de put
¹**downhill** (adj) **1** (af)hellend, neerwaarts
2 gemakkelijk: *it's all ~ from here* het is een
makkie vanaf hier
²**downhill** (adv) bergafwaarts, naar beneden: *go* ~ verslechteren
download downloaden
downplay afzwakken; bagatelliseren, relativeren
downpour stortbui, plensbui
¹**downright** (adj) **1** uitgesproken, overduidelijk: *a ~ liar* iem. die liegt dat het gedrukt
staat **2** eerlijk, oprecht
²**downright** (adv) volkomen, door en door
¹**downriver** (adj) stroomafwaarts (gelegen)
²**downriver** (adv) stroomafwaarts; met de
stroom mee
down-river racing het wildwatervaren
downshift [Am] **1** [car] terugschakelen
2 [fig] een stapje terug doen
downside 1 nadeelʰ; schaduwzijde, keer-

zijde **2** [Am] onderkant
downsizing inkrimping, bezuiniging
¹downstairs (adj) beneden, op de begane
grond
²downstairs (adv) (naar) beneden, de trap
af
downstream stroomafwaarts
down-to-earth nuchter, met beide benen
op de grond
downtown naar de binnenstad, de stad in
downtrodden onderdrukt
downward naar beneden gaand, neerwaarts, aflopend: ~ *spiral* neerwaartse spiraal
downwards see downward
downwind met de wind mee (gaand)
downy donzig, zacht
dowry bruidsschat
dowse (met een wichelroede) wateraders
(mineralen) opsporen, wichelroede lopen
dowsing-rod wichelroede
¹doze (n) sluimering, dutjeʰ
²doze (vb) sluimeren, dutten, soezen: ~ *off*
indutten, in slaap sukkelen
³doze (vb) (+ away) verdutten, versuffen
dozen 1 dozijnʰ, twaalftalʰ **2** groot aantalʰ,
heleboel: ~*s (and* ~*s) of people* een heleboel
mensen; *by the* ~ bij tientallen, bij bosjes || *it's
six of one and half a* ~ *of the other* het is lood
om oud ijzer
dozy slaperig, soezerig
¹drab (n) [vulg] slons, slet, hoer
²drab (adj) **1** [inform] vaalbruin **2** kleurloos,
saai
draconian draconisch; zeer streng: ~
measures uiterst harde maatregelen
¹draft (n) **1** klad(jeʰ), conceptʰ, schets: *in* ~ in
het klad **2** [Am] dienstplicht
²draft (vb) **1** ontwerpen, schetsen, een klad-
(je) maken van **2** [Am] indelen, detacheren
3 [Am] oproepen (voor militaire dienst)
draftsman 1 tekenaar, ontwerper **2** opsteller (van documenten)
¹drag (n) **1** het slepen, het trekken **2** het
dreggen **3** dreg, dregnetʰ, dregankerʰ **4** rem
[fig]; belemmering, vertraging, blok aan het
been: *it was a* ~ *on the proceedings* het belemmerde de werkzaamheden **5** saai gedoeʰ, saai figuurʰ, vervelend iets (iem.): *it was
such a* ~ het was stomvervelend **6** trekjeʰ [of
a cigarette]; haaltjeʰ **7** door een man gedragen vrouwenkleding: *in* ~ in travestie, als
man verkleed
²drag (vb) **1** dreggen: ~ *for* dreggen naar
2 zich voortslepen; kruipen [of time]; lang
duren, langdradig zijn: ~ *on* eindeloos duren
3 achterblijven
³drag (vb) afdreggen; afzoeken [river]
⁴drag (vb) (mee)slepen, (voort)trekken,
(voort)sleuren, (voort)zeulen: ~ *through the
mire* (or: *mud*) door het slijk halen [also fig];

don't ~ *my name in* laat mijn naam erbuiten
drag-and-drop sleep-
drag down 1 slopen, uitputten, ontmoedigen **2** neerhalen [also fig]; verlagen
draggy [inform] duf, saai, vervelend
dragon draak
dragonfly libel, waterjuffer
¹dragoon (n) dragonder [also fig]
²dragoon (vb) (+ into) (met geweld) dwingen tot
drag out 1 eruit trekken [truth etc] **2** rekken [meeting, story etc]; uitspinnen
drag queen [inform] mannelijke travestiet
¹drain (n) **1** afvoerkanaalʰ, afvoerbuis, ri-
oolʰ: *down the* ~ naar de knoppen, verloren
2 afvloeiing, onttrekking; [fig] druk; belasting: *it is a great* ~ *on his strength* het vergt
veel van zijn krachten
²drain (vb) **1** weglopen, wegstromen, (uit)-
lekken: ~ *away* wegvloeien; [fig] wegebben,
afnemen **2** leeglopen, afdruipen **3** afwate-
ren, lozen
³drain (vb) **1** afvoeren, doen afvloeien, afgieten; [fig] doen verdwijnen **2** leegmaken,
leegdrinken: ~ *off* afvoeren, leegmaken
3 droogleggen || *a face* ~*ed of all colour* een
doodsbleek gezicht
drainpipe regenpijp, afvoerpijp
drake mannetjeseend, woerd
dram 1 drachme, dram **2** neutjeʰ
drama toneelstukʰ, dramaʰ
dramatic 1 dramatisch, toneel-: ~ *irony*
tragische ironie **2** indrukwekkend, aangrijpend
dramatist toneelschrijver
¹dramatize (vb) zich aanstellen, dramatisch
doen, overdrijven
²dramatize (vb) dramatiseren, als drama
bewerken, aanschouwelijk voorstellen
¹drape (n) **1** draperie **2** [Am] gordijnʰ
²drape (vb) **1** bekleden, omhullen, versieren
2 draperen [also fig]
drapery 1 stoffen **2** manufacturenhandel
3 [Am] gordijnʰ
drastic drastisch, ingrijpend
drat verwensen, vervloeken: [inform] *that*
~*ted animal!* dat vervelende beest!
draught 1 tocht, trek, luchtstroom: [in-
form] *feel the* ~ op de tocht zitten; [fig] in
geldnood verkeren **2** teug; slok [of medi-
cine] **3** drankjeʰ, medicijnʰ, dosis **4** het aftappen: *beer on* ~ bier van 't vat **5** schets,
conceptʰ, kladʰ **6** damschijf: *(game of)* ~*s*
damspel, het dammen
draughtboard dambordʰ
draught-proof tochtdicht, tochtvrij [of
windows etc]
draughtsman 1 tekenaar, ontwerper
2 opsteller [of documents] **3** damschijf
¹draw (n) **1** trek, het trekken: *he is quick on
the* ~ hij kan snel zijn revolver trekken; [fig]

hij reageert snel **2** aantrekkingskracht, attractie, trekpleister **3** [lottery] trekking, (uit)loting, verloting **4** gelijkspel[h], remise
²draw (vb) **1** komen, gaan: ~ *to an end* (or: *a close*) ten einde lopen; ~ *level* gelijk komen [in race] **2** aantrekkingskracht uitoefenen, publiek trekken **3** [sport, game] gelijkspelen, in gelijkspel eindigen, remise maken **4** trekken [of tea]
³draw (vb) **1** (aan)trekken, (aan)lokken: ~ *attention to* de aandacht vestigen op **2** (in)halen: ~ *a deep breath* diep inademen, diep ademhalen **3** ertoe brengen, overhalen **4** (te voorschijn) halen, uittrekken; [fig] ontlokken; naar buiten brengen; (af)tappen [beer etc]: ~ *blood* bloed doen vloeien; [fig] iem. gevoelig raken; *he refused to be ~n* hij liet zich niet uit zijn tent lokken **5** van de ingewanden ontdoen **6** opstellen [text]; opmaken, formuleren; uitschrijven [cheque] **7** trekken [money, wages]; opnemen, ontvangen **8** [sport, game] in gelijkspel doen eindigen ‖ ~ *off* a) afleiden [attention]; **b)** weglokken; **c)** aftappen
⁴draw (vb) **1** trekken, slepen; tevoorschijn halen [weapon]; dichtdoen [curtain]: ~ *the blinds* de jaloezieën neerlaten; ~ *back the curtains* de gordijnen opentrekken; ~ *s.o. into a conversation* iem. in een gesprek betrekken **2** tekenen, schetsen: [fig] *one has to ~ the line somewhere* je moet ergens een grens trekken **3** loten, door loting verkrijgen **4** putten [also fig]: ~ *inspiration from* inspiratie opdoen uit; *I'll have to ~ upon my savings* ik zal mijn spaargeld moeten aanspreken ‖ ~ *a conclusion* een conclusie trekken
draw apart uit elkaar gaan, uit elkaar groeien
draw away 1 (+ from) wegtrekken (van), (zich) terugtrekken (van) **2** (+ from) uitlopen (op), een voorsprong nemen (op)
drawback nadeel[h], bezwaar[h]
draw back (+ from) (zich) terugtrekken (van), terugwijken (van/voor)
drawbridge ophaalbrug
drawer 1 lade: *a chest of ~s* een ladekast **2** (-s) (lange) onderbroek
draw in 1 binnenrijden, komen aanrijden **2** aan de kant gaan rijden **3** ten einde lopen [of day]; schemerig worden; korter worden [of days]
drawing 1 tekening **2** het tekenen, tekenkunst: *Yvonne is good at* ~ Yvonne is goed in tekenen
drawing board tekentafel: *back to the* ~! terug naar af!; overnieuw!
drawing-pin punaise
drawing-room salon, zitkamer
¹drawl (n) lijzige manier van praten
²drawl (vb) lijzig praten
drawn 1 vertrokken, strak; afgetobd [face]

2 onbeslist [match]
¹draw out (vb) **1** langer worden [of days] **2** wegrijden [of train etc]
²draw out (vb) **1** (uit)rekken, uitspinnen **2** aan de praat krijgen, eruit halen, uithoren
¹draw up (vb) stoppen, tot stilstand komen: ~ *to* naderen, dichter komen bij
²draw up (vb) **1** opstellen; plaatsen [soldiers] **2** opmaken, opstellen, formuleren **3** aanschuiven [chair]; bijtrekken ‖ *draw o.s. up* zich oprichten, zich lang maken
¹dread (n) (doods)angst, vrees, schrik
²dread (vb) vrezen, erg opzien tegen, doodsbang zijn (voor): *I ~ to think (of) what will happen to him* ik moet er niet aan denken wat hem allemaal zal overkomen
dreadful vreselijk, ontzettend
dreadlocks rastakapsel, rastavlechten
dreads [inform] *dreadlocks* dreads
¹dream (n) droom; [fig] ideaal[h]: *a ~ of a dress* een beeldige jurk
²dream (vb) dromen, zich verbeelden, zich indenken: ~ *up* verzinnen; *she wouldn't ~ of moving* zij piekerde er niet over om te verhuizen
dreamy 1 dromerig **2** [inform] beeldig
dreary 1 somber, treurig **2** saai
dredge (op)dreggen, (uit)baggeren: [fig] ~ *up old memories* herinneringen ophalen
dregs 1 bezinksel, droesem: *drink* (or: *drain*) *to the* ~ tot op de bodem ledigen **2** [depr] iets waardeloos, uitvaagsel: ~ *of society* uitschot van de maatschappij
drench doordrenken, doorweken, kletsnat maken: *sun-drenched beaches* zonovergoten stranden
¹dress (n) **1** jurk, japon **2** kleding, dracht
²dress (vb) **1** (aan)kleden, van kleding voorzien, kleren aantrekken: ~*ed to kill* opvallend gekleed; ~ *up* verkleden, vermommen **2** versieren, opsieren, optuigen: ~ *up* a) opdoffen; **b)** [also fig] mooi doen lijken, aanvaardbaar laten klinken (*or*: maken), leuk brengen **3** [med] verbinden; verzorgen [wound]; verband aanleggen op **4** opmaken, kammen en borstelen, kappen ‖ ~ *down* a) roskammen [horse]; **b)** een pak slaag geven, op z'n donder geven
³dress (vb) **1** zich (aan)kleden, gekleed gaan **2** zich verkleden: ~ *for dinner* zich verkleden voor het eten
dressage dressuur
dress circle balkon[h]
dresser 1 buffetkast, keukenkast **2** [Am] ladekast **3** kleder, kleedster
dressing 1 het (aan)kleden **2** [med] verband(materiaal)[h] **3** slasaus **4** [Am; culinary] vulling
dressing down schrobbering; uitbrander
dressing-gown 1 badjas **2** ochtendjas
dressmaker naaister, kleermaker

dress rehearsal generale repetitie
¹dribble (n) **1** stroompjeʰ; [fig] vleugjeʰ; druppeltjeʰ, beetjeʰ **2** [sport] dribbel **3** kwijlʰ, speekselʰ
²dribble (vb) **1** (weg)druppelen, langzaam wegstromen; [fig] haast ongemerkt verdwijnen: *the answers ~d in* de antwoorden kwamen binnendruppelen **2** kwijlen **3** [sport] dribbelen
³dribble (vb) (laten) druppelen, langzaam laten vloeien
dried droog, gedroogd: *~ milk* melkpoeder
drier droger, haardroger, wasdroger, droogmolen
¹drift (n) **1** afwijking, afdrijving, het zwerven **2** vlaag, sneeuwvlaag, regenvlaag, stofwolk **3** opeenhoping, berg, massa **4** ongeorganiseerde beweging, gang, trek: *the ~ from the country to the city* de trek van het platteland naar de stad **5** strekking, tendens, bedoeling: *the general ~ of the story* de algemene strekking van het verhaal
²drift (vb) **1** (af)drijven, uiteendrijven [also fig]; (zich laten) meedrijven, (rond)zwalken: *~ away* (or: *off*) geleidelijk verdwijnen **2** opwaaien; (zich) ophopen [of snow]
³drift (vb) **1** meevoeren, voortdrijven **2** bedekken [with snow, leaves]
driftwood drijfhoutʰ; wrakhoutʰ
¹drill (n) **1** boor(machine), drilboor **2** het drillen, exercitie, oefening **3** driloefening, het opdreunen, het erin stampen **4** gebruikelijke procedure, normale gang van zaken
²drill (vb) **1** boren, gaten boren **2** stampen, (mechanisch) leren **3** oefenen, exerceren
³drill (vb) **1** doorboren **2** aanboren **3** drillen, africhten, trainen **4** erin stampen, erin heien
drily droog(jes)
¹drink (n) **1** (iets te) drinken, slok, teug: *would you like a ~?* wilt u misschien iets drinken? **2** drank, sterkedrank, alcohol: *food and ~* eten en drinken
²drink (vb) **1** in zich opnemen, (in)drinken: *~ in s.o.'s words* iemands woorden in zich opnemen **2** drinken op, het glas heffen op: *they drank (to) his health* zij dronken op zijn gezondheid
³drink (vb) drinken, leegdrinken, opdrinken: *he ~s like a fish* hij zuipt als een ketter; *~ up* opdrinken, (het glas) leegdrinken
drink-driver alcomobilist, automobilist die te veel gedronken heeft
drink to toosten op, een dronk uitbrengen op
¹drip (n) **1** gedruppelʰ, druppel, het druppelen **2** infuusʰ, infusievloeistof **3** sukkel, slome (duikelaar)
²drip (vb) druipen, druppelen: *~ping wet* drijfnat, doornat
³drip (vb) laten druppelen
drip-dry kreukherstellend; strijkvrij

drippy flauw, onnozel
¹drive (n) **1** rit(jeʰ), rijtoer: *let's go for a ~* laten we een eindje gaan rijden **2** [psychology] drift, drang **3** actie, campagne **4** laan, oprijlaan, oprit **5** (groot) offensiefʰ, (zware) aanval **6** aandrijving, overbrenging: *front-wheel ~* voorwielaandrijving **7** drijfkracht, stuwkracht **8** energie, doorzettingsvermogenʰ **9** diskdrive || *right-hand ~* met het stuur rechts, (met) rechtse besturing
²drive (vb) **1** snellen, (voort)stormen, (blijven) doorgaan **2** gooien, schieten, lanceren
³drive (vb) **1** dwingen, brengen tot: *~ s.o. to despair* iem. wanhopig maken **2** aandrijven
⁴drive (vb) **1** drijven [also fig]; opjagen, bijeendrijven: *~ out* verdrijven, uitdrijven, verdringen **2** rijden, (be)sturen, vervoeren: *~ in* binnenrijden; *~ off* wegrijden; *~ up* voorrijden **3** voortdrijven, duwen; slaan [also sport]: *~ home* a) vastslaan, inhameren; b) volkomen duidelijk maken; *~ in* a) inslaan [nail etc]; b) inhameren [fig]
drive at doelen op, bedoelen: *what is he driving at?* wat bedoelt hij?
¹drive-in (n) drive-in, bioscoop, cafetaria
²drive-in (adj) drive-in, inrij-
¹drivel (n) gezwamʰ, kletskoek
²drivel (vb) zwammen, (onzin) kletsen, zeveren
driver 1 bestuurder, chauffeur, machinist **2** (vee)drijver
driveway oprijlaan, oprit
driving 1 aandrijvend; stuwend [also fig] **2** krachtig, energiek: *~ rain* slagregen
driving licence rijbewijsʰ
driving mirror achteruitkijkspiegel
¹drizzle (n) motregen
²drizzle (vb) motregenen, miezeren
droll komiek, humoristisch
dromedary dromedaris
¹drone (n) **1** hommel, dar **2** gegonsʰ, gezoemʰ, gebromʰ **3** dreun, eentonige manier van praten
²drone (vb) **1** gonzen, zoemen, brommen **2** (op)dreunen [also fig]; monotoon spreken: *~ on* (door)zeuren
drool 1 kwijlen: [inform, fig] *~ about* (or: *over*) dwepen met, weglopen met **2** [inform] zwammen, leuteren
¹droop (n) hangende houding, het (laten) hangen
²droop (vb) **1** neerhangen, (af)hangen, slap worden, krom staan **2** verflauwen, afnemen, verslappen
¹drop (n) **1** druppel, drupjeʰ, neutjeʰ; [fig] greintjeʰ; spoor(tje)ʰ: *he has had a ~ too much* hij heeft te diep in het glaasje gekeken **2** zuurtje **3** (-s) druppels, medicijnʰ: [inform] *knock-out ~s* bedwelmingsmiddel || *a ~ in a bucket* (or: *in the ocean*) een druppel op een gloeiende plaat; *at the ~ of a hat* meteen, bij

de minste aanleiding, zonder te aarzelen
²drop (vb) **1** druppelen, druipen **2** vallen, omvallen, neervallen, zich laten vallen; [fig] terloops geuit worden: ~ *dead!* val dood! **3** ophouden, verlopen, uitvallen: *they let the matter* ~ zij lieten de zaak verder rusten **4** dalen, afnemen, zakken: *the wind has ~ped* de wind is gaan liggen || ~ *back* (or: *behind*) achterblijven, achtergelaten worden; ~ *behind* achterraken bij
³drop (vb) **1** laten druppelen, laten druipen **2** laten vallen, laten zakken, neerlaten **3** laten varen, laten schieten, opgeven: ~ *(the) charges* een aanklacht intrekken **4** laten dalen, verminderen, verlagen: ~ *one's voice* zachter praten **5** terloops zeggen, laten vallen: ~ *s.o. a hint* iem. een wenk geven; ~ *me a line* schrijf me maar een paar regeltjes **6** afleveren, afgeven, afzetten: *he ~ped me at the corner* hij zette mij bij de hoek af
drop by langskomen; binnenvallen: *drop in on her* even bij haar aanlopen
drop-down menu dropdown, uitklapbaar keuzemenu[h]
drop in langskomen, binnenvallen: ~ *on s.o.* even aanlopen bij iem.
droplet druppeltje[h]
¹drop off (vb) **1** geleidelijk afnemen, teruglopen **2** [inform] in slaap vallen
²drop off (vb) **1** afzetten, laten uitstappen **2** afgeven
drop out 1 opgeven, zich terugtrekken **2** [Am] vroegtijdig verlaten
drop-out drop-out, voortijdige schoolverlater, verstotene
droppings uitwerpselen [of animals]; keutels
drought (periode van) droogte
drove horde; kudde [cattle]; menigte [people]: *people came in ~s* de mensen kwamen in drommen
drown 1 (doen) verdrinken, (doen) verzuipen: ~ *one's sorrows (in drink)* zijn verdriet verdrinken **2** (doen) overstromen, onder water zetten, (rijkelijk) overspoelen; [fig] overstemmen; overstelpen
¹drowse (vb) slaperig zijn, dommelen, loom zijn
²drowse (vb) slaperig maken, suf maken, sloom maken
drowsy 1 slaperig; loom **2** er slaperig uitziend: *a* ~ *hamlet* een ingeslapen gehuchtje
drubbing 1 pak[h] slaag, aframmeling **2** (zware) nederlaag
¹drudge (n) sloof, zwoeger, werkezel
²drudge (vb) zwoegen, zich afbeulen, eentonig werk doen
drudgery eentonig werk[h], slaafs werk[h]
¹drug (n) **1** geneesmiddel[h], medicijn[h] **2** drug, verdovend middel[h]
²drug (vb) medicijn(en) e.d. toedienen, be-

dwelmen, drogeren, verdoven
drug addict drugsverslaafde
drugstore [Am] klein warenhuis[h], apotheek, drogisterij
¹drum (n) **1** trom, trommel **2** getrommel[h], geroffel[h], roffel, het trommelen **3** (-s) slagwerk[h], drumstel[h], drums **4** drum, ton, vat[h]
²drum (vb) trommelen, drummen, slagwerker zijn, roffelen, ritmisch tikken || ~ *up* optrommelen, bijeenroepen; ~ *sth. into* s.o. (or: *s.o.'s head*) iets bij iem. erin hameren
drum major tamboer-majoor
drummer slagwerker, drummer, tamboer
drumstick 1 trommelstok **2** (gebraden) kippenpootje[h], drumstick
¹drunk (n) dronkaard, zuiplap
²drunk (adj) **1** dronken: ~ *and disorderly* in kennelijke staat; *blind* (or: *dead*) ~ stomdronken **2** door het dolle heen, (brood)dronken: ~ *with power* tiranniek, machtswellustig
drunkard [dated] dronkaard
drunk-driving [Am] het rijden onder invloed
drunken dronken, dronkenmans-
¹dry (adj) **1** droog: ~ *land* vaste grond **2** droog, (op)gedroogd; zonder beleg [bread]; drooggelegd [land; also fig]: *run* ~ opdrogen, droog komen te staan **3** [inform] dorstig **4** droog, op droge toon (gezegd), ironisch || ~ *cleaner('s)* stomerij; *(as)* ~ *as dust, bone*-~ gortdroog, kurkdroog; ~ *run* repetitie, het proefdraaien
²dry (vb) (op)drogen, droog worden, uitdrogen: *dried milk* melkpoeder || ~ *out* a) uitdrogen, grondig droog worden; b) afkicken [alcoholics]; ~ *up* a) opdrogen; b) [also fig] afnemen tot niets
³dry (vb) (af)drogen, laten drogen || ~ *out* a) grondig droog laten worden; b) laten afkicken [alcoholics]
dry-cleaning 1 het chemisch reinigen **2** chemisch gereinigde kleding
dryer see *drier*
DTP desktop publishing DTP
dual tweevoudig, tweeledig: ~ *carriageway* dubbele rijbaan; *dual-purpose* voor twee doeleinden geschikt
dub 1 tot ridder slaan, ridderen **2** noemen, (om)dopen (tot), de bijnaam geven van **3** (na)synchroniseren, dubben
dubbing het bijmixen [sound]; (na)synchronisatie
dubious 1 twijfelend, aarzelend, onzeker **2** onbetrouwbaar, twijfelachtig
duchess hertogin
duchy hertogdom[h]
¹duck (n) eend, eendvogel || *play ~s and drakes with, make ~s and drakes of* verkwanselen; *take to sth. like a* ~ *to water* in z'n ele-

ment zijn
²duck (vb) buigen, (zich) bukken, wegduiken
³duck (vb) **1** plotseling (onder)dompelen, kopje-onder duwen **2** ontwijken, vermijden **3** snel intrekken [head]
duckboard loopplank [across ditch or mud]
duckling jonge eend, eendjeʰ
duckweed eendenkroosʰ
duct buis [also biology]; kanaalʰ, goot, leiding
dud 1 prulʰ, nepdingʰ **2** blindganger [bomb, grenade]
dude 1 kerel, vent **2** stadsmens [as a holidaymaker on farm]
¹due (n) **1** datgene wat iem. toekomt: *give s.o. his* ~ iem. niet tekortdoen, iem. geven wat hem toekomt **2** (-s) schuld(en), rechten, contributie
²due (adj) **1** gepast, juist, terecht: *with* ~ *care* met gepaste zorgvuldigheid; *in* ~ *time, in* ~ *course (of time)* te zijner tijd **2** schuldig, verschuldigd, invorderbaar, verplicht: *postage* ~ ongefrankeerd; *the amount* ~ het verschuldigde bedrag; *fall* (or: *become*) ~ vervallen, verschijnen [instalment]; *our thanks are* ~ *to you* wij zijn u dank verschuldigd **3** verwacht: *the aircraft is* ~ *at 4.50 p.m.* het toestel wordt om 16 uur 50 verwacht || ~ *to* toe te schrijven aan
³due (adv) precies [only for points of the compass]: ~ *south* pal naar het zuiden
duel duelʰ
duet duetʰ
due to wegens, vanwege, door
duff waardeloos, slecht, kapot
duffle bag plunjezak
dugout 1 (boomstam)kano **2** schuilholʰ, uitgegraven schuilplaats **3** [sport] dug-out
duke hertog
dukedom hertogdomʰ
dull 1 saai, vervelend **2** dom, sloom **3** mat [of colour, sound, pain]; dof **4** bot, stomp **5** bewolkt, betrokken **6** [com] flauw: *the* ~ *season* de slappe tijd || *as* ~ *as ditchwater* (or: *dishwater*) oersaai
duly 1 behoorlijk, naar behoren, terecht **2** stipt, prompt
dumb 1 stom, niet kunnen spreken, zwijgzaam: *to be struck* ~ met stomheid geslagen zijn, sprakeloos zijn **2** dom, stom, suf
dumbfound verstomd doen staan
dumbo dombo, stomkop
dumb show gebarenspelʰ, pantomime
dumbstruck perplex; met stomheid geslagen
¹dummy (n) **1** dummy; blinde [cards]; pop; modelʰ [of book]; proefpagina, stroman, figurant **2** nepartikelʰ **3** fopspeen **4** [inform] sufferd, uilskuikenʰ
²dummy (adj) **1** namaak, schijn, nep **2** proef-: ~ *run* het proefdraaien, militaire oefening

¹dump (n) **1** hoop, (vuilnis)belt, (vuil)stortplaats **2** dump, tijdelijk depotʰ van legergoederen **3** [inform] puinhoop, vervallen woning, desolate stad, desolaat dorpʰ || [inform] *(down) in the* ~s in de put, somber
²dump (vb) **1** dumpen, storten, lozen, neersmijten **2** dumpen [goods on foreign market] **3** achterlaten, in de steek laten
Dumpster [Am] afvalcontainer
dumpy kort en dik
dunce [dated] domkop; langzame leerling
dune duin
dung mest, drek, gier
dungarees overall, jeans, tuinbroek
dungeon kerker
dunghill 1 mesthoop **2** puinhoop
dunk onderdompelen [also fig]; (in)dopen; soppen [bread in tea etc]
duodenum [med] twaalfvingerige darm
¹dupe (n) dupe, slachtofferʰ (van bedrog), bedrogene
²dupe (vb) bedriegen, benadelen, duperen
¹duplicate (n) **1** duplicaatʰ, kopie **2** duploʰ: *in* ~ in duplo, in tweevoud
²duplicate (adj) **1** dubbel, tweevoudig **2** gelijkluidend, identiek
³duplicate (vb) **1** verdubbelen, kopiëren, verveelvuldigen **2** herhalen
duplicity dubbelhartigheid, bedrogʰ
durability duurzaamheid
durable duurzaam, bestendig, onverslijtbaar
duration duur: *for the* ~ *of* zolang ... duurt, tijdens
duress [form] dwang
during tijdens, gedurende, onder: ~ *the afternoon* in de loop van de middag
dusk schemer(ing), duisterʰ, duisternis
dusky [form] duister; schemerig
¹dust (n) **1** stofʰ, poeder **2** stofwolk: [fig] *when the* ~ *had settled* toen de gemoederen bedaard waren
²dust (vb) (af)stoffen, stof afnemen
³dust (vb) **1** bestuiven, bestrooien: ~ *crops* gewas besproeien [from aeroplane] **2** afstoffen
dustbin vuilnisbak
duster 1 stoffer, plumeau **2** stofdoek
dust jacket stofomslagʰ
dustman vuilnisman
dust off afstoffen; [fig] opfrissen; ophalen [old knowledge]
dustpan blikʰ [dustpan and brush]
dust-up 1 handgemeenʰ **2** rel, oproerʰ
dusty 1 stoffig, bestoft, droog **2** als stof || *not so* ~ lang niet gek
¹Dutch (n) Nederlands, Hollands
²Dutch (n) Nederlanders, het Nederlandse volk || [Am; inform] *beat the* ~ een bijzondere prestatie leveren

[3]**Dutch** (adj) Nederlands, Hollands ‖ ~ *auction* veiling bij afslag; ~ *bargain* overeenkomst die met een dronk bezegeld wordt; ~ *comfort* schrale troost; ~ *courage* jenevermoed; ~ *door* boerderijdeur, onder- en bovendeur; ~ *treat* feest waarbij ieder voor zich betaalt; *talk like a* ~ *uncle* duidelijk zeggen waar het op staat; *go* ~ ieder voor zich betalen

Dutchman Nederlander, Hollander ‖ … *or I am a* ~ (or: *I am a* ~ *if* …) ik ben een boon als ik …

dutiful 1 plicht(s)getrouw **2** gehoorzaam, eerbiedigend

duty 1 plicht, verplichting, taak, functie, dienst: *do* ~ *for* dienstdoen als, vervangen; *off* ~ buiten (de) dienst(tijd), in vrije tijd; *on* ~ in functie, in diensttijd **2** belasting, accijns, invoerrecht(en), uitvoerrecht(en), recht(en) **3** mechanisch arbeidsvermogen[h]: *a heavy ~ drilling machine* een boormachine voor zwaar werk **4** (duties) functie, werkzaamheden **5** belasting, accijns, (invoer)rechten, uitvoer)rechten

duty-free belastingvrij

duvet dekbed[h]; donzen dekbed[h]

[1]**dwarf** (n) dwerg

[2]**dwarf** (adj) dwerg-, dwergachtig

[3]**dwarf** (vb) **1** in z'n groei belemmeren, klein(er) maken, klein houden: ~ *plants* miniatuurplanten kweken **2** klein(er) doen lijken: *the skyscraper ~ed all the other buildings* bij de wolkenkrabber verzonken alle andere gebouwen in het niet

dwell 1 wonen, verblijven, zich ophouden **2** blijven stilstaan, uitweiden: ~ *(up)on* (lang) blijven stilstaan bij, (lang) doorgaan over

dwelling woning

dwindle afnemen, achteruitgaan

[1]**dye** (n) verf(stof), kleurstof

[2]**dye** (vb) verven, kleuren

dyed-in-the-wool door de wol geverfd; door en door

dyke 1 dijk, (keer)dam **2** kanaaltje[h], sloot, (natuurlijke) waterloop **3** pot, lesbienne

dynamic 1 dynamisch, bewegend **2** voortvarend, actief, energiek

dynamics 1 [mus] dynamiek [also fig] **2** [physics] dynamica; bewegingsleer

dynamite dynamiet[h] ‖ *the news was really* ~ het nieuws sloeg in als een bom

dynamo dynamo

dynasty dynastie, (vorsten)huis[h]

dysentery bloeddiarree

dysfunctional verstoord; slecht functionerend: *a ~ family* een verstoord gezin(sleven)

dyslexia leesblindheid, dyslexie

E 1 [elec] *earth* aarde **2** *east(ern)* O., Oost(e-lijk)
each 1 elk, ieder afzonderlijk: ~ *year* he *grows weaker* ieder jaar wordt hij zwakker **2** elk; ieder [of a group]: *they are a dollar* ~ ze kosten een dollar per stuk
each other elkaar, mekaar: *they hate* ~'s *guts* ze kunnen elkaars bloed wel drinken
eager 1 vurig, onstuimig **2** (+ for) (hevig) verlangend (naar), begerig || [inform] ~ *beaver* (overdreven) harde werker
eagle adelaar, arend
eagle-eyed scherpziend; met arendsogen
e-alert e-mailnieuwsbrief
ear 1 oor[h]: [fig] *play it by* ~ improviseren, op z'n gevoel afgaan; *up to* one's ~s tot over zijn oren **2** gehoor[h], oor[h]: *have an* ~ *for* een gevoel hebben voor **3** (koren)aar **4** oor[h], lus, oog[h], handvat[h] || *keep an* ~ (or: one's ~(s)) *(close) to the ground* **a)** (goed) op de hoogte blijven [of trends, gossip]; **b)** de boel goed in de gaten houden; *prick up* one's ~s de oren spitsen; *be out on* one's ~ ontslagen worden; *be all* ~s een en al oor zijn
eardrum trommelvlies[h]
earful: [inform] *give* s.o. *an* ~ iem. onomwonden de waarheid zeggen
earl (Engelse) graaf
¹early (adj) **1** vroeg, vroegtijdig: ~ *bird* vroege vogel; ~ *retirement* VUT, vervroegd pensioen; *the* ~ *bird catches the worm* vroeg begonnen, veel gewonnen; *in the* ~ *1960s* in het begin van de jaren zestig **2** spoedig: *an* ~ *reply* een spoedig antwoord **3** oud, van lang geleden: *the* ~ *Celts* de oude Kelten
²early (adv) **1** vroeg, (in het) begin, tijdig: ~ *on (in)* al vroeg, al in het begin **2** te vroeg: *we were an hour* ~ we kwamen een uur te vroeg
earmark reserveren [funds etc]: ~ *for* opzijleggen om (… te)
earn 1 verdienen, (ver)krijgen **2** verwerven, (terecht) krijgen: *his behaviour* ~ed *him his nickname* zijn gedrag bezorgde hem zijn bijnaam
¹earnest (n) ernst: *in (real)* ~ menens; *I am in (real)* ~ ik méén het
²earnest (adj) ernstig, serieus, gemeend
earnings 1 inkomen, inkomsten, verdiensten **2** winst [of business]
earphones koptelefoon
earshot gehoorsafstand: *out of* (or: *within*) ~ buiten (*or:* binnen) gehoorsafstand
¹earth (n) **1** aarde **2** [zoology] hol[h]: *go* (or:

run) *to* ~ **a)** zijn hol invluchten; **b)** onderduiken || *promise the* ~ gouden bergen beloven; *down to* ~ met beide benen op de grond, nuchter, eerlijk; *why on* ~ waarom in vredesnaam
²earth (vb) aarden
earthenware aardewerk[h]
earthly aards, werelds: [inform] *no* ~ *use* absoluut geen zin, geen enkele zin
earthquake aardbeving
earthworm pier, regenworm
earthy 1 vuil (van aarde) **2** materialistisch, aards, grof
earwax oorsmeer[h]
earwig oorwurm
¹ease (n) **1** gemak[h], gemakkelijkheid **2** ongedwongenheid, gemak[h], comfort[h]: [mil] *stand at* ~ op de plaats rust; *at* one's ~ op zijn gemak, rustig **3** welbehagen[h]: *ill at* ~ niet op z'n gemak
²ease (vb) afnemen, minder worden, (vaart) minderen: ~ *off* (or: *up*) afnemen, verminderen, rustiger aan gaan doen
³ease (vb) **1** verlichten, doen afnemen: ~ *back the throttle* gas terugnemen **2** gemakkelijk(er) maken: [fig] ~ s.o.'s *mind* iem. geruststellen **3** voorzichtig bewegen: ~ *off the lid* voorzichtig het deksel eraf halen
easel (schilders)ezel
easily 1 moeiteloos, rustig, met gemak **2** ongetwijfeld, zonder meer, beslist
¹east (n) het oosten [point of the compass]; oost: *the East* het oostelijk gedeelte, de Oost, de Oriënt
²east (adj) oostelijk: ~ *wind* oostenwind
³east (adv) in, uit, naar het oosten: *sail due* ~ recht naar het oosten varen
Easter Pasen
Easter Bunny paashaas
¹easterly (n) oostenwind
²easterly (adj) oostelijk
eastern 1 oostelijk, oost(en)-: *Eastern Hemisphere* oostelijk halfrond; *the Eastern bloc* het Oostblok **2** oosters
¹easy (adj) **1** (ge)makkelijk, eenvoudig, moeiteloos: *have* ~ *access to sth.* makkelijk toegang hebben tot iets **2** ongedwongen: *have an* ~ *manner* ontspannen manier van doen **3** comfortabel, gemakkelijk: ~ *chair* leunstoel, luie stoel **4** welgesteld, bemiddeld: *in* ~ *circumstances* in goede doen; *have an* ~ *time (of it)* een gemakkelijk leventje hebben || *by* ~ *stages* stap voor stap; *on* ~ *terms* op gemakkelijke condities, op afbetaling
²easy (adv) **1** gemakkelijk, eenvoudig: *easier said than done* gemakkelijker gezegd dan gedaan **2** kalm, rustig: *take it* ~ het rustig aan doen; ~ *does it!* voorzichtig! (dan breekt het lijntje niet)
easygoing 1 laconiek, makkelijk **2** gemak-

zuchtig, laks
easy-peasy makkelijk, een eitje
¹**eat** (vb) eten: ~ *out* buitenshuis eten
²**eat** (vb) **1** (op)eten, vreten **2** verslinden, opvreten: *~en* **up** *with curiosity* verteerd door
nieuwsgierigheid **3** aantasten, wegvreten ‖
what's ~ing you? wat zit je zo dwars?
eavesdrop afluisteren, luistervinkje spelen
e-banking internetbankieren[h]
¹**ebb** (n) eb, laag water[h]: [fig] *be at a* **low** ~ in
de put zitten
²**ebb** (vb) afnemen, wegebben
ebony ebbenhout[h]
e-book *electronic book* e-boek[h]; internet-
boek[h], digitaal boek[h]
ebullient uitbundig, uitgelaten
EC *European Community* EG
¹**eccentric** (n) zonderling, excentriekeling
²**eccentric** (adj) zonderling, excentriek
ecclesiastical geestelijk, kerkelijk, kerk-
echelon rang; groep, echelon[h]
¹**echo** (n) echo, weerklank
²**echo** (vb) weerklinken, resoneren
³**echo** (vb) **1** echoën, herhalen, nazeggen
2 weerkaatsen
¹**eclipse** (n) eclips, verduistering: *a* **total** ~ *of
the sun* een volledige zonsverduistering
²**eclipse** (vb) **1** verduisteren **2** overschaduwen, in glans overtreffen
eco-car groene auto; elektrische auto
ecological ecologisch
ecology ecologie
e-commerce internethandel, e-commerce
economic 1 economisch **2** rendabel, lonend, winstgevend
economical 1 zuinig, spaarzaam **2** economisch, voordelig
economics economie (als wetenschap)
economist 1 zuinig iem. **2** econoom
economize (+ on) bezuinigen (op), spaarzaam zijn
economy 1 economie, economisch stelsel[h]:
all those strikes are damaging the French ~ al die
stakingen brengen de Franse economie veel
schade toe **2** besparing, bezuiniging, zuinig
gebruik: *we bought a smaller house for reasons
of* ~ we hebben een kleiner huis gekocht om
redenen van bezuiniging
economy class economyclass; toeristenklasse
economy size voordeelverpakking, voor-
deelpak[h]
ecstasy 1 extase, vervoering **2** ecstasy
[drug]
Ecuador Ecuador
¹**Ecuadorian** (n) Ecuadoraan(se)
²**Ecuadorian** (adj) Ecuadoraans
ecumenical oecumenisch
eczema eczeem[h]
ed *edition* uitg., uitgave
¹**eddy** (n) werveling, draaikolk

²**eddy** (vb) (doen) dwarrelen, (doen) kolken
¹**edge** (n) **1** snede, snijkant; scherpte [also
fig]; effectiviteit, kracht: *her* **voice** *had an ~ to
it* haar stem klonk scherp; **take** *the ~ off* het
ergste wegnemen **2** kant, richel **3** rand,
boord[h], oever, grens: *on the ~ of* op het punt
van ‖ [inform] *have an ~ over* een voorsprong
hebben op; *be on ~* gespannen zijn
²**edge** (vb) (langzaam/voorzichtig) bewegen:
~ *away* (or: *off*) voorzichtig wegsluipen; ~ *up*
dichterbij schuiven
³**edge** (vb) omranden: *~d* **with** *lace* met een
randje kant
edging rand, boord[h], bies
edgy 1 scherp **2** gespannen, prikkelbaar
edible eetbaar, niet giftig
edification stichting, zedelijke en godsdienstige opbouw
edifice gebouw[h], bouwwerk[h], bouwsel[h]
edify [form] stichten: *an ~ing* **homily** een
stichtelijke preek
edit bewerken, herschrijven: *an ~ed* **version**
een gekuiste versie; *~ed* **by** onder redactie
van [magazines etc]
edition uitgave, editie, oplage; [fig] versie
editor 1 bewerker, samensteller **2** redacteur **3** uitgever
¹**editorial** (n) hoofdartikel[h], redactioneel artikel[h]
²**editorial** (adj) redactioneel, redactie-, re-
dacteurs-
editor-in-chief hoofdredacteur
educate 1 opvoeden, vormen **2** opleiden,
onderwijzen: *an ~d* **person** een gestudeerd
iem., intellectueel **3** scholen, trainen
education 1 onderwijs[h], scholing, opleiding **2** opvoeding, vorming **3** pedagogie,
opvoedkunde
educational 1 onderwijs- **2** leerzaam;
educatief
eel paling ‖ *be as* **slippery** *as an ~* zo glad als
een aal zijn
eerie angstaanjagend, griezelig
efface 1 uitwissen **2** uit het geheugen bannen ‖ ~ *o.s.* zich wegcijferen
¹**effect** (n) **1** resultaat[h], effect[h], gevolg[h], uitwerking: **take** ~ resultaat hebben; *to no ~*
vruchteloos, tevergeefs **2** uitvoering, voltrekking: **put** *plans into* ~ plannen uitvoeren
3 inhoud, strekking: *words* **to** *that ~* woorden
van die strekking **4** werking, (rechts)geldig-
heid: *come* **into** ~, *take ~* van kracht worden
5 (-s) bezittingen, eigendommen ‖ *in ~* in
feite, eigenlijk
²**effect** (vb) bewerkstelligen, teweegbrengen, veroorzaken: ~ *a* **cure** *for s.o.* iem. genezen
effective 1 effectief, doeltreffend **2** indrukwekkend, treffend: ~ *speeches* indrukwekkende toespraken **3** van kracht [law etc]
effeminate verwijfd

effervescence 1 levendigheid, uitgelatenheid **2** het bruisen
effete verzwakt, slap, afgeleefd
efficacy werkzaamheid, doeltreffendheid
efficiency 1 efficiëntie, doeltreffendheid, doelmatigheid **2** bekwaamheid **3** productiviteit
efficient 1 efficiënt, doeltreffend, doelmatig **2** bekwaam **3** productief
effigy beeltenis
effluent 1 afvalwater^h, rioolwater^h **2** aftakking, zijrivier, afvoer
effort 1 moeite, inspanning, poging: *make an ~ (to do sth.)* zich inspannen iets te doen **2** prestatie: *he has made a jolly good ~* hij heeft geweldig zijn best gedaan
effrontery brutaliteit
effusion 1 ontboezeming **2** uitstroming
effusive overdadig [of utterances]; uitbundig
e.g. *exempli gratia* bijv.
egalitarian gelijkheids-, gelijkheid voorstaand
egg 1 ei^h: *fried ~* gebakken ei; *poached ~* gepocheerd ei; *scrambled ~s* roerei; *~ whisk* eierklopper **2** eierstruif **3** eicel ǁ *have* (or: *put) all one's ~s in one basket* alles op één kaart zetten; [inform] *have ~ on one's face* voor schut staan
eggbeater [Am] eierklopper
eggcup eierdopje^h
egghead [inform] intellectueel, gestudeerde
eggnog eierdrank
egg on [inform] aanzetten; aansporen
eggplant aubergine
ego 1 ego^h **2** ik-bewustzijn^h **3** eigenwaarde
egocentric 1 egocentrisch **2** egoïstisch, zelfzuchtig
egoism egoïsme^h
egotism eigenwaan
egret (kleine) zilverreiger
Egypt Egypte
¹Egyptian (n) Egyptenaar, Egyptische
²Egyptian (adj) Egyptisch
eiderdown 1 (donzen) dekbed^h **2** eiderdons^h
eight acht
eighteen achttien
eighth achtste: *the ~ fastest runner* de op zeven na snelste loper
eightieth tachtigste
eighty tachtig: *in the eighties* in de jaren tachtig
¹either (pron) **1** één van beide(n): *use ~ hand* gebruik een van je (twee) handen; *choose ~ of the colours* kies één van de twee kleuren **2** beide(n), alle twee, allebei: *in ~ case, ~ way* in beide gevallen, in elk geval; *on ~ side* aan beide kanten
²either (adv) evenmin, ook niet, bovendien

niet: *he can't sing, and I can't ~* hij kan niet zingen en ik ook niet
³either (conj) (+ or) of, ofwel, hetzij: *have ~ cheese or a dessert* neem kaas of een toetje
ejaculation 1 zaadlozing, ejaculatie **2** uitroep
eject uitgooien, uitzetten, uitstoten, uitwerpen
ejection 1 verdrijving, (ambts)ontzetting, uitzetting **2** uitwerping
ejector seat schietstoel
eke out 1 rekken [also supplies]; aanvullen **2** bijeenscharrelen: *~ a living* (met moeite) zijn kostje bijeen scharrelen
¹elaborate (adj) **1** gedetailleerd, uitgebreid, uitvoerig **2** ingewikkeld
²elaborate (vb) (+ up)on) uitweiden (over)
³elaborate (vb) **1** in detail uitwerken, uitvoerig behandelen, uitweiden over **2** (moeizaam) voortbrengen, ontwikkelen
elapse verstrijken, voorbijgaan
¹elastic (n) elastiek(je^h)
²elastic (adj) **1** elastieken: *~ band* elastiekje **2** elastisch, rekbaar **3** flexibel, soepel
elate verrukken, in vervoering brengen: *be ~d at* (or: *by) sth.* met iets verguld zijn
¹elbow (n) **1** elleboog, (scherpe) bocht **2** [techn] elleboog, knie(stuk^h) ǁ *give s.o. the ~* iem. de bons geven; *at s.o.'s ~* naast iem., bij iem. in de buurt
²elbow (vb) zich (een weg) banen, met de ellebogen duwen, werken
elbow-grease zwaar werk^h, poetswerk^h, schoonmaakwerk^h
elbow-room bewegingsvrijheid, armslag
¹elder (n) **1** oudere: *he is my ~ by four years* hij is vier jaar ouder dan ik **2** oudste [of two] **3** voorganger, ouderling
²elder (adj) oudste [of two]; oudere
elderberry vlierbes
elderly op leeftijd, bejaard: *a home for the ~* een bejaardentehuis
eldest oudste [of three or more]
¹elect (adj) gekozen [but not yet in office]: *the president ~* de nieuwgekozen president
²elect (vb) **1** kiezen, verkiezen (als) **2** besluiten: *~ to become a lawyer* besluiten jurist te worden
election verkiezing, keus: *municipal* (or: *local) ~(s)* gemeenteraadsverkiezingen
electioneer stemmen werven; op verkiezingscampagne gaan
electoral 1 kies-, kiezers-: *~ register* (or: *roll)* kiesregister **2** electoraal, verkiezings-: *~ campaign* verkiezingscampagne
electorate electoraat^h, de kiezers
electric 1 elektrisch: *~ chair* elektrische stoel; *~ storm* onweer **2** opwindend, opzwepend **3** gespannen [eg of atmosphere]
electrical elektrisch, elektro-
electrician elektricien, elektromonteur

electricity elektriciteit, elektrische stroom
electrify 1 onder spanning zetten **2** elektrificeren, voorzien van elektrische installaties **3** opwinden, geestdriftig maken
electrocute elektrocuteren, op de elektrische stoel ter dood brengen
electronic elektronisch: ~ *banking* elektronisch bankieren, internetbankieren; ~ *data processing* elektronische informatieverwerking; ~ *scrap* elektronisch afval, e-schroot
electronics elektronica
elegant elegant, sierlijk
elegy treurdicht[h], klaaglied[h]
element 1 element[h], onderdeel[h], (hoofd)-bestanddeel[h]: *out of one's* ~ als een vis op het droge **2** iets, wat: *there is an* ~ *of truth in it* er zit wel wat waars in **3** [chem, maths] element[h] **4** (-s) de elementen [of weather] **5** (-s) (grond)beginselen
elemental 1 essentieel; wezenlijk: ~ *needs* basisbehoeften **2** van de elementen [also of weather]: ~ *force* natuurkracht; elementaire kracht
elementary 1 eenvoudig, simpel: ~ *question* eenvoudige vraag **2** inleidend, elementair: ~ *school* lagere school, basisschool **3** [science, chem] elementair
elephant olifant || *white* ~ overbodig luxeartikel
elevate 1 opheffen, omhoogbrengen, verhogen **2** verheffen [only fig]; op een hoger plan brengen **3** promoveren, bevorderen: ~*d to the presidency* tot president verheven
elevation 1 hoogte, heuvel, ophoging **2** bevordering, promotie **3** verhevenheid
elevator [Am] lift
eleven elf; [sport] elftal; ploeg
elevenses [dated] elfuurtje[h]; hapje om elf uur
eleventh elfde: [fig] *at the* ~ *hour* ter elfder ure, op het laatste ogenblik
elf elf, fee
elicit 1 ontlokken, loskrijgen: ~ *an answer from s.o.* een antwoord uit iem. krijgen; *elicit a response* een reactie ontlokken **2** teweegbrengen, veroorzaken
eligible in aanmerking komend, geschikt, bevoegd: ~ *for* (a) *pension* pensioengerechtigd
eliminate 1 verwijderen **2** uitsluiten, buiten beschouwing laten: ~ *the possibility of murder* de mogelijkheid van moord uitsluiten **3** uitschakelen [in match etc] **4** [inform] van kant maken, uit de weg ruimen
elimination 1 verwijdering, eliminatie **2** uitschakeling [in match etc] **3** uitsluiting; het schrappen [of options]
elite elite
elitist elitair
elk eland
ellipse ellips, ovaal[h]

ellipsis 1 weglatingsteken[h] [three dots] **2** [linguistics] ellips
elm 1 iep, olm **2** iepenhout[h], olmenhout[h]
elocution voordrachtskunst, welbespraaktheid
elongate langer worden (maken), (zich) verlengen, in de lengte (doen) groeien
elope er vandoor gaan [with lover, or to get married in secret]
eloquence welsprekendheid, welbespraaktheid
eloquent welsprekend [of person, argument]
else anders, nog meer: *anything* ~? verder nog iets?; *little* ~ niet veel meer; *what* ~ *did you expect?* wat had jij anders verwacht?
elsewhere elders, ergens anders
elucidate (nader) toelichten, licht werpen op, ophelderen
elude 1 ontwijken, ontschieten, ontsnappen aan; [fig] ontduiken; zich onttrekken aan [duties]; uit de weg gaan: ~ *capture* weten te ontkomen **2** ontgaan [of fact, name]; ontschieten: *his name* ~*s me* ik ben zijn naam even kwijt
elusive 1 ontwijkend: ~ *answer* ontwijkend antwoord **2** moeilijk te vangen **3** onvatbaar, ongrijpbaar: *an* ~ *name* een moeilijk te onthouden naam
'em *see* them
emaciate uitgemergeld
e-mail *electronic mail* e-mail, elektronische post
emanate from [form] afkomstig zijn van
emancipate 1 vrijmaken [slaves etc]; emanciperen, zelfstandig maken: ~*d women* geëmancipeerde vrouwen **2** gelijkstellen voor de wet, emanciperen
emancipation 1 bevrijding [of slaves]; emancipatie **2** emancipatie, gelijkstelling voor de wet: *the* ~ *of women* de emancipatie van de vrouw
embalm balsemen
embankment 1 dijk, dam, wal **2** opgehoogde baan, spoordijk **3** kade
embargo embargo[h] [of ships, trade]; blokkade, beslag[h], beslaglegging, verbod[h], belemmering, uitvoerverbod[h]
embark 1 aan boord gaan (nemen), (zich) inschepen **2** beginnen, van start gaan: ~ *(up)on* zich begeven, beginnen (aan)
embarkation 1 inscheping, inlading, het aan boord gaan (brengen) **2** het beginnen
embarrass 1 in verlegenheid brengen **2** geldverlegenheid brengen, in financiële moeilijkheden brengen
embarrassing pijnlijk; beschamend; gênant
embarrassment 1 verlegenheid, onbehagen[h] **2** (geld)verlegenheid, (geld)probleem[h]
embassy ambassade, diplomatieke verte-

genwoordigers
emba̲ttled 1 (voortdurend) in moeilijkheden **2** omsingeld [by enemies]
embe̲d 1 (vast)zetten, vastleggen: *the arrow ~ded itself in his leg* de pijl zette zich vast in zijn been; *be ~ded in* vastzitten in **2** omsluiten, insluiten, omringen, omgeven **3** inbedden
embe̲llish verfraaien, versieren: *~ a story* een verhaal opsmukken
e̲mber 1 gloeiend stukje[h] kool **2** (-s) gloeiende as, smeulend vuur[h]; [fig] laatste vonken; resten
embe̲zzle verduisteren, achterhouden
embi̲tter verbitteren, bitter(der) maken
e̲mblem embleem[h], symbool[h]
emblema̲tic symbolisch: *be ~ of* het symbool zijn van
embo̲diment belichaming
embo̲dy 1 vorm geven (aan), uitdrukken: *~ one's principles in actions* zijn principes tot uiting laten komen in daden **2** inlijven: *his points of view were embodied in the article* zijn standpunten waren verwerkt in het artikel
¹embra̲ce (n) omhelzing, omarming
²embra̲ce (vb) elkaar omhelzen, elkaar omarmen
³embra̲ce (vb) **1** omhelzen, omarmen, omvatten **2** gebruikmaken van, aangrijpen: *~ an offer* gebruikmaken van een aanbod
embro̲ider 1 borduren **2** opsmukken, verfraaien
embro̲il verwikkelen; betrekken: *~ o.s. in* betrokken raken bij
e̲mbryo embryo[h]: *in ~* in de kiem (aanwezig), in wording, in de dop
eme̲nd corrigeren; verbeteringen aanbrengen [in text]
emenda̲tion correctie, verbetering
e̲merald 1 smaragd(groen) **2** smaragden, van smaragd
eme̲rge 1 verschijnen, tevoorschijn komen: *~ from* (or: *out of*) tevoorschijn komen uit **2** bovenkomen, opduiken **3** blijken, uitkomen: *after a long investigation it ~d that* een langdurig onderzoek wees uit dat
eme̲rgence 1 het bovenkomen **2** het uitkomen **3** het optreden
eme̲rgency 1 onverwachte gebeurtenis, onvoorzien voorval[h] **2** noodsituatie, noodtoestand, noodgeval[h]: *state of ~* noodtoestand; *~ exit* nooduitgang, nooddeur; *in case of ~* in geval van nood
eme̲rgency room [Am] eerstehulp(afdeling)
e̲migrant emigrant(e)
e̲migrate emigreren, het land verlaten
e̲minence 1 heuvel, hoogte **2** eminentie [also as title]; verhevenheid
e̲minent 1 uitstekend **2** hoog; verheven [also lit]; aanzienlijk

emi̲ssion afgifte, uitzending; afscheiding [of body]; [science] emissie; uitstoot [of (poisonous) gases]
emi̲t 1 uitstralen, uitzenden **2** afscheiden, afgeven; uitstoten [(poisonous) gases]: *~ a smell* stank afgeven
¹emo̲llient (n) verzachtend middel[h]
²emo̲llient (adj) verzachtend, zachtmakend
e̲-money *electronic money* elektronisch geld[h]; e-geld[h]
emo̲ticon emoticon[+h]
emo̲tion 1 (gevoels)aandoening, emotie, gevoelen[h], ontroering: *mixed ~s* gemengde gevoelens **2** het gevoel, de gevoelswereld **3** bewogenheid
emo̲tional 1 emotioneel, gevoels-, gemoeds-: *~ intelligence* emotionele intelligentie **2** ontroerend
emo̲tive roerend; gevoelig
e̲mpathy empathie
e̲mperor keizer
e̲mphasis 1 accent[h]; klemtoon [also fig]: *lay* (or: *place, put*) *an ~ on sth.* het accent leggen op iets **2** nadruk, klem, kracht
e̲mphasize benadrukken, de nadruk leggen op
empha̲tic 1 nadrukkelijk **2** krachtig **3** duidelijk
e̲mpire (keizer)rijk[h]; imperium[h] [also fig]; wereldrijk[h]
empi̲rical gebaseerd op ervaring
¹emplo̲y (n) (loon)dienst: *in the ~ of* in dienst van
²emplo̲y (vb) **1** in dienst nemen, tewerkstellen **2** gebruiken, aanwenden **3** bezighouden: *be ~ed in* bezig zijn, zich bezighouden met
emplo̲yable bruikbaar, inzetbaar
emplo̲yee werknemer
emplo̲yee participation medezeggenschap[+h]
emplo̲yer werkgever
emplo̲yment 1 beroep[h], werk[h], baan **2** bezigheid **3** werkgelegenheid: *full ~* volledige werkgelegenheid **4** gebruik[h], het gebruiken
empo̲wer 1 machtigen **2** in staat stellen
e̲mpress keizerin
e̲mptiness leegte
¹e̲mpty (n): *returned empties* geretourneerde lege flessen/kratten
²e̲mpty (adj) **1** leeg, ledig **2** nietszeggend, hol **3** onbewoond, leegstaand: [esp Am] *~ nest* [fig] leeg nest, kinderen het huis uit **4** leeghoofdig, oppervlakkig
³e̲mpty (vb) leeg raken, (zich) legen
⁴e̲mpty (vb) legen, leegmaken
e̲mu emoe
ena̲ble 1 in staat stellen, (de) gelegenheid geven **2** mogelijk maken
ena̲ct 1 bepalen, vaststellen **2** tot wet ver-

heffen
enamel 1 (email)lak^{+h}, glazuur^h, vernis^h
2 email^h, (tand)glazuur^h
enamour bekoren, charmeren: ~ed of (or:
with) dol, verliefd op
encampment kamp(ement)^h, legerplaats,
veldverblijf^h
encapsulate 1 (zich) inkapselen **2** samenvatten
enchant 1 betoveren, beheksen **2** bekoren, verrukken: be ~ ed by (or: with) verrukt
zijn over
encipher coderen
encircle omcirkelen, omsingelen, insluiten
encl enclosed, enclosure bijl., bijlage
enclose 1 omheinen, insluiten **2** insluiten;
bijsluiten [enclosure etc]
enclosure 1 (om)heining, schutting **2** omheind stuk land **3** vak^h, afdeling **4** bijlage
encode coderen
encompass 1 omringen, omgeven **2** bevatten, omvatten
encore toegift, encore^h: ~! bis!, nog eens!
¹encounter (n) **1** (onverwachte) ontmoeting **2** krachtmeting, confrontatie, treffen^h
²encounter (vb) **1** ontmoeten, (onverwacht) tegenkomen **2** ontmoeten, geconfronteerd worden met: ~ **difficulties** moeilijkheden moeten overwinnen
encourage 1 bemoedigen, hoop geven
2 aanmoedigen, stimuleren, in de hand werken
encroach opdringen, oprukken: the sea ~es
further **(up)on** the land de zee tast de kust
steeds verder aan
encroachment overschrijding; aantasting,
inbreuk
encrust 1 met een korst bedekken **2** bedekken, bezetten: ~ed with precious stones
bezet met edelstenen
encrypt coderen, in code weergeven; ver-
sleutelen [message, data]
encumber 1 beladen, (over)belasten: ~ed
with parcels met boodschappen beladen
2 hinderen, belemmeren: ~ o.s. **with** financial
responsibilities zich financiële verplichtingen
op de hals halen
encumbrance [form] last; belemmering
encyclop(a)edia encyclopedie
¹end (n) **1** einde^h, afsluiting, besluit^h: **come**
(or: **draw**) to an ~ ten einde lopen, ophou-
den; **put** an ~ to een eind maken aan, afschaffen; **in** the ~ ten slotte, op het laatst,
uiteindelijk; for weeks **on** ~ weken achtereen
2 einde^h, uiteinde^h: ~ **to** ~ in de lengte **3** ein-
de^h, verste punt^h, grens; [also fig] uiterste^h
4 kant, onderkant, bovenkant, zijde; [also
fig] afdeling; part^h: place **on** ~ rechtop zetten
5 einde^h, vernietiging, dood **6** doel^h, bedoeling, (beoogd) resultaat^h: the ~ **justifies** the
means het doel heiligt de middelen ‖ at the ~

of the **day** uiteindelijk, als puntje bij paaltje
komt; be at the ~ of one's tether aan het eind
van zijn krachten zijn; **make** (both) ~s **meet**
de eindjes aan elkaar knopen; that irritates me
no ~ dat irriteert me heel erg
²end (vb) **1** eindigen, aflopen: our efforts ~ed
in a total failure onze pogingen liepen op
niets uit **2** zijn einde vinden, sterven
³end (vb) **1** beëindigen, een eind maken aan,
ophouden met **2** conclusie vormen van
3 vernietigen, een eind maken aan: ~ **it** (all)
er een eind aan maken, zelfmoord plegen
endanger in gevaar brengen, een gevaar
vormen voor, bedreigen: ~ed **species** bedreigde diersoorten
endear geliefd maken
endearment 1 uiting van genegenheid
2 innemendheid: **terms** of ~ lieve woordjes
¹endeavour (n) poging, moeite, inspanning
²endeavour (vb) pogen, trachten, zich inspannen
endemic inheems; plaatsgebonden
ending 1 einde^h, beëindiging, afronding,
eindspel^h **2** einde^h, slot^h, afloop: **happy** ~
goede afloop
endive andijvie
endless 1 eindeloos **2** [inform] ontelbaar
endorse bevestigen, bekrachtigen, beamen
endorsement 1 bevestiging; bekrachtiging **2** aantekening [eg on driving licence]
endow 1 begiftigen, subsidiëren, bekostigen **2** schenken, geven aan: ~ed with great
musical talent begiftigd met grote muzikaliteit
endowment 1 gave, begaafdheid, talent^h
2 gift **3** het schenken
endue begiftigen, schenken
endurance 1 uithoudingsvermogen^h,
weerstand **2** duurzaamheid ‖ **beyond** (or:
past) ~ onverdraaglijk, niet uit te houden
endurance training duurtraining
¹endure (vb) **1** duren, blijven **2** het uithouden
²endure (vb) **1** doorstaan, uithouden, verdragen **2** ondergaan, lijden
enduring blijvend, (voort)durend
enema klysma^h; lavement^h
enemy vijand, vijandelijke troepen: the ~
were **thrown** back de vijand werd teruggeslagen
energetic 1 energiek, vurig, actief
2 krachtig; sterk [protest etc]
energy kracht, energie: **nuclear** ~ kernenergie
enervate ontkrachten, slap maken, verzwakken
enfeeble verzwakken, uitputten
enfold 1 wikkelen; hullen in **2** omsluiten: ~
in one's arms in de armen sluiten
enforce 1 uitvoeren, op de naleving toe-

zien van; de hand houden aan [rule, law] **2** (af)dwingen **3** versterken, benadrukken
enforcement 1 handhaving, uitvoering **2** dwang
¹engage (vb) **1** (+ in) zich bezighouden (met), zich inlaten (met), doen (aan) **2** zich verplichten, beloven, aangaan **3** [techn] in elkaar grijpen, gekoppeld worden **4** (+ with) [mil] de strijd aanbinden (met)
²engage (vb) **1** aannemen, in dienst nemen, contracteren **2** bezetten; in beslag nemen [also fig]: ~ s.o. *in conversation* een gesprek met iem. aanknopen **3** beloven, verplichten: ~ *o.s. to do sth.* beloven iets te doen **4** [mil] aanvallen **5** [techn] koppelen, inschakelen
engaged 1 verloofd: ~ *to* verloofd met **2** bezet, bezig, druk, gereserveerd: *I'm* ~ ik heb een afspraak; *the telephone is* ~ de telefoon is in gesprek **3** gecontracteerd
engagement 1 verloving **2** afspraak **3** belofte, verplichting: ~*s* financiële verplichting **4** gevecht **5** contract
engaging innemend, aantrekkelijk
engender veroorzaken, voortbrengen
engine motor, machine, locomotief
¹engineer (n) **1** ingenieur **2** machinebouwer **3** genieofficier, geniesoldaat: *the (Royal) Engineers* de Genie **4** technicus, mecanicien; [shipp] werktuigkundige **5** [Am] (trein)machinist
²engineer (vb) **1** bouwen, maken, construeren **2** bewerkstelligen, op touw zetten
engineering 1 techniek **2** bouw, constructie
England Engeland
¹English (n) Engels, de Engelse taal: *the* ~ de Engelsen
²English (adj) Engels, in het Engels: ~ *breakfast* Engels ontbijt, ontbijt met spek en eieren
Englishman Engelsman
English-speaking Engelstalig
Englishwoman Engelse; Engelse vrouw
engrave graveren
engraving 1 gravure **2** graveerkunst
engross geheel in beslag nemen, overheersen: *I was so* ~*ed in* my book that ik was zo in mijn boek verdiept, dat
engulf overspoelen: ~*ed by* fear door angst overmand; ~*ed in* the waves door de golven verzwolgen
enhance verhogen, versterken, verbeteren
enhancement verhoging, versterking, verbetering
enhancer prestatieverhogend middel, stimulerend middel
enigma mysterie, raadsel
enjoy genieten van, plezier beleven aan: *Dick* ~*s a* good *health* Dick geniet een goede gezondheid || ~ *o.s.* zich vermaken
enjoyable plezierig, prettig, fijn

enjoyment plezier; genot; genoegen
enkindle aansteken [fig]; doen oplaaien; opwekken [anger, passion]
¹enlarge (vb) **1** groeien, groter worden, zich uitbreiden **2** uitgebreid spreken, uitweiden: ~ *on*/*about a subject* uitweiden over een onderwerp **3** uitvergroot worden
²enlarge (vb) vergroten, groter maken
enlighten onderrichten, onderwijzen
enlightened verlicht, rationeel, redelijk: ~ *ideas* verlichte opvattingen
enlightenment opheldering, verduidelijking
the **Enlightenment** verlichting
¹enlist (vb) dienst nemen, vrijwillig in het leger gaan
²enlist (vb) werven, mobiliseren, in dienst nemen: ~ *s.o. in an enterprise* iem. bij een onderneming te hulp roepen
enmity vijandschap, haat(gevoel), onmin
enormity 1 gruweldaad, wandaad **2** gruwelijkheid, misdadigheid **3** enorme omvang; immense grootte [of problem etc]
enormous enorm, geweldig groot
¹enough (pron) genoeg, voldoende: *beer* ~ genoeg bier || *be* ~ *of a man to* wel zo flink zijn om te
²enough (adv) **1** genoeg: ~ *said* genoeg daarover; *oddly* (or: *strangely*) ~ merkwaardig genoeg **2** zeer, heel: *I'm having* ~ *problems with my own children* ik heb al genoeg problemen met mijn eigen kinderen **3** tamelijk, redelijk: *she paints* well ~ ze schildert vrij behoorlijk
enquire see ¹*inquire*
enquiry see *inquiry*
enrage woedend maken, tot razernij brengen
enrapture verrukken: ~*d at* (or: *by*) in vervoering om, door
enrich 1 verrijken, rijk(er) maken, uitbreiden **2** verrijken, de kwaliteit verhogen: ~*ed* *uranium* verrijkt uranium
¹enrol (vb) zich inschrijven, zich opgeven
²enrol (vb) **1** inschrijven, opnemen **2** werven, aanwerven, in dienst nemen
ensemble 1 geheel; totaal **2** [theatre, mus] ensemble; gezelschap **3** [fashion] ensemble
ensign 1 insigne, embleem **2** vlag, nationale vlag
enslave knechten, tot slaaf maken, onderwerpen
ensnare vangen, verstrikken; [also fig] in de val laten lopen
ensue 1 volgen: *the ensuing* month de volgende maand, de maand daarna **2** (+ from) voortvloeien (uit), voortkomen (uit)
ensure 1 veiligstellen, beschermen **2** garanderen, instaan voor: ~ *the safety of our guests* de veiligheid van onze gasten waar-

borgen **3** verzekeren van
entail met zich meebrengen, noodzakelijk
maken, inhouden
entangle verwarren, onontwarbaar maken; [also fig] verstrikken; vast laten lopen
entanglement 1 complicatie, het verstrikt
raken **2** gecompliceerde relatie; [esp] affaire
3 hindernis
¹enter (vb) **1** zich laten inschrijven, zich opgeven **2** [theatre] opkomen
²enter (vb) **1** gaan in/op/bij, zich begeven in,
zijn intrede doen in: ~ the **Church** priester
worden **2** inschrijven, bijschrijven, opschrijven, noteren, boeken, invoeren **3** opgeven,
inschrijven **4** toelaten; binnenlaten [as
member] **5** deelnemen aan; meedoen aan
[competition, fight] **6** inzenden: ~ sth. in the
competition iets inzenden voor de wedstrijd
³enter (vb) binnengaan; binnenlopen [of
ship]; binnendringen
enter into 1 beginnen; aanknopen [con-
versation] **2** zich verplaatsen in, zich inleven
in **3** deel uitmaken van, onderdeel vormen
van **4** ingaan op, onder de loep nemen
5 aangaan; sluiten [contract, treaty]
enterprise 1 onderneming **2** firma, zaak
3 ondernemingsgeest, ondernemingszin: we
need a **man** of ~ we hebben iem. met initiatief nodig
enterprising ondernemend
¹entertain (vb) **1** een feestje (etentje) geven, gasten hebben **2** vermaak bieden
²entertain (vb) **1** gastvrij ontvangen, aanbieden **2** onderhouden, amuseren **3** koesteren, erop nahouden: ~ **doubts** twijfels hebben **4** overdenken, in overweging nemen: ~
a **proposal** over een voorstel nadenken
entertainer iem. die het publiek vermaakt,
zanger, conferencier, cabaretier, goochelaar
entertaining onderhoudend, vermakelijk,
amusant
entertainment 1 iets dat amusement
biedt, opvoering, uitvoering, show, conference **2** feestᵸ, partij, feestmaalᵸ **3** gastvrijheid, gastvrij onthaalᵸ **4** vermaakᵸ, plezierᵸ,
amusementᵸ: greatly (or: much) to our ~ tot
onze grote pret **5** amusementswereld(jeᵸ),
amusementsbedrijfᵸ
enthralling betoverend, boeiend
enthrone op de troon zetten, kronen
¹enthuse (vb) (+ about, over) enthousiast
spreken/zijn (over)
²enthuse (vb) enthousiast maken
enthusiasm 1 (+ about, for) enthousias-
meᵸ (voor), geestdrift (voor/over), verrukking, vervoering **2** vurige interesse, passie
enthusiast 1 (+ about, for) enthousiaste-
ling (in), fan (van), liefhebber (van) **2** dweper
enthusiastic enthousiast
entice (ver)lokken, verleiden

entire 1 compleet, volledig **2** geheel, totaal
3 gaaf, heel, onbeschadigd
entirely 1 helemaal, geheel (en al), volkomen **2** alleen, enkel, slechts
entirety totaliteit: in its ~ in zijn geheel
entitle 1 betitelen, noemen: a **novel** ~d
'Enduring love' een roman met als titel 'Enduring love' **2** recht geven op: be ~d **to** compensation' recht hebben op schadevergoeding
entity bestaanᵸ, wezenᵸ, het zijn
entrails ingewanden, darmen
¹entrance (n) **1** ingang, toegang, entree
2 binnenkomst **3** opkomst [on stage] **4** entree, toelating; [by extension] toegangsgeldᵸ: ~ **fee** toegangsgeldᵸ; **no** ~ verboden
toegang
²entrance (vb) in verrukking brengen, meeslepen
entreat smeken (om), bidden (om), dringend verzoeken
¹entrench (vb) **1** zich verschansen, zich ingraven **2** (+ on, upon) inbreuk maken (op)
²entrench (vb) stevig vastleggen; verankeren [right, habit etc]
entrenchment loopgravenstelselᵸ; verschansing
entrepreneur 1 ondernemer **2** impresario
[stage]
entrust toevertrouwen: ~ sth. **to** s.o., ~ s.o.
with sth. iem. iets toevertrouwen
entry 1 intrede, entree, toetreding, intocht, binnenkomst; [theatre] opkomst
2 toegang: **no** ~ verboden in te rijden **3** ingang, toegang, halᵸ **4** notitie, inschrijving,
boeking
entwine ineenstrengelen **2** (zich) winden (om)
enumerate 1 opsommen **2** (op)tellen
enunciate (goed) articuleren, (duidelijk)
uitspreken
envelop inwikkelen, inpakken; [fig] omhullen; omgeven: a subject ~ed **in** mystery een
onderwerp omgeven met geheimzinnigheid
envelope 1 omhulling [also fig] **2** envelop:
padded ~ luchtkussenenvelop
enviable benijdenswaardig, begerenswaardig
envious (+ of) jaloers (op), afgunstig
environment 1 omgeving **2** milieuᵸ, omgeving
environmental milieu-; omgevings-: the ~
effects of using coal de gevolgen van het gebruik van steenkool voor het milieu
environmentalist 1 milieudeskundige,
milieubeheerder **2** milieuactivist, milieubewust iem.
envisage voorzien; zich voorstellen [in fu-
ture]
envoy (af)gezant, diplomatiek vertegenwoordiger

¹envy (n) afgunst: *he was filled with ~ at my new car* hij benijdde me mijn nieuwe wagen
²envy (vb) benijden
enzyme enzym[h]
ephemeral kortstondig, voorbijgaand
¹epic (n) epos[h], heldendicht[h]
²epic (adj) **1** episch, verhalend **2** heldhaftig **3** [inform] episch, enorm, geweldig: *~ fail* totale mislukking
epidemic epidemie
epidermis opperhuid
epigraph epigraaf; opschrift, inscriptie [esp on monument]
epilepsy epilepsie, vallende ziekte
¹epileptic (n) epilepticus
²epileptic (adj) epileptisch
epilogue 1 epiloog, slotrede **2** naschrift[h], nawoord[h]
episcopal bisschoppelijk
episode episode, (belangrijke) gebeurtenis, voorval[h]; aflevering [of serial]
epitaph grafschrift[h]
epithet 1 bijnaam **2** [Am] scheldwoord[h]
epitome belichaming; personificatie: *the ~ of* het toppunt van
epoch 1 keerpunt[h], mijlpaal **2** tijdvak[h], tijdperk[h]
epoch-making van grote betekenis; baanbrekend
equable gelijkmatig, gelijkmoedig
¹equal (n) gelijke, weerga
²equal (adj) **1** gelijk, overeenkomstig, hetzelfde: *on ~ terms* op voet van gelijkheid; *~ to* gelijk aan **2** onpartijdig, eerlijk, rechtvaardig: *~ opportunity* gelijkberechtiging **3** gelijkmatig, effen
³equal (vb) evenaren, gelijk zijn aan: *two and four ~s six* twee en vier is zes
equality gelijkheid, overeenkomst
¹equalize (vb) **1** gelijk worden **2** [sport] gelijkmaken
²equalize (vb) gelijkmaken, gelijkstellen
equally 1 eerlijk, evenzeer, gelijkmatig **2** in dezelfde mate
equanimity 1 gelijkmoedigheid **2** berusting
equate 1 (+ to, with) vergelijken (met) **2** (+ with) gelijkstellen (aan) **3** gelijkmaken, met elkaar in evenwicht brengen
equation vergelijking
equator evenaar, equator
equatorial 1 equatoriaal **2** tropisch
Equatorial Guinean Equatoriaal-Guineeër
equestrian ruiter
equilibrium evenwicht[h]
equip (+ with) uitrusten (met), toerusten (met)
equipment uitrusting, installatie, benodigdheden
equity 1 billijkheid, rechtvaardigheid

2 (equities) aandelen
¹equivalent (n) equivalent[h]
²equivalent (adj) (+ to) equivalent (aan), gelijkwaardig (aan)
equivocal 1 dubbelzinnig **2** twijfelachtig
equivocate 1 eromheen draaien, een ontwijkend antwoord geven **2** een slag om de arm houden
er eh [hesitation]
era era, tijdperk[h], jaartelling, hoofdtijdperk[h]
eradicate met wortel en al uittrekken; [fig] uitroeien; verdelgen
erase uitvegen, uitwissen
eraser 1 stukje vlakgom, gummetje[h] **2** bordenwisser
e-reader e-reader
¹erect (adj) recht, rechtop (gaand), opgericht
²erect (vb) **1** oprichten, bouwen, neerzetten **2** stichten, vestigen, instellen
erection 1 erectie **2** gebouw[h] **3** het oprichten, het bouwen, het optrekken **4** het instellen
ergonomic ergonomisch
Eritrea Eritrea
¹Eritrean (n) Eritreeër, Eritreese
²Eritrean (adj) Eritrees
ermine hermelijn[h]
¹erode (vb) wegspoelen
²erode (vb) **1** (also + away) uitbijten [of acid] **2** (also + away) uithollen [of water]; afslijpen, eroderen
erogenous erogeen: *~ zone* erogene zone
erosion erosie [also fig]
erotic erotisch
err 1 zich vergissen **2** afwijken: *~ on the side of caution* het zekere voor het onzekere nemen **3** zondigen
errand 1 boodschap: *go on* (or: *run*) *~s for s.o.* boodschappen doen voor iem. **2** doel[h] [of message]
errand-boy loopjongen
erratic 1 onregelmatig, ongeregeld, grillig **2** excentriek, onconventioneel **3** veranderlijk, wispelturig
error vergissing: *~ of judgement* beoordelingsfout; *human ~* menselijke fout; *be in ~* zich vergissen
error message foutmelding
erudition [form] uitgebreide kennis; eruditie
erupt 1 uitbarsten [of volcano, geyser etc]; (vuur) spuwen, spuiten **2** barsten [also fig]; uitbreken
¹escalate (vb) stijgen [of prices, wages]; escaleren
²escalate (vb) verhevigen, doen escaleren
escalator roltrap
escapade 1 escapade **2** dolle streek, wild avontuur[h]
¹escape (n) ontsnapping, vlucht: *make one's ~* ontsnappen

²**escape** (vb) **1** (+ from, out of) ontsnappen (uit/aan), ontvluchten: ~ *with* one's life het er levend afbrengen **2** naar buiten komen; ontsnappen [of gas, steam] **3** verdwijnen, vervagen, vergeten raken
³**escape** (vb) **1** vermijden, ontkomen aan: ~ *death* de dood ontlopen **2** ontschieten; (even) vergeten zijn [of name, etc] **3** ontgaan: ~ one's *attention* aan iemands aandacht ontsnappen **4** ontglippen, ontvallen
escape artist [roughly] boeienkoning
escape hatch 1 noodluikʰ, nooddeur [in ship, plane] **2** uitvlucht
¹**escort** (n) **1** escorteʰ, (gewapende) geleideʰ **2** begeleider, metgezel
²**escort** (vb) escorteren, begeleiden, uitgeleide doen
e-signature *electronic signature* elektronische (*or:* digitale) handtekening
esp *especially* i.h.b., in het bijzonder
especial speciaal, bijzonder
especially 1 speciaal: *bought* ~ *for you* speciaal voor jou gekocht **2** vooral, in het bijzonder, voornamelijk
espionage spionage
Esq *esquire* Dhr.
esquire de (Weledelgeboren) Heer
essay essayʰ, opstelʰ, (korte) verhandeling
essence 1 essentie, kern **2** wezenʰ, geest: he's the ~ *of* kindness hij is de vriendelijkheid zelf
¹**essential** (n) **1** het essentiële, essentie, wezenʰ **2** essentieel puntʰ, hoofdzaak **3** noodzakelijk iets, onontbeerlijke zaak: the *basic* ~s de allernoodzakelijkste dingen
²**essential** (adj) **1** (+ for, to) essentieel (voor), wezenlijk **2** (+ for, to) onmisbaar (voor), noodzakelijk (voor)
establish 1 vestigen [also fig]; oprichten, stichten: ~ed *custom* ingeburgerd gebruik; ~ o.s. zich vestigen **2** benoemen, aanstellen **3** vaststellen [facts]; bewijzen ‖ ~ed *church* staatskerk
establishment vestiging, oprichting, instelling
the **Establishment** staatskerk
estate 1 landgoedʰ, buiten(verblijf)ʰ **2** (land)bezitʰ, vastgoedʰ **3** woonwijk **4** stand, klasse **5** [law] boedel **6** plantage ‖ *industrial* ~ industrieterrein, industriegebied, industriewijk
estate agent makelaar in onroerend goed
estate car stationcar
¹**esteem** (n) achting, respectʰ, waardering: hold s.o. in *high* ~ iem. hoogachten
²**esteem** (vb) **1** (hoog)achten, waarderen, respecteren **2** beschouwen: ~ sth. a *duty* iets als een plicht zien
esthet- *see* aesthet-
estimable 1 achtenswaardig **2** schatbaar, taxeerbaar

¹**estimate** (n) **1** schatting: at a rough ~ ruwweg **2** (kosten)raming, begroting, prijsopgave **3** oordeelʰ
²**estimate** (vb) **1** schatten, berekenen: ~ sth. at £100 iets op 100 pond schatten **2** beoordelen [pers]
estimation 1 (hoog)achting: *hold* s.o. in ~ iem. (hoog)achten **2** schatting, taxatie
Estonia Estland
¹**Estonian** (n) Est(lander); Estlandse
²**Estonian** (adj) Estlands
estrangement vervreemding, verwijdering
estuary (wijde) riviermond
et al *et alia, et alii* e.a.
etc *et cetera* enz., etc., enzovoort
etch etsen
eternal eeuwig [also inform]
eternity 1 eeuwigheid [also inform] **2** onsterfelijkheid, het eeuwige leven
ethereal 1 etherisch [also fig]; hemels **2** ijl **3** vluchtig: ~ *oil* etherische olie
ethical ethisch
ethics 1 ethiek, zedenleer **2** gedragsnormen, gedragscode
Ethiopia Ethiopië
¹**Ethiopian** (n) Ethiopiër, Ethiopische
²**Ethiopian** (adj) Ethiopisch
ethnic etnisch: ~ *minority* etnische minderheid
ethnicity 1 het behoren tot een bepaald ras of volk **2** volkstrots
ethos ethosʰ
etiquette etiquetteʰ
EU *European Union* EU, Europese Unie
eucalyptus eucalyptus; gomboom
eulogy (+ of, on) lofprijzing (over)
euphemism eufemismeʰ
euphony welluidendheid
euphoria euforie, gevoelʰ van welbevinden, opgewektheid
euro euro
Europe Europa
¹**European** (n) Europeaan
²**European** (adj) Europees: ~ *Union* Europese Unie, EU
euro symbol euroteken
euthanasia euthanasie
euthanize in laten slapen; euthanasie plegen op
evacuate evacueren, ontruimen; [mil] terugtrekken uit
evacuation ontruiming, evacuatie
evade vermijden, (proberen te) ontkomen aan, ontwijken: ~ one's *responsibilities* zijn verantwoordelijkheden uit de weg gaan
evaluate 1 de waarde bepalen van, evalueren **2** berekenen
evaluation 1 waardebepaling, beoordeling, evaluatie **2** berekening
evangelical evangelisch

evangelist evangelist: *the four ~s* de vier evangelisten
evaporate verdampen, (doen) vervliegen; [fig] in het niets (doen) verdwijnen: *my hope has ~d* ik heb de hoop verloren
evasion ontwijking, uitvlucht: *~ of taxes* belastingontduiking
evasive ontwijkend
eve 1 vooravond: *on the ~ of* aan de vooravond van; *on the ~ of the race* de dag voor de wedstrijd **2** avond
¹even (adj) **1** vlak, gelijk, glad **2** gelijkmatig, kalm, onveranderlijk: *an ~ temper* een evenwichtig humeur **3** even: *~ and odd numbers* even en oneven getallen **4** gelijk, quitte: *get ~ with s.o. 't iem.* betaald zetten; *now we're ~ again* nu staan we weer quitte **5** eerlijk: *an ~ exchange* een eerlijke ruil
²even (vb) gelijk worden, glad worden
³even (vb) gelijk maken
⁴even (adv) **1** zelfs: *~ now* zelfs nu; *~ so* maar toch; *~ if* (or: *though*) zelfs al **2** [before comparative] nog: *that's ~ better* dat is zelfs nog beter
even-handed onpartijdig
evening avond; [fig] einde[h]: *good ~!* goedenavond!; *in* (or: *during*) *the ~ 's* avonds; *on Tuesday ~* op dinsdagavond
even out (gelijkmatig) spreiden, gelijk verdelen, uitsmeren
evensong avonddienst
event 1 gebeurtenis, evenement[h], manifestatie: *the normal* (or: *usual*) *course of ~s* de gewone gang van zaken; *happy ~* blijde gebeurtenis [birth] **2** geval[h]: *at all ~s* in elk geval; *in the ~ of his death* in het geval dat hij komt te overlijden **3** uitkomst, afloop: *in the ~, he decided to withdraw from the race* uiteindelijk besloot hij zich uit de wedstrijd terug te trekken **4** [sport] nummer[h], onderdeel[h]
eventful veelbewogen; rijk aan gebeurtenissen
eventual uiteindelijk
eventuality eventualiteit, mogelijke gebeurtenis
eventually ten slotte, uiteindelijk
even up gelijk worden, gelijkmaken, gelijkschakelen, evenwicht herstellen
ever 1 ooit: *faster than ~* sneller dan ooit **2** toch, in 's hemelsnaam: *how ~ could I do that?* hoe zou ik dat in 's hemelsnaam kunnen? **3** echt, erg, verschrikkelijk, zo ... als het maar kan: *it is ~ so cold* het is verschrikkelijk koud **4** immer, altijd, voortdurend: *an ever-growing fear* een steeds groeiende angst; *they lived happily ~ after* daarna leefden ze nog lang en gelukkig; *~ since* van toen af, sindsdien
¹evergreen (n) altijd jeugdig iem. (iets); onsterfelijke melodie [etc]; evergreen
²evergreen (adj) altijdgroen, groenblijvend;

[fig] onsterfelijk; altijd jeugdig
everlasting 1 eeuwig(durend), eindeloos **2** onsterfelijk; [fig] onverwoestbaar
every 1 elk(e), ieder(e), alle: [inform] *~ bit as good* in elk opzicht even goed; *~ which way* in alle richtingen; *~ (single) one of them is wrong* ze zijn stuk voor stuk verkeerd; *three out of ~ seven* drie op zeven; *~ other week* om de andere week, eens in de twee weken **2** alle, alle mogelijke: *she was given ~ opportunity* ze kreeg alle kansen || *~ now and again* (or: *then*), *~ so often* (zo) nu en dan, af en toe
everybody iedereen: *~ despises her* iedereen kijkt op haar neer
everyday (alle)daags, gewoon, doordeweeks
everyone see everybody
everyplace [Am; inform] overal
everything 1 alles, alle dingen: *~ but a success* allesbehalve een succes, bepaald geen succes **2** (+ and) van alles, dergelijke, zo, dat (alles), nog van die dingen: *with exams, holidays and ~ she had plenty to think of* met examens, vakantie en zo had ze genoeg om over te denken
everywhere 1 overal **2** overal waar, waar ook: *~ he looked he saw decay* waar hij ook keek zag hij verval
evict uitzetten, verdrijven
eviction order bevel tot uitzetting
evidence 1 aanduiding, spoor[h], teken[h]: *bear* (or: *show*) *~ of* sporen dragen van, getuigen van **2** bewijs[h], bewijsstuk[h], bewijsmateriaal[h]: *conclusive ~* afdoend bewijs; *on the ~ of* op grond van **3** getuigenis, getuigenverklaring: *call s.o. in ~* iem. als getuige oproepen **4** duidelijkheid, zichtbaarheid, opvallendheid: *be in ~* zichtbaar zijn, opvallen
evident duidelijk, zichtbaar, klaarblijkelijk
¹evil (n) **1** kwaad[h], onheil[h], ongeluk[h]: *choose the least* (or: *lesser*) *of two ~s* van twee kwaden het minste kiezen **2** kwaad[h], zonde: *speak ~ of* kwaadspreken over **3** kwaal
²evil (adj) **1** kwaad, slecht, boos: *put off the ~ day* (or: *hour*) iets onaangenaams op de lange baan schuiven **2** kwaad, zondig
evince tonen, aan de dag leggen
evocative (gevoelens) oproepend: *it is ~ of his earlier paintings* het doet denken aan zijn vroegere schilderijen
evoke oproepen, tevoorschijn roepen, (op)wekken
evolution evolutie, ontwikkeling, groei
evolutionary evolutie-
¹evolve (vb) zich ontwikkelen, zich ontvouwen, geleidelijk ontstaan
²evolve (vb) ontwikkelen, afleiden, uitdenken
e-wallet mobiele portemonnee
e-waste e-afval, e-schroot
ewe ooi, wijfjesschaap[h]

ex ex, ex-man, ex-vrouw, ex-verloofde
¹exact (adj) **1** nauwkeurig, accuraat **2** exact, precies: *the ~ time* de juiste tijd
²exact (vb) **1** vorderen [money, payment]; afdwingen, afpersen **2** eisen, vereisen
exacting veeleisend
exactly precies, helemaal, juist, nauwkeurig: *not ~* eigenlijk niet; [iron] niet bepaald
exaggerate 1 overdrijven, aandikken **2** versterken
exaggeration overdrijving
exalt 1 verheffen, verhogen, adelen **2** loven, prijzen **3** in vervoering brengen
exam *examination* examenʰ
examination 1 examenʰ: *sit for* (or: *take*) *an ~* examen doen **2** onderzoekʰ, inspectie, analyse: *a medical ~* een medisch onderzoek; *on closer ~* bij nader onderzoek; *under ~* nog in onderzoek
examine 1 onderzoeken, onder de loep nemen, nagaan **2** examineren: *~ s.o. in* (or: *on*) iem. examineren in
examiner 1 examinator **2** inspecteur
example voorbeeldʰ: *give* (or: *set*) *a good ~* een goed voorbeeld geven; *make an ~ of s.o.* een voorbeeld stellen; *for ~* bijvoorbeeld
exasperate 1 erger maken **2** boos maken, ergeren
exasperation ergernis, ergerlijkheid, kwaadheid
excavate 1 uitgraven, blootleggen, delven **2** uithollen
exceed 1 overschrijden **2** overtreffen, te boven gaan: *they ~ed us in number* zij overtroffen ons in aantal
exceedingly buitengewoon, bijzonder
¹excel (vb) uitblinken, knap zijn
²excel (vb) overtreffen, uitsteken boven
excellence 1 voortreffelijkheid, uitmuntendheid **2** uitmuntende eigenschap
Excellency excellentie: *His* (or: *Her*) *~* Zijne (*or*: Hare) Excellentie
excellent uitstekend, voortreffelijk
¹except (vb) uitzonderen, uitsluiten, buiten beschouwing laten
²except (prep) behalve, uitgezonderd, tenzij, op … na: *~ for Sheila* behalve Sheila
³except (conj) ware het niet dat, maar, echter, alleen: *I'd buy that ring for you, ~ I've got no money* ik zou die ring best voor je willen kopen, alleen heb ik geen geld
exception uitzondering, uitsluiting: *with the ~ of* met uitzondering van; *an ~ to the rule* een uitzondering op de regel ‖ *take ~ to* bezwaar maken tegen, aanstoot nemen aan
exceptionable 1 verwerpelijk **2** aanvechtbaar
exceptional uitzonderlijk, buitengewoon
excerpt 1 uittrekselʰ **2** stukjeʰ, fragmentʰ, passage
¹excess (n) **1** overmaat, overdaad: *in* (or: *to*)

~ overmatig **2** excesʰ, buitensporigheid, uitspatting **3** overschotʰ, surplusʰ, rest **4** eigen risicoʰ [of insurance] ‖ *in ~ of* meer dan, boven; *drink to ~* (veel te) veel drinken
²excess (adj) **1** bovenmatig, buitenmatig **2** extra-: *~ baggage* (or: *luggage*) overvracht, overgewicht; *~ postage* strafport
excessive 1 buitensporig **2** overdadig, overmatig
¹exchange (n) **1** ruil, (uit)wisseling, woordenwisseling, gedachtewisseling **2** beurs, beursgebouwʰ **3** telefooncentrale **4** het (om)ruilen, het (uit)wisselen: *in ~ for* in ruil voor **5** het wisselen [of money]
²exchange (vb) **1** ruilen, uitwisselen, verwisselen: *~ words with* een woordenwisseling hebben met **2** wisselen, inwisselen
exchequer schatkist, staatskas
the **Exchequer** ministerieʰ van Financiën
¹excise (n) accijns
²excise (vb) uitsnijden, wegnemen
excite 1 opwekken, uitlokken, oproepen **2** opwinden: *do not get ~d about it!* wind je er niet over op! **3** prikkelen; stimuleren [also sexually]
excited opgewonden, geprikkeld
excitement 1 opwindende gebeurtenis, sensatie **2** opwinding, opschudding, drukte
exciting 1 opwindend; spannend **2** stimulerend
exclamation 1 uitroep, schreeuw, kreet: *~ mark* uitroepteken **2** geroepʰ, geschreeuwʰ, luidruchtig commentaarʰ
exclude uitsluiten, weren, uitzonderen, verwerpen
excluding exclusief; niet inbegrepen
exclusion uitsluiting, uitzetting, verwerping, uitzondering: *to the ~ of* met uitsluiting van
exclusive exclusief: *mutually ~ duties* onverenigbare functies; *~ rights* alleenrecht, monopolie; *~ of* exclusief, niet inbegrepen
exclusively uitsluitend, enkel, alleen
excommunicate excommuniceren; in de ban doen
excrement uitwerpselʰ, uitwerpselen, ontlasting
excruciating tenenkrommend, vreselijk: *it was ~ly funny* het was om je ziek te lachen
excursion 1 excursie, uitstapjeʰ, pleziertochtjeʰ **2** uitweiding: *the teacher made a brief ~ into politics* de leraar hield een korte uitweiding over politiek
¹excuse (n) **1** excuusʰ, verontschuldiging: *make one's* (or: *s.o.'s*) *~s* zich excuseren (voor afwezigheid) **2** uitvlucht, voorwendselʰ
²excuse (vb) **1** excuseren, verontschuldigen, vergeven: *~ my being late* neem me niet kwalijk dat ik te laat ben; *~ me, can you tell me …?* pardon, kunt u me zeggen …?; *~ me!* sorry!, pardon! **2** vrijstellen, ontheffen **3** la-

ten weggaan, niet langer ophouden ‖ *may I be ~d*? mag ik van tafel af?, mag ik even naar buiten? [to go to the toilet]; *~ o.s.* zich excuseren [also for absence]
execute 1 uitvoeren [sentence]; afwikkelen [testament] **2** executeren, terechtstellen
execution 1 executie, terechtstelling **2** uitvoering; volbrenging [of sentence]; afwikkeling [of testament] **3** spel[h], (muzikale) voordracht, vertolking
executioner beul
[1]**executive** (n) **1** leidinggevend persoon, hoofd[h], directeur **2** uitvoerend orgaan[h], administratie, dagelijks bestuur[h]
[2]**executive** (adj) **1** leidinggevend: *~ director* lid van de raad van bestuur, directeur [who is member of the Board of Directors] **2** uitvoerend [also pol]
executor executeur(-testamentair)
exemplary voorbeeldig [of behaviour etc]
exemplification 1 voorbeeld[h], illustratie **2** toelichting
exemplify toelichten; illustreren [with an example]
[1]**exempt** (adj) vrij(gesteld), ontheven
[2]**exempt** (vb) (+ from) vrijstellen (van), ontheffen, excuseren
[1]**exercise** (n) **1** (uit)oefening, gebruik[h], toepassing **2** lichaamsoefening, training **3** (-s) militaire oefeningen, manoeuvres
[2]**exercise** (vb) **1** (zich) oefenen, lichaamsoefeningen doen, trainen **2** (uit)oefenen, gebruiken, toepassen: *~ patience* geduld oefenen; *~ power* macht uitoefenen **3** uitoefenen, waarnemen; bekleden [office, position] **4** [mil] laten exerceren, drillen
exercise bike hometrainer
exercise book schoolschrift[h]
exert uitoefenen, aanwenden, doen gelden: *~ pressure* pressie uitoefenen; *~ o.s.* zich inspannen
exertion 1 (zware) inspanning **2** uitoefening, aanwending: *the ~ of power* de uitoefening van macht
exhalation 1 uitblazing, uitademing **2** uitwaseming, verdamping, uitlaatgas[h]
exhale uitademen
[1]**exhaust** (n) **1** uitlaat, uitlaatbuis, uitlaatpijp **2** afzuigapparaat[h] **3** uitlaatstoffen, uitlaatgassen
[2]**exhaust** (vb) **1** opgebruiken, opmaken **2** uitputten, afmatten; [fig] uitputtend behandelen: *~ a subject* een onderwerp uitputten; *feel ~ed* zich uitgeput voelen
exhaust fume uitlaatgas[h]
exhaustion 1 het opgebruiken **2** uitputting
[1]**exhibit** (n) **1** geëxposeerd stuk[h] **2** geëxposeerde collectie **3** [law] officieel bewijsstuk: *~ A* eerste/belangrijkste bewijsstuk **4** [Am] tentoonstelling

[2]**exhibit** (vb) **1** tentoonstellen, uitstallen **2** vertonen, tonen, blijk geven van
exhibition 1 tentoonstelling, expositie **2** vertoning ‖ *make an ~ of o.s.* zich belachelijk aanstellen
exhilarate 1 opwekken, opvrolijken **2** versterken, stimuleren
exhilarating 1 opwekkend, opbeurend **2** versterkend, stimulerend
exhort aanmanen, oproepen
exhume opgraven; [fig] aan het licht brengen
exile 1 balling, banneling **2** ballingschap: *send into ~* in ballingschap zenden
exist 1 bestaan, zijn, voorkomen, gebeuren **2** (over)leven, bestaan, voortbestaan: *how can they ~ in these conditions?* hoe kunnen zij in deze omstandigheden overleven?
existence 1 bestaanswijze, levenswijze **2** het bestaan, het zijn: *come into ~* ontstaan
existent 1 bestaand **2** levend, in leven **3** huidig, actueel
existential existentieel; bestaans-
[1]**exit** (n) **1** uitgang **2** afslag; uitrit [of motorway] **3** vertrek[h]: *make one's ~* van het toneel verdwijnen
[2]**exit** (vb) afgaan; van het toneel verdwijnen [also fig]
exonerate 1 zuiveren, vrijspreken: *~ s.o. from all blame* iem. van alle blaam zuiveren **2** vrijstellen, ontlasten
exorbitant buitensporig, overdreven
exorcism uitdrijving, (geesten)bezwering
exotic exotisch, uitheems, vreemd
expand 1 opengaan, (zich) ontplooien, spreiden **2** (doen) uitzetten, (op)zwellen, (in omvang) doen toenemen **3** (zich) uitbreiden, (zich) ontwikkelen, uitgroeien: *she owns a rapidly ~ing chain of fast-food restaurants* zij bezit een snelgroeiende keten van fastfoodrestaurants **4** uitwerken, uitschrijven ‖ *~ on sth.* over iets uitweiden
expansion uitbreiding, uitgezet deel[h], vergroting: *sudden industrial ~* plotselinge industriële groei
expansion card uitbreidingskaart
expatriate (ver)banneling, iem. die in het buitenland woont
expect 1 verwachten, wachten op, voorzien: *I did not ~ this* ik had dit niet verwacht **2** rekenen op, verlangen: *~ too much of s.o.* te veel van iem. verlangen [3] [inform] aannemen, vermoeden: *I ~ you're coming too* jij komt zeker ook? ‖ *be ~ing (a baby)* in (blijde) verwachting zijn
expectancy verwachting, afwachting
expectant 1 verwachtend, (af)wachtend, vol vertrouwen: *~ crowds* menigte vol verwachting **2** toekomstige: *~ mother* aanstaande moeder
expectation verwachting, afwachting,

(voor)uitzicht[h]; vooruitzichten [of inheritance, money]: ~ *of life* vermoedelijke levensduur; *against* (or: *contrary to*) *(all)* ~*(s)* tegen alle verwachting in

expedient geschikt, passend

expedite 1 bevorderen, bespoedigen **2** (snel) afhandelen, afwerken

expedition expeditie, onderzoekingstocht; [by extension] plezierreis; excursie

expeditious snel, prompt

expel 1 verdrijven, verjagen **2** wegzenden, wegsturen, deporteren: ~ *from school* van school sturen

expend 1 besteden, uitgeven, spenderen **2** (op)gebruiken, verbruiken, uitputten

expenditure uitgave(n), kosten, verbruik[h]

expense 1 uitgave, uitgavenpost **2** kosten, uitgave(n), prijs; [fig] moeite; opoffering: *at the ~ of* op kosten van; [fig] ten koste van **3** (-s) onkosten **4** onkostenvergoeding ‖ *spare no ~* geen kosten sparen

expensive duur, kostbaar

[1]**experience** (n) ervaring, belevenis, ondervinding, praktijk

[2]**experience** (vb) ervaren, beleven, ondervinden: ~ *difficulties* op moeilijkheden stoten

experienced ervaren, geschikt, geroutineerd

[1]**experiment** (n) experiment[h], proef(neming), test

[2]**experiment** (vb) experimenteren, proeven nemen

experimental 1 experimenteel: ~ *stage* proefstadium **2** empirisch

experimentation proefneming

[1]**expert** (n) expert, deskundige

[2]**expert** (adj) bedreven, deskundig, bekwaam: ~ *job* a) vakkundig uitgevoerde klus; b) werkje voor een expert

expertise bekwaamheid; deskundigheid, (vak)kennis

expiration 1 uitademing **2** vervaltijd, expiratie **3** dood

expire 1 verlopen, verstrijken, aflopen, vervallen: *your ticket ~s* je kaart wordt ongeldig **2** [form] sterven

expiry einde[h], verval[h], vervaldag, afloop: ~ *date* vervaldatum

explain (nader) verklaren, uitleggen, uiteenzetten, toelichten, verantwoorden, rechtvaardigen: ~ *one's conduct* zijn gedrag verantwoorden; ~ *away* wegredeneren, goedpraten

explanation verklaring, uitleg, toelichting

explanatory verklarend; verhelderend

expletive krachtterm, vloek, verwensing

explicable verklaarbaar

explicit expliciet, duidelijk, uitvoerig, uitgesproken, uitdrukkelijk

[1]**explode** (vb) **1** exploderen, ontploffen,

(uiteen)barsten **2** uitbarsten, uitvallen: ~ *with laughter* in lachen uitbarsten

[2]**explode** (vb) **1** tot ontploffing brengen, opblazen **2** ontzenuwen, verwerpen: ~*d ideas* achterhaalde ideeën

[1]**exploit** (n) (helden)daad, prestatie, wapenfeit[h]

[2]**exploit** (vb) **1** benutten, gebruikmaken van **2** uitbuiten: ~ *poor children* arme kinderen uitbuiten

exploitation 1 exploitatie, gebruik[h], ontginning **2** uitbuiting

exploration onderzoek[h], studie

explore 1 een onderzoek instellen **2** onderzoeken, bestuderen: ~ *all possibilities* alle mogelijkheden onderzoeken **3** verkennen

explorer ontdekkingsreiziger, onderzoeker

explosion 1 explosie, ontploffing, uitbarsting **2** uitbarsting, losbarsting, uitval: ~ *of anger* uitval van woede

[1]**explosive** (n) explosief[h], ontplofbare stof, springstof

[2]**explosive** (adj) **1** explosief, (gemakkelijk) ontploffend: ~ *population increase* enorme bevolkingsgroei **2** opvliegend, driftig

exponent 1 exponent; vertegenwoordiger, verdediger **2** uitvoerder **3** [maths] exponent

[1]**export** (n) **1** export, uitvoer(handel) **2** exportartikel[h]

[2]**export** (vb) exporteren, uitvoeren

expose 1 blootstellen, blootgeven, introduceren aan **2** tentoonstellen, uitstallen, (ver)tonen: ~ *the goods* de waren uitstallen **3** onthullen, ontmaskeren, bekendmaken **4** [photo] belichten

exposé onthulling; ontmaskering

exposed blootgesteld, onbeschut, kwetsbaar: ~ *pipes* slecht geïsoleerde leidingen; *be ~ to* blootstaan aan

exposure 1 blootstelling [to weather, danger, light] **2** bekendmaking, uiteenzetting, onthulling: *the ~ of his crimes* de onthulling van zijn misdaden **3** [photo] belichting

expound uiteenzetten

[1]**express** (n) sneltrein, snelbus, exprestrein

[2]**express** (adj) **1** uitdrukkelijk, duidelijk (kenbaar gemaakt), nadrukkelijk: *it was his ~ wish it should be done* het was zijn uitdrukkelijke wens dat het gedaan werd **2** snel(gaand), expres-, ijl-: *an ~ train* een sneltrein

[3]**express** (vb) uitdrukken, laten zien, betuigen: *he ~ed his concern* hij toonde zijn bezorgdheid

[4]**express** (adv) **1** met grote snelheid, met spoed **2** per expresse, met snelpost **3** speciaal

expression 1 uitdrukking, zegswijze **2** (gelaats)uitdrukking, blik **3** [maths] (hoeveelheids)uitdrukking, symbool[h], symbolen-

(verzameling) **4** het uitdrukken: *that's be-yond* (or: *past*) ~ daar zijn geen woorden voor **5** expressie, uitdrukkingskracht
expressive expressief, betekenisvol, veelzeggend: *this poem is* ~ *of great sorrow* dit gedicht drukt groot verdriet uit
expressway [Am] snelweg
expulsion verdrijving, verbanning, uitwijzing
exquisite 1 uitstekend, prachtig, voortreffelijk **2** fijn, subtiel
extemporize improviseren
¹extend (vb) zich uitstrekken [of land, time]; voortduren
²extend (vb) **1** (uitt)rekken, langer (groter) maken, uitbreiden: *an ~ing* **ladder** schuifladder **2** uitstrekken, uitsteken, aanreiken **3** (aan)bieden, verlenen, betuigen, bewijzen: ~ *a warm* **welcome** *to s.o.* iem. hartelijk welkom heten
extension 1 aanvulling, verlenging, toevoeging: [comp] **file** ~ extensie **2** (extra) toestel(nummer)ʰ: **ask for** ~ *212* vraag om toestel 212 **3** uitstelʰ, langer tijdvakʰ **4** uitbreiding, vergroting, verlenging: *the* ~ *of a* **contract** de verlenging van een contract
extensive uitgestrekt, groot, uitgebreid: *an* ~ **library** een veelomvattende bibliotheek
extent 1 omvang, grootte, uitgestrektheid: *the full* ~ *of his* **knowledge** de volle omvang van zijn kennis **2** mate, graad, hoogte: *to a certain* ~ tot op zekere hoogte; *to a great* (or: *large*) ~ in belangrijke mate, grotendeels; *to what* ~ in hoeverre
extenuate verzachten, afzwakken: *extenuating* **circumstances** verzachtende omstandigheden
¹exterior (n) buitenkant, oppervlakte, uiterlijk: *do not* **judge** *people by their* ~s beoordeel mensen niet op hun uiterlijk
²exterior (adj) buiten-, aan buitenkant
exterminate uitroeien, verdelgen
external 1 uiterlijk, extern **2** (voor) uitwendig (gebruik) ‖ ~ **examination** (or: **examiner**) examen (or: examinator) van buiten de school
extinct 1 uitgestorven **2** niet meer bestaand, afgeschaft **3** uitgedoofd; (uit)geblust [also fig]; dood: *an* ~ **volcano** een uitgedoofde vulkaan
extinction 1 ondergang, uitroeiing: *be threatened by* (or: *with*) **complete** ~ bedreigd worden door totale uitroeiing **2** het doven
extinguish 1 doven, (uit)blussen **2** vernietigen, beëindigen
extinguisher 1 (brand)blusapparaatʰ, brandblusser **2** domper, kaarsendover
extol hoog prijzen, ophemelen, verheerlijken: ~ *s.o.'s talents to the skies* iemands talent hemelhoog prijzen
extort afpersen: ~ *a confession* **from** *s.o.*

iem. een bekentenis afdwingen
extortion afpersing; afzetterij
¹extra (n) **1** niet (in de prijs) inbegrepen zaak, bijkomend tariefʰ **2** figurant, dummy
²extra (adj) extra, bijkomend ‖ ~ **buses** *for football-supporters* speciaal ingezette bussen voor voetbalsupporters
³extra (adv) **1** extra, buitengewoon, bijzonder (veel): ~ **good** *quality* speciale kwaliteit **2** buiten het gewone tarief: **pay** ~ *for postage* bijbetalen voor portokosten
¹extract (n) **1** passage, fragmentʰ, uittrekselʰ **2** extractʰ, aftrekselʰ, afkookselʰ
²extract (vb) **1** (uit)trekken, (uit)halen, verwijderen; [fig] afpersen; weten te ontlokken: ~ *a* **confession** een bekentenis afdwingen **2** (uit)halen [minerals etc]; onttrekken, winnen
extraction 1 het winnen [of minerals etc] **2** afkomst, oorsprong: *Americans of Polish and Irish* ~ Amerikanen van Poolse en Ierse afkomst
extracurricular buitenschools
extradite 1 uitleveren [criminal] **2** uitgeleverd krijgen
extramarital buitenechtelijk
extraneous 1 van buitenaf, buiten-, extern **2** onbelangrijk
extraordinary 1 extra: *an* ~ **session** een extra zitting **2** buitengewoon, bijzonder
extraterrestrial buitenaards
extravagant 1 buitensporig, mateloos **2** verkwistend, verspillend: *she* **is** *rather* ~ zij smijt met geld
¹extreme (n) uitersteʰ, extremeʰ: **go** *from one* ~ *to the other* van het ene uiterste in het andere (ver)vallen; *in the* ~ uitermate, uiterst
²extreme (adj) **1** extreem, buitengewoon **2** uiterst, verst **3** grootst, hoogst: ~ **danger** het grootste gevaar
extremely uitermate, uiterst, buitengewoon
extremism extremismeʰ
extremity 1 uiteindeʰ **2** [always singular] uitersteʰ **3** lidmaat: *the* **upper** *and* **lower** *extremities* armen en benen **4** (extremities) handen en voeten **5** uiterste nood
extricate halen uit, bevrijden, losmaken: ~ *o.s. from difficulties* zich uit de nesten redden
exuberant 1 uitbundig, vol enthousiasme, geestdriftig **2** overdadig, overvloedig: ~ **growth** weelderige groei
exude 1 (zich) afscheiden, afgeven: ~ **sweat** zweet afscheiden **2** (uit)stralen, duidelijk tonen: ~ **happiness** geluk uitstralen
exultation uitgelatenheid, verrukking
¹eye (n) **1** oogʰ: ~s *gezichtsvermogenʰ*; blik; kijk; *as* **far** *as the* ~ *can see* zo ver het oog reikt; **catch** *s.o.'s* ~ iemands aandacht trekken; **close** (or: **shut**) *one's* ~s *to* oogluikend toestaan; **cry** (or: **weep**) *one's* ~s *out* hevig

huilen; **have** an ~ for kijk hebben op; **keep** an
~ on in de gaten houden; **keep** your ~s open
let goed op!; *there is more to it* (or: *in it*) *than
meets the* ~ er zit meer achter (dan je zo zou
zeggen); **open** s.o.'s ~s (to) iem. de ogen openen (voor); **set** (or: **lay**) ~s on onder ogen
krijgen; **under** (or: *before*) *his very* ~s vlak voor
(*or:* onder) zijn ogen; **with** an ~ **to** met het
oog op; **all** ~s een en al aandacht **2** oog[h];
opening [of needle]; oog[h]; ringetje[h] [for fas-
tener] **3** centrum[h], oog[h]; middelpunt[h] [of
storm] **4** [bot] kiem, oog[h] ‖ **do** s.o. in the ~
iem. een kool stoven; **make** ~s at s.o. lonken
naar iem.; **see** ~ to ~ *(with s.o.)* het eens zijn
(met iem.); *with one's* ~s **shut** met het grootste gemak; [inform] *that was* **one** *in the* ~ *for
him* dat was een hele klap voor hem
²**eye** (vb) bekijken, aankijken, kijken naar
  eyeball oogappel, oogbal, oogbol: [inform]
  ~ **to** ~ (vlak) tegenover elkaar
  eyebrow wenkbrauw: *raise* an ~ (or: *one's*)
  ~s de wenkbrauwen optrekken; *(be)* **up to**
  one's ~s *(in work)* tot over de oren (in het
  werk zitten)
  eye-catching opvallend
  eyeful 1 goede blik: *get* (or: *have*) an ~ *(of)*
  een goede blik kunnen werpen (op) **2** lust
  voor het oog: *Deborah is quite an* ~ Deborah
  ziet er heel erg goed uit
  eyelash wimper, ooghaartje[h]
  eyelet oogje[h]
  eye-opener openbaring, verrassing: *it was
  an* ~ *to him* daar keek hij van op
  eyesight gezicht(svermogen)[h]
  eyesore ontsiering: *be a* **real** ~ vreselijk lelijk zijn
  eyewash [inform] onzin; larie
  eyewitness ooggetuige
  eyrie 1 roofvogelnest[h] **2** arendsnest[h] [fig]

f

FA *Football Association*
fable 1 fabel, mythe, legende **2** verzinsel[h], verzinsels, fabeltje[h], praatje[h]
fabric 1 stof, materiaal[h], weefsel[h] **2** bouw, constructie
fabricate 1 bouwen, vervaardigen, fabriceren **2** verzinnen, uit de duim zuigen
fabrication 1 fabricage **2** verzinsel[h]
fabric softener wasverzachter
fabulous 1 legendarisch, verzonnen **2** fantastisch
façade gevel, front[h], voorzijde: [fig] *a ~ of friendliness* een façade van vriendelijkheid
¹face (n) **1** gezicht[h], gelaat[h]: *look s.o. in the ~* iem. recht aankijken [also fig]; *meet s.o. ~ to ~ iem.* onder ogen komen; *show one's ~* zijn gezicht laten zien; *in (the) ~ of* ondanks, tegenover **2** (gezichts)uitdrukking: *fall on one's ~* (plat) op zijn gezicht vallen; [also fig] zijn neus stoten **3** aanzien[h], reputatie, goede naam: *lose ~* zijn gezicht verliezen, afgaan; *save (one's) ~* zijn figuur redden **4** (belangrijkste) zijde, oppervlak[h]; bodem [earth]; gevel, voorzijde; wijzerplaat [clock]; kant; wand [mountain] ‖ *fly in the ~ of sth.* tegen iets in gaan; *on the ~ of it* op het eerste gezicht
²face (vb) uitzien, het gezicht (de voorkant) toekeren, uitzicht hebben
³face (vb) **1** onder ogen zien, (moedig) tegemoet treden: *let's ~ it,* ... laten we wel wezen, ... **2** confronteren: *Joe was ~d with many difficulties* Joe werd met vele moeilijkheden geconfronteerd **3** staan tegenover, uitzien op: *the picture facing the title page* de illustratie tegenover het titelblad ‖ *~ s.o. down* iem. overbluffen
face-cloth washandje[h]
faceless gezichtloos, grauw; anoniem [of crowd]
face-lift facelift [also fig]; opknapbeurt
facer 1 klap in het gezicht **2** onverwachte moeilijkheid, kink in de kabel, probleem[h]
facetious (ongepast) geestig; schertsend; spottend
face value 1 nominale waarde **2** ogenschijnlijke betekenis, eerste indruk: *take sth. at (its)* ~ iets kritiekloos accepteren
¹facial (n) [cosmetics] gezichtsbehandeling
²facial (adj) gezichts-
facile [oft depr] **1** oppervlakkig, luchtig **2** makkelijk, vlot **3** vlot, vaardig; vloeiend [style (of writing)]

facilitate vergemakkelijken, verlichten
facilities voorzieningen, faciliteiten
facility 1 voorziening, gelegenheid: *research facilities* onderzoeksfaciliteiten **2** vaardigheid, handigheid, talent[h] **3** simpelheid; gemakkelijkheid [of task, piece of music]
facing 1 bekleding [eg on wall, metal] **2** [fashion] beleg[h]
fact 1 feit[h], waarheid, zekerheid: *the ~s of life* de bloemetjes en de bijtjes; *know for a ~* zeker weten **2** werkelijkheid, realiteit: *in ~* in feite ‖ *in ~* bovendien, zelfs, en niet te vergeten
fact-finding: *he's on a ~ mission* hij is op onderzoeksreis om feitenmateriaal te verzamelen; hij is op inspectiereis
faction 1 (pressie)groep **2** partijruzie, interne onenigheid
factoid weetje[h], feitje[h]
factor 1 factor, omstandigheid **2** agent, vertegenwoordiger, zaakgelastigde
factory fabriek, werkplaats
factory farming bio-industrie
factual feitelijk, werkelijk
faculty 1 (geest)vermogen[h], functie, zin, zintuig[h]: *faculties* verstandelijke vermogens; *the ~ of hearing* (or: *speech*) de gehoorzin, het spraakvermogen **2** (leden van) faculteit, wetenschappelijk personeel[h], staf: *the Faculty of Law* de Juridische Faculteit
fad bevlieging, rage, gril
¹fade (vb) langzaam verdwijnen, afnemen; verflauwen [of enthusiasm]; vervagen [of colours, memories]; verbleken; verschieten [of colours]; verwelken [of flowers]: [film] *~ in* (in)faden, invloeien
²fade (vb) doen verdwijnen, laten wegsterven, laten vervagen: *~ in* (or: *up*) **a)** het volume (geleidelijk) laten opkomen; **b)** [film] (in)faden, invloeien
fade away (geleidelijk) verdwijnen; afnemen [of forces]; vervagen [of colours]; wegsterven [of sound]
fade out 1 langzaam (doen) wegsterven; wegdraaien [sound] **2** [film] geleidelijk (doen) vervagen; langzaam uitfaden
faeces [form] fecaliën; ontlasting
fag 1 saai werk[h] **2** [Am; inform] homo **3** [inform] peuk, sigaret
fagged (out) [inform] afgepeigerd, kapot
faggot 1 takkenbos, bundel (aanmaak)houtjes **2** bal gehakt **3** vervelend mens, (oude) zak **4** flikker, homo
¹fail (n) onvoldoende ‖ *without ~* zonder mankeren
²fail (vb) **1** tekortschieten, ontbreken, het begeven: *words ~ed me* ik kon geen woorden vinden **2** afnemen, opraken, verzwakken **3** zakken, een onvoldoende halen **4** mislukken, het niet halen, het laten afwe-

ten **5** faillet gaan
³fail (vb) **1** nalaten, niet in staat zijn, er niet in slagen: *I ~ to see your point* ik begrijp niet wat u bedoelt **2** in de steek laten, teleurstellen **3** zakken voor; niet halen [exam] **4** laten zakken, als onvoldoende beoordelen
¹failing (n) tekortkoming; zwakheid [in character]; fout [in construction]
²failing (prep) bij gebrek aan
failure 1 het falen, het zakken, afgang: *power ~* stroomstoring, stroomuitval **2** mislukking, fiasco[h], mislukkeling **3** nalatigheid, verzuim[h], onvermogen[h] **4** het uitblijven; mislukking [of crop] **5** storing, ontregeling
¹faint (n) flauwte, onmacht: *to fall down in a ~* flauwvallen
²faint (adj) **1** flauw, leeg, wee: *~ with hunger* flauw van de honger **2** halfgemeend, zwak: *damn with ~ praise* het graf in prijzen **3** laf **4** nauwelijks waarneembaar, vaag; onduidelijk [sound] **5** gering, vaag; zwak [idea, hope]: *I haven't the ~est idea* ik heb geen flauw idee
³faint (vb) flauwvallen
faint-hearted laf; angstig
¹fair (n) **1** markt, bazaar **2** beurs, (jaar)markt, tentoonstelling **3** kermis
²fair (adj) **1** eerlijk, redelijk, geoorloofd: *get a ~ hearing* een eerlijk proces krijgen; *by ~ means or foul* met alle middelen; *~ play* fair play, eerlijk spel; [inform] *~ enough!* dat is niet onredelijk!, oké! **2** behoorlijk, bevredigend, redelijk **3** mooi [weather]; helder [sky] **4** gunstig, veelbelovend: [shipp] *~ wind* gunstige wind **5** blank, licht(gekleurd); blond [hair, skin] || *the ~ sex* het schone geslacht
³fair (adv) **1** eerlijk, rechtvaardig: *play ~* eerlijk spelen, integer zijn; *to win ~ and square* overtuigend winnen **2** precies, pal, net: *~ and square* a) precies; b) rechtuit, open(hartig)
fairground kermisterrein[h]
fairly 1 eerlijk, billijk **2** volkomen, helemaal: *I was ~ stunned* ik stond compleet paf **3** tamelijk, redelijk
fair-minded rechtvaardig, eerlijk
fairness 1 eerlijkheid **2** lichte kleur [of hair, skin]
fair-trade eerlijke handel tussen rijke en arme landen: *~ agreement* prijsbinding(sovereenkomst)
fairy 1 (tover)fee, elf(je[h]) **2** [depr] homo, nicht
fairyland sprookjeswereld, sprookjesland[h]
fairy tale 1 sprookje[h] **2** verzinsel[h]
faith 1 geloof[h], geloofsovertuiging, vertrouwen[h]: *pin one's ~ on, put one's ~ in* vertrouwen stellen in **2** (ere)woord[h], gelofte **3** trouw, oprechtheid: *act in good ~* te goeder trouw handelen

faithful 1 gelovig, godsdienstig **2** trouw, loyaal **3** getrouw [replica] **4** betrouwbaar [worker]
faithfully 1 trouw **2** met de hand op het hart || *yours ~* hoogachtend
faith healer gebedsgenezer
faithless 1 ontrouw **2** onbetrouwbaar, vals
¹fake (n) **1** vervalsing, kopie **2** oplichter, bedrieger
²fake (adj) namaak-, vals; vervalst [jewel, painting]
³fake (vb) **1** voorwenden; doen alsof [illness, surprise]: *a ~d robbery* een in scène gezette overval **2** namaken; vervalsen [painting, signature]
falcon valk
¹fall (n) **1** val, smak, het vallen; [fig] ondergang; verderf[h]: *the Fall (of man)* de zondeval **2** afname, daling; verval[h] [of river]; het zakken [of prices, temperature] **3** (-s) waterval **4** [Am] herfst, najaar[h]
²fall (vb) **1** vallen, omvallen; invallen [nightfall]; afnemen; dalen [of prices, barometer, voice]; aflopen; afhellen [of land]: *~ to pieces* in stukken vallen [also fig]; *the wind fell* de wind nam af, de wind ging liggen; *~ apart* uiteenvallen; [inform] instorten; *sth. to ~ back on* iets om op terug te vallen; *~ over* omvallen; [inform] *~ over backwards* zich uitsloven, zich in allerlei bochten wringen; *~ through* mislukken **2** ten onder gaan, vallen, sneuvelen; ingenomen worden [of town, fortress]; zijn (hoge) positie verliezen: *~ from power* de macht verliezen **3** betrekken [of face] **4** terechtkomen, neerkomen; [fig] ten deel vallen: *it fell to me to put the question* het was aan mij de vraag te stellen **5** raken: *~ behind with* achterpraken met || *Easter always ~s on a Sunday* Pasen valt altijd op zondag; *~ asleep* in slaap vallen, mislukken; *~ flat* niet inslaan, mislukken; *~ short (of)* tekortschieten (voor), niet voldoen (aan)
³fall (vb) worden: *~ ill* ziek worden; *~ silent* stil worden
fallacy 1 denkfout, drogreden **2** vergissing
fall down 1 (neer)vallen, instorten, ten val komen **2** [inform] mislukken, tekortschieten: *~ on sth.* (or: *the job*) er niets van bakken
fallen 1 gevallen **2** zondig: *~ angel* (or: *woman*) gevallen engel (or: vrouw) **3** gesneuveld
fall guy [Am; inform] **1** slachtoffer[h] **2** zondebok
fall in 1 instorten, invallen **2** [mil] aantreden, zich in het gelid opstellen
falling-out [inform] ruzie
fall out 1 (+ with) ruzie maken (met) **2** gebeuren, terechtkomen, uitkomen
fall-out 1 radioactieve neerslag **2** het uitvallen, het ophouden

fallow braak, onbewerkt: *lie* ~ braak liggen [also fig]
fallow deer damhertʰ
fall to 1 de verantwoordelijkheid zijn van **2** [form] beginnen met
false 1 onjuist, fout, verkeerd: ~ *pride* ongerechtvaardigde trots; *true* or ~? waar of onwaar? **2** onecht, kunstmatig: ~ *teeth* kunstgebit; *a* ~ *beard* een valse baard **3** bedrieglijk, onbetrouwbaar: ~ *alarm* loos alarm; ~ *bottom* dubbele bodem; *under* ~ *pretences* onder valse voorwendsels
falsehood onwaarheid; leugen
falsify 1 vervalsen, falsificeren **2** verkeerd voorstellen [event] **3** weerleggen [prophecy]
falter 1 wankelen, waggelen **2** aarzelen, weifelen **3** stotteren, stamelen: *Vic's voice* ~*ed* Vics stem beefde
fame 1 roem, bekendheid **2** (goede) naam, reputatie: *of ill* ~ berucht
familiar 1 vertrouwd, bekend, gewoon: *doesn't that look* ~ *to you?* komt dat je niet bekend voor? **2** (+ with) op de hoogte (van), bekend (met) **3** informeel, ongedwongen **4** vrijpostig
familiarity 1 vertrouwdheid, bekendheid: ~ *breeds contempt* wat vertrouwd is wordt gemakkelijk doodgewoon **2** ongedwongenheid **3** vrijpostigheid, vrijheid
familiarize bekendmaken; vertrouwd maken: ~ *o.s. with* zich eigen maken
family 1 (huis)gezinʰ, kinderen, gezinsleden **2** familie(leden), geslachtʰ: *run in the* ~ in de familie zitten **3** afkomst, afstamming, familie
family doctor huisarts
famine 1 hongersnood **2** tekortʰ, schaarste, gebrekʰ
famish (laten) verhongeren, uitgehongerd zijn: *the men were* ~*ed* de mannen waren uitgehongerd
famous (+ for) beroemd (om), (wel)bekend
¹fan (n) **1** waaier **2** ventilator, fan **3** bewonderaar(ster), enthousiast, fan
²fan (vb) **1** (toe)waaien; blazen [air]; toewuiven [cool] **2** aanblazen; aanwakkeren [also fig]: ~ *the flames* het vuur aanwakkeren, olie op het vuur gooien
fanatic fanatiekeling(e)
fanaticism fanatismeʰ
fanciful 1 fantasievol; rijk aan fantasie [style, writer] **2** denkbeeldig, verzonnen, ingebeeld
¹fancy (n) **1** fantasie, verbeelding(skracht), inbeelding **2** voorkeur, voorliefde, zin: *a passing* ~ een bevlieging **3** veronderstelling, ideeʰ, fantasie
²fancy (adj) **1** versierd, decoratief, elegant: ~ *cakes* taartjes; ~ *dress* kostuum; ~ *goods* fantasiegoed, snuisterijen **2** grillig; buitensporig [prices] **3** verzonnen, denkbeeldig

³fancy (vb) **1** zich voorstellen, zich indenken **2** vermoeden, geloven: ~ *that!* stel je voor!, niet te geloven! **3** leuk vinden, zin hebben in: ~ *a girl* op een meisje vallen; ~ *some peanuts?* wil je wat pinda's?; ~ *o.s.* een hoge dunk van zichzelf hebben
fancy woman [inform] minnares
fang hoektand; snijtand [of dog or wolf]; giftand [of snake]; slagtand
fantasize fantaseren
fantastic 1 grillig, bizar **2** denkbeeldig **3** enorm, fantastisch, geweldig
fantasy 1 verbeelding, fantasie **2** illusie, fantasie
FAQ *frequently asked questions* vraagbaak; veelgestelde vragen
¹far (adj) ver, (ver)afgelegen: *at the* ~ *end of* the room aan het andere eind van de kamer
²far (adv) **1** ver: ~ *and near* overal; *so* ~ (tot) zó ver, in zoverre; ~ *from easy* verre van makkelijk; *in so* ~ *as*, *as* ~ *as* voor zover; *as* ~ *as I can see* volgens mij **2** lang; ver: *so* ~ tot nu toe; *so* ~ *so good* tot nu toe is alles nog goed gegaan **3** veel, verreweg: ~ *too easy* veel te makkelijk
faraway 1 (ver)afgelegen, ver **2** afwezig, dromerig; ver [of look]
farce 1 klucht **2** schijnvertoning, zinloos gedoeʰ
¹fare (n) **1** vervoerprijs, ritprijs, vervoerkosten, tariefʰ; [roughly] kaartjeʰ **2** kost, voedselʰ, voerʰ: *simple* ~ eenvoudige kost
²fare (vb) (ver)gaan ‖ *how did you* ~? hoe is het gegaan?; ~ *well* succes hebben, het goed maken
fare dodger [inform] zwartrijder
¹farewell (n) afscheidʰ, vaarwelʰ
²farewell (int) vaarwel, adieu, tot ziens
far-fetched vergezocht
¹farm (n) boerderij, landbouwbedrijfʰ
²farm (vb) boer zijn, boeren, een boerderij hebben
³farm (vb) bewerken, bebouwen; cultiveren [land] ‖ ~ *out a*) uitbesteden [work, child]; *b*) overdragen, afschuiven [responsibility]
farmer boer, landbouwer, agrariër
farmers' market [roughly] boerderijwinkel, [roughly] markt met producten van de boerderij
farm-hand boerenknecht, landarbeider
farmhouse boerenhoeve; boerderij
farming het boerenbedrijf
farmstead boerenhoeve
far-off ver(afgelegen), ver weg, lang geleden
far-out 1 afgelegen, ver weg **2** [inform] uitzonderlijk, uitheems; bizar **3** [inform] fantastisch
far-reaching verstrekkend; verreikend
far-sighted 1 vooruitziend **2** verziend
¹fart (n) [vulg] **1** scheet, wind **2** lul, klootzak

²fart (vb) [vulg] een scheet laten ‖ ~ *about* (or: *around*) klooien, rotzooien
¹farther (adj) verder (weg)
²farther (adv) verder, door, vooruit
farthest verst (weg)
farthing [hist] een vierde penny; [roughly] duit [also fig]
fascinate boeien, fascineren
fascination 1 aantrekkingskracht, charme, bekoring **2** geboeidheid
Fascism fascismeʰ
fascist fascist
¹fashion (n) **1** gebruikʰ, mode, gewoonte: *set* a ~ de toon aangeven; *come into* ~ in de mode raken **2** manier, stijl, trant: *did he change the nappies? yes, after* a ~ heeft hij de baby verschoond? ja, op zijn manier
²fashion (vb) vormen, modelleren, maken
fashionable modieus, in (de mode), populair
¹fast (n) vasten(tijd)
²fast (adj) **1** vast, stevig, hecht: ~ *colours* wasechte kleuren **2** snel, vlug; gevoelig [film]: ~ *food* gemaksvoedsel; ~ *lane* linker rijbaan, inhaalstrook **3** vóór [of clock] ‖ [inform] *make a ~ buck* snel geld verdienen; [inform] *pull* a ~ *one on s.o.* met iem. een vuile streek uithalen, iem. afzetten
³fast (vb) vasten
⁴fast (adv) **1** stevig, vast: ~ *asleep* in diepe slaap; *play* ~ *and loose (with)* het niet zo nauw nemen (met), spelen (met) [s.o.'s feelings] **2** snel, vlug, hard
fasten vastmaken, bevestigen, dichtmaken: ~ *up* one's coat zijn jas dichtdoen
fastener (rits)sluiting; haakjeʰ [of dress]
fastening sluiting, slotʰ; bevestiging [of window, door]
fastidious veeleisend, pietluttig, kieskeurig
fast-track snel; snel promotie makend
¹fat (n) vetʰ, bakvetʰ, lichaamsvetʰ ‖ *the ~ is in the fire* de poppen zijn aan het dansen; *chew the* ~ kletsen
²fat (adj) **1** dik, vet(gemest), weldoorvoed **2** vettig, zwaar; vet [of meat, food] **3** rijk; vruchtbaar [of land]; vet [of clay] **4** groot, dik, lijvig: [iron] a ~ *lot* of good that'll do you daar schiet je geen moer mee op, nou, daar heb je veel aan ‖ [inform] a ~ *cat* a) rijke pief; b) (stille) financier, geldschieter [pol]
fatal 1 (+ to) noodlottig (voor), dodelijk; fataal [of illness, accident] **2** rampzalig [of decision]
fatality 1 slachtofferʰ, dodelijk ongelukʰ **2** noodlottigheid
fatally: see fatal; ~ *injured* dodelijk gewond; *she tried,* ~, *to cross the river* haar poging de rivier over te steken werd haar noodlottig
fate lotʰ, noodlotʰ, bestemming: *as sure as* ~

daar kun je donder op zeggen
fateful noodlottig, rampzalig, belangrijk
fatfree vetarm, vetvrij
fathead sufferd
¹father (n) **1** vader, huisvader **2** grondlegger, stichter
²father (vb) **1** vader zijn van, voor **2** produceren; de geestelijke vader zijn van [eg of plan, book]
Father pater, priester: ~ *Christmas* de Kerstman
fatherhood vaderschapʰ
father-in-law schoonvader
fatherly vaderlijk
fathom vadem; vaam
¹fatigue (n) **1** vermoeidheid; moeheid **2** [mil] corvee
²fatigue (vb) afmatten, vermoeien
fatigues 1 [mil] gevechtstenueʰ **2** strafcorveeʰ
fatten dik(ker) maken: ~ *up* (vet)mesten
¹fatty (n) [inform] vetzak, dikke(rd)
²fatty (adj) vettig, vet(houdend): *(un)saturated* ~ *acids* (on)verzadigde vetzuren
fatuous dom, dwaas, stompzinnig
faucet [Am] kraan
¹fault (n) **1** fout, defectʰ, gebrekʰ **2** overtreding, misstap **3** foute service; fout [tennis] **4** schuld, oorzaak: *at* ~ schuldig **5** [geology] breuk, verschuiving
²fault (vb) aanmerkingen maken op, bekritiseren
fault-finding muggenzifterij
faulty 1 defect, onklaar **2** onjuist, verkeerd, gebrekkig
fauna fauna; dierenwereld
¹favour (n) **1** genegenheid, sympathie, goedkeuring: *be in* (or: *out of*) ~ *with* in de gunst (or: uit de gratie) zijn bij **2** partijdigheid, voorkeur, voortrekkerij **3** gunst, attentie, begunstiging: *do s.o. a* ~ iem. een plezier doen ‖ *do me a* ~! zeg, doe me een lol!
²favour (vb) **1** gunstig gezind zijn, positief staan tegenover, een voorstander zijn van **2** begunstigen, prefereren, bevoorrechten
favourable 1 welwillend, goedgunstig: *the weather is* ~ *to us* het weer zit ons mee **2** gunstig, veelbelovend, positief
¹favourite (n) **1** favoriet(e) **2** lieveling(e)
²favourite (adj) favoriet, lievelings-
favouritism voortrekkerij, vriendjespolitiek
fawn kwispelstaarten ‖ [fig] ~ *(up)on* vleien, kruipen voor
¹fax (n) **1** fax(apparaatʰ) **2** fax(berichtʰ)
²fax (vb) faxen, per fax verzenden
faze van streek maken, in de war doen geraken
¹fear (n) vrees, angst(gevoelʰ): *in* ~ *and trembling* met angst en beven; *go in* ~ *of* bang zijn voor; [inform] *no* ~ beslist niet, geen sprake

van
²fear (vb) **1** vrezen, bang zijn voor **2** vermoeden, een oergevoel hebben van, vrezen: ~ the **worst** het ergste vrezen
fearful 1 vreselijk, afschuwelijk, ontzettend **2** bang, angstig
fearsome afschrikwekkend, ontzaglijk
feasible 1 uitvoerbaar, haalbaar, doenlijk **2** aannemelijk, waarschijnlijk, geloofwaardig
¹feast (n) **1** feest[h] **2** feestmaal[h], banket[h]
²feast (vb) feesten, feestvieren
³feast (vb) onthalen; trakteren [also fig]: ~ one's **eyes** (on) zich verlustigen in de aanblik (van)
feat 1 heldendaad **2** prestatie, knap stuk werk[h]
feather veer; pluim || a ~ in one's cap iets om trots op te zijn, een eer
featherbrained onnozel
featherweight vedergewicht
¹feature (n) **1** (gelaats)trek: ~s gezicht[h] **2** (hoofd)kenmerk[h], hoofdtrek **3** hoogtepunt[h], specialiteit, hoofdnummer[h] **4** speciaal onderwerp[h]; [newspaper] hoofdartikel[h]
²feature (vb) een (belangrijke) plaats innemen, opvallen
feature film speelfilm, hoofdfilm
featureless kleurloos; saai, onopvallend
February februari
feckless lamlendig, futloos
fecundity 1 vruchtbaarheid **2** productiviteit
federal 1 federaal; bonds- **2** [esp Am] nationaal; regerings-: ~ **government** centrale regering; landsregering
Federal 1 federaal, bonds- **2** [Am] nationaal, lands-, regerings-
federation 1 federatie, statenbond **2** bond, federatie, overkoepelend orgaan[h]
fed up [inform] zat, beu, ontevreden: be ~ with sth. van iets balen, het zat (or: beu) zijn
fee 1 honorarium[h] [eg of doctor, lawyer] **2** inschrijfgeld[h], lidmaatschapsgeld[h] **3** (-s) schoolgeld[h], collegegeld[h]
feeble 1 zwak, teer; krachteloos [of creatures] **2** flauw, slap; zwak [eg of excuse, joke]: a ~ **effort** een halfhartige poging
feeble-minded 1 zwakzinnig, zwak begaafd **2** dom
¹feed (n) **1** voeding [of animal, baby]; voedering **2** (vee)voer[h], groenvoer[h]
²feed (vb) eten; zich voeden; grazen, weiden: ~ **on** leven van, zich voeden met [also fig]
³feed (vb) **1** voeren, (te) eten geven, voederen: ~ **up** vetmesten, volstoppen **2** voedsel geven aan; [fig] stimuleren [imagination] **3** [esp technology] aanvoeren [raw materials]; toevoeren: ~ coins **into** the pay phone munten in de telefoon stoppen

feedback terugkoppeling, antwoord[h], reactie, feedback
¹feel (n) **1** het voelen, betasting **2** aanleg, gevoel[h], feeling **3** routine: get the ~ of sth. iets in zijn vingers krijgen
²feel (vb) **1** (rond)tasten, (rond)zoeken **2** voelen **3** gevoelens hebben, een mening hebben
³feel (vb) **1** voelen, gewaarworden **2** voelen (aan), betasten: ~ s.o.'s **pulse** iem. de pols voelen [also fig]; ~ one's **way** op de tast gaan [also fig] **3** voelen, gewaarworden: ~ the **effects** of lijden onder de gevolgen van **4** voelen, aanvoelen, de indruk krijgen: I ~ it necessary to deny that ik vind het nodig dat te ontkennen **5** vinden, menen: it was felt that ... men was de mening toegedaan dat ...
⁴feel (vb) **1** zich voelen: I felt such a **fool** ik voelde me zo stom; ~ **cold** (or: **warm**) het koud (or: warm) hebben; ~ **small** zich klein voelen; I ~ **like** sleeping ik heb zin om te slapen; I ~ **like** a walk ik heb zin een wandelingetje **2** aanvoelen, een gevoel geven, voelen
feeler tastorgaan[h], voelhoorn, voelspriet; [fig] proefballonnetjes: put (or: throw) out ~s een balletje opgooien
feel-good positief; een goed gevoel gevend
feeling 1 gevoel[h], gewaarwording: a **sinking** ~ een benauwd gevoel **2** emotie, gevoel[h]: ~s gevoelens; **hurt** s.o.'s ~s iem. kwetsen; **mixed** ~s gemengde gevoelens **3** idee[h], gevoel[h], indruk **4** aanleg, gevoel[h]: a ~ **for** colour een gevoel voor kleur **5** opinie, mening, geloof[h] **6** opwinding, ontstemming, wrok: ~s **ran** high de gemoederen raakten verhit **7** gevoel[h]: have lost all ~ in one's **fingers** alle gevoel in zijn vingers kwijt zijn
feign veinzen, simuleren: ~ed **indifference** gespeelde onverschilligheid
felicitous [form] welgekozen; gelukkig
felicity geluk[h], gelukzaligheid || **express** o.s. with ~ zijn woorden goed weten te kiezen
feline 1 katachtig **2** katten-
fell omhakken, kappen; [fig] he ~ed his **opponent** at a blow hij velde zijn tegenstander met één klap
¹fellow (n) **1** kerel, vent **2** maat, kameraad **3** wederhelft; andere helft [of pair]: a sock and **its** ~ een sok en de bijbehorende (sok) **4** lid[h] van universiteitsbestuur
²fellow (adj) mede-, collega, -genoot
fellowship 1 genootschap[h] **2** broederschap, verbond[h] **3** omgang, gezelschap[h] **4** vriendschap, kameraadschap(pelijkheid): ~ in misfortune vriendschap in tegenspoed **5** [educ] beurs, toelage
felony (ernstig) misdrijf[h], zware misdaad
felt vilt[h]: ~ **pen** viltstift
felt-tip pen viltstift

fem *feminine* vrl., vrouwelijk
¹female (n) **1** vrouwelijk persoon, vrouw **2** wijfjeʰ, vrouwtjeʰ **3** vrouwspersoon
²female (adj) vrouwelijk, wijfjes- ‖ ~ *suffrage* vrouwenkiesrecht
¹feminine (n) de vrouwelijke vorm; vrouwelijkʰ
²feminine (adj) vrouwen-, vrouwelijk
feminism feminismeʰ
feminist feministe
fen moeras(land)ʰ
¹fence (n) **1** hekʰ, omheining, afscheiding: [fig] *be* (or: *sit*) *on the* ~ geen partij kiezen **2** heler
²fence (vb) [sport] schermen
³fence (vb) omheinen: ~ *in* afrasteren; [fig] inperken
fend: ~ *off* afweren [blow]; ontwijken [question]; ~ *for o.s.* voor zichzelf zorgen
fender 1 stootrand, stootkussenʰ; [Am] bumper **2** [Am] spatbordʰ **3** haardschermʰ
fennel venkel
feral wild
¹ferment (n) **1** gist(middelʰ) **2** onrust, opwinding
²ferment (vb) **1** (ver)gisten, (doen) fermenteren **2** in beroering zijn (brengen); onrustig zijn (maken)
fern varen
ferocious woest, ruw, wild, meedogenloos
ferocity woestheid, ruwheid, gewelddadigheid
¹ferret (n) fret
²ferret (vb) rommelen, snuffelen: ~ *about* (or: *around*) *among s.o.'s papers* in iemands papieren rondsnuffelen ‖ ~ *out* uitvissen, uitzoeken
Ferris wheel reuzenradʰ
¹ferry (n) **1** veerʰ, veerboot, pont **2** veerdienst; veer
²ferry (vb) **1** overzetten, overvaren **2** vervoeren: ~ *children* to and from a party kinderen naar een feestje brengen en ophalen
ferryboat veerboot
fertile 1 vruchtbaar **2** rijk (voorzien), overvloedig: ~ *imagination* rijke verbeelding
fertility vruchtbaarheid
fertilize 1 bevruchten, insemineren **2** vruchtbaar maken, bemesten
fertilizer (kunst)mest
fervent vurig, hartstochtelijk, fervent
fervour heftigheid, hartstocht, vurigheid
fester 1 zweren, etteren **2** knagen; irriteren
festival 1 feestʰ, feestelijkheid **2** muziekfeestʰ, festivalʰ
festive feestelijk: *the* ~ *season* de feestdagen
festivity feestelijkheid, festiviteit
festoon met slingers versieren
fetch 1 halen, brengen, afhalen **2** tevoor-

schijn brengen; trekken [audience, tears] **3** opbrengen [money]: *the painting* ~ed £100 het schilderij ging voor 100 pond weg
fetching leuk, aantrekkelijk, aardig
fete feestʰ, festijnʰ
fetish fetisj
fetter keten, boei, ketting
feud vete, onenigheid, ruzie
feudal feodaal, leen-
feudalism leenstelselʰ
fever 1 opwinding, agitatie, spanning: *in a* ~ *of anticipation* in opgewonden afwachting **2** koorts, verhoging
fever blister koortslip
few 1 weinige(n), weinig, enkele(n), een paar: *holidays are* ~ *and far between* feestdagen zijn er maar weinig; *a* ~ een paar, enkele(n) **2** weinig, een paar: *a* ~ *words* een paar woorden; *every* ~ *days* om de zoveel dagen ‖ [inform] *there were a good* ~ er waren er nogal wat; *quite a* ~ vrij veel; *quite a* ~ *books* nogal wat boeken
ff *following* e.v., en volgende(n)
fiancé verloofde
fiasco mislukking, fiascoʰ
fib leugentjeʰ; *tell* ~s jokken
fibre 1 vezel **2** draad **3** kwaliteit, sterkte, karakterʰ: *moral* ~ ruggengraat
fibreglass fiberglasʰ, glasvezel
fickle wispelturig, grillig
fiction verzinselʰ, verdichtselʰ, fictie
fictional roman-: ~ *character* romanfiguur
fictitious 1 onecht **2** verzonnen; bedacht [story]; gefingeerd [name, address] **3** denkbeeldig; fictief [event]
¹fiddle (n) viool, fiedel ‖ *play second* ~ *(to)* in de schaduw staan (van)
²fiddle (vb) [inform] **1** vioolspelen, fiedelen **2** lummelen: ~ *about* (or: *around*) rondlummelen **3** friemelen, spelen: ~ *with* morrelen aan, spelen met
³fiddle (vb) **1** spelen **2** [inform] foezelen met, vervalsen, bedrog plegen met: ~ *one's taxes* met zijn belastingaangifte knoeien
fiddlesticks lariekoek, kletskoek
fiddling onbeduidend, nietig: ~ *little screws* pietepeuterige schroefjes
fidelity 1 (natuur)getrouwheid, precisie **2** (+ to) trouw (aan/jegens), loyaliteit
¹fidget (n) zenuwlijer, iem. die niet stil kan zitten
²fidget (vb) de kriebels hebben, niet stil kunnen zitten: ~ *with one's pen* met zijn pen friemelen
¹field (n) **1** veldʰ, landʰ, weide, akker, vlakte, sportveldʰ, sportterreinʰ, gebiedʰ **2** arbeidsveldʰ, gebiedʰ, branche: ~ *of study* onderwerp (van studie) **3** [elec, physics] (kracht)veldʰ, draagwijdte, invloedssfeer, reikwijdte: *magnetic* ~ magnetisch veld **4** bezetting; veldʰ, alle deelnemers, jachtpartij, jachtstoet

5 concurrentie, veld[h]; andere deelnemers: *play* the ~ fladderen, van de een naar de ander lopen
²**field** (vb) [sport] in het veld brengen; uitkomen met
field day schooluitstapje[h], excursie || *have a* ~ volop genieten
field glasses veldkijker, verrekijker
field hockey hockey[h]
Field Marshal [mil] veldmaarschalk
field-test in de praktijk testen
field trip uitstapje[h], excursie
fiend 1 duivel, demon, kwade geest **2** [in compounds] fanaat, maniak
fierce 1 woest, wreed **2** hevig: ~ *dislike* intense afkeer
fiery 1 brandend, vurig **2** onstuimig, vurig, opvliegend: ~ *temperament* fel temperament
fifteen vijftien
fifteenth vijftiende
fifth vijfde; [mus] kwint
fiftieth vijftigste
fifty vijftig: *a man in his fifties* een man van in de vijftig
fifty-fifty half om half, fiftyfifty: *go* ~ *with s.o.* met iem. samsam doen
fig 1 vijg **2** vijgenboom || *not care* (or: *give*) *a* ~ *(for)* geen bal geven (om)
¹**fight** (n) **1** gevecht[h], strijd, vechtpartij: *a* ~ *to the finish* een gevecht tot het bittere einde **2** vechtlust, strijdlust: *(still) have plenty of* ~ *in one* zijn vechtlust (nog lang) niet kwijt zijn
²**fight** (vb) **1** vechten, strijden: ~ *to a finish* tot het bittere eind doorvechten **2** ruziën
³**fight** (vb) bestrijden, strijden tegen: ~ *off sth.* ergens weerstand tegen bieden; ~ *it out* het uitvechten
fighter vechter, strijder, vechtersbaas
¹**fighting** (n) het vechten, gevechten
²**fighting** (adj) strijdbaar, uitgerust voor de strijd: ~ *spirit* vechtlust || *he has a* ~ *chance* als hij alles op alles zet lukt het hem misschien
figment verzinsel[h]: ~ *of the imagination* hersenspinsel
figurative figuurlijk
¹**figure** (n) **1** vorm, contour, omtrek, gedaante, gestalte, figuur[h] **2** afbeelding; [maths] figuur[h]; motief[h]: [maths] *solid* ~ lichaam **3** personage[h]: ~ *of fun* mikpunt van plagerij **4** cijfer[h]: *double* ~*s* getal van twee cijfers **5** bedrag[h], waarde, prijs
²**figure** (vb) **1** voorkomen, een rol spelen, gezien worden: ~ *in a book* in een boek voorkomen **2** [Am; inform] vanzelf spreken, logisch zijn: *that* ~*s* dat ligt voor de hand, dat zit er wel in
³**figure** (vb) [Am; inform] denken, menen, geloven
figurehead 1 [shipp] boegbeeld[h] **2** [fig] leider in naam, stroman

figure out 1 berekenen, becijferen, uitwerken **2** [Am] uitpuzzelen, doorkrijgen: *be unable to figure a* **person** *out* geen hoogte van iem. kunnen krijgen
figure skating kunstrijden[h]
Fiji Fiji
¹**Fijian** (n) Fijiër, Fijische
²**Fijian** (adj) Fijisch
filament 1 fijne draad **2** [elec] gloeidraad
filch jatten, gappen
¹**file** (n) **1** vijl **2** dossier[h], register[h], legger **3** (dossier)map, ordner, klapper **4** [comp] bestand[h] **5** rij, file: *in single* ~ in ganzenmars
²**file** (vb) in een rij lopen, achter elkaar lopen
³**file** (vb) **1** vijlen, bijvijlen; bijschaven [also fig]: ~ *sth. smooth* iets gladvijlen **2** opslaan, archiveren: ~ *away* opbergen
filial kinder-: ~ *piety* respect voor de ouders
filibuster vertragingstactiek
¹**Filipino** (n) Filipino; Filipijn
²**Filipino** (adj) Filipijns
¹**fill** (n) vulling, hele portie: *eat one's* ~ zich rond eten
²**fill** (vb) **1** (op)vullen, vol maken: ~ *a gap* een leemte opvullen **2** vervullen, bezetten, bekleden: ~ *a vacancy* een vacature bezetten
filler vulling, vulsel[h], vulstof, plamuur[h]
fillet filet[+h], lendenstuk[h], haas: ~ *of pork* varkenshaas
fill in 1 invullen [form] **2** passeren: ~ *time* de tijd doden **3** (+ on) [inform] op de hoogte brengen (van), briefen (over) **4** dichtgooien, dempen
¹**filling** (n) vulling, vulsel[h]
²**filling** (adj) machtig, voedzaam: *that pancake was rather* ~ die pannenkoek lag nogal zwaar op de maag
filling station benzinestation[h], tankstation[h]
fill out 1 opvullen, groter (dikker) maken: ~ *a story* een verhaaltje uitbouwen **2** [Am] invullen [form]
¹**fill up** (vb) **1** zich vullen, vollopen, dichtslibben **2** benzine tanken
²**fill up** (vb) **1** (op)vullen; vol doen [tank]; bijvullen **2** invullen [form]
filly merrieveulen[h], jonge merrie
¹**film** (n) **1** dunne laag, vlies[h]: *a* ~ *of dust* een dun laagje stof **2** rolfilm, film **3** (speel)film
²**film** (vb) **1** filmen; opnemen **2** verfilmen, een film maken van
filmy dun, doorzichtig
¹**filter** (n) filter[h], filtertoestel[h], filtreertoestel[h]
²**filter** (vb) uitlekken, doorsijpelen, doorschemeren: *the news* ~*ed out* het nieuws lekte uit
³**filter** (vb) filtreren, zeven, zuiveren
filth 1 vuiligheid, vuil[h], viezigheid **2** vuile taal, smerige taal
filthy 1 vies, vuil, smerig **2** schunnig || ~ *lu-*

cre vuil gewin, poen
fin 1 vin **2** vinvormig voorwerp[h], zwemvlies[h], kielvlak[h], stabilisatievlak[h]
¹final (n) **1** finale, eindwedstrijd **2** (-s) (laatste) eindexamen[h]: *take one's ~s* eindexamen
doen
²final (adj) **1** definitief, finaal, beslissend
2 laatste, eind-, slot-: *give* (or: *put*) *the ~*
touch(es) *to* de laatste hand leggen aan
finalize tot een einde brengen, de laatste
hand leggen aan, afronden
finally 1 ten slotte, uiteindelijk **2** afdoend,
definitief, beslissend: *it was ~ decided* er
werd definitief besloten
¹finance (n) **1** financieel beheer[h], geldwe-
zen[h], financiën **2** (-s) geldmiddelen, fondsen
²finance (vb) financieren, bekostigen
financial financieel: *~ year* boekjaar
finch vink
¹find (n) (goede) vondst
²find (vb) [law] oordelen
³find (vb) **1** vinden, ontdekken, terugvinden:
*he was found **dead*** hij werd dood aangetroffen **2** (be)vinden, (be)oordelen (als), ontdekken; blijken; [law] oordelen; verklaren, uitspreken: *it was found that all the vases were
broken* alle vazen bleken gebroken te zijn; *be
found **wanting*** niet voldoen, tekortschieten,
te licht bevonden worden; *the jury found him
not **guilty*** de gezworenen spraken het onschuldig over hem uit
finder vinder: *~s **keepers*** wie wat vindt,
mag het houden
finding 1 vondst **2** [esp law] bevinding;
uitspraak
find out 1 ontdekken, erachter komen
2 betrappen ǁ *be found out* door de mand
vallen
¹fine (n) (geld)boete
²fine (adj) **1** fijn, dun, scherp: *the ~ **print*** de
kleine lettertjes **2** voortreffelijk, fijn: *that's all
very ~* allemaal goed en wel **3** fijn, goed: *~
workmanship* goed vakmanschap **4** in orde,
gezond: *I'm ~, thanks* met mij gaat het goed,
dank je ǁ *~ **arts*** beeldende kunst(en); *one of
these ~ **days*** vandaag of morgen; *not to put
too ~ a **point*** (or: *an **edge***) *on it* zonder er
doekjes om te winden
³fine (vb) beboeten
⁴fine (adv) **1** fijn, in orde: *it **suits** me ~* ik vind
het prima **2** fijn, dun: *cut up onions ~* uien
fijn snipperen
finery opschik, opsmuk, mooie kleren
fine-tooth comb stofkam; luizenkam:
[fig] *go over sth. **with** a ~* iets grondig onderzoeken
finger vinger ǁ [inform] ***work** one's ~s to the
bone* zich kapot werken; [inform] *have a ~ in
every **pie*** overal een vinger in de pap hebben;
*be all ~s and **thumbs*** twee linkerhanden hebben, erg onhandig zijn; ***burn** one's ~s* zijn

vingers branden; [inform] ***cross** one's ~s, keep
one's ~s **crossed*** duimen; *have one's ~s in the
till* geld stelen uit de kas (van de winkel waar
men werkt); *not be able to **put*** (or: ***lay***) *one's ~
on sth.* iets niet kunnen plaatsen; *not **lift*** (or:
move, raise, stir) *a ~* geen vinger uitsteken;
*let slip **through** one's ~s* door de vingers laten
glippen; ***twist*** (or: ***wind***) *s.o. **round** one's (little)
~ iem. om zijn vinger winden
fingermark (vuile) vinger(afdruk)
fingerprint vingerafdruk
fingertip vingertop ǁ *have sth. **at** one's ~s*
iets heel goed kennen
finicky 1 pietepeuterig **2** [depr] pietluttig;
kieskeurig
¹finish (n) beëindiging, einde[h], voltooiing:
*be in **at** the ~* [fig] bij het einde aanwezig zijn;
*(fight) **to** the ~* tot het bittere einde (doorvechten)
²finish (vb) **1** eindigen, tot een einde komen, uit zijn: *the film ~es **at** 11 p.m.* de film is
om 11 uur afgelopen; *~ **off*** eindigen
met; *we used to ~ **up** with a glass of port* we
namen altijd een glas port om de maaltijd af
te ronden **2** uiteindelijk terechtkomen, belanden: *he will ~ **up** in jail* hij zal nog in de gevangenis belanden
³finish (vb) **1** (often + off) beëindigen, afmaken, een einde maken aan: *~ a **book*** een
boek uitlezen **2** (often + off, up) opgebruiken, opeten, opdrinken **3** afwerken, voltooien, de laatste hand leggen aan: *~ (up)
cleaning* ophouden met schoonmaken
finished 1 (goed) afgewerkt, verzorgd,
kunstig **2** klaar, af: *those days are ~* die tijden
zijn voorbij **3** geruïneerd, uitgeput: *he is ~ **as**
a politician* als politicus is hij er geweest
finishing school etiquetteschool
finishing touch laatste hand: *put the ~es
to* de laatste hand leggen aan
finite eindig, begrensd, beperkt
finite verb [linguistics] persoonsvorm
Finland Finland
Finn Fin(se)
Finnish Fins
fir 1 spar(renboom) **2** sparrenhout[h], vurenhout[h]
¹fire (n) **1** vuur[h], haard(vuur[h]): *catch ~* vlam
vatten **2** brand: *set on ~, set ~ to* in brand
steken; *on ~* in brand; [fig] in vuur (en vlam)
3 het vuren, vuur[h]; schot[h] [of gun]: *be* (or:
come) ***under** ~* onder vuur genomen worden
[also fig] **4** kachel ǁ ***play** with ~* met vuur spelen; *~! brand!*
²fire (vb) **1** in brand steken; doen ontvlammen [also fig]: *it ~d him **with** enthusiasm* het
zette hem in vuur en vlam **2** [inform] de laan
uitsturen, ontslaan ǁ *~ **up*** bezielen, stimuleren
³fire (vb) **1** stoken, brandend houden: *oil-
fired**furnace*** oliekachel, petroleumkachel

2 bakken [pottery] **3** schieten; (af)vuren [also fig]: ~ *questions* vragen afvuren
firearm vuurwapen[h]
firebrand brandhout[h]
fire brigade brandweer(korps[h])
firecracker voetzoeker
fire drill brandweeroefening
fire engine brandspuit; brandweerauto
fire escape 1 brandtrap **2** brandladder
fire exit nooduitgang, branddeur
firefighter brandbestrijder, brandweerman
firefly glimworm
fire hydrant brandkraan
fireman 1 brandweerman **2** stoker
fireplace 1 open haard **2** schoorsteen, schouw
fireproof vuurbestendig, brandveilig
the **fireside** (hoekje bij de) haard ‖ ~ *chat* informeel gesprek
fire station brandweerkazerne
fire wall 1 brandmuur **2** [comp] firewall
fireworks vuurwerk
firing line vuurlinie, vuurlijn [also fig]
¹firm (n) firma
²firm (adj) **1** vast, stevig, hard: *be on ~ ground* vaste grond onder de voeten hebben [also fig] **2** standvastig, resoluut: ~ *decision* definitieve beslissing; *take a ~ line* zich (kei)hard opstellen
³firm (adv) stevig, standvastig: *stand ~ op* zijn stuk blijven
¹first (adv) **1** eerst: *he told her ~* hij vertelde het eerst aan haar; ~ *and foremost* in de eerste plaats, bovenal; ~ *of all* in de eerste plaats, om te beginnen **2** liever, eerder: *she'd die ~ rather than give in* ze zou eerder sterven dan toe te geven
²first (num) eerste deel, begin: *at ~* aanvankelijk, eerst ‖ *she came out ~* ze behaalde de eerste plaats; ~ *form* eerste klas, [roughly] brugklas [school]; *I'll take the ~ train* ik neem de eerstvolgende trein
first-aid eerstehulp-, EHBO-: ~ *box* (or: *kit*) EHBO-doos
first-degree eerstegraads: [law] ~ *murder* moord met voorbedachten rade
firsthand uit de eerste hand
first name voornaam: *be on ~ terms* elkaar bij de voornaam noemen
first-rate prima, eersterangs
first school [roughly] onderbouw
fiscal fiscaal, belasting(s)-: ~ *year* boekjaar; belastingjaar
¹fish (n) vis, zeedier[h]: ~ *and chips* (gebakken) vis met patat ‖ *like a ~ out of water* als een vis op het droge; [inform] *drink like a ~* drinken als een tempelier; *have other ~ to fry* wel wat anders te doen hebben
²fish (vb) vissen [also fig]; hengelen, raden
³fish (vb) (be)vissen: ~ *out a piece of paper*

from a bag een papiertje uit een tas opdiepen
fisherman visser, sportvisser
fish finger visstick
fishing rod hengel
fishing tackle vistuig[h], visbenodigdheden
fishmonger vishandelaar, visboer
fishwife visvrouw; [depr] viswijf[h]
fishy 1 visachtig **2** [inform] verdacht: *a ~ story* een verhaal met een luchtje eraan
fission splijting, deling; [biology] (cel)deling; [physics] (kern)splitsing
fissure spleet; kloof
fist vuist
¹fit (n) **1** vlaag, opwelling, inval: *by* (or: *in*) ~*s* *(and starts)* bij vlagen **2** aanval, stuip; toeval[h] [also fig]: *a ~ of coughing* een hoestbui; *give s.o. a ~* iem. de stuipen op het lijf jagen
²fit (adj) **1** geschikt, passend: *a ~ person to do sth.* de juiste persoon om iets te doen **2** gezond, fit, in (goede) conditie: *as ~ as a fiddle* kiplekker, zo gezond als een vis **3** gepast: *think* (or: *see*) ~ *to do sth.* het juist achten (om) iets te doen **4** [inform] knap; seksueel aantrekkelijk
³fit (adj) geschikt zijn, passen, goed zitten: *it ~s like a glove* het zit als gegoten
⁴fit (vb) **1** passen, voegen **2** aanbrengen, monteren: *have a new lock ~ted* een nieuw slot laten aanbrengen
¹fit in (vb) (goed) aangepast zijn, zich aanpassen aan: ~ *with your ideas* in overeenstemming zijn met jouw ideeën; ~ *with our plans* stroken met onze plannen
²fit in (vb) **1** inpassen, plaats (tijd) vinden voor **2** aanpassen: *fit sth. in with sth.* iets ergens bij aanpassen
fitness 1 het passend zijn: ~ *for a job* geschiktheid voor een baan **2** fitheid, goede conditie
fitness steps steps
fitted 1 (volledig) uitgerust, compleet: ~ *kitchen* volledig uitgeruste keuken; ~ *with* (uitgerust) met, voorzien van **2** vast: ~ *carpet* vaste vloerbedekking ‖ ~ *sheet* hoeslaken
fitter monteur, installateur
fitting 1 [techn] hulpstuk[h], accessoire[h] **2** [fashion] maat
fit up [inform] onderdak verlenen: *fit s.o. up with a bed* iem. onderdak verlenen
five vijf: *give me ~* geef me er vijf (van); [fig] geef me de vijf
fivefold vijfvoudig
fiver [inform] briefje[h] van vijf
¹fix (n) **1** moeilijke situatie, knel: *be in* (or: *get o.s. into*) *a ~* in de knel zitten (*or:* raken) **2** doorgestoken kaart, afgesproken werk[h]: *the election was a ~* de verkiezingen waren doorgestoken kaart **3** shot, dosis
²fix (vb) **1** vastmaken, bevestigen, monteren: ~ *sth. in the mind* (or: *memory*) iets in de geest (*or:* in het geheugen) prenten **2** vasthouden;

trekken [attention]; fixeren [eyes]: ~ *one's eyes* (or: *attention*) **(up)on** *sth.* de blik (*or:* aandacht) vestigen op iets **3** vastleggen, bepalen; afspreken [price, date, place] **4** regelen, schikken: [depr] *the whole thing was ~ed* het was allemaal doorgestoken kaart **5** opknappen, repareren, in orde brengen **6** [Am] bereiden; maken [meal, drink]: ~ *sth.* **up** iets klaarmaken

fixation 1 bevestiging, bepaling **2** [psychology] fixatie

fixed 1 vast: ~ *idea* idee-fixe **2** voorzien van: *how are you ~ for beer?* hoe staat het met je voorraad bier?

fixed-term voor bepaalde duur: ~ *contract* tijdelijk contract

fixer tussenpersoon

fixings [Am; inform] **1** uitrusting, toebehoren **2** garnering; versiering

fix up regelen, organiseren, voorzien van: *fix s.o. up with a job* iem. aan een baan(tje) helpen

1fizz (n) **1** gebruis[h], gesis[h], geschuim[h] **2** [inform] mousserende drank, champagne

2fizz (vb) sissen, (op)bruisen, mousseren

fizzle (zachtjes) sissen, (zachtjes) bruisen ‖ [inform] ~ *out* met een sisser aflopen

fizzy bruisend, sissend, mousserend

flabbergast [inform] verstomd doen staan, verbijsteren, overdonderen: *be ~ed at* (or: *by*) verstomd staan door

flabby slap; zwak

flaccid slap, zwak, zacht

1flag (n) **1** vlag, vaandel[h], vlaggetje[h]: ~ *of convenience* goedkope vlag; *show the* ~ [fig] je gezicht laten zien **2** lisbloem ‖ *keep the* ~ *flying* doorgaan met de strijd, volharden

2flag (vb) verslappen; verflauwen

3flag (vb) **1** met vlaggen versieren (markeren) **2** doen stoppen (met zwaaibewegingen), aanhouden, aanroepen: ~ *(down) a taxi* een taxi aanroepen

flag-day collectedag, speldjesdag

flagon 1 schenkkan, flacon **2** kan, fles

flagpole vlaggenstok, vlaggenmast

flagrant flagrant, in het oog springend

flagship vlaggenschip[h]; [fig also] paradepaardje[h]

flagstaff vlaggenstok, vlaggenmast

1flail (n) (dors)vlegel

2flail (vb) **1** dorsen **2** wild zwaaien (met): *the boy ~ed his arms in the air* de jongen maaide met zijn armen in de lucht

flair flair, feeling, fijne neus, bijzondere handigheid

flak 1 [mil] (granaten voor) luchtafweergeschut **2** [inform] scherpe kritiek

1flake (n) vlok, sneeuwvlok, schilfer; bladder

2flake (vb) (doen) (af)schilferen, (doen) pellen ‖ [inform] ~ *out* **a)** omvallen van vermoeidheid; **b)** gaan slapen; **c)** flauwvallen

flaky 1 vlokkig **2** schilferachtig **3** [Am; inform] geschift **4** [inform] onbetrouwbaar, onstabiel

flamboyant 1 bloemrijk **2** schitterend, vlammend **3** opzichtig, zwierig

1flame (n) **1** vlam, gloed: ~*s* vuur[h]; hitte; *burst into ~(s)* in brand vliegen **2** geliefde, liefde, passie

2flame (vb) vlammen, ontvlammen; opvlammen ‖ ~ *out* (or: *up*) (razend) opvliegen, (razend) opstuiven

flammable brandbaar, explosief

flan [roughly] kleine vla(ai)

Flanders Vlaanderen

1flank (n) zijkant, flank

2flank (vb) flankeren: ~*ed by* (or: *with*) *trees* met bomen erlangs

flannel 1 flanel[h] **2** (flanellen) doekje[h], washandje[h] **3** [inform] mooi praatje[h], vleierij, smoesjes

1flap (n) **1** geflapper[h], geklap[h] **2** klep, flap, (afhangende) rand; (neerslaand) blad[h] **3** [inform] staat van opwinding, paniek, consternatie

2flap (vb) flapp(er)en, klepp(er)en, slaan

3flap (vb) op en neer bewegen, slaan met

1flare (n) **1** flakkerend licht[h], flikkering **2** signaalvlam, vuursignaal[h]

2flare (vb) (op)flakkeren, (op)vlammen; [fig] opstuiven: ~ *up* **a)** opflakkeren; **b)** [also fig] woest worden

flare-up opflakkering, uitbarsting, hevige ruzie

1flash (n) **1** (licht)flits, vlam, (op)flikkering: ~*es of lightning* bliksemschichten; *quick as a* ~ razend snel; *in a* ~ in een flits **2** flits(licht[h]), flitsapparaat[h] **3** lichtsein[h], vlagsein[h] **4** kort (nieuws)bericht[h], nieuwsflits **5** opwelling, vlaag: *a ~ of inspiration* een flits van inspiratie

2flash (adj) **1** plotseling (opkomend): ~ *flood* (or: *fire*) plotselinge overstroming (or: brand) **2** [inform] opzichtig, poenig

3flash (vb) **1** opvlammen; (plotseling) ontvlammen [also fig] **2** plotseling opkomen: ~ *into view* (or: *sight*) plotseling in het gezichtsveld verschijnen **3** snel voorbijflitsen, (voorbij)schieten: ~ *past* (or: *by*) voorbijvliegen, voorbijflitsen

4flash (vb) **1** (doen) flitsen, (doen) flikkeren: ~ *the headlights* (*of a car*) met de koplampen flitsen **2** pronken met: ~ *money around* te koop lopen met zijn geld

flashback terugblik

flash card 1 (systeem)kaartje[h] **2** [comp] flashkaart, geheugenkaart

flasher 1 flitser, knipperlicht[h] **2** potloodventer [exhibitionist]

flashlight 1 flitslicht[h], lichtflits, signaallicht[h] **2** [Am] zaklantaarn

flashy opzichtig; poenig, opvallend

flask 1 fles, flacon; [chem] kolf **2** veldfles **3** thermosfles
¹flat (n) **1** vlakte, vlak terrein^h **2** flat, etage, appartement^h: *a block of ~s* een flatgebouw **3** platte kant, vlak^h, hand(palm) **4** [Am] lekke band **5** [mus] mol(teken^h); [Belg] b-molteken^h
²flat (adj) **1** vlak, plat **2** laag, niet hoog; plat [also of feet] **3** zonder prik; [Belg] plat [water]; verschaald [beer] **4** effen; gelijkmatig [colour, paint] **5** bot, vierkant; absoluut [negation, refusal] **6** leeg; plat [tyre] **7** saai, oninteressant, mat, smaakloos; flauw [food]: *fall ~* mislukken, geen effect hebben **8** [mus] te laag **9** [mus] mol, mineur
³flat (adv) **1** [inform] helemaal: *~ broke* helemaal platzak; *~ out* (op) volle kracht, met alle kracht [advance, work] **2** [inform] botweg, ronduit: *tell s.o. sth. ~* iem. botweg iets zeggen **3** [mus] (een halve toon) lager, te laag **4** rond, op de kop af, exact: *ten seconds ~* op de kop af tien seconden
flat-bottomed platboomd, met een platte bodem
flatfish platvis
flat-iron strijkijzer^h, strijkbout
flatly 1 uitdrukkingsloos, mat; dof [say, speak etc] **2** botweg; kortaf [eg refuse]: *Simon ~ refused to say where he had been* Simon vertikte het gewoon om te zeggen waar hij had gezeten **3** helemaal
flat rate uniform tarief^h; vast bedrag^h
flatten 1 afplatten, effenen: *~ out* afvlakken, effenen **2** flauw(er) maken, dof maken
flatter 1 vleien: *~ o.s.* zich vleien, zichzelf te hoog aanslaan; *I ~ myself that I'm a good judge of character* ik vlei mezelf met de hoop dat ik mensenkennis bezit **2** strelen [ears, eyes] **3** flatteren, mooier afschilderen
flattery 1 vleierij; [teasingly] slijm **2** gevlei^h, vleiende woorden
flatulence winderigheid
flaunt 1 pronken met, pralen met, tentoonspreiden: [mockingly] *if you've got it, ~ it!* wie het breed heeft, laat het breed hangen **2** doen opvallen, (zich) zeer opvallend uitdossen (gedragen)
flautist fluitist, fluitspeler
flavour 1 smaak, aroma^h, geur; [fig] bijsmaak **2** het karakteristieke, het eigene, het typische: *Camden has its own peculiar ~* Camden heeft iets heel eigens
flavouring smaakstof, aroma^h, kruid^h, kruiderij
flaw 1 barst, breuk, scheur **2** gebrek^h; fout [in jewel, stone, character]
flawless gaaf; vlekkeloos, onberispelijk
flax vlas^h [plant, fibre]
flaxen 1 als, van vlas **2** vlaskleurig: *~ hair* vlashaar; vlasblond haar
flay 1 villen, (af)stropen **2** afranselen; [fig]

hekelen
flea 1 vlo **2** watervlo ‖ *go off with a ~ in his ear* van een koude kermis thuiskomen; *~ market* vlooienmarkt, rommelmarkt
fleabite vlooienbeet; [fig] iets onbelangrijks; kleinigheid
¹fleck (n) vlek(je^h), plek(je^h), spikkel(tje^h)
²fleck (vb) (be)spikkelen, vlekken, stippen
fledgling (vliegvlugge) jonge vogel; [fig] beginneling
flee (ont)vluchten
¹fleece (n) **1** (schaaps)vacht **2** vlies^h **3** fleece^{+h}
²fleece (vb) **1** scheren [sheep] **2** [inform] afzetten; het vel over de oren halen [pers]
fleet 1 vloot, marine, luchtvloot **2** schare, verzameling, groep: *a ~ of cars* (or: *taxis*) een wagenpark
fleeting 1 vluchtig, vergankelijk **2** kortstondig: *a ~ glance* een vluchtige blik
Fleming Vlaming
Flemish Vlaams
flesh vlees^h: *~ and blood* het lichaam, een mens(elijk wezen); *one's own ~ and blood* je eigen vlees en bloed, je naaste verwanten
fleshy 1 vlezig **2** dik
¹flex (n) (elektrisch) snoer^h
²flex (vb) buigen, samentrekken
flexibility flexibiliteit; buigzaamheid; soepelheid
flexible 1 buigzaam [also fig]; soepel, flexibel: *~ working hours* variabele werktijd **2** meegaand, plooibaar
flexitime variabele werktijd(en)
flexiworker flexwerker
¹flick (n) **1** tik, mep, slag **2** ruk, schok: *a ~ of the wrist* een snelle polsbeweging **3** [inform] film **4** (the flicks) bios
²flick (vb) even aanraken, aantikken, afschudden; aanknippen [switch]: *~ crumbs from* (or: *off*) *the table* kruimels van de tafel vegen ‖ *~ through* a newspaper een krant doorbladeren
¹flicker (n) **1** trilling, (op)flikkering, flikkerend licht^h **2** sprankje^h: *a ~ of hope* een sprankje hoop
²flicker (vb) **1** trillen, fladderen, wapperen, flikkeren **2** heen en weer bewegen, heen en weer schieten
flick knife stiletto
flier *see* flyer
flight 1 vlucht, het vliegen; baan [of projectile, ball]; [fig] opwelling; uitbarsting: *put to ~* op de vlucht jagen **2** zwerm, vlucht, troep **3** trap: *a ~ of stairs* een trap
flight attendant steward(ess)
flight path 1 vliegroute **2** baan [of satellite]
flight recorder vluchtrecorder, zwarte doos
flighty grillig, wispelturig

¹**flimsy** (n) doorslag(papierʰ), kopie
²**flimsy** (adj) **1** broos, kwetsbaar, dun **2** on- benullig, onnozel
flinch [also fig] terugdeinzen; terugschrik- ken [with fear, pain]: *without ~ing* zonder een spier te vertrekken
¹**fling** (n) **1** worp, gooi **2** uitspatting, korte, hevige affaire ‖ *have one's ~* uitspatten
²**fling** (vb) **1** gooien, (weg)smijten, (af)wer- pen **2** wegstormen, (boos) weglopen
flint vuursteen(tjeʰ)
¹**flip** (n) tik, mep, (vinger)knip
²**flip** (adj) glad, ongepast, brutaal
³**flip** (vb) [inform] **1** flippen, maf worden **2** boos worden, door het lint gaan
⁴**flip** (vb) **1** wegtikken, wegschieten (met de vingers): *~ a coin* kruis of munt gooien **2** omdraaien
flip-chart flip-over, flap-over
flip-flop teenslipper
flippant oneerbiedig, spottend
flipper 1 vin, zwempoot **2** zwemvliesʰ
flip side 1 B-kant (van grammofoonplaat) **2** keerzijde [also fig]
flip through doorbladeren, snel doorlezen
¹**flirt** (n) flirt
²**flirt** (vb) flirten, koketteren
flirt with 1 flirten met; [fig] spelen met; overwegen: *we ~ the idea of* we spelen met de gedachte om **2** uitdagen, flirten met: *~ danger* een gevaarlijk spel spelen
¹**flit** (n) [inform] **1** snelle beweging **2** verhui- zing: *do a (moonlight) ~* met de noorderzon vertrekken
²**flit** (vb) fladderen; vliegen: *thoughts ~ted through his mind* gedachten schoten hem door het hoofd
¹**float** (n) **1** drijvend voorwerpʰ, vlotʰ, boei, dobber **2** drijver **3** kar, (praal)wagen **4** con- tanten, kleingeldʰ
²**float** (vb) **1** drijven, dobberen **2** vlot komen [of ship] **3** zweven
³**float** (vb) **1** doen drijven **2** vlot maken [ship etc] **3** over water vervoeren **4** in omloop brengen, voorstellen, rondvertellen: *~ an idea* met een idee naar voren komen
floating 1 drijvend: *~ bridge* a) ponton- brug; b) kettingpont **2** veranderlijk: *~ kidney* wandelende nier; *~ voter* zwevende kiezer
¹**flock** (n) **1** bosje, vlokjeʰ **2** troep, zwerm, kudde
²**flock** (vb) bijeenkomen, samenstromen: *people ~ed to the cities* men trok in grote groepen naar de steden
flog slaan, ervan langs geven
¹**flood** (n) **1** vloed **2** uitstorting, stroom, vloed: *~ of reactions* stortvloed van reacties **3** overstroming
²**flood** (vb) (doen) overstromen, overspoe- len, buiten zijn oevers doen treden: *we were ~ed (out) with letters* we werden bedolven

onder de brieven
floodgate sluisdeur [fig]; sluis: *open the ~s* de sluizen openzetten
flooding overstroming
floodlight 1 schijnwerper **2** strijklichtʰ, spotlichtʰ
flood tide vloed; hoogtijʰ
¹**floor** (n) **1** vloer, grond: *first ~* eerste ver- dieping; [Am] begane grond **2** verdieping, etage **3** vergaderzaal [of parliament]: *a mo- tion from the ~* een motie uit de zaal ‖ *wipe the ~ with s.o.* de vloer met iem. aanvegen
²**floor** (vb) **1** vloeren [also fig]; knock-out slaan, verslaan: *his arguments ~ed me* tegen zijn argumenten kon ik niet op **2** van de wijs brengen
floorboard 1 vloerplank **2** bodemplank
floor show floorshow, striptease
¹**flop** (n) **1** smak, plof **2** flop, mislukking
²**flop** (vb) **1** zwaaien, klappen, spartelen: *~ about in the water* rondspartelen in het water **2** smakken, ploffen: *~ down in a chair* neer- ploffen in een stoel **3** [inform] mislukken, floppen; zakken [at examination]
¹**floppy** (n) floppy (disk), diskette, flop
²**floppy** (adj) **1** slap(hangend) **2** [inform] zwak
flora flora
floral 1 gebloemd: *~ tribute* bloemenhulde **2** m.b.t. flora, plant-
florid 1 bloemrijk, (overdreven) sierlijk **2** in het oog lopend, opzichtig **3** blozend, hoog- rood
florin florijn, gulden
florist 1 bloemist **2** bloemkweker
flotilla 1 flottieltje, smaldeelʰ **2** vloot [of small ships]
flotsam 1 drijfhoutʰ, wrakhoutʰ: [fig] *~ and jetsam* uitgestotenen **2** rommel, rotzooi
¹**flounce** (n) **1** zwaai, ruk, schok **2** (gerim- pelde) strook [on article of clothing, curtain]
²**flounce** (vb) **1** zwaaien [of body]; schok- ken, schudden **2** ongeduldig lopen: *~ about the room* opgewonden door de kamer ijsbe- ren
flounder 1 ploeteren **2** stuntelen, van zijn stuk gebracht worden **3** de draad kwijtra- ken, hakkelen
flour meelʰ, (meel)bloem
¹**flourish** (n) **1** krul, krulletter **2** bloemrijke uitdrukking, stijlbloempjeʰ **3** zwierig ge- baarʰ **4** fanfare, geschalʰ
²**flourish** (vb) **1** gedijen, bloeien **2** floreren, succes hebben: *his family were ~ing* het ging goed met zijn gezin
³**flourish** (vb) tonen, zwaaien met: *he ~ed a letter in my face* hij zwaaide een brief onder mijn neus heen en weer
flout 1 beledigen, bespotten **2** afwijzen, in de wind slaan
¹**flow** (n) **1** stroom, stroming, het stromen

2 vloed, overvloed: *ebb and* ~ eb en vloed
²flow (vb) **1** (toe)vloeien, (toe)stromen
2 golven; loshangen [of hair, article of clothing] **3** opkomen [of high tide]: *swim with the* ~*ing tide* met de stroom meegaan
¹flo**wer** (n) **1** bloem, bloesem **2** bloei: *the orchids are in* ~ de orchideeën staan in bloei
²flo**wer** (vb) bloeien, tot bloei (ge)komen (zijn)
flo**wing 1** vloeiend **2** loshangend, golvend
fl. oz. *fluid ounce*
flu *influenza* griep
flub [Am] verknoeien
flu**ctuate** fluctueren, schommelen, variëren
flue schoorsteenpijp, rookkanaal[h]
flu**ency** spreekvaardigheid
flu**ent** vloeiend: *be* ~ *in English* vloeiend Engels spreken
¹fluff (n) pluis(jes), dons[h]
²fluff (vb) **1** verknallen, verprutsen **2** opschudden [pillow]
fluff o**ut 1** opschudden **2** opzetten
¹flu**id** (n) vloeistof
²flu**id** (adj) **1** vloeibaar, niet vast, vloeiend **2** instabiel, veranderlijk: *our plans are still* ~ onze plannen staan nog niet vast ‖ ~ *ounce* ounce
fluke bof, meevaller, mazzel: *by a* ~ door stom geluk
flu**mmox** in verwarring brengen, perplex doen staan
flunk [Am; inform] (doen) zakken [examination]; afwijzen [at examination]
flu**nkey** [oft depr] **1** lakei **2** strooplikker
flunk o**ut** [Am; inform] weggestuurd worden
fluore**scent** fluorescerend: ~ *lamp* tl-buis
fluor**ide** fluoride[h], fluorwaterstofzout[h]
flurr**y** vlaag [also fig]; windvlaag, windstoot, (korte) bui: *in a* ~ *of excitement* in een vlaag van opwinding
¹flush (n) **1** vloed, (plotselinge) stroom, vloedgolf **2** (water)spoeling **3** opwinding: *in the first* ~ *of victory* in de overwinningsroes **4** blos **5** flush, serie kaarten van dezelfde kleur
²flush (adj) **1** goed voorzien, goed bij kas: ~ *with money* goed bij kas **2** gelijk, vlak: ~ *with the wall* gelijk met de muur
³flush (vb) **1** doorspoelen; doortrekken [toilet] **2** kleuren, blozen
⁴flush (vb) **1** (schoon)spoelen: ~ *sth. away* (or: *down*) iets wegspoelen **2** opwinden, aanvuren: ~*ed with happiness* dolgelukkig **3** doen wegvliegen: ~ *s.o.* out of (or: *from*) *his hiding place* iem. uit zijn schuilplaats verjagen
¹flu**ster** (n) opwinding, verwarring: *be in a* ~ opgewonden zijn
²flu**ster** (vb) van de wijs brengen, zenuwachtig maken

flute fluit
fluti**st** [Am] fluitist
¹flu**tter** (n) **1** gefladder[h], geklapper[h] **2** opwinding, drukte: *be in a* ~ opgewonden zijn **3** [inform] gokje[h], speculatie
²flu**tter** (vb) **1** fladderen, klapwieken **2** dwarrelen [of leaf] **3** wapperen [of flag] **4** zenuwachtig rondlopen, ijsberen **5** snel slaan, (snel) kloppen
flux 1 vloed, het vloeien, stroom **2** voortdurende beweging, veranderlijkheid: *everything was in a state of* ~ er waren steeds nieuwe ontwikkelingen
¹fly (n) **1** vlieg: *die like flies* in groten getale omkomen; *not harm* (or: *hurt*) *a* ~ geen vlieg kwaad doen **2** gulp ‖ *a* ~ *in the ointment* een kleinigheid die het geheel bederft; *a* ~ *on the wall* een spion; [inform] *there are no flies on her* ze is niet op haar achterhoofd gevallen
²fly (vb) **1** vliegen [of bird, aeroplane etc]: ~ *away* wegvliegen; [fig] verdwijnen; ~ *in* (or: *out*) aankomen (or: vertrekken) per vliegtuig; ~ *past* (in formatie) over vliegen; ~ *at* a) aanvallen, zich storten op [of bird]; b) [fig] uitvallen tegen; ~ *into* landen op [airport] **2** wapperen [of flag, hair]; fladderen, vliegen **3** zich snel voortbewegen, vliegen, vluchten; omvliegen [of time]; wegvliegen [of money]: *let* ~ a) (af)schieten, afvuren; b) laten schieten; ~ *into a rage* (or: *passion, temper*) in woede ontsteken ‖ ~ *high* hoog vliegen [fig]; ambitieus zijn
³fly (vb) **1** vliegen, besturen: ~ *a plane in* een vliegtuig aan de grond zetten **2** vliegen (met) [airline company] **3** laten vliegen [pigeon]; oplaten [kite]: ~ *a kite* vliegeren; [fig] een balletje opgooien **4** voeren; laten wapperen [flag] **5** ontvluchten, vermijden
flyer 1 vlugschrift[h], folder, flyer **2** piloot, vlieger **3** vliegtuigpassagier
flying 1 vliegend: ~ *jump* (or: *leap*) sprong met aanloop; ~ *saucer* vliegende schotel **2** (zeer) snel, zich snel verplaatsend (ontwikkelend), vliegend: ~ *start* vliegende start [also fig] **3** kortstondig, van korte duur, tijdelijk
flying squad vliegende brigade, mobiele eenheid
flyover viaduct[h] [across motorway]
flysheet 1 (reclame)blaadje[h], folder, circulaire **2** informatieblad[h]; gebruiksaanwijzing [of catalogue, book]
fly **swatter** vliegenmepper
flyweight [boxing, wrestling] **1** worstelaar (bokser) in de vlieggewichtklasse, vlieggewicht **2** vlieggewicht[h]
foal veulen[h]
¹foam (n) **1** schuim[h] **2** schuimrubber
²foam (vb) **1** schuimen **2** schuimbekken: ~ *at the mouth* schuimbekken [also fig]
fob o**ff 1** wegwuiven, geen aandacht be-

steden aan **2** afschepen, zich afmaken van: *we won't be fobbed off this time* deze keer laten we ons niet met een kluitje in het riet sturen
fob watch zakhorloge[h]
focal m.b.t./van het brandpunt: ~ *distance* (or: *length*) brandpuntsafstand
focal point brandpunt[h] [also fig]; middelpunt[h]
¹focus (n) **1** brandpunt[h], focus; [fig] middelpunt[h]; centrum[h] **2** scherpte: *out of* ~ onscherp
²focus (vb) **1** in een brandpunt (doen) samenkomen **2** (zich) concentreren: ~ *on* zich concentreren op
fodder (droog) veevoeder[h]; voer[h] [also fig]
foe [form] vijand, tegenstander
foetus foetus
¹fog (n) mist; nevel [also fig]; onduidelijkheid, verwarring
²fog (vb) beslaan: *my glasses ~ged up* mijn bril besloeg
fogbound 1 door mist opgehouden **2** in mist gehuld
fogey ouderwets figuur[h], ouwe zeur
foggy mistig, (zeer) nevelig; [also fig] onduidelijk; vaag: [inform] *I haven't the foggiest (idea)* (ik heb) geen flauw idee
foible 1 zwak[h], zwakheid, zwak punt[h] **2** gril
¹foil (n) **1** (aluminium)folie, zilverpapier[h] **2** contrast, achtergrond: *be a ~ to* beter doen uitkomen
²foil (vb) verijdelen, verhinderen, voorkomen
foist opdringen
¹fold (n) **1** vouw, plooi, kronkel(ing), kreuk **2** schaapskooi **3** het vouwen **4** kudde; [fig] kerk; gemeente: *return to the* ~ in de schoot van zijn familie terugkeren
²fold (vb) [inform] **1** op de fles gaan, over de kop gaan **2** het begeven, bezwijken
³fold (vb) **1** (op)vouwen: ~ *away* opvouwen, opklappen; ~ *back* terugslaan, omslaan **2** (om)wikkelen, (in)pakken **3** (om)sluiten, omhelzen: ~ *s.o. in one's arms* iem. in zijn armen sluiten **4** hullen [in fog] **5** over elkaar leggen; kruisen [arms]; intrekken [wings]
folder 1 folder, (reclame)blaadje[h] **2** map(-je[h])
¹fold up (vb) **1** bezwijken, het begeven, het opgeven **2** failliet gaan, over de kop gaan
²fold up (vb) opvouwen, opklappen
foliage gebladerte[h], blad[h], loof[h]
folk [inform] **1** familie, gezin, oude lui: *her ~s were from New Jersey* haar familie kwam uit New Jersey **2** luitjes, jongens, mensen **3** mensen, lieden, lui: *some ~ never learn* sommige mensen leren het nooit
folklore 1 folklore **2** volkskunde
folk-tale volksverhaal[h], sage, sprookje[h]

follow volgen, achternalopen, aanhouden; gaan langs [road, direction, river]; achternazitten, vergezellen, bijwonen, komen na, opvolgen, aandacht schenken aan, in de gaten houden, begrijpen; bijhouden [news]; zich laten leiden door; uitvoeren [order, advice]; nadoen [example]; voortvloeien uit: ~ *the rules* zich aan de regels houden; ~ *s.o. about* (or: *around*) iem. overal volgen; ~ *on* verder gaan, volgen [after interruption]; ~ *up* a) (op korte afstand) volgen, in de buurt blijven van; b) vervolgen, een vervolg maken op; c) gebruikmaken van; d) nagaan; *the outcome is as ~s* het resultaat is als volgt; *to* ~ als volgend gerecht; *would you like anything to ~?* wilt u nog iets toe?
follower 1 aanhanger, volgeling **2** [also social networking] volger
¹following (n) aanhang, volgelingen
²following (adj) **1** volgend **2** mee, in de rug; gunstig [wind]
³following (prep) na, volgende op: ~ *the meeting* na de vergadering
follow-up vervolg[h], voortzetting, vervolgbrief, tweede bezoek[h]
folly 1 (buitensporig) duur en nutteloos iets **2** dwaasheid, dwaas gedrag[h]: *where ignorance is bliss, 'tis ~ to be wise* [roughly] wat niet weet, wat niet deert
foment aanstoken, aanmoedigen, stimuleren
fond 1 liefhebbend, teder, innig **2** dierbaar, lief: *his ~est wish was fulfilled* zijn liefste wens ging in vervulling **3** al te lief, al te toegeeflijk || *be ~ of* gek zijn op; [inform] er een handje van hebben te
fondle liefkozen, strelen, aaien
fondness 1 tederheid, genegenheid, warmte **2** voorliefde, hang: *his ~ for old proverbs is quite irritating at times* zijn voorliefde voor oude spreekwoorden is soms heel irritant
font 1 (doop)vont[h] **2** font[h], lettertype[h]
food 1 voedingsmiddel[h], voedingsartikel[h], levensmiddel[h]; eetwaar: *frozen ~s* diepvriesproducten **2** voedsel[h], eten[h]; voeding [also fig]: ~ *for thought* (or: *reflection*) stof tot nadenken
foodprocessor keukenmachine
foodstuff levensmiddel[h], voedingsmiddel[h], voedingsartikel[h]
¹fool (n) **1** dwaas, gek, zot(skap), stommeling: *more ~ him* hij had beter kunnen weten; *make a ~ of s.o.* iem. voor de gek houden **2** nar, zot: *act* (or: *play*) *the* ~ gek doen **3** dessert van stijf geklopte room, ei, suiker en vruchten || *he's nobody's* (or: *no*) ~ hij is niet van gisteren
²fool (vb) **1** gek doen: ~ *(about, around) with* spelen met, flirten met **2** lummelen, lanterfanten: ~ *about* (or: *around*) rondlummelen,

aanrommelen
³fool (vb) voor de gek houden, ertussen nemen: *he ~ed her into believing he's a guitarist* hij maakte haar wijs dat hij gitarist is
foolery dwaasheid
foolhardy onbezonnen, roekeloos
foolish 1 dwaas, dom, stom **2** verbouwereerd, beteuterd ‖ *penny wise, pound ~* [roughly] sommige mensen zijn zuinig als het om kleine bedragen gaat, terwijl ze grote bedragen over de balk gooien
foolproof 1 volkomen veilig **2** kinderlijk eenvoudig **3** onfeilbaar; waterdicht **4** bedrijfszeker
fool's errand vruchteloze onderneming: *send s.o. on a ~ iem.* voor niks laten gaan
¹foot (n) **1** voet [also of mountain, stocking]: *put one's feet up* (even) gaan liggen; *stand on one's own feet* op eigen benen staan; *on ~ te* voet, op handen **2** (vers)voet **3** poot [of table] **4** voeteneinde[h] [of bed] **5** onderste, laatste deel[h], (uit)einde[h] **6** [measure of length] voet [0.3048 metre] ‖ *have a ~ in both camps* geen partij kiezen; [fig] *feet of clay* fundamentele zwakte; *carry* (or: *sweep*) *s.o. off his feet* iem. meeslepen; [inform] *fall* (or: *land*) *on one's feet* mazzel hebben; *find one's feet* **a)** beginnen te staan [of child]; **b)** op eigen benen kunnen staan; *get to one's feet* opstaan; *put one's ~ down* streng optreden; [inform] plankgas rijden; [inform] *put one's ~ in it* (or: *one's mouth*) een blunder begaan; [inform] *be rushed off one's feet* zich uit de naad werken; *my ~!* kom nou!; *they say it's easy. Easy my ~!* ze zeggen dat het makkelijk is. Nou, vergeet het maar!
²foot (vb) betalen, vereffenen, dokken voor
³foot (vb): [inform] *~ it* **a)** dansen; **b)** de benenwagen nemen, te voet gaan
footage 1 lengte (in voeten) **2** (stuk) film
foot-and-mouth disease mond-en-klauwzeer[h]
¹football (n) **1** voetbal [ball] **2** rugbybal **3** speelbal [fig]
²football (n) [Am] Amerikaans football[h]
footbridge voetbrug
footer voettekst
foothill uitloper [of mountains]
foothold 1 steun(punt[h]) voor de voet, plaats om te staan **2** vaste voet, steunpunt[h], zekere positie
footing 1 steun (voor de voet), steunpunt[h], houvast[h]; [fig] vaste voet: *lose one's ~* wegglijden **2** voet, niveau[h], sterkte **3** voet, verstandhouding, omgang: *on the same ~* op gelijke voet
footlights voetlicht; [by extension] (toneel)carrière
footling 1 dwaas, stom **2** onbeduidend, waardeloos
footloose vrij, ongebonden

footman lakei, livreiknecht
footmark voetafdruk; voetstap
footnote voetnoot; [fig] kanttekening
footpath voetpad[h], wandelpad[h]
footprint voetafdruk, voetspoor[h], voetstap
footstep 1 voetstap, voetafdruk; voetspoor[h] [also fig]: *follow* (or: *tread*) *in s.o.'s ~s* in iemands voetsporen treden **2** pas, stap
foppish fatterig, dandyachtig
for 1 voor, om, met het oog op, wegens, bedoeld om, ten behoeve van: *act ~ the best* handelen om bestwil; *long ~ home* verlangen naar huis; *write ~ information* schrijven om informatie; *thank you ~ coming* bedankt dat je gekomen bent; *now ~ it* en nu erop los **2** voor, wat betreft, gezien, in verhouding met: *an ear ~ music* een muzikaal gehoor; *it's not ~ me* to het is niet aan mij om te; so much *~ that* dat is dat; *I ~ one will not do it* ik zal het in elk geval niet doen; *~ all I care* voor mijn part **3** ten voordele van, ten gunste van, vóór: *~ and against* voor en tegen **4** in de plaats van, tegenover, in ruil voor **5** als (zijnde): *left ~ dead* dood achtergelaten **6** over, gedurende, sinds, ver, met een omvang: *it was not ~ long* het duurde niet lang **7** dat ... zou ..., dat ... moet ...: *~ her to leave us is impossible* het is onmogelijk dat zij ons zou verlaten **8** opdat: *~ this to work it is necessary to* wil dit lukken, dan is het nodig te ‖ *anyone ~ coffee?* wil er iem. koffie?; *and now ~ sth. completely different* en nu iets anders
forage 1 naar voedsel zoeken, foerageren **2** doorzoeken: *~ about in s.o.'s bag* iemands tas doorsnuffelen
foray 1 [mil] inval; strooptocht **2** [inform] uitstapje[h], intrede: *John's ~ into science failed* Johns poging zich op het gebied van de wetenschap te wagen mislukte
forbear zich onthouden, zich inhouden, afzien: *he should ~ from quarrels* hij moet zich verre houden van ruzies
forbearance verdraagzaamheid; tolerantie
forbid 1 verbieden, ontzeggen **2** voorkomen, verhoeden, buitensluiten: *God ~!* God verhoede!
forbidden verboden, niet toegestaan
forbidding afstotelijk, afschrikwekkend
¹force (n) **1** kracht, geweld[h], macht: *by ~ of circumstances* door omstandigheden gedwongen; *join ~s (with)* de krachten bundelen (met); *by* (or: *from, out of*) *~ of habit* uit gewoonte **2** (rechts)geldigheid, het van kracht zijn: *a new law has come into ~* (or: *has been put into ~*) een nieuwe wet is van kracht geworden **3** macht, krijgsmacht, leger[h] **4** (the Forces) strijdkrachten
²force (vb) **1** dwingen, (door)drijven, forceren: *~ back* terugdrijven; *Government will ~ the prices up* de regering zal de prijzen op-

drijven **2** forceren, open-, doorbreken: *the burglar ~d an* **entry** de inbreker verschafte zich met geweld toegang
forced gedwongen, onvrijwillig, geforceerd: *~ labour* dwangarbeid; *~ landing* noodlanding
forcemeat gehakt[h]
forceps (verlos)tang: *two pairs of ~* twee tangen
forceps delivery tangverlossing
forcible 1 gewelddadig, gedwongen, krachtig **2** indrukwekkend, overtuigend
fore het voorste gedeelte: [fig] *come to the ~* op de voorgrond treden
[1]**forearm** (n) onderarm, voorarm
[2]**forearm** (vb): *forewarned is ~ed* een gewaarschuwd mens telt voor twee
forebear voorvader, voorouder
foreboding 1 voorteken[h], voorspelling **2** (akelig) voorgevoel[h]
[1]**forecast** (n) voorspelling; verwachting [of weather]
[2]**forecast** (vb) voorspellen, verwachten, aankondigen
foreclosure executie
forecourt voorplein[h]
forefather voorvader, stamvader
forefinger wijsvinger
forefront voorste deel[h], voorste gelid, front[h], voorgevel: *in the ~ of the fight* aan het (gevechts)front
foregather samenkomen, (zich) verzamelen
forego voorafgaan
foregoing voorafgaand, voornoemd, vorig
foregone conclusion uitgemaakte zaak
forehead voorhoofd[h]
foreign 1 buitenlands: *~ aid* ontwikkelingshulp; *~ exchange* deviezen; *Foreign Office* Ministerie van Buitenlandse Zaken **2** vreemd, ongewoon
foreigner buitenlander, vreemdeling
foreman 1 voorzitter van jury **2** voorman, ploegbaas
[1]**foremost** (adj) **1** voorst(e), eerst(e), aan het hoofd: *head ~* met het hoofd naar voren **2** opmerkelijkst, belangrijkst
[2]**foremost** (adv) voorop
forename voornaam
forensic gerechtelijk, (ge)rechts-, forensisch
foreplay voorspel[h]
forerunner 1 voorteken[h]; [fig] voorbode **2** voorloper
foresee voorzien, verwachten, vooraf zien
foreseeable 1 te verwachten, te voorzien **2** afzienbaar, nabij: *in the ~ future* in de nabije toekomst
foreshadow aankondigen, voorspellen
foresight 1 vooruitziende blik, het vooruitzien **2** toekomstplanning, voorzorg

foreskin voorhuid
forest woud[h] [also fig]; bos[h]
forestall 1 vóór zijn **2** vooruitlopen op **3** (ver)hinderen, dwarsbomen, voorkomen
forester boswachter, houtvester
foretaste voorproef(je[h])
foretell voorspellen, voorzeggen
forethought toekomstplanning, voorzorg, vooruitziende blik
forever 1 (voor) eeuwig, voorgoed, (voor) altijd **2** onophoudelijk, aldoor: *I was ~ dragging David away from the fireplace* ik moest David aldoor bij de open haard wegslepen
forewarn van tevoren waarschuwen || *~ed is forearmed* een gewaarschuwd man telt voor twee
foreword voorwoord[h]; woord[h] vooraf
[1]**forfeit** (n) het verbeurde, boete, straf
[2]**forfeit** (vb) verbeuren, verspelen, verbeurd verklaren
[1]**forge** (n) **1** smidse, smederij **2** smidsvuur[h]
[2]**forge** (vb) **1** vervalsing(en) maken, valsheid in geschrifte plegen **2** vooruitschieten: *~ ahead* gestaag vorderingen maken
[3]**forge** (vb) **1** smeden [also fig]; bedenken, beramen **2** vervalsen: *a ~d passport* een vals paspoort
forger vervalser, valsemunter
forgery 1 vervalsing, namaak **2** het vervalsen, oplichterij
[1]**forget** (vb) vergeten, nalaten, verwaarlozen: *~ to do sth.* iets nalaten te doen
[2]**forget** (vb) vergeten, niet denken aan, niet meer weten: [inform] *~ (about) it* laat maar, denk er maar niet meer aan; [inform] *So you want to borrow my car? ~ it!* Dus jij wil mijn auto lenen? Vergeet het maar!; *not ~ting* en niet te vergeten, en ook
forgetful vergeetachtig; verstrooid
forget-me-not vergeet-mij-nietje[h]
forgive vergeven || *Dick forgave his sister the money he had lent her* Dick schold zijn zus het geld kwijt dat hij haar geleend had
forgo zich onthouden van, afstand doen van, het zonder (iets) doen
[1]**fork** (n) **1** vork, hooivork, mestvork **2** tweesprong, splitsing
[2]**fork** (vb) **1** zich vertakken, zich splitsen, uiteengaan: *~ed tongue* gespleten tong **2** afslaan, een richting opgaan: *~ right* rechts afslaan
forklift truck vorkheftruck
fork out (geld) dokken
forlorn 1 verlaten, eenzaam **2** hopeloos, troosteloos || *~ hope* hopeloze onderneming, laatste hoop
[1]**form** (n) **1** (verschijnings)vorm, gedaante, silhouet[h] **2** vorm, soort, systeem[h] **3** vorm(geving), opzet, presentatiewijze **4** formulier[h], voorgedrukt vel[h] **5** formaliteit, vast gebruik[h], gewoonte: *true to ~* geheel in stijl,

zoals gebruikelijk **6** [sport] conditie, vorm: *be on ~, be in great ~* goed op dreef zijn **7** manier, wijze, vorm **8** (school)klas: *first ~* eerste klas

²form (vb) zich vormen, verschijnen, zich ontwikkelen

³form (vb) **1** vormen, modelleren, vorm geven **2** maken; opvatten [plan]; construeren, samenstellen: *~ (a) part of* deel uitmaken van

f̲o̲rmal formeel, officieel, volgens de regels

form̲a̲lity 1 vormelijkheid, stijfheid **2** formaliteit

¹f̲o̲rmat (n) **1** (boek)formaatʰ, afmeting, grootte, uitvoering **2** manier van samenstellen, opzet **3** (beschrijving van) opmaak; indeling [of data]

²f̲o̲rmat (vb) formatteren, opmaken; indelen [data etc]

form̲a̲tion 1 vorming **2** formatie, opstelling, verbandʰ: *fly in ~* in formatie vliegen

f̲o̲rmative vormend, vormings-: *the ~ years of his career* de beginjaren van zijn loopbaan

f̲o̲rmatting het formatteren, opmaak

¹f̲o̲rmer (n) leerling [of certain form]: *second-~* tweedeklasser

²f̲o̲rmer (dem pron) **1** eerste; eerstgenoemde [of two] **2** vroeger, voorafgaand, vorig: *in ~ days* in vroeger dagen

f̲o̲rmerly vroeger, eertijds, voorheen

f̲o̲rm feed paginadoorvoer; formuliertoevoer

f̲o̲rmidable 1 ontzagwekkend, gevreesd **2** formidabel, geweldig, indrukwekkend

f̲o̲rmula 1 formule, formulering, formulierʰ; [fig] clichéʰ **2** formule, samenstelling, receptʰ **3** [Am] babyvoeding

f̲o̲rmulate 1 formuleren **2** opstellen, ontwerpen, samenstellen

f̲o̲rnicate [form] overspel plegen

fors̲a̲ke verlaten, in de steek laten, opgeven

fort fortʰ, vesting, sterkte ‖ *hold the ~* de zaken waarnemen, op de winkel letten

forth voort, tevoorschijn: *bring ~* **a)** voortbrengen, veroorzaken; **b)** baren ‖ *hold ~* uitweiden; *and so ~* enzovoort(s)

forthc̲o̲ming 1 aanstaand, verwacht, aangekondigd: *her ~ album* haar binnenkort te verschijnen album **2** tegemoetkomend, behulpzaam **3** [also with negation] beschikbaar, ter beschikking: *an explanation was not ~* een verklaring bleef uit

f̲o̲rthright rechtuit, openhartig, direct

forthw̲i̲th onmiddellijk; terstond

f̲o̲rtieth veertigste

fortific̲a̲tion versterking, fortificatie

f̲o̲rtify versterken, verstevigen

f̲o̲rtitude standvastigheid, vastberadenheid

f̲o̲rtnight veertien dagen, twee weken: *a ~ on Monday* **a)** maandag over veertien da-

gen; **b)** maandag veertien dagen geleden; *Tuesday ~* dinsdag over veertien dagen

f̲o̲rtress vesting, versterkte stad, fortʰ

fort̲u̲itous 1 toevallig, onvoorzien **2** [inform] gelukkig

f̲o̲rtunate gelukkig, fortuinlijk, gunstig

f̲o̲rtune 1 fortuinʰ, voorspoed, gelukʰ **2** lotgevalʰ, (toekomstige) belevenis: *tell ~s* de toekomst voorspellen **3** fortuinʰ, vermogenʰ, rijkdom: *she spends a ~ on clothes* ze geeft een vermogen uit aan kleren

f̲o̲rtune hunter gelukzoeker

f̲o̲rtune-teller waarzegger

f̲o̲rty veertig: *a man in his forties* een man van in de veertig

¹f̲o̲rward (n) [sport] voorspeler: *centre ~* middenvoor

²f̲o̲rward (adj) **1** voorwaarts, naar voren (gericht) **2** vroegrijp: *a ~ girl* een vroegrijp meisje **3** arrogant, brutaal **4** voorst, vooraan gelegen **5** gevorderd, opgeschoten **6** vooruitstrevend, modern, geavanceerd **7** termijn-, op termijn: *~ planning* toekomstplanning

³f̲o̲rward (vb) **1** doorzenden; nazenden [mail] **2** zenden, (ver)sturen, verzenden

⁴f̲o̲rward (adv) **1** voorwaarts, vooruit; naar voren [in space; also fig]: *backward(s) and ~* vooruit en achteruit, heen en weer **2** vooruit, vooraf; op termijn [in time]: *from today ~* vanaf heden

f̲o̲rwarding address doorstuuradres

f̲o̲rwards voorwaarts, vooruit, naar voren

f̲o̲rward slash slash

¹f̲o̲ssil (n) fossielʰ

²f̲o̲ssil (adj) fossiel: *~ fuel* fossiele brandstof

f̲o̲ster 1 koesteren, aanmoedigen; [fig] voeden **2** opnemen in het gezin; als pleegkind opnemen [without adoption]: *~ parent* pleegouder

f̲o̲ster parent pleegouder

¹foul (n) [sport] overtreding, fout

²foul (adj) **1** vuil, stinkend, smerig, vies: *~ weather* smerig weer **2** vuil, vulgair: *a ~ temper* een vreselijk humeur; *~ language* vuile taal **3** [sport] onsportief, gemeen, vals: [oft fig] *~ play* onsportief spel, boze opzet, misdaad ‖ *fall ~ (of)* in aanvaring komen (met)

³foul (vb) [sport] een overtreding begaan, in de fout gaan

⁴foul (vb) **1** bevuilen, bekladden **2** [sport] een overtreding begaan tegenover

foul-m̲o̲uthed ruw in de mond, vulgair

foul-up 1 verwarring, onderbreking **2** blokkering, mechanisch defectʰ, storing

found 1 grondvesten; funderen [also fig] **2** stichten, oprichten, tot stand brengen: *this bakery was ~ed in 1793* deze bakkerij is in 1793 opgericht

found̲a̲tion 1 stichting, fondsʰ, oprichting

2 fundering [also fig]; fundament[h], basis: *the story is completely without ~* het verhaal is totaal ongegrond
found<u>a</u>tion course basiscursus
¹**f<u>ou</u>nder** (n) stichter, oprichter, grondlegger
²**f<u>ou</u>nder** (vb) **1** invallen, instorten, mislukken: *the project ~ed on the ill will of the government* het project mislukte door de onwil van de regering **2** zinken, vergaan, schipbreuk lijden
f<u>ou</u>nding f<u>a</u>ther grondlegger; stichter, oprichter
f<u>ou</u>ndling vondeling
f<u>ou</u>ndry (metaal)gieterij
f<u>ou</u>ntain 1 fontein: *~ pen* vulpen **2** bron [also fig]
f<u>ou</u>ntainhead [form] bron; diepe oorsprong
four vier, viertal, vierspan ‖ *be on all ~s* op handen en knieën lopen, kruipen
four-leaved cl<u>o</u>ver klavertjevier[h]
four-p<u>o</u>ster b<u>e</u>d hemelbed[h]
f<u>ou</u>rsome viertal[h], kwartet[h]
foursqu<u>a</u>re 1 vierkant, vierhoekig **2** resoluut, open en eerlijk, vastbesloten
fourt<u>ee</u>n veertien
fourt<u>ee</u>nth veertiende
fourth vierde, kwart
fowl kip, hoen[h], haan
¹**fox** (n) vos [also fig]
²**fox** (vb) doen alsof
³**fox** (vb) **1** beetnemen, bedriegen, te slim af zijn **2** in de war brengen
foxglove vingerhoedskruid[h]
foxhound jachthond
foxy 1 vosachtig **2** [esp Am; inform] sexy **3** sluw
fr<u>a</u>ction 1 breuk, gebroken getal[h]: *decimal ~* tiendelige breuk; *vulgar ~* (gewone) breuk **2** fractie, (zeer) klein onderdeel[h]
fr<u>a</u>ctious 1 onhandelbaar, dwars, lastig **2** humeurig, prikkelbaar
fr<u>a</u>cture 1 fractuur, (bot)breuk, beenbreuk **2** scheur, barst, breuk
fr<u>a</u>ctured [Am; inform] stomdronken; teut, lazarus
fragile breekbaar, broos
fragment fragment[h], deel[h], (brok)stuk
fragment<u>a</u>tion versplintering
fragrance geur, (zoete) geurigheid
frail breekbaar, zwak, tenger, teer
¹**frame** (n) **1** (het dragende) geraamte [of construction]; skelet[h] [wood construction]; frame[h] [of bicycle]; raamwerk[h], chassis[h] **2** omlijsting, kader[h], kozijn[h]; montuur [of glasses]; raam[h] [of window etc] **3** [oft fig] (gestructureerd) geheel[h], structuur, opzet: *~(s) of reference* referentiekader ‖ *~ of mind* gemoedsgesteldheid
²**frame** (vb) **1** vorm geven aan, ontwerpen,

uitdenken, formuleren, uitdrukken, vormen, vervaardigen, verzinnen, zich inbeelden **2** inlijsten, omlijsten, als achtergrond dienen voor **3** [inform] erin luizen, in de val laten lopen, (opzettelijk) vals beschuldigen: *the swindlers were ~d* de zwendelaars werden in de val gelokt
fr<u>a</u>me-up complot[h], gearrangeerde beschuldiging, valstrik
fr<u>a</u>mework 1 geraamte[h] **2** structuur; kader[h]
France Frankrijk
fr<u>a</u>nchise 1 stemrecht[h], burgerrecht[h] **2** concessie **3** franchise, systeemlicentie
¹**frank** (adj) (+ with) openhartig (tegen), oprecht, eerlijk: *~ly, I don't give a damn* eerlijk gezegd kan het me geen barst schelen
²**frank** (vb) **1** frankeren **2** stempelen, automatisch frankeren
fr<u>a</u>nkly eerlijk gezegd: *~, I don't like it* eerlijk gezegd vind ik het niet leuk
fr<u>a</u>ntic 1 dol, buiten zichzelf, uitzinnig: *the noise drove me ~* het lawaai maakte me hoorndol **2** [inform] verwoed, extreem: *~ efforts* verwoede pogingen
fr<u>a</u>ternal broederlijk [also fig]; vriendelijk
frat<u>e</u>rnity 1 broederlijkheid **2** genootschap[h], broederschap, vereniging: *the medical ~* de medische stand **3** [Am] studentencorps[h]; studentenclub [for men]
fr<u>a</u>ternize zich verbroederen
fr<u>a</u>tricide broedermoord, zustermoord
fraud 1 bedrog[h], fraude, zwendel **2** bedrieger, oplichter **3** vervalsing, bedriegerij, oplichterij: *the newly-discovered Rembrandt was a ~* de pas ontdekte Rembrandt was een vervalsing
fr<u>au</u>dster fraudeur
fr<u>au</u>dulence bedrog[h], bedrieglijkheid
fr<u>au</u>dulent [form] frauduleus, vals
fraught vol, beladen: *the journey was ~ with danger* het was een reis vol gevaren
¹**fray** (n) strijd, gevecht[h], twist: *eager for the ~* strijdlustig
²**fray** (vb) verzwakken, uitputten: *~ed nerves* overbelaste zenuwen
³**fray** (vb) (uit)rafelen, verslijten
¹**freak** (n) **1** gril, kuur, nuk **2** uitzonderlijk verschijnsel[h] **3** [inform] fanaticus, freak, fanaat
²**freak** (adj) abnormaal, uitzonderlijk, ongewoon: *a ~ accident* een bizar ongeval; *~ weather* typisch weer
³**freak** (vb): *~ out* door het lint gaan, helemaal gek worden, flippen
fr<u>ea</u>k <u>ou</u>t [inform] helemaal gek maken: *the pop star freaked out the audience* de popster bracht het publiek tot hysterie
fr<u>e</u>ckle (zomer)sproet
¹**free** (adj) **1** vrij, onafhankelijk, onbelemmerd: *a ~ agent* iem. die vrij kan handelen; ~

fight algemeen gevecht; *give* (or: *allow*) *s.o. a* ~ **hand** iem. de vrije hand laten; [socc] ~ **kick** vrije schop; ~ **speech** vrijheid van meningsuiting; **set** ~ vrijlaten, in vrijheid stellen; ~ **from** *care* vrij van zorgen, onbekommerd; ~ **of** *charge* gratis, kosteloos **2** vrij, gratis, belastingvrij: [inform] **for** ~ gratis, voor niets **3** vrij, zonder staatsinmenging: ~ **enterprise** (de) vrije onderneming; ~ **trade** vrije handel, vrijhandel **4** vrij, niet bezet, niet in gebruik; [science] ongebonden: *is this* **seat** ~? is deze plaats vrij? **5** vrijmoedig, vrijpostig: ~ *and* *easy* ongedwongen, zorgeloos ‖ ~ **pardon** gratie(verlening)
²free (vb) **1** bevrijden, vrijlaten **2** verlossen, losmaken, vrijstellen
³free (adv) **1** vrij, los, ongehinderd: *the dogs ran* ~ de honden liepen los **2** gratis
freebie [inform] weggevertje[h], iets dat je gratis krijgt
freebooter vrijbuiter [oft fig]; kaper
freedom 1 vrijheid, onafhankelijkheid: ~ *of the* **press** persvrijheid; ~ *of* **speech** vrijheid van meningsuiting **2** vrijstelling, ontheffing, vrijwaring
free-for-all [inform] **1** algemene ruzie; algemeen gevecht **2** vrij spel; wildweststituatie
freehold 1 volledig eigendomsrecht **2** vrij bezit
free house pub die (or: café[h] dat) niet onder contract staat bij een brouwerij
¹freelance (adj) freelance, onafhankelijk, zelfstandig
²freelance (vb) freelance werken, als freelancer werken
freeload klaplopen, profiteren, bietsen
freeman 1 vrij man **2** ereburger
freemason vrijmetselaar
freephone het gratis bellen [eg an 0800 number]
freepost antwoordnummer[h] ‖ ~ *no. 1111* antwoordnummer 1111
free-range scharrel-: ~ *eggs* scharreleieren
freesia fresia
freestyle 1 [swimming] vrije slag, (borst)-crawl **2** [wrestling etc] vrije stijl
freeway [Am] snelweg, autoweg
freewheel rustig aandoen [also fig]
¹freeze (n) **1** vorst, vorstperiode **2** bevriezing, blokkering, opschorting: *a* **wage** ~ een loonstop
²freeze (vb) vriezen: *it is freezing in here* het is hier om te bevriezen; *the government froze all* **contracts** de regering bevroor alle contracten
³freeze (vb) bevriezen [also fig]; verstijven, ijzig behandelen, opschorten: *make one's* **blood** ~ het bloed in de aderen doen stollen; ~ *out* [inform] uitsluiten ‖ *frozen* **with** *fear* verstijfd van angst
freezer 1 diepvries, diepvriezer **2** vriesvak[h]

freezing point vriespunt[h]
freight vracht(goederen)
freight car [Am] goederenwagon
¹French (n) Frans, de Franse taal: *the* ~ de Fransen
²French (adj) Frans: ~ **bread** (or: *loaf*) stokbrood ‖ ~ **bean** sperzieboon; ~ **fries** patat, friet; ~ **kiss** tongzoen; *take* ~ **leave** er tussenuit knijpen; ~ **windows** openslaande (bal-kon)deuren, openslaande (terras)deuren
¹French kiss (n) tongzoen
²French kiss (vb) tongzoenen
Frenchman Fransman
Frenchwoman Française, Franse
frenetic jachtig; woest; verwoed
frenzy (vlaag van) waanzin, razernij, staat van opwinding
frequency 1 frequentie, (herhaald) voorkomen[h] **2** [science] frequentie, trillingsgetal[h], periodetal[h] **3** [radio] frequentie, golflengte
¹frequent (adj) frequent, veelvuldig: *a* ~ *caller* een regelmatig bezoeker
²frequent (vb) regelmatig bezoeken
fresh 1 vers, pas gebakken, vers geplukt: ~ *from the oven* zo uit de oven, ovenvers **2** nieuw, ander, recent: *a* ~ *attempt* een hernieuwde poging **3** zoet [of water]; niet brak **4** zuiver, helder, levendig: ~ *air* frisse lucht **5** fris, koel, nogal koud: *a* ~ *breeze* een frisse bries [wind-force 5] **6** [inform] brutaal, flirterig
freshen in kracht toenemen, aanwakkeren
freshen up 1 opfrissen, verfrissen **2** zich opfrissen, zich verfrissen
fresher [inform] eerstejaars(student)
freshman eerstejaars(student), groene
freshwater zoetwater-
fret zich ergeren, zich opvreten (van ergernis), zich zorgen maken: *the child is* ~*ting* **for** *its mother* het kind zit om z'n moeder te zeuren
fretful geïrriteerd, zeurderig
fretsaw figuurzaag
friar monnik, broeder
friction wrijving [also fig]; frictie, onenigheid
Friday vrijdag: *on* ~(*s*) vrijdags, op vrijdag
fridge [inform] *refrigerator* koelkast, ijskast
fried gebakken: ~ *egg* spiegelei
friend 1 vriend(in), kameraad, kennis, collega: *make* ~*s with s.o.* bevriend raken met; *can we still be* ~*s?* kunnen we vrienden blijven?; *a* ~ *in need (is a* ~ *indeed)* in nood leert men zijn vrienden kennen **2** vriend(in), voorstander, liefhebber
friendly 1 vriendelijk, welwillend, aardig **2** vriendschappelijk, bevriend, gunstig gezind: ~ *nations* bevriende naties
friendship vriendschap
fries [esp Am] patat; [Belg] frieten

Friesian see Frisian
frieze fries+h, sierlijst
frigate fregath
fright angst, vrees, schrik: *give a ~* de schrik op 't lijf jagen; *he took ~ at the sight of the knife* de schrik sloeg hem om 't hart toen hij het mes zag
frighten bang maken, doen schrikken, afschrikken: *we were ~ed to **death*** we schrokken ons dood; *~ s.o. to **death*** iem. de stuipen op het lijf jagen; *be ~ed **of** snakes* bang voor slangen zijn
frightful 1 angstaanjagend **2** [inform] afschuwelijk: *I am ~ly **late*** ik ben vreselijk laat
frigid 1 koud [also fig]; koel, onvriendelijk **2** frigide
frill 1 (sier)strook **2** (-s) franje [also fig]; fraaiigheden, kouwe drukte
fringe 1 franje **2** randgroepering, randverschijnselh: *the ~s of **society*** de zelfkant van de maatschappij **3** pony(haarh)
fringe benefit secundaire arbeidsvoorwaarde
frisbee frisbee
Frisian Fries
¹frisk (vb) huppelen, springen
²frisk (vb) fouilleren
frisky vrolijk, speels
fritter away verkwisten, verspillen
frivolous 1 onbelangrijk, pietluttig, onnozel **2** frivool, lichtzinnig
frizz kroeskop, kroeshaarh, krul(len)
¹frizzle (vb) **1** krullen, kroezen **2** sissen; knetteren [in pan]
²frizzle (vb) **1** kroezend maken, doen krullen: *~ **up*** friseren **2** laten sissen; laten knetteren [in pan]; braden, bakken
fro see ¹to
frock jurk, japon
frog kikker, kikvors: *as mad as a **box** of ~s* zo gek als een deur ‖ *have a ~ in one's throat* een kikker in de keel hebben, schor/hees zijn
frogman kikvorsman
¹frolic (n) pret, lol, gekheid: *the little **boys** were having a ~* de jongetjes waren aan het stoeien
²frolic (vb) **1** (rond)dartelen, rondhossen **2** pret maken
from van, vanaf, vanuit: *~ one **day** to the next* van de ene dag op de andere; *judge ~ the **facts*** oordelen naar de feiten; *I heard ~ **Mary*** ik heb bericht gekregen van Mary; *recite ~ **memory*** uit het geheugen opzeggen; *~ **bad** to **worse*** van kwaad tot erger; *(in) a week ~ **now*** over een week
¹front (n) **1** voorkant, voorste gedeelteh: *the driver sits **in** (the) ~* de bestuurder zit voorin; *in ~ **of*** voor, in aanwezigheid van **2** [mil] fronth [also fig]; gevechtslinie **3** façade [also fig]; schijn, dekmantel: *show (or: put on) a **bold** ~* zich moedig voordoen **4** (strand)boulevard,

promenade langs de rivier **5** [meteorology] fronth
²front (adj) **1** voorst, eerst: *~ **garden*** voortuin; *~ **runner*** koploper **2** façade-, camouflage-: *~ **organisation*** mantelorganisatie ‖ *up ~* eerlijk, rechtdoorzee
frontage 1 fronth; voorgevel **2** voorterreinh
frontal frontaal, voor-: *~ **attack*** frontale aanval
front crawl borstcrawl
front door voordeur
frontier grens(gebiedh): *the ~s of **knowledge*** de grenzen van het weten
frontline frontlinie [also fig]
front page voorpagina [of newspaper]
front runner [athletics] koploper
¹frost (n) vorst, bevriezing: *there was five **degrees** of ~* het vroor vijf graden
²frost (vb) **1** bevriezen [plant etc] **2** glaceren [cake] **3** matteren [glas, metal]: *~ed **glass*** matglas
frostbite bevriezing
frosting [esp Am] eiwitglazuur
frosty vriezend, (vries)koud; [fig] ijzig; afstandelijk: *~ **welcome*** koele verwelkoming
¹froth (n) **1** schuimh **2** oppervlakkigheid, zeepbel **3** gebazelh
froth (vb) schuimen, schuimbekken
¹frown (n) frons, fronsende blik, afkeuring
²frown (vb) de wenkbrauwen fronsen, streng kijken, turen: [fig] *~ **at** (or: on)* afkeuren(d staan tegenover)
frozen 1 bevroren, vastgevroren, doodgevroren: *~ **over*** dichtgevroren **2** (ijs)koud [also fig]; ijzig, hard **3** diepvries-, ingevroren: *~ **food*** diepvriesvoedsel **4** [econ] bevroren, geblokkeerd: *~ **assets*** bevroren tegoeden
frugal 1 (+ of) zuinig (met), spaarzaam (met) **2** schraal, karig, sober
fruit 1 vrucht, stukh fruit **2** fruith, vruchten: [also fig] *bear ~* vrucht dragen **3** (-s) opbrengst, resultaath
fruiterer fruithandelaar, fruitkoopman
fruitful vruchtbaar [also fig]; productief, lonend
fruition vervulling, verwezenlijking, realisatie: *bring (or: come) to ~* in vervulling doen gaan
fruit machine fruitautomaat, gokautomaat
frumpish slonzig; t(r)uttig
frustrate frustreren, verijdelen: *~ s.o. **in** his plans, ~ s.o.'s **plans*** iemands plannen dwarsbomen
frustration 1 frustratie, teleurstelling **2** verijdeling, dwarsboming
¹fry (n) jong(e vis), broed(selh); [fig] kleintjeh; jonkieh.
²fry (vb) braden, bakken, frituren: *a fried **egg*** een spiegelei

frying pan koekenpan || *from* (or: *out*) *of the* ~ *into the fire* van de wal in de sloot
ft foot, feet ft, voet
¹fuck (vb) [vulg] neuken, naaien, wippen
²fuck (n): *what the* ~ *is going on here?* wat is hier verdomme aan de hand?
¹fuck off (vb) [vulg] opsodemieteren
²fuck off (vb) [vulg] pissig maken
fuck up [vulg] verkloten; verpesten
fuddled verward, in de war, beneveld, dronken
¹fudge (n) **1** onzin, larie **2** zachte karamel
²fudge (vb) **1** knoeien (met), vervalsen **2** er omheen draaien, ontwijken **3** in elkaar flansen
fuel brandstof; [fig] voedselʰ: ~ *for dissension* stof tot onenigheid
fuel oil stookolie
fug bedomptheid, mufheid
fugitive vluchteling, voortvluchtige
fugue fuga
fulfil volbrengen, vervullen, uitvoeren, voltooien: ~ *a condition* aan een voorwaarde voldoen; ~ *a purpose* aan een doel beantwoorden
fulfilment 1 vervulling **2** voldoening
¹full (n) totaalʰ, geheelʰ: *in* ~ volledig, voluit
²full (adj) vol, volledig: ~ *board* vol(ledig) pension; ~ *to the brim* boordevol; *come* ~ *circle* weer terugkomen bij het begin; [fig] *give* ~ *marks for sth.* iets hoog aanslaan, iets erkennen; ~ *moon* vollemaan; *(at)* ~ *speed* (in) volle vaart; ~ *stop* punt [punctuation mark]; *come to a* ~ *stop* (plotseling) tot stilstand komen; *in* ~ *swing* in volle gang; ~ *of o.s.* vol van zichzelf; *he was* ~ *of it* hij was er vol van
³full (adv) **1** volledig, ten volle: ~ *ripe* helemaal rijp **2** zeer, heel: *know sth.* ~ *well* iets zeer goed weten **3** vlak, recht: *hit s.o.* ~ *on the nose* iem. recht op zijn neus slaan
full-blooded 1 volbloed, raszuiver **2** volbloedig, energiek
full-blown 1 in volle bloei **2** goed ontwikkeld, volledig: ~ *war* regelrechte oorlog
full-grown volwassen, volgroeid
full-scale volledig, totaal, levensgroot
full-time fulltime, met volledige dagtaak
fully 1 volledig, geheel: ~ *automatic* volautomatisch **2** minstens, ten minste: ~ *an hour* minstens een uur
fully-fledged 1 geheel bevederd [of bird] **2** volwassen, ten volle ontwikkeld **3** (ras)echt, volslagen
fulminate foeteren; fulmineren; heftig uitvaren
fulsome overdreven
¹fumble (vb) struikelen, hakkelen, klunzen
²fumble (vb) **1** tasten, morrelen (aan), rommelen (in): ~ *about* rondtasten **2** [ball game] fumbelen
¹fume (n) (onwelriekende/giftige) damp, rook
²fume (vb) **1** roken, dampen **2** opstijgen [of fume] **3** [fig] koken [with rage]; branden: ~ *at* verbolgen zijn over
fumigate uitroken, zuiveren
¹fun (n) pret, vermaakʰ, plezierʰ: *figure of* ~ groteske figuur, schertsfiguur; ~ *and games* pretmakerij, iets leuks; *make* ~ *of, poke* ~ *at* voor de gek houden, de draak steken met; *for* ~, *for the* ~ *of it* (or: *the thing*) voor de aardigheid; *for* ~, *in* ~ voor de grap
²fun (adj) prettig, amusant, gezellig: *a* ~ *guy* een leuke kerel; *a* ~ *game* een leuk spelletje
¹function (n) **1** functie, taak, werking **2** plechtigheid, ceremonie, receptie, feestʰ: *I have a* ~ *tonight* ik ga vanavond naar een feest (receptie)
²function (vb) functioneren, werken: ~ *as* fungeren als
functional functioneel, doelmatig, bruikbaar
functionary functionaris, beambte
function key functietoets
function room zaal, receptiezaal, feestzaal
fund 1 fondsʰ **2** voorraad, bron, schat: *a* ~ *of knowledge* een schat aan kennis **3** (-s) fondsen, geldʰ, kapitaalʰ: *short of* ~s slecht bij kas
¹fundamental (n) (grond)beginselʰ, grondslag, fundamentʰ
²fundamental (adj) fundamenteel, grond-, basis-
fundamentalism fundamentalismeʰ
funding fondsgelden
fund raiser 1 benefiet **2** fondsenwerver
funeral 1 begrafenis(plechtigheid); [Am] rouwdienst **2** [Am] begrafenisstoet **3** [inform] zorg, zaak: *it's is your* ~ het is jouw zorg
funereal akelig, droevig, triest: *a* ~ *expression* begrafenisgezicht
funfair 1 pretparkʰ, amusementsparkʰ **2** reizende kermis
fungal schimmel-
fungus fungus, paddenstoel, schimmel
funicular kabelbaan(trein)
funk [inform] schrik, angst: *be in a (blue)* ~ in de rats zitten
funky 1 [Am; inform] funky, eenvoudig; gevoelsmatig [of music] **2** [inform] extravagant, cool **3** [Am] stinkend
¹funnel (n) **1** trechter **2** koker, pijp; schoorsteen(pijp) [of steamship]
²funnel (vb) afvoeren (als) door een trechter: ~ *off* doen afvloeien
funny 1 grappig, leuk **2** vreemd, gek **3** niet in orde, niet pluis: *there is sth.* ~ *about* er is iets niet pluis met **4** misselijk, onwel: *feel* ~ zich onwel voelen || ~ *bone* telefoonbotje [in elbow]
fur 1 vacht **2** bontʰ, pels(werkʰ), bontjas

3 aanslag, beslag^h
fu**rious 1** woedend, razend **2** fel, verwoed, heftig: a ~ **quarrel** een felle twist
fu**rlough** verlof(tijd): **on** ~ met verlof
fu**rnace** oven, verwarmingsketel, hoogoven
fu**rnish 1** verschaffen, leveren, voorzien van **2** uitrusten, meubileren, inrichten: a ~ed **house** een gemeubileerd huis
fu**rnishings** woninginrichting
fu**rniture** meubilair^h, meubels: a **piece** of ~ een meubelstuk
fu**rniture van** verhuiswagen
fu**rrow 1** voor^h, gleuf, groef, rimpel **2** zog^h; spoor^h [of ship]
¹fu**rther** (adj) verder, nader: on ~ **consideration** bij nader inzien; ~ **education** voortgezet onderwijs voor volwassenen
²fu**rther** (vb) bevorderen, stimuleren: ~ s.o. 's interests iemands belangen behartigen
³fu**rther** (adv) verder, nader, elders: **inquire** ~ nadere inlichtingen inwinnen
fu**rtherm**o**re** verder, bovendien
fu**rthermost** verst (verwijderd)
fu**rthest** verst, laatst, meest
fu**rtive** heimelijk
fu**ry** woede(aanval), razernij
¹fuse (n) **1** lont **2** (schok)buis, ontsteker **3** zekering, stop: a ~ has **blown** er is een zekering gesprongen
²fuse (vb) **1** (doen) fuseren [of businesses etc] **2** (doen) uitvallen [of electrical appliance]
fu**sion** fusie(proces^h), (samen)smelting, mengeling, coalitie, kernfusie
fu**sion bomb** waterstofbom
¹fuss (n) (nodeloze) drukte, omhaal, ophef: I don't understand what all the ~ is **about** ik snap niet waar al die heisa om gemaakt wordt; **kick** up (or: **make**) a ~ heibel maken, luidruchtig protesteren; make a ~ **of** (or: over) overdreven aandacht schenken aan
²fuss (vb) (+ about) zich druk maken (om), drukte maken, zich opwinden: ~ **about** zenuwachtig rondlopen
fu**ssy 1** (overdreven) druk, zenuwachtig, bemoeiziek **2** pietluttig, moeilijk: [inform] I'm not ~ het is mij om het even
fu**tile** vergeefs, doelloos
fu**tility** nutteloosheid, doelloosheid
¹fu**ture** (n) toekomst: in the **distant** ~ in de verre toekomst; **for** the (or: **in**) ~ voortaan, in 't vervolg
²fu**ture** (adj) toekomstig, aanstaande: ~ **tense** toekomende tijd
fu**zz 1** dons^h, pluis, donzig haar^h **2** [inform] smeris [policeman]; de smerissen [the police]
fu**zzy 1** donzig, pluizig **2** kroes, krullig **3** vaag **4** verward ‖ [maths] ~ **logic** fuzzy logic, vage logica
f-word vloekwoord^h

FYI for your information ter info(rmatie)

g

g *gram(s)* g, gram
gabble kakelen, kwebbelen: ~ *away* erop los kletsen
gable gevelspits, geveltop
gabled met gevelspits
Gabon Gabon
¹**Gabonese** (n) Gabonees, Gabonese
²**Gabonese** (adj) Gabonees
gadfly paardenvlieg, horzel
gadget (handig) dingetjeʰ, apparaatjeʰ, snufjeʰ
gadgetry snufjes
Gaelic Gaelisch
gaffe blunder; flater
gaffer chef-technicus [at TV or film shootings]
¹**gag** (n) **1** (mond)prop **2** (zorgvuldig voorbereid) komisch effectʰ **3** grap
²**gag** (vb) kokhalzen, braken: ~ *on sth.* zich in iets verslikken
³**gag** (vb) een prop in de mond stoppen
gaga 1 kierewiet: *go* ~ kinds worden **2** stapel: *be* ~ *about* stapel zijn op
gaggle 1 vlucht (ganzen) **2** (snaterend) gezelschap: *a* ~ *of girls* een stel snaterende meisjes
gaiety vrolijkheid, pret, opgewektheid
¹**gain** (n) **1** aanwinst **2** groei, stijging, verhoging **3** (-s) winst, opbrengst
²**gain** (vb) **1** winst maken **2** winnen: ~ *(up)on* terrein winnen op, inhalen **3** groeien **4** voorlopen [of timepiece]: *my watch* ~*s (three minutes a day)* mijn horloge loopt (elke dag drie minuten meer) voor
³**gain** (vb) winnen, verkrijgen, behalen: ~ *the victory* (or: *the day*) de overwinning behalen; ~ *weight* aankomen
gainful 1 winstgevend **2** bezoldigd; betaald
gait gang, pas, loop
¹**gal** (n) meid, meisjeʰ
²**gal** *gallon(s)*
galactic galactisch; van de Melkweg
galaxy Melkweg
gale storm, harde wind
¹**gall** (n) **1** gal(blaas) **2** bitterheid, rancune **3** galnoot, galappel **4** brutaliteit, lef
²**gall** (vb) (mateloos) irriteren, razend maken
gallant dapper, moedig; indrukwekkend [of ship, horse]
gallantry 1 moedige daad **2** moed, dapperheid **3** hoffelijkheid
gall bladder galblaas

galleon galjoenʰ
gallery 1 galerij, portiek, (zuilen)gang **2** galerij, balkonʰ **3** museumʰ, museumzaal **4** (kunst)galerie **5** engelenbak: [fig] *play to the* ~ op het publiek spelen, effect najagen; commercieel zijn
galley 1 galei **2** kombuis
Gallic Gallisch, Frans
gallicize verfransen
gallon gallon [measure of capacity]
¹**gallop** (n) galop: *at a* ~ in galop, op een galop; [fig] op een holletje
²**gallop** (vb) galopperen; [fig] zich haasten; vliegen
gallows galg
gallows humour galgenhumor
gallstone galsteen
galore in overvloed, genoeg: *examples* ~ voorbeelden te over
galvanic 1 galvanisch **2** opwindend, opzienbarend
galvanize prikkelen, opzwepen: ~ *s.o. into action* (or: *activity*) iem. tot actie aansporen
the **Gambia** Gambia
¹**Gambian** (n) Gambiaan(se)
²**Gambian** (adj) Gambiaans
¹**gamble** (n) gok(jeʰ) [also fig]; riskante zaak, speculatie: *take a* ~ *(on)* een gokje wagen (op); *it is a* ~ het is een gok
²**gamble** (vb) **1** gokken, spelen, dobbelen: ~ *on* gokken op **2** speculeren
³**gamble** (vb) op het spel zetten, inzetten: ~ *away* vergokken
gambler gokker
gambling gokkerij
¹**game** (n) **1** spelʰ [also fig]; wedstrijd, partij: ~ *of chance* kansspel; *play the* ~ eerlijk (spel) spelen, zich aan de regels houden; *it is all in the* ~ het hoort er (allemaal) bij **2** spelletjeʰ, tijdverdrijfʰ **3** [tennis] game: *(one)* ~ *all* gelijk(e stand); ~ *and (set)* game en set **4** plannetjeʰ: *two can play (at) that* ~ dat spelletje kan ik ook spelen; *none of your (little)* ~*s!* geen kunstjes!; *the* ~ *is up* het spel is uit, nu hangen jullie **5** jachtdierʰ; prooi [also fig] **6** (-s) spelenʰ, (atletiek)wedstrijden **7** (-s) gym(nastiek); sport [at school] ‖ *beat* (or: *play*) *s.o. at his own* ~ iem. een koekje van eigen deeg geven
²**game** (adj) **1** dapper, kranig, flink **2** bereid(willig), enthousiast: *be* ~ *to do sth.* bereid zijn om iets te doen; *I am* ~ ik doe mee **3** lam; kreupel [of arm, leg]
gamecock vechthaan
gamekeeper jachtopziener
games computer spelcomputer
game show spelshow
gammon 1 (gekookte) achterham **2** gerookte ham
gamut gamma⁺ʰ [also fig]; toonladder, scala, reeks: *the whole* ~ *of human experience*

het hele register van menselijke ervaringen
gander mannetjesgans || *have/take a ~ at*
een blik werpen op
gang groep mensen, (boeven)bende, troep;
ploeg [workers]: *violent street ~s* gewelddadige straatbendes; *a ~ of labourers removing graffiti* een ploeg werklui die graffiti verwijderen
gangling slungelig
gangplank loopplank
gangrene 1 koudvuurʰ **2** verrotting
¹gangsta (n) [Am; inform] gangster, bendelidʰ
²gangsta (adj) [Am; inform] heftig
gangsta rap [Am; inform] gangsterrap
gangster gangster, bendelidʰ
gang up een bende vormen, (samen)klieken, zich verenigen: *~ against* (or: *on*) samenspannen tegen, aanvallen; *~ with* zich aansluiten bij, samenspannen met
gangway 1 doorgang **2** (gang)padʰ [in theatre etc] **3** loopplank
gaol *see ¹jail*
gap (tussen)ruimte, opening, gatʰ, kloof, barst, ravijnʰ, tekortʰ: *bridge* (or: *close, fill*) *a ~* **a)** een kloof overbruggen; **b)** een tekort aanvullen; *some developing countries are quickly closing the ~* sommige ontwikkelingslanden lopen snel de achterstand in
gape 1 gapen, geeuwen **2** geopend zijn, gapen: *gaping wound* gapende wond **3** staren: *~ at* aangapen, aanstaren
gapper [educ] student die zijn studie een jaar onderbreekt
gap year tussenjaar: *take a ~* een jaartje ertussenuit gaan
garage garage, garagebedrijfʰ, benzinestationʰ
garb dracht, kledij
garbage 1 afvalʰ, huisvuilʰ **2** rommel
garbage can vuilnisbak, vuilnisvatʰ
garbage collector vuilnisman
garble onvolledige voorstelling geven van, verkeerd voorstellen, verdraaien: *~d account* verdraaide voorstelling
¹garden (n) tuin [also fig]; groenten, bloementuin: *the ~ of Eden* de hof van Eden, het Aards Paradijs; *lead up the ~ (path)* om de tuin leiden
²garden (vb) tuinieren
gardener tuinman, hovenier, tuinier
gardening het tuinieren, tuinbouw
garden party tuinfeestʰ
gargantuan gigantisch
gargle gorgelen
gargoyle waterspuwer
garish 1 fel, schel **2** bont, opzichtig
garland 1 slinger **2** lauwer(krans)
garlic knoflookʰ
garment kledingstukʰ: *~s* kleren
garner [form] opslaan; vergaren: *~ in* (or:

up) binnenhalen
¹garnish (n) garnering, versiering
²garnish (vb) garneren, verfraaien, opkloppen
¹garotte (n) wurgpaal; garrot
²garotte (vb) verwurgen
garret zolderkamertjeʰ
garrison garnizoenʰ, garnizoensplaats
garter kousenband, jarretelle
gas 1 gasʰ, gifgasʰ, lachgasʰ, mijngasʰ: *natural ~* aardgas **2** benzine: *step on the ~* gas geven, er vaart achter zetten **3** [inform] gezwamʰ, kletspraat, gekletsʰ
gasbag kletsmeier
gas chamber gaskamer
gas fitter gasfitter
gas guzzler [inform] benzineslokop
gash 1 jaap, gapende wond **2** kloof, breuk
gasket pakking
gaslight 1 gaslamp **2** gaslichtʰ
gas lighter gasaansteker, gasontsteker
gas main hoofd(gas)leiding
gasman meteropnemer
gas mark stand
gasoline 1 gasoline **2** benzine
¹gasp (n) snik: *at one's last ~* bij de laatste ademtocht
²gasp (vb) **1** (naar adem) snakken, naar lucht happen: *~ for breath* naar adem snakken **2** hijgen, puffen, snuiven
³gasp (vb) haperend uitbrengen, hijgend uitbrengen: *'call an ambulance!' she ~ed* 'bel een ziekenwagen!' hijgde ze
gas ring gaspit
gas station benzinestationʰ, tankstationʰ
gassy 1 met een hoog koolzuurgehalte, met veel prik **2** [Am] winderig
gastric maag-
gastronome fijnproever
gastronomy fijnproeverij
gasworks gasfabriek(en)
gate 1 poort(jeʰ), deur, hekʰ, ingang, afsluitboom, slagboom, sluis(deur), schuif; uitgang [at airport]; perronʰ: *anti-theft ~s* antidiefstalpoortjes **2** [sport] publiekʰ [number of paying spectators]: *a ~ of 2000* 2000 man publiek **3** entreegelden
gatecrash (onuitgenodigd) binnenvallen [at party etc]
gatecrasher onuitgenodigde gast, indringer
gatekeeper portierʰ
gate money entreegelden; recette
gatepost deurpost || *between you and me and the ~* onder ons gezegd en gezwegen
gateway poort: *the ~ to success* de poort tot succes; *the ~ to Europe* de toegangspoort tot Europa
¹gather (vb) **1** zich verzamelen, samenkomen: *~ round* bijeenkomen; *~ round s.o. (sth.)* zich rond iem. (iets) scharen **2** zich op(een)-

hopen, zich op(een)stapelen
²gather (vb) **1** verzamelen, samenbrengen, bijeenroepen, op(een)hopen, op(een)stapelen, vergaren, inzamelen, plukken, oogsten, oprapen: ~ *(one's) strength* op krachten komen; ~ *wood* hout sprokkelen; ~ *speed* op snelheid komen **2** opmaken, afleiden, concluderen: *your husband is not in I* ~ uw echtgenoot is niet thuis, begrijp ik; ~ *from* afleiden uit
gathering 1 bijeenkomst, vergadering **2** verzameling, op(een)stapeling, op(een)hoping
gauche onhandig, onbeholpen
gaudy opzichtig, schel, bont
¹gauge (n) **1** standaardmaat, ijkmaat, vermogen^h, capaciteit, inhoud; kaliber^h [also of firearms]: *narrow-~ film* smalfilm **2** meetinstrument^h, meter, kaliber^h
²gauge (vb) meten, uitmeten, afmeten, opmeten, peilen
gaunt 1 uitgemergeld, vel over been **2** somber
gauntlet kaphandschoen, sporthandschoen, werkhandschoen: *fling* (or: *throw*) *down the* ~ iem. uitdagen; *pick* (or: *take*) *up the* ~ de uitdaging aanvaarden; *run the* ~ spitsroeden (moeten) lopen
gauze gaas^h, verbandgaas^h, muggengaas^h
gavel voorzittershamer
gawk [inform] gapen: ~ *at sth.* naar iets staan gapen
gawky klungelig, onhandig
¹gay (n) homo(seksueel), nicht, lesbienne
²gay (adj) **1** homoseksueel: ~ *marriage* (or: *blessing*) homohuwelijk **2** vrolijk, opgeruimd **3** fleurig, bont: ~ *colours* bonte kleuren
gaze staren, aangapen: ~ *at* (or: *on*) aanstaren
gazelle gazel(le), antilope
gazette krant, dagblad^h
gazillion [esp Am; inform] onbepaald groot getal, massa, tig: *make ~s of dollars* zakken vol dollars verdienen
GB *Great Britain* Groot-Brittannië
GCE *General Certificate of Education* middelbareschooldiploma, havodiploma, vwo-diploma
GCSE *General Certificate of Secondary Education* eindexamen
¹gear (n) **1** toestel^h, mechanisme^h, apparaat^h, inrichting: *landing* ~ landingsgestel **2** transmissie, koppeling, versnelling: *bottom* ~ eerste versnelling; *reverse* ~ achteruit; *top* ~ hoogste versnelling; *change* ~ (over)schakelen **3** uitrusting, gereedschap^h, kledij, spullen: *hunting* ~ jagersuitrusting
²gear (vb) (over)schakelen, in (een) versnelling zetten: ~ *down* terugschakelen, vertragen; ~ *up* opschakelen, overschakelen

gearbox versnellingsbak
gearlever (versnellings)pook
gear to afstemmen op, instellen, afstellen op: *be geared to* ingesteld zijn op, berekend zijn op
gearwheel tandwiel^h, tandrad^h
gee jee(tje)!
geek sukkel, fanaat: *computer~* computerfanaat
geezer (ouwe) vent
¹gel (n) gel
²gel (vb) **1** gel(ei)achtig worden, stollen **2** vorm krijgen [of ideas etc]; goed kunnen samenwerken [of people]; lukken
gelatin gelatine(achtige stof)
geld castreren
gelding castraat, gecastreerd paard^h, ruin
gem 1 edelsteen, juweel^h **2** kleinood^h, juweeltje^h
Gemini [astrology] (de) Tweelingen
gemstone (half)edelsteen
gender (grammaticaal) geslacht^h
gene gen^h
genealogy genealogie, familiekunde
¹general (n) **1** algemeenheid, het algemeen: *in* ~ in het algemeen **2** generaal, veldheer
²general (adj) algemeen: ~ *anaesthetic* algehele verdoving; ~ *election* algemene, landelijke verkiezingen; *in the* ~ *interest* in het algemeen belang; *the* ~ *public* het grote publiek; *as a* ~ *rule* in 't algemeen, doorgaans ‖ ~ *delivery* poste restante; ~ *practitioner* huisarts
generality algemeenheid
generalize generaliseren, veralgemenen, (zich) vaag uitdrukken
generally 1 gewoonlijk, meestal **2** algemeen: ~ *known* algemeen bekend **3** in het algemeen, ruwweg: ~ *speaking* in 't algemeen
general-purpose voor algemeen gebruik; universeel
generate genereren, doen ontstaan, voortbrengen: ~ *electricity* elektriciteit opwekken; ~ *heat* warmte ontwikkelen
generation 1 generatie, (mensen)geslacht^h, mensenleven^h **2** generatie, voortplanting, ontwikkeling
generation gap generatiekloof
generator generator
generic 1 de soort betreffende, generiek **2** algemeen, verzamel- ‖ ~ *drugs* merkloze geneesmiddelen
generosity vrijgevigheid, gulheid
generous 1 grootmoedig, edel(moedig) **2** vrijgevig, royaal, gul **3** overvloedig, rijk(elijk)
genesis ontstaan^h, wording
Genesis (het bijbelboek) Genesis
genetic genetisch: ~ *engineering* geneti-

sche manipulatie; ~ *fingerprint* genenprint; ~*ally* *modified* genetisch gemodificeerd
geneticist geneticus
genetics genetica, erfelijkheidsleer
Geneva Genève
genial 1 mild, zacht, aangenaam; warm [of weather, climate etc] **2** vriendelijk, sympathiek
geniality hartelijkheid, sympathie, vriendelijkheid
genital genitaal, geslachts-, voortplantings-
genitalia genitaliën, geslachtsorganen
genitive genitief, tweede naamval
genius 1 genie[h] [pers]: *be a ~ at* geniaal zijn in **2** genialiteit, begaafdheid: *a woman of ~* een geniale vrouw **3** geest: *evil ~* kwade genius
Genoa Genua
genocide genocide, volkerenmoord
genre genre[h], soort, type[h]
gent gentleman, heer || [inform] *the Gents* het herentoilet
genteel 1 [oft iron] chic, elegant: ~ *poverty* fatsoenlijke/stille armoede **2** aanstellerig
[1]**gentile** (n) niet-jood, christen, heiden
[2]**gentile** (adj) niet-joods, christelijk, ongelovig
gentility deftigheid, voornaamheid
gentle 1 voornaam, van goede afkomst **2** zacht, licht, (ge)matig(d): ~ *pressure* lichte dwang; *hold it gently* hou het voorzichtig vast **3** zacht(aardig), teder, vriendelijk: *the ~ sex* het zwakke geslacht **4** kalm, bedaard, rustig
gentleman 1 (echte) heer: *Ladies and Gentlemen!* Dames en Heren! **2** edelman
gentleman's agreement herenakkoord[h]
gentry lage(re) adel, voorname stand: *landed ~* (groot)grondbezitters, lage landadel
genuflect [form] een kniebuiging maken
genuine 1 echt, zuiver, onvervalst: ~ *parts* oorspronkelijke onderdelen **2** oprecht, eerlijk
genus 1 soort, genre[h], klasse **2** genus[h], geslacht[h]
geographer aardrijkskundige, geograaf
geographic(al) aardrijkskundig, geografisch
geography aardrijkskunde, geografie: [inform] *the ~ of the house* de indeling van het huis
geological geologisch
geologist geoloog
geology geologie
geometric(al) meetkundig
geometry meetkunde
Georgia Georgië
Georgian 1 Georgisch [of Georgia] **2** Georgian [of or characteristic of the time of King

George]
gerbil woestijnrat
geriatric ouderdoms-; [depr] aftands; oud
geriatrics geriatrie, ouderdomszorg
germ 1 [biology] kiem, geslachtscel; [fig] oorsprong; begin[h] **2** [med] ziektekiem, bacil
[1]**German** (n) Duits[h], de Duitse taal
[2]**German** (n) Duitse(r)
[3]**German** (adj) Duits: ~ *shepherd* Duitse herder(shond) || ~ *measles* rodehond
Germanic 1 Germaans **2** Duits
Germany Duitsland
germ carrier bacillendrager, kiemdrager
germinate [also fig] ontkiemen, ontspruiten: *the idea ~d with him* het idee kwam bij hem op
germ warfare biologische oorlogvoering
gerontology ouderdomskunde
gestation dracht(tijd), zwangerschap(speriode)
gesticulate gebaren
[1]**gesture** (n) gebaar[h], geste, teken[h]: *a ~ of friendship* een vriendschappelijk gebaar
[2]**gesture** (vb) gebaren, (met gebaren) te kennen geven
[1]**get** (vb) **1** (ge)raken, (ertoe) komen, gaan, bereiken: ~ *rid of sth.* zich van iets ontdoen; *he is ~ting to be an old man* hij is een oude man aan het worden; *he never ~s to drive the car* hij krijgt nooit de kans om met de auto te rijden; ~ *lost* verdwalen; ~ *lost!* loop naar de maan!; ~ *to see s.o.* iem. te zien krijgen; ~ *ahead* vooruitkomen, succes boeken; ~ *behind* achterpraten; [fig] ~ *nowhere* (or: *somewhere*) niets (or: iets) bereiken; ~ *there* er komen, succes boeken; ~ *above o.s.* heel wat van zichzelf denken; ~ *at a)* bereiken, te pakken krijgen, komen aan, komen achter; **b)** [inform] bedoelen; **c)** bekritiseren; **d)** knoeien met; **e)** omkopen; **f)** ertussen nemen; ~ *at the truth* de waarheid achterhalen; *what are you ~ting at?* wat bedoel je daarmee?; ~ *in contact* (or: *touch*) *with* contact opnemen met; ~ *into the car* in de auto stappen; *what has got into you?* wat bezielt je?, wat heb je?; ~ *off a)* afstappen van [bicycle, pavement, lawn]; **b)** ontheven worden van [obligation]; ~ *onto s.o.* iem. te pakken krijgen; ~ *on(to) one's bike* op zijn fiets stappen; ~ *out of sth.* ergens uitraken, zich ergens uit redden; ~ *out of the way* uit de weg gaan, plaatsmaken; ~ *over* te boven komen, overwinnen; ~ *over an illness* genezen van een ziekte; *I still can't ~ over the fact that …* ik heb nog steeds moeite met het feit dat …, ik kan er niet over uit dat …; ~ *through* heen raken door [time, money, clothing, work]; ~ *through an exam* slagen voor een examen; ~ *to* bereiken, kunnen beginnen aan, toekomen aan; *where has he got to?* waar is hij naartoe?; ~ *to the top of the ladder* (or: *tree*)

de top bereiken **2** beginnen, aanvangen: ~ *going!* (or: *moving!*) vooruit!, begin (nu eindelijk)!; ~ *going* **a)** op dreef komen [of person]; **b)** op gang komen [of party, project, machine etc]; ~ *to like* sth. ergens de smaak van te pakken krijgen ‖ ~ *off the ground* van de grond raken; [inform] ~ *stuffed!* stik!, val dood!

²**get** (vb) **1** (ver)krijgen, verwerven: ~ *a glimpse of* vluchtig te zien krijgen; ~ *one's hands on* te pakken krijgen; ~ *leave* verlof krijgen; ~ *what is coming to one* krijgen wat men verdient; ~ sth. *out of* s.o. iets van iem. loskrijgen **2** (zich) aanschaffen, kopen: *my car was stolen, so I had to* ~ *a new one* mijn auto was gestolen, dus moest ik een nieuwe kopen **3** bezorgen, verschaffen, voorzien: ~ s.o. *some food* iem. te eten geven; ~ sth. *for* s.o. iem. iets bezorgen, iets voor iem. halen **4** doen geraken, doen komen, gaan, brengen, krijgen, doen: ~ sth. *going* iets op gang krijgen, iets op dreef helpen; ~ s.o. *talking* iem. aan de praat krijgen; [inform, fig] *it* ~s *you nowhere* je bereikt er niets mee; ~ sth. *into one's head* zich iets in het hoofd halen; ~ sth. *into* s.o.'s *head* iets aan iem. duidelijk maken; ~ s.o. *out of* sth. iem. aan iets helpen ontsnappen **5** maken, doen worden, bereiden, klaarmaken: ~ *dinner (ready)* het avondmaal bereiden; *let me* ~ *this clear* (or: *straight*) laat me dit even duidelijk stellen; ~ *ready* klaarmaken; ~ sth. *done* iets gedaan krijgen **6** nemen, vangen, opvangen, ontvangen, grijpen, (binnen)halen: *go and* ~ *your breakfast!* ga maar ontbijten! **7** overhalen, zover krijgen: ~ s.o. *to talk* iem. aan de praat krijgen **8** [inform] hebben, krijgen: *he got a mobile phone for his birthday* hij kreeg een mobieltje voor zijn verjaardag **9** vervelen, ergeren: *it really* ~s *me when* ik erger me dood wanneer **10** snappen, begrijpen, verstaan: *he has finally got the message* (or: *got it*) hij heeft het eindelijk door; ~ sth. *(s.o.) wrong* iets (iem.) verkeerd begrijpen

³**get** (aux vb) worden: ~ *killed (in an accident)* omkomen (bij een ongeluk); ~ *married* trouwen; ~ *punished* gestraft worden

⁴**get** (vb) (ge)raken, worden: ~ *better* beter worden; ~ *used to* wennen aan; ~ *even with* s.o. het iem. betaald zetten

get across 1 oversteken, aan de overkant komen **2** begrepen worden; aanslaan [of idea etc]; succes hebben **3** overkomen [of person]; bereiken, begrepen worden: ~ *to the audience* zijn gehoor weten te boeien

get along 1 vertrekken, voortmaken, weggaan **2** opschieten, vorderen: *is your work getting along?* schiet het al op met je werk? **3** (zich) redden, het stellen, het maken: *we can* ~ *without your help* we kunnen je hulp best missen **4** (+ with) (kunnen) opschieten

(met), overweg kunnen (met): *they* ~ *very well* ze kunnen het goed met elkaar vinden

get (a)round 1 op de been zijn; rondlopen [of person, after illness] **2** rondtrekken, rondreizen, overal komen **3** zich verspreiden; de ronde doen [of news]: *get (a)round to* s.o. iem. ter ore komen **4** gelegenheid hebben, toekomen: *get (a)round to* sth. **a)** aan iets kunnen beginnen; **b)** ergens de tijd voor vinden

getaway ontsnapping: *make one's* ~ ontsnappen

get away 1 wegkomen, weggaan: *did you manage to* ~ *this summer?* heb je deze zomer wat vakantie kunnen nemen? **2** ontsnappen, ontkomen: ~ *from* ontsnappen aan; *you can't* ~ *from this* hier kun je niet (meer) onderuit ‖ ~ *from it all* even alles achterlaten, er tussenuit gaan; *he'll never* ~ *with it* dat lukt hem nooit; *some students* ~ *with murder* sommige studenten mogen echt alles en niemand die er wat van zegt; *commit a crime and* ~ *with it* ongestraft een misdaad bedrijven

¹**get back** (vb) terugkomen, teruggaan, thuiskomen: ~! terug!, naar buiten! ‖ ~ *at* (or: *on*) s.o. het iem. betaald zetten

²**get back** (vb) **1** terugkrijgen, terugvinden **2** terugbrengen, terughalen, naar huis brengen ‖ *get one's own back (on* s.o.*)* het iem. betaald zetten

get by 1 zich er doorheen slaan, zich redden, het stellen: ~ *without* sth. het zonder iets kunnen stellen **2** (net) voldoen, er (net) mee door kunnen

¹**get down** (vb) dalen: ~ *on one's knees* op zijn knieën gaan (zitten) ‖ ~ *to* sth. aan iets kunnen beginnen, aan iets toekomen; ~ *to business* ter zake komen; ~ *to work* aan het werk gaan

²**get down** (vb) **1** doen dalen, naar beneden brengen; naar binnen krijgen [food] **2** deprimeren, ontmoedigen: *it is not just the work that gets you down* het is niet alleen het werk waar je depressief van wordt

¹**get in** (vb) **1** binnenkomen; toegelaten worden [to school, university]: ~ *on* sth. aan iets meedoen; [inform] ~ *on* the act mogen meedoen **2** instappen [into vehicle]

²**get in** (vb) binnenbrengen; binnenhalen [harvest]; inzamelen [money]: *get the doctor in* de dokter er bij halen; *I couldn't get a word in (edgeways)* ik kon er geen speld tussen krijgen, ik kreeg geen kans om ook maar iets te zeggen

¹**get off** (vb) **1** ontsnappen, ontkomen **2** afstappen, uitstappen: *you should* ~ *at Denmark Street* je moet bij Denmark Street uitstappen **3** vertrekken, beginnen: ~ *to a good start* flink van start gaan, goed beginnen **4** in slaap vallen **5** vrijkomen, er goed afkomen: ~ *lightly* er licht van afkomen ‖ ~ *with* het

aanleggen met, aanpappen met
²**get off** (vb) **1** doen vertrekken, doen beginnen **2** doen vrijkomen, er goed doen afkomen, vrijspraak krijgen voor: *he got me off with a fine* hij zorgde ervoor dat ik er met een bon af kwam **3** (op)sturen [letter]; wegsturen: *get s.o. off to school* iem. naar school sturen **4** eraf krijgen: *I can't get the lid off* ik krijg het deksel er niet af **5** uittrekken [clothing, shoes]; afnemen **6** leren, instuderen: *get sth. off by heart* iets uit het hoofd leren
¹**get on** (vb) **1** vooruitkomen, voortmaken, opschieten: *~ with one's work* goed opschieten met zijn werk **2** bloeien, floreren **3** (+ with) (kunnen) opschieten met, overweg kunnen met **4** oud (laat) worden: *he is getting on (in years)* hij wordt oud, hij wordt een dagje ouder **5** opstappen [horse, bicycle]; opstijgen; instappen [bus, aeroplane] ‖ *he is getting on for fifty* hij loopt tegen de vijftig; *~ to sth.* a) iets door hebben; b) iets op het spoor komen
²**get on** (vb) **1** aantrekken, opzetten: *~e's hat and coat on* zijn hoed opzetten en zijn jas aantrekken **2** erop krijgen: *I can't get the lid on* ik krijg het deksel er niet op
¹**get out** (vb) **1** uitlekken, bekend worden **2** naar buiten gaan, weggaan, eruit komen **3** ontkomen, maken dat je weg komt, ontsnappen: *no-one here gets out alive* niemand komt hier levend vandaan **4** afstappen, uitstappen
²**get out** (vb) eruit halen (krijgen) [splinter, stains; also fig]
¹**get over** (vb) begrepen worden [of joke, comedian]
²**get over** (vb) overbrengen [meaning etc]; duidelijk maken, doen begrijpen
¹**get through** (vb) (er) doorkomen, zijn bestemming bereiken; goedgekeurd worden [of bill]; aansluiting krijgen [by telephone etc]; begrepen worden: *~ to a)* bereiken, doordringen tot, contact krijgen met; *b)* begrepen worden door
²**get through** (vb) **1** zijn bestemming doen bereiken, laten goedkeuren; erdoor krijgen [also at exams] **2** duidelijk maken, aan zijn verstand brengen
get-together bijeenkomst
¹**get up** (vb) **1** opstaan, recht (gaan) staan **2** opsteken [of wind, storm etc] ‖ *~ to b)* bereiken; *b)* gaan naar, benaderen; *what is he getting up to now?* wat voert hij nu weer in zijn schild?
²**get up** (vb) **1** organiseren; op touw zetten [party, play] **2** maken, ontwikkelen, produceren: *~ speed* versnellen **3** instuderen, bestuderen ‖ *get one up on s.o.* iem. de loef afsteken; *~ to* doen bereiken
get-up 1 uitrusting, kostuumʰ **2** uitvoering,

formaatʰ **3** aankleding, decorʰ
geyser 1 geiser **2** (gas)geiser
Ghana Ghana
¹**Ghanaian** (n) Ghanees, Ghanese
²**Ghanaian** (adj) Ghanees
ghastly verschrikkelijk, afgrijselijk
gherkin augurk
ghetto gettoʰ
ghost 1 geest, spookʰ, spookverschijning **2** spook(beeld)ʰ, fata morgana **3** spoorʰ, greintjeʰ: *not have the ~ of a chance* geen schijn van kans hebben; *a ~ of a smile* een zweem van een glimlach ‖ *give up the ~* de geest geven, sterven
ghostly spookachtig
ghost town spookstad
ghost-writer spookschrijver
ghoul gruwelijk, morbide mens; monsterʰ
ghoulish 1 gruwelijk; morbide **2** satanisch
GHQ *General Headquarters* hoofdkwartierʰ
GI dienstplichtige
giant reus, kolos; [fig] uitblinker: *Shakespeare is one of the ~s of English literature* Shakespeare is een van de allergrootsten in de Engelse literatuur
giant killer reuzendoder [person who beats a favourite]
gibber brabbelen
gibberish gebrabbelʰ
gibbon gibbon
¹**gibe** (n) spottende opmerking
²**gibe** (vb) (be)spotten, schimpen: *~ at* de draak steken met
giddy 1 duizelig, draaierig, misselijk **2** duizelingwekkend **3** frivool, wispelturig, lichtzinnig
gift 1 cadeauʰ, geschenkʰ, gift: *free ~* gratis geschenk [by way of promotion] **2** gave, talentʰ, aanleg: *have the ~ of (the) gab* a) welbespraakt zijn; b) praatziek zijn
gifted begaafd, talentvol, intelligent
gift-horse gegeven paardʰ [fig]; geschenkʰ: *don't look a ~ in the mouth* je moet een gegeven paard niet in de bek zien
gift shop cadeauwinkel(tjeʰ)
giftwrap als cadeautje inpakken, in cadeaupapier inpakken
gift-wrapping geschenkverpakking
gig optredenʰ, concertʰ
gigantic gigantisch, reusachtig (groot)
¹**giggle** (n) gegiechelʰ: *have the ~s* de slappe lach hebben
²**giggle** (vb) giechelen (van)
gigolo gigolo
gild vergulden; [fig] versieren; opsmukken
gilded verguld; [fig] versierd; sierlijk: *today's ~ youth* de rijkeluisjeugd van deze tijd
gill kieuw
gilt 1 goudgerande schuldbrief [with government guarantee] **2** verguldselʰ
gilt-edged 1 goudgerand **2** met rijksga-

rantie: ~ *shares* goudgerande aandelen
gimme *give me* geef mij, toe (nou), kom op nou
gimmick truc(je^h), vondst
gimmicky op effect gericht [of products]
gin gin, jenever
ginger 1 gember(plant) **2** roodachtig bruin^h, rossig; [of person] rooie
ginger ale gemberbier^h
gingerbread gembercake, gemberkoek, peperkoek
gingerly (uiterst) voorzichtig
ginger up stimuleren, opvrolijken, oppeppen
ginseng ginseng(plant)
gipsy zigeuner(in)
giraffe giraf(fe)
gird 1 [form] omgorden **2** zich gereed maken: [form] ~ *o.s. up* zich vermannen; zich voorbereiden
girder steunbalk, draagbalk, dwarsbalk
girdle gordel, (buik)riem, korset^h
girl 1 meisje^h, dochter; [inform] vrouw(tje^h) **2** dienstmeisje^h **3** liefje^h, vriendinnetje^h
girlfriend vriendin(netje^h), meisje^h
Girl Guide padvindster
Girl Scout padvindster
giro 1 giro(dienst): *National* Giro postgiro **2** girocheque
girth 1 buikriem; singel **2** omtrek; omvang; [mockingly] dikke buik: *one metre in* ~ met een omtrek van één meter
the **gist** hoofdgedachte, essentie, kern
give 1 geven, schenken, overhandigen: ~ *him my best* **wishes** doe hem de groeten van mij; ~ *a* **dinner** een diner aanbieden **2** geven, verlenen, verschaffen, gunnen: ~ *a* **prize** een prijs toekennen; *we were* ~*n three hours' rest* we kregen drie uur rust; *he has been* ~*n two years* hij heeft twee jaar (gevangenisstraf) gekregen; ~ *s.o. to* **understand** (or: **know**) iem. te verstaan (or: kennen) geven **3** geven, opofferen, wijden: ~ *one's* **life** *for one's country* zijn leven geven voor zijn vaderland **4** [+ noun] doen: ~ *a* **beating** een pak slaag geven; ~ *a* **cry** een kreet slaken; ~ *s.o. a sly* **look** iem. een sluwe blik toewerpen **5** (op)geven, meedelen: *the teacher gave us three* **exercises** *(to do)* de onderwijzer heeft ons drie oefeningen opgegeven (als huiswerk); ~ *infor-mation* informatie verstrekken **6** produceren, voortbrengen: ~ *off* (af)geven, verspreiden, maken ‖ ~ *or* **take** *5 minutes* 5 minuten meer of minder; ~ *as* **good** *as one gets* met gelijke munt betalen; *don't* ~ *me that* (hou op met die) onzin; ~ *s.o. what for* iem. flink op zijn donder geven
give-and-take geven en nemen; compromis^h
give away 1 weggeven, cadeau doen **2** verraden, verklappen
give-away 1 cadeautje^h **2** onthulling, (ongewild) verraad^h
give in (+ to) toegeven (aan), zich gewonnen geven, zwichten (voor)
^1**given** (adj) **1** gegeven, gekregen, verleend **2** gegeven [also maths]; (wel) bepaald, vastgesteld: *under the* ~ **conditions** in de gegeven omstandigheden; *at any* ~ **time** om het even wanneer, op elk moment **3** geneigd: ~ *to drinking* verslaafd aan de drank
^2**given** (prep) gezien: ~ *the present* **situation** in het licht van de huidige situatie
^3**given** (conj) [often with 'that'] aangezien: ~ *(that) you don't like it* aangezien je het niet leuk vindt
given name voornaam, doopnaam
^1**give out** (vb) uitgeput raken, opraken
^2**give out** (vb) **1** afgeven, verspreiden, maken **2** verdelen, uitdelen, uitreiken
^1**give over** (vb) ophouden, stoppen
^2**give over** (vb) afzien van, stoppen, opgeven: *I asked the students to* ~ *chewing gum in class* ik verzocht de studenten om geen kauwgom meer te kauwen tijdens de les
^1**give up** (vb) opgeven, zich gewonnen geven: ~ *on* geen hoop meer hebben voor; *I* ~ *on you* je bent hopeloos
^2**give up** (vb) **1** opgeven, afstand doen van, niet langer verwachten, alle hoop opgeven voor; [inform] laten zitten: ~ *one's* **seat** zijn zitplaats afstaan; ~ *for* **dead** (or: **lost**) als dood (or: verloren) beschouwen [also fig]; ~ *smoking* stoppen met roken **2** ophouden **3** overgeven, overleveren, (toe)wijden: *give o.s. up* zich gevangen geven, zich melden
gizmo dingetje^h, apparaatje^h
glacial ijs- [also fig]; ijzig, ijskoud: ~ **detritus** gletsjerpuin; ~ *era* ijstijd(vak)
glacier gletsjer
glad blij, gelukkig, verheugd: *be* ~ *to see the back of s.o.* iem. gaarne zien vertrekken; *I'd be* ~ *to!* met plezier!; *I'll be* ~ *to* **help** ik wil je graag helpen [also iron]; ~ *about* (or: *at, of*) blij om, verheugd over
gladden blij maken
gladiator gladiator
gladiolus gladiool
gladly graag, met plezier
glam [inform] *glamorous* (zeer) aantrekkelijk; prachtig, glitter-
glamorous (zeer) aantrekkelijk, bekoorlijk, betoverend (mooi), prachtig, glitter-
glamour betovering, schone schijn
glamping *glamour camping* het luxe kamperen
^1**glance** (n) (vluchtige) blik, oogopslag, kijkje^h: *at a* ~ met één oogopslag, onmiddellijk
^2**glance** (vb) (vluchtige) kijken, een (vluchtige) blik werpen: ~ *at* even bekijken, een blik werpen op
gland klier: *sweat* ~*s* zweetklieren

¹glare (n) **1** woeste (dreigende) blik **2** verblindend licht[h] [also fig]; (felle) glans
²glare (vb) **1** fel schijnen, blinken, schitteren: *the sun ~d down on our backs* de zon brandde (fel) op onze rug **2** boos kijken, woest kijken
glaring 1 verblindend, schitterend, fel: *~ colours* schreeuwende kleuren **2** dreigend, woest: *~ eyes* vlammende ogen
glass 1 glas[h], (drink)glas[h], brillenglas[h], spiegel **2** lens **3** glas[h]; glaasje[h] [drink] **4** glas(-werk)[h] **5** (-es) bril: *two pairs of ~es* twee brillen **6** (-es) verrekijker, toneelkijker ‖ *people who live in ~ houses should not throw stones* wie in een glazen huisje zit, moet niet met stenen gooien
glass fibre glasvezel, glasdraad
glasshouse (broei)kas
glassworks glasfabriek, glasblazerij
glassy glasachtig, glazig, (spiegel)glad
glaucoma glaucoom[h]
¹glaze (n) glazuur[h], glazuurlaag
²glaze (vb) (also + over) glazig worden; breken [of eyes]
³glaze (vb) in glas zetten: *double-glazed windows* dubbele ramen
glazing 1 glazuur[h], glazuurlaag **2** beglazing, ruiten, ramen[h]: *double ~* dubbel glas, dubbele ramen
¹gleam (n) (zwak) schijnsel[h], glans, schittering; straal(tje[h]) [also fig]: *not a ~ of hope* geen sprankje hoop
²gleam (vb) (zwak) schijnen, glanzen, schitteren
glean 1 verzamelen, oprapen; vergaren [ears] **2** moeizaam vergaren; (bijeen) sprokkelen [information]: *~ ideas from everywhere* overal ideeën vandaan halen
glee leedvermaak[h], vreugde, opgewektheid
glib welbespraakt, vlot, rad van tong, glad, handig
glide 1 glijden, sluipen, zweven **2** [aviation] zweven
glider 1 zweefvliegtuig[h] **2** zweefvlieger
glimmer 1 zwak licht[h], glinstering, flikkering **2** straaltje[h] [fig]: *~ of hope* sprankje hoop
glimpse glimp: *catch* (or: *get*) *a ~ of* eventjes zien, een glimp opvangen van
glisten schitteren, glinsteren, glimmen: *~ with* schitteren van, fonkelen van
glitch out stoppen als gevolg van een storing
¹glitter (n) geschitter[h], glans, glinstering
²glitter (vb) schitteren, blinken, glinsteren: *~ with* blinken van ‖ *all that ~s is not gold* het is niet al goud wat er blinkt
glitz glitter
glitzy opzichtig, opvallend
gloat 1 wellustig staren, begerig kijken **2** zich verlustigen, zich vergenoegen: *~ over* (or: *on*) zich verkneukelen in

glob [inform] klont; klodder, kwak
global 1 wereldomvattend, wereld-: *~ warming* opwarming van de aarde ten gevolge van het broeikaseffect; *~ cloud* netwerk van over de hele wereld verspreide computers die rechtstreeks met elkaar verbonden zijn **2** algemeen, allesomvattend, globaal
globalization globalisering
globalize wereldomvattend, wereldwijd maken
globe globe, aarde, wereldbol
globefish kogelvis
globetrotter globetrotter, wereldreiziger
gloom 1 duisternis, halfduister[h]: *cast a ~ over sth.* een schaduw over iets werpen **2** zwaarmoedigheid, somberheid
gloomy 1 duister; donker **2** mistroostig, somber **3** hopeloos; weinig hoopgevend
glorify 1 verheerlijken, vereren **2** ophemelen, loven, prijzen: [inform] *this isn't a country house but a glorified hut* dit is geen landhuis, maar een veredeld soort hut **3** mooier voorstellen, verfraaien
glorious 1 roemrijk, glorierijk, glorieus, luisterrijk **2** prachtig, schitterend
glory 1 glorie, eer, roem: *I wrote that book for my own personal ~* ik heb dat boek geschreven voor mijn eigen roem **2** lof, dankzegging
glory in erg genieten van, trots zijn op
gloss 1 lippenglans **2** glans **3** glamour, schone schijn
glossary verklarende woordenlijst; glossarium[h]
glossy glanzend, blinkend, glad: *~ print* glanzende foto ‖ *~ magazine* duur blad, glossy
glove handschoen: *fit like a ~* als gegoten zitten ‖ *throw down the ~* de handschoen toewerpen
glove compartment dashboardkastje[h], handschoenenkastje[h]
¹glow (n) gloed; [fig] bezieling; enthousiasme[h]
²glow (vb) **1** gloeien, glimmen; [fig] bezield zijn; enthousiast zijn **2** blozen ‖ *~ with pride* zo trots als een pauw zijn
glowworm glimworm
glucose glucose, druivensuiker
¹glue (n) lijm
²glue (vb) lijmen, plakken; [fig] *his eyes were ~d to the girl* hij kon zijn ogen niet van het meisje afhouden
glum mistroostig
¹glut (n) **1** overvloed **2** overschot[h]
²glut (vb) **1** volstoppen: *~ o.s. with* zich volstoppen met **2** (over)verzadigen, overladen, overvoeren
glutton slokop, gulzigaard, (veel)vraat
gluttony gulzigheid; vraatzucht

gm *gram* g(r)
¹GM (adj) *genetically modified: GM* **foods** genetisch gemanipuleerd voedsel
²GM *general manager*
GMT *Greenwich Mean Time* GT, Greenwichtijd
gnarled knoestig, ruw, verweerd
gnash knarsetanden, tandenknarsen: ~ *one's* **teeth** tandenknarsen
gnat mug, muskiet
¹gnaw (vb) knagen [also fig]; knabbelen, smart veroorzaken, pijn doen
²gnaw (vb) **1** knagen aan [also fig]; kwellen **2** (uit)knagen, afknagen: *the* **mice** *have ~n a small hole* de muizen hebben een holletje uitgeknaagd
gnome gnoom, aardmannetjeʰ, kabouter
GNP *gross national product* bnp, bruto nationaal product
gnu gnoe
¹go (n) **1** poging: *have a go at sth.* eens iets proberen **2** beurt, keer: *at* (or: *in*) *one go* in één klap, in één keer **3** aanval || *make a go of it* er een succes van maken; *(it's)* **no** *go* het kan niet, het lukt nooit
²go (adj) goed functionerend, in orde, klaar: *all* **systems** *(are) go* (we zijn) startklaar
³go (vb) **1** gaan, starten, vertrekken, beginnen: *(right) from the* **word** *go* vanaf het begin; *go to* **find** *s.o.* iem. gaan zoeken; *get going* **a)** aan de slag gaan; **b)** op gang komen; *let go* laten gaan, loslaten; [fig] *I wouldn't go so* **far** *as to say that* dat zou ik niet durven zeggen; *go* **about** *sth.* **a)** iets aanpakken; **b)** zich bezighouden met; *go* **by** *sth.* zich baseren op, zich laten leiden door; *nothing to go* **by** niets om op af te gaan; *go* **off** afgaan van, afstappen van; *go* **on** *the* **pill** aan de pil gaan; *go* **over a)** doornemen, doorlezen [text]; **b)** herhalen [explanation]; **c)** repeteren [part, lesson]; *go* **through a)** nauwkeurig onderzoeken, doorzoeken; **b)** nagaan, checken [assertion etc]; **c)** doornemen [text]; *we go* **through** *a difficult time* we maken een moeilijke periode door; *ready, steady, go!* klaar voor de start? af! **2** gaan, voortgaan, lopen, reizen: *go by* **air** (or: **car**) met het vliegtuig (or: de auto) reizen; *go* **for** *a walk* een wandeling maken; *go* **abroad** naar het buitenland gaan; *go* **along** *that way* die weg nemen **3** gaan (naar), wijzen (naar/op); voeren (naar) [also fig]; reiken, zich uitstrekken: *go* **from** *bad to worse* van kwaad tot erger vervallen; *the difference goes* **deep** het verschil is erg groot **4** gaan; (voortdurend) zijn [in a particular condition]: *as* **things** *go* in het algemeen; *go* **armed** gewapend zijn; *how are* **things** *going?* hoe gaat het ermee? **5** gaan, lopen, draaien; werken [of appliance, system, factory etc]: *the* **clock** *won't go* de klok doet het niet; *go* **slow** een langzaamaanactie houden **6** gaan; afgaan [of gun]; aflopen; luiden [of bell etc] **7** verstrijken, (voorbij)gaan; verlopen [of time]: *ten* **days** *to go to* (or: *before*) *Easter* nog tien dagen (te gaan) en dan is het Pasen **8** gaan; afleggen [distance]: *five* **miles** *to go* nog vijf mijl af te leggen **9** gaan; luiden [of poem, story]; klinken [of tune]: *the tune goes like* **this** het wijsje klinkt als volgt **10** aflopen, gaan, uitvallen: *how did the* **exam** *go?* hoe ging het examen?; *go* **well** goed aflopen, goed komen **11** doorgaan, gebeuren, doorgang vinden: *what he says goes* wat hij zegt, gebeurt ook **12** vooruitgaan, opschieten: *how is the work going?* hoe vordert het (met het) werk? **13** gelden; gangbaar zijn [of money]; gezaghebbend zijn; gezag hebben [of judgement, person]: *that goes* **for** *all of us* dat geldt voor ons allemaal **14** wegkomen, er onderuitkomen, er vanaf komen: *go* **unpunished** ongestraft wegkomen **15** (weg)gaan; verkocht worden [of merchandise]: *go* **cheap** goedkoop verkocht worden; *going!, going!, gone!* eenmaal! andermaal! verkocht! **16** gaan; besteed worden [of money, time] **17** verdwijnen; verloren gaan [also fig]: *my complaints went* **unnoticed** mijn klachten werden niet gehoord **18** verdwijnen, wijken, afgeschaft worden, afgevoerd worden: *my* **car** *must go* mijn auto moet weg **19** weggaan, vertrekken; heengaan [also fig]; sterven, doodgaan: *we must* **be** *going* we moeten ervandoor **20** gaan, passen, thuishoren: *the* **forks** *go in the top drawer de vorken horen in de bovenste la; *where do you want this* **cupboard** *to go?* waar wil je deze kast hebben? **21** dienen, helpen, nuttig zijn, bijdragen: *this goes to* **prove** *I'm right* dit bewijst dat ik gelijk heb; *it only goes to* **show** zo zie je maar || *go by the* **book** volgens het boekje handelen; *go and* **get** *sth.* iets gaan halen; *let o.s.* **go a)** zich laten gaan, zich ontspannen; **b)** zich verwaarlozen; **anything** *goes* alles is toegestaan, alles mag; *go* **before** voorafgaan [in time]; *go one better* (één) meer bieden; [fig] het beter doen, overtreffen; *go* **easy** *on* geen druk uitoefenen op, matig (or: voorzichtig) zijn met; *go* **easy** *with* aardig zijn tegen; **here** *goes!* daar gaat ie (dan)!; *there* **you** *go* **a)** alsjeblieft; **b)** daar heb je het (al); *go* **west** het hoekje omgaan, de pijp uitgaan; *go* **wrong a)** een fout maken, zich vergissen; **b)** fout (or: mis) gaan, de mist in gaan; *not much evidence to go on* niet veel bewijs om op af te gaan; *to go* om mee te nemen [eg hot dishes]
⁴go (vb) **1** maken; gaan maken [trip etc] **2** afleggen, gaan: *go the shortest* **way** de kortste weg nemen || *go it alone* iets helemaal alleen doen
⁵go (vb) worden, gaan: *go* **bad** slecht worden, bederven; *go* **blind** blind worden; *go* **broke** al

zijn geld kwijtraken; *we'll have to go* **hungry** we moeten het zonder eten stellen; *the milk went* **sour** de melk werd zuur; *going* **fifteen** bijna vijftien (jaar), naar de vijftien toe
go ab<u>ou</u>t 1 rondlopen **2** (rond)reizen **3** de ronde doen; rondgaan [of rumour, gossip] **4** omgang hebben, verkering hebben: ~ *with s.o.* omgaan met iem.
go acr<u>o</u>ss oversteken, overgaan, gaan over
goad drijven; [fig] aanzetten; prikkelen, opstoken: *she ~ed him* **on** *to take revenge* ze stookte hem op wraak te nemen
go ag<u>ai</u>nst 1 ingaan tegen, zich verzetten tegen **2** indruisen tegen, in strijd zijn met, onverenigbaar zijn met
go ah<u>ea</u>d 1 voorafgaan, voorgaan, vooruitgaan: *Peter went ahead* **of** *the procession* Peter liep voor de stoet uit **2** beginnen, aanvangen: *we went ahead* **with** *our task* we begonnen aan onze taak; *~!* ga je gang!, begin maar! **3** verder gaan, voortgaan, vervolgen: *we went ahead* **with** *our homework* we gingen verder met ons huiswerk
the **¹go-ahead** (n) [inform] toestemming: *give the ~* het startsein geven, zijn fiat geven
²go-ahead (adj) [inform] voortvarend; ondernemend
goal 1 doelʰ: *one's ~ in* **life** iemands levensdoel **2** (eind)bestemming **3** doelʰ, goal: **keep** *~ het doel verdedigen, keepen* **4** doelpuntʰ, goal: *kick* (or: *make*) *a ~* een doelpunt maken
goal area doelgebiedʰ
goalie [inform] keeper, doelman
goalkeeper [sport] keeper, doelman, doelverdediger
goal kick doeltrap, uittrap, doelschop
go al<u>o</u>ng 1 meegaan: *she decided to ~* **with** *the children* ze besloot om met de kinderen mee te gaan **2** vorderen, vooruitgaan: *the work was going along nicely* het werk schoot lekker op
go al<u>o</u>ng with 1 meegaan met [also fig]; akkoord gaan met, bijvallen **2** samenwerken met, terzijde staan **3** deel uitmaken van, behoren tot, horen bij
goalpost doelpaal: *move the ~s* [fig, inform] de regels naar zijn hand zetten
go a(r)<u>ou</u>nd 1 rondgaan (in), rondlopen; de ronde doen [of rumour etc]; zich verspreiden [of disease]: *his words kept going round my head* zijn woorden bleven mij door het hoofd spelen; *you can't go a(r)ound complaining all of the time!* je kan toch niet de hele tijd lopen klagen! **2** voldoende zijn (voor): *there are enough chairs to go a(r)ound* er zijn genoeg stoelen voor iedereen
go-as-you-pl<u>ea</u>se: *~ ticket* algemeen abonnement; passe-partout
goat 1 geit **2** ezel, stomkop ‖ *get s.o.'s ~* iem. ergeren
go at 1 aanvallen, te lijf gaan; [fig] van leer

trekken tegen, tekeergaan tegen **2** verkocht worden voor
goatee sik
goatee beard sik(jeʰ)
go aw<u>ay</u> weggaan, vertrekken: ~ *with s.o.* (*sth.*) ervandoor gaan met iem. (iets)
gob 1 rochel, fluim **2** smoel, mond, bek: *shut your ~!* houd je waffel!, kop dicht!
go b<u>a</u>ck 1 teruggaan, terugkeren **2** teruggaan, zijn oorsprong vinden, dateren: *Louis and I ~ a long* **time** Louis en ik kennen elkaar al heel lang; *this tradition goes back* **to** *the Middle Ages* deze traditie gaat terug tot de middeleeuwen **3** teruggrijpen, terugkeren **4** teruggedraaid worden; teruggezet worden [of clock, watch]
go b<u>a</u>ck on 1 terugnemen; terugkomen op [word(s) etc] **2** ontrouw worden, verraden
gobble (op)schrokken: ~ *down* (or: *up*) naar binnen schrokken
gobbledygook [inform] ambtelijk jargon; onbegrijpelijke taal
go-between tussenpersoon, bemiddelaar
go bey<u>o</u>nd gaan boven, overschrijden, overtreffen, te buiten gaan: ~ *one's* **duty** buiten zijn boekje gaan, zijn bevoegdheid overschrijden; *their teasing is going beyond a joke* hun geplaag is geen grapje meer
goblet kelk, beker
gobsmacked met de mond vol tanden, stomverbaasd
go by 1 voorbijgaan [also fig]; passeren **2** verstrijken, verlopen, aflopen
god (af)god; [fig] invloedrijk persoon; idoolʰ
God God: *in ~'s* **name!**, *for ~'s* **sake!** in godsnaam!; ~ **bless** *you!* God zegene u!; *thank ~!* goddank!
godchild petekindʰ
goddaughter peetdochter
goddess godin
godfather [also fig] peetvader, peter, peetoom
godforsaken 1 (van) godverlaten **2** triest, ellendig, hopeloos
godmother meter, peettante
go d<u>o</u>wn 1 naar beneden gaan: ~ *to the Mediterranean* naar de Middellandse Zee afzakken **2** dalen [of price, temperature] **3** zinken; ondergaan [ship, person] **4** in de smaak vallen, ingang vinden: ~ *like a* **bomb** enthousiast ontvangen worden; ~ *with* in de smaak vallen bij, gehoor vinden bij **5** te boek gesteld worden: ~ *in history* de geschiedenis ingaan ‖ ~ *on one's knees* op de knieën vallen [also fig]; ~ *with measles* de mazelen krijgen
godsend meevaller; buitenkansjeʰ
godson peetzoon
godspeed: [Am; dated] *wish him ~* hem een goede reis toewensen
godwit grutto
go f<u>a</u>r 1 het ver schoppen, het ver brengen

2 toereiken(d zijn), veruit volstaan, lang meegaan || *far gone* ver heen
go for 1 gaan om, (gaan) halen, gaan naar: *Rob went for some more coffee* Rob ging nog wat koffie halen; ~ *a walk* een wandeling maken **2** gelden voor, van toepassing zijn op **3** verkocht worden voor, gaan voor: ~ *a song* voor een prikje van de hand gaan **4** aanvallen, te lijf gaan; [also fig; with words] van leer trekken tegen
go forward 1 vooruitgaan [also fig]; vorderen, vooruitgang boeken **2** zijn gang gaan, voortgaan, vervolgen
go-getter doorzetter
goggle staren, turen: ~ *at* aangapen
goggle-eyed met uitpuilende ogen
goggles veiligheidsbril, sneeuwbril, stofbril
go in 1 erin gaan, (erin) passen **2** naar binnen gaan
go in for 1 (gaan) deelnemen aan, opgaan voor; zich aanmelden voor [an exam, competition etc] **2** (gaan) doen aan; een gewoonte maken van [hobby, sport etc]
¹going (n) **1** vertrek[h]: *comings and ~s* komen en gaan [also fig] **2** gang, tempo[h]: *be heavy ~* moeilijk zijn, een hele klus zijn || *while the ~ is good* nu het nog kan
²going (adj) **1** voorhanden, in omloop: *there is a good job* ~ er is een goede betrekking vacant; *I've got some fresh coffee* ~ ik heb nog verse koffie staan **2** (goed) werkend **3** gangbaar, geldend: *the ~ rate* het gangbare tarief
going-over [inform] **1** onderzoek[h] **2** pak[h] slaag
goings-on [inform] voorvallen; gebeurtenissen: *there was all sorts of ~* er gebeurde van alles
go into 1 binnengaan (in), ingaan **2** gaan in, zich aansluiten bij, deelnemen aan: ~ *business* zakenman worden **3** (nader) ingaan op, zich verdiepen in, onderzoeken: ~ *(the) details* in detail treden
go-kart gocart; skelter
gold 1 goud[h] [also fig] **2** goud[h], goudstukken, rijkdom **3** goud[h], goudkleur: ~ *card* creditcard met speciale voordelen voor de houder **4** goud(en medaille): ~ *medallist* goudenmedaillewinnaar
goldcrest goudhaantje[h]
golden gouden; goudkleurig [also fig]: *the Golden Age* de gouden eeuw; ~ *handshake* gouden handdruk; ~ *rule* gulden regel; ~ *wedding (anniversary)* gouden bruiloft || ~ *oldie* gouwe ouwe
goldfinch putter, distelvink
goldfish goudvis
gold rush goudkoorts
golf golf[h] [game]
golfer golfspeler
goliath goliath, reus, krachtpatser
golly gossie(mijne)

gondola 1 gondel [Venetian boat] **2** gondola; open (hang)bak [for displaying articles]
gondolier gondelier
¹gone (adj) **1** verloren [also fig] **2** voorbij, vertrokken || *be three months* ~ in de derde maand zijn [of pregnancy]; *far* ~ ver heen
²gone (prep) over: *he is* ~ *fifty* hij is over de vijftig, hij is de vijftig voorbij; *it's* ~ *three* het is over drieën
goner [inform] gedoemde; de klos: *you are a* ~ je gaat eraan
gong 1 gong **2** medaille, lintje[h]
goo kleverig goedje[h]
¹good (n) **1** goed[h], welzijn[h], voorspoed: *for the common* ~ voor het algemeen welzijn; *he will come to no* ~ het zal slecht met hem aflopen; *for his (own)* ~ om zijn eigen bestwil **2** nut[h], voordeel[h]: *it's no* ~ *(my) talking to her* het heeft geen zin met haar te praten **3** goed werk[h], dienst: *be after (or: up to) no* ~ niets goeds in de zin hebben **4** goedheid, verdienste, deugd(zaamheid): ~ *and evil* goed en kwaad **5** (-s) goederen, (koop)waar, handelsartikelen: *deliver the ~s* de goederen (af)leveren; [fig] volledig aan de verwachtingen voldoen **6** (-s) bezittingen || *for ~ (and all)* voorgoed, voor eeuwig (en altijd)
²good (adj) **1** goed, knap, kundig: ~ *looks* knapheid; ~ *for (or: on) you* goed zo, knap (van je) **2** goed, correct, juist: ~ *English* goed Engels; *my watch keeps* ~ *time* mijn horloge loopt gelijk; *all in* ~ *time* alles op zijn tijd **3** goed, fatsoenlijk, betrouwbaar: *(in) ~ faith* (te) goede(r) trouw **4** aardig, lief, gehoorzaam: ~ *humour* opgewektheid; *put in a ~ word for, say a ~ word for* een goed woordje doen voor, aanbevelen; *be so ~ as to* wees zo vriendelijk, gelieve; *it's ~ of you to help him* het is aardig van u om hem te helpen **5** goed, aangenaam, voordelig, lekker, smakelijk, gezond: ~ *buy* koopje, voordeeltje; ~ *afternoon* goedemiddag; *feel* ~ a) zich lekker voelen; b) lekker aanvoelen; *too* ~ *to be true* te mooi om waar te zijn **6** afdoend, geldig: *this rule holds* ~ deze regel geldt **7** aanzienlijk, aardig groot, lang: *stand a* ~ *chance* een goede kans maken; *a* ~ *deal, a* ~ *many* heel wat; *a* ~ *hour (or: ten miles)* ruim een uur (or: tien mijl) || *all* ~ *things come to an end* aan alle goede dingen komt een einde; *one* ~ *turn deserves another* de ene dienst is de andere waard; *be in s.o.'s* ~ *books* bij iem. in een goed blaadje staan; *as* ~ *as gold* erg braaf, erg lief [of child]; *stroke of* ~ *luck* buitenkansje; *it's a* ~ *thing that* het is maar goed dat; *it's a* ~ *thing to* ... het is verstandig om ...; *a* ~ *thing too!* maar goed ook!; *too much of a* ~ *thing* te veel van het goede; *make* ~ *time* lekker opschieten; *as* ~ *as* zo goed als, nagenoeg; *be* ~ *at* goed zijn in; *be* ~ *for another couple of years* nog wel een paar jaar mee-

kunnen; ~*ies and* **baddies** de goeien en de slechteriken
¹**goodbye** (n) afscheidʰ, afscheidsgroet
²**goodbye** (int) tot ziens: [inform, fig] *you can kiss ~ to that* dat kan je wel vergeten, zeg maar dag met je handje
¹**good-for-nothing** (n) nietsnut
²**good-for-nothing** (adj) niet-deugend; waardeloos
goodish 1 tamelijk goed **2** behoorlijk, tamelijk groot, lang, veel: *a ~ number of people* een vrij groot aantal mensen
good-looking knap, mooi
goodness 1 goedheid: *have the ~ to answer, please* wees zo vriendelijk te antwoorden, a.u.b.; *~ (me)!, my ~!, ~ gracious!* wel, heb je ooit!; goeie genade!; *for ~' sake!* in 's hemelsnaam!; *thank ~!* goddank! **2** gezonde stoffen
good-tempered goedgehumeurd, opgewekt
good-time op amusement belust, gezelligheids-
good will 1 welwillendheid **2** goodwill; (goede) reputatie [part of assets] **3** klantenkring [commercial value of a business]; klanten, zakenrelaties
¹**goody** (n) lekkernij, zoetigheid
²**goody** (int) [child language] jippie!, leuk!
goody-goody schijnheilige
gooey [inform] **1** kleverig; zacht **2** sentimenteel
¹**goof** (n) **1** sufkop, stommeling **2** blunder, flater
²**goof** (vb) miskleunen, een flater slaan
go off 1 weggaan [also fig]; (van het toneel) afgaan: *~ with* ertussenuit knijpen met, ervandoor gaan met **2** afgaan [of alarm, gun]; ontploffen [of bomb]; aflopen [of alarm-clock]; losbarsten [also fig] **3** slechter worden, achteruit gaan; verwelken [of flowers]; zuur worden; bederven [of food]: *the veal has gone off* het kalfsvlees is niet goed meer
goofy [inform] **1** [Am] mal **2** met vooruitstekende tanden
google googelen, zoeken op internet
¹**go on** (vb) zich baseren op, afgaan op, zich laten leiden door
²**go on** (vb) **1** voortduren [also fig]; doorgaan (met), aanhouden: *he went on to say that* hij zei vervolgens dat **2** verstrijken, verlopen, voorbijgaan **3** (door)zaniken, (door)zagen: *~ about* doorzeuren over **4** gebeuren, plaatsvinden, doorgang vinden: *what is going on?* wat is er aan de hand? || *enough to be going* (or: *go*) *on with* genoeg om mee rond te komen
goose 1 gans **2** onbenulʰ || *he cannot say boo to a ~* hij brengt nog geen muis aan het schrikken

gooseberry kruisbes(senstruik) || *play ~* het vijfde wiel aan de wagen zijn
goose bumps [Am] [fig] kippenvelʰ
goose-flesh kippenvelʰ
goose pimples [fig] kippenvel
go out 1 uitgaan, van huis gaan, afreizen: *~ with* uitgaan met, verkering hebben met **2** uitgaan [of fire, light] **3** uit de mode raken **4** teruglopen; eb worden [of sea]: *the tide is going out* het is eb || *go (all) out for sth.* zich volledig inzetten voor iets
go out of 1 verlaten; uitgaan [a room]: *~ play* 'uit' gaan [of ball] **2** verdwijnen uit: *~ fashion* uit de mode raken; *~ sight* (or: *view*) uit het zicht verdwijnen; *~ use* in onbruik raken, buiten gebruik raken
go over 1 (+ to) overlopen (naar), overschakelen (op); overgaan (tot) [other party etc]: *we now ~ to our reporter on the spot* we schakelen nu over naar onze verslaggever ter plaatse **2** aanslaan, overkomen
Gordian: *cut the ~ knot* de (gordiaanse) knoop doorhakken
¹**gore** (n) [form] geronnen bloedʰ; gestold bloedʰ
²**gore** (vb) doorboren; spietsen
gorge kloof, bergengte || *my ~ rises at* ik walg van, ik heb tabak van
gorgeous schitterend, grandioos; prachtig [also of person]
gorilla gorilla
gormless stom, dom, onnozel
go round (+ to) langsgaan (bij) [s.o.] **2** (rond)draaien
gorse brem
gory bloederig, bloedig: *a ~ film* een film met veel bloed en geweld
goshawk havik
gospel evangelieʰ: *take sth. for ~* iets zonder meer aannemen
gossamer 1 herfstdraad, spinragʰ **2** gaasʰ, fijn en licht weefselʰ
¹**gossip** (n) **1** roddel, kletspraat, praatjes **2** roddelaar(ster), kletskous
²**gossip** (vb) roddelen
gotcha hebbes!; nou heb ik je!; gelukt!
Gothic 1 [linguistics] Gotisch **2** [architecture] gotisch
go through aangenomen worden [of proposal, bill etc]; erdoor komen || *~ with* doorgaan met
go to 1 gaan naar [also fig] **2** zich getroosten: *~ great* (or: *considerable*) *expense* er heel wat geld tegenaan gooien; *~ great lengths* zich de grootste moeite getroosten, alle mogelijke moeite doen
gouge (uit)gutsen, uitsteken: *~ out s.o.'s eyes* iem. de ogen uitsteken
goulash goulash
go under 1 ondergaan, zinken; [fig] er onder door gaan; bezwijken **2** failliet gaan,

bankroet gaan

go up 1 opgaan, naar boven gaan: ~ *in the world* in de wereld vooruitkomen 2 stijgen; omhooggaan [of price, temperature] 3 ontploffen, in de lucht vliegen: ~ *in smoke* (or: *flames*) in rook (or: vlammen) opgaan

gourmet lekkerbek

gout jicht

govern 1 regeren, besturen: ~*ing body* bestuurslichaam, raad van beheer 2 bepalen, beheersen, beïnvloeden

governance 1 bestuurʰ, beheerʰ 2 heerschappij, macht

governess gouvernante

government regering(svorm), (staats)bestuurʰ, kabinetʰ, leiding: *the Government has* (or: *have*) *accepted the proposal* de regering heeft het voorstel aanvaard

governor 1 gouverneur 2 bestuurder; president [of bank]; directeur [of prison]; commandant [of garrison] 3 [inform] ouwe, ouwe heer, baas

go with 1 meegaan met [also fig]; het eens zijn met: ~ *the times* met de tijd meegaan 2 samengaan, gepaard gaan met, passen bij: *your socks don't* ~ *your shirt* jouw sokken passen niet bij je overhemd

go without het stellen zonder || *it goes without saying* het spreekt vanzelf

gown 1 toga, tabbaard 2 nachthemdʰ, ochtendjas 3 lange jurk, avondjapon 4 operatieschort: *surgical* ~ operatieschort, operatiejas

goy niet-Jood; goj

GP *general practitioner* huisarts

GPO *General Post Office* hoofdpostkantoor

gr 1 *gram* gr. 2 *gross* gros

¹**grab** (n) greep, graai: *make a* ~ *at* (or: *for*) *sth.* ergens naar grijpen; *up for* ~*s* voor het grijpen

²**grab** (vb) graaien, grijpen, pakken

³**grab** (vb) 1 grijpen, vastpakken 2 bemachtigen, in de wacht slepen: ~ *s.o.'s seat* iemands plaats inpikken; *try to* ~ *the attention* proberen de aandacht op zich te vestigen

grace 1 gratie, charme 2 [goodness] vriendelijkheid, fatsoenʰ: *with bad* ~ onvriendelijk, met tegenzin 3 uitstelʰ, genade: *a day's* ~ een dag uitstel [of payment] 4 (dank)gebedʰ: *say* ~ dank zeggen, bidden (bij maaltijd) 5 genade, goedertierenheid; gunst [of God]: *fall from* ~ tot zonde vervallen; [fig] uit de gratie raken, in ongenade vallen || *his smile is his saving* ~ zijn glimlach maakt al het overige goed

graceful 1 gracieus, bevallig, elegant 2 aangenaam, correct, charmant

gracious hoffelijk || *good* ~! goeie genade!

grad [inform] *graduate* afgestudeerde

gradation 1 (geleidelijke) overgang, verloopʰ, gradatie 2 nuance(ring), stap, trede:

many ~*s of red* vele tinten rood

¹**grade** (n) 1 rang, niveauʰ, kwaliteit 2 klas [at elementary school] 3 cijferʰ [as a mark for work handed in at school]: *make the* ~ slagen, aan de eisen voldoen, carrière maken

²**grade** (vb) 1 kwalificeren, rangschikken; sorteren [size, quality etc]: ~*d eggs* gesorteerde eieren 2 een cijfer geven, beoordelen || ~*d reader* voor een bepaald niveau bewerkt boek

grader 1 [Am; educ] leerling uit de ... klas, ... jaars: *fourth* ~ leerling uit de vierde klas 2 iem. die cijfers geeft

grade school basisschool

gradient helling, stijging, hellingshoek: *on a* ~ op een helling

gradual geleidelijk, trapsgewijs

¹**graduate** (n) 1 afgestudeerde 2 gediplomeerde

²**graduate** (vb) een diploma behalen, afstuderen, een getuigschrift behalen: *he has* ~*d in law from Yale* hij heeft aan Yale een titel in de rechten behaald

graduate programme mastersopleiding

graduate school instituutʰ voor onderwijs aan masterstudenten of promovendi

graduate student 1 masterstudent (or: promovendus) 2 bachelor, doctorandus

graduation 1 schaalverdeling, maatstreep 2 uitreiking van diploma, het afstuderen

graffiti graffiti, opschriften, muurtekeningen

¹**graft** (n) 1 ent, griffel 2 (politiek) geknoeiʰ, omkoperij, smeergeldʰ 3 zwaar werkʰ

²**graft** (vb) 1 enten, samenbinden, inplanten 2 verenigen, aan elkaar voegen

grain 1 graankorrel 2 graanʰ, korenʰ 3 korrel(tjeʰ); [fig] greintjeʰ; zier: *take his words with a* ~ *of salt* neem wat hij zegt met een korreltje zout 4 textuur, vleug; draad [of fabric]; vlam; nerf [in wood]; korrel [of film, metal]; structuur [of rock]: *go against the* ~ tegen de draad in gaan [also fig]

gram gram

grammar 1 spraakkunst, grammatica 2 (correct) taalgebruikʰ

grammar school 1 atheneumʰ; gymnasiumʰ [with Latin and Greek] 2 voortgezet lagere school; [roughly] mavo

grammatical grammaticaal

gramme *see gram*

gramophone grammofoon, platenspeler

gran oma

¹**grand** (n) 1 vleugel(piano) 2 duizend pondʰ (dollar); [roughly] milleʰ: *it cost me two* ~ het kostte me twee mille

²**grand** (adj) 1 voornaam, gewichtig, groots: *live in* ~ *style* op grote voet leven 2 grootmoedig: *a* ~ *gesture* een grootmoedig gebaar 3 prachtig, indrukwekkend 4 reusachtig, fantastisch 5 hoofd-, belangrijkste; [in

titles] groot-: ~ **duke** groothertog ‖ ~ **piano** vleugel(piano); ~ **jury** jury van 12-23 personen die onderzoekt of het bewijsmateriaal voldoende is om arrestaties te verrichten
grandad opa, grootvader
grandchild kleinkindʰ
granddaughter kleindochter
grandeur grootsheid; pracht
grandfather grootvader
grandiose grandioos, groots, prachtig
grandma oma, grootmoeder
grandmaster [chess, draughts, bridge] grootmeester
grandmother grootmoeder
grandpa opa, grootvader
grandparent grootouder
grandson kleinzoon
grandstand tribune, hoofdtribune, eretribune
granite granietʰ
granny oma, opoe, grootjeʰ
granny flat aanleunwoning
¹grant (n) subsidie, toelage, beurs
²grant (vb) **1** toekennen, inwilligen, verlenen, toestaan: ~ a **request** een verzoek inwilligen; ~ a **discount** korting verlenen **2** toegeven, erkennen: I must ~ you that you've are a better driver than I ik moet toegeven dat je beter rijdt dan ik ‖ **take** sth. for ~ed iets als (te) vanzelfsprekend beschouwen
grape druif: a **bunch** of ~s een tros druiven
grapefruit grapefruit, pompelmoes
grape sugar druivensuiker
grapevine 1 wijnstok, wingerd **2** geruchtʰ **3** geruchtencircuitʰ: I heard it **on** the ~ het is me ter ore gekomen
graph grafiek, diagramʰ, grafische voorstelling
graphic 1 grafisch, m.b.t. tekenen, schrijven, drukken: the ~ **arts** de grafische kunsten **2** treffend, levendig: a ~ **description** een levendige beschrijving; ~ **designer** grafisch ontwerper
graphics grafiek, grafische kunst, grafische media
graphics card grafische kaart, videokaart
graphite grafietʰ
graphology handschriftkunde
graph paper millimeterpapierʰ
grapple (+ with) worstelen (met) [also fig]; slaags raken (met): ~ **with** a problem met een probleem worstelen
¹grasp (n) **1** greep [also fig]; macht **2** begripʰ, bevatting, beheersing: that is **beyond** my ~ dat gaat mijn pet te boven
²grasp (vb) grijpen, graaien
³grasp (vb) **1** grijpen, vastpakken **2** vatten, begrijpen: I ~ed half of what he said de helft van wat hij zei heb ik begrepen
grasping hebberig, inhalig
¹grass (n) **1** grasʰ **2** tipgever, verklikker

3 [inform] marihuana, weed ‖ **cut** the ~ from under s.o.'s feet iem. het gras voor de voeten wegmaaien
²grass (vb) klikken [to police]: ~ **on** s.o. iem. verraden, iem. aangeven
grasshopper sprinkhaan
grassroots 1 van gewone mensen, aan de basis: the ~ **opinion** de publieke opinie **2** fundamenteel
grass widow onbestorven weduwe, groene weduwe
grassy 1 grazig, grasrijk **2** grasachtig
¹grate (n) **1** roosterʰ, haardroosterʰ **2** traliewerkʰ **3** haard
²grate (vb) **1** knarsen **2** irriterend werken: the noise ~d **on** my nerves het lawaai werkte op mijn zenuwen
³grate (vb) raspen: ~d **cheese** geraspte kaas
grateful dankbaar
grater rasp
gratification voldoening, bevrediging
gratify 1 behagen, genoegen doen **2** voldoen, bevredigen
grating 1 roosterʰ, traliewerkʰ **2** rasterʰ
gratis gratis, kosteloos
gratitude dankbaarheid, dank
gratuitous 1 ongegrond, nodeloos **2** gratis, kosteloos
¹grave (n) grafʰ, grafkuil; [fig] dood; ondergang: from the **cradle** to the ~ van de wieg tot het graf; **dig** one's own ~ zichzelf te gronde richten; **rise** from the ~ uit de dood opstaan
²grave (adj) **1** belangrijk, gewichtig: ~ **issue** ernstige zaak **2** ernstig, plechtig: a ~ **look** on his face een ernstige uitdrukking op zijn gezicht
gravedigger doodgraver
gravel 1 grindʰ, kiezelʰ **2** kiezelzandʰ, grof zandʰ
graveyard kerkhofʰ, begraafplaats
gravitation zwaartekracht: **law** of ~ wet van de zwaartekracht
gravity 1 ernst, serieusheid **2** zwaarte, gewichtʰ, dichtheid: **centre** of ~ zwaartepunt [also fig] **3** zwaartekracht
gravy 1 jus, vleessaus **2** gemakkelijk verdiend geldʰ, voordeeltjeʰ
gravy boat juskom [with spout]
gravy train [inform] goudmijntjeʰ: **get** (a ride) on the ~ gemakkelijk geld verdienen
gray see ²grey
¹graze (n) **1** schampschotʰ **2** schaafwond, schram
²graze (vb) **1** grazen, weiden **2** schampen, schuren
³graze (vb) **1** laten grazen, weiden, hoeden **2** licht(jes) aanraken, schampen, schuren: he ~d his arm **against** the wall hij schaafde zijn arm tegen de muur
¹grease (n) vetʰ, smeerʰ
²grease (vb) invetten, oliën, smeren

¹great (n) groten, vooraanstaande figuren: *Hermans is one of the ~ of* Dutch literature Hermans is een van de groten van de Nederlandse literatuur
²great (adj) **1** groot; nobel [persons]: *a ~ man* een groot man **2** geweldig, fantastisch: *a ~ idea* een geweldig idee **3** groot, belangrijk, vooraanstaand: *Great Britain* Groot-Brittannië; *the Great Wall of China* de Chinese Muur **4** buitengewoon, groot; zwaar [emotions, situations etc] **5** groot, aanzienlijk; hoog [number]: *a ~ deal* heel wat; *a ~ many* heel wat, een heleboel **6** lang; hoog [age, time]: *live to a ~ age* een hoge leeftijd bereiken **7** groot, ijverig, enthousiast: *a ~ reader* een verwoed lezer **8** [inform] omvangrijk, dik, reuzen-, enorm: *a ~ big tree* een kanjer van een boom **9** goed, bedreven: *he is ~ at golf* hij is een geweldige golfer || *Great Dane* Deense dog; *at ~ length* uitvoerig; *be in ~ spirits* opgewekt zijn; *set ~ store by* (or: *on*) grote waarde hechten aan; *the ~est thing since sliced bread* iets fantastisch; *the Great War* de Eerste Wereldoorlog
Great Britain Groot-Brittannië
greatly zeer, buitengewoon: *~ moved* zeer ontroerd
grebe fuut
Grecian Grieks [in style etc]
Greece Griekenland
greed 1 hebzucht, hebberigheid, gulzigheid **2** gierigheid
greedy 1 gulzig; *~ eyes* gulzige blikken **2** hebzuchtig; begerig: *~ for* (or: *of*) *money* geldzuchtig
¹Greek (n) Griek(se)
²Greek (adj) Grieks: [fig] *that is ~ to me* daar snap ik niks van
¹green (n) **1** grasveldʰ, brink, dorpspleinʰ **2** [golf] green **3** groenʰ **4** loofʰ, groen gewasʰ **5** (-s) (blad)groenten **6** (de) Groenen, (de) milieupartij
²green (adj) **1** groen, met gras begroeid **2** groen, plantaardig: *~ vegetables* bladgroenten **3** groen, onrijp; [fig] onervaren; naïef **4** groen, milieu-: *the ~ party* de Groenen **5** jaloers, afgunstig: *~ with envy* scheel van afgunst
greenback [Am; inform] (Amerikaans) bankbiljet
greenery groenʰ, bladeren en groene takken
greenfinch groenling
green gas biogasʰ
greengrocer groenteboer, groenteman
greenhorn groentjeʰ, beginneling
greenhouse broeikas: *~ effect* broeikaseffect
Greenland Groenland
Greenlander Groenlander, Groenlandse
Greenlandic Groenlands

Greenwich Mean Time Greenwichtijd
greet 1 begroeten, groeten **2** onthalen, begroeten || *a cold air ~ed us* een vlaag koude lucht kwam ons tegemoet
greeting 1 groet, begroeting, wens: *exchange ~s* elkaar begroeten **2** aanhef [of letter]
gregarious 1 in kudde(n) levend: *a ~ animal* een kuddedier **2** van gezelschap houdend, graag met anderen zijnd
Gregorian gregoriaans: *~ calendar* gregoriaanse kalender
gremlin 1 pechduiveltjeʰ, zetduivel **2** kwelgeest, lastpak
grenade (hand)granaat
¹grey (n) **1** schimmel [horse] **2** grijsʰ
²grey (adj) **1** grijs(kleurig): *~ cells* grijze cellen, hersenen; *his face turned ~* zijn gezicht werd (as)grauw **2** grijs, bewolkt, grauw **3** somber, treurig, triest: *~ with age* grijs van de ouderdom; [fig] verouderd
greyhound 1 hazewind(hond) **2** greyhoundbus [large coach for long-distance travel]
grid 1 roosterʰ, traliewerkʰ **2** rasterʰ; coördinatenstelselʰ [of map] **3** netwerkʰ, hoogspanningsnetʰ
gridlock verkeersknoop, het muurvast zitten; [fig] impasse
grief leedʰ, verdrietʰ, smart: *come to ~* a) verongelukken; b) vallen; c) [also fig] mislukken, falen
grievance 1 grief, klacht **2** bitter gevoelʰ: *nurse a ~ against s.o.* wrok tegen iem. koesteren
¹grieve (vb) treuren, verdriet hebben: *~ for s.o.,* *~ over s.o.'s death* treuren om iemands dood
²grieve (vb) bedroeven, verdriet veroorzaken: *it ~s me to hear that* het spijt mij dat te horen
grievous 1 zwaar, ernstig, verschrikkelijk: [law] *~ bodily harm* zwaar lichamelijk letsel; *a ~ wound* een ernstige wond **2** pijnlijk
griffin griffioen
¹grill (n) **1** grill, roosterʰ **2** geroosterd (vlees)gerechtʰ
²grill (vb) verhoren, aan een kruisverhoor onderwerpen
³grill (vb) roosteren, grilleren; [fig] bakken: *grilling on the beach* op het strand liggen bakken
grille 1 traliewerkʰ, roosterʰ, rasterwerkʰ **2** traliehek(je)ʰ, kijkraampje **3** radiatorschermʰ [of car]; sierschermʰ, grille
grim 1 onverbiddelijk, meedogenloos: *~ determination* onwrikbare vastberadenheid **2** akelig, beroerd: *~ prospects* ongunstige vooruitzichten
grimace grimas, gezichtʰ, grijns: *make ~s* smoelen trekken

ground

grime vuil[h], roet[h]
grimy vuil; groezelig, goor
¹grin (n) **1** brede glimlach **2** grijns, grimas: *take that (silly) ~ off your face!* sta niet (zo dom) te grijnzen!
²grin (vb) grijnzen, grinniken, glimlachen: *~ and bear it* zich flink houden, op zijn tanden bijten
¹grind (n) **1** geknars[h], schurend geluid **2** inspanning, (vervelend) karwei[h]
²grind (vb) **1** blokken, ploeteren: *he is ~ing away at his maths* hij zit op zijn wiskunde te blokken **2** knarsen, schuren, krassen: *~ one's teeth* tandenknarsen; *~ to a halt* tot stilstand komen [also fig] **3** verbrijzelen, (ver)malen, verpletteren; [fig] onderdrukken: *~ coffee* koffie malen; *~ing poverty* schrijnende armoede **4** (uit)trappen [also fig]: *Joe ~ed his cigarette into the rug* Joe trapte zijn sigaret in het tapijt (uit) **5** (doen) draaien [(coffee) grinder, barrel organ etc]
grinder 1 molen **2** slijper, slijpmachine **3** maalsteen **4** kies
grind out uitbrengen, voortbrengen; opdreunen [continuously and mechanically]: *the pupil first had to ~ ten irregular verbs* de leerling moest eerst tien onregelmatige werkwoorden opdreunen
grindstone slijpsteen: *go back to the ~* weer aan het werk gaan
gringo vreemdeling
¹grip (n) **1** greep, houvast[h]: *keep a tight ~ on* stevig vasthouden **2** beheersing, macht, meesterschap[h]; [fig] begrip[h]; vat[h]: *come to ~s with a problem* een probleem aanpakken; *keep (or: take) a ~ on o.s.* zich beheersen, zichzelf in de hand houden **3** greep, handvat[h] **4** toneelknecht
²grip (vb) pakken [of brake etc]; grijpen [of anchor]
³grip (vb) vastpakken, grijpen, vasthouden; [fig] pakken; boeien: *a ~ping story* een boeiend verhaal
gripe klacht, bezwaar[h], kritiek
grip fastening klittenbandsluiting
grisly 1 griezelig, akelig **2** weerzinwekkend, verschrikkelijk
gristle kraakbeen[h] [in meat]
¹grit (n) **1** gruis[h], zand[h] **2** lef[h], durf
²grit (vb) **1** knarsen: *~ one's teeth* knarsetanden [also fig] **2** met zand bestrooien: *~ the icy roads* de gladde wegen met zand bestrooien
gritty 1 zanderig, korrelig **2** kranig, moedig, flink
grizzled 1 grijs, grauw **2** grijsharig
grizzly grizzly(beer)
¹groan (n) gekreun[h], gekerm[h], gesteun[h]
²groan (vb) **1** kreunen, kermen, steunen: *~ with pain* kreunen van de pijn **2** grommen, brommen

grocer kruidenier
groceries boodschappen
grocery 1 (groceries) kruidenierswinkel **2** kruideniersbedrijf[h], kruideniersvak[h] **3** (groceries) kruidenierswaren, levensmiddelen
grog grog
groggy 1 onvast op de benen, wankel **2** suf, versuft, verdoofd: *I feel ~* ik voel me suf
groin lies
¹groom (n) **1** bruidegom **2** stalknecht
²groom (vb) **1** verzorgen [horses]; roskammen **2** een keurig uiterlijk geven; uiterlijk verzorgen [pers] || *~ a candidate for the Presidency* een kandidaat voorbereiden op het presidentschap
groove 1 groef, gleuf, sponning **2** routine, sleur: *find one's ~, get into the ~* zijn draai vinden; *be stuck in the ~* in een sleur zitten
¹grope (vb) tasten, rondtasten; [fig] zoeken: *~ for an answer* onzeker naar een antwoord zoeken
²grope (vb) **1** al tastend zoeken: *~ one's way* zijn weg op de tast zoeken **2** betasten [esp with sexual intentions]
¹gross (n) gros[h], 12 dozijn, 144: *by the ~* bij dozijn, bij het gros
²gross (adj) **1** grof [also fig]; dik, lomp: *~ injustice* uitgesproken onrechtvaardigheid; *~ language* ruwe taal **2** bruto, totaal: *~ national product* bruto nationaal product
³gross (vb) een bruto winst hebben van, in totaal verdienen
grotesque zonderling, belachelijk
grotto grot
grotty [inform] rottig, vies, waardeloos
grouch mopperen, mokken: *he is always ~ing about his students* hij loopt altijd te mopperen over zijn studenten
¹ground (n) **1** terrein[h] **2** grond, reden; basis [of action, reasoning]: *on religious ~s* uit godsdienstige overwegingen **3** grond, aarde; bodem [also fig]: *go to ~* a) zich in een hol verschuilen [of animal]; b) onderduiken [of person]; *get off the ~* van de grond komen **4** gebied[h] [fig]; grondgebied[h], afstand: *break new (or: fresh) ~* nieuw terrein betreden, pionierswerk verrichten; *gain (or: make) ~* a) veld winnen; b) erop vooruit gaan; *give (or: lose) ~* terrein verliezen, wijken; *hold (or: keep, stand) one's ~* standhouden, voet bij stuk houden **5** (-s) gronden, domein[h]; park[h] [around bldg]: *a house standing in its own ~s* een huis, geheel door eigen grond omgeven || *cut the ~ from under s.o.'s feet* iem. het gras voor de voeten wegmaaien; *it suits him down to the ~* dat komt hem uitstekend van pas
²ground (vb) **1** op de grond terecht komen, de grond raken **2** aan de grond lopen, stranden

³ground (vb) **1** aan de grond houden [aeroplane, pilot]: *the planes* have been *~ed by the fog* de vliegtuigen moeten door mist aan de grond blijven **2** laten stranden [ship] **3** [Am; elec] aarden

groundbreaking baanbrekend; grensverleggend

ground control vluchtleiding

ground-floor benedenverdieping, parterre

ground frost vorst aan de grond, nachtvorst

grounding scholing, training, basisvorming

groundless ongegrond

groundnut aardnoot; pinda

ground plan plattegrond, grondplanʰ; [fig] ontwerpʰ; blauwdruk

groundsman 1 terreinknecht **2** tuinman

groundswell vloedgolf [also fig]; zware golving; nadeining [of sea, after storm or earthquake]

the **groundwork** grondslag; basis

¹group (n) groep, geheelʰ, verzameling, klasse, familie, afdeling, onderdeelʰ

²group (vb) zich groeperen

³group (vb) groeperen, in groepen plaatsen: *we ~ed ourselves round the guide* we gingen in een groep rond de gids staan

¹grouse (n) korhoenʰ, Schotse sneeuwhoen

²grouse (vb) mopperen, klagen

grovel kruipen [fig]; zich vernederen, zich verlagen: *~ before s.o.* voor iem. kruipen

¹grow (vb) **1** groeien, opgroeien, ontstaan: *~ wild* in het wild groeien; *~ up* **a)** opgroeien, volwassen worden; **b)** ontstaan; *~ up into* opgroeien tot, zich ontwikkelen tot, worden; *~ out of* **a)** ontstaan uit; **b)** ontgroeien [bad habit, friends]; *~ out of one's clothes* uit zijn kleren groeien **2** aangroeien, zich ontwikkelen, gedijen: *~ to become* uitgroeien tot; *~ into sth.* big tot iets groots uitgroeien || *~ up!* doe niet zo kinderachtig!

²grow (vb) **1** kweken, verbouwen, telen: *~ vegetables* groenten kweken **2** laten staan (groeien) [beard] **3** laten begroeien, bedekken

³grow (vb) worden, gaan: *she has ~n (into) a woman* ze is een volwassen vrouw geworden

grower kweker, teler, verbouwer

growing pains 1 groeistuipen, groeipijnen **2** kinderziekten [fig]

growl 1 grommen, brommen **2** snauwen, grauwen

grown 1 gekweekt, geteeld **2** volgroeid, rijp, volwassen

grown-up volwassen

growth 1 gewasʰ, productʰ **2** gezwelʰ, uitwas, tumor **3** groei, (volle) ontwikkeling: *reach full ~* volgroeid zijn **4** toename, uitbreiding **5** kweek, productie

growth area groeisector, (snel) groeiende bedrijfstak

grub 1 larve, made, rups **2** etenʰ, voerʰ, hap

grubby vuil, vies, smerig

¹grudge (n) wrok, grief: *bear s.o. a ~* een wrok tegen iem. koesteren

²grudge (vb) misgunnen, niet gunnen, benijden

grudgingly met tegenzin, niet van harte

gruelling afmattend, slopend

gruesome gruwelijk, afschuwelijk

gruff nors, bars

¹grumble (vb) rommelen [of thunder]

²grumble (vb) morren, mopperen, brommen: *~ at s.o. about sth.* tegen iem. over iets mopperen

grumpy knorrig, humeurig

grunge [Am] vuilʰ, smerigheid

grunt knorren, brommen, grommen

GSM *Global System for Mobile Communications* gsm

G-string g-strings, tangaslipjeʰ

¹guarantee (n) waarborg, garantie(bewijsʰ), zekerheid, belofte

²guarantee (vb) **1** garanderen, waarborgen, borg staan voor **2** verzekeren

¹guard (n) **1** bewaker, cipier, gevangenbewaarder **2** conducteur [on train] **3** beveiliging, beschermingʰ (middelʰ), schermʰ, kap **4** wacht, bewaking, waakzaamheid: *be on* (or: *keep, stand*) *~* de wacht houden, op wacht staan; *the changing of the ~* het aflossen van de wacht; *catch s.o. off* (*his*) *~* iem. overrompelen; *be on* (*one's*) *~ against* bedacht zijn op **5** garde, (lijf)wacht, escorteʰ

²guard (vb) **1** (zich) verdedigen, zich dekken **2** zich hoeden, zijn voorzorgen nemen: *~ against sth.* zich voor iets hoeden **3** op wacht staan

³guard (vb) **1** bewaken, beveiligen, bewaren [secret] **2** beschermen

guard dog waakhond

guarded voorzichtig; bedekt [terms]

guardian 1 bewaker, beschermer, oppasser **2** voogd(es), curator

guardian angel beschermengel, engelbewaarder

guardianship 1 bescherming **2** voogdij(schap)

guard rail 1 leuning, reling **2** vangrail

Guatemala Guatemala

¹Guatemalan (n) Guatemalaan(se), Guatemalteek(se)

²Guatemalan (adj) Guatemalaans, Guatemalteeks

guava guave

gue(r)rilla guerrilla(strijder)

¹guess (n) gis(sing), ruwe schatting: *your ~ is as good as mine* ik weet het net zo min als jij; *make* (or: *have*) *a ~* (*at sth.*) (naar iets) raden; *it is anybody's* (or: *anyone's*) *~* dat is niet te

zeggen; *at a* ~ naar schatting
²guess (vb) **1** raden, schatten, gissen: *keep s.o. ~ing* iem. in het ongewisse laten; ~ *at sth.* naar iets raden **2** denken, aannemen: *What is that? - That is his new car, I* ~ Wat is dat nou? - Dat is zijn nieuwe auto, neem ik aan
guesswork giswerkʰ; het raden
guest 1 gast, logé: ~ *of honour* eregast **2** genodigde, introducé || *be my ~!* ga je gang!
guesthouse pensionʰ
¹guffaw (n) bulderende lach
²guffaw (vb) bulderen van het lachen
guidance 1 leiding **2** raad, adviesʰ, hulp, begeleiding: *vocational* ~ beroepsvoorlichting
¹guide (n) **1** gids **2** leidraad **3** padvindster, gids
²guide (vb) **1** leiden, gidsen, de weg wijzen, (be)geleiden: *a ~d tour of the head office* een rondleiding in het hoofdkantoor **2** als leidraad dienen voor: *he was ~d by his feelings* hij liet zich leiden door zijn gevoelens
guide dog geleidehond
guideline richtlijn; richtsnoerʰ
guild gildeʰ
guilder gulden
guildhall 1 gildehuisʰ **2** raadhuisʰ, stadhuisʰ
guile slinksheid, bedrogʰ, valsheid: *he is full of* ~ hij is niet te vertrouwen
guillotine 1 guillotine, valbijl **2** papiersnijmachine
guilt schuld, schuldgevoelʰ
guilty schuldig, schuldbewust: *a* ~ *conscience* een slecht geweten; *plead not* ~ schuld ontkennen
guinea gienjeʰ [old gold coin with a value of 21 shillings]
Guinea Guinee
Guinea-Bissau Guinee-Bissau
guinea fowl parelhoenʰ
¹Guinean (n) **1** Guineeër, Guineese **2** Papoea-Nieuw-Guineeër, Papoea-Nieuw-Guineese
²Guinean (adj) **1** Guinees **2** Papoea-Nieuw-Guinees
guinea pig 1 cavia **2** proefkonijnʰ
guitar gitaar
gulf golf, (wijde) baai
the **Gulf stream** Golfstroom
gull meeuw
gullet keel(gatʰ), strot || *stick in s.o.'s* ~ onverteerbaar zijn voor iem.
gullible makkelijk beet te nemen, lichtgelovig, onnozel
gully geul, ravijnʰ, greppel
¹gulp (n) **1** teug, slok **2** slikbeweging
²gulp (vb) schrokken, slokken, slikken: *he ~ed down his drink* hij sloeg zijn borrel achterover
gum 1 (-s) tandvleesʰ **2** gom(hars) **3** kauwgom

gumdrop gombal
gumption [inform] **1** initiatiefʰ, ondernemingslust, vindingrijkheid **2** gewiekstheid, pienterheid
¹gun (n) **1** stukʰ geschut, kanonʰ **2** vuurwapenʰ, (jacht)geweerʰ, pistoolʰ **3** spuitpistoolʰ || *beat* (or: *jump*) *the* ~ te vroeg van start gaan; [fig] op de zaak vooruitlopen; *stick to one's* ~s voet bij stuk houden
²gun (vb) jagen, op jacht zijn (gaan)
³gun (vb) (also + down) neerschieten, neerknallen: *he was ~ned down from an ambush* hij werd vanuit een hinderlaag neergeknald
gunboat diplomacy machtspolitiek
gunfight vuurgevechtʰ
gunfire geweervuurʰ; (geweer)schoten
gunge smurrie
gunman gangster, (beroeps)moordenaar
gunmetal staalgrijsʰ
gunner 1 artillerist, kanonnier **2** boordschutter
gunpoint: *at* ~ onder bedreiging van een vuurwapen, onder schot
gunpowder buskruitʰ
gun-runner wapensmokkelaar
gunshot 1 schotʰ; geweerschotʰ, pistoolschotʰ **2** schootsafstand
¹gurgle (n) gekirʰ [of baby]; geklokʰ, gemurmelʰ
²gurgle (vb) kirren, klokken, murmelen
³gurgle (vb) kirrend zeggen
guru goeroe
¹gush (n) **1** stroom [also fig]; vloed, uitbarsting **2** uitbundigheid, overdrevenheid **3** sentimentaliteit
²gush (vb) **1** stromen, gutsen **2** dwepen (met), overdreven doen (over)
³gush (vb) spuiten, uitstorten, doen stromen
gust 1 (wind)vlaag, windstoot **2** uitbarsting: *a ~ of laughter* een lachsalvo
gusto animoʰ: *with (great)* ~ enthousiast
gusty stormachtig
¹gut (n) **1** darm **2** (-s) ingewanden **3** (-s) lefʰ, durf, moed || *hate s.o.'s ~s* grondig de pest hebben aan iem.; *sweat* (or: *work*) *one's ~s out* zich een ongeluk werken
²gut (adj) instinctief, onberedeneerd: *a* ~ *reaction* een (zuiver) gevoelsmatige reactie
³gut (vb) uitbranden [of bldg]
gutless laf; zonder durf
¹gutter (n) **1** goot [also fig]; geul, greppel, dakgoot: *he'll end up in the* ~ hij belandt nog in de goot
²gutter (vb) druipen [of candle]
the **gutter press** schandaalpers; roddelpers
guttural keel-; [linguistics] gutturaal
guv 1 baas [employer] **2** ouwe heer [father] **3** meneer
guy 1 kerel, vent, man **2** mens: ~s lui; jongens; mensen; *where are you ~s going?* waar

gaan jullie naartoe?
Guyana Guyana
¹Guyanese (n) Guyaan(se)
²Guyanese (adj) Guyaans
guzzler zwelger, brasser, zuiper
gym 1 gymlokaal[h], fitnesscentrum[h], sportschool **2** gymnastiek(les)
gymnasium gymnastieklokaal[h]
gymnast gymnast, turner
gymnastics gymnastiek, lichamelijke oefening, turnen[h]
gynaecologist gynaecoloog, vrouwenarts
gypsy zigeuner(in)
gyrate (rond)draaien, wentelen; (rond)tol-
len
gyroscope gyroscoop

h

haberdashery 1 fournituren, garen[h], band, fourniturenwinkel **2** [Am] herenmode(artikelen), herenmodezaak
habit 1 habijt[h], ordekleed[h] **2** rijkleding: *riding* ~ rijkleding **3** gewoonte, hebbelijkheid, aanwensel[h]: *fall* (or: *get*) *into the* ~ de gewoonte aannemen; *he has a* ~ *of changing the lyrics in mid-song* hij heeft de gewoonte om midden in het lied de tekst de veranderen; *get out of* (or: *kick*) *the* ~ *of doing sth.* (de gewoonte) afleren om iets te doen; *be in the* ~ *of doing sth.* gewoon zijn iets te doen
habitable bewoonbaar
habitat natuurlijke omgeving [of plant, animal]; habitat, woongebied[h]
habitation woning, bewoning
habitual 1 gewoon(lijk), gebruikelijk **2** gewoonte-: ~ *criminal* recidivist
¹hack (n) **1** huurpaard[h], knol **2** broodschrijver **3** houw, snee, jaap, trap(wond)
²hack (vb) **1** hakken, houwen, een jaap geven: ~ *off a branch* een tak afkappen; ~ *at sth.* in iets hakken, op iets in houwen **2** fijnhakken; bewerken [soil] **3** kraken, een computerkraak plegen, hacken
hacker 1 (computer)kraker, hacker **2** computermaniak
hackneyed afgezaagd; banaal [of saying]
hacksaw ijzerzaag, metaalzaag
haddock schelvis
haemophilia hemofilie, bloederziekte
haemorrhage bloeding: *massive* ~*s* zware bloedingen
haemorrhoids aambeien
hag (lelijke oude) heks
haggard verwilderd uitziend; wild [of look]; met holle ogen, afgetobd
haggle 1 kibbelen **2** pingelen, afdingen: ~ *with s.o. about* (or: *over*) *sth.* met iem. over iets marchanderen
Hague: *The* ~ Den Haag, 's-Gravenhage
¹hail (n) (welkomst)groet
²hail (n) hagel(steen); [fig] regen; stortvloed: *a* ~ *of bullets* een regen van kogels
³hail (vb) hagelen [also fig]; neerkomen (als hagel)
⁴hail (vb) **1** erkennen, begroeten als: *the people* ~*ed him (as) king* het volk haalde hem als koning in **2** aanroepen: ~ *a taxi* een taxi (aan)roepen
hail from afkomstig zijn van; komen uit
Hail Mary Ave Maria, weesgegroet(je[h])
hailstone hagelsteen

hailstorm hagelbui
hair haar[h], haren, hoofdhaar[h]: *let one's* ~ *down* het haar los dragen; [fig] zich laten gaan || *hang by a* ~ aan een zijden draadje hangen; *not harm a* ~ *on s.o.'s head* iem. geen haar krenken; [inform] *keep your* ~ *on!* maak je niet dik!; *split* ~*s* haarkloven; *tear one's* ~ *(out)* zich de haren uit het hoofd trekken; *without turning a* ~ zonder een spier te vertrekken
haircut 1 het knippen: *have a* ~ zijn haar laten knippen **2** kapsel[h]
hairdo kapsel[h]
hairdresser kapper; [Am] dameskapper
hairgrip (haar)speld(je[h])
hairline 1 haargrens **2** *hairline crack* haarscheurtje[h]
hairpin haarspeld: ~ *bend* haarspeldbocht
hair's breadth haarbreed(te) || *escape death by a* ~ op het nippertje aan de dood ontsnappen
hair-splitting haarkloverij
hairstyle kapsel[h], coiffure
hairy 1 harig, behaard **2** riskant
Haiti Haïti
¹Haitian (n) Haïtiaan(se)
²Haitian (adj) Haïtiaans
hake heek
halal halal
halcyon kalm, vredig, gelukkig
hale gezond, kras: ~ *and hearty* fris en gezond
¹half (n) helft, half(je[h]), de helft van: ~ *an hour, a* ~ *hour* een half uur; *two and a* ~ twee-en-een-half; *one* ~ een helft || [inform] *go halves with s.o. in sth.* de kosten van iets met iem. samsam delen; *he's too clever by* ~ hij is veel te sluw; [inform] *that was a game and a* ~ dat was me een wedstrijd
²half (pron) de helft: ~ *of six is three* de helft van zes is drie
³half (adv) half; [inform] bijna: *only* ~ *cooked* maar half gaar; *I* ~ *wish* ik zou bijna willen; ~ *as much* (or: *many*) again anderhalf maal zoveel; [inform] ~ *seven* half acht; *he didn't do* ~ *as badly as we'd thought* hij deed het lang zo slecht niet als we gedacht hadden; ~ *past* (or: *after*) *one* half twee; [inform] ~ *one*, ~ *two* etc half twee, half drie enz.; ~ *and* ~ half om half || [inform] *he didn't* ~ *get mad* hij werd me daar toch razend; [inform] *not* ~ *bad* lang niet kwaad, schitterend; *not* ~ *strong enough* lang niet sterk genoeg
half-baked [fig] halfbakken; halfgaar
half-breed halfbloed, bastaard-
half-caste [depr] halfbloed
halfhearted halfhartig; halfslachtig
half holiday vrije middag [at schools]
half-life [physics] halfwaardetijd, halveringstijd
half-term [school] korte vakantie

half-timbered vakwerk-
half-time 1 [sport] rust: *at* ~ tijdens de rust
2 halve werktijd, deeltijdarbeid, halve dagen: *be on* ~ halve dagen werken, een deeltijdbaan (*or:* halve baan) hebben
¹halfway (adj) **1** in het midden: [sport] ~
line middenlijn **2** tamelijk; beetje
²halfway (adv) halverwege: *meet* s.o. ~ iem.
tegemoet komen
halfway house 1 rehabilitatiecentrumʰ,
reclasseringscentrumʰ **2** compromisʰ
half-wit [depr] halvegare
halibut heilbot
halitosis slechte adem
hall 1 zaal, ridderzaal **2** openbaar gebouwʰ, paleisʰ **3** groot herenhuisʰ **4** vestibule, halʰ, gang **5** studentenhuisʰ: ~ *of residence* studentenhuis
hallelujah hallelujaʰ
hallmark stempelʰ [also fig]; gehaltemerkʰ,
waarmerkʰ, kenmerkʰ
hallo hallo!, hé!
hallowed gewijd, heilig
Hallowe'en avond voor Allerheiligen
hallstand staande kapstok
hallucinate hallucineren
hallucination hallucinatie, zinsbegoocheling
hallway portaalʰ, halʰ, vestibule
halo 1 halo **2** stralenkrans; [fig] glans
halogen halogeenʰ
¹halt (n) **1** [inform] (bus)halte, stopplaats;
stationnetjeʰ **2** halt, stilstand, rust: *call a* ~ *to*
een halt toeroepen; *come to a* ~ tot stilstand
komen
²halt (vb) halt (doen) houden, stoppen, pauzeren
halter 1 halsterʰ **2** strop
halting weifelend, aarzelend, onzeker: *a* ~
voice een stokkende stem
halve halveren, in tweeën delen, tot de
helft reduceren
¹ham (n) **1** ham **2** dij, bil: ~*s* achtersteʰ **3** [in-
form] amateur
²ham (vb) overacteren, overdrijven: ~ *up* zich
aanstellen
hamburger hamburger
ham-fisted onhandig
hamlet gehuchtʰ
¹hammer (n) hamer: *go* (or: *come*) *under the*
~ geveild worden ‖ *go at it* ~ *and tongs* er uit
alle macht tegenaan gaan
²hammer (vb) **1** hameren: ~ *(away) at* er op
losbeuken **2** [inform] zwoegen: ~ *(away) at*
sth. op iets zwoegen
³hammer (vb) **1** hameren, smeden **2** [in-
form] verslaan, inmaken, een zware nederlaag toebrengen **3** [inform] scherp bekritiseren, afkraken ‖ ~ *out* *a compromise solution*
(moeizaam) een compromis uitwerken
hammerhead hamerhaai

hammock hangmat
¹hamper (n) **1** (grote) sluitmand; pakmand
[for foodstuffs]: *Christmas* ~ kerstpakket
2 [Am] wasmand
²hamper (vb) belemmeren, storen; [fig] hinderen
hamster hamster
¹hamstring (n) **1** kniepees **2** hakpees, achillespees
²hamstring (vb) de achillespees doorsnijden
bij, kreupel maken; [fig] verlammen; frustreren
¹hand (n) **1** hand; voorpoot [of animals]:
bind (or: *tie*) s.o. ~ *and foot* iem. aan handen
en voeten binden [also fig]; *hold* (or: *join*) ~*s*
(elkaar) de hand geven; *shake* s.o.'s ~, *shake*
~*s with* s.o. iem. de hand drukken; *wring*
one's ~*s* ten einde raad zijn; ~*s off!* bemoei je
er niet mee!; *at* ~ dichtbij; [fig] op handen;
close (or: *near*) *at* ~ heel dichtbij; *by* ~ a) met
de hand (geschreven); b) in handen, per
bode [letter]; *make* (or: *earn*) *money* ~ *over fist*
geld als water verdienen **2** arbeider, werkman, bemanningslidʰ: ~*s needed* arbeidskrachten gevraagd; *all* ~*s on deck!* alle hens
aan dek! **3** vakman, specialist: *be a poor* ~ *at*
sth. geen slag van iets hebben **4** wijzer [of
clock]; naald [of meter] **5** kaart(en) [assigned
to a player]; hand: *overplay one's* ~ te veel
wagen, te ver gaan, zijn hand overspelen;
show (or: *reveal*) *one's* ~ zijn kaarten op tafel
leggen **6** handbreed(te) [approximately 10
cm] **7** kant, zijde, richting: *at my left* ~ aan
mijn linkerhand; *on the one* (or: *other*) ~ aan
de ene (*or:* andere) kant **8** handschriftʰ,
handtekening: *set* (or: *put*) *one's* ~ *to a document* zijn hand(tekening) onder een document plaatsen **9** hulp, steun, bijstand: *give*
(or: *lend*) s.o. *a (helping)* ~ iem. een handje
helpen **10** controle, beheersing, bedwangʰ:
have the situation well in ~ de toestand goed
in handen hebben; *take in* ~ onder handen
nemen; *get out of* ~ uit de hand lopen **11** (-s)
macht, beschikking, gezagʰ: *change* ~*s* in andere handen overgaan, van eigenaar veranderen; *put* (or: *lay*) *(one's)* ~*s on sth.* de hand
leggen op iets; *the children are off my* ~*s* de
kinderen zijn de deur uit; *have time on one's*
~*s* tijd zat hebben **12** toestemming, (huwelijks)belofte; (handels)akkoordʰ [with hand-
shake]: *ask for s.o.'s* ~ iem. ten huwelijk vragen **13** invloed, aandeelʰ: *have a* ~ *in sth.* bij
iets betrokken zijn **14** applausʰ, bijval: *the*
actress got a big (or: *good*) ~ de actrice kreeg
een daverend applaus **15** (-s) [sport] handsʰ,
handsbal ‖ *wait on* (or: *serve*) s.o. ~ *and foot*
iem. op zijn wenken bedienen; *they are* ~ *in*
glove ze zijn twee handen op één buik; *try*
one's ~ *at* (*doing*) *sth.* iets proberen; *get one's*
~ *in at* sth. iets onder de knie krijgen; *go* ~ *in* ~
samengaan; *force* s.o.'s ~ iem. tot handelen

dwingen; **lay** (or: **put**) one's ~ on de hand weten te leggen op; **strengthen** one's ~ zijn positie verbeteren; my ~s are **tied** ik ben machteloos; **turn** one's ~ to sth. iets ondernemen; [euph] where can I **wash** my ~s? waar is het toilet?; **wash** one's ~s of sth. zijn handen van iets aftrekken; win ~s **down** op één been winnen; **at** the ~ of s.o., **at** s.o.'s ~s van(wege) iem., door iem.; live **from** ~ **to** mouth van de hand in de tand leven; cash **in** ~ contanten in kas; we have plenty of time **in** ~ we hebben nog tijd genoeg; **out of** ~ **a)** voor de vuist weg; **b)** tactloos; have s.o. eating **out of** one's ~ iem. volledig in zijn macht hebben; **to** ~ bij de hand, dichtbij; a **hand-to-mouth** existence een leven van dag tot dag; [roughly] te veel om dood te gaan, te weinig om van te leven; **with** one ~ (tied) behind one's back zonder enige moeite; (at) **first** (or: **second**) ~ uit de eerste (or: tweede) hand
²**hand** (vb) **1** overhandigen, aanreiken, (aan)geven: ~ **back** teruggeven; ~ **round** ronddelen **2** helpen, een handje helpen, leiden || [inform] you have to ~ it **to** her dat moet je haar nageven
handbag handtas(je)
handball handbalʰ
hand blender staafmixer
handbrake handrem
handcuffs handboeien
hand down 1 overleveren [tradition etc]; overgaan [possession]: this watch has been handed down in our family for 130 years dit horloge gaat in onze familie al 130 jaar over van generatie op generatie **2** aangeven
handful 1 handvol **2** [inform] lastig kindʰ: that **child** is a ~ ik heb mijn handen vol aan dat kind
handicap 1 handicap, nadeelʰ, functiebeperking **2** [sport] handicap, (wedren met) voorgift
handicapped gehandicapt, invalide
handicraft handvaardigheid, handenarbeid, handwerkʰ
hand in 1 inleveren: please ~ your paper **to** your own teacher lever alsjeblieft je proefwerk in bij je eigen docent **2** voorleggen, aanbieden, indienen: ~ one's **resignation** zijn ontslag indienen
handkerchief zakdoek
¹**handle** (n) **1** handvatʰ, hendel, steel **2** knop, kruk, klink **3** heftʰ, greep **4** oorʰ, hengselʰ || [inform] **fly** off the ~ opvliegen, z'n zelfbeheersing verliezen
²**handle** (vb) **1** aanraken, betasten; bevoelen [with one's hands] **2** hanteren, bedienen, manipuleren: ~ **with** care! voorzichtig (behandelen)! **3** behandelen, omgaan met **4** verwerken, afhandelen **5** aanpakken; bespreken [problem]: can he ~ that **situation**? kan hij die situatie aan? **6** verhandelen, han-

delen in
handlebar stuurʰ [of bicycle]
handling 1 behandeling; hantering, verwerking **2** beheerʰ **3** rijgedragʰ [of car] **4** transportʰ
hand-me-down [Am] afdankertjeʰ
handout 1 gift, aalmoes **2** stencilʰ, folder
hand out ronddelen, uitdelen
hand over overhandigen [esp money]; overdragen
hand-pick 1 plukken met de hand **2** zorgvuldig uitkiezen, selecteren
handrail leuning
handsfree handsfree: you must **phone** ~ in a car in een auto moet je handsfree bellen
handshake handdruk
handsome 1 mooi, schoon; knap [man]; elegant, statig [woman] **2** royaal; gul [reward, prize]; overvloedig, ruim || **come** down ~(ly) flink over de brug komen
hands-on praktisch, praktijk-: ~ **training** praktijkgerichte training
handwriting (hand)schriftʰ || [Am] the ~ on the **wall** het teken aan de wand
handwritten met de hand geschreven
handy 1 bij de hand, binnen bereik **2** handig, praktisch: **come** in ~ van pas komen
handyman klusjesman, manusje-van-allesʰ
¹**hang** (n) het vallen; val [of material]; het zitten [of cloting] || [inform] **get** (or: **have**) the ~ of sth. de slag van iets krijgen (or: hebben)
²**hang** (vb) **1** hangen: ~ **loose a)** loshangen; **b)** kalm blijven **2** hangen, opgehangen worden **3** zweven, blijven hangen **4** aanhangen, zich vastklemmen, vast (blijven) zitten **5** onbeslist zijn: ~ in the **balance** (nog) onbeslist zijn || ~ **behind** achterblijven; [Am] ~ **in** (there) volhouden; she hung **on(to)** his every word zij was één en al oor; ~ **onto** sth. proberen te (be)houden; ~ **over** one's head iem. boven het hoofd hangen
³**hang** (vb) **1** (op)hangen [also as punishment]: he ~ed **himself** hij verhing zich **2** laten hangen: ~ one's **head** in shame het hoofd schuldbewust laten hangen **3** tentoonstellen [painting] || [inform] ~ **it** (all)! ze kunnen van mij allemaal in elkaar storten!; ~ sth. **on** s.o. iem. de schuld van iets geven
hangar hanga(a)r, vliegtuigloods
hang (a)round 1 rondhangen, rondlummelen **2** wachten, treuzelen
hang back aarzelen; dralen: ~ **from** doing sth. aarzelen iets te doen
hanger-on (slaafse) volgeling, parasiet, handlanger
hang-glider deltavlieger [appliance as well as user]; zeilvlieger, hangglider
¹**hanging** (n) **1** ophanging **2** wandtapijtʰ
²**hanging** (adj) hangend; hang-
hangman beul

hang on 1 zich (stevig) vasthouden, niet loslaten, blijven (hangen): ~ *tight!* hou (je) stevig vast!; ~ *to* zich vasthouden aan **2** volhouden, het niet opgeven, doorzetten **3** even wachten; aan de lijn blijven [telephone]: ~ *(a minute)!* ogenblikje!

hangout verblijf[h], stamkroeg, ontmoetingsplaats, hangplek

1hang out (vb) [inform] uithangen, zich ophouden: *where* were you hanging out? waar heb jij uitgehangen?; *I used to* ~ *with him* vroeger ben ik veel met hem opgetrokken

2hang out (vb) uithangen; ophangen [laundry]; uitsteken [flag]

hangover 1 kater, houten kop **2** overblijfsel[h]: *his style of driving is a* ~ *from his racing days* zijn rijstijl heeft hij overgehouden aan zijn tijd als autocoureur **3** ontnuchtering, ontgoocheling

1hang up (vb) **1** ophangen [telephone]: *and then she hung up* **on** *me* en toen gooide ze de hoorn op de haak **2** vastlopen

2hang up (vb) **1** ophangen **2** uitstellen, ophouden, doen vastlopen || [inform] *be hung up* **on** (or: *about*) *sth.* complexen hebben over iets

hang-up complex[h], obsessie, frustratie

hank streng [yarn]

hanker (+ after, for) hunkeren (naar)

hanky zakdoek

hanky-panky 1 hocus pocus, bedriegerij **2** gescharrel[h], overspel[h]

haphazard toevallig, op goed geluk (af), lukraak

hapless ongelukkig, onfortuinlijk

happen 1 (toevallig) gebeuren: *as it ~s* (or: ~ed) toevallig, zoals het nu eenmaal gaat; *should anything* ~ *to him* mocht hem iets overkomen **2** toevallig verschijnen, toevallig komen, gaan || *if you* ~ *to see him* mocht u hem zien; *I ~ed to notice it* ik zag het toevallig; *I ~ed (up)on it* ik trof het toevallig aan

happening gebeurtenis

happiness geluk[h]

happy 1 gelukkig, blij **2** gepast, passend; gelukkig [language, behaviour, suggestion] **3** voorspoedig, gelukkig: *Happy Birthday* hartelijk gefeliciteerd met je verjaardag; *Happy New Year* Gelukkig nieuwjaar **4** blij; verheugd [in polite phrases]: *I'll be* ~ *to accept your kind invitation* ik neem uw uitnodiging graag aan || *(strike) the* ~ *medium* de gulden middenweg (inslaan); [euph] ~ *event* blijde gebeurtenis, geboorte; *many* ~ *returns (of the day)!* nog vele jaren!

happy-go-lucky zorgeloos; onbezorgd

haram haram

harass 1 treiteren, pesten, kwellen **2** teisteren, voortdurend bestoken

harassment kwelling; pesterij

1harbour (n) **1** haven **2** schuilplaats

2harbour (vb) **1** herbergen; onderdak verlenen [criminal] **2** koesteren [emotions, ideas]

1hard (adj) **1** hard, vast(staand), krachtig, taai, robuust: ~ *cover* (boek)band, gebonden editie; ~ *currency* harde valuta; *a* ~ *winter* een strenge winter; ~ *and fast rule* (or: *line*) vaste regel, ijzeren wet **2** hard, hardvochtig: *drive a* ~ *bargain* keihard onderhandelen; *be* ~ *on* s.o. onvriendelijk zijn tegen iem. **3** moeilijk, hard, lastig: ~ *labour* dwangarbeid; *she gave him a* ~ *time* hij kreeg het zwaar te verduren van haar; ~ *of hearing* slechthorend, hardhorend **4** hard, ijverig, energiek: *a* ~ *drinker* een stevige drinker; *a* ~ *worker* een harde werker || ~ *cash* baar geld, klinkende munt; *they preferred* ~ *copy* to soft copy zij verkozen uitdraai boven beeldschermtekst; ~ *feelings* wrok(gevoelens), rancune; ~ *luck* pech, tegenslag; *as* ~ *as nails* ongevoelig, onverzoenlijk; ~ *shoulder* vluchtstrook; *play* ~ *to get* moeilijk doen, zich ongenaakbaar opstellen; ~ *by* vlakbij

2hard (adv) **1** hard, krachtig, inspannend, zwaar: *be* ~ *hit* zwaar getroffen zijn; *think* ~ diep nadenken; *be* ~ *on* s.o.'s heels (or: trail) iem. op de hielen zitten **2** met moeite, moeizaam: *be hard put (to it) to (do sth.)* het moeilijk vinden (om iets te doen); *old habits die* ~ vaste gewoonten verdwijnen niet gauw; *take* sth. ~ iets zwaar opnemen, zwaar lijden onder iets

hardback (in)gebonden [book]

hardboard (hard)board[h], houtvezelplaat

hard-boiled 1 hardgekookt **2** hard, ongevoelig

hard copy (computer)uitdraai, afdruk

1hard-core (adj) hard

2hard-core (adj) onbuigzaam

hard disk harde schijf, vaste schijf, harddisk

hard-earned zuurverdiend

harden 1 (ver)harden, ongevoelig worden, maken: *a ~ed criminal* een gewetenloze misdadiger **2** gewennen: *become ~ed to* sth. aan iets wennen

hard-hat 1 helm [helmet] **2** [inform] bouwvakker

hard-headed praktisch, nuchter, zakelijk

hard-hearted hardvochtig

hardline keihard, van een politiek van de harde lijn voerend

hardly nauwelijks, amper: *we had* ~ *arrived when it began to rain* we waren er nog maar net toen het begon te regenen; *I could* ~ *move* ik kon me haast niet bewegen; ~ *anything* bijna niets; ~ *anybody* vrijwel niemand; ~ *ever* bijna nooit

hard-pressed in moeilijkheden; sterk onder druk: *be* ~ *for time* in tijdnood zitten

hardship ontbering, tegenspoed

hard up slecht bij kas || *be* ~ *for sth.* grote behoefte aan iets hebben

hardware 1 ijzerwaren, (huis)gereed-schap[h] **2** apparatuur [also of computer]; hardware, bouwelementen
hardwood hardhout[h]
hardy 1 sterk, robuust **2** winterhard, wintervast: ~ *annual* winterharde plant; [fig; mockingly] onderwerp dat regelmatig aan de orde komt, oude bekende
hare haas
harebrained onbezonnen; dwaas
harelip hazenlip
harem harem
haricot snijboon
¹harm (n) kwaad[h], schade: *be* (or: *do*) *no* ~ geen kwaad kunnen; *she came to no* ~ er overkwam haar geen kwaad; *out of* ~'s *way* in veiligheid
²harm (vb) kwaad doen, schade berokkenen
harmful schadelijk, nadelig
harmless 1 onschadelijk, ongevaarlijk **2** onschuldig
¹harmonic (n) harmonische (toon), boven-toon
²harmonic (adj) harmonisch
harmonica harmonica; mondharmonica
harmonious 1 harmonieus **2** eensgezind
harmony 1 harmonie, eensgezindheid, overeenstemming: *be in* ~ *with* in overeenstemming zijn met **2** goede verstandhouding, eendracht: *live in* ~ in goede verstandhouding leven
¹harness (n) gareel[h], (paarden)tuig[h] || *get back into* ~ weer aan het werk gaan
²harness (vb) **1** optuigen; inspannen [horse]; in het gareel brengen **2** aanwenden, gebruiken; benutten [(natural) energy sources]
harp harp
harp on zaniken, zeuren: ~ *about sth.* doorzeuren over iets
harpoon harpoen
harpsichord klavecimbel[h]
harrow eg
harrowing aangrijpend
harsh 1 ruw, wrang; verblindend [light]; krassend [sound] **2** wreed, hardvochtig
¹harvest (n) oogst(tijd)
²harvest (vb) **1** oogsten, vergaren **2** verkrijgen, behalen (wat men verdient)
harvester oogstmachine
hash 1 hachee **2** mengelmoes[h] **3** hasj(iesj) || *make a* ~ *of it* de boel verknoeien
hashish hasjiesj
hash symbol hekje[h] (#)
hashtag hashtag
¹hassle (n) **1** gedoe[h]: *a real* ~ een zware opgave, een heel gedoe **2** ruzie
²hassle (vb) moeilijk maken, dwarszitten, lastigvallen
haste 1 haast, spoed: *make* ~ zich haasten **2** overhaasting

¹hasten (vb) zich haasten
²hasten (vb) versnellen, bespoedigen
hasty 1 haastig; gehaast **2** overhaast; onbezonnen
hat hoed: *at the drop of a* ~ bij de minste aanleiding, plotseling, zonder aarzeling || *knock into a cocked* ~ a) gehakt maken van, helemaal inmaken; **b)** in duigen doen vallen; *I'll eat my* ~ *if* … ik mag doodvallen als …; *keep sth. under one's* ~ iets geheim houden, iets onder de pet houden; *pass* (or: *send, take*) *the* ~ *(round)* met de pet rondgaan; [fig] *take off one's* ~ (or: *take one's* ~ *off*) *to s.o.* zijn pet(je) afnemen voor iem.; [inform] *talk through one's* ~ bluffen, nonsens verkopen; *throw* (or: *toss*) *one's* ~ *in(to) the ring* zich in de (verkiezings)strijd werpen; [comp] *black* ~ cracker; criminele hacker; [comp] *white* ~ hacker met goede bedoelingen die inbreekt om een bedrijf te wijzen op veiligheidslekken
¹hatch (n) **1** onderdeur **2** luik[h] **3** sluisdeur || *down the* ~ proost!
²hatch (vb) (also + out) uit het ei komen [of chick]; openbreken [of egg(shell)]
³hatch (vb) **1** (also + out) uitbroeden, broeden **2** beramen [plan]
hatchback 1 (opklapbare) vijfde deur **2** vijfdeursauto
hatchet 1 bijltje[h], (hand)bijl **2** tomahawk, strijdbijl || [inform] *bury the* ~ de strijdbijl begraven, vrede sluiten
hatchet man 1 huurmoordenaar, gangster **2** [depr] handlanger, trawant; [by extension] waakhond; ordehandhaver
hatchling pas uitgekomen jong[h]
¹hate (n) **1** gehate persoon, gehaat iets **2** haat
²hate (vb) **1** haten, grondig verafschuwen, een hekel hebben aan **2** [inform] het jammer vinden: *I ~ having to tell you* … het spijt me u te moeten zeggen …; *I ~ to say this, but* … ik zeg het niet graag, maar …
hateful 1 gehaat, weerzinwekkend **2** hatelijk [remark] **3** onsympathiek, onaangenaam, onuitstaanbaar
hatred haat, afschuw
haughty trots, arrogant
¹haul (n) **1** haal, trek, het trekken **2** vangst, buit **3** afstand, traject[h]: *in* (or: *over*) *the long* ~ op lange termijn **4** lading, vracht
²haul (vb) **1** halen, ophalen; inhalen [with effort]: ~ *down one's flag* (or: *colours*) de vlag strijken; [fig] zich overgeven; ~ *in the net* het net binnenhalen **2** vervoeren **3** slepen [take somebody to court]
haulage 1 het slepen, het trekken **2** vervoer[h], transport[h] **3** transportkosten, vervoerkosten: *all prices include* ~ bij alle prijzen zijn de vervoerkosten inbegrepen
haulier vrachtrijder, vervoerder, expedi-

teur
haunch lende, heup, bil, dij: *on one's ~es* op
zijn hurken
¹**haunt** (n) **1** trefpunt^h: *we went for a drink at
one of his favourite ~s* we gingen iets drinken
in een van de plaatsen waar hij graag kwam
2 hol^h; schuilplaats [of animals]
²**haunt** (vb) **1** vaak aanwezig zijn in, zich altijd ophouden in, regelmatig bezoeken: *he
~s that place* daar is hij altijd te vinden
2 rondspoken in, rondwaren in: *~ed castle*
spookkasteel **3** achtervolgen, niet loslaten,
(steeds) lastigvallen: *that tune has been ~ing
me all afternoon* dat deuntje speelt de hele
middag al door mijn kop
have 1 hebben, bezitten, beschikken over,
houden: *he has (got) an excellent memory* hij
beschikt over een voortreffelijk geheugen; *~
mercy on us* heb medelijden met ons; *I've got
it* ik heb het, ik weet het (weer); *you ~ sth.*
there daar zeg je (me) wat, daar zit wat in; *~
sth. about* (or: on, with) one iets bij zich hebben; *what does she ~ against me?* wat heeft
ze tegen mij? **2** [as part of a whole] bevatten, bestaan uit: *the book has six chapters* het
boek telt zes hoofdstukken **3** krijgen, ontvangen: *we've had no news* we hebben geen
nieuws (ontvangen); *you can ~ it back tomorrow* je kunt het morgen terugkrijgen **4** nemen, pakken; gebruiken [food, drink etc]: *~
breakfast* ontbijten; *~ a drink* iets drinken,
een drankje nemen **5** hebben, genieten van,
lijden aan: *~ a good time* het naar zijn zin
hebben **6** hebben, laten liggen, leggen, zetten: *let's ~ the rug in the hall* laten we het tapijt in de hal leggen **7** hebben, maken, nemen: *~ a bath* (or: *shower*) een bad (or: douche) nemen; *~ a try* iets proberen **8** toelaten,
accepteren: *I won't ~ such conduct* ik accepteer zulk gedrag niet; *I'm not having any* ik
pik het niet, ik pieker er niet over **9** hebben
te: *I still ~ quite a bit of work to do* ik heb nog
heel wat te doen **10** laten, doen, opdracht
geven te: *~ one's hair cut* zijn haar laten
knippen **11** krijgen [child]: *~ a child by* een
kind hebben van **12** zorgen voor: *can you ~
the children tonight?* kun jij vanavond voor
de kinderen zorgen? **13** [inform] te pakken
hebben [lit and fig]; het winnen van: *you've
got me there* a) jij wint; b) geen idee, daar
vraag je me wat **14** [inform] bedriegen, bij
de neus nemen: *John's been had* ze hebben
John beetgenomen **15** hebben, zijn: *I ~
worked* ik heb gewerkt; *he has died* hij is gestorven; *I had better* (or: *best*) *forget it* ik
moest dat maar vergeten; *I'd just as soon die*
ik zou net zo lief doodgaan ‖ *he had it coming to him* hij kreeg zijn verdiende loon; *rumour has it that ...* het gerucht gaat dat ...; *~
it (from s.o.)* het (van iem.) gehoord hebben;
[inform] *~ had it a)* hangen, de klos zijn;

b) niet meer de oude zijn, dood zijn; c) het
beu zijn, er de brui aan geven; *~ it in for s.o.*
een hekel hebben aan iem., het op iem. gemunt hebben, de pik hebben op iem.; *~ it* (or:
the matter) *out with s.o.* het (probleem) uitpraten met iem.; *~ s.o. up (for sth.)* iem. voor
de rechtbank brengen (wegens iets); *~ nothing on* niet kunnen tippen aan
haven beschutte haven, veilige haven [also
fig]; toevluchtsoord^h
have-nots armen
have on 1 aanhebben; dragen [clothes];
ophebben [hat] **2** gepland hebben, op zijn
agenda hebben: *I've got nothing on tonight*
vanavond ben ik vrij **3** [inform] voor de gek
houden, een loopje nemen met: *are you having me on?* zit je mij nou voor de gek te houden?
have to moeten, verplicht zijn om te, (be)-
hoeven: *we have (got) to go now* we moeten
nu weg; *he didn't ~ do that* dat had hij niet
hoeven doen
havoc verwoesting, vernieling, ravage; [fig]
verwarring: *play ~ among* (or: *with*), *make ~
of, wreak ~ on* a) totaal verwoesten; b) grondig in de war sturen, een puinhoop maken
van
hawk havik; [fig] oorlogszuchtig persoon:
watch like a ~ zeer nauwlettend in de gaten
houden
hawker (straat)venter, marskramer
hawthorn haagdoorn, meidoorn
hay hooi^h ‖ *hit the ~* gaan pitten; *make ~
while the sun shines* men moet het ijzer smeden als het heet is
hay fever hooikoorts
hay-stack hooiberg
haywire in de war, door elkaar: *my plans
went ~* mijn plannen liepen in het honderd
¹**hazard** (n) **1** gevaar^h, risico^h: *smoking and
drinking are health ~s* roken en drinken zijn
een gevaar voor de gezondheid **2** kans, mogelijkheid, toeval^h **3** [golf] (terrein)hindernis
²**hazard** (vb) **1** in de waagschaal stellen, wagen, riskeren **2** zich wagen aan, wagen: *~ a
guess* een gok wagen
hazardous gevaarlijk, gewaagd, riskant
¹**haze** (n) nevel, damp, waas^h; [fig] vaagheid;
verwardheid
²**haze** (vb) (+ over) nevelig worden
hazel hazelaar, hazelnotenstruik
hazelnut hazelnoot
hazy nevelig, wazig; [fig] vaag: *a ~ idea*
vaag idee
he hij, die, dat, het: *'Who is he?' 'He's John'*
'Wie is dat?' 'Dat is John'
¹**head** (n) **1** hoofd^h, kop, hoofdlengte: *~ and
shoulders above* met kop en schouders erbo-
venuit; [fig] verreweg de beste; *~s or tails?*
kruis of munt?; *~ first* (or: *foremost*) voorover **2** hoofd^h, verstand^h: *it never entered* (or:

came *into*) *his* ~ het kwam niet bij hem op; **get** (or: **take**) *sth. into one's* ~ zich iets in het hoofd zetten; *the success has* **gone** *to* (or: **turned**) *his* ~ het succes is hem naar het hoofd gestegen; **put** *one's* ~*s together* de koppen bij elkaar steken; *a* ~ *for mathematics* een wiskundeknobbel **3** persoon, hoofd[h]: *£1 a* ~ £1 per persoon **4** uiteinde[h], kop **5** hoofdje[h], korfje[h], kruin **6** top, bovenkant **7** breekpunt[h], crisis: *that* **brought** *the matter to a* ~ daarmee werd de zaak op de spits gedreven **8** boveneinde[h], hoofd(einde)[h] **9** voorkant, kop, spits; hoofd[h] [also of team] **10** meerdere, leider, hoofd[h]: ~ *of* **state** staatshoofd **11** stuk[h] (vee); kudde; aantal[h] dieren: *50* ~ *of* **cattle** 50 stuks vee || *have one's* ~ *in the* **clouds** met het hoofd in de wolken lopen; *from* ~ *to* **foot** van top tot teen; *bury one's* ~ *in the* **sand** de kop in het zand steken; *I could not make* ~ *or* **tail** *of it* ik kon er geen touw aan vastknopen; *keep one's* ~ *above* **water** het hoofd boven water houden; *keep* *one's* ~ zijn kalmte bewaren; *laugh* *one's* ~ *off* zich een ongeluk lachen; *lose* *one's* ~ het hoofd verliezen; **scream** (or: **shout**) *one's* ~ *off* vreselijk tekeergaan; *have one's* ~ **screwed** *on straight* (or: *right*) verstandig zijn, niet gek zijn
²head (vb) gaan, gericht zijn, koers zetten: *the plane* ~*ed* **north** het vliegtuig zette koers naar het noorden
³head (vb) **1** aan het hoofd staan van, voorop lopen: *the general* ~*ed the* **revolt** de generaal leidde de opstand **2** bovenaan plaatsen, bovenaan staan op **3** overtreffen, voorbijstreven **4** [socc] koppen **5** richten, sturen
headache 1 hoofdpijn **2** probleem[h], vervelende kwestie: *finding reliable staff has* **become** *a major* ~ het vinden van betrouwbaar personeel is een groot probleem geworden
head butt kopstoot
headcase [inform] halvegare
headdress hoofdtooi
header 1 [socc] kopbal **2** duik(eling): *take a* ~ een duikeling maken **3** koptekst
head for afgaan op, koers zetten naar: *he was already heading for the bar* hij liep al in de richting van de bar; *you are heading for* **trouble** als jij zo doorgaat krijg je narigheid
headgear hoofddeksel[h]
headhunting 1 het koppensnellen **2** headhunting
heading opschrift[h], titel, kop
headlamp koplamp
headland kaap; landtong
headlight koplamp
headline (kranten)kop, opschrift[h]: **make** (or: **hit**) *the* ~*s* volop in het nieuws komen || *where do we go* **from** ~ hoofdpunten van het nieuws
headlong 1 voorover, met het hoofd voorover **2** haastig, halsoverkop

headmaster schoolhoofd[h], rector
headmistress schoolhoofd[h]
head off 1 onderscheppen, van richting doen veranderen **2** voorkomen
head-on frontaal, van voren: *a* ~ **collision** een frontale botsing
headphones koptelefoon
headquarters hoofdbureau, hoofdkantoor, hoofdkwartier
headrest hoofdsteun [eg in car]
headset koptelefoon
head start (+ on, over) voorsprong (op) [also fig]; goede uitgangspositie
headstone grafsteen
headstrong koppig, eigenzinnig
heads-up [Am; inform] alert
headway voortgang; vaart [of ship]: [fig] **make** ~ vooruitgang boeken
headwind tegenwind
heady 1 opwindend, wild **2** bedwelmend; dronken makend [wine]
heal (also + over) genezen, (doen) herstellen; dichtgaan [of wound]; [fig] bijleggen; vereffenen
healer genezer || *time is the great* ~ de tijd heelt alle wonden
health gezondheid, gezondheidstoestand: *have* (or: *be in*, *enjoy*) *good* ~ een goede gezondheid genieten || *drink (to) s.o.'s* ~ op iemands gezondheid drinken
health food gezonde (natuurlijke) voeding
healthy gezond, heilzaam: *he has a* ~ **respect** *for my father* hij heeft een groot ontzag voor mijn vader
¹heap (n) **1** hoop, stapel, berg **2** boel, massa, hoop: *we've got* ~*s of* **time** we hebben nog zeeën van tijd
²heap (vb) **1** (+ up) ophopen, (op)stapelen, samenhopen **2** (+ on, with) vol laden (met), opladen (met) **3** overladen, overstelpen: *she* ~*ed reproaches* **(up)on** *her mother* zij overstelpte haar moeder met verwijten
¹hear (vb) **1** luisteren naar, (ver)horen, behandelen; verhoren [prayer]; overhoren, gehoor geven aan: *please* ~ *me* **out** laat mij uitspreken **2** vernemen, kennisnemen van, horen: *we are* **sorry** *to* ~ *that* het spijt ons te (moeten) horen dat
²hear (vb) horen: ~ *from* bericht krijgen van, horen van; ~ *of* (or: *about*) horen van (or: over) || ~*!* ~*!* bravo!
hearing 1 gehoor[h], hearing, hoorzitting: *he would not even give us a* ~ hij wilde zelfs niet eens naar ons luisteren **2** behandeling [of a case] **3** [Am; law] verhoor[h] **4** gehoor[h]: *she is* **hard** *of* ~ zij is hardhorend **5** gehoorsafstand: *out of* (or: *within*) ~ *distance* buiten (or: binnen) gehoorsafstand
hearing aid (ge)hoorapparaat[h]
hearsay praatjes, geruchten: *I know it* **from**

~ ik weet het van horen zeggen
hearse lijkwagen
heart 1 hart[h], hartspier, binnenste[h], gemoed[h]: *from* (or: *to*) *the **bottom** of my* ~ uit de grond van mijn hart; *they **have** their own interests at* ~ zij hebben hun eigen belangen voor ogen; *set one's* ~ *on sth.* zijn zinnen op iets zetten, iets dolgraag willen; *she **took** it to* ~ zij trok het zich aan, zij nam het ter harte; *in one's* ~ *of hearts* in het diepst van zijn hart; *with all one's* ~ van ganser harte **2** boezem, borst **3** geest, gedachten, herinnering: *a **change** of* ~ verandering van gedachten; *(learn) **by*** ~ uit het hoofd (leren) **4** kern, hart[h], essentie **5** moed, durf: *not **have** the* ~ de moed niet hebben; ***lose*** ~ de moed verliezen; ***take*** ~ moed vatten, zich vermannen || *my* ~ ***bleeds*** ik ben diepbedroefd; [iron] oh jee, wat heb ik een medelijden; ***cry*** (or: ***weep***) *one's* ~ *out* tranen met tuiten huilen; *eat one's* ~ *out* wegkwijnen (van verdriet/verlangen)
heart attack hartaanval; hartinfarct[h]
heartbeat hartslag
heartbreaking 1 hartbrekend, hartverscheurend **2** frustrerend [work]
heart condition hartkwaal
hearten bemoedigen, moed geven
heartfelt hartgrondig, oprecht
hearth haard(stede); [fig] huis[h]; woning: ~ *and **home*** huis en haard
heartily 1 van harte, oprecht, vriendelijk **2** flink, hartig: *eat* ~ stevig eten **3** hartgrondig: *I* ~ ***dislike*** *that fellow* ik heb een hartgrondige hekel aan die vent
heart-rending hartverscheurend
heart-stopping adembenemend
heartstrings diepste gevoelens; [iron] sentimentele gevoelens: *tug at s.o.'s* ~ iem. zeer (ont)roeren
heart-to-heart openhartig gesprek[h]
hearty 1 hartelijk, vriendelijk **2** gezond, flink, hartig: *a* ~ ***meal*** een stevig maal; *hale and* ~ kerngezond **3** [inform] (al te) joviaal
¹heat (n) **1** warmte, hitte **2** vuur[h], drift, heftigheid: *in the* ~ *of the conversation* in het vuur van het gesprek **3** [inform] druk, dwang, moeilijkheden: *turn* (or: *put*) *the* ~ *on s.o.* iem. onder druk zetten **4** loopsheid: *on* ~ loops, tochtig **5** voorwedstrijd, serie, voorronde
²heat (vb) warm worden: ~ *up* heet worden
³heat (vb) verhitten, verwarmen: ~ *up* opwarmen
heater kachel, verwarming(stoestel[h])
heath 1 heideveld[h], open veld[h] **2** dopheide, erica
heathen 1 heiden, ongelovige **2** barbaar
heather heide(kruid[h]), struikheide
heating verwarming(ssysteem[h])
heat wave hittegolf

¹heave (n) **1** hijs, het op en neer gaan: *the* ~ *of the sea* de deining van de zee **2** ruk: *he gave a **mighty*** ~ hij gaf een enorme ruk
²heave (vb) **1** (op)zwellen, rijzen, omhooggaan: *his **stomach** ~d* zijn maag draaide ervan om **2** op en neer gaan **3** trekken, sjorren: ~ *at* (or: *on*) trekken aan
³heave (vb) **1** opheffen, (op)hijsen **2** slaken: *she ~d a **sigh*** ze zuchtte diep, ze liet een diepe zucht **3** [inform] gooien, smijten **4** [shipp] hijsen, takelen
heaven hemel; [fig] gelukzaligheid; Voorzienigheid: *in Heaven's **name***, *for Heaven's **sake*** in hemelsnaam; ***thank** ~(s)!* de hemel zij dank!
heavenly 1 hemels; goddelijk **2** hemel-: ~ ***bodies*** hemellichamen
heavy 1 zwaar: ~ ***industry*** zware industrie; ~ ***with*** zwaar beladen met; ~ ***with*** *the smell of roses* doortrokken van de geur van rozen **2** zwaar, hevig, aanzienlijk: ~ ***traffic*** druk verkeer, vrachtverkeer **3** moeilijk te verteren [also fig]: *I **find** it* ~ *going* ik schiet slecht op **4** serieus [newspaper, part in play]; zwaar op de hand **5** streng **6** zwaar, drukkend **7** zwaarmoedig || *play the* ~ ***father*** een (donder)preek houden; *make* ~ ***weather*** *of sth.* moeilijk maken wat makkelijk is; [inform] *be* ~ *on* veel gebruiken [petrol, makeup]; *time **hung*** ~ *on her hands* de tijd viel haar lang
heavy-footed 1 log **2** moeizaam; stroef
heavy-handed 1 onhandig; log, onbeholpen **2** tactloos
heavyset zwaargebouwd
heavyweight 1 zwaar iem. **2** worstelaar (bokser) in de zwaargewichtklasse **3** kopstuk[h], zwaargewicht
Hebrew Hebreeuws, Joods
heckle steeds onderbreken [speaker]
hectic koortsachtig [also fig]; jachtig, druk, hectisch
¹hedge (n) heg, haag
²hedge (vb) een slag om de arm houden, ergens omheen draaien
³hedge (vb) **1** omheinen: ~ *about* (or: *around, in*) *with* omringen met **2** dekken [bets, speculations]
hedgehog egel
hedge in omheinen; [fig] omringen; belemmeren: *hedged in by **rules** and regulations* door regels en voorschriften omringd
hedgerow haag
hedge sparrow heggenmus
heed aandacht, zorg: *give* (or: *pay*) ~ *to* aandacht schenken aan; *take* ~ *of* nota nemen van, letten op
heedless 1 achteloos, onoplettend: *be* ~ *of* niet letten op, in de wind slaan **2** onvoorzichtig
heel 1 hiel [also of stocking]; hak [also of shoe] **2** uiteinde[h], onderkant; korst [of

cheese]; kapje^h [of bread] ‖ **bring** to ~ kleinkrijgen, in het gareel brengen; **dig** one's ~s in
het been stijf houden; he **took** to his ~s hij
koos het hazenpad; **turn** on one's ~ zich plotseling omdraaien; **down** at ~ met scheve
hakken, afgetrapt; [fig] haveloos; **at** (or: on)
the ~s op de hielen, vlak achter
he̲fty 1 fors, potig **2** zwaar, lijvig
hege̲mony hegemonie; overwicht^h
hei̲fer vaars(kalf^h)
height 1 hoogte, lengte, peil^h, niveau^h: it is
only 4 feet **in** ~ het is maar 4 voet hoog
2 hoogtepunt^h, toppunt^h: the ~ of **summer**
hartje zomer; **at** its ~ op zijn hoogtepunt
3 top, piek **4** terreinverheffing, hoogte
hei̲ghten 1 hoger (doen) worden, verhogen **2** (doen) toenemen, verhevigen
hei̲nous gruwelijk
heir 1 erfgenaam: ~s erven; **sole** ~ enige
erfgenaam **2** opvolger: ~ **to** the throne
troonopvolger
hei̲ress erfgename [of fortune]
hei̲rloom erfstuk^h, familiestuk^h
heist [Am; inform] roof(overval)
he̲licopter helikopter
he̲lium helium^h
hell hel [also fig]: she drove ~ for **leather** zij
reed in vliegende vaart ‖ come ~ and (or: or)
high **water** wat er zich ook voordoet
he̲ll-bent (+ on, for) vastbesloten (om)
he̲llhole [inform] hel; afschuwelijk oord^h
hello̲ 1 hallo **2** hé [to express surprise]
helm helmstok; [also fig] stuurrad^h; roer^h: **at**
the ~ aan het roer; **take** the ~ het roer in
handen nemen
he̲lmet helm
he̲lmsman roerganger, stuurman
¹help (n) **1** hulp, steun, bijstand: that's a **big**
~! nou, daar hebben we wat aan!, daar
schieten we mee op, zeg!; can we **be** of any ~?
kunnen wij ergens mee helpen? **2** help(st)er,
dienstmeisje^h, werkster **3** huishoudelijk per-
soneel^h **4** remedie: there is **no** ~ for it er is
niets aan te doen
²help (vb) **1** helpen, bijstaan, (onder)steu-
nen, baten: ~ **along** (or: forward) vooruithel-
pen, bevorderen; ~ **out** a) bijspringen;
b) aanvullen **2** opscheppen, bedienen: ~
yourself ga je gang, tast toe **3** verhelpen,
helpen tegen: it can't be ~ed er is niets aan te
doen **4** voorkomen, verhinderen: if I can ~ it
als het aan mij ligt **5** [+ negation] nalaten,
zich weerhouden van: we **could** not ~ but
smile wij moesten wel glimlachen, of we wilden of niet
he̲lp desk helpdesk
he̲lpful 1 nuttig **2** behulpzaam
¹he̲lping (n) portie [food]
²he̲lping (adj) steunend: lend a ~ **hand** een
handje helpen
he̲lpless 1 hulpeloos: ~ **with** laughter slap

van de lach **2** onbeholpen
helter-ske̲lter holderdebolder, halsoverkop, kriskras
¹hem (n) boord^h, zoom: **take** the ~ up (of sth.)
(iets) korter maken
²hem (vb) (om)zomen: ~ **about** (or: around)
omringen; feel ~med **in** zich ingekapseld voelen
he̲-man mannetjesputter
he̲misphere halve bol; [geography] half-
rond^h: the **northern** (or: **southern**) ~ het
noordelijk (or: zuidelijk) halfrond
hemp hennep, cannabis
hen 1 hoen^h, hen, kip **2** pop [of bird] **3** [in-
form] pop [of bird]
hence 1 van nu (af): five **years** ~ over vijf
jaar **2** vandaar
hencefo̲rth van nu af aan, voortaan
he̲nchman 1 volgeling, aanhanger **2** trawant
he̲nna henna
he̲n-party vrijgezellenfeest^h (voor vrouwen)
he̲npecked onder de plak (zittend): a ~
husband een pantoffelheld
hepati̲tis geelzucht; hepatitis
¹her (pers pron) **1** haar, aan haar: he **gave** ~ a
watch hij gaf haar een horloge **2** zij: that's ~
dat is ze
²her (poss pron) haar: it's ~ **day** het is haar
grote dag
¹he̲rald (n) **1** heraut, gezant **2** (voor)bode
²he̲rald (vb) aankondigen: ~ **in** inluiden
he̲raldry heraldiek, wapenkunde
herb kruid^h: ~s and **spices** kruiden en spece-
rijen
herba̲ceous kruidachtig: ~ **border** border
van overblijvende (bloeiende) planten
he̲rbal kruiden-
he̲rbivore herbivoor, planteneter
Hercule̲an herculisch
¹herd (n) **1** kudde, troep, horde; [depr] massa:
the **common** (or: **vulgar**) ~ de massa
²herd (vb) samendrommen, bij elkaar hokken: ~ **with** omgaan met
³herd (vb) hoeden: ~ **together** samendrijven
here hier, op deze plaats, hierheen: w~ do
we go **from** ~? hoe gaan we nu verder?; **near**
~ hier in de buurt; [inform] ~ we **are** daar zijn
we dan, (zie)zo; ~ **you are** hier, alsjeblieft; ~
and **now** nu meteen; **over** ~ hier(heen); ~,
there and everywhere overal; that's is neither ~
nor there dat slaat nergens op, dat heeft er
niets mee te maken
here̲abouts hier in de buurt; hieromtrent
¹herea̲fter (n) hiernamaals^h
²herea̲fter (adv) **1** hierna; voortaan, verderop **2** [form] na de dood
hereby̲ 1 hierbij **2** hierdoor
here̲ditary erfelijk, erf-
here̲dity 1 erfelijkheid **2** overerving

heresy ketterij
heretic ketter
heretical ketters
herewith hierbij, bij deze(n)
heritage 1 erfenis; erfgoed[h] [also fig]
2 erfdeel[h]
hermaphrodite 1 hermafrodiet **2** [bot] tweeslachtige plant
hermit kluizenaar
hermit crab heremietkreeft
hernia hernia, (lies)breuk
hero 1 held **2** hoofdpersoon, hoofdrolspeler
heroic 1 heroïsch, heldhaftig **2** helden-: ~ *age* heldentijd **3** groots, gedurfd
heroin heroïne
heroine 1 heldin **2** hoofdrolspeelster
heroism heldenmoed
heron reiger
herring haring
herring gull zilvermeeuw
hers van haar, de (*or:* het) hare: *my books and* ~ mijn boeken en die van haar; *a friend of* ~ een vriend van haar
herself zichzelf, zich, zelf: *she cut* ~ ze sneed zich; *she did it* ~ ze deed het zelf
hesitate aarzelen, weifelen: ~ *about* (*or: over*) aarzelen over
hesitation aarzeling
hessian jute, zaklinnen[h]
heterogeneous heterogeen, ongelijksoortig
heterosexual heteroseksueel
hew houwen, sabelen, (be)kappen: ~ *down* a) kappen, omhakken [trees]; b) neermaaien [people]
hexagon regelmatige zeshoek
hexameter hexameter
heyday hoogtijdagen, bloei, beste tijd
hi 1 hé **2** hallo, hoi
hibernate een winterslaap houden [also fig]
hiccup 1 hik **2** [inform] probleempje[h]
the **hiccups** de hik
hidden verborgen, geheim: ~ *agenda* geheime agenda
¹hide (n) (dieren)huid, vel[h]
²hide (vb) zich verbergen: ~ *away* (*or: out*) zich schuil houden
³hide (vb) verbergen, verschuilen: ~ *from view* aan het oog onttrekken
hide-and-seek verstoppertje[h]: *play* ~ verstoppertje spelen
hideaway [inform] (geheime) schuilplaats
hidebound bekrompen
hideous afschuwelijk, afzichtelijk
hideout schuilplaats
hiding 1 het verbergen **2** het verborgen zijn: *come out of* ~ tevoorschijn komen; *go into* ~ zich verbergen **3** [inform] pak[h] rammel || [inform] *be on a* ~ *to nothing* voor een on-

mogelijke taak staan, geen schijn van kans maken
hiding place schuilplaats, geheime bergplaats
hierarchy hiërarchie
hieroglyph hiëroglief
hi-fi *high fidelity* hifi-geluidsinstallatie, stereo
¹high (n) **1** (hoogte)record[h], hoogtepunt[h], toppunt[h]: *hit a* ~ een hoogtepunt bereiken; *an all-time* ~ een absoluut hoogtepunt, een absolute topper **2** hogedrukgebied[h] || *from on* ~ uit de hemel
²high (adj) **1** hoog, hooggeplaatst, verheven: ~ *command* opperbevel; *a* ~ *opinion of* een hoge dunk van; *have friends in* ~ *places* een goede kruiwagen hebben; ~ *pressure* a) [meteorology] hoge druk; b) [inform] agressiviteit [of salesmanship]; ~ *society* de hogere kringen; ~ *tide* hoogwater, vloed; [fig] hoogtepunt; ~ *water* hoogwater **2** intens, sterk, groot: ~ *hopes* hoge verwachtingen **3** belangrijk: ~ *treason* hoogverraad **4** vrolijk: *in* ~ *spirits* vrolijk **5** gevorderd, hoog, op een hoogtepunt: ~ *season* hoogseizoen; *it's* ~ *time we went* het is de hoogste tijd om te gaan **6** aangeschoten, zat || *get on one's* ~ *horse* een hoge toon aanslaan; *the* ~ *sea(s)* de volle zee; ~ *tea* vroeg warm eten, vaak met thee; ~ *and dry* gestrand; [fig] zonder middelen; ~ *and mighty* uit de hoogte
³high (adv) **1** hoog, zeer **2** schel || *hold one's head* ~ zijn hoofd niet laten hangen; *feelings ran* ~ de emoties liepen hoog op; *ride* ~ succes hebben; *search* ~ *and low* in alle hoeken zoeken
¹highbrow (n) (semi-)intellectueel
²highbrow (adj) geleerd, intellectueel
high-class 1 eersteklas, prima, eerlijk **2** hooggeplaatst, voornaam
high-definition met hoge resolutie
highfalutin [inform] hoogdravend
high-flyer hoogvlieger, ambitieus persoon
high-grade hoogwaardig
high-handed eigenmachtig, aanmatigend, autoritair
highland hoogland[h]
the **Highlands** de Schotse Hooglanden
high-level op hoog niveau
¹highlight (n) **1** lichtste deel[h]; [fig] opvallend kenmerk[h] **2** hoogtepunt[h] **3** (-s) coupe soleil
²highlight (vb) naar voren halen, doen uitkomen: *use this pen to* ~ *the relevant passages* gebruik deze pen maar om de relevant passages te markeren
highly 1 hoog: ~ *paid officials* goed betaalde ambtenaren **2** zeer, erg, in hoge mate **3** met lof: *speak* ~ *of* loven, roemen
high-minded hoogstaand, verheven
highness 1 hoogheid: *His* (*or: Her*) *Royal*

Highness Zijne (*or:* Hare) Koninklijke Hoogheid **2** hoogte, verhevenheid
high-pitched 1 hoog, schel **2** steil [roof]
high-powered krachtig; met groot vermogen: *a ~ car* een auto met een krachtige motor; *a ~ manager* een dynamische manager; een topmanager
high-profile opvallend; op de voorgrond tredend
high-rise [Am] hoog: ~ *flats* torenflats
high road hoofdweg, grote weg; [fig] (directe) weg
high school [Am] middelbare school
high-sounding hoogdravend; klinkend
high-speed snel: ~ *rail link* hogesnelheidslijn
high street hoofdstraat: *High-Street fashion* mode voor het grote publiek
high-strung nerveus, overgevoelig
high-tech geavanceerd technisch
high-technology geavanceerde technologie
highway grote weg, verkeersweg; [fig] (directe) weg
highwayman struikrover
highway patrol [Am] verkeerspolitie
hijab hoofddoek, hidjab
¹hijack (n) kaping
²hijack (vb) kapen
hijacker kaper
¹hike (n) lange wandeling, trektocht
²hike (vb) lopen, wandelen, trekken
³hike (vb) **1** (+ up) ophijsen, optrekken **2** [Am] verhogen
hiker wandelaar
hilarious 1 heel grappig, dolkomisch **2** vrolijk, uitgelaten
hilarity hilariteit, vrolijkheid
hill heuvel ‖ *it is up ~ and down dale* het gaat heuvelop, heuvelaf; *over the ~* over zijn hoogtepunt heen
hillbilly [Am; depr] boerenkinkel, boerentrien
hillock 1 heuveltjeʰ **2** bergjeʰ [earth]
hillside helling
hilly heuvelachtig
hilt gevestʰ, handvatʰ ‖ *(up)to the ~* volkomen, tot over de oren
him 1 hem, aan hem **2** hij: ~ *and his jokes* hij met zijn grapjes
himself zichzelf, zich, zelf: *he cut ~* hij sneed zich; *he did it ~* hij deed het zelf
¹hind (n) hinde
²hind (adj) achterst ‖ *talk the ~ leg(s) off a donkey* iem. de oren van het hoofd kletsen
hinder 1 belemmeren, hinderen **2** (+ from) beletten (te), verhinderen, tegenhouden
hindmost achterst
hindquarters achterdeel; achterlijf [of horse]
hindrance belemmering, beletselʰ, hinder-

nis
hindsight kennis, inzichtʰ achteraf: *with ~* achteraf gezien
¹Hindu (n) hindoe
²Hindu (adj) Hindoes
hinge scharnierʰ; [fig] spil
¹hint (n) **1** wenk, hint, tip: *drop a ~* een hint geven; *take a ~* een wenk ter harte nemen **2** vleugjeʰ, tikjeʰ
²hint (vb) aanwijzingen geven: ~ *at* zinspelen op
³hint (vb) laten doorschemeren
¹hip (n) heup
²hip (adj) hip, modern ‖ ~, ~, *hurrah!* hiep, hiep, hoera!
hippie hippie
hippo nijlpaardʰ
hippopotamus nijlpaardʰ
¹hire (n) huur, (dienst)loonʰ: *for* (*or: on*) ~ te huur
²hire (vb) **1** huren: ~ *out* verhuren **2** inhuren, (tijdelijk) in dienst nemen
hireling huurling
hire purchase huurkoop: *on* ~ op afbetaling
his zijn, van hem, het zijne, de zijne: *these boots are* ~ deze laarzen zijn van hem; *a hobby of* ~ een hobby van hem; *it was* ~ *day* het was zijn grote dag
hiss 1 sissen **2** uitfluiten: ~ *off* (*or: away, down*) van het podium fluiten
historian historicus
historic historisch, beroemd
historical historisch, geschiedkundig
history 1 geschiedenis: *ancient* (*or: past*) ~ verleden tijd **2** historisch verhaalʰ
¹hit (n) **1** klap, slag **2** treffer **3** hit, succes-(nummer)ʰ **4** buitenkansjeʰ, treffer **5** goede zet: *make a ~ (with)* succes hebben (bij)
²hit (vb) **1** aanvallen **2** hard aankomen ‖ ~ *home* doel treffen
³hit (vb) treffen [also fig]; raken: *be hard ~* zwaar getroffen zijn ‖ [inform] ~ *it off (with)* het (samen) goed kunnen vinden (met)
⁴hit (vb) **1** slaan; geven [a blow]: [fig] ~ *a man when he is down* iem. een trap nageven; ~ *and run* doorrijden na aanrijding; ~ *back (at)* terugslaan; [fig] van repliek dienen **2** stoten (op), botsen (tegen)
hit-and-run 1 m.b.t. het doorrijden [after collision] **2** [mil] verrassings- [attack]
¹hitch (n) **1** ruk, zet, duw **2** storing: *go off without a ~* vlot verlopen
²hitch (vb) **1** vastmaken, vasthaken: ~ *a horse to a cart* een paard voor een wagen spannen **2** liften: [inform] ~ *a ride* liften ‖ *get ~ed* trouwen; ~ *up* optrekken
hitchhiker lifter
hither herwaarts: ~ *and thither* her en der
hitherto tot nu toe, tot dusver
hit list [inform] **1** dodenlijst **2** zwarte lijst

hit man [Am; inform] huurmoordenaar
hit out 1 krachtig slaan **2** aanvallen || ~ *at*
uithalen naar
hit (up)on bedenken; komen op [an idea];
bij toeval ontdekken
HIV *human immunodeficiency virus* hiv-vi-
rus[h]
hive 1 bijenkorf [also fig] **2** zwerm; [fig]
menigte **3** (-s) netelroos
HM 1 *Her Majesty* H.M., Hare Majesteit
2 *His Majesty* Z.M., Zijne Majesteit
HMU *hit me up* bel of mail me even
Ho 1 *Honorary* Ere- **2** *Hono(u)rable* Hoog-
(wel)geboren [title for noblemen]
[1]**hoard** (n) **1** (geheime) voorraad, schat
2 opeenhoping
[2]**hoard** (vb) hamsteren: ~ *up* oppotten
hoarding 1 (tijdelijke) schutting **2** recla-
mebord[h]
hoarfrost rijp
hoarse 1 hees, schor **2** met een hese stem
hoary 1 grijs **2** grijsharig, witharig **3** (al)-
oud, eerbiedwaardig: *a ~ joke* een ouwe bak
[1]**hoax** (n) bedrog[h]: *the bomb scare turned out
to be a ~* de bommelding bleek vals (alarm)
[2]**hoax** (vb) om de tuin leiden: ~ *s.o. into believing that* iem. laten geloven dat ...
hob kookplaat [of cooker]
hobble (doen) strompelen; [fig] moeizaam
(doen) voortgaan
hobby hobby, liefhebberij
hobby-horse 1 hobbelpaard[h] **2** stokpaardje[h] [also fig]
hobgoblin 1 kobold **2** boeman
hobnob (also + with) vriendschappelijk omgaan (met): *he is always ~bing with the manager* hij papt altijd met de directeur aan
hobo [Am] zwerver
hockey 1 hockey[h] **2** [Am] ijshockey[h]
hocus-pocus hocus pocus, gegoochel[h], bedriegerij
hoe schoffel
hog 1 varken[h] **2** zwijn[h] [also fig]; veelvraat ||
[inform] *go the whole ~* iets grondig doen
hogwash lariekoek; flauwekul
the **hoi polloi** het volk; het gepeupel
[1]**hoist** (n) hijstoestel[h], tillift
[2]**hoist** (vb) hijsen, takelen: ~ *one's flag* zijn
vlag in top hijsen
hoity-toity [inform, dated] hooghartig
hokum [Am; inform] onzin; klets
[1]**hold** (n) **1** greep, houvast[h]; [fig] invloed:
catch/get (or: *grab, take*) ~ *of* (vast)grijpen,
(vast)pakken; *get a ~ on* vat krijgen op; *have
a ~ over s.o.* macht over iem. hebben; *keep*
(or: *leave*) ~ *of* vasthouden, loslaten; *take ~*
vastgrijpen; [fig] aanslaan **2** (scheeps)ruim[h] ||
on ~ uitgesteld, vertraagd, in afwachting;
put a project on ~ een project opschorten; *no
~s barred* alle middelen zijn toegestaan, alles
mag

[2]**hold** (vb) **1** houden, het uithouden, standhouden: ~ *by* (or: *to*) zich houden aan **2** van
kracht zijn, gelden, waar zijn: ~ *good* (or:
true) *for* gelden voor, van toepassing zijn op
3 doorgaan, aanhouden; goed blijven [of
weather]
[3]**hold** (vb) **1** vasthouden (aan), beethouden;
[fig] boeien: *will you ~ the line?* wilt u even
aan het toestel blijven?; ~ *together* bijeen-
houden; ~ *s.o. to his promise* iem. aan zijn belofte houden **2** hebben: ~ *a title* een titel
dragen **3** bekleden [eg position] **4** doen
plaatsvinden, beleggen, houden: ~ *a conversation* een gesprek voeren **5** in bedwang
houden, weerhouden: *there is no ~ing her* zij
is niet te stuiten **6** [inform] ophouden met,
stilleggen, stoppen: ~ *everything!* stop!
7 menen, beschouwen als: ~ *sth. cheap* (or:
dear) weinig (or: veel) waarde aan iets hechten; ~ *sth. against s.o.* iem. iets verwijten **8** in
hechtenis houden, vasthouden || ~ *it!* houen
zo!, stop!; ~ *one's own* a) het (alleen) aankunnen; b) zich handhaven, niet achteruitgaan [of a sick person]; ~ *one's own with* opgewassen zijn tegen
holdall reistas, weekendtas
[1]**hold back** (vb) aarzelen, schromen, iets
verzwijgen: ~ *from* zich weerhouden van
[2]**hold back** (vb) **1** tegenhouden, inhouden,
in de weg staan **2** achterhouden, voor zich
houden
holder 1 houder, bezitter; drager [of a ti-
tle] **2** bekleder [of an office]
holding 1 pachtgoed[h]: *small ~s* kleine boe-
renbedrijfjes **2** bezit[h] [of shares etc]; eigendom[h]
[1]**hold off** (vb) uitblijven, wegblijven
[2]**hold off** (vb) **1** uitstellen **2** weerstaan, tegenstand bieden aan
hold on 1 volhouden **2** zich vasthouden
3 aanhouden **4** [inform] wachten; niet op-
hangen [telephone] || [inform] ~*!* stop!,
wacht eens even!
hold on to 1 vasthouden, niet loslaten:
whatever you do, ~ *your dreams* wat je ook
doet, geef nooit je dromen op **2** [inform]
houden
[1]**hold out** (vb) **1** standhouden, volhouden,
het uithouden **2** weigeren toe te geven || ~
for blijven eisen; ~ *on* a) weigeren toe te geven aan; b) iets geheim houden voor
[2]**hold out** (vb) uitsteken [hand]
hold over 1 aanhouden **2** verdagen, uitstellen
[1]**hold up** (vb) standhouden, het uithouden
[2]**hold up** (vb) **1** (onder)steunen **2** omhoog
houden; opsteken [hand]: ~ *as an example*
tot voorbeeld stellen; ~ *to ridicule* (or: *scorn*)
bespotten **3** ophouden, tegenhouden, vertragen **4** overvallen
hold-up 1 oponthoud[h] **2** roofoverval; [fig]

overval
hole 1 gatʰ, holte, kuil **2** gatʰ, opening, bres: **make** a ~ in een gat slaan in; [fig] duchtig aanspreken; [fig] **pick** ~s in ondergraven [eg argument] **3** holʰ [of animal]; legerʰ **4** hokʰ, krotʰ; [Am] isoleercel **5** penibele situatie: **in** a ~ in het nauw, in de knel **6** kuiltjeʰ [in ballgames]; knikkerpotjeʰ; [billiards] zak **7** [golf] hole
hole-in-the-wall [inform] **1** flappentap; geldautomaat **2** [Am] duister tentjeʰ
¹holiday (n) **1** feestdag: **public** ~ officiële feestdag **2** vakantiedag: ook ~s vakantie; vrije tijd; **take** a ~ vrijaf nemen; **on** ~, **on** one's ~s op vakantie
²holiday (vb) met vakantie zijn
holiday-maker vakantieganger
holiness heiligheid
holler [inform; Am] schreeuwen; roepen, blèren
¹hollow (n) **1** holte, kuil **2** leegte
²hollow (adj) **1** hol **2** zonder inhoud, leeg, onoprecht **3** hol [of sound] ‖ **beat** s.o. ~ iem. totaal verslaan
holly hulst
holocaust holocaust, vernietiging
holster holster
holy heilig, gewijd, vroom, godsdienstig: the Holy **Ghost** (or: **Spirit**) de Heilige Geest; Holy **Writ** de Heilige Schrift; [Roman Catholicism] the Holy **See** de Heilige Stoel; ~ **water** wijwater; Holy **Week** de Goede Week
homage hulde: **pay** (or: **do**) ~ to eer bewijzen aan
¹home (n) **1** huisʰ, woning, verblijfʰ, woonhuisʰ **2** thuisʰ, geboortegrond: **arrive** (or: **get**) ~ thuiskomen; **leave** ~ het ouderlijk huis verlaten; **at** (or: **back**) ~ bij ons thuis, in mijn geboortestreek, geboorteplaats; **be at** ~ a) thuis zijn; b) ontvangen; **make yourself at** ~ doe alsof je thuis bent; (away) **from** ~ van huis; it's a ~ **from** ~ het is er zogoed als thuis **3** bakermat, zetel, haard: **strike** ~ doel treffen **4** (te)huisʰ, inrichting **5** [sport, game] eindstreep, finish, (thuis)honkʰ ‖ **drive** a nail ~ een spijker er helemaal inslaan; ~ (in) **on** a) zich richten op [of aeroplane etc]; b) koersen op [a beacon]
²home (adj) **1** huis-, thuis-: ~ **base** (thuis)basis; [sport, game] doel, honk; ~ **brew** zelf gebrouwen bier; ~ **help** gezinshulp; ~ **movie** zelf opgenomen film; ~ **remedy** huismiddel(tje) **2** huiselijk: ~ **life** het huiselijk leven **3** lokaal: the Home **Counties** de graafschappen rondom Londen
Home binnenlands, uit eigen land: the ~ **Office** het Ministerie van Binnenlandse Zaken; the ~ **Secretary** de minister van Binnenlandse Zaken
homeless dakloos
homely 1 eenvoudig **2** alledaags **3** [Am]

lelijk [of persons]
homemade zelfgemaakt: ~ **jam** zelfgemaakte jam
homemaker [Am] [roughly] huismoeder, [roughly] huisvrouw
home shopping het thuiswinkelen
homesick: **be** (or: **feel**) ~ heimwee hebben
homespun 1 zelfgesponnen **2** eenvoudig
homestead hofstede, boerderij
homeward(s) (op weg) naar huis, terugkerend, huiswaarts: homeward **bound** op weg naar huis
home watch buurtpreventie, buurtwacht
homework huiswerkʰ; [fig] voorbereiding: **do** ~ huiswerk maken; **do** ~ ~ zich (grondig) voorbereiden
homey huiselijk, gezellig, knus
homicidal moorddadig: ~ **tendencies** moordneigingen
homicide doodslag, moord
homoeopathy homeopathie
homogeneity homogeniteit, gelijksoortigheid
homogeneous homogeen, gelijksoortig
homosexual homoseksueel
¹Honduran (n) Hondurees, Hondurese
²Honduran (adj) Hondurees
Honduras Honduras
hone slijpen, wetten; [fig] verbeteren
honest 1 eerlijk, oprecht: **earn** (or: **turn**) an ~ **penny** een eerlijk stuk brood verdienen **2** braaf
honestly echt: ~, did you believe him? eerlijk, geloofde je hem?
honesty eerlijkheid, oprechtheid: ~ is the best **policy** eerlijk duurt het langst
honey 1 honing; [fig] zoetheid; liefelijkheid **2** [Am] schat; liefjeʰ [as form of address]
honeybee honingbij
¹honeycomb (n) **1** honingraat **2** honingraatmotiefʰ
²honeycomb (vb) doorboren, doorzeven: ~ed **with** doorzeefd met, doortrokken van
honeymoon 1 huwelijksreis **2** wittebroodsdagen
honeysuckle kamperfoelie
¹honk (vb) schreeuwen [of goose]
²honk (vb) (doen) toeteren, (doen) claxonneren: he ~ed the **horn** hij toeterde
honorary honorair, ere-, onbezoldigd
¹honour (n) eer(bewijsʰ), hulde, aanzienʰ, reputatie: **code** of ~ erecode; it **does** him ~, it is **to** his ~ het strekt hem tot eer; **in** ~ bound, **on** one's ~ moreel verplicht; **do** the ~s als gastheer optreden ‖ **Your** (or: **His**) Honour Edelachtbare [form of address for judges]
²honour (vb) **1** eren, in ere houden, eer bewijzen: ~ **with** vereren met **2** honoreren
honourable 1 eerzaam, respectabel **2** eervol: ~ **mention** eervolle vermelding **3** eerbaar **4** hooggeboren, edelachtbaar: **Most**

(or: **Right**) *Honourable* edel(hoog)achtbaar [in titles]
honour killing eerwraak
honours degree [educ] universitaire graad
hooch sterkedrank
hood 1 kap, capuchon **2** overkapping, huif; vouwdak[h] [of car]; kap [of carriage, pram] **3** beschermkap, wasemkap
hoodlum 1 gangster; bendelid[h], crimineel **2** (jonge) vandaal
hoodwink bedriegen, voor de gek houden
hoody [inform] **1** hoody **2** straat-, hangjongere **3** bonte kraai
hooey onzin, nonsens, kletskoek
hoof hoef
1hook (n) **1** (telefoon)haak: ~ *and eye* haak en oog; *off the* ~ van de haak [telephone] **2** vishoek, vishaak **3** hoek, kaap, landtong || ~, *line and sinker* helemaal, van a tot z; *by* ~ *or by crook* hoe dan ook, op eerlijke of oneerlijke wijze; *get* (or: *let*) *s.o. off the* ~ iem. uit de puree halen
2hook (vb) vastgehaakt worden
3hook (vb) **1** vasthaken, aanhaken: ~ *on* vasthaken **2** aan de haak slaan [also fig]; strikken, bemachtigen
hooked 1 haakvormig: *a* ~ *nose* een haakneus, haviksneus **2** met een haak **3** vast(gehaakt), verstrikt: *her skirt got* ~ *on a nail* ze bleef met haar rok achter een spijker haken **4** (+ on) verslaafd (aan) [drugs]: [fig] *he is completely* ~ *on that girl* hij is helemaal bezeten van dat meisje
hooker [Am; inform] hoer
hook up 1 (+ with) aansluiten (op), verbinden (met) **2** aanhaken, vasthaken
hooligan (jonge) vandaal, herrieschopper, hooligan
hoop 1 hoepel, ring **2** [sport] hoepel; [croquet] hoop; ijzeren poortje[h] || *put s.o. through the* ~*(s)* iem. het vuur na aan de schenen leggen
1hoot (n) **1** gekras[h] [of owl] **2** getoet[h] **3** (ge)boe[h], gejouw[h] **4** [inform] giller || [inform] *he doesn't give* (or: *care*) *a* ~ het kan hem geen zier schelen
2hoot (vb) **1** krassen, schreeuwen **2** toeteren (met) **3** schateren, bulderen van het lachen
3hoot (vb) uitjouwen: ~ *at s.o.*, ~ *s.o. off the stage* iem. uitjouwen, iem. wegjouwen
hooter sirene, fabrieksfluit, fabriekssirene
hoover stofzuigen
1hop (n) **1** hink(el)sprong(etje[h]), huppelsprong(etje[h]) **2** dansje[h], dansfeest[h] **3** reisje[h] **4** (-s) hop(plant), hopbel || *catch s.o. on the* ~ iem. verrassen, bij iem. binnenvallen; *on the* ~ druk in de weer
2hop (vb) hinkelen, huppen, wippen: ~ *in* (or: *out*) instappen, uitstappen
3hop (vb) **1** overheen springen **2** springen in

[on bus, train] || [inform] ~ *it!* smeer 'em!, donder op!
1hope (n) hoop(volle verwachting), vertrouwen[h]; [Belg] betrouwen[h]: ~ *against hope* tegen beter weten in blijven hopen; *lay/set* (or: *pin, put*) *one's* ~*s on* zijn hoop vestigen op; *live in* ~*(s)* (blijven) hopen
2hope (vb) (+ for) hopen (op): ~ *for the best* er het beste (maar) van hopen
1hopeful (n) veelbeloved persoon, belofte
2hopeful (adj) hoopvol, hoopgevend, veelbelovend, optimistisch: *I'm not very* ~ *of success* ik heb niet veel hoop op een geslaagde afloop
hopefully 1 hoopvol **2** hopelijk: ~, *he will come* het is te hopen dat hij komt
hopeless hopeloos, wanhopig, uitzichtloos: ~ *at* hopeloos slecht in
horizon horizon [also fig]
horizontal horizontaal, vlak
hormone hormoon[h]
horn 1 hoorn, gewei[h], (voel)hoorn **2** toeter, claxon, trompet: *blow* (or: *sound*) *the* ~ toeteren || *draw* (or: *pull*) *in one's* ~*s* a) terugkrabbelen; b) de buikriem aanhalen
hornet horzel
hornet's nest wespennest[h] || *stir up a* ~ zich in een wespennest steken
hornrimmed met hoornen montuur
horny 1 [inform] geil **2** [inform] sexy **3** eeltig **4** van hoorn
horoscope horoscoop: *cast a* ~ een horoscoop trekken
horrendous afgrijselijk, afschuwelijk
horrible afschuwelijk, vreselijk, verschrikkelijk
horrid 1 vreselijk, verschrikkelijk **2** akelig
horrific weerzinwekkend, afschuwelijk
horrify met afschuw vervullen, schokken, ontstellen
horror 1 (ver)schrik(king), gruwel, ontzetting **2** (-s) kriebels || *you little* ~! klein kreng dat je bent!
horse 1 paard[h]: *eat* (or: *work*) *like a* ~ eten (or: werken) als een paard **2** (droog)rek[h], schraag, ezel **3** bok [gymnastic apparatus]; paard[h] **4** heroïne || *a* ~ *of another* (or: *a different*) *colour* een geheel andere kwestie; (straight) from the ~'s *mouth* uit de eerste hand; *hold your* ~*s!* rustig aan!, niet te overhaast!
horse about [inform] dollen; stoeien
horseback paardenrug: *three men on* ~ drie mannen te paard
horseman ruiter, paardrijder
horseplay stoeipartij, lolbroekerij
horsepower paardenkracht
horse racing paardenrennen[h]
horseradish 1 mierik(swortel) **2** mierikswortelsaus
horseshoe (hoef)ijzer[h]

horticulture 1 tuinbouw 2 hovenierskunst

¹hose (n) 1 brandslang, tuinslang 2 kousen, panty's, sokken

²hose (vb) (met een slang) bespuiten, schoonspuiten: ~ *down* a car een auto schoonspuiten

hospice 1 verpleeghuisʰ voor terminale patiënten 2 [Am] wijkverpleger, wijkverpleegster 3 gastenverblijfʰ [in monastery]

hospitable gastvrij, hartelijk

hospital ziekenhuisʰ: *in* ~, [Am] *in the* ~ in het ziekenhuis

hospitality gastvrijheid

hospitalize (laten) opnemen in een ziekenhuis

¹host (n) 1 gastheer 2 waard 3 massa, menigte: ~s *of tourists* horden toeristen

²host (vb) ontvangen, optreden als gastheer bij, op: ~ *a television* **programme** een televisieprogramma presenteren

hostage gijzelaar: *take* s.o. ~ iem. gijzelen

hostel 1 tehuisʰ, studentenhuisʰ, pensionʰ 2 jeugdherberg

hostess 1 gastvrouw 2 hostess 3 stewardess

host family gastgezinʰ

hostile 1 vijandelijk 2 vijandig, onvriendelijk

hostilities vijandelijkheden, oorlogshandelingen

hostility 1 vijandschap 2 vijandelijkheid, vijandige daad

hot 1 heet, warm, gloeiend, scherp, pikant, vurig, hartstochtelijk, heetgebakerd; [inform] geil; opgewonden; [inform; techn] radioactief: ~ *flushes* opvliegen, opvlieging; *with two policemen in* ~ *pursuit* met twee agenten op zijn hielen; *am* / *getting* ~? word ik warm? [while guessing] 2 vers [of track]; recent; heet (van de naald) [of news]: ~ *off the press* vers van de pers ‖ ~ *air* blabla, gezwets; *like a cat on* ~ *bricks,* [Am] *like a cat on a* ~ *tin roof* benauwd, niet op zijn gemak; *sell like* ~ *cakes* als warme broodjes de winkel uitvliegen; *strike while the iron is* ~ het ijzer smeden als het heet is; *a* ~ *potato* een heet hangijzer; ~ *stuff* a) bink; b) prima spul; c) (harde) porno; d) buit, gestolen goed; *be* ~ *on s.o.'s* **track** (or: **trail**) iem. na op het spoor zijn; *be in* (or: *get into*) ~ *water* in de problemen zitten (or: raken); *make* it (or: *the place, things*) *(too)* ~ *for s.o.* iem. het vuur na aan de schenen leggen; *not* so ~ niet zo goed; ~ *on astrology* gek op astrologie; *blow* ~ *and cold* nu eens voor dan weer tegen zijn

hotbed 1 broeikas 2 broeinestʰ

hotblooded 1 vurig, hartstochtelijk 2 opvliegend

hotchpotch hutspot, ratjetoeʰ; [fig] mengelmoesʰ; allegaartjeʰ

hotel hotelʰ

hothouse (broei)kas

hotkey sneltoets

hotplate kookplaat(jeʰ), warmhoudplaat(-jeʰ)

hot-tempered heetgebakerd, heethoofdig

¹hot up (vb) [inform] warm(er) worden, hevig(er) worden

²hot up (vb) [inform] verhevigen, intensiveren

¹hound (n) (jacht)hond, windhond

²hound (vb): [inform] *be* ~ed *out by envious colleagues* door jaloerse collega's weggepest worden

hour 1 uurʰ: *after* ~s na sluitingstijd, na kantoortijd; *on the* ~ op het hele uur; *out of* ~s buiten de normale uren; *at the eleventh* ~ ter elfder ure, op het allerlaatste ogenblik 2 momentʰ, huidige tijd: *the* ~ *has come* de tijd is gekomen, het is zover

hourglass zandloper

¹hourly (adj) 1 ieder uur; uurlijks 2 per uur: ~ *pay* uurloon

²hourly (adv) ieder uur: *three* ~ elke drie uur

¹house (n) 1 huisʰ, woning, behuizing, (handels)huisʰ: ~ *of cards* kaartenhuis [also fig]; ~ *of God* godshuis, huis des Heren; *eat* s.o. *out of* ~ *and home* iem. de oren van het hoofd eten; *move* ~ verhuizen; [fig] *put* (or: *set*) *one's* ~ *in order* orde op zaken stellen; *set up* ~ op zichzelf gaan wonen; *on the* ~ van het huis, (rondje) van de zaak 2 (vorstelijk/adellijk) geslachtʰ, koningshuisʰ, vorstenhuisʰ, adellijke familie 3 bioscoopzaal, schouwburgzaal, voorstelling: [fig] *bring the* ~ *down* staande ovaties oogsten ‖ *like a* ~ *on fire* a) krachtig; b) (vliegens)vlug; c) prima, uitstekend; *keep* ~ het huishouden doen

²house (vb) huisvesten, onderdak bieden aan

House volksvertegenwoordiging, kamer: *the* ~ *of Commons* het Lagerhuis; *the* ~ *of Lords* het Hogerhuis; *the* ~s *of Parliament* het parlement, de parlementsgebouwen; *the* ~ *of Representatives* het Huis van Afgevaardigden

house agent makelaar (in onroerend goed)

housebreaking inbraak

housebroken [Am] zindelijk

¹household (n) (de gezamenlijke) huisbewoners, huisgenoten, huisgezinʰ

²household (adj): *a* ~ *name* begrip, bekende naam; *a* ~ *word* gangbare uitdrukking

householder gezinshoofdʰ; bewoner

housekeeper huishoudster

housekeeping huishouding, huishoudenʰ

houseman 1 (intern) assistent-arts [in hospital] 2 (huis)knecht

house-proud [depr] (overdreven) proper

houseroom onderdak[h], (berg)ruimte: [fig] *I wouldn't give such a chair* ~ ik zou zo'n stoel niet eens gratis willen hebben
house-to-house huis-aan-huis-
housetrained [of animals] zindelijk
housewarming inwijdingsfeest[h] [of house]
housewife huisvrouw
housework huishoudelijk werk[h]
housing 1 huisvesting, woonruimte **2** [techn] huis[h], omhulsel[h]
housing association woningbouwvereniging
housing estate 1 nieuwbouwproject[h] **2** woonwijk
hovel krot[h], bouwval
hover 1 hangen (boven); (blijven) zweven [of birds etc] **2** rondhangen, blijven hangen || [fig] ~ *between* life and death tussen leven en dood zweven
hovercraft hovercraft
[1]**how** (adv) **1** hoe, hoeveel, hoever: ~ *are things?* hoe gaat het ermee?; [inform] ~ *idiotic can you get?* kan het nog gekker?; *she knows* ~ *to cook* ze kan koken; ~ *do you like my hat?* wat vind je van mijn hoed?; ~ *do you do?* aangenaam, hoe maakt u het?; ~ *is she (off) for clothes?* heeft ze genoeg kleren?; ~ *about John?* wat doe je (dan) met John? **2** hoe, waardoor, waarom: ~ *come she is late?* hoe komt het dat ze te laat is? || ~ *about going home?* zouden we niet naar huis gaan?; ~ *about an ice-cream?* wat vind je van een ijsje?
[2]**how** (conj) zoals: *colour it* ~ *you like* kleur het zoals je wilt
[1]**however** (adv) **1** hoe ... ook, hoe dan ook, op welke wijze ook: ~ *you travel*, you will be tired hoe je ook reist, je zult moe zijn **2** echter, nochtans, desondanks: *this time, ~, he meant what he said* deze keer echter meende hij het **3** hoe in 's hemelsnaam: ~ *did you manage to come?* hoe ben je erin geslaagd te komen?
[2]**however** (conj) hoe ... maar, zoals ... maar: ~ *he tried, it wouldn't go in* hoe hij het ook probeerde, het wilde er niet in
[1]**howl** (n) gehuil[h], brul, gil: ~*s of derision* spotgelach, hoongelach
[2]**howl** (vb) huilen, jammeren, krijsen: *the wind* ~*ed* de wind gierde; ~ *with laughter* gieren van het lachen || *the speaker was* ~*ed down* de spreker werd weggehoond
howler giller, flater, blunder
howling gigantisch, enorm
howsoever *see* [1]*however*
hp 1 horsepower pk, paardenkracht **2** hire purchase huurkoop: *on (the) hp* op huurkoopbasis; [roughly] op afbetaling
HQ headquarters hoofdbureau, hoofdkwartier
HRH Her Royal Highness H.K.H., Z.K.H., Hare

(Zijne) Koninklijke Hoogheid
hr(s) hour(s) uur, uren
hub 1 naaf **2** centrum[h], middelpunt[h] **3** overstapluchthaven
hubbub 1 gedruis[h]; kabaal[h] **2** straatrumoer[h]; drukte
[1]**huddle** (n) **1** (dicht opeengepakte) groep, kluwen, menigte **2** samenraapsel[h], bos[h], troep || *go into a* ~ de koppen bij elkaar steken
[2]**huddle** (vb) bijeenkruipen: ~ *together* bij elkaar kruipen; *the singers* ~*d together around the microphone* de zangeressen stonden dicht bijeen rond de microfoon
hue kleur [also fig]; tint || *raise a* ~ *and cry against a new measure* luid protesteren tegen een nieuwe maatregel
huff boze bui: *in a* ~ nijdig, beledigd
[1]**hug** (n) omhelzing, knuffel
[2]**hug** (vb) **1** omarmen, omhelzen, tegen zich aandrukken **2** (zich) vasthouden aan
huge reusachtig, kolossaal, enorm: ~*ly overrated* zwaar overschat
hulk 1 (scheeps)casco[h], scheepsromp, hulk **2** vleesklomp, kolos
hull 1 (scheeps)romp **2** (peulen)schil; [fig] omhulsel[h]
hullabaloo kabaal[h]; herrie
hullo hallo
[1]**hum** (n) zoemgeluid[h], bromgeluid[h], brom, gebrom[h], gezoem[h]
[2]**hum** (vb) **1** zoemen, brommen **2** bruisen, (op volle toeren) draaien: *things are beginning to* ~ er komt schot in; ~ *with activity* gonzen van de bedrijvigheid
[3]**hum** (vb) neuriën: *he was just* ~*ming a tune to himself* hij zat in zichzelf een deuntje te neuriën
[1]**human** (n) mens
[2]**human** (adj) menselijk, mensen-: ~ *being* mens; ~ *interest* het menselijk element, de gevoelsinbreng [in newspaper articles etc]; ~ *nature* de menselijke natuur; *the* ~ *race* de mensheid; ~ *rights* mensenrechten; *I'm only* ~ ik ben (ook) maar een mens
humane humaan, menselijk
humanistic humanistisch
humanitarian humanitair, menslievend
humanity 1 mensdom[h] **2** menselijkheid, mensheid, mens-zijn[h], menslievendheid: *crimes against* ~ misdaden tegen de menselijkheid **3** (humanities) geesteswetenschappen
humankind [form] mensheid
[1]**humble** (adj) bescheiden, onderdanig, nederig, eenvoudig: *my* ~ *apologies* mijn nederige excuses || *eat* ~ *pie* een toontje lager zingen, inbinden
[2]**humble** (vb) vernederen
humbug 1 bedrieger, oplichter **2** pepermuntballetje[h], kussentje[h] **3** onzin, nonsens,

larie **4** bluf

humdrum saai, vervelend, eentonig

humid vochtig

humidity vochtigheid

humiliate vernederen, krenken

humiliation vernedering

humility nederigheid, bescheidenheid

hummingbird kolibrie

humorous humoristisch, grappig, komisch

¹**humour** (n) **1** humor, geestigheid: *sense* of ~ gevoel voor humor **2** humeurʰ, stemming: *in a bad* ~ slechtgeluimd, in een slechte bui

²**humour** (vb) tegemoetkomen (aan), paaien, toegeven: ~ *a child* een kind zijn zin geven

¹**hump** (n) **1** bult, bochel **2** [inform] landerigheid: *it gives* me the ~ ik baal ervan ‖ *be over the* ~ het ergste achter de rug hebben

²**hump** (vb) **1** welven, bol maken, ronden **2** [inform] torsen, (mee)zeulen

¹**hunch** (n) voorgevoelʰ, vaag idee

²**hunch** (vb) krommen; optrekken [shoulders]; (krom)buigen

hunchback gebochelde, bultenaar

hundred honderd; [fig] talloos: *one* ~ *per cent* honderd percent, helemaal; *I'm not feeling one* ~ *per cent* ik voel me niet helemaal honderd procent

hundredth honderdste

¹**Hungarian** (n) Hongaar(se)

²**Hungarian** (adj) Hongaars

Hungary Hongarije

¹**hunger** (n) honger, trek; [fig] hunkering; dorst: *a* ~ *for* sth. een hevig verlangen naar iets

²**hunger** (vb) hongeren, honger hebben; [fig] hunkeren; dorsten

hungover katterig; met een kater

hungry 1 hongerig, uitgehongerd: *feel* ~ honger hebben **2** (+ for) [fig] hunkerend (naar)

hunk 1 homp, brokʰ **2** [fig] stukʰ

hunky-dory [inform] prima

¹**hunt** (n) jacht(partij), vossenjacht; [fig] speurtocht, zoektocht

²**hunt** (vb) **1** jagen (op), jacht maken (op) **2** zoeken, speuren: ~ *high* and low for sth. overal zoeken naar iets **3** opjagen: *a ~ed look* een (op)gejaagde blik

hunt down opsporen, najagen

hunter 1 jager [also fig] **2** jachtpaardʰ

hunting jacht, vossenjacht

hunt out opdiepen, opsporen

huntsman 1 jager **2** jachtmeester

hunt up opzoeken, natrekken

hurdle 1 horde, hindernis; obstakelʰ [also fig] **2** schotʰ, horde **3** (-s) horde(loop)

hurl smijten, slingeren: ~ *reproaches at one another* elkaar verwijten naar het hoofd slingeren; *the dog ~ed itself at* (or: on) *the postman* de hond stortte zich op de postbode

hurray hoera(atjeʰ), hoezeeʰ, hoerageroepʰ ‖ *hip, hip,* ~! hiep, hiep, hoera!

hurricane orkaan, cycloon

hurried haastig, gehaast, gejaagd

¹**hurry** (n) haast: *I'm rather in a* ~ ik heb nogal haast

²**hurry** (vb) zich haasten, haast maken, opschieten: *he hurried along* hij snelde voort; ~ *up!* schiet op! vooruit!

³**hurry** (vb) **1** tot haast aanzetten, opjagen **2** verhaasten, bespoedigen: ~ *up a job* haast maken met een klus **3** haastig vervoeren

¹**hurt** (n) **1** pijn(lijke zaak) **2** letselʰ, wond

²**hurt** (vb) pijn doen: *my feet* ~ mijn voeten doen pijn; *it won't* ~ *to cut down on spending* het kan geen kwaad om te bezuinigen

³**hurt** (vb) **1** bezeren, verwonden, blesseren: *I* ~ *my knee* ik heb mijn knie bezeerd **2** krenken, kwetsen, beledigen: *feel* ~ zich gekrenkt voelen

hurtful 1 schadelijk **2** kwetsend

hurtle kletteren, razen, suizen

husband man, echtgenoot: ~ *and wife* man en vrouw

husbandry landbouw en veeteelt, het boerenbedrijf: *animal* ~ veehouderij, veeteelt

¹**hush** (n) stilte

²**hush** (vb) verstommen, tot rust komen ‖ ~! stil!, sst!

³**hush** (vb) tot zwijgen brengen, doen verstommen: ~ *up* verzwijgen, doodzwijgen

hush-hush [inform] (diep) geheim

hush money zwijggeldʰ

husk 1 schil(letjeʰ), (mais)vliesʰ: *rice* in the ~ ongepelde rijst **2** (waardeloos) omhulselʰ, lege dop

husky eskimohond

hussy brutaaltjeʰ: *brazen* (or: *shameless*) ~ brutaal nest

¹**hustle** (n) gedrangʰ, bedrijvigheid, drukte: ~ *and bustle* drukte, bedrijvigheid

²**hustle** (vb) **1** dringen, duwen **2** zich haasten, hard werken, druk in de weer zijn

³**hustle** (vb) **1** (op)jagen, duwen: *she ~d him out of the house* ze werkte hem het huis uit **2** [Am; inform] bewerken [eg customers]

hustler [Am; inform] **1** ritselaar **2** hoer

hut 1 hut(jeʰ), huisjeʰ, keet **2** [mil] barak

hyacinth hyacint

¹**hybrid** (n) kruising

²**hybrid** (adj) hybride: ~ *car* hybride, hybrideauto

hydrant brandkraan

hydraulic hydraulisch: ~ *engineering* waterbouw(kunde)

hydroelectric hydro-elektrisch

hydrofoil draagvleugel, (draag)vleugelboot

hydrogen waterstofʰ

hydroplane 1 glijboot; speedboot **2** wa-

tervliegtuig[h]
hyena hyena
hygiene hygiëne, gezondheidsleer, gezondheidszorg
hygienic hygiënisch
hymn hymne, lofzang, kerkgezang[h]
[1]**hype** (n) **1** kunstje[h], truc, list **2** opgeblazen zaak [by media, advertising]; schreeuwerige reclame, aanprijzing
[2]**hype** (vb) enthousiasmeren: ~ *up an audience* een publiek opzwepen
hyperbole [form] hyperbool, overdrijving
hypermarket hypermarkt, weidewinkel
hypersensitivity hypergevoeligheid
hypertension verhoogde bloeddruk; hypertensie
hypertext hypertekst
hyperventilate hyperventileren
hyphen verbindingsstreepje[h], afbrekingsteken[h], koppelteken[h]
hyphenate afbreken, door een koppelteken verbinden
hypnosis hypnose
hypnotic 1 hypnotisch; hypnotiserend **2** slaapopwekkend
hypnotism hypnotisme[h]
hypnotize hypnotiseren [also fig]; biologeren, fascineren
[1]**hypochondriac** (n) hypochonder, zwaarmoedig mens
[2]**hypochondriac** (adj) hypochondrisch, zwaarmoedig
hypocrisy hypocrisie
hypocrite hypocriet, huichelaar
hypocritical hypocriet; schijnheilig
hypodermic onderhuids: ~ *needle* injectienaald
hypothesis hypothese, veronderstelling
hypothetical hypothetisch, verondersteld
hysteria hysterie
hysterical hysterisch

i

I ik, zelf, eigen persoon

Iberian Iberisch

¹ice (n) **1** ijsʰ: [fig] *put sth.* on ~ iets in de ijskast zetten, iets uitstellen **2** vruchtenijsʰ, waterijs(je)ʰ **3** ijs(je)ʰ ‖ *break the* ~ het ijs breken; *cut no* (or: *not much*) ~ *(with s.o.)* geen (or: weinig) indruk maken (op iem.)

²ice (vb) bevriezen, dichtvriezen: ~ *over* dichtvriezen ‖ ~*d drinks* (ijs)gekoelde dranken

ice age ijstijd

iceberg ijsberg: [esp fig] *the tip of the* ~ het topje van de ijsberg

icebound ingevroren, door ijs ingesloten

icebreaker ijsbreker

ice cream ijs(je)ʰ, roomijs(je)ʰ

ice cube ijsblokjeʰ

ice floe ijsschots

Iceland IJsland

Icelander IJslander, IJslandse

Icelandic IJslands

ice rink (overdekte) ijsbaan

ice skate schaatsen

ice tea icetea

icicle ijskegel, ijspegel

icing suikerglazuurʰ, glaceerselʰ ‖ *(the)* ~ *on the cake* tierelantijntje(s)

icing sugar poedersuiker

icky goor, vies, smerig

icon ico(o)nʰ; [comp] pictogramʰ; icoon

iconoclast beeldenstormer

icy 1 ijzig, ijskoud, ijsachtig: *an* ~ *look* een ijzige blik **2** met ijs bedekt, bevroren, glad

¹ID *identification* ID; legitimatie(bewijs): *get a positive ID on* de identiteit achterhalen van

²ID (vb) de identiteit vaststellen van: *positively ID s.o.* iem. herkennen

ID card legitimatie(bewijsʰ), identiteitsbewijsʰ

idea idee⁺ʰ, denkbeeldʰ, begripʰ, gedachte: *is this your* ~ *of a pleasant evening?* noem jij dit een gezellige avond?

¹ideal (n) ideaalʰ

²ideal (adj) **1** ideaal **2** ideëel, denkbeeldig **3** idealistisch

idealism idealismeʰ

idealist idealist

idealize idealiseren

identical identiek, gelijk(luidend), gelijkwaardig: ~ *twins* eeneiige tweeling

identifiable identificeerbaar; herkenbaar

identification 1 identificatie [also psychology]; legitimatie **2** identiteitsbewijsʰ

¹identify (vb) (+ with) zich identificeren (met), zich vereenzelvigen (met)

²identify (vb) **1** identificeren, de identiteit vaststellen van, in verband brengen: *I can't* ~ *your accent* ik kan uw accent niet thuisbrengen; *s.o. who is identified* **with** *a fascist party* iem. die in verband gebracht wordt met een fascistische partij **2** erkennen, vaststellen

identity 1 identiteit, persoon(lijkheid): *a case of mistaken* ~ een geval van persoonsverwisseling **2** volmaakte gelijkenis

identity card legitimatie(bewijsʰ), identiteitsbewijsʰ

ideological ideologisch

ideology ideologie

idiocy idiotie, dwaasheid

idiom 1 idiomatische uitdrukking **2** idioomʰ, taaleigenʰ, taaleigenaardigheid

idiosyncrasy eigenaardigheid, typerend kenmerkʰ

idiosyncratic eigenaardig

idiot idioot

¹idle (adj) **1** werkloos, inactief: *he has been* ~ *all day* hij heeft de hele dag niets uitgevoerd **2** lui, laks **3** doelloos, zinloos, vruchteloos: *an* ~ *attempt* een vergeefse poging; ~ *gossip* loze kletspraat **4** ongebruikt, onbenut: ~ *machines only cost money* stilstaande machines kosten alleen maar geld

²idle (vb) **1** nietsdoen, luieren: ~ *about* luieren, rondhangen **2** stationair draaien [of engine]

idle away verdoen; verlummelen [time]

idler leegloper; lanterfanter

idly see ¹*idle*

idol 1 afgod(sbeeldʰ), idoolʰ **2** favoriet

idolatry 1 verafgoding, blinde verering **2** afgoderij

idolize verafgoden

idyl(l) idylle

idyllic idyllisch

i.e. *id est* d.w.z., dat wil zeggen

¹if (n) onzekere factor, voorwaarde, mogelijkheid ‖ *ifs and buts* maren, bedenkingen

²if (conj) **1** indien, als, zo, op voorwaarde dat: *if anything* indien dan al iets, dan …; *if anything* this is even worse dit is zo mogelijk nog slechter; *if not* zo niet; *if so* zo ja **2** telkens als, telkens wanneer **3** of: *I wonder if she is happy* ik vraag mij af of ze gelukkig is **4** zij het, (al)hoewel, al: *a talented if arrogant young man* een begaafde, zij het arrogante, jongeman; *protest, if only to pester them* protesteer, al was het maar om hen te pesten; *if we failed we did all we could* we hebben wel gefaald maar we hebben gedaan wat we konden **5** warempel, zowaar: *if that isn't Mr Smith!* als dat niet meneer Smith is! ‖ *if only* als … maar, ik wou dat

iffy onzeker, dubieus

igloo iglo, Eskimohut, sneeuwhut

ignite

¹ignite (vb) ontbranden, vlam vatten
²ignite (vb) aansteken
ignition 1 ontsteking(sinrichting) [of car]: *turn* the ~, *switch* the ~ *on* het contactsleuteltje omdraaien, starten **2** ontbranding, ontsteking
ignition key contactsleuteltjeʰ
ignoble laag(hartig), onwaardig
ignominious schandelijk, oneervol
ignorance onwetendheid, onkunde, onkundigheid: *keep in* ~ in het ongewisse laten
ignorant 1 onwetend, onkundig: ~ *of* onkundig van; *I'm very* ~ *of politics* ik heb helemaal geen verstand van politiek **2** dom, onontwikkeld
ignore negeren
¹ill (n) **1** tegenslag **2** kwaadʰ, onheilʰ, vloek: *speak* ~ *of* kwaadspreken van
²ill (adj) **1** ziek, beroerd, ongezond: *fall* (or: *be taken*) ~ ziek worden **2** slecht, kwalijk: ~ *fame* slechte naam; ~ *health* slechte gezondheid **3** schadelijk, nadelig, ongunstig: ~ *effects* nadelige gevolgen **4** vijandig, onvriendelijk: ~ *feeling* haatdragendheid
³ill (adv) **1** slecht, kwalijk, verkeerd: ~ *at ease* slecht op zijn gemak **2** nauwelijks, amper, onvoldoende: *I can* ~ *afford* the money ik kan het geld eigenlijk niet missen
ill-advised onverstandig
ill-bred onopgevoed, ongemanierd
ill-considered ondoordacht; onbezonnen
ill-disposed 1 kwaadgezind, kwaadwillig **2** afkerig, onwillig: ~ *towards* a plan gekant tegen een plan
illegal onwettig, illegaal, onrechtmatig
illegality onwettigheid, onrechtmatigheid
illegible onleesbaar
illegitimate 1 onrechtmatig, illegaal **2** onwettig [of child]; buitenechtelijk **3** ongewettigd, ongeldig
ill-fated 1 gedoemd te mislukken **2** noodlottig
ill-gotten onrechtmatig verkregen: ~ *gains* vuil geld; gestolen goed
illicit onwettig, illegaal, ongeoorloofd
illiteracy analfabetismeʰ, ongeletterdheid
illiterate ongeletterd, analfabeet
ill-mannered ongemanierd
ill-natured onvriendelijk
illness ziekte, kwaal
illogical onlogisch, ongerijmd, tegenstrijdig
ill-tempered slecht gehumeurd, humeurig
ill-timed misplaatst, op een ongeschikt ogenblik
ill-treat slecht behandelen; mishandelen
illuminate 1 [also fig] verlichten, licht werpen op **2** met feestverlichting versieren
illumination 1 verlichting; [fig] geestelijke verlichting **2** opheldering, verduidelijking **3** (-s) feestverlichting

illusion 1 illusie, waandenkbeeldʰ: *optical* ~ gezichtsbedrog; *cherish* the ~ *that* de illusie koesteren dat; *be under an* ~ misleid zijn **2** (zins)begoocheling, zelfbedrogʰ
illusory denkbeeldig, bedrieglijk
illustrate illustreren, verduidelijken, toelichten
illustration illustratie, toelichting, afbeelding
illustrious illuster, vermaard, gerenommeerd
image 1 beeldʰ, afbeelding, voorstelling **2** imagoʰ, reputatie: *corporate* ~ bedrijfsimago
imagery beeldspraak
imaginable voorstelbaar, denkbaar, mogelijk
imaginary denkbeeldig; imaginair
imagination verbeelding(skracht), voorstelling(svermogenʰ), fantasie
imagine 1 zich verbeelden, zich indenken, fantaseren: *just* ~ *that!* stel je voor! **2** veronderstellen, aannemen
imaginings [form] waandenkbeelden; waanideeën
imam imam
imbalance onevenwichtigheid, wanverhouding
¹imbecile (n) imbeciel, zwakzinnige, stommeling
²imbecile (adj) imbeciel, zwakzinnig, dwaas
imbecility stommiteit, idioterie
imbroglio gecompliceerde situatie; verwikkeling
imbue (door)drenken [also fig]; verzadigen, doordringen: ~*d with* hatred van haat vervuld
imitate 1 nadoen, imiteren: *you should* ~ *your brother* neem een voorbeeld aan je broer **2** lijken op: *it is wood, made to* ~ *marble* het is hout dat eruitziet als marmer
imitation imitatie, navolging, namaak: ~ *leather* kunstleer
immaculate 1 vlekkeloos, onbevlekt, zuiver: [Roman Catholicism] *Immaculate Conception* onbevlekte ontvangenis **2** onberispelijk
immaterial 1 onstoffelijk, immaterieel **2** onbelangrijk, irrelevant: *all that is* ~ *to me* dat is mij allemaal om het even
immature onvolgroeid, onrijp, onvolwassen
immaturity onvolgroeidheid; onrijpheid, onvolwassenheid
immeasurable onmetelijk, immens, oneindig
immediacy 1 nabijheid **2** dringendheid, urgentie, directheid
immediate 1 direct, onmiddellijk, rechtstreeks: *an* ~ *reply* een onmiddellijk antwoord **2** nabij, dichtstbijzijnd, naast: *my* ~

family mijn naaste familie
¹**immediately** (adv) meteen, onmiddellijk
²**immediately** (conj) zodra
immemorial onheuglijk, eeuwenoud, oeroud: *from time ~* sinds mensenheugenis
immense immens, onmetelijk, oneindig: *enjoy o.s. ~ly* zich kostelijk amuseren
immerse 1 (onder)dompelen **2** verdiepen, absorberen, verzinken: *he ~s himself completely in his work* hij gaat helemaal op in zijn werk
immigrant immigrant
immigrate immigreren
immigration immigratie
imminence dreiging, nabijheid; nadering [of danger]
imminent dreigend, op handen zijnd: *a storm is ~* er dreigt onweer
immobile onbeweeglijk, roerloos
immobilize onbeweeglijk maken, stilleggen, lamleggen, inactiveren
immoderate onmatig, overmatig, buitensporig
immodest 1 onbescheiden, arrogant **2** onfatsoenlijk, onbeschaamd
immodesty 1 onbescheidenheid **2** onfatsoenlijkheid
immoral immoreel, onzedelijk, verdorven
immortal onsterfelijk
immortality onsterfelijkheid
immortalize vereeuwigen
immune immuun, onvatbaar, bestand: *~ against* (or: *from, to*) immuun voor; *~ from punishment* vrijgesteld van straf
immune system immuunsysteem[h], natuurlijk afweersysteem[h]
immunity onschendbaarheid: *~ from taxation* vrijstelling van belasting
immunization immunisatie, immunisering
immutable onveranderbaar, onveranderlijk
imp 1 duiveltje[h] **2** deugniet
impact 1 schok, botsing, inslag: *on ~* op het moment van een botsing **2** schokeffect[h], (krachtige) invloed, impact
impair schaden, benadelen, verslechteren: *~ one's health* zijn gezondheid schaden
impaired beschadigd, verzwakt: *visually ~* visueel gehandicapt
impairment beschadiging, afbreuk, verslechtering, verzwakking
impart 1 verlenen, verschaffen **2** meedelen, onthullen
impartial onpartijdig, neutraal, onbevooroordeeld
impassable onbegaanbaar
impasse impasse; dood spoor[h]: *talks have reached an ~* de onderhandelingen zitten muurvast
impassioned bezield, hartstochtelijk

impassive ongevoelig, gevoelloos, onbewogen; [sometimes depr] hardvochtig; kil
impatient 1 ongeduldig, geërgerd, onlijdzaam **2** begerig: *the child is ~ to see his mother* het kind popelt van ongeduld om zijn moeder te zien
impeachment beschuldiging, aanklagingsprocedure
impeccable 1 foutloos, feilloos, vlekkeloos **2** onberispelijk, smetteloos
impede belemmeren, (ver)hinderen
impediment 1 beletsel[h], belemmering **2** (spraak)gebrek[h]
impel 1 aanzetten, aanmoedigen **2** voortdrijven, voortstuwen
impending dreigend, aanstaand
impenetrable ondoordringbaar, ontoegankelijk; [fig] ondoorgrondelijk; onpeilbaar
¹**imperative** (n) gebiedende wijs
²**imperative** (adj) **1** noodzakelijk, vereist **2** verplicht, dwingend **3** gebiedend, autoritair
imperceptible onwaarneembaar, onmerkbaar, onzichtbaar
imperfect onvolmaakt, onvolkomen, gebrekkig
imperfection onvolkomenheid, gebrek[h], gebrekkigheid, onvolmaaktheid
imperial keizerlijk, rijks-, m.b.t. het Britse rijk: *~ eagle* keizerarend
imperialism imperialisme[h], expansiedrang
¹**imperialist** (n) imperialist [also depr]
²**imperialist** (adj) imperialistisch [also depr]
imperious [form] **1** heerszuchtig **2** dwingend
impermeable ondoordringbaar, waterdicht
impersonal 1 onpersoonlijk, zakelijk **2** niet menselijk ‖ [linguistics] *~ pronoun* onbepaald voornaamwoord
impersonate 1 vertolken, (de rol) spelen (van), imiteren **2** zich uitgeven voor
impertinent onbeschaamd, brutaal
imperturbable onverstoorbaar, onwankelbaar
impervious 1 ondoordringbaar **2** onontvankelijk, ongevoelig: *~ to* ongevoelig voor
impetuous onstuimig, impulsief, heetgebakerd
impetus 1 impuls, stimulans **2** drijvende kracht, drijfkracht, stuwkracht, drijfveer
impinge (up)on 1 treffen, raken, inslaan in **2** beroeren, van invloed zijn op **3** inbreuk maken op
impish ondeugend, schelms
implacable onverbiddelijk, onvermurwbaar
implant 1 (in)planten, (in de grond) steken **2** inprenten, inhameren
implausible onaannemelijk, onwaarschijnlijk

¹implement (n) werktuig^h, gereedschap^h, instrument^h
²implement (vb) ten uitvoer brengen, toepassen, verwezenlijken: ~ *a new computer network* een nieuw computernetwerk in gebruik nemen
implicate betrekken, verwikkelen
implication 1 implicatie, (onuitgesproken) suggestie: *by* ~ bij implicatie **2** verwikkeling, betrokkenheid
implicit 1 impliciet, onuitgesproken, stilzwijgend **2** onvoorwaardelijk: ~ *faith* onvoorwaardelijk geloof
implore smeken, dringend verzoeken
imply 1 impliceren, met zich meebrengen: *his refusal implies that ...* uit zijn weigering blijkt dat ... **2** suggereren, duiden op: *are you ~ing that you're going to resign?* wil je daarmee zeggen dat je ontslag gaat nemen?
impolite onbeleefd, onhoffelijk
imponderable onvoorspelbaar
¹import (n) **1** invoerartikel^h **2** invoer, import
²import (vb) invoeren, importeren: ~ *cars from Japan into Europe* auto's uit Japan invoeren in Europa
importance belang(rijkheid); gewicht^h, betekenis: *place no ~ on sth.* geen belang aan iets hechten
important belangrijk, gewichtig: ~ *to* belangrijk voor
importation invoer(artikel^h), import(goederen)
impose 1 opleggen, heffen, afdwingen: ~ *a task* een taak opleggen **2** opdringen: ~ *o.s.* (or: *one's company*) *(up)on* zich opdringen aan
impose (up)on gebruik maken van, tot last zijn, een beroep doen op
imposing imponerend, indrukwekkend, ontzagwekkend
imposition 1 heffing, belasting **2** (opgelegde) last, (zware) taak, druk **3** straf(taak), strafwerk^h
impossibility onmogelijkheid
impossible onmogelijk: *an* ~ *situation* een hopeloze situatie; *that chap is* ~ *to get along with* die gozer is onmogelijk om mee om te gaan
impostor bedrieger, oplichter
impotence 1 onvermogen^h; machteloosheid **2** impotentie
impotent 1 machteloos, onmachtig **2** impotent
impound 1 beslag leggen op **2** in een asiel opsluiten
impoverish verarmen, verpauperen
impracticable onuitvoerbaar, onrealiseerbaar
impractical onpraktisch, onhandig
imprecise onnauwkeurig
impregnable onneembaar, onaantastbaar

impregnate 1 doordrenken, impregneren **2** zwanger maken **3** bevruchten
impress 1 bedrukken, afdrukken, indrukken, opdrukken **2** (een) indruk maken op, imponeren: *your boyfriend ~es us unfavourably* je vriendje maakt geen beste indruk op ons; ~*ed at* (or: *by, with*) geïmponeerd door, onder de indruk van **3** inprenten
impression 1 afdruk, indruk **2** indruk, impressie: *make an ~ (on)* indruk maken (op); *under the ~ that ...* in de veronderstelling dat ...
impressive indrukwekkend, ontzagwekkend
imprint (af)drukken, indrukken, stempelen; [fig] griffen; inprenten
imprison in de gevangenis zetten
imprisonment gevangenneming, gevangenschap
improbability onwaarschijnlijkheid
improbable onwaarschijnlijk, onaannemelijk
¹impromptu (adj) onvoorbereid, geïmproviseerd
²impromptu (adv) voor de vuist (weg), spontaan
improper 1 ongepast, misplaatst **2** onfatsoenlijk, oneerbaar
impropriety 1 ongepastheid **2** onfatsoenlijkheid
improve vooruitgaan, beter worden: *his health is improving* zijn gezondheid gaat vooruit
improvement verbetering, vooruitgang: *that is quite an* ~ dat is een stuk beter; *an* ~ *in the weather* een weersverbetering
improve (up)on overtreffen: *improve (up)on a previous performance* een eerdere prestatie overtreffen
improvident zorgeloos, verkwistend
improvisation improvisatie
improvise improviseren, in elkaar flansen
imprudent onvoorzichtig; ondoordacht
impudent schaamteloos, brutaal
impulse 1 impuls, puls, stroomstoot **2** opwelling, inval, impuls(iviteit): *act on* ~ impulsief handelen
impulsive impulsief
impunity straffeloosheid: *with* ~ straffeloos, ongestraft
impure 1 onzuiver, verontreinigd **2** onzedig
impute toeschrijven, wijten, aanwrijven
¹in (adj) **1** intern, inwonend, binnen- **2** populair, modieus, in **3** exclusief: *in-crowd* kliekje, wereldje
²in (adv) binnen, naar binnen, erheen: *built-in* ingebouwd; *fit sth. in* iets (er)in passen; *the police moved in* de politie kwam tussenbeide
³in (prep) **1** in: *in my opinion* naar mijn mening; *play in the street* op straat spelen **2** [di-

rection; also fig] in, naar, ter: *in aid of* ten
voordele van **3** [time] in, binnen: *in a few
minutes* over enkele minuten; *in all those
years* gedurende al die jaren **4** [activity, pro-
fession] wat betreft, in: *the latest thing in
computers* het laatste snufje op het gebied
van computers **5** [proportion, size, degree]
in, op, uit: *sell in ones* per stuk verkopen; *one
in twenty* één op twintig **6** [in the shape of]
als: *buy in instalments* op afbetaling kopen
7 in zover dat, in, met betrekking tot, doordat, omdat: *he resembles you in being* very
practical hij lijkt op jou in zoverre dat hij heel
praktisch is || *he was in charge of* hij was ver-
antwoordelijk voor; *in honour of* ter ere van
inability onvermogen^h, onmacht
inaccessible ontoegankelijk, onbereikbaar
inaccurate 1 onnauwkeurig **2** foutief
inaction inactiviteit
inactive 1 inactief; passief **2** ongebruikt;
buiten werking
inactivity inactiviteit
inadequacy ontoereikendheid, tekort^h, tekortkoming, gebrek^h
inadequate ontoereikend, onvoldoende,
ongeschikt
inadmissible ontoelaatbaar, ongeoorloofd: ~ *evidence* ontoelaatbaar bewijs
inadvertent 1 onoplettend, nonchalant
2 onopzettelijk: *I dropped it ~ly* ik heb het
per ongeluk laten vallen
inalienable onvervreemdbaar [of right]
inane leeg, inhoudloos, zinloos
inanimate levenloos, dood
inapplicable ontoepasselijk, ontoepas-
baar, onbruikbaar
inappropriate ongepast, onbehoorlijk,
misplaatst
inapt 1 ontoepasselijk, ongeschikt **2** onbekwaam, on(des)kundig, onhandig
inarticulate 1 onduidelijk (uitgesproken),
onverstaanbaar, onsamenhangend **2** onduidelijk sprekend
inasmuch as aangezien, omdat
inattentive onoplettend, achteloos
inaudible onhoorbaar
inaugurate installeren, inaugureren, (in
een ambt/functie) bevestigen
inauguration installatie(plechtigheid), inauguratie, inhuldiging
inauspicious onheilspellend; ongunstig
inborn aangeboren
inbound [Am] binnenkomend, thuisko-
mend, inkomend, binnenlopend
inbox postvak in
inbreeding inteelt
inc incl.
Inc [Am] *Incorporated* nv, naamloze vennootschap
incalculable 1 onberekenbaar **2** onvoor-

spelbaar
incandescent 1 gloeiend: ~ *lamp* gloeilamp **2** kwaad, woedend
incapable onbekwaam, machteloos: *drunk
and* ~ dronken en onbekwaam; *be* ~ *of* niet
in staat zijn tot, niet kunnen
incapacitate uitschakelen; ongeschikt maken: *his age* ~s *him for* work door zijn leeftijd
is hij niet in staat te werken
incapacity onvermogen^h, onmacht: ~ *for
work* arbeidsongeschiktheid
incarnate vleesgeworden, lijfelijk: *the devil*
~ de duivel in eigen persoon
incarnation incarnatie; belichaming
incautious onvoorzichtig
^1**incendiary** (n) **1** brandstichter **2** opruier
^2**incendiary** (adj) **1** brandgevaarlijk, (licht)
ontvlambaar: ~ *bomb* brandbom **2** opruiend
^1**incense** (n) wierook(geur)
^2**incense** (vb) kwaad, boos maken: ~*d at* (or:
by) zeer boos over
incentive 1 stimulans, aansporing, motief^h
2 (prestatie)premie, toeslag, aanmoedi-
gingspremie
incessant onophoudelijk, voortdurend,
aanhoudend
incest incest, bloedschande
^1**inch** (n) (Engelse) duim [24.5 mm]; inch: *not
budge* (or: *give, yield)* an ~ geen duimbreed
wijken; *every* ~ *a gentleman* op-en-top een
heer || *give* him an ~ *and he'll take a mile* als je
hem een vinger geeft neemt hij de hele
hand; ~ *by* ~ beetje bij beetje; *we came within an* ~ *of death* het scheelde maar een haar
of we waren dood geweest
^2**inch** (vb) schuifelen, langzaam voortgaan: ~
forward through a crowd zich moeizaam een
weg banen door een menigte
incidence (mate van) optreden, frequentie: *a high* ~ *of disease* een hoog ziektecijfer
incident incident^h, voorval^h, gebeurtenis
incidental bijkomend, begeleidend, bijkomstig: ~ *expenses* onvoorziene uitgaven;
~ *to* samenhangend met, gepaard gaande
met
incidentally 1 terloops **2** overigens, trouwens, tussen twee haakjes
incident room meldkamer
incinerate (tot as) verbranden, verassen
incipient beginnend, begin-
incision insnijding, inkerving, snee; [med]
incisie
incisive 1 scherp(zinnig) **2** doortastend
incisor snijtand
incite 1 opwekken, aanzetten, aansporen
2 bezielen, opstoken, ophitsen
inclement guur, stormachtig
inclination 1 neiging, voorkeur: *have* an ~
to get fat aanleg hebben om dik te worden
2 geneigdheid, zin
^1**incline** (n) helling, glooiing

²**incline** (vb) neigen, geneigd zijn, een neiging hebben: *I ~ to think so* ik neig tot die gedachte
³**incline** (vb) **1** (neer)buigen, neigen: *~ one's head* het hoofd neigen **2** beïnvloeden, aanleiding geven: *I am ~d to think so* ik neig tot die gedachte
¹**inclined** (adj) **1** geneigd; bereid: *if you feel so ~* als u daar zin in heeft **2** aangelegd
²**inclined** (adj) hellend: *~ plane* hellend vlak
inclose see *enclose*
include 1 omvatten, bevatten, insluiten: *the price ~s freight* de prijs is inclusief vracht; [mockingly] *~ out* uitsluiten, niet meerekenen **2** (mede) opnemen, bijvoegen, toevoegen
including inclusief: *10 days ~ today* 10 dagen, vandaag meegerekend; *up to and ~* tot en met
inclusive inclusief: *pages 60 to 100 ~* pagina 60 tot en met 100
incoherent incoherent, onsamenhangend
income inkomenʰ, inkomsten: *live within one's ~* niet te veel uitgeven, rondkomen
income tax inkomstenbelasting
incoming 1 inkomend, aankomend, binnenkomend: *~ tide* opkomend tij **2** opvolgend, komend: *the ~ tenants* de nieuwe huurders
incomparable onvergelijkelijk, onvergelijkbaar
incompatible onverenigbaar, (tegen)strijdig, tegengesteld
incompetence incompetentie; onbekwaamheid
incompetent onbevoegd, onbekwaam
incomplete 1 onvolledig, incompleet **2** onvolkomen, onvoltooid
incomprehensible onbegrijpelijk, ondoorgrondelijk
inconceivable onvoorstelbaar, ondenkbaar
inconclusive 1 niet doorslaggevend, onovertuigend **2** onbeslist
incongruity ongerijmdheid
incongruous 1 ongerijmd, strijdig **2** ongelijksoortig
inconsiderable onaanzienlijk, onbetekenend
inconsiderate onattent, onnadenkend
inconsistency 1 inconsistentie **2** onverenigbaarheid
inconsistent 1 inconsistent, onlogisch **2** onverenigbaar, strijdig
inconsolable ontroostbaar
inconspicuous onopvallend
incontinence incontinentie
incontinent incontinent
incontrovertible onweerlegbaar, onomstotelijk
¹**inconvenience** (n) ongemakʰ, ongeriefʰ

²**inconvenience** (vb) overlast bezorgen, ongelegen komen
inconvenient storend, ongelegen
incorporate 1 opnemen, verenigen, incorporeren **2** omvatten, bevatten: *this theory ~s new ideas* deze theorie omvat nieuwe ideeën
incorporated als naamloze vennootschap erkend: *Jones ~* [roughly] Jones nv
incorrect incorrect, onjuist, verkeerd, ongepast
incorrigible onverbeterlijk
¹**increase** (n) **1** toename, groei, aanwas: *be on the ~* toenemen **2** verhoging, stijging
²**increase** (vb) toenemen, (aan)groeien, stijgen
³**increase** (vb) vergroten, verhogen
increasingly in toenemende mate; meer en meer: *~ worse* hoe langer hoe erger
incredible ongelofelijk, ongeloofwaardig; [inform] verbluffend (goed)
incredulity ongelovigheid
incredulous ongelovig: *be ~ of* geen geloof hechten aan, sceptisch staan tegenover
increment 1 toename, (waarde)vermeerdering **2** periodiekʰ [of salary]; periodieke verhoging
incriminate 1 beschuldigen, aanklagen **2** bezwaren, als de schuldige aanwijzen: *incriminating statements* bezwarende verklaringen
incubation 1 uitbroeding **2** broedperiode **3** incubatie(tijd)
¹**incumbent** (n) bekleder van een kerkelijk ambt
²**incumbent** (adj) zittend, in functie zijnd: [Am] *the ~ governor* de zittende gouverneur
incur oplopen, zich op de hals halen: *~ large debts* zich diep in de schulden steken; *~ expenses* onkosten maken
incurable ongeneeslijk: *~ pessimism* onuitroeibaar pessimisme
incursion inval, invasie, strooptocht; [fig] *an ~ upon s.o.'s privacy* een inbreuk op iemands privacy
indebted schuldig, verschuldigd: *be ~ to s.o. for ...* iem. dank verschuldigd zijn voor ...
indecency onfatsoenlijkheid
indecent onfatsoenlijk, onbehoorlijk, indecent: *~ assault* aanranding; *~ exposure* openbare schennis der eerbaarheid, (geval van) exhibitionisme
indecipherable niet te ontcijferen; onleesbaar
indecision 1 besluiteloosheid **2** aarzeling
indecisive 1 niet afdoend: *the battle was ~* de slag was niet beslissend **2** besluiteloos, weifeland
indeed 1 inderdaad: *is it blue? ~ it is* is het blauw? inderdaad **2** in feite, sterker nog: *I don't mind. ~, I would be pleased* ik vind het best. Sterker nog, ik zou het leuk vinden

3 [after a word to be emphasised] echt: *that's a surprise* ~ dat is echt een verrassing ‖ *very kind* ~ werkelijk zeer vriendelijk
indefatigable onvermoeibaar
indefinite 1 onduidelijk, onbestemd, vaag: *postponed* ~*ly* voor onbepaalde tijd uitgesteld **2** onbepaald [also linguistics]: ~ *article* onbepaald lidwoord; [linguistics] ~ *pronoun* onbepaald voornaamwoord **3** onzeker, onbeslist
indelible onuitwisbaar
indelicate 1 onbehoorlijk **2** smakeloos, grof **3** tactloos
indemnity 1 schadeloosstelling, herstelbetaling(en) **2** garantie, (aansprakelijkheids)verzekering **3** vrijstelling [of punishment]; vrijwaring
¹indent (n) **1** inspringing **2** orderbrief
²indent (vb) een schriftelijke bestelling doen
³indent (vb) kartelen, kerven, inkepen: *an* ~*ed coastline* een grillige kustlijn
⁴indent (vb) (laten) inspringen [line]
indentation 1 keep, snee **2** inspringing **3** inham, fjord **4** karteling, insnijding
independence onafhankelijkheid
independent 1 onafhankelijk, partijloos: *of* ~ *means* financieel onafhankelijk; ~ *school* particuliere school **2** vrijstaand
indescribable onbeschrijfelijk, niet te beschrijven
indestructible onverwoestbaar
indeterminate 1 onbepaald, onbeslist **2** onbepaalbaar **3** onduidelijk, vaag
index 1 index [also science]; indexcijferʰ, verhoudingscijferʰ **2** (bibliotheek)catalogus **3** registerʰ, index ‖ ~ *finger* wijsvinger
India 1 India **2** Brits-Indië, Voor-Indië
¹Indian (n) **1** Indiër, Indiase **2** indiaan: *American* ~ indiaan; *Red* ~ indiaan
²Indian (adj) **1** Indiaas **2** indiaans ‖ ~ *corn* mais; *in* ~ *file* in ganzenmars; ~ *ink* Oost-Indische inkt; ~ *summer* Indian summer
indicate 1 duiden op, een teken zijn van, een teken zijn voor **2** te kennen geven **3** de noodzaak aantonen van: *surgery seemed to be* ~*d* een operatie leek wenselijk **4** aangeven, aanwijzen: *the cyclist* ~*d left* de fietser stak zijn linkerhand uit
indication aanwijzing, indicatie, tekenʰ: *there is little* ~ *of improvement* er is weinig dat op een verbetering duidt
indicator richtingaanwijzer
indict aanklagen
indictment 1 (aan)klacht **2** (staat van) beschuldiging
indie onafhankelijke platen-, filmmaatschappij
indifference onverschilligheid
indifferent 1 onverschillig: ~ *to hardship* ongevoelig voor tegenspoed **2** (middel)matig

indigenous 1 inheems: *plants* ~ *to this island* op dit eiland thuishorende planten **2** aangeboren, geboren
indigestion indigestie
indignant verontwaardigd
indignation verontwaardiging
indignity vernedering, belediging, hoon
indirect indirect, niet rechtstreeks: [linguistics] ~ *object* meewerkend voorwerp
indiscreet indiscreet
indiscretion indiscretie, onbescheidenheid: *an* ~ *of his youth* een misstap uit zijn jeugd
indiscriminate 1 kritiekloos, onzorgvuldig **2** lukraak: *deal out* ~ *blows* in het wilde weg om zich heen slaan
indispensable onmisbaar, essentieel
indisposition 1 ongesteldheid, onpasselijkheid **2** ongenegenheid, onwil(ligheid)
indisputable onbetwistbaar
indistinct onduidelijk, vaag
indistinguishable niet te onderscheiden
¹individual (n) individuʰ; [inform] figuurᵗʰ; typeʰ
²individual (adj) **1** individueel, persoonlijk, eigen: *I can't thank you all* ~*ly* ik kan u niet ieder afzonderlijk bedanken **2** afzonderlijk: *give* ~ *attention to* persoonlijke aandacht besteden aan
individualism individualismeʰ
individuality individualiteit: *she's a girl of marked* ~ ze is een uitgesproken persoonlijkheid
indivisible ondeelbaar
indocility hardleersheid
indoctrinate indoctrineren
indolence traagheid, sloomheid
indomitable ontembaar, onbedwingbaar
Indonesia Indonesië
¹Indonesian (n) Indonesiër, Indonesische
²Indonesian (adj) Indonesisch
indoor binnen-: ~ *aerial* kamerantenne; *sports* zaalsporten
indoors binnen: *let's go* ~ laten we naar binnen gaan
indubitably zonder twijfel
induce 1 bewegen tot, brengen tot: *our reduced prices will* ~ *people to buy* onze verlaagde prijzen zullen de mensen tot kopen bewegen; *nothing will* ~ *me to give in* nooit zal ik toegeven **2** teweegbrengen, veroorzaken, leiden tot; opwekken [contractions]
inducement aansporing; stimulans
induction 1 installatie, inhuldiging, bevestiging **2** opwekking [of contractions] **3** opgewekte geboorte **4** introductie(cursus)
inductive 1 aanleiding gevend, veroorzakend **2** inductief
¹indulge (vb) zich laten gaan, zich te goed doen; [inform] zich te buiten gaan aan drank (eten): ~ *in* zich (de luxe) permitteren (van)

²**indulge** (vb) **1** toegeven aan **2** (zich) uitleven (in)

indulgence 1 mateloosheid: ~ *in strong drink* overmatig drankgebruik **2** toegeeflijkheid

indulgent toegeeflijk, inschikkelijk

industrial 1 industrieel **2** geïndustrialiseerd: *the ~ nations* de industrielanden **3** de industriearbeid(ers) betreffende: ~ *dispute* arbeidsconflict

industrialization industrialisatie

industrious vlijtig, arbeidzaam

industry 1 industrie **2** bedrijfsleven[h] **3** vlijt, (werk)ijver

inedible oneetbaar

ineffective 1 ineffectief **2** inefficiënt, ondoelmatig, onbekwaam

ineffectual 1 vruchteloos, vergeefs **2** ongeschikt

inefficient inefficiënt, ondoelmatig, onpraktisch

ineligible ongeschikt: ~ *to vote* niet stemgerechtigd

inept 1 absurd, dwaas **2** onbeholpen, onbekwaam

ineptitude onbekwaamheid

inequality ongelijkheid, verschil[h]

inequitable onrechtvaardig

inequity onrechtvaardigheid

ineradicable onuitroeibaar, onuitwisbaar

inert inert, traag, mat: ~ *gas* edel gas

inescapable onontkoombaar; onvermijdelijk

inestimable onschatbaar

inevitability onvermijdelijkheid; onontkoombaarheid

inevitable onvermijdelijk, onontkoombaar, onafwendbaar

inexact onnauwkeurig

inexcusable onvergeeflijk

inexhaustible 1 onuitputtelijk **2** onvermoeibaar

inexorable onverbiddelijk

inexpensive voordelig, goedkoop

inexperienced onervaren

inexplicable onverklaarbaar

infallible 1 onfeilbaar **2** feilloos: *infallibly, she makes the wrong choice* ze doet steevast de verkeerde keus

infamous 1 berucht **2** schandelijk

infamy 1 beruchtheid **2** schanddaad

infancy 1 kindsheid, eerste jeugd **2** beginstadium[h]: *in its ~* in de kinderschoenen

¹**infant** (n) jong kind[h]

²**infant** (adj) kinder-: ~ *prodigy* wonderkind

infanticide kindermoord

infantile 1 infantiel, kinderachtig, onvolwassen **2** kinder-: ~ *paralysis* kinderverlamming

infantry infanterie, voetvolk[h]

infant school kleuterschool

infatuated gek, dol, (smoor)verliefd: *be ~ with s.o.* (sth.) gek zijn op iem.

infatuation verliefdheid

infect 1 besmetten [also fig]; infecteren: [fig] *an ~ed computer* een besmette computer **2** vervuilen, bederven

infection infectie, infectieziekte

infectious 1 besmettelijk **2** aanstekelijk

infer 1 (+ from) concluderen (uit), afleiden, opmaken **2** impliceren, inhouden

inference gevolgtrekking

¹**inferior** (n) ondergeschikte

²**inferior** (adj) **1** lager, minder, ondergeschikt **2** inferieur, minderwaardig: ~ *goods* goederen van mindere kwaliteit; *be ~ to* onderdoen voor

inferiority minderwaardigheid

infernal 1 hels, duivels **2** afschuwelijk, vervloekt

inferno inferno[h]; vuurzee

infertile onvruchtbaar

infest teisteren, onveilig maken: *be ~ed with* vergeven zijn van

infestation teistering, het onveilig-zijn/onveilig-worden, plaag

infidel ongelovige

infidelity ontrouw

infiltrate (+ into) infiltreren (in), tersluiks binnendringen

¹**infinite** (n) oneindigheid: *the ~* het heelal; *the Infinite* God

²**infinite** (adj) **1** oneindig, onbegrensd **2** buitengemeen groot

infinitesimal oneindig klein || ~ *calculus* infinitesimaalrekening

infinitive infinitief

infinity oneindigheid, grenzeloosheid

infirm zwak: ~ *of purpose* besluiteloos

infirmary ziekenhuis[h], ziekenafdeling, ziekenzaal

infirmity 1 zwakheid **2** gebrek[h], kwaal

¹**inflame** (vb) opwinden, kwaad maken: ~*d with rage* in woede ontstoken

²**inflame** (vb) **1** ontsteken, ontstoken raken: *an ~d eye* een ontstoken oog

inflammable ontvlambaar, zeer brandbaar; [fig] opvliegend

inflammation ontsteking, ontbranding

inflatable opblaasbaar

inflate 1 opblazen, doen zwellen **2** inflateren; kunstmatig opdrijven [eg prices]

inflation 1 het opblazen **2** [econ] inflatie: *galloping ~* wilde inflatie

inflect [linguistics] verbuigen, vervoegen

inflexible onbuigbaar [also fig]; onbuigzaam

inflict 1 opleggen, opdringen: ~ *a penalty (up)on s.o.* iem. een straf opleggen **2** toedienen, toebrengen: ~ *a blow (up)on s.o.* iem. een klap geven **3** teisteren

in-flight tijdens de vlucht: ~ *movie* tijdens

de vlucht vertoonde film
inflow toevloed; instroom, toestroom
¹**influence** (n) **1** invloed, inwerking, macht: ~ *on* (or: *upon*) (onbewuste) invloed op **2** protectie; [inform] kruiwagen ‖ [inform] *under the* ~ onder invloed
²**influence** (vb) beïnvloeden, invloed hebben op
influential invloedrijk
influenza influenza, griep
influx toevloed, instroming
info *information* info, informatie
inform 1 informeren, op de hoogte stellen: ~ *s.o. about* (or: *of*) iem. inlichten over **2** berichten, meedelen
informal 1 informeel, niet officieel **2** ongedwongen: ~ *speech* spreektaal
informant informant, zegsman
informatics informatica
information informatie, inlichting(en), voorlichting: *obtain* ~ informatie inwinnen
informative informatief, leerzaam
informed ingelicht: *ill-*~ slecht op de hoogte
informer geheim agent, politiespion
infrastructure infrastructuur
infrequent zeldzaam
¹**infringe** (vb) (+ (up)on) inbreuk maken (op)
²**infringe** (vb) schenden; overtreden [agreement etc]
infuriate razend maken
infuse 1 (in)gieten, ingeven **2** bezielen, inprenten, storten: ~ *courage into s.o.*, ~ *s.o. with courage* iem. moed inblazen
ingenious ingenieus, vernuftig
ingenuity 1 vindingrijkheid, vernuft^h **2** ingenieuze uitvinding
ingenuous 1 argeloos, naïef, onschuldig, ongekunsteld **2** eerlijk, openhartig
inglorious eerloos; schandelijk
ingot baar, (goud)staaf, ingot
ingrained 1 ingeworteld **2** verstokt, doortrapt
ingratiate bemind maken: ~ *o.s. with s.o.* bij iem. in de gunst trachten te komen
ingratitude ondankbaarheid
ingredient ingrediënt^h
ingrown ingegroeid [of nails]: [fig] ~ *habit* vaste gewoonte
inhabit bewonen, wonen in
inhabitant bewoner, inwoner
inhalation inhalatie, inademing
inhale inademen, inhaleren
inhaler inhaleertoestel^h
inherent inherent, intrinsiek, eigen: *violence is* ~ *in a dictatorship* geweld is inherent aan een dictatuur
inherit erven, erfgenaam zijn; meekrijgen [vices and virtues etc]
inheritance 1 erfenis, nalatenschap **2** (over)erving

inheritance tax successierecht^h
inhibit 1 verbieden, ontzeggen **2** hinderen, onderdrukken: ~ *s.o. from doing sth.* iem. beletten iets te doen
inhibited geremd
inhibition 1 geremdheid; verlegenheid **2** remming; vertraging
inhospitable ongastvrij
inhuman onmenselijk; wreed
inhumane onmenselijk; inhumaan
inhumanity wreedheid
inimical 1 vijandig **2** (+ to) schadelijk (voor)
inimitable onnavolgbaar, weergaloos
iniquity onrechtvaardigheid, ongerechtigheid, zonde
¹**initial** (n) initiaal, beginletter, hoofdletter, voorletter: ~*s* paraaf
²**initial** (adj) begin-, eerste, initiaal: ~ *capital* grondkapitaal; ~ *stage* beginstadium
initially aanvankelijk, eerst, in het begin
initiate 1 beginnen, in werking stellen **2** (+ into) inwijden (in)
initiative initiatief^h: *on one's own* ~ op eigen initiatief
inject 1 injecteren **2** inbrengen, introduceren: ~ *a little life into a community* een gemeenschap wat leven inblazen
injection injectie [also fig]; stimulans
in-joke grapje voor ingewijden
injudicious [form] onverstandig; onoordeelkundig
injure 1 (ver)wonden, kwetsen, blesseren: *twelve people were* ~*d* er vielen twaalf gewonden **2** kwaad doen, benadelen, beledigen
injury 1 verwonding, letsel^h, blessure: *suffer minor injuries* lichte verwondingen oplopen **2** mishandeling **3** schade, onrecht^h
injustice onrechtvaardigheid: *do s.o. an* ~ iem. onrecht doen
ink inkt [also of octopus]; drukinkt
inkling flauw vermoeden^h, vaag idee^h: *he hasn't an* ~ *of what goes on* hij heeft geen idee van wat er gebeurt
¹**inland** (adj) binnenlands: ~ *navigation* binnen(scheep)vaart
²**inland** (adv) landinwaarts
Inland Revenue 1 staatsbelastinginkomsten **2** belastingdienst
in-law aangetrouwd familielid^h: *my* ~*s* mijn schoonouders, mijn schoonfamilie
inlay 1 inlegsel^h, inlegwerk^h, mozaïek^h **2** informatieblad^h, informatieboekje^h bij cd
inlet 1 inham, kreek **2** inlaat [for liquids]; toegang
in-line skate skate
inmate gevangene; opgenomen patiënt
inmost 1 binnenst **2** diepst, geheimst
inn 1 herberg **2** taveerne, kroeg
innards ingewanden

innate aangeboren, ingeboren: ~*ly kind* vriendelijk van nature
inner 1 binnenst, innerlijk: ~ *city* a) binnenstad; b) verpauperde stadskern; ~ *tube* binnenband **2** verborgen, intiem: ~ *life* gemoedsleven; *the* ~ *meaning* de diepere betekenis
innings slagbeurt, innings || *have a good* ~ een lang en gelukkig leven leiden
innkeeper waard
innocence onschuld
innocent onschuldig, schuldeloos
innocuous onschadelijk
innovate vernieuwen
innovation vernieuwing, innovatie
innuendo (bedekte) toespeling
innumerable ontelbaar, talloos
inoculation inenting [with vaccine]
inoffensive onschuldig, onschadelijk, geen ergernis wekkend
inoperable 1 [med] inoperabel **2** onuitvoerbaar; onbruikbaar
inopportune ongelegen (komend)
inordinate [form] buitensporig
inorganic anorganisch
in-patient (intern verpleegd) patiënt
input 1 toevoer, invoer, inbreng **2** invoer, input
inquest 1 gerechtelijk onderzoek[h], lijkschouwing **2** jury voor lijkschouwing
¹inquire (vb) (+ into) een onderzoek instellen (naar)
²inquire (vb) (na)vragen, onderzoeken: ~ *after* (or: *for*) s.o. naar iemands gezondheid informeren; ~ *of* s.o. bij iem. informeren
inquiry (+ into) onderzoek[h] (naar), (na)vraag, enquête, informatie: *make inquiries* inlichtingen inwinnen; *on* ~ bij navraag
inquisition (gerechtelijk) onderzoek[h], ondervraging: *the Inquisition* de inquisitie
inquisitive nieuwsgierig, benieuwd
inroad inbreuk; aantasting: *the holidays make* ~*s* *(up)on my budget* de vakantie vormt een aanslag op mijn portemonnee
ins: *the* ~ *and outs* de fijne kneepjes (van het vak), de details
insane krankzinnig [also fig]; onzinnig
insanitary 1 ongezond **2** smerig, besmet
insanity krankzinnigheid, waanzin
insatiable onverzadigbaar
inscribe 1 (+ in(to), on) inschrijven (in), graveren; [fig] inprenten **2** opdragen; van een opdracht voorzien [book etc]
inscription 1 inscriptie, opschrift[h] **2** opdracht [in book etc]
inscrutable ondoorgrondelijk, raadselachtig
insect 1 insect[h] **2** (nietig) beestje[h]; [fig] onderkruiper
insecticide insecticide[h], insectenvergif[h]
insecure 1 onveilig, instabiel, wankel

2 onzeker, bang
insecurity onzekerheid; onveiligheid
insemination bevruchting, inseminatie: *artificial* ~ kunstmatige inseminatie
insensible 1 onwaarneembaar, onmerkbaar **2** gevoelloos, bewusteloos **3** ongevoelig, onbewust: *be* ~ *of the danger* zich niet van het gevaar bewust zijn
insensitive ongevoelig, gevoelloos: ~ *to the feelings of others* onverschillig voor de gevoelens van anderen
inseparable on(af)scheidbaar, onafscheidelijk
¹insert (n) tussenvoegsel[h], bijlage, inzetstuk[h], bijsluiter
²insert (vb) inzetten, inbrengen; [comp] invoegen: ~ *a coin* een muntstuk inwerpen
insertion 1 insertie, inplanting **2** tussenvoeging; plaatsing [in newspaper] **3** tussenzetsel[h], inzetstuk[h]
in-service training bijscholing
inset 1 bijvoegsel[h], (losse) bijlage, inlegvel[h], inlegvellen **2** inzetsel[h], tussenzetsel[h]
¹inside (n) binnenkant, binnenste[h]; huizenkant [of pavement or road]
²inside (adj) **1** binnen-: *the* ~ *track* de binnenbaan; [Am] voordelige positie, voordeel **2** van ingewijden, uit de eerste hand: ~ *information* inlichtingen van ingewijden || ~ *job* inbraak door bekenden
³inside (adv) **1** [place and direction; also fig] (naar) binnen, aan de binnenkant: *turn sth.* ~ *out* iets binnenstebuiten keren **2** [inform] in de bak
⁴inside (prep) **1** [place] (binnen)in **2** [time] binnen, (in) minder dan: ~ *an hour* binnen een uur
insider ingewijde
insidious verraderlijk, geniepig, bedrieglijk
insight (+ into) inzicht (in), begrip[h] (van)
insignia insignes, onderscheidingstekenen
insignificant onbeduidend, onbelangrijk, gering
insincere onoprecht, hypocriet
insinuate insinueren, toespelingen maken, indirect suggereren: *what are you insinuating?* wat wil je daarmee zeggen? || *he was trying to* ~ *himself into the minister's favour* hij probeerde bij de minister in de gunst te komen
insinuation bedekte toespeling; insinuatie
insipid 1 smakeloos, flauw **2** zouteloos, banaal, nietszeggend
insist (+ (up)on) (erop) aandringen, volhouden, erop staan: *I* ~ *(up)on an apology* ik eis een verontschuldiging
insistence 1 aandrang, eis **2** volharding, vasthoudendheid
insistent vasthoudend, dringend, hardnekkig
insofar in zoverre: ~ *as* voor zover

insofar as voor zover

insolent onbeschaamd, schaamteloos, brutaal

insoluble onoplosbaar

insolvent insolvent, niet in staat om geldelijke verplichtingen na te komen

insomnia slapeloosheid

insomuch as zodanig dat, aangezien, daar

insouciance zorgeloosheid, onverschilligheid

inspect inspecteren, onderzoeken, keuren

inspection inspectie, onderzoek[h], controle: *on ~ a)* ter inzage; *b)* bij nader onderzoek

inspector inspecteur, opzichter, controleur

inspiration 1 inspiratie **2** [inform] inval, ingeving

inspire 1 inspireren, bezielen **2** opwekken, doen ontstaan

instability onvastheid, instabiliteit

install 1 installeren; plechtig bevestigen [in office, dignity] **2** installeren, aanbrengen, plaatsen: *~ central **heating*** centrale verwarming aanleggen || *~ o.s.* zich installeren, zich nestelen

installation 1 toestel[h], installatie, apparaat[h] **2** installatie; plechtige bevestiging [in office, dignity] **3** installering, vestiging **4** aanleg, installering, montage

instalment 1 (afbetalings)termijn **2** aflevering [of story, TV programme etc]

instance geval[h], voorbeeld[h]: *for ~* bijvoorbeeld || *in the **first** ~* in eerste instantie, in de eerste plaats

[1]**instant** (n) moment[h], ogenblik(je[h]): *the ~ (that) I saw her* zodra ik haar zag

[2]**instant** (adj) **1** onmiddellijk, ogenblikkelijk: *an ~ **replay*** een herhaling [of television recordings] **2** kant-en-klaar, instant

instantaneous onmiddellijk, ogenblikkelijk

instantly onmiddellijk, dadelijk

instead in plaats daarvan: *~ of* in plaats van

instep 1 wreef [of foot] **2** instap [of shoes]

instigate 1 aansporen, aanstichten, teweegbrengen **2** aanzetten, uitlokken, ophitsen: *~ s.o. **to** steal* iem. aanzetten tot diefstal

instigation aandrang, instigatie: *at Peter's ~* op aandrang van Peter

instil geleidelijk doen doordringen, bijbrengen, langzaamaan inprenten

instinct instinct[h], intuïtie

instinctive instinctief, intuïtief

[1]**institute** (n) instituut[h], instelling

[2]**institute** (vb) stichten, invoeren, op gang brengen, instellen || *~ proceedings **against** s.o.* een rechtszaak tegen iem. aanspannen

institution 1 instelling, stichting, invoering **2** gevestigde gewoonte, (sociale) institutie, regel **3** instituut[h], instelling, genootschap[h] **4** inrichting, gesticht[h]

instruct 1 onderwijzen, onderrichten, instrueren **2** opdragen, bevelen

instruction 1 onderricht[h], instructie, les **2** voorschrift[h], order, opdracht: *~s for use* handleiding

instructive instructief, leerzaam

instructor instructeur, docent

instrument instrument[h], gereedschap[h]; werktuig[h] [also fig]: *~ of **fate*** speelbal van het lot

instrumental 1 (+ in) behulpzaam (bij), hulpvaardig: *be ~ in* een cruciale rol spelen bij **2** instrumentaal

insubordinate ongehoorzaam, opstandig

insufferable on(ver)draaglijk, onuitstaanbaar

insufficient ontoereikend, onvoldoende, te weinig

insular 1 eiland-, geïsoleerd **2** bekrompen, kortzichtig

insulate 1 (+ from) isoleren (van), afschermen (van), beschermen (tegen) **2** isoleren [heat, sound]

insulation 1 isolatie, afzondering **2** isolatiemateriaal[h]

[1]**insult** (n) belediging: *add ~ to **injury*** de zaak nog erger maken

[2]**insult** (vb) beledigen

insuperable onoverkomelijk, onoverwinnelijk

insupportable on(ver)draaglijk, onuitstaanbaar

insurance 1 verzekering, assurantie, verzekeringspolis **2** [Am] zekerheid, bescherming

insure 1 (laten) verzekeren **2** [Am] garanderen, veiligstellen

insurer verzekeraar

insurgence oproer[h], opstand

insurmountable onoverkomelijk, onoverwinnelijk

insurrection oproer[h], opstand

intact intact, ongeschonden, gaaf

intake 1 inlaat, toevoer(opening), opgenomen hoeveelheid **2** opneming, opname, toegelaten aantal[h], voeding: *an ~ of **breath*** een inademing

intangible 1 immaterieel: *~ **assets*** immateriële activa **2** ongrijpbaar, ondefinieerbaar

integer [maths] geheel getal[h]

integral 1 wezenlijk **2** geheel, volledig, integraal

[1]**integrate** (vb) geïntegreerd worden, integreren, deel gaan uitmaken (van)

[2]**integrate** (vb) **1** integreren, tot een geheel samenvoegen **2** als gelijkwaardig opnemen [eg minorities]; integreren

integration integratie

integrity 1 integriteit, rechtschapenheid: *a **man** of ~* een integer man **2** ongeschonden toestand, eenheid

intellect intellect[h], verstand(elijk vermogen)[h]
¹intellectual (n) intellectueel
²intellectual (adj) intellectueel; verstandelijk
intelligence 1 intelligentie, verstand(elijk vermogen)[h] **2** informatie, nieuws[h], inlichtingen **3** (geheime) informatie, inlichtingendienst
intelligent intelligent, slim
intelligible begrijpelijk, verstaanbaar
intemperate 1 onmatig, buitensporig, heftig, drankzuchtig **2** guur [of climate, wind]; extreem
intend 1 van plan zijn, bedoelen, in de zin hebben: *I ~ to cancel the order* ik ben van plan de order te annuleren; *we ~ them to repair it* we willen dat zij het repareren **2** (voor)bestemmen, bedoelen: *their son was ~ed for the Church* hun zoon was voorbestemd om priester te worden
intense intens, sterk, zeer hevig
¹intensify (vb) intens(er) worden, versterken, toenemen
²intensify (vb) verhevigen, versterken, intensiveren
intensity intensiteit, sterkte, (mate van) hevigheid
intensive intensief, heftig, (in)gespannen: *~ care* intensieve verpleging, intensive care
¹intent (n) bedoeling, intentie, voornemen[h] || *to all ~s and purposes* feitelijk, in (praktisch) alle opzichten
²intent (adj) **1** (in)gespannen, aandachtig **2** vastbesloten, vastberaden: *be ~ on revenge* zinnen op wraak
intention 1 bedoeling, oogmerk[h], voornemen[h]: *have no ~ of doing so* (or: *to do so*) er niet over peinzen dat te doen **2** (-s) [inform] bedoelingen, (huwelijks)plannen
intentional opzettelijk; expres
inter ter aarde bestellen, begraven
interact op elkaar inwerken, met elkaar reageren
interaction wisselwerking
interactive interactief
interbreed (onderling) kruisen
intercede 1 ten gunste spreken, een goed woordje doen **2** bemiddelen, tussenbeide komen
intercept onderscheppen, afsnijden
intercession tussenkomst, bemiddeling, voorspraak
¹interchange (n) **1** uitwisseling, ruil(ing), verwisseling **2** knooppunt[h] [of motorways]; verkeersplein[h]
²interchange (vb) **1** uitwisselen, ruilen **2** (onderling) verwisselen, afwisselen
interchangeable 1 uitwisselbaar, ruilbaar **2** (onderling) verwisselbaar
the **intercom** intercom

intercourse 1 omgang, sociaal verkeer[h], betrekking(en) **2** (geslachts)gemeenschap[h]: *sexual ~* geslachtsgemeenschap
interdenominational oecumenisch
interdependent onderling afhankelijk, afhankelijk van elkaar
interest 1 interesse, (voorwerp[h] van) belangstelling: *show an ~ in* belangstelling tonen voor; *take a great ~ in* zich sterk interesseren voor **2** (eigen)belang[h], interesse, voordeel[h]: *it's in the ~ of the community* het is in het belang van de gemeenschap **3** rente [also fig]; interest: *the rate of ~, the ~ rate* de rentevoet; *lend money at 7% ~* geld lenen tegen 7% rente
interested 1 belangstellend, geïnteresseerd, vol interesse **2** belanghebbend, betrokken: *the ~ party* de betrokken partij
interesting interessant, belangwekkend
interface 1 raakvlak[h] [also fig]; grensvlak[h], scheidingsvlak[h] **2** [comp] koppeling, aansluiting, interface
interfaith oecumenisch, van meerdere religies: *the commemoration was an ~ service* de herdenkingsdienst werd geleid door vertegenwoordigers van verschillende religies
interfere hinderen, in de weg staan: *don't ~* hou je erbuiten
interference 1 (ver)storing, belemmering **2** inmenging, tussenkomst, bemoeienis
interfere with 1 aankomen, betasten, knoeien met: *don't ~ that bike* blijf met je handen van die fiets af **2** zich bemoeien met **3** [euph] aanranden, zich vergrijpen aan
¹interim (n) interim, tussentijd: *in the ~* intussen, ondertussen
²interim (adj) tijdelijk, voorlopig: *an ~ report* een tussentijds rapport
interior 1 inwendig, binnen- **2** binnenshuis, interieur- **3** innerlijk: *~ monologue* monologue intérieur, inwendige monoloog **4** binnenlands
interior decorator binnenhuisarchitect(e)
interject (zich) ertussen werpen, tussenbeide komen, opmerken
interjection 1 tussenwerpsel[h], interjectie **2** uitroep, kreet
¹interlock (vb) in elkaar grijpen, nauw met elkaar verbonden zijn: *these problems ~* deze problemen hangen nauw met elkaar samen
²interlock (vb) met elkaar verbinden, aaneenkoppelen
interloper indringer
interlude 1 onderbreking, pauze **2** tussenstuk[h], tussenspel[h]
intermarry 1 een gemengd huwelijk aangaan **2** onderling trouwen, binnen de eigen familie trouwen
¹intermediary (n) tussenpersoon, bemiddelaar, contactpersoon

²**intermediary** (adj) bemiddelend, optredend als tussenpersoon
intermediate tussenliggend, tussengelegen, tussentijds: ~ *course* aanvullende cursus
interminable oneindig (lang), eindeloos
intermingle (zich) (ver)mengen, (vrijelijk) met elkaar omgaan
intermission onderbreking [also in play etc]; pauze, rust: *without* ~ ononderbroken
intermittent met tussenpozen (verschijnend/werkend), onderbroken, met onderbrekingen
¹**intern** (n) [Am] **1** intern, inwonend (co)assistent **2** hospitant(e), stagiair(e)
²**intern** (vb) interneren, gevangen zetten; vastzetten [during wartime]
internal 1 inwendig, innerlijk, binnen-: *the ~ ear* het inwendige oor **2** binnenlands, inwendig
internalize zich eigen maken
¹**international** (n) **1** interland(wedstrijd) **2** international, interlandspeler
²**international** (adj) internationaal
internee (politieke) gevangene
the **Internet** het internet
internet account internetaansluiting
internet banking internetbankierenʰ
internet café internetcaféʰ
internment internering
interpersonal intermenselijk
interplay interactie, wisselwerking
interpose 1 tussenplaatsen, invoegen **2** interrumperen, onderbreken **3** naar voren brengen, aanvoeren
¹**interpret** (vb) als tolk optreden, tolken
²**interpret** (vb) **1** interpreteren, uitleggen, opvatten **2** vertolken, interpreteren **3** (mondeling) vertalen
interpretation 1 interpretatie, uitleg **2** het tolken **3** vertolking, interpretatie
interpreter tolk
interracial tussen (verschillende) rassen, voor verschillende rassen
interregnum tussenregering
¹**interrelate** (vb) met elkaar in verband staan, met elkaar verbonden zijn
²**interrelate** (vb) met elkaar in verband brengen
interrogation ondervraging, verhoorʰ
¹**interrogative** (n) vragend (voornaam)-woordʰ
²**interrogative** (adj) vragend; vraag- [also linguistics]: ~ *pronoun* vragend voornaamwoord
¹**interrupt** (vb) storen, onderbreken, in de rede vallen
²**interrupt** (vb) **1** onderbreken, afbreken, belemmeren **2** interrumperen, in de rede vallen, storen
interruption 1 onderbreking, afbreking **2** interruptie, het storen

intersection 1 (weg)kruising, kruispuntʰ, snijpuntʰ **2** doorsnijding, kruising
intersperse 1 verspreid zetten, (hier en daar) strooien: *a speech ~d with posh words* een met deftige woorden doorspekte toespraak **2** afwisselen, variëren, van tijd tot tijd onderbreken
interstate highway autosnelweg
interstice nauwe tussenruimte, spleet, reet
¹**intertwine** (vb) zich in elkaar strengelen, (met elkaar) verweven zijn
²**intertwine** (vb) ineenstrengelen, dooreenvlechten
interval 1 tussenruimte, interval, tussentijd: *trams go at 15-minute ~s* er rijdt iedere 15 minuten een tram **2** pauze, rust **3** interval, toonsafstand
intervene 1 tussenbeide komen, zich erin mengen, ertussen komen **2** ertussen liggen: *in the intervening* ***months*** in de tussenliggende maanden
intervention tussenkomst, inmenging; ingreep [also med]
¹**interview** (n) **1** (persoonlijk) onderhoudʰ, sollicitatiegesprekʰ **2** interviewʰ, vraaggesprekʰ
²**interview** (vb) interviewen, een vraaggesprek houden met, een sollicitatiegesprek voeren met
interviewer 1 interviewer **2** ondervrager
¹**interweave** (vb) zich in elkaar strengelen
²**interweave** (vb) in elkaar vlechten; verweven
intestine darm(kanaalʰ), (buik)ingewanden: *large* ~ dikke darm; *small* ~ dunne darm
intimacy 1 intimiteit, vertrouwelijkheid, intieme mededeling **2** innige verbondenheid, vertrouwdheid: *they were on* ***terms*** *of* ~ er bestond een sterke vriendschapsband tussen hen **3** intimiteit, intieme omgang, geslachtsverkeerʰ
¹**intimate** (adj) **1** intiem [also sexually]; innig (verbonden) **2** vertrouwelijk, privé: ~ *secrets* hartsgeheimen; *they are on* ~ ***terms*** zij zijn goede vrienden
²**intimate** (vb) suggereren, een hint geven, laten doorschemeren
intimation aanduiding, suggestie, hint
intimidate intimideren, bang maken
into 1 in, binnen-: *look* ~ *the matter* de zaak bestuderen; [inform] *he's* ~ *Zen these days* tegenwoordig interesseert hij zich voor zen **2** [change of circumstance] tot, in: *translate* ~ *Japanese* in het Japans vertalen **3** [duration or distance] tot … in: *far* ~ *the* ***night*** tot diep in de nacht ‖ *run* ~ *an old friend* een oude vriend tegen het lijf lopen; *talk somebody* ~ *leaving* iem. ompraten om te gaan
intolerable on(ver)draaglijk, onuitstaanbaar
intolerance onverdraagzaamheid; [also

med] intolerantie: *lactose* ~ lactose-intolerantie

intolerant (+ of) onverdraagzaam (tegenover), intolerant

intonation intonatie, stembuiging

[1]**intoxicant** (n) bedwelmend middel[h], alcoholische drank, sterkedrank

[2]**intoxicant** (adj) bedwelmend, alcoholisch

intoxication 1 bedwelming, dronkenschap **2** vervoering

intractable 1 lastig **2** onhandelbaar

intransigent onbuigzaam, onverzoenlijk, onverzettelijk

intransitive onovergankelijk

intravenous in de ader(en); intraveneus

intrepid onverschrokken, dapper

intricate ingewikkeld, complex, moeilijk

[1]**intrigue** (n) intrige, gekonkel[h], samenzwering

[2]**intrigue** (vb) intrigeren, samenzweren

[3]**intrigue** (vb) intrigeren, nieuwsgierig maken, boeien

intrinsic intrinsiek, innerlijk, wezenlijk

introduce 1 introduceren, voorstellen, inleiden: ~ *to* **a)** voorstellen aan [s.o.]; **b)** kennis laten maken met [sth.] **2** invoeren, introduceren, naar voren brengen: ~ *a new subject* een nieuw onderwerp aansnijden

introduction 1 inleiding, introductie, voorwoord[h]: *an ~ to* the *Chinese language* een inleiding tot de Chinese taal **2** introductie, voorstelling, inleiding

introductory inleidend: ~ *offer* introductieaanbieding; ~ *remarks* inleidende opmerkingen

introspection introspectie; zelfreflectie

[1]**intrude** (vb) **1** (zich) binnendringen, zich opdringen: *intruding* **into** *conversations* zich ongevraagd in gesprekken mengen **2** zich opdringen, ongelegen komen, storen: *let's not ~ on his time any longer* laten wij niet langer onnodig beslag leggen op zijn tijd

[2]**intrude** (vb) **1** binnendringen, indringen, opdringen **2** opdringen, lastigvallen, storen

intruder indringer, insluiper

intrusion binnendringing, indringing, inbreuk: *an ~* **(up)on** *my privacy* een inbreuk op mijn privacy

intuition intuïtie, ingeving: *she had an ~ that things were wrong* ze had een plotselinge ingeving dat de zaak fout zat

intuitive intuïtief

inundate onder water zetten, overstelpen, overstromen

inure gewennen, harden

invade 1 binnenvallen, een inval doen in, binnendringen **2** overstromen: *hundreds of people ~d the newly-opened shopping centre* honderden mensen overstroomden het pas geopende winkelcentrum **3** inbreuk maken op; schenden [privacy]

invader indring(st)er

[1]**invalid** (n) invalide

[2]**invalid** (adj) **1** ongerechtvaardigd, ongegrond, zwak **2** ongeldig, onwettig, nietig: *this will is* ~ dit testament is ongeldig

[3]**invalid** (adj) **1** invalide, gebrekkig **2** invaliden-, zieken-: ~ *chair* rolstoel

invalidate ongeldig maken (verklaren), nietig maken: *this automatically ~s the guarantee* hierdoor komt de garantie automatisch te vervallen; *his arguments were ~d* zijn argumenten werden ontzenuwd

invaluable onschatbaar

invariable onveranderlijk, constant, vast

invariably steevast; steeds, altijd

invasion 1 invasie [also fig]; inval, het binnenvallen **2** inbreuk, schending

invasive 1 invasie-; binnendringend **2** zich verspreidend [of illness]

invective scheldwoord[h], scheldwoorden, getier[h]

inveigh krachtig protesteren, uitvaren, tieren

inveigle verleiden, overhalen: ~ *s.o.* **into** *stealing* iem. ertoe brengen om te stelen

invent 1 uitvinden, uitdenken **2** bedenken, verzinnen

invention 1 uitvinding, vinding **2** bedenksel[h], verzinsel[h]

inventive inventief, vindingrijk, creatief

inventor uitvinder

inventory 1 inventaris(lijst), inventarisatie, boedelbeschrijving **2** overzicht[h], lijst

inverse omgekeerd, tegenovergesteld, invert: ~ *ratio* omgekeerd evenredigheid

invert omkeren, inverteren: ~*ed commas* aanhalingstekens

[1]**invertebrate** (n) ongewerveld dier[h]

[2]**invertebrate** (adj) ongewerveld

[1]**invest** (vb) geld beleggen, (geld) investeren

[2]**invest** (vb) investeren, beleggen: *they ~ed all their spare time* **in** *the car* ze staken al hun vrije tijd in de auto

[1]**investigate** (vb) een onderzoek instellen

[2]**investigate** (vb) onderzoeken, nasporen

investigation onderzoek[h]

investigative onderzoeks-; onderzoekend: ~ *journalism* onderzoeksjournalistiek

investigator onderzoeker, detective

investment investering, (geld)belegging

inveterate 1 ingeworteld, diep verankerd **2** verstokt, aarts-: ~ *liars* onverbeterlijke leugenaars

invidious 1 aanstootgevend, ergerlijk **2** hatelijk, beledigend

invigilate surveilleren [at examination]

invigorate (ver)sterken, kracht geven

invincible onoverwinnelijk, onomstotelijk || ~ *belief* onwankelbaar geloof

inviolable onschendbaar

invisible onzichtbaar [also fig]; verborgen

invitation uitnodiging, invitatie: *an ~ to a party* een uitnodiging voor een feest
invite 1 uitnodigen, inviteren: *~ s.o. over* (or: *round*) iem. vragen langs te komen **2** uitnodigen, verzoeken **3** vragen om, uitlokken
invoice factuur
invoke 1 aanroepen, inroepen **2** zich beroepen op, een beroep doen op
involuntary onwillekeurig, onopzettelijk, onbewust: *an ~ movement* een reflexbeweging
involve 1 betrekken, verwikkelen: *whose interests are ~d?* om wiens belangen gaat het?; *the persons ~d* de betrokkenen **2** (met zich) meebrengen, betekenen: *large sums of money are ~d* er zijn grote bedragen mee gemoeid; *this job always ~s a lot of paperwork* dit werk brengt altijd veel administratieve rompslomp met zich mee
involvement 1 betrokkenheid **2** deelname **3** inmenging **4** verhouding; relatie
invulnerable onkwetsbaar [also fig]; onaantastbaar
¹inward (adj) **1** innerlijk, inwendig **2** binnenwaarts, naar binnen gericht
²inward (adv) **1** binnenwaarts, naar binnen **2** innerlijk, in de geest
I/O *input/output*
iodine jodium(tinctuurʰ)
iota jota; [fig] greintjeʰ: *not an ~* geen jota
IOU *I owe you* schuldbekentenis
IP *Internet Protocol* IPʰ
IQ *Intelligence Quotient* IQʰ, intelligentiequotiëntʰ
Iran Iran
¹Iranian (n) Iraniër, Iraanse
²Iranian (adj) Iraans
Iraq Irak
¹Iraqi (n) Irakees, Irakese
²Iraqi (adj) Irakees
irascible prikkelbaar, opvliegend
irate ziedend, woedend
ire [form] toorn; woede
Ireland Ierland
iris 1 iris; regenboogvliesʰ [of eye] **2** lis, iris
¹Irish (n) Iers, de Ierse taal, (Iers-)Gaelisch
²Irish (adj) Iers, van Ierland
Irishman Ier
Irishwoman Ierse
iris scan irisscan
irk ergeren, hinderen: *it ~s me to do this job* deze klus staat me tegen
irksome ergerlijk; hinderlijk
¹iron (n) ijzerʰ, strijkijzerʰ, brandijzerʰ: *rule with a rod of ~* met ijzeren vuist regeren; *cast ~* gietijzer; *wrought ~* smeedijzer ‖ *have too many ~s in the fire* te veel hooi op z'n vork genomen hebben
²iron (adj) **1** ijzeren **2** ijzersterk: *~ constitution* ijzeren gestel ‖ *the Iron Curtain* het IJzeren Gordijn

³iron (vb) strijken: [fig] *~ out problems* problemen gladstrijken
the **Iron Age** ijzertijd
ironic ironisch: *~ally* ironisch genoeg
ironing het strijken, strijkgoedʰ
ironmonger ijzerhandelaar
¹irony (n) ironie, spot: *life's ironies* de tegenstrijdigheden van het leven
²irony (adj) ijzerachtig: *this food has an ~ taste* er zit een ijzersmaak aan dit eten
irradiate 1 schijnen op, verlichten: *their faces were ~d with happiness* hun gezicht straalde van geluk **2** bestralen [also with x-rays etc] **3** doen stralen, doen schitteren
¹irrational (n) onmeetbaar getalʰ
²irrational (adj) irrationeel, onredelijk: *~ behaviour* onberekenbaar gedrag
irreconcilable 1 onverzoenlijk **2** onverenigbaar, onoverbrugbaar
irrecoverable 1 onherstelbaar, hopeloos **2** onherroepelijk **3** oninbaar, oninvorderbaar
irrefutable onweerlegbaar, onbetwistbaar
¹irregular (n) lidʰ van ongeregelde troepen, partizaan, guerrillastrijder
²irregular (adj) **1** onregelmatig, abnormaal, afwijkend: *in spite of his ~ passport* hoewel zijn paspoort niet in orde was **2** ongeregeld, ongeordend: *she studies very ~ly* ze studeert zeer onregelmatig ‖ *~ verbs* onregelmatige werkwoorden
irrelevance irrelevantie, irrelevant(e) opmerking, vraag …
irrelevant irrelevant, niet ter zake (doend)
irremediable onherstelbaar
irreparable onherstelbaar, niet te verhelpen
irreplaceable onvervangbaar
irrepressible onbedwingbaar, ontembaar, onstuitbaar: *~ laughter* onbedaarlijk gelach
irresistible onweerstaanbaar, onbedwingbaar, onweerlegbaar
irresolute besluiteloos, weifelend, aarzelend
irrespective toch, sowieso: *~ of* ongeacht; *~ of whether it was necessary or not* of het nu noodzakelijk was of niet
irresponsible 1 onverantwoord(elijk) **2** ontoerekenbaar, niet aansprakelijk
irretrievable onherstelbaar, niet meer ongedaan te maken, reddeloos (verloren)
irreverent oneerbiedig, zonder respect
irreversible onomkeerbaar, onherroepelijk, onveranderlijk
irrevocable onherroepelijk, onomkeerbaar
irrigate irrigeren, bevloeien, begieten
irrigation irrigatie, bevloeiing, besproeiing
irritable lichtgeraakt, prikkelbaar, opvliegend
irritant 1 irriterend (or: prikkelend) mid-

del^h **2** ergernis
irritate 1 irriteren, ergeren, boos maken:
be ~d at (or: *by, with*) geërgerd zijn door **2** irriteren; prikkelen [skin etc]
irritation 1 irritatie, ergernis **2** irritatie,
branderigheid, branderige plek
IRS *Internal Revenue Service* belastingdienst; fiscus
Is *Island(s), Isle(s)* Eiland(en)
Isaiah Jesaja, Isaias
ISDN *integrated services digital network*
ISDN
Islam islam, islamitische wereld
Islamic islamitisch
island 1 eiland^h [also fig] **2** vluchtheuvel
islander eilander, eilandbewoner
isle [in specific combinations] eiland^h
islet eilandje^h
isn't *is not*
isolate isoleren, afzonderen, afsluiten
isolation isolatie, afzondering, isolement^h:
in ~ in afzondering, op zichzelf
Israel Israël
^1**Israeli** (n) Israëli, bewoner van Israël
^2**Israeli** (adj) Israëlisch
^1**Israelite** (n) Israëliet, nakomeling van Israël
^2**Israelite** (adj) Israëlitisch
^1**issue** (n) **1** uitgave, aflevering; nummer^h [of
magazine] **2** kwestie, (belangrijk) punt^h,
probleem^h: *force the ~* een beslissing forceren; *make an ~ of sth.* ergens een punt van
maken **3** publicatie, uitgave, emissie: *the day
of ~* de dag van publicatie
^2**issue** (vb) uitkomen, verschijnen: *~ forth*
(or: *out*) tevoorschijn komen
^3**issue** (vb) **1** uitbrengen, publiceren, in circulatie brengen, uitvaardigen: *they ~d a new
series of stamps* ze gaven een nieuwe serie
postzegels uit **2** uitlenen [books] **3** uitstorten, uitspuwen: *a volcano issuing dangerous
gases* een vulkaan die gevaarlijke gassen
uitspuwt
isthmus istmus, nauwe verbinding, landengte
it 1 het: *I dreamt it* ik heb het gedroomd; *it is
getting on* het wordt laat; *it says in this book
that ...* er staat in dit boek dat ...; *it is reported that* volgens de berichten; *I've got it* ik heb
een idee; *she let him have it* ze gaf hem ervan
langs; *who is it?* wie is het? **2** hét, het neusje
van de zalm, het probleem: *that is it, I've finished* dat was het dan, klaar is Kees; *that is it*
dat is 't hem nu juist
IT *information technology* IT, informatietechnologie
^1**Italian** (n) Italiaan(se)
^2**Italian** (adj) Italiaans
italic 1 cursief, cursieve drukletter: *the
words in ~* de schuingedrukte woorden
2 schuinschrift^h, lopend schrift^h
italicize cursiveren

Italy Italië
^1**itch** (n) **1** jeuk, kriebel **2** verlangen^h, hang
^2**itch** (vb) **1** jeuken, kriebelen: *the wound
keeps ~ing* de wond blijft maar jeuken **2** jeuk
hebben **3** graag willen: *she was ~ing to tell
her* ze zat te popelen om het haar te vertellen
itchy 1 jeukend **2** rusteloos: *get ~ feet* de
reiskriebels krijgen
item 1 item^h, punt^h, nummer^h **2** onderdeel^h,
bestanddeel^h **3** artikel^h, (nieuws)bericht^h
itemize specificeren
itinerant rondreizend, (rond)trekkend: *~
preacher* rondtrekkend prediker
itinerary 1 routebeschrijving, reisbeschrijving **2** reisroute
its zijn, haar, ervan: *this coat has had ~ day*
deze mantel heeft zijn tijd gehad; *the government has lost ~ majority* de regering is
haar meerderheid kwijt; *~ strength frightens
me* de kracht ervan maakt mij bang
itself 1 zich, zichzelf: *the animal hurt ~* het
dier bezeerde zich; *by ~* alleen, op eigen
kracht; *in ~* op zichzelf **2** zelf: *the watch ~
was not in the box* het horloge zelf zat niet in
de doos
ivory ivoor^h
the **Ivory Coast** Ivoorkust
ivy klimop

j

¹jab (n) **1** por, steek **2** [inform] prik, injectie
²jab (vb) porren, stoten, stompen: *he ~bed his elbow into my side* hij gaf me een por in de ribben
jabber brabbelen, kwebbelen: *~ away* erop los kwebbelen
jack 1 toestel[h], hefboom, vijzel, krik, stut, stellage, (zaag)bok **2** dier[h], mannetje[h] **3** [cards] boer: *~ of hearts* hartenboer
jackal jakhals
jackass ezel [also fig]
jackboot 1 kaplaars [boot] **2** totalitarisme[h]
jackdaw kauw, torenkraai
jacket 1 jas(je[h]), colbert(je)[h] **2** omhulsel[h], bekleding, mantel, huls **3** stofomslag[h] [of book] ‖ *potatoes cooked in their ~s* aardappelen in de schil bereid
jacket potato aardappel in de schil
jack-in-the-box duveltje in een doosje
¹jackknife (n) (groot) knipmes[h]
²jackknife (vb) scharen [of articulated vehicles]
jack-of-all-trades manusje-van-alles[h]
jack off [vulg] zich aftrekken
jackpot pot [at games of hazard]; jackpot: *hit the ~* **a)** (de pot) winnen [at poker etc]; **b)** [fig] een klapper maken, het helemaal maken
jack up opkrikken; [inform, fig also] opvijzelen; opdrijven [prices etc]
jade 1 knol [old horse] **2** jade, bleekgroen
jaded 1 afgemat, uitgeput **2** afgestompt
jagged getand, gekarteld, puntig: *~ edge* scherpe rand
¹jail (n) gevangenis, huis[h] van bewaring
²jail (vb) gevangen zetten
jailbird bajesklant
jailbreak ontsnapping uit de gevangenis; uitbraak
jailer cipier, gevangenbewaarder
¹jam (n) **1** opstopping, blokkering, stremming **2** knel, knoei, moeilijkheden: *be in* (or: *get into*) *a ~* in de nesten zitten (or: raken) **3** jam, marmelade **4** jamsessie
²jam (vb) vast (blijven) zitten, klemmen, blokkeren, vastraken: *the door ~med* de deur raakte klem
³jam (vb) **1** vastzetten, klemmen, knellen **2** (met kracht) drijven, dringen, duwen: *~ the brakes on* op de rem gaan staan **3** (vol)proppen: *he ~med all his clothes into a tiny case* hij propte al zijn kleren in een piepklein koffertje **4** blokkeren, verstoppen, versperren: *the*

crowds ~med the streets de massa versperde de straten **5** [radio] storen
Jamaica Jamaica
¹Jamaican (n) Jamaicaan(se)
²Jamaican (adj) Jamaicaans
jam-packed propvol, barstensvol
¹jangle (n) **1** metaalklank, gerinkel[h] **2** wanklank
²jangle (vb) **1** kletteren, rinkelen, rammelen **2** vals klinken, wanklank geven: *the music ~d on my ears* de muziek schetterde in mijn oren
³jangle (vb) irriteren, van streek maken: *it ~d his nerves* het vrat aan zijn zenuwen
janitor 1 portier[h], deurwachter **2** [Am] conciërge, huisbewaarder
January januari
Japan Japan
¹Japanese (n) Japanner, Japanse
²Japanese (adj) Japans
¹jar (n) **1** (zenuw)schok, onaangename verrassing, ontnuchtering: *suffer a nasty ~* flink ontnuchterd worden **2** pot, (stop)fles, kruik; [inform] glas[h] [beer etc]
²jar (vb) **1** knarsen, vals klinken: [also fig] *~ring note* valse noot, dissonant **2** botsen, in strijd zijn: *~ring opinions* botsende meningen
jargon jargon[h], vaktaal; [depr] koeterwaals[h]; taaltje[h]
jasmin(e) jasmijn
¹jaundice (n) geelzucht
²jaundice (vb) afgunstig maken, verbitteren: *take a ~d view of the matter* een scheve kijk op de zaak hebben
jaunt uitstapje[h], tochtje[h], snoepreisje[h]
jaunty 1 zwierig, elegant **2** vrolijk, zelfverzekerd: *a ~ step* een kwieke tred
javelin 1 speer, werpspies **2** [athletics] speerwerpen[h]
¹jaw (n) **1** kaak: *lower* (or: *upper*) *~* onderkaak, bovenkaak **2** praat, geklets[h], gezwam[h], geroddel[h] **3** tegenspraak, brutale praat: *don't give me any ~!* hou je gedeisd! **4** (-s) bek; muil [of animal]
²jaw (vb) **1** kletsen, zwammen, roddelen **2** preken: *~ at s.o.* iem. de les lezen
jawbreaker [Am] toverbal
jay Vlaamse gaai
jazz 1 jazz **2** gesnoef[h] **3** onzin, larie ‖ *and all that ~* en nog meer van die dingen
jazz up opvrolijken, opfleuren, verfraaien: *they jazzed it up* ze brachten wat leven in de brouwerij
jealous 1 jaloers, afgunstig: *~ of* jaloers op **2** (overdreven) waakzaam, nauwlettend: *guard ~ly* angstvallig bewaken
jealousy jaloersheid, afgunst, jaloezie
jeans spijkerbroek, jeans
jeep jeep
¹jeer (n) hatelijke opmerking: *~s* gejouw[h]; hoon

jeer 852

²**jeer** (vb) jouwen: ~ *at* s.o. iem. uitlachen
³**jeer** (vb) uitjouwen
jell 1 (doen) opstijven, geleiachtig (doen) worden 2 vorm krijgen (geven), kristalliseren: *my ideas are beginning to* ~ mijn ideeën beginnen vorm te krijgen
jelly gelei, gelatine(pudding), jam: *beat* s.o. *to* ~ iem. tot moes slaan
jellyfish kwal
jemmy koevoet, breekijzer[h]
jeopardize in gevaar brengen, riskeren, op het spel zetten: ~ *one's life* zijn leven wagen
jeopardy gevaar[h]: *put one's future in* ~ zijn toekomst op het spel zetten
¹**jerk** (n) 1 ruk, schok, trek 2 [vulg] lul, zak
²**jerk** (vb) schokken, beven: ~ *to a halt* met een ruk stoppen
³**jerk** (vb) rukken aan, stoten, trekken aan: *he ~ed the fish out of the water* hij haalde de vis met een ruk uit het water
jerk off [Am; vulg] zich aftrekken
jerky schokkerig, spastisch, hortend: *move along jerkily* zich met horten en stoten voortbewegen
jest 1 grap, mop 2 scherts, gekheid: *in* ~ voor de grap
jester nar
Jesus Jezus
¹**jet** (n) 1 straal [of water etc] 2 (gas)vlam, pit 3 [inform] jet, straalvliegtuig[h], straalmotor
²**jet** (vb) 1 spuiten, uitspuiten, uitwerpen: ~ *(out) flames* vlammen werpen; ~ *out* eruit spuiten 2 [inform] per jet reizen || ~ *out* vooruitspringen
jet-black gitzwart
jetfoil draagvleugelboot
jetsam strandgoed[h]
jettison werpen [ship's cargo]; [fig] overboord gooien; prijsgeven
jetty pier, havendam, havenhoofd[h], golfbreker
Jew 1 Jood 2 [rel] jood[h]
jewel 1 juweel[h] [also fig]; edelsteen, sieraad[h] 2 steen [in timepiece]
jeweller juwelier
jewellery juwelen, sieraden
Jewess 1 Jodin 2 [rel] jodin
Jewish 1 Joods 2 [rel] joods
Jewry Jodendom[h], de Joden
jib 1 weigeren (verder te gaan) [of horse] 2 terugkrabbelen: ~ *at* terugdeinzen voor, zich afkerig tonen van
¹**jibe** (n) spottende opmerking
²**jibe** (vb) spotten; schimpen: ~ *at* de draak steken met
jiffy momentje[h]: *I won't be a* ~ ik kom zo; *in a* ~ in een mum van tijd, in een wip
¹**jig** (n) 1 sprongetje[h] 2 jig, gigue [dance]
²**jig** (vb) op en neer (doen) wippen, (doen) huppelen, (doen) hossen
¹**jiggle** (vb) schommelen, wiegen

²**jiggle** (vb) doen schommelen, (zacht) rukken aan, wrikken
jigsaw figuurzaag
jigsaw (puzzle) (leg)puzzel
jilt afwijzen; de bons geven [lover]
¹**jingle** (n) 1 geklingel[h], gerinkel[h], getinkel[h] 2 [depr] rijmelarij, rijmpje[h] 3 jingle [on radio]
²**jingle** (vb) (laten) klingelen, (doen) rinkelen
jinks aan iets de handen vol hebben; *make a* ~ dolle pret
jinx 1 onheilsbrenger 2 doem, vloek: *put a* ~ *on* s.o. iem. beheksen
jitters kriebels, zenuwen: *give* s.o. *the* ~ iem. nerveus maken
jittery [inform] zenuwachtig; nerveus
jnr *junior* jr.
job 1 karwei[h], klus, job: *have a* ~ *to get* sth. *done* aan iets de handen vol hebben; *make a (good)* ~ *of* sth. iets goed afwerken; *on the* ~ aan het werk, bezig 2 baan(tje[h]), vak[h], job, taak: [euph] *between* ~s zonder werk, werkloos; [euph] *op zoek naar een nieuwe uitdaging*; ~s *for the boys* vriendjespolitiek 3 [inform] geval[h], ding[h]: *that new car of yours is a beautiful* ~ die nieuwe auto van jou is een prachtslee 4 [inform] toestand: *make the best of a bad* ~ ergens het beste van maken; *he has gone, and a good* ~ *too* hij is weg, en maar goed ook || *that should do the* ~ zo moet het lukken
jobbery ambtsmisbruik[h], (ambtelijke) corruptie
jobbing klusjes-: *a* ~ *gardener* een klusjesman voor de tuin
jobless zonder werk, werkloos
job satisfaction arbeidsvreugde
job-sharing het werken met deeltijdbanen
jock [inform] 1 [Am] atleet, atlete 2 Schot 3 dj
¹**jockey** (n) jockey
²**jockey** (vb) manoeuvreren: ~ *for position* met de ellebogen werken
jocular schertsend, grappig
jodhpurs rijbroek: *a pair of* ~ een rijbroek
¹**jog** (n) 1 duw(tje[h]), schok, stootje[h] 2 sukkeldraf(je[h]) 3 een stukje joggen
²**jog** (vb) 1 joggen, trimmen 2 op een sukkeldraf(je) lopen, sukkelen: ~ *along* (or: *on*) voortsukkelen
³**jog** (vb) (aan)stoten, een duw(tje) geven, (aan)porren || ~ s.o.'s *memory* iemands geheugen opfrissen
⁴**jog** (vb) hotsen, op en neer (doen) gaan, schudden
joggle hotsen, heen en weer (op en neer) (doen) gaan, schudden
jogtrot sukkeldraf(je[h]), lichte draf
john 1 [Am; inform] wc 2 [Am; inform] klant [of whore]; hoerenloper
johnny kerel, man, vent
¹**join** (n) verbinding(sstuk[h]), voeg, las, naad

²**join** (vb) **1** samenkomen, zich verenigen, verenigd worden, elkaar ontmoeten, uitkomen op: ~ *up (with)* samensmelten (met) **2** zich aansluiten, meedoen, deelnemen: *can I ~ in?* mag ik meedoen?; ~ *up* dienst nemen (bij het leger), lid worden, zich aansluiten (bij)

³**join** (vb) **1** verenigen, verbinden, vastmaken: ~ *the main road* op de hoofdweg uitkomen; ~ *up (with)* samenvoegen (met) **2** zich aansluiten bij, meedoen met, deelnemen aan: ~ *the army* dienst nemen (bij het leger); *will you ~ us?* doe je mee?, kom je bij ons zitten?

joiner 1 schrijnwerker, meubelmaker **2** nieuw lid

¹**joint** (n) **1** verbinding(sstukʰ), voeg, las, naad **2** gewrichtʰ, geleding, scharnierʰ: *out of* ~ [also fig] ontwricht, uit het lid, uit de voegen **3** braadstukʰ, gebraadʰ, (groot) stukʰ vlees **4** [inform] tent, kroeg **5** [inform] joint, stickieʰ

²**joint** (adj) gezamenlijk, gemeenschappelijk: ~ *account* gezamenlijke rekening; ~ *owners* mede-eigenaars; ~ *responsibility* gedeelde verantwoordelijkheid

joist (dwars)balk, bintʰ, (horizontale) steunbalk

¹**joke** (n) **1** grap(jeʰ), mop: *practical* ~ poets, practical joke; *crack* (or: *tell*) ~s moppen tappen; *be* (or: *go*) *beyond a* ~ te ver gaan, niet leuk zijn; [inform] *no* ~ geen grapje **2** mikpuntʰ [of mockery, wittiness]; spot

²**joke** (vb) grappen maken, schertsen: *you must be joking!* dat meen je niet!; *joking apart* in alle ernst, nee, nou even serieus

joker 1 grapjas, grappenmaker **2** [cards] joker; [fig] (laatste) troef **3** kerel, (rot)vent

jollity uitgelatenheid, joligheid

¹**jolly** (adj) **1** plezierig, prettig **2** [also iron] vrolijk, jolig: *a ~ fellow* een lollige vent **3** [inform; euph] (lichtelijk) aangeschoten, dronken ‖ [inform] *it's a ~ shame* het is een grote schande; *Jolly Roger* piratenvlag

²**jolly** (vb) vleien, bepraten: ~ *along* (or: *up*) zoet houden, bepraten; ~ *s.o. into sth.* iem. tot iets overhalen

³**jolly** (adv) [inform] heel, zeer: *you ~ well will!* en nou en of je het doet!

¹**jolt** (n) schok, ruk, stoot; [fig also] verrassing; ontnuchtering

²**jolt** (vb) (+ along) (voort)schokken, horten, botsen, stoten

³**jolt** (vb) schokken; [fig] verwarren: ~ *s.o. out of a false belief* iem. plotseling tot een beter inzicht brengen

Jordan 1 Jordaan [river] **2** Jordanië

¹**Jordanian** (n) Jordaniër, Jordaanse

²**Jordanian** (adj) Jordaans

josh plagen, voor de gek houden

jostle (ver)dringen, (weg)duwen, (weg)stoten

¹**jot** (n) jota [only fig]: *I don't care a* ~ het kan me geen moer schelen

²**jot** (vb) (+ down) (vlug) noteren, neerpennen, opkrabbelen

jotter blocnote, notitieboekjeʰ

journal 1 dagboekʰ, journaalʰ, kasboekʰ **2** dagbladʰ, krant **3** tijdschriftʰ

journalese journalistieke stijl, krantentaal, sensatiestijl

journalism journalistiek

journalist journalist(e)

journalistic journalistiek: ~*ally speaking* vanuit journalistiek oogpunt

¹**journey** (n) (dag)reis; tocht [over land]

²**journey** (vb) reizen, trekken

journey planner reisplanner

joust aan een steekspel deelnemen; een steekspel houden [also fig]: ~ *with s.o.* met iem. in het krijt treden

Jove Jupiter

jovial joviaal, vrolijk

jowl kaak, kaaksbeenʰ, wang

joy 1 bron van vreugde: *she's a great ~ to her parents* ze is de vreugde van haar ouders **2** vreugde, genotʰ, blijdschap: *be filled with ~* overlopen van vreugde

joyous [form] blij, opgewekt

joypad gamepad

joyride joyride

joystick 1 knuppel; stuurstang [of aeroplane] **2** bedieningspookjeʰ; joystick [of videogames, computer etc]

JP *Justice of the Peace* politierechter

Jr *Junior* jr.

jubilant 1 uitbundig, triomfantelijk: ~ *shout* vreugdekreet; ~ *at* in de wolken over **2** jubelend, juichend

jubilee jubileumʰ: *diamond ~* diamanten jubileum

judder (heftig) vibreren, trillen, schudden

¹**judge** (n) **1** rechter **2** scheidsrechter, arbiter, jurylidʰ; beoordelaar [at competition etc] **3** kenner, expert: *good ~ of character* mensenkenner, iem. met veel mensenkennis

²**judge** (vb) **1** rechtspreken, vonnis vellen **2** arbitreren, als scheidsrechter optreden; [at match] punten toekennen **3** oordelen, een oordeel vellen: *judging by* (or: *from*) *his manner* naar zijn houding te oordelen

³**judge** (vb) **1** rechtspreken over, berechten **2** beoordelen, achten, schatten: ~ *s.o. by his actions* iem. naar zijn daden beoordelen

judg(e)ment 1 oordeelʰ, uitspraak, vonnisʰ, schatting: *sit in judg(e)ment on* rechter spelen over; *in my judg(e)ment* naar mijn mening **2** inzichtʰ: *use one's judg(e)ment* zijn (gezond) verstand gebruiken; *against one's better judg(e)ment* tegen beter weten in

Judg(e)ment Day dag des oordeels; laatste oordeel

judicial gerechtelijk, rechterlijk, rechter(s)-: ~ *branch* rechterlijke macht; ~ *system* gerechtelijk apparaat
judiciary 1 rechtswezen[h] **2** rechterlijke macht
judicious verstandig, voorzichtig
judo judo[h]
¹jug (n) **1** kan(netje[h]) **2** [Am] kruik
²jug (vb) stoven [hare, rabbit]: ~*ged hare* gestoofde haas, hazenpeper
juggernaut grote vrachtwagen, bakbeest[h]
juggle 1 (+ with) jongleren (met) **2** goochelen, toveren **3** (+ with) knoeien (met), frauderen
juggler 1 jongleur **2** goochelaar
Jugoslav see ¹*Yugoslav*
jugular vein halsader: [inform] *go for the* ~ naar de keel vliegen
juice sap[h], levenssap[h] ‖ *let s.o.* **stew** *in their own* ~ iem. in zijn eigen vet gaar laten koken
juicer fruitpers, vruchtenpers
July juli
¹jumble (n) **1** warboel, janboel, troep **2** mengelmoes[h], allegaartje[h]
²jumble (vb) dooreengooien, dooreenhaspelen, samenflansen
jumble sale liefdadigheidsbazaar, rommelmarkt
¹jumbo (n) **1** kolos, reus **2** jumbo(jet)
²jumbo (adj) kolossaal, jumbo-, reuzen-
jumbotron [Am; inform] [roughly] zeer groot videoscherm[h]
¹jump (n) sprong; [fig] (plotselinge/snelle) stijging; schok, ruk: [fig] *stay one* ~ *ahead* één stap vóór blijven
²jump (vb) **1** springen; [bicycle racing] wegspringen; demarreren: ~ *in* naar binnen springen, vlug instappen; [fig] tussenbeide komen; [fig] *he* ~*ed at the offer* hij greep het aanbod met beide handen aan; ~ *on s.o.* iem. te lijf gaan; [fig] uitvaren tegen iem. **2** opspringen, opschrikken, een schok krijgen: *he* ~*ed at the noise* hij schrok op van het lawaai; ~ *to one's feet* opspringen **3** zich haasten, overhaast komen (tot): ~ *to conclusions* overhaaste conclusies trekken
jumper 1 springer **2** pullover, (dames)trui, jumper **3** [Am] overgooier
jumper cable [Am] startkabel
jumping jack hansworst; trekpop [toy]
jump lead startkabel
jump-start 1 starten met startkabels **2** [fig] een duwtje in de rug geven
jump suit overall
jumpy 1 gespannen **2** lichtgeraakt, prikkelbaar
junction verbinding(spunt[h]), kruispunt[h]; knooppunt[h] [of motorways, railways]
juncture tijdsgewricht[h], toestand: *at this* ~ onder de huidige omstandigheden
June juni

jungle 1 jungle, oerwoud[h] **2** warboel, warwinkel, chaos: *a* ~ *of tax laws* een doolhof van belastingwetten
¹junior (n) **1** junior **2** jongere, kleinere: *he's my* ~ *by two years, he's two years my* ~ hij is twee jaar jonger dan ik **3** mindere, ondergeschikte
²junior (adj) **1** jonger, klein(er); junior [after names] **2** lager geplaatst, ondergeschikt, jonger: ~ *clerk* jongste bediende
junior college [Am] universiteit [with only the first two years of the course]
junior high (school) [Am] middenschool, brugschool
juniper jeneverbes(struik)
junk 1 (oude) rommel, rotzooi, schroot[h] **2** jonk
junk food junkfood[h], ongezonde kost, vette hap
junkie junkie, (drugs)verslaafde
junk mail huis-aan-huispost, ongevraagde post, reclamedrukwerk[h]
jurisdiction 1 rechtspraak **2** (rechts)bevoegdheid, jurisdictie, competentie: *have* ~ *of* (or: *over*) bevoegd zijn over
juror jurylid[h]
jury jury
¹just (adj) **1** billijk, rechtvaardig, fair **2** (wel)verdiend: *get* (or: *receive*) *one's* ~ *deserts* zijn verdiende loon krijgen **3** gegrond, gerechtvaardigd
²just (adv) **1** precies, juist, net: ~ *about* zowat, wel zo'n beetje, zo ongeveer; ~ *now* net op dit moment, daarnet **2** amper, ternauwernood, (maar) net: ~ *a little* een tikkeltje (maar) **3** net, zo-even, daarnet: *they've (only)* ~ *arrived* ze zijn er (nog maar) net **4** gewoon, (alleen) maar, (nu) eens, nu eenmaal: *it* ~ *doesn't* **make** *sense* het slaat gewoon nergens op; ~ *wait and see* wacht maar, dan zul je eens zien **5** gewoonweg, in één woord, (toch) even ‖ ~ *the* **same** toch, niettemin
justice 1 rechter: *Justice of the* **Peace** kantonrechter, politierechter; [Belg] vrederechter **2** gerechtigheid, rechtmatigheid, recht[h], rechtvaardigheid, Justitia: *do* ~ *(to)* recht laten wedervaren; *do* ~ *to s.o.*, *do o.s.* ~ zich (weer) waarmaken, aan de verwachtingen voldoen; *to* **do** *him* ~ ere wie ere toekomt **3** gerecht[h], rechtspleging, justitie: *bring s.o. to* ~ iem. voor het gerecht brengen
justifiable 1 gerechtvaardigd, verantwoord, rechtmatig **2** te rechtvaardigen, verdedigbaar
justification 1 rechtvaardiging; verantwoording: *there are few* ~*s* **for** *a war* er zijn weinig redenen die een oorlog rechtvaardigen **2** [printing] het opvullen, uitvullen
justify 1 rechtvaardigen, bevestigen: *we were clearly justified* **in** *sacking him* we hebben

hem terecht ontslagen **2** [esp in passive voi-
ce] in het gelijk stellen, rechtvaardigen, staven: *am I justified in thinking that …* heb ik gelijk als ik denk dat …
jut (also + out) uitsteken, (voor)uitspringen
jute jute
¹**juvenile** (n) jongere, jeugdig persoon
²**juvenile** (adj) jeugdig, kinderlijk: ~ *court*
kinderrechter; ~ *delinquency* jeugdcriminali-
teit
juvenilia jeugdwerk(en)
juxtapose naast elkaar plaatsen

k

K 1 *1000* 1000: *he earns £30K a year* hij verdient £30.000 per jaar **2** *1024 bytes* KB
kale (boeren)kool
kaleidoscope caleidoscoop
kangaroo kangoeroe
kangaroo court onwettige rechtbank
kapok kapok
karaoke karaoke
karting karting[h], gocarting
kayak kajak [of Eskimos]; kano
¹Kazakh (n) Kazach(se)
²Kazakh (adj) Kazachs
Kazakhstan Kazachstan
keel [shipp] kiel
keelhaul 1 kielhalen, kielen **2** op z'n nummer zetten, op z'n donder geven: *Julian was ~ed by his boss* Julian kreeg flink op z'n donder van zijn baas
keen 1 scherp [also fig]; bijtend, fel; hevig [of wind, frost, etc; also of fight]: *we're facing ~ competition from small businesses* we kampen met felle concurrentie van kleine ondernemingen **2** scherp; helder [of senses, intelligence etc]: *~ sight* scherp gezichtsvermogen **3** vurig, enthousiast: *a ~ golfer* een hartstochtelijk golfer; *~ on* gespitst op, gebrand op **4** spotgoedkoop
¹keep (n) **1** (hoofd)toren **2** bolwerk[h], bastion[h] **3** (levens)onderhoud[h], kost, voedsel[h]: *earn your ~* de kost verdienen || *for ~s* voor altijd, voorgoed
²keep (vb) **1** blijven, doorgaan met: *~ left* links houden; *will you please ~ still!* blijf nou toch eens stil zitten!; *how is Richard ~ing?* hoe gaat het met Richard?; *~ abreast of* bijhouden; [fig] op de hoogte blijven van; *~ back* op een afstand blijven; *~ indoors* in huis blijven; *if the rain ~s off* als het droog blijft; *~ off!* (or: *out!*) verboden toegang!; *~ off* uit de buurt blijven van, vermijden; *~ out of* a) zich niet bemoeien met; b) niet betreden; c) zich niet blootstellen aan **2** goed blijven; vers blijven [of food]: [fig] *your news will have to ~ a bit* dat nieuwtje van jou moet maar even wachten
³keep (vb) **1** houden, zich houden aan, bewaren: *~ a promise* een belofte nakomen; *~ a secret* een geheim bewaren **2** houden, onderhouden, eropna houden, (in dienst) hebben: *~ chickens* kippen houden **3** (in bezit) hebben, bewaren, in voorraad hebben, verkopen: *~ the change* laat maar zitten **4** houden, ophouden, vasthouden, tegenhouden:

~ within bounds binnen de perken houden; *~ it clean* houd het netjes; *~ sth. going* iets aan de gang houden; *~ s.o. waiting* iem. laten wachten; *what kept you (so long)?* wat heeft je zo (lang) opgehouden?, waar bleef je (nou)?; *~ back* a) tegenhouden, op een afstand houden; b) achterhouden, geheimhouden; *~ down* a) binnenhouden [food]; b) omlaaghouden, laag houden; c) onder de duim houden; d) onderdrukken, inhouden [rage]; *~ one's weight down* z'n gewicht binnen de perken houden; *~ your head down!* bukken!; *~ off* op een afstand houden; *~ s.o. out* iem. buitensluiten; *he tried to ~ the bad news from his father* hij probeerde het slechte nieuws voor z'n vader verborgen te houden; *he couldn't ~ his eyes off the girl* hij kon z'n ogen niet van het meisje afhouden; *~ your hands off me!* blijf met je poten van me af!; *~ them out of harm's way* zorg dat ze geen gevaar lopen; *he kept it to himself* hij hield het voor zich **5** bijhouden [book, diary etc]; houden: *Mary used to ~ (the) accounts* Mary hield de boeken bij **6** houden, aanhouden, blijven in: *~ your seat!* blijf (toch) zitten!
keep at door blijven gaan met: *~ it!* ga zo door!
keeper 1 bewaarder **2** keeper, doelverdediger; [cricket] wicketkeeper
¹keep in (vb) binnen blijven
²keep in (vb) na laten blijven
keeping 1 bewaring, hoede: *in safe ~* in veilige bewaring **2** overeenstemming, harmonie: *in ~ with* in overeenstemming met
keep in with (proberen) op goede voet (te) blijven met: *now that she's old she wishes she had kept in with her children* nu ze oud is, wilde ze dat ze op goede voet was gebleven met haar kinderen
¹keep on (vb) **1** volhouden, doorgaan: *he keeps on telling me these awful jokes* hij blijft me maar van die vreselijke grappen vertellen **2** doorgaan, doorrijden, doorlopen, verder gaan **3** blijven praten, doorkletsen
²keep on (vb) **1** aanhouden, ophouden; blijven dragen [clothing, hat]: *please ~ your safety helmet throughout the tour* houd u alstublieft tijdens de rondleiding uw veiligheidshelm op **2** aanlaten [light]
keepsake aandenken[h], souvenir[h]: *for a ~* als aandenken
keep to 1 blijven bij, (zich) beperken tot, (zich) houden (aan): *~ the point* bij het onderwerp blijven; *she always keeps (herself) to herself* ze is erg op zichzelf **2** houden, rijden: *~ the left* links houden
¹keep up (vb) **1** overeind blijven, blijven staan **2** hoog blijven [of price, standard; also fig] **3** (in dezelfde/goede staat) blijven, aanhouden: *I do hope that the weather keeps up* ik hoop wel dat het weer mooi blijft **4** op-

blijven **5** bijblijven, bijhouden: ~ **with** *one's neighbours* niet bij de buren achterblijven; ~ **with** *the Joneses* z'n stand ophouden; ~ **with** *the times* bij de tijd blijven

²**keep up** (vb) **1** omhooghouden, ophouden **2** hooghouden: ~ *the* **costs** de kosten hoog houden; *keep* **morale** *up* het moreel hooghouden **3** doorgaan met, handhaven, volhouden: ~ *the* **conversation** de conversatie gaande houden; ~ *the good* **work!** ga zo door!

keg vaatje^h: ~ **beer** bier van het vat

kelp kelp; zeewier^h

ken kennis, bevattingsvermogen^h, begrip^h: *that is* **beyond** (or: **outside**) *my* ~ dat gaat boven mijn pet

kennel 1 hondenhok^h **2** kennel, hondenfokkerij

Kenya Kenia

¹**Kenyan** (n) Keniaan(se)

²**Kenyan** (adj) Keniaans

kerb stoeprand, trottoirband

kerchief [dated] hoofddoek^h; halsdoek^h

kerfuffle opschudding

kernel 1 pit, korrel **2** kern, essentie

kerosene kerosine, (lampen)petroleum^h, lampolie, paraffineolie

kestrel torenvalk

kettle ketel: *put the* ~ *on* theewater opzetten

kettledrum keteltrom(mel), pauk

¹**key** (n) **1** sleutel; [fig] toegang; oplossing, verklaring: ~ *to the* **mystery** sleutel van het raadsel **2** toon; [mus] toonaard, toonsoort; tonaliteit, stijl: *out of* ~, *off* ~ vals **3** toets [of piano, typewriter etc]; klep [of wind instrument]

²**key** (adj) sleutel-, hoofd-, voornaamste: ~ **figure** sleutelfiguur; ~ **question** hamvraag; ~ **witness** hoofdgetuige, voornaamste getuige

³**key** (vb) (+ in) invoeren [by means of keyboard]; intikken

keyboard 1 toetsenbord^h **2** klavier^h **3** klavierinstrument^h, toetsinstrument^h; keyboard^h

key card sleutelkaart

keyhole sleutelgat^h || ~ **surgery** kijkoperatie

keyhole surgery kijkoperatie

keynote 1 grondtoon, hoofdtoon **2** hoofdgedachte, grondgedachte

keynote address thematoespraak; programmaverklaring

keypad (druk)toetsenpaneel(tje)^h [of remote control unit, pocket calculator etc]

key signature voortekening

keystone 1 sluitsteen [of arch] **2** hoeksteen, fundament^h

key up opwinden, gespannen maken: *the boy* **looked** *keyed up* de jongen zag er gespannen uit

kg *kilogram(s)* kg

khaki kaki(kleur), kakistof

kibbutz kibboets

¹**kick** (n) **1** schop, trap **2** terugslag [of gun] **3** kick, stimulans, impuls: *do sth.* **for** ~*s* iets voor de lol doen **4** kracht, fut, energie || *a* ~ *in the* **pants** een schop onder zijn kont [fig]; *a* ~ *in the* **teeth** een slag in het gezicht [fig]

²**kick** (vb) **1** schoppen, trappen: [socc] ~ *off* aftrappen **2** terugslag hebben [of gun] **3** er tegenaan schoppen, protesteren: ~ **against** (or: *at*) protesteren tegen || ~ *off* sterven

³**kick** (vb) **1** schoppen, trappen, wegtrappen: ~ *o.s.* zich voor zijn kop slaan; ~ *out* eruit schoppen, ontslaan **2** stoppen met [addiction etc] || ~ *a* **person** *when he is down* iem. nog verder de grond in trappen; ~ **upstairs** wegpromoveren

¹**kick around** (vb) **1** rondslingeren: *his old bicycle has been kicking around in the garden for weeks now* zijn oude fiets slingert al weken rond in de tuin **2** in leven zijn, bestaan, rondhollen

²**kick around** (vb) **1** sollen met, grof behandelen **2** commanderen, bazen

kickback smeergeld^h

kick back relaxen, ontspannen

kick in in werking treden, beginnen (te werken); (plotseling) beginnen mee te spelen [eg of fear]: *but when she saw the rhino at close range,* **fear** *kicked in* maar toen ze de neushoorn van dichtbij zag, werd ze ineens bang

kick-off 1 [socc] aftrap **2** begin^h

kick-start 1 snel op gang brengen, een impuls geven aan **2** aantrappen; starten [engine]

kickstart(er) trapstarter

¹**kid** (n) **1** jong geitje^h, bokje^h **2** kind^h, joch^h **3** geitenleer^h

²**kid** (adj) **1** jonger: ~ **brother** (or: **sister**) jonger broertje (or: zusje) **2** van geitenleer, glacé: *handle* (or: *treat*) *(s.o.) with* ~ **gloves** (iem.) met fluwelen handschoentjes aanpakken

³**kid** (vb) plagen, in de maling nemen: *no* ~*ding?* meen je dat?; *no* ~*ding!* echt waar!

kiddie jong^h, joch^h, knul

kiddo [Am; inform] jochie^h

kidnap ontvoeren, kidnappen

kidney nier

kidult kidult

¹**kill** (n) buit, vangst, (gedode) prooi || *be in at the* ~ erbij zijn als de vos gedood wordt; [fig] er (op het beslissende moment) bij zijn

²**kill** (vb) **1** [also fig] doden, moorden, ombrengen: *my* **feet** *are* ~*ing me* ik verga van de pijn in mijn voeten; ~ *o.s.* **laughing** (or: *with laughter*) zich een ongeluk lachen; ~ *off* afmaken, uit de weg ruimen, uitroeien; *be* ~*ed* om het leven komen **2** [socc] doodmaken, doodleggen, stoppen || *dressed to* ~ piek-

fijn uitzien
killer moordenaar
killer whale orka
¹killing (n) **1** moord, doodslag **2** groot (financieel) succesʰ: *make a ~ zijn slag slaan,* groot succes hebben
²killing (adj) **1** dodelijk, fataal **2** slopend, uitputtend
killjoy spelbreker
kiln (steen)oven
kilo 1 kilo(gram) **2** kilometer
kilobyte kilobyte
kilogramme kilogram
kilometre kilometer
kilowatt kilowatt
kilt kilt
kin familie, verwanten: *kith and ~* vrienden en verwanten; *next of ~* naaste verwanten
¹kind (n) **1** soort, typeʰ, aard: *nothing of the ~* niets van dien aard, geen sprake van; *three of a ~* drie gelijke(n), drie dezelfde(n); *a ~ of* een soort; *all ~s of* allerlei; *I haven't got that ~ of money* zulke bedragen heb ik niet **2** wijze, manier van doen **3** wezenʰ, karakterʰ, soort || *pay in ~* in natura betalen; [fig] met gelijke munt terugbetalen
²kind (adj) vriendelijk, aardig: *with ~ regards* met vriendelijke groeten; *would you be ~ enough to* (or: *so ~ as to*) *open the window* zou u zo vriendelijk willen zijn het raam open te doen
kinda [inform] wel; best, nogal: *he's ~ cute* hij is wel leuk; *I was ~ scared* ik was een beetje bang
kindergarten kleuterschool
¹kindle (vb) ontbranden, (op)vlammen, vlam vatten: *such dry wood ~s easily* zo'n droog hout vat gemakkelijk vlam
²kindle (vb) **1** ontsteken **2** opwekken, doen stralen, gloeien: *I don't know what ~d their hatred of him* ik weet niet waardoor ze hem zijn gaan haten
kindling aanmaakhoutʰ
¹kindly (adj) vriendelijk, (goed)aardig: *in a ~ fashion* vriendelijk
²kindly (adv) alstublieft: *~ move your car* zet u a.u.b. uw auto ergens anders neer || *he did not take ~ to all those rules* hij kon niet zo goed tegen al die regels
kindness 1 vriendelijke daad, iets aardigs, gunst **2** vriendelijkheid: *out of ~* uit goedheid
¹kindred (n) **1** verwantschap **2** verwanten, familie(leden)
²kindred (adj) verwant: *a ~ spirit* een verwante geest
king koning; [card game also] heer
kingcup boterbloem
kingdom koninkrijkʰ, rijkʰ, domeinʰ
kingfisher ijsvogel
kingpin 1 [bowling] koning **2** spil [fig]; lei-

dende figuur
King's English standaard Engels, BBC-Engels
king-size(d) extra lang, extra groot
kink 1 kink; knik [in wire etc] **2** kronkel, eigenaardigheid
kinky 1 pervers **2** sexy; opwindend [of clothes]
kinship verwantschap; [also fig] overeenkomst; verbondenheid: *she felt a deep ~ with the other students in her group* ze voelde een diepe verbondenheid met de andere studenten in haar groep
kinsman (bloed)verwant
kiosk 1 kiosk, stalletjeʰ **2** reclamezuil **3** telefooncel
¹kip (n) **1** slaapplaats, bedʰ **2** dutjeʰ, slaap(-jeʰ)
²kip (vb) (also + down) (gaan) pitten, (gaan) slapen
kipper gerookte haring
¹Kirghiz (n) Kirgies, Kirgizische
²Kirghiz (adj) Kirgizisch
Kirghizistan Kirgizië
¹kiss (n) kus(jeʰ), zoen(tjeʰ): *blow a ~* een kushandje geven, een kus toewerpen || *~ of life* mond-op-mondbeademing
²kiss (vb) **1** kussen, elkaar kussen, (elkaar) zoenen: *~ and be friends* het afzoenen, het weer goedmaken **2** (even/licht) raken; [billiards] klotsen (tegen); een klos maken
kisser snoet, waffel: *he smacked the thief in the ~* hij gaf de dief een klap voor zijn kanis
the **kissing disease** knuffelziekte, ziekte van Pfeiffer
kit 1 (gereedschaps)kist, doos, (plunje)zak **2** bouwdoos, bouwpakketʰ **3** uitrusting, spullen: *did you remember to bring your squash ~?* heb je eraan gedacht je squashspullen mee te brengen?
kitbag plunjezak
kitchen keuken
kitchen garden moestuin, groentetuin
kitchen sink aanrechtʰ
kite 1 vlieger: *fly a ~* vliegeren, een vlieger oplaten; [fig] een balletje opgooien **2** wouw || *go fly a ~* maak dat je weg komt
kitten katjeʰ, poesjeʰ || *have ~s* de zenuwen hebben, op tilt slaan
kitty 1 katjeʰ, poesjeʰ **2** pot; inzet [in card game]; kas
kiwi 1 kiwi(vrucht) **2** Nieuw-Zeelander
klaxon claxon
kleptomaniac kleptomaan
km kilometre(s) km
knack 1 vaardigheid, handigheid, slag: *get the ~ of sth.* de slag te pakken krijgen van iets **2** truc, handigheidjeʰ: *there's a ~ in it* je moet de truc even doorhebben
knacker sloper
knackered bekaf, doodop

knapsack knapzak, plunjezak
knave 1 [cards] boer **2** schurk
knead 1 (dooreen)kneden: *make sure you ~ the dough properly* zorg ervoor dat je het deeg goed kneedt **2** kneden; masseren [eg muscle]
knee 1 knie: *bring s.o. to his ~s* iem. op de knieën krijgen **2** kniestuk[h] ‖ *his ~s were knocking together* hij stond te trillen op zijn benen
kneecap 1 knieschijf **2** kniebeschermer
¹knee-deep (adj) kniehoog, kniediep
²knee-deep (adj) diep [fig]: *be ~ in debt* tot over de oren in de schulden zitten
knee-jerk [inform] automatisch: *a ~ reaction* een voorspelbare reactie
kneel (also + down) knielen, geknield zitten
knees-up knalfuif, feest[h]
knell doodsklok [also fig]
knickers slipje[h]; onderbroek [of woman]
knick-knack prul(letje[h]), snuisterij
¹knife (n) mes[h] ‖ *turn* (or: *twist*) *the ~* nog een trap nagaven
²knife (vb) (door)steken, aan het mes rijgen
knight 1 ridder: *~ errant* dolende ridder; ridderlijk persoon **2** [chess] paard[h]
knighthood ridderorde: *confer a ~ on s.o.* iem. tot ridder slaan
¹knit (vb) één worden, vergroeien: *the broken bones ~ readily* de gebroken botten groeien weer snel aan elkaar
²knit (vb) **1** breien **2** fronsen, samentrekken **3** verweven, verbinden: *(their interests are) closely ~* (hun belangen zijn) nauw verweven
knitting breiwerk[h]
knob 1 knop, hendel, handvat[h], schakelaar **2** knobbel, bult: *the ~ on her leg was quite visible* de bult op haar been was goed te zien **3** brok(je[h]), klontje[h]
knobbly knobbelig
knobby knobbelig
¹knock (n) **1** slag, klap, klop, tik **2** oplazer: *take a lot of ~s* heel wat te verduren krijgen
²knock (vb) **1** (hard) slaan, meppen, stoten (tegen): *~ a hole* (or: *nail*) *in* een gat (or: spijker) slaan in **2** (af)kraken **3** met stomheid slaan, versteld doen staan
³knock (vb) kloppen, tikken: *~ at* (or: *on*) *a door* op een deur kloppen ‖ *~ against sth.* tegen iets (op) botsen; *~ into s.o.* iem. tegen het lijf lopen
knockabout 1 gooi-en-smijt- [of films] **2** rouwdouw
knock about 1 rondhangen, lanterfanten **2** (rond)slingeren **3** rondzwerven, rondscharrelen, van de hand in de tand leven: *~ with* optrekken met, scharrelen (or: rotzooien) met

3 teleurstellen **4** versteld doen staan
knockdown 1 verpletterend, vernietigend **2** afbraak-, spotgoedkoop
knock down 1 neerhalen, tegen de grond slaan; [fig] vloeren **2** slopen, tegen de grond gooien **3** aanrijden, omverrijden, overrijden **4** naar beneden krijgen, afdingen, afpingelen: *knock s.o. down a pound* een pond bij iem. afdingen **5** verkopen [at auction]: *the chair was knocked down at three pounds* de stoel ging weg voor drie pond
knocker 1 deurklopper **2** [inform] negatieveling **3** (-s) [inform] tiet
knock-kneed met X-benen
knock off 1 (af)nokken (met), kappen; stoppen [work] **2** goedkoper geven, korting geven **3** in elkaar draaien **4** afmaken, nog doen **5** [inform] jatten, beroven
knock-on domino(-effect)
knockout 1 [boxing] knock-out **2** [sport] eliminatietoernooi[h]; [roughly] voorronde **3** spetter, juweel[h]: *you look a ~* je ziet eruit om te stelen
knock out 1 vloeren, knock-out slaan **2** verdoven; bedwelmen [of drug] **3** [sport] uitschakelen, elimineren **4** in elkaar flansen: *we knocked out a programme for the festivities* we flansten snel een programma voor de festiviteiten in elkaar
knock over 1 omgooien, neervellen, aanrijden, overrijden, omverrijden **2** versteld doen staan **3** overvallen, beroven
knock together in elkaar flansen, (slordig/haastig) in elkaar zetten
¹knock up (vb) [tennis] inslaan
²knock up (vb) **1** afbeulen, slopen **2** bij elkaar verdienen [money] **3** zwanger maken
¹knot (n) **1** knoop; strik [as decoration] **2** knoop [fig]; moeilijkheid **3** kwast, knoest, noest **4** kluitje mensen **5** band, verbinding, huwelijksband **6** knoop, zeemijl per uur, zeemijl ‖ *get tied (up) into ~s (over)* van de kook raken door, de kluts kwijtraken (van/over)
²knot (vb) **1** (vast)knopen, (vast)binden, een knoop leggen in **2** dichtknopen, dichtbinden
knotty 1 vol knopen, in de knoop (geraakt) **2** kwastig; knoestig [of wood] **3** ingewikkeld, lastig
¹know (n) *in the ~* ingewijd, (goed) op de hoogte
²know (vb) **1** weten, kennis hebben (van), beseffen: *if you ~ what I mean* als je begrijpt wat ik bedoel; *for all I ~ he may be in China* misschien zit hij in China, wie weet; *you ~* weet je (wel), je weet wel; *not that I ~ of* niet dat ik weet **2** kennen, bekend zijn met: *~ one's way* de weg weten **3** herkennen, (kunnen) thuisbrengen: *I knew Jane by her walk* ik herkende Jane aan haar manier van lopen ‖ *don't I ~ it* moet je mij vertellen; *~ backwards*

(and forwards) kennen als zijn broekzak, kunnen dromen; ~ *better* than to do sth. (wel) zo verstandig zijn iets te laten
know-how handigheid, praktische vaardigheid, technische kennis
knowing 1 veelbetekenend: ~ *glance* (or: *look*) blik van verstandhouding **2** bewust: *~ly hurt* s.o. iem. bewust pijn doen
know-it-all wijsneus; betweter
knowledge kennis, wetenschap, informatie, geleerdheid: *to the **best*** of one's ~ *(and belief)* naar (zijn) beste weten; *without* s.o.'s ~ buiten iemands (mede)weten; *be **common*** ~ algemeen bekend zijn
knowledgeable goed geïnformeerd, goed op de hoogte: *be ~ **about*** verstand hebben van
known 1 bekend, algemeen beschouwd, erkend **2** gegeven, bekend || *make **o.s.*** ~ *to* zich voorstellen aan
knuckle knokkel || *rap* on (or: *over*) *the ~s* op de vingers tikken; *near the* ~ op het randje [of joke]
knuckle down (+ to) zich serieus wijden (aan) [job, chore]; aanpakken, aanvatten: *it's high time you knuckled down to some hard study* het wordt hoog tijd dat je eens flink gaat studeren
knuckle under (+ to) buigen (voor), zwichten (voor)
KO [inform] *knockout* ko
koala koala(beer)
kooky verknipt, geschift
the **Koran** Koran
kosher koosjer, jofel, in orde
kowtow (+ to) door het stof gaan (voor), zich vernederen
kph *kilometres per hour* km/u, kilometer per uur
Kurd Koerd
Kurdish Koerdisch
Kuwait Koeweit
¹**Kuwaiti** (n) Koeweiter, Koeweitse
²**Kuwaiti** (adj) Koeweits
kW *kilowatt(s)* kW
¹**Kyrgyz** (n) Kirgies, Kirgizische
²**Kyrgyz** (adj) Kirgizisch
Kyrgyzstan Kirgizië

l

l 1 *left* links **2** *litre(s)* l, liter(s)
L *learner driver* leerling-automobilist
LA *Los Angeles*
lab [inform] *laboratory* lab^h; laboratorium^h
¹label (n) **1** etiket^h, label^h **2** label^h [of CD]; platenmaatschappij **3** etiket^h
²label (vb) **1** etiketteren, labelen, merken **2** een etiket opplakken, bestempelen als
laboratory laboratorium^h, proefruimte
laborious 1 afmattend, bewerkelijk **2** moeizaam
¹labour (n) **1** arbeid; werk^h [in employment] **2** (krachts)inspanning, moeite **3** arbeidersklasse, arbeidskrachten **4** (barens)weeën **5** bevalling: *be in* ~ bevallen
²labour (vb) **1** arbeiden, werken **2** zich inspannen, ploeteren: ~ *at* (or: *over*) sth. op iets zwoegen **3** moeizaam vooruitkomen, zich voortslepen
laboured 1 moeizaam **2** gekunsteld
labourer (hand)arbeider, ongeschoolde arbeider: *agricultural* ~ landarbeider
labour force beroepsbevolking
labour market arbeidsmarkt
labour under te kampen hebben met, last hebben van: ~ *the delusion* (or: *illusion*) *that* in de waan verkeren dat
labyrinth doolhof; labyrint^h [also fig]
¹lace (n) **1** veter, koord^h **2** kant(werk^h)
²lace (vb) **1** rijgen, dichtmaken met veter **2** (door)vlechten, (door)weven **3** een scheutje sterkedrank toevoegen aan: ~ *tea with* rum een scheutje rum in de thee doen
lacerate (ver)scheuren
¹lack (n) **1** gebrek^h, tekort^h: *die for* (or: *through*) ~ *of food* sterven door voedselgebrek **2** behoefte
²lack (vb) **1** missen, niet hebben: *he simply ~s courage* het ontbreekt hem gewoon aan moed **2** gebrek hebben aan, te kort komen
lackadaisical lusteloos; futloos
lackey 1 lakei, livreiknecht **2** kruiper
lacking afwezig, ontbrekend: *be* ~ *in* gebrek hebben aan
lacklustre dof, glansloos; mat [of eyes]
laconic kort en krachtig, laconiek
lacquer 1 lak **2** (blanke) lak, vernis^h **3** (haar)lak
lactation 1 het zogen, melkvoeding **2** lactatie(periode), zoogperiode
lad jongen, knul, jongeman ‖ *be one of the ~s* erbij horen
ladder 1 ladder [also fig]; trap(leer), touw-

ladder **2** ladder [in stocking] **3** [sport] ladder, ranglijst
laden zwaar beladen; vol: [fig] ~ *with anxieties* onder zorgen gebukt
Ladies(') dames(toilet^h)
¹ladle (n) soeplepel
²ladle (vb) **1** opscheppen, oplepelen: ~ *out soup* soep opscheppen **2** (+ out) rondstrooien, smijten met
lady 1 dame: *ladies and gentlemen* dames en heren; [Am] *First Lady* presidentsvrouw **2** lady ‖ ~ *doctor* vrouwelijke arts
ladybird lieveheersbeestje^h
ladybug [Am] lieveheersbeestje^h
lady-in-waiting hofdame
ladykiller vrouwenjager, (ras)versierder
ladylike 1 ladylike, zoals een dame past, beschaafd **2** elegant
ladyship lady: *her, your* ~ mevrouw de barones, gravin enz.
¹lag (vb) (+ behind) achterblijven, achteraan komen
²lag (vb) bekleden, betimmeren; isoleren [pipes etc]
lager (blond) bier^h; [fig] pils^h
laggard treuzelaar, laatkomer, slome duikelaar^h
lagging bekleding(smateriaal^h), isolatie(-materiaal^h), het bekleden
lagoon lagune
la(h)-di-da(h) bekakt
laid-back relaxed, ontspannen
lair 1 hol^h; leger^h [of wild animal] **2** hol^h [fig]; schuilplaats
laity 1 leken(dom^h), de leken **2** leken(publiek^h), de leken
lake meer^h, vijver
lamb 1 lam(metje)^h, lamsvlees^h **2** lammetje^h, lief kind^h, schatje^h
lame 1 mank, kreupel **2** onbevredigend, nietszeggend: ~ *excuse* zwak excuus ‖ ~ *duck* slappeling, zielige (or: behoeftige) figuur
¹lament (n) **1** jammerklacht **2** klaaglied^h
²lament (vb) **1** (+ over) klagen (over), jammeren (over) **2** treuren: ~ *for* a *brother* treuren om een broer
³lament (vb) (diep) betreuren, treuren om, bewenen
lamentable 1 betreurenswaardig, beklagenswaard(ig) **2** erbarmelijk (slecht), bedroevend (slecht)
lamentation 1 geweeklaag^h; jammerklacht **2** leed^h
laminate 1 in dunne lagen splijten **2** lamineren, tot dunne platen pletten, bedekken met (metalen) platen: ~d *wood* triplex, multiplex
lamp lamp
¹lampoon (n) satire, schotschrift^h
²lampoon (vb) hekelen
lamp-post lantaarnpaal

lampshade lampenkap

lance lans, spies, speer

lancet lancet[h] [surgical knife]

¹land (n) **1** (vaste)land[h] **2** landstreek, staat, gebied[h]: *native* ~ vaderland **3** bouwland[h], aarde, grond, grondgebied[h], lap grond, weiland[h] || *the promised* ~ het beloofde land

²land (vb) **1** landen, aan land gaan **2** (be)-landen, neerkomen, terechtkomen: ~ *in a mess* in de knoei raken || [inform] *I ~ed up in Rome* uiteindelijk belandde ik in Rome

³land (vb) **1** aan wal zetten **2** doen landen; aan de grond zetten [aeroplane] **3** doen belanden, brengen: ~ *s.o. in a mess* iem. in de knoei brengen **4** vangen; binnenhalen, binnenbrengen [fish] **5** in de wacht slepen, bemachtigen

land agent 1 rentmeester **2** onroerend-goedhandelaar

landed 1 land-, grond-, uit land bestaand: ~ *property* grondbezit **2** land bezittend: ~ *gentry* (or: *nobility*) landadel

land forces landstrijdkrachten, landmacht

landing 1 landingsplaats, steiger, aanlegplaats **2** landing [of aeroplane]; het aan wal gaan; aankomst [of ship] **3** overloop, (trap)-portaal[h]

landing craft landingsvaartuig[h], landingsschip[h]

landing gear landingsgestel[h], onderstel[h]

landing net schepnet[h]

landing stage (aanleg)steiger, aanlegplaats, losplaats

landlady 1 hospita, pensionhoudster, waardin **2** huisbazin, vrouw van de huisbaas

landlord 1 landheer **2** huisbaas, pensionhouder, waard

landmark 1 grenspaal **2** oriëntatiepunt[h] [also fig]; markering, baken[h] **3** mijlpaal, keerpunt[h]

landowner landeigenaar; grondbezitter

landscape landschap[h], panorama[h]

landslide aardverschuiving [also fig]: *win by a* ~ een verpletterende overwinning behalen

lane 1 (land)weggetje[h], laantje[h], paadje[h] **2** (voorgeschreven) vaarweg, vaargeul **3** luchtcorridor, luchtweg, (aan)vliegroute **4** [traf] rijstrook **5** [sport] baan

language 1 taal: *foreign* ~s vreemde talen **2** taalgebruik[h], woordgebruik[h], stijl **3** (groeps)taal, vaktaal, jargon[h] **4** communicatiesysteem[h], gebarentaal, (programmeer)-taal, computertaal **5** taalbeheersing, spraak(vermogen[h])

language acquisition taalverwerving

languid lusteloos, (s)loom, slap

languish (weg)kwijnen, verslappen, verzwakken

languor 1 apathie, lusteloosheid, matheid **2** lome stilte, zwoelheid, drukkendheid

languorous 1 loom; lusteloos **2** zwoel

lank 1 schraal, (brood)mager, dun **2** krachteloos, slap; sluik [of hair] **3** lang en buigzaam [eg of hair]

lanky slungelachtig

lantern lantaarn

Laos Laos

¹Laotian (n) Laotiaan(se)

²Laotian (adj) Laotiaans

¹lap (n) **1** schoot [also of article of clothing] **2** overlap(ping), overlappend deel[h], overslag **3** [sport] baan, ronde **4** etappe [of trip]

²lap (vb) (+ against) kabbelen (tegen), klotsen (tegen)

³lap (vb) likken, oplikken: ~ *up* oplikken, opslorpen; [fig] verslinden

¹lapse (n) **1** kleine vergissing, fout(je[h]) **2** misstap **3** (tijds)verloop[h], verstrijken van tijd **4** periode, tijd(je[h]); poos(je[h]) [in past]

²lapse (vb) **1** (gaandeweg) verdwijnen, achteruitgaan, afnemen: *my anger had soon ~d* mijn boosheid was weldra weggeëbd **2** vervallen, terugvallen, afglijden: ~ *into silence* in stilzwijgen verzinken **3** verstrijken, verlopen

lapsed 1 afvallig, ontrouw **2** [law] verlopen, vervallen

laptop (computer) schootcomputer, laptop

lapwing kievit

larceny diefstal

¹lard (n) varkensvet[h], (varkens)reuzel

²lard (vb) larderen [also fig]; doorspekken, doorrijgen met spek

larder provisiekamer, provisiekast

large 1 groot, omvangrijk, ruim **2** veelomvattend, ver(re)gaand **3** onbevangen, gedurfd **4** edelmoedig, vrijgevig || *as* ~ *as life* a) in levenden lijve, hoogstpersoonlijk; b) onmiskenbaar; ~*r than life* overdreven, buiten proporties; *the murderer is still at* ~ de moordenaar is nog steeds op vrije voeten

largely grotendeels, hoofdzakelijk, voornamelijk

lark 1 grap: *for a* ~ voor de gein **2** leeuwerik

larva larve, larf

larynx strottenhoofd[h]

lascivious wellustig, geil

laser laser: ~ *beams* laserstralen

¹lash (n) **1** zweepkoord[h], zweepeinde[h] **2** zweepslag **3** wimper

²lash (vb) **1** opzwepen, ophitsen: ~ *s.o. into a fury* iem. woedend maken **2** vastsnoeren, (stevig) vastbinden; [shipp] sjorren

³lash (vb) **1** een plotselinge beweging maken (met), slaan; zwiepen [eg of tail] **2** met kracht slaan (tegen), geselen, teisteren; striemen [of rain]; beuken [of waves]

lash out 1 (+ at) (heftig) slaan, schoppen (naar), uithalen (naar), een uitval doen (naar) **2** (+ at, against) uitvallen (tegen) **3** met geld smijten

lass meisje[h]
lassie meisje[h]
lassitude vermoeidheid, uitputting
¹lasso (n) lasso, werpkoord[h]
²lasso (vb) met een lasso vangen
¹last (n) (schoenmakers)leest ‖ *stick* to one's ~ zich bij zijn leest houden
²last (vb) **1** duren, aanhouden **2** meegaan, intact blijven, houdbaar zijn: *his irritation won't* ~ zijn ergernis gaat wel over; ~ *out* **a)** niet opraken; **b)** het volhouden **3** toereikend zijn
³last (vb) toereikend zijn voor, voldoende zijn voor
⁴last (adv) **1** als laatste; [in compounds] laatst-: *come in* ~ als laatste binnenkomen; *last-mentioned* laatstgenoemde; ~ *but not least* (als) laatstgenoemde, maar daarom niet minder belangrijk **2** (voor) het laatst, (voor) de laatste keer: *when did you see her* ~? (or: ~ *see her?*) wanneer heb je haar voor het laatst gezien?
⁵last (num) laatste [of a series]; laatstgenoemde: *breathe one's* ~ zijn laatste adem uitblazen; *fight to* (or: *till*) *the* ~ vechten tot het uiterste; *I don't think we have seen the* ~ *of him* ik denk dat we nog wel terugzien ‖ *at (long)* ~ (uit)eindelijk, ten slotte
⁶last (num) laatste [also fig]; vorige, verleden: *at the* ~ *minute* (or: *moment*) op het laatste ogenblik; ~ *night* gister(en)avond, vannacht; ~ *Tuesday* vorige week dinsdag; *the* ~ *but one* de voorlaatste; *the* ~ *few days* de laatste paar dagen ‖ *that's the* ~ *straw* dat doet de deur dicht; *the* ~ *word in cars* het nieuwste snufje op het gebied van auto's; *down to every* ~ *detail* tot in de kleinste details
last-ditch: ~ *effort* (or: *attempt*) laatste wanhopige poging
lasting blijvend, aanhoudend, duurzaam: *a* ~ *solution* een definitieve oplossing
lastly ten slotte, in de laatste plaats, tot slot
last-minute allerlaatst, uiterst
latch klink [of door, gate]: *on the* ~ op de klink [not locked]
latchkey huissleutel
latchkey child sleutelkind[h]
latch on to 1 snappen, (kunnen) volgen **2** hangen aan, zich vastklampen aan
¹late (adj) **1** te laat, verlaat, vertraagd: *five minutes* ~ vijf minuten te laat **2** laat, gevorderd: *in the* ~ *afternoon* laat in de middag; *at a* ~ *hour* laat (op de dag), diep in de nacht; *at the* ~*st* uiterlijk, op zijn laatst **3** recent, van de laatste tijd, nieuw: *her* ~*st album* haar nieuwste album **4** voormalig, vorig **5** (onlangs) overleden, wijlen: *his* ~ *wife* zijn (onlangs) overleden vrouw
²late (adv) **1** te laat, verlaat, vertraagd: *better* ~ *than never* beter laat dan nooit **2** laat,

op een laat tijdstip, gevorderd: ~ *in (one's) life* op gevorderde leeftijd; ~*r on* **a)** later, naderhand; **b)** verderop ‖ *of* ~ onlangs, kort geleden
lately onlangs, kort geleden: *have you been there* ~? ben jij er/daar de laatste tijd nog geweest?
late-night laat(st), nacht-: ~ *shopping* koopavond
latent latent; verborgen, sluimerend
lateral zij-, aan, vanaf, naar de zijkant
lath **1** tengel(lat), latwerk[h] **2** lat
lather (zeep)schuim[h], scheerschuim[h]
¹Latin (n) Latijn [language]
²Latin (n) Romaan, iem. die een Romaanse taal spreekt
³Latin (adj) Latijns: ~ *America* Latijns-Amerika
Latin-American Latijns-Amerikaans
latitude 1 hemelstreek, luchtstreek, zone **2** (geografische) breedte, poolshoogte **3** speelruimte, (geestelijke) vrijheid
latrine latrine, wc (van kamp/kazerne)
latte koffie verkeerd
latter 1 laatstgenoemde [of two] **2** laatst-(genoemd) [of two]: *the* ~ *part of the year* het tweede halfjaar; *in his* ~ *years* in zijn laatste jaren
lattice raster(werk)[h], vak-, raam-, traliewerk[h], rooster[h]: ~ *window* glas-in-loodraam
Latvia Letland
¹Latvian (n) Let(lander); Letlandse
²Latvian (adj) Lets, Letlands
laudable prijzenswaardig
¹laugh (n) **1** lach, gelach[h], lachje[h] **2** geintje[h], lolletje[h], lachertje[h]: *for* ~*s* voor de lol ‖ *have the last* ~ het laatst lachen
²laugh (vb) **1** lachen: ~ *to o.s.* inwendig lachen **2** in de lach schieten, moeten lachen
³laugh (vb) **1** lachend zeggen **2** belachelijk maken, uitlachen, weglachen: ~ *off* met een grapje afdoen
laughable lachwekkend, belachelijk
laugh at 1 uitlachen, belachelijk maken **2** lachen om **3** maling hebben aan
laughing 1 lachend, vrolijk, opgewekt **2** om te lachen: *no* ~ *matter* een serieuze zaak, geen gekheid
laughing stock mikpunt[h] (van spot) [also of things]
laughter 1 gelach[h]: *burst into* ~ in lachen uitbarsten, het uitschateren; *roar with* ~ bulderen van het lachen **2** plezier[h], pret, lol
¹launch (n) **1** motorsloep **2** rondvaartboot, pleziarboot **3** tewaterlating **4** lancering
²launch (vb) (also + out) (energiek) iets (nieuws) beginnen: ~ *out into business for o.s.* voor zichzelf beginnen; ~ *into* zich storten op
³launch (vb) **1** lanceren, afvuren, (weg)werpen, (weg)smijten **2** te water laten **3** op

gang brengen, (doen) beginnen, op touw zetten
launching pad lanceerplatform^h; [fig] springplank
launder 1 wassen (en strijken) **2** witmaken [black money]
launderette wasserette
laundry 1 wasserij, wasinrichting **2** was, wasgoed^h
laundry list waslijst [also fig]; wenslijst
laurel 1 laurier **2** lauwerkrans, erepalm **3** (-s) lauweren, roem, eer: *rest on one's ~s* op zijn lauweren rusten
lava lava
lavatory 1 toilet^h, wc, openbaar toilet^h **2** toiletpot
lavender lavendel
¹lavish (adj) **1** kwistig, gul, verkwistend **2** overvloedig, overdadig: *~ praise* overdadige lof
²lavish (vb) kwistig schenken
law 1 wet, recht^h, rechtsregel, wetmatigheid, natuurwet: *~ and order* orde en gezag, recht en orde; *be a ~ unto o.s.* zijn eigen wetten stellen, eigenmachtig optreden **2** wet(geving), rechtsstelsel^h **3** rechten(studie), rechtsgeleerdheid **4** recht^h, rechtsgang, justitie, gerecht^h: *go to ~* naar de rechter stappen, een proces aanspannen **5** (gedrags)code, (spel)regel, norm, beroepscode, sportcode, kunstcode **6** [inform] politie, sterke arm ‖ *take the ~ into one's own hands* het recht in eigen hand nemen; *~ of the jungle* recht van de sterkste; *lay down the ~* **a)** de wet voorschrijven; **b)** snauwen, blaffen
law-abiding gezagsgetrouw, gehoorzaam aan de wet
law centre wetswinkel
law court rechtscollege^h, rechtbank, gerechtshof^h
lawful 1 wettig, legaal, rechtsgeldig **2** rechtmatig, geoorloofd, legitiem
lawless 1 wetteloos **2** onstuimig, losbandig, wild
lawmaker wetgever
lawn 1 gazon^h, grasveld^h **2** batist^h, linnen^h
lawnmower grasmaaier, grasmaaimachine
lawsuit proces^h, (rechts)geding^h, (rechts)zaak
lawyer 1 advocaat, (juridisch) raadsman **2** jurist, rechtsgeleerde
lax laks, nalatig: *~ about keeping appointments* laks in het nakomen van afspraken
¹laxative (n) laxeermiddel^h
²laxative (adj) laxerend
¹lay (n) ligging, positie: *[Am] the ~ of the land* de natuurlijke ligging van het gebied; [fig also] de stand van zaken
²lay (adj) leken-, niet-priesterlijk, wereldlijk
³lay (vb) wedden ‖ *~ into* ervan langs geven

[also fig]
⁴lay (vb) **1** leggen, neerleggen (= neervlijen) **2** installeren, leggen, plaatsen, zetten; dekken [table]: *the scene of the story is laid in Oxford* het verhaal speelt zich af in Oxford **3** (eieren) leggen **4** in een bepaalde toestand brengen/leggen/zetten, brengen: *~ bare* blootleggen; [fig] aan het licht brengen; *~ low* **a)** tegen de grond werken; **b)** (vernietigend) verslaan; **c)** [fig] vellen [eg of disease]; *~ waste* verwoesten **5** riskeren, op het spel zetten, (ver)wedden: *~ a wager* een weddenschap aangaan ‖ *~ in* **a)** inslaan; **b)** opslaan
layabout nietsnut
lay about wild (om zich heen) slaan, te lijf gaan; ervan langs geven [also fig]
lay aside 1 opzijleggen, sparen, wegleggen, bewaren **2** laten varen; opgeven [plan, hope]
lay down 1 neerleggen: *~ one's tools* staken **2** vastleggen, voorschrijven, bepalen: *~ a procedure* een procedure uitstippelen **3** opgeven, laten varen; neerleggen [office]
layer 1 laag: *~ of sand* laag zand **2** legger [chicken]; leghen
layman leek, amateur, niet-deskundige
¹lay off (vb) stoppen, ophouden, opgeven: *~, will you?* laat dat, ja?
²lay off (vb) (tijdelijk) ontslaan, op non-actief stellen, laten afvloeien
lay-off 1 (tijdelijk) ontslag **2** (periode van) tijdelijke werkloosheid
lay on zorgen voor, regelen, organiseren: *~ a car* een auto regelen ‖ *lay it on (thick)* **a)** (sterk/flink) overdrijven, het er dik opleggen; **b)** slijmen
layout indeling, ontwerp^h, bouwplan^h
lay out 1 uitgeven, investeren **2** uitspreiden, etaleren; klaarleggen [clothing] **3** afleggen; opbaren [corpse]
lay up 1 opslaan, een voorraad aanleggen van, inslaan **2** uit de roulatie halen, het bed doen houden: *he was laid up with the flu* hij moest in bed blijven met de griep
laze luieren, niksen: *~ about* (or: *around*) aanklooien, rondlummelen
lazy 1 lui **2** loom, drukkend: *~ day* lome dag
lazybones [inform] luiwammes
lb *libra* lb., Engels pond, 454 gram
L-driver *learner-driver* leerling-automobilist
¹lead (n) **1** lood^h **2** (diep)lood^h, peillood^h, paslood^h **3** (potlood)stift, grafiet^h ‖ *swing the ~* zich drukken, lijntrekken
²lead (n) **1** leiding, het leiden: *take the ~* de leiding nemen, het initiatief nemen **2** aanknopingspunt^h, aanwijzing, suggestie: *give s.o. a ~* iem. op weg helpen, iem. een hint geven **3** leiding, koppositie, eerste plaats **4** voorsprong **5** hoofdrol; [by extension]

hoofdrolspeler **6** (honden)lijn, hondenriem
³lead (vb) **1** (weg)leiden; (mee)voeren [by
the hand, on a rope etc] **2** brengen tot,
overhalen, aanzetten tot: ~ *s.o. to* **think** *that*
iem. in de waan brengen dat **3** leiden [exis-
tence, life]: ~ *a* **life** *of luxury* een weelderig
leven leiden ‖ ~ *away* meeslepen, blind(e-
lings) doen volgen; ~ *(s.o.)* **on a)** (iem.) overhalen (tot); **b)** iem. iets wijsmaken; ~ *up* to
a) (uiteindelijk) resulteren in; **b)** een inleiding (*or:* voorbereiding) zijn tot
⁴lead (vb) **1** leiden, voorgaan, de weg wijzen, begeleiden **2** aan de leiding gaan, aanvoeren, op kop liggen; [sport] voorstaan; een
voorsprong hebben op; [fig] de toon aangeven: *Liverpool ~s with sixty* **points** Liverpool
staat bovenaan met zestig punten **3** voeren;
leiden [of road, route]; [fig] resulteren in: ~
to disaster tot rampspoed leiden **4** leiden,
aanvoeren, het bevel hebben (over) ‖ ~ *off*
(with) beginnen (met)
leaden 1 loden, van lood **2** loodgrijs, lood-
kleurig
leader 1 leider, aanvoerder, gids **2** eerste
man, partijleider, voorman; [mus] concertmeester; eerste violist; [Am; mus] dirigent
3 [journalism] hoofdcommentaar[h]
leadership 1 leiderschap[h] **2** leiding: *the ~*
are (or: *is*) *divided* de leiding is verdeeld
lead-in inleiding
leading 1 voornaam(st), hoofd-, toonaangevend: ~ *actor* hoofdrolspeler **2** leidend,
(be)sturend ‖ ~ *question* suggestieve vraag
leading-edge allermodernst; allernieuwst
lead singer leadzanger
¹leaf (n) **1** blad[h] [of tree, plant]; (bloem)blad[h]
2 blad[h], bladzijde [of book] **3** uitklapbare
klep; insteekblad[h], uitschuifblad[h] [of table]
4 [as second part in compounds] folie; blad-
[of metal]: *gold* ~ bladgoud
²leaf (vb) bladeren: ~ *through* (snel) doorbladeren
leaflet 1 blaadje[h] **2** foldertje[h], brochure
league 1 [sport] bond, competitie, divisie
2 klasse, niveau[h]: *she's not in my* ~ ik kan niet
aan haar tippen ‖ *in* ~ *with* in samenwerking
met, samenspannend met
¹leak (n) **1** lek[h], lekkage, ongewenste ontsnapping: *spring a* ~ lek raken; [inform] *take*
a ~ pissen **2** uitlekking; ruchtbaarheid [of secret data]
²leak (vb) lekken, lek zijn, (lekkend) doorlaten; [information] onthullen: ~ *information*
(out) to the papers gegevens aan de kranten
doorspelen; [fig] ~ *out* (laten) uitlekken,
(onbedoeld) bekend worden
leakage lekkage, lek[h]
¹lean (adj) mager, schraal, karig
²lean (vb) **1** leunen **2** steunen, staan (tegen)
3 zich buigen: ~ *down* zich bukken; ~ *over to*
s.o. zich naar iem. overbuigen **4** hellen,

scheef staan ‖ ~ *over backwards* zich in (de
gekste) bochten wringen, alle mogelijke
moeite doen; ~ *on* onder druk zetten; ~ *to*
(or: *towards*) **a)** neigen tot; **b)** prefereren; ~
(up)on steunen op, afhankelijk zijn van
³lean (vb) **1** laten steunen, zetten (tegen)
2 buigen, doen hellen: *the Leaning* **Tower** *of*
Pisa de scheve toren van Pisa; ~ *one's head*
back zijn hoofd achteroverbuigen **3** mager,
schraal **4** arm(zalig), weinig opleverend: ~
years magere jaren
lean-to aanbouw, afdak[h]
¹leap (n) sprong, gesprongen afstand, plotselinge toename, hindernis, obstakel[h] ‖ *by ~s*
and **bounds** halsoverkop; [fig] *a* ~ *in the* **dark**
een sprong in het duister
²leap (vb) (op)springen, vooruitspringen: ~
for joy dansen van vreugde ‖ *her heart* ~*ed* **up**
haar hart maakte een sprongetje; ~ *at* met
beide handen aangrijpen [chance etc]
¹leapfrog (n) haasje-over[h], bokspringen[h]
²leapfrog (vb) sprongsgewijs vorderen
³leapfrog (vb) haasje-over spelen, bosksprin-
gen
leap year schrikkeljaar[h]
¹learn (vb) **1** leren, studeren: ~ *how to play*
the piano piano leren spelen; ~ *from* experience door ervaring wijzer worden **2** horen,
vernemen, te weten komen: ~ *about* (or: *of*)
sth. from the papers iets uit de krant te weten
komen
²learn (vb) **1** leren, zich eigen maken, bestuderen **2** vernemen, horen van, ontdekken: *I*
~*t it from the papers* ik heb het uit de krant
learned 1 onderlegd, ontwikkeld, geleerd
2 belezen **3** wetenschappelijk, academisch:
~ *periodical* wetenschappelijk tijdschrift
learner 1 leerling **2** beginner, beginneling
3 leerling-automobilist
learner's permit [Am] voorlopig rijbewijs
learning 1 studie; onderwijs[h], het leren
2 kennis; geleerdheid
¹lease (n) **1** pacht, pachtcontract[h] **2** (ver)-
huur, (ver)huurcontract[h], (ver)huurovereen-
komst **3** pachttermijn, huurtermijn, pacht-
duur ‖ *a (new)* ~ *of* **life** een nieuw leven, een
tweede kans
²lease (vb) **1** (ver)pachten **2** (ver)huren, leasen
leaseholder 1 pachter **2** huurder
leash (honden)lijn, riem: *always* **keep** *Sarah*
on the ~ houd Sarah altijd aangelijnd ‖ *strain*
at the ~ trappelen van ongeduld
¹least (adj) kleinste, geringste: *I haven't the* ~
idea ik heb er geen flauw idee van; *the line of*
~ **resistance** de weg van de minste weerstand
²least (adv) minst(e): *the* ~ **popular** *leader* de
minst populaire leider; *to say the* ~ *(of it)* om
het zachtjes uit te drukken; *at (the)* ~ *seven*
ten minste zeven; *it didn't bother me* **in** *the* ~

het stoorde mij helemaal niet
¹leather (n) leerʰ
²leather (adj) leren, van leer
¹leave (n) **1** toestemming, permissie, verlofʰ:
~ *of absence* verlof, vakantie; *by* (or: *with*)
your ~ met uw permissie **2** verlofʰ, vrij, vakantie: *on* ~ met verlof ‖ *take one's* ~ *of s.o.*
a) iem. gedag zeggen; b) afscheid nemen
van iem.
²leave (vb) **1** laten liggen, laten staan, achterlaten, vergeten: ~ *about* (or: *around*) laten
(rond)slingeren **2** laten staan, onaangeroerd
laten: ~ *(sth.) undone* (iets) ongedaan laten;
be left with (blijven) zitten met, opgescheept
worden met **3** overlaten, doen overblijven:
four from six ~s two zes min vier is twee **4** afgeven, achterlaten: ~ *a note for s.o.* een
boodschap voor iem. achterlaten **5** toevertrouwen, in bewaring geven **6** nalaten, achterlaten ‖ ~ *it at that* het er (maar) bij laten; ~
(people) to themselves zich niet bemoeien met
(mensen)
³leave (vb) weggaan (bij/van), verlaten, vertrekken (bij/van): *it's time for you to* ~, *it's
time you left* het wordt tijd dat je weggaat
leave behind 1 thuis laten, vertrekken
zonder, vergeten (mee te nemen) **2** (alleen)
achterlaten, in de steek laten: *John was left
behind* John werd (alleen) achtergelaten
3 achter zich laten, passeren
¹leave off (vb) ophouden, stoppen
²leave off (vb) **1** uit laten [not wear any
longer]; niet meer dragen **2** staken, stoppen
met
leave out 1 buiten laten (liggen/staan)
2 weglaten, overslaan, niet opnemen **3** buitensluiten: *feel left out* zich buitengesloten
voelen
leavings overschot, overblijfsel(en), etensresten
¹Lebanese (n) Libanees, Libanese
²Lebanese (adj) Libanees
Lebanon Libanon
lecherous 1 wellustig, liederlijk **2** geil, hitsig
¹lecture (n) **1** lezing, verhandeling, voordracht **2** (hoor)collegeʰ, (openbare) les
3 preek, berisping: *read s.o. a* ~ iem. de les
lezen
²lecture (vb) de les lezen
³lecture (vb) **1** spreken (voor), lezing(en)
geven (voor) **2** college geven (aan), onderrichten
lecturer 1 spreker, houder van lezing **2** docent [in higher educ]
LED *light-emitting diode* led
ledge richel, (uitstekende) rand
ledger [bookkeeping] grootboekʰ; [Am
also] registerʰ
lee 1 luwte, beschutting, beschutte plek
2 [shipp] lij(zijde)

leech bloedzuiger; [fig] uitzuiger; parasiet ‖
cling (or: *stick*) *like a* ~ *(to)* niet weg te branden zijn (bij)
leek prei
¹leer (n) **1** wellustige blik **2** wrede grijns,
vuile blik
²leer (vb) **1** loeren, grijnzen **2** verlekkerd kijken, wellustige blikken werpen
lees droesem; bezinkselʰ
leeway (extra) speelruimte, speling; [Am]
veiligheidsmarge
¹left (n) **1** linkerkant, linksʰ, linkerhand:
keep to the ~ links (aan)houden; *turn to the* ~
links afslaan **2** [pol] linksʰ, de progressieven
²left (adj) **1** linker, links **2** [pol] links
³left (adv) **1** links, aan de linkerzijde **2** naar
links, linksaf, linksom: *turn* ~ links afslaan
left-back linksachter
left-hand links, linker: ~ *bend* bocht naar
links; ~ *drive* linkse besturing [of car]
left-handed 1 links(handig) **2** links, onhandig **3** dubbelzinnig, dubieus: ~ *compliment* twijfelachtig compliment
left luggage office bagagedepotʰ
leftover over(gebleven); resterend, ongebruikt
leftovers 1 (etens)restjes, kliekje(s)
2 kliekjesmaaltijd
left-wing links; progressief
lefty [inform] **1** [pol] lid van de linkervleugel **2** [Am] linkshandige
leg 1 beenʰ **2** poot [of animal]; achterpoot
3 beengedeelteʰ van kledingstuk; beenʰ [of
stocking]; (broeks)pijp **4** poot [of furniture
etc] **5** gedeelteʰ (van groter geheelʰ); etappe
[of trip, competition etc]; estafetteonder-
deelʰ; manche [of competition] **6** bout [of
calf, lam]: ~ *of mutton* schapenbout **7** schenkel: ~ *of veal* kalfsschenkel ‖ *give s.o. a* ~ *up*
iem. een voetje geven; [fig] iem. een handje
helpen; *pull s.o.'s* ~ iem. voor de gek houden;
run s.o. off his ~s a) iem. geen seconde met
rust laten; b) iem. uitputten; *shake a* ~ opschieten; *not have a* ~ *to stand on* geen poot
hebben om op te staan; *stretch one's* ~s de
benen strekken [by means of a walk]; *walk
s.o. off his* ~s iem. laten lopen tot hij erbij
neervalt
legacy erfenis [also fig]; nalatenschap
legal 1 wettig, legaal, rechtsgeldig: ~ *tender* wettig betaalmiddel **2** wettelijk, volgens
de wet **3** juridisch: *(free)* ~ *aid* kosteloze
rechtsbijstand
legality rechtsgeldigheid, rechtmatigheid
legalize legaliseren, wettig maken
legend 1 (volks)overlevering, legende(n)
2 onderschriftʰ, opschriftʰ
legendary legendarisch [also fig]
legging 1 beenkap, beenbeschermer,
scheenbeschermer **2** legging
legible leesbaar

¹**legion** (n) legioenʰ
²**legion** (adj) talrijk: *books on this subject are* ~ er zijn veel/legio boeken over dit onderwerp
¹**legionary** (n) legionair, legioensoldaat
²**legionary** (adj) legioens-
legislation wetgeving
legislative 1 wetgevend, bevoegd tot wetgeving **2** wets-, m.b.t. wetgeving
legislator wetgever, lidʰ van een wetgevend lichaam
legit *legitimate* wettig, legaal, oké
legitimacy 1 wettigheid; rechtmatigheid, legitimiteit **2** geldigheid
legitimate 1 wettig, rechtmatig, legitiem **2** geldig: ~ *purpose* gerechtvaardigd doel
leg-pull plagerij, beetnemerij
leg-up steuntjeʰ, duwtjeʰ; zetjeʰ [in the right direction]
¹**leisure** (n) (vrije) tijd, gelegenheid: *at* ~ vrij, zonder verplichtingen, ontspannen; *at one's* ~ in zijn vrije tijd, als men tijd heeft, als het schikt
²**leisure** (adj) **1** vrij: ~ *hours* (or: *time*) vrije uren (*or:* tijd) **2** vrijetijds-
leisure centre [roughly] recreatiecentrumʰ, [roughly] sportcentrumʰ
leisurely zonder haast (te maken), ontspannen, op zijn gemak
leisurewear vrijetijdskleding
lemon 1 citroen **2** [inform] idioot **3** miskoop, maandagochtendexemplaarʰ
lemonade (citroen)limonade
lemon squash 1 citroensiroop **2** citroenlimonade
lemur maki
lend 1 (uit)lenen: ~ *s.o. a book* iem. een boek lenen **2** verlenen, schenken, geven: ~ *assistance to* steun verlenen aan || ~ *itself to* a) zich (goed) lenen tot; b) vatbaar zijn voor
lender geldschieter
length 1 lengte, omvang, (lichaams)lengte, grootte, gestalte: ~ *of a book* omvang van een boek; *three centimetres in* ~ drie centimeter lang **2** lengte, duur: *for the* ~ *of our stay* voor de duur van ons verblijf **3** eind(je)ʰ, stuk(je)ʰ: ~ *of rope* eindje touw || *go to considerable* (or: *great*) ~s erg z'n best doen, zich veel moeite getroosten; *at* ~ a) langdurig; b) uitvoerig; c) ten slotte; *go to all* ~s (or: *any* ~(s)) er alles voor over hebben; *at some* ~ uitvoerig
lengthen verlengen, langer maken: ~ *a dress* een jurk langer maken
lengthy 1 langdurig **2** langdradig
lenience toegevendheid, mildheid
lenient 1 tolerant, toegevend **2** mild, genadig: ~ *verdict* mild vonnis
lens lens
lentil linze
Leo [astrology] (de) Leeuw

leopard luipaard, panter
leotard tricotʰ, balletpakjeʰ, gympakjeʰ
leper lepralijder, melaatse
leprosy lepra, melaatsheid
leprous melaats
¹**lesbian** (n) lesbienne
²**lesbian** (adj) lesbisch
lesion verwonding; letselʰ
¹**less** (adj) kleiner: *no* ~ *a person than* niemand minder dan
²**less** (adv) minder: ~ *money* minder geld; *he couldn't care* ~ het kon hem geen barst schelen; *more or* ~ min of meer || *none the* ~ niettemin
³**less** (prep) zonder, verminderd met, op ... na: *a year* ~ *one month* een jaar min één maand
lessen (ver)minderen, (doen) afnemen
lesser minder, kleiner, onbelangrijker: *to a* ~ *extent* in mindere mate
lesson 1 les, leerzame ervaring: *let this be a* ~ *to you* laat dit een les voor je zijn **2** leerstof **3** lesuurʰ **4** Schriftlezing, Bijbellezing || *teach s.o. a* ~ iem. een lesje leren
lest (voor het geval/uit vrees) dat, opdat niet: *she was afraid* ~ *he leave her* ze vreesde dat hij haar zou verlaten
¹**let** (n) **1** [sport, esp tennis] let(bal), overgespeelde bal **2** beletselʰ, belemmering: *without* ~ *or hindrance* vrijelijk, zonder (enig) beletsel
²**let** (vb) **1** verhuurd worden **2** uitbesteed worden || [inform] ~ *on (about, that)* verklappen, doorvertellen (dat); [inform] ~ *on (that)* net doen (alsof)
³**let** (vb) **1** laten, toestaan: ~ *sth. be known* iets laten weten; *please,* ~ *me buy this round* laat mij nu toch dit rondje aanbieden **2** laten: ~ *me hear* (or: *know*) hou me op de hoogte; ~ *me see* eens kijken; ~ *'s not talk about it* laten we er niet over praten **3** [maths] stellen, geven: ~ *x be y+z* stel x is y +z, gegeven x is y+z **4** verhuren, in huur geven **5** aanbesteden || ~ *s.o. be* iem. met rust laten; ~ *fly (at)* uithalen (naar); ~ *s.o. go* get on with it iem. zijn gang laten gaan; ~ *go (of)* loslaten, uit zijn hoofd zetten, ophouden (over); ~ *o.s. go* zich laten gaan; ~ *s.o. have it* iem. de volle laag geven, iem. ervan langs geven; ~ *slip* a) laten uitlekken; b) missen, voorbij laten gaan [chance]; ~ *through* laten passeren, doorlaten; ~ *into* a) binnenlaten in, toelaten tot; b) in vertrouwen nemen over, vertellen
let down 1 neerlaten, laten zakken, laten vallen **2** teleurstellen, in de steek laten: *don't let me down* laat me niet in de steek **3** leeg laten lopen [tyre]
let-down afknapper, teleurstelling
lethal dodelijk, fataal
lethargy lethargie, (s)loomheid, loomheid,

sloomheid
let in binnenlaten, toelaten: *let o.s. in zich
toegang verschaffen* ‖ ~ *for* opschepen met,
laten opdraaien voor; *let o.s. in for* zich op de
hals halen; ~ *on* **a)** in vertrouwen nemen
over, inlichten over; **b)** laten meedoen met
let off 1 afvuren, afsteken, af laten gaan: ~
fireworks vuurwerk afsteken **2** excuseren,
vrijuit laten gaan, vrijstellen van: *the judge
let him off* de rechter liet hem vrijuit gaan; *be
~ with* er afkomen met
¹let out (vb) **1** uithalen, van leer trekken: ~
at s.o. naar iem. uithalen, tegen iem. uitvaren **2** dichtgaan, sluiten; uitgaan [of school
etc]
²let out (vb) **1** uitnemen; wijder maken
[clothing] **2** laten uitlekken, verklappen,
openbaar maken, bekendmaken **3** laten
ontsnappen, vrijlaten, laten gaan: *let the air
out of a balloon* een ballon laten leeglopen
4 geven [scream] **5** de laan uitsturen, ontslaan, (van school) sturen
letter 1 letter: *to the ~* naar de letter, tot in
detail, tot de kleinste bijzonderheden
2 brief: ~ *to the editor* ingezonden brief; ~ *of
introduction* aanbevelingsbrief; *covering ~*
begeleidend schrijven; *by* ~ per brief, schriftelijk **3** (-s) letteren, literatuur
letter bomb bombrief
letterbox brievenbus
letterhead 1 briefhoofdʰ **2** postpapierʰ
met briefhoofd
lettuce sla, salade: *a head of ~* een krop sla
let up 1 minder worden, afnemen, gaan
liggen: *I hope the wind's going to ~ a little* ik
hoop dat de wind wat gaat liggen **2** het
kalm aan doen, gas terugnemen **3** pauzeren, ophouden (met werken)
leukaemia leukemie, bloedkanker
levee [Am] (rivier)dijk, waterkering
¹level (n) **1** peilʰ, niveauʰ, hoogte, natuurlijke plaats: ~ *of achievement* (or: *production*)
prestatiepeil, productiepeil; *find one's ~* zijn
plaats vinden **2** vlakʰ, (vlak) oppervlakʰ,
vlakte, vlak landʰ **3** horizontaal **4** [Am] waterpas: [inform] *on the ~* rechtdoorzee,
goudeerlijk **5** niveauʰ: *at ministerial ~* op ministerieel niveau
²level (adj) **1** waterpas, horizontaal **2** vlak,
egaal, zonder oneffenheden: ~ *teaspoon* afgestreken theelepel **3** (op) gelijk(e hoogte),
even hoog: ~ *crossing* gelijkvloerse kruising,
overweg; *draw ~ with* op gelijke hoogte komen met **4** gelijkmatig, evenwichtig, regelmatig: *in a ~ voice* zonder stemverheffing
5 bedaard, kalm: *keep a ~ head* zijn verstand
erbij houden **6** gelijkwaardig, op gelijke
voet **7** strak [of look]; doordringend: *give s.o.
a ~ look* iem. strak aankijken ‖ *(do) one's ~
best* zijn uiterste best (doen)
³level (vb) **1** egaliseren, effenen **2** nivelle-

ren, op gelijk niveau brengen; opheffen [dis-
tinction]: ~ *down* tot hetzelfde niveau omlaag brengen; ~ *up* tot hetzelfde niveau omhoog brengen
⁴level (vb) (horizontaal) richten, aanleggen,
afvuren; uitbrengen [cricism etc]: ~ *a charge
against* (or: *at*) *s.o.* een beschuldiging tegen
iem. uitbrengen
⁵level (adv) vlak, horizontaal, waterpas
level-headed nuchter, afgewogen
¹lever (n) **1** hefboom, koevoet, breekijzerʰ
2 werktuigʰ [only fig]; pressiemiddelʰ, in-
strumentʰ **3** hendel, handgreep, handvatʰ
²lever (vb) opheffen d.m.v. hefboom, tillen,
(los)wrikken: ~ *s.o. out of his job* iem. weg-
manoeuvreren
leverage 1 hefboomwerking, hefboom-
kracht **2** macht, invloed, pressie: *even small
groups can exert enormous political ~* zelfs
kleine groeperingen kunnen enorme politieke pressie uitoefenen
levitate zweven; levitatie ondergaan
levity lichtzinnigheid, lichtvaardigheid, oneerbiedigheid
¹levy (n) heffing, vordering, belastingheffing: *make a ~ on* een heffing instellen op
²levy (vb) **1** heffen, opleggen: ~ *a fine* een
boete opleggen **2** vorderen, innen **3** (aan)-
werven, rekruteren
lewd 1 wellustig **2** obsceen, schunnig
lexicography lexicografie, het samenstellen van woordenboeken
lexicology lexicologie [study of words]
lexicon woordenboekʰ
liability 1 (wettelijke ver)plicht(ing): ~ *to
pay taxes* belastingplichtigheid **2** (liabilities)
passiva, lasten, schulden **3** blok aan het been
liability insurance aansprakelijkheidsverzekering
liable 1 (wettelijk) verplicht: ~ *for tax* belas-
tingplichtig **2** (+ for) aansprakelijk (voor),
(wettelijk) verantwoordelijk (voor) **3** vatbaar, vaak lijdend: ~ *to colds* vaak verkouden
4 de neiging hebbend, het risico lopend: *it
isn't ~ to happen* dat zal niet zo gauw gebeuren
liaison 1 liaison [also mil]; verbinding; [by
extension] samenwerkingsverbandʰ **2** bui-
tenechtelijke verhouding
liana liaan
liar leugenaar
¹libel (n) **1** smaadschriftʰ **2** smaad, laster,
belastering
²libel (vb) **1** belasteren, valselijk beschuldigen **2** een smaadschrift publiceren tegen
¹liberal (n) liberaal, ruimdenkend iem.
²liberal (adj) **1** ruimdenkend, onbevooroordeeld, liberaal **2** royaal, vrijgevig **3** overvloedig, welvoorzien ‖ ~ *arts* vrije kunsten
liberalism liberalismeʰ
liberate bevrijden

liberated bevrijd; geëmancipeerd [socially, sexually]
liberation bevrijding, vrijlating
Liberia Liberia
¹Liberian (n) Liberiaan(se)
²Liberian (adj) Liberiaans
libero [socc] vrije verdediger
libertarian vrijheidsgezinde
libertine 1 losbol **2** libertijn
liberty 1 vrijheid, onafhankelijkheid: ~ *of conscience* gewetensvrijheid; *at* ~ **a)** in vrijheid, op vrije voeten; **b)** vrij, onbezet; **c)** ongebruikt, werkloos **2** vrijheid, vrijmoedigheid: *take liberties with s.o.* zich vrijheden veroorloven tegen iem.
Libra [astrology] (de) Weegschaal
librarian bibliothecaris
library bibliotheek, (openbare) leeszaal; uitleenverzameling [of films, CDs etc]
Libya Libië
¹Libyan (n) Libiër, Libische
²Libyan (adj) Libisch
licence 1 vergunning, licentie, verlofʰ **2** verlofʰ, permissie, toestemming **3** vrijheid **4** losbandigheid, ongebondenheid **5** (artistieke) vrijheid
license 1 (een) vergunning verlenen (aan): ~*d to sell* **tobacco** met tabaksvergunning; ~*d* **victualler** caféhouder met drankvergunning **2** (officieel) toestemming geven voor
licensee vergunninghouder; licentiehouder [of liquor licence, tobacco licence]
license plate [Am] nummerbordʰ
licentious wellustig
lichen korstmosʰ
¹lick (n) **1** lik, veeg; [by extension] ietsjeʰ; klein beetjeʰ: *a ~ of* **paint** een kwastje (verf) **2** (vliegende) vaart: *(at)* **full** ~*, at a* **great** ~ met een noodgang
²lick (vb) **1** likken **2** [inform] een pak slaag geven [also fig]; ervan langs geven, overwinnen: ~ *a* **problem** een probleem uit de wereld helpen
³lick (vb) lekken; (licht) spelen (langs) [of waves, flames]: *the* **flames** ~*ed (at) the walls* de vlammen lekten (aan) de muren
licking pakʰ rammel: *the team* **got** *a ~* het team werd ingemaakt
lid 1 deksel⁺ʰ, klep **2** (oog)lidʰ ‖ *take the ~ off* onthullingen doen; *that* **puts** *the ~ on* dat doet de deur dicht
¹lie (n) **1** leugen: *tell a ~* liegen **2** ligging, situering, positie: *the ~ of the* **land** de natuurlijke ligging van het gebied; [fig] de stand van zaken ‖ *give the ~ to* weerleggen
²lie (vb) liegen, jokken
³lie (vb) **1** (plat/uitgestrekt/vlak) liggen, rusten **2** (begraven) liggen, rusten: **here** ~*s ...* hier ligt ... **3** gaan liggen, zich neerleggen **4** zich bevinden [in a place, situation]; liggen, gelegen zijn: ~ **fallow** braak liggen; *my*

sympathy ~*s* **with** … mijn medeleven gaat uit naar … ‖ *I don't know what* ~*s in store* **for** *me* ik weet niet wat me te wachten staat
lie about 1 luieren, niksen **2** (slordig) in het rond liggen; rondslingeren [of objects]
Liechtenstein Liechtenstein
Liechtensteiner Liechtensteiner, Liechtensteinse
lie down (gaan) liggen: [fig] *we won't take this lying down* we laten dit niet over onze kant gaan
lie-down [inform] dutjeʰ
liege 1 leenheer **2** leenman, vazal
lie in [inform] uitslapen, lang in bed blijven liggen
lie over overstaan, blijven liggen, uitgesteld worden: *let sth. ~* iets uitstellen
lieu: *in ~ of* in plaats van
lie up 1 zich schuilhouden, onderduiken **2** het bed houden, platliggen
lieutenant [mil] luitenant
lie with zijn aan, de verantwoordelijkheid zijn van, afhangen van: *the* **choice** *lies with her* de keuze is aan haar
life 1 levend wezenʰ, levenʰ: *several lives were* **lost** verscheidene mensen kwamen om het leven **2** levenʰ, bestaanʰ, levendigheid, bedrijvigheid, levensduur, levensbeschrijving: *a* **matter** *of ~ and death* een zaak van leven of dood; *make ~* **easy** niet moeilijk doen; *you (can)* **bet** *your ~* nou en of!, wat dacht je!; **bring** *to ~* (weer) bijbrengen; [fig] tot leven wekken; **come** *to ~* **a)** bijkomen, tot leven komen; **b)** [fig] geïnteresseerd raken; **save** *s.o.'s ~* iemands leven redden; *take one's (own) ~* zelfmoord plegen; **for** *~* voor het leven, levenslang; *for the ~ of me I couldn't remember it* al sla je me dood, ik weet het echt niet meer; *this is the ~!* dit noem ik nog eens leven! **3** levenslang(e gevangenisstraf) ‖ *take one's ~ in one's (own) hands* zijn leven in de waagschaal stellen; *the ~ (and soul) of the* **party** de gangmaker van het feest; **start** *~* zijn carrière beginnen; *not on your ~* nooit van z'n leven
lifebelt redding(s)gordel
lifebuoy redding(s)boei
life-course savings scheme levensloopregeling
lifeguard 1 badmeester, strandmeester **2** lijfwacht
life insurance levensverzekering
life jacket redding(s)vestʰ
lifeless levenloos; dood; [fig] futloos, lusteloos
lifeline 1 redding(s)lijn **2** vitale verbindingslijn; navelstreng [fig]
lifelong levenslang; voor het leven
life preserver [Am] reddingsboei, reddingsvestʰ
lifer [inform] tot levenslang veroordeelde

life-raft redding(s)vlot^h
lifesaver 1 levensreddend middel^h **2** [inform] redder in de nood
lifespan (potentiële) levensduur
lifestyle levensstijl
lifetime levensduur, mensenleven^h: *the chance of a ~* een unieke kans
^{1}**lift** (n) **1** lift **2** lift, gratis (auto)rit **3** (ver)-heffing
^{2}**lift** (vb) **1** (op)stijgen, opgaan, opkomen, omhooggaan, omhoogkomen: *~ off* opstijgen, starten **2** optrekken [of mist etc]
^{3}**lift** (vb) **1** optillen, optrekken, ophijsen: *not ~ a hand* (or: *finger*) geen hand (or: vinger) uitsteken **2** opheffen, afschaffen: *~ a blockade* een blokkade opheffen **3** verheffen, op een hoger plan brengen: *this news will ~ his spirits* dit nieuws zal hem opbeuren **4** rooien, uit de grond halen **5** verheffen, luider doen klinken: *~ up one's voice* zijn stem verheffen
lift-off lancering
ligament gewrichtsband
^{1}**light** (n) **1** licht^h, verlichting, openbaarheid: *bring* (or: *come*) *to ~* aan het licht brengen (or: komen); *reversing ~* achteruitrijlicht; *see the ~* het licht zien, tot inzicht komen; *shed* (or: *throw*) *~ (up)on* licht werpen op, klaarheid brengen in **2** vuurtje^h, vlammetje^h: *can you give me a ~, please?* heeft u misschien een vuurtje voor me? || *set (a) ~ to sth.* iets in de fik steken; *see the ~ at the end of the tunnel* licht in de duisternis zien; *a shining ~* een lichtend voorbeeld; *in (the) ~ of this statement* gezien deze verklaring
^{2}**light** (adj) **1** licht, niet zwaar: *~ clothing* lichte kleding; *~ food* licht (verteerbaar) voedsel; light; dieetproducten; *~ of heart* licht-, luchthartig; [sport] *~ heavyweight* halfzwaargewicht; *~ opera* operette; *make ~ work of* zijn hand niet omdraaien voor; *make ~ of* niet zwaar tillen aan **2** licht, verlicht, helder
^{3}**light** (vb) **1** ontbranden, vlam vatten **2** aangaan; gaan branden [of lamp etc] **3** opklaren; oplichten [also of face, eyes]
^{4}**light** (vb) **1** aansteken: *~ a fire* (or: *lamp*) een vuur (or: lamp) aansteken **2** verlichten, beschijnen; *~ed* (or: *lit*) *by electricity* elektrisch verlicht
^{5}**light** (adv) licht: *sleep ~* licht slapen; *travel ~* weinig bagage bij zich hebben
light-armed lichtgewapend
light bulb (gloei)lamp
^{1}**lighten** (vb) **1** lichter worden, afnemen in gewicht **2** opleven, opfleuren **3** ophelderen, opklaren **4** klaren, dagen **5** bliksemen, (weer)lichten
^{2}**lighten** (vb) **1** verlichten, ontlasten; [fig] opbeuren **2** verlichten, verhelderen
lighter aansteker

light-headed licht-, warhoofdig
light-hearted luchthartig
lighthouse vuurtoren
lighting verlichting
lightly 1 licht(jes), een ietsje **2** licht(jes), gemakkelijk **3** luchtig, lichtvaardig || *~ come, ~ go* zo gewonnen, zo geronnen
lightness lichtheid [also fig]
lightning bliksem, weerlicht^h: *forked ~* vertakte bliksem(straal); *like (greased) ~* als de (gesmeerde) bliksem; *~ conductor* bliksemafleider
^{1}**light up** (vb) **1** (ver)licht(ing) aansteken, de lamp(en) aandoen **2** [inform] (een sigaar/sigaret/pijp) opsteken || *his eyes lit up with greed* zijn ogen begonnen te glimmen van hebzucht
^{2}**light up** (vb) **1** aansteken, ontsteken **2** verlichten
lightweight lichtgewicht [also fig]
^{1}**like** (n) **1** (-s) voorkeuren: *~s and dislikes* sympathieën en antipathieën **2** soortgenoot, (soort)gelijke: [inform] *the ~s of us* mensen als wij, ons soort (mensen) || *I've never seen* (or: *heard*) *the ~ of it* zoiets heb ik nog nooit meegemaakt (or: gehoord)
^{2}**like** (adj) soortgelijk, (soort)verwant: *they are as ~ as two peas (in a pod)* ze lijken op elkaar als twee druppels water
^{3}**like** (vb) willen, wensen: *if you ~* zo u wilt, als je wilt
^{4}**like** (vb) houden van, (prettig) vinden, (graag) willen: *would you ~ a cup of tea?* wilt u een kopje thee?; *I'd ~ to do that* dat zou ik best willen; *how do you ~ your egg?* hoe wilt u uw ei?
^{5}**like** (adv) **1** [inform] weet je, wel: *he thinks he's clever* – hij vindt zichzelf best wel slim **2** [inform] nou, zoiets als: *her request was ... ~ ... unusual, you know* haar verzoek was ... nou ja ... ongebruikelijk, weet je
^{6}**like** (prep) **1** als, zoals, gelijk aan: *cry ~ a baby* huilen als een kind; *it is just ~ John to forget it* echt iets voor John om het te vergeten; *~ that* zo, op die wijze; *just ~ that* zo maar (even); *what is he ~?* wat voor iem. is hij?; *what is it ~?* hoe voelt dat nou?; *more ~ ten pounds than nine* eerder tien pond dan negen **2** (zo)als: *take a science ~ chemistry* neem nou scheikunde || *it hurts ~ anything* het doet erg veel pijn; *that's more ~ it* dat begint er op te lijken; *there's nothing ~ a holiday* er gaat niets boven een vakantie; *sth. ~ five days* om en nabij vijf dagen
^{7}**like** (conj) **1** zoals, op dezelfde wijze als: [inform] *they ran ~ crazy* ze liepen zo hard zij konden; *it was ~ in the old days* het was zoals vroeger **2** [inform] alsof: *it looks ~ he will win* het ziet ernaar uit dat hij zal winnen
likeable innemend, aardig, sympathiek
likelihood waarschijnlijkheid: *in all ~* naar

alle waarschijnlijkheid
¹likely (adj) waarschijnlijk, aannemelijk; [by extension] kansrijk: *he is the most ~* **candidate** *for the job* hij komt het meest in aanmerking voor de baan; *he* **is** *~ to become suspicious* hij wordt allicht achterdochtig
²likely (adv) waarschijnlijk: *not ~! kun je net* denken!; *as ~ as not* eerder wel dan niet
like-minded gelijkgestemd
likeness gelijkenis, overeenkomst: *it's a* **good** *~* het lijkt er goed op [eg of photo]
likewise 1 evenzo, insgelijks **2** evenzeer
liking voorkeur, voorliefde: *have a ~ for* houden van, gek zijn op || *is your room* **to** *your ~?* is uw kamer naar wens?
lilac 1 sering **2** lila^h
lily lelie || *gild the ~* iets mooier, beter maken dan nodig
limb 1 lid(maat) [plural: ledematen]; arm, been^h **2** (dikke/grote) tak || *out on a ~* op zichzelf aangewezen
limbo 1 voorportaal^h (der hel) **2** vergetelheid **3** opsluiting **4** onzekerheid, twijfel: *be* **in** *~* in onzekerheid verkeren
lime 1 limoen **2** linde **3** gebrande kalk
limelight kalklicht^h: *in the ~* in de schijnwerpers
limestone kalksteen^+h
limey [Am; inform] Brit, Engelsman
¹limit (n) limiet, (uiterste) grens: [Am] *go the ~* tot het uiterste gaan; [Am; esp mil] *off ~s* **(to)** verboden terrein (voor); **within** *~s* binnen bepaalde grenzen; *you're the ~* je bent onmogelijk
²limit (vb) begrenzen, beperken: *~ing* **factors** beperkende factoren; *~* **to** beperken tot
limitation beperking, begrenzing: *he* **has** (or: **knows**) *his ~s* hij heeft (or: kent) zijn beperkingen
limited beperkt, gelimiteerd || *~ (liability)* **company** naamloze vennootschap
limitless onbegrensd
¹limp (n) kreupele (slepende) gang, mankheid: *he* **walks** *with a ~* hij trekt met zijn been
²limp (adj) (ver)slap(t)
³limp (vb) **1** mank lopen, slecht ter been zijn **2** haperen, horten
limpid (glas)helder
linchpin spil [fig]; hoeksteen
¹line (n) **1** lijn, snoer^h, koord^h: *the ~ is* **bad** de verbinding is slecht [telephone] **2** smalle streep, lijn: *we must* **draw** *the ~ somewhere* we moeten ergens een grens trekken; *in ~ with* in het verlengde van; [fig] in overeenstemming met **3** rij (naast/achter elkaar); [mil] linie; stelling: **come** (or: **fall**) *into ~* op één lijn gaan zitten, zich schikken; *read between the ~s* tussen de regels door lezen; *all* **along** *the ~* **a)** over de (ge)hele linie; **b)** [also fig] van begin tot eind **4** kort briefje^h, krabbeltje^h: **drop** *s.o. a ~* iem. een briefje schrijven

5 beleidslijn, gedragslijn: *~ of* **thought** zienswijze, denkwijze **6** koers, route; weg [also fig]: *~ of* **least** *resistance* weg van de minste weerstand **7** lijndienst **8** spoorweglijn, spoor^h **9** terrein^h [fig]; vlak^h, branche: **banking** *is his ~* hij zit in het bankwezen **10** assortiment^h, soort artikel^h **11** lint^h, lont, band **12** (-s) (straf)regels, strafwerk^h **13** (-s) trouwakte **14** (-s) methode, aanpak: *do sth.* **along** (or: **on**) *the wrong ~s* iets verkeerd aanpakken || **lay** (or: **put**) *it on the ~* a) betalen; **b)** open kaart spelen; **sign** *on the dotted ~* a) (een contract) ondertekenen; **b)** [inform] niet tegenstribbelen; **c)** in het huwelijksbootje stappen; **toe** *the ~* in het gareel blijven; **on** *~* aan het werk, functionerend; **out of** *~* uit de pas, over de schreef
²line (vb) **1** liniëren: *~d* **paper** gelinieerd papier **2** flankeren: *a road ~d* **with** *trees* een weg met (rijen) bomen erlangs **3** voeren, (van binnen) bekleden: *~d* **with** *fur* met bont gevoerd || *~ one's* **nest** (or: **pocket, purse**) zijn zakken vullen, zijn beurs spekken
lineage 1 geslacht^h, nageslacht^h **2** afkomst
linear 1 lineair, lengte-, recht(lijnig): *~* **measure** lengtemaat
linen 1 linnen^h, lijnwaad^h **2** linnengoed^h
liner 1 lijnboot **2** lijntoestel^h
linesman 1 [sport] grensrechter, lijnrechter **2** lijnwerker
¹line up (vb) in de rij gaan staan: [fig] *~* **alongside** (or: **with**) zich opstellen naast
²line up (vb) **1** opstellen in (een) rij(en) **2** op een rij zetten, samenbrengen
linger 1 treuzelen, dralen: *~* **over** *details* lang stilstaan bij details **2** (zwakjes) voortleven: *the memory ~s* **on** de herinnering leeft voort
lingo taal(tje)^h, (vak)jargon^h: *at least I master the* **commercial** *~ they use over there* in elk geval beheers ik het handelstaaltje dat ze daar spreken
linguist 1 talenkenner, talenwonder^h **2** taalkundige, linguïst
linguistic taalkundig, linguïstisch
linguistics taalkunde, linguïstiek: *applied ~* toegepaste taalkunde
lining voering(stof), (binnen)bekleding || *every cloud has a silver ~* achter de wolken schijnt de zon
¹link (n) **1** schakel [also fig]; verbinding, verband^h: *missing ~* ontbrekende schakel **2** presentator **3** (-s) [sport] (golf)links, golfbaan
²link (vb) een verbinding vormen, zich verbinden, samenkomen: *~* **up** zich aaneensluiten
³link (vb) verbinden, koppelen: *~* **hands** de handen ineenslaan
linkman 1 presentator **2** middenvelder **3** bemiddelaar, tussenpersoon
link-up verbinding, koppeling

linoleum linoleum[h]
linseed lijnzaad[h]
lion 1 leeuw 2 idool[h]
lioness leeuwin
lionhearted moedig (als een leeuw)
lionize als een beroemdheid behandelen; op een voetstuk plaatsen
the **lion's share** leeuwendeel
lip 1 lip: [fig] *hang on s.o.'s ~s* aan iemands lippen hangen; *my ~s are sealed* ik zwijg als het graf 2 rand 3 praatjes, grote mond: *we don't want any of your ~* hou jij je praatjes maar voor je
lip-service lippendienst: *give* (or: *pay*) *~ to* lippendienst bewijzen aan
lipstick lippenstift
liquefy smelten, vloeibaar worden (maken)
liqueur likeur(tje[h])
[1]**liquid** (n) vloeistof, vocht[h]
[2]**liquid** (adj) 1 vloeibaar 2 [com] liquide, vlottend: *~ assets* liquide middelen
liquidate elimineren, uit de weg ruimen
liquidity 1 vloeibaarheid 2 [com] liquiditeit
liquidizer mengbeker, sapcentrifuge
liquor alcoholische drank, alcohol; [Am] sterkedrank
liquorice 1 zoethout[h], zoethoutwortel 2 drop
[1]**lisp** (n) slissende uitspraak, geslis[h]: *he speaks with a ~* hij slist
[2]**lisp** (vb) 1 brabbelen; krompraten [of child] 2 lispelen, slissen
[1]**list** (n) 1 lijst, tabel 2 [shipp] slagzij 3 (-s) strijdperk[h], ring: *enter the ~s (against)* in het krijt treden (tegen)
[2]**list** (vb) [shipp] slagzij maken
[3]**list** (vb) 1 een lijst maken van, rangschikken in een lijst 2 op een lijst zetten: *~ed buildings* op de monumentenlijst geplaatste gebouwen
listen luisteren: *~ in (to)* (mee)luisteren (naar), afluisteren; *~ to* luisteren naar
listener luisteraar
listless lusteloos, futloos
lit 1 aan(gestoken), brandend 2 verlicht, beschenen
litany litanie [also fig]
lite light, dieet-: *~ ice cream* halfvol ijs
literacy alfabetisme[h], het kunnen lezen en schrijven
literal letterlijk, letter-
literary 1 literair, letterkundig 2 geletterd: *~ man* geletterd man, letterkundige
literate geletterd: *only half the children in this group are ~* niet meer dan de helft van de kinderen in deze groep kan lezen en schrijven
literature 1 literatuur, letterkunde: *the ~ of* (or: *on*) *a subject* de literatuur over een onderwerp 2 [inform] voorlichtingsmateri-

aal[h]
lithe soepel; buigzaam, lenig
Lithuania Litouwen
[1]**Lithuanian** (n) Litouwer, Litouwse
[2]**Lithuanian** (adj) Litouws
litigation proces[h], procesvoering, rechtszaak
litmus paper lakmoespapier(tje)[h]
litre liter
litter 1 rommel, rotzooi, troep 2 (stal)stro[h]; afdekstro[h] [for plants]; stalmest 3 nest[h] (jongen), worp: *have a ~ of kittens* jongen, jongen krijgen
litterbin afvalbak, prullenmand
[1]**little** (adj) 1 klein: *a ~ bit* een (klein) beetje; *~ finger* pink; *his ~ sister* zijn jongere zusje; *her ~ ones* haar kinderen; *its ~ ones* haar jongen 2 klein(zielig), kleintjes: *~ minds* kleingeestigen; *~ things please ~ minds* kleine mensen, kleine wensen
[2]**little** (pron) weinig, beetje: *he got ~ out of it* het bracht hem maar weinig op; *make ~ of sth.* ergens weinig van begrijpen; *~ or nothing* weinig of niets; *~ by ~* beetje bij beetje; *every ~ helps* alle beetjes helpen
[3]**little** (adv) 1 weinig, amper, gering: *~ more than an hour* iets meer dan een uur 2 volstrekt niet: *~ did he know that ...* hij had er geen flauw benul van dat ...
liturgy liturgie
[1]**live** (adj) 1 levend, in leven (zijnd): *~ bait* levend aas; *a real ~ horse!* een heus paard! 2 direct, rechtstreeks: *~ broadcast* directe uitzending 3 levendig, actief: *a ~ topic* een actueel onderwerp 4 onder spanning staand: *~ wire* onder spanning staande draad; [fig] energieke figuur || *~ ammunition* (or: *cartridges*) scherpe munitie (or: patronen)
[2]**live** (vb) 1 leven, bestaan: *~ and let ~* leven en laten leven; *long ~ the Queen!* (lang) leve de koningin!; *~ together* samenleven, samenwonen; *~ above* (or: *beyond*) *one's means* boven zijn stand leven; *~ for a)* leven voor; *b)* toeleven naar; *~ with a situation* (hebben leren) leven met een situatie 2 wonen: *~ in* inwonen, intern zijn; *~ on one's own* op zichzelf wonen 3 voortleven: *you haven't ~d yet!* je hebt nog helemaal niet van het leven genoten!
[3]**live** (vb) 1 leven: *~ a double life* een dubbelleven leiden 2 beleven, doormaken, meemaken || *~ it up* het ervan nemen, de bloemetjes buiten zetten
liveable 1 bewoonbaar 2 leefbaar
live-in 1 samenwonend 2 inwonend
livelihood levensonderhoud[h]: *earn* (or: *gain*) *one's ~* de kost verdienen
lively levendig: *~ colours* sprekende kleuren
liven verlevendigen, opfleuren: *~ up* op-

fleuren, opvrolijken
liver lever
livery livrei, uniform[h]
live-screen rechtstreeks uitzenden
livestock vee[h], levende have
live up to naleven, waarmaken: ~ one's reputation zijn naam eer aan doen
livid 1 hels, des duivels: ~ at razend op **2** lijkbleek, asgrauw **3** loodgrijs, blauwgrijs
¹living (n) **1** inkomen[h], kostwinning: *earn/gain* (or: *get, make*) a ~ (as, out of, by) de kost verdienen (als) **2** leven[h], levensonderhoud[h]
²living (adj) **1** levend, bestaand: *(with)in ~ memory* bij mensenheugenis **2** levendig ‖ he's the ~ *image of his father* hij is het evenbeeld van zijn vader
living room woonkamer; huiskamer
lizard hagedis
llama lama(wol)
LL B *Bachelor of Laws* bachelor (in de rechten)
¹load (n) **1** lading; last [also fig]: *that takes a ~ off my mind* dat is een pak van mijn hart **2** belasting, massa **3** (elektrisch) vermogen[h], kracht **4** [inform] hoop, massa's: *they have ~s of money* ze barsten van het geld
²load (vb) laden [firearms, camera]
³load (vb) laden, geladen worden, bevrachten: *the table was ~ed with presents* de tafel stond vol met cadeaus
loaded 1 geladen, emotioneel geladen **2** [inform] stomdronken **3** [Am; inform] stoned **4** venijnig, geniepig: *a ~ question* een strikvraag
loaf 1 brood[h]: *a ~ of brown bread* een bruin brood **2** brood(suiker)[h] **3** kop, hersens: *use your ~ for once* denk nu eens een keer na
loaf about rondhangen, lummelen
loafer 1 leegloper, lanterfanter **2** [Am] lage schoen, loafer
loam leem[+h]
¹loan (n) **1** lening: *apply for a ~ with a bank* een lening bij een bank aanvragen **2** leen[h], tijdelijk gebruik[h]: *have sth. on ~ from s.o.* iets van iem. te leen hebben; *thank you for the ~ of your car* bedankt voor het lenen van je auto
²loan (vb) (uit)lenen: ~ *money to a friend* geld aan een vriend lenen
loan shark [inform] woekeraar; uitzuiger
loanword leenwoord[h]
loath ongenegen, afkerig: *the elderly couple were ~ to leave the house at night* het oudere echtpaar ging 's avonds niet graag de deur uit
loathe verafschuwen
loathing afkeer
loathsome walgelijk, weerzinwekkend
lob 1 [tennis] lobben **2** [inform] gooien, smijten
¹lobby (n) **1** hal[h], portaal[h] **2** foyer **3** lobby,

pressiegroep
²lobby (vb) lobbyen, druk uitoefenen op de politieke besluitvorming
³lobby (vb) in de wandelgangen bewerken; onder druk zetten [MPs]
lobbyist lobbyist; lid van pressiegroep
lobe (oor)lel **2** kwab; lob [of brain, lung]
lobster zeekreeft
¹local (n) **1** plaatselijke bewoner, inboorling **2** [inform] stamcafé[h], stamkroeg
²local (adj) plaatselijk, lokaal, buurt-, streek-: ~ *authority* plaatselijke overheid; ~ *call* lokaal gesprek; ~ *government* plaatselijk bestuur
locality plaats, district[h], buurt
localize lokaliseren, tot een bepaalde plaats beperken, een plaats toekennen: *they hoped to ~ the outbreak of polio* ze hoopten de uitbarsting van polio tot een klein gebied te beperken
¹locate (vb) [Am] zich vestigen, gaan wonen, een zaak opzetten
²locate (vb) **1** de positie bepalen van, opsporen: *I can't ~ that village anywhere* ik kan dat dorp nergens vinden **2** vestigen, plaatsen, stationeren: *the estate was ~d on the bank of a river* het landgoed was gelegen aan de oever van een rivier
location 1 plaats, ligging, positie **2** terrein[h], afgebakend land[h] **3** locatie: *filmed on ~ in Australia* op locatie gefilmd in Australië
loch 1 meer[h] **2** smalle (ingesloten) zeearm
¹lock (n) **1** (haar)lok **2** slot[h] [also of firearms]; sluiting: *under ~ and key* achter slot en grendel; [fig] in de gevangenis **3** vergrendeling **4** (schut)sluis **5** houdgreep ‖ ~, *stock, and barrel* in zijn geheel, alles inbegrepen
²lock (vb) sluiten, vergrendeld (kunnen) worden: *the doors wouldn't ~* de deuren wilden niet sluiten
³lock (vb) **1** (af)sluiten, op slot doen **2** wegsluiten; opsluiten [also fig]: *don't forget to ~ away your valuables* vergeet niet je kostbaarheden op te bergen
locker kast(je[h]); kluis [eg for clothing, luggage]
locker room kleedkamer
lock gate sluisdeur
locksmith slotenmaker
¹lock up (vb) afsluiten, alles op slot doen
²lock up (vb) **1** op slot doen, afsluiten **2** opbergen, wegsluiten: ~ *one's gold and silver* zijn goud en zilver veilig opbergen **3** opsluiten; wegstoppen [in prison, madhouse]
lock-up 1 arrestantenhok[h], cachot[h], nor, bajes **2** afsluitbare ruimte, kiosk, dagwinkel, opbergbox
locomotion (voort)beweging(svermogen[h])
locomotive locomotief
locust 1 sprinkhaan **2** [Am] cicade
lodestar leidster [also fig]; poolster

¹lodge (n) **1** (schuil)hut **2** personeelswoning, portierswoning **3** afdeling, (vrijmetselaars)-loge

²lodge (vb) **1** verblijven, (tijdelijk) wonen, logeren: ~ *at* a friend's, ~ *with* a friend bij een vriend wonen **2** vast komen te zitten, blijven steken: *the bullet ~d in the ceiling* de kogel bleef in het plafond steken

³lodge (vb) **1** onderdak geven, logeren, (tijdelijk) huisvesten **2** indienen, voorleggen: ~ a *complaint* een aanklacht indienen

lodger kamerbewoner, (kamer)huurder

lodgings (gehuurde) kamer(s)

loft zolder(kamer), vliering, hooizolder

lofty 1 torenhoog **2** verheven, edel: ~ *ideals* hooggestemde idealen **3** hooghartig, arrogant: *behave loftily to s.o.* (erg) uit de hoogte doen tegen iem.

¹log (n) **1** blok(hout)ʰ, boomstronk, boomstam **2** logboekʰ, scheepsjournaalʰ || *sleep like a ~* slapen als een os

²log (vb) in het logboek opschrijven || ~ *off* uitloggen; *the truck driver had ~ged up 700 miles* de vrachtrijder had er 700 mijl op zitten; ~ *into* a computer system inloggen

logarithm logaritme

logbook 1 logboekʰ, scheepsjournaalʰ, journaalʰ van een vliegtuig, werkverslagʰ, dagboekʰ, reisjournaalʰ **2** registratiebewijsʰ [of car]

log cabin blokhut

logger [Am] houthakker

loggerhead: *they are always at ~s with each other* ze liggen altijd met elkaar overhoop

logic logica, redeneerkunde

logical logisch, steekhoudend, vanzelfsprekend (volgend uit)

logistics logistiek

logjam impasse; knelpuntʰ

logo 1 logotypeʰ, woordmerkʰ **2** logoʰ, beeldmerkʰ, firma-embleemʰ

loin lende

loincloth lendendoekʰ

¹loiter (vb) treuzelen: ~ *about* (or: *around*) rondhangen; ~ *with intent* zich verdacht ophouden

²loiter (vb) verdoen, verlummelen: ~ *away* one's time zijn tijd verdoen

LOL *laughing out loud* lol [lach me rot]

loll (rond)hangen, lummelen, leunen

lollipop (ijs)lolly: ~ *man* klaar-over

lolly 1 lolly **2** [inform] poen

lone alleen, verlaten, eenzaam: *be* (or: *play*) a ~ *hand* [fig] met niemand rekening houden; ~ *wolf* iem. die zijn eigen weg gaat

lonely eenzaam, verlaten, alleen

loner eenzame, eenling

lonesome eenzaam, alleen: *by* (or: *on*) *his ~* in zijn (dooie) eentje

¹long (adj) lang, langgerekt, langdurig, ver, langlopend: *a ~ haul* a) een hele ruk [eg a

long trip]; **b)** een lange tijd (*or:* termijn); *to cut a ~ story short* om kort te gaan, samengevat; *in the ~ term* op den duur, op de lange duur; ~ *vacation* zomervakantie; *it won't take ~* het zal niet lang duren; *before* ~ binnenkort, spoedig; *he won't stay for ~* hij zal niet (voor) lang blijven || *the ~ arm of the law* de lange arm der wet; *not by a ~ chalk* op geen stukken na, bijlange (na) niet; *make* (*or:* pull) a ~ *face* ongelukkig kijken; [roughly] een lang gezicht trekken; *in the ~ run* uiteindelijk; ~ *shot* a) kansloos deelnemer; **b)** gok, waagstuk; [Am] *by a ~ shot* veruit, met gemak; [Am] *not by a ~ shot* op geen stukken na, bijlange na niet; ~ *in the tooth* lang in de mond, aftands; *take a ~ view* dingen op de lange termijn bekijken; *go a ~ way* (towards) voordelig (in het gebruik) zijn, veel helpen, het ver schoppen

²long (vb) (also + for) hevig verlangen (naar), hunkeren: *after two weeks we were ~ing for the city again* na twee weken verlangden we alweer naar de stad

³long (adv) lang, lange tijd: *all night* ~ de hele nacht; *be ~ in doing sth.* lang over iets doen

longboat barkas; (grote) sloep

longbow (grote) handboog

longevity lang levenʰ, lange levensduur

longhand (gewoon) handschrift

¹longing (n) verlangenʰ, hunkering

²longing (adj) vol verlangen, smachtend

longitude (geografische) lengte, longitude

long-lasting langdurig

long-life 1 met een lange levensduur **2** langer houdbaar || ~ *batteries* batterijen met een lange levensduur

long-lived 1 lang levend **2** van lange duur, hardnekkig

long-sighted 1 verziend **2** vooruitziend

long-tailed tit staartmees

long-term langlopend, op lange termijn: *the ~ unemployed* de langdurig werklozen

long-winded langdradig

loo wc, plee

¹look (n) **1** blik, kijkjeʰ: *let's have a ~* laten we even een kijkje nemen **2** (gelaats)uitdrukking, blik **3** uiterlijkʰ, (knap) voorkomenʰ, aanzienʰ: *by the ~ of it* (or: things) zo te zien **4** mode **5** uitzichtʰ **6** (-s) uiterlijkʰ, schoonheid: *lose one's ~s* minder mooi worden

²look (vb) **1** kijken, (proberen te) zien, aandachtig kijken: ~ *about* (or: *around*) om zich heen kijken, rondkijken; ~ *ahead* vooruitzien [also fig]; ~ *on* toekijken; ~ *at* kijken naar, beschouwen, onderzoeken; *not ~ at* niet in overweging nemen, niets willen weten van; ~ *beyond* verder kijken dan; ~ *down the road* de weg af kijken; ~ *round* the town een kijkje in de stad nemen; ~ *before you leap* bezint eer gij begint **2** uitkijken, uitzien, liggen: ~

to *the south* op het zuiden liggen **3** wijzen [in particular direction]; (bepaalde kant) uitgaan || ~ **down** *(up)on* neerkijken op; ~ **forward** *to* tegemoet zien, verlangen naar; ~ **here!** kijk eens (even hier)!, luister eens!; ~ **in** aanlopen, aanwippen; [inform] tv kijken; ~ **in** *on s.o.* bij iem. langskomen; ~ **after** passen op, toezien op; ~ **after** *o.s.*, ~ **after** *one's own interests* voor zichzelf zorgen; ~ **for** zoeken (naar); ~ **for** *trouble* om moeilijkheden vragen; ~ **into** a) even bezoeken; **b)** onderzoeken; ~ **(up)on** *s.o. as* iem. beschouwen als
³look (vb) **1** zijn blik richten op, kijken (naar), zien: ~ *what you've* **done** kijk nou (eens) wat je gedaan hebt **2** eruitzien als: ~ *one's* **age** aan iem. zijn leeftijd afzien
⁴look (vb) lijken (te zijn), uitzien, de indruk wekken te zijn: [Am] ~ **good** goed lijken te gaan, er goed uitzien; *it* ~s *like* snow er is sneeuw op komst; *he* ~s *as if he has a hangover* hij ziet eruit alsof hij een kater heeft
lookalikeʰ evenbeeldʰ, dubbelganger
looker [inform] schoonheid
looker-on toeschouwer, kijker
look-in [inform] **1** kijkjeʰ; bezoekjeʰ **2** kans (op succes)
looking-glass spiegel
lookout 1 het uitkijken: *keep a* ~ een oogje in het zeil houden; *be* **on** *the* ~ **for** op zoek zijn naar **2** uitkijkpost **3** uitzichtʰ
look over doornemen [eg letters]; doorkijken
look through goed bekijken; grondig/helemaal doornemen, een voor een doornemen [eg documents] || *look* **right** (or: **straight**) *through s.o.* straal langs iem. heen kijken, doen alsof iem. lucht is
look to 1 zorgen voor, bekommeren over: ~ *it that ...* zorg ervoor, dat ... **2** vertrouwen op, rekenen op: *don't* ~ *her* **for** *help* (or: *to help you*) verwacht van haar geen hulp
¹look up (vb) **1** opkijken, de ogen opslaan **2** beter worden [eg of business]; vooruitgaan: *prices are looking up* de prijzen stijgen || ~ **to** opkijken naar, bewonderen
²look up (vb) **1** opzoeken, naslaan **2** raadplegen **3** (kort) bezoeken, opzoeken
¹loom (n) weefgetouwʰ
²loom (vb) opdoemen [also fig]; dreigend verschijnen, zich flauw aftekenen: ~ *large* onevenredig belangrijk lijken, nadrukkelijk aanwezig zijn
¹loony (n) gek, dwaas
²loony (adj) geschift, gek, getikt
loony-bin gekkenhuisʰ
¹loop (n) **1** lus, strop, bocht **2** beugel, handvatʰ **3** spiraaltjeʰ || [inform] *be* **in** *the* ~ tot de incrowd/trendsetters behoren
²loop (vb) een lus vormen
³loop (vb) **1** een lus maken in, met een lus vastmaken **2** door een lus halen

loophole uitvlucht, uitweg: *~s in the law* mazen in de wet(geving)
¹loose (n) (staat van) vrijheid, losbandigheid: *there's a killer* **on** *the* ~ er loopt een moordenaar vrij rond
²loose (adj) **1** los, slap, open: ~ **ends** losse eindjes; [fig] onvolkomenheden, onafgewerkte zaken **2** vrij, bevrijd, ongehinderd: *break* (or: *get*) ~ uitbreken, ontsnappen; *cut* ~ a) (met moeite) weggaan, zich losmaken; **b)** op gang komen; *let* ~ vrij laten, de vrije hand laten, ontketenen **3** wijd, ruim, soepel **4** ongedisciplineerd, lichtzinnig: *have a* ~ *tongue* loslippig zijn || *be at a* ~ *end* niets omhanden hebben; *have a* **screw** ~ ze zien vliegen, een beetje geschift zijn
³loose (vb) losmaken, bevrijden
⁴loose (adv) losjes
loose-leaf losbladig
loosely losjes, vaag, in het wilde weg
¹loosen (vb) losgaan, ontspannen, verslappen: ~ *up* een warming-up doen, de spieren losmaken
²loosen (vb) los(ser) maken, laten verslappen: *drink ~s the* **tongue** drank maakt spraakzaam; ~ *up* doen ontspannen
¹loot (n) **1** (oorlogs)buit, gestolen goedʰ, prooi **2** poet, poen, geldʰ
²loot (vb) plunderen, roven
lop afsnoeien, afkappen
lop-eared met hangende oren: *a* ~ *rabbit* een hangoor(konijn)
lopsided 1 scheef, overhellend **2** ongebalanceerd, eenzijdig
¹lord (n) **1** heer, vorst, koning **2** lord, edelachtbare, excellentie: *live like a* ~ als een vorst leven; *My* Lord edelachtbare, heer **3** (the Lords) het Hogerhuis, de leden van het Hogerhuis
²lord (vb) de baas spelen: ~ *it over s.o.* over iem. de baas spelen
Lord (de) Heer, God: *the ~'s* **Prayer** het Onze Vader
Lord Chancellor voorzitter van het Hogerhuis
lordship Lord [form of address for lord and judge]; edele heer, edelachtbare
lore traditionele kennis, overlevering
lorry vrachtauto
¹lose (vb) **1** verliezen, verlies lijden, er op achteruit gaan: *you can't* ~ daar heb je niets bij te verliezen; ~ *out on sth.* er (geld) bij inschieten **2** achterlopen [of watch etc]
²lose (vb) **1** verliezen, kwijtraken, verspelen: [inform] ~ *one's* **cool** z'n kalmte verliezen; ~ *count* de tel kwijtraken; ~ *sight* of uit het oog verliezen; ~ *one's* **temper** boos worden; ~ *no* **time** *in (doing sth.)* geen tijd verspillen met (iets); ~ *o.s.* **in** geheel opgaan in **2** doen verliezen, kosten: *her stupid mistake lost us a major customer* haar stomme fout kostte ons

een grote klant **3** missen, niet winnen
loser verliezer: *born* ~ geboren verliezer; *a good* (or: *bad*) ~ een goede (or: slechte) verliezer
loss 1 verlies[h] **2** nadeel[h], schade **3** achteruitgang, teruggang ‖ *be at a ~ (what to do)* niet weten wat men doen moet; *be at a ~ for words* met de mond vol tanden staan
lost 1 verloren, weg, kwijt: ~ *property (department, office)* (afdeling/bureau) gevonden voorwerpen **2** gemist: ~ *chance* gemiste kans **3** in gedachten verzonken, afwezig, er niet bij: ~ *in thought* in gedachten verzonken **4** verspild: *sarcasm is ~ (up)on him* sarcasme raakt hem niet ‖ *get ~!* donder op!
lot 1 portie, aandeel[h] **2** kavel, perceel[h], partij, (veiling)nummer[h] **3** lot[h], loterijbriefje[h]: *cast* (or: *draw*) ~*s* loten **4** (nood)lot[h], levenslot[h]: *cast* (or: *throw*) *in one's* ~ *with* mee gaan doen met **5** [Am] stuk grond, terrein[h]: *parking* ~ parkeerterrein **6** groep, aantal dingen (mensen), een hoop, een heleboel: ~*s and lots* ontzettend veel, hopen; *a* ~ *of books*, ~*s of books* een heleboel boeken; *that's the ~* dat is alles; *things have changed quite a* ~ er is nogal wat veranderd
lotion lotion, haarwater[h], gezichtswater[h]
lottery loterij
¹loud (adj) **1** luid(ruchtig), hard **2** opzichtig; schreeuwend [of colour]
²loud (adv) luid(ruchtig), hard, schreeuwerig: ~ *and clear* erg duidelijk, overduidelijk; *out* ~ hardop
loudmouth luidruchtig persoon
loudspeaker luidspreker, box
¹lounge (n) **1** lounge, hal[h], foyer **2** zitkamer, conversatiezaal
²lounge (vb) **1** luieren, (rond)hangen: ~ *about* (or: *around*) rondhangen **2** slenteren, kuieren
louse luis
louse up grondig bederven, verpesten
lousy 1 vol luizen **2** [inform] waardeloos, vuil, beroerd **3** [inform] armzalig [of amount, number etc]
lout lummel, hufter
lovable lief; beminnelijk
¹love (n) **1** liefde, verliefdheid: *mother sends her* ~ moeder laat je groeten; *fall in ~ with s.o.* verliefd worden op iem. **2** plezier[h], genoegen[h]: *music is a great* ~ *of his* muziek is een van zijn grote liefdes **3** liefje[h] **4** [inform] snoes; geliefd persoon [also man] **5** groeten **6** [tennis] love, nul: ~ *all* nul-nul ‖ *not for* ~ *or money* niet voor geld of goeie woorden; *there is no* ~ *lost between them* ze kunnen elkaar niet luchten of zien
²love (vb) liefde voelen, verliefd zijn
³love (vb) **1** houden van, liefhebben, graag mogen: ~ *dearly* innig houden van **2** dol zijn op, heerlijk vinden: *he* ~*s (to go) swimming* hij

is dol op zwemmen
lovebird 1 dwergpapegaai **2** (-s) [inform] tortelduifjes
lovelorn [form] vol liefdesverdriet
lovely 1 mooi, lieftallig, aantrekkelijk **2** [inform] leuk, prettig, fijn, lekker
love match huwelijk[h] uit liefde
love potion liefdesdrank(je[h])
lover 1 (be)minnaar **2** liefhebber, enthousiast **3** (-s) verliefd paar[h] **4** (-s) minnaars, stel[h]
lover boy loverboy
lovesick smachtend van liefde, smoorverliefd
lovey liefje[h], schatje[h]
¹low (n) **1** laag terrein[h], laagte **2** dieptepunt[h], laag punt[h]: *an all-time* ~ een absoluut dieptepunt **3** geloei[h], gebulk[h] **4** lagedrukgebied[h]
²low (adj) **1** laag, niet hoog, niet intensief: *the Low Countries* de lage landen; ~*est common denominator* kleinste gemene deler; ~*est common multiple* kleinste gemene veelvoud; ~ *point* minimum, dieptepunt; ~ *tide* laagwater, eb **2** laag(hartig): ~ *trick* rotstreek **3** plat, ordinair: ~ *expression* ordinaire uitdrukking **4** zacht, stil, niet luid; laag [tone]: *speak in a* ~ *voice* zacht praten **5** ongelukkig, depressief: ~ *spirits* neerslachtigheid **6** verborgen, onopvallend: *lie* ~ zich gedeisd houden **7** zwak, slap, futloos ‖ *keep a* ~ *profile* zich gedeisd houden; *bring* ~ a) aan lagerwal brengen; b) uitputten; c) ziek maken
³low (vb) loeien
⁴low (adv) **1** laag, diep: *aim* ~ laag mikken **2** zacht, stil **3** diep [of sound]; laag **4** bijna uitgeput: *run* ~ opraken, bijna op zijn
¹lowbrow (n) [inform; depr] niet-intellectueel
²lowbrow (adj) [inform; depr] niet intellectueel; ordinair
lowcut laag uitgesneden
the **¹low-down** (n) fijne[h] van de zaak, feiten, inzicht[h]: *have the* ~ *on* het fijne weten over
²low-down (adj) laag, gemeen
¹lower (adj) **1** lager, lager gelegen, onder-, van lage(r) orde: ~ *classes* lagere stand(en); ~ *deck* benedendek **2** neder-, beneden-: *the Lower Rhine* de Neder-Rijn ‖ *Lower Chamber* (or: *House*) Lagerhuis
²lower (vb) afnemen, minder worden, dalen, zakken
³lower (vb) **1** verlagen, doen zakken **2** neerlaten, laten zakken: ~ *one's eyes* de ogen neerslaan **3** verminderen, doen afnemen: ~ *one's voice* zachter praten
lower-case onderkast; in, met kleine letters
low-fat met laag vetgehalte, mager, halva-, halfvol: ~ *margarine* halvarine; ~ *milk* magere melk

low-key rustig, ingehouden
lowland laagland[h]
the **Lowlands** de Schotse Laaglanden
lowlife proleet, schooier, iem. van lage stand
lowly 1 bescheiden; laag [in rank] **2** eenvoudig, nederig
low-minded laag(hartig)
loyal trouw, loyaal
loyalist (regerings)getrouwe, loyalist
loyalty 1 loyaliteit, trouw: *customer* ~ klantentrouw; ~ *card* klantenpas **2** (loyalties) banden, binding
lozenge 1 ruit, ruitvormig iets[h] **2** (hoest)tablet[h]
LP *long-playing record* lp, elpee
LP gas *liquified petroleum gas* lpg[h], autogas[h]
Lt *Lieutenant* lt., luitenant
Ltd *limited* [roughly] nv; naamloze vennootschap
lubricant 1 smeermiddel[h] **2** glijmiddel[h]
lubricate (door)smeren, oliën
lucid 1 helder; duidelijk [also fig] **2** bij zijn verstand
luck geluk[h], toeval[h], succes[h]: *bad* (or: *hard*) ~ pech; *good* ~ succes; *push* one's ~ te veel risico's nemen, overmoedig worden; *try* one's ~ zijn geluk beproeven; *let's do it once more for* ~ laten we het nog een keer doen, misschien brengt dat geluk; *be out of* ~, *be down on* one's ~ pech hebben; *with* ~ als alles goed gaat; *no such* ~ helaas niet; *as* ~ *would have it* (on)gelukkig, toevallig
luckily gelukkig: ~ *for you, I found your keys* je hebt geluk dat ik je sleutels heb gevonden
luckless onfortuinlijk
lucky 1 gelukkig, fortuinlijk, toevallig juist: *a* ~ *thing no-one got hurt* gelukkig raakte er niemand gewond **2** gelukbrengend, geluks-: ~ *charm* talisman; ~ *dip* grabbelton; [fig] loterij; ~ *star* geluksster || *strike* ~ boffen
lucrative winstgevend, lucratief
lucre gewin[h]: *filthy* ~ vuil gewin
ludicrous belachelijk, bespottelijk
[1]**lug** (n) uitsteeksel[h], handvat[h], oor[h]
[2]**lug** (vb) (voort)trekken, (voort)zeulen: ~ *sth. along* iets meesleuren
luggage bagage: *left* ~ afgegeven bagage, bagage in depot
lugubrious luguber, naargeestig, treurig
lukewarm 1 lauw **2** niet erg enthousiast
[1]**lull** (n) korte rust: *a* ~ *in the storm* een korte windstilte tijdens de storm
[2]**lull** (vb) **1** sussen, kalmeren: ~ *to sleep* in slaap sussen **2** in slaap brengen
lullaby slaapliedje[h]
lumbago spit
[1]**lumber** (n) **1** rommel, afgedankt meubilair[h] **2** [Am] half bewerkt hout[h], timmerhout[h], planken

[2]**lumber** (vb) sjokken, zich log voortbewegen: ~ *along* voortsjokken
[3]**lumber** (vb) [inform] (met iets vervelends/moeilijks) opzadelen: ~ *(up) with* opzadelen met
lumberjack [Am] bosbouwer, houthakker
lumber-room rommelkamer
luminous lichtgevend; [fig] helder; duidelijk
[1]**lump** (n) **1** klont, klomp, brok[h]: [fig] *with a* ~ *in my throat* met een brok in mijn keel **2** bult, knobbel
[2]**lump** (vb) klonteren
[3]**lump** (vb) **1** tot een geheel samenvoegen, bij elkaar gooien: ~ *together* onder één noemer brengen **2** slikken: *you'll have to* **like** *it or* ~ *it* je hebt het maar te slikken
lump sum bedrag[h] ineens, ronde som
lunacy waanzin
lunar van de maan, maan-: ~ *eclipse* maansverduistering
[1]**lunatic** (n) krankzinnige
[2]**lunatic** (adj) krankzinnig, gestoord || *the* ~ *fringe* het extremistische deel [of a group]
[1]**lunch** (n) lunch
[2]**lunch** (vb) lunchen
lunch break lunchpauze; middagpauze
luncheon 1 lunch **2** [Am] lichte maaltijd
lung long
[1]**lunge** (n) stoot, uitval
[2]**lunge** (vb) (+ at) uitvallen (naar), een uitval doen
[3]**lunge** (vb) stoten
[1]**lurch** (n) ruk, plotselinge slingerbeweging || [inform] *leave s.o. in the* ~ iem. in de steek laten
[2]**lurch** (vb) slingeren, strompelen
[1]**lure** (n) **1** lokmiddel[h], lokaas[h] **2** aantrekking, verleiding, aantrekkelijkheid
[2]**lure** (vb) (ver)lokken, meetronen: ~ *away (from)* weglokken (van); ~ *into* verlokken tot
lurid 1 schril, zeer fel (gekleurd), vlammend **2** luguber, choquerend
lurk 1 op de loer liggen, zich schuilhouden **2** latent (aanwezig) zijn, verborgen zijn
luscious 1 heerlijk: *a* ~ *peach* een overheerlijke perzik **2** weelderig
[1]**lush** (n) [Am; inform] zuiplap
[2]**lush** (adj) **1** weelderig; overdadig groeiend **2** [inform] luxueus
lust 1 sterk verlangen[h], lust, aandrift: *a* ~ *for power* een verlangen naar macht **2** wellust(igheid), (zinnelijke) lust: *his* **eyes,** *full of* ~ zijn ogen, vol wellust
lust after hevig verlangen naar; begeren
lustre glans, schittering, luister, roem: *add* ~ *to* glans geven aan
lustrous glanzend, schitterend: ~ *eyes* stralende ogen
lusty 1 krachtig, flink, gezond **2** wellustig
lute luit

Luxembourg Luxemburg
Luxembourger Luxemburger, Luxemburgse
luxuriance overvloed, weelderigheid
luxuriant 1 weelderig, overdadig: ~ *flora* weelderige flora **2** vruchtbaar [also fig]: ~ *imagination* rijke verbeelding
luxurious luxueus, weelderig; duur [eg of habits]
luxury 1 weelde, luxe, overvloed: *a life of* ~ een luxueus leven **2** luxe(artikel[h]) **3** weelderigheid
lymph lymfe, weefselvocht[h]
lymph gland lymfklier; lymfknoop
lynch lynchen
lynx lynx
lyre lier
[1]**lyric** (n) **1** lyrisch gedicht[h] **2** (-s) tekst [of song]
[2]**lyric** (adj) lyrisch [of poem, poet]
lyrical lyrisch

m

m 1 *married* geh., gehuwd **2** *masculine* m., mannelijk **3** *metre(s)* m, meter(s) **4** *mile(s)* mijl(en) **5** *million(s)* mln., miljoen(en) **6** *minute(s)* min, minuut, minuten
ma ma
MA *Master of Arts* Master of Arts, drs., doctorandus
ma'am *madam* mevrouw
mac *mackintosh* regenjas
macabre macaber, griezelig
macaroon bitterkoekje[h]
mace 1 goedendag, strijdknots, knuppel **2** scepter; staf [of speaker in House of Commons] **3** foelie
Macedonia Macedonië
¹Macedonian (n) Macedoniër, Macedonische
²Macedonian (adj) Macedonisch
machination intrige
machine 1 machine [also fig]; werktuig[h], apparaat[h] **2** aandrijfmechanisme[h]
machine gun machinegeweer[h]
machinery machinerie [also fig]; machinepark[h], systeem[h], apparaat[h]
machinist monteur, werktuigkundige, machinebankwerker, vakman voor werktuigmachines
¹macho (n) macho
²macho (adj) macho
mackerel makreel
mackintosh regenjas
macrobiotic macrobiotisch
mad 1 gek, krankzinnig: *go ~* gek worden; *drive s.o. ~* iem. gek maken **2** dwaas, onzinnig: *~ project* dwaze onderneming **3** wild, razend; hevig [eg of wind]: *make a ~ run for ...* als een gek rennen naar ... **4** hondsdol **5** (+ about, after, for, on) verzot (op) **6** (+ at, about sth.; at, with s.o.) boos (op), woedend (op/om) || *~ as a* **hatter**, *~ as a March* **hare** stapelgek
¹Madagascan (n) Malagassiër, Malagassische
²Madagascan (adj) Malagassisch
Madagascar Madagaskar
madam mevrouw, juffrouw: *excuse me, ~, can I help you?* pardon, mevrouw, kan ik u van dienst zijn?
madcap dol, roekeloos: *~ ideas* dwaze ideeën
mad cow disease gekkekoeienziekte
madden gek worden/maken, woedend worden/maken, irriteren

maddening erg vervelend: *~ waste of time* ergerlijk tijdverlies
madhouse gekkenhuis[h] [also fig]
madly 1 als een bezetene **2** heel (erg): *~ in love* waanzinnig verliefd
madman gek
madness 1 krankzinnigheid, waanzin(nigheid) **2** dwaasheid, gekte **3** enthousiasme[h]
maelstrom 1 (enorme) draaikolk **2** maalstroom [also fig]
mafia maffia
mag *magazine* tijdschrift[h]
magazine 1 magazine[h], tijdschrift[h]; radiomagazine, tv-magazine[h] **2** magazijn[h] [of gun]
maggot made
¹magic (n) magie [also fig]; toverkunst, betovering: *as if by ~*, *like ~* als bij toverslag
²magic (adj) **1** magisch, tover- **2** betoverend || *~ carpet* vliegend tapijt
magical wonderbaarlijk, magisch
magician 1 tovenaar **2** goochelaar [also fig]; kunstenaar
magisterial 1 gezaghebbend [also fig] **2** autoritair **3** magistraal
magistrate 1 magistraat, (rechterlijk) ambtenaar **2** politierechter, vrederechter
magnanimity grootmoedigheid
magnanimous edelmoedig, grootmoedig
magnate magnaat
magnet magneet [also fig]
magnetic 1 magnetisch: *~ compass* kompas; *~ needle* magneetnaald; *~ north* magnetische noordpool **2** onweerstaanbaar
magnetism 1 magnetisme[h] **2** aantrekkingskracht
magnetize 1 magnetiseren **2** boeien, fascineren
magnificence 1 pracht, weelde **2** grootsheid
magnificent 1 prachtig, groots **2** weelderig **3** prima
¹magnify (vb) overdrijven, opblazen
²magnify (vb) **1** vergroten [of lens etc]; uitvergroten **2** versterken [sound]
magnifying glass vergrootglas[h]
magnitude 1 belang[h], belangrijkheid **2** omvang, grootte **3** [astronomy] helderheid
magnum anderhalveliterfles
magpie 1 ekster **2** verzamelaar, hamsteraar
mahogany mahonie[h]
maid 1 hulp, dienstmeisje[h] **2** meisje[h], juffrouw **3** maagd || *~ of* **honour** (ongehuwde) hofdame
¹maiden (n) **1** meisje[h], juffrouw **2** maagd
²maiden (adj) **1** maagdelijk, van een meisje **2** ongetrouwd [of woman]: *~ name* meisjesnaam **3** eerste [eg of trip, flight]: *the Titanic sank on her ~* **voyage** de Titanic zonk tijdens

haar eerste reis

m<u>ai</u>denhead 1 maagdenvlies[h] **2** maagdelijkheid [also fig]

¹mail (n) **1** post, brieven **2** maliënkolder

²mail (vb) **1** posten, per post versturen **2** (be)pantseren

m<u>ai</u>lbox [Am] brievenbus

m<u>ai</u>ling list adressenlijst, verzendlijst

m<u>ai</u>lman [Am] postbode

maim verminken [also fig]; kreupel maken

¹m<u>ai</u>n (n) **1** hoofdleiding, hoofdbuis, hoofdkabel **2** (-s) (elektriciteits)net[h], elektriciteit, lichtnet[h]: *connected to the ~s* (op het elektriciteitsnet) aangesloten **3** (open) zee ‖ *in the ~* voor het grootste gedeelte, in het algemeen

²m<u>ai</u>n (adj) hoofd-, belangrijkste, voornaamste: *~ course* hoofdgerecht; *~ line* **a)** hoofdlijn [of railways]; **b)** [Am] hoofdstraat; *~ street* hoofdstraat

m<u>ai</u>nframe mainframe[h], hoofdcomputer

m<u>ai</u>nland vasteland[h]

m<u>ai</u>nly hoofdzakelijk, voornamelijk, grotendeels

m<u>ai</u>nstay steunpilaar, pijler

m<u>ai</u>nstream 1 heersende stroming **2** hoofdstroom [of river] **3** mainstream [jazz]

maint<u>ai</u>n 1 handhaven, in stand houden: *he ~ed his calm attitude* hij bleef rustig; *~ order* de orde bewaren **2** onderhouden [eg house, family]; zorgen voor, een onderhoudsbeurt geven **3** beweren, stellen: *the suspect ~s his innocence* de verdachte zegt dat hij onschuldig is **4** verdedigen, opkomen voor: *~ an opinion* een mening verdedigen

m<u>ai</u>ntenance 1 handhaving [eg of law] **2** onderhoud[h] [of house, machine] **3** levensonderhoud[h], levensbehoeften **4** toelage [of woman, child]; alimentatie

maison<u>e</u>tte 1 huisje[h], flatje[h] **2** maisonnette

maize mais

maj<u>e</u>stic majestueus, verheven

M<u>aj</u>esty Majesteit, Koninklijke Hoogheid ‖ *on Her* (or: *His*) *~'s service* dienst [on envelope]

¹m<u>aj</u>or (n) **1** meerderjarige **2** majoor **3** [Am] hoofdvak[h] [of study] **4** [Am] hoofdvakstudent

²m<u>aj</u>or (adj) **1** groot, groter, voornaamste: *a ~ breakthrough* een belangrijke doorbraak; *the ~ part of* de meerderheid van; *~ road* hoofdweg **2** ernstig, zwaar: *~ operation* zware operatie **3** meerderjarig, volwassen **4** [mus] in majeur: *C ~* C grote terts **5** senior, de oudere: *Rowland ~* Rowland senior

m<u>aj</u>or in [Am] als hoofdvak(ken) hebben, (als hoofdvak) studeren

maj<u>o</u>rity 1 meerderheid: *the ~ of people* de meeste mensen; *the ~ world* de derde wereld, de ontwikkelingslanden **2** meeste: *in*

the ~ in de meerderheid

m<u>aj</u>orly [inform] uiterst, heel erg: *he is ~ insane* hij is compleet gestoord

¹make (n) **1** merk[h] **2** fabricage, vervaardiging ‖ *on the ~* **a)** op (eigen) voordeel uit, op winst uit; **b)** op de versiertoer

²make (vb) **1** doen, zich gedragen, handelen: *~ as if* (or: *though*) **a)** doen alsof; **b)** op het punt staan **2** gaan, zich begeven: *we were making toward(s) the woods* wij gingen naar de bossen ‖ *you'll have to ~ do with this old pair of trousers* je zult het met deze oude broek moeten doen; *~ away* (or: *off*) 'm smeren, ervandoor gaan; *~ away with o.s.* zich van kant maken; *~ off with* wegnemen, meenemen, jatten

³make (vb) **1** maken, bouwen, fabriceren, scheppen, veroorzaken, bereiden; opstellen [law, testament]: *~ coffee* (or: *tea*) koffie (or: thee) zetten; *God made man* God schiep de mens; *~ over a dress* een jurk vermaken; *show them what you are made of* toon wat je waard bent **2** maken, vormen, maken tot, benoemen tot: *the workers made him their spokesman* de arbeiders maakten hem tot hun woordvoerder **3** (ver)krijgen, (be)halen; binnenhalen [profit]; hebben [success]; lijden [loss]; verdienen, scoren, maken [point etc]: *~ a lot of money* veel geld verdienen; [cards] *~ a trick* een slag maken; *he made a lot on this deal* hij verdiende een hoop aan deze transactie **4** laten, ertoe brengen, doen, maken dat: *don't ~ me laugh* laat me niet lachen; *she made the food go round* ze zorgde ervoor dat er genoeg eten was voor iedereen; *you can't ~ me* je kunt me niet dwingen **5** schatten (op), komen op: *what time do you ~ it?* hoe laat heeft u het? **6** worden, maken, zijn: *three and four ~ seven* drie en vier is zeven **7** (geschikt) zijn (voor), (op)leveren, worden: *this student will never ~ a good doctor* deze student zal nooit een goede arts worden; *the man is made for this job* de man is perfect voor deze baan **8** bereiken, komen tot; halen [speed]; gaan; pakken [train]; zien; in zicht krijgen [land]; worden, komen in: *~ an appointment* op tijd zijn voor een afspraak; *~ the front pages* de voorpagina's halen; *~ it* op tijd zijn, het halen; [fig] succes hebben, slagen; *have it made* geslaagd zijn, op rozen zitten **9** doen, verrichten; uitvoeren [research]; geven [promise]; nemen [test]; houden [speech]: *~ an effort* een poging doen, pogen; *~ a phone call* opbellen **10** opmaken [bed] **11** tot een succes maken, het hem doen, de finishing touch geven *of o.s.* succes hebben [in life] ‖ *this fool can ~ or break the project* deze gek kan het project maken of breken; *~ sth. do* zich met iets behelpen; *let's ~ it next week* (or: *Wednesday*) laten we (voor) volgende week (or: woensdag) afspreken; ~ *the **most** of* a) er het beste van maken; **b)** zoveel mogelijk profiteren van; ~ **much** *of* a) belangrijk vinden; **b)** veel hebben aan; **c)** veel begrijpen van; ~ **nothing** *of* a) gemakkelijk doen (over), geen probleem maken van; **b)** niets begrijpen van; *they couldn't* ~ *anything **of** my notes* ze konden niets met mijn aantekeningen beginnen

make-believe schijn, fantasie, het doen alsof: *this **fight** is just* ~ dit gevecht is maar spel

make for 1 gaan naar, zich begeven naar: *we made for the nearest **pub*** we gingen naar de dichtstbijzijnde kroeg **2** bevorderen, bijdragen tot, zorgen voor

¹make out (vb) klaarspelen, het maken, zich redden: *the European **industry** is not making out as bad as everybody says* met de Europese industrie gaat het niet zo slecht als iedereen zegt

²make out (vb) **1** uitschrijven, invullen: ~ *a **cheque** to* (or: *in favour of*) een cheque uitschrijven op naam van (*or:* ten gunste van) **2** beweren, verkondigen: *she makes **herself** out to be very rich* zij beweert dat ze erg rijk is **3** onderscheiden, zien **4** ontcijferen [eg handwriting] **5** begrijpen, snappen, hoogte krijgen van: *I can't* ~ *this **message*** ik snap dit bericht niet

makeover opknapbeurt, metamorfose

maker maker, fabrikant ‖ *meet one's* ~ sterven, dood gaan

¹makeshift (n) tijdelijke vervanging, noodoplossing

²makeshift (adj) voorlopig, tijdelijk, nood-

¹make up (vb) **1** zich opmaken, zich schminken **2** zich verzoenen, weer goedmaken ‖ ~ *for* weer goedmaken, vergoeden; ~ *to s.o.* bij iem. in de gunst zien te komen; ~ *to s.o. for sth.* a) iem. iets vergoeden; **b)** iets goedmaken met iem (*or:* bij) iem.

²make up (vb) **1** opmaken, schminken **2** bijleggen; goedmaken [quarrel]: *make **it** up (with s.o.)* het weer goedmaken (met iem.) **3** volledig maken, aanvullen: *father made up the difference of three pounds* vader legde de ontbrekende drie pond bij **4** vergoeden, goedmaken, teruggeven, terugbetalen: ~ *lost **ground*** de schade inhalen **5** verzinnen: ~ *an **excuse*** een excuus verzinnen **6** vormen, samenstellen: *the group was made up **of** four musicians* de groep bestond uit vier muzikanten **7** maken, opstellen; klaarmaken [medicine]; bereiden, maken tot (pakje), (kleren) maken (van), naaien **8** opmaken [bed]

make-up 1 make-up, schmink **2** aard, karakterʰ, natuur **3** samenstelling, opbouw

making 1 (-s) verdiensten **2** (-s) ingrediënten [also fig]; (juiste) kwaliteiten: *have the ~s of a surgeon* het in zich hebben om chirurg te worden ‖ *in the* ~ in de maak, in voorberei-

ding

maladjusted 1 [psychology] onaangepast **2** [econ] onevenwichtig

malady kwaal, ziekte: *a **social** ~* een sociale plaag

¹Malagasy (n) Malagassiër, Malagassische

²Malagasy (adj) Malagassisch

malaise 1 malaise **2** wee gevoel

malapropism grappige verspreking

malaria malaria

Malawi Malawi

¹Malawian (n) Malawiër, Malawische

²Malawian (adj) Malawisch

Malaysia Maleisië

¹Malaysian (n) Maleisiër, Maleisische

²Malaysian (adj) Maleisisch

malcontent ontevredene, ontevreden mens

¹male (n) **1** mannelijk persoon **2** mannetjeʰ [animal]

²male (adj) **1** mannelijk [also fig]: ~ *chauvinism* (mannelijk) seksisme; ~ *choir* mannenkoor **2** mannetjes-

malefactor boosdoener

malevolence kwaadwilligheid, boosaardigheid

malevolent [esp form] kwaadwillig

malformed misvormd

malfunction storing, defectʰ

Mali Mali

¹Malian (n) Malinees, Malinese

²Malian (adj) Malinees

malice 1 kwaadwilligheid, boosaardigheid: *bear* ~ *towards* (or: *to, against*) *s.o.* (een) wrok tegen iem. koesteren **2** boos opzet

malicious 1 kwaadwillig; kwaadaardig **2** [law] opzettelijk

malign kwaadaardig; maligne

malignant 1 schadelijk, verderfelijk **2** kwaadwillig, boosaardig **3** kwaadaardig [of disease]: *a ~ **tumour*** een kwaadaardig gezwel

mall 1 wandelgalerij, promenade **2** winkelpromenade, groot winkelcentrumʰ **3** [Am] middenberm

mallard wilde eend

malleable [fig] kneedbaar

mall rat [roughly] hangjongere

malnourished ondervoed

malnutrition slechte voeding, ondervoeding

malpractice 1 [med] medische fout, nalatigheid **2** [law] misdrijfʰ

malt mout, malt

Malta Malta

¹Maltese (n) Maltees, Maltese

²Maltese (adj) **1** Maltees; Maltezer: ~ *Cross* Maltezer kruis **2** Maltezisch

maltreatment mishandeling

malversation malversatie, verduistering, wanbeheerʰ

malware malware
mam mammy mam(s)
mammal zoogdier[h]
mammoth mammoet
¹man (n) **1** man, de man, echtgenoot, minnaar, partner: ~ *of letters* schrijver, geleerde; ~ *of means* (or: *property*) bemiddeld (*or:* vermogend) man; *the* ~ *in the street* de gewone man, jan met de pet; ~ *about town* man van de wereld, playboy; ~ *and wife* man en vrouw; ~ *of the world* iem. met mensenkennis; *the very* ~ de persoon die men nodig heeft, net wie men zocht; *be* ~ *enough to* mans genoeg zijn om **2** mens, het mensdom: *the rights of Man* de mensenrechten; *to the last* ~ tot op de laatste man; *every* ~ *for himself* ieder voor zich; *as a* ~ als één man; *one* ~, *one vote* enkelvoudig stemrecht **3** ondergeschikte, soldaat: *men* manschappen; *officers and men* officieren en manschappen; *I'm your* ~ op mij mag (*or:* kan) je rekenen ‖ *be enough of a* ~ *to* wel zo flink zijn om te; *(all) to a* ~ eensgezind
²man (vb) **1** bemannen, bezetten: *~ned crossing* bewaakte overweg **2** vermannen: ~ *o.s.* zich vermannen
³man (int) [Am] sjonge!
¹manacle (n) **1** handboei **2** belemmering
²manacle (vb) in de boeien slaan, aan elkaar vastketenen
¹manage (vb) **1** rondkomen, zich behelpen **2** slagen, het klaarspelen: *can you* ~? gaat het?, lukt het (zo)?; *I'll* ~ het lukt me wel **3** als beheerder optreden
²manage (vb) **1** slagen in, weten te, kunnen, kans zien te: *the* ~*d to escape* hij wist te ontsnappen **2** leiden, besturen; beheren [business]; hoeden [cattle] **3** beheersen, weten aan te pakken, manipuleren **4** hanteren **5** aankunnen, aandurven, in staat zijn tot: *I cannot* ~ *another mouthful* ik krijg er geen hap meer in
manageable handelbaar, beheersbaar
management 1 beheer[h], management[h], bestuur[h], administratie **2** overleg[h], beleid[h]: *more luck than (good)* ~ meer geluk dan wijsheid **3** werkgevers
manager 1 bestuurder, chef; directeur [of business]; manager [of sports team]; impresario [of singer] **2** manager, bedrijfsleider: *general* ~ algemeen directeur
managerial bestuurs-, directeurs-, leidinggevend
manatee lamantijn
mandarin 1 mandarijntje[h] **2** bureaucraat
Mandarin Mandarijns[h] [language]; Chinees
mandarin orange mandarijntje[h]
mandate mandaat[h], machtiging om namens anderen te handelen
mandatory 1 bevel-: ~ *sign* gebodsbord **2** verplicht: ~ *subject* verplicht (school)vak

mandolin mandoline
mane manen
manège 1 manege, (paard)rijschool **2** rijkunst
mange schurft[+h], scabiës
manger trog, krib
mange-tout peul(tje[h])
¹mangle (n) **1** mangel **2** wringer
²mangle (vb) **1** mangelen, door de mangel draaien **2** verscheuren, verminken, havenen; [fig] verknoeien: *~d bodies* verminkte lichamen
mango mango
mangy 1 schurftig **2** sjofel
manhandle 1 toetakelen, afranselen **2** door mankracht verplaatsen
manhood 1 mannelijkheid **2** volwassenheid
mania 1 manie, waanzin, zucht: *Beatle* ~ Beatlemania, Beatlegekte **2** (+ for) rage (om/voor)
maniac maniak, waanzinnige
manic 1 manisch **2** erg opgewonden, bezeten
¹manicure (n) manicure
²manicure (vb) manicuren
¹manifest (adj) zichtbaar, duidelijk, klaarblijkelijk
²manifest (vb) zichtbaar maken, vertonen: ~ *one's interest* blijk geven van belangstelling
manifestation 1 manifestatie **2** verkondiging, openbaring **3** uiting
manifesto manifest[h]
manifold veelvuldig, verscheiden
manipulate 1 hanteren [appliance] **2** manipuleren [also med] **3** knoeien met [text, figures]
manipulation manipulatie
manipulative manipulatief
mankind het mensdom, de mensheid
manly mannelijk, manhaftig
man-made door de mens gemaakt, kunstmatig: ~ *fibre* kunstvezel
mannequin 1 mannequin **2** etalagepop
manner 1 manier, wijze: *in a* ~ in zekere zin; *in a* ~ *of speaking* bij wijze van spreken **2** houding, gedrag[h] **3** stijl, trant **4** soort, slag: *all* ~ *of* allerlei **5** (-s) manieren, goed gedrag[h]: *bad* ~*s* slechte manieren; *it's bad* ~*s* dat is onbeleefd **6** (-s) zeden, sociale gewoonten
mannerism 1 aanwensel[h] **2** gekunsteldheid
mannish manachtig; mannelijk [of women]
¹manoeuvre (n) manoeuvre
²manoeuvre (vb) manoeuvreren; [fig] slinks handelen: ~ *s.o. into a good job* een goed baantje voor iem. versieren
manor manor, groot (heren)huis[h] met om-

liggende gronden
manpower 1 arbeidskrachten **2** beschikbare strijdkrachten
mansion herenhuis[h]
man-size flink, kolossaal
manslaughter doodslag
mantelpiece schoorsteenmantel
mantra mantra
[1]manual (n) **1** handboek[h], handleiding **2** [mus] manuaal[h]
[2]manual (adj) hand-: ~ *labour* handenarbeid; ~ *worker* handarbeider
[1]manufacture (n) **1** fabricaat[h], product[h], goederen **2** vervaardiging, fabricage, productie(proces[h]), makelij
[2]manufacture (vb) **1** vervaardigen, verwerken, produceren: *manufacturing industry* verwerkende industrie **2** verzinnen
manufacturer fabrikant
[1]manure (n) mest
[2]manure (vb) bemesten, gieren
manuscript manuscript[h], handschrift[h]
many 1 vele(n), menigeen: ~ *'s the time* vaak; *a good* (or: *great*) ~ vele(n), menigeen; *and as* ~ *again* (or: *more*) en nog eens zoveel; *have had one too* ~ een glaasje te veel op hebben; ~ *of* the pages were torn veel bladzijden waren gescheurd; *as* ~ *as* thirty wel dertig **2** veel, een groot aantal: *a good* ~ *raisins* een flinke hoeveelheid rozijnen; *ten mistakes in as* ~ *lines* tien fouten in tien regels **3** (+ a(n)) menig(e): ~ *a time* vaak
[1]map (n) **1** kaart **2** plan[h], grafische voorstelling || *put on the* ~ de aandacht vestigen op
[2]map (vb) in kaart brengen: ~ *out* in kaart brengen; [fig] plannen, indelen; *I've got my future* ~ped *out for me* mijn toekomst is al uitgestippeld
maple esdoorn
maple leaf esdoornblad[h]
mapping afbeelding
mar bederven, verstoren: *make* (or: *mend*) or ~ *a plan* een plan doen slagen of mislukken
[1]marathon (n) marathon(loop)
[2]marathon (adj) marathon, ellenlang
maraud plunderen, roven
[1]marble (n) **1** marmer[h] **2** knikker: *play (at)* ~s knikkeren || *he has lost his* ~s er zit bij hem een steekje los
[2]marble (adj) marmeren, gemarmerd
[1]march (n) **1** mars **2** opmars: *on the* ~ in opmars || *steal a* ~ *on s.o.* iem. te vlug af zijn
[2]march (vb) (op)marcheren, aanrukken: *quick* ~! voorwaarts mars!
[3]march (vb) **1** doen marcheren **2** leiden; voeren [on foot]: *be* ~ed *away* (or: *off*) weggeleid worden
March maart
marching order 1 [mil] marsorder **2** ontslag[h]; [mockingly] afwijzing
march past defilé[h], parade

mare merrie
margarine margarine
margin 1 marge; [Stock Exchange] surplus[h]: ~ *of error* foutenmarge **2** kantlijn
marginal 1 in de kantlijn geschreven: ~ *notes* kanttekeningen **2** miniem, onbeduidend, bijkomstig: *of* ~ *importance* van ondergeschikt belang
marguerite margriet
marigold 1 goudsbloem **2** afrikaantje[h]
marijuana marihuana
marina jachthaven
[1]marinade (n) marinade
[2]marinade (vb) marineren
[1]marine (n) **1** marine, vloot **2** marinier
[2]marine (adj) zee-: ~ *biology* mariene biologie
mariner zeeman, matroos
marionette marionet
marital echtelijk, huwelijks-: ~ *status* burgerlijke staat
maritime maritiem: ~ *law* zeerecht
marjoram marjolein
[1]mark (n) **1** teken[h], leesteken[h]; [fig] blijk: *as a* ~ *of my esteem* als blijk van mijn achting **2** teken[h], spoor[h], vlek; [fig] indruk: *bear the* ~s *of* de sporen dragen van; *make one's* ~ zich onderscheiden **3** (rapport)cijfer[h], punt[h] **4** peil[h], niveau[h]: *above* (or: *below*) *the* ~ boven (or: beneden) peil; *I don't feel quite up to the* ~ ik voel me niet helemaal fit **5** start-(streep): *not quick off the* ~ niet vlug (van begrip); *on your* ~s, *get set, go!* op uw plaatsen! klaar? af! **6** doel[h], doelwit[h]: [fig] *hit the* ~ in de roos schieten; [fig] *miss* (or: *overshoot*) *the* ~ het doel missen, te ver gaan, de plank misslaan || *keep s.o. up to the* ~ zorgen dat iem. zijn uiterste best doet; *overstep the* ~ over de schreef gaan
[2]mark (vb) **1** vlekken (maken/krijgen) **2** cijfers geven
[3]mark (vb) **1** merken, tekenen, onderscheiden: ~ *the occasion* de gelegenheid luister bijzetten **2** beoordelen, nakijken; cijfers geven voor [schoolwork] **3** letten op [words etc]: ~ *how it is done* let op hoe het gedaan wordt **4** te kennen geven, vertonen **5** bestemmen, opzijzetten **6** vlekken; tekenen [animal] **7** [sport] dekken
Mark model[h], type[h], rangnummer[h]
mark down 1 noteren, opschrijven **2** afprijzen **3** een lager cijfer geven
marked 1 duidelijk: *a* ~ *preference* een uitgesproken voorkeur **2** gemarkeerd; gemerkt [eg money] **3** bestemd, uitgekozen
marker 1 teller **2** teken[h], merk[h], kenteken[h], mijlpaal, kilometerpaal, baken[h], boekenlegger, scorebord[h] **3** markeerstift
[1]market (n) **1** markt, handel, afzetgebied[h]: *be in the* ~ *for sth.* iets willen kopen; *price o.s. out of the* ~ zich uit de markt prijzen

2 marktprijs **3** markt, beurs
²**market** (vb) inkopen doen, winkelen
³**market** (vb) **1** op de markt brengen **2** verkopen, verhandelen
marketable 1 verkoopbaar **2** markt-: ~ *value* marktwaarde
market-driven marktgestuurd
market garden moestuin
marketing 1 markthandel **2** marketing, marktonderzoekʰ
marketplace marktpleinʰ
marking 1 tekening [of animal etc] **2** (ken)tekenʰ **3** het nakijken van huiswerk
mark out 1 afbakenen, markeren **2** uitkiezen, bestemmen: *marked out as a candidate for promotion* uitgekozen als promotiekandidaat
marksman scherpschutter
mark up in prijs verhogen
marmalade marmelade
marmot marmot
¹**maroon** (n) **1** vuurpijl, lichtseinʰ **2** kastanjebruinʰ
²**maroon** (vb) **1** achterlaten; [fig] aan zijn lot overlaten **2** isoleren, afsnijden: ~ed by the *floods* door de overstromingen ingesloten
marquee grote tent, feesttent
marquis markies
marriage huwelijkʰ, echt(verbintenis): ~ *of convenience* verstandshuwelijk; *her* ~ *to* haar huwelijk met; ~ *settlement* huwelijksvoorwaarden
marriageable huwbaar
marriage vows trouwbeloften
married gehuwd: *a* ~ *couple* een echtpaar
marrow 1 (eetbare) pompoen: *vegetable* ~ eetbare pompoen **2** mergʰ **3** kern, pit
marry trouwen (met), in het huwelijk treden (met): ~ *money* (or: *wealth*) een rijk huwelijk sluiten; *get married* trouwen ‖ *married to* verknocht aan; *he is married to his work* hij is met zijn werk getrouwd; *he is married with three children* hij is getrouwd en heeft drie kinderen
marsh moerasʰ
¹**marshal** (n) **1** (veld)maarschalk **2** hofmaarschalk **3** hoofdʰ van ordedienst **4** [Am] hoofdʰ van politie; [roughly] sheriff **5** [Am] brandweercommandant
²**marshal** (vb) **1** (zich) opstellen **2** leiden, (be)geleiden
¹**marsupial** (n) buideldierʰ
²**marsupial** (adj) buideldragend
mart handelscentrumʰ
marten 1 [animal] marter **2** [fur] marter(-bont)ʰ
martial 1 krijgs-: ~ *arts* (oosterse) vechtkunsten [karate, judo etc] **2** krijgshaftig
¹**Martian** (n) Marsbewoner
²**Martian** (adj) Mars-
¹**martyr** (n) martelaar [also fig]: *make a* ~ *of*

o.s. zich als martelaar opwerpen
²**martyr** (vb) de marteldood doen sterven; martelen [also fig]; kwellen
martyrdom 1 martelaarschapʰ **2** marteldood **3** marteling, lijdensweg
¹**marvel** (n) wonderʰ: *do* (or: *work*) ~*s* wonderen verrichten
²**marvel** (vb) (+ at) zich verwonderen (over), zich verbazen (over)
marvellous prachtig, fantastisch
marzipan marsepein(tje)ʰ
masc *masculine* mnl., mannelijk
mascot mascotte
masculine 1 mannelijk **2** manachtig
¹**mash** (n) (warm) mengvoerʰ
²**mash** (vb) **1** fijnstampen, fijnmaken: ~*ed potatoes* (aardappel)puree **2** mengen, hutselen
¹**mask** (n) maskerʰ [also fig]; momʰ
²**mask** (vb) zich vermommen, een masker opzetten; [fig] zijn (ware) gelaat verbergen
³**mask** (vb) **1** maskeren, vermommen **2** verbergen, verhullen
masked gemaskerd
masking tape afplakbandʰ
masochist masochist
mason 1 metselaar **2** vrijmetselaar
¹**masquerade** (n) **1** maskerade **2** vermomming
²**masquerade** (vb) (+ as) zich vermommen (als), zich voordoen (als)
¹**mass** (n) massa, hoop, menigte: *in the* ~ in massa; *a* ~ *of* één en al; *the* ~*es* de massa
²**mass** (n) [Roman Catholicism] mis
³**mass** (vb) (zich) verzamelen: ~ *troops* troepen concentreren
¹**massacre** (n) **1** bloedbadʰ **2** [fig] afslachting
²**massacre** (vb) **1** uitmoorden **2** in de pan hakken
¹**massage** (n) massage
²**massage** (vb) **1** masseren **2** manipuleren; knoeien met [data etc]
massive 1 massief, zwaar **2** groots, indrukwekkend **3** massaal **4** aanzienlijk, enorm
mass-produce in massa produceren
mast mast
¹**master** (n) **1** meester, heer, baas, schoolmeester: ~ *of the* *house* heer des huizes **2** origineelʰ, matrijs, master(tape) ‖ *Master of Arts* [roughly] doctorandus, [roughly] Master of Arts, [roughly] Master of Science; *Master of Ceremonies* ceremoniemeester
²**master** (adj) hoofd-, voornaamste
³**master** (vb) overmeesteren; de baas worden [also fig]; te boven komen
master bedroom grootste slaapkamer
master card hoogste kaart; hoge troef
masterful 1 meesterachtig **2** meesterlijk
master key loper, passe-partoutʰ
mastermind uitdenken: *he* ~*ed the* *project*

hij was het brein achter het project
masterpiece meesterstuk[h], meesterwerk[h]
masterstroke meesterzet
mastery 1 meesterschap[h]: *the ~ over* de overhand op **2** beheersing, kennis
masticate kauwen
masturbate masturberen
¹mat (n) **1** mat(je[h]) [also fig; sport]; deurmat **2** tafelmatje[h], onderzettertje[h] **3** klit: *a ~ of hair* een wirwar van haren
²mat (adj) mat, dof
³mat (vb) klitten, in de war raken
⁴mat (vb) verwarren, doen samenklitten
¹match (n) **1** gelijke: *find* (or: *meet*) *one's ~* zijns gelijke vinden; *be more than a ~ for s.o.* iem. de baas zijn **2** wedstrijd **3** lucifer **4** huwelijk[h]
²match (vb) (bij elkaar) passen: *~ing clothes* (or: *colours*) bij elkaar passende kleren (or: kleuren)
³match (vb) **1** evenaren, niet onderdoen voor: *can you ~ that?* kan je dat net zo goed doen?; *they are well ~ed* zij zijn aan elkaar gewaagd **2** passen bij: *they are well ~ed* ze passen goed bij elkaar **3** doen passen; aanpassen [colour]: *~ jobs and applicants* het juiste werk voor de juiste kandidaten uitzoeken
matchbox lucifersdoosje[h]
matchless weergaloos, niet te evenaren
matchmaking het koppelen, het tot stand brengen van huwelijken
¹mate (n) **1** maat, kameraad **2** (huwelijks)partner, gezel(lin), mannetje[h]; wijfje[h] [of birds] **3** helper [of craftsman]; gezel **4** stuurman **5** [chess] mat[h]
²mate (vb) paren, huwen, zich voortplanten
³mate (vb) **1** koppelen, doen paren **2** schaken, mat zetten
¹material (n) **1** materiaal[h], grondstof; [fig] gegevens; stof **2** soort
²material (adj) **1** materieel, lichamelijk: *~ damage* materiële schade **2** belangrijk, wezenlijk: *a ~ witness* een belangrijke getuige
materialism materialisme[h]
materialist(ic) materialistisch
¹materialize (vb) **1** werkelijkheid worden: *his dreams never ~d* zijn dromen werden nooit werkelijkheid **2** tevoorschijn komen [of ghost]
²materialize (vb) **1** verwezenlijken, realiseren, uitvoeren **2** materialiseren
maternal moeder-: *~ love* moederliefde || *~ grandfather* grootvader van moederszijde
maternity moederschap[h]: *~ home* kraamkliniek
maternity blues [inform] babyblues, postnatale depressie
maternity leave zwangerschapsverlof[h]
matey vriendschappelijk: *be ~ with s.o.* beste maatjes met iem. zijn
math [Am] wiskunde

mathematical 1 wiskundig **2** precies, exact
mathematician wiskundige
mathematics wiskunde
maths *mathematics* wiskunde
mating season paartijd, bronst
matriarchal matriarchaal
matricide moedermoord(enaar)
matriculation inschrijving, toegang tot universiteit
matrimony huwelijk[h], echt(elijke staat)
matrix 1 gietvorm, matrijs **2** matrix
matron 1 matrone **2** directrice, hoofdverpleegster || *~ of honour* getrouwd bruidsmeisje
matt mat, niet glanzend
¹matter (n) **1** materie, stof **2** stof, materiaal[h], inhoud **3** stof [in, of body] **4** belang[h]: *no ~* het maakt niet uit, laat maar **5** kwestie: *just a ~ of time* slechts een kwestie van tijd; *no laughing ~* niets om te lachen; *for that ~,* wat dat betreft || *as a ~ of course* vanzelfsprekend; *as a ~ of fact* eigenlijk; *what is the ~ with him?* wat scheelt hem?
²matter (vb) van belang zijn, betekenen: *it doesn't ~* het geeft niet, het doet er niet toe; *what does it ~?* wat zou het?
matter-of-fact zakelijk, nuchter
matting matwerk[h]; matten [as floor covering etc]
mattress matras[+h]
¹mature (adj) **1** rijp, volgroeid **2** volwassen: *behave ~ly* zich gedragen als een volwassene **3** weloverwogen **4** belegen [cheese, wine]
²mature (vb) **1** rijpen, tot rijpheid komen: *~d cheese* belegen kaas **2** volgroeien, zich volledig ontwikkelen, volwassen worden **3** vervallen [of Bill of Exchange etc]
maturity 1 rijpheid **2** volgroeidheid, volwassenheid
maul 1 verscheuren; aan stukken scheuren [also fig] **2** ruw behandelen
Maundy Thursday Witte Donderdag
Mauritania Mauritanië
¹Mauritanian (n) Mauritaniër, Mauritaanse
²Mauritanian (adj) Mauritaans
¹Mauritian (n) Mauritiaan(se)
²Mauritian (adj) Mauritiaans
Mauritius Mauritius
maverick [Am] **1** non-conformist **2** ongebrandmerkt kalf, veulen
maw 1 pens; maag [of animal] **2** krop [of bird] **3** muil; bek [fig]
mawkish 1 walgelijk; flauw [of taste] **2** overdreven sentimenteel
max *maximum* max.: [inform] *to the ~* absoluut, compleet, totaal
maxim spreuk
maximally hoogstens, maximaal
maximize maximaliseren: *~ one's experience* zo veel mogelijk munt slaan uit zijn er-

varing
¹maximum (n) maximumʰ: *at its* ~ op het hoogste punt
²maximum (adj) maximaal, hoogste: ~ *speed* topsnelheid
may 1 mogen: ~ *I ask why you think so?* mag ik vragen waarom je dat denkt?; *you* ~ *not leave yet* je mag nog niet vertrekken **2** [possibility] kunnen: *they* ~ *arrive later* ze komen misschien later; *come what* ~ wat er ook gebeurt; ~ *I help you?* kan ik u helpen?; *I hope he* ~ *recover, but I fear he* ~ *not* ik hoop dat hij beter wordt, maar ik vrees van niet **3** [in wishes] mogen: ~ *you stay forever young* moge jij altijd jong blijven
May mei
maybe misschien, wellicht: *as soon as* ~ zo vlug mogelijk
mayday mayday, noodsignaalʰ
May Day 1 mei, dag van de arbeid
mayfly eendagsvlieg
mayhem rotzooi: *cause* (or: *create*) ~ herrie schoppen
mayonnaise mayonaise
mayor burgemeester
maypole meiboom
maze doolhof [also fig]
MBA *Master of Business Administration*
me mij, voor mij, ik: *he liked her better than me* hij vond haar aardiger dan mij; *poor me* arme ik; *it is me* ik ben het
mead mede
meadow wei(de), graslandʰ
meagre schraal [meal, result etc]
meal 1 maalʰ, maaltijd **2** meelʰ
meals-on-wheels [roughly] tafeltje-dek-jeʰ
mealy 1 melig **2** bleek [complexion]
¹mean (n) **1** (-s) middelʰ: *by ~s of* door middel van; *by no* ~*, not by any (manner of)* ~*s* in geen geval; *a ~s to an end* een middel om een doel te bereiken **2** (-s) middelen (van bestaan): *live beyond one's ~s* boven zijn stand leven **3** middelmaat; [fig] middenweg **4** gemiddelde (waarde)
²mean (adj) **1** gemeen, laag, ongemanierd: ~ *tricks* ordinaire trucs **2** gierig **3** armzalig, armoedig **4** [Am] kwaadaardig, vals **5** gemiddeld, doorsnee- **6** gebrekkig, beperkt: *no* ~ *cook* een buitengewone kok, geen doorsneekok **7** laag; gering [origin]
³mean (vb) het bedoelen: ~ *ill* (or: *well*) *(to, towards, by s.o.)* het slecht (or: goed) menen (met iem.)
⁴mean (vb) **1** betekenen, willen zeggen: *it ~s nothing to me* het zegt me niets **2** bedoelen: *what do you* ~ *by that?* wat bedoel je daarmee? **3** de bedoeling hebben: ~ *business* vastberaden zijn, zeer serieus zijn; *I* ~ *to leave tomorrow* ik ben van plan morgen te vertrekken **4** menen **5** bestemmen **6** bete-

kenen, neerkomen op: *those clouds* ~ *rain* die wolken voorspellen regen
meander 1 zich (in bochten) slingeren; kronkelen [of river] **2** (rond)dolen [also fig]
meanderings slingerpad, kronkelpad, gekronkel
¹meaning (n) **1** betekenis, zin, inhoud: [disapprovingly] *what's the* ~ *of this?* wat heeft dit te betekenen? **2** bedoeling, strekking
²meaning (adj) veelbetekenend, veelzeggend
meaningful 1 van (grote) betekenis, gewichtig **2** zinvol
meaningless 1 zonder betekenis, nietszeggend **2** zinloos
means test inkomensonderzoekʰ
means-tested inkomensafhankelijk
meantime tussentijd: *in the* ~ ondertussen
meanwhile ondertussen
measles 1 mazelen **2** rodehond
measly 1 met mazelen **2** [inform] armzalig: ~ *tip* hondenfooi
measurable 1 meetbaar: *within a* ~ *distance of* dicht in de buurt van **2** van betekenis, belangrijk
¹measure (n) **1** maatregel, stap: *take strong ~s* geen halve maatregelen nemen **2** maat [also music]; maateenheid, maat(beker); maat(streep) [mus]; mate, gematigdheid: *a* ~ *of wheat* een maat tarwe; *in (a) great* (or: *large*) ~ in hoge (or: ruime) mate; *made to* ~ op maat gemaakt **3** maatstaf **4** maatstok, maatlat, maatlintʰ **5** ritmeʰ, melodie
²measure (vb) **1** beoordelen, taxeren **2** opnemen, met de ogen afmeten **3** letten op, overdenken: ~ *one's words* zijn woorden wegen
³measure (vb) meten, afmeten, opmeten, toemeten, uitmeten, de maat nemen: *the room ~s three metres by four* de kamer is drie bij vier (meter); ~ *off* (or: *out*) afmeten [material etc]; ~ *out* toemeten
measured weloverwogen, zorgvuldig
measurement 1 afmeting, maat **2** meting
measure up voldoen: ~ *to* a) voldoen aan; b) berekend zijn op (or: voor), opgewassen zijn tegen
meat 1 vleesʰ: *white* ~ wit vlees [eg poultry] **2** [Am] eetbaar gedeelteʰ [of fruit, crustacean, egg]; (vrucht)vleesʰ **3** essentie: *there is no real* ~ *in the story* het verhaal heeft weinig om het lijf **4** fortʰ, sterke kant ‖ *one man's* ~ *is another man's poison* de een traag, de ander graag
meatball gehaktbal
meaty 1 lijvig **2** vleesachtig **3** stevig: *a* ~ *discussion* een pittige discussie
mechanic mecanicien, technicus, monteur
mechanical 1 mechanisch, machinaal; [fig] ongeïnspireerd **2** ambachtelijk, handwerk- **3** werktuig(bouw)kundig: ~ *engineering*

werktuig(bouw)kunde
mechanics 1 mechanica, werktuigkunde
2 mechanisme **3** techniek
mechanism 1 mechanisme[h], mechaniek[h]
2 werking **3** techniek
mechanization mechanisering
medal medaille
medallion 1 (grote) medaille **2** medaillon[h]
medallist medaillewinnaar
meddle in zich bemoeien met, zich inlaten
met: *don't ~ my affairs* bemoei je met je eigen
zaken
meddlesome bemoeiziek
media media
median middel-, midden-, middelst: *~ point*
zwaartepunt
¹mediate (vb) overbrengen
²mediate (vb) bemiddelen, bijleggen: *~ between* bemiddelen tussen
mediation bemiddeling
mediator bemiddelaar, tussenpersoon
medic [inform] medisch student; dokter
¹medical (n) (medisch) onderzoek[h], keuring
²medical (adj) medisch: *~ certificate* dok-
tersverklaring
medicament medicijn[h]
Medicare ziektekostenverzekering
medication 1 medicament[h], medicijn[h],
medicijnen **2** medicatie
medicinal 1 geneeskrachtig **2** geneeskundig, medisch
medicine 1 geneesmiddel[h]: *she takes too
much ~* ze slikt te veel medicijnen **2** tovermiddel[h] **3** geneeskunde, medicijnen
medieval middeleeuws
mediocre middelmatig
mediocrity middelmatigheid
¹meditate (vb) **1** diep nadenken, in gedachten verzonken zijn: *~ (up)on* overpeinzen
2 mediteren
²meditate (vb) van plan zijn: *~ revenge* zinnen op wraak
meditation 1 overpeinzing, bespiegeling:
deep in ~ in gepeins verzonken **2** meditatie
Mediterranean m.b.t. de Middellandse
Zee, m.b.t. het Middellandse Zeegebied
¹medium (n) **1** middenweg, compromis[h]
2 gemiddelde[h], midden[h] **3** medium[h], middel[h]: *through the ~ of* door middel van **4** tussenpersoon **5** (natuurlijke) omgeving, milieu[h] **6** uitingsvorm, kunstvorm **7** [spiritism]
medium[h]
²medium (adj) gemiddeld, doorsnee-: *in the
~ term* op middellange termijn; [radio] *~
wave* middengolf
medlar mispel
medley 1 mengelmoes(je)[h] **2** [mus] potpourri, medley
meek 1 gedwee **2** bescheiden **3** zachtmoedig
¹meet (n) **1** samenkomst; trefpunt[h] [for

hunt] **2** jachtgezelschap[h] **3** [Am; athletics]
ontmoeting, wedstrijd
²meet (vb) **1** elkaar ontmoeten, elkaar tegenkomen: *~ up* elkaar (toevallig) treffen; *~
up with* tegen het lijf lopen **2** samenkomen,
bijeenkomen **3** kennismaken **4** sluiten; dicht
gaan [of article of clothing]
³meet (vb) **1** ontmoeten, treffen, tegenkomen: *run to ~ s.o.* iem. tegemoet rennen;
[fig] *~ s.o. halfway* a) iem. tegemoetkomen;
b) het verschil (samen) delen **2** (aan)raken
3 kennismaken met: *pleased to ~ you* aangenaam **4** afhalen: *I'll ~ your train* ik kom je van
de trein afhalen **5** behandelen, het hoofd
bieden: *~ criticism* kritiek weerleggen **6** tegemoetkomen (aan), voldoen (aan), vervullen: *~ the bill* de rekening voldoen **7** beantwoorden, (onvriendelijk) bejegenen **8** ondervinden, ondergaan, dragen: *~ one's
death* de dood vinden
meeting 1 ontmoeting [also sport]; wedstrijd **2** bijeenkomst, vergadering, bespreking: *meeting-house* kerk
meet with 1 ondervinden, ondergaan: *~
approval* instemming vinden **2** tegen het lijf
lopen **3** [Am] een ontmoeting hebben met
megabyte megabyte [1 million bytes]
megalomania grootheidswaanzin
megaphone megafoon
megawatt megawatt
meh [inform] bleh, waardeloos
melancholic melancholisch, zwaarmoedig
¹melancholy (n) melancholie, zwaarmoedigheid
²melancholy (adj) **1** melancholisch, zwaarmoedig **2** droevig, triest
mellow 1 rijp; sappig [of fruit] **2** zacht,
warm; vol [of sound, colour, taste] **3** gerijpt,
zacht(moedig), mild
melodious melodieus, welluidend
melodrama melodrama[h] [also fig]
melody melodie
melon meloen
melt smelten: *~ in the mouth* smelten op de
tong; *~ down* omsmelten
meltdown het afsmelten [at nuclear power plant]
meltingpoint smeltpunt[h]
melting pot smeltkroes [also fig]: *in the ~*
onstabiel
member lid[h], lidmaat, (onder)deel[h], element[h], zinsdeel[h], lichaamsdeel[h]: *~ of Parliament* parlementslid; *~ state* lidstaat
membership 1 lidmaatschap[h] **2** ledental[h],
de leden
membrane membraan[h]
meme 1 [biology] meme **2** [comp] inter-
nethype
memento gedenkteken[h]
memo *memorandum* memo[h]
memoir 1 biografie **2** verhandeling

memoirs memoires, autobiografie
memorable gedenkwaardig
memorandum memorandum[h], informele nota: ~ *of association* akte van oprichting
[1]**memorial** (n) gedenkteken[h], monument[h]
[2]**memorial** (adj) herdenkings-: ~ *service* herdenkingsdienst
memorize 1 uit het hoofd leren **2** onthouden
memory 1 geheugen[h], herinnering: *to the best of my* ~ voor zover ik mij kan herinneren; *within living* ~ bij mensenheugenis; *from* ~ van buiten, uit het hoofd **2** herinnering, aandenken[h]: *in* ~ *of, to the* ~ *of* ter (na)gedachtenis aan
memory lane: *go down* ~ terug in je herinnering gaan
[1]**menace** (n) **1** (be)dreiging: *filled with* ~ vol dreiging **2** lastpost, gevaar[h]
[2]**menace** (vb) (be)dreigen
[1]**mend** (n) herstelling, reparatie || *he's on the* ~ hij is aan de beterende hand
[2]**mend** (vb) er weer bovenop komen, herstellen, zich (ver)beteren
[3]**mend** (vb) **1** herstellen, repareren: ~ *stockings* kousen stoppen **2** goedmaken **3** verbeteren
mendicant 1 bedelmonnik **2** bedelaar
[1]**menial** (n) [oft depr] dienstbode, knecht, meid
[2]**menial** (adj) [oft depr] ondergeschikt, oninteressant: *a* ~ *job* een min baantje
menopause menopauze
men's room [Am] herentoilet[h]
menstrual 1 menstrueel: ~ *cycle* menstruatiecyclus; ~ *period* menstruatie **2** maandelijks
menstruate menstrueren, ongesteld zijn
menstruation menstruatie, ongesteldheid
menswear herenkleding
mental 1 geestelijk, mentaal, psychisch: ~ *illness* zenuwziekte; ~*ly defective* (or: *deficient, handicapped*) geestelijk gehandicapt; ~*ly retarded* achterlijk **2** hoofd-, met het hoofd: ~ *arithmetic* hoofdrekenen; ~ *gymnastics* hersengymnastiek; *make a* ~ *note of sth.* iets in zijn oren knopen **3** psychiatrisch: ~ *hospital* psychiatrische inrichting
mentality mentaliteit
[1]**mention** (n) vermelding, opgave: *honourable* ~ eervolle vermelding; *make* ~ *of* vermelden
[2]**mention** (vb) vermelden: *not to* ~ om (nog maar) niet te spreken van || *don't* ~ *it* geen dank
mentor mentor
menu menu[h], (menu)kaart, maaltijd: *set* ~, *fixed price* ~ keuzemenu
menu bar menubalk
mercantile handels-, koopmans-
[1]**mercenary** (n) huurling

[2]**mercenary** (adj) **1** op geld belust **2** gehuurd: ~ *troops* huurtroepen
merchandise koopwaar, artikelen, producten
[1]**merchant** (n) groothandelaar, koopman
[2]**merchant** (adj) **1** koopvaardij-: ~ *shipping* koopvaardij **2** handels-, koopmans-
merciful genadig; mild: ~*ly, he came just in time* gelukkig kwam hij net op tijd
merciless genadeloos: *a* ~ *ruler* een meedogenloos heerser
mercury kwik(zilver)[h]
mercy 1 genade, barmhartigheid **2** daad van barmhartigheid, weldaad: *be thankful for small mercies* wees maar blij dat het niet erger is **3** vergevensgezindheid: *throw o.s. on a person's* ~ een beroep doen op iemands goedheid; [oft iron] *left to the (tender)* ~ *of* overgeleverd aan de goedheid van || *at the* ~ *of* in de macht van
mercy killing [euph] euthanasie, de zachte dood
mere louter, puur: *by the* ~*st chance* door stom toeval; *at the* ~ *thought of it* alleen al de gedachte eraan
merely slechts, enkel, alleen
merge 1 (+ with) opgaan (in), samengaan (met), fuseren (met) **2** (geleidelijk) overgaan (in elkaar): *the place where the rivers* ~ de plaats waar de rivieren samenvloeien
merger 1 samensmelting **2** [econ] fusie
meridian meridiaan, middaglijn
[1]**merit** (n) **1** verdienste, waarde: *the* ~*s and demerits of sth.* de voors en tegens van iets; *reward each according to his* ~*s* elk naar eigen verdienste belonen; *judge sth. on its (own)* ~*s* iets op zijn eigen waarde beoordelen **2** (-s) intrinsieke waarde
[2]**merit** (vb) verdienen, waard zijn
meritocracy meritocratie
mermaid (zee)meermin
merriment 1 vrolijkheid **2** pret, plezier[h], hilariteit
merry 1 vrolijk, opgewekt: *Merry Christmas* Vrolijk kerstfeest **2** aangeschoten || *lead s.o. a* ~ *dance* a) iem. het leven zuur maken; b) iem. voor de gek houden; *make* ~ pret maken; *make* ~ *over* zich vrolijk maken over
merry-go-round draaimolen, carrousel; [fig] maalstroom; roes
merrymaking 1 pret(makerij), feestvreugde **2** feestelijkheid
[1]**mesh** (n) **1** maas, steek; [fig also] strik **2** net(werk)[h]: *a* ~ *of lies* een netwerk van leugens
[2]**mesh** (vb) **1** (+ with) ineengrijpen, ingeschakeld zijn; [fig] harmoniëren (met) **2** verstrikt raken
mesmerize magnetiseren, (als) verlammen: ~*d at his appearance* gebiologeerd door zijn verschijning

¹mess (n) **1** puinhoop, troep, (war)boel, knoeiboel: *his **life** was a ~ zijn leven was een mislukking;* **clear** up *the* ~ de rotzooi opruimen **2** vuile boel **3** moeilijkheid: *get o.s.* **into** *a ~ zichzelf in moeilijkheden brengen* **4** mess, kantine
²mess (vb) zich bemoeien met iets, tussenkomen: *~ **in** other people's business z'n neus in andermans zaken steken* || **no** *~ing echt waar*
¹mess about (vb) prutsen, (lui) rondhangen: *don't ~ **with** people like him laat je met mensen zoals hij niet in; he spent the weekend messing about hij lummelde wat rond tijdens het weekend*
²mess about (vb) **1** rotzooien met: *stop messing my daughter about blijf met je poten van mijn dochter af* **2** belazeren
¹message (n) **1** boodschap: *the ~ of a **book** de kerngedachte van een boek; (I) **got** the ~ begrepen, ik snap het al; send s.o. **on** a ~ iem. om een boodschap sturen* **2** bericht[h] **3** sms
²message (vb) sms'en
messenger boodschapper, koerier: *~ from **Heaven** gezant des hemels*
Messiah Messias, Heiland
Messrs 1 (de) Heren **2** Fa., Firma: *~ **Smith & Jones** de Firma Smith & Jones*
mess up 1 in de war sturen, verknoeien: *mess **things** up ergens een potje van maken* **2** smerig maken **3** ruw aanpakken, toetakelen **4** in moeilijkheden brengen
mess-up [inform] warboel: *they **made** a complete ~ of it ze hebben de boel grondig verknoeid*
mess with lastigvallen: *don't ~ me laat me met rust*
messy 1 vuil, vies **2** slordig, verward
metabolism metabolisme[h], stofwisseling
¹metal (n) **1** metaal[h] **2** steenslag [for road]
²metal (adj) metalen
metallic 1 metalen: *~ **lustre** metaalglans* **2** metaalhoudend
metamorphosis metamorfose, gedaanteverwisseling
metaphor metafoor, beeld[h], beeldspraak
metaphorical metaforisch
metaphysical 1 metafysisch, bovennatuurlijk **2** [oft depr] abstract, te subtiel
meteor meteoor
meteorite meteoriet
meteorologist weerkundige
mete out toedienen: *~ **rewards and punishments** beloningen en straffen uitdelen*
meter meter, meettoestel[h]
methadone methadon[h]
method methode, procedure: *~s of **payment** wijzen van betaling*
methodical methodisch, zorgvuldig
methodology methodologie
meticulous uiterst nauwgezet, pietepeuterig

metre 1 meter **2** metrum[h]
metric metriek: *~ **system** metriek stelsel*
metrical metrisch, ritmisch
metro metro, ondergrondse
metropolis metropool
¹metropolitan (n) bewoner van een metropool
²metropolitan (adj) hoofdstedelijk
mettle 1 moed, kracht: *a **man** of ~ een man met pit; **show** (or: **prove**) one's ~ zijn karakter tonen* **2** temperament[h], aard
mew 1 miauwen **2** krijsen
¹Mexican (n) Mexicaan(se)
²Mexican (adj) Mexicaans || [Am; inform] *~ **promotion** bevordering zonder salarisverhoging*
Mexico Mexico
mg *milligram(s)*
¹miaow (n) miauw, kattengejank[h] [also fig]
²miaow (vb) m(i)auwen
Michaelmas term herfsttrimester[h]
microbe microbe
microchip microchip
microfilm microfilm
microloan microlening
micrometer micrometer
micron micron, micrometer
microphone microfoon
microprocessor microprocessor [central processing unit of computer]
microscope microscoop: *put* (or: *examine*) *under the ~ onder de loep nemen [also fig]*
microscopic microscopisch (klein)
microwave 1 magnetron; [Belg] microgolfoven **2** microgolf
microwave oven magnetron
mid- midden, het midden van: *in **mid-air** in de lucht; from **mid-June** to **mid-August** van half juni tot half augustus; in **mid-ocean** in volle zee*
midday middag
midden mesthoop, afvalhoop
¹middle (n) **1** midden[h], middelpunt[h], middellijn, middelvlak[h]: *in the ~ (of) middenin; be caught in the ~ tussen twee vuren zitten* **2** middel[h], taille || *keep to the ~ of the **road** de (gulden) middenweg nemen*
²middle (adj) middelst, midden, tussen-: *~ **age** middelbare leeftijd; Middle **Ages** middeleeuwen; ~ **class** a) bourgeoisie; b) kleinburgerlijk; ~ **finger** middelvinger || ~ **distance** [athletics] middenafstand; the Middle **East** het Midden-Oosten*
middle-aged van middelbare leeftijd
middle-class kleinburgerlijk
middleman tussenpersoon, bemiddelaar, makelaar
middlename 1 tweede voornaam **2** tweede natuur: *bad **luck** is our ~ we zijn voor het ongeluk geboren; **sobriety** is his ~ hij is de soberheid zelve*

middle-of-the-road gematigd
middling middelmatig, tamelijk (goed), redelijk; [inform] tamelijk gezond
midge mug
¹midget (n) dwerg, lilliputter
²midget (adj) lilliputachtig, mini-: ~ *golf* midgetgolf
midland binnenland^h, centraal gewest^h
the **Midlands** Midden-Engeland: *a ~ town* een stad in Midden-Engeland
midlife middelbare leeftijd: *a ~ crisis* een crisis op middelbare leeftijd
midnight middernacht: *at ~* om middernacht
the **midnight oil**: *burn the ~* werken tot diep in de nacht
midriff 1 middenrif^h **2** maagstreek
midst midden^h: *in the ~ of the fight* in het heetst van de strijd
midterm midden van een politieke ambtstermijn
midway halverwege: *stand ~ between* het midden houden tussen
midweek het midden van de week
midwife vroedvrouw
mien [form] voorkomen^h, gelaatsuitdrukking
miffed op de tenen getrapt
¹might (n) macht, kracht: *with ~ and main* met man en macht
²might (aux vb) **1** mocht(en), zou(den) mogen: *~ I ask you a question?* zou ik u een vraag mogen stellen? **2** [possibility] kon(den), zou(den) (misschien) kunnen: *he told her he ~ arrive later* hij zei dat hij misschien later kwam; *it ~ be a good idea to ...* het zou misschien goed zijn te ...; *you ~ have warned us* je had ons wel even kunnen waarschuwen
mighty 1 machtig, krachtig **2** indrukwekkend, kolossaal **3** geweldig
migraine migraine(aanval)
¹migrant (n) seizoenarbeider
²migrant (adj) migrerend, trek-: *~ seasonal workers* rondtrekkende seizoenarbeiders
migrate trekken, verhuizen
migration migratie, volksverhuizing
migratory zwervend: *~ bird* trekvogel
mike [inform] *microphone* microfoon
mil milliliter: *an alcohol level of .8 per ~* een alcoholgehalte van 0,8 pro mille
milady 1 milady **2** elegante vrouw
¹mild (n) licht bier^h
²mild (adj) **1** mild, zacht(aardig), welwillend: *only ~ly interested* maar matig geïnteresseerd; *to put it ~ly* om het zachtjes uit te drukken **2** zwak, licht, flauw: *~ flavoured tobacco* tabak met een zacht aroma
mildew 1 schimmel(vorming) **2** meeldauw(schimmel)
mile mijl [1,609.34 metres]; [fig] grote afstand: *she is feeling ~s better* ze voelt zich

stukken beter; *stick out a ~* in het oog springen; *my thoughts were ~s away* ik was met mijn gedachten heel ergens anders; *recognize s.o. a ~ off* iem. van een kilometer afstand herkennen || *run a ~ from s.o.* met een boog om iem. heenlopen
mileage 1 totaal aantal afgelegde mijlen **2** profijt^h: *he has got a lot of political ~ out of his proposal* met dat voorstel heeft hij heel wat politiek voordeel gehaald
milestone mijlpaal
milieu milieu^h, sociale omgeving
¹militant (n) militant
²militant (adj) militant, strijdlustig
militarism militarisme^h
¹military (n) leger^h, soldaten, strijdkrachten
²military (adj) militair, krijgs- || *~ service* (leger)dienst; *~ tribunal* krijgsraad
militate pleiten: *~ against* pleiten tegen; *~ for* (or: *in favour of*) pleiten voor (or: ten gunste van)
militia militie(leger^h), burgerleger
¹milk (n) melk; [bot] melk(sap^h): *attested ~* kiemvrije melk; *semi-skimmed ~* halfvolle melk; *skim(med) ~* magere, afgeroomde melk || *~ run* routineklus, makkie; *~ and honey* melk en honing [abundance]; *(it's no use) cry(ing) over spilt milk* gedane zaken nemen geen keer
²milk (vb) **1** melken **2** (ont)trekken; sap aftappen van [tree, snake etc] **3** exploiteren, uitbuiten **4** ontlokken [information]; (uit)melken
milking machine melkmachine
milkman melkboer
milksop bangerik, huilebalk
milk tooth melktand
milky 1 melkachtig, troebel **2** melkhoudend || *the Milky Way* de Melkweg
¹mill (n) **1** molen, pers **2** fabriek || *put s.o. through the ~* iem. flink onder handen nemen; *have been through the ~* het klappen van de zweep kennen
²mill (vb) **1** malen **2** (metaal) pletten, walsen
mill about krioelen, wemelen
millennium millennium^h, periode van duizend jaar
miller molenaar
milligram(me) milligram
millimetre millimeter
million miljoen; [fig] talloos: [Am] *thanks a ~* reuze bedankt; *a chance in a ~* een kans van één op duizend || *feel like a ~ (dollars)* zich kiplekker voelen
millionaire miljonair
millionth miljoenste
millipede duizendpoot
millstone molensteen [also fig]
milometer mijlenteller, kilometerteller
milord milord
¹mime (n) **1** mime, (panto)mimespeler, mi-

mekunst **2** nabootsing
²mime (vb) mimen, optreden in mimespel
¹mimic (n) **1** mime, mimespeler **2** na-aper [also animals]
²mimic (adj) **1** mimisch: ~ *art* mimiek **2** nabootsend, na-apend
³mimic (vb) nabootsen, na-apen
mimicry 1 nabootsing **2** mimiek
min 1 *minimum* **2** *Ministry* **3** *minute(s)*
minaret minaret
¹mince (n) **1** gehakt[h], gehakt vlees[h] **2** [Am] gehakt voedsel[h]
²mince (vb) **1** aanstellerig spreken **2** trippelen
³mince (vb) **1** fijnhakken: *~d meat* gehakt (vlees) **2** aanstellerig uitspreken: *she didn't ~ her words* zij nam geen blad voor de mond, ze zei waar het op stond **3** vergoelijken: *not ~ the matter* er geen doekjes om winden
mincemeat pasteivulling || *make ~ of* in de pan hakken, geen stukje heel laten van [an argument]
mincer gehaktmolen
¹mind (n) **1** geest, gemoed[h]: *set s.o.'s ~ at ease* iem. geruststellen; *have sth. on one's ~* iets op zijn hart hebben **2** verstand[h]: *be clear in one's ~ about sth.* iets ten volle beseffen **3** mening, opinie: *have a ~ of one's own* er zijn eigen ideeën op na houden; *speak one's ~* zijn mening zeggen, zeggen wat je op je hart hebt; *be in two ~s (about)* het met zichzelf oneens zijn over; *to my ~* volgens mij **4** bedoeling: *nothing is further from my ~!* a) ik denk er niet aan!, ik pieker er niet over!; b) dat is helemaal niet mijn bedoeling; *have half a ~ to* min of meer geneigd zijn om; [iron] veel zin hebben om; *change one's ~* zich bedenken; *make up one's ~* tot een besluit komen, een beslissing nemen **5** wil, zin(nen): *have sth. in ~* a) iets van plan zijn; b) iets in gedachten hebben **6** aandacht, gedachte(n): *bear in ~* in gedachten houden; *cross (or: enter) one's ~* bij iem. opkomen; *give (or: put, turn) one's ~ to sth.* zijn aandacht richten op; *set one's ~ on sth.* zich ergens op concentreren; *it'll take my ~ off things* het zal mij wat afleiden **7** denkwijze **8** herinnering: *bring (or: call) sth. to ~* aan iets herinneren; *come (or: spring) to ~, come into one's ~* te binnen schieten; *keep in ~* niet vergeten; *it slipped my ~* het is mij ontschoten; *who do you have in ~?* aan wie denk je?
²mind (vb) opletten, oppassen: *~ (you), I would prefer not to* maar ik zou het liever niet doen
³mind (vb) **1** denken aan, bedenken, letten op: *~ one's own business* zich met zijn eigen zaken bemoeien; *never ~* maak je geen zorgen, het geeft niet; *never ~ the expense* de kosten spelen geen rol; *never ~ what your fa-*

ther said ongeacht wat je vader zei; [when leaving] *~ how you go* wees voorzichtig **2** zorgen voor, oppassen, bedienen: *he couldn't walk, never ~ run* hij kon niet lopen, laat staan rennen || *~ you go to the dentist* denk erom dat je nog naar de tandarts moet
⁴mind (vb) **1** bezwaren hebben (tegen), erop tegen zijn, zich storen aan: *he doesn't ~ the cold weather* het koude weer deert hem niet; *would you ~?* zou je 't erg vinden?, vindt u het erg? **2** gehoorzamen
mind-blowing fantastisch, duizelingwekkend
mind-boggling verbijsterend
minded geneigd: *he could do it if he were so ~* hij zou het kunnen doen als hij er (maar) zin in had
minder 1 kinderoppas **2** bodyguard
mindful 1 bedachtzaam **2** opmerkzaam **3** denkend aan: *~ of one's duties* zijn plichten indachtig
mindless 1 dwaas, dom **2** niet lettend op: *~ of danger* zonder oog voor gevaar || *~ violence* zinloos geweld
mind out (+ for) oppassen (voor)
mindreader gedachtelezer
mindset 1 denkrichting **2** obsessie
mind's eye 1 geestesoog[h], verbeelding **2** herinnering
¹mine (n) mijn; [fig] goudmijn: *a ~ of information* een rijke bron van informatie
²mine (vb) **1** in een mijn werken, een mijn aanleggen: *~ for gold* naar goud zoeken **2** mijnen leggen
³mine (vb) uitgraven
⁴mine (poss pron) **1** van mij: *that box is ~* die doos is van mij **2** de mijne(n), het mijne: *a friend of ~* een vriend van me
minefield mijnenveld[h] [also fig]
miner mijnwerker
¹mineral (n) **1** mineraal[h] **2** (-s) mineraalwater[h]
²mineral (adj) delfstoffen-, mineraal-: *~ ores* mineraalertsen
mineralogy mineralogie
minesweeper mijnenveger
mingle 1 zich (ver)mengen **2** zich mengen onder: *they didn't feel like mingling* ze hadden geen zin om met de anderen te gaan praten [at party]
mingy krenterig
miniature miniatuur
minibar minibar
minicab minitaxi
minimal minimaal
minimize minimaliseren, zo klein mogelijk maken, vergoelijken
minimum minimum[h]: *keep sth. to a ~* iets tot het minimum beperkt houden; *~ wage* minimumloon
mining mijnbouw

minion gunsteling, slaafs volgeling, hielenlikker
miniscooter scootmobiel
minister 1 minister: *Minister of the Crown* minister (van het Britse kabinet); *Minister of State* onderminister **2** geestelijke, predikant **3** gezant
ministerial 1 ministerieel **2** geestelijk
minister to [form] bijstaan, verzorgen
ministry 1 ministerie[h] **2** dienst, verzorging **3** geestelijk ambt[h] [priest, vicar]: *enter the ~* geestelijke worden
mink 1 nertsbont[h] **2** nertsmantel
¹minor (n) **1** minderjarige **2** bijvak[h] [at Am university]
²minor (adj) **1** minder, kleiner, vrij klein **2** minder belangrijk, lager, ondergeschikt: *~ poet* minder belangrijke dichter; *~ road* secundaire weg **3** minderjarig **4** [mus] mineur: *in a ~ key* in mineur [also fig]
minority 1 minderheid **2** minderjarigheid
minster kloosterkerk
minstrel minstreel
¹mint (n) **1** munt [bldg]; [inform] bom duiten; smak geld; [fig] bron **2** pepermuntje[h] **3** [bot] munt
²mint (vb) munten, tot geld slaan; [fig] smeden: *~ a new expression* een nieuwe uitdrukking creëren
mint condition perfecte staat: *in ~* puntgaaf
minuet menuet[h]
¹minus (n) **1** minteken[h] **2** minus[h], tekort[h]; [fig] nadeel[h]
²minus (adj) **1** negatief [maths, science] **2** [educ] -min, iets minder goed dan: *a B-~* [roughly] een 8 min
³minus (prep) **1** min(us), min, onder nul: *wages ~ taxes* loon na aftrekking van belastingen; *~ six (degrees centigrade)* zes graden onder nul **2** minder dan: *~ two cm in diameter* minder dan twee cm doorsnede **3** [inform] zonder: *a teapot ~ a spout* een theepot zonder tuit
¹minute (n) **1** minuut, ogenblik[h]: *~ hand* grote wijzer; *wait a ~* wacht eens even; *I won't be a ~* ik ben zo klaar, ik ben zo terug; *just a ~!* moment!, ogenblik(je)!; *in a ~* zo dadelijk; *the ~ (that) I saw him* zodra ik hem zag **2** aantekening, notitie **3** nota, memorandum[h] **4** (-s) notulen
²minute (adj) **1** onbeduidend **2** minutieus, gedetailleerd
minx brutale meid
miracle mirakel[h], wonder[h]
miraculous miraculeus, wonderbaarlijk
mirage 1 luchtspiegeling, fata morgana **2** droombeeld[h], hersenschim
mire [form] **1** moeras[h] **2** slijk[h] || *be in the ~* in de knoei (*or:* puree) zitten
¹mirror (n) spiegel; [fig] weerspiegeling

²mirror (vb) (weer)spiegelen, afspiegelen, weerkaatsen
mirror version spiegelsite, mirrorsite
mirth vrolijkheid, lol
misadventure tegenspoed, ongeluk[h]: *death by ~* dood door ongeluk
misanthrope misantroop, mensenhater
misapply 1 verkeerd toepassen **2** verduisteren [money]
misapprehension misverstand[h], misvatting: *under the ~ that ...* in de waan dat ...
misbehave zich misdragen, zich slecht gedragen
¹miscalculate (vb) zich misrekenen
²miscalculate (vb) verkeerd schatten, onjuist berekenen: *I had ~d the distance* ik had de afstand fout geschat
miscarriage 1 mislukking [of plan]: *~ of justice* rechterlijke dwaling **2** miskraam
miscarry 1 mislukken, falen **2** een miskraam krijgen
miscegenation rassenvermenging
miscellaneous 1 gemengd, gevarieerd: *~ articles* artikelen over uiteenlopende onderwerpen **2** veelzijdig
miscellany mengeling, mengelwerk[h]
mischance ongeluk[h], tegenslag: *by ~, through ~* bij ongeluk
mischief 1 kattenkwaad[h]: *her eyes were full of ~* haar ogen straalden ondeugd uit; *get into ~* kattenkwaad uithalen **2** ondeugendheid **3** onheil[h], schade: *the ~ had been done* het kwaad was al geschied
mischievous 1 schadelijk, nadelig **2** ondeugend, speels
misconception verkeerde opvatting
misconduct 1 wangedrag[h], onfatsoenlijkheid **2** ambtsmisdrijf[h], ambtsovertreding
misconstrue verkeerd interpreteren
misdemeanour misdrijf[h]
miser vrek
miserable 1 beroerd, ellendig **2** armzalig: *live on a ~ pension* van een schamel pensioentje rondkomen **3** waardeloos
miserly vrekkig
misery 1 ellende, nood: *put an animal out of its ~* een dier uit zijn lijden helpen **2** tegenslag, beproeving **3** pijn, ziekte
misfire 1 ketsen, niet afgaan **2** weigeren **3** niet aanslaan
misfit 1 onaangepast iem. **2** niet-passend kledingstuk
misfortune ongeluk[h], tegenspoed
misgiving onzekerheid, bang vermoeden[h]: *they had serious ~s about employing him* ze twijfelden er ernstig aan of ze hem in dienst konden nemen
misguided 1 misleid, verblind **2** ondoordacht
mishandle verkeerd behandelen, slecht regelen

mishap ongeluk(je)ʰ, tegenvaller(tjeʰ): *a journey without* ~ een reis zonder incidenten
mishmash mengelmoesʰ, rommeltjeʰ
misinform verkeerd inlichten (*or:* informeren)
misinterpret verkeerd interpreteren, verkeerd begrijpen
misinterpretation verkeerde interpretatie: *open to* ~ voor verkeerde uitleg vatbaar
misjudge verkeerd (be)oordelen: ~ *s.o.* zich in iem.
mislay zoekmaken, verliezen: *I've mislaid my glasses* ik kan mijn bril niet vinden
mislead misleiden, bedriegen, op 't verkeerde spoor brengen
misleading misleidend, bedrieglijk
mismanagement wanbeheerʰ, wanbestuurʰ, -beleidʰ
mismatch verkeerde combinatie, verkeerd huwelijkʰ
misogynist vrouwenhater
misplace misplaatsen: *a ~d remark* een misplaatste opmerking
¹misprint (n) drukfout, zetfout
²misprint (vb) verkeerd drukken: ~ *a word* een drukfout maken
misread verkeerd lezen: ~ *s.o.'s feelings* zich in iemands gevoelens vergissen
misrepresent 1 verkeerd voorstellen **2** slecht vertegenwoordigen
¹misrule (n) **1** wanbestuurʰ **2** wanorde, anarchie
²misrule (vb) slecht (*or:* verkeerd) besturen
¹miss (n) misser, misslag: *give sth. a* ~ iets laten voorbijgaan; *I think I'll give it a* ~ *this year* ik denk dat ik het dit jaar maar eens oversla
²miss (vb) **1** missen: *his shots all ~ed* hij schoot er telkens naast **2** [in ing-form] ontbreken: *the book is ~ing* het boek is zoek **3** mislopen, falen
³miss (vb) **1** missen, niet raken **2** mislopen, te laat komen voor: ~ *s.o.* een afspraak mislopen **3** ontsnappen aan: *he narrowly ~ed the accident* hij ontsnapte ternauwernood aan het ongeluk **4** vermissen, afwezigheid opmerken: *they'll never* ~ *it* ze zullen nooit merken dat het verdwenen is
Miss 1 Mejuffrouw, Juffrouw: *the ~es Brown* de (jonge)dames Brown **2** [also 'miss'] jongedame
missile 1 raket: *guided* ~ geleide raket **2** projectielʰ
missing 1 ontbrekend: *the* ~ *link* de ontbrekende schakel **2** vermist: *killed, wounded or* ~ gesneuveld, gewond of vermist **3** verloren, weg
mission 1 afvaardiging, legatie: [Am] *foreign* ~ gezantschap **2** roeping, zending: *her* ~ *in life* haar levenstaak **3** opdracht: ~ *accomplished* taak volbracht, opdracht uitgevoerd

¹missionary (n) missionaris, zendeling
²missionary (adj) **1** zendings-: ~ *work* zendingswerk **2** zendelings-: [fig] *with ~ zeal* met toewijding; met hartstocht
mission control controlecentrumʰ
mission statement doelstellingen, missie
¹miss out (vb) over het hoofd gezien worden: *she always misses out* ze vist altijd achter het net ‖ ~ *on the fun* de pret mislopen
²miss out (vb) **1** vergeten **2** overslaan
the **missus** [mockingly] moeder de vrouw
¹mist (n) **1** mist [also fig]; nevel: *lost in the ~ of antiquity* verloren in de nevelen der oudheid **2** waasʰ: *see things through a* ~ alles in een waas zien
²mist (vb) **1** misten **2** (+ over, up) beslaan **3** beneveld worden, wazig worden
¹mistake (n) fout, dwaling: *and make no* ~ a) en vergis je niet; b) en houd jezelf niet voor de gek; *my* ~ ik vergis me, mijn fout; *by* ~ per ongeluk; *and no* ~, *there's no ~ about it* daar kun je van op aan, en dat is zeker
²mistake (vb) **1** verkeerd begrijpen **2** verkeerd kiezen **3** niet herkennen: *there's no mistaking him with his orange hat* je kunt hem eenvoudig niet mislopen met zijn oranje hoed **4** (+ for) verwarren (met)
mistaken verkeerd (begrepen), mis: ~ *identity* persoonsverwisseling; *be* ~ *about* zich vergissen omtrent
mister [without surname] meneer: *what's the time, ~?* hoe laat is het, meneer?
mistletoe maretak
mistress 1 meesteres; bazin [eg of dog, shop]: *she is her own* ~ zij is haar eigen baas; ~ *of the house* vrouw des huizes **2** lerares **3** maîtresse
¹mistrust (n) wantrouwenʰ
²mistrust (vb) wantrouwig zijn (over), wantrouwen
misty mistig, nevelig
misunderstand 1 niet begrijpen: *a misunderstood artist* een onbegrepen kunstenaar **2** verkeerd begrijpen
misunderstanding 1 misverstandʰ **2** geschilʰ **3** onbegripʰ
¹misuse (n) **1** misbruikʰ: ~ *of funds* verduistering van gelden **2** verkeerd gebruikʰ
²misuse (vb) **1** misbruiken **2** verkeerd gebruiken
mitigate 1 lenigen, verlichten **2** matigen, verzachten: [law] *mitigating circumstances* verzachtende omstandigheden
mitt 1 want **2** [baseball] (vang)handschoen
¹mix (n) **1** mengeling, mix **2** mengselʰ
²mix (vb) zich (laten) (ver)mengen: ~ *with* omgaan met
³mix (vb) **1** (ver)mengen **2** bereiden, mixen: *he was ~ing a salad* hij was een slaatje aan het klaarmaken **3** mixen [sound] ‖ ~ *it (up)* elkaar in de haren zitten, knokken

mixed gemengd, vermengd: ~ *bag* allegaartje, ratjetoe, een bonte verzameling; *technology is a ~ blessing* de technologie heeft voor- en nadelen; [tennis] ~ *doubles* gemengd dubbel
mixed up 1 in de war, versuft **2** betrokken, verwikkeld
mixer mengtoestel[h], (keuken)mixer || *a good ~* een gezellig mens
mixture mengsel[h], mengeling
mix up 1 verwarren: *I kept mixing up the names of those twins* ik haalde steeds de namen van die tweeling door elkaar **2** in de war brengen
mm *millimetre(s)* mm
mnemonic ezelsbruggetje[h], geheugensteuntje[h]
¹moan (n) **1** gekreun[h], gekerm[h] **2** geklaag[h], gejammer[h]
²moan (vb) **1** kermen, kreunen **2** klagen, jammeren: *what's he ~ing about now?* waarover zit ie nu weer te zeuren?
moat slotgracht
¹mob (n) **1** gepeupel[h] **2** menigte **3** bende
²mob (vb) samenscholen
³mob (vb) **1** in bende aanvallen, lastigvallen **2** omstuwen, drommen rondom
¹mobile (n) **1** mobile **2** mobieltje[h] || ~ *phone* mobieltje, gsm
²mobile (adj) **1** beweeglijk, mobiel, los, levendig **2** rondtrekkend [of vehicle, shop]: *a ~ home* een stacaravan
mobility beweeglijkheid, mobiliteit
mobility scooter scootmobiel
mobilize mobiliseren: *he ~d all his forces* hij verzamelde al zijn krachten
mobster bendelid[h]; gangster
¹mock (adj) onecht, nagemaakt: ~ *trial* schijnproces
²mock (vb) spotten, zich vrolijk maken
³mock (vb) **1** bespotten **2** (minachtend) trotseren, tarten
mockery 1 namaaksel[h] **2** aanfluiting, schijnvertoning **3** bespotting, hoon: *make a ~ of* de spot drijven met
modal modaal: [linguistics] ~ *auxiliary* modaal hulpwerkwoord
mod cons *modern conveniences* modern comfort[h]: *house with all ~* huis dat van alle gemakken is voorzien
mode 1 wijze, manier, methode **2** gebruik[h], procedure
¹model (n) **1** model[h], maquette, evenbeeld[h] **2** type[h] [eg of car] **3** exclusief model[h] [article of clothing] **4** toonbeeld[h], voorbeeld[h]
²model (adj) **1** model- **2** perfect: *a ~ husband* een modelechtgenoot
³model (vb) mannequin zijn
⁴model (vb) **1** modelleren, boetseren **2** vormen naar een voorbeeld: *he ~led his main character on one of his teachers* voor de

hoofdpersoon gebruikte hij een van zijn leraren als voorbeeld
modem *modulator-demodulator* modem[h]
¹moderate (n) gematigde
²moderate (adj) gematigd, matig: ~ *prices* redelijke prijzen
³moderate (vb) **1** (zich) matigen: *the strikers have ~d their demands* de stakers hebben hun eisen bijgesteld **2** afnemen, verminderen
moderation gematigdheid || ~ *in all things* alles met mate
modern modern: ~ *history* nieuwe geschiedenis; ~ *languages* levende talen
modern-day hedendaags, modern
modernism modernisme[h]
modernize moderniseren, (zich) vernieuwen
modest 1 bescheiden **2** niet groot **3** redelijk
modification 1 wijziging **2** verzachting
modify 1 wijzigen **2** verzachten
modular modulair
module 1 module; [architecture] bouwelement[h]: *lunar ~* maanlandingsvoertuig **2** modulus, maat(staf)
moist vochtig, klam
moisten bevochtigen, natmaken
moisture vocht[h], vochtigheid
molar kies
Moldova Moldavië
¹Moldovan (n) Moldaviër, Moldavische
²Moldovan (adj) Moldavisch
mole 1 mol **2** (kleine) moedervlek, vlekje[h] **3** pier, golfbreker **4** spion, mol
molecular moleculair: ~ *weight* moleculegewicht
molecule molecule[+h]
molehill molshoop
molest lastigvallen, molesteren
mollify 1 bedaren **2** vertederen, vermurwen: *be mollified by s.o.'s flatteries* zich laten vermurwen door iemands vleierij **3** matigen, verzachten
mollusc weekdier[h]
molten gesmolten
mom mamma
moment 1 (geschikt) ogenblik[h], moment[h]: *for the ~* voorlopig; *in a ~* ogenblikkelijk; *just a ~, please* een ogenblikje alstublieft **2** tijdstip[h]: *at the ~* op het ogenblik **3** belang[h], gewicht[h]: *of (great) ~* van (groot) belang
momentarily [Am] zo meteen, spoedig
momentary kortstondig, vluchtig
momentous gewichtig, ernstig
momentum 1 impuls, hoeveelheid van beweging **2** vaart [also fig]; (stuw)kracht: *gain* (or: *gather*) ~ aan stootkracht winnen
¹Monacan (n) Monegask(ische)
²Monacan (adj) Monegaskisch
Monaco Monaco
monarch monarch: *absolute ~* absoluut

vorst
monarchy monarchie
monastery (mannen)klooster[h]
Monday maandag: *on* ~*(s)* maandags, op
maandag
monetary monetair
money 1 geld[h]: *one's* ~*'s* **worth** waar voor
je geld; *made of* ~ stinkend rijk; *I'm not made
of* ~ het geld groeit me niet op de rug; *there is*
~ *in it* er valt geld aan te verdienen **2** welstand, rijkdom: ~ *talks* met geld open je (alle)
deuren ‖ *for my* ~ wat mij betreft
moneyed 1 [form] welgesteld **2** [form]
geldelijk: ~ *assistance* geldelijke ondersteuning
money-grubber geldwolf
moneylender financier, geldschieter
moneymaking winstgevend
money-washing witwassen[h]
Mongolia Mongolië
[1]**Mongolian** (n) Mongoliër, Mongolische
[2]**Mongolian** (adj) Mongolisch
mongrel 1 bastaard(hond) **2** mengvorm
[1]**monitor** (n) **1** monitor, leraarshulpje[h]
2 controleapparaat[h], monitor
[2]**monitor** (vb) controleren, meekijken (mee-
luisteren) met, afluisteren, toezicht houden
op
monk (klooster)monnik
monkey 1 aap: [inform] *make a* ~ *(out) of
s.o.* iem. voor aap/voor schut zetten **2** deugniet
monkey business [inform] apenstreken,
kattenkwaad[h]
monkey-nut apennoot(je[h])
monkey-puzzle apenboom
monochrome monochroom; zwart-wit
monogamous monogaam
monogram monogram[h], naamteken[h]
monologue monoloog, alleenspraak
mononucleosis (ziekte van) Pfeiffer
monopolize monopoliseren
monopoly monopolie[h], alleenrecht[h]
monosyllable eenlettergrepig woord[h]:
speak in ~*s* kortaf spreken
monotonous monotoon, eentonig, slaapverwekkend
monsoon 1 moesson(wind), passaatwind
2 (natte) moesson, regenseizoen[h]
monster 1 monster[h], gedrocht[h] **2** onmens,
beest[h] **3** bakbeest[h], kanjer: ~ *potatoes* enorme aardappelen
monstrosity monstruositeit, wanproduct[h]
monstrous 1 monsterlijk **2** enorm
Montenegro Montenegro
month maand ‖ *I won't do it in a* ~ *of Sundays* ik doe het in geen honderd jaar
[1]**monthly** (n) maandblad[h]
[2]**monthly** (adj, adv) maandelijks
monument monument[h], gedenkteken[h]
monumental 1 monumentaal **2** kolossaal

[1]**moo** (n) boe(geluid)[h] [of cow]
[2]**moo** (vb) loeien
moobs [inform] mannentieten, spiertieten
mooch 1 jatten, gappen **2** [Am] bietsen,
schooien
mood 1 stemming, bui: *in no* ~ *for* (or: *to*)
niet in de stemming voor (*or:* om) **2** wijs: *imperative* ~ gebiedende wijs
moody 1 humeurig, wispelturig **2** slechtgehumeurd
moon maan, satelliet (van andere planeten) ‖ *promise s.o. the* ~ iem. gouden bergen
beloven; *be over the* ~ in de wolken zijn, in
de zevende hemel zijn
moonbeam manestraal
[1]**moonlight** (n) maanlicht[h]
[2]**moonlight** (vb) **1** een bijbaantje hebben,
bijverdienen, klussen **2** zwartwerken
moonlighter iem. die een bijbaantje
heeft, schnabbelaar
moonlight flit [inform] vertrek met de
noorderzon
moonlit maanbeschenen, met maanlicht
overgoten
moon over dagdromen over, mijmeren
moonshine 1 maneschijn **2** geklets[h], dro-
merij **3** [esp Am] illegaal gestookte sterkedrank
moonstruck 1 maanziek **2** warhoofdig,
geschift
[1]**moor** (n) **1** hei(de), woeste grond **2** [Am]
veenmoeras[h]
[2]**moor** (vb) meren, aanmeren, afmeren,
vastmeren, vastleggen
moorhen waterhoen[h]
mooring ligplaats, ankerplaats ‖ *lose one's*
~*s* zijn houvast verliezen
Moorish Moors, Saraceens
moorland heide(landschap[h])
moose eland [North America]
moot onbeslist, onuitgemaakt: *a* ~ *point*
(*or:* **question**) een onopgeloste kwestie
[1]**mop** (n) **1** zwabber, stokdweil **2** haarbos,
ragebol
[2]**mop** (vb) **1** (aan)dweilen, zwabberen
2 droogwrijven, (af)vegen: ~ *one's* **brow** zich
het zweet van het voorhoofd wissen **3** betten, opnemen
[1]**mope** (n) **1** kniesoor, brompot **2** kniesbui:
have a ~ klagerig zeuren **3** (the mopes)
neerslachtigheid
[2]**mope** (vb) kniezen, chagrijnen: ~ *about,* ~
(a)round lusteloos rondhangen
moped bromfiets, brommertje[h], snorscooter
mop up 1 opdweilen, opnemen **2** opslokken **3** zuiveren, verzetshaarden opruimen:
mopping-up **operations** zuiveringsacties
[1]**moral** (n) **1** moraal, (zeden)les: *the* ~ *of the
story* de moraal van het verhaal **2** stelregel,
principe[h] **3** (-s) zeden

²**moral** (adj) **1** moreel, zedelijk, ethisch: *it's a* ~ *certainty* het is zogoed als zeker **2** deugdzaam, kuis
morale moreel[h], mentale veerkracht: *the* ~ *of the troops was excellent* het moreel van de soldaten was uitstekend
moralist moralist
moralistic moralistisch, moraliserend
morality zedenleer, moraal
moralize moraliseren
morass moeras[h]; [fig] poel; [fig] uitzichtloze situatie
moratorium 1 moratorium[h], algemeen uitstel van betaling **2** tijdelijk verbod of uitstel, opschorting
morbid 1 morbide, ziekelijk: *a* ~ *imagination* een ziekelijke fantasie **2** zwartgallig, somber
¹**more** (pron) meer: *$50,* ~ *or less* ongeveer vijftig dollar; *a few* ~ nog een paar; *there was much* ~ er was nog veel meer; *there were many* ~ er waren er nog veel meer; *one* ~ *try* nog een poging; *the* ~ *people there are the happier he feels* hoe meer mensen er zijn, hoe gelukkiger hij zich voelt; *I was just one* ~ *candidate* ik was niet meer dan de zoveelste kandidaat ‖ *and what's* ~ en daarbij komt nog dat
²**more** (adv) **1** meer, veeleer, eerder: ~ *or less* min of meer, zo ongeveer; *once* ~ nog eens, nog een keer; *that's* ~ *like it* dat begint er al op te lijken, dat is al beter; *I will be* ~ *than happy to help you* ik zal je met alle liefde en plezier helpen **2** -er, meer: ~ *difficult* moeilijker; ~ *easily* makkelijker **3** bovendien
moreover bovendien, daarnaast
morgue mortuarium[h]
moribund stervend, ten dode opgeschreven
morning ochtend, morgen; [fig] begin[h]: *good* ~ goedemorgen; *he works* ~*s* hij werkt 's morgens; *in the* ~ **a)** 's morgens; **b)** morgenochtend; *at two o'clock in the* ~ 's nachts om twee uur; ~*!* morgen!
morning coat jacquet[h]
morning dress 1 jacquetkostuum[h] **2** colbertkostuum[h]
¹**Moroccan** (n) Marokkaan(se)
²**Moroccan** (adj) Marokkaans
Morocco Marokko
moron [inform] **1** zwakzinnige, debiel **2** imbeciel, zakkenwasser
morose 1 chagrijnig **2** somber
morph veranderen: ~ *into* veranderen in
morphine morfine
morsel hap, mondvol, stuk(je)[h]: *he hasn't got a* ~ *of sense* hij heeft geen greintje hersens
mortal 1 sterfelijk: *the* ~ *remains* het stoffelijk overschot **2** dodelijk, moordend; fataal [also fig] **3** doods-, dodelijk, zeer hevig

(groot): ~ *enemy* aartsvijand, doodsvijand; *it's a* ~ *shame* het is een grof schandaal **4** (op aarde) voorstelbaar: *she did every* ~ *thing to please him* ze wrong zich in de gekste bochten om het hem naar de zin te maken
mortality 1 sterftecijfer[h] **2** sterfelijkheid
mortally 1 dodelijk **2** doods-, enorm: ~ *wounded* dodelijk gewond
¹**mortar** (n) **1** vijzel **2** mortier[+h] **3** mortel, (metsel)specie
²**mortar** (vb) (vast)metselen
mortar bomb mortiergranaat
¹**mortgage** (n) hypotheek(bedrag[h])
²**mortgage** (vb) (ver)hypothekeren; [also fig] verpanden
mortgage interest relief hypotheekrenteaftrek
mortician [Am] begrafenisondernemer
mortification 1 zelfkastijding, versterving **2** gekwetstheid: *to his* ~ tot zijn schande
mortify 1 tuchtigen, kastijden: ~ *the flesh* het vlees doden **2** krenken, kwetsen
mortuary lijkenhuis[h], mortuarium[h]
mosaic mozaïek[h]
mosque moskee
mosquito mug, muskiet: ~ *net* klamboe, muskietennet
moss mos[h]
¹**most** (pron) meeste(n), grootste gedeelte van: *twelve at (the)* ~, *twelve at the very* ~ hoogstens twaalf; *this is the* ~ *I can do* meer kan ik niet doen; *for the* ~ *part* grotendeels
²**most** (adv) **1** meest, hoogst, zeer: ~ *complicated* zeer ingewikkeld; ~ *of all I like music* voor alles houd ik van muziek **2** -st(e), meest: *the* ~ *difficult problem* het moeilijkste probleem **3** [Am] bijna, haast: ~ *every evening* bijna elke avond
mostly grotendeels, voornamelijk, meestal
MOT [inform] *Ministry of Transport* verplichte jaarlijkse autokeuring
motel motel[h]
moth 1 mot: *this sweater has got the* ~ *in it* de mot zit in deze trui **2** nachtvlinder
¹**mother** (n) **1** moeder [also fig]; bron, oorsprong: *expectant* (or: *pregnant*) ~ aanstaande moeder **2** moeder(-overste) ‖ *shall I be* ~? zal ik (even) opscheppen?
²**mother** (vb) (be)moederen, betuttelen
motherboard moederbord[h]
motherhood moederschap[h]
mother-in-law schoonmoeder
mother-of-pearl paarlemoer[h]
Mother's Day [Am] Moederdag
mother tongue moedertaal
motif (leid)motief[h], (grond)thema[h]
¹**motion** (n) **1** beweging, gebaar[h], wenk **2** beweging(swijze), gang, loop: *the film was shown in slow* ~ de film werd vertraagd afgedraaid; *put* (or: *set*) *sth. in* ~ iets in beweging zetten **3** motie **4** mechaniek[h], bewe-

gend mechanisme[h] ‖ **go** *through the* ~s plichtmatig verrichten, net doen alsof
²**motion** (vb) wenken, door een gebaar te
kennen geven: *the policeman* ~*ed the* **crowd**
to keep moving de agent gebaarde de mensen door te lopen
motion picture speelfilm
motivate motiveren
motivation 1 motivering **2** motivatie
motive 1 motief[h], beweegreden: *without* ~
ongegrond, zonder reden(en) **2** leidmotief[h]
motley 1 samengeraapt **2** bont, (veel)kleu-
rig: *a* ~ **collection** een bonte verzameling
motor 1 motor **2** auto
motorbike 1 motor(fiets) **2** [Am] bromfiets, brommer
motorcycle motor(fiets)
motor home kampeerauto, camper
motorist automobilist
motorman 1 wagenbestuurder **2** chauffeur
motor scooter scooter
motortruck [Am] vrachtwagen
motorway autosnelweg
MOT-test verplichte jaarlijkse keuring [for
cars over 3 years old]; apk
mottled gevlekt, gespikkeld
motto lijfspreuk
¹**mould** (n) **1** vorm, mal, matrijs, pudding-
(vorm); [fig] aard; karakter[h]: *cast in one* (or:
the same) ~ uit hetzelfde hout gesneden
2 afgietsel[h] **3** schimmel **4** teelaarde, blad-
aarde
²**mould** (vb) vormen, kneden: ~ *a person's*
character iemands karakter vormen
moulder (tot stof) vergaan, vermolmen,
verrotten
moulding 1 afgietsel[h], afdruk **2** lijstwerk[h],
profiel[h]
mouldy 1 beschimmeld, schimmelig **2** muf
3 afgezaagd; oud
¹**moult** (n) rui
²**moult** (vb) ruien, verharen, vervellen
mound 1 hoop aarde, (graf)heuvel; [fig]
berg; hoop **2** wal, dam, dijk
¹**mount** (n) **1** berg, heuvel **2** rijdier[h] **3** pla-
teautje[h]; zetting [of jewels]; opplakkarton[h],
opzetkarton[h] [of photo, picture]
²**mount** (vb) **1** (op)stijgen, (op)klimmen: *the*
expenses kept ~*ing* **up** de uitgaven liepen
steeds hoger op **2** een paard bestijgen
³**mount** (vb) **1** bestijgen, beklimmen, opgaan: *he* ~*ed the* **stairs** hij liep de trap op **2** te
paard zetten, laten rijden: ~*ed* **police** bereden politie **3** zetten op; opplakken [photos]
4 organiseren, in beeld brengen: ~ *an* **ex-**
hibition een tentoonstelling organiseren
mountain berg, heuvel, hoop: ~ **bike**
mountainbike; ~ **range** bergketen ‖ *make a* ~
out of a **molehill** van een mug een olifant
maken

mountaineer 1 bergbeklimmer **2** bergbe-
woner
mountainous 1 bergachtig, berg- **2** gigantisch, reusachtig
mountainside berghelling
mountebank 1 kwakzalver **2** charlatan
¹**mourn** (vb) **1** (+ for, over) rouwen (om), in
de rouw zijn, treuren **2** rouw dragen
²**mourn** (vb) betreuren, bedroefd zijn over
mourner 1 rouwdrager, rouwdraagster
2 rouwklager, rouwklaagster
mournful bedroefd, triest
mourning 1 rouw, rouwdracht: *go into* ~
de rouw aannemen **2** rouwtijd
mouse muis
mousetrap muizenval
moustache snor
¹**mouth** (n) **1** mond, muil, bek: *a big* ~ een
grote bek; *keep one's* ~ **shut** niets verklappen; *it makes my* ~ **water** het is om van te
watertanden; *out of s.o.'s own* ~ met iemands eigen woorden; **mouth-to-mouth**
mond op mond **2** opening, ingang, toegang;
(uit)monding [of river]; mond [of port etc] ‖
shoot *one's* ~ *off* zijn mond voorbijpraten;
down *in the* ~ terneergeslagen, ontmoedigd
²**mouth** (vb) **1** declameren, geaffecteerd
(uit)spreken **2** (voor zich uit) mompelen
mouthful 1 mondvol, hapje[h] **2** [inform]
hele mond vol, een lang woord: *a large* ~ *to*
swallow moeilijk te geloven
mouthpiece 1 mondstuk[h] **2** spreekbuis,
woordvoerder
mouthwash mondspoeling
movable 1 beweegbaar, beweeglijk, los: ~
scene coulisse **2** verplaatsbaar, verstelbaar ‖
~ **property** roerend goed
¹**move** (n) **1** beweging: *get a* ~ *on* **a)** in beweging komen, aanpakken; **b)** opschieten;
large forces were **on** *the* ~ grote strijdkrachten
waren op de been **2** verhuizing, trek: *be* **on**
the ~ op reis zijn, aan het zwerven zijn, op
trek zijn [of birds] **3** zet, beurt, slag: *make a*
~ een zet doen; *it's* **your** ~ jij bent aan zet
4 stap, maatregel, manoeuvre: *make a* ~
a) opstaan [from table]; **b)** opstappen, het
initiatief nemen; **c)** maatregelen treffen, in
actie komen
²**move** (vb) **1** (zich) bewegen, zich verplaatsen, van positie veranderen: *it's* **time** *to be*
moving het is tijd om te vertrekken; ~ **along**
doorlopen, opschieten; ~ **over** inschikken,
opschuiven **2** vooruitkomen, opschieten:
suddenly things **began** *to* ~ plotseling kwam
er leven in de brouwerij; **keep** *moving*! blijf
doorgaan!, doorlopen! **3** [board game] een
zet doen, zetten, aan zet zijn **4** verkeren,
zich bewegen: *he* ~s **in** *the highest circles* hij
beweegt zich in de hoogste kringen **5** verhuizen, (weg)trekken, zich verzetten: *they* ~*d*
into *a flat* ze betrokken een flat **6** een voor-

stel doen: ~ *for* adjournment verdaging voorstellen

³move (vb) **1** bewegen, (ver)roeren, in beweging brengen: *the police* ~d them *along* de politie dwong hen door te lopen **2** verplaatsen; [board game] zetten; verschuiven **3** opwekken, (ont)roeren, raken, aangrijpen: *he is* ~d to *tears* hij is tot tranen toe geroerd **4** aanzetten, aansporen: *be* ~d to zich geroepen voelen om te

¹move ab<u>ou</u>t (vb) **1** zich (voortdurend) bewegen, rondlopen, ronddrentelen **2** dikwijls verhuizen

²move ab<u>ou</u>t (vb) **1** vaak laten verhuizen, vaak verplanten **2** vaak verplaatsen, rondsjouwen

move <u>i</u>n 1 intrekken, gaan wonen; betrekken [house, flat etc]: ~ *with* s.o. bij iem. intrekken **2** binnenvallen, optrekken, aanvallen, tussenbeide komen: *the police moved in* on *the crowd* de politie reed op de menigte in

m<u>o</u>vement 1 beweging, voortgang, ontwikkeling, impuls, trend, tendens; [med] stoelgang; ontlasting **2** beweging, organisatie: *the feminist* ~ de vrouwenbeweging **3** mechaniek[h] **4** [mus] beweging; deel[h] [of symphony etc]

¹move <u>o</u>n (vb) **1** verder gaan, opschieten, doorgaan **2** vooruitkomen, promotie maken

²move <u>o</u>n (vb) iem. gebieden door te gaan

move <u>ou</u>t verhuizen, vertrekken

m<u>o</u>ver 1 indiener van een voorstel **2** verhuizer

move <u>u</u>p 1 in een hogere klas komen, in rang opklimmen **2** stijgen, toenemen

m<u>o</u>vie 1 film: *go to the* ~s naar de film gaan **2** bioscoop **3** (the movies) filmindustrie

m<u>o</u>ving 1 ontroerend **2** bewegend: [Am] ~ *picture* film

m<u>o</u>ving van verhuiswagen

mow maaien: ~ *down* soldiers soldaten neermaaien

m<u>o</u>wer 1 maaier **2** maaimachine, grasmaaier

¹Mozamb<u>i</u>can (n) Mozambikaan(se)

²Mozamb<u>i</u>can (adj) Mozambikaans

Mozamb<u>i</u>que Mozambique

MP 1 *Member of Parliament* **2** *military police(man)*

mpg *miles per gallon* mijlen per gallon

mph *miles per hour* mijlen per uur

MPV *multipurpose vehicle* MPV, spacewagon, ruimtewagen

Mr *mister* dhr., de heer

Mrs Mevr.

Ms Mw. [instead of Miss or Mrs]

Mt *Mount* Berg

¹much (adv) veel: *how* ~ *is it?* hoeveel kost het?; *it's not up to* ~ het is niet veel soeps; *her contribution didn't amount to* ~ haar bijdrage stelde niet veel voor; *that's not* ~ *use to me*

now daar heb ik nu niet veel aan || *there isn't* ~ *in it* het maakt niet veel uit; *it was as* ~ *as I could do to keep from laughing* ik had de grootst mogelijke moeite om niet te lachen; *he's* **not** ~ *of a singer* als zanger stelt hij niet veel voor; *well,* *so* ~ *for that* dat was dan dat

²much (adv) **1** [degree] veel, zeer, erg: *she was* ~ *the oldest* zij was verreweg de oudste; *as* ~ *as $2 million* (maar) liefst 2 miljoen dollar; ~ *as he would have liked to go* hoe graag hij ook was gegaan; ~ *to my surprise* tot mijn grote verrassing **2** veel, vaak, dikwijls, lang: *she didn't stay* ~ ze bleef niet lang **3** ongeveer, bijna: *they were* ~ *the* **same** *size* ze waren ongeveer even groot

m<u>u</u>chness hoeveelheid, grootte: *much of a* ~ lood om oud ijzer

¹muck (n) **1** troep, rommel, rotzooi: *make a* ~ *of a job* niets terecht brengen van een klus, er niets van bakken **2** (natte) mest, drek **3** slijk[h]; viezigheid [also fig]

²muck (vb) bemesten || ~ *out* uitmesten; ~ *up* verknoeien

¹muck ab<u>ou</u>t (vb) **1** niksen, lummelen **2** vervelen, klieren: ~ *with* knoeien met

²muck ab<u>ou</u>t (vb) **1** pesten **2** knoeien met

m<u>u</u>ckraking vuilspuiterij

m<u>u</u>cous slijm-: ~ *membrane* slijmvlies

mud modder, slijk[h]; [fig] roddel; laster: *drag* s.o.'s *name through the* ~ iem. door het slijk halen; *fling* (or: *sling, throw*) ~ *at* s.o. iem. door de modder sleuren

¹m<u>u</u>ddle (n) verwarring, warboel: *in a* ~ in de war

²m<u>u</u>ddle (vb) wat aanknoeien, wat aanmodderen: ~ *along* (or: on) voortmodderen; ~ *through* met vallen en opstaan het einde halen

³m<u>u</u>ddle (vb) **1** (also + up) door elkaar gooien, verwarren **2** in de war brengen: *a bit* ~d een beetje in de war

muddle-h<u>ea</u>ded warrig, dom

m<u>u</u>ddy 1 modderig **2** troebel, ondoorzichtig **3** vaal, dof

m<u>u</u>dguard spatbord[h]

m<u>ue</u>sli muesli

¹muff (n) **1** mof **2** misser [originally at ball game]; fiasco[h]

²muff (vb) **1** [sport] missen: ~ *an easy* **catch** een makkelijke bal missen **2** verknoeien: *I know I'll* ~ *it* ik weet zeker dat ik het verpest

m<u>u</u>ffle 1 warm inpakken, warm toedekken: ~ *up* goed inpakken **2** dempen [sound]: ~d **curse** gedempte vloek

m<u>u</u>ffler 1 das, sjaal **2** geluiddemper; [Am] knalpot

¹mug (n) **1** mok, beker **2** kop, smoel **3** sufferd, sul

²mug (vb) aanvallen en beroven

m<u>u</u>gger straatrover

mugging aanranding; straatroof
muggins sul, sufferd
muggy benauwd, drukkend
mugshot portretfoto [for police file]
mug up uit je hoofd leren, erin stampen
mulberry moerbeiboom
mule 1 muildier^h, muilezel: *obstinate* (or: *stubborn*) *as a* ~ koppig als een ezel **2** stijfkop, dwarskop
mullet 1 [zoology] zeebarbeel: *red* ~ mul **2** matje^h [hair style]
multicultural multicultureel
multidimensional gecompliceerd; met veel kanten [eg problem]
multilateral 1 veelzijdig **2** multilateraal
multinational multinationaal
¹multiple (n) [maths] veelvoud^h: *least* (or: *lowest*) *common* ~ kleinste gemene veelvoud
²multiple (adj) **1** veelvoudig: ~ *choice* meerkeuze-; ~ *shop* (or: *store*) grootwinkelbedrijf **2** divers, veelsoortig **3** [bot] samengesteld
multiplex megabioscoop
multiplication vermenigvuldiging
multiplication table tafel van vermenigvuldiging
multiplicity 1 veelheid, massa **2** veelsoortigheid: *a* ~ *of ideas* een grote verscheidenheid aan ideeën
¹multiply (vb) **1** zich vermeerderen, aangroeien **2** zich vermenigvuldigen **3** een vermenigvuldiging uitvoeren
²multiply (vb) **1** vermenigvuldigen: ~ *three by four* drie met vier vermenigvuldigen **2** vergroten: ~ *one's chances* zijn kansen doen stijgen
multipurpose veelzijdig, voor meerdere doeleinden geschikt
multiracial multiraciaal
multistorey car park parkeergarage
multitask multitasken, verschillende taken tegelijkertijd uitvoeren
multitude 1 massa: *a* ~ *of ideas* een grote hoeveelheid ideeën **2** menigte
¹mum (n) mamma
²mum (adj) stil: *keep* ~ zijn mondje dicht houden
³mum (int) mondje dicht!, sst!, niets zeggen!: ~ *'s the word!* mondje dicht!, niks zeggen!
mumble 1 mompelen **2** knauwen op, mummelen op
mummify mummificeren, balsemen
mummy 1 mummie **2** mammie, mam(s)
mumps de bof
munch kauwen (op): ~ *(away at) an apple* aan een appel knagen
mundane gewoon: ~ *matters* routinezaken
Munich München
municipal gemeentelijk

municipality 1 gemeente **2** gemeentebestuur^h
munition 1 munitie **2** (-s) wapens; bommen, granaten
¹mural (n) muurschildering, fresco^h
²mural (adj) muur-, wand-: ~ *painting* muurschildering
¹murder (n) **1** moord: *get away with* ~ a) alles kunnen maken; b) precies kunnen doen wat men wil **2** beroerde toestand
²murder (vb) **1** vermoorden, ombrengen **2** verknoeien, ruïneren
murderer moordenaar
murky 1 duister, donker **2** vunzig, kwalijk: ~ *affairs* weinig verheffende zaken
¹murmur (n) **1** gemurmel^h; geruis^h [of brook] **2** gemopper^h **3** gemompel^h
²murmur (vb) **1** mompelen **2** ruisen, suizen **3** mopperen: ~ *against* (or: *at*) mopperen op, klagen over
Murphy's Law de wet van Murphy
muscle 1 spier: *flex one's* ~*s* de spieren losmaken **2** (spier)kracht, macht
muscular 1 spier-: ~ *dystrophy* spierdystrofie **2** gespierd, krachtig
¹muse (n) muze; [fig also] inspiratie: *The Muses* de (negen) muzen, kunsten en wetenschappen
²muse (vb) (+ about, over, on) peinzen (over), mijmeren
museum museum^h
mush 1 moes^h, brij **2** sentimenteel gekletsh, kletspraat **3** [advertising] geruis^h
¹mushroom (n) **1** champignon **2** (eetbare) paddenstoel
²mushroom (vb) **1** zich snel ontwikkelen, als paddenstoelen uit de grond schieten **2** paddenstoelvormig uitwaaieren [of smoke]
mushrooming snelle groei, explosieve toename
mushy 1 papperig, zacht: ~ *peas* erwtenpuree **2** [inform] halfzacht, sentimenteel
music 1 muziek: ~ *hall* variété(theater) **2** bladmuziek, partituur ‖ *face the* ~ de consequenties aanvaarden; *piped* ~ ingeblikte muziek [in restaurant etc]
¹musical (n) musical
²musical (adj) **1** muzikaal **2** welluidend **3** muziek-: ~ *sound* klank [as opposed to noise] ‖ ~ *chairs* stoelendans
musician musicus, muzikant
music stand muziekstandaard
musk 1 muskus **2** muskusdier^h **3** muskusplant
muskrat muskusrat
Muslim moslim
¹muss (n) [Am] wanorde
²muss (vb) [Am] in de war maken; verknoeien [hair, clothing]: ~ *up one's suit* zijn pak ruïneren

mussel mossel
¹must (n) noodzaak, vereiste^h, must: *the Millennium Dome is a* ~ je moet beslist naar de Millennium Dome toe
²must (aux vb) **1** [command, obligation and necessity] moeten; [in indirect speech also] moest(en); [condition] zou(den) zeker: *you* ~ *come and see us* je moet ons beslist eens komen opzoeken; *if you* ~ *have your way, then do* als je per se je eigen gang wil gaan, doe dat dan; ~ *you have your way again?* moet je nu weer met alle geweld je zin krijgen?
2 [prohibition; with negation] mogen: *you* ~ *not go near the water* je mag niet dicht bij het water komen **3** [supposition] moeten; [Am also; with negation] kunnen: *you* ~ *be out of your mind to say such things* je moet wel gek zijn om zulke dingen te zeggen; *s.o.* ~ *have seen sth., surely?* er moet toch iem. iets gezien hebben?
mustard mosterd: [Am; inform] *cut the* ~ het 'm flikken, het maken
¹muster (n) **1** inspectie: *pass* ~ ermee door kunnen **2** verzameling
²muster (vb) zich verzamelen; bijeenkomen [for inspection]
³muster (vb) **1** verzamelen, bijeenroepen **2** bijeenrapen; verzamelen [courage, powers]: ~ *up one's courage* al zijn moed bijeenrapen
must-have iets dat iedereen moet (*or:* wil) hebben: *three* ~ *books for parents* drie boeken die elke ouder gelezen moet hebben
musty 1 muf: ~ *air* bedompte lucht **2** schimmelig
mutation 1 verandering, wijziging **2** mutatie
¹mute (n) (doof)stomme
²mute (adj) **1** stom **2** zwijgend, stil, sprakeloos || ~ *swan* knobbelzwaan
mutilate verminken; toetakelen [also fig]
mutilation verminking
mutineer muiter
¹mutiny (n) muiterij, opstand
²mutiny (vb) muiten
mutt halvegare, idioot
¹mutter (n) **1** gemompel^h **2** gemopper^h
²mutter (vb) **1** mompelen: *he* ~*ed an oath* hij vloekte zachtjes **2** mopperen: ~ *against* (*or:* *at*) mopperen over
mutton schapenvlees^h
muttonhead stomkop
mutual 1 wederzijds, wederkerig: ~ *consent* wederzijds goedvinden **2** gemeenschappelijk, onderling: ~ *interests* gemeenschappelijke belangen
muzak achtergrondmuziek, muzak
¹muzzle (n) **1** snuit; muil [of animal] **2** mond; tromp [of gun] **3** muilkorf
²muzzle (vb) muilkorven [also fig]; de mond snoeren

muzzy 1 duf, saai, dof **2** wazig, vaag **3** beneveld, verward
¹my (pron) mijn: *my dear boy* beste jongen; *he disapproved of my going out* hij vond het niet goed dat ik uitging
²my (int) **1** o jee **2** wel: *my, my* welwel
Myanmar Myanmar
myopic 1 bijziend, kippig **2** kortzichtig
myself 1 mij, me, mezelf: *I am not* ~ *today* ik voel me niet al te best vandaag **2** zelf: *I'll go* ~ ik zal zelf gaan
mysterious geheimzinnig, mysterieus
mystery 1 geheim^h, mysterie^h, raadsel^h **2** geheimzinnigheid
¹mystic (n) mysticus
²mystic (adj) **1** mystiek **2** occult, esoterisch, alleen voor ingewijden **3** raadselachtig
mystical 1 mystiek **2** occult, esoterisch
mystification mystificatie, misleiding
mystify verbijsteren, verwarren, voor een raadsel stellen: *her behaviour mystified me* ik begreep niets van haar gedrag
mystique 1 aura **2** geheime techniek
myth 1 mythe, mythologie **2** fabel, allegorie **3** verzinsel^h, fictie
mythical 1 mythisch **2** fictief, verzonnen
mythological 1 mythologisch **2** mythisch
mythology mythologie

n

N *North* N., Noord(en)
n/a *not applicable* n.v.t., niet van toepassing
nab (op)pakken, inrekenen
naff niks waard, waardeloos
¹nag (n) **1** klein paard(je^h), pony **2** knol, slecht renpaard^h **3** zeurpiet
²nag (vb) **1** zeuren: *a ~ging headache* een zeurende hoofdpijn; *~ (at)* s.o. iem. aan het hoofd zeuren **2** treiteren
¹nail (n) **1** nagel **2** spijker: *hit the ~ on the head* de spijker op de kop slaan ‖ *pay on the ~* contant betalen
²nail (vb) **1** (vast)spijkeren **2** vastnagelen: *he was ~ed to his seat* hij zat als vastgenageld op zijn stoel **3** te pakken krijgen: *he ~ed me as soon as I came in* hij schoot me direct aan toen ik binnenkwam **4** betrappen
nail-biter razend spannende film, razend spannend boek^h
nail down 1 vastspijkeren **2** nauwkeurig vaststellen, bepalen: *John had nailed him down* John had hem precies door **3** vastleggen, houden aan: *it's difficult to nail him down on any subject* hij zegt niet gauw wat hij ergens van denkt; *we nailed him down to his promise* we hielden hem aan zijn belofte **4** zich verzekeren van, veiligstellen: *they've already nailed down the championship* ze zijn al zeker kampioen
nail up 1 dichtspijkeren **2** (op)hangen
naive 1 naïef **2** onnozel, dom
naivety naïviteit, onschuld, onnozelheid
naked 1 naakt, bloot **2** onbedekt, onnozelheid ‖ *the ~ eye* het blote oog; *~ truth* naakte waarheid
¹name (n) **1** naam, benaming: *enter* (or: *put down*) *one's ~ for* zich opgeven voor; *what's-his-~?* hoe heet hij ook alweer?, dinges; *I only know him by ~* ik ken hem alleen van naam; *a man by* (or: *of*) *the ~ of Jones* iem. die Jones heet, een zekere Jones; *he hasn't a penny to his ~* hij heeft geen cent; *I can't put a ~ to it* ik weet niet precies hoe ik het moet zeggen; *first ~* voornaam; *second ~* achternaam **2** reputatie, naam: *make* (or: *win*) *a ~ for o.s.*, *win o.s. a ~* naam maken ‖ *the ~ of the game is …* waar het om gaat is …; *call s.o. ~s* iem. uitschelden; *lend one's ~ to* zijn naam lenen aan; *in the ~ of* in (de) naam van
²name (vb) **1** noemen, benoemen, een naam geven: *she was ~d after her mother*, [Am also] *she was ~d for her mother* ze was naar haar moeder genoemd **2** dopen [ship]

3 (op)noemen: *~ your price* noem je prijs **4** benoemen, aanstellen **5** vaststellen: *~ the day* de trouwdag vaststellen ‖ *you ~ it* noem maar op
name-calling het schelden, scheldpartij
namedropping opschepperij, indruk willen maken door met namen te strooien
namely namelijk
namesake naamgenoot
Namibia Namibië
¹Namibian (n) Namibiër, Namibische
²Namibian (adj) Namibisch
nan [child language] oma
¹nancy (n) [depr] mietje^h, nicht, flikker
²nancy (adj) [depr] verwijfd
nanny kinderjuffrouw
the **nanny state** [depr] [roughly] betuttelende verzorgingsstaat
¹nap (n) **1** dutje^h, tukje^h **2** vleug [of fabric]
²nap (vb) dutten, dommelen: *catch s.o. ~ping* iem. betrappen
nape (achterkant van de) nek
napkin 1 servet^h, doekje^h **2** luier
nappy luier
narcissus (witte) narcis
¹narcotic (n) verdovend middel^h, slaapmiddel^h
²narcotic (adj) verdovend, slaapverwekkend
¹nark (n) verklikker, tipgever
²nark (vb) kwaad maken, irriteren: *she felt ~ed at* (or: *by*) *his words* zijn woorden ergerden haar
narrate vertellen, beschrijven
narration verhaal^h, vertelling, verslag^h
¹narrative (n) verhaal^h, vertelling
²narrative (adj) verhalend, verhaal-, narratief: *~ power* vertelkunst
narrator verteller
¹narrow (n) engte, zee-engte, bergengte
²narrow (adj) **1** smal, nauw, eng: *by a ~ margin* nog net, op het nippertje **2** beperkt, krap: *a ~ majority* een kleine meerderheid **3** bekrompen **4** nauwgezet, precies: *a ~ examination* een zorgvuldig onderzoek ‖ *it was a ~ escape* het was op het nippertje; *in the ~est sense* strikt genomen
narrow down beperken, terugbrengen: *it narrowed down to this* het kwam (ten slotte) hierop neer
narrowly 1 net, juist: *the sailor ~ escaped drowning* de zeeman ontkwam maar net aan de verdrinkingsdood **2** zorgvuldig
narrow-minded bekrompen, kleingeestig
nasal neus-, nasaal: *~ spray* neusspray
nasality neusgeluid^h, nasaliteit
nasturtium Oost-Indische kers
nasty 1 smerig, vuil, vies **2** onaangenaam, onprettig: *the bill was a ~ shock* de rekening zorgde voor een onaangename verrassing **3** lastig, hinderlijk, vervelend **4** gemeen, hatelijk: *a ~ look* een boze blik; *he turned ~*

when *I refused to leave* hij werd giftig toen ik niet wilde weggaan **5** ernstig, hevig: *a ~ accident* een ernstig ongeluk; *a ~ blow* a) een flinke klap; **b)** een tegenvaller **nation 1** natie, volk[h] **2** land[h], staat
¹national (n) **1** landgenoot **2** staatsburger, onderdaan
²national (adj) **1** nationaal, rijks-, staats-, volks-: ~ *anthem* volkslied; ~ *debt* staatsschuld; ~ *monument* historisch monument; ~ *service* militaire dienst; *National Trust* [roughly] monumentenzorg **2** landelijk, nationaal
nationalism nationalisme[h]
nationalist(ic) nationalistisch
nationality nationaliteit
nationalize 1 nationaliseren **2** naturaliseren **3** tot een natie maken
nationwide landelijk, door het hele land
¹native (n) **1** inwoner, bewoner: *a ~ of Dublin* een geboren Dubliner **2** [oft depr] inboorling, inlander **3** inheemse diersoort, plantensoort
²native (adj) **1** geboorte-: *Native American* indiaan; *a ~ speaker of English* iem. met Engels als moedertaal **2** natuurlijk **3** autochtoon, inheems, binnenlands; [oft depr] inlands: *go ~* zich aanpassen aan de plaatselijke bevolking
nativity geboorte
the **Nativity** geboorte(feest[h]) van Christus, Kerstmis
nativity play kerstspel[h]
NATO *North Atlantic Treaty Organization* NAVO, Noord-Atlantische Verdragsorganisatie
natty 1 sjiek, netjes, keurig **2** handig, bedreven
¹natural (n) natuurtalent[h], favoriet, meest geschikte persoon: *John's a ~ for the job* John is geknipt voor die baan
²natural (adj) **1** natuurlijk, natuur-: ~ *forces* natuurkrachten; ~ *gas* aardgas; ~ *history* natuurlijke historie, biologie **2** geboren, van nature: *he's a ~ linguist* hij heeft een talenknobbel **3** aangeboren **4** normaal **5** ongedwongen
naturalist 1 naturalist **2** natuurkenner
naturalization 1 naturalisatie **2** inburgering **3** het inheems maken [plants, animals]
naturalize 1 naturaliseren **2** doen inburgeren, overnemen **3** inheems maken; uitzetten [plants, animals]: *rabbits have become ~d in Australia* konijnen zijn in Australië een inheemse diersoort geworden
naturally 1 natuurlijk, vanzelfsprekend, uiteraard **2** van nature || *it comes ~ to her* het gaat haar gemakkelijk af
nature 1 wezen[h], natuur, karakter[h]: *he is stubborn by ~* hij is koppig van aard; *in the (very) ~ of things* uit de aard der zaak **2** soort,

aard: *sth. of that ~* iets van dien aard **3** de natuur: ~ *reserve* natuurreservaat; [fig] *let ~ take its course* de zaken op hun beloop laten; *contrary to ~* wonderbaarlijk, onnatuurlijk
nature conservation natuurbeheer[h]
naturism naturisme[h], nudisme[h]
naught nul, niets: *come to ~* op niets uitlopen
naughty 1 ondeugend, stout **2** slecht, onfatsoenlijk
nausea 1 misselijkheid **2** walging, afkeer
nauseate misselijk maken: *he was ~d at the sight of such cruelty* het zien van zoveel wreedheid vervulde hem met afschuw; *a nauseating taste* een walgelijke smaak
nauseous 1 [esp Am] misselijk **2** [form] misselijk makend, walgelijk [also fig]
nautical nautisch, zee(vaart)-: ~ *mile* a) (Engelse) zeemijl [1,853.18 metres]; **b)** internationale zeemijl [1,852 metres]
naval 1 zee-, scheeps-: ~ *architect* scheepsbouwkundig ingenieur **2** marine-, vloot-: ~ *battle* zeeslag; ~ *officer* marineofficier; ~ *power* zeemacht
nave schip[h] [of church] **2** naaf [of wheel]
navel 1 navel **2** middelpunt[h]
navigable 1 bevaarbaar **2** zeewaardig **3** bestuurbaar
¹navigate (vb) een schip/vliegtuig besturen; [also comp] navigeren
²navigate (vb) **1** bevaren **2** oversteken, vliegen over **3** besturen **4** loodsen [fig]; (ge)leiden **5** [comp] navigeren op
navigation navigatie, stuurmanskunst, scheepvaart: *inland ~* binnen(scheep)vaart
navigator 1 [aviation] navigator **2** [shipp] navigatieofficier
navvy 1 grondwerker **2** graafmachine
navy 1 marine **2** oorlogsvloot, zeemacht
nay 1 nee(n) **2** tegenstemmer, stem tegen: *the ~s have it* de motie/het (wets)voorstel is verworpen **3** weigering
NE *north-east* N.O., noordoost
¹near (adj) **1** dichtbij(gelegen): *Near East* Nabije Oosten **2** kort [road] **3** nauw verwant **4** intiem; persoonlijk [friend] **5** krenterig, gierig || *he had a ~ escape,* [inform] *it was a ~ thing* het was maar op het nippertje; *it was a ~ miss* het was bijna raak [also fig]
²near (vb) naderen
³near (adv) dichtbij, nabij: *from far and ~* van heinde en ver; *nowhere ~ as clever* lang niet zo slim; *she was ~ to tears* het huilen stond haar nader dan het lachen
⁴near (prep) dichtbij, nabij, naast: *he lived ~ his sister* hij woonde niet ver van zijn zuster; *go* (or: *come*) ~ *to doing sth.* iets bijna doen, op het punt staan iets te doen
nearby dichtbij, nabij gelegen
nearly 1 bijna, vrijwel: *is his book ~ finished?* is zijn boek nu al bijna af? **2** nauw, na, van

nabij: ~ *related* nauw verwant ‖ *not* ~ (nog) lang niet, op geen stukken na

nearside linker: *the* ~ *wheel* het linker wiel

near-sighted bijziend

neat 1 net(jes), keurig, proper **2** puur; zonder ijs [of drink] **3** handig, vaardig, slim **4** sierlijk, smaakvol **5** [Am] schoon, netto **6** [Am] gaaf, prima **7** kernachtig

nebulous nevelig [also fig]; troebel, vaag

necessarily noodzakelijk(erwijs), onvermijdelijk, per definitie

¹**necessary** (n) **1** behoefte: *the* ~ a) het benodigde; b) geld **2** (necessaries) benodigdheden, vereisten **3** (necessaries) (levens)behoeften

²**necessary** (adj) noodzakelijk, nodig, vereist, essentieel: ~ *evil* noodzakelijk kwaad

necessitate 1 noodzaken **2** vereisen, dwingen tot

necessity 1 noodzaak, dwang: *in case of* ~ in geval van nood **2** noodzakelijkheid **3** behoefte, vereiste^h **4** nood, armoede

¹**neck** (n) **1** hals, nek: [sport] ~ *and* ~ nek aan nek **2** hals(vormig voorwerp^h); [eg] flessenhals **3** zee-engte, landengte, bergengte: *a* ~ *of land* een landengte ‖ [Am] ~ *of the woods* buurt, omgeving; *breathe* down *s.o.'s* ~ a) iem. op de hielen zitten; b) iem. op de vingers kijken; *get it in the* ~ hoer zijn kiezen krijgen; *risk one's* ~ zijn leven wagen; *stick one's* ~ *out* zijn nek uitsteken; *up to one's* ~ *in (debt)* tot zijn nek in (de schuld)

²**neck** (vb) vrijen (met), kussen

necklace halsband^h, halssnoer^h, (hals)ketting

necktie [esp Am] stropdas

nectar nectar, godendrank

nectarine nectarine

née geboren

¹**need** (n) **1** noodzaak: *there's no* ~ *for you to leave yet* je hoeft nog niet weg (te gaan) **2** behoefte, nood: *as* (or: *if, when*) *the* ~ *arises* als de behoefte zich voordoet; *have* ~ *of* behoefte hebben aan; *people in* ~ *of* help hulpbehoevenden **3** armoede: *a friend in* ~ een echte vriend ‖ *if* ~ *be* desnoods, als het moet

²**need** (vb) nodig hebben, behoefte hebben aan, vereisen: *they* ~ *more room to play* ze hebben meer speelruimte nodig; *this* ~*s to be done urgently* dit moet dringend gedaan worden

³**need** (aux vb) hoeven, moeten; [+ negation] had (niet) hoeven: *all he* ~ *do is* ... al wat hij moet doen is ...; *we* ~ *not have worried* we hadden ons geen zorgen hoeven te maken

needful noodzakelijk

¹**needle** (n) **1** naald, breinaald, magneetnaald, injectienaald, dennennaald: *look for a* ~ *in a haystack* een speld in een hooiberg zoeken **2** sterke rivaliteit: ~ *match* wedstrijd op het scherp van de snede ‖ [inform] *get the*

~ *pissig worden*

²**needle** (vb) **1** naaien, een naald halen door, (door)prikken **2** zieken, pesten

needless onnodig: ~ *to say* ... overbodig te zeggen ...

needlework naaiwerk^h, handwerk(en)

needs noodzakelijkerwijs: *he* ~ *must* hij kan niet anders; *at a moment like this, he must* ~ *go* uitgerekend op een moment als dit moet hij zo nodig weg

needy arm, noodlijdend

nefarious misdadig, schandelijk

negate 1 tenietdoen **2** ontkennen

negation ontkenning

¹**negative** (n) **1** afwijzing, ontkenning: *the answer is in the* ~ het antwoord luidt nee **2** weigering **3** [photo] negatief^h

²**negative** (adj) **1** negatief: *the* ~ *sign* het minteken **2** ontkennend, afwijzend: ~ *criticism* afbrekende kritiek

¹**neglect** (n) **1** verwaarlozing **2** verzuim^h: ~ *of duty* plichtsverzuim

²**neglect** (vb) **1** verwaarlozen **2** verzuimen, nalaten

negligence nalatigheid, slordigheid

negligible verwaarloosbaar, niet noemenswaardig

¹**negotiate** (vb) onderhandelen

²**negotiate** (vb) **1** (na onderhandeling) sluiten, (na onderhandeling) afsluiten **2** nemen, passeren, doorkomen, tot een goed einde brengen: ~ *a sharp bend* een scherpe bocht nemen

negotiation 1 onderhandeling, bespreking: *enter into* (or: *open, start*) ~*s with* in onderhandeling gaan met **2** (af)sluiting

negotiator onderhandelaar

negress negerin

negro neger

¹**neigh** (n) (ge)hinnik^h

²**neigh** (vb) hinniken

neighbour 1 buurman, buurvrouw: *my* ~ *at dinner* mijn tafelgenoot **2** medemens, naaste: *duty to one's* ~ (ver)plicht(ing) ten opzichte van zijn naaste

neighbourhood 1 buurt, wijk **2** nabijheid, omgeving ‖ *I paid a sum in the* ~ *of 150 dollars* ik heb rond de 150 dollar betaald

neighbouring aangrenzend

¹**neither** (pron) geen van beide(n): ~ *of us wanted him to come* we wilden geen van beiden dat hij kwam; ~ *candidate* geen van beide kandidaten

²**neither** (adv) evenmin, ook niet: *she cannot play and* ~ *can I* zij kan niet spelen en ik ook niet

³**neither** (conj) noch: *she could* ~ *laugh nor cry* ze kon (noch) lachen noch huilen

neologism neologisme^h, nieuw woord^h

neon neon^h

Nepal Nepal

¹Nepalese (n) Nepalees, Nepalese
²Nepalese (adj) Nepalees
nephew neef(je^h), zoon van broer of zus
nepotism nepotisme^h, vriendjespolitiek, begunstiging van familieleden en vrienden
nerd sul, klungel, nerd
nerve 1 zenuw: [fig] *hit* (or: *touch*) *a* ~ een zenuw raken **2** moed, durf, lef^h, brutaliteit: *you've got a* ~*!* jij durft, zeg!; *lose one's* ~ de moed verliezen **3** (-s) zenuwen, zelfbeheersing: *get on s.o.'s* ~*s* op iemands zenuwen werken
nerve-racking zenuwslopend
nervous 1 zenuwachtig, gejaagd **2** nerveus, zenuw-: ~ *breakdown* zenuwinstorting, zenuwinzinking; *(central)* ~ *system* (centraal) zenuwstelsel **3** angstig, bang: ~ *of* bang voor
nervy 1 [inform] zenuwachtig, schrikkerig **2** [Am; inform] koel(bloedig), onverschillig
nest 1 nest^h: *a* ~ *of robbers* een roversnest **2** broeinest^h, haard || *feather one's* ~ zijn zakken vullen
nest egg appeltje^h voor de dorst
¹nestle (vb) **1** zich nestelen, lekker (gaan) zitten (liggen) **2** (half) verscholen liggen **3** schurken, (dicht) aankruipen: ~ *up against* (or: *to*) *s.o.* dicht tegen iem. aankruipen
²nestle (vb) **1** neerleggen **2** tegen zich aan drukken, in zijn armen nemen
¹net (n) **1** net^h; [fig] web^h; (val)strik **2** netmateriaal^h, mousseline, tule || *surf the Net* internetten, surfen op internet
²net (n) nettobedrag^h
³net (adj) netto, schoon, zuiver: ~ *profit* nettowinst
⁴net (vb) (in een net) vangen; [also fig] (ver)strikken
⁵net (vb) **1** (als winst) opleveren, (netto) opbrengen **2** winnen, opstrijken, (netto) verdienen
nether onder-, neder-, beneden-: ~ *world* schimmenrijk, onderwereld
the **Netherlands** Nederland
netiquette nettiquette
netizen netizen, internetburger
netting net(werk)^h
¹nettle (n) (brand)netel || *grasp the* ~ de koe bij de hoorns vatten
²nettle (vb) irriteren, ergeren
network 1 net(werk)^h **2** radio- en televisiemaatschappij, omroep **3** computernetwerk^h
networking 1 het werken met een netwerk(systeem) **2** [Am] het netwerken
neural neuraal, zenuw-
neurology neurologie
¹neurotic (n) neuroot, zenuwlijder
²neurotic (adj) neurotisch
¹neuter (adj) onzijdig [of word, plant, animal]
²neuter (vb) helpen, castreren; steriliseren

[animal]
neutral 1 neutraal [also chem]; onpartijdig **2** onzijdig, geslachtloos || *in* ~ *gear* in z'n vrij
neutrality neutraliteit
neutralize neutraliseren
never nooit: *never-ending* altijddurend, oneindig (lang); *never-to-be-forgotten* onvergetelijk || *this'll* ~ *do* dit is niks, hier kun je niks mee; *he* ~ *so looked!* hij keek niet eens!
nevermore nooit meer
the **never-never** [inform] huurkoop(systeem): *on the* ~ op afbetaling
nevertheless niettemin, desondanks, toch
new nieuw, ongebruikt, recent: ~ *bread* vers brood; ~ *moon* (eerste fase van de) wassende maan, nieuwemaan; ~ *town* nieuwbouwstad; *the New World* de Nieuwe Wereld, Noord- en Zuid-Amerika; ~ *year* a) jaarwisseling; b) nieuw jaar || ~ *broom* frisse wind; *turn over a* ~ *leaf* met een schone lei beginnen; *break* ~ *ground* [fig] nieuwe wegen banen; *that's* ~ *to me* dat is nieuw voor me; *I'm* ~ *to the job* ik werk hier nog maar pas
newbie nieuwkomer (or: groentje) op internet
newborn 1 pasgeboren **2** herboren
newcomer nieuwkomer, beginner
newly 1 op nieuwe wijze, anders **2** onlangs, pas, recentelijk: ~ *wed* pasgetrouwd **3** opnieuw
newlywed jonggehuwde, pasgetrouwde
news 1 nieuws^h: *break the* ~ *to s.o.* (als eerste) iem. het (slechte) nieuws vertellen; *that is* ~ *to me* dat is nieuw voor mij **2** nieuws^h, nieuwsberichten, journaal^h, journaaluitzending
newsagent krantenverkoper, tijdschriftenverkoper
newscast nieuwsuitzending, journaal^h
newsflash nieuwsflits
newsletter nieuwsbrief, mededelingenblad^h
newspaper krant, dagblad^h
newsprint krantenpapier^h
newsreader nieuwslezer
newsreel bioscoopjournaal^h
newsroom redactiekamer
newsstand kiosk
New Year's Day nieuwjaarsdag
New Year's Eve oudejaarsdag, oudejaarsavond
New Zealand Nieuw-Zeeland
¹next (adj) **1** volgend [of place]; na, naast, dichtstbijzijnd: *she lives* ~ *door* ze woont hiernaast; *the* ~ *turn past the traffic lights* de eerste afslag na de verkeerslichten; *the* ~ *best* het beste op één na, de tweede keus; *the* ~ *but one* de volgende op één na **2** volgend [of time]; aanstaand: *the* ~ *day* de volgende dag, de dag daarop; ~ *Monday* aanstaande maandag; *the* ~ *few weeks* de ko-

mende weken
²next (dem pron) (eerst)volgende: ~, *please* volgende graag ‖ ~ *of kin* (naaste) bloedverwant(en), nabestaande(n)
³next (adv) **1** daarnaast: *what* ~? **a)** wat (krijgen we) nu?; **b)** [depr] kan het nog gekker? **2** [time; also fig] daarna, daaropvolgend, de volgende keer: *the* ~ *best* thing op één na het beste ‖ ~ *to impossible* bijna onmogelijk; *for* ~ *to nothing* bijna voor niks **next-door** aangrenzend: *we are* ~ *neighbours* we wonen naast elkaar
NGO *non-governmental organization* ngo
NHS *National Health Service* nationaal ziekenfonds
nib pen, kroontjespen
¹nibble (n) hapje^h
²nibble (vb) knabbelen (aan), knagen (aan): ~ *away* (or: *off*) wegknabbelen, afknabbelen, wegknagen, afknagen
Nicaragua Nicaragua
¹Nicaraguan (n) Nicaraguaan(se)
²Nicaraguan (adj) Nicaraguaans
nice 1 aardig, vriendelijk: *you're a* ~ *friend!* mooie vriend ben jij! **2** mooi, goed: ~ *work!* goed zo! **3** leuk, prettig: *have a* ~ *day* nog een prettige dag, tot ziens **4** genuanceerd, verfijnd **5** kies(keurig), precies ‖ ~ *and warm* (or: *fast*) lekker warm (or: hard)
nicety 1 detail^h, subtiliteit, nuance **2** nauwkeurigheid, precisie ‖ *to a* ~ precies, tot in de puntjes
niche 1 nis **2** stek, plek(je^h), hoekje^h: *he has found his* ~ hij heeft zijn draai gevonden
¹nick (n) **1** kerf, keep **2** snee(tje^h), kras **3** bajes, nor **4** politiebureau^h **5** staat, vorm: *in good* ~ in prima conditie, in goede staat ‖ *in the* ~ *of time* op het nippertje
²nick (vb) **1** inkepen, inkerven, krassen **2** jatten **3** in de kraag grijpen, arresteren
nickel 1 vijfcentstuk [in Canada and Am]; stuiver **2** nikkel
¹nickname (n) **1** bijnaam **2** roepnaam
²nickname (vb) een bijnaam geven (aan)
nicotine nicotine
niece nicht(je^h), oomzegster, tantezegster, dochter van broer of zus
niff lucht, stank
nifty 1 jofel, tof **2** handig
Niger Niger
Nigeria Nigeria
¹Nigerian (n) Nigeriaan(se)
²Nigerian (adj) Nigeriaans
¹Nigerien (n) Nigerees, Nigerese
²Nigerien (adj) Nigerees
niggard vrek
nigger [depr] nikker, neger
¹niggle (vb) muggenziften, vitten
²niggle (vb) **1** knagen aan, irriteren **2** vitten op
night nacht, avond: ~ *and day* dag en nacht;

stay the ~ blijven logeren; *at* (or: *by*) ~ 's nachts, 's avonds; *first* ~ première(avond); *last* ~ gisteravond, vannacht; ~ *owl* nachtbraker, nachtmens ‖ *make a* ~ *of it* nachtbraken, doorhalen
nightcap slaapmuts(je^h) [also drink]
nightclub nachtclub
nightclubbing: *go* ~ (de) nachtclubs afgaan
nightdress nachthemd^h, nachtjapon
nightfall vallen van de avond
nightie [inform] nachtpon
nightingale nachtegaal
nightly nachtelijk, elke nacht (avond), 's nachts, 's avonds
nightmare nachtmerrie
night shift 1 nachtdienst **2** nachtploeg
night-time nacht(elijk uur^h)
nightwear nachtkleding, nachtgoed^h
nighty nachthemd^h, nachtjapon
nil nihil, niets^h, nul: *three-*~ drie-nul
nimble 1 behendig, vlug **2** alert, gevat, spits
nimby [inform] *not in my backyard* niet-in-mijn-achtertuinprotesteerder: ~ *syndrome* blijf-uit-mijn-buurtsyndroom
nine negen ‖ *he was dressed (up) to the* ~*s* hij was piekfijn gekleed
ninepins kegelen^h, kegelspel^h
nineteen negentien
nineteenth negentiende
ninetieth negentigste
ninety negentig: *he was in his nineties* hij was in de negentig
ninny imbeciel, sukkel
ninth negende
¹nip (n) **1** stokje^h, borreltje^h **2** kneep **3** (bijtende) kou: *there was a* ~ *in the air* het was nogal fris(jes)
²nip (vb) nippen, in kleine teugjes nemen
³nip (vb) **1** (+ out) eventjes (weg)gaan, vliegen, rennen: ~ *in* **a)** binnenwippen; **b)** naar links (or: rechts) schieten [in traf]
⁴nip (vb) **1** knijpen, beknellen; bijten [also of animal] **2** in de groei stuiten: ~ *in the bud* in de kiem smoren
nipper 1 peuter **2** (-s) tang, nijptang, buigtang
nipple 1 tepel **2** [Am] speen [of feeding bottle] **3** (smeer)nippel
nippy 1 vlug, rap **2** fris(jes), koud
niqab (gezichts)sluier, nikab
nit 1 neet, luizenei^h **2** stommeling
¹nitpicking (n) muggenzifterij
²nitpicking (adj) muggenzifterig
nitrogen stikstof^h
nitrous salpeterachtig: ~ *acid* salpeterigzuur; ~ *oxide* lachgas
the **nitty-gritty** kern, essentie: *let's get down to the* ~ laten we nu de harde feiten eens bekijken

nitwit idioot, stommeling
¹nix (n) niks, niets^h, nop
²nix (vb) een streep halen door, niet toestaan
¹no (n) **1** neen^h, weigering **2** tegenstemmer: *I won't take no for an answer* ik sta erop, je kunt niet weigeren, ik wil geen nee horen
²no (pron) **1** geen, geen enkele, helemaal geen: *on no account* onder geen enkele voorwaarde; *there's no milk* er is geen melk in huis; *I'm no expert* ik ben geen deskundige **2** haast geen, bijna geen, heel weinig, een minimum van: *it's no distance* het is vlakbij; *in no time* in een mum van tijd
³no (adv) **1** nee(n): *oh no!* 't is niet waar!; *did you tell her?* no I didn't* heb je het tegen haar gezegd? neen; *no! neen* toch! **2** niet, in geen enkel opzicht: *he told her in no uncertain terms* hij zei het haar in duidelijke bewoordingen; *let me know whether or no you are coming* laat me even weten of je komt of niet; *the mayor himself, no less* niemand minder dan de burgemeester zelf
nob 1 kop, hoofd^h **2** hoge ome
nobble 1 [sport] uitschakelen [horse, dog; esp through doping] **2** omkopen; bepraten [pers] **3** (weg)kapen; jatten [money, prize]
nobility 1 adel, adelstand **2** adeldom **3** edelmoedigheid, nobelheid
¹noble (n) edele, edelman, edelvrouw
²noble (adj) **1** adellijk, van adel **2** edel, nobel: *~ savage* edele wilde || [chem] *~ gas* edelgas
nobleman edelman, lid^h van de adel
nobody niemand, onbelangrijk persoon, nul
no-brainer 1 fluitje van een cent, koud kunstje, makkie; vanzelfsprekendheid **2** iem. zonder hersens, dombo
nocturnal nachtelijk, nacht-
¹nod (n) knik(je^h), wenk(je^h): *give (s.o.) a ~* (iem. toe)knikken || *on the ~* **a)** op de lat, op krediet; **b)** zonder discussie (*or:* formele) stemming
²nod (vb) **1** knikken [as greeting, order]; ja knikken [indicating approval]: *have a ~ding acquaintance with s.o. (sth.)* iem. (iets) oppervlakkig kennen **2** (+ off) indutten, in slaap vallen **3** (zitten te) suffen, niet opletten, een fout maken
³nod (vb) **1** knikken met [head] **2** door knikken te kennen geven [approval, greeting, permission]: *~ approval* goedkeurend knikken
nodding oppervlakkig: *have a ~ acquaintance with s.o.* iem. oppervlakkig kennen; *have a ~ acquaintance with sth.* een vage notie hebben van iets
node 1 knoest, knobbel **2** [science, comp] knoop
Noel [form] Kerstmis
no-frill(s) zonder franje, eenvoudig

nohow op geen enkele manier, helemaal niet, van geen kant: *we couldn't find it ~* we konden het helemaal nergens vinden
noise 1 geluid^h **2** lawaai^h, rumoer^h **3** [techn] geruis^h, ruis, storing
noise nuisance geluidshinder, geluidsoverlast
noisy lawaaierig, luidruchtig, gehorig
nomad 1 nomade **2** zwerver [also fig]
nomadic nomadisch, (rond)zwervend
no-man's-land niemandsland
nominal 1 in naam (alléén), theoretisch, niet echt **2** zogoed als geen, niet noemenswaardig; symbolisch [eg amount]: *at (a) ~ price* voor een spotprijs
nominate 1 (+ as, for) kandidaat stellen (als/voor), (als kandidaat) voordragen, nomineren **2** benoemen: *~ s.o. to be* (*or:* as) iem. benoemen tot
nomination 1 kandidaatstelling, voordracht, nominatie **2** benoeming
nominee 1 kandidaat **2** benoemde
non-aggression non-agressie, (belofte van) het niet aanvallen: *~ pact* (*or:* agreement*) niet-aanvalsverdrag
non-aligned niet-gebonden; neutraal [country, politics]
nonchalant nonchalant, onverschillig
non-commissioned zonder officiersaanstelling: *~ officer* onderofficier
non-committal neutraal; vrijblijvend [reply]
nondescript 1 non-descript, moeilijk te beschrijven **2** nietszeggend, onbeduidend
¹none (pron) geen (enkele), niemand, niets: *I'll have ~ of your tricks* ik pik die streken van jou niet; *there is ~ left* er is niets meer over; *~ other than the President* niemand anders dan de president; *~ of the students* niemand van de studenten
²none (adv) helemaal niet, niet erg, niet veel: *she was ~ the wiser* ze was er niets wijzer op geworden; *she is none too bright* ze is niet al te slim
nonentity onbelangrijk persoon (ding^h)
nonetheless niettemin, echter, toch
non-event afknapper
non-existent niet-bestaand
non-iron zelfstrijkend
no-nonsense 1 zakelijk, no-nonsense **2** zonder franjes [eg dress]
nonplussed verbijsterd
nonproliferation non-proliferatie
non-returnable zonder statiegeld
nonsense onzin, nonsens, flauwekul: *make (a) ~* tenietdoen, het effect bederven van; *stand no ~* geen flauwekul dulden; *what ~* wat een flauwekul
nonsensical onzinnig, absurd
non-smoking rookvrij
non-stick antiaanbak-, met een antiaan-

baklaag
non-stop non-stop, zonder te stoppen; doorgaand [train]; zonder tussenlandingen [flight]; direct [connection]; doorlopend [performance]
non-U [inform; mockingly] niet gebruikelijk bij de upper class
noob [inform] leek, dombo, nitwit
noodles (soort eier)vermicelli, (soort) mi, noedels
nook (rustig) hoekje^h, veilige plek: *search every ~ and cranny* in elk hoekje en gaatje zoeken, overal zoeken
noon middag(uur^h), twaalf uur 's middags
no-one niemand
noose lus, strik, strop
nootropic smartdrug
nope [inform] nee
nor 1 evenmin, ook niet: *you don't like melon? ~ do I* je houdt niet van meloen? ik ook niet **2** [often after neither] noch, en ook niet, en evenmin: *neither Jill ~ Sheila* noch Jill noch Sheila; *she neither spoke ~ smiled* ze sprak noch lachte
Nordic noords, Noord-Europees, Scandinavisch
norm norm, standaard
¹normal (n) het normale, gemiddelde^h, normale toestand: *above* (or: *below*) *~* boven (*or:* onder) normaal
²normal (adj) normaal, gewoon, standaard
normalization 1 normalisatie **2** het normaal worden
normalize normaal worden (maken), herstellen, normaliseren
Norman Normandisch
normative normatief, bindend
Norseman Noorman
¹north (n) het noorden [point of the compass]; noord: *face (the) ~* op het noorden liggen; *the North* het Noordelijk gedeelte
²north (adj) noordelijk: *the North Pole* de noordpool; *the North Sea* de Noordzee
³north (adv) van, naar, in het noorden: *face ~* op het noorden liggen
northbound iem. die naar het noorden gaat, iets dat naar het noorden gaat [traf, road]
north-east noordoostelijk
northeastern uit het noordoosten, noordoostelijk
¹northerly (n) noordenwind
²northerly (adj) noordelijk
northern noordelijk, noorden-, noord(-): *the ~ lights* het noorderlicht
North Korea Noord-Korea
¹North Korean (n) Noord-Koreaan(se)
²North Korean (adj) Noord-Koreaans
northward noord(waarts), noordelijk
north-west noordwestelijk
northwestern noordwest(elijk)

Norway Noorwegen
¹Norwegian (n) Noor(se)
²Norwegian (adj) Noors
nos *numbers* nummers
¹nose (n) **1** neus, reukorgaan^h; [fig] reukzin; speurzin: *(right) under s.o.'s (very) ~* vlak voor zijn neus **2** punt^h; neus [of aeroplane, car, shoe] ‖ *cut off one's ~ to spite one's face* woedend zijn eigen glazen ingooien; *follow one's ~* zijn instinct volgen; *have a ~ for sth.* ergens een fijne neus voor hebben; *keep one's ~ to the grindstone* zwoegen, voortdurend hard werken; *keep one's ~ out of s.o.'s affairs* zich met zijn eigen zaken bemoeien; *look down one's ~ at s.o.* de neus voor iem. ophalen, neerkijken op iem.; *pay through the ~ (for)* zich laten afzetten (voor); *poke one's ~ into s.o.'s affairs* zijn neus in andermans zaken steken; *put s.o.'s ~ out of joint* **a)** iem. voor het hoofd stoten; **b)** iem. jaloers maken; *rub s.o.'s ~ in it* (or: *the dirt*) iem. iets onder de neus wrijven; *turn up one's ~ at sth. (s.o.)* zijn neus ophalen voor iets (iem.); *(win) by a ~* een neuslengte vóór zijn
²nose (vb) zich (voorzichtig) een weg banen [of ship, car]
nose about rondneuzen (in), rondsnuffelen (in)
nosebleed bloedneus
¹nosedive (n) **1** duikvlucht **2** plotselinge (prijs)daling
²nosedive (vb) **1** een duikvlucht maken **2** plotseling dalen, vallen
nosegay ruiker(tje^h), boeketje^h
nose job [inform] neuscorrectie
nose out ontdekken, erachter komen
¹nosh (n) eten^h
²nosh (vb) bikken, eten
nosiness bemoeizucht, nieuwsgierigheid
nostalgia nostalgie, verlangen^h (naar het verleden)
nostril 1 neusgat^h **2** neusvleugel
nosy nieuwsgierig: *Nosey Parker* bemoeial, nieuwsgierig aagje
not niet, geen, helemaal niet: *~ a thing* helemaal niets; *I hope ~* ik hoop van niet; *~ to say* misschien zelfs, om niet te zeggen; *~ at all* helemaal niet; *~ least* vooral; *as likely as ~* waarschijnlijk; *~ only ... but (also)* niet alleen ..., maar (ook); *~ a bus but a tram* geen bus maar een tram; *~ that I care* niet (om)dat het mij iets kan schelen
¹notable (n) belangrijk persoon; notabele
²notable (adj) opmerkelijk, opvallend
notably in het bijzonder, met name: *others, ~ the Americans and the English, didn't want to talk about it* anderen, met name de Amerikanen en Engelsen, wilden er niet over praten
notary notaris: *~ public* notaris
notation 1 notatie [music, chess etc]; schrijfwijze: *chemical ~* chemische symbolen

notch

2 [Am] aantekening, noot
¹notch (n) **1** keep [also fig]; kerf, inkeping
2 graad; stukjeʰ
²notch (vb) **1** (in)kepen, (in)kerven, insnijden **2** (also + up) (be)halen [victory, points]; binnenhalen: *we ~ed* **up** *nine victories in a row* we behaalden negen overwinningen op rij
¹note (n) **1** aantekening, notitie: *make ~s* aantekeningen maken; *make a ~ of your expenses* houd bij wat voor onkosten je maakt **2** briefjeʰ, berichtjeʰ, (diplomatieke) nota, memorandumʰ **3** (voet)noot, annotatie **4** (bank)biljetʰ, briefjeʰ **5** [mus] toon, noot **6** (onder)toon, klank: *sound* (or: *strike*) *a ~ of warning* een waarschuwend geluid laten horen **7** aanzienʰ, belangʰ, gewichtʰ: *of ~ van* belang, met een reputatie, algemeen bekend **8** aandacht, nota: *take ~ of* notitie nemen van || *compare ~s* ervaringen uitwisselen
²note (vb) **1** nota nemen van, aandacht schenken aan, letten op **2** (op)merken, waarnemen **3** aandacht vestigen op, opmerken **4** (+ down) opschrijven, noteren
notebook 1 notitieboekjeʰ **2** notebook
noted (+ for) beroemd (om/wegens), bekend
notepaper postpapierʰ
noteworthy vermeldenswaardig, opmerkelijk
¹nothing (pron) niets; [pers] nul; waardeloos iem.; [matter] kleinigheid; niemendalletje: *she did ~ but grumble* ze zat alleen maar te mopperen || *there was ~ for it but to call a doctor* er zat niets anders op dan een dokter te bellen; *for ~* **a)** tevergeefs; **b)** gratis, voor niets; *there's ~ to it* er is niets aan, het is een makkie; [sport] *there's ~ in it* zij zijn gelijk
²nothing (adv) helemaal niet, lang niet: *my painting is ~ like* (or: *near) as good as yours* mijn schilderij is bij lange na niet zo goed als het jouwe
¹notice (n) **1** aankondiging, waarschuwing; opzegging [of contract]: *give one's ~* zijn ontslag indienen; *we received three month's ~* de huur is ons met drie maanden opgezegd; *at a moment's ~* direct, zonder bericht vooraf **2** aandacht, belangstelling, attentie: *I'd like to bring this book to your ~* ik zou dit boek onder uw aandacht willen brengen; *take (no) ~ of* (geen) acht slaan op **3** mededeling, berichtʰ
²notice (vb) (op)merken, zien, waarnemen: *she didn't ~ her friend in the crowd* zij zag haar vriendin niet in de menigte
noticeable 1 merkbaar, zichtbaar, waarneembaar **2** opmerkelijk, opvallend, duidelijk
notice board mededelingenbordʰ, prikbordʰ
notification 1 aangifte **2** informatie, mededeling
notify informeren, bekendmaken, op de hoogte stellen
notion 1 begripʰ **2** ideeʰ, mening, veronderstelling: *she had no ~ of what I was talking about* ze had geen benul waar ik het over had; *the ~ that the earth is flat* het denkbeeld dat de aarde plat is
notoriety beruchtheid
notorious algemeen (ongunstig) bekend, berucht
¹notwithstanding (adv) desondanks, ondanks dat, toch
²notwithstanding (prep) ondanks, in weerwil van: *the road was built ~ fierce opposition* de verkeersweg werd gebouwd ondanks de felle tegenstand
nougat noga
nought nul || *~s and crosses* boter, kaas en eieren, kruisje nulletje
the **noughties** de jaren nul
noun zelfstandig naamwoordʰ
nourish 1 voeden [also fig]; *~ing food* voedzaam eten **2** koesteren: *~ the hope to* de hoop koesteren om te
nourishment 1 voeding [also fig]; het voeden, het gevoed worden **2** voedselʰ, etenʰ
¹novel (n) roman
²novel (adj) nieuw, onbekend: *~ ideas* verrassende ideeën
novelist romanschrijver, schrijver
novelty nieuwigheid, nieuwsʰ, iets onbekends, aardigheidjeʰ: *the ~ soon wore off* het nieuwe was er al snel af, de nieuwigheid was er al gauw af
November november
novice 1 novice **2** beginneling, nieuweling
¹now (n) nuʰ, dit momentʰ: *before ~* vroeger, tot nu toe; *by ~* ondertussen, inmiddels; *for ~* voorlopig; *as from ~, from ~ on* van nu af aan; *until ~, up till ~, up to* tot nu toe
²now (adv) **1** nu, tegenwoordig, onder deze omstandigheden: *they'll be here any minute ~* ze kunnen nu elk ogenblik aankomen; *~ what do you mean?* maar wat bedoel je nu eigenlijk?; *(every) ~ and again* (or: *then)* zo nu en dan, af en toe, van tijd tot tijd; *just ~* **a)** zo-even, daarnet; **b)** nu, op dit ogenblik; *~ then, where do you think you're going?* zo, en waar dacht jij heen te gaan? **2** nu (dat), gezien (dat): *~ you are here I will show you* nu je hier (toch) bent zal ik het je laten zien
nowadays tegenwoordig, vandaag de dag
nowhere nergens [also fig]; nergens heen: *it got him ~* het leverde hem niets op; *she is ~ near as bright as him* ze is lang niet zo intelligent als hij; *he started from ~ but became famous* hij kwam uit het niets maar werd beroemd
noxious [also fig] schadelijk, ongezond

nozzle 1 tuit, pijp **2** (straal)pijp, mondstukʰ, straalbuis
nub 1 brokʰ, klompjeʰ, stomp(jeʰ) **2** [singular] kern(puntʰ), essentie: *the ~ of* the matter de kern van de zaak
nuclear 1 m.b.t. de kern(en), kern- **2** nucleair, kern-, atoom-: *~ disarmament* nucleaire ontwapening; *~ waste* kernafval
nucleus kern [also fig]
¹**nude** (n) naakt iem.: *in the ~* naakt, in zijn nakie
²**nude** (adj) naakt
¹**nudge** (n) stoot(jeʰ), por, duwtjeʰ
²**nudge** (vb) **1** (zachtjes) aanstoten [with elbow] **2** zachtjes duwen, schuiven **3** [fig] een duwtje in de rug geven
nudist nudist, naturist
nudity naaktheid
nugget 1 (goud)klompjeʰ **2** juweel(tje)ʰ [only fig]: *~ of information* informatie die goud waard is
nuisance 1 lastig iem. (iets), lastpost, lastpak: *make a ~ of o.s.* vervelend zijn **2** (over)last, hinder: *what a ~* wat vervelend
nuke [esp Am; inform] **1** atoombom **2** kernwapenʰ
null: *~ and void* van nul en gener waarde
nullify 1 nietig verklaren, ongeldig verklaren **2** opheffen, tenietdoen
¹**numb** (adj) (+ with) verstijfd (van), verdoofd, verkleumd
²**numb** (vb) **1** verlammen [also fig]; doen verstijven **2** verdoven: *medicines ~ed the pain* medicijnen verzachtten de pijn
¹**number** (n) **1** getalʰ: *~ 10 bus* (bus)lijn 10 **2** aantalʰ: *a ~ of problems* een aantal problemen; *in ~* in aantal, in getal; *any ~ of* ontelbaar veel **3** nummerʰ: *published in ~s* in afleveringen verschenen **4** gezelschapʰ, groep **5** (-s) aantallen, hoeveelheid, grote aantallen: *win by ~s* winnen door getalsterkte || *have s.o.'s ~* iem. doorhebben; *always think of ~ one* altijd alleen maar aan zichzelf denken; *my ~ one problem* mijn grootste probleem
²**number** (vb) nummeren, nummers geven
³**number** (vb) **1** tellen **2** vormen [number]; bedragen: *we ~ed eleven* we waren met ons elven **3** tellen, behoren tot: *I ~ him among my best friends* hij behoort tot mijn beste vrienden || *his days are ~ed* zijn dagen zijn geteld
number crunching getallenkrakenʰ
numberless ontelbaar, talloos
number plate nummerplaat, nummerbordʰ
num(b)skull sufferd, stomkop
¹**numeral** (n) **1** cijferʰ: *Roman ~s* Romeinse cijfers **2** telwoordʰ
²**numeral** (adj) getal(s)-, van getallen
numerate met een wiskundige basiskennis, gecijferd: *some of my students are hardly ~* enkele van mijn studenten kunnen nauwelijks rekenen
numerical 1 getallen-, rekenkundig **2** numeriek, in aantal, getals-
numerous talrijk(e), groot, vele
nun non
nunnery [form] vrouwenkloosterʰ, nonnenkloosterʰ
nuptial huwelijks-
¹**nurse** (n) **1** verpleegster, verpleger, verpleegkundige: *male ~* verpleger, ziekenbroeder; *~!* zuster! **2** kindermeisjeʰ **3** voedster
²**nurse** (vb) zuigen, aan de borst zijn: *be nursing at one's mother's breast* de borst krijgen
³**nurse** (vb) **1** verplegen, verzorgen **2** zogen, borstvoeding geven: *nursing mother* zogende moeder **3** behandelen, genezen: *~ s.o. back to health* iem. weer gezond krijgen **4** bevorderen, koesteren: *~ a grievance* (or: *grudge*) *against s.o.* een grief (*or:* wrok) tegen iem. koesteren
nursemaid 1 kindermeisjeʰ **2** verzorgster
nursery 1 kinderkamer **2** crèche, kinderdagverblijfʰ **3** kwekerij
nurseryman kweker
nursery rhyme kinderversjeʰ
nursery school peuterklas
nursing verpleging, verzorging, verpleegkunde
nursing home 1 verpleegtehuisʰ **2** particulier ziekenhuisʰ
¹**nurture** (n) [form] opvoeding, vorming
²**nurture** (vb) [form] **1** voeden **2** koesteren, verzorgen **3** opvoeden
nut 1 noot **2** moer **3** fanaat, gek || *~s and bolts* grondbeginselen, hoofdzaken; *do one's ~* woedend zijn; *she can't sing for ~s* ze kan totaal niet zingen; *off one's ~* niet goed bij zijn hoofd
nutcase mafkees
nutcracker notenkraker: *(a pair of) ~s* een notenkraker
nutmeg 1 muskaatnoot **2** nootmuskaat
¹**nutrient** (n) voedingsstof, bouwstof
²**nutrient** (adj) voedend, voedings-
nutrition 1 voeding **2** voedingsleer
nutritional voedings-
nutritious voedzaam
nuts gek, getikt: *go ~* gek worden
nutshell notendop [also fig]
nutty 1 met (veel) noten, vol noten **2** naar noten smakend **3** gek, getikt, gestoord: *as ~ as a fruitcake* stapelgek, mesjokke
nuzzle 1 (be)snuffelen **2** (zich) nestelen
nylon nylon⁺ʰ: *~s* nylonkousen
nymph nimf
¹**nymphomaniac** (n) nymfomane
²**nymphomaniac** (adj) nymfomaan

O

o' of van: *five o'clock* vijf uur
oaf klungel, lomperd
¹oak (n) eik
²oak (adj) eiken, eikenhout
oak-apple galappel, galnoot
OAP *old age pension* AOW, Algemene Ouderdomswet
oar roeispaan, (roei)riem ‖ *put* (or: *shove*) *one's ~ in* zich ermee bemoeien, zijn neus erin steken
oarsman roeier
oasis oase [also fig]
oat haver, haverkorrel ‖ *feel one's ~s* bruisen van energie; [Am also] zelfgenoegzaam doen; *off one's ~s* zonder eetlust
oath 1 eed: *make* (or: *take, swear*) *an ~* een eed afleggen; *under ~* onder ede **2** vloek
oatmeal 1 havermeelʰ, havervlokken **2** havermout(pap)
obdurate 1 onverbeterlijk **2** onverzettelijk
obedience 1 gehoorzaamheid: *passive ~* onvoorwaardelijke gehoorzaamheid **2** [rel] obediëntie
obedient 1 gehoorzaam **2** onderworpen
obeisance 1 buiging **2** eerbied, respectʰ
obese zwaarlijvig
obesity obesitas, zwaarlijvigheid
obey gehoorzamen (aan), opvolgen, toegeven aan
obituary overlijdensberichtʰ [with short biography]
¹object (n) **1** voorwerpʰ, objectʰ **2** doelʰ **3** [linguistics] voorwerpʰ: *direct ~ (of a verb)* lijdend voorwerp; *indirect ~ (of a verb)* meewerkend voorwerp ‖ *money is no ~* geld speelt geen rol
²object (vb) bezwaar hebben (maken): *he ~ed to being called a coward* hij wou niet voor lafaard doorgaan
objection bezwaarʰ: *raise ~s* bezwaren maken
objectionable 1 bedenkelijk **2** ongewenst, onaangenaam
¹objective (n) **1** doelʰ, doelstelling, doelwitʰ, operatiedoelʰ **2** objectiefʰ
²objective (adj) objectief, onpartijdig
obligation 1 plicht, (zware) taak **2** verplichting, verbintenis: *lay* (or: *place, put*) *s.o. under an ~* iem. aan zich verplichten
obligatory verplicht
¹oblige (vb) het genoegen doen, ten beste geven: *~ with a song* een lied ten beste geven

²oblige (vb) **1** aan zich verplichten: *(I'm) much ~d (to you)* dank u zeer **2** verplichten; (ver)binden [by promise, contract]: *I feel ~d to say that …* ik voel me verplicht te zeggen dat …
obliging attent, voorkomend, behulpzaam
oblique 1 schuin, scheef: *~ stroke* schuine streep **2** indirect, ontwijkend
obliterate uitwissen, wegvagen
obliteration 1 uitroeiing, vernietiging **2** uitwissing, verwijdering **3** afstempeling [of stamps]
oblivion vergetelheid: *fall* (or: *sink*) *into ~* in vergetelheid raken
oblivious 1 vergeetachtig **2** onbewust: *~ of* niet lettend op, vergetend; *~ of* (or: *to*) zich niet bewust van
¹oblong (n) rechthoek, langwerpige figuur
²oblong (adj) rechthoekig
obnoxious [form] **1** aanstootgevend **2** uiterst onaangenaam: *an ~ child* een stierlijk vervelend kind
oboe hobo
obscene obsceen, onzedelijk
obscenities obsceniteiten, schunnige taal
obscenity obsceniteit, vies woord
¹obscure (adj) **1** obscuur, onduidelijk, onbekend **2** verborgen, onopgemerkt
²obscure (vb) **1** verduisteren **2** overschaduwen **3** verbergen
obscurity 1 duisterʰ, duisternis **2** onbekendheid: *live in ~* een obscuur leven leiden **3** onduidelijkheid, onbegrijpelijkheid
obsequious kruiperig, onderdanig
observable waarneembaar, merkbaar
observant 1 opmerkzaam, oplettend **2** in acht nemend; nalevend [law, duty, rites]
observation 1 waarneming, observatie: *keep s.o. under ~* iem. in de gaten (blijven) houden **2** opmerking, commentaarʰ
observatory sterrenwacht
observe 1 opmerken, zeggen: *he ~d that* hij merkte op dat **2** naleven, in acht nemen **3** waarnemen, observeren
observer 1 toeschouwer **2** waarnemer [also aviation]; observeerder, observator
obsess obsederen: *~ed by* (or: *with*) geobsedeerd door
obsession 1 obsessie, dwanggedachte: *have an ~ about sth.* bezeten zijn door iets **2** bezetenheid, het bezeten-zijn
obsessive 1 obsederend **2** bezeten
obsolete verouderd, in onbruik (geraakt), achterhaald
obstacle obstakelʰ, belemmering: *form an ~ to sth.* een beletsel vormen voor iets
obstacle course hindernisbaan: *he had to run an ~* hij moest allerlei hindernissen overwinnen
obstetrician verloskundige
obstetrics obstetrie, verloskunde

obstinate 1 halsstarrig **2** hardnekkig; koppig

obstruct 1 versperren, blokkeren **2** belemmeren, hinderen **3** [sport, esp football] obstructie plegen tegen

obstruction 1 belemmering, hindernis **2** versperring, obstakelʰ **3** obstructie [also sport, med]

obtain (ver)krijgen, behalen

¹**obtrude** (vb) opdringerig zijn, zich opdringen

²**obtrude** (vb) (+ (up)on) opdringen (aan), ongevraagd naar voren brengen

obtuse 1 stomp: *an ~ angle* een stompe hoek **2** traag van begrip

obviate ondervangen, voorkomen: *~ the necessity* (or: *need*) *of sth.* iets overbodig maken

obvious 1 duidelijk, zonneklaar: *an ~ lie* een aperte leugen **2** voor de hand liggend, doorzichtig **3** aangewezen, juist: *the ~ man for the job* de aangewezen man voor het karweitje

obviously duidelijk, kennelijk

¹**occasion** (n) **1** gebeurtenis, voorvalʰ **2** evenementʰ, gelegenheid, feestʰ: *he seemed to be equal to the ~* hij leek tegen de situatie opgewassen te zijn; *we'll make an ~ of it* we zullen het vieren; *on the ~ of your birthday* ter gelegenheid van je verjaardag **3** aanleiding, reden: *give ~ to* aanleiding geven tot; *you have no ~ to leave* jij hebt geen reden om weg te gaan

²**occasion** (vb) veroorzaken, aanleiding geven tot

occasional 1 incidenteel, nu en dan voorkomend: *~ showers* verspreide buien **2** gelegenheids-

occasionally nu en dan, af en toe

occidental westers

occult occult, geheim, verborgen: *the ~* het occulte

occupant 1 bezitter, landbezitter **2** bewoner **3** inzittende [of car] **4** bekleder [of office]

occupation 1 beroepʰ **2** bezigheid, activiteit **3** bezetting (door vijand)

occupational m.b.t. een beroep, beroeps-: *~ hazard* beroepsrisico

occupy 1 bezetten, bezit nemen van: *~ a building* een gebouw bezetten **2** in beslag nemen: *it will ~ a lot of his time* het zal veel van zijn tijd in beslag nemen **3** bezighouden: *~ o.s. with* zich bezighouden met **4** bewonen, betrekken

occur 1 voorkomen, aangetroffen worden **2** opkomen, invallen: *it simply did not ~ to him* het kwam eenvoudigweg niet bij hem op **3** gebeuren

occurrence 1 voorvalʰ, gebeurtenis **2** het voorkomen

ocean oceaan: *the Pacific Ocean* de Stille Zuidzee; *~s of time* zeeën van tijd

ochre oker

o'clock uur: *ten ~* tien uur

octagon achthoek

octave octaaf

October oktober

octogenarian tachtigjarige

octopus inktvis

oculist oogarts

odd 1 oneven: *~ and even numbers* oneven en even getallen **2** vreemd, ongewoon: *an ~ habit* een gekke gewoonte **3** overblijvend: *the ~ man at the table* de man die aan tafel overschiet [after the others have formed pairs] **4** toevallig, onverwacht: *he drops in at ~ times* hij komt zo nu en dan eens langs **5** los, niet behorend tot een reeks: *an ~ glove* een losse handschoen; *~ job* klusje **6** [after noun, cardinal number] iets meer dan: *five pounds ~* iets meer dan vijf pond; *60-~ persons* ruim 60 personen ‖ *~ man out* vreemde eend; *which is the ~ man out in the following list?* welke hoort in het volgende rijtje niet thuis?

oddball [Am] gekke vent, rare

oddity 1 eigenaardigheid, vreemde eigenschap **2** gekke vent **3** iets vreemds, vreemd voorwerpʰ, vreemde gebeurtenis **4** curiositeit

odd-job man manusje-van-allesʰ, klusjesman

oddment overschotʰ, overblijfselʰ, restantʰ

odds 1 ongelijkheid, verschil: *that makes no ~* dat maakt niets uit; *what's the ~?* wat doet dat ertoe? **2** onenigheid: *be at ~ with* in onenigheid leven met **3** (grote) kans, waarschijnlijkheid: *the ~ are that she will do it* de kans is groot dat ze het doet **4** verhouding tussen de inzetten bij weddenschap: *take ~ of one to ten* een inzet accepteren van één tegen tien ‖ *~ and ends* prullen; *~ and sods* rommel; *against all (the) ~* tegen alle verwachtingen in; *over the ~* meer dan verwacht

odious hatelijk, weerzinwekkend

odour 1 geur, stank, lucht(jeʰ): *an ~ of sanctity* een geur van heiligheid **2** reputatie, naam: *be in good ~ with* goed aangeschreven staan bij

oestrogen oestrogeenʰ

oeuvre (kunst)werkʰ; oeuvreʰ

of 1 van, van ... vandaan: *go wide of the mark* ver naast het doel schieten **2** (afkomstig) van, (afkomstig) uit, (veroorzaakt, gemaakt) door: *a colour of your own choice* een kleur die u zelf kunt kiezen; *that's too much to ask of Jane* dat is te veel van Jane gevraagd; *of necessity* uit noodzaak **3** [composition, contents, amount] bestaande uit, van: *a box of chocolates* een doos chocola **4** over,

van, met betrekking tot: *quick of under-standing* snel van begrip **5** van, te, bij, met: *men of courage* mannen met moed; *be of importance* (or: *value*) van belang (or: waarde) zijn **6** van, behorend tot: *it's that dog of hers again* het is die hond van haar weer **7** van, tot, naar, voor: *fear of spiders* angst voor spinnen **8** van, onder: *a pound of flour* een pond bloem; *five of us* vijf mensen van onze groep || *the month of May* de maand mei; *an angel of a husband* een engel van een man
¹off (adj) **1** vrij: *my husband is ~ today* mijn man heeft vandaag vrij **2** minder (goed), slecht(er): *her singing was a bit ~ tonight* ze zong niet zo best vanavond **3** verder (gelegen), ver(ste) **4** rechter(-) [of side of horse, vehicle]; rechts **5** rustig, stil: *during the ~ season* buiten het (hoog)seizoen **6** (hoogst) onwaarschijnlijk: *~ chance* kleine kans **7** bedorven [of food]; zuur: *this sausage is ~* dit worstje is bedorven **8** van de baan, afgelast, uitgesteld: *the meeting is ~* de bijeenkomst gaat niet door **9** weg, vertrokken, gestart: *get ~ to a good start* goed beginnen **10** uit-(geschakeld), buiten werking, niet aan: *the water is ~* het water is afgesloten **11** mis, naast: *his guess was slightly ~* hij zat er enigszins naast
²off (adv) **1** verwijderd, weg, (er)af, ver, hiervandaan: *three miles ~* drie mijl daarvandaan; *send ~ a letter* een brief versturen **2** af, uit, helemaal, ten einde: *a day ~* een dagje vrij; *kill ~* uitroeien; *turn ~ the radio* zet de radio af **3** ondergeschikt, minder belangrijk: *5% ~* met **5%** korting || *~ and on* af en toe, nu en dan; *be well* (or: *badly*) *~* rijk (or: arm) zijn
³off (prep) **1** van, van af: *he got ~ the bus* hij stapte uit de bus **2** van de baan, van ... af, afgestapt van: *~ duty* vrij (van dienst), buiten dienst; *I've gone ~ fish* ik lust geen vis meer **3** van ... af, naast, opzij van, uit: *it was ~ the mark* het miste zijn doel [also fig]; *an alley ~ the square* een steegje dat op het plein uitkomt **4** onder, beneden, achter zijn, minder dan: *a year or two ~ sixty* een jaar of wat onder de zestig
offal afval^h, vuil^h, vuilnis, slachtafval^h; [fig] uitschot^h
offbeat [inform] ongebruikelijk, onconventioneel
off-colour onwel, niet lekker
off day ongeluksdag
offence 1 overtreding, misdrijf^h, delict^h, misdaad: *commit an ~* een overtreding begaan **2** belediging: *cause* (or: *give*) *~ to s.o.* iem. beledigen; *take ~ at* aanstoot nemen aan, zich ergeren aan; *he is quick to take ~* hij is gauw op z'n teentjes getrapt
¹offend (vb) kwaad doen: *the verdict ~s against all principles of justice* het vonnis is een aanfluiting van alle rechtsprincipes

²offend (vb) beledigen [also fig]; boos maken
offender overtreder, zondaar: *first ~* niet eerder veroordeelde
¹offensive (n) aanval, offensief^h; [fig] campagne; beweging: *take* (or: *go into*) *the ~* aanvallen, in het offensief gaan
²offensive (adj) **1** offensief, aanvallend **2** beledigend, aanstootgevend
¹offer (n) aanbod^h, aanbieding, offerte, voorstel^h: *be on ~* in de aanbieding zijn, te koop zijn; *this house is under ~* op dit huis is een bod gedaan
²offer (vb) voorkomen, gebeuren, optreden: *as occasion ~s* wanneer de gelegenheid zich voordoet
³offer (vb) **1** (aan)bieden, geven, schenken: *~ one's hand* zijn hand uitsteken; *he ~ed to drive me home* hij bood aan me naar huis te brengen **2** te koop aanbieden, tonen, laten zien
offering 1 offergave **2** aanbieding, aanbod^h: *foreign ~s on the market* buitenlandse koopwaar op de markt
offertory-box offerblok^h, collectebus
offhand 1 onvoorbereid, geïmproviseerd: *avoid making ~ remarks* maak geen ondoordachte opmerkingen **2** nonchalant
office 1 ambt^h, openbare betrekking, functie: *hold ~* een ambt bekleden **2** dienst, hulp, zorg: *good ~s* goede diensten **3** kantoor^h, bureau^h || *the Foreign ~* het ministerie van Buitenlandse Zaken
office manager officemanager
officer 1 ambtenaar, functionaris, medewerker: *policy ~* beleidsmedewerker **2** iem. die een belangrijke functie bekleedt, directeur, voorzitter: *clerical* (or: *executive*) *~* (hoge) regeringsfunctionaris **3** politieagent **4** officier
¹official (n) beambte, functionaris, (staats)ambtenaar; [sport] official; wedstrijdcommissaris
²official (adj) officieel; ambtelijk
officialese stadhuistaal, ambtenarenlatijn^h
officiate 1 officieel optreden: *~ as chairman* (officieel) als voorzitter dienstdoen **2** [sport] arbitreren
officious bemoeiziek, opdringerig
off-key vals; uit de toon [also fig]
off-licence 1 slijtvergunning **2** slijterij, drankzaak
off-line offline, niet-gekoppeld
offload 1 lossen [vehicle, esp aeroplane] **2** dumpen
off-peak buiten het hoogseizoen, de spits [of use, traf]; goedkoop, rustig: *in the ~ hours* tijdens de daluren
offprint overdruk
off-putting ontmoedigend
offset compenseren, opwegen tegen, te-

nietdoen: ~ *against* zetten tegenover
offshoot uitloper [also fig]; scheut, zijtak
offshore 1 in zee, voor de kust, buiten-
gaats: ~ *fishing* zeevisserij **2** aflandig: ~ *wind*
aflandige wind
¹offside (n) **1** [sport] buitenspel^h, buiten-
spelpositie **2** rechterkant [of car, horse, road
etc] **3** verste kant
²offside (adj) [sport] buitenspel-: *the ~ rule*
de buitenspelregel
offspring kroost^h, nakomeling(en)
offstage 1 achter (de schermen) **2** onzichtbaar
off-the-record onofficieel, binnenskamers
often vaak: *as ~ as not* de helft van de keren, vaak; *he was late once too ~* hij kwam
één keer te veel te laat ǁ *every so ~* nu en dan
ogre menseneter
oh o!, och!, ach!: *oh no!* dat niet!, o nee!; *oh
yes!* o ja!, jazeker!; *oh yes?* zo?, o ja?; *oh well*
och, och kom
¹oil (n) **1** (aard)olie; [Belg] petroleum **2** petroleum, kerosine, stookolie, diesel(brandstof), smeerolie **3** olieverf ǁ ~ *and vinegar*
(or: *water*) water en vuur; *strike* ~ olie aanboren; [fig] plotseling rijk worden
²oil (vb) smeren, oliën, insmeren, invetten
oilcake lijnkoek(en), oliekoek(en)
oil-change olieversing: *do an* ~ de olie
verversen
oilcloth wasdoek^h
oil-fired met olie gestookt
oil painting olieverfschilderij^h ǁ [mocking-
ly] *he's no* ~ hij is geen adonis
oil rig booreiland^h
oilskin 1 oliejas **2** (-s) oliepak^h **3** geolied
doek^h, wasdoek^h
oil slick olievlek [on water]
oily 1 olieachtig, geolied, vettig **2** kruiperig, vleiend
ointment zalf, smeersel^h
¹OK (n) goedkeuring, akkoord^h, fiat^h
²OK (adj, adv) oké, OK, in orde, voldoende,
akkoord, afgesproken: *it looks OK now* nu
ziet het er goed uit
³OK (vb) goedkeuren, akkoord gaan met
¹old (n) vroeger tijden, het verleden: *heroes
of* ~ helden uit het verleden
²old (adj) **1** oud, bejaard, antiek, verouderd,
ouderwets, in onbruik geraakt: ~ *age* ouderdom, hoge leeftijd; ~ *maid* oude vrijster; *as ~
as the hills* zo oud als de weg naar Rome
2 voormalig, ex-: *the good ~ days* (or: *times*)
de goede oude tijd; *pay off* ~ *scores* een oude
rekening vereffenen **3** lang bekend: *good ~
John* die beste Jan **4** oud, van de leeftijd van:
*a **17-year-**~ girl* een zeventienjarig meisje
5 ervaren, bekwaam: *an* ~ *hand at shoplifter*
een doorgewinterde winkeldief ǁ *a chip off
the ~ block* helemaal haar moeder; *money for
~ rope* iets voor niets, gauw verdiend geld; ~

country a) land in de Oude Wereld; **b)** [with
the] moederland, geboorteland; *the ~ man*
a) **de ouwe** [also ship's captain]; **b)** de baas
[also husband]; **c)** mijn ouweheer; *in any ~
place* waar je maar kan denken; *any ~ thing
will do* alles is goed; *the Old **World*** de Oude
Wereld; [Am] (continentaal) Europa, de
Oude Wereld
old-age pension ouderdomspensioen^h,
AOW
olden: [form] *in ~ days* eertijds, voorheen
old-fashioned ouderwets, verouderd,
conservatief
oldie 1 oude grap (grammofoonplaat): *a
golden ~* een gouwe ouwe **2** oudje^h [pers]
oldish ouwelijk, nogal oud
old-school ouderwets
oldster oudje^h, ouder lid^h
old-time oud, van vroeger, ouderwets
old-timer [Am] **1** oudgediende, oude rot
2 oude bewoner **3** iets ouds, oude auto
old-world ouderwets, verouderd, van
vroeger
Old-World van de Oude Wereld
O level *ordinary level* Brits (examenvak^h op)
eindexamenniveau^h [compare 'havo']
¹olive (n) olijf(boom), olijfhout^h
²olive (adj) **1** olijfkleurig **2** olijfgroen; olijf-
bruin [complexion]
olive branch olijftak ǁ *hold out an* ~ de
hand reiken
¹Olympian (n) olympiër [also fig]
²Olympian (adj) **1** Olympisch [also fig];
goddelijk, verheven **2** olympisch, van de
Olympische Spelen
Olympic olympisch: *the ~ **Games*** de Olympische Spelen
the **Olympics** Olympische Spelen
Oman Oman
¹Omani (n) Omaniet, Omanitische
²Omani (adj) Omanitisch
ombudsman ombudsman
omega omega; [fig] slot^h, besluit^h
omelet(te) omelet
omen voorteken^h
ominous 1 veelbetekenend **2** onheilspellend, dreigend
omission weglating, verzuim^h
omit 1 weglaten, overslaan **2** verzuimen,
nalaten, verwaarlozen
omnibus 1 (auto)bus **2** omnibus(uitgave)
omnipotent almachtig
omnipresence alomtegenwoordigheid
omnipresent alomtegenwoordig
omniscient alwetend
omnivorous alleseetend: *an ~ reader* iem.
die alles wat los en vast zit leest
¹on (adj) **1** aan(gesloten), ingeschakeld;
open [appliance, tap etc] **2** aan de gang,
gaande: *the **match** is on* de wedstrijd is aan
de gang **3** op [stage]: *you're on in five minutes*

je moet over vijf minuten op **4** aan de beurt, dienstdoend || *I'm* on! oké, ik doe mee; *the wedding is* on het huwelijk gaat door
²on (adv) **1** in werking, aan, in functie: *the music came* on de muziek begon; *have you anything on tonight?* heb je plannen voor vanavond?; *leave the light* on het licht aan laten **2** [of clothes] aan: *put* on *your new dress* trek je nieuwe jurk aan **3** verder, later, voort, door: *five years* on vijf jaar later; *send* on doorsturen, nazenden; *later* on later; *and so* on enzovoort; *(talk)* on *and* on zonder onderbreking (praten); *from that moment* on vanaf dat ogenblik **4** [indicating place or direction; also fig] op, tegen, aan, toe: *they collided head* on ze botsten frontaal
³on (prep) **1** [indicating place or direction; also fig] op, in, aan, bovenop: *I have it* on *good authority* ik heb het uit betrouwbare bron; *hang* on *the wall* aan de muur hangen **2** bij, nabij, aan, verbonden aan: *on your right* aan de rechterkant; *just* on *sixty people* amper zestig mensen **3** [time] op, bij: *arrive* on *the hour* op het hele uur aankomen; *come* on *Tuesday* kom dinsdag; *on opening the door* bij het openen van de deur **4** [condition] in, met: *the patient is* on *antibiotics* de patiënt krijgt antibiotica; *be* on *duty* dienst hebben; *on trial* op proef **5** over: *take pity* on *the poor* medelijden hebben met de armen **6** ten koste van, op kosten van: *this round is* on *me* dit rondje is voor mij, ik betaal dit rondje
on-board aan boord: ~ *computer* boordcomputer
¹once (adv) **1** eenmaal, eens, één keer: ~ *again* (or: *more*) opnieuw, nog eens; ~ *too often* één keer te veel; ~ *or twice* zo nu en dan, van tijd tot tijd; *(all) at* ~ tegelijk(ertijd), samen; *(just) for (this)* ~ (voor) deze ene keer; ~ *and for all* voorgoed, definitief, voor de laatste keer; ~ *in* a *while* een enkele keer; *he only said it the* ~ hij zei het maar één keer **2** vroeger, (ooit) eens: *the* ~ *popular singer* de eens zo populaire zanger; ~ *upon* a *time there was ...* er was eens ... || *at* ~ onmiddellijk, meteen; *all at* ~ plots(eling), ineens, opeens
²once (conj) eens (dat), als eenmaal, zodra: ~ *you are ready, we'll leave* zodra je klaar bent, zullen we gaan
once-over kijkje͏ʰ, vluchtig overzicht͏ʰ: *give s.o. the* ~ iem. globaal opnemen, iem. vluchtig bekijken
oncoming 1 naderend, aanstaand **2** tegemoetkomend [also fig]: ~ *traffic* tegenliggers
¹one (n) één: *the figure* ~ het cijfer één; *by* ~*s and twos* alleen of in groepjes van twee; [fig] heel geleidelijk
²one (pron) **1** (er) een, (er) eentje: *the best* ~*s* de beste(n); *you are a fine* ~ jij bent me d'r eentje; *give him* ~ geef hem er een van, geef

hem een knal; *let's have (a quick)* ~ laten we er (gauw) eentje gaan drinken; *the* ~ *that I like best* degene die ik het leukst vind; *he was* ~ *up* on me hij was me net de baas; *this* ~*'s on me* ik trakteer!; *this* ~ deze hier **2** men: ~ *must never pride o.s. on one's achievements* men mag nooit prat gaan op zijn prestaties **3** een zeker(e), één of ander(e), ene: ~ *day* he left op een goeie dag vertrok hij; ~ *Mr Smith* called for you een zekere meneer Smith heeft voor jou gebeld **4** één, enig; [fig] dezelfde, hetzelfde; [as intensifier] hartstikke: *this is* ~ *good book* dit is een hartstikke goed boek; *from* ~ *chore to another* van het ene klusje naar het andere; *they are all* ~ *colour* ze hebben allemaal dezelfde kleur; ~ *day out of six* één op de zes dagen, om de zes dagen; *my* ~ *and only friend* mijn enige echte vriend || *for* ~ *thing* a) ten eerste; b) (al was het) alleen maar omdat; *neither* ~ *thing* nor *the other* vlees noch vis, halfslachtig
³one (num) één: ~ *after another* een voor een, de een na de andere; ~ *by* ~ een voor een, de een na de ander; ~ *to* ~ één op één, één tegen één || ~ *and all* iedereen, jan en alleman; *I was* ~ *too many for him* ik was hem te slim af; *like* ~ *o'clock* als een gek, energiek; *l, for* ~, *will refuse* ik zal in ieder geval weigeren
one another elkaar, mekaar: *they loved* ~ ze hielden van elkaar
one-armed eenarmig: ~ *bandit* eenarmige bandiet [gambling machine]
one-horse 1 met één paard [carriage etc] **2** derderangs, slecht (toegerust): ~ *town* gat
oneliner oneliner
one-man eenmans-: ~ *show* solovoorstelling
one-night stand [inform] **1** eenmalig optreden **2** affaire, sekspartner voor één nacht
one-off exclusief, uniek, eenmalig
one-on-one 1 [sport] één tegen één **2** [Am] individueel [eg of education]
one-parent family eenoudergezin͏ʰ
onerous lastig, moeilijk
oneself 1 zich(zelf): *be* ~ zichzelf zijn; *by* ~ in z'n eentje, alleen **2** zelf: *one should do it* ~ men zou het zelf moeten doen
one-sided 1 eenzijdig **2** bevooroordeeld, partijdig
one-time voormalig, vroeger, oud-
one-track beperkt [fig]; eenzijdig: *he has a* ~ *mind* hij denkt altijd maar aan één ding
one-upmanship slagvaardigheid, kunst de ander steeds een slag voor te zijn
one-way in één richting: ~ *street* straat met eenrichtingsverkeer
ongoing voortdurend, doorgaand: ~ *research* lopend onderzoek
onion ui || *know one's* ~*s* zijn vak verstaan, van wanten weten
online online, via het internet: ~ *auction*

onlineveiling, internetveiling; ~ *banking* elektronisch bankieren, internetbankieren; ~ *dating* onlinedating
onlooker toeschouwer, (toe)kijker
¹**only** (adj) **1** enig: *an ~ child* een enig kind; *we were the ~ people wearing hats* we waren de enigen met een hoed (op) **2** best, (meest) geschikt, juist
²**only** (adv) **1** slechts, alleen (maar): *she was ~ too* glad ze was maar al te blij; *~ five minutes more* nog vijf minuten, niet meer; *if ~ als …* maar, ik wou dat …; *if ~ to, if ~ because* al was het alleen maar om **2** [with expressions of time] pas, (maar) eerst, nog: *the train has ~ just left* de trein is nog maar net weg; *he arrived ~ yesterday* hij is gisteren pas aangekomen; *I like it, ~ I cannot afford it* ik vind het mooi, maar ik kan het niet betalen
onrush 1 toeloop, toestroming **2** aanval, bestorming
onset 1 aanval, (plotselinge) bestorming **2** begin^h, aanvang, aanzet: *the ~ of scarlet fever* de eerste symptomen van roodvonk
¹**onshore** (adj) **1** aanlandig, zee-: *~ breeze* zeebries **2** kust-, aan de kust gelegen, op de kust gelegen, binnenlands: *~ fishing* kustvisserij
²**onshore** (adv) **1** land(in)waarts, langs de kust **2** aan land
onside [sport] niet buitenspel
on-site plaatselijk, ter plekke
onslaught (hevige) aanval, (scherpe) uitval, aanslag
on-the-job-training opleiding in de praktijk
onus 1 last, plicht: *the ~ of proof rests with the plaintiff* de bewijslast ligt bij de eiser **2** blaam, schuld: *put (or: shift) the ~ onto* de blaam werpen op
onward voorwaarts, voortgaand: *the ~ course of events* het verdere verloop van de gebeurtenissen
onwards voorwaarts, vooruit: *move ~* voortgaan, verder gaan
oompah hoempageluid^h, (eentonig) gehoempapa
oomph [inform] **1** charme **2** geestdrift, animo
oops oei, jee(tje), nee maar, pardon
oops-a-daisy hup(sakee), hoepla(la), hop
¹**ooze** (n) modder, slijk^h, drab
²**ooze** (vb) **1** binnensijpelen, doorsijpelen, insijpelen, druipen, druppelen: *~ out of (or: from)* sijpelen uit **2** (uit)zweten, vocht afscheiden, lekken, bloed opgeven || *his courage ~d away* de moed zonk hem in de schoenen
³**ooze** (vb) afscheiden, uitwasemen; [fig] druipen van; doortrokken zijn van, uitstralen: *her voice ~d sarcasm* er klonk sarcasme in haar stem

op *operation* operatie
opacity 1 onduidelijkheid, ondoorgrondelijkheid **2** ondoorschijnendheid
opal 1 opaal^+h, opaalsteen **2** opaalglas^h, melkglas^h
opaque 1 ondoorschijnend, ondoorzichtig; dekkend [of paint, colour] **2** onduidelijk, onbegrijpelijk **3** [fig] stompzinnig, dom, traag van begrip
¹**open** (n) (de) open ruimte, openlucht, open veld, open zee; [fig] openbaarheid: *bring into the ~* aan het licht brengen, bekendmaken; *come (out) into the ~* **a)** open kaart spelen [of someone]; **b)** aan het licht komen, ruchtbaarheid krijgen [of something]
²**open** (adj) **1** open, geopend, met openingen, onbedekt, niet (af)gesloten, vrij: *keep one's eyes ~* goed opletten; [fig] *with one's eyes ~* bij zijn volle verstand, weloverwogen; *~ prison* open gevangenis; *~ to the public* toegankelijk voor het publiek **2** open(staand), beschikbaar, onbeslist, onbepaald: *~ cheque* ongekruiste cheque; *it is ~ to you to* het staat je vrij te; *lay o.s. (wide) ~ to* zich (helemaal) blootstellen aan **3** openbaar, (algemeen) bekend, duidelijk, openlijk: *~ hostilities* openlijke vijandigheden; *~ secret* publiek geheim **4** open(hartig), oprecht, mededeelzaam: *admit ~ly* eerlijk uitkomen voor; *be ~ with* open kaart spelen met **5** open(baar), vrij toegankelijk || *keep ~ house* erg gastvrij zijn; *have (or: keep) an ~ mind* onbestaan voor; *lay o.s. ~ to ridicule* zich belachelijk maken
³**open** (vb) **1** opengaan, (zich) openen, geopend worden: *~ into (or: onto) the garden* uitkomen in (or: op) de tuin **2** openen, beginnen; van wal steken [of speaker] **3** opendoen, (een boek) opensaan
⁴**open** (vb) **1** openen: *~ a tin* een blik opendraaien **2** openen, voor geopend verklaren, starten: *~ the bidding* het eerste bod doen [at auction, at cardgame]; *~ fire at (or: on)* het vuur openen op
open-air openlucht-, buiten-, in de openlucht
open-and-shut (dood)eenvoudig: *an ~ case* een uitgemaakte zaak
opencast bovengronds, in dagbouw: *~ mining* dagbouw
open-ended open, met een open einde: *~ discussion* vrije discussie
opener openingsnummer, openingsronde; eerste manche, ronde: *a standard ~* een klassiek begin
openhanded gul, vrijgevig
open-hearted 1 openhartig, eerlijk **2** hartelijk, open
opening 1 opening, begin(fase), inleiding; [chess, draughts] opening(szet); beginspel^h **2** opening, kans, (gunstige) gelegenheid:

new ~s for trade nieuwe afzetgebieden **3** vacature **4** opening, het opengaan, geopend worden, bres, gat[h], uitweg: *hours* of ~ are *Tuesdays 1 to 5* openingsuren dinsdag van 1 tot 5

openly open, openhartig: *you can speak* ~ u kunt vrijuit spreken

open-minded onbevooroordeeld, ruimdenkend

open-mouthed met de mond wijd open- (gesperd); [also fig] sprakeloos [with surprise]

[1]**open out** (vb) **1** verbreden, breder worden, zich uitbreiden: ~ *into* uitmonden in [of river] **2** opengaan, (naar buiten) openslaan

[2]**open out** (vb) openvouwen, openleggen

open-plan met weinig tussenmuren: *an ~ office* een kantoortuin

open season open seizoen[h], jachtseizoen[h], hengelseizoen[h]

[1]**open up** (vb) **1** opengaan, zich openen, zich ontplooien; [fig] loskomen; vrijuit (gaan) spreken: *in the second half the game opened up* in de tweede helft werd er aantrekkelijker gespeeld **2** (de deur) opendoen

[2]**open up** (vb) openen, openmaken, toegankelijk maken, opensnijden

opera opera

operable 1 opereerbaar **2** uitvoerbaar, realiseerbaar

opera glasses toneelkijker

opera house opera(gebouw[h])

[1]**operate** (vb) **1** in werking zijn, functioneren; lopen [also of train]; draaien [of engine]; te werk gaan **2** (de juiste) uitwerking hebben, werken; (het gewenste) resultaat geven [of tariff, treaty, law]: *the new cutbacks will not ~ till next month* de nieuwe bezuinigingsmaatregelen gaan pas volgende maand in **3** te werk gaan, opereren; [med also] een operatie doen; ingrijpen

[2]**operate** (vb) **1** bewerken **2** bedienen [machine, appliance]; besturen [also car, ship]: *be ~d by* werken op, (aan)gedreven worden door [steam, electricity] **3** [Am; med] opereren

operating system besturingssysteem[h]

operating theatre operatiekamer

operation 1 operatie, handeling, onderneming, campagne, militaire actie, chirurgische ingreep **2** werking: *bring* (or: *put*) *sth. into* ~ iets in werking brengen (or: zetten); *come into* ~ in werking treden, ingaan [of law] **3** bediening

operational operationeel, gebruiksklaar, bedrijfsklaar, gevechtsklaar: ~ *costs* bedrijfskosten

operations room controlekamer [at manoeuvres]; commandopost, hoofdkwartier[h]

operative 1 werkzaam, in werking, van kracht: *the ~ force* de drijvende kracht; *be-*

come ~ in werking treden, ingaan [of law] **2** meest relevant, voornaamste

operator 1 iem. die een machine bedient, operateur, telefonist(e), telegrafist(e), bestuurder **2** [inform] gladjanus

operetta operette

ophthalmic oogheelkundig

ophthalmologist oogheelkundige, oogarts

ophthalmology oogheelkunde

opiate opiaat[h], slaapmiddel[h], pijnstiller

opinion 1 mening, oordeel[h], opinie, opvatting: *a matter* of ~ een kwestie van opvatting; *in the* ~ *of most people* gaar het oordeel van de meeste mensen; *in my* ~ naar mijn mening; *be of (the)* ~ *that* van oordeel zijn dat **2** (hoge) dunk, waardering, (gunstig) denkbeeld[h]: *have a high* ~ *of* een hoge dunk hebben van **3** advies[h], oordeel[h]; mening [of expert]: *have a second* ~ advies van een tweede deskundige inwinnen

opinionated koppig, eigenwijs

opinion poll opinieonderzoek[h], opiniepeiling

opium opium[h]

opponent opponent, tegenstander, tegenspeler

opportune geschikt, gunstig (gekozen)

opportunism opportunisme[h], het steeds handelen naar de omstandigheden

[1]**opportunist** (n) opportunist, iem. die steeds van gunstige gelegenheden gebruik probeert te maken

[2]**opportunist** (adj) opportunistisch

opportunity (gunstige/geschikte) gelegenheid, kans: *take* (or: *seize*) *the* ~ to van de gelegenheid gebruikmaken om; *she had ample* ~ *for doing that* ze had ruimschoots de gelegenheid (om) dat te doen

oppose 1 tegen(over)stellen, contrasteren, tegenover elkaar stellen **2** zich verzetten tegen, bestrijden

opposed 1 tegen(over)gesteld: *be* ~ *to* tegen(over)gesteld zijn aan **2** tegen, afkerig: *be* ~ *to* (gekant) zijn tegen, afkeuren ‖ *as* ~ *to* in tegenstelling met

opposing 1 tegenoverliggend **2** tegenwerkend; [sport] vijandig: *the* ~ *team* de tegenpartij

[1]**opposite** (n) tegen(over)gestelde[h], tegendeel[h]: *be* ~*s* elkaars tegenpolen zijn

[2]**opposite** (adj) **1** tegen(over)gesteld, tegenover elkaar gelegen, tegen-: ~ *number* ambtgenoot, collega **2** [after noun] tegenover, aan de overkant: *the houses* ~ de huizen hier tegenover

[3]**opposite** (adv) tegenover (elkaar), aan de overkant: *she lives* ~ ze woont hiertegenover; ~ *to* tegenover

[4]**opposite** (prep) tegenover: *she sat* ~ *a fat boy* ze zat tegenover een dikke jongen

opposition 1 oppositie, het tegen(over)-stellen: *in ~ to* tegen(over), verschillend van, in strijd met **2** oppositie, verzet[h]: *meet with strong ~* op hevig verzet stuiten **3** oppositie-(groep), oppositiepartij
oppress 1 onderdrukken **2** benauwen: *~ed by anxiety* doodsbenauwd
oppression 1 benauwing, neerslachtigheid **2** onderdrukking(smaatregel), verdrukking
oppressive 1 onderdrukkend, tiranniek **2** benauwend, deprimerend
oppressor onderdrukker, tiran
opt (+ for) opteren (voor), kiezen, besluiten
optic gezichts-, oog-, optisch: *~ nerve* oogzenuw
optical 1 optisch: *~ illusion* optisch bedrog, gezichtsbedrog **2** gezichtkundig || *~ fibre* glasvezel
optician opticien
optics optica
optimal optimaal, best, gunstigst
optimism optimisme[h]
optimist optimist
optimistic optimistisch
optimum optimum[h]
option 1 keus, keuze, alternatief[h]: *have no ~ but to go* geen andere keus hebben dan te gaan **2** [fin] optie
optional keuze-, facultatief, vrij: *an ~ extra* accessoire, leverbaar tegen meerprijs
opt out niet meer (willen) meedoen, zich terugtrekken: *~ of* a) niet meer (willen) meedoen aan [idea, plan]; **b)** afschuiven [responsibility]; **c)** opzeggen [contract]
opulence (enorme) rijkdom, overvloed, weelde
opulent overvloedig, (schat)rijk
or 1 of, en, ofwel, anders gezegd, of misschien, nog, ook: *would you like tea or coffee* wil je thee of koffie **2** of (anders): *tell me or I'll kill you!* vertel het mij of ik vermoord je!
oracle orakel[h]
¹oral (n) mondeling[h], mondeling examen[h]
²oral (adj) mondeling, oraal, gesproken: *~ agreement* mondelinge overeenkomst; *~ tradition* mondelinge overlevering
¹orange (n) sinaasappel
²orange (adj) oranje(kleurig)
orange juice jus d'orange, sinaasappelsap[h]
orang-utan orang-oetan(g)
oration (hoogdravende) rede(voering): *a funeral ~* een grafrede
orator (begaafd) redenaar
oratorical retorisch; [sometimes depr] hoogdravend
oratory 1 oratorium[h] **2** redenaarskunst
orb bolvormig iets, globe, hemellichaam[h]
¹orbit (n) **1** kring; (invloeds)sfeer, interessesfeer **2** baan [of planet etc]; omloop, kring(loop)

²orbit (vb) een (cirkel)baan beschrijven (rond)
orchard boomgaard
orchestra orkest[h]
orchestral orkestraal; orkest-
orchestrate orkestreren, voor orkest arrangeren; [fig] (harmonieus/ordelijk) samenbrengen; organiseren
orchestration orkestratie
orchid orchidee
ordain 1 (tot geestelijke of priester) wijden **2** (voor)beschikken [by God, fate] **3** verordenen
ordeal 1 beproeving, bezoeking; [fig] vuurproef; pijnlijke ervaring **2** godsoordeel[h]: *~ by fire* vuurproef
¹order (n) **1** orde, stand, rang, (sociale) klasse, soort, aard: *~ of magnitude* orde (van grootte); *in the ~ of* in de orde (van grootte) van, ongeveer, om en (na)bij **2** (rang)orde, volgorde, op(een)volging: *in alphabetical ~* alfabetisch gerangschikt; *in ~ of importance* in volgorde van belangrijkheid **3** ordelijke inrichting, orde(lijkheid), ordening, geregeldheid, netheid; [mil] opstelling; stelsel[h], (maatschappij)structuur: *in good ~* piekfijn in orde; *out of ~* defect, buiten gebruik **4** (dag)orde, agenda; reglement[h] [of meeting etc]: *call s.o. to ~* iem. tot de orde roepen; *be out of ~* a) buiten de orde gaan [of speaker]; **b)** (nog) niet aan de orde zijn **5** orde, tucht, gehoorzaamheid: *keep ~* de orde bewaren **6** (klooster)orde, ridderorde **7** bevel[h], order, opdracht, instructie: *on doctor's ~s* op doktersvoorschrift **8** bedoeling, doel[h]: *in ~ to* om, teneinde **9** bestelling, order: *be on ~* in bestelling zijn, besteld zijn **10** [fin] (betalings)opdracht, order(briefje[h]): *postal ~* postwissel || *~s are orders* (een) bevel is (een) bevel; *made to ~* op bestelling gemaakt; [fig] perfect
²order (vb) **1** bevelen, het bevel hebben **2** bestellen, een order plaatsen
³order (vb) **1** ordenen, in orde brengen, (rang)schikken **2** (een) opdracht geven (om), het bevel geven (tot), verzoeken om; voorschrijven [of doctor]: *he ~ed the troops to open fire* hij gaf de troepen bevel het vuur te openen **3** bestellen, een order plaatsen voor || *~ s.o. about* (or: *around*) iem. (steeds) commanderen, iem. voortdurend de wet voorschrijven
order book orderboek[h], bestel(lingen)boek[h]
ordered geordend, ordelijk
order form bestelformulier[h]
¹orderly (n) **1** ordonnans **2** (zieken)oppasser, hospitaalsoldaat
²orderly (adj) ordelijk, geordend, geregeld
order out wegsturen, de deur wijzen
¹ordinal (n) rangtelwoord[h]

²**ordinal** (adj) rang-: ~ *numbers* rangtel-
woorden
ordinance verordening, bepaling, voor-
schrift^h
¹**ordinary** (n) het gewone: *out of the* ~ ongewoon, bijzonder
²**ordinary** (adj) **1** gewoon, gebruikelijk,
normaal, vertrouwd **2** ordinair, middelmatig
ordination [rel] wijding
ordnance 1 (zwaar) geschut^h **2** militaire
voorraden en materieel, oorlogsmateriaal^h
ordnance survey map topografische
kaart, stafkaart
ore erts^h
organ 1 orgel^h **2** orgaan^h: ~s *of speech*
spraakorganen **3** orgaan^h, instrument^h, instelling
organ grinder orgeldraaier
organic 1 wezenlijk, essentieel **2** (orga-
nisch-)biologisch, natuurlijk: ~ *food* natuurvoeding; ~ *waste* [roughly] gft-afval
organism organisme^h
organist organist, orgelspeler
organization organisatie, structuur, vereniging
¹**organize** (vb) zich organiseren, zich verenigen
²**organize** (vb) **1** organiseren, regelen, tot
stand brengen, oprichten **2** lid worden van
[trade union]; zich verenigen in
organizer 1 organisator **2** systematische
agenda
orgasm orgasme^h
orgy orgie, uitspatting; [fig] overdaad
oriel (window) erker, erkervenster^h
orient 1 richten **2** oriënteren, situeren: ~
o.s. zich oriënteren
Orient Oriënt, Oosten^h
oriental oosters, oostelijk, oriëntaal: ~ *rug*
(or: *carpet*) oosters tapijt
orientation 1 oriëntatie **2** oriënterings-
vermogen^h
origin oorsprong, origine, ontstaan^h, bron,
afkomst, herkomst, oorzaak: *country of* ~
land van herkomst
¹**original** (n) origineel, oorspronkelijke versie
²**original** (adj) origineel, oorspronkelijk, authentiek: *an* ~ *mind* een creatieve geest; ~ *sin*
erfzonde
originality originaliteit, oorspronkelijkheid
originate ontstaan, beginnen, voortkomen: ~ *from* (or: *in*) sth. voortkomen uit iets
¹**ornament** (n) **1** ornament^h, sieraad^h **2** versiering, decoratie
²**ornament** (vb) (ver)sieren
ornamental sier-, decoratief: ~ *painter* de-
coratieschilder
ornate sierlijk
ornithologist ornitholoog, vogelkenner

ornithology vogelkunde
¹**orphan** (n) wees
²**orphan** (vb) tot wees maken
orphanage weeshuis^h
orthodontics orthodontie
orthodox 1 orthodox, rechtgelovig **2** conservatief, ouderwets
orthodoxy 1 orthodoxe praktijk, gewoonte **2** orthodoxie, rechtzinnigheid
orthography spellingleer
orthopaedic orthopedisch
oscillate 1 trillen, (heen en weer) slingeren: *oscillating current* wisselstroom **2** weifelen
oscillation 1 schommeling, trilling **2** besluiteloosheid
osprey visarend
ossify (doen) verbenen; [fig] verharden; afstompen
ostentation vertoon^h
ostentatious opzichtig
osteopath orthopedist
ostracize verbannen; [fig] uitstoten
ostrich struisvogel [also fig]
other 1 ander(e), nog een, verschillend(e):
every ~ *week* om de (andere) week, eens in
de twee weken; *on the* ~ *hand* daarentegen
2 (nog/weer) andere(n), overige(n), nieuwe:
someone or ~ iemand; *one after the* ~ na elkaar; *among* ~s onder andere **3** anders, verschillend: *none* ~ *than John* niemand anders
dan John ‖ *the* ~ *week* een paar weken geleden
other than behalve, buiten: *there was no-
one else* ~ *his sister* er was niemand behalve
zijn zuster
¹**otherwise** (adj) anders, verschillend, tegengesteld: *mothers, married and* (or: *or*) ~
moeders, al dan niet gehuwd
²**otherwise** (adv) anders, overigens: *be* ~
engaged andere dingen te doen hebben; *go
now;* ~ *it'll be too late* ga nu, anders wordt het
te laat
otter (vis)otter
ought to 1 [command, prohibition, obliga-
tion] (eigenlijk) moeten, zou (eigenlijk)
moeten: *you* ~ *be grateful* je zou dankbaar
moeten zijn **2** [supposition] moeten, zullen,
zou moeten: *this* ~ *do the trick* dit zou het
probleem moeten oplossen, hiermee zou het
moeten lukken
ounce (Engels, Amerikaans) ons^h; [fig] klein
beetje^h: *an* ~ *of common sense* een greintje
gezond verstand
our ons, onze, van ons
ours van ons, de (or: het) onze: *the decision
is* ~ de beslissing ligt bij ons; *a friend of* ~ een
vriend van ons
ourselves 1 ons, onszelf: *we busied* ~ *with
organizing the party* we hielden ons bezig met
het organiseren van het feestje **2** zelf, wij

zelf, ons zelf: *we went ~ we gingen zelf*
oust 1 verdrijven, uitdrijven, ontzetten, afzetten: *~ s.o. from* (or: *of*) *iem.* ontheffen van **2** verdringen, vervangen
¹out (adj) **1** uit [of equipment] **2** voor uitgaande post: *~ box* (or: *tray*) brievenbak voor uitgaande post
²out (adv) **1** [place, direction; also fig; also sport] uit, buiten, weg: *inside ~* binnenste buiten; *~ in Canada* daarginds in Canada **2** buiten bewustzijn, buiten gevecht, in slaap, dronken **3** niet (meer) in werking, uit **4** uit, openbaar, tevoorschijn: *the sun is ~* de zon schijnt; *~ with it!* vertel op!, zeg het maar!, voor de dag ermee! **5** ernaast [of estimates] || *~ and about* (weer) op de been, in de weer; *~ and away* veruit; *she is ~ for trouble* ze zoekt moeilijkheden
³out (prep) uit, naar buiten: *from ~ the window* vanuit het raam
out-and-out volledig, door en door: *an ~ supporter of the programme* een verdediger van het programma door dik en dun
outback [Austr] binnenlandʰ
outbalance zwaarder wegen dan, belangrijker zijn dan
outbid meer bieden dan, overtroeven
outbound uitgaand, op de uitreis, vertrekkend: *~ traffic* uitgaand verkeer
outbox postvak uit
outbreak uitbarsting, het uitbreken
outburst uitbarsting, uitval
outcast verschoppeling, verworpene
¹outcaste (n) paria, kasteloze
²outcaste (adj) kasteloos, paria-
outclass overtreffen
outcome resultaatʰ, gevolgʰ, uitslag
outcry 1 schreeuw, kreet **2** (publiek) protestʰ, tegenwerping: *public ~ against* (or: *over*) publiek protest tegen
outdated achterhaald, ouderwets
outdo 1 overtreffen **2** overwinnen, de loef afsteken
outdoor 1 openlucht-, buiten(shuis)-: *~ advertising* buitenreclame **2** buiten een instelling, thuis zittend, zijnd
outdoors buiten(shuis), in de openlucht
outer buitenste: *~ garments* (or: *wear*) bovenkleding; *~ space* de ruimte; *the ~ world* de buitenwereld
outermost buitenste, uiterste
outfit 1 uitrusting, toerusting **2** groep, (reis)gezelschapʰ, teamʰ, ploeg
outflow 1 uitloop, afvoer **2** uitstroming, uitvloeiing, afvloeiing
outgoing 1 hartelijk, vlot **2** vertrekkend, uitgaand: *~ tide* aflopend tij **3** uittredend, ontslag nemend
outgoings uitgaven, onkosten
outgrow 1 ontgroeien (aan), afleren, te boven komen: *~ one's strength* uit zijn krach-

ten groeien **2** boven het hoofd groeien, groter worden dan
outhouse bijgebouwʰ, aanbouw
outing 1 uitstapjeʰ, excursie **2** wandeling, ommetjeʰ
outlandish vreemd, bizar, excentriek
outlast langer duren (meegaan) dan, overleven
¹outlaw (n) vogelvrijverklaarde, bandiet
²outlaw (vb) verbieden, buiten de wet stellen, vogelvrij verklaren
outlet 1 uitlaat(klep), afvoerkanaalʰ **2** afzetgebiedʰ, markt **3** vestiging, verkooppuntʰ **4** [Am] (wand)contactdoos, stopcontactʰ
¹outline (n) **1** omtrek(lijn), contour **2** schets, samenvatting, overzichtʰ, ontwerpʰ: *in broad ~* in grote trekken **3** (-s) (hoofd)trekken, hoofdpunten
²outline (vb) **1** schetsen, samenvatten **2** omlijnen, de contouren tekenen van
outlive overleven, langer leven dan
outlook 1 uitkijk(post): *be on the ~ for* uitzien, uitkijken naar **2** uitzichtʰ, gezichtʰ **3** vooruitzichtʰ, verwachting **4** kijk, oordeelʰ: *a narrow ~ on life* een bekrompen levensopvatting
outmatch overtreffen
outmoded 1 uit de mode **2** verouderd
outnumber in aantal overtreffen, talrijker zijn dan: *be ~ed* in de minderheid zijn
out of 1 [place and direction; also fig] buiten, uit (… weg): *turned ~ doors* de straat opgejaagd, op straat gezet; *~ the ordinary* ongewoon; *feel ~* it zich buitengesloten voelen; *one ~ four* een op vier **2** uit, vanuit, komende uit: *act ~ pity* uit medelijden handelen **3** zonder, -loos: *~ breath* buiten adem
out-of-date achterhaald, ouderwets
out-patient poliklinisch patiënt
out-patient clinic polikliniek
out-patient treatment poliklinische behandeling
outperform overtreffen, beter doen dan
outpost 1 voorpost **2** buitenpost
outpouring 1 uitvloeiing, afvloeiing, stroom **2** ontboezeming
output opbrengst, productie, prestatie, nuttig effectʰ, vermogenʰ, uitgangsvermogenʰ, uitgangsspanning, uitvoer, output
¹outrage (n) **1** geweld(daad), wandaad, misdaad, misdrijfʰ, aanslag, belediging, schandaalʰ **2** [Am] verontwaardiging
²outrage (vb) **1** geweld aandoen, zich vergrijpen aan, overtreden, beledigen **2** [Am] verontwaardigd maken: *I felt ~d by what they had done* ik was buiten mezelf over wat ze gedaan hadden
outrageous 1 buitensporig **2** gewelddadig **3** schandelijk, schaamteloos, afschuwelijk
outrank hoger zijn in rang dan, belangrij-

ker zijn dan
¹outright (adj) **1** totaal, volledig, grondig **2** volstrekt: ~ *nonsense* volslagen onzin **3** onverdeeld, onvoorwaardelijk **4** direct
²outright (adv) **1** helemaal, voor eens en altijd **2** ineens: *kill* ~ ter plaatse afmaken **3** openlijk
outrun 1 harder (verder) lopen dan, inhalen **2** ontlopen, ontsnappen aan
outset beginʰ, aanvang: *from the (very)* ~ van meet af aan, vanaf het (allereerste) begin
outshine in glans overtreffen; [fig] overschaduwen
¹outside (n) **1** buitenkant, buitensteʰ, uiterlijkʰ **2** buitenwereld **3** uiersteʰ, grens: *at the (very)* ~ uiterlijk, op zijn laatst
²outside (adj) **1** buiten-, van buiten(af), buitenstaand **2** gering, klein: *an* ~ *chance* een hele kleine kans
³outside (adv) buiten, buitenshuis
outsider 1 buitenstaander **2** zonderling **3** [sport] outsider [horse]
outsize extra groot
outskirts buitenwijken, randgebied: *on the* ~ *of town* aan de rand van de stad
outsmart te slim af zijn
outsourcing uitbesteding, outsourcing
outspoken open(hartig), ronduit
outstanding 1 opmerkelijk, voortreffelijk **2** onbeslist, onbetaald: ~ *debts* uitstaande schulden
outstation buitenpost, afgelegen standplaats
outstay langer blijven dan: ~ *one's welcome* langer blijven dan men welkom is
outstrip 1 achter zich laten, inhalen **2** overtreffen
outward 1 buitenwaarts, naar buiten (gekeerd), uitgaand: ~ *passage* (or: *journey*) heenreis **2** uitwendig, lichamelijk: *to all* ~ *appearances* ogenschijnlijk
outwardly klaarblijkelijk, ogenschijnlijk
outwards naar buiten, buitenwaarts: ~ *bound* uitgaand, op de uitreis
outweigh 1 zwaarder wegen dan **2** belangrijker zijn dan
outwit te slim af zijn, beetnemen
outwork 1 thuiswerkʰ **2** buitenwerkʰ
outworn 1 versleten, uitgeput **2** verouderd, afgezaagd
¹oval (n) ovaalʰ
²oval (adj) ovaal(vormig), eivormig: *the Oval Office* [fig] het presidentschap
ovary eierstok; [bot] vruchtbeginselʰ
ovation ovatie, hulde(betoonʰ)
oven (bak)oven, fornuisʰ: *like an* ~ snikheet
oven glove ovenwant
oven mitt ovenwant
¹over (adv) **1** [direction; also fig] over-, naar de overkant, omver: *he called her* ~ hij riep

haar bij zich **2** [place] daarover, aan de overkant, voorbij: ~ *in France* (daarginds) in Frankrijk; ~ *here* hier, in dit land; ~ *there* daarginds; ~ *against* tegenover; ~ *(to you)* [fig] jouw beurt **3** [degree] boven, meer, te: *some apples were left* ~ er bleven enkele appelen over **4** [place] boven, bedekt: *he's mud all* ~ hij zit onder de modder **5** ten einde, af, over **6** ten einde, helemaal, volledig: *they talked the matter* ~ de zaak werd grondig besproken **7** opnieuw: ~ *and over again* telkens weer || *that's him all* ~ dat is typisch voor hem
²over (prep) **1** [place] over, op, boven … uit: *chat* ~ *a cup of tea* (even) (bij)kletsen bij een kopje thee; *buy nothing* ~ *fifty francs* koop niets boven de vijftig frank; ~ *and above these problems there are others* behalve deze problemen zijn er nog andere **2** [length, surface etc] doorheen, door, over: *speak* ~ *the phone* over de telefoon spreken; ~ *the past five weeks* gedurende de afgelopen vijf weken **3** [direction] naar de overkant van, over **4** [place] aan de overkant van, aan de andere kant van **5** betreffende, met betrekking tot, over, om: *all this fuss* ~ *a trifle* zo'n drukte om een kleinigheid **6** [maths] gedeeld door: *eight* ~ *four equals two* acht gedeeld door vier is twee
overact overdrijven, overacteren
¹overall (n) **1** (-s) overal **2** (werk)kiel
²overall (adj) **1** totaal, geheel, alles omvattend: ~ *efficiency* totaal rendement **2** globaal, algemeen
³overall (adv) **1** in totaal, van kop tot teen **2** globaal
¹overbalance (vb) het evenwicht verliezen, kapseizen, omslaan
²overbalance (vb) uit het evenwicht brengen
overbearing dominerend, bazig: ~ *manner* arrogante houding
overboard overboord: *throw* ~ overboord gooien [also fig]
overburden [also fig] overbelasten, overladen
¹overcast (n) bewolking
²overcast (adj) **1** betrokken, bewolkt **2** donker
¹overcharge (vb) overvragen, te veel vragen
²overcharge (vb) **1** overdrijven: ~*d with emotion* te emotioneel geladen **2** overvragen, te veel in rekening brengen (voor): ~ *a person* iem. te veel laten betalen
overcoat overjas
¹overcome (adj) overwonnen, overmand: ~ *by the heat* door de warmte bevangen; ~ *by* (or: *with*) *grief* door leed overmand
²overcome (vb) overwinnen, zegevieren (over), te boven komen: ~ *a temptation* een verleiding weerstaan

overcrowded 1 overvol, stampvol **2** overbevolkt

overdo 1 overdrijven, te veel gebruiken: ~ *things* (or: *it*) te hard werken, overdrijven **2** te gaar koken, overbakken: ~*ne meat* overgaar vlees

¹overdose (n) overdosis

²overdose (vb) een overdosis toedienen, nemen van

¹overdraw (vb) overdisponeren: ~ *one's account* overdisponeren, zijn tegoed overschrijden

²overdraw (vb) overdrijven

overdress (zich) te netjes kleden, (zich) opzichtig kleden

overdrive overversnelling, overdrive

overdue te laat, over (zijn) tijd, achterstallig

overestimate overschatten

overexpose te lang blootstellen; [photo] overbelichten

¹overflow (n) **1** overstroming **2** overschotʰ, overvloed

²overflow (vb) overstromen, (doen) overlopen: *full to ~ing* boordevol

overgrow 1 overgroeien **2** overwoekeren **3** te groot worden voor, ontgroeien

¹overhang (n) overhang(end gedeelteʰ), uitsteekselʰ

²overhang (vb) overhangen, uitsteken

³overhang (vb) boven het hoofd hangen, voor de deur staan, dreigen

¹overhaul (n) revisie, controlebeurt

²overhaul (vb) **1** grondig nazien, reviseren; [by extension] repareren **2** [shipp] inhalen, voorbijsteken, voorbijvaren

overhead 1 hoog (aangebracht), in de lucht: ~ *railway* luchtspoorweg **2** algemeen, vast: ~ *charges* (or: *expenses*) vaste bedrijfsuitgaven

overheads algemene onkosten

overhear 1 toevallig horen **2** afluisteren

overjoyed (+ at) in de wolken (over)

overkill overkill

¹overlap (n) overlap(ping)

²overlap (vb) elkaar overlappen, gedeeltelijk samenvallen

³overlap (vb) overlappen, gedeeltelijk bedekken

overlay 1 bekleding, bedekking, (bedden)-overtrek **2** deklaagjeʰ

overleaf aan ommezijde

overload te zwaar (be)laden, overbelasten

overlook 1 overzien, uitkijken op **2** over het hoofd zien, voorbijzien **3** door de vingers zien

overly [Am, Scotland] (al) te, overdreven: ~ *protective* overdreven beschermend

¹overnight (adj) **1** van de vorige avond **2** nachtelijk: ~ *journey* nachtelijke reis **3** plotseling [eg success]

²overnight (adv) **1** de avond tevoren **2** tijdens de nacht: *stay* ~ overnachten **3** in één nacht, zomaar ineens: *become famous* ~ van de ene dag op de andere beroemd worden

overpass viaductʰ

overpopulation overbevolking

overpower 1 bedwingen, onderwerpen **2** overweldigen **3** bevangen

overrate overschatten, overwaarderen

¹overreach (vb) te ver reiken

²overreach (vb) verder reiken dan, voorbijschieten, voorbijstreven: ~ *o.s.* te veel hooi op zijn vork nemen

overreaction te sterke reactie

overriding doorslaggevend, allergrootst

overrule 1 verwerpen, afwijzen; terzijde schuiven [eg objection] **2** herroepen, intrekken, nietig verklaren: ~ *a decision* een beslissing herroepen

¹overrun (vb) **1** overstromen **2** [fig] uitlopen

²overrun (vb) **1** overstromen [also fig] **2** onder de voet lopen, veroveren **3** overschrijden [time limit] **4** overgroeien

¹overseas (adj) overzees, buitenlands: ~ *trade* overzeese handel

²overseas (adv) overzee, in (de) overzeese gebieden

oversee toezicht houden (op)

overseer opzichter, voorman

overshadow overschaduwen; [fig] domineren

overshoot voorbijschieten, verder gaan dan: ~ *the runway* doorschieten op de landingsbaan

oversight 1 onoplettendheid, vergissing **2** supervisie

over-sixties zestigplussers

oversize(d) bovenmaats, te groot

oversleep (zich) verslapen, te lang slapen

overspill 1 overloop, gemorst waterʰ **2** surplusʰ **3** overloop; migratie [of surplus of population]

overstate overdrijven

overstay langer blijven dan: ~ *one's welcome* langer blijven dan de gastvrouw of gastheer lief is

overstep overschrijden: ~ *one's authority* zijn boekje te buiten gaan

overt open(lijk): ~ *hostility* openlijke vijandigheid

overtake inhalen

over-the-counter 1 [com] incourant: ~ *securities* incourante fondsen **2** [med] zonder (dokters)recept verkrijgbaar

overthrow om(ver)werpen, omgooien **2** omverwerpen, ten val brengen

¹overtime (n) **1** (loonʰ voor) overuren, overwerk(geld)ʰ **2** [Am; sport] (extra) verlenging: *go into* ~ verlengd worden

²overtime (adv) over-: *work* ~ overuren ma-

overtone

922

ken
overtone 1 [mus] boventoon **2** [fig] ondertoon, suggestie
overture [mus] ouverture, inleiding, voorstel[h]: [fig] *make* ~s *(to)* toenadering zoeken
(tot)
[1]**overturn** (vb) omslaan, verslagen worden
[2]**overturn** (vb) doen omslaan, ten val brengen
overview overzicht[h], samenvatting
[1]**overweight** (n) over(ge)wicht[h]; te zware
last [also fig]
[2]**overweight** (adj) te zwaar, te dik
[3]**overweight** (vb) **1** overladen **2** te zeer benadrukken
overwhelm bedelven, verpletteren: ~ed
with grief door leed overmand
overwhelming overweldigend, verpletterend: ~ *majority* overgrote meerderheid
[1]**overwork** (vb) te hard werken
[2]**overwork** (vb) **1** te hard laten werken, uitputten **2** te vaak gebruiken, tot cliché maken: *an ~ed* **expression** een afgesleten uitdrukking
ovulate ovuleren
[1]**owe** (vb) schuld(en) hebben: ~ *for* everything
one has voor alles wat men heeft nog (ten
dele) moeten betalen
[2]**owe** (vb) **1** schuldig zijn, verplicht zijn, verschuldigd zijn **2** (+ to) te danken hebben
(aan), toeschrijven (aan)
owing 1 verschuldigd, schuldig, onbetaald:
how much is ~ *to* you? hoeveel heeft u nog te
goed? **2** (+ to) te danken (aan), te wijten
(aan)
owing to wegens, ten gevolge van
owl uil [also fig]
[1]**own** (adj) eigen, van ... zelf, eigen bezit (familie): an ~ **goal** een doelpunt in eigen doel;
be one's ~ **man** (or: **master**) heer en meester
zijn, onafhankelijk zijn; not have a moment
(or: minute, second) to **call** one's ~ geen moment voor zichzelf hebben; you'll have a room
of your ~ je krijgt een eigen kamer ‖ beat s.o.
at his ~ **game** iem. met zijn eigen wapens
verslaan; in his ~ (good) **time** wanneer het
hem zo uitkomt; **hold** one's ~ **a)** standhouden; **b)** niet achteruitgaan [of health]; **on**
one's ~ in zijn eentje, op eigen houtje
[2]**own** (vb) bekennen, toegeven: ~ *up* (to) opbiechten
[3]**own** (vb) bezitten, eigenaar zijn van
owner eigenaar
ownership 1 eigendom[h], bezit[h] **2** eigen-
dom(srecht)[h]: **land** of uncertain ~ grond met
onbekende eigenaar
ox os, rund[h]
Oxbridge Oxford en Cambridge
oxidation oxidatie
oxide oxide[h]
oxtail soup ossenstaartsoep

oxygen zuurstof[h]
oyster oester
oystercatcher scholekster
oz ounce(s) ons
ozone 1 ozon **2** frisse lucht
ozone depletion ozonafbraak

p

¹p (n) p, P ‖ *mind one's p's and q's* op zijn woorden passen
²p 1 *page* p., blz.

¹pa (n) pa
²pa *per annum* p.j., per jaar
¹pace (n) **1** pas, stap, schrede, gang **2** tempoʰ, gang, tred: *force the ~* het tempo opdrijven; *keep ~ (with)* gelijke tred houden (met) ‖ *put s.o. through his ~s* iem. uittesten, iem. laten tonen wat hij kan
²pace (vb) stappen, kuieren: *~ up and down* ijsberen
³pace (vb) (also + off, out) afstappen, afpassen, met stappen afmeten
pacemaker 1 [sport] haas **2** [med] pacemaker
pacific vreedzaam, vredelievend ‖ *the Pacific Ocean* de Grote Oceaan
pacifier [Am] fopspeen
pacifist pacifist
pacify kalmeren, de rust herstellen in
¹pack (n) **1** pakʰ, (rug)zak, last, verpakking, pakketʰ **2** pakʰ, hoop, pakʰ kaarten; [Am] pakjeʰ [cigarettes]: *~ of lies* pak leugens; *~ of nonsense* hoop onzin **3** (veldʰ van) pakijsʰ **4** kompresʰ **5** troep, bende, horde, meute; [sport] pelotonʰ [rugby]
²pack (vb) **1** (in)pakken, zijn koffer pakken **2** inpakken, zich laten inpakken ‖ *~ into* zich verdringen in; *~ up* ermee uitscheiden
³pack (vb) **1** (in)pakken, verpakken; inmaken [fruit etc]: [fig] *~ one's bags* zijn biezen pakken; *~ed lunch* lunchpakket **2** samenpakken, samenpersen: *the theatre was ~ed with people* het theater was afgeladen **3** wegsturen: *~ s.o. off* iem. (ver) wegsturen **4** bepakken, volproppen: *~ed out* propvol **5** [Am] op zak hebben [eg pistol]; bij de hand hebben ‖ *~ it in* (or: *up*) ermee ophouden
¹package (n) **1** pakketʰ, pak(jeʰ), bundel; [comp] programmapakketʰ; standaardprogrammaʰ **2** verpakking
²package (vb) **1** verpakken, inpakken **2** groeperen, ordenen
package deal 1 speciale aanbieding **2** packagedeal, koppelverkoop
package holiday pakketreis, geheel verzorgde reis
packed 1 opeengepakt: *~ (in* (or: *together*)) *like sardines* als haringen opeengepakt

2 volgepropt, overvol: *the theatre was ~ with people* het theater was afgeladen
packet 1 pak(jeʰ), stapeltjeʰ: *a ~ of cigarettes* een pakje sigaretten; *~ soup* soep uit een pakje **2** bom geld
packing 1 verpakking **2** pakking, dichtingsmiddelʰ
pact verdragʰ
¹pad (n) **1** kussen(tje)ʰ, vulkussenʰ, opvulselʰ, stootkussenʰ, onderlegger, stempelkussenʰ; [sport] beenbeschermer **2** schrijfblok, blocnote **3** (lanceer)platformʰ **4** bedʰ, verblijfʰ, huisʰ
²pad (vb) **1** draven, trippelen **2** lopen, stappen
³pad (vb) (also + out) (op)vullen: *~ded envelope* luchtkussenenveloppe
padding opvulling, (op)vulselʰ
¹paddle (n) **1** peddel, roeispaan, schoep **2** vin [eg of seal]; zwempoot ‖ *go for a ~* gaan peddelen
²paddle (vb) **1** pootje baden **2** (voort)peddelen
paddle boat rader(stoom)boot
paddling pool pierenbadʰ, kinder(zwem)badʰ
paddock kraal; omheinde weide [near stable or racecourse]
paddy woedeaanval
Paddy Ier
paddy field rijstveldʰ
padlock hangslotʰ
padre aal(moezenier)
¹pagan (n) heiden
²pagan (adj) heidens
¹page (n) **1** pagina, bladzijde **2** page, (schild)knaap
²page (vb) oproepen, oppiepen
pageant 1 vertoning, spektakelstukʰ **2** historisch schouwspelʰ
page boy 1 page **2** pagekop(je)
page break harde paginaovergang
pager pieper, semafoon
paid betaald, voldaan ‖ *put ~ to* afrekenen met, een eind maken aan
pail emmer
¹pain (n) **1** pijn, leedʰ, lijdenʰ: *be in ~* pijn hebben **2** lastpost: *he's a real ~ (in the neck)* hij is werkelijk onuitstaanbaar **3** (-s) (barens)weeën, pijnen **4** (-s) moeite, last: *be at ~s (to do sth.)* zich tot het uiterste inspannen (om iets te doen)
²pain (vb) pijn doen, leed doen
pained pijnlijk, bedroefd
painful 1 pijnlijk **2** moeilijk **3** [inform] verschrikkelijk (slecht)
painkiller pijnstiller
painstaking nauwgezet, ijverig
¹paint (n) kleurstof, verf: *wet ~!* pas geverfd!
²paint (vb) **1** verven, (be)schilderen **2** (af)-

schilderen, beschrijven, portretteren **3** (zich) verven, (zich) opmaken: ~ a **picture** of een beeld schetsen van
painter 1 (kunst)schilder, huisschilder **2** vanglijn, meertouw^h
painting 1 schilderij **2** schilderkunst, schilderwerk^h
paintwork lak, verfwerk^h; verflaag [of car etc]
^1**pair** (n) **1** paar^h, twee(tal^h): a ~ of **gloves** een paar handschoenen; the ~ of **them** allebei; in ~s twee aan twee **2** tweespan^h || ~ of **scissors** schaar; ~ of **spectacles** bril; ~ of **trousers** broek
^2**pair** (vb) paren, een paar (doen) vormen, (zich) verenigen, koppelen, huwen, in paren rangschikken: ~ **off** in paren plaatsen, koppelen; ~ **up** paren (doen) vormen [work, sport etc]
Pakistan Pakistan
^1**Pakistani** (n) Pakistaan(se)
^2**Pakistani** (adj) Pakistaans
pal makker
palace 1 paleis^h **2** het hof
palatable 1 smakelijk, eetbaar **2** aangenaam, aanvaardbaar: a ~ **solution** een bevredigende oplossing
palate 1 gehemelte^h, verhemelte^h **2** smaak, tong
palatial paleisachtig, schitterend
palaver gewauwel^h
^1**pale** (n) **1** (schutting)paal, staak **2** (omheind) gebied^h, omsloten ruimte; grenzen [also fig]
^2**pale** (adj) **1** (ziekelijk) bleek, licht-, flets: ~ **blue** lichtblauw **2** zwak, minderwaardig
^3**pale** (vb) (doen) bleek worden, (doen) verbleken
^1**Palestinian** (n) Palestijn(se)
^2**Palestinian** (adj) Palestijns
palette (schilders)palet^h
palisade 1 palissade, (paal)heining **2** (-s) (steile) kliffen
^1**pall** (n) **1** lijkkleed^h **2** [Am] doodkist **3** mantel; sluier: ~ of **smoke** rooksluier
^2**pall** (vb) vervelend worden, zijn aantrekkelijkheid verliezen: his stories began to ~ **on** us zijn verhaaltjes begonnen ons te vervelen
pall-bearer slippendrager
pallet 1 strozak **2** spatel; strijkmes^h [of potter] **3** pallet, laadbord^h, stapelbord^h
^1**palliative** (n) pijnstiller
^2**palliative** (adj) **1** verzachtend, pijnstillend **2** vergoelijkend
pallid (ziekelijk) bleek, flets **2** mat, flauw
pallor (ziekelijke) bleekheid, bleke gelaatskleur
pally vriendschappelijk, vertrouwelijk: be ~ **with** beste maatjes zijn met

palm || have (or: hold) s.o. in the ~ of one's **hand** iem. geheel in zijn macht hebben; **grease** (or: oil) s.o.'s ~ iem. omkopen
^2**palm** (vb) (in de hand) verbergen, wegpikken, achteroverdrukken
palmistry handlijnkunde, handleeskunst
palm off 1 aansmeren, aanpraten: palm sth. off **on** s.o. iem. iets aansmeren **2** afschepen, zoet houden: ~ s.o. **with** some story iem. zoet houden met een verhaaltje
palmy 1 palmachtig, vol palmbomen **2** voorspoedig, bloeiend: [fig] ~ **days** bloeitijd
palpable tastbaar, voelbaar; [fig] duidelijk
palpitation hartklopping, klopping; het bonzen [of heart]
paltry 1 waardeloos, onbetekenend: two ~ **dollars** twee armzalige dollars **2** verachtelijk, walgelijk: ~ **trick** goedkoop trucje
pal up vriendjes worden: ~ **with** s.o. goede maatjes worden met iem.
pamper (al te veel) toegeven aan, verwennen
pamphlet pamflet^h, folder, boekje^h
^1**pan** (n) pan, braadpan, koekenpan, vat^h, ketel; schaal [of scales]; toiletpot
^2**pan** (vb) **1** (goud)erts wassen **2** [film] pannen; laten meedraaien [camera]
^3**pan** (vb) **1** wassen in goudzeef **2** afkammen, (af)kraken **3** [film] pannen; doen meedraaien [camera]
panacea wondermiddel^h
Panama Panama
^1**Panamanian** (n) Panamees, Panamese
^2**Panamanian** (adj) Panamees
pancake pannenkoek, flensje^h: as **flat** as a ~ zo plat als een dubbeltje
pancreas pancreas^{+h}, alvleesklier
pandemonium 1 hel, hels spektakel^h **2** heksenketel, chaos, tumult^h
pane (venster)ruit, glasruit
panel 1 paneel^h, vlak^h, (muur)vak^h, (wand)plaat **2** (gekleurd) inzetstuk^h [of carpet] **3** controlebord^h, controlepaneel^h **4** naamlijst **5** panel^h, comité^h, jury
panelling lambrisering, paneelwerk^h
pang plotselinge pijn, steek, scheut: ~s of **remorse** hevige gewetenswroeging
^1**panic** (n) paniek: get **into** a ~ **(about)** in paniek raken (over)
^2**panic** (vb) in paniek raken (brengen), angstig worden (maken)
panic button noodknop
pannier 1 (draag)mand, (draag)korf **2** fietstas
panorama panorama^h, vergezicht^h
panoramic panoramisch
pansy 1 [bot] (driekleurig) viooltje^h **2** [inform] verwijfde man, jongen; nicht, flikker
^1**pant** (n) hijgende beweging, snak
^2**pant** (vb) **1** hijgen **2** snakken, hunkeren

3 snuiven, blazen; puffen [of steam train]
³pant (vb) hijgend uitbrengen, uitstoten: ~ *out a few words* enkele woorden uitbrengen
panther panter, luipaard, poema
panties slipje[h], (dames)broekje[h]: *a pair of ~* een (dames)slipje
pantomime 1 (panto)mime[h], gebarenspel[h] **2** (humoristische) kindermusical, sprookjesvoorstelling
pantry provisiekast, voorraadkamer
pants 1 [Am] (lange) broek: [fig] *wear the ~* de broek aanhebben; *wet one's ~* het in zijn broek doen, doodsbenauwd zijn **2** damesonderbroek, kinderbroek(je), panty's ‖ *scare s.o.'s ~ off* iem. de stuipen op het lijf jagen; *with one's ~ down* onverhoeds, met de broek op de enkels
pantyhose [Am] panty
pap 1 pap, brij, moes[h] **2** leesvoer[h]
papa papa, vader
papacy 1 pausdom[h] **2** pausschap[h]; pauselijk gezag[h]
papal 1 pauselijk, van de paus: *~ bull* pauselijke bul **2** rooms-katholiek
¹paper (n) **1** (blad[h]/vel[h]) papier[h], papiertje[h]: *on ~* op papier, in theorie **2** dagblad[h], krant(je[h]) **3** (schriftelijke) test: *set a ~* een test opgeven **4** verhandeling, voordracht: *read* (or: *deliver*) *a ~* een lezing houden **5** document[h]: *your ~s, please* uw papieren, alstublieft
²paper (vb) behangen, met papier beplakken: *~ over* a) (met papier) overplakken; b) verdoezelen
paperback paperback, pocket(boek[h])
paperclip paperclip
paper feed papierdoorvoer
paperhanger behanger
paper money papiergeld[h], bankbiljetten; cheques
paperweight presse-papier
papist pausgezinde
pappy pappie
paprika paprika(poeder)
Pap test paptest
Papua New Guinea Papoea-Nieuw-Guinea
¹Papua New Guinean (n) Papoea-Nieuw-Guinees, -Guineeër
²Papua New Guinean (adj) Papoea-Nieuw-Guinees
par 1 gelijkheid, gelijkwaardigheid: *be on* (or: *to*) *a ~ (with)* gelijk zijn (aan), op één lijn staan (met); *put (up)on a ~* gelijkstellen, op één lijn stellen **2** gemiddelde toestand: *be up to ~* zich goed voelen, voldoende zijn ‖ *~ for the course* de gebruikelijke procedure, wat je kunt verwachten
parable parabel, gelijkenis
parabola parabool
¹parachute (n) parachute
²parachute (vb) aan een parachute neerko-

men, parachuteren, aan een parachute neerlaten
¹parade (n) **1** parade, (uiterlijk) vertoon[h], show: *make a ~ of* paraderen met **2** stoet, optocht, defilé[h], modeshow **3** paradeplaats
²parade (vb) **1** paraderen, een optocht houden **2** [fig] paraderen: *old ideas parading as new ones* verouderde ideeën opgepoetst tot nieuwe **3** aantreden, parade houden
paradigm voorbeeld[h], model[h]
paradise paradijs[h]
paradox paradox, (schijnbare) tegenstrijdigheid
paraffin 1 paraffine **2** kerosine; paraffineolie
paraffin oil kerosine; paraffineolie
paragliding paragliding[h], schermvliegen[h]
paragon toonbeeld[h], voorbeeld[h], model[h]: *~ of virtue* toonbeeld van deugd
paragraph 1 paragraaf, alinea; [law] lid[h] **2** krantenbericht(je)[h]
Paraguay Paraguay
¹Paraguayan (n) Paraguayaan(se)
²Paraguayan (adj) Paraguayaans
parakeet parkiet
¹parallel (n) **1** parallel, evenwijdige lijn; [fig] gelijkenis; overeenkomst: *draw a ~ (between)* een vergelijking maken (tussen); *without (a) ~* zonder weerga **2** parallel, breedtecirkel
²parallel (adj) parallel, evenwijdig; [fig] overeenkomend; vergelijkbaar: [gymnastics] *~ bars* brug met gelijke leggers; *~ to* (or: *with*) a) parallel met, evenwijdig aan; b) vergelijkbaar met
the **Paralympics** Paralympische Spelen, Paralympics
paralyse verlammen [also fig]; lamleggen
paralysis verlamming; [fig] machteloosheid; onmacht
paramedic paramedicus
paramount opperst, voornaamst: *of ~ importance* van het grootste belang
paranoia [med] paranoia, vervolgingswaanzin, (abnormale) achterdochtigheid
paranoid paranoïde
parapet balustrade, (brug)leuning, muurtje[h]
paraphernalia uitrusting, toebehoren, accessoires: *photographic ~* fotospullen
¹paraphrase (n) omschrijving, parafrase
²paraphrase (vb) omschrijven, in eigen woorden weergeven
¹paraplegic (n) iem. die gedeeltelijk verlamd is
²paraplegic (adj) verlamd in de onderste ledematen
parasite 1 parasiet, woekerdier[h], woekerplant, woekerkruid[h] **2** klaploper, profiteur
parasol parasol, zonnescherm[h]
paratroops para(chute)troepen, parachutisten

parcel 1 pak(je^h), pakket^h, bundel **2** perceel^h, lap grond: *a ~ of land* een lap grond
parcel up inpakken
parch verdorren, uitdrogen: *~ed with thirst* uitgedroogd (van de dorst)
parchment perkament(papier)^h
¹pardon (n) **1** vergeving, pardon^h **2** kwijtschelding (van straf), gratie(verlening), amnestie: *free ~* gratie(verlening); *general ~* amnestie || *(l) beg (your) ~* neemt u mij niet kwalijk [also iron]; *~ pardon, wat zei u?*
²pardon (vb) **1** vergeven, genade schenken, een straf kwijtschelden **2** verontschuldigen: *~ me for coming too late* neemt u mij niet kwalijk dat ik te laat kom
pare 1 (af)knippen, schillen, afsnijden **2** reduceren, besnoeien: *~ down the expenses* de uitgaven beperken
parent 1 ouder, vader, moeder **2** moederdier^h, moederplant
parentage 1 ouderschap^h: *child of unknown ~* kind van onbekende ouders **2** afkomst, geboorte
parental ouderlijk, ouder-: *~ leave* ouderschapsverlof
parental leave ouderschapsverlof^h
parenthesis 1 uitweiding, tussenzin **2** ronde haak, haakje(s): *in ~* tussen (twee) haakjes [also fig]
parenthetic tussen haakjes: *~ remark* verklarende opmerking
parenthood ouderschap^h
parenting 1 het ouderschap **2** opvoeding
pariah 1 paria [member of the lowest class in India] **2** verschoppeling
parish 1 parochie, kerkelijke gemeente **2** gemeente, dorp^h, district^h
parishioner parochiaan, gemeentelid^h
¹Parisian (n) Parijzenaar, Parisienne
²Parisian (adj) Parijs, m.b.t. Parijs
parity 1 gelijkheid, gelijkwaardigheid: *~ of pay* gelijke wedde **2** overeenkomst, gelijkenis **3** pari(teit), omrekeningskoers, wisselkoers
¹park (n) **1** (natuur)park^h, domein^h, natuurreservaat^h: *national ~* nationaal park, natuurreservaat **2** parkeerplaats
²park (vb) **1** parkeren **2** (tijdelijk) plaatsen, deponeren, (achter)laten: *~ o.s.* gaan zitten
parka parka, anorak
parking het parkeren, parkeergelegenheid: *no ~* verboden te parkeren
parking lot parkeerterrein^h
parking meter parkeermeter
parkland 1 open grasland^h [full of trees] **2** parkgrond
parkway [Am] snelweg [through beautiful landscape]
parlance zegswijze, uitdrukking: *in legal ~* in rechtstaal
parley onderhandelen

parliament parlement, volksvertegenwoordiging
parliamentarian parlementslid^h
parliamentary parlementair, parlements-: *~ party* kamerfractie
parlour salon, woonkamer, zitkamer: *ice cream ~* ijssalon
parlour game gezelschapsspel^h, woordspel^h
parlous gevaarlijk, hachelijk
parochial 1 parochiaal, parochie-, gemeentelijk, dorps- **2** bekrompen, provinciaal
¹parody (n) parodie, karikatuur, nabootsing: *this trial is a ~ of justice* dit proces is een karikatuur van rechtvaardigheid
²parody (vb) imiteren, nadoen, navolgen
parole 1 erewoord^h, parool^h, woord^h **2** voorwaardelijke vrijlating, parooltijd: *on ~* voorwaardelijk vrijgelaten
paroxysm (gevoels)uitbarsting, uitval: *~ of anger* woedeaanval; *~ of laughter* hevige lachbui
parquet parket^h, parketvloer
parricide 1 vadermoordenaar, moedermoordenaar **2** vadermoord, moedermoord
¹parrot (n) papegaai [also fig]; naprater
²parrot (vb) papegaaien, napraten: *~ the teacher's explanation* als een papegaai de uitleg van de leraar opzeggen
¹parry (vb) een aanval afwenden [also fig]
²parry (vb) **1** afwenden, (af)weren: *~ a blow* een stoot afwenden **2** ontwijken, (ver)mijden: *~ a question* zich van een vraag afmaken
¹parse (vb) (zich laten) ontleden, (zich laten) analyseren: *the sentence did not ~ easily* de zin was niet makkelijk te ontleden
²parse (vb) taalkundig ontleden [word, sentence]
parsimonious spaarzaam, krenterig
parsley peterselie
parsnip pastinaak
parson predikant [in Church of England]; dominee, pastoor
parsonage pastorie
¹part (n) **1** (onder)deel^h, aflevering, gedeelte^h, stuk^h, deel^h, verzameling: *two ~s of flour* twee delen bloem **2** rol: *play a ~* een rol spelen, doen alsof **3** aandeel^h, part^h, functie: *have a ~ in* iets te maken hebben met, een rol spelen in **4** houding, gedragslijn **5** zijde, kant: *take the ~ of* de zijde kiezen van **6** (-s) streek, gebied^h, gewest^h **7** (-s) bekwaamheid, talent^h, talenten || *~ and parcel of* een essentieel onderdeel van; *in ~(s)* gedeeltelijk, ten dele; *for the most ~* meestal, in de meeste gevallen; *b)* vooral
²part (vb) van elkaar gaan, scheiden: *~ (as) friends* als vrienden uit elkaar gaan
³part (vb) **1** scheiden, (ver)delen, breken **2** scheiden, afzonderen: *he wouldn't be ~ed*

from his money hij wilde niet betalen
⁴part (adv) deels, gedeeltelijk, voor een deel
partake (+ of) deelnemen (aan), deelhebben (aan): *~ in the festivities* aan de festiviteiten deelnemen
partial 1 partijdig, bevooroordeeld **2** gedeeltelijk, deel-, partieel: *~ solar eclipse* gedeeltelijke zonsverduistering **3** (+ to) verzot (op), gesteld (op)
partiality partijdigheid, bevoorrechting
participant deelnemer
participate (+ in) deelnemen (aan), betrokken zijn (bij)
participation 1 aandeelʰ **2** participatie, deelname, medezeggenschap⁺ʰ **3** [econ] winstdeling
participle deelwoordʰ: *past ~* voltooid deelwoord; *present ~* onvoltooid deelwoord
particle 1 deeltjeʰ, partikelʰ **2** beetjeʰ, greintjeʰ
¹particular (n) **1** bijzonderheid, detailʰ: *in ~* in het bijzonder, vooral **2** (-s) feiten, (volledig) verslagʰ **3** (-s) personalia, persoonlijke gegevens
²particular (adj) **1** bijzonder, afzonderlijk, individueel: *this ~ case* dit specifieke geval **2** (+ about, over) nauwgezet (in), kieskeurig (in/op): *he's not over ~* hij neemt het niet zo nauw **3** bijzonder, uitzonderlijk: *of ~ importance* van uitzonderlijk belang; *for no ~ reason* zomaar, zonder een bepaalde reden **4** intiem, persoonlijk: *~ friend* intieme vriend
particularly (in het) bijzonder, vooral, voornamelijk: *not ~ smart* niet bepaald slim
parting scheiding [also: in hair]
partisan 1 partijganger, aanhanger **2** partizaan
¹partition (n) **1** (ver)deling, scheiding **2** scheid(ing)smuur, tussenmuur
²partition (vb) (ver)delen, indelen: *~ off* afscheiden [by means of dividing wall]
partly gedeeltelijk: *~ …, ~ …* [also] enerzijds …, anderzijds …
partner partner, huwelijkspartner, vennoot, compagnon: *silent* (or: *sleeping*) *~* stille vennoot ‖ *~ in crime* medeplichtige
partnership 1 partnerschapʰ: *enter into ~ with* met iem. in zaken gaan **2** vennootschap
partridge patrijs
part-time in deeltijd
part with 1 afstand doen van, opgeven **2** verlaten
party 1 partij, medeplichtige: *be a ~ to* deelnemen aan, medeplichtig zijn aan; *third ~* derde **2** (politieke) partij **3** gezelschapʰ, groep: *a coach ~* een busgezelschap **4** feest(je)ʰ, partijtjeʰ: *that was quite a ~,* [Am] *that was some ~* dat was me het feestje wel
party line 1 gemeenschappelijke (telefoon)lijn **2** partijlijn, partijprogrammaʰ: *follow the ~* het partijbeleid volgen

party piece vast nummerʰ [at parties etc]
party-pooper [Am; inform] spelbreker
¹pass (n) **1** passage, (berg)pas, doorgang, vaargeul **2** geslaagd examenʰ, voldoende **3** (kritische) toestand: *it* (or: *things*) *had come to such a ~ that …* het was zo ver gekomen dat … **4** pas, toegangsbewijsʰ **5** [socc] pass **6** [baseball] vrije loop **7** [tennis] passeerslag **8** [cards] pas ‖ *make a ~ at a girl* een meisje proberen te versieren
²pass (vb) **1** (verder) gaan, (door)lopen, voortgaan: *~ along* doorlopen; *~ to other matters* overgaan naar andere zaken **2** voorbijgaan, passeren, voorbijkomen, overgaan, eindigen: *~ unnoticed* niet opgemerkt worden **3** passeren, er door(heen) raken **4** circuleren; gangbaar zijn [eg of coins]; algemeen bekendstaan (als): *~ by* (or: *under*) *the name of* bekendstaan als; *~ as* (or: *for*) doorgaan voor, dienen als **5** aanvaard worden; slagen [(part of) examination]; door de beugel kunnen [eg rude language] **6** gebeuren, plaatsvinden: *come to ~* gebeuren **7** [cards] passen **8** overgemaakt worden: *the estate ~ed to the son* het landgoed werd aan de zoon overmaakt **9** [sport] passeren, een pass geven; [tennis] een passeerslag geven
³pass (vb) **1** passeren, voorbijlopen: *~ a car* een auto inhalen **2** (door)geven, overhandigen; uitgeven [money]: *could you ~ me that book, please?* kun je mij even dat boek aangeven?; *~ in* inleveren **3** slagen in: *~ an exam* voor een examen slagen **4** komen door, aanvaard worden door: *the bill ~ed the senate* het wetsvoorstel werd door de senaat bekrachtigd **5** overschrijden, te boven gaan; overtreffen [eg expectations]: *this ~es my comprehension* dit gaat mijn petje te boven **6** laten glijden, (doorheen) laten gaan: *~ one's hand across* (or: *over*) *one's forehead* met zijn hand over zijn voorhoofd strijken **7** [sport] passeren, toespelen, doorspelen **8** uiten; leveren [criticism]: *~ judgement (up)on* een oordeel vellen over **9** vermaken, overdragen **10** doorbrengen [eg time]; spenderen
passable 1 passabel, begaanbaar, doorwaadbaar **2** redelijk, tamelijk, vrij goed
passage 1 doortocht, verloopʰ **2** (rechtop) doortocht, vrije doorgang **3** passage, kanaalʰ, doorgang, (zee)reis, overtocht: *work one's ~* voor zijn overtocht aan boord werken **4** gang, corridor **5** passage; plaats [eg in book]
passageway gang, corridor
¹pass away (vb) **1** sterven, heengaan **2** voorbijgaan, eindigen: *the storm passed away* het onweer ging voorbij
²pass away (vb) verdrijven [time]
¹pass by (vb) voorbijgaan; voorbijvliegen [time]

²**pass by** (vb) over het hoofd zien, geen aandacht schenken aan: *life passes her by* het leven gaat aan haar voorbij
pass down overleveren, doorgeven
passenger 1 passagier, reiziger **2** profiteur [in group]; klaploper
passer-by (toevallige) voorbijganger
¹**passing** (n) **1** het voorbijgaan, het verdwijnen: *in* ~ terloops **2** [euph] het heengaan, dood
²**passing** (adj) **1** voorbijgaand, voorbijtrekkend **2** vluchtig, oppervlakkig, terloops
passion 1 passie, (hartstochtelijke) liefde, enthousiasme^h: *he's got a* ~ *for skiing* hij is een hartstochtelijk skiër **2** (hevige) gevoelsuitbarsting, woedeaanval
the **Passion** passie(verhaal^h)
passionate 1 hartstochtelijk, vurig: ~ *plea* vurig pleidooi **2** begerig **3** opvliegend
passive 1 passief: ~ *resistance* lijdelijk verzet; ~ *smoker* meeroker, passieve roker **2** [linguistics] passief, lijdend: *the active and* ~ *voices* de bedrijvende en lijdende vorm
passkey 1 privésleutel, huissleutel **2** loper
¹**pass off** (vb) (geleidelijk) voorbijgaan, weggaan, verlopen ‖ ~ *as* doorgaan voor
²**pass off** (vb) **1** negeren **2** uitgeven: *pass s.o. off as* (or: *for*) iem. laten doorgaan voor
¹**pass on** (vb) **1** verder lopen, doorlopen: ~ *to* overgaan tot **2** sterven, heengaan
²**pass on** (vb) doorgeven, (verder)geven: ~ *the decreased costs to the consumer* de verlaagde prijzen ten goede laten komen aan de consument; *pass it on* zegt het voort
¹**pass out** (vb) **1** flauw vallen, van zijn stokje gaan **2** promoveren [at mil academy]; zijn diploma behalen
²**pass out** (vb) verdelen, uitdelen, verspreiden
¹**pass over** (vb) sterven, heengaan
²**pass over** (vb) **1** laten voorbijgaan, overslaan: ~ *an opportunity* een kans laten schieten **2** voorbijgaan aan, over het hoofd zien **3** overhandigen, aanreiken
Passover Pascha [jewish Easter]
passport 1 paspoort^h **2** vrijgeleide^h
pass through 1 ervaren, doormaken: ~ *police training* de politieopleiding doorlopen **2** passeren, reizen door
pass up 1 laten voorbijgaan, laten schieten **2** (naar boven) aangeven
password wachtwoord^h
¹**past** (n) verleden (tijd): *in the* ~ in het verleden, vroeger
²**past** (adj) **1** voorbij(gegaan), over, gepasseerd **2** vroeger, gewezen **3** verleden: ~ *participle* voltooid deelwoord; ~ *tense* verleden tijd **4** voorbij(gegaan), geleden: *in times* ~ in vroegere tijden **5** voorbij, vorig, laatst: *for some time* ~ al enige tijd ‖ *that is all* ~ *history now* dat is nu allemaal voltooid verleden tijd

³**past** (adv) voorbij, langs: *a man rushed* ~ een man kwam voorbijstormen
⁴**past** (prep) voorbij, verder dan, later dan: *he cycled* ~ *our house* hij fietste langs ons huis; *it is* ~ *my understanding* het gaat mijn begrip te boven; *he is* ~ *it* hij is er te oud voor, hij kan het niet meer; *half* ~ *three* half vier
¹**paste** (n) **1** deeg^h [for pastry] **2** pastei, paté, puree **3** stijfsel^h, stijfselpap, plaksel^h **4** pasta, brij(achtige massa)
²**paste** (vb) **1** kleven; plakken [also comp] **2** uitsmeren **3** pasta maken van
pastel pastel^h, pastelkleur
paste up aanplakken, dichtplakken
pasteurize pasteuriseren
pastille pastille
pastime tijdverdrijf^h
pastor predikant, dominee, pastoor
pastoral 1 herders- **2** uiterst lieflijk **3** pastoraal, herderlijk: ~ *care* zielzorg, geestelijke (gezondheids)zorg
pastry 1 (korst)deeg^h **2** gebak^h, gebakjes, taart **3** gebakje^h
pastrycook pasteibakker; banketbakker
pasture weiland^h, grasland^h
¹**pat** (n) **1** klopje^h **2** stukje^h; klontje^h [butter] **3** geklop^h, getik^h ‖ ~ *on the back* (goedkeurend) (schouder)klopje; [fig] aanmoedigend woordje
²**pat** (adj) **1** passend: *a* ~ *solution* een pasklare oplossing **2** ingestudeerd, (al te) gemakkelijk
³**pat** (vb) tikken
⁴**pat** (vb) **1** tikken op, (zachtjes) kloppen op, aaien **2** (zacht) platslaan
⁵**pat** (adv) **1** paraat, gereed: *have one's answer* ~ zijn antwoord klaar hebben **2** perfect (aangeleerd), exact (juist): *have* (or: *know*) *sth. (off)* ~ iets uit het hoofd kennen
patch 1 lap(je^h), stuk (stof), ooglap, (hecht)pleister, schoonheidspleister(tje^h) **2** vlek **3** lapje^h grond, veldje^h **4** stuk(je)^h, flard: ~*es of fog* mistbanken, flarden mist ‖ *not a* ~ *on* helemaal niet te vergelijken met
patch pocket opgenaaide zak
patch up 1 (op)lappen, verstellen **2** (haastig) bijleggen [quarrel etc] **3** in elkaar flansen, aan elkaar lappen
patchwork 1 lapjeswerk^h, patchwork^h: *a* ~ *of fields* een bonte lappendeken van velden **2** lapwerk^h, knoeiwerk^h
pate kop, hersens: *bald* ~ kale knikker
¹**patent** (n) patent^h, octrooi^h: ~ *law* octrooiwet, octrooirecht; ~ *medicine* a) patentgeneesmiddel(en); b) wondermiddel
²**patent** (adj) **1** open(baar) **2** duidelijk ‖ ~ *leather* lakleer
patentee patenthouder
paternal 1 vaderlijk [also fig] **2** van vaderszijde: ~ *grandmother* grootmoeder van vaders kant

paternalism paternalisme[h]
paternity vaderschap[h]
paternity leave vaderschapsverlof[h]
path 1 pad[h], weg, paadje[h]: *beat* (or: *clear*) *a*
~ zich een weg banen [also fig] **2** baan [eg of
bullet, comet]; route; [fig] weg; pad[h]
pathetic zielig, erbarmelijk: ~ *sight* treurig
gezicht
pathfinder 1 verkenner, padvinder **2** pionier, baanbreker
pathological pathologisch; ziekelijk [also
fig]: ~ *liar* pathologische/ziekelijke leugenaar
pathos aandoenlijkheid
pathway pad[h]
patience geduld[h]: ~ *of Job* jobsgeduld; *lose
one's* ~ zijn geduld verliezen
[1]patient (n) patiënt
[2]patient (adj) geduldig, verdraagzaam
patio patio, terras[h]
patriarch patriarch; [fig] grondlegger
[1]patrician (n) patriciër, aanzienlijk burger
[2]patrician (adj) patricisch, aanzienlijk, vooraanstaand
patricide 1 vadermoordenaar **2** vadermoord
patrimony patrimonium[h], erfdeel[h]
patriot patriot
patriotic patriottisch
patriotism patriottisme[h], vaderlandsliefde
[1]patrol (n) **1** (verkennings)patrouille **2** patrouille, (inspectie)ronde: *on* ~ op patrouille
[2]patrol (vb) patrouilleren, de ronde doen
[3]patrol (vb) afpatrouilleren, de ronde doen
van
patrolman 1 wegenwachter **2** [Am] politieagent
patron 1 patroon[h]: ~ *of the arts* iem. die
kunst of kunstenaars ondersteunt **2** (vaste)
klant
patronage 1 steun, bescherming **2** klandizie, clientèle
patroness patrones, beschermheilige
patronize 1 beschermen **2** klant zijn van,
vaak bezoeken **3** uit de hoogte behandelen,
kleineren
patronizing neerbuigend
[1]patter (n) **1** jargon[h], taaltje[h]: *salesman's* ~
verkoperspraat **2** geklets[h], gekakel[h] **3** gekletter[h]; getrippel[h] [of feet]
[2]patter (vb) **1** kletsen **2** kletteren **3** trippelen
[1]pattern (n) **1** model[h], prototype[h] **2** patroon[h], dessin[h], (giet)model[h], mal, plan[h],
schema[h]: *geometric(al)* ~s geometrische figuren **3** staal[h], monster[h]
[2]pattern (vb) een patroon vormen
[3]pattern (vb) vormen, maken, modelleren: ~
after (or: *on*) modelleren naar; ~ *o.s.* *on s.o.*
iem. tot voorbeeld nemen
paucity geringheid, schaarste

paunch 1 buik(je[h]), maag **2** pens
pauper arme
[1]pause 1 (n) pauze, onderbreking, rust(punt[h]),
weifeling: ~ *to take* a breath adempauze
[2]pause (vb) **1** pauzeren, pauze houden
2 talmen, blijven hangen **3** aarzelen, nadenken over
pave bestraten [also fig]; plaveien: ~ *with
flowers* met bloemen bedekken
paved 1 bestraat, geplaveid **2** vol (van),
vergemakkelijkt (door)
pavement 1 bestrating, wegdek[h], plavei-
sel[h] **2** trottoir[h], voetpad[h], stoep **3** [Am] rijweg, straat
pavement café terrasje[h]
pavilion paviljoen[h], cricketpaviljoen[h], clubhuis[h]
[1]paw (n) **1** poot, klauw **2** [inform] hand
[2]paw (vb) **1** krabben **2** onhandig rondtasten
[3]paw (vb) **1** ruw aanpakken, betasten **2** be-
krabben
[1]pawn (n) **1** (onder)pand[h]: *at* (or: *in*) ~ ver-
pand **2** [chess] pion; [fig] marionet: *he was
only a* ~ *in their game* hij was niet meer dan
een pion in hun spel
[2]pawn (vb) verpanden, in pand geven; [fig]
op het spel zetten [life]: ~ *one's word* (or:
honour) plechtig beloven op zijn woord van
eer
pawnbroker pandjesbaas
pawnshop pandjeshuis[h], bank van lening
[1]pay (n) **1** betaling **2** loon[h], salaris[h]: *on full* ~
met behoud van salaris
[2]pay (vb) **1** betalen; [fig] boeten: *make* s.o. ~
iem. laten boeten; ~ *down* contant betalen
2 lonend zijn: *it* ~s *to be honest* eerlijk duurt
het langst
[3]pay (vb) **1** betalen, afbetalen, vergoeden: ~
cash contant betalen; ~ *over* (uit)betalen
2 belonen [fig]; vergoeden, schadeloosstellen, betaald zetten: ~ *s.o. for his loyalty* iem.
voor zijn trouw belonen **3** schenken, verlenen: ~ *attention* opletten, aandacht schenken **4** lonend zijn (voor): *it didn't* ~ *him at all*
het bracht hem niets op || ~ *as you earn* loon-
belasting
payable betaalbaar, verschuldigd: *make* ~
betaalbaar stellen [Bill of Exchange]; ~ *to* ten
gunste van
pay-as-you-go prepaid
pay back terugbetalen, vergoeden; [fig]
betaald zetten: *she paid him back his infideli-
ties* ze zette hem zijn avontuurtjes betaald
paycheck [Am] looncheque, salaris[h]
PAYE *pay as you earn* loonbelasting
payee begunstigde; ontvanger [of Bill of
Exchange etc]
payer betaler
pay for betalen (voor), de kosten betalen
van; [fig] boeten voor
paying lonend, rendabel

payload 1 betalende vracht [in ship, aeroplane] **2** nuttige last; springlading [in bomb, rocket] **3** netto lading
payment 1 (uit)betaling, honorering, loon[h], (af)betaling **2** vergoeding, beloning, (verdiende) loon[h] **3** betaalde som, bedrag[h], storting: *make monthly ~s on the car* de auto maandelijks afbetalen || *deferred ~, ~ on deferred terms* betaling in termijnen, afbetaling
payment-in-kind betaling in natura
¹pay off (vb) renderen, (de moeite) lonen
²pay off (vb) **1** betalen en ontslaan **2** (af)betalen, vereffenen, aflossen
pay-off 1 [fig] afrekening, vergelding **2** resultaat[h], inkomsten, winst **3** climax, ontknoping
payola [Am] **1** omkoperij **2** steekpenning(en)
¹pay out (vb) **1** terugbetalen, met gelijke munt betalen **2** vieren [rope, cable]
²pay out (vb) **1** uitbetalen **2** (+ on) (geld) uitgeven (voor)
pay phone munttelefoon, telefooncel
payroll 1 loonlijst **2** loonkosten
payslip loonstrookje[h]
pay station [Am] (publieke) telefooncel
pay train trein met kaartverkoop (en onbemande stations)
pay up betalen, (helemaal) afbetalen; volstorten [shares]: *paid-up capital* gestort kapitaal
PC 1 *Personal Computer* pc **2** *police constable* politieagent
PCB 1 *polychlorinated biphenyl* pcb **2** *Printed Circuit Board* printplaat
PE *physical education* gymnastiek
pea erwt: *green ~s* erwtjes || *as like as two ~s (in a pod)* (op elkaar lijkend) als twee druppels water
peace 1 vrede, periode van vrede **2** openbare orde: *keep the ~* de openbare orde handhaven **3** rust, kalmte, tevredenheid, harmonie: *~ of mind* gemoedsrust; *hold (or: keep) one's ~* zich koest houden; *make one's ~ with* zich verzoenen met || *be at ~* de eeuwige rust genieten
peaceful 1 vredig **2** vreedzaam
peacekeeping force vredesmacht
peacemaker vredestichter
peace operation vredesoperatie
¹peach (n) **1** perzik [also colour] **2** perzikboom **3** prachtexemplaar[h], prachtmeid: *a ~ of a dress* een schattig jurkje
²peach (vb) klikken, een klikspaan zijn: *~ against* (or: *on*) *an accomplice* een medeplichtige verraden
peacock (mannetjes)pauw [also fig]; dikdoener
¹peak (n) **1** piek, spits, punt[h]; [fig] hoogtepunt[h]; toppunt[h] **2** (berg)piek, (hoge) berg, top **3** klep [of hat]

²peak (vb) een piek (*or:* hoogtepunt) bereiken: *the traffic ~s at 6* om 6 uur is het spitsuur
peak hour spitsuur[h]
peak load piekbelasting
peak performance topprestatie
peaky ziekelijk
¹peal (n) **1** klokkengelui[h], klokkenspel[h], carillon[h] **2** luide klank: *~s of laughter* lachsalvo's; *a ~ of thunder* een donderslag
²peal (vb) **1** luiden **2** galmen, (doen) klinken, luid verkondigen: *~ out* weergalmen
peanut 1 pinda; [also] pindaplant **2** (-s) onbeduidend iets, kleinigheid, een schijntje
peanut butter pindakaas
pear peer
pearl 1 parel **2** paarlemoer[h] || *cast ~s before swine* paarlen voor de zwijnen werpen
peasant 1 (kleine) boer **2** plattelander **3** lomperik, (boeren)kinkel
peasantry 1 plattelandsbevolking **2** boerenstand
pea soup erwtensoep
peat turf, (laag)veen[h]
pebble kiezelsteen, grind[h]
pebble-dash grindpleister, grindsteen
¹peck (n) **1** pik (met snavel) **2** vluchtige zoen
²peck (vb) (+ at) pikken (in/naar): *~ at a)* vitten op; *b)* met lange tanden eten van
³peck (vb) **1** oppikken, wegpikken **2** vluchtig zoenen
pecker [Am; vulg] lul, pik || [inform] *keep your ~ up* kop op!
pecking order pikorde, hiërarchie: *be at the bottom of the ~* niets in te brengen hebben
peckish 1 hongerig **2** [Am] vitterig
pecs [inform] *pectorals* borstspieren
pectoral borst-: *~ cross* borstkruis; *~ fin* borstvin
peculiar 1 vreemd, eigenaardig, excentriek, raar: *I feel rather ~* ik voel me niet zo lekker **2** bijzonder: *of ~ interest* van bijzonder belang **3** (+ to) eigen (aan), typisch (voor): *a habit ~ to the Dutch* een gewoonte die Nederlanders eigen is
peculiarity 1 eigenaardigheid, bijzonderheid, merkwaardigheid **2** eigenheid, (typisch) kenmerk[h]
pecuniary [form] **1** financieel: *~ loss* geldverlies **2** [law] met geldboete
pedagogic(al) 1 opvoedkundig, pedagogisch **2** schoolmeesterachtig
pedagogy pedagogiek
¹pedal (n) pedaal[h], trapper
²pedal (vb) **1** peddelen, fietsen **2** trappen, treden
pedant 1 muggenzifter, betweter **2** boekengeleerde **3** geleerddoener
pedantic pedant, schoolmeesterachtig, frikkerig
¹peddle (vb) leuren, venten

²**peddle** (vb) **1** (uit)venten, aan de man brengen: ~ **dope** (or: **drugs**) drugs verkopen **2** verspreiden, verkondigen: ~ **gossip** roddel(praatjes) verkopen
pedestal voetstuk[h], sokkel: [fig] **knock** s.o. **off** his ~ iem. van zijn voetstuk stoten
pedestrian voetganger: ~ **crossing** voetgangersoversteekplaats; ~ **precinct** autovrij gebied
pediatrician kinderarts
pedicure pedicure
pedigree 1 stamboom, afstamming, goede komaf **2** stamboek[h] [of animals]: ~ **cattle** stamboekvee
pedlar 1 venter, straathandelaar **2** drugsdealer **3** verspreider [of gossip]
¹**pee** (n) plas, urine: **go** for (or: **have**) a ~ een plasje gaan doen
²**pee** (vb) plassen, een plas(je) doen
¹**peek** (n) (vluchtige) blik, kijkje[h]: **have** a ~ **at** een (vlugge) blik werpen op
²**peek** (vb) **1** gluren **2** (+ at) vluchtig kijken (naar)
peekaboo kiekeboe
¹**peel** (n) schil
²**peel** (vb) **1** (also + off) afpellen; afbladderen [of paint]; vervellen: **my nose** ~ed mijn neus vervelde; ~ **off** afschilferen van **2** (+ off) zich uitkleden
³**peel** (vb) schillen, pellen: ~ **off** a) lostrekken, losmaken; b) uittrekken [clothes]; ~ **the skin off** a banana de schil van een banaan afhalen
peeling (aardappel)schil
¹**peep** (n) **1** piep, tjilp(geluid[h]) **2** [child language] toeter, claxon **3** kik, woord[h], nieuws[h] **4** (vluchtige) blik, kijkje[h]: **take** a ~ **at** vluchtig bekijken
²**peep** (vb) **1** (+ at) gluren (naar), loeren (naar), (be)spieden **2** (+ at) vluchtig kijken (naar), een kijkje nemen (bij) **3** tevoorschijn komen: ~ **out** opduiken; **the flowers** are already ~ing **through** the soil de bloemen steken hun kopjes al boven de grond uit **4** piepen, tjirpen ‖ ~ing Tom voyeur, gluurder
peephole kijkgaatje[h]
¹**peer** (n) **1** gelijke, collega **2** edelman ‖ ~ **of** the **realm** edelman die lid is van het Hogerhuis
²**peer** (vb) turen, staren, spieden
peerage 1 adel, adeldom[h] **2** adelstand
peeress 1 vrouwelijke peer, edelvrouw **2** vrouw van een peer
peer group (groep van) gelijken, leeftijdgenoten, collega's
peerless weergaloos, ongeëvenaard
peer pressure groepsdruk
peeve ergeren, irriteren
peevish 1 chagrijnig, slechtgehumeurd **2** weerbarstig, dwars
¹**peg** (n) **1** pin, pen, plug **2** schroef [of string instrument] **3** (tent)haring **4** kapstok [also

fig]: **buy** clothes **off** the ~ confectiekleding kopen **5** wasknijper ‖ **take** s.o. **down** a ~ (or: two) iem. een toontje lager laten zingen
²**peg** (vb) **1** vastpennen, vastpinnen: he is hard to ~ **down** je krijgt moeilijk vat op hem **2** stabiliseren, bevriezen
¹**peg out** (vb) zijn laatste adem uitblazen, het hoekje omgaan
²**peg out** (vb) afbakenen: ~ a **claim** (een stuk land) afbakenen
¹**pejorative** (n) pejoratief, woord met ongunstige betekenis
²**pejorative** (adj) pejoratief, ongunstig
pelican pelikaan
pelican crossing oversteekplaats
pellet 1 balletje[h], bolletje[h], prop(je[h]) **2** kogeltje[h], hagelkorrel: ~s hagel
pellucid doorzichtig; helder [also fig]
¹**pelt** (n) vacht, huid, vel[h]
²**pelt** (vb) **1** (neer)kletteren, (neer)plenzen: ~ing **rain** kletterende regen; it is ~ing (down) **with** rain het regent dat het giet **2** hollen: ~ **down** a hill een heuvel afrennen
³**pelt** (vb) bekogelen, beschieten; bestoken [also fig]
pelvis bekken[h], pelvis[h]
¹**pen** (n) **1** pen, balpen, vulpen **2** hok[h], kooi, cel
²**pen** (vb) **1** op papier zetten, (neer)pennen **2** opsluiten [also fig]; afzonderen: all the sheep were ~ned **in** alle schapen zaten in de schaapskooi
penal 1 strafbaar: ~ **offence** strafbaar feit **2** zwaar, (heel) ernstig: ~ **taxes** zware belastingen **3** straf-: ~ **code** wetboek van strafrecht ‖ ~ **servitude** dwangarbeid
penalize 1 straffen **2** een achterstand geven, benadelen **3** een strafschop toekennen **4** strafbaar stellen, verbieden
penalty 1 straf, geldstraf, gevangenisstraf, (geld)boete: **on** (or: under) ~ **of** op straffe van **2** (nadelig) gevolg[h], nadeel[h], schade: **pay** the ~ **of** de gevolgen dragen van **3** handicap, achterstand, strafpunt[h] **4** strafschop
penalty area [socc] strafschopgebied[h]
penalty box [ice hockey] strafbank, strafhok(je[h])
penalty kick [socc] strafschop
penance boete(doening), straf
penchant hang, neiging, voorliefde
¹**pencil** (n) **1** potlood[h], vulpotlood[h], stift **2** (maquilleer)stift
²**pencil** (vb) **1** (met potlood) kleuren, met potlood merken: ~led **eyebrows** zwartgemaakte wenkbrauwen **2** schetsen; tekenen [also fig]
pencil sharpener puntenslijper
pendant hanger(tje[h]), oorhanger
pendent 1 (neer)hangend **2** overhangend, uitstekend
¹**pending** (adj) hangend, onbeslist, in be-

handeling: *patent* ~ octrooi aangevraagd
²**pending** (prep) in afwachting van [eg arrival]
pendulum slinger, slingerbeweging: *a clock with a* ~ een slingeruurwerk
¹**penetrate** (vb) doordringen, penetreren, binnendringen, indringen
²**penetrate** (vb) **1** doordringen, dringen door, zich boren in, (ver)vullen **2** doorgronden, penetreren **3** dringen door, zien door: *our eyes couldn't* ~ *the darkness* onze ogen konden niet door de duisternis heendringen
penetrating doordringend, scherp(zinnig); snijdend [of wind]; scherp; luid [of sound]
pen-friend penvriend(in), correspondentievriend(in)
penguin pinguïn
penicillin penicilline
peninsula schiereiland^h
penis penis
penitence 1 boete(doening) **2** berouw^h
penitent berouwvol ‖ *be* ~ boete doen
¹**penitentiary** (n) federale gevangenis
²**penitentiary** (adj) **1** straf-, boet(e)- **2** heropvoedings-, verbeterings-
penknife zak(knip)mes^h
penmanship kalligrafie, schoonschrijfkunst
pen-name schrijversnaam, pseudoniem^h
penniless 1 zonder geld, blut, platzak **2** arm, behoeftig
penny penny, stuiver, cent, duit: *it costs 30 pence* het kost 30 penny ‖ *not have* (or: *be without*) *a* ~ *to one's name* geen rooie duit bezitten; *a* ~ *for your thoughts* waar zit jij met je gedachten?; *the* ~ *has dropped* het kwartje is gevallen, ik snap 't; *spend a* ~ een kleine boodschap doen [to the toilet]; *ten a* ~ dertien in een dozijn; *in for a* ~, *in for a pound* wie A zegt, moet ook B zeggen
penny-pinching vrekkig
penny-wise op de kleintjes lettend ‖ ~ *and pound-foolish* zuinig met muntjes maar kwistig met briefjes
pension pensioen^h: *retire on a* ~ met pensioen gaan
pensioner gepensioneerde
pension off 1 pensioneren, met pensioen sturen **2** afdanken, afschaffen
pensive 1 peinzend, (diep) in gedachten **2** droefgeestig, zwaarmoedig
pentagon vijfhoek
the **Pentagon** ministerie^h van defensie van de USA
pentathlon vijfkamp
Pentecost 1 [Am] pinksterzondag, Pinksteren **2** [Judaism] pinksterfeest, Wekenfeest
penthouse dakappartement^h, penthouse^h
pent-up 1 opgesloten, ingesloten, vastzittend **2** opgekropt, onderdrukt: ~ *emotions*

opgekropte gevoelens
penultimate voorlaatst, op één na laatst
penury grote armoede, (geld)nood
peony pioen
¹**people** (n) **1** volk^h, gemeenschap, ras^h, stam: *nomadic* ~*s* nomadische volken **2** staat, natie **3** mensen, personen, volk^h, lui **4** de mensen, ze, men: ~ *say* ... men zegt ... **5** (gewone) volk^h, massa **6** huisgenoten, ouwelui, (naaste) familie
²**people** (vb) bevolken [also fig]; voorzien van (inwoners), bewonen
pep [inform] fut, vuur^h, energie
¹**pepper** (n) **1** peper [powder, plant, fruit] **2** paprika [plant, fruit]
²**pepper** (vb) **1** (in)peperen, flink kruiden: ~ *a speech with witty remarks* een toespraak doorspekken met grappige opmerkingen **2** bezaaien, bespikkelen: ~*ed with* bezaaid met **3** bekogelen; bestoken [also fig]
peppercorn peperkorrel, peperbol
peppermint pepermunt(je)^h
pepper spray pepperspray
pep up oppeppen, opkikkeren, doen opleven; pikanter maken [dish]
per 1 via, per, door **2** per, voor, elk(e): *60 km* ~ *hour* zestig km per uur
perceivable 1 waarneembaar **2** begrijpelijk
perceive 1 waarnemen, bespeuren, (be)merken **2** bemerken, beseffen
per cent procent^h, percent^h ‖ *I'm one hundred* ~ *in agreement with you* ik ben het volledig met je eens
percentage 1 percentage^h **2** procent^h, commissie(loon^h)
perceptible waarneembaar, merkbaar: *he worsened perceptibly* hij ging zienderogen achteruit
perception 1 waarneming, gewaarwording **2** voorstelling **3** (in)zicht^h, besef^h, visie: *a clear* ~ *of* een duidelijk inzicht in
perceptive 1 opmerkzaam, oplettend **2** scherp(zinnig), verstandig
¹**perch** (n) **1** stok(je^h), stang; staaf [for bird] **2** baars ‖ *knock s.o. off his* ~ iem. op zijn nummer zetten
²**perch** (vb) **1** neerstrijken; neerkomen [of birds]; plaatsnemen, zich neerzetten **2** (neer)zetten, (neer)plaatsen, (neer)leggen: *the boy was* ~*ed on the wall* de jongen zat (hoog) bovenop de muur
percolator koffiezetapparaat^h
percussion slagwerk^h, percussie, slaginstrumenten
perdition verdoemenis, hel
¹**perennial** (n) overblijvende plant
²**perennial** (adj) **1** het hele jaar durend **2** vele jaren durend, langdurig, eeuwig, blijvend: ~ *snow* eeuwige sneeuw **3** [bot] overblijvend

¹perfect (adj) **1** perfect, volmaakt, uitstekend, volledig, (ge)heel, onberispelijk: *have a ~ set of teeth* een volkomen gaaf gebit hebben; *~ly capable of* heel goed in staat om **2** zuiver, puur: *~ blue* zuiver blauw **3** [linguistics] voltooid: *~ participle* voltooid deelwoord; *~ tense* (werkwoord in de) voltooide tijd **4** volslagen, volledig, totaal: *a ~ stranger* een volslagen onbekende || *have a ~ right (to do sth.)* het volste recht hebben (om iets te doen)

²perfect (vb) **1** perfectioneren, vervolmaken **2** voltooien, beëindigen **3** verbeteren: *~ one's English* zijn Engels verbeteren

perfection 1 perfectie, volmaaktheid: *the dish was cooked to ~* het gerecht was voortreffelijk klaargemaakt **2** hoogtepuntʰ, toonbeeldʰ

perfectionist perfectionist

perfidious trouweloos, verraderlijk

perforate doorprikken: *stamps with ~d edges* postzegels met tandjes

¹perform (vb) **1** optreden, een uitvoering geven, spelen **2** presteren, werken; functioneren [of machines]: *the car ~s well* de auto loopt goed **3** presteren, het goed doen **4** doen, handelen

²perform (vb) **1** uitvoeren, volbrengen, ten uitvoer brengen: *~ miracles* wonderen doen **2** uitvoeren, opvoeren, (ver)tonen, presenteren

performance 1 voorstelling, opvoering, uitvoering, tentoonstelling: *theatrical ~* toneelopvoering **2** prestatie, succesʰ: *a peak ~* een topprestatie **3** uitvoering, volbrenging, vervulling **4** prestaties, werking: *a car's ~* de prestaties van een auto

performer 1 uitvoerder **2** artiest

performing 1 gedresseerd, afgericht **2** uitvoerend: *~ arts* uitvoerende kunsten

¹perfume (n) parfumʰ, (aangename) geur

²perfume (vb) parfumeren

perfunctory plichtmatig (handelend): *a ~ visit* een routinebezoek, een verplicht bezoekje

perhaps misschien, mogelijk(erwijs), wellicht

peril (groot) gevaarʰ, risicoʰ: *you do it at your ~* je doet het op eigen verantwoordelijkheid

perilous (levens)gevaarlijk, riskant

perimeter omtrek

¹period (n) **1** periode, tijdperkʰ, fase: *bright ~s* opklaringen **2** lestijd, les(uurʰ) **3** (menstruatie)periode, ongesteldheid: *she is having her ~* ze is ongesteld **4** puntʰ [punctuation mark]: *I won't do it, ~!* ik doe het niet, punt uit!

²period (adj) historisch, stijl-: *~ costumes* historische klederdrachten; *~ furniture* stijlmeubelen

periodical tijdschriftʰ

periodic(al) periodiek, regelmatig terugkerend, cyclisch, kring-

peripatetic rondreizend, rondzwervend, (rond)trekkend

peripheral 1 ondergeschikt, marginaal **2** perifeer, rand- [also fig]: [comp] *~ equipment* randapparatuur; *~ shops* winkels aan de rand van de stad

periphery (cirkel)omtrek, buitenkant, rand

periscope periscoop

perish 1 omkomen **2** vergaan, verteren

¹perishable (n) beperkt houdbaar (voedsel)productʰ: *~s* snel bedervende goederen

²perishable (adj) **1** kortstondig **2** (licht) bederfelijk, beperkt houdbaar

perishing beestachtig, moordend: *~ cold* beestachtige kou

perjury meineed

perk extra verdienste: *~s* extraatjes; (extra) voordeelʰ

perk up opleven, herleven, opfleuren

perky 1 levendig, opgewekt, geestdriftig **2** verwaand

perm 1 permanent **2** combinatie; selectie [football pools]

permanence 1 duurzaamheid **2** permanent iem. (iets), vast elementʰ: *is your new address a ~ or merely temporary?* is je nieuwe adres permanent of slechts tijdelijk?

permanent blijvend, duurzaam: *~ address* vast adres; *~ wave* permanent

permeate (door)dringen, (door)trekken, zich (ver)spreiden (over): *a revolt ~d the country* een opstand verspreidde zich over het land

permissible toelaatbaar

permission toestemming, vergunning, goedkeuring: *without* (or: *with*) *my ~* zonder (or: met) mijn toestemming

permissive verdraagzaam, tolerant: *the ~ society* de tolerante maatschappij

¹permit (n) **1** verlofbrief, pasjeʰ, permissiebriefjeʰ; geleidebiljetʰ [of goods] **2** (schriftelijke) vergunning, toestemming, machtiging

²permit (vb) toestaan, toelaten, veroorloven: *weather ~ting* als het weer het toelaat

pernicious 1 schadelijk, kwaadaardig **2** dodelijk, fataal

¹perpendicular (n) loodlijn, verticaal, loodrechte lijn: *be out of (the) ~* niet in het lood staan

²perpendicular (adj) loodrecht, heel steil: *~ to* loodrecht op

perpetrate plegen, begaan: *~ a crime* een misdaad plegen

perpetration het plegen, het uitvoeren

perpetual eeuwig(durend), blijvend, permanent, langdurig, onafgebroken: *~ check* eeuwig schaak

perplex 1 verwarren, van zijn stuk brengen, van streek brengen **2** ingewikkeld(er)

maken, bemoeilijken, compliceren: *a ~ing task* een hoofdbrekend karwei
perplexity 1 verbijsterend iets **2** verbijstering
perquisite 1 faciliteit, (extra/meegenomen) voordeel[h] **2** extra verdienste
persecute vervolgen, achtervolgen; [fig] kwellen; vervelen: ~ *s.o.* *with questions* iem. voortdurend lastigvallen met vragen
persecution vervolging; [fig] kwelling
perseverance volharding, doorzetting(svermogen[h])
persevere volhouden, doorzetten: ~ *at* (or: *in, with*) volharden in; ~ *in doing sth.* volharden in iets, iets doorzetten
Persian Perzisch, Iraans: ~ *cat* Perzische kat, pers
persist 1 (koppig) volhouden, (hardnekkig) doorzetten: ~ *in* (or: *with*) (koppig) volharden in, (hardnekkig) doorgaan met **2** (blijven) duren, voortduren, standhouden: *the rain will ~ all day* de regen zal de hele dag aanhouden
persistence 1 volharding, vasthoudendheid **2** hardnekkigheid
persistent 1 vasthoudend **2** voortdurend, blijvend, aanhoudend: ~ *rain* aanhoudende regen
person 1 persoon, individu[h], mens: *you are the ~ I am looking for* jij bent degene die ik zoek; *in* ~ in eigen persoon **2** persoonlijkheid, karakter[h], persoon
persona 1 persona, imago[h] **2** (personae) personage[h], rol, karakter[h]
personable knap, voorkomend
personage 1 personage[h], belangrijk persoon **2** personage[h], rol, karakter[h]
personal 1 persoonlijk, individueel: *from ~ experience* uit eigen ervaring **2** persoonlijk, vertrouwelijk, beledigend: ~ *remarks* persoonlijke opmerkingen
personality 1 persoonlijkheid, karakter[h], sterk karakter[h] **2** persoonlijkheid, bekende figuur, beroemdheid
personalize 1 verpersoonlijken **2** merken [with a sign]: ~*d stationery* postpapier voorzien van de naam of de eigenaar
personally 1 persoonlijk, in (eigen) persoon, zelf **2** voor mijn part, wat mij betreft **3** van persoon tot persoon: *speak ~ to s.o. about sth.* iets onder vier ogen met iem. bespreken
personal organizer agenda, palmtop (computer)
personification verpersoonlijking, personificatie
personify verpersoonlijken, belichamen, symboliseren
personnel 1 personeel[h], staf, werknemers: *most of the ~ work* (or: *works*) *from 9 to 6* het meeste personeel werkt van 9 tot 6 **2** perso-

nele hulpmiddelen, troepen, manschappen
perspective 1 perspectief[h] [also fig]; verhouding, dimensie **2** vergezicht[h], uitzicht[h], perspectief[h] **3** gezichtspunt[h] [also fig]; standpunt[h]: *see* (or: *look*) *at sth. in its/the right* ~ een juiste kijk op iets hebben **4** toekomstperspectief[h], vooruitzicht[h] **5** perspectief[h], perspectivisch tekenen; dieptezicht[h] [also fig]: *see* (or: *look*) *at sth. in* ~ iets relativeren, iets in het juiste perspectief zien
perspex plexiglas[h]
perspicuous doorzichtig, helder, duidelijk
perspiration transpiratie, zweet[h]
perspire transpireren, zweten
persuade overreden, overtuigen, bepraten: ~ *s.o. to do sth.* iem. tot iets overhalen; ~ *o.s. of sth.* a) zich met eigen ogen van iets overtuigen; b) zichzelf iets wijsmaken
persuasion 1 overtuiging, mening, geloof[h]: *people of different ~s* mensen met verschillende (geloofs)overtuiging **2** overtuiging(skracht), overreding(skracht)
persuasive overtuigend
pert vrijpostig, brutaal
pertain to 1 behoren tot, deel uitmaken van **2** eigen zijn aan, passend zijn voor **3** betrekking hebben op, verband houden met
pertinence [form] pertinentie, relevantie
pertinent relevant, toepasselijk: ~ *to* betrekking hebbend op
perturb in de war brengen [also fig]; van streek brengen
Peru Peru
peruse 1 doorlezen, nalezen, (grondig) doornemen **2** bestuderen, analyseren
[1]Peruvian (n) Peruaan(se)
[2]Peruvian (adj) Peruaans
pervade doordringen [also fig]; zich verspreiden in, vervullen: *the author ~s the entire book* de auteur is in het hele boek aanwezig
pervasive 1 doordringend [also fig]; diepgaand **2** alomtegenwoordig
perverse 1 pervers, verdorven, tegennatuurlijk **2** eigenzinnig, koppig, dwars
perversion 1 perversiteit, perversie **2** verdraaiing, vervorming: *a ~ of the law* een valse uitlegging van de wet; *a ~ of the truth* een verdraaiing van de waarheid
[1]pervert (n) pervers persoon [sexually]; viezerik
[2]pervert (vb) **1** verkeerd gebruiken, misbruiken: ~ *the course of justice* verhinderen dat het recht zijn loop heeft **2** verdraaien, vervormen: *his ideas had been ~ed* zijn opvattingen waren verkeerd voorgesteld **3** perverteren, corrumperen, bederven
pesky [Am; inform] verduiveld; hinderlijk, irriterend
pessimism pessimisme[h], zwartkijkerij
pessimist pessimist, zwartkijker
pessimistic pessimistisch; zwartgallig

pest 1 lastpost **2** schadelijk dier^h, schadelijke plant: ~s ongedierte^h; ~ *control* ongediertebestrijding
pest control ongediertebestrijding
pester kwellen, lastigvallen, pesten: ~ *s.o. into doing sth.* iem. door te blijven zeuren dwingen tot het doen van iets
pesticide pesticide^h, verdelgingsmiddel^h, bestrijdingsmiddel^h
pestiferous 1 schadelijk **2** verderfelijk **3** vervelend, irriterend
pestilence pest, (pest)epidemie
pestilent (dood)vervelend, irriterend
pestle stamper
¹pet (n) **1** huisdier^h, troeteldier^h **2** lieveling, favoriet
²pet (adj) **1** tam, huis-: ~ *snake* huisslang **2** favoriet, lievelings-: *politicians are my ~ aversion* (or: *hate*) aan politici heb ik een hartgrondige hekel; ~ *topic* stokpaardje
³pet (vb) vrijen: *heavy ~ting* stevige vrijpartij
petal bloemblad^h, kroonblad^h
peter out 1 afnemen, slinken **2** uitgeput raken, opraken, uitgaan, doven
petite klein en tenger, fijn; sierlijk [of woman]
¹petition (n) **1** verzoek^h, smeekbede **2** petitie, smeekschrift^h, verzoek(schrift)^h **3** verzoek(schrift)^h, aanvraag: *file a ~ for divorce* een aanvraag tot echtscheiding indienen
²petition (vb) een verzoek richten tot
petitioner 1 petitionaris, verzoeker **2** [law] eiser [in divorce]
¹petrify (vb) verstenen; tot steen worden [also fig]
²petrify (vb) **1** (doen) verstenen, tot steen maken **2** doen verstijven, verlammen: *be petrified by* (or: *with*) *terror* verstijfd zijn van schrik
petrol benzine
petroleum aardolie
petroleum jelly vaseline
petrol station tankstation^h, benzinestation^h
pet shop dierenwinkel
petticoat onderrok
pettifogging 1 muggenzifterig **2** nietig, onbelangrijk
pettish humeurig
petty 1 onbetekenend, onbelangrijk: ~ *details* onbelangrijke details **2** klein, tweederangs, ondergeschikt: *the ~ bourgeoisie* de lagere middenstand; [shipp] ~ *officer* onderofficier **3** klein, gering: ~ *larceny* gewone diefstal, kruimeldiefstal
petulant prikkelbaar, humeurig
petunia petunia
pew kerkbank
pewit kieviet
¹pewter (n) tin^h, tinnegoed^h
²pewter (adj) tinnen: ~ *mugs* tinnen kroezen

¹phantom (n) spook^h [also fig]; geest(verschijning)
²phantom (adj) **1** spook-, spookachtig, schimmig: ~ *ship* spookschip **2** schijn-, denkbeeldig: ~ *withdrawals* spookopnames
pharaoh farao
pharisee 1 een van de farizeeën **2** farizeeër, schijnheilige
pharma de farmaceutische industrie
pharmaceutical farmaceutisch: ~ *chemist* apotheker
pharmaceuticals farmaceutica, geneesmiddelen
pharmaceutics farmacie
pharmacist apotheker
pharmacy apotheek
pharyngitis keelholteontsteking
phase fase, stadium^h, tijdperk^h: *the most productive ~ in the artist's life* de meest productieve periode in het leven van de kunstenaar; *in* ~ **a)** in fase; **b)** corresponderend; *out of* ~ niet in fase
phase in geleidelijk introduceren
phase out geleidelijk uit de productie nemen, geleidelijk opheffen
PhD *Doctor of Philosophy* dr., doctor in de menswetenschappen
pheasant fazant
phenomenal 1 waarneembaar: *the ~ world* de waarneembare wereld **2** fenomenaal, schitterend: ~ *strength* uitzonderlijke kracht
phenomenon fenomeen^h, (natuur)verschijnsel^h
philanthropist mensenvriend
philatelist postzegelverzamelaar
philharmonic filharmonisch
Philippine Filipijns
the **Philippines** Filipijnen
¹philistine (n) cultuurbarbaar
²philistine (adj) acultureel
philosopher filosoof, wijsgeer
philosophical 1 filosofisch, wijsgerig **2** kalm, wijs
philosophy filosofie, levensbeschouwing, opvatting
phlegm 1 slijm^h, fluim **2** flegma^h, onverstoorbaarheid **3** onverschilligheid, apathie
phlegmatic flegmatisch, onverstoorbaar
phobia fobie, (ziekelijke) vrees
phoenix feniks
¹phone (n) telefoon: *on the ~* aan de telefoon
²phone (vb) (op)bellen: ~ *back* terugbellen; ~ *up* opbellen
phone call telefoontje^h
phone-in belprogramma^h
phonetics fonetiek
¹phoney (n) [inform] **1** onecht persoon, bedrieger **2** namaak(sel^h), nep, bedrog^h

²**phoney** (adj) vals, onecht, nep
phosphorus fosfor[h]
photo foto
photo booth pasfotoautomaat
photocopier fotokopieerapparaat[h]
photocopy fotokopie
photodegrade afbreken onder invloed van zonlicht
photogenic fotogeniek
¹**photograph** (n) foto
²**photograph** (vb) fotograferen, foto's maken, een foto nemen van
photographer fotograaf
photography fotografie
photon foton[h]
photosensitize lichtgevoelig maken
photo shoot fotosessie
¹**phrase** (n) 1 gezegde[h], uitdrukking, woordgroep, zinsdeel[h] 2 uitdrukkingswijze, bewoordingen: *a turn of* ~ een uitdrukking; *he has quite a turn of* ~ hij kan zich heel goed uitdrukken || *coin a* ~ een uitdrukking bedenken
²**phrase** (vb) uitdrukken, formuleren, onder woorden brengen
phrase book (ver)taalgids
phraseology idioom[h], woordkeus: *scientific* ~ wetenschappelijk jargon
physical 1 fysiek, natuurlijk, lichamelijk: ~ *education* lichamelijke oefening, gymnastiek; ~ *exercise* lichaamsbeweging **2** materieel **3** natuurkundig, fysisch || *a* ~ *impossibility* absolute onmogelijkheid
physician arts; geneesheer [oft as opposed to surgeon]; internist
physicist natuurkundige
physics natuurkunde
physio 1 fysiotherapeut(e) **2** fysio(therapie)
physiognomy 1 gezicht[h] **2** kenmerk[h], kenteken[h]
physiology 1 fysiologie, leer van de lichaamsfuncties van mensen en dieren **2** levensfuncties
physiotherapist fysiotherapeut(e)
physique lichaamsbouw
pi pi [also maths]
pianist pianist(e)
piano piano
pic 1 *picture* foto, plaatje[h], illustratie **2** *picture* film
¹**pick** (n) **1** pikhouweel[h] **2** keus: *take your* ~ zoek maar uit, kies maar welke je wilt; *the* ~ het beste, het puikje; *the* ~ *of the bunch* het neusje van de zalm
²**pick** (vb) **1** hakken (in), prikken; opensteken [lock]: ~ *a hole in* een gat maken in **2** peuteren in [eg teeth]; wroeten in; pulken in [nose] **3** afkluiven, kluiven op; ontdoen van [meat] || ~ *off* één voor één neerschieten
³**pick** (vb) **1** (zorgvuldig) kiezen, selecteren,

uitzoeken: ~ *one's* **words** zijn woorden zorgvuldig kiezen; ~ *and* **choose** kieskeurig zijn **2** plukken, oogsten **3** pikken [of birds] **4** met kleine hapjes eten, peuzelen (aan): ~ *at a meal* zitten te kieskauwen || ~ *over* a) de beste halen uit; **b)** doorzeuren; ~ *at a* plukken aan; **b)** vitten (*or:* hakken) op; ~ *on* vitten op
pickaxe pikhouweel[h]
¹**picket** (n) **1** paal, staak **2** post(er), een staker die werkwilligen tegenhoudt
²**picket** (vb) posten, postend bewaken: ~ *a factory* (*or:* *people*) een bedrijf (*or:* mensen) posten
picket line groep posters [at strike]
pickings 1 restjes, kliekjes, overschot[h] **2** extraatjes: *there are easy* ~ *to be made* daar valt wel wat te snaaien
pickle 1 pekel [also fig]; moeilijk parket[h], knoei: *be in a* **sorry** (*or:* *fine*) ~ zich in een moeilijk parket bevinden **2** zuur[h], azijn: *vegetables in* ~ groenten in het zuur **3** (-s) tafelzuur[h], zoetzuur[h]
pickled 1 ingelegd (in zuur/zout) **2** in de olie, lazarus
pick-me-up [inform] opkikkertje[h]
pick out 1 (uit)kiezen, eruit halen, uitpikken **2** onderscheiden, zien, ontdekken **3** doen uitkomen, afsteken
pickpocket zakkenroller
¹**pick up** (vb) vaart krijgen; aanwakkeren [of wind]
²**pick up** (vb) **1** oppakken, opnemen, oprapen: ~ *your* **feet** til je voeten op; *pick o.s. up* overeind krabbelen **2** opdoen, oplopen, oppikken: ~ *speed* vaart vermeerderen; *he picked her up in a bar* hij heeft haar in een bar opgepikt; *where did you pick that up?* waar heb je dat geleerd? **3** ontvangen; opvangen [radio or light signals] **4** ophalen, een lift geven, meenemen: *I'll pick you up at seven* ik kom je om zeven uur ophalen **5** (terug)vinden, terugkrijgen: ~ *the trail* het spoor terugvinden **6** (bereid zijn te) betalen [account] **7** draad weer opnemen, hervatten: ~ *the threads* de draad weer opvatten **8** beter worden, opknappen, er bovenop komen; [econ] opleven; aantrekken: *the weather is picking up* het weer wordt weer beter
pick-up 1 (taxi)passagier, lifter; [inform] scharreltje[h] **2** open bestelauto
pick-up truck open bestelauto
picky kieskeurig
¹**picnic** (n) picknick || *it is no* ~ het valt niet mee, het is geen pretje
²**picnic** (vb) picknicken
¹**picture** (n) **1** afbeelding, schilderij, plaat, prent, schets, foto **2** plaatje[h], iets beeldschoons **3** toonbeeld[h]: *he is the (very)* ~ *of health* hij blaakt van gezondheid **4** (speel)film: *go to the* ~*s* naar de bioscoop gaan **5** beeld[h] [on TV] || *come into the* ~ een rol

gaan spelen; *put s.o. in the* ~ iem. op de hoogte brengen
²**picture** (vb) **1** afbeelden, schilderen, beschrijven: ~ *to s.s.* zich voorstellen **2** zich voorstellen, zich inbeelden
picture gallery schilderijenkabinet^h, galerie voor schilderijen
picture postcard prentbriefkaart, ansichtkaart
picturesque schilderachtig
piddle een plasje doen || *stop piddling around* schiet toch eens op
piddling belachelijk (klein), onbenullig, te verwaarlozen
pidgin mengtaal [on basis of English]
pie 1 pastei **2** taart
¹**piebald** (n) gevlekt dier^h, bont paard^h
²**piebald** (adj) gevlekt [esp black and white]; bont
¹**piece** (n) **1** stuk^h, portie, brok^h, onderdeel^h; deel^h [also techn]; stukje^h (land), lapje^h, eindje^h, schaakstuk^h, damschijf, muntstuk^h, geldstuk^h, artikel^h, muziekstuk^h, toneelstuk^h; [mil] kanon^h; geweer^h: *five cents a* ~ vijf cent per stuk; *a good* ~ *of advice* een goede raad; ~ *of (good) luck* buitenkansje; *that is a fine* ~ *of work* dat ziet er prachtig uit; *come* (or: *go*) *(all) to* ~s (helemaal) kapot gaan, instorten, in (or: uit) elkaar vallen; *say* (or: *speak, state*) *one's* ~ zijn zegje doen, zeggen wat men te zeggen heeft; *in* ~s in stukken; *be all of a* ~ *with* ... helemaal van hetzelfde slag zijn als ..., uit hetzelfde hout gesneden zijn als ...; *of a* ~ in één stuk **2** staaltje^h, voorbeeld^h || ~ *(nasty)* ~ *of work* (gemene) vent (or: griet); *give s.o. a* ~ *of one's mind* iem. flink de waarheid zeggen; *pick up the* ~s de stukken lijmen
²**piece** (vb) samenvoegen, in elkaar zetten: ~ *together* aaneenhechten, aaneenvoegen, in elkaar zetten [story]
piecemeal stuksgewijs, geleidelijk, bij stukjes en beetjes
piecework stukwerk^h
pie chart cirkeldiagram^h, taartdiagram^h
pied bont, gevlekt || *the Pied Piper (of Hamelin)* de rattenvanger van Hameln
pier 1 pier, havenhoofd^h **2** pijler, brugpijler
pierce doordringen, doorboren: ~*d ears* gaatjes in de oren
¹**piercing** (n) piercing, gaatje^h
²**piercing** (adj) **1** doordringend; onderzoekend [also of look] **2** scherp; snijdend [wind, cold]; stekend [pain]; snerpend [sound]
piety vroomheid; trouw [to parents, relatives]
piffle [inform] nonsens, kletskoek, onzin
piffling belachelijk (klein), waardeloos, onbenullig
pig 1 varken^h, (wild) zwijn^h **2** [inform] varken^h [term of abuse]; gulzigaard, hufter **3** [Am] big **4** smeris || *be* ~*(gy) in the middle*

tussen twee vuren zitten; *bleed like a (stuck)* ~ bloeden als een rund; *buy a* ~ *in a poke* een kat in de zak kopen; *and* ~*s might fly!* ja, je kan me nog meer vertellen!; *make a* ~ *of o.s.* overdadig eten (en drinken), schranzen
pigeon 1 duif **2** kleiduif || *it is not my* ~ het zijn mijn zaken niet
¹**pigeon-hole** (n) loket^h, hokje^h, (post)vakje^h
²**pigeon-hole** (vb) **1** in een vakje leggen [document]; opbergen **2** in de ijskast stoppen, opzijleggen, op de lange baan schuiven **3** in een hokje stoppen, een etiket opplakken
piggery 1 varkensfokkerij **2** varkensstal, zwijnerij
piggy big, varkentje^h || *be* ~ *in the middle* tussen twee vuren zitten
piggyback ritje^h op de rug
piggy bank spaarvarken^h
pig-headed koppig, eigenwijs
piglet big, biggetje^h
pigment pigment^h
pigmentation 1 huidkleuring **2** kleuring
pigsty varkensstal [also fig]
pigtail (haar)vlecht, staartje^h
pike 1 piek, spies **2** snoek
¹**pile** (n) **1** (hei)paal, staak, pijler **2** stapel, hoop: ~*s of books* stapels boeken **3** hoop geld, fortuin^h: *he has made his* ~ hij is binnen **4** aambei **5** (kern)reactor **6** pool [on velvet, carpet]; pluis^h
²**pile** (vb) zich ophopen: ~ *in* binnenstromen, binnendrommen; ~ *up* zich opstapelen
³**pile** (vb) (op)stapelen, beladen || ~ *it on (thick)* overdrijven
pile driver 1 heimachine **2** harde slag [in boxing]; (harde) trap
pile-up 1 opeenstapeling, op(een)hoping **2** kettingbotsing
pilfer stelen, pikken
pilferer kruimeldief
pilgrim pelgrim
pilgrimage bedevaart, pelgrimstocht
pill 1 pil [also fig]; bittere pil: *sweeten the* ~ de pil vergulden **2** (anticonceptie)pil: *be on the* ~ aan de pil zijn **3** bal
¹**pillage** (n) **1** plundering, roof **2** buit
²**pillage** (vb) plunderen, (be)roven
pillar 1 (steun)pilaar; zuil [also fig] **2** zuil; kolom [smoke, water, air] || *driven from* ~ *to post* van het kastje naar de muur gestuurd
pillar box brievenbus [of Post Office]
pillbox 1 pillendoosje^h **2** klein rond (dames)hoedje^h **3** [mil] bunker
¹**pillory** (n) blok^h, schandpaal: *in the* ~ aan de schandpaal
²**pillory** (vb) aan de kaak stellen, hekelen
pillow (hoofd)kussen^h
pillowcase kussensloop
¹**pilot** (n) **1** loods **2** piloot, vlieger: *on automatic* ~ op de automatische piloot **3** gids,

leider
²**pilot** (vb) loodsen, (be)sturen, vliegen; (ge)leiden [also fig]: ~ a bill **through** Parliament een wetsontwerp door het parlement loodsen
pilot light 1 waakvlam(metjeʰ) **2** controlelamp(jeʰ)
pilot project proefprojectʰ
pilot scheme proefprojectʰ
pimp pooier
pimple puist(jeʰ), pukkel
¹**pin** (n) **1** speld, sierspeld, broche **2** pin, pen, stift; [techn] splitpen; bout, spie, nagel **3** kegel [bowling] **4** vlaggenstok [in a hole at golf] || I have ~s and **needles** in my arm mijn arm slaapt
²**pin** (vb) **1** (vast)spelden; vastmaken [with pin] **2** doorboren, doorsteken **3** vasthouden, knellen, drukken: ~ s.o. **down** iem. neerdrukken, iem. op de grond houden || ~ s.o. **down** on sth. iem. ergens op vastpinnen, iem. ergens aan ophangen
PIN personal identification number persoonlijk identificatienummerʰ, pincode
pinafore (kinder)schortʰ
pinball flipper(spelʰ)
pinball machine flipperkast
pincers 1 (nijp)tang: a **pair** of ~ een nijptang **2** schaar [of lobster]
¹**pinch** (n) **1** kneep **2** klem, nood(situatie): feel the ~ de nood voelen **3** snuifjeʰ, klein beetjeʰ: take sth. with a ~ of **salt** iets met een korreltje zout nemen || **at** a ~ desnoods, in geval van nood
²**pinch** (vb) **1** knijpen, dichtknijpen, knellen, klemmen: ~ed **with** anxiety door zorgen gekweld **2** verkleumen, verschrompelen: ~ed with cold verkleumd van de kou **3** jatten, pikken, achterover drukken **4** inrekenen, in de kraag grijpen **5** knellen, pijn doen: these shoes ~ my toes mijn tenen doen pijn in deze schoenen **6** krenterig zijn, gierig zijn: ~ and save (or: scrape) kromliggen
pin-cushion speldenkussenʰ
¹**pine** (n) **1** pijn(boom) **2** vurenhoutʰ, grenenhoutʰ, dennenhoutʰ
²**pine** (vb) **1** kwijnen, treuren: ~ away (from sth.) wegkwijnen (van iets) **2** (+ after) smachten (naar), verlangen, hunkeren: ~ to do sth. ernaar hunkeren iets te doen
pineapple ananas
pine cone dennenappel, pijnappel
¹**ping** (n) ping, kort tinkelend geluidʰ
²**ping** (vb) 'ping' doen [make a short jingling sound]
ping-pong pingpongʰ, tafeltennisʰ
pinhead 1 speldenkop **2** kleinigheid **3** sufferd
pin-hole speldenprik; speldengaatjeʰ
¹**pinion** (n) **1** vleugelpuntʰ **2** [techn] rondselʰ, klein(ste) tandwielʰ

²**pinion** (vb) **1** kortwieken **2** binden; vastbinden [arms]; boeien [hands]
¹**pink** (n) **1** anjelier, anjer **2** roze(rood)ʰ **3** puikjeʰ, toppuntʰ, toonbeeldʰ: in the ~ (of health) in blakende gezondheid
²**pink** (adj) **1** roze: ~ elephants witte muizen, roze olifanten [a drunk's hallucinations] **2** gematigd links **3** homoseksueel: the ~ pound koopkracht van homoseksuelen || be tickled ~ bijzonder in zijn schik zijn
pinnacle 1 pinakel, siertorentjeʰ **2** (berg)top, spits, piek; [fig] toppuntʰ
pinny schortʰ
¹**pinpoint** (n) **1** speldenpunt **2** stipjeʰ, kleinigheid, puntjeʰ
²**pinpoint** (vb) uiterst nauwkeurig aanduiden
pinstripe(d) met dunne streepjes [on material, suit]; krijtstreep
pin-striped met krijtstrepen
pint 1 pint [for liquid 0.568 litre, (Am) 0.473 litre] **2** pint, grote pils
pint-size(d) nietig, klein, minuscuul
pin-up pin-up; [Belg] prikkelpop
¹**pioneer** (n) pionier, voortrekker
²**pioneer** (vb) pionieren, pionierswerk verrichten (voor), de weg bereiden (voor)
pious 1 vroom **2** hypocriet, braaf **3** vroom, onvervulbaar, ijdel: ~ hope (or: wish) ijdele hoop, vrome wens
¹**pip** (n) **1** oogʰ [on dice etc] **2** pit [of fruit] **3** b(l)iep, tikjeʰ, toontjeʰ **4** ster [on uniform] **5** aanval van neerslachtigheid, humeurigheid: she gives me the ~ ze werkt op mijn zenuwen
²**pip** (vb) **1** neerknallen, raken **2** verslaan
¹**pipe** (n) **1** pijp, buis, leiding(buis), orgelpijp, tabakspijp: ~ of peace vredespijp **2** (-s) doedelzak(ken) || put that in your ~ and smoke it die kun je in je zak steken
²**pipe** (vb) **1** fluiten, op de doedelzak spelen **2** door buizen leiden **3** door kabelverbinding overbrengen [music, radio programme]: ~d music muziek in blik || ~ down zijn mond houden; ~ up beginnen te zingen
pipe dream droombeeldʰ, luchtkasteelʰ
pipeline 1 pijpleiding, oliepijpleiding **2** toevoerkanaalʰ, informatiebron || in the ~ onderweg, op komst
piper fluitspeler, doedelzakspeler || pay the ~ het gelag betalen
¹**piping** (n) **1** pijpleiding, buizennetʰ **2** het fluitspelen, fluitspelʰ
²**piping** (adj) schril [voice] || ~ hot kokend heet
piquant pikant, prikkelend
¹**pique** (n) gepikeerdheid, wrevel: in a fit of ~ in een kwaaie bui
²**pique** (vb) kwetsen [pride]; irriteren || ~ o.s. (up)on sth. op iets prat gaan
piracy zeeroverij; piraterij [also fig]

piranha piranha
¹pirate (n) **1** piraat [also fig]; zeerover **2** zeeroversschip^h
²pirate (vb) aan zeeroverij doen
³pirate (vb) **1** plunderen **2** plagiëren, nadrukken, illegale kopieën maken van: ~*d edition* roofdruk
pirate copy illegale kopie
Pisces [astrology] (de) Vissen
¹piss (n) [vulg] pis ‖ *take* the ~ *out of s.o.* iem. voor de gek houden; *are you taking* the ~? zit je mij nou in de maling te nemen?
²piss (vb) [vulg] (be)pissen ‖ ~ *about* (or: *around*) rotzooien; *it is* ~*ing (down)* het stortregent; ~ *off* oprotten
pissed 1 bezopen **2** kwaad: *be* ~ *off at s.o.* woest zijn op iem.
piste skipiste
pistil [bot] stamper
pistol pistool^h
piston [techn] zuiger
¹pit (n) **1** kuil, put, (kolen)mijn(schacht) **2** dierenkuil **3** kuiltje^h, putje^h **4** werkkuil; pits [at racetrack] **5** orkestbak; parterre [theatre] **6** nest^h [bed] **7** [Am] pit; steen [of fruit] **8** (the pits) (een) ramp, (een) verschrikking: *do you know that town? it's the* ~*s!* ken je die stad? erger kan niet!
²pit (vb) als tegenstander opstellen, uitspelen: ~ *one's strength against s.o.* zijn krachten met iem. meten
¹pitch (n) **1** worp: [fig] *make* a ~ *for sth.* een gooi naar iets doen **2** hoogte, intensiteit, top(punt^h); [mus] toon(hoogte): *perfect* ~ absoluut gehoor **3** [sport] (sport)terrein^h, veld^h; [cricket] grasmat **4** (slim) verkoopverhaal^h, verkooppraat(je^h) **5** standplaats, stalletje^h, stek **6** schuinte, (dak)helling **7** pek^{+h}
²pitch (vb) **1** afhellen; aflopen [of roof] **2** strompelen, slingeren ‖ ~ *in(to)* aan het werk gaan
³pitch (vb) **1** opslaan [tent, camp] **2** doen afhellen [roof]: ~*ed roof* schuin dak **3** op toon stemmen, (toon) aangeven
pitch-dark pikdonker
pitcher 1 grote (aarden) kruik; [Am] kan **2** [baseball] werper
pitchfork hooivork
piteous meelijwekkend, zielig
pitfall valkuil; [fig] valstrik
pith merg^h; het wit en de velletjes [of citrus fruit] ‖ *the* ~ *(and marrow) of the matter* de kern van de zaak
pitiful 1 zielig **2** armzalig
pitiless meedogenloos
pittance hongerloon^h: *a mere* ~ een bedroevend klein beetje
¹pity (n) **1** medelijden^h **2** betreurenswaardig feit^h: *it is a thousand pities* het is ontzettend jammer; *what* a ~! wat jammer!; *more's the* ~ jammer genoeg

²pity (vb) medelijden hebben met: *she is much to be pitied* zij is zeer te beklagen
¹pivot (n) spil, draaipunt^h; [fig] centrale figuur
²pivot (vb) om een spil draaien; [fig] draaien: ~ *(up)on* sth. om iets draaien
pivotal 1 spil-, als spil dienend **2** centraal: ~ *question* cruciale vraag
pix 1 foto's **2** film, de filmindustrie
pixelated met zichtbare pixels (*or:* beeldpuntjes)
pixie fee, elf
pizza pizza
pizzazz pit, lef^h
pl 1 *place* plaats **2** *plural* mv., meervoud
placard plakkaat^h, aanplakbiljet^h; protestbord^h [of protester]
placate tot bedaren brengen, gunstig stemmen
¹place (n) **1** plaats, ruimte: *change* ~*s with* s.o. met iem. van plaatsen verwisselen; *fall into* ~ duidelijk zijn; *lay* (or: *set*) a ~ *for s.o.* voor iem. dekken; *put* (or: *keep*) *s.o.* in his ~ iem. op zijn plaats zetten (*or:* houden); *take* ~ plaatsvinden; *take s.o.'s* ~ iemands plaats innemen; *out of* ~ misplaatst, niet passend (*or:* geschikt); *all over the* ~ overal (rondslingerend); *in the first* ~ in de eerste plaats **2** (woon)plaats, woning: *come round to my* ~ *some time* kom eens (bij mij) langs **3** gelegenheid [pub etc]: ~ *of worship* kerk, kapel, e.d. **4** passage [in book] **5** stand, rang, positie: *know one's* ~ zijn plaats kennen **6** taak, functie
²place (vb) **1** plaatsen, zetten: ~ *an order for goods* goederen bestellen **2** aanstellen, een betrekking geven **3** thuisbrengen, identificeren
placebo placebo^h, nepgeneesmiddel^h, zoethoudertje^h
placement plaatsing
placid vreedzaam, kalm
plagiarism plagiaat^h: *copy-and-paste* ~ (plagiaat door) knippen en plakken
plagiarist plagiaris, plagiator
¹plagiarize (vb) plagiaat plegen
²plagiarize (vb) plagiëren
¹plague (n) **1** plaag, teistering **2** pest: *avoid s.o. (sth.) like the* ~ iem. (iets) schuwen als de pest; *bubonic* ~ (builen)pest **3** lastpost
²plague (vb) **1** teisteren, treffen **2** (+ with) lastigvallen (met), pesten
plaice 1 schol **2** [Am] platvis
¹plaid (n) plaid
²plaid (adj) plaid-, met Schots patroon
¹plain (n) vlakte, prairie
²plain (adj) **1** duidelijk: *in* ~ *language* in duidelijke taal **2** simpel, onvermengd; puur [water, whisky etc]: ~ *flour* bloem [without baking powder] **3** ronduit, oprecht: ~ *dealing* eerlijk(heid) **4** vlak, effen **5** recht [knit-

ting stitch] **6** volslagen; totaal [nonsense]: *it's ~ foolishness* het is je reinste dwaasheid || *it was ~ sailing* all the way het liep allemaal van een leien dakje
³**plain** (adv) **1** duidelijk **2** ronduit
plain-clothes in burger(kleren)
plainly 1 ronduit: *speak ~* ronduit spreken **2** zonder meer: *it is ~ clear* het is zonder meer duidelijk
plaintiff aanklager, eiser
plaintive 1 klagend **2** treurig, triest
¹**plait** (n) vlecht
²**plait** (vb) vlechten
¹**plan** (n) **1** plan^h: *what are your ~s for tonight?* wat ga je vanavond doen? **2** plattegrond **3** ontwerp^h, opzet: *~ of action* (or: *campaign, battle*) plan de campagne **4** schema^h, ontwerp^h
²**plan** (vb) plannen maken: *he hadn't ~ned for* (or: *on*) *so many guests* hij had niet op zoveel gasten gerekend; *~ on doing sth.* er op rekenen iets te (kunnen) doen
³**plan** (vb) **1** in kaart brengen, schetsen, ontwerpen **2** plannen, van plan zijn: *he had it all ~ned out* hij had alles tot in de details geregeld
¹**plane** (n) **1** plataan^h **2** schaaf **3** vlak^h, draagvlak^h; vleugel [of aeroplane] **4** niveau^h; plan^h **5** vliegtuig^h
²**plane** (adj) vlak, plat: *~ geometry* vlakke meetkunde
³**plane** (vb) **1** glijden; zweven [of aeroplane] **2** schaven, effen maken
plane crash vliegtuigongeluk^h
planet planeet
planetarium planetarium^h
plank (zware) plank: [fig] *walk the ~* gedwongen ontslag nemen, het veld ruimen
plankton plankton^h
planner ontwerper; [urban development] planoloog
planning planning, ordening
¹**plant** (n) **1** plant, gewas^h **2** fabriek, bedrijf^h; [elec] centrale **3** machinerie, uitrusting, installatie **4** doorgestoken kaart, vals bewijsmateriaal^h
²**plant** (vb) **1** planten; poten [also fish]; aanplanten **2** (met kracht) neerzetten [feet]; plaatsen: *with one's feet ~ed (firmly) on the ground* met beide voeten (stevig) op de grond **3** zaaien **4** onderschuiven; verbergen [stolen goods]; laten opdraaien voor: *~ false evidence* vals bewijsmateriaal onderschuiven
plantain weegbree
plantation 1 beplanting, aanplant **2** plantage
planter 1 planter, plantagebezitter **2** bloembak, bloempot
plaque 1 plaat, gedenkplaat **2** vlek [on skin] **3** tandaanslag

plasma plasma^h
plasma screen plasmascherm^h
plasma TV plasma-tv
¹**plaster** (n) **1** (hecht)pleister **2** pleister(kalk) **3** gips^h: *~ of Paris* (gebrande) gips
²**plaster** (vb) **1** (be)pleisteren, bedekken: *~ make-up on one's face* zich zwaar opmaken, z'n gezicht plamuren; *~ over* (or: *up*) dichtpleisteren **2** verpletteren, inmaken
plastered [inform] lazarus
plasterer stukadoor
plastering 1 bepleistering **2** [inform; sport] verpletterende nederlaag
¹**plastic** (n) plastic^h, kunststof
²**plastic** (adj) **1** plastisch **2** plastic, synthetisch **3** kunstmatig || *~ money* plastic geld [with cheque card, credit card]; *~ surgery* plastische chirurgie
plate 1 plaat(je^h), naambordje^h, nummerbord^h, nummerplaat; [geology] plaat [large piece of the earth's crust] **2** bord^h; bordvol^h [food] **3** collecteschaal **4** zilveren (gouden) bestek^h, verzilverd bestek^h, pleet^h || *give s.o. sth. on a ~* iem. iets in de schoot werpen; *have enough on one's ~* genoeg omhanden hebben
plateau plateau^h, tafelland^h; [fig also] stilstand [in growth] || *the pink ~* het roze plafond
plateful bordvol^h
platform 1 platform^h **2** podium^h **3** balkon^h [of bus, tram] **4** perron^h **5** partijprogramma^h, politiek programma^h
platinum platina^h
platitude open deur, afgezaagde waarheid
platoon peloton^h
platter plat bord^h, platte schotel || *on a ~* op een gouden schotel
plausible 1 plausibel, aannemelijk **2** bedrieglijk overtuigend
¹**play** (n) **1** spel^h: *~ (up)on words* woordspeling; *allow full* (or: *free*) *~ to sth.* iets vrij spel laten **2** toneelstuk^h: *the ~s of Shakespeare* de stukken van Shakespeare **3** beurt, zet; [Am; esp sport] manoeuvre: *make a ~ for sth.* iets proberen te krijgen **4** actie, activiteit, beweging: *bring* (or: *call*) *into ~* erbij betrekken **5** [techn] speling || *make great ~ of* erg de nadruk leggen op, sterk benadrukken
²**play** (vb) **1** spelen: *a smile ~ed on her lips* een glimlach speelde om haar lippen; *~ hide-and-seek, ~ at soldiers* verstoppertje (or: soldaatje) spelen; *~ by ear* op het gehoor spelen; [fig] op zijn gevoel afgaan **2** werken; spuiten [fountain] **3** zich vermaken **4** aan zet zijn [chess] **5** glinsteren; flikkeren [light] || *~ about* (or: *around*) stoeien, aanklooien; *what on earth are you ~ing at?* wat heeft dit allemaal te betekenen?; *~ (up)on s.o.'s feelings* op iemands gevoelens werken

³play (vb) **1** spelen, bespelen; opvoeren [play]; draaien [gramophone record, CD]: ~ *back* a tape een band afspelen **2** richten; spuiten [water] **3** uitvoeren; uithalen [joke]: ~ *s.o. a trick* iem. een streek leveren **4** verwedden, inzetten **5** [sport] opstellen [player] ‖ ~ *s.o. along* iem. aan het lijntje houden; ~ *sth. down* iets als minder belangrijk voorstellen

playabílity speelbaarheid
play-act doen alsof, toneelspelen
playback 1 opname op tape **2** weergavetoets
playbill afficheʰ [for theatre performance]
playboy playboy
player speler
playful speels, vrolijk
playgoer schouwburgbezoeker
playground speelplaats
playgroup peuterklasjeʰ
playhouse 1 schouwburg **2** poppenhuisʰ
playing field 1 speelveldʰ, sportveldʰ **2** speelweide
playmate 1 speelkameraad **2** pin-up
¹play off (vb) de beslissingsmatch spelen
²play off (vb) uitspelen: *he played his parents off (against each other)* hij speelde zijn ouders tegen elkaar uit
play-off beslissingsmatch
play out 1 beëindigen [game; also fig]: ~ *time* op veilig spelen, geen risico's nemen **2** helemaal uitspelen **3** uitbeelden ‖ *played out* afgedaan, uitgeput
playpen box [for small children]
playtime speelkwartierʰ
play up 1 last bezorgen: *my leg is playing up again* ik heb weer last van mijn been **2** benadrukken ‖ ~ *to s.o.* iem. vleien, iem. naar de mond praten
playwright toneelschrijver
PLC *Public Limited Company* nv, naamloze vennootschap
plea 1 smeekbede **2** verweerʰ, pleidooiʰ
plea bargaining [esp Am] het bepleiten van strafvermindering in ruil voor schuldbekentenis
¹plead (vb) **1** pleiten, zich verdedigen: ~ *guilty* (or: *not guilty*) schuld bekennen (or: ontkennen) **2** smeken, dringend verzoeken: ~ *with s.o. for sth.* (or: *to do sth.*) iem. dringend verzoeken iets te doen
²plead (vb) **1** bepleiten **2** aanvoeren [as defence, apology]; zich beroepen op: ~ *ignorance* onwetendheid voorwenden
pleading pleidooiʰ; betoogʰ
pleasant 1 aangenaam: ~ *room* prettige kamer **2** aardig, sympathiek **3** mooi [weather]
pleasantry grapjeʰ, aardigheidjeʰ: *exchange pleasantries* beleefdheden uitwisselen

¹please (vb) **1** naar de zin maken, tevredenstellen **2** wensen: *do as you* ~*!* doe zoals je wilt!; ~ *yourself!* ga je gang!
²please (int) **1** alstublieft: *may I come in,* ~*?* mag ik alstublieft binnenkomen? **2** alstublieft, wees zo goed: *do come in,* ~*!* komt u toch binnen, alstublieft! **3** graag (dank u): 'A beer?' 'Yes, ~' 'Een biertje?' 'Ja, graag'
pleased tevreden, blij: *he was pleased as Punch* hij was de koning te rijk
pleasing 1 aangenaam, innemend **2** bevredigend
pleasure genoegenʰ, plezierʰ: *take great ~ in sth.* plezier hebben in iets; *with* ~ met genoegen, graag
¹pleat (n) platte plooi, vouw
²pleat (vb) plooien: ~*ed skirt* plooirok
¹plebeian (n) proleet
²plebeian (adj) proleterig, onbeschaafd
¹pledge (n) **1** pandʰ, onderpandʰ **2** plechtige belofte, gelofte
²pledge (vb) **1** verpanden, belenen **2** een toost uitbrengen op, toosten op **3** plechtig beloven, (ver)binden: ~ *allegiance to* trouw zweren aan; ~ *o.s.* zich (op erewoord) verbinden
plenary 1 volkomen, volledig: *with ~ powers* met volmacht(en) **2** plenair, voltallig: ~ *assembly* (or: *session*) plenaire vergadering (or: zitting)
plentiful overvloedig
¹plenty (n) overvloed ‖ *he has ~ going for him* alles loopt hem mee
²plenty (adj) overvloedig, genoeg
³plenty (adv) ruimschoots
pliable buigzaam, plooibaar; [fig] gedwee
pliant buigzaam, soepel; [fig] gedwee
pliers buigtang, combinatietang: *a pair of ~* een buigtang
plight (benarde) toestand: *a sorry* (or: *hopeless*) ~ een hopeloze toestand
plimsoll gymschoen, gympieʰ
¹plod (vb) ploeteren, zwoegen: ~ *away at one's work all night* de hele nacht door zwoegen
²plod (vb) afsjokken: ~ *one's way* zich voortslepen
plodding moeizaam
¹plop (n) plons, floep; plof [in water]
²plop (vb) met een plons (doen) neervallen, (laten) plonzen
³plop (adv) met een plons
¹plot (n) **1** stukʰ grond, perceelʰ **2** intrige; plot [of play, novel]; complotʰ **3** [Am] plattegrond, kaart, diagramʰ
²plot (vb) samenzweren, plannen smeden
³plot (vb) **1** in kaart brengen, intekenen; uitzetten [graph, diagram] **2** (also + out) in percelen indelen [land] **3** beramen; smeden [conspiracy]
¹plough (n) ploeg

²**plough** (vb) ploegen; [fig] ploeteren; zwoegen: ~ **through** *the snow* zich door de sneeuw heen worstelen
³**plough** (vb) (om)ploegen: ~ *one's* **way** *through sth.* zich (moeizaam) een weg banen door iets ‖ ~ **back** *profits into equipment* winsten in apparatuur (her)investeren
plow [Am] ploeg
ploy truc(je^h), list
¹**pluck** (n) **1** moed, durf, lef^h **2** het plukken [of chicken etc]
²**pluck** (vb) **1** (+ at) rukken (aan), trekken (aan) **2** tokkelen
³**pluck** (vb) **1** plukken [chicken etc; also flowers]; trekken **2** tokkelen op
plucky dapper, moedig
¹**plug** (n) **1** stop, prop, pen **2** stekker **3** pruim, pluk tabak **4** aanbeveling, reclame, spot; gunstige publiciteit [on radio, TV] ‖ *pull the* ~ *on sth.* iets niet laten doorgaan, een eind maken aan iets
²**plug** (vb) **1** (also + up) (op)vullen, dichtstoppen **2** neerknallen, neerschieten, beschieten **3** pluggen, reclame maken voor; populair maken [on radio, TV]; voortdurend draaien [gramophone records] ‖ ~ *in* aansluiten, de stekker insteken
plughole afvoer, gootsteengat^h
plum 1 pruim **2** pruimenboom **3** donkerrood^h, donkerpaars^h **4** iets heel goeds, iets begerenswaardigs, het neusje van de zalm
plumage veren(kleed^h) [of bird]
¹**plumb** (n) (loodje^h van) schietlood^h, paslood^h: *off* (or: *out*) *of* ~ niet loodrecht, niet in het lood
²**plumb** (adj) **1** loodrecht **2** [Am] uiterst: ~ *nonsense* je reinste onzin
³**plumb** (vb) **1** loden, peilen met dieplood, meten met schietlood **2** verticaal zetten, loodrecht maken **3** (trachten te) doorgronden, peilen
⁴**plumb** (adv) **1** loodrecht, precies in het lood: ~ *in the* **middle** precies in het midden **2** [Am] volkomen
plumber loodgieter, gas- en waterfitter
plumbing loodgieterswerk^h, (het aanleggen van een) systeem van afvoerbuizen
plumb line loodlijn
plumcake rozijnencake, krentencake
plume 1 pluim, (sier)veer, vederbos **2** pluim, sliert, wolkje^h: *a* ~ *of* **smoke** een rookpluim
¹**plummet** (n) (loodje^h van) loodlijn, (gewicht^h van) dieplood^h, schietlood^h
²**plummet** (vb) (also + down) pijlsnel vallen, scherp dalen, instorten, neerstorten: *prices* ~*ed* de prijzen kelderden
plummy 1 (zeer) goed, begerenswaardig: *a* ~ *job* een vet baantje **2** vol [of voice]; te vol, geaffecteerd
plump stevig [oft euph]; rond, mollig

¹**plump down** (vb) neerploffen, neervallen, neerzakken
²**plump down** (vb) (plotseling) neergooien, neerploffen, neerkwakken, laten vallen
¹**plunder** (n) **1** plundering, roof, beroving **2** buit
²**plunder** (vb) (be)stelen, (be)roven, plunderen
¹**plunge** (n) duik, sprong ‖ *take the* ~ de knoop doorhakken, de sprong wagen
²**plunge** (vb) **1** zich werpen, duiken, zich storten **2** (plotseling) neergaan, dalen, steil aflopen **3** (+ into) binnenvallen
³**plunge** (vb) werpen, (onder)dompelen, storten: *he was* ~*d into grief* hij werd door verdriet overmand
¹**plunk** (vb) neerploffen, luidruchtig (laten) vallen: ~ *down* neersmijten, neergooien
²**plunk** (adv) **1** met een plof **2** precies, juist: ~ *in the* **middle** precies in het midden
¹**plural** (n) meervoud^h, meervoudsvorm
²**plural** (adj) meervoudig, meervouds-
¹**plus** (n) **1** plus, plusteken^h **2** pluspunt^h, voordeel^h
²**plus** (adj) **1** [maths] plus, groter dan nul **2** [elec] plus, positief **3** ten minste, minimaal, meer (ouder) dan: *she has got* **beauty** ~ ze is meer dan knap; *you have to be* **twelve** ~ *for this* hier moet je twaalf of ouder voor zijn
³**plus** (prep) plus, (vermeerderd) met, en, boven nul: *he paid back the loan* ~ *interest* hij betaalde de lening terug met de rente; ~ *six (degrees centigrade)* zes graden boven nul
¹**plush** (n) pluche^h
²**plush** (adj) **1** pluchen, van pluche **2** sjiek, luxueus
plus sign plus, plusteken^h, het symbool +
¹**ply** (n) **1** [often in compounds] laag [of wood or double material]; vel^h [of thin wood]: *three-*~ *wood* triplex **2** streng, draad [of rope, wool]
²**ply** (vb) (+ between) een bepaalde route regelmatig afleggen [of bus, ship etc]; pendelen (tussen), geregeld heen en weer rijden (varen) (tussen) ‖ ~ *for* **hire** passagiers opzoeken [of taxi]
³**ply** (vb) geregeld bevaren, pendelen over
ply with (voortdurend) volstoppen met [food, drink]; (doorlopend) voorzien van ‖ *they plied the MP with questions* ze bestookten het kamerlid met vragen
plywood triplex^+h, multiplex^+h
p.m. *post meridiem* nm., 's middags
PM *Prime Minister* MP, minister-president
pneumatic pneumatisch, lucht(druk)-: ~ *drill* lucht(druk)boor
pneumonia longontsteking
po po
¹**poach** (vb) stropen, illegaal vissen (jagen): ~ *on s.o.'s preserve(s)* zich op andermans gebied begeven; [fig] aan iemands bezit (*or*: zaken/

werk) komen

²poach (vb) **1** pocheren [egg, fish] **2** stropen [game, fish] **3** [sport] afpakken [ball]

PO Box *Post Office Box* postbus

¹pocket (n) **1** zak **2** (opberg)vak^h, voorvakje^h, map **3** financiële middelen, portemonnee, inkomen^h **4** ertsader, olieader **5** klein afgesloten gebied^h; [mil] haard **6** zakformaat^h ‖ *have s.o. in one's ~* iem. volledig in zijn macht hebben; *have sth. in one's ~* ergens (bijna) in geslaagd zijn; *I was twenty dollars out of ~* ik ben twintig dollar kwijtgeraakt

²pocket (vb) **1** in zijn zak steken, in eigen zak steken **2** opstrijken; (op oneerlijke wijze) ontvangen [money]

pocketbook 1 zakboekje^h, notitieboekje^h **2** portefeuille **3** [Am] pocket(boek^h), paperback **4** [Am] (dames)handtas

pocketful zak vol [also fig]

pocket money zakgeld^h

pockmark 1 pokput **2** put, gat^h, holte

pockmarked 1 pokdalig **2** vol gaten, met kuilen of holen

pod peul(enschil), (peul)dop, huls

podgy rond, klein en dik, propperig

podium podium^h, (voor)toneel^h

poem gedicht^h, vers^h

poet dichter

poetess dichteres

poetic(al) dichterlijk, poëtisch: *poetic licence* dichterlijke vrijheid

poetry poëzie, dichtkunst

poignancy 1 scherpheid **2** ontroering, gevoeligheid

poignant 1 scherp [of taste, emotions]; schrijnend **2** aangrijpend, ontroerend, gevoelig

¹point (n) **1** punt^h, stip, plek, decimaalteken^h, komma: *in English a decimal ~ is used to indicate a fraction: 8.5* in het Engels wordt een decimaalpunt gebruikt om een breuk aan te geven: 8.5 **2** (waarderings)punt^h, cijfer^h: *be beaten on ~s* op punten verliezen **3** (puntig) uiteinde^h, (land)punt; tak [antlers]; uitsteeksel^h **4** punt^h, kwestie: *the main ~* de hoofdzaak **5** karakteristiek, eigenschap: *that's his strong ~* dat is zijn sterke kant **6** zin, bedoeling, effect^h: *get (or: see) the ~ of sth.* iets snappen **7** (kompas)streek **8** punt^h [exact location, time etc]; kern, essentie: *the ~ of the joke* de clou van de grap; *~ of view* gezichtspunt, standpunt; *come (or: get) to the ~* ter zake komen; *you have a ~ there* daar heb je gelijk in, daar zit iets in; *I always make a ~ of being in time* ik zorg er altijd voor op tijd te zijn; *I take your ~, ~ taken* ik begrijp wat je bedoelt; *that's beside the ~* dat heeft er niets mee te maken, dat staat er buiten; *on the ~ of* op het punt van; *that's (not) to the ~* dat is (niet) relevant; *up to a (certain) ~* tot op zeke-

re hoogte **9** (-s) [railways] wissel **10** contactpunt^h, stopcontact^h ‖ *in ~ of fact* **a)** in werkelijkheid; **b)** bovendien, zelfs; *stretch a ~* niet al te nauw kijken, van de regel afwijken

²point (vb) **1** (+ at, towards) gericht zijn (op), aandachtig zijn (op) **2** (+ at, to) wijzen (naar), bewijzen: *~ to sth.* ergens naar wijzen, iets suggereren, iets bewijzen

³point (vb) **1** scherp maken **2** (+ at, towards) richten (op), (aan)wijzen: *~ out a mistake* een fout aanwijzen, een fout onder de aandacht brengen **3** voegen [brickwork]

point-blank 1 van vlakbij, korte afstands-, regelrecht: *fire ~ at s.o.* van dichtbij op iem. schieten **2** rechtstreeks, (te) direct, bot: *a ~ refusal* een botte weigering

pointed 1 puntig, puntvormig **2** scherp, venijnig: *a ~ answer* een bits antwoord **3** nadrukkelijk, duidelijk, opvallend

pointer 1 wijzer [on scales etc] **2** aanwijsstok **3** aanwijzing, suggestie, advies^h **4** pointer, staande hond

pointless zinloos, onnodig, onbelangrijk

point out wijzen naar: *~ sth. to s.o.* iem. op iets attenderen **2** naar voren brengen, in het midden ter sprake brengen: *~ s.o.'s responsibilities* iem. zijn plichten voorhouden

poise evenwicht^h; [fig] zelfverzekerdheid; zelfvertrouwen^h

poised 1 evenwichtig, stabiel, verstandig **2** zwevend; [fig] in onzekerheid; balancerend: *he was ~ between life and death* hij zweefde tussen leven en dood **3** stil (in de lucht hangend) **4** klaar, gereed: *be ~ for victory* op het punt staan om te winnen

¹poison (n) vergif^h, gif^h; [fig] schadelijke invloed

²poison (vb) **1** vergiftigen **2** bederven [atmosphere, mentality]; verzieken: *their good relationship was ~ed by jealousy* hun goede verhouding werd door jaloezie verpest

¹poke (n) **1** por, prik, duw **2** vuistslag

²poke (vb) **1** (+ out, through) tevoorschijn komen, uitsteken **2** (+ about) (rond)lummelen **3** (+ about) zoeken, snuffelen, (rond)neuzen, zich bemoeien met iets

³poke (vb) **1** porren, prikken, stoten: *~ one's nose into sth.* zijn neus ergens insteken **2** (op)poken; (op)porren [fire]

¹poker (n) kachelpook, pook

²poker (n) poker^h [cards]

poker face pokergezicht^h, pokerface

poky benauwd, klein

Poland Polen

polar pool-, van de poolstreken: *~ bear* ijsbeer

polarize 1 [physics] polariseren [also fig]; in tweeën splijten **2** sturen, richten: *society today is ~d towards material prosperity* de maatschappij is tegenwoordig gericht op materiële welvaart

pole 1 pool; [fig] tegenpool **2** paal, mast, stok, vaarboom || *drive* s.o. up the ~ iem. razend maken; *be ~s apart* onverzoenlijk zijn
Pole Pool(se), iem.; van Poolse afkomst
polecat 1 bunzing [in Europe] **2** stinkdier[h]; skunk [in America]
polemic woordenstrijd, pennenstrijd, twist
pole star Poolster
pole vault polsstoksprong, het polsstok-(hoog)springen
¹police (n) politie, politiekorps[h], politieapparaat[h]
²police (vb) **1** onder politiebewaking stellen **2** controleren, toezicht uitoefenen op
police constable [form] politieman, politievrouw
police force politie, politiekorps[h]
policeman politieagent || *sleeping* ~ verkeersdrempel
police station politiebureau[h]
policy 1 beleid[h], gedragslijn, politiek **2** polis, verzekeringspolis **3** tactiek, verstand[h]
policy day heidedag, beleidsdag
policymaker beleidsmaker
polio polio, kinderverlamming
¹polish (n) **1** poetsmiddel[h] **2** glans, glimmend oppervlak[h] **3** beschaving, verfijning
²polish (vb) gaan glanzen, glanzend worden
³polish (vb) (also + up) (op)poetsen; polijsten [also fig]; bijschaven: *a ~ed performance* een perfecte voorstelling
Polish Pools
polish off wegwerken, afraffelen
polite 1 beleefd, goed gemanierd **2** verfijnd, elegant
politic diplomatiek, verstandig: *the body* ~ de staat, het staatslichaam
political 1 politiek, staatkundig: *~ prisoner* politieke gevangene **2** overheids-, rijks-, staats- **3** politiek geëngageerd: *he is not a very ~ person* hij is niet zo erg in politiek geïnteresseerd
politician (partij)politicus
politics 1 politiek **2** politieke wetenschappen, politicologie **3** politieke overtuiging
¹poll (n) **1** stemming, het stemmen: *go to the ~s* stemmen **2** aantal (uitgebrachte) stemmen, opkomst **3** opiniepeiling **4** (-s) stembureau[h]
²poll (vb) zijn stem uitbrengen
³poll (vb) **1** krijgen; behalen [(preference) vote]: *he ~ed thirty per cent of the votes* hij kreeg dertig procent van de stemmen **2** ondervragen, een opiniepeiling houden
pollard 1 geknotte boom **2** [cattle breeding] hoornloos dier[h]
pollen stuifmeel[h]
pollination bestuiving
polling booth stemhokje[h]
pollster enquêteur
poll tax personele belasting

pollute 1 vervuilen, verontreinigen **2** verderven [fig]; verpesten [atmosphere]
pollution 1 vervuiling, (milieu)verontreiniging **2** bederf[h], verderf[h]
polo [sport] polo[h]
poltergeist klopgeest
poly polytechnic school voor hoger beroepsonderwijs
polygamy veelwijverij
polygon veelhoek, polygoon
polysyllabic veellettergrepig
polytechnic [dated] hogeschool
polythene polyethyleen[h], plastic[h]: *~ bag* plastic tas
pomegranate granaatappel(boom)
pomp prachtvertoon[h], praal: *~ and circumstance* pracht en praal
pomposity gewichtigdoenerij, hoogdravendheid
pompous gewichtig, hoogdravend
ponce 1 pooier, souteneur **2** verwijfd type[h]
pond vijver
¹ponder (vb) (+ on, over) nadenken (over), piekeren (over)
²ponder (vb) overdenken, overwegen
ponderous 1 zwaar, massief, log **2** zwaar op de hand, moeizaam, langdradig
¹pong (n) stank, ruft
²pong (vb) stinken, ruften
pontiff paus
pontifical 1 pauselijk **2** [fig] autoritair, plechtig
pontoon 1 ponton, brugschip[h] **2** eenentwintig[h]
pony 1 pony, ponypaardje[h] **2** renpaard[h] **3** [Am] klein model[h]
ponytail paardenstaart
¹poo (n) [inform] poep
²poo (vb) [inform] poepen
poodle poedel(hond)
poof(ter) [inform] **1** nicht, flikker, poot **2** slappeling, zijig ventje[h]
¹pool (n) **1** poel, plas **2** (zwem)bassin[h], zwembad[h] **3** pot [at games of chance]; (gezamenlijke) inzet **4** (the pools) (voetbal)toto, voetbalpool
²pool (n) poulespel[h] [American form of billiards]
³pool (vb) samenvoegen, bij elkaar leggen; verenigen [money, ideas, means]
pool room biljartgelegenheid, biljartlokaal[h], goklokaal[h]
poop achtersteven, achterdek[h]
pooped uitgeput, vermoeid: *~ out* uitgeteld, uitgeput
poop scoop hondenpoepschepje[h]
poor 1 arm **2** slecht, schraal, matig: *~ results* slechte resultaten **3** armzalig, bedroevend: *cut a ~ figure* een armzalig figuur slaan **4** zielig, ongelukkig: *~ fellow!* arme kerel!
poorhouse armenhuis[h]

¹**poorly** (adj) niet lekker, ziek ‖ ~ *off* a) in slechte doen; b) slecht voorzien

²**poorly** (adv) **1** arm, armoedig **2** slecht, matig, onvoldoende: *think* ~ *of* geen hoge pet ophebben van

¹**pop** (n) **1** knal, plof **2** pop(muziek): *top* of the ~s (tophit) nummer één **3** pap, pa, papa **4** prik(limonade), frisdrank

²**pop** (vb) **1** knallen, klappen, ploffen **2** plotseling, onverwacht bewegen, snel komen, snel gaan: ~ *off* opstappen [also inform, in sense of dying]; ~ *open* uitpuilen [of eyes]; ~ *out* a) tevoorschijn schieten; b) uitpuilen; ~ *up* opduiken, (weer) boven water komen, omhoog komen [of illustrations, greetings cards etc] **3** (neer)schieten, (af)vuren: ~ *off* a) afschieten; b) afgeschoten worden **4** laten knallen, laten klappen **5** snel zetten, leggen, brengen, steken: *I'll just* ~ *this letter into the post* ik gooi deze brief even op de bus **6** plotseling stellen; afvuren [questions] **7** slikken, spuiten [drugs, pills]

popcorn popcorn, gepofte mais

pope paus

pop-eyed met uitpuilende ogen, met grote ogen, verbaasd

popgun speelgoedpistooltje^h

poplar populier, populierenhout^h

popper drukknoop(je^h)

poppet schatje^h

poppy papaver, klaproos

poppycock klets(praat)

Poppy Day [in Great Britain] herdenkingsdag voor de gevallenen

poppy seed maanzaad^h

popsy liefje^h, schatje^h

the **populace** (gewone) volk^h, massa

popular 1 geliefd, populair, gezien: ~ *with* geliefd bij **2** algemeen, veel verbreid **3** volks-, van, voor het volk: ~ *belief* volksgeloof; ~ *front* volksfront

popularity populariteit, geliefdheid

popularization popularisering

popularly 1 geliefd **2** algemeen, gewoon-(lijk): ~ *known* as in de wandeling bekend als

populate bevolken, bewonen: *densely* ~d dichtbevolkt

population 1 bevolking, inwoners, bewoners **2** bevolkingsdichtheid

populist populist; opportunist

pop-up pop-upscherm^h

pop-up book uitklapboek^h

pop-up menu pop-upmenu^h

pop-up toaster broodrooster^{+h}

porcelain porselein^h

porch 1 portaal^h, portiek **2** [Am] veranda

porcupine stekelvarken^h

pore porie

pore over zich verdiepen in, aandachtig bestuderen

pork varkensvlees^h

porn *pornography* porno

pornographic pornografisch

pornography porno(grafie)

porous poreus, waterdoorlatend

porpoise 1 bruinvis **2** dolfijn

porridge 1 (havermout)pap **2** bajes: *do* ~ in de bak zitten

port 1 haven, havenstad; [fig] veilige haven; toevluchtsoord^h **2** bakboord^h, links **3** port(wijn) ‖ *any* ~ *in a storm* nood breekt wet(ten)

portable 1 draagbaar **2** overdraagbaar: ~ *pension* meeneempensioen

portal (ingangs)poort, portaal^h, ingang

portent voorteken^h, voorbode ‖ *a matter of great* ~ een gewichtige zaak

porter 1 kruier, sjouwer, drager **2** portier^h

portfolio portefeuille

porthole patrijspoort

portico portiek, zuilengang

portion gedeelte^h, (aan)deel^h, portie

portion out verdelen, uitdelen

portly [mockingly] gezet, stevig

portmanteau word porte-manteauwoord^h, samentrekking

portrait portret^h, foto; schildering [also in words]

portray portretteren, (af)schilderen, beschrijven

portrayal portrettering, afbeelding, beschrijving

Portugal Portugal

¹**Portuguese** (n) Portugees, Portugese

²**Portuguese** (adj) Portugees

¹**pose** (n) houding, vertoon^h

²**pose** (vb) poseren, doen alsof, een pose aannemen: ~ *as* zich voordoen als, zich uitgeven voor

³**pose** (vb) **1** stellen, voorleggen: ~ *a question* een vraag stellen **2** vormen: ~ *a threat* (or: *problem*) een bedreiging (or: probleem) vormen

poser moeilijke vraag, lastig vraagstuk^h

¹**posh** (adj) chic, modieus

²**posh** (adv) bekakt, kakkineus: *talk* ~ bekakt

position 1 positie, plaats(ing), ligging, situatie: *be in* a ~ *to do sth.* in staat zijn iets te doen **2** positie, juiste plaats **3** standpunt^h, houding, mening: *define* one's ~ zijn standpunt bepalen **4** rang, (maatschappelijke) positie, stand **5** betrekking, baan

¹**positive** (n) **1** positief^h [of photo] **2** positief getal^h

²**positive** (adj) **1** positief **2** duidelijk, nadrukkelijk: *a* ~ *assertion* een uitspraak die niets aan duidelijkheid te wensen overlaat **3** overtuigd, absoluut zeker: *'Are you sure?'* *'Positive'* 'Weet je het zeker?' 'Absoluut' **4** echt, volslagen, compleet: *a* ~ *nuisance* een ware plaag **5** zelfbewust, (te) zelfverzekerd **6** wezenlijk, (duidelijk) waarneembaar:

a ~ *change* for the better een wezenlijke verbetering ‖ ~ *sign* plusteken
posse troep, (politie)macht; groep [with
common purpose]
possess 1 bezitten, hebben, beschikken
(over) **2** beheersen, meester zijn van, zich
meester maken van: *what could have ~ed him?*
wat kan hem toch bezield hebben?
possessed 1 bezeten, geobsedeerd: *like
one* ~ als een bezetene; ~ *with rage* buiten
zichzelf van woede **2** [form] bezittend: *be ~
of* bezitten
possession 1 bezit[h], eigendom[h], bezitting:
take ~ *of* in bezit nemen, betrekken **2** (bal)-
bezit[h] **3** bezetenheid
possessive 1 bezitterig, hebberig **2** dominerend, alle aandacht opeisend ‖ ~ *(pronoun)* bezittelijk voornaamwoord
possessor eigenaar, bezitter
possibility mogelijkheid, kans, vooruitzicht[h]: *there is no* ~ *of his coming* het is uitgesloten dat hij komt
possible 1 mogelijk, denkbaar, eventueel:
do everything ~ al het mogelijke doen; *if* ~
zo mogelijk **2** acceptabel, aanvaardbaar, redelijk
possibly 1 mogelijk, denkbaar, eventueel: *I
cannot* ~ *come* ik kan onmogelijk komen
2 misschien, mogelijk(erwijs), wellicht: *'Are
you coming too?' 'Possibly'* 'Ga jij ook mee?'
'Misschien'
possum opossum, buidelrat ‖ *play* ~ doen
alsof je slaapt
[1]post (n) **1** paal, stijl, post **2** [equestrian
sports] startpaal, finishpaal, vertrekpunt[h],
eindpunt[h] **3** (doel)paal **4** post(bestelling),
postkantoor[h], brievenbus: *by return of* ~ per
kerende post, per omgaande **5** post, (stand)-
plaats, (leger)kamp[h]: *be at one's* ~ op zijn
post zijn **6** betrekking, baan, ambt[h]
[2]post (vb) **1** (also + up) aanplakken, beplakken **2** posteren, plaatsen, uitzetten **3** (over)-
plaatsen, stationeren, aanstellen tot **4** (also
+ off) posten, op de post doen, (ver)sturen
5 op de hoogte brengen, inlichten: *keep s.o.
~ed* iem. op de hoogte houden
postage porto[+h]
postage stamp 1 postzegel **2** [inform]
iets kleins; vierkante millimeter, postzegel
postcard briefkaart, ansichtkaart
postdate postdateren, een latere datum
geven
poster affiche[h], aanplakbiljet[h], poster
poster colour plakkaatverf, gouache
posterior later, volgend: ~ *to* komend na,
volgend op, later dan
posterity nageslacht[h]
[1]postgraduate (n) afgestudeerde [contin-
ues studies at university]; masterstudent
[2]postgraduate (adj) postuniversitair, na de
universitaire opleiding komend, postdocto-

raal
posthumous postuum, (komend/verschij-
nend) na de dood
posting stationering, (over)plaatsing
post-it (note) memobriefje[h], geeltje[h]
postman postbode
postmark poststempel[h], postmerk[h]
post-mortem 1 lijkschouwing, sectie
2 nabespreking [esp to find out what went
wrong]
post office 1 postkantoor[h] **2** post, posterijen
postpaid franco, port betaald
postpone (+ until, to) uitstellen (tot), opschorten (tot)
postscript postscriptum[h]; naschrift[h] [in let-
ter]
post-traumatic posttraumatisch: ~ *stress
disorder* posttraumatisch stresssyndroom
postulate (zonder bewijs) als waar aannemen, vooronderstellen
[1]posture (n) **1** (lichaams)houding, postuur[h],
pose **2** houding, standpunt[h]
[2]posture (vb) **1** poseren, een gemaakte
houding aannemen **2** (+ as) zich uitgeven
(voor)
postwar naoorlogs
posy boeket(je)[h]
[1]pot (n) **1** pot, (nacht)po, potvormig voorwerp[h] (van aardewerk), (gemeenschappelijke) pot, gezamenlijk (gespaard) bedrag[h]
2 hoop [money]; bom **3** hasj(iesj), marihuana **4** aardewerk[h] ‖ *keep the* ~ *boiling* de kost
verdienen, het zaakje draaiende houden; *go
(all) to* ~ op de fles gaan, in de vernieling zijn
[2]pot (vb) schieten: ~ *at* (zonder mikken)
schieten op
[3]pot (vb) **1** (+ up) potten, in een bloempot
planten **2** in de zak stoten [billiard ball] **3** op
het potje zetten [child]
potato aardappel(plant): *mashed* ~*(es)*
aardappelpuree
potato crisp chips
pot-belly dikke buik, buikje[h], dikzak
potency invloed, kracht
potent 1 krachtig, sterk, effectief **2** (seksueel) potent **3** machtig, invloedrijk
potentate absoluut heerser; [fig] iem. die
zich zeer laat gelden
[1]potential (n) mogelijkheid: *he hasn't realized his full* ~ *yet* hij heeft de grens van zijn
kunnen nog niet bereikt
[2]potential (adj) potentieel, mogelijk, in
aanleg aanwezig
pothole 1 gat[h], put; kuil [in road surface]
2 grot
potion drankje[h] [medicine, magic potion,
poison]
potluck: [inform] *take* ~ eten wat de pot
schaft
pot-roast smoren, stoven, braden

practice

pot-shot schot^h op goed geluk af, schot in het wilde weg; [fig] schot in het duister

potted 1 pot-: ~ *plant* kamerplant, potplant **2** ingemaakt, in een pot bewaard **3** (erg) kort samengevat

^{1}**potter** (n) pottenbakker

^{2}**potter** (vb) **1** (+ about) rondscharrelen, rondslenteren, aanrommelen, prutsen **2** (+ away) je tijd verdoen, rondlummelen, lanterfanten

pottery 1 pottenbakkerij **2** aardewerk^h, keramiek

^{1}**potty** (n) (kinder)po, potje^h

^{2}**potty** (adj) **1** knetter, niet goed snik, dwaas: ~ *about* helemaal wég van **2** onbenullig, pietluttig

potty trained zindelijk

pouch 1 zak(je^h) **2** (zakvormige) huidplooi, buidel, wangzak: *she had ~es under her eyes* zij had wallen onder haar ogen

pouf 1 poef, zitkussen^h **2** [inform] flikker, homo

poulterer poelier

poultry gevogelte^h, pluimvee^h

^{1}**pounce** (n) het stoten [of bird of prey]; het zich plotseling (neer)storten; [fig] plotselinge aanval: *make a ~ at* (or: *on*) zich storten op

^{2}**pounce** (vb) **1** zich naar beneden storten; (op)springen [to seize sth.] **2** plotseling aanvallen; [fig] kritiek uitbrengen

pounce (up)on 1 (weg)graaien, inpikken, begerig grijpen **2** plotseling aanvallen; zich storten op [also fig]

^{1}**pound** (n) **1** pond^h [of weight, currency] **2** depot^h; [for seized goods, towed-away cars etc] asiel^h; omheinde ruimte || *have one's ~ of flesh* het volle pond krijgen

^{2}**pound** (vb) **1** hard (toe)slaan, flinke klappen uitdelen **2** (herhaaldelijk) zwaar bombarderen, een spervuur aanleggen **3** bonzen [of heart]

^{3}**pound** (vb) **1** (fijn)stampen, verpulveren **2** beuken op, stompen op

pounding 1 (ge)dreun, (ge)bons **2** [inform] afstraffing, pak^h slaag

pound note bankbiljet van één pond

pound sign 1 pondteken^h **2** [Am] hekje^h [hash]

pound sterling [form] pond sterling^h

pound symbol pondteken^h; [also] hekje^h

^{1}**pour** (vb) **1** stromen; (rijkelijk) vloeien [also fig]: *the money kept ~ing in* het geld bleef binnenstromen **2** stortregenen, gieten **3** (thee/koffie) inschenken

^{2}**pour** (vb) (uit)gieten, doen (neer)stromen

pout (de lippen) tuiten, pruilen (over)

poverty armoede, behoeftigheid

poverty-stricken straatarm

powder 1 poeder, (kool)stof **2** talkpoeder^h, gezichtspoeder^h **3** (bus)kruit^h

powdered 1 gepoederd, met poeder bedekt **2** in poedervorm (gemaakt/gedroogd): ~ *milk* melkpoeder; ~ *sugar* poedersuiker

powder keg kruitvat^h [also fig]; tijdbom, explosieve situatie

powder puff poederdonsje^h, poederkwastje^h

powder room [euph] damestoilet^h

powdery 1 poederachtig, kruimelig, brokkelig **2** (als) met poeder bedekt, gepoederd

power 1 macht, vermogen^h, mogelijkheid **2** kracht, sterkte **3** invloed, macht, controle: *come in* (or: *into*) ~ aan het bewind komen **4** (vol)macht, recht^h, bevoegdheid: ~ *of attorney* volmacht **5** invloedrijk iem. (iets), mogendheid, autoriteit: *the Great Powers* de grote mogendheden **6** (-s) (boze) macht(en), (hemelse) kracht(en) **7** (drijf)kracht, (elektrische) energie, stroom: *electric* ~ elektrische stroom **8** macht: *to the ~ (of)* tot de … macht **9** grote hoeveelheid, groot aantal^h, hoop: *it did me a ~ of good* het heeft me ontzettend goed gedaan || *a ~ behind the throne* een man achter de schermen; *more ~ to your elbow* veel geluk, succes

powerboat motorboot

power brakes rembekrachtiging

power cut stroomonderbreking, stroomuitval

powerful 1 krachtig, machtig, invloedrijk **2** effectief, met een sterke (uit)werking: *a ~ speech* een indrukwekkende toespraak

powerless machteloos, zwak

power nap hazenslaap

power point stopcontact^h

power station elektriciteitscentrale^h

power steering stuurbekrachtiging

powwow 1 indianenbijeenkomst **2** [inform] lange conferentie, rumoerige bespreking, overleg^h

pp *pianissimo* pp **2** *pages* pp., bladzijden **3** *per pro(curationem)* p.p., bij volmacht, namens

PR *public relations* pr

practicable 1 uitvoerbaar, haalbaar **2** bruikbaar; begaanbaar [of road]

^{1}**practical** (n) practicum^h, praktijkles, praktijkexamen^h

^{2}**practical** (adj) **1** praktisch, in de praktijk, handig **2** haalbaar, uitvoerbaar **3** zinnig, verstandig || *for all ~ purposes* feitelijk, alles welbeschouwd

practicality 1 praktisch aspect **2** bruikbaarheid

practically 1 bijna, praktisch, zogoed als **2** in de praktijk, praktisch gesproken

practice 1 praktijk, toepassing: *put sth. in(to)* ~ iets in praktijk brengen **2** oefening, training, ervaring: *be out of* ~ uit vorm zijn, het verleerd zijn **3** gewoonte, gebruik^h, normale gang van zaken: *make a ~ of sth.* ergens een gewoonte van maken **4** uitoefening,

beoefening, het praktiseren; praktijk [of lawyer, doctor etc]
practise 1 praktiseren, uitoefenen, beoefenen: ~ *black magic* zwarte magie bedrijven; *he* ~*s as a lawyer* hij werkt als advocaat **2** in de praktijk toepassen, uitvoeren **3** oefenen, instuderen, repeteren
practitioner beoefenaar, beroeps(kracht): *medical* ~*s* de artsen
pragmatic zakelijk, praktisch
Prague Praag
prairie prairie, grasvlakte
¹praise (n) **1** lof, het prijzen, aanbeveling **2** glorie, eer, lof ‖ ~ *be (to God)!* God zij geloofd!
²praise (vb) prijzen, vereren
praiseworthy loffelijk, prijzenswaardig
pram kinderwagen
prance 1 steigeren **2** (vrolijk) springen, huppelen, dansen: ~ *about* (or: *around*) rondspringen, rondlopen
prank streek, grap
prankster [inform] grappenmaker
prat [inform] idioot, zak, eikel
¹prattle (n) kinderpraat, gebabbelʰ
²prattle (vb) babbelen, kleppen, keuvelen
prawn (steur)garnaal
pray 1 bidden, (God) aanroepen **2** hopen, wensen: *we're* ~*ing for a peaceful day* we hopen op een rustige dag ‖ *he is past* ~*ing for* hij is niet meer te redden
prayer 1 gebedʰ, het bidden **2** (smeek)bede, verzoekʰ ‖ *he doesn't have a* ~ hij heeft geen schijn van kans
prayer book gebedenboekʰ
preach preken; [fig] een zedenpreek houden
preacher predikant
preachy preek-, moraliserend: ~ *in tone* prekerig van toon
preamble inleiding, voorwoordʰ
pre-arrange vooraf regelen, vooraf overeenkomen
precarious 1 onzeker, onbestendig: *he made a* ~ *living* hij had een ongewis inkomen **2** onveilig, gevaarlijk **3** twijfelachtig, niet op feiten gebaseerd
precaution voorzorgsmaatregel, voorzorg: *take* ~*s* voorzorgsmaatregelen treffen
precede voorgaan, vooraf (laten) gaan, de voorrang hebben: *the years preceding his marriage* de jaren voor zijn huwelijk
precedence voorrang, prioriteit, het voorgaan: *give* ~ *to* laten voorgaan, voorrang verlenen aan
precedent 1 precedentʰ, vroegere beslissing waarom men zich kan beroepen: *create* (or: *establish, set*) *a* ~ een precedent scheppen; *without* ~ zonder precedent, ongekend **2** traditie, gewoonte, gebruikʰ
preceding voorafgaand

precept 1 voorschriftʰ, principeʰ, grondregel **2** het voorschrijven
precinct 1 (-s) omsloten ruimte [around church, university]; (grond)gebiedʰ, terreinʰ **2** stadsgebiedʰ: *pedestrian* ~ voetgangersgebied; *shopping* ~ winkelcentrum **3** [Am] districtʰ
the **precincts** buurt: *the* ~ *of Bond Street* de omgeving van Bond Street
¹precious (adj) **1** kostbaar, waardevol: ~ *metals* edele metalen **2** dierbaar: *her family is very* ~ *to her* haar familie is haar zeer dierbaar **3** gekunsteld, gemaakt **4** kostbaar, waardeloos
²precious (adv) bar: *he had* ~ *little money* hij had nauwelijks een rooie cent
precipice steile rotswand, afgrond
¹precipitate (adj) overhaast, plotseling
²precipitate (vb) **1** (neer)storten [also fig]; (neer)werpen **2** versnellen, bespoedigen
precipitous 1 (vreselijk) steil **2** als een afgrond, duizelingwekkend hoog **3** overijld; plotseling
precise nauwkeurig, precies: *at the* ~ *moment that* juist op het moment dat
precisely 1 precies: *we'll arrive at 10.30* ~ we komen precies om half elf aan **2** inderdaad, juist, precies
¹precision (n) nauwkeurigheid, juistheid
²precision (adj): ~ *bombing* precisiebombardement, nauwkeurig gericht bombardement
preclude uitsluiten: ~ *from* voorkomen, verhinderen, beletten
precocious vroeg(rijp), vroeg wijs
preconceived vooraf gevormd, zich vooraf voorgesteld: *a* ~ *opinion* een vooropgezette mening
preconception vooroordeelʰ
precondition eerste vereisteʰ, allereerste voorwaarde
precook van tevoren bereiden: ~*ed potatoes* voorgekookte aardappelen
precursor voorloper, voorganger
predation 1 plundering, roof **2** [zoology] predatie
predator roofdierʰ
predatory 1 roof-: ~ *bird* roofvogel **2** plunderend: ~ *incursions* strooptochten, plundertochten **3** [depr] roofdierachtig: *a* ~ *female* een mannenverslindster
predecessor 1 voorloper, voorganger **2** voorvader
predestination voorbeschikking
predetermine vooraf bepalen, voorbeschikken: *the colour of s.o.'s eyes is* ~*d by that of his parents* de kleur van iemands ogen wordt bepaald door die van zijn ouders
predicament hachelijke situatie, kritieke toestand
predicate [linguistics] gezegdeʰ

predict voorspellen, als verwachting opgeven
predictable voorspelbaar, zonder verrassing, saai
prediction voorspelling
predilection voorliefde; voorkeur
predisposition neiging, vatbaarheid, aanleg
predominant overheersend, belangrijkst
predominantly hoofdzakelijk
predominate heersen, regeren, overheersen, de overhand hebben, beheersen
pre-eminent uitstekend, superieur
pre-empt 1 beslag leggen op, zich toe-eigenen, de plaats innemen van 2 overbodig
maken, ontkrachten
pre-emptive preventief, voorkomend
preen 1 gladstrijken [feathers] 2 (zich) opknappen, (zich) mooi maken ‖ *he ~ed himself
on his intelligence* hij ging prat op zijn intelligentie
pre-exist eerder bestaan
prefab montagewoning, geprefabriceerd
gebouw
prefabricate in onderdelen gereedmaken,
volgens systeembouw maken
¹**preface** (n) voorwoord[h], inleiding
²**preface** (vb) 1 van een voorwoord voorzien, inleiden 2 leiden tot, het begin zijn van
prefect [English educ] oudere leerling als
ordehandhaver
prefer 1 (+ to) verkiezen (boven), de voorkeur geven (aan), prefereren: *she ~s tea* **to**
coffee ze drinkt liever thee dan koffie; *he
~red to leave rather than to wait* hij wilde liever
weggaan dan nog wachten 2 promoveren,
bevorderen
preferable verkieslijk, te prefereren: *everything is ~* **to** alles is beter dan
preference voorkeur, voorliefde: *in ~ to*
liever dan
preferment bevordering, promotie
prefix voorvoegsel[h]
pregnancy zwangerschap
pregnant 1 zwanger; drachtig [of animals]
2 vindingrijk, vol ideeën 3 vruchtbaar, vol
4 veelbetekenend: *a ~ silence* een veelbete-
kenende stilte
prehistoric prehistorisch
prehistory 1 prehistorie 2 voorgeschiedenis
prejudge veroordelen [without trail or in-
terrogation]; vooraf beoordelen
¹**prejudice** (n) 1 vooroordeel[h], vooringenomenheid: *without ~* onbevooroordeeld
2 nadeel[h]
²**prejudice** (vb) 1 schaden, benadelen: *~ a
good* **cause** afbreuk doen aan een goede
zaak 2 innemen, voorinnemen
prelate kerkvorst, prelaat
prelim *preliminary examination* tentamen[h]

¹**preliminary** (n) voorbereiding, inleiding:
the preliminaries de voorronde(s)
²**preliminary** (adj) inleidend, voorbereidend
prelude 1 voorspel[h], inleiding 2 prelude;
ouverture [of opera]
premarital voorechtelijk, voordat het huwelijk gesloten is: *~ sex* seks voor het huwelijk
premature 1 te vroeg, voortijdig: *a ~ baby*
een te vroeg geboren baby; *his ~ death* zijn
vroegtijdige dood 2 voorbarig, overhaast
premeditated opzettelijk, beraamd: *~
murder* moord met voorbedachten rade
premeditation opzet
¹**premier** (n) eerste minister, minister-president, premier
²**premier** (adj) eerste, voornaamste
premiership eredivisie
premise 1 vooronderstelling 2 (-s) huis[h] (en
erf), zaak: *licensed ~s café*; *the shopkeeper
lives* **on** *the ~s* de winkelier woont in het pand
premium 1 beloning, prijs 2 (verzeke-
rings)premie 3 toeslag, extra[h], meerprijs
4 [fig] hoge waarde: *put s.o.'s work* **at** *a ~* iemands werk hoog aanslaan
premonition voorgevoel[h]
prenatal prenataal, voor de geboorte
preoccupation 1 hoofdbezigheid, (voornaamste) zorg 2 het volledig in beslag genomen zijn
preoccupied in gedachten verzonken, volledig in beslag genomen
¹**prep** (n) huiswerk[h], voorbereiding(stijd)
²**prep** (adj) voorbereidend: *~ school* voorbereidingsschool
preparation 1 voorbereiding: *make ~s* **for**
voorbereidingen treffen voor 2 preparaat[h]
3 voorbereiding(stijd), huiswerk[h], studie
¹**prepare** (vb) voorbereidingen treffen: *~* **for**
the worst zich op het ergste voorbereiden
²**prepare** (vb) 1 voorbereiden, gereedmaken, prepareren, bestuderen, instuderen
2 klaarmaken, (toe)bereiden
prepared 1 voorbereid, gereed 2 bereid:
be ~ to do sth. bereid zijn iets te doen
prepay vooruitbetalen
preponderant overwegend, overheersend, belangrijkst
preposition voorzetsel[h]
prepossess 1 inspireren 2 in beslag nemen, bezighouden 3 bevooroordeeld maken, gunstig stemmen
preposterous onredelijk, absurd
¹**preppy** (n) [Am; inform] (ex-)leerling van
voorbereidingsschool; kakmeisje[h]
²**preppy** (adj) bekakt
prerequisite eerste vereiste[h]: *a ~ of* (or: *for,
to*) een noodzakelijke voorwaarde voor
¹**prerogative** (n) voorrecht[h]
²**prerogative** (adj) bevoorrecht

¹**Presbyterian** (n) presbyteriaan
²**Presbyterian** (adj) presbyteriaans
presbytery 1 priesterkoor^h **2** (gebied bestuurd door) raad van ouderlingen [Presbyterian Church] **3** pastorie
pre-schooler peuter, kleuter, (nog) niet schoolgaand kind^h
prescience 1 voorkennis **2** vooruitziendheid
¹**prescribe** (vb) **1** voorschriften geven, richtlijnen geven **2** (+ for) een advies geven (over), een remedie voorschrijven (tegen)
²**prescribe** (vb) **1** voorschrijven, opleggen, bevelen **2** aanbevelen: ~ a recipe for (or: to) s.o. iem. een recept voorschrijven
prescription 1 voorschrift^h [also fig] **2** recept^h, geneesmiddel^h
presence 1 aanwezigheid, tegenwoordigheid: ~ of mind tegenwoordigheid van geest **2** nabijheid, omgeving: in the ~ of in tegenwoordigheid van **3** presentie, (indrukwekkende) verschijning, bovennatuurlijk iem. (iets) **4** persoonlijkheid
¹**present** (n) **1** geschenk^h, cadeau^h, gift **2** het heden: at ~ op dit ogenblik, tegenwoordig; for the ~ voorlopig
²**present** (adj) **1** onderhavig, in kwestie: in the ~ case in dit geval **2** huidig, tegenwoordig **3** [linguistics] tegenwoordig: ~ participle onvoltooid deelwoord; ~ tense tegenwoordige tijd **4** tegenwoordig, aanwezig
³**present** (vb) **1** voorstellen, introduceren, voordragen **2** opvoeren, vertonen: ~ a show een show presenteren **3** (ver)tonen: ~ no difficulties geen problemen bieden **4** aanbieden, schenken, uitreiken: ~ s.o. with a prize iem. een prijs uitreiken **5** presenteren: ~ arms! presenteer geweer!
presentable toonbaar, fatsoenlijk
presentation 1 voorstelling **2** schenking, gift, geschenk^h: make a ~ of aanbieden
present-day huidig, modern, gangbaar
presenter presentator
presentiment (angstig) voorgevoel^h
presently 1 dadelijk, binnenkort **2** [Am] nu, op dit ogenblik
preservation 1 behoud^h, bewaring **2** staat
preservationist milieubeschermer, natuurbeschermer
preservative 1 bewaarmiddel^h, conserveringsmiddel^h **2** voorbehoedmiddel^h
¹**preserve** (n) **1** jam **2** (natuur)reservaat^h, wildpark^h ‖ poach on another's ~ in iemands vaarwater zitten
²**preserve** (vb) **1** bewaren; levend houden [for future generations]: only two copies have been ~d slechts twee exemplaren zijn bewaard gebleven **2** behouden, in stand houden: well ~d goed geconserveerd **3** inmaken: ~d fruits gekonfijt fruit **4** in leven houden, redden

pre-set vooraf instellen, afstellen
preside 1 als voorzitter optreden **2** (+ over) de leiding hebben (van)
presidency presidentschap^h, presidentstermijn
president 1 voorzitter **2** president **3** [Am] leidinggevende, directeur
presidential presidentieel: ~ year jaar met presidentsverkiezingen
¹**press** (n) **1** pers, het drukken, journalisten: freedom (or: liberty) of the ~ persvrijheid; get a good ~ een goede pers krijgen **2** drukpers: at (or: in) (the) ~ ter perse **3** drukkerij **4** pers(toestel^h) **5** menigte, gedrang^h
²**press** (vb) **1** druk uitoefenen: ~ ahead with onverbiddelijk doorgaan met **2** persen, strijken **3** dringen, haast hebben: time ~es de tijd dringt **4** zich verdringen
³**press** (vb) **1** drukken, duwen, klemmen **2** platdrukken **3** bestoken [also fig]; op de hielen zitten: ~ s.o. hard iem. het vuur na aan de schenen leggen **4** druk uitoefenen op, aanzetten: ~ for an answer aandringen op een antwoord; be ~ed for money (or: time) in geldnood (or: tijdnood) zitten **5** persen, strijken ‖ [law] ~ charges een aanklacht indienen; ~ home one's point of view zijn zienswijze doordrijven
Press uitgeverij
press agency persbureau^h
press baron [inform] krantenmagnaat
press cutting krantenknipsel^h
press gallery perstribune
pressie cadeau(tje)^h, geschenk^h
pressing 1 dringend, urgent **2** (aan)dringend, opdringerig
pressman journalist
press release persbericht^h
press-stud drukknoopje^h
¹**pressure** (n) **1** druk, gewicht^h: the ~ of taxation de belastingdruk **2** stress, spanning: work under ~ werken onder druk **3** dwang: a promise made under ~ een afgedwongen belofte
²**pressure** (vb) onder druk zetten
pressure cooker snelkookpan
pressure group pressiegroep; lobby
pressurize 1 onder druk zetten [also fig] **2** de (lucht)druk regelen van: ~d cabin drukcabine
prestige prestige^h, aanzien^h
prestigious gerenommeerd; prestigieus
presto presto, onmiddellijk: hey ~! hocus pocus pas!
presumable aannemelijk, vermoedelijk
¹**presume** (vb) zich vrijheden veroorloven
²**presume** (vb) **1** zich veroorloven, de vrijheid nemen **2** veronderstellen, vermoeden, aannemen
presume (up)on misbruik maken van: presume (up)on s.o.'s kindness misbruik maken

van iemands vriendelijkheid
presumption 1 (redelijke) veronderstelling **2** reden om te veronderstellen **3** arrogantie, verwaandheid
presumptuous aanmatigend, arrogant
presupposition vooronderstelling, voorwaarde, vereiste[h]
pretence 1 aanspraak, pretentie: ~ *to* aanspraak op **2** valse indruk, schijn: *she made a* ~ *of laughing* ze deed alsof ze lachte **3** uiterlijk vertoon[h], aanstellerij: *devoid of all* ~ zonder enige pretentie **4** huichelarij
[1]**pretend** (vb) **1** voorgeven, (ten onrechte) beweren **2** voorwenden
[2]**pretend** (vb) doen alsof, komedie spelen
pretender 1 (troon)pretendent **2** huichelaar, schijnheilige
pretension 1 aanspraak **2** pretentie, aanmatiging
pretentious 1 pretentieus, aanmatigend **2** opzichtig
pretext voorwendsel[h], excuus[h]: *under the* ~ *of* onder voorwendsel van
[1]**pretty** (adj) **1** aardig [also iron]; mooi, aantrekkelijk: *a* ~ *mess* een mooie boel **2** groot, aanzienlijk, veel: *it cost him a* ~ *penny* het heeft hem een flinke duit gekost || *a* ~ *kettle of fish* een mooie boel
[2]**pretty** (adv) **1** nogal, vrij: ~ *nearly* zogoed als; *I have* ~ *well* finished my essay ik heb mijn opstel bijna af **2** erg, zeer **3** [Am] aardig, behoorlijk
prevail 1 de overhand krijgen, zegevieren: [form] *the author was* ~*ed* *upon* *to* write an occasional poem de auteur werd overgehaald om een gelegenheidsgedicht te schrijven **2** wijd verspreid zijn, heersen, gelden
prevailing gangbaar, heersend
prevalent 1 heersend, gangbaar, wijd verspreid **2** (over)heersend
prevarication draaierij, uitvlucht
[1]**prevent** (vb) in de weg staan
[2]**prevent** (vb) voorkomen, verhinderen
preventable vermijdbaar
prevention preventie || ~ *is better* than cure voorkomen is beter dan genezen
[1]**preventive** (n) **1** obstakel[h], hindernis **2** voorbehoedmiddel[h]
[2]**preventive** (adj) preventief, voorkomend: ~ *detention* voorlopige hechtenis
preview voorvertoning
previous voorafgaand, vorig, vroeger: ~ *conviction* eerdere veroordeling
pre-war vooroorlogs
[1]**prey** (n) prooi [also fig]; slachtoffer[h]: *beast* (or: *bird*) *of* ~ roofdier, roofvogel; *become* (or: *fall*) *(a)* ~ *to* ten prooi vallen aan
[2]**prey** (vb): ~ *(up)on* a) uitzuigen; b) aantasten; c) jagen op; *it* ~*s on* his mind hij wordt erdoor gekweld
[1]**price** (n) **1** prijs [also fig]; som: *set* a ~ *on* een

prijs vaststellen voor; *at* a low ~ voor weinig geld; *at* any ~ tot elke prijs **2** notering **3** waarde || *every man has* his ~ iedereen is te koop
[2]**price** (vb) prijzen, de prijs vaststellen van: ~ *o.s. out of* the market zich uit de markt prijzen
price cut prijsverlaging
priceless onbetaalbaar, onschatbaar; [fig] kostelijk
price tag prijskaartje[h] [also fig]
pricey prijzig, duur
[1]**prick** (n) **1** prik: [fig] ~*s of conscience* wroeging, berouw **2** [inform] lul, eikel, schoft **3** [inform] pik
[2]**prick** (vb) prikken, steken
[3]**prick** (vb) prikken, (door)steken; prikkelen [also fig]
[1]**prickle** (n) stekel, doorn, prikkel
[2]**prickle** (vb) prikkelen, steken, kriebelen
pride 1 trots, verwaandheid, hoogmoed: *take* (a) ~ in fier zijn op **2** eergevoel[h]: *false* ~ misplaatste trots, ijdelheid **3** troep [lions]
pride (up)on prat gaan op, trots zijn op
priest priester, pastoor
prig verwaande kwast
prim 1 keurig: ~ *and proper* keurig netjes **2** preuts
primacy voorrang, vooraanstaande plaats
primal [form] **1** oer-; oorspronkelijk **2** voornaamst
primarily hoofdzakelijk, voornamelijk
[1]**primary** (n) **1** hoofdzaak **2** [Am] voorverkiezing
[2]**primary** (adj) **1** voornaamste: *of* ~ *importance* van het allergrootste belang **2** primair, eerst **3** elementair, grond-: ~ *care* eerstelijnsgezondheidszorg; ~ *colour* primaire kleur; ~ *education* (or: *school*) basisonderwijs, basisschool
primate primaat[h]
Primate aartsbisschop
[1]**prime** (n) **1** hoogste volmaaktheid, bloei, hoogtepunt[h], puikje[h]: *in the* ~ *of life* in de kracht van zijn leven; *she is well past her* ~ ze is niet meer zo jong, ze heeft haar beste jaren achter de rug **2** priemgetal[h]
[2]**prime** (adj) **1** eerst, voornaamst: ~ *suspect* hoofdverdachte **2** uitstekend, prima: [radio, TV] ~ *time* primetime; ~ *quality* topkwaliteit **3** oorspronkelijk, fundamenteel || ~ *number* priemgetal
[3]**prime** (vb) **1** klaarmaken, prepareren **2** laden [firearm] **3** op gang brengen [by pouring water or oil]; injecteren [engine]
[1]**primer** (n) **1** eerste leesboek[h], abc[h] **2** beknopte handleiding, inleiding
[2]**primer** (n) grondverf
primeval 1 oorspronkelijk, oer-: ~ *forest* ongerept woud **2** oeroud
primitive 1 primitief **2** niet comfortabel,

ouderwets: *our accommodation there will* ~ onze huisvesting daar zal gebrekkig zijn
primrose 1 sleutelbloem **2** lichtgeel[h]
primula primula, sleutelbloem
prince 1 prins: ~ *royal* kroonprins **2** vorst [also fig]; heerser || *he is my Prince Charming* hij is mijn droomprins
princedom 1 prinsdom[h], vorstendom[h] **2** prinselijke waardigheid
princess prinses
princess royal 1 kroonprinses **2** titel van de oudste dochter van de Britse koning(in)
[1]principal (n) **1** directeur, directrice **2** hoofd[h], hoofdpersoon: ~s hoofdrolspelers **3** schoolhoofd[h] **4** [fin] kapitaal[h], hoofdsom, geleende som
[2]principal (adj) voornaamste
principality prinsdom[h], vorstendom[h]
the **Principality** Wales
principally voornamelijk, hoofdzakelijk
principle 1 (grond)beginsel[h], uitgangspunt[h]: *in* ~ in principe **2** principe[h], beginsel[h] || *live up* (or: *stick to*) *one's* ~s aan zijn principes vasthouden
prink (zich) mooi maken, (zich) optutten: ~ *up* zich chic kleden
[1]print (n) **1** afdruk; [fig] spoor[h]: *a* ~ *of a tyre* een bandenspoor **2** [art] prent **3** (foto)afdruk, druk: *in* ~ gedrukt, verkrijgbaar **4** stempel **5** gedrukt exemplaar[h], krant, blad[h] **6** patroon[h]
[2]print (vb) **1** (+ off) een afdruk maken van; afdrukken [also photo] **2** inprenten || ~ed *circuit* gedrukte bedrading
[3]print (vb) **1** (af)drukken: ~ed *papers* drukwerk; ~ *out* een uitdraai maken (van) **2** publiceren **3** in blokletters (op)schrijven **4** (be)stempelen
printer 1 (boek)drukker **2** printer
printing oplage, druk
printing press drukpers
printout uitdraai
print preview [comp] afdrukvoorbeeld[h]
prior vroeger, voorafgaand
priority prioriteit, voorrang: *get one's priorities right* de juiste prioriteiten stellen
prior to vóór, voorafgaande aan
prism prisma[h]
prison 1 gevangenis **2** gevangenisstraf
prison camp interneringskamp[h]
prisoner gevangene, gedetineerde: ~ *of war* krijgsgevangene
prissy preuts, stijf
pristine [form] **1** oorspronkelijk **2** ongerept
privacy 1 persoonlijke levenssfeer **2** geheimhouding, stilte, beslotenheid **3** afzondering
[1]private (n) soldaat, militair
[2]private (adj) **1** besloten, afgezonderd: ~ *celebration* viering in familiekring; ~ *hotel*

familiehotel **2** vertrouwelijk, geheim: ~ *conversation* gesprek onder vier ogen; *in* ~ in het geheim **3** particulier, niet openbaar: ~ *enterprise* particuliere onderneming; [fig] ondernemingslust; ~ *life* privéleven; ~ *property* privé-eigendom, particulier eigendom; ~ *school* particuliere school **4** persoonlijk, eigen: ~ *detective* privédetective || ~ *eye* privédetective; ~ *means* a) inkomsten anders dan uit loon; b) eigen middelen; ~ *practice* particuliere praktijk; ~ *parts* geslachtsdelen
privation ontbering, gebrek[h]
privatize privatiseren
privet liguster(heg)
[1]privilege (n) **1** voorrecht[h], privilege[h] **2** onschendbaarheid, immuniteit: *breach of* ~ inbreuk op de parlementaire gedragsregels **3** bevoorrechting
[2]privilege (vb) **1** bevoorrechten, een privilege verlenen **2** machtigen, toestaan **3** vrijstellen
[1]prize (n) **1** prijs, beloning **2** prijs(schip[h]), (oorlogs)buit
[2]prize (vb) **1** waarderen, op prijs stellen **2** openen [with instrument]: ~ *a crate open* een krat openbreken
prize money prijzengeld[h]
prizewinner prijswinnaar
[1]pro (n) **1** *professional* prof, beroeps **2** argument[h], stem vóór iets: *the ~s and cons* de voor- en nadelen
[2]pro (adj) **1** pro, voor **2** beroeps-
[3]pro (adv) (er)vóór, pro
[4]pro (prep) vóór, ter verdediging van
probability waarschijnlijkheid; kans: *in all* ~ hoogstwaarschijnlijk; [maths] *theory of* ~ kansberekening
probable waarschijnlijk, aannemelijk
probably 1 waarschijnlijk **2** ongetwijfeld, vast wel: ~ *the greatest singer of all* misschien wel de grootste zanger van allemaal
probation proef(tijd), onderzoek[h], onderzoeksperiode: *on* ~ a) op proef; b) voorwaardelijk in vrijheid gesteld
probation officer reclasseringsambtenaar
[1]probe (n) **1** sonde **2** ruimtesonde **3** (diepgaand) onderzoek[h]
[2]probe (vb) **1** (met een sonde) onderzoeken **2** (goed) onderzoeken, diep graven (in): ~ *into* graven naar
problem 1 probleem[h], vraagstuk[h], kwestie **2** opgave, vraag
problematic(al) 1 problematisch **2** twijfelachtig
procedure procedure, methode, werkwijze
proceed 1 beginnen, van start gaan **2** verder gaan, doorgaan: *work is* ~ing *steadily* het werk vordert gestaag **3** te werk gaan, handelen: *how shall we* ~ welke procedure zullen

we volgen? **4** plaatsvinden, aan de gang zijn **5** zich bewegen, gaan, rijden **6** ontstaan: ~ *from* voortkomen uit

proceeding 1 handeling, maatregel **2** optreden^h, handelwijze **3** (-s) gebeurtenissen, voorvallen **4** (-s) notulen; handelingen [of society etc]; verslag^h **5** (-s) gerechtelijke actie: *take* (or: *start*) *legal* ~*s* gerechtelijke stappen ondernemen

proceeds opbrengst

proceed to overgaan tot, verder gaan met

¹**process** (n) **1** proces^h, ontwikkeling **2** methode **3** (serie) verrichting(en), handelwijze, werkwijze **4** (voort)gang, loop, verloop^h: *in the* ~ en passant; *in (the)* ~ *of* doende met

²**process** (vb) (als) in processie gaan, een optocht houden

³**process** (vb) **1** bewerken, verwerken **2** ontwikkelen (en afdrukken)

procession 1 stoet, optocht, processie: *walk in* ~ in optocht lopen **2** opeenvolging

processor processor; verwerkingseenheid

proclaim 1 afkondigen, verklaren **2** kenmerken: *his behaviour* ~*ed him a liar* uit zijn gedrag bleek duidelijk dat hij loog

proclamation afkondiging

procrastination uitstel^h, aarzeling

¹**procreate** (vb) zich voortplanten

²**procreate** (vb) **1** voortbrengen **2** scheppen

procurable verkrijgbaar, beschikbaar

¹**procure** (vb) koppelen, tot ontucht overhalen

²**procure** (vb) verkrijgen, verwerven

¹**prod** (n) **1** por, steek **2** zet [also fig]; duwtje^h

²**prod** (vb) **1** porren, prikken, duwen **2** aansporen, opporren

¹**prodigal** (n) verkwister: *the* ~ *has returned* de verloren zoon is teruggekeerd

²**prodigal** (adj) **1** verkwistend: *the* ~ *son* de verloren zoon **2** vrijgevig

prodigious wonderbaarlijk

prodigy 1 wonder^h, bovennatuurlijk verschijnsel^h **2** wonderkind^h

¹**produce** (n) opbrengst, productie: *agricultural* ~ landbouwproducten

²**produce** (vb) **1** produceren, voortbrengen, opbrengen **2** produceren, vervaardigen **3** tonen, produceren, tevoorschijn halen, voor de dag komen met: ~ *evidence* (or: *reasons*) bewijzen (*or:* redenen) aanvoeren **4** uitbrengen, het licht doen zien: ~ *a play* een toneelstuk op de planken brengen **5** veroorzaken, teweegbrengen

producer 1 producent, fabrikant **2** [film; TV] producer, productieleider **3** regisseur **4** [radio, TV] samensteller

product 1 product^h, voortbrengsel^h: *agricultural* ~*s* landbouwproducten **2** resultaat^h, gevolg^h **3** product^h, uitkomst van een vermenigvuldiging

production 1 product^h, schepping **2** [theatre, film] productie **3** productie, vervaardiging, opbrengst **4** het tonen: *on* ~ *of your tickets* op vertoon van uw kaartje

production line productiestraat; lopende band

productive productief, vruchtbaar

productivity 1 productiviteit **2** rendement^h

prof *professor* prof, professor

¹**profane** (adj) niet kerkelijk, werelds || ~ *language* godslasterlijke taal, gevloek

²**profane** (vb) ontheiligen

profanity 1 godslastering; (ge)vloek **2** blasfemie

profess 1 beweren, voorwenden **2** verklaren, betuigen: *he* ~*ed his ignorance on the subject* hij verklaarde dat hij niets van het onderwerp afwist **3** aanhangen

professed 1 voorgewend, zogenaamd **2** openlijk, verklaard, naar eigen zeggen

profession 1 verklaring, uiting **2** beroep^h, vak^h, alle beoefenaren van het vak

¹**professional** (n) **1** beroeps, deskundige **2** professional, prof: *turn* ~ beroeps worden

²**professional** (adj) **1** professioneel, beroeps-, prof-: ~ *jealousy* broodnijd **2** vakkundig, bekwaam **3** met een hogere opleiding **4** professioneel; opzettelijk [of foul]

professor professor, hoogleraar; [Am also] docent: ~ *of chemistry* hoogleraar in de scheikunde

proffer aanbieden, aanreiken

proficiency vakkundigheid, bekwaamheid

proficient vakkundig, bekwaam

¹**profile** (n) **1** profiel^h, zijaanzicht^h: *in* ~ en profil, van opzij **2** silhouet^h, doorsnede **3** profiel^h, karakterschets || *keep a low* ~ zich op de achtergrond houden

²**profile** (vb) **1** van opzij weergeven, aftekenen, in silhouet weergeven, een dwarsdoorsnede geven van **2** een karakterschets geven van

¹**profit** (n) **1** winst, opbrengst **2** rente **3** nut^h, voordeel^h, profijt^h: *I read the book much to my* ~ ik heb veel aan het boek gehad

²**profit** (vb) **1** nuttig zijn **2** (+ by, from) profiteren (van), profijt trekken

profitable 1 nuttig, voordelig **2** winstgevend

¹**profiteer** (n) woekeraar

²**profiteer** (vb) woekerwinst maken

profligacy 1 losbandigheid **2** verkwisting

¹**profligate** (n) **1** losbol **2** verkwister

²**profligate** (adj) **1** losbandig, lichtzinnig **2** verkwistend

profound 1 wijs, wijsgerig, diepzinnig: *a* ~ *thinker* een groot denker **2** diepgaand, moeilijk te doorgronden **3** diep, grondig: *silence* diepe stilte

profundity 1 diepzinnigheid, wijsgerig-

heid **2** ondoorgrondelijkheid
profuse 1 gul, kwistig: *be ~ in one's apolo-gies* zich uitputten in verontschuldigingen **2** overvloedig, overdadig: *bleed ~ly* hevig bloeden
progenitor voorvader
progeny 1 nageslacht[h], kinderen **2** volgelingen
prognosis prognose, voorspelling
¹program (n) (computer)programma[h]
²program (vb) programmeren
¹programme (n) programma[h]
²programme (vb) programmeren, een schema opstellen voor
programmer programmeur
¹progress (n) voortgang, vooruitgang; [fig] vordering: *the patient is making ~* de patiënt gaat vooruit; *in ~* in wording, aan de gang, in uitvoering
²progress (vb) vorderen, vooruitgaan, vooruitkomen; [fig also] zich ontwikkelen
progression 1 opeenvolging, aaneenschakeling **2** voortgang, vooruitgang
¹progressive (n) vooruitstrevend persoon
²progressive (adj) **1** toenemend, voortschrijdend, voorwaarts; progressief [tax] **2** progressief, vooruitstrevend **3** [linguistics] progressief, duratief: *the ~ (form)* de duurvorm, de bezigheidsvorm
prohibit verbieden: *smoking ~ed* verboden te roken
prohibition verbod[h], drankverbod[h]
¹project (n) **1** plan[h], ontwerp[h] **2** project[h], onderneming **3** project[h], onderzoek[h]
²project (vb) vooruitspringen, uitsteken: *~ing shoulder blades* uitstekende schouderbladen
³project (vb) **1** ontwerpen, uitstippelen **2** werpen, projecteren: *~ slides* dia's projecteren **3** afbeelden, tonen **4** schatten
projectile projectiel[h], raket
projection 1 uitstekend deel[h], uitsprong **2** projectie, beeld[h] **3** raming, plan[h], projectie
projector projector, filmprojector, diaprojector
¹proletarian (n) proletariër
²proletarian (adj) proletarisch
proletariat proletariaat[h]; arbeidersklasse: *dictatorship of the ~* dictatuur van het proletariaat
pro-life antiabortus(-)
proliferation 1 woekering, snelle groei **2** verspreiding
prolific vruchtbaar; [fig] met overvloedige resultaten; rijk: *a ~ writer* een productief schrijver
prologue proloog, voorwoord[h], inleiding
prolong 1 verlengen, langer maken **2** verlengen, aanhouden: *a ~ed silence* langdurige stilte
prom 1 promenadeconcert[h]; [Am] school-

bal[h], universiteitsbal[h]; dansfeest[h] **2** promenade, boulevard
¹promenade (n) **1** wandeling, het flaneren **2** promenade, boulevard
²promenade (vb) **1** wandelen (langs), flaneren **2** wandelen met, lopen te pronken met
prominence 1 verhoging, uitsteeksel[h] **2** het uitsteken **3** opvallendheid, bekendheid, belang[h]: *bring sth. into ~* iets bekendheid geven
prominent 1 uitstekend, uitspringend: *~ teeth* vooruitstekende tanden **2** opvallend **3** vooraanstaand, prominent: *a ~ scholar* een eminent geleerde
promiscuity 1 willekeurige vermenging **2** onzorgvuldigheid **3** vrij seksueel verkeer[h], promiscuïteit
promiscuous 1 ongeordend **2** willekeurig **3** promiscue; met willekeurige seksuele relaties
¹promise (n) belofte, toezegging: *break one's ~* zich niet aan zijn belofte houden
²promise (vb) **1** een belofte doen, (iets) beloven **2** verwachtingen wekken, veelbelovend zijn
³promise (vb) **1** beloven, toezeggen; [inform] verzekeren: *the ~d land* het Beloofde Land **2** beloven, doen verwachten: *it ~d to be a severe winter* het beloofde een strenge winter te worden
promising veelbelovend
promontory kaap, klip, voorgebergte[h]
promote 1 bevorderen, in rang verhogen **2** bevorderen, stimuleren **3** steunen [eg bill] **4** ondernemen, in gang zetten **5** reclame maken voor
promoter 1 begunstiger, bevorderaar **2** organisator, financier van een manifestatie
promotion 1 bevordering, promotie **2** aanbieding, reclame
promotional 1 bevorderings-: *~ opportunities* promotiekansen **2** reclame-; advertentie-
¹prompt (n) geheugensteuntje[h], het voorzeggen, hulp van de souffleur
²prompt (adj) prompt, onmiddellijk, vlug, alert: *~ payment* prompte betaling
³prompt (vb) **1** bewegen, drijven: *what ~ed you to do that?* hoe kwam je erbij dat te doen? **2** opwekken, oproepen **3** herinneren, voorzeggen, souffleren
⁴prompt (adv) precies, stipt: *at twelve o'clock ~* om twaalf uur precies
prompter souffleur
prone 1 voorover, voorovergebogen **2** vooroverliggend, uitgestrekt **3** geneigd, vatbaar: *he is ~ to tactlessness* hij is geneigd tot tactloosheid
prong 1 punt[h], piek, vorktand **2** tak, ver-

takking
pronoun [linguistics] voornaamwoord^h
¹**pronounce** (vb) **1** spreken, articuleren
2 oordelen, zijn mening verkondigen: ~
(up)on uitspraken doen over, commentaar
leveren op
²**pronounce** (vb) **1** uitspreken **2** verklaren,
verkondigen: ~ *judgement* (or: *verdict*) uitspraak doen
pronounced 1 uitgesproken **2** uitgesproken, onmiskenbaar
pronto meteen, onmiddellijk
pronunciation uitspraak
¹**proof** (n) **1** toets, proefneming: *bring* (or:
put) *to the* ~ op de proef stellen **2** bewijs^h: *in*
~ *of his claim* om zijn stelling te bewijzen
3 drukproef **4** proefafdruk
²**proof** (adj) bestand [also fig]; opgewassen:
~ *against water* waterdicht, waterbestendig
-proof -bestendig, -vast, -dicht: *bulletproof*
kogelvrij; *childproof* onverwoestbaar [of
toys]
proofread proeflezen; drukproeven corrigeren
¹**prop** (n) **1** stut, pijler, steun, steunpilaar
2 rekwisiet^h, benodigd voorwerp^h bij toneelvoorstelling
²**prop** (vb) ondersteunen [also fig]; stutten
propaganda propaganda, propaganda-
materiaal^h, propagandacampagne
¹**propagate** (vb) **1** verspreiden, bekendmaken **2** voortzetten; doorgeven [to next gen-
eration] **3** fokken, telen
²**propagate** (vb) (zich) voortplanten
propel voortbewegen, aandrijven ‖ *~ling
pencil* vulpotlood
¹**propellant** (n) **1** drijfgas^h **2** [fuel] aandrijf-
brandstof
²**propellant** (adj) voortdrijvend [also fig];
stuwend
propeller propeller
propensity neiging
proper 1 gepast, fatsoenlijk **2** juist, passend: *the* ~ *treatment* de juiste behandeling
3 juist, precies: *the* ~ *time* de juiste tijd **4** geweldig, eersteklas: *a* ~ *spanking* een geweldig pak slaag **5** behorend [tot]; eigen [to]: ~
to behorend tot, eigen aan **6** eigenlijk,
strikt: *London* ~ het eigenlijke Londen ‖ ~
noun (or: *name*) eigennaam
properly 1 goed, zoals het moet **2** eigenlijk, strikt genomen **3** correct, fatsoenlijk
4 volkomen, volslagen
property 1 eigenschap, kenmerk^h **2** per-
ceel^h, onroerend goed^h **3** rekwisiet^h, benodigd voorwerp^h bij een toneelvoorstelling
4 bezit^h, eigendom^h: *lost* ~ gevonden voorwerpen **5** bezit^h, vermogen^h, onroerend
goed^h
prophecy 1 voorspelling **2** profetie
¹**prophesy** (vb) **1** voorspellingen doen **2** als

een profeet spreken
²**prophesy** (vb) **1** voorspellen, voorzeggen
2 aankondigen
prophet profeet
prophetic profetisch; voorspellend
proponent voorstander, verdediger
¹**proportion** (n) **1** deel^h, gedeelte^h, aan-
deel^h **2** verhouding, relatie: *bear no* ~ *to* in
geen verhouding staan tot **3** proportie,
evenredigheid: *out of all* ~ buiten alle verhoudingen
²**proportion** (vb) **1** aanpassen, in de juiste
verhouding brengen **2** proportioneren: *well*
~*ed* goed geproportioneerd
proportional verhoudingsgewijs, proportioneel, evenredig
proposal 1 voorstel^h **2** huwelijksaanzoek^h
¹**propose** (vb) **1** een voorstel doen **2** een
huwelijksaanzoek doen
²**propose** (vb) **1** voorstellen, voorleggen: ~ *a
motion* een motie indienen **2** van plan zijn,
zich voornemen **3** een dronk uitbrengen
(op)
¹**proposition** (n) **1** bewering **2** voorstel^h,
plan^h **3** probleem^h, moeilijk geval^h: *he's a
tough* ~ hij is moeilijk te hanteren
²**proposition** (vb) oneerbare voorstellen
doen aan
propound voorstellen
proprietary 1 eigendoms-, van de eigenaar, particulier: ~ *name* (or: *term*) gedeponeerd handelsmerk **2** bezittend, met bezittingen als een eigenaar, bezittend: *he always has this* ~ *air* hij gedraagt zich altijd alsof
alles van hem is
proprietor eigenaar
propriety juistheid, geschiktheid **2** correctheid, fatsoen^h, gepastheid
propulsion 1 drijfkracht **2** voortdrijving,
voortstuwing
prop up overeind houden, ondersteunen
prosaic 1 zakelijk **2** alledaags
proscribe 1 verbieden, als gevaarlijk verwerpen **2** verbannen [also fig]; verstoten
prose proza^h
prosecute 1 voortzetten, volhouden
2 (gerechtelijk) vervolgen, procederen tegen: *trespassers will be* ~*d* verboden voor
onbevoegden
prosecution 1 gerechtelijke vervolging;
proces^h **2** [law] eiser
prosecutor 1 eiser, eisende partij **2** [Am]
openbare aanklager: *public* ~ openbare aanklager
¹**prospect** (n) **1** vergezicht^h, panorama^h
2 idee^h, denkbeeld^h **3** ligging, uitzicht^h
4 hoop, verwachting, kans, vooruitzicht^h
5 potentiële klant, prospect^h
²**prospect** (vb) naar bodemschatten zoeken:
~ *for gold* goud zoeken
prospective 1 voor de toekomst, nog niet

in werking **2** toekomstig: *a ~ buyer* een gegadigde, een mogelijke koper; *~ student* as-
pirant-student
prospector goudzoeker
prosper bloeien, slagen, succes hebben
prosperity voorspoed, succes[h]
prosperous 1 bloeiend; voorspoedig
2 welvarend **3** gunstig
[1]**prostitute** (n) prostitué [man]; prostituee
[2]**prostitute** (vb) **1** prostitueren, tot prostitué (prostituee) maken: *~ o.s.* zich prostitueren **2** vergooien, verlagen, misbruiken: *~
one's honour* zich verlagen, z'n eer te grabbel gooien
prostitution prostitutie
[1]**prostrate** (adj) **1** ter aarde geworpen
2 liggend, uitgestrekt, languit **3** verslagen,
gebroken: *~ with grief* gebroken van verdriet
[2]**prostrate** (vb) neerwerpen, neerslaan: *~
o.s.* zich ter aarde werpen, in het stof knielen
prosy saai, vervelend
protagonist 1 voorvechter **2** voorstander
3 [literature; theatre] protagonist; hoofdfi-
guur
protect 1 beschermen **2** beveiligen, bevei-
ligingen aanbrengen
protection 1 beschermer, bescherming,
beschutting **2** vrijgeleide[h]
protection money protectiegeld[h], be-
schermgeld[h]
protective beschermend, beschermings-: *~
colouring* schutkleur; *~ sheath* condoom
protector 1 beschermer, beschermheer
2 beschermend middel[h]
protectorate protectoraat[h], land dat onder bescherming van een ander land staat
protein proteïne, eiwit[h]
[1]**protest** (n) protest[h], bezwaar[h]: *enter* (or:
lodge, make) a ~ against sth. ergens protest
tegen aantekenen
[2]**protest** (vb) protesteren, bezwaar maken
[3]**protest** (vb) **1** bezweren, betuigen: *~ one's
innocence* zijn onschuld betuigen **2** [Am]
protesteren tegen: *they are ~ing nuclear
weapons* ze protesteren tegen kernwapens
Protestant protestant(s)
protocol 1 protocol[h] **2** officieel verslag[h],
akte, verslag[h] van internationale onderhandelingen
proton proton[h]
prototype prototype[h], oorspronkelijk model[h]
protract voortzetten, verlengen, rekken
protractor gradenboog, hoekmeter
protrude uitpuilen, uitsteken: *protruding
eyes* uitpuilende ogen
protuberant gezwollen, uitpuilend
proud 1 trots, fier, zelfverzekerd, hoog-
moedig, arrogant **2** trots, vereerd: *I'm ~ to
know her* ik ben er trots op dat ik haar ken
3 imposant [of thing]

provable bewijsbaar; aantoonbaar
[1]**prove** (vb) **1** blijken: *our calculations ~d incorrect* onze berekeningen bleken onjuist te
zijn **2** [culinary] rijzen
[2]**prove** (vb) bewijzen, (aan)tonen: *of ~n
authenticity* waarvan de echtheid is bewezen
provenance herkomst
proverb gezegde[h], spreekwoord[h], spreuk
proverbial spreekwoordelijk
[1]**provide** (vb) **1** voorzieningen treffen: *~
against flooding* maatregelen nemen tegen
overstromingen **2** in het onderhoud voorzien, verzorgen: *~ for children* kinderen onderhouden
[2]**provide** (vb) **1** bepalen, eisen, vaststellen: *~
that ...* bepalen dat ... **2** voorzien, uitrusten,
verschaffen: *they ~d us with blankets and food*
zij voorzagen ons van dekens en voedsel
provided op voorwaarde dat, (alleen) indien, mits: *~ that* op voorwaarde dat, mits
providence voorzorg, zorg voor de toekomst, spaarzaamheid
Providence de Voorzienigheid, God
provident 1 vooruitziend **2** zuinig, spaarzaam
providential wonderbaarlijk
provider 1 leverancier **2** kostwinner
providing op voorwaarde dat, (alleen) indien, mits: *~ (that) it is done properly* mits het
goed gebeurt
province 1 provincie, gewest[h] **2** vakgebied[h], terrein[h]: *outside one's ~* buiten zijn
vakgebied **3** (-s) platteland[h], provincie
[1]**provincial** (n) **1** provinciaal, iem. uit de
provincie **2** provinciaaltje[h], bekrompen mens
[2]**provincial** (adj) provinciaal, van de provincie; [depr] bekrompen
provision 1 bepaling, voorwaarde **2** voorraad, hoeveelheid, rantsoen[h] **3** levering,
toevoer, voorziening **4** voorzorg, voorbereiding, maatregelen: *make ~ for the future* voor
zijn toekomst zorgen **5** (-s) levensmiddelen,
provisie, proviand[h]
provisional tijdelijk, voorlopig
proviso voorwaarde, beperkende bepaling
provocation provocatie, uitdaging: *he did
it under ~* hij is ertoe gedreven
provocative provocerend, prikkelend: *~
clothes* uitdagende kleding
provoke 1 tergen, prikkelen: *his behaviour
~d me into beating him* door zijn gedrag werd
ik zo kwaad dat ik hem een pak slaag gaf
2 uitdagen, provoceren, ophitsen **3** veroorzaken, uitlokken
prow voorsteven
prowess 1 dapperheid **2** bekwaamheid
[1]**prowl** (n) jacht, roof(tocht), het rondsluipen
[2]**prowl** (vb) **1** jagen, op roof uit zijn **2** lopen
loeren, rondsluipen, rondsnuffelen: *s.o. is*

~ing **about** (or: *around*) *on the staircase* er sluipt iem.

prowl car [Am] surveillancewagen [of police]

proximity nabijheid: *in the* ~ in de nabijheid, in de nabije toekomst

proxy 1 gevolmachtigde, afgevaardigde: *stand* ~ *for s.o.* als iemands gemachtigde optreden **2** (bewijs van) volmacht, volmachtbrief: *marry by* ~ bij volmacht trouwen

prude preuts mens

prudence 1 voorzichtigheid, omzichtigheid: *fling* (or: *throw*) ~ *to the winds* alle voorzichtigheid overboord gooien **2** beleid[h], wijsheid

prudent voorzichtig, met inzicht, verstandig

prudential verstandig

[1]**prune** (n) pruimedant, gedroogde pruim

[2]**prune** (vb) (be)snoeien [also fig]; korten, reduceren

prurient 1 wellustig **2** obsceen, pornografisch

[1]**pry** (vb) **1** gluren: ~ *about* rondneuzen **2** nieuwsgierig zijn: *I wish you wouldn't* ~ *into my affairs* ik wou dat je je niet met mijn zaken bemoeide

[2]**pry** (vb) [Am] (open)wrikken: ~ *open a chest* een kist openbreken

PS *postscript* PS, post scriptum

psalm psalm, hymne, kerkgezang[h]

pseudo- pseudo-; schijn-

pseudonym pseudoniem[h]; schuilnaam

psyche psyche, ziel

psychiatric psychiatrisch

psychiatrist psychiater

psychiatry psychiatrie

psychic 1 psychisch, geestelijk **2** paranormaal, bovennatuurlijk **3** paranormaal begaafd

psycho [inform] psychopaat, gek

psychoanalysis 1 psychoanalyse **2** (leer der) psychoanalyse

psychoanalyst psychoanalyticus

psychological psychologisch: ~ *warfare* psychologische oorlogvoering

psychologist psycholoog

[1]**psychology** (n) karakter[h], aard, psyche

[2]**psychology** (n) **1** (wetenschap der) psychologie **2** mensenkennis

psychopath psychopaat, geestelijk gestoorde

psychosis psychose

psychosomatic psychosomatisch

psychotic psychotisch

[1]**psych out** (vb) [Am] in de war raken

[2]**psych out** (vb) [Am] **1** analyseren, hoogte krijgen van **2** doorkrijgen, begrijpen: *I couldn't psych him out* ik kon er niet achter komen wat voor iem. hij was **3** intimideren [opponent]

PTO *please turn over* z.o.z., zie ommezijde

pub *public house* café[h], bar, pub, kroeg

puberty puberteit

pubescence 1 beharing **2** begin[h] van de puberteit

pubic van de schaamstreek, schaam-

[1]**public** (n) publiek[h], mensen, geïnteresseerden: *in* ~ in het openbaar

[2]**public** (adj) **1** openbaar, publiek, voor iedereen toegankelijk, algemeen bekend: ~ *bar* zaaltje in Brits café met goedkoop bier; ~ *conveniences* openbare toiletten; ~ *footpath* voetpad, wandelpad; ~ *house* café, bar, pub; ~ *transport* openbaar vervoer; ~ *utility* nutsbedrijf **2** algemeen, gemeenschaps-, nationaal, maatschappelijk: ~ *holiday* nationale feestdag; ~ *interest* het algemeen belang; ~ *opinion* publieke opinie; ~ *school* particuliere kostschool; [Scotland, Am] gesubsidieerde lagere school **3** overheids-, regerings-, publiek-, staats-: ~ *assistance* sociale steun, uitkering; ~ *spending* overheidsuitgaven

publication 1 uitgave, publicatie, boek[h], artikel[h] **2** publicatie, bekendmaking

publicity 1 publiciteit, bekendheid, openbaarheid **2** publiciteit, reclame

publicize bekendmaken, adverteren

public relations officer perschef, persvoorlichter

publish 1 publiceren, schrijven **2** uitgeven, publiceren **3** bekendmaken, aankondigen, afkondigen

publisher uitgever(ij)

publishing house uitgeverij

puck 1 kwelduivel **2** ondeugend kind[h] **3** [ice hockey] puck

[1]**pucker** (n) vouw, plooi, rimpel

[2]**pucker** (vb) samentrekken, rimpelen

pudding 1 pudding [also fig] **2** dessert[h], toetje[h]

puddle plas, (modder)poel

pudgy kort en dik, mollig

puerile 1 kinder-, kinderlijk **2** kinderachtig

[1]**Puerto Rican** (n) Porto Ricaan(se)

[2]**Puerto Rican** (adj) Porto Ricaans

Puerto Rico Porto Rico

[1]**puff** (n) **1** ademstoot, puf **2** rookwolk **3** trek, haal; puf [on cigarette etc] **4** puf, puffend geluid[h] **5** (poeder)dons[h]

[2]**puff** (vb) **1** puffen, hijgen, blazen **2** roken, dampen: ~ (*away*) *at* (or: *on*) *a cigarette* een sigaret roken **3** puffen, in wolkjes uitgestoten worden **4** (also + out) opzwellen, zich opblazen

[3]**puff** (vb) **1** uitblazen, uitstoten: ~ *smoke into s.o.'s eyes* iem. rook in de ogen blazen **2** roken; trekken [on cigarette etc] **3** (also + out) opblazen, doen opzwellen: ~*ed up with pride* verwaand, opgeblazen

puffy opgezet, gezwollen, opgeblazen

pug 1 mopshond **2** klei(mengsel[h])

pugilist [form] vuistvechter, bokser
pugnacious strijdlustig
puke overgeven, (uit)braken, kotsen: *it makes me ~* ik word er kotsmisselijk van
¹pull (n) **1** ruk, trek, stoot; [fig] klim; inspanning, moeite: *a long ~ across the hills* een hele klim over de heuvels **2** trekkracht **3** teug; slok [drink]; trek [on cigar] **4** (trek)knop, trekker, handvatʰ **5** invloed, macht: *have a ~ on s.o.* invloed over iemand hebben **6** het trekken, het rukken
²pull (vb) **1** trekken, getrokken worden, plukken, rukken: *~ at* (or: *on*) *a pipe* aan een pijp trekken **2** zich moeizaam voortbewegen: *~ away from* achter zich laten **3** gaan [of vehicle, rowing boat]; gedreven worden, roeien, rijden: *the car ~ed ahead of us* de auto ging voor ons rijden; *the train ~ed into Bristol* de trein liep Bristol binnen
³pull (vb) **1** trekken (aan), (uit)rukken, naar zich toetrekken, uit de grond trekken, tappen, zich verzekeren van, (eruit) halen: *~ customers* klandizie trekken; *he ~ed a gun on her* hij richtte een geweer op haar; *the current ~ed him under* de stroming sleurde hem mee **2** doen voortgaan, voortbewegen **3** verrekken [muscle] **4** (be)roven ‖ *~ the other one* maak dat een ander wijs
pull-down menu rolmenu*ʰ
pulley 1 katrol **2** riemschijf
¹pull in (vb) **1** aankomen, binnenlopen, binnenvaren **2** naar de kant gaan (en stoppen) [of vehicle]
²pull in (vb) **1** binnenhalen [money]; opstrijken **2** aantrekken, lokken: *Paul Simon always pulls in many people* Paul Simon trekt altijd veel mensen **3** inhouden: *~ your stomach* houd je buik in **4** in zijn kraag grijpen [eg thief]; inrekenen
pull off 1 uittrekken, uitdoen **2** bereiken, slagen in: *~ a deal* in een transactie slagen; *he has pulled it off again* het is hem weer gelukt, hij heeft het weer klaargespeeld
¹pull out (vb) **1** (zich) terugtrekken; [fig] terugkrabbelen: *~ of politics* uit de politiek gaan **2** vertrekken, wegrijden **3** gaan inhalen, uithalen: *the driver who pulled out had not seen the oncoming lorry* de bestuurder die zijn baan verliet had de naderende vrachtauto niet gezien
²pull out (vb) verwijderen, uitdoen, uittrekken: *~ a tooth* een kies trekken
pullover pullover
¹pull over (vb) **1** opzijgaan, uit de weg gaan **2** [Am] (naar de kant rijden en) stoppen
²pull over (vb) **1** naar de kant rijden **2** stoppen [vehicle]
pull round 1 bij bewustzijn komen **2** zich herstellen
pull tab lipjeʰ
pull through erdoor getrokken worden,

erdoor komen: *the patient pulls through* de patiënt komt er doorheen
pull together 1 samentrekken **2** samenwerken ‖ *pull yourself together* beheers je
¹pull up (vb) stoppen: *the car pulled up* de auto stopte
²pull up (vb) **1** uittrekken **2** (doen) stoppen: *~ your car at the side* zet je auto aan de kant **3** tot de orde roepen, op zijn plaats zetten
pull-up 1 rustplaats, wegrestaurantʰ **2** optrekoefening [on bar]
pulp 1 moesʰ, pap **2** vruchtvleesʰ **3** pulp, houtpap **4** rommel **5** sensatiebladʰ, sensatieboekʰ, sensatieverhaalʰ ‖ *beat s.o. to a ~* iem. tot moes slaan
pulpit preekstoel, kansel
pulp magazine sensatiebladʰ, pulpbladʰ
pulsate kloppen, ritmisch bewegen, trillen
pulse 1 hartslag, pols(slag): *feel* (or: *take*) *s.o.'s ~* iemands hartslag opnemen; [fig] iem. polsen **2** (afzonderlijke) slag, stoot, trilling **3** ritmeʰ [eg in music] **4** peul(vrucht) **5** peulenʰ, peulvruchten
¹pulverize (vb) verpulveren, verpulverd worden
²pulverize (vb) verpulveren; [fig] vernietigen; niets heel laten van
puma poema
¹pump (n) **1** pomp **2** dansschoen; [Am] galaschoen
²pump (vb) **1** pompen, pompend bewegen **2** bonzen [of heart]
³pump (vb) **1** pompen: *~ money into an industry* geld investeren in een industrie **2** (krachtig) schudden [hand] **3** met moeite gedaan krijgen, (erin) pompen, (eruit) stampen: *~ a witness* een getuige uithoren
pumpkin pompoen
¹pun (n) woordspeling
²pun (vb) woordspelingen maken
¹punch (n) **1** werktuigʰ om gaten te slaan, ponsmachine, ponstang, perforator, kniptang **2** (vuist)slag: [boxing] *pull one's ~es* zich inhouden [also fig] **3** slagvaardigheid, kracht, pit: *his speech lacks ~* er zit geen pit in zijn toespraak **4** punch, bowl(drank)
²punch (vb) **1** ponsen **2** slaan: *~ up* op de vuist gaan **3** [Am] inslaan, een prikklok gebruiken: *~ in* (or: *out*) klokken bij binnenkomst (or: vertrek)
³punch (vb) **1** slaan, een vuistslag geven **2** gaten maken in, perforeren; knippen [ticket]; ponsen
Punch Jan Klaassen: *~ and Judy* Jan Klaassen en Katrijn
punchbag [boxing] stootzak, zandzak, stootkussenʰ
punchball boksbal
punch-drunk versuft; [fig] verward
punch line clou
punch-up knokpartij

punchy [inform] versuft, bedwelmd
punctilious zeer precies, plichtsgetrouw, nauwgezet
punctual punctueel, stipt, nauwgezet
¹**punctuate** (vb) onderbreken: *a speech ~d by* (or: *with*) *jokes* een toespraak doorspekt met grappen
²**punctuate** (vb) leestekens aanbrengen
punctuation interpunctie(tekens)
punctuation mark leesteken^h
¹**puncture** (n) gaatje^h [eg in tyre]; lek^h, lekke band
²**puncture** (vb) lek maken, doorboren; [fig] vernietigen
pundit 1 pandit **2** expert
pungent 1 scherp: ~ *remarks* stekelige opmerkingen **2** prikkelend, pikant: *a ~ smell* een doordringende geur
punish 1 (be)straffen **2** zijn voordeel doen met [somebody's weakness]; afstraffen
punishing slopend, erg zwaar: *a ~ climb* een dodelijk vermoeiende beklimming
punishment 1 straf, bestraffing: *corporal ~* lijfstraf **2** ruwe behandeling, afstraffing
punitive 1 straf- **2** zeer hoog [eg of tax]
¹**punk** (n) **1** punk(er) **2** (jonge) boef, relschopper
²**punk** (adj) **1** waardeloos **2** punk-, van (een) punk(s)
punnet (spanen) mand(je^h) [for fruit, vegetables]; (plastic) doosje^h
¹**punt** (n) punter, platte rivierschuit
²**punt** (vb) **1** bomen, varen in een punter **2** gokken [eg at horse races]
puny nietig, miezerig, onbetekenend
¹**pup** (n) **1** pup(py), jong hondje^h **2** jong^h [eg of otter, seal]
²**pup** (vb) jongen; werpen [of dog]
pupil 1 leerling **2** pupil [of eye]
puppet marionet [also fig]; (houten) pop
puppy 1 puppy, jong hondje^h **2** snotneus
puppy fat [inform] babyvet^h
¹**purchase** (n) **1** (aan)koop: ~s inkoop; aanschaf; *make ~s* inkopen doen **2** vat^h, greep: *get a ~ on a rock* houvast vinden aan een rots
²**purchase** (vb) zich aanschaffen, (in)kopen
purchaser (in)koper
purchasing power koopkracht
pure 1 puur, zuiver, onvervalst: *a ~ Arab horse* een rasechte arabier; *~ and simple* niets dan, eenvoudigweg **2** volkomen, zuiver, puur
purebred rasecht [of animals]; volbloed-
purée moes^h, puree
purely uitsluitend, volledig, zonder meer: *a ~ personal matter* een zuiver persoonlijke aangelegenheid
purgation zuivering, reiniging
purgatory vagevuur^h, (tijdelijke) kwelling
¹**purge** (n) **1** zuivering **2** laxeermiddel^h
²**purge** (vb) zuiveren, louteren, verlossen

purification zuivering, verlossing, bevrijding
¹**purify** (vb) zuiver worden
²**purify** (vb) zuiveren, louteren
purism purisme^h, (taal)zuivering
¹**puritan** (n) puritein, streng godsdienstig persoon
²**puritan** (adj) puriteins, moraliserend, streng van zeden
purity zuiverheid, puurheid, onschuld
purler smak, harde val: *come* (or: *take*) *a ~* een flinke smak maken
purloin [form] stelen; ontvreemden
purple 1 purper, donkerrood, paarsrood: *he became ~ with rage* hij liep rood aan van woede **2** (te) sierlijk, bombastisch: *a ~ passage* (or: *patch*) een briljant gedeelte [in tedious text]
¹**purport** (n) strekking, bedoeling
²**purport** (vb) **1** beweren: *he ~s to be the inventor of the electric blanket* hij beweert de uitvinder van de elektrische deken te zijn **2** kennelijk bedoelen **3** van plan zijn
purpose 1 doel^h, bedoeling, plan^h, voornemen^h: *accidentally on ~* per ongeluk expres; *he did it on ~* hij deed het met opzet **2** zin, (beoogd) effect^h, resultaat^h, nut^h: *all your help will be to no ~* al je hulp zal tevergeefs zijn **3** de zaak waarom het gaat: *his remark is (not) to the ~* zijn opmerking is (niet) ter zake **4** vastberadenheid
purposeful 1 vastberaden **2** met een doel, opzettelijk
¹**purr** (n) **1** spinnend geluid^h; gespin^h [of cat] **2** zoemend geluid^h; gesnor^h [of machine]
²**purr** (vb) **1** spinnen [of cat] **2** gonzen; zoemen [of machine]
¹**purse** (n) **1** portemonnee **2** [Am] damestas(je^h)
²**purse** (vb) samentrekken, rimpelen, tuiten: *indignantly, she ~d her lips* ze tuitte verontwaardigd de lippen
purse strings geldbuidelkoordjes; [fig] financiële macht: *loosen the ~* de uitgaven verhogen; *tighten the ~* bezuinigen; de buikriem aanhalen
pursuance uitvoering, voortzetting: *in (the) ~ of his duty* tijdens het vervullen van zijn plicht
pursuant (ver)volgend, uitvoerend || *~ to your instructions* overeenkomstig uw instructies
pursue 1 jacht maken op, achtervolgen **2** volgen; achternalopen [also fig]; lastigvallen: *this memory ~d him* deze herinnering liet hem niet los **3** doorgaan met, vervolgen: *it is wiser not to ~ the matter* het is verstandiger de zaak verder te laten rusten
pursuer achtervolger; doorzetter
pursuit 1 achtervolging; jacht [also fig]: *in ~ of happiness* op zoek naar het geluk **2** be-

zigheid, hobby
purvey bevoorraden met; leveren [food]
pus pus, etter
¹push (n) **1** duw, stoot, zet, ruk: *give that door a* ~ geef die deur even een zetje **2** grootscheepse aanval [of army]; offensief^h; [fig] energieke poging **3** energie, doorzettingsvermogen^h, fut **4** druk, nood, crisis: *if* (or: *when*) *it comes to the* ~ als het erop aankomt || *give s.o. the* ~ **a)** iem. ontslaan; **b)** iem. de bons geven; *at a* ~ als het echt nodig is, in geval van nood
²push (vb) **1** duwen, stoten, dringen **2** vorderingen maken, vooruitgaan, verder gaan: ~ *ahead* (or: *forward, on*) (rustig) doorgaan; ~ *ahead/along* (or: *forward, on*) *with* vooruitgang boeken met **3** pushen, dealen
³push (vb) **1** (weg)duwen, een zet geven, voortduwen; [fig] beïnvloeden; dwingen: ~ *the button* op de knop drukken; *he ~es the matter too far* hij drijft de zaak te ver door; ~ *s.o. about* (or: *around*) iem. ruw behandelen, iem. commanderen, iem. met minachting behandelen; ~ *back the enemy* de vijand terugdringen; ~ *o.s. forward* zich op de voorgrond dringen; *that ~ed prices up* dat joeg de prijzen omhoog **2** druk uitoefenen op, lastigvallen, aandringen bij: *don't* ~ *your luck (too far)!* stel je geluk niet te veel op de proef!; *he ~ed his luck and fell* hij werd overmoedig en viel **3** pushen [drugs]
push button drukknop
pushcart handkar
pushchair wandelwagen, buggy
pusher 1 (te) ambitieus iem., streber **2** (illegale) drugsverkoper, (drugs)dealer
push in 1 een gesprek ruw onderbreken, ertussen komen, iem. in de rede vallen **2** voordringen
pushing 1 opdringerig **2** vol energie, ondernemend
push off 1 ervandoor gaan, weggaan, ophoepelen: *now* ~, *will you* hoepel nu alsjeblieft eens op **2** uitvaren, van wal steken
push through doordrukken, er doorheen slepen: *we'll push this matter through* we zullen deze zaak erdoor krijgen
pushy 1 opdringerig **2** streberig
puss 1 poes [esp used to call animal]: *Puss in boots* de Gelaarsde Kat **2** poesje^h, liefje^h, schatje^h
pussy 1 poes(je^h), kat(je^h) **2** [Am] watje^h; ei^h **3** [vulg] kutje
pussycat [inform] **1** poesje^h; katje^h **2** schatje^h; liefje^h
pustule puistje^h
¹put (vb) varen, koers zetten: *the ship* ~ *into the port* het schip voer de haven binnen || *his sickness* ~ *paid to his plans* zijn ziekte maakte een eind aan zijn plannen; ~ *(up)on s.o.* iem. last bezorgen

²put (vb) **1** zetten, plaatsen, leggen, steken; stellen [also fig]; brengen [in a situation]: ~ *pressure (up)on* pressie uitoefenen op; ~ *a price on sth.* een prijskaartje hangen aan; ~ *sth. behind o.s.* zich over iets heen zetten, met iets breken; ~ *the children to bed* de kinderen naar bed brengen; ~ *to good use* goed gebruikmaken van **2** onderwerpen; dwingen, drijven: ~ *s.o. through it* iem. een zware test afnemen, iem. zwaar op de proef stellen **3** (in)zetten, verwedden: ~ *money on* geld zetten op; [fig] zeker zijn van **4** voorleggen, ter sprake brengen: ~ *a proposal before* (or: *to*) *a meeting* een vergadering een voorstel voorleggen **5** uitdrukken, zeggen, stellen: *how shall I* ~ *it?* hoe zal ik het zeggen || *you'll be hard* ~ *to think of a second example* het zal je niet meevallen om een tweede voorbeeld te bedenken; ~ *it* (or: *one, sth.*) *across s.o.* het iem. flikken, iem. beetnemen; *not* ~ *it past s.o. to do sth.* iem. ertoe in staat achten iets te doen; ~ *stay* ~ blijven waar je bent, op zijn plaats blijven
¹put about (vb) laveren, van richting veranderen
²put about (vb) **1** van richting doen veranderen [ship] **2** verspreiden [rumour, lies]
put across overbrengen [also fig]; aanvaardbaar maken, aan de man brengen: *know how to put one's ideas across* zijn ideeën weten over te brengen
put aside opzijzetten, wegzetten; opzijleggen [also of money]; sparen
putative vermeend; vermoedelijk
put back 1 terugzetten, terugdraaien: *put the clock back* de klok terugzetten [also fig] **2** vertragen, tegenhouden: *production has been* ~ *by a strike* de productie is door een staking vertraagd
put by opzijzetten; wegzetten [money]
¹put down (vb) landen [of aeroplane]
²put down (vb) **1** neerzetten, neerleggen **2** onderdrukken [rebellion, crime etc] **3** opschrijven, noteren: *put sth. down to ignorance* iets toeschrijven aan onwetendheid **4** een spuitje geven [sick animal]; uit zijn lijden helpen **5** afzetten; uit laten stappen [passengers] **6** aanbetalen **7** kleineren, vernederen; [fig] op zijn plaats zetten
¹put in (vb) **1** een verzoek indienen, solliciteren: ~ *for* zich kandidaat stellen voor; ~ *for leave* verlof (aan)vragen **2** binnenlopen: ~ *at a port* een haven binnenlopen
²put in (vb) **1** (erin) plaatsen, zetten, inlassen, invoegen: ~ *an appearance* zich (eens) laten zien **2** opwerpen: ~ *a (good) word for s.o.* een goed woordje voor iem. doen **3** besteden [time, work, money]; doorbrengen [time]: *he* ~ *a lot of hard work on the project* hij heeft een boel werk in het project gestopt **4** indienen, klacht, document: ~ *a claim for*

damages een eis tot schadevergoeding indienen

put off 1 uitstellen, afzeggen **2** afzetten; uit laten stappen [passengers] **3** afschrikken, (van zich) afstoten: *the **smell** of that food put me off* de reuk van dat eten deed me walgen **4** afschepen, ontmoedigen **5** van de wijs brengen: *the **speaker** was ~ by the noise* de spreker werd door het lawaai van zijn stuk gebracht **6** uitdoen, uitdraaien; afzetten [light, gas, radio etc]

put on 1 voorwenden; aannemen [attitude]: *~ a brave **face*** flink zijn **2** toevoegen, verhogen: *~ **weight*** aankomen, zwaarder worden; *put it on* **a)** aankomen [weight]; **b)** overdrijven **3** opvoeren, op de planken brengen: *~ a **play*** een toneelstuk op de planken brengen; *put it on* doen alsof **4** aantrekken [clothing]; opzetten [glasses, hat] **5** inzetten; inleggen [extra train etc] **6** in werking stellen; aandoen [light]; aanzetten [radio etc]; opzetten [record, kettle]: *~ a **brake*** (or: *the **brakes***) afremmen [fig] **7** in contact brengen, doorverbinden: *who put the police on **to** me?* wie heeft de politie op mijn spoor gezet?

¹put out (vb) uitvaren: *~ **to** sea* zee kiezen

²put out (vb) **1** uitsteken, tonen: *~ **feelers*** zijn voelhoorns uitsteken **2** aanwenden, inzetten, gebruiken **3** uitdoen, doven, blussen: *~ the **fire*** (or: *light*) het vuur (or: licht) doven **4** van zijn stuk brengen **5** storen: *put o.s. out* zich moeite getroosten, moeite doen **6** buiten zetten [garbage]; eruit gooien, de deur wijzen **7** uitvaardigen, uitgeven; uitzenden [message]: *~ an official **statement*** een communiqué uitgeven **8** uitbesteden [work]: *~ a job **to** a subcontractor* een werk aan een onderaannemer uitbesteden

¹put over (vb) overvaren

²put over (vb) **1** overbrengen [also fig]; aan de man brengen: *put (a fast) one* (or: *sth.*) *over on s.o.* iem. iets wijsmaken **2** [Am] uitstellen

putrefy (doen) (ver)rotten, (doen) bederven

putrid (ver)rot, vergaan, verpest

putsch staatsgreep; putsch

put through (door)verbinden [telephone call]

put together 1 samenvoegen, samenstellen, combineren: *more than all the **others** ~* meer dan alle anderen bij elkaar **2** verzamelen, verenigen ‖ *put **two** and two together* **a)** zijn conclusies trekken; **b)** logisch nadenken

putty 1 stopverf **2** plamuur[h] ‖ *be ~ in s.o.'s hands* als was in iemands handen zijn

¹put up (vb) logeren: *~ **at** an inn* in een herberg logeren ‖ *I wouldn't ~ **with** it any longer* ik zou het niet langer meer slikken

²put up (vb) **1** opzetten, oprichten; bouwen

[tent, statue etc]: *~ a **smokescreen*** een rookgordijn leggen **2** opsteken, hijsen, ophangen: *put one's **hands** up* de handen opsteken [indicating surrender] **3** bekendmaken, ophangen: *~ a **notice*** een bericht ophangen **4** verhogen, opslaan: *~ the **rent*** de huurprijs verhogen **5** huisvesten, logeren **6** beschikbaar stellen [funds]; voorschieten: *who will ~ **money** for new research?* wie stelt geld beschikbaar voor nieuw onderzoek? **7** bieden, tonen: *the rebels ~ strong **resistance*** de rebellen boden hevig weerstand **8** (te koop) aanbieden: *they ~ their house **for** sale* zij boden hun huis te koop aan **9** kandidaat stellen, voordragen: *they put him up **for** chairman* zij droegen hem als voorzitter voor ‖ *put s.o. up to sth.* **a)** iem. opstoken tot iets; **b)** iem. op de hoogte brengen van iets

put-up afgesproken: *it's a ~ **job*** het is een doorgestoken kaart

¹puzzle (n) **1** raadsel[h], probleem[h] **2** puzzel: *crossword ~* kruiswoordraadsel

²puzzle (vb) peinzen, piekeren

³puzzle (vb) **1** voor een raadsel zetten, verbazen, verbijsteren **2** in verwarring brengen **3** overpeinzen: *~ one's **brains** (about, over)* zich het hoofd breken (over); *~ sth. out* iets uitpluizen

puzzled in de war, perplex

puzzler 1 puzzelaar(ster) **2** probleem[h], moeilijke vraag

puzzling onbegrijpelijk; raadselachtig

¹pygmy (n) pygmee, dwerg; [fig] nietig persoon

²pygmy (adj) heel klein, dwerg-

pyjamas pyjama: *four pairs of ~* vier pyjama's

pyramid piramide

pyre brandstapel

pyromaniac pyromaan

pyrotechnic vuurwerk-: *a ~ **display*** een vuurwerk(show)

pyrrhic: *Pyrrhic **victory*** pyrrusoverwinning

python python

q

Qatar Qatar
¹Qatari (n) Qatarees, Qatarese
²Qatari (adj) Qatarees
Q-tip [Am] wattenstaafje[h]
¹quack (n) **1** kwakzalver, charlatan **2** kwak [of duck]; gekwaak[h]
²quack (vb) **1** kwaken [of duck] **2** zwetsen, kletsen
quad bike quad
quadrangle 1 vierhoek, vierkant[h], rechthoek **2** (vierhoekige) binnenplaats, vierkant plein[h] (met de gebouwen eromheen)
¹quadrilateral (n) vierhoek
²quadrilateral (adj) vierzijdig
quadruped viervoeter, (als) van een viervoeter
¹quadruple (n) viervoud[h]
²quadruple (adj) vierdelig, viervoudig
quadruplet één van een vierling: ~s vierling
quagmire moeras[h] [also fig]; poel
¹quail (n) kwartel
²quail (vb) (terug)schrikken, bang worden
quaint 1 apart, curieus, ongewoon: *a ~ old building* een bijzonder, oud gebouw **2** vreemd, grillig
¹quake (n) **1** schok **2** aardbeving
²quake (vb) schokken, trillen, bibberen
qualification 1 beperking, voorbehoud[h]: *a statement with many ~s* een verklaring met veel kanttekeningen **2** kwaliteit, verdienste, kwalificatie **3** (bewijs[h] van) geschiktheid: *a medical ~* een medische bevoegdheid **4** beschrijving, kenmerking
qualified 1 beperkt, voorwaardelijk, voorlopig: *~ optimism* gematigd optimisme **2** bevoegd, geschikt: *a ~ nurse* een gediplomeerde verpleegster
¹qualify (vb) zich kwalificeren, zich bekwamen, geschikt zijn, worden: *~ for membership* in aanmerking komen voor lidmaatschap
²qualify (vb) **1** beperken, kwalificeren, (verder) bepalen: *a ~ing exam* een akte-examen **2** geschikt maken, het recht geven **3** verzachten, matigen
qualitative kwalitatief
quality 1 kwaliteit, deugd, capaciteit: *~ of life* leefbaarheid, kwaliteit van het bestaan **2** eigenschap, kenmerk[h], karakteristiek **3** kwaliteit, waarde, gehalte[h]: *~ newspaper* kwaliteitskrant; *~ time* kwaliteitstijd
qualm 1 (gevoel van) onzekerheid, ongemakkelijk gevoel[h]: *she had no ~s about going*

on her own ze zag er niet tegenop om alleen te gaan **2** (gewetens)wroeging
quandary moeilijke situatie, dilemma[h], onzekerheid: *we were in a ~ about how to react* we wisten niet goed hoe we moesten reageren
quantify kwantificeren, in getallen uitdrukken, meten, bepalen
quantity 1 hoeveelheid, aantal[h], som, portie **2** grootheid; [fig] persoon; ding[h]: *an unknown ~* een onbekende (grootheid), een nog niet doorgronde (or: berekenbare) persoon **3** kwantiteit, hoeveelheid, omvang
¹quantum (n) kwantum[h], (benodigde/wenselijke) hoeveelheid
²quantum (adj) spectaculair: *~ leap* spectaculaire stap vooruit, doorbraak, omwenteling
¹quarantine (n) quarantaine, isolatie
²quarantine (vb) in quarantaine plaatsen; [fig also] isoleren
quark quark
¹quarrel (n) **1** ruzie, onenigheid: *start* (or: *pick*) *a ~* (*with s.o.*) ruzie zoeken (met iem.) **2** kritiek, reden tot ruzie: *I have no ~ with him* ik heb niets tegen hem
²quarrel (vb) **1** ruzie maken, onenigheid hebben **2** kritiek hebben, aanmerkingen hebben
quarrelsome ruziezoekend
quarry 1 (nagejaagde) prooi, wild[h] **2** (steen)groeve
quart quart[h], kwart gallon; twee pints [measure of capacity] ‖ *put a ~ into a pint pot* het onmogelijke proberen
quarter 1 kwart[h], vierde deel[h]: *a ~ of an hour* een kwartier; *three ~s of the people* voted driekwart van de mensen stemde **2** kwart dollar, kwartje[h] **3** kwartaal[h]; [Am] collegeperiode; academisch kwartaal[h] **4** kwartier[h] [of time, moon]: *for an hour and a ~* een uur en een kwartier (lang); *it's a ~ past* (or: *to*) *eight* het is kwart over (*or:* voor) acht **5** quarter; kwart[h] [weight, size, measure] **6** (wind)richting; windstreek [of compass]; hoek, kant: *I expect no help from that ~* ik verwacht geen hulp uit die hoek **7** (stads)deel[h], wijk, gewest[h] **8** genade, clementie: *ask for* (or: *cry*) *~* om genade smeken **9** (-s) [oft mil] kwartier[h], verblijf[h], woonplaats, legerplaats, kamer(s); [fig] kring: *this information comes from the highest ~s* deze inlichtingen komen uit de hoogste kringen
quarterdeck [shipp] **1** (officiers)halfdek[h] **2** (marine)officieren
quarter-final kwartfinale
¹quarterly (n) driemaandelijks tijdschrift[h], kwartaalblad[h]
²quarterly (adj) driemaandelijks, viermaal per jaar, kwartaalsgewijs
quartermaster intendant; kwartiermaker

quartet kwartet[h], viertal[h]
quarto kwarto[h]
quartz kwarts[h]
quasi quasi, zogenaamd
[1]**quaver** (n) **1** trilling **2** [mus] achtste (noot)
[2]**quaver** (vb) trillen, beven, sidderen: *in a ~ing voice* met bevende stem
quay kade
queasy 1 misselijk, onpasselijk **2** overgevoelig, kieskeurig: *he has a ~ conscience* hij neemt het erg nauw
[1]**queen** (n) **1** koningin **2** [chess] koningin, dame **3** [cards] vrouw, dame: *~ of hearts* hartenvrouw **4** nicht, verwijfde flikker
[2]**queen** (vb): *~ it over s.o.* de mevrouw spelen ten opzichte van iem.
queen consort gemalin van de koning; koningin
Queen's English standaard Engels, BBC-Engels
[1]**queer** (n) homo, flikker
[2]**queer** (adj) **1** vreemd, raar, zonderling: *a ~ customer* een rare snuiter **2** verdacht, onbetrouwbaar **3** onwel, niet lekker **4** homoseksueel ‖ *be in Queer Street* **a)** in moeilijkheden zitten; **b)** schulden hebben
quell onderdrukken, een eind maken aan, onderwerpen
quench 1 doven, blussen **2** lessen [thirst]
querulous 1 klagend **2** klagerig
[1]**query** (n) vraag, vraagteken[h]
[2]**query** (vb) **1** vragen (naar), informeren (naar) **2** in twijfel trekken; een vraagteken plaatsen bij [also lit]; betwijfelen
query language zoektaal
quest zoektocht: *the ~ for the Holy Grail* de zoektocht naar de Heilige Graal
[1]**question** (n) **1** vraag: *a leading ~* een suggestieve vraag **2** vraagstuk[h], probleem[h], kwestie: *that is out of the ~* er is geen sprake van, daar komt niets van in; *that is not the ~* daar gaat het niet om **3** twijfel, onzekerheid, bezwaar[h]: *call sth. into ~* iets in twijfel trekken; *beyond (all)* (or: *without*) *~* ongetwijfeld, stellig ‖ *beg the ~* het punt in kwestie als bewezen aanvaarden; *pop the ~ (to her)* (haar) ten huwelijk vragen
[2]**question** (vb) **1** vragen, ondervragen, uithoren: *~ s.o. about* (or: *on*) *his plans* iem. over zijn plannen ondervragen **2** onderzoeken **3** betwijfelen, zich afvragen: *I ~ whether* (or: *if*) ... ik betwijfel het of ...
questionable 1 twijfelachtig **2** verdacht
question mark vraagteken[h] [also fig]; mysterie[h], onzekerheid
questionnaire vragenlijst
question time vragenuurtje[h]
[1]**queue** (n) rij, file ‖ *jump the ~* voordringen, voor je beurt gaan
[2]**queue** (vb) een rij vormen, in de rij (gaan) staan

[1]**quibble** (n) spitsvondigheid, haarkloverij
[2]**quibble** (vb) uitvluchten zoeken, bekvechten: *we don't have to ~ about the details* we hoeven niet over de details te harrewarren
quiche quiche, hartige taart
[1]**quick** (n) **1** levend vlees[h] [under skin, nail] **2** hart[h], kern, essentie: *cut s.o. to the ~* iemands gevoelens diep kwetsen **3** [Am] kwik[h]
[2]**quick** (adj) **1** snel, gauw, vlug: *be as ~ as lightning* bliksemsnel zijn; *~ march!* voorwaarts mars!; *in ~ succession* snel achter elkaar; *he is ~ to take offence* hij is gauw beledigd **2** gevoelig, vlug (van begrip), scherp **3** levendig, opgewekt
quicken 1 levend worden, (weer) tot leven komen: *his pulse ~ed* zijn polsslag werd weer sterker **2** leven beginnen te vertonen; tekenen van leven geven [of child in womb]
quickie vluggertje[h], haastwerk[h], prutswerk[h]
quicksand drijfzand[h]
quicksilver kwik(zilver)[h]; [fig] levendig temperament[h]
quickstep quickstep, snelle foxtrot
quick-tempered lichtgeraakt; opvliegend
quick-witted vlug van begrip, gevat, scherp
quid 1 pond[h] [sterling] **2** (tabaks)pruim[h]
quid pro quo vergoeding; compensatie
quiescence rust, stilte
[1]**quiet** (n) **1** stilte **2** rust, kalmte: *they lived in peace and ~* zij leefden in rust en vrede
[2]**quiet** (adj) **1** stil, rustig: *~ as a mouse* muisstil **2** heimelijk, geheim: *keep ~ about last night* hou je mond over vannacht **3** zonder drukte, ongedwongen: *a ~ dinner party* een informeel etentje
[1]**quieten** (vb) (also + down) tot bedaren brengen, kalmeren, tot rust brengen: *my reassurance didn't ~ her fear* mijn geruststelling verminderde haar angst niet
[2]**quieten** (vb) (also + down) rustig worden, bedaren, kalmeren
quietude kalmte, (gemoeds)rust, vrede
quilt 1 gewatteerde deken, dekbed[h]: *a continental ~* een dekbed **2** sprei
quinine kinine
quintessence 1 kern, hoofdzaak **2** het beste, het fijnste
quintet vijftal[h], (groep van) vijf musici, kwintet[h]
quip 1 schimpscheut, steek **2** geestigheid, woordspeling
quirk 1 spitsvondigheid, uitvlucht **2** geestigheid, spotternij **3** gril, nuk: *a ~ of fate* een gril van het lot **4** (rare) kronkel, eigenaardigheid
quirky 1 spitsvondig **2** grillig; eigenzinnig
[1]**quit** (adj) vrij, verlost, bevrijd: *we are well ~ of those difficulties* goed, dat we van die moeilijkheden af zijn
[2]**quit** (vb) **1** ophouden, stoppen: *I've had*

enough, I ~ ik heb er genoeg van, ik kap ermee **2** opgeven **3** vertrekken, ervandoor gaan, zijn baan opgeven: *the neighbours have already had **notice** to ~* de buren is de huur al opgezegd
³quit (vb) **1** ophouden met, stoppen met: ~ *complaining about the cold!* hou op met klagen over de kou! **2** verlaten, vertrekken van, heengaan van
quite 1 helemaal, geheel, volledig, absoluut: ~ *possible* best mogelijk; *you're ~ **right*** je hebt volkomen gelijk; *that's ~ another matter* dat is een heel andere zaak **2** nogal, enigszins, tamelijk: *it's ~ **cold** today* het is nogal koud vandaag **3** werkelijk, echt, in feite: *they seem ~ **happy** together* zij lijken echt gelukkig samen **4** erg, veel: *there were ~ a **few** people* er waren flink wat mensen; *that was ~ a **party*** dat was me het feestje wel
quits quitte: *now we **are** ~* nu staan we quitte
¹quiver (n) **1** pijlkoker **2** trilling, siddering, beving
²quiver (vb) (doen) trillen, (doen) beven, sidderen
¹quiz (n) **1** ondervraging, verhoor[h] **2** test, kort examen[h] **3** quiz
²quiz (vb) **1** ondervragen, uithoren **2** mondeling examineren
quizzical 1 komisch, grappig **2** spottend, plagerig **3** vorsend, vragend: *she gave me a ~ **look*** ze keek me met een onderzoekende blik aan
quota 1 quota, evenredig deel[h], aandeel[h] **2** (maximum) aantal[h]
quotation 1 citaat[h], aanhaling, het citeren **2** notering [of Stock Exchange, exchange rate, price] **3** prijsopgave
quotation mark aanhalingsteken[h]
¹quote (n) **1** citaat[h], aanhaling **2** notering [of Stock Exchange etc] **3** aanhalingsteken[h]: *in ~s* tussen aanhalingstekens
²quote (vb) **1** citeren, aanhalen **2** opgeven [price]
quotient quotiënt[h]

r

rabbi rabbi, rabbijn

¹rabbit (n) konijn[h], konijnenbont[h], konijnen-vlees[h]

²rabbit (vb) **1** op konijnen jagen **2** kletsen, zeuren

rabbit hole konijnenhol[h]

rabbit warren 1 konijnenveld[h] **2** doolhof, wirwar van straatjes

rabble kluwen, troep, bende: *the* ~ het gepeupel

rabid 1 razend, woest **2** fanatiek **3** dol, hondsdol

rabies hondsdolheid

raccoon *see* racoon

¹race (n) **1** wedren, wedloop, race: ~ *against time* race tegen de klok; *the* ~*s* de (honden)-rennen, de paardenrennen **2** sterke stroom **3** ras[h] **4** volk[h], natie, stam, slag, klasse

²race (vb) **1** wedlopen, aan een wedloop deelnemen, een wedstrijd houden **2** rennen, hollen, snellen **3** doorslaan [of screw, wheel]; doordraaien [of engine]

³race (vb) **1** een wedren houden met, om het hardst lopen met: *I'll* ~ *you* **to** *that tree* laten we doen wie het eerst bij die boom is **2** (zeer) snel vervoeren: *they* ~*d the child* **to** *hospital* ze vlogen met het kind naar het ziekenhuis **3** laten doordraaien [engine]

racecourse renbaan

racehorse renpaard[h]

racer 1 renner, hardloper **2** renpaard[h] **3** racefiets **4** renwagen **5** raceboot **6** wedstrijdjacht[h] **7** renschaats: ~*s* noren

racetrack (ovale) renbaan, circuit[h]

racial raciaal: ~ *discrimination* ras(sen)discriminatie

¹racing (n) het wedrennen, het deelnemen aan wedstrijden

²racing (n) rensport

racism 1 racisme[h] **2** rassenhaat

¹racist (n) racist

²racist (adj) racistisch

¹rack (n) **1** rek[h], (bagage)rek[h] **2** ruif **3** pijnbank: [fig] *be* **on** *the* ~ op de pijnbank liggen, in grote spanning (*or:* onzekerheid) verkeren **4** kwelling, marteling **5** verwoesting, afbraak, ondergang: *go to* ~ *and* **ruin** geheel vervallen, instorten

²rack (vb) kwellen, pijnigen, teisteren: ~ *one's* **brains** zijn hersens pijnigen; ~*ed with* **jealousy** verteerd door jaloezie

racket 1 [sport] racket[h] **2** sneeuwschoen **3** lawaai[h], herrie, kabaal[h]: *kick up a* ~ een rel

(*or:* herrie) schoppen **4** bedriegerij, bedrog[h], zwendel **5** [inform] gangsterpraktijken, misdadige organisatie, afpersing, intimidatie

racketeer gangster, misdadiger, afperser

racoon 1 wasbeer **2** wasberenbont[h]

racy 1 markant; krachtig [style, person(ality)] **2** pittig, kruidig, geurig **3** pikant; gewaagd [story]

radar radar

radial radiaal, stervormig, straal-: ~ *tyre* radiaalband

radiance straling, schittering, pracht

radiant 1 stralend, schitterend: *he was* ~ *with joy* hij straalde van vreugde **2** stervormig **3** stralings-: ~ *heat* stralingswarmte

¹radiate (vb) **1** stralen, schijnen **2** een ster vormen: *streets radiating* **from** *a square* straten die straalsgewijs vanaf een plein lopen

²radiate (vb) **1** uitstralen, (naar alle kanten) verspreiden: ~ *confidence* vertrouwen uitstralen **2** bestralen

radiation 1 straling **2** bestraling

radiation sickness stralingsziekte

radiator radiator, radiatorkachel, radiateur; koeler [of engine]

¹radical (n) **1** basis(principe[h]) **2** wortel(teken[h]) **3** radicaal

²radical (adj) **1** radicaal, drastisch **2** fundamenteel, wezenlijk, essentieel **3** wortel-: ~ *sign* wortelteken

radio radio(toestel[h])

radioactive radioactief

radio button checkbox; hokje dat aangevinkt kan worden

radiogram röntgenfoto

radiography radiografie

radiologist radioloog

radiotherapy [med] bestraling

radish radijs

radium radium[h]

radius straal, radius; halve middellijn [of circle]: *within a* ~ *of four miles* binnen een straal van vier mijl

RAF *Royal Air Force*

raffish liederlijk, losbandig, wild

¹raffle (n) loterij, verloting

²raffle (vb) (also + off) verloten

raft 1 vlot[h], drijvende steiger **2** reddingvlot[h] **3** grote verzameling: *he worked his way through a whole* ~ *of* **letters** hij werkte zich door een hele berg brieven heen

rafter dakspant[h]

¹rag (n) **1** versleten kledingstuk[h], lomp, vod[h]: *from* ~*s to* **riches** van armoede naar rijkdom **2** lapje[h], vodje[h], stuk[h], flard: *I haven't a* ~ *to* **put** *on* ik heb niets om aan te trekken **3** vlag, gordijn[h], krant, blaadje[h]: *the local* ~ het plaatselijke blaadje **4** herrie, keet, (studenten)lol ‖ *chew the* ~ mopperen, kankeren

²rag (vb) **1** pesten, plagen: *they* ~*ged the teacher* zij schopten keet bij de leraar **2** te

grazen nemen, een poets bakken
ragamuffin schooiertjeʰ
ragbag allegaartjeʰ
rag doll lappenpop
¹rage (n) **1** manie, passie, bevlieging: *short hair is (all) the ~ now* kort haar is nu een rage **2** woede, woede-uitbarsting, razernij: *be in a ~* woedend zijn
²rage (vb) woeden, tieren, razen; [fig] tekeergaan: *a raging fire* een felle brand
ragged 1 haveloos, gescheurd, gerafeld: *~ trousers* een kapotte broek **2** ruig, onverzorgd: *a ~ beard* een ruige baard **3** ongelijk, getand, knoestig: *~ rocks* scherpe rotsen
ragtag gepeupelʰ, grauwʰ || *~ and bobtail* uitschot, schorem
¹raid (n) **1** inval, (verrassings)overval **2** rooftocht, roofoverval: *a ~ on a bank* een bankoverval **3** politieoverval, razzia
²raid (vb) **1** overvallen, binnenvallen **2** (be)roven, plunderen, leegroven: *they have been ~ing the fridge as usual* ze hebben zoals gewoonlijk de koelkast geplunderd
raider 1 overvaller **2** kaper(schipʰ) **3** rover
¹rail (n) **1** lat, balk, stang **2** leuning **3** omheining, hek(werk)ʰ, slagboom **4** rail, spoorstaaf; [fig] trein; spoorwegen: *travel by ~* sporen, per trein reizen **5** reling || *run off the ~s* uit de band springen, ontsporen
²rail (vb) (+ against, at) schelden (op), uitvaren (tegen), tekeergaan (tegen)
railcard treinabonnementʰ
railing 1 traliewerkʰ; spijlen [of gate] **2** leuning, reling, hekʰ, balustrade **3** gescheldʰ
raillery scherts, grap(pen), gekheid
rail pass treinabonnementʰ
railroad 1 [Am] per trein vervoeren **2** jagen, haasten, drijven: *~ a bill through Congress* een wetsvoorstel erdoor jagen in het Congres
railway 1 spoorweg, spoorlijn **2** spoorwegmaatschappij, de spoorwegen
railway station spoorwegstationʰ
¹rain (n) **1** regen, regenbui, regenval: *it looks like ~* het ziet er naar uit dat het gaat regenen **2** (stort)vloed, stroom: *a ~ of blows* een reeks klappen **3** (the rains) regentijd, regenseizoenʰ
²rain (vb) **1** regenen **2** neerstromen **3** doen neerdalen, laten neerkomen: *the father ~ed presents upon his only daughter* de vader overstelpte zijn enige dochter met cadeaus || *it ~s invitations* het regent uitnodigingen
rainbow regenboog
rain check nieuw toegangsbewijsʰ [for match, event]: *I don't want a drink now, but I'll take a ~ on it* ik wil nu niets drinken, maar ik hou het van je tegoed
raincoat regenjas
rain down neerkomen, neerdalen (in gro-

ten getale): *blows rained down (up)on his head* een regen van klappen kwam neer op zijn hoofd
rainfall regen(val), neerslag
rain forest regenwoudʰ
rainproof regendicht, tegen regen bestand
rainstorm stortbui
rainy regenachtig, regen-: *save (up)/provide (or: put away, keep) sth. for a ~ day* een appeltje voor de dorst bewaren
raise 1 wekken; opwekken [from death]; wakker maken: *~ expectations* verwachtingen wekken **2** opzetten, tot opstand bewegen **3** opwekken, opbeuren: *the news of her arrival ~d his hopes* het nieuws van haar aankomst gaf hem weer hoop **4** bouwen, opzetten, stichten **5** kweken, produceren, verbouwen **6** grootbrengen, opvoeden: *~ a family* kinderen grootbrengen **7** uiten, aanheffen, ter sprake brengen, opperen: *~ objections to sth.* bezwaren tegen iets naar voren brengen **8** doen ontstaan, beginnen, in het leven roepen: *his behaviour ~s doubts* zijn gedrag roept twijfels op **9** (op)heffen, opnemen; opslaan [eyes]; omhoog doen **10** bevorderen, promoveren **11** versterken, vergroten; verheffen [voice]; vermeerderen, verhogen: *~ the temperature* de verwarming hoger zetten; [fig] de spanning laten oplopen **12** heffen; innen [money]; bijeenbrengen, inzamelen: *~ taxes* belastingen heffen **13** op de been brengen; werven [eg army] **14** opheffen, beëindigen: *~ a blockade* een blokkade opheffen **15** [maths] verheffen tot [power]
raisin rozijn
¹rake (n) **1** hark, riek: *as lean as a ~* zo mager als een lat **2** losbol **3** schuinte; val [of mast,]; helling **4** hellingshoek
²rake (vb) **1** harken **2** zoeken, snuffelen: *the customs officers ~d through my luggage* de douanebeambten doorzochten mijn bagage van onder tot boven **3** oplopen, hellen
³rake (vb) **1** (bijeen)harken [also fig]; vergaren, bijeenhalen: *you must be raking it in* je moet wel scheppen geld verdienen **2** rakelen, poken; [fig] oprakelen: *~ over old ashes* oprakelen, oude koeien uit de sloot halen **3** doorzoeken, uitkammen: *~ one's memory* zijn geheugen pijnigen
rake up 1 bijeenharken, aanharken **2** [inform] optrommelen, opscharrelen **3** oprakelen [also fig]: *~ old stories* oude koeien uit de sloot halen
rakish 1 liederlijk, losbandig **2** zwierig, vlot **3** smalgebouwd, snel, snelvarend
¹rally (n) **1** bijeenkomst, vergadering **2** opleving, herstelʰ **3** [tennis] rally **4** rally, sterrit **5** herstelʰ [of share prices]
²rally (vb) **1** bijeenkomen, zich verzamelen

ransom

2 zich aansluiten: ~ *round* the flag zich om de vlag scharen 3 (zich) herstellen, opleven, weer bijkomen 4 weer omhooggaan; zich herstellen [of share prices]
³**rally** (vb) 1 verzamelen, ordenen, herenigen 2 bijeenbrengen, verenigen, op de been brengen 3 doen opleven, nieuw leven inblazen 4 plagen, voor de gek houden
rally (a)round te hulp komen, helpen, bijspringen
¹**ram** (n) 1 ram [male sheep] 2 stormram
²**ram** (vb) 1 aanstampen, vaststampen 2 heien 3 doordringen, overduidelijk maken 4 persen, proppen 5 rammen, bonken, beuken, botsen op
RAM *random-access memory* RAMʰ
Ramadan ramadan; vastenmaand
¹**ramble** (n) zwerftocht, wandeltocht, uitstapjeʰ
²**ramble** (vb) 1 dwalen, zwerven, trekken 2 afdwalen, bazelen: *once he gets started he ~s on* als hij eenmaal begonnen is, blijft hij maar doorzeuren 3 wild groeien; woekeren [of plants] 4 kronkelen [of path, river]
rambler 1 wandelaar, trekker, zwerver 2 klimroos
rambling 1 rondtrekkend, ronddolend 2 onsamenhangend, verward: *he made a few ~ remarks* hij maakte een paar vage opmerkingen 3 wild groeiend; kruipend [of plants] 4 onregelmatig, grillig: ~ *passages* gangetjes die alle kanten op gaan
rambunctious [Am; inform] 1 onstuimig, onbesuisd, luidruchtig 2 (lekker) eigenzinnig
ramification afsplitsing, vertakking, onderverdeling, implicaties: *all ~s of the plot were not yet known* alle vertakkingen van de samenzwering waren nog niet bekend
ramp 1 helling, glooiing 2 oprit; afrit [also of lorries etc]; hellingbaan 3 verkeersdrempel
¹**rampage** (n) dolheid, uitzinnigheid: *be on the* ~ uitzinnig tekeergaan
²**rampage** (vb) (uitzinnig) tekeergaan, razen
rampant 1 wild, woest, verwoed 2 (te) weelderig, welig tierend || *crime* was ~ *in that neighbourhood* de misdaad vierde hoogtij in die buurt
rampart 1 borstwering, wal 2 verdediging, bolwerkʰ
ram-raid [inform] ramkraak
ramrod laadstok [to tamp down gunpowder]: *as stiff as a* ~ kaarsrecht
ramshackle bouwvallig, vervallen
ranch boerderij, ranch
rancher boer; veefokker
rancid ranzig
rancour wrok, haat
¹**random** (n): *at* ~ op goed geluk af; *fill in answers at* ~ zomaar wat antwoorden invullen

²**random** (adj) willekeurig, toevallig, op goed geluk: ~ *check* steekproef
random-access [comp] directe toegang [of memory]: ~ *file* direct toegankelijk bestand
randy [inform] geil, wellustig
¹**range** (n) 1 rij, reeks, keten: *a ~ of mountains* een bergketen 2 woeste (weide)grond 3 schietterreinʰ; testgebiedʰ [of rockets, projectiles] 4 gebiedʰ, kring, terreinʰ 5 sortering, collectie, assortimentʰ 6 groot keukenfornuisʰ 7 bereikʰ, draagkracht, draagwijdte: *the man had been shot at close* ~ de man was van dichtbij neergeschoten; *(with)in* ~ binnen schootsafstand, binnen bereik
²**range** (vb) 1 zich uitstrekken 2 voorkomen [of plant, animal]; aangetroffen worden 3 verschillen, variëren: *ticket prices ~ from three to eight pound* de prijzen van de kaartjes liggen tussen de drie en acht pond 4 zwerven, zich bewegen, gaan: *his new book ~s over too many subjects* zijn nieuwe boek omvat te veel onderwerpen
³**range** (vb) 1 rangschikken, ordenen, (op)stellen 2 doorkruisen, zwerven over, aflopen; [fig] afzoeken; gaan over: *his eyes ~d the mountains* zijn ogen zochten de bergen af 3 weiden, hoeden, houden
ranger 1 boswachter 2 gids; padvindster [14-17 years old] 3 [Am] commandoʰ [soldier]
¹**rank** (n) 1 rij, lijn, reeks 2 gelidʰ, rij: *the ~ and file* de manschappen; [fig] de gewone man; *close (the) ~s* de gelederen sluiten 3 taxistandplaats 4 rang, positie, graad, de hogere stand: *raised to the ~ of major* tot (de rang van) majoor bevorderd; *pull* ~ op zijn strepen gaan staan || *pull* ~ *on s.o.* misbruik maken van zijn macht ten opzichte van iem.
²**rank** (adj) 1 (te) weelderig, (te) welig: ~ *weeds* welig tierend onkruid 2 te vet [of soil] 3 stinkend 4 absoluut: [fig] ~ *injustice* schreeuwende onrechtvaardigheid
³**rank** (vb) 1 zich bevinden [in a certain position]; staan, behoren: *this book ~s among (or: with) the best* dit boek behoort tot de beste; ~ *as* gelden als 2 [Am] de hoogste positie bekleden
⁴**rank** (vb) 1 opstellen, in het gelid plaatsen 2 plaatsen, neerzetten, rangschikken: ~ *s.o. with Stan Laurel* iem. op één lijn stellen met Stan Laurel
ranking classificatie, (positie in een) rangorde
rankle steken, knagen, woekeren
ransack 1 doorzoeken, doorsnuffelen 2 plunderen, leegroven, beroven
¹**ransom** (n) 1 losgeldʰ, losprijs, afkoopsom 2 vrijlating [for ransom money] || *hold s.o. to* ~ een losgeld voor iem. eisen [under threat of violence]

²ransom (vb) **1** vrijkopen **2** vrijlaten [for ransom money] **3** losgeld voor iem. eisen
¹rant (n) bombast, holle frasen
²rant (vb) **1** bombast uitslaan **2** tieren, tekeergaan: *the schoolmaster started to ~ and rave* de meester begon te razen en te tieren
¹rap (n) **1** tik, slag: *get a ~ over the knuckles* een tik op de vingers krijgen; [fig] op de vingers getikt worden **2** geklopʰ, klop **3** zier, beetjeʰ: *he doesn't give a ~ for her* hij geeft helemaal niets om haar **4** schuld, straf: *I don't want to take the ~ for this* ik wil hier niet voor opdraaien **5** [inform; mus] rap [rhythmic lyrics to music]
²rap (vb) **1** kloppen, tikken: *~ at a door* op een deur kloppen **2** praten, erop los kletsen
³rap (vb) **1** slaan, een tik geven **2** bekritiseren, op de vingers tikken
rapacious hebzuchtig; inhalig
rapacity hebzucht, roofzucht
¹rape (n) **1** verkrachting **2** koolzaadʰ, raapzaadʰ
²rape (vb) verkrachten, onteren
¹rapid (n) stroomversnelling
²rapid (adj) snel, vlug: *~ fire* snelvuur; *in ~ succession* snel achter elkaar; [Am] *~ transit* snelverkeer [train, tram, underground]
rapidity vlugheid
rapist verkrachter
rap out 1 eruit gooien, er uitflappen **2** door kloppen meedelen, door kloppen te kennen geven: *~ an SOS* met klopsignalen een SOS doorgeven
rapport 1 verstandhouding: *be in ~ with s.o.* een goede verstandhouding met iem. hebben **2** contactʰ
rapt 1 verrukt, in vervoering: *they listened to the new record with ~ attention* helemaal gegrepen luisterden zij naar de nieuwe plaat **2** verdiept, verzonken
rapture 1 vervoering, verrukking, extase **2** (-s) extase, vervoering: *she was in ~s about* (or: *over*) *her meeting with the poet* zij was lyrisch over haar ontmoeting met de dichter
rapturous hartstochtelijk, meeslepend
rare 1 ongewoon, ongebruikelijk, vreemd **2** zeldzaam **3** halfrauw, niet gaar; kort gebakken [of meat]
rarefied 1 ijl, dun **2** verheven
rarely 1 zelden: *he ~ comes home before eight* hij komt zelden voor achten thuis **2** zeldzaam, ongewoon, uitzonderlijk: *a ~ beautiful woman* een zeldzaam mooie vrouw
raring dolgraag, enthousiast
rarity zeldzaamheid, rariteit, schaarsheid
rascal 1 schoft, schurk **2** schavuit, deugniet, rakker
¹rash (n) (huid)uitslag
²rash (adj) **1** overhaast, te snel **2** onstuimig **3** ondoordacht: *in a ~ moment* op een onbewaakt ogenblik

¹rasp (n) **1** rasp **2** raspgeluidʰ, graspʰ
²rasp (vb) schrapen, krassen: *with ~ing voice* met krakende stem
³rasp (vb) raspen, vijlen, schuren
raspberry 1 frambozenstruik **2** framboos **3** [inform] afkeurend pf!
rat 1 rat **2** deserteur, overloper **3** [Am] verrader, klikspaan || *smell a ~* lont ruiken, iets in de smiezen hebben
¹rate (n) **1** snelheid, vaart, tempoʰ **2** prijs, tariefʰ, koers: *~ of exchange* wisselkoers; *~ of interest* rentevoet **3** (sterfte)cijferʰ, geboortecijferʰ **4** (kwaliteits)klasse, rang, graad **5** (-s) gemeentebelasting, onroerendgoedbelasting || *at any ~* in ieder geval, ten minste; *at this ~* in dit geval, op deze manier
²rate (vb) gerekend worden, behoren, gelden: *he ~s as one of the best writers* hij geldt als een van de beste schrijvers
³rate (vb) **1** schatten, bepalen; waarderen [also fig]: *~ s.o.'s income at* iemands inkomen schatten op **2** beschouwen, tellen, rekenen: *~ among* (or: *with*) rekenen onder (or: tot)
rateable 1 te schatten, taxeerbaar **2** belastbaar, schatbaar
ratepayer 1 belastingbetaler **2** huiseigenaar
rather 1 liever, eerder: *I would ~ not invite your brother* ik nodig je broer liever niet uit **2** juister (uitgedrukt), liever gezegd: *she is my girlfriend, or ~ she was my girlfriend* zij is mijn vriendin, of liever: ze was mijn vriendin **3** enigszins, tamelijk, nogal, wel: *a ~ shocking experience, ~ a shocking experience* een nogal schokkende ervaring **4** meer, sterker, in hogere mate: *they depend ~ on Paul's than on their own income* zij zijn meer van Pauls inkomen afhankelijk dan van het hunne **5** [inform] jazeker, nou en of
ratify bekrachtigen; goedkeuren [treaty]
rating 1 taxering [rated value, assessment] **2** waarderingscijferʰ [of TV programme]; kijkcijferʰ **3** naam, positie, status
ratio (evenredige) verhouding
¹ration (n) **1** rantsoenʰ; portie [also fig] **2** (-s) proviandʰ, voedselʰ, rantsoenen
²ration (vb) rantsoeneren, op rantsoen stellen, distribueren, uitdelen: *petrol is ~ed* de benzine is op de bon
rational 1 rationeel, redelijk **2** (wel)doordacht, logisch **3** verstandig: *man is a ~ being* de mens is een redelijk wezen
rationale grond(reden), grondgedachte(n), beweegreden(en)
¹rationalist (n) rationalist
²rationalist (adj) rationalistisch
rationality 1 rationaliteit **2** rede; denkvermogenʰ **3** redelijkheid
¹rationalize (vb) rationaliseren; efficiënter inrichten [business etc]
²rationalize (vb) rationaliseren, aanneme-

lijk maken, verklaren, achteraf beredeneren
rat on laten vallen, verraden, in de steek laten

the **rat race** moordende competitie, carrière-jacht

rattan 1 rotanʰ, Spaans rietʰ **2** rotting, wandelstok

¹**rattle** (n) **1** geratelʰ, gerammelʰ, gerinkelʰ **2** rammelaar, ratel

²**rattle** (vb) **1** rammelen, ratelen, kletteren **2** (+ away, on) (door)ratelen, (blijven) kletsen ‖ ~ **through** sth. iets afraffelen, iets gauw afmaken

³**rattle** (vb) **1** heen en weer rammelen, schudden, rinkelen met **2** [inform] op stang jagen, opjagen, van streek maken

rattlesnake ratelslang

¹**rattling** (adj) levendig, stevig, krachtig: a ~ **trade** een levendige handel

²**rattling** (adv) uitzonderlijk, uitstekend: a ~ **good match** een zeldzaam mooie wedstrijd

ratty 1 ratachtig, vol ratten, rat(ten)- **2** geïrriteerd

raucous rauw, schor

raunchy [inform] **1** geil, wellustig **2** rauw, ruig, ordinair **3** [Am] vies, smerig, goor

¹**ravage** (n) **1** verwoesting(en), vernietiging **2** (-s) vernietigende werking: the ~s of **time** de tand des tijds

²**ravage** (vb) **1** verwoesten, vernietigen, teisteren: she came from a country ~d **by** war zij kwam uit een door oorlog verwoest land **2** leegplunderen, leegroven

¹**rave** (n) **1** juichende bespreking **2** wild feestʰ, dansfeestʰ ‖ be **in** a ~ **about** helemaal weg zijn van

²**rave** (vb) **1** (+ against, at) razen (tegen/op), ijlen, (als een gek) tekeergaan (tegen) **2** (+ about) opgetogen zijn, raken (over), lyrisch worden (over), dwepen (met)

³**rave** (vb) wild uiting geven aan, zich gek maken

raven raaf

ravenous uitgehongerd, begerig, roof-zuchtig

raver [inform] **1** snel figuur; swinger **2** raver [of house party]

ravine ravijnʰ

¹**raving** (adj) malend, raaskallend

²**raving** (adv) stapel-: stark ~ **mad** knotsknet-tergek

ravings wartaal, geraaskalʰ

ravish 1 verrukken, in vervoering brengen, betoveren **2** verkrachten, onteren

ravishing verrukkelijk, betoverend

raw 1 rauw; ongekookt [of vegetables, meat] **2** onuitgewerkt [figures etc]; grof, on-af(gewerkt), onrijp: ~ **material** grondstof; ~ **silk** ruwe zijde **3** groen, onervaren, onge-traind **4** ontveld, rauw, open **5** guur, ruw; rauw [of weather] ‖ ~ **deal** oneerlijke behan-

deling; touch s.o. **on** the ~ iem. tegen het zere been schoppen; **in** the ~ ongeciviliseerd, pri-mitief, naakt

rawboned broodmager, vel over been

rawhide 1 ongelooide huid **2** zweep

ray 1 straal [of light etc] **2** sprankjeʰ, glimp, lichtpuntjeʰ: a ~ of **hope** een sprankje hoop **3** [zoology] rog, vleet

raze met de grond gelijk maken, volledig verwoesten

razor (elektrisch) scheerapparaatʰ, scheer-mesʰ

razor-billed auk alk

razor blade (veiligheids)scheermesjeʰ

razor-sharp vlijmscherp [also fig]

razzle braspartij, lol, stappen: **go** on the ~ aan de rol gaan, de bloemetjes buiten zetten

RC 1 Red Cross Rode Kruis **2** Roman Catholic r.-k.

Rd road str., straat

¹**reach** (n) **1** bereikʰ [of arm, power etc; also fig]; reikwijdte: **above** (or: beyond, out **of**) ~ buiten bereik, onbereikbaar, onhaalbaar, niet te realiseren; **within** easy ~ **of** gemakke-lijk bereikbaar van(af) **2** recht stuk rivier [between two bends]

²**reach** (vb) **1** reiken, (zich) (uit)strekken, (een hand) uitsteken, bereiken; dragen [of sound]; halen: the forests ~ **down to** the sea de bossen strekken zich uit tot aan de zee **2** pakken, (ergens) bij kunnen, grijpen: ~ **down** sth. from a shelf iets van een plank af-pakken **3** aanreiken, geven, overhandigen **4** komen tot [also fig]; bereiken, arriveren: ~ a **decision** tot een beslissing komen

react 1 reageren [also fig]; ingaan (op) **2** (+ (up)on) uitwerking hebben (op), z'n weer-slag hebben (op), veranderen

reaction 1 reactie, antwoordʰ, reflex **2** te-rugslag, weerslag, terugkeer

¹**reactionary** (n) reactionair, behoudend persoon

²**reactionary** (adj) reactionair, behoudend

reactivate 1 weer actief maken **2** nieuw leven inblazen

reactor 1 atoomreactor, kernreactor **2** re-actievatʰ, reactor

¹**read** (vb) **1** studeren, leren: ~ **for** a degree in Law rechten studeren **2** zich laten lezen, le-zen, klinken: your **essay** ~s like a **translation** je opstel klinkt als een vertaling ‖ he ~ more **into** her words than she'd ever meant hij had meer in haar woorden gelegd dan zij ooit had bedoeld

²**read** (vb) **1** lezen, kunnen lezen, begrijpen, weten te gebruiken: ~ **over** (or: through) doorlezen, overlezen; ~ **up** on sth. a) zijn kennis over iets opvijzelen; b) zich op de hoogte stellen van iets; **widely** ~ zeer bele-zen; ~ **up** bestuderen **2** oplezen, voorlezen: ~ **out** the instructions de instructies voorlezen

3 uitleggen, interpreteren; voorspellen [future]; [fig] doorgronden; doorzien **4** aangeven, tonen, laten zien: *the thermometer ~s twenty degrees* de thermometer geeft twintig graden aan **5** studeren: *~ Economics* economie studeren
readability leesbaarheid
readable 1 lezenswaard(ig), leesbaar **2** leesbaar, te lezen
reader 1 lezer [also fig] **2** leesboek^h, bloemlezing **3** lector [at university]; [Belg] [roughly] docent
readership lezerspubliek^h; aantal lezers [of newspaper etc]: *a newspaper with a ~ of ten million* een krant met tien miljoen lezers
readily 1 graag, bereidwillig **2** gemakkelijk, vlug, dadelijk: *his motives will be ~ understood* zijn motivatie is zonder meer duidelijk
readiness 1 bereid(willig)heid, gewilligheid **2** vlugheid, vaardigheid, gemak^h: *~ of tongue* rapheid van tong **3** gereedheid: *all is in ~* alles staat klaar
reading 1 het (voor)lezen **2** belezenheid **3** (voor)lezing, voordracht **4** stand; waarde [as read on instrucment]: *the ~s on the thermometer* de afgelezen temperaturen **5** lectuur, leesstof: *these novels are required ~* deze romans zijn verplichte lectuur
reading comprehension leesvaardigheid
¹readjust (vb) zich weer aanpassen, weer wennen
²readjust (vb) weer aanpassen, opnieuw instellen, bijstellen
read-only onuitwisbaar; niet schrijfbaar, alleen-lezen-: *~ memory* ROM
¹ready (n): *at the ~* klaar om te vuren [of firearm]
²ready (adj) **1** klaar, gereed, af: *~, steady, go!* klaar? af! **2** bereid(willig), graag: *I am ~ to pay for it* ik wil er best voor betalen **3** vlug, gevat || *~ cash* (or: *money*) baar geld, klinkende munt; *find a ~ sale* goed verkocht worden
ready-made kant-en-klaar, confectie-
ready meal kant-en-klaarmaaltijd
ready-to-wear confectie-
¹real (n): *for ~* in werkelijkheid, echt, gemeend
²real (adj) echt, werkelijk, onvervalst: [inform] *the ~ thing* het echte, je ware || *in ~ terms* in concrete termen, in de praktijk
real estate 1 onroerend goed^h **2** [Am] huizen in verkoop
real-estate agent [Am] makelaar in onroerend goed
realism realisme^h, werkelijkheidszin
realist realist
realistic 1 realistisch, m.b.t. realisme, natuurgetrouw **2** realistisch, praktisch, werkelijkheidsbewust

reality werkelijkheid, realiteit, werkelijk bestaan^h: *in ~* in werkelijkheid, in feite
realization 1 bewustwording, besef^h, begrip^h **2** realisatie, realisering, verwezenlijking
realize 1 beseffen, zich bewust zijn of worden, zich realiseren: *don't you ~ that ...?* zie je niet in dat ...? **2** realiseren, verwezenlijken, uitvoeren **3** realiseren, verkopen, te gelde maken
¹really (adv) **1** werkelijk, echt, eigenlijk: *I don't ~ feel like it* ik heb er eigenlijk geen zin in; *(O) ~?* O ja?, Echt waar? **2** werkelijk, echt, zeer: *it is really cold today* het is ontzettend koud vandaag
²really (int) waarachtig!, nou, zeg!: *~, Mike! Mind your manners!* Mike toch! Wat zijn dat voor manieren!; *well ~!* nee maar!
realm 1 koninkrijk^h, rijk^h **2** rijk^h, sfeer; gebied^h [fig]: *the ~ of science* het domein van de wetenschap
reanimation reanimatie
reap maaien, oogsten, verwerven; opstrijken [profit]
reappear weer verschijnen, opnieuw tevoorschijn komen, weer komen opdagen
reappraisal heroverweging
¹rear (n) achtergedeelte^h, achterstuk^h; [fig] achtergrond || *at the ~*, [Am] *in the ~* achteraan, aan de achterkant
²rear (adj) achter-, achterste: *~ door* achterdeur
³rear (vb) (also + up) steigeren
⁴rear (vb) grootbrengen, fokken, kweken
rear-admiral schout-bij-nacht
the **rearguard** achterhoede
rearmament herbewapening
rearmost achterste, allerlaatste
rearrange herschikken, herordenen, anders rangschikken
rearview mirror achteruitkijkspiegel
¹reason (n) **1** reden, beweegreden, oorzaak: *by ~ of* wegens; *with (good) ~* terecht **2** redelijkheid, gezond verstand^h: *it stands to ~ that* het spreekt vanzelf dat; *anything (with)in ~* alles wat redelijk is
²reason (vb) **1** redeneren, logisch denken **2** (+ with) redeneren (met), argumenteren (met)
³reason (vb) door redenering afleiden, beredeneren, veronderstellen: *~ sth. out* iets beargumenteren
reasonable 1 redelijk, verstandig: *beyond ~ doubt* zonder gerede twijfel **2** redelijk, schappelijk, billijk
reasonably vrij, tamelijk, nogal: *it is in a ~ good state* het is in vrij behoorlijke staat
reasoning redenering
¹reassemble (vb) opnieuw vergaderen; opnieuw samenkomen
²reassemble (vb) **1** opnieuw samenbren-

gen **2** opnieuw samenvoegen
reassert 1 bevestigen **2** (opnieuw) handhaven
reassure geruststellen, weer (zelf)vertrouwen geven
reassuring geruststellend
rebate korting: *tax* ~ belastingteruggave
¹**rebel** (n) rebel, opstandeling
²**rebel** (vb) (+ against) rebelleren (tegen), zich verzetten (tegen), in opstand komen (tegen)
rebellion opstand, opstandigheid, rebellie
rebellious opstandig
rebirth 1 wedergeboorte **2** herleving, wederopleving
¹**reboot** (n) reboot; herstart
²**reboot** (vb) rebooten; herstarten
¹**rebound** (n) **1** terugkaatsing [of ball] **2** terugwerking, reactie: *on the* ~ van de weeromstuit, als reactie
²**rebound** (vb) terugkaatsen, terugspringen, terugstuiten
¹**rebuff** (n) afwijzing; weigering [of help, proposal etc]: *he met with* (or: *suffered*) *a* ~ hij kwam van een koude kermis thuis
²**rebuff** (vb) afwijzen, weigeren, afschepen
rebuild 1 opnieuw bouwen, verbouwen, opknappen **2** vernieuwen
¹**rebuke** (n) berisping, standjeʰ
²**rebuke** (vb) (+ for) berispen (om/voor), een standje geven (voor)
rebut weerleggen
¹**recalcitrant** (n) weerspannige, tegenstribbelaar, ongehoorzame
²**recalcitrant** (adj) opstandig, weerspannig
¹**recall** (n) **1** rappelʰ; terugroeping [of officers, envoy etc] **2** herinnering, geheugenʰ: *total* ~ absoluut geheugen; *beyond* (or: *past*) ~ onmogelijk te herinneren
²**recall** (vb) **1** terugroepen; rappelleren [envoy] **2** terugnemen [present, merchandise etc]; terugroepen [product, by manufacturer]: *millions of cans of soft drink have been ~ed* er zijn miljoenen blikjes frisdrank teruggehaald
³**recall** (vb) zich herinneren
¹**recap** (n) recapitulatie, korte opsomming
²**recap** (vb) recapituleren, kort samenvatten, samenvattend herhalen
recapitulate recapituleren, kort samenvatten
recapture 1 heroveren **2** oproepen; (zich) in herinnering brengen **3** doen herleven
recede achteruitgaan, zich terugtrekken, terugwijken; [also fig] teruglopen [of value etc]: *a receding* **forehead** een terugwijkend voorhoofd; *a receding* **hairline** een kalend hoofd
¹**receipt** (n) **1** reçuʰ, ontvangstbewijsʰ, kwitantie **2** ontvangst
²**receipt** (vb) kwiteren; voor ontvangst teke-

nen [bill etc]
receive 1 ontvangen, verwelkomen, gasten ontvangen **2** ontvangen, krijgen, in ontvangst nemen **3** opvangen, toelaten, opnemen: *be at* (or: *on*) *the receiving* **end** al de klappen krijgen
received algemeen aanvaard, standaard-: *Received Standard* **English** Algemeen Beschaafd Engels
receiver 1 ontvanger [person, appliance] **2** hoorn [of telephone] **3** bewindvoerder **4** heler **5** tuner-versterker
recent 1 recent, van de laatste tijd: *in* ~ *years* de laatste jaren; *a* ~ **book** een onlangs verschenen boek **2** nieuw, modern: ~ **fashion** nieuwe mode
recently 1 onlangs, kort geleden **2** de laatste tijd: *he has* **been** *moody,* ~ hij is de laatste tijd humeurig (geweest)
receptacle vergaarbak, container, vatʰ, kom
reception 1 ontvangst [also fig]; onthaalʰ, welkomʰ: *the* ~ *of his book was* **mixed** zijn boek werd met gemengde gevoelens ontvangen **2** receptie [at party; in hotel etc] **3** opname [in hospital]
reception centre opvangcentrumʰ
reception desk balie [of hotel, library etc]
receptionist 1 receptionist(e) [eg in hotel] **2** assistent(e) [of doctor etc]
reception room 1 ontvangkamer; receptiezaal **2** [in private house] woonvertrekʰ
receptive ontvankelijk, vatbaar, open
recess 1 vakantie; onderbreking [parliament etc] **2** [Am] (school)vakantie **3** [Am] pauze [between classes] **4** nis, uitsparing, holte **5** uithoek
recession 1 recessie, economische teruggang **2** terugtrekking, terugtreding
recharge herladen; weer opladen [battery etc]
recipe receptʰ, keukenreceptʰ
recipient ontvanger
reciprocal wederkerig, wederzijds: ~ **action** wisselwerking
reciprocate 1 beantwoorden [feelings]; vergelden, op gelijke manier behandelen **2** uitwisselen
recital 1 relaasʰ, verhaalʰ **2** recital [music] **3** voordracht [poem, text]
recite 1 reciteren, opzeggen: *Simon can already* ~ *the* **alphabet** Simon kan het alfabet al opzeggen **2** opsommen
reckless 1 roekeloos **2** zorgeloos: ~ *of danger* zonder zich zorgen te maken over gevaar
¹**reckon** (vb) **1** (+ on) rekenen (op), afgaan (op) **2** (+ with) rekening houden (met): *she is a woman to be ~ed* **with** dat is een vrouw met wie je rekening moet houden **3** (+ with) afrekenen (met)
²**reckon** (vb) **1** berekenen, (op)tellen **2** mee-

rekenen, meetellen, rekening houden met **3** beschouwen, aanzien (voor), houden (voor): *I ~ him among my friends* ik beschouw hem als één van mijn vrienden **4** aannemen, vermoeden, gissen: *I ~ that he'll be home soon* ik neem aan dat hij gauw thuiskomt **reckoner** rekenaar: *ready ~* rekentabel **reckoning 1** berekening, schatting **2** afrekening: *day of ~* dag van de afrekening; [fig] dag des oordeels
¹reclaim (n): *he is beyond ~* hij is onverbeterlijk
²reclaim (vb) **1** terugwinnen, recupereren, regenereren: *~ed paper* kringlooppapier **2** droogleggen [land]: *land ~ed from the sea* op de zee teruggewonnen land **3** terugvorderen
reclamation 1 terugwinning **2** terugvordering
¹recline (vb) achterover leunen, (uit)rusten, op de rug liggen
²recline (vb) doen leunen, doen rusten
reclining seat stoel met verstelbare rugleuning
recluse kluizenaar
recognition 1 erkenning **2** waardering, erkentelijkheid **3** herkenning: *change beyond* (or: *out of*) *all ~* onherkenbaar worden
recognizable herkenbaar
recognize 1 herkennen **2** erkennen **3** inzien
¹recoil (n) terugslag, terugloop, terugsprong; terugstoot [of firearm]
²recoil (vb) **1** (+ from) terugdeinzen (voor), terugschrikken (voor), zich terugtrekken **2** terugslaan, teruglopen, terugspringen; terugstoten [of firearm]
recollect zich (moeizaam) herinneren, zich voor de geest halen
recollection herinnering: *to the best of my ~* voor zover ik mij herinner
recommend 1 aanbevelen, aanraden, adviseren: *I can ~ the self-service in this hotel* ik kan u de zelfbediening in dit hotel aanbevelen; *~ed price* adviesprijs **2** tot aanbeveling strekken **3** toevertrouwen, overgeven, (aan)bevelen
recommendation 1 aanbeveling, aanprijzing, advies[h] **2** aanbevelingsbrief
¹recompense (n) vergoeding, schadeloosstelling, beloning: *in ~ for* als vergoeding voor
²recompense (vb) vergoeden, schadeloosstellen: *~ s.o. for sth.* iem. iets vergoeden
reconcile verzoenen, in overeenstemming brengen, verenigen: *become ~d to sth.* zich bij iets neerleggen
reconciliation verzoening, vereniging
reconnaissance verkenning
reconnoitre op verkenning uitgaan, verkennen

reconsider 1 opnieuw bekijken, opnieuw in overweging nemen: *may I ask you to ~ the matter?* mag ik u vragen er nog eens over na te denken? **2** herroepen, herzien, terugkomen op
reconstruct 1 opnieuw opbouwen, herbouwen **2** reconstrueren [events]
reconstruction 1 reconstructie [of event] **2** wederopbouw
¹record (n) **1** verslag[h], rapport[h], aantekening: *for the ~* openbaar, officieel; *off the ~* vertrouwelijk, onofficieel; *all this is off the ~* dit alles blijft tussen ons **2** document[h], archiefstuk[h], officieel afschrift[h] **3** vastgelegd feit[h], het opgetekend zijn **4** staat van dienst, antecedenten, verleden[h] **5** plaat, opname
²record (adj) record-: *a ~ amount* een recordbedrag
³record (vb) **1** zich laten opnemen, opnamen maken **2** optekenen, noteren, te boek stellen: *~ed delivery* aangetekend [mail] **3** vastleggen; opnemen [on tape, record]
recorder 1 rechter; voorzitter van Crown Court **2** (tape)recorder **3** blokfluit
recording opname, opgenomen programma[h]: *a studio ~* een studio-opname
record-player platenspeler, grammofoon
recount (uitvoerig) vertellen, weergeven
recoup 1 vergoeden, compenseren, schadeloosstellen **2** terugwinnen, inhalen: *~ expenses from a company* onkosten verhalen op een maatschappij
recourse toevlucht, hulp: *have ~ to* zijn toevlucht nemen tot
¹recover (vb) herstellen, genezen, er weer bovenop komen
²recover (vb) terugkrijgen, terugvinden: *~ consciousness* weer bijkomen
recovery 1 herstel[h], recuperatie, genezing: *make a quick ~ from an illness* vlug van een ziekte herstellen **2** het terugvinden, het terugwinnen, het terugkrijgen, herwinning
recreation recreatie, ontspanning, hobby
recreational recreatief, recreatie-, ontspannings-
recreation ground speelterrein[h], recreatieterrein[h]
recrimination tegenbeschuldiging, recriminatie, tegeneis: *mutual ~s* beschuldigingen over en weer
¹recruit (n) **1** rekruut **2** nieuw lid[h]
²recruit (vb) rekruten (aan)werven
³recruit (vb) rekruteren, (aan)werven, aantrekken
recruiter recruiter
recruitment 1 rekrutering; werving **2** versterking
rectangle rechthoek
rectangular rechthoekig
rectification rectificatie
rectify rectificeren, rechtzetten, verbeteren

rectitude 1 rechtschapenheid **2** oprechtheid, eerlijkheid

rector 1 [Anglican Church] predikant, dominee **2** rector [head of university]

rectory predikantswoning; pastorie

rectum rectum^h, endeldarm

¹recumbent (n) ligfiets

²recumbent (adj) **1** liggend; achteroverleunend: ~ *bike* ligfiets **2** nietsdoend

recuperate herstellen, opknappen, er weer bovenop komen

recur terugkomen, terugkeren, zich herhalen: *a ~ring* ***dream*** een steeds terugkerende droom; *~ring* ***decimal*** repeterende breuk

recurrent terugkomend, terugkerend

recycle recyclen, weer bruikbaar maken: *~d* ***paper*** kringlooppapier

¹red (n) **1** rood^h, rode kleur **2** iets roods **3** rode, communist ‖ *be in the* ~ rood staan

²red (adj) **1** rood: *~* ***currant*** rode aalbes; *like a ~* ***rag*** *to a bull* als een rode lap op een stier **2** rood, communistisch ‖ *~* ***herring*** bokking; [fig] vals spoor, afleidingsmanoeuvre; *Red* ***Indian*** indiaan, roodhuid; *~* ***lead*** (rode) menie; *~* ***tape*** bureaucratie, ambtenarij, papierwinkel; *paint the* ***town*** *~* de bloemetjes buiten zetten; *see* ~ buiten zichzelf raken (van woede)

red-blooded levenskrachtig

redbreast roodborst

redcurrant rode aalbes

redden rood worden (maken), (doen) blozen

reddish roodachtig, rossig

redecorate opknappen; opnieuw schilderen, behangen

redeem 1 terugkopen, afkopen, inlossen; [fig] terugwinnen: *~ a* ***mortgage*** een hypotheek aflossen **2** vrijkopen, loskopen **3** goedmaken, vergoeden: *a ~ing* ***feature*** een verzoenende trek **4** verlossen, bevrijden, redden

Redeemer Verlosser, Heiland

redemption 1 redding, verlossing, bevrijding: ***beyond*** (or: *past*) *~* reddeloos (verloren) **2** afkoop, aflossing

redevelop renoveren: *~ a slum* ***district*** een krottenwijk renoveren

redevelopment 1 nieuwe ontwikkeling **2** renovatie

red-handed op heterdaad

redhead roodharige, rooie

red-hot 1 roodgloeiend; [fig] enthousiast **2** heet van de naald, zeer actueel: *~* ***news*** allerlaatste nieuws

rediscovery herontdekking

redistribution herdistributie; herverdeling

red-light district rosse buurt

redneck [Am; inform; depr] (blanke) landarbeider; conservatieveling

redo 1 overdoen, opnieuw doen **2** opknappen

redouble verdubbelen

redress herstellen, vergoeden, goedmaken: *~ the* ***balance*** het evenwicht herstellen

redskin roodhuid

reduce 1 verminderen, beperken, verkleinen, verlagen, reduceren **2** herleiden, reduceren, omzetten, omsmelten **3** (+ to) terugbrengen (tot), degraderen (tot): *be ~d to* ***tears*** alleen nog maar kunnen huilen **4** (+ to) verpulveren (tot), fijnmalen; klein maken [also fig]: *his accusations were ~d* ***to*** *nothing* van zijn beschuldigingen bleef niets overeind

reduction reductie, vermindering, korting

redundancy 1 overtolligheid, overbodigheid **2** ontslag^h; [by extension] werkloosheid

redundancy money afvloeiingspremie

redundant 1 overtollig, overbodig **2** werkloos: *all the workers were* ***made*** *~* al de werknemers moesten afvloeien

reduplicate 1 verdubbelen **2** (steeds) herhalen

reduplication 1 verdubbeling **2** herhaling

reed 1 riet^h, rietsoort **2** riet^h; tong [in wind instrument or organ pipe]

re-education 1 omscholing, herscholing **2** heropvoeding

¹reef (n) **1** rif^h **2** klip **3** [sailing] reef^h, rif^h

²reef (vb) [sailing] reven, inhalen, inbinden

reefer 1 jekker **2** marihuanasigaret

¹reek (n) stank

²reek (vb) **1** (slecht) ruiken; [fig] stinken: *his statement ~s* ***of*** *corruption* zijn verklaring riekt naar corruptie **2** roken, dampen, wasemen

¹reel (n) **1** haspel, klos, spoel, (garen)klosje^h **2** (film)rol

²reel (vb) **1** duizelen, draaien **2** wervelen, warrelen **3** wankelen, waggelen: *~* ***back*** terugdeinzen, terugwijken

re-enact 1 weer invoeren **2** weer opvoeren **3** re-ensceneren [crime]; naspelen [battle]

re-entry terugkeer, terugkomst: *the ~ of a spacecraft into the* ***atmosphere*** de terugkeer van een ruimtevaartuig in de atmosfeer

re-examine 1 opnieuw onderzoeken **2** [law] opnieuw verhoren

¹ref (n) [inform] *referee* scheids; scheidsrechter

²ref (abbrev) *reference* ref.

refer 1 (+ to) verwijzen (naar), doorsturen (naar) **2** (+ to) toeschrijven (aan), terugvoeren (tot)

¹referee (n) **1** scheidsrechter; [fig] bemiddelaar **2** (vak)referent, expert **3** referentie [person giving the reference]

²referee (vb) als scheidsrechter optreden (bij)

reference 1 referentie, getuigschrift^h, pers die referentie geeft **2** verwijzing: *be* ***outside***

our terms of ~ buiten onze competentie vallen **3** zinspeling: *make no* ~ *to* geen toespeling maken op **4** raadpleging: *make* ~ *to a dictionary* een woordenboek naslaan **5** betrekking, verband[h]: *in* (or: *with*) ~ *to* in verband met
reference book naslagwerk[h]
reference work naslagwerk[h]
referendum referendum[h], volksstemming
refer to 1 verwijzen naar, betrekking hebben op, van toepassing zijn op **2** zinspelen op, refereren aan, vermelden **3** raadplegen, naslaan: ~ *a* **dictionary** iets opzoeken in een woordenboek; *she kept referring to her home town* ze had het steeds weer over haar geboorteplaats
¹refill (n) (nieuwe) vulling, (nieuw) (op)vulsel[h], inktpatroon: *would you* **like** *a* ~? zal ik je nog eens inschenken?
²refill (vb) opnieuw vullen, (opnieuw) aanvullen, (opnieuw) bijvullen, (opnieuw) opvullen
refill pack navulpak[h]
refine zuiveren, raffineren; [fig] verfijnen; verbeteren
refined verfijnd, geraffineerd; [fig] verzorgd; beschaafd: ~ *manners* goede manieren; ~ *sugar* geraffineerde suiker
refinement 1 verbetering, uitwerking **2** raffinage **3** verfijning, raffinement[h], (over)beschaafdheid
refinery raffinaderij
¹refit (n) herstel[h], nieuwe uitrusting
²refit (vb) hersteld worden, opnieuw uitgerust worden
³refit (vb) herstellen, opnieuw uitrusten
reflect 1 nadenken, overwegen: *he ~ed that* ... hij bedacht dat ... **2** weerspiegelen, weerkaatsen, reflecteren; [fig] weergeven; getuigen van
reflection 1 weerspiegeling, weerkaatsing, reflectie **2** overdenking, overweging: *on* ~ bij nader inzien
reflective 1 weerspiegelend, reflecterend **2** bedachtzaam
reflector reflector
reflect (up)on 1 nadenken over, overdenken **2** zich ongunstig uitlaten over, een ongunstig licht werpen op: *your impudent behaviour reflects only on* **yourself** je brutale gedrag werkt alleen maar in je eigen nadeel
¹reflex (n) **1** weerspiegeling: ~*es* afspiegeling **2** reflex[h], reflexbeweging: *his* ~*es* zijn reactievermogen
²reflex (adj) weerkaatst, gereflecteerd: ~ *camera* spiegelreflexcamera ‖ ~ *action* reflexbeweging
reflexive [linguistics] reflexief, wederkerend: ~ *pronoun* (or: *verb*) wederkerend voornaamwoord (or: werkwoord)
¹refloat (vb) weer vlot raken

²refloat (vb) vlot krijgen
¹reform (n) hervorming, verbetering
²reform (vb) verbeteren, hervormen: *Reformed Church* hervormde kerk
reformation hervorming, verbetering
the **Reformation** de Reformatie
reformer hervormer
refract breken [beams, rays]
refraction (straal)breking: *angle of* ~ brekingshoek
refractory (stijf)koppig, halsstarrig: *a* ~ *fever* een hardnekkige koorts
¹refrain (n) refrein[h]
²refrain (+ from) zich onthouden (van), ervan afzien, het nalaten: *kindly* ~ *from smoking* gelieve niet te roken
¹refresh (vb) zich verfrissen, zich opfrissen
²refresh (vb) **1** verfrissen: ~ *s.o.'s* **memory** iemands geheugen opfrissen **2** aanvullen, herbevoorraden
refresher course herhalingscursus, bijscholingscursus
refreshing 1 verfrissend, verkwikkend: *a* ~ *breeze* een lekker koel briesje **2** aangenaam, verrassend
refreshment 1 verfrissing [also fig]; verkwikking, verademing **2** (-s) iets te drinken met een hapje daarbij
refreshment station verzorgingspost
¹refrigerate (vb) invriezen
²refrigerate (vb) koelen
refrigeration 1 invriezing, het diepvriezen **2** afkoeling
refrigerator 1 koelruimte, koelkast, ijskast **2** koeler
¹refuel (vb) (bij)tanken
²refuel (vb) opnieuw voltanken
refuge 1 toevlucht(soord[h]) [also fig]; schuilplaats, toeverlaat: ~ *from* bescherming tegen **2** vluchtheuvel
refugee vluchteling
¹refund (n) terugbetaling, geld[h] terug
²refund (vb) terugbetalen, restitueren: ~ *the cost of postage* de verzendkosten vergoeden
refurbish opknappen; [fig] opfrissen: ~ *the office* het kantoor opknappen
refusal 1 weigering, afwijzing **2** optie, (recht[h] van) voorkeur: *have (the) first* ~ *of a house* een optie op een huis hebben
¹refuse (n) afval[h], vuil[h], vuilnis
²refuse (vb) weigeren, afslaan, afwijzen: ~ *a request* op een verzoek niet ingaan
refuse collector vuilnisophaler, vuilnisman
refuse dump vuilnisbelt
refutation weerlegging
refute weerleggen
regain 1 herwinnen, terugwinnen: ~ *consciousness* weer tot bewustzijn komen **2** opnieuw bereiken: *I helped him* ~ *his* **footing** ik hielp hem weer op de been [also fig]

regal koninklijk
regale (+ on, with) vergasten (op), onthalen (op), trakteren (op): ~ o.s. **on** (or: **with**) zich te goed doen aan
regalia 1 rijksinsigniën, regalia **2** onderscheidingstekenen: *the mayor in full* ~ de burgemeester in vol ornaat **3** staatsiegewaad
¹**regard** (n) **1** achting, respectʰ: *hold s.o. in high* ~ iem. hoogachten **2** betrekking, verbandʰ, opzichtʰ: *in this* ~ op dit punt **3** aandacht, zorg: *give* (or: *pay*) *no* ~ *to* zich niet bekommeren om; *have little* ~ *for* weinig rekening houden met **4** (-s) groeten, wensenʰ || *kind* ~*s to you all* ik wens jullie allemaal het beste
²**regard** (vb) **1** beschouwen, aanzien: ~ *s.o. as* iem. aanzien voor **2** betreffen, betrekking hebben op, aangaan: *as* ~*s* met betrekking tot
regarding betreffende, aangaande
regardless hoe dan ook || *they did it* ~ ze hebben het toch gedaan
regardless of ongeacht, zonder rekening te houden met: ~ *expense* zonder op een cent te letten
regency regentschapʰ
¹**regenerate** (adj) **1** herboren, bekeerd **2** geregenereerd, hernieuwd
²**regenerate** (vb) [biology] opnieuw (aan)groeien
³**regenerate** (vb) **1** verbeteren, bekeren, vernieuwen **2** nieuw leven inblazen, doen herleven
regeneration regeneratie
regent 1 regent(es) **2** [Am] curator; bestuurslidʰ [of university]
reggae reggae
regicide 1 koningsmoord **2** koningsmoordenaar
regime regimeʰ
regimen 1 regimeʰ, verloopʰ **2** regimeʰ, kuur
regiment regimentʰ; [fig] groot aantalʰ
region 1 streek, gebiedʰ: ~*s* sfeer; terreinʰ; *the Arctic* ~*s* de Arctica; *in the* ~ *of* in de buurt van [also fig] **2** gewestʰ: ~*s* provincie; regio
regional van de streek, regionaal
¹**register** (n) **1** registerʰ, (naam)lijst, rol, gastenboekʰ, kiezerslijst: *the Parliamentary Register* de kiezerslijst **2** (kas)registerʰ
²**register** (vb) **1** zich (laten) inschrijven: ~ *at a hotel* inchecken; ~ *with the police* zich aanmelden bij de politie **2** doordringen tot, (in zich) opnemen
³**register** (vb) **1** (laten) registreren, (laten) inschrijven; [fig] nota nemen van: ~ *a protest against* protest aantekenen tegen **2** registreren; aanwijzen [eg degrees] **3** uitdrukken, tonen: *her face* ~*ed surprise* op haar gezicht viel verwondering af te lezen **4** (laten) aan-

tekenen; aangetekend versturen [mail]
registered 1 geregistreerd, ingeschreven: ~ *trademark* (wettig) gedeponeerd handelsmerk **2** gediplomeerd, erkend, bevoegd: [Am] ~ *nurse* gediplomeerd verpleegkundige; *State Registered nurse* gediplomeerd verpleegkundige **3** aangetekend [of letter]
register office 1 registratiebureauʰ **2** (bureau van de) burgerlijke stand
registrar 1 registrator, ambtenaar van de burgerlijke stand **2** archivaris **3** administratief hoofdʰ [of university] **4** [law] gerechtssecretaris, griffier **5** [med] stagelopend specialist
registration registratie, inschrijving, aangifte
registry 1 archiefʰ, registratiekantoorʰ **2** (bureau van de) burgerlijke stand **3** registerʰ **4** registratie
registry office (bureau van de) burgerlijke stand: *married at a* ~ getrouwd voor de wet
regress achteruitgaan, teruggaan
regressive regressief, teruglopend
¹**regret** (n) **1** spijt, leed(wezen)ʰ, berouwʰ: *greatly* (or: *much*) *to my* ~ tot mijn grote spijt **2** (-s) (betuigingen van) spijt, verontschuldigingen: *have no* ~*s* geen spijt hebben
²**regret** (vb) betreuren, spijt hebben van, berouw hebben over: *we* ~ *to inform you* tot onze spijt moeten wij u meedelen
regretful bedroefd, vol spijt
regrettable betreurenswaardig, te betreuren
regrettably 1 bedroevend, teleurstellend: ~ *little response* bedroevend weinig respons **2** helaas, jammer genoeg
¹**regular 1** beroeps(militair): *the* ~*s* de geregelde troepen **2** vaste klant, stamgast
²**regular** (adj) **1** regelmatig: *a* ~ *customer* een vaste klant; *a* ~ *job* vast werk; *keep* ~ *hours* zich aan vaste uren houden **2** [Am] gewoon, standaard-: *the* ~ *size* het gewone formaat **3** professioneel: *the* ~ *army* het beroepsleger **4** echt, onvervalst: *a* ~ *fool* een volslagen idioot
regularity regelmatigheid
regularize regulariseren, regelen
regulate regelen, reglementeren, ordenen || *a regulating effect* een regulerende werking
regulation regeling, reglementʰ, reglementering, (wettelijk) voorschriftʰ, bepaling: *rules and* ~*s* regels en voorschriften
regulator regelaar; kompassleutel [of timepiece]
rehab [Am] *rehabilitation* afkickenʰ; ontwenning: *in* ~ in een ontwenningskliniek
rehabilitation 1 rehabilitatie, eerherstelʰ **2** herstelling: *economic* ~ economisch herstel
rehabilitation centre revalidatiecentrumʰ

¹rehash (n) herbewerking; [fig] opgewarmde kost: *his latest book is a ~ of one of his earlier ones* zijn jongste boek is een herbewerking van een van zijn eerdere boeken
²rehash (vb) herwerken, opnieuw bewerken
rehearsal repetitie: *dress ~* generale repetitie
¹rehearse (vb) herhalen
²rehearse (vb) repeteren, (een) repetitie houden
¹reign (n) regering: *~ of terror* schrikbewind; *in the ~ of Henry* toen Hendrik koning was
²reign (vb) regeren; heersen [also fig]: *the ~ing champion* de huidige kampioen
reiki reiki⁺ʰ
reimburse terugbetalen, vergoeden
¹rein (n) teugel: [fig] *give free ~ to s.o. (sth.)* iem. (iets) de vrije teugel laten; [fig] *keep a tight ~ on s.o.* bij iem. de teugels stevig aanhalen
²rein (vb) inhouden [also fig]; beteugelen, in bedwang houden: *~ back* (or: *in, up*) halt doen houden
reincarnation reïncarnatie, wedergeboorte
reindeer rendierʰ
reinforce versterken: *~d concrete* gewapend beton
reinforcement versterking
reinstate herstellen
reinsurance herverzekering
reiterate herhalen
reiteration herhaling
reiterative herhalend
¹reject (n) afgekeurd persoon (voorwerpʰ); afgekeurde [for military service]; uitschotʰ: *~s are sold at a discount* tweedekeusartikelen worden met korting verkocht
²reject (vb) **1** verwerpen, afwijzen, weigeren **2** uitwerpen
rejection 1 verwerping, afkeuring, afwijzing **2** uitwerping
reject shop winkel met tweedekeusartikelen
rejoice (+ at, over) zich verheugen (over): *I ~ to hear* het verheugt me te vernemen
rejoicing vreugde, feestviering
¹rejoin (vb) **1** (zich) weer verenigen **2** weer lid worden (van) **3** zich weer voegen bij: *I thought he would ~ his friends, but he went to sit by himself* ik dacht dat hij weer bij zijn vrienden zou gaan staan, maar hij ging apart zitten
²rejoin (vb) antwoorden
rejoinder repliek, (vinnig) antwoordʰ
rejuvenate verjongen; vernieuwen
rejuvenation verjonging
rekindle opnieuw ontsteken, opnieuw aanwakkeren
¹relapse (n) instorting; terugval [into evil]: *have a ~* opnieuw achteruitgaan

²relapse (vb) terugvallen; weer vervallen [into evil]; (weer) instorten: *~ into poverty* weer tot armoede vervallen
¹relate (vb) (+ to) in verband staan (met), betrekking hebben (op)
²relate (vb) **1** verhalen, berichten: *strange to ~ ...* hoe onwaarschijnlijk het ook moge klinken, maar ... [at beginning of incredible story] **2** (met elkaar) in verband brengen, relateren
related verwant, samenhangend, verbonden: *drug-~ crime* misdaad waarbij drugs een rol spelen; *I'm ~ to her by marriage* zij is aangetrouwde familie van me
relation 1 bloedverwant, familielidʰ **2** bloedverwantschapʰ, verwantschap **3** betrekking, relatie, verbandʰ: *bear no ~ to* geen verband houden met, geen betrekking hebben op; *in* (or: *with*) *~ to* met betrekking tot, in verhouding tot
relationship 1 betrekking, verhouding **2** bloedverwantschapʰ, verwantschap
¹relative (n) familielidʰ, (bloed)verwant(e)
²relative (adj) **1** betrekkelijk, relatief: *~ pronoun* betrekkelijk voornaamwoord **2** toepasselijk, relevant
relativity betrekkelijkheid, relativiteit
¹relax (vb) **1** verslappen, verminderen; [fig] ontdooien **2** zich ontspannen, relaxen
²relax (vb) ontspannen, verslappen, verminderen: *~ one's efforts* zich minder inspannen
relaxation ontspanning(svorm)
relaxing rustgevend, ontspannend
¹relay (n) **1** aflossing, verse paarden, nieuwe ploeg, verse voorraad **2** estafettewedstrijd
²relay (vb) heruitzenden; doorgeven [information]
relay race estafettewedstrijd
¹release (n) **1** bevrijding, vrijgeving, verlossing **2** ontslagʰ; ontheffing [of obligation]; vrijspreking **3** nieuwe film/video/cd/release; het uitbrengen [of film, video, CD]: *on general ~* in alle bioscopen (te zien) **4** (artikelʰ voor) publicatie
²release (vb) **1** (+ from) bevrijden (uit), vrijlaten, vrijgeven **2** (+ from) ontslaan (van), vrijstellen; ontheffen (van) [obligation] **3** uitbrengen [film, video]; in de handel brengen [CD]
relegate 1 (+ to) verwijzen (naar) **2** overplaatsen **3** [sport] degraderen
relent minder streng worden, toegeven; [fig] afnemen; verbeteren
relentless 1 meedogenloos, zonder medelijden **2** gestaag, aanhoudend
relevance relevantie
relevant (+ to) relevant (voor): *I've marked the ~ passages* ik heb de desbetreffende passages aangegeven
reliability betrouwbaarheid
reliable betrouwbaar, te vertrouwen, ge-

loofwaardig
reliance vertrouwen[h]
reliant vertrouwend: *be ~ on s.o.* vertrouwen stellen in iem.

relic 1 relikwie **2** overblijfsel[h], souvenir[h]
relief 1 reliëf[h]; [fig] levendigheid; contrast[h]: *bring* (or: *throw*) *into ~* doen contrasteren [also fig] **2** verlichting, opluchting, ontlasting: *it was a* **great** *~* het was een pak van mijn hart **3** afwisseling, onderbreking: *provide a little light ~* voor wat afwisseling zorgen **4** ondersteuning, steun, hulp **5** ontzet[h]; bevrijding [of city under siege]
relief fund ondersteuningsfonds[h], hulpfonds[h]
relief map reliëfkaart
relief worker hulpverlener, hulpverleenster
relieve 1 verlichten, opluchten, ontlasten: *~ one's* **feelings** zijn hart luchten; *~ o.s.* zijn behoefte doen; *~ of* **a)** ontlasten van, afhelpen van; **b)** [inform] afhandig maken; **c)** ontslaan uit, ontheffen van **2** afwisselen, onderbreken: *a dress ~d with lace* een jurk met kant afgezet **3** ondersteunen, helpen, troosten, bemoedigen **4** aflossen, vervangen **5** [mil] ontzetten, bevrijden
relieved opgelucht
religion 1 godsdienst **2** vroomheid **3** gewetenszaak, heilige plicht: *make a ~ of sth.* van iets een erezaak maken
religious godsdienstig, religieus, vroom
religiously 1 godsdienstig **2** gewetensvol, nauwgezet
relinquish 1 opgeven; prijsgeven [eg religion] **2** afstand doen van [claim, right] **3** loslaten
[1]relish (n) **1** genoegen[h], lust, plezier[h], zin: *read with great ~* met veel plezier lezen **2** smaak [also fig]; trek: *add* (or: *give*) *(a) ~ to* prikkelen; *eat with (a) ~* met smaak eten **3** saus **4** pikant smaakje[h]
[2]relish (vb) **1** smakelijk maken, kruiden **2** genieten van, genoegen scheppen in, zich laten smaken **3** tegemoet zien, verlangen naar: *~ the* **prospect** (or: **idea**) het een prettig vooruitzicht (or: idee) vinden; *I do not exactly ~ the* **idea** *of going on my own* ik kijk er niet echt naar uit om alleen te gaan
[1]relocate (vb) zich opnieuw vestigen
[2]relocate (vb) opnieuw vestigen; verplaatsen
relocation vestiging elders, verhuizing naar elders
reluctance tegenzin, weerzin, onwil: *with great ~* met grote tegenzin
reluctant onwillig, aarzelend
rely (up)on vertrouwen (op), zich verlaten op, steunen op: *can he be relied upon?* kun je op hem rekenen?

remain 1 blijven, overblijven: *it ~s to be*

seen het staat te bezien; *~* **behind** achterblijven, nablijven **2** verblijven, zich ophouden **3** voortduren, blijven bestaan
[1]remainder (n) **1** rest, overblijfsel[h], restant[h] **2** ramsj [of books] **3** verschil[h] [of subtraction]
[2]remainder (vb) opruimen; uitverkopen [books at reduced prices]
remaining overgebleven
remains 1 overblijfselen, ruïnes, resten **2** stoffelijk overschot
[1]remake (n) remake, nieuwe versie
[2]remake (vb) opnieuw maken, omwerken, een nieuwe versie maken
[1]remand (n) **1** terugzending [in preventive custody] **2** voorarrest[h]: *on ~* in voorarrest
[2]remand (vb) **1** terugzenden **2** terugzenden in voorlopige hechtenis: *~ into* **custody** terugzenden in voorlopige hechtenis
remand centre observatiehuis[h]; [roughly] huis[h] van bewaring [for preventive custody]
[1]remark (n) opmerking: *make a ~* een opmerking maken
[2]remark (vb) (+ (up)on) opmerkingen maken (over)
[3]remark (vb) opmerken, bemerken
remarkable 1 merkwaardig, opmerkelijk **2** opvallend
[1]remarry (vb) hertrouwen
[2]remarry (vb) opnieuw trouwen met
remedial beter makend, genezend, herstellend, verbeterend
[1]remedy (n) remedie, (genees)middel[h], hulpmiddel[h]: *beyond* (or: *past*) *~* ongeneeslijk, onherstelbaar, niet te verhelpen
[2]remedy (vb) verhelpen [also fig]; voorzien in, genezen
[1]remember (vb) **1** bedenken [in testament; by tipping] **2** gedenken [the dead; in prayers] **3** (+ to) de groeten doen (aan)
[2]remember (vb) (zich) herinneren, onthouden, van buiten kennen, denken aan
remembrance 1 herinnering: *in ~ of* ter herinnering aan **2** herinnering, aandenken[h], souvenir[h] **3** (-s) groet
Remembrance Day dodenherdenking
remind herinneren, doen denken: *will you ~ me?* help me eraan denken, wil je?
reminder 1 herinnering **2** betalingsherinnering **3** geheugensteuntje[h]
reminisce herinneringen ophalen
reminiscence herinnering: *~s* memoires
remiss nalatig: *be ~ in one's duties* in zijn plichten tekortschieten
remission 1 vergeving **2** kwijtschelding **3** vermindering [eg of sentence]
[1]remit (vb) afnemen
[2]remit (vb) **1** vergeven [sins] **2** kwijtschelden; schenken [debt, sentence]; vrijstellen van **3** doen afnemen/verminderen; laten verslappen [attention]; verzachten; verlichten [pain] **4** terugzenden, zenden, sturen

5 overmaken; doen overschrijven [money]
remittance overschrijving [of money];
overmaking, betalingsopdracht, overgemaakt bedrag^h
remnant 1 restant^h, rest, overblijfsel^h
2 coupon [material]
remonstrate protesteren: ~ *with s.o.*
(up)on sth. iem. iets verwijten
remorse 1 wroeging **2** medelijden^h
remorseless meedogenloos
remote 1 ver (weg), ver uiteen: ~ *control*
afstandsbediening; *the* ~ *past* het verre verleden **2** afgelegen **3** gereserveerd, terughoudend **4** gering, flauw: *I haven't the ~st*
idea ik heb er geen flauw benul van
removal 1 verwijdering **2** verplaatsing
3 afzetting, overplaatsing **4** verhuizing
removal van verhuiswagen
¹**remove** (vb) verhuizen, vertrekken
²**remove** (vb) **1** verwijderen, wegnemen;
opheffen [doubt, fear]; afnemen [hat]; uitwissen [traces]; schrappen; afvoeren [from
list]; uitnemen, uittrekken **2** afzetten, ontslaan, wegzenden: ~ *s.o. from office* iem. uit
zijn ambt ontslaan **3** verhuizen, verplaatsen,
overplaatsen
removed verwijderd, afgelegen, ver: *far ~*
from the truth ver bezijden de waarheid ‖ *a*
first cousin once ~ een achterneef
remover verhuizer
remuneration 1 beloning **2** vergoeding
remunerative winstgevend
renaissance renaissance, herleving
rename herdopen, een andere naam geven
rend 1 scheuren, verscheuren: ~ *apart* van-
eenscheuren **2** doorklieven, kloven, splijten:
[fig] *a cry rent the skies* (or: *air*) een gil door-
kliefde de lucht **3** kwellen; verdriet doen
[heart]
render 1 (terug)geven, geven, vergelden,
verlenen; verschaffen [assistance]; bewijzen
[service]; betuigen [thanks]; uitbrengen [re-
port]; uitspreken [verdict]: ~ *good for evil*
kwaad met goed vergelden; *services ~ed* bewezen diensten **2** overgeven, overleveren
3 vertalen, omzetten, overzetten: ~ *into*
German in het Duits vertalen **4** maken, veranderen in
rendering 1 vertolking, weergave **2** vertaling
rendition 1 vertolking **2** vertaling **3** teruggave
renegade afvallige, overloper
renege 1 een belofte verbreken: ~ *on one's*
word zijn woord breken **2** [cards] verzaken
renew 1 vernieuwen, hernieuwen; oplappen [coat]; verversen; bijvullen [water]; vervangen [tyres] **2** doen herleven, verjongen
3 hervatten; weer opnemen [conversation];
herhalen **4** verlengen [contract]
renewable 1 vernieuwbaar, herwinbaar,

recycleerbaar: ~ *energy* zonne- en windenergie **2** verlengbaar
renewal 1 vernieuwing, vervanging **2** verlenging
renounce afstand doen van, opgeven, laten varen
renovate 1 vernieuwen, opknappen, renoveren, verbouwen **2** doen herleven
renovation vernieuwing, renovatie
renown faam, roem
renowned vermaard; beroemd
¹**rent** (n) **1** huur, pacht: [Am] *for* ~ te huur
2 (meer)opbrengst van landbouwgrond
3 scheur(ing), kloof, barst
²**rent** (vb) **1** huren: ~ *to buy* huurkopen
2 (also + out) verhuren
rental 1 huuropbrengst **2** huur(pennin-
gen), pacht(geld) **3** [Am] het gehuurde; het
verhuurde [eg rented house]
rent arrears achterstallige huur
renunciation 1 afstand, verwerping, verstoting **2** zelfverloochening
reopen 1 opnieuw opengaan, opnieuw
openen, weer beginnen; heropenen [of shop
etc] **2** hervatten [discussion]
reorganize reorganiseren
¹**repair** (n) herstelling, reparatie, herstel^h: *in*
(a) good (state of) ~ in goede toestand, goed
onderhouden; *under* ~ in reparatie
²**repair** (vb) **1** herstellen, repareren **2** ver-
goeden, (weer) goedmaken
repairer hersteller, reparateur
reparation 1 herstel^h, herstelling, reparatie **2** vergoeding, schadeloosstelling: ~*s* her-
stelbetaling
repartee 1 gevatte reactie **2** gevatheid
repatriation repatriëring
repay 1 terugbetalen, aflossen **2** beantwoorden: ~ *kindness by* (or: *with*) *ingratitude*
goedheid met ondankbaarheid beantwoor-
den **3** vergoeden, goedmaken **4** betaald
zetten
repayment 1 terugbetaling, aflossing
2 vergoeding, vergelding, beloning
¹**repeal** (n) herroeping, afschaffing, intrek-
king
²**repeal** (vb) herroepen, afschaffen, intrek-
ken
¹**repeat** (n) **1** herhaling **2** heruitzending: *in*
summer there are endless ~s of American soaps
in de zomer krijg je eindeloze herhalingen
van Amerikaanse soaps
²**repeat** (vb) **1** zich herhalen, terugkeren:
history ~s itself de geschiedenis herhaalt zich
2 repeteren [eg timepiece, firearm]: ~*ing*
decimal repeterende breuk
³**repeat** (vb) **1** herhalen: ~ *a course* (or: *year*)
blijven zitten [at school] **2** nazeggen, naver-
tellen: *his words will not bear ~ing* zijn woorden laten zich niet herhalen
repeatedly herhaaldelijk, steeds weer, tel-

kens
repeater zittenblijver
repeat order nabestelling
¹repel (vb) afkeer opwekken
²repel (vb) afweren, terugdrijven; afslaan
[offer, attack(er)]; afstoten [damp]
¹repellent (n) **1** afweermiddelʰ, insecten-
werend middelʰ **2** waterafstotend middelʰ
²repellent (adj) **1** afwerend, afstotend
2 weerzinwekkend, walgelijk **3** onaantrekkelijk
repent berouw hebben (over), berouwen
repentance berouwʰ
repercussion 1 terugslag, (onaangename)
reactie, repercussie **2** weerkaatsing, echo
3 terugstoot
repertory company repertoiregezel-
schapʰ
repetition herhaling, repetitie
repetitive (zich) herhalend, herhaald, her-
halings-: [med] ~ *strain injury* repetitive
strain injury, RSI; muisarm
repine morren, klagen
replace 1 terugplaatsen, terugleggen, terugzetten **2** vervangen, in de plaats stellen
3 de plaats innemen van, verdringen
replacement 1 vervanging **2** vervanger,
plaatsvervanger, opvolger **3** vervangstukʰ,
nieuwe aanvoer; versterking [mil]
replacement cost vervangingswaarde;
nieuwwaarde
replay 1 opnieuw spelen, overspelen **2** terugspelen, herhalen
replenish weer vullen, aanvullen, bijvullen
replete (+ with) vol (van), gevuld, volgepropt
replica 1 replica, kopie **2** reproductie; [fig]
evenbeeldʰ
replicate 1 herhalen **2** een kopie maken
van
¹reply (n) antwoordʰ, repliek
²reply (vb) antwoorden: ~ *to* antwoorden
op, beantwoorden
repo man [inform] iem. van een incassobu-
reau voor autobedrijven
¹report (n) **1** rapportʰ, verslagʰ, berichtʰ,
schoolrapportʰ **2** knal, slag, schotʰ **3** geruchtʰ, praatjeʰ, praatjes: *the ~ goes that ...*, ~
has it that ... het gerucht doet de ronde dat
...
²report (vb) **1** rapporteren, berichten, melden: ~ *progress* over de stand van zaken berichten **2** opschrijven, noteren; samenvatten
[reports, proceedings] **3** rapporteren, doorvertellen: ~ *s.o. to the police* iem. bij de politie
aangeven **4** verslag uitbrengen, verslag
doen, rapport opstellen: ~ *back* verslag komen uitbrengen; ~ *(up)on sth.* over iets verslag uitbrengen **5** zich aanmelden, verantwoording afleggen: ~ *to s.o. for duty* (or:
work) zich bij iem. voor de dienst (*or:* het

werk) aanmelden
reportedly naar verluidt, naar men zegt
reporter reporter, verslaggever
¹repose (n) **1** rust, slaap, ontspanning
2 kalmte
²repose (vb) **1** rusten, uitrusten **2** (+ on) berusten (op), steunen
³repose (vb) stellen; vestigen [faith, hope]: ~
confidence (or: *trust*) *in sth.* vertrouwen stellen in iets
repository 1 magazijnʰ, pakhuisʰ, opslagplaats **2** schatkamer [fig]; bron; centrumʰ [of
information]
repossess weer in bezit nemen, terugnemen; gedwongen verkopen
represent 1 voorstellen, weergeven, afbeelden **2** voorhouden, onder het oog brengen **3** aanvoeren, beweren: ~ *o.s. as* zich uitgeven voor **4** verklaren, uitleggen, duidelijk
maken **5** symboliseren, staan voor, betekenen **6** vertegenwoordigen
representation 1 voorstelling, afbeelding, uitbeelding, opvoering **2** vertegenwoordiging **3** protestʰ
¹representative (n) **1** vertegenwoordiger,
agent **2** afgevaardigde, gedelegeerde, gemachtigde **3** volksvertegenwoordiger: [Am]
House of Representatives Huis van Afgevaardigden
²representative (adj) **1** representatief, typisch **2** voorstellend, symboliserend ‖ *be ~ of*
typisch zijn voor
repress 1 onderdrukken [also fig]; verdrukken, in bedwang houden, smoren **2** verdringen
repression 1 onderdrukking, verdrukking
2 verdringing
repressive onderdrukkend; hardvochtig
en wreed [of regime]
¹reprieve (n) **1** (bevelʰ tot) uitstelʰ; opschorting [of death penalty] **2** kwijtschelding,
gratie; omzetting [of death penalty] **3** res-
pijtʰ, verlichting, verademing: *temporary ~*
(voorlopig) uitstel van executie
²reprieve (vb) **1** uitstel/gratie verlenen
[death penalty] **2** respijt geven [fig]; een
adempauze geven
¹reprimand (n) (officiële) berisping, uitbrander
²reprimand (vb) (officieel) berispen
¹reprint (n) **1** overdruk(jeʰ) **2** herdruk
²reprint (vb) herdrukken
reprisal represaille, vergelding(smaatregel)
¹reproach (n) **1** schande, smaad, blaam:
above (or: *beyond*) ~ onberispelijk, perfect
2 verwijtʰ, uitbrander, berisping: *a look of* ~
een verwijtende blik
²reproach (vb) verwijten, berispen, afkeuren: *I have nothing to* ~ *myself with* ik heb
mezelf niets te verwijten
reprocess recyclen, terugwinnen; opwer-

ken [nuclear fuel]

¹**reproduce** (vb) zich voortplanten, zich vermenigvuldigen

²**reproduce** (vb) **1** weergeven, reproduceren, vermenigvuldigen **2** voortbrengen **3** opnieuw voortbrengen, herscheppen; [biology] regenereren

reproduction 1 reproductie, weergave, afbeelding **2** voortplanting

reproductive 1 reproductief **2** voortplantings-: ~ *organs* voortplantingsorganen

reprove berispen, terechtwijzen

reptile 1 reptielʰ **2** (lage) kruiper [fig]

republic republiek [also fig]

¹**republican** (n) republikein

²**republican** (adj) republikeins

repudiate 1 verstoten [woman, child] **2** verwerpen; niet erkennen [debt etc]; afwijzen; ontkennen [accusation]

repudiation 1 verstoting **2** verwerping, (ver)loochening

repugnance afkeer; weerzin: *feel ~ towards* sth. weerzin voelen tegen iets

repugnant weerzinwekkend

repulse 1 terugdrijven; terugslaan [enemy]; afslaan [attack]; [fig] verijdelen **2** afslaan; afwijzen [assistance, offer]

repulsive afstotend, weerzinwekkend, walgelijk

reputable achtenswaardig, fatsoenlijk

reputation reputatie, (goede) naam, faam: *have the ~ for* (or: *of*) *being corrupt* de naam hebben corrupt te zijn

¹**repute** (n) reputatie, (goede) naam, faam: *know s.o. by ~* iem. kennen van horen zeggen

²**repute** (vb) beschouwen (als), houden voor: *be highly ~d* een zeer goede naam hebben

reputed 1 befaamd **2** vermeend

reputedly naar men zegt, naar het heet

¹**request** (n) verzoekʰ, (aan)vraag, verzoeknummerʰ: *at the ~ of* op verzoek van; *on ~* op verzoek

²**request** (vb) verzoeken, vragen (om)

request programme verzoekprogrammaʰ

require 1 nodig hebben, behoeven **2** vereisen, eisen, vorderen: *two signatures are ~d* er zijn twee handtekeningen nodig; ~ *sth. from* (or: *of*) *s.o.* iets van iem. vereisen

requirement 1 eis, (eerste) vereiste: *meet* (or: *fulfil*) *the ~s* aan de voorwaarden voldoen **2** behoefte, benodigdheid

¹**requisite** (n) **1** vereisteʰ **2** rekwisietʰ, benodigdheid

²**requisite** (adj) vereist, essentieel, nodig

requisition (op)vorderen

requite 1 vergelden, betaald zetten, wreken **2** belonen **3** beantwoorden: ~ *s.o.'s love* iemands liefde beantwoorden

reread herlezen

¹**rerun** (n) herhaling [of film, play etc]

²**rerun** (vb) opnieuw (laten) spelen; herhalen [film, TV programme]

reschedule verplaatsen

¹**rescue** (n) **1** redding, verlossing, bevrijding **2** hulp, bijstand, steun

²**rescue** (vb) redden, verlossen, bevrijden

rescuer redder

rescue-team reddingsploeg

¹**research** (n) (wetenschappelijk) onderzoekʰ

²**research** (vb) onderzoekingen doen, wetenschappelijk werk verrichten, wetenschappelijk onderzoeken: *this book has been well ~ed* dit boek berust op gedegen onderzoek

researcher onderzoeker

research student postdoctoraal student; promovendus

resemblance gelijkenis, overeenkomst: *show great ~ to* s.o. een grote gelijkenis met iem. vertonen

resemble lijken op

resent kwalijk nemen, verontwaardigd zijn over, zich storen aan: *I ~ that remark* ik neem je die opmerking wel kwalijk

resentful 1 boos, verontwaardigd, ontstemd **2** wrokkig, haatdragend

resentment 1 verontwaardiging **2** wrok, haat

reservation 1 middenberm; middenstrook [of motorway]: *central ~* middenberm **2** [Am] reservaatʰ [for indians] **3** gereserveerde plaats **4** reserve, voorbehoudʰ, bedenking: *without ~(s)* zonder voorbehoud **5** reservering, plaatsbespreking: *do you have a ~?* heeft u gereserveerd?

¹**reserve** (n) **1** reserve, (nood)voorraad: *have* (or: *keep*) sth. *in ~* iets in reserve hebben (or: houden) **2** reservaatʰ: *nature ~* natuurreservaat **3** reservespeler, invaller **4** reservist **5** reserve, voorbehoudʰ, bedenking: *without ~* zonder enig voorbehoud **6** gereserveerdheid, reserve, terughoudendheid

²**reserve** (vb) **1** reserveren, achterhouden, in reserve houden **2** (zich) voorbehouden [right]: *all rights ~d* alle rechten voorbehouden **3** bespreken [seat]; openhouden, laten vrijhouden

reserved 1 gereserveerd, terughoudend, gesloten **2** gereserveerd; besproken [of seat]

reservist reservist

reservoir (water)reservoirʰ, stuwmeerʰ

reset 1 opnieuw zetten [jewel, leg, plant, book] **2** resetten, opnieuw instellen [also comp]; terugzetten op nul [meter]

reshape een nieuwe vorm geven

reside wonen, zetelen

residence 1 residentie, verblijfʰ, verblijfplaats, woonplaats: *take up ~ in* gaan wonen in **2** (voorname) woning, villa, herenhuisʰ **3** ambtswoning [of governor]

residence permit verblijfsvergunning
¹resident (n) ingezetene, (vaste) inwoner, bewoner
²resident (adj) **1** woonachtig, inwonend, intern: [Am] ~ *alien* vreemdeling met een verblijfsvergunning **2** vast [on inhabitant] **residential** woon-, van een woonwijk: ~ *area* (or: *district, quarter*) (deftige/betere) woonwijk; ~ *hotel* familiehotel
residents' association buurtcomité
¹residual (n) **1** residuᵸ; rest [also maths, chem] **2** [chem] bijproductᵸ
²residual (adj) achterblijvend; rest-**residue** residuᵸ, overblijfselᵸ, rest(antᵸ)
¹resign (vb) **1** berusten, zich schikken **2** afstand doen van een ambt, aftreden, ontslag nemen; bedanken [for position]; opgeven [chess]
²resign (vb) **1** berusten in, zich schikken in, zich neerleggen bij: ~ *o.s.* *to sth., be ~ed to sth.* zich bij iets neerleggen **2** afstaan; afstand doen van [right, claim, ownership]; overgeven **3** opgeven [hope]
resignation 1 ontslagᵸ, ontslagbrief, aftreding, ontslagneming: *hand in/offer* (or: *send in, tender*) *one's* ~ zijn ontslag indienen **2** afstand **3** berusting, overgave
resigned gelaten, berustend
resilience veerkracht [also fig]; herstellingsvermogenᵸ
resilient veerkrachtig [also fig]
resin (kunst)harsᵸ: *synthetic* ~ kunsthars
resist 1 weerstaan, weerstand bieden (aan), tegenhouden; bestand zijn tegen [cold, heat, damp]; resistent zijn tegen [disease, infection]: ~ *temptation* de verleiding weerstaan **2** zich verzetten (tegen), bestrijden: *this novel ~s* **interpretation** deze roman laat zich niet interpreteren
resistance 1 weerstand, tegenstand, verzetᵸ: *make* (or: *offer*) *no* ~ geen weerstand bieden; [fig] *take the line of least* ~ de weg van de minste weerstand kiezen **2** weerstandsvermogenᵸ
the **Resistance** verzetsbeweging, verzetᵸ
resistance fighter verzetsstrijder
resistant weerstand biedend, resistent, bestand: *heat-*~ hittebestendig
¹resit (n) herexamenᵸ
²resit (vb) opnieuw afleggen [examination]
resolute resoluut, vastberaden, beslist
resolution 1 resolutie, motie, voorstelᵸ, planᵸ **2** besluitᵸ, beslissing, voornemenᵸ: *good* ~s goede voornemens **3** oplossing, ontbinding, ontleding **4** vastberadenheid, beslistheid, vastbeslotenheid
¹resolve (n) **1** besluitᵸ, beslissing, voornemenᵸ: *a firm* ~ *to stay* een vast voornemen om te blijven **2** [Am] resolutie, motie, voorstelᵸ **3** vastberadenheid, beslistheid
²resolve (vb) **1** een besluit nemen, beslui-

ten, zich voornemen: *they ~d (up)on doing sth.* zij besloten iets te doen **2** zich oplossen, zich ontbinden, uiteenvallen
³resolve (vb) **1** beslissen, besluiten: *he ~d to leave* hij besloot weg te gaan **2** oplossen, een oplossing vinden voor **3** opheffen; wegnemen [doubt] **4** ontbinden, (doen) oplossen **5** ertoe brengen, doen beslissen: *that ~d us to ...* dat deed ons besluiten om ... **6** besluiten, beëindigen; bijleggen [dispute]
resolved vastbesloten, beslist
resonance resonantie, weerklank, weergalm
resonant 1 resonerend, weerklinkend, weergalmend **2** vol; diep [of voice]
resort 1 hulpmiddelᵸ, redmiddelᵸ, toevlucht: *in the last* ~, *as a last* ~ in laatste instantie, in geval van nood **2** drukbezochte plaats, (vakantie)oordᵸ: *without* ~ *to* zonder zijn toevlucht te nemen tot
resort to zijn toevlucht nemen tot: ~ *violence* zijn toevlucht nemen tot geweld
resound weerklinken [also fig]; weergalmen
resounding 1 (weer)klinkend **2** zeer groot, onmiskenbaar: *a* ~ *success* een daverend succes
resource 1 hulpbron, redmiddelᵸ: *left to one's own ~s* aan zijn lot overgelaten **2** toevlucht, uitweg **3** vindingrijkheid: *he is full of* ~ (or: *a man of* ~) hij is (zeer) vindingrijk **4** (-s) rijkdommen, (geld)middelen, voorraden: *natural* ~s natuurlijke rijkdommen
resourceful vindingrijk
¹respect (n) **1** opzichtᵸ, detailᵸ, (oog)puntᵸ: *in all* (or: *many*) ~s in alle (or: vele) opzichten; *in some* ~ in zeker opzicht, enigermate **2** betrekking, relatie: *with* ~ *to* met betrekking tot, wat betreft **3** aandacht, zorg, inachtneming: *without* ~ *to* zonder te letten op, ongeacht **4** eerbied, achting, ontzagᵸ: *be held in the greatest* ~ zeer in aanzien zijn; *with* (all due) ~ als u mij toestaat **5** (-s) eerbetuigingen, groeten, complimenten: *give her my* ~s doe haar de groeten; *pay one's last* ~s to s.o. iem. de laatste eer bewijzen [at someone's death]
²respect (vb) **1** respecteren, eerbiedigen, (hoog)achten **2** ontzien, ongemoeid laten
respectability fatsoenᵸ, fatsoenlijkheid
respectable 1 achtenswaardig, eerbiedwaardig **2** respectabel, (tamelijk) groot, behoorlijk: *a* ~ *income* een behoorlijk inkomen **3** fatsoenlijk [also iron]
respectful eerbiedig: *yours* ~*ly* met de (meeste) hoogachting
respectively respectievelijk
respiration ademhaling
³respirator 1 ademhalingstoestelᵸ **2** gasmaskerᵸ, rookmaskerᵸ, stofmaskerᵸ
respiratory ademhalings-

respite 1 respijt[h], uitstel[h], opschorting: *work without* ~ zonder onderbreking werken **2** verlichting
resplendent schitterend, prachtig
respond 1 antwoorden **2** (+ to) reageren (op), gehoor geven (aan), gevoelig zijn (voor)
respondent 1 gedaagde [in appeal of divorce proceedings] **2** ondervraagde, geënquêteerde
response 1 antwoord[h], repliek, tegenzet **2** reactie, gehoor[h], weerklank, respons: *meet with no* ~ geen weerklank vinden
responsibility verantwoordelijkheid, aansprakelijkheid: *on one's own* ~ op eigen verantwoordelijkheid
responsible 1 betrouwbaar, degelijk, solide **2** verantwoordelijk; belangrijk [of job] **3** (+ for) verantwoordelijk (voor), aansprakelijk (voor): *be* ~ *to* verantwoording verschuldigd zijn aan
responsive (+ to) ontvankelijk (voor), gevoelig (voor), vlug reagerend (op)
¹rest (n) **1** rustplaats, verblijf[h], tehuis[h] **2** steun, standaard, houder, statief[h]; [billiards] bok **3** [mus] rust(teken[h]) **4** rust, slaap, pauze: *come to* ~ tot stilstand komen; *set s.o.'s mind at* ~ iem. geruststellen **5** de rest, het overige, de overigen: *and the* ~ *of it, all the* ~ *of it* en de rest
²rest (vb) **1** rusten, stil staan, slapen, pauzeren: *I feel completely* ~*ed* ik voel me helemaal uitgerust **2** blijven [in a certain condition]: ~ *assured* wees gerust, wees ervan verzekerd **3** braak liggen
³rest (vb) **1** laten (uit)rusten, rust geven **2** doen rusten, leunen, steunen
¹restart (vb) opnieuw beginnen, starten
²restart (vb) weer op gang brengen; [sport] hervatten
restaurant restaurant[h]
restful 1 rustig, kalm, vredig **2** rustgevend, kalmerend
resting-place rustplaats [also fig]
restitution restitutie, teruggave, schadeloosstelling
restive 1 weerspannig, onhandelbaar, dwars; koppig [of horse] **2** ongedurig, onrustig; rusteloos [of person]
restless rusteloos, onrustig, ongedurig
restoration 1 restauratie(werk[h]), reconstructie **2** herstel[h], herinvoering, rehabilitatie **3** teruggave
restore 1 teruggeven, terugbetalen, terugbrengen **2** restaureren **3** reconstrueren **4** in ere herstellen, rehabiliteren **5** herstellen, weer invoeren, vernieuwen
restrain 1 tegenhouden, weerhouden: ~ *from* weerhouden van **2** aan banden leggen, beteugelen, beperken, in toom houden
restrained 1 beheerst, kalm **2** ingetogen,

sober; gematigd [of colour]
restraint 1 terughoudendheid, gereserveerdheid, zelfbeheersing: *without* ~ vrijelijk, in onbeperkte mate **2** ingetogenheid, soberheid
restrict beperken, begrenzen, aan banden leggen: ~ *to* beperken tot
restriction beperking, (beperkende) bepaling, restrictie, voorbehoud[h]
restrictive beperkend: ~ *trade practices* beperkende handelspraktijken
rest room [Am] toilet[h] [in restaurant, office etc]
rest (up)on (be)rusten op, steunen op
rest with berusten bij
¹result (n) **1** resultaat[h], uitkomst; uitslag [of sporting events] **2** gevolg[h], effect[h], uitvloeisel[h]: *as a* ~ dientengevolge, als gevolg waarvan; *as a* ~ *of* ten gevolge van **3** uitkomst [of sum]; antwoord[h]
²result (vb) **1** volgen, het gevolg zijn: ~ *from* voortvloeien uit **2** aflopen, uitpakken: ~ *in* tot gevolg hebben
resultant resulterend, eruit voortvloeiend
resume 1 opnieuw beginnen, hervatten, hernemen **2** terugnemen, terugkrijgen **3** voortzetten, vervolgen, doorgaan
résumé 1 (korte) samenvatting **2** [Am] cv, curriculum vitae[h]
resumption hervatting, voortzetting
resurgence heropleving, opstanding
resurrect 1 (doen) herleven, (doen) herrijzen **2** opgraven, weer voor de dag halen
resurrection herleving, opleving, opstanding
the **Resurrection** de verrijzenis, de opstanding
resuscitate 1 weer bijbrengen, reanimeren **2** doen herleven
¹retail (n) kleinhandel, detailhandel
²retail (vb) in een winkel verkocht worden: ~ *at* (or: *for*) *fifty cents* in de winkel voor vijftig cent te koop zijn
³retail (vb) in een winkel verkopen
⁴retail (vb) omstandig vertellen
retailer 1 winkelier, kleinhandelaar **2** slijter
retain 1 vasthouden, binnenhouden: *a* ~*ing wall* steunmuur **2** houden, handhaven, bewaren: *we* ~ *happy memories of those days* wij bewaren goede herinneringen aan die dagen
retainer 1 voorschot[h] [of fee] **2** volgeling, bediende: *an old* ~ een oude getrouwe
retaliate wraak nemen
retard ophouden, tegenhouden, vertragen
retarded achtergebleven, achterlijk, geestelijk gehandicapt
retch kokhalzen
retention 1 het vasthouden, het binnenhouden **2** handhaving, behoud[h]
¹rethink (n) heroverweging, het opnieuw

doordenken
²**rethink** (vb) heroverwegen, opnieuw bezien
reticence 1 terughoudendheid, gereserveerdheid **2** het verzwijgen, het achterhouden **3** zwijgzaamheid, geslotenheid
reticent 1 terughoudend, gereserveerd
2 zwijgzaam, gesloten
retina netvliesʰ, retina
retinue gevolgʰ, hofstoet
retire 1 zich terugtrekken, weggaan, heengaan, zich ter ruste begeven: ~ *for the night*
(or: *to bed*) zich ter ruste (*or:* te bed) begeven
2 met pensioen gaan
retired 1 teruggetrokken, afgezonderd,
afgelegen **2** gepensioneerd, stil levend, ren-
tenierend
retirement 1 pensionering, het gepensioneerd worden, het met pensioen gaan: *to*
take early ~ met de vut gaan; [Belg] op brugpensioen gaan **2** afzondering, eenzaamheid
retirement pension ouderdomspensi-
oenʰ; AOW
retiring 1 teruggetrokken, niet opdringerig **2** pensioen-: ~ *age* de pensioengerech-
tigde leeftijd
¹**retort** (n) **1** weerwoordʰ, repliek, antwoordʰ: *say (sth.) in ~* (iets) als weerwoord
gebruiken **2** distilleerkolf
²**retort** (vb) een weerwoord geven, antwoorden
³**retort** (vb) (vinnig) antwoorden; [fig] de bal
terugkaatsen
retrace 1 herleiden, terugvoeren tot
2 weer nagaan [in memory] **3** terugkeren: ~
one's steps (or: *way*) op zijn schreden terugkeren
retract intrekken [also fig]; herroepen, afstand nemen van
¹**retreat** (n) **1** toevluchtsoordʰ, schuilplaats
2 tehuisʰ, asielʰ **3** terugtocht, aftocht: *beat a*
(hasty) ~ zich (snel) terugtrekken; [fig] (snel)
de aftocht blazen **4** retraite
²**retreat** (vb) teruggaan, zich terugtrekken
¹**retrench** (vb) bezuinigen
²**retrench** (vb) besnoeien, inkrimpen, bekorten
retrial nieuw onderzoekʰ; revisie
retribution vergelding, straf
retrieval 1 herwinning, het terugvinden
2 herstelling, het verhelpen **3** het ophalen
[data from files] || *beyond* (or: *past*) ~ **a)** voor-
goed verloren; **b)** onherstelbaar
retrieve 1 terugwinnen, terugvinden, terugkrijgen **2** herstellen, weer goedmaken,
verhelpen **3** ophalen [data from files]
retrospect terugblik: *in* ~ achteraf gezien
retrospection terugblik, retrospectiefʰ
retrospective 1 retrospectief, terugblik-
kend **2** met terugwerkende kracht
¹**return** (n) **1** terugkeer, terugkomst, thuis-

komst, terugreis: *the point of no* ~ punt
waarna er geen weg terug is **2** retourtjeʰ
3 teruggave [also of tax]; teruggezonden artikelʰ: *on sale and* ~ op commissie **4** opbrengst, winst, rendementʰ: ~ *on capital* (or:
investment) kapitaalopbrengst, resultaat
van de investering **5** aangifte, officieel rapportʰ **6** verkiezing, afvaardiging **7** terugslag,
return, terugspeelbal **8** return(wedstrijd),
revanche || *by* ~ *(of post)* per omgaande, per
kerende post; *in* ~ *for* in ruil voor
²**return** (adj) **1** retour-: ~ *ticket* retour(tje)
2 tegen-, terug-: *a* ~ *visit* een tegenbezoek
³**return** (vb) terugkeren, terugkomen, teruggaan: ~ *to* **a)** terugkeren op; **b)** vervallen
in
⁴**return** (vb) **1** retourneren, terugbrengen,
teruggeven **2** opleveren, opbrengen **3** beantwoorden, terugbetalen: ~ *like for like* met
gelijke munt terugbetalen **4** [sport] terugslaan, retourneren, terugspelen **5** kiezen,
verkiezen, afvaardigen
⁵**return** (vb) antwoorden
return key returntoets, entertoets
¹**retweet** (n) retweet
²**retweet** (vb) retweeten, doorsturen
reunion reünie, hereniging, samenkomst
reunite (zich) herenigen, weer bij elkaar
komen
reusable geschikt voor hergebruik
reuse opnieuw gebruiken
rev Reverend Eerw., Eerwaarde
revaluation herwaardering; revaluatie
[also fin]
revamp opknappen, vernieuwen
reveal openbaren, onthullen, bekendmaken
revealing onthullend, veelzeggend
revel pret maken, feestvieren: ~ *in* erg genieten van, zich te buiten gaan aan
revelation bekendmaking, openbaring,
onthulling: *it was quite a* ~ *to me* dat was een
hele openbaring voor mij
revelry pret(makerij), uitgelatenheid
¹**revenge** (n) wraak(neming), vergelding:
take ~ *on s.o. for sth.* wraak nemen (*or:* zich
wreken) op iem. vanwege iets **2** [sport,
game] revanche(partij)
²**revenge** (vb) wreken, vergelden, wraak
nemen
revengeful wraakzuchtig
revenue 1 inkomenʰ, opbrengst; inkomsten [from property, investment etc] **2** inkomsten
revenue tariff belastingtariefʰ
reverberate weerkaatsen [sound, light,
heat]; terugkaatsen, echoën, weerklinken: ~
upon terugwerken op [also fig]
reverberation weerklank, weerkaatsing
revere (ver)eren, respecteren, eerbied hebben voor

reverence verering, respect[h], (diepe) eerbied, ontzag[h]: *hold s.o. (sth.) in* ~ eerbied koesteren voor iem.

the **(iets) reverend** eerwaard(ig)
Reverend Eerwaarde: *the* ~ *Mr Johnson* de Weleerwaarde Heer Johnson
reverent eerbiedig, respectvol
reversal omkering, om(me)keer
¹reverse (n) **1** tegenslag, nederlaag **2** keerzijde [of coins; also fig]; rugzijde, achterkant **3** achteruit [of car]: *put a car into* ~ een auto in zijn achteruit zetten **4** tegendeel[h], omgekeerde, tegengestelde[h]: *but the* ~ *is also true* maar het omgekeerde is ook waar || *in* ~ omgekeerd, in omgekeerde volgorde
²reverse (adj) tegen(over)gesteld, omgekeerd, achteraan: ~ *gear* achteruit [of car]; *in* ~ *order* in omgekeerde volgorde
³reverse (vb) achteruitrijden [of car]; achteruitgaan
⁴reverse (vb) **1** (om)keren, omdraaien, omschakelen; achteruitrijden [car]: ~ *one's policy* radicaal van politiek veranderen **2** herroepen [decision]; intrekken; [law] herzien
revert 1 (+ to) terugkeren (tot) [previous condition]; terugvallen (in) [habit] **2** (+ to) terugkomen (op) [earlier topic of conversation] **3** terugkeren [of property to owner]
¹review (n) **1** terugblik, overzicht[h], bezinning: *be under* ~ opnieuw bekeken worden **2** parade, inspectie **3** recensie, (boek)bespreking **4** tijdschrift[h]
²review (vb) **1** opnieuw bekijken, herzien **2** terugblikken op, overzien **3** parade houden, inspecteren **4** recenseren, bespreken, recensies schrijven
reviewer recensent
revile (uit)schelden
revise 1 herzien, verbeteren, corrigeren: ~*d edition* herziene uitgave [of book]; *enclosed you will find our* ~*d invoice* bijgesloten vindt u onze gecorrigeerde factuur **2** repeteren [lesson]; herhalen; studeren [for examination]
revision 1 revisie, herziening, wijziging **2** herhaling [of lesson]; het studeren [for examination]
revitalize nieuwe kracht geven, nieuw leven geven
revival 1 reveil[h] **2** (her)opleving, wedergeboorte, hernieuwde belangstelling **3** herstel[h] [of strengths] || *the* ~ *of a play* de heropvoering van een toneelstuk
¹revive (vb) **1** herleven, bijkomen, weer tot leven (op krachten) komen **2** weer in gebruik komen, opnieuw ingevoerd worden
²revive (vb) **1** doen herleven, vernieuwen, weer tot leven brengen **2** opnieuw invoeren [old custom]
¹revoke (vb) [cards] verzaken
²revoke (vb) herroepen; intrekken [order, promise, licence]

¹revolt (n) opstand, oproer[h]: *stir people to* ~ mensen opruien
²revolt (vb) **1** (+ against) in opstand komen (tegen), rebelleren, muiten **2** walgen: ~ *at* (or: *against, from*) walgen van
³revolt (vb) doen walgen, afstoten; afkerig maken van [also fig]: *be* ~*ed by sth.* van iets walgen
revolting walgelijk, onsmakelijk, weerzinwekkend
revolution 1 (om)wenteling; draaiing [around centre] **2** rotatie; draai(ing) [around axis]; toer, slag **3** revolutie, (staats)omwenteling **4** ommekeer, omkering: *a* ~ *in thought* algehele verandering in denkbeelden
revolutionary revolutionair
revolve (rond)draaien, (doen) (rond)wentelen: *the discussion always* ~*s around* (or: *about*) *money* de discussie draait altijd om geld
revolver revolver
revolving draaiend, roterend: ~ *door* draaideur
revulsion walging, afkeer, weerzin: *a* ~ *against* (or: *from*) een afkeer van, een weerzin tegen
¹rev up (vb) **1** draaien, op toeren komen **2** [fig] opstarten, op gang komen
²rev up (vb) **1** op toeren laten komen **2** [fig] opvoeren, uitbreiden: ~ *one's computer* zijn computer versnellen
¹reward (n) beloning, compensatie, loon[h]: *the* ~*s of popularity* de voordelen van populariteit
²reward (vb) belonen
rewarding lonend, de moeite waard; dankbaar [of work, task]
rewind opnieuw opwinden, terugspoelen
¹rewrite (n) **1** bewerking **2** bewerkt boek, artikel
²rewrite (vb) bewerken, herschrijven
rhapsody verhalend gedicht[h]
rhetoric 1 redekunst, retoriek, retorica **2** welsprekendheid, bombast, holle frasen
rhetorical retorisch, gekunsteld || ~ *question* retorische vraag
¹rheumatic (n) reumapatiënt
²rheumatic (adj) reumatisch: ~ *fever* acute reuma
rheumatism reuma(tiek), reumatisme[h], gewrichtsreumatiek
the **Rhine** Rijn
rhino *rhinoceros* neushoorn
rhinoceros neushoorn
rhododendron rododendron
rhubarb rabarber
¹rhyme (n) **1** rijm(woord)[h] **2** (berijmd) gedicht[h], vers[h] || *without* ~ *or reason* zonder enige betekenis, onzinnig
²rhyme (vb) **1** rijmen, rijm hebben: ~*d verses* rijmende verzen **2** dichten, rijmen

³**rhyme** (vb) **1** laten rijmen **2** berijmen
rhyming rijmend, op rijm: ~ *slang* rijmend
slang
rhythm ritmeʰ, maat
rhythmic(al) ritmisch, regelmatig
¹**rib** (n) **1** rib **2** balein [of umbrella] **3** blad-
nerf **4** ribstukʰ **5** ribbelpatroonʰ [in knitting]
²**rib** (vb) plagen, voor de gek houden
ribaldry schunnige taal
ribbed geribd: ~ *material* geribbelde stof
ribbon 1 lint(je)ʰ, onderscheiding **2** (-s)
flard: [fig] *cut to* ~s in de pan hakken
3 (schrijfmachine)lintʰ
rib cage ribbenkast
rice rijst
rich 1 rijk: ~ *in* rijk aan; *the* ~ de rijken
2 kostbaar, luxueus **3** rijkelijk, overvloedig
4 vruchtbaar: ~ *soil* vruchtbare aarde
5 machtig [of food] **6** vol [of sounds]; warm
[of colour] **7** [inform; oft iron] kostelijk [of
joke]: *that's (pretty)* ~*!* a) dat is een goeie!;
b) wat een flater! ‖ *strike it* ~ een goudmijn
ontdekken, fortuin maken
riches 1 rijkdom, het rijk-zijn **2** kostbaarheden, weelde
richly volledig, dubbel en dwars: ~ *deserve*
volkomen verdienen
¹**rick** (n) hooimijt
²**rick** (vb) **1** ophopen **2** verdraaien, verstuiken
rickety gammel, wankel
rickshaw riksja
ricochet (doen) ricocheren, (laten) afketsen: *the bullet* ~*ted off the wall* de kogel ketste
af op de muur
rid bevrijden, ontdoen van: *be well* ~ *of s.o.*
goed van iem. af zijn; *get* ~ *of* kwijtraken,
van de hand doen
riddance bevrijding, verwijdering: *they've
just left. Good* ~*!* ze zijn net weg. Mooi zo,
opgeruimd staat netjes!
-**ridden 1** gedomineerd door, beheerst
door: *conscience-ridden* gewetensbezwaard
2 vergeven van: *this place is* *vermin-ridden*
het wemelt hier van het ongedierte
¹**riddle** (n) **1** raadselʰ, mysterieʰ **2** (grove)
zeef
²**riddle** (vb) **1** zeven [also fig]; schiften, natrekken **2** doorzeven: *the body was* ~*d with*
bullets het lichaam was met kogels doorzeefd
riddled gevuld, vol, bezaaid: *the translation
was* ~ *with errors* de vertaling stond vol fouten
¹**ride** (n) **1** rit(jeʰ), tocht(jeʰ) **2** rijpadʰ, ruiterpadʰ ‖ *take s.o. for a* ~ iem. voor de gek hou-
den, iem. in de maling nemen
²**ride** (vb) **1** rijden, paardrijden **2** rijden, voor
anker liggen ‖ ~ *roughshod over s.o. (sth.)*
nergens naar kijken, niet al te zachtzinnig te
werk gaan; ~ *up* omhoogkruipen, opkruipen

³**ride** (vb) **1** berijden, doorrijden **2** (be)rijden,
rijden met: ~ *a bicycle* (or: *bike*) op de fiets
rijden, fietsen **3** beheersen, tiranniseren: *the
robber was ridden by* *fears* de dief werd door
schrik bevangen **4** [Am] jennen, kwellen
ride out overleven [also fig]; heelhuids
doorkomen: *the ship rode out the* *storm* het
schip doorstond de storm
rider (be)rijder, ruiter
ridge 1 (berg)kam, richel, bergketen **2** nok
[of roof] **3** ribbel **4** golftop **5** rug, (uitgerekt)
hogedrukgebiedʰ
¹**ridicule** (n) spot, hoon
²**ridicule** (vb) ridiculiseren, bespotten
ridiculous ridicuul, belachelijk
riding boot rijlaars
rife 1 wijdverbreid, vaak voorkomend: *violence is* ~ *in westerns* er is veel geweld in
cowboyfilms **2** (+ with) goed voorzien (van),
legio
riffle through vluchtig doorbladeren
riff-raff uitschotʰ, schoremʰ
¹**rifle** (n) geweerʰ, karabijn
²**rifle** (vb) doorzoeken, leeghalen: *the burglar
had* ~*d every* *cupboard* de dief had iedere
kast overhoop gehaald
rifle range 1 schietbaan **2** schootsafstand,
draagwijdte: *within* ~ binnen schot(bereik)
rift 1 spleet, kloof **2** onenigheid, tweedracht
¹**rig** (n) **1** tuigʰ, tuigage, takelage **2** uitrusting, (olie)booruitrusting **3** plunje, uitrusting: *in full* ~ in vol ornaat
²**rig** (vb) **1** (op)tuigen, optakelen **2** uitrusten,
uitdossen **3** knoeien met, sjoemelen met: *the
elections were* ~*ged* de verkiezingen waren
doorgestoken kaart
the **rigging** tuigʰ, tuigage, takelage, het optuigen
¹**right** (n) **1** rechterkant: *keep to the* ~ rechts
houden; *on* (or: *to*) *your* ~ aan je rechterkant
2 rechterhand; rechtse [in boxing]; rechter-
(hand)schoen **3** rechtsʰ, de conservatieven
4 rechtʰ, voorrechtʰ, (gerechtvaardigde) eis:
the ~ *of free* *speech* het recht op vrije meningsuiting; ~ *of way* recht van overpad;
[traf] voorrang(srecht); *all* ~s *reserved* alle
rechten voorbehouden; *he has a* ~ *to the*
money hij heeft recht op het geld; *within
one's* ~s in zijn recht **5** rechtʰ, gerechtigheid:
he is *in* *the* ~ hij heeft gelijk, hij heeft het
recht aan zijn kant ‖ *put* (or: *set*) *to* ~s in orde
brengen, rechtzetten
²**right** (adj) **1** juist, correct, rechtmatig: *you
were* ~ *to tell her* je deed er goed aan het
haar te vertellen; *put* (or: *set*) *the clock* ~ de
klok juist zetten **2** juist, gepast, recht: *strike
the* ~ *note* de juiste toon aanslaan; *on the* ~
side of fifty nog geen vijftig (jaar oud); *keep
on the* ~ *side of the law* zich (keurig) aan de
wet houden; [fig] *be on the* ~ *track* op het

goede spoor zitten; ~ **angle** rechte hoek **3** in goede staat, in orde: *let me see if I've* **got** *this* ~ even kijken of ik het goed begrijp **4** rechts, conservatief **5** eerlijk, betrouwbaar: *the ~ sort* het goede soort (mensen); **Mister** Right de ware Jakob; *(as)* ~ *as* **rain** perfect in orde, kerngezond; **put** (or: **set**) *s.o.* ~ iem. terechtwijzen; **see** *s.o.* ~ zorgen dat iem. aan zijn trekken komt; ~ **enough** bevredigend, ja hoor **6** waar, echt, heus: *it's a* ~ **mess** het is een puinzooi **7** gelijk: *you* **are** ~ je hebt gelijk **8** rechtvaardig, gerechtvaardigd: *it* **seemed** *only* ~ *to tell you this* ik vond dat je dit moest weten
³**right** (vb) **1** rechtmaken, recht(op) zetten: *the* **yacht** *~ed itself* het jacht kwam weer recht te liggen **2** genoegdoening geven, rehabiliteren **3** verbeteren; rechtzetten [mistakes]: ~ *a* **wrong** een onrecht herstellen ‖ ~ *o.s.* zich herstellen
⁴**right** (adv) **1** naar rechts, aan de rechterzijde: ~ **arm** (or: **hand**) rechterhand, assistent; *keep on the* ~ **side** rechts houden; ~ *and* **left** aan alle kanten, overal, links en rechts; *~, left and centre,* **left**, *~, and centre* aan alle kanten **2** juist, vlak, regelrecht: ~ **ahead** recht vooruit; ~ **behind** *you* vlak achter je **3** onmiddellijk, direct: *I'll be* ~ **back** ik ben zó terug **4** juist, correct: *nothing seems to* **go** ~ *for her* niets wil haar lukken **5** helemaal, volledig: *she turned* ~ **round** zij maakte volledig rechtsomkeert **6** zeer, heel, recht ‖ ~ **away** onmiddellijk; ~ **off** onmiddellijk; ~ **on** zo mogen wij het horen
Right Zeer [in forms of address]
right-about in tegenovergestelde richting ‖ *(do a)* ~ **turn** (or: **face**) rechtsomkeert (maken) [also fig]
right-angled rechthoekig, met rechte hoek(en)
righteous 1 rechtvaardig, deugdzaam **2** gerechtvaardigd, gewettigd: ~ **indignation** gerechtvaardigde verontwaardiging
rightful 1 wettelijk, rechtmatig: *the ~* **owner** de rechtmatige eigenaar **2** gerechtvaardigd, rechtvaardig
right-hand rechts, m.b.t. de rechterhand: ~ **man** rechterhand, onmisbare helper; ~ **turn** bocht naar rechts
right-handed 1 rechtshandig **2** met de rechterhand toegebracht **3** voor rechtshandigen
rightly 1 terecht **2** rechtvaardig, oprecht
right-minded weldenkend
right-to-life antiabortus-
right-wing van de rechterzijde, conservatief
right-winger 1 lidʰ van de rechterzijde, conservatief **2** rechtsbuiten, rechtervleugelspeler
rigid 1 onbuigzaam, stijf, stug, strak **2** star,

verstard
rigidity 1 onbuigzaamheid **2** starheid
rigmarole 1 onzin, gewauwelʰ **2** rompslomp
rigorous 1 onbuigzaam, streng, ongenadig **2** rigoureus, nauwgezet, zorgvuldig
rigour 1 gestrengheid, strikte toepassing: *with the utmost* ~ *of the* **law** met strenge toepassing van de wet **2** hardheid, meedogenloosheid **3** accuratesse, uiterste nauwkeurigheid
rig out 1 uitrusten, van een uitrusting voorzien **2** uitdossen: *he had* **rigged** *himself out as a general* hij had zich als generaal uitgedost
rig-out plunje, (apen)pakʰ
rig up [esp inform] **1** monteren, opstellen **2** in elkaar flansen
rile op stang jagen, nijdig maken, irriteren
rim rand, boordʰ, velg; montuur [of glasses]
rime rijp, aangevroren mist
rimless montuurloos [of glasses]
rind schil, korst, zwoerdʰ
¹**ring** (n) **1** ring, kring, piste, arena **2** groepering, bende **3** gerinkelʰ, klank; [inform] telefoontjeʰ: **give** *s.o. a* ~ iem. opbellen **4** bijklank, ondertoon: *her offer has a* **suspicious** ~ er zit een luchtje aan haar aanbod **5** het boksen, bokswereld, ring **6** circus, circuswereld, piste ‖ **make** (or: **run**) *~s round s.o.* iem. de loef afsteken
²**ring** (vb) **1** rinkelen, klinken; (over)gaan [of bell]; bellen: ~ **true** oprecht klinken **2** bellen, de klok luiden, aanbellen **3** tuiten [of ears]; weerklinken **4** telefoneren, bellen: ~ **off** opleggen, ophangen [telephone] **5** (+ with) weergalmen (van), gonzen
³**ring** (vb) **1** doen rinkelen, luiden **2** opbellen, telefoneren naar: *I'll* ~ *you* **back** *in a minute* ik bel je dadelijk terug
⁴**ring** (vb) **1** omringen, omcirkelen **2** ringelen; ringen [animals]
ring-binder ringband
ring finger ringvinger
ringleader leider [of group of agitators]
ringlet lange krul
ringmaster circusdirecteur
ringtone beltoon
¹**ring up** (vb) **1** (al luidend) optrekken [bell] **2** registreren; aanslaan [on cash register]
²**ring up** (vb) opbellen, telefoneren
rink 1 (kunst)ijsbaan **2** rolschaatsbaan
¹**rinse** (n) (kleur)spoeling
²**rinse** (vb) **1** spoelen **2** een kleurspoeling geven aan
¹**riot** (n) **1** ordeverstoring, ongeregeldheid **2** braspartij, uitbundig feestʰ **3** overvloed, weelde: *a* ~ *of* **colour** een bonte kleurenpracht **4** oproerʰ, tumultʰ **5** dolle pret, pretmakerij ‖ **run** ~ **a)** relletjes trappen, uit de band springen; **b)** woekeren [of plants]

²**r**i**ot** (vb) **1** relletjes trappen **2** er ongebreideld op los leven, uitspatten
ri**oter** relschopper
ri**otous 1** oproerig, wanordelijk **2** luidruchtig, uitgelaten: ~ *assembly* het oproerkraaien **3** denderend
ri**ot police** ME, mobiele eenheid
¹**rip** (n) **1** (lange) scheur, snee **2** losbol, snoeper
²**rip** (vb) **1** scheuren, splijten **2** vooruitsnellen; scheuren [fig]: *let* it (or: *her*) ~ plankgas geven ‖ *let sth.* ~ iets op zijn beloop laten
³**rip** (vb) **1** openrijten, losscheuren, afscheuren, wegscheuren: *the bag had been ~ped open* de zak was opengereten; ~ *up* aan stukken rijten **2** jatten, pikken: ~ *off* a) te veel doen betalen, afzetten; b) stelen
ripe 1 rijp [also fig]; volgroeid; belegen [of cheese, wine] **2** wijs, verstandig: *of ~ age* volwassen, ervaren; *a ~ judgement* een doordacht oordeel **3** op het kantje af, plat **4** klaar, geschikt: *the time is ~ for action* de tijd is rijp voor actie
ripen rijpen, rijp worden, wijs worden, doen rijpen
rip-off 1 afzetterij **2** diefstal, roof
¹**ripple** (n) **1** rimpeling, golfjeʰ, deining **2** gekabbelʰ, geruisʰ: *a ~ of laughter* een kabbelend gelach
²**ripple** (vb) kabbelen, ruisen
³**ripple** (vb) rimpelen, (doen) golven
rip-roaring lawaaierig, totaal uitgelaten
¹**rise** (n) **1** helling, verhoging, hoogte **2** stijging [also fig]; verhoging; [Stock Exchange] hausse **3** loonsverhoging **4** het rijzen, het omhooggaan **5** het opgaan, opgang; opkomst [of celestial body]: *the ~ of fascism* de opkomst van het fascisme **6** oorsprong, beginʰ: *give ~ to* aanleiding geven tot **7** opkomst, groei ‖ *get a ~ out of s.o.* iem. op de kast jagen
²**rise** (vb) **1** opstaan [also from bed]: ~ *to one's feet* opstaan **2** (op)stijgen [also fig]; (op)klimmen: [fig] ~ *to the occasion* zich tegen de moeilijkheden opgewassen tonen **3** opkomen, opgaan; rijzen [of celestial body] **4** promotie maken, bevorderd worden: ~ *in the world* vooruitkomen in de wereld **5** opdoemen, verschijnen **6** toenemen [also fig]; stijgen [of prices] **7** in opstand komen, rebelleren: ~ *in arms* de wapens opnemen **8** ontstaan, ontspringen
riser 1 stootbordʰ **2** iem. die opstaat: *a late ~* een langslaper; *an early ~* een vroege vogel, iem. die vroeg opstaat
risible 1 lacherig, lachziek **2** lachwekkend
¹**rising** (n) opstand, revolte
²**rising** (adj) **1** opkomend, aankomend: *a ~ politician* een opkomend politicus **2** stijgend, oplopend: ~ *damp* opstijgend grondwater **3** opstaand, rijzend: *the land of the ~*

sun het land van de rijzende zon
¹**risk** (n) **1** verzekerd bedragʰ **2** risicoʰ, kans, gevaarʰ: *at ~* in gevaar; *I don't want to run the ~ of losing my job* ik wil mijn baan niet op het spel zetten
²**risk** (vb) **1** wagen, op het spel zetten **2** riskeren, gevaar lopen
risky 1 gewaagd, gevaarlijk **2** gedurfd, gewaagd
rite rite [also fig]; ritus, (kerkelijke) ceremonie
ritual ritueelʰ [also fig]; ritus, riten, kerkelijke plechtigheid
¹**rival** (n) rivaal
²**rival** (adj) rivaliserend, mededingend
³**rival** (vb) **1** naar de kroon steken, wedijveren met **2** evenaren
rivalry rivaliteit
river rivier [also fig]; stroom: ~*s of blood* stromen bloed; *the ~ Thames* de (rivier de) Theems ‖ *sell s.o. down the ~* iem. bedriegen
river bank rivieroever
riverfront rivieroever, waterkant
¹**riverside** (n) rivieroever, waterkant
²**riverside** (adj) aan de oever(s) (van de rivier)
¹**rivet** (n) klinknagel
²**rivet** (vb) **1** vastnagelen [also fig]: *he stood ~ed to the ground* hij stond als aan de grond genageld **2** vastleggen, fixeren **3** boeien [also fig]; richten; concentreren [attention, eyes]
riveting geweldig, meeslepend, opwindend: *a ~ story* een pakkend verhaal
rivulet riviertjeʰ, beek(je)ʰ)
roach voorn, witvis
road 1 weg, straat, baan: *on the ~ to recovery* aan de beterende hand, herstellende; *rule(s) of the ~* verkeersregels, scheepvaartreglement; *the main* ~ de hoofdweg; *subsidiary ~s* secundaire wegen; *hit the ~* a) gaan reizen; b) weer vertrekken; *one for the ~* een afzakkertje, eentje voor onderweg **2** (-s) [shipp] rede
road accident verkeersongevalʰ
roadblock wegversperring
road hog wegpiraat, snelheidsmaniak
roadhouse pleisterplaats, wegrestaurantʰ
road rage agressie in het verkeer; [Belg] verkeersagressie
road safety verkeersveiligheid
roadshow 1 drive-inshow [of radio broadcasting company] **2** (hit)teamʰ [providing the drive-in show] **3** (band/theatergroep op) tournee **4** promotietour
roadside kant van de weg: ~ *restaurant* wegrestaurant
roadsign verkeersbordʰ, verkeerstekenʰ
road tax wegenbelasting
road test 1 testrit **2** [Am] rijexamenʰ
road user weggebruik(st)er

roadway rijweg
roadworks wegwerkzaamheden, werk in uitvoering
roam ronddolen, zwerven: ~ *about* (or: *around*) ronddwalen
roaming roaming
¹**roar** (n) **1** gebrulʰ, gebulderʰ; geronkʰ [of machine]; het rollen [of thunder] **2** schaterlach, gegierʰ
²**roar** (vb) **1** brullen, bulderen, schreeuwen; rollen [of thunder]; ronken [of machine]; weergalmen **2** schateren, gieren: ~ *with laughter* brullen van het lachen
¹**roaring** (adj) **1** luidruchtig, stormachtig **2** voorspoedig, gezond: *a* ~ *success* een denderend succes; *do a* ~ *trade* gouden zaken doen
²**roaring** (adv) zeer, erg: ~ *drunk* straalbezopen
¹**roast** (n) braadstukʰ
²**roast** (adj) geroosterd, gegril(leer)d, gebraden: ~ *beef* rosbief, roastbeef
³**roast** (vb) de mantel uitvegen, een uitbrander geven
⁴**roast** (vb) **1** roosteren, grill(er)en; poffen [potatoes] **2** branden [coffee]
roasting uitbrander: *give s.o. a good* (or: *real*) ~ iem. een flinke uitbrander geven
rob (be)roven [also fig]; (be)stelen: [inform] ~ *s.o. blind* iem. een poot uitdraaien
robber rover, dief
robbery diefstal, roof, beroving
robe 1 robe, gewaadʰ **2** ambtsgewaadʰ, toga **3** kamerjas, badjas **4** [Am] plaid, reisdeken
robin roodborstjeʰ
robot robot [also fig]
robust 1 krachtig, robuust, fors, gezond **2** onstuimig, ruw
¹**rock** (n) **1** rots, klip, rotsblokʰ, vast gesteenteʰ, mineraal gesteenteʰ: *as firm as a* ~ **a)** muurvast; **b)** betrouwbaar; **c)** kerngezond **2** steun, toeverlaat **3** rock(muziek), rock-'n-roll **4** zuurstok, kaneelstok ‖ *be on the* ~*s* **a)** op de klippen gelopen zijn, gestrand zijn; **b)** naar de knoppen zijn; **c)** (financieel) aan de grond (zitten)
²**rock** (vb) **1** schommelen, wieg(el)en, deinen **2** (hevig) slingeren, schudden **3** rocken, op rock-'n-roll muziek dansen
³**rock** (vb) **1** (doen) heen en weer schommelen/wiegen **2** heen en weer slingeren, doen wankelen **3** schokken, doen opschrikken
rock-bottom (absoluut) dieptepuntʰ: *fall to* ~ een dieptepunt bereiken
rocker schommelstoel ‖ *off one's* ~ knetter(gek)
¹**rocket** (n) **1** raket, vuurpijl **2** raket [self-propelling missile] **3** [inform] uitbrander: *give s.o. a* ~ iem. een uitbrander geven
²**rocket** (vb) omhoog schieten, flitsen: *prices*

~ *up* de prijzen vliegen omhoog
rocket launch raketlancering
rocking chair schommelstoel
rocky 1 rotsachtig **2** steenhard, keihard **3** wankel, onvast
rod 1 stok; scepter [also fig]; heerschappij **2** roe(de), gesel **3** stang **4** stok, hengel, maatstok **5** [Am; inform] blaffer ‖ *rule with a* ~ *of iron* met ijzeren vuist regeren
rodent knaagdierʰ
rodeo rodeo
roe 1 ree **2** kuit: *hard* ~ kuit; *soft* ~ hom
roebuck reebok, mannetjesree
rogue 1 schurk, bandiet **2** [mockingly] snuiter, deugniet **3** solitair: *a* ~ *elephant* een solitaire olifant
roguery schurkenstreek, gemene streek
rogue state schurkenstaat
roguish 1 schurkachtig, gemeen **2** kwajongensachtig
roisterer lawaaimaker, druktemaker
role 1 rol, toneelrol **2** rol, functie, taak
roleplay rollenspelʰ
¹**roll** (n) **1** rol, rolletjeʰ: *a* ~ *of paper* een rol papier **2** rol, perkament(rol) **3** rol, registerʰ, (naam)lijst: *the* ~ *of honour* de lijst der gesneuvelden **4** broodjeʰ **5** buiteling, duikeling **6** schommelgang, waggelgang **7** wals, rol **8** rollende beweging; geslingerʰ [of ship]; deining [of water]; [fig] golving [of landscape] **9** geroffelʰ, roffel [eg on drum]; gerommelʰ; gedreunʰ [of thunder, guns]
²**roll** (vb) **1** rollen, rijden, lopen; draaien [of press, camera etc]: [fig] *the years* ~*ed by* de jaren gingen voorbij; ~ *on the day this work is finished!* leve de dag waarop dit werk af is! **2** zich rollend bewegen, buitelen; slingeren [of ship]; [fig] rondtrekken; zwerven: [inform] *be* ~*ing in it* (or: *money*) bulken van het geld, zwemmen in het geld **3** dreunen; roffelen [of drum]
³**roll** (vb) **1** rollen, laten rollen: ~ *on one's stockings* zijn kousen aantrekken **2** een rollende beweging doen maken; rollen [with eyes]; doen slingeren [ship]; gooien [dice]; laten lopen [camera] **3** een rollend geluid doen maken; roffelen [drum]; rollen [r sound]: ~ *one's r's* de r rollend uitspreken **4** oprollen, draaien: [inform] ~ *one's own* shag roken **5** rollen, walsen, pletten **6** [Am; inform] rollen, beroven
rollator rollator
roll back terugrollen, terugdrijven, terugdringen: ~ *the hood of a car* de kap van een wagen achteruitschuiven **2** weer oproepen, weer voor de geest brengen **3** [Am] terugschroeven [prices]
roll-call appelʰ, naamafroeping
roller 1 rol(letjeʰ), wals, cilinder, krulspeld **2** roller; breker [heavy wave]
rollerblade skeeleren

ro**ller coaster** roetsjbaan, achtbaan
¹**r**o**ller skate** (n) rolschaats
²**r**o**ller skate** (vb) rolschaatsen
ro**llicking** uitgelaten, vrolijk, onstuimig
ro**lling** rollend, golvend
ro**lling pin** deegrol(ler)
ro**ll-neck** rolkraag
ro**ll-on 1** licht korsetʰ **2** (deodorant)roller
ro**ll-on roll-off** rij-op-rij-af-, roll-on-roll-off-, roro-: a ~ **ferry** een rij-op-rij-afveerboot [carrying loaded lorries]
¹**roll** o**ver** (vb) zich omdraaien
²**roll** o**ver** (vb) **1** over de grond doen rollen **2** verlengen [loan, debt]
¹**roll** u**p** (vb) **1** zich oprollen **2** (komen) aanrijden; [fig] opdagen ‖ ~! ~! *The best show in London!* Komt binnen, komt dat zien! De beste show in Londen!
²**roll** u**p** (vb) oprollen, opstropen: *roll one's* **sleeves** *up* zijn mouwen opstropen; [fig] de handen uit de mouwen steken
ro**ll-up** [inform] sjekkieʰ
¹**r**o**ly-poly** (n) kort en dik persoon, propjeʰ
²**r**o**ly-poly** (adj) kort en dik
ROM *read-only memory* ROM
ro**man** romein(s), niet cursief
¹**R**o**man** (n) **1** Romein(se) **2** rooms-katholiek ‖ *when in Rome do as the ~s do* 's lands wijs, 's lands eer
²**R**o**man** (adj) **1** Romeins: ~ **numerals** Romeinse cijfers **2** rooms-katholiek: ~ *Catholic* rooms-katholiek
¹**r**o**mance** (n) **1** middeleeuws ridderverhaalʰ, romantisch verhaalʰ, avonturenroman, (romantisch) liefdesverhaalʰ, geromantiseerd verhaalʰ; [fig] romantische overdrijving **2** romance, liefdesavontuurʰ **3** romantiek
²**r**o**mance** (vb) avonturen vertellen; [fig] fantaseren: ~ *about one's love-affairs* sterke verhalen vertellen over zijn liefdesavonturen
Ro**mance** Romaans
Ro**mania** Roemenië
¹**R**o**manian** (n) Roemeen(se)
²**R**o**manian** (adj) Roemeens
ro**mantic** romantisch
ro**manticism** romantiek [as trend in art]
ro**manticize** romantiseren: *a heavily ~d* **version** *of the early years of Hollywood* een sterk geromantiseerde versie van de beginjaren van Hollywood
Ro**many** zigeuner-, van de zigeuners
¹**romp** (n) stoeipartij
²**romp** (vb) **1** stoeien **2** flitsen, (voorbij)-schieten ‖ ~ *through* an exam met gemak voor een examen slagen
ro**mper** kruippakjeʰ, speelpakjeʰ: a *pair of* ~s een kruippakje
roof dakʰ; [fig] dakʰ; hoogste puntʰ: ~ *of the* **mouth** gehemelte, verhemelte; *go through* (or: *hit*) *the* ~ a) ontploffen, woedend wor-

den; **b)** de pan uit rijzen, omhoogschieten [of prices]
roof box dakkofferʰ
ro**ofing** dakwerkʰ, dakbedekking
ro**ofless** dakloos, zonder onderdak
roof-rack imperiaal
ro**oftop 1** top van het dak **2** dakʰ [flat]: *shout* sth. *from the ~s* iets van de daken schreeuwen
¹**rook** (n) **1** valsspeler, bedrieger **2** roek **3** [chess] toren
²**rook** (vb) **1** bedriegen, afzetten **2** bedriegen door vals spel
ro**okie** [mil] rekruut, nieuweling, groentjeʰ; [Am] nieuwe speler [at baseball etc]
¹**room** (n) **1** kamer, vertrekʰ, zaal: ~s appartementʰ; flat **2** ruimte, plaats: *make* ~ plaatsmaken **3** ruimte, gelegenheid, kans: *there is still ample* ~ *for* **improvement** er kan nog een heel wat aan verbeterd worden
²**room** (vb) [Am] een kamer bewonen, inwonen, op kamers wonen: *she ~ed* **with** *us for six months* ze heeft een half jaar bij ons (in)gewoond
ro**omer** [Am] kamerbewoner, huurder
ro**om-mate** kamergenoot
ro**om service** bediening op de kamer [in hotel]; room service
ro**omy** ruim, groot, wijd
roost 1 roest, stok, kippenhokʰ **2** nestʰ, bedʰ; slaapplaats [of birds] ‖ *it will* **come** *home to* ~ je zult er zelf de wrange vruchten van plukken, het zal zich wreken; *rule the* ~ de baas zijn, de lakens uitdelen
ro**oster** [Am] haan
¹**root** (n) **1** oorsprong, wortel, basis: *money is the ~ of all* **evil** geld is de wortel van alle kwaad **2** kern, het wezenlijke: *get to the* ~ *of the* **problem** tot de kern van het probleem doordringen ‖ *strike* ~, *take* ~ a) wortel schieten; **b)** [fig] ingeburgerd raken [of ideas]; ~ *and* **branch** met wortel en tak, grondig; *strike at the ~s of* een vernietigende aanval doen op
²**root** (vb) **1** wortelschieten, wortelen; [fig] zich vestigen; zijn oorsprong hebben **2** wroeten, graven, woelen: *the pigs were ~ing* **about** *in the earth* de varkens wroetten rond in de aarde ‖ ~ *for the team* het team toejuichen
³**root** (vb) vestigen, doen wortelen: *a* **deeply** *~ed love* een diepgewortelde liefde ‖ *she stood ~ed to the* **ground** (or: *spot*) ze stond als aan de grond genageld
ro**otless** ontworteld, ontheemd
root o**ut 1** uitwroeten, uitgraven; [fig] tevoorschijn brengen **2** vernietigen, uitroeien
root sign worteltekenʰ
¹**rope** (n) **1** (stukʰ) touwʰ, koordʰ, kabel: [boxing] *on* **the** *~s* in de touwen **2** snoerʰ, streng: *a* ~ *of* **garlic** een streng knoflook ‖

money for old ~ een fluitje van een cent; *know* (or: *learn*) *the* ~s de kneepjes van het vak kennen (or: leren)
²**rope** (vb) **1** vastbinden **2** met touwen afzetten **3** [Am] vangen [with a lasso] ‖ ~ s.o. *in to help* (or: *join*) iem.

zover krijgen dat hij komt helpen (or: meedoet)
rope-ladder touwladder
ropy armzalig, miezerig, beroerd
rosary 1 rozentuin **2** rozenkrans
rose 1 roos, rozenstruik **2** roos, rozet **3** sproeidop, sproeier **4** rozerood[h], dieproze[h] ‖ *it is not all* ~s het is niet allemaal rozengeur en maneschijn; *under the* ~ onder geheimhouding
rose-bed rozenperk[h]
rose-coloured rooskleurig [also fig]; optimistisch: ~ *spectacles* [fig] een optimistische kijk, een roze bril
rose-hip rozenbottel
rosemary rozemarijn
rose-tinted *see rose-coloured*
rosette rozet
rosewater rozenwater[h]
rose-window roosvenster[h]
rosin hars[h]; [mus] snarenhars[h]
¹**roster** (n) rooster[h], werkschema[h], dienstrooster[h]
²**roster** (vb) inroosteren: ~ed *day off* roostervrije dag
rostrum podium[h], spreekgestoelte[h]
rosy 1 rooskleurig, rozig, blozend, gezond **2** rooskleurig, optimistisch
¹**rot** (n) **1** verrotting, bederf[h], ontbinding; [fig] verval[h]; de klad: *then the* ~ *set in* toen ging alles mis, toen kwam er de klad in **2** vuur[h] [in wood] **3** onzin, flauwekul: *talk* ~ onzin uitkramen
²**rot** (vb) **1** rotten, ontbinden, bederven **2** vervallen, ten onder gaan **3** wegkwijnen, wegteren
³**rot** (vb) **1** laten rotten, doen wegrotten **2** aantasten, bederven
rota rooster[h], aflossingsschema[h]
rotary roterend: ~ *press* rotatiepers
¹**rotate** (vb) **1** roteren, om een as draaien **2** elkaar aflossen **3** rouleren
²**rotate** (vb) **1** ronddraaien, laten rondwentelen **2** afwisselen
rotation 1 omwenteling, rotatie **2** het omwentelen, rotatie **3** het afwisselen, het aflossen: *the* ~ *of crops* de wisselbouw; *by* (or: *in*) ~ bij toerbeurt
rotatory 1 rotatie-, omwentelings-, ronddraaiend **2** afwisselend, beurtelings
rote het mechanisch leren (herhalen), het opdreunen, stampwerk[h]: *learn sth. by* ~ iets uit het hoofd leren
rotten 1 rot, verrot, bedorven **2** vergaan, verteerd **3** verdorven, gedegenereerd **4** waardeloos, slecht **5** ellendig, beroerd: *she*

felt ~ ze voelde zich ellendig
rotund 1 rond, cirkelvormig **2** diep, vol **3** breedsprakig, pompeus **4** dik, rond, mollig
rouble roebel
¹**rough** (n) **1** gewelddadige kerel, agressieveling **2** ruw terrein[h] **3** tegenslag, onaangename kanten: [fig] *take the* ~ *with the smooth* tegenslagen voor lief nemen **4** ruwe staat: *write sth. in* ~ iets in het klad schrijven
²**rough** (adj) **1** ruw, ruig, oneffen **2** wild, woest: ~ *behaviour* wild gedrag; [fig] *give s.o. a* ~ *passage* (or: *ride*) het iem. moeilijk maken **3** ruw, scherp, naar: ~ *luck* pech, tegenslag; *a* ~ *time* een zware tijd; *it is* ~ *on him* het is heel naar voor hem **4** ruw, schetsmatig, niet uitgewerkt: *a* ~ *diamond* een ruwe diamant; [fig] een ruwe bolster; ~ *copy* eerste schets; ~ *justice* min of meer rechtvaardige behandeling ‖ *live* ~ zwerven, in de openlucht leven
³**rough** (vb): ~ *it* zich behelpen, op een primitieve manier leven
rough-and-tumble 1 knokpartij **2** ruwe ordeloosheid
¹**roughen** (vb) ruw worden
²**roughen** (vb) ruw maken
rough-hewn 1 ruw (uit)gehakt, ruw (uit)gesneden **2** onbehouwen, lomp
rough-house 1 een rel schoppen, geweld plegen **2** ruw aanpakken
roughly ruwweg, ongeveer, zo'n beetje: ~ *speaking* ongeveer
roughneck [Am; inform] gewelddadig iem., ruwe klant
rough out een ruwe schets maken van, (in grote lijnen) schetsen
roughshod onmenselijk, wreed ‖ *ride* ~ *over s.o.* over iem. heen lopen
rough up 1 ruw maken [hair etc] **2** aftuigen, afrossen
roulette roulette
¹**round** (n) **1** bol, ronding **2** ronde, rondgang, toer: *go the* ~s de ronde doen, doorverteld worden **3** schot[h], geweerschot[h] **4** kring, groep mensen **5** [mus] driestemmige (vierstemmige) canon[h] **6** rondheid **7** volledigheid **8** rondte: *in the* ~ a) losstaand, vrijstaand [of statue]; b) alles welbeschouwd ‖ *a* ~ *of applause* een applaus
²**round** (adj) **1** rond, bol, bolvormig: ~ *cheeks* bolle wangen **2** rond, gebogen, cirkelvormig: ~ *trip* rondreis; [Am] retour **3** rond, compleet; afgerond [of number]: *in* ~ *figures* in afgeronde getallen ‖ ~ *robin* petitie
³**round** (vb) **1** ronden, rond maken; [also fig] afronden: ~ *down* naar beneden afronden; ~ *off sharp edges* scherpe randen rond afwerken; ~ *off* besluiten, afsluiten [evening etc] **2** ronden, om(heen) gaan: ~ *a corner* een hoek omgaan ‖ ~ *out* afronden [story, study];

~ *(up)on* s.o. tegen iem. van leer trekken, zich woedend tot iem. keren
⁴round (adv) **1** [direction; also fig] rond, om: *next time* ~ de volgende keer; *he* **talked** *her* ~ hij praatte haar om **2** [place; also fig] rond-om, in het rond: *all* ~ **a)** rondom; **b)** voor alles en iedereen; **c)** in alle opzichten **3** bij, bij zich: *they* **asked** *us* ~ *for tea* ze nodigden ons bij hen uit voor de thee; *they* **brought** *her* ~ ze brachten haar weer bij (bewustzijn) **4** [time] doorheen: *all (the)* **year** ~ het hele jaar door
⁵round (prep) **1** om, rondom, om … heen: ~ *the* **corner** om de hoek **2** omstreeks: ~ *8* **o'clock** omstreeks acht uur
¹roundabout (n) **1** draaimolen **2** rotonde, verkeersplein[h]
²roundabout (adj) indirect, omslachtig: *we heard of it in a* ~ **way** we hebben het via via gehoord
roundly 1 ronduit, onomwonden **2** volkomen, volslagen
round-the-clock de klok rond, dag en nacht
round-trip [Am] retour-: ~ *ticket* retourtje, retourbiljet
round up 1 bijeenjagen, bijeendrijven **2** grijpen; aanhouden [criminals]; oprollen [gang] **3** naar boven toe afronden
¹rouse (vb) **1** ontwaken, wakker worden **2** in actie komen
²rouse (vb) **1** wakker maken, wekken; [fig] opwekken: ~ *o.s.* *to action* zichzelf tot actie aanzetten **2** prikkelen **3** oproepen, tevoorschijn roepen: *his conduct* ~*d* **suspicion** zijn gedrag wekte argwaan
rousing 1 opwindend, bezielend **2** levendig, krachtig: *a* ~ *cheer* luid gejuich
¹rout (n) totale nederlaag, aftocht, vlucht: *put to* ~ een verpletterende nederlaag toebrengen
²rout (vb) **1** verslaan, verpletteren **2** (+ out) eruit jagen, wegjagen: ~ *out of bed* uit bed jagen **3** (+ out) opduike(le)n, opsnorren
route 1 route, weg: *en* ~ onderweg **2** [Am] ronde, dagelijkse route
route planner routeplanner
router 1 [comp] router **2** iem. die routes uitstippelt; sorteerder
routine 1 routine, gebruikelijke procedure **2** sleur
¹rove (vb) zwerven, dolen, dwalen: *he has a roving* **eye** hij kijkt steeds naar andere vrouwen
²rove (vb) doorzwerven, dolen, dwalen
rover zwerver
¹row (n) **1** rel, ruzie **2** herrie, kabaal[h]: *kick up* (or: *make*) *a* ~ luidkeels protesteren
²row (n) **1** rij, reeks: *three days in a* ~ drie dagen achtereen **2** huizenrij, straat met (aan weerszijden) huizen; Straat [in street name]

3 roeitochtje[h]
³row (vb) roeien, in een roeiboot varen, per roeiboot vervoeren
⁴row (vb) **1** ruzie maken **2** vechten, een rel schoppen
rowanberry lijsterbes
¹rowdy (n) lawaaischopper
²rowdy (adj) ruw, wild, ordeloos
rower roeier
row house [Am] rijtjeshuis[h]
rowing-boat roeiboot
rowing-machine roeitrainer
¹royal (n) lid[h] van de koninklijke familie
²royal (adj) **1** koninklijk, van de koning(in): *Royal* **Highness** Koninklijke Hoogheid **2** koninklijk, vorstelijk || *treat s.o.* ~*ly* iem. als een vorst behandelen
royalist royalist, monarchist
royalty 1 iem. van koninklijken bloede, koning(in), prins(es) **2** royalty, aandeel[h] in de opbrengst **3** koningschap[h] **4** leden van het koninklijk huis
rpm *revolutions per minute* omwentelingen per minuut, -toeren
RPM *revolution(s) per minute* rpm; -toeren
R rating [Am] [roughly] niet geschikt voor jeugdige kijkers
RSI *Repetitive Strain Injury* RSI; muisarm
RSS *really simple syndication* RSS
RT *retweet* retweet
¹rub (n) **1** poetsbeurt, wrijfbeurt **2** hindernis, moeilijkheid: *there's the* ~ daar zit de moeilijkheid, dat is het hem juist
²rub (vb) **1** schuren langs, wrijven **2** slijten, dun/ruw/kaal worden || ~ *up* **against** *s.o.* tegen iem. aanlopen
³rub (vb) **1** wrijven, afwrijven, inwrijven, doorheen wrijven, poetsen, boenen: ~ *one's* **hands** zich in de handen wrijven **2** schuren **3** beschadigen, afslijten: ~ *away* wegslijten, afslijten
rub along 1 zich staande houden, het net klaarspelen **2** het goed samen kunnen vinden
rubber 1 rubber[h], synthetisch rubber[h], rubberachtig materiaal[h] **2** wrijver, wisser, gum **3** [Am] overschoen **4** [sport, game] robber, reeks van drie partijen **5** condoom
rubber band elastiekje[h]
rubber bullet rubberkogel
rubberneck [Am] nieuwsgierige, zich vergapende toerist
rubber stamp 1 stempel **2** marionet [fig]
rubber-stamp automatisch goedkeuren, gedachteloos instemmen met
rubbery rubberachtig, taai
¹rubbish (n) **1** vuilnis, afval[h] **2** nonsens, onzin: *talk* ~ zwetsen, kletsen
²rubbish (vb) afbrekende kritiek leveren op, afkraken
rubbish bin vuilnisbak

rubbishy waardeloos, onzinnig
rubble puin[h], steengruis[h], steenbrokken
rubella rodehond
rub in inwrijven, (in)masseren ‖ *there's no need to rub it in* je hoeft er niet steeds op terug te komen
¹rub off (vb) **1** weggewreven worden **2** overgaan op, overgenomen worden: *his stinginess has rubbed off on you* je hebt zijn krenterigheid overgenomen **3** afslijten, minder worden: *the novelty has rubbed off a bit* de nieuwigheid is er een beetje af
²rub off (vb) **1** wegvegen, afwrijven **2** afslijten, afschuren
rubric 1 rubriek; titel [of (chapter in) code] **2** rubriek, categorie
rub up 1 oppoetsen, opwrijven **2** ophalen, bijvijlen: *~ one's Italian* zijn Italiaans ophalen ‖ *rub s.o. up the wrong way* iem. tegen de haren instrijken, iem. irriteren
ruby 1 robijn[+h] **2** robijnrood[h]
ruck 1 de massa **2** de gewone dingen, dagelijkse dingen **3** vouw, kreukel, plooi
rucksack rugzak
ruck up in elkaar kreuke(le)n
ruckus tumult[h], ordeverstoring
ruction kabaal[h], luid protest[h]
rudder roer[h]
rudderless stuurloos [also fig]
ruddy 1 blozend, gezond **2** rossig, rood(achtig) **3** verdraaide
rude 1 primitief [people]; onbeschaafd **2** ruw, primitief, eenvoudig **3** ongemanierd, grof: *be ~ to s.o.* onbeleefd tegen iem. zijn ‖ [fig] *a ~ awakening* een ruwe teleurstelling; *~ health* onverwoestbare gezondheid
rudiment 1 [biology] rudiment[h] **2** (-s) beginselen, grondslagen
rudimentary 1 rudimentair, elementair, wat de grondslagen betreft **2** in een beginstadium
rue spijt hebben van, berouw hebben van: *you'll ~ the day you said this* je zal de dag berouwen dat je dit gezegd hebt
rueful berouwvol, treurig, bedroefd
¹ruff (n) **1** plooikraag **2** kraag, verenkraag, kraag van haar
²ruff (vb) [cards] troeven
ruffian bruut, woesteling, bandiet
¹ruffle (n) ruche [along collar, cuff]; geplooide rand
²ruffle (vb) **1** verstoren, doen rimpelen, verwarren: *~ s.o.'s hair* iemands haar in de war maken **2** (+ up) opzetten [feathers] **3** ergeren, kwaad maken, opwinden
rug 1 tapijt[h], vloerkleed[h] **2** deken, plaid
rugby rugby[h]
rugged 1 ruw, ruig, grof **2** onregelmatig van trekken, doorploegd
rugger rugby[h]
¹ruin (n) **1** ruïne, vervallen bouwwerk[h] **2** ondergang, verval[h]: *this will be the ~ of him* dit zal hem nog kapot maken **3** (-s) ruïne, bouwval, overblijfsel[h]: *in ~s* vervallen, tot een ruïne geworden
²ruin (vb) **1** verwoesten, vernietigen **2** ruïneren, bederven: *his story has ~ed my appetite* zijn verhaal heeft me mijn eetlust ontnomen **3** ruïneren, tot de ondergang brengen
ruinous 1 vervallen, ingestort, bouwvallig **2** rampzalig, ruïneus
¹rule (n) **1** regel, voorschrift[h]: *~s of the road* verkeersregels, verkeerscode; *according to* (or: *by*) *~* volgens de regels, stipt **2** gewoonte, gebruik[h], regel: *as a ~* gewoonlijk, in het algemeen **3** duimstok, meetlat **4** regering, bewind[h], bestuur[h]: *under British ~* onder Britse heerschappij ‖ *~ of thumb* vuistregel, nattevingerwerk
²rule (vb) **1** heersen, regeren, de zeggenschap hebben **2** een bevel uitvaardigen, bepalen, verordenen
³rule (vb) **1** beheersen [also fig]; heersen over, regeren: *be ~d by* zich laten leiden door **2** beslissen, bepalen, bevelen: *~ sth. out* iets uitsluiten, iets voor onmogelijk verklaren **3** trekken [line] ‖ *~d paper* gelinieerd papier
ruler 1 heerser, vorst **2** liniaal
¹ruling (n) regel, bepaling: *give a ~* uitspraak doen
²ruling (adj) (over)heersend, dominant
¹rum (n) rum
²rum (adj) vreemd, eigenaardig
¹rumble (n) **1** gerommel[h], rommelend geluid[h] **2** [Am] tip, informatie **3** [Am] knokpartij, straatgevecht[h]
²rumble (vb) **1** rommelen, donderen: *my stomach is rumbling* mijn maag knort **2** voortdonderen, voortrollen, ratelen
³rumble (vb) **1** mompelen, mopperen, grommen **2** doorhebben, doorzien, in de gaten hebben
rumbling 1 gerommel[h] **2** praatje[h], gekrets[h]
rumbustious onstuimig, onbesuisd, uitgelaten
¹ruminant (n) herkauwer
²ruminant (adj) herkauwend
ruminate 1 herkauwen **2** peinzen, nadenken, piekeren
¹rummage (n) **1** onderzoek[h], het doorzoeken: *I'll have a ~ in the attic* ik zal eens op zolder gaan zoeken **2** [Am] rommel, oude spullen, troep
²rummage (vb) (+ about, through, among) rondrommelen (in), snuffelen (in), (door)zoeken
rummage sale rommelmarkt
¹rumour (n) gerucht[h], geruchten, praatjes, verhalen: *~ has it that you'll be fired* er gaan geruchten dat je ontslagen zult worden

²**rumour** (vb) geruchten verspreiden, praatjes rondstrooien

rump 1 achterdeelʰ; bout [of animal]; stuit [of bird] **2** achtersteʰ **3** rest(ant)ʰ); armzalig overblijfselʰ [of parliament, administration]

rumple kreuken, door de war maken, verfrommelen

rump steak lendenbiefstuk

rumpus tumultʰ, ruzie, geschreeuwʰ: *cause* (or: *kick up, make*) *a* ~ ruzie maken

¹**run** (n) **1** looppas, het rennen: *make a* ~ *for it* het op een lopen zetten; *on the* ~ **a)** op de vlucht; **b)** druk in de weer **2** tocht, afstand, eindje hollen, vlucht, rit, trajectʰ, route; uitstapjeʰ [of train, boat]; [skiing] baan; helling; [cricket, hockey] run [a score of 1 point] **3** opeenvolging, reeks, serie; [theatre] looptijd; [mus] loopjeʰ: *a* ~ *of success* een succesvolle periode **4** (+ on) vraag (naar), stormloop (op): [com] *a* ~ *on copper* een plotselinge grote vraag naar koper **5** terreinʰ, veldʰ; ren [for animals] **6** eindʰ, stukʰ; lengte [of material] **7** [Am] ladder [in stocking] || *we'll give them a (good)* ~ *for their money* we zullen ze het niet makkelijk maken; *give s.o. the* ~ *of iem.* de (vrije) beschikking geven over; *a* ~ *on the bank* een run op de bank

²**run** (vb) **1** rennen, hollen, hardlopen **2** gaan, (voort)bewegen, lopen, (hard) rijden, pendelen; heen en weer rijden (varen) [of bus, ferry etc]; voorbijgaan; aflopen [of time]; lopen; werken [of machines]; (uit)lopen, (weg)stromen, druipen; [fig] (voort)duren; zich uitstrekken, gelden: ~ *afoul* (or: *foul*) *of* [fig] stuiten op, in botsing komen met; [shipp] ~ *aground* aan de grond lopen; *feelings ran high* de gemoederen raakten verhit **3** rennen, vliegen, zich haasten **4** lopen, zich uitstrekken; gaan [also fig]: *prices are* ~*ning high* de prijzen zijn over het algemeen hoog; ~ *to extremes* in uitersten vervallen **5** wegrennen, vluchten **6** luiden, klinken: *the third line* ~*s as follows* de derde regel luidt als volgt **7** kandidaat zijn **8** [Am] ladderen [of stocking] || ~ *along!* vooruit!, laat me eens met rust!; ~ *across s.o. (sth.)* iem. tegen het lijf lopen, ergens tegen aan lopen; ~ *for it* op de vlucht slaan, het op een lopen zetten; ~ *through the minutes* de notulen doornemen

³**run** (vb) **1** rijden (lopen) over; volgen [road]; afleggen [distance]: ~ *a race* een wedstrijd lopen; ~ *s.o. over* iem. overrijden **2** doen bewegen, laten gaan, varen, rijden, doen stromen, gieten, in werking stellen, laten lopen; [fig] doen voortgaan; leiden, runnen: ~ *a business* een zaak hebben; ~ *s.o. close* (or: *hard*) iem. (dicht) op de hielen zitten; [fig] weinig voor iem. onderdoen **3** smokkelen **4** ontvluchten, weglopen van **5** kandidaat stellen || ~ *a (traffic-)light* door rood rijden

runabout wagentjeʰ, (open) autootjeʰ

run-around het iem. afschepen, het iem. een rad voor ogen draaien: *give s.o. the* ~ een spelletje spelen met iem., iem. bedriegen

runaway vluchteling, ontsnapte || ~ *inflation* galopperende inflatie

run away weglopen, vluchten, op de loop gaan || *don't* ~ *with the idea* geloof dat nu maar niet te snel

rundown 1 vermindering, afname **2** opsomming, zeer gedetailleerd verslagʰ

run down 1 reduceren, verminderen in capaciteit **2** aanrijden **3** opsporen, vinden, te pakken krijgen: *run a criminal down* een misdadiger opsporen **4** kritiseren, naar beneden halen, afkraken: *how dare you run her down?* hoe durf je haar te kleineren?

run-down 1 vervallen; verwaarloosd [of things] **2** uitgeput, verzwakt, doodmoe

rung sport, trede

¹**run in** (vb) binnen (komen) lopen

²**run in** (vb) **1** oppakken, aanhouden, inrekenen **2** inrijden [car]

run-in 1 aanloop **2** ruzie, twist, woordenwisseling

run into 1 stoten op, in botsing komen met, botsen tegen **2** terechtkomen in: ~ *difficulties* (or: *debts*) in de problemen (or: schulden) raken **3** tegen het lijf lopen, onverwacht ontmoeten **4** bedragen, oplopen: *the costs* ~ *thousands of pounds* de kosten lopen in de duizenden

runner 1 agent, vertegenwoordiger, loopjongen, bezorger **2** glijijzerʰ [of skate, sleigh]; glijgoot, glijplank **3** loper, tafelloper, traploper, vloerloper **4** slingerplant **5** uitloper **6** deelnemer [eg runner, racehorse] || [inform] *do a* ~ zich uit de voeten maken, ervandoor gaan

runner-up tweede, wie op de tweede plaats eindigt: *runners-up* de overige medaillewinnaars

¹**running** (n) het rennen; [sport] hardlopenʰ: *out of* (or: *in*) *the* ~ kansloos (or: met een goede kans) (om te winnen) || *make the* ~ het tempo bepalen; [fig] de toon aangeven, de leiding hebben

²**running** (adj) **1** hardlopend, rennend, hollend **2** lopend: ~ *water* stromend water **3** (door)lopend, continu, opeenvolgend: ~ *commentary* direct verslag || [Am; pol] ~ *mate* kandidaat voor de tweede plaats; *in* ~ *order* goed werkend

running event loopnummerʰ

runny vloeibaar, dun, gesmolten: ~ *nose* loopneus

¹**run off** (vb) weglopen, wegvluchten: ~ *with s.o.* er vandoor gaan met iem.

²**run off** (vb) **1** laten weglopen, laten wegstromen, aftappen **2** reproduceren, afdraai-

en, fotokopiëren
run-of-the-mill doodgewoon, niet bijzonder, alledaags
run on doorgaan, doorlopen, voortgaan: *time ran on* de tijd ging voorbij
¹run out (vb) **1** opraken, aflopen: *our supplies have* ~ onze voorraden zijn uitgeput **2** niets meer hebben, te weinig hebben: *we are running out of time* we komen tijd te kort **3** weglopen, wegstromen
²run out (vb) uitrollen, afwikkelen; laten aflopen [rope]
¹run over (vb) overlopen, overstromen ‖ ~ *with energy* overlopen van energie
²run over (vb) **1** overrijden, aanrijden: *Marco ran over an old lady* Marco reed een oude dame aan **2** doornemen, nakijken, repeteren
run through 1 doorboren, doorsteken **2** repeteren, doorlopen
¹run up (vb) (+ against) (toevallig) tegenkomen: ~ *against difficulties* op moeilijkheden stuiten
²run up (vb) (doen) oplopen, snel (doen) toenemen, opjagen: *her debts ran up, she ran up debts* ze maakte steeds meer schulden
run-up voorbereiding(stijd), vooravond: ~ *to an election* verkiezingsperiode
runway startbaan, landingsbaan
rupee [fin] roepie [Asian coin, esp of India and Pakistan]
¹rupture (n) **1** breuk, scheiding, onenigheid **2** breuk, hernia, ingewandsbreuk
²rupture (vb) **1** verbreken, verbroken worden **2** scheuren [of muscle etc] **3** een breuk krijgen: ~ *o.s. lifting sth.* zich een breuk tillen
rural landelijk, plattelands, dorps
ruse list, truc
¹rush (n) **1** heftige beweging, snelle beweging, stormloop, grote vraag, toevloed **2** haast, haastige activiteiten **3** (rushes) [film] eerste afdruk [before editing] **4** rus, bies **5** (rushes) biezen [for twining baskets, mats etc]
²rush (vb) **1** stormen, vliegen, zich haasten **2** ondoordacht handelen, overijld doen: ~ *into marriage* zich overhaast in een huwelijk storten
³rush (vb) **1** meeslepen, haastig vervoeren, meesleuren **2** opjagen, tot haast dwingen **3** haastig behandelen, afraffelen: ~ *out* massaal produceren
rush delivery spoedbestelling
rush hour spitsuurʰ: *evening* ~ avondspits; *morning* ~ ochtendspits
rush-hour spits-: ~ *traffic* spitsverkeer
rusk (harde) beschuit, scheepsbeschuit
¹russet (n) **1** roodbruinʰ **2** winterappel
²russet (adj) roodbruin
Russia Rusland
¹Russian (n) Rus(sin)

²Russian (adj) Russisch
¹rust (n) **1** roest, oxidatie **2** roestkleur, roestbruinʰ
²rust (vb) roesten, oxideren
¹rustic (n) plattelander, buitenman, boer
²rustic (adj) **1** boers, simpel, niet beschaafd **2** rustiek, uit grof materiaal gemaakt: ~ *bridge* rustieke brug [of unprocessed wood] **3** landelijk, dorps, provinciaal
¹rustle (n) geruisʰ, geritselʰ
²rustle (vb) ruisen, ritselen, een ritselend geluid maken
³rustle (vb) **1** [Am] roven [cattle, horses] **2** weten te bemachtigen, bij elkaar weten te krijgen: ~ *up a meal* een maaltijd in elkaar draaien
rustler [Am] veedief
¹rustproof (adj) roestvrij
²rustproof (vb) roestvrij maken
rusty 1 roestig, verroest **2** verwaarloosd; [fig] verstoft; niet meer paraat: *my French is a bit* ~ mijn Frans is niet meer wat het geweest is
rut 1 voorʰ, groef, spoorʰ **2** vaste gang van zaken, sleur: *get into a* ~ vastroesten in de dagelijkse routine **3** bronst, paartijd
ruthless meedogenloos, wreed, hard
rutting bronstig, in de bronsttijd, paartijd
Rwanda Rwanda
¹Rwandan (n) Rwandees, Rwandese
²Rwandan (adj) Rwandees
rye 1 rogge **2** whisky, roggewhisky

S

s *second* sec., seconde
S *South* Z., Zuid(en)
sabbath sabbat, rustdag: *keep* (or: *break*) *the* ~ de sabbat houden (*or:* schenden)
¹sabbatical (n) sabbatsverlof^h; verlof^h [at university]
²sabbatical (adj): ~ *year* sabbatsjaar, verlofjaar
¹sabotage (n) sabotage
²sabotage (vb) saboteren, sabotage plegen (op)
sabre sabel
sabre-rattling sabelgekletter^h, (het dreigen met) militair geweld^h
saccharine 1 suikerachtig, sacharine-, mierzoet **2** [fig] suikerzoet, zoet(sappig)
sachet 1 reukzakje^h **2** (plastic) ampul [for shampoo] ‖ ~ *of sugar* suikerzakje
¹sack (n) **1** zak, baal, jutezak **2** zak, ontslag^h: *get the* ~ ontslagen worden; *give s.o. the* ~ iem. de laan uitsturen **3** bed^h: *hit the* ~ gaan pitten, onder de wol kruipen
²sack (vb) **1** plunderen **2** de laan uitsturen, ontslaan
sackcloth jute ‖ *in* ~ *and ashes* in zak en as, in rouw
sack race zakloopwedstrijd
sacrament sacrament^h
sacramental tot het sacrament behorend, offer-: ~ *wine* miswijn
sacred 1 gewijd, heilig: ~ *cow* heilige koe **2** plechtig, heilig, oprecht: *a* ~ *promise* een plechtige belofte **3** veilig, onschendbaar
¹sacrifice (n) **1** offer^h, het offeren **2** opoffering, offer^h, het opgeven, prijsgeven
²sacrifice (vb) offeren, een offer brengen
³sacrifice (vb) **1** offeren, aanbieden, opdragen **2** opofferen, opgeven, zich ontzeggen: *he sacrificed his life to save her children* hij gaf zijn leven om haar kinderen te redden
sacrilege heiligschennis
sacrilegious heiligschennend, onterend
sacristan koster
sacristy sacristie
sacrosanct heilig, onaantastbaar: *his spare time is* ~ *to him* zijn vrije tijd is hem heilig
sad 1 droevig, verdrietig, ongelukkig, zielig: *to be* ~*ly mistaken* er totaal naast zitten **2** schandelijk, bedroevend (slecht)
sadden bedroeven, verdrietig maken, somber stemmen
¹saddle (n) **1** zadel^h: *be in the* ~ te paard zitten; [fig] de baas zijn, het voor het zeggen

hebben **2** lendenstuk^h, rugstuk^h: ~ *of lamb* lamszadel
²saddle (vb) **1** (+ up) zadelen, opzadelen: ~ *up one's horse* zijn paard zadelen **2** (+ with, (up)on) opzadelen (met), opschepen (met), afschuiven op: *he ~d all responsibility on her* hij schoof alle verantwoordelijkheid op haar af
saddlebag zadeltas(je^h)
saddle-sore doorgereden, met zadelpijn
saddo [inform] stumper, sukkel
sadism sadisme^h
sadist sadist(e)
sadistic sadistisch
sadly helaas
safari safari, jachtexpeditie, filmexpeditie: *on* ~ op safari
¹safe (n) brandkast, (bewaar)kluis, safe(loket^h)
²safe (adj) **1** veilig, beschermd: ~ *from attack* beveiligd tegen aanvallen **2** veilig, zeker, gevrijwaard: *as* ~ *as houses* zo veilig als een huis; *be on the* ~ *side* het zekere voor het onzekere nemen; *better (to be)* ~ *than sorry* je kunt beter het zekere voor het onzekere nemen; *play it* ~ op veilig spelen, geen risico nemen **3** betrouwbaar, gegarandeerd: *the party has twenty* ~ *seats* de partij kan zeker rekenen op twintig zetels **4** behouden, ongedeerd: *she arrived* ~ *and sound* ze kwam heelhuids aan
safe conduct vrijgeleide^h, vrije doorgang
safe deposit (brand)kluis, bankkluis
¹safeguard (n) waarborg, bescherming, voorzorg(smaatregel)
²safeguard (vb) beveiligen, beschermen, waarborgen
safehouse safehouse^h; onderduikadres^h [in war]
safe-keeping (veilige) bewaring
safety veiligheid, zekerheid: ~ *first* veiligheid vóór alles; *let's not split up, there's* ~ *in numbers* laten we ons niet opsplitsen, in een groep is het veiliger
safety belt veiligheidsgordel, veiligheidsriem
safety catch veiligheidspal
safety curtain brandscherm^h
safety glass veiligheidsglas^h
safety island vluchtheuvel
safety net vangnet^h [for acrobats]; [fig; econ] buffer
safety pin veiligheidsspeld
saffron saffraan, oranjegeel
¹sag (n) verzakking, doorzakking, doorbuiging
²sag (vb) **1** (also + down) verzakken, doorzakken, doorbuigen **2** dalen, afnemen, teruglopen: *her spirits* ~*ged* de moed zonk haar in de schoenen
saga 1 familiekroniek **2** (lang) verhaal^h
sagacious scherpzinnig, verstandig

sagacity scherpzinnigheid, wijsheid, in-zicht[h]

[1]**sage** (n) **1** wijze (man), wijsgeer **2** salie

[2]**sage** (adj) wijs(gerig), verstandig

Sagittarius [astrology] (de) Boogschutter

said (boven)genoemd, voornoemd

[1]**sail** (n) **1** zeil[h], de zeilen: *set* ~ de zeilen hijsen, onder zeil gaan **2** zeiltocht(je[h]), boottocht(je[h]): *take s.o. for a* ~ met iem. gaan zeilen **3** molenwiek, zeil[h]

[2]**sail** (vb) **1** varen, zeilen, per schip reizen: ~ *close to* (or: *near*) *the wind* scherp bij de wind zeilen; [fig] bijna zijn boekje te buiten gaan **2** afvaren, vertrekken, uitvaren: *we're ~ing for Ireland tomorrow* we vertrekken morgen naar Ierland **3** glijden, zweven, zeilen: *she ~ed through her finals* ze haalde haar eindexamen op haar sloffen

[3]**sail** (vb) **1** bevaren **2** besturen [ship]

sailing 1 bootreis **2** afvaart, vertrek[h], vertrektijd **3** navigatie, het besturen van een schip **4** zeilsport

sailing ship zeilschip[h]

sailor zeeman, matroos: *Andy is a good* (or: *bad*) ~ Andy heeft nooit (*or:* snel) last van zeeziekte

saint 1 heilige, sint: *All Saints' Day* Allerheiligen **2** engel; [fig] iem. met engelengeduld

Saint sint, heilig

saintly heilig: *lead a* ~ *life* als een heilige leven

saint's day heiligendag, naamdag

sake 1 belang[h], (best)wil: *for the* ~ *of the company* in het belang van het bedrijf; *we're only doing this for your* ~ we doen dit alleen maar ter wille van jou **2** doel[h], oogmerk[h]: *I'm not driving around here for the* ~ *of driving* ik rijd hier niet rond voor de lol

salaam oosterse groet [low bow with right hand on forehead]

salacious 1 geil **2** obsceen, schunnig

salad 1 salade, slaatje[h] **2** sla

salad cream slasaus

salamander salamander

salami slicing [fig] kaasschaafmethode

salaried per maand betaald, gesalarieerd

salary salaris[h]

salary scale salarisschaal

sale 1 verkoop, afzet(markt): *for* ~ te koop **2** verkoping, veiling, bazaar **3** uitverkoop, opruiming

saleroom veilinglokaal[h]

salesclerk winkelbediende

salesgirl winkelmeisje[h], verkoopster

saleslady verkoopster

salesman 1 verkoper, winkelbediende **2** vertegenwoordiger, agent, handelsreiziger || *traveling* ~ handelsreiziger

salesmanship verkoopkunde, verkooptechniek

sales pitch verkooppraatje[h]

sales representative vertegenwoordiger

sales tax omzetbelasting

saleswoman 1 verkoopster, winkelbediende **2** vertegenwoordigster, agente, handelsreizigster

salient opvallend, belangrijkste

saline zout(houdend), zoutachtig, zilt

saliva speeksel[h]

salivate kwijlen [also fig]; speeksel produceren

[1]**sallow** (n) wilg

[2]**sallow** (adj) vaal(geel)

sally 1 uitval: *the army made a successful sally* het leger deed een succesvolle uitval **2** uitbarsting, opwelling **3** kwinkslag, (geestige) inval

sally forth 1 een uitval doen **2** erop uit gaan, op stap gaan, naar buiten rennen

salmon 1 zalm **2** zalmkleur

salmon trout zalmforel

saloon 1 zaal, salon **2** bar, café[h] **3** sedan, gesloten vierdeursauto

[1]**salt** (n) (keuken)zout[h] || ~ *cellar* zoutvaatje; *the* ~ *of the earth* het zout der aarde; *he's not worth his* ~ hij is het zout in de pap niet waard

[2]**salt** (adj) **1** zout, zilt **2** gepekeld, gezouten: ~ *fish* gezouten vis

[3]**salt** (vb) **1** zouten, pekelen, inmaken **2** pekelen [roads]; met zout bestrooien **3** [fig] kruiden || *he's got quite some money ~ed away* (or: *down*) hij heeft aardig wat geld opgepot

saltpetre salpeter[+h]

saltshaker zoutvaatje[h], zoutstrooier

saltwater zoutwater-

salty 1 zout(achtig) **2** gezouten, gekruid; pikant [of language]

salubrious heilzaam, gezond

salutary weldadig, heilzaam, gunstig, gezond

salutation 1 aanhef [in letter] **2** begroeting, groet, begroetingskus

[1]**salute** (n) **1** saluut[h], militaire groet, saluutschot[h]: *take the* ~ de parade afnemen **2** begroeting, groet

[2]**salute** (vb) **1** groeten, begroeten, verwelkomen **2** salueren, een saluutschot lossen (voor)

[3]**salute** (vb) eer bewijzen aan, huldigen: *there were several festivals to* ~ *the country's 50 years of independence* er waren verschillende festivals om de vijftigjarige onafhankelijkheid van het land eer te bewijzen

[1]**salvage** (n) **1** berging, redding, het in veiligheid brengen **2** geborgen goed[h], het geborgene: *the divers were not entitled to a share in the salvage* de duikers hadden geen recht op een aandeel in de geborgen goederen **3** bruikbaar afval[h], recycling, hergebruik[h]

[2]**salvage** (vb) **1** bergen, redden, in veiligheid brengen **2** terugwinnen, verzamelen

voor hergebruik
salvation 1 redding: *that **was** my* ~ dat was mijn redding **2** verlossing
the **Salvation Army** Leger des Heils
¹**salve** (n) zalf [also fig]; smeersel^h, balsem
²**salve** (vb) sussen, kalmeren, tevreden stellen: ~ *one's **conscience*** zijn geweten sussen
salvia salie
salvo salvo^h, plotselinge uitbarsting: *a* ~ *of **applause*** een daverend applaus
¹**same** (dem pron) dezelfde, hetzelfde: *the* ~ *applies to you* hetzelfde geldt voor jou; ~ *here* ik ook (niet), met mij precies zo, idem dito; *they are **much** the* ~ ze lijken (vrij) sterk op elkaar; *it's all the* ~ *to me* het is mij om het even, het maakt me niet uit; *(the)* ~ *to you* insgelijks, van 't zelfde; *at the* ~ ***time*** tegelijkertijd; ***much** the* ~ *problem* vrijwel hetzelfde probleem
²**same** (adv) net zo, precies hetzelfde: *he found nothing, (the)* ~ ***as** my own dentist* hij vond niets, net als mijn eigen tandarts
sameness 1 gelijkheid, overeenkomst **2** eentonigheid, monotonie
same-sex homo-: ~ ***marriage*** homohuwelijk
¹**sample** (n) **1** (proef)monster^h, staal^h, voorbeeld^h: *take a* ~ *of **blood*** een bloedmonster nemen **2** steekproef
²**sample** (vb) **1** een steekproef nemen uit, monsters trekken uit **2** (be)proeven, testen, keuren
sample copy proefexemplaar^h, proefnummer^h
sanatorium sanatorium^h, herstellingsoord^h
sanctify 1 heiligen **2** rechtvaardigen, heiligen **3** heilig maken, verlossen van zonde(schuld)
sanctimonious schijnheilig
¹**sanction** (n) **1** toestemming, goedkeuring **2** sanctie, dwang(middel^h), strafmaatregel: *apply ~s against racist regimes* sancties instellen tegen racistische regimes
²**sanction** (vb) **1** sanctioneren, bekrachtigen, bevestigen **2** goedkeuren, toestaan, instemmen met
sanctity heiligheid, vroomheid
sanctuary 1 omtrek van (hoog)altaar, priesterkoor^h **2** vogelreservaat^h, wildreservaat^h **3** asiel^h, vrijplaats, wijkplaats, toevlucht(soord^h): *he got up and **took** ~ in his study* hij stond op en zocht zijn toevlucht in zijn studeerkamer
¹**sand** (n) **1** zand^h **2** (-s) zandvlakte, strand^h, woestijn
²**sand** (vb) **1** met zand bestrooien: ~ *slippery **roads*** gladde wegen met zand bestrooien **2** (+ down) (glad)schuren, polijsten
sandal sandaal
¹**sandbag** (n) zandzak

²**sandbag** (vb) **1** met zandzakken versterken **2** [Am; inform] dwingen: *he was ~ged **into** leaving* hij werd gedwongen te vertrekken
sandbank zandbank, ondiepte
sandblast zandstralen
sandbox zandbak
sandcastle zandkasteel^h
sander schuurmachine
sanding machine schuurmachine
the **sandman** zandmannetje^h, Klaas Vaak
¹**sandpaper** (n) schuurpapier^h
²**sandpaper** (vb) schuren
sandpit 1 zandgraverij, zandgroeve **2** zandbak
sandstone zandsteen^{+h}
¹**sandwich** (n) sandwich, dubbele boterham
²**sandwich** (vb) klemmen, vastzetten, plaatsen: *I'll* ~ *her **in** between two other appointments* ik ontvang haar wel tussen twee andere afspraken door
sandwich-board advertentiebord^h; reclamebord^h [carried on chest and back]
sandwich course cursus waarin theorie en praktijk afwisselend aan bod komen
sandwich man sandwichman
sandy 1 zand(er)ig, zandachtig **2** ros(sig) [of hair]; roodachtig
sane 1 (geestelijk) gezond, bij zijn volle verstand **2** verstandig [of ideas etc]; redelijk
sanguine 1 optimistisch, hoopvol, opgewekt **2** blozend, met een gezonde kleur
sanitarium sanatorium^h, herstellingsoord^h
sanitary 1 sanitair, m.b.t. de gezondheid **2** hygiënisch, schoon: ~ ***fittings*** het sanitair || ~ ***stop*** sanitaire stop
sanitary napkin [Am] maandverband^h
sanitary towel maandverband^h
sanitation 1 bevordering van de volksgezondheid **2** afvalverwerking, rioolzuivering
sanity 1 (geestelijke) gezondheid **2** verstandigheid, gezond verstand^h
Santa Claus kerstman(netje)
¹**sap** (n) **1** (planten)sap^h **2** levenskracht, energie, vitaliteit: *the* ~ *of **youth*** jeugdige levenskracht **3** slagwapen^h, knuppel **4** sul, sukkel, oen
²**sap** (vb) aftappen [also fig]; sap onttrekken aan; [fig] levenskracht onttrekken aan; uitputten: *the tension at the office was ~ping my **energy*** de spanning op kantoor vrat al mijn energie
sapless futloos
sapphire 1 saffier^{+h} **2** saffierblauw^h
sarcasm sarcasme^h, bijtende spot
sarcastic sarcastisch, bijtend
sarcophagus sarcofaag, stenen doodskist
sardine sardine: *(packed) like ~s* als haringen in een ton
sardonic boosaardig spottend, cynisch
sarky sarcastisch

sash 998

sash 1 sjerp 2 raam^h, schuifraam^h
sashay nonchalant lopen, paraderen: *the models ~ed down the catwalk* de modellen paradeerden over het podium
¹sass (n) tegenspraak, brutaliteit: *I'm not accepting such ~ from anybody* ik accepteer zulke brutale opmerkingen van niemand
²sass (vb) brutaal zijn tegen, brutaliseren
¹Sassenach (n) Engelsman
²Sassenach (adj) Engels
satanic 1 van de duivel 2 satanisch, duivels, hels
satchel (school)tas [oft with shoulder strap]; pukkel
satellite 1 satelliet 2 voorstad, randgemeente: *New Malden is one of the many ~s of London* New Malden is een van de vele voorsteden van Londen 3 satellietstaat, vazalstaat
satellite dish schotelantenne
satellite town satellietstad
satiate (over)verzadigen, bevredigen, overvoeden, overladen: *be ~d with* a) verzadigd zijn van; b) zijn buik vol hebben van
¹satin (n) satijn^h
²satin (adj) satijnachtig, satijnen, satijnzacht: *~ finish* satijnglans
satire 1 satire, hekeldicht^h, hekelroman 2 satire, bespotting
satiric(al) satirisch
satirize 1 hekelen, bespotten 2 een satire schrijven op
satisfaction 1 genoegen^h, plezier^h, tevredenheid 2 voldoening, bevrediging, zekerheid: *prove sth. to s.o.'s ~* iets tot iemands volle tevredenheid bewijzen 3 genoegdoening, eerherstel^h, voldoening: *demand ~* genoegdoening eisen 4 (af)betaling, terugbetaling, voldoening
satisfactory 1 voldoende, (goed) genoeg 2 voldoening schenkend, bevredigend 3 geschikt
¹satisfy (vb) 1 voldoen, toereikend zijn, (goed) genoeg zijn 2 voldoen, genoegen schenken, tevreden stemmen
²satisfy (vb) 1 tevredenstellen, genoegen schenken, bevredigen: *be satisfied with* tevreden zijn over 2 vervullen, voldoen aan, beantwoorden aan: *~ the conditions* aan de voorwaarden voldoen 3 nakomen [an obligation]; vervullen 4 bevredigen, verzadigen: *~ one's curiosity* zijn nieuwsgierigheid bevredigen 5 overtuigen, verzekeren: *be satisfied that* ervan overtuigd zijn dat, de zekerheid (verkregen) hebben dat
satsuma mandarijntje^h
saturate 1 doordrenken [also fig]; doordringen, onderdompelen 2 (over)verzadigen, volledig vullen: *the computer market will soon be ~d* de afzetmarkt voor computers zal weldra verzadigd zijn 3 [science, chem] ver-

zadigen: *~d fats* verzadigde vetten
Saturday zaterdag
Saturn Saturnus
satyr halfgod
¹sauce (n) 1 saus [also fig]; sausje^h 2 brutaliteit, tegenspraak, vrijpostigheid
²sauce (vb) brutaal zijn tegen, een brutale mond opzetten tegen: *don't you ~ me, young man* niet zo'n grote mond tegen mij opzetten, jongeman
sauce boat sauskom
saucepan steelpan
saucer 1 (thee)schoteltje^h 2 schotelantenne
saucy 1 brutaal; (lichtjes) uitdagend [also sexually]: *don't be ~ with me* wees niet zo brutaal tegen mij 2 vlot, knap, tof: *a ~ hat* een vlot hoedje
Saudi Arabia Saudi-Arabië
¹Saudi Arabian (n) Saudiër, Saudische
²Saudi Arabian (adj) Saudisch; Saudi-Arabisch
sauna sauna
¹saunter (n) 1 wandeling(etje^h) 2 slentergang
²saunter (vb) drentelen, slenteren: *we spent the afternoon ~ing up and down the pier* de hele middag slenterden we heen en weer op de pier
sausage worst, saucijs
sausage roll saucijzenbroodje^h
¹savage (n) 1 wilde, primitieve (mens) 2 woesteling, wildeman 3 barbaar
²savage (adj) 1 primitief, onbeschaafd 2 wreed(aardig), woest: *a ~ dog* een valse hond 3 heftig, fel: *~ criticism* meedogenloze kritiek 4 lomp, ongemanierd
savagery wreedheid, ruwheid, gewelddadigheid
savanna(h) savanne
¹save (n) redding: *the goalkeeper made a brilliant ~* de doelverdediger wist met een prachtige actie de bal uit het doel te houden
²save (vb) 1 sparen (voor), geld opzijleggen, zuinig zijn 2 [sport] een doelpunt (weten te) voorkomen 3 verlossing brengen, redden, verlossen
³save (vb) 1 redden, bevrijden, verlossen: *~ the situation* de situatie redden, een fiasco voorkomen 2 (be)sparen, bewaren, opslaan: *~ time* tijd (uit)sparen 3 overbodig maken, voorkomen, besparen: *I've been ~d a lot of trouble* er werd me heel wat moeite bespaard 4 [sport] redden 5 [sport] voorkomen [goal]; stoppen [penalty, kick] ‖ *God ~ the Queen* God behoede de koningin
⁴save (prep) behalve, met uitzondering van: *everyone ~ Gill* allemaal behalve Gill
saving 1 redding, verlossing 2 besparing: *a ~ of ten dollars* een besparing van tien dollar
savings spaargeld

savings account 1 spaarrekening **2** [Am] depositorekening

savings bank spaarbank, spaarkas

saviour 1 redder, bevrijder **2** (de) Verlosser; (de) Heiland [Jesus Christ]

¹savour (n) **1** bijsmaak [also fig]; zweem: *I detected a certain ~ of **garlic** ik bespeurde een bijsmaak van knoflook* **2** smaak [also fig]; aroma^h, geur: *the ~ **of** local life* de eigenheid van het plaatselijke leven

²savour (vb) met smaak proeven, genieten (van)

savour of geuren naar [also fig]; rieken naar, iets weg hebben van

¹savoury (n) hartig voorgerecht^h (nagerecht^h), hartig hapje^h

²savoury (adj) **1** smakelijk, lekker **2** hartig, pikant **3** eerbaar, respectabel, aanvaardbaar: *I'll spare you the less ~ **details** ik zal je de minder fraaie bijzonderheden besparen*

savvy (gezond) verstand^h

¹saw (n) zaag(machine): *circular ~* cirkelzaag

²saw (vb) zagen, gezaagd worden, zich laten zagen

³saw (vb) zagen, in stukken zagen: *~ **down** a tree* een boom omzagen

sawdust zaagsel^h

sawmill houtzagerij

sax *saxophone* sax

Saxon 1 Angelsaksisch, Oudengels **2** Saksisch

saxophone saxofoon

¹say (n) **1** invloed, zeggen^h, zeggenschap: *have a ~ in the matter* iets in de melk te brokkelen hebben, een vinger in de pap hebben **2** zegje^h, mening: *have* (or: *say*) *one's ~* zijn zegje doen

²say (vb) zeggen, praten, vertellen: *I couldn't ~* ik zou het niet kunnen zeggen; *so to ~* bij wijze van spreken; *I'd rather not ~* dat zeg ik liever niet, dat houd ik liever voor me; *a man, they ~, of bad reputation* een man, (zo) zegt men, met een slechte reputatie

³say (vb) **1** (op)zeggen, uiten, (uit)spreken: *~ **grace*** (or: *one's*) ***prayers*** dank zeggen, bidden; *I dare ~ that* het zou zelfs heel goed kunnen dat; *~ **no more!*** geen woord meer!, praat er mij niet van!, dat zegt al genoeg!; *to ~ **nothing** of* om nog maar te zwijgen over; *to ~ to o.s.* bij zichzelf denken; *that **is** to ~* met andere woorden, dat wil zeggen, tenminste **2** zeggen, vermelden, verkondigen: *to ~ the **least*** op zijn zachtst uitgedrukt; *she is said to **be** very rich* men zegt dat ze heel rijk is; *it ~s on the bottle* op de fles staat **3** zeggen, aanvoeren, te kennen geven: *what do you ~ **to** this?* wat zou je hiervan vinden? **4** zeggen, aannemen, veronderstellen: *let's ~, shall we ~* laten we zeggen; *~ **seven** a.m.* pakweg zeven uur ('s ochtends) **5** aangeven, tonen, zeggen: *what time does your **watch** ~?* hoe

laat is het op jouw horloge? || *when all is said and **done*** alles bij elkaar genomen, al met al; *no sooner said than **done*** zo gezegd, zo gedaan; *it goes without ~ing* het spreekt vanzelf; *you can ~ that **again**, you said it* zeg dat wel, daar zeg je zoiets, en of!; *~ **when*** zeg het als 't genoeg is, zeg maar ho

saying gezegde^h, spreekwoord^h, spreuk: *as the ~ **goes*** zoals het spreekwoord zegt

say-so 1 bewering, woord^h: *why should he believe you **on** your ~?* waarom zou hij je op je woord geloven? **2** toestemming, permissie

scab 1 onderkruiper, werkwillige, stakingsbreker **2** zwartwerker [non-union member] **3** korst(je^h): *a ~ had **formed** on her knee* er had zich een korstje gevormd op haar knie

scabbard 1 schede [for sword, knife] **2** holster

scabby schurftig

scabies schurft

scads massa's, hopen: *~ **of** people* massa's mensen

scaffold 1 schavot^h **2** (bouw)steiger, stellage

scaffolding steiger(constructie), stelling(en), stellage

¹scald (n) brandwond, brandblaar, brandvlek

²scald (vb) zich branden [by hot water, steam]

³scald (vb) **1** branden, (doen) branden **2** (uit)wassen, (uit)koken, steriliseren **3** bijna tot kookpunt verhitten [milk]

scalding [also adverb] kokend(heet)

¹scale (n) **1** schub, schaal, (huid)schilfer: [fig] *the ~s **fell** from her eyes* de schellen vielen haar van de ogen **2** (weeg)schaal: *a **pair** of ~s* een weegschaal **3** aanslag, ketelsteen **4** schaal(verdeling), schaalaanduiding, maatstok, meetlat: *the ~ of the **problem*** de omvang van het probleem; *at ~* op grote schaal; [fig] *on a large* (or: *small*) *~* op grote (or: kleine) schaal; *draw **to** ~* op schaal tekenen **5** [mus] toonladder **6** [maths] schaal

²scale (vb) (af)schilferen, (af)bladderen

³scale (vb) (be)klimmen, (op)klauteren; opgaan [ladder] || *~ **back*** (or: *down*) verlagen, verkleinen, terugschroeven; *~ **up*** verhogen, vergroten, opschroeven

scale drawing schaaltekening

scale model schaalmodel^h

scalene ongelijkzijdig [of triangle]

scallywag deugniet, rakker, schavuit

¹scalp (n) hoofdhuid

²scalp (vb) scalperen

scalpel scalpel, ontleedmes^h, operatiemes^h

scamp boef(je^h), rakker, deugniet: *you ~!* (jij) boef!

scamper hollen, rennen, draven

¹scan (n) **1** onderzoekende blik **2** scan, het aftasten, het onderzoeken

²scan (vb) zich laten scanderen [of poem]; metrisch juist zijn: *some of the lines of this song* **don't** ~ sommige regels van dat liedje kloppen metrisch niet
³scan (vb) **1** scanderen, in versvoeten verdelen: *the audience were ~ning his* **name:** *'John-son, John-son'* het publiek scandeerde zijn naam: 'John-son, John-son' **2** nauwkeurig onderzoeken, afspeuren, afzoeken **3** snel/vluchtig doorlezen **4** aftasten; scannen [with radar]
scandal 1 schandaalʰ, schande **2** achterklap, laster(praat)
scandalize choqueren, ergernis geven: *he didn't know whether to laugh or* **be** *~d* hij wist niet of hij nou moest lachen of zich moest ergeren
scandalmonger kwaadspreker, lasteraar(ster)
scandalous schandelijk, schandalig, aanstootgevend
¹Scandinavian (n) Scandinaviër, Scandinavische
²Scandinavian (adj) Scandinavisch
scanner aftaster, scanner, (draaiende) radarantenne
scant weinig, spaarzaam, gering: *do ~* **justice** *to sth.* iets weinig recht doen
scanty karig, krap, gering
scapegoat zondebok
¹scar (n) littekenʰ, schram, kras
²scar (vb): *~* **over** een litteken vormen; helen
scarab mestkever
scarce schaars [of food, money, etc]; zeldzaam: **make** *o.s. ~* zich uit de voeten maken
scarcely 1 nauwelijks, met moeite: *~* **ever** haast nooit **2** [iron] zeker niet: *that's ~ the point here* dat is nou niet helemaal waar het hier om gaat
scarcity schaarste, gebrekʰ
¹scare (n) schrik, vrees, paniek: *give s.o. a ~* iem. de stuipen op het lijf jagen
²scare (vb) **1** doen schrikken, bang maken: *~d* **out of** *one's wits* buiten zichzelf van schrik, doodsbang **2** (+ off, away) wegjagen, afschrikken
scarecrow vogelverschrikker [also fig]
scare up 1 optrommelen, bij elkaar scharrelen **2** klaarmaken, vervaardigen: *~ a meal* **from** *leftovers* uit restjes een maaltijd in elkaar flansen
scarf sjaal(tjeʰ), sjerp
scarlatina roodvonk
scarlet scharlaken(rood) ‖ *~* **fever** roodvonk
scarper 'm smeren
scar tissue littekenweefselʰ
scary 1 eng, schrikaanjagend **2** (snel) bang, schrikachtig
scat snel vertrekken: *~!* ga weg!
scathing vernietigend; bijtend [eg sarcasm]
¹scatter (n) (ver)spreiding, verstrooiing: *a ~*

of houses een paar huizen hier en daar
²scatter (vb) verstrooid raken, zich verspreiden
³scatter (vb) verstrooien [also science]; verspreiden [also fig]: *all his CDs were ~ed* **through** *the room* al zijn cd's lagen verspreid door de kamer; *~* **about** (or: *around*) rondstrooien
scatterbrain warhoofdʰ
scattered verspreid (liggend), ver uiteen: *~ showers* hier en daar een bui
scattering verspreiding
scatty gek, warrig
scavenge 1 afval doorzoeken **2** aas eten
scenario scenarioʰ; draaiboekʰ [also fig]; (film)scriptʰ
scene 1 plaats van handeling, locatie, toneelʰ: *change of ~* verandering van omgeving **2** scène [also theatre]; ophef, misbaarʰ **3** decorʰ, coulisse(n): *behind the ~s* achter de schermen [also fig] **4** landschapʰ ‖ *set the ~ (for sth.)* (iets) voorbereiden; *steal the ~* de show stelen
scene change decorwisseling [also fig]
scenery 1 decors, coulissen **2** landschapʰ: *change of ~* verandering van omgeving
scenic 1 schilderachtig **2** van de natuur, landschap(s)- ‖ *~* **railway** miniatuurspoorbaan
¹scent (n) **1** geur; lucht [also hunt] **2** spoorʰ [also fig]: *on a* **false** (or: *wrong*) *~* op een verkeerd spoor **3** parfumʰ, luchtjeʰ, geurtjeʰ **4** reuk(zin); neus [also fig]
²scent (vb) **1** ruiken [also fig]; geuren, lucht krijgen van **2** parfumeren: *~* **soap** geparfumeerde zeep
sceptic twijfelaar
sceptical (+ about, of) sceptisch (over), twijfelend
scepticism kritische houding
sceptre scepter
schedule 1 programmaʰ: *be* **behind** *~* achter liggen op het schema, vertraging hebben; *on ~* op tijd **2** (inventaris)lijst **3** dienstregeling, roosterʰ
scheduled 1 gepland, in het rooster opgenomen **2** op een lijst gezet **3** lijn- [service, flight]
¹scheme (n) **1** stelselʰ, ordening, systeemʰ **2** programmaʰ **3** oogmerkʰ, projectʰ **4** planʰ, complotʰ **5** ontwerpʰ
²scheme (vb) plannen maken, plannen smeden: *~* **for** *sth.* iets plannen
³scheme (vb) **1** beramen [plans]; smeden **2** intrigeren: *he was always scheming* **against** *her* hij was altijd bezig complotten tegen haar te smeden
schemer 1 plannenmaker **2** intrigant, samenzweerder
scheming sluw
schism scheuring [in church]; afscheiding

schizophrenia schizofrenie
¹schizophrenic (n) schizofreen
²schizophrenic (adj) schizofreen
schmalzy sentimenteel
scholar 1 geleerde: *not much* of a ~ geen studiehoofd **2** beursstudent
scholarly wetenschappelijk, geleerd
scholarship 1 (studie)beurs **2** wetenschappelijkheid **3** wetenschap, geleerdheid
scholastic 1 school- **2** schools
¹school (n) **1** school [also of fish etc]; [of thoughts] richting: ~ of *thought* denkwijze, (filosofische) school **2** school; [fig] leerschool: *lower* (or: *upper*) ~ onderbouw, bovenbouw; *modern* ~ [roughly] mavo; *keep in after* ~ na laten blijven; *quit* ~ van school gaan; *after* ~ na school(tijd); *at* ~ op school **3** collegeruimte, examengebouwʰ, leslokaalʰ **4** studierichting **5** (universitair) instituutʰ, faculteit: *medical* ~ faculteit (der) geneeskunde **6** scholing, (school)opleiding
²school (vb) scholen, trainen; africhten [horse]: ~ed *in* opgeleid tot
schoolboy schooljongen, scholier
school certificate einddiplomaʰ
school crossing patrol klaar-overbrigade
schooldays schooltijd
school friend schoolvriend(in)
schoolgirl schoolmeisjeʰ
schooling 1 scholing, onderwijsʰ **2** dressuur
school-marm 1 schooljuffrouw **2** schoolfrik
schoolmaster schoolmeester
schoolmate schoolkameraad
schoolmistress schooljuffrouw
school superintendent 1 schooldirecteur **2** onderwijsinspecteur
schoolteacher 1 onderwijzer(es) **2** leraar
school yard schoolpleinʰ
schooner 1 schoener **2** groot bierglasʰ **3** groot sherryglasʰ (portglasʰ)
science 1 (natuur)wetenschap: *applied* ~ toegepaste wetenschap **2** techniek, vaardigheid
science fiction sciencefiction
scientific 1 wetenschappelijk **2** vakkundig: *a* ~ *boxer* een bokser met een goede techniek
scientist natuurwetenschapper
sci-fi *science fiction*
scintillate 1 schitteren, fonkelen **2** vonken **3** sprankelen, geestig zijn: *scintillating humour* tintelende humor
scissors schaar: *a pair of* ~ een schaar
¹scoff (n) **1** spottende opmerking: *he was used to* ~s *about his appearance* hij was gewend aan spottende opmerkingen over zijn uiterlijk **2** mikpuntʰ van spotternij **3** vretenʰ
²scoff (vb) (+ at) spotten (met): *they* ~ed *the*

idea ze maakten spottende opmerkingen over het idee
³scoff (vb) schrokken, vreten
¹scold (vb) (+ at) schelden (op)
²scold (vb) uitvaren tegen: ~ *s.o. for sth.* iem. om iets berispen
scolding standjeʰ, uitbrander
scone scone [small, solid cake]
¹scoop (n) **1** schep, lepel, bak: *three* ~s *of ice cream* drie scheppen ijs **2** primeur [in newspaper]; sensationeel nieuwtjeʰ
²scoop (vb) **1** scheppen, lepelen: ~ *out* opscheppen; ~ *up* opscheppen [with hands, spoon] **2** uithollen, (uit)graven **3** binnenhalen; grijpen [money]; in de wacht slepen
scoot rennen, vliegen: *is that the time? I'd better* ~ is het al zo laat? Ik moet rennen
scooter 1 autoped **2** (brom)scooter
scope 1 bereikʰ, gebiedʰ, omvang: *that is beyond* (or: *outside*) *the* ~ *of this book* dat valt buiten het bestek van dit boek **2** ruimte, armslag, gelegenheid: *this job gives you* ~ *for your abilities* deze baan geeft je de kans je talenten te ontplooien
¹scorch (vb) razendsnel rijden, vliegen, scheuren
²scorch (vb) **1** (ver)schroeien, (ver)zengen, verbranden **2** verdorren
scorcher 1 snikhete dag **2** scherpe kritiek, scherpe uithaal **3** snelheidsduivel
scorching 1 verschroeiend, verzengend: *a* ~ *summer afternoon* op een snikhete zomermiddag **2** vernietigend, bijtend
¹score (n) **1** stand, puntentotaalʰ, score: *level the* ~ gelijkmaken **2** (doel)puntʰ [also fig]; rake opmerking, succesʰ: [fig] ~ *off one's opponent* een punt scoren tegen zijn tegenstander **3** getrokken lijn, kerf, kras, striem, schram, lijn **4** reden, grond: *on the* ~ *of* vanwege **5** grief: *pay off* (or: *settle*) *old* ~s een oude rekening vereffenen **6** onderwerpʰ, themaʰ, puntʰ: *on that* ~ wat dat betreft **7** [mus] partituur; [by extension] muziek [for musical etc] || *know the* ~ weten hoe de zaken er voorstaan
²score (vb) **1** scoren, (doel)punt maken; puntentotaal halen [eg in test] **2** de score noteren **3** succes hebben **4** geluk hebben || ~ *off s.o.* iem. aftroeven
³score (vb) **1** lijn(en) trekken, (in)kerven, schrammen: ~ *out* (or: *through*) doorstrepen **2** scoren; maken [point]; [fig] behalen; boeken [success]; winnen **3** tellen voor; waard zijn [of point, run] **4** toekennen [points]; geven **5** een score halen van [eg in test] **6** fel bekritiseren, hekelen
scoreboard scorebordʰ
scorer 1 scoreteller **2** (doel)puntenmaker
¹scorn (n) (voorwerpʰ van) minachting, geringschatting: *pour* ~ *on* verachten
²scorn (vb) **1** minachten, verachten **2** ver-

smaden, beneden zich achten
scornful negatief: ~ *of sth.* met minachting
voor iets
Scorpio [astrology] (de) Schorpioen
scorpion schorpioen
Scot Schot
scotch 1 een eind maken aan; ontzenuwen
[theory]; de kop indrukken [rumour] **2** verijdelen [plan]
¹**Scotch** (n) **1** Schotse whisky **2** de Schotten
²**Scotch** (adj) Schots: ~ *whisky* Schotse whis-
ky || ~ *broth* Schotse maaltijdsoep
Scotch tape sellotape, plakbandᵗʰ
scot-free 1 ongedeerd **2** ongestraft
Scotland Schotland
Scotland Yard Scotland Yard; opsporingsdienst
¹**Scots** (n) Schots
²**Scots** (adj) Schots
Scotsman Schot
Scotswoman Schotse
¹**Scottish** (n) de Schotten
²**Scottish** (adj) Schots
scoundrel schoft
¹**scour** (vb) rennen: ~ *about after* (or: *for*) *sth.*
rondrennen op zoek naar iets
²**scour** (vb) **1** (door)spoelen, uitspoelen **2** (+
out) uitschuren, uithollen **3** doorkruisen
4 afzoeken, doorzoeken, afstropen: ~ *the
shops for a CD* de winkels aflopen voor een
cd
³**scour** (vb) schuren, schrobben
¹**scourge** (n) gesel
²**scourge** (vb) **1** geselen **2** teisteren: *for sev-
en years the country was ~d by war* zeven jaar
lang werd het land door oorlog geteisterd
scouring powder schuurmiddelʰ
¹**scout** (n) **1** verkenner **2** talentenjager;
scout [in the world of football, film] **3** verkenner, padvinder, gids
²**scout** (vb) **1** zoeken: ~ *(about, around) for
sth.* naar iets op zoek zijn **2** terrein verkennen
³**scout** (vb) **1** verkennen **2** minachtend afwijzen: *every offer of help was ~ed* elk aanbod
om te helpen werd met minachting van de
hand gewezen
scoutmaster hopman
¹**scowl** (n) norse blik
²**scowl** (vb) (+ at) het voorhoofd fronsen (tegen), stuurs kijken (naar)
¹**scrabble** (n) gegraaiʰ
²**scrabble** (vb) graaien, grabbelen, scharrelen: ~ *about for sth.* naar iets graaien
scrag 1 hals **2** halsstukʰ
scraggy broodmager
scram: ~*!* maak dat je wegkomt!
¹**scramble** (n) **1** klauterpartij: *it was a bit of a
~ to reach the top* het was een hele toer om
de top te bereiken **2** gedrangʰ, gevechtʰ
3 motorcross

²**scramble** (vb) **1** klauteren, klimmen **2** (+
for) vechten (om), zich verdringen **3** zich
haasten: ~ *to one's feet* overeind krabbelen
³**scramble** (vb) **1** door elkaar gooien, in de
war brengen **2** roeren [egg] **3** afraffelen
4 vervormen [to encode radio or telephone
message]; verdraaien
¹**scrap** (n) **1** stukjeʰ, beetjeʰ, fragmentʰ:
there's not a ~ of truth in what they've told you
er is niets waar van wat ze je verteld hebben
2 knipselʰ **3** vechtpartij(tjeʰ), ruzie **4** afvalʰ,
schrootʰ **5** (-s) restjes
²**scrap** (vb) ruziën, bakkeleien
³**scrap** (vb) **1** afdanken, dumpen; laten varen
[ideas, plans] **2** slopen, tot schroot verwerken
scrapbook plakboekʰ
¹**scrape** (n) **1** geschraapʰ, geschuurʰ **2** ge-
krasʰ, kras **3** schaafwond **4** netelige situatie:
get into ~s in moeilijkheden verzeild raken
²**scrape** (vb) **1** schuren, strijken, krassen: *the
sound of chairs scraping on a tiled floor* het geluid van stoelen die over een tegelvloer
schrapen **2** schrapen; zagen [eg on violin]
3 met weinig rondkomen, sober leven **4** het
op het kantje af halen [also examination]: ~
through in maar net een voldoende halen
voor || ~ *along on money from friends* het uit
weten te zingen met geld van vrienden
³**scrape** (vb) **1** (af)schrapen, (af)krabben,
uitschrapen **2** schaven [eg knee]: ~ *the
paintwork* de verf beschadigen || ~ *together*
(or: *up*) bij elkaar schrapen [money]
scraper 1 schraper; (verf)krabber **2** flessen-
likker
scrap heap vuilnisbelt, schroothoop: [fig]
throw s.o. (sth.) on the ~ iem. (iets) afdanken
scrap iron schrootʰ, oud ijzerʰ
scrap paper kladpapierʰ
scrappy fragmentarisch
¹**scratch** (n) **1** krasjeʰ, schram: *without a ~*
ongedeerd **2** startstreep: *start from ~* a) [fig]
bij het begin beginnen; b) met niets begin-
nen || *up to ~* in vorm, op het vereiste niveau;
come up to ~ het halen
²**scratch** (adj) samengeraapt: *a ~ meal* een
restjesmaaltijd
³**scratch** (vb) scharrelen, wroeten || ~ *along*
het hoofd boven water weten te houden
⁴**scratch** (vb) **1** (zich) schrammen **2** krabbelen [letter] **3** schrappen, doorhalen **4** terugtrekken **5** (+ together, up) bijeenschrapen
[money; information]
⁵**scratch** (vb) krassen, (zich) krabben
scratch card kraslotʰ
scratch paper kladpapierʰ
¹**scrawl** (n) **1** krabbeltjeʰ **2** poot, onbeholpen handschriftʰ
²**scrawl** (vb) krabbelen, slordig schrijven
scrawny broodmager
¹**scream** (n) **1** gil, krijs **2** giller, dolkomisch

iets (iem.): *do you know Ernest?* **He's** *a* ~ ken jij Ernest? Je lacht je gek
²**scream** (vb) tieren, razen, tekeergaan
³**scream** (vb) gillen, schreeuwen: ~ *for* water om water schreeuwen; ~ *with laughter* gieren van het lachen
¹**screech** (n) gil, krijs, schreeuw: *a* ~ *of* **brakes** gierende remmen
²**screech** (vb) knarsen, kraken, piepen
³**screech** (vb) gillen, gieren
¹**screen** (n) **1** scherm[h]; koorhek[h] [in church] **2** beschutting, bescherming; afscherming [of electrical equipment etc]; muur: *under* ~ *of* **night** onder dekking van de nacht **3** doek[h], projectiescherm[h], beeldscherm[h] **4** het witte doek, de film **5** hor, venstergaas[h] **6** zeef, rooster[h]; [fig] selectie(procedure)
²**screen** (vb) **1** afschermen [also from radiation]; afschutten, beschermen; dekken [soldier]: ~ *off one corner of the room* een hoek van de kamer afschermen **2** beschermen, de hand boven het hoofd houden **3** doorlichten, op geschiktheid testen, screenen **4** vertonen, projecteren: *the feature film will* **be** *~ed at 8.25* de hoofdfilm wordt om 8.25 uur vertoond **5** verfilmen
screening 1 filmvertoning **2** doorlichting **3** afscherming
screenplay scenario[n], script
screen print zeefdruk
screen saver schermbeveiliger; screensaver
screen test screentest, proefopname
screenwriter scenarioschrijver
¹**screw** (n) **1** schroef **2** propeller, scheepsschroef **3** vrek **4** cipier
²**screw** (vb) zich spiraalsgewijs bewegen
³**screw** (vb) **1** schroeven, aandraaien: *I could* ~ *his* **neck** ik zou hem zijn nek wel kunnen omdraaien; ~ *down* vastschroeven; ~ *on* vastschroeven **2** verfrommelen **3** afzetten: *he's so stupid, no wonder he* **gets** *~ed all the time* hij is zo stom, geen wonder dat hij iedere keer wordt afgezet **4** belazeren, verneuken **5** [vulg] neuken ‖ ~ *you!* val dood!
screwball 1 idioot **2** [baseball] omgekeerde curve
screwdriver schroevendraaier
screwed-up 1 verpest **2** verknipt, opgefokt
screw out of afpersen, uitzuigen: *screw* **money** *out of s.o.* iem. geld afhandig maken; *screw* **s.o.** *out of sth.* zorgen dat iem. iets niet krijgt
screw up 1 verwringen, verdraaien, verfrommelen: *she screwed up her* **eyes** zij kneep haar ogen dicht **2** verzieken, verknoeien **3** bij elkaar rapen; verzamelen [courage] **4** nerveus maken
screwy excentriek, zonderling
¹**scribble** (n) **1** gekrabbel[h] **2** briefje[h], kladje[h]

²**scribble** (vb) krabbelen
scribe 1 schrijver, klerk **2** schriftgeleerde
scrimmage schermutseling
¹**scrimp** (vb) zich bekrimpen: ~ *and* **save** heel zuinig aan doen
²**scrimp** (vb) beknibbelen op
script 1 geschrift[h] **2** script, manuscript[h], draaiboek[h], tekst **3** schrijfletters, handschrift[h]
script girl regieassistente
scripture heilig geschrift[h]: *the* **(Holy)** *Scripture* de Heilige Schrift
scriptwriter scenarioschrijver
scroll schuiven [moving text on computer screen]; scrollen
scroll 1 rol, perkamentrol, geschrift[h] **2** krul
scroll bar [comp] schuifbalk
scrolling scrollen[h]
¹**scrounge** (vb) schooien, bietsen
²**scrounge** (vb) **1** in de wacht slepen, achteroverdrukken **2** bietsen
scrounger klaploper, bietser, profiteur
¹**scrub** (n) **1** met struikgewas bedekt gebied[h] **2** struikgewas[h], kreupelhout[h] **3** het boenen
²**scrub** (vb) een schrobber gebruiken, schrobben ‖ *the surgeon was* ~*bing* **up** de chirurg was zijn handen aan het schrobben
³**scrub** (vb) **1** schrobben, boenen **2** (also + out) schrappen, afgelasten, vergeten
scrubby 1 miezerig **2** met struikgewas bedekt
scrub nurse [Am] operatiezuster
scruff nekvel[h]: *take by the* ~ *of the* **neck** bij het nekvel grijpen
scruffy smerig, vuil, slordig
¹**scruple** (n) scrupule, gewetensbezwaar[h]: **make** *no* ~ *about doing sth.* er geen been in zien om iets te doen
²**scruple** (vb) aarzelen
scrupulous nauwgezet: *~ly* **clean** kraakhelder
scrutinize in detail onderzoeken, nauwkeurig bekijken
scrutiny 1 nauwkeurig toezicht[h] **2** kritische blik
scud voortscheren, ijlen, snellen: *the children were ~ding* **downhill** *on their sledges* de kinderen raasden van de heuvel af op hun sleeën
¹**scuff** (n) slijtplek
²**scuff** (vb) **1** sloffen **2** versleten zijn [of shoe, floor]
³**scuff** (vb) schuren, slepen
¹**scuffle** (n) knokpartij, schermutseling
²**scuffle** (vb) bakkeleien, knokken
¹**scull 1** korte (roei)riem **2** sculler, éénpersoonsroeiboot met twee korte riemen
²**scull** (vb) roeien
scullery bijkeuken
sculptor beeldhouwer
¹**sculpture** (n) beeldhouwwerk[h], plastiek[h],

beeldhouwkunst
²**sculpture** (vb) 1 beeldhouwen 2 met sculptuur versieren, bewerken
scum 1 schuimʰ [on water] 2 uitschotʰ [also fig]; afvalʰ: *the ~ of humanity* (or: *the earth*) het schorem, uitschot
¹**scupper** (n) spuigatʰ
²**scupper** (vb) 1 tot zinken brengen 2 (overvallen en) in de pan hakken, (overvallen en) afmaken: *be ~ed* eraan gaan
scurf roos [of skin]
scurrility 1 grofheid 2 grove taal
scurrilous grof
scurry dribbelen, zich haasten: *~ for shelter* haastig een onderdak zoeken
¹**scurvy** (n) scheurbuik
²**scurvy** (adj) gemeen
¹**scuttle** (n) 1 luik(gat)ʰ, ventilatieopening 2 kolenbak 3 overhaaste vlucht
²**scuttle** (vb) zich wegscheren: *~ off* (or: *away*) zich uit de voeten maken
³**scuttle** (vb) doen zinken [by making holes]
scuzzy [inform] smerig
¹**scythe** (n) zeis
²**scythe** (vb) (af)maaien [also fig]
SE *southeast* Z.O., zuidoost
sea 1 zee, oceaan; [fig] massa; overvloed: *put (out) to ~* uitvaren; *at ~* op zee; *the seven ~s* de zeven (wereld)zeeën 2 zeegolf, sterke golfslag: *heavy ~* zware zee 3 kust, strandʰ || *be (all) at ~* a) verbijsterd zijn; b) geen notie hebben
sea battle zeeslag
seabed zeebedding, zeebodem
seabird zeevogel
seaborne over zee (vervoerd/aangevoerd): *~ supplies* bevoorrading overzee
sea breeze 1 zeebries 2 wind op zee
sea change ommekeer
sea dog zeebonk, zeerob
seafaring zeevarend
seafood eetbare zeevis en schaal- en schelpdieren
seafront strandboulevard; zeekant [of town]
seagoing zeevarend
seagull zeemeeuw
¹**seal** (n) 1 zegelʰ; stempelʰ [also fig]; lakzegelʰ, (plak)zegel; [fig] kenmerkʰ; [fig] bezegeling: *set the ~ on* a) bezegelen; b) [also fig] afsluiten; *under ~ of secrecy* onder het zegel van geheimhouding 2 dichting, dichtingsmateriaalʰ, (luchtdichte/waterdichte) afsluiting, stankafsluiting 3 (zee)rob, zeehond, zeeleeuw
²**seal** (vb) 1 zegelen; verzegelen [verdict, orders etc]; [fig] opsluiten 2 dichten, verzegelen, (water)dicht maken; dichtschroeien [meat]: *my lips are ~ed* ik zal er niets over zeggen; *~ off an area* een gebied afgrendelen 3 bezegelen, bevestigen: *~ s.o.'s doom*

(or: *fate*) iemands (nood)lot bezegelen
sea lane vaarroute
sea legs zeebenen: *get* (or: *find*) *one's ~* zeebenen krijgen
sea level zeeniveauʰ, zeespiegel
sealing wax zegelwas
sea lion zeeleeuw
seal ring zegelring
sealskin robbenvelʰ, sealskin
seam 1 naad, voeg 2 scheurtjeʰ [in metal] 3 (steenkool)laag || *burst at the ~s* tot barstens toe vol zitten
seaman zeeman, matroos
seamanship zeemanschapʰ, zeevaartkunde
sea mile zeemijl [international: 1,852 metres, British: 1,853.18 metres]
seamless naadloos
seamstress naaister
seamy 1 met een naad 2 minder mooi: *the ~ side of life* de zelfkant van het leven
seaplane watervliegtuigʰ
seaport zeehaven
sear 1 schroeien, verschroeien, (dicht)branden 2 (doen) verdorren, opdrogen, uitdrogen; [fig] verharden
¹**search** (n) grondig onderzoekʰ, opsporing, speurwerkʰ; [comp] zoekbewerking, zoekfunctie: *in ~ of* op zoek naar
²**search** (vb) (+ for) grondig zoeken (naar), speuren
³**search** (vb) grondig onderzoeken, fouilleren, naspeuren || *~ me!* weet ik veel!
search engine zoekmachine [on the Internet]
searching 1 onderzoekend [glance] 2 grondig
searchlight zoeklichtʰ, schijnwerper
search party opsporingsteamʰ
search warrant bevel(schrift)ʰ tot huiszoeking
seascape zeegezichtʰ [painting]
seashell zeeschelp
seashore zeekust
seasick zeeziek
the **seaside** kust, zee(kust)
¹**season** (n) 1 seizoenʰ; [fig] jaarʰ: *rainy ~* regentijd 2 geschikte tijd, seizoenʰ, jachtseizoenʰ, vakantieperiode: *cherries are in ~* het is kersentijd; *a word in ~* een woord op het passende moment, een gepast woord; *in and out of ~* te pas en te onpas 3 feesttijd, kersten nieuwjaarstijd: *the ~ of good cheer* de gezellige kerst- en nieuwjaarstijd
²**season** (vb) 1 kruiden [also fig] 2 (ge)wennen, harden: *~ed troops* doorgewinterde troepen 3 laten liggen [wood]
seasonable 1 passend bij het seizoen 2 tijdig 3 passend
seasonal volgens het seizoen; seizoengevoelig [com]: *~ employment* seizoenarbeid

seasonal affective disorder winterde-pressie
seasoning 1 het kruiden **2** specerij
season's greetings [roughly] Gelukkig Nieuwjaar[h]
season ticket seizoenkaart, abonnement[h]
[1]seat (n) **1** (zit)plaats, stoel: *the back* ~ *of a car* de achterbank van een auto; *have* (or: *take*) *a* ~ neem plaats **2** zitting [of chair]; wc-bril **3** zitvlak[h] **4** zetel [fig]; centrum[h]; haard [of disease, fire]: *a* ~ *of learning* een zetel van wetenschap **5** landgoed[h] **6** zetel, lidmaat-schap[h]: *have a* ~ *on a board* zitting hebben in een commissie **7** kiesdistrict[h]
[2]seat (vb) zetten, doen zitten, zetelen: *be* ~*ed* ga zitten; *be* **deeply** ~*ed* diep ingewor-teld zijn [of feeling, illness etc]
seat belt veiligheidsgordel
seating 1 plaatsing, het geven van een plaats **2** plaatsruimte, zitplaatsen
seawall zeedijk
seaward zeewaarts
seawater zeewater[h]
seaweed 1 zeewier[h] **2** zeegras[h]
seaworthy zeewaardig
sec *second* seconde: *just a* ~ een ogenblikje
secateurs snoeischaar, tuinschaar
secession afscheiding, het afscheiden
secluded afgezonderd, teruggetrokken, stil: *a* ~ *life* een teruggetrokken leven; *a* ~ *house* een afgelegen huis
seclusion afzondering, eenzaamheid, rust
[1]second (n) **1** seconde; [fig] momentje[h]; ogenblikje[h]: *I'll be back in a* ~ ik ben zo terug **2** secondant; getuige [at boxing, duel] **3** (-s) tweede kwaliteitsgoederen, tweede keus (klas) **4** (-s) tweede keer [at meal]: *who would like* ~*s?* wie wil er nog?
[2]second (vb) **1** steunen, bijstaan, meewer-ken **2** ondersteunen, goedkeuren; bijvallen [proposal etc]
[3]second (vb) tijdelijk overplaatsen, detache-ren
[4]second (adv) **1** op één na: ~ *best* op één na de beste **2** ten tweede
[5]second (num) tweede, ander(e); [fig] twee-derangs; minderwaardig: ~ *class* tweede klas [also of mail]; ~ *nature* tweede natuur; *in the* ~ *place* ten tweede, bovendien; *he was* ~ *to none* hij was van niemand de mindere; *every* ~ *day* om de andere dag
secondary 1 secundair, bijkomend, bij-komstig, ondergeschikt: ~ *to* ondergeschikt aan **2** secundair, tweederangs: ~ *to* inferieur aan **3** [school] secundair, middelbaar: ~ *edu-cation* middelbaar onderwijs; ~ *school* mid-delbare school; ~ *modern (school)*, [inform] ~ *mod* middelbare school; [roughly] mavo; ~ *technical school* middelbare technische school
second-class 1 tweedeklas-: ~ *mail* twee-

deklaspost **2** tweederangs, inferieur, min-derwaardig
second-degree tweedegraads-: ~ *burn* tweedegraadsverbranding
second-guess [esp Am] achteraf bekritise-ren
second hand secondewijzer
second-hand 1 tweedehands: *a* ~ *car* een tweedehands auto **2** uit de tweede hand: *a* ~ *report* een verslag uit de tweede hand
secondly ten tweede, op de tweede plaats
secondment detachering: *he's here on* ~ hij is bij ons gedetacheerd
second-rate tweederangs, inferieur, mid-delmatig
secrecy geheimhouding, geheimzinnig-heid
[1]secret (n) geheim[h], mysterie[h], sleutel: *in* ~ in het geheim; *let s.o. into a* ~ iem. in een ge-heim inwijden
[2]secret (adj) **1** geheim, verborgen, vertrou-welijk: *a* ~ *admirer* een stille aanbidder; ~ *ballot* geheime stemming; ~ *service* geheime dienst; *keep sth.* ~ *from s.o.* iets voor iem. ge-heim houden **2** gesloten, discreet **3** verbor-gen, afgezonderd
secretarial van een secretaresse, secretari-aats-
secretariat secretariaat[h]
secretary 1 secretaresse **2** secretaris; secre-taris-generaal [of department]
Secretary minister: ~ *of State* minister
secretary-general secretaris-generaal
secrete 1 verbergen, verstoppen, wegstop-pen: ~ *sth. about one's person* iets op zijn li-chaam verstoppen **2** afscheiden [of organs, glands]
secretion afscheiding(sproduct[h])
secretive geheimzinnig, gesloten, gereser-veerd
secretly 1 in het geheim **2** stiekem
sect sekte, geloofsgemeenschap
[1]sectarian (n) sektariër, lid van een sekte
[2]sectarian (adj) sekte-: *a* ~ *killing* een sekte-moord
section 1 sectie, (onder)deel[h], afdeling, lid[h], stuk[h], segment[h], partje[h], wijk, district[h], stadsdeel[h], landsdeel[h]; baanvak[h] [of railway]: *all* ~*s of the population* alle lagen van de be-volking **2** groep [within society] **3** (onder)af-deling, paragraaf, lid[h], sectie; katern[h] [of newspaper, book] **4** (dwars)doorsnede [also in maths]; profiel[h] **5** een vierkante mijl [640 acres] **6** (chirurgische) snee, incisie, (in)snij-ding, sectie: *c(a)esarean* ~ keizersnede ‖ *in* ~ in profiel
sectional 1 uitneembaar, demonteerbaar: ~ *furniture* aanbouwmeubilair **2** sectioneel, m.b.t. een bepaalde bevolkingsgroep: ~ *in-terests* (tegenstrijdige) groepsbelangen
section mark paragraafteken[h]

sector sector, (bedrijfs)tak, afdeling, terrein[h], branche

secular 1 wereldlijk, niet-kerkelijk: ~ *music* wereldlijke muziek **2** vrijzinnig, niet aan vaste leerstellingen gebonden

secularize verwereldlijken

¹secure (adj) **1** veilig, beschut, beveiligd: ~ *against* (or: *from*) veilig voor **2** veilig, stevig, zeker: *a* ~ *method of payment* een veilige manier van betalen **3** vol vertrouwen

²secure (vb) **1** beveiligen, in veiligheid brengen **2** bemachtigen, zorgen voor: ~ *the biggest **number** of orders* het grootste aantal orders in de wacht slepen **3** stevig vastmaken, vastleggen, afsluiten

security 1 veiligheid(sgevoel[h]) **2** veiligheidsvoorziening, verzekering **3** beveiliging, (openbare) veiligheid: *tight* ~ *is in force* er zijn strenge veiligheidsmaatregelen getroffen **4** obligatie(certificaat[h]), effect[h], aandeel[h] **5** borg [pers]: *be s.o.'s* ~ zich voor iem. borg stellen **6** (waar)borg, onderpand[h]: *give as (a)* ~ in onderpand geven

security check veiligheidscontrole

Security Council Veiligheidsraad [of United Nations]

security forces politietroepen

security prison bewaakte gevangenis: *maximum, minimum* ~ zwaar-, lichtbewaakte gevangenis

security reason veiligheidsoverweging: *for* ~*s* uit veiligheidsoverwegingen

¹sedate (adj) bezadigd, onverstoorbaar, kalm

²sedate (vb) kalmeren, tot rust brengen, een kalmerend middel toedienen aan

¹sedative (n) kalmerend middel[h]

²sedative (adj) kalmerend, pijnstillend

sedentary (stil)zittend: ~ *work* zittend werk; ~ *bird* standvogel

sediment sediment[h], neerslag, bezinksel[h]; afzetting(smateriaal[h]) [by water, wind etc]

sedimentation het neerslaan, afzetting, sedimentatie

sedition ongehoorzaamheid, ordeverstoring

seditious opruiend, oproerig, opstandig

seduce verleiden [also fig]; overhalen: ~ *s.o. into sth.* iem. tot iets overhalen

seducer verleider

seduction verleiding(spoging)

seductive verleidelijk

¹see (n) **1** (aarts)bisdom[h] **2** (aarts)bisschopszetel: *the Holy See* de Heilige Stoel

²see (vb) nadenken, bekijken, zien: *let me* ~ wacht eens, even denken; *we will* ~ *about that* dat zullen we nog wel (eens) zien

³see (vb) **1** voor zich zien, zich voorstellen **2** lezen [newspaper etc]; zien: *have you* ~*n today's papers?* heb je de kranten van vandaag gezien? **3** tegenkomen, ontmoeten: ~ *you (later)!*, *(I'll) be* ~*ing you!* tot ziens!, tot kijk!; ~ *a lot of s.o.* iem. vaak zien **4** ontvangen, spreken met: *Mrs Richards can* ~ *you now* Mevr. Richards kan u nu even ontvangen; *can I* ~ *you for a minute?* kan ik u even spreken? **5** bezoeken, opzoeken, langs gaan bij: ~ *the town* de stad bezichtigen; ~ *over* (or: *round*) *a house* een huis bezichtigen **6** raadplegen, bezoeken: ~ *a doctor* een arts raadplegen **7** meemaken, ervaren, getuige zijn van: *have* ~*n better days* betere tijden gekend hebben **8** begeleiden, (weg)brengen: ~ *a girl home* een meisje naar huis brengen; ~ *s.o. out* iem. uitlaten; *I'll* ~ *you through* ik help je er wel doorheen || ~ *sth. out* (or: *through*) iets tot het einde volhouden

⁴see (vb) **1** zien, kijken (naar), aankijken tegen: *worth* ~*ing* de moeite waard, opmerkelijk; *I cannot* ~ *him doing it* ik zie het hem nog niet doen; *we shall* ~ we zullen wel zien, wie weet; ~ *through s.o. (sth.)* iem. (iets) doorhebben **2** zien, begrijpen, inzien: *I don't* ~ *the fun of doing that* ik zie daar de lol niet van in; *as far as I can* ~ volgens mij; *as I* ~ *it* volgens mij **3** toezien (op), opletten, ervoor zorgen, zorgen voor: ~ *to it that* ervoor zorgen dat

¹seed (n) **1** zaad(je)[h]; kiem [fig]; zaad[h], begin[h]: *go* (or: *run*) *to* ~ uitbloeien, doorschieten; [fig] verlopen, aftakelen **2** korreltje[h], bolletje[h] **3** [sport, esp tennis] geplaatste speler

²seed (vb) zaad vormen, uitbloeien, doorschieten

³seed (vb) **1** zaaien, zaad uitstrooien **2** bezaaien [also fig]; bestrooien **3** [sport, esp tennis] plaatsen

seedbed zaaibed[h] **2** [fig] voedingsbodem

seedless zonder zaad

seedling zaailing

seedsman zaadhandelaar

seedy 1 slonzig, verwaarloosd, vervallen **2** niet lekker, een beetje ziek, slap

seeing aangezien, in aanmerking genomen dat: ~ *(that) there is nothing I can do* aangezien ik niets kan doen

¹seek (vb) (+ after, for) zoeken (naar): ~ *for a solution* een oplossing zoeken

²seek (vb) **1** nastreven, proberen te bereiken, zoeken **2** vragen, wensen, verlangen **3** opzoeken: ~ *s.o. out* naar iem. toekomen, iem. opzoeken **4** proberen (te), trachten (te): ~ *to escape* proberen te ontsnappen

seem (toe)schijnen, lijken, eruitzien: *he* ~*s (to be) the leader* hij schijnt de leider te zijn; *he* ~*s to have done it* het ziet ernaar uit dat hij het gedaan heeft; *it would* ~ *to me that* (or: *as if*) het lijkt mij dat (or: alsof); *he is not satisfied, it would* ~ hij is niet tevreden, naar het schijnt; *it* ~*s to me* mij dunkt

seeming schijnbaar, ogenschijnlijk, onoprecht: *in* ~ *friendship* onder schijn van

vriendschap
seemly correct, fatsoenlijk
seep (weg)sijpelen, lekken, doorsijpelen; [fig] doordringen: *the water ~s into the* ***ground*** het water sijpelt weg in de grond
seer 1 ziener, profeet **2** helderziende
¹**seesaw** (n) wip
²**seesaw** (vb) **1** wippen, op en neer wippen, op de wip spelen **2** schommelen, zigzaggen, veranderlijk zijn: *~ing* ***prices*** schommelende prijzen
seethe koken, zieden, kolken: *he was seething* ***with*** *rage* hij was witheet van woede
see-through [inform] **1** doorzichtig **2** doorkijk-, doorschijnend: *~* ***blouse*** doorkijkbloes
segment deelʰ, segmentʰ, part(je)ʰ
segregate afzonderen, scheiden, rassenscheiding toepassen op
segregation afzondering, scheiding, rassenscheiding, apartheid
seismic seismisch, aardbevings-
seismograph seismograaf
seize 1 grijpen, pakken, nemen: *~ the* ***occasion*** *with both hands* de kans met beide handen aangrijpen; *~d* ***with*** *fear* door angst bevangen **2** in beslag nemen, afnemen **3** bevatten, begrijpen, inzien: *she never seemed to ~ the* ***point*** ze scheen helemaal niet te begrijpen waar het om ging
seize up vastlopen [of machine]; blijven hangen; [fig also] blijven steken; niet verder kunnen
seize (up)on aangrijpen [chance, cause]
seizure 1 confiscatie, inbeslagneming, beslaglegging **2** aanval
seldom zelden, haast nooit: *~ if* ***ever,*** *~ or* ***never*** zelden of nooit
¹**select** (adj) **1** uitgezocht, zorgvuldig gekozen, geselecteerd **2** exclusief
²**select** (vb) een keuze maken
³**select** (vb) (uit)kiezen, uitzoeken, selecteren
selection keuze, selectie, verzameling
selection committee sollicitatiecommissie
selective selectief, uitkiezend
selector 1 lidʰ van selectiecommissie/benoemingscommissie **2** kiezer, keuzeschakelaar
self 1 het zelf, het eigen wezen, het ik **2** persoonlijkheid, karakterʰ: *he is still not quite his* ***old*** *~* hij is nog steeds niet helemaal de oude **3** de eigen persoon, zichzelf, het eigenbelang: *he never thinks of anything* ***but*** *~* hij denkt altijd alleen maar aan zichzelf
-self 1 -zelf: ***oneself*** zichzelf **2** [with emphasis] zelf: *I did it* ***myself*** ik heb het zelf gedaan
self-absorbed in zichzelf verdiept
self-addressed aan zichzelf geadresseerd:

~ ***envelope*** antwoordenvelop
self-appointed opgedrongen, zichzelf ongevraagd opwerpend (als): *a ~* ***critic*** *iem.* die zich een oordeel aanmatigt
self-assured zelfverzekerd, vol zelfvertrouwen
self-awareness zelfbewustzijnʰ
self-build doe-het-zelfbouw
self-catering zelf voor eten zorgend, maaltijden niet inbegrepen
self-centred egocentrisch, zelfzuchtig
self-confidence zelfvertrouwenʰ, zelfverzekerdheid
self-confident zelfverzekerd
self-conscious 1 bewust, zich van zichzelf bewust **2** verlegen, niet op zijn gemak
self-contained 1 onafhankelijk **2** vrij; met eigen keuken en badkamer [apartment]
self-contradictory tegenstrijdig
self-control zelfbeheersing
self-defeating zichzelf hinderend, zijn doel voorbijstrevend
self-defence zelfverdediging: *in ~* uit zelfverdediging
self-denial zelfopoffering, zelfverloochening
self-destruct zichzelf vernietigen
self-determination zelfbeschikking(srechtʰ)
self-doubt onzekerheid
self-educated autodidactisch: *a ~* ***man*** een autodidact
self-effacing bescheiden
self-employed zelfstandig, met een eigen onderneming, eigen baas
self-esteem gevoelʰ van eigenwaarde, trots
self-evident vanzelfsprekend
self-explanatory duidelijk, onmiskenbaar, wat voor zichzelf spreekt
self-fulfilling zichzelf vervullend: *a ~* ***prophecy*** een zichzelf vervullende voorspelling
self-governing autonoom
self-harm zichzelf verwonden
self-help zelfhulp
self-importance gewichtigheid, eigendunk
self-imposed (aan) zichzelf opgelegd
self-indulgence genotzucht
self-inflicted zelf veroorzaakt
self-interest eigenbelangʰ
selfish zelfzuchtig, egoïstisch
selfless onbaatzuchtig, onzelfzuchtig
self-made 1 zelfgemaakt **2** opgewerkt, opgeklommen: *a ~* ***man*** een man die alles op eigen kracht bereikt heeft
self-pity zelfmedelijdenʰ
self-preservation zelfbehoudʰ
self-raising zelfrijzend
self-reliant onafhankelijk, zelfstandig

self-respecting zichzelf respecterend
self-righteous vol eigendunk, intolerant
self-righting zichzelf oprichtend [after capsizing]
self-sacrifice zelfopoffering
selfsame precies dezelfde (hetzelfde), identiek
self-satisfaction eigendunk
self-satisfied zelfvoldaan
self-service zelfbediening: ~ *restaurant* zelfbedieningsrestaurant
self-serving uit eigenbelang
self-starter zelfstarter
self-styled zogenaamd, zichzelf noemend: ~ *professor* iem. die zich voor professor uitgeeft
self-sufficient onafhankelijk
self-supporting zelfstandig
self-taught 1 zelf geleerd, zichzelf aangeleerd **2** autodidactisch, zichzelf opgeleid
self-willed eigenwijs
¹sell (n) bedrogʰ, verlakkerij, zwendel
²sell (vb) **1** verkocht worden, verkopen, kosten, in de handel zijn **2** handel drijven, verkopen ‖ ~ *up* zijn zaak sluiten
³sell (vb) **1** verkopen, in voorraad hebben, handelen in, verkwanselen: ~ *off* uitverkopen; ~ *at five pounds* (or: *at a loss*) voor vijf pond (or: met verlies) verkopen **2** aanprijzen: ~ *o.s.* zichzelf goed verkopen **3** overhalen, warm maken voor, aanpraten: *be sold on sth.* ergens helemaal weg van zijn **4** misleiden, bedriegen, bezwendelen ‖ ~ *s.o. short* iem. tekortdoen
sell-by date uiterste verkoopdatum
seller 1 verkoper **2** succesʰ, artikelʰ dat goed verkoopt
selling point [com] verkoopargumentʰ, voordeelʰ, aanbeveling
selling price verkoopprijs
sellotape plakbandʰ
sell out 1 door de voorraad heen raken **2** verkocht worden, uitverkocht raken **3** zijn aandeel in een zaak verkopen **4** verraad plegen: ~ *to the enemy* samenwerken met de vijand
sell-out 1 volle zaal, uitverkochte voorstelling **2** verraadʰ
semblance 1 schijn, uiterlijkʰ, vorm: *put on a* ~ *of enthousiasm* geestdriftig doen **2** gelijkenis **3** afbeelding, beeldʰ, kopie ‖ *without a* ~ *of guilt* zonder ook maar een zweem van schuldgevoel
semen spermaʰ, zaadʰ
semester semesterʰ [university]
semicircle 1 halve cirkel **2** halve kring
semicircular halfrond
semicolon puntkomma
semiconductor halfgeleider
semi-conscious halfbewust
¹semi-detached (n) halfvrijstaand huisʰ,

huisʰ van twee onder een kap
²semi-detached (adj) halfvrijstaand
semi-final halve finale
seminal 1 sperma-; zaad- **2** embryonaal; [fig also] in wording **3** vruchtbaar [fig]: *a* ~ *mind* een oorspronkelijke geest
seminar 1 werkgroep, cursus **2** congresʰ
seminary seminarieʰ, kweekschool voor priesters
semi-skimmed halfvolle melk
Semite Semiet
Semitic Semitisch
senate 1 senaat, Amerikaanse Senaat **2** senaat, universitaire bestuursraad
senator senator, senaatslidʰ, lidʰ van de Amerikaanse Senaat
¹send (vb) bericht sturen, laten weten: *I sent to warn her* ik heb haar laten waarschuwen
²send (vb) **1** (ver)sturen, (ver)zenden **2** sturen, zenden; (doen) overbrengen [by extension]; dwingen tot: ~ *to bed* naar bed sturen; *she ~s her love* je moet de groeten van haar hebben; ~ *ahead* vooruit sturen; ~ *in* **a)** inzenden, insturen [for evaluation]; **b)** indienen **3** teweegbrengen, veroorzaken: *the news sent us into deep distress* het nieuws bracht diepe droefenis bij ons teweeg **4** maken, doen worden: *this rattle ~s me crazy* ik word gek van dat geratel **5** opwinden, meeslepen: *this music really ~s me* ik vind die muziek helemaal te gek ‖ ~ *packing* de laan uit sturen, afschepen
³send (vb) (uit)zenden: ~ *s.o. after her* stuur iem. achter haar aan; ~ *s.o. off the field* iem. uit het veld sturen
send down 1 naar beneden sturen; doen dalen [prices, temperature] **2** verwijderen (wegens wangedrag) [from university] **3** opsluiten [in prison]
sender afzender, verzender: *return to* ~ retour afzender
send for 1 (schriftelijk) bestellen **2** (laten) waarschuwen, laten komen: ~ *help* hulp laten halen
¹send off (vb) een bestelbon opsturen: ~ *for* schriftelijk bestellen
²send off (vb) **1** versturen, op de post doen **2** op pad sturen, de deur uit laten gaan **3** wegsturen; [sport] uit het veld sturen
send-off uitgeleideʰ, afscheidʰ, het uitzwaaien: *give s.o. a* ~ iem. uitzwaaien
send on 1 vooruitsturen, (alvast) doorsturen **2** doorsturen [mail]
send out 1 weg sturen, eruit sturen **2** uitstralen, afgeven; uitzenden [signal]
send up 1 opdrijven, omhoogstuwen, doen stijgen: ~ *prices* de prijzen opdrijven **2** parodiëren, de draak steken met **3** opsluiten [in prison]
send-up parodie, persiflage
Senegal Senegal

¹Senegalese (n) Senegalees, Senegalese
²Senegalese (adj) Senegalees
senile 1 ouderdoms- **2** seniel, afgetakeld
senility seniliteit
¹senior (n) **1** oudere, iem. met meer dienstjaren: *she is four **years** my ~, she is my ~ **by** four
years* ze is vier jaar ouder dan ik **2** oudgediende, senior **3** laatstejaars **4** oudere leerling
²senior (adj) **1** oud, op leeftijd, bejaard,
oudst(e): *a ~ **citizen*** een 65-plusser, een bejaarde **2** hooggeplaatst, hoofd-: *a ~ **position***
een leidinggevende positie **3** hoger geplaatst, ouder in dienstjaren **4** hoogst in
rang **5** laatstejaars **6** ouderejaars **7** senior:
Jack Jones Senior Jack Jones senior || ~ **service**
marine
senior high (school) laatste vier jaar van
de middelbare school
seniority 1 (hogere) leeftijd **2** anciënniteit, aantal dienstjaren, voorrang op grond
van dienstjaren (leeftijd): *their names were
listed in the **order** of ~* hun namen waren gerangschikt op volgorde van het aantal
dienstjaren
senior school middelbare school [for children of 14-17 years old]
sensation 1 gevoelʰ, (zintuiglijke) gewaarwording, sensatie, beroering:
cause (or: *create*) *a ~* voor grote opschudding zorgen
sensational 1 sensationeel, opzienbarend,
te gek, fantastisch **2** sensatie-, sensatiebelust
¹sense (n) **1** bedoeling, strekking **2** betekenis, zin: *in a ~* in zekere zin **3** (vaag) gevoelʰ,
begripʰ, (instinctief) besefʰ: *~ of **duty*** plichtsbesef, plichtsgevoel; *~ of **humour*** gevoel
voor humor **4** (zintuiglijk) vermogenʰ, zin,
zintuigʰ: *~ of **smell*** reuk(zinvermogen)
5 (gezond) verstandʰ, benulʰ: *there was a **lot**
of ~ in her words* er stak heel wat zinnigs in
haar woorden **6** zin, nutʰ: *what's the ~?* wat
heeft het voor zin? **7** (groeps)mening, (algemene) stemming **8** (-s) positieven, gezond
verstandʰ: *bring s.o. to his ~s* **a)** iem. tot bezinning brengen; **b)** iem. weer bij bewustzijn
brengen || *make ~* **a)** zinnig zijn; **b)** ergens op
slaan, steekhoudend zijn; *it just doesn't **make**
~* het klopt gewoon niet, het slaat gewoon
nergens op; *make ~ of sth.* ergens uit wijs
kunnen (worden); *talk ~* verstandig praten
²sense (vb) **1** (zintuiglijk) waarnemen, gewaar worden **2** zich (vaag) bewust zijn, voelen **3** begrijpen, door hebben: *at last he was
beginning to ~ what the trouble was* eindelijk
begon hij door te krijgen wat het probleem
was
senseless 1 bewusteloos **2** gevoelloos
3 onzinnig, idioot
sense-organ zintuigʰ
sensibility 1 (over)gevoeligheid [for im-

pressions, art]: *offend s.o.'s sensibilities* iemands gevoelens kwetsen **2** lichtgeraakt-
heid **3** gevoelʰ, gevoeligheid, waarnemings-
vermogenʰ, bewustzijnʰ; erkenning [of
problem]
sensible 1 verstandig, zinnig **2** praktisch;
functioneel [of clothes etc] **3** merkbaar,
waarneembaar **4** (+ to) gevoelig (voor), ontvankelijk (voor)
sensitive 1 gevoelig, ontvankelijk **2** precies; gevoelig [of instrument] **3** (fijn)gevoe-
lig, smaakvol **4** lichtgeraakt **5** [photo]
(licht)gevoelig **6** gevoelig, geheim: *~ **post***
vertrouwenspost || *~ **plant** a)* gevoelige
plant; **b)** kruidje-roer-mij-niet
sensitivity 1 gevoeligheid **2** (fijn)gevoe-
ligheid, smaak
sensor aftaster, sensor, verklikker
sensory zintuiglijk
sensual sensueel, zinnelijk, wellustig
sensualism genotzucht, wellust
sensuous 1 zinnelijk, zintuiglijk **2** aangenaam, behaaglijk: *with ~ **pleasure*** vol behagen, behaaglijk
¹sentence (n) **1** (vol)zin: *complex* (or: *compound*) ~ samengestelde zin **2** vonnisʰ, von-
nissing, (rechterlijke) uitspraak, veroordeling, straf: *under ~ of death* ter dood veroordeeld
²sentence (vb) veroordelen, vonnissen: *be
~d to **pay** a fine* veroordeeld worden tot een
geldboete
sententious moraliserend, prekerig
sentient (+ of) bewust (van)
sentiment 1 gevoelʰ, mening, opvatting:
*(those are) **my** ~s exactly* zo denk ik er ook
over, precies wat ik zou zeggen **2** (geluk)-
wens **3** gevoelʰ, gevoelens; stemming [also
on Stock Exchange, market]; emotie, voorkeur: *be **swayed** by ~* zich laten leiden door
zijn gevoel
sentimental sentimenteel, (over)gevoelig:
*~ **value*** gevoelswaarde
sentimentality sentimentaliteit
sentry schildwacht: *stand* (or: *keep*) ~ op
wacht staan
sepal blaadje van een bloemkelk
separable (af)scheidbaar, verdeelbaar: *in
his poems form is not ~ **from** content* in zijn
gedichten is de vorm niet los te zien van de
inhoud
¹separate (adj) afzonderlijk, (af)gescheiden,
apart, verschillend, alleenstaand: *~ **ownership*** particulier eigendom(srecht); *keep ~
from* afgezonderd houden van
²separate (vb) **1** zich (van elkaar) afscheiden, zich afzonderen, zich verdelen, uiteenvallen: *~ **from*** zich afscheiden van **2** scheiden, uit elkaar gaan
³separate (vb) afzonderen, losmaken, verdelen: *legally ~d* gescheiden van tafel en

bed; **widely** ~d ver uit elkaar gelegen
separates afzonderlijk combineerbare kle-
dingstukken
separation (af)scheiding, afzondering, af-
scheuring, verschil^h, onderscheid^h, het uiteengaan, vertrek^h, (tussen)ruimte, afstand:
judicial (or: **legal**) ~ scheiding van tafel en
bed
separation allowance alimentatie
separatist separatist, iem. die zich af-
scheidt; [pol] autonomist; nationalist
sepia sepia
September september
septic 1 (ver)rottings-: ~ **matter** etter
2 ontstoken, geïnfecteerd
sepulchral graf-, begrafenis-; [fig] somber;
akelig: in a ~ **voice** met een grafstem
sepulchre graf^h, graftombe
sequel 1 gevolg^h, resultaat^h, afloop: as a ~
to als gevolg van **2** vervolg^h [to a book];
voortzetting
sequence 1 reeks [poems, plays]; opeenvolging, rij, volgorde: the ~ of **events** de loop
der gebeurtenissen; **in** ~ op volgorde, de een
na de ander **2** episode, fragment^h, (onder)-
deel^h, (film)opname, scène
sequester 1 afzonderen, verborgen houden **2** in bewaring stellen, beslag leggen op
seraglio harem
^1**Serb** (n) Serviër, Servische
^2**Serb** (adj) Servisch
Serbia Servië
^1**Serbian** (n) Serviër, Servische
^2**Serbian** (adj) Servisch
serenade serenade(muziek)
serene sereen, helder: a ~ summer **night** een
kalme zomeravond
serenity helderheid, kalmte, rust
serf lijfeigene, slaaf
serfdom lijfeigenschap^h, slavernij
sergeant 1 sergeant, wachtmeester **2** brigadier (van politie)
^1**serial** (n) **1** feuilleton^h, vervolgverhaal^h, (televisie)serie **2** seriepublicatie
^2**serial** (adj) serieel, in serie, opeenvolgend: ~
number volgnummer, serienummer
serialize 1 als feuilleton publiceren
2 rangschikken, ordenen in reeksen
serial killer seriemoordenaar
series 1 reeks, serie, rij, verzameling,
groep: **arithmetical** ~ rekenkundige reeks
2 [elec] serie(schakeling): **in** ~ in serie (geschakeld)
serious 1 ernstig, serieus: ~ **damage** aan-
zienlijke schade; after ~ **thought** na rijp beraad **2** oprecht, gemeend
seriously 1 ernstig, serieus, belangrijk,
aanzienlijk: ~ **ill** ernstig ziek **2** echt, heus,
zonder gekheid: but ~, are you really thinking
of moving? maar serieus, ben je echt van plan
te verhuizen?

seriousness ernst: in all ~ in alle ernst,
zonder gekheid
sermon preek [also fig]; vermaning: Sermon
on the **Mount** Bergrede
seropositive seropositief
serotonin serotonine^h
serpent 1 slang, serpent^h **2** onderkruiper
serpentine 1 slangachtig, slangen- **2** kronkelig
serrated zaagvormig, getand, gezaagd: a ~
knife een kartelmes
serum serum^h
servant 1 dienaar, bediende, (huis)knecht,
dienstbode **2** (-s) personeel^h
^1**serve** (vb) **1** dienen, voorzien in, volstaan,
vervullen: ~ a **purpose** een bepaald doel dienen; ~ the **purpose** of dienstdoen als **2** behandelen, bejegenen: that ~s him **right!** dat is
zijn verdiende loon!, net goed! **3** ondergaan, vervullen, (uit)zitten: he ~d ten **years** in
prison hij heeft tien jaar in de gevangenis gezeten **4** dagvaarden, betekenen: ~ a **writ** on
s.o., ~ s.o. **with** a writ iem. dagvaarden
^2**serve** (vb) **1** dienen (bij), in dienst zijn van:
[fig] ~ two **masters** twee heren dienen **2** serveren, opdienen: ~ **dinner** het eten opdienen; ~ **at** table bedienen, opdienen **3** dienen,
dienstdoen, helpen, baten: that **excuse** ~d
him well dat smoesje is hem goed van pas gekomen; are you being ~d? wordt u al geholpen? **4** [sport] serveren, opslaan
serve out 1 verdelen, ronddelen **2** uitdie-
nen, uitzitten
server 1 ober, kelner, serveerster **2** opscheplepel **3** dienblad^h **4** [comp] server
servery 1 buffet^h [in self-service restau-
rant] **2** doorgeefluik^h [between kitchen and
dining room]
^1**service** (n) **1** dienst, (overheids)instelling,
bedrijf^h: **secret** ~ geheime dienst **2** krijgs-
machtonderdeel^h [army, navy or airforce]: **on**
(active) ~ in actieve dienst **3** hulp, bijstand,
dienst(verlening): **do** s.o. a ~ iem. een dienst
bewijzen **4** (kerk)dienst **5** verbinding; dienst
[by bus, train or boat] **6** onderhoudsbeurt,
onderhoud^h, service **7** servies^h **8** nutsbedrijf^h
9 [sport] opslag, service(beurt) **10** gasleiding, waterleiding [in house]; huisaanslui-
ting **11** dienstbaarheid, dienst, het dienen,
het dienstbaar zijn: **in** ~ in dienst [eg of bus
or train] **12** nut^h, dienst: **at** your ~ tot uw
dienst **13** bediening, service
^2**service** (vb) **1** onderhouden, een (onder-
houds)beurt geven **2** (be)dienen, voorzien
van
serviceable 1 nuttig, bruikbaar, handig
2 sterk, stevig, duurzaam
service area wegrestaurant^h [with filling
station]
service charge 1 bedieningsgeld^h **2** administratiekosten

service flat verzorgingsflat
serviceman militair, soldaat
service provider 1 dienstverlener
2 [comp] provider
service road ventweg, parallelweg
services wegrestaurant[h] (met benzinestation)
service station 1 benzinestation[h], pompstation[h] **2** wegrestaurant[h]
serviette servet(je)[h], vingerdoekje[h]
servile slaafs, onderdanig, kruiperig: ~ *imitation* slaafse navolging
servility slaafsheid, kruiperige houding
serving portie: *three ~s of ice-cream* drie porties ijs
servitude slavernij, onderworpenheid
sesame sesam(kruid[h]), sesamzaad[h] ‖ *Open ~!* Sesam, open u!
session 1 zitting [court of law, administration, committee]; vergadering, sessie: *secret ~* geheime zitting **2** zittingsperiode, zittingstijd **3** academiejaar[h], semester[h], halfjaar[h] **4** schooltijd **5** bijeenkomst, partij, vergadering **6** (opname)sessie: *recording ~* opnamesessie (in studio)
¹set (n) **1** stel[h], span[h], servies[h]; set [pots, pans etc]; reeks: *~ of (false)* **teeth** een (vals) gebit **2** kring, gezelschap[h], groep, kliek: *the jet ~* de elite; *the* **smart** *~* de chic, de hogere standen (*or:* kringen) **3** toestel[h], radiotoestel[h], tv-toestel[h] **4** stek, loot, jonge plant **5** set, spel[h], partij **6** [maths] verzameling **7** vorm; houding [of head]; ligging [of hills]: *the ~ of her* **head** de houding van haar hoofd **8** toneelopbouw, scène, (film)decor[h]; [by extension] studiohal; set: *on (the) ~* op de set, bij de (film)opname
²set (adj) **1** vast, bepaald, vastgesteld, stereotiep, routine-, onveranderlijk: *~* **phrase** stereotiepe uitdrukking; *~* **purpose** vast vooropgesteld doel **2** voorgeschreven; opgelegd [book, subject] **3** strak, onbeweeglijk; stijf [face]; koppig, hardnekkig: *~ in one's ways* met vaste gewoonten; *~* **fair** a) bestendig [weather]; **b)** prettig, goed [prospect] **4** klaar, gereed: *get ~, ready, steady, go* op uw plaatsen, klaar voor de start, af; *be all ~ for* sth. (*or:* **to do** *sth.*) helemaal klaar zijn voor iets (*or:* om iets te doen) **5** volledig en tegen vaste prijs [meal in restaurant]: *~* **dinner** dagschotel, dagmenu **6** geplaatst, gevestigd: *eyes ~ deep in the head* diepliggende ogen **7** vastbesloten: *her mind is ~ on pleasure* ze wil alleen plezier maken ‖ *~* **square** tekendriehoek
³set (vb) **1** vast worden; stijf worden [of cement, jelly]; verharden, stollen, een vaste vorm aannemen; bestendig worden [of weather] **2** ondergaan [of sun, moon]: *the sun had nearly ~* de zon was bijna onder **3** aan elkaar groeien [of broken leg]

⁴set (vb) **1** zetten, plaatsen, stellen, leggen, doen zitten: *~ a* **trap** een val zetten; *~* **free** vrijlaten, bevrijden; *~ pen* **to** *paper* beginnen te schrijven **2** gelijkzetten [clock, timepiece] **3** opleggen, opdragen, opgeven; geven [example]; stellen, opstellen; (samen)stellen [questions etc]: *~ s.o. a good* **example** iem. het goede voorbeeld geven; *~ s.o. a* **task** iem. een taak opleggen; *~* **to** *work* zich aan het werk zetten, beginnen te werken **4** bepalen [date]; voorschrijven; aangeven [size, pace, tone]; vaststellen: *~ the* **fashion** de mode bepalen; *~ a* **price** *on* sth. de prijs van iets bepalen **5** brengen, aanleiding geven tot, veroorzaken: *that ~ me* **thinking** dat bracht me aan het denken **6** stijf doen worden [cement, jelly etc] **7** instellen [camera, lens, appliance] **8** dekken [table]: *~ the* **table** de tafel dekken **9** zetten [letters, text] **10** uitzetten [watch, nets]; posteren: *~ a* **watch** een schildwacht uitzetten **11** zetten [broken leg]; bij elkaar voegen, samenvoegen **12** op muziek zetten [text]: *~* **to** *music* op muziek zetten **13** situeren [story, play]: *the novel is ~ in the* **year** *2020* de roman speelt zich af in het jaar 2020 **14** vestigen [record]: *~ a new* **record** een nieuw record vestigen ‖ *~* **(up)on** *s.o.* iem. aanvallen; **against** *that fact you must ~ that …* daartegenover moet je stellen dat …; *~ s.o.* **against** *s.o.* iem. opzetten tegen iem.; *~ s.o.* **beside** *s.o. else* iem. met iem. anders vergelijken
set about 1 beginnen (met/aan), aanpakken: *the next day they ~* **cleaning** *the house* de dag daarop begonnen ze met het schoonmaken van het huis **2** aanvallen
set apart terzijde leggen, reserveren
set aside 1 terzijde zetten, reserveren; sparen [money]: *~* **for** reserveren voor **2** buiten beschouwing laten, geen aandacht schenken aan: *setting aside the* **details** afgezien van de details
setback 1 inzinking **2** tegenslag, nederlaag
set back terugzetten, achteruitzetten: *the accident has set us back by about four weeks* door het ongeluk zijn we ongeveer vier weken achter (op schema) geraakt
set down 1 neerzetten **2** afzetten; laten afstappen [from vehicle] **3** neerschrijven, opschrijven
set in intreden [season, reaction]; invallen [darkness, thaw]; beginnen: *rain has ~* het is gaan regenen
¹set off (vb) zich op weg begeven, vertrekken: *~ in pursuit of* in de achtervolging inzetten
²set off (vb) **1** versieren **2** doen uitkomen [colours]: *she wore a dress that ~ her complexion quite* **well** ze droeg een jurk die haar teint goed deed uitkomen **3** doen ontbranden; tot ontploffing brengen [bomb] **4** doen op-

wegen, goedmaken: ~ *against* doen opwegen tegen **5** doen [laugh, talk]; stimuleren:
set s.o. off laughing iem. aan het lachen
brengen **6** afzetten, afpassen: *a small area
was ~ for the smokers* er was een kleine ruimte afgezet voor de rokers
set on ertoe brengen, aansporen
¹**set out** (vb) **1** zich op weg begeven, vertrekken: ~ *for Paris* vertrekken met bestemming Parijs **2** zich voornemen, het plan opvatten
²**set out** (vb) **1** uitzetten, klaarzetten; opzetten [chessmen]: *if you ~ the white pieces, I'll
do the black ones* als jij de witte stukken opzet, doe ik de zwarte **2** tentoonstellen; uitstallen [goods] **3** verklaren, uiteenzetten
set point setpuntʰ
set square tekendriehoek
sett 1 (dassen)burcht **2** vierkante straatkei
setting 1 ondergang [sun, moon] **2** stand;
instelling [of instrument, machine] **3** omlijsting, achtergrond: *the story has its ~ in Sydney*
het verhaal speelt zich af in Sydney **4** mon-
tering; aankleding [film, play]
settings instellingen; *see setting*
¹**settle** (vb) **1** gaan zitten, zich neerzetten,
neerstrijken: ~ *back in a chair* gemakkelijk
gaan zitten in een stoel **2** neerslaan; bezinken [of dust, dregs] **3** zich vestigen, gaan
wonen ‖ ~ *in* a) zich installeren [in house];
b) zich inwerken; ~ *for sth.* genoegen nemen
met iets; ~ *(down) to sth.* zich ergens op concentreren, zich ergens toe zetten
²**settle** (vb) **1** regelen, in orde brengen
2 vestigen [in place of residence, society]
3 koloniseren: *their forefathers ~d the land in
1716* hun voorvaderen koloniseerden het
land in 1716 **4** zetten, plaatsen, leggen: *she
~d herself in the chair* zij nestelde zich in haar
stoel **5** (voorgoed) beëindigen; beslissen [ar-
gument, doubts]; de doorslag geven: *that ~s
it!* dat doet de deur dicht!, dat geeft de
doorslag!; *let's ~ this once and for all* laten we
dit nu eens en altijd regelen **6** schikken, bijleggen, tot een schikking komen ‖ ~ *into* zich
thuis doen voelen in; ~ *on* vastzetten op
³**settle** (vb) **1** kalmeren, (doen) bedaren
2 opklaren [liquid]; helderder worden (maken) **3** (+ (up)on) overeenkomen (m.b.t.),
een besluit nemen, afspreken: ~ *(up)on a
date* een datum vaststellen **4** betalen [eg
bill]; voldoen, vereffenen: ~ *a claim* schade
uitbetalen; ~ *up* verrekenen [among each
other]; ~ *(an account, old score) with s.o.* het
iem. betaald zetten
settled vast, onwrikbaar; gevestigd [opin-
ion]; bestendig [weather]; onveranderlijk
¹**settle down** (vb) **1** een vaste betrekking
aannemen, zich vestigen **2** wennen, zich
thuis gaan voelen, ingewerkt raken **3** (+ to)
zich concentreren (op), zich toeleggen (op):

he finally settled down to his studies eindelijk
ging hij zich toeleggen op zijn studie **4** vast
worden [of weather]
²**settle down** (vb) kalmeren, tot rust komen
(brengen)
settlement 1 nederzetting, kolonie,
groepje kolonisten, plaatsjeʰ **2** kolonisatie
3 schikking, overeenkomst **4** afrekening: *in
~ of* ter vereffening van
settler kolonist
set-to 1 vechtpartij **2** ruzie: *there was a bit of
a ~ outside the pub* er ontstond ruzie buiten
de kroeg
¹**set up** (vb) zich vestigen: ~ *as a dentist* zich
als tandarts vestigen
²**set up** (vb) **1** opzetten [eg tent]; opstellen,
monteren, stichten; oprichten [school]; beginnen; aanstellen [committee]; opstellen
[rules]; organiseren **2** aanheffen; verheffen
[voice] **3** veroorzaken **4** er bovenop helpen,
op de been helpen **5** vestigen: *set s.o. up in
business* iem. in een zaak zetten **6** beramen
[hold-up] **7** belazeren, de schuld in de
schoenen schuiven
set-up 1 opstelling [at film shooting] **2** opbouw, organisatie
seven zeven
sevenfold 1 zevenvoudig **2** zevendelig
seven-league: ~ *boots* zevenmijlslaarzen
seventeen zeventien
seventeenth zeventiende
seventh zevende
seventieth zeventigste
seventy zeventig: *he is in his seventies* hij is
in de zeventig
¹**sever** (vb) **1** breken, het begeven, losgaan
2 uiteen gaan, scheiden
²**sever** (vb) **1** afbreken: ~ *the rope* het touw
doorsnijden **2** (af)scheiden: ~ *o.s. from* zich
afscheiden van **3** verbreken [relationship
etc]
several 1 verscheidene, enkele, een aantal
(ervan): *she has written ~ books* ze heeft verscheidene boeken geschreven; ~ *of my friends*
verscheidene van mijn vrienden **2** apart(e),
respectievelijk(e), verschillend(e): *after their
studies the students went their ~ ways* na hun
studie gingen de studenten elk hun eigen
weg
severally 1 afzonderlijk, hoofdelijk: *the
partners are ~ liable* de vennoten zijn hoofdelijk aansprakelijk **2** elk voor zich, respectievelijk
severance 1 verbreking; opzegging [of re-
lations] **2** scheiding, (ver)deling **3** ontslagʰ,
verbreking van arbeidscontract
severe 1 streng, strikt **2** hevig, bar: ~ *conditions* barre omstandigheden **3** zwaar,
moeilijk, ernstig: ~ *requirements* zware eisen
‖ *leave* (or: *let*) *sth. ~ly alone* ergens z'n handen niet aan willen vuilmaken

severity 1 strengheid, hardheid **2** hevigheid, barheid **3** soberheid, strakheid

sew naaien; hechten [wound]

sewage afvalwater[h], rioolwater[h]: *raw* ~ ongezuiverd afvalwater

sewage works rioolzuiveringsinstallatie

¹sewer (n) riool(buis)

²sewer (n) naaister

sewerage 1 riolering, rioolstelsel[h] **2** (afval)waterafvoer

sewing naaiwerk[h]

sewing machine naaimachine

sew up 1 dichtnaaien, hechten **2** succesvol afsluiten, beklinken, regelen

¹sex (n) **1** geslacht[h], sekse: *the second* ~ de tweede sekse, de vrouw(en) **2** seks, erotiek **3** seksuele omgang, geslachtsgemeenschap: *have* ~ *with s.o.* met iem. naar bed gaan, vrijen

²sex (vb) seksen, het geslacht vaststellen van

¹sexagenarian (n) zestigjarige, zestiger

²sexagenarian (adj) zestigjarig

sexism seksisme[h], ongelijke behandeling in verband met sekse

¹sexist (n) seksist

²sexist (adj) seksistisch

sexless 1 onzijdig, geslachtloos **2** niet opwindend

sex life seksleven[h]

sex object 1 seksobject[h], lustobject[h] **2** sekssymbool[h]

sex offender zedendelinquent

sextant sextant [navigation instrument]

sexual 1 seksueel, geslachts-: ~ *harassment* ongewenste intimiteiten [at work]; ~ *intercourse* geslachtsgemeenschap **2** geslachtelijk, m.b.t. het geslacht

sexuality seksualiteit

sex up [inform] **1** [sth.] opleuken, oppimpen **2** [s.o.] opgeilen

sexy sexy, opwindend

sf *sciencefiction* sf

Sgt *sergeant*

sh sst

shabby 1 versleten, af(gedragen), kaal **2** sjofel, armoedig **3** min, gemeen: *what a* ~ *way* to treat an old friend! wat een laag-bij-de-grondse manier om een oude vriend te behandelen!

shack 1 hut **2** hok[h], keet, schuurtje[h]

shacked up [inform] [roughly] samenwonend: *to be* ~ het bed delen

¹shackle (n) **1** (hand)boei, keten, kluister **2** (-s) belemmering **3** schakel, sluiting

²shackle (vb) **1** boeien, ketenen **2** koppelen, vastmaken **3** belemmeren, hinderen || *be* ~*d with sth.* met iets opgezadeld zitten

shack up hokken, samenwonen, samenleven: ~ *together* (samen)hokken, samenwonen

¹shade (n) **1** schaduw, lommer[h]: *put* s.o. (sth.)

in the ~ iem. (iets) overtreffen **2** schaduwplek(je[h]) **3** schakering, nuance: ~*s of meaning* (betekenis)nuances **4** (zonne)scherm[h], (lampen)kap, zonneklep **5** schim, geest, spook[h] **6** tikkeltje[h], ietsje[h], beetje[h] **7** (rol)-gordijn[h] **8** (-s) duisternis, schemerduister[h] **9** (-s) zonnebril

²shade (vb) **1** beschermen, beschutten; [fig] in de schaduw stellen: ~ *one's eyes* zijn hand boven de ogen houden **2** afschermen [light]; dimmen **3** arceren, schaduw aanbrengen in

³shade (vb) geleidelijk veranderen, (doen) overgaan || ~ *away* (or: *off*) geleidelijk aan (laten) verdwijnen

shading arcering

¹shadow (n) **1** schaduw, duister[h], duisternis, schemerduister[h] **2** schaduw(beeld[h]) [also fig]; silhouet[h]: *afraid* of one's own ~ zo bang als een wezel; *cast* a ~ *on sth.* een schaduw werpen op iets [also fig] **3** schaduwplek, schaduwhoek, arcering; schaduw [in painting] **4** iem. die schaduwt, spion, detective || *he is the* ~ *of his former self* hij is bij lange na niet meer wat hij geweest is; *without the* ~ *of a doubt* zonder ook maar de geringste twijfel

²shadow (vb) schaduwen; volgen [by detective]

shadow-boxing het schaduwboksen

shadow cabinet schaduwkabinet[h]

shadowy 1 onduidelijk, vaag, schimmig **2** schaduwrijk, in schaduw gehuld

shady 1 schaduwrijk **2** onbetrouwbaar, verdacht, louche

¹shaft (n) **1** schacht [of arrow, spear] **2** steel, stok **3** lichtstraal, lichtbundel, bliksemstraal, lichtflits **4** koker; schacht [lift, mine] **5** (drijf)as || *get the* ~ te grazen genomen worden

²shaft (vb) te grazen nemen, belazeren

¹shag (n) **1** warboel, kluwen **2** shag **3** [inform] wip, seks

²shag (vb) [inform] neuken; naaien, wippen

shagged (out) bekaf, uitgeteld

shaggy 1 harig, ruigbehaard **2** ruig, wild, woest

shah sjah

¹shake (n) **1** het schudden, handdruk: *he said no with a* ~ *of the head* hij schudde (van) nee **2** milkshake **3** ogenblikje[h], momentje[h]: *in two* ~*s* (of a lamb's tail) zo, direct, in een seconde

²shake (vb) **1** schudden, schokken, beven, (t)rillen: ~ *with* laughter schudden van het lachen **2** wankelen **3** de hand geven: ~ *(on it)!* geef me de vijf!, hand erop!

³shake (vb) **1** doen schudden, schokken, doen beven **2** (uit)schudden, zwaaien, heen en weer schudden: ~ *dice* dobbelstenen schudden; ~ *off* a) (van zich) afschudden; b) [also fig] ontsnappen aan; ~ *before use* (or:

using) schudden voor gebruik **3** geven; schudden [hand] **4** schokken, verontrusten, overstuur maken: *mother was tremendously ~n by Paul's death* moeder was enorm getroffen door de dood van Paul **5** aan het wankelen brengen [fig]; verzwakken, verminderen: *these stories have ~n the firm's credit* deze verhalen hebben de firma in diskrediet gebracht

shakedown afpersing, geld-uit-de-zak-klopperij

¹shake down (vb) **1** gewend raken, ingewerkt raken **2** goed gaan lopen, werken, goed afgesteld zijn

²shake down (vb) **1** (af)schudden, uitschudden **2** (op de grond) uitspreiden **3** afpersen, geld uit de zak kloppen

shake up 1 (door elkaar) schudden; hutselen **2** wakker schudden; opschrikken; overstuur raken **3** reorganiseren, orde op zaken stellen in

shake-up radicale reorganisatie ‖ *they need a thorough ~* ze moeten eens flink wakker geschud worden

shaky 1 beverig, trillerig, zwak(jes) **2** wankel [also fig]; gammel, onbetrouwbaar: *my Swedish is rather ~* mijn Zweeds is nogal zwak

shale gas schaliegas[h]

shall 1 zullen: *how ~ I recognize her?* hoe zal ik haar herkennen? **2** [command; also promise, threat, plan etc] zullen, moeten: *you ~ do as I tell you* doe wat ik zeg **3** zullen, moeten: *~ I open the window?* zal ik het raam openzetten?

shallot sjalot

shallow 1 ondiep: *~ dish* plat bord **2** licht; niet diep [of breathing] ‖ *~ arguments* oppervlakkige argumenten

shallows ondiepte, ondiepe plaats, wad[h]

¹sham (n) **1** komedie, schijn(vertoning), bedrog[h]: *the promise was a ~* de belofte was maar schijn **2** imitatie **3** bedrieger, hypocriet

²sham (adj) **1** namaak-, imitatie-, vals **2** schijn-, gesimuleerd, pseudo-: *a ~ fight* een schijngevecht

³sham (vb) voorwenden, doen als of: *~ illness* doen alsof je ziek bent

¹shamble (n) schuifelgang(etje[h])

²shamble (vb) schuifelen; sloffen [also fig]: *a shambling gait* een sukkelgangetje

shambles janboel, troep, bende, zooi: *the house is a complete ~* het huis is een echte varkensstal

¹shame (n) **1** schande, schandaal[h] **2** zonde: *what a ~!* het is een schande!, wat jammer! **3** schaamte(gevoel[h]): *have no sense of ~* zich nergens voor schamen **4** schande, smaad, vernedering: *put to ~* a) in de schaduw stellen; b) beschaamd maken (or: doen staan); *to my ~* tot mijn (grote) schande; *~ on you!*

schaam je!, je moest je schamen!; [to speaker] *~!* schandalig!, hoe durft u!

²shame (vb) **1** beschamen: *it ~s me to say this* ik schaam me ervoor dit te (moeten) zeggen **2** schande aandoen, te schande maken **3** in de schaduw stellen, overtreffen: *your translation ~s all the other attempts* jouw vertaling stelt alle andere pogingen in de schaduw

shamefaced 1 beschaamd **2** beschroomd

shameful 1 beschamend **2** schandelijk, schandalig

shameless schaamteloos, onbeschaamd

¹shampoo (n) shampoo

²shampoo (vb) shamponeren; met shampoo reinigen [car, carpet]

shamrock klaver

shandy shandy

shank 1 (onder)been[h], scheenbeen[h], schenkel **2** schacht [of anchor, column, key] **3** steel

shanks'(s) pony: *go on* (or: *ride*) *shanks'(s) pony* met de benenwagen gaan

shanty 1 barak, hut, keet **2** zeemansliedje[h]

shanty town sloppenwijk, barakkenkamp[h]

¹shape (n) **1** vorm, gestalte, gedaante, verschijning: *take ~* (vaste/vastere) vorm aannemen; *in the ~ of* in de vorm van **2** bakvorm, gietvorm, model[h], sjabloon **3** (goede) conditie, (goede) toestand, vorm: *in bad* (or: *good*) *~* in slechte (or: goede) conditie ‖ [+ negation] *in any ~ or form* in welke vorm dan ook, van welke aard dan ook; *knock* (or: *lick*) *sth. into ~* iets fatsoeneren

²shape (vb) (also + up) zich ontwikkelen, zich vormen, vorm aannemen: *we'll see how things ~ (up)* we zullen zien hoe de dingen zich ontwikkelen

³shape (vb) **1** vormen, maken, ontwerpen: *~d like a pear* in de vorm van een peer, peervormig **2** bepalen, vormen, vorm (richting) geven aan: *his theories, which ~d mathematical thinking in the 1980s* zijn theorieën, die het wiskundig denken in de jaren tachtig richting gaven

shapeless 1 vorm(e)loos, ongevormd **2** misvormd, vervormd

shapely goedgevormd, welgevormd

¹share (n) **1** aandeel[h], effect[h] **2** (onder)deel[h], aandeel[h], part[h], gedeelte[h], portie: *get one's fair ~* zijn rechtmatig (aan)deel krijgen ‖ *go ~s (with s.o. in sth.)* de kosten (van iets met iem.) delen

²share (vb) **1** (ver)delen: *~ a bedroom* een slaapkamer delen; *~ (out) among* (or: *between*) verdelen onder (or: over) **2** deelgenoot maken van: *~ a secret with s.o.* iem. deelgenoot maken van een geheim

³share (vb) delen, deelnemen: *~ and share alike* eerlijk delen

shareholder aandeelhouder

share-out verdeling

shareware shareware

shark 1 haai **2** afzetter, woekeraar
¹sharp (n) (noot met) kruis^h || **F** ~ f-kruis, fa
kruis, fis
²sharp (adj) **1** scherp, spits, puntig: *a ~ angle*
een scherpe hoek **2** schril: *a ~ contrast* een
schril contrast **3** abrupt, plotseling, steil: *a ~
fall* (or: *rise*) *in prices* een scherpe daling (or:
stijging) van de prijzen **4** bijtend, doordringend, snijdend: *~ frost* bijtende vrieskou
5 scherp, pikant, sterk: *a ~* **flavour** een
scherpe smaak **6** hevig, krachtig: *a ~* **blow**
een hevige klap **7** streng, vinnig: *a ~* **reproof**
een scherp verwijt **8** scherpzinnig, bijdehand, pienter, vlug: *keep a ~* **look-out** scherp
uitkijken; *be too ~* **for** *s.o.* iem. te slim af zijn
9 geslepen, sluw: *a ~* **salesman** een gehaaid
verkoper **10** stevig, flink, vlug: *at a ~* **pace** in
een stevig tempo || *~* **practice** oneerlijke
praktijken, een vuil zaakje
³sharp (adv) **1** stipt, precies, klokslag: *three
o'clock ~* klokslag drie uur **2** opeens, plotseling, scherp: *turn ~* **right** scherp naar rechts
draaien || *look ~!* schiet op, haast je!
sharpen scherp(er) worden (maken), (zich)
(ver)scherpen, slijpen
sharpener (punten)slijper
sharper afzetter, oplichter
sharp-eyed scherpziend, waakzaam, alert
sharpish snel, (nu) meteen, direct
sharpshooter scherpschutter
¹shatter (vb) uiteenspatten, barsten, in
stukken (uiteen)vallen
²shatter (vb) **1** aan gruzelementen slaan,
(compleet) vernietigen: *his death ~ed our
hopes* zijn dood ontnam ons alle hoop
2 schokken, in de war brengen: *~ed* **nerves**
geschokte zenuwen **3** afmatten, totaal uitputten: *I feel* **completely** *~ed* ik ben doodop
¹shave (n) scheerbeurt: *I badly* **need** *a ~* ik
moet me nodig weer eens scheren; *a* **close** *~*
op het nippertje
²shave (vb) **1** (zich) scheren **2** (also + off)
(af)schaven, afraspen **3** scheren langs,
schampen, rakelings gaan langs
shaver scheerapparaat^h
shaving 1 het scheren, scheerbeurt
2 schijfje^h: *~s* spaanders; schaafkrullen
shawl sjaal(tje^h), omslagdoek, hoofddoek
she zij, ze; [in some constructions] die; dat,
het || *is it a* **he** *or a ~?* is het een jongen of een
meisje?
sheaf 1 schoof **2** bundel: *he produced a ~ of
papers from a plastic bag* hij haalde uit een
plastic tasje een stapel papieren tevoorschijn
shear 1 (af)scheren: *~ing* **sheep** schapen
scheren **2** ontdoen, plukken, villen: *shorn of*
ontdaan van
shears (grote) schaar, heggenschaar: *a* **pair**
of ~ een schaar
sheath 1 schede, (bescherm)huls, koker
2 nauwaansluitende jurk **3** condoom^h, ka-

potje^h
sheathe in de schede steken, van een omhulsel voorzien: *he carefully ~d the* **knife** hij
stak het mes zorgvuldig in de schede
sheathing 1 (beschermende) bekleding,
omhulling, mantel **2** bekleding
sheath knife steekmes
shebang zootje^h, zaak(je^h), santenkraam:
the **whole** *~* het hele zootje
¹shed (n) schuur(tje^h), keet, loods
²shed (vb) **1** afwerpen, verliezen, afleggen,
afschudden: *the tree had ~ its* **leaves** de boom
had zijn bladeren laten vallen; *the lorry ~ its
load* de vrachtwagen verloor zijn lading
2 storten, vergieten: *~ hot* **tears** hete tranen
schreien
she-devil duivelin [also fig]
sheen glans, schittering, (weer)schijn
sheep schaap^h [also fig]; onnozel kind^h, gedwee persoon: *the* **black** *~* het zwarte schaap
|| *separate the ~ and the* **goats** de goeden van
de slechten scheiden, het koren van het kaf
scheiden
sheepdog (schaap)herdershond [collie]
sheepfold schaapskooi
sheepish verlegen, onnozel, dom
¹sheer (adj) **1** dun, doorschijnend, transparant: *~ nylon* dun nylon **2** erg steil, loodrecht
3 volkomen, je reinste: *that's ~* **nonsense** dat
is klinkklare onzin!
²sheer (vb) [shipp] scherp uitwijken, zwen-
ken || *~ off* uit 't roer lopen; [inform] 'm sme-
ren; *~ away* **from** mijden
sheet 1 (bedden)laken^h: *fitted ~* hoeslaken;
between the ~s in bed, tussen de lakens
2 blad^h; vel^h [paper] **3** plaat: *a ~ of* **glass** een
glasplaat, een stuk glas **4** gordijn^h, muur,
vlaag: *a ~ of* **flame** een vuurzee
sheet feeder papierinvoer
sheet ice 1 ijs^h, ijslaag [on water] **2** ijzel
sheeting 1 lakenstof^h **2** bekleding(smate-
riaal^h)
sheet iron bladstaal^h, plaatijzer^h
sheet lightning weerlicht^h, bliksem
sheet music bladmuziek
sheik(h) sjeik
shelf 1 (leg)plank, boekenplank **2** (rots)-
richel || *be (put, left)* **on** *the ~* **a)** afgeschreven
worden, in onbruik raken, afgedankt wor-
den; **b)** blijven zitten, niet meer aan een man
raken [of woman]
shelf-life houdbaarheid: *most dairy products
have a* **limited** *~* de meeste zuivelproducten
zijn beperkt houdbaar
shelfload: *~s of* **reports** planken vol rap-
porten
¹shell (n) **1** geraamte^h [of bldg]; skelet^h;
romp [of ship]; chassis^h **2** deegbakje^h, pastei-
korst **3** huls, granaat^h, patroon^h **4** hard om-
hulsel^h, schelp, slakkenhuis^h, dop, schaal,
schulp: *come out of one's ~* loskomen, ont-

dooien
²**shell** (vb) **1** van zijn schil ontdoen, schillen, doppen, pellen **2** beschieten, onder vuur nemen, bombarderen
shellfish schaaldierʰ, schelpdierʰ
shell out dokken, neertellen, ophoesten
shellproof bomvrij
¹**shelter** (n) **1** schuilgelegenheid, schuilkelder, bushokjeʰ, tramhuisjeʰ **2** schuilplaats, toevluchtsoordʰ, tehuisʰ, asielʰ: ~ *for battered* **women** opvang(te)huis voor mishandelde vrouwen **3** (+ from) beschutting (tegen), bescherming: *give* ~ onderdak verlenen
²**shelter** (vb) (+ from) schuilen (voor/tegen)
³**shelter** (vb) **1** (+ from) beschutten (tegen), beschermen **2** huisvesten, onderdak verlenen
sheltered accommodation woon-zorgcomplexʰ
¹**shelve** (vb) geleidelijk aflopen [of bottom]; glooien, (zacht) hellen
²**shelve** (vb) **1** op een plank zetten **2** op de lange baan schuiven, opschorten
shenanigan 1 trucjeʰ, foefjeʰ **2** kattenkwaadʰ, bedriegerij
¹**shepherd** (n) (schaap)herder
²**shepherd** (vb) hoeden, leiden, in de gaten houden
shepherdess herderin
shepherd's pie gehakt met een korst van aardappelpuree
sherbet [Am] sorbet
sheriff sheriff
sherry sherry
¹**shield** (n) **1** schildʰ **2** beveiliging, bescherming
²**shield** (vb) (+ from) beschermen (tegen), in bescherming nemen
¹**shift** (n) **1** verschuiving, verandering **2** ploeg [workmen] **3** werktijd, arbeidsduur **4** redmiddelʰ, hulpmiddelʰ ‖ *make* ~ *without* het stellen zonder
²**shift** (vb) **1** van plaats veranderen, zich verplaatsen, schuiven: ~*ing* **sands** drijfzand **2** wisselen, veranderen: *the* **scene** ~*s* de achtergrond van het verhaal verandert **3** zich redden, zich behelpen, het klaarspelen: ~ *for* **o.s.** het zelf klaarspelen
³**shift** (vb) **1** verplaatsen, verschuiven, verzetten: ~ *the* **blame** *onto* de schuld schuiven op **2** verwisselen, verruilen, veranderen; schakelen [acceleration]: ~ *one's* **ground** plotseling een ander standpunt innemen
shift key hoofdlettertoets
shiftless niet vindingrijk, inefficiënt, onbeholpen
shift work ploegendienst
shifty niet rechtdoorzee, stiekem, onbetrouwbaar
Shiite sjiiet
shilling shilling

shilly-shally dubben, weifelen, aarzelen
¹**shimmer** (n) flikkering, flauw schijnselʰ
²**shimmer** (vb) glinsteren, flakkeren
¹**shin** (n) scheen: *Joe got kicked on the* ~*s during the match* Joe werd tijdens de wedstrijd tegen zijn schenen geschopt
²**shin** (vb) klauteren; klimmen [using hands and feet]: ~ *up a tree* in een boom klimmen
shinbone scheenbeenʰ
shindy herrie, tumultʰ, opschudding: *kick up a* ~ herrie schoppen
¹**shine** (n) **1** schijn(selʰ), lichtʰ, uitstraling **2** glans, schittering: *take the* ~ *out of* van zijn glans beroven, maken dat de aardigheid af gaat van **3** poetsbeurt; het poetsen [of shoes] ‖ *take a* ~ *to s.o.* iem. zomaar aardig vinden
²**shine** (vb) **1** glanzen, glimmen, blinken **2** schitteren, uitblinken: ~ *out* duidelijk naar voren komen
³**shine** (vb) poetsen [shoes]
⁴**shine** (vb) schijnen, lichten, gloeien: *he shone his* **light** *in my face* hij scheen met zijn lantaarn in mijn gezicht
shingle 1 dakspaan, panlat **2** [Am] naambord van arts e.d. **3** kiezelʰ, grindʰ, kiezelstrandʰ **4** (-s) gordelroos
shiny glanzend, glimmend
¹**ship** (n) **1** schipʰ, vaartuigʰ: *on* **board** ~ aan boord **2** vliegtuigʰ, kist **3** ruimteschipʰ
²**ship** (vb) **1** verschepen, (per schip) verzenden (vervoeren): ~ *off* (or: *out*) verschepen **2** aan boord nemen, laden **3** binnenkrijgen: ~ **water** water maken ‖ ~ *off* wegsturen, wegzenden
shipboard scheepsboordʰ: *on* ~ aan boord
shipbuilding scheepsbouw
shipload scheepslading, scheepsvracht
shipmate scheepsmaat, medebemanningslidʰ
shipment 1 zending, vracht, scheepslading **2** vervoerʰ [not only by ship]
shipowner reder
shipper expediteur, verzender
shipping 1 verscheping, verzending **2** scheepvaart
shipping company scheepvaartmaatschappij
shipshape netjes, in orde, keurig
¹**shipwreck** (n) schipbreuk; [fig] ondergang; mislukking
²**shipwreck** (vb) schipbreuk (doen) lijden, (doen) mislukken
shipyard scheeps(timmer)werf
shire graafschapʰ
¹**shirk** (vb) zich drukken
²**shirk** (vb) zich onttrekken aan
shirt overhemdʰ ‖ *keep one's* ~ *on* zich gedeisd houden; *put one's* ~ *on sth.* al zijn geld op iets zetten [horses]

shirtsleeve hemdsmouw: *in* one's ~s in hemdsmouwen

shirty nijdig, kwaad, geërgerd

¹**shit** (n) **1** stront, kak, poep, het poepen: *have* a ~ gaan kakken **2** rommel, rotzooi **3** zeurkous **4** gezeikʰ, gekletsʰ, onzin **5** hasj

²**shit** (vb) [vulg] schijten, poepen

³**shit** (vb) schijten op: ~ o.s. het in zijn broek doen [also fig]

shitty [vulg] **1** lullig **2** rot-

¹**shiver** (n) rilling [also fig]; siddering, gevoelʰ van angst (afkeer): *give* s.o. the ~s iem. de rillingen geven

²**shiver** (vb) rillen [with fear, cold]; sidderen

shivery 1 rillerig, beverig **2** kil [of weather]

shoal 1 ondiepte **2** zandbank **3** menigte, troep; school [of fish]

¹**shock** (n) **1** aardschok **2** dikke bosʰ [of hair] **3** schok, schrik, (onaangename) verrassing: *come upon* s.o. *with* a ~ een (grote) schok zijn voor iem. **4** (elektrische) schok **5** shock: *in a state of* ~ in shocktoestand

²**shock** (vb) een schok veroorzaken

³**shock** (vb) **1** schokken, choqueren, laten schrikken: *be ~ed at* (or: *by*) geschokt zijn door **2** een schok geven [also elec]; een shock veroorzaken bij

shocking 1 stuitend, schokkend, weerzinwekkend **2** vreselijk, erg: ~ *weather* rotweer

shockproof schokvast

shock therapy shocktherapie

shock wave schokgolf

shoddy prullig, niet degelijk

shoe 1 schoen **2** hoefijzerʰ **3** remschoen, remblok ‖ *know where the ~ pinches* weten waar de schoen wringt, weten waar de pijn zit; *put* o.s. *in* s.o.'s ~s zich in iemands positie verplaatsen

shoehorn schoenlepel

shoelace (schoen)veter

shoemaker schoenmaker

shoe polish schoensmeer⁺ʰ

shoestring 1 (schoen)veter **2** (te) klein budgetʰ: *on* a ~ met erg weinig geld

¹**shoo** (vb) ks(t) roepen, wegjagen: ~ *sth. away* (or: *off*) iets wegjagen

²**shoo** (int) ks(t)

¹**shoot** (n) **1** (jonge) spruit, loot, scheut **2** jacht(partij)

²**shoot** (vb) **1** snel bewegen, (weg)schieten, voortschieten: ~ *ahead* vooruitschieten **2** schieten [with weapon]: ~ *at* (or: *for*) a) schieten op; b) (zich) richten op **3** afgaan [of weapon] **4** steken [of pain, wound]: *the pain shot through* (or: *up*) *his arm* een stekende pijn ging door zijn arm **5** uitlopen, ontspruiten **6** [sport] (op doel) schieten **7** plaatjes schieten, foto's nemen, filmen ‖ ~! zeg op!, zeg het maar!

³**shoot** (vb) **1** (af)schieten [bullet, arrow etc]; afvuren [also fig; questions etc]: ~ *down* neerschieten; [fig] afkeuren; ~ *off* a) afschieten, afsteken [fireworks]; b) afvuren [gun] **2** jagen (op) **3** doen bewegen; schuiven [bolt]; spuiten [drugs] **4** (naar doel) schieten [ball]; schieten **5** snel passeren: *he shot the traffic lights* hij ging met hoge snelheid door de verkeerslichten **6** schieten [pictures]; opnemen [film] **7** spelen [billiards etc]

¹**shooting** (n) **1** jacht **2** het schieten **3** opname [film, sequence]

²**shooting** (adj) **1** schietend **2** stekend: ~ *pains* pijnscheuten ‖ ~ *star* vallende ster

shooting gallery schietbaan

shooting match schietwedstrijd: *the whole* ~ het hele zaakje

¹**shoot out** (vb) naar buiten schieten: *the branches are beginning to* ~ de takken beginnen al uit te schieten

²**shoot out** (vb) een vuurgevecht leveren over: *they're going to shoot it out* ze gaan het uitvechten (met de revolver)

shoot-out gevechtʰ [with small arms]

¹**shoot up** (vb) omhoog schieten [of plants, children]; snel groeien [of temperature, prices]

²**shoot up** (vb) kapot schieten, overhoop schieten

¹**shop** (n) **1** winkel, zaak: *mind the* ~ de winkel runnen; [fig] de touwtjes in handen hebben **2** werkplaats, atelierʰ **3** werkʰ, zaken, beroepʰ: *set up* ~ een zaak opzetten; *talk* ~ over zaken praten ‖ *all over the* ~ door elkaar, her en der verspreid

²**shop** (vb) winkelen: ~ *around* rondkijken, zich oriënteren (alvorens te kopen) [also fig]

³**shop** (vb) verlinken [to police]

shopaholic koopziek persoon: *he's* a ~ hij is koopziek

shop assistant winkelbediende

shopbot prijsvergelijker

the **shop floor 1** werkplaats, werkvloer **2** arbeiders

shopkeeper winkelier

shoplifter winkeldief

shopper iem. die winkelt: *the* ~s het winkelpubliek

shopping boodschappen, het boodschappen doen: *Mary always does her* ~ *in Leeds* Mary doet haar boodschappen altijd in Leeds

shopping arcade (overdekte) winkelgalerij

shopping bag boodschappentas

shopping street winkelstraat

shop-soiled minder geworden [of goods, because they have lain too long; also fig]; smoezelig

shop steward vakbondsvertegenwoordiger

shoptalk gepraat over het werk

shopwalker (afdelings)chef

shop window etalage

¹shore (n) **1** kust; oever [of lake]: *off the* ~ voor de kust; *on* ~ aan (de) wal, op het land **2** steunbalk

²shore (vb) [also fig] steunen, schragen: ~ *up* (onder)steunen

shoreline waterlijn, oever, kustlijn

¹short (n) **1** korte (voor)film **2** borrel **3** (-s) korte broek, onderbroek

²short (adj) **1** kort, klein, beknopt: ~ *and sweet* kort en bondig; *little* ~ *of* weinig minder dan, bijna; ~ *for* een afkorting van; *in* ~ in het kort **2** kort(durend): *(at)* ~ *notice* (op) korte termijn; ~ *order* snelbuffet; *in* ~ *order* onmiddellijk; *make* ~ *work of* snel een einde maken aan **3** te kort, onvoldoende, karig, krap: ~ *of breath* kortademig; ~ *change* te weinig wisselgeld; ~ *of money* krap bij kas; *in* ~ *supply* schaars, beperkt leverbaar; ~ *weight* ondergewicht; *(be)* ~ *of* (or: *on*) tekort (hebben) aan **4** kortaf, bits **5** bros; kruimelig [eg dough] **6** onverdund [hard liquor]: *a* ~ *drink* (or: *one*) een borrel ‖ ~ *circuit* kortsluiting; ~ *temper* drift(igheid)

³short (adv) **1** niet (ver) genoeg: *four inches* ~ vier inches te kort; *come* (or: *fall*) ~ tekortschieten; [fig] *cut s.o.* ~ iem. onderbreken **2** plotseling: *stop* ~ plotseling ophouden; *be taken* (or: *caught*) ~ nodig moeten ‖ *sell s.o.* ~ iem. tekortdoen; *nothing* ~ *of* a) slechts, alleen maar; b) niets minder dan; ~ *of* behalve, zonder

shortage gebrek[h], tekort[h], schaarste

shortbread zandkoek

shortcake 1 theebeschuit **2** [Am] zandgebak[h]

short-change 1 te weinig wisselgeld geven aan: *be* ~*d* te weinig (wisselgeld) terugkrijgen **2** afzetten

¹short-circuit (vb) kortsluiting veroorzaken

²short-circuit (vb) **1** kortsluiten **2** verkorten [procedure etc]; vereenvoudigen

shortcoming tekortkoming

short cut korte(re) weg, sluiproute

shorten verkorten: ~*ed form* verkorting

shortfall tekort[h]

shorthand steno(grafie)

short-handed met te weinig personeel

shortish vrij kort, aan de korte kant

¹shortlist (n) aanbevelingslijst [of applicants, candidates]; shortlist

²shortlist (vb) voordragen, op de voordracht plaatsen, nomineren

short-lived kortdurend, kortlevend

shortly 1 spoedig, binnenkort, kort: ~ *after* ... korte tijd na ...; ~ *afterwards* korte tijd later **2** kortaf

short-sighted 1 bijziend **2** kortzichtig

short-tempered opvliegend

short-term op korte termijn, kortetermijn-

short-wave kortegolf-

short-winded 1 kortademig **2** kortdurend

shorty [inform] kleintje[h]

¹shot (n) **1** schot[h] [also sport]; worp, stoot **2** (snedige) opmerking **3** gok, poging: *it's a long* ~, *but certainly worth trying* het is een hele gok, maar zeker de moeite van het proberen waard; *have* (or: *make*) *a* ~ *(at sth.)* (ergens) een slag (naar) slaan **4** [photo] opname, kiekje[h] **5** injectie, shot **6** [athletics] (stoot)kogel **7** borrel **8** lading [of firearm]; schroot[h] ‖ ~ *in the arm* a) stimulans, injectie; b) borrel(tje); *a* ~ *across the bows* een schot voor de boeg, waarschuwing; *a* ~ *in the dark* een slag in de lucht; *call the* ~*s* de leiding hebben, het voor het zeggen hebben; *(do sth.) like a* ~ onmiddellijk (iets doen)

²shot (adj) doorweven, vol: ~ *(through) with* doorspekt met ‖ *be* ~ *of* klaar zijn met, af zijn van

¹shotgun (n) (jacht)geweer[h]

²shotgun (adj) gedwongen: ~ *wedding* (or: *marriage*) moetje

should zou(den), zou(den) moeten, moest(en), mochten: ~ *you need any help, please ask the staff* mocht u hulp nodig hebben, wendt u zich dan tot het personeel; *why* ~ *I listen to him?* waarom zou ik naar hem luisteren?; *the teacher told Sheila that she* ~ *be more careful* de docent zei tegen Sheila dat zij voorzichtiger moest zijn; *he hoped that he* ~ *be accepted* hij hoopte dat hij aangenomen zou worden; *if Sheila came, I* ~ *come too* als Sheila kwam, dan kwam ik ook; *it* ~ *be easy for you* het moet voor jou gemakkelijk zijn; *yes, I* ~ *love to* ja, dat zou ik echt graag doen; *I suggest that we* ~ *leave* ik stel voor dat wij naar huis (zouden) gaan; [sometimes untranslated] *it's surprising he* ~ *be thought so attractive* het is verbazingwekkend dat hij zo aantrekkelijk wordt gevonden

¹shoulder (n) **1** schouder: *stand head and* ~*s above* met kop en schouders uitsteken boven [also fig] **2** (weg)berm: *hard* ~ vluchtstrook **3** schoft [of animal] ‖ *put* (or: *set*) *one's* ~ *to the wheel* zich schouders ergens onder zetten, ergens hard aan werken; *rub* ~*s with* omgaan met; *(straight) from the* ~ op de man af, recht voor z'n raap

²shoulder (vb) **1** op zich nemen, op zijn schouders nemen: ~ *a great burden* (or: *responsibility*) een zware last (or: verantwoording) op zich nemen **2** duwen, (met de schouders) dringen: *he* ~*ed his way through the crowd* hij baande zich een weg door de menigte

shoulder blade schouderblad[h]

shoulder pad schoudervulling

¹shout (n) schreeuw, kreet, gil: ~ *of joy* vreugdekreet

²shout (vb) schreeuwen, (uit)roepen, brullen, gillen: ~ *o.s. hoarse* zich schor schreeu-

wen; *the audience ~ed* **down** *the speaker* het publiek joelde de spreker uit; *~ for joy* het uitroepen van vreugde
shout-out groet: *I want to give a ~ to …* ik wil de groeten doen aan …
¹**shove** (n) duw, zet, stoot
²**shove** (vb) (weg)duwen, dringen (tegen), een zet geven, stoppen, leggen: *~ along* heen en weer duwen, vooruitdringen; *~ it in the drawer* stop het in de la ‖ *~ off* a) afschuiven; b) afduwen [in boat]; *let's ~ off* laten we er vandoor gaan
¹**shovel** (n) 1 schop, spade, schep 2 schoep [of machine] 3 laadschop
²**shovel** (vb) (op)scheppen, schuiven, opruimen (met een schep): *~ food into one's mouth* eten in zijn mond proppen; *~ a path through the snow* een pad graven door de sneeuw
¹**show** (n) 1 vertoning, show, uitzending, (televisie)programma, concert, opvoering: *a ~ in the theatre* een toneelopvoering 2 spektakel(stuk), grootse vertoning: *a ~ of force* (or: *strength*) een machtsvertoon; *make a ~ of one's learning* te koop lopen met zijn geleerdheid 3 tentoonstelling 4 poging, gooi, beurt: *a bad* (or: *poor*) *~* een slechte beurt; *good ~!* goed geprobeerd!; *put up a good ~* een goede prestatie leveren 5 uiterlijk, schijn, opschepperij: *this is all empty ~* dit is allemaal slechts schijn 6 pracht (en praal) 7 vertoning, demonstratie: *objects on ~* de tentoongestelde voorwerpen ‖ *vote by (a) ~ of hands* handopsteking stemmen; *give the (whole) ~ away* de hele zaak verraden; *steal the ~* de show stelen
²**show** (vb) (zich) (ver)tonen [of film]: *your slip is ~ing* je onderjurk komt eruit; *time will ~* de tijd zal het leren ‖ *it just goes to ~!* zo zie je maar!
³**show** (vb) 1 (aan)tonen, laten zien, tentoonstellen, vertonen: *~ one's cards* (or: *hand*) open kaart spelen [also fig]; *~ (s.o.) the way* a) iem. de weg wijzen; b) [also fig] een voorbeeld stellen; *~ o.s.* je (gezicht) laten zien, je ware aard tonen; *he has nothing to ~ for all his work* zijn werk heeft helemaal niets opgeleverd 2 uitleggen, demonstreren, bewijzen: *he ~ed me how to write* hij leerde me schrijven 3 te kennen geven, tentoonspreiden: *~ bad taste* van een slechte smaak getuigen 4 (rond)leiden: *~ s.o. about* (or: *(a)round*) iem. rondleiden; *~ her into the waiting room* breng haar naar de wachtkamer; *~ s.o. over the factory* iem. een rondleiding geven door de fabriek 5 aanwijzen: *the clock ~s five minutes past* de klok staat op vijf over
show business amusementsbedrijf, show business
¹**showcase** (n) vitrine [in shop, museum]; uitstalkast
²**showcase** (vb) [Am] onder de aandacht

brengen, goed laten uitkomen
showdown 1 [poker] het tonen van zijn kaarten [also fig] 2 directe confrontatie, krachtmeting
¹**shower** (n) 1 bui: *occasional ~s* hier en daar een bui 2 douche: *have a ~* douchen, een douche nemen 3 stroom, toevloed, golf: *a ~ of arrows* (or: *bullets*) een regen van pijlen (or: kogels)
²**shower** (vb) 1 zich douchen 2 (toe)stromen: *apples ~ed down the tree* het regende appels uit de boom
³**shower** (vb) 1 (+ with) overgieten (met), uitstorten, doen neerstromen 2 (+ with) overladen (met), overstelpen: *~ questions on s.o.* een heleboel vragen op iem. afvuren
shower cap douchemuts
showery buiig, regenachtig
showgirl revuemeisje
show house modelwoning
showing vertoning, voorstelling, voorkomen, figuur: *make a good ~* een goed figuur slaan; *a poor ~* een zwakke vertoning [eg of football team] ‖ *on present ~* zoals de zaak er nu voor blijkt te staan
showman 1 impresario [organiser of concerts, shows] 2 aansteller
¹**show off** (vb) opscheppen, indruk proberen te maken
²**show off** (vb) 1 pronken met, etaleren: *don't ~ your knowledge* loop niet zo te koop met je kennis 2 goed doen uitkomen: *your white dress shows off your tanned skin* je witte jurk doet je gebruinde huid goed uitkomen
show-off opschepper
showpiece pronkstuk, paradepaardje
showroom toonzaal
show stopper uitsmijter, hoogtepunt
show trial schijnproces
¹**show up** (vb) opdagen, verschijnen
²**show up** (vb) 1 ontmaskeren, aan het licht brengen: *~ an impostor* een bedrieger ontmaskeren 2 zichtbaar maken: *only strong light shows up her wrinkles* slechts sterk licht toont haar rimpeltjes 3 in verlegenheid brengen: *the pupil's remark showed him up* de opmerking van de scholier zette hem voor gek
show-window etalage
showy opvallend, opzichtig
shrapnel 1 (soort) granaat 2 granaatscherven
¹**shred** (n) 1 stukje, reepje, snipper: *not a ~ of clothing* geen draadje kleding; *tear sth. to ~s* a) iets aan flarden scheuren; b) [also fig] niets heel laten van 2 greintje: *not a ~ of evidence* niet het minste bewijs, geen enkel bewijs
²**shred** (vb) verscheuren, versnipperen, in stukjes snijden
shredder 1 (grove keuken)schaaf [for veg-

etables, cheese]; rasp **2** papierversnipperaar
shrew 1 spitsmuis **2** feeks
shrewd slim: ~ *guess* intelligente gok; ~
observer scherp waarnemer
¹shriek (n) schreeuw, gil, (schrille) kreet
²shriek (vb) schreeuwen, gillen: ~ *out* uitschreeuwen; ~ *with laughter* gieren van het
lachen
shrift: *make short* ~ *of* korte metten maken
met
shrill schel, schril, doordringend; [fig] fel: ~
contrast schril contrast
shrimp garnaal; [inform] klein opdonder-
tjeʰ
shrine 1 (heiligen)tombe **2** heiligdomʰ;
[fig] gedenkplaats
¹shrink (n) zielenknijper [psychiatrist]
²shrink (vb) **1** krimpen, afnemen, slinken
2 wegkruipen, ineenkrimpen; [fig] huiveren:
~ *back* terugdeinzen
³shrink (vb) doen krimpen, kleiner maken,
doen slinken
shrivel verschrompelen, uitdrogen, inkrimpen
shrooms paddo's
¹shroud (n) **1** lijkwade, doodskleedʰ **2** [fig]
sluier: *wrapped in a* ~ *of mystery* in een sluier
van geheimzinnigheid gehuld
²shroud (vb) (om)hullen, verbergen: *mountains ~ed in mist* in mist gehulde bergen
Shrove Tuesday Vastenavond; vette dinsdag [Tuesday before Ash Wednesday]
shrub struik, heester
¹shrug (n) schouderophalenʰ
²shrug (vb) (de schouders) ophalen
shrug off van zich afschudden [clothing];
geen belang hechten aan: *she shrugged off all
criticism* zij liet alle kritiek langs haar heen
gaan
shrunken gekrompen, verschrompeld
shucks! 1 onzin! **2** krijg nou wat!
¹shudder (n) huivering, rilling
²shudder (vb) **1** huiveren, sidderen, beven: /
~ *to think* ik huiver bij de gedachte **2** trillen
¹shuffle (n) **1** schuifelgang **2** [dance]
schuifelpas **3** het schudden [of cards, domi-
noes]
²shuffle (vb) **1** mengen, door elkaar halen;
schudden [cards] **2** heen en weer bewegen,
herverdelen: ~ *one's papers* in zijn papieren
rommelen **3** schuiven: *try to* ~ *off one's responsibility* zijn verantwoordelijkheid proberen af te schuiven
³shuffle (vb) schuifelen, sloffen: ~ *one's feet*
met de voeten schuifelen
shufti kijkjeʰ: *have* (or: *take*) *a* ~ *at* een blik
werpen op
shun mijden, schuwen
shunt afleiden, afvoeren, rangeren; op een
dood spoor zetten [pers]: ~ *a train onto a siding* een trein op een zijspoor rangeren

shush sst!, stilte!
¹shut (adj) dicht, gesloten: *slam the door* ~ de
deur dichtsmijten
²shut (vb) sluiten, dichtgaan: *the shop ~s on
Sundays* de winkel is 's zondags gesloten
³shut (vb) **1** sluiten, dichtdoen, dichtslaan,
dichtdraaien; [fig] stopzetten: ~ *one's eyes*
(or: *ears*) *to sth.* iets niet willen zien (*or:* horen); ~ *in by mountains* door bergen ingesloten; ~ *down a plant* een fabriek (voorgoed)
sluiten; ~ *out of* de toegang ontzeggen tot
2 opsluiten; ~ *sth. away* iets (veilig) opbergen; ~ *o.s. in* zichzelf opsluiten [eg in room]
shutdown sluiting; stopzetting [of busi-
ness]
shut-eye slaap, dutjeʰ: *have a bit of* ~ een
dutje doen
¹shutter (n) **1** blind, (rol)luikʰ: *put up the ~s*
de zaak sluiten [temporarily or permanently]
2 sluiter [also of camera]
²shutter (vb) met (een) luik(en) sluiten: *~ed
windows* (or: *houses*) vensters (*or:* huizen)
met gesloten luiken
¹shuttle (n) **1** schuitjeʰ [of sewing machine]
2 pendeldienst
²shuttle (vb) pendelen
³shuttle (vb) heen en weer vervoeren
shuttlecock pluimbal; shuttle [badminton]
shuttle service pendeldienst
¹shut up (vb) **1** zwijgen: ~*!* kop dicht! **2** sluiten [shop etc]
²shut up (vb) **1** sluiten, (zorgvuldig) afsluiten: *they* ~ *the house before they left* ze sloten
het huis af voordat ze weggingen; ~ *shop* de
zaak sluiten **2** opsluiten, achter slot en grendel zetten, opbergen **3** doen zwijgen, de
mond snoeren: *turn the television on, that usually shuts them up* zet de tv maar aan, meestal
houden ze dan hun mond dicht
¹shy (n) **1** gooi, worp **2** gooi, poging, experi-
mentʰ: *have a* ~ *at sth.* een gooi doen naar
iets, het (ook) eens proberen
²shy (adj) **1** verlegen: *give s.o. a* ~ *look* iem.
verlegen aankijken **2** voorzichtig, behoedzaam: *fight* (or: *be*) ~ *of* uit de weg gaan
3 schuw; schichtig [animals]
³shy (vb) **1** schichtig opspringen: ~ *at sth.*
schichtig worden voor iets [of horses] **2** terugschrikken: ~ *away from sth.* iets vermijden, voor iets terugschrikken
⁴shy (vb) gooien, slingeren
shyster gewetenloos mens [esp lawyer or
politician]
Siamese Siamees
Siberian Siberisch
sibling [form] broer, zus
¹sick (n) braakselʰ, spuugselʰ
²sick (adj) **1** ziek, sukkelend: *fall* ~ ziek worden; *go* (or: *report*) ~ zich ziek melden
2 misselijk; [fig also] met walging vervuld: *be
* ~ overgeven, braken; *be worried* ~ doodon-

gerust zijn; *you* **make** *me ~!* ik word niet goed van jou! **3** wee, onpasselijk makend: *a ~ feeling* een wee gevoel **4** ziekelijk, ongezond, morbide; wrang [mockery]: *a ~ joke* een lugubere grap; *a ~ mind* een zieke geest **5** beu, moe: *I am ~ (and tired) of it* ik ben het spuugzat **6** [inform] vet, gaaf ‖ *~ to* **death** *of s.o. (sth.)* iem. (iets) spuugzat zijn

sickbay ziekenboeg

sickbed ziekbed[h]

sick benefit ziekengeld[h]

sick call ziekenbezoek[h] [by doctor or clergyman]

¹sicken (vb) **1** ziek worden **2** misselijk worden **3** (+ for) smachten (naar) **4** de eerste tekenen (van een ziekte) vertonen, onder de leden hebben: *be ~ing* **for** *measles* de mazelen onder de leden hebben

²sicken (vb) ziek maken, doen walgen

sickening 1 ziekmakend, ziekteverwekkend **2** walgelijk, weerzinwekkend

sickle sikkel

sick leave ziekteverlof[h]: *on ~* met ziekteverlof

sick list ziekenlijst: *on the ~* afwezig wegens ziekte

sickly 1 ziekelijk, sukkelend **2** bleek [face, complexion]; flauw [smile] **3** walgelijk [smell]; wee [smell, air]

sickness 1 ziekte **2** misselijkheid

sickness benefit ziektegeld[h], uitkering wegens ziekte

sick pay ziekengeld[h]

¹side (n) **1** zij(de), (zij)kant, flank; helling [of mountain]; oever [of river]; richting, aspect[h]; trek [of character]: *always look on the* **bright** *~ of life* bekijk het leven altijd van de zonnige kant; *take ~s with s.o.* partij voor iem. kiezen; *this ~* **up** deze kant boven [on boxes before shipping]; *at* (or: *by*) *my ~* naast mij; *~ by ~* zij aan zij; *whose ~ are you on, anyway?* aan wiens kant sta jij eigenlijk? **2** bladzijde **3** gedeelte[h], deel[h]: *he went to the* **far** *~ of the room* hij liep tot achter in de kamer **4** gezichtspunt[h] **5** ploeg, team[h]: *let the ~ down* niet aan de verwachtingen van de anderen voldoen ‖ *know (on) which ~ one's* **bread** *is buttered* weten waar men zijn kaarsje moet laten branden; *the other ~ of the* **coin** de keerzijde van de medaille; *laugh on the other ~ of one's face* (or: *mouth*) lachen als een boer die kiespijn heeft; *put on* (or: *to*) *one ~,* *set on one ~* terzijde leggen, sparen, reserveren; *take on* (or: *to*) *one ~* terzijde nemen [for a talk]; *on the ~* **a)** als bijverdienste, zwart; **b)** in het geniep

²side (adj) **1** zij-: *~ entrance* zijingang **2** bij-, neven-

³side (vb) (+ against, with) partij kiezen (tegen, voor)

sideboard 1 buffet[h] **2** dientafel **3** (-s) bakkebaarden

sideburns bakkebaarden

sidecar zijspan[h]

side dish bijgerecht[h]

side effect 1 bijwerking [of medicine or therapy] **2** neveneffect[h]

sidekick handlanger, ondergeschikte partner

sidelight 1 zijlicht[h]; stadslicht[h] [of car] **2** [fig] toevallige informatie: *that throws some* **interesting** *~s on the problem* dat werpt een interessant licht op de zaak

¹sideline (n) **1** bijbaan, nevenactiviteit **2** (-s) [sport] zijlijnen ‖ *be* (or: *sit, stand*) **on** *the ~s* de zaak van een afstand bekijken

²sideline (vb) van het veld sturen; [fig] buiten spel zetten; negeren

sidelong zijdelings

side-saddle dameszadel[h]

sideshow bijkomende voorstelling; extra attractie [at fairground; in circus]

side-slip zijwaartse slip [of car, aeroplane, skier]

¹sidestep (vb) opzijgaan, uitwijken

²sidestep (vb) ontwijken; uit de weg gaan [also fig; responsibility, problems]

sidestroke zijslag [swimming]

¹sideswipe (n) **1** zijslag, zijstoot **2** schimpscheut, hatelijke opmerking

²sideswipe (vb) schampen (langs), zijdelings raken

sidetrack 1 op een zijspoor zetten [also fig]; rangeren, opzijschuiven **2** van zijn onderwerp afbrengen, afleiden

sidewalk [Am] stoep, trottoir[h]

sideward zijwaarts, zijdelings

sideways zijwaarts, zijdelings

siding 1 rangeerspoor[h], wisselspoor[h] **2** afbouwmateriaal[h]; buitenbekleding [of wall]

sidle zich schuchter bewegen: *~ up to s.o., ~ away from s.o.* schuchter naar iem. toelopen, schuchter van iem. weglopen

siege beleg[h], belegering, blokkade: *lay ~ to* belegeren; *raise the ~* het beleg opbreken

Sierra Leone Sierra Leone

¹Sierra Leonian (n) Sierra Leoner, Sierra Leoonse

²Sierra Leonian (adj) Sierra Leoons

¹sieve (n) zeef: *a memory like a ~* een geheugen als een zeef

²sieve (vb) ziften [also fig]; zeven, schiften

sift 1 ziften [also fig]; strooien [sugar]: *~ out* uitzeven **2** uitpluizen, doorpluizen: *he ~ed through his papers* hij doorzocht zijn papieren

¹sigh (n) zucht

²sigh (vb) zuchten: *~ for* smachten naar

¹sight (n) **1** (aan)blik, (uit)zicht[h], schouwspel[h], bezienswaardigheid: *I cannot* **stand** (or: *bear*) *the ~ of him* ik kan hem niet luchten of zien; *catch ~ of, get a ~ of* in het oog krijgen, een glimp opvangen van; *lose ~ of* uit het oog verliezen [also fig]; *see the* ~s de bezienswaardigheden bezoeken **2** vizier^h: *have one's* ~*s* **set** *on*, **set** *one's* ~*s* on op het oog hebben, erg willen **3** boel: *he is a* ~ *too clever for me* hij is me veel te vlug af **4** (ge)zicht^h, gezichtsvermogen^h: *loss of* ~ het blind worden **5** gezicht^h, het zien: *at first* ~ op het eerste gezicht; *know s.o. by* ~ iem. van gezicht kennen **6** (uit)zicht^h, gezicht(sveld)^h: *come into* (or: *within*) ~ zichtbaar worden; *keep in* ~ of binnen het gezichtsveld blijven van; *out of* ~, *out of mind* uit het oog, uit het hart; *we are (with)in* ~ *of the end* het einde is in zicht; *stay* (or: *keep*) *out of* ~ blijf uit het gezicht ‖ *raise* (or: *lower*) *one's* ~*s* meer (or: minder) verwachten; *out of* ~! fantastisch!, te gek!; *second* ~ helderziendheid

²**sight** (vb) **1** in zicht krijgen, in het vizier krijgen **2** waarnemen, zien: *he was last* ~*ed in London* hij werd voor het laatst gezien in Londen

sighting waarneming: *there have been numerous* ~*s of UFO's lately* er zijn de laatste tijd veel vliegende schotels gezien

sightread [mus] van blad spelen (or: zingen)

sightseeing het bezoeken van bezienswaardigheden

sightseer toerist

¹**sign** (n) **1** teken^h, symbool^h **2** aanwijzing, (ken)teken^h, blijk, voorteken^h **3** wenk, teken^h, seintje^h **4** (uithang)bord^h **5** (ken)teken^h: ~ *of the times* teken des tijds **6** sterrenbeeld^h: ~ *of the zodiac* sterrenbeeld

²**sign** (vb) **1** (onder)tekenen: ~ *one's name* tekenen; ~ *in* tekenen bij aankomst, intekenen; ~ *on at the Job Centre* inschrijven op het arbeidsbureau; ~ *up for a course* zich voor een cursus inschrijven **2** signeren, ondertekenen: ~*ed copies are available within* gesigneerde exemplaren zijn binnen verkrijgbaar **3** wenken, een teken geven, gebaren **4** (+ on, up) contracteren [player]

¹**signal** (n) **1** signaal^h [also fig; also of radio, TV]; teken^h, sein^h: ~ *of distress* noodsignaal **2** sein(apparaat^h), signaal^h **3** verkeerslicht^h

²**signal** (adj) buitengewoon, glansrijk: *a* ~ *victory* een glansrijke overwinning

³**signal** (vb) aankondigen, te kennen geven

⁴**signal** (vb) (over)seinen, een teken geven

signal box seinhuisje^h

signalize doen opvallen, de aandacht vestigen op, opluisteren

signalman seiner; [railways also] sein(huis)wachter

signatory ondertekenaar

signature handtekening

signature campaign handtekeningenactie

signature tune herkenningsmelodie; tune [of radio, TV]

signboard 1 uithangbord^h **2** bord^h met opschrift

signet zegel^h

signet ring zegelring

significance betekenis, belang^h: *a meeting of great historical* ~ een ontmoeting van grote historische betekenis

significant belangrijk, veelbetekenend: *be* ~ *of* aanduiden, kenmerkend zijn voor

signify 1 betekenen, beduiden **2** te kennen geven: *the teacher rose,* ~*ing that the class was over* de docent stond op, daarmee gaf hij te kennen dat de les afgelopen was

sign language gebarentaal

sign-on herkenningsmelodie [of radio or TV programme]; tune

signpost wegwijzer

¹**silence** (n) stilte, stilzwijgen^h, stilzwijgendheid, zwijgzaamheid: *put* (or: *reduce*) *s.o. to* ~ iem. tot zwijgen brengen; *in* ~ in stilte, stilzwijgend; ~! stil!, zwijg!

²**silence** (vb) tot zwijgen brengen, het stilzwijgen opleggen, stil doen zijn

silencer 1 geluiddemper [on firearm] **2** knalpot

silent stil, (stil)zwijgend, zwijgzaam, onuitgesproken, stom, rustig: *a* ~ *film* een stomme film; *keep* ~ rustig blijven

silhouette silhouet^h, beeltenis, schaduwbeeld^h, omtrek

silicone silicone^h

¹**silk** (n) **1** zij(de), zijdedraad **2** King's (Queen's) Counsel

²**silk** (adj) zijden, zijde-

silken 1 zij(de)achtig **2** zacht

silkworm zijderups

sill 1 vensterbank **2** drempel

¹**silly** (n) domoor: *of course you're coming with us,* ~! natuurlijk mag je met ons mee, dommerdje!

²**silly** (adj) **1** dwaas, dom, onverstandig **2** verdwaasd, suf, murw: *knock s.o.* ~ iem. murw slaan

silly season komkommertijd

silo silo, voederkuil, (betonnen) voedersleuf

silt slib^h, slik

silt up dichtslibben, verzanden

¹**silver** (n) **1** zilver^h **2** zilvergeld^h **3** zilver(-werk)^h; [fig] tafelgerei^h

²**silver** (adj) **1** van zilver, zilveren, zilver-: ~ *foil* zilverfolie **2** verzilverd: ~ *plate* verzilverd vaatwerk **3** zilverachtig ‖ ~ *wedding* (anniversary) zilveren bruiloft

silverfish zilvervisje^h, papiermot

silversmith zilversmid

silvery zilverachtig, zilverkleurig

SIM card simkaart

simian (mens)aap

similar (+ to) gelijk (aan), vergelijkbaar, hetzelfde; [maths] gelijkvormig: *in* ~ *cases* in vergelijkbare gevallen

similarity 1 vergelijkbaarheid, overeenkomst **2** punt[h] van overeenkomst, gelijkenis
similarly 1 op dezelfde manier, op een vergelijkbare manier **2** [at beginning of sentence] evenzo
simile vergelijking; gelijkenis [figure of speech]
[1]**simmer** (n) gesudder[h], gepruttel[h]
[2]**simmer** (vb) **1** sudderen, pruttelen **2** zich inhouden [of rage, laughter]: ~ *down* bedaren
[3]**simmer** (vb) aan het sudderen brengen/houden
[1]**simper** (n) onnozele glimlach, zelfvoldane grijnslach
[2]**simper** (vb) onnozel glimlachen, zelfvoldaan grijnslachen
simple 1 eenvoudig, eerlijk, simpel: *the* ~ *life* het natuurlijke leven; *the* ~ *truth* de nuchtere waarheid **2** dwaas, onnozel **3** eenvoudig, gemakkelijk: ~ *solution* eenvoudige oplossing **4** enkel(voudig): ~ *forms of life* eenvoudige levensvormen
simple-minded 1 argeloos, onnadenkend **2** zwakzinnig
simpleton dwaas, sul
simplicity 1 eenvoud, ongecompliceerdheid: *it is* ~ *itself* het is een koud kunstje **2** simpelheid
simplification vereenvoudiging
simplify 1 vereenvoudigen **2** (te) eenvoudig voorstellen, simplificeren
simplistic simplistisch
simply 1 eenvoudig, gewoonweg **2** stomweg **3** enkel, maar, slechts: *if you want to call the nurse,* ~ *push the red button* als u de zuster wilt roepen, hoeft u alleen maar op de rode knop te drukken
simulate 1 simuleren, voorwenden, doen alsof **2** imiteren, nabootsen: ~*d gold* namaakgoud
simulation 1 voorwending, veinzerij **2** nabootsing, imitatie
simultaneity gelijktijdigheid
simultaneous gelijktijdig, simultaan: ~*ly with* tegelijk met
[1]**sin** (n) zonde; [fig also] misdaad: *live in* ~ in zonde leven, in zonde samenwonen; *for my* ~*s* voor mijn straf
[2]**sin** (vb) (+ against) zondigen (tegen)
[1]**since** (adv) **1** sindsdien, van toen af, ondertussen: *I've lived here ever* ~ ik heb hier sindsdien de hele tijd gewoond **2** geleden: *he left some years* ~ hij is enige jaren geleden weggegaan
[2]**since** (prep) sinds, sedert, van ... af: *he has never been the same* ~ *his wife's death* hij is nooit meer dezelfde geweest sinds de dood van zijn vrouw
[3]**since** (conj) **1** sinds, vanaf de tijd dat: *I haven't* seen you ~ *you were a child* ik heb je

niet meer gezien sinds je klein was **2** aangezien, daar: ~ *you don't want me around I might as well leave* aangezien je me niet in de buurt wilt hebben, kan ik net zo goed weggaan
sincere eerlijk, oprecht, gemeend
sincerely eerlijk, oprecht, gemeend: *yours* ~ met vriendelijke groeten [complimentary close in letter to acquaintances]
sincerity eerlijkheid, gemeendheid: *in all* ~ in alle oprechtheid
sine sinus
sinew 1 pees **2** (spier)kracht
sinful 1 zondig, schuldig **2** slecht: *a* ~ *waste of money* een schandalige geldverspilling
[1]**sing** (vb) **1** zingen; suizen [of wind]; fluiten [of bullet] **2** gonzen [of ear] || ~ *sth. out* iets uitroepen; ~ *out (for)* schreeuwen (om)
[2]**sing** (vb) bezingen
[3]**sing** *singular* enk, enkelvoud
Singapore Singapore
[1]**Singaporean** (n) Singaporees, Singaporese
[2]**Singaporean** (adj) Singaporees
[1]**singe** (n) **1** schroeiing **2** schroeiplek
[2]**singe** (vb) **1** (ver)schroeien **2** krullen; golven [hair]
singer zanger(es)
singing 1 (ge)zang[h], het zingen **2** zangkunst
[1]**single** (n) **1** enkeltje[h], enkele reis **2** vrijgezel **3** [mus] single **4** (-s) enkel(spel)[h] [at tennis]
[2]**single** (adj) **1** enkel(voudig) **2** ongetrouwd, alleenstaand **3** enig **4** afzonderlijk, individueel: *not a* ~ *man* helped niet één man hielp **5** eenpersoons-: ~ *bed* eenpersoonsbed **6** enkele reis: *a* ~ *ticket* een (kaartje) enkele reis || *in* ~ *file* achter elkaar (in de rij)
single-handed alleen, zonder steun
single-minded 1 doelbewust **2** vastberaden
singleness concentratie || ~ *of purpose* doelgerichte toewijding
single out uitkiezen, selecteren
single-parent family eenoudergezin[h]
singlet (onder)hemd[h], sporthemd[h]
[1]**sing-song** (n) **1** dreun: *say sth. in a* ~ iets opdreunen **2** samenzang
[2]**sing-song** (adj) eentonig, zangerig
[1]**singular** (n) [linguistics] enkelvoud[h], enkelvoudsvorm
[2]**singular** (adj) **1** bijzonder, uitzonderlijk **2** ongewoon, vreemd: ~ *event* eigenaardige gebeurtenis
singularity bijzonderheid, eigenaardigheid
Sinhalese Singalees, Singalese [inhabitant of Sri Lanka]
sinister 1 boosaardig, onguur **2** onheilspellend, duister, sinister
[1]**sink** (n) **1** gootsteen(bak) **2** wasbak **3** poel (van kwaad): ~ *of iniquity* poel van verderf

²**sink** (vb) **1** (weg)zinken, (weg)zakken, verzakken: *her spirits sank* de moed zonk haar in de schoenen; *his voice sank* **to** *a whisper* zijn stem daalde tot op fluisterniveau **2** (neer)-dalen: ~ *in one's estimation* in iemands achting dalen **3** afnemen, verflauwen, verdwijnen **4** achteruit gaan, zwakker worden: *the sick man is ~ing fast* de zieke man gaat snel achteruit **5** doordringen, indringen (in): *his words will ~ in* zijn woorden zullen inslaan ‖ ~ *or swim* pompen of verzuipen

³**sink** (vb) **1** laten zinken, doen zakken: ~ *a ship* een schip tot zinken brengen **2** vergeten, laten rusten: ~ *the differences* de geschillen vergeten **3** graven, boren: ~ *a well* een put boren **4** bederven [plan etc]; verpesten ‖ *be sunk in thought* in gedachten verzonken zijn; *be sunk* reddeloos verloren zijn

sinner zondaar

sinuous 1 kronkelend, bochtig **2** lenig, buigzaam

sinus holte, opening; [anatomy] sinus

sinusitis voorhoofdsholteontsteking

¹**sip** (n) slokjeʰ, teugjeʰ

²**sip** (vb) **1** met kleine teugjes drinken **2** (+ at) nippen (aan)

siphon (also + off, out) (over)hevelen [also fig]; overtappen: *management ~ed millions into plans for the building of a new head office* de directie hevelde miljoenen over naar plannen voor de bouw van een nieuw hoofdkantoor

sir meneer; mijnheer [form of address]: *Dear Sir* geachte heer; *Dear Sirs* mijne heren [in letter]; *no ~!* geen sprake van!

sire 1 vader van dier [of horse] **2** Sire; heer [form of address of emperor, king]

siren 1 (alarm)sirene **2** [mythology] sirene **3** verleidster

sirloin (steak) lendenbiefstuk

sis [inform] *sister* zusjeʰ

sissy mietjeʰ, watjeʰ

sister 1 zus(ter) **2** non, zuster **3** (hoofd)verpleegster

sisterhood 1 zusterschap, nonnenorde **2** vrouwenbeweging

sister-in-law schoonzus(ter)

¹**sit** (vb) **1** zitten: ~ *tight* rustig blijven zitten, volhouden **2** zijn, zich bevinden, liggen, staan: ~ *heavy on the stomach* zwaar op de maag liggen **3** poseren, model staan: ~ *for a portrait* voor een portret poseren **4** (zitten te) broeden **5** zitting hebben ‖ ~ *pretty* op rozen zitten; ~ *about* (or: *around*) lanterfanten; ~ *back* gemakkelijk gaan zitten; [fig] zijn gemak nemen, zich terugtrekken; ~ *by* rustig toe zitten te kijken; ~ *down* gaan zitten; ~ *in* als vervanger optreden; ~ *in on* als toehoorder bijwonen; ~ *for an exam* een examen afleggen

²**sit** (vb) **1** laten zitten **2** berijden [horse]

3 afleggen [examination]

sitcom *situation comedy* komische tv-serie

sit-down zittend: ~ *meal* zittend genuttigde maaltijd

¹**site** (n) **1** plaats, locatie **2** (bouw)terreinʰ

²**site** (vb) plaatsen, situeren: *the farm is beautifully ~d* de boerderij is prachtig gelegen

sit on 1 zitting hebben in **2** onderzoeken **3** laten liggen, niets doen aan **4** terechtwijzen, op z'n kop zitten

sit out 1 uitzitten [eg concert] **2** niet meedoen aan [eg dance]

sitter 1 modelʰ, iem. die poseert **2** broedende vogel, broedhen **3** *babysitter* kinderoppas, babysit

sitter-in (baby)oppas

¹**sitting** (n) **1** zitting, vergadering **2** tafel, gelegenheid om te eten **3** het zitten **4** het poseren ‖ *he read the story at one ~* hij las het verhaal in één ruk uit

²**sitting** (adj) zittend: ~ *duck* (or: *target*) makkelijk doel(wit), weerloos slachtoffer; ~ *tenant* huidige huurder

sitting room zitkamer, woonkamer, huiskamer

situated 1 geplaatst **2** gelegen, gesitueerd

situation 1 toestand, situatie, omstandigheden **2** ligging, plaats **3** betrekking, baan: ~ *vacant* functie aangeboden, vacature

situation comedy komische tv-serie

sit up 1 rechtop (gaan) zitten: *that will make him ~ and take notice!* daar zal hij van opkijken! **2** opblijven; waken [with sick person]

six zes: *arranged by ~es* per zes geschikt ‖ *everything is at ~es and sevens* alles is helemaal in de war; *it's ~ of one and half a dozen of the other, it's ~ and two threes* het is lood om oud ijzer

sixfold zesvoudig

six-shooter revolver

sixteen zestien

sixteenth zestiende

sixth zesde

sixth form bovenbouw vwo

sixthly ten zesde, op de zesde plaats

sixtieth zestigste

sixty zestig: *in the sixties* in de jaren zestig

sixty-four thousand dollar question hamvraag

size 1 afmeting, formaatʰ, grootte, omvang: *trees of various ~s* bomen van verschillende grootte **2** maat: *she takes ~ eight* ze heeft maat acht ‖ *cut down to ~* iem. op zijn plaats zetten

sizeable vrij groot, flink

¹**sizzle** (n) gesisʰ, geknetterʰ

²**sizzle** (vb) sissen, knetteren

sizzling snik-: *a ~ hot day* een snikhete dag

skanking [inform] dansstijl met wilde (arm)bewegingen

¹**skate** (n) **1** schaats: *get* (or: *put*) *one's ~s on*

opschieten **2** rolschaats
²skate (vb) **1** schaatsen(rijden) **2** rolschaatsen ‖ ~ **over** (or: *round*) *sth.* ergens luchtig
overheen lopen
skateboard skateboardʰ, rol(schaats)plank
skateboarding skateboarden
skater 1 schaatser **2** rolschaatser
skating rink 1 ijsbaan, schaatsbaan **2** rolschaatsbaan
skedaddle ervandoor gaan, 'm smeren
skeleton 1 skeletʰ, geraamteʰ: *the ~ of the*
building het geraamte van het gebouw
2 uitgemergeld persoon (dierʰ) **3** schemaʰ,
schets ‖ ~ *in the* **cupboard** (or: **closet**) onplezierig (familie)geheim, lijk in de kast
skeleton key loper
¹sketch (n) **1** schets, tekening, beknopte beschrijving **2** sketch, kort toneelstukjeʰ (verhaalʰ)
²sketch (vb) schetsen, tekenen
³sketch (vb) (also + in, out) schetsen, kort
beschrijven
sketchy schetsmatig, ruw; [fig] oppervlakkig
skew schuin, scheef
¹skewer (n) vleespen, spies
²skewer (vb) doorsteken [(as if) with skewer]
¹ski (n) ski
²ski (vb) skiën, skilopen
¹skid (n) **1** steunblokʰ, steunbalk **2** glijbaan,
glijplank **3** remschoen, remblokʰ **4** schuiver,
slip, slippartij: *the car went* **into** *a* ~ de wagen
raakte in een slip ‖ **put** *the ~s under one's*
plans **a)** iem. (iets) ruïneren; **b)** iem. achter
zijn vodden zitten
²skid (vb) slippen [also of wheel]; schuiven
skidmark remspoorʰ [also fig]
skid row achterbuurt
skier skiër
skiff skiff
skiing skisport; skiënʰ
skilful bekwaam, (des)kundig, vakkundig,
ervaren
skill bekwaamheid, vakkundigheid, vaardigheid
skilled bekwaam, vakkundig: ~ **worker** geschoolde arbeider, vakman
skim 1 vluchtig inkijken: ~ *over a* **book** een
boek vlug doornemen **2** afromen [milk]
3 scheren
skimmed afgeroomd: ~ *milk* taptemelk
¹skimp (vb) (+ on) bezuinigen (op), beknibbelen: *whatever you do, don't* ~ **on** *your food*
wat je ook doet, ga in ieder geval niet bezuinigen op het eten
²skimp (vb) **1** karig (toe)bedelen, zuinig zijn
met **2** kort houden
skimpy karig, schaars
¹skin (n) huid [also of aeroplane, ship]; velʰ,
pels: *have a* **thick** ~ een olifantshuid hebben;

have a **thin** ~ erg gevoelig zijn ‖ ~ *and* **bone(s)**
vel over been; *escape by the* ~ *of one's* **teeth**
op het nippertje ontsnappen; **get** *under s.o.'s*
~ **a)** iem. irriteren; **b)** bezeten zijn van iem.;
save one's ~ er heelhuids afkomen
²skin (vb) **1** villen; (af)stropen [also fig]
2 schillen, pellen **3** oplichten, afzetten ‖
keep *one's eye* ~*ned* alert zijn, wakker blijven
skin-deep oppervlakkig [also fig]: *his politeness* **is** *only* ~ zijn beleefdheid is alleen
maar buitenkant
skin diver sportduiker
skinflint vrek
skinful genoeg drank om dronken van te
worden: *he has* **had** *quite a* ~ *by the look of him*
hij heeft zo te zien al het nodige op
skin game 1 oneerlijk gokspelʰ **2** afzetterij, zwendel
skinhead skinhead
skinny broodmager: *a* ~ *latte* een koffie
verkeerd met magere melk
skin patch huidpleister, slimme pleister
skint platzak, blut
¹skip (n) **1** sprongetjeʰ **2** afvalcontainer
²skip (vb) **1** huppelen, (over)springen
2 touwtjespringen ‖ ~ **over** overslaan, luchtig overheen gaan
³skip (vb) overslaan, weglaten, wegblijven
van
skipper 1 kapitein, schipper **2** [sport] aanvoerder van een team
¹skirmish (n) **1** schermutseling [also fig]
2 woordenwisseling
²skirmish (vb) **1** schermutselen **2** (rede)twisten
¹skirt (n) **1** rok **2** rand, zoom, uiteindeʰ
3 [inform] stukʰ: *what a* **piece** *of* ~! wat een
stuk!
²skirt (vb) **1** begrenzen, lopen langs **2** ontwijken, omzeilen
skirting board plint
skittish 1 schichtig [of horse]; nerveus
2 grillig **3** frivool
skittle kegel
skive zich aan het werk onttrekken, zich
drukken: *were you skiving or were you really ill?*
was je je aan het drukken, of was je echt
ziek?
skulk 1 zich verschuilen **2** sluipen
skull schedel, doodshoofdʰ: ~ *and* **crossbones** doodshoofd met gekruiste beenderen; *he couldn't* **get** *it into his* ~ het drong niet
tot zijn hersenen door
skullcap petjeʰ, kalotjeʰ, keppeltjeʰ
skunk 1 stinkdierʰ **2** schoft, schooier
sky hemel, lucht: *praise s.o. to the skies* iem.
de hemel in prijzen ‖ *the* ~ *is the* **limit** het kan
niet op [of money]
sky-blue hemelsblauw
skydive [parachuting] vrije val maken: *skydiving* vrije val

sky-high hemelhoog; [fig] buitensporig hoog [eg prices]: *blow* ~ in de lucht laten vliegen, opblazen; [fig] geen spaan heel laten van
skyjacking (vliegtuig)kaping
¹skylark (n) veldleeuwerik
²skylark (vb) **1** stoeien **2** pret maken
skylight dakraamʰ
skyline 1 horizon **2** skyline; silhouetʰ [seen against sky]
skyrocket omhoogschieten [of prices]: *fuel prices have ~ed again* de brandstofprijzen zijn weer huizenhoog gestegen
skyscraper wolkenkrabber
slab 1 plaat [eg iron] **2** plat rechthoekig stukʰ steen
¹slack (n) **1** los (hangend) deel van zeil of touw: *take* up (or: *in*) *the* ~ **a)** aantrekken [rope etc]; **b)** [fig] de teugel(s) kort houden **2** steenkoolgruisʰ **3** (-s) sportpantalon, lange broek **4** slappe tijd
²slack (adj) **1** slap, los: *reign with a* ~ *hand* met slappe hand regeren **2** zwak, laks **3** lui, traag ‖ ~ *water* stil water, dood getijde
³slack (vb) **1** verslappen, (zich) ontspannen **2** los(ser) maken, (laten) vieren **3** de kantjes ervan af lopen, traag werken ‖ ~ *off* verslappen [in one's work]
¹slacken (vb) **1** verslappen, (zich) ontspannen **2** langzamer lopen (rijden) **3** verminderen, afnemen
²slacken (vb) los(ser) maken, (laten) vieren: ~ *speed* vaart minderen
slacker luilak
slacklining slacklinenʰ
slag-heap heuvel van mijnafval
¹slam (n) **1** harde slag; [baseball] rake slag **2** slemʰ [bridge]; alle slagen: *grand* ~ groot slem
²slam (vb) **1** met een klap dichtslaan, (neer)smijten, dichtsmijten: ~ *the door* (*in s.o.'s face*) de deur (voor iemands neus) dichtslaan; ~ *down* neersmijten **2** harde klap met de hand geven **3** scherp bekritiseren
¹slander (n) laster(praat)
²slander (vb) (be)lasteren
slanderous lasterlijk
slang zeer informele taal, jargonʰ/taal van bepaalde sociale klasse of beroep
¹slant (n) **1** helling, schuinte **2** gezichtspuntʰ, kijk, optiek ‖ *the top shelf was on a* ~ de bovenste plank hing scheef
²slant (vb) hellen, schuin aflopen
³slant (vb) **1** laten hellen, scheef houden **2** niet objectief weergeven: ~*ed news* nieuwsberichten waarin partij wordt gekozen
¹slap (n) klap, mep: ~ *on the back* vriendschappelijke klap op de rug; [fig] schouderklopje; ~ *in the face* klap in het gezicht [also fig]; ~ *on the wrist* vermaning, lichte straf; ~

and tickle geflirt
²slap (vb) **1** een klap geven, meppen: ~ *s.o. on the back* iem. op zijn schouder kloppen, iem. feliciteren **2** smijten, kwakken: ~ *down* **a)** neersmijten; **b)** [inform] hard aanpakken [eg a wrong]
³slap (adv) **1** met een klap, regelrecht **2** eensklaps
slapdash nonchalant, lukraak
slap-happy 1 uitgelaten **2** nonchalant
slapstick 1 gooi-en-smijtfilm **2** grove humor
slap-up super-de-luxe, eersteklas
¹slash (n) **1** houw, slag **2** snee, jaap **3** schuine streep
²slash (vb) **1** houwen **2** snijden **3** striemen **4** drastisch verlagen [prices] **5** scherp bekritiseren **6** een split maken in: ~*ed sleeve* mouw met split
¹slate (n) **1** lei [rock, writing tablet]; daklei **2** kandidatenlijst
²slate (vb) **1** beleggen [eg meeting]; vaststellen **2** scherp bekritiseren **3** (als kandidaat) voordragen, voorstellen
slatternly slonzig
¹slaughter (n) slachting, bloedbadʰ
²slaughter (vb) **1** slachten, vermoorden **2** totaal verslaan, inmaken
slaughterhouse slachthuisʰ, abattoirʰ
¹Slav (n) Slaaf, Slavische
²Slav (adj) Slavisch
¹slave (n) slaaf, slavin
²slave (vb) zich uitsloven, zwoegen: ~ *away* (*at sth.*) zwoegen (op iets), ploeteren [eg for examination]
slaver kwijlen [also fig]: *that dog is ~ing at the mouth* het kwijl loopt die hond zijn bek uit
slavery 1 slavernij **2** slavenarbeid
Slavic Slavisch
slavish slaafs, onderdanig
slay doden, afmaken, slachten
sleaze goorheid, viesheid
sleazy 1 goor, vies **2** armoedig, goedkoop: ~ *excuse* waardeloos excuus
¹sled (n) slee
²sled (vb) sleeën
sledge slee
sledgehammer voorhamer, moker: ~ *blow* keiharde slag
¹sleek (adj) **1** zacht en glanzend [of hair] **2** (te) keurig verzorgd, opgedoft, opgedirkt **3** mooi gestroomlijnd [of car]
²sleek (vb) gladmaken **2** glanzend maken
¹sleep (n) **1** slaap, nachtrust: *my foot has gone to* ~ mijn voet slaapt; *not lose* ~ *over sth.* niet wakker liggen van iets; *put to* ~ **a)** in slaap brengen; **b)** wegmaken [anaesthetic]; **c)** een spuitje geven [animal] **2** rust(periode), winterslaap **3** slaap, oogvuilʰ
²sleep (vb) slapen, rusten: ~ *round the clock*

de klok rond slapen; ~ *late* uitslapen; ~ *in*
a) in huis slapen [eg as housesitter]; **b)** uitslapen; ~ *on* (or: *over*) *sth.* een nachtje over iets
slapen || *let* ~*ing* *dogs* *lie* men moet geen sla-
pende honden wakker maken; ~ *around* met
jan en alleman naar bed gaan; ~ *with* *s.o.*
met iem. naar bed gaan
³sleep (vb) slaapplaats hebben voor: *this hotel* ~*s eighty (guests)* dit hotel biedt plaats
voor tachtig gasten || ~ *off* one's hangover zijn
roes uitslapen
sleeper 1 slaper, slaapkop **2** dwarsbalk [of
railway]; biel(s) **3** slaapwagen, slaaptrein
sleeping bag slaapzak
sleepover logeerpartij
sleepwalker slaapwandelaar
sleepy 1 slaperig **2** loom
¹sleet (n) natte sneeuw(bui), natte hagel-
(bui)
²sleet (vb) sneeuwen en regenen tegelijk
sleeve 1 mouw **2** koker, mof **3** hoes [of
gramophone record] || *have* *sth.* *up one's* ~
iets achter de hand houden; *laugh* *in* (or: *up*)
one's ~ in zijn vuistje lachen; *roll* *up one's* ~*s*
de handen uit de mouwen steken
sleeveless mouwloos
sleigh arrenslee
sleight-of-hand 1 goochelarij; gegoo-
chelʰ [also fig] **2** vingervlugheid
slender 1 slank, tenger **2** schaars, karig: *a* ~
income een karig inkomen **3** zwak, teer
sleuth 1 speurhond **2** [mockingly] detective, speurneus
¹slew (n) [Am] massa, hoop: *there have been a
whole* ~ *of* *shooting incidents* er is weer een
hele reeks schietpartijen geweest
²slew (vb) (rond)zwenken, met kracht omdraaien
¹slice (n) **1** plak(jeʰ), snee(tjeʰ), schijf(jeʰ): ~
of cake plakje cake **2** deelʰ **3** schep || ~ *of luck*
meevaller
²slice (vb) **1** (also + up) in plakken snijden
2 snijden: ~*d bread* gesneden brood **3** (+ off)
afsnijden
³slice (vb) kappen [hit (ball) with spin]
¹slick (n) olievlek [on surface of sea]
²slick (adj) [inform] **1** glad, glibberig, glanzend **2** glad, uitgeslapen, gehaaid **3** oppervlakkig, zich mooi voordoend **4** goed (uitgevoerd), kundig, soepel (draaiend/verlopend)
slicker 1 gladjanus **2** waterafstotende regenjas
¹slide (n) **1** glijbaan **2** sleehelling **3** val; achteruitgang [also fig]: *a dangerous* ~ *in* *oil prices* een gevaarlijke daling van de olieprijzen
4 (stoom)schuif **5** dia(positiefʰ) **6** (aard)ver-
schuiving, lawine **7** haarspeld
²slide (vb) **1** schuiven: *sliding door* schuifdeur; *sliding scale* variabele schaal, glijdende
(loon)schaal **2** slippen **3** (uit)glijden
4 (voort) laten glijden || ~ *over* *sth.* luchtig

over iets heen praten
slide rule rekenliniaal
¹slight (adj) **1** tenger, broos **2** gering, klein,
onbeduidend: ~ *cold* lichte verkoudheid; *not
in the* ~*est* niet in het minst
²slight (vb) geringschatten, kleineren: ~*ing
remarks about his teacher* geringschattende
opmerkingen over zijn docent
slightly een beetje, enigszins: ~ *longer* een
beetje langer
¹slim (adj) **1** slank, tenger **2** klein, gering: ~
chance geringe kans
²slim (vb) afslanken, aan de (slanke) lijn
doen
slime slijmʰ
slimy 1 slijmerig [also fig]; glibberig **2** kruiperig
¹sling (n) **1** slinger **2** zwaai, slingering **3** katapult **4** draagdoek, mitella **5** draagriem,
draagband **6** lus, (hijs)strop
²sling (vb) **1** (weg)slingeren, zwaaien, smijten: ~ *s.o. out* iem. eruit smijten **2** ophangen
slink (weg)sluipen: ~ *away* (or: *off, out*) zich
stilletjes uit de voeten maken; ~ *in* heimelijk
binnensluipen
¹slip (n) **1** misstap [also fig]; vergissing, on-
gelukjeʰ: ~ *of the pen* verschrijving; ~ *of the
tongue* verspreking **2** hoesjeʰ, (kussen)sloop
3 onderrok, onderjurk **4** strookjeʰ (papier)
5 stek(jeʰ), ent || *give* *s.o. the* ~ aan iem. ont-
snappen
²slip (vb) **1** (uit)glijden, slippen: ~*ped* *disc*
hernia; *time* ~*s away* (or: *by*) de tijd gaat ongemerkt voorbij; ~ *through* doorschieten
2 glippen, (snel) sluipen: ~ *away* wegglip-
pen; ~ *in* (or: *out*) naar binnen (or: buiten)
glippen; ~ *through* *one's fingers* door zijn
vingers glippen **3** afglijden, vervallen || *let* ~
zich verspreken; ~ *up* zich vergissen; ~ *into*
(or: *out*) *of a dress* een jurk aanschieten (or:
uittrekken)
³slip (vb) **1** schuiven, slippen, laten glijden: ~
in a remark een opmerking tussendoor plaatsen **2** ontglippen, ontschieten: ~ *one's attention* ontgaan; ~ *one's memory* (or: *mind*)
vergeten; *let* ~ **a)** zich laten ontvallen; **b)** laten ontsnappen **3** (onopvallend) toestoppen
slip-knot 1 schuifknoop **2** slipsteek
slipover 1 slip-over **2** pullover
slipper pantoffel, slipper
slippery 1 glad, glibberig **2** moeilijk te
pakken te krijgen, ontwijkend; [fig also]
moeilijk te begrijpen **3** glibberig, riskant
4 onbetrouwbaar, vals || ~ *slope* glibberig
pad, gevaarlijke koers
slip road oprit, afrit; invoegstrook, uitvoegstrook
slipshod onzorgvuldig, slordig
slipstream 1 schroefwind, luchtbeweging
door de propeller veroorzaakt **2** zuiging
[behind car]

slip-up vergissing, fout(je[h])
¹slit (n) **1** spleet, gleuf, lange snee **2** split [eg in dress]
²slit (vb) **1** snijden **2** scheuren
slither glijden, glibberen
sliver 1 splinter, scherf **2** dun plakje[h]
slob smeerlap, slons, luie stomkop
slobber 1 kwijlen **2** sentimenteel doen, zwijmelen: ~ *over sth.* zwijmelig doen over iets
¹slog (n) **1** geploeter[h], gezwoeg[h] **2** [cricket, boxing] harde klap, woeste slag, uithaal
²slog (vb) **1** (+ at) zwoegen (op), noest doorwerken (aan): ~ *away (at)* ijverig doorworstelen (met) **2** ploeteren, sjokken
³slog (vb) [cricket, boxing] hard stoten, uithalen naar, een ontzettende mep geven || ~ *it out* het uitvechten
slogan 1 strijdkreet **2** motto[h] **3** slagzin [in advertisement]
¹slop (n) **1** waterige soep, slappe kost **2** spoeling, dun varkensvoer[h] **3** (-s) vuil waswater[h]
²slop (vb) **1** (+ over) overstromen: ~ *about* (or: *around*) rondklotsen **2** plassen, kliederen **3** sloffen **4** morsen (op), kliederen (op) || ~ *about* (or: *around*) rondhannesen
¹slope (n) helling
²slope (vb) hellen, schuin aflopen, schuin oplopen, glooien: ~ *down (to)* aflopen (naar) || ~ *off* er vandoor gaan
sloppy 1 slordig, slonzig, onzorgvuldig **2** melig, sentimenteel **3** vies en nat
¹slosh (vb) **1** plassen, ploeteren **2** klotsen
²slosh (vb) **1** klotsen met: ~ *about* rondklotsen **2** meppen, een dreun verkopen || ~ *the paint on the wall* de verf op de muur kwakken
slot 1 groef, geul, gleuf **2** plaatsje[h], ruimte, zendtijd: *find a* ~ *for* een plaats inruimen voor [in programme]
sloth 1 luiaard **2** luiheid
slot machine 1 automaat **2** [game] fruitmachine
¹slouch (n) **1** slappe houding, ronde rug **2** zoutzak: *be no* ~ *at* handig zijn in
²slouch (vb) **1** hangen, erbij hangen **2** een slappe houding hebben
¹slough (n) **1** moeras[h] **2** modderpoel
²slough (n) afgeworpen huid [of snake etc]
¹Slovak (n) Slowaak(se)
²Slovak (adj) Slowaaks
Slovakia Slowakije
¹Slovene (n) Sloveen(se)
²Slovene (adj) Sloveens
Slovenia Slovenië
slovenly slonzig, slordig
¹slow (adj) **1** langzaam, traag, geleidelijk: ~ *handclap* traag handgeklap [as sign of boredom]; ~ *train* boemeltrein **2** saai, flauw **3** laat || ~ *on the uptake* traag van begrip

²slow (vb) vertragen, inhouden: ~ *(the car) down* snelheid minderen; ~ *down* het kalmer aan doen
³slow (adv) langzaam: *be four minutes* ~ vier minuten achterlopen; *go* ~ het langzaamaan doen
slowdown vertraging, vermindering, productievermindering
sludge 1 slijk[h], modder **2** olieklont, oliekorst
slug 1 naaktslak **2** metaalklomp **3** kogel **4** slok
sluggard luiaard
sluggish traag
¹sluice (n) **1** (afwaterings)sluis **2** sluiskolk **3** sluisdeur
²sluice (vb) (also + out) uitstromen
³sluice (vb) **1** laten uitstromen **2** (also + out, down) overspoelen, water laten stromen over
sluice-gate sluisdeur
¹slum (n) achterbuurt, slop[h]
²slum (vb): ~ *it* armoedig leven
slumber slaap, sluimer
slumdog sloppenwijkbewoner
¹slump (n) ineenstorting, snelle daling: *a* ~ *in sales of violent videogames* een sterke daling in de verkoop van gewelddadige videospelletjes
²slump (vb) **1** in elkaar zakken: ~ *down to the floor* op de vloer in elkaar zakken **2** instorten, mislukken; [fin] vallen
¹slur (n) smet, blaam
²slur (vb) brabbelen, onduidelijk (uit)spreken || *that fact was* ~*red over* aan dat feit werd achteloos voorbij gegaan
slurp slobberen, (op)slurpen
slush 1 sneeuwbrij **2** dunne modder **3** gezwijmel[h], sentimentele onzin
slut [inform] **1** slons **2** slet, slettebak
sluttish [inform] **1** slonzig **2** sletterig
sly 1 sluw, geslepen **2** geniepig **3** pesterig || *on the* ~ in het geniep
¹smack (n) **1** smaak **2** vleugje[h] **3** trek: *he has a* ~ *of inflexibility in him* hij heeft iets onverzettelijks **4** smakkend geluid[h], smak **5** klap **6** klapzoen || *have a* ~ *at sth.* een poging wagen (te)
²smack (vb) (+ of) rieken (naar)
³smack (vb) **1** slaan **2** smakken met [lips] **3** met een smak neerzetten
⁴smack (adv) **1** met een klap: *hit s.o.* ~ *on the head* iem. een rake klap op zijn kop geven **2** recht, precies: ~ *in the middle* precies in het midden
smacker 1 klap, smak **2** klapzoen **3** pond[h], dollar
¹smacking (n) pak[h] slaag
²smacking (adj) energiek, vlug: *at a* ~ *pace* in een stevig tempo
¹small (n) **1** het smalste gedeelte: *the* ~ *of the*

back lenden(streek) **2** (-s) kleine was
²**small** (adj) **1** klein, gering, jong, fijn, onbelangrijk: ~ *arms* handvuurwapens; ~ *business* kleinbedrijf; ~ *change* kleingeld; ~ *print* kleine druk; [fig] de kleine lettertjes; ~ *wonder* geen wonder; *feel* (or: *look*) ~ zich schamen **2** bescheiden: *in a* ~ *way* op kleine schaal **3** slap, licht: ~ *beer* [fig] onbelangrijke zaken || *the* ~ *hours* de kleine uurtjes
sm**a**ll **ad** rubrieksadvertentie
sm**a**ll **fry** [inform] onbelangrijke mensen
sm**a**llholder [Am] kleine boer
small-mi**nded** kleingeestig
sm**a**llpox pokken
small-sca**le** kleinschalig
sm**a**ll **talk** geklets[h], informeel gesprekje[h]
small-ti**me** gering, onbelangrijk
small-town 1 van een kleine stad **2** [esp Am] bekrompen
sm**a**rmy zalvend, vleierig: *be polite and helpful, but never be* ~ wees beleefd en hulpvaardig, maar doe nooit kruiperig
¹**smart** (adj) **1** heftig, fel: *at a* ~ *pace* met flinke pas **2** bijdehand, slim, gevat **3** sluw **4** keurig, knap: *how* ~ *you look!* wat zie je er mooi uit! || ~ *aleck* wijsneus
²**smart** (vb) **1** pijn doen, steken **2** pijn hebben, lijden: ~ *over* (or: *under*) *an insult* zich gekwetst voelen door een belediging
sm**a**rt **bomb** precisiebom
sm**a**rt **card** chipkaart, chipknip, bankpas (met pincode en chip)
sm**a**rt **drug** smartdrug
sm**a**rten (also + up) opknappen, (zichzelf) opdoffen
¹**smash** (n) **1** slag, gerinkel[h] **2** klap, slag, dreun **3** ineenstorting, krach, bankroet[h] **4** topper, groot succes[h] **5** [tennis] smash
²**smash** (vb) **1** slaan op, beuken tegen **2** (also + up) vernielen, in de prak rijden: ~ *in* in elkaar slaan, inslaan **3** uiteenjagen; verpletteren [enemy] **4** [tennis] smashen
³**smash** (vb) (also + up) breken, kapot vallen
⁴**smash** (vb) **1** razen, beuken, botsen: *the car* ~*ed into the garage door* de auto vloog met een klap tegen de garagedeur **2** geruïneerd worden, failliet gaan **3** [tennis] een smash slaan
sm**a**sh-and-gr**a**b **raid** etalagediefstal
sm**a**shed dronken
sm**a**sher **1** iets geweldigs, kanjer: *Lisa is a real* ~ Lisa is echt een wereldmeid **2** dreun, vernietigend antwoord[h]
sm**a**sh **hit** geweldig succes[h]
sm**a**shing geweldig
sm**a**sh-up klap, dreun, botsing
sm**a**ttering beetje[h]: *have a* ~ *of* **French** een paar woordjes Frans spreken
¹**smear** (n) **1** smeer[h], vlek **2** verdachtmaking **3** uitstrijkje[h]
²**smear** (vb) **1** vies worden, uitlopen **2** afgeven

³**smear** (vb) **1** smeren, uitsmeren, besmeren **2** vlekken maken op **3** verdacht maken
sm**ea**r **test** uitstrijkje[h]
¹**smell** (n) **1** reuk, geur; [fig] sfeer **2** vieze lucht || *take a* ~ *at this* ruik hier eens even aan
²**smell** (vb) **1** (+ of) ruiken (naar), geuren (naar) **2** snuffelen **3** (+ of) stinken (naar); ruiken (naar) [also fig] **4** (+ at) ruiken (aan)
sm**e**lling-salts reukzout[h]
smell **out** opsporen, op het spoor komen: *they use sniffer dogs to* ~ *drug* **traffickers** ze zetten snuffelhonden in om drugshandelaren op te sporen
sm**e**lly vies, stinkend
¹**smelt** (n) spiering
²**smelt** (vb) **1** uitsmelten [ore] **2** uit erts uitsmelten [metal]
¹**smile** (n) glimlach: *wipe the* ~ *off s.o.'s face* iem. het lachen doen vergaan; *be all* ~*s* stralen, van oor tot oor glimlachen
²**smile** (vb) **1** (+ at) glimlachen (naar/tegen) **2** er stralend uitzien [nature]
³**smile** (vb) glimlachend uiten: *she* ~*d her approval* ze glimlachte goedkeurend
sm**i**ley smiley
¹**smirch** (n) vlek; [fig] smet
²**smirch** (vb) **1** bevuilen **2** [fig] een smet werpen op
¹**smirk** (n) zelfgenoegzaam lachje[h]
²**smirk** (vb) zelfgenoegzaam glimlachen
smite **1** slaan, verslaan, vellen **2** straffen **3** raken, treffen: *smitten with s.o.* smoorverliefd op iem.
smith **1** smid **2** maker, smeder
smither**ee**ns: *smash into* (or: *to*) ~ aan diggelen gooien
sm**i**thy smederij
smock **1** kieltje[h], schortje[h] **2** jak[h], kiel
¹**smoke** (n) **1** rook **2** rokertje[h], sigaret **3** damp **4** trekje[h] || *go up in* ~ in rook opgaan; [fig] op niets uitlopen
²**smoke** (vb) roken: ~*d ham* gerookte ham; *no smoking* verboden te roken
sm**o**ke **alarm** rookmelder
sm**o**ke-free rookvrij
sm**o**ke **out 1** uitroken [from hole etc] **2** te weten komen [eg plans]
sm**o**ker **1** roker **2** rookcoupé, rookrijtuig[h] **3** mannenbijeenkomst
sm**o**kescreen rookgordijn[h]; [also fig] afleidingsmanoeuvre
¹**smoking** (n) het roken
²**smoking** (adj) [inform] spetterend
sm**o**king **gun** [fig] hard bewijs[h]
smooch vrijen, knuffelen
¹**smooth** (adj) **1** glad **2** soepel, gelijkmatig **3** gemakkelijk **4** rustig **5** overmatig vriendelijk, glad: ~ *operator* gladjanus **6** zacht smakend **7** zacht; strelend [of voice, sound] || *in* ~ *water* in rustig vaarwater

²**smooth** (vb) **1** gladmaken, effen maken **2** (also + out) gladstrijken; [fig] (onregelmatigheden/verschillen) wegnemen: ~ *down one's clothes* zijn kleren gladstrijken
smoothie gladde/handige prater
¹**smother** (vb) (ver)stikken, (ver)smoren
²**smother** (vb) **1** (uit)doven **2** smoren, onderdrukken: *all opposition was ~ed* elke vorm van tegenstand werd onderdrukt **3** (+ in) overladen (met); overdekken (met) [fig]; verstikken: *~ed in cream* rijkelijk met room bedekt
smoulder (na)smeulen, gloeien
¹**smudge** (n) vlek; [fig] smet
²**smudge** (vb) vlekken
³**smudge** (vb) **1** (be)vlekken, vuilmaken **2** [fig] een smet werpen op, bezoedelen
smudgy 1 vlekkerig, besmeurd **2** wazig
smug zelfvoldaan
smuggle smokkelen
smuggler smokkelaar
smut 1 vuiltje^h, stofje^h **2** roetdeeltje^h **3** roet^h, kolenstof **4** vuiligheid: *talk* ~ vuile taal uitslaan
smutty vuil, goor, vies
snack snack, hapje^h, tussendoortje^h
snack bar snackbar, cafetaria^{+h}
¹**snag** (n) **1** uitsteeksel^h, punt^h, stomp **2** probleem^h, tegenvaller: *there's a ~ in it somewhere* er schuilt ergens een addertje onder 't gras **3** (winkel)haak, scheur, haal **4** boom(stronk)
²**snag** (vb) **1** blijven haken met **2** scheuren [clothing] **3** te pakken krijgen
snail (huisjes)slak [also fig]; slome: ~ *mail* slakkenpost, gewone post
snail mail [mockingly] gewone post, slakkenpost
snail's pace slakkengangetje
snake slang || *a ~ in the grass* een addertje onder het gras
¹**snap** (n) **1** klap: *shut a book* (or: *lid*) *with a ~* een boek (or: deksel) met een klap dichtdoen **2** hap, beet **3** knip [with fingers, scissors] **4** foto **5** karweitje^h van niets, kleinigheid **6** pit, energie: *put some ~ into it!* een beetje meer fut!
²**snap** (adj) **1** impulsief: ~ *decision* beslissing van 't moment (zelf) **2** onverwacht, onvoorbereid: ~ *check* (onverwachte) controle
³**snap** (vb) **1** (weg)grissen, grijpen, (weg)rukken: ~ *up* op de kop tikken **2** knippen met [fingers] **3** kieken, een foto maken van || ~ *it up* vooruit, aan de slag
⁴**snap** (vb) **1** (also + at) happen (naar), bijten **2** (af)breken, (af)knappen; het begeven [also fig] **3** (dicht)klappen, dichtslaan: *the door ~ped to* (or: *shut*) de deur sloeg dicht **4** (also + out) snauwen || ~ *at a)* grijpen naar; *b)* aangrijpen [chance etc]; *I was only ~ped at* ik werd alleen maar afgesnauwd; ~ *out of it*

ermee ophouden; ~ *to it* vooruit, schiet 'ns op
⁵**snap** (int) klap, knal
snapdragon [bot] leeuwenbek
snap election vervroegde verkiezingen
snap fastener [Am] drukknoopje^h
snappy 1 pittig, levendig **2** chic, net **3** snauwerig, prikkelbaar || *look ~!*, *make it ~!* schiet op!
snapshot kiekje^h, snapshot^h, momentopname
snare (val)strik, val: *lay a ~ for s.o.* voor iem. een valstrik leggen
¹**snarl** (n) **1** grauw^h, snauw **2** knoop [also fig]; wirwar || *be in a ~* in de war zijn
²**snarl** (vb) **1** (+ at) grauwen (tegen), grommen, snauwen **2** in de war raken (brengen)
snarl up 1 in de war raken (brengen), in de knoop raken (brengen): *get snarled up* verstrikt raken **2** vastlopen [of traf]
snarl-up 1 (verkeers)knoop **2** warboel
¹**snatch** (n) **1** greep, ruk: *make a ~ at* een greep doen naar **2** brok^h, stuk^h, fragment^h: *a ~ of conversation* een flard van een gesprek || *sleep in ~es* met tussenpozen slapen
²**snatch** (vb) rukken || ~ *at* grijpen naar, (dadelijk) aangrijpen
³**snatch** (vb) **1** (weg)rukken, (weg)grijpen, bemachtigen: ~ *a kiss* een kus stelen; ~ *away* wegrukken, wegpakken; *she ~ed the letter out of my hand* ze rukte de brief uit mijn hand **2** aangrijpen, gebruikmaken van
snazzy 1 chic **2** opzichtig
¹**sneak** (n) **1** gluiper(d) **2** klikspaan
²**sneak** (adj) onverwacht, verrassings-: *a ~ preview* een onaangekondigde voorvertoning
³**sneak** (vb) sluipen: ~ *away* wegsluipen; ~ *(up)on s.o.* naar iem. toesluipen || ~ *on s.o.* over iem. klikken, iem. verraden
⁴**sneak** (vb) heimelijk doen, smokkelen: ~ *a smoke* stiekem roken
sneaker 1 sluiper **2** gluiperd **3** klikspaan **4** (-s) gympies
sneaking 1 gluiperig **2** heimelijk **3** vaag: *a ~ suspicion* een vaag vermoeden
sneak-thief insluiper
¹**sneer** (n) **1** grijns(lach) **2** (+ at) spottende opmerking (over), hatelijkheid
²**sneer** (vb) **1** (+ at) grijnzen (naar), spottend lachen **2** spotten (met)
¹**sneeze** (n) nies(geluid^h): *~s* genies
²**sneeze** (vb) niezen || *not to be ~d at* de moeite waard, niet niks
snick knip(je^h), inkeping
¹**snicker** (n) **1** hinnikgeluid^h **2** giechel
²**snicker** (vb) **1** (zacht) hinniken **2** giechelen
snide hatelijk
¹**sniff** (n) **1** snuivend geluid^h **2** luchtje^h, snuifje^h: *get a ~ of sea air* de zeelucht opsnuiven

²**sniff** (vb) **1** snuiven, snuffen **2** snuffelen ‖ *not to be ~ed at* niet te versmaden
³**sniff** (vb) **1** snuiven **2** besnuffelen **3** ruiken, de geur opsnuiven van
sniffer dog snuffelhond [for explosives, drugs]
¹**sniffle** (n) gesnuifʰ, gesnotterʰ
²**sniffle** (vb) snuffen, snotteren
sniffy arrogant, hooghartig
¹**snigger** (n) giechel
²**snigger** (vb) gniffelen
¹**snip** (n) **1** knip: *one ~ of the scissors and 99 balloons flew up into the air* een knip met de schaar en 99 ballonnen gingen de lucht in **2** snipper, stukjeʰ, fragmentʰ **3** koopjeʰ, buitenkans
²**snip** (vb) snijden, knippen
³**snip** (vb) (also + off) (af)knippen, doorknippen, versnipperen
¹**snipe** (n) snip
²**snipe** (vb) (+ at) sluipschieten, uit een hinderlaag schieten (op) ‖ *he got tired of critics sniping at him* hij was het beu door critici aangevallen te worden
sniper sluipschutter
snippet stukjeʰ, fragmentʰ, knipselʰ
¹**snitch** (vb) klikken: *he ~ed on John* hij verklikte John
²**snitch** (vb) gappen
snivel 1 een loopneus hebben, snotteren **2** grienen, janken
snob snob
snobbery snobismeʰ
snobbish snobistisch
snog vrijen
¹**snooker** (n) snooker(biljart)ʰ
²**snooker** (vb) in het nauw drijven, in een moeilijke positie brengen, dwarsbomen
snoop [inform] (+ about, around) rondsnuffelen
snooty verwaand
¹**snooze** (n) dutjeʰ
²**snooze** (vb) dutten, een uiltje knappen
¹**snore** (n) gesnurkʰ, snurk
²**snore** (vb) snurken
¹**snort** (n) gesnuifʰ: *he gave a ~ of contempt* hij snoof minachtend
²**snort** (vb) snuiven: *Ian ~ed with rage* Ian snoof van woede
snot snotʰ
snotty 1 snotterig, met snot **2** verwaand, snobistisch
snout snuit
¹**snow** (n) **1** sneeuw [also on TV screen] **2** sneeuwbui **3** sneeuw, cocaïne
²**snow** (vb) **1** sneeuwen **2** neerdwarrelen
³**snow** (vb) ondersneeuwen, overdonderen ‖ *be ~ed in* (or: *up*) ingesneeuwd zijn; *be ~ed under* ondergesneeuwd worden, bedolven worden
¹**snowball** (n) sneeuwbal

²**snowball** (vb) een sneeuwbaleffect hebben, escaleren
³**snowball** (vb) **1** (met sneeuwballen) bekogelen **2** doen escaleren
snowbound ingesneeuwd
snowdrift sneeuwbank
snowdrop sneeuwklokjeʰ
snowflake sneeuwvlok(jeʰ)
snowman sneeuwman, sneeuwpop
snowstorm sneeuwstorm
snow-white sneeuwwit
Snowwhite Sneeuwwitje
snowy 1 besneeuwd, sneeuwachtig **2** sneeuwwit
Snr Senior sr.
¹**snub** (n) bitse afwijzing: *her remark was clearly meant as a ~* haar opmerking was duidelijk bedoeld om te katten
²**snub** (vb) afstoten, afkatten, met de nek aanzien
¹**snuff** (n) snuif(tabak): *take ~* snuiven
²**snuff** (vb) snuiven [tobacco, cocaine]
³**snuff** (vb) **1** snuiten **2** opsnuiven **3** besnuffelen ‖ *~ it* 't hoekje omgaan; *~ out* een eind maken aan [expectation, uprising etc]
snuffle snotteren
¹**snug** (n) gelagkamer
²**snug** (adj) **1** behaaglijk, beschut, knus: *be as ~ as a bug in a rug* een lekker leventje leiden **2** goed ingericht **3** nauwsluitend **4** ruim [income]
snuggle zich nestelen: *~ up to s.o.* lekker tegen iem. aan gaan liggen ‖ *~ down* lekker onder de dekens kruipen
¹**so** (adj) **1** zo, waar: *is that really so?* is dat echt waar?; *if* so als dat zo is **2** dat, het: *she was skinny but not extremely* so ze was wel mager maar niet extreem; *'She's the prettiest' 'Yes, so she is'* 'Ze is de knapste' 'Dat is ze inderdaad'
²**so** (dem pron) **1** dusdanig, dat: *'You were cheating' 'But so were you'* 'Je hebt vals gespeeld' 'Maar jij ook' **2** iets dergelijks, zo(iets): *six days or so* zes dagen of zo
³**so** (adv) **1** zo, aldus: *(would you) be so kind as to leave* zou u zo goed willen zijn weg te gaan; *but even so* maar toch; *so far it hasn't happened* tot nu toe is het niet gebeurd; *so long as you don't tell anybody* als je 't maar aan niemand vertelt; *if* so als dat zo is **2** zozeer, zo erg: *she is not so stupid* ze is niet zo dom; *so many came* er kwamen er zo veel **3** daarom, zodoende: *so what?* dan?, wat dan nog?; *so here we are!* hier zijn we dan!; *so there you are* daar ben je dus ‖ *so long!* tot ziens!; *every so often* nu en dan; *so there* nu weet je het
⁴**so** (conj) **1** zodat, opdat, om: *be careful so you don't get hurt* pas op dat je je geen pijn doet **2** zodat, (en) dus: *he is late, so (that) we can't start yet* hij is te laat, zodat we nog niet

kunnen beginnen
⁵so (int) ziezo
¹soak (n) **1** week maken, het nat maken **2** zuipschuit, drankorgelʰ
²soak (vb) sijpelen, doortrekken: ~ *through the paper* het papier doordrenken
³soak (vb) **1** doorweken, (door)drenken: *~ed to the skin* doornat; *~ed through* kletsnat **2** (onder)dompelen: *~ o.s.* in zich verdiepen in **3** afzetten: *~ the rich* de rijken plukken
⁴soak (vb) weken, in de week zetten: *~ off* losweken
soaking door en door: *~ wet* doorweekt
soak up 1 opnemen, absorberen **2** kunnen incasseren [criticism, blow]
so-and-so 1 die en die, dinges **2** dit en dit **3** je-weet-wel: *a real ~* een rotzak
¹soap (n) **1** zeep **2** soap
²soap (vb) (in)zepen
soapbox 1 zeepdoos **2** zeepkist, geïmproviseerd platformʰ
soap opera soap (opera)
soapsuds zeepsop
soar 1 hoog vliegen; [fig] een hoge vlucht nemen **2** (omhoog) rijzen, stijgen: *prices ~ed* de prijzen vlogen omhoog **3** zweven
¹sob (n) snik
²sob (vb) snikken
³sob (vb) snikkend vertellen: *~ one's heart out* hartverscheurend snikken
¹sober (adj) **1** nuchter, niet beschonken: *as ~ as a judge* volkomen nuchter **2** matig, ingetogen: *~ colours* gedekte kleuren **3** beheerst, kalm **4** verstandig, afgewogen: *in ~ fact* in werkelijkheid **5** ernstig
²sober (vb) (+ down, up) nuchter worden (maken), (doen) bedaren
sobriety 1 nuchterheid, gematigdheid **2** kalmte, ernst
sob story zielig verhaalʰ, tranentrekker
so-called zogenaamd
soccer voetbalʰ
sociability gezelligheid
sociable gezellig, vriendelijk
¹social (n) gezellige bijeenkomst, feestjeʰ
²social (adj) **1** sociaal, maatschappelijk: *man is a ~ animal* de mens is een sociaal wezen **2** gezellig, vriendelijk **3** gezelligheids-: *a ~ club* een gezelligheidsvereniging
social bookmarking het delen van favoriete links op internet
socialism socialismeʰ
¹socialist (n) socialist
²socialist (adv) socialistisch
socialize gezellig doen, zich aanpassen: *~ with* omgaan met
social network sociaal netwerk
social science 1 sociale wetenschap(pen) **2** (-s) maatschappijwetenschappen
social service 1 liefdadig werkʰ **2** (-s) sociale voorzieningen

social work maatschappelijk werkʰ
social worker maatschappelijk werk(st)er
society 1 vereniging, genootschapʰ **2** de samenleving, de maatschappij **3** gezelschapʰ: *I try to avoid his ~* ik probeer zijn gezelschap te ontlopen **4** society, hogere kringen
sociological sociologisch
sociologist socioloog
sociology sociologie
¹sock (n) **1** sok **2** inlegzool(tjeʰ) **3** (vuist)slag, oplawaai **4** windzak ‖ *pull one's ~s up* er tegen aan gaan; *put a ~ in it* kop dicht
²sock (vb) meppen, slaan, dreunen ‖ *~ it to s.o.* **a)** iem. op zijn donder geven; **b)** grote indruk op iem. maken
socket 1 holte, (oog)kas, gewrichtsholte **2** kandelaar **3** sok, mof, buis **4** stopcontact, contactdoos, fitting, lamphouder
¹sod (n) **1** vent **2** rotklus, ellende **3** (gras)zode: *under the ~* onder de (groene) zoden ‖ *I don't give a ~* het interesseert me geen barst
²sod (vb): *~ it!* verdomme!
soda 1 soda, natriumcarbonaatʰ: *baking ~* zuiveringszout **2** soda(water)ʰ **3** priklimonade, frisʰ
soda water spuitwaterʰ
sodden 1 doorweekt, doordrenkt **2** klef [of bread etc] **3** opgeblazen; opgezwollen [through drink]: *~ features* opgeblazen gezicht
sodium natriumʰ
Sod's Law de wet van 'Sod' [if anything can go wrong, it will]
sofa bank, sofa
soft 1 zacht; gedempt [light] **2** slap [also fig]; week, sentimenteel: *(have) a ~ spot for s.o.* een zwak voor iem. hebben **3** niet-verslavend; soft [drugs] **4** eenvoudig: *~ option* gemakkelijke weg **5** onnozel: *have gone ~ in the head* niet goed wijs zijn geworden **6** niet-alcoholisch; fris [drink]: *~ drink* fris(drank) **7** zwak, gek, verliefd: *be ~ about* (or: *on*) gek (or: verliefd) zijn op, een zwak hebben voor ‖ *~ loan* lening op gunstige voorwaarden
soft-boiled 1 zachtgekookt [of egg] **2** [fig] weekhartig
soft copy tekst(en) in elektronische vorm [not on paper]
soft drink fris(drank)
¹soften (vb) **1** zacht(er) worden **2** vertederd worden
²soften (vb) **1** zacht(er) maken; dempen [light]; ontharden [water] **2** verwennen, verslappen **3** vertederen
softener waterontharder; [esp] wasverzachter
soften up 1 mild stemmen **2** verzwakken, murw maken
softie slappeling, goedzak, dwaas

soft-soap stroop smeren bij, vleien
software software, (computer)programmatuur
software package softwarepakket[h]
soggy 1 doorweekt **2** drassig **3** klef [of bread etc]
¹soil (n) **1** grond, land[h], teelaarde **2** (vader)-land[h]: *on Dutch ~* op Nederlandse bodem; *native ~* geboortegrond **3** (ver)vuil(ing) **4** afval[h] **5** aarde, grond, land[h]
²soil (vb) vuil worden
³soil (vb) vuilmaken
¹solace (n) troost, bemoediging
²solace (vb) troosten, opbeuren: *~ o.s. (with sth.)* zich troosten (met iets)
solar van de zon, zonne-: *~ eclipse* zonsverduistering
solar farm zonnepark[h]
solar system zonnestelsel[h]
soldering iron soldeerbout
soldier 1 militair, soldaat **2** strijder, voorvechter
soldier on volhouden
¹sole (n) **1** zool [of foot and shoe] **2** tong [fish and dish]
²sole (adj) **1** enig, enkel **2** exclusief, uitsluitend: *~ agent* alleenvertegenwoordiger
solely 1 alleen **2** enkel, uitsluitend
solemn 1 plechtig **2** ernstig: *look as ~ as a judge* doodernstig kijken **3** (plecht)statig **4** belangrijk, gewichtig: *~ warning* dringende waarschuwing
solemnity 1 plechtigheid **2** plechtstatigheid, ceremonieel[h] **3** ernst
¹solicit (vb) **1** een verzoek doen **2** tippelen
²solicit (vb) **1** (dringend) verzoeken: *~ s.o.'s attention* iemands aandacht vragen **2** aanspreken [by prostitute]
solicitor 1 procureur **2** rechtskundig adviseur; advocaat [at lower court] **3** notaris
solicitous 1 (+ about, for) bezorgd (om), bekommerd **2** aandachtig, nauwgezet
solicitude 1 zorg, bezorgdheid, angst **2** aandacht, nauwgezetheid
¹solid (n) **1** vast lichaam[h] **2** (driedimensionaal) lichaam[h] **3** (-s) vast voedsel[h]
²solid (adj) **1** vast, stevig, solide: *~ rock* vast gesteente **2** ononderbroken [of time]: *Brugman talked ~ly for three hours* Brugman sprak drie uur aan één stuk **3** betrouwbaar [financially] **4** driedimensionaal: *~ geometry* stereometrie **5** unaniem: *~ vote* eenstemmigheid **6** gegrond, degelijk: *~ reasons* gegronde redenen **7** zuiver, massief, puur: *~ gold* puur goud
solidarity solidariteit
solidify hard(er) (doen) worden, (doen) verharden
solidity 1 hardheid **2** dichtheid, compactheid
soliloquy alleenspraak, monoloog: *teach-*

*ing involves more than **holding** a ~ for fifty minutes* lesgeven houdt meer in dan vijftig minuten lang een monoloog houden
solitary 1 alleen(levend), solitair **2** eenzelvig **3** afgezonderd, eenzaam: *~ confinement* eenzame opsluiting **4** enkel: *give me one ~ example* geef mij één enkel voorbeeld
solitude eenzaamheid
¹solo (n) solo-optreden[h], solovlucht
²solo (adv) solo, alleen: *fly ~* solo vliegen; *go ~* een solocarrière beginnen, op de solotoer gaan
soloist solist(e)
so long tot ziens
solstice zonnestilstand, zonnewende
soluble 1 oplosbaar **2** verklaarbaar
solution oplossing, solutie; [fig] uitweg: *~ for* (or: *of, to*) *a problem* oplossing van een probleem
solve 1 oplossen, een uitweg vinden voor **2** verklaren
solvency solvabiliteit, financiële draagkracht
solvent oplosmiddel[h]
¹Somali (n) Somaliër, Somalische
²Somali (adj) Somalisch
Somalia Somalië
sombre somber, duister, zwaarmoedig
¹some (pron) **1** wat, iets, enkele(n), sommige(n), een aantal, een of ander(e), een: *she bought ~ oranges* ze kocht een paar sinaasappels; *~ day you'll understand* ooit zul je het begrijpen; *I've made a cake; would you like ~?* ik heb een cake gebakken, wil je er wat van (or: een stukje)?; *~ say* so er zijn er die dat zeggen **2** geweldig, fantastisch: *that was ~ holiday* tjonge/nou dat was een fijne vakantie
²some (adv) **1** ongeveer, zo wat: *it costs ~ fifty pounds* het kost zo'n vijftig pond **2** [Am; inform] enigszins, een beetje: *he was annoyed ~* hij was een tikje geïrriteerd
somebody iemand
some day op een dag, ooit: *we all must die ~* we moeten allemaal eens sterven
somehow 1 op de een of andere manier, hoe dan ook, ergens: *~ (or other) you'll have to tell him* op de een of andere wijze zul je het hem moeten vertellen **2** om de een of andere reden, waarom dan ook
someone iemand
someplace [Am] ergens, op een of ander plaats: *do it ~ else* doe het ergens anders
¹somersault (n) salto (mortale), buiteling: *turn* (or: *do*) *a ~* een salto maken
²somersault (vb) een salto maken
something 1 iets, wat: *he dropped ~* hij liet iets vallen; *seventy ~* zeventig en nog wat; *there is ~ in* (or: *to*) *it* daar is iets van aan **2** (+ of) iets, enigszins: *it came as ~ of a surprise* het kwam een beetje als een verrassing

sometime ooit, eens: *I'll show it to you* ~ ik zal het je weleens laten zien
sometimes soms, af en toe, bij gelegenheid
somewhat enigszins, een beetje: *the soil is ~ moist* de aarde is een beetje vochtig
somewhere 1 ergens (heen): *we're getting ~ at last* dat lijkt er al meer op **2** ongeveer: *~ about sixty* zo'n zestig
somnolence slaperigheid
son zoon, jongen
sonata sonate
song 1 lied(jeʰ), wijsjeʰ **2** gezangʰ || *don't make such a ~ and **dance** about those old records* maak toch niet zo'n drukte om die oude platen; *go for a ~* bijna voor niets van de hand gaan; *on ~* op dreef, op volle toeren, in topvorm
songbird zangvogel
song contest songfestivalʰ: *the **Eurovision** ~* het Eurovisie songfestival
songwriter liedjesschrijver, liedjesschrijfster
sonic m.b.t. geluid(sgolven), geluids-: *~ boom* (or: *bang*) supersone knal
son-in-law schoonzoon
sonnet sonnetʰ
sonny jochieʰ, mannetjeʰ
soon 1 spoedig, gauw, snel (daarna): *speak too ~* te voorbarig zijn; *the ~er the **better*** hoe eerder hoe beter; *as ~ as* zodra (als), meteen toen; *no ~er had he arrived than she left* nauwelijks was hij aangekomen of zij ging al weg **2** graag, bereidwillig: *I'd ~er **walk*** ik loop liever; *I'd (just) as ~ **stay** home* ik blijf net zo lief thuis
soothe kalmeren, geruststellen, troosten
soothsayer waarzegger
sooty 1 roetig, (als) met roet bedekt **2** roetkleurig
sop doorweken, soppen
sophisticated 1 subtiel, ver ontwikkeld: *a ~ taste* een verfijnde smaak **2** wereldwijs, ontwikkeld **3** ingewikkeld
sophistication 1 subtiliteit, raffinementʰ **2** wereldwijsheid **3** complexiteit
sophomore [Am] tweedejaarsstudent
sopping doorweekt, doornat: *~ with rain* kletsnat van de regen
soppy sentimenteel, zoetig
soprano sopraan(zangeres)
sorcerer tovenaar
sorcery tovenarij
sordid 1 vuil [also fig]; vies: *the ~ details* de smerige details **2** armzalig, beroerd
¹sore (n) **1** pijnlijke plek, zweer, wond **2** (-s) zeerʰ, pijnlijk onderwerpʰ: *recall* (or: *reopen*) *old ~s* oude wonden openrijten
²sore (adj) **1** pijnlijk, irriterend: *a ~ throat* keelpijn **2** onaangenaam, pijnlijk: *a ~ point* een teer punt **3** beledigd, kwaad, nijdig:

*don't **get** ~ about the money you lost* maak je niet zo nijdig over het geld dat je verloren hebt || *a sight for ~ eyes* een aangenaam iets (iem.)
sorehead zeur(kous)
sorely ernstig, in belangrijke mate, pijnlijk: *he was ~ **tempted*** hij werd in grote verleiding gebracht
sorrel zuring, soort moeskruidʰ
sorrow verdrietʰ, leedʰ: *drown one's ~s* zijn verdriet verdrinken
sorrowful 1 treurig **2** bedroefd
¹sorry (adj) **1** droevig, erbarmelijk: *he came home in a ~ **condition*** hij kwam thuis in een trieste toestand **2** naar, ellendig: *be in a ~ plight* in een ellendige situatie verkeren **3** waardeloos [excuse etc] **4** bedroefd **5** medelijdend: *be* (or: *feel*) *~ for s.o.* medelijden hebben met iem. **6** berouwvol: *you'll **be** ~* het zal je berouwen, daar krijg je spijt van
²sorry (int) **1** sorry, het spijt me, pardon **2** wat zegt u?
¹sort (n) **1** soort, klasse, typeʰ: *just buy him an ice cream, that ~ of **thing*** koop maar een ijsje voor hem, of zoiets; *a ~ of (a)* een soort van, een of andere; *he is a lawyer of ~s* hij is een soort advocaat, hij is zo'n beetje advocaat; *'I'm going alone' 'you'll do nothing of the ~!'* 'ik ga alleen' 'daar komt niets van in!'; *all ~s of* allerlei **2** persoon, typeʰ, slag: *he is a **bad** ~* deugt niet **3** [comp] sortering || *be out of ~s* zich niet lekker voelen
²sort (vb) sorteren, klasseren: *~ **letters*** brieven sorteren; *~ **over*** (or: *through*) sorteren, klasseren
¹sorted (adj) [inform] in orde gemaakt; voor elkaar: *that's your ticket ~* je ticket is geregeld
²sorted (int) geregeld
sort of min of meer, zo ongeveer, een beetje: *I feel ~ **ill*** ik voel me een beetje ziek; *'are you in charge here?' 'well yes, ~'* 'heeft u hier de leiding?' 'nou, min of meer, ja'
sort out 1 sorteren, indelen, rangschikken **2** ordenen, regelen: *things will sort **themselves** out* de zaak komt wel terecht; *sort o.s. out* met zichzelf in het reine komen **3** te pakken krijgen, een opdonder geven: *stop that or I'll come and sort you out* hou daarmee op of je krijgt het met mij aan de stok
so-so zozo, middelmatig
sot dronkaard
sought after veelgevraagd
soul 1 ziel, geest: *poor ~!* (arme) stakker!; *with heart and ~* met hart en ziel; *All Souls' Day* Allerzielen; *not a (living) ~* geen levende ziel, geen sterveling **2** soul || *the (life and) ~ of the party* de gangmaker van het feest; *she is the ~ **of** kindness* zij is de vriendelijkheid zelf
soul-destroying geestdodend, afstompend
soul mate boezemvriend(in), minnaar,

minnares
soul-searching het geweten onderzoekend
¹**sound** (n) **1** geluidʰ, klank, toon: *I don't like the ~ of it* het bevalt me niet, het zit me niet lekker; *by the ~ of it* (or: *things*) zo te horen **2** gehoorsafstand **3** zee-engte, zeestraat **4** inham, baai, golf
²**sound** (adj) **1** gezond, krachtig, gaaf, fit: *be (as) ~ as a bell* **a)** (zo) gezond als een vis zijn; **b)** perfect functioneren [machine]: *a ~ mind in a ~ body* een gezonde geest in een gezond lichaam **2** correct, logisch; gegrond [argument]; wijs [advice] **3** financieel gezond, evenwichtig, betrouwbaar **4** vast [sleep] **5** hard, krachtig: *a ~ thrashing* een flink pak ransel
³**sound** (vb) klinken [also fig]; luiden, galmen: *that ~s reasonable* dat klinkt redelijk || *~ off* **a)** opscheppen; **b)** zijn mening luid te kennen geven
⁴**sound** (vb) **1** laten klinken: *~ a warning* een waarschuwing laten horen **2** uiten, uitspreken **3** blazen [alarm, retreat]; blazen op [eg trumpet] **4** testen [by percussing lungs] **5** peilen [also fig]; onderzoeken, polsen: *~ s.o. out about* (or: *on*) *sth.* iem. over iets polsen
⁵**sound** (adv) vast; diep [sleep]: *~ asleep* vast in slaap
sound barrier geluidsbarrière
sound bite soundbite [korte, kernachtige uitspraak]
sound card geluidskaart
sounding peiling [also fig]: *make* (or: *take*) *~s* poolshoogte nemen, opiniepeilingen houden
sounding board 1 klankbordʰ [also fig]; spreekbuis **2** klankbodem
soundly 1 gezond, stevig **2** vast [asleep]
sound-proof geluiddicht
soundtrack 1 geluidsspoorʰ [of film with sound] **2** (cd met) opgenomen filmmuziek
soup soep || *in the ~* in de puree
soup kitchen 1 gaarkeuken [for poor, homeless] **2** veldkeuken
soup up opvoeren [engine, power]
sour 1 zuur, wrang **2** onvriendelijk; scherp [tongue] **3** guur; onaangenaam [weather] || *~ grapes* de druiven zijn zuur; *go* (or: *turn*) *~* slecht aflopen
source bron [also fig]; oorsprong, oorzaak
source language brontaal
sourpuss zuurpruim
souse 1 doornat maken, (een vloeistof) gieten (over iets) **2** pekelen, marineren
soused bezopen, dronken
¹**south** (n) het zuiden [point of compass]; zuid: *(to the) ~ of* ten zuiden van; *the South* het zuidelijk gedeelte
²**south** (adj) zuidelijk

³**south** (adv) in, uit, naar het zuiden: *down ~* in het zuiden
South Africa Zuid-Afrika: *the Republic of ~* de Republiek Zuid-Afrika
¹**South African** (n) Zuid-Afrikaan(se)
²**South African** (adj) Zuid-Afrikaans: *~ Dutch* Afrikaans [language]
southbound op weg naar het zuiden
south-east zuidoostelijk
south-eastern zuidoostelijk
¹**southerly** (n) zuidenwind
²**southerly** (adj, adv) zuidelijk
southern zuidelijk: *~ lights* zuiderlicht, aurora australis
southerner zuiderling, Amerikaan uit de zuidelijke staten
South Korea Zuid-Korea
¹**South Korean** (n) Zuid-Koreaan(se)
²**South Korean** (adj) Zuid-Koreaans
South Pole zuidpool
South Sudan Zuid-Sudan
¹**South Sudanese** (n) Zuid-Sudanees, Zuid-Sudanese
²**South Sudanese** (adj) Zuid-Sudanees
southward zuid(waarts), zuidelijk
south-west zuidwestelijk
south-western zuidwestelijk
¹**sovereign** (n) soeverein, vorst
²**sovereign** (adj) **1** soeverein, onafhankelijk, heersend, oppermachtig **2** doeltreffend, efficiënt; krachtig [remedy]
sovereignty soevereiniteit, zelfbeschikking, heerschappij
Soviet Sovjet-; Russisch
¹**sow** (n) zeug
²**sow** (vb) opwekken, de kiem leggen van: *~ the seeds of doubt* twijfel zaaien
³**sow** (vb) **1** zaaien [also fig]; verspreiden **2** zaaien, (be)planten, poten
soy soja
spa 1 minerale bron **2** badplaats [near spring]; kuuroordʰ
¹**space** (n) **1** ruimte **2** afstand, interval **3** plaats, ruimte, gebiedʰ: *clear a ~ for s.o. (sth.)* ruimte maken voor iem. (iets) **4** tijdspanne: *during the ~ of three years* binnen het bestek van drie jaar; *vanish into ~* in het niet verdwijnen
²**space** (vb) uit elkaar plaatsen, over de tijd verdelen: *~ out* over meer ruimte verdelen, spreiden; *~ out payments* betalen in termijnen
space centre ruimtevaartcentrumʰ
spacecraft ruimtevaartuigʰ
spaced out 1 zweverig, high, onder invloed **2** wereldvreemd, excentriek
space flight ruimtevlucht
spaceman ruimtevaarder
space probe ruimtesonde
spaceship ruimteschipʰ
spacing spatie: *single* (or: *double*) *~* met

enkele (*or:* dubbele) regelafstand
spacious ruim, groot
spade 1 spade, schop **2** [cards] schoppen(s):
the five of ~s schoppenvijf || *call a* ~ *a* ~ de
dingen bij hun naam noemen
Spain Spanje
spam 1 [culinary] vlees, smac **2** [comp]
spam, reclamemail
¹**span** (n) **1** breedte, wijdte, vleugelbreedte;
spanwijdte [of aeroplane] **2** (tijd)span(ne)
3 overspanning, spanwijdte
²**span** (vb) overspannen [also fig]; overbruggen
¹**spangle** (n) lovertjeʰ, dun blaadjeʰ klatergoud
²**spangle** (vb) met lovertjes versieren: ~*d*
with stars met sterren bezaaid
Spaniard Spanjaard, Spaanse
Spanish Spaans || ~ *chestnut* tamme kas-
tanje(boom)
spank (een pak) voor de broek geven, een
pak slaag geven
¹**spanking** (n) pakʰ voor de broek
²**spanking** (adj) **1** kolossaal, prima: ~ *new*
spiksplinternieuw **2** vlug, krachtig
spanner moersleutel: *adjustable* ~ Engelse
sleutel || *throw a* ~ *into the works* een spaak in
het wiel steken
¹**spar** (n) lange paal, rondhoutʰ
²**spar** (vb) **1** boksen **2** redetwisten
¹**spare** (n) reserve, dubbel, reserveonder-
deelʰ, reservewielʰ
²**spare** (adj) **1** extra, reserve: ~ *room* logeerkamer; ~ *tyre* reservewiel; [mockingly]
zwembandje **2** vrij [time] **3** mager || *go* ~ ra-
zend worden
³**spare** (vb) **1** het stellen zonder, missen,
overhebben: *enough and to* ~ meer dan genoeg; *can you* ~ *me a few moments?* heb je
een paar minuten voor mij? **2** sparen, ontzien: ~ *s.o.'s feelings* iemands gevoelens sparen **3** sparen, bezuinigen op: *no expense* ~*d*
het mag wat kosten
sparing zuinig; spaarzaam
¹**spark** (n) vonk; [fig] sprank(jeʰ); greintjeʰ: *a*
~ *of compassion* een greintje medelijden ||
some bright ~ *left the tap running* één of andere slimmerik heeft de kraan open laten
staan
²**spark** (vb) vonken
³**spark** (vb) **1** ontsteken, doen ontbranden
2 aanvuren, aanwakkeren **3** uitlokken: ~ *off*
a war een oorlog uitlokken
¹**sparkle** (n) fonkeling, glinstering, gefon-
kelʰ
²**sparkle** (vb) **1** fonkelen, glinsteren: *sparkling with wit* sprankelend van geest(igheid)
2 parelen, (op)bruisen: *sparkling water* spuitwater; *sparkling wine* mousserende wijn
3 sprankelen, geestig zijn
spark plug bougie

sparring partner sparringpartner [also
fig]; trainingspartner, oefenmaat
sparrow mus
sparrow hawk sperwer
sparse dun, schaars, karig: *a* ~*ly populated
area* een dunbevolkt gebied
sparsity schaarsheid
Spartan spartaans; [fig] zeer hard
spasm 1 kramp, huivering, spasmeʰ: ~*s of
laughter* lachkrampen **2** aanval, opwelling:
~*s of grief* opwellingen van smart
spastic spastisch, krampachtig
spat klappen, ruzietjeʰ
spate 1 hoge waterstand [of river]: *the rivers
are in* ~ de rivieren zijn gezwollen **2** toevloed, overvloed, stroom: *a* ~ *of publications*
een stroom publicaties
spatial ruimtelijk, ruimte-
¹**spatter** (n) **1** spat(jeʰ), vlekjeʰ **2** gespatʰ
²**spatter** (vb) **1** (be)spatten, (be)sprenkelen,
klateren: *the lorry* ~*ed my clothes with mud* de
vrachtauto bespatte mijn kleren met modder **2** bekladden; besmeuren [also fig]
spatula spatel
¹**spawn** (n) **1** kuit [of fish] **2** kikkerdrilʰ
²**spawn** (vb) kuit schieten
¹**speak** (vb) spreken, een toespraak houden:
so to ~ (om) zo te zeggen, bij wijze van spreken; *strictly* ~*ing* strikt genomen; ~ *out
against sth.* zich tegen iem. uitspreken; ~ *up
for s.o. (sth.)* het voor iem. (iets) opnemen;
nothing to ~ *of* niets noemenswaard(ig)s; ~ *ill*
(*or: well*) *of s.o.* (*sth.*) kwaad (*or:* gunstig)
spreken over iem. (iets); ~ *to s.o.* (*about sth.*)
iem. (over iets) aanspreken; [telephone]
~*ing!* spreekt u mee! || *that* ~*s for itself* dat
spreekt voor zich; *could you* ~ *up* please kunt
u wat harder spreken, a.u.b.; ~ *for sth.* **a)** iets
bestellen; **b)** van iets getuigen; **c)** een toespraak houden (*or:* pleiten) voor [also fig]
²**speak** (vb) (uit)spreken, zeggen, uitdrukken: ~ *one's mind* zijn mening zeggen
speaker spreker
Speaker voorzitter van het Lagerhuis
speaking sprekend, levensecht, treffend: *a*
~ *likeness* een sprekende gelijkenis
speaking engagement spreekbeurt
speaking terms: *not be on* ~ *with s.o.* niet
(meer) spreken tegen iem., onenigheid met
iem. hebben
¹**spear** (n) speer, lans
²**spear** (vb) (met een speer) doorboren,
spietsen
¹**spearhead** (n) speerpunt; [fig] spits, leider
²**spearhead** (vb) de spits zijn van [also fig];
leiden; aanvoeren [eg action, campaign]
¹**special** (n) iets bijzonders, extra-editie, speciaal gerechtʰ op menu, speciale attractie,
(tv-)special, speciaal programmaʰ
²**special** (adj) speciaal, bijzonder, apart, ex-
tra || *Special Branch* Politieke Veiligheidspoli-

tie; ~ *delivery* expressebestelling

specialism specialisme[h], specialisatie

specialist specialist

speciality 1 bijzonder kenmerk[h], bijzonderheid, detail[h] **2** specialiteit [subject, product etc]

specialization specialisatie

[1]**specialize** (vb) **1** zich specialiseren, gespecialiseerd zijn **2** in bijzonderheden treden

[2]**specialize** (vb) **1** specificeren, speciaal vermelden **2** beperken

specially speciaal, op speciale wijze, bijzonder: *he is not ~ interesting* hij is niet bepaald interessant

species soort, type[h]: *the (human) ~, our ~* het mensdom, de menselijke soort

specific 1 specifiek, duidelijk: *be ~ de* dingen bij hun naam noemen, er niet omheen draaien **2** specifiek, soortelijk: *~ gravity* soortelijk gewicht

specification 1 specificatie, gedetailleerde beschrijving **2** (-s) technische beschrijving

specify specificeren, precies vermelden

specimen 1 monster[h], staaltje[h] **2** (mooi) exemplaar[h], (rare) knakker, eigenaardige kerel

speck vlek, stip, plek(je[h]); [fig] greintje[h]

[1]**speckle** (n) spikkel, stippel, vlekje[h]

[2]**speckle** (vb) bespikkelen, stippelen

specs *spectacles* bril

spectacle 1 schouwspel[h], vertoning **2** aanblik, gezicht[h] **3** (-s) bril: *a pair of ~s* een bril

spectacular spectaculair, sensationeel

spectator toeschouwer, kijker

spectral 1 spookachtig **2** [physics] spectraal

spectre spook[h], geest; schim [also fig]

speculate speculeren, berekenen: *~ about* (or: *on*) overdenken, overpeinzen; *~ in* speculeren in

speculation 1 beschouwing, overpeinzing **2** speculatie

speculative speculatief, theoretisch, op gissingen berustend

speech 1 toespraak, rede(voering), speech: *Queen's* (or: *King's*) *~* troonrede; *maiden ~* eerste redevoering die iem. houdt, redenaarsdebuut **2** opmerking, uitlating **3** rede: *(in)direct ~* (in)directe rede; *reported ~* indirecte rede **4** spraak(vermogen[h]), uiting, taal: *freedom of ~* vrijheid van meningsuiting

speech day prijsuitdeling(sdag) [at school]

speech defect spraakgebrek[h]

speechless 1 sprakeloos, verstomd **2** onbeschrijfelijk: *~ admiration* woordeloze bewondering

speech recognition spraakherkenning

speech therapist logopedist

[1]**speed** (n) **1** spoed, haast **2** (rij)snelheid, vaart, gang: *(at) full ~* met volle kracht, in volle vaart **3** versnelling [of bicycle] **4** versnelling(sbak) [of car] **5** (sluiter)snelheid **6** speed, amfetamine

[2]**speed** (vb) **1** (te) snel rijden, de maximumsnelheid overschrijden: *~ up* sneller gaan rijden, gas geven **2** (voorbij)snellen [also fig]

[3]**speed** (vb) **1** opjagen, haast doen maken: *it needs ~ing up* er moet schot in worden gebracht, er moet tempo in komen **2** versnellen, opvoeren: *~ up (production)* (de productie) opvoeren **3** (+ away) (snel) vervoeren

speedboat speedboot

speed bump verkeersdrempel

speed camera flitspaal

speeding het te hard rijden

speed limit topsnelheid, maximumsnelheid

speedometer snelheidsmeter

speedway 1 (auto)renbaan, speedway-(baan) **2** autosnelweg

speedy snel, vlug, prompt

[1]**spell** (n) **1** bezwering(sformule), ban, betovering: *put a ~ on* (or: *over*) betoveren; *fall under the ~ of* in de ban raken van **2** periode, tijd(je[h]), (werk)beurt **3** vlaag, aanval, bui: *cold ~* koudegolf

[2]**spell** (vb) **1** (voor)spellen, betekenen, inhouden: *these measures ~ the ruin of* deze maatregelen betekenen de ondergang van

[3]**spell** (vb) spellen: *~ out* (or: *over*) uitleggen, nauwkeurig omschrijven

spellbound geboeid, gefascineerd: *hold one's audience ~* het publiek in zijn ban houden

spell-checker spellingcontrole

spelling spelling(wijze)

spend 1 uitgeven, spenderen, besteden: *~ money on* geld spenderen aan **2** doorbrengen, wijden: *~ the evening watching TV* de avond doorbrengen met tv kijken **3** uitputten: *the storm had soon spent its force* de storm was spoedig uitgeraasd

spending cut bezuinigingsmaatregel

spending money [esp Am] zakgeld[h]

spending power koopkracht

spendthrift verkwister, verspiller

spent 1 (op)gebruikt, af, leeg: *~ cartridge* lege huls **2** uitgeput, afgemat

sperm 1 spermacel, zaadcel **2** sperma[h], zaad[h]

sperm bank spermabank

sperm whale potvis

spew (uit)braken, spuwen: *~ out* uitspugen; *~ up* overgeven

sphere 1 bol, bal, kogel **2** hemellichaam[h], globe, wereldbol **3** sfeer, kring, gebied[h], terrein[h]: *~ of influence* invloedssfeer

spherical (bol)rond, bol-

sphinx sfinx

spice kruid[h], kruiden, specerij(en): *add ~ to* kruiden, smaak geven aan

spick and span 1 brandschoon, keurig, in de puntjes **2** (spik)splinternieuw
spicy 1 gekruid, heet **2** geurig **3** pikant [fig]; pittig: ~ *story* gewaagd verhaal
spider spin, spinnenkop
spidery 1 spinachtig; [fig] krabbelig [handwriting] **2** broodmager: ~ *legs* spillebenen **3** ragfijn
spiel 1 woordenstroom, (breedsprakig) verhaal[h]: *the* **saleman's** ~ het verkooppraatje **2** reclametekst [radio]
¹spike (n) **1** (scherpe) punt, pin, piek; prikker [for bills, loose notes etc] **2** (koren)aar **3** (-s) spikes [sports shoe]
²spike (vb) **1** (vast)spijkeren **2** van spijkers (punten) voorzien: ~*d* **shoes** spikes **3** alcohol toevoegen aan: ~ *coffee with cognac* wat cognac in de koffie doen
spike heel naaldhak
¹spill (n) **1** val(partij), duik **2** stukje papier (hout) [to light lamp or stove] **3** het afwerpen [of horseman] **4** verspilling
²spill (vb) overlopen, overstromen, uitstromen: *the* **milk** ~*ed* de melk liep over
³spill (vb) **1** doen overlopen, laten overstromen, morsen (met), omgooien, verspillen: ~ *the* **wine** met wijn morsen **2** vergieten [blood]; doen vloeien
spillage lozing [eg of oil into sea]
spillway 1 overlaat **2** afvoerkanaal[h]
¹spin (n) **1** draaibeweging, rotatie; [sport] spin; effect[h] [on ball] **2** ritje[h], tochtje[h]: *let's* **go** *for a* ~ laten we 'n eindje gaan rijden **3** (terug)val; duik [also fig] **4** spin, tolvlucht || *in a (flat)* ~ in paniek, van de kaart
²spin (vb) tollen, snel draaien: *make s.o.'s* **head** ~ iemands hoofd doen tollen
³spin (vb) **1** spinnen [also fig] **2** in elkaar draaien, verzinnen; produceren [story] **3** spineffect geven [ball] **4** snel laten ronddraaien: ~ *a* **coin** kruis of munt gooien; ~ *a* **top** tollen [game] || ~ *out* **a)** uitspinnen [story]; **b)** rekken [time]; **c)** zuinig zijn met [money]
spinach spinazie
spindle 1 spindel, (spin)klos, spoel **2** as, spil **3** stang, staaf, pijp
spindly spichtig, stakig
spin doctor spindoctor
spin-drier centrifuge
spin-dry centrifugeren
spine 1 ruggengraat **2** stekel, doorn **3** rug [of book]
spine-chiller horrorfilm, horrorroman, horrorverhaal[h], griezel-, gruwelfilm
spineless 1 zonder ruggengraat [also fig] **2** karakterloos, slap
spin-off (winstgevend) nevenproduct[h] (resultaat[h]), bijproduct[h]
spinster 1 oude vrijster **2** ongehuwde vrouw

¹spiral (n) spiraal, schroeflijn
²spiral (adj) **1** spiraalvormig, schroefvormig: ~ *staircase* wenteltrap **2** kronkelend
spire (toren)spits, piek, punt[h]
¹spirit (n) **1** geest, ziel, karakter[h], bovennatuurlijk wezen[h]: *the* **Holy** *Spirit* de Heilige Geest; *kindred* ~*s* verwante zielen **2** levenskracht, energie **3** levenslust, opgewektheid **4** moed, durf, lef[h] **5** zin, diepe betekenis: *the* ~ *of the law* de geest van de wet **6** spiritus, alcohol; [sometimes singular] sterkedrank(en): *methylated* ~ (brand)spiritus **7** (-s) gemoedsgesteldheid, geestesgesteldheid, stemming: *be in* **great** (or: **high**) ~*s* opgewekt zijn **8** mens met karakter, karakter[h] **9** (-s) spiritus, geest || **public** ~ gemeenschapszin
²spirit (vb) (+ away, off) wegtoveren, ontfutselen; [fig] heimelijk laten verdwijnen
spirited 1 levendig, geanimeerd **2** bezield, vol energie
spiritless 1 lusteloos, moedeloos **2** levenloos, doods, saai
spirit level waterpas
spiritual 1 geestelijk, spiritueel **2** mentaal, intellectueel **3** godsdienstig, religieus || ~ *healing* geloofsgenezing
spiritualism 1 spiritualisme[h] **2** spiritisme[h]
spirituality 1 spiritualiteit **2** vroomheid
¹spit (n) **1** spuug[h], speeksel[h] **2** spit[h], braadspit[h] **3** landtong **4** spade, schop: *dig a hole two* ~*(s)* **deep** een gat twee spaden diep graven **5** geblaas[h]; gesis[h] [of cat] || ~ *and polish* (grondig) poetswerk [eg in army]
²spit (vb) **1** spuwen, spugen **2** sputteren; blazen [eg cat] **3** lichtjes neervallen; druppelen [rain] || *he is the* ~*ting* **image** *of his father* hij lijkt als twee druppels water op zijn vader
³spit (vb) (also + out) (uit)spuwen, (uit)spugen, opgeven || ~ *it out!* voor de dag ermee!
¹spite (n) wrok, boosaardigheid: *from* (or: *out of*) ~ uit kwaadaardigheid || *in* ~ *of* o.s. of men wil of niet
²spite (vb) treiteren, pesten
spiteful hatelijk
spitfire heethoofd, driftkop
spittle speeksel[h], spuug[h]
¹splash (n) **1** plons **2** vlek, spat **3** gespetter[h], gespat[h] || *make a* ~ opzien baren
²splash (vb) **1** (rond)spatten, uiteenspatten: ~ *about* rondspatten **2** rondspetteren **3** klateren, kletteren
³splash (vb) **1** (be)spatten **2** laten spatten **3** met grote koppen in de krant zetten
⁴splash (adv) met een plons
splatter 1 spetteren, (be)spatten **2** poedelen **3** klateren, kletteren
¹splay (vb) naar buiten staan [of foot]
²splay (vb) **1** (also + out) (zich) verwijden, (zich) verbreden **2** (also + out) (zich) uitspreiden
spleen 1 milt **2** zwaarmoedigheid, neer-

slachtigheid **3** boze bui ‖ *vent* one's ~ zijn gal spuwen

splendid 1 schitterend, prachtig **2** groots, indrukwekkend **3** voortreffelijk, uitstekend

splendour 1 pracht, praal **2** glorie, grootsheid

¹splice (n) **1** las, verbinding **2** splits [of rope] **3** houtverbinding

²splice (vb) **1** verbinden, aan elkaar verbinden, een verbinding maken **2** lassen; koppelen [film, sound tape] ‖ *get* ~*d* trouwen

splint 1 metaalstrook, metaalstrip **2** spalk

¹splinter (n) splinter, scherf

²splinter (vb) versplinteren, splinteren

¹split (n) **1** spleet, kloof; [fig] breuk; scheiding **2** splitsing **3** (-s) spagaat: *do the* ~*s* een spagaat maken

²split (adj) **1** gespleten, gebarsten **2** gesplitst, gescheurd: [sport] ~ *decision* niet-eenstemmige beslissing; ~ *level* met halve verdiepingen; ~ *pea* spliterwt; ~ *second* onderdeel van een seconde, flits

³split (vb) (+ on) verraden

⁴split (vb) **1** splijten, splitsen; [fig] afsplitsen; scheuren: *George and I have* ~ *up* George en ik zijn uit elkaar gegaan; ~ *up into groups* (zich) in groepjes verdelen **2** delen, onder elkaar verdelen: *let's* ~ *(the bill)* laten we (de kosten) delen

splitting fel, scherp, hevig: ~ *headache* barstende hoofdpijn

split-up breuk [after quarrel]; echtscheiding, het uit elkaar gaan

splodge vlek, plek, veeg

splurge 1 uitspatting, het zich te buiten gaan **2** spektakelʰ

¹splutter (n) gesputterʰ, gespetterʰ

²splutter (vb) **1** sputteren, stamelen, hakkelen **2** sputteren, sissen **3** proesten, spetteren

¹spoil (n) **1** buit, geplunderde goederen **2** (-s) voordelen, winst

²spoil (vb) **1** bederven, (doen) rotten, beschadigen, verpesten: ~ *the fun* het plezier vergallen **2** bederven, verwennen, vertroetelen ‖ *be* ~*ing for a fight* staan te trappelen om te vechten

spoils buit

spoilsport spelbreker

spoke 1 spaak **2** sport, trede ‖ *put a* ~ *in s.o.'s wheel* iem. een spaak in het wiel steken

spokesman woordvoerder, afgevaardigde

spokesperson woordvoerder

¹sponge (n) **1** klaploper **2** spons: [boxing] *throw in the* ~ de spons opgooien; [fig] de strijd opgeven **3** wondgaasʰ

²sponge (vb) klaplopen, parasiteren: ~ *on s.o.* op iem. (parasi)teren

³sponge (vb) **1** sponzen, schoon-, afsponzen **2** afspoelen met een spons

sponge bag toilettasjeʰ

sponger 1 sponzenduiker **2** klaploper

¹sponsor (n) **1** sponsor, geldschieter **2** peter, meter

²sponsor (vb) propageren, steunen, bevorderen, sponsoren

sponsorship sponsoring

spontaneity spontaniteit

spontaneous 1 spontaan, natuurlijk, ongedwongen **2** uit zichzelf, vanzelf: ~ *combustion* zelfontbranding

¹spoof (n) **1** poets, bedrogʰ **2** parodie

²spoof (vb) **1** voor de gek houden, een poets bakken **2** parodiëren

spook geest, spookʰ

spooky spookachtig, griezelig, eng

spool 1 spoel **2** klos, garenklos

¹spoon (n) lepel: *slotted* ~ schuimspaan

²spoon (vb): ~ *out* opscheppen, uitdelen

spoon-feed 1 voeren, met een lepel voeren **2** iets met de lepel ingieten, iem. iets voorkauwen

spoonful lepel (vol)

¹sport (n) **1** pret, spelʰ, plezierʰ: *in* ~ voor de grap **2** spelʰ, tijdverdrijfʰ **3** sport **4** jacht **5** sportieve meid (kerel)

²sport (vb) spelen [of animals]; zich vermaken

³sport (vb) pronken met, vertonen, te koop lopen met: *he was* ~*ing a bowler hat* hij liep met een hoge hoed

sporting 1 sportief, eerlijk, fair: ~ *chance* redelijke kans **2** sport-

sports 1 sport **2** sportdag, sportevenement **3** atletiek

sports car sportwagen

sports centre sportcomplexʰ

sports event sportmanifestatie

sportsman 1 sportieve man **2** sportman

sportsmanlike sportief

sportsmanship sportiviteit, zich als een goede winnaar (verliezer) gedragen

sportswear [Am] sportieve kleding

sportswoman 1 sportieve vrouw **2** sportvrouw

sporty 1 sportief, sport- **2** zorgeloos, vrolijk **3** opvallend; bijzonder [of clothes]

¹spot (n) **1** plaats, plek: *they were on the* ~ ze waren ter plaatse **2** vlekjeʰ, stip **3** puistjeʰ **4** positie, plaats, functie **5** spot(jeʰ) [advertising etc] **6** spot(lightʰ) **7** beetjeʰ, wat: *a* ~ *of bother* een probleempje **8** onmiddellijke levering ‖ *now he is in a (tight)* ~ nu zit hij in de penarie; *he had to leave on the* ~ hij moest op staande voet vertrekken; *put s.o. on the* ~ iem. in het nauw brengen, iem. voor het blok zetten

²spot (vb) **1** verkleuren, vlekken krijgen **2** vlekken **3** spetteren, licht regenen: *it is* ~*ting with rain* er vallen dikke regendruppels

³spot (vb) **1** vlekken maken in, bevlekken **2** herkennen, eruit halen: ~ *a mistake* een fout ontdekken

⁴spot (adv) precies: *arrive ~ on time* precies op tijd komen
spot check (onverwachte) steekproef
spotless brandschoon, vlekkeloos; [fig also] onberispelijk
¹spotlight (n) **1** bundellichtʰ, spotlightʰ **2** bermlichtʰ [of car] ‖ *be in the ~, hold the ~* in het middelpunt van de belangstelling staan
²spotlight (vb) **1** beschijnen **2** onder de aandacht brengen
spot-on [inform] precies (goed)
spotty 1 vlekkerig **2** ongelijkmatig, onregelmatig **3** puisterig
spouse echtgenoot, echtgenote
¹spout (n) **1** pijp, buis **2** tuit **3** stortkoker **4** straal, opspuitende vloeistof, opspuitend zandʰ ‖ *up the ~* **a)** naar de knoppen, verknald [eg money, life]; **b)** totaal verkeerd [eg figures]; **c)** hopeloos in de knoei, reddeloos verloren [of person]; **d)** zwanger
²spout (vb) **1** spuiten, met kracht uitstoten: *the water ~ed from the broken pipe* het water spoot uit de gebarsten leiding **2** galmen, spuien: *she was always ~ing German verses* ze liep altijd Duitse verzen te galmen
¹sprain (n) verstuiking
²sprain (vb) verstuiken
sprat sprot
¹sprawl (n) **1** nonchalante houding **2** slordige massa, vormeloos geheelʰ: *the ~ of the suburbs* de uitdijende voorsteden
²sprawl (vb) **1** armen en benen uitspreiden, nonchalant liggen, onderuit zakken **2** zich uitspreiden, alle kanten op gaan: *~ing suburbs* naar alle kanten uitgroeiende voorsteden
¹spray (n) **1** takjeʰ [also as corsage]; twijg **2** verstuiver, spuitbus **3** straal, wolk **4** nevel, wolk van druppels
²spray (vb) (be)sproeien, (be)spuiten, (een vloeistof) verstuiven
spray-gun spuitpistoolʰ; verfspuit
¹spread (n) **1** wijdte, breedte; [fig also] reikwijdte **2** uitdijing **3** verbreiding, verspreiding **4** stuk land, landbezitʰ van één boer **5** smeerselʰ **6** (feest)maalʰ, onthaalʰ **7** dubbele pagina, spread
²spread (vb) **1** zich uitstrekken, zich uitspreiden **2** zich verspreiden, overal bekend worden: *the disease ~ quickly to other villages* de ziekte breidde zich snel uit naar andere dorpen **3** uitgespreid worden: *cold butter does not ~ easily* koude boter smeert niet gemakkelijk
³spread (vb) **1** uitspreiden, verbreiden, verspreiden; [fig also] spreiden; verdelen: *~ out one's arms* zijn armen uitspreiden **2** uitsmeren, uitstrijken **3** bedekken, beleggen, besmeren **4** klaarzetten [meal]; dekken [table]
spreadeagle 1 (zich) met armen en benen

wijd neerleggen **2** volkomen verslaan, verpletteren
spreadsheet spreadsheet
spree pret(jeʰ), lol: *spending ~* geldsmijterij
sprig 1 twijgjeʰ, takjeʰ **2** telg, spruit
¹spring (n) **1** bron [also fig]; oorsprong, herkomst **2** (metalen) veer, springveer **3** sprong **4** lente, voorjaarʰ: *in (the) ~* in het voorjaar (*or*: de lente)
²spring (vb) **1** (op)springen: *the first thing that ~s to one's mind* het eerste wat je te binnen schiet; *~ to one's feet* opspringen **2** (terug)veren **3** (also + up) ontspringen, ontstaan, voortkomen: *~ from* afstammen van; *~ from* (*or*: *out of*) voortkomen uit
³spring (vb) **1** springen over [of horse, obstacle] **2** plotseling bekendmaken: *~ sth. on s.o.* iem. met iets verrassen
springboard [also fig] springplank; duikplank
spring-clean voorjaarsschoonmaak, grote schoonmaak
spring roll loempia
spring tide springtijʰ, springvloed
springtime lente(tijd), voorjaarʰ
springy 1 veerkrachtig **2** elastisch
¹sprinkle (n) **1** regenbuitjeʰ **2** kleine hoeveelheid ‖ *a ~ of houses* enkele (verspreid liggende) huizen
²sprinkle (vb) **1** sprenkelen [also fig]; strooien **2** bestrooien [also fig]; besprenkelen: *~ with* bestrooien met
sprinkler 1 (tuin)sproeier **2** blusinstallatie
sprinkling kleine hoeveelheid, greintjeʰ
¹sprint (n) sprint, spurt
²sprint (vb) sprinten
sprinter 1 [sport] sprinter **2** sprinter [train]
sprite 1 (boze) geest **2** elf(jeʰ)
¹sprout (n) **1** spruit, loot, scheut **2** spruitjeʰ [vegetable]
²sprout (vb) **1** (ont)spruiten, uitlopen **2** de hoogte in schieten, groeien: *~ up* de hoogte in schieten
³sprout (vb) doen ontspruiten
¹spruce (n) spar, sparrenhoutʰ
²spruce (adj) net(jes), keurig
³spruce (vb) opdoffen, opdirken, verfraaien
spry levendig, actief: *a ~ old man* een vitale oude man
spud pieper, aardappel
spunk pit, lefʰ, durf
¹spur (n) **1** spoorʰ [of horseman]: *win one's ~s* **a)** zijn sporen verdienen; **b)** [also fig] zich onderscheiden **2** aansporing, prikkel, stimulans: *act on the ~ of the moment* spontaan iets doen **3** uitloper [of mountain]
²spur (vb) **1** de sporen geven **2** aansporen, aanmoedigen: *~ on (to)* aanzetten (tot), aansporen (tot)
spurious 1 onecht, vals, vervalst **2** onlogisch: *~ argument* verkeerd argument

spurn 1 (weg)trappen **2** afwijzen, van de hand wijzen
¹spurt (n) **1** uitbarsting, losbarsting, vlaag, opwelling: *a ~ of flames* een plotselinge vlammenzee **2** sprint(je^h), spurt: *put on a ~* een sprintje trekken **3** (krachtige) straal, stroom, vloed
²spurt (vb) **1** spurten, sprinten **2** spuiten, opspatten: *the blood ~ed out* het bloed gutste eruit
¹sputter (n) gesputter^h, gestamel^h
²sputter (vb) sputteren, proesten, stamelen, brabbelen
¹spy (n) spion(ne), geheim agent(e)
²spy (vb) spioneren, spieden, loeren, een spion zijn: *~ (up)on* bespioneren, bespieden; *~ into* bespioneren, zijn neus steken in
³spy (vb) **1** bespioneren, bespieden **2** ontwaren, in het oog krijgen || *I ~ (with my little eye)* ik zie, ik zie, wat jij niet ziet
spyhole kijkgat^h
spy out 1 verkennen, onderzoeken **2** opsporen
spyware spyware
sq *square* kwadraat^h
¹squabble (n) schermutseling, gekibbel^h
²squabble (vb) kibbelen, overhoop liggen
squad 1 [sport] selectie **2** sectie **3** (politie)brigade: *drugs ~* narcoticabrigade
squad car patrouilleauto
squadron 1 eskadron^h **2** [navy, airforce] eskader^h
squadron leader majoor; eskadercommandant [in airforce]
squalid 1 smerig, vuil, vies, gemeen, laag **2** ellendig, beroerd
¹squall (n) **1** vlaag, rukwind, windstoot, bui, storm **2** kreet, gil, schreeuw
²squall (vb) gillen, krijsen, (uit)schreeuwen
squally 1 buiig, regenachtig, winderig **2** stormachtig
squalor 1 misère **2** smerigheid
squander (+ on) verspillen (aan): *~ money* met geld smijten
¹square (n) **1** vierkant^h **2** kwadraat^h, tweede macht **3** plein^h **4** veld^h, hokje^h; ruit [on games' board] **5** (huizen)blok^h **6** oefenplein^h, oefenterrein^h **7** ouderwets persoon || *be back to ~ one* van voren af aan moeten beginnen; *on the ~* **a)** rechtdoorzee; **b)** in een rechte hoek
²square (adj) **1** vierkant, kwadraat-, in het vierkant, fors; breed [of figure]: *~ brackets* vierkante haakjes; *one ~ metre* één vierkante meter; *three metres ~* drie meter in het vierkant **2** recht(hoekig) **3** eerlijk, fair; open-(hartig) [eg answer]; regelrecht [eg refusal]: *a ~ deal* een rechtvaardige behandeling, een eerlijke transactie **4** ouderwets **5** stevig [of meal] **6** [sport, esp golf] gelijk: *be (all) ~* gelijk staan || *a ~ peg (in a round hole)* de verkeerde

persoon (voor iets); *be ~ with* quitte staan met, op gelijke hoogte (*or:* voet) staan met; *all ~* we staan quitte; [sport] gelijke stand
³square (vb) **1** overeenstemmen, kloppen **2** in een rechte hoek staan
⁴square (vb) **1** vierkant maken **2** rechthoekig maken **3** rechten [shoulders]; rechtzetten **4** in orde brengen, regelen: *~ up* vereffenen; *~ up one's debts* zijn schuld(en) voldoen **5** omkopen **6** kwadrateren, tot de tweede macht verheffen: *three ~d equals nine* drie tot de tweede (macht) is negen **7** [sport] op gelijke stand brengen
⁵square (adv) **1** recht(hoekig), rechtop **2** (regel)recht: *look s.o. ~ in the eye* iem. recht in de ogen kijken **3** eerlijk, rechtvaardig: *play ~* eerlijk spelen **4** rechtuit, open(hartig): *come ~ out with an answer* onomwonden antwoorden
square-built vierkant, hoekig, breed
square dance quadrille
squarely 1 recht(hoekig), rechtop **2** (regel)recht **3** eerlijk: *act ~* eerlijk handelen
square up 1 in gevechtshouding gaan staan: *~ to reality* de werkelijkheid onder ogen zien **2** afrekenen, orde op zaken stellen
¹squash (n) **1** kwast, vruchtendrank **2** gedrang^h, oploop **3** pulp
²squash (vb) **1** geplet worden **2** dringen, zich persen: *can I ~ in next to you?* kan ik er nog bij, naast u?
³squash (vb) **1** pletten, platdrukken **2** verpletteren; de mond snoeren **3** de kop indrukken **4** wringen: *~ in* erin persen
squashy 1 zacht, overrijp **2** drassig || *a ~ pillow* een zacht kussen
¹squat (n) **1** hurkende houding, het hurken **2** ineengedoken houding [of animal] **3** kraakpand^h **4** het kraken [of house]
²squat (adj) **1** gedrongen, plomp **2** gehurkt
³squat (vb) **1** (also + down) (neer)hurken **2** zich tegen de grond drukken [of animal] **3** zich illegaal vestigen [on a stretch of land] **4** als kraker een leegstaand pand bewonen
squatter 1 (illegale) kolonist, landbezetter **2** kraker
¹squawk (n) schreeuw, gekrijs^h
²squawk (vb) krijsen, schril schreeuwen
¹squeak (n) **1** gepiep^h, geknars^h **2** klein kansje^h || *that was a narrow ~* dat was op het nippertje, dat ging nog net
²squeak (vb) **1** piepen, knarsen, gilletjes slaken **2** doorslaan || *~ through* (*or:* by) het nog net halen
squeaky piepend, krakend || *~ clean* brandschoon
¹squeal (n) **1** gil, schreeuw, gepiep^h **2** klacht
²squeal (vb) **1** krijsen, piepen **2** klikken, doorslaan: *~ on s.o.* iem. aanbrengen
squeamish 1 (gauw) misselijk **2** teerge-

voelig, overgevoelig **3** (al te) kieskeurig ‖ *this film is not for ~ viewers* deze film is niet geschikt voor al te gevoelige kijkers
squeegee rubber wisserʰ, schuiver, trekker
¹squeeze (n) **1** samendrukking, pressie, druk: *she gave his hand a little ~* ze kneep even in zijn hand; *put the ~ on s.o.* iem. onder druk zetten **2** gedrangʰ **3** (stevige) handdruk, (innige) omarming **4** beperking, schaarste ‖ *it was a close* (or: *narrow, tight*) *~* we zaten als haringen in een ton
²squeeze (vb) dringen, zich wringen: *~ through* zich erdoorheen wurmen [also fig]
³squeeze (vb) **1** drukken (op), knijpen (in), (uit)persen, uitknijpen: *~ a lemon* een citroen uitpersen **2** duwen, wurmen: *how can she ~ so many things into one single day?* hoe krijgt ze zoveel dingen op één dag gedaan? **3** tegen zich aan drukken, stevig omhelzen
squelch een zuigend geluid maken, ploeteren
squib 1 voetzoeker **2** blindganger **3** schotschriftʰ
squid pijlinktvis
squidgy klef
squiggle kronkel(lijn), krabbel
squillion [mockingly] ziljoenʰ, ontelbaar veel
¹squint (n) **1** scheel oogʰ, turend oogʰ **2** (vluchtige) blik: *have* (or: *take*) *a ~ at sth.* een blik werpen op iets
²squint (vb) **1** scheel kijken **2** gluren, turen: *~ at sth.* een steelse blik op iets werpen
squire 1 landjonker; landheer [in England] **2** meneer [form of address among men]
squirm 1 kronkelen, zich in bochten wringen **2** wel door de grond kunnen gaan: *be ~ing with embarrassment* zich geen raad weten van verlegenheid
¹squirrel (n) eekhoorn
²squirrel (vb): *he ~ed away* more than he needed hij hamsterde meer dan hij nodig had
¹squirt (n) **1** straal [of liquid etc] **2** spuit(jeʰ), waterpistoolʰ
²squirt (vb) (krachtig) naar buiten spuiten
³squirt (vb) (uit)spuiten, uitspuwen
sr *senior* sr., sen.
Sri Lanka Sri Lanka
¹Sri Lankan (n) Sri Lankaan(se)
²Sri Lankan (adj) Sri Lankaans
St 1 *Saint* St., H., Sint, Heilige **2** *Street* str., straat **3** *strait* zee-engte, straat
¹stab (n) **1** steek(wond), stoot, uithaal **2** pijnscheut, plotse opwelling **3** poging, gooi: *have* (or: *make*) *a ~ at* eens proberen ‖ *a ~ in the back* dolkstoot in de rug
²stab (vb) (+ at) (toe)stoten (naar), steken, uithalen (naar): *a ~bing pain* een stekende pijn
³stab (vb) (door)steken, neersteken, doorboren: *be ~bed to death* doodgestoken worden

stability stabiliteit, duurzaamheid
stabilize (zich) stabiliseren, in evenwicht blijven (brengen)
¹stable (n) **1** stal; [fig] ploeg; groep **2** (ren)stal ‖ *it is no use shutting the ~ door* after the horse has bolted als het kalf verdronken is, dempt men de put
²stable (adj) **1** stabiel, vast, duurzaam **2** standvastig
¹stack (n) **1** (hooi)mijt, houtmijt **2** stapel, hoop: *~s of money* bergen geld **3** schoorsteen
²stack (vb) **1** (op)stapelen, op een hoop leggen, volstapelen **2** arrangeren: *~ the cards* de kaarten vals schikken
¹stack up (vb) **1** een file vormen [of cars, aeroplanes]; aanschuiven **2** ervoor staan
²stack up (vb) **1** opstapelen **2** ophouden: *traffic* was stacked up for miles het verkeer werd kilometers lang opgehouden
stadium stadionʰ
¹staff (n) **1** staf [also fig]; steun **2** vlaggenstok **3** notenbalk **4** staf [also mil]; personeelʰ, korpsʰ ‖ *the ~ of life* brood
²staff (vb) bemannen, van personeel voorzien
staff manager personeelschef
staff member staflidʰ
¹stag (n) **1** hertenbok **2** man die alleen op stap is
²stag (adj) mannen-: *~ party* vrijgezellenfeest, hengstenbal
¹stage (n) **1** toneelʰ [also fig]; podiumʰ, platformʰ: *put on the ~* opvoeren; *be on the ~* aan het toneel verbonden zijn **2** fase, stadiumʰ: *at this ~* op dit punt, in dit stadium **3** stopplaats, halte aan het eind van een tariefzone **4** etappe, trajectʰ, tariefzone: *by easy ~s* in korte etappes; *in ~s* gefaseerd **5** postkoets ‖ *set the ~ for* de weg bereiden voor
²stage (vb) **1** opvoeren, ten tonele brengen **2** produceren **3** regisseren **4** organiseren
stagecoach postkoets
stage door artiesteningang
stage fright plankenkoorts
stage-manage in scène zetten, opzetten
stage manager toneelmeester
¹stagger (n) wankeling
²stagger (vb) wankelen: *~ along* moeizaam vooruitkomen
³stagger (vb) **1** doen wankelen; [fig] onthutsen **2** zigzagsgewijs aanbrengen: *a ~ed road* crossing een kruising met verspringende zijwegen **3** spreiden [holidays]: *~ed office hours* glijdende werktijden
staggering 1 wankelend **2** onthutsend, duizelingwekkend
staging 1 steiger; platformʰ **2** opvoering
stagnant 1 stilstaand **2** stagnerend
stagnate stilstaan, stagneren, stremmen
stag party bokkenfuif; hengstenbalʰ

staid 1 bezadigd **2** vast, stellig
¹stain (n) **1** vlek, smet, schandvlek **2** kleurstof
²stain (vb) vlekken
³stain (vb) **1** bevlekken **2** kleuren: *~ed glass* gebrandschilderd glas
stainless roestvrij [steel]
stair 1 trap: *a winding ~* een wenteltrap **2** trede
staircase trap: *a moving ~* een roltrap
stairway trap
stairwell trappenhuisʰ
¹stake (n) **1** staak, paal **2** brandstapel: *go to the ~* op de brandstapel sterven **3** inzet; [fig] belangʰ: *have a ~ in sth.* zakelijk belang hebben bij iets ‖ *be at ~* op het spel staan
²stake (vb) **1** (+ off, out) afpalen [eg land]; afbakenen: *~ out a claim* aanspraak maken op **2** spietsen **3** (+ on) verwedden (om), inzetten (op); [fig] op het spel zetten: *I'd ~ my life on it* ik durf er mijn hoofd om te verwedden ‖ *~ out* posten bij, in de gaten houden
stakeholder 1 beheerder van de inzet **2** [econ] stakeholder; belanghebbende
stalactite stalactiet, druipsteenpegel
stalagmite stalagmiet, druipsteenkegel
stale 1 niet vers, oud(bakken) **2** afgezaagd **3** mat, afgemat, machinaal
stalemate 1 [chess] patʰ **2** patstelling, dood puntʰ
¹stalk (n) **1** [bot] stengel, steel **2** stronk
²stalk (vb) (+ out) (uit) schrijden: *the chairman ~ed out in anger* de voorzitter stapte kwaad op
³stalk (vb) **1** besluipen **2** achtervolgen, stalken **3** rondwaren door
stalker 1 iem. die wild besluipt; jager **2** stalker
¹stall (n) **1** box, hokʰ, stal **2** stalletjeʰ, stand, kraam, tent: *coffee ~* koffietentje **3** stallesplaats: *~s* stalles
²stall (vb) **1** blijven steken, ingesneeuwd zijn **2** afslaan [of engine] **3** uitvluchten zoeken, tijd rekken
³stall (vb) **1** stallen **2** ophouden, blokkeren
stallion (dek)hengst
¹stalwart (n) trouwe aanhanger
²stalwart (adj) **1** stevig, stoer **2** flink **3** standvastig, trouw
stamen meeldraad
stamina uithoudingsvermogenʰ
stammer stotteren, stamelen ‖ *speak with a ~* stotteren
¹stamp (n) **1** stempel; [fig] (ken)merkʰ **2** zegel, postzegel, waarmerkʰ **3** kenmerkʰ
²stamp (vb) stampen, trappen
³stamp (vb) **1** stempelen, persen, waarmerken: *be ~ed on one's memory* in zijn geheugen gegrift zijn **2** frankeren, een postzegel plakken op: *~ed addressed envelope* antwoordenvelop **3** fijnstampen: *~ out* uitroei-

en; *~ on* onderdrukken
stamp collector postzegelverzamelaar
¹stampede (n) **1** wilde vlucht; op hol slaan [of animals]; paniek **2** stormloop
²stampede (vb) op de vlucht slaan, op hol slaan
³stampede (vb) op de vlucht jagen; [fig] het hoofd doen verliezen: *don't be ~d into selling your house* ga nou niet halsoverkop je huis verkopen
stance 1 houding, stand **2** pose, gezindheid: *an obvious anti-American ~* een duidelijke anti-Amerikaanse gezindheid
¹stand (n) **1** stilstand, halt: *bring to a ~* tot staan brengen **2** stelling [also mil]; [fig] standpuntʰ **3** plaats, positie, post **4** statiefʰ, standaard **5** stand, kraam **6** standplaats [of taxis etc] **7** tribune, podiumʰ, getuigenbank
²stand (vb) **1** (rechtop) staan, opstaan: *~ clear of* vrijlaten [door etc] **2** zich bevinden, staan, liggen **3** stilstaan, halt houden; stoppen [of vehicles] **4** blijven staan, stand houden: *~ and deliver!* je geld of je leven! **5** gelden, opgaan: *the offer still ~s* het aanbod is nog van kracht **6** zijn, (ervoor) staan, zich in een bepaalde situatie bevinden: *I want to know where I ~* ik wil weten waar ik aan toe ben **7** kandidaat zijn, zich kandidaat stellen: *~ for president against ...* kandidaat zijn voor het presidentschap met ... als tegenkandidaat ‖ *I ~ corrected* ik neem mijn woorden terug; *~ to lose sth.* waarschijnlijk iets zullen verliezen; *~ aloof* zich op een afstand houden; *~ apart* zich afzijdig houden; *~ easy!* op de plaats rust!; *~ in (for s.o.)* (iem.) vervangen
³stand (vb) **1** plaatsen, rechtop zetten: *~ everything on its head* alles op zijn kop zetten **2** verdragen, uitstaan, doorstaan, ondergaan **3** weerstaan **4** trakteren (op): *~ s.o. a drink* iem. op een drankje trakteren
stand-alone standalone; autonoom
¹standard (n) **1** peilʰ, niveauʰ: *~ of living* levensstandaard; *below ~* beneden peil, beneden de norm **2** vaandelʰ [also fig]; standaard, vlag **3** maat(staf), norm **4** standaard(maat) **5** houder [eg candlestick] **6** (munt)standaard: *the gold ~* de gouden standaard **7** staander, steun, paal **8** hoogstammige plant (struik)
²standard (adj) **1** normaal, gebruikelijk: *~ size* standaardmaat, standaardgrootte **2** staand: *~ rose* stamroos
standardization standaardisering, normalisering
standardize standaardiseren, normaliseren
stand aside 1 opzijgaan **2** zich afzijdig houden
stand back 1 achteruit gaan **2** op een afstand liggen **3** afstand nemen **4** zich op de achtergrond houden

¹standby (n) **1** reserve **2** stand-by
²standby (adj) reserve-, nood-
stand by 1 erbij staan **2** werkloos toezien
3 gereed staan **4** bijstaan, steunen **5** zich
houden aan [promise]; trouw blijven aan
[somebody]
stand down zich terugtrekken, aftreden
stand for 1 staan voor, betekenen **2** goedvinden, zich laten welgevallen
stand-in vervanger
¹standing (n) **1** status, rang, positie: s.o. of ~
iem. van aanzien **2** reputatie **3** (tijds)duur:
friendship of **long** ~ oude vriendschap
²standing (adj) **1** blijvend, van kracht, vast:
~ **committee** permanente commissie; ~ **joke**
vaste grap; ~ **order** a) doorlopende order;
b) automatische overschrijving; ~ **orders** statuten **2** staand, stilstaand: ~ **ovation** staande
ovatie **3** zonder aanloop [of jump etc]
standing room staanplaatsen
stand-off 1 impasse, patstelling **2** even-
wichtʰ **3** (periode van) nietsdoen
standoffish afstandelijk
standout [Am; inform] uitblinker, schoonheid: Helen's translation **was** a ~ Helens vertaling stak met kop en schouder boven de rest
uit
stand out 1 duidelijk uitkomen, in het oog
vallen **2** zich onderscheiden **3** blijven volhouden: ~ **for** verdedigen
standpoint standpuntʰ [also fig]: **from** a
commercial ~ commercieel gezien
standstill stilstand: **at** a ~ tot stilstand gekomen
¹stand up (vb) **1** overeind staan **2** gaan
staan: ~ and be **counted** voor zijn mening
uitkomen; ~ **for** opkomen voor **3** standhouden, overeind blijven; [fig] doorstaan: that
won't ~ in **court** daar blijft niets van overeind
in de rechtszaal ‖ ~ **to** trotseren
²stand up (vb) laten zitten: she stood **me** up
zij is niet op komen dagen
stand-up 1 rechtop staand **2** lopend [of
supper etc] **3** flink [fight]; stevig ‖ ~ **comedian** conferencier
stanza coupletʰ, strofe
¹staple (n) **1** nietjeʰ **2** krammetjeʰ **3** hoofd-
bestanddeelʰ [also fig]; hoofdschotel
²staple (adj) **1** voornaamste: ~ **diet** hoofd-
voedsel; ~ **products** stapelproducten **2** belangrijk
³staple (vb) (vast)nieten, hechten
stapler nietmachine
¹star (n) **1** ster: Star of **David** davidster;
shooting ~ vallende ster; **thank** one's (lucky)
~s zich gelukkig prijzen **2** asterisk, sterretjeʰ
3 uitblink(st)er, beroemdheid, (film)ster, vedette: all-~ **cast** sterbezetting ‖ the Stars and
Stripes (or: **Bars**) Amerikaanse vlag
²star (vb) (als ster) optreden
³star (vb) **1** met een sterretje aanduiden

2 als ster laten optreden: a **film** ~ring Eddy
Murphy een film met (in de hoofdrol) Eddy
Murphy
starboard stuurboordʰ, rechts
starch 1 zetmeelʰ **2** stijfselʰ
starchy 1 zetmeelrijk: ~ **food** meelkost
2 gesteven **3** stijfjes
stardom sterrendomʰ; roem
¹stare (n) starende blik
²stare (vb) (+ at) staren (naar)
³stare (vb) staren naar: it is staring you in the
face het ligt voor de hand; ~ s.o. **down** (or:
out) iem. aanstaren tot hij de ogen neerslaat
starfish zeester
stargazer 1 [mockingly] sterrenkijker
2 dromer
¹staring (adj) (te) fel [colour]
²staring (adv) volledig: stark ~ **mad** knettergek
¹stark (adj) **1** grimmig **2** stijf, onbuigzaam
3 [fig] schril: ~ **contrast** schril contrast **4** verlaten [of landscape]; kaal ‖ ~ **poverty** bittere
armoede
²stark (adv) volledig: ~ **naked** spiernaakt
starkers poedelnaakt
starlet (film)sterretjeʰ
starling spreeuw
starry-eyed [inform] te idealistisch, wereldvreemd
star-spangled met sterren bezaaid ‖ the
Star-Spangled **Banner** a) het Amerikaanse
volkslied; b) de Amerikaanse vlag
¹start (n) **1** schok, ruk: **give** s.o. a ~ iem. laten
schrikken, iem. doen opkijken; **wake** up with
a ~ wakker schrikken **2** start: **from** ~ to **finish**
van begin tot eind; **false** ~ valse start [also
fig]; get off to a **good** ~ goed beginnen, een
goede start maken; **make** a ~ on beginnen
met; make a **fresh** (or: **new**) ~ opnieuw beginnen; **for** a ~ om te beginnen; **from** the
(very) ~ vanaf het (allereerste) begin **3** start-
seinʰ **4** voorsprong, voordeelʰ: **give** s.o. a ~ (in
life) iem. op gang helpen
²start (vb) **1** beginnen, starten, beginnen te
lopen: ~ing **next month** vanaf volgende
maand; ~ **out** vertrekken; [fig] zijn loopbaan
beginnen; ~ (all) **over** again (helemaal) opnieuw beginnen; ~ **at** beginnen bij; ~ **from**
beginnen bij; [fig] uitgaan van; **to** ~ (off) **with**
om (mee) te beginnen, in het begin, in de
eerste plaats **2** vertrekken, opstijgen, afvaren: ~ (out) **for** op weg gaan naar **3** (op)-
springen, (op)schrikken: ~ **back** (from) terugdeinzen (voor); ~ **at** (op)schrikken van
4 (plotseling) bewegen; losspringen [of
wood]; aanslaan [of engine]; tevoorschijn
springen: ~ **for** the door richting deur gaan
5 startsein geven **6** uitpuilen [of eyes]
³start (vb) **1** (doen) beginnen, aan de gang
brengen, aanzetten; starten [engine]; aansteken [fire]; op touw zetten; opzetten

[business etc]; naar voren brengen [subject] **2** brengen tot, laten: *the dust ~ed me cough-ing* door het stof moest ik hoesten **3** aanne-men, laten beginnen

starter 1 beginner: *a slow ~* iem. die lang-zaam op gang komt **2** startmotor **3** vooraf-je^h, voorgerecht^h || *for ~s* om te beginnen

starting block startblok^h

starting pistol startpistool^h

starting point uitgangspunt^h [also fig]

¹**startle** (vb) (op)schrikken

²**startle** (vb) **1** doen schrikken, opschrikken **2** schokken

startling verrassend

¹**start off** (vb) **1** beginnen: *he started off (by) saying that* hij begon met te zeggen dat **2** vertrekken **3** beginnen te zeggen

²**start off** (vb) (+ on) aan de gang laten gaan (met), laten beginnen (met)

¹**start up** (vb) **1** opspringen **2** een loopbaan beginnen: *~ in business* in zaken gaan **3** ont-staan, opkomen

²**start up** (vb) aan de gang brengen; opzet-ten [business]; starten [engine]

start-up pas opgericht (internet)bedrijf

star turn hoofdnummer^h, hoofdattractie

starvation 1 hongerdood **2** verhongering

starvation wages hongerloon^h

¹**starve** (vb) **1** verhongeren: *~ to death* ver-hongeren **2** honger lijden **3** sterven van de honger

²**starve** (vb) **1** uithongeren **2** doen kwijnen; [also fig] laten hunkeren; onthouden: *be ~d of* behoefte hebben aan **3** door uithonge-ring dwingen: *be ~d into surrender* door uit-hongering tot overgave gedwongen worden

stash (also + away) verbergen, opbergen

¹**state** (n) **1** toestand, staat: *~ of affairs* stand van zaken; *a poor ~ of health* een slechte ge-zondheidstoestand **2** (gemoeds)toestand, stemming: *be in a ~* in alle staten zijn **3** staat, natie, rijk^h **4** staatsie, praal: *~ banquet* staatsiebanket || *lie in ~* opgebaard liggen

²**state** (vb) **1** (formeel) verklaren, uitdrukken **2** aangeven, opgeven: *at ~d intervals* op ge-zette tijden, met regelmatige tussenpozen **3** vaststellen, specificeren

state benefit uitkering

stateless staatloos

stately 1 statig **2** waardig **3** formeel || *~ home* landhuis

statement 1 verklaring **2** (bank)afschrift^h

state-of-the-art hypermodern, uiterst ge-avanceerd

stateroom 1 staatsiezaal **2** passagiershut **3** (privé)coupé

the **States** Verenigde Staten

statesman staatsman

statesmanlike als een staatsman

statesmanship staatsmanschap^h

statewide over de gehele staat

static 1 statisch, stabiel: *~ electricity* stati-sche elektriciteit **2** in rust **3** atmosferisch

¹**station** (n) **1** station^h [also of railway, radio, TV]; goederenstation^h **2** standplaats, plaats, post **3** brandweerkazerne **4** politiebureau^h **5** [mil] basis, post **6** positie, rang, status: *marry above* (or: *beneath*) *one's ~* boven (or: beneden) zijn stand trouwen

²**station** (vb) plaatsen, stationeren: *~ o.s.* postvatten

stationary stationair, stilstaand, vast

stationer handelaar in kantoorbenodigd-heden, kantoorboekhandel

stationery 1 kantoorbenodigdheden **2** kantoorboekhandel **3** briefpapier^h en en-veloppen: *printed ~* voorbedrukt briefpapier

stationmaster stationschef

statistic statistisch gegeven

statistical statistisch

statistics statistiek(en), cijfers, percentages

statue (stand)beeld^h: *Statue of Liberty* Vrij-heidsbeeld

statuesque 1 als een standbeeld **2** plas-tisch

statuette beeldje^h

stature 1 gestalte, (lichaams)lengte **2** [fig] formaat^h

status status

status seeker statuszoeker

statute statuut^h, wet

statutory statutair, volgens de wet

¹**staunch** (adj) **1** betrouwbaar, trouw **2** soli-de

²**staunch** (vb) **1** stelpen **2** tot staan brengen **3** waterdicht maken

stave 1 duig **2** stok, knuppel **3** stang, staaf **4** sport [of ladder, chair]

stave in 1 in duigen slaan **2** een gat slaan in, indrukken, kapotslaan

stave off 1 van zich afhouden, op een af-stand houden **2** voorkomen

¹**stay** (n) **1** verblijf^h, oponthoud^h **2** steun [also fig] **3** verbindingsstuk^h [eg in aero-plane] **4** balein^h

²**stay** (vb) **1** blijven: *come to ~, be here to ~* blijven; [fig] zich een blijvende plaats ver-werven; *~ for s.o.* wachten op iem. **2** verblij-ven, logeren: *~ the night* de nacht doorbren-gen **3** stilhouden, ophouden **4** overblijven

³**stay** (vb) **1** (also + up) (onder)steunen **2** uit-houden [sport]: *~ the course* tot het einde toe volhouden

⁴**stay** (vb) blijven: *~ seated* blijven zitten; *~ ahead of the others* de anderen voorblijven; *~ away* wegblijven; *~ behind* (achter)blijven; *~ in* (after school) nablijven; *~ indoors* binnen blijven; *~ on a)* erop blijven; **b)** aanblijven [of light etc]; **c)** (aan)blijven [in office]; *~ up late* laat opblijven

stayer 1 blijver **2** volhouder, doorzetter, langeafstandsloper, langeafstandszwemmer

staying power uithoudingsvermogen^h
steadfast 1 vast, standvastig **2** trouw
¹steady (n) vrijer, vaste vriend(in)
²steady (adj) **1** vast, vaststaand, stabiel: *(as)* ~ *as a rock* rotsvast **2** gestaag, geregeld; vast [of job, income etc]; regelmatig [of life]; sterk [of nerves] **3** kalm, evenwichtig: ~ *on!* kalm aan!, langzaam! **4** betrouwbaar, oppassend **5** gematigd [of climate]; matig
³steady (vb) **1** vast/bestendig worden **2** kalm worden
⁴steady (vb) **1** vastheid geven, steunen: ~ *o.s.* zich staande houden **2** bestendigen, stabiliseren
⁵steady (adv) vast, gestaag ‖ *go* ~ vaste verkering hebben
⁶steady (int) **1** kalm aan, rustig **2** [shipp] recht zo
steak 1 (lapje) vlees^h, runderlapje^h **2** (vis)moot **3** visfilet
steak tartare tartaar
¹steal (vb) **1** stelen **2** sluipen: ~ *away* er heimelijk vandoor gaan; ~ *up on s.o.* iem. besluipen; ~ *over s.o.* iem. bekruipen [of feeling, thought]
²steal (vb) (ont)stelen, ontvreemden: ~ *a ride* stiekem meerijden
stealth heimelijkheid, geheim^h: *by* ~ stiekem, in het geniep
stealthy heimelijk, stiekem
¹steam (n) stoom(kracht), wasem, condensatie; [fig] kracht(ige gevoelens); vaart: *blow* (or: *let, work*) *off* ~ stoom afblazen, zijn agressie kwijtraken; *run out of* ~ zijn energie verliezen, futloos worden
²steam (vb) **1** stomen, dampen: ~*ing hot milk* gloeiend hete melk **2** opstomen; [fig] energiek werken: ~ *ahead* (or: *away*) doorstomen, er vaart achter zetten
³steam (vb) (gaar) stomen, klaarstomen: ~*ed fish* (or: *rice*) gestoomde vis (or: rijst)
steamboat stoomboot
steam engine stoommachine
steamer 1 stoompan, stoomketel **2** stoomschip^h, stoomboot
¹steamroller (n) stoomwals [also fig]
²steamroller (vb) **1** met een stoomwals platwalsen **2** verpletteren, vernietigen: ~ *all opposition* alle verzet de kop indrukken
¹steam up (vb) beslaan, met condensatie bedekt worden: *my glasses* are steaming up mijn bril beslaat
²steam up (vb) **1** doen beslaan, met condensatie bedekken **2** opgewonden maken, opwinden, ergeren: *don't get steamed up about it* maak je er niet druk om
steamy 1 m.b.t. stoom, dampig **2** heet, sensueel
steed (strijd)ros^h, paard^h
¹steel (n) **1** staal^h [also fig] **2** stuk^h staal: *a man of* ~ een man van staal, een sterke man

²steel (vb) stalen; pantseren [also fig]; harden, sterken: ~ *o.s. to do sth.* zich dwingen iets te doen
steelworks staalfabriek
steely stalen, (als) van staal; [fig] onbuigzaam: ~ *composure* ijzige kalmte
¹steep (adj) **1** steil, sterk hellend: *a* ~ *slope* een steile helling **2** scherp (oplopend), snel (stijgend): *a* ~ *rise in prices* scherpe prijsstijgingen **3** onredelijk [eg of claim]; sterk [story]
²steep (vb) (in)trekken, weken
³steep (vb) onderdompelen [also fig]
steeple (toren)spits, bovenste deel^h van een toren
steeplechase [equestrian sport, athletics] steeplechase, hindernisren, hindernisloop
¹steer (n) **1** jonge os **2** stierkalf^h
²steer (vb) sturen, koers (doen) zetten: *he* ~*ed for home* hij ging op huis aan ‖ ~ *clear of sth.* uit de buurt blijven van iets
steering committee stuurgroep
steering wheel stuurwiel^h
steersman stuurman, roerganger
stellar 1 van, m.b.t. de sterren **2** [Am; inform] top-: ~ *year* gloriejaar
¹stem (n) **1** stam [of tree, word]; basisvorm **2** (hoofd)stengel [of flower]; steel(tje^h) **3** stamvormig deel^h; steel [of glass, pipe] **4** voorsteven, boeg: *from* ~ *to stern* van de voor- tot de achtersteven; [fig] van top tot teen
²stem (vb) **1** doen stoppen, stelpen **2** het hoofd bieden aan, weerstand bieden aan: ~ *the tide* (of public opinion) tegen het getijde (van de publieke opinie) ingaan
stem from stammen uit, voortkomen uit: *his bitterness stems from all his disappointments* zijn verbittering komt door al zijn teleurstellingen
stench stank
stencil 1 stencil^h, stencilafdruk **2** modelvorm, sjabloon
stenography [Am; dated] steno(grafie)
¹step (n) **1** stap, voetstap, (dans)pas: *break* ~ uit de pas gaan; *fall into* ~ *with* zich aansluiten bij, in de pas lopen met; ~ *by* ~ stapje voor stapje, geleidelijk; *out of* ~ **a)** uit de pas; **b)** [also fig] niet ermee eens; **c)** uit de toon **2** stap, daad: *watch* (or: *mind*) *your* ~ wees voorzichtig, pas op **3** (trap)trede, stoepje^h **4** (-s) (stenen) trap, stoep(je^h) **5** (-s) trap(ladder)
²step (vb) stappen, gaan: ~ *forward* naar voren komen, zich aanbieden als vrijwilliger; ~ *inside* komt u binnen; ~ *on the gas* (or: *it*) flink gas geven; [fig] opschieten; ~ *out of line* uit het gareel raken
step aside 1 opzij stappen, uit de weg gaan **2** zijn plaats afstaan
stepbrother stiefbroer, halfbroer

stepdaughter stiefdochter
step down 1 aftreden **2** zijn plaats afstaan
stepfather stiefvader
step in 1 binnenkomen **2** tussenbeide komen, inspringen
stepladder trapje^h, keukentrap
stepmother stiefmoeder
step off beginnen, starten: ~ *on the wrong foot* op de verkeerde manier beginnen
step out 1 snel(ler) gaan lopen, flink doorstappen **2** (even) naar buiten gaan
stepping stone 1 stapsteen [eg to wade through river] **2** springplank, hulp: *a ~ to success* een springplank naar het succes
steps steps
stepsister stiefzuster
stepson stiefzoon
¹step up (vb) naar voren komen, opstaan
²step up (vb) doen toenemen, opvoeren: ~ *production* de productie opvoeren
stereo system stereo-installatie
stereotype stereotype, stereotiep beeld^h
sterile 1 steriel, onvruchtbaar; [fig] weinig creatief: *a ~ discussion* een zinloze discussie **2** steriel, kiemvrij
sterility onvruchtbaarheid, steriliteit
sterilize steriliseren, onvruchtbaar maken, kiemvrij maken
¹sterling (n) pond^h sterling
²sterling (adj) echt, zuiver, onvervalst; [fig] degelijk; betrouwbaar: *a ~ friend* een echte vriend; ~ *silver* 92,5% zuiver zilver
¹stern (n) achterschip^h, achtersteven
²stern (adj) streng, hard, onbuigzaam, strikt
steroid steroïde^h: *anabolic ~s* anabole steroïden
stethoscope stethoscoop
stetson (breedgerande) cowboyhoed
¹stew (n) stoofpot, stoofschotel || *be in* (or: *get into*) *a ~* opgewonden zijn (or: raken)
²stew (vb) stoven, smoren || *let s.o. ~ (in one's own juice)* iem. in zijn eigen vet gaar laten koken
steward 1 rentmeester, beheerder **2** steward, hofmeester **3** ceremoniemeester, zaalwachter **4** wedstrijdcommissaris, official
¹stick (n) stok, tak, stuk^h hout **2** staf, stok(-je^h) **3** staaf(je^h), reep(je^h), stuk^h: *a ~ of chalk* een krijtje **4** stok, knuppel **5** stick, hockey-stick, (polo)hamer: [fig] *wield the big ~* dreigen **6** stengel; steel [celeriac] **7** figuur^{+h}, snuiter, droogstoppel **8** afranseling [also fig]: *give s.o. some ~* iem. een pak slaag geven
²stick (vb) **1** klem zitten, vastzitten **2** blijven steken, (blijven) vastzitten **3** plakken [also fig]; (vast)kleven; [inform] blijven: *it will always ~ in my mind* dat zal me altijd bijblijven; ~ *together* bij elkaar blijven; ~ *around* rondhangen, in de buurt blijven; ~ *to the point* bij het onderwerp blijven; ~ *to one's principles*

trouw blijven aan zijn principes
³stick (vb) **1** (vast)steken, (vast)prikken, bevestigen, opprikken **2** doodsteken, neersteken **3** steken, zetten, leggen: ~ *it in your pocket* stop het in je zak **4** (vast)kleven, vastlijmen, vastplakken **5** [only negative] pruimen, uitstaan, verdragen: *I can't ~ such people* ik heb de pest aan zulke mensen
stick at 1 opzien tegen, terugdeinzen voor: ~ *nothing* nergens voor terugdeinzen **2** doorgaan (met), volhouden
sticker 1 plakkertje^h, zelfklevend etiket^h, sticker **2** doorzetter, volhouder
sticking plaster kleefpleister
stick-in-the-mud conservatieveling, vastgeroest iem.
stickleback stekelbaars
stickler (+ for) (hardnekkig) voorstander (van), ijveraar: ~ *for accuracy* pietje-precies
stick out 1 overduidelijk zijn **2** volhouden, doorbijten: ~ *for sth.* zich blijven inzetten voor iets **3** uitsteken, vooruit steken
¹stick up (vb) **1** omhoogstaan, uitsteken **2** opkomen: ~ *for s.o.* het voor iem. opnemen
²stick up (vb) omhoogsteken, uitsteken: *stick 'em up, stick your hands up* handen omhoog
stick-up overval
sticky 1 kleverig, plakkerig **2** pijnlijk, lastig: *he will come to (or: meet) a ~ end* het zal nog slecht met hem aflopen **3** zwoel, broeierig, drukkend || *she has got ~ fingers* ze heeft lange vingers, zij jat
¹stiff (n) [inform] lijk^h, dooie
²stiff (adj) **1** stijf, stug, gereserveerd **2** vastberaden, koppig: *put up (a) ~ resistance* hardnekkig weerstand bieden **3** stram, stroef: *a ~ neck* een stijve nek **4** zwaar, moeilijk, lastig: *a ~ climb* een flinke klim(partij) **5** sterk, stevig, krachtig: *a ~ breeze* een stevige bries **6** (te) groot, overdreven, onredelijk: ~ *demands* pittige eisen **7** sterk [alcoholic drink]: *a ~ drink* een stevige borrel || *keep a ~ upper lip* zich flink houden, geen emoties tonen
³stiff (adv) door en door, intens: *bore s.o. ~* iem. gruwelijk vervelen; *scare s.o. ~* iem. de stuipen op het lijf jagen
¹stiffen (vb) **1** verstijven **2** verstevigen, in kracht toenemen
²stiffen (vb) **1** dikker maken, doen verdikken **2** verstevigen, krachtiger maken; [also fig] versterken; vastberadener maken
stiff-necked 1 koppig, eigenzinnig **2** verwaand
¹stifle (vb) stikken; smoren [also fig]
²stifle (vb) **1** verstikken, doen stikken, smoren; [fig also] in de doofpot stoppen: *a stifling heat* een verstikkende hitte **2** onderdrukken: ~ *one's laughter* zijn lach inhouden

stigma brandmerk^h, (schand)vlek, stigma^h
stigmatize stigmatiseren, brandmerken
stile 1 overstap **2** draaihekje^h
stiletto heel naaldhak
¹**still** (n) **1** filmfoto, stilstaand (film)beeld^h
2 distilleertoestel^h
²**still** (adj) **1** stil, onbeweeglijk, rustig, kalm:
~ *picture* filmfoto, stilstaand (film)beeld
2 stil, geluidloos, gedempt **3** niet mousserend: ~ *water* mineraalwater zonder prik;
plat water; ~ *wine* niet-mousserende wijn
³**still** (adv) **1** stil: *keep* ~ (zich) stilhouden; *my
heart stood* ~ mijn hart stond stil [with fright]
2 nog (altijd): *is he* ~ *here?* is hij hier nog?
3 nog (meer): *he is* ~ *taller, he is taller* ~ hij is
nog groter **4** toch, niettemin: ... *but he* ~
agreed ... maar hij stemde er toch mee in
stillborn doodgeboren
still life stilleven^h
stilt 1 stelt **2** paal, pijler
stilted 1 (als) op stelten **2** stijf, gekunsteld
stimulant stimulans, opwekkend middel^h;
[fig] prikkel
stimulate stimuleren, opwekken: ~ *s.o.
(in)to more efforts* iem. tot meer inspanningen aanmoedigen
stimulation stimulering
stimulus stimulus; prikkel; [fig] aanmoediging
¹**sting** (n) **1** angel **2** giftand **3** brandhaar^{+h}
4 steek, beet, prikkel(ing)
²**sting** (vb) **1** steken, bijten; [fig] grieven: *a
bee* ~s een bij steekt; *his conscience stung him*
zijn geweten knaagde **2** prikkelen, branden;
[fig] aansporen: *that stung him (in)to action*
dat zette hem tot actie aan **3** afzetten, oplichten: ~ *s.o. for a few dollars* iem. een paar
dollar lichter maken
stinging 1 stekend, bijtend: *a* ~ *reproach*
een scherp verwijt **2** prikkelend
stinging nettle brandnetel
stingy vrekkig, gierig
¹**stink** (n) **1** stank **2** herrie: *create/kick up* (or:
make, raise) a ~ *about sth.* herrie schoppen
over iets
²**stink** (vb) **1** stinken: *it* ~s *to high heaven* het
stinkt uren in de wind **2** oerslecht zijn, niet
deugen: *this plan* ~s dit plan deugt van geen
kanten
stink-bomb stinkbom
stinker 1 stinker(d) **2** iets beledigends, iets
slechts, moeilijke opdracht, lastig examen^h
stinking 1 stinkend [also fig]: ~ *rich* stinkend rijk **2** oerslecht, gemeen
¹**stint** (n) portie, karwei(tje)^h, taak: *do one's
daily* ~ zijn dagtaak volbrengen || *without* ~
onbeperkt
²**stint** (vb) zich bekrimpen, zich beperken
³**stint** (vb) **1** beperken, inperken **2** zuinig
toebedelen, krap houden: ~ *o.s. of food* zichzelf karig voedsel toebedelen

stipulate bedingen, bepalen, als voorwaarde stellen: ~ *for the best conditions* de
beste voorwaarden bedingen
¹**stir** (n) **1** het roeren, het poken: *give the fire
a* ~ pook het vuur even op **2** beroering, opwinding, sensatie: *cause* (or: *make*) *quite a* ~
(veel) opzien baren, (veel) ophef veroorzaken
²**stir** (vb) **1** (zich) (ver)roeren, (zich) bewegen
2 opstaan, op zijn
³**stir** (vb) **1** (+ up) (op)poken, opporren; [fig]
aanwakkeren; [fig] aanstoken, opstoken: ~
one's curiosity iemands nieuwsgierigheid
prikkelen **2** (also + up) (om)roeren
stir-fry roerbakken, wokken
stirring opwekkend, stimulerend, bezielend
stirrup (stijg)beugel
¹**stitch** (n) **1** steek in de zij **2** steek: *drop a* ~
een steek laten vallen **3** lapje^h, stukje^h (stof);
[fig] beetje^h: *not do a* ~ *of work* geen lor uitvoeren; *not have a* ~ *on* spiernaakt zijn
4 [med] hechting || *in* ~es slap van het la-
chen, in een deuk (van het lachen)
²**stitch** (vb) **1** stikken, (vast)naaien, dichtnaaien: ~ *up* a *wound* een wond hechten
2 borduren
stoat 1 hermelijn **2** wezel
¹**stock** (n) **1** moederstam [from which grafts
are taken] **2** steel **3** familie, ras^h, geslacht^h,
afkomst: *be* (or: *come*) *of good* ~ van goede
komaf zijn **4** aandeel^h, effect^h **5** voorraad: ~
in trade a) voorhanden voorraad; b) kneep
(van het vak), truc; *while* ~s *last* zolang de
voorraad strekt; *take* ~ de inventaris opmaken; [fig] *take* ~ *(of the situation)* de toestand
bekijken; *out of* ~ niet in voorraad **6** bouillon **7** aandelen(bezit^h), effecten, fonds^h: *his* ~
is falling zijn ster verbleekt **8** materiaal^h, ma-
terieel^h, grondstof: *rolling* ~ rollend materieel [of railways] **9** vee(stapel)^h **10** (-s) [shipp]
stapel(blokken), helling: *on the* ~s op stapel;
[fig] in voorbereiding
²**stock** (adj) **1** gangbaar: ~ *sizes* gangbare
maten **2** stereotiep, vast: *a* ~ *remark* een stereotiepe opmerking
³**stock** (vb) voorraad inslaan, zich bevoorraden, hamsteren: ~ *up on sugar* suiker inslaan
⁴**stock** (vb) **1** van het nodige voorzien: *a well-
stocked department store* een goed voorzien
warenhuis **2** in voorraad hebben
stockade 1 houten omheining **2** met houten afzetting omheind terrein^h
stockbroker effectenmakelaar
stock exchange effectenbeurs, beurs(ge-
bouw^h): *the* Stock Exchange de (Londense)
Beurs
stockholder aandeelhouder
stocking kous
stock-in-trade 1 (goederen)voorraad
2 gereedschap^h || *that joke is part of his* ~ dat

is één van zijn standaardgrappen
stockist leverancier (uit voorraad)
stock market (effecten)beurs
¹**stockpile** (n) voorraad, reserve
²**stockpile** (vb) voorraden aanleggen (van)
stockroom 1 magazijn[h] **2** showroom [eg in hotel]
stock size vaste maat, confectiemaat
stock-still doodstil
stocky gedrongen, kort en dik, stevig
stodge zware kost, onverteerbaar eten[h]; [fig] moeilijke stof
stodgy 1 zwaar; onverteerbaar [food]; [fig] moeilijk; droog **2** saai, vervelend
stoic stoïcijn
stoic(al) stoïcijns, onaangedaan
¹**stoke** (vb) **1** (also + up) het vuur opstoken **2** (+ up) zich met eten volproppen
²**stoke** (vb) (also + up) aanstoken, opstoken [fire]; opvullen [stove]
stole stola
stolid onverstoorbaar, standvastig
¹**stomach** (n) **1** maag: *on an **empty** ~* op een nuchtere maag **2** buik: *lie on one's ~* op zijn buik liggen **3** eetlust, trek **4** zin: *I have **no** ~ for a fight* ik heb geen zin om ruzie te maken
²**stomach** (vb) slikken, pikken, aanvaarden: *you **needn't** ~ such a remark* zo'n opmerking hoef je niet zomaar te slikken
stomach-ache 1 maagpijn **2** buikpijn
¹**stomp** (n) stomp [jazz dance, jazz music]
²**stomp** (vb) stampen
stone 1 steen [also as hard mineral]; pit [of fruit]: *(semi-)**precious** ~* (half)edelsteen **2** stone, 14 Engelse pond[h]: *he **weighs** 14 ~(s)* hij weegt 90 kilo || *leave no ~ unturned* geen middel onbeproefd laten, alles proberen; *rolling ~* zwerver
Stone Age stenen tijdperk[h]
stone-cold steenkoud || *~ **sober*** broodnuchter; *~ **dead*** morsdood
stoned 1 stomdronken **2** stoned, high
stoneless pitloos, zonder pit
stonemason steenhouwer
stone's throw steenworp: *within a ~* op een steenworp afstand
stony 1 steenachtig, vol stenen **2** keihard, steenhard; [fig] gevoelloos
stony-broke platzak, blut
stooge 1 [theatre] mikpunt[h], aangever **2** knechtje[h], slaafje[h] **3** stroman
stool 1 kruk, bankje[h] **2** voetenbank(je[h]) **3** ontlasting
¹**stoop** (n) **1** gebukte houding **2** ronde rug, kromme rug
²**stoop** (vb) **1** (zich) bukken, voorover buigen **2** zich verwaardigen **3** zich vernederen, zich verlagen: *he wouldn't ~ **to** lying about his past* hij vond het beneden zijn waardigheid om over zijn verleden te liegen **4** gebogen lopen, met ronde rug lopen

³**stoop** (vb) buigen: *~ one's **head*** het hoofd buigen
¹**stop** (n) **1** einde[h], beëindiging, pauze, onderbreking: *bring to a ~* stopzetten, een halt toeroepen; *put a ~ to* een eind maken aan **2** halte, stopplaats **3** afsluiting, blokkade, belemmering **4** punt[h] **5** diafragma[h], lensopening **6** pal, plug, begrenzer || *pull out all the ~s* alle registers opentrekken, alles uit de kast halen
²**stop** (vb) **1** ophouden, tot een eind komen, stoppen **2** stilhouden, tot stilstand komen: *~ **short*** plotseling halt houden; *they ~ped **short** of actually smashing the windows* ze gingen niet zover, dat ze de ramen daadwerkelijk ingooiden; *~ **at** nothing* tot alles in staat zijn, nergens voor terugschrikken **3** blijven, verblijven, overblijven: *~ **by*** (even) langskomen; *~ **in*** binnenblijven; *~ **off*** zijn reis onderbreken; *~ **over*** de (vlieg)reis onderbreken
³**stop** (vb) **1** (af)sluiten, dichten, dichtstoppen: *~ **up** a leak* een lek dichten **2** verhinderen, afhouden, tegenhouden: *~ **thief!*** houd de dief! **3** blokkeren, tegenhouden: *~ a **cheque*** een cheque blokkeren **4** een eind maken aan, stopzetten, beëindigen, ophouden met, staken: *~ **work*** het werk neerleggen; *~ **it!*** hou op!
stopgap 1 noodoplossing **2** invaller **3** stoplap
stopoff kort verblijf[h]
stopover reisonderbreking, kort verblijf[h]
stoppage 1 verstopping, stremming **2** inhouding: *~ of **pay*** inhouden van loon **3** staking, (werk)onderbreking, prikactie
stoppage time (extra) bijgetelde tijd [to make up for interruptions of play]
stopper stop, plug, kurk: *put the ~(s) on sth.* ergens een eind aan maken
stopping distance afstand tot voorligger
storage opslag, bewaring
storage chip geheugenchip
storage space opslagruimte
¹**store** (n) **1** voorraad: *in ~* in voorraad; *there's a surprise in ~ for you* je zult voor een verrassing komen te staan **2** opslagplaats, magazijn[h], pakhuis[h] **3** (-s) [mil] provisie, goederen, proviand[h] **4** [Am] winkel, zaak **5** warenhuis[h] || *set (great) ~ by* veel waarde hechten aan
²**store** (vb) bevoorraden, inslaan
store brand huismerk[h]
storehouse pakhuis[h], opslagplaats: *Steve is a ~ of information* Steve is een grote bron van informatie
storekeeper 1 [Am] winkelier **2** hoofd van het magazijn
storeroom opslagkamer, voorraadkamer
storey verdieping, woonlaag: *the second ~* de eerste verdieping
stork ooievaar

¹storm (n) **1** (hevige) bui, noodweer[h]
2 storm(wind), orkaan: ~ *in a teacup* storm in
een glas water, veel drukte om niks **3** uitbarsting, vlaag: ~ *of protests* regen van protesten
²storm (vb) **1** stormen, waaien, onweren
2 (+ at) tekeergaan (tegen), uitvallen, razen
3 rennen, denderen: ~ *in* binnen komen
stormen
³storm (vb) [mil] bestormen, stormlopen op
storm cloud regenwolk, onweerswolk;
[fig] donkere wolk; teken[h] van onheil
storm surge stormvloed
storm trooper stoottroeper
storm window voorzetraam[h]
stormy 1 stormachtig, winderig **2** heftig,
ruw: *a ~ meeting* een veelbewogen bijeenkomst
story 1 verhaal[h], relaas[h]: *cut a long ~ short*
om kort te gaan; *the (same) old ~* het oude
liedje **2** (levens)geschiedenis, historie **3** vertelling, novelle, verhaal[h] **4** [journalism] (materiaal voor) artikel[h], verhaal[h] **5** smoesje[h],
praatje[h]: *tell stories* jokken **6** verdieping
¹storybook (n) verhalenboek[h]
²storybook (adj) als in een sprookje,
sprookjesachtig: *a ~ ending* een gelukkige
afloop, een happy end
story line intrige; plot[h]
storyteller 1 verteller **2** [inform] praatjesmaker
¹stout (n) stout, donker bier[h]
²stout (adj) **1** moedig, vastberaden: ~ *resistance* krachtig verzet **2** solide, stevig **3** gezet, dik
stout-hearted dapper, moedig, kloek
stove 1 (elektrische) kachel, gaskachel, ko-
lenkachel **2** (elektrisch) fornuis[h], gasoven,
gasfornuis[h]
stow opbergen, inpakken || ~ *it!* kap er-
mee!, hou op!
stowaway verstekeling
¹stow away (vb) zich verbergen [on ship,
aeroplane]
²stow away (vb) opbergen, wegbergen
straddle schrijlings zitten (op), met ge-
spreide benen zitten (op), wijdbeens staan
(boven)
straggle 1 (af)dwalen, achterblijven, van
de groep af raken **2** (wild) uitgroeien, verspreid groeien: *straggling houses* verspreid
liggende huizen
straggly 1 (onregelmatig) verspreid, verstrooid, schots en scheef **2** verwilderd; verward [hair, beard]
¹straight (n) recht stuk[h] [of racecourse]
²straight (adj) **1** recht, steil; sluik [hair];
rechtop: *(as) ~ as a die* kaarsrecht; [fig] goudeerlijk **2** puur, onverdund; [fig] zonder franje; serieus: *a ~ rendering of the facts* een letterlijke weergave van de feiten; ~ *whisky*

whisky puur **3** open(hartig), eerlijk, rechtdoorzee: ~ *answer* eerlijk antwoord **4** strak,
in de plooi, correct: *keep a ~ face* zijn gezicht
in de plooi houden; *keep (s.o.) to the ~ and
narrow path* (iem.) op het rechte pad houden
5 ordelijk, geordend, netjes: *put* (or: *set*) *the
record ~* een fout herstellen **6** direct, rechtstreeks **7** hetero(seksueel)
³straight (adv) **1** rechtstreeks, meteen, zonder omwegen: *come ~ to the point* meteen
ter zake raken **2** recht, rechtop: ~ *on* recht-
door || *think ~* helder denken; *tell s.o.* ~ iem.
eerlijk de waarheid zeggen
straightaway onmiddellijk
¹straighten (vb) recht worden, rechttrekken; bijtrekken [also fig]: ~ *up* overeind gaan
staan
²straighten (vb) rechtzetten; rechttrekken
[also fig]: ~ *one's legs* de benen strekken; ~
the room de kamer aan kant brengen; ~ *o.s.
up* zich oprichten
straighten out 1 recht leggen, rechtmaken **2** op orde brengen: *things will soon
straighten themselves out* alles zal gauw op
zijn pootjes terechtkomen
straightforward 1 oprecht, open, eerlijk
2 duidelijk
straight-up eerlijk (waar), serieus
¹strain (n) **1** spanning, druk, trek; [fig] belasting; inspanning **2** overbelasting, uitputting **3** verrekking [of muscles]; verstuiking
4 (-s) flard [of music, poem]; melodie **5** stijl;
toon [of expression] **6** (karakter)trek, element[h] **7** stam, ras[h], soort
²strain (vb) **1** zich inspannen, moeite doen,
zwoegen **2** (+ at) rukken (aan), trekken: ~ *at
the leash* aan de teugels trekken, zich los willen rukken [fig]
³strain (vb) **1** spannen, (uit)rekken **2** inspannen, maximaal belasten: ~ *one's eyes* turen,
ingespannen kijken **3** overbelasten; [fig] geweld aandoen: ~ *one's voice* zijn stem forceren **4** verrekken [muscles]; verdraaien
5 vastklemmen **6** zeven, laten doorsijpelen
7 afgieten
strained gedwongen, geforceerd, onnatuurlijk: ~ *relations* gespannen verhoudingen
strainer 1 zeef **2** vergiet[h] **3** filter(doek)[h]
strait 1 zee-engte, (zee)straat: *the Straits of
Dover* het Nauw van Calais **2** lastige omstandigheden, moeilijkheden: *be in dire ~s*
ernstig in het nauw zitten
straitened behoeftig
straitjacket dwangbuis; keurslijf[h] [also fig]
strait-laced puriteins, bekrompen, preuts
strand streng, snoer[h], draad: *a ~ of pearls*
een parelsnoer
stranded gestrand, aan de grond; vast(gelopen) [also fig]
strange 1 vreemd, onbekend, nieuw: *he is*

~ *to* the business hij heeft nog geen ervaring in deze branche **2** eigenaardig, onverklaarbaar: ~ *to say* vreemd genoeg

stranger vreemde(ling), onbekende, buitenlander: *be a* ~ *to* ergens part noch deel aan hebben

strangle 1 wurgen **2** onderdrukken; smoren [tendency, cry]

stranglehold wurggreep; verstikkende greep [also fig]: *have a* ~ *on* in zijn greep hebben

[1]**strap** (n) **1** riem, band(je[h]) **2** strop, band; reep [also of metal]

[2]**strap** (vb) **1** vastbinden, vastgespen **2** (also + up) verbinden, met pleisters afdekken

strapless strapless

strapping flink, potig, stoer

stratagem strategie, truc, plan[h]

strategic strategisch

strategist strateeg

strategy strategie, plan[h], methode, beleid[h]

stratification 1 laagvorming **2** gelaagdheid, verdeling in lagen

straw 1 stro[h] **2** strohalm, strootje[h]: *a* ~ *in the wind* een voorteken, een teken aan de wand; *the last* ~, *the* ~ *that broke the camel's back* de druppel die de emmer deed overlopen; *clutch at* ~s zich aan iedere strohalm vastklampen **3** rietje[h] [for drinking]

strawberry 1 aardbei(plant) **2** donkerroze[h]

straw man [esp Am] stropop; [fig also] marionet

[1]**stray** (n) **1** zwerver; verdwaalde [also fig]; zwerfdier[h] **2** dakloos kind[h]

[2]**stray** (adj) verdwaald, zwervend: ~ *bullet* verdwaalde kogel; ~ *cats* zwerfkatten

[3]**stray** (vb) dwalen; rondzwerven [also fig]: ~ *from the subject* van het onderwerp afdwalen

[1]**streak** (n) **1** streep, lijn, strook: *a* ~ *of light* een streepje licht **2** (karakter)trek, tikje[h]: *there's a* ~ *of madness in Mel* er zit (ergens) een draadje los bij Mel || *like a* ~ *of lightning* bliksemsnel

[2]**streak** (vb) **1** (weg)schieten, flitsen, snellen **2** streaken, naakt rondrennen

[3]**streak** (vb) strepen zetten op, strepen maken in: ~ed *with grey* met grijze strepen

streaker [inform] streaker

streaky gestreept, met strepen; doorregen [of bacon]

[1]**stream** (n) **1** stroom, water[h], beek, stroomrichting **2** (stort)vloed, stroom

[2]**stream** (vb) **1** stromen [also fig]; vloeien, druipen: *his face was* ~ing *with sweat* het zweet liep hem langs het gezicht **2** wapperen, waaien, fladderen

[3]**stream** (vb) doen stromen, druipen van: *the wound was* ~ing *blood* het bloed gutste uit de wond

streamer wimpel, lint[h], serpentine

streaming directe weergave; streaming

streamline stroomlijnen; [fig] lijn brengen in; vereenvoudigen: ~ *an organization* een organisatie efficiënter maken

street straat, weg, straatweg: *dead-end* ~ doodlopende straat; *be* ~s *ahead (of)* ver voorliggen op; *in the* ~, [Am] *on the* ~ op straat; *that's (right) up my* ~ dat is precies in mijn straatje, dat is net iets voor mij

streetcar [Am] tram

street level gelijkvloers[h]

street lighting straatverlichting

street smarts [Am; inform] straatwijsheid

streetwalker tippelaarster

streetwise door het (straat)leven gehard, door de wol geverfd, slim

strength 1 sterkte [also fig]; kracht(en), vermogen[h]: *on the* ~ *of* op grond van, uitgaand van **2** (getal)sterkte, macht, bezetting: *(bring) up to (full)* ~ op (volle) sterkte (brengen) **3** gehalte[h], concentratie; zwaarte [of tobacco]; sterkte || *go from* ~ *to* ~ het ene succes na het andere behalen

[1]**strengthen** (vb) sterk(er) worden, in kracht toenemen

[2]**strengthen** (vb) sterk(er) maken, versterken, verstevigen

strenuous 1 zwaar, inspannend, vermoeiend **2** vol energie, onvermoeibaar, ijverig

[1]**stress** (n) **1** spanning, druk, stress, belasting: *(be) under great* ~ onder (grote) druk staan, zwaar belast worden **2** klem(toon), nadruk, accent[h]; [fig] gewicht[h]; belang[h]: *lay* ~ *on* benadrukken **3** [techn] spanning, druk, (be)last(ing)

[2]**stress** (vb) **1** benadrukken, de nadruk leggen op: *we can't* ~ *enough that* we kunnen er niet voldoende de nadruk op leggen dat **2** de klemtoon leggen op **3** belasten, onder druk zetten

stressful stressvol, veeleisend

stress mark klemtoonteken[h], accent[h]

[1]**stretch** (n) **1** (groot) stuk[h] [land, road, sea etc]; uitgestrektheid, vlakte, eind(je[h]), stuk[h]: ~ *of road* stuk weg **2** tijd, periode; [inform] straftijd: *ten hours at a* ~ tien uur aan een stuk **3** rek(baarheid), elasticiteit || *not by any* ~ *of the imagination* met de beste wil van de wereld niet; *at full* ~ met inspanning van al zijn krachten; *at a* ~ desnoods, als het moet

[2]**stretch** (vb) **1** (+ out) zich uitstrekken, (languit) gaan liggen **2** zich uitstrekken (tot), reiken (tot), zich uitrekken **3** rekbaar zijn, elastisch zijn **4** (+ over) duren, zich uitspreiden (over) **5** (uit)rekken [also fig]: ~ *s.o.'s patience* iemands geduld op de proef stellen **6** (aan)spannen, opspannen, strak trekken: ~ *a rope* een touw spannen **7** (uit)strekken, reiken: ~ *o.s.* zich uitrekken **8** tot het uiterste inspannen, forceren: *be fully* ~ed

zich helemaal geven **9** ruim interpreteren; het niet zo nauw nemen (met) [rules]; geweld aandoen, overdrijven: ~ *the rules* de regels vrij interpreteren **10** verrekken [muscles]
stretcher brancard, draagbaar
stretch limousine verlengde limousine
stretch mark zwangerschapsstriem
stretchy [inform] elastisch
strew 1 (+ on, over) uitstrooien (over): *books were ~n all over his desk* zijn bureau was bezaaid met boeken **2** (+ with) bestrooien (met) **3** verspreid liggen op
stricken getroffen, geslagen, bedroefd: ~ *look* verslagen blik
strict strikt, nauwkeurig: ~ *parents* strenge ouders; *~ly speaking* strikt genomen
stricture aanmerking, afkeuring: *pass ~s (up)on* kritiek uitoefenen op
¹stride (n) **1** pas, stap, schrede: *get into one's* ~ op dreef komen; *take sth. in (one's)* ~ a) ergens makkelijk overheen stappen; **b)** iets spelenderwijs doen (*or:* klaren) **2** gang || *make great ~s* grote vooruitgang boeken
²stride (vb) (voort)stappen, grote passen nemen
strident schel, schril, scherp
strife ruzie, conflictʰ: *industrial* ~ industriële onrust
¹strike (n) **1** slag, klap **2** (lucht)aanval **3** staking: *(out) on* ~ in staking **4** vondst [of oil etc]; ontdekking; [fig] succesʰ; vangst
²strike (vb) **1** strijken; neerlaten [flag]; opbreken [camp, tent] **2** bereiken, sluiten, halen: ~ *a bargain with* het op een akkoordje gooien met **3** aannemen [pose]: ~ *a pose* een houding aannemen **4** ontdekken, vinden, stoten op: ~ *oil* olie aanboren; [fig] fortuin maken **5** een indruk maken op, opvallen, lijken: *did it ever* ~ *you that* heb je er weleens aan gedacht dat, is het jou weleens opgevallen dat **6** opkomen bij; invallen [idea] || ~ *terror into s.o.'s heart* iem. de schrik op het lijf jagen
³strike (vb) **1** slaan, uithalen, treffen, raken, botsen (met/op), stoten (op/tegen), aanvallen, toeslaan; aanslaan [string, note]; aansteken [match]: ~ *a blow* een klap uitdelen; *the clock ~s* de klok slaat; *struck dumb* met stomheid geslagen; ~ *down* a) neerslaan; **b)** [also fig] vellen; **c)** branden [of sun]; ~ *(up)on* a) treffen, slaan op; **b)** stoten op, ontdekken; **c)** krijgen, komen op [idea]; *struck by lightning* door de bliksem getroffen **2** staken, in staking gaan **3** (op pad/weg) gaan, beginnen (met): ~ *for home* de weg naar huis inslaan || ~ *home* to s.o. grote indruk maken op iem., geheel doordringen tot iem. [of remark]; *struck on* smoor(verliefd) op
strikebreaker stakingsbreker
strike-call stakingsoproep

strike force aanvalsmacht; [esp] (direct inzetbare) aanvalstroepen
strike off 1 schrappen, royeren **2** afdraaien, drukken
¹strike out (vb) **1** (fel) uithalen [also fig]; (fel) tekeergaan **2** nieuwe wegen inslaan: ~ *on one's own* zijn eigen weg inslaan
²strike out (vb) schrappen, doorhalen
strike pay stakingsuitkering
striker 1 staker **2** slagman **3** [socc] spits
strike up 1 gaan spelen (zingen), inzetten, aanheffen **2** beginnen: ~ *a conversation (with)* een gesprek aanknopen (met)
striking opvallend, treffend, aantrekkelijk
striking distance bereikʰ: *within* ~ binnen het bereik, binnen loopafstand
¹string (n) **1** koordʰ, touw(tje)ʰ, garenʰ: *pull ~s* invloed uitoefenen **2** draad, band **3** snaar **4** (-s) strijkinstrumenten, strijkers **5** aaneenschakeling, reeks, sliert, streng: ~ *of cars* rij auto's || *have two ~s* (or: *a second* ~) *to one's bow* op twee paarden wedden, meer pijlen op zijn boog hebben; *with no ~s attached* a) zonder kleine lettertjes; **b)** zonder verplichtingen (achteraf)
²string (vb) **1** (vast)binden **2** (aan elkaar) rijgen, ritsen, aaneenschakelen: ~ *words together* woorden aan elkaar rijgen **3** (+ up) opknopen, ophangen **4** bespannen, besnaren: *highly strung* fijnbesnaard, overgevoelig || *strung up* zenuwachtig, gespannen, opgewonden
¹string along (vb) (+ with) zich aansluiten (bij)
²string along (vb) belazeren, misleiden, aan het lijntje houden
string band strijkjeʰ
string bass [Am] contrabas
string bean [Am] snijboon
stringency strengheid, striktheid: *the ~ of the law* de bindende kracht van de wet
stringent stringent, streng, dwingend: ~ *rule* strikte regel
string orchestra strijkorkestʰ
string quartet strijkkwartetʰ
stringy 1 draderig, pezig: ~ *arm* pezige arm **2** mager, lang en dun
¹strip (n) **1** strook, strip, reep **2** kleur(en) [of sports team] || *tear s.o. off a* ~, *tear a* ~ (or: *~s*) *off s.o.* iem. uitfoeteren
²strip (vb) **1** (also + off) zich uitkleden: *~ped to the waist* met ontbloot bovenlijf **2** een striptease opvoeren
³strip (vb) **1** uitkleden **2** (also + off) van iets ontdoen, pellen, (af)schillen, verwijderen, afscheuren; afhalen [bed]; afkrabben [paint]: ~ *down* uit elkaar halen, ontmantelen [machines]
strip cartoon stripverhaalʰ, beeldverhaalʰ
strip club striptent
stripe 1 streep, lijn, strook **2** streep [deco-

ration] **3** opvatting, mening: *of all* **political** *~s* van alle politieke kleuren

striped gestreept

strip-lighting tl-verlichting, buisverlichting

stripper [inform] stripper

stripy streperig, met strepen

strive 1 (+ after, for) (na)streven, zich inspannen (voor) **2** vechten

¹**stroke** (n) **1** slag, klap, stoot: *at a ~ in één klap; on the ~ of twelve* klokslag twaalf (uur), op slag van twaalven **2** aanval, beroerte **3** haal, streep **4** schuine streep **5** streling, aai **6** [rowing] slag(roeier) ‖ *~ of (good)* **luck** buitenkansje, geluk(je); *he has not done a ~ of* **work** hij heeft geen klap uitgevoerd

²**stroke** (vb) **1** aaien, strelen, (glad)strijken **2** [rowing] de slag aangeven in, slag(roeier) zijn

¹**stroll** (n) wandeling(etjeʰ), blokjeʰ om: *go for a ~* een blokje om lopen

²**stroll** (vb) wandelen, kuieren, slenteren

stroller 1 wandelaar **2** [Am] wandelwagen(tjeʰ), buggy

strong sterk, krachtig, fors, stevig; zwaar [beer, cigar]; geconcentreerd [solution]; scherp [odour, taste]; drastisch [measure]; hoog [fever, price etc]; onregelmatig [verb]; kras [language]: *~* **arm** *of the law* (sterke) arm der wet; *~* **language** (or: **stuff**) krasse taal, gevloek; *~* **nerves** stalen zenuwen; *hold ~* **views** er een uitgesproken mening op nahouden; *(still) going ~* nog steeds actief; *two* **hundred** *~ in* uitblinken in

strong-arm hardhandig, ruw, gewelddadig: *~* **methods** grove middelen

strongbox brandkast, geldkist, safe(loketʰ)

stronghold [also fig] bolwerkʰ, vesting

strongly 1 sterk: *feel ~ about sth.* iets uitgesproken belangrijk vinden **2** met klem, nadrukkelijk

strongman sterke man; machthebber

strong-minded vastberaden, stijfkoppig

strongroom (bank)kluis

strong-willed wilskrachtig, vastberaden

structural structureel, bouw-, constructie-: *~* **alterations** verbouwing

structure 1 bouwwerkʰ, constructie, (op)-bouw **2** structuur, samenstelling, constructie

¹**struggle** (n) **1** worsteling, gevechtʰ, strijd: *put up a ~* zich verzetten **2** (kracht)inspanning: *quite a ~* een heel karwei

²**struggle** (vb) worstelen, vechten; [also fig] strijden; zich inspannen: *~* **to** *one's feet* overeind krabbelen

strum betokkelen, tingelen

¹**strut** (n) **1** pompeuze gang **2** stut, steun

²**strut** (vb) pompeus schrijden (op/over), paraderen, heen en weer stappen (op)

¹**stub** (n) **1** stomp(jeʰ), eindjeʰ, peuk **2** reçu-

strook; controlestrook [of voucher or cheque book]

²**stub** (vb) **1** stoten: *~ one's* **toe** zijn teen stoten **2** (+ out) uitdrukken, uitdoven: *~ out a cigarette* een sigaret uitmaken

stubble 1 stoppel(s) **2** stoppelveldʰ **3** stoppelbaard

stubborn 1 koppig, eigenwijs **2** weerbarstig: *~* **lock** stroef slot

¹**stucco** (n) stucʰ, pleister(kalk), gipspleister

²**stucco** (vb) pleisteren, stukadoren

stuck 1 vast [also fig]; klem, onbeweeglijk, ten einde raad: *be ~* **for** *an answer* met zijn mond vol tanden staan; *get ~* **with** *s.o.* met iem. opgezadeld zitten **2** vastgekleefd, vastgeplakt

stuck-up bekakt, verwaand

¹**stud** (n) **1** (sier)spijker, sierknopjeʰ **2** knoop(jeʰ), overhemdsknoopjeʰ, boordenknoopjeʰ, manchetknoopjeʰ **3** (ren)stal, fokbedrijfʰ **4** fokhengst; dekhengst [also fig] **5** nop [under football shoe]; [Belg] stud

²**stud** (vb) **1** (+ with) beslaan (met), voorzien van spijkers/knopjes **2** bezetten, bedekken: *~ded* **with** *quotations* vol citaten

student 1 student(e): *~ of* **law, law** *~* student in de rechten, rechtenstudent **2** kenner: *~ of* **bird-life** vogelkenner

student loan studielening

students' union studentenvereniging

student teacher 1 (leraar-)stagiair(e) **2** iem. die studeert voor onderwijzer

stud farm fokbedrijfʰ

studied weloverwogen, (wel)doordacht: *~* **insult** opzettelijke belediging; *~* **smile** gemaakte glimlach

studio 1 studio, werkplaats; atelierʰ [of artist] **2** (-s) filmstudio

studio flat eenkamerappartementʰ, studio

studious 1 leergierig, ijverig **2** nauwgezet **3** bestudeerd, weloverwogen, opzettelijk: *~* **politeness** bestudeerde beleefdheid

¹**study** (n) **1** studie, onderzoekʰ, aandacht, attentie **2** studeerkamer; [Belg] bureauʰ **3** (studies) studie(vakʰ): *graduate studies* postkandidaatsstudie; masteropleiding; [Belg] derde cyclus

²**study** (vb) studeren, les(sen) volgen, college lopen: *~ to be a doctor* voor dokter studeren

³**study** (vb) **1** (be)studeren, onderzoeken: *~ law* rechten studeren **2** instuderen, van buiten leren

¹**stuff** (n) **1** materiaalʰ, (grond)stof, elementen: *she* **has** *the ~ of an actress in her* er zit een actrice in haar **2** spulʰ, goed(jeʰ), waar: *a drop of the* **hard** *~* een lekker neutje; *do you* **call** *this ~ coffee?* noem jij deze troep koffie? **3** troep, rommel: *throw that ~ away!* gooi die rommel weg! ‖ *do your ~* eens tonen wat je kan; *know one's ~* zijn vak verstaan; *that's the ~!* (dat is) je ware!, zo mag ik 't horen

²**stuff** (vb) **1** (op)vullen, volproppen, volstoppen: ~ *o.s.* zich volproppen, zich over-
eten; ~ *full* volproppen; *my mind is ~ed with
facts* mijn denkraam zit vol (met) feiten
2 (vol)stoppen, dichtstoppen: *~ed nose* verstopte neus; *my nose is completely ~ed up* mijn
neus is helemaal verstopt **3** proppen, stoppen, steken, duwen: ~ *sth. in(to)* iets proppen
in **4** opzetten: ~ *a bird* een vogel opzetten
5 farceren, vullen: *~ed pepper* gevulde pa-
prika || *(you can)* ~ *yourself!* je kan (van mij)
de pot op!; *he can ~ his job!* hij kan de pot op
met zijn baan
stuffing (op)vulsel[h], vulling, farce || *knock*
(or: *take*) *the ~ out of s.o.* iem. tot moes slaan,
iem. uitschakelen
stuffy 1 bedompt, benauwd, muf **2** saai,
vervelend **3** bekrompen, preuts
¹**stumble** (n) struikeling, misstap; [fig] blunder
²**stumble** (vb) **1** struikelen, vallen **2** hakkelen, haperen, stamelen: ~ *in* one's speech
hakkelen
stumble across tegen het lijf lopen, toevallig ontmoeten, stuiten op, toevallig vinden
stumble into door een toeval belanden in;
terechtkomen in: *he stumbled into that job* hij
kreeg die baan in de schoot geworpen
stumbling block 1 struikelblok[h] **2** steen
des aanstoots
¹**stump** (n) **1** stomp(je[h]), (boom)stronk,
eindje[h], peukje[h] **2** [cricket] wicketpaaltje[h]
²**stump** (vb) stampen
³**stump** (vb) voor raadsels stellen, moeilijke
vragen stellen: *that ~ed me* daar had ik geen
antwoord op
stumper moeilijke vraag
stump up dokken, betalen, neertellen
stumpy gedrongen, kort en dik
stun 1 bewusteloos slaan **2** schokken, verwarren, verdoven **3** versteld doen staan,
verbazen: *be ~ned into speechlessness* met
stomheid geslagen zijn
stunner schoonheid
stunning ongelofelijk mooi, verrukkelijk,
prachtig
¹**stunt** (n) **1** stunt, (acrobatische) toer, kunstje[h] **2** (reclame)stunt, attractie **3** stuntvlucht
²**stunt** (vb) (in zijn groei) belemmeren
stunt man stuntman
stupefaction verbijstering, (stomme) verbazing
stupefy 1 bedwelmen, verdoven: *be stupefied by drink* door de drank versuft zijn
2 verbijsteren, versteld doen staan
stupendous fantastisch, enorm: *a ~ effort*
een ongelofelijke inspanning
¹**stupid** (n) sufferd
²**stupid** (adj) **1** dom, stom, stompzinnig
2 suf, versuft

stupidity domheid, stommiteit, domme
opmerking, traagheid (van begrip)
stupor (toestand van) verdoving: *in a
drunken ~* in benevelde toestand
sturdy 1 sterk, flink, stevig (gebouwd)
2 vastberaden, krachtig
sturgeon steur
¹**stutter** (n) gestotter[h]: *have a ~* stotteren
²**stutter** (vb) stotteren, stamelen: ~ *out* stot-
terend uitbrengen
sty 1 varkensstal, varkenshok[h] **2** strontje[h]
[small sore on eyelid]
style 1 genre[h], type[h], model[h], vorm: *in all
sizes and ~s* in alle maten en vormen **2** benaming, (volledige) (aanspreek)titel, (firma)-
naam: *trade under the ~ of Young & Morris*
handel drijven onder de firmanaam Young &
Morris **3** (schrijf)stijl, (schrijf)wijze: *spaghetti
Italian ~* spaghetti op zijn Italiaans **4** stijl,
stroming, school: *the new ~ of building* de
nieuwe bouwstijl **5** manier van doen, levenswijze, stijl: *the balloon sailed into the air in
great ~* de ballon ging zonder enig probleem
schitterend omhoog **6** mode, stijl: *in ~* in de
mode || *cramp s.o.'s style* iem. in zijn doen en
laten belemmeren
stylish 1 modieus, naar de mode (gekleed)
2 stijlvol, elegant, deftig, chic
stylist 1 stilist(e), auteur met (goede) stijl
2 ontwerp(st)er
stylistic stilistisch: *a ~ change* een stijlver-
andering
stylize stileren: *~d representations* gesti-
leerde afbeeldingen
suave hoffelijk, beleefd; [depr] glad
sub 1 voorschot[h] [wages] **2** duikboot **3** wis-
sel(speler)
sub- ondergeschikt, bijkomend, hulp-: *sub-
post office* hulppostkantoor
subclass subklasse; onderklasse
¹**subconscious** (n) onderbewustzijn[h], onderbewuste[h]
²**subconscious** (adj) onderbewust
subcontractor onderaannemer
subculture subcultuur
subdivide opsplitsen
subdivision (onder)verdeling, onderafdeling
subdue 1 onderwerpen, beheersen: ~ *one's
passions* zijn hartstochten beteugelen **2** matigen, verzachten
subdued getemperd, gematigd, gedempt,
ingehouden, stil: *~ colours* zachte kleuren
¹**subject** (n) **1** onderdaan, ondergeschikte
2 onderwerp[h], thema[h]: *on the ~ of* omtrent,
aangaande, over **3** (studie)object[h], (school)-
vak[h] **4** aanleiding, omstandigheid, reden
5 [linguistics] onderwerp[h]
²**subject** (adj) **1** onderworpen: ~ *to foreign
rule* onder vreemde heerschappij **2** afhankelijk: ~ *to your consent* behoudens uw toe-

stemming **3** onderhevig, blootgesteld: ~ *to change* vatbaar voor wijziging(en)
³subject (vb) (+ to) onderwerpen (aan), doen ondergaan
subject index 1 klapper, systematisch register[h] **2** trefwoordenregister[h]
subjection onderwerping, afhankelijkheid, onderworpenheid
subjective subjectief
subject matter onderwerp[h]; inhoud [of book]
subjugation onderwerping, overheersing
subjunctive [linguistics] aanvoegende wijs
sublet onderverhuren
sublime subliem, verheven: *(from) the ~ to the ridiculous* (van) het sublieme tot het potsierlijke
submachine gun machinepistool[h]
submarine duikboot, onderzeeër
submerge 1 (doen) duiken [of submarine]; onderduiken **2** (doen) zinken, (doen) ondergaan, overstromen: *~d rocks* blinde klippen
submersion onderdompeling, overstroming
submission 1 onderwerping, onderdanigheid: *starve the enemy into ~* de vijand uithongeren **2** voorstel[h]
submissive onderdanig, onderworpen
¹submit (vb) toegeven, zwichten, zich overgeven: *~ to s.o.'s wishes* iemands wensen inwilligen; *~ to defeat* zich gewonnen geven
²submit (vb) **1** (+ to) voorleggen (aan): *~ s.o.'s name for appointment* iem. ter benoeming voordragen **2** onderwerpen, overgeven: *~ o.s. to* zich onderwerpen aan
subnormal beneden de norm
¹subordinate (adj) (+ to) ondergeschikt (aan), onderworpen, afhankelijk: *~ clause* bijzin, ondergeschikte zin
²subordinate (vb) (+ to) ondergeschikt maken (aan), achterstellen (bij)
subordination 1 ondergeschiktheid **2** [linguistics] onderschikking
¹subpoena (n) dagvaarding
²subpoena (vb) dagvaarden
¹subscribe (vb) **1** (+ to) intekenen (voor); zich abonneren (op) [magazine]: *~ for* (vooraf) bestellen **2** (+ to) onderschrijven [opinion] **3** (+ to) (geldelijk) steunen
²subscribe (vb) **1** (onder)tekenen, zijn handtekening zetten onder: *~ one's name (to sth.)* (iets) ondertekenen **2** inschrijven (voor)
subscriber 1 ondertekenaar **2** intekenaar, abonnee
subscription 1 ondertekening **2** abonnement[h], intekening, inschrijving: *take out a ~ to sth.* zich op iets abonneren **3** contributie, bijdrage, steun
subscription rate abonnementsprijs
subsequent (+ to) volgend (op), later, aansluitend

subsequently vervolgens, nadien, daarna
subservient 1 bevorderlijk, nuttig: *~ to* bevorderlijk voor **2** ondergeschikt **3** kruiperig, onderdanig
subside 1 (be)zinken, (in)zakken, verzakken **2** slinken, inkrimpen, afnemen **3** bedaren
subsidence instorting, verzakking, het wegzakken
subsidiary 1 helpend, steunend, aanvullings-: *~ troops* hulptroepen **2** (+ to) ondergeschikt (aan), afhankelijk (van): *~ subject* bijvak
subsidize subsidiëren
subsidy subsidie
subsist (in) leven (blijven): *~ on welfare* van een uitkering leven
subsistence 1 bestaan[h], leven[h] **2** onderhoud[h], kost, levensonderhoud[h]
subsistence farming landbouw voor eigen gebruik
subsistence level bestaansminimum[h]: *live at ~* nauwelijks rondkomen
subsoil ondergrond
subspecies ondersoort
substance substantie, wezen[h], essentie, stof, materie, kern, hoofdzaak: *the ~ of his remarks* de kern van zijn opmerkingen; *a man of ~* een rijk man
substantial werkelijk, aanzienlijk, stoffelijk, degelijk: *~ meal* stevige maaltijd
substantiate van gronden voorzien, bewijzen, verwezenlijken: *~ a claim* een bewering hard maken
substantive 1 substantief [also linguistics]; zelfstandig **2** wezenlijk **3** belangrijk || *~ law* materieel recht
¹substitute (n) vervanger, plaatsvervanger; [also sport] invaller, wisselspeler
²substitute (adj) plaatsvervangend
³substitute (vb) in de plaats stellen (voor), invallen (voor), wisselen: *~ A by* (or: *with*) *B* A door B vervangen; *~ A for B* B vervangen door A
substitution vervanging, wissel
subtenant onderhuurder
subterfuge 1 uitvlucht, voorwendsel[h] **2** trucje[h], list
subterranean onderaards, ondergronds
subtitle ondertitel
subtle subtiel, fijn, nauwelijks merkbaar, scherp(zinnig): *smile subtly* fijntjes lachen
subtlety subtiliteit, scherpzinnigheid, subtiel onderscheid[h]
subtract (+ from) aftrekken (van), in mindering brengen (op)
subtraction aftrekking, vermindering
subtropical subtropisch
suburb voorstad, buitenwijk
suburban van de voorstad; [fig] bekrompen

suburbia suburbia; (bewoners van de) voorsteden

subversion 1 ontwrichting **2** ondermijning

subversive ontwrichtend, ondermijnend

subway 1 (voetgangers)tunnel, ondergrondse (door)gang **2** [Am] metro

¹**succeed** (vb) (op)volgen: ~ *to the property* de bezittingen overerven

²**succeed** (vb) slagen, gelukken, succes hebben: ~ *in (doing) sth.* slagen in iets, erin slagen iets te doen

success succesʰ, goede afloop, bijval: *be a ~, meet with* ~ succes boeken; *make a ~ of it* het er goed afbrengen

successful succesvol, geslaagd

succession 1 reeks, serie, opeenvolging: ~ *of defeats* reeks nederlagen **2** (troon)opvolging: *law of* ~ successiewet ‖ *in quick* ~ vlak na elkaar

successive opeenvolgend

successor opvolger: ~ *to the throne* troonopvolger

succinct beknopt, kort, bondig

succour hulp, steun

¹**succulent** (n) vetplant

²**succulent** (adj) sappig

succumb (+ to) bezwijken (aan/voor): ~ *to one's enemies* zwichten voor zijn vijanden

¹**such** (adj) **1** zulk(e), zodanig, dergelijke, zo'n: ~ *clothes as he would need* de kleren die hij nodig zou hebben; ~ *as* zoals; *a man* ~ *as Paul* een man als Paul; *I have accepted his help,* ~ *as it is* ik heb zijn hulp aangenomen, ook al is die vrijwel niets waard; *there's no* ~ *thing as automatic translation* automatisch vertalen is onmogelijk **2** die en die, dat en dat: *at* ~ *(and* ~*) a place and at* ~ *(and* ~*) a time* op die en die plaats en op dat en dat uur

²**such** (dem pron) zulke, zo iem. (iets), dergelijke(n), zulks: ~ *was not my intention* dat was niet mijn bedoeling ‖ ~ *being the case* nu de zaken er zo voorstaan

suchlike zo'n, zulk(e), dergelijke: *worms and* ~ *creatures* wormen en dergelijke beestjes

¹**suck** (n) slokjeʰ, teugjeʰ

²**suck** (vb) **1** zuigen (aan/op): ~ *sweets* op snoepjes zuigen; ~ *in* opzuigen, in zich opnemen; ~ *up* opzuigen; [fig] ~ *it up* slikken of stikken **2** likken, vleien: ~ *up (to) s.o.* iem. likken, iem. vleien

sucker 1 zuiger, uitloper, scheut **2** onnozele hals, sukkel: *I am a* ~ *for red-headed women* ik val nu eenmaal op vrouwen met rood haar

suckle de borst krijgen (geven), zuigen, zogen

suckling 1 zuigeling **2** jongʰ: ~ *pig* speenvarken

suction zuiging, (kiel)zogʰ

the **Sudan** Sudan

¹**Sudanese** (n) Sudanees, Sudanese

²**Sudanese** (adj) Sudanees

sudden plotseling, haastig, snel, scherp: ~ *death (play-off)* beslissende verlenging; *all of a* ~ plotseling, ineens

suddenly plotseling, opeens, ineens

suds (zeep)sop, schuim

sue 1 (gerechtelijk) vervolgen, dagvaarden: ~ *for divorce* (echt)scheiding aanvragen **2** verzoeken, smeken: ~ *for mercy* (iem.) om genade smeken

suede suède

¹**suffer** (vb) **1** lijden, schade lijden, beschadigd worden: ~ *from* lijden aan **2** (+ for) boeten (voor)

²**suffer** (vb) verdragen, dulden: *not* ~ *fools (gladly)* weinig geduld hebben met dwazen

sufferer lijder; patiënt

suffering pijn, lijdenʰ: *severe* ~*s* zware pijn(en)

suffice genoeg zijn (voor), volstaan, voldoen: *your word will* ~ *(me)* uw woord is me voldoende; ~ *(it) to say that* het zij voldoende te zeggen dat

sufficiency 1 voldoende voorraad, toereikende hoeveelheid **2** toereikendheid

sufficient voldoende, genoeg

suffocate (doen) stikken, verstikken

suffocation (ver)stikking

suffrage stemrechtʰ, kiesrechtʰ

suffuse bedekken: *eyes* ~*d with tears* ogen vol tranen; ~*d with light* overgoten door licht

¹**sugar** (n) **1** suiker **2** schat(jeʰ), liefjeʰ **3** zoete woordjes, vleierij

²**sugar** (vb) **1** zoeten, suiker doen in **2** aangenamer maken, verzoeten: ~ *the pill* de pil vergulden

sugar beet suikerbiet

sugarcane suikerrietʰ

sugar caster suikerstrooier, strooibus

sugar daddy [Am; inform] rijke (oudere) mainteneur

sugary 1 suikerachtig, suiker- **2** suikerzoet [fig]; stroperig

suggest suggereren, doen denken aan, duiden op, influisteren, ingeven, opperen, aanvoeren, voorstellen, aanraden: ~ *doing sth.* voorstellen iets te doen; ~ *sth. to s.o.* iem. iets voorstellen

suggestion 1 suggestie, aanduiding, aanwijzing, mededeling, ideeʰ, overweging, voorstelʰ, raad: *at the* ~ *of* op aanraden van **2** zweem, tikjeʰ: *a* ~ *of anger* een zweem van woede

suggestion box ideeënbus

suggestive 1 suggestief, suggererend, veelbetekenend **2** gewaagd, van verdacht allooi, schuin

suicidal 1 zelfmoord- **2** met zelfmoordneigingen

suicide 1 zelfmoord, zelfdoding: *commit* ~

zelfmoord plegen; *assisted* ~ hulp bij zelfdoding **2** zelfmoordenaar

suicide attack zelfmoordaanslag

suicide attempt zelfmoordpoging

suicide mission zelfmoordaanslag

suicide squad zelfmoordcommando[h]

¹suit (n) **1** kostuum[h], pak[h]: *bathing* ~ badpak **2** [cards] kleur, kaarten van één kleur: *follow* ~ kleur bekennen; [fig] iemands voorbeeld volgen **3** stel[h], uitrusting: ~ *of armour* wapenrusting **4** (rechts)geding[h], proces[h], rechtszaak: *criminal* (or: *civil*) ~ strafrechtelijke (or: civiele) procedure

²suit (vb) **1** aanpassen, geschikt maken: ~ *one's style to one's audience* zijn stijl aan zijn publiek aanpassen **2** goed zijn voor: *I know what ~s me best* ik weet wel wat voor mij het beste is **3** voldoen, aanstaan, bevredigen: ~ *s.o.'s needs* aan iemands behoeften voldoen; ~ *yourself!* a) ga je gang maar!; b) moet je zelf weten!

³suit (vb) **1** passen (bij), geschikt zijn (voor), staan (bij): *this colour ~s her complexion* deze kleur past bij haar teint; ~ *s.o.* (*down*) *to the ground* a) voor iem. geknipt zijn, precies bij iem. passen; b) iem. uitstekend van pas komen **2** gelegen komen (voor), uitkomen (voor), schikken: *that date will* ~ (*me*) die datum komt (me) goed uit

suitability geschiktheid, gepastheid

suitable (+ to, for) geschikt (voor), gepast, passend

suitcase koffer; [Belg] valies[h]

suite 1 stel[h], rij, suite, ameublement[h]: ~ *of rooms* suite; *three-piece* ~ driedelige zitcombinatie **2** suite, gevolg[h]

suited 1 geschikt, (bij elkaar) passend: *well* ~ *to one another* voor elkaar gemaakt **2** gericht (op), beantwoordend (aan)

suitor [form] **1** [law] aanklager; eiser **2** [dated] huwelijkskandidaat

¹sulk (n) boze bui: *have a* ~, *have* (*a fit of*) *the* ~*s* een chagrijnige bui hebben

²sulk (vb) mokken, chagrijnig zijn

sulky chagrijnig

sullen 1 nors, stuurs **2** somber: ~ *sky* sombere hemel

sulphur zwavel: ~ *dioxide* zwaveldioxide

sulphuric zwavelachtig, zwavelhoudend: ~ *acid* zwavelzuur

sultan sultan

sultry 1 zwoel, drukkend **2** wellustig, sensueel

sum 1 som, totaal[h], geheel[h], bedrag[h] **2** (reken)som, berekening, optelling: *good at* ~*s* goed in rekenen **3** samenvatting, kern, strekking: *in* ~ in één woord

summarily 1 summier, in het kort: *deal* ~ *with* summier behandelen **2** terstond, zonder vorm van proces

summarize samenvatten

¹summary (n) samenvatting, korte inhoud, uittreksel[h]

²summary (adj) summier, beknopt, samenvattend: ~ *account* beknopt overzicht; ~ *statement* verzamelstaat, recapitulatie; ~ *jurisdiction* korte procesgang, snelrecht; ~ *execution* standrechtelijke executie

summation 1 optelling **2** som; totaal[h] **3** samenvatting

summer zomer; [fig] bloeitijd: *in* (*the*) ~ in de zomer

summer house zomerhuis[h]

summer school zomercursus; vakantiecursus [at university]

summertime zomerseizoen[h], zomer(tijd)

summer time zomertijd

summery zomers

summing-up samenvatting [by judge]

summit 1 top, hoogste punt[h] **2** toppunt[h], hoogtepunt[h]: *at the* ~ op het hoogste niveau **3** topconferentie

summit meeting topconferentie

summit talks topconferentie

summon 1 bijeenroepen, oproepen **2** dagvaarden

¹summons (n) **1** oproep **2** aanmaning **3** dagvaarding: *serve a* ~ *on s.o.* iem. dagvaarden

²summons (vb) **1** dringend aanmanen **2** dagvaarden

summon up vergaren, verzamelen: ~ *one's courage* (*to do sth.*) zich vermannen, al zijn moed verzamelen (om iets te doen)

sumptuous weelderig, luxueus, rijk

sum total 1 totaal[h] **2** resultaat[h]

¹sum up (vb) beoordelen, doorzien: *sum s.o. up as a fool* iem. voor gek verslijten

²sum up (vb) samenvatten

sun zon, zonlicht[h], zonneschijn: *a place in the* ~ een plaatsje in de zon; [fig] een gunstige positie; *beneath* (or: *under*) *the* ~ onder de zon, op aarde

sunbaked 1 zongedroogd **2** zonovergoten

sunbathe zonnebaden

sunbeam zonnestraal

sunblind zonnescherm[h]

sunburn zonnebrand, roodverbrande huid

sunburnt 1 gebruind **2** [Am] verbrand

sundae ijscoupe

Sunday zondag, feestdag, rustdag

Sunday best zondagse kleren: *in one's* ~ op zijn zondags

Sunday clothes zondagse kleren: *in one's* ~ op zijn zondags

sun deck 1 zonnedek[h] **2** dakterras[h]

sundial zonnewijzer

sundown zonsondergang: *at* ~ bij zonsondergang

sundry divers, allerlei, verschillend: *all and* ~ iedereen, jan en alleman

sunflower zonnebloem

sunglasses zonnebril: *a pair of* ~ een zonnebril
sunken 1 gezonken, onder water, ingevallen: ~ *eyes* diepliggende ogen **2** verzonken, ingegraven, verlaagd: ~ *road* holle weg
sunlamp hoogtezon
sunlight zonlicht[h]
sunlit door de zon verlicht, in het zonlicht, zonovergoten
[1]**Sunnite** (n) soenniet
[2]**Sunnite** (adj) soennitisch
sunny zonnig, vrolijk: *on the* ~ *side of forty* nog geen veertig
sunny-side up [Am] aan één kant gebakken: *two eggs* ~ twee spiegeleieren
sunray zonnestraal
sunrise zonsopgang
sun roof 1 plat dak[h] [to sunbathe] **2** schuifdak[h] [of car]
sunscreen 1 zonnescherm[h] **2** zonnefilter[h] [eg in sun lotion]
sunset zonsondergang, avondrood[h]: *at* ~ bij zonsondergang
sunshade zonnescherm[h], parasol, zonneklep
sunshine zonneschijn; [fig] zonnetje[h]
sunstroke zonnesteek
suntan (bruine) kleur
suntanned gebruind, bruin
sunup zonsopgang
super super, fantastisch
superabundant zeer overvloedig, al te overvloedig, rijkelijk (aanwezig)
superannuated 1 gepensioneerd **2** verouderd, ouderwets
superannuation 1 pensionering, pensioen[h] **2** pensioen[h], lijfrente
superb groots, prachtig, voortreffelijk
superbug resistente bacterie
supercilious uit de hoogte, verwaand
superconductivity supergeleiding
superduper [inform] super; je van het
superficial oppervlakkig, niet diepgaand, vluchtig: ~ *wound* ondiepe wond
superfluous overbodig
superglue secondelijm
superhuman bovenmenselijk, buitengewoon
superimpose bovenop leggen, opleggen
superintend toezicht houden (op), controleren, toezien (op)
superintendent 1 (hoofd)opzichter, hoofd[h], directeur **2** hoofdinspecteur [of police]
[1]**superior** (n) **1** meerdere, superieur, hogere in rang, chef **2** overste: *Mother Superior* moeder-overste
[2]**superior** (adj) **1** superieur, beter, bovenst, opperst; [fig also] hoger; hoofd-: ~ *to* a) beter [quality]; b) hoger [rank]; *be* ~ *to* verheven zijn boven, staan boven **2** hoger, voor-

naam, deftig **3** verwaand, arrogant: ~ *smile* hooghartig lachje ‖ ~ *court* hogere rechtbank
superiority superioriteit, grotere kracht, hogere kwaliteit
[1]**superlative** (n) superlatief [also linguistics]; overtreffende trap
[2]**superlative** (adj) voortreffelijk, prachtig ‖ [linguistics] ~ *degree* superlatief, overtreffende trap
superman superman, supermens
supermarket supermarkt
supernatural bovennatuurlijk
supernaturalistic bovennatuurlijk, supernaturalistisch
supernumerary 1 extra[h], reserve **2** figurant
superpower grootmacht, supermacht
superscript superscript (teken)
supersede vervangen, de plaats doen innemen van, afschaffen
superserver krachtige server
supersonic supersonisch, sneller dan het geluid
superstition bijgeloof[h]
superstitious bijgelovig: ~ *beliefs* bijgeloof
supervise 1 aan het hoofd staan (van), leiden **2** toezicht houden (op), controleren
supervision supervisie, leiding, toezicht[h]
supervisor 1 opzichter, controleur, inspecteur, chef **2** coördinator
supine 1 achteroverliggend, op de rug liggend **2** lui, traag
supper (licht) avondmaal[h], avondeten[h], souper[h]
supplant verdringen, vervangen
supple soepel [also fig]; buigzaam, lenig
[1]**supplement** (n) aanvulling, bijvoegsel[h], supplement[h]: *pay a* ~ bijbetalen
[2]**supplement** (vb) aanvullen, van een supplement voorzien: ~ *by* (or: *with*) aanvullen met
supplementary aanvullend, toegevoegd, extra
supplication smeekbede
supplier leverancier
[1]**supply** (n) **1** voorraad: *supplies* (mond)voorraad; proviand[h]; benodigdheden **2** bevoorrading, aanvoer, toevoer, levering **3** aanbod[h]: ~ *and demand* vraag en aanbod
[2]**supply** (vb) **1** leveren, verschaffen, bezorgen, voorzien van: ~ *sth. to s.o.,* ~ *s.o. with sth.* iem. iets bezorgen, iem. van iets voorzien **2** voorzien in, verhelpen, vervullen: ~ *a need* voorzien in een behoefte
[1]**support** (n) **1** steun, hulp, ondersteuning: *in* ~ *of* tot steun van **2** steun(stuk[h]), stut, drager, draagbalk **3** onderhoud[h], levensonderhoud[h], middelen van bestaan
[2]**support** (vb) **1** (onder)steunen, stutten,

dragen **2** steunen, helpen, bijstaan, verdedigen, bijvallen, subsidiëren **3** onderhouden, voorzien in de levensbehoeften van: ~ o.s. (or: *one's family*) zichzelf (*or:* zijn familie) onderhouden **4** verdragen, doorstaan, verduren || ~*ing programme* bijfilm, voorfilm(pje); ~*ing part* (or: *role*) bijrol
supporter 1 verdediger, aanhanger, voorvechter **2** supporter
support group praatgroep
supportive steunend, helpend, aanmoedigend
suppose (ver)onderstellen, aannemen, denken: *he is ~d to be in London* hij zou in Londen moeten zijn; *I'm not ~d to tell you this* ik mag je dit (eigenlijk) niet vertellen; *I ~ so* (or: *not*) ik neem aan van wel (*or:* niet); ~ *it rains* stel dat het regent, en als het nou regent?
supposed vermeend, vermoedelijk, zogenaamd: *his ~ wealth* zijn vermeende rijkdom
supposedly vermoedelijk, naar alle waarschijnlijkheid, naar verluidt
supposing indien, verondersteld dat: ~ *it rains, what then?* maar wat als het regent?
supposition (ver)onderstelling, vermoedenʰ, gissing: *in* (or: *on*) *the ~ that* in de veronderstelling dat
suppository zetpil
suppress onderdrukken, bedwingen, achterhouden: ~ *evidence* (or: *facts*) bewijsstukken (*or:* feiten) achterhouden; ~ *feelings* gevoelens onderdrukken
suppression onderdrukking
suppressor onderdrukker
supranational supranationaal, bovennationaal
supremacy overmacht, superioriteit
supreme opperst, hoogst: *Supreme Being* Opperwezen, God; *Supreme Court* hooggerechtshof
¹**surcharge** (n) **1** toeslag, strafport **2** extra belasting
²**surcharge** (vb) **1** extra laten betalen **2** overladen, overbelasten
¹**sure** (adj) **1** zeker, waar, onbetwistbaar: *one thing is ~* één ding staat vast **2** zeker, veilig, betrouwbaar: ~ *proof* waterdicht bewijs **3** zeker, verzekerd, overtuigd: ~ *of o.s.* zelfverzekerd, zelfbewust; *you can be ~ of it* daar kan je van op aan || ~ *card* iem. (iets) waar men op kan bouwen; ~ *thing* a) feit, zekerheid; b) [exclamation] natuurlijk!; *be ~ to tell her* vergeet vooral niet het haar te vertellen; *it is ~ to be a girl* het wordt vast een meisje; *just to make ~* voor alle zekerheid
²**sure** (adv) zeker, natuurlijk, ongetwijfeld: ~ *enough!* natuurlijk!; *he promised to come and ~ enough he did* hij beloofde te komen en ja hoor, hij kwam ook; *I don't know for ~* ik ben er niet (zo) zeker van

sure-fire onfeilbaar, zeker: ~ *winner* zekere winnaar
surely 1 zeker, ongetwijfeld, toch: *slowly but ~* langzaam maar zeker; ~ *I've met you before?* ik heb je toch al eens eerder ontmoet?; ~ *you are not suggesting it wasn't an accident?* je wilt toch zeker niet beweren dat het geen ongeluk was? **2** natuurlijk; ga je gang [in reply to request]
surety 1 borgsteller **2** borg(som): *stand ~ for s.o.* zich borg stellen voor iem.
¹**surf** (n) branding
²**surf** (vb) surfen: ~ *the Net* internetten, (op het net) surfen
¹**surface** (n) oppervlakʰ, oppervlakte [also fig]: *come to the ~* tevoorschijn komen, bovenkomen
²**surface** (vb) aan de oppervlakte komen [also fig]; opduiken, verschijnen
³**surface** (vb) bedekken, bestraten, asfalteren
surface mail landpost, zeepost
surfboard surfplank
surfeit overdaad; overlading [of stomach]: *have a ~ of* zich ziek eten aan
surfer (branding)surfer
surfing (branding)surfen
¹**surge** (n) **1** (hoge) golf **2** opwelling, vlaag, golf
²**surge** (vb) **1** golven, deinen, stromen: ~ *by* voorbijstromen **2** dringen, duwen: *surging crowd* opdringende massa **3** opwellen; opbruisen [of feelings]
surgeon 1 chirurg **2** scheepsdokter
surgery 1 behandelkamer; spreekkamer [of doctor] **2** spreekuurʰ **3** chirurgie, heelkunde: *be in* (or: *have, undergo*) ~ geopereerd worden
surgical chirurgisch, operatief || ~ *stocking* steunkous, elastische kous
¹**Surinam** (n) Suriname
²**Surinam** (adj) Surinaams
¹**Surinamese** (n) Surinamer, Surinaamse
²**Surinamese** (adj) Surinaams
surly knorrig, nors
surmise gissing, vermoedenʰ
surmount 1 overwinnen, te boven komen **2** bedekken, overdekken: *peaks ~ed with snow* met sneeuw bedekte toppen
surname achternaam
surpass overtreffen, te boven gaan: ~ *all expectations* alle verwachtingen overtreffen
¹**surplus** (n) overschotʰ, teveelʰ, rest(antʰ)
²**surplus** (adj) overtollig, extra: ~ *grain* graanoverschot
¹**surprise** (n) verrassing, verbazing, verwondering: *come as a ~ (to s.o.)* totaal onverwacht komen (voor iem.); *to my great ~* tot mijn grote verbazing
²**surprise** (vb) verrassen, verbazen, overvallen, betrappen: *you'd be ~d!* daar zou je van

opkijken!
surprised verrast, verbaasd: *be* ~ *at* zich
verbazen over
surprise visit onwerwacht bezoekʰ
surprising verrassend, verbazingwekkend
surreal onwerkelijk
surrealism surrealismeʰ
¹**surrender** (n) overgave
²**surrender** (vb) zich overgeven, capituleren
³**surrender** (vb) overgeven, uitleveren, afstaan, afstand doen van
surreptitious heimelijk, stiekem: ~ *glance*
steelse blik
¹**surrogate** (n) **1** plaatsvervanger, substi-
tuut **2** vervangend middelʰ, surrogaatʰ
²**surrogate** (adj) plaatsvervangend, surro-
gaat- ‖ ~ *mother(hood)* draagmoeder(schap)
surround omringen, omsingelen: ~*ed by*
(or: *with*) omringd door
surroundings omgeving, buurt, streek,
omtrek
surveillance toezichtʰ, bewaking: *under*
(close) ~ onder (strenge) bewaking
surveillance airplane verkenningsvlieg-
tuigʰ
¹**survey** (n) **1** overzichtʰ: *a* ~ *of major Dutch*
writers een overzicht van belangrijke Nederlandse schrijvers **2** onderzoekʰ **3** taxering;
taxatierapportʰ [of house] **4** opmeting, opname; kartering [of terrain]
²**survey** (vb) **1** overzien, toezien op **2** onderzoeken **3** taxeren [house] **4** opmeten,
karteren
surveyor **1** opziener, opzichter, inspecteur
2 landmeter **3** taxateur
survival **1** overleving, het overleven: ~ *of*
the fittest natuurlijke selectie, (het verschijnsel dat) de sterkste(n) overleven **2** overblijfselʰ
survival kit nooduitrusting
survive overleven, voortbestaan, bewaard
blijven, langer leven dan; [fig] zich (weten
te) handhaven: ~ *an earthquake* een aardbeving overleven; ~ *one's children* zijn kinderen
overleven
survivor overlevende
susceptibility **1** gevoeligheid **2** (suscepti-
bilities) zwakke plek: *wound s.o. in his sus-*
ceptibilities iem. op zijn zwakke plek raken
susceptible (+ to) vatbaar (voor), gevoelig
(voor), onderhevig (aan)
¹**suspect** (n) verdachte
²**suspect** (adj) verdacht
³**suspect** (vb) **1** vermoeden, vrezen, geloven, denken **2** (+ of) verdenken (van), wantrouwen
suspend **1** (op)hangen **2** uitstellen: ~*ed*
sentence voorwaardelijke straf **3** schorsen
suspender **1** (sok)ophouder **2** (-s) [Am]
bretels: *a pair of* ~*s* bretels
suspense spanning, onzekerheid: *hold* (or:

keep) in ~ in onzekerheid laten
suspension **1** opschorting [of verdict, sentence etc]; onderbreking, uitstelʰ [of pay-
ment] **2** vering
suspension bridge hangbrug, ketting-
brug
suspicion **1** vermoedenʰ, veronderstelling:
have a ~ *that* vermoeden dat **2** verdenking:
above ~ boven alle verdenking verheven
3 zweempjeʰ: *a* ~ *of irony* een zweempje ironie
suspicious **1** verdacht: *feel* ~ *about* (or: *of*)
s.o. iem. wantrouwen **2** wantrouwig, achterdochtig
suss out **1** doorkrijgen [sth.]: *I can't* ~ *how*
to remove that wheel clamp ik kan er maar niet
achter komen hoe ik die wielklem eraf moet
halen **2** doorhebben [somebody]
sustain **1** (onder)steunen, dragen, staven,
bevestigen: ~*ing food* versterkend voedsel
2 volhouden, aanhouden: ~ *a note* een noot
aanhouden **3** doorstaan: ~ *an attack* een
aanval afslaan **4** ondergaan, lijden, oplopen:
~ *a defeat* (or: *an injury*) een nederlaag (or:
letsel) oplopen
sustainable **1** verdedigbaar **2** duurzaam
sustained voortdurend, aanhoudend
sustenance voedselʰ [also fig]
¹**suture** (n) hechting
²**suture** (vb) hechten
SW *South-West(ern)* Z.W., zuidwest
¹**swab** (n) **1** zwabber, stokdweil **2** prop
(watten), wattenstokjeʰ **3** uitstrijk(jeʰ): *take*
a ~ een uitstrijkje maken
²**swab** (vb) zwabberen, (op)dweilen, opnemen
¹**swagger** (n) **1** geparadeerʰ, zwier(ige
gang) **2** opschepperij
²**swagger** (vb) **1** paraderen, lopen als een
pauw **2** opscheppen, pochen
¹**swallow** (n) **1** zwaluw **2** slok ‖ *one* ~ *doesn't*
make a summer één zwaluw maakt nog geen
zomer
²**swallow** (vb) slikken
³**swallow** (vb) **1** (door)slikken, inslikken,
binnenkrijgen **2** opslokken, verslinden: ~ *up*
opslokken, inlijven **3** [fig] slikken, geloven: ~
a story een verhaal slikken **4** inslikken
[words or sounds] **5** herroepen, terugnemen: ~ *one's words* zijn woorden terugnemen **6** onderdrukken, verbijten: ~ *one's*
pride zijn trots terzijde schuiven; ~ *hard* zich
vermannen
swallow-tailed zwaluwstaartvormig, ge-
vorkt: ~ *coat* rok(jas)
¹**swamp** (n) moeras(land)ʰ
²**swamp** (vb) **1** doen vollopen **2** onder water doen lopen, overstromen **3** bedelven,
overspoelen: ~ *with* work (or: *letters*) bedelven onder het werk (or: de brieven)
swan zwaan ‖ *the Swan of Avon* Shake-

speare
¹swank (n) **1** opschepper **2** opschepperij
²swank (vb) opscheppen, zich aanstellen: ~
about in a new fur coat rondparaderen in een
nieuwe bontmantel
swanky 1 opschepperig **2** chic, modieus,
stijlvol
swan song zwanenzang
¹swap (n) ruil: *do* (or: *make*) *a* ~ ruilen
²swap (vb) ruilen, uitwisselen: ~ *jokes* moppen tappen onder elkaar; ~ *over* (or: *round*)
van plaats verwisselen; ~ *for* (in)ruilen tegen
¹swarm (n) zwerm, massa: ~ *of bees* bijen-
zwerm; ~*s of children* drommen kinderen
²swarm (vb) **1** (uit)zwermen, samendrommen: ~ *in* (or: *out*) naar binnen (or: buiten)
stromen; ~ *about* (or: *round*) samendrommen
rond **2** (+ with) krioelen (van), wemelen
3 klimmen: ~ *up a tree* in een boom klauteren
swarthy donker, bruin, zwart(achtig)
swastika hakenkruis^h
swat meppen, (dood)slaan: ~ *a fly* een vlieg
doodmeppen
swathe 1 zwad(e), hoeveelheid met één
maai afgesneden gras (koren) **2** (gemaaide)
strook, baan: *cut a wide* ~ *through* flinke sporen achterlaten in
¹sway (n) **1** slingering, zwaai; schommeling
[of ship etc] **2** invloed, druk, overwicht^h,
dwang: *under the* ~ *of his arguments* overgehaald door zijn argumenten
²sway (vb) beïnvloeden: *be* ~*ed by* zich laten
leiden door
³sway (vb) slingeren, (doen) zwaaien; [fig
also] (doen) aarzelen: ~ *to the music* deinen
op de maat van de muziek
swear 1 (+ at, about) vloeken (op/over)
2 zweren, een eed afleggen, met kracht beweren, wedden; ~ *an oath* een eed afleggen;
~ *to do sth.* plechtig beloven iets te zullen
doen; ~ *by s.o. (sth.)* bij iem. (iets) zweren,
volkomen op iem. (iets) vertrouwen **3** beëdigen, de eed afnemen: *sworn translator* beëdigd vertaler; *sworn enemies* gezworen vijanden; ~ *in* beëdigen; ~ *to secrecy* (or: *silence*)
een eed van geheimhouding afnemen van
swearword vloek, krachtterm
¹sweat (n) **1** zweet^h: *he was in a cold* ~ het
klamme zweet brak hem uit **2** inspanning,
karwei^h: *a frightful* ~ een vreselijk karwei
3 eng gevoel^h, angst, spanning: *in a* ~ benauwd, bang **4** (oude) rot: *old* ~ oude rot
²sweat (vb) zweten, (doen) (uit)zweten: ~
blood water en bloed zweten; ~ *it out* (tot
het einde) volhouden, standhouden, zweten
sweated door uitbuiting verkregen, uitgebuit: ~ *labour* slavenarbeid
sweater sweater, sportvest^h, (wollen) trui
sweatshop slavenhok^h
sweat suit trainingspak^h, joggingpak^h

sweaty 1 zwetend, bezweet, zweterig
2 broeierig, heet
Swede Zweed(se)
Sweden Zweden
¹Swedish (n) Zweeds^h [language]
²Swedish (adj) Zweeds
¹sweep (n) **1** (schoonmaak)beurt, opruiming: *make a clean* ~ schoon schip maken
2 veger, schoorsteenveger, straatveger
3 veeg, haal (met een borstel), streek
4 zwaai, slag, draai, bocht: *wide* ~ wijde
draai || *a* ~ *of mountain country* een stuk
bergland, een berglandschap
²sweep (vb) **1** vegen: ~ *the seas* de zeeën
schoonvegen; *be swept from sight* aan het
gezicht onttrokken worden; ~ *up* aanvegen,
uitvegen, bijeenvegen **2** (laten) slepen
3 (toe)zwaaien, slaan: ~ *aside* (met een
zwaai) opzijschuiven; [fig] naast zich neerleggen; ~ *off* (met een zwaai) afnemen [hat]
4 meesleuren, wegsleuren, meevoeren, afrukken: ~ *along* meesleuren, meeslepen; *be
swept off one's feet* **a)** omvergelopen worden; **b)** [fig] overdonderd worden; **c)** versteld
staan, halsoverkop verliefd worden; *be swept
out to sea* in zee gesleurd worden **5** doorkruisen, teisteren, razen over: *the storm swept
the country* de storm raasde over het land
6 afzoeken **7** bestrijken **8** (volledig) winnen
9 zich (snel) (voort)bewegen, vliegen: ~
along voortsnellen; ~ *by* (or: *past*) voorbijschieten; ~ *down on* aanvallen; ~ *on* voortij-
len; ~ *round* zich (met een zwaai) omdraai-
en; ~ *from* (or: *out of*) *the room* de kamer uit
stuiven; ~ *into power* aan de macht komen
10 zich uitstrekken: ~ *down to the sea* zich
uitstrekken tot aan de zee
sweeper 1 veger, straatveger, schoorsteenveger **2** tapijtenroller, (straat)veegma-
chine **3** [socc] vrije verdediger, laatste man
sweeping 1 veelomvattend, ingrijpend: ~
changes ingrijpende veranderingen **2** radicaal, veralgemenend: ~ *condemnation* radicale veroordeling **3** geweldig, kolossaal: ~
reductions reusachtige prijsverlagingen
¹sweet (n) **1** lieveling, schatje^h **2** snoepje^h,
lekkers^h **3** dessert^h, toetje^h
²sweet (adj) zoet, lekker, heerlijk, geurig,
melodieus: ~ *nature* zachte natuur, beminnelijk karakter; *keep s.o.* ~ iem. te vriend
houden; *be* ~ *on s.o.* gek zijn op iem.; *how* ~
of you wat aardig van je || ~ *nothings* lieve
woordjes; *have a* ~ *tooth* een zoetekauw zijn
sweetbread zwezerik
¹sweeten (vb) zoet(er) worden
²sweeten (vb) **1** zoeten, zoet(er) maken
2 verzachten, verlichten, veraangenamen
3 sussen, omkopen, zoet houden
sweetener 1 zoetstof **2** smeergeld^h, fooi,
steekpenning
sweetheart 1 schat **2** liefje^h, vriend(in)

sweetie 1 liefje[h], schatje[h] **2** snoepje[h]
sweetmeat 1 snoepje[h] **2** (-s) snoepgoed[h]
sweetness zoetheid: *yesterday Sarah was all ~ and light* gisteren was Sarah een en al beminnelijkheid
sweet pepper paprika
sweet-talk vleien
[1]swell (n) **1** zwelling, het zwellen, volheid **2** deining
[2]swell (adj) voortreffelijk, prima: *a ~ teacher* een prima leraar
[3]swell (vb) (op)zwellen, bol gaan staan: *~ out* bollen; *~ up* (op)zwellen; *~ with pride* zwellen van trots
[4]swell (vb) doen zwellen, bol doen staan: *~ one's funds* wat bijverdienen
swelling zwelling, het zwellen
sweltering smoorheet, drukkend
[1]swerve (n) zwenking, wending
[2]swerve (vb) **1** zwenken, plotseling uitwijken: *~ from the path* van het pad afdwalen [also fig] **2** afwijken, afdwalen
[3]swerve (vb) **1** doen zwenken, opzij doen gaan **2** doen afwijken
swift vlug, snel, rap
[1]swig (n) slok
[2]swig (vb) met grote teugen drinken
[3]swig (vb) naar binnen gieten, leegzuipen
[1]swill (n) **1** spoeling, spoelbeurt: *give a ~* uitspoelen **2** afval[h] **3** varkensdraf, varkensvoer[h]
[2]swill (vb) zuipen, gretig drinken
[3]swill (vb) **1** afspoelen, doorspoelen, uitspoelen: *~ down* afspoelen; *~ out* uitspoelen **2** opzuipen, gretig opdrinken: *~ down* opzuipen
[1]swim (n) zwempartij: *have* (or: *go*) *for a ~* gaan zwemmen, een duik (gaan) nemen || *be in* (or: *out of*) *the ~* (niet) op de hoogte zijn, (niet) meedoen
[2]swim (vb) **1** zwemmen [also fig]; baden **2** vlotten, drijven, zweven: *~ming in butter* drijvend in de boter **3** duizelen, draaierig worden: *my head is ~ming* het duizelt mij
[3]swim (vb) (over)zwemmen: *~ a river* een rivier overzwemmen
swim-bladder zwemblaas
swimmer zwemmer
swimming de zwemsport
swimming costume zwempak[h], badpak[h]
swimmingly vlot, moeiteloos, als van een leien dakje: *everything goes on* (or: *off*) *~* alles loopt gesmeerd
swimming pool zwembad[h]
swimming trunks zwembroek
[1]swindle (n) (geval[h] van) zwendel, bedrog[h], oplichterij
[2]swindle (vb) oplichten, afzetten, bedriegen: *~ money out of s.o., ~ s.o. out of money* iem. geld afhandig maken
swindler zwendelaar(ster), oplichter

swine zwijn[h], varken[h]
[1]swing (n) **1** schommel **2** schommeling, zwaai, slingerbeweging, forse beweging: *~ in public opinion* kentering in de publieke opinie **3** (fors) ritme[h] **4** swing(muziek) **5** actie, vaart, gang: *in full ~* in volle actie; *get into the ~ of things* op dreef komen **6** inspiratie || *go with a ~* van een leien dakje gaan
[2]swing (vb) **1** met veerkrachtige tred gaan, met zwaaiende gang lopen: *~ along* (or: *by, past*) met veerkrachtige gang voorbijlopen **2** swingen **3** opgehangen worden: *~ for it* ervoor gestraft worden **4** slingeren, schommelen, zwaaien: [fig] *~ into action* in actie komen **5** draaien, (doen) zwenken: *~ round* (zich) omdraaien, (zich) omgooien; *~ to* dichtslaan [door etc] **6** (op)hangen: *~ from the ceiling* aan het plafond hangen **7** beïnvloeden, bepalen, manipuleren: *what swung it was the money* wat de doorslag gaf, was het geld **8** wijsmaken: *you can't ~ that sort of stuff on her* zoiets maak je haar niet wijs
swing bridge draaibrug
swing door klapdeur, tochtdeur
swingeing geweldig, enorm: *~ cuts* zeer drastische bezuinigingen
swinger [inform] **1** snelle jongen **2** iem. die aan partnerruil doet **3** biseksueel
swinging 1 schommelend, slingerend, zwaaiend **2** veerkrachtig: *~ step* veerkrachtige tred **3** ritmisch, swingend
[1]swipe (n) **1** mep, (harde) slag: *have* (or: *take*) *a ~ at* uithalen naar **2** verwijt[h], schimpscheut
[2]swipe (vb) gappen, jatten, stelen
swipe card magneetkaart
[1]swirl (n) **1** (draai)kolk, maalstroom **2** werveling
[2]swirl (vb) **1** (doen) wervelen, (doen) dwarrelen: *~ about* rondwervelen, ronddwarrelen **2** (doen) draaien
[1]swish (n) **1** zwiep, slag **2** zoevend geluid[h], geruis[h]: *the ~ of a cane* het zoeven van een rietje
[2]swish (adj) chic, modieus
[3]swish (vb) **1** zoeven, suizen, ruisen: *~ past* voorbijzoeven **2** zwiepen
[4]swish (vb) doen zwiepen, slaan met: *~ing tail* zwiepende staart
[1]Swiss (n) Zwitser(se)
[2]Swiss (adj) Zwitsers: *~ cheese* a) emmentaler; b) [fig] gatenkaas || *~ roll* opgerolde cake met jam
[1]switch (n) **1** schakelaar **2** [railways] wissel **3** ommezwaai, verandering **4** twijgje[h], loot **5** (valse) haarlok, (valse) haarvlecht
[2]switch (vb) **1** verwisselen: *~ (a)round* verwisselen **2** ontsteken
[3]switch (vb) **1** (om)schakelen, veranderen (van), overgaan (op): *~ places* van plaats veranderen; *~ off* a) uitschakelen, afzetten;

b) versuffen; ~ *over* **a)** overschakelen; **b)** [radio, TV] een ander kanaal kiezen; ~ *through* *(to)* doorverbinden; ~ *to* overgaan naar **2** draaien, (doen) omzwaaien: ~ *round* omdraaien
switchback 1 bochtige, heuvelige weg **2** achtbaan
switchblade [esp Am] stiletto
switchboard schakelbord[h]
switched-on 1 levendig, alert **2** bij (de tijd), vooruitstrevend **3** high
switch on 1 inschakelen, aanzetten, aandoen **2** stimuleren, doen opleven, inspireren
switch-over 1 overschakeling, omschakeling **2** overgang, verandering
Switzerland Zwitserland
[1]**swivel** (n) (ketting)wartel
[2]**swivel** (vb) (rond)draaien: ~ *round* in one's chair ronddraaien in zijn stoel
swivel chair draaistoel
swizz 1 bedrog[h] **2** ontgoocheling
swizzle stick [inform] roerstokje[h]
swollen gezwollen [also fig]; opgeblazen
swollen-headed 1 verwaand, arrogant **2** overmoedig
swoon 1 in vervoering geraken **2** bezwijmen, in onmacht vallen
[1]**swoop** (n) **1** duik **2** veeg, haal: *at* one (fell) ~ met één slag, in één klap
[2]**swoop** (vb) stoten [of bird of prey]; (op een prooi) neerschieten; zich storten op [also fig]: ~ *down* stoten
[1]**swop** (n) ruil
[2]**swop** (vb) ruilen, uitwisselen: ~ *for* (in)ruilen tegen
sword zwaard[h] ‖ *cross* ~s (with) in conflict komen (met); *put* to the ~ over de kling jagen, vermoorden
swordfish zwaardvis
swordsman 1 zwaardvechter **2** schermer
sword swallower degenslikker
sworn 1 gezworen: ~ *enemies* gezworen vijanden **2** beëdigd: ~ *statement* verklaring onder ede
[1]**swot** (n) **1** blokker, stuud, studie(bol) **2** geblok[h], gezwoeg[h]
[2]**swot** (vb) blokken op: ~ *sth. up,* ~ *up on sth.* iets erin stampen, iets repeteren; ~ *for* an exam blokken voor een examen
sycamore 1 esdoorn **2** plataan[h]
syllable lettergreep
syllabus samenvatting, leerplan[h]
sylph 1 luchtgeest **2** tengere/elegante dame
symbol symbool[h], (lees)teken[h]
symbolic(al) symbolisch: *be* symbolic *of* voorstellen
symbolism 1 symbolisme[h] **2** symboliek, symbolische betekenis
symbolize symboliseren, symbool zijn van: *a white dove* ~s *peace* een witte duif is het

symbool van vrede
symmetry symmetrie
sympathetic 1 sympathiek, welwillend: *be* (or: *feel*) ~ *to/toward(s)* s.o. iem. genegen zijn **2** meevoelend, deelnemend
sympathize 1 sympathiseren: ~ *with* sympathiseren met, meevoelen met **2** meevoelen, deelneming voelen
sympathizer sympathisant
sympathy sympathie, genegenheid, deelneming: *letter of* ~ condoleancebrief; *feel* ~ *for* meeleven met; *be in* ~ *with* gunstig staan tegenover, begrip hebben voor
symphony symfonie
symphony orchestra symfonieorkest[h]
symptom symptoom[h], (ziekte)verschijnsel[h], indicatie
symptomatic symptomatisch: *be* ~ *of* symptomatisch zijn voor, wijzen op
synagogue synagoge
sync synchronisatie: *be* out of ~ with niet gelijk lopen met
synchronic synchroon
[1]**synchronize** (vb) **1** gelijktijdig gebeuren, samenvallen **2** gelijk staan [of clock]
[2]**synchronize** (vb) **1** synchroniseren [also film]; (doen) samenvallen (in de tijd): ~ *with* synchroniseren met **2** gelijk zetten [clock]
syndicate 1 syndicaat[h], belangengroepering **2** perssyndicaat[h], persbureau[h]
syndrome syndroom[h], complex[h] van kenmerkende (ziekte)verschijnselen
synod synode
synonym synoniem[h]
synonymous synoniem
synopsis korte inhoud(sbeschrijving), samenvatting, overzicht[h]
syntax syntaxis, zinsbouw
synth *synthesizer*
synthesize 1 maken, samenstellen **2** bijeenvoegen, tot een geheel maken **3** synthetisch bereiden, langs kunstmatige weg maken
synthetic synthetisch, op synthese berustend, kunstmatig vervaardigd
syphilis syfilis
Syria Syrië
[1]**Syrian** (n) Syriër, Syrische
[2]**Syrian** (adj) Syrisch
[1]**syringe** (n) (injectie)spuit
[2]**syringe** (vb) **1** inspuiten, een injectie geven **2** uitspuiten, schoonspuiten
syrup siroop, stroop
system 1 stelsel[h], systeem[h] **2** geheel[h], samenstel[h] **3** methode **4** gestel[h], lichaam[h], lichaamsgesteldheid **5** systematiek ‖ *get* sth. out of one's ~ iets verwerken
systematic systematisch, methodisch
systematize systematiseren, tot een systeem maken
systems analyst systeemanalist(e)

t

t t, T ‖ *cross one's t's (and dot one's i's)* de puntjes op de i zetten, op de details letten; *to a T* precies, tot in de puntjes
ta [inform, child language] dank je
tab 1 lus, ophanglusjeʰ **2** etiketjeʰ, labelʰ **3** klepjeʰ, flapjeʰ; lipjeʰ [of tin] **4** [inform] rekening: *pick up the ~* betalen **5** tabtoets **6** tabblad ‖ *keep ~s* (or: *a ~*) *on* in de gaten houden
tabby 1 cyperse kat **2** poes, vrouwtjeskat
tabernacle [rel] tabernakelʰ, (veld)hut, tent
tab key tabtoets
table 1 tafel: *lay the ~* de tafel dekken; *at ~* aan tafel **2** tabel, lijst, tafel: *learn one's ~s* de tafels van vermenigvuldiging leren ‖ *turn the ~s (on s.o.)* de rollen omdraaien; *under the ~* dronken; *drink s.o. under the ~* iem. onder de tafel drinken
tablecloth tafelkleedʰ
table-manners tafelmanieren
table-mat onderzetter
tablespoon opscheplepel, eetlepel
tablet 1 (gedenk)plaat, plaquette **2** tabletʰ, pil
table-talk tafelgesprekken
table tennis tafeltennisʰ
tabletop tafelbladʰ
tabloid krant(jeʰ) [half size of regular newspaper]
tabloid press sensatiepers
taboo taboeʰ: *put sth. under ~* iets taboe verklaren
tabs [inform] *tabloids* de roddelpers
tacit stilzwijgend: *~ agreement* stilzwijgende overeenkomst
taciturn zwijgzaam, (stil)zwijgend
¹tack (n) **1** kopspijker(tjeʰ), nageltjeʰ; [Am] punaise **2** koers; boeg [while navigating] **3** koers(verandering), strategie, aanpak
²tack (vb) van koers veranderen, het anders aanpakken
³tack (vb) **1** vastspijkeren: [fig] *~ on* toevoegen aan **2** rijgen
¹tackle (n) **1** takel **2** [sport] tackle **3** [Am football] tackle, stopper **4** uitrusting, benodigdheden **5** [shipp] takelage, takelwerkʰ
²tackle (vb) **1** aanpakken, onder de knie proberen te krijgen: *~ a problem* een probleem aanpakken **2** aanpakken, een hartig woordje spreken met **3** tackelen, (de tegenstander) neerleggen
tacky 1 plakkerig, kleverig **2** haveloos, sjo-

fel **3** smakeloos, ordinair
tact tact
tactful tactvol, omzichtig
tactic 1 tactische zet, tactiek, manoeuvre **2** (-s) tactiek
tactical tactisch [also mil]; diplomatiek: *~ voting* strategisch stemgedrag
tactician tacticus
tactile 1 tast-: *~ organs* tastorganen **2** tastbaar, voelbaar
tactless tactloos
tad klein beetjeʰ: *just a ~ depressing* een klein beetje deprimerend
Tadzhikistan Tadzjikistan
¹tag (n) **1** etiketʰ [also fig]; insigneʰ, labelʰ **2** tag **3** stiftjeʰ [at end of shoe-lace etc] **4** afgezaagd gezegdeʰ, clichéʰ **5** flard, rafel, los uiteindeʰ **6** klit haar **7** elektronische enkelband
²tag (vb) (+ along) dicht volgen, slaafs achternalopen ‖ *the children were ~ging along behind their teacher* de kinderen liepen (verveeld) achter hun onderwijzer aan
³tag (vb) **1** van een etiket voorzien [also fig]; etiketteren, merken **2** vastknopen, toevoegen: *a label had been ~ged on at the top* aan de bovenkant was een kaartje vastgemaakt
¹tail (n) **1** staart **2** onderste, achterste deelʰ, uiteindeʰ, pandʰ; sleep [of clothing]; staart [of comet, aeroplane] **3** (-s) munt(zijde) **4** (-s) rokkostuumʰ ‖ *with one's ~ between one's legs* met hangende pootjes; *turn ~ and run* hard weglopen; *be on s.o.'s ~* iem. op de hielen zitten
²tail (vb) schaduwen, volgen
tailback file, verkeersopstopping
tailboard laadklep, achterklep
tailcoat jacquetʰ, rok, rokkostuumʰ
tail end uiteindeʰ
¹tailgate (n) [Am] achterklep, laadklep; vijfde deur [of car]
²tailgate (vb) geen afstand houden, bumperkleven
tailgater bumperklever
tail light (rood) achterlichtʰ
tail off 1 geleidelijk afnemen, verminderen **2** verstommen **3** uiteenvallen
¹tailor (n) kleermaker
²tailor (vb) **1** maken [clothes]; op maat snijden en aan elkaar naaien **2** aanpassen, op maat knippen: *we ~ our insurance to your needs* wij stemmen onze verzekering af op uw behoeften
tailor-made 1 maat-: *~ suit* maatkostuum **2** geknipt, precies op maat
tailwind rugwind
¹taint (n) smet(jeʰ), vlekjeʰ
²taint (vb) bederven, rotten, ontaarden
³taint (vb) besmetten
Taiwan Taiwan
¹Taiwanese (n) Taiwanees, Taiwanese

²**Taiwanese** (adj) Taiwanees
¹**Tajik** (n) Tadzjiek(se)
²**Tajik** (adj) Tadzjieks
Tajikistan Tadzjikistan
¹**take** (n) **1** vangst **2** opbrengst, ontvangst(en) **3** [film] opname
²**take** (vb) **1** pakken, aanslaan, wortel schieten **2** effect hebben, inslaan, slagen **3** bijten [of fish] **4** worden: *he was ~n ill* hij werd ziek **5** vlam vatten ‖ *Gerard ~s after his father* Gerard lijkt op zijn vader; *I took against him at first sight* ik mocht hem meteen al niet
³**take** (vb) **1** nemen, grijpen, (beet)pakken: [fig] *~ my grandfather, he is still working* neem nou mijn opa, die werkt nog steeds **2** veroveren, innemen, vangen; [chess, draughts] slaan: [chess] *he took my bishop* hij sloeg mijn loper; *he took me unawares* hij verraste mij **3** winnen, (be)halen **4** nemen, zich verschaffen, gebruiken: *~ the bus* de bus nemen; *this seat is ~n* deze stoel is bezet; *do you ~ sugar in your tea?* gebruikt u suiker in de thee? **5** vereisen, in beslag nemen: *it won't ~ too much time* het zal niet al te veel tijd kosten; *have what it ~s* aan de eisen voldoen **6** meenemen, brengen: *that bus will ~ you to the station* met die bus kom je bij het station; *~ s.o. around* iem. rondleiden; *~ s.o. aside* iem. apart nemen **7** weghalen, wegnemen: *~ five from twelve* trek vijf van twaalf af **8** krijgen, vatten, voelen: *she took an immediate dislike to him* zij kreeg onmiddellijk een hekel aan hem; *~ fire* vlam vatten; *~ it into one's head* het in zijn hoofd krijgen **9** opnemen, noteren, meten: *let me ~ your temperature* laat mij even je temperatuur opnemen **10** begrijpen: *~ for granted* als vanzelfsprekend aannemen; *I ~ it that he'll be back soon* ik neem aan dat hij gauw terugkomt; *~ it badly* het zich erg aantrekken; *what do you ~ me for?* waar zie je me voor aan? **11** aanvaarden, accepteren: *~ sides* partij kiezen; *you may ~ it from me* je kunt van mij aannemen **12** maken, doen; nemen [school subject]: *~ a decision* een besluit nemen; *~ an exam* een examen afleggen; *~ notes* aantekeningen maken; *she took a long time over it* zij deed er lang over **13** raken, treffen **14** behandelen [problem etc] **15** gebruiken, innemen ‖ *~ it or leave it* graag of niet; *~ aback* verrassen, van zijn stuk brengen, overdonderen; *she was rather ~n by* (or: *with*) *it* zij was er nogal mee in haar schik; *~ it (up)on o.s.* het op zich nemen, het wagen
take apart 1 uit elkaar halen, demonteren **2** een vreselijke uitbrander geven
¹**takeaway** (n) afhaalrestaurantʰ, afhaalmaaltijd
²**takeaway** (adj) afhaal-, meeneem-
take away 1 aftrekken **2** weghalen **3** verminderen, verkleinen, afbreuk doen aan: *it*

takes sth. away *from* the total effect het doet een beetje afbreuk aan het geheel
take back 1 terugbrengen; [fig] doen denken aan: *it took me back to my childhood* het deed me denken aan mijn jeugd **2** terugnemen, intrekken
take down 1 afhalen, naar beneden halen **2** opschrijven, noteren **3** uit elkaar halen, demonteren, slopen
take-home afhaal-, meeneem-: *~ dinners* afhaalmaaltijden; *~ exam* tentamen dat je thuis maakt
take-home pay nettoloonʰ
take in 1 in huis nemen, kamers verhuren aan **2** naar binnen halen, meenemen **3** omvatten, betreffen **4** innemen [clothing]; [shipp] oprollen [sailing] **5** begrijpen, doorzien **6** (in zich) opnemen [surroundings etc]; bekijken **7** bedriegen **8** geabonneerd zijn op
¹**take off** (vb) **1** zich afzetten **2** opstijgen; starten [also fig; of project etc] **3** (snel) populair worden, succes hebben
²**take off** (vb) **1** uittrekken, uitdoen **2** meenemen, wegvoeren: *she took the children off to bed* zij bracht de kinderen naar bed **3** afhalen, weghalen, verwijderen **4** verlagen [price] **5** nadoen, imiteren **6** vrij nemen ‖ *take o.s. off* ervandoor gaan, zich uit de voeten maken
take-off 1 start, het opstijgen, vertrekʰ **2** parodie, imitatie
¹**take on** (vb) tekeergaan, zich aanstellen
²**take on** (vb) **1** op zich nemen, als uitdaging accepteren **2** krijgen; aannemen [colour]; overnemen, in dienst nemen **3** het opnemen tegen, vechten tegen **4** aan boord nemen
take out 1 mee naar buiten nemen, mee uit nemen, naar buiten brengen; [Am] *~ food* een afhaalmaaltijd meenemen; *take s.o. out for a walk* (or: *meal*) iem. mee uit wandelen nemen, iem. mee uit eten nemen **2** verwijderen, uithalen **3** tevoorschijn halen **4** nemen, aanschaffen: *an insurance (policy)* een verzekering afsluiten **5** buiten gevecht stellen [opponent] ‖ *take it out of s.o.* veel van iemands krachten vergen; *don't take it out on him* reageer het niet op hem af
takeover overname
take over 1 overnemen, het heft in handen nemen **2** navolgen, overnemen
take to 1 beginnen te, gaan doen aan, zich toeleggen op **2** aardig vinden, mogen: *he did not take kindly to it* hij moest er niet veel van hebben **3** de wijk nemen naar, vluchten naar: *~ one's bed* het bed houden
¹**take up 1** verder gaan [of story, chapter] ‖ *~ with* bevriend raken met
²**take up** (vb) **1** optillen, oppakken: *~ the hatchet* de strijdbijl opgraven **2** absorberen [also fig]; opnemen, in beslag nemen: *it near-*

ly took up all the room het nam bijna alle ruimte in beslag **3** oppikken [passengers] **4** ter hand nemen, gaan doen aan: ~ *a cause* een zaak omhelzen; ~ *gardening* gaan tuinieren **5** vervolgen [story]; hervatten **6** aannemen, aanvaarden, ingaan op: *he took me up on my offer* hij nam mijn aanbod aan **7** innemen [position]; aannemen [attitude] || *I'll take you up on that* daar zal ik je aan houden
taking: *for the* ~ voor het grijpen
takings verdiensten, recette, ontvangsten
talcum powder talkpoeder[h]
tale 1 verhaal(tje)[h]: *thereby hangs a* ~ daar zit een (heel) verhaal aan vast; *tell* ~*s* kletsen, roddelen **2** sprookje[h], legende **3** leugen, smoes(je[h]) **4** gerucht[h], roddel, praatje[h]
talent 1 talent[h], (natuurlijke) begaafdheid, gave **2** talent[h], begaafde persoon
talented getalenteerd, talentvol
taleteller 1 kwaadspreker **2** roddelaar(ster)
¹talk (n) **1** praatje[h]; lezing [on radio] **2** gesprek[h]: *have a* ~ *(to, with s.o.)* (met iem.) spreken **3** (-s) besprekingen, onderhandelingen **4** gepraat[h] **5** gerucht[h], praatjes: *there is* ~ *of* er is sprake van (dat), het gerucht gaat dat **6** geklets[h]: *be all* ~ praats hebben [but achieving nothing]
²talk (vb) **1** spreken, praten: *now you're* ~*ing* zo mag ik het horen, dat klinkt al (een stuk) beter; *you can* (or: *can't*) ~ moet je horen wie het zegt; *do the* ~*ing* het woord voeren; [at beginning of sentence] ~*ing of plants* over planten gesproken **2** roddelen, praten: *people will* ~ de mensen roddelen toch (wel) || ~ *to s.o.* eens ernstig praten met iem.
³talk (vb) **1** spreken (over), discussiëren over, bespreken: ~ *s.o.'s head off* iem. de oren van het hoofd praten; ~ *one's way out of sth.* zich ergens uitpraten **2** zeggen, uiten || ~ *s.o. round to sth.* iem. ompraten tot iets; ~ *s.o. into (doing) sth.* iem. overhalen iets te doen; ~ *s.o. out of (doing) sth.* iem. iets uit het hoofd praten
talk about 1 spreken over, bespreken, het hebben over: ~ *problems!* over problemen gesproken!; *know what one is talking about* weten waar men het over heeft **2** roddelen over: *be talked about* over de tong gaan **3** spreken van, zijn voornemen uiten (om): *they're talking about emigrating to Australia* zij overwegen naar Australië te emigreren
talkative praatgraag, praatziek
talk back (brutaal) reageren: ~ *to s.o.* iem. van repliek dienen
talk down neerbuigend praten: ~ *to one's audience* afdalen tot het niveau van zijn gehoor
talking point discussiepunt[h]
talking-to uitbrander: *(give s.o.) a good* ~ een hartig woordje (met iem. spreken)

talk of 1 spreken over, bespreken: [at beginning of sentence] *talking of plants* over planten gesproken **2** spreken van, het hebben over: ~ *doing sth.* van plan zijn iets te doen
talk out 1 uitvoerig spreken over: ~ *a bill* door lange redevoeringen het aannemen van een wet verhinderen **2** uitpraten
talk over (uitvoerig) spreken over, uitvoerig bespreken: *talk things over with s.o.* de zaak (uitvoerig) met iem. bespreken
talk show praatprogramma[h]; talkshow [on TV]
tall 1 lang [of person]; groot; hoog [of tree, mast etc]: *Peter is 6 feet* ~ Peter is 1,80 m (lang); *the pole is 10 feet* ~ de paal is 3 m hoog **2** overdreven, te groot: ~ *order* onredelijke eis; ~ *story* sterk verhaal || ~ *talk* opschepperij
¹tally (n) **1** rekening **2** inkeping **3** label[h], etiket[h], merk[h] **4** score(bord[h]) **5** aantekening: *keep (a)* ~ *(of)* aantekening houden (van)
²tally (vb) (+ with) overeenkomen (met), gelijk zijn, kloppen
talon klauw [of bird of prey]
tambour 1 trom(mel) **2** schuifklep [of desk]
¹tame (adj) **1** tam, mak **2** meegaand **3** oninteressant, saai
²tame (vb) temmen; [fig] bedwingen
tamper with 1 knoeien met, verknoeien: ~ *documents* documenten vervalsen **2** zich bemoeien met **3** komen aan, zitten aan **4** omkopen
tampon tampon
¹tan (adj) geelbruin, zongebruind
²tan (vb) bruin worden [sun]
³tan (vb) **1** bruinen [sun] **2** looien, tanen || ~ *s.o.'s hide*, ~ *the hide off s.o.* iem. afranselen
tandem tandem || *in* ~ achter elkaar
tang 1 scherpe (karakteristieke) lucht, indringende geur **2** scherpe smaak; smaakje[h] [fig]; zweem, tikje[h]
tangent raaklijn, tangens || *fly* (or: *go*) *off at a* ~ een gedachtesprong maken, plotseling van koers veranderen
tangerine 1 feloranje[h] **2** tangerine [fruit]
tangible tastbaar [also fig]; voelbaar, concreet: [law] ~ *assets* activa
¹tangle (n) **1** knoop; klit [in hair, wool etc]: *in a* ~ in de war **2** verwarring, wirwar
²tangle (vb) **1** in de knoop raken, klitten **2** in verwarring raken, in de war raken: ~ *with s.o.* verwikkeld raken in een ruzie met iem.
tank 1 (voorraad)tank, reservoir[h] **2** tank, pantserwagen
tankard bierpul
tanker tanker
tank up 1 tanken, (bij)vullen **2** zich volgieten, zuipen

tannery looierij
tannin looizuur[h], tannine
tanning pak[h] slaag: *give him a good ~!* geef hem een goed pak slaag!
tantalize 1 doen watertanden, kwellen **2** verwachtingen wekken
tantalizing (heel) verleidelijk, aantrekkelijk
tantamount (+ to) gelijk(waardig) (aan): *be ~ to* neerkomen op
tantrum woede-uitbarsting; driftbui [pl, of small child]: *get into a ~, throw a ~* een woedeaanval krijgen
Tanzania Tanzania
¹Tanzanian (n) Tanzaniaan(se)
²Tanzanian (adj) Tanzaniaans
¹tap (n) **1** kraan, tap(kraan); stop [of vat]: *turn the ~ on* (or: *off*) doe de kraan open (or: dicht); *on ~* uit het vat, van de tap; [fig] met-een voorradig, zo voorhanden **2** tik(je[h]), klopje[h]: *a ~ on a shoulder* een schouderklopje **3** afluisterapparatuur
²tap (vb) tikken, kloppen: *~ at* (or: *on*) *the door* op de deur tikken
³tap (vb) **1** doen tikken: *~ s.o. on the shoulder* iem. op de schouder kloppen **2** (af)tappen, afnemen: *her telephone was ~ped* haar telefoon werd afgeluisterd; [fig] *~ a person for information* informatie aan iem. ontfutselen **3** openen; aanbreken [also fig]; aanboren, aansnijden; [fig also] gebruiken: *~ new sources of energy* nieuwe energiebronnen aanboren
tap dancing het tapdansen
¹tape (n) **1** lint[h], band[h], koord[h]: *insulating ~* isolatieband **2** meetlint[h], centimeter **3** (magneet)band, geluidsband, videoband **4** (plak)band[h]: *adhesive ~* plakband
²tape (vb) **1** (vast)binden, inpakken, samenbinden **2** [Am] verbinden, met verband omwikkelen: *his knee was ~d up* zijn knie zat in het verband || *have s.o. ~d* iem. helemaal doorhebben
³tape (vb) opnemen, een (band)opname maken (van)
tape measure meetlint[h], centimeter
¹taper (n) **1** (dunne) kaars **2** (was)pit, lontje[h] **3** (geleidelijke) versmalling [eg of long object]; spits toelopend voorwerp[h]
²taper (vb) **1** taps toelopen, geleidelijk smaller worden: *this stick ~s off to a point* deze stok loopt scherp toe in een punt **2** (+ off) (geleidelijk) kleiner worden, verminderen, afnemen
³taper (vb) smal(ler) maken, taps doen toelopen
tape recorder bandrecorder
tape recording bandopname
tapestreamer tapestreamer
tapestry 1 wandtapijt[h] **2** bekledingsstof van muren

tapeworm lintworm
taproom tapperij, gelagkamer
tap water kraanwater[h]
¹tar (n) teer[h]
²tar (vb) teren, met teer insmeren; [fig] zwartmaken: *~ and feather s.o.* iem. met teer en veren bedekken [as punishment]
tarantula vogelspin, tarantula
tardy 1 traag, sloom: *~ progress* langzame vooruitgang; *he is ~ in paying* hij is slecht van betalen **2** (te) laat **3** weifelend, onwillig
tare 1 tarra(gewicht[h]) [difference between gross and net weight] **2** leeg gewicht[h] [of lorry etc]
tares onkruid[h]
¹target (n) **1** doel[h], roos, schietschijf; [fig] streven[h]; doeleinde[h]: *on ~* op de goede weg, in de goede richting **2** doelwit[h] [of mockery, criticism]; mikpunt[h]
²target (vb) mikken op: *he ~s his audiences carefully* hij neemt zijn publiek zorgvuldig op de korrel
target date streefdatum
tariff (tol)tarief[h], invoerrechten, uitvoerrechten: *postal ~s* posttarieven
¹tarmac (n) asfalt[h]
²tarmac (vb) asfalteren
¹tarnish (n) glansverlies[h], dofheid; [fig] smet
²tarnish (vb) dof worden, verkleuren; aanslaan [of metal]; [fig] aangetast worden
³tarnish (vb) dof maken, doen aanslaan; [fig] bezoedelen: *a ~ed reputation* een bezoedelde naam
tarragon dragon
tarry 1 treuzelen, op zich laten wachten **2** (ver)blijven, zich ophouden
¹tart (n) [inform] **1** slet, del **2** (vruchten)-taart(je[h])
²tart (adj) **1** scherp(smakend), zuur, wrang **2** scherp, sarcastisch
tartan 1 Schotse ruit **2** doek[h] in Schotse ruit **3** tartan[h], (geruite) Schotse wollen stof
tartar 1 woesteling **2** tandsteen
Tartar Tataar
tart up opdirken, optutten: *~ a house* een huis kitscherig inrichten
task taak, karwei[h], opdracht || *take s.o. to ~ (for)* iem. onder handen nemen (vanwege)
task bar [comp] taakbalk
task force speciale eenheid [of army, police]; gevechtsgroep
task-juggling multitasking
taskmaster opdrachtgever: *a hard ~* een harde leermeester
¹taste (n) **1** kleine hoeveelheid, hapje[h], slok-je[h], beetje[h], tikkeltje[h]: *have a ~ of this cake* neem eens een hapje van deze cake **2** ervaring, ondervinding: *give s.o. a ~ of the whip* iem. de zweep laten voelen **3** smaak, smaak-je[h], voorkeur, genoegen[h]: *leave a unpleasant ~ in the mouth* een onaangename nasmaak

hebben [also fig]; *everyone to his* ~ ieder zijn meug; *add sugar to* ~ suiker toevoegen naar smaak **4** smaak, smaakzin, schoonheidszin; gevoel[h] [for proper behaviour, fashion, style etc]: *in good* ~ *a)* smaakvol; *b)* behoorlijk; *sweet to the* ~ zoet van smaak
²**taste** (vb) smaken: *the pudding* ~*d of garlic* de pudding smaakte naar knoflook
³**taste** (vb) **1** proeven, keuren **2** ervaren, ondervinden: ~ *defeat* het onderspit delven
taste bud smaakpapil
tasteful smaakvol
tasteless 1 smaakloos (m.b.t. water enz.) **2** smakeloos (van een slechte smaak)
tasty 1 smakelijk **2** hartig
ta-ta dáág
tatter flard, lomp, vod[h]: *in* ~*s* aan flarden, kapot [also fig]
tattered 1 haveloos; aan flarden [clothes] **2** in lompen gekleed [pers]
¹**tattle** (n) **1** geklets[h], geroddel[h] **2** geklik[h]
²**tattle** (vb) kletsen, roddelen
¹**tattoo** (n) **1** tatoeage **2** taptoe [drumbeat or clarion call]: *beat* (or: *sound) the* ~ taptoe slaan (*or:* blazen) **3** tromgeroffel[h]
²**tattoo** (vb) tatoeëren
tatty slordig, slonzig, sjofel
¹**taunt** (n) hatelijke opmerking, bespotting: ~*s* spot, hoon
²**taunt** (vb) hekelen: *they* ~*ed him into losing his temper* ze tergden hem tot hij in woede uitbarstte
Taurus [astrology] (de) Stier
taut strak, gespannen
tautology tautologie
tavern taveerne, herberg
tawdry opzichtig, smakeloos, opgedirkt
¹**tax** (n) **1** last, druk, gewicht[h]: *be a* ~ *on* veel vergen van **2** belasting, rijksbelasting: *value added* ~ belasting op de toegevoegde waarde, btw
²**tax** (vb) **1** belasten, belastingen opleggen **2** veel vergen van, zwaar op de proef stellen: ~ *your memory* denk eens goed na
taxation 1 belasting(gelden) **2** belastingsysteem[h]
tax bracket belastingschijf
tax collector (belasting)ontvanger
tax cut belastingverlaging
tax-deductible aftrekbaar van de belastingen
tax evasion belastingontduiking
tax exemption belastingvrijstelling
tax-free belastingvrij
tax haven belastingparadijs[h]
¹**taxi** (n) taxi
²**taxi** (vb) **1** (doen) taxiën **2** in een taxi rijden (vervoeren)
taxicab taxi
taxi driver taxichauffeur
taxiway taxibaan

taxman 1 belastingontvanger **2** belastingen, fiscus
taxonomic taxonomisch
taxpayer belastingbetaler
tax rebate belastingteruggave
tax return belastingaangifte
tax with 1 beschuldigen van, ten laste leggen **2** rekenschap vragen voor, op het matje roepen wegens
TB *tuberculosis* tb(c)
tea 1 thee: *make* ~ theezetten; [mockingly] *not for all the* ~ *in China* voor geen goud, voor niets ter wereld **2** lichte maaltijd om 5 uur 's middags **3** theeplant, theebladeren
teabag theezakje[h], theebuiltje[h]
¹**teach** (vb) **1** leren, afleren: *I will* ~ *him to betray our plans* ik zal hem leren onze plannen te verraden **2** doen inzien, leren: *experience taught him that ...* bij ondervinding wist hij dat ...
²**teach** (vb) onderwijzen, leren, lesgeven: ~ *s.o.* **chess,** ~ **chess** *to s.o.* iem. leren schaken; *John* ~*es me (how) to swim* John leert mij zwemmen; ~ *school* onderwijzer zijn
teacher 1 leraar, docent(e) **2** onderwijzer(es)
teacher training (college) lerarenopleiding
teaching 1 het lesgeven **2** onderwijs[h] **3** leer, leerstelling
tea cloth theedoek, droogdoek
tea-cosy theemuts
teacup theekopje[h]
teak teakhout[h]
tea leaf theeblad[h] ‖ *read the tea leaves* de toekomst voorspellen
¹**team** (n) **1** team[h], (sport)ploeg, elftal[h] **2** span[h] [of draught animals]
²**team** (vb) (+ up) een team vormen: ~ *up with* samenwerken met, samenspelen met
team bench spelersbank
team-mate teamgenoot
team spirit teamgeest
teamster 1 voerman, menner **2** vrachtwagenchauffeur
teamwork groepsarbeid, samenwerking, samenspel[h]
teapot theepot
¹**tear** (n) **1** traan: *move s.o. to* ~*s* iem. aan het huilen brengen; *shed* ~*s over* tranen storten over [sth. not worthy of tears] **2** drup(pel)
²**tear** (n) **1** scheur **2** flard
³**tear** (vb) **1** scheuren, stuk gaan: *silk* ~*s easily* zijde scheurt makkelijk **2** rukken, trekken: ~ *at sth.* aan iets rukken **3** rennen; [fig] stormen; vliegen: *the boy tore across the street* de jongen stormde de straat over
⁴**tear** (vb) **1** (ver)scheuren [also fig]: *the girl tore a hole in her coat* het meisje scheurde haar jas; ~ *up* verscheuren; [fig] tenietdoen; [fig] *be torn between love and hate* tussen

liefde en haat in tweestrijd staan; ~ *in half*
(or: *two*) in tweeën scheuren **2** (uit)rukken,
(uit)trekken || ~ *down* a building een gebouw
afbreken
tear apart 1 verscheuren [fig]; zich vernietigend uitlaten over **2** overhoop halen **3** [in-
form] uitschelden || *the critics tore his latest
novel apart* de critici schreven zijn laatste roman de grond in
tearaway herrieschopper
tear away aftrekken, wegtrekken, afscheuren; [fig] verwijderen: [fig] *I could hardly
tear myself away* **from** *the party* ik kon het
feest maar met tegenzin verlaten
teardrop traan
tearful 1 huilend **2** huilerig
tear gas traangas[h]
tear into in alle hevigheid aanvallen, heftig
tekeergaan tegen
tear-jerker tranentrekker, smartlap, sentimentele film, sentimenteel liedje[h]
tear off afrukken, aftrekken, afscheuren;
[fig] verwijderen
tearoom tearoom, theesalon
¹tease (n) **1** plaaggeest, kwelgeest **2** plagerij, geplaag[h], flirt
²tease (vb) **1** plagen, lastigvallen, pesten: ~
s.o. for sth. iem. lastigvallen om **2** opgewon-
den maken, opwinden **3** ontlokken || ~ *out*
ontwarren [also fig]
teaser 1 plaaggeest, plager **2** moeilijke
vraag, probleemgeval[h]
teaspoon theelepeltje[h]
teastrainer theezeefje[h]
teat 1 tepel **2** speen
tea towel theedoek, droogdoek
tea-trolley theewagen
tech [inform] *technical college, school*
technical technisch
technicality 1 technische term **2** technisch
detail[h], (klein) formeel punt[h]: *he lost the case
on a* ~ hij verloor de zaak door een vormfout
technician technicus, specialist: *dental* ~
tandtechnicus
technique techniek, werkwijze, vaardigheid
technological technologisch: ~ *university*
technische universiteit
technology technologie, techniek
tech-savvy technisch onderlegd: *even if
you're* **not** ~ zelfs als je geen techneut bent
teddy bear teddybeer
tedious vervelend, langdradig, saai
tedium 1 verveling **2** saaiheid, eentonigheid, langdradigheid
tee [golf] tee || *to a* ~ precies, tot in de punt-
jes
teem 1 wemelen, krioelen, tieren: ~*ing
with* krioelen van; *his head ~s with new ideas*
zijn hoofd zit vol nieuwe ideeën; *those forests
~ with snakes* die bossen krioelen van de

slangen **2** stortregenen, gieten: *it was ~ing
down* (or: *with*) *rain* het goot
teen 1 tiener **2** (-s) tienerjaren: *boy* (or: *girl*)
in his (or: *her*) ~*s* tiener
teenage tiener-: ~ *boy* (or: *girl*) tiener
teenager tiener
teeny(-weeny) piepklein
teeter 1 wankelen, waggelen: [fig] ~ *on the
edge of collapse* op de rand van de ineenstorting staan **2** wippen, op de wip spelen
teethe tandjes krijgen [esp milk teeth]
teething troubles kinderziekten [fig]
teetotaller geheelonthouder
telebanking het telebankieren
¹telecast (n) tv-uitzending
²telecast (vb) op tv uitzenden
telecommunications 1 telecommunica-
tietechniek **2** (telecommunicatie)verbindin-
gen
teleconference teleconferentie
telefax telefax
telegram telegram[h]: *by* ~ per telegram
telegraph telegraaf, telegrafie: *by* ~ per
telegraaf
telemarketing telefonische verkoop, telemarketing
telepathic telepathisch
telepathy telepathie
¹telephone (n) telefoon, (telefoon)toestel[h]:
by ~ telefonisch; *on* (or: *over*) *the* ~ telefonisch
²telephone (vb) telefoneren, (op)bellen: *he
has just ~d* **through** *from Beirut* hij heeft zojuist uit Beiroet opgebeld
telephone booth telefooncel
telephone call telefoongesprek[h]
telephone directory telefoongids
telephoto lens telelens
teleprinter telex, telexapparaat[h]: *by* ~ per
telex
Teleprompter [Am] autocue
¹telescope (n) telescoop, (astronomische)
verrekijker
²telescope (vb) **1** in elkaar schuiven **2** ineengedrukt worden: *two cars ~d* **together** *in
the accident* twee auto's werden bij het ongeval ineengedrukt
³telescope (vb) in elkaar schuiven, ineen-
drukken, samendrukken
telescopic telescopisch, ineenschuifbaar: ~
lens telelens
teleselling telefonische verkoop, telemarketing
teleshopping het telewinkelen, het teleshoppen
television televisie, tv(-toestel[h]): *watch* ~
tv kijken; *on* (*the*) ~ op de televisie
television audience 1 televisiekijkers
2 publiek bij een tv-opname
television broadcast televisie-uitzending

television commercial reclamespot
television programme televisieprogramma[h]
television set televisietoestel[h]
teleworking telewerken[h], het thuiswerken
¹telex (n) **1** telex, telexbericht[h]: *by* ~ per telex **2** telexdienst
²telex (vb) telexen
¹tell (vb) **1** spreken, zeggen, vertellen: *as far as we can* ~ voor zover we weten; *you can never* ~ je weet maar nooit **2** het verklappen, het verraden: *don't* ~*!* verklap het niet!; ~ *on s.o.* iem. verklikken **3** (mee)tellen, meespelen, van belang zijn: *his age will* ~ *against him* zijn leeftijd zal in zijn nadeel pleiten
²tell (vb) **1** vertellen, zeggen, spreken: ~ *a secret* een geheim verklappen; [inform] ~ *s.o. where he gets off,* ~ *s.o. to get off* iem. op zijn plaats, iem. op zijn nummer zetten; *you're* ~*ing me!* vertel mij wat! **2** weten, kennen, uitmaken: *can you* ~ *the difference?* weet (*or:* zie) jij het verschil?; *can she* ~ *the time yet?* kan ze al klok kijken?; *there is no* ~*ing what will happen* je weet maar nooit wat er gebeurt; *how can I* ~ *if* (or: *whether*) *it is true or not?* hoe kan ik weten of het waar is of niet? **3** onderscheiden, uit elkaar houden: ~ *truth from lies* de waarheid van leugens onderscheiden **4** zeggen, bevelen, waarschuwen: *I told you so!* ik had het je nog gezegd! ‖ *all told* alles bij elkaar (genomen), over het geheel; *I'll* ~ *you what: let's call him now* weet je wat?: laten we hem nu opbellen; [inform] ~ *s.o. off for sth.* iem. om iets berispen
teller 1 verteller **2** (stemmen)teller [eg in House of Commons] **3** kassier
telling 1 treffend, raak: *a* ~ *blow* een rake klap **2** veelbetekenend, veelzeggend
telling-off uitbrander
tell-tale 1 roddelaar(ster) **2** verklikker **3** teken[h], aanduiding: [fig] *a* ~ *nod* een veelbetekenend knikje
telly teevee, tv, buis
temerity roekeloosheid
¹temp (n) *temporary employee* tijdelijk medewerk(st)er, uitzendkracht
²temp (vb) als uitzendkracht werken, werken via een uitzendbureau
¹temper (n) **1** humeur[h], stemming: *be in a bad* ~ in een slecht humeur zijn, de pest in hebben **2** kwade bui **3** driftbui, woedeaanval: *fly* (or: *get*) *into a* ~ een woedeaanval krijgen **4** opvliegend karakter[h], drift: *have a* ~ opvliegend zijn **5** kalmte, beheersing: *keep* (or: *lose*) *one's* ~ zijn kalmte bewaren (*or:* verliezen)
²temper (vb) temperen, matigen
temperament 1 temperament[h] [also fig]; aard, gestel[h], vurigheid **2** humeurigheid
temperamental 1 natuurlijk, aangeboren

2 grillig, onberekenbaar, vol kuren
temperance 1 gematigdheid, matigheid, zelfbeheersing **2** geheelonthouding
temperate 1 matig, gematigd: ~ *zone* gematigde luchtstreek **2** met zelfbeheersing
temperature temperatuur, verhoging, koorts: *have* (or: *run*) *a* ~ verhoging hebben
tempest (hevige) storm [also fig]
tempestuous stormachtig [also fig]; hartstochtelijk
template mal, sjabloon
temple 1 tempel, kerk **2** slaap [on head]
tempo tempo[h]
temporary tijdelijk, voorlopig: ~ *buildings* noodgebouwen; ~ *employment agency* uitzendbureau
tempt 1 verleiden, in verleiding brengen: *I am* ~*ed to believe that it's true* ik ben geneigd te geloven dat het waar is **2** tarten, tergen: ~ *Providence* het noodlot tarten
temptation 1 verleidelijkheid **2** verleiding, verzoeking: *lead us not into* ~ leid ons niet in verzoeking
tempter verleider
tempting verleidelijk
temptress verleidster
ten tien: *I bet you* ~ *to one she'll come* ik wed tien tegen één dat ze komt
tenable verdedigbaar, houdbaar
tenacious 1 vasthoudend, hardnekkig **2** krachtig; goed [of memory]
tenacity 1 vasthoudendheid, hardnekkigheid **2** kracht [of memory]
tenancy 1 huur(termijn), pacht(termijn) **2** bewoning, gebruik[h], genot[h]
tenant 1 huurder, pachter **2** bewoner
¹tend (vb) **1** gaan [in certain direction]; zich richten, zich uitstrekken: *prices are* ~*ing downwards* de prijzen dalen **2** neigen, geneigd zijn: *John* ~*s to get angry* John wordt gauw boos; *it* ~*s to get hot in here in summer* het wordt hier vaak erg warm in de zomer ‖ ~ *to* zwemen naar; [Am] aandacht besteden aan
²tend (vb) **1** verzorgen, zorgen voor, passen op: ~ *sheep* schapen hoeden **2** [Am] bedienen: *who's* ~*ing bar?* wie staat er achter de bar?
tendency 1 neiging, tendens, trend **2** aanleg: *he has a* ~ *to grow fat* hij heeft een aanleg tot dik worden
tendentious partijdig, vooringenomen
¹tender (n) **1** verzorger, oppasser, tender **2** tender [of locomotive] **3** offerte, inschrijving: *put out to* ~ aanbesteden (voor inschrijving)
²tender (adj) **1** mals [of meat] **2** gevoelig: ~ *spot* gevoelige plek **3** broos, teer **4** liefhebbend, teder **5** pijnlijk, zeer: ~ *place* gevoelige plek **6** jong, onbedorven: *of* ~ *age* van prille leeftijd

³**tender** (vb) inschrijven: ~ *for* the building of a road inschrijven op de aanleg van een weg
⁴**tender** (vb) aanbieden: ~ *one's* **resignation** zijn ontslag indienen
tenderfoot groentjeʰ, nieuwkomer
tender-hearted teerhartig
tenderize mals maken [meat]
tendon (spier)pees
tendril 1 (hecht)rank [of plant] **2** streng, sliert
tenement 1 pachtgoedʰ **2** (huur)kamer, appartementʰ
tenement house huurkazerne, etagewoning, flatgebouwʰ
tenfold tienvoudig
tenner tientjeʰ, (briefjeʰ van) tien pond (dollar)
tennis tennis(spel)ʰ
tennis court tennisbaan
tennis racket tennisracketʰ
tenor 1 tenor [singer, part, voice, instrument] **2** gang [of one's life]; loop, verloopʰ, (algemene) richting **3** teneur [of text, conversation]; strekking: *get* the ~ of what is being said in grote lijnen begrijpen wat er wordt gezegd
tenpin bowling kegelspelʰ; bowling
¹**tense** (n) tijd, werkwoordstijd
²**tense** (adj) gespannen, in spanning: a face ~ *with* anxiety een van angst vertrokken gezicht
³**tense** (vb) (+ up) zenuwachtig worden
⁴**tense** (vb) (+ up) gespannen maken: ~ *one's* **muscles** zijn spieren spannen
tension 1 spanning, gespannenheid; strakheid [eg of rope]; zenuwachtigheid: *suffer from* **nervous** ~ overspannen zijn **2** gespannen toestand: *racial* ~s rassenonlusten **3** trekspanning [of solid substance] **4** (elektrische) spanning
tent tent: [also fig] *pitch* one's ~ zijn tent opslaan
tentacle tentakel, tastorgaanʰ, voelspriet, vangarm
tentative 1 voorlopig: a ~ **conclusion** een voorzichtige conclusie **2** aarzelend
tenterhooks: *on* ~ ongerust, in gespannen verwachting
tenth tiende
tenuous 1 dun, (rag)fijn **2** (te) subtiel **3** vaag, zwak: a ~ **argument** een zwak argument
tenure 1 pachtregeling **2** ambtstermijn **3** beschikkingsrechtʰ, eigendomsrechtʰ **4** vaste aanstelling
tepid lauw, halfwarm; [fig] koel; mat
terabyte terabyte
term 1 onderwijsperiode, trimesterʰ, semesterʰ, kwartaalʰ **2** termijn, periode, duur, tijd, ambtstermijn; zittingsperiode [of court of law, parliament]; huurtermijn, aflossings-

termijn, (af)betalingstermijn: *in the* **short** ~ op korte termijn **3** [maths] term, lidʰ **4** (vak)term, woordʰ, uitdrukking: ~s bewoordingen; manier van uitdrukken; *tell s.o. in no* **uncertain** ~s in niet mis te verstane bewoordingen te kennen geven **5** (-s) voorwaarden [of agreement, contract]; condities, bepalingen ǁ ~s of **reference** taakomschrijving [eg of committee]; *on* **equal** ~s als gelijken; *to be* **on** *friendly* ~s *with* s.o. op vriendschappelijke voet met iem. staan; *come* to ~s with zich verzoenen met, zich neerleggen bij; *in* ~s *of* money financieel gezien, wat geld betreft; *they are not on* speaking ~s ze spreken niet meer met elkaar, ze hebben onenigheid
¹**terminal** (n) **1** contactklem **2** eindpuntʰ, eindhalte, eindstationʰ **3** (computer)terminal
²**terminal** (adj) **1** eind-, slot-, laatste: ~ **sta**tion eindstation **2** terminaal, ongeneeslijk **3** van (onderwijs)periode, termijn-: ~ **examinations** trimesterexamens, semesterexamens
¹**terminate** (vb) eindigen, aflopen
²**terminate** (vb) beëindigen, eindigen, een eind maken aan, (af)sluiten: ~ a **contract** een contract opzeggen; ~ a **pregnancy** een zwangerschap onderbreken
terminology terminologie, (systeemʰ van) vaktermen
terminus eindpuntʰ [of bus route, railway line]; eindstationʰ, eindhalte
termite termiet
¹**terrace** (n) **1** verhoogd vlak oppervlakʰ, (dak)terrasʰ **2** bordesʰ, (open) tribune, staanplaatsen **3** rij huizen, huizenblokʰ
²**terrace** (vb) tot terras(sen) vormen, terrasgewijs aanleggen: ~d **garden** terrastuin ǁ ~d **house** rijtjeshuis
terrain terreinʰ; gebiedʰ [also fig]
terrestrial van de aarde, van het land, aards: *the* ~ **globe** de aardbol
terrible 1 verschrikkelijk, vreselijk **2** ontzagwekkend, enorm: a ~ **responsibility** een zware verantwoordelijkheid
terribly verschrikkelijk
terrier terriër
terrific geweldig, fantastisch: *at a* ~ **speed** razendsnel
terrify schrik aanjagen: *be terrified* **of** s.o. (sth.) doodsbang zijn voor iem. (iets)
terrifying angstaanjagend, afschuwelijk
territorial territoriaal: ~ **waters** territoriale wateren, driemijlszone
territory 1 territoriumʰ, (stuk) grondgebiedʰ **2** territoriumʰ, (eigen) woongebiedʰ, (grond)gebiedʰ **3** (stukʰ) landʰ, gebiedʰ; terreinʰ [also fig]; districtʰ, werkterreinʰ; [com] rayonʰ; handelsgebiedʰ: *unknown* ~ onbekend gebied
terror 1 verschrikking, plaag: *the* ~ of the

neighbourhood de schrik van de buurt **2** lastig iem.

, rotjoch[h], rotmeid **3** (gevoel van) schrik: *run away in* ~ in paniek wegvluchten
terrorism terrorisme[h]
¹terrorist (n) terrorist
²terrorist (adj) terroristisch, terreur-
terrorize terroriseren, schrik aanjagen
terse beknopt, kort
tertiary tertiair: *a* ~ *burn* derdegraadsverbranding
¹test (n) **1** test, toets(ing), proef, toets, proefwerk[h]; [chem] reactie: *put sth. to the* ~ iets op de proef stellen, iets testen **2** toets, criterium[h], maat(staf) **3** [chem] reageermiddel[h]
²test (vb) **1** toetsen, testen, aan een test onderwerpen, nagaan, nakijken, onderzoeken **2** veel vergen van, hoge eisen stellen aan: ~ *s.o.'s patience* iemands geduld zwaar op de proef stellen; ~*ing times* zware tijden
³test (vb) (d.m.v. een test) onderzoeken: ~ *for* onderzoeken (op), het gehalte bepalen van
testament testament[h]: *last will and* ~ uiterste wil(sbeschikking), testament
the **Testament** Testament[h] [part of bible]
testator testateur, erflater
test ban treaty kernstopverdrag[h]
test card testbeeld[h]
test case proefproces[h]
test-drive een proefrit maken
tester tester [pers]; testapparaat[h]
testicle teelbal, zaadbal, testikel
testify (+ against, for) getuigen (tegen/voor): ~ *to* a) bevestigen; b) getuigenis afleggen van; c) een teken (*or:* bewijs) zijn van
testimonial 1 getuigschrift[h], aanbevelingsbrief **2** huldeblijk, eerbewijs[h]
testimony getuigenverklaring, bewijs[h], blijk[h]: *bear* ~ *to* getuigen; bevestigen; blijk geven van, wijzen op
testosterone testosteron[h]
test tube reageerbuis
test-tube baby reageerbuisbaby
testy 1 prikkelbaar, opvliegend **2** geërgerd, geïrriteerd: *a* ~ *remark* een knorrige opmerking
tetchy prikkelbaar [pers]; lichtgeraakt
¹tether (n) tuier [rope used to secure grazing animal] ‖ *at the end of one's* ~ uitgeteld, aan het eind van zijn Latijn
²tether (vb) vastmaken, tuien, (aan een paal) vastleggen, (vast)binden; [fig] aan banden leggen
¹text (n) **1** tekst(gedeelte[h]), gedrukte tekst, inhoud **2** tekst, onderwerp[h], Bijbeltekst **3** sms(-bericht[h])
²text (vb) sms'en: ~ *me when you know* stuur mij maar een sms als je het weet
textbook leerboek[h], studieboek[h], schoolboek[h] ‖ ~ *example* schoolvoorbeeld

text editing tekstverwerking
text editor teksteditor
text file tekstbestand[h]
textile weefsel[h], textielproduct[h], stof[h] ‖ ~*s* textielindustrie
texture textuur, weefselstructuur; [by extension] structuur; samenstelling: *the smooth* ~ *of ivory* de gladheid van ivoor
¹Thai (n) Thai(se)
²Thai (adj) Thais
Thailand Thailand
the **Thames** Theems ‖ *she won't set the* ~ *on fire* ze heeft het buskruit niet uitgevonden
than 1 dan, als: *she's better* ~ *I am* (or: ~ *me*) zij is beter dan ik; *he would sooner die* ~ *give in* hij zou (nog) liever sterven dan toegeven; *none other* ~ *Joe* niemand anders dan Joe **2** of, dan, en, toen
thank 1 (be)danken, dankbaar zijn: ~ *you* dank u (wel), (ja) graag, alstublieft; *no,* ~ *you* (nee) dank u **2** danken, (ver)wijten, verantwoordelijk stellen: *she has herself to* ~ *for that* het is haar eigen schuld, dat heeft ze aan zichzelf te danken
thankful dankbaar, erkentelijk, blij
thankfully gelukkig: ~, *he's not coming* gelukkig komt hij niet
thankless ondankbaar
thanks dankbaarheid, dankbetuiging, (kort) dankgebed: *a letter of* ~ een schriftelijk bedankje; *received with* ~ in dank ontvangen; [inform] ~*!* bedankt!, merci!; *no,* ~ (nee) dank je (wel), laat maar (zitten)
thanksgiving dankbetuiging, dankzegging
Thanksgiving (Day) [Am] Thanksgiving Day [national holiday; fourth Thursday in November]
thanks to dankzij, door (toedoen van)
thank-you bedankje[h], woord[h] van dank: *a* ~ *letter* een bedankbriefje
¹that (dem pron) **1** die, dat: ~*'s Alice* dat is Alice; ~*'s life* zo is het leven; *at* ~ *point* toen; *do you see* ~ *house?* zie je dat huis daar?; *don't yell like* ~ schreeuw niet zo; *he isn't as stupid as all* ~ zo stom is hij ook weer niet; *that's* ~ dat was het dan, zo, dat zit erop **2** diegene, datgene, hij, zij, dat: *those going by train* diegenen die met de trein gaan **3** die, dat, wat, welke: *the chair(s)* ~ *I bought* de stoel(en) die ik gekocht heb **4** dat, waarop, waarin, waarmee: *the house* ~ *he lives in* het huis waarin hij woont ‖ [inform] *that's it* a) dat is 't hem nu juist, dat is (nu juist) het probleem; b) dat is wat we nodig hebben, dat is de oplossing; c) dit (*or:* dat) is het einde; *we left it at* ~ we lieten het daarbij
²that (adv) **1** zo(danig): *she's about* ~ *tall* ze is ongeveer zo groot **2** heel, heel erg, zo: *its not all* ~ *expensive* het is niet zo heel erg duur
³that (conj) **1** dat, het feit dat: *it was only*

then ~ *I found out* ~ … pas toen ontdekte ik dat …; *she* **knew** ~ *he was ill* ze wist dat hij ziek was **2** [purpose] opdat, zodat **3** [reason or cause] omdat: **not** ~ *I care, but* … niet dat het mij iets kan schelen, maar … **4** [consequence] dat, zodat: *so high* ~ *you cannot see the top* zo hoog dat je de top niet kan zien

¹thatch (n) **1** strodakʰ, rieten dakʰ **2** dakstroʰ, dekrietʰ, dakbedekking

²thatch (vb) (een dak) (met stro) bedekken: ~*ed* **roof** strodak

¹thaw (n) dooi

²thaw (vb) (ont)dooien, smelten; [fig] ontdooien; vriendelijker worden

¹the (adv) **1** [with comparative] hoe, des te: *so much* ~ **better** des te beter; ~ **sooner** ~ *better* hoe eerder hoe beter **2** [with superlative] de, het: *he finished* ~ **fastest** hij was het eerste klaar

²the (art) **1** de, het: *she looks after* ~ **children** zij zorgt voor de kinderen; ~ **Italians** *love spaghetti* (de) Italianen zijn dol op spaghetti; *play* ~ **piano** piano spelen; *ah, this is* ~ *life!* ah, dit is pas leven!; *help* ~ **blind** help de blinden **2** mijn, jouw [etc]: *I've got a pain in* ~ **leg** ik heb pijn in mijn been **3** per, voor elk: *paid by* ~ **week** per week betaald

theatre 1 theaterʰ, schouwburg **2** toneelʰ, toneelstukken, dramaʰ **3** collegezaal, gehoorzaal, auditoriumʰ **4** operatiekamer **5** toneelʰ, (actie)terreinʰ, operatieterreinʰ: ~ *of* **war** oorlogstoneel

theatrical 1 toneel-, theater- **2** theatraal, overdreven

thee u, gij

theft diefstal

their 1 hun, haar: *they studied* ~ **French** ze leerden hun Frans; ~ *eating biscuits annoyed her* (het feit) dat zij koekjes aten irriteerde haar **2** zijn, haar: *no-one gave* ~ **address** niemand gaf zijn adres

theirs 1 de hunne, het hunne, van hen: *a friend* **of** ~ een vriend van hen **2** de zijne, het zijne, van hem, de hare, het hare, van haar: *I forgot my book, could somebody* **lend** *me* ~? ik ben mijn boek vergeten, kan iem. mij het zijne lenen?

them 1 hen, hun, aan hen, ze: *I* **bought** ~ *a present* (or: *a present* **for** ~) ik heb een cadeau voor hen gekocht **2** zij (ze): *I* **hate** ~ **worrying** *like that* ik vind het vreselijk als ze zich zulke zorgen maken; *it* ~ zij zijn het

thematic thematisch: ~ *analysis* thematische analyse

theme 1 themaʰ, onderwerpʰ, gegevenʰ **2** [Am] opstelʰ, essayʰ **3** [mus] themaʰ, hoofdmelodie, herkenningsmelodie

theme park themaparkʰ, pretparkʰ

theme song herkenningsmelodie

themselves 1 zich, zichzelf: *the students kept it* **to** ~ de studenten hielden het voor

zich **2** zelf, zij zelf, hen zelf: **they** ~ *started* zij zelf zijn ermee begonnen

¹then (adj) toenmalig: *the* ~ **chairman** de toenmalige voorzitter

²then (adv) **1** toen, op dat ogenblik, destijds: *before* ~ voor die tijd; *by* ~ dan, toen, ondertussen **2** dan, (onmiddellijk) daarna, verder: ~ *they went home* daarna zijn ze naar huis gegaan **3** dan (toch), in dat geval: *why did you go* ~? waarom ben je dan gegaan? || ~ *and* **there** onmiddellijk, dadelijk; *but* ~, *why did you do it?* maar waarom heb je het dan toch gedaan?

thence 1 vandaar, van daaruit **2** daarom, dus, daaruit

theologian theoloog, godgeleerde

theological theologisch, godgeleerd

theology theologie, godgeleerdheid

theorem (grond)stelling, principeʰ, theorie

theoretical 1 theoretisch **2** denkbeeldig, fictief: ~ *amount* fictief bedrag

theoretician theoreticus

theorize theoretiseren

theory theorie, leer, veronderstelling: ~ *of evolution* evolutietheorie; *in* ~ in theorie, op papier; [maths] ~ *of chances* kansrekening

therapeutic(al) therapeutisch, genezend

therapy therapie, geneeswijze, (psychiatrische) behandeling

¹there (adv) **1** daar, er, ginds; [fig] op dat punt; wat dat betreft: *there's no rush* er is geen haast bij; ~ *I don't* **agree** *with you* op dat punt ben ik het niet met je eens; ~ *they* **come** daar komen ze; *he lives* **over** ~ hij woont daarginds **2** daar(heen), daarnaartoe: ~ *and* **back** heen en terug || ~ *you* **are** a) alstublieft, alsjeblieft; b) zie je wel, wat heb ik je gezegd; *and* **then** onmiddellijk, ter plekke

²there (int) daar, zie je, nou: ~, *what did I tell you!* nou, wat heb ik je gezegd!

thereabouts daar ergens, (daar) in de buurt, daaromtrent; [fig] rond die tijd; (zo) ongeveer: *twenty years* **or** ~ zo ongeveer twintig jaar

thereafter daarna

thereby daardoor || ~ *hangs a tale* daar zit nog een (heel) verhaal aan vast

therefore daarom, om die reden, dus

therein [form] daarin

thereof daarvan, ervan

thereto [form] daaraan

thereupon daarop

thermal 1 thermisch, warmte- **2** thermaal: ~ *springs* warmwaterbronnen

thermals [inform] thermisch ondergoed

thermometer thermometer

thermonuclear thermonucleair

thermos thermosfles, thermoskan

thermostat thermostaat, warmteregulator

thesaurus thesaurus; [esp] synoniemen-

woordenboek^h
th<u>e</u>sis thesis, (hypo)these, (academisch)
proefschrift^h
they 1 zij, ze: ~ *chased each other* ze zaten
elkaar achterna; *so* ~ *say* dat zeggen ze toch
2 hij (of zij): *everyone is proud of the work* ~ *do
themselves* iedereen is trots op het werk dat
hij zelf doet
¹thick (n) dichtste, drukste gedeelte^h, druk-
te: *be in the* ~ *of it* er midden in zitten ||
through ~ *and thin* door dik en dun
²thick (adj) **1** dik; breed [line]; vet [letter,
font]; zwaar(gebouwd), (op)gezwollen; dubbel [tongue]: *two inches* ~ twee inch dik
2 dik, dicht; dicht bezaaid; druk; vol; overvloedig, weinig vloeibaar, weinig doorzichtig, mistig; betrokken [weather]: ~ *on the
ground* zeer talrijk; *the sky was* ~ *with planes*
de lucht zag zwart van vliegtuigen **3** zwaar
[accent] **4** dom, traag van begrip **5** [inform]
intiem, dik bevriend: *be as* ~ *as thieves* de
beste maatjes met elkaar zijn **6** [inform]
sterk, sterk overdreven: *a bit* ~ al te kras ||
give s.o. a ~ *ear* iem. een oorveeg geven; *have
a* ~ *skin* een olifantshuid hebben; *lay it on* ~
flink overdrijven
³thick (adv) **1** dik, breed, vet **2** dik, dicht,
dicht opeengepakt, dicht op elkaar, talrijk:
blows came ~ *and fast* het regende slagen
¹th<u>i</u>cken (vb) dik(ker) worden; gebonden
worden [of liquid]; toenemen (in dikte/aan-
tal)
²th<u>i</u>cken (vb) dik(ker) maken, indikken,
doen toenemen (in dikte/aantal): ~ *gravy
with flour* saus binden met bloem
th<u>i</u>cket (kreupel)bosje^h, struikgewas^h
thickh<u>ea</u>ded dom, bot (van verstand)
th<u>i</u>ckness 1 dikte, afmeting in de dikte, dik
gedeelte, troebelheid, mistigheid: *length,
width, and* ~ lengte, breedte en dikte **2** laag
th<u>i</u>ckset 1 dicht (beplant/bezaaid) **2** zwaar
(gebouwd), dik, gedrongen
thick-sk<u>i</u>nned dikhuidig; [fig] ongevoelig
thick-w<u>i</u>tted dom, bot (van verstand)
thief dief || *there is honour among thieves*
dieven stelen niet van elkaar
thieve stelen
th<u>ie</u>vish steels, dieven-, heimelijk
thigh dij
th<u>i</u>mble vingerhoed
¹thin (adj) **1** dun, smal, fijn, schraal, mager,
slank: ~ *air* ijle lucht **2** dun (bezet/gezaaid),
dunbevolkt: *a* ~ *audience* een klein publiek;
[inform] ~ *on top* kalend **3** dun (vloeibaar),
slap, waterig: ~ *beer* schraal bier **4** zwak,
armzalig: *a* ~ *excuse* een mager excuus || *dis-
appear* (or: *vanish*) *into* ~ *air* spoorloos (or:
volledig) verdwijnen; *the* ~ *end of the wedge*
het eerste (kleine) begin; *skate on* ~ *ice* zich
op glad ijs wagen; *have a* ~ *skin* erg gevoelig
zijn; *have a* ~ *time (of it)* **a)** een moeilijke tijd

doormaken; **b)** weinig succes boeken
²thin (vb) (ver)dunnen, uitdunnen, vermageren
thine van u, uw, de uwe, het uwe
thing 1 ding^h, dingetje^h, zaak(je^h), voor-
werp^h, iets: *a good* ~ *too!* (dat is) maar goed
ook!; *it's a good* ~ *that* het is maar goed dat;
it's a good ~ *to* je doet er goed aan (om); *a
lucky* ~ *no-one got caught* gelukkig werd (er)
niemand gepakt; *make a* ~ *of* ergens moeilijk
over doen; *not a* ~ *to wear* niks om aan te
trekken; *it doesn't mean a* ~ *to me* het zegt
me totaal niets; *and another* ~ bovendien,
meer nog; *for one* ~ **a)** in de eerste plaats, om
te beginnen; **b)** immers **2** schepsel^h, wezen^h,
ding^h: *the poor* ~ de (arme) stakker **3** (favoriete) bezigheid: *do one's (own)* ~ doen waar
men zin in heeft **4** (dat) wat gepast is: *the
very* ~ *for you* echt iets voor jou; *be not (quite)
the* ~ niet passen **5** (dat) wat nodig is: *just the*
~ *I need* juist wat ik nodig heb **6** het belangrijkste (punt, kenmerk): *the* ~ *is that* de
kwestie is dat, waar het om gaat is dat **7** (-s)
spullen: *pack one's* ~s zijn boeltje bijeenpak-
ken **8** (-s) (algemene) toestand: *that would
only make* ~s *worse* dat zou het allemaal alleen maar verergeren; *how are* ~s?, [inform]
how's ~s? hoe gaat het (ermee)? || *have a* ~
about **a)** geobsedeerd zijn door; **b)** dol zijn
op; **c)** als de dood zijn voor; *not know the first*
~ *about* niet het minste verstand hebben van;
know a ~ *or two about* het een en ander weten over; *let* ~s *rip* (or: *slide*) de boel maar laten waaien; *well, of all* ~s! wel heb ik ooit!; *I'll
do it first* ~ *in the morning* ik doe het morgenochtend meteen; *the first* ~ *I knew she had hit
him* voor ik wist wat er gebeurde had ze hem
een mep gegeven
th<u>i</u>ngamajig dingetje^h, hoe-heet-'t-ook-al-
weer^h
¹think (n) **1** gedachte **2** bedenking, overweging: *have a hard* ~ *about* diep nadenken over
|| *have got another* ~ *coming* het lelijk mis
hebben
²think (vb) **1** denken, (erover) nadenken,
zich (goed) bedenken: ~ *for o.s.* zelfstandig
denken; ~ *to o.s.* bij zichzelf denken; ~ *back
to* terugdenken aan; *yes, I* ~ *so* ja, ik denk van
wel; ~ *twice* er (nog eens) goed over nadenken; ~ *about* **a)** denken aan, nadenken over;
b) overwegen [idea, proposal, plan]; **c)** (terug)denken aan; ~ *about moving* er ernstig
over denken om te verhuizen **2** menen,
hebben: *I thought as much* dat was te verwachten, ik vermoedde al zoiets, dat dacht
ik al
³think (vb) **1** denken, vinden, geloven: ~ *s.o.
pretty* iem. mooi vinden; ~ *out for o.s.* voor
zichzelf beslissen **2** (na)denken over: ~ *out*
overdenken, goed (na)denken over; ~ *over*

overdenken, in overweging houden; ~ *through* doordenken, (goed) nadenken over; ~ *up* bedenken, verzinnen; *and to* ~ *(that)* en dan te moeten bedenken dat; ~ *what* you're doing bedenk wat je doet **3** overwegen **4** denken aan, zich herinneren: *he didn't* ~ *to switch off the headlights* hij vergat de koplampen uit te doen **5** (in)zien, zich voorstellen, begrijpen: *she couldn't* ~ *how he did it* ze begreep niet hoe hij het voor elkaar had gekregen **6** verwachten, vermoeden, bedacht zijn op: *she never thought to see us here* ze had nooit verwacht ons hier te treffen || ~ *nothing of sth.* iets niets bijzonders vinden, zijn hand voor iets niet omdraaien

thinker denker, geleerde, filosoof
thinking 1 het (na)denken: *way of* ~ denkwijze, zienswijze **2** mening, oordeelʰ
thinking cap: *put on one's* ~ diep nadenken
think of 1 denken aan, rekening houden met: *(just, to) think of it!* stel je (eens) voor! **2** (erover) denken om, van plan zijn: *be thinking of doing sth.* van plan zijn iets te doen; *he would never* ~ *(doing) such a thing* zoiets zou nooit bij hem opkomen **3** [after cannot, could not, try, want etc] zich herinneren **4** bedenken, voorstellen, verzinnen, (uit)vinden: ~ *a number* neem een getal in gedachten **5** aanzien, aanslaan: *think highly of* een hoge dunk hebben van || *think better of it* zich bedenken, ervan afzien
think-tank denktank, groep specialisten
thin-skinned overgevoelig, lichtgeraakt
third derde; [mus] terts: ~ *in line* (als) derde op de lijst; *in* ~ *(gear)* in zijn drie, in zijn derde versnelling
third-degree derdegraads-
thirdly op de derde plaats
third-party tegenover derden: ~ *insurance* aansprakelijkheidsverzekering, WA-verzekering
third-rate derderangs
Third World derde wereld
¹thirst (n) dorst [also fig]; sterk verlangenʰ
²thirst (vb) sterk verlangen: ~ *after* (or: *for*) snakken naar; ~ *after revenge* op wraak belust zijn
thirsty 1 dorstig: *be* (or: *feel*) ~ dorst hebben **2** verlangend: *be* ~ *for* snakken naar
thirteen dertien
thirteenth dertiende
thirtieth dertigste
thirty dertig: *he's in his early* (or: *late*) *thirties* hij is voor (*or:* achter) in de dertig
¹this (dem pron) **1** dit, deze, die, dat: *these are my daughters* dit zijn mijn dochters; *what's all* ~? wat is hier allemaal aan de hand?, wat heeft dit allemaal te betekenen?; ~ *is where I live* hier woon ik; *do it like* ~

doe het zo **2** nu, dit: ~ *is a good moment to stop* dit is een goed moment om te stoppen; *after* ~ hierna; *at* ~ op dit ogenblik; *for all* ~ ondanks dit alles **3** [what is just over] laatste, voorbije: *she's so grumpy these days* ze is tegenwoordig zo humeurig; ~ *morning* vanmorgen **4** [what is coming] komende, aanstaande: *where are you travelling* ~ *summer?* waar ga je de komende zomer naartoe? **5** [inform] een (zekere), zo'n: ~ *fellow came cycling along* er kwam een kerel aanfietsen
²this (adv) zo: *I know* ~ *much,* that the idea is crazy ik weet in elk geval dat het een krankzinnig idee is
thistle distel
thither daarheen, ginds
thong 1 (leren) riempjeʰ **2** (-s) [Am] (teen)slipper; sandaal **3** string [underware]
thorn 1 doorn **2** doornstruik || *a* ~ *in one's flesh* (or: *side*) een doorn in het vlees (*or:* oog)
thorny 1 doorn(acht)ig, stekelig **2** lastig **3** ergerlijk
thorough 1 grondig, diepgaand: *a* ~ *change* een ingrijpende verandering **2** echt, volmaakt: *a* ~ *fool* een volslagen idioot
¹thoroughbred (n) rasdierʰ, raspaardʰ
²thoroughbred (adj) volbloed, rasecht; ras- [also fig]
thoroughfare 1 (drukke) verkeersweg, verkeersader, belangrijke waterweg **2** doorgang, doortocht, doorreis: *no* ~ geen doorgaand verkeer, verboden toegang, doodlopende weg
thoroughgoing 1 zeer grondig, volledig: ~ *cooperation* verregaande samenwerking **2** echt, volmaakt
thou gij: ~ *shalt not kill* gij zult niet doden
¹though (adv) niettemin, desondanks, toch wel: *I really liked the first part,* ~ maar het eerste deel vond ik echt heel goed
²though (conj) hoewel: ~ *he smiles I do not trust him* hoewel hij glimlacht vertrouw ik hem niet; ~ *only six, he is a bright lad* hoewel hij nog maar zes jaar is, is hij een slim jongetje || *as* ~ alsof
thought 1 gedachte: *perish the* ~! ik moet er niet aan denken! **2** bedoeling, planʰ: *she had no* ~ *of hurting him* het was niet haar bedoeling om hem pijn te doen **3** ideeʰ, opinie **4** het denken, gedachte: *in* ~ in gedachten verzonken **5** denkwijze **6** de rede, het denkvermogen **7** het nadenken, de aandacht: *after serious* ~ na rijp beraad **8** hoop, verwachting: *I had given up all* ~ *of ever getting away from there* ik had alle hoop opgegeven er nog ooit vandaan te komen || *have second* ~s zich bedenken
thoughtful 1 nadenkend **2** diepzinnig **3** attent, zorgzaam
thoughtless 1 gedachteloos **2** onnaden-

kend **3** roekeloos **4** onattent, zelfzuchtig
tho̲usand duizend; [fig] talloos
tho̲usandth duizendste
thrash 1 geselen, aframmelen **2** verslaan,
niets heel laten van ‖ ~ *out a solution* tot een
oplossing komen
thra̲shing 1 pak^h rammel **2** nederlaag
¹**thread** (n) **1** draad; [fig also] lijn: *lose the ~
of one's story* de draad van zijn verhaal kwijtraken; *take up* (or: *pick up*) *the ~s* de draad
weer opnemen **2** garen^h **3** schroefdraad ‖
hang by a (single) ~ aan een zijden draad
hangen
²**thread** (vb) **1** een draad steken in [needle]
2 rijgen [beads] **3** inpassen; inleggen [film,
sound tape etc] **4** zich een weg banen door;
[fig] zich heen worstelen door **5** banen, zoeken, vinden: *~ one's way through the crowd*
zich een weg banen door de menigte
thre̲adbare 1 versleten, kaal **2** armoedig:
a ~ joke een afgezaagde grap
threat 1 dreigement^h, bedreiging: *under ~
of* onder bedreiging met **2** gevaar^h, bedreiging: *they are a ~ to society* ze vormen een
gevaar voor de maatschappij
¹**thre̲aten** (vb) **1** dreigen (te gebeuren) **2** er
dreigend uitzien: *the weather is ~ing* de lucht
ziet er dreigend uit
²**thre̲aten** (vb) **1** bedreigen, een dreigement uiten tegen, een gevaar vormen voor:
peace is ~ed de vrede is in gevaar **2** dreigen
(met): *they ~ed to kill him* ze dreigden hem te
doden
three drie, drietal, drietje, maat drie, drie
uur: *~ parts* drie vierde, driekwart
three-co̲rnered 1 driehoekig **2** driehoeks-
, tussen drie partijen
¹**three-D** (n) driedimensionale vorm
²**three-D** (adj) driedimensionaal
three-dime̲nsional 1 driedimensionaal
2 stereoscopisch
thre̲efold drievoudig
thre̲e-peat [Am; inform] derde overwinning op rij: *pull off a ~* drie keer achterelkaar
winnen
thre̲e-piece driedelig: *~ suit* driedelig pak
three-qua̲rter driekwart
thre̲esome drietal^h, driemanschap^h
thre̲shing machine dorsmachine
thre̲shold 1 drempel [also fig]; aanvang,
begin^h: *~ of pain* pijndrempel **2** ingang
thrice drie maal
thrift zuinigheid, spaarzaamheid
thri̲fty zuinig, spaarzaam
¹**thrill** (n) **1** beving, golf van ontroering
2 huivering [of fear, horror]: *he felt a ~ of
horror* hij huiverde van afgrijzen **3** opwindende gebeurtenis: *it was quite a ~* het was
heel opwindend
²**thrill** (vb) **1** beven, aangegrepen worden
2 huiveren

³**thrill** (vb) **1** doen beven, opwinden: *be ~ed
(to bits) with sth.* ontzettend gelukkig met
iets zijn **2** doen huiveren, angst aanjagen
thri̲ller iets opwindends, thriller, spannend
misdaadverhaal^h
thri̲lling spannend, opwindend
thrive gedijen, floreren, bloeien: *he seems
to ~ on hard work* hard werken schijnt hem
goed te doen
throat 1 hals **2** keel, strot: *clear one's ~* zijn
keel schrapen ‖ *be at each other's ~s* elkaar in
de haren vliegen; *force* (or: *ram, thrust*) *sth.
down s.o.'s ~* iem. iets opdringen
¹**throb** (n) klop, geklop^h, gebons^h
²**throb** (vb) **1** kloppen **2** bonzen; bonken [of
heart]
throe heftige pijn ‖ [fig] *in the ~s of* worste-
lend met
thrombo̲sis trombose
throne troon, zetel; [fig also] macht; heerschappij
¹**throng** (n) menigte, mensenmassa
²**throng** (vb) zich verdringen, toestromen
³**throng** (vb) vullen, overstelpen, overvol
maken: *people ~ed the streets* de straten zagen zwart van de mensen
¹**thro̲ttle** (n) [techn] smoorklep
²**thro̲ttle** (vb) **1** doen stikken, (ver)smoren;
[fig also] onderdrukken **2** wurgen **3** gas
minderen [car]
thro̲ttle ba̲ck afremmen [also fig]; (vaart)
minderen
¹**through** (adj) doorgaand, doorlopend: *~
train* doorgaande trein; *no ~ road* geen
doorgaand verkeer
²**through** (adv) **1** door, verder: *go ~ with*
doorgaan met **2** door(heen): *read sth. ~*
a) iets doornemen; b) iets uitlezen **3** klaar,
erdoorheen **4** helemaal, van begin tot eind:
get soaked (or: *wet*) *~* doornat worden; *~
and through* door en door, in hart en nieren
‖ *are you ~?* a) heeft u verbinding? [tele-
phone]; b) [Am] bent u klaar?; *I will put you ~*
ik zal u doorverbinden
³**through** (prep) **1** (helemaal) door, via,
langs, over, gedurende: *seen ~ a child's eyes*
gezien met de ogen van een kind; *he remained calm ~ the whole trial* hij bleef kalm
gedurende het hele proces; *~ and through*
helemaal door(heen) [also fig] **2** [manner]
door middel van: *he spoke ~ his representative* hij sprak via zijn vertegenwoordiger
3 [cause] door, wegens, uit: *he could not travel ~ illness* hij kon wegens ziekte niet reizen
4 [Am] tot en met: *Monday thru Thursday* van
maandag tot en met donderdag
¹**througho̲ut** (adv) helemaal, door en door,
steeds: *our aim has been ~ …* ons doel is
steeds geweest …
²**througho̲ut** (prep) (helemaal) door, door
heel: *~ the country* door/in heel het land

throughput 1 verwerkte hoeveelheid; productie **2** [also comp] verwerkingscapaciteit
throughway [Am] snelweg
¹throw (n) worp, gooi
²throw (vb) met iets gooien/werpen
³throw (vb) **1** werpen, gooien; [fig also] terecht doen komen: ~ *dice* dobbelstenen gooien, dobbelen; *the **horse** threw him* het paard wierp hem af; ~ *o.s. into sth.* zich ergens op werpen, zich enthousiast ergens in storten; *be ~n (back) upon one's own resources* op zichzelf worden teruggeworpen **2** richten, (toe)werpen, toezenden: *he threw us a sarcastic **look*** hij wierp ons een sarcastische blik toe **3** afschieten [missile] **4** omzetten, veranderen in **5** draaien [wood, earthenware] **6** snel op zijn plaats brengen/leggen, maken: ~ *the switch **to** 'off'* de schakelaar op 'uit' zetten **7** maken, hebben, organiseren: [inform] ~ *a **party*** een fuif geven **8** [inform] verwarren, van de wijs brengen ‖ ~ *open* openstellen; ~ *s.o. **into** confusion* iem. in verwarring brengen
throw about rondsmijten: *throw one's **money** about* met geld smijten
throw away 1 weggooien **2** verspelen, missen: ~ *a **chance*** een kans verspelen **3** vergooien: *throw one's money away **on*** zijn geld weggooien aan
throw-away 1 wegwerp- **2** zonder nadruk: *a ~ **remark*** een quasinonchalante opmerking
throwback 1 terugslag **2** terugkeer
throw back 1 teruggooien **2** openslaan, opzij werpen: ~ *the **blankets*** de dekens terugslaan ‖ *be thrown back **on*** moeten terugrijpen naar, weer aangewezen zijn op
throw down 1 neergooien **2** afbreken
throw in 1 erin gooien, inwerpen **2** gratis toevoegen: *I'll ~ an extra **battery*** ik doe er nog een gratis batterij bij **3** terloops opmerken **4** [sport] ingooien
throw-in [sport] inworp
throw off 1 zich bevrijden van, van zich af schudden **2** uitgooien, haastig uittrekken: ~ *one's **mask*** zijn masker afwerpen [also fig] **3** uitstoten; [also fig] produceren
throw out 1 weggooien, wegdoen **2** verwerpen, afwijzen **3** uiten, suggereren **4** geven, uitzenden: ~ *heat* warmte uitstralen **5** in de war brengen: *now all our **calculations** are thrown out* nu zijn al onze berekeningen fout **6** wegsturen, eruit gooien
throw over in de steek laten: *he threw **her** over* hij heeft haar laten zitten
throw together bij elkaar brengen, samenbrengen: *throw **people** together* mensen met elkaar in contact brengen
¹throw up (vb) **1** omhoog gooien, optillen: ~ *one's **eyes*** de ogen ten hemel slaan

2 voortbrengen **3** optrekken, opbouwen: ~ *barricades* barricaden opwerpen **4** opgeven, opzeggen: ~ *one's **job*** zijn baan vaarwel zeggen
²throw up (vb) [inform] overgeven, kotsen
thru *see* **¹through**
thrum 1 tokkelen (op); pingelen (op) [guitar] **2** ronken, brommen, dreunen
thrush lijster
¹thrust (n) **1** stoot, duw, zet **2** steek [also fig] **3** druk, (drijf)kracht **4** beweging, strevenʰ, richting **5** [mil] uitval
²thrust (vb) **1** uitvallen, toestoten **2** dringen, worstelen: ~ *in* zich een weg banen naar binnen
³thrust (vb) **1** stoten **2** steken, stoppen: *he ~ his hands **into** his pockets* hij stak zijn handen in zijn zakken **3** duwen, dringen: *she ~ her way **through** the crowd* ze worstelde zich door de menigte heen ‖ ~ *sth. **upon** s.o.* iem. ergens mee opschepen
¹thud (n) plof, slag, bons
²thud (vb) (neer)ploffen, bonzen
thug misdadiger, moordenaar
thuggery gewelddadigheid
¹thumb (n) duim ‖ *give the ~s up* (or: *down*) goedkeuren, afkeuren; *twiddle one's ~s* duimendraaien; *~s **down*** afgewezen; *~s **up!*** a) prima!; b) kop op!, hou je taai; *be **under** s.o.'s ~* bij iem. onder de plak zitten
²thumb (vb) (+ through) (door)bladeren [eg book]
³thumb (vb) **1** beduimelen, vuile vingerafdrukken achterlaten in **2** vragen [lift]; liften: ~ *a **ride*** liften
thumbnail 1 duimnagel **2** [comp] thumbnail, postzegel
thumb tack [Am] punaise
¹thump (n) dreun, klap
²thump (vb) dreunen, bonzen
³thump (vb) **1** dreunen op, beuken: *he was ~ing **out** a well-known song* timmerend op de toetsen speelde hij een bekend liedje **2** stompen **3** een pak slaag geven
⁴thump (adv) met een dreun: *the boy **ran** ~ with his head against the bookcase* de jongen liep 'bam' met zijn hoofd tegen de boekenkast
thumping geweldig
¹thunder (n) **1** donder, onweerʰ **2** gedonderʰ [also fig] ‖ *steal s.o.'s ~* met de eer gaan strijken
²thunder (vb) **1** donderen, onweren **2** denderen, dreunen **3** donderen, razen, tekeergaan
³thunder (vb) uitbulderen, brullen: ~ *out curses* verwensingen uitschreeuwen
thunderbolt 1 bliksemflits **2** donderslag, schok, klap
thunderclap donderslag [also fig]
thunder-cloud onweerswolk

thundering 1 donderend 2 kolossaal
thunderstorm onweersbui
thunderstruck (als) door de bliksem getroffen
thundery 1 onweerachtig 2 dreigend
Thursday donderdag
thus (al)dus, zo || ~ *far* tot hier toe, tot nu
toe
thwart 1 verijdelen, dwarsbomen 2 tegenwerken, tegenhouden
THX *thanks* dank je
thy uw
thyme tijm
thyroid gland schildklier
¹**tick** (n) 1 tik, getikʰ [of clock] 2 momentjeʰ,
ogenblikjeʰ: *in two ~s* in een wip 3 vink(jeʰ);
(merk)teken(tjeʰ) [used on checklist] 4 kre-
dietʰ, pof: *on ~* op de pof
²**tick** (vb) tikken: ~ *away* (or: *by*) a) tikken;
b) voorbijgaan [time] || *what makes* s.o. *(sth.)*
~ wat iem. drijft; ~ *over* a) stationair draaien
[of engine]; b) [inform] zijn gangetje gaan
³**tick** (vb) aanstrepen [on list] || ~ *off* een uit-
brander geven
ticker 1 horlogeʰ, klok 2 hartʰ, rikketik
ticker-tape serpentine
¹**ticket** (n) 1 kaart(jeʰ), toegangsbewijsʰ,
plaatsbewijsʰ: ~ *tout* zwarthandelaar in
kaartjes 2 prijskaartjeʰ, etiketʰ 3 bon, bekeuring: *parking* ~ bon voor foutparkeren;
speeding ~ bon voor te hard rijden 4 [Am]
kandidatenlijst || *that's just the* ~ dát is het
(precies), dát is precies wat we nodig hebben, dát is wat we zoeken
²**ticket** (vb) 1 etiketteren, prijzen 2 bestemmen, aanduiden 3 [Am] een bon geven
ticket collector (kaartjes)controleur; conducteur
ticketing kaartverkoop
ticket office kassa [eg in theatre]; loketʰ
[eg in station]
¹**tickle** (n) gekietelʰ, kietelend gevoelʰ
²**tickle** (vb) 1 kietelen, kriebelen; [fig] (aangenaam) prikkelen 2 amuseren, aan het lachen maken: *amuseren: ~d to death* zich kostelijk
amuseren
ticklish 1 kietelig: *be* ~ niet (*or:* slecht) tegen kietelen kunnen 2 netelig
tidal getijden-: ~ *river* getijdenrivier
tidal wave getijdengolf, vloedgolf; [fig]
golf van emotie
tiddler 1 visjeʰ 2 klein kindʰ; [fig] klein
broertjeʰ
tiddly 1 aangeschoten 2 klein
tiddlywinks vlooienspel
tide 1 getij(de)ʰ, tijʰ: *high* ~ vloed; *low* ~ eb;
[fig] *turn the* ~ het getijde doen keren
2 stroom; stroming [also fig]: [inform, fig]
swim (or: *go*) *with the* ~ met de stroom mee
gaan
tidemark hoogwaterlijn

¹**tide over** (vb) helpen over: *she gave me £15
to tide me over the next two days* ze gaf me £15
om me door de volgende twee dagen te helpen
²**tide over** (vb) (iem.) verder helpen, (iem.)
voorthelpen [financially]
tideway 1 stroombedʰ 2 eb in stroombed
tidings tijding(en)
¹**tidy** (n) opbergdoosjeʰ voor prulletjes
²**tidy** (adj) 1 netjes, keurig, op orde 2 proper
3 aardig (groot): ~ *income* aardig inkomen
³**tidy** (vb) opruimen, schoonmaken: ~ *away*
opruimen; ~ *up* opruimen, in orde brengen
¹**tie** (n) 1 touw(tje)ʰ, koordʰ 2 (strop)das
3 band, verbondenheid 4 [sport, game] gelijk spelʰ 5 [sport] (afval)wedstrijd, voorronde
²**tie** (vb) 1 vastgemaakt worden 2 een knoop
leggen 3 [sport] gelijk eindigen: *they ~d for a
second place* ze deelden de tweede plaats || ~
in (with) verband houden (met); [fig] kloppen
³**tie** (vb) 1 (vast)binden, (vast)knopen: *his
hands are ~d* zijn handen zijn gebonden
[fig]; ~ *a knot* een knoop leggen; ~ *back* op-
binden, bijeen binden [eg hair] 2 (ver)bin-
den 3 binden, beperken: ~ *down* de handen
binden, bezighouden; ~ s.o. *down to* iem.
zich laten houden aan 4 [sport] gelijk spelen,
staan met: ~*d game* gelijkspel
tiebreak(er) beslissingswedstrijd; [tennis]
tiebreak(er)
tied (vast)gebonden: ~ *house* gebonden
café [selling beer from one particular brew-
ery]
tie-dye met de tie-and-dyetechniek verven
tie-on hang-: ~ *label* hangetiket
tiepin dasspeld
tier rij, verdieping; rang [eg in theatre]
¹**tie up** (vb) 1 afgemeerd worden 2 verband
houden 3 kloppen || ~ *with* verband houden
met, kloppen met
²**tie up** (vb) 1 vastbinden, verbinden, dichtbinden: ~ *a dog* een hond vastleggen; [fig]
be tied up with verband houden met 2 afmeren 3 (druk) bezighouden, ophouden, stopzetten: *be tied up* bezet zijn 4 vastzetten,
vastleggen [money]
tiff ruzietjeʰ
tiger tijger
¹**tight** (adj) 1 strak, nauw(sluitend), krap: ~
shoes te nauwe schoenen 2 propvol: *a* ~
schedule een overladen programma 3 potdicht 4 beklemmend: *be in a* ~ *corner* (or:
place, spot) in een lastig parket zitten
5 schaars, krap 6 gierig 7 stevig, vast
8 streng: *keep a* ~ *grip* (or: *hold*) *on* s.o. iem.
goed in de hand houden 9 [inform] dronken
|| *a* ~ *squeeze* een hele toer
²**tight** (adv) vast, stevig: *hold me* ~ hou me
stevig vast; *good night, sleep* ~ goedenacht,
welterusten

¹**tighten** (vb) **1** zich spannen, strakker worden **2** krap worden

²**tighten** (vb) **1** aanhalen, spannen, vastsnoeren: ~ *one's belt* de buikriem aanhalen [fig] **2** vastklemmen, vastdraaien **3** verscherpen [measure]: ~ *up* verscherpen

tight-fisted krenterig

tight-fitting nauwsluitend

tightknit hecht: *a ~ society* een hechte maatschappij

tight-lipped 1 met opeengeklemde lippen **2** gesloten, stil

tightrope walker koorddanser

tights panty: *(a pair of)* ~ een panty

tightwad vrek

tigress tijgerin

tile tegel, (dak)pan || *he has a ~ loose* d'r zit een steekje los bij hem; *be (out) on the ~s* aan de zwier zijn

¹**till** (n) geldlade, kassa

²**till** (vb) bewerken [soil]

³**till** (prep) [time] tot (aan), voor: ~ *tomorrow* tot morgen; *not ~ after dinner* niet vóór het middageten

⁴**till** (conj) [time] tot(dat), voordat: *he read ~ Harry arrived* hij las tot Harry (aan)kwam; *it was a long time ~ she came home* het duurde lang voor zij thuis kwam

tiller roerʰ, roerpen, helmstok

¹**tilt** (n) **1** schuine stand: *he wore his hat at a ~* hij had zijn hoed schuin op **2** steekspelʰ; [fig] woordenwisseling

²**tilt** (vb) **1** scheef staan, (over)hellen: ~ *over* wippen, kantelen **2** op en neer gaan, wiegelen, schommelen

³**tilt** (vb) scheef houden/zetten, doen (over)hellen, kantelen

timber 1 balk **2** (timmer)houtʰ || ~*!* van onderen!

timbered in vakwerk uitgevoerd: *a ~ house* een huis in vakwerk

¹**time** (n) **1** tijd, tijdsduur: *gain ~* tijd winnen; *kill ~* de tijd doden; *lose no ~* geen tijd verliezen, direct doen; *take one's ~* zich niet haasten; ~ *and (~)* again steeds opnieuw; *in next to no ~* in een mum van tijd; *let's take some ~ off* (or: ~ *out*) laten we er even tussenuit gaan; *I'm working against ~* ik moet me (vreselijk) haasten, het is een race tegen de klok; *for a ~* een tijdje; *all the ~* **a)** de hele tijd, voortdurend; **b)** altijd **2** tijdstipʰ, tijd: *do you have the ~?* weet u hoe laat het is?; *keep (good) ~* goed lopen [of clock]; *at the ~* toen, indertijd; *by the ~ the police arrived ...* tegen de tijd dat de politie arriveerde ...; *what ~ is it?, what's the ~?* hoe laat is het? **3** (-s) tijdperkʰ, periode: *move with the ~s* met zijn tijd meegaan; *at one ~* vroeger, eens; *be behind the ~s* achterlopen, niet meer van deze tijd zijn; *once upon a ~* er was eens **4** gelegenheid, momentʰ: *have ~ on one's hands* ge-

noeg vrije tijd hebben; *any ~* altijd, om 't even wanneer; *every ~* elke keer, altijd, steeds (*or:* telkens) (weer); *many ~s, many a ~* vaak, dikwijls **5** keer, maal⁺ʰ: *nine ~s out of ten* bijna altijd, negen op de tien keer **6** [mus] maat: *keep ~* in de maat blijven, de maat houden **7** tempoʰ: ~ *signature* maataanduiding || *pass the ~ of day with s.o.* iem. goedendag zeggen, even met iem. staan praten; *I had the ~ of my life* ik heb ontzettend genoten; *since ~ out of mind* sinds onheuglijke tijden; *do ~* zitten [in prison]; *I have no ~ for him* ik mag hem niet, ik heb een hekel aan hem; *mark ~* [mil] pas op de plaats maken; [fig] een afwachtende houding aannemen; *play for ~* tijd rekken; ~ *will tell* de tijd zal het uitwijzen; ~*'s up!* het is de hoogste tijd!; *(and) about ~ too!* (en) het werd ook tijd; ~ *after ~* keer op keer; *at all ~s* altijd, te allen tijde; *one at a ~* één tegelijk; *at the same ~* **a)** tegelijkertijd; **b)** toch; *at ~s* soms; *for the ~ being* voorlopig; *from ~ to ~* van tijd tot tijd; *in ~* **a)** op tijd; **b)** na verloop van tijd; *on ~* **a)** op tijd; **b)** op afbetaling

²**time** (vb) **1** vaststellen, berekenen [time, duration]: *the train is ~d to leave at four o'clock* de trein moet om vier uur vertrekken **2** het juiste moment kiezen voor (om te): *his visit was ill ~d* zijn bezoek kwam ongelegen **3** klokken

time bomb tijdbom [also fig]

time clock prikklok

time-consuming tijdrovend

time exposure tijdopname

time-honoured traditioneel

timekeeper 1 uurwerkʰ: *my watch is a good ~* mijn horloge loopt altijd op tijd **2** tijdwaarnemer, tijdopnemer

time lag pauze [between two consecutive occurrences]; tijdsverloopʰ, vertraging, tijdsinterval

timeless 1 oneindig, eeuwig **2** tijd(e)loos

time limit tijdslimiet

timeline tijdbalk; tijdlijn

timely 1 tijdig **2** van pas komend, gelegen

time out time-out, onderbreking

timepiece uurwerkʰ, klok, horlogeʰ

timer 1 timer [eg on video] **2** tijdopnemer **3** tijdwaarnemer

timeserving opportunistisch

timeshare deeltijdeigenaarschapʰ

time-sharing deeltijdeigenaarschapʰ

time switch tijdschakelaar

¹**timetable** (n) **1** dienstregeling **2** (les)roosterʰ

²**timetable** (vb) plannen, inroosteren

³**timetable** (vb) een rooster maken

time trialist tijdrijder

time warp vervorming van de tijd, tijdsvervorming

time-wasting het tijdrekken, het tijdwin-

nen, spelbederf[h]
time-worn 1 versleten, oud **2** afgezaagd
time zone tijdzone
timid 1 bang, angstig **2** timide, verlegen
timidity 1 angst **2** bedeesdheid
timing timing
timorous 1 bang, angstig **2** timide, bedeesd
timpani pauk(en)
timpanist paukenist
[1]**tin** (n) **1** tin[h] **2** blik[h] **3** blik(je[h]), conservenblik[h] **4** bus
[2]**tin** (adj) **1** tinnen: ~ *soldier* tinnen soldaatje
2 blikken: ~ *can* (leeg) blikje; ~ *whistle* blikken fluitje **3** prullerig
[3]**tin** (vb) inblikken
tincture 1 tinctuur **2** [form] vleugje[h] **3** tint
tinder 1 tondel **2** olie op het vuur
tinderbox 1 tondeldoos **2** [fig] kruitvat[h]
tine 1 scherpe punt[h]; tand [of (pitch)fork]
2 geweitak
tinfoil aluminiumfolie[h]
[1]**tinge** (n) tint(je[h]) [also fig]
[2]**tinge** (vb) **1** tinten **2** doortrekken: *comedy*
~d with tragedy tragikomedie
[1]**tingle** (n) tinteling
[2]**tingle** (vb) **1** opgewonden zijn, popelen
2 (laten) tintelen; (doen) suizen [of ears]
[1]**tinker** (n) ketellapper
[2]**tinker** (vb) **1** ketellappen **2** (+ at, with)
prutsen (aan)
[1]**tinkle** (n) **1** gerinkel[h] **2** plasje[h] **3** telefoontje[h]
[2]**tinkle** (vb) **1** rinkelen, tingelen **2** plassen
[3]**tinkle** (vb) laten rinkelen
tinny 1 tin-, blikachtig **2** metaalachtig [of
sound] **3** waardeloos
tin-opener blikopener
tinplate blik[h]
tinpot waardeloos
tinsel klatergoud[h] [also fig]
[1]**tint** (n) **1** (pastel)tint **2** kleurshampoo
[2]**tint** (vb) kleuren
tiny heel klein, nietig
[1]**tip** (n) **1** tipje[h], topje[h], punt[h]; filter[h] [of ciga-
rette]; pomerans [on billiard cue]: *the ~ of the*
iceberg het topje van de ijsberg **2** stort[h],
stortplaats; [fig] zwijnenstal **3** fooi **4** tip,
raad: *give s.o. a ~ on* iem. een tip geven over
5 tik(je[h]), duwtje[h] || *have sth. on the ~ of one's*
tongue iets voor op de tong hebben liggen
[2]**tip** (vb) **1** kiep(er)en, kantelen: *these bunks ~*
up deze slaapbanken klappen omhoog
2 omkantelen: ~ *over* omvallen **3** fooien uitdelen
[3]**tip** (vb) **1** doen overhellen: ~ *sth. up* iets
schuin houden **2** doen omslaan, omvergooi-
en: ~ *over* omgooien **3** (weg)kieperen
4 overgieten **5** aantikken, eventjes aanraken **6** tippen, (als fooi) geven **7** tippen, als
kanshebber aanwijzen

tip off waarschuwen, een tip geven
tip-off waarschuwing, hint
tipper 1 fooiengever **2** kiepauto
tipping point omslagpunt[h]
[1]**tipple** (n) (sterke)drank, drankje[h]
[2]**tipple** (vb) aan de drank zijn, pimpelen
tipster tipgever, informant
tipsy aangeschoten
tiptoe op zijn tenen lopen || *on* ~ a) op zijn
tenen, stilletjes; b) vol verwachting
tip-top 1 tiptop, piekfijn **2** chic
tip-up: *a ~ seat* een klapstoeltje
tirade tirade; scheldkanonnade
[1]**tire** (n) **1** hoepel **2** band
[2]**tire** (vb) **1** moe worden **2** (+ of) beu worden: *I never ~ of it* het verveelt me nooit
[3]**tire** (vb) **1** (also + out) afmatten, vermoeien
2 vervelen
tired 1 moe: ~ *out* doodop **2** afgezaagd ||
be ~ of sth. iets beu zijn
tireless 1 onvermoeibaar **2** onophoudelijk
tiresome 1 vermoeiend **2** vervelend, saai
tiro beginneling, beginner
tissue 1 doekje[h], gaasje[h] **2** papieren (zak)-
doekje[h], velletje vloeipapier[h] **3** web[h], netwerk[h]: ~ *of lies* aaneenschakeling van leugens **4** (cel)weefsel[h]
tissue paper zijdepapier[h]
tit 1 mees **2** [inform] tiet, tepel **3** sukkel,
klier
titan 1 [mythology] titan **2** kolos
titanic reusachtig
titbit 1 lekker hapje[h] **2** interessant nieuwtje[h], roddeltje[h]
tit-for-tat vergeldings-, uit wraak
tit-for-tat policy lik-op-stukbeleid[h]
tithe tiend[+h]
titillate prikkelen, aangenaam opwinden
titivate mooi maken, opdirken
title titel, titelblad[h]; [sport] kampioen-
(schap); [law] eigendomsrecht[h]; ondertitel,
aftiteling [of film]
titled met een (adellijke) titel
title deed eigendomsakte
title-holder titelhouder, titelhoudster
title page titelpagina
titmouse [form] mees
[1]**titter** (n) gegiechel[h]
[2]**titter** (vb) (onderdrukt/nerveus) giechelen
tittle tittel [also fig]; puntje[h]
[1]**tittle-tattle** (n) kletspraat, roddelpraat
[2]**tittle-tattle** (vb) kletsen
T-junction 1 T-kruising **2** T-stuk[h]
[1]**to** (adv) **1** [direction] (er)heen: *to and fro*
heen en weer **2** [place; also fig] tegen, bij,
eraan: *bring s.o. to* iem. bijbrengen
[2]**to** (prep) **1** naar, naar … toe, tot: *pale to clear*
blue bleek tot hel blauw; *drink to her health*
op haar gezondheid drinken; *they remained*
loyal to a man ze bleven stuk voor stuk
trouw; *to my mind* volgens mij; *travel to Rome*

naar Rome reizen; *from bad to* **worse** van kwaad tot erger **2** [place; also fig] tegen, op, in: *I've been to my* **aunt's** ik ben bij mijn tante gaan logeren; *we beat them eleven to* **seven** we hebben ze met elf (tegen) zeven verslagen **3** [in comparison] met, ten opzichte van, voor: *use 50* **lbs.** *to the acre* gebruik 50 pond per acre; *superior to synthetic* **fabric** beter dan synthetische stof; *compared to* **Jack** vergeleken bij Jack; *true to* **nature** natuurgetrouw; *I'm new to the* **place** ik ben hier nieuw; *made to* **size** op maat gemaakt **4** [time] tot, tot op, op: *three years ago to the* **day** precies drie jaar geleden; *stay to the* **end** tot het einde blijven; *five (minutes) to* **three** vijf (minuten) voor drie **5** bij, aan, van: *the* **key** *to the house* de sleutel van het huis; *there's more to* **it** er zit meer achter
³to [often untranslated] **1** te: *I don't* **want** *to apologize* ik wil mij niet verontschuldigen **2** dat, het: *I don't* **want** *to* dat wil ik niet
toad [zoology] pad
toadstool paddenstoel
¹toady (n) vleier
²toady (vb) vleien: ~ *to s.o.* iem. vleien
to-and-fro heen en weer (gaand), schommelend
¹toast (n) **1** toost, (heil)dronk: **propose** *a ~ to s.o.* een toost uitbrengen op iem. **2** geroosterde boterham, toast || **have** *s.o. on ~* iem. helemaal in zijn macht hebben
²toast (vb) **1** roosteren, toast maken van: [fig] ~ *o.s. at the fire* zich warmen bij het vuur **2** toosten op
toaster broodrooster[h]
toastmaster ceremoniemeester [at dinner]
tobacco tabak
tobacconist tabakshandelaar
¹toboggan (n) slee
²toboggan (vb) sleeën, rodelen
tod: *on one's* ~ in z'n uppie
today vandaag, tegenwoordig
toddle 1 waggelen **2** kuieren: ~ **round** (or: *over*) even aanlopen **3** (also + along) opstappen
toddler dreumes, hummel
to-die-for [inform; mockingly] voortreffelijk; om je vingers bij af te likken
to-do drukte, gedoe[h], ophef
toe teen, neus, punt[h] || **turn** *up one's ~s* de pijp uitgaan; *on one's ~s* alert
toecap neus [of shoe]
toehold steunpuntje[h]; [fig] houvast[h]; opstapje[h]
toenail teennagel
toff fijne meneer: *the ~s* de rijkelui
toffee toffee
toffee-nosed snobistisch, verwaand
tofu tofoe, tahoe
toga toga

together 1 samen, bijeen: *come* ~ samenkomen **2** tegelijk(ertijd): *all* ~ *now* nu allemaal tegelijk **3** aaneen, bij elkaar, tegen elkaar: *tie* ~ aan elkaar binden **4** [inform] voor elkaar, geregeld: *get things* ~ de boel regelen **5** achtereen, zonder tussenpozen: *for* **hours** ~ uren aan een stuk, uren achter elkaar || ~ *with* met
togetherness saamhorigheid
toggle 1 knevel, pin **2** houtje[h] [on duffel coat]
Togo Togo
¹Togolese (n) Togolees, Togolese
²Togolese (adj) Togolees
togs kloffie, plunje
¹toil (n) gezwoeg[h]
²toil (vb) **1** (+ at, on) hard werken (aan): ~ *away* ploeteren **2** moeizaam vooruitkomen
toilet 1 wc, toilet[h] **2** toilet[h], gewaad[h]: **make** *one's* ~ toilet maken **3** toilettafel, kaptafel
toilet bag toilettas
toilet paper wc-papier[h]
toilet roll closetrol, wc-rol
toiletry 1 toiletartikel[h] **2** toiletgerei[h]
¹token (n) **1** teken[h], blijk, bewijs[h]: *in* ~ *of* ten teken van **2** herinnering, aandenken[h] **3** bon, cadeaubon **4** munt, fiche[h], penning
²token (adj) symbolisch: ~ *resistance* symbolisch verzet
tolerable 1 draaglijk **2** toelaatbaar **3** redelijk
tolerance 1 verdraagzaamheid, tolerantie: ~ *of* (or: *to*) *hardship* het verdragen van ontberingen **2** toegestane afwijking, tolerantie, speling
tolerant verdraagzaam
tolerate 1 tolereren, verdragen **2** (kunnen) verdragen
toleration verdraagzaamheid
¹toll (n) **1** tol; [fig] prijs: **take** *a heavy* ~ een zware tol eisen **2** kosten van een interlokaal telefoongesprek **3** (klok)gelui[h]
²toll (vb) **1** luiden [of bell] **2** slaan [the hour]
toll bridge tolbrug
toll call [Am] interlokaal telefoongesprek[h]
toll-free [Am] gratis; zonder kosten [of call]: ~ *800* **service** gratis telefoonnummer
toll road tolweg
tom kater || *(every)* Tom, **Dick** *and Harry* Jan, Piet en Klaas; *peeping* Tom gluurder
Tom Tom; Thomas || *(every)* ~, **Dick** *and* **Harry** Jan, Piet en Klaas; *peeping* ~ voyeur
tomahawk tomahawk; strijdbijl
tomato tomaat
tomb (praal)graf[h], (graf)tombe, grafmonument[h]
tombola tombola [lottery game]
tomboy wilde meid, wildebras, robbedoes
tombstone grafsteen
tomcat kater
tome (dik) boekdeel[h]

tomfool stom
tomfoolery 1 dwaasheid, flauw gedrag[h]
2 onzin
tommy gun [inform] tommygun; pistool-mitrailleur
tommyrot [inform] volslagen onzin
tomorrow morgen: *the day after* ~ over-morgen; ~ *week* morgen over een week
tomtom tamtam, trommel
ton 1 (metrieke) ton [weight; approx 1,016 kg]: [fig] *it weighs (half) a* ~ het weegt lood-zwaar **2** grote hoeveelheid **3** honderd pond, honderd mijl per uur: *do the* ~ honderd mijl per uur rijden || *come down like a* ~ *of bricks* flink tekeergaan
¹tone (n) **1** toon, klank, stem(buiging), tint: *speak in an angry* ~ op boze toon spreken **2** intonatie, accent[h] **3** [photo] toon, tint **4** [mus] (hele) toon, grote seconde **5** geest; stemming [also of market]: *set the* ~ de toon aangeven
²tone (vb) overeenstemmen: ~ *(in) with* kleuren bij
³tone (vb) **1** tinten **2** doen harmoniëren: ~ *(in) with* doen harmoniëren met, laten passen bij
tone-deaf geen (muzikaal) gehoor hebbend
tone down 1 afzwakken [also fig]: ~ *one's language* op zijn woorden passen **2** verzachten
toneless 1 toonloos, monotoon **2** kleurloos
toner inkt [for printers and copiers]
tongs tang: *pair of* ~ tang
tongue 1 tong, spraak **2** taal **3** tongvormig iets; lipje[h] [of shoe]; landtong; klepel [of bell] || *(speak) with* ~ *in cheek* spottend (spreken); *hold your* ~*!* houd je mond!; *have lost one's* ~ zijn tong verloren hebben; *set* ~*s wagging* de tongen in beweging brengen
tongue-in-cheek ironisch, spottend
tongue-tied met de mond vol tanden
tongue-twister tongbreker, moeilijk uit te spreken woord[h]/zin
tonic versterkend middel[h] [also fig]
tonic water tonic
tonight 1 vanavond **2** vannacht
tonsil (keel)amandel: *have one's* ~*s out* zijn amandelen laten knippen
tonsil(l)itis amandelontsteking
tonsure tonsuur
too 1 te (zeer): ~ *good to be true* te mooi om waar te zijn **2** [inform] erg, al te: *it's* ~ *bad* (het is) erg jammer **3** ook, eveneens: *he,* ~*, went to Rome* híj ging ook naar Rome; *he went to Rome,* ~ hij ging ook naar Róme **4** bovendien: *they did it; on Sunday* ~*!* zij hebben het gedaan; en nog wel op zondag!
¹tool (n) **1** handwerktuig[h], (stuk[h]) gereed-schap[h], instrument[h]: *down* ~*s* het werk neer-

leggen [in protest] **2** werktuig[h]
²tool (vb) toeren, rijden: ~ *along* rondtoeren, voortsnorren
³tool (vb) bewerken
toolbar [comp] werkbalk
toolbox gereedschapskist
toolkit (set) gereedschappen
tool-shed gereedschapsschuurtje[h]
¹toot (n) **1** (hoorn)stoot **2** getoeter[h]
²toot (vb) toeteren, blazen (op)
tooth 1 tand [also of comb, saw]; kies: *teeth* gebit[h]; [fig] *(fight)* ~ *and nail* met hand en tand (vechten); [fig] *armed to the teeth* tot de tanden gewapend; [fig] *get one's teeth into sth.* ergens zijn tanden in zetten **2** (teeth) [inform] kracht, effect[h] || [inform] *be fed up to the (back) teeth* er schoon genoeg van hebben; *kick in the teeth* voor het hoofd stoten; *the sound set his teeth on edge* het geluid ging hem door merg en been
toothache tandpijn, kiespijn
toothbrush tandenborstel
toothed 1 getand **2** met tanden
toothless 1 tandeloos **2** krachteloos
toothpaste tandpasta
toothpick tandenstoker
toothsome lekker
toothy 1 met grote, vooruitstekende tanden **2** getand
¹tootle (n) getoeter[h]
²tootle (vb) (rond)toeren
³tootle (vb) blazen (op); toeteren (op) [instrument]
tootsy [child language] voet(je[h])
¹top (n) **1** top, hoogste punt[h]: *from* ~ *to bottom* van onder tot boven; *from* ~ *to toe* van top tot teen; *(shout) at the* ~ *of one's voice* luidkeels (schreeuwen); *on* ~ boven(aan) **2** bovenstuk[h], bovenkant, tafelblad[h]; dop [of bottle, fountain pen]; top(je[h]) [article of clothing]; deksel[+h], kroonkurk; room [on milk]; bovenrand [of page] **3** beste; belang-rijkste[h] [of form, organisation]: *be* (or: *come out*) *(at the)* ~ *of the form* de beste van de klas zijn **4** oppervlakte **5** tol [toy] || *off the* ~ *of one's head* onvoorbereid [speaking]; *(feel) on* ~ *of the world* (zich) heel gelukkig (voelen); [inform] *blow one's* ~ in woede uitbarsten; *come out on* ~ overwinnen; *get on* ~ *of sth.* iets de baas worden; *go over the* ~ **a)** te ver gaan; **b)** uit de loopgraven komen; *on* ~ *of that* daar komt nog bij, bovendien
²top (adj) hoogste, top-: ~ *drawer* bovenste la; [fig] *out of the* ~ *drawer* van goede komaf; ~ *prices* hoogste prijzen; *at* ~ *speed* op top-snelheid
³top (vb) **1** van top voorzien, bedekken: [fig] ~ *off* (or: *up*) *sth.* iets bekronen **2** de top be-reiken van [eg mountain; also fig] **3** aan de top staan [also fig]; aanvoeren [list, team] **4** overtreffen: *to* ~ *it all* tot overmaat van

ramp ‖ ~ and *tail* afhalen, doppen; ~ *up* bijvullen

topaz topaas[+h]

top boot kaplaars

topcoat 1 overjas **2** bovenste verflaag, deklaag

top copy origineel[h]

topdog [inform] heer en meester: *be* ~ het voor het zeggen hebben

top-down van boven af; van boven naar beneden [of corporate structure]

top-drawer van goede komaf

top-dress bestrooien [of sand, manure etc]

top-end van hoge kwaliteit

top flight 1 eersteklas, uitstekend **2** best mogelijk

top-gear 1 hoogste versnelling **2** topconditie: *he's back into* ~ hij draait weer op volle toeren

top hat hoge hoed

top-heavy [also fig] topzwaar

topiary 1 vormboom **2** vormsnoei

topic onderwerp[h] (van gesprek): ~ *of conversation* gespreksthema

topical 1 actueel **2** plaatselijk [also med] **3** naar onderwerp gerangschikt, thematisch

topicality actualiteit

topknot 1 (haar)knotje[h] **2** strik [in hair] **3** kam [of cock]

topless 1 zonder bovenstuk(je) **2** met topless bediening **3** topless

topmost (aller)hoogst

topnotch eersteklas

top-of-the-bill bekendst; belangrijkst

topper hoge hoed

topping toplaag(je[h]), sierlaagje[h]

[1]topple (vb) (bijna) omvallen, kantelen: ~ *down* (or: *over*) omtuimelen

[2]topple (vb) (bijna) doen omvallen, omkieperen

top-ranking van de hoogste rang; hoogstgeplaatst

tops je van het: *come out* ~ als de beste uit de bus komen

topsail marszeil[h]

top secret uiterst geheim

topside 1 bovenkant **2** [roughly] biefstuk

topsoil bovenste laag losse (teel)aarde, bovengrond

topsy-turvy ondersteboven (gekeerd), op zijn kop: *the world is going* ~ de wereld wordt op zijn kop gezet

[1]top-up (n) aanvulling

[2]top-up (adj) aanvullend

top-up card prepaidkaart

[1]torch (n) **1** toorts; fakkel [also fig] **2** zaklamp **3** soldeerlamp ‖ *carry a* (or: *the*) ~ *for s.o.* hopeloos verliefd zijn op iem.

[2]torch (vb) in brand steken

torchlight 1 fakkellicht[h] **2** licht[h] van een zaklantaarn

[1]torment (n) kwelling

[2]torment (vb) kwellen, plagen: ~*ed by mosquitoes* bestookt door muggen

tornado tornado

[1]torpedo (n) torpedo

[2]torpedo (vb) [also fig] torpederen

torpid 1 gevoelloos **2** traag **3** in winterslaap

torrent [also fig] stortvloed: *the rain fell in* ~*s* het stortregende

torrential [also fig] als een stortvloed: ~ *rains* stortregens

torrid 1 zeer heet, tropisch; verzengend [heat]: *the* ~ *zone* de tropen **2** intens

torsion torsie; wringing

torso [also fig] torso

tort onrechtmatige daad

tortoise landschildpad

tortoiseshell 1 lapjeskat **2** schildpad [as material]

tortuous 1 kronkelend; slingerend [of road] **2** omslachtig, gecompliceerd, misleidend, bedrieglijk

[1]torture (n) marteling, zware kwelling

[2]torture (vb) martelen: ~*d by doubt* (or: *jealousy*) gekweld door twijfel (or: jaloezie)

torture chamber martelkamer, folterkamer

torturer folteraar, beul

Tory conservatief, lid[h] van de conservatieve partij in Groot-Brittannië

tosh onzin

[1]toss (n) **1** worp **2** beweging, knik, slinger, zwaai, val: *take a* ~ van het paard geslingerd worden; [fig] vallen **3** opgooi: *argue the* ~ een definitieve beslissing aanvechten; *lose* (or: *win*) *the* ~ verliezen (or: winnen) bij het tossen

[2]toss (vb) tossen, een munt opgooien, loten: *we'll have to* ~ *for* it we zullen erom moeten tossen

[3]toss (vb) **1** slingeren: *the ship was* ~*ed about* het schip werd heen en weer geslingerd **2** schudden, (doen) zwaaien, afwerpen **3** gooien, aangooien, opgooien, in de lucht werpen: ~ *hay* hooi keren **4** een munt opgooien met: *I'll* ~ *you for* it we loten erom

toss off 1 achteroverslaan [drink] **2** razendsnel produceren: ~ *a speech* voor de vuist weg een toespraak houden

toss up tossen, kruis of munt gooien

toss-up 1 opgooi **2** [inform] twijfelachtige zaak, onbesliste zaak: *it's a* ~ *whether* het is een gok of, het is nog maar de vraag of

tot 1 dreumes: *a tiny* ~ een kleine hummel **2** scheutje[h] [of hard liquor]

[1]total (n) totaal[h]

[2]total (adj) totaal, volledig: ~ *abstainer* geheelonthouder; *in* ~ *ignorance* in absolute onwetendheid; *sum* ~ totaalbedrag

[3]total (vb) (+ (up) to) oplopen (tot)

⁴**total** (vb) **1** bedragen, oplopen tot **2** (also +
up) het totaal vaststellen van
totalitarian totalitair
totality 1 totaalʰ **2** totaliteit
tote (bij zich) dragen [eg gun]; meevoeren
tote bag (grote) draagtas
totter 1 wankelen [also fig] **2** wankelend
overeind komen: ~ *to* one's feet wankelend
opstaan
totty [inform] lekkere wijven
¹**tot up** (vb) (+ to) oplopen (tot), bedragen
²**tot up** (vb) optellen
toucan toekan
¹**touch** (n) **1** aanraking, tik(jeʰ); contactʰ
[also fig]: *I felt a ~ on my shoulder* ik voelde
een tikje op mijn schouder; *be* (or: *keep*) *in ~
with* contact hebben (*or:* onderhouden) met;
lose ~ with uit het oog verliezen **2** gevoelʰ bij
aanraking, tastzin **3** vleugjeʰ; snufjeʰ [eg
salt]; lichte aanval [of disease]: *a ~ of the sun*
een lichte zonnesteek **4** stijl, manier: *put the
finishing ~(es) to sth.* de laatste hand leggen
aan iets; *lose one's ~* achteruitgaan, het verleren **5** [mus] aanslag **6** [sport] deelʰ van
veld buiten de zijlijnen [football, rugby] ‖
play at ~ tikkertje spelen
²**touch** (vb) (elkaar) raken, aan elkaar grenzen
³**touch** (vb) **1** raken [also fig]; aanraken: *you
haven't ~ed your **meal*** je hebt nog geen hap
gegeten **2** een tikje geven, aantasten; [fig]
aankunnen: *he ~ed his **cap*** hij tikte zijn pet
aan **3** raken, ontroeren: *~ed with pity* door
medelijden bewogen **4** treffen, betreffen:
*he does not want to ~ **politics*** hij wil zich niet
met politiek inlaten **5** benaderen, bereiken;
[fig] evenaren: *the thermometer ~ed **50°*** de
thermometer liep tot 50° op; *~ s.o. for a fiver*
iem. vijf pond aftroggelen
¹**touch-and-go** (n) **1** een dubbeltje op zijn
kant, kantje boord **2** veranderlijkheid
²**touch-and-go** (adj) riskant: *it's a ~ state of
affairs* het is een dubbeltje op zijn kant
touch at aandoen: *the ship touched at Port
Said* het schip deed Port Said aan
touchdown 1 landing [aeroplane] **2** [rug-
by, Am football] touchdown
¹**touch down** (vb) landen
²**touch down** (vb) [rugby, Am football] aan
de grond brengen achter de doellijn [ball; by
opponent]
touched 1 ontroerd **2** getikt
touching ontroerend
touchline zijlijn
touch off 1 afvuren, doen ontploffen **2** de
stoot geven tot
touchpaper lont [eg of fireworks]
touchscreen aanraakschermʰ
touchstone maatstaf
touch-tone toets-, drukknop-: *~ phone*
toetstelefoon

touch-type blind typen
touch up 1 retoucheren **2** bijschaven; [fig]
opfrissen [memory]
touch (up)on terloops behandelen
touchy 1 overgevoelig, prikkelbaar **2** netelig
touchy-feely [inform] **1** knuffelig; aanhalig **2** soft; klef
¹**tough** (n) woesteling, zware jongen
²**tough** (adj) **1** taai, stoer: *as ~ as old boots*
a) vreselijk taai; b) keihard; *~ as nails* spijkerhard **2** moeilijk, lastig: *a ~ job* een lastig karwei **3** onbuigzaam: *a ~ guy* (or: *customer*)
een keiharde; *get ~ with* hard optreden tegen **4** ruw **5** tegenvallend, hard: *it's your ~
luck* het is je eigen stomme schuld; *it's ~ on
him* het is een grote tegenvaller voor hem; *~
(luck)!* pech!, jammer!
³**tough** (adv) hard, onverzettelijk: *talk ~* zich
keihard opstellen [during negotations]
toughen taai, hard (doen) worden: *~ up*
sterker worden
toughie 1 rouwdouw **2** lastig probleemʰ
toupee haarstukjeʰ
¹**tour** (n) **1** reis, rondreis **2** (+ of) (kort) bezoekʰ (aan): *a guided ~ of* (or: *round*) *the castle*
een rondleiding door het kasteel **3** tournee:
on ~ op tournee **4** verblijfʰ: *the ambassador
did a four-year ~ in Washington* de ambassadeur heeft vier jaar Washington als standplaats gehad
²**tour** (vb) **1** (be)reizen, rondreizen **2** op
tournee gaan door
tourism toerismeʰ
tourist toerist
tourist class toeristenklasse
tourist office VVV-kantoorʰ
tournament toernooiʰ, steekspelʰ
tour operator reisorganisator
tousle in de war maken [hair]
¹**tout** (n) **1** klantenlokker **2** scharrelaar; handelaar [esp in illegal tickets and information
about racehorses]
²**tout** (vb) **1** klanten lokken, werven: *~ for
business* klanten ronselen **2** (aan)prijzen; handelen [in information about racehorses]
³**tout** (vb) **1** verhandelen [information about
racehorses] **2** op de zwarte markt verkopen
[tickets]
¹**tow** (n) **1** sleep: *take a car in ~* een auto slepen **2** het (mee)slepen
²**tow** (vb) (weg)slepen, op sleeptouw nemen,
(weg)trekken
towards 1 naar, tot, richting: *her window
faced ~ the sea* haar raam keek uit op de zee;
he walked ~ the signpost hij ging op de wegwijzer af; *we're saving ~ buying a house* we
sparen om later een huis te kunnen kopen
2 ten opzichte van, met betrekking tot: *her
attitude ~ her parents* haar houding ten opzichte van haar ouders **3** [to express time]

voor, vlak voor, naar … toe: ~ *six (o'clock)* tegen zessen

tow bar 1 trekhaak **2** [skiing] sleepbeugel [of ski lift]; anker[h]

towel handdoek: *throw in the ~* de handdoek in de ring gooien; [fig] het opgeven

towelling badstof

[1]**tower** (n) **1** toren, (zend)mast **2** torenflat, kantoorflat ‖ *~ of strength* steun en toeverlaat, rots in de branding

[2]**tower** (vb) (+ over, above) uittorenen (boven), (hoog) uitsteken

tower block torengebouw[h], torenflat

towering 1 torenhoog **2** enorm, hevig: *he's in a ~ rage* hij is razend

towing zone wegsleepzone

town 1 stad **2** gemeente ‖ *go to ~ on sth.* zich inzetten, veel werk maken van iets; [inform] uitspatten, zich uitleven; *(out) on the ~* (aan het) stappen, (een avondje) uit; *he went up to ~ from Nottingham* hij is vanuit Nottingham naar Londen gegaan

town clerk gemeentesecretaris

town council gemeenteraad

town councillor (gemeente)raadslid[h]

town hall stadhuis[h]

town house 1 huis in de stad **2** huis in stadswijk

townscape stadsgezicht[h]

township 1 gemeente **2** kleurlingenwijk, woonstad

townspeople 1 stedelingen, ingezetenen **2** stadsmensen

towpath jaagpad[h]

towrope sleeptouw[h]

toxic toxisch, giftig, vergiftigings-

toxin toxine; giftige stof

[1]**toy** (n) speeltje[h], (stuk[h]) speelgoed[h]; [fig] speelbal

[2]**toy** (vb) (+ with) spelen (met), zich amuseren (met): *he ~ed with the idea of buying a new car* hij speelde met de gedachte een nieuwe auto te kopen

toyshop speelgoedwinkel

[1]**trace** (n) spoor[h], voetspoor[h]; [also fig] overblijfsel[h]; vleugje[h]: *not a ~ of humour* geen greintje humor; *lose ~ of* uit het oog verliezen; *lost without ~* spoorloos verdwenen ‖ *kick over the ~s* uit de band springen

[2]**trace** (vb) **1** (+ out) (uit)tekenen, schetsen; trekken [line] **2** overtrekken **3** volgen, nagaan **4** (+ back) nagaan, naspeuren, opsporen, terugvoeren: *the rumour was ~d back to his aunt* men kwam erachter dat het gerucht afkomstig was van zijn tante **5** vinden, ontdekken: *I can't ~ that book* ik heb dat boek niet kunnen vinden

trace element spoorelement[h]

tracer lichtspoorkogel

tracing paper overtrekpapier[h]

[1]**track** (n) **1** spoor[h]: *on the right (or: wrong) ~*

op het goede (*or:* verkeerde) spoor [also fig]; *go off the beaten ~* ongebaande wegen bewandelen [fig]; *be on s.o.'s ~* iem. op het spoor zijn **2** voetspoor[h], (voet)afdruk; prent [of animals]: [fig] *cover (up) one's ~s* zijn sporen uitwissen **3** pad[h], bosweg, landweg; [fig also] weg; baan **4** renbaan, racebaan, wielerbaan **5** (spoor)rails **6** rupsband **7** nummer[h] [on CD, gramophone record]; (opname)spoor[h] [on (cassette) tape] ‖ *the wrong side of the (railroad) ~s* de achterbuurten; *lose ~ of* uit het oog verliezen, niet meer op de hoogte blijven van; [inform] *make ~s 'm smeren; across the ~s* in de achterbuurten; [inform] *in one's ~s* ter plaatse, ter plekke

[2]**track** (vb) **1** het spoor volgen van, volgen **2** (+ down) (op)sporen, ontdekken, naspeuren

tracker 1 spoorvolger **2** speurhond

track events [athletics] loopnummers

tracksuit trainingspak[h]

tract 1 uitgestrekt gebied[h], landstreek **2** traktaat[h]; verhandeling [rel, ethics] **3** [anatomy] kanaal[h]: *digestive ~* spijsverteringskanaal

traction 1 trekking, het (voort)trekken **2** trekkracht, aandrijving

tractor tractor, (landbouw)trekker

[1]**trade** (n) **1** handel, zaken: *Department of Trade and Industry* [roughly] Ministerie van Economische Zaken; *do a good ~* goede zaken doen **2** bedrijfstak, branche **3** handel, (mensen van) het vak, handelaars **4** vak[h], ambacht[h], beroep[h]: *a butcher by ~* slager van beroep **5** passaat(wind)

[2]**trade** (vb) handel drijven, handelen, zaken doen ‖ *~ (up)on s.o.'s generosity* misbruik maken van iemands vrijgevigheid

[3]**trade** (vb) verhandelen, uitwisselen, (om)ruilen: *~ in an old car for a new one* een oude auto voor een nieuwe inruilen

trade association beroepsvereniging

trade deficit handelstekort[h]

trade fair handelsbeurs

trade-in 1 inruilobject[h] **2** inruil

trademark handelsmerk[h]; [fig] typisch kenmerk[h] [of person]

trade-off 1 inruil [as a compromise] **2** wisselwerking

trade price (groot)handelsprijs

trader 1 handelaar **2** koopvaardijschip[h]

trade relations handelsbetrekkingen

tradesman 1 winkelier **2** leverancier

tradespeople winkeliers [as group]

trade(s) union (vak)bond, vakvereniging

trade unionist vakbondslid[h], aanhanger van een vakbond

trade wind passaatwind

trading estate industriegebied[h]

trading partner handelspartner

trading post handelsnederzetting

tradition traditie, overlevering
traditional traditioneel, vanouds gebruikelijk
traditionally traditiegetrouw; vanouds
¹**traffic** (n) **1** verkeerʰ, vervoerʰ, transportʰ **2** handel, koophandel: ~ *in drugs* drugshandel
²**traffic** (vb) **1** handel drijven (in), handelen (in), zaken doen (in) **2** zwarte handel drijven (in), sjacheren (met) ‖ ~ *in arms* wapenhandel drijven
traffic calming snelheidsbeperkende maatregelen
traffic circle rotonde, (rond) verkeerspleinʰ
traffic island vluchtheuvel
traffic jam (verkeers)opstopping
trafficker zwarthandelaar, sjacheraar; dealer [in drugs etc]
traffic lane rijstrook
traffic sign verkeerstekenʰ, verkeersbordʰ
traffic warden parkeercontroleur, parkeerwachter
tragedy tragedie, dramaʰ, tragiek, het tragische
tragic tragisch, droevig
¹**trail** (n) **1** sliert, stroom, rij: ~*s of smoke* rookslierten **2** spoorʰ, padʰ: *a ~ of destruction* een spoor van vernieling; *blaze a ~* [fig] de weg banen, baanbrekend werk verrichten **3** spoorʰ; prent [of animal]; geur(vlag) [as trace]: *be hard* (or: *hot*) *on s.o.'s ~* iem. op de hielen zitten
²**trail** (vb) **1** slepen, loshangen: *her gown was ~ing along on the ground* haar japon sleepte over de grond **2** zich (voort)slepen, strompelen **3** kruipen [of plants] **4** (+ behind) [sport] achterliggen, achterstaan, achteraankomen ‖ *his voice ~ed off* zijn stem stierf weg
³**trail** (vb) **1** slepen, sleuren **2** volgen, schaduwen **3** [sport] achterliggen op, achterstaan op
trailer 1 aanhangwagen, oplegger **2** caravan **3** [film] trailer
¹**train** (n) **1** trein: *by ~* per trein **2** sleep [of dress]; [fig] nasleep **3** gevolgʰ, stoet, sleep **4** rij, reeks, opeenvolging; [fig] aaneenschakeling: *a ~ of thought* een gedachtegang; *preparations are in ~* de voorbereidingen zijn aan de gang
²**train** (vb) **1** (zich) trainen, (zich) oefenen **2** een opleiding volgen, studeren: *he is ~ing to be a lawyer* hij studeert voor advocaat
³**train** (vb) **1** trainen, oefenen; africhten [animal] **2** opleiden, scholen **3** leiden [plant] **4** richten, mikken
trained getraind; ervaren: ~ *nurse* gediplomeerd verpleegster
trainee stagiair(e)
trainer 1 trainer, africhter, dompteur **2** (-s) trainingsschoenen

training training, oefening, opleiding: *physical ~* conditietraining
training college pedagogische academie
traipse sjouwen, slepen ‖ ~ *about* rondslenteren
trait trek(je ʰ), karaktertrek, karaktereigenschap
traitor (land)verrader, overloper: *turn ~* een verrader worden
trajectory baan [of missile]
tram tram: *by ~* met de tram
tramline 1 tramrail **2** (-s) dubbele zijlijnen [in tennis court]
¹**tramp** (n) **1** getrappelʰ, gestampʰ **2** voettocht, trektocht **3** zwerver, landloper **4** tramp(boot), vrachtzoeker, schip van de wilde vaart
²**tramp** (vb) **1** stappen, marcheren, stampen **2** lopen, trekken, een voettocht maken
³**tramp** (vb) **1** aflopen, doorlopen **2** trappen op, stampen op: ~ *down* plattrappen
¹**trample** (vb) **1** stampen, trappelen, stappen: ~ *(up)on* trappen op; [fig] met voeten treden; ~ *on s.o.'s feelings* iemands gevoelens kwetsen
²**trample** (vb) vertrappen, trappen op
trampoline trampoline
trance trance: *be in a ~* in trance zijn
tranquil kalm, vredig, rustig
tranquillity kalmte, rust(igheid)
tranquillize kalmeren, tot bedaren brengen
tranquillizer tranquillizer, kalmerend middelʰ
transact verrichten, afhandelen, afwikkelen: ~ *business with s.o.* met iem. zaken doen
transaction 1 transactie, zaak, handelsovereenkomst **2** afhandeling, afwikkeling
transatlantic trans-Atlantisch
transceiver [radio] zendontvanger
transcend 1 te boven gaan **2** overtreffen: *he ~s himself* hij overtreft zichzelf
transcendent superieur, alles (allen) overtreffend, buitengewoon
transcendental transcendentaal, bovenzintuiglijk
transcribe transcriberen, overschrijven, (in een andere spelling) overbrengen; [mus] bewerken: ~ *the music for organ* de muziek voor orgel bewerken
transcript afschriftʰ; kopie
transcription transcriptie, het overschrijven; [mus] bewerking; arrangementʰ
¹**transfer** (n) **1** overplaatsing, overdracht; [sport] transfer **2** overgeplaatste; [sport] transfer(speler) **3** [fin] overdracht, overschrijving, overboeking **4** overdrukplaatjeʰ **5** overstapkaartjeʰ
²**transfer** (vb) **1** overstappen: ~ *from the train to the bus* van de trein op de bus overstappen **2** overgeplaatst worden; verande-

ren [of place, work, school]
³transfer (vb) **1** overmaken, overhandigen, overdragen: ~ *one's rights* **to** *s.o.* zijn rechten aan iem. (anders) overdragen **2** overplaatsen, verplaatsen, overbrengen **3** overdrukken **4** [sport] transfereren [player] **transferable 1** verplaatsbaar **2** overdraagbaar **3** inwisselbaar; verhandelbaar [cheque etc]
transference overplaatsing, overbrenging
transfix 1 doorboren; doorsteken [eg with lance] **2** (vast)spietsen **3** als aan de grond nagelen, verlammen
¹transform (vb) (van vorm/gedaante/karakter) veranderen, een gedaanteverwisseling ondergaan
²transform (vb) **1** (van vorm/gedaante/karakter) veranderen, hervormen, omvormen: *stress ~ed him* **into** *an aggressive man* door de stress veranderde hij in een agressief man **2** [also elec] omzetten, transformeren
transformation transformatie
transformer [elec] transformator
transfuse een transfusie geven (van)
transfusion transfusie
transgenic transgenetisch [of crop etc]: ~ *mice* transgene muizen
¹transgress (vb) **1** een overtreding begaan **2** zondigen
²transgress (vb) overtreden, inbreuk maken op, schenden
transient 1 voorbijgaand, kortstondig **2** doorreizend, doortrekkend
transistor transistor
transit doorgang, doortocht: *in* ~ tijdens het vervoer, onderweg
transit camp doorgangskampʰ
transition overgang: *period of* ~ overgangsperiode
transitional tussenliggend, overgangs-, tussen-
transitive transitief, overgankelijk
transit visa doorreisvisumʰ
translate 1 vertalen: ~ *a sentence* **from** *English* **into** *Dutch* een zin uit het Engels in het Nederlands vertalen **2** interpreteren, uitleggen, vertolken **3** omzetten; omvormen [also biology]: ~ *ideas into actions* ideeën in daden omzetten
translation vertaling
translator 1 vertaler **2** tolk
translucent doorschijnend
transmission 1 uitzending, programmaʰ **2** overbrenging; overdracht [also of disease, heredity] **3** transmissie, overbrenging, versnellingsbak **4** het doorgeven, overlevering
transmit 1 overbrengen; overdragen [also of disease, heredity]: ~ *a message* een boodschap overbrengen **2** overleveren; doorgeven [traditions etc]
transmitter 1 overbrenger, overdrager

2 seintoestelʰ, seingever **3** microfoon [of telephone] **4** zender [radio, TV]
transparency 1 dia(positiefʰ), projectieplaatjeʰ, overhead(sheet) **2** doorzichtigheid
transparent 1 doorzichtig [also fig]; transparant: *a* ~ *lie* een doorzichtige leugen **2** eenvoudig/gemakkelijk te begrijpen
¹transpire (vb) **1** transpireren; waterdamp verdampen [of human being, animal] **2** uitlekken, aan het licht komen, bekend worden: *it ~d that the president himself was involved* het lekte uit dat de president er zelf bij betrokken was
²transpire (vb) uitwasemen, uitzweten
¹transplant (n) **1** getransplanteerd orgaanʰ (weefselʰ), transplantaatʰ **2** transplantatie
²transplant (vb) **1** verplanten, overplanten **2** overbrengen, doen verhuizen **3** transplanteren, overplanten
¹transport (n) vervoer(middel)ʰ, transportʰ: *public* ~ openbaar vervoer; *I'd like to come, but I've no* ~ ik zou wel mee willen, maar ik heb geen vervoer
²transport (vb) vervoeren, transporteren, overbrengen
transport aircraft transportvliegtuigʰ
transportation 1 vervoermiddelʰ, transportmiddelʰ **2** vervoerʰ, transportʰ, overbrenging
transport cafe wegcaféʰ, chauffeurscaféʰ
transporter 1 transporteur **2** transportmiddelʰ
transpose 1 anders schikken, (onderling) verwisselen, omzetten **2** [mus] transponeren
transvestite travestiet
¹trap (n) **1** val, (val)strik, hinderlaag, strikvraag (or: *set*) *a* ~ een val (op)zetten, een strik spannen **2** sifon; stankafsluiter [in drainpipe] **3** [inform] smoel, waffel, bek: *shut your* ~! hou je kop!
²trap (vb) **1** (ver)strikken, (in een val) vangen; [fig] in de val laten lopen: ~ *s.o.* **into** *a confession* iem. door een list tot een bekentenis dwingen **2** opsluiten: *be ~ped* opgesloten zitten, in de val zitten, vastzitten **3** opvangen [eg energy]
trapdoor valdeur, val, (val)luikʰ
trapeze trapeze
trapper vallenzetter, pelsjager
trappings (uiterlijke) sieraden, (uiterlijk) vertoon
¹trash (n) **1** rotzooi, (oude) rommel, troep **2** onzin, gekletsʰ **3** afvalʰ, vuilʰ, vuilnis **4** nietsnut(ten), uitschotʰ, tuigʰ
²trash (vb) kritiseren; afkraken [book, film etc]
trash can vuilnisemmer
trash talking [Am] ophitsende taal; gescheldʰ
trashy waardeloos, kitscherig: ~ *novel* flutroman

trauma 1 wond, verwonding, letsel[h]
2 [psychology] trauma[h]
traumatic traumatisch, beangstigend
¹travel (n) **1** (lange/verre) reis, rondreis, het reizen: *on our ~s* tijdens onze rondreis **2** (-s) reisverhaal[h], reisverhalen, reizen, reisbeschrijving: *Gulliver's Travels* Gullivers Reizen
²travel (vb) **1** reizen, een reis maken: *~ling circus* rondreizend circus **2** vertegenwoordiger zijn: *~ in electrical appliances* vertegenwoordiger in huishoudelijke apparaten zijn **3** zich (voort)bewegen, zich voortplanten, gaan: *news ~s fast* nieuws verspreidt zich snel ‖ *flowers ~ badly* bloemen kunnen slecht tegen vervoer
³travel (vb) **1** doorreizen, doortrekken; afreizen [also as commercial traveller] **2** afleggen: *~ 500 miles a day* 500 mijl per dag afleggen
travel agency reisbureau[h]
traveller 1 reiziger, bereisd man **2** handelsreiziger, vertegenwoordiger **3** zigeuner, zwerver
traveller's cheque reischeque
travelog(ue) (geïllustreerd) reisverhaal[h], reisfilm
¹traverse (vb) schuins klimmen
²traverse (vb) **1** (door)kruisen, oversteken, (dwars) trekken door, doorsnijden **2** dwars beklimmen [slope]
travesty travestie, karikatuur, parodie: *~ of justice* karikatuur van rechtvaardigheid
¹trawl (n) **1** sleepnet[h], trawl **2** zoektocht, speurtocht [eg for talent]
²trawl (vb) met een sleepnet vissen (naar); [fig] uitkammen; uitpluizen: [fig] *~ for* zorgvuldig doorzoeken
trawler treiler, trawler
tray 1 dienblad[h], (presenteer)blad[h] **2** bakje[h], brievenbak(je[h])
treacherous verraderlijk, onbetrouwbaar: *~ ice* verraderlijk ijs; *~ memory* onbetrouwbaar geheugen
treachery verraad[h], ontrouw, onbetrouwbaarheid
treacle (suiker)stroop [also fig]
treacly stroperig, kleverig; [fig] (honing)zoet; vleiend
¹tread (n) **1** tred, pas, gang: *a heavy ~* een zware stap **2** trede, opstapje[h] **3** loopvlak[h] [of tyre] **4** profiel[h] [of tyre]
²tread (vb) treden, stappen, lopen, wandelen: *~ in the mud* in de modder trappen
³tread (vb) **1** betreden, bewandelen, begaan **2** trappen, vertrappen, intrappen, stuktrappen, uittrappen, vasttrappen; [fig] onderdrukken: *~ grapes* (met de voeten) druiven persen; *~ water* watertrappelen **3** heen en weer lopen in, lopen door **4** (zich) banen, platlopen
treadle trapper, pedaal[h]

treadmill tredmolen [also fig]
treason hoogverraad[h], landverraad[h]
¹treasure (n) **1** schat, kostbaarheid; [inform] juweel[h]; parel: *my secretary is a ~* ik heb een juweel van een secretaresse **2** schat(ten), rijkdom: *~ of ideas* schat aan ideeën
²treasure (vb) **1** (+ up) verzamelen, bewaren **2** waarderen, op prijs stellen
treasure house schatkamer: *the museum is a ~ of paintings* dit museum heeft een schat aan schilderijen
treasurer penningmeester
treasure trove (gevonden) schat, (waardevolle) vondst; rijke bron [also fig]
treasury schatkamer, schatkist; [fig] bron
the **Treasury** Ministerie[h] van Financiën
¹treat (n) traktatie, (feestelijk) onthaal[h], feest[h], plezier[h]: *it's my ~* ik trakteer
²treat (vb) **1** trakteren **2** (+ with) onderhandelen (met), (vredes)besprekingen voeren (met), zaken doen (met)
³treat (vb) **1** behandelen [also med]: *~ s.o. kindly* iem. vriendelijk behandelen **2** beschouwen, afdoen: *~ sth. as a joke* iets als een grapje opvatten **3** aan de orde stellen; behandelen [subject] **4** trakteren, onthalen
treatable behandelbaar
treatise verhandeling, beschouwing
treatment behandeling, verzorging
treaty verdrag[h], overeenkomst
¹treble (n) jongenssopraan
²treble (adj) driemaal, drievoudig, driedubbel ‖ *~ recorder* altblokfluit
³treble (vb) verdrievoudigen, met drie vermenigvuldigen
treble clef sopraansleutel
tree boom: *family ~* stamboom
tree-house boomhut
trefoil [bot] klaver(blad[h])
¹trek (n) tocht; lange reis
²trek (vb) (te voet) trekken
trellis latwerk[h], traliewerk[h]
¹tremble (n) trilling, huivering, rilling: *be all of a ~* over zijn hele lichaam beven
²tremble (vb) **1** beven, rillen, bibberen: *in fear and trembling* met angst en beven **2** schudden [bldg, earth]; trillen **3** huiveren, in angst zitten: *I ~ to think* ik moet er niet aan denken, ik huiver bij de gedachte
tremendous 1 enorm, geweldig **2** fantastisch
tremor 1 aardschok, lichte aardbeving **2** huivering, siddering
tremulous 1 trillend, sidderend **2** schuchter, nerveus: *~ voice* onvaste stem
trench 1 geul, greppel **2** loopgraaf **3** [geology] trog
trenchant scherp, krachtig: *~ remark* spitse opmerking
trench coat trenchcoat; regenjas
¹trend (n) tendens, neiging, trend: *set the ~*

de toon aangeven
²**trend** (vb) overhellen, geneigd zijn: *prices are ~ing downwards* de prijzen lijken te gaan zakken
trendsetter trendsetter, voorloper
trendy in, modieus, trendy
trepidation ongerustheid, angst
¹**trespass** (n) **1** overtreding, inbreuk, schending **2** [rel] zonde, schuld
²**trespass** (vb) **1** op verboden terrein komen **2** [rel] een overtreding begaan, zondigen
trespasser overtreder: *~s will be prosecuted* verboden toegang voor onbevoegden
trespass (up)on 1 wederrechtelijk betreden [grounds] **2** beslag leggen op, inbreuk maken op; misbruik maken van [time, hospitality]
trestle schraag, onderstel[h]
trestle table schragentafel
triad 1 [mus] drieklank **2** drietal[h], triade
trial 1 (gerechtelijk) onderzoek[h], proces[h], rechtszaak **2** proef, experiment[h]: *give sth. a ~* iets testen; *by ~ and error* met vallen en opstaan **3** poging **4** beproeving [also fig]; probleem[h]: *~s and tribulations* zorgen en problemen
trial balloon proefballon(netje[h])
trial period proeftijd
triangle driehoek, triangel
triangular 1 driehoekig **2** driezijdig: *~ contest* driehoeksverkiezing
tribal stam-, stammen-, van een stam
tribe 1 stam, volksstam **2** groep; geslacht[h] [related things]
tribesman 1 stamlid[h] **2** stamgenoot
tribulation 1 bron van ellende **2** beproeving, rampspoed
tribunal 1 rechtbank, gerecht[h], tribunaal[h] **2** [roughly] commissie, [roughly] raad, [roughly] raad van onderzoek
tribune 1 volksleider, demagoog **2** podium[h], tribune
tributary 1 schatplichtige; belastingplichtige [state, person] **2** zijrivier
tribute 1 bijdrage, belasting **2** hulde, eerbetoon[h]: *pay (a) ~ to s.o.* iem. eer bewijzen
trice ogenblik[h], moment[h]: *in a ~* in een wip
¹**trick** (n) **1** truc [also fig]; foefje[h], kneep: *know the ~s of the trade* het klappen van de zweep kennen; *magic ~s* goocheltrucs **2** handigheid, slag: *get* (or: *learn*) *the ~ of it* de slag te pakken krijgen (van iets) **3** streek, kattenkwaad[h]: *play a ~ (up)on s.o.*, *play s.o. a ~* iem. een streek leveren **4** aanwensel[h], tic: *you have the ~ of pulling your hair when you're nervous* je hebt de vreemde gewoonte om aan je haren te trekken als je zenuwachtig bent **5** [cards] slag ‖ *this poison should do the ~* met dit vergif moet het lukken; *not* (or: *never*) *miss a ~* overal van op de hoogte zijn; *be up to s.o.'s ~s* iem. doorhebben; *how's ~s?*

hoe staat het ermee?
²**trick** (vb) **1** bedriegen, misleiden: *~ s.o. into sth.* iem. iets aanpraten, iem. ergens inluizen **2** oplichten, afzetten: *~ s.o. out of his money* iem. zijn geld afhandig maken
trickery bedrog[h]
¹**trickle** (n) **1** stroompje[h], straaltje[h] **2** het druppelen
²**trickle** (vb) **1** druppelen **2** druppelsgewijs komen (gaan): *the first guests ~d in at ten o'clock* om tien uur druppelden de eerste gasten binnen
trick question strikvraag
trickster oplichter, bedrieger
tricky 1 sluw, listig **2** lastig, moeilijk: *~ question* lastige vraag
tricycle driewieler
trident drietand
tried beproefd, betrouwbaar
triennial 1 driejaarlijks, om de drie jaar terugkomend **2** driejarig, drie jaar durend
trier volhouder; doorzetter
trifle 1 kleinigheid, wissewasje[h] **2** habbekrats, prikje[h], schijntje[h] **3** beetje[h]: *he's a ~ slow* hij is ietwat langzaam
trifle with 1 niet serieus nemen: *she is not a woman to be trifled with* zij is geen vrouw die met zich laat spotten **2** spelen met
trifling 1 onbelangrijk: *of ~ importance* van weinig belang **2** waardeloos
¹**trigger** (n) trekker; pal [of pistol]: *pull the ~* de trekker overhalen; [fig] het startschot geven
²**trigger** (vb) teweegbrengen, veroorzaken: *~ off* a) op gang brengen; b) ten gevolge hebben
trigger-happy 1 schietgraag, snel schietend **2** strijdlustig
trigonometry trigonometrie, driehoeksmeting
¹**trill** (n) **1** roller; triller [of birds] **2** met trilling geproduceerde klank; rollende medeklinker [eg rolling r]
²**trill** (vb) trillen, kwinkeleren, vibreren ‖ *~ the r* een rollende r maken
trillion 1 triljoen; [fig] talloos **2** [Am] biljoen; miljoen maal miljoen; [fig] talloos
trilogy trilogie
¹**trim** (n) **1** versiering; sierstrip(pen) [on car] **2** het bijknippen **3** staat (van gereedheid), conditie: *the players were in (good) ~* de spelers waren in (goede) vorm
²**trim** (adj) **1** net(jes), goed verzorgd: *a ~ garden* een keurig onderhouden tuin **2** in vorm, in goede conditie
³**trim** (vb) **1** in orde brengen, net(jes) maken; (bij)knippen [eg of hair] **2** afknippen; [fig] besnoeien: *~ (down) the expenditure* de uitgaven beperken **3** versieren: *a coat ~med with fur* een jas afgezet met bont **4** naar de wind zetten [of sails]; [fig] aanpassen; schik-

ken: *he ~s his opinions* **to** *the circumstances* hij past zijn mening aan de omstandigheden aan
tr<u>i</u>mmer 1 snoeimes^h, tuinschaar, tondeuse **2** weerhaan [fig]; opportunist
tr<u>i</u>mmings 1 garnituur, toebehoren^h **2** (af)snoeisel^h, afknipsel^h **3** opsmuk, franje: *tell us the story without* **the** *~* vertel ons het verhaal zonder opsmuk
Tr<u>i</u>nity Drie-eenheid
tr<u>i</u>nket 1 kleinood^h **2** prul^h, snuisterij
tr<u>i</u>o 1 drietal^h, trio^h **2** [mus] trio^h
¹trip (n) **1** tocht, reis, uitstapje^h **2** misstap [also fig]; val, vergissing **3** trip [on LSD; also fig]; reuze-ervaring
²trip (vb) **1** (also + up) struikelen, uitglijden **2** huppelen, trippelen: *the girl ~ped* **across** *the room* het meisje huppelde door de kamer **3** (+ up) een fout begaan: *the man ~ped* **up** *after a few questions* de man versprak zich na een paar vragen
³trip (vb) **1** (also + up) laten struikelen, beentje lichten **2** (also + up) op een fout betrappen **3** (also + up) erin laten lopen, strikken, zich laten verspreken
tripe 1 pens **2** [inform] onzin
¹triple (adj) drievoudig, driedubbel
²triple (vb) verdrievoudigen
triple-play tripleplay-, 3-in-1-
tr<u>i</u>plet 1 één van een drieling: *~s* drieling **2** drietal^h, drie, trio^h
tr<u>i</u>plets drieling
tr<u>i</u>plicate triplicaat^h, derde exemplaar^h: *in ~* in drievoud
tr<u>i</u>pod driepoot, statief^h
tr<u>i</u>pper dagjesmens
tr<u>i</u>ptych drieluik^h
tr<u>i</u>pwire struikeldraad, valstrik
tr<u>i</u>te afgezaagd, cliché
¹tr<u>i</u>umph (n) triomf, overwinning, groot succes^h
²tr<u>i</u>umph (vb) zegevieren: *~* **over** *difficulties* moeilijkheden overwinnen
tr<u>i</u>umphal triomf-, zege-: *~* **arch** triomfboog
tr<u>i</u>umphant 1 zegevierend **2** triomfantelijk
tr<u>i</u>vet drievoet; [Am] onderzetter [for pots and pans etc]
tr<u>i</u>vial 1 onbelangrijk **2** gewoon, alledaags **3** oppervlakkig
triv<u>ia</u>lity 1 iets onbelangrijks **2** onbelangrijkheid
¹Tr<u>o</u>jan (n) Trojaan || *work like a ~* werken als een paard
²Tr<u>o</u>jan (adj) Trojaans: *~* **Horse** paard van Troje [also fig]; [comp] Trojaans paard
troll 1 sleeplijn [fishing gear] **2** trol [in mythology, comp]
tr<u>o</u>lley 1 tweewielig (vierwielig) karretje^h, winkelwagentje^h **2** tram **3** theewagen || *off*

one's ~ (stapel)gek
tr<u>o</u>lley bus trolleybus
tr<u>o</u>lley car tram
tr<u>o</u>llop [inform] **1** slons, sloddervos **2** slet, sloerie
tromb<u>o</u>ne trombone, schuiftrompet
¹troop (n) **1** troep, menigte **2** [mil] troep, peloton^h **3** (-s) troepen(macht), strijdmachten
²troop (vb) **1** als groep gaan: *his children ~ed in* zijn kinderen marcheerden naar binnen **2** samenscholen
tr<u>oo</u>per 1 cavalerist **2** gewoon soldaat **3** (staats)politieagent || *swear like a ~* vloeken als een ketter
tr<u>o</u>phy 1 prijs, trofee **2** trofee; zegeteken^h [also fig]; aandenken^h
tr<u>o</u>pic keerkring: *~ of* **Cancer** Kreeftskeerkring; *~ of* **Capricorn** Steenbokskeerkring; *the ~s* de tropen
tr<u>o</u>pical tropisch; [fig] heet; drukkend
¹trot (n) **1** draf(je^h), haastige beweging: *be on the ~* ronddraven, niet stilzitten **2** (-s) [inform] diarree: *have the ~s* aan de dunne zijn
²trot (vb) **1** draven [also of person] **2** [inform] lopen, (weg)gaan
³trot (vb): *~* **out** voor de dag komen met
tr<u>o</u>tter 1 draver [horse] **2** varkenspoot
¹tr<u>ou</u>ble (n) **1** zorg, bezorgdheid: *that is the least of my ~s!* dat is mij een zorg! **2** tegenslag, narigheid, probleem^h: *get into ~* in moeilijkheden raken **3** ongemak^h, overlast: *I do not want to be any ~* ik wil (u) niet tot last zijn **4** moeite, inspanning: *save o.s. the ~* zich de moeite besparen **5** kwaal, ongemak^h: *he suffers from* **back** *~* hij heeft rugklachten **6** onlust, onrust **7** pech, mankement^h: *the car has* **got** *engine ~* de wagen heeft motorpech
²tr<u>ou</u>ble (vb) moeite doen: *do not ~ to* **explain** doe geen moeite het uit te leggen
³tr<u>ou</u>ble (vb) **1** verontrusten: *what ~s me is …* wat me dwars zit is … **2** lastigvallen, storen: *I hope I'm not troubling you* ik hoop dat ik niet stoor **3** kwellen
tr<u>ou</u>blemaker onruststoker, herrieschopper
tr<u>ou</u>bleshooter probleemoplosser, puinruimer
tr<u>ou</u>blesome lastig
trough 1 trog, drinkbak, eetbak **2** goot **3** laagte(punt^h); diepte(punt^h) [on meter, in statistics etc]
trounce afrossen, afstraffen; [sport; fig] inmaken
troupe troep; groep [esp actors, artists]
tr<u>ou</u>ser broek(s)-: *~* **buttons** broeksknopen
tr<u>ou</u>ser-leg broekspijp
tr<u>ou</u>sers (lange) broek: *a* **pair** *of ~* een (lange) broek; *wear the ~* de broek aan hebben
tr<u>ou</u>sseau uitzet
trout (zee)forel || *old ~* oude tang

trowel troffel ‖ *lay* it on with a ~ het er dik op leggen, aandikken
Troy Troje
truant 1 spijbelaar: *play* ~ spijbelen **2** lijntrekker
truce (tijdelijke) wapenstilstand ʰ
truck vrachtwagen, truck ‖ *have* no ~ with geen zaken doen met
trucker [Am] vrachtwagenchauffeur
truckle kruiperig doen: ~ *to* s.o. voor iem. kruipen
truckle bed [roughly] bed op wieltjes dat onder een ander bed geschoven kan worden
truckload wagenlading, trucklading
truck stop chauffeurscaféʰ
truculence 1 vechtlust, agressiviteit **2** gewelddadigheid
truculent vechtlustig, agressief
¹trudge (n) trektocht, mars
²trudge (vb) sjokken: ~ *along* zich voortslepen
¹true (adj) **1** waar, juist: *come* ~ werkelijkheid worden **2** echt, waar: ~ *to* life levensecht **3** trouw: *a* ~ *friend* een trouwe vriend
²true (adv) **1** waarheidsgetrouw: *ring* ~ echt klinken **2** juist
true-blue 1 betrouwbaar, eerlijk **2** onwrikbaar; aarts- [of conservative politician]
true-born rasecht, geboren
true-life waargebeurd
truelove lief(ste)
truffle truffel [also bonbon]
truism 1 waarheid als een koe **2** clichéʰ
truly 1 oprecht: *I am* ~ *grateful* to you ik ben u oprecht dankbaar **2** echt, werkelijk **3** trouw, toegewijd ‖ *yours* ~ a) hoogachtend [complimentary close in letters]; b) de ondergetekende, [roughly] ik
¹trump (n) troef(kaart) [also fig]: *spades are* ~s schoppen is troef ‖ *come* (or: *turn*) up ~s geluk hebben met
²trump (vb) troeven, troef (uit)spelen ‖ ~ *up* verzinnen; *the charge was clearly* ~ed *up* de beschuldiging was duidelijk verzonnen
trump card troefkaart [also fig]: *that was my* ~ dat was mijn laatste redmiddel
¹trumpet (n) **1** trompet: [fig] *blow* one's own ~ zijn eigen lof zingen **2** getrompetterʰ [eg of elephant]
²trumpet (vb) **1** trompet spelen **2** trompetteren
truncate beknotten [also fig]; aftoppen: ~ *a story* een verhaal inkorten
truncheon wapenstok
trunk 1 (boom)stam **2** romp, torso **3** hutkoffer [oft also piece of furniture] **4** slurf; snuit [of elephant] **5** kofferbak [of car] **6** (-s) korte broek; zwembroek [for men]
trunk call interlokaal telefoongesprekʰ
trunk road hoofdweg
¹truss (n) **1** dakkap, dakspantʰ **2** breukband

3 bundel, bosʰ, pakʰ
²truss (vb) (stevig) inbinden: ~ *up* a) inbinden, opmaken [chicken]; b) knevelen
¹trust (n) **1** vertrouwenʰ: *a position* of ~ een vertrouwenspositie **2** (goede) hoop, verwachting **3** zorg, hoede: *commit a child to* s.o.'s ~ een kind aan iemands zorgen toevertrouwen **4** trust, kartelʰ **5** [law] trust, machtiging tot beheer van goederen voor een begunstigde: *hold property in* (or: *under*) ~ eigendom in bewaring hebben
²trust (vb) **1** vertrouwen: *you should not* ~ *in* him je mag hem niet vertrouwen **2** vertrouwen hebben, hopen
³trust (vb) **1** vertrouwen op, aannemen, hopen: *I* ~ *everything is all right with him* ik hoop maar dat alles met hem in orde is **2** toevertrouwen: *he* ~ed *his car to a friend* hij gaf zijn auto bij een vriend in bewaring
trustee beheerder; bewindvoerder [of capital, estate]; bestuurder, commissaris [of institution, school]
trust fund beheerd fonds
trusting vertrouwend, vriendelijk
trustworthy betrouwbaar
truth 1 waarheid: *to tell the* ~ … om de waarheid te zeggen … **2** echtheid **3** oprechtheid
truthful 1 eerlijk, oprecht **2** waar, (waarheids)getrouw
¹try (n) **1** poging: *give* it a ~ het eens proberen, een poging wagen **2** [rugby] try
²try (vb) **1** proberen, uitproberen, op de proef stellen; [also fig] vermoeien: ~ s.o.'s *patience* iemands geduld op de proef stellen; ~ *to be* on time proberen op tijd te komen; *tried and found* wanting gewogen en te licht bevonden; ~ *on* aanpassen [clothes]; ~ *out* testen, de proef nemen met; ~ sth. *on* s.o. iets op iem. uitproberen; *just* ~ *and stop me!* probeer me maar eens tegen te houden! **2** berechten, verhoren: ~ s.o. *for murder* iem. voor moord berechten
trying moeilijk, zwaar: ~ *person* to deal with lastige klant
try-out test, proef: *give* s.o. a ~ het met iem. proberen
tsar tsaar
tsarina tsarina
T-shirt T-shirtʰ
tsunami tsunami, vloedgolf
TT 1 *teetotaller* geheelonthouder **2** *Tourist Trophy* TT [motorcycle race]
tub 1 tobbe, ton: *have a* ~ een bad nemen **2** kuipjeʰ
tuba tuba
tubby tonvormig, rond, dik
tube 1 buis(je)ʰ, pijp, slang, huls, koker, tube **2** binnenband **3** metro **4** [Am] televisie, buis
tuberculosis tuberculose

tube station metrostation[h]
tubular buisvormig: ~ *bells* buisklokken,
klokkenspel
¹tuck (n) **1** plooi **2** zoetigheid
²tuck (vb) plooien maken ‖ ~ *in!* val aan, tast
toe!; ~ *into* flink smullen van
³tuck (vb) **1** plooien **2** inkorten, innemen
3 (+ up) opstropen, optrekken **4** intrekken:
with his legs ~ed up under him in kleermakerszit **5** (also + away) (ver)stoppen, wegstop-
pen, verschuilen: ~ *away* (or: *in)* verorberen
6 (+ in) instoppen: ~ *s.o. in* (or: *up)* iem. toedekken; ~ *one's shirt into one's trousers* zijn
hemd in zijn broek stoppen
tucked gehurkt
tuck-in smulpartij
tuck shop snoepwinkeltje[h]
Tuesday dinsdag
tuft bosje[h], kwastje[h], kuifje[h]
tufted 1 in bosjes groeiend **2** met, vol bosjes **3** [esp zoology] gekuifd
¹tug (n) **1** ruk, haal: *give* a ~ *at* (heftig) rukken aan **2** (felle) strijd, conflict[h]: [inform] ~ *of*
love touwtrekkerij om (de voogdij over) een
kind [between divorced parents] **3** sleepboot
²tug (vb) (+ at) rukken (aan)
³tug (vb) **1** rukken aan **2** slepen [tug boat]
tugboat sleepboot
tuition 1 schoolgeld[h], lesgeld[h] **2** onderwijs[h]
tulip tulp
¹tumble (n) **1** val(partij): *have* (or: *take)* a ~
vallen **2** warboel: *in* a ~ overhoop
²tumble (vb) **1** vallen, tuimelen, struikelen:
~ *down* neerploffen; ~ *down the stairs* van de
trap rollen **2** rollen, woelen: ~ *about* rond-
tollen **3** stormen, lopen: ~ *into* (or: *out of)*
bed in zijn bed ploffen, uit zijn bed springen
4 (snel) zakken, kelderen: *tumbling prices*
dalende prijzen ‖ ~ *to* snappen
³tumble (vb) **1** doen vallen, omgooien **2** in
de war brengen **3** drogen [in tumble drier]
tumbledown bouwvallig
tumble-dryer droogtrommel
tumbler 1 duikelaar **2** acrobaat **3** tuimel-
glas[h], (groot) bekerglas[h] **4** [techn] tuimelaar
[of lock] **5** droogtrommel
tummy buik(je[h])
tummy button navel
tumour tumor
tumult tumult[h]: *in* a ~ totaal verward
tumultuous tumultueus, wanordelijk
tun vat[h]
tuna tonijn
tundra toendra
¹tune (n) **1** wijsje[h], melodie; [fig] toon **2** juiste toonhoogte: *sing out of* ~ vals zingen
3 overeenstemming: *it is in* ~ *with the spirit of*
the time het is in overeenstemming met de
tijdgeest ‖ *call the* ~ de lakens uitdelen;
change one's ~, *sing* another (or: *dance* to an-

other) ~ een andere toon aanslaan, een
toontje lager gaan zingen; *to the* ~ *of £1000*
voor het bedrag van £1000
²tune (vb) **1** (+ with) harmoniëren (met)
2 zingen
³tune (vb) **1** stemmen **2** afstemmen [also
fig]; instellen: ~ *o.s. to* zich aanpassen aan;
~*d to* afgestemd op **3** afstellen [engine]
tune in afstemmen, de radio (televisie)
aanzetten: ~ *to* afstemmen op
tuner 1 [mus] stemmer **2** tuner [separate
radio]
¹tune up (vb) stemmen [of orchestra]
²tune up (vb) in gereedheid brengen, afstellen
tunic 1 tunica **2** tuniek, (korte) uniformjas
tuning fork stemvork
Tunisia Tunesië
¹Tunisian (n) Tunesiër, Tunesische
²Tunisian (adj) **1** Tunesisch **2** Tunisch
tunnel 1 tunnel **2** onderaardse gang [of
mole etc]
tunny tonijn
turban tulband
turbid 1 troebel, drabbig **2** verward: ~
emotions verwarde emoties
turbine turbine
turbot tarbot
turbulence 1 wildheid **2** beroering, onrust
turbulent 1 wild **2** woelig, oproerig: ~
crowd oproerige menigte
turd 1 drol **2** verachtelijk persoon
¹turf (n) **1** graszode, plag **2** gras(veld)[h]: *play*
on home ~ een thuiswedstrijd spelen **3** renbaan, racebaan, paardenrennen[h]
²turf (vb): [inform] ~ *s.o. out* iem. eruit knikkeren
turgid 1 [med] (op)gezwollen **2** hoogdravend
Turk Turk(se)
turkey 1 kalkoen **2** [Am] flop ‖ *talk* ~ geen
blad voor de mond nemen
Turkey Turkije
Turkish Turks ‖ ~ *bath* Turks bad; ~ *delight*
Turks fruit; ~ *towel* ruwe badhanddoek
¹Turkmen (n) Turkmeen(se)
²Turkmen (adj) Turkmeens
Turkmenistan Turkmenistan
turmoil beroering: *the whole country was in*
(a) ~ het gehele land was in opschudding
¹turn (n) **1** draai, slag, omwenteling; [fig]
ommekeer; kentering [of season]; wisseling:
a few ~s of the screwdriver will do een paar
slagen met de schroevendraaier is genoeg; ~
of the tide getijwisseling, kentering; ~ *of the*
century eeuwwisseling **2** bocht, draai, kromming, afslag: *the next right* ~ de volgende afslag rechts **3** wending, draai, (verandering
van) richting: *take a* ~ *for the worse* een ongunstige wending nemen **4** beurt: *take* ~s *at*
sth. iets om beurten doen, elkaar aflossen

met iets; ~ *and* ~ *about* om en om, om de beurt; *by* ~s om en om, om de beurt; *in* ~ om de beurt, achtereenvolgens, op zijn beurt; *take it in* ~(s) *to do sth.* iets om beurten doen; *out of* ~ a) vóór zijn beurt, niet op zijn beurt; b) op een ongeschikt moment **5** dienst, daad: *do s.o. a bad* (or: *ill*) ~ iem. een slechte dienst bewijzen **6** aanleg, neiging: *be of a musical* ~ *(of mind)* muzikaal aangelegd zijn **7** korte bezigheid, wandelingetjeʰ, ommetjeʰ, ritjeʰ, tochtjeʰ; nummer(tje)ʰ [in circus, show]; artiest [in show] **8** korte tijd [of participation, work]; poos: *take a* ~ *at the wheel* het stuur een tijdje overnemen **9** slag; winding [in rope etc] **10** schok, draai, schrik: *she gave him quite a* ~ zij joeg hem flink de stuipen op het lijf **11** aanval; vlaag [of rage, illness] ‖ ~ *of phrase* formulering; *at every* ~ bij elke stap, overal

²**turn** (vb) **1** woelen, draaien: *toss and* ~ *all night* de hele nacht (liggen) draaien en woelen **2** zich richten, zich wenden: *his thoughts* ~ed *to his mother* hij dacht aan zijn moeder; ~ *away (from)* zich afwenden (van), weggaan (van); ~ *to drink* aan de drank raken **3** van richting veranderen, afslaan, een draai maken, (zich) omkeren: *the aeroplane* ~ed *sharply* het vliegtuig maakte een scherpe bocht; ~ *about* zich omkeren; *about* ~! rechtsom(keert)! [order to troops]; ~ *(a)round* a) zich omdraaien; b) een ommekeer maken, van gedachten (*or:* mening) veranderen; ~ *back* terugkeren, omkeren **4** draaien [of head, stomach]; tollen, duizelen: *my head is* ~*ing* het duizelt mij **5** gisten, bederven ‖ ~ *to* aan het werk gaan; ~ *into* veranderen in, worden; ~ *on* a) draaien om, afhangen van; b) gaan over [of conversation]; *water* ~s *to ice* water wordt ijs; ~ *(up)on s.o.* iem. aanvallen, zich tegen iem. keren

³**turn** (vb) **1** (rond)draaien, doen draaien: *the wheels* ~ *fast* de wielen draaien snel **2** omdraaien, (doen) omkeren, omploegen, omspitten, omslaan; keren [collar]; omvouwen: *the car* ~ed de auto keerde; ~ *about* omkeren, omdraaien; ~ *(a)round* ronddraaien, omkeren; ~ *back* omvouwen, omslaan; ~ *sth. inside out* iets binnenstebuiten keren; [fig] grondig doorzoeken, overhoophalen; ~ *upside down* ondersteboven keren; ~ *to page seven* sla bladzijde zeven op **3** draaien [on lathe, at pottery etc]; vormen, maken: ~ *a phrase* iets mooi zeggen **4** verzuren, zuur worden (maken): *the warm weather* ~ed *the milk* door het warme weer verzuurde de melk **5** maken, draaien; beschrijven [circle etc] **6** overdenken, overwegen **7** omgaan [corner]; omdraaien; omzeilen [cape]; omtrekken **8** (doen) veranderen (van), omzetten, verzetten, (ver)maken; een wending geven aan [conversation]; bocht laten maken,

draaien, afwenden, omleiden: ~ *the car into the garage* de auto de garage indraaien; ~ *into* veranderen in, (ver)maken tot, omzetten in; ~ *the conversation to sth.* different het gesprek op iets anders brengen **9** richten, wenden: ~ *your attention to the subject* richt je aandacht op het onderwerp **10** doen worden, maken: *the sun* ~ed *the papers yellow* de zon maakte de kranten geel; [Am] ~ *loose* loslaten, vrijlaten **11** verdraaien; verzwikken [ankle etc] **12** misselijk maken: *Chinese food* ~s *my stomach* Chinees eten maakt mijn maag van streek **13** worden [time, age]; passeren, geweest zijn: *it is* (or: *has*) ~ed *six o'clock* het is zes uur geweest **14** (weg)sturen, (weg)zenden: ~ *s.o. adrift* iem. aan zijn lot overlaten; ~ *away* wegsturen, wegjagen, ontslaan; [fig] verwerpen, afwijzen; *we were* ~ed *back at the entrance* bij de ingang werden we teruggestuurd **15** zetten, doen, brengen, laten gaan: ~ *s.o. into the street* iem. op straat zetten **16** omzetten, draaien, een omzet hebben van; maken [profit]

⁴**turn** (vb) worden: ~ *traitor* verrader worden; *the milk* ~ed *sour* de melk werd zuur

turnabout ommekeer

turncoat overloper, afvallige, deserteur

¹**turn down** (vb) achteruitgaan, een recessie doormaken: *our economy is turning down* onze economie gaat achteruit

²**turn down** (vb) **1** omvouwen, omslaan: *the sheets* de lakens omslaan **2** (om)keren; omdraaien [card] **3** afwijzen [plan, person]; verwerpen: *they turned your suggestion down* ze wezen je voorstel van de hand **4** lager zetten [gas, light]; zachter zetten [radio, volume]

¹**turn in** (vb) **1** binnengaan, indraaien **2** naar binnen staan: *his feet* ~ zijn voeten staan naar binnen **3** onder de wol kruipen, erin duiken

²**turn in** (vb) **1** naar binnen vouwen, naar binnen omslaan **2** overleveren; uitleveren [to police] **3** inleveren, geven

turning afsplitsing, aftakking, zijstraat, afslag, bocht: *the next* ~ *on* (or: *to*) *the right* de volgende straat rechts

turning circle draaicirkel

turning point keerpuntʰ [also fig]: ~ *in* (or: *of*) *s.o.'s life* keerpunt in iemands leven

turnip raap; knol [fodder]

¹**turn off** (vb) **1** afslaan **2** [inform] interesse verliezen, afhaken

²**turn off** (vb) **1** afsluiten [gas, water]; ~ *the gas* draai het gas uit **2** uitzetten, afzetten; uitdoen [eg light] **3** weerzin opwekken bij, doen afknappen: *it really turns me off* ik word er niet goed van

turn-off 1 afslag **2** afknapper

¹**turn on** (vb) enthousiast raken

²**turn on** (vb) **1** aanzetten; aandoen [radio

etc]; [fig] laten werken **2** opendraaien; openzetten [water, gas] **3** enthousiast maken, opwinden
t̲u̲rn-on [inform] opwindend persoon, ding
t̲u̲rnout 1 opkomst, publiek[h], menigte **2** kleding **3** opruimbeurt: *your kitchen needs a good ~* jouw keuken heeft een flinke schoonmaakbeurt nodig **4** productie
¹turn o̲u̲t (vb) **1** (op)komen, verschijnen **2** zich ontwikkelen, aflopen: *things will ~ all right* het zal goed aflopen **3** naar buiten staan [of feet etc] **4** [mil] aantreden [of watch]
²turn o̲u̲t (vb) **1** uitdoen; uitdraaien [light, stove etc] **2** eruit gooien, wegsturen **3** produceren, afleveren **4** leegmaken, opruimen, een beurt geven: *~ your **handbag*** je handtas omkeren **5** uitrusten, kleden **6** optrommelen, bijeenroepen
³turn o̲u̲t (vb) blijken (te zijn), uiteindelijk zijn: *the man turned out to **be** my neighbour* de man bleek mijn buurman te zijn
t̲u̲rnover 1 omzetsnelheid [of articles] **2** omzet **3** verloop[h] [of staff] **4** (appel)flap
¹turn o̲ver (vb) **1** zich omkeren **2** kantelen, omvallen **3** aanslaan; starten [of (car) engine]
²turn o̲ver (vb) **1** omkeren, omdraaien, op zijn kop zetten **2** omslaan [page]; doorbladeren: ***please*** *~* zie ommezijde **3** starten [car etc] **4** overwegen: *turn sth. over in one's mind* iets (goed) overdenken **5** overgeven; uitleveren, overleveren [to police]
t̲u̲rnover rate omzetsnelheid
t̲u̲rnpike 1 [Am] tolweg **2** [hist] tolweg; tolhek[h]
t̲u̲rn signal [Am] richtingaanwijzer
t̲u̲rnstile tourniquet[h], draaihek[h]
t̲u̲rntable 1 draaischijf [for locomotives] **2** draaischijf [of record player]; platenspeler
¹turn u̲p (vb) **1** verschijnen, komen (opdagen), tevoorschijn komen, voor de dag komen: *your **brooch** has turned up* je broche is terecht **2** zich voordoen: *the **opportunity** will ~* de gelegenheid doet zich wel voor **3** naar boven gedraaid zijn
²turn u̲p (vb) **1** vinden **2** blootleggen, aan de oppervlakte brengen **3** naar boven draaien; opzetten [collar]; omslaan [sleeve, pipe]; omhoogslaan, om(hoog)vouwen; opslaan [eyes]: *turn one's **collar** up* zijn kraag opzetten **4** hoger draaien; harder zetten [radio]
t̲u̲rpentine terpentijn(olie)
t̲u̲rquoise turkoois⁺[h]
t̲u̲rret 1 torentje[h] **2** geschutskoepel
t̲u̲rtle 1 (zee)schildpad **2** [Am] zoetwaterschildpad
t̲u̲rtledove tortelduif
t̲u̲rtleneck 1 col **2** coltrui
tusk 1 slagtand **2** scherp uitsteeksel
¹t̲u̲ssle (n) vechtpartij, worsteling

²t̲u̲ssle (vb) (+ with) vechten (met), worstelen (met)
t̲u̲telage voogdijschap[h]
¹t̲u̲tor (n) **1** privéleraar **2** studiebegeleider; [roughly] mentor **3** [Am] docent
²t̲u̲tor (vb) **1** als privéleraar werken **2** [Am] college krijgen van een docent
³t̲u̲tor (vb) (+ in) (privé)les geven (in)
tut̲o̲rial 1 werkgroep **2** [Am; esp technology] handleiding
tux̲e̲do [Am] smoking(kostuum[h])
TV *television* tv
¹twang (n) **1** tjing; ploink [of string] **2** neusgeluid[h]: *speak with a ~* door de neus praten
²twang (vb) **1** geplukt worden [of string] **2** snorren; zoeven [of arrow] **3** spelen [on instrument]; rammen; zagen [on violin]: *~ing on a guitar* jengelend op een gitaar
³twang (vb) **1** scherp laten weerklinken **2** nasaal uitspreken **3** bespelen, jengelen op, krassen op
¹tweak (n) ruk [on ear, nose]
²tweak (vb) beetpakken (en omdraaien), knijpen in; trekken aan [ear, nose]
twee 1 fijntjes, popperig **2** zoetelijk
tweeds tweed kleding
tweep volger
¹tweet (n) **1** tjiep, tjilp; getjilp[h] [of bird] **2** [social networking] twitterbericht
²tweet (vb) tjilpen, tjirpen
³tweet (vb) [social networking] twitteren
tw̲e̲eter tweeter; hogetonenluidspreker
tw̲e̲etup twitterbijeenkomst
tw̲e̲ezers pincet: *a pair of ~* een pincet
twelfth twaalfde
Twelfth N̲i̲ght driekoningenavond
twelve twaalf
tw̲e̲ntieth twintigste
tw̲e̲nty twintig: *in the twenties* in de jaren twintig
twice tweemaal, twee keer: *~ a **day*** tweemaal per dag; *~ as **good*** (or: *much*) dubbel zo goed (or: veel); *once or ~* een keer of twee
¹tw̲i̲ddle (n) draai, krul, kronkel
²tw̲i̲ddle (vb) zitten te draaien (met/aan), spelen (met), friemelen (met)
¹twig (n) twijg, takje[h]
²twig (vb) snappen, begrijpen
tw̲i̲light 1 schemering [also fig]; vage voorstelling **2** schemerlicht[h]
¹twin (n) **1** (een van een) tweeling **2** bijbehorende, tegenhanger **3** (-s) tweeling
²twin (adj) tweeling-: *~ **beds*** lits-jumeaux; *~ **towers*** twee identieke torens naast elkaar
¹twine (n) streng, vlecht
²twine (vb) **1** wikkelen, winden, vlechten: *she ~d her arms **(a)round** my neck* zij sloeg haar armen om mijn nek **2** omwikkelen
³twine (vb) zich wikkelen, zich winden: *the vines ~d (themselves) **round** the tree* de ranken slingerden zich om de boom

twin-engined tweemotorig
twinge 1 scheut, steek **2** [fig] knaging [of conscience]; kwelling: ~s of *conscience* gewetenswroeging
¹**twinkle** (n) **1** schittering, fonkeling: *a mischievous* ~ een ondeugende flikkering **2** knipoog **3** trilling ‖ *in a* ~ in een oogwenk
²**twinkle** (vb) **1** schitteren; fonkelen [of star]: *his eyes ~d with amusement* zijn ogen schitterden van plezier **2** trillen
³**twinkle** (vb) knipperen met [eyes]
twinkling: *in the* ~ *of an eye* in een ogenblik (*or:* mum van tijd)
twins tweeling
¹**twirl** (n) **1** draai, pirouette **2** krul
²**twirl** (vb) snel (doen) draaien, (doen) tollen, (doen) krullen: ~ *one's hair around* one's fingers zijn haar rond zijn vingers krullen
¹**twist** (n) **1** draai, draaibeweging, bocht, kromming; [fig] wending: *a road full of ~s and turns* een weg vol draaien en bochten; *give the truth a* ~ de waarheid een beetje verdraaien **2** verdraaiing; vertrekking [of face] **3** afwijking; [of character] trek
²**twist** (vb) **1** draaien, zich wentelen: *the corners of his mouth ~ed down* zijn mondhoeken trokken naar beneden **2** kronkelen, zich winden **3** zich wringen
³**twist** (vb) **1** samendraaien, samenstrengelen; [tobacco] spinnen: ~ *flowers into a garland* bloemen tot een krans samenvlechten **2** vlechten [eg rope] **3** winden, draaien om: ~ *the lid off a jar* het deksel van een jampot afdraaien **4** draaien, verwringen; vertrekken [face]; verrekken [muscle]; verstuiken [foot]; omdraaien [arm] **5** [fig] verdraaien [story, words etc]: *a ~ed mind* een verwrongen geest **6** wringen, afwringen, uitwringen
twister 1 bedrieger **2** [Am] wervelwind
¹**twit** (n) sufferd, domkop
²**twit** (vb) **1** bespotten **2** verwijten: ~ *s.o. about* (or: on) *his clumsiness* iem. (een beetje spottend) zijn onhandigheid verwijten
¹**twitch** (n) **1** trek, kramp **2** ruk
²**twitch** (vb) **1** trekken, trillen: *a ~ing muscle* een trillende spier **2** (+ at) rukken (aan)
³**twitch** (vb) **1** vertrekken: [fig] *he didn't ~ an eyelid* hij vertrok geen spier **2** trekken aan
¹**twitter** (n) getjilpʰ, gekwetterʰ ‖ *all of a* ~ opgewonden
²**twitter** (vb) tjilpen, kwetteren
twitterer twitteraar
two twee, tweetal: ~ *years* old twee jaar oud; ~ *or three* een paar, een stuk of wat; ~ *by* ~ twee aan twee; *arranged in* ~s per twee gerangschikt; *cut in* ~ in tweeën gesneden; *an apple or* ~ een paar appelen ‖ *in* ~ *twos* in een paar tellen
two-bit [Am] klein, waardeloos
two-dimensional tweedimensionaal

two-earner tweeverdiener(s)-: ~ *couple* tweeverdieners
two-edged [also fig] tweesnijdend
two-faced met twee gezichten; [fig] onoprecht
twofold tweevoudig
two-handed 1 voor twee handen: ~ *sword* tweehandig zwaard **2** voor twee personen: ~ *saw* trekzaag
two-income family tweeverdienersgezinʰ
twopence (Brits muntstuk van) twee pence ‖ *I don't care* ~ ik geef er geen zier om
twopenny twee pence kostend (waard)
¹**two-piece** (n) **1** deux-pièces **2** bikini
²**two-piece** (adj) tweedelig
twosome 1 tweetalʰ **2** spelʰ voor twee
two-stroke tweetakt-
¹**two-time** (vb) dubbel spel spelen
²**two-time** (vb) bedriegen, ontrouw zijn
two-way 1 tweerichtings-: ~ *traffic* tweerichtingsverkeer **2** wederzijds
tycoon magnaat
¹**type** (n) **1** typeʰ, soort, modelʰ **2** zetselʰ: *in* ~ gezet; *in italic* ~ in cursief (schrift) **3** drukletter, typeʰ
²**type** (vb) typen, tikken: ~ *out* uittikken
typecast steeds eenzelfde soort rol geven [actor]: *be* ~ *as a villain* altijd maar weer de schurk spelen
typeface fontʰ, lettertypeʰ
typescript getypte kopij
typewriter schrijfmachine
typhoid tyfus
typhoon tyfoon
typhus vlektyfus
typical typisch, typerend, kenmerkend: *be* ~ *of* karakteriseren, kenmerkend zijn voor
typify 1 typeren, karakteriseren **2** symboliseren
typography typografie
tyrannical tiranniek
¹**tyrannize** (vb) (+ over) als een tiran regeren (over); [fig] de tiran spelen
²**tyrannize** (vb) tiranniseren
tyranny 1 tirannie **2** tirannieke daad
tyrant tiran
tyre band
tyre-gauge bandspanningsmeter

U

u u, U
U [inform; mockingly] typisch upper class
ubiquitous overal aanwezig, alomtegenwoordig
U-boat U-boot; onderzeeër
udder uier
UFO *unidentified flying object* ufo, vliegende schotel
Uganda Uganda
¹Ugandan (n) Ugandees, Ugandese
²Ugandan (adj) Ugandees
ugh bah
ugly 1 lelijk, afstotend: [fig] ~ *duckling* lelijk eendje; [inform] *(as)* ~ *as sin* (zo) lelijk als de nacht 2 dreigend: *an* ~ *look* een dreigende blik 3 [inform] vervelend; lastig [of character]: *an* ~ *customer* een lastig mens
uh eh
UK *United Kingdom* UK, VK, Verenigd Koninkrijk
Ukraine Oekraïne
¹Ukrainian (n) Oekraïner, Oekraïense
²Ukrainian (adj) Oekraïens
ulcer (open) zweer, maagzweer
ulterior verborgen: *an* ~ *motive* een bijbedoeling
¹ultimate (n) maximumʰ; [fig] toppuntʰ; eindeʰ
²ultimate (adj) 1 ultiem, uiteindelijk, laatst 2 fundamenteel 3 uiterst, maximaal: *the* ~ *chic* het toppunt van chic
ultimately uiteindelijk
ultimatum ultimatumʰ
ultra extremistisch, radicaal
ultramarine ultramarijnʰ, lazuur(blauw)ʰ
ultramodern hypermodern
ultrasound scan echoscopie
ultraviolet ultravioletʰ
Ulysses Odysseus
um hm, ahum
umbilical navel-: ~ *cord* navelstreng
umbrage ergernis: *give* ~ ergeren; *take* ~ *at* (or: *over*) zich ergeren aan
¹umbrella (n) 1 paraplu; [fig] bescherming; overkoepelende organisatie: *under the* ~ *of the EU* onder de bescherming van de EU 2 (tuin)parasol, zonneschermʰ
²umbrella (adj) algemeen, verzamel-: ~ *term* overkoepelende term
¹umpire (n) scheidsrechter, umpire
²umpire (vb) als scheidsrechter optreden (in)
umpteen [inform] een hoop, heel wat, tig
umpteenth [inform] zoveelste

UN *United Nations* VN, Verenigde Naties
unabated onverminderd
unable niet in staat: *he was* ~ *to come* hij was verhinderd
unabridged onverkort, niet ingekort
unacceptable onaanvaardbaar
unaccompanied 1 onvergezeld 2 [mus] zonder begeleiding
unaccountable onverklaarbaar
unaccustomed 1 ongewoon, ongebruikelijk 2 niet gewend: *he is* ~ *to writing letters* hij is niet gewend brieven te schrijven
unaffected 1 ongedwongen, natuurlijk 2 onaangetast; [fig] niet beïnvloed; ongewijzigd
unafraid niet bang
unaided zonder hulp
unalloyed onvermengd [also fig]; zuiver: ~ *metal* niet gelegeerd metaal
unambiguous ondubbelzinnig
unanimity 1 eenstemmigheid, unanimiteit 2 eensgezindheid
unanimous 1 eenstemmig, unaniem 2 eensgezind
unannounced onaangekondigd
unanswerable 1 onweerlegbaar 2 niet te beantwoorden
unanswered onbeantwoord
unapproachable ontoegankelijk, onbenaderbaar
unarmed ongewapend
unashamed 1 zich niet schamend 2 onbeschaamd
unasked ongevraagd
unassuming pretentieloos; bescheiden
unattached 1 los, niet gebonden, onafhankelijk 2 alleenstaand, ongetrouwd
unattended 1 niet begeleid 2 onbeheerd: *leave sth.* ~ iets onbeheerd laten (staan)
unauthorized 1 onbevoegd 2 ongeoorloofd 3 niet geautoriseerd, onofficieel: *an* ~ *biography* een onofficiële biografie
unavailable niet beschikbaar
unavailing vergeefs, nutteloos
unavoidable onvermijdelijk
unaware (+ of) zich niet bewust (van): *be* ~ *that* niet weten dat
unawares 1 onverwacht(s): *catch* (or: *take*) *s.o.* ~ iem. verrassen (*or:* overrompelen) 2 onbewust
unbalance uit zijn evenwicht brengen, in verwarring brengen
unbalanced 1 niet in evenwicht, onevenwichtig 2 in de war
unbar ontgrendelen; [fig] openstellen; vrij maken
unbearable 1 ondraaglijk 2 onuitstaanbaar
unbeaten 1 niet verslagen; ongeslagen [sport] 2 onovertroffen; ongebroken [record]

unbecoming 1 niet (goed) staand **2** ongepast, onbehoorlijk: *your conduct is ~ for* (or: *to) a gentleman!* zo gedraagt een heer zich niet!

unbelief ongeloof^h, ongelovigheid
unbelievable ongelofelijk
unbeliever ongelovige
unbending onbuigzaam, onverzettelijk
unbias(s)ed 1 onbevooroordeeld **2** zuiver, niet vertekend
unbind 1 losmaken **2** bevrijden
unblushing 1 schaamteloos **2** niet blozend
unborn 1 (nog) ongeboren **2** toekomstig
unbosom uiten: *~ o.s. (to)* zijn hart uitstorten (bij)
unbowed 1 ongebogen **2** ongebroken [fig]; niet onderworpen
unbridled ongebreideld: *~ tongue* losse tong
unbroken 1 ongebroken, heel **2** ongedresseerd **3** ononderbroken **4** onovertroffen; ongebroken [record]
unbuckle losgespen
unburden 1 ontlasten, van een last bevrijden: *~ one's conscience* zijn geweten ontlasten; *~ o.s.* (or: *one's heart) to s.o.* zijn hart uitstorten bij iem. **2** zich bevrijden van, opbiechten
uncalled-for 1 ongewenst, ongepast **2** onnodig: *that remark was ~* die opmerking was nergens voor nodig **3** ongegrond
uncanny geheimzinnig, griezelig
uncaring onverschillig, ongevoelig
unceasing onophoudelijk
unceremonious 1 informeel, ongedwongen **2** niet erg beleefd
uncertain 1 onzeker: *in no ~ terms* in niet mis te verstane bewoordingen; *be ~ of* (or: *about) s.o.'s intentions* twijfelen aan iemands bedoelingen **2** onbepaald, vaag **3** veranderlijk: *a woman with an ~ temper* een wispelturige vrouw
uncertainty 1 onzekerheid, twijfel(achtigheid) **2** onduidelijkheid, vaagheid **3** veranderlijkheid, onbetrouwbaarheid
unchallenged onbetwist, zonder tegenspraak: *we cannot let this pass ~* we kunnen dit niet zomaar laten passeren
unchanging niet veranderend; standvastig
uncharitable harteloos, liefdeloos: *an ~ judg(e)ment* een hard oordeel
unchecked 1 ongehinderd **2** ongecontroleerd
uncivil onbeleefd
uncivilized onbeschaafd
unclaimed 1 niet opgeëist **2** niet afgehaald [letter, luggage]
unclassified 1 ongeordend, niet ingedeeld **2** niet geheim (vertrouwelijk)
uncle oom

unclean 1 vuil; bevuild [fig]; bevlekt **2** onkuis **3** [rel] onrein: *~ meat* onrein vlees
unclear onduidelijk
Uncle Sam [inform] Uncle Sam, de Amerikaanse regering, het Amerikaanse volk
uncoil (zich) ontrollen
uncoloured ongekleurd [also fig]; objectief
uncomfortable 1 ongemakkelijk, oncomfortabel: *~ situation* pijnlijke situatie **2** niet op zijn gemak, verlegen
uncommitted 1 niet-gebonden, neutraal: *he wants to remain ~* hij wil zich niet vastleggen **2** zonder verplichting(en)
uncommon ongewoon, buitengewoon: *~ly rude* hoogst onbeleefd
uncompromising 1 onbuigzaam, niet toegeeflijk **2** vastberaden
unconcerned 1 onbezorgd **2** onverschillig
unconditional onvoorwaardelijk
¹unconscious (n) het onbewuste, het onderbewuste
²unconscious (adj) **1** onbewust, niet wetend: *be ~ of sth.* zich ergens niet bewust van zijn **2** bewusteloos
uncontested onbetwist: *~ election* verkiezing zonder tegenkandidaten
uncontrollable 1 niet te beheersen, onbedwingbaar **2** onbeheerst: *~ laughter* onbedaarlijke gelach
unconventional 1 onconventioneel, ongebruikelijk **2** natuurlijk **3** niet-conventioneel, nucleair, atoom-
unconvincing niet overtuigend
uncool [inform] niet cool; stom
uncork ontkurken
uncouple ontkoppelen, afkoppelen, loskoppelen
uncouth ongemanierd, grof
¹uncover (vb) zijn hoofddeksel afnemen
²uncover (vb) **1** het (hoofd)deksel afnemen van, opgraven **2** aan het licht brengen, ontdekken
uncritical 1 onkritisch **2** kritiekloos
unction zalving
unctuous zalvend, vleierig
uncut 1 ongesneden, ongemaaid **2** onverkort; ongecensureerd [book, film] **3** ongeslepen [diamond]
undaunted onverschrokken: *~ by* niet ontmoedigd door
undecided 1 onbeslist: *the match was left ~* de wedstrijd eindigde onbeslist **2** weifelend, besluiteloos: *be ~ about* in tweestrijd staan over
undeniable onbetwistbaar: *that is undeniably true* dat is ontegenzeglijk waar
¹under (adv) **1** onder, eronder, hieronder, daaronder, (naar) beneden, omlaag: *groups of nine and ~* groepen van negen en minder **2** in bedwang, onder controle **3** bewuste-

loos: *the drug* **put** *her* ~ *for the day* door het verdovingsmiddel raakte zij de hele dag buiten bewustzijn
²under (prep) **1** [place] onder; [fig] onder het gezag van; onder toezicht van: ~ *the cliffs* aan de voet van de klippen; *he wrote* ~ *another* **name** hij schreef onder een andere naam; *a place* ~ *the* **sun** een plekje onder de zon **2** [circumstance] onder, in, in een toestand van, krachtens, tijdens: ~ *construction* in aanbouw; *the issue* ~ *discussion* het probleem dat ter discussie staat; *collapse* ~ *the* **strain** het onder de spanning begeven **3** minder dan: ~ *age* minderjarig; *just* ~ *a* **minute** net iets minder dan een minuut, net binnen de minuut; *children* ~ *six* kinderen beneden de zes jaar
under-age minderjarig
¹underarm (n) [euph] oksel
²underarm (adj, adv) onderhands [esp sport]
undercarriage 1 onderstelʰ [of wagon]; chassisʰ **2** landingsgestelʰ
underclothes ondergoed
undercoat grond(verf)laag
undercover geheim: ~ *man* spion; stille, detective
undercurrent onderstroom [also fig]; verborgen gedachten, gevoelens
underdeveloped onderontwikkeld [also econ, photo]; (nog) onvoldoende ontwikkeld
underdog underdog, (verwachte) verliezer
underdone niet (helemaal) gaar
underestimate onderschatten, te laag schatten
underexpose onderbelichten
underexposure onderbelichting
underfloor onder de vloer: ~ *heating* vloerverwarming
underfoot 1 onder de voet(en), op de grond; [fig] onderdrukt: *crush* (or: *trample*) *sth.* ~ iets vertrappen **2** in de weg, voor de voeten
undergo ondergaan, doorstaan
undergraduate [inform] student(e) [who does not have a degree yet]; bachelorstudent
¹underground (n) metro, ondergrondse: *by* ~ met de ondergrondse
²underground (adj) ondergronds, (zich) onder de grond (bevindend); [fig] clandestien
³underground (adv) ondergronds, onder de grond; [fig] clandestien: *go* ~ onderduiken, ondergronds gaan werken
undergrowth kreupelhoutʰ
underhand 1 onderhands, clandestien **2** achterbaks
underhanded 1 onderhands **2** achterbaks
underlie 1 liggen onder, zich bevinden on-

der **2** ten grondslag liggen aan, verklaren: *underlying* **principles** grondprincipes **3** schuil gaan achter: *underlying* **meaning** werkelijke betekenis
underline onderstrepen [also fig]; benadrukken
undermanned onderbezet
undermine ondermijnen; ondergraven [also fig]; verzwakken
¹underneath (n) onderkant
²underneath (adv) [place; also fig] onderaan, eronder, aan de onderkant: *what's written* ~? wat staat er aan de onderkant geschreven?
³underneath (prep) [place] beneden, (vlak) onder: ~ *his coat* he wore a suit onder zijn jas droeg hij een pak
underpants onderbroek
underpass tunnel(tjeʰ): *take the* ~! ga door het tunneltje!
underpopulated onderbevolkt
underprivileged (kans)arm, sociaal zwak
underrate 1 te laag schatten [costs] **2** onderschatten, onderwaarderen
underscore onderstrepen [also fig]; benadrukken
undersea onderzees, onderzee-, onderwater-
under-secretary 1 ondersecretaris, tweede secretaris **2** staatssecretaris: *permanent* ~ [roughly] secretaris-generaal [of ministry]
underside onderkant, onderzijde
undersigned ondertekend (hebbend): *I, the* ~ ik, ondergetekende
undersized te klein, onder de normale grootte
understaffed onderbezet
understand 1 begrijpen, inzien, verstand hebben van, (goed) op de hoogte zijn: *give s.o. to* ~ *that* iem. te verstaan geven dat; ~ *each other* (or: *one another*) elkaar begrijpen, op één lijn zitten; *I simply don't* ~ ik snap het gewoon niet; ~ *about* verstand hebben van **2** begrijpen, (er) begrip hebben voor: *he begged her to* ~ hij smeekte haar begrip voor de situatie te hebben **3** begrijpen, (er)uit opmaken, vernemen: *I understood* *that you knew him* ik had begrepen dat je hem kende **4** verstaan [language] **5** opvatten: *as I* ~ *it* zoals ik het zie **6** als vanzelfsprekend aannemen: *that is understood!* (dat spreekt) vanzelf!
understandable begrijpelijk
understandably 1 begrijpelijk **2** begrijpelijkerwijs: ~, *we were all annoyed* begrijpelijkerwijs waren we allemaal geïrriteerd
¹understanding (n) **1** afspraak, overeenkomst: *come* to (or: *reach*) *an* ~ het eens worden; *on the* ~ *that* met dien verstande dat **2** (onderling) begripʰ, verstandhouding **3** verstandʰ, intelligentie, begripʰ **4** inter-

pretatie, beoordeling, opvatting: *a wrong ~ of the situation* een verkeerde beoordeling van de situatie
²**understanding** (adj) begripvol, welwillend
understate 1 (te) zwak uitdrukken **2** te laag opgeven [eg age, income]
understatement understatementʰ: *that's an ~* dat is zwak uitgedrukt
understudy understudy, invaller
undertake 1 ondernemen **2** op zich nemen, beloven, zich verplichten tot **3** garanderen, instaan voor
undertaker begrafenisondernemer
¹**undertaking** (n) het verzorgen van begrafenissen
²**undertaking** (n) **1** onderneming: *translating the Bible is quite an ~* het is een hele onderneming om de Bijbel te vertalen **2** (plechtige) belofte, garantie
under-the-counter onder de toonbank; clandestien
undertone 1 gedempte toon: *speak in ~s* (or: *an ~*) met gedempte stem spreken **2** ondertoon [fig] **3** lichte tint, zweem: *red with a slight ~ of yellow* rood met een klein beetje geel erin
undervalue onderwaarderen
underwater onder water
underwear ondergoedʰ
underworld onderwereld
underwrite 1 ondertekenen [policy]; afsluiten [insurance]; (door ondertekening) op zich nemen [risk, liability] **2** verzekeren [shipp]; zich garant stellen voor **3** onderschrijven, goedvinden
undeserved onverdiend; onterecht
¹**undesirable** (n) ongewenst persoon; persona non grata
²**undesirable** (adj) ongewenst; onwenselijk: *~ discharge* oneervol ontslag
undeterred niet ontmoedigd
undies [inform] (dames)ondergoed
undisputed onbetwist
undistinguished niet bijzonder, alledaags, gewoon
undisturbed ongestoord
undivided onverdeeld
¹**undo** (vb) losgaan
²**undo** (vb) **1** losmaken, losknopen **2** uitkleden **3** tenietdoen, ongedaan maken: *this mistake can never be ~ne* deze fout kan nooit goedgemaakt worden
undoing ondergang
undomesticated 1 ongetemd, wild **2** niet huishoudelijk (aangelegd)
undone 1 ongedaan, onafgemaakt **2** los(gegaan): *come ~* losgaan, losraken
undoubted ongetwijfeld
undreamed onvoorstelbaar: *~ of* onvoorstelbaar

undress (zich) uitkleden
undue 1 overmatig: *exercise ~ influence upon s.o.* te grote invloed op iem. uitoefenen **2** onbehoorlijk
unduly 1 uitermate, overmatig **2** onbehoorlijk **3** onrechtmatig
undying onsterfelijk, eeuwig
unearth 1 opgraven; [fig] opdiepen **2** onthullen
unearthly 1 bovenaards **2** bovennatuurlijk, mysterieus **3** angstaanjagend, eng **4** [inform] onmogelijk [time]: *wake s.o. up at an ~ hour* iem. op een belachelijk vroeg uur wakker maken
uneasy 1 onbehaaglijk: *~ conscience* bezwaard geweten; *be ~ with* zich niet op zijn gemak voelen met **2** bezorgd: *be ~ about, grow ~ at* zich zorgen maken over **3** onrustig [eg during sleep] **4** verontrustend
uneconomic(al) 1 oneconomisch, onrendabel **2** verkwistend
uneducated ongeschoold, onontwikkeld
unemployed 1 ongebruikt **2** werkloos, zonder werk
unemployment werkloosheid: *~ benefit* werkloosheidsuitkering
unemployment benefit werkloosheidsuitkering
unending 1 oneindig, eindeloos **2** onophoudelijk
unenviable niet benijdenswaard(ig); onplezierig [task]
unequal ongelijk(waardig); *~ in size* ongelijk in grootte
unequivocal ondubbelzinnig; duidelijk
unerring onfeilbaar: *~ devotion* niet aflatende toewijding
UNESCO *United Nations Educational, Scientific, and Cultural Organization* Unesco
unethical onethisch
uneven 1 ongelijk; oneffen [eg surface]; onregelmatig **2** van ongelijke kwaliteit
uneventful onbewogen, rustig, saai: *~ day* dag zonder belangrijke gebeurtenissen
unexceptional niet ongewoon; gewoon
unexpected onverwacht
unfailing onuitputtelijk, onophoudelijk
unfair oneerlijk, onrechtvaardig: *~ competition* oneerlijke concurrentie
unfaithful ontrouw, overspelig
unfaltering 1 zonder te aarzelen **2** onwankelbaar; standvastig: *~ love* onwankelbare liefde
unfamiliar 1 onbekend, niet vertrouwd **2** ongewoon, vreemd
unfashionable niet modieus
¹**unfasten** (vb) losgaan
²**unfasten** (vb) losmaken, losknopen
unfavourable ongunstig
unfeeling gevoelloos [also fig]; hardvochtig

unfettered ontketend [also fig]; vrij
unfinished 1 onaf, onvoltooid: ~ *business* onafgedane kwestie(s) **2** onbewerkt [eg of wood]
unfit 1 ongeschikt **2** in slechte conditie
unflinching 1 onbevreesd **2** vastberaden
unfold 1 (zich) openvouwen **2** (zich) uitspreiden **3** (zich) openbaren, (zich) ontvouwen
unforeseeable onvoorspelbaar
unforgettable onvergetelijk
unforgivable onvergeeflijk
unforgiving 1 onverzoenlijk **2** keihard: *business is* ~ het zakenleven is meedogenloos
unfortunate ongelukkig, betreurenswaardig
unfounded ongegrond
unfriend ontvrienden
unfriendly onvriendelijk, vijandig: ~ *area* onherbergzaam gebied; ~ *reception* koele ontvangst
unfulfilled onvervuld
unfurl (zich) ontrollen; (zich) ontvouwen [eg of flag]
ungainly lomp
unget-at-able [inform] onbereikbaar
ungodly 1 goddeloos **2** [inform] afgrijselijk
ungracious 1 onhoffelijk; lomp **2** onaangenaam: ~ *task* ondankbare taak
ungrateful ondankbaar
unguarded 1 onbewaakt: *in an* ~ *moment* op een onbewaakt ogenblik **2** onbedachtzaam **3** achteloos
unguent zalf
unhappy 1 ongelukkig, bedroefd **2** ongepast
unharmed ongedeerd, onbeschadigd
unhealthy ongezond [also fig]; ziekelijk
unheard niet gehoord, ongehoord: *his advice went* ~ naar zijn raad werd niet geluisterd
unheard-of ongekend, buitengewoon
unheeded genegeerd, in de wind geslagen: *his remark went* ~ er werd geen acht geslagen op zijn opmerking
unhinge 1 uit de scharnieren tillen [door] **2** [inform] uit zijn evenwicht brengen: *his mind is* ~*d* hij is geestelijk uit evenwicht
unholy 1 goddeloos **2** [inform] verschrikkelijk: [inform] *at an* ~ *hour* op een onchristelijk tijdstip; ~ *noise* heidens lawaai
unhook loshaken
unhurt ongedeerd
unicorn eenhoorn
unidentified niet geïdentificeerd: ~ *flying object* vliegende schotel
unification eenmaking, unificatie
¹**uniform** (n) uniformʰ
²**uniform** (adj) uniform, eensluidend

uniformity 1 uniformiteit **2** gelijkmatigheid
unify (zich) verenigen, tot één maken
unilateral eenzijdig, van één kant
unimaginable onvoorstelbaar
unimpeachable 1 onbetwistbaar **2** onberispelijk
unimportant onbelangrijk
unimpressed niet onder de indruk
unimpressive weinig indrukwekkend; saai
unintentional onbedoeld, onopzettelijk
uninterested 1 ongeïnteresseerd **2** zonder belangen
uninteresting oninteressant
uninterrupted onbonderbroken, doorlopend
union 1 verbondʰ, unie **2** (vak)bond, vakvereniging **3** studentenvereniging **4** huwelijkʰ **5** verbinding, koppelstukʰ
unionist vakbondslidʰ
Union Jack Britse vlag
union leader vakbondsleider
unique uniek; [inform] opmerkelijk
unisex uniseks-
unison 1 koorʰ, het tegelijk spreken: *speak in* ~ in koor spreken **2** harmonie: *work in* ~ eendrachtig samenwerken
unit 1 eenheid, onderdeelʰ, afdeling, meetgrootheid; [techn] apparaatʰ; module: ~ *of account* rekeneenheid **2** combineerbaar onderdeelʰ [of furniture]; unit, blokʰ
¹**unite** (vb) **1** zich verenigen, samenwerken, fuseren: *they* ~*d in fighting the enemy* samen bestreden zij de vijand **2** zich verbinden, aaneengroeien **3** zich mengen
²**unite** (vb) **1** verbinden, verenigen, tot een geheel maken **2** in de echt verbinden
united 1 verenigd: *the United* **Kingdom** het Verenigd Koninkrijk; *the United* **Nations** de Verenigde Naties; *the United* **States** de Verenigde Staten **2** saamhorig, hecht, harmonieus **3** gezamenlijk: *with their* ~ *powers* met vereende krachten
the **United Arab Emirates** Verenigde Arabische Emiraten
unity 1 geheelʰ, eenheid, samenhang **2** samenwerking **3** harmonie: *at* (or: *in*) ~ eendrachtig, eensgezind
universal 1 universeel, algemeen: ~ *rule* algemeen geldende regel **2** algeheel, alomvattend: ~ *agreement* algemene instemming
universally overal: ~ *present* alomtegenwoordig
universe 1 heelalʰ **2** wereld; [also] gebiedʰ
university universiteit, hogeschool
unjust onrechtvaardig
unjustifiable niet te verantwoorden
unkempt 1 ongekamd **2** onverzorgd
unkind 1 onaardig, onvriendelijk **2** ruw
unknown onbekend: ~ *quantity* onbeken-

de grootheid; [fig] onzekere factor ‖ ~ **to** us buiten ons medeweten, zonder dat wij het wisten
unl̲awful onwettig, illegaal
unl̲eaded loodvrij
unl̲eash losmaken van de riem [dog]; [also fig] ontketenen: ~ *one's rage (up)on* s.o. zijn woede op iem. koelen
unl̲ess tenzij, behalve, zonder dat: *I won't go ~ you come with me* ik ga niet tenzij jij meekomt
unl̲icensed 1 zonder vergunning **2** zonder goedkeuring
¹**unl̲ike** (adj, adv) **1** verschillend, niet gelijkend **2** ongelijkwaardig **3** [maths] tegengesteld
²**unl̲ike** (prep) **1** anders dan, in tegenstelling tot **2** niet typisch voor: *that's ~ John* dat is niets voor John
unl̲ikely 1 onwaarschijnlijk **2** weinig belovend, niet hoopgevend: *he is ~ to succeed* hij heeft weinig kans van slagen
unl̲imited onbeperkt, ongelimiteerd
unl̲isted 1 niet geregistreerd: ~ *number* geheim telefoonnummer **2** [fin] incourant
unl̲oad 1 lossen, uitladen, leegmaken **2** wegdoen, zich ontdoen van: ~ *responsibilities onto* s.o. de verantwoordelijkheid op iem. afschuiven **3** ontladen [firearm; also fig]; afreageren
unl̲ock 1 openmaken, opendoen, van het slot doen: ~ *the truth* de waarheid onthullen **2** losmaken, bevrijden, de vrije loop laten
unl̲ooked-for onverwacht
unl̲oose(n) 1 losmaken, losknopen, vrijlaten: *old memories were unloose(ne)d* oude herinneringen kwamen boven **2** ontspannen
unl̲ucky ongelukkig: *be* ~ pech hebben
unm̲ade onopgemaakt: ~ *bed* onopgemaakt bed
unm̲anageable 1 onhandelbaar **2** onhanteerbaar, niet te besturen
unm̲annerly ongemanierd, ruw, onbeschaafd
unm̲arked 1 ongemerkt; zonder merkteken **2** zonder cijfer; onbeoordeeld ‖ *a novel ~ by psychological insight* een roman die niet uitblinkt door psychologisch inzicht
unm̲arried ongetrouwd
unm̲ask het masker afnemen, ontmaskeren, onthullen
unm̲entionable 1 taboe **2** niet (nader) te noemen **3** niet te beschrijven
unm̲indful zorgeloos, vergeetachtig: ~ *of* zonder acht te slaan op
unmist̲akable onmiskenbaar, ondubbelzinnig
unm̲itigated 1 onverminderd, onverzacht **2** absoluut, volkomen: ~ *disaster* regelrechte ramp

unn̲atural onnatuurlijk, abnormaal
unn̲ecessary 1 onnodig, niet noodzakelijk **2** overbodig
unn̲erve 1 van zijn stuk brengen, ontmoedigen **2** nerveus maken
unn̲erving zenuwslopend; verontrustend
unn̲oticed onopgemerkt
UNO *United Nations Organisation* VN, Verenigde Naties
unobtr̲usive 1 onopvallend **2** discreet, voorzichtig
unocc̲upied 1 leeg, onbezet, vrij **2** niet bezig, werkeloos
unoff̲icial onofficieel, officieus, niet bevestigd ‖ ~ *strike* wilde staking
unp̲ack uitpakken: ~ *one's suitcase* (or: *clothes*) zijn koffer (or: kleren) uitpakken
unp̲aid onbetaald
unp̲aralleled zonder weerga, ongeëvenaard
unp̲ick lostornen: ~ *a seam* (or: *stitches*) een naad (or: steken) lostornen
unpl̲easant onaangenaam, onplezierig
unpl̲easantness 1 onaangenaam voorvalʰ **2** wrijving, woorden, ruzie **3** onaangenaamheid
unpl̲ug de stekker uittrekken van: ~ *the phone* de telefoonstekker eruit trekken; [mus] *an ~ged set* een akoestische set
unp̲olished 1 onopgelijst [also style]; ongepeld [rice] **2** ruw; onbeschaafd [manners]
unp̲opular impopulair
unpr̲ecedented ongekend, nooit eerder voorgekomen
unpred̲ictable onvoorspelbaar
unprep̲ared 1 onvoorbereid, geïmproviseerd **2** onverwacht(s)
unpr̲incipled gewetenloos
unprof̲essional 1 niet professioneel, onprofessioneel, niet beroeps, amateur- **2** amateuristisch
unpr̲oved niet bewezen
unprov̲ided onvoorzien: *he left his family ~ for* hij liet zijn gezin onverzorgd achter; *the cabin was ~ with kitchen utensils* in de hut was geen keukengerei aanwezig
unprov̲oked niet uitgelokt, zonder aanleiding
unqu̲alified 1 niet gekwalificeerd, onbevoegd **2** onvoorwaardelijk: ~ *success* onverdeeld succes
unqu̲estionable onbetwistbaar
unqu̲estionably ongetwijfeld, zonder twijfel: *they are ~ the best team of the USA* dat ze het beste team van Amerika zijn, staat buiten kijf
unqu̲estioned 1 niet ondervraagd **2** onbetwistbaar **3** onbetwist, niet tegengesproken
unqu̲estioning onvoorwaardelijk
unqu̲ote een citaat beëindigen, aanha-

lingstekens sluiten: *he said (quote) 'Over my dead body' (~)* hij zei (aanhalingstekens openen) 'Over mijn lijk' (aanhalingstekens sluiten)

¹**unravel** (vb) rafelen, rafelig worden
²**unravel** (vb) ontrafelen [also fig]; uithalen; [fig also] uitzoeken; oplossen
unreal 1 onwerkelijk, denkbeeldig 2 onecht, onwaar, vals
unrealistic onrealistisch
unreasonable 1 redeloos, verstandeloos 2 onredelijk 3 buitensporig, overdreven
unreasoning redeloos, irrationeel, onnadenkend
unrecognized 1 niet herkend 2 niet erkend
unrelated 1 niet verwant 2 geen verband houdend met
unrelenting 1 onverminderd, voortdurend 2 meedogenloos, onverbiddelijk
unreliable onbetrouwbaar
unrelieved 1 eentonig, vlak, saai: *~ by* niet afgewisseld met 2 hevig, sterk, intens
unrequited onbeantwoord: *~ love* onbeantwoorde liefde
unreserved 1 onverdeeld, geheel, onvoorwaardelijk 2 openhartig, eerlijk
unresolved 1 onopgelost; onbeantwoord 2 besluiteloos
unrest onrust, beroering
unrewarding niet lonend, niet de moeite waard; [fig] ondankbaar
unrivalled ongeëvenaard
unroll (zich) uitrollen, (zich) ontrollen; [also fig] (zich) tonen; (zich) onthullen
unruffled kalm, onverstoord
unruly onhandelbaar, weerspannig
unsatisfactory onbevredigend
unsavoury 1 onsmakelijk, vies; [also fig] weerzinwekkend 2 smakeloos, flauw
unscathed ongedeerd, onbeschadigd: *return ~* heelhuids terugkeren
unscientific onwetenschappelijk
unscramble 1 ontcijferen, decoderen 2 ontwarren, uit elkaar halen
¹**unscrew** (vb) 1 losraken 2 losgeschroefd worden
²**unscrew** (vb) 1 losschroeven 2 losdraaien, eraf draaien: *can you ~ this bottle?* krijg jij deze fles open?
unscrupulous zonder scrupules, immoreel, gewetenloos
unseasonable abnormaal voor het seizoen: *an ~ summer* een slechte zomer
unseat 1 afwerpen, uit het zadel werpen, doen vallen, ten val brengen 2 zijn positie afnemen; [pol] zijn zetel doen verliezen
unsecured 1 onbeveiligd 2 [fin] ongedekt: *~ loan* ongedekte lening
unseeing niet(s) ziend, wezenloos
unseemly 1 onbehoorlijk 2 onaantrekke-

lijk, lelijk
unseen 1 onzichtbaar 2 onvoorbereid: *questions on an ~ text* vragen over een niet bestudeerde tekst
¹**unsettle** (vb) 1 onvast worden; (aan het) wankelen (slaan) [fig]; op losse schroeven komen te staan, onzeker worden 2 van streek raken 3 wisselvallig worden [of weather]
²**unsettle** (vb) 1 doen loskomen, los maken 2 doen wankelen [fig]; op losse schroeven zetten: *unsettling changes* veranderingen die alles op losse schroeven zetten 3 van streek maken
unsettled 1 onzeker, verwar(ren)d: *~ times* onzekere tijden 2 wisselvallig; veranderlijk [weather] 3 onbeslist, (nog) niet uitgemaakt: *this issue is still ~* deze kwestie is nog niet afgedaan 4 in de war
unshrinkable krimpvrij
unsightly onooglijk
unskilled 1 ongeschoold 2 onervaren, onbedreven
unsociable 1 terughoudend, teruggetrokken 2 ongezellig
unsocial asociaal, onmaatschappelijk: *~ hours* ongebruikelijke werktijden
unsolicited ongevraagd
unsophisticated 1 onbedorven, echt, eerlijk 2 onervaren, naïef 3 ongedwongen, ongecompliceerd
unsound 1 ongezond, ziek(elijk): *of ~ mind* krankzinnig, ontoerekeningsvatbaar 2 ongaaf 3 onstevig, zwak 4 ondeugdelijk 5 ongegrond, ongeldig 6 onbetrouwbaar, vals
unsparing 1 kwistig, gul, vrijgevig: *~ of* kwistig met 2 meedogenloos, ongenadig
unspeakable 1 onuitsprekelijk, onuitspreekbaar, onbeschrijf(e)lijk 2 afschuwelijk
unspecified ongespecificeerd; niet nader omschreven
unspoilt onaangetast
unspoken stilzwijgend; onuitgesproken
unsprayed onbespoten
unstable 1 veranderlijk, wisselvallig, onevenwichtig, wispelturig 2 onstabiel [also science, chem]; labiel: *~ equilibrium* wankel evenwicht 3 onvast, los
unstamped ongefrankeerd
unsteady 1 onvast, wankel: *her voice was ~* haar stem was onvast 2 veranderlijk, wisselvallig 3 onregelmatig
unstinted royaal, gul, kwistig
unstoppable onstuitbaar, niet te stoppen
unstuck los ‖ [inform] *come (badly) ~* in het honderd lopen, mislukken
unstudied 1 ongekunsteld, natuurlijk 2 ongestudeerd, ongeschoold
unsubstantiated onbewezen; ongefundeerd
unsuccessful 1 niet succesvol, zonder suc-

ces **2** niet geslaagd, afgewezen: *be ~* niet slagen, mislukken
unsuited ongepast: *~ for* ongeschikt voor
unsure 1 onzeker, onvast **2** onbetrouwbaar, twijfelachtig
unsuspected 1 onverdacht **2** onverwacht; onvermoed
unsuspecting 1 nietsvermoedend **2** niet achterdochtig, argeloos
unswerving 1 recht, rechtdoor, rechtaan **2** onwankelbaar
untangle 1 ontwarren **2** ophelderen, oplossen
untenable onhoudbaar [also fig]; niet te verdedigen
unthinkable 1 ondenkbaar, onvoorstelbaar **2** onaanvaardbaar: *it's ~!* geen sprake van!, daar komt niets van in! **3** onwaarschijnlijk
unthinking 1 onnadenkend: *~ moment* onbewaakt ogenblik **2** onbewust, onbedoeld
untidy slordig
untie 1 losknopen, losmaken **2** bevrijden [person who is tied up]; vrijlaten
until tot, totdat, voor; [+ negation] niet voor: *I cannot leave ~ Sunday* ik kan niet voor zondag vertrekken, ik kan pas zondag vertrekken; *I did not know about it ~ today* ik wist er tot vandaag niets van; *I was very lonely ~ I met Karen* ik was erg eenzaam tot ik Karen ontmoette
untimely 1 ongelegen, ongeschikt **2** voortijdig, te vroeg: *~ death* te vroege dood
untold 1 niet verteld **2** onnoemelijk, onmetelijk
¹untouchable (n) onaanraakbareʰ; paria
²untouchable (adj) **1** onaanraakbaar, onrein **2** onaantastbaar
untouched onaangeroerd
untoward 1 ongelegen, ongewenst: *~ circumstances* ongunstige omstandigheden **2** ongepast
untried 1 niet geprobeerd, onbeproefd **2** niet getest
untroubled 1 ongestoord **2** kalm, rustig
untrue 1 onwaar, niet waar **2** ontrouw, niet loyaal **3** afwijkend [from norm]; onzuiver, scheef: *~ tone* onzuivere toon
untruthful 1 leugenachtig; oneerlijk **2** onwaar
¹unused (adj) ongebruikt, onbenut: *~ opportunity* onbenutte gelegenheid
²unused (adj) niet gewend: *~ to hard work* er niet aan gewend hard te (moeten) werken
unusual 1 ongebruikelijk, ongewoon **2** opmerkelijk, buitengewoon
unusually bijzonder; erg
unutterable onuitsprekelijk [also fig]; onbeschrijfelijk: *~ idiot* volslagen idioot
unvarnished onverbloemd

¹unveil (vb) de sluier afdoen, de sluier laten vallen
²unveil (vb) onthullen, ontsluieren; [fig] openbaren; aan het licht brengen
unwanted 1 ongewenst **2** onnodig
unwarranted ongerechtvaardigd, ongewettigd, ongegrond
unwelcome niet welkom; ongewenst
unwell onwel, ziek
unwieldy 1 onhandelbaar, onhandig, onpraktisch, niet gemakkelijk te hanteren **2** onbehouwen, lomp
unwilling onwillig, niet bereid
¹unwind (vb) **1** zich afwikkelen [also fig]; zich ontrollen **2** [inform] zich ontspannen
²unwind (vb) **1** afwikkelen, ontrollen **2** ontwarren
unwise onverstandig
unwitting 1 onwetend, onbewust **2** onopzettelijk, ongewild
unworkable (bijna) onuitvoerbaar; onpraktisch
unworthy 1 onwaardig **2** ongepast: *that attitude is ~ of you* die houding siert je niet
unwrap openmaken, uitpakken
unwritten 1 ongeschreven **2** mondeling overgeleverd ‖ *~ law* ongeschreven wet, gewoonterecht
unzip 1 openritsen, losmaken **2** [comp] uitpakken, unzippen
¹up (n) **1** (opgaande) helling **2** opwaartse beweging ‖ *ups and downs* wisselvalligheden, voor- en tegenspoed; [inform] *on the up-and-up* gestaag stijgend; [Am] eerlijk, openhartig
²up (adj) **1** omhoog-, opgaand, hoog, hoger-(geplaatst): *an up stroke* opwaartse uithaal [with pen] **2** op, uit bed, wakker **3** actief, gezond **4** gestegen, omhooggegaan: *the temperature is up eight degrees* de temperatuur ligt acht graden hoger **5** naar een hoger gelegen plaats gaand [of train]: *the up line* de Londenlijn **6** in aanmerking komend (voor), ter studie: *the house is up for sale* het huis staat te koop **7** verkiesbaar gesteld, kandidaat: *Senator Smith is up for re-election* senator Smith stelt zich herkiesbaar **8** om, voorbij: *time is up* de tijd is om **9** met voorsprong, vóór op tegenstrever **10** duurder (geworden), in prijs gestegen: *coffee is up again* de koffie is weer eens duurder geworden **11** [after noun] naar boven lopend, omhooggericht ‖ *what is up?* wat gebeurt er (hier)?; *up and about* (or: *around*) weer op de been, (druk) in de weer; *road up* werk in uitvoering [warning sign]
³up (vb) [inform] onverwacht doen, plotseling beginnen: *she upped and left* zij vertrok plotseling
⁴up (vb) [inform] (plotseling) de hoogte in jagen, verhogen, (abrupt) doen stijgen: *he up-*

ped the **offer** hij deed een hoger bod
⁵up (adv) **1** [place or direction] omhoog, op-,
uit-: *six* **floors** *up* zes hoog; *up the* **republic**
leve de republiek; *live up in the hills* boven in
de bergen wonen; *turn up the music* zet de
muziek harder; *he went up* **north** hij ging
naar het noorden; *up and* **down** op en neer,
heen en weer; *up* **till** (or: *to*) *now* tot nu toe;
up **to** *and including* tot en met; *from £4 up*
vanaf vier pond; *children* **from** *six years up*
kinderen van zes jaar en ouder **2** tevoorschijn, zichtbaar: *it will* **turn** *up* het zal wel
aan het licht komen **3** helemaal, op, door-:
full *up* (helemaal) vol **4** [place or direction]
in, naar: *he* **went** *up to Cambridge* hij ging in
Cambridge studeren ‖ [sport] *be* **two** *(goals)*
up twee goals voorstaan; *I don't feel up* **to** *it* ik
voel er mij niet toe in staat
⁶up (prep) **1** [place or direction] op, boven in,
omhoog: *up (the)* **river** stroomopwaarts;
[theatre] *up* **stage** achter op de scène; *up the*
stairs de trap op **2** [direction towards a central point] naar, in: *up the* **street** verderop in
de straat; *up the* **valley** (verder) het dal in ‖ *up*
and **down** *the country* door het gehele land
up-and-coming [inform] veelbelovend
upbeat vrolijk, optimistisch
upbraid verwijten, een (fikse) uitbrander
geven: *~ s.o.* **for** *doing sth.* (or: *with sth.*) iem.
iets verwijten
upbringing opvoeding
upcoming [Am] voor de deur staand, aanstaande
up-country 1 in/naar/uit het binnenland
2 achtergebleven, naïef
¹update (n) herziening, moderne versie
²update (vb) moderniseren, bijwerken, herzien
upend 1 op zijn kop zetten, ondersteboven
zetten **2** omverslaan
¹upgrade (n) (oplopende) helling ‖ *on the ~*
a) oplopend, toenemend; b) vooruitgang
boekend
²upgrade (vb) **1** bevorderen, promotie geven **2** verbeteren, opwaarderen
upheaval omwenteling, opschudding: *so-*
cial ~ sociale beroering
¹uphill (adj) **1** hellend, oplopend, (berg)op-
waarts **2** (uiterst) moeilijk, zwaar
²uphill (adv) **1** bergop, naar boven, omhoog
2 moeizaam, tegen de stroom in
uphold 1 ophouden, rechthouden, hooghouden **2** (moreel) steunen, goedkeuren
3 (her)bevestigen, blijven bij
upholster stofferen [room, seats]; bekleden
upholstery stoffering, bekleding
upkeep onderhoudskosten
upland 1 hoogland^h, plateau^h **2** binnen-
land^h
upload [comp] uploaden

upmarket voor de betere inkomensklasse,
uit de duurdere prijsklasse: *an ~* **bookshop**
een exclusieve boekhandel
upon *see ³on*
¹upper (n) **1** bovenleer^h [of footwear]
2 [Am; inform] pepmiddel^h; [fig] stimulans;
leuke ervaring ‖ [inform] *be (down)* **on** *one's*
~s berooid zijn, straatarm zijn
²upper (adj) **1** hoger, boven-, opper-: *~* **arm**
bovenarm; *~* **atmosphere** hogere atmosfeer
[above troposphere]; *~* **lip** bovenlip **2** hoger
gelegen: *~* **reaches** *of the Nile* bovenloop van
de Nijl **3** belangrijker, hoger geplaatst, superieur ‖ *the ~* **class** de hogere stand, de aristocratie; *have the ~ hand* de overhand hebben; *the Upper* **House** het Hogerhuis, de Senaat, de Eerste Kamer; [inform] *he is wrong in*
the ~ **storey** hij is niet goed bij zijn hoofd
upper-class uit de hogere stand, aristocratisch
uppermost hoogst, bovenst, belangrijkst
uppish [inform] verwaand, arrogant
¹upright (n) stijl, staander, stut
²upright (adj) **1** recht(opstaand), loodrecht
staand, kaarsrecht **2** oprecht, rechtdoorzee ‖
~ **piano** pianino, gewone piano
³upright (adv) rechtop, verticaal
uprising opstand
¹upriver (adj) stroomopwaarts (gelegen)
²upriver (adv) stroomopwaarts; tegen de
stroom in
uproar tumult^h, rumoer^h, herrie
uproarious 1 luidruchtig, uitgelaten
2 lachwekkend
uproot 1 ontwortelen [also fig]; uit zijn
vertrouwde omgeving wegrukken [persons]
2 uitroeien
¹upset (n) **1** omverwerping, verstoring, totale ommekeer **2** ontsteltenis: *Sheila has had*
a **terrible** *~* Sheila heeft een flinke klap gekregen **3** lichte (maag)stoornis **4** [sport] verrassende nederlaag (wending)
²upset (adj) van streek, overstuur, geërgerd
³upset (vb) **1** omkantelen, omslaan, omvallen **2** overlopen **3** verstoord worden, in de
war raken
⁴upset (vb) **1** omstoten, omverwerpen, omgooien **2** doen overlopen **3** in de war sturen,
verstoren, van zijn stuk brengen: *a very ~ting*
experience een heel nare ervaring **4** ziek
maken; van streek maken [stomach]
the **upshot** (eind)resultaat^h; uitkomst
upside 1 voordeel^h; pluspunt^h **2** bovenkant
upside down 1 ondersteboven, omgekeerd **2** compleet in de war
upskill bijscholen
¹upstage (adj) [inform] hooghartig, afstandelijk
²upstage (vb) [inform] meer aandacht trekken dan, de show stelen van, in de schaduw
stellen

¹upstairs (adj) m.b.t. de bovenverdiepin-
g(en), boven-
²upstairs (adv) naar de bovenverdiepin-
g(en), de trap op, naar boven
upstanding 1 recht overeind (staand)
2 flinkgebouwd **3** eerlijk, oprecht
¹upstate (adj) [Am] meer naar het binnenland gelegen, provinciaal, provincie-, afgelegen
²upstate (adv) uit/naar/in het binnenland,
noordelijk
upstream tegen de stroom in(gaand),
stroomopwaarts
upsurge 1 opwelling, vlaag **2** plotselinge
toename
uptake opname [of food, liquid] ‖ *slow* (or:
quick) *on the* ~ niet zo vlug van begrip
uptight [inform] **1** zenuwachtig, gespannen **2** kwaad
up-to-date 1 bijgewerkt, op de hoogte
2 modern, bij(detijds), hedendaags
uptown 1 in/naar/van de bovenstad **2** [Am]
in/naar/van de betere woonwijk(en)
upturn 1 beroering **2** verbetering, ommekeer
upward stijgend, opwaarts, toenemend
upwards (naar) omhoog, naar boven, in
stijgende lijn: *from* the knees ~ boven de
knieën; ~ *of* twenty people meer dan twintig
mensen
Ural Mountains Oeral
uranium uranium^h: *depleted* ~ verarmd
uranium
urban stedelijk, stads-: [Am] ~ *renewal*
stadsvernieuwing; ~ *sprawl* suburbanisatie
urbanize verstedelijken, urbaniseren
urban myth broodjeaapverhaal^h
urchin rakker, boefje^h, kwajongen
¹urge (n) drang, impuls, neiging, behoefte
²urge (vb) **1** drijven, aansporen: ~ *on* voortdrijven **2** dringend verzoeken, bidden, smeken **3** bepleiten, aandringen op **4** trachten
te overtuigen: she ~d *(up)on* us the need for
secrecy zij drukte ons de noodzaak van geheimhouding op het hart
urgency 1 (aan)drang, pressie **2** urgentie,
dringende noodzaak
urgent 1 urgent, dringend **2** aanhoudend,
hardnekkig
urinal 1 urinaal^h, (pis)fles **2** urinoir^h, openbare waterplaats
urinary urine-
urinate urineren, wateren
urine urine, plas
urine sample urinemonster^h
URL *Universal Resource Locator* URL;
[roughly] internetadres^h
urn urn
Uruguay Uruguay
¹Uruguayan (n) Uruguayaan(se)
²Uruguayan (adj) Uruguayaans

us 1 (voor/aan) ons: *all of* us enjoyed it wij
genoten er allen van; he helps them more
than us hij helpt hen meer dan ons **2** wij,
ons: us *girls* refused to join in wij meisjes wei-
gerden mee te doen; they are stronger *than* us
ze zijn sterker dan wij **3** [referring to 1st
person singular] mij: *let* us hear it again laat
het nog eens horen
US *United States* VS, Verenigde Staten
USA 1 *United States of America* VS, Verenigde Staten **2** *United States Army* leger
van de Verenigde Staten
usable bruikbaar
usage gebruik^h, behandeling, gewoonte,
taalgebruik^h
USB *Universal Serial Bus* USB: ~ *flash drive*
geheugenstick, USB-stick
¹use (n) **1** gebruik^h, toepassing: *make* a good
~ of goed gebruikmaken van; *in* ~ in gebruik;
out of ~ in onbruik **2** nut^h, bruikbaarheid:
have no ~ for a) niet kunnen gebruiken;
b) niets moeten hebben van; this will be of ~
dit zal goed van pas komen; it is *no* ~ arguing
tegenspreken heeft geen zin; what is *the* ~ of
it? wat heeft het voor zin?
²use (vb) **1** gebruiken: ~ *up* opmaken **2** behandelen: he was *ill* ~d hij werd slecht behandeld
use-by date houdbaarheidsdatum
used gebruikt, tweedehands
¹used to (adj) gewend aan, gewoon aan
²used to (vb) had(den) de gewoonte te,
deed, deden: the winters ~ *be* colder de winters waren vroeger kouder; my father ~ *say*:
'Money doesn't buy you happiness.' mijn vader
zei altijd: 'Met geld koop je geen geluk.'
useful bruikbaar, nuttig: *come* in ~ goed
van pas komen; *make* o.s. ~ zich verdienstelijk maken
useless 1 nutteloos, vergeefs **2** onbruikbaar, waardeloos, hopeloos
user gebruiker, verbruiker; verslaafde [alco-
hol, drugs]
user-friendly gebruikersvriendelijk
user ID gebruikers-ID; gebruikersnaam
user interface gebruikersinterface
¹usher (n) **1** portier^h, zaalwachter **2** plaats-
aanwijzer **3** ceremoniemeester
²usher (vb) **1** als portier/plaatsaanwijzer optreden voor, voorgaan, brengen naar: ~ *out*
uitlaten, naar buiten geleiden; ~ *into* bin-
nenleiden in **2** (+ in) aankondigen; [fig] inluiden; de voorbode zijn van
usual gebruikelijk, gewoon: *business* as ~
de zaken gaan gewoon door, alles gaat zijn
gangetje; *as* ~ zoals gebruikelijk; it is ~ *to* het
is de gewoonte om
usually gewoonlijk
usurer woekeraar
usurp onrechtmatig in bezit nemen, zich
toe-eigenen, zich aanmatigen

usury woeker, woekerrente
utensil 1 gebruiksvoorwerp[h]: *cooking* ~s keukengerei **2** (-s) werktuigen [also fig]; gereedschap[h]
uterine 1 uterus-, baarmoeder- **2** met, van dezelfde moeder: ~ *sister* halfzus met dezelfde moeder
uterus baarmoeder
utilitarian 1 utilitair; nuttigheids- **2** utilitaristisch
utility 1 (openbare) voorziening, nutsbedrijf[h], waterleidings-, gas-, elektriciteitsbedrijf[h] **2** nut[h], nuttigheid
utility company openbaar nutsbedrijf[h]
utility program hulpprogramma[h]
utility room [roughly] bijkeuken
utility value gebruikswaarde
utilize gebruiken, gebruikmaken van
[1]**utmost** (n) **1** uiterste (grens) **2** uiterste best, al het mogelijke: *do one's* ~ zijn uiterste best doen
[2]**utmost** (adj) uiterst, hoogst: *of the* ~ *importance* van het (aller)grootste belang
utopia utopie; droombeeld[h]
[1]**utter** (adj) uiterst, absoluut, volslagen
[2]**utter** (vb) **1** uiten; slaken [eg sigh, cry] **2** uitspreken, zeggen **3** in omloop brengen [counterfeit money]
utterance uiting [also linguistics]; uitlating, woorden: *give* ~ *to* uitdrukking geven aan
utterly 1 uiterst, absoluut **2** volkomen, volslagen: ~ *mad* volslagen krankzinnig
U-turn (totale) ommezwaai: [traf] *no* ~s keren verboden
uvula huig
uxorious 1 dol op zijn echtgenote **2** slaafs [towards wife]
Uzbek Oezbeeks
Uzbekistan Oezbekistan

V

v *versus* van
V *volt(s)* V
vacancy 1 vacature **2** lege plaats, leegte, ruimte: *no vacancies* vol [in hotel] **3** afwezigheid
vacant 1 leeg; leeg(staand) [of house]; onbewoond; vrij [of toilet]: ~ *possession* leeg te aanvaarden **2** vacant [of position]; open(staand) **3** afwezig [of mind]
vacate 1 vrij maken; ontruimen [house] **2** opgeven [position]; neerleggen [office]
¹**vacation** (n) **1** vakantie [esp of court of law and universities]: *long* ~ zomervakantie **2** ontruiming [of house]
²**vacation** (vb) [Am] vakantie hebben/houden
vaccinate (+ against) vaccineren (tegen), inenten
vaccination (koepok)inenting, vaccinatie
vaccine vaccinʰ, entstof
vacillate (+ between) aarzelen (tussen), onzeker zijn
vacuity 1 leegheid **2** saaiheid **3** dwaasheid
¹**vacuum** (n) vacuümʰ, leegte: ~ *cleaner* stofzuiger
²**vacuum** (vb) stofzuigen
vacuum-packed vacuümverpakt
vagabond vagebond, landloper
vagina vagina
vagrancy landloperij
¹**vagrant** (n) landloper, zwerver
²**vagrant** (adj) (rond)zwervend, rondtrekkend
vague 1 vaag, onduidelijk, onscherp: *be* ~ *about* sth. vaag zijn over iets **2** gering: *I haven't the* ~*st idea* ik heb geen flauw idee
vain 1 ijdel, verwaand **2** zinloos, nutteloos; vals [hope]; vergeefs [effort, attempt]: *in* ~ tevergeefs **3** triviaal, leeg || *take God's name in* ~ Gods naam ijdel gebruiken
vale vallei, dalʰ
valedictorian [Am; school] afscheidsredenaar
valentine 1 liefjeʰ [chosen on St Valentine's Day, 14 February] **2** valentijnskaart
valerian valeriaan
valet 1 lijfknecht, (persoonlijke) bediende **2** hotelbediende
valiant moedig, heldhaftig
valid 1 redelijk [of arguments etc]; steekhoudend, gegrond **2** geldig [of ticket]
validate bevestigen, bekrachtigen
validity 1 (rechts)geldigheid, het van

kracht zijn **2** redelijkheid [of arguments etc]
valley dalʰ, vallei
valour (helden)moed, dapperheid
¹**valuable** (n) kostbaarheid
²**valuable** (adj) **1** waardevol, nuttig **2** kostbaar
valuation 1 schatting **2** waarde, beoordeling
¹**value** (n) **1** (gevoels)waarde, betekenis **2** maatstaf, waarde **3** (gelds)waarde, valuta, prijs: *(get)* ~ *for money* waar voor zijn geld (krijgen); *to the* ~ *of* ter waarde van **4** nutʰ, waarde: *of great* ~ erg nuttig
²**value** (vb) **1** (+ at) taxeren (op), schatten **2** waarderen, op prijs stellen
value added tax belasting op de toegevoegde waarde, btw
valueless waardeloos
valve 1 klep; ventielʰ [also music]; schuif **2** klep(vliesʰ) [of heart, blood vessels]
vamp: ~ *up* opkalefateren, opknappen
vampire 1 vampier: ~ *bat* vampier [kind of bat] **2** uitzuiger [fig]
van 1 bestelwagen, busjeʰ; [in compounds often] wagen **2** (goederen)wagon || *in the* ~ *of* in de voorhoede van
vandal vandaal
vandalism vandalismeʰ, vernielzucht
vane 1 vin, bladʰ; schoep [of screw]; vleugel **2** windwijzer, weerhaantjeʰ
vanguard voorhoede [also fig]; spits
¹**vanilla** (n) vanille
²**vanilla** (adj) [fig] doorsnee: *plain* ~ *model* basismodel
vanish (plotseling) verdwijnen
vanishing act grote verdwijntruc || *do a* ~ *with* sth. iets snel wegmoffelen
vanishing point 1 verdwijnpuntʰ **2** [fig] punt waarop iets ophoudt (te bestaan); eindeʰ
vanity 1 ijdelheid, verbeelding **2** leegheid
vanity bag damestasjeʰ
vanquish overwinnen [also fig]; verslaan, bedwingen
vantage [Am] voordeelʰ [tennis]; voorsprong
vantage point (voordeel)positie, gunstige ligging
vapid 1 duf, flauw **2** smakeloos; verschaald [beer]
vaporize (laten) verdampen
vaporizer verstuiver
vapour damp, gasʰ, wasem
variability veranderlijkheid, onbestendigheid
¹**variable** (n) variabele (grootheid), variabele waarde
²**variable** (adj) veranderlijk, wisselend, onbestendig
variance verschilʰ, afwijking; [fig] verschilʰ van mening: *be at* ~ het oneens zijn; *at* ~

with in strijd met, in tegenspraak met
¹variant (n) variant, afwijkende vorm
²variant (adj) afwijkend, alternatief
variation variatie [also music]; (af)wisseling, afwijking
varicoloured veelkleurig
varicose vein spatader
varied gevarieerd, afwisselend
variegated (onregelmatig) gekleurd, (bont) geschakeerd
variety 1 verscheidenheid, afwisseling, variatie, verandering, assortimentʰ: *they sell a* **wide** *~ of toys* ze verkopen allerlei verschillende soorten speelgoed **2** variëteit [biology]; verscheidenheid, rasʰ, (onder)soort: *~ is* *the* **spice** *of life* verandering van spijs doet eten **3** variétéʰ
various 1 gevarieerd, uiteenlopend, verschillend (van soort): *their ~ social* **backgrounds** hun verschillende sociale achtergrond **2** verscheiden, divers: *he mentioned ~* **reasons** hij noemde diverse redenen
¹varnish (n) vernis⁺ʰ, vernislaag [also fig]; lak; glazuurʰ [of earthenware]: *a ~ of* **civilization** een dun laagje beschaving
²varnish (vb) vernissen, lakken; [fig] mooier voorstellen: *she tried to ~* **over** *his misbehaviour* ze probeerde zijn wangedrag te verbloemen
varsity 1 universiteit [Oxford and Cambridge] **2** [Am] universiteitsteamʰ [eg of sport]
vary variëren, (doen) veranderen: *with ~ing* **success** met wisselend succes; *prices ~* **from** *15* **to** *95 pounds* de prijzen lopen uiteen van 15 tot 95 pond
vase vaas
vasectomy vasectomie
vast enorm (groot), geweldig: *~* **auditorium** kolossale aula; *~ly* **exaggerated** vreselijk overdreven
vat vatʰ, ton, kuip
VAT *value added tax* btw, belasting op de toegevoegde waarde
the **¹Vatican** (n) Vaticaan
²Vatican (adj) Vaticaans: *the ~* **Council** het Vaticaans concilie; *a ~* **decree** een pauselijk besluit
¹vault (n) **1** gewelfʰ, boog, (gewelfde) grafkelder (wijnkelder) **2** (bank)kluis **3** sprong; [athletics] polsstoksprong
²vault (vb) [also fig] springen (op/over), een sprong maken; [athletics] polsstokhoogspringen
vaunt opscheppen (over) ‖ *her* **much-vaunted** *secretary* haar veelgeprezen secretaris
VCR videorecorder
VD *venereal disease* soa, seksueel overdraagbare aandoening
VDU *visual display unit* [roughly] beeld-

schermʰ, [roughly] terminal
veal kalfsvleesʰ
veer van richting (doen) veranderen, omlopen; (met de klok mee)draaien [of wind]; [fig] een andere kant (doen) opgaan: *the car* *~ed* **off** (or: *across*) *the road* de auto schoot (plotseling) van de weg af (*or:* dwars over de weg)
vegan veganist
¹vegetable (n) **1** groente, eetbaar gewasʰ **2** plant; [fig] vegeterend mens
²vegetable (adj) plantaardig, groente- ‖ *~* **marrow** pompoen
the **vegetable kingdom** plantenrijkʰ
¹vegetarian (n) vegetariër
²vegetarian (adj) vegetarisch
vegetarianism vegetarismeʰ
vegetate 1 groeien; spruiten [(as if) of plant] **2** vegeteren [fig]
vegetation 1 vegetatie, (planten)groei **2** [med] vegetatie, woekering
veggie [inform] vegetariër
veggieburger groenteburger
veggies [Am; inform] groente
vehemence felheid, hevigheid
vehement fel, heftig, krachtig: *~* **protests** hevige protesten
vehicle 1 voertuigʰ [also fig]; middelʰ, mediumʰ: *language is the ~ of* **thought** taal is het voertuig van de gedachte **2** oplosmiddelʰ, bindmiddelʰ **3** drager, overbrenger
¹veil (n) sluier: *draw a ~* **over** *sth.* een sluier over iets trekken; [also fig] iets in de doofpot stoppen; *take the ~* non worden
²veil (vb) (ver)sluieren [also fig]: *~ed* **threat** verholen dreigement
vein 1 ader, bloedvatʰ, ertsader, nerf **2** vleugjeʰ, klein beetjeʰ: *a ~ of* **irony** een vleugje ironie **3** gemoedstoestand, bui ‖ *in* *the same ~* in dezelfde geest, van hetzelfde soort
velcro klittenbandʰ
velocity snelheid
¹velvet (n) fluweelʰ
²velvet (adj) fluwelen
vend 1 verkopen **2** venten, aan de man brengen
vendetta bloedwraak
vendetta killing eerwraak
vending machine automaat [for soft drinks, sweets, cigarettes etc]
vendor verkoper
¹veneer (n) **1** fineerʰ **2** [fig] vernisjeʰ, dun laagjeʰ (vernis)
²veneer (vb) **1** fineren **2** [fig] een vernisje geven
venerable 1 eerbiedwaardig **2** hoogeerwaarde [title of archdeacon] **3** [Roman Catholicism] eerwaardig
venerate aanbidden
veneration verering, diepe eerbied

Venetian Venetiaans || ~ *blind* jaloezie
Venezuela Venezuela
¹Venezuelan (n) Venezolaan(se)
²Venezuelan (adj) Venezolaans
vengeance wraak: *take* ~ *(up)on s.o.* zich op iem. wreken || *work* **with** *a* ~ werken dat de stukken eraf vliegen
venial vergeeflijk, onbetekenend
Venice Venetië
venom 1 vergifʰ **2** venijnʰ, boosaardigheid
venomous 1 (ver)giftig **2** venijnig, boosaardig
¹vent (n) **1** (lucht)opening, (ventilatie)gatʰ, luchtgatʰ **2** [also fig] uitlaat, uitweg: *give* ~ *to one's feelings* zijn hart luchten **3** split [in coat etc]
²vent (vb) **1** uiten [feelings]; luchten **2** afreageren: ~ *sth.* **on** *s.o.* (*sth.*) iets afreageren op iem. (iets)
ventilate 1 ventileren, luchten **2** (in het openbaar) bespreken; naar buiten brengen [opinion]
ventilation 1 ventilatie, luchtverversing, ventilatie(systeemʰ) **2** openbare discussie **3** uiting; het naar buiten brengen [of opinion etc]
ventilator ventilator
ventriloquist buikspreker
¹venture (n) (gevaarlijke) onderneming, gewaagd projectʰ, speculatie, avontuurlijke reis/stap
²venture (vb) **1** (aan)durven, wagen (iets te doen), durven (te beweren) **2** (zich) wagen, riskeren: ~ *one's* **life** zijn leven op het spel zetten; *nothing* ~*d, nothing gained* wie niet waagt, die niet wint; ~ *out of doors* zich op straat wagen
venture capital risicodragend kapitaalʰ
venue 1 plaats van samenkomst, ontmoetingsplaats, trefpuntʰ **2** plaats van handeling, locatie, terreinʰ, toneelʰ
veracity 1 oprechtheid, eerlijkheid **2** geloofwaardigheid, nauwkeurigheid
veranda verandaʰ
verb werkwoordʰ
verbal 1 mondeling, gesproken, verbaal: ~ *agreement* mondelinge overeenkomst **2** van woorden, woord(en)- **3** woordelijk, woord voor woord: ~ *translation* letterlijke vertaling
verbalize onder woorden brengen; formuleren
verbatim woordelijk, woord voor woord
verbose breedsprakig
verdant 1 grasgroen **2** met gras bedekt
verdict 1 oordeelʰ, vonnisʰ, beslissing: ~ *on* oordeel over **2** (jury)uitspraak: *bring* *in a* ~ uitspraak doen
verge rand; kant [fig]; berm: *bring s.o.* **to** *the* ~ *of despair* iem. op de rand van de wanhoop brengen

verge on grenzen aan: *verging on the* **tragic** op het randje van het tragische
verifiable verifieerbaar: *his story is* **hardly** ~ de waarheid van zijn verhaal kan moeilijk bewezen worden
verification 1 verificatie, onderzoekʰ **2** bevestiging
verify 1 verifiëren, de juistheid nagaan van **2** waarmaken, bevestigen
veritable waar, echt, werkelijk
vermilion vermiljoenʰ
vermin 1 ongedierteʰ **2** gespuisʰ
verminous 1 vol (met) ongedierte **2** door ongedierte overgebracht [disease] **3** vies
¹vernacular (n) landstaal, streektaal
²vernacular (adj) in de landstaal
versatile 1 veelzijdig; [also] flexibel [of mind] **2** ruim toepasbaar, veelzijdig bruikbaar
versatility 1 veelzijdigheid **2** ruime toepasbaarheid
verse 1 versʰ, versregel, dichtregel, Bijbelversʰ **2** versʰ, coupletʰ, strofe **3** versvorm, verzen, gedichten: *blank* ~ onberijmde verzen
versed bedreven, ervaren
versification 1 verskunst **2** versbouw
¹versify (vb) **1** rijmen, dichten **2** rijmelen
²versify (vb) op rijm zetten
version versie, variant, interpretatie, lezing, vertaling
Version Bijbelvertaling
versus 1 tegen, contra **2** vergeleken met, tegenover
vertebra (ruggen)wervel
vertebral 1 gewerveld **2** wervel-: ~ *column* wervelkolom
¹vertebrate (n) gewerveld dierʰ
²vertebrate (adj) gewerveld
¹vertical (n) **1** loodlijn **2** loodrecht vlakʰ **3** loodrechte stand: *out of the* ~ niet loodrecht, uit het lood
²vertical (adj) verticaal, loodrecht
vertigo duizeligheid, draaierigheid
verve vuurʰ, geestdrift
¹very (adj) **1** absoluut, uiterst: *from the* ~ *beginning* vanaf het allereerste begin **2** zelf, juist, precies: *the* ~ *man he needed* precies de man die hij nodig had; *he died in this* ~ *room* hij stierf in deze zelfde kamer; *this is the* ~ *thing for me* dat is net iets voor mij **3** enkel, alleen (al): *the* ~ *fact that ...* alleen al het feit dat ...
²very (adv) **1** heel, erg: *that is* ~ *difficult* dat is erg moeilijk; *the* ~ *last day* de allerlaatste dag **2** helemaal: *keep this for your* ~ *own* houd dit helemaal voor jezelf **3** precies: *in the* ~ *same hotel* in precies hetzelfde hotel
vessel 1 vaartuigʰ, schipʰ **2** [anatomy, bot] vatʰ, kanaalʰ; buis [for blood, fluid] **3** vatʰ [for liquid]

¹**vest** (n) **1** (onder)hemdʰ **2** [Am] vestʰ
²**vest** (vb) toekennen, bekleden: ~*ed* *inter-ests* gevestigde belangen
vestibule 1 vestibule, halʰ **2** kerkportaalʰ
vestige spoorʰ: *not a ~ of regret* geen spoor van spijt
vestment 1 (ambts)kleedʰ, ambtsgewaadʰ **2** [rel] liturgisch gewaadʰ, misgewaadʰ
¹**vet** (n) *veterinary surgeon* dierenarts, veearts
²**vet** (vb) **1** medisch behandelen [animal] **2** grondig onderzoeken, (medisch) keuren; [fig] doorlichten
¹**veteran** (n) veteraan; oudgediende [also fig]; oud-soldaat
²**veteran** (adj) **1** door en door ervaren **2** veteranen- ǁ ~ *car* oldtimer [from before 1916]
Veterans Day [Am] 11 november
veterinarian [Am] dierenarts, veearts
veterinary veeartsenij-: ~ *surgeon* dierenarts, veearts
¹**veto** (n) veto(recht)ʰ
²**veto** (vb) zijn veto uitspreken over, zijn toestemming weigeren
vex 1 ergeren, plagen, irriteren **2** in de war brengen
vexation 1 ergernis, irritatie **2** kwelling
vexatious vervelend, ergerlijk
vexed 1 geërgerd, geïrriteerd **2** hachelijk, netelig: ~ *question* lastige kwestie
VHF *very high frequency* FM
via 1 via, door, langs: *he left ~ the garden* hij vertrok door de tuin **2** [means] door middel van
viability 1 levensvatbaarheid **2** doenlijkheid, uitvoerbaarheid
viable 1 levensvatbaar [also fig] **2** uitvoerbaar
viaduct viaductʰ
vial medicijnflesjeʰ
vibes *vibrations* vibraties, uitstralende gevoelens
vibrant 1 trillend **2** helder [of colour] **3** levendig; krachtig [of voice]
vibrate (doen) trillen [also fig]
vibration trilling
vibrator vibrator
vicar 1 predikant; dominee [Anglican Church] **2** [Roman Catholicism] plaatsvervanger, vicaris
vicarage pastorie
vicarious 1 afgevaardigd **2** indirect
vice 1 gebrekʰ, onvolmaaktheid, slechte gewoonte **2** ondeugd **3** ontucht, prostitutie **4** handschroef, bankschroef
vice-chairman vicepresident, vicevoorzitter
vice-chancellor 1 vicekanselier [of court of law] **2** rector magnificus [of university]
vice-president vicepresident; vicevoorzitter

viceroy onderkoning
vice squad zedenpolitie
vicinity 1 buurt, wijk **2** nabijheid, buurt, omgeving
vicious 1 wreed, boosaardig, gemeen: ~ *blow* gemene mep **2** gevaarlijk, gevelddadig: ~*(-looking) knife* gevaarlijk (uitziend) mes **3** vol kuren [of animals] ǁ ~ *circle* a) vicieuze cirkel; b) [also fig] cirkelredenering
vicissitudes wisselvalligheden
victim 1 slachtofferʰ, dupe: *fall ~ to s.o.* (*sth.*) aan iem. (iets) ten prooi vallen **2** offerʰ [human, animal]
victimize 1 slachtofferen, doen lijden **2** represailles nemen tegen [eg a few persons]; (onverdiend) straffen
victor overwinnaar, winnaar
Victorian victoriaans, negentiende-eeuws; [roughly] (overdreven) preuts; schijnheilig
victorious 1 zegevierend: *be ~* overwinnen, de overwinning behalen **2** overwinnings-
victory overwinning, zege
victualler leverancier van levensmiddelen ǁ *licensed ~* caféhouder met vergunning
victuals levensmiddelen, proviand
¹**video** (n) video(film), videorecorder: ~ *on demand* video (*or:* tv, film) op aanvraag; ~ *cartridge* (*or:* *cassette*) videocassette
²**video** (vb) op (de) video opnemen
videodisc videoplaat, beeldplaat
videophone beeldtelefoon
video recorder videorecorder
¹**videotape** (n) videoband
²**videotape** (vb) op videoband opnemen
vie rivaliseren
Vienna Wenen
¹**Viennese** (n) Wener, Weense
²**Viennese** (adj) Weens
Vietnam Vietnam
¹**Vietnamese** (n) Vietnamees, Vietnamese
²**Vietnamese** (adj) Vietnamees
¹**view** (n) **1** bezichtiging, inspectie; [fig] overzichtʰ: *a general ~ of the subject* een algemeen overzicht van het onderwerp **2** zienswijze, opvatting: *take a dim* (*or:* *poor*) ~ *of s.o.'s conduct* iemands gedrag maar matig waarderen; *in my ~* volgens mij, zoals ik het zie **3** uitzichtʰ, gezichtʰ; [fig] vooruitzichtʰ **4** gezichtʰ, afbeelding; [fig] beeldʰ **5** bedoeling: *with a ~ to doing sth.* met de bedoeling iets te doen **6** zichtʰ, gezicht(svermogen)ʰ **7** zichtʰ, uitzichtʰ, gezichtsveldʰ: *come into ~* in zicht komen ǁ *have in ~* op het oog hebben; *in ~ of* vanwege, gezien
²**view** (vb) tv kijken
³**view** (vb) **1** bekijken; beschouwen [also fig]: ~ *a house* een huis bezichtigen **2** inspecteren
viewer 1 kijker, tv-kijker **2** viewer [for viewing slides]
viewpoint gezichtspuntʰ; oogpuntʰ [also

fig]
vigil waak, (nacht)wake: *keep* ~ waken
vigilance waakzaamheid, oplettendheid
vigilant waakzaam, oplettend, alert
vigorous 1 krachtig, sterk, vol energie
2 krachtig; gespierd [language] **3** groeizaam; gezond [plants]
vigour 1 kracht, sterkte **2** energie, vitaliteit
3 groeikracht; levenskracht [of plants, ani-
mals]
Viking Viking, Noorman
vile 1 gemeen **2** walgelijk; afschuwelijk [eg
food] **3** gemeen; beroerd [weather]
villa villa, landhuis^h
village dorp^h: ~ *green* a) dorpsplein;
b) dorpsweide
villager dorpsbewoner
villain 1 boef, schurk, slechterik: *heroes
and* ~s helden en schurken **2** rakker, deugniet
villainous schurkachtig, gemeen, doortrapt, heel slecht
villainy 1 schurkenstreek **2** schurkachtig-
heid, doortraptheid
vim fut, pit
vindicate 1 rechtvaardigen **2** van verdenking zuiveren, rehabiliteren
vindication 1 rechtvaardiging **2** rehabilitatie
vindictive straffend, rancuneus, wraakzuchtig
vine 1 wijnstok, wingerd **2** [Am] kruiper,
klimplant
vinegar azijn
vineyard wijngaard
¹vintage (n) **1** wijnoogst, wijnpluk **2** wijn-
tijd, (goed) wijnjaar^h **3** jaar^h, jaargang,
bouwjaar^h, lichting: *they belong* to the 1960 ~
zij zijn van de lichting van 1960
²vintage (adj) **1** uitstekend, voortreffelijk: *a
~ silent film* een klassieke stomme film
2 oud, antiek: ~ *car* auto uit de periode
1916-1930, klassieke auto
vinyl vinyl^h
viola altviool
violate 1 overtreden, inbreuk maken op,
breken: ~ *a treaty* een verdrag schenden
2 schenden, ontheiligen **3** verkrachten
violation 1 overtreding [also sport]
2 schending, schennis **3** verkrachting
violence 1 geweld^h: *acts of* ~ gewelddda-
digheden **2** gewelddadigheid: *crimes of* ~
geweldmisdrijven **3** hevigheid, heftigheid
violent 1 hevig, heftig, wild: ~ *contrast*
schril contrast **2** gewelddadig: ~ *death* gewelddadige dood **3** hel; schreeuwend [col-
our]
¹violet (n) viooltje^h
²violet (adj) violet, paars(achtig blauw)
violin 1 viool **2** violist(e)
violinist violist(e)

violist altviolist
violoncello (violon)cello
VIP *very important person* vip, hooggeplaatst persoon, beroemdheid
viper adder [also fig]; serpent^h, verrader
viral viraal, virus-
virally viraal, als een virus: *spread* ~ zich razendsnel verspreiden
¹virgin (n) maagd [also of man]
²virgin (adj) maagdelijk, ongerept: ~ *snow*
vers gevallen sneeuw
the **Virgin Islands** Maagdeneilanden: *the British* ~ de Britse Maagdeneilanden
virginity maagdelijkheid, het (nog) maagd
zijn; [fig] ongereptheid
Virgo [astrology] (de) Maagd
virile 1 mannelijk **2** potent
virility 1 mannelijkheid, kracht **2** potentie
virtual feitelijk, eigenlijk, praktisch: *to them
it was a* ~ *defeat* voor hen kwam het neer op
een nederlaag || ~ *reality* virtuele werkelijk-
heid
virtually praktisch, feitelijk: *my work is* ~
finished mijn werk is zogoed als af
virtue 1 deugd: *make a* ~ *of necessity* van
de nood een deugd maken **2** verdienste,
goede eigenschap || *by* (or: *in*) ~ *of* op grond
van
virtuosity virtuositeit, meesterschap^h
virtuous 1 deugdzaam **2** kuis
virulence 1 kwaadaardigheid, virulentie
2 venijnigheid
virulent 1 (zeer) giftig; dodelijk [poison]
2 kwaadaardig [disease] **3** venijnig, kwaadaardig
virus virus^h
virus scanner virusscanner
visa visum^h
visceral 1 [anatomy] m.b.t. de ingewanden, inwendig; visceraal **2** [fig] diepgeworteld
viscosity kleverigheid, taaiheid, stroperigheid
viscount burggraaf [title between baron
and earl]
viscountess burggravin
viscous 1 kleverig **2** taai [also fig]
visibility 1 zicht^h [meteorology] **2** zichtbaarheid
visible zichtbaar, waarneembaar, merkbaar
vision 1 gezicht(svermogen)^h, het zien:
field of ~ gezichtsveld **2** visie, inzicht^h: *a man
of* ~ een man met visie **3** visioen^h, droom(-
beeld^h) **4** (droom)verschijning **5** (vluchtige)
blik, glimp
¹visionary (n) **1** ziener, profeet **2** dromer,
idealist
²visionary (adj) **1** visioenen hebbend **2** dromerig, onrealistisch **3** denkbeeldig
¹visit (n) bezoek^h; visite [also of doctor]; (tij-

delijk) verblijf^h: *pay s.o. a ~ iem.* een bezoek-(je) brengen
²**v<u>i</u>sit** (vb) **1** een bezoek afleggen, op bezoek gaan **2** [Am] logeren, verblijven ‖ [Am] *~ with* een praatje (gaan) maken met
³**v<u>i</u>sit** (vb) **1** bezoeken, op visite gaan bij **2** [Am] logeren bij, verblijven bij **3** inspecteren, onderzoeken **4** bezoeken, treffen, teisteren: *the village was ~ed by the plague* het dorp werd getroffen door de pest
visit<u>a</u>tion 1 (officieel) bezoek^h, huisbezoek^h **2** beproeving
v<u>i</u>siting bezoekend, gast-: *~ professor* gasthoogleraar; [sport] *the ~ team* de gasten
v<u>i</u>siting hours bezoekuur, bezoektijd
v<u>i</u>sitor bezoeker, gast, toerist
v<u>i</u>sitor's book gastenboek
v<u>i</u>sor 1 klep [of hat] **2** zonneklep [of car] **3** vizier^h [of helmet]
v<u>i</u>sta 1 uitzicht^h, doorkijk(je^h), (ver)gezicht^h **2** perspectief^h, vooruitzicht^h: *open up new ~s* (or: *a new ~*) nieuwe perspectieven openen
v<u>i</u>sual 1 visueel: *~ aids* visuele hulpmiddelen; *~ arts* beeldende kunsten; *~ display unit* (beeld)scherm, monitor **2** gezichts-, oog- **3** zichtbaar **4** optisch
v<u>i</u>sualize 1 zich voorstellen **2** visualiseren, zichtbaar maken
v<u>i</u>tal 1 essentieel, van wezenlijk belang, onmisbaar: *of ~ importance* van vitaal belang **2** vitaal, levenskrachtig, levens-: *~ parts* vitale delen ‖ *~ statistics* a) bevolkingsstatistiek; b) belangrijkste feiten
vit<u>a</u>lity vitaliteit, levenskracht
v<u>i</u>tamin vitamine
v<u>i</u>tiate 1 schaden, schenden, verzwakken **2** bederven; vervuilen [also fig]
v<u>i</u>treous glas-, glazen, van glas, glasachtig, glazig: *~ enamel* email
v<u>i</u>triol [chem] zwavelzuur^h; [fig] venijn^h
vitri<u>o</u>lic 1 vitrioolachtig, vitriool- **2** bijtend, venijnig
v<u>i</u>va mondeling (her)examen^h
viv<u>a</u>cious levendig, opgewekt
viv<u>a</u>city levendigheid, opgewektheid
v<u>i</u>vid 1 helder [colour, light]; sterk **2** levendig, krachtig: *a ~ imagination* een levendige fantasie
vivis<u>e</u>ction vivisectie
v<u>i</u>xen 1 wijfjesvos **2** feeks
viz *videlicet* nl., namelijk, te weten, d.w.z.
V-neck V-hals
voc<u>a</u>bulary woordenlijst, woordenschat
¹**v<u>o</u>cal** (n) **1** lied(je^h), (pop)song **2** (-s) zang: *~s: Michael Jackson* zang: Michael Jackson
²**v<u>o</u>cal** (adj) **1** gesproken, mondeling, vocaal, gezongen: *~ group* zanggroep **2** zich duidelijk uitend, welbespraakt **3** stem-: *~ cords* (or: *chords*) stembanden
v<u>o</u>calist vocalist(e), zanger(es)
vocaliz<u>a</u>tion 1 het uitspreken; stemge-

bruik^h **2** [linguistics] vocalisatie
v<u>o</u>calize (met de stem) uiten; zingen
voc<u>a</u>tion 1 beroep^h, betrekking **2** roeping **3** aanleg, talent^h: *have a ~ for* aanleg hebben voor
voc<u>a</u>tional beroeps-, vak-: *~ training* beroepsonderwijs
voc<u>i</u>ferate schreeuwen, heftig protesteren
voc<u>i</u>ferous schreeuwend, lawaaierig, luidruchtig
v<u>o</u>dka wodka
vogue 1 mode: *be in ~* in de mode zijn, in zijn **2** populariteit
¹**v<u>o</u>ice** (n) **1** stem, (stem)geluid^h, uiting, mening: *speak in a low ~* op gedempte toon spreken; *give ~ to* uitdrukking geven aan; *raise one's ~* a) zijn stem verheffen; b) protest aantekenen; *in (good) ~* goed bij stem **2** vorm: *active* (or: *passive*) *~* bedrijvende (or: lijdende) vorm
²**v<u>o</u>ice** (vb) uiten, verwoorden
v<u>o</u>ice mail voicemail
v<u>o</u>ice-over commentaarstem [with film, documentary]
¹**v<u>o</u>id** (n) leegte, (lege) ruimte, vacuüm^h
²**v<u>o</u>id** (adj) **1** leeg, verlaten: *~ of* zonder, vrij van **2** nietig, ongeldig: *null and ~* ongeldig, van nul en gener waarde
vol *volume* (boek)deel^h
v<u>o</u>latile 1 vluchtig, (snel) vervliegend **2** veranderlijk, wispelturig
volc<u>a</u>nic vulkanisch [also fig]; explosief: *~ eruption* vulkaanuitbarsting
volc<u>a</u>no vulkaan [also fig]; explosieve situatie: *dormant ~* sluimerende vulkaan; *extinct ~* uitgedoofde vulkaan
vol<u>i</u>tion wil, wilskracht: *by* (or: *of*) *one's own ~* uit eigen wil, vrijwillig
¹**v<u>o</u>lley** (n) **1** salvo^h [also fig]; (stort)vloed, regen: *a ~ of oaths* (or: *curses*) een scheldkanonnade **2** [sport] volley^h; [socc] omhaal
²**v<u>o</u>lley** (vb) **1** (gelijktijdig) losbranden; een salvo afvuren [also fig] **2** in een salvo afgeschoten worden, (tegelijk) door de lucht vliegen **3** [sport] volleren, een volley maken; [socc] omhalen
³**v<u>o</u>lley** (vb) **1** [sport] uit de lucht slaan (schieten); [socc] direct op de slof nemen **2** [tennis] volleren, met een volley passeren
¹**v<u>o</u>lleyball** (n) volleybal^h [sport]
²**v<u>o</u>lleyball** (n) volleybal [ball]
volt volt
v<u>o</u>ltage voltage^h
v<u>o</u>lume 1 (boek)deel^h, band, bundel: *speak ~s* boekdelen spreken **2** jaargang **3** hoeveelheid, omvang, volume^h **4** volume^h, inhoud **5** volume^h, (geluids)sterkte: *turn down the ~* het geluid zachter zetten
v<u>o</u>lume control volumeknop
vol<u>u</u>minous omvangrijk, lijvig; wijd [eg clothing, book]

vulture

voluntary 1 vrijwillig, uit eigen beweging: ~ *worker* vrijwilliger **2** vrijwilligers-: ~ *organization* [roughly] stichting **3** gefinancierd door vrijwillige giften [church, school]
¹**volunteer** (n) vrijwilliger
²**volunteer** (vb) zich (als vrijwilliger) aanmelden, uit eigen beweging meedoen
³**volunteer** (vb) **1** (vrijwillig) aanbieden, (uit eigen beweging) aanbieden **2** uit zichzelf zeggen [remark, information]
voluntourism vrijwilligerstoerisme[h]
voluptuous 1 sensueel, wellustig **2** weelderig, overvloedig
¹**vomit** (n) braaksel[h], overgeefsel[h]
²**vomit** (vb) (uit)braken [also fig]; overgeven
voodooism voodoocultus
voracious vraatzuchtig [also fig]: *a ~ reader* een alleslezer
vortex werveling [also fig]; maalstroom
¹**vote** (n) **1** stem, uitspraak: *cast* (or: *record*) *one's* ~ zijn stem uitbrengen; *casting* ~ beslissende stem [by chairman, when votes are equally divided] **2** stemming: ~ *of censure* motie van afkeuring; ~ *of confidence* (or: *no-confidence*) motie van vertrouwen (or: wantrouwen); *put sth. to the* ~ iets in stemming brengen **3** stemmenaantal[h]: *the floating* ~ de zwevende kiezers **4** stemrecht[h] **5** stembriefje[h]
²**vote** (vb) stemmen, een stemming houden
³**vote** (vb) **1** bij stemming verkiezen, stemmen op **2** bij stemming bepalen, beslissen: ~ *s.o. out of office* (or: *power*) iem. wegstemmen **3** (geld) toestaan **4** uitroepen tot, het ermee eens zijn dat: *the play was ~d a success* het stuk werd algemeen als een succes beschouwd **5** voorstellen: *I ~ we leave now* ik stel voor dat we nu weggaan
vote down afstemmen, (bij stemming) verwerpen: ~ *a proposal* een voorstel verwerpen
vote in verkiezen: *the Conservatives were voted in again* de conservatieven werden opnieuw verkozen
voter 1 kiezer: *floating* ~ zwevende kiezer **2** stemgerechtigde
vouch borg staan: ~ *for* instaan voor; garanderen
voucher bon, waardebon, cadeaubon, consumptiebon
vouch for instaan voor, waarborgen, borg staan voor
¹**vow** (n) gelofte, eed, plechtige belofte: *make* (or: *take*) *a* ~ plechtig beloven
²**vow** (vb) (plechtig) beloven, gelofte afleggen van, zweren
vowel [linguistics] klinker
vox pop [inform] [roughly] straatinterview[h]
¹**voyage** (n) lange reis, zeereis, bootreis: ~ *home* thuisreis, terugreis; ~ *out* heenreis
²**voyage** (vb) reizen

voyager (ontdekkings)reiziger
voyeur voyeur; gluurder
voyeurism voyeurisme[h]
vs *versus* van, vs.
vulcanization vulkanisatie
vulgar 1 vulgair, laag bij de gronds, ordinair **2** alledaags, gewoon **3** algemeen (bekend/aangenomen), van het volk: ~ *tongue* volkstaal ‖ ~ *fraction* gewone breuk
vulgarity 1 (vulgarities) platte uitdrukking, grove opmerking **2** (vulgarities) smakeloze, onbeschaafde daad **3** platheid, vulgair gedrag[h]
vulgarize 1 populariseren, gemeengoed maken **2** verlagen, onbeschaafd maken
vulnerable kwetsbaar [also fig]; gevoelig
vulture 1 gier **2** aasgier

W

W 1 *watt(s)* W **2** *west(ern)* W
¹wacko (n) [esp Am; inform] idioot
²wacko (adj) [esp Am; inform] lijp, gestoord
wacky mesjogge, kierewiet
wad 1 prop [cotton wool, paper etc]; dot, (op)vulselʰ **2** pakʰ [letters, money etc] **3** pak(jeʰ); rolletjeʰ [banknotes]
¹waddle (n) waggelende gang, eendengang
²waddle (vb) waggelen
wade waden: ~ *through* a boring book een vervelend boek doorworstelen || ~ *in* aanpakken; ~ *into* s.o. (sth.) iem. (iets) hard aanpakken
wader 1 wader **2** waadvogel **3** (-s) lieslaarzen
wading bird waadvogel
wafer 1 wafel(tjeʰ) **2** hostie, ouwel
¹waffle (n) **1** wafel **2** gewauwelʰ, gezwetsʰ, onzin
²waffle (vb) wauwelen, kletsen
¹waft (vb) zweven, drijven, waaien
²waft (vb) voeren, dragen, doen zweven
¹wag (n) **1** waggeling, kwispeling **2** grappenmaker
²wag (vb) **1** waggelen, wiebelen; schommelen [while walking]: *set* the tongues ~ging de tongen in beweging brengen **2** kwispelen
³wag (vb) **1** schudden [head]; heen en weer bewegen: *wag* one's finger at s.o. iem. met de vinger dreigen **2** kwispelen [tail]
¹wage (n) loonʰ, arbeidsloonʰ: *minimum* ~ minimumloon
²wage (vb) voeren [war, campaign]: ~ *war against* (or: *on*) oorlog voeren tegen
wage-cut loonsverlaging
wage demand looneis
wage earner 1 loontrekker **2** kostwinner
wage freeze loonstop
¹wager (n) weddenschap: *lay* (or: *make*) a ~ een weddenschap aangaan
²wager (vb) **1** een weddenschap aangaan **2** verwedden, wedden (om/met), op het spel zetten: *I'll* ~ (you £10) that he'll come ik wed (tien pond met u) dat hij komt
wage settlement loonakkoordʰ
wages floor minimumloonʰ
waggish guitig, ondeugend
¹waggle (n) waggeling, schommeling
²waggle (vb) **1** waggelen, wiebelen, schommelen **2** kwispelen
³waggle (vb) **1** schudden [head]; heen en weer bewegen **2** kwispelen (met)
waggoner vrachtrijder, voerman

wagon 1 wagen, boerenwagen; [Am] wagentjeʰ; kar [with ice cream, hot dogs etc] **2** dienwagen(tjeʰ), theewagen **3** [Am] stationcar [type of car] **4** goederenwagon **5** vrachtwagen || *go on* the (water) ~ geheelonthouder worden
wagtail kwikstaart
¹wail (n) **1** geweeklaagʰ, gejammerʰ **2** geloeiʰ; gehuilʰ [of siren]
²wail (vb) **1** klagen, jammeren; huilen [also of wind] **2** loeien; huilen [of siren]
waist 1 middelʰ; taille [also of article of clothing]: stripped *to* the ~ met ontbloot bovenlijf **2** smal(ler) gedeelteʰ, vernauwing
waistcoat vestʰ [of suit]
waist-deep tot aan het middel (reikend)
waistline middelʰ; taille [also of article of clothing]
¹wait (n) **1** wachttijd, oponthoudʰ **2** hinderlaag: lie in ~ *for* s.o. voor iem. op de loer liggen
²wait (vb) **1** wachten: ~ a *minute!* wacht even!; *I'll* do it *while* you ~ het is zo klaar, u kunt erop wachten **2** bedienen (aan tafel): ~ *on* s.o. iem. bedienen || ~ *and see* (de dingen) afwachten; ~ *for* me! niet zo vlug!
³wait (vb) afwachten, wachten op: ~ *one's turn* zijn beurt afwachten
waiter kelner
waiting 1 wachttijd **2** bediening: *do* the ~ bedienen **3** dienst: *in* ~ dienstdoend || *no* ~ verboden stil te staan
waiting game afwachtende houding: *play* a ~ de kat uit de boom kijken
waiting list wachtlijst
waiting room wachtkamer
waitress serveerster
waive 1 afzien van; afstand doen van [rights, privileges] **2** uitstellen; opschorten [problem]
¹wake (n) **1** kielwaterʰ, kielzogʰ **2** [fig] spoorʰ, nasleep: *in* the ~ *of* in het spoor van, in de voetstappen van
²wake (vb) ontwaken; wakker worden [also fig]: in his waking *hours* wanneer hij wakker is; ~ *up* ontwaken, wakker worden; ~ *up to* sth. iets gaan inzien
³wake (vb) **1** (also + up) wekken; wakker maken [also fig] **2** bewust maken, doordringen: ~ s.o. *up to* sth. iem. van iets doordringen
wakeful 1 wakend, waakzaam **2** slapeloos: ~ *nights* slapeloze nachten
¹waken (vb) ontwaken, wakker worden
²waken (vb) **1** wekken, wakker maken **2** opwekken
wake-up call 1 wektelefoontjeʰ **2** waarschuwing
¹walk (n) **1** gang, manier van gaan **2** stap; stapvoetse gang [of horse] **3** wandeling: *have* (or: *take*) a ~, *go* for a ~ een wandeling

(gaan) maken **4** levenswandel: ~ *of* **life** a) beroep, roeping; **b)** (maatschappelijke) rang (*or:* stand) **5** wandelgang, voetpad[h] **6** wandelafstand: *it is ten* **minutes'** ~ het is tien minuten lopen
²walk (vb) **1** lopen: ~ *in* one's sleep slaapwandelen **2** stappen; stapvoets gaan [of horse] **3** (rond)waren, verschijnen ‖ ~ *away* (*or:* off) *with* **a)** er vandoor gaan met, stelen; **b)** gemakkelijk winnen; ~ *off* opstappen, er vandoor gaan; ~ *out* **a)** het werk onderbreken, staken; **b)** opstappen, weglopen [eg at consultation]; ~ *out* on s.o. iem. in de steek laten; ~ *tall* het hoofd hoog dragen, trots zijn; ~ *up!* kom erin!, komt dat zien! [eg at circus]; ~ *up* to s.o. op iem. afgaan; [inform] ~ *over* met gemak achter zich laten; ~ *(all)* *over* s.o. met iem. de vloer (aan)vegen
³walk (vb) **1** lopen, gaan; te voet afleggen [distance] **2** lopen door/langs/op, bewandelen **3** meelopen met: ~ s.o. *home* iem. naar huis brengen **4** laten lopen; uitlaten [eg dog]; stapvoets laten lopen [horse]: ~ s.o. *off* his feet iem. de benen uit zijn lijf laten lopen
walker 1 wandelaar, voetganger **2** [Am] looprek[h], rollator; loopstoel [for child]
walking papers ontslag(brief): *get* one's ~ zijn ontslag krijgen
walkout 1 staking, werkonderbreking **2** het weglopen [from a meeting by way of protest]
walkover gemakkelijke overwinning
walkway 1 gang, wandelgang **2** wandelweg, promenade
¹wall (n) muur, wand: [fig] a *writing* on the ~ een teken aan de wand ‖ *drive* (*or:* push) s.o. to the ~ iem. in het nauw drijven; *drive* s.o. up the ~ iem. stapelgek maken
²wall (vb) **1** ommuren **2** dichtmetselen
wallet portefeuille
wallflower 1 muurbloem **2** muurbloempje[h]
¹Walloon (n) Waal(se) [inhabitant of the Walloon provinces in Belgium]
²Walloon (adj) Waals
¹wallop (n) **1** dreun, mep **2** bier[h]
²wallop (vb) aframmelen, hard slaan
¹walloping (n) **1** aframmeling **2** zware nederlaag
²walloping (adj) reusachtig, enorm
wallow 1 (zich) wentelen, (zich) rollen: ~ *in* the *mud* zich in het slijk wentelen [fig]; [fig] ~ *in* self-pity zwelgen in zelfmedelijden **2** rollen; slingeren [of ship]
wall painting 1 muurschildering, fresco[h] **2** muurschilderkunst
wallpaper behang[h]
wall-to-wall kamerbreed [eg carpet]
wally sukkel, stommeling
walnut walnoot
walrus walrus

¹waltz (n) wals [dance (music)]
²waltz (vb) walsen, de wals dansen; [fig] (rond)dansen ‖ ~ *off* with er vandoor gaan met
wan 1 bleek; flets [complexion] **2** flauw; zwak [light, smile]
wand toverstokje[h], toverstaf
wander 1 (rond)zwerven, (rond)dwalen: ~ *about* rondzwerven **2** kronkelen; (zich) slingeren [of river, road] **3** verdwalen; op de verkeerde weg raken [also fig] **4** afdwalen [also fig]: ~ *from* (*or:* off) one's subject van zijn onderwerp afdwalen **5** kuieren
wanderer zwerver
wanderings zwerftochten
¹wane (n): *on* the ~ aan het afnemen [also fig]
²wane (vb) afnemen, verminderen; [fig] vervallen
¹wangle (n) (slinkse) streek, smoesje[h]
²wangle (vb) weten los te krijgen, klaarspelen: ~ a *well-paid job* out of s.o. een goed betaalde baan van iem. weten los te krijgen
³wangle (vb) zich eruit draaien, zich redden: ~ (o.s.) out of a situation zich uit een situatie weten te redden
¹want (n) **1** behoefte: *meet* a long-felt ~ in een lang gevoelde behoefte voorzien **2** gebrek[h], gemis[h]: *drink water* **for** ~ of anything better water drinken bij gebrek aan iets beters **3** tekort[h], nood **4** armoede, behoeftigheid: *live* **in** ~ in armoede leven
²want (vb) behoeftig zijn ‖ he does not ~ *for* anything, he ~s *for* nothing hij komt niets te kort
³want (vb) **1** (graag) willen, wensen: *I* ~ it (to be) *done* today ik wil dat het vandaag gedaan wordt; ~ *in* (*or:* out) naar binnen (*or:* buiten) willen **2** moeten, hoeven: *you* ~ to *see* a psychiatrist je moet naar een psychiater; *in that case you* ~ *room 12A, it's just around the corner* in dat geval moet u kamer 12A hebben, die is net om de hoek **3** nodig hebben, vergen, vereisen **4** zoeken; vragen [pers]: ~*ed*, experienced *mechanic* gevraagd: ervaren monteur; ~*ed by the police* (**for** a crime) gezocht door de politie (voor een misdaad)
wanting 1 te kort, niet voorhanden: a few pages are ~ er ontbreken een paar bladzijden **2** onvoldoende: *be* ~ **in** sth. **a)** in iets tekortschieten; **b)** iets missen
wanton 1 lichtzinnig [of woman] **2** moedwillig **3** buitensporig, onverantwoord
WAP wireless application protocol WAP
¹war (n) oorlog: ~ *of* **nerves** zenuw(en)oorlog; *wage* ~ *on* (*or:* against) oorlog voeren tegen iem. [also fig] ‖ *have* been in the ~s er gehavend uitzien
²war (vb) strijd voeren; strijden [oft fig]: ~ *against* strijden tegen
war baby oorlogsbaby

¹warble (n) gekweel^h, gezang^h
²warble (vb) **1** kwelen **2** zingen [of bird]
war crime oorlogsmisdaad
ward 1 (ziekenhuis)afdeling **2** (stads)wijk [as part of consituency] **3** pupil [minor under guardianship]; [fig] beschermeling: ~ of court onder bescherming van het gerecht staande minderjarige **4** voogdijschap^h, hoede, curatele **5** afdeling van gevangenis
warden 1 hoofd^h, beheerder; bestuurder [of schools, hospitals etc] **2** [Am] gevangenisdirecteur **3** wachter, opzichter, bewaker, suppoost, conciërge, portier^h
warder cipier, gevangenbewaarder
ward off afweren, afwenden
wardrobe 1 kleerkast, hangkast **2** garderobe [also in theatre]
wardroom officierenkajuit, officiersmess
ware 1 (koop)waar, goederen **2** aardewerk^h
warehouse pakhuis^h, opslagplaats, magazijn^h
warfare oorlog(voering); strijd [also fig]
war game oorlogsspel
warhead kop van raket, torpedo; kernkop
warhorse 1 oorlogspaard^h, strijdros^h **2** ijzervreter **3** oude rot [in politics]
warlike 1 krijgshaftig, strijdlustig **2** militair, oorlogs-
warlord militair leider
¹warm (n) warmte: come in and have a ~! kom binnen en warm je wat!
²warm (adj) **1** warm [also fig]; innemend: ~ greetings hartelijke groeten; give a ~ welcome to hartelijk welkom heten; keep a place ~ for s.o. een plaats voor iem. openhouden **2** warmbloedig, hartstochtelijk, vurig: a ~ supporter een vurig aanhanger **3** verhit [also fig]; geanimeerd, heftig: a ~ discussion een geanimeerde discussie || make things ~ for s.o. a) het iem. moeilijk maken; b) iem. straffen
³warm (vb) warm worden [also fig]; in de stemming (ge)raken: ~ to (or: toward(s)) s.o. iets gaan voelen voor iem.
⁴warm (vb) **1** (ver)warmen **2** opwarmen [also fig]; warm maken
warm-hearted warm, hartelijk
warmonger oorlogs(aan)stoker
warmth [also fig] warmte, hartelijkheid, vuur^h
¹warm up (vb) **1** warm(er) worden [also fig]; op temperatuur komen; [fig] in de stemming raken **2** [sport] een warming-up doen, de spieren losmaken
²warm up (vb) **1** opwarmen [also fig]; warm maken, in de stemming brengen **2** (ver)warmen
warm-up opwarming(stijd)
warn 1 waarschuwen: ~ s.o. of sth. iem. op iets opmerkzaam maken, iem. voor iets

waarschuwen **2** waarschuwen: the doctor ~ed him off drink de dokter waarschuwde hem geen alcohol te drinken || ~ s.o. off iem. weren
warning waarschuwing(steken^h); [fig] afschrikwekkend voorbeeld^h: give a ~ waarschuwen
¹warp (n) **1** schering [in weaving] **2** kromtrekking [in wood]
²warp (vb) krom trekken [of wood]
³warp (vb) **1** krom trekken [wood] **2** scheeftrekken, bevooroordeeld maken: his past has ~ed his judgment zijn verleden heeft zijn oordeelsvermogen verwrongen
warpath oorlogspad^h: go on the ~ op het oorlogspad gaan
¹warrant (n) **1** bevel(schrift)^h, aanhoudingsbevel^h: ~ of arrest arrestatiebevel **2** machtiging, volmacht **3** (waar)borg **4** rechtvaardiging, grond: no ~ for geen grond tot
²warrant (vb) **1** rechtvaardigen **2** machtigen
³warrant (vb) **1** garanderen: ~ed pure gegarandeerd zuiver **2** verzekeren: I (or: I'll) ~ (you) dat kan ik je verzekeren
warranty (schriftelijke) garantie
warren 1 konijnenpark^h **2** doolhof [of streets]; wirwar
warrior 1 strijder, krijger **2** soldaat
Warsaw Warschau
warship oorlogsschip^h
wart wrat: ~s and all met alle gebreken
wartime oorlogstijd
war victim oorlogsslachtoffer^h
wary 1 omzichtig, alert: ~ of op zijn hoede voor **2** voorzichtig
¹wash (n) **1** wasbeurt, het wassen: have a ~ zich wassen **2** vieze, waterige troep, slootwater^h, slappe thee **3** was(goed^h) **4** golfslag **5** zog^h, kielwater^h **6** spoelwater^h || it'll come out in the ~ het zal wel loslopen
²wash (vb) **1** zich wassen, zich opfrissen **2** gewassen (kunnen) worden **3** geloofwaardig zijn: that argument won't ~ dat argument gaat niet op **4** breken [of wave] || the stain will ~ off de vlek gaat er (in de was) wel uit
³wash (vb) **1** wassen; [fig] zuiveren: ~ clean schoonwassen; ~ off (eraf) wassen **2** wassen, de was doen **3** meesleuren [of water]; wegspoelen: be ~ed overboard overboord slaan
washable wasbaar
wash away afwassen, wegspoelen, uitwassen; [fig] reinigen; zuiveren: ~ s.o.'s sins iem. reinigen van zijn zonden
wash cloth [Am] washandje^h
wash down 1 wegspoelen [food, with drink] **2** (helemaal) schoonmaken: ~ with ammonia schoonmaken met ammonia
washed-out 1 verbleekt [in the wash] **2** uitgeput **3** [sport] afgelast (wegens regen)
washed-up verslagen, geruïneerd

washer 1 wasser **2** (sluit)ring, afdichtings-
ring **3** leertje^h **4** wasmachine, wasautomaat
washing was(goed^h)
washing-machine wasmachine
washing-up afwas, vaat: *it's your turn to do
the ~* jij bent aan de beurt om af te wassen
washing-up liquid afwasmiddel^h
washing-up machine afwasmachine,
vaatwasser
wash-leather zeem, zeemleer^h
¹**wash out** (vb) (in de was) eruit gaan [of
stains]
²**wash out** (vb) **1** uitwassen, uitspoelen
2 wegspoelen **3** onmogelijk maken [of rain,
the match]
wash-out flop, mislukking
wash rag [Am] washandje^h
washroom 1 wasruimte, waslokaal^h
2 [Am] toilet^h
washstand wastafel
¹**wash up** (vb) **1** [Am] zich opfrissen **2** afwassen, de vaat doen
²**wash up** (vb) doen aanspoelen [of tide]
washy 1 waterig [of liquid]; slap **2** bleek,
kleurloos
wasp wesp
waspish [oft depr] **1** wespachtig **2** giftig,
nijdig **3** dun; slank [like a wasp]
wassup [inform] hé, hoe is ie
wastage 1 verspilling; verlies^h [through
leakage] **2** verloop^h [of staff]
¹**waste** (n) **1** woestenij; woestijn [also fig]
2 verspilling **3** afval(product)^h, puin^h, vuilnis:
go to ~, run to ~ verloren gaan, verspild worden
²**waste** (adj) **1** woest, braak(liggend), verlaten: *lay ~* verwoesten **2** afval-, overtollig
³**waste** (vb) **1** verspild worden **2** (+ away)
wegteren, wegkwijnen
⁴**waste** (vb) **1** verspillen, verkwisten: *you
didn't ~ time* je liet er geen gras over groeien;
~ time on sth. tijd verspillen aan iets **2** verwoesten
wastebasket [Am] afvalbak, prullenmand
wasteful verspillend, spilziek
wasteland woestenij, onbewoonbaar ge-
bied^h: [fig] *a cultural ~* een cultureel onderontwikkeld gebied
wastepaper papierafval^h
wastepaperbasket prullenmand
wastepipe afvoer(buis)
waste product afvalproduct^h
¹**watch** (n) **1** horloge^h **2** (watches) (nacht)-
wake **3** bewaker, wachtpost, nachtwaker
4 waaktijd, wachtkwartier^h, wacht(dienst),
bewaking, uitkijk: *keep ~ over* waken over
5 wacht, waakzaamheid, hoede: *keep (a)
close ~ on* (nauwlettend) in de gaten houden, de wacht houden over
²**watch** (vb) **1** (toe)kijken **2** wachten: *~ for*
one's chance zijn kans afwachten **3** uitkijken:

~ out uitkijken, oppassen; *~ (out) for* uitkijken naar, loeren op **4** de wacht houden
³**watch** (vb) **1** bekijken, kijken naar **2** afwachten [chance, opportunity]: *~ one's
chance* zijn kans afwachten **3** gadeslaan, letten op: *~ one's weight* op zijn gewicht letten;
~ it! pas op!, voorzichtig!; *~ yourself* pas op!
4 bewaken; hoeden [cattle] **5** verzorgen,
zorgen voor
watchdog waakhond [also fig]; (be)waker
watchful waakzaam, oplettend
watchmaker horlogemaker
watchman bewaker, nachtwaker
watchword 1 wachtwoord^h **2** leus, slogan
¹**water** (n) **1** water^h: *tread ~* watertrappelen;
spend money like ~ geld uitgeven als water
2 water^h, waterstand: *at high* (or: *low*) *~* bij
hoogwater; *at low ~* bij laagwater **3** urine:
make (or: *pass*) *~* wateren **4** water^h **5** (-s) mi-
neraalwater^h; [fig] (water)kuur: *drink* (or:
take) *the ~s* een kuur doen || *~ on the brain*
waterhoofd; *run like ~ off a duck's back* niet
het minste effect hebben; *hold ~* steek houden; *fish in troubled ~s* in troebel water vissen
²**water** (vb) **1** tranen, lopen, wateren: *my
eyes ~ed* mijn ogen traanden **2** watertanden: *make the mouth ~* doen watertanden
3 water drinken [of animals]
³**water** (vb) **1** water geven, begieten: *~ the
plants* de planten water geven **2** van water
voorzien, bespoelen, besproeien: *~ down*
aanlengen; [fig] afzwakken; *a watered-
down version* een verwaterde versie
water biscuit (cream)cracker
water-borne 1 drijvend, vlot **2** over water
vervoerd, zee-: *~ trade* zeehandel
water-butt regenton
watercolour 1 aquarel, waterverfschilde-
rij^h **2** waterverf
waterfall waterval
waterfowl watervogel
waterfront waterkant [of city district etc]:
on the ~ aan de waterkant
water heater boiler; [Am] geiser
water hole waterpoel
watering can gieter
watering place 1 waterplaats **2** kuur-
oord^h, badplaats
water level (grond)waterpeil^h
waterline waterlijn [of ship]
waterlogged 1 vol water (gelopen) [ship]
2 met water doortrokken [soil, wood]
Waterloo (verpletterende) nederlaag, beslissende slag: *meet one's ~* verpletterend
verslagen worden
waterman veerman
watermark 1 watermerk^h [in paper] **2** wa-
terpeil^h
water-meadow uiterwaard
water-power waterkracht, hydraulische

kracht
¹waterproof (n) (waterdichte) regenjas
²waterproof (adj) waterdicht
³waterproof (vb) waterdicht maken
watershed 1 waterscheiding **2** [fig] keerpuntʰ
the **waterside** waterkant
¹water-ski (n) waterski
²water-ski (vb) waterskiën
water snake ringslang
waterspout 1 waterspuwer, spuier **2** waterhoos
water-table grondwaterspiegel
watertight [also fig] waterdicht
waterway 1 waterweg **2** vaarwaterʰ
waterwheel waterradʰ
water wings (zwem)vleugels
waterworks 1 waterleiding(bedrijfʰ) **2** waterlanders, tranen: *turn* on the ~ in tranen uitbarsten
watery 1 waterachtig, water-, vol water **2** nat, vochtig, tranend: ~ *eye* waterig oog, traanoog **3** waterig, smakeloos, flauw, slap, bleek
watt watt
wattle 1 lel; halskwab [esp of birds] **2** hordewerkʰ, gevlochten rijswerkʰ: ~ *and daub* met leem opgevuld vlechtwerk
¹wave (n) **1** golf [also fig]; vloed; [fig] opwelling: ~ *of violence* golf van geweld **2** (haar)golf **3** wuivend gebaarʰ **4** golf(beweging), verkeersgolf, aanvalsgolf
²wave (vb) **1** golven, fluctueren **2** wapperen [of flag]
³wave (vb) **1** (toe)wuiven, zwaaien: [fig] ~ *sth. aside* iets van tafel vegen; ~ *s.o. on* iem. gebaren verder te gaan; ~ *at* (or: *to*) *s.o.* naar iem. zwaaien **2** krullen, golven
wavelength golflengte [λ; also fig]: *be on the same* ~ op dezelfde golflengte zitten [fig]
waver 1 onzeker worden, wankelen **2** aarzelen: ~ *between* aarzelen tussen **3** flikkeren [of light]; flakkeren [of candle]
wavy golvend, deinend
¹wax (n) **1** (bijen)was: [fig] *be* ~ *in s.o.'s hands* als was in iemands handen zijn **2** (boen)was **3** oorsmeerʰ
²wax (vb) wassen, opkomen; toenemen [of water, moon]
waxen 1 glad als was **2** week als was
waxwork 1 wassen beeldʰ **2** (-s) wassenbeeldententoonstelling, wassenbeeldenmuseumʰ
waxy 1 wasachtig, bleek **2** woedend, opvliegend
¹way (n) **1** weg, route: [fig] *things are going his* ~ het zit hem mee; *lose* the (or: *one's*) ~ verdwalen, de weg kwijtraken; [fig] *pave* the ~ *(for sth., s.o.)* de weg effenen (voor iets/iem.); [fig] *pay one's* ~ geen schulden maken, zonder verlies werken; *work one's* ~ *through*

college werkstudent zijn; ~ *in* ingang; ~ *out* uitgang; [fig] uitweg; *better weather is on the* ~ er is beter weer op komst; *on the* ~ *out* op weg naar buiten; [inform, fig] uit (de mode) rakend; *that's the* ~ *(it is, goes)* zo gaat het nu eenmaal **2** manier, wijze, gewoonte, gebruikʰ; [depr] hebbelijkheid: ~ *of life* levenswijze; ~ *of thinking* denkwijze; *in a big* ~ a) op grote schaal; b) grandioos; c) met enthousiasme; *go the right* (or: *wrong*) ~ *about sth.* iets op de juiste (or: verkeerde) wijze aanpakken; [fig] *find a* ~ een manier vinden, er raad op weten; *set in one's* ~s met vast(geroest)e gewoontes; *one* ~ *and another* alles bij elkaar (genomen); *one* ~ *or another* (or: *the other*) op de een of andere manier; *there are no two* ~s *about it* er is geen twijfel (over) mogelijk **3** richting: *look the other* ~ de andere kant opkijken [also fig]; [fig] *I don't know which* ~ *to turn* ik weet me geen raad; *the other* ~ *around* (or: *about*) andersom **4** opzichtʰ: *in a* ~ in zekere zin; *in more* ~s *than one* in meerdere opzichten **5** afstand, eindʰ, stukʰ: *a long* ~ *away* (or: *off*) een heel eind weg, ver weg; *go a long* ~ *to meet s.o.* iem. een heel eind tegemoetkomen [also fig] **6** (voort)gang, snelheid, vaart: *be under* ~ onderweg zijn; *gather* (or: *lose*) ~ vaart krijgen (or: minderen) [of ship]; *negotiations are well under* ~ onderhandelingen zijn in volle gang **7** ruimte [also fig]; plaats, gelegenheid: *clear the* ~ a) de weg banen; b) [also fig] ruim baan maken; *give* ~ a) toegeven, meegeven; b) [also fig] wijken, voorrang geven; c) doorzakken, bezwijken; *make* ~ *for* plaats maken voor; *put s.o. in the* ~ *of sth.* iem. op weg helpen (met iets), iem. aan iets helpen; *out of the* (or: *one's*) ~ uit de weg [also fig]; *get sth. out of the* ~ iets uit de weg ruimen, iets afhandelen ‖ ~s *and means* geldmiddelen; *make* ~ opschieten [also fig]; *make one's (own)* ~ *(in life, in the world)* in de wereld vooruitkomen; [fig] *go one's own* ~ zijn eigen weg gaan; *go out of one's* (or: *the*) ~ *to ...* zijn (uiterste) best doen om ...; *have a* ~ *with elderly people* met ouderen om weten te gaan; *you can't have it both* ~s óf het een óf het ander; *see one's* ~ *(clear) to doing sth.* zijn kans schoon zien om iets te doen; *by the* ~ terloops, trouwens, à propos; *they had done nothing out of the* ~ zij hadden niets bijzonders gedaan; *by* ~ *of example* als voorbeeld; *any* ~ in ieder geval, hoe dan ook; *either* ~ hoe dan ook; [inform] *every which* ~ overal, in alle hoeken en gaten; [Am; inform] *no* ~! geen sprake van!
²way (adv) ver, lang, een eind: ~ *back* ver terug, (al) lang geleden
wayfarer [form] trekker; (voet)reiziger
waylay 1 belagen, opwachten **2** onderscheppen

way-out te gek, geavanceerd, excentriek
wayside kant van de weg, berm: [fig] *fall by the* ~ afvallen, uitvallen
wayward eigenzinnig, koppig
WC *water closet* wc
we wij, we
weak 1 zwak, slap; week [constitution]; broos: *a* ~ *argument* een zwakke redenering; *go* ~ *at the knees* a) slappe knieën krijgen [when in love]; **b)** op zijn benen staan te trillen [with fear]; ~ *at* (or: *in*) *physics* zwak in natuurkunde **2** flauw, zwak; matig [offer, market, Stock Exchange]: *a* ~ *demand (for)* weinig vraag (naar) ‖ *have a* ~ *spot for* een speciaal plekje in zijn hart hebben voor
¹weaken (vb) toegeven, zwichten
²weaken (vb) verzwakken, afzwakken, (doen) verslappen
weak-kneed 1 besluiteloos, slap, niet wilskrachtig **2** bangelijk, timide, laf
weakling zwakkeling, slappeling
weak-minded 1 zwakzinnig; [fig] achterlijk **2** zwak [of will, character]
weakness 1 zwakte, slapheid, zwakheid **2** zwak punt^h **3** zwakheid, zonde, fout **4** zwak^h, voorliefde: *he has a* ~ *for* blonde *women* hij valt op blonde vrouwen
weal striem, streep ‖ *for the public* ~ voor het algemeen welzijn
wealth 1 overvloed, rijkdom **2** rijkdom(men), bezit^h, bezittingen, vermogen^h
wealthy rijk, vermogend
wean spenen [child, young] ‖ ~ *s.o. (away) from sth.* iem. iets afleren
weapon wapen^h
weaponry wapentuig^h
¹wear (n) **1** dracht; het aanhebben [clothing] **2** het gedragen worden [of clothing]; gebruik^h **3** slijtage: *show (signs of)* ~ slijtageplekken vertonen **4** sterkte, kwaliteit **5** (passende) kleding, tenue^h: *sports*~ sporttenue ‖ *normal* ~ *and tear* normale slijtage
²wear (vb) **1** goed blijven [also fig]: *this sweater* ~*s well* deze trui ziet er nog goed uit **2** (also + on, away) voortkruipen [of time]; voortduren: *the meeting wore on* (or: *away*) de vergadering ging maar door
³wear (vb) **1** dragen [on one's body]; aan hebben **2** vertonen, hebben, tentoonspreiden; voeren [colour, flag]: *he* ~*s a beard* hij heeft een baard **3** uitputten **4** [inform; often with negation] aanvaarden, toestaan: *they won't* ~ *it* zij nemen het niet
⁴wear (vb) [also fig] verslijten, (af)slijten, uitslijten: *worn clothes* afgedragen kleren; ~ *thin* dun worden, slijten; *my patience is* ~*ing thin* mijn geduld is aan het opraken
wearable draagbaar
wear down 1 (af)slijten, verslijten **2** verzwakken, afmatten: ~ *resistance* tegenstand (geleidelijk) overwinnen

wearing vermoeiend, slopend
wearisome 1 vermoeiend **2** vervelend, langdradig
¹wear off (vb) (geleidelijk) minder worden: *the novelty will soon* ~ het nieuwtje zal er (wel) gauw af gaan
²wear off (vb) verslijten, afslijten
¹wear out (vb) afgemat raken: *his patience wore out* zijn geduld raakte op
²wear out (vb) uitputten: *wear o.s. out* uitgeput raken, zich uitsloven
³wear out (vb) verslijten, afdragen
¹weary (adj) **1** moe, lusteloos: ~ *of* moe van [also fig] **2** vermoeiend
²weary (vb) moe worden: ~ *of* moe worden, genoeg krijgen van
³weary (vb) vermoeien
¹weasel (n) wezel
²weasel (vb) (also + out) zich drukken, er tussenuit knijpen: ~ *out (of one's duty)* zich onttrekken (aan zijn plicht); ~ *words* dubbelzinnig spreken
¹weather (n) weer^h: *wet* ~ nat weer ‖ *(be, feel) under the* ~ a) (zich) niet lekker (voelen); **b)** dronken (zijn)
²weather (vb) verweren
³weather (vb) **1** doen verweren **2** doorstaan [storm; also fig]; te boven komen
weather-beaten 1 (door storm) beschadigd (geteisterd) **2** verweerd [of face]
weatherboard 1 waterdorpel **2** houten buitenbekleding [of overlapping planks]
weathercock weerhaan, windwijzer; [fig] draaier; opportunist
weather eye *keep a* ~ *open (for)* op zijn hoede zijn (voor), oppassen (voor)
weather forecast weersvoorspelling, weerbericht^h
weatherglass barometer
weatherproof weerbestendig, tegen weer en wind bestand
weathers weersomstandigheden: *in all* ~ weer of geen weer
weathervane windwijzer
¹weave (n) **1** weefsel^h **2** (weef)patroon^h
²weave (vb) zigzaggen, (zich) slingeren; [traf] weven; van rijstrook wisselen
³weave (vb) zich slingerend banen: *they were weaving their way through the full hall* zij baanden zich zigzaggend een weg door de volle hal
⁴weave (vb) **1** vlechten, weven **2** verweven, verwerken **3** maken [story]; ophangen
web 1 (spinnen)web^h **2** web^h, weefsel^h; net(werk)^h [also fig] **3** val, netten **4** weefsel^h **5** (zwem)vlies^h
the **Web** het web
web address webadres^h, internetadres^h
webbing 1 singel(band), geweven band **2** omboordsel^h
webcam webcamera, webcam

¹webcast (n) (live-)uitzending via internet; webcast
²webcast (vb) (live) uitzenden via internet; webcasten
web designer websiteontwerper
webhead [inform] internetverslaafde; internettalent[h]
weblog weblog, blog[+h]
web page internetpagina
website website
web store webwinkel
web traffic webverkeer
¹wed (vb) paren: ~ *to* paren aan
²wed (vb) trouwen, huwen: ~*ded couple* getrouwd paar
wedded 1 huwelijks-, van het huwelijk: ~ *life* huwelijksleven **2** verslingerd, getrouwd: [fig] ~ *to his job* getrouwd met zijn werk
wedding 1 huwelijk[h], huwelijksplechtigheid, bruiloft **2** koppeling, het samengaan: *the ~ of two great minds* het samengaan van twee grote geesten
wedding anniversary trouwdag: *celebrate one's 25th* ~ zijn 25-jarig huwelijk vieren
wedding breakfast bruiloftsmaal[h], maaltijd of lunch na trouwerij
wedding day trouwdag
wedding gift huwelijkscadeau[h]
wedding ring trouwring
¹wedge (n) **1** wig [also fig]: *drive a ~ between the parties* tweedracht zaaien tussen de partijen **2** wigvorm **3** hoek; punt[h] [of cheese, cake]
²wedge (vb) vastzetten, vastklemmen: *we were ~d (in) between the police and the rioters* we zaten ingeklemd tussen de politie en de relschoppers
wedlock huwelijk[h], huwelijkse staat || *born out of ~* buiten huwelijk geboren, onecht
Wednesday woensdag
wee klein: *a ~ bit* een klein beetje, ietsje, een pietsje [also iron]
¹weed (n) **1** onkruid[h] **2** tabak, marihuana, hasj, sigaret **3** lange slapjanus
²weed (vb) **1** wieden, verwijderen, schoffelen **2** wieden; zuiveren: *the manager ~ed out the most troublesome employees* de manager zette de lastigste werknemers aan de kant
weedkiller onkruidverdelger
weedy 1 vol onkruid **2** slungelig
week week, werkweek: *a ~ (on) Sunday, Sunday* ~ zondag over een week; *yesterday* ~ gisteren een week geleden; *most people work a 38-hour* ~ de meeste mensen hebben een 38-urige werkweek || *~ in, ~ out* week in, week uit, wekenlang
weekday doordeweekse dag, werkdag, weekdag
weekend weekend[h], weekeinde[h]
¹weekly (n) weekblad[h]

²weekly (adj) wekelijks: *she earns £150* ~ zij verdient 150 pond in de week
weeny heel klein, piepklein
¹weep (n) huilbui: *let them have their* ~ laat ze maar (uit)huilen
²weep (vb) wenen, huilen: ~ *for* (or: *with*) *joy* van vreugde schreien; *no-one will* ~ *over his resignation* niemand zal een traan laten om zijn vertrek
³weep (vb) **1** storten; schreien [tears] **2** huilen, schreien: ~ *o.s. to sleep* zichzelf in slaap huilen
weeping met hangende takken, treur-: ~ *willow* treurwilg
weepy 1 huilerig, snotterig **2** sentimenteel
wee(-wee) plasje[h]: *do (a) wee(-wee), have a wee(-wee)* een plasje plegen
¹weigh (vb) drukken, een last zijn: *his unemployment ~s (up)on him* hij gaat gebukt onder zijn werkloosheid || ~ *in with* aan komen zetten met, te berde brengen
²weigh (vb) **1** wegen: *it ~s four kilos* het weegt vier kilo; *the greengrocer ~ed a bag of potatoes* de groenteman woog een zak aardappelen; ~ *in* (laten) wegen, zich laten wegen; ~ *out* afwegen **2** overwegen, afwegen: ~ *one's words* zijn woorden wegen; ~ *up* a) wikken en wegen; b) schatten; c) zich een mening vormen over; ~ *up the situation* de situatie opnemen **3** lichten [anchor, ship] || ~ *down* beladen; [fig] deprimeren; *his marriage problems ~ him down* hij gaat gebukt onder zijn huwelijksproblemen
weighbridge weegbrug
weigh-in gewichtscontrole [of boxer before fight; of jockey after race]; wegen na de wedren
¹weight (n) **1** gewicht[h] [for scales]; gewichtsklasse, zwaarte: ~*s and measures* maten en gewichten; *lose* ~ afvallen, vermageren; *put on* ~ aankomen, zwaarder worden; *over* ~ te zwaar; *under* ~ te licht **2** gewicht[h], zwaar voorwerp[h] **3** (zware) last; [fig] druk; belasting: *his departure is a* ~ *off my mind* zijn vertrek is een pak van mijn hart **4** belang[h], invloed: *worth one's* ~ *in gold* zijn gewicht in goud waard **5** grootste deel[h], hoofddeel[h], grootste nadruk: *the ~ of evidence is against them* het grootste gedeelte van het bewijsmateriaal spreekt in hun nadeel || *carry* ~ gewicht in de schaal leggen, van belang zijn; *give* ~ *to* versterken, extra bewijs leveren voor; *pull one's* ~ [fig] (ieder) zijn steentje bijdragen; *throw one's* ~ *about* (or: *around*) zich laten gelden, gewichtig doen
²weight (vb) **1** verzwaren [also of material] **2** beladen [also fig]; gebukt doen gaan: ~*ed down with many parcels* beladen met veel pakjes
weightlifter gewichtheffer
weight-watcher lijner, iem. die goed op

zijn lichaamsgewicht let
weighty 1 zwaar 2 belangrijk, zwaarwegend 3 invloedrijk, gezaghebbend
weir 1 (stuw)dam 2 (vis)weer[h]
weird raar, gek, vreemd, eng: ~ *and* **wonderful** nieuwerwets
weirdo rare (snuiter)
¹**welcome** (n) 1 welkom[h], verwelkoming 2 onthaal[h]: *they gave the speaker a* **hearty** ~ zij heetten de spreker hartelijk welkom; *bid s.o.* ~ iem. welkom heten ‖ *outstay* one's ~ langer blijven dan men welkom is, blijven plakken
²**welcome** (adj) 1 welkom, aangenaam: ~ *change* welkome verandering 2 [roughly] vrij: *you're* ~ *to the use of my books* je mag mijn boeken gerust gebruiken ‖ *'thank you' -* *'you're* ~*' '*dank u' - 'geen dank'; ~ *home,* ~ *back* welkom thuis
³**welcome** (vb) 1 verwelkomen, welkom heten 2 (gunstig) onthalen: *we'd* ~ *a* **change** we zouden een verandering toejuichen
¹**weld** (n) las(naad)
²**weld** (vb) 1 lassen 2 samenvoegen, aaneensmeden ‖ *this* **iron** ~*s well* dit ijzer laat zich goed lassen
welfare 1 welzijn[h], welvaart, voorspoed 2 maatschappelijk werk[h], welzijnszorg 3 bijstand: *be* **on** ~ van de bijstand leven
welfare state verzorgingsstaat, welvaartsstaat
welfare work maatschappelijk werk[h], welzijnszorg
¹**well** (n) 1 put, diepe ruimte, diepte, kuil 2 boorput, oliebron 3 koker, schacht
²**well** (adj) 1 gezond, goed, beter, wel: *she's* *feeling* ~ *again* zij voelt zich weer goed 2 goed, in orde, naar wens: *all's* ~ *that ends* ~ eind goed, al goed; ~ *enough* goed genoeg 3 raadzaam, wenselijk: *it would be (just) as* ~ *to confess your little accident* je kan het beste je ongelukje maar opbiechten ‖ *all* **very** ~ *(,* *but)* alles goed en wel (maar), dat kan wel zijn (maar); *she's* ~ *in* **with** *my boss* zij staat in een goed blaadje bij mijn baas
³**well** (vb) vloeien, (op)wellen
⁴**well** (adv) 1 op de juiste manier, goed, naar wens: *behave* ~ zich goed gedragen 2 zorgvuldig, grondig, door en door: ~ *cooked* goed gaar 3 ver, ruim, zeer, een eind: ~ *in* *advance* ruim van tevoren; *the exhibition was* ~ *worth visiting* de tentoonstelling was een bezoek meer dan waard 4 gunstig, vriendelijk, goedkeurend: *treat s.o.* ~ iem. vriendelijk behandelen 5 redelijkerwijze, met recht: *I* **cannot** *very* ~ *refuse to help him* ik kan moeilijk weigeren om hem te helpen 6 verstandig ‖ *be* ~ *off* **a)** met warmpjes bijzitten; **b)** geluk hebben; ~ *and* **truly** helemaal; *be* ~ *out of* it er goed van af komen [of sth. unpleasant]; *as* ~ ook, evenzeer, net zo lief, net zo goed; *as* ~ *as* zowel … als, en, niet alleen … maar ook; *in*

theory as ~ *as in practice* zowel in theorie als in de praktijk; *wish s.o.* ~ iem. succes toewensen; *leave* (or: *let*) ~ *alone* laat maar zo, het is wel goed zo
⁵**well** (int) 1 zo, nou, wel: ~, *what a surprise* zó, wat een verrassing 2 nou ja, goed dan; jawel [but]: ~, *if she loves the boy* nou ja, als ze van de jongen houdt 3 goed, nu ‖ *oh* ~, *you can't win them all* nou ja, je kan niet altijd winnen; ~ *then?* wel?, nu?
well-advised verstandig, raadzaam
well-appointed goed ingericht, goed voorzien
well-being welzijn[h], gezondheid, weldadig gevoel[h]
well-born van goeden huize
well-bred welopgevoed, beschaafd, welgemanierd
well-disposed (+ towards) welwillend (jegens), vriendelijk (tegen), gunstig gezind
well-done goed doorbakken
well-endowed [inform] fors, weelderig geschapen
well-established 1 voldoende bewezen [eg of principle] 2 reeds lang gevestigd [business]
well-fed 1 goed gevoed 2 weldoorvoed, dik, gezet
well-heeled rijk, vermogend
wellie rubberlaars
well-informed 1 goed op de hoogte, onderlegd 2 goed ingelicht, welingelicht
wellington rubberlaars, kaplaars
well-kept 1 goed onderhouden [of building, garden] 2 goed bewaard [of secret]
well-known bekend, overal bekend
well-matched 1 goed bij elkaar passend 2 aan elkaar gewaagd, tegen elkaar opgewassen
well-meaning goedbedoeld, welgemeend
well-nigh bijna, vrijwel: *it's* ~ *impossible* het is vrijwel onmogelijk
well off rijk, welgesteld: *you don't know* *when you're* ~ je hebt geen idee hoe goed je 't hebt
well-oiled dronken, in de olie
well-preserved goed geconserveerd [of elderly person]: *grandfather* **looks** ~ *at 93* grootvader ziet er nog goed uit op zijn 93e
well-read belezen
wellspring (onuitputtelijke) bron
well-timed op het juiste moment (gedaan / gezegd/komend)
well-to-do rijk, bemiddeld
well-tried beproefd
well-turned-out piekfijn gekleed
well-wisher iem. die iem. het beste toewenst
well-worn afgezaagd, cliché(matig), alledaags

welsh zijn woord niet houden, verplichtingen niet nakomen: ~ *on debts* schulden niet (af)betalen

¹**Welsh** (n) bewoners van Wales

²**Welsh** (adj) Wels, van Wales, in het Wels ‖ ~ *rabbit*, ~ *rarebit* toast met gesmolten kaas

welsher bedrieger; oplichter [of bookmaker]

Welshman bewoner van Wales

¹**welter** (n) mengelmoesʰ, enorm aantalʰ, enorme hoeveelheid

²**welter** (vb) zich rollen; zich wentelen [also fig]

welterweight (bokser uit het) weltergewicht

¹**west** (n) het westen: *the West* het westelijk gedeelte

²**west** (adj) westelijk, west(en)-: ~ *wind* westenwind

³**west** (adv) in/uit/naar het westen, ten westen

westbound in westelijke richting (gaand/reizend)

West Country het zuidwesten van Engeland

¹**westerly** (n) westenwind

²**westerly** (adj) westelijk

¹**western** (n) western, wildwestfilm, wildwestroman

²**western** (adj) westelijk, west(en)-

westerner westerling

westward(s) westwaarts, westelijk

¹**wet** (n) **1** nat weerʰ, regen **2** nattigheid, vochtʰ, vochtigheid **3** sukkel, doetjeʰ

²**wet** (adj) **1** nat, vochtig: ~ *paint* nat, pas geverfd; ~ *through, wringing* ~ kletsnat, helemaal doorweekt **2** regenachtig, nat **3** [inform] slap, sullig, sloom ‖ ~ *blanket* **a)** domper, koude douche; **b)** spelbreker; ~ *dream* natte droom; *he is still* ~ *behind the ears* hij is nog niet droog achter de oren

³**wet** (vb) **1** nat maken, bevochtigen **2** plassen in [bed etc]: ~ *the bed* bedwateren; *he has* ~ *his pants again* hij heeft weer in zijn broek geplast

wetting het nat (gemaakt) worden: *get a* ~ een bui op zijn kop krijgen

¹**whack** (n) **1** klap, mep, dreun **2** (aan)deelʰ, portie **3** poging: *let me have a* ~ *at it* laat mij het eens proberen

²**whack** (vb) een mep geven, een dreun verkopen

whacked doodmoe, uitgeteld, kapot

whacking [inform] enorm, kolossaal

whale walvis ‖ *a* ~ *of a time* een reusachtige tijd; *they had a* ~ *of a time* ze hebben een geweldige lol gehad

whalebone baleinʰ

whaler walvisvaarder

whaling walvisvangst

wham klap, slag, dreun ‖ ~*!* knal!, boem!

wharf kade, aanlegsteiger

whassup [inform] hé, hoe is ie

what 1 wat: ~*'s the English* for *'gezellig'?* wat is 'gezellig' in het Engels?; *no matter* ~ hoe dan ook; ~ *do you call that?* hoe heet dat?; *books, clothes, records and* ~ *have you* boeken, kleren, platen en wat nog allemaal; ~ *of it?* en wat (zou dat) dan nog?; ~ *about an ice-cream?* wat zou je denken van een ijsje?; ~ *did he do that for?* waarom deed hij dat?; ~ *if I die?* stel dat ik doodga, wat dan? **2** wat, dat(gene) wat, hetgeen: ~*'s more* bovendien, erger nog; *say* ~ *you will* wat je ook zegt **3** welke, wat voor, welke (ook), die, dat: ~ *work we did was worthwhile* het beetje werk dat we deden was de moeite waard; ~ *books do you read?* wat voor boeken lees je? **4** [in exclamations] wat (voor), welk (een): ~ *a delicious meal!* wat een lekkere maaltijd! ‖ ~ *and* ~ *not* en wat al niet, enzovoorts enzovoorts; *so* ~*?* nou en?, wat dan nog?

whatchamacallit hoe-heet-het-ook-alweerʰ, dingetjeʰ

whatever 1 alles wat, wat ook: *I'll stay* ~ *happens* ik blijf, wat er ook gebeurt **2** om het even wat (welke), wat (welke) dan ook: *have you found your scarf or* ~ heb je je sjaal of wat je ook kwijt was gevonden; *any colour* ~ om het even welke kleur **3** [in questions and negations] helemaal, totaal, überhaupt: *no-one* ~ helemaal niemand **4** wat (toch): ~ *happened?* wat is er in 's hemelsnaam gebeurd?; ~ *for?* waarom toch?

whatnot wat al niet, noem maar op: *she bought books, records and* ~ ze kocht boeken, platen en noem maar op

whatsisname hoe-heet-ie-ook-alweer, dinges

whatsoever helemaal, absoluut: *no doubt* ~ geen enkele twijfel

wheat tarwe ‖ *separate the* ~ *from the chaff* het kaf van het koren scheiden

wheaten tarwe-: ~ *products* tarweproducten

wheatmeal tarwemeelʰ, volkoren tarwemeelʰ

¹**wheedle** (vb) flikflooien, vleien

²**wheedle** (vb) **1** (+ into) met gevlei overhalen (tot) **2** (+ out of) aftroggelen, afvleien: ~ *a promise out of s.o.* iem. zover krijgen dat hij een belofte doet

¹**wheel** (n) **1** wielʰ, radʰ, draaischijf **2** stuurʰ, stuurradʰ, stuurwielʰ, roerʰ: *at* (or: *behind*) *the* ~ aan het roer, achter het stuur; [fig] aan de leiding **3** auto, kar: *on* ~*s* per auto, met de wagen ‖ *there are* ~*s within* ~*s* het zit zeer ingewikkeld in elkaar

²**wheel** (vb) **1** rollen, rijden **2** (also + (a)round, about) zich omkeren, zich omdraaien, van richting veranderen **3** cirkelen; in rondjes vliegen [of birds] ‖ ~*ing and deal-*

ing ritselen, gesjacher, gemarchandeer
³**wheel** (vb) duwen, trekken [sth. on wheels]; (ver)rijden, rollen: *they ~ed the **patient** back to his room* ze reden de patiënt terug naar zijn kamer
wheelbarrow kruiwagen
wheelchair rolstoel
wheel clamp wielklem
wheeler-dealer [esp Am; inform] ritselaar, handige jongen
wheelhouse stuurhut, stuurhuisʰ
¹**wheeze** (n) **1** gepiepʰ [of breathing] **2** grap, geintjeʰ **3** plannetjeʰ, ideeʰ
²**wheeze** (vb) **1** piepen, fluiten, fluitend ademhalen **2** hijgen, puffen
whelp jongʰ, puppy, welp
¹**when** (adv) **1** [interrogative] wanneer: *~ will I see you?* wanneer zie ik je weer? **2** wanneer, waarop, dat: *the day ~ I went to Paris* de dag waarop ik naar Parijs ging || [when pouring] *say ~* zeg maar ho; *since ~ has he been here?* sinds wanneer is hij al hier?
²**when** (conj) **1** toen: *she came ~ he called* ze kwam toen hij riep; *~ I was a little girl* toen ik een klein meisje was **2** als, wanneer: *he laughs ~ you tickle him* hij lacht (telkens) als je hem kietelt **3** als (het zo is dat): *why use gas ~ it can explode?* waarom gas gebruiken als (je weet dat) het kan ontploffen? **4** hoewel, terwijl, ondanks (het feit) dat: *the part was plastic ~ it ought to have been made of leather* het onderdeel was van plastic hoewel het van leer had moeten zijn
whence [dated] van waar; waar vandaan; waaruit [also fig]: *dreams ~ poetry springs* dromen waaruit dichtkunst ontspringt
whenever 1 telkens wanneer, wanneer ook, om het even wanneer: *~ we meet he turns away* iedere keer als wij elkaar tegenkomen, draait hij zich om **2** wanneer (toch, in 's hemelsnaam): *~ did I say that?* wanneer in 's hemelsnaam heb ik dat gezegd?
where 1 [interrogative] waar; waarheen, waarin, waarop [also fig]: *~ are you going?* waar ga je naartoe? **2** waar, alwaar, waarheen: *Rome, ~ once Caesar reigned* Rome, alwaar eens Caesar heerste **3** daar waar, in die omstandigheden waar, waarbij: *nothing has changed ~ Rita is concerned* er is niets veranderd wat Rita betreft **4** terwijl, daar waar: *she was shy her brother was talkative* terwijl zij verlegen was, was haar broer spraakzaam
whereabouts verblijfplaats, plaats waar iem. (iets) zich bevindt
whereas hoewel, daar waar, terwijl
whereby [form] waardoor
wherefore [form] waarom; om welke reden
whereof waarvan: *the things ~ he spoke* de dingen waarover hij sprak
whereupon waarna, waarop: *he emptied*

his glass, ~ he left hij dronk zijn glas leeg, waarna hij vertrok
wherever 1 waar (toch, in 's hemelsnaam): *~ can John be?* waar kan John toch zijn? **2** waar ook, overal waar: *I'll think of you ~ you go* ik zal aan je denken waar je ook naartoe gaat
wherewithal middelen, (benodigde) geldʰ: *I don't have the ~* ik heb er geen geld voor
whet wetten, slijpen, (aan)scherpen
whether 1 of: *she wondered ~ he would be in* ze vroeg zich af of hij thuis zou zijn; *he wasn't sure ~ to buy it* hij wist niet of hij het wel zou kopen **2** (+ or) of, ofwel, zij het, hetzij: *~ he is ill **or** not I shall tell him* of hij nu ziek is of niet, ik zal het hem zeggen
whetstone wetsteen, slijpsteen
which 1 welk(e): *~ colour do you prefer?* welke kleur vind je het mooist? **2** welke (ervan), wie, wat: *he could not tell ~ was which* hij kon ze niet uit elkaar houden **3** die, dat, welke, wat: *the clothes ~ you **ordered** de kleren die je besteld hebt **4** wat, hetgeen, (iets) wat: *he said they were spying on him, ~ is sheer nonsense* hij zei dat ze hem bespioneerden, wat klinkklare onzin is
whichever om het even welk(e), welk(e) ook, die(gene) die: *~ **way** you do it* hoe je het ook doet
¹**whiff** (n) **1** vleug [of smell]; zweem; flard [of smoke]; zuchtjeʰ [of air, wind]; spoorʰ [also fig] **2** teug, het opsnuiven, het inademen **3** sigaartjeʰ
²**whiff** (vb) (onaangenaam) ruiken, rieken
¹**while** (n) tijd(jeʰ), poos(jeʰ): *a **good** ~* geruime tijd; *worth* ~ de moeite waard; *they will make it **worth** your ~* je zult er geen spijt van hebben; *(every) **once** in a ~* af en toe, een enkele keer; *we haven't seen her **for** a long ~* wij hebben haar lang niet gezien; *(for) a ~* een tijdje, een ogenblik
²**while** (conj) **1** terwijl, zolang als: *~ I cook the meal you can clear up* terwijl ik het eten maak kun jij opruimen **2** [contrast] terwijl, hoewel, daar waar: *~ she has the talent she does not have the perseverance* hoewel ze het talent heeft, zet ze niet door
while away verdrijven
whilst see ²*while*
whim gril, opwelling, bevlieging
¹**whimper** (n) zacht gejankʰ, gejammerʰ: *without a ~* zonder een kik te geven
²**whimper** (vb) janken, jammeren
whimsical grillig, eigenaardig, fantastisch
whimsicality 1 gril, kuur **2** grilligheid
whimsy 1 gril, kuur, opwelling **2** eigenaardigheid
¹**whine** (n) gejammerʰ, gejengelʰ
²**whine** (vb) **1** janken, jengelen **2** zeuren, zaniken

whinge mopperen, klagen, zeuren
¹whinny (n) hinnikend geluidʰ, gehinnikʰ
²whinny (vb) hinniken
¹whip (n) zweep, karwats, gesel
²whip (vb) **1** snel bewegen, snellen, schieten: *she ~ped off her coat* zij gooide haar jas uit; ~ *up* **a)** snel oppakken; **b)** snel in elkaar draaien (or: flansen); *he ~ped round the corner* hij schoot de hoek om **2** overhands naaien **3** zwepen [also fig]; (met de zweep) slaan, ranselen: *the rain ~ped the windows* de regen striemde tegen de ramen **4** kloppen [fresh cream etc]; stijf slaan: *~ped cream* slagroom **5** verslaan, kloppen, in de pan hakken
whip hand: *have (got) the ~ of* (or: *over*) de overhand hebben over
whiplash injury zweepslagtraumaʰ
whipping pakʰ slaag, aframmeling
whipping cream slagroom
whippy veerkrachtig, buigzaam
whip-round inzameling: *have a ~* de pet laten rondgaan
¹whirl (n) **1** werveling, draaikolk **2** verwarring, roes: *my thoughts are in a ~* het duizelt mij **3** drukte, gewoelʰ, maalstroom: *a ~ of activity* koortsachtige bedrijvigheid **4** poging: *give it a ~* probeer het eens een keer
²whirl (vb) **1** tollen, rondtuimelen: *my head ~s* het duizelt mij **2** stormen, snellen, stuiven
³whirl (vb) ronddraaien, wervelen, (doen) dwarrelen: *he ~ed round* hij draaide zich vliegensvlug om
whirligig 1 tol [toy]; molentjeʰ **2** draaimolen, carrousel **3** [fig] mallemolen
whirlpool 1 draaikolk **2** wervelbadʰ, bubbelbadʰ
¹whirlwind (n) wervelwind, windhoos
²whirlwind (adj) bliksem-, zeer snel: *a ~ campaign* een bliksemcampagne
¹whirr (n) gegonsʰ, gezoemʰ, gesnorʰ
²whirr (vb) gonzen, zoemen, snorren
¹whisk (n) **1** kwast, plumeau, borstel **2** garde, (eier)klopper
²whisk (vb) **1** zwaaien, zwiepen **2** (also + up) (op)kloppen, stijf slaan
whisk away 1 wegvegen, wegslaan **2** snel wegvoeren, snel weghalen: *the children were whisked off to bed* de kinderen werden snel in bed gestopt
whisker 1 snorhaarʰ; snorharen [of cat etc] **2** (-s) bakkebaard(en) ‖ *win by a ~* met een neuslengte winnen
whiskey [Am, Ireland] (glasʰ) whisky
whisky (glasʰ) whisky
¹whisper (n) **1** gefluisterʰ; geruisʰ [of wind]: *in a ~*, *in ~s* fluisterend **2** geruchtʰ, insinuatie **3** het fluisteren, fluistering
²whisper (vb) fluisteren, ruisen, roddelen
¹whistle (n) **1** fluit, fluitjeʰ **2** gefluitʰ, fluitend geluidʰ ‖ *wet one's ~* de keel smeren

[with drink]; *blow the ~ on sth.* **a)** een boekje opendoen over iets; **b)** een eind maken aan
²whistle (vb) fluiten, een fluitsignaal geven ‖ ~ *up* in elkaar flansen, uit het niets tevoorschijn roepen
whistle-blower klokkenluider
whit greinʰ, sikkepit: *not a* ~ geen zier, geen steek
¹white (n) **1** witʰ [also chess, draughts]; het witte **2** oogwitʰ **3** blanke
²white (adj) **1** wit, bleek, blank: ~ *Christmas* witte kerst; ~ *coffee* koffie met melk; ~ *as a sheet* lijkbleek, wit als een doek; ~ *tie* **a)** wit strikje [of dress suit]; **b)** rokkostuum **2** blank [of human being] ‖ ~ *ant* termiet; ~ *elephant* **a)** witte olifant; **b)** kostbaar maar nutteloos bezit (or: geschenk); **c)** weggegooid geld; ~ *ensign* Britse marinevlag; *show the ~ feather* zich lafhartig gedragen; ~ *hope* iem. van wie men grote verwachtingen heeft; ~ *lie* leugentje om bestwil; *White Paper* witboek; ~ *spirit* terpentine; *bleed s.o.* ~ iem. uitkleden, iem. het vel over de oren halen
whiteboard whiteboardʰ, schoolbordʰ
white-collar witte boorden-, hoofd-: ~ *job* kantoorbaan; ~ *staff* administratief personeel
Whitehall Whitehall; [fig] de (Britse) regering; Londen
white-hat hacker hacker met goede bedoelingen
white-hat hacking [roughly] computerkraken met goede bedoelingen
white-hot witheet, witgloeiend
White House Witte Huis; [fig] Amerikaanse president
¹whiten (vb) wit worden, opbleken
²whiten (vb) witten, bleken
¹whitewash (n) **1** witkalk, witselʰ **2** vergoelijking, dekmantel
²whitewash (vb) **1** witten **2** vergoelijken **3** witwassen
whither 1 [interrogative] waarheen, waarnaartoe **2** naar daar waar, naar ergens waar: *he knew ~ she had gone* hij wist waar zij heengegaan was
Whit Monday pinkstermaandag, tweede pinksterdag
Whitsun Pinksteren
Whit Sunday pinksterzondag
whittle (+ away, down) (af)snijden [wood]; snippers afsnijden van, besnoeien; [fig] reduceren; beknibbelen: ~ *away* kleiner maken
¹whiz(z) (n) gefluitʰ, het zoeven, gesuisʰ
²whiz(z) (vb) zoeven, fluiten, suizen: *they whiz(z)ed past* zij zoefden voorbij
whiz(z)kid briljant jongmensʰ, genieʰ, wonderʰ
who 1 die, wie: *anyone ~ disagrees* wie niet akkoord gaat **2** om het even wie, wie dan

ook **3** wie: ~ *cares* wat maakt het uit; ~ *knows* *what he'll do next* wie weet wat hij nog zal doen

whod<u>u</u>n(n)it detective(roman), detectivefilm

who<u>e</u>ver 1 wie (toch): ~ *can that be?* wie kan dat toch zijn? **2** om het even wie, wie (dan) ook, al wie: ~ *you meet, don't speak to them* wie je ook tegenkomt, spreek hen niet aan

¹whole (n) geheel[h], totaal[h]: *on the* ~ alles bij elkaar, in het algemeen; *the* ~ *of Boston* heel Boston

²whole (adj) **1** heel, geheel, totaal, volledig: ~ *number* heel getal; *swallow sth.* ~ iets in zijn geheel doorslikken; [fig] iets voor zoete koek aannemen **2** geheel, gaaf, gezond || *go (the)* ~ *hog* tot het einde toe doorgaan, geen half werk doen; *a* ~ *lot of people* een heleboel mensen; [Am] *the* ~ *shebang* het hele zootje

³whole (adv) totaal, geheel: *a* ~ *new life* een totaal nieuw leven

wholeh<u>ea</u>rted hartgrondig

wh<u>o</u>lemeal volkoren

¹wh<u>o</u>lesale (n) groothandel

²wh<u>o</u>lesale (adj) **1** in het groot, groothandel-, grossiers-: *sell* ~ in het groot verkopen **2** massaal, op grote schaal: ~ *slaughter* massamoord

wh<u>o</u>lesaler groothandelaar, grossier

wh<u>o</u>lesome 1 gezond, heilzaam **2** nuttig [advice]

wh<u>o</u>lewheat volkoren

wh<u>o</u>lly geheel, volledig, totaal

whom 1 wie: *tell* ~ *you like* zeg het aan wie je wil **2** die, wie: *your father is a man for* ~ *I have immense respect* jouw vader is iem. voor wie ik enorm veel respect heb

whom<u>e</u>ver [form] wie ook, om het even wie: *tell* ~ *you meet* zeg het aan iedereen die je tegenkomt

¹whoop (n) uitroep; kreet [with joy]

²whoop (vb) schreeuwen, roepen; een kreet slaken [with joy] || ~ *it up* uitbundig feestvieren

wh<u>oo</u>pee: *make* ~ keet maken, aan de zwier gaan

wh<u>oo</u>ping cough kinkhoest

¹whoosh (n) gesuis[h], geruis[h], gesis[h]

²whoosh (vb) suizen, ruisen, sissen

whop afranselen, slaan; [fig] verslaan

wh<u>o</u>pper 1 kanjer **2** grove leugen

wh<u>o</u>pping [inform] kolossaal, geweldig: *a* ~ *(great) lie* een kolossale leugen

whore [inform] hoer

wh<u>o</u>rehouse bordeel[h]

whorl 1 krans [of leaves around stem] **2** spiraal [of shell, fingerprint]

whose van wie, wat, welke, waarvan, wiens, wier: ~ *cap is this?* wiens pet is dit?,

wie zijn pet is dit?; *a writer* ~ *books are all bestsellers* een schrijver wiens boeken allemaal bestsellers zijn; *children* ~ *parents work at home* kinderen van wie de ouders thuis werken, kinderen wier de ouders thuis werken

¹why (adv) waarom, om welke reden: ~ *not ask him?* waarom vraag je het (hem) niet gewoon? || *the* ~*s and wherefores* het hoe en waarom

²why (int) [when surprised] wel allemachtig: ~, *if it isn't Mr Smith* wie we daar hebben! Meneer Smith! || ~, *a child could answer that* nou zeg, een kind zou dat weten

wick wiek, pit; kousje[h] [of lamp]; katoen[h] || *get on s.o.'s* ~ iem. op de zenuwen werken

w<u>i</u>cked 1 slecht, verdorven, zondig: ~ *prices* schandelijk hoge prijzen **2** kwaadaardig; gemeen [tongue] **3** schadelijk; kwalijk [cough]; gevaarlijk [storm]; streng [winter]

w<u>i</u>cker vlechtwerk[h]

w<u>i</u>cker basket rieten mand

w<u>i</u>cker ch<u>ai</u>r rieten stoel

w<u>i</u>cket deurtje[h], hekje[h] || [fig] *bat (or: be) on a sticky* ~ zich in een moeilijk parket bevinden

¹wide (adj) **1** wijd, breed **2** ruim, uitgestrekt, veelomvattend; rijk [experience]; algemeen [knowledge]: *he has* ~ *interests* hij heeft een brede interesse **3** wijd open [eyes]: *keep your eyes* ~ houd je ogen wijd open **4** ernaast, mis; ver naast [shot, guess]: ~ *of the mark* compleet ernaast, irrelevant; *the dart went* ~ *of the target* het pijltje ging ver naast het doel || ~ *boy* gladde jongen; *give s.o. (sth.) a* ~ *berth* iem. (iets) uit de weg blijven

²wide (adv) **1** wijd, breed **2** helemaal, volledig

wide-<u>a</u>ngle groothoek-

w<u>i</u>de-aw<u>a</u>ke klaarwakker; [inform, fig] uitgeslapen

w<u>i</u>dely 1 wijd (uiteen), ver uit elkaar **2** breed, over een groot gebied; [also fig] op vele gebieden: ~ *known* wijd en zijd bekend **3** sterk, heel, erg: *differ* ~ sterk verschillen

w<u>i</u>den breder worden, breder maken

wide-r<u>a</u>nging breed opgezet, van grote omvang

w<u>i</u>descreen breedbeeld(formaat)

w<u>i</u>de-screen breedbeeld-: ~ *TV* breedbeeldtelevisie

widespr<u>ea</u>d wijdverspreid, wijdverbreid

w<u>i</u>dget 1 [inform] dingetje[h], apparaatje[h] **2** [comp] widget

¹widow (n) weduwe

²widow (vb) tot weduwe (weduwnaar) maken: *her* ~*ed father* haar vader, die weduwnaar is

w<u>i</u>dower weduwnaar

width breedte

wield 1 uitoefenen; bezitten [power, influ-

ence] **2** hanteren; gebruiken [tools]
wife vrouw, echtgenote: [inform] *the ~*
vrouwlief, mijn vrouw
wi-fi *wireless fidelity* wifi
wig pruik
¹wiggle (n) gewiebel^h
²wiggle (vb) **1** wiebelen **2** wriemelen, kronkelen
³wiggle (vb) doen wiebelen, op en neer bewegen, heen en weer bewegen: *~ one's toes*
zijn tenen bewegen
¹wild (n) **1** woestenij, wildernis: *(out) in the*
~s in de wildernis **2** (vrije) natuur, natuurlijke staat: *in the ~* in het wild
²wild (adj) **1** wild, ongetemd: *~ flower* wilde
bloem **2** barbaars, onbeschaafd: *the Wild*
West het wilde westen; *run ~* verwilderen
[eg of garden] **3** onbeheerst, losbandig
4 stormachtig; guur [of weather, sea]
5 woest; onherbergzaam [of region] **6** dol,
waanzinnig: *the ~est nonsense* je reinste onzin **7** woest, woedend: *~ with anger* razend
van woede **8** wanordelijk; verward [of hair]
9 fantastisch [of idea]; buitensporig: *the ~est*
dreams de stoutste dromen **10** roekeloos,
gewaagd **11** woest, enthousiast: *she's ~*
about him ze is weg van hem ‖ *a ~ guess* een
gok in het wilde weg; *~ horses* wouldn't drag
it from me! voor geen geld ter wereld vertel
ik het; *~ camping* vrij kamperen
wild card jokerteken^h
¹wildcat (n) **1** wilde kat, boskat **2** heethoofd; kat [woman]
²wildcat (adj) **1** onsolide [bank, firm]; (financieel) onbetrouwbaar **2** wild; onofficieel
[of strike]
wilderness wildernis [also fig]
wildfire: *spread like ~* als een lopend vuurtje (rondgaan)
wildfowl wild gevogelte^h [waterfowl]
wild-goose chase dwaze onderneming:
be on a ~ met een dwaze onderneming bezig
zijn; *send* s.o. on a ~ iem. misleiden
wildlife dieren in het wild
wile list, (sluwe) streek
wilful 1 koppig, eigenzinnig **2** opzettelijk,
expres: *~ murder* moord met voorbedachten
rade
wiliness sluwheid
¹will (n) **1** testament^h: *his last ~ (and testa-*
ment) zijn laatste wilsbeschikking; *she has a ~*
of her own ze heeft een eigen willetje; *he did*
it of his own free ~ hij deed het uit vrije wil
2 wil, wilskracht, wens, verlangen^h: *good* (or:
ill) ~ goede (or: slechte) wil ‖ *at ~* naar goeddunken; *with a ~* vastberaden, enthousiast
²will (vb) **1** willen, wensen, verlangen: *God*
~ing als God het wil; *whether she ~ or no* of ze
wil of niet **2** willen, zullen: [emphatically] *I*
said I would do it and I ~ ik heb gezegd dat ik
het zou doen en ik zal het ook doen; *~ you*

hurry up, please? wil je opschieten, alsjeblieft?; *that ~ be John* dat zal John wel zijn; *I ~*
lend you a hand ik zal je een handje helpen
3 [habit, repetition] plegen, kunnen: *acci-*
dents ~ happen ongelukken zijn niet te vermijden **4** kunnen, in staat zijn te: *this ~ do* zo
is het genoeg **5** zullen, moeten: *you ~ do as I*
say je zult doen wat ik zeg
willful *see* wilful
willies kriebels, de zenuwen: *give* s.o. *the ~*
iem. op de zenuwen werken
willing gewillig, bereid(willig): *~ workers*
werkwilligen; *I am ~ to admit that ...* ik geef
grif toe dat ...
willow wilg
willowy slank, soepel, elegant
will power wilskracht: *by sheer ~* door louter wilskracht
willy plasser, piemel
willy-nilly goedschiks of kwaadschiks: *~,*
he was sent to Spain for a year hij werd voor
een jaar naar Spanje gestuurd, of hij nu wilde of niet
wilt 1 (doen) verwelken, (doen) verdorren
2 hangerig worden, lusteloos worden
wily sluw, listig, slim
wimp sul, doetje^h
¹win (n) overwinning
²win (vb) **1** winnen, zegevieren, de overwinning behalen: *~ hands down* op zijn gemak
winnen; *~ out* (or: *through*) zich erdoorheen
slaan, het (uiteindelijk) winnen
³win (vb) **1** winnen [competition, prize etc]:
you can't ~ 'em all je kunt niet altijd winnen
2 verkrijgen, verwerven; behalen [victory,
fame, honour]; winnen [friendship, confi-
dence]; ontginnen [mine, vein]; winnen [ore,
oil]: *~ back* terugwinnen **3** overreden, overhalen: *~* s.o. *over* iem. overhalen
¹wince (n) huivering [of pain, fear]
²wince (vb) huiveren; ineenkrimpen [of pain
etc]; terugdeinzen: *~ at* s.o.'s words van iemands woorden huiveren
¹winch (n) windas, lier
²winch (vb) opwinden met een windas
¹wind (n) **1** wind, luchtstroom, tocht, rukwind: [fig] *take the ~ from* (or: *out of*) s.o.'s
sails iem. de wind uit de zeilen nemen; *fair ~*
gunstige wind **2** windstreek, windrichting
3 adem(haling), lucht: *get back* (or: *recover*)
one's ~ (weer) op adem komen **4** (buik)wind,
darmgassen: *break ~* een wind laten **5** (-s)
blazers(sectie) ‖ *get ~ of* sth. ergens lucht van
krijgen; *(see) how the ~ blows* (or: *lies*) (kijken)
uit welke hoek de wind waait; [inform] *get*
(or: *have*) *the ~ up* hem knijpen, in de rats
zitten; [inform] *put the ~ up* de stuipen op
het lijf jagen; *(sail) near the ~* scherp (bij de
wind) (zeilen); [fig] de grens van het toelaat-
bare (raken); *there's* sth. *in the ~* er is iets aan
de hand; *second ~* het weer op adem komen,

(nieuwe) energie (voor tweede krachtsinspanning)
²**wind** (vb) **1** kronkelen, zich slingeren: *the
river ~s through the landscape* de rivier kron-
kelt door het landschap **2** spiralen, zich
draaien: *~ing staircase* (or: *stairs*) wenteltrap
³**wind** (vb) buiten adem brengen; naar adem
laten snakken [after thump]
⁴**wind** (vb) **1** winden, wikkelen, (op)rollen: ~
back terugspoelen; ~ *in* binnenhalen, inhalen [of (fishing) line] **2** omwinden, omwikkelen **3** opwinden: ~ *one's watch* zijn horloge
opwinden
⁵**wind** (vb) winden, spoelen, draaien ‖ ~ *on (a
film)* (een filmpje) doorspoelen
windbag [inform] kletsmajoor
windbreak beschutting (tegen de wind)
windbreaker [Am] windjackʰ
windchill gevoelstemperatuur, windverkil-
ling
¹**wind down** (vb) zich ontspannen, uitrusten
²**wind down** (vb) **1** omlaagdraaien: ~ *a car
window* een portierraampje naar beneden
draaien **2** terugschroeven, verminderen
windfall 1 afgewaaide vrucht **2** meevaller,
mazzeltjeʰ, erfenisjeʰ
wind farm windmolenparkʰ
winding-up liquidatie, opheffing
wind instrument blaasinstrumentʰ
windless windstil
windmill 1 windmolen, windturbine
2 (speelgoed)molentjeʰ ‖ *fight* (or: *tilt*) *at ~s*
tegen windmolens vechten
window 1 raamʰ, vensterʰ, ruit: ~ *on the
world* venster op de wereld **2** etalage
3 [comp] vensterʰ ‖ *a ~ of opportunity for
peace* een kleine kans op vrede, de deur naar
vrede staat op een kier; [inform] *out of the ~*
niet meer meetellend, afgeschreven
window dressing 1 het etaleren, etalage
2 etalage, etalage-inrichting, etalagemate-
riaalʰ **3** gunstige voorstelling, het mooier
presenteren dan het is
window-pane (venster)ruit
window-shop etalages kijken: *go ~ping*
etalages gaan kijken
windowsill vensterbank, raamkozijnʰ
windpipe luchtpijp
windscreen voorruit [of car]
windshield 1 windschermʰ [of motorcycle,
scooter] **2** [Am] voorruit [of car]
windshield wiper [Am] ruitenwisser
windsock windzak [at airport]
windsurfing windsurfen
windswept 1 winderig, door de wind geteisterd **2** verwaaid, verfomfaaid
¹**wind up** (vb) **1** eindigen (als), terechtkomen (in), worden (tot): *he'll ~ in prison* hij
belandt nog eens in de gevangenis **2** sluiten,
zich opheffen

²**wind up** (vb) **1** opwinden; opdraaien [of
spring mechanism]: ~ *an alarm* een wekker
opwinden **2** omhoogdraaien, ophalen, ophijsen **3** opwinden, opzwepen: *get wound up*
opgewonden raken
³**wind up** (vb) besluiten, beëindigen, afronden: ~ *a conversation* (or: *project*) een gesprek (*or:* project) beëindigen; *winding up* tot
besluit, samenvattend
¹**windward** (n) loef(zijde)
²**windward** (adj) **1** loef-, wind-: ~ *side* loefzijde, windzijde **2** windwaarts, tegen de
wind (in)
³**windward** (adv) windwaarts, tegen de
wind in
windy 1 winderig, open, onbeschut **2** winderig, opgeblazen; gezwollen [of words]
3 bang
¹**wine** (n) wijn: *sparkling* ~ mousserende
wijn, schuimwijn
²**wine** (vb): ~ *and dine* uitgebreid dineren
¹**wing** (n) **1** vleugel: [fig] *spread* (or: *stretch*)
one's ~s op eigen benen gaan staan; [fig]
take under one's ~s onder zijn vleugels nemen **2** [architecture] vleugel, zijstukʰ **3** [mil]
vleugel, flank **4** [pol; fig] (partij)vleugel
5 [football, rugby; fig] vleugel(speler) **6** (-s)
coulisse: *in the ~s* achter de schermen ‖ *clip
s.o.'s ~s* iem. kortwieken; *on the ~* in de
vlucht
²**wing** (vb) **1** van vleugels voorzien; [fig]
vleugels geven; voortjagen **2** vleugellam
maken, aan de vleugel verwonden
³**wing** (vb) vliegen, (als) op vleugels gaan
winger [football, rugby] vleugelspeler, bui-
tenspeler
wing mirror buitenspiegel, zijspiegel
wing nut vleugelmoer
wingspan vleugelspanning; [aviation]
spanwijdte
¹**wink** (n) **1** knipperbeweging [with eyes];
knipoog(jeʰ): *give s.o. a ~* iem. een knipoog
geven **2** ogenblikʰ [of sleep]: *not get a ~ (of
sleep), not sleep a ~* geen oog dichtdoen ‖ *tip
s.o. the ~* iem. een hint geven; *forty ~s* dutje
²**wink** (vb) **1** knipperen (met) (de ogen),
knipogen: ~ *at s.o.* iem. een knipoog geven
2 twinkelen
winker richtingaanwijzer, knipperlichtʰ
winkle out lospeuteren, uitpersen: *winkle
information out of s.o.* informatie van iem.
lospeuteren
winner 1 winnaar **2** (kas)succesʰ: *be onto a
~* een lot uit de loterij hebben
winning 1 winnend, zegevierend **2** innemend; aantrekkelijk [smile etc]
winnow 1 wannen, van kaf ontdoen: ~ *the
chaff (from the grain)* het kaf (uit het koren)
wannen **2** (uit)ziften, schiften
wino zuiplap, dronkenlap
winsome aantrekkelijk, charmant

winter winter: *in (the)* ~ 's winters, in de winter; *last* (or: *this*) ~ afgelopen (*or:* komende) winter
winter sports wintersporten
wintertime wintertijd, winterseizoen[h]: *in (the)* ~ in de winter
wintry winters, winter-, guur
win-win win-win-, met alleen maar voordelen: *it's a* ~ *situation* het is een win-winsituatie, je zit altijd goed
¹**wipe** (n) veeg: *give sth. a* ~ iets even afvegen
²**wipe** (vb) **1** (af)vegen, (weg)wrijven, (uit)wissen: ~ *one's feet* (or: *shoes*) zijn voeten vegen; ~ *away* wegvegen, wrijven; ~ *down*, *give a* ~-*down* afnemen [with damp cloth]; *please* ~ *that grin off your face* haal die grijns van je gezicht **2** (af)drogen, droog wrijven: ~ *one's hands* zijn handen afdrogen
wipe off 1 afvegen, wegvegen, uitwissen **2** tenietdoen [debt etc]
wipe out 1 uitvegen, uitdrogen, (van binnen) schoonmaken **2** vereffenen, uitwissen **3** wegvagen, met de grond gelijk maken, uitroeien, vernietigen **4** uitvegen, wegvegen, uitwissen ‖ *Jane was wiped out* Jane was bekaf
wiper 1 veger **2** ruitenwisser
wipe up 1 afdrogen: *help to* ~ *(the dishes)* helpen met afdrogen **2** opnemen, opdweilen
¹**wire** (n) **1** metaalkabel, telefoon-, telegraafkabel, telefoonlijn **2** [Am] telegram[h]: *by* ~ telegrafisch, per telegram **3** metaaldraad: *barbed* ~ prikkeldraad
²**wire** (vb) [Am] telegraferen: ~ *(to) s.o.* iem. een telegram sturen
³**wire** (vb) **1** met een draad vastmaken **2** bedraden
wire-cutters draadschaar
wired 1 (met draad) verstevigd [of clothing] **2** op het alarmsysteem aangesloten **3** voorzien van afluisterapparatuur
¹**wireless** (n) **1** radiotelefonie **2** radio: *on* (or: *over*) *the* ~ op (*or:* via) de radio
²**wireless** (adj) draadloos, radio-
wiretapping het afluisteren
wiring bedrading
wiry 1 draad-, als draad **2** taai, buigzaam als draad; weerbarstig [hair] **3** pezig
wisdom wijsheid
wisdom tooth verstandskies
wise wijs, verstandig ‖ *it is easy to be* ~ *after the event* achteraf is het (altijd) makkelijk praten; *be* ~ *to sth.* iets in de gaten hebben; *without anyone's being the* ~*r* onopgemerkt, zonder dat er een haan naar kraait; *come away none the* ~*r* (or: *not much* ~*r*) niets (*or:* weinig) wijzer zijn geworden
¹**wisecrack** (n) grappige opmerking
²**wisecrack** (vb) een grappige opmerking

maken
wiseguy wijsneus, betweter
wisely wijselijk: *he* ~ *kept his mouth shut* hij hield wijselijk zijn mond
¹**wise up** (vb) [Am] in de gaten krijgen, doorkrijgen: ~ *to what is going on* in de smiezen krijgen wat er gaande is
²**wise up** (vb) [Am] uit de droom helpen: *get wised up* uit de droom geholpen worden
¹**wish** (n) **1** verlangen[h], behoefte, zin **2** wens: *best* (or: *good*) ~*es* beste wensen; *express a* ~ *to* de wens te kennen geven te; *make a* ~ een wens doen
²**wish** (vb) **1** wensen, willen, verlangen: *what more can you* ~ *for?* wat wil je nog meer? **2** (toe)wensen: ~ *s.o. well* iem. het beste wensen ‖ ~ *away* wegwensen, wensen dat iets niet bestond; *I wouldn't* ~ *that on my worst enemy* dat zou ik mijn ergste vijand nog niet toewensen
wishful wensend, verlangend: ~ *thinking* wishful thinking; [roughly] vrome wens, [roughly] ijdele hoop
wish list verlanglijstje[h]
wishy-washy 1 waterig, slap, dun **2** krachteloos, slap, armzalig
wisp 1 bosje[h], bundeltje[h]: ~ *of hay* bosje hooi **2** pluimpje[h], plukje[h]: ~ *of hair* plukje haar, piek **3** sliert, kringel, (rook)pluim(pje[h]): ~*s of music* flarden muziek
wistful 1 weemoedig, droefgeestig **2** smachtend
¹**wit** (n) **1** gevat iemand **2** scherpzinnigheid **3** geestigheid **4** (-s) verstand[h], benul[h], intelligentie: *have enough* ~ (or: *have the* ~*(s)*) *to say no* zo verstandig zijn nee te zeggen ‖ *at one's* ~*s' end* ten einde raad; *have* (or: *keep) one's* ~*s about one* alert zijn, bijdehand (*or:* pienter) zijn; *live by* (or: *on) one's* ~*s* op ongeregelde manier aan de kost komen
²**wit** (vb): *to* ~ te weten, namelijk, dat wil zeggen
witch heks
witchcraft tove(na)rij, hekserij
witch doctor medicijnman
witchery 1 betovering, bekoring, charme **2** tovenarij
with 1 met: *a conversation* ~ *Jill* een gesprek met Jill; *compared* ~ *Mary* vergeleken bij Mary; *angry* ~ *Sheila* kwaad op Sheila **2** [direction] mee met, overeenkomstig (met): *it changes* ~ *the seasons* het verandert met de seizoenen; *sail* ~ *the wind* met de wind zeilen; *come* ~ *me* kom met mij mee **3** [accompaniment, cohesion, characteristic] (samen) met, bij, inclusief, hebbende: *she can sing* ~ *the best of them* ze kan zingen als de beste; *I like it* ~ *sauce* ik eet het graag met saus; *what is* ~ *him?* wat is er met hem (aan de hand)?; *spring is* ~ *us* het is lente; *it's all right* ~ *me* ik vind het goed, mij is het om het even

4 [place; also fig] bij, toevertrouwd aan: *she stayed* ~ *her aunt* ze logeerde bij haar tante **5** [contrast] niettegenstaande, ondanks: *a nice girl,* ~ *all her faults* een leuk meisje, ondanks haar gebreken **6** [means or cause] met, met behulp van, door middel van: *they woke her* ~ *their noise* zij maakten haar wakker met hun lawaai; *pleased* ~ *the results* tevreden over de resultaten; *filled* ~ *water* vol water; *sick* ~ *worry* ziek van de zorgen **7** [time] bij, tegelijkertijd met, samen met: ~ *his death all changed* met zijn dood veranderde alles; *he arrived* ~ *Mary* hij kwam tegelijkertijd met Mary aan; *she's not* ~ *it* **a)** ze heeft geen benul; **b)** ze is hopeloos ouderwets ‖ *I'm* ~ *you there* dat ben ik met je eens; *away* (or: *down*) ~ *him!* weg met hem!; *it's all over* ~ *him* het is met hem afgelopen; *what's up* ~ *him?* wat heeft hij?

¹withdraw (vb) **1** uit de weg gaan, opzijgaan **2** zich terugtrekken: *the army withdrew* het leger trok terug **3** zich onttrekken aan, niet deelnemen

²withdraw (vb) **1** terugtrekken: ~ *one's hand* zijn hand terugtrekken **2** onttrekken aan, niet laten deelnemen: ~ *a team from a tournament* een ploeg uit een toernooi terugtrekken **3** terugnemen [remark, promise]; herroepen: ~ *an offer* (or: *a promise*) op een aanbod (or: belofte) terugkomen **4** opnemen [from bank account]: ~ *a hundred pounds* honderd pond opnemen

withdrawal terugtrekking, terugtocht, het (zich) terugtrekken **2** intrekking [eg of promise] **3** opname [from bank account] **4** ontwenning [from drug]

withdrawal symptom ontwenningsverschijnsel[h]

withdrawn 1 teruggetrokken, op zichzelf (levend) **2** (kop)schuw, bescheiden, verlegen

¹wither (vb) **1** verwelken, verdorren: ~*ed leaves* dorre bla(de)ren **2** vergaan: *my hopes* ~*ed (away)* mijn hoop vervloog

²wither (vb) **1** doen verwelken, doen vergaan **2** vernietigen, wegvagen

withhold onthouden, niet geven, toestaan, inhouden: ~ *one's consent* zijn toestemming weigeren

within [place] binnen in, in: ~ *the organization* binnen de organisatie; *he came to* ~ *five feet from the goal* hij kwam tot op anderhalve meter van het doel; *he returned* ~ *an hour* hij kwam binnen het uur terug ‖ *inquire* ~ informeer binnen

without zonder: *she left* ~ *a word* zij vertrok zonder een woord te zeggen; *it goes* ~ *saying* het spreekt vanzelf ‖ *he had to do* ~ hij moest het zonder stellen

withstand 1 weerstaan, het hoofd bieden: ~ *an attack* een aanval weerstaan **2** bestand zijn tegen, opgewassen zijn tegen: ~ *wind*

and weather bestand zijn tegen weer en wind

¹witness (n) **1** (oog)getuige, medeondertekenaar **2** getuigenis, getuigenverklaring, (ken)teken[h], bewijs[h]: *bear* (or: *give*) ~ *(on behalf of s.o.)* getuigen (ten gunste van iem.) ‖ *bear* ~ *of* (or: *to*) staven, bewijzen

²witness (vb) getuigen, als getuige verklaren: ~ *against s.o.* getuigen tegen iem.

³witness (vb) **1** getuige zijn van, bij: ~ *an accident* getuige zijn van een ongeluk; ~ *a signature* (als getuige) medeondertekenen **2** getuigen van, een teken zijn van

witness box getuigenbank

witter on kletsen, wauwelen

witticism geestige opmerking

witty geestig

¹wizard (n) **1** tovenaar: *he's a* ~ *with a microwave oven* hij kan toveren met een magnetron **2** genie[h]

²wizard (adj) waanzinnig, te gek, eindeloos

wizened verschrompeld, gerimpeld, verweerd

wk week

¹wobble (n) **1** schommeling, afwijking **2** beving, trilling

²wobble (vb) waggelen, wankelen

³wobble (vb) wiebelen (met): *don't* ~ *your chair* zit niet met je stoel te wiebelen

wobbly wankel, onvast, wiebelig

woe 1 ramp(spoed), narigheid, ellende **2** smart, wee[h]: *tale of* ~ smartelijk verhaal

woeful smartelijk, verdrietig

¹wolf (n) **1** wolf **2** versierder ‖ *keep the* ~ *from the door* (nog) brood op de plank hebben; ~ *in sheep's clothing* wolf in schaapskleren; *cry* ~ *(too often)* (te vaak) (lichtvaardig) loos alarm slaan

²wolf (vb) (also + down) (op)schrokken; naar binnen schrokken [food]

wolf cub wolfsjong[h], wolfje[h]

wolf whistle lokfluitje[h]

woman 1 vrouw, vrouwspersoon, de vrouw, het vrouwelijke geslacht **2** werkster, (dienst)meid **3** maîtresse: *kept* ~ maîtresse **4** vrouw, echtgenote

womanhood 1 vrouwelijkheid, het vrouw-zijn **2** de vrouwen, het vrouwelijk geslacht

womanish 1 vrouwelijk, vrouw(en)- **2** [depr] verwijfd

womanizer rokkenjager, versierder

womankind de vrouwen, het vrouwelijke geslacht

womanly vrouwelijk

womb baarmoeder; [also fig] schoot

Women's Lib *Women's Liberation* vrouwenemancipatiebeweging; [roughly] Dolle Mina

women's refuge blijf-van-mijn-lijfhuis; [Belg] vluchthuis

¹wonder (n) **1** wonder[h], volmaakt voor-

werp^h **2** wonder^h, mirakel^h: [fig] *do* (or: *work*) ~s wonderen doen; ~s never *cease* de wonderen zijn de wereld nog niet uit **3** verwondering, verbazing, bewondering || *it is little* (or: *no*) ~ *that* het is geen wonder dat
2 wonder (vb) **1** (+ at) verbaasd staan (van), verrast zijn, zich verbazen, (vreemd) opkijken: *I don't* ~ *at* her hesitation haar aarzeling verbaast me niet; *I shouldn't* ~ *if* het zou me niet verbazen als **2** benieuwd zijn, zich iets afvragen: *I* ~ *who* will win ik ben benieuwd wie er gaat winnen; *I* ~ *whether* she noticed ik vraag me af of ze het gemerkt heeft **3** iets betwijfelen, zich iets afvragen: *Is that so? I* ~ O ja? Ik betwijfel het (ten zeerste), O ja? Ik moet het nog zien
wonder boy wonderkind^h
wonderful schitterend, geweldig, fantastisch
wonderland sprookjesland^h, wonderschoon gebied^h
wondrous wonder(baarlijk): ~ *tales* wondere vertellingen
wonky krakkemikkig, wankel; [fig] slap
woo 1 dingen naar (de gunst van), voor zich trachten te winnen: ~ *the voters* dingen naar de gunst van de kiezers **2** het hof maken, dingen naar de hand van
1 wood (n) **1** hout^h: *I haven't had the flu this winter yet, touch* ~ ik heb deze winter nog geen griep gehad, laat ik het afkloppen **2** bos^h: *a walk* in the ~s een wandeling in het bos || *he can't see the* ~ *for the trees* hij ziet door de bomen het bos niet meer; *out of the* ~(s) in veilige haven, buiten gevaar, uit de problemen
2 wood (adj) houten
woodcarving houtsnijwerk^h
woodcraft houtsnijkunst, houtbewerking
woodcut 1 houtsnede **2** hout(snede)blok^h
woodcutter houthakker
wooded bebost, bosrijk
wooden 1 houten: ~ *horse* houten paard, paard van Troje; ~ *shoe* klomp **2** houterig, stijf, harkerig
wooden-headed dom, stom
woodland bosrijke streek
woodlouse pissebed
woodman 1 houtvester, boswachter **2** houthakker
woodpecker specht
wood pigeon houtduif
woodpile houtstapel; stapel brandhout
woodsman 1 houtvester, boswachter **2** houthakker
woodwinds hout^h
woodwork 1 houtbewerking, timmermanskunst **2** houtwerk^h || *crawl (come) out of the* ~ plotseling tevoorschijn komen
woof 1 woef(geluid^h), waf, geblaf^h **2** inslag [of fabric]

woofer woofer, lagetonenluidspreker
1 wool (n) wol || *pull the* ~ over s.o.'s eyes iem. zand in de ogen strooien
2 wool (adj) wollen, van wol
1 wool-gathering (n) verstrooidheid, afwezigheid
2 wool-gathering (adj) verstrooid, afwezig, aan het dagdromen
woollen wollen, van wol
1 woolly (n) wolletje^h, trui, wollen kledingstuk^h, ondergoed^h
2 woolly (adj) **1** wollen, wollig, van wol **2** onduidelijk, vaag, wollig, warrig
woozy wazig, licht in het hoofd
1 word (n) **1** woord^h, (gesproken) uiting: ~s tekst; woorden [to song]; *have a* ~ in s.o.'s ear iem. iets toefluisteren; *by* ~ of *mouth* mondeling; *put* ~s in(to) s.o.'s mouth iem. woorden in de mond leggen; *right from the* ~ *go* vanaf het begin; ~s *fail* me woorden schieten mij tekort; *say the* ~ een seintje geven; *take* s.o. at his ~ iem. aan zijn woord houden; ~ *for* ~ woord voor woord, woordelijk; *in* other ~s met andere woorden; *put* into ~s onder woorden brengen; *have a* ~ *with* s.o. iem. (even) spreken; *have* ~s *with* s.o. woorden hebben met iem. **2** (ere)woord^h, belofte: *he is as good as his* ~ wat hij belooft doet hij; *I give* you my ~ *for it* ik verzeker het je op mijn erewoord; *keep* one's ~ (zijn) woord houden; *take* s.o.'s ~ *for it* iem. op zijn woord geloven **3** (wacht)woord^h, bevel^h: *his* ~ is *law* zijn wil is wet **4** nieuws^h, bericht^h, boodschap: *the* ~ *got* round that het bericht deed de ronde dat; *send* ~ of berichten || *eat* one's ~s zijn woorden inslikken, iets terugnemen; *I could not get* a ~ in edgeways ik kon er geen speld tussen krijgen; *weigh* one's ~s zijn woorden wegen
2 word (vb) verwoorden, onder woorden brengen: *I received a carefully* ~ed letter ik kreeg een brief die in zorgvuldige bewoordingen gesteld was
word blindness woordblindheid
wording formulering, woordkeus
wordless woordloos; onuitgesproken
wordplay woord(en)spel^h, woordspelingen
word processor tekstverwerker
word wrap woordomslag, automatische tekstoverloop naar volgende regel op scherm
wordy omslachtig; langdradig
1 work (n) **1** werk(stuk)^h, arbeid: *a* ~ of *art* een kunstwerk; *have one's* ~ *cut out* (for one) ergens de handen aan vol hebben; *set to* ~ aan het werk gaan; *set about* one's ~ in the wrong way verkeerd te werk gaan; *at* ~ aan het werk, op het werk; *men at* ~ werk in uitvoering; *out of* ~ werkloos **2** borduurwerk^h, handwerk^h, naaldwerk^h **3** (~s) oeuvre^h, wer-

ken, verzameld werk[h]: *Joyce's* **collected** *~s* de verzamelde werken van Joyce **4** (-s) mechanisme[h] [of clock etc] **5** (-s) zooi, bups, mikmak **6** (-s) fabriek, bedrijf[h], werkplaats ‖ *give s.o. the ~s* a) iem. flink onder handen nemen; b) iem. om zeep helpen; [inform] *gum up the ~s* de boel in de war sturen; *shoot the ~s* alles op alles zetten, alles riskeren

[2]**work** (vb) **1** werken, functioneren: *the scheme **didn't** ~* het plan werkte niet; *~ **away*** (druk) aan het werk zijn; *~ **at*** werken aan, zijn best doen op; *it ~s **by** electricity* het loopt op elektriciteit; *~ **on*** werken aan iets, bezig zijn met iets; *~ **to*** werken volgens **2** gisten, werken **3** raken [in a condition]: *the boy's socks ~ed **down*** de sokken van de jongen zakten af; *~ **round to*** toewerken naar, aansturen op

[3]**work** (vb) **1** verrichten, tot stand brengen, bewerkstelligen: *~ **miracles** (or: **wonders**)* wonderen verrichten **2** laten werken, aan het werk hebben: *~ s.o. **hard*** iem. hard laten werken **3** in werking zetten, aanzetten, bedienen, bewerken, in bedrijf houden: *~ a **mine*** een mijn exploiteren **4** zich banen [a path through sth.]: *~ one's way **to** the top* zich naar de top werken **5** bewerken, kneden, werken met: *~ **clay*** kleien, boetseren

workable 1 bedrijfsklaar, gebruiksklaar, bruikbaar **2** uitvoerbaar, haalbaar, werkbaar

workaholic werkverslaafde, workaholic
workaround alternatief[h], alternatieve oplossing
workbench werkbank
workbook 1 werkboek(je[h]) **2** handleiding, instructieboekje[h]
workday werkdag
worker werker, arbeider, werknemer
workflow workflow, werkstroom
work force personeelsbestand[h]
workhorse werkpaard[h] [also fig]; werkezel
work in 1 insteken **2** verwerken: *try to ~ some more details* probeer nog een paar bijzonderheden op te nemen ‖ *~ **with*** (kunnen) samenwerken met
working werkend, werk-: *the ~ **class*** de arbeidersklasse; *~ **man*** arbeider; *~ **mother*** buitenshuis werkende moeder
working day werkdag
working drawing constructietekening, werktekening
working knowledge praktijkkennis, praktische beheersing: *~ **of** German* voldoende beheersing van het Duits
working week werkweek
workload werk[h], werklast, werkbelasting
workman werkman, arbeider
workmanlike ambachtelijk
workmanship 1 vakmanschap[h], vakkundigheid **2** (hand)werk[h], afwerking

work off wegwerken: *~ **steam*** stoom afblazen
workout 1 training **2** intensieve conditietraining, work-out
[1]**work out** (vb) **1** zich ontwikkelen, verlopen, (gunstig) uitvallen **2** oplosbaar zijn, uitkomen **3** trainen ‖ *~ **at** (or: to)* uitkomen op, bedragen
[2]**work out** (vb) **1** uitwerken; opstellen [plan etc] **2** uitrekenen, uitwerken, berekenen, uitzoeken: *work **things** out* de dingen op een rijtje zetten; *try if you can work it out **for** yourself* probeer eens of je er zelf achter kunt komen **3** hoogte krijgen van, doorgronden, doorzien
work permit werkvergunning
workplace werk[h], werkplek: *at (or: in) the ~* op het werk
work placement stage: *do a ~ at a department store* stage lopen bij een warenhuis
worksheet kladje[h]; kladblaadje[h], kladpapiertje[h]
workshop 1 werkplaats, atelier[h] **2** workshop **3** werkgroep
workstation 1 werkplek **2** werkstation[h]
work stoppage werkonderbreking; staking
worktop werkblad[h], aanrecht[h]
work-to-rule stiptheidsactie
[1]**work up** (vb) (+ to) toewerken (naar)
[2]**work up** (vb) **1** opbouwen, uitbouwen **2** stimuleren: *~ an **appetite*** zich inspannen zodat men honger krijgt **3** woedend (nerveus) maken: *don't **get** worked up* maak je niet druk **4** opwerken, omhoogwerken: *work one's way up **from*** zich omhoogwerken vanuit **5** (om)vormen: *he's working up his notes **into** a book* hij is bezig zijn aantekeningenmateriaal uit te werken tot een boek ‖ *work **s.o.** (or: **o.s.**) up* iem. (*or:* zichzelf) opjuinen

world wereld; [fig] hoop, boel, menigte: *make a ~ of **difference*** een hoop verschil uitmaken; *it will do you a ~ of **good*** daar zul je reuze van opknappen; *come into the ~* geboren worden; *all the ~ **knows**, the whole ~ knows* de hele wereld weet het; *why **in** the ~ did you do this?* waarom heb je dat in 's hemelsnaam gedaan?; *out of this ~* a) niet van deze wereld; b) te gek; *the **other** ~* het hiernamaals; *the **Third** World* de derde wereld ‖ *I'd **give** the ~ to …* ik zou er alles (ter wereld) voor over hebben om …; *think the ~ of s.o.* een zeer hoge dunk van iem. hebben, iem. op handen dragen; *they are ~s **apart*** ze verschillen als dag en nacht; *not **for** (all) the ~* voor geen goud; *it is **for** all the ~ like (or: as if)* het lijkt sprekend op
world-beater superkampioen
World Cup wereldbeker, wereldkampioenschap(pen) [socc]

world-famous wereldberoemd
world-leader 1 [pol] wereldleider **2** [econ] toonaangevend bedrijf[h]
worldly werelds, aards, wereldwijs: ~ *wisdom* wereldwijsheid; ~ *goods* wereldse goederen
worldly-wise wereldwijs
world power wereldmacht
world record wereldrecord[h]
world war wereldoorlog
world-weary levensmoe
worldwide wereldwijd, over de hele wereld
1worm (n) **1** worm, hazelworm **2** schroefdraad
2worm (vb) **1** ontwormen [dog, cat etc] **2** wurmen: ~ *one's way into* zich weten in te dringen in **3** ontfutselen, ontlokken: ~ *a secret out of* s.o. iem. een geheim ontfutselen
worn-out 1 afgedragen, (tot op de draad) versleten **2** uitgeput, doodop, bekaf
worried bezorgd, ongerust: *a* ~ *look* een zorgelijk gezicht
worrisome 1 zorgwekkend, onrustbarend **2** zorgelijk, tobberig
1worry (n) **1** (voorwerp[h] van) zorg **2** zorgenkind[h], bron van zorgen **3** (be)zorg(dheid), ongerustheid
2worry (vb) (+ about, over) zich zorgen maken (over): *I should* ~ (zal) mij een zorg (zijn) || *not to* ~! maak je geen zorgen!; ~ *at* **a)** zich het hoofd breken over [problem]; **b)** aandringen bij [somebody]
3worry (vb) lastigvallen, hinderen, storen: *the rain doesn't* ~ *him* de regen deert hem niet; *oh, that doesn't* ~ *me* o, daar zit ik niet (zo) mee, o, daar geef ik niks om; *you'll* ~ *yourself to death* je maakt je veel te druk
worrying zorgwekkend, zorgelijk
1worse (n) iets slechters, slechtere dingen: *a change for the* ~ een verandering ten kwade, een verslechtering
2worse (adj, adv) **1** slechter, erger, minder (goed): *to make things* ~ tot overmaat van ramp; ~ *still* erger nog **2** zieker, zwakker: *today mother was much* ~ *than yesterday* vandaag was moeder zieker dan gisteren || *the* ~ *for drink* (or: *liquor*) aangeschoten; *he is none the* ~ *for* hij is niet minder geworden van, hij heeft niet geleden onder; *I like him none the* ~ *for it* ik mag hem er niet minder om
worsen verergeren, verslechteren, bemoeilijken
1worship (n) **1** verering, aanbidding **2** eredienst, godsdienst(oefening) || *Your* Worship Edelachtbare
2worship (vb) **1** naar de kerk gaan **2** van eerbied vervuld zijn, in aanbidding verzonken zijn
3worship (vb) [also fig] aanbidden, vereren
worshipper 1 kerkganger, gelovige

2 aanbidder, vereerder
worst 1 slechtst, ergst: *come off* ~ aan het kortste eind trekken **2** ziekst, zwakst || *if the* ~ *comes to the* ~ in het ergste geval; *so you want to fight, OK, we'll fight. Do your* ~! dus jij wil vechten, goed, dan vechten we. Kom maar op!; *at (the)* ~ in het ergste geval
1worth (n) **1** waarde, kwaliteit: *of great* ~ van grote waarde **2** markt-, tegenwaarde: *I want a dollar's* ~ *of apples* mag ik voor een dollar appels?
2worth (adj) waard: *land* ~ *100,000 dollars* land met een waarde van 100.000 dollar; *it is* ~ *(one's) while* het is de moeite waard; ~ *seeing* bezienswaardig; *for what it's* ~ voor wat het waard is; *it's* ~ *it* het is de moeite waard || *for all one is* ~ uit alle macht
worthwhile de moeite waard, waardevol, nuttig
worthy 1 waardig, waardevol **2** waard: *in clothes* ~ *of the occasion* in bij de gelegenheid passende kleding; *he isn't* ~ *of her* hij is haar niet waard **3** [oft iron] achtenswaardig, braaf
would 1 willen, zullen, wensen: *he* ~ *not hear of it* hij wilde er niet van horen; *I wish he* ~ *leave me alone* ik wilde dat hij me met rust liet; *I* ~ *like to show you this* ik zou je dit graag laten zien; *he* ~ *sooner die than surrender* hij zou liever sterven dan zich overgeven **2** gewoonlijk, steeds, altijd: *we* ~ *walk to school together* we liepen gewoonlijk samen naar school **3** zou(den): *I* ~ *try it anyway (if I were you)* ik zou het toch maar proberen (als ik jou was); *he was writing the book that* ~ *bring him fame* hij was het boek aan het schrijven dat hem beroemd zou maken **4** [supposition] moeten, zullen, zou(den), moest(en): *he* ~ *be in bed by now* hij zal nu wel in bed liggen; ~ *you please shut the door?* wil je de deur sluiten alsjeblieft? **5** [doubt or uncertainty] zou kunnen: *we* ~ *suggest the following* we zouden het volgende willen voorstellen
would-be 1 [depr] zogenaamd **2** toekomstig, potentieel, mogelijk: *a* ~ *buyer* een mogelijke koper, een gegadigde
1wound (n) wond, verwonding; [fig] belediging || *lick one's* ~s zijn wonden likken [after defeat]
2wound (vb) (ver)wonden; [fig] grieven; krenken: *when he suddenly left her, she felt* ~*ed and betrayed* toen hij plotseling bij haar wegging, voelde ze zich gekwetst en verraden
wow 1 klapper, groot succes[h], sensatie **2** wow [of stereo equipment]
wrack verwoesting, verval[h], ruïne
wraith (geest)verschijning, schim, spook[h], spookgestalte
1wrangle (n) ruzie
2wrangle (vb) ruzie maken, ruziën: ~ *with*

s.o. about (or: *over*) *sth.* met iem. om (*or:* over) iets ruziën

¹wrap (n) **1** omslag(doek^h), omgeslagen kledingstuk^h, sjaal, stola **2** (reis)deken || *take the ~s off* onthullen; ***under** ~s* geheim

²wrap (vb) zich wikkelen

³wrap (vb) **1** inpakken, verpakken **2** wikkelen, omslaan, vouwen **3** (om)hullen, bedekken: *~ped **in** mist* in nevelen gehuld

wrapper 1 (stof)omslag^h, kaft **2** adresband(je^h) **3** papiertje^h, pakpapier^h, wikkel

wrapping paper inpakpapier^h

¹wrap up (vb) **1** zich (warm) (aan)kleden **2** zijn mond houden: *~!* kop dicht!

²wrap up (vb) **1** verpakken, inpakken **2** warm aankleden, (goed/stevig) inpakken **3** afwikkelen, afronden, sluiten: *~ a **deal*** een overeenkomst sluiten || *be wrapped up **in*** opgaan in; *wrap it up!* hou op!

wrath [form] toorn; woede

wrathful woedend

wreak 1 uitstorten: *~ vengeance **(up)on*** wraak nemen op **2** veroorzaken, aanrichten

wreath (rouw)krans, (ere)krans || *~ of smoke* kringetje rook

¹wreathe (vb) kringelen, kronkelen

²wreathe (vb) **1** omkransen, om(k)ringen, omhullen: *~d **in** om(k)ringd door, gehuld in; [fig] *a face ~ **in** smiles* een in glimlachen gehuld gelaat **2** (om)wikkelen, (om)strengelen **3** (be)kransen, met een krans tooien

¹wreck (n) **1** wrak^h [also fig]; ruïne **2** schipbreuk [also fig]; ondergang, vernietiging

²wreck (vb) **1** schipbreuk doen lijden, doen stranden, aan de grond doen lopen; [fig] doen mislukken [plan etc]: *the **ship** was ~ed on the rocks* het schip liep op de rotsen **2** ruïneren, verwoesten, te gronde richten

wreckage wrakgoed^h, wrakstukken, brokstukken, restanten

wrecked [inform] **1** straalbezopen **2** zeer high

wrecker 1 berger, bergingsmaatschappij **2** [Am] sloper, sloopbedrijf^h **3** [Am] takelwagen

wren winterkoninkje^h

¹wrench (n) **1** ruk, draai **2** verrekking, verstuiking **3** moersleutel

²wrench (vb) **1** (los)wringen, (los)wrikken, een ruk geven aan: *~ **open** openwrikken, openrukken; *~ **away** (or: *off*) losrukken, wegrukken, loswrikken **2** verzwikken, verstuiken **3** verdraaien [facts etc]

wrest 1 (los)rukken, (los)wringen, (los)wrikken: [fig] *~ a confession **from** s.o.* een bekentenis uit iem. persen **2** zich meester maken van, zich toe-eigenen **3** verdraaien; geweld aandoen [meaning, facts]

wrestle worstelen (met/tegen) [also fig]: *~ **with** problems* met problemen kampen

wrestler worstelaar

wrestling worstelen^h

wretch 1 stakker, zielenpoot **2** ellendeling, klier **3** schurk, boef, schooier

wretched 1 beklagenswaardig, zielig, droevig **2** ellendig, ongelukkig **3** verachtelijk, laag **4** waardeloos, beroerd, rot-

¹wriggle (n) kronkelbeweging, gekronkel^h, gewriemel^h

²wriggle (vb) kronkelen, wriemelen; [fig] zich in allerlei bochten wringen: *~ **out of** sth.* ergens onderuit proberen te komen

³wriggle (vb) **1** wriemelen met, wriemelend heen en weer bewegen **2** kronkelend afleggen

wring 1 omdraaien: *~ a hen's **neck*** een kip de nek omdraaien **2** (uit)wringen, (uit)persen, samenknijpen: *~ s.o.'s **hand*** iem. stevig de hand drukken **3** afpersen, afdwingen: *~ a confession **from** (or: *out **of***) s.o.* iem. een bekentenis afdwingen

¹wrinkle (n) **1** rimpel, plooi, kreuk **2** foefje^h, kunstje^h **3** tip, idee^h

²wrinkle (vb) rimpelen, rimpels (doen) krijgen, kreuke(le)n

wrinkly rimpelig, gerimpeld; kreukelig

wrist 1 pols(gewricht^h) **2** pols(stuk^h) [of clothing]; manchet

wristband 1 horlogebandje^h, pols(arm)band **2** manchet

wristlet 1 horlogeband(je^h) **2** polsband(je^h) [sport] **3** armband(je^h)

wristwatch polshorloge^h

writ 1 bevelschrift^h, dwangbevel^h, gerechtelijk schrijven^h: *serve a ~ on* een dagvaarding betekenen aan **2** de Schrift [Bible]

write schrijven, (weg)schrijven: *~ a **cheque*** een cheque uitschrijven; *~ **back** terugschrijven, antwoorden; *~ **about** (or: *on*) *a subject* over een onderwerp schrijven; *~ away **for*** over de post bestellen || *nothing to ~ **home** about* niet(s) om over naar huis te schrijven; *envy was written all **over** his face* de jaloezie stond hem op het gezicht te lezen

write down 1 neerschrijven, opschrijven, op papier vastleggen **2** beschrijven, uitmaken voor, beschouwen (als): *write s.o. down (as) a **bore*** iem. uitmaken voor een vervelende vent

¹write in (vb) schrijven, schriftelijk verzoeken: *~ **for** a free catalogue* schrijven om een gratis catalogus

²write in (vb) bijschrijven, invoegen, toevoegen, inlassen

¹write off (vb) schrijven, over de post bestellen: *~ **for** sth., ~ to order sth.* schrijven om iets te bestellen

²write off (vb) **1** afschrijven [also fig]; afvoeren: *~ **losses** (or: *a **car***) verliezen (or: auto) afschrijven **2** (op)schrijven, in elkaar draaien

write-off 1 afschrijving **2** total loss; weggooier [fig]

write out 1 uitschrijven, voluit schrijven
2 schrijven; uitschrijven [cheque etc]
3 schrappen; uitschrijven [part in TV series]:
*her **part** was written out* haar rol werd geschrapt

writer schrijver, schrijfster, auteur: *the (present)* ~ ondergetekende

writer's block writer's block

write up 1 bijwerken [diary] **2** uitwerken,
uitschrijven

writhe wringen, kronkelen, (ineen)krim-
pen: ~ *with pain* kronkelen van de pijn

writing 1 schrijvenʰ: *in* ~ schriftelijk
2 (hand)schriftʰ **3** schriftʰ, schriftuur: **put** *sth.
down in* ~ iets op schrift stellen **4** (-s) werken,
geschriften || *the* ~ *on the **wall*** het teken aan
de wand

writing desk schrijfbureauʰ

writing pad schrijfblokʰ, blocnote

¹**wrong** (n) **1** kwaadʰ, onrechtʰ: *right and* ~
juist en onjuist **2** misstand, wantoestand
3 onrechtmatige daad || *be **in** the* ~ **a)** het mis
hebben; **b)** de schuldige zijn, het gedaan
hebben

²**wrong** (adj) **1** verkeerd, fout, onjuist: ~
number verkeerd verbonden; *(the)* ~ ***way***
round achterstevoren, de verkeerde kant op;
go down the ~ ***way*** in het verkeerde keelgat
schieten [of food] **2** slecht, verkeerd, niet
goed: ***you're*** ~ *to do this,* ***it's*** ~ *of you to do this*
u doet hier verkeerd aan **3** in de verkeerde
richting, de verkeerde kant op || *get hold of
the* ~ ***end*** *of the stick* het bij het verkeerde
eind hebben; *come to the* ~ ***shop*** aan het verkeerde adres (gekomen) zijn; *get on the* ~
side *of s.o.* iemands sympathie verliezen; *on
the* ~ ***side*** *of sixty* de zestig gepasseerd; [Am]
the ~ ***side*** *of the tracks* de achterbuurten, de
zelfkant; *bark up the* ~ ***tree*** op het verkeerde
spoor zijn, aan het verkeerde adres zijn;
you're ~ je hebt ongelijk, je vergist je

³**wrong** (vb) **1** onrecht doen, onrechtvaardig
behandelen, onredelijk zijn tegen: ~ *a **person*** iem. tekortdoen **2** onbillijk beoordelen

wrongdoer wetsovertreder; misdadiger

wrongdoing 1 wandaad, overtreding
2 wangedragʰ, misdadigheid

wrongful 1 onterecht, onbillijk **2** onrechtmatig, onwettig

wrong-headed 1 dwars(liggerig), eigenwijs **2** foutief, verkeerd

wrought-up gespannen, nerveus, opgewonden

wry 1 (ver)zuur(d), wrang: ~ ***mouth*** zuinig
mondje **2** (licht) ironisch, spottend, droog;
laconiek [of humour]: ~ ***smile*** spottend lachje

wt *weight* gewicht

WWW *World Wide Web* www

WYSIWYG *What You See Is What You Get*
wysiwyg

X

xenophobe xenofoob, vreemdelingenhater

xenophobia xenofobie, vreemdelingenhaat, vreemdelingenangst

XL *extra large* XL; extra groot [clothing]

Xmas Kerstmis, kerst

X-rated [roughly] (voor) boven de achttien

X-rating keuring boven de 18

¹**X-ray** (n) **1** röntgenstraal **2** röntgenfoto

²**X-ray** (vb) **1** doorlichten [also fig] **2** bestralen

xylophone xylofoon

y

yacht jacht[h] [ship]
yachting (wedstrijd)zeilen[h]
yachtsman zeiler
yackety-yack [inform] geouwehoer[h], ge-lul[h]
yada yada yada [Am; inform] blablabla
yahoo varken[h], schoft
yak jak, knorbuffel
yammer 1 jammeren **2** kakelen
¹yank (n) ruk, sjor
²yank (vb) een ruk geven aan, trekken
Yank see Yankee
Yankee [Am] **1** yankee, yank; [hist] noor-derling **2** [depr] Amerikaan
¹yap (n) gekef[h]
²yap (vb) **1** keffen **2** [inform] kleppen, kake-len
yard 1 Engelse el [91.4 cm]: *by the ~* per yard; [fig] ellenlang **2** [shipp] ra **3** (omheind) terrein[h], binnenplaats, erf[h] **4** [Am] plaatsje[h], (achter)tuin, gazon[h] || *the* Yard Scotland Yard
yardage 1 aantal yards **2** lengte
yardstick meetlat; [fig] maatstaf
yarn 1 lang verhaal[h], (langdradig) verhaal[h] **2** garen[h], draad || *spin a ~* een lang verhaal vertellen
¹yawn (n) geeuw, gaap
²yawn (vb) geeuwen; gapen [also fig]; wijd geopend zijn: *~ing hole* gapend gat
yd *yard*
yds *yards*
¹ye (pers pron) gij, u, jullie, jij
²ye (art) de: *ye olde Spanish Inn* de oude Spaanse herberg
yea 1 stem vóór: *~s and nays* stemmen vóór en tegen **2** voorstemmer
year 1 jaar[h]: *a ~ from today* vandaag over een jaar; *all the ~ round* het hele jaar door; *for many ~s* sinds jaar en dag; *over the ~s* met de jaren **2** lange tijd; [fig] eeuw **3** (-s) jaren, leeftijd **4** (-s) eeuwigheid; eeuwen: *it has been ~s* het is eeuwen geleden
yearling eenjarig dier[h], eenjarig renpaard[h]
yearly jaarlijks, elk jaar: *a ~ income* een jaarinkomen
yearn smachten, verlangen: *~ after* (or: *for*) smachten naar
yeast gist; [fig] desem
¹yell (n) gil, kreet, schreeuw, aanmoedi-gingskreet
²yell (vb) gillen, schreeuwen: *~ one's **head** off* tekeergaan, tieren
¹yellow (n) **1** geel[h] **2** eigeel[h], dooier

²yellow (adj) **1** geel(achtig) **2** laf || [socc] *show s.o. a ~ **card*** iem. een gele kaart geven; *~ pages* gouden gids
¹yelp (n) **1** gekef[h] **2** gejank[h] **3** gil
²yelp (vb) **1** keffen **2** janken **3** gillen
Yemen Jemen
¹Yemeni (n) Jemeniet, Jemenitische
²Yemeni (adj) Jemenitisch
yen 1 yen [Japanese currency] **2** verlangen[h]
yeoman kleine landeigenaar
yep [Am; inform] ja
¹yes (n) ja[h]: *say ~* ja zeggen, het jawoord ge-ven
²yes (adv) ja; jawel [after negative sentence]
yesterday gisteren: *the day **before** ~* eer-gisteren; *~'s weather was terrible* het weer van gisteren was afgrijselijk || *I saw him ~ **week*** ik heb hem gisteren een week geleden gezien
¹yet (adv) **1** nog, tot nu toe, nog altijd: *she has ~ to ring up* ze heeft nog steeds niet op-gebeld; *as ~* tot nu toe **2** [in interrogative sentences] al **3** opnieuw, nog: *~ **again*** nog een keer **4** toch nog, uiteindelijk: *he'll beat you ~* hij zal jou nog wel verslaan **5** toch: *and ~ she refused* en toch weigerde zij
²yet (conj) maar (toch), doch: *strange ~ true* raar maar waar
yeti yeti, verschrikkelijke sneeuwman
yew taxus(boom), taxushout[h]
Yid [depr] Jood[h], jid
Yiddish Jiddisch
¹yield (n) opbrengst, productie, oogst, ren-dement[h]
²yield (vb) **1** opbrengst hebben; vrucht dra-gen [of tree] **2** zich overgeven [to enemy] **3** toegeven, wijken: *~ **to** temptation* voor de verleiding bezwijken **4** voorrang verlenen
³yield (vb) **1** voortbrengen [fruit; also fig: profit, results]; opleveren, opbrengen **2** overgeven, opgeven, afstaan: *~ (up) one's position to the enemy* zijn positie aan de vij-and overgeven **3** toegeven
yielding 1 meegevend, buigzaam **2** mee-gaand **3** productief, winstgevend
yippee [inform] jippie
yob [inform] vandaal
yobbish baldadig, vernielzuchtig; onbe-schoft, hondsbrutaal
yobbo vandaal
yodel jodelen
yoga yoga
yogurt yoghurt
¹yoke (n) **1** juk[h] [also fig]; heerschappij, sla-vernij: *throw off the ~* zich van het juk bevrij-den **2** koppel[h], span[h], paar[h] **3** draagjuk[h] **4** verbintenis; juk[h] [of marriage]
²yoke (vb) **1** onder het juk brengen, inspan-nen, voorspannen **2** koppelen, verbinden: *~d in marriage* in de echt verbonden
yokel boerenkinkel
yolk dooier

yonder ginds, daar ginder

yore: *of* ~ (van) vroeger, uit het verleden

you 1 jij, jou, je; [form] u: *I saw* ~ *chasing her* ik heb gezien hoe je haar achterna zat; *Mrs Walters* **to** ~ voor jou ben ik mevr. Walters **2** jullie, u: *what* **are** ~ *two* **up to?** wat voeren jullie twee uit? **3** je, men: ~ *can't always get what* ~ *want* je kunt niet altijd krijgen wat je wilt; *that's fame* **for** ~ dat noem ik nou nog eens beroemd zijn

¹young (n) **1** de jongelui, de jeugd **2** jongen [of animal]

²young (adj) **1** jong, pasgeboren, klein, nieuw, vers, fris: ~ *child* klein kind, kindje; *a* ~ *family* een gezin met kleine kinderen **2** vroeg, net begonnen: *the* **day** (or: **night**) *is (still)* ~ het is nog vroeg **3** junior, jong(er)e: *the* ~*er* **Smith, Smith** *the* ~*er* de jongere Smith **4** jeugdig: *one's* ~ *day(s)* iemands jonge jaren || ~ *blood* nieuw bloed, vers bloed, nieuwe ideeën; *Young* **Turk** revolutionair, rebel; ~ *turk* wildebras

youngster 1 jongmens[h] **2** jochie[h], kereltje[h]

your 1 jouw, jullie, uw, van jou, jullie: *this is* ~ **day** dit is jullie grote dag; *I was surprised at* ~ **leaving** *so hastily* ik was verbaasd dat je zo haastig vertrok **2** zo'n (fameuze), een: *so this is* ~ **Hyde** *Park!* dit is dus dat (beroemde) Hyde Park van jullie!

yours van jou, van jullie, de, het jouwe, de, het uwe: *take* **what** *is* ~ neem wat van jou is; *a friend* **of** ~ een vriend van jou || *sincerely* ~ met vriendelijke groeten

yourself 1 je, zich: *you are not* ~ je bent niet in je gewone doen; *then you came* **to** ~ toen kwam je bij **2** je zelf, zelf: *it's easier to* **do** *it* ~ het is gemakkelijker om het zelf te doen; *you* ~ *told me* je hebt het me zelf gezegd

yourselves 1 zich, jullie: *you ought to be ashamed* **of** ~ jullie zouden je moeten schamen **2** zelf: *finish it* ~ maak het zelf af

youth 1 jeugd, jonge jaren **2** jongeman, jongen **3** tiener: ~*s* jongelui

youthful jeugdig, jong, jeugd-

youth hostel jeugdherberg

¹yowl (n) gejank[h] [of animals]

²yowl (vb) janken [of animals]

yrs 1 *years* **2** *yours*

yuck bah, gadsie

yucky smerig

¹Yugoslav (n) Joegoslaaf, Joegoslavische

²Yugoslav (adj) Joegoslavisch, van Joegoslavië

Yugoslavia Joegoslavië

yuletide kersttijd

Yuletide Kerstmis, kerst

yummy 1 lekker, heerlijk **2** prachtig [eg of colours]

yuppie *young urban professional* yup(pie)

Z

z z, Z
¹Zaïrean (n) Zaïrees, Zaïrese
²Zaïrean (adj) Zaïrees
Zambia Zambia
¹Zambian (n) Zambiaan(se)
²Zambian (adj) Zambiaans
¹zany (n) idioot, halvegare
²zany (adj) **1** grappig, zot, leuk **2** idioot, krankzinnig, absurd
¹zap (n) pit, pep ‖ ~! zoef!, flits!, wam!
²zap (vb) [inform] **1** snel gaan, zoeven, racen: *he was ~ping off in his car to Cardiff* hij scheurde weg in zijn wagen naar Cardiff **2** zappen; kanaalzwemmen [TV]
³zap (vb) raken, treffen
zeal ijver, geestdrift: *show ~ for sth.* voor iets enthousiast zijn
zealot fanatiekeling
zealous 1 ijverig, vurig, enthousiast **2** verlangend, gretig
zebra zebra: *~ crossing* zebra(pad)
Zen zen, zenboeddhisme^h
zenith toppunt^h, top, piek: *at the ~ of his fame* op het toppunt van zijn roem
¹zero (vb) het vizier instellen, scherp stellen: *~ in on* a) het vuur richten op; b) zijn aandacht richten op [problem]; c) inhaken op [eg on new market]
²zero (num) nul, nulpunt, laagste punt, beginpunt: *his chances of recovery were ~* hij had geen enkele kans op herstel
zero economic growth nulgroei
zero hour 1 [mil] uur nul [of operation] **2** kritiek moment, beslissend tijdstip
zest 1 iets extra's, jeu, pit: *give* (or: *add*) *~ to* meer smaak geven aan, wat meer pit geven **2** animo^h, enthousiasme^h: *~ for life* levenslust, levensvreugde
Zeus Zeus ‖ *by ~!* wel verdorie!, drommels!
¹zigzag (n) zigzag
²zigzag (vb) zigzaggen: *the road ~ged down to the valley* de weg zigzagde naar de vallei toe
³zigzag (adv) zigzag, in een zigzaglijn
zillion eindeloos groot getal^h
Zimbabwe Zimbabwe
¹Zimbabwean (n) Zimbabwaan(se)
²Zimbabwean (adj) Zimbabwaans
Zimmer frame looprek(je)^h, rollator
zinc zink^h
zine *magazine* tijdschrift^h, blad^h
¹zip (n) **1** snerpend geluid^h; gescheur^h [of clothing] **2** rits(sluiting) **3** pit, fut: *she's still*

full of ~ zij zit nog vol energie
²zip (vb) **1** zoeven, scheuren: *bullets ~ped over them* kogels floten over hen heen **2** snel gaan: *~ by* voorbijsnellen **3** vastgeritst worden, losgeritst worden, ingeritst worden
³zip (vb) **1** ritsen: *~ up* dichtritsen **2** [comp] inpakken, comprimeren
Zip code [Am] postcode
zip file zipbestand^h, gecomprimeerd bestand^h
zipper rits(sluiting)
zippy energiek, levendig, vitaal
zip up comprimeren, inpakken
zit [inform] puistje^h, pukkel
zodiac dierenriem
zombie levenloos iem., robot, automaat, zoutzak
¹zone (n) **1** streek, gebied^h, terrein^h, zone: *demilitarized ~* gedemilitariseerde zone **2** luchtstreek **3** ring, kring, streep **4** [Am] postdistrict^h, telefoondistrict^h, treindistrict^h
²zone (vb) bestemmen: *~ a part of the town as residential* een deel van de stad voor bewoning bestemmen
zoning zonering, indeling in zones; [esp] ruimtelijke ordening, bestemmingsplan^h
zoo *zoological garden* dierentuin
zookeeper dierenverzorger
zoological zoölogisch, dierkundig
zoologist zoöloog, dierkundige
zoology 1 dierkunde, zoölogie **2** dierenleven^h, fauna; dierenwereld [in certain region]
¹zoom (n) **1** gezoem^h **2** [photo] zoom
²zoom (vb) **1** zoemen, snorren **2** snel stijgen [also fig]; de hoogte in schieten **3** [inform] zoeven, hard rijden **4** [photo] zoomen: *~ in (on)* inzoomen (op); *~ out* uitzoomen
zoom lens zoomlens, zoomobjectief^h
zucchini [Am] courgette